FILING REQUIREMENTS

For 1998, Code Sec. 6012 requires a tax return to be filed if gross income for the year is at least as much as the amount shown for the categories in the table below.

Filing Status	Gross Income 1998
Single	
Under 65	$ 6,950
65 or older	8,000
Dependent with unearned income	700
Dependent with no unearned income	4,250
Married Filing Joint Return	
Both spouses under 65	$12,500
One spouse 65 or older	13,350
Both spouses 65 or older	14,200
Married Filing Separate Return	
All	$ 2,700
Head of Household	
Under 65	$ 8,950
65 or older	10,000
Surviving Spouse	
Under 65	$ 9,800
65 or older	10,650

PERSONAL EXEMPTION

The personal exemption reduces taxable income by $2,700 in 1998.

High-Income Taxpayers. The deduction for personal exemptions is reduced or even eliminated for certain high-income taxpayers. When adjusted gross income exceeds one of the following threshold amounts, the deduction for exemptions is reduced by 2 percent for each $2,500 ($1,250 for a married person filing separately) or fraction thereof by which adjusted gross income exceeds the threshold amount.

Filing Status	Adjusted Gross Income Threshold Amount 1998
Single	$124,500
Married Filing Joint Return	186,800
Married Filing Separate Return	93,400
Head of Household	155,650
Surviving Spouse	186,800

The deduction for personal exemptions is fully eliminated when adjusted gross income exceeds the threshold amount by more than $122,500; in no case can the deduction for exemptions be reduced by more than 100 percent.

CCH Federal Taxation

Comprehensive Topics

1999

Coordinating Author: **Ephraim P. Smith**
California State University, Fullerton

Technical Review Authors: **Philip J. Harmelink**
University of New Orleans

James R. Hasselback
Florida State University

Contributing Authors: **Rolf K. Auster**
Florida International University

Ted D. Englebrecht
Old Dominion University

Edward C. Foth
DePaul University

Lawrence A. Kreiser
Cleveland State University

Thomas M. Porcano
Miami University (Ohio)

CCH INCORPORATED
Chicago

Editorial Staff

Diane L. McComb

ISBN 0-8080-0244-9

© 1998, **CCH** INCORPORATED

4025 W. Peterson Ave., Chicago IL 60646-6085
1-800-248-3248
http://www.cch.com

Material from *Uniform CPA Examination Questions and Unofficial Answers,* Copyright © 1980 and 1982–1985, by the American Institute of Certified Public Accountants, Inc., is reprinted (or adapted) with permission.

Chapters 2 through 11 are from *CCH Federal Taxation—Basic Principles (1999).*

Printed in the United States of America

Preface

CCH Federal Taxation—Comprehensive Topics introduces students of accounting to the complex and absorbing study of federal taxation. *Comprehensive Topics* covers a broad range of subjects from the definition of income to corporate reorganizations.

The order in which topics are introduced in this book represents a simple and clear division among the basic taxable entities. The initial eleven chapters deal with topics affecting individual taxpayers. As the cornerstone for the foundation of federal taxation, these topics constitute an extensive outline of the basics. This book distills the major ideas and operational techniques for dealing with problems encountered in these areas. The second major focus of the book covers corporations and partnerships. Eight chapters examine the tax complexities of these entities. In addition, three chapters cover the taxation of estates, gifts, and trusts and the techniques for retirement planning. Chapter 24, "Tax Research, Practice, and Procedure," is pertinent to all tax entities and acquaints the student with the fundamentals necessary for understanding complex tax issues.

The seventh edition of *Comprehensive Topics* has been prepared to ensure that all material presented is complete and current through the Taxpayer Relief Act of 1997. *Comprehensive Topics* is designed to be used either in a one-semester class or in a two-semester sequence. This book was not prepared as a restatement of the Internal Revenue Code and related tax law. Many such works currently exist. It was designed as a learning device to present federal tax information in a way that will stimulate thought and planning as well as mastery of the difficult, tightly interwoven intricacies of federal tax law in a sequence different from that presented in the Code. This was done so that common ideas and underlying similarities could be linked in the mind of the student and unifying characteristics could be drawn together to present a clearer and more functional picture of the whole.

The contributing authors of this volume wish to thank many of their colleagues for helpful suggestions and for the time and energy they have given to improving the manuscript. We wish to express our sincere appreciation to Professor Terry L. Crain of the University of Oklahoma for his special assistance in the preparation of this edition.

Ephraim P. Smith

February 1998

How to Use This Book

CCH Federal Taxation—Comprehensive Topics has been organized to make it easy to study the fundamental concepts of federal tax laws affecting individuals. Special features, end-of-chapter materials, an appendix, and supplementary materials are provided to further assist in the learning process.

Chapter Openings

All chapters begin with the same elements: a list of the learning objectives and an overview. This information provides an understanding of the material that will be studied in the chapter.

Special Features

Special features—Keystone Problems, Tax Planning Pointers, and Tax Blunders—appear throughout the book. Their purpose is to make familiar the specific applications of the tax law, suggest tax-saving strategies, and illustrate methods of avoiding undesired tax consequences. Additionally, vivid and realistic examples to illustrate salient points are included within the chapters to show application of the law and accounting techniques.

End-of-Chapter Materials

Every chapter ends with a summary of the material covered. Questions and Problems follow for applying the principles learned and allowing the instructor to evaluate recall of the main ideas discussed in the chapter. The problems are sequenced in the order in which the topics are presented in the chapter. Also included are Comprehensive Problems and Research Problems. Comprehensive Problems are designed to develop computational skills, while the purpose of the Research Problems is to provide an opportunity to learn and utilize the methodology of tax research.

End-of-Book Materials

In addition to the Topical Index, other useful research materials are found at the end of the book. The Appendix covers various Tax Rate Schedules, and the Glossary of Tax Terms contains over 200 definitions. In addition, the Finding Lists and Table of Cases detail the textbook's citations by Internal Revenue Code Sections, Regulations Sections, Revenue Procedures, Revenue Rulings, and court cases.

Supplementary Materials

A *Study Guide*, sold separately, outlines and highlights the in-depth textbook presentation and contains Objective Questions (and Answers) for self-evaluation. It also includes a series of Tax Return Problems designed to complement conceptual study of federal taxation and to provide exposure to various aspects of tax return preparation.

To order the *STUDY GUIDE* for this volume, contact your bookstore or write or call: **CCH** INCORPORATED, 4025 W. Peterson Ave., Chicago, Illinois 60646-6085 (1-800-248-3248; http://www.cch.com).

Contents

A detailed Table of Contents for each chapter begins on page ix.

Table of Contents

Paragraph

CHAPTER 1 INTRODUCTION TO FEDERAL TAXATION AND UNDERSTANDING THE FEDERAL TAX LAW

FUNDAMENTAL ASPECTS OF FEDERAL TAXATION
Sources of Revenue 1101
Tax Collection and Penalties 1121
Taxpayer Obligations 1131
Brief History of the Federal Income Tax 1151
Federal Tax Legislative Process.............. 1161
Tax Reform 1165

UNDERLYING RATIONALE OF THE FEDERAL INCOME TAX
Objectives of the Tax Law 1171
Economic Factors 1175
Social Factors 1181
Political Factors 1185
Tax Policy and Reform Measures 1187

BASIC TAX CONCEPTS
Essential Tax Terms Defined............... 1195

CHAPTER 2 INDIVIDUAL TAXATION— AN OVERVIEW

COMPONENTS OF THE TAX FORMULA
Gross Income........................... 2001
Deductions for Adjusted Gross Income 2015
Adjusted Gross Income 2025
Itemized Deductions v. Standard Deduction ... 2035
Personal Exemptions 2045
Tax Rates 2055
Tax Credits and Prepayments 2065
Net Tax Due or Refund 2075
Classification of Taxpayers 2085

PERSONAL EXEMPTIONS
Taxpayer and Spouse 2201
Dependents 2225
High-Income Taxpayers—Phaseout of
    Exemptions 2227

FILING STATUS AND REQUIREMENTS
Married Individuals Filing Jointly 2301
Married Individuals Filing Separate Returns ... 2315
Single Individuals 2325

CHAPTER   3   GROSS INCOME

THE CONCEPT OF INCOME

ECONOMIC BENEFIT, CONSTRUCTIVE
RECEIPT, AND ASSIGNMENT OF
INCOME DOCTRINES

ITEMS INCLUDED IN GROSS INCOME

CHAPTER   4   GROSS INCOME—EXCLUSIONS

COMMON EXCLUSIONS FROM GROSS
INCOME

EMPLOYEE BENEFITS

Chapter 1

Introduction to Federal Taxation and Understanding the Federal Tax Law

Learning Objectives

After completing Chapter 1, you should be able to:

1. Identify types of taxes used by federal and state governments to raise revenues.
2. Understand the methods of tax collection and the trends shown by tax collection statistics.
3. Differentiate between tax avoidance and tax evasion.
4. Recall the underlying rationale of the federal income tax and its historical development.
5. Describe the route a tax bill takes until enacted into law.
6. Define the basic tax concepts and terms of federal income taxation.

INTRODUCTION

Taxes are big business. Unfortunately, many business decisions are made in the United States today without regard to federal tax consequences. Individuals are concerned with personal income tax decisions and gift and estate tax decisions, while corporations concern themselves with corporate taxes, personal holding company taxes, and accumulated earnings tax decisions. Further, businesspersons must concern themselves with the choice of business entity: corporation, partnership, or S corporation. Differences in tax costs can be considerable. Advantages and disadvantages are virtually unlimited. This book presents information which is required knowledge if you make business decisions.

While most businesspersons (and many advisors) think about how to make decisions in nontax terms, the tax accountant bears the burden of introducing tax considerations. The topics presented in this book must be viewed in terms of decision-making—therefore, tax planning and tax research are of the utmost importance. Tax decisions are not made in a vacuum. Lawyers, accountants, financial managers, and a host of other experts work as a team in the decision-making process. This book is intended to serve as a guide for accounting students and for MBA students interested in gaining insight into and expertise in the tax complexities of business decision-making.

OVERVIEW OF CHAPTER

This chapter presents information on the magnitude of federal taxes collected and on taxpayer obligations. Then, a brief historical account is presented of federal tax collections prior to and after the adoption of the Sixteenth Amendment to the Constitution, which enabled Congress to levy "taxes on incomes, from whatever source derived." Following this is an introductory discussion of the federal legislative process and an analysis of the social, political, and economic rationale underlying the federal tax law. Finally, basic tax concepts are explained.

Fundamental Aspects of Federal Taxation

¶ 1101   SOURCES OF REVENUE

Types of Taxes

From the very beginning, with the ratification of the Sixteenth Amendment to the Constitution, through various Revenue Acts and many court cases, a set of tax laws has evolved that raised over $1.49 trillion on the 208.9 million tax returns processed by the IRS in 1996. The federal government uses a number of different types of taxes to generate the cash flow it needs for operating the government. The following is a listing of the various types of federal taxes:

Income taxes	Corporations, individuals, fiduciaries
Employment taxes	Old age, survivors, disability, and hospital insurance (federal insurance contributions, self-employment insurance contributions), unemployment insurance, railroad retirement
Estate and gift taxes	Estate, gift, and generation-skipping transfers
Excise and customs taxes	Alcohol, tobacco, gasoline, other

Over the years individuals have borne the burden in the arena of tax payments. Individual taxes account for over 50 percent of total tax collections. Individual and corporate income tax collections account for over 62 percent of total tax receipts.

Historically, Americans have been staunch supporters of the federal government's tax efforts. The rate of participation and compliance is one of the highest in the world. Realistically, the impact of estimating withholding provisions and the threat of government audits have aided in the outstanding record of the Internal Revenue Service.

Individual Income Taxes

Presently the United States government taxes income, transfers, and several transaction-type items (excise, customs, etc.). The major source of revenues is the tax on individuals (see Table 2). In 1996, individuals contributed 50.1 percent of the gross internal revenue collected. Since 1943, the U.S. has been on a pay-as-you-go system. In 1996, approximately 63 percent of the income tax collected came from tax withheld on wages.

Corporate Income Taxes

Corporate income taxes accounted for 12.7 percent of the total revenue collected by the U.S. government in 1996. The Tax Reform Act of 1986 reduced the top corporate income tax rate from 46 percent to 34 percent. The Revenue Reconciliation Act of 1993 raised the corporate income tax rate to 35 percent. The corporate tax rate has changed from 1 percent in 1913 to a high of 52 percent between 1952 and 1962. Generally, corporations are subject to tax based on net income without regard to dividends distributed to their shareholders.

Estate and Gift Taxes

Estate and gift taxes accounted for only 1.2 percent of the total revenue collected by the government in 1996. The estate tax, as we know it today, was enacted on September 8, 1916, and is levied on the transfer of property. The gift tax was originally enacted in 1924, was repealed in 1926, and then was restored in 1932.

Excise and Customs Taxes

Excise and customs taxes are levied on transactions, not on income or wealth. Examples of excise taxes are the taxes on alcohol, tobacco, and gasoline. The government collects the tax, usually at an early stage of production. In 1996, 2.8 percent of the government's revenue, or $42.22 billion, came from excise taxes.

Customs taxes are levied on certain goods entering the country. There are several reasons why the government levies this tax but by far the most important reason is the protection of U.S. industry from foreign competition.

State and Local Taxes

Just as the federal government needs an ever-increasing amount of dollars to satisfy its requirements, so do the states and local communities. State and local taxes are also big business. The major source of revenue for state governments is the income tax and the sales tax. For local communities, the property tax is a major source of revenue. Combined state and local collection totalled over $1.1 trillion in 1994. This is a slight increase from 1993. California collected the most in state and local taxes at $103 billion. New York and Texas followed at $84 and $47.3 billion, respectively.

Value-Added Tax

The value-added tax (VAT) is of fairly recent origin and much more popular overseas than in the United States. The concept of a VAT was first proposed by a German industrialist and government consultant, Dr. Wilhelm von Siemens, in 1918. In the next three decades much discussion took place. France was the first major country to adopt the VAT. In 1919, France instituted a general sales tax. This stayed in place until 1948, when it was replaced with a tax on production at each stage of the manufacturing process.

There are many forms of taxation, but basically all taxes can be categorized as direct taxes or indirect taxes. The federal income tax on individuals and corporations is a direct tax. Indirect taxes are those levied on producers or distributors with the expectation that these taxes will be passed on to the ultimate consumer. The VAT is an example of an indirect tax. It is merely a sales tax assessed at any or all levels of production and distribution. It is applied only on the value added to the product in an early stage of production or distribution. Notice that the VAT is a tax on products, not on business entities. The major drawback of the VAT is that it is extremely regressive.

> *Example 1.1.* A sweater is produced at a cost of $10. If the VAT is 5 percent, then each taxpayer, regardless of income level or ability to pay, must pay the fifty cents for VAT.

The VAT continues to be discussed as an attractive source of revenue in the United States. Each 1 percent of VAT would be expected to raise $12 billion. Even with the exclusions for food and medicine, $7.6 billion would be raised per percentage point of tax. Despite these attractions, the VAT worries many Americans. First, it is a very regressive tax. Second, there is some concern that ultimately the VAT will partially replace the personal income tax. Proponents of the VAT, however, maintain that its use would help shrink the "tax gap" (discussed at ¶ 1121). That is, the element of the population not currently paying taxes would have to pay a VAT tax, since it is a layered sales tax.

Flat Tax

The past several years have seen heated discussions about using a flat tax. Proponents of a flat tax point to the lower cost of administration and the ease of preparation by Americans as the major benefits. A flat tax would take an individual's total income minus an allowance for family size and apply one tax rate. This rate would apply to all individuals. There would be no deductions.

Various senators and representatives have presented proposals for consideration. Rep. Dick Armey, R-Texas, and Sen. Richard Shelby, R-Ala., have proposed a flat tax composed of two tax forms—one for individuals and one for businesses. Their proposal would tax individuals on total income minus an allowance based on family size and then apply a 17 percent tax rate. For businesses, the tax rate would be the same 17 percent, but it would be applied against the firm's gross revenue minus costs of purchases, wages, salaries, capital equipment, structures, land, and pensions.

KEYSTONE PROBLEM

The federal government currently uses many forms of taxation, both direct and indirect, to raise revenue. Would it not be more effective and less burdensome just to employ a single tax? What would you consider to be a more effective and efficient system of raising revenue?

¶ 1121   TAX COLLECTION AND PENALTIES

Returns

The Internal Revenue Service processed 208.9 million federal tax returns and supplementary documents in 1996—a small increase over the 205.7 million processed in 1995. This is in comparison to over 143 million tax returns processed in 1980. It collected $1.49 trillion in 1996, an increase of $110.8 billion, up almost 8.1 percent from 1995. Taxes and tax collections are indeed big business. Table 1, derived from the 1980 Annual Report of the Commissioner of the Internal Revenue Service and the 1996 Internal Revenue Service Data Book, details the magnitude of work required to support our government. Over 56 percent of all returns are filed by individuals. In 1996, individuals filed over 118 million returns, for a total of approximately $745 billion.

Table 1   NUMBER OF RETURNS FILED BY PRINCIPAL TYPE OF RETURN

(Figures in Thousands)

Type of Return	1980	1995	1996	Increase or Decrease Between 1980 and 1996 Amount	Percent
Grand total	143,446	205,747	208,938	65,492	45.66
Income tax, total	107,827	161,898	165,297	57,470	53.30
Individual	93,143	116,298	118,833	25,690	27.58
Declaration of estimated tax	8,699	35,475	36,044	27,345	314.35
Fiduciary	1,877	3,187	3,259	1,382	73.63
Partnership	1,390	1,572	1,623	233	16.76
Corporation	2,718	4,781	4,874	2,156	79.32
Estate tax	148	83	86	(62)	− 41.89
Gift tax	216	215	226	10	4.63
Employment tax	26,499	29,006	28,562	2,063	7.79
Exempt organizations	444	560	573	129	29.05
Employee plans	792	1,262	855	63	7.95
Excise tax	909	787	765	(144)	− 15.84
Supplemental documents	6,064	11,937	12,573	6,509	107.34

Sources: 1980 Annual Report of the Commissioner of the Internal Revenue Service and Internal Revenue Service Data Book 1996.

Tax Collections

Tax collections have increased dramatically between 1980 and 1996. This was due in part to the growth in the economy. Table 2 gives data on tax collections from 1980, 1995, and 1996. Obviously, the increase in tax collections from 1980 to 1996 in billions of dollars is staggering—$967,171,401,000. Now, notice the detail. Corporate taxes have increased 161 percent between 1980 and 1996, while personal income taxes have increased 159 percent. Estate and gift taxes have increased 170 percent in the same period. Keep these figures in mind as you read the chapters that follow.

Just as the dollar amounts have increased in tax collections, so has the number of returns filed. From 1980 to 1996, the number of corporate income tax returns increased by 79.3 percent. During the same time period, the number of individual income tax returns increased by 27.6 percent. The number of individuals requesting a refund increased to 88 million in 1996.

Table 2   GROSS INTERNAL REVENUE COLLECTIONS

(In thousands of dollars)

Source	Percent of 1996 Collections	1980	1995	1996	Increase or Decrease Between 1980 and 1996	
					Amount	Percent
Grand total.....	100.00	519,375,273	1,375,731,835	1,486,546,674	967,171,401	186.22
Income taxes, total	62.85	359,927,392	850,201,510	934,368,067	574,440,675	159.60
Corporation ..	12.72	72,379,610	174,422,173	189,054,791	116,675,181	161.20
Individual	50.14	287,547,782	675,779,337	745,313,276	457,765,494	159.20
Employment taxes, total ...	33.12	128,330,480	464,405,305	492,365,178	364,034,698	283.67
Old-age, survivors, disability, and hospital insurance	32.43	122,486,499	455,271,459	482,080,772	359,594,273	293.58
Unemployment insurance	0.40	3,309,000	5,803,748	5,957,025	2,648,025	80.02
Railroad retirement ...	0.29	2,534,981	4,330,098	4,327,382	1,792,401	70.71
Estate and gift taxes	1.18	6,498,381	15,144,394	17,591,817	11,093,436	170.71
Excise taxes, total	2.84	24,619,021	44,980,627	42,221,611	17,602,590	71.50

Sources: 1980 Annual Report of the Commissioner of the Internal Revenue Service and Internal Revenue Service Data Book 1996.

Tax Audits and Penalties

The U.S. tax system is a voluntary compliance tax system. The total number of federal tax returns filed in 1996 was 208,938,000, of which 118,833,000 were filed by individual taxpayers. The IRS conducted examinations of 2,136,819 returns, and on the basis of these examinations, it recommended additional tax and penalties of $28.1 billion, up from $27.84 billion in 1995.

Although audits of individual returns made up the bulk of the examinations (1,941,546 returns), they resulted in only $7.6 billion of the total recommended collections, while audits of corporate returns yielded $18 billion. Of course, audits do not always favor the IRS, as evidenced by the fact that, of the individual returns examined, 60,678 resulted in refunds; however, this amount was down from 66,311 in 1995.

Until recently, there had been an upsurge in the number of taxpayers who illegally sought, either openly or covertly, to reduce or eliminate their tax obligation. However, the IRS has responded to the challenge by taking advantage of the developing computer technology. Computers already scrutinize tax returns, check errors, and perform a number of routine, repetitive tasks with speed, efficiency, and great accuracy. The IRS continues to match almost all information returns that businesses are required to submit on magnetic media to verify that correct amounts are reported on taxpayers' returns. Information returns include W-2 Forms listing salary and 1099 Forms listing other income.

In 1996, the IRS audited 1.9 million individual income tax returns or 1.64 percent of all individual tax returns. This is approximately the same number of returns and percent that were audited in 1995. Table 3 presents information on the percentage of returns audited by type of return.

Table 3   PERCENTAGE OF RETURNS AUDITED

Type of Return	Percentage Audited	
	1995	1996
Individual	1.67	1.64
Partnership	0.46	0.49
Corporation	2.05	2.34
Estate	14.20	14.47
Gift	0.88	0.89
Excise	3.72	4.17
Employment	0.18	0.17

Sources: Internal Revenue Service Data Book 1996.

Because of severe budget deficits during the late 1980s, the personnel needed to audit the growing number of returns filed have not been added. A hiring freeze at the IRS in the enforcement departments started in 1980 and extended through 1991. In its 1995 appropriation, the IRS received an additional $405 million to hire 5,000 personnel. This allowed the IRS to conduct approximately 450,000 additional audits. The current mood in Congress is anti-IRS. Table 4 graphically depicts the percentage of returns audited by the Internal Revenue Service.

Table 4   PERCENTAGE OF RETURNS AUDITED—1980–1996

Sources: 1980 Annual Report of the Commissioner of the Internal Revenue Service and Internal Revenue Service Data Book 1996.

A review of the IRS data reveals a geographical disparity in audits. A taxpayer living in the Western Region of the United States had a greater chance of being audited than a taxpayer residing in the other three regions. Table 5 presents information on the number of returns audited by geographic region.

Table 5   IRS AUDITS BY GEOGRAPHIC REGION— 1996 INDIVIDUAL RETURNS

Region	Filed	Examined by Revenue Agent or Tax Auditor	Percentage
		NUMBER OF RETURNS	
Northeast	33,005,583	144,897	0.44
Southeast	32,709,603	184,125	0.56
Midstates	26,604,611	162,185	0.61
Western	25,210,512	268,990	1.07
International	1,050,686	1,653	0.16
Region Total	118,580,995 *	761,850	0.64
		Examined at Service Centers	
	118,580,995 *	1,179,696	1.00
Grand Total	118,580,995 *	1,941,546	1.64

Source: Internal Revenue Service Data Book 1996. * The 1996 transition to new geographic regions caused a slight discrepancy in the total for number of returns filed.

Naturally, for certain types of taxpayers and those with higher incomes, the probability of audit is much greater. Individuals with income of over $100,000 were most likely to be audited. Table 6 presents information on examination coverage by the amount of income earned.

Table 6   IRS AUDITS BY AMOUNT OF INCOME AND TYPE OF RETURN

CLASSIFICATION	PERCENT AUDITED	
No Schedule C		
Income Level	1995	1996
Under $25,000 (1040A)	1.30	2.00
$25,000–$50,000	0.90	0.95
$50,000–$100,000	1.05	1.16
Over $100,000	2.79	2.35
With Schedule C		
Income Level		
Under $25,000	5.85	4.21
$25,000–$100,000	3.08	2.85
Over $100,000	3.47	4.09

Source: Internal Revenue Service Data Book 1996.

The Internal Revenue Service has acknowledged that the problem of tax evasion is indeed a serious one. The "tax gap," that is, the total revenue lost through tax evasion, has increased from $81 billion in 1981 to $127 billion in 1992. The IRS had estimated the tax gap to be more than $150 billion in 1992, when excise and employment taxes are included. The IRS estimated that $94 billion of the tax gap was caused by individuals and $33 billion by corporations. Today, the voluntary compliance rate is estimated by the Commissioner of Internal Revenue to be 83 to 85 percent. Each percentage point of noncompliance costs the government $7 billion in lost revenue. Currently, 9 to 10 million Americans required to file returns do not file.

The Tax Reform Act of 1986 closed many of the loopholes associated with tax shelters. Since 1988 the IRS has been using a revised audit-selection formula that is aimed at high-income returns. Further, the Tax Acts of 1986 and 1987, the Technical and Miscellaneous Revenue Act of 1988, and the Revenue Reconciliation Acts of 1989, 1990, and 1993 changed the penalties imposed on taxpayers for not complying with the tax laws.

The Improved Penalty and Compliance Act, which was incorporated into the Revenue Reconciliation Act of 1989, revamped the civil tax penalty provisions of the Internal Revenue Code. The goal was to create a fairer, less complex, and more effective penalty system. The Act made changes in the following broad areas:

1. Document and information return penalties
2. Accuracy-related penalties
3. Preparer, promoter, and protestor penalties
4. Penalties for failures to file or pay tax

¶ 1131   TAXPAYER OBLIGATIONS

Tax accountants, lawyers, and businesspersons, since the inception of the first federal income tax law, have concerned themselves with choosing among the various forms a transaction may take. There is an acute awareness among tax accountants that tax consequences of an action may differ depending upon procedural variations and alternative approaches to a business decision. The increasing complexity of the modern tax laws serves only to accentuate the problem.

Because of the extreme difficulty experienced in trying to differentiate between tax avoidance and tax evasion, Congress enacted, in the 1954 Internal Revenue Code, a provision which illustrates circumstances that constitute prima facie evidence of the tainted purpose. The 1986 Code contends with the problem of criminal tax evasion in Section 7201, entitled "Attempt to Evade or Defeat Tax." It reads:

> Any person who willfully attempts in any manner to evade or defeat any tax imposed by this title or the payment thereof shall, in addition to other penalties provided by law, be guilty of a felony and, upon conviction thereof, shall be fined not more than $100,000 ($500,000 in the case of a corporation), or imprisoned not more than five years, or both, together with the costs of prosecution.

The goal of every businessperson should be profit maximization. The government endorses this goal. Tax avoidance is legal and a legitimate pursuit of a business entity.

Tax Avoidance

All citizens have the prerogative to arrange their transactions and affairs in such a manner as to reduce their tax liabilities. A good businessperson is obligated to search out those transactions and to time those events which will lower the tax liability. Judge Learned Hand, in *S.R. Newman,* declared many years ago:

> Over and over again courts have said that there is nothing sinister in so arranging one's affairs as to keep taxes as low as possible. Everybody does so, rich or poor; and all do right, for nobody owes any public duty to pay more than the law demands: taxes are enforced extractions, not voluntary contributions. To demand more in the name of morals is mere cant. CA-2, 47-1 USTC ¶ 9175, 159 F.2d 848.

There is a clear demarcation between tax avoidance and tax evasion. The saving of tax dollars requires specific actions so as to avoid the tax liability prior to the time it would have occurred according to law. It requires the proper handling of affairs so that items of income are subjected to a lower tax rate than would apply if no action had been taken. In some instances, it requires the postponing of income which is subject to taxation until a time when the individual's tax bracket would be lower.

Tax Evasion

To be guilty of evading taxes, the individual must already have a tax liability. All actions must be definitely complete, and in spite of this liability, the taxpayer does not report income. The courts have ruled that it is not wrong to find a form of a transaction that does not lead to any tax liability. However, there is a legal obligation to disclose a tax liability based on completed transactions, and the refusal to report the tax liability is illegal.

The Tax Court in *Berland's Inc. of South Bend* (16 TC 182, acq., 1951-2 CB 1, CCH Dec. 18,057) said that the purpose of tax evasion must be the "principal" purpose, and the taxpayer is not guilty of tax evasion merely because the tax consequences of the particular transaction are considered. Furthermore, the Tax Court said:

> The consideration of the tax aspects of the plan was no more than should be expected of any business bent on survival under the tax rates then current. Such consideration is only part of ordinary business prudence.

What frequently distinguishes tax avoidance from tax evasion is the intent of the taxpayer. The intent to evade tax occurs when a taxpayer knowingly misrepresents the facts. Intent is a mental process, a state of mind. A taxpayer's intent is judged by his or her actions. The taxpayer who knowingly understates income leaves evidence in the form of identifying earmarks, referred to as "badges" of fraud. Internal revenue agents are on the lookout for these badges of fraud. The more common badges are:

1. *Understatement of income.* The IRS considers the failure to report entire sources of income, such as tips, or specific items where similar items are included in income, such as dividends received, as an indication that there may have been an understatement of income. Other such indications include the unexplained failure to report substantial amounts of income determined by the IRS to have been received, the concealment of bank accounts or other property, and the failure to deposit receipts to a business account contrary to normal practices.

2. *Claiming of fictitious or improper deductions.* To the IRS, a substantial overstatement of deductions is a badge of fraud that could warrant a further look at the taxpayer's books. Other indications of improper deductions are the inclusion of obviously unallowable items in unrelated accounts and the claiming of fictitious deductions or dependency deductions for nonexistent, deceased, or self-supporting persons.

3. *Accounting irregularities.* Accounting practices that are considered a badge of fraud include the keeping of two sets of books or no books, false entries, backdated or postdated docu-

ments, inadequate records, and discrepancies between book and return amounts.

4. *Allocation of income.* The distribution of profits to fictitious partners and the inclusion of income or deductions in the return of a related taxpayer with a lower tax rate than that of the taxpayer are indications of an intentional misstatement of taxable income.

5. *Acts and conduct of the taxpayer.* Aside from the improper reporting of income or deductions, a taxpayer's conduct can give the IRS reason to question the propriety of a return. For example, false statements, attempts to hinder an examination of a return, the destruction of books or records, the transfer of assets for purposes of concealment, or the consistent underreporting of income over a period of years are badges of fraud.

The presence of one or more of these badges of fraud does not in itself mean that the return is fraudulent. However, it should alert an examiner that additional probing and inquiry are necessary. *Internal Revenue Manual, Part IV—Audit,* IRM 4231, Sec. 940.

Corporate Tax Avoidance

Normally, the Commissioner and the courts accept a corporation as being distinct from its shareholders. However, if it appears that a sham transaction has taken place, then the Commissioner has grounds for taking action. Judge Learned Hand, in summarizing many cases on the subject of tax avoidance v. tax evasion, stated in *National Investors Corp. v. Hoey:*

> To be a separate jural person for purposes of taxation, a corporation must engage in some industrial, commercial, or other activity besides avoiding taxation: in other words, that the term "corporation" will be interpreted to mean a corporation which does some "business" in the ordinary meaning; and that escaping taxation is not "business" in the ordinary meaning. 44-2 USTC ¶ 9407, 144 F.2d 466, 467-68 (CA-2 1944).

Section 269 of the Internal Revenue Code provides the Commissioner with a very important tool in judging whether or not a corporate acquisition is tax avoidance or merely a sham. If the Commissioner feels that there is no principal purpose for the tax-free acquisition, "such deduction, credit, or other allowance" may be disallowed. The key defense by the taxpayer is to substantiate that there was indeed a "principal purpose." If there is a principal purpose, nothing stops the taxpayer from having other purposes, such as the saving of taxes. *Kershaw Mfg. Co., Inc.,* 24 TCM 228, TC Memo. 1965-44, CCH Dec. 27,268(M).

Taxpayer's Assessment of Tax Liability

In order to decrease potential tax liability, the taxpayer must choose the action that will allow the greatest tax savings. An example of a tax savings device is investment in municipal bonds instead of corporate bonds. The interest derived from corporate bonds is taxable income, whereas the interest received from municipal bonds is tax free. In the above example, the taxpayer does not have to hide the fact that there is a lower tax liability on the profit.

When contemplating a transaction, the taxpayer makes an assessment of the tax liability. Naturally, any doubtful issues are resolved in the taxpayer's own favor. Certainly, there is nothing fraudulent about using this procedure. On the other hand, if the taxpayer knowingly overstates expenses, thereby reducing the tax liability, then the taxpayer is guilty of tax evasion.

¶ 1151   BRIEF HISTORY OF THE FEDERAL INCOME TAX

The origin of taxation in the United States dates back to the Constitution and, therefore, the Constitution is the ultimate source of the power to tax. Originally, the Constitution empowered Congress "to lay and collect taxes, duties, imports and excises, to pay the debts and provide for the common defense and general welfare of the United States." In granting this power, Congress also limited the power of taxation in that "all duties, imports, and excises shall be uniform throughout the United States, that direct taxes should be laid in proportion to the population." It was within these confinements that many cases tested the constitutionality of the early tax laws—a test many of the taxes did not pass. During the late 1800s, the terms "uniform" and "direct taxes" were very important concepts.

Income Tax Law of 1894

In the late 1880s, support was mounting at the state level for an income tax. In Ohio, the State Democratic Convention approved a graduated income tax in the summer of 1891. Reflecting on the mood of the country at that time, William Jennings Bryan supported an income tax as preferential to a tax on tobacco and beer which he felt would put an unfair hardship on the poor. Although this proposed tax and others like it were never passed, they encouraged others to investigate the possibilities of a federal income tax. Ultimately this led to the actual passage of the Wilson Tariff Bill of 1894. This bill was not an income tax bill; however, an amendment was attached to the bill which allowed for an income tax. The provisions of this income tax law stated that the tax would commence on January 1, 1895, and continue until January 1, 1900. It was a 2 percent tax on all "gains, profits, and income" over $4,000 "derived from any kind of property, rents, interest, dividends, or salaries, or from any profession, trade, employment, or vocation." Income was defined to include interest on all securities except federal bonds which were exempt by law of their issuance from any federal taxation. The Act also imposed a 2 percent tax on net profits of corporations but not on partnerships.

There was much criticism of this law. Concerns arose that provisions such as the $4,000 exemption made the law discriminatory against certain groups. Consequently, many cases were brought before the courts. The major point raised by opponents of the Act was whether or not such a tax on income derived from property was a "direct tax" in the sense commonly understood in the Constitution. A direct tax was held to be a tax on the land and, therefore, had to be apportioned among the states.

The Supreme Court declared the law unconstitutional in the famous *Pollock v. Farmers' Loan & Trust Co.* case, 157 U.S. 429, 15 S.Ct. 673 (1895). It characterized the income tax as a "direct tax" and stated that the Constitution provides that "no direct tax shall be laid, unless in proportion to the census or enumeration hereinbefore directed to be taken." Therefore, the Court invalidated a significant portion of the law and rendered income tax apportionment impossible. Further, the Court considered the property tax a direct tax and excise and duties taxes as indirect taxes. The Court stated, in a five-to-four decision, that a tax on real estate and on personal property is a direct tax and, therefore:

> unconstitutional and void, because not apportioned according to representation, all these sections constituting one entire scheme of taxation, are necessarily invalid.

The Court expressed, in one of its longest opinions, no opinion on whether or not the income tax provisions were unconstitutional. Thus, with this decision, the first federal income tax law since the Civil War in the United States was declared to be unconstitutional.

Corporation Excise Tax of 1909

Support for an income tax was growing even though the courts had voided all attempts made by Congress. Government was becoming more costly and new sources of revenue were essential. The Spanish American War produced a great need for funds, and many believed that an income tax was the only solution. In the *Pollock* decision, the Supreme Court voted five to four that the tax was unconstitutional. By late 1908, it was abundantly clear that only by passage of a constitutional amendment would the government receive the power needed to impose a federal income tax. Therefore, an amendment was passed by Congress in 1909. However, because of the length of time required to ratify a constitutional amendment, Congress simultaneously passed the Corporation Excise Tax of 1909. The Supreme Court had ruled in the *Pollock* case that an "excise tax" was not required to be apportioned. Further, the Court indicated in several cases that an income tax on corporations would be upheld if it were deemed an excise tax levied on corporations for the privilege of carrying on or doing business as a corporation, granted the amount of tax due was based upon the net income of the corporation.

The Tax Act of 1909 was the first Act to be upheld by the courts that taxed corporate profits. Prior to this time, corporate profits were tax free except for a short period of time during the Civil War. The 1909 Act provided that corporations would pay an annual special excise tax. This tax amounted to 1 percent on net income over $5,000 exclusive of dividends from other corporations.

As can be imagined, many influential people objected to the 1909 Act. By 1910, fifteen cases challenging the Act had reached the Supreme Court. In a unanimous decision, the Supreme Court upheld that the Tax Act of 1909 was not a direct tax, but an indirect tax and "an excise upon the particular privilege of doing business as a corporate entity."

The Revenue Act of 1909 was a tax for the privilege of doing business as a corporation, even though the assessment was on the net income of the corporation. A unanimous Supreme Court upheld the law in *Flint v. Stone Tracy Co., 220* U.S. 107, 31 S.Ct. 342 (1911).

When examining the differences between the 1895 law which was held to be unconstitutional and the 1909 law which was upheld as constitutional, the difference is indeed in only a few words, changing a tax *upon* income to a tax *measured* by income. Justice Day wrote the opinion for the Supreme Court and stated that the difference was "not merely nominal, but rests upon substantial difference between the mere ownership of property and the actual doing of business in a certain way."

Sixteenth Amendment and the Revenue Act of 1913

Taxation laws as we know them today derive their authority from the Sixteenth Amendment as passed by Congress on July 12, 1909. The amendment stated:

> The Congress shall have power to lay and collect taxes on incomes, from whatever source derived, without apportionment among the several States, and without regard to any census or enumeration.

Alabama became the first state to ratify the amendment in the same year that it was passed—1909. On February 25, 1913, the final vote for ratification was received.

Congress now was given the clear authority to enact a tax on income from whatever source derived. Taxes could be either direct or indirect and could be imposed without regard to any census or enumeration.

On October 3, 1913, pursuant to the power granted by the Sixteenth Amendment, Congress enacted the Revenue Act of 1913 which imposed a tax on the net income of individuals and corporations. The Revenue Act of 1913 was retroactive to March 1, 1913. This date is important for tax purposes because this is the date which is sometimes used as a basis for computing gains and losses. Simultaneous to the enactment of the Revenue Act, the Corporation Excise Tax was repealed.

The Revenue Act of 1913 serves as the basis for the income tax laws of the United States. However, it would never have been passed without its two precedents, the Income Tax Law of 1894 and the Corporation Excise Tax of 1909. These two laws laid the foundation and framework for an income tax. The Supreme Court ruling in the *Pollock* case made it mandatory that an amendment to the Constitution be passed to allow for a direct tax on income.

1913 to Date

Following the passage of the Sixteenth Amendment, there have been many changes in the tax law. Many of the more important changes in our federal taxing system are outlined below. Some of the data for 1916–1962 came from *World Tax Series: Taxation in the United States,* CCH (Commerce Clearing House), 1963, pp. 117–118.

1913	The Revenue Act of 1913—Normal tax and surtax approved. Personal exemptions established.
1916	The Revenue Act of 1916—Established the estate tax.
1917	Charitable contributions granted tax deductible status. Federal income taxes were disallowed as a tax deduction. Credit for dependents allowed for first time.
1918	Tax preferences and exemptions established. Tax credit was granted for foreign income taxes paid. Carryforward provisions adopted for net operating losses. Depletion deductions for mines and oil and gas wells were instituted. Tax-free corporate mergers and other reorganizations permitted.
1921	Capital gains rates established. Profit-sharing and pension trusts exempted from tax.
1924	Gift tax enacted to prevent avoidance of the estate tax.
1926	January 1, 1926—Gift tax repealed.
1932	Gift tax restored in more effective form.
1934	The personal exemption and exemption for dependents were made deductible in determining net income for the purpose of surtax as well as normal tax.
1935	Federal Social Security Act enacted.
1936	Mutual investment companies allowed deduction for dividends distributed by them.
1938	LIFO adopted as an acceptable inventory method.
1939	Internal Revenue Code of 1939—Set out to codify separately the Internal Revenue laws.
1942	Net operating losses were allowed to be carried back. Provisions were made or changed for medical expenses, alimony, capital gains, and a standard deduction in lieu of itemized deductions.
1943	Current Tax Payment Act—Pay-as-you-go system adopted.
1948	Marital deduction originated for estate and gift tax. Split-income treatment approved for married couples.
1950	Self-employment tax enacted.
1954	Internal Revenue Code of 1954—Successor to the 1939 Code. Completely overhauled federal tax laws. Largest piece of federal legislation enacted to date. Broad changes were made in an attempt to codify income, estate, gift, and excise tax laws along with administration and procedure rules into one document.

1962   The Revenue Act of 1962—Granted a tax credit of 7 percent for investment in Section 38 Property. Further, the concept of "depreciation recapture" was introduced.

1964   The Revenue Act of 1964—Intended to stimulate sagging economy. Largest corporate and individual tax rate reduction since the Act of 1913.

The Act extended depreciation recapture to business realty. Foreign investment income subjected to increased taxation.

1966   The Tax Adjustment Act of 1966—Suspended the 7 percent investment credit. It was reinstituted six months later.

Graduated withholding replaced flat-rate. Corporations required to pay estimated tax more quickly.

1969   The Tax Reform Act of 1969—Investments in commercial and industrial buildings were significantly affected when depreciation allowances were reduced and the recapture rules changed. Investment tax credit repealed.

1971   The Revenue Act of 1971—Restored investment credit at 7 percent.

1974   Employee Retirement Income Security Act of 1974 (ERISA)—Major changes to the entire private pension system.

1975   The Tax Reduction Act of 1975—Reduced taxes for both individuals and corporations. Changed the investment tax credit from seven to 10 percent for a two-year period.

1976   The Tax Reform Act of 1976—Established at-risk rules for tax shelters and eliminated many tax shelters. Also, the Act made extensive changes in the treatment of foreign income.

1977   The Tax Reduction and Simplification Act of 1977—Attempted to simplify the system. Established zero-bracket amount exemption deductions.

1978   The Revenue Act of 1978—Revised corporate rate structures. New structure taxes the first $100,000 of income on a graduated scale, ranging from 17 to 40 percent, and at a 46 percent rate on all taxable income over $100,000. The Act made the 10 percent investment credit permanent.

The Act also made changes to capital gains, tax shelter rules, employee benefits, and estate and gift taxes.

1978   The Energy Tax Act of 1978—Instituted a tax credit for residential energy savings.

1980   The Bankruptcy Act of 1980—Added a seventh type of tax-free reorganization, the "G" type. Clarified rules for tax treatment of bad debts.

1980   The Windfall Profit Tax Act—Excise tax levied on domestic oil.

1980   The Installment Sales Revision Act of 1980—Revised installment sales rules.

1981   Economic Recovery Tax Act (ERTA)—Largest tax cut bill ever passed. Top individual tax rates decreased from 70 to 50 percent. All property placed in service after December 31, 1980, eligible for the Accelerated Cost Recovery System (ACRS). Increased allowable contributions to Keoghs, SEPs, and other retirement systems. Permitted two-earner married couples a deduction to reduce the inequity of the "marriage penalty." Extended the investment credit to include a wider array of investments.

1982   Tax Equity and Fiscal Responsibility Act (TEFRA)—Largest revenue-raising bill ever passed. Tightened up on itemized deductions. New rules on partial liquidations and for the taxation of distributed appreciated property. Tightened up pension rules. Corporate deductions for certain tax preferences cut by 15 percent. Required that basis of depreciated property must be reduced by 50 percent of investment credit. ACRS modified for 1985 and 1986 and Federal Unemployment Tax Act (FUTA) notes increased.

1982   Technical Corrections Act of 1982—Made changes to: ACRS, the investment credit, targeted jobs credit, the credit for research costs, and incentive stock options. Made changes to the Windfall Profit Tax Act.

1982   Subchapter S Revision Act of 1982—Enacted many new provisions for S corporations.

1983   Social Security Act Amendments of 1983—Bailed out the Social Security System.

1984   Deficit Reduction Act of 1984—Composed of two parts: first, the Tax Reform Act of 1984 and second, the Spending Reduction Act of 1984. The Tax Reform Act of 1984 provided for reducing the holding period on capital gains from more than one year to more than six months, extending the ACRS recovery period for 15-year real property to 18 years, taxing interest-free loans between family members, and drastically slashing the income-averaging provisions.

1986   The Tax Reform Act of 1986—The most significant and complex tax revision in the history of this country. The scope of the changes was so comprehensive that the tax law was redesignated the Internal Revenue Code of 1986.

1987   Revenue Act of 1987—Focused primarily on business tax rules. Areas affected included accounting for long-term contracts, limitations on the use of the installment method, application of corporate tax rates to master limited partnerships, and changes in the estimated tax rules for corporations. The Act postponed for five years the reduction to 50 percent of the top estate and gift tax rate.

1988   Family Support Act of 1988—Provided for major reform in the area of modifying the principal welfare program, Aid to Families with Dependent Children (AFDC). Also included in the Act was the modification of employee business expense reimbursement rules. Beginning in 1989 additional amounts will have to be deducted as miscellaneous itemized deductions.

1988   Technical and Miscellaneous Revenue Act of 1988—TAMRA contained a number of substantive provisions. Included in the Act were the taxpayer's bill of rights, limitations on the completed-contract accounting method, and extension of the exclusions for employee-provided educational assistance and the business energy credits.

1989   P.L. 101-140. Repealed Code Sec. 89. The nondiscrimination and qualification rules for employee benefit plans were repealed. Prior law nondiscrimination rules were reinstated.

1989   Medicare Catastrophic Coverage Repeal Act of 1989—Repealed the medicare surtax retroactively.

1989   Revenue Reconciliation Act of 1989—The Act achieved a deficit reduction of about $17.8 billion and accelerated the rate of collection of withholding and payroll tax. The Act also changed the partial interest exclusion on ESOPs. Modifications were also made to the like-kind exchange rules.

1990   Revenue Reconciliation Act of 1990—The Act contains a number of significant changes, including a deficit reduction of about $40 billion in 1991. The Act also increased from two to three the number of statutory rates, 15 percent, 28 percent, and 31 percent. Also, a maximum capital gain rate of 28 percent was established.

1991   Tax Extension Act of 1991—The Act extended, for six months only, 11 tax provisions that were to expire on December 31, 1991.

1992   Energy Policy Act of 1992—The Act greatly increases the amount of employer-provided transportation benefits excludable by employees.

1993   Revenue Reconciliation Act of 1993—The Act raised the tax rates for high-income earners. Changes also were made to the AMT, passive losses, and Section 179. Corporate tax rates increased by 1 percent.

1994   Social Security Domestic Employment Reform Act of 1994—The Act raises the threshold for paying Social Security and federal unemployment taxes on domestic workers from $50 per quarter to $1,000 annually, retroactive to the beginning of 1994.

1994   General Agreement on Tariffs and Trade (GATT)—To offset the loss of revenue from the reduction in tariffs, Congress passed several tax and revenue provisions. The major revenue items are: estimated tax treatment for Code Sec. 936 and subpart F income; increased premiums for employers with underfunded pension plans; and reduced interest rates on large corporate tax refunds.

1996   Taxpayer Bill of Rights 2—The Act includes more than 40 separate provisions, many of which will provide useful tools for tax practitioners representing clients before the IRS.

1996   Small Business Job Protection Act—The major portion of tax law changes passed in 1996 is contained in this Act. It also contains many technical corrections. The balance of the Act can be divided into four major categories: small business provisions, S corporation reform, pension simplification, and revenue-raising offsets.

1996   Health Insurance Portability and Accountability Act—The focus of this Act is on portability of health insurance. However, this Act contains tax provisions that focus on a variety of health-related issues, as well as several revenue-raising provisions unrelated to health care.

1996   Personal Responsibility and Work Opportunity Reconciliation Act—The tax impact of this Act is primarily limited to the earned income tax credit.

1997   Taxpayer Relief Act of 1997—The Act provides significant tax cuts for many taxpayers. Major features include a reduction in capital gains tax rates, expanded IRAs, educational tax incentives, estate tax relief, and a child tax credit.

¶ 1161   FEDERAL TAX LEGISLATIVE PROCESS

When reviewing the tax acts since the mid to late 1970s, it becomes obvious that tax reform is a yearly event. Tax bills are passed for numerous reasons (i.e., revenue needs, incentive for economic development, or to slow down the economy). Further, each year certain provisions of the Internal Revenue Code expire and must be renewed. Tax bills in this country have not followed a uniform path. Normally, major tax legislation originates with the President sending a message to Congress. An alternative approach is for congressional initiative on a tax bill.

The Constitution requires that revenue legislation originate in the House of Representatives. Therefore, the first step is for hearings before the House of Representatives Ways and Means Committee. Many influential bodies present recommendations to this Committee— the Secretary of the Treasury, the Office of Management and Budget, etc. After meeting with various bodies, the Committee meets in executive session, and a tax bill is transmitted by means of a Committee report to the House.

The House of Representatives debates the bill usually under a "closed rule" procedure, which permits amendments to come only if approved by the Ways and Means Committee. If the bill is defeated it may be referred back to committee; if it passes, it is sent to the Senate where it is first discussed in the Senate Finance Committee.

Hearings are held by the Finance Committee which might result in amendments to the House bill. The amendments may range from insignificant to totally changing the bill. The bill is then transmitted to the whole Senate. One significant difference between the House and the Senate is that, in the Senate, any Senator may offer amendments from the floor of the Senate. After passage, if there are any differences between the House and Senate versions of the bill, it goes to the Joint Conference Committee, which is composed of ranking members of the House Ways and Means Committee (seven members) and the Senate Finance Committee (five members) for resolution. The Conference

Committee version of the bill must be accepted or rejected—it cannot be changed by either the House or the Senate. Assuming passage by the House and the Senate, the bill becomes law when approved by the President. If it is vetoed, both the Senate and the House must vote affirmatively by a two-thirds majority to override the President's veto.

Exhibit 1 illustrates the sequence of events whereby a tax bill is introduced before the House Ways and Means Committee, passes through the House of Representatives, the Senate Finance Committee, and the Senate. As indicated in the final portion of Exhibit 1, if approved by the President, the tax bill will be incorporated into the Internal Revenue Code.

Exhibit 1   THE LEGISLATIVE PROCESS

Tax Bill is screened by House Ways
and Means Committee
↓
Consideration by the House of
Representatives
↓
Referred to Senate Finance Committee
↓
Consideration by the Senate ⟶ Sent to Joint Conference
Committee (if the House and
Senate differ)
↓
Consideration by the House and
Senate

Approval or Veto by the President ⟵
↓
Incorporation into the Code
(if approved by the President
or his veto is overridden)

¶ 1165   TAX REFORM

The year 1986 was a most interesting year for tax legislation. Both political parties, Democrats and Republicans, were "demanding" tax reform. The Treasury Department presented to President Reagan a massive tax reform plan that would impact the tax liability of most individuals and corporations. President Reagan, in his 1986 budget, called for a tax system that would be "simpler, more neutral, and more conducive to economic growth."

Tax Reform Act of 1986

The Senate passed a bill with only two rate brackets, 15 and 27 percent (28 percent was the final figure approved). Like that of the House of Representatives, their bill called for the removal of many tax deductions. One new feature added in the Senate bill was the drastic reduction in the number of people eligible for Individual Retirement Accounts (IRAs). After much debate, compromising, and political maneuvering, the Tax Reform Act of 1986 was passed and signed into law by President Reagan on October 22, 1986. The Tax Reform Act of 1986 carries the label of the most extensive overhaul of the U.S. tax code in almost 40 years, as well as the most fundamental reform of the U.S. tax structure. The scope of the changes was so comprehensive that the tax code was renamed the Internal Revenue Code of 1986.

One of the measures adopted in the Tax Reform Act of 1986 was that inflation adjustments would be provided annually for several specific items such as the standard deduction, tax brackets, personal exemption amounts, and the earned income credit. Indexing was designed to protect individuals from "bracket creep"—that is, where an individual's income increases only by the inflationary rate but the taxpayer moves into a higher tax bracket. Table 7 presents comparative data for the inflation-indexed items for 1997 and 1998.

Table 7   1997–1998 PARTIAL COMPARISON OF TAX CHANGES FOR INDIVIDUALS

Item	1997	1998
Filing requirements If filing status is:	Children and other dependents should see Chapter 2 for special rules.	
	A return was required if gross income was at least:	A return is required if gross income was at least:
Single		
Under 65	$ 6,800	$ 6,950
65 or older	7,800	8,000
Head of Household		
Under 65	$ 8,700	$ 8,950
65 or older	9,700	10,000
Married Filing Jointly		
Both under 65	$12,200	$12,500
One spouse 65 or older	13,000	13,350
Both 65 or older	13,800	14,200
Not living with spouse at end of year (or on date spouse died)		
Married Filing Separately		
All	2,650	2,700
Qualifying Widow(er)	$ 2,650	$ 2,700
Under 65	$ 9,550	$ 9,800
65 or older	10,350	10,650

Table 7   1997–1998 PARTIAL COMPARISON OF TAX CHANGES FOR INDIVIDUALS—Continued

Item	1997	1998
Tax rates		
Married filing jointly or surviving spouse	15% 0 to $ 41,200 28% $ 41,200 to $ 99,600 31% $ 99,600 to $151,750 36% $151,750 to $271,050 39.6% Over $271,050	15% 0 to $ 42,350 28% $ 42,350 to $102,300 31% $102,300 to $155,950 36% $155,950 to $278,450 39.6% Over $278,450
Single	15% 0 to $ 24,650 28% $ 24,650 to $ 59,750 31% $ 59,750 to $124,650 36% $124,650 to $271,050 39.6% Over $271,050	15% 0 to $ 25,350 28% $ 25,350 to $ 61,400 31% $ 61,400 to $128,100 36% $128,100 to $278,450 39.6% Over $278,450
Married filing separately	15% 0 to $ 20,600 28% $ 20,600 to $ 49,800 31% $ 49,800 to $ 75,875 36% $ 75,875 to $135,525 39.6% Over $135,525	15% 0 to $ 21,175 28% $ 21,175 to $ 51,150 31% $ 51,150 to $ 77,975 36% $ 77,975 to $139,225 39.6% Over $139,225
Head of household	15% 0 to $ 33,050 28% $ 33,050 to $ 85,350 31% $ 85,350 to $138,200 36% $138,200 to $271,050 39.6% Over $271,050	15% 0 to $ 33,950 28% $ 33,950 to $ 87,700 31% $ 87,700 to $142,000 36% $142,000 to $278,450 39.6% Over $278,450
Itemized deductions	High-income taxpayers whose AGI exceeded the threshold amount of $121,200 must reduce itemized deductions by 3% of the excess over that threshold. The reduction may be no more than 80% of itemized deductions, excluding deductions for medical expenses, investment interest, casualty losses, or wagering losses.	Threshold amount increased to $124,500.
Social Security wage base	The maximum amount of taxable and creditable annual earnings subject to the Social Security and self-employment income tax is $65,400.	The Social Security Administration raised the base to $68,400.

Table 7   1997–1998 PARTIAL COMPARISON OF TAX CHANGES FOR INDIVIDUALS—Continued

Item	1997	1998
Personal exemptions	$2,650, indexed for inflation; reduced or eliminated at high-income levels. Phaseout begins when adjusted gross income exceeds: $181,800 Joint returns or surviving spouses 151,500 Heads of households 121,200 Single taxpayers 90,900 Married persons filing separate returns Exemptions are reduced by 2 percent for each $2,500 ($1,250 for married person filing separately) by which AGI exceeds the threshold amount.	$2,700, indexed for inflation; reduced or eliminated at high-income levels. Phaseout begins when adjusted gross income exceeds: $186,800 Joint returns or surviving spouses 155,650 Heads of households 124,500 Single taxpayers 93,400 Married persons filing separate returns Exemptions are reduced by 2 percent for each $2,500 ($1,250 for married person filing separately) by which AGI exceeds the threshold amount.
Standard deduction		
Basic standard deduction		
Single	$4,150	$4,250
Head of household	6,050	6,250
Married filing jointly or qualifying widow(er)	6,900	7,100
Married filing separately	3,450	3,550
Additional standard deduction for blindness or 65		
Married (filing jointly or separately) or qualifying widow(er)	$ 800	$ 850
Single or head of household	$1,000	$1,050
Dependent's standard deduction	Cannot exceed the greater of (A) $650 or (B) the individual's earned income (usually limited to $4,150).	Cannot exceed the greater of (A) $700 or (B) earned income plus $250 (limited to $4,250).
Nanny tax	Wage threshold for paying Social Security and federal unemployment taxes on domestic workers is $1,000 annually.	Wage threshold for paying Social Security and federal unemployment taxes on domestic workers raised to $1,100 annually.

Revenue Reconciliation Act of 1990

After much-publicized posturing, confrontation, and negotiation, Congress passed the Act on October 27 and President Bush signed the measure on November 5. The emphasis was on increased taxes for the wealthy, with the top regular tax rate set at 31 percent. Moreover, high-income individuals were faced with the reduction or elimination of their personal exemption deductions. For consumers, a 10 percent luxury excise tax was established for high-priced items such as cars, boats, airplanes, furs, and jewelry. And if tax preferences abound for an individual, the alternative minimum tax rate was increased from 21 to 24 percent. Low-income taxpayers received some tax relief by an increase in the earned income tax credit; however, all taxpayers must bear the burden of significant increases in the excise taxes on alcoholic beverages, tobacco, and gasoline.

Revenue Reconciliation Act of 1993

President Clinton signed into law the Revenue Reconciliation Act of 1993 in August 1993. The Act significantly raised the tax rates for high-income taxpayers. A 36 percent bracket was created and a 39.6 percent rate was imposed on taxable incomes in excess of $250,000. Also, the cap of $135,000 on the Medicare Hospital Insurance tax was removed. The 2.9 percent tax is now imposed on all wages and self-employment income.

Tax Bills of 1996

A number of tax bills were signed into law in 1996. President Clinton signed:

1. Taxpayer Bill of Rights 2, July 30, 1996.
2. Small Business Job Protection Act, August 20, 1996.
3. Health Insurance Portability and Accountability Act, August 21, 1996.
4. Personal Responsibility and Work Opportunity Reconciliation Act, August 22, 1996.

The Small Business Job Protection Act contains a number of important provisions. The Act provides for more generous equipment write-offs for small business, a new type of pension plan for companies employing 100 or fewer employees, and changes in spousal IRAs to put them in compliance with those for working spouses. The law also extends several expired or expiring provisions.

Taxpayer Relief Act of 1997

On August 5, 1997, President Clinton signed into law the Taxpayer Relief Act of 1997. The Act creates 285 new Code sections and amends 824 Code sections. Highlights of TRA '97 include:

1. Lowering the capital gains tax rates for individuals
2. Changing the long-term holding period of capital assets from more than 12 months to more than 18 months to obtain the most advantageous rate (maximum of 20 percent)

3. Instituting an exclusion of gain of up to $500,000 (joint return) in the sale of a principal residence

4. Instituting a $500 per child tax credit

5. Creating the Hope scholarship credit and lifetime learning credit

6. Expanding IRAs to include a Roth IRA and an education IRA

7. Allowing withdrawals, without penalty, from IRAs for first-time homebuyers and for qualified higher education expenses

8. Increasing the $600,000 exemption for estates to $1 million over the next nine years (to 2006)

Table 8 presents the major changes in the new tax laws that affect individuals.

Table 8   TAXPAYER RELIEF ACT OF 1997

Item	Old Law	New Law
Capital Gains	Capital assets held for more than 12 months were taxed at 28%.	The top capital gains rate of 28% is lowered to 20%. For taxpayers in the 15% bracket, the maximum long-term capital gains tax rate is 10%. Not all gains benefit from the new rate. Gain from sale of collectibles continues to be taxed at 28%. Also, gain attributable to depreciation deductions on sale of nonresidential real estate must be recaptured at 25%.
Sale of a Principal Residence	The gain on the sale of a personal residence could be rolled over to a new residence if the taxpayer was trading-up. A once in a lifetime exclusion of $125,000 was available to taxpayers age 55 or over.	The $125,000 exclusion is no longer available on sales of principal residences on or after August 5, 1997, unless there was a binding contract in effect on or before August 5, 1997, or the taxpayer had purchased a new residence on or before August 5, 1997. Effective for sales originating after May 6, 1997, homeowners of any age may exclude from income up to $500,000 (joint return), and the exclusion is reusable every two years. Also, there is no age requirement for this exclusion.
Individual Retirement Accounts (IRAs)	A 10% penalty for withdrawals before age 59-1/2.	Early withdrawals (pre-age 59-1/2) are allowed, without penalty, for first-time homebuyers and for qualified higher education expenses.
Roth IRA	Not included under old law.	A Roth IRA allows for the tax-free buildup of an IRA. Contributions to the Roth IRA are with after-tax dollars. However, qualified withdrawals from the Roth IRA are tax-free and are available to middle- and upper-middle-income taxpayers. Up to $4,000 per year per couple may be contributed to the Roth IRA.

Table 8   TAXPAYER RELIEF ACT OF 1997—Continued

Item	Old Law	New Law
Education Tax Incentives	Not included under old law.	*Hope Scholarship Credit*—Allowed for the first two years of postsecondary education for qualified tuition and related expenses. The maximum credit is $1,500 for each eligible student for the first two years of postsecondary education. *Lifetime Learning Credit*—For expenses paid after June 30, 1998, a credit of 20% that could be applied to the first $5,000 of qualified expenses through the year 2002 and to the first $10,000 thereafter. The tax credit applies to college juniors and seniors, graduate students, or working Americans pursuing job-skill training. *Education IRA*—Allows taxpayers to make non-deductible contributions of up to $500 per child per year, subject to a phase-out range, to an education IRA. The buildup would be tax free, as would be the withdrawal.
Child Tax Credit	Not included under old law.	Taxpayers will be allowed a tax credit of $400 beginning in 1998 and $500 thereafter. The credit is available for dependent children under age 17. The credit is phased out for taxpayers at higher levels.
Estate Tax	An estate was allowed a $600,000 unified tax exemption.	The $600,000 exemption increases to $1 million over the next nine years (to 2006). For decedents dying in 1998, the exemption is $625,000.

Underlying Rationale of the Federal Income Tax

¶ 1171   OBJECTIVES OF THE TAX LAW

The federal income tax is comprised of a complicated and continually evolving blend of legislative provisions, administrative pronouncements, and judicial decisions. The primary purpose of the tax law is obviously to raise revenue, but social, political, and economic objectives are also extremely important. These various objectives, which frequently work at cross-purposes with the revenue raising objective of the law, must be examined and understood to gain an appreciation of the rationale underlying the immense multipurpose body of law known as the federal income tax.

It is easy to criticize the entire tax law for being too complex. However, any time one law attempts to raise revenue and achieve a variety of social, political, and economic objectives, while simultaneously attempting to be equitable to all income levels and administratively feasible for the government to enforce, it cannot avoid being complex.

Tax loopholes are frequently attacked as being counterproductive to the revenue raising objective of the Treasury because they cost the U.S. government billions of dollars in lost revenue. However, some of these so-called loopholes can be thought of as tax incentives, enacted by Congress to encourage certain types of investment, or to achieve specified social, economic, or political objectives.

For example, the tax law provides that interest from municipal bonds is generally excluded from gross income, while interest received from all other sources, including savings accounts and corporate obligations, is subject to taxation. The municipal bond provision thus offers excellent tax benefits for individuals with available resources to invest, but these bonds typically provide a lower yield than corporate obligations.

Primarily because of this tax benefit, municipal bonds are a popular type of investment for wealthy taxpayers. To better evaluate the criticism that municipal bonds are a tax loophole, the probable tax consequences of this type of investment can be examined in the case of a taxpayer in the 39.6 percent marginal tax bracket.

Example 1.2. The taxpayer has $50,000 available to invest. After evaluating the pros and cons of stocks, bonds, money market certificates, and other types of investments, the taxpayer's decision is limited to the following two choices:

Freemont Highway municipal bonds, rate of interest 9%
Data-Search Inc., corporate bonds, rate of interest 12%

	Freemont	Data-Search
Interest income (before taxes)	$4,500	$6,000
Income taxes	0	2,376
Yield (after taxes)	$4,500	$3,624

Result. The taxpayer will select the Freemont municipal bonds. Even with a lower rate of interest than the corporate obligations, Freemont provides a larger after-tax yield.

A common but simplistic criticism of this tax provision is that the wealthy individual has used a loophole to avoid $1,672 of taxes ($4,500 interest × 39.6 percent tax rate), thereby depriving the U.S. government of a corresponding amount of revenue. However, this criticism must be weighed against the underlying purpose of the municipal bond provision which is encouraging taxpayers to invest in state and local obligations and allowing the various municipalities to compete for resources in the bond market at a lower rate of interest than corporate bonds.

¶ 1175 ECONOMIC FACTORS

Over the years, numerous provisions of the tax law have been employed to help stimulate the economy, to encourage capital investment, or to direct resources to selected business activities. Perhaps the most well-known provision of the tax law, designed to serve as a stimulus to the economy, was the investment tax credit. This credit, which served to encourage investment in qualified property, primarily tangible personal property used in a trade or business, had been suspended for a period of time, repealed, reinstated, and again repealed.

Similar to its use of the investment credit, Congress has used depreciation write-offs as a means of controlling the economy. Viewed as a popular stimulus for business investment is the tax benefit resulting from the accelerated cost recovery methods of depreciation. Additionally, the related election to expense allows the taxpayer to deduct as much as $18,500 of the cost of qualifying property in the year of purchase. However, where the cost of qualified property placed in service during the year exceeds $200,000, the $18,500 ceiling is reduced by the amount of such excess.

Various other tax provisions have been employed to help stimulate selected industries. Thus, unique tax benefits, such as the provisions for percentage depletion, apply to the mining of natural resources. Correspondingly, farming activities benefit from special elections to expense rather than capitalize soil and water conservation expenditures under an approved conservation plan.

Small business investment has been encouraged by various provisions. For example, certain types of small businesses may elect to file as an S corporation, which essentially provides the limited liability protection of corporate status, while treating most items of income as if the entity were a partnership. Correspondingly, a special rule allows ordinary loss treatment for small business stock.

Even the tax rate structure for regular corporations encourages small business. The current corporate tax brackets are as follows:

Taxable Income					
Over	But not over:	Pay	+	%	of Excess over:
$ 0	$ 50,000	$ 0	15		$ 0
50,000	75,000	7,500	25		50,000
75,000	100,000	13,750	34		75,000
100,000	335,000	22,250	39		100,000
335,000	10,000,000	113,900	34		335,000
10,000,000	15,000,000	3,400,000	35		10,000,000
15,000,000	18,333,333	5,150,000	38		15,000,000
18,333,333	—	6,416,667	35		18,333,333

Phaseout of graduated rate benefits. An additional 5 percent rate is incorporated into the rate schedule above in order to phase out benefits of the graduated rates up to 34 percent. Thus, the graduated rate benefits are phased out between $100,000 and $335,000 of taxable income by increasing the maximum 34 percent rate to 39 percent. Similarly, to phase out the benefit of the 34 percent bracket, the tax rate on income between $15,000,000 and $18,333,333 increases from the maximum rate of 35 percent to 38 percent.

¶ 1181　SOCIAL FACTORS

Numerous tax provisions can best be explained in light of their underlying social objectives. For example, premiums paid by an employer on group-term insurance plans are not treated as additional compensation to the employees. This provision encourages business investment in group-term insurance and provides benefits to the family of a deceased employee. Also, social considerations provide the rationale for excluding employer-paid premiums on accident and health plans or the premiums on medical benefit plans from an employee's gross income.

Deferred compensation plans allow an individual to defer taxation on current income until retirement. The preferential tax treatment is an attempt to encourage private retirement plans to supplement the Social Security benefits. Other socially motivated tax provisions include the deduction for charitable contributions, the child care credit for working parents, and the credit for the elderly.

Frequently, social considerations help to explain a tax provision that discourages certain types of activities. For example, even though an individual may have incurred a fine or a penalty while engaged in a regular business activity, no deduction is allowed for this type of expenditure. The basis underlying this Congressional policy is that by allowing such a deduction, the law would be implicitly condoning and encouraging such activities. Correspondingly, bribes to government officials and illegal kickbacks or rebates are not deductible, even if related to the active conduct of one's trade or business.

¶ 1185　POLITICAL FACTORS

Since the tax law is created by Congress, and Congress consists of several hundred elected officials, political factors play a major role in the development of tax legislation. Special interest groups frequently seek to influence tax legislation, while Congressmen themselves are often likely to introduce legislation which would be of particular benefit to their own district or, perhaps, to selected constituents. Of course, special interest legislation does invite widespread criticism if it does not also serve a useful economic or social objective.

As with the economic and social objectives, many politically inspired provisions have been designed in a negative context to discourage certain types of activities. Thus, provisions such as the alternative minimum tax, which imposes an alternative tax rate on taxable income increased by tax preference items, the limitation on investment interest expense, or the accumulated earnings restrictions on corporations can be explained on this basis.

¶ 1187   TAX POLICY AND REFORM MEASURES

If there has been a trend through the years in tax statutes, it has been toward reform. The word "reform" itself first appeared in the popular name of the tax act entitled Tax Reform Act of 1969, but the concept of reform had begun to take shape long before and the enactment of reform measures has continued unabated through the years.

During the later part of the 1980s, various changes in the tax law, especially the passage of the Tax Reform Act of 1986, have resulted in the most dramatic tax modifications in tax policy since the enactment of the Internal Revenue Code of 1913. For the first time in 73 years, Congress attempted to address the broad public-policy implications of the entire tax law. In undertaking the revision of 1986, Congress sorted through a massive panorama of loopholes, inequities, and antiquated provisions and eliminated provisions that had lost much of their original social, political, or economic purpose.

Clearly, the tax policy implications of the 1986 revision will be under examination for some time to come. A major impact can be expected on the manner in which individuals and businesses save, invest, earn, and spend their money. For example, with the curtailment of the deduction for contributions to individual retirement accounts (IRAs), high-yield securities such as dividend-paying blue chip stocks, corporate bonds, and "municipals" might become more attractive investments than growth stocks. In fact, many wage earners may find it advantageous to pay taxes on their entire salary, rather than investing in a deferred compensation plan if they anticipate future increases in their marginal tax rates. Correspondingly, with the elimination of the consumer interest deduction, many individuals may shift to making cash purchases instead of incurring nondeductible obligations. Of course, some homeowners may be tempted to circumvent these restrictive provisions by using home equity loans to finance consumer purchases.

The Taxpayer Relief Act of 1997 cut taxes in a fashion that had not been seen since 1981. The reduction of capital gains tax rates will have a significant impact on investment strategies.

The student of tax law can anticipate frequent if not annual changes to the way individuals and businesses are taxed. The source of tax revenue to finance the operation of the federal government during the next decade will be a hotly debated issue. Some tax policymakers will promote new taxation schemes, such as a consumption tax, while others will advocate a tax policy that is revenue-neutral and neutral as to its impact on various income groups.

Basic Tax Concepts

¶ 1195　ESSENTIAL TAX TERMS DEFINED

When studying federal income taxation, it is important to keep in mind several basic tax concepts. By understanding these basic concepts unique to federal taxation, the course will be more interesting and meaningful. Because some of the terms set out below have definitions peculiar to income taxation, it is advisable that they be carefully examined before proceeding to the discussion of specific topics. Refer to the Glossary of Tax Terms in the back of the book for a comprehensive listing of tax terms discussed throughout the text.

Accrual basis of accounting

The *accrual* basis is distinguished from the *cash* basis. On the accrual basis, income is accounted for as and when it is earned, whether or not it has been collected. Expenses are deducted when they are incurred, whether or not paid in the same period. In determining when the expenses of an accrual-basis taxpayer are incurred, the all-events test is applied. Such test provides that the expenses are deductible in the year in which all of the events have occurred that determine the fact of liability and the amount of the liability can be determined with reasonable accuracy. Generally, all of the events that establish liability for an amount, for the purpose of determining whether such amount has been incurred, are treated as not occurring any earlier than the time that economic performance occurs.

Assignment of income doctrine

The assignment of income by an individual who retains the right of ownership to the property has generally proved ineffective as a tax-shifting procedure. For the assignment to be effective, a gift of the property would be necessary. For example, Ben is preparing to attend Major State College. As a means of paying for room and board, his father assigns to Ben his salary. This is an invalid assignment of income and Ben's father would be liable for the tax. In *Lucas v. Earl*, 2 USTC ¶ 496, 281 U.S. 111-115, 50 S.Ct. 241 (1930), the Supreme Court ruled that the government could "tax salaries to those who earned them and provide that the tax could not be escaped by anticipatory arrangements and contracts however skillfully devised to prevent the salary when paid from vesting even for a second in the man who earned it." Also, in this case the Court stated that "no distinction can be taken according to the motives leading to the arrangement by which the fruits are attributed to a different tree from that on which they grew."

Basis

The basis of property is the cost of such property. It usually means the amount of cash paid for the property and the fair market value of other property provided in the transaction.

Example 1.3. An individual paid $4,000 for an automobile and assumed a $1,500 loan on the car; thus, the basis in the automobile is $5,500.

Example 1.4. An individual paid $500,000 for a tract of land and a building. Purchase commissions, legal and recording fees, surveys, transfer taxes, title insurance, and charges for installation of utilities amounted to $70,000. The basis of the property would be $570,000. Any amounts owed by the seller and assumed by the buyer are included in the basis of the property.

The definition and the determination of "basis" are of utmost importance because it is that figure which is usually used for depreciation and the determination of gain or loss. If property was acquired by gift, inheritance, or in exchange for other property, special rules for finding its basis apply.

Business purpose

When a transaction occurs it must be grounded in a business purpose other than tax avoidance. Tax avoidance is not a proper motive for being in business. The concept of business purpose was originally set forth in *Gregory v. Helvering,* 35-1 USTC ¶ 9043, 293 U.S. 465, 55 S.Ct. 266 (1935). In this case, the Supreme Court ruled that a transaction aiming at tax-free status had no business purpose. Further, the Court stated that merely transferring assets from one corporation to another under a plan which can be associated with neither firm was invalid. This was merely a series of legal transactions that when viewed by the Court in its entirety had no business purpose.

Capital asset

Everything owned and used for personal purposes, pleasure, or investment is a capital asset. Examples of capital assets are stocks, bonds, a residence, household furnishings, a pleasure automobile, gems and jewelry, gold, silver, etc. Capital assets do not include inventory, accounts or notes receivable, depreciable property, real property, works created by personal efforts (copyrights), and U.S. publications.

Cash basis

The cash basis is one of the two principal recognized methods of accounting. It must be used by all taxpayers who do not keep books. As to all other taxpayers (except corporations, certain partnerships, and tax-exempt trusts) it is elective, except that it may not be used if inventories are necessary in order to reflect income. On the cash basis, income is reported only as it is received, in money or other property having a fair market value, and expenses are deductible only in the year that they are paid.

Claim of right

The term claim of right asks whether cash or property received by an individual to which the individual does not have full claim and which the individual might have to return in the future must be included in income. The question here is whether the taxpayer must report the income when received or wait until the taxpayer has full right to it. In *North American Oil Consolidated v. Burnet,* 3 USTC ¶ 943, 286 U.S. 417 (1932), the Supreme Court resolved the question by stating that amounts received by an individual under a claim of right must be included in gross income even though the individual might have to refund the amount at a later time.

Conduits

Some entities are not tax paying. They pass through their income (loss) to owners (beneficiaries). A partnership is an example of a conduit. Partnerships do not pay taxes; they merely report the partnership's taxable income or losses. The income (loss) flows directly to the partners. However, partnerships do compute partnership taxable income. Other types of conduits are grantor trusts and S corporations.

Constructive-receipt doctrine

When a cash-basis individual receives income, or it is credited to an account the individual may draw upon, or it is set aside for the individual, the courts have ruled that the individual has constructively received the income. This concept was developed to stop taxpayers from choosing the year in which to recognize income. Once an individual has an absolute right to the income, it must be recognized. A good example of the constructive receipt doctrine is interest earned on a bank account. If interest is credited to the taxpayer's account, it is of no consequence that the taxpayer does not withdraw the money. The day the interest is credited to the account is the day the taxpayer must include the amount in income.

Entity

Generally, for tax purposes there are four types of entities: individuals, corporations, trusts, and estates. Each entity determines its own tax and files its own tax return. Each tax entity has its specific rules to follow for the determination of taxable income. Basically the concept of "entity" answers the question "Who is the taxpayer?" Note that partnerships were not in the list of entities. For tax purposes, partnerships are not tax-paying entities. The income (loss) flows directly to the partners.

Gross income

Gross income, for income tax purposes, refers to all income that is taxable. The law enumerates specific items of income that are not to be included in gross income and, therefore, are nontaxable. With these exceptions, all income is includible in gross income.

Holding period

The holding period of property is the length of time that the property has been held by the taxpayer, or the length of time that the taxpayer is treated for income tax purposes as having held it. The term is most important for income tax purposes as it relates to capital gains transactions. Whether a capital gain or loss is short or long term depends on whether the asset sold or exchanged has been held by the taxpayer for more than 12 months or 18 months. The maximum tax rate for property held more than 18 months is 20 percent, while the maximum rate of 28 percent is applied to property held more than 12 months but not more than 18 months.

Income

The fundamental concept of income is set forth in the Sixteenth Amendment—"incomes, from whatever source derived." It is the gain derived from capital, labor, or both. For tax purposes the term "income" is not used alone. The most common usages are gross income, adjusted gross income, and taxable income.

Income-shifting

Income-shifting is the transfer of income from one family member to another who is subject to a lower tax rate or the selection of a form of business that decreases the tax liability for its owners.

Pay-as-you-go tax system

The American tax system is often referred to as a pay-as-you-go tax system. Much of the federal government's tax collections come from withholdings and estimated taxes. The various types of taxpayers pay tax throughout the year, not just at year-end. The United States has been on a pay-as-you-go system since 1943.

Realized v. recognized gain or loss

A gain or loss is realized when a transaction is completed. However, not all realized gains and losses are taxed (recognized). A recognized gain or loss occurs when a taxpayer is obligated to pay tax on a completed transaction.

Substance v. form

Individuals should arrange their financial transactions in a manner that will minimize their tax liability. If a transaction is all it purports to be and not merely a transaction to avoid taxes, then it is valid. If the transaction is solely to avoid taxes and there is no business purpose to the transaction, then it is invalid. The fact that a taxpayer uses one form of transaction rather than another to minimize taxes does not invalidate the transaction. A good example of when substance v. form is a significant issue is in the area of leases. Payments under a lease are tax deductible. Payments under a purchase agreement are not tax deductible. Therefore, it is of utmost importance to determine the true "substance" of this type of transaction. Questions to be asked might include: Do any equity rights transfer to the lessee at the end of the lease period? May the lessee buy the property at a nominal purchase price? With a lease transaction it is immaterial that the parties refer to the transaction as a lease. The true substance of the transaction controls over the form.

Tax benefit rule

A recovery is includible in income only to the extent that the deduction reduced tax in any prior year by any amount. Therefore, where a deduction reduced taxable income but did not reduce tax, the recovery amount is excludable from income. This rule applies to both corporate and noncorporate taxpayers.

Taxable income

Taxable income for a corporation is gross income minus all deductions allowable, including special deductions such as the one for dividends received. Taxable income for individuals who itemize deductions is equal to adjusted gross income minus personal exemptions, minus the greater of itemized deductions or the standard deduction amount. For taxpayers who do not itemize, taxable income is adjusted gross income minus personal exemptions minus the standard deduction.

Wherewithal to pay

The concept that the taxpayer should be taxed on a transaction when he or she has the means to pay the tax. For example, a taxpayer owns property that is increasing in value. The IRS does not tax the increased value until the taxpayer sells the property. At the time of sale, the taxpayer has the wherewithal to pay.

SUMMARY OF CHAPTER 1

✓   Taxes are indeed big business. The Internal Revenue Service collected $1,486,546,674 in 1996.

✓   Individuals contributed over 50 percent of all taxes raised by the IRS.

✓   Corporations contributed approximately 13 percent of all taxes raised by the IRS.

✓   The Taxpayer Relief Act of 1997 had a major impact on the taxation of capital gains, individual retirement accounts, estate taxes, education credits, and the sale of a personal residence.

✓   A basic understanding of tax terminology will help business leaders run their corporations.

CHAPTER 1 QUESTIONS AND PROBLEMS

1. Clearly, individuals are carrying a much heavier tax burden than corporations. Is this justified?

2. Some economists have argued that corporate taxes should be eliminated and only individuals should be taxed. Explain.

3. Discuss excise tax when used as a measure for social control (i.e., tax on alcohol and gasoline).

4. Why is the value-added tax (VAT) considered regressive?

5. How might the VAT be used to balance the budget?

6. What is the test which distinguishes between tax avoidance and tax evasion?

7. If your interest is in tax avoidance, name several types of investments that will lower your tax liability.

8. "The tax evader is a criminal." Support or refute this statement.

9. Discuss the badges of fraud.

10. What is meant by the term "tax gap"?

11. Why is income-shifting considered such a major tax planning concept?

12. What was the constitutional impediment to income taxation prior to the Sixteenth Amendment?

13. The federal taxing system has tried to reflect changes in society and lifestyles. Give three examples.

14. What was the purpose of the Sixteenth Amendment?

15. Of what importance is the date March 1, 1913?

16. Where must revenue legislation originate?

17. Which committees of Congress are responsible for revenue legislation?

18. What is the purpose of the Joint Conference Committee?

19. The legislative process of a tax bill begins with the:
    a. House Ways and Means Committee
    b. President
    c. Senate Finance Committee
    d. Any of the above

20. The Sixteenth Amendment granted Congress the right to:
    a. Create progressive tax rates
    b. Create a value-added tax
    c. Tax income from whatever source derived
    d. Impose a national property tax

21. The value-added tax has great appeal to politicians because:

     a.   It has the potential to raise large sums of money.

     b.   It taxes the rich and not the poor.

     c.   It is progressive in nature.

     d.   All of the above.

22. An attractive characteristic of the personal income tax is:

     a.   It does not tax the poor.

     b.   It is equitable.

     c.   It is free from loopholes.

     d.   It has the ability to raise a considerable amount of money.

23. The Tax Reform Act of 1986:

     a.   Amended the Internal Revenue Code of 1954

     b.   Replaced the Internal Revenue Code of 1954 with the Internal Revenue Code of 1986

     c.   Replaced the Internal Revenue Code of 1954 with the Internal Revenue Code of 1987

     d.   Was found to be unconstitutional by the Supreme Court in 1987

24. The Tax Reform Act of 1986 did all of the following except:

     a.   Reduce the number of corporate tax rates

     b.   Reduce the number of individual tax brackets

     c.   Institute a taxpayer's bill of rights

     d.   Index "bracket creep"

25. The Revenue Reconciliation Act of 1993 did all of the following except:

     a.   Increase individual tax rates

     b.   Increase corporate tax rates

     c.   Increase the alternative minimum tax

     d.   Eliminate the phaseout of personal exemptions

26. The Taxpayer Relief Act of 1997 did all of the following except:

     a.   Create multiple capital gain tax rates

     b.   Create an education tax credit

     c.   Reduce individual tax rates

     d.   Create the Roth IRA

27. Which item listed below is *not* a capital asset?

     a.   Stocks

     b.   Pleasure automobile

     c.   Bonds

     d.   Depreciable property

28. Major features of conduits are:
    a. Pass through their income to owners
    b. Need not file income tax returns
    c. Need not pay taxes
    d. Both (a) and (c) above

29. What are the five major provisions of the Taxpayer Relief Act of 1997?

30. What is the Hope credit?

31. *Research Problem.* The following case highlights the right of the taxpayer to select among legitimate business alternatives in order to avoid taxes. Read the case and prepare a written brief.

    Peterson & Pegau Baking Co., 2 BTA 637 (1925), CCH Dec. 775.

Chapter 2

Individual Taxation—
An Overview

Learning Objectives

After completing Chapter 2, you should be able to:

1. Understand the components of the tax formula.
2. Apply the standard deduction to each filing status.
3. Determine whether an individual qualifies as a personal exemption.
4. Distinguish among the five different filing statuses.
5. Apply the tax tables and the tax rate schedules to taxable income.

OVERVIEW OF CHAPTER

This chapter discusses the components of the tax formula and studies the implications of the standard deduction to the taxpayer. Additionally, the qualifications for the personal exemption are analyzed. Finally, the basic filing statuses are examined as well as the role of the tax tables and the tax rate schedules.

Components of the Tax Formula

Taxable income is computed using one of the two overall accounting methods, the cash method or the accrual method. It is also possible to use a combination of the two overall methods. Under the cash method, income is reported when it is received and deductions are taken when the expense is paid. The accrual method requires income to be reported when all the events necessary to fix the right to receive payment have occurred and there is reasonable certainty regarding the amount. Likewise, accrual basis taxpayers usually claim a deduction in the year in which all events that fix the liability have occurred, provided the amount of the liability is reasonably determinable.

A basic understanding of the method used to calculate the tax liability is a necessity in the study of federal income taxation. That method is as follows:

> Gross Income
> — Deductions for Adjusted Gross Income
>
> = Adjusted Gross Income
> — Greater of Itemized Deductions or Standard Deduction
> — Personal Exemptions
>
> = Taxable Income
> × Tax Rate
>
> = Tax Liability
> — Tax Credits and Prepayments
>
> = Net Tax Due or Refund

¶ 2001   GROSS INCOME

Gross income includes all items of income from whatever source unless specifically excluded. Examples of gross income include compensation for services, interest, rents, royalties, dividends, and annuities. An individual's income from business is included in gross income after deducting the cost of goods sold.

The receipt of income can be in different forms such as cash, property, services, or even a forgiveness of an indebtedness. However, income is not reported by a taxpayer until it is realized.

Gross income and inclusions and exclusions will be discussed in further detail in Chapters 4 and 5.

¶ 2015   DEDUCTIONS FOR ADJUSTED GROSS INCOME

To arrive at adjusted gross income, all deductions specifically allowed by law are subtracted from gross income. Some of the items allowed as deductions for adjusted gross income include:

1. Trade or business expenses, such as advertising, depreciation, and utilities.
2. Certain reimbursed employee expenses, such as travel, transportation, and entertainment expenses.
3. Moving expenses.
4. Losses from sale or exchange of property.

These deductions are sometimes referred to as "deductions from gross income" or, since almost all the allowable deductions in this section are business expenses, the deductions are sometimes referred to as "business deductions." These deductions are discussed in Chapter 6.

¶ 2025   ADJUSTED GROSS INCOME

In the tax formula there are deductions for adjusted gross income and then deductions from adjusted gross income. It is important to take these deductions in the proper categories. Adjusted gross income is an important subtotal because certain other items are based on the amount of adjusted gross income. The credit for child and dependent care expenses along with itemized deductions for medical expenses, charitable contributions, personal casualty losses, and miscellaneous expenses are all based on adjusted gross income. The phaseouts of itemized deductions and personal exemptions are also based on adjusted gross income.

¶ 2035   ITEMIZED DEDUCTIONS v. STANDARD DEDUCTION

Itemized deductions are certain expenses of a personal nature that are specifically allowed as a deduction. Items included in this group are: medical expenses, state and local income taxes, property taxes, home mortgage interest, charitable contributions, personal casualty losses, and miscellaneous employee expenses.

Taxpayers receive the benefit of a minimum amount of itemized deductions called the standard deduction. The standard deduction is a fixed amount used to simplify the computation of the tax liability. It is also designed to eliminate lower-income individuals from the tax rolls. All taxpayers subtract the larger of their itemized deductions or the standard deduction.

The standard deduction is based on the filing status of the taxpayer and is made up of the "basic standard deduction" plus any "additional standard deduction." The standard deduction is adjusted annually, if necessary, for inflation.

Filing Status	Basic Standard Deduction 1998
Single	$4,250
Married Filing Jointly	7,100
Married Filing Separately	3,550
Head of Household	6,250
Surviving Spouse	7,100

The standard deduction is of principal benefit to moderate and low income level taxpayers since the amount is usually more than the total itemized deductions, which means that such taxpayers need not report their itemized deductions. Thus, the need to audit such returns by the IRS is substantially reduced since the opportunities for error or misstatement of taxable income are lessened.

Overall Limitation on Itemized Deductions

For tax years beginning after 1990, an individual whose adjusted gross income exceeds a threshold amount is required to reduce the amount allowable for itemized deductions by 3 percent of the excess over that threshold. For 1998, the threshold amount is $124,500 for single and joint taxpayers ($62,250 for married persons filing a separate return). These thresholds are indexed for inflation after 1991.

In no event, however, may the reduction be more than 80 percent of allowable itemized deductions, not counting the deductions for medical expenses, investment interest, casualty losses, or wagering losses to the extent of wagering gains. The reduction is applied only after first taking into account the other Code provisions that determine how much of a particular type of expense may be deducted, such as the 2 percent limitation on miscellaneous deductions.

Example 2.1. Mark and Sylvia Ward are married taxpayers who file a joint return. In 1998, they have adjusted gross income of $174,500 and preliminary itemized deductions of $18,000. Their itemized deductions consist of medical expenses ($8,000), state and local taxes ($7,000), and charitable contributions ($3,000). Their adjusted itemized deductions on their return would be $16,500, computed as follows:

Medical expenses		$ 8,000
State and local taxes	$ 7,000	
Charitable contributions	3,000	
	$10,000	
Less: 3% of AGI in excess of $124,500	1,500	8,500
Adjusted itemized deductions		$16,500

Additional Standard Deduction for Age and Blindness

An additional standard deduction is allowed aged or blind taxpayers. The additional standard deduction is the total of the additional amounts allowed for age and blindness. The dollar value of an additional amount will depend on the taxpayer's filing status. The extra standard deduction became effective for 1988 and is adjusted for inflation.

Filing Status	*Dollar Value of One Additional Amount 1998*
Single	$1,050
Married Filing Jointly............................	850
Married Filing Separately	850
Head of Household	1,050
Surviving Spouse	850

Taxpayers can receive an additional standard deduction for being both aged and blind. Thus, a married couple, both of whom are aged and blind, receive an additional standard deduction of $3,400 ($850 × 4).

Example 2.2. Rebecca Greene, 55, qualifies as a head of household in 1998. Her basic standard deduction is $6,250. She is not entitled to an additional standard deduction.

Example 2.3. Assume the same facts as in Example 2.2, except that Rebecca is 67 and legally blind. Her basic standard deduction for 1998 is $6,250. She is also entitled to an additional standard deduction of $2,100 ($1,050 for her age and $1,050 for her blindness). Her total standard deduction is $8,350.

Example 2.4. Jeffrey and Donna Dirk are both 72 and file a joint return for 1998. Donna is blind. Their basic standard deduction is $7,100. They are entitled to an additional standard deduction of

$2,550 ($850 × 2 for their age plus $850 for Donna's blindness). Their total standard deduction is $9,650.

To qualify for the old-age additional standard deduction, the taxpayer and/or spouse must be age 65 before the close of the year. For purposes of the old-age additional standard deduction, an individual attains the age of 65 on the day preceding the 65th birthday. Thus, an individual whose 65th birthday falls on January 1 in a given year attains the age of 65 on the last day of the calendar year immediately preceding.

A person is considered blind for the extra standard deduction if that person's central visual acuity does not exceed 20/200 in the better eye with correcting lenses, or if visual acuity is greater than 20/200 but is accompanied by a limitation in the fields of vision such that the widest diameter of the visual field subtends an angle no greater than 20 degrees.

If the taxpayer or spouse dies during the year, the number of additional standard deduction amounts for age or blindness is determined as of the date of death. Thus, the additional standard deduction for age will not be allowed for an individual who dies before attaining the age of 65 even though the individual would have been 65 before the close of the year.

The additional standard deductions for age 65 or older and blindness apply only to taxpayers and their spouses. No additional standard deduction amounts are allowed to taxpayers who claim an exemption for dependents who are aged or blind.

Example 2.5. Darren Davidson is single and fully supports his 70-year-old father. Darren qualifies as a head of household. Darren's regular standard deduction is $6,250 for 1998. Darren may claim a dependency exemption for his father but may not claim the additional standard deduction amount for his dependent father.

Married Taxpayers Filing Separately

All taxpayers may not be able to take the larger of itemized deductions or the standard deduction. Rules require both spouses to either itemize or use the standard deduction. If one spouse takes itemized deductions the other spouse is required to also itemize even if itemized deductions are less than the standard deduction for married individuals filing separately.

Example 2.6. Joe and Mary Bloome are married but decide to file separate returns for 1998. Joe has adjusted gross income of $30,000 and $4,800 of itemized deductions, while Mary has $25,000 of adjusted gross income and $2,500 of itemized deductions. Joe and Mary can elect not to itemize, in which case they will each use the standard deduction of $3,550. However, if they decide to itemize, Joe will have itemized deductions of $4,800 and Mary will have $2,500 of itemized deductions. Since Joe itemizes, Mary is also required to itemize.

TAX PLANNING POINTER ▼

In situations where total itemized deductions are approximately equal to the standard deduction, it is possible for cash basis taxpayers to obtain a deduction for itemized deductions in one year and to use the standard deduction the next year by proper timing of payments. For example, an individual may pay two years' church pledges in one year and nothing the next year. It may also be possible to pay real estate or city and state income tax estimated payments prior to the end of the year.

¶ 2045   PERSONAL EXEMPTIONS

From 1979 through 1984, the personal exemption was $1,000. The application of the index for inflation raised the personal exemption to $1,040 for 1985 and $1,080 for 1986. The Tax Reform Act of 1986 raised the personal exemption to $1,900 for 1987, $1,950 for 1988, and $2,000 for 1989. The personal exemption as adjusted for inflation after 1989 was raised to $2,050 for 1990, $2,150 for 1991, $2,300 for 1992, $2,350 for 1993, $2,450 for 1994, $2,500 for 1995, $2,550 for 1996, $2,650 for 1997, and becomes $2,700 for 1998.

No personal exemption amount is allowable on the return of an individual who is eligible to be claimed as a dependent on another taxpayer's return. For example, a child will not be allowed the personal exemption on his or her own return if that child is eligible to be claimed on the parent's return.

The deduction for personal exemptions is reduced or even eliminated for certain high-income taxpayers. Taxpayers whose adjusted gross income exceeds the appropriate threshold amount (based on filing status) have to reduce exemptions by 2 percent for each $2,500 of adjusted gross income or fraction thereof in excess of the threshold amount. The phaseout of the tax benefit for personal exemptions began in 1991, and the threshold amounts are adjusted for inflation (cost-of-living index adjustment). For a detailed explanation of the phaseout of personal exemptions, see ¶ 2227.

¶ 2055   TAX RATES

The tax formula implies that the "Taxable Income" figure is multiplied by the appropriate tax rate to arrive at the "Tax Liability." In reality, the "Tax Liability" is either derived from the appropriate column of the tax tables or is computed from the appropriate line in the tax rate schedules.

Prior to 1986 the maximum tax rate was 50 percent. The tax rate schedules for 1987 ranged from 11 percent to 38.5 percent. The tax rate schedules (reproduced in the Appendix) include only five tax brackets after 1992: 15 percent, 28 percent, 31 percent, 36 percent, and 39.6 percent.

¶ 2065 TAX CREDITS AND PREPAYMENTS

Any tax credits are applied against the income tax. It is significant to note the difference between a credit and a tax deduction. A deduction reduces income to which the rate applies and indirectly reduces the tax liability. A credit directly reduces the tax liability.

The principal credits include the earned income credit, child tax credit, credit for the elderly, general business credit, dependent care credit, and foreign tax credit. These credits will be discussed in further detail in Chapter 8.

The tax liability is further reduced by the amounts withheld on income and by any estimated payments made during the year. Income taxes may be withheld on the various sources of income that a taxpayer receives during the year. Employers are required to withhold income tax on compensation paid to their employees. In addition, estimated payments may be necessary if enough taxes have not been withheld.

¶ 2075 NET TAX DUE OR REFUND

The tax result after applying the credits and prepayments to the "Tax Liability" is the amount that must be paid to the Internal Revenue Service or the amount overpaid and to be refunded to the taxpayer.

¶ 2085 CLASSIFICATION OF TAXPAYERS

The Internal Revenue Code defines the term "taxpayer" as any person subject to any internal revenue act. The term "person" includes an individual, a trust, estate, partnership, association, company, or corporation. A "partnership" includes a syndicate, group, pool, joint venture, or other unincorporated venture, through or by means of which any business, financial operation, or venture is carried on and which is not a trust or estate or a corporation. The term "corporation" is not defined but is stated to include associations, joint-stock companies, and insurance companies.

A proper classification of taxpayers is essential in determining the type of tax return to be filed. Individuals have little trouble choosing the right tax return, but problems often arise with artificial entities such as trusts, estates, partnerships, corporations, and associations.

Taxpayers are usually classified according to the type of tax return that they are required to file. Excluding most information returns, which are not tax returns in the strict sense of the term, and returns for organizations exempt from income tax, almost all tax returns will fall into one of the following four categories:

TYPE OF RETURN	FORM	FILED BY
Individual	1040	Every natural person with income of statutory minimums
Corporation	1120	Corporations, including organizations taxed as corporations
Fiduciary	1041	Trusts and estates with income in excess of statutory minimums
Partnership	1065	Partnerships or joint ventures (information return only)

Personal Exemptions

In computing taxable income an individual is allowed a deduction for each personal exemption allowed. The personal exemption is $2,700 for 1998. After 1989, the personal exemption amount is indexed for inflation.

Such exemptions are (1) the exemptions for an individual taxpayer and spouse, and (2) the exemptions for dependents of the taxpayer. However, no personal exemption amount is allowed on the return of an individual who is eligible to be claimed as a dependent on another taxpayer's return.

¶ 2201   TAXPAYER AND SPOUSE

Since there are two taxpayers on a joint return, two exemptions are allowed on the return even though there may be only one individual earning income. Where a joint return is filed by the taxpayer and spouse, no other person is allowed an exemption for the spouse even if the spouse otherwise qualifies as a dependent of another person.

The taxpayer is allowed an exemption for the spouse of the taxpayer if a joint return is not filed. However, the spouse must have no income for the year and must not be the dependent of another taxpayer. Thus, a taxpayer is not entitled to an exemption for the spouse on a separate return for the year in which the spouse has any gross income even though the income is not sufficient to require the spouse to file a return.

¶ 2225   DEPENDENTS

Taxpayers are allowed to claim a personal exemption and receive a $2,700 deduction in 1998 for each dependent. To qualify as a dependent, all the following tests must be met:

1. support
2. relationship or member of the household

3. gross income
4. citizen or resident of the United States
5. no joint return filed
6. Social Security number

Support Test

Over one-half of the support of a dependent must be furnished by the taxpayer. In determining whether the taxpayer has provided over half of the support, the support received from the taxpayer as compared to the entire amount of support which the individual receives from all sources, including support which the individual supplies, will be taken into account.

In computing the amount which is contributed for the support of an individual, there must be included any amount which is contributed by the individual for his or her own support, including receipts which are excludable from gross income, such as benefits received under Social Security or money withdrawn from a savings account. However, it is only the amount actually spent on support which is taken into consideration, not the total amount available for support.

The term "support" includes food, shelter, clothing, medical and dental care, education, and similar items. Generally, the amount of an item of support will be the amount of expense incurred by the one furnishing the item. If the item of support furnished by an individual is in the form of property or lodging, it will be necessary to measure the amount of the item of support in terms of its fair market value. The value of personal services is not included in support determination. *F. Markarian*, 65-2 USTC ¶ 9755, 352 F.2d 870 (CA-7 1965), cert. denied, 384 U.S. 988, 86 S.Ct. 1886.

Where the taxpayer owns the home in which the dependent lives, the fair rental value of the lodging furnished is part of the total support. However, this does not mean an equal allocation between parents and children. It is recognized that an adult has certain minimum base housing costs which cannot be treated as equal to the minimum housing costs of minor children. In one case, the court allocated 60 percent of the housing costs to the mother and 40 percent to be divided equally among three children. *J.D.M. Cameron*, 33 TCM 725, CCH Dec. 32,654(M), T.C. Memo. 1974-166. Amounts paid to others to care for children while working are included as part of support. *T. Lovett*, 18 TC 477, CCH Dec. 19,018 (1952), acq., 1952-2 CB 2. The amount paid may also qualify for the dependent care credit.

Some capital expenditures may qualify as items of support. The cost of an automobile is counted in determining who furnished over half of a dependent's support. A television set furnished and set apart in the child's bedroom is also an item of support. Rev. Rul. *77-282, 1977-2 CB 52*.

Welfare payments made by a state agency to or on behalf of a dependent child are attributable to the agency rather than the parents. *H. Johnson*, 33 TCM 659, CCH Dec. 32,630(M), T.C. Memo. 1974-150;

H.M. Lutter, 75-1 USTC ¶ 9439, 514 F.2d 1095 (CA-7 1975), cert. denied, 423 U.S. 931, 96 S.Ct. 283. This may deny a dependency exemption to the parents since the agency may have provided more than half the support of a child. However, amounts expended by a state for training and education of handicapped children are not taken into account in determining support. This rule applies only if the institution qualifies as an "educational institution" and the residents qualify as "students." Rev. Rul. 59-379, 1959-2 CB 51, clarified by Rev. Rul. 60-190, 1960-1 CB 51. Social Security Medicare benefits are disregarded in the computation of support. Rev. Rul. 79-173, 1979-1 CB 86.

Amounts received as scholarships for study at an educational institution are not considered in determining whether the taxpayer furnishes more than one-half the support of the student. Amounts received for tuition payments and allowances by a veteran are not considered scholarships in determining the support test.

> *Example 2.7.* John has a child who receives a $4,000 scholarship to Academic University for one year. John contributes $3,000, which constitutes the balance of the child's support for that year. John may claim the child as a dependent, as the $4,000 scholarship is not counted in determining the support of the child and, therefore, John is considered as providing all the support of the child.

Relationship or Member of the Household Test

The dependent must be a relative of the taxpayer or a member of the taxpayer's household. Individuals considered to be related to the taxpayer and eligible for the dependency exemption include: an adopted child; a son or daughter or a descendant of either; stepson or stepdaughter; brother, sister, stepbrother or stepsister; father or mother or ancestor of either; stepfather or stepmother; son or daughter of a brother or sister; brother or sister of father or mother; and son-in-law, daughter-in-law, father-in-law, mother-in-law, brother-in-law, or sister-in-law. A nonrelated person must be a member of the taxpayer's household for the entire year to qualify as a dependent. The taxpayer must maintain and occupy the household. An individual is not a member of the taxpayer's household if at any time during the year the relationship between the individual and the taxpayer is in violation of local law.

The taxpayer and the dependent will be considered as occupying the household for the entire year notwithstanding temporary absences from the household due to special circumstances. A nonpermanent failure to occupy the common abode by reason of illness, education, business, vacation, military service, or a custody agreement under which the dependent is absent for less than six months in the tax year, will be considered temporary absence due to special circumstances.

The fact that the dependent dies during the year will not deprive the taxpayer of the deduction if the dependent lived in the household for the entire part of the year preceding death. Similarly, the period during the year preceding birth of an individual will not prevent the individual from qualifying as a dependent.

Gross Income Test

A taxpayer is allowed an exemption for each dependent whose gross income for the year is less than the personal exemption amount ($2,700 for 1998) or who is a child of the taxpayer and who (1) has not attained the age of 19 at the year-end or (2) is a student. The student exception applies only to students who are under the age of 24 by the year-end.

Example 2.8. Colleen Drew, age 21, earns $3,000 working part-time while attending school full-time. Her parents pay more than one-half of her support. Colleen's parents will be able to claim Colleen on their tax return even though she earned more than $2,700 in 1998 since she is under age 24.

The term "child" means a son, daughter, stepchild, adopted child, or a foster child who is a member of an individual's household if the child was placed with the individual by an authorized placement agency for legal adoption pursuant to a formal application filed by the individual with the agency.

The term "student" means an individual who, during each of five calendar months during the calendar year, is a full-time student at an educational institution. A full-time student is one who is enrolled for some part of five calendar months for the number of hours or courses which is considered to be full-time attendance. The five calendar months need not be consecutive. School attendance exclusively at night does not constitute full-time attendance. However, full-time attendance may include some attendance at night in connection with a full-time course of study.

The gross income amount is determined before the deduction for any expenses, such as materials, taxes, and depreciation. Thus, a taxpayer would not be able to claim his grandmother for 1998 if she received $2,900 in rental income, even though her expenses reduced the net income to less than $2,700. However, cost of goods sold is subtracted from gross receipts to determine gross income. Receipts which are excludable from gross income are not counted in applying the gross income test.

Citizen or Resident Test

The term "dependent" does not include any individual who is not a citizen or national of the United States unless such individual is a resident of the United States or a resident of American Samoa, Canada, or Mexico.

No Joint Return Test

No exemption will be allowed for any dependent who has filed a joint return with the dependent's spouse. However, the dependency exemption will still be allowed where a joint return is filed by a dependent and spouse merely as a claim for refund and where no tax liability would exist for either spouse on the basis of separate returns. Rev. Rul. 65-34, 1965-1 CB 86.

Social Security Number

Social Security numbers are required for all individuals who are claimed as dependents. Failure to include the Social Security number or other required information can result in the loss of the exemption.

Multiple Support Agreements

Special rules allow a taxpayer to be treated as having contributed over half of the support of an individual where two or more taxpayers contributed to the support of the individual if (1) no one person contributed over half of the individual's support, (2) each member of the group which collectively contributed more than half of the support of the individual would have been entitled to claim the individual as a dependent except for the fact that they did not contribute more than one-half of the support, (3) the member of the group claiming the individual as a dependent contributed more than 10 percent of the individual's support, and (4) each other person in the group who contributed more than 10 percent of the support files a written declaration that they will not claim the individual as a dependent for the year.

> *Example 2.9.* Brothers Alfred, Bill, Chuck, and Don contributed the entire support of their mother in the following percentages: Alfred, 30 percent; Bill, 20 percent; Chuck, 29 percent; and Don, 21 percent. Any one of the brothers, except for the fact that he did not contribute more than half of her support, would have been entitled to claim his mother as a dependent. Consequently, any one of the brothers could claim a deduction for the exemption of the mother provided a written declaration from each of the brothers is attached to the return.

If, in the above example, Don were a neighbor instead of a brother, he would not qualify as a member of the group for multiple support agreement purposes. He would not be eligible to claim the mother since she was not a member of Don's household. Don would not be required to sign the multiple support agreement.

Divorced or Separated Parents

When taxpayers are divorced or legally separated, special rules apply to determine which one is entitled to exemptions for their children. These rules may result in a taxpayer who did not provide more than half of the support of the child being entitled to the exemption.

To qualify, the parents must be divorced or legally separated under a decree of divorce or separate maintenance, separated under a written separation agreement, or lived apart at all times during the last six months of the year. In addition, both parents together must provide more than one-half of the child's support. The child must be in the custody of one or both parents for more than one-half of the calendar year. Thus, a dependency exemption may not be claimed by one of the parents if a person other than the parents provides one-half or more for the support of the child during the year or has custody of the child for one half or more of the year.

As a general rule, a child will be treated as receiving over half of the support from the parent having custody for a greater portion of the year. If the parents of the child are divorced or separated for only a portion of a year after having joint custody for the prior portion of the year, the parent who has custody for the greater portion of the remainder of the year after divorce or separation will be treated as having custody for a greater portion of the year.

Example 2.10. Bill, a child of Jim and Cathy Durell, who were divorced on June 1, received $5,000 for support during the year, of which $2,200 was provided by Jim and $1,900 by Cathy. No multiple support agreement was entered into. Prior to the divorce, Jim and Cathy jointly had custody of Bill. For the remainder of the year, Jim had custody of Bill for the months of October through December, while Cathy had custody of Bill for the months of June through September. Since Cathy had custody for four of the seven months following the divorce, she is the custodial parent for the year and is treated as having provided over half of the support for Bill for the year.

Post-1984 Divorces

For divorces taking place in years after 1984, the custodial parent is entitled to the exemption in all cases unless he or she expressly waives the right to the exemption. This may be done by the custodial parent signing a written declaration that he or she will not claim the exemption. The noncustodial parent is required to attach this declaration to his or her tax return each year when claiming the exemption. Failure to attach Form 8332, Release of Claim to Exemption for Child of Divorced or Separated Parents, means that the noncustodial parent cannot claim the exemption, regardless of the amount of support furnished.

Form **8332** (Rev. June 1996) Department of the Treasury Internal Revenue Service	**Release of Claim to Exemption for Child of Divorced or Separated Parents** ▶ ATTACH to noncustodial parent's return **EACH YEAR** exemption claimed.	OMB No. 1545-0915 Attachment Sequence No. **51**
Name(s) of parent claiming exemption		Social security number

Part I Release of Claim to Exemption for Current Year

I agree not to claim an exemption for_____
                                          Name(s) of child (or children)

for the tax year 19_____ .

_____   _____   _____
Signature of parent releasing claim to exemption   Social security number   Date

If you choose not to claim an exemption for this child (or children) for future tax years, complete Part II.

Part II Release of Claim to Exemption for Future Years *(If completed, see Noncustodial Parent below.)*

I agree not to claim an exemption for_____
                                          Name(s) of child (or children)

for the tax year(s)_____ .
                   (Specify. See instructions.)

_____   _____   _____
Signature of parent releasing claim to exemption   Social security number   Date

Pre-1985 Divorces

For divorces taking place prior to 1985, a child is treated as receiving over half of the support from the parent who is not the custodial parent and the noncustodial parent is entitled to the dependency exemption if certain conditions are met. A noncustodial parent who provides at least $600 for the support of a child during the year is treated as having provided more than half the support of the child if the decree of divorce or of separate maintenance or an applicable written agreement between the parents provides that the noncustodial parent is entitled to the personal exemption. The noncustodial parent must provide at least $600 for the support of each child claimed as a dependent.

> *Example 2.11.* Ricky Reeves received all of his support of $1,000 during the year from his parents, Mike and Nancy, who are separated under a written separation agreement allowing Mike the personal exemption for Ricky. Nancy had custody of Ricky for the entire year, but under the agreement Mike was to provide $600 for the support of Ricky. Mike, in fact, provided only $550 for the support of Ricky during the year. Nancy is treated as having provided over half the support for Ricky for the year. Even though Mike paid over half of Ricky's support, Mike did not meet the $600 requirement for a noncustodial parent.

> *Example 2.12.* Darlene and Steve Morgan were divorced in 1982. Darlene has custody of their only child for the entire year. The divorce decree states that Steve must pay the entire support of the child but does not mention which parent is entitled to the personal exemption. Darlene is entitled to claim the personal exemption for the child because she is the custodial parent, even though Steve paid the entire support of the child. However, Darlene can sign a Form 8332 to allow Steve to claim the personal exemption for the child.

Amounts expended for the support of a child are treated as received from the noncustodial parent to the extent that the noncustodial parent provided amounts for the support of the child. This rule applies whether or not the amounts are actually expended for child support.

> *Example 2.13.* The parents of a child are divorced in 1983 with the mother having custody of the child. The father provides the mother with $3,500 in child support payments. The divorce decree gives the personal exemption to the father. He is entitled to the personal exemption whether or not the mother uses the $3,500 toward the child's support.

KEYSTONE PROBLEM

The personal exemption reduces taxable income by $2,700 in 1998. In certain situations, such as multiple support agreements and children of divorced parents, it is possible to assign the personal exemption for a dependent to one of the eligible parties. What should be taken into consideration in determining which party should receive the personal exemption?

¶ 2227 HIGH-INCOME TAXPAYERS—PHASEOUT OF EXEMPTIONS

For tax years beginning after 1990, the deduction for personal exemptions is reduced or even eliminated for certain high-income taxpayers. If a taxpayer's adjusted gross income exceeds the appropriate threshold amount (based on filing status) below, the deduction for exemptions is reduced by 2 percent for each $2,500 or fraction thereof by which the adjusted gross income exceeds the threshold amount. In the case of a married person filing separately, the exemption deduction is reduced by 2 percent for each $1,250 or fraction thereof by which such adjusted gross income exceeds the threshold amount. In no case will the deduction for exemptions be reduced by more than 100 percent.

For 1998, the threshold amounts (adjusted annually for inflation) are as follows:

Joint return or a surviving spouse	$186,800
Head of household	155,650
Single taxpayer	124,500
Married person filing a separate return..........	93,400

The deduction for personal exemptions will be fully eliminated when adjusted gross income exceeds the threshold amount by more than $122,500.

Example 2.14. Assume a married couple with four personal exemptions has $230,300 in adjusted gross income. The couple's personal exemption deduction would be computed as follows:

Adjusted gross income......................	$	230,300
Threshold for phaseout		− 186,800
Excess over threshold	$	43,500
Each $2,500.............................		÷ 2,500
Number of $2,500s		17.4
Number of $2,500s or fractions thereof		18
Phaseout rate		2%
Reduction in personal exemptions		36%
Personal exemption amount	$	2,700
Personal exemptions (4)		× 4
Initial personal exemption deduction	$	10,800
Personal exemption percent allowed		× 64%
Personal exemption deduction	$	6,912

Filing Status and Requirements

The tax liability of an individual not only varies with the amount of income but also depends upon marital status.

Taxpayers must determine their income tax liability from among five different filing statuses:

1. Married individuals filing jointly
2. Married individuals filing separate returns
3. Single individuals
4. Heads of households
5. Surviving spouses

Filing Status			
	1		Single
	2		Married filing joint return (even if only one had income)
	3		Married filing separate return. Enter spouse's social security no. above and full name here. ▶ _____
Check only one box.	**4**		Head of household (with qualifying person). (See page 10.) If the qualifying person is a child but not your dependent, enter this child's name here. ▶ _____
	5		Qualifying widow(er) with dependent child (year spouse died ▶ 19____). (See page 10.)

A married taxpayer meeting the "abandoned spouse" requirements may be considered as an unmarried person for tax purposes. These requirements are: (1) the taxpayer must file a separate return, (2) the taxpayer's spouse cannot be a member of the household during the last six months of the year, (3) the taxpayer must furnish over half the cost of maintaining the taxpayer's home, and (4) the taxpayer's home must be the principal residence of a dependent child for more than one-half of the year.

> *Example 2.15.* Melvin Moore left Esther and their two children on April 15, 1998, and has not been heard from since. Esther furnishes the entire cost of the household and the support of the two children for the remainder of the year. For 1998, Esther would qualify as an abandoned spouse and thus be considered as unmarried. If Melvin had left during the last half of the year, or if there were no children, Esther would not qualify as unmarried under the abandoned spouse rules. She would file as married filing separately.

An individual qualifying as an abandoned spouse will qualify for head of household status. Head of household status provides the spouse with a lower rate than the tax rate for a married person filing a separate return or a single individual.

Married persons are taxed at the lowest rate if they file jointly, and at the highest rates if they file separately. Unmarried taxpayers who are heads of households use a set of rates between those for single people and those for married couples filing jointly. Surviving spouses use the same rates as those married filing jointly. All unmarried taxpayers who do not qualify for another filing status must file as single taxpayers.

¶ 2301 MARRIED INDIVIDUALS FILING JOINTLY

A married couple may file a joint return including their combined incomes, or each spouse may file a separate return reflecting his or her income only. A joint return is not allowed if either the husband or wife is a nonresident alien at any time during the tax year, or if the husband and wife have different tax years. However, if at the end of a tax year one spouse is a U.S. citizen or a resident alien and the other spouse is a nonresident alien, a special election may be made to treat the nonresident spouse as a U.S. resident. If no election is made, the taxpayer's status is married filing separately unless there is a dependent which would allow head of household status to be used.

Joint returns were originally enacted to establish equity for married taxpayers in common law states since in community property states married taxpayers are able to split their income. Therefore, the progressive rates are constructed upon the assumption that income is earned equally by the two spouses. A joint return may be filed and the splitting device may be used even if one spouse has no income.

If a joint return is filed, the income and deductions of both spouses are combined. The exemptions to which either spouse is entitled are combined, and both spouses sign the return. In a joint return, the general rule is that both spouses are jointly and severally liable for any deficiency in tax, interest, and penalties.

A joint return may be made for the survivor and a deceased spouse or for both deceased spouses. The tax year of such spouses must begin on the same day and end on different days only because of the death of either or both spouses. The surviving spouse must not remarry before the close of the tax year and the spouses must have been cligible to file a joint return on the date of death.

The determination of whether an individual is married is made as of the close of the tax year, unless the spouse dies during the year, in which case the determination will be made as of the time of death. A married couple does not have to be living together on the last day of the tax year in order to file a joint return, but an individual legally separated under a decree of divorce or separate maintenance will not be considered married.

¶ 2315   MARRIED INDIVIDUALS FILING SEPARATE RETURNS

If a husband and wife file separate returns, they should each report only their own income and claim only their own exemptions and deductions on their individual returns.

Separate returns will result in approximately the same tax liability as a joint return where both spouses have approximately equal amounts of income. However, when the incomes are unequal, it is generally advantageous for married taxpayers in noncommunity property states to file a joint return since the combined amount of tax on separate returns is higher than the tax on a joint return.

Special circumstances may warrant the use of separate returns. Where one spouse incurs significant medical expenses, the smaller adjusted gross income of a separate return results in a larger medical deduction since medical expenses are allowed only to the extent they exceed 7.5 percent of adjusted gross income. It may be desirable to file separate returns to protect against a potential deficiency on the other spouse's return where there is some concern over the tax liability or there is a questionable item on the return itself.

In community property states, a married couple's income is treated as earned equally by the two spouses. Income earned on capital investment made from a spouse's separate property in most community property states remains the separate property of that spouse. There are three community property states in which income from separate property is treated as community property (Texas, Idaho, and Louisiana). See discussion of the "Texas Rule" at ¶ 3215. Community property income and deductions must be accounted for on the same basis. Deductions pertaining to the separate property of one spouse must be taken by that spouse. However, where the income from that property is taxable one-half to each spouse, the deductions must be divided between the husband and wife.

The Code places numerous limitations upon deductions, credits, etc., where married taxpayers file separately. If both husband and wife have income, they should generally figure their tax both jointly and separately to insure they are using the method resulting in less tax.

If an individual has filed a separate return for a year for which a joint return could have been filed and the time for filing the return has expired, a joint return by the husband and wife may still be filed. The joint return must be filed within three years of the due date of the original return for which a change is requested. All payments, credits, refunds, or other payments made or allowed on the separate return of either spouse are taken into account in determining the extent to which the tax based on the joint return has been paid.

If a joint return has been filed for a year, the spouses may not thereafter file separate returns for that year after the time for filing the return for that year has expired.

¶ 2325   SINGLE INDIVIDUALS

A single individual for tax purposes is an unmarried person who does not qualify as head of household. Generally, if only one of the two individuals is working, it is advantageous from a tax standpoint to enter into marriage. However, where the incomes are approximately equal, the total tax will be smaller if they are not married.

¶ 2345   HEADS OF HOUSEHOLDS

Unmarried individuals who maintain a household for dependents are entitled to use the head of household rates. Although a taxpayer may secure dependency exemptions for unrelated persons living in the household, they cannot qualify a taxpayer for head of household status. Only relatives serve this purpose. Over one-half of the cost of maintaining the household must be furnished by the taxpayer. The unmarried child or grandchild of the taxpayer does not have to be the taxpayer's dependent. However, if the child or grandchild is married, the taxpayer must be able to claim the dependency exemption. The household must be the principal abode for more than one-half of the year. Any other relative must qualify as the taxpayer's dependent. A dependent relative who is a dependent only because of a multiple-support agreement cannot qualify a taxpayer for head of household status. A legally adopted child of a taxpayer is considered a child of the taxpayer by blood. A dependent foster child is treated like a dependent blood son or daughter, rather than as an unrelated individual. However, the foster child must be a dependent to enable the parent to use head of household status. Rev. Rul. 84-89, 1984-1 CB 5.

Example 2.16. Sara Shuster is unmarried and maintains a household in which she and her son reside. The son is claimed by his father as a dependent. Since Sara is not required to claim the dependency exemption on her child, she may use the head-of-household tax rate schedule. If the son is married, Sara must be able to claim him as a dependent in order to file as head of household.

The taxpayer's dependent parents need not live with the taxpayer to enable the taxpayer to qualify as a head of household. The household maintained by the taxpayer must actually constitute the principal place of abode of the father or mother or both of them. The father or mother must occupy the household for the entire year. A rest home or home for the aged qualifies as a household for this purpose.

Example 2.17. Meg Morgan, an unmarried individual living in Baltimore, maintains a household in Los Angeles for her dependent mother. Meg may use the head-of-household tax rate schedule even though her mother does not live with her.

Although generally a married couple cannot file a joint return if one of them is a nonresident alien, the taxpayer who is a U.S. citizen will qualify as a head of household if the taxpayer is the one providing the maintenance of the household and if there is a related dependent living with the taxpayer the entire year. The law provides that, for purposes of the head of household status, the taxpayer is treated as unmarried.

A taxpayer does not qualify for head of household status if the only other person living in his household is a nonresident alien spouse because the spouse does not qualify as a dependent. However, a taxpayer having a nonresident alien spouse may qualify if an unmarried dependent or unmarried stepchild lives with the taxpayer. Rev. Rul. 55-711, 1955-2 CB 13, amplified by Rev. Rul. 74-370, 1974-2 CB 7.

A physical change in the location of a home will not prevent a taxpayer from qualifying as a head of household. The fact that the individual qualifying the taxpayer for head of household status is born or dies within the tax year will not block a claim for head of household status. The household must have been the principal place of abode of the individual for the remaining or preceding part of the year.

A nonpermanent failure to occupy the common abode by reason of illness, education, business, vacation, military service, or a custody agreement under which a child or stepchild is absent for less than six months in a year will not bar the head of household status. However, it must be reasonable to assume that the household member will return to the household and the taxpayer continues to maintain the household or a substantially equivalent household in anticipation of such return.

The costs of maintaining a household are the expenses incurred for the mutual benefit of the occupants. They include property taxes, mortgage interest, rent, utility charges, upkeep and repairs, property insurance, and food consumed on the premises. Such expenses do not include the cost of clothing, education, medical treatment, vacations, life insurance, and transportation. In addition, the cost of maintaining a household does not include any amount which represents the value of services rendered in the household by the taxpayer or by a person qualifying the taxpayer as a head of household. The taxpayer, for example, cannot impute a value for services provided by the taxpayer for cooking, cleaning, and doing laundry.

It is possible for a household to be a portion of a home. The Tax Court held that a widow and her unmarried daughter occupying one level of a four-level house and sharing two levels constituted a household. *J.F. Fleming Est.*, 33 TCM 619, CCH Dec. 32,611(M), T.C. Memo. 1974-137. Since the widow paid more than one-half of the household maintenance expenses attributable to her and her daughter, she qualified as a head of household.

¶ 2355   SURVIVING SPOUSES

Special tax benefits are extended to a surviving spouse. In addition to the right to file a joint return for the year in which a spouse dies, a taxpayer whose spouse died in either of the two years preceding the tax year, and who has not remarried, may file as a surviving spouse provided the surviving spouse maintains a household for a dependent child or stepchild.

Surviving spouses use the same tax rate schedules and tax tables as married taxpayers filing joint returns. The surviving spouse provisions do not authorize the surviving spouse to file a joint return; they only make the joint return tax rates available.

The surviving spouse must provide over half the cost of maintaining the household in which both the surviving spouse and dependent live. Of course, an exemption for the deceased spouse is available in the year of death but is not available on the return of the surviving spouse in the two years following death.

Example 2.18. Albert Olm's wife died in 1998, leaving a child who qualifies as Albert's dependent. In the year of death, Albert and his deceased wife are entitled to file a joint return and claim three exemptions—one each for Albert, his deceased spouse, and the dependent child. If the child continues to live with Albert in a household provided by him and be his dependent, Albert will be allowed to file as a surviving spouse for 1999 and 2000. Only two exemptions will be allowed in those years—one for Albert and one for the dependent child.

¶ 2365 DEPENDENTS

The standard deduction for an individual who can be claimed as a dependent on the tax return of another taxpayer is the greater of the individual's earned income plus $250 (up to the maximum allowable standard deduction) or $700. However, an individual over 18 or a full-time student over 23 will not qualify as a dependent if income exceeds $2,700.

An individual may not claim a personal exemption if the individual can be claimed as a dependent on another taxpayer's return. It does not matter whether the other taxpayer actually claims the exemption.

Example 2.19. Michael Turner, who is single, is claimed as a dependent on his parents' 1998 tax return. He receives $1,500 in interest income from a savings account. In addition, he earns $1,800 while working part-time after school. The standard deduction for a single individual for 1998 is $4,250. However, Michael is limited to a standard deduction of $2,050, the larger of his earned income plus $250 or $700.

Example 2.20. Sonya Ross is single and claimed as a dependent on her parents' 1998 tax return. She has $1,200 in interest income and also earns $350 from part-time employment. Her standard deduction is limited to $700, the larger of her earned income of $350 plus $250 or $700.

Example 2.21. Tom Moss, a 22-year-old, full-time college student, is claimed as a dependent on his parents' 1998 return. Tom is married and files a separate return. Tom has $1,500 in interest income and wages of $3,700. His standard deduction is $3,550, because the greater of $700 or his earned income ($3,700 plus $250) is $3,950, but his standard deduction cannot be more than the $3,550 maximum allowable standard deduction

If a dependent child is under 14 years of age at the end of the tax year and has more than $1,400 of net unearned (investment) income for the year, his or her net unearned income is taxed to the child at the additional rate of tax that the parent would be required to pay if the child's net unearned income were included in the parents' taxable income. This applies regardless of the source of the assets creating the child's net unearned income as long as the child has at least one living parent as of the close of the tax year. The income of the custodial parent is used for the tax computation in the case of parents that are not married. The parent with the greater taxable income is to be used when married parents file separately.

Net unearned income is unearned income (such as interest, dividends, capital gains, and certain trust income) less the sum of $700 (referred to as the first $700 clause) and the greater of: (1) $700 of the standard deduction or $700 of itemized deductions, or (2) the amount of allowable deductions which are directly connected with the production of unearned income. Thus, unearned income is reduced by $1,400 unless the child has itemized deductions connected with the production of unearned income exceeding $700. The amount of net unearned income cannot exceed taxable income for the year.

The child in each of the following examples is under 14 and a dependent of his or her parents. In each of the examples no personal exemption is allowed since the child is a dependent of another taxpayer.

Example 2.22. Amy Acorn has $300 of unearned income and no earned income. Amy will have no tax liability since her standard deduction of $700 will reduce taxable income to zero.

Example 2.23. Bill Barnes has $900 of unearned income and no earned income. Bill will have $200 of taxable income ($900 gross income — $700 standard deduction). His net unearned income is reduced to zero by the first $700 clause and the $700 standard deduction. The $200 taxable income is taxed at Bill's tax rate.

Example 2.24. Charles Clewis has $1,500 of unearned income and no earned income. His $700 standard deduction reduces taxable income to $800. The $1,500 of unearned income is reduced by (1) the first $700 clause and (2) the $700 standard deduction, leaving $100 of net unearned income. The $100 of net unearned income is taxed at the additional rate of the parents while the remaining $700 of taxable income is taxed at Charles's rate.

Example 2.25. Dave Drummer has $800 of earned income and $400 of unearned income. Dave's standard deduction is $1,050 (the amount of earned income plus $250). His taxable income is $150 ($1,200 gross income — $1,050 standard deduction). Since the unearned income is less than $1,400, there is no net unearned income. The taxable income is taxed at Dave's tax rate.

Example 2.26. Frank Fisher has $400 of earned income and $1,600 of unearned income. His taxable income is $1,300 ($2,000 gross income — $700 standard deduction). Frank's $1,600 unearned income is reduced by $1,400 (the first $700 clause + the $700 standard deduction), leaving $200 of net unearned income. The $200 of net unearned income is taxed at the parent's rate. Frank is taxed at his rate on the remaining $1,100 taxable income ($1,300 taxable income — $200 taxed at parent's rate).

Example 2.27. Gene Gambol has $1,000 of earned income plus $2,400 of unearned income. He has $900 of itemized deductions (net of the 2 percent floor) which are directly connected with the production of the unearned income. Gene has $500 of other itemized deductions. His taxable income is $2,000 ($3,400 gross income — $1,400 of itemized deductions). Gene's net unearned income of $800 is taxed at his parents' rate. The unearned income is reduced by $1,600 (the first $700 clause + the entire $900 of deductions relating to the production of unearned income since it exceeds $700). Gene is taxed at his rate on $1,200 ($1,000 of earned income + $1,600 net unearned income and reduced by $1,400 itemized deductions).

TAX PLANNING POINTER ▼

___

Parents can avoid having a dependent's income taxed at their rate by making gifts to children of assets that will not generate income until after the child becomes age 14. The tax on the income would then be taxed at the child's tax rate. Examples of such assets include single premium ordinary life insurance policies, Series EE savings bonds, and property expected to appreciate over time.

___

A parent may elect to include on his or her return the unearned income of a child whose income is between $700 and $6,500. The child's income must consist solely of interest and dividends. The child is treated as having no gross income and does not have to file a tax return if the election is made.

The electing parent must include the gross income of the child in excess of $1,400 on the parent's tax return for the year, resulting in the taxation of that income at the parent's highest marginal rate. There is an additional tax liability equal to the lesser of (1) $105 or (2) 15 percent of the child's income exceeding $700. This liability reflects the child's unearned income from $700 to $1,400 that would otherwise be taxed to the child at the 15 percent tax rate.

¶ 2375   FILING REQUIREMENTS

The obligation to file a return depends on the amount of gross income, marital status during the year, and age. Only income which is taxable is included in the computation of gross income in order to determine whether or not a return must be filed.

With certain exceptions, the gross income level at which taxpayers must file returns is determined by adding the standard deduction to the personal exemptions allowed for the taxpayer. Because married individuals filing separately must both itemize or both use the standard deduction, the standard deduction amount is not added to the personal exemption to determine the gross income filing figure. The old-age additional standard deduction entitles an individual to increase the gross income level filing requirement by $850 or $1,050. However, no increase is permitted for blindness or for exemptions for dependents.

For 1998, Code Sec. 6012 requires a tax return to be filed if gross income for the year is at least as much as the amount shown for the categories in the table on the next page.

Filing Status	Gross Income
Single	
Under 65 and not blind.................................	$ 6,950
Under 65 and blind	6,950
65 or older	8,000
Dependent with unearned income	700
Dependent with no unearned income	4,250
Married Filing Joint Return	
Both spouses under 65 and neither blind	$12,500
Both spouses under 65 and one or both spouses blind	12,500
One spouse 65 or older..............................	13,350
Both spouses 65 or older	14,200
Married Filing Separate Return	
All—whether 65 or older or blind......................	$ 2,700
Head of Household	
Under 65 and not blind.................................	$ 8,950
Under 65 and blind	8,950
65 or older	10,000
Surviving Spouse	
Under 65 and not blind.................................	$ 9,800
Under 65 and blind	9,800
65 or older	10,650

Even if the aforementioned gross income requirements are not met, a return nevertheless must be filed if an individual had net earnings from self-employment of $400 or more.

A return should be filed by any taxpayer eligible for the earned income credit even though the taxpayer does not meet any of the above filing requirements. A refund can result even if no income tax has been withheld.

Taxpayers must record their identifying number (Social Security number) on their returns. Returns filed by taxpayers claiming exemptions for dependents must include the dependents' Social Security numbers.

¶ 2385 TAX TABLES

The tables are based on taxable income. The tables apply to taxpayers with taxable income of less than $100,000. Separate tables are provided for single taxpayers, married taxpayers filing jointly and surviving spouses, married taxpayers filing separately, and heads of households.

Each line of the tax tables represents an interval of taxable incomes. Under $3,000 the intervals are $25 and above $3,000 the intervals are $50. The tax given in the tables is based on the midpoint taxable income of each interval. Thus, the tax from the tables for the interval $40,000–$40,050 is the same as the tax determined from the tax rate schedules for $40,025.

The tax tables may not be used by the following taxpayers:

1. estates or trusts

2. taxpayers claiming the exclusion for foreign earned income

3. taxpayers who file a short period return

4. taxpayers whose income exceeds the ceiling amount

It is expected that 95 percent of all individual taxpayers will be able to determine their tax liability from the tables.

To find the income tax from the tax tables, the taxpayer must (1) find the line that includes the taxable income and (2) read down the column until the taxable income line is reached. For a married couple filing jointly with taxable income of $32,623, the income tax would be $4,894.

SAMPLE TAX TABLE FOR 1998

At Least	But Less Than	Single	Married Filing Jointly	Married Filing Separately	Head of a Household
$32,500	$32,550	$5,812	$4,879	$6,354	$4,879
32,550	32,600	5,826	4,886	6,368	4,886
32,600	32,650	5,840	4,894	6,382	4,894
32,650	32,700	5,854	4,901	6,396	4,901

¶ 2395   TAX RATE SCHEDULES

Taxpayers using the tax rate schedules must compute their tax based on taxable income. The tax rate schedules are used by those not eligible to use the tax tables. The tax rate schedules are presented in the Appendix.

¶ 2405   SELF-EMPLOYMENT TAX

The tax on net self-employment income is levied to provide the self-employed with the same benefits that employees receive through their payment of the Social Security tax (FICA). In general, the tax is levied, assessed, and collected as part of the regular income tax.

The tax is imposed for the purposes of insuring the self-employed individual for old-age, survivors, and disability benefits and for hospitalization benefits under the Social Security program. For 1998, the tax rate is 15.3 percent, made up of two parts: (1) an old-age, survivors, and disability insurance (OASDI) rate of 12.4 percent and (2) a medicare hospital insurance (HI) rate of 2.9 percent.

In general, net self-employment income equals the gross income derived by an individual from a trade or business carried on as a sole proprietor, less any allowable deductions, plus the distributive share of a partnership's net income. If a self-employed individual has more than one business, the net self-employment income is the total of the net earnings of all businesses. A loss in one business is deductible from the earnings of the other businesses.

Not all self-employment income is subject to tax. Remuneration paid for the services of a newsboy under age 18 is exempt from the tax. Dividends are included only by a dealer in stock and securities. Interest is included only if on business loans. Rental income is included only by a real estate dealer or in cases in which services are rendered to the occupants. Generally, self-employment income does not include any item that is excluded from gross income. Wages received by a child under 18 from a parent are not subject to the self-employment tax.

The self-employment tax is imposed on "net earnings from self-employment." Net earnings from self-employment is net self-employment income less a special deduction. The actual deduction, however, is not subtracted from a taxpayer's net self-employment income in computing net earnings from self-employment. Instead, a taxpayer reduces net self-employment income by an amount (termed a "deemed deduction") equal to net self-employment income multiplied by one-half of the self-employment tax rate, or 7.65 percent. This deduction is incorporated into Schedule SE by multiplying the net self-employment income by .9235. (This gives the same deduction as multiplying net self-employment income by .0765 and then subtracting the result.)

A taxpayer is allowed a deduction for one-half of the self-employment tax as a deduction from gross income.

Example 2.28. In 1998 Pierre Painter, a self-employed artist, had $45,000 in self-employment income. His deductible business expenses amounted to $15,000. Pierre's self-employment tax is computed as follows:

Gross income from self-employment	$45,000
Less: Business expense deductions	15,000
Net self-employment income	$30,000
Less: Deemed deduction ($30,000 × 7.65%)	2,295
Net earnings from self-employment	$27,705
Self-employment tax ($27,705 × 15.3%)	$ 4,239

On Form 1040, Schedule SE, Pierre would simply multiply his net self-employment income of $30,000 by .9235.

The cap on wages and self-employment income that is taken into account in calculating the portion of the FICA tax applicable to old-age, survivors, and disability insurance (OASDI) is $68,400 for 1998. This also applies to wages, self-employment income, and income derived under the Railroad Retirement Act. There is no longer a cap on wages and self-employment income that is taken into account in calculating the medicare hospital insurance (HI) portion of the self-employment tax. For 1993 the cap on the medical hospital insurance was set at $135,000.

Example 2.29. Katie Adams has $150,000 in self-employment income for the year. Her net earnings from self-employment is $138,525 ($150,000 × .9235). She will be subject to an OASDI tax of $8,481.60 ($68,400 × 12.4%) and an HI tax of $4,017.23 ($138,525 × 2.9%). Thus, her total self-employment tax is $12,498.83.

Thus, self-employment and Social Security (FICA) tax rate parity is achieved between self-employed persons and employees. Both employees and their employers are liable for Social Security tax and the employer must contribute 6.2 cents per dollar earned by the employee up to the cap limitation ($68,400 for 1998) for OASDI and another 1.45 cents per dollar without a cap for HI.

The net earnings from self-employment subject to the OASDI portion of the self-employment tax are limited to the self-employment base ($68,400 for OASDI and unlimited for HI in 1998) less any wages from which Social Security tax was withheld during the year. Thus, the tax is applied to the lesser of (1) the self-employment base ($68,400) minus income subject to Social Security taxes or (2) the net earnings from self-employment.

> *Example 2.30.* In 1998, Margaret Moore has $66,000 in income from self-employment and receives $8,000 in wages that are subject to Social Security taxes. Margaret's net earnings from self-employment are $60,951 ($66,000 × .9235). Her net earnings from self-employment subject to OASDI self-employment tax for the year are $60,400 ($68,400 − $8,000, the wages on which Social Security tax was withheld), which is less than net earnings from self-employment. Her net earnings from self-employment subject to the HI self-employment tax are $60,951, the full amount of the net earnings from self-employment. Thus, her total self-employment tax is $9,257 ($60,400 × 12.4% + $60,951 × 2.9%).

One-half of the self-employment tax liability for the year is allowed as a deduction on the tax return. This deduction is taken as a deduction from gross income on the front of Form 1040.

> *Example 2.31.* Jim Jergens has $40,000 in self-employment income. His net earnings from self-employment are $36,940 ($40,000 × .9235). The self-employment tax is $5,651.82 ($36,940 × 15.3%). One half of this amount, $2,825.91, is allowed as a deduction from gross income.

If the net earnings from self-employment are less than $400, there is no self-employment tax. However, this does not mean that the first $400 of net earnings from self-employment is not subject to the self-employment tax.

> *Example 2.32.* Sylvia Knight's only source of income for 1998 is $433.14 from self-employment. The net earnings from self-employment are $400 ($433.14 × .9235). The self-employment tax is $61.20 ($400 × 15.3%). Sylvia has a deduction from gross income of one half the self-employment tax, or $30.60. If Sylvia had managed to earn less than $433.14, there would have been no self-employment tax.

An optional method of computing self-employment income may be used by persons whose net income from a trade or business is relatively low. The details are omitted, but the method enables taxpayers to obtain greater credit for Social Security benefits than their income would normally allow.

TAX BLUNDERS

1. Sara Michaels and Tommy Tooks marry on December 31. Sara earned $40,000 for the year, and Tommy earned $35,000. If Sara and Tommy had waited until the beginning of the following year to marry they would have realized a significant tax savings. Each filing as single taxpayers will result in less total tax than filing jointly.

2. Assume Sara earned $75,000 and Tommy earned $5,000 because he attended school most of the year and they marry at the beginning of the next year. There would be a significant tax savings in marrying at the end of the first year and filing jointly over each filing as single taxpayers.

SUMMARY OF CHAPTER 2

✓   The standard deduction eliminates low- to moderate-level tax-payers from the tax rolls. The standard deduction is made up of two parts: the basic standard deduction and the additional standard deduction. Both of these parts are adjusted each year for inflation. The standard deduction differs depending upon filing status.

✓   Taxpayers are allowed a personal exemption for themselves and their spouse, plus an exemption for each qualified dependent. Taxpayers who are dependents are not allowed a personal exemption for themselves.

✓   High-income taxpayers will find both their itemized deductions and their personal exemptions reduced based on adjusted gross income.

✓   Taxpayers must determine their tax liability from among five different filing statuses.

✓   Special taxation rules are imposed on returns filed by individuals that are dependents of other taxpayers.

✓   In general, filing requirements are based on a taxpayer's gross income, filing status, and age.

✓   Self-employed individuals are required to pay a self-employment tax that is equivalent to the Social Security taxes paid by employees.

CHAPTER 2 QUESTIONS

1. What is the purpose in knowing and understanding the components of the tax formula?

2. What is the distinction between deductions for adjusted gross income and deductions from adjusted gross income?

3. How does a tax deduction differ from a tax credit?

4. What other terms are used to describe deductions for adjusted gross income?

5. Analyze any differences between increasing the standard deduction and increasing the exemption allowed.

6. Explain the rationale behind an individual's arranging financial affairs to use the standard deduction one year and itemized deductions in another year.

7. What is the reason that some taxpayers are not entitled to the standard deduction or are entitled to only part of it? Explain.

8. How is the standard deduction computed for a dependent child with unearned income?

9. George files a separate return. His wife's only source of income is $600 in interest income. Can George claim an exemption for his wife on his separate return?

10. Are taxpayers allowed to claim the additional old-age or blindness standard deduction for dependents?

11. In determining the dependency exemption, how is the value of lodging provided a dependent computed for the support test?

12. Bill and Becky had a child born on April 15. The child died within three hours of birth. Can they claim an exemption for the child?

13. Can a student attending a class in night school qualify as a full-time student?

14. Rhoda and Mike are both full-time students who married late in the year. Rhoda had $1,800 in wages from a part-time job and Mike had $900 in dividend income. They filed a joint return and received a refund of the $175 that had been withheld on Rhoda's wages. Rhoda's parents paid over one-half of Rhoda's support. Can Rhoda's parents claim her as a dependent?

15. Explain the concept of the "multiple support agreement." What are the requirements for such an agreement?

16. During the year, Alice Johnson was supported by her four sons, Amos, Luther, Bennet, and Ivan, in the following percentages:

Amos	8%
Luther	32%
Bennet	18%
Ivan	42%

Which of the brothers is entitled to claim his mother as a dependent, providing a multiple support agreement exists?

17. Homer and Wilma received a divorce in 1983. During the year, Homer contributed $900 support for their only child in the custody of Wilma. Absent any written agreement relative to the receipt of the dependency exemption, who should be entitled to the exemption?

18. What conditions must exist in Problem 17 for Homer to take the dependency exemption?

19. Tom and Jane were legally separated during the preceding year under a written separation agreement. Jane had custody of their two children for the entire year while Tom contributed $2,000 support for each child. Absent any written agreement relative to the receipt of the dependency exemption, who should be entitled to the exemptions?

20. How do the pre-1985 rules differ from the post-1984 rules for dependency exemptions following divorce?

21. Calculate the number of exemptions and the standard deduction that the taxpayer is entitled to take in 1998 in each of the following independent cases:

    a. John, age 66, and his wife, age 64, file a joint return.

    b. Jack, age 62 and blind, and his wife, who became 65 on January 1 of the following year, file a joint return.

    c. Jim and Mary, both 52, contribute more than half the support for Jim's father, who lives with them. Jim's father is 72 and blind. Jim and Mary file a joint return.

    d. Harry, age 66, is a widower who maintains a home for himself and his 22-year-old son who attends college full time. Harry provided more than one half of his son's support.

    e. Jackson is 28 and his wife, Joan, is 27. They have two children, one three-year-old and the other seven years old. On March 29 of this year, Joan gave birth to a daughter, who died the next day. Jackson and Joan file a joint return.

    f. Joe, age 65, and his wife, JoAnne, age 64, maintain a home for their unmarried daughter, age 23, who earned $4,000 and attends college on a part-time basis. Joe and JoAnne contributed $6,000 toward her support. Joe and JoAnne file a joint return.

    g. William, a 42-year-old bachelor, pays $450 per month support for his 75-year-old mother who is disabled and is living in a rest home. She receives a taxable pension of $100 per month and uses the entire $550 per month for routine living expenses.

    h. Same as (g), except William's mother also receives $400 per month from dividends on stock she owns. She also uses this amount for routine living expenses.

    i. Billy Bob and his wife, Mary Sue, both 45, maintain a home for Mary Sue's friend, Jackie Jo, age 17, who came to dinner one night several years ago and has lived with them since. Jackie Jo attends school and has no income. Billy Bob and Mary Sue file a joint return.

j. Benson, a 45-year-old widower, maintains a home for his 22-year-old son, Chester, who attends college full-time on a $4,000-per-year scholarship. Chester also works part-time while at school, earning $1,500 per year. Benson contributes $2,000, which constitutes the balance of Chester's support for the year.

k. Same as (j), except Chester contributes the $4,000 per year from his savings account instead of receiving it from the scholarship award.

l. Richard, a bachelor under 65, maintains a home in which a son of a deceased friend has lived the entire year. Richard furnishes over one half of the support of the young man, who attends school. The young man also works part time after school, earning $2,000 per year.

m. Dan and his wife, Pam, maintain a household for and completely support three foster children. The children have been living in Dan and Pam's home all year. On December 31 of the tax year, Pam gives birth to a son.

22. What is meant by filing status?

23. What filing status options are available to Darlene, assuming she separated from her husband in March? Darlene is the sole support of her daughter, who lives with Darlene.

24. How do head of household expenses differ from the expenses used in the support test?

25. Are all individuals required to file an income tax return?

26. Charles has interest income of $950 and no other income. He is claimed as a dependent by his parents. Is he required to file an income tax return?

27. Why might an individual file an income tax return even though not required to do so?

28. Under what circumstances must a return be filed by an individual even though there is only $750 in taxable income?

29. What is the difference between the tax tables and the tax rate schedules?

30. What is the limit for self-employment tax?

CHAPTER 2 PROBLEMS

31. Tom and Linda are married taxpayers who file a joint return. They have itemized deductions of $9,700 and four exemptions. Assuming an adjusted gross income of $40,000, what is their taxable income for 1998?

32. Compute Marie's taxable income for 1998, assuming she is single and claims two dependent children. Her adjusted gross income is $70,000, and she has itemized deductions of $9,000.

33. Which of the following taxpayers should itemize? Explain.

    a. Robert is a single taxpayer. He has itemized deductions of $4,800.

    b. Jane qualifies as head of household. Her itemized deductions total $2,400.

    c. Brian is married and files a separate return. He has itemized deductions of $3,900.

    d. Lisa is a surviving spouse. Her itemized deductions are $4,600.

34. John and Mary are married taxpayers filing a joint return. They have adjusted gross income of $200,000. Their preliminary itemized deductions total $20,000. What is the amount of itemized deductions allowed on their joint tax return?

35. Compute the taxable income for 1998 under each of the following circumstances:

    a. Jim is married and files a joint return. Jim and his wife have two dependent children. They have adjusted gross income of $19,000 and itemized deductions of $4,600.

    b. Jim is single with no dependents. His adjusted gross income is $20,000 with itemized deductions of $2,800.

    c. Jim is a full-time college student under 24 supported by his father. Jim earned $2,200 from a part-time job and had $500 of interest income. His itemized deductions were $600.

    d. Jim is married but files separately and claims two dependent children. His adjusted gross income is $65,000 and he claims $8,900 of itemized deductions. Jim's wife also itemizes on her return.

    e. Assume the same situation as in (d), but Jim's itemized deductions are only $1,500.

36. Duke and Pat Collins have adjusted gross income of $500,000. They have itemized deductions of $20,000 consisting of $8,000 in medical expenses, $3,000 in property taxes, $4,000 in housing interest, and $5,000 in miscellaneous itemized deductions that exceed 2 percent of adjusted gross income. What is the amount of their itemized deductions?

37. What is Mary's taxable income for 1998, assuming she has $4,400 of earned income and $800 of unearned income and is claimed as a dependent by her parents?

38. Compute Stanley's taxable income for 1998, assuming he has $1,000 in wages from working in a grocery store and $1,700 in

interest income from some bonds he owns. Stanley is claimed as a dependent on his parents' return.

39. Bradford is 12 years old and is claimed as a dependent on his parents' return. In 1998, he received unearned income of $1,500. Bradford's itemized deductions totaled $150. Determine Bradford's taxable income.

40. What is the standard deduction and the number of exemptions that a married couple will be allowed, assuming that they are not over 65 or blind, that they fully support the husband's 82-year-old blind mother, and that they have no other dependents?

41. Has Jodi provided more than 50 percent of the support in the following situations?

    a. Jodi contributed $4,200 to her mother's support during the year. Her mother received $5,300 in Medicare payments that were used to pay her medical expenses.

    b. Jodi's daughter was a full-time student. Jodi paid $2,000 towards her daughter's living expenses. The daughter earned $1,800 from a part-time job and spent that plus $600 from her savings to help support herself.

42. Margaret is attending school full-time for the year. Her parents paid $3,000 toward her support. She earned $2,000 from a part-time job which she used toward her support. In addition, Margaret withdrew $1,500 from her savings account to help in her support. Have her parents provided over one-half of Margaret's support?

43. Myrtle is fully supported by her three children and Fred, a close friend of the family. Mark paid $4,000 toward Myrtle's support, while Nancy, Opel, and Fred paid $3,200, $800, and $2,000, respectively. Which individuals are eligible to claim Myrtle under a multiple support agreement?

44. Annie was divorced in 1984. She provided over half the cost of maintaining the home that she and her 12-year-old son lived in the entire year. Her former husband provided more than half of the son's total support, and he claims the son as a dependent. What is Annie's best filing status for the year? Would the filing status change if Annie had been divorced in 1985?

45. A single taxpayer with one dependent has $160,000 of adjusted gross income. What is the amount of the deduction for personal exemptions allowed this taxpayer?

46. What is the best filing status in each of the following situations?

    a. Phillip and Catherine were married on December 31, 1998.

    b. John and Sandra were married in 1987. John left Sandra in March 1998, and she has not heard from him since that time.

    c. Melody and Werner were married during the year. Werner is a resident and citizen of Germany.

47. What is the taxpayer's filing status for 1998 in each of the following situations?

    a. Bill's wife died in 1997. Bill maintained a household for his two dependent children in 1998.

    b. Bill is unmarried and lives in an apartment. He supported his aged parents, who live in a separate home. Bill provided over half of the cost of maintaining his parents' home and also provided over half of each of his parents' support.

    c. Bill is unmarried and maintains a household for his 18-year-old daughter and her husband. Bill pays over half of the support of his daughter. The daughter files a joint return with her husband.

48. Indicate the filing status and the number of exemptions allowed to Sandy for 1998, 1999, 2000, and 2001, assuming her husband died in 1998 and Sandy has been the sole support of her son since that time.

49. Mike and Ellen Evans decide to part in April. Mike moves into an apartment two blocks away. The children spend each weekend with Mike. What filing statuses are available to Mike and Ellen, assuming they are not divorced before the end of the year?

50. Which of the following individuals are required to file a tax return for 1998? Assume no tax has been withheld.

    a. Rebecca, single and with no dependents, earned $4,500 for the year.

    b. Hugh and Jane are married and file a joint return. They have four children. Their gross income is $14,000 and they have itemized deductions of $8,000.

    c. Peter has self-employment income of $450. He is a full-time college student and is claimed as a dependent on his parents' return.

51. Julian and Georgia file a joint return. They have adjusted gross income of $110,000 and itemized deductions of $9,000. Are they required to use the Tax Rate Schedules or the Tax Tables in computing their income tax?

52. Eric is single and has no dependents for 1998. He earned $30,000 and had deductions from gross income of $1,800 and itemized deductions of $4,500. Compute Eric's income tax for the year using the Tax Rate Schedules.

53. Allen has taxable income of $43,475 for 1998. Using the Tax Rate Schedules in the Appendix, compute Allen's income tax liability before tax credits and prepayments for each of the following filing statuses.

    a. Married filing jointly

    b. Married filing separately

    c. Single

    d. Head of household

54. Determine the amount of self-employment tax due for 1998, assuming that Lynette earned $30,000 in wages and also earned $20,000 from a business that she owned.

55. What is the total tax due for 1998, including self-employment tax, for Stuart, assuming that he earned $20,000 in wages, earned $24,000 in self-employment income from his first business, had a loss of $10,000 from his second business, received $3,000 in interest income, and had $5,100 in dividend income?

56. Mr. Smith died early in the year. Mrs. Smith remarried in December and, therefore, was unable to file a joint return with Mr. Smith. What is the filing status of the decedent, Mr. Smith?

    a. Single

    b. Married filing separate return

    c. Married filing joint return

    d. Head of household

    e. Surviving spouse

57. Which of the following is not considered when determining the total support test for a child?

    a. Fair rental value of lodging

    b. Medical insurance premiums

    c. Birthday presents

    d. Scholarship

    e. Recreation

58. Which relative does not have to live in the same household of the taxpayer claiming head of household filing status?

    a. Aunt

    b. Son

    c. Granddaughter

    d. Father

    e. Brother

59. To qualify for head of household rates, which of the following must be present?

    a. You must be unmarried on the last day of your tax year.

    b. You must maintain a household and contribute over 50 percent of the cost of maintaining the household.

    c. The person for whom the household is maintained has to be a relative.

    d. (a) and (b).

    e. All of the above.

60. *Comprehensive Problem.* Richard and Jennifer were married in 1982. They have a five-year-old child and a son born November 15, 1998. Richard's 67-year-old father lived in a nursing home until his death on May 23, 1998. Richard and Jennifer provided all of his support until his death. Richard earned $43,000 in salary during the year. They also received $1,350 in interest from the credit union. They incurred $4,900 in itemized deductions during the year. Compute Richard and Jennifer's income tax for 1998 using the Tax Rate Schedules.

61. *Comprehensive Problem.* Scott and Glenna are married with two dependent children. They have $75,000 in wage income and $3,000 in interest income on some bonds they own. They have deductions for adjusted gross income of $4,000 and itemized deductions of $9,000. Neither of the children has any income. Determine the tax savings for the family if Scott and Glenna were to transfer the bonds to the children, both under 14.

62. *Research Problem.* Sidney and Angelene were married in 1994. During 1998, they were both employed, each earning $32,000 for the year. They discovered that there was a significant tax savings if they could file as single taxpayers and thus arranged a vacation trip and a divorce before the end of the year. Early in 1999 they remarried. What is their filing status for 1998? See Rev. Rul. 76-255.

Chapter 3

Gross Income

Learning Objectives

After completing Chapter 3, you should be able to:

1. Define and distinguish among the various concepts of income: economic, accounting, and legal.
2. Recognize the various items included in gross income.
3. Determine when items are included in income.
4. Understand the rules governing alimony.
5. Differentiate alimony from child support.
6. Comprehend the rules for recapturing alimony.
7. Understand the rules governing the discharge of indebtedness for both solvent and insolvent taxpayers.

OVERVIEW OF CHAPTER

Gross income, according to the Internal Revenue Code, includes all income unless specifically exempted by law. This comprehensive definition requires a more probing discussion of what must be included in income. Further, we must concern ourselves with "how much" must be included in income and what portion of total income may be excluded.

The Concept of Income

A frustrating characteristic of the English language is that a single term can be used to express a variety of concepts. Take the concept of income: economists, the courts, and accountants use this term, but for each, the definition imparts a singular *view*.

¶ 3001 ECONOMIC INCOME

The economic concept of income is more general than the accounting definition. The most commonly accepted definition of economic income is that of J. R. Hicks. He defines economic income as being "the maximum amount a person can consume during a week and still expect to be as well-off at the end of the week as he was at the beginning." J. R. Hicks, *Value and Capital* (Oxford: Clarendon Press, 1946), p. 172. This assumes that there were no capital contributions or withdrawals during the period measured. The economist's definition is not practical for tax purposes because the concept of "well-being" is not capable of objective measurement. The economic concept of income places a heavy emphasis on the future. No objective rules exist for determining well-being at any moment in time. Economists must deal in terms of real wealth, which includes holding gains and losses rather than monetary wealth alone. H. C. Simons maintained, "The precise, objective measurement of income implies the existence of perfect markets from which one, after ascertaining quantities, may obtain the prices necessary for routine valuation of all possible inventories of commodities, services, and property rights." *Personal Income Taxation* (Chicago: University of Chicago Press, 1921), p. 50. Since no such markets exist where the necessary prices for valuation may be obtained, the economic concept is an inappropriate measure of taxable income.

¶ 3015   THE LEGAL/TAX CONCEPT OF INCOME

The legal concept of income is also less precise than that of the accountant. Congress has not defined income, but has specified how particular items of income are to be taxed. The concept of income has crystalized through a series of court cases. The legal concept is different from the economic and accounting concepts. Gross income includes "all income from whatever source derived" unless specifically exempted by law. Code Sec. 61(a).

Eisner v. Macomber

In the case of *Eisner v. Macomber,* 1 USTC ¶ 32, 252 U.S. 189, 40 S.Ct. 189 (1920), the Supreme Court dealt at great length with the problem of defining income. The Court stated:

After examining dictionaries in common use . . . , we find little to add to the succinct definition adopted in two cases arising under the Corporation Tax Act of 1909 . . . "Income may be defined as the gain derived from capital, from labor, or from both combined," provided it be understood to include profit gained through sale or conversion of capital assets. . . .

Here we have the essential matter: *not* a gain *accruing* to capital; not a *growth* or *increment* of value in the investment; but a gain, a profit, something of exchangeable value, *proceeding* from the property, severed from the capital, however invested or employed, and *coming in,* being *"derived"*—that is, *received* or *drawn* by the recipient (the taxpayer) for his separate use, benefit and disposal; that is income derived from property.

The same fundamental conception is clearly set forth in the Sixteenth Amendment—"incomes, from whatever source derived"—the essential thought being expressed with a conciseness and lucidity entirely in harmony with the form and style of the Constitution.

Like the accountants' concept, the legal concept does not embrace holding gains or losses. The legal definition of income is close to the accountants', but not identical, as will be highlighted in the remainder of the chapter.

Example 3.1. Rachel owned 300 shares of Imperial Soap which she purchased for $1,000. She sold the stock this year for $1,200. Rachel realized a gain of $200, not the $1,200 proceeds she received from the sale. Only the $200 is included in gross income. The $1,000 is Rachel's return of capital.

¶ 3025 ACCOUNTING INCOME

The accountant desires to measure income over a specified period of time. Income, from an accounting point of view, is the excess of revenues over the costs incurred in producing those revenues. The emphasis for the accountant is on completed transactions. Therefore, unlike the economist, the accountant does not recognize holding gains. The accountant deals exclusively with objectively measurable forms such as monetary transactions.

Realization of Income

As in financial accounting all gains must be "realized" before they are includible in income. This usually occurs at the time of an arm's-length transaction.

Example 3.2. Tom Spears buys a parcel of real estate for $1,000 in 1985. In 1998, he has it appraised and finds that the property's market value is $1,500. He has a paper gain of $500, but he has no taxable income. Also in 1998, he sells the property for $1,500, at which time the income is "realized" and "recognized."

Under the accrual method of accounting, income is recognized when a transaction is consummated. Under the cash method of accounting, income is recognized only when cash is received. The cash method and accrual method of accounting are discussed in Chapter 12. To prevent cash basis taxpayers from choosing the year in which to recognize income, the Internal Revenue Service applies the constructive receipt doctrine.

Economic Benefit, Constructive Receipt, and Assignment of Income Doctrines

This chapter discusses three doctrines: the economic benefit doctrine, the constructive receipt doctrine, and the assignment of income doctrine. The doctrines focus on the following questions: what is income, when is it taxable, and to whom is it taxable?

In determining "what" is income and "when" an item must be included in the taxable income of a cash basis taxpayer, two concepts were conceived: the economic benefit doctrine and the constructive receipt doctrine. Over time the courts have tended to blur the distinction between these two doctrines. *F. Bowden,* 61-1 USTC ¶ 9382, 289 F.2d 20 (CA-5 1961), reversing 32 TC 853 (1959).

¶ 3101   ECONOMIC BENEFIT DOCTRINE

The economic benefit doctrine addresses the "what" and the constructive receipt doctrine addresses the "when." Any amount of compensation granted or paid to the individual for services rendered, be it cash, bonus, profit sharing, compensation in kind, or any other ingenious method of payment, must be included in gross income. Gross income is defined under the broad language of Code Sec. 61(a) of the Internal Revenue Code as "all income from whatever source derived." Thus, taxable income may consist of cash, receivables, property, land, or any other form of economic benefit.

¶ 3125   CONSTRUCTIVE RECEIPT DOCTRINE

The second doctrine, that of constructive receipt, was defined in the case of *Ross.* In this case, the Circuit Court of Appeals stated that the doctrine of constructive receipt was conceived "in order to prevent the taxpayer from choosing the year in which to reduce it (income) to possession." *L.W. Ross,* 48-2 USTC ¶ 9341, 169 F.2d 483 (CA-1 1948).

The Regulations explain the doctrine of constructive receipt, based upon the fact that income is:

> credited to [the taxpayer's] account, or set apart for him, or otherwise made available so that he may draw upon it at any time. ... However, income is not constructively received if the taxpayer's control of its receipt is subject to substantial limitations or restrictions. Reg. § 1.451-2.

A distinctive feature of the constructive receipt doctrine is that it affects only cash basis taxpayers, since they are deemed to have received income prior to the time of actual receipt. Because the accrual basis taxpayer is assumed to have recognized income at the moment it is "earned," there is no need to apply the constructive receipt doctrine. It is of no consequence if an individual refuses compensation. The courts have ruled that once the individual has an "absolute right" to the compensation, the amount of the remuneration must be included in the taxpayer's income. However, where the individual has only a conditional right, the courts hold that no present income was received. Generally, any compensation granted to an individual to which the individual has an absolute right is regarded as constructively received income. The taxpayer must include in current income any amounts of compensation which the taxpayer has refused to accept.

> *Example 3.3.* Leah was an employee of Loss Leaders Inc. On December 2, 1998, Loss Leaders announced a year-end bonus for all employees. Checks would be available for pickup at the cashier's desk December 29, 1998. Leah called in sick on December 29, 1998, and she did not stop by the cashier's desk until January 5, 1999. Leah must include her bonus on her 1998 tax return. She had a right to the bonus on December 29, 1998. It is immaterial that she chose not to collect her bonus on December 29, 1998.

As between the two doctrines, economic benefit and constructive receipt, logically the applicability of the economic benefit doctrine comes first. If the taxpayer has not received economic benefit, then it is not necessary to determine whether the taxpayer is in constructive receipt of income. Now that the concepts of "what" is income and "when" an item must be included in taxable income have been explained, it is necessary to determine "to whom" the income is taxable.

¶ 3201   ASSIGNMENT OF INCOME DOCTRINE

Compensation, interest, rents, dividends, and other forms of income usually must be included in the gross income of the recipient. A tax problem arises when an individual attempts to limit tax liability by assigning income. For example, a taxpayer has the employer forward a portion of the salary to one of the taxpayer's creditors instead of to the taxpayer. The taxpayer would have to recognize this as income inasmuch as the taxpayer received benefit from the proceeds and had control of the income.

In *Helvering v. Horst,* 40-2 USTC ¶ 9787, 311 U.S. 112, 61 S.Ct. 144 (1940), the Supreme Court ruled that a father who gave his son interest coupons, detached from bonds prior to their maturity, was liable for the tax on the interest even though the interest was received by his son. The Court stated:

> Income is "realized" by the assignor because he, who owns or controls the source of income, also controls the disposition of that which he could have received himself and diverts the payment from himself to others as the means of procuring the satisfaction of his wants. The taxpayer has equally enjoyed the fruits of his labor or investment and obtained the satisfaction of his desires whether he collects and uses the income to procure those satisfactions, or whether he disposes of his right to collect it as the means of procuring them.

In the preceding case, if the father wished to avoid the tax liability, he would have had to transfer the property which produced the income.

Generally, the courts have felt that a person should not be allowed to reduce tax liability by the voluntary assignment of income. This is referred to as the "fruit-of-the-tree" doctrine. Income (fruit) is taxable to the individual who has earned it. Thus, assignment of income will be disregarded, for tax purposes, unless the source of the income (tree) is also assigned. In *Lucas v. Earl,* 2 USTC ¶ 496, 281 U.S. 111, 50 S.Ct. 241 (1930), the Court stated that the "fruit" may not be "attributed to a different tree from that on which it grew."

If a person only has physical possession over the income of another person, he or she has no tax liability. Regardless of whether or not the person received it as an agent or creditor, it is taxed to the owner of the property. The rules which govern the assignment of income apply both to income from property as well as to income from services.

> *Example 3.4.* Jack Smith owns a warehouse complex and assigns the rents to his daughter Linda. Jack remains liable for the tax on the rental income, even though Linda is receiving the rental income.

Example 3.5. Linda Katz, a recent college graduate, earns $350 per week. In an effort to repay a college loan to her uncle she assigns half of her pay to him. Linda is taxed on the full $350 per week.

The question of tax liability for married persons filing separate returns arises frequently during discussions concerning to whom is income taxable. Various states treat this problem differently so that there is no solution which is universally applicable. The existence of community property laws in several states requires treatment of tax liability which is significantly different from those states in which there are no community property laws.

¶ 3215   COMMUNITY PROPERTY INCOME

In the eight community property states (Arizona, California, Idaho, Louisiana, Nevada, New Mexico, Texas, and Washington), all property acquired by a husband and wife *after* marriage is considered as owned by them in community, and, as such, is referred to as community property. Any income from these properties is automatically considered joint or community income, and if taxpayers are filing separate tax returns, the income would be shared equally between them on their separate returns. In 1985, Wisconsin implemented a marital property act; therefore, for federal income tax purposes it is considered a community property state.

Property acquired *before* marrriage or inherited by one spouse during marriage is considered to be that spouse's separate property. In California, Arizona, Nevada, New Mexico, Washington, and Wisconsin, any income from these separate properties is considered separate income; thus, if the spouses are filing separately, the income would not be shared and would be reported on that spouse's separate return. This is called the "California Rule." Conversely, in Texas, Idaho, and Louisiana, income from these separate properties is considered community income; thus, if the spouses are filing separately, the income would be shared between them on their separate returns. This is called the "Texas Rule."

Section 66 of the Internal Revenue Code sets forth a specific rule for treatment of community income where the spouses live apart. Section 66 was passed by Congress in 1980 and was effective 1981 and thereafter. The need for this section arose because in community property states each spouse is liable for one-half the tax on income. Generally, when spouses are living apart, the spouse that earns the income will keep it.

If two individuals are married to each other at some time during a calendar year, but live apart for the *entire* tax year, do not file a joint return, and one or both have earned income, none of which is transferred between them, the following rules cover the reporting of income on their separate tax returns:

1. Earned income (other than trade or business income and partnership income) is treated as income of the spouse who rendered the personal services.

2. Trade or business income is treated as the husband's income unless the wife exercises substantially all of the management and control of the business.

3. Community income derived from the separate property of one spouse is treated as the income of such spouse.

4. All other community income is taxed in accordance with the applicable community property law. Code Sec. 879(a).

¶ 3225 TENANCY BY THE ENTIRETY

If property is held by a married couple as tenants by the entirety, all income from the property must be included by the husband in his return or must be shared equally by husband and wife, depending on state law. In states which have abolished the common law rule, such as Delaware, Florida, Indiana, Maryland, Michigan, Missouri, New York, Oregon, Pennsylvania, and the District of Columbia, one-half of the income is reported on the husband's tax return and one-half on the wife's tax return.

¶ 3235 JOINT TENANTS AND TENANTS IN COMMON

Parties holding property as joint tenants each report income from the property in direct proportion to their interest in the property. When one of the parties dies, the interest in the property is automatically passed to the surviving joint tenant. Upon the death of a tenant in common, the deceased's interest is automatically transferred to the heirs. Parties holding property as tenants in common are taxed on their proportionate share of income based on their contribution of ownership of the property.

Items Included in Gross Income

Having discussed the concept of income, what it is, when it is taxable, and to whom it is taxable, attention now will be focused on the types of items which are included in gross income.

¶ 3301 LIST OF INCOME ITEMS

As has been explained, the concept of income is broad and general. Section 61(a) of the Code simply lists fifteen items which must be included in gross income. Remember, gross income is in no way limited to these fifteen income items.

1. Compensation for services, including fees, commissions, fringe benefits, and similar items

2. Gross income derived from business

3. Gain derived from dealings in property (discussed in Chapters 9–11)

4. Interest

5. Rents

6. Royalties

7. Dividends

8. Alimony and separate maintenance payments

9. Annuities (discussed in Chapter 4)

10. Income from life insurance and endowment contracts

11. Pensions (discussed in Chapter 23)

12. Income from discharge of indebtedness

13. Distributive share of partnership gross income (discussed in Chapter 19)

14. Income in respect of a decedent (discussed in Chapter 22)

15. Income from an interest in an estate or trust (discussed in Chapter 22)

Section 61(a) clearly points out that gross income is not limited to these items, but that these are merely the most typical sources of income. It is irrelevant whether or not the above items are received in money, goods, or services. Note that items such as gifts or inheritances are not included. On the other hand, illegal gains such as gambling gains and income from swindling or extortion must be included in income. Sections 71–90 of the Internal Revenue Code concern themselves with items to be included as gross income. Obviously there are a number of items that are specifically exempted from gross income. Chapter 4 discusses these items. They can be found in Sections 101–136 of the Internal Revenue Code.

¶ 3315   COMPENSATION FOR SERVICES

All compensation received by the individual is included in gross income. This would include salary, bonuses, tips, commissions, director's fees, and any other amounts received for personal services. This compensation is taxed when received and not when earned unless the individual reports income under the accrual method. Generally, the individual includes as income the fair market value of property received. If the taxpayer receives corporate stock as compensation for services, the fair market value of the stock, at the time of transfer, must be included in gross income.

> *Example 3.6.* Charlotte Moss, a cash basis taxpayer, received a paycheck on Friday, January 2, 1999. The pay period covered is for the previous two weeks' work. This money is included on her 1999 tax return, not her 1998 return. However, if Charlotte had had the option of receiving her paycheck on December 31, 1998, by simply requesting it, then, under the constructive receipt doctrine, her salary would have been taxed in 1998.

Year-end bonuses are included in the tax return for the year they are received. Voluntary payments such as severance pay and Christmas bonuses also must be included. Meals and living quarters which an employee receives constitute gross income unless they are furnished for the convenience of the employer. Further, they must be furnished on the employer's premises. With respect to lodging, it must be a condition of employment. See ¶ 4185 for a complete discussion of meals and lodging as compensation.

> *Example 3.7.* Charlotte's employer, IBC Inc. informed employees on December 15, 1998, that a 5 percent cash bonus, based on 1998

earnings, would be paid to all employees on February 9, 1999. Charlotte would have to include her bonus in her 1999 tax return.

Bartering is becoming a more common practice in the United States today. Bartering is the exchange of your property or services for another's property or services. The fair market value of property or services received must be included in gross income.

Example 3.8. Robert Jones, owner of Jones' Dry Cleaning, was discussing his income tax problems with one of his best customers, Sam Owen. Sam is an accountant and is self-employed. During the course of their conversation, they struck a deal. Jones would do all of Owen's cleaning and Owen would do Jones's accounts and tax returns. No money would exchange hands. In this instance, both Jones and Owen must include in their income the fair market value of services received.

Small items given by the employer to the employee, such as a turkey at Thanksgiving or a ham at Christmas, are not taxable to the employee even though the employer is allowed a deduction for the item as a business expense. However, a small cash stipend, such as a $20 bill at Christmas or a gift certificate, would be considered as taxable and includible in gross income.

¶ 3325 COMPENSATION v. GIFT

Section 102(a) explicitly excludes the value of property acquired by gift from being included in gross income. However, Section 102(b) does not exclude the income earned on the property after it is received.

In determining whether or not a payment or transfer is in the form of compensation or a gift, the Supreme Court has said that it is necessary to consider all the relevant surrounding circumstances and especially to determine the intent of the parties involved. *A.G. Bogardus,* 37-2 USTC ¶ 9534, 302 U.S. 34, 58 S.Ct. 61 (1937). The Fifth Circuit Court of Appeals said that a gift is "not intended as a return of value or made because of any intent to repay another what is his due, but bestowed only because of personal affection or regard or pity, or from general motives of philanthropy or charity." *C. Schall,* 49-1 USTC ¶ 9298, 174 F.2d 893 (CA-5 1949).

A payment or transfer can be considered compensation by one party and a gift by the other. However, the Supreme Court stated in *Bogardus:*

The statute definitely distinguishes between compensation on the one hand and gifts on the other hand, the former being taxable and the latter free from taxation. The two terms are, and were meant to be, mutually exclusive; and a bestowal of money cannot, under the statute, be both a gift and a payment of compensation.

When determining if the payment was compensation or a gift, the courts look to see if the transferor took a tax deduction for the payment. If the transferor did, then it indicates that the payment was meant to be compensation. On the other hand, if the transferor did not take a tax deduction for the sum, it is not conclusive, but it is evidence that a gift was intended. The mere fact that an employer was not legally obliged to make a payment is not, in itself, evidence of a gift. Code Sec. 102(c).

In the landmark case of *Duberstein,* the Supreme Court reiterated the statement that a gift proceeds from "detached and disinterested generosity." *M. Duberstein,* 60-2 USTC ¶ 9519, 363 U.S. 278, 80 S.Ct. 1190 (1960). Duberstein received a Cadillac from the president of a company with whom he had done business for quite some time. Duberstein had on several occasions given business leads to this other company. Naturally, the Commissioner insisted Duberstein must include the fair market value in gross income and Duberstein insisted it was a gift. The Supreme Court stated:

> despite the characterization of the transfer of the Cadillac by the parties and the absence of any obligation, even of a moral nature, to make it, it was at bottom a recompense for Duberstein's past services, or an inducement for him to be of further service in the future.

The *Duberstein* case concludes with the general premise that corporations ordinarily just do not make gifts without receiving some economic benefit in return.

¶ 3331   JURY DUTY PAY

Jury duty pay must be included in gross income. However, any jury duty pay remitted to an employer in exchange for compensation for the period the employee was on jury duty is deductible from gross income. Code Sec. 62(a)(13).

¶ 3335   PRIZES AND AWARDS

Gross income includes amounts received as prizes and awards from radio and television give-away and quiz shows, lotteries, door prizes, and awards from contests. Where the prize or award is not made in money but in the form of property, the fair market value of such property must be included in gross income.

Scientific and Charitable Prizes and Awards

Prizes and awards in the fields of science, charity, and the arts (such as the Pulitzer Prize and the Nobel Peace Prize) are includible in gross income unless the recipient assigns the prize or award to a governmental agency or tax-exempt charitable organization. This assignment must be made prior to the recipient's using the item that is awarded. To be eligible for the exclusion the recipient (1) must have been selected without any action on the recipient's part to enter the contest and (2) must not be required to render any substantial future services as a condition to receiving the prize or award. Code Sec. 74(b). If a proper assignment is made, none of the winnings need be included in the recipient's gross income. However, the recipient is not allowed a charitable contribution deduction.

Employee Achievement Awards

Employee awards for length of service or safety achievement are excludable from gross income by the employee and are deductible by the employer if they are awarded as part of a meaningful presentation, and:

1. The awards do not exceed a total of $400 for all *nonqualified plan awards* received by any one employee during the tax year, or

2. The awards do not exceed $1,600 for all *qualified plan awards* received by any one employee during the tax year.

However, the $1,600 limitation applies in the aggregate. Thus, the $400 limitation and the $1,600 limitation cannot be added together to allow deductions exceeding $1,600. Code Sec. 274(j)(2).

A qualified plan award is one awarded as part of an established written plan or program by the employer that does not discriminate in favor of highly compensated employees. An employee achievement award will not be considered a qualified plan award if the average cost of all employee achievement awards provided by the employer during the tax year exceeds $400. The average cost does not include awards of nominal value. Code Sec. 274(j)(3)(B). The following example illustrates the tax status of employee achievement awards.

Example 3.9. Ben Smith received three employee achievement awards during 1998. Two were qualified awards of a tennis racket valued at $200 and a television/stereo valued at $1,300. The third was a nonqualified award of a briefcase valued at $250. Ben's employer satisfies all the requirements for qualified plan awards. Inasmuch as Ben's total of awards received exceeds $1,600, he must include the excess $150 ($1,750 − $1,600) in gross income.

A length of service award does not qualify if it was received by an employee within the first five years of employment or if the recipient received a length of service award within the previous four years. Safety achievement awards cannot be given to more than 10 percent of the employees. Managers, administrators, clerical employees, and other professional employees are not eligible for safety achievement awards.

¶ 3345 SCHOLARSHIPS AND FELLOWSHIPS

Generally, gross income does not include any amount received as a qualified scholarship by an individual who is a degree candidate at an educational organization. The amount received by a degree candidate is excludable up to the aggregate amount incurred by the candidate for tuition and course-related expenses, such as books, supplies, and equipment. No exclusion is allowed for room, board, or incidental expenses.

Non-degree candidates must include in income scholarships and fellowships. The exclusion provision applies only to degree candidates. Under special rules the exclusion provision extends to tuition reductions provided for the education (below the graduate level) of employees of an educational institution. The rules do not affect the exclusion for employer-provided educational assistance to an employee (see ¶ 4201).

Example 3.10. Mary Smart is a full-time undergraduate student at State University. Mary is an honor student and received a $3,000-per-year scholarship. The scholarship award pays for Mary's tuition ($2,000), books ($200), equipment ($300), and incidental expenses ($500). Mary would have to include in her gross income only the $500 for incidental expenses.

¶ 3355 GROSS INCOME DERIVED FROM BUSINESS

Gross income is defined by the Code as including gross income derived from a business. Gross income means total sales revenues less cost of goods sold, plus income from investments and any other incidental income. The Regulations state that gross income shall be determined as follows:

without subtraction of selling expenses, losses or other items not ordinarily used in computing costs of goods sold . . . . The cost of goods sold should be determined in accordance with the method of accounting consistently used by the taxpayer. Reg. § 1.61-3(a).

Example 3.11. The income statement of ABC, a manufacturing enterprise, shows the following information:

Gross Sales		$162,000
Less: Cost of Goods Sold:		
Inventory, January 1	$ 30,000	
Purchases	160,000	
Goods Available for Sale	$190,000	
Less: Inventory, December 31	45,000	
Cost of Goods Sold		$145,000
Gross Profit (Gross Income)		$ 17,000

The taxpayer, in this example, would include $17,000 in gross income. The net profit or loss of a business is determined by subtracting from gross profit (income) all selling, as well as general and administrative, expenses. Continuing on from the previous calculations:

Gross Profit (Income)		$17,000
Less: Selling Expenses	$4,000	
General and Administrative Expenses	8,000	
Total Operating Expenses		$12,000
Net Profit (Income)		$ 5,000

In the determination of penalties and additional tax due to the omission of items of income, gross income is defined in Code Sec. 6501(e)(1)(A)(i) as total income received or accrued "prior to diminution by the cost of such sales."

¶ 3375 PARTNERSHIPS AND S CORPORATIONS

Partnerships and S corporations are not taxed, but their taxable income is taxed to the individual partners or shareholders. Each partner or shareholder absorbs a proportionate share of the firm's income, whether or not distributed. An S corporation is a small business corporation desiring not to be taxed at the corporate level. A corporation desiring S corporation status must meet various requirements, including valid stockholder approval of S status.

¶ 3385 INTEREST

Interest received by a taxpayer or credited to the taxpayer must be included in gross income. Interest income includes interest on bank accounts, loans, notes, corporate bonds, and U.S. savings bonds. Interest income received on obligations of states, territories, or a possession of the United States is generally wholly exempt from taxation.

Example 3.12. Leo Lionstone has a savings account at First National Bank that pays him interest on June 30 and December 31 of each year. In 1998, $25 of interest income was credited to his account in June and $28 of interest income on December 31. Even though Leo makes no withdrawals during the year, he must include $53 of interest income in his 1998 gross income. He had an absolute right to the money; therefore, he must recognize the income.

A cash basis taxpayer reports interest income when received. Interest earned on bank accounts is considered received, under the constructive receipt doctrine, when credited to the account. An accrual basis taxpayer reports interest income as it accrues. Interest on U.S. Series EE savings bonds may be reported each year or the taxpayer may elect to report the entire amount in the year that the bond matures. Once the taxpayer chooses a method, all of the taxpayer's Series EE savings bonds must be reported in the same manner. Code Sec. 454.

Below-Market Interest Loans

For many years individuals have been making use of below-market interest rate loans. This was especially popular among family members. To remedy this tax-avoidance scheme the Tax Reform Act of 1984 imputed interest on interest-free or below-market demand and term loans. A below-market interest demand loan is defined as a demand loan with an interest rate below the applicable federal short-term rate. A demand loan is defined as any loan payable in full on demand of the lender. A term loan is a below-market loan if the amount loaned exceeds the present value of all payments due under the loan. Imputed interest is computed by using the statutory federal rate of interest. The federal rate is adjusted monthly and published by the IRS. In an effort to simplify the computation of forgone interest on below-market demand loans, the IRS established a "blended annual rate." For the year 1997, the blended annual rate was set at 5.85 percent and, for 1996, it was 5.77 percent.

Section 7872(c), relating to loans with below-market interest rates, applies to:

1. gift loans,
2. compensation-related loans,

3.   corporation-shareholder loans,

4.   "tax-avoidance" loans (i.e., tax avoidance being the principal purpose of the loan),

5.   other below-market loans in which the interest arrangements have a significant effect on federal tax liability, and

6.   loans by elderly individuals to qualified continuing care facilities.

A below-market loan is treated as a gift, dividend, contribution to capital, payment of compensation, or other payment depending on the substance of the transaction. For below-market loans that are not gift loans, "forgone interest" is deductible by the borrower and must be included in the lender's gross income. In an employer-employee relationship it is treated as additional compensation. With respect to a corporation-shareholder relationship it is treated as if the corporation paid a dividend. The forgone interest on a gift loan is treated as a taxable gift. Forgone interest may be defined as the additional interest which would have been paid had the loan been granted at "the market rate" rather than at the artificially low rate created for the below-market rate loan.

Example 3.13. *Prior to June 7, 1984:* On January 1, 1983, Philip made a $200,000 loan to his daughter, Leah, for two years at a simple interest rate of 2 percent. Leah is in the 15 percent tax bracket and Philip is in the 36 percent tax bracket. Further, assume both Philip and Leah earn 10 percent simple interest on the $200,000. Before making the loan, Philip would have been taxed $7,200 ($200,000 × .10 × .36). After the loan, their family tax obligation would be $3,840.

Calculations:

Philip:	Income ($200,000 × .02)	$ 4,000	
	Tax at 36 percent		$1,440
Leah:	Income ($200,000 × .10)	$20,000	
	Interest Expense	4,000	
	Net Interest Income	$16,000	
	Tax at 15 percent		2,400
	Total Tax Liabilities of Philip and Leah		$3,840

Notice a savings to Philip and Leah of $3,360 per year ($7,200 less $3,840).

Current rule: Assume the loan was made this year and assume a blended annual rate of 5.85 percent. The imputed interest on the $200,000 loan would be $11,700.

In this case, Leah would have been deemed to have made an additional interest payment of $7,700 ($11,700 − $4,000), and Philip would have been deemed to have received $11,700 in interest income. Further, Philip would be deemed to have made a gift of $7,700 to Leah.

Gift, Employee, and Commercial Loans

The rules for below-market loans do not apply to:

1. Gift loans between individuals if:

    a. the aggregate outstanding amount of loans between such individuals does not exceed $10,000, and

    b. the loan is not attributable to the purchase or carrying of income-producing assets; or

2. Compensation-related or corporation-shareholder loans if:

    a. the aggregate outstanding amount of loans between the borrower and the lender does not exceed $10,000, and

    b. the avoidance of federal tax is not a principal purpose of the loan. Code Sec. 7872(c).

Special rules exist for gift loans between individuals that do not exceed $100,000. The imputed interest is limited to the borrower's net investment income for the tax year. However, if the borrower uses the proceeds for investment purposes and the borrower's investment income is in excess of $1,000, interest is imputed. If the borrower has net investment income of $1,000 or less for the year, the borrower's net investment income is deemed to be zero.

Some loans are specifically excluded from the rules for below-market loans, such as:

1. loans made available by lenders to the general public on the same terms and conditions;

2. loans subsidized by a federal, state, or municipal government that are made available to the general public;

3. certain employee-relocation loans;

4. loans to or from a foreign person, unless the interest would be effectively connected with the conduct of a U.S. trade or business and not exempt from U.S. tax under an income tax treaty; and

5. loans on which the interest arrangement can be shown to have no significant effect on the federal tax liability of the lender or the borrower.

If a taxpayer structures a transaction to be similar to a loan not subject to the rules and one of the principal purposes of structuring the transaction is the avoidance of federal tax, the loan will be considered a tax-avoidance loan and subject to the rules for below-market loans.

Whether an interest arrangement has a significant effect on the federal tax liability (item 5, above) will be determined by all the facts and circumstances. Some factors to be considered are:

1. whether items of income and deduction generated by the loan offset each other,

2. the amount of such items,

3. the cost of complying with the below-market loan provisions if they applied, and

4. any reasons, other than taxes, for structuring the transaction as a below-market loan.

These rules apply to term loans made after June 6, 1984, and to demand loans outstanding after that date.

Bond Transactions

When a bond is sold between interest dates and the accrued interest is added to the selling price, the seller must recognize the interest as income. All interest earned from the date of purchase is taxable to the buyer.

Example 3.14. Aaron Adams purchases a $1,000 bond of the Rhody Corporation from Baron Ziegler at face value. Interest is paid at a rate of 9 percent on April 1 and October 1. The bond was purchased on June 1 for $1,015 ($15 representing accrued interest). Baron, the seller, must report $15 as interest income. On October 1 Aaron will receive $45 interest of which $30 ($45 − $15) will be taxable.

"Flat" Basis Bonds

Occasionally, a taxpayer will buy a bond with defaulted interest included in the purchase price. In this case, the entire amount is considered a capital investment. However, if after the purchase date interest accrues on the bond, this would be considered interest income when received. Recovery of defaulted interest on a flat bond results in no income. All interest in excess of basis, but less than the face amount of the bonds, is taxable as a capital gain.

Example 3.15. Aaron Adams purchases a $1,000 bond of the Rhody Corporation for $700 "flat." Interest is paid at the rate of 9 percent on April 1 and October 1. On June 1, when Adams bought the bond, there was $105 accrued interest in default. On October 1, Adams received $135 interest from Rhody Corporation. The $105 of defaulted interest is considered a return of investment and the $30 ($135 − $105) is interest income. Adams's basis in the bond is now $595 ($700 − $105).

¶ 3395   RENT AND ROYALTY INCOME

Rental income is the amount received by the owner of property for allowing someone else to use it. Rental income must be included in gross income. All expenses (i.e., depreciation, taxes, repairs, and other ordinary and necessary expenses attributable to the rental property) are deductible from gross income. If the tenant instead of paying rent pays off obligations of the landlord, then this amount must be included in the gross income of the landlord. However, the landlord may deduct these expenses if they would otherwise be deductible. For example, if the tenant pays the property taxes in lieu of rent, the landlord may deduct this sum from gross income. However, the landlord may deduct this sum from gross income in the year received, whether the taxpayer is on the cash or accrual basis, but anticipated expenses may not be deducted until actually paid. The tenant, if rent is paid in advance, is not allowed a tax deduction for rent expense until the year in which the payment is due even though the cash basis is used. Rent received in advance is always taxable when received.

Royalty income received for allowing someone the use of copyrights, patents, licenses, and rights to oil, gas, or other mineral properties is includible in gross income. Security deposits received from tenants are not included in gross income if they are to be returned to the tenant. If the security deposit is to be used as a final payment of rent, then it is advance rent and must be included in gross income when it is received.

Lessee Improvements

Improvements made by the lessee are not income to the lessor either at the time the improvements are made or upon termination of the lease. Code Sec. 1019. Gain or loss will be recognized only at the time the property is sold.

However, where the lessee makes repairs which are the responsibility of the lessor or makes improvements in lieu of rent, the lessor has rental income to the extent of the market value of the improvements.

Example 3.16. Robert Wolf entered into a 50-year lease with Cleveland Inc. on January 7, 1985. Wolf remodeled the building at a cost of $50,000. The building has a book value of $20,000 to Cleveland Inc. In 1998, Wolf defaulted and Cleveland Inc. took back the building. The improvements made by Wolf are not income to Cleveland Inc. in 1998. Only when the building is sold would Cleveland Inc. recognize gain on the improvements.

Example 3.17. Robert Wolf and Cleveland Inc. agreed that Mr. Wolf would make improvements to the building amounting to $10,000. In exchange for making these improvements, Cleveland Inc. will not charge Mr. Wolf rent of $10,000 in 1998. In this case, Cleveland Inc. has $10,000 of rental income for 1998.

Lease Cancellations and Bonuses

Bonuses received for the granting of a lease are considered rental income. Also, payments received by a landlord to cancel or modify a lease must be included in gross income. However, payments made to a tenant to cancel a lease are considered as "amounts received in exchange for such lease or agreement." Code Sec. 1241. Further, Section 1241 applies to amounts received for the cancellation of a distributor's agreement if the distributor has a substantial capital investment in the distributorship. Usually, the payment received by a tenant results in capital gain income because the lease is considered a capital asset (see ¶ 11,155).

¶ 3401 DIVIDEND INCOME

The term "dividend" means "any distribution of property made by a corporation to its shareholders out of its earnings and profits." Code Sec. 316(a). In the above definition, dividends were defined in terms of "property." The term property is defined as "money, securities, and any other property." Code Sec. 317(a). Notice, it does not include stock or rights to acquire stock.

Distributions from a corporation in the form of a dividend only come after they have been authorized by the board of directors. The distribution may take the form of cash or other assets, but a true dividend must come from earnings accumulated after February 28, 1913. Code Sec. 316; Reg. § 1.316-1. Retained earnings are the corporation's taxable income that has been retained in the business and not previously distributed. Usually, the directors, when desiring to make a distribution to the stockholders, award cash. Basically there are two common types of dividends:

1. cash
2. stock (dividends and rights)

Cash Dividend

When dealing with dividends, one must be cognizant of four dates:

1. declaration
2. record
3. payment
4. receipt

Example 3.18. The board of directors of the Rhody Corporation declares on March 3, 1998, a cash dividend of $1.00 per share to be paid on May 27, 1998, to each stockholder of record as of April 28, 1998. The stockholder received the dividend on June 9, 1998. The four dates in the example were:

1. Declaration Date—March 3, 1998
2. Record Date—April 28, 1998
3. Payment Date—May 27, 1998
4. Receipt Date—June 9, 1998

Anyone who owns shares of stock of Rhody Corporation on April 28, 1998, is entitled to a $1.00 per share cash dividend. Therefore, the market value of the stock from March 1 until April 28 should reflect the $1.00 per share dividend. If a share of stock is sold on May 5, 1998, the stockholder still will receive the dividend because he or she was a shareholder on the date of record. The person receiving the cash dividend must recognize ordinary income for that amount. The shareholder having the unqualified right to demand payment must recognize taxable income. Reg. § 1.301-1. The date the dividend is received by the taxpayer, not the date the dividend is declared, determines taxability. Unlike accrued interest income on bonds, no part of the purchase may be allocated to dividend income.

Although from a theoretical viewpoint in the above example, the $1.00 dividend can be identified from the purchase price, in reality this is not always the case. With interest on bonds, the interest can be readily determined at any time. A person who has a stockbroker collect the dividend is still required to pay tax on it under the rules of the constructive receipt doctrine. Also, if a dividend is declared and a person dies before the payment date, the dividend income is not included in the final income tax return, but in the estate tax return. *M. Putnam Est.*, 57-1 USTC ¶ 9200, 352 U.S. 82, 77 S.Ct. 175 (1956).

Mutual Funds

Individuals holding an interest in a mutual fund may receive any combination of three types of distribution: ordinary dividends, return of capital, and capital gains dividends. Taxpayers are notified within 45 days after the close of the tax year of the distribution into the above three classes from dividends distributed during the year. For example, the stockholders will be informed of the portion of the dividends received to be treated as a long-term capital gain. Further, they will be apprised of the portion of the mutual fund's established capital gains they must report as long-term capital gains even though the company has retained them. Ordinary dividends of a mutual fund are reported as dividend income to the recipient.

Life Insurance and Annuity Contracts

Dividends on life insurance and annuity contracts are excludable from gross income and are considered a reduction in the cost of the policy. Code Sec. 301. If it is a fully paid-up life insurance policy and the dividend exceeds the net premiums paid, then the excess is fully taxable. Also, once payment of the proceeds under the contract has commenced, then any dividend received is fully taxable.

Example 3.19. Leah Lambert and her husband receive the following dividends during 1998:

	Leah	Husband
Able Auto Parts	$300	
Get Rich REIT		$450
Canadian Exploration	$250	
Live Long Insurance		$200

For the year 1998, all of the above-listed dividends are includible in gross income except the dividend from Live Long Insurance, which is considered a reduction in premium cost. Therefore, Leah has $550 of dividend income and her husband has $450 in dividend income, for a total of $1,000. This total amount of $1,000 must be included in gross income.

Example 3.20. Leah and her husband purchased a 10-year endowment policy. The policy commences payments on January 1, 1999. Therefore, any dividends issued by the company in 1998 would not be taxable. Any dividends issued by the company after January 1, 1999, would be fully taxable.

Example 3.21. Assume in Example 3.20 that Leah and her husband paid $25,000 for the policy. Over the years, they had received $2,200 in dividends. Therefore, their basis in the policy is $22,800 ($25,000 − $2,200).

The above rules concerning life insurance and annuity contracts apply regardless of whether the taxpayer receives the dividend in cash or lets it accumulate to purchase additional insurance.

Stock Dividends

A stock dividend is defined as a distribution by a corporation of its own stock, including treasury stock. Reg. § 1.305-1. Stock dividends usually are not included in the gross income of the recipient. However, there are certain exceptions to this rule. They are as follows:

1. Distributions in lieu of money. If the stockholder has the option of receiving stock in lieu of money, then the corporate distribution is taxable to the recipient.

2. Disproportionate distributions. If some shareholders receive property and other shareholders receive stock so as to alter the individual stockholder's proportionate interest in the corporation, then the distribution is included as gross income.

3. Distributions of common and preferred stock. If some stockholders receive common stock and other stockholders receive preferred stock, then the distribution is considered part of gross income.

4. Distributions on preferred stock. A stock dividend on preferred stock is taxable to the recipient unless it increases the conversion ratio of convertible preferred stock made specifically to take into account a stock dividend or stock split on the convertible preferred stock in which case it is tax free. Code Sec. 305(b)(4).

5. Distributions of convertible preferred stock. A distribution of convertible preferred stock is taxable to the recipient unless it can be proven to the Commissioner that the individual stockholder's equity in the corporation remains constant.

Upon receipt of a nontaxable stock dividend, the stockholder must allocate the original cost over all the shares the stockholder presently owns.

Example 3.22. Aaron Adams owns 100 shares of Rhody Corporation common stock which he purchased for $11 per share in 1994 for a total cost of $1,100. Rhody Corporation pays a 10 percent stock dividend in June 1998, and Aaron receives 10 shares (10 percent of 100 shares) of stock. Therefore, he now owns 110 shares of stock and his basis remains at $1,100 or $10 per share ($1,100/110 shares). At the time any of the 110 shares is sold, its basis is $10 per share.

Example 3.23. If, in Example 3.22, instead of receiving the common stock, Aaron received 20 shares of Rhody Corporation preferred stock as a stock dividend and it had a fair market value of $10 per share and the 100 original shares of Rhody Corporation common stock at this time had a fair market value of $2,000, then the following computations would be necessary:

Computations:

Basis of original stock $1,100

Fair market value of original stock $2,000
Fair market value of the new preferred stock 200

Fair market value of preferred and common $2,200

Basis of original 100 shares after stock dividend 1,100 × 2,000/2,200 .... $1,000
Basis of new stock after the dividend 1,100 × 200/2,200 .... $ 100

To determine whether or not the sale should be treated as a long-term capital gain, the date when the original shares were purchased is the controlling factor. To be classified as a long-term gain, a capital asset must be held for more than one year. For 1998, the maximum tax on capital gains is 20 percent if held greater than 18 months.

The new shares take on the basis of the old shares. If lots of the old shares were purchased on different dates and the dividend shares cannot be identified with any particular lot, then the new shares take the basis of the earliest purchased stock. Reg. § 1.1012-1(c).

Stock Rights

A stock right is defined as a distribution by a corporation to its shareholders of *rights* to purchase corporate stock. Usually, the shareholder has a right to buy the stock at less than fair market value. Therefore, the stock rights have a market value. The stockholder receiving the rights has three alternative courses of action. The stockholder may exercise, sell, or hold the stock rights.

If the market value of the stock rights is less than 15 percent of the market value of the stock with respect to which it is distributed, then the basis of the rights is zero unless the shareholder irrevocably elects to allocate the basis between the stock and the rights. Code Sec. 307(b)(1). Where the market value of the rights is 15 percent or greater, the basis must be allocated between the stock and rights according to their respective values on the date on which the rights are distributed to the stockholder, not the record date. In Chapter 9, at ¶ 9125, a full discussion appears on the allocation of basis for taxable and nontaxable stock rights.

¶ 3451 DIVORCE AND SEPARATION

Pre-1985 Agreements

Prior to the Tax Reform Act of 1984, Code Sec. 71 defined alimony as a series of support payments received after divorce or legal separation. If the following four conditions exist, then the recipient must include the alimony payments in gross income and the person making the payments is entitled to a tax deduction for adjusted gross income. The conditions are as follows:

1. Payments are required under the terms of the decree of divorce or separate maintenance or a written separation agreement or a decree of support.

2. Payments must be to discharge the legal obligation of support.

3. Payments must be periodic.

4. Payments must not be for child support.

The following payments would not qualify:

1. lump-sum settlements,

2. payments not required under the decree or agreement,

3. payments not arising out of a marital relationship (repayment of a loan), and

4. payments made before the decree.

Determining whether or not payments are periodic or lump-sum in nature can be quite difficult. If the installments are to be paid over an indefinite period of time, or where the period of time exceeds 10 years, by the terms of the decree, then the payments will qualify. It is not necessary that the payments come in regular intervals. However, only 10 percent of the total sum specified qualifies for alimony treatment. If more than 10 percent is paid in any year, that excess is considered a property settlement.

Example 3.24. The decree provides for the wife to receive $200,000 over 20 years at a rate of $10,000 per year. The $10,000 payment each year would qualify as alimony and the husband would receive the tax deduction. However, assume the wife received $55,000 in each of the first two years and the remaining $90,000 ($200,000 − $110,000) equally ($5,000 per year) over the following 18 years. The husband, in this situation, can deduct only $20,000 (10% of $200,000) in each of the first two years. During the remaining years, he may deduct $5,000 a year.

If the payments are in installments over a period of 10 or fewer years, then they do not qualify as alimony. However, there is an exception to this 10-year rule when payments are subject to certain contingencies. The payments will qualify for a tax deduction if state law or the divorce decree specifies that alimony will cease at the death of either spouse, remarriage of the spouse receiving alimony, or a change of economic status of either spouse.

Alimony and separate maintenance payments received by the taxpayer are included in gross income. Further, the payer is allowed a tax deduction.

Post-1984 Agreements

Payments under instruments executed after December 31, 1984, that meet the following requirements are deductible as alimony:

1. Payments must be made in cash.

2. Payments must be made under a divorce or separation instrument.

3. Parties must live in separate households after a divorce or separation decree is entered.

4. Alimony must end at the payee's death. (This provision need not be expressly stated in the divorce decree.)

5. Parties involved may not file a joint return.

If the above conditions are met, it is of no consequence that the payments may be designated as consideration for property or that they may be in discharge of a fixed dollar obligation.

A special feature was added that the parties could designate by written agreement payments otherwise qualifying as alimony payments as excludable by the payee and nondeductible by the payer. Code Sec. 71(b)(1)(B).

The Tax Reform Act of 1986 changed only a few rules with respect to divorces. However, because of the lower tax rates and increased exemptions for dependents, tax planning for pending divorces is essential and tax planning for divorces executed after 1986 is highly recommended.

Alimony termination on payee's death. Under the 1986 law, the requirement that the "instrument must state" that payments must terminate on the payee's death has been repealed. This amendment is effective for divorce or separation instruments executed after December 31, 1984.

Front-loading limitation. The Tax Reform Act of 1986 fixed the amount of annual payments exempt from recapture at $15,000. The front-loading requirement under the recapture rules was set at three post-separation years.

Recapture rules. Under the revised recapture rules the tax treatment of past payments has been changed to require the inclusion of previously deducted alimony or separate maintenance payments in income. The revised recapture rules also allow the recipient spouse, who previously included the alimony in income, to deduct the recaptured amount.

Under the recapture rules adopted by the Tax Reform Act of 1986, payments will be recaptured if:

1. Payments made in the second post-separation year exceed the payments in the third post-separation year by more than $15,000, and/or

2. Payments made in the first post-separation year exceed the average alimony payments of the second post-separation year and the third post-separation year by more than $15,000.

The excess amounts in the first and second post-separation years only may be recaptured in the third post-separation year. The following examples illustrate the alimony recapture rules.

Example 3.25. Bob and Mary Barnsen were divorced on January 13, 1998. Mary pays Bob the following amounts of alimony under the terms of her divorce decree.

Year	Amount
1998 (1st post-separation year)	$70,000
1999 (2nd post-separation year)	40,000
2000 (3rd post-separation year)	20,000

Mary computes her amount to be recaptured as follows:

Year 2 Calculation

Payments in the second year	$40,000
Less: Payments in the third year	20,000
	$20,000
Less: $15,000	15,000
Amount of second-year payments subject to recapture in 2000	$ 5,000

The amount of second-year payments used in computing the recapture for the first post-separation year is $35,000 ($40,000 − $5,000).

Year 1 Calculation

Payments in the first year	$70,000
Less: Average payments made in the second and third year (($35,000 + $20,000) ÷ 2)	27,500
	$42,500
Less: $15,000	15,000
Amount of first-year payments subject to recapture in 2000	$27,500

Therefore, Bob has gross income of $70,000 and $40,000 in 1998 and 1999, respectively. In 2000, the recapture of $32,500 exceeds the $20,000 alimony received; therefore, Bob has a deduction of $12,500. Mary deducts alimony of $70,000 in the first post-separation year and $40,000 in the second. In year three, she must recapture $32,500 ($5,000 + $27,500) which exceeds her third year payment of $20,000. Therefore, she has income of $12,500 in 2000.

Example 3.26. Bill and Alice Bailey were divorced on January 6, 1998. Bill makes the following alimony payments to Alice under a divorce decree.

Year	Amount
1998 (1st post-separation year)	$50,000
1999 (2nd post-separation year)	18,000
2000 (3rd post-separation year)	0

Year 2 Calculation

Payments in the second year	$18,000
Less: Payments in the third year	0
	$18,000
Less: $15,000	15,000
Amount of second-year payments subject to recapture in 2000	$ 3,000

Year 1 Calculation

Payments in the first year	$50,000
Less: Average payments made in the second and third year	
(($15,000 + $0) ÷ 2)	7,500
	$42,500
Less: $15,000	15,000
Amount of first-year payments subject to recapture in 2000 ..	$27,500

Note that in calculating the recapture amount for the first year, only $15,000, rather than $18,000, is treated as paid in the second year. This is because the average of payments made in the second and third years does not include the $3,000 payment made in the second year that is recaptured in the third year.

Bill will show $30,500 as income on his 2000 tax return and Alice will show a tax deduction of $30,500 on her 2000 tax return.

Bill deducts as alimony $50,000 in 1998 and $18,000 in 1999 and Alice includes in her gross income $50,000 and $18,000 in those two years.

Exceptions to the recapture rule. There are three exceptions to the recapture rule (in addition to the $15,000 floor).

1. Payments cease by reason of death or remarriage prior to the end of the third post-separation year.

2. Payments received under a temporary support order before the divorce or separation.

3. Payments pursuant to a continuing liability to pay a fixed part of your income from a business or property or from compensation for employment or self-employment.

If the payer stops or reduces the amount of alimony or separate maintenance during any of the first three post-separation years for any other than the above listed reasons then the payments are subject to recapture.

Example 3.27. Randy Reeves is required under the terms of a divorce decree to make payments to Candy of $25,000 in 1998, $30,000 in 1999, and $35,000 in 2000. Randy makes the first payment in 1998 and one-half the second payment when Candy remarries. Randy immediately stops making alimony payments. The recapture rule does not apply.

Exemption for Dependent Child

Under prior law, the spouse who had custody of the child was generally entitled to the personal exemption, provided the parents together furnished over half of the child's support. For years beginning after 1984, the custodial parent is entitled to the exemption unless the right to claim it is expressly waived. Code Sec. 152(e). For the custodial parent to transfer the exemption, the custodial parent must sign a written declaration transferring the exemption to the noncustodial parent. This written declaration may be made annually, for more than one year, or permanently. Even when the custodial parent transfers the exemption to the noncustodial parent, the custodial parent is still eligible for head of household filing status, the earned income credit, and the child and dependent care credit.

TAX BLUNDERS

1. Bob and Judy are in the middle of a divorce case. After the divorce Judy will be in the 31 percent tax bracket, and Bob will be in the 15 percent bracket. Judy wants to pay Bob $20,000 per year as alimony. Bob is insisting he receive $10,000 as alimony and $10,000 as child support. Bob will be the custodial parent. In this case it would benefit Judy to pay Bob's tax on the additional $10,000 alimony. She will save $1,600 by counting all $20,000 as alimony. ($3,100 tax savings less $1,500 payment of Bob's tax on $10,000).

2. Same facts as above. Judy would be wise to pay Bob for the personal exemption for the child. The savings to Bob is at the 15 percent rate. Judy would benefit from the 31 percent rate.

3. The lower tax rates drastically reduce the net after-tax value for alimony payments. The payer's net after-tax cost of alimony increases as the individual's tax bracket decreases.

    Assume Frank and Robin Forkes were divorced in 1982. Frank makes annual alimony payments of $15,000. In 1987, Frank had $75,000 of taxable income, which placed him in the 38.5 percent tax bracket. Therefore, his net after-tax cost for alimony was $9,225. In 1998, with the same taxable income his after-tax cost for alimony payments increased to $10,350 because Frank is in the 31 percent tax bracket in 1998.

Just as the lower tax rates prove disadvantageous to the payer of alimony, the increased exemption for dependents ($2,700 in 1998) makes the dependency exemption all the more important. Under present law, the custodial parent is automatically entitled to the dependency exemption.

Legal Fees

If a spouse is collecting alimony, legal fees incurred to enforce the payment are deductible as an itemized deduction by that spouse. Legal fees incurred in arranging the divorce settlement are not deductible. The payer-spouse cannot deduct any legal fees for the arrangement of the divorce or for the adjustment of alimony payments.

Payment in Arrears

Payments of amounts in arrears are deductible when paid. When a lump-sum settlement occurs for payment in arrears, even this is deductible.

Medical and Dental Expenses

Payments made for medical and dental expenses of the payee-spouse by the payer-spouse must be included in the gross income of the payee-spouse if they qualify as alimony. In addition, the payee-spouse is allowed to deduct these two expenses if the payee-spouse itemizes deductions.

Payments made for medical expenses of children of divorced parents may be deducted by the spouse making the payment. In this case, the children will be treated as dependents of both parents.

Transfer of Property Between Spouses

Under prior law, property transfers between divorcing spouses were taxable when they involved the release of support or marital rights. The 1984 tax law provides that no gain or loss will be recognized for property transfers between spouses during marriage, or former spouses incident to a divorce on transfers taking effect after July 18, 1984. The basis the property will carry is the same in the hands of the receiving spouse as it was in the hands of the transmitting spouse. Incident to a divorce means the transfer must occur within one year after the marriage ceases.

Example 3.28. Tom and Roberta Thorne are finishing up the terms of their divorce settlement. Roberta insists Tom turn over to her stock Tom purchased three years ago at a cost of $5,000. The current fair market value of this stock is $9,000. Under the pre-1985 tax law, Tom would have a $4,000 taxable gain, but under the 1984 tax law, the transfer of property between spouses results in no tax liability. Roberta will assume the stock with a tax basis of $5,000.

Child Support

Payments made by one spouse which are specifically identified for the support of minor children are not taxable to the other spouse and are not deductible by the first spouse. The support must be for the children of the parent making the payment. Under prior law, the spouse that contributed over 50 percent for the maintenance was allowed a dependency exemption for the child. Under the 1984 law, effective January 1, 1985, the custodial parent is entitled to the exemption unless he or she signs a waiver.

Example 3.29. By the terms of the divorce settlement, Bob Barter is directed to pay alimony of $800 per month and child support of $300 per month. Assume that $300 per month is more than 50 percent of the child's support. Bob is not allowed an exemption for support of his child. Under prior law, since Bob was providing more than half the support for the child, he was entitled to a dependency exemption if the divorce decree granted him the exemption. Under the 1984 tax law, the custodial parent is entitled to the exemption.

When the instrument sets forth one amount for alimony and one amount for child support and a particular payment is less than the total of the two, the payment will first apply towards the child support. Child support payments, if in arrears, must be paid before any future amounts may be considered as alimony.

Where the divorce decree, for example, requires the husband to pay $300 a month to his divorced wife and $150 a month for the support of a minor child and the husband pays only $150, it is nevertheless considered to be payment for the support of the child. Reg. § 1.71-1(e).

An important change was made in the area of child support payments. Under prior law, child support payments had to be "specifically designated." *J. Lester,* 61-1 USTC ¶ 9463, 366 U.S. 299, 81 S.Ct. 1343 (1961). If the divorce or separation agreement did not specify the amount for child support, then the entire amount is to be treated as alimony. The Tax Reform Act of 1984 changed this so as to allow for contingencies specified in the instrument relating to the child. For example, payments might change when the child leaves school, marries, etc.

Reporting Requirements

The taxpayer paying alimony must furnish the payee's taxpayer identification number on the tax return. Code Sec. 215(c). A $50 penalty in a calendar year will be levied for failure to comply with the reporting requirement unless it can be shown that failure to comply was due to reasonable cause and not to willful neglect. Code Sec. 6724(d)(3).

Life Insurance Proceeds and Annuities

Premiums paid on a life insurance policy by the payer spouse will be treated as alimony if the policy is owned by the payee spouse. Often a payer spouse will purchase a life insurance policy to provide for the continuation of alimony payments after the payer's death. Under prior law, such proceeds, if they met strict requirements, were indeed treated as alimony and the payments were includible in the gross income of the payee. Section 101(e) authorized such a procedure. Therefore, life insurance proceeds are no longer subject to alimony treatment. Rather, life insurance proceeds are treated as a transfer of a contract, and the payee assumes the carryover basis of the policy.

¶ 3485   DISCHARGE OF DEBT

When a debt is cancelled for a consideration, in whole or in part, the debtor realizes taxable income for the amount of the debt discharged. Code Sec. 61(a)(12). For example, if the debtor performed a personal service for the creditor and the debt was fully or partially cancelled, the debtor would have to realize as income the cancelled amount as compensation for services. Reg. § 1.61-12(a).

Creditor's Gifts

If a creditor gratuitously cancels a debt, then the amount forgiven is not income but a nontaxable gift. Code Sec. 102(a). The Supreme Court ruled that the cancellation of a debt by the creditor for "no consideration" is a gift and, therefore, no taxable income is involved. *Helvering v. American Dental Co.,* 43-1 USTC ¶ 9318, 318 U.S. 322, 63 S.Ct. 577 (1935). However, where consideration of any kind or amount is given for cancellation of the debt, it may be extremely difficult to prove the cancellation was gratuitous.

Bankruptcy and Insolvency

Generally, income from a nongratuitous discharge of indebtedness is includible in gross income unless it is excludable under Code Sec. 108. For discharges after 1986, two types of exclusions are provided in the following priority order (Code Sec. 108(a)):

1. The discharge occurs in a bankruptcy case under Title 11 of the U.S. Code.

2. The discharge occurs when the taxpayer is insolvent outside of bankruptcy. An insolvent taxpayer is one who has an excess of liabilities over the fair market value of assets immediately prior to the discharge. The exclusion is limited to the insolvent amount.

Discharge or reduction of debt in bankruptcy does not generate income. If the debt was incurred in connection with property used in a trade or business, the amount of debt that was discharged reduces certain tax attributes that could otherwise provide benefits in the future. Section 108(b)(5) allows the taxpayer to elect to apply any portion of the cancellation of debt to reduce the basis in depreciable property or real property held as inventory before reducing other tax attributes. This election by the taxpayer is available regardless of whether the debt is evidenced by a security. If the taxpayer does not elect to reduce the basis in depreciable property, then the amount excluded from gross income (the portion of the debt that was cancelled) reduces tax attributes in the order given in Code Sec. 109(b)(2)):

1. Net operating losses and carryovers

2. General business credit

3. Capital loss carryovers

4. Reduction of basis of the property of the taxpayer

5. Foreign tax credit carryovers

Tax attributes other than credit carryovers are reduced one dollar for each dollar of debt discharge excluded. Code Sec. 108(b)(3)(A). Where a taxpayer excludes income from the discharge of indebtedness in a Title 11 bankruptcy case or the discharge occurs when the taxpayer is insolvent and the taxpayer is required to apply such excluded income to reduce its tax attributes, the reduction for post-1986 tax years in foreign tax credit, research credit, and the general business credit carryovers is to be made at a rate of 33⅓ cents per dollar excluded. Code Sec. 108(b)(3)(B).

An insolvent taxpayer is allowed to exclude from gross income any discharge of indebtedness except that the amount excluded cannot exceed the amount by which the taxpayer is insolvent. Code Sec. 108(a)(3).

Example 3.30. Mike Merchant has assets of $50,000 and liabilities of $85,000. If one of Mike's creditors forgives him of $40,000 worth of debt, then Mike must recognize $5,000 ($50,000 − ($85,000 − $40,000)) of taxable income.

Purchase Money Debts

If a debt owed to the seller for the purchase of property is reduced by the seller, then no income is recognized by the purchaser. The reduction is a purchase price adjustment, not a discharge in indebtedness. Consequently, the purchaser recognizes no income even though the obligation has been reduced. In order for this rule to apply, there must be a "pure" cancellation of indebtedness income; the only relationship between the parties must be that of debtor and creditor, and the debt forgiveness must not simply be the method by which the creditor makes a payment to the debtor for services or property. Code Sec. 108(e)(5).

Corporate Debts

A shareholder's gratuitous forgiveness of the corporation's indebtedness or cancellation of the corporation's indebtedness to the shareholder is usually considered a contribution of capital to the corporation to the extent of the principal debt. Code Sec. 108(e)(6); Reg. § 1.61-12(a).

Example 3.31. Benjamin Warren is sales manager and shareholder of Cleveland Widget Inc. The company is in bankruptcy and Benjamin has not been paid for several months. Benjamin agrees to cancel the debt for the unpaid wages. Cleveland Widget Inc. recognized no income; instead, the cancellation is treated as a contribution of capital. Benjamin, who is on the cash basis, recognizes no income from the unpaid wages.

Student Loans

A special income exclusion applies to the discharge of all or part of a student loan under a governmental agency student loan program if, pursuant to the loan agreement, the discharge is made because the individual works for a specified period of time in certain geographical areas for certain classes of employers (e.g., as a doctor or nurse in a rural area). Code Sec. 108(f). The amount of the loan that is forgiven is excluded from gross income.

KEYSTONE PROBLEM

Roy and Ann are students at one of the country's finest state universities and wish to marry in the near future. Roy has inherited a potato farm from his late grandfather. Both have scholarships and part-time jobs. They will receive as gifts, property (a small house), and some stocks and bonds. Further, both have cash from savings and investments (about $10,000). Roy is also in debt ($5,000) to his uncle for a defunct rock band he had started as a freshman. His uncle will forgive the debt if Roy marries and settles down. The young couple have come to you for advice on financial planning. What are the principal considerations you feel they would need to take into account in planning their financial future? What steps would you advise them to take in setting up their affairs? Consider such concerns as terms of property ownership, whether to file a tax return jointly or separately, whether to choose the cash or accrual basis for paying tax, how to minimize tax liability, and other factors which you feel are relevant to the problem.

SUMMARY OF CHAPTER 3

✓ The economic benefit doctrine and the constructive receipt doctrine were conceived to explain what constitutes income and when an item of income is taxable.

✓ Under the accrual method of accounting, income is recognized when a transaction is consummated; under the cash method of accounting, income is recognized only when cash is received or constructively received.

✓ Section 61(a) of the Internal Revenue Code provides a list of 15 items that are includible in gross income. Gross income, however, is not limited to these items. (See checklist on the next page.)

✓ Several rules, including the alimony recapture rules, govern when alimony payments should be included in the recipient's gross income and when they are deuctible by the payer.

✓ Alimony is support payment made from one spouse to the other after divorce or legal separation. Child support consists of payments made by one spouse that are specifically identified for the support of minor children. Alimony and child support payments are subject to different tax treatments.

✓ When a debt is cancelled for a consideration, the debtor realizes taxable income for the amount of the debt discharged. Special rules govern the discharge of indebtedness for insolvent taxpayers.

SUMMARY CHECKLIST
Inclusions in Gross Income

Agreement not to Compete
Alimony
Annuities
Awards

Back Pay
Bad Debt Recoveries
Bargain Purchase from Employer
Bonuses
Breach of Contract Damages
Buried Treasure
Business Income

Cancellation of Debts
Cancellation of Lease
Christmas Bonuses
Commissions
Compensation for Personal Services

Debts Forgiven
Director's Fees
Discounts
Dividends

Embezzlement Proceeds
Employee Death Benefits
Employee's Awards
Employee's Bonuses
Estate and Trust Income
Executor's Fees

Fees

Gain from Sale of Property
Gain from Sale of Securities (including government securities)
Gambling Winnings

Hobby Income

Illegal Transactions (gains from gambling, betting, lotteries, embezzlement, protection money, etc.)
Insider's Profits
Interest

Jury Duty Fees

Kickbacks

Mileage Allowance
Military Pay

Notary Fees

Partnership Income
Pensions
Per Diem Allowance
Prizes
Professional Fees
Punitive Damages

Rents
Retirement Pay
Rewards
Royalties

Salaries
Severance Pay
Social Security Benefits for the Well-to-Do
Supplemental Unemployment Benefits

Tips and Gratuities
Travel Allowances

Unemployment Compensation
U.S. Savings Bonds (interest)

Wages

CHAPTER 3 QUESTIONS

1. Explain and differentiate between the three concepts of income: economic, legal, and accounting.

2. Compare and contrast the economic benefit doctrine and the constructive receipt doctrine.

3. Explain the fruit-of-the-tree doctrine and why it was established by the courts.

4. Mr. Whaley is short of money, so he asks his boss for an advance of $25. Is this taxable income to Whaley?

5. Mr. Randolph directs his employer to deduct $50 per week from his pay for the purchase of U.S. savings bonds. Can Mr. Randolph exclude this amount from his gross income? Explain.

6. Distinguish between compensation and gifts and identify the tax consequence associated with each.

7. Under what conditions will scholarships or fellowships granted by an educational institution not be included in gross income.

8. Are selling and administrative expenses of a business deducted before or after gross income?

9. In a rental agreement, when are improvements to the property made by the lessee regarded as income?

10. Describe under what terms a stock dividend would not be included in gross income.

11. An elderly woman gives stocks and bonds to her son for management and safekeeping. She keeps the stocks and bonds in her own name. He is to manage the portfolio at his choosing. To whom are the dividends and capital gains taxable at year-end?

12. Under what conditions are alimony payments from post-1984 divorces included in the recipient's gross income?

13. Give some examples of payments not qualifying as alimony.

14. Describe the intent of the "front-loading" provisions with respect to alimony payments.

15. Explain the tax status of child support payments.

16. Are payments for a life insurance policy that is owned by a former spouse who is the beneficiary of the policy deductible as alimony by the payer?

17. John and Jane divorced in 1998. They have two children, ages 6 and 11. The divorce decree requires John to pay $800 a month to Jane and does *not* specify the use of the money. According to the decree, the payments will stop after the children reach 18 or graduate from high school, whichever comes first. May John deduct the payments as alimony?

18. All of the following would be *excluded* from income as a qualified scholarship by an individual who is a candidate for a degree at a qualified educational institution, except:

    a. Tuition

    b. Student fees

    c. Course books

    d. Room and board

19. On January 1, 1994, John made a loan of $6,000 to his neighbor. The loan was evidenced by a written promise to repay the principal within three years and was to bear interest at a rate of 6% per annum. John's neighbor paid interest for the first year only and then his financial condition deteriorated. In 1998, John learned that he would only be able to recover $3,000 of the loan. The loan was *not* made in the course of John's business. May John deduct $3,000 of the loan on his tax return?

20. If another person cancels or pays your debts, but not as a loan or gift, have you constructively received this amount, and generally must you include it in your gross income for the year?

CHAPTER 3 PROBLEMS

21. Leah Sarah is employed at Cleveland Inc. at an annual salary of $45,000. Leah received $35,000 in salary in 1998 from Cleveland Inc., a prosperous company. They credited the unpaid salary to Leah Sarah's account. Leah only had to stop by the payroll office to receive her money. In January 1999, Leah Sarah requested and received the remaining $10,000 of her salary. How much income must Leah Sarah report on her 1998 income tax return?

22. Cal Corey and his wife are living in Las Vegas, Nevada, and own an apartment house from which they receive $20,000 a year in net rental income. Cal's wife also owns an apartment house, which she purchased as an investment while she was working before their recent marriage. The net rental income from this building is $15,000 a year. If the Coreys file separate returns what would each file for rental income on their tax returns?

23. Fred Miller, a teacher, had several additional sources of income during 1998. He received a $500 gift as a result of his helping a friend build a house, and he was assigned $300 of interest due his uncle on bonds his uncle owns. He also had the use of a van (value of $1,000) for the year from his parents who were traveling. Further, he received free, $600 of gasoline for the van because he tutored the son of the station owner free of charge. What of the additional income must be included in his income tax return?

24. Helen Troy, a student seeking a Master's degree in accounting, was awarded a 50 percent scholarship to graduate school (valued at $3,000) and a $6,000 per year teaching assistant-ship (not required of Master's level students). She also, because of her great beauty, won first prize in the Miss International Beauty Pageant. The prize included $14,000 in cash, a $25,000 car, a $10,000 scholarship, and travel expenses of $2,000 relating to the pageant. What must she include as gross income?

25. Billy Dent, as the owner of an apartment building, receives and makes the following payments during 1998:

Received in January 1998 rent that
   was due in December 1997 .... $5,000
Received in December 1998 rent
   not due until January 1999 4,000
Security deposit which is to be refunded
   when tenant vacates the apartment 500

How much rental income must Billy Dent include on his 1998 income tax return?

26. On February 1, 1998, Sarah Sugarman makes a $100,000 loan to Stephen Spears for a term of four months. The loan is to be repaid on May 31, 1998. Assume the applicable federal rate on February 1, 1998, for a loan of this term is 5 percent. Determine the amount of interest that must be paid on May 31, 1998, if the loan is not to be considered a below-market loan.

27. Judd Harrison owns 200 shares of stock in the Widget Company for which he paid $1,600 in 1989. The board of directors of the company decided to pay a 10 percent stock dividend in April 1998, for which Judd received 20 shares of stock. Was this a taxable stock dividend? Explain.

28. In January 1999, Judd Harrison decides to sell 100 shares in the Widget Company. Since April 1998, no stock dividends had been paid by the company. On the date the stock is sold the market price is $12 a share. What is the basis per share that Judd must use in computing any gains or losses? (Refers back to Problem 27.)

29. In 1998, Ollie Lingo and his wife have several endowment life insurance policies. On the first, which begins payment in 1999, but was fully paid by 1985, a dividend of $200 is declared and paid. On the second, which began payment in 1986, a $500 dividend is paid. On the third, which has two more years before it is paid up, a dividend of $100 is paid. How much of dividends received, if anything, is to be excluded from gross income? (In none of the cases cited above has the taxpayer received dividends in excess of premiums paid.)

30. Robin Redd sells his car to his son for $2,000 to be paid back at the rate of $100 per month. After seven payments Robin decides to give the car to his son as a birthday present. How much income must the son report from this transaction?

31. R.E. Lee entered into a 10-year lease in 1992 with Mr. Grant. In addition to the $6,000 a year rent he paid in 1998, he prepaid two months of 1999 rent totaling $1,000. Also, in 1998, Mr. Lee remodeled the kitchen at a cost of $1,500. How much rental income must Mr. Grant include in gross income in 1998? What is the tax status to Mr. Grant of the remodeling work completed by Mr. Lee?

32. Arnold and Barbara Cane were divorced in June 1998. Pursuant to the divorce decree, Arnold is obliged to perform as follows:

    a. Transfer title of their personal home to Barbara. They purchased the house in 1986 and their basis today is $40,000. The fair market value of the house is $50,000. The house is subject to a 25-year, $25,000 mortgage.

    b. Arnold is to continue making payments on the house until it is fully paid off. In 1998, Arnold made payments totaling $1,800.

    c. Arnold is to make $300 per month payments to Barbara. Of this amount one-half is for child support. The divorce decree further states that alimony is to cease upon the death of the wife. In 1998, he made six payments.

    How do the transactions in the divorce agreement affect Arnold's and Barbara's taxable income?

33. John and Mary Johnson were divorced in January 1998. By terms of their divorce decree John had to pay alimony to Mary at the rate of $50,000 in 1998, $25,000 in 1999, and zero in 2000. For the first three years of the agreement, determine what portions of the payments are deductible by John and includible in Mary's gross income.

34. Roy Rainer will pay his wife, Mae, alimony according to the following schedule:

    Year 1—$50,000
    Year 2—$40,000
    Year 3–Year 8—$20,000

    Roy and Mae were divorced on January 6, 1998.

    For the first three years of the agreement, what portions are excludable and includible in Mae's gross income?

35. Richard and Sally Murphy were divorced in 1988. By the terms of their decree Richard pays Sally $600 a month for alimony and child support. When Jane, their 14-year-old daughter, reaches age 18, the payments will be reduced by $150 per month.

    Explain to Richard and Sally their tax status for 1998.

36. John Izzy and his wife have had marital problems, so they verbally agree to a trial marital separation. Since Mrs. Izzy does not work, her husband has agreed to give her $500 a week to live on. Is this payment deductible by Mr. Izzy, and is it income for his wife?

37. Robert and Roberta Moss have decided to obtain a divorce. Robert is willing to pay Roberta $3,000 for marital rights. Further, he is going to transfer $3,500 worth of property which has a $2,500 basis. What are the tax consequences of this arrangement?

38. Robert Reed, a bachelor, maintains his parents in a nursing home. They have no income of their own and are completely dependent on their son. His parents are 75 and 72 years of age. Robert has the following sources of income:

Salary	$45,000
Interest on Municipal Bonds	750
Interest on Bank Accounts	800
Dividends on Common Stock of U.S. Corporation	500

Robert has itemized deductions of $6,500. Robert owns several apartment buildings. His net rental income was $3,000 for the year. Then, on December 31 one of his best tenants brought in a check for $500. This money covers the months of December and January. Robert is confused on how to account for this rental income. It is not included in the $3,000 listed above. Compute Robert's taxable income.

39. Fran Finery's boutique has assets of $10,000 and liabilities of $14,000. Fran's major creditor cancels $5,000 in liabilities.

Discuss the tax ramifications of this forgiveness of debt. Assume the majority of Fran's assets are depreciable property. Discuss the tax ramifications facing the Finery Corporation assuming it is not in bankruptcy. Then, discuss the ramifications assuming the Finery Corporation is in bankruptcy.

40. If Mack Mudd becomes insolvent with assets of $35,000 and liabilities of $65,000 and one of his creditors cancels a debt of $10,000, what amount must Mack recognize as income?

41. *IRS Adapted Problem.* Mr. Wolf, a cash-basis taxpayer, owns an apartment building. His records reflect the following information for 1998:

Tenant G paid cost of floor repairs that were Mr. Wolf's responsibility	$ 950
Security deposits to be returned to tenants upon expiration of their leases in 2001	1,350
Advance rents received in December for the first six months of 1999	3,000

What is the amount of gross rental income Mr. Wolf should include in his gross income?

a. $2,300

b. $3,000

c. $3,950

d. $4,350

e. $5,300

42. *IRS Adapted Problem.* Roger signed for a ten-year lease to rent office space from Doug. In the first year, Roger paid Doug $5,000 for the first year's rent and $5,000 as rent for the last year of the lease. How much must Doug include in income in the first year of the lease?

a. $0

b. $5,000

c. $5,500

d. $10,000

43. *IRS Adapted Problem.* Each of the following would be one of the requirements for a payment to be alimony under instruments executed after 1984 except:

a. Payments are required by a divorce or separation instrument.

b. Payments can be a noncash property settlement.

c. Payments are *not* designated in the instrument as *not* alimony.

d. Payments are *not* required after death of the recipient spouse.

44. *IRS Adapted Problem.* Under Pete's divorce decree, he must pay $500 a month to Laura, his former spouse, for the support of their two children. In 1997, he paid $5,500 instead of the $6,000 he was required to pay. In 1998, he paid $6,000 child support for 1998 and $500 toward child support he neglected to pay in 1997. For purposes of determining whether Pete may claim his children as dependents, which of the following statements accurately represents the amount of support attributable to each year?

a. $5,500 for 1997; $6,500 for 1998

b. $6,000 for 1997; $6,000 for 1998

c. $5,500 for 1997; $6,000 for 1998

d. $5,500 for 1997; $6,000 for 1998; $500 for 1996

45. *IRS Adapted Problem.* Robert divorced Laura in 1997. During 1998, per the divorce decree, Robert made the following payments:

The entire mortgage payment on house (jointly owned) $10,800
Tuition for their child .... $ 6,000
Child support .... $ 4,500
Life insurance policy premiums on policy owned by Lisa ...... $ 3,000

What is the amount Robert can deduct as alimony on his 1998 tax return?

   a. $3,000

   b. $5,400

   c. $8,400

   d. $10,800

46. *IRS Adapted Problem.* In which of the following situations will the divorced custodial parent be entitled to the dependency exemption for the child?

   a. The noncustodial parent provides $1,500 of support for the child and the custodial parent provides $1,200.

   b. The custodial and noncustodial parent both provide $1,500 of support for the child.

   c. The custodial parent provides $1,500 of support for the child and the noncustodial parent provides $1,200.

   d. All of the above.

47. *IRS Adapted Problem.* Which of the following is not considered "constructive receipt" income in 1998?

   a. Andrew Mason was informed that his check for services rendered was available on December 15, 1998, but he waited until January 16, 1999, to pick up the check.

   b. A payment on a sale of real property placed in escrow on December 16, 1998, but not received by Benjamin Miles until January 12, 1999, when the transaction was closed.

   c. Earned Income of Candice Cord was received by her agent on December 30, 1998, but was not received by her until January 5, 1999.

   d. Daniel Dryer received a check on December 30, 1998, for services rendered, but was unable to make a deposit until January 5, 1999.

   e. Ellen Elks received stock on December 30, 1998, for services rendered, but was unable to find a buyer for the stock until January 20, 1999.

48. *IRS Adapted Problem.* A distribution of stock or stock rights is generally considered a taxable dividend unless it is which of the following:

   a. A distribution in lieu of money

   b. A proportionate distribution

   c. A distribution with respect to preferred stock

   d. A distribution of convertible preferred stock

49. *Comprehensive Problem.* David and Doris Kelley were divorced on February 3, 1998. They lived apart during 1998. The divorce decree required David to make the following payments:

    a. Transfer full title to their jointly owned family home to Doris. Fair market value of the home is $80,000, basis $50,000.

    b. $1,000 per month mortgage payments on the house, above. The mortgage has 20 years remaining before being fully paid off.

    c. $2,000 per month for 10 years' support payments to Doris, of which $600 per month is child support.

    d. Doris insisted that the children attend private schools. In 1998, David paid $1,500 in tuition for the children's private high school.

David paid his lawyer $5,000 to represent him in the divorce proceedings. David and Doris agreed that Doris would maintain a home for the children. Further, Doris agreed to allow David to claim one child as a dependency exemption. This agreement was put in writing and signed by Doris.

Besides the divorce, David has had a big year financially. He owns an apartment house and he requires each new tenant to place a $750 security deposit with him before moving into the apartment. When the tenant ultimately vacates the apartment, David will refund the deposit. In 1998, David collected $3,750 in security deposits and rental income of $15,000.

David entered a local raffle in 1998. David won first prize, which was a new automobile with a window price of $20,000. He checked with several local car dealers and was positive that if he had purchased a similar car on his own, the price would have been $18,200.

David loaned his sister Lois $5,000. Lois was repaying the loan at $100 per month plus interest of $40. Since Lois was about to depart on an extended vacation on December 2, 1998, she gave David $200 plus interest of $80 to cover the months of December and January.

David has a good job that pays an annual salary of $50,000. In 1998, business was very good and in December 1998 bonuses were announced for the employees. David earned a $4,000 bonus for 1998. Bonuses would be mailed to the employees during the first week of January 1999. David has itemized deductions of $20,000.

Determine David's 1998 taxable income.

50. *Comprehensive Problem.* Bert and Barbara Longfelt support in nursing homes both Bert's parents and Barbara's parents. Bert's parents are 70 and 68 years of age respectively and have no income except for the $3,600 in Social Security they

receive annually. Barbara's parents, both 72 years of age, have the following sources of income:

Social Security $9,800
Interest Income (Joint Ownership) $2,600
Dividend Income .... $ 900

Bert's annual salary is $35,000 and his wife's annual salary is $40,000. They have two small children who live at home. Also, they own an apartment house from which they derive $6,000 net rental income. Two items from their rental property confused them so they did not include them in their rental income:

Security deposits received and to be
    used against final month's rent $500
Two tenants paid rent in advance in
    December 1998. The rent was due
    January 1, 1999.. $600

Barbara owned stock prior to her marriage to Bert and received the following cash dividends:

General Corp. common stock dividend
    (U.S. corporation) $300
Live Forever Life Insurance Co.
    (dividends on life insurance policy) $100

Bert and Barbara have several sources of interest income:

Interest income from savings accounts $850
Interest income from State of Tennessee Highway Bonds $400

Barbara entered the local area bake-off, won first place for her cherry pie, and received a $1,000 cash prize.

Bert, who is an accountant, made an arrangement with Harold the dentist. Bert would do Harold's tax work if Harold would take care of Bert and his family's dental work. During the year, Bert estimated that the value of his services to Harold was $500 and that Harold gave Bert and his family $600 worth of dental services. In December, Bert did a consulting assignment on a weekend and received $700. No Social Security or taxes were withheld.

During the year, they had $17,000 withheld for federal taxes.

During 1998, Bert and Barbara have $8,000 of itemized deductions. Compute Bert and Barbara's net tax due, including self-employment tax.

51. *Research Problem.* Robert Olsen was a very successful college basketball player. Knowing that he would be offered a multimillion dollar contract, he established a corporation assigning to it his services in professional sports in exchange for a monthly salary. Upon audit the IRS challenged this assignment of contract. Who will prevail? See *C. Johnson,* 78 TC 882, CCH Dec. 39,069 (1982).

Chapter 4

Gross Income—Exclusions

Learning Objectives

After completing Chapter 4, you should be able to:

1. List the items specifically excluded from gross income.
2. Distinguish between exclusions and deductions.
3. Determine the nontaxable portion of life insurnace and annuities.
4. Determine the nontaxable portion of Social Security benefits.
5. Distinguish between taxable and nontaxable interest income.
6. Determine the tax status of various fringe benefits.
7. Understand the tax status of various educational assistance plans.

OVERVIEW OF CHAPTER

Gross income is defined in the Internal Revenue Code as including "all income from whatever source derived." It includes all income unless expressly exempted by law. The exempted classes are referred to as "exclusions from gross income." This chapter discusses those items that have been specifically excluded from gross income. In addition to several cash considerations, a major portion of the chapter will be dedicated to a discussion of various types of fringe benefits. Finally, the tax status of these elements of income and their relative value to employees will be discussed.

No matter what the type of job, taxes take a significant portion of each weekly paycheck. Therefore, the proper arrangement of income to derive the greatest benefit from sources which are includible and excludable in gross income is of great importance.

Sections 101 through 139 of the Internal Revenue Code list "Items Specifically Excluded from Gross Income." Selected sections are as follows:

Sec. 101.   Certain death benefits
Sec. 102.   Gifts and inheritances
Sec. 103.   Interest on state and local bonds
Sec. 104.   Compensation for injuries or sickness
Sec. 105.   Amounts received under accident and health plans
Sec. 106.   Contributions by employer to accident and health plans
Sec. 107.   Rental value of parsonages
Sec. 108.   Income from discharge of indebtedness
Sec. 109.   Improvements by lessee on lessor's property
Sec. 111.   Recovery of tax benefit items
Sec. 112.   Certain combat pay of members of the Armed Forces
Sec. 115.   Income of States, municipalities, etc.
Sec. 117.   Qualified scholarships
Sec. 118.   Contributions to the capital of a corporation
Sec. 119.   Meals or lodging furnished for the convenience of the employer
Sec. 120.   Amounts received under qualified group legal services plans
Sec. 121.   Exclusion of gain from sale of principal residence
Sec. 122.   Certain reduced uniformed services retirement pay
Sec. 123.   Amounts received under insurance contracts for certain living expenses
Sec. 125.   Cafeteria plans
Sec. 126.   Certain cost-sharing payments
Sec. 127.   Educational assistance programs
Sec. 129.   Dependent care assistance programs
Sec. 130.   Certain personal injury liability assignments
Sec. 131.   Certain foster care payments
Sec. 132.   Certain fringe benefits
Sec. 133.   Repealed
Sec. 134.   Certain military benefits
Sec. 135.   Income from United States savings bonds used to pay higher education tuition and fees
Sec. 136.   Energy conservation subsidies provided by public utilities
Sec. 137.   Adoption assistance programs
Sec. 138.   Medicare+Choice MSA
Sec. 139.   Cross references to other Acts

Note that the items listed are exclusions from gross income. Do not confuse exclusions from gross income with deductions from gross income, a subject discussed in later chapters. Basically, an exclusion does not appear on the individual's tax return, whereas deductions must appear. It should be noted that even though some income sources may be considered exclusions and are not reported on an individual's 1040 tax return, they may still be subject to tax (i.e., a gift which requires a gift tax return by the donor). This chapter provides an overview of commonly encountered exclusions. Not all types of exclusions are discussed in this chapter. For example, Sections 107 and 118 are not discussed. The exclusions from income which will be discussed more fully include cafeteria plans, life insurance, fringe benefits, and retirement plans.

Common Exclusions from Gross Income

¶ 4001   GIFTS AND INHERITANCES

A gift, bequest, or inheritance is excluded from gross income. Code Sec. 102(a). Therefore, it follows that the donor does not receive a tax deduction for the property transmitted. A gift transpires when there is a valid transfer of property from one individual to another for no consideration. If property received by gift or inheritance later produces income, the income is taxable. Although the recipient of a gift pays no tax on receipt of the gift, the donor may be required to pay a transfer tax, known as the gift tax. See Chapter 21.

¶ 4015   LIFE INSURANCE PROCEEDS

Generally, life insurance proceeds received by the beneficiary are not included in gross income if such amounts are paid by reason of death of the insured. Code Sec. 101(a)(1). Premiums on life insurance policies are not deductible by the insured; therefore, it logically follows that the proceeds from the policy would be excluded from gross income. It is immaterial who the beneficiary is or whether the policy was part of a "group" life insurance plan or was individually purchased. If, however, the payment is delayed and the total amount when received includes some interest, the interest is taxable. For spouses dying prior to October 23, 1986, where the beneficiary was the decedent's surviving spouse (widow or widower), up to $1,000 per year of such interest could be excluded from gross income. It was immaterial whether the decedent had multiple policies in effect; only $1,000 per year total could be excluded. Further, if the surviving spouse later remarried, $1,000 per year of interest from gross income could continue to be excluded. The $1,000 per year exclusion is not allowable with regard to amounts received by an individual whose spouse died after October 22, 1986.

> *Example 4.1.* Millie Rose received an option to receive as benefici-ary of her husband's life insurance policy (date of death, May 1, 1983) $25,000 in a lump sum or $3,500 per year for 10 years. If she chose the $25,000 lump-sum payment, it would have been totally excludable. If she chose the $3,500 per year for 10 years, she could have excluded $2,500, which is 1/10 of the face value, plus the special widow's allowance of $1,000 per year. Therefore, all $3,500 per year would have been excludable. Note, if Millie Rose had been the sister of the deceased, then she would have had to include in gross income $1,000 per year.

> *Example 4.2.* Millie Rose remarried two years after her first husband's death. Shortly thereafter, her second husband died in an automobile accident. Millie Rose is the beneficiary of a $100,000 life insurance policy. She elected a 10-year installment payout. Therefore, she receives $10,000 per year plus interest. In this case, the interest amounts to $1,000 per year. Millie Rose is allowed a $1,000-a-year interest exclusion for *each* deceased spouse.

> *Example 4.3.* Millie Rose remarried, in 1987, after her second husband's death. Within one year, husband number three died unexpectedly. Millie Rose was the sole beneficiary of a $50,000 life insurance policy. She elected a 10-year installment payment. Thus, she would receive $5,000 per year plus interest of $500. Because husband number three died after October 22, 1986, the $500 per year of interest is fully taxable.

Where the proceeds are received by the beneficiary in installments, the annuity exclusion ratio (discussed later) is used. The face amount of the policy is the cost and only the interest is included in income.

When the proceeds are received for reasons other than death, such as surrender of a life insurance policy, the insured is allowed to recover tax free the amount actually paid for the contract. Code Sec. 72(e)(2)(B). If the cost of the policy exceeds the proceeds, the loss is not deductible. *London Shoe Co., Inc.*, 35-2 USTC ¶ 9664, 80 F.2d 230 (CA-2 1935), cert. denied, 298 U.S. 663, 56 S.Ct. 747.

In computing the premiums paid under the policy, all dividends received must be subtracted from the amounts paid in.

Example 4.4. Ralph Rogers surrendered an endowment policy and received $25,000 from the insurance company. Over time, Ralph had paid in $14,500 in premiums. He must recognize $10,500 ($25,000 − $14,500) of income. He may exclude from income only the amount of his total premiums paid.

¶ 4025 SALE OF RESIDENCE

Gross income may not include all the gain realized from the sale or exchange of a principal residence. The gain to be excluded is limited to a maximum of $500,000 ($250,000 for married individual filing a separate return). For detailed discussion, see Chapter 10.

¶ 4055 RETIREMENT INCOME

Historically, Social Security benefits, both monthly and lump-sum, had been excluded from tax. The exclusion extended to benefits received under the Railroad Retirement Act. Benefits received from retirement systems of other countries are not excluded from the federal income tax.

However, for tax years after 1983 and before 1994, a portion of the Social Security benefits or railroad retirement benefits must be included in taxable income for taxpayers whose modified adjusted gross income plus one-half the Social Security benefits received exceeds a base of $25,000 for a single taxpayer ($32,000 for a married taxpayer filing a joint return and zero for a married person filing a separate return). Modified adjusted gross income for purposes of determining the base also includes interest on tax-exempt bonds. The amount of Social Security benefits includible in taxable income is the lesser of one half of the benefits or one half of the excess of the taxpayer's combined income over the base.

Example 4.5. Bill and Linda Peterson, both over age 65, have the following sources of income:

Interest Income (taxable)	$19,000
Dividend Income	4,000
Net Rental Income	6,000
Adjusted Gross Income	$29,000
Social Security Benefits	$10,500

Computations:

Adjusted Gross Income	$29,000
½ of Social Security Benefits	5,250
Modified Adjusted Gross Income + ½ Social Security Benefits..	$34,250
Base Amount for Married Couple.........................	32,000
Excess	$ 2,250
50 Percent of Excess	$ 1,125

Of the $10,500 Bill and Linda received in Social Security benefits, they must include $1,125 in their gross income. Remember, the maximum amount to be included in gross income is the lesser of 50 percent of the "excess" or 50 percent of the Social Security benefit received.

Example 4.6. Assume the same facts as in Example 4.5, except that Bill and Linda also have $9,000 of interest income from tax-exempt bonds.

Computations:

Adjusted Gross Income from Above Problem	$29,000
Plus: Tax-Exempt Interest	9,000
1/2 of Social Security Benefits	5,250
Modified Adjusted Gross Income + ½ Social Security Benefits..	$43,250
Less: Base Amount for Married Couples	32,000
Excess	$11,250
50 Percent of Excess	$ 5,625

In this instance, Bill and Linda must include $5,250 in their gross income. This is because 50 percent of their Social Security benefits is the maximum amount that can be included in gross income.

Social Security benefits are taxable to the individual who receives the benefits. Therefore, if a child receives Social Security benefits, the benefits are taxable to the child using the same formulas that are discussed above.

The Revenue Reconciliation Act of 1993 created a second threshold for years after 1993. This second threshold applies to taxpayers with provisional income greater than $34,000 for a single taxpayer and $44,000 for a married taxpayer filing a joint return. Provisional income is defined as the sum of adjusted gross income, exempt interest earnings, certain foreign source income, and one-half of the Social Security benefits received during the year. Taxpayers with provisional income exceeding the second threshold will be taxed up to 85 percent of their Social Security benefits.

Taxpayers with provisional income exceeding these amounts will include the lesser of:

A. 85 percent of the taxpayer's Social Security benefits, or

B. the total of the following calculation:

1.   85 percent of the amount that provisional income exceeds the new threshold amounts, plus

2.   the smaller of: (a) the amount of Social Security benefits included under prior law; or (b) $4,500 for an unmarried taxpayer, or $6,000 for married taxpayers filing jointly.

Married taxpayers filing separate returns have no base amount and must include in gross income the lesser of: (a) 85 percent of their Social Security benefits; or (b) 85 percent of their provisional income.

Example 4.7. Norm, a single taxpayer, has modified AGI of $50,000 in 1998 and he received $14,000 of Social Security benefits. Norm's provisional income is therefore $57,000. He must include $11,900 of his Social Security benefits in his gross income. This is computed as follows:

A. $14,000 × 85% = $11,900

B.   [($57,000 − $34,000) × 85%] + $4,500 = $24,050

Example 4.8. Pat, a single taxpayer, has modified AGI of $36,000 in 1998 and she received $10,000 in Social Security benefits. Pat's provisional income is therefore $41,000. Pat must include in her AGI $8,500 of her Social Security benefits. This is computed as follows:

A. $10,000 × 85% = $8,500

B.   [($41,000 − $34,000) × 85%] + $4,500 = $10,450

Example 4.9. Linda, a single taxpayer, has AGI of $26,000 and Social Security benefits of $8,000. Linda's provisional income is $30,000 and she must include in her AGI $2,500 of her Social Security benefits. Inasmuch as her provisional income is below the threshold amount ($34,000), she includes in AGI the lesser of 50 percent of her Social Security benefits or one-half the excess of combined income over the base. This is computed as follows:

Adjusted Gross Income	$26,000
Plus: ½ of Social Security Benefits	4,000
Modified AGI + ½ Social Security Benefits	$30,000
Less: Base Amount for Single Taxpayer	25,000
Excess	$ 5,000
50 Percent of Excess	$ 2,500

Example 4.10. Ron, a single taxpayer, has AGI of $32,000 of income and $8,000 of Social Security benefits. Ron's provisional income is $36,000 and he must include $5,700 of his Social Security benefits in his income. This is computed as follows:

A. $8,000 × 85% = $6,800

B.   [($36,000 − 34,000) × 85%] + 4,000 = $5,700

Example 4.11. Norm and Pat, a married couple filing a joint return, have AGI of $40,000 and Social Security benefits of $12,000. Norm and Pat have provisional income of $46,000 and they must include $7,700 of Social Security benefits in their AGI. This is computed as follows:

A. $12,000 × 85% = $10,200

B.   [($46,000 − 44,000) × 85%] + $6,000 = $7,700

Example 4.12. Philip and Linda, a married couple filing a joint return, have AGI of $30,000 and Social Security benefits of $14,000. Therefore their provisional income is $37,000. Philip and Linda must include in their AGI $2,500 of their Social Security benefits. It is computed as follows:

Provisional Income $37,000
Base Amount Old Law   32,000
Excess .... $ 5,000
50 Percent of Excess .... $ 2,500

Inasmuch as provisional income, $37,000, does not exceed the threshold amount ($44,000), only $2,500 is included in the AGI of Philip and Linda.

¶ 4075   INTEREST ON GOVERNMENT OBLIGATIONS

Savings Bonds

Interest earned on United States savings bonds is fully taxable. On Series EE bonds, no interest per se is paid each year, but the bond is issued at a discount and each year increases in value until maturity. The difference between the purchase price of the bond and the redemption value is taxable interest income. Cash basis taxpayers have the choice of reporting interest income on a yearly basis or reporting all interest income when the bonds finally mature, while accrual basis taxpayers must accrue the increase in the redemption value each year as interest. If cash basis taxpayers exercise the election to report the interest currently, all such bonds owned by them must be similarly treated for all subsequent years.

Taxpayers who elected to defer recognizing income until the bonds mature may change their method of reporting income on a yearly basis without permission from the IRS. However, in the year of change all interest accrued to date, not previously reported, must be included in gross income.

Series EE bonds were first issued in 1980. Prior to 1980, Series E bonds were issued. Series HH bonds replaced Series H bonds in 1980, as well. Series HH and Series H bonds are treated identically for tax purposes. These bonds are issued at face value and interest is paid twice a year by check. Cash basis taxpayers must report interest income in the year it is received.

Example 4.13. Robert and Mary Moore had the following interest income in 1998:

1.   Interest on Series EE bonds, $300

2.   Interest on bank savings account, $400

3.   Interest on municipal bond, $500

Robert and Mary have taxable interest income of $700. If they elect, they can defer the recognition of income on the Series EE bonds until the bonds mature. In that case, then total interest to be included in gross income totals $400.

Taxpayers who owned Series E bonds prior to 1980 and did not report interest income on a yearly basis could trade their E bonds for Series H bonds and not realize taxable income unless they received cash on the trade. The same rules hold for Series EE bonds as for Series HH bonds today. The taxpayer defers the recognition of income until the taxpayer disposes of the bonds or they mature, then the taxpayer reports as interest income the difference between the redemption value and the total cost of traded bonds, plus any amount received at the time of trade.

Example 4.14. Bruce Bronson trades in Series E bonds that have a redemption value of $2,800 for Series HH bonds. Bruce receives $2,500 of Series HH bonds and $300 in cash. Therefore, he must report $300 of taxable income.

Educational Savings Bonds

For tax years beginning after 1989, a tax exemption is provided for interest earned on U.S. savings bonds used to finance the higher education of the taxpayer, the taxpayer's spouse, or dependents. Code Sec. 135. The bonds must be purchased after December 31, 1989, and the exclusion is available only to the individual who purchased the bonds. The purchaser of the bonds must have reached the age of 24 and be the sole owner of the bonds. The bonds must be redeemed during the same tax year in which the qualified educational expenses are incurred by the taxpayer, the taxpayer's spouse, or any dependents.

Qualified higher education expenses include tuition and fees, net of scholarships and other tuition reduction amounts. Room and board and expenses incurred for sports, games, or hobbies other than as part of a degree program are not covered.

The key to computing the exclusion is the amount of qualified higher education expenses that the individual incurs in the year the bonds are redeemed. If these expenses exceed the aggregate redemption amount (principal plus interest), then all of the interest may be excluded, subject to an income-linked phase-out discussed below. If the redemption amount is larger than the qualified educational expenses, however, the exclusion is reduced on a pro rata basis.

Example 4.15. During 1998, Mary Adams, age 50, redeems Series EE bonds and receives $5,000 of principal and $2,500 of accrued interest. Mary's daughter attends college and has qualified expenses of $8,000. Mary may exclude from her gross income the entire $2,500 of interest.

Example 4.16. Same facts as in Example 14.15, except Mary's daughter incurred only $6,000 in qualified expenses. Mary may exclude from gross income only $2,000. This is calculated as follows:

$$\frac{\text{Qualified Expenses}}{\text{Series EE Proceeds}} = \text{Percentage Exclusion}$$

Percentage Exclusion × Series EE Interest = Interest Exclusion

Percentage Exclusion = $6,000/$7,500 = 80%

Interest Exclusion $2,500 × 80% = $2,000

The exclusion for accrued interest is subject to phaseout provisions. The phaseout ranges for 1998 are as follows:

Filing Status	Modified AGI
Married filing jointly	$78,350 — $108,350
Single (including head of household)	$52,250 — $ 67,250

Married individuals filing separately are not eligible for the exclusion.

For those falling within the phaseout range, the amount of interest otherwise excludable will be reduced (but not below zero) by multiplying that interest by a fraction that is determined by dividing the excess of modified AGI (that is, the excess of modified AGI over the bottom figure of the phaseout range) by the number of dollars in the phaseout range ($30,000 for joint returns and $15,000 for single taxpayers).

Example 4.17. Same facts as in Example 4.15, but also assume that Mary is a single mother and that her modified AGI is $63,750. Mary may exclude from her gross income $583. This amount is computed as follows:

$$\$2,500 - (\$2,500 \times \$11,500/\$15,000) = \$583$$

The $11,500 is the excess of modified AGI over the phaseout range.

Qualified higher education expenses must be further reduced by expenses taken into account for the Hope Scholarship and Lifetime Learning credits.

State and Municipal Bonds

Interest received on state and local government bonds is generally excludable from gross income. Code Sec. 103(a). The term "state or local bond" means an obligation of a state or political subdivision, and the term "state" includes the District of Columbia and any possession of the U.S. Code Sec. 103(c). Tax-exempt bonds are an attractive investment for many well-to-do investors because the after-tax return on such bonds is considerably higher than taxable bonds.

Example 4.18. David Smith, a highly paid corporate executive, was in the 39.6 percent marginal tax bracket. He was contemplating buying some bonds, but could not decide whether to buy corporate bonds, paying 12 percent interest, or a municipal bond, paying 9 percent. Since Mr. Smith is in the 39.6 percent marginal tax bracket, the 12 percent corporate bond nets Mr. Smith only 7.25 percent. Therefore, the 9 percent tax-free interest income from the municipal bonds is a better decision.

Example 4.19. Sam Roberts, a well-to-do banker, has the following securities in his portfolio:

1. One $5,000, 10 percent corporate bond, annual interest income, $500

2. Ten shares of ABC Inc. stock, no dividends paid

3. One $10,000 bond issued by the Port Authority of N.Y. in 1984 at 8 percent

4. Dividend on life insurance policy, $100

5. One $10,000, 9 percent State of Ohio bond issued in 1985, annual interest, $900

Of the items listed above, the interest on the corporate bond must be included in gross income. The shares of stock paid no dividend; therefore, there is no dollar amount to be included in gross income. However, if a dividend had been paid, it would have been includible in Sam Roberts's gross income. The $800 interest on the Port Authority bond is fully tax-exempt as is the interest on the State of Ohio bond. The life insurance dividend is considered a reduction in premium and is not includible in gross income.

Interest received on state or local bonds is generally excludable from gross income when bond proceeds are used exclusively for traditional government purposes. However, interest on state and local bonds used to benefit other persons is not tax free when it is from (1) private activity bonds that are not exempt, (2) state or local bonds that have not been issued in registered form, or (3) arbitrage bonds.

Private Activity Bonds. Private activity bonds that qualify for tax exemption include (1) exempt-facility bonds (e.g., proceeds used to finance airports, water facilities, waste disposal facilities, electric energy or gas facilities), (2) qualified mortgage bonds (proceeds used to finance certain owner-occupied residences), (3) qualified veteran's mortgage bond (issued only by five states), (4) qualified small issue bonds (face amount of bond issue is $1 million or less), (5) qualified student loan bonds, (6) qualified redevelopment bonds (proceeds used to redevelop blighted areas), or (7) qualified tax-exempt organization bonds. Code Sec. 141(e).

Registered Bonds. In order to restrict the number of long-term bearer obligations and to maintain liquidity in the financial markets, certain obligations must be issued in a registered form in order to be tax-exempt. This applies to certain bonds issued after August 15, 1986. A registration-required bond means any bond other than a bond which (1) is not of a type offered to the public, (2) has a maturity (at issue) of not more than one year, or (3) is issued abroad with safeguards to ensure that the obligations are sold and resold only to persons who are not U.S. persons and that no interest or principal is payable to any U.S. person. Code Sec. 149.

Arbitrage Bonds. Arbitrage bonds are generally denied tax-exempt status unless a special tax or rebate is paid to the United States. Code Sec. 148. Arbitrage bonds are used for speculative purposes by state or local issuing authorities. A bond issue becomes an arbitrage issue if the proceeds are used to buy other obligations, frequently federal obligations, that have a higher yield than the state issue.

Employee Benefits

¶ 4101 FRINGE BENEFITS

In the United States today fringe benefits are a very significant part of the worker's compensation package. Compensation experts maintain that approximately one-third of a worker's gross compensation is composed of fringe benefits. From a tax viewpoint, there are two types of fringe benefits: statutory and nonstatutory. A statutory fringe benefit is specifically excluded by some provision of the law. An example of a statutory fringe benefit would be employees' accident and health plans, which are covered by Section 105 of the Internal Revenue Code. A nonstatutory fringe benefit is one not specifically mentioned in the law. Examples of nonstatutory fringe benefits are free parking for employees and an employer-subsidized cafeteria. In an effort to clear the air concerning fringe benefits, the Tax Reform Act of 1984 codified the tax treatment of a number of nonstatutory fringe benefits. Gross income specifically does not include:

1. No-additional-cost services

2. Qualified employee discounts

3. Working condition fringe benefits

4. De minimis fringe benefits (property or service, the value of which is so small as to make the accounting for it unreasonable or administratively impracticable)

Nondiscrimination rules, as set forth in Section 132, must be met for the above-listed fringe benefits.

No-Additional-Cost Services

The value of no-additional-cost services provided to employees or their spouses or dependent children by employers is excludable from income. This exclusion applies whether the service is provided directly for no charge, at a reduced price, or through a cash rebate of all or part of the amount paid for the service. Reg. § 1.132-2. In order for the exclusion to apply, however, the employer must not incur any significant additional costs in providing the service to the employee (disregarding any amounts paid by the employee for the service) and the service provided to the employee must be one that is offered for sale to customers in the ordinary course of the line of business of the employer for which the employee is working.

For determining whether a fringe benefit qualifies as an excludable no-additional-cost service, transportation of passengers by air and transportation of cargo by air are treated as the same service. Thus, an employee performing services in the air cargo industry may receive air travel as a no-additional-cost service. This also includes passenger travel provided through reciprocal agreements with other airlines. Code Sec. 132(h)(8).

In determining the cost of a service, the employer must include revenue that is forgone because the service is provided to an employee rather than to a nonemployee.

Example 4.20. Regional Airlines provides its employees with seats on flights it runs. Assuming Regional provides these seats only if, at the time the plane is ready to depart, there are empty seats for the employees to occupy, no cost is attributed to this service because of forgone revenue. However, if Regional permits its employees to book no-additional-cost seats in advance of a flight's departure and then does not offer these seats for sale to the public, forgone revenue would be attributed to the cost of providing this benefit.

In addition, an employer must include the cost of labor incurred in providing no-additional-cost services to employees for purposes of determining whether substantial additional costs have been incurred. However, labor cost is not included if the services are merely incidental to the primary services being provided.

The no-additional-cost services exclusion is available to employees of one employer for services provided to them by an unrelated employer (another employer not under common control) under a reciprocal arrangement between the two employers. For the services to qualify they must be: (1) of the same type, (2) under a written reciprocal agreement between employers, and (3) no substantial additional cost to either employer.

An employee working for an employer in multiple lines of business is limited to the line of business of the employer for which the employee works. For example, a company that owns both an airline and a hotel could not offer an employee of the airline a free hotel room. However, an important exception exists to employees who service more than one line of business. Therefore, the C.E.O. of the company or the V.P. for Finance could exclude fringes from both lines of business since they both render service to both businesses.

Examples of no-additional-cost services are excess capacity services such as hotel accommodations, telephone services, and transportation by aircraft, train, bus, subway, and cruise line.

Services that are not eligible for treatment as no-additional-cost services are nonexcess capacity services such as the use of a stock brokerage firm or a mutual fund to purchase stock or an interest in the mutual fund. However, if you receive nonexcess capacity services, the value of the benefit may be a qualified employee discount.

Qualified Employee Discounts

Certain employee discounts provided to employees on the selling price of qualified property or services of the employer are excludable from gross income. In order to be excludable, the discounts must be available to employees on a nondiscriminating basis. The employee discount may not exceed the gross profit percentage normally offered by the employer to customers. In the case of qualified services, the excludable amount cannot exceed 20 percent of the price offered to nonemployee customers.

> ***Example 4.21.*** Smith's Cut-Rate had total sales of $1,000,000 for 1998. The cost of merchandise for this period was $500,000. Therefore, the gross profit percentage was 50 percent. The employees were offered a 60 percent discount on merchandise purchased from the company. In this case, the employees had to include 10 percent of the value of the merchandise they purchased in their gross income.

> ***Example 4.22.*** Mary Ray works for a computer manufacturer. She bought a portable computer from a local computer store and received the usual employee discount. Mary also received a one-year parts and labor warranty. Normally, the computer shop does not give one-year warranties on machines. Mary need not include the value of the discount in her income but she must include the value of the warranty.

The value of the discounts can be excluded from the income of officers, owners, or highly compensated employees only if these discounts are made available on substantially the same terms to each member of a group of employees which is defined under a reasonable classification set up by the employer that does not discriminate in favor of officers, owners, or highly compensated employees. Code Sec. 132(h).

Working Condition Fringe Benefits

The fair market value of any property or service provided to an employee by an employer as a working condition fringe benefit is excludable from the gross income of the employee to the extent that the employer can deduct the costs as an ordinary and necessary business expense.

The following are examples of working condition fringe benefits that would be excludable:

1. Value of use of an employer-provided car or plane for business purposes

2. Subscriptions to business periodicals by an employer for employees

3. Safety precautions provided by an employer for employees

4. Employer expenditures for on-the-job training or travel by an employee

5. Fair market value of the use of consumer products manufactured for sale to nonemployee customers but provided to employees for product testing and evaluation outside the employer's workplace

De Minimis Fringe Benefits

De minimis fringes result when the value of the property or service provided to the employee is so minimal that accounting for it would be unreasonable. Examples of de minimis fringes include:

1. Typing of personal letters by company secretaries
2. Occasional personal use of the company copying machine
3. Monthly transit passes provided to employees at a discount (not to exceed $65 per month)
4. Employer-provided parking valued up to $170 per month, even if you choose it instead of cash
5. Occasional parties or picnics for employees
6. Traditional holiday gifts (small fair market value)
7. Tickets occasionally given out for entertainment events
8. Coffee and donuts furnished to employees
9. Occasional supper money or taxi fare due to overtime work

Any cash benefit or its equivalent (such as the use of a company credit card) cannot be excluded as a de minimis benefit under any circumstances. In addition, season tickets to sporting or theatrical events, the commuting use of an employer-provided car or other vehicle more than once a month, membership in a private country club or athletic facility, and use of employer-owned or leased facilities, such as an apartment or hunting lodge, for a weekend are never excludable as de minimis fringe benefits.

While many of these employee benefits are typically not included in an employee's gross income, in most circumstances, the employer is allowed a deduction for costs incurred.

¶ 4115 GROUP-TERM LIFE INSURANCE

An employee is allowed to exclude from gross income all of the cost of a group-term life insurance policy provided by an employer if the face amount of the policy does not exceed $50,000. Code Sec. 79. When over $50,000 of group-term life insurance is purchased, the cost of the premium for the amount of insurance over $50,000 must be included in gross income of the employee.

The $50,000 coverage limitation is eliminated and the total cost of group-term life insurance coverage in any amount is excluded from the gross income of the employee where (1) the employee is disabled, (2) the employer is directly or indirectly the beneficiary of the insurance, or (3) a charitable organization is the sole beneficiary. Some retired employees may also be entitled to a full exclusion.

For a group-term policy to be covered by Code Sec. 79, it must not discriminate in favor of highly compensated employees. It is perfectly acceptable to have a group plan where coverage is directly proportional to salary.

The cost of group-term life insurance provided to an employee during any taxable period for inclusion in the employee's gross income is to be determined under the uniform premium table method. Under this method the cost of group-term life insurance protection in excess of the excludable amount is determined on the basis of uniform premiums computed on the basis of five-year age brackets. The age of the employee for purposes of the age brackets used in the table is the employee's age on the last day of the tax year. The amount that must be included under the uniform premium table is generally less than the actual cost of the insurance.

Example 4.23. Nine Lives Corp. purchased group-term life insurance for all its employees. The company pays 100 percent of the premiums for all employees, equal to twice the employee's salary. Otto Olson, age 52 and vice president of Nine Lives, earns $37,500 per year. Therefore, the company paid premiums on a $75,000 group-term policy. For an individual 50–54 years of age, the premium is assumed to be $5.76 (see Table 1) per $1,000 of coverage.

Total coverage	$75,000
Tax-free group insurance	50,000
Insurance subject to tax	$25,000
Cost per thousand dollars per year of insurance for 52-year-old	$ 5.76
Taxable income to Otto (25 × $5.76)	$ 144

Table 1 UNIFORM PREMIUMS FOR $1,000 OF GROUP-TERM LIFE INSURANCE PROTECTION

5-Year Age Bracket	Cost Per $1,000 of Protection for 1-Month Period
Under 30	$ .08
30 to 34	.09
35 to 39	.11
40 to 44	.17
45 to 49	.29
50 to 54	.48
55 to 59	.75
60 to 64	1.17
65 to 69	2.10
70 and above	3.76

Source: Table 1, Reg. § 1.79-3(d)(2).

Example 4.24. Assume in Example 4.23, that Otto contributes $1 per thousand dollars of protection per year. The amount includible in his gross income is $69 ($144 cost of $75,000 coverage less employee contribution of $75).

A company may have a group term life insurance plan where the employee pays the entire premium. If the employees are charged a uniform premium, it is still possible that some of the older workers will be subject to tax on coverage over $50,000.

Example 4.25. Alfred Ajax is 62 years old and elects group-term insurance of $100,000 and there are no employer contributions. His employer established a uniform rate of $.50 per $1,000 per month. Alfred would have to include $102 in his gross income. The cost of the coverage over the $50,000 group policy is $702 ($1.17 × 12 months × 50). Alfred's annual contribution is $600 (.50 × 12 months × 100).

TAX PLANNING POINTER ▼

The fact that premiums on group-term insurance for coverage of over $50,000 are taxable to the employee need not mean that such compensation is not valuable. Usually group plans are far more attractive than policies that can be obtained individually, and therefore, may be extremely beneficial as part of a total employee compensation package.

¶ 4125   ANNUITIES

An annuity is a contract that pays a fixed income at set regular intervals for a specific period of time. The amount of income depends upon the premium paid, the life expectancy of the annuitant, and the number of years payments are to be received. When income is received as an annuity under an annuity, endowment, or life insurance contract, the amount received generally consists of two separate parts: (1) a nontaxable return of the annuitant's investment in the contract and (2) a taxable amount representing a gain on the investment (interest). Code Sec. 72(a).

Under special rules for the taxation of amounts received as an annuity and paid out for reasons other than the death of the insured, the tax-free portion of annuity income is spread evenly over the annuitant's lifetime. This annuity method is not limited to payments that are to be received during the taxpayer's lifetime. It also applies to payments that are to be made for a prescribed number of years.

Exclusion Ratio Formula

The excludable portion of an annuity payment is the annuity payment times the exclusion ratio. The exclusion ratio is the "investment in the contract" divided by the "expected return" under the contract as of the "annuity starting date." These terms are further defined below. The formula for determining the excludable portion may be stated as follows:

$$\text{Amount of exclusion} = \frac{\text{Total payment}}{\text{for the year}} \times \frac{\text{Investment in the contract}}{\text{Expected return for life of contract}}$$

The following example illustrates the computation of the exclusion ratio.

Example 4.26. Sam Sterling purchased an annuity contract that provided for payments of $100 per month. He paid $12,650 for the annuity. Sam's expected return under the contract is assured to be $16,000.

Annual annuity payments ($100 × 12)	$ 1,200
Investment in the contract	12,650
Expected return	16,000
Exclusion ratio $\frac{\$12,650}{\$16,000}$	79.1%
Monthly exclusion ($100 × 79.1%)	79.10
Monthly amount to be included in gross income	20.90

Once the exclusion ratio is determined, one of two sets of rules is applied depending on the taxpayer's annuity starting date.

1. *Annuity starting date before 1987.* The exclusion ratio is applied every year there is a payment, regardless of whether the annuitant lives beyond the life expectancy. If this happens, the annuitant may exclude, over the life of the contract, more than the cost. On the other hand, if the annuitant dies at an age earlier than that of the life expectancy, the total of the yearly exclusions will be less than the cost.

2. *Annuity starting date after 1986.* The exclusion ratio is applied to payments until the total exclusions equal the investment in the contract. All later payments are fully taxable. On the other hand, if the annuitant dies before the investment in the contract is fully recovered tax free through the annuity exclusion, a deduction is provided for the last tax year in an amount equal to the unrecovered portion of the investment.

Annuity Starting Date Defined

The annuity starting date is the first day of the first period for which an amount is received as an annuity under the contract. The first day of the first period for which an amount is received as an annuity is the later of (1) the date upon which the obligations of the contract become fixed or (2) the first day of the period that ends on the date of the first annuity payment. If, however, that date fell before 1954, then the annuity starting date is January 1, 1954.

Example 4.27. Gene Smith purchased a deferred single life annuity on January 1, 1998, payable in monthly installments on the first of each month, beginning August 1 of that year for the preceding calendar month. The August 1 payment is for the period beginning July 1. The annuity starting date is July 1.

Investment in the Contract Defined

The investment in the contract is, generally, the total amount of premiums or other consideration paid for the contract less amounts, if any, received prior to the annuity starting date that are excludable from gross income. Accordingly, if a taxpayer paid premiums of $5,000 for an annuity contract and had recovered $1,000 tax free as of the annuity starting date, the investment in the contract for purposes of the exclusion ratio formula would be $4,000. Once payments have started and the tax-free amount of each annuity payment is determined then any increases in annuity payments are fully taxable.

Expected Return Under the Contract

The expected return under the contract is limited to amounts receivable as an annuity or as annuities. If no life expectancy is involved (as in the case of installment payments for a fixed number of years), the expected return is found by multiplying the total amount payable from the annuity installments by the number of payments to be received. Code Sec. 72(c)(3); Reg. § 1.72-5(c) and (d).

To determine the expected return under contracts involving life expectancy, actuarial tables prescribed by the IRS must be used (see Tables 2–6 following Example 4.33). The tables provide a multiplier (based on life expectancy) that is applied to the annual payment in order to obtain the expected return under the contract. This procedure can become quite complex since annuities may be based, variously, on one life, joint lives only, joint lives and continuing to the last survivor, and for life or term certain.

Single Life Annuities

To demonstrate the general principles note the following example of a single life annuity.

Example 4.28. Marvin Mariner retires at age 65. His annuity contract provides for him to receive $100 per month for life. His total premiums under the policy had been $14,400.

Annual annuity payment ($100 × 12 months) . . . . $ 1,200
Multiple from Table 2, Age 65 . . . . 20.0
Expected return ($1,200 × 20.0) $24,000

Marvin had an investment cost of $14,400 in the annuity and an expected return of $24,000. Therefore, the exclusion ratio was $14,400/$24,000 = 60%. Since he receives $1,200 a year, he may exclude from gross income $720 ($1,200 × 60%). Where payments are made quarterly, semiannually, or annually, the applicable multiple shown in Table 5 may be used.

In the preceding example, if Marvin received his first semiannual payment six full months after the annuity starting date, the adjusted multiple would be 19.8 (20.0 − .2). If Marvin were to receive $600 six months after his annuity starting date, his expected return would be $23,760 ($1,200 × 19.8). See Table 5.

Joint and Survivor Annuities

Under a joint and survivor annuity two individuals receive periodic payments for life. Some policies adjust the amount of the payment after the death of the first annuitant.

Example 4.29. Robert and Betty Moss purchased a joint and survivorship annuity contract. The contract provided for the couple to receive $200 per month for life. Upon the death of one spouse, the surviving spouse would continue to receive $200 per month. Robert Moss was 69 years old and his wife was 66. The cost of the policy was $36,825.

Computations:

Annual annuity payments ($200 × 12)	$ 2,400
Multiple from Table 3	22.9
Expected return ($2,400 × 22.9)	$54,960
Investment in annuity contract	$36,825

Exclusion ratio $\dfrac{\$36,825}{\$54,960} = 67\%$

Annual exclusion ($2,400 × 67%)	$ 1,608

Example 4.30. Assume the same facts as in Example 4.29, except that when the first spouse dies the surviving spouse will receive only $150 per month. The cost of the annuity is $29,450.

Computations:

Multiple from Table 3, Ages 69 and 66	22.9
Multiple from Table 4	13.1
Expected return after first death ($1,800 × 22.9)	$41,220
Expected return differential after first death ($600 × 13.1)	$ 7,860
Expected return from annuity	$49,080
Cost of annuity	$29,450

Exclusion ratio $\dfrac{\$29,450}{\$49,080} = 60\%$

Therefore, while both individuals are alive they can exclude $120 ($200 × 60%) per month. After the death of one spouse, the exclusion will be only $90 ($150 × 60%).

Example 4.31. Assume the same facts as in Example 4.30, except that Robert purchases the annuity and the annuity contract provides that if Robert dies first, Betty will receive only $150 per month instead of $200. The cost of the annuity is $29,450.

Computations:

Multiple from Table 3	22.9
Multiple from Table 2	16.8
Multiple applicable to second annuitant	6.1
Expected return (first annuitant) ($2,400 × 16.8)	$40,320
Expected return (second annuitant) ($1,800 × 6.1)	$10,980
Expected return from annuity	$51,300

Exclusion ratio $\dfrac{\$29,450}{\$51,300} = 57.4\%$

Therefore, while both individuals are alive, they can exclude $114.80 ($200 × 57.4%) per month. After the death of Robert, the exclusion will be $86.10 ($150 × 57.4%) per month.

Example 4.32. Assume the same facts as in Example 4.31, except that Robert purchases the annuity and the annuity contract provides that if Betty dies first, Robert will receive only $150 per month instead of $200. The cost of the annuity is $29,450.

Computations:

Multiple from Table 3	22.9
Multiple from Table 2	19.2
Multiple applicable to second annuitant	3.7
Expected return (first annuitant) ($2,400 × 19.2)	$46,080
Expected return (second annuitant) ($1,800 × 3.7)	$ 6,660
Expected return from annuity	$52,740

Exclusion ratio $\dfrac{\$29,450}{\$52,740} = 55.8\%$

Therefore, while both individuals are alive, they can exclude $111.60 ($200 × 55.8%) per month. After the death of Betty, the exclusion will be $83.70 ($150 × 55.8%) per month.

Employee Annuities

If the employer paid in all of the cost of the pension or annuity, the payments received by the employee are fully taxable to the employee. If the employee made contributions, the total amount that an employee may exclude from income is the total amount of the employee's contributions. The employee uses the exclusion ratio until the investment in the contract is recovered. Thereafter, all proceeds are included in income. Also, if the employee's benefits cease prior to the date the employee's total contributions have been recovered, the amount of unrecovered contributions is allowed as a deduction on the annuitant's last tax return.

The Small Business Job Protection Act of 1996 provides for a simplified method for determining the portion of an annuity distribution from a qualified retirement plan. For further discussion, see "*Safe-Harbor Method of Calculation*" at ¶ 23,415.

Refund Annuities

When payments are received under a guaranteed refund provision, the value of such payments reduces the investment in the contract. Obviously, where a refund has been received, an adjustment to the "investment in the contract" must be made so as to determine the excludable portion. The adjustment required to the "investment in the contract" is determined as follows:

1. Divide maximum amount guaranteed by the amount to be received annually and round off to the nearest whole year.

2. Refer to the actuarial table entitled "Percent Value of Refund Feature" to determine the appropriate percentage figure to be employed (see Table 6).

3. Multiply percentage found in the table by the smaller of (a) original investment in the contract, or (b) the total amount guaranteed.

4. Subtract the amount determined in Step 3 from the original "investment in the contract."

The following example illustrates the above provisions.

Example 4.33. Jerome Jackson, 65, purchased for $25,000 an immediate installment refund annuity, payable $100 per month for life. The contract provided that, in the event the husband did not live long enough to recover the full purchase price, payments were to be made to his wife until the total payments under the contract equaled the purchase price. Jerome's investment in the contract adjusted for the purpose of determining the exclusion ratio is computed in the following manner:

Investment in Contract

Cost of the annuity contract (investment in the contract, unadjusted)	$25,000
Amount to be received annually	$ 1,200
Number of years for which payment guaranteed ($25,000 divided by $1,200)	20.8
Rounded to nearest whole number of years	21
Percentage located in Table 6 for age 65 (age of the annuitant as of the annuity starting date) and 21 (the number of whole years)	20%
Subtract value of the refund feature to the nearest dollar (20% of $25,000)	$ 5,000
Investment in the contract adjusted for the present value of the refund feature without discount for interest	$20,000

Monthly Exclusion

Adjusted investment in contract	$20,000
Annual payments	1,200
Multiple from Table 2, Age 65	20.0
Expected return ($1,200 × 20)	24,000
Exclusion ratio $\frac{\$20,000}{\$24,000} = 83.3\%$	
Monthly exclusion (83.3% of $100)	$ 83.33

IRS Actuarial Tables

Gender-neutral annuity tables used to compute that portion of an annuity that is includible in gross income have been adopted. These tables apply to amounts received as an annuity after June 30, 1986.

Table 2   ORDINARY LIFE ANNUITIES—ONE LIFE—EXPECTED RETURN MULTIPLES

Age	Multiple	Age	Multiple
57	26.8	72	14.6
58	25.9	73	13.9
59	25.0	74	13.2
60	24.2	75	12.5
61	23.3	76	11.9
62	22.5	77	11.2
63	21.6	78	10.6
64	20.8	79	10.0
65	20.0	80	9.5
66	19.2	81	8.9
67	18.4	82	8.4
68	17.6	83	7.9
69	16.8	84	7.4
70	16.0	85	6.9
71	15.3	86	6.5

Source: Table V, Reg. § 1.72-9.

Table 3   ORDINARY JOINT LIFE AND LAST SURVIVOR ANNUITIES—TWO LIVES—EXPECTED RETURN MULTIPLES

Age	65	66	67	68	69	70	71	72	73	74
65	25.0	24.6	24.2	23.8	23.4	23.1	22.8	22.5	22.2	22.0
66	24.6	24.1	23.7	23.3	22.9	22.5	22.2	21.9	21.6	21.4
67	24.2	23.7	23.2	22.8	22.4	22.0	21.7	21.3	21.0	20.8
68	23.8	23.3	22.8	22.3	21.9	21.5	21.2	20.8	20.5	20.2
69	23.4	22.9	22.4	21.9	21.5	21.1	20.7	20.3	20.0	19.6
70	23.1	22.5	22.0	21.5	21.1	20.6	20.2	19.8	19.4	19.1
71	22.8	22.2	21.7	21.2	20.7	20.2	19.8	19.4	19.0	18.6
72	22.5	21.9	21.3	20.8	20.3	19.8	19.4	18.9	18.5	18.2
73	22.2	21.6	21.0	20.5	20.0	19.4	19.0	18.5	18.1	17.7
74	22.0	21.4	20.8	20.2	19.6	19.1	18.6	18.2	17.7	17.3
75	21.8	21.1	20.5	19.9	19.3	18.8	18.3	17.8	17.3	16.9
76	21.6	20.9	20.3	19.7	19.1	18.5	18.0	17.5	17.0	16.5
77	21.4	20.7	20.1	19.4	18.8	18.3	17.7	17.2	16.7	16.2
78	21.2	20.5	19.9	19.2	18.6	18.0	17.5	16.9	16.4	15.9
79	21.1	20.4	19.7	19.0	18.4	17.8	17.2	16.7	16.1	15.6
80	21.0	20.2	19.5	18.9	18.2	17.6	17.0	16.4	15.9	15.4

Source: Table VI, Reg. § 1.72-9.

Table 4   ANNUITIES FOR JOINT LIFE ONLY—TWO LIVES—EXPECTED RETURN MULTIPLES

Age	65	66	67	68	69	70	71	72	73	74
65	14.9	14.5	14.1	13.7	13.3	12.9	12.5	12.0	11.6	11.2
66	14.5	14.2	13.8	13.4	13.1	12.6	12.2	11.8	11.4	11.0
67	14.1	13.8	13.5	13.1	12.8	12.4	12.0	11.6	11.2	10.8
68	13.7	13.4	13.1	12.8	12.5	12.1	11.7	11.4	11.0	10.6
69	13.3	13.1	12.8	12.5	12.1	11.8	11.4	11.1	10.7	10.4
70	12.9	12.6	12.4	12.1	11.8	11.5	11.2	10.8	10.5	10.1
71	12.5	12.2	12.0	11.7	11.4	11.2	10.9	10.5	10.2	9.9
72	12.0	11.8	11.6	11.4	11.1	10.8	10.5	10.2	9.9	9.6
73	11.6	11.4	11.2	11.0	10.7	10.5	10.2	9.9	9.7	9.4
74	11.2	11.0	10.8	10.6	10.4	10.1	9.9	9.6	9.4	9.1
75	10.7	10.5	10.4	10.2	10.0	9.8	9.5	9.3	9.1	8.8
76	10.3	10.1	9.9	9.8	9.6	9.4	9.2	9.0	8.8	8.5
77	9.8	9.7	9.5	9.4	9.2	9.0	8.8	8.6	8.4	8.2
78	9.4	9.2	9.1	9.0	8.8	8.7	8.5	8.3	8.1	7.9
79	8.9	8.8	8.7	8.6	8.4	8.3	8.1	8.0	7.8	7.6
80	8.5	8.4	8.3	8.2	8.0	7.9	7.8	7.6	7.5	7.3

Source: Table VI A, Reg. § 1.72-9.

Table 5   MULTIPLE ADJUSTMENTS

If the number of whole months from the annuity starting date to the first payment date is—

	0-1	2	3	4	5	6	7	8	9	10	11	12
And payments under the contract are to be made:												
Annually	+0.5	+0.4	+0.3	+0.2	+0.1	0	0	−0.1	−0.2	−0.3	−0.4	−0.5
Semiannually	+ .2	+ .1	0	0	− .1	− .2	...	...	...	...	...	...
Quarterly	+ .1	0	− .1	...	...	...	...	...	...	...	...	...

Source: Reg. § 1.72-5(a)(2)(i).

Table 6   PERCENT VALUE OF REFUND FEATURE

Age	Years—									
	21	22	23	24	25	26	27	28	29	30
55	8	9	9	10	11	12	13	14	15	16
56	9	9	10	11	12	13	14	15	16	18
57	9	10	11	12	13	14	15	17	18	19
58	10	11	12	13	14	16	17	18	19	21
59	11	12	13	15	16	17	18	20	21	22
60	12	14	15	16	17	19	20	21	23	24
61	14	15	16	17	19	20	22	23	25	26
62	15	16	18	19	20	22	23	25	27	28
63	16	18	19	21	22	24	25	27	29	30
64	18	19	21	23	24	26	28	29	31	33
65	20	21	23	25	26	28	30	31	33	35
66	21	23	25	27	28	30	32	34	35	37
67	23	25	27	29	31	32	34	36	38	40
68	25	27	29	31	33	35	37	38	40	42
69	28	29	31	33	35	37	39	41	43	44
70	30	32	34	36	38	40	42	43	45	47
71	32	34	36	38	40	42	44	46	47	49
72	35	37	39	41	43	45	46	48	50	51
73	37	39	41	43	45	47	49	51	52	54
74	40	42	44	46	48	50	51	53	54	56
75	42	44	46	48	50	52	54	56	57	58
76	45	47	49	51	53	54	56	58	59	60
77	47	50	51	53	55	57	58	60	61	62
78	50	52	54	56	57	59	61	62	63	64
79	53	55	56	58	60	61	63	64	65	66
80	55	57	59	60	62	63	65	66	67	68

Source: Table VII, Reg. § 1.72-9.

¶ 4140   ADOPTION EXPENSES

There is a limited exclusion from gross income of up to $5,000 of adoption expenses per child, or $6,000 for each child with special needs where such expenses are paid or incurred by the taxpayer's employer under a qualified adoption assistance program. To be eligible, the child must be under the age of 18. Qualified adoption expenses include ordinary and necessary adoption expenses, court costs, attorney fees, and other expenses incurred for the principal purpose of the legal adoption of an eligible child. This exclusion is available for tax years beginning after 1996 and before 2002. A deduction for adoption expenses must be coordinated with the adoption credit. (See ¶ 8031.)

Example 4.34. Ron and Roberta begin adoption proceedings in 1998 for an infant through a U.S.-based agency. During 1998 they incurred $3,000 of legal fees. During 1999 they incur $2,000 of additional adoption fees, and on November 16, 1999, they finalize the adoption. The $5,000 in expenses were incurred through Ron's employer's adoption assistance program. Ron and Roberta have

$60,000 of adjusted gross income in 1999. They may exclude from gross income the $5,000 paid by Ron's employer in 1999.

¶ 4145 COMPENSATION FOR INJURIES AND SICKNESS

The law specifically excludes from gross income:

1. Amounts received under workers' compensation acts as compensation for personal injuries or sickness

2. Amount of any damages received (whether by suit or agreement and whether as lump sums or as periodic payments) on account of personal injuries or sickness

3. Amounts received for personal injuries or sickness through accident and health insurance which the worker purchased

4. Amounts received as a pension, annuity, or similar allowance for personal injuries or sickness resulting from active service in the armed forces of any country or in the Coast and Geodetic Survey or the Public Health Service, or as a disability annuity payable under the provisions of Section 808 of the Foreign Service Act of 1980

5. Amounts received as disability income attributable to injuries incurred as a direct result of violent attack which the Secretary of State determines to be a terrorist attack and which occurred while such individual was an employee of the United States engaged in the performance of official duties outside the United States (Code Sec. 104(a))

Note the above-mentioned exclusions from gross income under workers' compensation acts cover occupational injury and sickness. Nonoccupational injuries and sicknesses are *not* covered. Further, payments received in excess of applicable workers' compensation laws are *not* excludable. However, benefits received under an accident and health insurance plan due to taxpayer's contributions are excludable from gross income. "No fault" insurance disability benefits received under the owner's insurance policy are excluded from gross income as well.

Example 4.35. Dixie Barnes worked for Cleveland Inc. for many years and was covered by workers' compensation and an accident and health plan that she personally purchased. On April 15, Dixie was seriously injured when a light fixture fell and broke her neck. She collected $4,000 for medical expenses incurred and $3,000 from her insurance company for her lost wages. Dixie may exclude from her gross income both the $4,000 received for medical expenses incurred and the $3,000 from her insurance company.

Damages compensating an injured person for personal injuries or sickness are excludable from gross income. These damages are often excludable even when measured by the amount of wages that might have been earned but for the injuries. However, amounts received specifically for lost wages are taxable. Damages received for nonphysical injuries are not excludable from gross income, and emotional distress is not considered a physical injury or sickness. However, an exclusion from gross income is allowed to the extent damages received are used to pay medical expenses attributable to emotional distress.

Punitive damages are taxable as ordinary income, regardless of whether or not they are derived from physical or nonphysical injury. This restriction is effective for amounts received after August 20, 1996, but does not apply to punitive damages awarded in wrongful death actions if applicable state law in effect on September 13, 1995, provides that only punitive damages may be awarded.

Damages received from actions based on age, injury to reputation, emotional distress, race, or sex discrimination violations are includible in gross income if received after August 20, 1996.

Example 4.36. Joan Jacobs was seriously injured in an automobile accident. The driver of the other car was charged and convicted of reckless driving. Joan received the following payments.

Reimbursement for medical and hospital expenses	$ 6,500
Loss of income reimbursement due to accident	2,500
Punitive damages	8,000
Payments for pain and suffering	3,000
Total payments received	$20,000

From the above payments, Joan may exclude from income all but the $8,000 received for punitive damages.

Compensatory damages received by the individual are excludable from income under Code Sec. 104(a)(2). Where the awards by the court, or, for that matter, the damages received in an out-of-court settlement, are really for lost profits in a business, then the amounts are included in income. When reimbursement for medical expenses incurred is received, the individual cannot take an itemized deduction for the same expenses. Further, if, for example, the taxpayer incurred medical expenses in 1998 and deducted them on the 1998 tax return and in June 1999 received reimbursement for the same expenses, the reimbursement must be included in gross income to the extent of the previous deduction.

¶ 4155 ACCIDENT AND HEALTH PLANS

Benefits received by an employee under an accident and health plan where premiums are paid by the employer are excludable from gross income if they come under the following conditions:

1. Permanent injury or loss of bodily function if amounts are paid on the nature of the injury and not on work time lost by employee

2. Reimbursement for medical expenses of employee, spouse, or dependents (Code Sec. 105(b) and (c))

To qualify the plan must not discriminate in favor of highly compensated executives, shareholders, or certain officers. Further, reimbursements are deductible only to the extent of actual medical expenses.

Example 4.37. Bea Safe was seriously injured while working on the job in June 1998. During the course of the year she received the following payments on account of her injury:

Workers' compensation	$ 750
Medical expense reimbursement	6,000
Damages for loss of limb	10,000

In the example, all three items are excluded from gross income.

The premiums the employer pays to fund an accident and health plan for employees are not taxed to the employee. It is immaterial whether or not payment is for an insured plan. Further, the plan can cover the employee for personal injuries or sickness, the employee's spouse, or any dependents. Code Sec. 106; Reg. § 1.106-1.

It does not matter if the employer contributions for health and accident insurance are purchased as a group policy or an individual policy. However, if the policy provides for benefits beyond health and accident insurance then only the portion of the employer's contribution associated with the health and accident insurance is excluded.

Amounts received by the employee for sickness or injury through the employer-paid health and accident plan are excluded from gross income as long as they are for medical care reimbursement. Amounts paid under the plan that are not medical care reimbursement must be included in the employee's gross income.

¶ 4165   QUALIFIED LONG-TERM CARE INSURANCE

Beginning January 1, 1997, qualified long-term care insurance contracts will generally be treated as accident and health insurance contracts. Amounts received as benefits under the contract may be excluded from gross income as amounts received for personal injury or sickness.

¶ 4185   MEALS AND LODGING

Meals furnished to an employee or the employee's family are considered compensation to the employee. However, employees may exclude the value of meals furnished by the employer if (1) the meals are furnished on the business premises of the employer, and (2) they are furnished for the convenience of the employer. Code Sec. 119(a)(1). For example, a waitress in a luncheonette works from 6 a.m. to 2 p.m. Her employer provides for her breakfast and lunch at the luncheonette free of charge. Further, she is required to have her meals on the premises. Under the circumstances, the meals are not income to the waitress. If the waitress had the right to free lunches on her days off, they would be included in her gross income.

The value of lodging may be excluded from gross income if (1) the lodging is on the employer's premises, (2) the lodging is for the convenience of the employer, and (3) the employee must accept the lodging as a condition of employment. Code Sec. 119(a)(2). Normally such lodging is provided for employees who must be available to respond to emergencies, as in the case of ambulance drivers. The required lodging must be a condition of employment to be excluded from gross income. If the above tests are not met, the value of the meals and lodging is income to the employee. Reg. § 1.61-2(d)(3).

Example 4.38. Dr. Bruce Key works at Metro General Hospital and is required to be on the premises because he is on call from Friday at 6:00 p.m. to Monday at 8:00 a.m. Dr. Key is not required to report the value of meals and lodging received while on duty.

Qualified campus lodging furnished by an educational institution to faculty and other employees may be eligible for exclusion from gross income where an adequate rental is charged. For rental to be considered adequate, applicable appraisal tests must be met. Code Sec. 119(d).

¶ 4195   CAFETERIA PLANS

Cafeteria plans are employer-sponsored benefit packages that offer employees a choice between taking cash and qualified benefits (such as accident and health coverage or group-term life insurance coverage). Code Sec. 125; Reg. § 1.125-1. No amount is included in the gross income of a cafeteria plan participant solely because he or she may choose among the benefits of the plan; but, if the participant chooses cash, it would be includible in gross income as compensation. If qualified benefits are chosen, they are excludable to the extent allowed by the law.

The cafeteria plan must limit its offering of benefits only between cash and qualified benefits to employees. A qualified benefit is any benefit that is not includible in the gross income of the employee by reason of an express provision of the law. The only taxable benefit that a cafeteria plan may offer is cash. The menu of items in the plan might include such nontaxable benefits as group-term life insurance, disability benefits, and accident and health benefits. This is not meant to be an exhaustive list of benefits includible in a cafeteria plan. Other fringes which may be included are dental plans, vacation days, and qualified dependent care assistance. Unused benefits from one plan year may not be accumulated by an employee and carried over to succeeding years.

However, the following plans have been expressly prohibited from inclusion: qualified scholarships (Code Sec. 117), educational assistance programs (Code Sec. 127), or excludable fringe benefits (Code Sec. 132). An exception is made for employer contributions to profit-sharing or stock bonus plans under a qualified cash or deferred arrangement as defined by Code Sec. 401(k)(2). The beauty of the cafeteria approach to fringe benefit management is that the employer is allowed a tax deduction for providing the fringe benefits offered in the plan while the employee participants recognize no income if they choose the nontaxable benefits. Further, the employees select fringe benefit plans they desire and need and not plans of no interest to them or plans already available to their spouses.

Participation in the cafeteria plan must be restricted to employees. The maximum number of years that can be required by the employer of the employee before allowing an employee to partake in the plan is three years. Further, the rules must be the same for all employees. The plan must not discriminate in favor of highly compensated individuals, shareholders owning more than 5 percent of the voting power or value of the stock, or certain key employees. Unless the cafeteria plan meets the above-stated anti-discrimination rules, the highly paid individuals or shareholders must include in gross income the maximum benefits they are entitled to receive. However, the plan will remain intact for the participants not included in the prohibited class. Code Sec. 125(b) and (e).

The reporting requirements for cafeteria plans are quite stringent. Employers must report to the IRS the name and address of and the amount of benefits provided to highly compensated employees. Also, they must report the number of highly compensated employees, along with a list of the number eligible to participate in the plan, the number who actually participate, and the amount of fringe benefits includible in income, and the total cost of the plan during the year.

Example 4.39. Ralph Jones works for Lorain Inc. and earns $30,000 per year. His employer has a basic cafeteria plan. Prior to the beginning of the benefit year, the employee must select the coverage desired. Ralph may choose among the following: $2,000 in cash or medical coverage up to $2,000 for the year, group-term life insurance, and day care facilities. Any unused benefit is forfeited. Therefore, if Ralph selects medical coverage and uses only $1,200, he forfeits the remaining $800.

Why choose medical coverage over cash? If Ralph chooses to receive the $2,000 in cash, he will immediately be taxed on the amount. Then, when he purchases a medical plan, he would be using after-tax dollars. Usually, group plans are considerably less expensive than privately purchased plans. By selecting group medical coverage, Ralph recognizes no income; therefore, he is selecting a nontaxable benefit plan with before-tax dollars. Remember this risk—if Ralph does not use all of his $2,000 covered medical expenses, he loses the dollars.

TAX PLANNING POINTER ▼

Cafeteria plans prove quite advantageous for married couples. If both spouses work for companies having cafeteria plans, they should arrange their affairs so as to provide themselves with full coverage. Typically, married couples find themselves with two medical plans and no dental plan. Cafeteria plans correct this drawback and are of great benefit to families.

¶ 4201   EDUCATIONAL ASSISTANCE PLANS

Payments of up to $5,250 per year received by an employee for tuition, fees, books, and supplies under an employer's assistance program may be excluded from gross income. Code Sec. 127. Any excess is includible in the employee's gross income and is subject to employment and income tax withholding.

The exclusion for educational assistance benefits expired on June 30, 1997. The provision was extended to expenses for courses beginning before June 1, 2000. This provision applies whether or not the educational courses are work-related. However, no exclusion is allowed for graduate level courses beginning after June 30, 1996.

Expenses disallowed because they exceed the $5,250 limit may be excludable if they meet the working condition fringe benefit rules under Code Sec. 132. Excludable assistance payments may not cover tools or supplies that the employee retains after completion of the course or the cost of meals, lodging, or transportation. Although the courses covered by the plan need not be job-related, courses involving sports, games, or hobbies may be covered only if they involve the employer's business. Reg. § 1.127-2(c).

The plan must be written. The employer may pay the expenses directly, reimburse the employees for their expenses, or provide the education directly. The plan need not be funded and prior approval of the plan by the IRS is not required, but the plan must not discriminate in favor of highly compensated employees. Further, not more than 5 percent of the total amount paid out during the year may be paid to or for employees who are shareholders or owners who own at least 5 percent of the business. An employer who maintains an educational plan must maintain records and file a return with respect to the plan. Code Sec. 6039D.

¶ 4215   TUITION REDUCTION PLANS

Qualified tuition reductions (QTRs) made available to employees (and their families) of qualified educational institutions are excludable from the employee's gross income. A QTR is the amount of reduction in tuition for education that is furnished by an educational institution to an employee (or an employee's dependent children or certain other individuals) provided certain requirements are met. The tuition reduction must be for education below the graduate level. Code Sec. 117(d). However, under a special rule, tuition reduction benefits paid to graduate teaching and research assistants employed by qualified educational institutions may be excluded from gross income. Code Sec. 117(d)(5).

¶ 4235   DEPENDENT CARE ASSISTANCE PROGRAMS

An employee receiving dependent care assistance payments provided under an employer's written nondiscriminatory plan generally may exclude such payments from gross income. Code Sec. 129. The exclusion for employer-provided dependent care assistance is limited to $5,000 a year ($2,500 in the case of a separate return by a married individual). Also, the exclusion is subject to an earned income limitation. Thus, an unmarried taxpayer may not exclude from gross income more than his or her earned income for the tax year, and a married taxpayer may not exclude more than the lesser of his or her earned income or the spouse's earned income. In applying the earned income test for a married taxpayer, the earned income of an incapacitated or student spouse is deemed to be $200 per month if one qualifying dependent is involved or $400 if two or more qualifying dependents are involved.

The employer's plan must be for the exclusive use of its employees and must not discriminate in favor of employees who are officers, owners, or highly compensated employees or their dependents. The purpose of the service provided must be to enable an individual to work. An employee who excludes the value of child or dependent care services from income may not claim any income tax deduction or credit with respect to such amounts.

Qualifying expenses include amounts paid for household services and care of the qualifying person. A qualifying person is any child under age 13, a disabled spouse, or any disabled person, provided that the qualifying person is a dependent of the taxpayer. The person who provides the care may not be the taxpayer's spouse or a person claimed by the taxpayer as a dependent. Further, if the taxpayer's child provides the care, the child must be age 19 or older by the end of the tax year.

The exclusion for employer-provided dependent care assistance may not be claimed unless the taxpayer reports the dependent care provider's correct name, address, and taxpayer identification number on the tax return. The exclusion may be claimed even though the information is not provided if it can be shown that the taxpayer exercised due diligence in attempting to provide this information. Code Sec. 129(e)(9). Similar information reporting requirements also apply to employers that provide dependent care programs for their employees.

¶ 4255   MILITARY BENEFITS

Qualified military benefits are excluded from gross income. Qualified military benefits are benefits that are received either in cash or in kind by members of the armed services or their dependents by reason of military service and that, as of September 9, 1986, were excludable from gross income by law, regulation, or administrative practice. However, the personal use of a car is not excludable as a qualified military benefit. Code Sec. 134.

Military retirement pay based on years of service and/or age must be included in gross income. Code Sec. 61(a)(11). However, veterans' benefits administered by the Veterans Administration are excludable from gross income. This includes amounts paid to veterans or their families in the form of educational, training, or subsistence allowances, disability compensation and pension payments for disabilities, and veterans' pensions.

Military personnel are allowed to deduct mortgage interest and taxes on homes even though they receive a military allowance that is excludable from gross income. Code Sec. 256(a)(6). However, such interest is subject to the qualified residence rules.

KEYSTONE PROBLEM

Commonwealth Medicine Company, a hospital supply firm, has had difficulty attracting new personnel, particularly at the executive level. They feel that the company is competitive in the area of salary, but that total compensation packages should be examined more carefully. Of course, many factors will determine the final list. However, you are asked to examine one consideration in developing these packages, which is to reduce the tax impact on the employee. Therefore, you wish to devise a plan that will provide benefits for employees that will not be included in their taxable income. Include in your examination the concept of cafeteria plans. Also investigate the consequences of limiting the plans to selected levels of personnel.

SUMMARY OF CHAPTER 4

✓   Sections 101 through 139 of the Internal Revenue Code list "Items Specifically Excluded from Gross Income."

✓   A portion of Social Security benefits must be included in taxable income for taxpayers who meet certain requirements described by the Revenue Reconciliation Act of 1993.

✓   For tax years beginning after 1989, a tax exemption is provided for interest earned on U.S. savings bonds used to finance the higher education of the taxpayer, the taxpayer's spouse, or the taxpayer's dependents.

✓   Certain employee discounts provided to employees on the selling price of qualified property or services of the employer are excludable from gross income, provided that the discount meets certain qualifications.

✓   Cafeteria plans offer employees a choice between taking cash and qualified benefits, which are any benefits that are not includible in the gross income of the employee by reason of an express provision of law.

✓   Educational assistance plans are subject to a number of tax status rules for determining exclusion.

From Gross Income to Taxable Income—Simplified

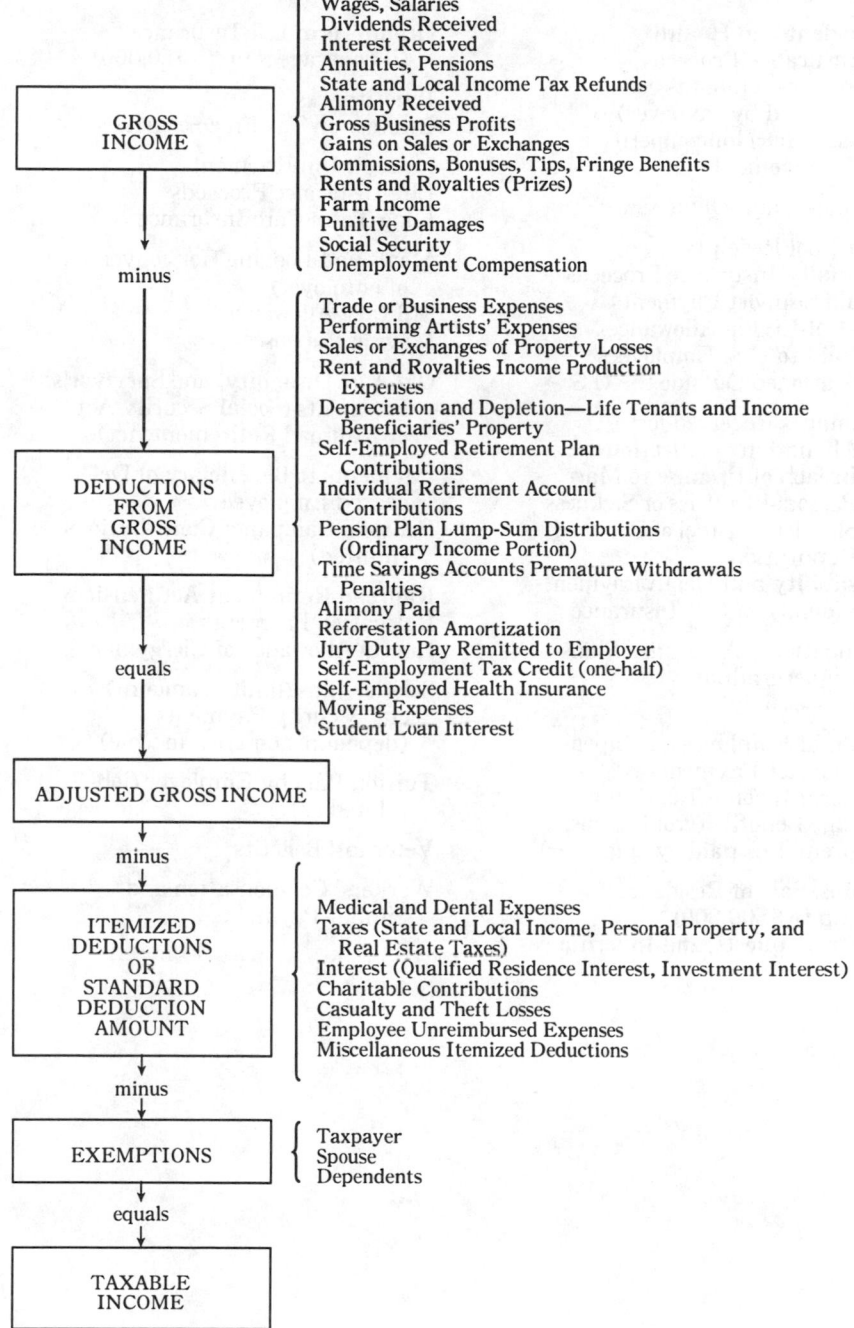

GROSS INCOME
- Wages, Salaries
- Dividends Received
- Interest Received
- Annuities, Pensions
- State and Local Income Tax Refunds
- Alimony Received
- Gross Business Profits
- Gains on Sales or Exchanges
- Commissions, Bonuses, Tips, Fringe Benefits
- Rents and Royalties (Prizes)
- Farm Income
- Punitive Damages
- Social Security
- Unemployment Compensation

minus

DEDUCTIONS FROM GROSS INCOME
- Trade or Business Expenses
- Performing Artists' Expenses
- Sales or Exchanges of Property Losses
- Rent and Royalties Income Production Expenses
- Depreciation and Depletion—Life Tenants and Income Beneficiaries' Property
- Self-Employed Retirement Plan Contributions
- Individual Retirement Account Contributions
- Pension Plan Lump-Sum Distributions (Ordinary Income Portion)
- Time Savings Accounts Premature Withdrawals Penalties
- Alimony Paid
- Reforestation Amortization
- Jury Duty Pay Remitted to Employer
- Self-Employment Tax Credit (one-half)
- Self-Employed Health Insurance
- Moving Expenses
- Student Loan Interest

equals

ADJUSTED GROSS INCOME

minus

ITEMIZED DEDUCTIONS OR STANDARD DEDUCTION AMOUNT
- Medical and Dental Expenses
- Taxes (State and Local Income, Personal Property, and Real Estate Taxes)
- Interest (Qualified Residence Interest, Investment Interest)
- Charitable Contributions
- Casualty and Theft Losses
- Employee Unreimbursed Expenses
- Miscellaneous Itemized Deductions

minus

EXEMPTIONS
- Taxpayer
- Spouse
- Dependents

equals

TAXABLE INCOME

¶ 4255

SUMMARY CHECKLIST
Exclusions from Gross Income

Accident and Health
  Insurance Proceeds
Annuities (amounts con-
  tributed by taxpayer)
Awards for Noncompetitive
  Achievements

Bequests and Devises

Car Pool Receipts
Casualty Insurance Proceeds
Child Support Payments
Cost-of-Living Allowances
  Paid to U.S. Employees
  Stationed Outside the U.S.

Damages Received for:
  Alienation of Affection
  Breach of Promise to Marry
  Personal Injuries or Sickness
  Slander or Libel of Personal
  Reputation
Disability and Death Payments
Dividends on Life Insurance

Educational Assistance Plans
  (undergraduate
  classes only)

Federal Employees' Compensation Act Payments
Federal Income Tax Refunds
Fringe Benefits (group plans,
  premiums paid by employer)

Gains: Sale of Residence
  (up to $500,000)
Gifts, Bequests, and Inheritances

Group-Term Life Insurance
  (if coverage is up to $50,000)

Inheritances
Interest on Tax-Free Securities

Lessee's Improvements
Life Insurance Proceeds
Long-Term Care Insurance

Meals and Lodging (for convenience
  of employer)
Military Allowances
Moving Expenses

Old Age, Disability, and Survivor's
  Payments (Social Security Act
  or Railroad Retirement Act)

Payments to Beneficiary of Deceased Employee
Political Campaign Contributions
  (limited)

Railroad Retirement Act Pensions
Relocation Payments
Rental Allowance of Clergymen

Scholarships (limited amount)
Social Security Payments
  (depending on gross income)

Tuition Paid by Employer (job-
  related only)

Veterans' Benefits

Workers' Compensation and
  Similar Payments

CHAPTER 4 QUESTIONS

1. How does a tax exclusion differ from a tax deduction?

2. An individual surrenders, for $20,000, an endowment life insurance policy in which he had a $15,000 investment. How much of the $20,000 of proceeds must be included in gross income?

3. Explain under which conditions the death benefit exclusion of $5,000 applies.

4. How is the amount of Social Security benefits included in taxable income calculated?

5. On Series EE U.S. savings bonds, what different tax consequences arise from the two choices in reporting interest?

6. List several social justifications for issuing private activity bonds.

7. What is an annuity, and what features determine the amount of income associated with such a contract?

8. How is the excludable portion of an annuity calculated?

9. What five categories of compensation for injuries and sickness are excluded from gross income?

10. How are employer contributions to accident and health and group legal services plans treated by employees on their own income tax returns?

11. Describe the elements of a cafeteria plan and what are the beneficial aspects of such a plan for employers and employees.

12. How does a joint and survivor annuity differ from a single person annuity? How is the computation of the exclusion different for the joint annuity?

13. Name two types of fringe benefits, discussed in this chapter, that cannot be included in a cafeteria plan?

14. Mrs. George is the beneficiary of her husband's life insurance policy. When Mr. George died in 1984, she elected to have the payments spread out over several years in order to have some income every month. Must she pay any taxes on the amount received? Explain. How would your answer differ if Mr. George had died in 1998?

15. Indicate whether the following income sources must be included or may be excluded from gross income:
    a. Insurance proceeds for loss of finger
    b. Prizes
    c. Embezzlement proceeds
    d. Interest on all savings deposits
    e. Child support
    f. Interest on Series HH bonds
    g. Receipt of alimony by divorced husband

    h.   Income produced from property acquired by gift

    i.   Gifts and inheritances

    j.   Scholarship grants for tuition

    k.   Compensation for injuries or sickness

    l.   Interest income on bonds issued by State of Ohio

    m. Life insurance proceeds from a group plan

16. Give an example of when meals provided to an employee by an employer may be excluded form income.

17. Mary Jane received $6,000 from her employer as reimbursement for her expenditures on tuition, fees, and books while attending State University. Mary Jane is working toward an undergraduate degree in business administration. Must Mary Jane recognize the $6,000 as income?

18. If an employee is covered by a group-term life insurance plan that pays the entire premium of the policy, must the employee include the premium coverage in income if her salary is over $50,000 per year?

CHAPTER 4 PROBLEMS

19. In January 1998, Leon McLeod received a gift of a beach cottage valued at $25,000 from his great-uncle who owned a number of such buildings. The cottage was rented each year to college students who occupied it during the school year. The annual net rental income received is $2,000 per year. The 1998 tax return of McLeod would include what elements of this transaction?

20. The Hightown Council refused to increase the town budget. Robert Read was laid off from work on August 4, 1998. Earlier in the year he had been temporarily disabled from a job-related injury and had received disability benefits. At year-end Robert Read and his wife have the following sources of income:

Disability income	$ 2,500
Unemployment compensation	5,000
Salary—January 1-August 4, 1998	10,000
Wife's salary	9,000
Supplemental unemployment compensation—employer provided	3,000

What amount of Read's family income was includible in gross income?

21. In 1998, Windsor Knott, an employee of the Victoria Tie Company, was seriously injured in the factory stockroom. He was hospitalized for 30 days and lost partial use of his left hand. During his hospitalization and recovery period, he received the following:

Workers' compensation	$ 9,000
Medical expenses reimbursement	10,000
Disability insurance benefits (insurance paid by taxpayer)	4,000
Accident and health insurance benefits (company policy benefits based on the degree of permanent injury)	9,500

Determine Knott's tax liability with regard to these payments. If the medical expenses had been deducted from Knott's 1998 tax return and reimbursement was received in 1999, how would the reimbursement be reflected in the 1999 return?

22. David and Renee Kimberly, ages 75 and 65, respectively, have the following sources of income:

Private pension receipts	$15,000
Social Security	12,000
Interest on bank deposits	2,000
Dividends from domestic corporations	1,500
Interest on tax-exempt securities	700

Their itemized deductions total $7,000. Compute their taxable income.

23. Lee Elder retires in 1998 at the age of 72. At retirement she decides to devote full time to her hobby of making stuffed dolls. She markets them as Lettuce Leaf Cuties and is an immediate success. Her income as company president is $60,000 in 1998; however, she continues to receive her Social Security payments of $6,000. Her husband, Arthur, also retired, receives $8,000 in Social Security and $3,000 in interest on tax-exempt bonds in his own name. For many years the couple had been filing separate tax returns and have continued this practice. Calculate their income tax liabilities. Would this change if their method of filing changed? How?

24. Charles Adams, who is single, retired on March 3, 1998, at the age of 65. For the year 1998, he receives the following income:

Salary	$14,000
Interest income	2,000
Dividend income	1,000
Tax-exempt income	1,000
Social Security benefits	5,000
Net rental income	6,000

What amount, if any, of his Social Security benefits must Charles include in his 1998 gross income? What is Charles' taxable income for 1998?

25. Felix Boots, a 35-year-old male, is vice president of the Kitty-Lit Pet Products Company and earns $50,000 per year. The company provides paid group-term life insurance of twice the officers' salaries for all officers of the company. The cost of the policy to the company for Mr. Boots is $650 per year. How much of the $650 must Felix include in his gross income? If Kitty-Lit changed its policy so as to enable all employees to be covered at twice their annual salary, what would Felix have to include in his gross income?

26. A. Fluent, an investor in stocks and bonds, wanted to increase his portfolio but wanted to minimize his tax liability on the income from the bonds. He is presented with the following alternative investments: U.S. Series EE bonds, U.S. Series HH bonds, bonds for industrial development for mass transit, and qualified veterans' mortgage bonds. Which should he choose for his investment? Why?

27. Norm and Pat, a married couple filing a joint return, have the following sources of income:

Wages	$35,000
Interest income	4,000
Dividend income	3,000
Social Security benefits	9,000

Both Norm and Pat are over 65 years of age. Determine their taxable income.

28. Ron and Gayle, both over 65 years of age, have the following sources of income:

Consulting income	$36,000
Interest income	4,000
Tax-exempt interest	4,000
Social Security benefits	12,000

Ron and Gayle have itemized deductions of $10,000. Compute their taxable income.

29. Robert Provider purchases a joint and survivor annuity providing for payments of $200 per month for his life and upon his death for his wife, Robin, for the remainder of her life. As of the annuity starting date Robert is 68 and Robin is 66. The annuity cost Robert $36,000. Determine the exclusion ratio for the annuity.

30. On September 23, 1998, Mary Jones bought an annuity contract for $22,050 that will give her $125 a month for life, beginning October 30. Mary is 61 years old. Determine the exclusion ratio and the amount of the pension to be included in Mary Jones's 1998 gross income.

31. Don Smith's wife died in January while still employed and, as her beneficiary, he began receiving an annuity of $147 per month. There was no investment in the contract after June 30, 1989. The investment in the contract was $7,938. Don Smith, age 65, received his first monthly annuity check as of February 3, 1998. Determine the amount of his pension to be included in his gross income.

32. Assume the same facts as in Problem 31, except that in January 1999, because of a cost-of-living increase, Don's annuity payment was increased to $175 per month. Determine the amount of the 1999 annuity payment to be included in Don's gross income.

33. Philip Southerly purchases a joint and survivor annuity providing for payments of $200 per month for his life and, after his death, $100 per month for his wife's life. As of the annuity starting date he is 70 years old and his wife is 67. The annuity cost Philip $28,000. Determine the exclusion ratio for the annuity Philip purchased and the amount of the pension to be included in gross income.

34. Peter Seaman, at age 45, purchased an annuity which will pay him $250 a month for life once he reaches age 65. He paid in $25,000. At retirement, he will have quarterly payments from the annuity. Peter receives his first annuity payment three months after the starting date (January 20). Perform the calculations and determine what amount he may exclude from gross income. What was the exclusion ratio? What was the adjusted multiple used to calculate the exclusion?

35. Beth, who is single, redeems her Series EE bonds. She receives $12,000, consisting of $8,000 principal and $4,000 interest. Beth's qualified educational expenses total $16,500. Further, Beth's adjusted gross income for the year is $40,000. Determine what, if any, interest income Beth must include in her gross income.

36. Linda Sue Carr worked for a large food brokerage firm. In January of this year she was terminated. After a court battle Linda Sue was reinstated in her job and received from the firm in November $7,500 in punitive damages. Must Linda Sue include the $7,500 in punitive damages in her 1998 gross income?

37. Steven Spokesman, a high school teacher in a local school district, was fired for publicly criticizing the local school district. The court ruled that Steven's freedom of speech had been violated and the school district was required to pay $24,000 in damages. Steven paid his lawyer $8,000 to defend him. Determine: (1) whether Steven must include the $24,000 in gross income and (2) whether he can deduct the $8,000 in legal fees?

38. Actress Nola Talent sued her coworker, actor Burt Dirt, for slander, citing his speech at a press interview where he labeled her a "floozy" and an "incompetent excuse for an actress." In her suit she claimed that as a consequence of this slander she not only felt degraded but was denied further acting roles. The court awarded her $100,000 in compensatory damages for damage to her acting career and $20 in punitive damages for the slander of her character. How is this reflected in her income tax return?

39. Robert Careless was injured while working on the production line on July 8, 1998. He received the following payments as a result of his serious injury:

Workers' compensation	$6,000
Medical expense reimbursement	2,000
Damages for personal injury	5,000

During 1998, Robert earned $16,000 in wages. How much of the above-listed amounts must Robert include in his gross income?

40. Roger Corby, a student, was employed seven nights a week at the Campus Inn as a desk clerk. He was required to be on duty from 11 p.m. to 6 a.m. and on call at various other hours, although he was rarely called after 12 p.m. His employer also required that he live on the premises and furnished him with a room free of charge, adjacent to the desk. Roger used the room as his permanent living quarters. Roger also ate all his meals free in the Inn dining room. Roger excluded the value of all these benefits from his tax return. What was the response of the IRS examiner?

41. Mrs. Betty Grant was the beneficiary of her late husband's $100,000 (face amount) life insurance policy. Mrs. Grant has been receiving payments of $5,200 per year since her husband's death on July 1, 1986. Based on her life expectancy, she will receive payments for 25 years. What amount, if any, should Betty include in her gross income for 1998?

    a. $ 200
    b. $1,200
    c. $4,200
    d. $5,200

42. *IRS Adapted Problem.* Ms. Green is single and over 65 years old. She received the following income in 1998:

Interest from certificates of deposit	$ 3,000
Tax-exempt interest	6,000
Taxable dividends	5,000
Taxable pension	15,000
Wages from consulting work	9,000
Social Security	14,000

She did not have any adjustments to income. What is the taxable amount of Ms. Green's Social Security?

    a. $7,000
    b. $9,350
    c. $11,000
    d. $11,900
    e. $13,850

43. *IRS Adapted Problem.* All of the following fringe benefits can be excluded from the employee's income except:

    a. Transportation up to $65 per month for combined commuter highway vehicle transportation and transit passes, and $175 per month for qualified parking.

b. Holiday gifts, other than cash, with a low fair market value.

c. Qualified employee discounts given employees on certain property and services offered to customers in the ordinary course of the line of business in which the employees perform services.

d. Memberships to municipal athletic facilities for employees, their spouses, and their dependent children.

44. *IRS Adapted Problem.* In December 1998, Mr. Stone cashed qualified Series EE U.S. Savings Bonds, which he had purchased in January 1993. The proceeds were used for his son's college education. All of the following statements are correct concerning the exclusion of the interest received except:

a. He cannot file as married filing separate.

b. Eligible expenses include room and board.

c. If the proceeds are *more* than the expenses, he will be able to exclude only part of the interest.

d. Before he figures his interest exclusion, he must reduce his qualified higher education expenses by certain benefits.

45. *IRS Adapted Problem.* Unemployment compensation generally includes any amount received under unemployment compensation laws of the United States or of a state. All of the following statements are correct, except:

a. Benefits received from a company-financed fund, to which you did not contribute, are *not* unemployment compensation, but are taxable wages.

b. Benefits paid to you as an unemployed member of a union out of regular union dues are *not* included in your gross income.

c. You may be liable for estimated taxes if you receive unemployment compensation.

d. Payments you receive from your employer during periods of unemployment, under a union agreement that guarantees you full pay during the year, are taxable as wages.

46. On January 4, 1998, Ralph Stuart, an employee of Hard Manufacturing Inc., enrolled for the spring semester at State University where he is a candidate for an undergraduate degree in accounting. His employer reimbursed him for the following expenses: $2,000 for tuition, $600 for books and $100 for transportation to State University. What amount should Ralph exclude from his gross income in 1998?

a. $0

b. $2,000

c. $2,600

d. $2,700

47. *IRS Adapted Problem.* Mr. Hines received a $6,200 grant from a local university for the fall of 1998. Mr. Hines was a candidate for a degree, and was required to be a research assistant, for which services he received payment under the grant. The $6,200 grant provided the following:

Tuition	$3,600
Books and supplies	500
Pay for services as research assistant	2,100

Mr. Hines spent the entire $6,200 on tuition, books, and supplies. What amount must Mr. Hines include in his income for 1998?

   a. $2,100

   b. $2,600

   c. $3,200

   d. $3,600

48. *IRS Adapted Problem.* The following items were received as court awards and damages during 1998. All should be included in ordinary income for 1998 by the taxpayer who received them except:

   a. Compensation for lost wages

   b. Compensatory damages for physical injury

   c. Damages for breach of contract

   d. Interest on damages for breach of contract

49. *Comprehensive Problem.* Rodney and Alice Jones have three small children, ranging in age from 5 to 10. One child is blind and needs special care. Rodney works as an accountant for a large CPA firm and has gross income of $45,000. Alice is a lawyer with a national law firm and earns $48,000. Rodney's parents are quite old, and he and his two brothers entirely support them according to the following percentages:

Rodney	45%
Steven	40%
Robert	15%

The brothers decide that in 1998 Rodney should be allowed to declare his parents as dependents.

Rodney's employer provides group-term life insurance at twice the employee's annual salary. Rodney is 40 years of age.

During 1998, Rodney and Alice receive the following dividends on their jointly held investments:

Dividends from Mexico Inc. (Mexican Corp.)	$700
Dividends from Widget Steel Corp.	150

They received interest income from the following investments:

Interest on State of Ohio highway bonds	$800
Interest on deposits in savings and loans	400

The Joneses have itemized deductions of $14,000. Compute their taxable income.

50. *Comprehensive Problem.* Mr. and Mrs. Sam Morris retired on February 10, 1998, and call you in for tax advice. Both Sam and his wife Sarah have worked for many years and are both 65 years of age.

Facts:

Dependent children: Three—Ages 21, 17, 16

Social Security Benefits	$9,900
Salaries: Sam (January 1-February 10)	6,000
Sarah (January 1-February 10)	5,000
Interest Income:	
Port Authority of N.Y. Bonds	400
Interest from Bank Deposits	900
Corporate Bonds	900
Highway Bonds of Ohio	1,000
City of Cleveland Bonds	1,000
Dividend Income:	
General Motors Common Stock	4,000
General Electric Common Stock	2,000
AGA Ltd. of England	1,000
Net Rental Income	4,000

One of their tenants moved out on July 14, 1998, and Sam determines that they had damaged the stove, and therefore returned only $50 of their $150 security deposit.

The Morrises' eldest son borrowed $10,000 two years ago to purchase a new automobile. He has made payments to his parents and on September 1, 1998, only $2,500 was still outstanding on the loan. On their son's birthday, they told him he no longer had to make payments.

Sam was Vice President of a very large corporation. As part of his fringe benefit package, the corporation purchased for him $50,000 of group-term life insurance. The corporation continues to pay for his life insurance even after retirement.

The Morrises' three children gave their parents a gala retirement party. Many friends and relatives were invited. Gifts valued at over $1,000 were received by the couple.

In October, Mrs. Morris entered a contest being run by a local bank. She submitted drawings for a bank logo. Her drawing was selected and she received $500.

Many years ago, Sam purchased an annuity policy for $9,000. Starting on March 3, 1998, he began receiving lifelong monthly payments of $60.

The Morrises' 21-year-old daughter is in college. She worked during the summer and earned $2,500. Interest on her savings accounts amounted to $500. Her parents paid for the college tuition of $4,000.

The Morrises have itemized deductions of $9,500.

Determine the Morrises' taxable income for 1998.

51. *Research Problem.* Larry Sorich, as part of his estate planning, assigned his $100,000 group-term life insurance policy to his niece. Larry's employer provided for only $50,000 of coverage; therefore, the niece paid for the premiums on the supplemental insurance. Larry did not include in gross income the premiums for the supplemental insurance. Larry's accountant challenged him on this arrangement. Who prevailed? See Rev. Rul. 71-587, 1971-2 CB 89.

Chapter 5

Deductions: General Concepts and Trade or Business Deductions

Learning Objectives

After completing Chapter 5, you should be able to:

1. Name the three categories of deductions allowable to individual taxpayers: (1) trade or business, (2) production of income, and (3) personal.

2. List allowable deductions for losses.

3. Discuss criteria for determining whether taxpayer expenditures are deductible.

4. Explain common business deductions, such as advertising, salaries and wages, fringe benefits, bad debts, etc.

5. Identify allowable business deductions related to capital expenditures, such as depreciation, amortization, depletion, repairs, and improvements, etc.

6. Understand restricted business deductions for lobbying activities and business start-up costs.

7. Discuss allowable deductions for transportation, travel, entertainment, employee moving expenses, and student loan interest.

OVERVIEW OF CHAPTER

Tax deductions are allowed to taxpayers only if specifically authorized by the Internal Revenue Code. In some instances, the Code is very general in allowing certain types of deductions, as for example the deduction of all ordinary and necessary expenses paid or incurred in carrying on a trade or business. In other instances, the Code is quite specific in allowing a certain type of deduction, as for example the deduction allowed to individual taxpayers for hobby expenses. The Code may also place limits on certain deductions. Business gifts are deductible by a business but only up to twenty-five dollars per year, per individual recipient. Furthermore, limitations may be placed on some deductions in one taxable year, but provision may be made to allow a carryback of the disallowed portion of a deduction to an earlier tax year or a carryover of the disallowed deduction to a later tax year. Business losses which appear on a tax return in the current year can be carried back to preceding tax returns to offset past taxable income and/or carried forward to future tax returns to offset future taxable income. Additionally, some Code sections specifically disallow the deduction of certain types of expenditures. For example, expenses relating to tax-exempt income are specifically disallowed even though the specific expenditure may be authorized by another provision of the Code.

Deductions allowable to individual taxpayers fall into three categories: trade or business deductions (including business-related expenses of employees), production of income deductions, and personal deductions. This chapter examines the general concepts of taxation underlying these three categories of allowable deductions for individuals and includes an introduction to trade or business deductions, including allowable deductions for transportation, travel, entertainment, and employee moving expenses.

Section 162 allows as a deduction all the ordinary and necessary expenses paid or incurred during the taxable year in carrying on any trade or business. Although Code Sec. 162 appears to be all-inclusive in allowing all business expenditures as tax deductions, the requirements for the deductibility of business expenditures place well-defined limitations on business deductions. For this reason, a basic knowledge of allowable business deductions is of value to an informed businessperson.

With some notable exceptions, trade or business deductions are the same for all business taxpayers regardless of whether the business is organized as a corporation, partnership, or sole proprietorship. Although the income tax form used to report deductions is different, the allowable deductions generally are the same. This chapter is concerned mainly with business deductions as they appear on a sole proprietor's Schedule C, which is included as part of the taxpayer's individual income tax return.

Categories of Allowable Deductions

¶ 5001   CLASSIFICATION OF TAX DEDUCTIONS

Three categories of tax deductions are allowable to individual taxpayers. These three categories are:

1. *Trade or business deductions.* Deductions applicable to trade or business including the business-related expenses of employees (Code Sec. 162).

2. *Production of income deductions.* Production of income deductions related to the production of nonbusiness income: (1) incurred for the production or collection of income; (2) for the

management, conservation, or maintenance of property held for the production of income; and (3) in connection with the determination, collection, or refund of any tax (Code Sec. 212).

3. *Personal deductions.* Selected personal expenditures (various Code sections).

In addition, taxpayers are allowed deductions for certain losses (Code Sec. 165).

Once an individual taxpayer has determined that a valid tax deduction exists, the deduction must then be classified as either a deduction for adjusted gross income (AGI) or a deduction from AGI (itemized deduction). For an individual taxpayer, trade or business deductions are deductible for AGI with the exception of some unreimbursed business-related expenses of employees. Production of income deductions for an individual taxpayer are deductible from AGI as itemized deductions with the exception of expenses connected with rents and royalties which are deductible for AGI. Personal deductions are also deductible from AGI as itemized deductions. Deductions for losses are deductible for AGI with the exception of personal casualty losses as explained later.

It is important for an individual taxpayer to differentiate properly between deductions "for" and "from" AGI. Deductions for AGI are always deductible on an individual's tax return. Deductions from AGI may or may not be deductible depending on whether they exceed the taxpayer's standard deduction. Since the standard deduction is a flat allowance allowed to all individual taxpayers, deductions from AGI (itemized deductions) which do not exceed the standard deduction are of no value to the taxpayer. Properly categorizing deductions as "for" or "from" AGI is also important in that deductions for AGI actually determine the AGI figure. AGI is used to determine the deductible amount of some itemized deductions such as charitable contributions, medical expenses, casualty losses, and miscellaneous itemized deductions as well as the phaseout of personal exemptions, the phaseout of (or limit on) itemized deductions, and the child care credit.

AGI as determined on a taxpayer's federal income tax return is also frequently used as the starting place for preparing a state income tax return. Improper classification of a deduction as "for" or "from" AGI on the federal tax return can result in the taxpayer's state income tax liability being determined incorrectly.

¶ 5011   TRADE OR BUSINESS DEDUCTIONS

In general, taxpayers are allowed a tax deduction for all the ordinary and necessary expenses paid or incurred during a tax year in carrying on a trade or business. This is true, with some exceptions, whether the taxpayer is a sole proprietor, a partner in a partnership, or a corporation. The income tax form used to report the deductions is different, but the allowable deductions are generally the same. Typical trade or business deductions allowable to a sole proprietor and reported on Schedule C of Form 1040 are included in Table 1.

Table 1   TYPICAL BUSINESS DEDUCTIONS ALLOWABLE TO SOLE PROPRIETOR—REPORTED ON SCHEDULE C OF FORM 1040
(Subject to various limitations)

Advertising	Interest on indebtedness
Bad debts from sales or services	Legal and professional services
Bank service charges	License fees
Car and truck expenses	Office expenses
Commissions	Pension and profit-sharing plans
Cost of goods sold	Rent on business property
Depletion	Repairs
Depreciation	Supplies
Dues and publications	Taxes
Employee benefit programs	Travel, meals, and entertainment
Freight charges	Utilities and telephone
Insurance (other than health)	Wages

Criteria for Determining Trade or Business Deductions

In determining whether an expenditure is an allowable tax deduction for a trade or business, certain criteria must be met. These criteria are as follows:

1. The expense must be ordinary and necessary.

2. The expense must be reasonable in amount.

3. The expense must be related to an activity which is deemed to be a trade or business.

4. The expenditure must be for a business-related purpose rather than be a personal expenditure.

5. The expenditure cannot be a capital expenditure.

6. The expenditure cannot be related to the generation of tax-exempt income.

7. The expenditure is not against public policy.

Expense Must Be Ordinary and Necessary

To be deductible for tax purposes, a trade or business expenditure must be ordinary and necessary. An ordinary expenditure is an expenditure which is commonly incurred by other businesses. It may be incurred infrequently by a particular business but if the expenditure is commonly incurred by other businesses, it is a valid tax deduction. A necessary expenditure is an expenditure which is appropriate for a particular business. Again, frequency of the expenditure for a particular business is not relevant. Whether the expenditure was needed is relevant.

Example 5.1. James Kincaid was the sole owner of Kincaid Corporation when it went bankrupt in 1994. Various creditors lost significant amounts of money due to the bankruptcy. In 1998,

James sets up a new business and incorporates it as the Second Time Around Corporation. In order to establish good credit, James has the new corporation pay in full all the former creditors of Kincaid Corporation who lost money in the 1994 bankruptcy. James had no legal obligation to make these payments. The Second Time Around Corporation deducts these payments on its tax return as ordinary and necessary business expenses. James could argue that the payments made to the former creditors of Kincaid Corporation were necessary payments in order to establish credit for the new corporation, but he probably would have difficulty establishing that the payments were ordinary since they were not typical expenditures that would be made by other taxpayers in a similar situation. Example based on facts in *Welch v. Helvering,* 3 USTC ¶ 1164, 290 U.S. 111, 54 S.Ct. 8 (1933).

TAX BLUNDER

In Example 5.1, James Kincaid made business payments that were, in his opinion, necessary business expenditures. They were not, however, ordinary business expenditures. If James had discussed his plans with a competent tax adviser before making the payments, he may well have taken a different course of action.

Expense Must Be Reasonable in Amount

Implicit in the statement "ordinary and necessary business expenditures" is the presumption that the expenditures are reasonable. *Lincoln Electric Co.,* 49-2 USTC ¶ 9388, 176 F.2d 815 (CA-6 1949), cert. denied, 338 U.S. 949, 70 S.Ct. 488. Reasonableness of an expenditure is of main concern to closely held corporations where a payment may include a portion of a disguised dividend.

> *Example 5.2.* John Mason is the president and sole owner of Sign Corporation. During the year, Sign Corporation paid John a salary of $300,000. Sign Corporation claimed a tax deduction on its tax return for the full salary payment. The Internal Revenue Service (IRS), when auditing Sign Corporation's tax return, could argue that the salary payment to John was unreasonable in amount and included a portion of a disguised dividend. The rationale behind the IRS's argument is that dividend payments are not an allowable deduction for a corporation. It may be that by paying an unreasonably high salary to John, Sign Corporation was attempting to get a tax deduction for a payment which, in effect, was a nondeductible dividend payment. The same logic could also apply to unreasonably large lease payments and rental payments to stockholders in closely held corporations.

TAX PLANNING POINTER ▼

In order to lessen the chance of a tax deduction being considered unreasonable by the IRS, the officials of a closely held corporation should substantiate the reasonableness of deductible payments made to owners of the corporation. The reasonableness of an expenditure could be substantiated by documenting similar payments made by closely held corporations of comparable size and type. If other comparable businesses are paying similar amounts, the reasonableness of the payments would appear more evident.

Expense Must Be Related to an Activity Which Is Deemed to Be a Trade or Business

A concern to the IRS in regard to the tax return of a trade or business is whether the activities carried on by the taxpayer actually represent bona fide trade or business activities or are merely personal activities of the taxpayer or represent investing activities which do not constitute a trade or business. Consider the following situations.

Situation 1. Larry James has collected stamps for over 20 years. He attends many stamp shows and buys and sells stamps on a regular basis. Do Larry's stamp collecting activities constitute a trade or business or is Larry merely engaged in the pursuit of a hobby?

Situation 2. Jason Jackson buys and sells stocks on a regular basis and generally has a portfolio of over 15 stocks at any one time. Is Jason engaged in a trade or business in relation to his stock activities or is he merely engaged in investing activities?

Deciding whether an activity is a trade or business activity, investing activity, or personal (hobby) activity is important since the type of activity will determine the amount and type of allowable deductions. Generally, a trade or business must involve two main features: (1) an intent to make a profit on the part of the taxpayer and, (2) entrepreneurial effort on the part of the taxpayer. Both trade or business features are necessary. Investing activities such as buying and selling stock and the maintenance of a stock portfolio include an intent to make a profit; however, investing activities usually are considered to lack entrepreneurial effort and, therefore, do not constitute a trade or business activity.

The distinction between a trade or business activity and a personal (hobby) activity can be blurred at times. A personal (hobby) activity can involve an intent to make a profit and can include entrepreneurial effort. Due to this difficulty in differentiating between a trade or business activity and a personal (hobby) activity, the Code states that if an activity results in a profit in any three out of five consecutive tax years (two out of seven consecutive tax years for the breeding and racing of horses), it is presumed to be a business for determining tax deductions. Code Sec. 183(d). The IRS can refute this presumption based on a preponderance of the evidence. If the taxpayer's activity does not result in a profit in three out of five consecutive tax years, the burden of proof shifts to the taxpayer to prove that the activity is still a trade or business. A taxpayer can elect to suspend the application of the three-out-of-five-year profit presumption until enough consecutive tax years exist after the start of the activity in order to determine whether the presumption has been met. Code Sec. 183(e).

Example 5.3. Hank Herringbone operates a small fishing resort which he has owned for 10 years. The resort has yet to earn a profit in any tax year during the period that Hank has owned it. The resort has not met the three-out-of-five-year profit test and the presumption is that it is a personal (hobby) activity. The personal (hobby) activity presumption can be refuted, however, if the taxpayer can demonstrate clearly by a review of the evidence that the activity truly is a trade or business.

TAX PLANNING POINTER ▼

If a taxpayer does not meet the three-out-of-five-year profit test, there are still other ways to demonstrate that the activity is a trade or business. The taxpayer could show that the activity was operated in a businesslike manner and not like a hobby, that good business records existed, and that there was an intent to make a profit, as demonstrated by specific example. Reg. § 1.183-2(b).

As mentioned earlier, the determination of whether an activity is a trade or business activity or personal (hobby) activity is important in determining allowable deductions. Hobby expenditures are deductible only to the extent of hobby gross income. In addition, personal deductions which are available to all taxpayers (taxes, home mortgage interest, or casualty losses) first have to be deducted from the hobby gross income before any other deductions are allowable. Also, any deductible hobby expenditures other than taxes, home mortgage interest, or casualty losses are treated as miscellaneous itemized deductions on a taxpayer's return and are subject to the 2 percent of adjusted gross income limitation which applies to these deductions. The 2 percent of adjusted gross income limitation on miscellaneous itemized deductions is discussed in greater detail in Chapter 7.

Example 5.4. John Sebastian collects coins as a hobby. During the current tax year, John made $12,000 gross income from the sale of coins, after deducting the cost of the coins, paid $10,000 of travel expenses related to his coin hobby, and incurred $3,000 of miscellaneous expenses going to various coin shows. John may deduct the $10,000 of travel expenses from the $12,000 of hobby gross income leaving a net remainder of $2,000. The $3,000 of hobby-related miscellaneous expenses is then deducted from the remaining hobby gross income of $2,000 leaving a remainder of $1,000 of hobby-related expenses which is not deductible on John's tax return. In addition, the $12,000 of deductible hobby expenses ($10,000 travel expenses + $2,000 deductible miscellaneous expenses) is subject to the 2 percent of adjusted gross income limitation which applies to miscellaneous itemized deductions. If John could prove that his coin activities constituted a trade or business, he would then be able to deduct the $1,000 of expenses in excess of gross income.

Expenditure Must Be for a Business-Related Purpose Rather Than a Personal Expenditure

No tax deduction is allowed for personal living or family expenses unless expressly permitted. Code Sec. 262. In some instances, however, it is not clear-cut whether an expenditure is a business-related deductible expenditure or whether it is a nondeductible personal expenditure. Entertainment is a gray area where business and personal motives can blend together and cause a problem in deciding the proper amount of a tax deduction. In the entertainment area there are explicit rules to make it easier to determine a valid tax deduction, but, even with a set of rules, uncertainty about the amount of tax deduction may still remain. Code Sec. 274.

In some cases, an expenditure might be part business-related and part personal. The business-related portion of the expenditure is deductible while the personal portion is not deductible. A reasonable method of allocation of the expenditure between business-related and personal portions must be devised in order to determine the deductible portion.

> *Example 5.5.* During 1998, Kathy Krupp used her car for both business-related and personal purposes. Kathy is allowed to deduct automobile expenses connected with the business-related use of the car. A reasonable allocation formula to determine the deductible business-related automobile expenses is to take the total automobile expenses for the year times the ratio of total business miles for the year divided by total miles driven in the car during the year.

Expenditure Cannot Be a Capital Expenditure

No deduction is allowed for capital expenditures for buildings, improvements, or restorations. Code Sec. 263(a). This does not mean, however, that capital expenditures can never be deducted for tax purposes. It does mean that capital expenditures must be capitalized and depreciated or amortized for tax purposes over a period of years. In 1998, it is possible to get an immediate tax deduction for up to $18,500 of capital expenditures on tangible personal property. Code Sec. 179. See ¶ 5401 for an expanded discussion.

Expenditure Cannot Be Related to the Generation of Tax-Exempt Income

Any expenditure related to tax-exempt income is not deductible. Code Sec. 265. The logic for this provision is that since the tax-exempt income is not subject to taxation, then any deduction related to the tax-exempt income should also not be deductible.

> *Example 5.6.* Jill Jackson, sole proprietor of Jill Jackson & Co., borrowed $100,000 at an annual interest rate of 9 percent and immediately invested the proceeds of the loan in tax-exempt securities yielding 10 percent. Since the $10,000 of annual income on

the securities is tax-exempt, the related $9,000 of interest expense on the loan used to buy the securities is not deductible on Jill's tax return. If the interest expense on loans to buy tax-exempt securities were an allowable tax deduction it would be possible to convert an uneconomic transaction into an economic one through the related tax effects.

Assume, in the above situation, that Jill borrowed $100,000 at an annual interest rate of 11 percent and immediately invested the proceeds of the loan in tax-exempt securities yielding 10 percent. The annual interest cost of $11,000 on the loan appears to make the transaction uneconomic since only $10,000 of annual tax-exempt interest would be earned. If Jill, however, was in the 28 percent tax bracket for tax purposes and was allowed to deduct the $11,000 of interest expense on her return, the uneconomic transaction would become economic after considering the tax effects. The $11,000 interest expense deduction would save Jill $3,080 in taxes ($11,000 interest deduction times the 28 percent tax rate). The after-tax cost of the interest would be $7,920 ($11,000 interest less $3,080 tax savings through interest deduction). The tax-exempt interest earned of $10,000 less the $7,920 after-tax interest cost would leave a net positive return on the transaction of $2,080.

TAX PLANNING POINTER ▼

In deciding whether a particular business transaction is bona-fide for tax purposes, it is important that the transaction have some economic substance apart from related tax effects in order to justify a tax deduction.

Expenditure Is Not Against Public Policy

Although a trade or business payment may be ordinary and necessary, reasonable, and meet other criteria for a proper deduction, it is not deductible if allowing the deduction will hinder public policy. The following payments are disallowed as tax deductions:

1. Fines and penalties paid to the government for the violation of a law. Code Sec. 162(f).

2. Direct or indirect payments to government officials if the payment is an illegal bribe or kickback including illegal payments under the Foreign Corrupt Practices Act of 1977. Code Sec. 162(c)(1).

3. Direct or indirect payments to any person if the payment constitutes an illegal bribe or kickback under enforced U.S. laws which subject the payer to a criminal penalty, loss of license, or loss of privilege to engage in a trade or business. Code Sec. 162(c)(2).

4. Kickbacks, rebates, and bribes made by physicians and other providers of goods or services in connection with Medicare and Medicaid. Code Sec. 162(c)(3). The Internal Revenue Code does not state that the payments have to be illegal under any law in order to not be deductible.

5. Two-thirds of any damages paid for violation of federal anti-trust laws. Code Sec. 162(g).

The above payments are disallowed as tax deductions under the argument that the allowance of a tax deduction for these items is to aid and abet activity which is contrary to the public good.

Example 5.7. Stronghold Trucking Company regularly pays traffic fines for excessive speeding which are levied against the company's trucks. The president of Stronghold Trucking Company argues that the speeding fines are ordinary and necessary business expenditures and, therefore, deductible on the company's tax return because the company cannot make a profit unless company trucks exceed speed limits on a regular basis. Even though an argument could be made in support of the president's position, that the speeding fines are ordinary and necessary business expenditures, to allow a tax deduction for the speeding fines is to aid and abet illegal activity; therefore, the deduction is disallowed.

Although the above payments involving illegal activity are not deductible since they hinder public policy, the regular trade or business expenses of an illegal activity are proper deductions on the tax return of the illegal activity. One exception to this policy is made for the ordinary and necessary business expenses of drug dealers. All ordinary and necessary business expenses of dealers in illegal drugs, with the exception of cost of goods sold, are disallowed for tax purposes. Code Sec. 280E.

Employee Business-Related Expenses

Employment-related expenses of employees are allowed as itemized deductions to the employee. In order to be deductible by the employee, however, an employment-related expense must be directly related to the performance of employment duties or be required by an employment agreement. Code Sec. 62; *F.M. Magill,* 4 BTA 272, CCH Dec. 1499 (1926).

Employee business expenses are allowed as miscellaneous itemized deductions. Miscellaneous deductions are only deductible to the extent they exceed 2 percent of the taxpayer's adjusted gross income. Business expenses incurred by an employee under a reimbursement arrangement with the employer are normally not shown on the tax return. The reimbursement arrangement must require the employee to substantiate the expenses to the employer and must not allow the employee to keep the excess reimbursement. If full reimbursement is not made, the unreimbursed expenses are only allowable as miscellaneous itemized deductions, limited to amounts in excess of 2 percent of the taxpayer's adjusted gross income. See ¶ 7601 for an expanded discussion.

Commuting expenses incurred going to and from work are assumed to be personal expenses incurred by all employees and, therefore, are not deductible. Work uniforms suitable for everyday use, such as a suit and tie, are also considered to be personal expenses incurred by all taxpayers and not deductible since they can be used by taxpayers at other times besides work. Expenses incurred in purchasing work uniforms which are not suitable for everyday use, such as a fire fighter's uniform or a police officer's uniform, are proper tax deductions.

If an employee accounts to an employer for business-related expenses and is reimbursed by the employer, the employee does not normally have to report the expenses on the tax return.

Table 2   TYPICAL EMPLOYMENT-RELATED EXPENSES DEDUCTIBLE AS TRADE OR BUSINESS DEDUCTIONS
(SUBJECT TO VARIOUS LIMITATIONS)

Expenses not shown on return
  Reimbursed expenses
Expenses deductible from AGI (miscellaneous itemized
  deductions subject to 2% of AGI limitation)
    Away-from-home travel expenses
    Employment agency fees
    Employment-related education
    Entertainment expenses (limited)
    Job-hunting expenses
    Office at home (limited)
    Outside salesperson's expenses
    Professional society dues
    Small tools and supplies
    Subscriptions to professional journals
    Transportation expenses
    Union dues
    Work clothes and uniforms

A topic associated with employee business-related expenses is the classification of an individual as an employee or an independent contractor. An independent contractor is an individual who sells services to the public and is, in effect, self-employed. If an individual is self-employed, all trade or business expenses are deductible for AGI, whereas, if the individual is an employee, any unreimbursed employment-related trade or business expenses are deductible as miscellaneous itemized deductions subject to the 2 percent limitation. In determining whether an individual is an employee or is self-employed, an analysis should be made of the individual's employment activity. Factors such as the following should be considered: (1) does the individual work for many firms or clients or just work for one firm or client, (2) does the individual make services available to the public, (3) does the individual determine work hours and schedules, and (4) does the individual receive regular payments from one firm or from a variety of firms. To determine whether an individual is an employee or is self-employed no one factor should be considered as controlling, but rather all these factors should be reviewed.

> *Example 5.8.* Sally Swiss is a lawyer who has practiced law for over 10 years. During this period, she has served many clients but, for the past several years, she is spending most of her time with only one client, Randall Corporation. In fact, in 1998 she did not receive fees from any client other than Randall, she moved her office into the Randall Corporation headquarters building, and she abides by the Randall Corporation full-time work schedule. Also, she no longer seeks business from other clients. Is Sally still self-employed in 1998 or is she now an employee of Randall Corporation? An analysis of the facts in this example would seem to indicate that Sally is now an employee of Randall. She receives fees from only one source (Randall), she no longer seeks business from other clients, and she spends her full time at Randall Corporation.

¶ 5025   PRODUCTION OF INCOME EXPENSES DEDUCTION

Production of income expenses are deductible if they are incurred:

1.   For the production or collection of income

2.   For the management, conservation, or maintenance of property held for the production of income

3.   In connection with the determination, collection, or refund of any tax

The term "production of income" refers to expenses which do not qualify as trade or business expenses yet are still deductible expenses. Code Sec. 212. Production of income expenses are investment expenses and tax planning and compliance expenses. Production of income expenses must meet the same criteria for deductibility as previously discussed for trade or business expenditures with the exception that the expenditure does not have to relate to a trade or business. To be deductible, production of income expenses must be ordinary and necessary, reasonable, cannot be capital expenditures, cannot relate to the generation of tax-exempt income, and cannot frustrate public policy. Production of income expenses are deductible from AGI as miscellaneous itemized deductions with the exception of rents and royalty expenses which are deductible for AGI. Code Sec. 62(a)(4).

Investment Expense Deductions

Typical investment expenses which are deductible include safe deposit box rentals, rent and royalty expenses, investment counsel fees, subscriptions to investment-related journals, newspapers, and other publications, investment custodial fees, legal and accounting fees related to investments, and investment-related clerical fees and office rent. Code Sec. 212. There is an annual investment-related interest expense deduction which is limited to net investment income. This deduction is discussed in Chapter 7. Code Sec. 163(d).

Tax Planning and Compliance Expenses

All expenses incurred by individual taxpayers in connection with the determination, collection, or refund of any tax are also deductible as nonbusiness expenses. Deductions in this area apply to tax planning expenses and tax compliance expenses of individuals and are properly classified as miscellaneous itemized deductions on the tax return. Businesses classify tax planning and compliance expenses as trade or business deductions. The cost of having a tax return prepared by a CPA or tax service is deductible as well as the legal fees incurred in contesting a tax liability in court. Deductions for tax planning and compliance expenses are not limited to the income tax area but also extend to gift and estate tax returns. Fees paid for tax advice regarding estate planning as well as divorce proceedings are also deductible. Rev. Rul. 72-545, 1972-2 CB 179.

> *Example 5.9.* Barbara Bramble is involved in divorce proceedings. Some of the legal advice she has received regarding the divorce involves advice on minimizing her future tax liability. If the part of the legal fee related to tax advice can be separated from the total legal fee for the divorce and, if it can be substantiated, Barbara may deduct this amount on her tax return as a tax planning expense.

TAX BLUNDER

In Example 5.9, Barbara Bramble gets a bill from her lawyer that states "Legal Services — $3,000." She does not request a breakout of the portion of the legal fee relating to tax planning advice. Barbara has lost the opportunity for a tax planning advice deduction on her tax return.

¶ 5045   PERSONAL DEDUCTIONS

Personal, living, and family expenses are not deductible on a tax return unless expressly permitted. Code Sec. 262. Many of the personal expenses which are allowed as tax deductions are listed in Table 3 on the next page.

Although many personal expenditures are not deductible for tax purposes, there is some logic and rationale behind allowing certain personal expenditures to be deductions and credits on an individual's tax return. Some personal deductions are allowed as tax deductions because they are involuntary payments which place a burden on the taxpayer's finances and inhibit the ability to pay income taxes. Deductions allowed for medical and dental expenses, casualty and theft losses, and alimony fall into this category. Other personal deductions and credits are allowed in order to encourage certain types of behavior on the part of taxpayers. For example, the allowance of a charitable deduction for tax purposes encourages the giving of gifts to charity and thereby promotes the public good. Certainly the deduction for state and local income taxes lessens to some degree the problems associated with double and triple taxation of the same income.

Table 3 TYPICAL PERSONAL EXPENDITURES DEDUCTIBLE OR NOT DEDUCTIBLE ON TAX RETURN
(SUBJECT TO VARIOUS LIMITATIONS)

Expenditures deductible for AGI
> Alimony
> Individual retirement accounts (IRAs) (limited)
> Moving expenses
> Interest paid on qualified education loans

Expenditures deductible from AGI (itemized deductions)
> Charitable contributions
> Gambling losses but only to extent of gambling winnings
> Hobby losses to extent of hobby income
> Interest expense (limited)
> Medical and dental expenses
> Personal casualty and theft losses
> State and local taxes (except sales taxes)

Expenditures eligible for tax credit
> Adoption expenses
> Child and disabled dependent care expenses

Expenditures not deductible
> Commuting expenses
> Depreciation on property held for personal use
> Funeral expenses
> Household living expenses
> Life insurance premiums
> Political contributions

To reiterate, all personal deductions and credits which are currently allowable can be justified in some way. Whether the justification for a certain deduction or credit is in line with current national goals and priorities is an issue which must be reviewed by Congress on a continuous basis.

¶ 5055 LOSSES DEDUCTIONS

In general, a deduction is allowed for losses sustained during the taxable year and not compensated for by insurance or otherwise. Code Sec. 165(a). For a business, all losses are deductible except as otherwise restricted.

For individual taxpayers, losses are limited to the following three categories:

1. Losses incurred in a trade or business

2. Losses incurred in transactions entered into for profit, though not connected with a trade or business

3. Losses of property not connected with a trade or business if such losses arise from fire, storm, shipwreck, or other casualty, or from theft

The limitations placed on losses of individual taxpayers, in effect, restrict individual losses to business losses, investment losses, and personal casualty or theft losses.

To be deductible, a loss must be sustained or realized by the taxpayer during the taxable year. Unrealized losses normally are not deductible.

Example 5.10. Janet Jurgens owns 100 shares of Clinton Corporation stock which she purchased on January 4, 1998, at $84 per share. On December 31, 1998, Clinton Corporation stock was selling at $52 per share. Janet cannot deduct the $32 per share decline in value in 1998 on her 1998 tax return since it is an unrealized loss. Janet would have to sell her stock in 1998 in order to recognize a loss for tax purposes.

Various losses which are deductible by individual taxpayers are listed in Table 4. All of the losses listed in Table 4 are deductible for AGI with the exception of personal casualty and theft losses, gambling losses, and hobby losses which are itemized deductions. Tax losses are discussed in greater detail in Chapter 6.

Table 4   LOSSES DEDUCTIBLE ON AN INDIVIDUAL'S TAX RETURN
(SUBJECT TO VARIOUS LIMITATIONS)

Losses deductible for AGI
    Business net operating loss carryback or carryforward
    Business or investment-related casualty or theft loss
    Loss on sale or exchange of business property
    Loss on sale or exchange of investment property
    Worthless securities
Losses deductible from AGI
    Gambling losses but only to extent of gambling winnings
    Hobby losses to extent of hobby income
    Personal casualty or theft loss

Factors Affecting Allowance of Deductions

In preceding sections of this chapter, various criteria have been reviewed which could cause a limitation or disallowance of a tax deduction to a taxpayer. Some additional factors which may affect the amount of an allowable tax deduction are the tax accounting method used, substantiation of deductions, and deductible amounts paid on behalf of another taxpayer.

¶ 5115   TAX ACCOUNTING METHOD

As a beginning point in computing tax deductions, taxable income, which consists of gross income less deductions, must be computed under the method of accounting which the taxpayer regularly uses to compute income in keeping books. Code Sec. 446(a). Differences between tax accounting and financial accounting for various deductions do exist in actual practice, however, and, in fact, are required in many instances because of divergencies between the tax accounting rules and generally accepted accounting principles (GAAP). The differences between tax accounting rules and financial accounting rules can usually be justified because of the different objectives which exist for tax and financial accounting.

TAX PLANNING POINTER ▼

Tax accounting methods chosen by taxpayers for various deductions do not have to be the same as the accounting methods used for financial accounting purposes. In choosing a tax accounting method for a deduction, the taxpayer can have as an objective the minimizing of tax liability, while for financial accounting purposes, the main objective in choosing an accounting method for a deduction might be to select the method which most fairly presents accounting income.

For tax purposes, the most common accounting methods are the cash method and the accrual method. Under the cash method of accounting, tax deductions are taken when expenditures are made, while under the accrual method of accounting, tax deductions are taken when there is a fixed and determinable liability regardless of when cash is paid. In some instances, tax deductions must be accounted for on the accrual method by cash method taxpayers. Prepaid interest, prepaid rent, purchases of capital equipment, and substantial purchases of merchandise are expenditures which must be accounted for on the accrual method of accounting even by a cash method taxpayer. The reason why the IRS requires the accrual method of accounting in the above instances is that allowing the cash method of accounting for these items could result in a material distortion of taxable income in any one year.

In other instances, tax deductions must be accounted for on the cash method by accrual method taxpayers. Warranty expense is an example of a deduction where the cash method of accounting is required by all taxpayers since, according to the IRS's position, there is no fixed liability present before actual cash payment with which to estimate the amount of the warranty expense.

Most individuals, small businesses, and professionals use the cash method of accounting for tax purposes. Most corporations, partnerships with corporations as partners, and some tax-exempt trusts must use the accrual method of accounting.

¶ 5125   SUBSTANTIATION OF TAX DEDUCTIONS

As noted earlier, tax deductions are allowed to taxpayers only if they are specifically authorized. In addition, taxpayers must be able to substantiate the deductions claimed on their tax returns if requested by the IRS through the audit process. Taxpayers can normally substantiate tax deductions by providing documentary evidence such as receipts, invoices, and cancelled checks. In some instances, oral testimony of the taxpayer or other persons in support of the taxpayer may be of some value. In the past, the IRS has argued in court that if a taxpayer fails to substantiate a deduction, then the entire deduction should be disallowed. In an important trend-setting case, however, the court held that if substantiation for a tax deduction was lacking but it was reasonable to assume that some amount of expense had been incurred, then it is reasonable to assume that some estimated tax deduction should be allowed. *G.M. Cohan*, 2 USTC ¶ 489, 39 F.2d 540 (CA-2 1930). The reasoning applied in the *Cohan* case to justify a reasonable deduction when substantiation for a deduction is lacking has become known as the *Cohan* rule for tax purposes. The *Cohan* rule applies to all tax deductions with the exception of travel and entertainment expenses, business gifts, and a few other expenditures where substantiation is required before a deduction will be allowed.

> *Example 5.11.* Leonard Lerner attends church each Sunday and always puts a twenty-dollar bill in the church collection basket. Leonard does not use church envelopes and does not make a charitable contribution by check. Leonard claims charitable contributions to his church of $1,040 on his 1998 tax return. In an audit of his 1998 tax return by the IRS, Leonard is questioned on the amount of his charitable contributions. Leonard has no documentary evidence or oral testimony other than his own to support his charitable contribution deduction of $1,040. Following the *Cohan* rule, the IRS may allow Leonard an estimated amount of two to three dollars a week for charitable contributions to church.

TAX BLUNDER

In Example 5.11, Leonard Lerner should have used church envelopes and had the church notify him in writing of his total charitable contributions at the end of the year.

A taxpayer must be able to substantiate tax deductions claimed on the return. If a tax return is audited by the IRS, documentary evidence such as invoices, paid receipts, and cancelled checks are very important in substantiating deductions. Oral evidence of other individuals may be of some value. Oral evidence of the taxpayer may also be of some value, but the IRS is certainly aware that many taxpayers, when questioned, merely declare that their deductions were computed correctly. The *Cohan* rule is of some use to taxpayers in that it generally provides a floor for tax deductions. The *Cohan* rule, however, will rarely result in a taxpayer's being allowed a tax deduction equal to the amount originally claimed. Also, the *Cohan* rule is no longer applicable as to travel and entertainment expenses, business gifts, and a few other selected areas.

¶ 5145   DEBTS OF ANOTHER TAXPAYER

In general, if a taxpayer pays a tax deductible expense which is the obligation of another taxpayer, neither taxpayer is entitled to a tax deduction. The payer-taxpayer is not entitled to a deduction since the payer had no obligation to make the payment. The payee-taxpayer is not entitled to the deduction since the payee did not actually pay the obligation.

> *Example 5.12.* On January 4, 1998, John Jenkins borrowed money from a bank to purchase a new home. The home loan required monthly payments. John lost his job in June 1998 and his father made John's home payments for the months of July through December 1998. John is not entitled to a tax deduction for the interest included in the home payments made by his father since he did not actually make the payments himself. Neither is John's father entitled to deduct the interest included in each of John's home payments since John's father had no obligation to make the payments. In effect, the manner in which the payments were made would result in a loss of an interest deduction to both taxpayers.

TAX PLANNING POINTER   ▼

If an individual is contemplating the payment of a tax deductible expense on behalf of another taxpayer, the proper way to structure the transaction is to make a loan to the other taxpayer or gift the amounts needed to make the tax deductible expenditures and let the other taxpayer actually make the required payments. By handling the transaction in this way, a tax deduction has been preserved for the other taxpayer.

Common Business Deductions

Common business deductions which are discussed in this section are: advertising, bad debts, salaries, wages, fringe benefits, interest payments, taxes, rental payments, insurance premiums, and legal and accounting fees.

¶ 5201   ADVERTISING

Advertising expenditures are deductible for tax purposes if they are reasonably related to the business activities in which the taxpayer is engaged or if they are related to production-of-income activities, such as renting of property. Goodwill advertising generally is deductible as reasonably related to a taxpayer's trade or business but advertising which is intended to influence public reaction to proposed legislation is not normally deductible. Reg. § 1.162-20.

> *Example 5.13.* The Lower Basin Electric Utility Co. runs a full-page advertisement in the local newspaper extolling the high quality of life in the Lower Basin service area. The cost of this

advertisement is tax deductible since it relates to goodwill advertising. Two weeks later, the Lower Basin Electric Utility Co. runs another full page advertisement in the local newspaper. This advertisement requests that voters in the Lower Basin service area contact their elected state legislators and ask that they vote against proposed legislation which, if adopted, might have an adverse effect on Lower Basin's ability to make a reasonable profit. The cost of this advertisement is not deductible for tax purposes since the advertising is intended to influence public reaction to proposed legislation.

¶ 5215   BAD DEBTS

Business or nonbusiness debts becoming worthless during the year are deductible. Code Sec. 166(a). Business bad debts are debts arising in connection with a trade or business, while nonbusiness bad debts are debts of a personal nature.

The amount of a bad debt deduction always is limited to the adjusted basis of the debt in the hands of the taxpayer. For a business taxpayer using the cash basis of accounting, the adjusted basis of business accounts receivable is normally zero in view of the fact that the receivables have not been recognized for tax purposes because income is recorded only when cash is collected from the receivables.

Example 5.14. On September 16, 1998, Roscoe Accounting Services, a cash basis taxpayer, sells $300 of accounting services to Ron Ranger on credit. One month later, Ron is declared bankrupt and cannot pay any of the $300 debt to Roscoe. Since Roscoe uses the cash basis of accounting, income is not recognized for tax purposes until cash is collected and, therefore, its accounts receivable have a zero basis. Roscoe is not entitled to a bad debt deduction for the $300 bad account receivable since the receivable has a zero basis for tax purposes.

Rules for Deduction

To be deductible as a bad debt, the debt must be a valid and enforceable obligation arising in a proper debtor-creditor relationship. In determining whether a bad debt was originally a bona fide debt, the following factors are considered: (1) did a valid debtor-creditor relationship exist, (2) was the transfer of money from the creditor to the debtor a gift rather than a debt, and (3) was there ever an intent on the part of the creditor to collect the debt.

An additional requirement for establishing a bad debt deduction is worthlessness of the debt. A business bad debt deduction can be taken by proving only partial worthlessness of a debt while full worthlessness of a debt must be proven in order to claim a nonbusiness bad debt deduction. Worthlessness of a debt is established by reviewing the facts existing in each case. Reg. § 1.166-2(b). The debtor's bankruptcy, death of the debtor, and unsuccessful court action against the debtor to collect the debt may be indications of the worthlessness of a debt. A taxpayer does not have to take legal action against a debtor to prove worthlessness of a debt. The facts may suggest that legal action would not have resulted in recovery of any of the debt.

Business Bad Debts

Business bad debts, which arise from the taxpayer's trade or business, differ from nonbusiness bad debts in that they can be deducted to the extent of their worthlessness at any time when they become partly or totally worthless and they can, generally, be deducted from gross income as an ordinary business deduction in the year incurred. Such tax treatment is not available to shareholders who have advanced money to a corporation as a contribution to capital or to creditors who hold a debt that is evidenced by a bond, debenture, note, or other evidence of indebtedness that is issued by a corporation or by a governmental unit, with interest coupons or in registered form. A business debt is a debt (1) created or acquired in connection with the trade or business of the taxpayer who is claiming the deduction, or (2) the worthlessness of which has been incurred in the taxpayer's trade or business. Reg. § 1.166-5(b).

> *Example 5.15.* John Henry owes $1,000 to the Sioto Lumber Company, an accrual basis taxpayer, for lumber purchased from the company. Sioto Lumber Co. estimates that it will eventually collect from John Henry only $300 of the $1,000 debt. Since the debt to Sioto is a business debt, Sioto is entitled to a $700 bad debt deduction this year for partial worthlessness of the business debt.

A cash basis taxpayer can deduct a business bad debt only if an actual cash loss has been sustained or if the amount deducted was included in income. Nearly all accrual basis taxpayers must use the specific charge-off method to deduct business bad debts; the reserve method for computing and deducting bad debts may be used only by small banks and thrift institutions. Under the specific charge-off method, when a specific debt, or portion thereof, becomes worthless it is written off as an ordinary deduction for tax purposes.

Since the tax treatment accorded business bad debts and nonbusiness bad debts differs, the taxpayer must show that the dominant motivation in making the payment was business related in order to obtain the more favorable tax treatment. Specific charge-off is based on actual worthlessness and is not applicable merely because the taxpayer gives up attempts to collect. A worthless debt arising from unpaid rent, interest, or a similar item is not deductible unless the income that such item represents has been reported for income tax purposes by a taxpayer on the accrual basis.

Nonbusiness Bad Debts

Nonbusiness bad debts do not include debts created or acquired in connection with a trade or business. Loans to relatives and friends are the most common type of nonbusiness debt. Nonbusiness bad debts can be deducted for tax purposes only if full worthlessness of the debt has been determined and then only by the specific charge-off method. The deduction is allowed in the year when full worthlessness takes place, regardless of how old the debt is. In contrast to a business bad debt which is deductible as an ordinary loss in the year incurred, a nonbusiness bad debt deduction is always treated as a short-term capital loss and is subject to the $3,000 limitation applicable to the deduction for capital losses (discussed in greater detail in Chapter 11). Code Sec. 166(d)(1)(B).

> *Example 5.16.* John Henry owes $1,000 to Mike Mackey on a personal loan. Mike estimates that he will only collect $300 of his $1,000 loan to John. Mike is not entitled to a $700 bad debt deduction at this time since total worthlessness must be proven before a bad debt deduction can be taken for a nonbusiness bad debt. If John paid $300 to Mike and the remaining $700 of debt was correctly determined to be worthless, a $700 nonbusiness bad debt deduction could be claimed by Mike since total worthlessness of the remaining debt has been established.

¶ 5225   SALARIES, WAGES, AND FRINGE BENEFITS

Expenditures for salaries and wages are deductible for tax purposes when paid or incurred by a taxpayer. If the taxpayer uses the cash basis of accounting, salaries and wages are deductible when paid. Taxpayers using the accrual basis of accounting take a deduction for salaries and wages when they are incurred. A deduction for salaries and wages can include bonus payments and payments for services performed in prior years. Advance payments for services to be performed in future years, however, are not deductible until the services are actually performed. A sole proprietor is not entitled to a tax deduction for amounts withdrawn as his or her own salary or compensation since, for tax purposes, the proprietor and the proprietor's business are indivisible. A sole proprietor can deduct for tax purposes reasonable salary payments to minor children and relatives for services actually performed by the related parties. Rev. Rul. 72-23, 1972-1 CB 43.

Employer expenditures for fringe benefits provided for the benefit of employees generally are deductible for tax purposes as trade or business expenses. Some common tax deductible employee fringe benefits include payments into employee pension plans, employee accident and health plan premiums, educational assistance program payments, and expenditures related to physical fitness rooms and clubhouses for employee use. To be deductible, many of these fringe benefit expenditures must meet eligibility requirements.

¶ 5235   INTEREST PAYMENTS

Most interest payments are deductible for tax purposes by taxpayers when incurred in a trade or business. Interest payments incurred in a trade or business are deductible in computing adjusted gross income.

Prepaid interest payments generally are not deductible in the year of payment but must be allocated over the periods to which the interest amounts apply regardless whether the taxpayer is on the cash basis or accrual basis of accounting. Code Sec. 461(g). Interest payments made on debts incurred to purchase tax-exempt securities are not deductible for tax purposes. Code Sec. 265. To be deductible, interest payments must be for the taxpayer's own debt and not the debt of another party.

Example 5.17. Mary Michael, the owner of Bea Manufacturing Co., pays an interest payment on a loan payable of Abco Foundry Co. Bea purchases a critical part used in its manufacturing process from Abco. Mary had no obligation to make the interest payment but did so in order to prevent Abco from being forced into bankruptcy by creditors and, thereby, losing a source of supply for the critical part needed by her company. Mary is not entitled to an interest deduction for the interest payment on Abco's loan payable since the payment was not her obligation.

¶ 5245   TAXES

Most taxes incurred by a trade or business with the exception of federal income taxes are deductible for tax purposes as business expenses. Federal income taxes are not deductible on the federal income tax return since the return is being prepared to compute the amount of federal income taxes due. Taxes withheld from employee wages such as federal, state, and local income taxes payable and F.I.C.A. taxes are not a proper business deduction to an employer since the employer has merely withheld these amounts from employee wages and remitted the amounts to the appropriate governmental authorities.

State and local sales taxes incurred in a business or investment activity in connection with the acquisition or disposition of property are not deductible. Instead, such taxes are treated as part of the cost of the acquired property or as a reduction in the amount realized on the disposition of the property.

If business property is sold during the year, the property tax deduction related to the property is allocated between the buyer and seller based on the number of days during the tax year that each party held the property. Code Sec. 164(d). This allocation formula is required regardless of which party actually pays the property tax and whether the buyer and seller use the cash or accrual method of accounting.

Example 5.18. Adams Co. sells land to Bevis Co. on June 28, 1998. Adams Co. and Bevis Co., sole proprietorships, are both calendar year and cash basis taxpayers. Property taxes of $2,000 were paid on the land by Adams Co. on February 2, 1998, to cover the property tax year of January 1, 1998, through December 31, 1998. Adams Co. is entitled to a property tax deduction of $975.34 and Bevis Co. is entitled to a property tax deduction of $1,024.66 based on the number of days during the year that each party held the property (178 days and 187 days, respectively), regardless of the fact that Adams actually paid the full amount of taxes on February 2, 1998, and is on the cash method of accounting.

¶ 5255   RENTAL PAYMENTS

Rental payments for property used in a trade or business are proper tax deductions. Code Sec. 162(a)(3). If rental payments are paid in advance, they usually are deductible by a taxpayer in the period covered by the payments and not in the period the payments are made regardless of whether the taxpayer uses the cash or accrual method of accounting. If payments characterized as rental payments are, in substance, payments for the purchase of property, no rental expense deduction is allowed for tax purposes. Instead, the taxpayer treats the rental payments as installment payments on the purchase of the property and qualify for possible interest expense and depreciation expense deductions. In determining whether a rental or lease agreement is, in substance, a purchase of property, the IRS examines the transaction to see if the taxpayer is building equity in the property or will, with a high degree of certainty, take title to the property at some future date.

Example 5.19. In 1998, ABC Manufacturing Co. leases manufacturing equipment for a five-year period with a $150,000 yearly lease payment stipulated in the contract. The equipment has an estimated five-year life and the lease contract states that ABC Manufacturing Co. can buy the equipment at the end of the lease period for a token $100 cash payment. ABC Manufacturing Co. is not entitled to a $150,000 rental expense deduction on its 1998 tax return since the lease agreement is, in substance, a purchase contract for the manufacturing property. The lease agreement covers the estimated life of the property and the company will, with a high degree of certainty, purchase the property for a nominal $100 cash payment at the end of the lease period. Instead of being allowed a rental deduction, ABC Manufacturing Co. is treated as the owner of the property for tax purposes and is entitled to owner-related deductions such as interest expense and depreciation expense.

¶ 5275   INSURANCE PREMIUMS

Insurance premiums for fire, casualty, and burglary insurance coverage on business property are all properly deductible for tax purposes as trade or business expenses. If a business taxpayer has a self-insurance plan, however, all payments into the self-insurance reserve are not deductible for tax purposes, but actual losses incurred by the taxpayer are proper business tax deductions. Code Sec. 165.

Insurance premiums paid by a business on life insurance coverage provided to employees as a fringe benefit are tax deductible, but premiums paid on a life insurance policy covering the life of an officer, employee, or other key person are not deductible if the business is a direct or indirect beneficiary under the policy. Code Sec. 264. Premiums paid on a life insurance policy where the business is a beneficiary are not deductible since life insurance proceeds do not have to be included in taxable income when received by the company.

Example 5.20. Adams Company carries a $100,000 life insurance policy on the life of John Adams, president and owner of the company. Adams Company, the named beneficiary on the policy, would use the proceeds from the policy, if received, to help lessen the impact of any business disruption due to the death of John

Adams. The $5,000 annual premium on the life insurance policy paid by Adams Company is not deductible for tax purposes. Likewise, the $100,000 life insurance proceeds, if received by Adams Company in the future, are excluded from taxable income.

¶ 5285   LEGAL AND ACCOUNTING FEES

For tax purposes, legal and accounting fees normally are deductible by a business in the year paid or incurred. If a legal fee is incurred in connection with the acquisition of a capital asset, it is considered a capital expenditure for tax purposes and not deductible currently.

In smaller businesses, legal and accounting fees may be incurred which are part-business and part-personal in nature.

> *Example 5.21.* Jim Jables, CPA, prepares tax returns and gives tax planning advice to both ABC Manufacturing Co. and Mark Merchant, the sole owner of ABC. To the extent possible, billings from Jim Jables, CPA, should separately designate whether a particular professional service was performed for ABC Manufacturing Co. and was business-related or was performed for Mark Merchant and was personal in nature.

TAX PLANNING POINTER

Tax work performed for a business by a CPA and legal work performed by an attorney may be of importance to the business and, at the same time, be of personal significance to the owner of the business. To the extent possible, cost of the business portion of a professional service should be kept separate from the personal portion of a professional service on any billing prepared by a professional person rendering a professional service. Documentation of a business portion of a professional service versus a personal portion may be beneficial in substantiating a business tax deduction for professional services.

Business Deductions Related to Capital Expenditures

A capital expenditure for tax purposes is an expenditure which is expected to benefit more than one tax year. Generally, capital expenditures do not qualify as tax deductions in the year the expenditures are made but must be allocated to the tax years which will receive some benefit from the expenditures. This process of allocating the cost of a capital expenditure to various tax periods is called depreciation, amortization, or depletion depending on the type of capital expenditure involved in the allocation process. The term "depreciation" is usually connected with tangible (physical presence) property, "amortization" with intangible (no physical presence) property, and "depletion" with natural resources.

In this section, depreciation of tangible property is reviewed, amortization of intangible assets and other expenditures is discussed, and depletion of natural resources is analyzed.

¶ 5401 DEPRECIATION OF TANGIBLE PROPERTY

Depreciation is the process of allocating the cost of a tangible asset to expense over its estimated useful life. To be depreciable, tangible property must have a limited life. Tangible property can be divided into two parts: real property and personal property. Real property is land, land improvements, buildings, and building improvements. Land does not have a limited life; therefore, it does not qualify for depreciation. Personal property is usually business machinery and equipment and office furniture and fixtures. The term "personal property" should not be confused with property owned by an individual for personal use.

A tax deduction for depreciation of the cost of tangible property has been allowed for tax purposes since the inception of the federal income tax in 1913. In 1981, the tax depreciation system was dramatically changed and simplified by adoption of the Accelerated Cost Recovery System (ACRS).

Accelerated Cost Recovery System (ACRS)

ACRS applies to most tangible property, new or used, placed in service for business or investment purposes after 1980 and before 1987. Property which is not eligible for ACRS includes property placed in service before 1981, property depreciated using a method not expressed in terms of years (units of production method), property which is amortized, and certain public utility property. Code Sec. 168(e). ACRS was substantially modified by the Tax Reform Act of 1986. Thus, most tangible property placed in service after 1986 must now be depreciated under the Modified Accelerated Cost Recovery System (MACRS).

Modified Accelerated Cost Recovery System (MACRS)

The general MACRS rules classify property based on class life for purposes of determining the applicable depreciation method, the applicable recovery period, and applicable convention. Absent an election out of MACRS, the IRS-established class lives must be used to determine the applicable MACRS recovery period even though a longer period may be desired. Rev. Proc. 87-56, 1987-2 CB 674, clarified and modified by Rev. Proc. 88-22, 1988-1 CB 785; IRS Letter Ruling 9015014, January 9, 1990. Salvage value is disregarded in computing the MACRS deduction. Asset recovery classifications are provided by statute. Code Sec. 168(c).

1. *3-year property.* This class includes over-the-road tractor units, dies, molds, and small tools.

2. *5-year property.* This class includes autos, light-duty trucks, computers, and office equipment, such as typewriters, or calculators.

3. *7-year property.* This class includes most manufacturing equipment, furniture, and fixtures.

4. *10-year property.* This class includes mainly public utility property.

5. *15-year property.* This class includes public utility personal property.

6. *20-year property.* This class includes public utility personal property.

7. *27.5-year property.* This class includes residential rental property.

8. *39-year property.* This class includes nonresidential real property, such as office buildings, shopping centers, warehouses, and manufacturing facilities.

9. *50-year property.* Railroad gradings or tunnel bores.

MACRS also specifies the standard cost recovery methods for each of the classes of assets. The cost of property in the 3-, 5-, 7-, and 10-year classes is recovered using the 200 percent declining-balance method of depreciation. Fifteen- and 20-year assets are depreciated using the 150 percent declining-balance depreciation method. The cost of 27.5-year and 39-year real property assets is recovered using the straight-line depreciation method. For all asset classes, the cost of the property or unadjusted basis is not reduced by salvage value in making the depreciation computation. When the declining-balance method is used, a switch to the straight-line method is allowed at the appropriate time to maximize the tax deduction.

Instead of computing MACRS depreciation in the above manner, optional MACRS depreciation tables are available for taxpayer use. These tables contain annual percentage depreciation rates which can be applied to the unadjusted basis of property in each tax year. An example of a MACRS depreciation table for 3-, 5-, 7-, 10-, 15-, and 20-year life property is shown in Table 5.

Under MACRS, a half-year convention applies to personal property. Under this convention, property placed in service or disposed of during a taxable year is considered placed in service or disposed of at the midpoint of that year. A midquarter convention applies when more than 40 percent of the cost of all personal property is placed in service during the last quarter of the taxable year. Under the midquarter convention, personal property is treated as placed in service (or disposed of) in the middle of the quarter. In determining whether 40 percent of the aggregate basis of MACRS property is placed in service during the last three months of a tax year, property placed in service and disposed within the same tax year is disregarded. Code Sec. 168(d)(3). For real property, both residential and nonresidential, depreciation is based on the number of months the property is in service during the taxable year with a midmonth convention applying in the first month of service and in the last month of service.

Table 5 MACRS DEPRECIATION TABLE

General Depreciation System
Applicable Depreciation Method: 200 or 150 Percent
Declining Balance Switching to Straight Line
Applicable Recovery Periods: 3, 5, 7, 10, 15, 20 years
Applicable Convention: Half-year

If the Recovery Year is:	3-year	5-year	7-year	10-year	15-year	20-year
			and the Recovery Period is: the Depreciation Rate is:			
1	33.33	20.00	14.29	10.00	5.00	3.750
2	44.45	32.00	24.49	18.00	9.50	7.219
3	14.81	19.20	17.49	14.40	8.55	6.677
4	7.41	11.52	12.49	11.52	7.70	6.177
5		11.52	8.93	9.22	6.93	5.713
6		5.76	8.92	7.37	6.23	5.285
7			8.93	6.55	5.90	4.888
8			4.46	6.55	5.90	4.522
9				6.56	5.91	4.462
10				6.55	5.90	4.461
11				3.28	5.91	4.462
12					5.90	4.461
13					5.91	4.462
14					5.90	4.461
15					5.91	4.462
16					2.95	4.461
17						4.462
18						4.461
19						4.462
20						4.461
21						2.231

Source: Rev. Proc. 87-57, 1987-2 CB 117, Table 1.

Example 5.22. In 1998, Max Book Company, a calendar year taxpayer, purchased the following assets:

1. April 1998—Business equipment, cost $14,000, salvage value $3,000
2. July 1998—Car, cost $11,000, salvage value $2,000
3. September 1998—Office building, cost $85,000

Based on the above information, MACRS depreciation for 1998 on these assets would be:

Depreciation

1. Business equipment ($14,000 cost × 28⁴/7% × ½ or 14.29% from the table) (7-year life, 200% DB) $2,000
2. Car ($11,000 cost × 40% × ½ or 20% from the table) (5-year life, 200% DB) 2,200
3. Office building ($85,000 cost/39-year life × 3½ months/12 months) (straight-line depr.) 636

Total $4,836

Example 5.23. Refer to Example 5.22 and assume the business equipment purchased in April 1998 was instead purchased in November 1998. Based on these facts, depreciation on all personal property purchased in 1998 would be based on the midquarter convention since more than 40 percent of all personal property placed in service was placed in service during the last quarter of the taxable year. Based on this information, MACRS depreciation for 1998 on the assets in Example 5.22 is:

		Depreciation
1.	Business equipment ($14,000 cost × 28⁴/7% × ⅛) (7-year life, 200% DB)	$ 500
2.	Car ($11,000 × 40% × ⅜) (5-year life, 200% DB)	1,650
3.	Office building (Same as Example 5.22)	636
	Total	$2,786

MACRS applies for determining depreciation for business use cars placed in service after 1986. Taxpayers who use the actual cost method for claiming deductions in lieu of the standard mileage rate are subject to specific limits on the depreciation amount (adjusted annually for inflation) that they can claim for cars in any particular year. Code Sec. 280F.

For cars placed in service during calendar year 1997, the maximum allowable depreciation deduction is $3,160 for the first year, $5,000 for the second year, $3,050 for the third year, and $1,775 for each succeeding year. Rev. Proc. 97-20, 1997-11 IRB 10. If a passenger automobile is used less than 100 percent for business purposes, the depreciation deduction limits are determined by multiplying the limitation amount by the percentage of business use. In addition, if the business use percentage for any year is less than 50 percent, MACRS depreciation must be computed using the alternative MACRS method (straight-line method over a five-year life).

Example 5.24. On January 23, 1997, Milly Hudson purchased a car for $25,000. During the year, she used it 70 percent for business. Without the specific car rules, her maximum depreciation deduction would be $3,500 ($25,000 × 70% business use × 20% depreciation (40% double-declining-balance rate for a five-year property × 50%)). However, under the specific car rules, the maximum MACRS depreciation may not exceed $3,160 for the first year even if Milly uses the car 100 percent for business. In addition, this amount must be reduced to reflect the actual business use percentage. Thus, the maximum depreciation deduction, including the Section 179 expense deduction, that Milly could have claimed for 1997 is $2,212 ($3,160 maximum depreciation × 70% business use). For 1998, Millie may claim $3,500 ($5,000 (maximum allowance for second year) × 70%). For 1999, the figure is $2,135 ($3,050 (maximum allowance for third year) × 70%).

Alternative MACRS System

MACRS deductions are reduced for certain property by requiring that an alternative MACRS method, based on the Asset Depreciation Range System (ADR) class lives, be used for (1) tangible property used predominantly outside the United States, (2) tax-exempt use property, (3) tax-exempt bond-financed property, (4) property imported from a foreign country for which an Executive Order is in effect because the country maintains trade restrictions or engages in other discriminatory acts, and (5) property for which an alternative MACRS election has been made (see below). Mixed-use property (property used for both business and personal purposes) that is used 50 percent or more for personal use is also required to be depreciated under the alternative MACRS rules. Code Sec. 168(g). Under the alternative MACRS rules, the applicable depreciation method for all property is the straight-line method. The deduction is computed by applying the straight-line method (without regard to salvage value), the applicable convention, and the applicable prescribed longer recovery period for the respective class of property.

Special Election. Instead of the regular MACRS deduction, taxpayers may irrevocably elect to apply the alternative MACRS system to any class of property for any tax year and depreciate assets using the straight-line method or the 150 percent declining method of depreciation. If elected, the alternative system applies to all property in the MACRS class placed in service during the tax year. For residential rental property and nonresidential real property, the election may be made on a property-by-property basis.

Example 5.25. In September 1998, Max Cracker Co., a calendar year taxpayer, purchased two pieces of equipment. One piece of equipment cost $25,000 and has a salvage value of $4,000. The other piece of equipment cost $20,000 and has a salvage value of $2,000. Max Cracker Co. elects to depreciate the equipment using the alternative depreciation system and to depreciate the assets over the MACRS class lives using straight-line depreciation. Both pieces of equipment are seven-year assets under MACRS. Salvage value is ignored in the depreciation computation and only one-half-year depreciation is allowed in the year of acquisition. For 1998 depreciation for the two pieces of property is $3,214 ($45,000 cost/7 years × ½).

Election to Expense Certain Depreciable Assets

Taxpayers are allowed to treat a limited amount of expenditures for business property as a current deduction (expense) for tax purposes rather than a capital expenditure subject to depreciation. Code Sec. 179. In 1998, the amount of capital expenditures eligible for immediate deduction by a taxpayer is $18,500. A taxpayer can elect to expense the cost of an entire asset or only a portion of the cost of an asset as long as the yearly expensing limitation is not exceeded in any one tax year. To qualify for the immediate expensing election, eligible property generally must be tangible personal property used in a trade or business and be eligible for MACRS. Code Sec. 179(d)(2). Buildings and property held for the production of income do not qualify for the immediate expensing election.

Example 5.26. In 1998, Brooks Tea Co., a calendar year taxpayer, purchases one business machine for $25,000 and elects to apply the immediate expensing of business assets provision (Code Sec. 179) to the maximum extent possible. In 1998, Brooks may take a current tax deduction for $18,500 of the cost of the machine using the expensing election. The remaining cost of the asset ($6,500) is eligible for MACRS depreciation.

The $18,500 immediate expensing limit is reduced dollar for dollar for amounts invested in personal property in excess of $200,000 in any year. The expense deduction is also limited in any tax year to the amount of taxable income derived by the taxpayer from any active trade or business in which the taxpayer is engaged. Unused deductions can be carried forward to subsequent tax years. If expensed property is converted to nonbusiness use at any time before the end of the property's recovery period, the difference between the amount expensed and the MACRS deductions that would have been allowed is recaptured as ordinary income.

> *Example 5.27.* In 1998, Brooks Tea Co., a calendar year taxpayer, purchases one business machine for $205,000 and elects to apply the immediate expensing of business assets provision (Code Sec. 179) to the maximum extent possible. In 1998, Brooks may take a current tax deduction for $13,500 of the cost of the machine using the expensing election. The remaining cost of the asset ($191,500) is eligible for MACRS depreciation.

Other Depreciation Considerations

A number of other factors may affect the amount of a depreciation deduction for a particular business taxpayer. Some of these other factors are briefly noted here.

Property placed in service prior to 1981 and some other miscellaneous categories of property are not eligible for MACRS depreciation. Pre-1981 property is normally depreciated using the straight-line, declining balance, or sum of the years-digits methods. Life estimates on these assets are longer than the life estimates allowed when using MACRS. Salvage value on these assets usually has to be taken into consideration when figuring depreciation, and the assets cannot be depreciated below a reasonable salvage value.

The following guidelines apply to expenditures for repairs and improvements to capital assets. Expenditures which add to the permanent value of capital assets are considered to be capital assets subject to depreciation for tax purposes. Reg. § 1.162-4. If expenditures do not extend the life of property beyond its original condition but merely maintain and preserve the property, the expenditures are deductible currently as normal maintenance and repair expenditures.

If property used for personal purposes is later converted to business use or held for the production of income, the basis of the property to be used for computing depreciation for tax purposes is the lesser of the fair market value of the property at the date of conversion to business or investment use or its adjusted basis at the date of conversion. Reg. § 1.167(g)-1.

A depreciation deduction must be taken by a taxpayer in the tax year that it is allowable. If a taxpayer forgets or chooses to not take an allowable depreciation deduction in a particular tax year, the taxpayer cannot compensate for the lost depreciation deduction by overdepreciating the asset in a later tax year. Reg. §1.167(a)-10. The taxpayer does have the option to file an amended tax return for the year when the proper depreciation deduction was not taken and correct the deduction to its proper amount.

KEYSTONE PROBLEM

The property ledger used for tax purposes by Able Garment Co., a calendar year taxpayer, is shown below. Compute the amount of the 1998 and 1999 depreciation deductions allowable to Able Garment Co. for these assets on its tax returns based on regular MACRS depreciation percentage rates.

Able Garment Co.
Property Ledger
as of December 31, 1998

	Asset	Year Purchased	Cost	Salvage Value
1.	Car	1998	$ 9,000	$1,000
2.	Car	1998	12,000	1,500
3.	Office furniture	1998	14,250	1,000
4.	Business equipment	1998	38,950	5,000
5.	Building (Office) Sept.	1998	95,000	—

¶ 5425   AMORTIZATION

In financial accounting, the term "amortization" is normally defined as the process of allocating the cost of an intangible asset to expense over its estimated useful life. The Code is not as precise in the use of the term "amortization." The Regulations actually refer to the process of allocating the cost of an intangible asset to expense as depreciation instead of amortization. Reg. § 1.167(a)-3. In other sections of the Code, reference is made to amortizing the cost of tangible assets, a process which is usually referred to as depreciation in financial accounting. In this part, the tax treatment of intangible assets is reviewed, the election to expense or amortize research and experimentation expenses is discussed, and other tax amortizable expenditures are briefly mentioned.

Intangible Assets

Intangible assets used in a trade or business and having limited useful lives subject to reasonable estimation can be amortized over an appropriate useful life. The straight-line depreciation method is used to compute the amortization deduction. Code Sec. 197 provides for a 15-year amortization period for specified intangible assets referred to as "section 197" intangibles. A section 197 intangible includes goodwill, going concern value, licenses or permits granted by a governmental agency, covenants not to compete, franchises, trademarks, trade names, patents, and copyrights.

Other Allowable Amortization Deductions

In some instances, amortization deductions are allowed for capital expenditures which are more favorable to a taxpayer than the normal depreciation allowances applicable to the property. These amortization deductions are provided to taxpayers as tax incentives to participate in investment activities which are considered to have some public interest attached to them. For example, taxpayers may elect to amortize the cost of pollution control facilities over a 60-month period. Code Sec. 169.

¶ 5435   RESEARCH AND EXPERIMENTAL EXPENDITURES

The term "research and experimental" expenditures (R&E) includes all experimental and laboratory costs connected with the development of an experimental or pilot model, plant process, product, or formula, invention, or similar property. It does not include expenditures for ordinary testing or inspection of materials or products for quality control or for efficiency surveys, management studies, consumer surveys, advertising, or promotion. Reg. § 1.174-2(a). R&E connected with a trade or business can be treated as a current deduction for tax purposes or, if elected by the taxpayer, be deferred and amortized over a period of not less than 60 months starting in the period when benefits from the R&E are first realized. Code Sec. 174(a) and (c). Any R&E involving the purchase of property which would normally be subject to depreciation such as equipment or the purchase of land cannot be deducted immediately but must be handled in accordance with its regular treatment for tax purposes. Code Sec. 174(c).

A taxpayer can choose to expense R&E in the first taxable year in which these expenditures are paid or incurred or can capitalize R&E and amortize the expenditures when paid or incurred over a period of 60 months or more. Subsequent changes in treatment require approval of the IRS.

Example 5.28. In 1998, Jones Ribbon Co. incurs R&E for the first time. R&E included the following amounts:

R&E Salaries	$350,000
R&E Materials	150,000
Total R&E	$500,000

If Jones Ribbon Co. chooses to treat all R&E incurred in 1998 as a current deduction, the amount of the deduction would be:

R&E Salaries	$350,000
R&E Materials	150,000
R&E Deduction	$500,000

If Jones Ribbon Co. elects to capitalize and amortize 1998 R&E, the monthly amortization deduction, assuming a 60-month amortization period, would be:

$500,000/60 = \$8,333.33$ per month amortization in 1998 starting with the month when benefits from the R&E are first realized.

TAX PLANNING POINTER ▼

Generally, immediate expensing of R&E is advantageous to a taxpayer for tax purposes as compared to capitalization and amortization of R&E. This is true because immediate expensing results in larger tax deductions in earlier years and lower tax payments.

¶5451 DEPLETION OF NATURAL RESOURCES

Depletion is normally defined as the process of allocating the cost of a natural resource to expense over its estimated useful life. For tax purposes, however, it is possible that depletion deductions for a natural resource may exceed the cost of the natural resource. Some natural resources which are subject to depletion include metals such as gold, silver, and copper, and minerals like coal, clay, sand, and oil.

The owner of a natural resource is entitled to the depletion deduction. Reg. § 1.611-1(b). Land on which the natural resource is located is not subject to depletion.

Two methods are available to taxpayers for computing the depletion deduction: the cost depletion method and the percentage depletion method. The taxpayer would normally compute the proper deductions using both depletion methods and then claim the higher deduction for tax purposes. Reg. § 1.611-1(a).

Cost Depletion Method

The cost depletion computation involves dividing the basis of the natural resource by the estimated units to be recovered from the natural resource to determine the depletion amount per unit. The depletion amount per unit is then multiplied by the units of the natural resource sold during the year which gives the cost depletion deduction for the tax year.

Example 5.29. In 1998, Basil Natural Resource Development Company acquires the rights to a natural resource for $5,000,000. The estimated recoverable units from the natural resource at the time of purchase amount to 250,000 units. The depletion amount per unit is $5,000,000/250,000 = $20 depletion amount per unit. If 40,000 units of the natural resource were sold during 1998, the depletion deduction using the cost depletion method would be $800,000 (40,000 units sold during year × $20 depletion amount per unit).

Percentage Depletion Method

Percentage depletion is computed by taking a specified depletion percentage and applying it to the gross income for the year derived from the sale of the natural resource. Some depletion percentages specified in the Code include 5 percent for sand and gravel, 10 percent for coal, 15 percent for gold, silver, and copper, and 22 percent for uranium. Code Sec. 613. The deduction for percentage depletion is limited on a property basis to 50 percent of the taxpayer's taxable net income derived from the natural resource for the year before deducting the depletion deduction. For oil and gas properties, the net income limitation on percentage depletion is 100 percent of net income from the property.

> *Example 5.30.* Referring to the previous example, Basil Natural Resource Development Company sells 40,000 units of its natural resource during 1998 at an average price of $160 per unit. Assuming a specified depletion percentage of 15 percent stated for the natural resource and operating expenses of $95 per unit of natural resource, the percentage depletion deduction is computed as follows:
>
> 1. Gross income derived from natural resource
>
> | | |
> |---|---:|
> | (40,000 units × $160) . . . . | $6,400,000 |
> | Code specified depletion percentage . . . . | 15% |
> | Percentage depletion deduction subject to limitation . . . . | $ 960,000 |
>
> 2. Taxable income limitation
>
> | | |
> |---|---:|
> | Gross income . . . . | $6,400,000 |
> | Operating expenses before depletion | |
> | (40,000 units × $95) . . . . | 3,800,000 |
> | Taxable income before depletion deduction . . . . | $2,600,000 |
> | Limitation percentage . . . . | 50% |
> | Percentage depletion deduction limitation . . . . | $1,300,000 |
> | Percentage depletion deduction, lesser of (1) or (2) . . . . . . | $ 960,000 |

As mentioned earlier, a taxpayer should compare the computed cost depletion deduction with the computed percentage depletion deduction and deduct the higher amount. In the two examples, the cost depletion deduction was $800,000 and the percentage depletion deduction was $960,000. Thus, taxpayer would deduct the $960,000 percentage depletion deduction amount.

The basis of the natural resource is reduced by any depletion deduction taken by a taxpayer. If the basis of the natural resource property is reduced to zero, after being reduced by depletion deductions, depletion can still be claimed by a taxpayer using the percentage depletion method since it is not based on the cost of the taxpayer's investment in natural resource property.

Restricted Business Deductions

Some business expenditures are restricted by the Code as to the types and amounts which are deductible for tax purposes. Restricted business deductions which are discussed in this section are: deductions for political contributions and lobbying activities, business start-up expenditures, and deductions for business gifts.

¶ 5501 POLITICAL CONTRIBUTIONS AND LOBBYING ACTIVITIES

Political contributions by businesses are not deductible for tax purposes. Specifically, amounts paid for advertising in political convention programs, tickets to political dinners, and tickets to inaugural balls are not deductible.

Lobbying expenditures of a business taxpayer, including the expenses of a professional lobbyist, are not deductible for tax purposes with some exceptions. Lobbying expenditures which are not deductible include amounts paid in connection with the election of a political candidate and grass roots lobbying of the general public. In addition, lobbying expenditures are not deductible for amounts paid in connection with influencing federal or state legislation through communication with legislators, government officials, and government employees who participate in the formulation of legislation and for amounts paid in connection with direct communication with top executive branch officials of the federal government for the purpose of influencing their official actions or positions. The executive officials included are the President, the Vice-President, cabinet members and their immediate deputies, and other senior level officers. An important exception allows the deduction of lobbying expenses incurred at the local governmental level for influencing legislation of direct interest to the taxpayer.

The deduction limitation does not apply in the case of any local council or similar governing body. In addition, a deduction for lobbying expenses is permitted for carrying on a trade or business in direct connection with appearances before, submissions or statements to, or sending communications to, the committees or individual members of local councils or similar bodies with respect to local legislation or proposed local legislation of direct interest to the taxpayer. A deduction is also permitted for expenses in direct connection with communication between the taxpayer and an organization of which the taxpayer is a member with respect to any local legislation or proposed local legislation of direct interest to the taxpayer. A taxpayer can deduct the portion of dues paid or incurred to an organization of which the taxpayer is a member which is attributable to those local legislation activities.

¶ 5515 BUSINESS START-UP EXPENDITURES

Business start-up expenditures include both business investigation expenses and business start-up costs. Business investigation expenses are costs incurred in investigating the creation or acquisition of a business prior to when a decision is made whether to acquire or enter the business. Business investigation expenses include costs such as travel, marketing surveys, legal, accounting, and engineering fees. Business start-up costs are expenses incurred prior to when a business becomes operational but after a decision has been made to enter the business. Business start-up costs include pre-operational advertising, employee training costs, and other pre-operational expenditures.

The deductibility of business investigation expenses depends on whether the taxpayer is currently in a line of business similar to the one being investigated or whether the investigated business is a new business for the taxpayer. If the taxpayer is currently in a similar line of business, all business investigation expenses are deductible for tax purposes in the year paid or incurred regardless of whether the taxpayer actually purchases the investigated business. If the investigated business is a new business for the taxpayer, the deductibility of the related business investigation expenses depends on whether the new business is actually purchased. If the new business is not purchased, the related business investigation expenses are not deductible for tax purposes since the taxpayer is not in a trade or business in regard to the new business. Rev. Rul. 57-418, 1957-2 CB 143. If the new business is purchased by the taxpayer, the related business investigation expenses must be capitalized for tax purposes and, if elected by the taxpayer, amortized over a period of not less than 60 months. Code Sec. 195.

Business start-up costs are treated the same as business investigation expenses for tax purposes. Start-up costs are deductible in the year paid or incurred if the taxpayer is currently in a similar line of business as the start-up business. If the start-up business is a new business, the start-up costs are capitalized for tax purposes and, if elected by the taxpayer, amortized over a period of not less than 60 months. Code Sec. 195.

Example 5.31. Raymond James owns a chain of four restaurants in Cleveland, Ohio. In 1998, Raymond incurs $7,000 of travel, legal, and accounting expenses related to the investigation of the possibility of buying a chain of seven restaurants in Miami, Florida. The $7,000 of business investigation expenses are deductible for tax purposes in 1998 regardless of whether Raymond purchases the chain of restaurants in Miami since the investigated business is similar to Raymond's current trade or business.

Example 5.32. Fred Matthews is currently a junior high school teacher in Cleveland, Ohio. In 1998, Fred incurs $6,000 of travel, legal, and accounting expenses related to an investigation of the possibility of buying a chain of five restaurants in Denver, Colorado. If, after the investigation, Fred decides not to buy the chain of restaurants, the $6,000 of business investigation expenses are not deductible for tax purposes since Fred is not in a trade or business similar to the investigated new business. If, after the investigation, Fred decides to buy the new chain of restaurants, the $6,000 of investigation expenses are capitalized for tax purposes and, if Fred elects, may be amortized over a period of not less than 60 months.

¶ 5555   BUSINESS GIFTS

A business tax deduction for business gifts is restricted to $25 per individual donee per year. Code Sec. 274(b). A business gift normally does not have to be included in the gross income of the recipient. The following items are specifically excluded from the definition of business gifts:

1. Items costing $4 or less which have the name of the taxpayer permanently imprinted on them

2. Signs, display racks, and other promotional materials to be used on the business premises of the recipient

3. Tangible personal property awarded to an employee by reason of length of service or safety achievement that does not exceed $400 in value (nonqualified plans) or $1,600 in value if awarded according to a qualified plan award where the average award does not exceed $400

Example 5.33. During 1998, the salesperson for ABC Vending Co. gave the owner of Video Games Co. a total of five bottles of high quality wine as business gifts at various times during the year. The five bottles of wine were purchased by ABC Vending Co. for a total of $150. ABC Vending Co. is entitled to a maximum deduction of $25 for the business gifts. The remaining $125 cost of the business gifts is not deductible for tax purposes.

Transportation, Travel, Entertainment, Moving Expenses, and Student Loan Interest

Tax deductions for transportation, travel, entertainment, moving expenses, and student loan interest are discussed in the following sections.

¶ 5601 TRANSPORTATION EXPENSES

Transportation expenses are defined for tax purposes as the costs of transporting a taxpayer from one location to another when the taxpayer is not in a travel status. Reg. § 1.62-1(g). A taxpayer is in a travel status when away from home for an extended period of time, which generally means overnight. If transportation expenses are incurred when in travel status, the expenses are considered to be travel expenses rather than transportation expenses. Included in transportation expenses are air fares, taxi fares, automobile expenses, parking fees, turnpike tolls, etc.

Transportation expenses of a self-employed taxpayer are deductible for AGI as trade or business expenses. Unreimbursed employee transportation expenses are deductible from AGI as miscellaneous itemized deductions subject to the 2 percent of AGI limitation (see discussion at ¶ 7601, 7603, and 7605). In order for transportation expenses to be deductible by an employee, however, the expenses must be paid or incurred in connection with services performed as an employee. Commuting expenses of an employee going from home to work and back have generally been held to be nondeductible expenses. The length of commute is considered irrelevant for tax purposes and only a matter of personal preference. If a taxpayer has a temporary work assignment beyond the general work area, however, and chooses to return home each night, the transportation expenses related to the round trip are deductible if not reimbursed by the employer. Work assignments with a duration in excess of one year are considered nontemporary and related transportation costs are nondeductible commuting expenses. Code Sec. 162.

> *Example 5.34.* John Jason is the manager of a retail store in the city of Clyde. He drives 10 miles to and from work each day. Transportation costs associated with his drive to and from work each day would not be deductible since they are ordinary commuting expenses. In August 1998, John's employer requests that he be the temporary manager for two weeks at the company store in Sidney while the regular manager is on vacation. The Sidney store is approximately 120 miles round-trip from John's home. His employer does not reimburse him for his transportation expenses in going to the Sidney store. The transportation expenses incurred by John during the two-week period when he returned home each night are deductible on John's tax return as transportation expenses incurred in going to a temporary work assignment beyond his general work area.

Another deductible employee transportation expense is the expense of going from one job to another job on the same workday. The cost of going to the first job and home from the second job is not deductible. *R. Paolini,* 43 TCM 513, CCH Dec. 38,784(M), T.C. Memo. 1982-69. Where an employee incurs additional transportation expenses beyond what would normally be incurred in commuting to work because the employee has to transport heavy and bulky tools to work, these additional expenses are also deductible as transportation expenses. Rev. Rul. 75-380, 1975-2 CB 59.

Computing Automobile Expenses

Automobile expenses are deductible as transportation expenses if incurred in connection with a trade or business or by an employee in connection with employment duties to the extent not reimbursed by the employer. Two methods are available for figuring automobile expenses: the taxpayer can keep records of the actual operating costs of the automobile, including an allowance for depreciation, or, in certain instances, can deduct a standard mileage rate. The 1998 rate for business use of an automobile is 32.5 cents per mile.

If the taxpayer uses the actual operating cost method of determining deductible automobile expenses, records must be kept of the actual costs of operation of the automobile, which include gas, oil, repairs, insurance, depreciation, licenses, and other costs. The taxpayer deducts the portion of these expenses that applies to the business use of the automobile.

The other method for figuring automobile expenses is the standard mileage rate method. The 1998 rate for business use of an automobile is 32.5 cents per mile. Parking fees, tolls, and state and local taxes can be deducted in addition to the standard mileage rate. Rev. Rul. 73-91, 1973-1 CB 71. Certain restrictions apply to the use of the standard mileage rate method, some of which are: if the taxpayer uses two or more cars for business purposes at the same time, the standard mileage rate method cannot be used; or if the taxpayer depreciates the automobile using MACRS depreciation in the first year of its life, the standard mileage rate method cannot be used in subsequent years. Also, the standard mileage rate applies to all business miles driven during the year. For 1998, the basis of a vehicle is reduced (but not below zero) by 12 cents per mile for all business miles to which the standard mileage rate applied.

TAX PLANNING POINTER ▼

The actual cost method of figuring automobile expenses will usually result in a larger deduction for tax purposes than the standard mileage rate method. The disadvantage of the actual cost method as compared to the standard mileage rate method is the additional recordkeeping requirements.

¶ 5635   TRAVEL EXPENSES

Travel expenses are defined for tax purposes as costs incurred while away from home in the pursuit of a trade or business including employment activities of an employee. Code Sec. 162(a)(2). Travel expenses include transportation expenses, 50 percent of business meal costs, lodging expenses, and other incidental expenses such as laundry and dry cleaning expenses. A requirement related to travel expenses is that meals and lodging must not be lavish or extravagant under the circumstances.

Travel expenses of self-employed taxpayers are deductible for AGI as trade or business expenses. Unreimbursed employee travel expenses are deductible from AGI, subject to the 2 percent floor applicable to miscellaneous itemized deductions (see discussion at ¶ 7601, 7603, and 7605). To be deductible, however, travel expenses must be incurred by a taxpayer while away from home. The IRS has interpreted the term "away from home" to mean "away from home overnight." Rev. Rul. 75-168, 1975-1 CB 58. Overnight does not mean a full 24-hour period but a period substantially longer than a normal work day where it is reasonable to need sleep or rest to meet normal job requirements.

Example 5.35. Linda James, a CPA, drives from Columbus, Ohio to Cincinnati, Ohio, a distance of 100 miles, on Thursday night in order to attend a business meeting in Cincinnati on Friday morning at 9 a.m. The meeting ends at 11 a.m. and Linda drives back to Columbus. Linda can deduct the travel expenses related to her trip even though it did not cover a 24-hour period.

The term "away from home" also raises the question of where the taxpayer's home is. The IRS takes the position that a taxpayer's tax home, for purposes of travel expenses, is at the location of the taxpayer's principal place of business or employment and not at the location of the taxpayer's personal residence. IRS Publication No. 463, Travel, Entertainment, and Gift Expenses. Normally a taxpayer lives in the same area where he or she works. If a taxpayer chooses to live in an area other than where he or she works, it is considered to be a personal preference and related travel costs are not deductible for tax purposes.

The travel expense provision is designed to lessen the burden on taxpayers who incur duplicate living expenses for sound business reasons. Two areas where problems arise are when a taxpayer works in a different location from where he or she lives for possible business reasons and when a taxpayer has two places of business in different areas. If a taxpayer's work away from the tax home is temporary, travel expenses are deductible for tax purposes. A temporary work assignment is one that is not indefinite or does not extend for more than one year. If a temporary work assignment is indefinite or extends for more than one year, travel expenses normally are not deductible. If a taxpayer has one or more places of business, the taxpayer may take a business deduction for daily transportation expenses paid or incurred in traveling between the taxpayer's residence and a temporary work location, regardless of the distance travelled. Rev. Rul. 90-23, 1990-1 CB 28. The IRS usually considers the following three factors in determining the principal place of business: (1) length of time spent at each location; (2) degree of business activity at each location; and (3) amount of income derived from each location. The more important location when measured against these three criteria is the taxpayer's principal place of business.

> *Example 5.36.* Larry Robinson, a CPA and a single taxpayer, works for a CPA firm in Cleveland, Ohio, from June through October each year and works for a CPA firm in Miami, Florida, from November through May. Larry makes approximately $20,000 in salary from his work in Cleveland and approximately $35,000 in salary from his work in Miami. Which area is Larry's tax home, Cleveland or Miami? Consideration of the length of time spent at each location indicates Miami as the tax home (seven months versus five months). Amount of income derived from each location also indicates Miami as the tax home ($35,000 versus $20,000). Since Miami is Larry's tax home, living costs in the Miami area are not deductible on Larry's tax return. Travel expenses incurred when traveling to and from and working in Cleveland are deductible as temporary living expenses. Another factor to consider in this case is that the IRS might argue that Larry has two tax homes, Cleveland and Miami. This issue could be refuted, however, if Larry can demonstrate that his travel expenses in Cleveland duplicate some of the living expenses he incurs in Miami when he is living in Cleveland. Apartment or motel expenses incurred in Cleveland while, at the same time, Larry still maintains an apartment in Miami are duplicate living expenses.

Combining Business and Personal Travel

Travel expenses are deductible for tax purposes if a taxpayer is away from home in pursuit of a trade or business including employment activities and attending a convention. A person may, however, combine personal activities such as sightseeing with a business trip. If the primary purpose of the trip is business, travel expenses including all transportation expenses are deductible as business expenses even though some time is spent on personal activities. Any direct costs associated with the personal activity, however, are not deductible. If the primary purpose of the trip is personal, travel expenses are not deductible even though some business activities are conducted during the trip. Direct costs of any business activity conducted on a personal trip such as renting a car to attend a business meeting are deductible by the taxpayer. Costs associated with taking a spouse along on a business trip are not deductible unless it can be shown that the presence of the spouse had a business purpose and the spouse is also employed by the person paying or reimbursing the expenses. Reg. § 1.162-2(c).

More restrictive travel requirements apply to travel outside of the United States. Travel expenses including transportation expenses incurred on foreign trips must be allocated between business and personal activities unless travel outside of the United States does not exceed seven days or time attributable to personal activities is less than 25 percent of the total travel time. Code Sec. 274(c). Additional travel restrictions apply to attendance at foreign conventions and attendance at business meetings on cruise ships. Code Sec. 274(h).

Substantiation of Travel Expenses

Taxpayers must substantiate expenditures for travel and transportation expenses by adequate records or by sufficient evidence corroborating the taxpayer's statements as to (1) amount, (2) time and place, (3) business purpose, and (4) business relationship to the taxpayer. Taxpayers must have documentary evidence for any lodging expense while traveling away from home and for any other expenditure of $75 or more, except transportation charges if documentary evidence is not readily available.

In lieu of substantiating actual travel-related meal and lodging costs, employers and employees may utilize optional IRS per diem allowances. The federal per diem rate is equal to the sum of the federal lodging expense allowance and the federal meal and incidental expense (M&IE) rate for the locality of travel. In 1998, the M&IE rates are $40 per day for any high-cost locality and $32 per day for other localities within the United States. The M&IE rate for travel outside the United States is equal to 40 percent of the per diem rate for the locality of travel. In 1998, the maximum per diem rate is $180 for high-cost localities, while for all other localities the maximum per diem rate is $113. The per diem amount is subject to the 50 percent limit on meals and entertainment expenses, which is discussed in the next section. Rev. Proc. 97-59, 1997-52 IRB 31.

¶ 5655   MEALS AND ENTERTAINMENT EXPENSES

Under regular rules, entertainment expenses are deductible by a taxpayer if the expenditures can be substantiated and are "directly related to" or "associated with" a taxpayer's business. Code Sec. 274(a). An entertainment expenditure is directly related to a taxpayer's business if the taxpayer can show that there was some general expectation of deriving some income or specific benefit from the expenditure and business was discussed or engaged in during the entertainment. A taxpayer can also show that an entertainment expenditure is directly related to the business if it is provided in a clear business setting where the guest may recognize the business motive of the taxpayer in incurring the expenditure. An entertainment expenditure is associated with a taxpayer's business if the entertainment immediately precedes or is followed by a substantial business discussion. Reg. § 1.274-2(d)(4) and (5).

> *Example 5.37.* Linda James, an insurance agent, takes Paul Mason, president of Mason Furniture Co., to dinner in order to discuss new types of insurance coverage. Linda pays the bill for dinner. Linda can deduct the dinner expense as an entertainment expense directly related to her business. If, after the dinner, Linda takes Paul to see a professional baseball game and pays for the tickets, the cost of the tickets is deductible by Linda as an entertainment expense associated with her business since the entertainment followed a substantial business discussion.

A business entertainment activity where substantial distractions occur such as a professional sporting event or night club entertainment usually does not qualify under the regular rules as being directly related to the taxpayer's business since the presumption is that the distractions preclude the conduct of business activity. Expenditures on activities of this type usually qualify as entertainment expense deductions if such activities are associated with the taxpayer's business and immediately precede or follow substantial business discussions as noted in the preceding example. The "immediately preceding or following" requirement is generally met if the entertainment activity takes place on the same day as the business discussion.

Only 50 percent of the amount of otherwise allowable meals and entertainment expenses is deductible subject to certain exceptions. The exceptions allowing full deductibility include meal and entertainment expenses fully taxed as compensation to the recipient, traditional recreational expenses paid by employers for employees, and expenditures for samples and promotional items made available to the general public. In addition, in 1998 and 1999, the business meals deduction of transportation workers is increased to 55 percent of the otherwise allowable amount. Items subject to the 50 percent rule are food, beverages, taxes, tips, tickets, and cover charges. Transportation expenses such as taxicab fares are 100 percent deductible. Entertainment expenses of a self-employed taxpayer are deductible for AGI as trade or business expenses subject to the 50 percent rule. Entertainment expenses incurred by the taxpayer as an employee and not reimbursed by an employer are deductible from AGI as itemized deductions subject to the 50 percent limitation and the 2 percent floor on miscellaneous itemized deductions.

Entertainment Facilities

Expenditures by a taxpayer relating to the ownership of entertainment facilities such as yachts, hunting lodges, and fishing camps are generally not deductible as entertainment expenses. Out-of-pocket costs related to the use of entertainment facilities of this type, however, if directly related to or associated with the taxpayer's business are deductible for tax purposes. In addition, deductions for club dues are no longer allowed. This restriction applies to any club, whether organized for business, pleasure, recreation, or any other social purpose. The restriction, however, does not apply to professional organizations such as bar associations, business organizations such as trade associations, and civic organizations such as Kiwanis, Lions, and Rotary.

Substantiation of Entertainment Expenses

No entertainment deduction is allowed for tax purposes unless the taxpayer substantiates by adequate records or by other sufficient evidence corroborating the taxpayer's own statements the amount of the expense, the time and place of the entertainment, the business purpose of the entertainment, and the business relationship of the persons entertained to the taxpayer. Adequate substantiation for the entertainment expense deduction includes an account book or expense statement with all pertinent information maintained by the taxpayer during the year and documentary evidence including itemized receipts, paid bills, etc., for each expenditure of $75 or more made during the year. Reg. § 1.274-5.

¶ 5675 MOVING EXPENSES—QUALIFICATION REQUIREMENTS

A deduction is allowed for moving expenses paid or incurred in connection with the commencement of work by a taxpayer as an employee or as a self-employed individual at a new principal place of work. Code Sec. 217. In order to qualify for the moving expense deduction, a taxpayer must move because of a new job location. It is not necessary that the taxpayer have a prior job location. Moving expenses incurred without changing job locations would not be deductible.

¶ 5681 MOVING EXPENSES—TIME AND DISTANCE REQUIREMENTS

In order for moving expenses to be deductible, the taxpayer also must meet a time requirement and a distance requirement. The time requirement states that an employee must work full-time at the new job location for at least 39 weeks in the 12-month period following the move in order for the moving expenses to be deductible. If self-employed, the taxpayer must work in the new location for 78 weeks during the two-year period following the move for the expenses to be deductible with 39 of the weeks required to be in the first 12 months. The time requirement does not apply if a worker dies, is discharged from work, becomes disabled, or is transferred by the employer. Reg. § 1.217-2(d)(1).

If a taxpayer has not completed the time requirement when filing an income tax return, the moving expense deduction can be taken in the year the expenses are paid assuming that the taxpayer will meet the time requirement in the following tax year. If the time requirement is not met in the following year, the moving expense deduction taken in the prior year normally may be recognized as income in the year the time requirement is not met or amended on the previous year's return.

The distance requirement states that the distance between the taxpayer's old residence and new job location must be at least 50 miles farther than the distance between the old residence and the old job location. If the taxpayer has no old job location (new worker, unemployed), the distance test is met if the new job location is at least 50 miles from the old residence. Code Sec. 217(c)(1).

> *Example 5.38.* Robert Long is transferred by his employer from Kenton to Westchester. Robert also moves his family from Kenton to Westchester. Robert's old residence was 10 miles from his old job location. Robert's new job location is 75 miles from his old residence. Robert satisfies the 50-mile distance requirement since the distance between his old residence and new job location is 65 miles farther than the distance between the old residence and the old job location.

¶ 5685   CLASSIFICATION OF MOVING EXPENSES

Moving expenses include two parts: (1) expenses incurred to move household goods and personal effects and (2) travel and lodging expenses incurred by the taxpayer in moving the family from the old residence to the new residence. The cost of meals is not deductible. If family travel to the new residence is accomplished by automobile, the taxpayer can deduct actual car expenses or an optional allowance of 10 cents per mile.

> *Example 5.39.* Robert Long incurs the following moving expenses in connection with his move from Kenton to Westchester:

Expenses of moving household goods	$ 3,500
Travel and lodging for family in moving from old residence to new location	450
Pre-move house-hunting trips	1,400
Temporary living expenses in new location	1,200
Real estate commission on sale of old home	4,000
Total moving expenses	$10,550

The expenses of moving household goods and of moving Robert's family to the new location are deductible in full. Pre-move house-hunting trips, temporary living expenses, and qualified residence expenses are no longer deductible. The overall moving expense deduction is $3,950.

¶ 5695   MOVING EXPENSES—YEAR OF DEDUCTION

The moving expense deduction generally is taken by a cash basis taxpayer in the year the expenses are paid. The moving expense deduction is treated as a deduction from gross income to arrive at adjusted gross income. Code Sec. 62(a). Qualified moving expenses reimbursed by an employer are excludable from an employee's gross income as a qualified fringe benefit to the extent they meet the requirements for a qualified moving expense reimbursement. Qualified moving expense reimbursements include any amount received, directly or indirectly, by an employee from an employer as a payment for, or a reimbursement of, expenses that would be deductible as moving expenses under Code Sec. 217 if directly paid or incurred by the employee. Qualified moving expense reimbursements do not include payments for, or reimbursements of, expenses that were deducted by the taxpayer in a prior tax year.

¶ 5700   STUDENT LOAN INTEREST

Interest payments on student loans due and paid after December 31, 1997, are deductible "above-the-line." That means that a taxpayer can deduct the interest whether or not the standard deduction or itemized deduction is used. In 1998, up to $1,000 of interest may be deducted. The deduction increases to $1,500 in 1999; $2,000 in 2000; and $2,500 in 2001 and thereafter. The deduction is phased out for single taxpayers with adjusted gross income between $40,000 and $55,000 and for joint filers with adjusted gross income between $60,000 and $75,000. Married taxpayers filing separately may not take the deduction. Also, an individual is not entitled to the deduction if the taxpayer can be claimed as a dependent by another taxpayer for the tax year beginning in the calendar year in which the individual's tax year begins.

To be eligible for the deduction the education loan must be used to pay for any of the following expenses: tuition, fees, room and board, books and supplies, and other related expenses. The deduction for interest paid on a student loan is allowed for any of the first 60 months in which interest payments are required. The 60 months need not be consecutive. Therefore, months in which the loan is deferred do not count against the 60 month limit.

SUMMARY OF CHAPTER 5

✓ Allowable tax deductions are divided into three categories: trade or business, production of income, and personal. Certain losses are also allowable tax deductions. Basic personal living expenses of an individual taxpayer normally are not deductible with the exception of certain personal expenditures that have been justified by Congress for various reasons as proper tax deductions.

✓ In order to be deductible, trade or business expenditures must (1) be ordinary and necessary, (2) be reasonable in amount, (3) be related to an activity which is deemed to be a trade or business, (4) not be personal expenditures, (5) not be capital expenditures, (6) not be related to the generation of tax-exempt income, and (7) not hinder public policy. Certain employment related expenses of employees are deductible as trade or business deductions if they are directly related to the performance of the employees' duties or are required by an employment agreement.

✓ More common trade or business deductions allowable under the criteria discussed above include advertising, bad debts, salaries, interest payments, rental payments, insurance, and legal fees. Allowable business deductions related to capital expenditures include depreciation, amortization, and depletion. Business start-up expenditures and business gifts are restricted deductions.

✓ Production of income deductions include investment expenses which, to be deductible, must meet the same seven criteria noted above for trade or business deductions except that investment expenditures do not have to be related to an activity that is deemed to be a trade or business.

✓ All expenses incurred by individual taxpayers in connection with the determination, collection, or refund of any tax are deductible.

✓ Individual taxpayers are allowed deductions for losses but are limited to business losses, investment losses, and casualty or theft losses. Personal losses other than casualty and theft losses are not deductible. With the exception of some selected expenditures, basic personal living expenses of a taxpayer are not deductible.

✓ Some additional factors that may affect the amount of an allowable tax deduction are tax accounting method used, substantiation of deductions, and deductible amounts paid on behalf of another taxpayer.

CHAPTER 5 QUESTIONS

1. Tax deductions for an individual taxpayer can be divided into what three categories?

2. What are production of income tax deductions? What allowable deductions are included in the production of income deductions category?

3. Explain the difference between a deduction for AGI and a deduction from AGI. Which type of deduction would be more advantageous for tax purposes?

4. How might an improper classification of a deduction as for or from AGI affect the itemized deductions on a taxpayer's return? How might this improper classification have an effect on a taxpayer's state income tax liability?

5. List the seven criteria that must be met before an expenditure can be considered as an allowable trade or business tax deduction.

6. Explain why the IRS would be interested in the reasonableness of a salary payment to an employee/owner of a closely held corporation.

7. How can the owner of a small business activity prove to the IRS that the activity is truly a business even though it has not made a profit since its inception over nine years ago?

8. If an activity of a taxpayer is determined to be a hobby for tax purposes, what tax deductions are available to the taxpayer? Are there any limitations on these deductions?

9. If an expenditure is part business-related and part personal, how does the taxpayer determine the business-related amount that is deductible for tax purposes?

10. What is the logical argument that supports the statutory disallowance of a deduction for any expenditure related to tax-exempt income?

11. Explain the difference between an employee and an independent contractor from a tax standpoint. What difference does it make for tax purposes if someone is characterized as an employee or independent contractor?

12. What losses are tax deductible for individual taxpayers?

13. How can a taxpayer substantiate a tax deduction if called on to do so by the IRS in an audit of the taxpayer's return?

14. Are all advertising expenditures deductible for tax purposes? What about goodwill advertising?

15. What is the difference between a business and nonbusiness bad debt for tax purposes?

16. What are the basic requirements for a bad debt deduction on a tax return? Do any of these requirements differ between business and nonbusiness bad debts?

17. Can a current tax deduction for salaries and wages include payments for services performed in past years and for services to be performed in future years? Why is a sole proprietor not entitled to a tax deduction for salary payments to himself or herself?

18. How could it be determined whether payments characterized as rental payments are, in substance, payments for the purchase of property? What difference would it make for tax purposes as to how the payments are characterized?

19. Is salvage value ever considered when using MACRS depreciation? When using MACRS, is depreciation ever allowed on an asset in the year of disposal?

20. To qualify for the immediate expensing election (Code Sec. 179), an asset must meet what qualifications?

21. From a tax standpoint, what difference does it make to a business if a payment made to purchase a business is labeled as a goodwill payment rather than a covenant not to compete payment?

22. What is the difference between the cost depletion method and the percentage depletion method for tax purposes? Which method does a taxpayer use if the taxpayer is eligible for both methods?

23. What restrictions apply to tax deductions for business gifts?

24. Define the term "transportation expenses" as used for tax purposes. Give three examples of transportation expenses which are deductible by employees.

25. Define the term "travel expenses" as used for tax purposes. Define the term "away from home" as interpreted by the IRS.

26. In order for entertainment expenses to be deductible, the expenses must be "directly related to" or "associated with" a taxpayer's business. Define the terms "directly related to" and "associated with."

27. With regard to moving expenses paid or incurred by a taxpayer in connection with the commencement of work, what time and distance requirements must be met by the taxpayer in order to justify a moving expense deduction?

CHAPTER 5 PROBLEMS

28. Jacob Blue is a stamp collector who regularly attends stamp shows throughout the United States. During 1998, Jacob sold stamps for $20,000 which had cost him $8,000, bought stamps for $14,000, incurred travel expenses of $11,000 attending stamp shows, and had miscellaneous expenses of $4,000 related to his stamp collecting activities. Which of the above expenditures are valid tax deductions for Jacob on his 1998 tax return?

29. Mary Johnson owns and operates Big Mountain Ski Resort in Colorado. Big Mountain's taxable income/(loss) for the past seven years (the period of time that it has been owned by Mary) is as follows:

Year	Profit/(Loss)
1	$ 8,000
2	(18,000)
3	(3,000)
4	(5,000)
5	(9,000)
6	4,000
7	(3,000)

Based on only these facts:

a. Is Big Mountain Ski Resort a trade or business or a hobby to Mary?

b. Ignoring your answer to (a), in what way can Mary demonstrate that Big Mountain Ski Resort is a trade or business instead of a hobby besides meeting a rigid profits test?

30. In 1998, Al Johnson used his personal car for both business and personal purposes. He drove 18,000 miles in the car during the year: 10,000 miles were for business-related purposes and 8,000 miles were for personal purposes. He incurred the following car expenses during 1998:

Expense	Amount
Gas	$3,900
Maintenance	900
Repairs and depreciation	900
Car washes	500
Total	$6,200

Based on this information, what part of the above car expenses is deductible as business-related expenses on Al's 1998 income tax return?

31. Refer to the facts in Problem 30 and assume that Al's total car expenses for 1998 amounted to only $3,700. What is the amount of Al's car expense deduction on his 1998 tax return?

32. Indicate whether the following expenditures are trade or business deductions (T), production of income deductions (PI), personal deductions (P), or are not deductible (X). Also indicate if the deductible expenditures are deductible "for" or "from" AGI.

a. Business advertising

b. Interest expense on home mortgage

c. Union dues of employee

d. Bank service charges on business checking account

e. Entertainment expenses of employee not reimbursed by employer

33. Indicate whether the following expenditures are trade or business deductions (T), production of income deductions (PI), personal deductions (P), or are not deductible (X). Also indicate if the deductible expenditures are deductible "for" or "from" AGI.

    a. Interest expense on business loan

    b. Hobby expenses in excess of hobby income

    c. Commuting expenses of individual taxpayer

    d. Rent payments by illegal gambling business

    e. Payment to bribe government official made by a business

34. Are any of the following losses deductible on an individual's income tax return? If so, is the loss deductible "for" or "from" AGI? Explain each loss.

Loss	Amount
Loss on sale of stock by individual's business	$ 4,000
Hobby loss in excess of hobby gross income	3,000
Gambling losses in excess of gambling winnings	8,000
Loss on sale of stock on individual's investment portfolio	9,000
Decline in value of stock held in individual's investment portfolio	7,000
Loss on sale of personal automobile	2,000
Total	$33,000

35. Which of the following 1998 trade or business expenditures of Ajax Corporation are deductible on its 1998 tax return? If an expenditure is not deductible, explain why it is not a valid deduction.

Expenditure	Amount
Salaries and wages to employees	$400,000
Purchase of new office building	250,000
Payment of illegal parking fines of President	1,400
Payment of wedding expenses for President's wedding	16,000
Entertainment expenses related to company business	24,000
Interest on money borrowed to buy tax-exempt securities	9,000
Total expenditures	$700,400

36. Indicate whether the following expenditures are deductible for AGI or from AGI.

    a. Medical expenses of individual taxpayer

    b. Safe deposit box rental for business

    c. Interest expense on business loan

    d. Investment counseling fees incurred by individual investor

    e. Gambling losses to extent of gambling winnings of individual gambler not involved in gambling business

37. Indicate whether the following expenditures are deductible for AGI or from AGI.

    a. Entertainment expenses of employee not reimbursed by employer

    b. Moving expenses of employee

    c. Transportation expenses of employee not reimbursed by employer

    d. Hobby losses to extent of hobby income

38. Are any of the following expenditures deductible on an individual taxpayer's income tax return? Explain each item.

Expenditure	Amount
Cost of having income tax return prepared by a CPA	$ 100
Legal fee for divorce proceeding of which 20 percent related to tax planning advice	3,000
Lost wages for time missed from work while having income tax return prepared	250
Legal fee for estate planning advice of which 35 percent related to tax planning advice	900
Cost of having federal gift tax return prepared by a CPA	100
Total expenditures.....................................	$4,350

39. In 1998, Fred Peters paid $10,000 of business interest expense on a loan made to his son Jack, age 30, during the year. Jack was planning to file for bankruptcy and avoid making the interest payment, but Fred made the payment in order to avoid embarrassment for the family. Can Fred claim a business interest expense deduction on his individual income tax return for the payment of his son Jack's business interest expense?

40. In 1998, Jackson Cement Co. makes the following salary payments to James Warner, an employee of the company:

Regular salary payment	$42,000
Bonus for current year.................................	6,000
Advance compensation for future services	9,000
Total...	$57,000
Less: Amounts withheld for taxes	18,000
Net Payment	$39,000

What amount can Jackson Cement Co., an accrual basis taxpayer, deduct in 1998 for the above salary payments to James Warner?

41. Bevis Bag Co., a calendar year and cash basis taxpayer, buys land on September 29, 1998. Property taxes of $9,000 were paid on the land by the previous owner on March 1, 1998, to cover the property tax year of January 1, 1998, to December 31, 1998. Is Bevis Bag Co. entitled to a property tax deduction for this land on its 1998 tax return? If so, what is the amount of the deduction?

42. Compute MACRS depreciation for the following qualified assets for the calendar years 1998 and 1999:

Asset	Year Purchased		Cost	Salvage Value
Business equipment (7-year property)	March	1998	$85,500	$10,000
Car	May	1998	7,760	1,000
Office furniture (7-year property)	July	1998	18,050	3,000
Building (Office)	January	1998	85,000	5,000

43. Refer to the facts in Problem 42 and assume that the straight-line method under the alternative MACRS system was elected over the MACRS recovery period for all the assets listed. Based on these facts, compute the 1998 and 1999 depreciation deduction for each of the assets listed.

44. Refer to the facts in Problem 42 and assume that the office building purchased in January 1998 and the car purchased in 1998 were both sold in June 1999. How much depreciation can be claimed as a deduction on these two assets in 1999 for the portion of the year they were held by the taxpayer? Assume MACRS depreciation is used.

45. Refer to the facts in Problem 42 and assume the business equipment purchased in March 1998 was instead purchased in November 1998. Based on these facts, compute the MACRS depreciation for the business equipment, car, and office furniture for calendar years 1998 and 1999.

46. In 1998, Jason Products Co., a calendar year taxpayer, purchased business equipment (7-year property) for $40,000. Jason wants to take the largest possible tax deduction in 1998 related to this property. Compute the largest tax deduction possible in 1998 for the business equipment.

47. Refer to the facts in Problem 46 and assume Jason purchased $210,000 of business equipment. Compute the largest tax deduction possible in 1998 for the business equipment.

48. In 1998, James Jar Co., a calendar year taxpayer, incurred the following research and experimentation expenditures (R&E): Salaries—$150,000; and Materials—$100,000.

    a. If James Jar Co. treats R&E as a current deduction, what is the amount of the current deduction in 1998?

    b. If James Jar Co. capitalizes R&E and amortizes it over a 60-month period, what is the amount of deduction on a monthly basis that James can take in 1998, starting with the month when benefits from the R&E are first realized?

49. In 1998, NRD Company purchased the rights to a natural resource for $10,000,000. The estimated recoverable units from the natural resource amount to 3,500,000 units. During 1998, NRD sold 1,000,000 units of the natural resource for $10 per unit and incurred operating costs other than depletion of $5 per unit. Based on these facts:

a. Compute the depletion deduction for 1998 using the cost depletion method.

b. Compute the depletion deduction for 1998 using the percentage depletion method. Assume a 15 percent specified depletion percentage.

c. Which depletion deduction, cost or percentage, does NRD use in 1998?

50. In 1998, Mary Kelly drove her personal car 2,800 miles for business purposes. She also incurred $182 in parking fees and $191 in turnpike tolls connected with her business trips. None of her automobile expenses were reimbursed by her employer. Compute Mary's deduction for automobile expenses on her 1998 tax return, assuming all of the above expenses are valid and she elects to use the standard mileage allowance method to figure her automobile expenses.

51. Herman Welbe owns one car dealership in Ohio and one in Florida. Each year, Herman lives eight months in Ohio and four months in Florida. In 1998, Herman received $90,000 net income from his Ohio dealership and $25,000 net income from his Florida dealership. Based on these facts, is Herman entitled to any travel expenses for tax purposes in relation to his trips between his two dealerships and for living expenses incurred at either location? Explain.

52. On Monday, Harvey Leonard travels from Chicago to New York on a business trip. The trip lasts five days. Three days of the trip are spent conducting business activities and two days are spent on personal sightseeing activities. Harvey incurs $550 in airfare costs in going to and returning from New York, $50 a day in expenses for meals, and $100 a day for lodging while in New York.

a. What amount is deductible on Harvey's tax return for travel expenses related to the above activities? Assume Harvey is self-employed.

b. Assume Harvey is an employee and is reimbursed $700 by his employer for the trip. What amount is deductible on Harvey's tax return for unreimbursed travel expenses related to the above activities?

53. In 1998, Peter Poppins incurs the following employment-related moving expenses:

Expenses related to moving household goods.................. $4,000
Expenses to drive from old location to new location 45
Temporary living expenses in new location 1,800
Real estate commission on sale of old home.................. 2,200

Total expenses... $8,045

Peter receives no reimbursement from his employer for his moving expenses. Based on the above facts, and assuming that Peter meets the time and distance requirements, compute

Peter's moving expense deduction that would appear on his 1998 tax return.

54. For an individual taxpayer, expenses connected with rents and royalties are normally deducted:

    a. For AGI

    b. From AGI

    c. Either for or from AGI

    d. For AGI but limited to a maximum percentage amount

55. An ordinary trade or business expenditure is one which is:

    a. Reasonable in amount

    b. Commonly incurred by other businesses

    c. Appropriate for a particular business

    d. Not a capital expenditure

56. A necessary trade or business expenditure is one which is:

    a. Reasonable in amount

    b. Commonly incurred by other businesses

    c. Appropriate for a particular business

    d. Not a capital expenditure

57. In 1998, the maximum amount of capital expenditures eligible for immediate expensing is:

    a. $1,000

    b. $17,500

    c. $18,500

    d. $10,000

58. *Comprehensive Problem.* John Stantus, a single taxpayer and calendar year taxpayer, is sole owner of Stantus Accounting Services Company, a sole proprietorship. In 1998, Stantus Accounting Services reports revenues of $240,000 and deductions of $165,000. Included in the deductions are $14,000 of illegal payments to government officials to secure additional government business for the firm. For tax purposes, John reports the revenue and expenses of his company on Schedule C of Form 1040—Individual Income Tax Return. If John has no other taxable income, deductions, or credits in 1998, other than those items mentioned above, what is his tax liability on his 1998 individual income tax return? Ignore liability for self-employment taxes.

59. *Comprehensive Problem.* Peter Nerf, who is single and a calendar year taxpayer, received a salary of $45,000 from his employer in 1998. During 1998, Peter made an employment-related move and incurred the following moving expenses:

Expenses to move household furniture	$1,000
Travel from old residence to new location	700
Temporary living expenses in new location	2,100
Real estate commission on sale of old home	5,000
Total moving expenses	$8,800

In 1998, Peter's employer did not reimburse him for the moving expenses. In 1998, Peter also incurred $4,000 of medical expenses, $5,000 of charitable contributions, and $3,000 of miscellaneous itemized deductions subject to the 2 percent of AGI floor limitation. If Peter has no other taxable income, deductions, or credits in 1998, other than those items mentioned above, and assuming that the above moving expenses qualify for a tax deduction subject to stated limitations, what is Peter's taxable income on his 1998 individual income tax return?

60. *Research Problem.* The following selected court cases have helped to shape the tax law in regard to allowable trade or business tax deductions. Read the following court cases and prepare a brief written abstract for each case.

   a.   *New Colonial Ice Co.,* 4 USTC ¶ 1292, 292 U.S. 435.

   b.   *T.H. Welch v. Helvering,* 3 USTC ¶ 1164, 290 U.S. 111.

61. *Research Problem.* Prepare a brief written abstract for each of the following additional selected court cases relating to allowable trade or business deductions.

   a.   *A. Trujillo,* 68 TC 670, CCH Dec. 34,554.

   b.   *Illinois Terminal Railroad Co.,* 67-1 USTC ¶ 9374, 179 Ct.Cls. 674, 375 F.2d 1016 (Ct.Cls. 1967).

   c.   *I.R. Wharton,* 53-2 USTC ¶ 9597, 207 F.2d 526 (CA-5 1953).

Chapter 6

Deductions: Business/ Investment Losses and Passive Activity Losses

Learning Objectives

After completing Chapter 6, you should be able to:

1. Determine the amount and classification of losses originating from business operations.

2. Ascertain the amount and classification of losses from investment-related activities.

3. Understand tax shelters and the rationale for at-risk rules.

4. Achieve a thorough understanding of the intricacies of the passive activity rules.

5. Identify and determine the amount of allowable business and theft losses.

6. Calculate the amount of a net operating loss and determine the amounts to be carried back and forward.

7. Understand the allowable home office expenses and determine the limitation on the deduction for such losses.

8. Achieve an understanding of the vacation home rental rules and the limitation on such losses.

OVERVIEW OF CHAPTER

Deductions are provided in the Code for losses resulting from unprofitable investment-related activities, dispositions of certain assets, and unprofitable business operations. In each of these cases certain limitations or adjustments may apply, thus limiting the amount of deductible loss. Generally, deductible losses from a business, property held for production of income, or investment property are deductible for adjusted gross income. Losses derived from personal-use property, if deductible, are usually deducted from adjusted gross income as itemized deductions.

This chapter deals with losses originating from business operations and certain investment-related activities. Tax shelters, at-risk rules, passive activity rules, business casualty and theft losses, net operating losses, hobby losses, home office expenses, and vacation homes are among the topics addressed. Casualty losses derived from personal-use properties are discussed in Chapter 7, and losses resulting from the sale of capital assets (e.g., stocks and bonds) and business-use assets (Code Sec. 1231) are discussed in Chapter 11.

Tax Shelters and At-Risk Rules

¶ 6001 TAX SHELTERS

A tax shelter is an activity providing deductions and/or credits to an investor which will reduce tax liability with respect to income from other sources. Prior to the Tax Reform Act of 1986, tax shelters played an unreasonably influential role in the financial planning of many individuals. A Treasury study revealed that in 1983, 21 percent of tax returns reporting total positive income greater than $250,000 paid taxes equaling *10 percent or less* of total positive income (which is composed of salary, interest, dividends, and income from profitable businesses and investments). S. Rept. No. 313, 99th Cong., 2d Sess. (1986), p. 714.

Congress recognized the undesirable consequences that tax shelters created, which included declining federal tax revenues, diverting investment capital from productive activities to tax avoidance schemes, and perhaps most importantly, the loss of faith in the federal tax system. The Senate Finance Committee went so far as to say: "Extensive shelter activity contributes to public concerns that the tax system is unfair and to the belief that tax is paid only by the naive and unsophisticated." The reason Congress had allowed tax shelters to exist in the first place was to encourage investment in certain areas in order to promote economic growth.

Example 6.1. Arthur Johnson, a corporate executive, had income of $275,000 during 1983 (before passive loss rules). He took advantage of the tax laws (legally) by purchasing a shopping center in January 1983. The price was $500,000. He paid $25,000 down and financed the balance over 20 years. Rental income averaged $3,500 a month, while payment on the $475,000 note was $6,000 a month. Maintenance, taxes, and repairs averaged $1,500 a month. Initially, it appears that Mr. Johnson was losing $4,000 a month ($3,500 − $6,000 − $1,500) during his first year of ownership ($48,000 a year). But after considering his tax bracket (50 percent) and depreciation (12 percent for 1983), his net cash flow actually increased by $5,000 for the year because of preferential tax rules:

Net Cash Flow Before Tax Benefit	$ (48,000)
Depreciation (12% × $500,000)	(60,000)
Principal Payment Adjustment *	2,000
Net Deductible Loss	$(106,000)
Times Tax Bracket	× .50
Tax Benefit	$ 53,000
Net Cash Flow Before Tax Benefit	(48,000)
Net Cash Flow	$ 5,000

* $2,000 of the note payments were applied to principal (*i.e.*, not deductible), all other monthly expenses were deductible.

Notice that the tax benefit in the preceding example was treated as an immediate cash inflow. It simply reduced the taxpayer's tax liability by the tax benefit amount, which, essentially, represented taxes that would have been paid on income from other sources, such as salary, dividends, interest, etc. When coupled with the possibility that the property could increase in value, this was a popular form of investment and an easy concept for tax shelter salesmen to sell. However, most such investments never provided a net cash flow as illustrated in the example.

Practically all tax shelters were formed as limited partnerships. Limited partnerships were used because they allowed losses and credits to be passed through to the partners' individual tax returns. A limited partner is a partner who is not personally liable for the debts of the partnership. More importantly, a limited partner can utilize deductions and/or credits that "flow through" from the partnership. Some examples of the activities tax shelter limited partnerships engaged in included equipment leasing, real estate, oil and gas, movie productions, cattle breeding, cattle feeding, and farming. Even though most tax shelters never made a profit, thousands of taxpayers bought into them for the sole purpose of avoiding income taxes. Thus, genuine economic value was rarely considered in making an investment decision to acquire an interest in a tax shelter activity.

The Tax Reform Act of 1986 significantly impacted such investment decisions with the passage of the passive activity rules. Code Sec. 469. *Essentially all limited partnership investments, rental properties, and businesses in which an owner does not materially participate have been affected.* The general rule is that losses arising from a passive activity are not deductible, except against income from a passive activity. The unused portion of the loss, however, is not lost but is suspended (i.e., carried over) until offset by passive income in a future tax year or until the entire activity is disposed of in a fully taxable transaction.

Example 6.2. Assume the same facts as in the preceding example, except that if Arthur Johnson purchased the shopping center in 1998, his investment would fall under the passive activity rules, which would allow no deduction (i.e., no tax benefit) for the loss in 1998. The entire disallowed loss would become a suspended loss until passive income is later received or he appropriately disposes of the rental property. For instance, if in 1999 the shopping center yields $25,000 in income, then the loss from 1998 would be used to offset the income and any unused balance of suspended loss would be carried over to 2000.

¶ 6125   AT-RISK RULES

Prior to the 1986 Act, Congress made a rather weak attempt to curb tax shelter abuse by enacting the at-risk provisions (Code Sec. 465) in 1976. The at-risk rules disallow losses that are in excess of an investor's amount at risk. In a general sense, at risk is the amount of investment that an investor could possibly lose. The rules apply to individuals as well as closely held corporations. An investor's amount at risk is computed as follows:

Cash invested
+   Adjusted basis of other property invested
+   Borrowings for which investor is personally liable
+   Borrowings for which investor has pledged collateral
+   Allocated portion of income
−   Allocated portion of losses
−   Withdrawals
=   Amount at risk

The formula does not indicate to what extent the allocated losses are deductible for tax purposes, because the amount at risk is reduced (but not below zero) regardless of the extent to which the losses are deductible. The deductible portion of any possible losses is calculated *after* applying the at-risk rules.

An investor is not at risk for nonrecourse borrowings, stop-loss arrangements, no-loss guarantees, or borrowings in which the lender has an interest (as in seller financing). Code Sec. 465. A nonrecourse loan is a loan that is secured by the property purchased, rather than the personal assets of the borrower (i.e., the borrower is not personally liable). A recourse loan, on the other hand, is one where the borrower is personally liable for repayment.

Example 6.3. Betty Smith gave $10,000 cash, pledged $10,000 for security of a partnership loan, and gave a computer with an adjusted basis of $5,000 for her interest in a limited partnership. Her amount at risk is $25,000. The activity allocated a $40,000 loss (passive loss) to her. Only $25,000 (the amount at risk) of the $40,000 loss can be used to offset income from other passive activities during the year. Since she is not at risk for the remaining $15,000, it is carried over into a future tax year until she becomes at risk, which would then free up this amount to be offset against passive income.

Example 6.4. Assume Betty Smith gave $10,000 cash and signed a nonrecourse note for property that the limited partnership was acquiring. Ms. Smith would only be at risk for her $10,000 cash investment, and, consequently, only $10,000 of the $40,000 could be used to offset income from other passive activities. The remaining $30,000 is carried over until she becomes at risk.

Generally, taxpayers are not considered at risk with regard to nonrecourse loans. However, a partner is considered to be at risk for certain *qualified* nonrecourse loans on real property. A qualified nonrecourse loan is one acquired from:

1.   a person who is actively and regularly engaged in the business of lending money, or

2.   any federal, state, or local government (including loans guaranteed by such governments) (Code Sec. 465(b)(6)(B))

An exception to this rule applies for loans acquired from:

1.   related parties,

2.   the seller of the property, or

3.   a person who receives a fee due to the taxpayer's investment in the property.

A partner would not be at risk for such loans. Code Sec. 49(a)(1)(D)(iv).

Because losses reduce the amount at risk, such losses usually may be recaptured if the investor's amount at risk is less than zero at the close of a taxable year. Code Sec. 465(e). Thus, when an individual's amount at risk drops below zero, the taxpayer will include in gross income the amount of the excess. A drop in at risk, for example, can occur when a debt arrangement is changed from recourse to nonrecourse.

Passive Activity Loss Rules

¶ 6201   APPLICATION OF RULES

The at-risk rules are still in effect and are applied before passive loss restrictions. Once the at-risk rules are satisfied, a passive loss can then be used in the following ways: offset passive income, offset other income (under certain conditions), and/or become suspended. Passive income and losses are "before AGI" items.

Example 6.5. Bob McKeown contributed $35,000 cash and signed a $15,000 nonrecourse note to invest in Limited Partnership A (LPA). He is at risk for $35,000 in the partnership. Bob is also at risk for $50,000 in Limited Partnership B (LPB). Both activities are considered to be passive activities. During the year, LPA experienced a loss and allocated to him his portion of the loss, $65,000. LPB had a better year and allocated $25,000 of income to Bob. Because Bob is at risk for only $35,000 for LPA, only $35,000 of the $65,000 loss is considered as a passive loss. As a result, $25,000 of the $35,000 passive loss from LPA can be used to offset the $25,000 of passive income (before AGI) from LPB. Ten thousand dollars ($35,000 − $25,000) of the passive loss from LPA is suspended under the passive loss rules. At the end of the year, Bob's amount at risk for LPA will be zero ($35,000 − $35,000).

The remaining $30,000 ($65,000 − $35,000) loss from LPA is carried over under the at-risk rules until Bob increases his amount at risk in LPA. Once Bob satisfies the at-risk rules, this amount will become a passive loss and may be used to offset future passive gains. Bob will be at risk for $75,000 ($50,000 + $25,000) for LPB at the end of the year.

Partnership	Initial Amount At Risk	Allocated Gain (Loss)	Passive Income (Loss)	Loss Carryover Under At-Risk Rules	Suspended Passive Loss	Ending Amount At Risk
A	$35,000	($65,000)	($35,000)	($30,000)	($10,000)	$ 0
B	$50,000	$25,000	$25,000	—	—	$75,000

If Bob had received $45,000 of passive income from LPB (instead of $25,000), his results would be different. He could offset the passive income with $35,000 of passive losses from LPA, resulting in $10,000 of net passive income, and have no suspended passive loss. His amount at risk for LPA is still zero and he still has a loss carryover under the at-risk rules of $30,000. His ending amount at risk for LPB would be $95,000 ($50,000 + $45,000).

Partnership	Initial Amount At Risk	Allocated Gain (Loss)	Passive Income (Loss)	Loss Carryover Under At-Risk Rules	Suspended Passive Loss	Ending Amount At Risk
A	$35,000	($65,000)	($35,000)	($30,000)	$0	$ 0
B	$50,000	$45,000	$45,000	—	—	$95,000

¶ 6205   CLASSIFICATION OF INCOME

Because of the passive activity rules, income is required to be classified as active, passive, or portfolio. Ordinarily, active income is attributable to the direct efforts of the taxpayer, such as salary, commissions, wages, etc. Passive income is income derived from a passive activity. Portfolio income is interest, dividends, annuities, and royalties not derived in the ordinary course of a trade or business. The gain from the sale of property that produces portfolio income (e.g., stocks and bonds) is also classified as portfolio income. Code Sec. 469(e). The reason for the classification is to keep separate the types of income that passive losses can offset. As previously mentioned, passive losses can only offset passive income and cannot be used as a deduction against active or portfolio income (except in certain instances). Similarly, tax credits from passive activities can only offset taxes incurred from passive income.

Portfolio income received by a limited partnership and allocated to the partners is not passive income, and the partners cannot offset the portfolio income by passive losses from this partnership or any other passive activity. Thus, limited partnerships that receive portfolio income and experience net income (or loss) from operations must separately allocate income (loss) generated from operations and portfolio income to its partners.

¶ 6211   DISALLOWANCE OF PASSIVE LOSSES AND CREDITS

For tax years after 1990, no passive activity losses or credits may be deducted against active and portfolio income. Interests in passive activities acquired by the taxpayer on or before October 22, 1986 (the date on which the Tax Reform Act of 1986 was enacted), were eligible for a special deduction and credit phaseout of losses for a five-year period. Code Sec. 469(m)(2). The applicable percentage was 65 percent (1987), 40 percent (1988), 20 percent (1989), 10 percent (1990), and 0 percent after 1990. Thus, after 1990, passive losses in excess of passive gains are not deductible and must be carried forward.

¶ 6215   SUSPENDED LOSSES

Generally, any loss or credit from a passive activity which is disallowed by the passive loss rules is treated as a deduction or credit allocable to such activity in the next taxable year. Code Sec. 469(b). Suspended losses can become deductible against future income from passive activities or against nonpassive income upon the fully taxable disposition of an entire interest. Keeping suspended losses for each passive activity separate is necessary in order to determine the amount of an activity's deductible portion of suspended loss whenever an event qualifying for the deduction occurs (e.g., a fully taxable disposition).

Example 6.6. Linda Helmsly owned the following passive activities during 1998 (all were acquired after 1986, and she was at risk for all losses):

Activity	Income/(Loss)	Suspended (Loss) *
ABC	$ 35,000	$ 0
XYZ	(45,000)	(20,000)
BBD	(60,000)	(80,000)
	$(70,000)	

* Suspended losses from previous years.

The amount of net loss experienced in 1998, $70,000, is not deductible but is suspended. It must be allocated, however, between all activities showing a loss for the year (XYZ and BBD):

Activity	Allocation	Suspended (Loss)	Total Suspended (Loss)
ABC	N/A	$ 0	$ 0
XYZ	$45,000/$105,000 × $70,000	(30,000)	(50,000)
BBD	$60,000/$105,000 × $70,000	(40,000)	(120,000)

APPLICATION OF THE AT-RISK AND PASSIVE LOSS RULES

Step 1.   Determine the amount at risk for each passive activity (before considering gain or loss for that year).

Step 2.   Determine whether each passive activity results in a gain or loss for the tax year.

Step 3.   If an activity results in a gain:

(a)   increase the amount at risk for that activity.

(b)   treat gain as passive gain.

Step 4.   If an activity results in a loss:

(a)   reduce the amount at risk for that activity (but not below zero) by the amount of the loss.

(b)   any excess losses are carried over under the at-risk rules.

(c)   treat losses (except for amounts carried over) as passive losses.

Step 5.   Add up all passive gains.

Step 6.   Add up all passive losses.

Step 7.   Reduce passive gains (but not below zero) by passive losses and any passive loss credits. Include any net passive gain in gross income.

Step 8.   Carry over excess passive losses as suspended passive losses.

(a)   If more than one activity results in a passive loss, allocate suspended passive losses between the activities in proportion to the amount of their passive losses.

(b)   In future tax years, use suspended passive losses to offset passive income.

¶ 6225   DISPOSITION OF A PASSIVE ACTIVITY

If a passive activity is disposed of in a fully taxable transaction, any losses (including suspended losses from prior years) may be recognized by the taxpayer in the year of disposition. Such losses can offset active and portfolio income (nonpassive income). However, losses from the sale of passive activities to related parties generally are not deductible. See Chapter 9.

The excess of the sum of Items 1 + 2 over 3 will be treated as a loss which is not from a passive activity (i.e., deductible against nonpassive income):

1.   Any loss from the activity for the tax year, including suspended losses from prior years, plus

2.   Any loss realized from the disposition of the activity, over

3.   Net income or gain from all passive activities (determined without regard to losses from the disposition or losses from the activity). Code Sec. 469(g)(1).

Passive activity interests that are capital assets and are appropriately disposed of are subject to the capital asset rules for losses (Code Sec. 1211) after applying the passive loss rules. See Chapter 11. A limited partnership interest held as an investment is a capital asset.

Example 6.7. Rob Williams had gross income of $125,000 in 1998 and owned the following passive activities during the year:

Activity	Gain/(Loss)	Suspended (Loss)
ZZZ	$15,000	$(50,000)
XXX........................	(10,000)	(28,000)
YYY	(22,500)	(45,000)

All activities were acquired after 1986, and Rob was at risk for all losses. He sold his entire interest in ZZZ in a fully taxable transaction. ZZZ was a limited partnership in which Rob was a limited partner. He acquired the limited partnership interest in 1987. The selling price was $22,000, while his basis in the interest was $55,000. The result is computed as follows:

Selling price	$ 22,000
Adjusted basis	(55,000)
Realized loss..	$(33,000)

The $50,000 of suspended losses will first offset the $15,000 gain from ZZZ, and the balance ($35,000) will be deductible against active and portfolio income. The $33,000 realized loss resulting from the sale of the limited partnership interest will become a long-term capital loss.

Death, Gift, and Other Transfers

If an interest in a passive activity is transferred by reason of death, suspended losses are deductible on a decedent's income tax return to the extent that the excess of the stepped-up basis in the hands of the transferee over the decedent's adjusted basis is less than the amount of suspended loss.

Example 6.8. Zeb McFarland died and left a passive activity to his nephew. Zeb's basis in the activity was $25,000, while the nephew's basis was "stepped up" to $40,000. Suspended losses amounted to $21,000. The amount of passive loss deduction that can offset nonpassive income is $6,000, the $21,000 suspended loss minus the $15,000 step-up in basis.

If an interest in a passive activity is transferred by gift, the suspended losses are not deductible but are added to the recipient's basis.

Example 6.9. Jennie Franklin gave her daughter a limited partnership interest in a real estate activity. Suspended losses amounted to $20,000. The mother's adjusted basis at the time of the gift was $30,000. The daughter's basis would be the mother's adjusted basis plus the amount of suspended losses, or $50,000 (assuming fair market value was greater than $30,000).

¶ 6231   TAXPAYERS AFFECTED BY PASSIVE LOSS RULES

The passive loss limitations apply to individuals, estates, trusts, closely held corporations, and personal service corporations. Code Sec.

469(a)(2). This list describes taxpayers that would otherwise be entitled to the tax benefits of losses or credits from a passive activity. Partnerships and S corporations are not included. Limitations on losses or credits from activities operated by these entities are passed through and applied at the level of the partners and shareholders, respectively.

Personal Service Corporations

The application of the passive activity loss rules to personal service corporations is intended to prevent taxpayers from sheltering personal service income simply by incorporating as a personal service corporation and acquiring passive activity investments at the corporate level. In general, a corporation is a personal service corporation if (1) it is a C corporation, (2) its principal activity is the performance of personal services, (3) the services are substantially performed by employee-owners, and (4) such employee-owners own more than 10 percent of the fair market value of the corporation's outstanding stock. Whether these qualifications are satisfied is determined during a testing period for the tax year, which is generally the corporation's prior tax year. Temp. Reg. § 1.469-1T(g)(2).

Closely Held Corporations

A closely held corporation's losses and credits from a passive activity may be limited if (1) it is a C corporation that is not a personal service corporation, and (2) more than 50 percent of its stock is owned directly or indirectly by (or for) not more than five individuals. Noting the distinction between taxpayers is worthwhile because closely held corporations are able to offset passive losses with net active income, but not portfolio income. Code Sec. 469(e)(2). Consequently, a closely held corporation is the only entity affected by the passive loss rules that can deduct losses from a passive activity that it owns.

> *Example 6.10.* Jasper Corporation, a closely held corporation, generated $150,000 of income from operations during the year. It also received passive losses of $200,000 and interest of $30,000. (Jasper Corporation was fully at risk for the amount of loss.) The corporation's taxable income is $30,000 because it can offset passive losses with active income, but not with portfolio income. The remaining $50,000 of passive losses will become suspended.

Oil and Gas Working Interests

A working interest which a taxpayer holds in oil and gas properties is not subject to the passive activity rules. Code Sec. 469(c)(3). The working interest cannot be held through any entity that limits the taxpayer's liability (e.g., limited partnership interest or stock in a corporation). A working interest is a working or operating mineral interest in any tract or parcel of land. Temp. Reg. § 1.469-1T(e)(4)(iv).

¶ 6235   MATERIAL PARTICIPATION

A passive activity is defined as "any activity which involves the conduct of a trade or business, and in which the taxpayer does not materially participate." Code Sec. 469(c)(1). Also included in the definition are rental activities, without regard to the extent of taxpayer participation. Temp. Reg. § 1.469-1T(e)(1)(ii). As a consequence, trade or business activities in which a taxpayer does materially participate are not passive activities. Nevertheless, rental of real estate properties is generally classified as a passive activity regardless of the level of participation.

"Material participation" requires a taxpayer to be involved in the operations of the activity on a regular, continuous, and substantial basis. Code Sec. 469(h)(1). When making this rule, Congress was aware that many taxpayers would accumulate suspended losses from tax shelter investments as a result of the passive loss rules. Moreover, some of these taxpayers might own profitable businesses that could be turned into passive activities (which would then be used to offset passive losses). The change from an active business to a passive activity could possibly be achieved by lowering a taxpayer's level of participation in the active business. The result of such maneuvering would impede the overall effectiveness of the passive loss provisions. Material participation, then, was devised to include virtually all "passive" business owners but at the same time exclude certain "active" business owners from being brought into the passive loss arena.

On the other hand, a business in which an individual materially participates is not a passive activity. Therefore, if the business experiences a loss, the loss will be deductible against all other types of income (passive, active, and/or portfolio) without regard to the passive loss restrictions. Additional guidance in making the determination as to who qualifies as a material participant is provided under the regulations by furnishing seven tests. Temp. Reg. § 1.469-5T(a). Thus, an individual will be treated as materially participating in an activity for the tax year if any of the following tests apply:

Test 1. The individual participates in the activity for more than 500 hours during the tax year.

Test 2. The individual's participation in the activity constitutes substantially all of the participation in such activity of all individuals (including individuals who are not owners) for the tax year.

Test 3. The individual participates in the activity for more than 100 hours during the tax year, and such individual's participation for the tax year is not less than the participation in the activity of any other individual (including nonowners) for the tax year.

Test 4. The activity is a "significant participation" activity for the tax year, and the individual's aggregate participation in all significant participation activities during such year exceeds 500 hours (see below).

Test 5. The individual materially participated in the activity for any five tax years, whether or not consecutive, during the 10 tax years that immediately preceded the tax year.

Test 6.   The activity is a personal service activity and the individual materially participated in the activity for any three tax years, whether or not consecutive, preceding the tax year.

Test 7.   Based on all of the facts and circumstances, the individual participates in the activity on a regular, continuous, and substantial basis during the tax year.

Also note that in determining whether a taxpayer materially participates, the participation of a taxpayer's spouse will be taken into account. Code Sec. 469(h)(5).

Significant Participation

An individual is treated as significantly participating in an activity for a tax year if and only if the individual participates in the activity for more than 100 hours during the year. A significant participating activity is a trade or business in which an individual significantly participates, but not to the extent of material participation as determined by the other six tests. Temp. Reg. § 1.469-5T(c). In other words, an individual may have ownership interests in several businesses, but participates infrequently (less than material participation in each). If the hours of participation for each activity exceed 100, and the total number of hours in all such businesses exceeds 500, then the individual is treated as materially participating in all such businesses.

Example 6.11. David Jones owns an interest in six businesses. His level of participation is as follows:

Activity	Hours
A	100
B	125
C	90
D	135
E	140
F	100
Total	690

David is not a material participant in any one of the activities above. In addition, he is not significantly participating in activities A, C, and F (not more than 100 hours of participation in each). The aggregate amount of participation in the significant participating activities is 400 hours from activities B, D, and E. Therefore, David is not treated as materially participating under Test 4, and *all activities* fall under the passive loss rules.

Example 6.12. Assume the same facts as in Example 6.11, except that activity C had 105 hours of participation. Because the number of participation hours is in excess of 100, activity C is a significant participation activity. This brings the aggregate number of hours in significant participating activities to 505. David would now be considered to be a material participant, and therefore only activities A and F would fall under the passive loss rules.

Limited Partners

Limited partners, by the very nature of their relationship to the partnership, are not considered to be material participants. As a general rule, limited partners are not involved in the day-to-day management of partnership affairs. However, if limited partners participate in the activity, they may become material participants in the partnership if one of the following applies:

1. The limited partner holds a general partnership interest at all times during the partnership's tax year ending with or within the individual's tax year (or the portion of the partnership's tax year during which the individual—directly or indirectly— owns such limited partnership interest).

2. The limited partner participates more than 500 hours (Test 1).

3. The limited partner participates for any five years during the 10 tax years immediately preceding the tax year at issue (Test 5).

4. For a personal service activity, the limited partner materially participated in the activity for any three years preceding the year at issue (Test 6). Temp. Reg. § 1.469-5T(e).

Participation Standard

The Internal Revenue Service considers an individual to be participating when any work is done by such individual in connection with an activity in which the individual owns an interest at the time the work is done. Individuals are not considered as participating in the following situations:

1. Work not customarily done by an owner if one of the principal purposes for the work is to avoid the disallowance of any loss or credit from such activity under the passive loss rules.

2. Work done in the individual's capacity as an investor (such as studying and reviewing financial statements of the activity, preparing or compiling summaries or analyses of the finances or operations of the activity for the individual's own use, and monitoring the finances or operations in a nonmanagerial role). Temp. Reg. § 1.469-5T(f).

¶ 6261 IDENTIFYING AN ACTIVITY

Determining the scope of a particular activity is important for identifying whether a taxpayer has two or more separate activities or one activity having two or more undertakings. Two situations in which this determination is vital occur when material participation is involved and upon disposition of the activity. For example, if an owner is involved in an activity that has two separate and distinct undertakings, such as rental property and retail sales, then a determination must be made as to whether the two undertakings will be treated as one activity or two activities. If the sales/rental business is treated as one activity, then the individual will only have to satisfy the material participation rules for one activity. A disposition of one of the undertakings, however, will not qualify as a "disposition of an entire interest" for purposes of recognizing a loss against nonpassive income. But if the sales/rental business is treated as two separate activities, then the material participation requirements must be met for each separate activity. In addition, because each undertaking is a separate activity, a disposition of an entire interest is allowed if one of the undertakings (now an activity) is sold.

Proposed Regulations were issued in 1992 which provide guidance for grouping a taxpayer's trade or business activities and rental activities under the passive activity rules. The regulations define trade or business activities as activities that:

1. Involve the conduct of a trade or business (within the meaning of Code Sec. 162);

2. Are conducted in anticipation of the commencement of a trade or business; or

3. Involve research or experimental expenditures that are deductible under Code Sec. 174 (or would be deductible if the taxpayer adopted the method described in Code Sec. 174(a)). Prop. Reg. § 1.469-4(b)(1).

Rental activities are defined as activities constituting rental activities within the meaning of Temporary Regulation § 1.469-1T(e)(3). They are discussed in detail in the next section of this chapter.

Under the Regulations, a taxpayer may treat one or more trade or business activities or rental activities as a single activity. To qualify for such treatment, the activities must constitute an appropriate economic unit for determining gain or loss for purposes of Code Sec. 469.

A facts and circumstances approach is used to determine whether or not various activities may be treated as a single activity. Any reasonable method of applying the relevant facts and circumstances may be used for this purpose. Certain factors are considered the most important in determining whether separate activities constitute an appropriate economic unit. However, not all factors need be present. They are:

1. similarities and differences in types of businesses;

2. the extent of common control;

3. the extent of common ownership;

4. geographical location; and

5. interdependence between activities.

Interdependence between activities may exist if firms buy or sell goods to one another, have customers in common, provide products or services together, share employees, or are accounted for on the same set of books and records. Prop. Reg. § 1.469-4(c)(1) and (2).

Example 6.13. Ernie operates a bookstore and a restaurant in a shopping mall in Atlanta and a bookstore and a restaurant in Miami. Depending upon how Ernie applies the facts and circumstances test, he may end up with one to four activities for purposes of the passive activity rules. Both bookstores and restaurants could be grouped into one activity. Alternatively, he may have two separate activities, one constituting the bookstores and one constituting the restaurants. He may also have an Atlanta activity and a Miami activity. Finally, he may treat each business as a separate activity. Prop. Reg. § 1.469-4(c)(3)

Example 6.14. Ted owns a large retail business. He is the sole proprietor of a firm that provides bookkeeping services to businesses. The retail business is the primary client of the bookkeeping firm. Because the two activities are under common control, Ted could treat the retail activity and the bookkeeping activity as a single activity. Prop. Reg. § 1.469-4(c)(3).

The Regulations generally prohibit the grouping of rental activities with nonrental trade or business activities. However, such groupings are permissible if the income generated by one activity is insubstantial in relation to the income generated by the other activity. No guidance is provided in the Proposed Regulations on the meaning of the word "insubstantial" in this context. Prop. Reg. § 1.469-4(d). But prior temporary regulations indicate that an activity providing 20 percent or less of the total revenue of two activities may be considered insubstantial.

Two separate rental activities, one involving personal property and the other involving real property, may not be grouped into one activity. An exception to this rule arises when personal property is rented in connection with real property. Prop. Reg. § 1.469-4(e).

Limited partners in partnerships are generally prohibited from grouping the limited partnership activity with other activities. However, such groupings are permitted with other activities in which the taxpayer is a limited partner and which carry on the same type of business. If the taxpayer is not a limited partner in the second activity, the grouping may still be achieved by applying the facts and circumstances test. Prop. Reg. § 1.469-4(f)(1) and (2).

Activities that have been grouped under any of the above criteria may not be regrouped in subsequent taxable years unless it can be demonstrated that the original grouping was clearly inappropriate. Alternatively, a material change in the facts and circumstances (such as a change in ownership) may occur that would justify a regrouping of activities. Prop. Reg. § 1.469-4(g).

The Commissioner has the authority to regroup a taxpayer's activities. This will occur if the grouping does not result in appropriate economic units under the facts and circumstances test and one of the primary purposes of the taxpayer's grouping is to avoid the passive loss rules. Prop. Reg. § 1.469-4(h).

Example 6.15. Bob and three friends each own separate retail businesses, and they invested in limited partnerships years ago that generate annual passive losses. Bob and his friends acquire limited partner interests in a partnership created to provide janitorial services to their respective retail businesses. The janitorial service is run by a general partner selected by Bob and the others. The janitorial service is set up to insure that it generates a profit. The four limited partners plan to treat the janitorial service as a separate activity and use losses from their other limited partnership to offset the net profit from the janitorial service.

Applying the facts and circumstances test, each partner's interest in the janitorial service and the partner's respective business would constitute one appropriate economic activity, rather than two. In addition, it is obvious that the partners created the janitorial service and treated it as a separate activity in order to circumvent the passive loss rules. Hence, the Commissioner would likely require the partners to treat their respective interests in the janitorial service and their individual businesses as one activity instead of two. Penalties may also be levied against them under Code Sec. 6662. Prop. Reg. § 1.469-4(h).

Activities carried on by a partnership or S corporation are first grouped by the partnership or S corporation by applying these rules. After the activities are grouped by the partnership or corporation, the individual partner or shareholder then groups the activities with other activities, as appropriate, in which the partner or shareholder is personally involved. Prop. Reg. § 1.469-4(j).

Under certain circumstances, a taxpayer who disposes of a substantial part of an activity during a taxable year may treat the part disposed of as a separate activity. To do so, the taxpayer must establish the following with reasonable certainty:

1. The amount of disallowed deductions and credits carried over from prior years that are allocable to that part of the activity for the taxable year; and

2. The amount of gross income and any other deductions and credits allocable to that part of the activity for the taxable year. Prop. Reg. § 1.469-4(k).

¶ 6273 RENTAL ACTIVITIES

An activity is a rental activity if during the year: (1) tangible property held in connection with the activity is used by customers or is held for use by customers, and (2) gross income attributable to the conduct of the activity represents amounts paid principally for the use of the property. Temp. Reg. § 1.469-1T(e)(3). Generally, any rental activity is a passive activity, without regard to material participation. Code Sec. 469(c)(2) and (4).

The following tests and examples are exceptions to rental activity status (i.e., if any test is met, then the activity is not a rental activity);

1. The average period of customer use for rental property is seven days or less.

   Example 6.16. George Lee owns a home video movie rental store. The average period of customer use is two days. The store is not a rental activity.

2. The average period of customer use is 30 days or less, and significant personal services are provided by or on behalf of the owner in connection with making the property available for use by customers. Significant personal services include services performed by individuals. In making the determination, factors such as the frequency with which the service is provided, type and amount of labor required, and the value of the services relative to the amount charged for the use of property will be weighed.

    Example 6.17. Monica Sellers owns a computer leasing service. The average period of customer use is more than seven days but less than 30 days. Pursuant to the lease agreements, skilled technicians and programming consultants employed by her maintain and service malfunctioning equipment as well as implement programs for no additional charge. The value of the maintenance, repair, and implementation services exceeds 50 percent of the amount charged for the use of the equipment. Significant personal services are provided and the activity is not a passive activity.

3. Extraordinary personal services are provided by or on behalf of the owner in connection with making the property available for use by customers. Extraordinary personal services are services provided to customers so that use of the property is actually incidental to the receipt of such services.

    Example 6.18. The use of a hospital's boarding facilities generally is incidental to the receipt of personal services provided by the hospital's medical staff. The hospital's boarding operations are not rental activities.

4. The rental of such property is treated as incidental to a nonrental activity of the taxpayer.

    Example 6.19. Bob Townson owns 3,000 acres of unimproved land for the principal purpose of realizing gain from appreciation. In order to defray the cost of carrying the land, he leases it to a rancher who allows cattle to graze on it. If the gross rental income is less than 2 percent of the lesser of the land's fair market value or the adjusted basis (incidental to the nonrental activity), then the land is not a rental activity. Assuming that the land is worth $600,000 and his adjusted basis is $450,000, the rent must be less than $9,000 (2% × $450,000) in order for it to be incidental.

5. The taxpayer customarily makes the property available during defined business hours for nonexclusive use by various customers.

    Example 6.20. Operating a golf course that is available during prescribed business hours for nonexclusive use by various golfers is not a rental activity.

6. The taxpayer provides property for use in an activity conducted by a partnership, S corporation, or joint venture in

which the taxpayer owns an interest, but the activity is not a rental activity. Temp. Reg. § 1.469-1T(e)(3)(B)(ii).

Example 6.21. Patricia Bowers is a partner in a law firm. She provides to the firm the use of expensive, sophisticated audio equipment for the purpose of analyzing a case. The equipment is unloaded in the firm's office and used for a specified period of time for a fee. The law firm is not engaged in a rental activity. None of her distributive share of partnership income will be considered as income from a rental activity.

TAX PLANNING POINTER

Even though an activity is not classified as a rental activity, it may still fall into passive activity status if the material participation requirements are not met.

¶ 6281   RENTAL REAL ESTATE ACTIVITIES

An individual is allowed to avoid the passive loss limitations for all rental real estate activities in which the individual *actively participates.* A $25,000 offset against nonpassive income can be attained if the taxpayer's modified adjusted gross income (AGI computed without regard to any passive activity loss, taxable Social Security benefits, or deductions for IRA contributions) is $100,000 or less. Code Sec. 469(i). The offset is before AGI.

Example 6.22. Alex Alexander owned three rental houses and had modified AGI of $77,500 for the year. The combined loss of the rental houses was $28,000. He was an active participant in the management of the rental properties. Alex qualifies for the $25,000 offset and will be able to reduce nonpassive income by that amount. The remaining $3,000 loss will become a suspended loss and will be allocated among all properties experiencing a loss.

Active participation, as opposed to material participation, need not be regular, continuous, and substantial. Active participation by an individual can include making some of the management decisions (such as approving prospective tenants, setting the terms of rental arrangements, and approving the costs of repairs or capital improvements). An outside property management firm, then, can be hired to provide appropriate management services on a day-to-day basis without jeopardizing active participation status. In addition, a taxpayer must hold a 10 percent or more interest in the property at all times during the year to be an active participant. Generally, a limited partner does not actively participate in a rental real estate activity that is owned through an interest in a limited partnership. As in the case of material participation, the participation of a taxpayer's spouse will be taken into account in determining whether the taxpayer actively participated.

Single individuals and married taxpayers filing jointly can qualify for the maximum $25,000 amount. Married individuals who live apart from their spouses at all times during the year can qualify for $12,500 each. Married individuals who do not live apart for the entire year and file separately cannot qualify for any part of the $25,000 offset.

The maximum level of modified AGI is $100,000 in qualifying for the full $25,000 ($12,500 for qualified married individuals filing separately) deduction. However, when modified AGI exceeds $100,000, the excess is subject to a phaseout of the full offset: For every dollar of modified AGI in excess of $100,000, the $25,000 ($12,500) offset is reduced by 50 cents (or 50 percent of the excess). Thus, the $25,000 offset is fully phased out at a modified AGI of $150,000.

Example 6.23. Ron Reingold owned two rental properties during the year and actively participated in the management of the properties. His modified AGI was $140,000. Ron's loss from the rental activities is $10,000. Ron is entitled to a $5,000 offset. Ron's deduction is limited to the $5,000 offset, and the remaining $5,000 becomes a suspended loss, figured as follows:

Modified AGI	$140,000
Maximum level allowed	(100,000)
Excess	$ 40,000
Excess	$ 40,000
Times reduction %	× .50
Offset reduction	$ 20,000
Maximum offset	$ 25,000
Offset reduction	(20,000)
Offset after phaseout	$ 5,000

Revenue Reconciliation Act of 1993 Changes to Benefit Real Estate Professionals

Additional relief was provided by the Revenue Reconciliation Act of 1993 for individuals and closely held C corporations that materially participate in rental real estate activities. After 1993, provided certain requirements are met, losses and credits from rental real estate activities will not be subject to the passive loss limitations. These requirements are designed to demonstrate that the taxpayer is a material participant in the activity, and commits a minimum amount of time, on an annual basis, to the activity.

Individuals are eligible if:

1. More than half of the personal services they perform during the year are for real property trades or business;
2. They are material participants in the real estate trade or business; and
3. They perform more than 750 hours of service per year in the real estate activities.

For closely held C corporations to qualify:

1. The corporation must materially participate in rental real estate activities; and

2. The corporation must derive more than 50 percent of its gross receipts for the taxable year from such activities.

The criteria for determining material participation are the same as under previous law. Furthermore, as under prior law, a limited partner in a limited partnership is generally not considered to be a material participant in the partnership.

These changes in the law were intended to benefit real estate professionals, those who commit the majority of their time to performing real estate activities. Thus, the average passive investor in such activities will not qualify for relief under these provisions.

However, a couple filing jointly could benefit from the new rules if at least one spouse satisfies the requirements. For example, one spouse may work as a real estate broker or as a real estate leasing agent and the other spouse could own rental property. Losses incurred on the rental property may be treated as losses from an activity in which the taxpayer materially participates (i.e., not as passive losses) if the real estate broker spouse satisfies the new requirements.

Example 6.24. During 1998, Beth Miller participated in the following personal service activities: 800 hours as a personal estate planner, 450 hours in rental real estate activities, and 600 hours as a real estate broker. Beth devoted more than one-half of her personal services to real property trades or businesses, and her material participation in those real estate activities exceeded 750 hours. Hence, any loss incurred by Beth in either real estate activity will not be subject to the passive loss rules. She will be able to offset any losses from either real estate activity against active or portfolio income.

¶ 6287 CHANGE OF ACTIVITY STATUS

Under the passive activity rules, it is quite possible for an activity to change from passive to nonpassive. For example, an individual may not materially participate in a business for a previous tax year, but in later years may become a material participant. Thus, while the taxpayer was not a material participant, the business was a passive activity. Then when the taxpayer becomes a material participant, circumstances would appear to terminate the application of passive activity rules. A passive activity could become a "former passive activity" if any of the following apply:

1. The taxpayer qualifies as a material participant.

2. The activity no longer qualifies as a trade or business or rental activity.

Example 6.25. Fred Manson's real estate activities consisted of five rental properties located on a 25-acre tract. For each rental property, an acre was carved out of the larger tract and was sold last year, leaving Fred with 20 acres of unproductive land. His real estate activities no longer qualify as a rental activity for the current year and, therefore, will be characterized as a former passive activity.

Generally, the passive loss rules do not apply to a former passive activity, except for the former passive activity's suspended losses. A former passive activity's suspended losses will continue to be suspended, but can be offset against (1) passive income from other passive activities or (2) nonpassive income from the former passive activity. Code Sec. 469(f).

Example 6.26. Sally Dennison was not a material participant for the past few years in SSS, a partnership. The partnership was engaged in the business of selling, constructing, maintaining, and repairing fireplaces, fireplace equipment, and chimneys. Sally became a partner in the business during 1990, and her share of allocated losses for 1990–1997 was $55,000. Because she owned no other passive activities, the $55,000 was a suspended loss. In 1998, she became a material participant, and SSS significantly improved its operating position. Her share of the net income amounted to $29,500 for the year, which is now characterized as nonpassive income. The $55,000 suspended loss will offset the $29,500 of nonpassive income from SSS, while the remaining $25,500 continues to be suspended.

KEYSTONE PROBLEM

Kim Boles, single and 38 years old, owned the following passive activities during 1998:

Activity	1998 Gain/(Loss)	Acquired
XYZ	($10,000)	10/05/86
LMN	($12,500)	06/22/87
TUV	$11,000	09/01/88

She was the sole proprietor of a small business that had gross revenues of $35,000 and expenses of $72,000. She participated in the business 2,000 hours. The business had a computer stolen from its office. The computer's basis was $12,000, and its fair market value was $7,500 at the time of the theft. The amount of the theft is not included in expenses as stated above.

Kim also owned a condo in Vail, Colorado. She used it 17 days for personal purposes and rented it 150 days. Gross rentals were $1,300, while all expenses other than interest and taxes were $1,700. Interest and taxes amounted to $6,500.

Kim received $15,000 salary from a part-time job, received $1,500 in dividends, and had total itemized deductions of $3,000. Compute Kim's taxable income for 1998 and any other tax consequences that are appropriate.

Business and Investment Losses

¶ 6301   BUSINESS CASUALTY AND THEFT LOSSES

Business and investment casualty losses which receive similar tax treatment are discussed in this section. Personal casualty losses are reviewed in greater detail at ¶ 7501.

The following losses can be deducted by an individual taxpayer (Code Sec. 165(c)):

1.   Losses incurred in a trade or business;

2.   Losses incurred in any transaction entered into for profit though not connected with a trade or business; or

3.   Losses of property not connected with a trade or business, if such losses arise from fire, storm, shipwreck, or other casualty, or from theft.

Casualty losses usually are losses from fire, storm, or other catastrophe. Theft losses are losses arising from robbery, embezzlement, or larceny. Reg. § 1.165-8(d). Generally, all casualty and theft losses are deductible if incurred in a trade or business or in connection with an investment with the exception of losses caused by a taxpayer's willful act or willful negligence. Reg. § 1.165-7(a)(3)(i).

Proper Year of Deduction

A casualty loss is normally deductible in the year it occurs. If a casualty loss is incurred in an area designated as a disaster area by the President of the United States, the taxpayer can elect to deduct the casualty loss in the tax year preceding the year of the loss. The intent behind permitting a taxpayer to deduct a disaster area casualty loss in the tax year preceding the loss is to lessen the immediate tax burden on the taxpayer and, thereby, lessen the financial burden related to the casualty loss.

Example 6.27. Greenwood Paper Co. incurred a casualty loss of $10,000 in 1998. The $10,000 loss is normally deductible on Greenwood's 1998 income tax return. Because the casualty occurred in an area designated as a disaster area by the President of the United States, Greenwood may elect to deduct the casualty loss on its 1997 tax return. Since the 1997 tax return was already filed, an amended return would be filed for 1997 to claim a tax refund.

No casualty loss can be taken in the year of loss if a reasonable prospect exists that full reimbursement of the loss from insurance or other source will be received in some future tax year. Reg. § 1.165-1(d)(2)(i). The casualty loss deduction is limited to the actual expected loss after expected insurance reimbursement. If the actual insurance reimbursement is less than the amount anticipated in past tax years, the difference can be deducted as a casualty loss deduction in the year the claim is settled.

A theft loss is different from a casualty loss in that a theft loss is deductible in the year the theft is discovered (which may not necessarily be the same as the year of theft). As with casualty losses, a theft loss deduction is limited to the actual expected loss after expected reimbursement. If the reimbursement is less than the amount anticipated in past tax years, the difference can be deducted in the year the claim is settled.

Computation of Deduction

A deduction resulting from the *partial destruction* of business property is limited to the lesser of the following:

1. The adjusted basis of the casualty property, or
2. The decline in fair market value of the casualty property.

Any insurance or other form of compensation will reduce the amount deductible. If such property is *completely destroyed or stolen,* the deductible loss is the adjusted basis of the property less any reimbursement (regardless of decline in the fair market value).

As a general rule, if reimbursement is less than the property's adjusted basis, then no gain can be realized. If reimbursement is less than adjusted basis but more than the amount of loss (computed using decline in FMV), then a taxpayer experiences neither a gain nor a loss.

Example 6.28. The following casualty and theft losses occurred at Turnkey Construction Company during 1998:

| | | Fair Market Value | | |
Event	Adjusted Basis	Before Casualty	After Casualty	Insurance Reimburse.
1. Stolen Equip.	$12,000	$ 6,000	$ 0	$ 6,000
2. Fire—Bldg.	$77,000	$95,000	$45,000	$35,000
3. Wreck—Truck	$21,000	$18,500	$10,000	$10,000

The loss deduction for each casualty and theft is figured as follows:

1. Stolen equipment (theft loss—treated the same way as complete casualty loss)

Adjusted basis	$12,000
Less: Insurance	6,000
Theft loss deduction	$ 6,000

2. Fire in building (partial business casualty—lesser of adjusted basis or decline in fair market value)

Decline in FMV	$50,000
Less: Insurance	35,000
Casualty loss deduction	$15,000

3. Wrecked truck (partial business casualty with insurance proceeds greater than amount of loss)

Decline in FMV	$ 8,500
Less: Insurance	10,000
Net	$(1,500)

The net amount of $1,500 is not a realized gain because the property's adjusted basis was $21,000 (the formula used to compute realized gain is insurance proceeds less adjusted basis, which would provide a $11,000 loss). On the other hand, the difference between the property's adjusted basis and insurance proceeds ($11,000 loss) is not a deductible loss because a partial casualty loss deduction requires the lesser of adjusted basis or decline in FMV in determining the amount of loss. Thus, a partial casualty where insurance proceeds are greater than the amount of loss yields neither a gain nor a loss (because the property's adjusted basis is greater than the insurance proceeds).

In some instances, however, a casualty or theft may result in a taxpayer realizing a gain. This could occur when the insurance coverage, which is normally based on fair market value, exceeds the cost basis of the property (i.e., insurance proceeds less adjusted basis equals realized gain).

Basis Adjustment

Whenever a taxpayer has a partial or complete casualty, the following items will reduce the property's adjusted basis if there was no gain realized:

1. Amount of reimbursement

2. Amount of deductible loss

Example 6.29. Jack Caldwell's business office was partially destroyed by a tornado. His adjusted basis in the building was $210,000, and the decline in FMV was $150,000. Insurance proceeds amounted to $100,000. Mr. Caldwell's adjusted basis in the property is computed as follows:

Decline in FMV	$150,000
Less: Insurance	100,000
Deductible loss	$ 50,000
Adjusted basis before casualty	$210,000
Less: Insurance	100,000
Less: Deductible loss	50,000
Adjusted basis after casualty	$ 60,000

In determining a casualty property's decline in value, appraisals establishing the property's fair market value before the casualty as well as after the casualty are important evidence for defending the amount of a casualty loss deduction. The cost of repairs to restore the casualty property to its condition before the casualty may also be sufficient evidence to indicate the amount of the loss deduction. Reg. § 1.165-1(d)(2)(ii).

¶ 6331   NET OPERATING LOSSES (NOLs)

Prior to the Taxpayer Relief Act of 1997, a business that had a net operating loss in one taxable year could carry the loss back to offset taxable income in the three preceding tax years or carry the loss forward to offset future taxable income for up to 15 years. Code Sec. 172.

For tax years beginning after August 5, 1997, the NOL carryback period is shortened to two years, and the NOL carryforward period is extended to 20 years. (Special carryback rules exist in relation to: (1) real estate investment trusts that do not receive carrybacks; (2) specified liability losses that are subject to a ten-year carryback; (3) excess interest losses that do not receive carrybacks; and (4) corporate capital losses that are not affected by the changes.)

Further, the three-year carryback period is retained for the portion of the NOL that relates to casualty and theft losses of individual taxpayers and to NOLs that are attributable to Presidentially declared disasters *and* are incurred by taxpayers engaged in farming or by a small business (gross receipts of $5 million or less for a three-tax-year period).

Example 6.30. Able Box Company has a net operating loss of $50,000 in 1998. The loss can be carried back to offset previous taxable income in 1996 and 1997. If any of the 1998 net operating loss remains after being carried back two years, the remainder can be carried forward to offset future taxable income for up to 20 years (1999–2018).

The objective of the net operating loss deduction is to increase tax fairness regarding the taxation of business income. A 12-month tax accounting period is an arbitrary period of time to tax business enterprises. Business affairs cannot be arranged into arbitrary 12-month periods. In order to alleviate the arbitrariness of a 12-month accounting period, the net operating loss deduction allows a business to offset tax losses against taxable income over a longer period of time which would normally include an entire business cycle of up and down periods.

The net operating loss deduction is available only for losses connected with a trade or business. An excess of nonbusiness and personal deductions over nonbusiness and personal income, with the exception of personal casualty and theft losses, is not eligible for NOL treatment. Personal casualty and theft losses, however, are considered to be business losses for purposes of computing the net operating loss deduction. The three-year carryback period is retained for the portion of the NOL that relates to casualty and theft losses of individual taxpayers.

Carryback and Carryforward Procedures

A business incurring a net operating loss in a taxable year can carry the loss back two years and forward 20 years. The net loss shown on a taxpayer's return usually requires adjustment in several ways before becoming a net operating loss. A business can elect to forgo the NOL carryback and carry it forward only.

TAX PLANNING POINTER

In deciding whether to carry a net operating loss back or to just carry it forward, the taxpayer has to analyze the advantages and disadvantages of each approach. A carryback results in an immediate tax refund. Due to the time value of money, it is advantageous to forgo a carryback in favor of a carryforward only when the estimated marginal tax rate to be applied to future income is expected to be substantially higher than the tax rate which applied to the income subject to the carryback.

If a net operating loss is carried back, it must be carried back two years first. Next, if any NOL remains it is carried forward to the next year (in other words, back one year). Then if any balance remains, it is carried forward until used up or lost because of the passage of time.

Example 6.31. Able Box Company has a net operating loss in 1998. If Able elects to carry back the NOL, it must carry back the loss to 1996. If any NOL remains, then the balance is applied against 1997 income and so on until it is used up or expires.

Taxpayers are required to file amended returns for the tax years in which they carry back net operating losses. The operating loss deduction is a deduction for adjusted gross income. Certain itemized deductions which are limited by adjusted gross income such as medical expenses and certain miscellaneous itemized deductions may have to be recomputed in the carryback year due to the change in adjusted gross income caused by the inclusion of the NOL. Charitable contributions are excluded from recomputation due to the carryback of a NOL. Code Sec. 170(b).

Computation of Net Operating Loss

The term "net operating loss" is defined as the "excess of deductions over gross income." Code Sec. 172(c). This excess of deductions over gross income is subject to modifications which limit the net operating loss to only business losses. A loss reported on a tax return by an individual taxpayer with business income is modified in the following ways in order to determine a net operating loss deduction:

Taxable Income/Loss

- \+   Any NOL deduction from another year
- \+   Deductions for personal and dependency exemptions
- \+   Nonbusiness capital losses exceeding nonbusiness capital gains
- \+   Nonbusiness deductions in excess of nonbusiness income
- =   Net operating loss

Nonbusiness deductions include all itemized deductions (less personal casualty and theft losses and unreimbursed employee business expenses) plus self-employed retirement plan contributions. Nonbusiness income is all income not derived from a trade or business, such as dividends, interest, and nonbusiness capital gains. Salary and wages are considered to be trade or business income for purposes of computing an NOL.

Example 6.32. Larry Watkins owns and operates a pizza parlor. In 1998, Larry had the following income and deductions listed on his individual tax return.

Business income	$45,000	
Salary from second job	15,000	
Interest	5,000	
Dividends	2,000	
Long-term capital gain (LTCG)	1,000	$68,000

Less:

Business deductions	$70,000	
Personal exemption	2,700	
Itemized deductions (included $10,000 personal casualty)	19,000	91,700
Taxable income		($23,700)

Larry's net operating loss for 1998 is computed as follows:

Taxable income (negative amount)			($23,700)
Add:			
Personal exemption		$2,700	
Nonbusiness deductions in excess of nonbusiness income:			
Itemized deductions	$19,000		
Less: Personal casualty	10,000		
Nonbusiness deductions	$ 9,000		
Less: Nonbusiness income			
Interest	5,000		
Dividends	2,000		
LTCG	1,000	1,000	
			3,700
Net operating loss deduction			($20,000)

If only the "business-related" items were considered, then the NOL could be figured as follows:

Business income	$45,000	
Salary from second job	15,000	
Total business income		$60,000
Business deductions	$70,000	
Personal casualty loss	10,000	
Total business deductions		$80,000
Net operating loss deduction		($20,000)

Recomputation of Tax Liability in Carryback Year

After the net operating loss is computed for the tax year in which the loss is incurred, the loss is then carried back two years to the appropriate tax year unless an election is made to only carry the loss forward. As previously mentioned, adjustments may have to be made for items relying on adjusted gross income in determining their deduction.

If including the net operating loss deduction in the carryback year results in a tax loss in the carryback year, required adjustments have to be made to the tax loss to determine the amount of net operating loss deduction that can be carried forward to the next year. The required adjustments are similar to the adjustments discussed previously which were required to determine the original amount of the net operating loss.

¶ 6345   HOBBY LOSSES

Special rules apply to expenses and losses incurred in pursuing an activity not engaged in for profit. Hobby losses are generally deductible only to the extent of income produced by the activity. Under Code Sec. 183, expenses that are otherwise deductible under the Code without regard to the existence of a business or profit motive (taxes, interest, casualty losses, etc.) are still deductible regardless of the amount of hobby income. However, such deductions reduce the amount of hobby income available to offset other hobby deductions. Other hobby expenses are deductible in an amount equal to the excess of hobby income over deductions otherwise allowable without regard to profit motive.

In determining whether an activity is engaged in for profit, reference is made to objective standards, taking into account the facts and circumstances of each case. Although a reasonable expectation of profit is not required, the circumstances should indicate that the taxpayer entered into, or continued, the activity with the objective of making a profit.

Among the factors considered in determining whether activities are engaged in for profit are (Reg. § 1.183-2(b)):

1. The taxpayer's history of income or losses with respect to the activity.

2. The amount of occasional profits, if any, which are earned.

3. The cause of the losses.

4. The success of the taxpayer in carrying on other similar or dissimilar activities.

5. The financial status of the taxpayer.

6. The time and effort expended by the taxpayer in carrying on the activity.

7. The expertise of the taxpayer or advisors.

8. The manner in which the taxpayer carries on the activity.

9. Expectation of profit by the taxpayer.

10. Expectation that assets used in the activity may appreciate in value.

11. Elements of personal pleasure or recreation.

If any activity is not engaged in for profit, deductions are allowable in the following order and only to the following extent (Reg. § 1.183-1(b)(1)):

1. Amounts deductible without regard to whether the activity giving rise to such amounts was engaged in for profit are allowable in full. Examples of these expenses include interest under Code Sec. 163 and realty taxes under Code Sec. 164.

2. Amounts deductible if the activity had been engaged in for profit, but only if the deduction does not result in an adjustment to the basis of property. Such deductions are allowed only to the extent the gross income of the activity exceeds the deduction under (1).

3. Amounts which result in an adjustment to the basis of property are deductible only to the extent that income exceeds the deductions allowed under (1) and (2). Deductions falling within this category include such items as depreciation, partial losses with respect to property, partially worthless debts, amortization, and amortizable bond premiums. If such expenses exceed the remaining hobby income, then the deductible amount (equal to remaining hobby income) is prorated among such properties in the ratio of the bases of all property. Basis of the property is reduced only by the amount actually deductible under Code Sec. 183.

The deduction for the allowed hobby expenses is an itemized deduction subject to the 2 percent floor on miscellaneous itemized deductions. For example, the feed expense incurred by a person who earns hobby income from the breeding, training, and showing of dogs is deductible only to the extent that the deduction, when aggregated with other miscellaneous deductions, exceeds 2 percent of the taxpayer's adjusted gross income. Hobby expenses that are deductible without reference to whether they are incurred in an activity designed to produce income, such as certain taxes, remain fully deductible.

Example 6.33. Gene Allison operates a fishing boat during three months of the year and is not engaged in this activity for profit. He used the boat for his own personal use for one month and leased it to another person for two months. He has income from such operations of $3,000, taxes of $1,400, utilities of $900, maintenance expenses of $600, and depreciation of $1,200. His deductions are limited to $3,000, the amount of the income from the boat, as follows:

Category 1—Taxes	$1,400
Category 2—Two-thirds of $1,500 utilities and maintenance	1,000
Category 3—Two-thirds of $1,200 depreciation limited to excess of $3,000 boat income over $2,400 total of Category 1 and 2 deductions	600
Total deductions	$3,000

The $1,400 is itemized as part of the taxes deduction, and the $1,600 is placed in the miscellaneous itemized deduction section of Schedule A that is reduced by 2 percent of adjusted gross income.

If profit results from the activity in three out of five consecutive years ending with the tax year in question, a rebuttable presumption is created that an activity was not engaged in as a hobby. This permits the taxpayer to avoid the restrictions on the deduction of hobby losses. In the case of horse racing, breeding, and showing, a rebuttable presumption is created if profit results from the activity in two out of seven consecutive years.

A taxpayer may elect to delay a determination as to whether the presumption applies until the close of the fourth (or sixth, in the case of horse racing, breeding, or showing) tax year after the tax year in which the taxpayer first engages in the activity. A taxpayer is required to execute a waiver of the statute of limitations in order to make the election.

¶ 6351   HOME OFFICE EXPENSES

If a taxpayer uses a portion of a personal residence for business-related activities, expenses allocable to the portion of the home used for business purposes may qualify as a tax deduction. For personal home expenses to be tax deductible, however, a portion of the home must be used exclusively on a regular basis as:

1. The principal place of business for any trade or business of the taxpayer;

2. A place of business which is used by patients, clients, or customers in meeting or dealing with the taxpayer in the normal course of a trade or business; or

3. In the case of a separate structure which is not attached to the dwelling unit, in connection with the taxpayer's trade or business (Code Sec. 280A(c)).

For tax years beginning after December 31, 1998, the Taxpayer Relief Act of 1997 expands the definition of a "principal place of business." A home office qualifies as a taxpayer's principal place of business under the Act if:

1. the office is used by the taxpayer to conduct administrative or management activities of the taxpayer's trade or business; and

2. there is no other fixed location of the trade or business where the taxpayer conducts substantial administrative or management activities of the trade or business.

If the taxpayer is an employee, the exclusive use test mentioned above must be for the convenience of the employer and not merely for the convenience of the employee. In other words, if an employee has an office on the employer's premises, then the likelihood of having a home office for the same purpose in a personal residence is greatly reduced.

The exclusive use test means that if the portion of the home used for business activities is also used for personal (nonbusiness) activities, then no deduction will be allowed. An exception to the exclusive use test applies when personal residences are used to provide day care services for children, handicapped individuals, and elderly persons. The day care facility exception applies only if the taxpayer has applied for, been granted, or is exempt from having a license, certification, registration, or approval under applicable state law. Personal family use of the day care facilities is acceptable but, in determining the allowable deduction, expenses allocable to the personal use time are not deductible. Code Sec. 280A(c). The regular basis test means that the portion of the home used for business purposes must be used for business on a regular basis, not occasionally.

> *Example 6.34.* Roger Blaine, a physician, uses a portion of his personal home as his principal medical office on an exclusive and regular basis. Expenses related to the portion of the home used for business purposes are deductible on Roger's tax return. If Roger occasionally meets patients in the family living room, which is also used regularly for family activities, then none of the expenses allocable to the living room are deductible since the room is not used exclusively and on a regular basis for business.

TAX PLANNING POINTER

Exclusive use of a portion of a home for business purposes is required to qualify for a business use of home deduction. Exclusive use for business purposes does not require, however, that the portion of the home used for business purposes be physically separated from the remainder of the home. A specified space within a room can qualify for the deduction as long as the exclusive use test is met. *G. Weightman,* 42 TCM 104, CCH Dec. 37,986(M), T.C. Memo. 1981-301.

Typical expenses deductible for a portion of a personal home used for business activities are heating, water, electricity, maintenance and repairs, depreciation, real estate taxes, and interest on a home mortgage. The portion of these expenses allocated to the business use of the home usually is based on the square feet used for business in relation to the total square feet available in the home. In no instance can the deduction for the business use of a home exceed the gross income derived from the business activities carried on at home and from the amount of income generated from rental activity of the home reduced by all related tax deductions other than the business use of home deduction. If the expenses of the business use of the home exceed the gross income derived from the business activity less related deductions, expenses normally allowable as deductions to all taxpayers (such as real estate taxes and interest on a home mortgage loan) are deducted first. If any income remains, other expenses are then deducted to the extent of the remaining income.

Any excess expenses that are not deductible in the current year can be carried forward to offset income from the same home office business activities in succeeding years. Code Sec. 280A(c). Also, for any home office deduction related to work as an *employee,* the deduction is categorized as a miscellaneous itemized deduction subject to the 2 percent of adjusted gross income limitation which applies to miscellaneous itemized deductions (except for mortgage interest and property taxes, which are fully deductible).

Example 6.35. Esther Simcox, a self-employed management consultant, maintains an office in her home on an exclusive and regular basis. The business office space accounts for one-fifth of the total space in her home. In 1998, Esther had gross income of $25,000 from her consulting business. Deductions related to her management consulting income, other than the business use of home deduction, amounted to $5,000. During 1998, Esther incurs the following home expenses:

Real estate taxes	$3,600	
Interest on mortgage loan	4,200	
Tax deductions normally allowable to all taxpayers		$ 7,800
Maintenance on home	$1,200	
Utilities (water, electricity, gas, sewer)	2,500	
Other expenses (repairs, maid service, etc.)	3,000	
Operating expenses		6,700
Total depreciation (straight-line)		2,500
Total		$17,000

Esther's home office deduction for 1998 is $3,400, determined by taking the $17,000 of home expenses times 1/5, the portion of the home used for business purposes. If Esther's gross income from the consulting business less related deductions, other than the business use of home deduction, amounted to only $2,000 in 1998, then the business use of home deduction is limited to $2,000. In calculating the business use of home deduction, tax deductions normally allowable to all taxpayers are deducted first.

¶ 6371   VACATION HOME EXPENSES

Special rules limit the amount of rental expense deductions that may be taken by an individual taxpayer (investor) on a residence that is rented out for part of a year and used for personal purposes during other parts of the year. Code Sec. 280A. If a personal residence is rented out for less than 15 days during the year, any rental income received is excluded from gross income and no rental expense deductions are allowed. Code Sec. 280A(g). However, regular expense deductions attributable to all personal residences (such as mortgage interest, property taxes, and personal casualty losses) are still available. If a residence is rented out during the year for more than 14 days, then the property will either be a personal residence (personal-use property) or rental property (which could provide a deductible loss subject to the passive loss rules).

A vacation home becomes a personal residence when its owner uses it excessively for personal purposes. Excessive personal use is measured by the greater of 14 days or 10 percent of the number of rental days. That is, if the owner personally uses the residence *more than the greater of* (1) 14 days or (2) 10 percent of rental days, then the dwelling will be a personal residence and rental losses are not deductible. If rental expenses exceed rental income, then regular expenses (mortgage interest, property taxes, and casualty losses) are deducted first. (Any remaining regular expenses are deductible as itemized deductions.) Other rental expense deductions (maintenance, repairs, depreciation, etc.) are limited to the remaining amount of rental income (after it is reduced by the amount of regular expenses that were deducted first).

Example 6.36. Joel Harris owned a condo in a resort area. During the year, he personally used it for 17 days, and it was rented for 100 days. Because he used the condo for more than either 14 days or 10 percent of rental days (10 days), the vacation home will be treated as a personal residence and losses will not be allowed.

However, if an individual rents out a vacation home for more than 14 days and does not use it excessively for personal purposes, then it will be treated as rental property. That is, if the taxpayer does not use it for personal purposes for the greater of 14 days or 10 percent of rental days, then losses are allowed to be deducted for AGI (subject to the passive activity rules). If an individual actively participates in the rental real estate activity, then up to $25,000 of losses can be used to offset nonpassive income.

Example 6.37. John Henderson owns a vacation home in Palm Springs. His expenses related to the home during the year are as follows:

Mortgage interest and taxes	$20,000
Utilities, maintenance, and repairs	5,000
Depreciation	15,000
Total expenses	$40,000

Assume Mr. Henderson rents out the home for less than 15 days during the year and uses it personally for more than 14 days. He receives rental income of $4,000. None of the rental income is reported on his income tax return, and no rental expenses are deductible on his tax return. The mortgage interest and taxes of $20,000, however, are allowable.

In determining rental expense deductions, the allocation formulas used to compute rental expenses differ depending on the type of expense being allocated and interpretation of the tax law by the Tax Court and the IRS. For regular expenses allowable to all taxpayers, the Tax Court allocation formula is based on a full year (365 days). *D.D. Bolton*, 82-2 USTC ¶ 9699, 694 F.2d 556 (CA-9 1982). The IRS prefers to allocate regular expenses based on total usage of the residence. For other expenses, the allocation formula is based on total usage of the residence.

Example 6.38. Assume Mr. Henderson rents out the vacation home for 25 days during the year and receives rental income of $10,000. He uses the dwelling for personal purposes for 30 days during the year. Under these assumptions, the rental income of $10,000 is included in his income because he rented the home out for more than 14 days. The dwelling will be treated as a personal residence because he used it for personal purposes for the greater of (1) 14 days, or (2) 10 percent of the rental days. The rental expense deductions are computed using both the IRS method and the Tax Court method as follows:

	Tax Court	IRS
Rental income	$10,000	$10,000
Less: Mortgage interest payments and property taxes		
($20,000 × 25 rental days/365 days a year)	1,370	
($20,000 × 25 rental days/55 total use days)		9,091
Less: Utility expenses, maintenance, and repair expenses, etc. ($5,000 × 25 rental days/55 total use days)	2,272	
($5,000 × 25 rental days/55 total use days, but limited to $909—cannot create a loss)		909
Amount remaining for depreciation	$ 6,358	$ 0
Less: Depreciation ($15,000 × 25 rental days/55 total use days = $6,818, but limited to $6,358)	6,358	0
Net Rental Loss	$ 0	$ 0

Example 6.39. Assume Mr. Henderson rents out the home for 25 days during the year and receives rental income of $10,000. He uses the home for personal purposes for seven days during the year. Under these assumptions, all rental income is recognized on his income tax return since the dwelling was rented out for more than 14 days. Because the residence will be treated as rental property (personal use was less than 14 days or 10 percent of rental days), losses are allowed. His rental income and rental expenses are computed as follows:

	Tax Court	IRS
Rental income	$10,000	$10,000
Less: Mortgage interest and property taxes		
($20,000 × 25 rental days/365 days a year)	1,370	
($20,000 × 25 rental days/32 total use days)		15,625
Less: Utility expenses, maintenance, and repair expenses, etc. ($5,000 × 25 rental days/32 total use days)	3,906	3,906
Income or loss before depreciation	$ 4,724	($ 9,531)
Less: Depreciation ($15,000 × 25 rental days/32 total use days)	11,718	11,718
Net Rental Loss	($ 6,994)	($21,249)

Under either the Tax Court or the IRS approach, the loss is less than the $25,000 loss allowed for rental property in which there is active participation. In this case, the remainder of the mortgage interest is not deductible because the vacation home is not considered a second residence. Therefore, the IRS approach is more favorable to the taxpayer.

Personal use days of a vacation home by an owner generally include the following: days of personal use by the owner or by a member of the owner's family including spouse, ancestors, lineal descendants, children, brothers, and sisters; and days of use under an arrangement to exchange one residence for another for a period of time; and days of use by any individual if not rented at a fair rental. Code Sec. 280A(d)(2)(A). Time spent at a vacation home by an owner while making repairs usually does not count as days of personal use if at least two-thirds of each day, up to eight hours a day, is spent making repairs.

SUMMARY OF CHAPTER 6

✓   Deductions arising from tax shelters are subject to the at-risk rules and the passive activity rules. The at-risk provisions are structured to deny taxpayers from deducting losses in excess of their actual economic investment in the endeavor. In general, deductions or expenses incurred by passive activities can only be deducted against passsive income, and any unused passive losses are suspended and carried forward to future years to offset passive income in those years.

✓   Net operating losses from business endeavors may be carried back two years and forward 20 years.

✓   Hobby losses require that expenses can only be deducted up to the amount of gross income derived from the activity.

✓   Business casualty or theft losses are the lesser of the decline in fair market value or the adjusted basis, but will equal adjusted basis when the property is totally destroyed. The three-year carryback period is retained for the portion of the NOL that relates to casualty and theft losses of individual taxpayers.

✓   Losses from ownership of a vacation home may be dedcutible if the home qualifies as rental property. The excessive use test is used in making the rental property determination (i.e., the greater of 14 days or 10 percent of the rental days). Once a home is determined to be rental, the losses are subject to the passive loss rules.

CHAPTER 6 QUESTIONS

1. What is a tax shelter? Generally, what two limitations apply to the deductibility of most tax shelter loss deductions?

2. Why were tax shelters popular before the Tax Reform Act of 1986? Briefly explain why tax shelter investments are not as popular today.

3. Generally, what is "at risk"?

4. What is a nonrecourse loan? Will a nonrecourse loan given by the seller of real estate to the buyer increase the amount the buyer has at risk? Explain.

5. What is the general rule for the deductibility of passive losses?

6. Briefly, how do the at-risk rules and passive activity rules function together?

7. Differentiate between the following: active income, passive income, and portfolio income.

8. On what date was the Tax Reform Act of 1986 enacted, and what significance does this date have for losses derived from passive activities in 1998?

9. What is a "suspended loss"? How can suspended losses offset nonpassive income?

10. Generally, how will a suspended loss attributable to a passive activity that is transferred by reason of death be treated for federal income tax purposes?

11. Generally, how will a suspended loss attributable to a passive activity that is transferred by gift be treated for federal income tax purposes?

12. What type of taxpayers (entities) are affected by the passive loss rules? What is the significance of a closely held corporation with regard to the deductibility of passive losses?

13. Briefly, what is "material participation"? Why is the determination of whether a taxpayer materially participates important?

14. What are the seven tests that help to establish material participation?

15. What is "significant participation," and why is it notable?

16. What is an undertaking? What is a "separate source of income production," and why is this meaningful?

17. How are both business and rental operations usually treated when carried on at the same location by the same owner? How can both undertakings be treated as one activity?

18. How can a taxpayer combine real estate undertakings?

19. How can nonrental undertakings be combined?

20. Identify the six tests concerning rental properties that help to establish a nonrental activity.

21. What relief from passive loss restrictions is provided to help taxpayers deduct losses from rental real estate activities? What are the qualifications?

22. What is "active participation"?

23. What consequences does a taxpayer face when one of several activities is no longer a passive activity?

24. Explain the tax treatment of the following business casualty losses: complete destruction of the property and partial destruction of the property.

25. How does an expected insurance reimbursement for a business casualty loss affect the amount of a casualty loss deduction? Does it make a difference whether an expected insurance reimbursement for business casualty loss differs from the actual insurance reimbursement when the claim is settled?

26. How will a business property's basis be adjusted as a result of a casualty loss?

27. Generally, are net operating losses available for personal-use expenditures? Explain.

28. What carryback and carryforward procedures apply to business net operating losses?

29. What qualifications must be met before a taxpayer is allowed a home office deduction?

30. How can a vacation home become rental property? What is the difference between "rental property" and "personal residence"?

CHAPTER 6 PROBLEMS

31. Billy Bob is at risk for $10,000 in Partnership A and $22,000 in Partnership B on January 1, 1998. Both partnerships are passive activities to Billy Bob. Billy Bob's share of net income from Partnership A during 1998 was $8,000. His share of losses from Partnership B was $12,000. What are the tax consequences to Billy Bob for 1998? How much is he at risk for each activity on January 1, 1999? Does he have any loss carryovers under the at-risk rules? Does he have any suspended losses under the passive loss rules?

32. What would be your answer to Problem 31 if Billy Bob's share of net income from Partnership A was $9,000 and his loss from Partnership B was $25,000?

33. In 1998, Wilmah Lansing invested in the Triple-K Limited Partnership by paying $15,000 cash and signing a $40,000 nonrecourse note. She also pledged $25,000 worth of securities for a loan obtained by the partnership. Her basis in the securities was $10,000. What amount does Wilmah have at risk in Triple-K as of January 1, 1999, if the partnership broke even (no income or loss)?

34. Refer to the facts in Problem 33 and assume that Triple-K allocated to Wilmah net income of $10,000 from operations in 1998. What amount does Wilmah have at risk as of January 1, 1999? Would your answer be different if she also withdrew $5,000? Explain.

35. Refer to the facts in Problem 33 and assume instead that Triple-K allocated to her a loss of $60,000 in 1998. What amount does Wilmah have at risk as of January 1, 1999?

36. In 1996, Keith Jackson invested in a partnership known as Astonishing Discoveries, Ltd. He was a limited partner. Mr. Jackson paid $25,000 cash and, along with all other partners, signed a nonrecourse note with which Astonishing Discoveries acquired an office park. The loan was made by the seller, a large financial institution that customarily made such loans. Jackson's allocated portion of the note was $100,000. In 1998, he received a $45,000 allocated loss from the partnership and had net passive income of $35,000 from other passive activities for the year. His adjusted gross income for 1998 was $145,000. Compute the following items for 1998:

    a.   Amount at risk

    b.   Passive loss deductions (against nonpassive income)

    c.   Suspended loss.

37. Tammy Faye Jones owned three passive activities in 1998 (she had no suspended losses prior to 1998):

Activity	Date Acquired	1998 Allocated Gain/(Loss)
One	7/20/83	(60,000)
Two	9/01/87	40,000
Three	3/10/88	(30,000)

    How much is her passive loss deduction (against nonpassive income) and suspended loss for each activity and the manner in which it is allocated?

38. Brent Fullback owned four passive activity interests in 1998:

Activity	Date Acquired	1998 Allocated Gain/(Loss)	Pre-1998 Suspended Loss
A-1	11/22/82	14,000	(27,000)
B-2	01/25/85	(22,000)	(25,000)
C-3	07/03/87	(5,000)	(8,000)
D-4	08/01/89	(3,000)	(1,000)

    On March 2, 1998, Fullback sold his entire interest in A-1 for $15,000. His basis in the activity on January 1, 1998, was $11,000. Compute the following:

    a.   Gain or loss realized from the sale of A-1

    b.   Passive loss deduction (against nonpassive income) and type (i.e., ordinary income (loss) or capital income (loss))

    c.   Suspended losses and how they are allocated

39. Jean Kelley owned three limited partnership interests in 1998:

Partnership	Date Acquired	1998 Allocated Gain/(Loss)	Pre-1998 Suspended Loss
MNO	05/03/87	(4,000)	(14,000)
OSD	10/14/87	10,000	(3,000)
CMP	11/15/88	(6,000)	(2,000)

How much is her passive loss deduction (against nonpassive activities) and suspended loss for each activity?

40. Thomas Settleton owned an interest as a general partner in LBO partnership. Settleton was not a material participant in the activity. His basis was $25,000 on the date he gifted the LBO partnership interest to his son, Willard. Suspended losses amounted to $40,000 as of that date. What are the federal income tax consequences of the gift to the son?

41. Teri Frazier owned three businesses and rental properties in 1998. During the year, her hair salon business experienced a $32,000 net loss. She participated 200 hours in the hair salon business. All of the salon's employees worked more than 600 hours for 1998. Her second business was a coin-operated laundry. She did not participate over 100 hours in the laundry operation. It had a net loss of $14,500. The third business was a flower shop, which had net income of $45,000 for 1998. She participated well over 1,000 hours in the flower shop business. None of the activities was located within one-half mile of each other. She also received dividends of $12,000 from her IBM stock, and interest of $14,000 from her AT&T bonds. In addition, Frazier had a net loss of $18,000 from her real estate rentals. Compute her adjusted gross income.

42. Darian Basemore owned an interest in five businesses in 1998. His level of participation and percentage of ownership in each enterprise is as follows:

Activity	Hours of Participation	Ownership Percentage
Ven-Tale	180	22%
MovERent	88	17
AZ Airlines	950	33
Sadd Books	135	12
Kingdom Autos	185	25

In which activity, if any, will Darian be considered a material participant?

43. Janice Hoplin, MD, owned her own medical clinic. She also owned the office building in which the clinic was located. The medical activity generated $125,000 of net income. She managed the building, which had 15 other medical professionals (tenants), from her medical office. The office rental activity provided her with a $12,000 net loss for the year. What is Janice's adjusted gross income?

44. Dave Eichoff had adjusted gross income for 1998 of $122,000 before any passive losses or other rental activities. He owned a mountain cabin in Idaho, which he rented for 125 days and which was not used by him at all during the year. The property will experience a net loss of $12,500. He also had a limited partnership interest that was purchased in 1985 and yielded a loss of $22,000. What is Dave's adjusted gross income after considering the passive activity and rental losses?

45. Diane Parker acquired an interest in a movie theater in June 1989. The theater broke even from 1989 to 1993. Parker did not actively participate in the activity during those years. She participated in the activity for 350, 400, 450, and 420 hours during 1994, 1995, 1996, and 1997, respectively. This was well below all other employees. The theater had losses allocated to her of $21,000, $6,000, $19,000, and $12,000 for 1994, 1995, 1996, and 1997, respectively. In 1998, however, she participated 750 hours in the business, and her share of the movie theater net income was $24,000. Her income from other sources (portfolio income) was $27,500. What are the income tax consequences to Diane for 1998?

46. Mary Beth is a CPA, devoting 3,000 hours per year to her practice. She also owns an office building in which she rents out space to tenants. She devotes none of her time to the management of the office building. She has a property management firm make all management decisions for her. During 1998, she incurred a loss, for tax purposes, of $30,000 on the office building. How must Mary Beth treat this loss on her 1998 tax return?

47. Assume the same facts as in Problem 46, except that Mary Beth is a real estate agent. She works 1,000 hours per year as a real estate agent and 1,200 hours per year managing her office building. How may she treat the loss on the office building?

48. Max Computer Center incurred the following casualty and theft losses in 1998:

| | | Fair Market Value | | |
	Adjusted Basis	Before Casualty	After Casualty	Insurance Reimbursement
a. Robbery-Equip.	$8,000	$9,000	$ 0	$7,500
b. Fire-Truck	$4,000	$5,000	$2,000	$3,500
c. Fire-Equip.	$9,000	$6,000	$ 0	$6,000

Compute the casualty and theft loss for each item listed.

49. In 1998, Mary Jackson had the following income and deductions listed on her individual income tax return:

Business income	$ 25,000
Interest income on personal investments	2,000
Less: Business expenses	45,000
Less: Personal exemption	2,700
Less: Nonbusiness deductions	3,000
Loss shown on tax return	$(23,700)

Compute the amount of Mary's 1998 net operating loss.

50. Ralph Sample had the following income and deductions listed on his 1998 income tax return:

Salary	$ 25,000
Business income	65,000
Interest income on personal investments	10,000
Less: Business expenses	102,000
Less: Personal exemption	2,700
Less: Nonbusiness deductions	12,000
Loss shown on tax return	$ (16,700)

Compute the amount of Ralph's 1998 net operating loss.

51. During 1998, Jane Mason incurred the following home expenses:

Real estate taxes	$ 4,000
Interest on home mortgage	7,000
Maintenance on home	2,000
Other home expenses including depreciation	4,000
Total	$17,000

Assume that Jane qualified for the home office deduction, all of the above expenditures qualified for the deduction as home office expenses, 8 percent of the space in the home was used for the business activity, and Jane earned $9,000 in 1998 after all deductions other than home office expenses.

     a.   Compute Jane's home office deduction for 1998.

     b.   Assume instead that Jane earned only $1,000 after all deductions other than home office expenses. What is her home office deduction?

52. In 1998, Joan Cannon incurred the following expenses relating to her vacation home:

Mortgage interest	$ 6,000
Property taxes	4,000
Utility expenses	4,000
Depreciation	6,000
Total expenses	$20,000

During 1998, Joan personally used the vacation home for 20 days. Determine the rental expense deduction that she is entitled to claim on her 1998 tax return in each of the following cases. Use the Tax Court method of allocating normal expenses allowable to all taxpayers.

a. Joan rents out the vacation home for 10 days during the year and receives $800 in rental income.

b. Joan rents out the vacation home for 30 days during the year and receives $1,500 in rental income.

c. Joan rents out the vacation home for 230 days during the year and receives $9,000 in rental income.

53. Refer to Problem 52, Part (c) and assume the IRS approach to allocating normal expenses allowable to all taxpayers is used. Based on these facts, what rental expense deductions are allowable in 1998?

54. Which of the following is not a passive activity?

a. Owning a limited partnership interest in an oil and gas limited partnership

b. Having rental residential properties

c. Owning a business and not materially participating

d. Being a material participant in a small-tool rental business (averaging three days use)

55. Benson Company experienced partial destruction of a warehouse from a tornado. The warehouse had a basis of $200,000 at the time of the casualty. Its fair market value before the accident was $1,000,000 and afterward, $600,000. How has this event changed the basis of the warehouse?

a. No effect

b. Decrease by $200,000

c. Decrease by $400,000

d. Decrease by $100,000 plus insurance proceeds received

56. Which of the following taxpayers would be least likely to qualify for a home office deduction?

a. Self-employed individual

b. Employee with an office on the employer's premises

c. Owner of property held for production of income

d. Employee whose home office is for the employer's convenience

57. Net operating losses can be increased by which of the following?

a. Personal casualty losses

b. Business casualty losses

c. Unreimbursed employee business expenses

d. All of the above

58. Bob White owned a cabin in the Great Smoky Mountains. He used it for 16 days and rented it out for 190 days during the year. Which of the following is true?

a. All allocated expenses are deductible (subject to the passive loss rules).

b. Only allocated expenses up to gross rentals are deductible.

c. The vacation home qualifies as a principal residence.

d. All rentals are received tax free and no expenses, other than taxes and interest, are deductible.

59. *Comprehensive Problem.* Harvey and Betty Duran, both age 37, are married with one dependent child. Determine their taxable income from the following information for 1998, and their tax liability. Both the ABC and XYZ partnerships are passive activities.

Harvey's salary	$ 45,000
Betty's salary	62,000
Dividends received from domestic corporations	11,000
Interest	7,000
Itemized deductions	6,920
Net loss from ABC Partnership (acq. 1983)	(14,200)
Net loss from XYZ Partnership (acq. 1988)	(6,000)
Harvey's business income (moonlighting)	7,700
Harvey's business deductions (before home office expenses)	22,000
Harvey's home office expenses	10,500
Net loss on rental property	(31,000)

60. *Comprehensive Problem.* Michael Rambo, single and calendar year taxpayer, is the sole owner of Slice-It Pizza Company, a sole proprietorship. Michael materially participated in the activity. In 1998 Slice-It Pizza reported revenues of $600,000 and deductions of $410,000, exclusive of a net operating loss deduction of $150,000.

The NOL was carried forward from 1997. For tax purposes, Michael reports revenues and expenses of Slice-It Pizza on Schedule C of Form 1040—Individual Income Tax Return. If Michael has no other taxable income, deductions or credits in 1998, other than those listed above, what tax effect does the $150,000 NOL have on his 1998 tax return? Ignore liability for self-employment taxes.

61. *Research Problem.* Clients Buddy and Debbie Jamison are considering converting their private vacation home to rental property. They have asked for advice as to the tax aspects of owning such property. The only real estate they own is their principal residence and the vacation home. Some of the following sources may prove to be helpful in preparing a report for the clients: Code Sec. 280A; Code Sec. 469; Reg. § 1.165-9(b); *A.B. Wood,* (CA-5) 52-2 USTC ¶ 9374, 197 F.2d 859; *E.G. McKinney,* 42 TCM 468, CCH Dec. 36,077(M), T.C. Memo. 1981-377, aff'd (CA-10) 83-2 USTC ¶ 9655; *T.B. Jefferson,* 50 TC 963, CCH Dec. 29,153; *L.M. McAuley,* 35 TCM 1236, CCH Dec. 34,005(M), T.C. Memo. 1976-276.

Chapter 7

Deductions: Itemized Deductions

Learning Objectives

After completing Chapter 7, you should be able to:

1. List items making up the medical expense deduction.
2. Apply rules for the interest expense deduction.
3. Explain requirements for the charitable contribution deduction.
4. Explain requirements for personal casualty and theft losses deduction.
5. Identify deductions for employee business expenses and investment expenses, as well as other miscellaneous itemized deductions.

OVERVIEW OF CHAPTER

In computing taxable income, personal, living, or family expenses are disallowed by Code Sec. 262. However, legislative sanction does allow some deductions for expenses which are essentially personal in nature. The expenses are deductible from adjusted gross income and are referred to as itemized deductions. If the Code does not expressly provide that a personal nonbusiness expense is deductible, no deduction is allowed. These deductions are taken on Schedule A of the individual tax return.

This chapter discusses those expenses that are specifically allowed as itemized deductions. These deductions include: medical expenses, taxes, interest, charitable contributions, casualty and theft losses, employee business expenses, investment expenses, and other miscellaneous itemized deductions.

There is an overall limitation on itemized deductions. High-income taxpayers whose AGI exceeds a threshold amount are required to reduce the allowable itemized deductions by a designated percent. This provision is detailed in Chapter 2.

Medical Expenses

¶ 7001   REQUIREMENTS FOR THE DEDUCTION

An itemized deduction is allowed for certain medical expenses. The deduction is allowable only to individuals and only for medical expenses actually paid during the year, regardless of when the expenses were incurred or the method of accounting used by the taxpayer. The expense must not be compensated for by insurance or otherwise. Only such medical expenses as exceed 7.5 percent of adjusted gross income for the year are deductible. Code Sec. 213.

Example 7.1. Jerome Jenkins with an adjusted gross income of $10,000 incurred the following medical expenses:

Medical insurance	$320
Medicines and drugs	175
Other medical expenses	500

The medical deduction is computed as follows:

Medicines and drugs	$175
Medical insurance	320
Other medical expenses	500
Total Medical Expenses	$995
Less 7.5% of $10,000 (adjusted gross income)	750
Total Medical Expense Deduction	$245

For medical expenses to be deductible, they must be for medical care of the taxpayer, spouse, or a dependent of the taxpayer. A child of divorced parents is treated as the dependent of both for purposes of the medical expense deduction. The gross income requirement for the dependency exemption is waived for purposes of a medical care deduction.

Example 7.2. John Farley incurs medical expenses for the care of his father. John pays over half of the support of his father but is unable to claim his father as a dependent because his father has $2,800 of income for the year. The income ceiling for dependents in 1998 is $2,700. Thus, John may include the medical expenses for the care of his father in his medical expense computation.

¶ 7015   MEDICAL CARE EXPENSES

The medical expense deduction is specifically limited for amounts spent for medical care. The term "medical care" is broadly defined to include amounts paid for the diagnosis, cure, mitigation, treatment, or prevention of disease. Further, expenses paid for "medical care" include those paid for the purpose of affecting any structure or function of the body or for transportation primarily for and essential to medical care. Amounts expended for illegal operations or treatments are not deductible. An expenditure which is merely beneficial to the general health of an individual, such as an expenditure for a vacation or health club fees, is not an expenditure for medical care. Amounts paid for accident or health insurance that constitute expenses paid for medical care are deductible as medical expenses. Payments for the following are payments for medical care: hospital services, nursing services, medical, laboratory, surgical, dental and other diagnostic and healing services, X-rays, medicines and drugs, and ambulance hire.

Payments for unnecessary cosmetic surgery directed solely at improving the patient's appearance do not qualify as a medical expense deduction for tax purposes. The rule does not apply to cosmetic surgery necessary to ameliorate a deformity arising from a congenital abnormality, a personal injury arising from an accident, or a disfiguring disease. Any reimbursements for unnecessary cosmetic surgery by an employer under a medical expense reimbursement plan must be included in the gross income of the employee in the year received.

Example 7.3. In June 1998, Jane Martin undergoes a liposuction operation solely to improve her physical appearance. All expenses related to this operation would not be deductible for tax purposes on her 1998 income tax return.

¶ 7025 CAPITAL EXPENDITURES

Capital expenditures for home improvements and additions which are added primarily for the medical care of an individual generally qualify for a medical expense deduction only to the extent that the cost of the improvement or addition exceeds any increase in the value of the affected property. The entire cost of additions or improvements that do not increase the value of the home is deductible as a medical expense. Medical expense deductions have been allowed for the costs of installing elevators in the homes of persons suffering from heart disease, air condition devices for persons suffering from an allergy, and specially built swimming pools for persons suffering from polio.

Example 7.4. Gary Greene is advised by a physician to install an elevator in the residence so that his wife, who is afflicted with heart disease, will not be required to climb stairs. If the cost of installing the elevator is $1,500 and the increase in the value of the residence is only $1,100, the difference of $400, which is the amount in excess of the value enhancement, is deductible as a medical expense. However, if the value of the residence is not increased by the addition, the entire cost of installing the elevator qualifies as a medical expense.

Specific types of capital expenditures incurred to accommodate a personal residence to the needs of a physically handicapped individual, such as construction of entrance ramps, widening of doorways, or installation of railings to allow use of wheelchairs, are fully deductible medical expenses since these types of expenditures do not increase the fair market value of the residence.

Capital expenditures which are related only to the sick person and not related to permanent improvement or betterment of property are deductible if such expenditures otherwise qualify as expenditures for medical care. For example, expenditures for eye glasses, handicapped service animal, dentures, artificial limbs, wheel chair, crutches, inclinator, or air conditioner which is detachable from the property and purchased only for the use of a sick person are deductible.

¶ 7035   TRANSPORTATION AND LODGING EXPENSES

Expenses paid for transportation primarily for and essential to the rendition of medical care are expenses paid for medical care. However, the transportation deduction does not include the cost of any meals while away from home receiving medical treatment. If a doctor prescribes an operation or other medical care, and the taxpayer chooses for purely personal considerations to travel to another locality for the medical care, neither the cost of transportation nor the cost of meals and lodging is an expenditure for medical care. In lieu of a deduction for actual expenses incurred, a standard mileage rate of $.10 per mile for 1998 is allowed in computing the cost of operating an automobile where transportation expenses are deductible as medical expenses. Parking fees and tolls may be taken as additional deductions.

Lodging while away from home under circumstances in which such lodging is primarily for and essential to medical care is deductible. The deduction is not allowed for amounts paid for lodging that is lavish or extravagant under the circumstances. No deduction is allowed for any amount of lodging expenses if there is any significant element of personal pleasure, recreation, or vacation in the travel away from home.

The amount of the deduction for lodging is subject to a limitation of $50 per night for each eligible person. The deduction is allowed not only for the patient but also for a person who must travel with the patient. Thus, if a parent accompanies a dependent child on a trip away from home for medical treatment, the parent could deduct up to $100 per day for lodging expenses.

Example 7.5. Corola Combs travels out of state for special surgery for her daughter. She travels 400 miles in the round trip and incurs $12 in parking fees and tolls. Corola spends three nights in a hotel while her daughter is in the hospital. The lodging expense totals $165. Her qualifying medical expenses are:

Lodging limited to $150 ($50 per night × 3 nights)	$150
Mileage 400 miles × $.10 per mile	40
Parking fees and tolls	12
Qualifying medical expenses from trip	$202

¶ 7045   HOSPITAL AND OTHER INSTITUTIONAL CARE

The cost of in-patient hospital care, including the cost of meals and lodging, is an allowable deduction for medical care. The extent to which expenses for care in an institution other than a hospital (e.g., a nursing home, home for the aged, or therapeutic center for alcohol or drug addiction) qualify as a deduction for medical care is primarily a question of fact depending on the condition of the individual and the nature of the services received. If an individual is in the institution because the physical condition and the availability of medical care in such institution is the principal reason for the patient's presence there, the entire cost of the maintenance, including meals and lodging furnished as a necessary incident to such care, is deductible. However, if an individual is placed in such institution primarily for personal or family reasons, then only that portion of the cost attributable to medical or nursing care (excluding meals and lodging) is deductible.

Example 7.6. Alexis Amberson is elderly, totally disabled, and suffers from a chronic ailment. Her family places her in a nursing home equipped to provide medical and nursing care services. The nursing home expenses are $25,000 a year. Of this amount, $8,500 is directly attributable to medical and nursing care. Since Alexis is in need of intensive medical and nursing care and has been placed in the nursing home facility for this purpose, all $25,000 is deductible (subject to the 7.5 percent of AGI limitation). Had Alexis been placed in the nursing home primarily for personal or family considerations, only $8,500 would be deductible.

While ordinary education is not medical care, special schooling for a mentally or physically handicapped individual is deductible, if the individual's condition is such that the resources of the institution for alleviating such mental or physical handicap are the principal reason for the individual's presence there. In such a case, the cost of attending such a special school includes the cost of meals and lodging, if supplied, and the cost of ordinary education furnished which is incidental to the special services furnished by the school.

¶ 7055   MEDICINES AND DRUGS

Only amounts paid for insulin and prescription medicines or drugs are deductible as a medical expense. Pharmaceutical items acquired without a prescription do not qualify even though they are used for a particular illness, disease, or medical condition. Cosmetics and toiletries are not considered medicines and drugs.

Example 7.7. Larry James had adjusted gross income of $12,000 in 1998. He paid a doctor $800 for medical expenses, a hospital $600, $200 for prescription drugs, and $150 for over-the-counter cold remedies and vitamins during 1998. His 1998 medical expenses are as follows:

Doctor	$ 800
Hospital	600
Medicine and drugs	200
Over-the-counter cold remedies and vitamins	0
Medical expenses	$1,600
Less: 7.5% of $12,000 (adjusted gross income)	900
Allowable medical expense deduction	$ 700

¶ 7065   MEDICAL INSURANCE PREMIUMS

A medical expense deduction is allowed for premiums paid for medical care insurance (including contact lens insurance), subject to the 7.5 percent limitation. If amounts are payable under an insurance contract for other than medical care (such as indemnity for loss of income or, life, limb, or sight), no amount paid for the insurance is deductible unless the medical care charge is stated separately in the contract or furnished in a separate statement. Prepaid long-term health care insurance premiums paid by a taxpayer before age 65 for medical care for the taxpayer, spouse, or any dependent, effective after age 65 are considered to be medical expenses in the year paid if the premiums are payable in equal yearly installments, or more often, under the contract (1) for a period of 10 years or more or (2) until the year the taxpayer reaches age 65 (but in no case for a period of less than five years). Reg. § 1.213-1(e).

Amounts paid as self-employment tax or as employee tax for hospital insurance under the Medicare program are not medical expenses. Similarly, the basic cost of Medicare insurance (Medicare Part A) is not deductible, unless voluntarily paid by the taxpayer for coverage. However, the cost of extra Medicare (Medicare Part B) is deductible. Self-employed persons are allowed to deduct 45 percent of amounts paid for health insurance in 1998 when calculating their adjusted gross income. Code Sec. 162(l)(6). The remaining 55 percent will qualify as a medical expense itemized deduction.

Medical expenses are deductible only in the year paid. If medical expenses are reimbursed under a medical care insurance plan in the same year as paid, then the reimbursement merely reduces the amount that would otherwise qualify for the medical expense deduction. However, where reimbursement, from insurance or otherwise, for medical expenses is received in a year subsequent to a year in which a deduction was claimed, the reimbursement must be included in gross income in the year received to the extent attributable to deductions allowed in the prior year.

Example 7.8. Morris Masters had adjusted gross income of $60,000 in 1998. He had a medical operation and, as a result, paid $5,000 in 1998 for hospitalization and $700 in doctors' bills. His transportation mileage for medical reasons totaled 300 miles. He also paid $640 for prescription medicines and drugs, $275 for contact lenses, and a $900 medical insurance premium in 1998. Under the medical insurance policy carried by the taxpayer, there is an allowance for the operation of only the first $1,000, which amount Morris received in 1998. His deduction for medical expenses is computed as follows:

Hospitalization (medical operation)	$5,000	
Less: Reimbursement from insurance company	1,000	$4,000
Premium on medical insurance policy		900
Doctors' bills		700
Prescription medicines and drugs		640
Contact lenses		275
Transportation for medical purposes (300 miles × $.10)		30
Total		$6,545
Less: 7.5% of $60,000 (adjusted gross income)		4,500
Total medical expenses deduction		$2,045

Taxes

¶ 7101 SUMMARY OF DEDUCTIBLE TAXES

The following taxes are deductible as itemized deductions (Code Sec. 164(a)):

1.   State, local, or foreign real property taxes

2.   State or local personal property taxes

3.   State, local, or foreign income taxes

Other state, local, and foreign taxes not listed above are deductible only if they are trade or business expenses or are incurred in the production of income. The following discussion of taxes relates only to the deductibility of nonbusiness taxes by individuals.

¶ 7105 PROPERTY TAXES

Local, state, and foreign real property taxes are generally deductible only by the person upon whom they are imposed in the year in which they were paid or accrued. Real property taxes are taxes imposed on interests in real property and levied for the general public welfare. Such taxes do not include taxes assessed against local benefits. Reg. § 1.164-3(b).

A tax paid for local benefits such as street, sidewalk, and other like improvements is not deductible if imposed because of and measured by some benefit inuring directly to the property against which the assessment is levied. A tax is considered assessed against local benefits when the property subject to the tax is limited to property benefited. Special assessments are not deductible, even though the incidental benefit may flow to the public welfare. Special assessments, however, can be added to the basis of the property.

Insofar as assessments against local benefits are made for the purpose of maintenance or repair or for the purpose of meeting interest charges with respect to such benefits, they are deductible. The burden is on the taxpayer to show the allocation of the amounts assessed to the different purposes.

If real property is sold during the year, the real property tax deduction must be allocated between the buyer and the seller based on the number of days during the year that each party held the property. This allocation is required regardless of which party actually pays the property tax or the method of accounting used by the taxpayers.

Example 7.9. William Wasserman sold land to David Deere on March 31. Property taxes of $1,460 were paid by David on November 27 to cover the real property taxes for the calendar year. William is entitled to a $360 real property tax deduction ($1,460/365 = $4 per day × 90 days). David is entitled to a $1,100 real property tax deduction ($4 per day × 275 days).

A tenant-stockholder in a cooperative housing corporation may deduct amounts paid or accrued to the corporation to the extent that they represent the tenant-stockholder's proportional share of the real property taxes on the apartment building or houses and land on which situated. Similarly, a taxpayer who owns an apartment in a condominium apartment complex may deduct the taxes assessed on the taxpayer's interest in the property and paid by the taxpayer each year, provided the taxpayer itemizes deductions in filing a federal income tax return.

To be deductible, personal property taxes must be ad valorem (i.e., a tax that is substantially in proportion to the value of the personal property.) A tax which is based on criteria other than value does not qualify as ad valorem. For example, a motor vehicle tax based on weight, model year, and horsepower, or any of these characteristics, is not an ad valorem tax. However, a tax which is partly based on value and partly based on other criteria may qualify in part.

> *Example 7.10.* Gayla Gopher paid $135 for motor vehicle license plates. The license plate fee is based on a combination of value and weight of the automobile. If $75 of the $135 fee is based on the value of the automobile, then $75 is deductible as a tax.

Taxes imposed by some states on intangible personal property or the income therefrom are deductible.

¶ 7115   INCOME TAXES

State or city income taxes, including franchise taxes measured by net income, are deductible as itemized deductions by individuals. State and local income taxes on interest income that is exempt from federal income tax are also deductible. However, state and local income taxes on other exempt income are not deductible.

Taxpayers may deduct state and local income taxes withheld from their salary. They may also deduct payments made on taxes for an earlier year in the year they were withheld or paid.

> *Example 7.11.* During 1998, Carl Castor had $1,200 in state income taxes withheld from his salary. In addition, he paid an additional $325 in 1998 when he filed his 1997 state income tax return. Carl's state income tax deduction for 1998 is $1,525, the amount he paid during 1998.

Any estimated state tax payments made that are in fact not required to be made are not deductible. For example, if a taxpayer made an estimated state income tax payment but the estimate of the state tax liability for the year shows that the taxpayer will receive a refund of the full amount of the estimated payment, then the taxpayer was not required to make the payment and may not deduct it as an itemized deduction.

If a taxpayer receives a refund of state, local, or foreign income taxes in a later year, all or part of the refund may need to be included in income in the year received. The tax benefit rule requires the taxpayer to include a recovery in gross income of the recovery year to the extent that a tax benefit resulted from the deduction of the item in the earlier year. This includes refunds resulting from taxes that were overwithheld, not determined correctly, or determined again as a result of an amended return. A refund of state, local, or foreign taxes may not be used to reduce the amount of taxes paid during the year to lower the deduction. The taxes paid and the refund received must be reported separately.

> *Example 7.12.* Paul Plymouth, a single taxpayer, received a refund of $270 in 1998 from his 1997 state income tax return. Paul had total itemized deductions in 1997 of $4,250, including $1,525 for state income taxes. The amount to be included in gross income for 1998 is $100. The amount included is the lesser of the refund received ($270) or the excess itemized deductions taken in 1997 ($100).

Itemized deductions for 1997	$ 4,250
Less: Standard deduction for 1997	4,150
Excess itemized deductions for 1997	$ 100

Interest

¶ 7201　REQUIREMENTS FOR DEDUCTION

Interest is the amount which one has contracted to pay for the use of borrowed money. The term has the usual ordinary, everyday meaning given to it in the business world. *Old Colony R.R. Co.,* 3 USTC ¶ 880, 284 U.S. 552, 52 S.Ct. 211 (1932). Interest incurred in a trade or business is deductible. However, as discussed in Chapter 5, interest incurred to purchase assets on which the income is tax exempt is not deductible.

It is not necessary that the parties to a transaction label a payment made for the use of money as interest for it to be so treated. The method of computation also does not control its deductibility, so long as the amount in question is an ascertainable sum contracted for the use of borrowed money.

Interest deductions for tax purposes can be separated into six types: personal (consumer) interest, qualified residence interest, investment interest, trade or business interest, passive investment interest, and qualified education loan interest. Each of these six types of interest deductions is explained in the following sections.

¶ 7205　PERSONAL (CONSUMER) INTEREST

Generally, interest on personal loans is nondeductible by individual taxpayers. Personal interest is any interest other than interest incurred in connection with a trade or business, investment interest, or qualified residence interest and interest taken into account in computing the taxpayer's income or loss from passive activities for the year. Personal interest also includes interest on tax deficiencies. Consumer debt is included in the definition of personal interest. Thus, the interest on auto loans and credit card debt is not deductible.

> *Example 7.13.* Sara Short incurs personal interest of $1,000 on an auto loan. Sara is not allowed an itemized deduction for the auto loan interest in 1998.

¶ 7210　QUALIFIED EDUCATION LOAN INTEREST

Starting in 1998, taxpayers will be allowed an interest deduction of up to $1,000 for interest paid on qualified education loans. Qualified education loans are loans incurred to pay expenses for undergraduate and graduate tuition, room and board, and related expenses. The deduction is phased out for single taxpayers with AGI between $40,000 and $55,000 and married taxpayers filing joint returns with AGI between $60,000 and $75,000. The deduction will be allowed in figuring adjusted gross income. The maximum deduction will increase to $1,500 in 1999, $2,000 in 2000, and $2,500 in 2001.

¶ 7215　QUALIFIED RESIDENCE INTEREST

Taxpayers may deduct interest on loans secured by first or second homes but certain restrictions apply. The homes must be "qualified residences." A home is a qualified residence if it is the taxpayer's principal residence or if it is a second residence designated for this purpose that is used for personal purposes for more than the greater of 14 days or 10 percent of the number of days it is rented (such as a vacation home). Taxpayers having more than two residences can designate each year which residence is to be considered the second residence. If the second residence is not used by the taxpayer or rented at any time during the year, the taxpayer need not meet the requirements that the residence be used for personal (nonrental) purposes for more than 14 days. Code Sec. 163(h).

Qualified residence interest is deductible to the extent of interest on up to $1 million of acquisition indebtedness. Acquisition indebtedness is debt incurred to acquire, construct, or substantially improve any qualified residence and is secured by the residence. If a residence is refinanced, the amount qualifying as acquisition indebtedness is limited to the amount of acquisition debt existing at the time of refinancing plus any of the amount of the new loan which is used to substantially improve the residence. A taxpayer can also borrow up to $100,000 of the equity in a home (home equity loan) and deduct the interest on the loan. No restrictions are placed on the use of the home equity loan funds. Home equity loans are defined for tax purposes as indebtedness other than acquisition indebtedness secured by a qualified residence to the extent that it does not exceed the fair market value of the residence reduced by any acquisition indebtedness on the home. Interest attributable to the amount of debt equal to or under the above limits is fully deductible while interest attributable to debt over such limits is not deductible.

TAX BLUNDER

Tim Johnson borrowed $20,000 on a car loan to finance the purchase of a new car. Tim also owns a home on which he has no mortgage. He did not consider a home equity loan when he purchased his car. The interest payments on his car do not qualify for an interest deduction on his tax return. Tim should have considered a home equity loan to finance the purchase of his car.

Taxpayers can turn nondeductible personal (consumer) interest into deductible qualified residence interest by taking out a home equity loan on their personal residence and using the proceeds to pay off personal loans, automobile loans, and credit card balances.

¶ 7225 INVESTMENT INTEREST

The deduction for investment interest is limited to the amount of net investment income. Interest disallowed is carried forward and treated as investment interest in the succeeding tax year. Interest disallowed is allowed in a subsequent year only to the extent the taxpayer has net investment income in such later year.

Definition of Investment Interest

Interest that is subject to the investment interest limitation is defined as interest on debt incurred or continued to purchase or carry property held for investment. Property held for investment includes any property that produces income of the following types: interest, dividends, annuities, or royalties not derived in the ordinary course of a trade or business. It also includes any interest in an activity involving the conduct of a trade or business that is not a passive activity and in which the taxpayer does not materially participate.

An investment activity is considered to be passive if it involves the conduct of any trade or business in which the taxpayer does not materially participate or if it involves the rental of tangible property. Passive investment activities are discussed in greater detail in Chapter 6.

Investment income includes gross income from property held for investment such as dividends, interest, and royalties. A taxpayer has the option of giving up capital gain rate treatment on the sale of capital assets in order to have the gains included as net investment income, thereby increasing the allowable deductible investment interest expense. If the taxpayer is in the 28 percent tax bracket for tax purposes and incurs a long-term capital gain on the sale of property that is also subject to a 28 percent tax rate, the taxpayer has the option of treating the capital gain as an ordinary gain and, thereby, increasing net investment income. The taxpayer should elect this option if it would result in the deduction of a greater amount of investment interest expense.

Net investment income is investment income net of investment expenses. Investment expenses are deductible expenses (other than interest) directly connected with the production of investment income.

Example 7.14. Roberta Ramsey has $17,000 of investment interest expense and $4,000 of net investment income in 1998. The amount disallowed is $13,000. Thus, $4,000 is allowed for 1998. The disallowed interest may be carried over to 1999 and deducted in that year to the extent that it, together with 1999 investment interest and other investment interest carryovers, does not exceed the investment interest limitation.

¶ 7235   TRADE OR BUSINESS INTEREST

Most interest payments incurred in a trade or business are fully deductible for tax purposes. Trade or business interest payments are deductible in computing adjusted gross income and are discussed at ¶ 5235.

¶ 7245   PASSIVE INVESTMENT INTEREST

Passive investment interest is the interest incurred on money borrowed to invest in a passive activity. The amount of passive investment interest is subtracted from any gain or added to any loss from the passive activity. Losses from passive activities are subject to the passive loss limitation rules explained at ¶ 6201.

¶ 7255   PAYMENTS FOR SERVICES

Payments for specific services which the lender performs in connection with the borrower's account are not deductible as interest. For example, interest does not include the separate charges made for investigation of the prospective borrower and the borrower's security, closing costs of the loan and the papers drawn in connection with the closing, or fees paid to a third party for servicing and collecting the particular loan. Rev. Rul. 69-188, 1969-1 CB 54.

¶ 7265   PREPAID INTEREST

Taxpayers on either the accrual or cash method of accounting are allowed to deduct prepaid interest only over the period of the loan to the extent the interest represents the cost of using the borrowed funds during each year. Interest deducted in advance from the proceeds of a loan is not considered paid until the loan payments are made.

> *Example 7.15.* On July 1, 1998, Horace Holmes borrows $5,000 from the bank on a one-year, 10 percent loan. The bank deducts the interest in advance and remits $4,500 to Horace. He pays the due amount of $5,000 on July 1, 1999. Horace has an interest expense deduction of $500 for 1999. He has not prepaid the interest in 1998.

Points are additional interest charges which are usually paid when a loan is closed and which are generally imposed by the lender in lieu of a higher interest rate. Where points are paid as compensation for the use of borrowed money, rather than as payment for the lender's services, the points substitute for a higher stated annual interest rate. As such, points are similar to a prepayment of interest, and are to be treated as paid over the term of the loan. An exception allows the current deduction of points paid in connection with a mortgage incurred in the purchase or improvement of, and secured by, the taxpayer's principal residence. This exception applies only if points are generally charged in the geographical area where the loan is made and to the extent of the number of points generally charged in that area for a home loan. Points paid on refinancing must be spread over the life of the loan. Any unamortized points are deductible when the loan is paid off.

Charitable Contributions

Contributions made to or for the use of qualified domestic organizations by individuals and corporations are deductible. Code Sec. 170. Any charitable contribution actually paid during the year is allowable as a deduction irrespective of the method of accounting used by the taxpayer.

Ordinarily, a contribution is made at the time delivery is effected. The unconditional delivery or mailing of a check which subsequently clears in due course will constitute an effective contribution on the date of delivery or mailing.

¶ 7301   QUALIFIED ORGANIZATIONS

To qualify for the deduction, a contribution must be made to or for the use of one of the following organizations:

1. The United States, a state, a possession of the United States, or any political subdivision of the foregoing

2. Corporation, trust, community chest, fund, or foundation that is created or organized in the United States or any possession and is organized and operated exclusively for religious, charitable, scientific, literary, or educational purposes, or to foster national or international amateur sports competition, or for the prevention of cruelty to children or animals

3. Veterans' organization organized in the United States or its possession

4. Domestic fraternal society operating under the lodge system

5. Nonprofit cemetery company

Generally, contributions made to foreign organizations are not deductible. No deduction is allowed for amounts paid to an organization which has as a substantial part of its activities the carrying on of propaganda or otherwise attempting to influence legislation. Organizations which participate in or intervene in any political campaign activities on behalf of or in opposition to any candidate for public office also do not qualify.

Gifts made to individuals generally are not deductible. For a contribution to be deductible, a donor cannot earmark it for the benefit of a specific individual.

Example 7.16. Fred Fromm made donations to needy individuals. The payments were made by Fred from personal funds directly to the individuals after an investigation of their needs. There was no specific fund established or maintained by Fred or any other person for the purpose of distributing the money to the needy individuals. Fred is not allowed a charitable contribution deduction for his donations to the individuals.

TAX BLUNDER

Referring to the facts in Example 7.16, Fred should have made donations to qualified charitable organizations who help needy individuals instead of making the contribution directly to needy individuals. In this way, Fred would have preserved a charitable contribution deduction on his federal income tax return.

An organization must meet specific requirements in order to be exempt from taxation. Code Sec. 501. However, this does not necessarily mean that a contribution to that organization is deductible by the donor. The IRS publishes a list of organizations which have applied for and received rulings or determination letters holding contributions to them to be deductible. Unless an organization has received a determination letter, it is not recognized as an organization to which contributions are deductible unless it is an organization described in (1), above.

Qualified charitable organizations are divided into two categories: public charities and private charities. Public charities include:

1. Church or a convention or association of churches

2. Educational organization which normally maintains a regular faculty and curriculum and a regularly enrolled body of students in attendance

3. Hospitals and medical research organizations

4. Organization supported by the government which is organized to administer property to or for the benefit of a college or university described in (2), above

5. Governmental units

6. Corporation, trust, or community chest, fund, or foundation that is created or organized in the United States or any possession and is organized and operated exclusively for religious, charitable, scientific, literary, or educational purposes, or to foster national or international amateur sports competition, or for the prevention of cruelty to children or animals

7. Certain types of private foundations

Private foundations are organizations which do not normally receive donations from the general public. There are two types of private foundations: operating and nonoperating. A private operating foundation is an organization that distributes substantially all of its income for the conduct of its charitable purposes. Private operating foundations are treated as public charities.

Most private foundations fall into the nonoperating foundation classification. Private nonoperating foundations that distribute all of their contributions to public charities are also treated as public charities. Thus, a public charity is any qualified charity except for private nonoperating foundations that do not distribute all of their income to public charities. These private nonoperating foundations not contributing all income are classified as private charities.

¶ 7315 VALUATION OF CHARITABLE DONATIONS

If a charitable contribution is made in property other than money, the amount of the contribution is normally the fair market value of the property at the time of the contribution. The fair market value is the price at which the property would change hands between a willing buyer and a willing seller, neither being under any compulsion to buy or sell and both having a reasonable knowledge of relevant facts. No charitable deduction is allowed for the contribution of services.

Where the taxpayer receives some benefit in return for payment to a charitable organization, the deduction is limited to the excess of the amount given over the value of the benefit received. Where a charitable organization sponsors charity balls, bazaars, banquets, shows, or athletic events, the presumption is that the price of admission is not a gift. The payment is for an item of value. The burden is on the taxpayer to show that the amount paid exceeds the fair market value of the admission or other privileges associated with the event. The fact that the full payment or a portion of the payment made by the taxpayer is used by the organization exclusively for charitable purposes has no bearing upon the determination to be made as to the value of the admission, dinner, or other privileges and the amount qualifying as a contribution.

> *Example 7.17.* Members of a charitable organization undertake a program of selling candy to raise funds for the charity. The candy is purchased at $5 per box, normally sells for $8 a box, but is sold at $10 per box. The organization promotes the sale as a "tax-deductible donation." Only $2 per box qualifies as a charitable contribution.

Taxpayers who make a payment to a college or university for the right to purchase tickets to an athletic event are entitled to deduct only 80 percent of the payment as a charitable deduction regardless of whether the tickets would have been available without making the payment.

Unreimbursed expenditures made incident to the rendering of services to an organization may constitute a deductible contribution. These expenses include reasonable expenditures for meals and lodging while away from home in the course of performing donated services.

Automobile expenses incurred in travel or transportation to perform charitable services are deductible. A standard mileage rate of $.14 per mile or the actual expenses of operating the automobile may be used. Rev. Proc. 97-58, 1997-52.24. Parking fees and tolls are added to either method of computation. General repairs or maintenance expenses, depreciation, insurance, or registration fees are not deductible. The costs of meals for the volunteers or the costs of child care for the volunteer's own children while the individual is performing services are not deductible.

TAX BLUNDER

> John Adams does volunteer work for a number of charitable organizations. He uses his car in connection with his volunteer work but does not keep track of the miles driven while performing his charitable duties. John has foregone a $.14 per mile charitable contribution deduction for all of the miles driven while performing his volunteer work.

¶ 7325   LIMITATIONS ON CHARITABLE CONTRIBUTIONS

An individual's charitable contribution deduction is subject to 20 percent, 30 percent, and 50 percent limitations. If a husband and wife file a joint return, the deduction for contributions is the aggregate of the contributions made by the spouses.

Individuals are limited to a deduction of 50 percent of adjusted gross income for charitable contributions made to public charities. Contributions of appreciated capital gain property to public charities and contributions of cash and ordinary income property to private charities are limited to 30 percent of adjusted gross income. An individual may deduct charitable contributions made to certain private charities to the extent the contributions do not exceed 20 percent of adjusted gross income. In addition, the total charitable deduction is limited to 50 percent of adjusted gross income. For purposes of the charitable contribution deduction limitations, adjusted gross income is computed before any deduction for net operating loss carrybacks.

Ordinary Income Property

When ordinary income property is contributed, the amount of the deduction must be reduced by the amount that would have been recognized as ordinary income if the property had been sold by the donor at its fair market value at the time of the contribution. Essentially, the deduction for ordinary income property is limited to the basis of the property.

"Ordinary income property" means property that if sold at the time of contribution would trigger income other than long-term capital gains. For example, ordinary income property includes property held by the donor primarily for sale to customers in the ordinary course of trade or business, a work of art created by the donor, a manuscript prepared by the donor, letters and memorandums prepared by or for the donor, and capital assets not held long-term by the donor.

> *Example 7.18.* Donna Fairfield contributes an ordinary income asset to a public charity. The asset has a basis of $10,000 and a fair market value of $12,000. Her charitable deduction is limited to $10,000 ($12,000 fair market value − $2,000 ordinary income).

Capital Gain Property

Capital gain property is appreciated property where the sale would result in a long-term capital gain if the property were sold at fair market value at the time of the contribution. Section 1231 property which is discussed in Chapter 11 is considered capital gain property for charitable contributions purposes. If the contributed property would have produced both ordinary income and long-term capital gain if sold, the fair market value must be reduced by the amount which would have been ordinary income.

> *Example 7.19.* Brent Bates contributed an asset to a qualified charity. The asset has a fair market value of $1,000 and a basis to him of $400. If the sale would result in a $600 gain of which $250 would be classified as ordinary income and $350 as long-term

capital gain, the asset is considered to be capital gain property. However, the charitable contribution deduction is limited to $750 ($1,000 FMV − $250 ordinary income element).

Capital gain property contributed to a private charity or tangible personal property contributed which has unrelated use to the organization receiving it must be reduced by the long-term capital gain. The reduced contributions amount would be the basis of the property.

"Unrelated use" means a use which is unrelated to the purpose or function constituting the basis of the charitable organization. For example, if a painting contributed to an educational institution is used by the organization for educational purposes by being placed in its library for display and study by art students, the use is not unrelated, but if the painting is sold and the proceeds used by the organization for educational purposes, the use of the property is unrelated.

> *Example 7.20.* Lois Lacey contributes an antique lamp to a qualified charity. The lamp has a fair market value of $5,000 and a basis to her of $3,000. The charity intends to sell the lamp and use the proceeds for charitable purposes. Lois's charitable deduction is limited to $3,000.

For the period through June 30, 1998, contributions of "qualified appreciated stock" to private charities are deductible at the full fair market value of the stock. "Qualified appreciated stock" is any stock of a corporation (1) for which market quotations are readily available on an established securities market as of the date of the contribution, and (2) which is a capital asset that, if sold at its fair market value on the date of contribution, would have produced long-term capital gain. After June 30, 1998, the contribution amount for this type of property will be the basis of the property.

TAX PLANNING POINTER

If the property to be contributed has not appreciated over the taxpayer's basis, the contribution is valued at fair market value. It is not wise to contribute property that would otherwise create a deductible loss if sold. The taxpayer should sell the property and donate the proceeds to the charitable organization.

Charitable Contribution Percentage Limits

Charitable contributions are subject to several limitations that are based on adjusted gross income. There are 50 percent, 30 percent, and 20 percent category limits that are determined by the type of property contributed and the type of charity receiving the donated property. In addition, there is an overall limit on total charitable contributions that is 50 percent of adjusted gross income.

A carryover of any unused charitable contributions is allowed. The carryover rules apply even if the taxpayer does not itemize for the year. The unused charitable contributions may be carried forward for up to five years. Current charitable contributions are considered first and then carryforwards are considered on a first-in, first-out basis.

50 Percent Limitation Category

Contributions of cash and ordinary income property made to public charities may not exceed 50 percent of an individual's adjusted gross income for the year. The 50 percent limited amount is the smaller of (1) the 50 percent category amount or (2) the limit as applied.

Example 7.21. Beatrice Bold donates $10,000 to State University, a public charity. Her adjusted gross income for the year is $17,000. She would be limited to a charitable deduction of $8,500 ($17,000 × 50%).

30 Percent Limitation Category

The 30 percent limit category is comprised of two distinct 30 percent limits that must be kept separate. The 30 percent public category consists of contributions of capital gain property made to any public charitable organization—30 percent public limit amount. The 30 percent private category consists of contributions of cash or ordinary income property to private charities. The 30 percent private limit amount is the lesser of (1) the 30 percent private contribution amount or (2) 30 percent of adjusted gross income minus the 30 percent public contribution amount.

An individual may elect to reduce 30 percent capital gain property by the long-term capital gain and have the contribution qualify as 50 percent limitation category charitable contributions. This "reduced contribution election" may be applied to all contributions of 30 percent capital gain property made during the year or carried over to such year, even though the individual has not made any contribution of 30 percent capital gain property for the year. Normally, the "reduced contribution election" is only tax advantageous to the taxpayer if the contributed property has appreciated only a small amount.

Capital assets reduced because of the "reduced contribution election" or because of unrelated use are not considered 30 percent capital gain property, but instead are placed in the 50 percent limitation category.

Example 7.22. Assume Teri Rogers contributes $5,000 of common stock to a public charitable organization. The stock has a basis to her of $4,800. Teri could now elect to reduce the 30 percent capital gain property by the long-term capital gain and classify the contribution as 50 percent limitation category property. If Teri has AGI of $10,000, a "reduced contribution election" would allow her to deduct a $4,800 charitable contribution deduction (with zero carryover) instead of a $3,000 charitable contribution deduction (with $2,000 carryover) with no election. If the basis of the stock to her was $3,400, a "reduced contribution election" would result in a deduction of $3,400 (with zero carryover) instead of a $3,000 deduction (with $2,000 carryover) with no election. Clearly, the tax advantage of the "reduced contribution election" is greater if the property has appreciated only a small amount.

20 Percent Limitation Category

An individual may deduct charitable contributions made during the year to any qualified charitable organization not included as a public charity. Such contributions are limited to 20 percent of adjusted gross income—20 percent limited amount. The 20 percent limitation generally applies to private charities and to certain other organizations, such as war veterans' organizations, domestic fraternal societies, and nonprofit cemeteries.

Capital gain property donated to a private charity must be reduced by the long-term capital gain. Donations of "qualified appreciated stock," however, are deductible at full fair market value through June 30, 1998.

> *Example 7.23.* Joyce Jeans has adjusted gross income for the year of $100,000. On February 1, 1998, she donates stock to a private charity. The stock has a fair market value of $25,000 and a basis to her of $10,000. She must reduce the fair market value by the long-term capital gain, leaving a charitable contribution deduction of $10,000. If the stock were qualified appreciated stock, her donation would be $20,000. She would be able to use the full fair market value but would be limited to 20 percent of adjusted gross income.

50 Percent Overall Limitation

There is an overall limitation placed on charitable contributions equal to 50 percent of adjusted gross income—maximum charitable deduction. This limitation is applied after the individual limitations are computed. In applying the overall limitation, the 50 percent contribution amount, 30 percent public limited amount, 30 percent private limited amount, and 20 percent limited amount must be taken in that order.

The application of the 50 percent overall limitation to the 50 percent limit amount would result in no further reduction. If the 50 percent limit amount exceeds the maximum deduction allowed there would be no further deductions allowed from the other categories.

The 30 percent public limit deduction is determined by taking the smaller of (1) the 30 percent public limit amount or (2) the maximum charitable deduction minus the 50 percent limit amount.

The 30 percent private limit deduction is determined by taking the smaller of (1) the 30 percent private limit amount or (2) the maximum charitable deduction minus the 50 percent contribution amount and minus the 30 percent public contribution amount. The contribution amounts are used rather than the limited amounts.

The 20 percent limit deduction is determined by taking the smaller of (1) the 20 percent limit amount or (2) the maximum charitable deduction minus the 50 percent contribution amount, the 30 percent public contribution amount, and the 30 percent private contribution amount.

Example 7.24. Darin Drum has adjusted gross income for the year of $100,000. On March 1, 1998, he makes two charitable contributions. His 30 percent public charity contribution amount is $42,000. He also contributes $23,000 in qualified appreciated stock to a private charity. His charitable contribution deduction for the year is limited to $38,000. His $42,000 contribution amount is limited to $30,000 ($100,000 × 30%). His $23,000 contribution is first limited to $20,000 ($100,000 × 20%) and further limited to $8,000 ($50,000 maximum charitable deduction minus $42,000 30 percent contribution amount).

STEPS IN DETERMINING INDIVIDUAL CHARITABLE CONTRIBUTIONS

Step 1. Determine the contribution amounts. The contribution amount is the fair market value reduced by any ordinary income and by the long-term capital gain deduction required because of unrelated use, reduced contribution election, or contribution to a private charity.

Step 2. Place all contributions into 50 percent, 30 percent public, 30 percent private, and 20 percent limitation categories.

Step 3. Determine each percent limit amount based on the 50 percent, 30 percent public, 30 percent private, and 20 percent maximums of adjusted gross income.

Property Given	Contribution Amount	Limitation Category
Cash		
Public Charity	Cash	50%
Private Charity	Cash	30% Private
Ordinary Income Property		
Public Charity	Basis	50%
Private Charity	Basis	30% Private
Capital Gain Property		
Public Charity	FMV-OI	30% Public
Public Reduced Contribution Election	Basis	50%
Private Charity	Basis	20%
Appreciated Tangible Personal Property with Unrelated Use		
Public Charity	Basis	50%
Private Charity	Basis	20%
Qualified Appreciated Stock		
Public Charity	FMV	30% Public
Private Charity		
(through June 30, 1998)	FMV	20%
(after June 30, 1998)	Basis	20%

Step 4. Determine each percent limit deduction. Any difference between the contribution amount and the deduction allowed in each category is carried over for five years.

  a. The 50 percent limit deduction is limited to 50 percent of adjusted gross income.

  b. The 30 percent public limit deduction is limited to the maximum contribution amount minus the 50 percent contribution amount.

  c. The 30 percent private limit deduction is limited to the maximum contribution amount minus the 50 percent and 30 percent public contribution amounts.

  d. The 20 percent limit deduction is limited to the maximum contribution amount minus the 50 percent, 30 percent public, and 30 percent private contribution amounts.

Step 5. Add the respective percent limit deductions to arrive at the charitable contribution deduction.

Example 7.25. Grace Goodheart has $100,000 of adjusted gross income and made charitable contributions as follows: $13,000 cash to the Red Cross, $24,000 fair market value stock to the Boy Scouts, $9,000 in cash to a private charity, and $23,000 in qualified appreciated stock on May 1, 1998, to a private charity. The charitable contribution deduction is computed as follows:

Limitation Category	Contribution Amounts	% Limit Amounts	% Limit Deductions	Carryover
50%	$13,000	$13,000	$13,000	$ 0
30% Public	24,000	24,000	24,000	0
30% Private	9,000	6,000	6,000	3,000
20%	23,000	20,000	4,000	19,000
Total Charitable Deduction			$47,000	

There are no reductions to arrive at the contribution amounts for each category.

The percent limit amounts are determined as follows:

1. The 50 percent limit amount is the smaller of the $13,000 valued contribution or $50,000 ($100,000 × 50 percent).

2. The 30 percent public limit amount is the smaller of the $24,000 contribution amount or $30,000 ($100,000 × 30 percent).

3. The 30 percent private limit amount is limited to $6,000 because the 30 percent public is taken against the 30 percent limit first ($30,000 − $24,000).

4. The 20 percent limit amount is reduced to $20,000 ($100,000 × 20 percent).

The steps in computing the 50 percent overall limitation are as follows:

1. The maximum contribution deduction is $50,000 ($100,000 × 50 percent overall limitation).

2. The 50 percent limit deduction is always the same as the 50 percent limit amount.

3. The 30 percent public limit deduction is the lesser of the 30 percent public limit amount or the $50,000 maximum contribution deduction minus the $13,000 50 percent contribution amount.

4. The 30 percent private limit deduction is the lesser of the 30 percent private limit amount or the $50,000 maximum contribution deduction minus the $13,000 50 percent contribution amount and the 30 percent public contribution amount.

5. The 20 percent limit deduction is the lesser of the 20 percent limit amount or the $50,000 maximum contribution deduction minus the $13,000 50 percent contribution amount, the 30 percent public contribution amount, and the 30 percent private contribution amount.

The charitable deduction is the total of Steps 2–5.

¶ 7355 FILING AND SUBSTANTIATION REQUIREMENTS

The deduction for contributions is made on Schedule A of Form 1040 as an itemized deduction. The taxpayer is required to state the name of each organization to which a contribution of over $3,000 was made. If the contribution is made in property other than money and is over $500, the taxpayer is required to state the kind of property contributed, the method used in determining the fair market value of the property at the time the contribution was made, and whether or not the amount of the contribution was reduced.

For contributed property for which the claimed value of one item or group of similar items exceeds $5,000, the taxpayer claiming the deduction must attach an appraisal of the donated property's fair market value to the income tax return. The appraisal must be obtained from a qualified appraiser. If the donee sells the property within two years, the donee must furnish the IRS and the donor with a statement regarding the sale.

Regulations cite specific evidence and records that must be available in order to substantiate deductions for charitable contributions. The rules, which apply to corporate and individual taxpayers claiming itemized deductions, require that contributions of money be substantiated by a cancelled check, receipt, or other reliable written evidence showing the amount and date of the contribution and the name of the donee. Similar evidence of contributions of property must be maintained, and the property must be described in sufficient detail to allow its identification. No deduction is allowed for any charitable contribution of $250 or more unless the taxpayer substantiates the contribution by a contemporaneous written acknowledgment of the contribution from the donee organization. Substantiation is not required if the donee organization files a return with the IRS which includes the information required on the written acknowledgment. The written acknowledgment should include the amount of cash contributed and/or a description of the property contributed.

Personal Casualty and Theft Losses

¶ 7501   CASUALTY LOSSES

This section discusses personal casualty and theft losses. Business casualty losses are discussed in Chapter 6. Personal casualty and theft losses are deductible as itemized deductions while business casualty and theft losses are deductible from gross income.

Criteria for Deduction

Any uninsured loss arising from fire, storm, shipwreck, or other casualty is allowable as a deduction in the year in which the loss is sustained. Code Sec. 165(c)(3). The IRS position is that the loss must be the result of sudden, unexpected, identifiable, and provable events of an unusual nature, such as an accident, mishap, or sudden invasion by a hostile agency, the cause of which was unknown, or was an unusual effect of a known cause, which occurred by chance and unexpectedly.

Loss through progressive deterioration of property through a steadily operating cause or a normal process is not deductible. The following have been found not to qualify as casualty losses: destruction of trees by disease or insects (*J.A. Appleman,* 64-2 USTC ¶ 9860, 338 F.2d 729 (CA-7 1964); *H.F. Burns,* 59-2 USTC ¶ 9514, 174 F.Supp. 203 (DC Ohio 1959), aff'd per curiam, 61-1 USTC ¶ 9127, 284 F.2d 436 (CA-6 1960); Rev. Rul. 57-599, 1957-2 CB 42); death of livestock; dry rot damage; gradual damage to pilings by storms, tides, and worms; various automobile breakdowns; accumulated water damage to basement walls; freeze and thaw road damage (*H. Stacy,* 29 TCM 542, CCH Dec. 30,132(M), T.C. Memo. 1970-127); and damage from termites (*J.A. Austra,* 25 TCM 178, CCH Dec. 27,837(M), T.C. Memo. 1966-28).

Determination of Amount of Loss

In determining the amount of loss deductible, the fair market value of the property immediately before and immediately after the casualty generally must be ascertained by competent appraisal. This appraisal must recognize the effects of any general market decline affecting undamaged as well as damaged property, which may occur simultaneously with the casualty, in order that any deduction be limited to the actual loss resulting from damage to the property.

Cleanup expenses are deductible as a part of the casualty loss. Costs of photographs and appraisal fees are not deductible as part of the casualty loss, but are deductible as an itemized expense in the determination of correct tax liability. Costs incurred to protect damaged property from future losses are not deductible as part of the casualty loss. Personal living expenses, such as temporary housing, rentals, medical care, lights, fuel, food and drink, or moving expenses are also not deductible as casualty losses.

The cost of repairs of the property damaged is acceptable as evidence of the loss of value. The taxpayer must show that (1) the repairs are necessary to restore the property to its condition immediately before the casualty, (2) the amount spent for such repairs is not excessive, (3) the repairs do not call for more than the damage suffered, and (4) the value of the property after the repairs does not, as a result of the repairs, exceed the value of the property immediately before the casualty.

A casualty loss occurs when an automobile owned by the taxpayer is damaged and the damage results from the faulty driving of the taxpayer or other person operating the automobile but is not due to the willful act or willful negligence of the taxpayer or of one acting on the taxpayer's behalf. Damage resulting from the faulty driving of the operator of the vehicle with which the taxpayer collides is also eligible for the casualty deduction.

The amount of loss to be taken into account is the lesser of either (1) the amount equal to the fair market value of the property immediately before the casualty reduced by the fair market value of the property immediately after the casualty, or (2) the amount of the adjusted basis of the property.

Limitations on Losses

Each personal casualty loss must be reduced by $100. Personal casualty losses are those not incurred in a trade or business or an investment transaction. Where the recognized losses exceed the recognized gains, the deduction is limited to that portion of the net loss which is in excess of 10 percent of adjusted gross income. If the recognized losses exceed the recognized gains after reductions, all gains and losses are ordinary. Where the recognized gains exceed the recognized losses each gain or loss is treated as a capital gain or loss. The $100 and 10 percent of adjusted gross income reductions apply separately to each individual taxpayer who sustains a loss even though the property damaged or destroyed is owned by two or more individuals. However, a husband and wife filing a joint return are treated as one individual taxpayer.

Example 7.26. Roberta Reynolds has $60,000 of adjusted gross income, a casualty loss of $8,500, and a casualty gain of $12,000. The casualty loss of $8,500 is reduced by $100 to $8,400 and netted against the $12,000 gain. The 10 percent reduction does not apply since a gain results from the netting. The $12,000 casualty gain is treated as a capital gain and the $8,400 casualty loss is treated as capital loss.

Example 7.27. James Thomasen has $40,000 of adjusted gross income, a $9,000 casualty loss after the $100 reduction, and a $3,000 casualty gain. The casualty loss deduction is limited to $2,000. The casualty loss must be reduced by the casualty gain and then reduced by 10 percent of adjusted gross income ($9,000 − $3,000 − $4,000).

If a loss is sustained in respect of property used partially for business and partially for nonbusiness purposes, the 10 percent and $100 reductions apply only to that portion of the loss properly attributable to the nonbusiness use.

Casualty losses are deductible in the year incurred. However, no portion of the loss with respect to which reimbursement may be received can be taken until it can be ascertained with reasonable certainty whether or not such reimbursement will be received. If, in the year of the casualty or other event, a portion of the loss is not covered by a claim for reimbursement with respect to which there is a reasonable prospect of recovery, then such portion of the loss is deductible in the year in which the casualty or other event occurs.

Example 7.28. Robert Rayer's personal use property having a basis of $20,000 and a fair market value of $23,000 is completely destroyed by fire in 1998. Robert has an insurance claim for $8,000, which is settled in 1999. He had adjusted gross income of $17,000 in 1998. Robert's 1998 loss equals $10,200 ($20,000 − $8,000 − $100 − $1,700 (10 percent of adjusted gross income)). The loss is deductible in 1998, the year incurred, because the loss can be ascertained with reasonable accuracy.

For casualty losses sustained, a taxpayer is not permitted to deduct a casualty loss for damage to insured property unless a timely insurance claim is filed with respect to the damage to that property. This rule applies to the extent that any insurance policy provides for full or partial reimbursement of the loss. If the loss is covered by insurance, it is immaterial whether or not the taxpayer is the primary beneficiary of the insurance policy so long as the filing of the claim is within the taxpayer's control.

Example 7.29. Tom Tower's automobile was damaged when Tom struck a tree during a snow storm. The damage amounted to $2,300. Rather than notify his automobile insurer because of fear of an increase in the cost of his insurance or cancellation of his policy, Tom paid for the repair costs. Tom may not deduct any casualty loss for the damage to his automobile.

Special Disaster Election

Under certain circumstances, a taxpayer who has sustained a disaster loss may elect to deduct the loss for the tax year immediately preceding the year in which the loss actually occurred. The special provision applies only to disasters occurring in an area determined by the President of the United States to warrant assistance by the federal government. In addition, in Presidentially declared disaster areas, taxpayers will never have to recognize gain on the receipt of insurance proceeds for personal property contained in personal residences.

If an election is made, the disaster to which the election relates is deemed to have occurred in the tax year immediately preceding the year in which the disaster actually occurred, and the loss to which the election applies is deemed to have been sustained in such preceding tax year. An election to claim the disaster deduction must be made by filing a return, an amended return, or a claim for refund clearly showing that the election has been made.

¶ 7525   THEFT LOSSES

Any loss arising from theft is treated as sustained in the year in which the taxpayer discovers the loss. However, if in the year of discovery there exists a claim for reimbursement with respect to which there is a reasonable prospect of recovery, no portion of the loss for which reimbursement may be received is sustained until the year in which it can be ascertained with reasonable certainty whether or not such reimbursement will be received.

The amount deductible in respect of a theft loss is determined in the same manner as a casualty loss. The fair market value of the property immediately after the theft is considered to be zero. Theft losses of nonbusiness personal property are limited by the same $100 and 10 percent of adjusted gross income reductions that apply to casualty losses.

Miscellaneous Itemized Deductions

Miscellaneous itemized deductions allowable for tax purposes include the following items: employee business expenses, job-seeking expenses, education expenses, investment expenses, wagering losses, and tax counsel and return preparer fees. Most miscellaneous itemized deductions, with some exceptions, are grouped together on a tax return and are deductible to the extent that the total of all of the miscellaneous items exceeds 2 percent of the taxpayer's adjusted gross income. All of these miscellaneous itemized deductions are discussed in more detail in the following sections.

¶ 7601   EMPLOYEE BUSINESS EXPENSES

The tax treatment of employee business expenses depends on whether the expenses are categorized as reimbursed expenses or nonreimbursed expenses. Business expenses incurred by an employee under a reimbursement arrangement with an employer are normally not shown on the tax return. Unreimbursed business expenses are deductible as miscellaneous itemized deductions, limited to amounts in excess of 2 percent of the taxpayer's adjusted gross income.

¶ 7603   REIMBURSED EMPLOYEE EXPENSES

Reimbursed expenses of employees are handled differently on a tax return depending on whether or not the employee makes an adequate accounting to the employer for the expenses. An adequate accounting by an employee to an employer would normally include filing an expense report listing time, place, and nature of an expense along with any supporting documentary evidence. Reg. § 1.162-17(b)(4). Also, the reimbursement arrangement must not allow the employee to keep any excess reimbursement.

If an employee makes an adequate accounting to the employer and reimbursement equals expenses, neither the reimbursement nor the expenses have to be shown on the employee's tax return. If an employee makes an adequate accounting to the employer and expenses exceed reimbursement and the employee desires to deduct the excess expenses, all employee expenses and all reimbursement must be listed on the employee's tax return, with the excess unreimbursed expenses being deductible as miscellaneous itemized deductions subject to the 2 percent nondeductible floor.

Example 7.30. Mary Turner incurs the following employee expenses which she submits to her employer for reimbursement under an adequate accounting reimbursement plan.

Travel expenses	$1,100
Transportation expenses	300
Entertainment expenses	600
Total expenses	$2,000

If Mary receives $2,000 in reimbursement from her employer, neither the expenses nor the reimbursement would have to be shown on her return. If Mary receives $1,400 in reimbursement from her employer, she would have to show the $2,000 of expenses and the $1,400 of reimbursement on her return in order to claim the $600 of excess employee expenses as an itemized deduction. The $600 deduction would be allocated proportionately to each type of expense incurred ($600/$2,000 = 30%). The allocation would be $330 to travel, $90 to transportation, and $180 to entertainment expenses. The $180 deduction for entertainment expenses would be subject to a 50 percent limitation, which would then put the entertainment deduction at $90. The $330 travel, the $90 transportation and the $90 entertainment deductions would be subject to the 2 percent of AGI limitation on miscellaneous itemized deductions.

If an employee does not make an adequate accounting to an employer, all employee expenses and any reimbursement would have to be listed on the employee's return. Reg. § 1.162-17(b). Employee business expenses paid or incurred under "nonaccountable plans" are deductible by an employee only as miscellaneous itemized deductions subject to the 2 percent of AGI floor. "Nonaccountable plans" are arrangements that: (1) do not require the employee to substantiate the reimbursed expenses to the employer, or (2) permit the employee to retain amounts in excess of the substantiated expenses covered under the arrangement. Code Sec. 62(c); Temp. Reg. § 1.62-1T(f).

¶ 7605   UNREIMBURSED EMPLOYEE EXPENSES

Unreimbursed employee expenses are allowed only as miscellaneous itemized deductions to the extent they exceed 2 percent of adjusted gross income. Major categories of employee expenses, which, if unreimbursed, must be taken as itemized deductions subject to the 2 percent of AGI floor, include the following: transportation expenses, travel expenses, entertainment expenses, job-seeking expenses, and qualifying educational expenses.

Other allowable employee expenses (subject to the 2 percent of AGI limitation if the expenses are unreimbursed) include professional society dues, employment agency fees, cost of small tools and supplies needed on the job, subscriptions to professional journals, union dues, and work clothes and uniforms not suitable for everyday use. Transportation, travel, and entertainment expenses are discussed in Chapter 5. Job-seeking expenses, education expenses, and other miscellaneous itemized deductions are discussed in greater detail in the following sections of this chapter.

KEYSTONE PROBLEM

Ralph Unit incurs the following qualified employee (business) expenses:

Travel expenses (Business meals included at 50 percent of cost) .	$ 5,000
Transportation expenses	2,600
Entertainment expenses	2,400
Total expenses	$10,000

What amounts of the above employee (business) expenses are deductible for AGI on Ralph's tax return and what amounts are deductible from AGI as itemized deductions based on each of the following assumptions? (Treat each assumption independently from the other assumptions.)

Assumption 1: Ralph is self-employed.

Assumption 2: Ralph is a business executive and receives reimbursement of $8,000 from his employer for these expenses under an adequate accounting reimbursement plan.

¶ 7655   JOB-SEEKING EXPENSES

Job-seeking expenses incurred by an individual are deductible for tax purposes if the individual is employed in a particular trade or business and is looking for work in the same trade or business (e.g., a teacher looking for work as a teacher, an accountant looking for work as an accountant, etc.) Rev. Rul. 75-120, 1975-1 CB 55, clarified by Rev. Rul. 77-16, 1977-1 CB 37. Job-seeking expenses include travel and transportation expenses incurred while going to and from different job locations, expenses of preparing a resume, mailing expenses, and employment agency fees. If deductible, job-seeking expenses are deductible from AGI as miscellaneous itemized deductions subject to the 2 percent of AGI limitation.

Job-seeking expenses are deductible by an individual looking for work in the same trade or business regardless of whether the individual is successful in finding a job. Job-seeking expenses are not deductible if the individual is looking for work in a new trade or business or if the expenses relate to the individual's first job. If an individual is unemployed when incurring the job seeking expenses, the expenses are deductible if the individual is looking for work in the same trade or business in which the individual was employed prior to unemployment.

Example 7.31. Larry Kap, a high school business teacher in Michigan, is looking for a high school teaching position in another state. He incurs travel expenses, employment agency fees, and some other miscellaneous expenses in his search for a new position. Larry eventually finds a teaching position in Iowa. Larry's job-seeking expenses are deductible since he was looking for work in the same trade or business. Even if Larry had been unsuccessful in finding a new job, the expenses would have been deductible since he was looking for work in the same trade or business.

If, instead, Larry was planning to leave the teaching profession and was looking for work as a public accountant, none of his job-seeking expenses would have been deductible since he was looking for work in a new trade or business. This is true regardless of whether Larry was successful or unsuccessful in finding a job as a public accountant.

If an individual combines job-seeking trips in the same trade or business with other personal activities, such as vacationing, the travel and transportation costs incurred on the trip are deductible only if the primary purpose of the trip was to seek new employment. Rev. Rul. 75-120, 1975-1 CB 55. If the purpose of the trip was primarily personal in nature, only the actual expenses incurred at the destination in seeking new employment are deductible for tax purposes.

¶ 7665 EDUCATION EXPENSES

Education expenses incurred by an individual taxpayer for continuing professional education and vocational education courses, professional development courses, and, in some instances, college degree programs are deductible for tax purposes if the following requirements are met. Education expenses are deductible by an individual taxpayer if incurred (1) to maintain or improve skills required in a present job or (2) to meet expressed requirements of an employer or applicable law to retain an employment position or rate of compensation. Reg. § 1.162-5(a). However, even though either of these two requirements are met, education expenses are not deductible if they are personal expenditures. The two categories of nondeductible education expenses are those that (1) are required of the individual in order to meet the *minimum education* requirements for qualification in present employment, trade, or business or (2) qualify the individual for a *new trade or business.*

Maintaining or Improving Skills

Education expenses incurred by an individual taxpayer to maintain or improve skills required in a present job such as a business executive taking a continuing education course in management techniques normally are deductible for tax purposes by the taxpayer. If education expenses incurred by an individual to maintain or improve existing skills also qualify the individual for a new trade or business, the education expenses are not deductible for tax purposes.

Example 7.32. Joan Mackey, a business executive, takes a three-day continuing professional education management course entitled "Advanced Management Techniques" which is relevant to her current management position. The $400 cost of the course is paid by Joan from her personal funds and is not reimbursed by her employer. The $400 payment is deductible on Joan's tax return as an education expense deduction. Joan is also attending law school at the present time and plans to get a law degree since knowledge of legal affairs will be of considerable help to her in her present management position. Joan is paying the cost of law school from her personal funds. The costs associated with attending law school are not deductible by Joan as education expenses since a law degree will qualify her for a new trade or business. It does not matter that knowledge of legal affairs will help Joan in her present management position.

Employer Requirements or Minimum Standards

Education expenses incurred by an individual taxpayer to meet expressed requirements of an employer or applicable law to retain an employment position or rate of compensation normally are deductible for tax purposes. If the education expenses are incurred, however, to meet minimum education standards for qualification in the individual taxpayer's existing trade or business, the expenses are not deductible.

Example 7.33. The Trotwood School System normally requires that all school teachers have, as a minimum, a bachelor's degree in education before they can teach in the school system. An exception to this rule is made for Jane Prim, who is hired in her senior year of college. Education expenses incurred by Jane to finish her senior year of college are not deductible on her individual income tax return since they are incurred to meet minimum education standards for qualification in Jane's trade or business which is teaching.

One year after Jane receives her bachelor's degree in education, the Trotwood school board adopts a requirement that all teachers in the school system must have a master's degree in education within six years in order to continue to teach in the system. If Jane decides to pursue her master's degree in education, the education expenses related to the degree are deductible on Jane's individual income tax return since Jane would incur the expenses in attempting to meet expressed requirements of her employer to retain her employment position.

New Trade or Business

Normally, education expenses incurred by an individual taxpayer to obtain a bachelor's degree are not deductible for tax purposes since the degree either is needed to meet minimum education requirements for the job the college graduate takes after graduation or qualifies the graduate for a new trade or business. Education expenses incurred by an individual relating to a master's degree may or may not be deductible depending on whether the degree qualifies the recipient for a new trade or business. For such expenses to be deductible, the individual usually has to establish a connection between the courses taken and the taxpayer's present business position. If the master's degree qualifies the individual for a new trade or business, education expenses incurred while working on the degree are not deductible even if there is a connection between the courses taken and the person's present position. Education expenses incurred when working on professional degrees such as the M.D. degree and J.D. degree normally are not deductible by an individual since, in each instance, the degree qualifies the individual for a new trade or business.

A review of all surrounding facts should be made in deciding whether certain education expenditures have qualified an individual for a new trade or business. A change in duties such as an elementary school teacher taking courses to become a high school teacher is not considered to be a new trade or business. Reg. § 1.162-5(b)(3). Education expenses related to bar exam review courses and CPA review courses have been considered to be nondeductible since they prepare an individual for a new trade or business. Rev. Rul. 69-292, 1969-1 CB 84.

Classification of Education Expenses

Deductible education expenses include tuition, books, other miscellaneous education expenses, and any related travel and transportation costs. Transportation costs include the costs of going from a work location to school for a night school student. If an individual taxpayer is self-employed, all education expenses are deductible for AGI. If the taxpayer is an employee, all education expenses are deductible from AGI as miscellaneous itemized deductions, subject to the 2 percent floor. Reg. § 1.162-6.

¶ 7675 WORK CLOTHES AND UNIFORMS

Taxpayers generally may not deduct the cost and upkeep of work clothing. Taxpayers may deduct the cost and upkeep of special equipment or work clothes only if they are required as a condition of employment and are not suitable for everyday use. Both conditions must be met to qualify such expenses as miscellaneous itemized deductions, subject to the 2 percent of AGI limitation.

The cost of uniforms that must be worn by ballplayers, fire fighters, police officers, letter carriers, nurses, jockeys, and civilian faculty members of a military school is deductible. Generally, the cost of uniforms of full-time active duty personnel in the armed forces is not deductible.

¶ 7685 MISCELLANEOUS EMPLOYEE EXPENSES

Other employee expenses allowable as miscellaneous itemized deductions subject to the 2 percent of AGI limitation are as follows:

1. Dues to professional societies
2. Union dues and expenses
3. Subscriptions to professional journals
4. Small tools and supplies

Investment Expenses

Deductions for investment expenses are allowed if the expenses are incurred for the production or collection of income or for the management, conservation, or maintenance of property held for the production of income. To be deductible, investment expenses must be ordinary and necessary, must be reasonable in amount, cannot be capital expenditures, cannot relate to the generation of tax-exempt income, and cannot frustrate public policy.

Most investment expenses are categorized as miscellaneous itemized deductions and are deductible by individuals only if the aggregate amount of miscellaneous itemized deductions exceeds 2 percent of the taxpayer's adjusted gross income. Code Sec. 67(a). One exception is deductions attributable to property held for the production of rents or royalties, which are deductible for adjusted gross income. Code Sec. 62(a)(4).

In this section, the following investment expense deductions are reviewed: rent and royalty expenses and miscellaneous investment expenses.

¶ 7701   RENT AND ROYALTY EXPENSES

Rents and royalties are closely related for tax purposes. Rents generally involve payments for the use of land, buildings, and other tangible property whereas royalties usually involve payments for copyrights, patents, and oil, gas, or mineral property. Rental income and expenses are normally related to investment property if only minimal services are provided to the tenants. Minimal service usually is limited to providing heat, light, and trash pickup. If additional services are provided to tenants, such as maid service, rental income and expenses may have to be considered as business income and expenses. If royalty income and expenses are derived from royalty property where the taxpayer has an operating interest or if the taxpayer is self-employed and created the royalty property, such as a writer with a copyright on a book, royalty income and expenses are trade or business income and expenses instead of investment income and expenses.

All rent and royalty expenses are deductible for AGI. Code Sec. 62(a)(4). Normal rent and royalty expenses include depreciation, depletion, repairs and maintenance expenditures, insurance, interest, taxes, and other items. If one piece of property is part rental property and part personal property, expenses must be allocated between the investment portion of the property and the personal portion with only the investment portion of the expenses being deductible for tax purposes.

¶ 7745   MISCELLANEOUS INVESTMENT EXPENSES

Typical investment expenses which are deductible under Code Sec. 212 were mentioned previously in Chapter 5. These included safe deposit box rentals, rent and royalty expenses, investment counseling fees, subscriptions to investment-related journals, newspapers, and other publications, investment custodial fees, legal and accounting fees related to investments, investment interest expense subject to limitations previously discussed, investment-related clerical fees, and investment-related office rents. Expenses of attending conventions, seminars, or similar meetings for investment purposes, however, are not deductible for tax purposes.

Investment-related expenses allowed under Code Sec. 212 are deductible from adjusted gross income as miscellaneous itemized deductions, subject to the 2 percent of AGI limitation. Rent and royalty expenses, however, are an exception and are deductible for adjusted gross income.

¶ 7765   TAX COUNSEL AND RETURN PREPARER FEES

Expenses paid or incurred by an individual in connection with the determination, collection, or refund of any tax are deductible. The deduction is allowed whether the taxing authority is federal, state, or municipal, and whether the tax is income, estate, gift, property, or any other tax. Thus, expenses paid or incurred by a taxpayer for tax counsel or expenses paid or incurred in connection with the preparation of returns or in connection with any proceedings involved in determining the extent of the tax liability or in contesting a tax liability are deductible as miscellaneous itemized deductions, subject to the 2 percent floor.

¶ 7775   WAGERING LOSSES

Losses sustained during the year on wagering transactions are allowed as an itemized deduction but only to the extent of the gains during the year from wagering. In the case of a husband and wife filing a joint return, the combined wagering losses of the spouses are allowed to the extent of the combined wagering gains. Code Sec. 165(d).

The Supreme Court has ruled that a professional gambler is entitled to deduct gambling losses as a trade or business expense. The fact that the taxpayer did not offer goods or services to others did not preclude characterization of the activities as a trade or business, rather, the appropriate "business" test was that the taxpayer must be involved in the activity with continuity and regularity and the taxpayer's primary purpose for engaging in the activity must be for income or profit. *R.P. Groetzinger,* 87-1 USTC ¶ 9191 480 U.S. 23, 107 S.Ct. 980 (1987), aff'g 85-2 USTC ¶ 9622, 771 F.2d 269 (CA-7 1985).

Thus, if gambling is conducted as a business, the losses are deductible as business losses, but only to the extent of gains. Losses of nonprofessional gamblers are nonbusiness losses and are deductible (to the extent of gains) only if itemized on Schedule A of Form 1040. They are not subject to the 2 percent floor on miscellaneous itemized deductions.

SUMMARY OF CHAPTER 7

✓ Personal expenditures are generally disallowed as deductions on the tax return. However, certain personal expenses, as listed in the Internal Revenue Code, are specifically allowed as itemized deductions. These deductions are taken on Schedule A of Form 1040. Itemized deductions are beneficial to a taxpayer only if the total of the itemized deductions exceeds the standard deduction.

✓ Only medical expenses actually paid during the year are allowed as an itemized deduction. The total of the allowable medical expenses must be reduced by 7.5 percent of adjusted gross income. Medical expenses must be for the medical care of the taxpayer, spouse, or a dependent of the taxpayer.

✓ State, local, and foreign property taxes and income taxes make up the taxes category of itemized deductions. Federal income, estate, gift, and Social Security taxes imposed on the taxpayer are not deductible.

✓ Certain interest paid or accrued on indebtedness qualifies as a deduction in computing taxable income. Prepaid interest is not deductible when paid but must be allocated to the periods for which it represents the cost of borrowing funds. Interest expense incurred to purchase tax-exempt income-producing assets is not deductible.

✓ Charitable contributions must be made to qualified organizations in order to qualify for the deduction. Only contributions made during the year are deductible. There are limits imposed on charitable contributions equal to 50 percent, 30 percent, and 20 percent of adjusted gross income, depending on the type of property given and the charity to which it is given.

✓ Certain personal casualty and theft losses may qualify as itemized deductions. Generally, the loss is equal to the smaller of the reduction in fair market value or the basis of the asset, reduced by (1) insurance proceeds, (2) 10 percent of adjusted gross income, and (3) $100.

✓ Miscellaneous itemized deductions are deductible only to the extent they exceed 2 percent of adjusted gross income. However, some miscellaneous itemized deductions are not subject to the 2 percent floor.

CHAPTER 7 QUESTIONS

1. What limits are imposed on the medical expense deduction?

2. When are capital expenditures incurred for medical reasons deductible?

3. When is the cost of transportation deductible as a medical expense?

4. Harry and Mary Holmes had the following health expenses. Which expenses are deductible as medical expenses?

   a. Nonprescription vitamins for Harry

   b. Trip to Florida for general health reasons

   c. Trip to Hawaii for specialized surgery only performed by one doctor located in Hawaii

   d. Crutch rental for period after surgery

   e. Cost of transportation to and from doctor

5. Ron and Judy Rupert have the following health expenses. Which expenses are deductible as medical expenses?

   a. Toothpaste and dental floss for cavity prevention

   b. Acupuncture treatments for Ron

   c. Medical insurance premiums

   d. Contact lenses for Judy

   e. Cosmetic surgery (liposuction operation) for Judy

6. What criteria must be met for personal property taxes to qualify as an itemized deduction?

7. When is a refund of a state or local income tax reported as income?

8. Which of the following taxes are deductible for federal income tax purposes as an itemized deduction?

   a. Personal property tax

   b. FICA tax imposed on employees

   c. Federal gift tax

   d. Sales taxes imposed on purchase of living room furniture

9. Which of the following taxes are deductible for federal income tax purposes as an itemized deduction?

   a. Federal income tax

   b. Federal gasoline tax

   c. State income tax

   d. Excise tax imposed on cigarettes

10. What special rules apply to prepaid interest?

11. What items are included in "net investment income" for purposes of the investment interest limitation?

12. Briefly describe the two major categories of qualified charitable organizations for tax purposes.

13. Distinguish between private operating foundations and private nonoperating foundations.

14. Dana Davenport donates eight hours of her time on a Saturday to help out a qualified charity. What is her charitable deduction?

15. If an asset is given to a charitable organization and the asset is sold, what is the effect on the charitable contribution deduction?

16. What happens to any unused charitable contributions?

17. When is the taxpayer required to attach an appraisal of a charitable contribution to his or her return?

18. What is the definition of a casualty loss?

19. When is a theft loss deductible?

20. In order for employee expenses to be deductible for tax purposes, what basic requirement(s) must be met?

21. What are nonaccountable employee reimbursement plans?

22. What conditions must be present before an individual taxpayer can deduct job seeking expenses? What types of expenditures are included in job seeking expenses for tax purposes?

23. When would education expenses be deductible for tax purposes by an individual taxpayer?

CHAPTER 7 PROBLEMS

24. Oliver Olms pays all of his father's medical expenses for the year, which total $3,800. Oliver also pays over half of his father's support but is unable to claim his father as a dependent because his father has $3,000 in gross income. Will Oliver be able to claim the $3,800 as a medical expense deduction on his individual income tax return?

25. You have a heart ailment. On the advice of your doctor, you install an elevator in your home so you will not have to climb the stairs. It costs $1,000 to install the elevator. The elevator has a 20-year life and increases the fair market value of your home by $600. What is the medical deduction for the elevator assuming the 7.5 percent limitation has been met?

26. Tom and Shannon Shores filed a joint return and paid the following medical expenses:

Hospital costs	$1,200
Doctor's bills	600
Medicine and drugs	200
Hospitalization insurance premiums	400

In addition, they incurred the following medical expenses for Tom's mother who is totally dependent upon and lives with Tom and Shannon:

Cosmetic surgery (face-lift operation)	$1,400
Doctor's bills	600
Medicines and drugs	100

They live 10 miles from the medical center and made 20 trips there for doctor office visits and hospital stays this year. Tom and Shannon's adjusted gross income is $25,000. What is Tom and Shannon's medical expense deduction for this year?

27. Assume the same facts as in Problem 26, except that the insurance company reimbursed Tom and Shannon $1,400 of their hospital and doctor's bills. Determine the medical expense deduction.

28. Carlos Diego paid the following expenses during the current tax year:

State sales tax	$ 600
Sales tax on purchase of automobile	800
License plate "tax" based on weight of vehicles	35
State income tax paid	6,000
Federal income tax paid	16,000

What is Carlos's tax expense deduction for the current tax year?

29. During 1998, Stacy Strong had withheld from her salary $925 for state income taxes. She received a refund of $85 during 1998 from an overpayment of 1997 state income taxes. She also received a refund in 1999 of $115 from an overpayment of her 1998 state income taxes. Assuming Stacy is on the cash basis and her itemized deductions exceed the standard deduction by more than the refund, what is the amount of state income taxes she may claim as a deduction on her 1998 federal income tax return?

30. On December 1, Raphael Renoir borrows $20,000 from the bank on a 15 percent, one-year business loan. Raphael prepays the interest of $3,000 at the time of the loan. What is the interest deduction allowed Raphael, assuming he is a cash basis, calendar year taxpayer?

31. In 1998, Sally Morris, a single taxpayer, pays $1,500 of interest on qualified student loans. Her AGI is $40,000. What is her qualified student loan interest deduction in 1998?

32. Assume the same facts as in Problem 31, except that Sally has AGI of $50,000. What is her qualified student loan interest deduction in 1998?

33. The interest paid on Josephine Young's personal residence for the year 1998 totals $4,800; the interest paid to her life insurance company is $80; the interest paid on a note to the National Bank (to buy state and municipal bonds) is $1,000. What is Josephine's total interest deduction for the year?

34. Mike and Sally Card file a joint return for the 1998 tax year. Their adjusted gross income is $65,000 and they incur the following interest expenses:

Qualified education loans	$ 1,500
Personal loan	1,000
Home mortgage loan	4,000
Loan used to purchase a variety of stocks, bonds, and securities	15,000

Investment income and related expenses amount to $7,000 and $500, respectively. What is Mike and Sally's interest deduction for the 1998 tax year?

35. Greg Grove pays $21,600 interest in 1998 on a home equity loan with an interest rate of 12 percent and an average balance of $180,000 during the year. How much of this interest is deductible on Greg's tax return for 1998?

36. Matilda Moore has $21,000 of investment interest expense and $7,000 of net investment income in 1998. How much of the investment interest expense is deductible for tax purposes in 1998?

37. Frank Freshman mailed a check for $200 on December 30, 1998, in part payment of a $350 pledge he made to State University on November 1. The University did not deposit the check until January 3, 1999. What is the amount of the charitable contribution deduction allowed Frank for 1998?

38. Mark Moody has adjusted gross income of $60,000 for the year. During the year, he gave his church $3,000 cash and land having a fair market value of $40,000 and a basis of $20,000. The land was held long-term. A contribution of $8,000 in cash was also made to a private charity. How much may be deducted as contributions if Mark does not elect to reduce the fair market value by the appreciation in value of the land donated? How much is the charitable contributions carryover?

39. Elmore Eisner made the following contributions during the current tax year:

Cash to United Way	$ 5,000
Land to Boy Scouts to be used as a summer camp:	
Cost	20,000
Fair market value	30,000
Painting to a 20 percent charity for permanent display in foundation's public gallery:	
Cost	5,000
Fair market value	7,000
Cash to individual needy families around town	3,000

a. Assuming Elmore's adjusted gross income is $80,000, what is his charitable contribution deduction for the year and carryover?

b. What is the charitable contribution and carryover if the cost and fair market value of the painting are $25,000 and $27,000, respectively?

40. In each of the following independent cases determine the amount of charitable contributions allowed the individual before consideration of any percentage limitations.

    a. Charlie Chubbs contributed an item of inventory from his sole proprietorship to a public charity for its use. The fair market value of the asset was $800 and his basis was $600.

    b. Durwood Dodson contributed some shares of common stock that he had held long-term to a private charity. The basis of the stock was $8,000 and it had a fair market value of $7,000.

    c. Esther Ensign contributed tangible personal property that she had held long-term to a public charity. The asset had a fair market value of $10,000 and a basis of $6,000. The charity intended to sell the asset and use the proceeds for charitable purposes.

41. Ralph Reeves gave some stock that he owned to charity. The stock had a FMV of $40,000 and a basis of $32,000. His adjusted gross income is $100,000. Determine the allowed charitable contribution deduction and carryover under the following assumptions:

    a. Given to a public charity

    b. Elects the reduced contribution election

    c. Given to private charity

    d. Qualified appreciated stock given to private charity

42. Jackson Jumper has owned a beach house at Padre Island for the last 20 years. While swimming in the surf at Padre one afternoon, someone stole his billfold (containing $50 cash), his wristwatch (cost $250; FMV $200) and, worst of all, his ice chest full of beer (cost – FMV = $25). As if that were not enough, later that day his beach house was completely destroyed by fire. His adjusted basis in the house was $25,000 but the FMV was $35,000 because of the resort areas developing around his property. The house was insured for only $15,000. What is Jackson's casualty and theft loss for the year assuming a $20,000 adjusted gross income?

43. Billy Pilgrim owned a car which he used two-thirds for business and one-third for personal use. The car had cost $6,000 and he had taken $2,000 depreciation on the business-use portion of the car. He was involved in a wreck for which repairs for the damage to the car amounted to $1,200. He had no insurance. What is Billy's casualty loss for the current tax year assuming a $15,000 adjusted gross income?

44. In 1998, Pablo Peso was involved in an auto collision which totally destroyed his new car. He sued the other driver for damages and his lawyer was confident of relief. The FMV of the car immediately before the accident was $4,000. In 1999, the

other driver died penniless, but up to that date Pablo has received only $1,000 of the damage award. What is Pablo's casualty loss for each year, assuming his adjusted gross income each year is $20,000?

45. Sam Slow was involved in a collision while driving his automobile. The automobile, which originally cost $8,000 and was used solely for his personal use, had an appraised value of $5,200 for trade-in purposes just before the accident. After the collision, the car was traded in on a new car, but the trade-in value was only $1,300. Assuming that Sam has adjusted gross income of $15,000 and carried no collision insurance, what amount can he deduct as a net casualty loss for the year?

46. In 1998, Carl Carp incurs the following qualified employee expenses, which he submits to his employer for reimbursement under an adequate accounting reimbursement plan.

Travel expenses (business meals included at 50 percent of cost)	$2,400
Entertainment expenses (100 percent of cost)	1,200
Total expenses	$3,600

How would these employee expenses and reimbursement be treated on Peter's individual tax return if he receives the following reimbursement from his employer?

a. $3,000
b. $3,600

47. Kearney Kramer donated to his church stock which he had held for five months. The stock had a fair market value of $1,000 at the time of the gift, but had only cost Kearney $700. What is the amount deductible as a charitable contribution?

a. $1,000
b. $880
c. $700
d. $300
e. None of the above

48. Which of the following unreimbursed employee expenses is deductible for adjusted gross income?

a. Transportation expenses
b. Union dues
c. Travel expenses
d. None of the above

49. If an employee does not make an adequate accounting to the employer and employer reimbursement of employee expenses exceeds the expenses, the employee business expenses are:

a. Not shown on the employee's tax return
b. Shown as miscellaneous itemized deductions subject to the 2 percent nondeductible floor

   c. Shown as miscellaneous itemized deductions not subject to the 2 percent nondeductible floor

   d. None of the above

50. If an employee makes an adequate accounting to the employer and employer reimbursement of employee expenses is less than the expenses, the excess expenses are:

   a. Not deductible on the employee's tax return

   b. Deductible as miscellaneous itemized deductions subject to the 2 percent nondeductible floor

   c. Deductible as miscellaneous itemized deductions not subject to the 2 percent nondeductible floor

   d. None of the above

51. *Comprehensive Problem.* Andy and Marcia Tufts, both age 35, are married with two dependent children and file a joint return. From the following information, compute their taxable income for 1998.

Andy's salary	$40,000
Marcia's salary	32,000
Andy's contribution to an IRA (assume IRA is deductible for AGI)	2,000
Dividends received from domestic corporations	950
Medical expenses for doctors and hospitals	4,200
Premiums for health insurance	2,600
Prescription drugs and medicines	800
Eyeglasses for one of the children	175
Interest on home mortgage	6,800
Interest on credit cards	300
Real property taxes on residence	1,300
Sales taxes	600
Fee for preparation of tax returns	125
Union dues and subscriptions	480

52. *Research Problem.* Mary Sage's daughter has a serious medical problem. Mary must take her daughter to a distant city to be treated. Mary and her daughter stay for seven days to receive treatment. Mary incurs $1,000 in transportation costs, $800 in motel costs, and $240 for meals. What amount is deductible as a medical expense deduction before the 7.5 percent limitation?

53. *Research Problem.* The following selected court cases have helped to shape the tax law in regard to travel expense deductions. Read the following cases and prepare a brief written abstract for each case.

   a. *Burns v. Gray,* 61-1 USTC ¶ 9294, 287 F.2d 698 (CA-6 1961).

   b. *R. Rosenspan,* 71-1 USTC ¶ 9241, 438 F.2d 905 (CA-2 1971), cert. denied, 404 U.S. 864, 92 S.Ct. 54.

   c. *H.A. Stidger,* 67-1 USTC ¶ 9309, 386 U.S. 287, 87 S.Ct. 1065 (1967).

Chapter 8

Tax Credits, Prepayments, and Special Methods

Learning Objectives

After completing Chapter 8, you should be able to:

1. Understand tax credits, both nonrefundable and refundable.
2. Compute estimated tax payments.
3. Apply the alternative minimum tax rules to individual taxpayers.

OVERVIEW OF CHAPTER

After completing this chapter, a student should be able to distinguish between the various types of tax credits available to taxpayers and to determine which credits represent a reduction of the income tax, which credits represent a return of a taxpayer overpayment of other types of taxes, and which credits can be used in other years if not fully used in the present year. This chapter will also provide tax planning hints on avoiding the alternative minimum tax provisions.

Nonrefundable Tax Credits

¶ 8001   TYPES OF CREDITS

A tax credit is a direct reduction of the tax due. It differs from a deduction which is a reduction in income subject to tax. For this reason, a credit is more valuable than the same amount of deduction. For example, a tax credit of $100 saves $100 in tax; a deduction of $100 saves $28 of tax for a taxpayer in the 28 percent marginal tax bracket and $15 for a taxpayer in the 15 percent marginal tax bracket.

Credits are divided into two types: (1) nonrefundable and (2) refundable. In the case of nonrefundable credits, there have been no payments to the government and therefore a taxpayer cannot obtain a refund of a credit if the credit exceeds the gross tax. Nonrefundable credits cannot be used to offset the recapture of any other credit or to offset taxes other than the income tax.

With the exception of the credit for earned income, refundable credits are prepayments. Refundable credits can be offset against the recapture of other credits and against other taxes.

The credits must be computed in the order in which they are presented to insure that any limitations are properly applied. The limitations are stated in terms of the gross tax reduced by previously computed credits.

¶ 8015   HOUSEHOLD AND DEPENDENT CARE CREDIT

A credit is allowed up to 30 percent of employment-related expenses for care of qualifying individuals. Job-related expenses are allowed up to $2,400 (maximum $720 credit) for one individual and up to $4,800 (maximum $1,440 credit) for two or more individuals. The credit is reduced by one percentage point for each $2,000 of adjusted gross income, or fraction thereof, above $10,000. Code Sec. 21(a)(2) and (c). The credit is not reduced below 20 percent. Thus, taxpayers with adjusted gross income of over $28,000 will have a credit of 20 percent.

		Credit Limitation	
Adjusted Gross Income	Applicable Percentage	One Person	Two or More Persons
$ 0 to $10,000	30%	$720	$1,440
10,001 to 12,000	29	696	1,392
12,001 to 14,000	28	672	1,344
14,001 to 16,000	27	648	1,296
16,001 to 18,000	26	624	1,248
18,001 to 20,000	25	600	1,200
20,001 to 22,000	24	576	1,152
22,001 to 24,000	23	552	1,104
24,001 to 26,000	22	528	1,056
26,001 to 28,000	21	504	1,008
28,001 and above	20	480	960

Employment-related expenses are those expenses paid for household and personal care of qualifying individuals which are necessary for the taxpayer to be gainfully employed or in active search for gainful employment. Code Sec. 21(b)(2); Reg. § 1.44A-1(c)(1). Gainful employment includes working for others, either full time or part time, or employment in one's own business or partnership. Volunteer work for a nominal salary does not constitute gainful employment.

If the taxpayer is not employed or actively seeking employment during any part of the year, expenses allocable to that part of the year are not considered for the credit. Thus, for example, a teacher who does not teach during the summer months could not use child care expenses incurred during the summer in computing the credit.

The maximum expenses eligible for the credit must be reduced by amounts excludable from income under an employer-provided dependent care assistance program. The name, address, and the taxpayer identification number of the person providing the dependent care must be shown on the return of the taxpayer receiving the credit.

A "qualifying individual" is a child under age 13, a mentally or physically incapacitated dependent, or a mentally or physically incapacitated spouse. Code Sec. 21(b)(1). In order to take the tax credit, a taxpayer must furnish over half the cost of maintaining a home that is the principal residence of the taxpayer as well as the principal residence of a qualified individual. Code Sec. 21(e)(1). Thus, the taxpayer must furnish over half of the cost of maintaining the household during the period the employment-related expenses are incurred.

The credit is available to a divorced or separated parent who has custody of a child who is under age 13 or who is physically or mentally incapable of self-care, even though the parent may not be entitled to a dependency exemption under the terms of a divorce decree or settlement agreement. Code Sec. 21(e)(5). The child will not be a qualifying individual for the other parent.

Only employment-related expenses qualify for the credit. These include ordinary and necessary household services to maintain a home. Any taxes required to be paid for FICA and federal unemployment or similar state payroll taxes on wages paid to an individual for providing household and personal care that constitutes employment are considered to be employment-related expenses. Disabled dependent or spouse care expenses for services performed outside the taxpayer's home are includible only if the disabled spouse or disabled dependent regularly spent at least eight hours a day in the taxpayer's home. Child care expenses are not confined to services performed within the taxpayer's home and include those for household services, day care centers, nursery school, and kindergarten. Expenditures for services provided by a dependent care center not in compliance with state or local regulations are not eligible for this credit. Expenses incurred to send a dependent to an overnight camp may not be claimed. Code Sec. 21(b)(2). No credit is allowed for any amounts paid to an individual for which the taxpayer is allowed a personal exemption deduction or who is a child of the taxpayer and has not reached the age of 19 at the close of the tax year. Code Sec. 21(e)(6).

Employment-related expenses cannot exceed the earned income of a single taxpayer. In the case of married taxpayers, expenses are limited to the earned income of the spouse with the lower income. Code Sec. 21(d)(1).

Example 8.1. Bob and Linda are married taxpayers filing a joint return with two dependents. They incurred $3,600 of employment-related child care expenses. Linda worked part time and had earnings of $2,700. Bob had earnings of $26,000. Since Linda's income was less than the amount of the employment-related expenses, the credit was based on her earnings. Since their adjusted gross income exceeds $28,000, the credit is reduced to 20 percent. The credit would be $540 ($2,700 × 20%).

In case of married taxpayers where, for any month, one spouse is either a full-time student at an educational institution or incapable of self-care, that spouse will be considered to have earned income of $200 per month if there is one qualifying individual in the household, and $400 per month if there are two or more qualifying individuals. Code Sec. 21(d)(2). If both spouses are students or are incapable of self-care, this rule applies to only one spouse for any one month. The $200 and $400 figures are used only in computing the lower income of the two spouses and are not included in the income of the taxpayers.

Married couples must file a joint return to claim the credit. The taxpayer who (1) has not lived with the other spouse for over six months at the end of the year, (2) lives with a qualifying dependent, and (3) provides over one-half of the cost of maintaining the household will be considered as single for the purpose of this credit. Code Sec. 21(e)(2) and (4). The taxpayer will not have to take the other spouse's income into consideration or file a joint return. There is no carryover of any unused household and dependent care credit.

¶ 8025   ELDERLY AND DISABLED PERSONS CREDIT

An important tax benefit for the elderly is the retirement income credit. This provision was added in 1954 because of concern that persons receiving Social Security benefits were favored over persons receiving comparable forms of retirement income. In 1976, changes were made to eliminate what was viewed as discrimination against those who are required to support themselves by working in their later years. Beginning in 1984, the credit was expanded to include the permanently and totally disabled. This expansion of the credit for the elderly was coupled with the repeal of the disability income exclusion effective for years after 1983.

Individuals can receive a 15 percent credit to be applied against their tax on all types of income, including earned income. To qualify for the credit for the elderly, an individual must (1) have reached age 65 before the end of the tax year or (2) have retired on disability before the close of the tax year and must have been permanently and totally disabled when he or she retired. The maximum base amount against which the 15 percent credit can be claimed is $5,000 for a single person and married persons filing jointly where only one spouse qualifies. The maximum is $7,500 when both spouses are qualified individuals and file a joint return. The figure is $3,750 when a married individual files a separate return. Code Sec. 22(a)-(c).

Where a qualified individual has not attained age 65 before the end of the tax year, the maximum base amount cannot exceed that individual's disability income for the year. Married individuals must file a joint return to receive the credit unless the spouses lived apart for the entire year. Nonresident aliens are not eligible for the credit. Code Sec. 22(c), (e)(1), and (f).

The maximum base amount must be reduced by Social Security, railroad retirement benefits, or other exempt pension benefits. Code Sec. 22(c)(3). Social Security and railroad retirement benefits also may be partially taxed under Section 86. Any amounts included in gross income will not reduce the maximum base amount. No reduction is required for pension or annuity payments from a tax-qualified pension plan, even though the amounts may be excluded from gross income. The maximum base amount is also reduced by one-half of the amount of adjusted gross income above certain income levels: $10,000 for married persons filing jointly, $5,000 for married persons filing separately, and $7,500 for single persons. Code Sec. 22(d)(1). Thus, for a single person, the credit would no longer be available when adjusted gross income reaches $17,500 ($7,500 plus two times $5,000). For the joint return the credit would be available up to an income level of $20,000 if only one spouse qualifies and up to $25,000 if both spouses qualify. On a joint return, the reduction is based on amounts received by either spouse.

> *Example 8.2.* Larry and Donna Douglas are both over 65 and report $12,000 of adjusted gross income on a joint return. In addition, they received Social Security benefits of $1,500 for the year. Their credit for the elderly will be computed as follows:

Maximum Base Amount		$7,500
Less: Social Security	$1,500	
½ (AGI in excess of $10,000)	1,000	2,500
Balance available for credit		$5,000
Credit allowed ($5,000 × 15%)		$ 750

The amount of the credit cannot exceed the income tax due for the year. There are no provisions for carryovers of any unused credit. Thus, if the credit exceeds the tax due, any remaining credit is lost.

¶ 8031   ADOPTION ASSISTANCE CREDIT AND EXCLUSION

A nonrefundable tax credit of up to $5,000 of qualified adoption expenses per child ($6,000 in the case of a child with special needs) has been provided for tax years beginning after 1996. Qualified expenses include adoption fees, court costs, attorney fees, and other expenses related to the legal adoption of an eligible child. Also, employees are entitled to exclude from income up to $5,000 of adoption expenses per adopted child ($6,000 in the case of a child with special needs) where such amounts are paid or incurred by their employers under a qualified adoption assistance program. The exclusion applies for tax years beginning after 1996 and before 2002. Special rules apply to foreign adoptions and adoptions of children with special needs, and the credit and exclusion are phased out beginning at modified adjusted gross income levels between $75,000 and $115,000. No credit is allowed for any expenses reimbursed by the employer or by a federal, state, or local program.

Expenses may include the cost of construction, renovations, alterations, or purchases specifically required by the state to meet the needs of the child. The increase in basis of the property that would result from such an expenditure must be reduced by the amount of credit allowed. Expenses incurred in carrying out a surrogate parenting arrangement or in adopting a spouse's child do not qualify for the credit. The child must be under age 18 or incapable of self-care in order to qualify for the credit.

The credit is taken in the year of adoption and includes expenses incurred in previous years. A carryforward period of five years is allowed for any credit disallowed because of limitation based on tax liability. Code Sec. 23.

Example 8.3. In 1998 a married couple incurs $8,000 in adoption expenses for a child with special needs. Their modified adjusted gross income is $100,000. They would be allowed a credit of $2,250 ($6,000 − (($100,000 − $75,000)/$40,000 × $6,000).

Example 8.4. A married couple incurs $7,000 in adoption expenses for a child without special needs. The employer reimburses the couple for $4,500 of the expenses under a qualified adoption assistance program. The couple will be eligible for an adoption credit of $500 ($5,000 maximum credit minus $4,500 exclusion from employer plan).

¶ 8032   CHILD TAX CREDIT

Beginning in 1998, taxpayers are allowed a credit for qualifying children under age 17. The credit is $400 per child for 1998 and $500 per child after 1998. The credit phases out when modified adjusted gross income exceeds $75,000 for single taxpayers, $110,000 for married taxpayers filing a joint return, and $55,000 for married taxpayers filing separately. The credit is reduced by $50 for each $1,000, or fraction thereof, of modified adjusted gross income above the threshold levels. Modified adjusted gross income is determined without regard to the exclusions from gross income for foreign earned income and foreign housing costs and income of residents of Guam, American Samoa, the Northern Mariana Islands, and Puerto Rico.

A "qualifying child" is a child, descendant, stepchild, or eligible foster child for whom the taxpayer may claim a dependency exemption and who is less than 17 years old at the close of the tax year. The child must be a U.S. citizen.

Taxpayers who qualify for the child tax credit may qualify for a refundable credit known as the supplemental child credit. Generally, a supplemental child credit will result only when the taxpayer's earned income credit exceeds the taxpayer's employee share of FICA. The amount treated as a supplemental child credit reduces the amount of the child tax credit but does not change the total amount of the child tax credits allowed and has no effect on determining the amount of any other credit for any tax year.

Example 8.5. Arleta Kern has two qualifying children. She is allowed an earned income credit of $1,300 and has a $500 regular tax liability, no other personal credits, and pays Social Security taxes of $1,000. Her child tax credit of $800 ($400 × 2 children) is limited to $500, her regular tax liability. However, $300 of the $500 credit will be taken as a supplemental child credit, which is the excess of the $1,300 earned income credit over the $1,000 in Social Security taxes. The child tax credit will be $200. The total credit is still $500, with $200 as a child tax credit and $300 as a supplemental child credit.

Taxpayers who have three or more qualifying children may also be entitled to an additional credit. Those taxpayers will be able to receive the full benefit of the child tax credit without being limited to their share of the FICA tax. This portion of the credit will be a refundable credit.

¶ 8033   HOPE AND LIFETIME LEARNING CREDITS

Beginning in 1998 new tax credits may be elected by low- and middle-income individuals for tuition expenses incurred by students pursing college or graduate degrees or vocational training. The credit phases out for AGI between $40,000 and $50,000 for singles; and $80,000 and $100,000 on a joint return.

The Hope Scholarship Credit provides a maximum nonrefundable tax credit of $1,500 per student for each of the first two years of post-secondary education. The $1,500 per year limitation is made up of 100 percent of the first $1,000 of qualified expenses plus 50 percent of next $1,000 of qualified expenses. The Hope Scholarship Credit applies for the first two years of higher education. The credit is applicable to the taxpayer, spouse, and dependents. The credit cannot be taken if an exclusion for education IRA or state tuition program is claimed. The credit applies only to expenses paid after 1997.

The Lifetime Learning Credit allows a credit of 20 percent of qualified tuition expenses paid by the taxpayer for any year the Hope Credit is not claimed. The credit is 20 percent of the first $5,000 of qualified tuition and fees paid for taxpayer, spouse, and/or dependent ($10,000 of qualified expenses after 2002). It is figured on a per-taxpayer basis. The credit applies for any number of years of higher education, and it only applies to expenses paid after June 30, 1998.

Example 8.6. Joe and Sheila Ames have three children in college. Joni, a freshman, incurs $2,100 in tuition expenses during 1998. Mike, a junior, incurs $3,000 in tuition expenses after June 30, 1998. Sally, in graduate school, incurs $3,500 in tuition expenses after June 30, 1998. Joe and Sheila paid all of the tuition expenses, and their adjusted gross income does not exceed $80,000. They will be allowed a credit on their 1998 tax return of $2,500. The Hope Credit applies to Joni and is limited to 100 percent of the first $1,000 of expenses and 50 percent of the next $1,000. The Lifetime Learning Credit applies to both Mike and Sally and is limited to 20 percent of the first $5,000 of expenses.

¶ 8035   FOREIGN TAX CREDIT

Both individuals and corporations may claim a credit against the United States tax for certain income taxes of foreign countries and possessions of the United States. Code Sec. 27(a). The foreign tax credit is the method employed by the United States and many other economically developed countries to deal with the problem of double taxation that arises whenever two taxing jurisdictions have a reasonable claim to impose a tax on the same income.

For example, a United States citizen is subject to tax on his or her worldwide income simply because of his or her citizenship. But if he or she were employed in Canada, the Canadian government has at least an equal right to tax the income. To avoid the possibility that combined taxes may exceed 100 percent, the usual rule is that "home yields to source." Thus, the U.S. citizen would be required to include and pay tax to Canada. To avoid double taxation, a credit is allowed for the Canadian tax against the U.S. liability.

As an alternative to the credit, a deduction of foreign income taxes may be taken under Code Sec. 164. A credit against the tax ordinarily results in a greater tax benefit than a deduction from gross income. However, in a few instances the limitation on the allowable credit will cause the deduction to be of greater benefit. All foreign taxes must be treated the same way—they must all be deducted or all claimed as a credit. The credit does not apply to payment of royalties made in the guise of a tax, such as under an oil production sharing agreement made after 1977. Code Sec. 901(e).

The credit is equal to the lesser of the actual tax paid to the foreign country or a limitation. Taxpayers are required to compute the limitation on the amount of foreign tax that can be used to reduce U.S. tax under the overall limitation. A taxpayer totals the taxes paid to all foreign countries and possessions. This total is then subjected to a limitation computed by multiplying the U.S. tax liability by a fraction consisting of taxable income from foreign sources over the worldwide taxable income. Code Sec. 904(a). For individuals, worldwide taxable income is computed as adjusted gross income less total itemized deductions or standard deduction (personal exemptions are not deducted). Thus, the credit cannot exceed that proportion of the U.S. tax which U.S. taxable income from sources within that country bear to the entire U.S. taxable income for the same year.

> **Example 8.7.** Anco, a domestic corporation, had worldwide taxable income of $500,000 and a tentative U.S. tax liability of $170,000. From its operations in a foreign country, Anco had $100,000 of taxable income on which a $45,000 tax was imposed. Anco's foreign tax credit is limited to $34,000 (($100,000/$500,000) × $170,000 = $34,000). If the actual tax paid the foreign country was less than the computed limitation, the credit would be the actual tax paid.

> **Example 8.8.** Allen Armstrong has worldwide taxable income (not including personal exemptions) of $250,000 for 1998 and a tentative U.S. tax liability of $78,458. Included in his worldwide income was $100,000 taxable income from a foreign country on which a $35,000 tax was imposed. Allen's foreign tax credit is limited to $31,383 (($100,000/$250,000) × $78,458).

Unused foreign taxes may be carried back two years and then forward five years. The credit is first carried to the earliest year and then to the next earliest year. There is no carryover to the year the foreign tax is deducted.

TAX BLUNDER

John Jones worked part of the year in a foreign country. He paid $20,000 in income taxes to the foreign country. On his tax return he took an itemized deduction for the income taxes paid. Unless the limitation reduced the credit significantly, it is very likely that taking a credit for the foreign income taxes paid will provide a much larger tax benefit to John than will an itemized deduction.

¶ 8040   CREDIT FOR QUALIFIED ELECTRIC VEHICLES

A taxpayer may claim a credit for investments in qualified electric vehicles placed in service after June 30, 1993, and before 2005. Code Sec. 30. The amount of the credit is 10 percent of costs up to $40,000. No credit is permitted for any portion of a vehicle's cost that is expensed under Section 179. The basis for depreciation of the vehicles must be reduced by the amount of the credit.

The credit applies to a motor vehicle powered primarily by an electric motor drawing current from rechargeable batteries, fuel cells, or other portable sources of electric current. The original use of the vehicle must begin with the taxpayer. For vehicles placed in service in 2002 through 2004, the credit is reduced 25 percent each year.

The credit is recaptured as an increase in tax in the year in which the vehicle ceases to be a qualified electric vehicle. The credit must be recaptured if the motor vehicle ceases to be a qualified electric vehicle within three full years from the date the electric vehicle is placed in service. A vehicle ceases to be a qualified electric vehicle if (1) the vehicle is modified so that it is no longer primarily powered by electricity; (2) the vehicle is used outside the U.S., or is property used as lodging, property used by certain tax-exempt organizations, or property used by governmental units or foreign persons or entities; or (3) the taxpayer sells or disposes of the vehicle and knows or has reason to know that the vehicle will be modified or have its use changed in a manner described in (2) or (3).

> *Example 8.9.* Sue Smith purchases an electric vehicle for $45,000 on January 22, 1998. She receives a $4,000 credit upon purchase ($40,000 limit x 10%). On March 27, 1999, Sue sells the vehicle to a tax-exempt entity. She must recapture $2,667 ($4,000 x 66 2/3%) in 2000 because it was held less than two years.

¶ 8045   GENERAL BUSINESS CREDIT

In order to provide a uniform limitation on the amounts of business credits that may be offset against tax liability and uniform rules for carrybacks and carryforwards, the 13 business credits listed below have been combined into a single credit called the general business credit. The amount of the current year business credit is the sum of the following credits determined for the tax year:

1.   Investment credit

2.   Work opportunity credit

3.   Welfare-to-work credit

4. Alcohol fuels credit

5. Research credit

6. Low-income housing credit

7. Enhanced oil recovery credit

8. Disabled persons access credit

9. Renewable electricity production credit

10. Empowerment zone credit

11. Indian employment credit

12. Employer Social Security credit

13. Orphan drug credit

The ceiling limitations, carryover, and recapture provisions apply to the total of the 13 general business credits.

Investment Credit

Taxpayers purchasing "qualified investments" are allowed a credit against the tax liability for a portion of the amount of their investment for the year the property is placed in service. Under Section 46(a) the investment credit is the sum of:

1. Rehabilitation credit

2. Energy credit

3. Reforestation credit

Rehabilitation Credit

A two-tier investment credit for qualified rehabilitated buildings makes up the rehabilitation credit. The credit is (1) 20 percent for rehabilitations of certified historic structures and (2) 10 percent for rehabilitations of other buildings originally placed in service before 1936. The 20 percent credit applies to both residential and nonresidential buildings and the 10 percent credit applies to nonresidential property. Code Sec. 47(a).

Certain expenditures do not qualify for the credit. The costs of acquiring a building or an interest in a building, such as a leasehold interest, are not considered as qualifying expenditures. The costs of facilities related to an existing building, such as a parking lot, also are not considered as qualifying expenditures. Expenditures incurred by a lessee do not qualify for the credit unless the remaining lease term on the date the rehabilitation is completed is at least as long as the applicable recovery period under the general depreciation rules (generally, 27.5 years for residential property and 39 years for nonresidential property). Straight-line depreciation must be used to qualify for the rehabilitation credit.

In addition, the cost of constructing a new building, or of completing a new building after it has been placed in service, will not qualify. Construction costs are considered to be for rehabilitation and not for new construction if (1) at least 50 percent of the existing external walls are retained as external walls, (2) at least 75 percent of existing external walls are retained as internal or external walls, and (3) at least 75 percent of the existing internal structure framework is retained in place. These tests do not apply to certified historic structures. Code Sec. 47(c).

The basis of a rehabilitated building must be reduced for the full rehabilitation credit.

Energy Credit

An energy credit is available for a taxpayer's investment in energy property. The eligible property and rates are shown in the table below.

Solar energy property 10%
Geothermal property 10%

The energy property must be depreciable property built or acquired by the taxpayer and must be either depreciable or amortizable. The energy property basis must be reduced by 50 percent of the credit taken. Code Sec. 48(a).

Reforestation Credit

The reforestation credit for any year is 10 percent of the portion of the amortizable basis of any qualified timber property which was acquired during the year. The basis of the timber property acquired must be reduced by 50 percent of the credit taken. Code Sec. 48(b).

Recapture of Credit

If qualified property is disposed of by sale or exchange, gift, or involuntary conversion before the close of the recapture period, the investment credit may be recaptured. For recovery property, the amount of increase in tax is determined by applying the recapture percentage to the amount of investment credit taken on the asset. Code Sec. 50.

If Property Ceases To Be Investment Credit Property Within	Recapture Percentage
First Year	100
Second Year	80
Third Year	60
Fourth Year	40
Fifth Year	20

Example 8.10. Billingsly Corporation purchased qualified business energy investment property with a MACRS life of five years for $30,000. Billingsly claimed an investment credit of $3,000 ($30,000 × 10%). If Billingsly sold the asset after four years of useful service, 20 percent of the $3,000, or $600, would be the increase in tax due because of the recapture.

If property with a basis reduced is disposed of in a transaction that triggers the recapture of an investment credit, then the basis "immediately before the event resulting in such recapture" is increased by 50 or 100 percent of the recaptured amount. Code Sec. 50(c)(3). The basis adjustment will affect gain or loss on disposition of the asset and also depreciation recapture.

> *Example 8.11.* Jerome Jackson purchased five-year Section 38 depreciable property for $30,000. After holding the asset for more than four years, Jerome sells it. A 10 percent investment credit of $3,000 was taken in the year of purchase and the asset basis was reduced by 50 percent of the credit taken. On disposition, investment credit would be recaptured in the amount of $600. The basis of the asset would be increased by one-half of this amount, or $300, for purposes of determining gain or loss and depreciation recapture.

Any increase in income tax because of recapture is treated as income tax imposed on the taxpayer even though the taxpayer has no income tax liability, has a net operating loss for the year, or no income tax return is otherwise required for the year. The investment credit recapture is not reduced by other nonrefundable tax credits.

If the investment credit allowable has not been used as a tax reduction, but is reflected in an unused carryover, the recapture will result in an adjustment of the carryover.

In determining the actual useful life of qualified property, the property is treated as placed in service on the first day of the month in which the property is placed in service. If property ceases to be qualified property, the cessation is treated as occurring on the actual date of the disqualification (i.e., sale, transfer, retirement). When the cessation is for any reason other than the occurrence of an event of a specific date, the cessation is treated as occurring on the first day of the tax year.

> *Example 8.12.* Bare Corporation purchases energy equipment with a life of five years on June 15, 1993, for $12,000. On June 7, 1998, the equipment is sold. Even though the asset was held for less than five years, for investment credit purposes, the asset was held more than five years (considered placed in service June 1, 1993, and sold June 7, 1998). None of the investment credit taken will be recaptured.

Taxpayers using an averaging convention in computing depreciation for qualified property may use the assumed dates of additions and retirements in determining the actual useful life of the property. This election must be used consistently and may not result in a substantial distortion of investment credit.

The death of a taxpayer does not trigger investment tax credit recapture. Moreover, recapture does not apply to the transfer caused by death of a partner's interest in a partnership, a beneficiary's interest in an estate or trust, or a shareholder's shares of stock in an S corporation. The property is treated as if it had actually been held for the entire useful life.

> *Example 8.13.* Benjamin Burr purchased $9,000 worth of energy equipment for his sole proprietorship, taking a $900 investment tax credit. He died four years later, leaving the equipment to his

daughter. There is no recapture of the credit and the daughter can dispose of the equipment immediately without recapture.

Recapture does not occur when property is transferred in a tax-free transfer by a corporation pursuant to a reorganization or a liquidation of a controlled subsidiary. Also, recapture does not occur when property is transferred in connection with a mere change in the form of carrying on a trade or business, provided that the taxpayer maintains a substantial interest in the business. Recapture will still occur if an early disposition occurs in a subsequent transaction that is not exempt.

TAX PLANNING POINTER ▼

Since recapture is affected by the holding period of the asset, care should be taken to dispose of an asset at the optimum time. Delaying the sale or disposition of property can reduce the amount of recapture.

TAX BLUNDER

Alvin Armend purchased energy equipment for $20,000 on June 1, 1993, taking the investment credit of $2,000. He sold the equipment on May 18, 1998. Since he sold the equipment before the five-year holding period, he must recapture $400 of the investment credit. Had Alvin held on to the asset for two more weeks he would have saved $400 in taxes.

At-Risk Limitations

The Economic Recovery Tax Act of 1981 contained an investment credit at-risk limitation which applies to businesses which are subject to loss limitations under Section 465. Generally, the taxpayer is allowed an investment credit for only that portion of an investment for which the taxpayer is at risk. A taxpayer is generally not at risk for nonrecourse debt. Where the taxpayer's at-risk amount increases, additional investment credit is allowed on the increase. If the taxpayer's at-risk amount decreases, the investment credit may be subject to recapture.

The investment credit at-risk rules do not apply to amounts borrowed for qualified energy property. In order to qualify under the exception, the taxpayer must have an investment in the property that is at risk in an amount that is at least 25 percent of the unadjusted basis of the property. In addition, any nonrecourse financing for the property must be a level payment loan. A level payment loan is a loan repaid in substantially equal installments including both principal and interest. Code Sec. 49.

Work Opportunity Credit

The work opportunity tax credit may be elected by employers who hire individuals for certain target groups suffering from unusually high unemployment. The credit is taken with respect to first-year wages paid to eligible individuals who begin work after September 30, 1997, and before October 1, 1998. The work opportunity credit equals 40 percent of the first $6,000 of wages for the first year of employment. The $6,000 limit is computed on each eligible employee for wages attributable to services rendered during the one-year period beginning with the day the individual begins work for the employer (maximum credit of $2,400 per employee). Code Sec. 51(a) and (b). The employee must complete a minimum of 120 hours of service for the credit to apply. If the employee completes at least 120 hours of service but less than 400 hours of service, the employer is entitled to a credit of 25 percent rather than the 40 percent.

> *Example 8.14.* Astabula Corp. hires Maxine Brown, a certified targeted group member, on December 1, 1997. The company pays $1,200 of wages to Maxine in December 1997 and $14,000 in 1998. The work opportunity credit for 1997 is $480 ($1,200 × 40%). The first $4,800 of wages paid in 1998 are also eligible for the credit of $1,920.

An employer's deduction for wages is reduced by the amount of the work opportunity credit. Also, wages taken into account in computing the work opportunity credit are not taken into account in computing any empowerment zone employment credit allowed by Code Sec. 1396.

The following individuals are members of targeted groups eligible for the work opportunity credit: (1) a qualified IV-A (Aid to Families with Dependent Children (AFDC)) recipient, (2) a qualified veteran, (3) a qualified ex-felon, (4) a high-risk youth, (5) a vocational rehabilitation referral, (6) a qualified summer youth employee, (7) a qualified food stamp recipient, or (8) a qualified SSI recipient.

An employer must obtain certification from a state employment security agency that an individual is a member of a targeted group. An individual may be treated as a member of a targeted group unless an employer either obtains written certification from the designated local agency on or before the day the individual begins work indicating that the individual is a member of a targeted group or completes a prescreening notice on or before the day employment is offered.

The work opportunity credit is elective with the taxpayer. If the credit is elected, the employer's deduction for wages is reduced by the amount of the tentative credit before application of the various limitations. Therefore, the employer has the option of taking the credit or the deduction.

> *Example 8.15.* Bertram Ross hired a qualified work opportunity credit employee. The employee begins work on March 2, 1998, and is paid $8,800 during the year. The targeted jobs credit allowed is $2,400 ($6,000 maximum amount × 40%). The taxpayer's tax deduction for wages is $6,400 ($8,800 wages paid − $2,400 work opportunity credit).

Welfare-to-Work Credit

This credit is available for employers for wages paid to long-term family assistance recipients who begin work after 1997. Code Sec. 51A. The amount of the credit for a tax year is 35 percent of the qualified first-year wages plus 50 percent of the qualified second-year wages. The credit applies only to the first $10,000 of wages in each year with respect to any individual. Thus, the maximum total credit per qualified employee is $8,500 for the two years.

> *Example 8.16.* Dewey Corporation hires Nina Alexis on June 5, 1998. Dewey pays Nina $7,000 in wages in 1998. Dewey Corporation can take a credit of $2,450 ($7,000 × 35%) in 1998. Dewey will also be eligible for a 35 percent credit on any wages paid Nina before June 5, 1999, but limited to $1,050 ($3,000 × 35%). The first $10,000 of wages paid Nina during the period of June 5, 1999, and June 4, 2000, will be eligible for a 50 percent credit.

If a welfare-to-work credit is allowed to an employer with respect to an individual for any tax year, the individual is not treated as a member of a targeted group for such tax year for the purposes of the work opportunity credit.

Alcohol Fuels Credit

To foster the production of gasohol, an income tax credit for alcohol and alcohol blended rules applies to fuel sales and uses. There is a 60-cent-per-gallon credit for alcohol of at least 190 proof and a 40-cent-per-gallon credit for alcohol of at least 150 but less than 190 proof for persons producing alcohol fuels or using them in a trade or business. Further, the amount of the allowable tax credit must be reduced to the extent that the alcohol is used in gasohol and other alcohol fuels for which there is an excise tax exemption for fuel taxes. Code Sec. 40.

The alcohol fuels credit is claimed as one of the components of the general business credit. Thus, it is subject to the maximum tax liability rules and the carryback and carryforward rules.

Taxpayers may elect to have the alcohol fuels credit not apply for any tax year. The election may be made or revoked at any time before the three-year period beginning on the last date for filing a return for such tax year, without regard to extensions.

Research Credit

A tax credit is allowed for qualifying research and development expenditures paid or incurred after June 30, 1996, and before July 1, 1998. The research credit is equal to the sum of (1) 20 percent of the excess (if any) of the *qualified research expenses* for the tax year over the base amount and (2) 20 percent of the *basic research payments.* Code Sec. 41(a). Thus, the research activities credit has two components: an incremental credit and a basic research credit.

Incremental research activities credit. The credit for increasing research activities applies only to research expenditures incurred in carrying on a trade or business in which a taxable entity is already engaged. Expenditures incurred, for example, in developing or improving a product, a formula, an invention, a plant process, or an experimental model are eligible for the credit. No credit is available for expenses relating to a potential trade or business. Thus, new businesses conducting research for future production that undertake research geared to the development of a new business activity may not claim the credit.

Qualified research expenses are the same as those costs eligible for a deduction under Code Sec. 174 (see ¶ 5435) other than expenses for foreign research, research in the social sciences, arts or humanities, or subsidized research. Credit-eligible research is limited to research undertaken to discover information that is (1) technological in nature and (2) intended to be useful in the development of a new or improved business component. Further, the research must be elements of a process of experimentation for a functional purpose (i.e., it must relate to a new or improved function, performance, reliability, or quality). Qualified research expenses cover in-house expenses for the taxpayer's own research (wages for substantially engaging in or directly supervising or supporting research activities, supplies, and computer use charges) and 65 percent of amounts paid or incurred for qualified research done by a person other than an employee of the taxpayer. Prepaid contract research expenses are to be taken into account over the period in which the research is conducted.

The incremental credit is 20 percent of the excess of a taxpayer's qualified research expenditures for the current tax year over its "base amount" for that year. The term "base amount" is defined as the product of (1) the taxpayer's "fixed-base" percentage and (2) the average annual gross receipts of the taxpayer for the four tax years preceding the credit year. The base amount may not be less than 50 percent of the qualified research expenses for the credit year.

The fixed-base percentage of an existing firm is the same as the percentage of the taxpayer's aggregate qualified research expenses for taxable years beginning after December 31, 1983, and before January 1, 1989, over the aggregate gross receipts of the taxpayer for these tax years. The percentage is rounded to 1/100 of 1 percent. In no event may the fixed-base percentage exceed 16 percent. The fixed-base percentage of start-up companies is set at 3 percent. Start-up companies are those with fewer than three tax years beginning after December 31, 1983, and before January 1, 1989, in which the taxpayer had both gross receipts and qualified research expenses. Qualified research expenses and gross receipts for periods prior to a change of business ownership are treated as transferred with the trade or business that gave rise to those expenditures and receipts for purposes of recomputing a taxpayer's fixed-base percentage.

Example 8.17. James Zorch, a calendar year taxpayer, has $1,000,000 in average gross receipts and a fixed-base percentage of 12 percent. It incurs qualified research expenditures of $260,000. The amount of the taxpayer's research credit is $26,000, determined as follows:

Qualified research expenditures incurred		$260,000
Less: The larger of:		
(1) Base amount ($1,000,000 × 12%) $120,000		
(2) Minimum average base period research expenses (50% of $260,000 qualified research expenditures) 130,000		130,000
Remainder of qualified research expenditures available for credit		$130,000
Research credit (20% of $130,000)		$ 26,000

Basic research credit. The second element of the research credit computation is 20 percent of the basic research payments. This is sometimes referred to as the university research credit because the credit is available to corporations for basic research to be performed by universities, colleges, and other qualified organizations (scientific research organizations, organizations promoting scientific research, and organizations that make basic research grants). The amount of basic research payments taken into account is the excess of such basic research expenditures over the qualified organization base period amount. Those expenses that do not exceed such base period amount are treated as contract research expenses and are subject to the 65-percent rule.

The qualified organization base period amount for the above purpose is equal to the sum of the minimum basic research amount and the maintenance-of-effort amount. The minimum basic research amount is equal to the greater of (1) 1 percent of the average of amounts paid or incurred during the base period for any in-house research expenses and any contract research expenses or (2) the amounts treated as contract research expenses during the base period. The maintenance-of-effort amount is the excess of the average of the nondesignated university contributions paid by the taxpayer during the base period multiplied by the cost-of-living adjustment for the calendar year in which such tax year begins over the amount of nondesignated university contributions paid by the taxpayer during the tax year.

The term "basic research" means any original investigation for the advancement of scientific knowledge not having a specific commercial objective. However, expenditures for basic research do not include amounts paid for such research conducted outside the United States or amounts paid for basic research in the social sciences or humanities (including the arts). Basic research must be performed pursuant to a written research agreement between the corporate taxpayer and a qualified organization.

Any business deduction for qualified research expenses or basic research payments must be reduced by 100 percent of the research credit. An election permits a taxpayer to avoid reducing the deduction by electing to reduce the research credit by the product of (1) 50 percent of the credit and (2) the maximum corporate tax rate. The election is made for each tax year. It is irrevocable and must be made no later than the time for filing the taxpayer's return for the year of the election.

Low-Income Housing Credit

A nonrefundable income tax credit applies to newly constructed or substantially rehabilitated qualified low-income housing projects placed in service after 1986. The credit is claimed over a credit period which is the 10 tax years beginning with the tax year in which the building is placed in service. First-year credits must be prorated to reflect a partial year of qualification. If the credit is prorated, the balance of the first year's credit is available in the eleventh year. The basis for purposes of depreciation is not reduced by the amount of low-income credit claimed. Code Sec. 42(a).

The applicable credit rate is the appropriate percentage issued by the IRS for the month in which the building is placed in service. For newly constructed units or rehabilitation expenditures exceeding specified minimum amounts per low-income unit that are not federally subsidized, the credit rate is computed so that the present value of the 10 annual credit amounts at the beginning of the credit period equals 70 percent of the qualified basis of the low-income units. For qualified federally subsidized units the rate is such that the present value equals 30 percent.

The credit rate equal to the 30 percent present value also applies to the cost of acquisition of certain existing low-income units. The credit for acquisition cost may be claimed only if the property was placed in service more than 10 years before the acquisition and there is substantial rehabilitation. Rehabilitation expenditures during any 24-month period must constitute a qualified basis equaling the greater of $3,000 per low-income unit or 10 percent of the unadjusted basis of the building. Rehabilitation expenses for any building are treated as a separate new building. If such test is satisfied and the substantial rehabilitation expenditures are not federally subsidized, such expenditures are eligible for the credit determined under the 70 percent present value applicable credit rate. A 30 percent present value applicable credit rate would apply to the existing portion of such building.

Example 8.18. Mildred Meridian incurs $100,000 in qualifying costs to rehabilitate low-income property on January 1, 1998. The expenditures are not federally subsidized. Assume that the applicable credit rate is 9 percent. Mildred is eligible for a $9,000 credit for each year from 1998 through 2007.

The amount of the credit is the product of the applicable credit rate and the taxpayer's share of the qualified basis of the property allocable to the units occupied by low-income tenants. A separate calculation to compute the qualified basis must be made for property qualifying for each of the credits. Each qualified basis amount is equal to the total basis of the low-income property multiplied by the percentage of units occupied by tenants with the appropriate income level.

A low-income housing project qualifies for the credit if it is residential rental property, if the units are used on a nontransient basis, and if a minimum occupancy requirement is met. Hotels, dormitories, nursing homes, hospitals, life-care facilities, and retirement homes do not qualify for the credit. At least 20 percent of a project's units must be occupied by individuals having incomes of 50 percent or less of the area median income (adjusted for family size) or at least 40 percent of the units must be occupied by individuals having incomes of 60 percent or less of area median income (again adjusted for family size). The taxpayer must irrevocably elect which of the two requirements (the 20 percent or the 40 percent test) will apply to the project. The gross rent paid by families in units qualifying for the credit cannot exceed 30 percent of the income limitation applicable to the tenants, based on family size.

Qualified low-income housing projects must maintain their qualification for a minimum of 15 years from the beginning of the year in which the project first qualifies for the credit. If not, a portion of the credits must be recaptured with interest. The allowable credits are reduced to two-thirds per year prior to recapture in determining the recapture amount.

The credit receives special treatment under the passive activity loss limitations. Qualifying projects are considered "active real estate rentals" regardless of the form of ownership or the investor's actual participation in the operations. The "active" status covers only the credit and does not extend to any income or loss from the project. There is no phaseout of the credit benefits as adjusted gross income exceeds $100,000. The credit is subject to the general business credit limitation and is subject to the carryback and carryforward rules.

Enhanced Oil Recovery Credit

The enhanced oil recovery credit for any year is an amount equal to 15 percent of the taxpayer's enhanced oil recovery cost for that year. Code Sec. 43. The taxpayer must reduce the amount otherwise deductible or required to be capitalized to the extent that a credit is allowed. The amount of the credit is to be reduced in a tax year following a calendar year during which the reference price of crude oil exceeds $28.

Disabled Persons Access Credit

A tax credit is available to an eligible small business for expenditures incurred to make the business accessible to disabled individuals. An eligible small business is defined as any person (including any predecessor) that either (1) had gross receipts for the preceding tax year that did not exceed $1 million or (2) had no more than 30 full-time employees during the preceding tax year. The amount of the credit is equal to 50 percent of the amount of the eligible access expenditures for that year that exceed $250 but that do not exceed $10,250. The amount of the credit must reduce the expenditures otherwise eligible for deduction or basis increase. Code Sec. 44.

Example 8.19. Dana Corporation, an eligible small business, spends $8,750 to install ramps to its building to make the building accessible to handicapped individuals. Dana is allowed a credit of

$4,250 (($8,750 − $250) × 50%). Only $4,500 is eligible for depreciation as the $8,750 expenditure must be reduced by the $4,250 credit.

A taxpayer may elect to currently deduct up to $15,000 annually of barrier removal expenses. Code Sec. 190. A deduction is not allowed to the extent that a credit is taken for these expenditures.

Renewable Electricity Production Credit

The renewable electricity production credit is an amount determined by the kilowatt hours of electricity produced by the taxpayer from qualified energy resources. The production must take place at a qualified facility during the 10-year period beginning on the date the facility was originally placed in service. The electricity production must be sold to an unrelated person during the year. Code Sec. 45.

Empowerment Zone Employment Credit

The general business credit includes an empowerment zone employment credit for employers. The credit is generally equal to 20 percent of the first $15,000 of wages paid during the year to each employee who is a resident of a designated empowerment zone and who performs substantially all employment services within the zone in a taxpayer's trade or business. Code Sec. 1396. The deduction that the employer would normally be allowed for wages is reduced by the amount of the empowerment zone credit claimed for the tax year. Several empowerment zones have been designated by the Secretary of Housing and Urban Development and the Secretary of Agriculture from urban and rural areas nominated by state and local governments.

Indian Employment Credit

The amount of the Indian employment credit is an amount equal to 20 percent of the excess of qualified wages paid or incurred during the year plus qualified employee health insurance costs paid or incurred over the sum of the qualified wages and qualified employee health insurance costs paid or incurred during the calendar year 1993. Code Sec. 45A. A qualified employee must be a member of an Indian tribe or the spouse of an enrolled member of an Indian tribe. Substantially all of the services performed must be performed within an Indian reservation. The principal place of abode of the employee while performing the services must be on or near the reservation in which the services are performed.

Employer Social Security Credit

A business credit is allowed to food and beverage establishments for the amount equal to the employer's Federal Insurance Contribution Act (FICA) obligation (7.65 percent) attributable to tips in excess of those treated as wages for purposes of satisfying the minimum wage provisions of the Fair Labor Standards Act. To prevent a double benefit, no deduction is allowed for any amount taken into account in determining the credit. Carrybacks attributable to unused employer Social Security credits are not allowed to a tax year ending before 1994.

Orphan Drug Credit

The orphan drug tax credit is available for amounts paid or incurred after June 30, 1996. The credit is an amount equal to 50 percent of the qualified clinical testing expenses for the taxable year. Code Sec. 45C(a). Basically, the term "clinical testing" means any human clinical testing that is carried out under an exemption for a drug being tested for a rare disease.

Limitation on General Business Credit

The general business credit may not exceed "net income tax" minus the greater of (1) the tentative minimum tax or (2) 25 percent of "net regular tax liability" above $25,000. Code Sec. 38(c). The term "net income tax" means the sum of the regular tax plus the alternative minimum tax and minus all other nonrefundable credits, except the credit for prior year minimum tax. "Net regular tax" is the regular tax liability reduced by such credits.

> *Example 8.20.* Lindy Corporation has purchases that entitle it to $62,000 in general business credits. Its tax liability before the deduction of the general business credit is $45,000. Except for the ceiling, Lindy's credit for the year would be $62,000. However, the ceiling on the credit yields a maximum credit of $40,000 ($45,000 − 25% × ($45,000 − $25,000)).

Where a husband and wife file separately, the $25,000 amount becomes $12,500. However, this reduction will not apply if the spouse of the taxpayer has no qualified investment for the tax year and no carryback or carryover to the tax year. The $25,000 is apportioned among component members of a controlled corporation. Each partner in a partnership takes the $25,000 figure into account separately, as do beneficiaries of estates and trusts and shareholders in S corporations.

Carryback and Carryforward of Unused Credits

When the general business credit exceeds the above limitation in any year, the excess or unused credit may be carried back for one year and forward for 20 years. The entire amount of the unused credit must be carried back and then forward to each of the 20 remaining carryover years in order. Credits carried over are used first and then credits earned currently; after that, any carryback credits are applied. Unused credits from two or more years are used up in the order they occurred—the oldest first. The credit for investment in the current year, plus any carryover credits, cannot exceed the general limitations in effect for that year.

The first-in, first-out method of investment credit carryover reduces the potential loss of investment credits from the expiration of credit carryovers, since the earliest years are used before the credit for the current year. Code Sec. 39.

Refundable Tax Credits

Since refundable credits generally represent payments that have been made to the government, fewer difficulties are encountered in carryback and carryover, recapture, limitations, and sequencing.

¶ 8105   WITHHOLDING OF TAX ON WAGES CREDIT

The tax deducted and withheld on wages is allowable as a credit against the tax. If the tax has actually been withheld, credit or refund will be made even though the tax has not been paid to the government by the employer. However, the IRS may credit any overpayment against any outstanding tax, interest, or penalty owed by the taxpayer. Code Sec. 31(a).

¶ 8115   SOCIAL SECURITY TAX REFUNDS CREDIT

Where an employee receives wages from more than one employer during the year, amounts may be deducted and withheld as employee Social Security tax on amounts exceeding $68,400 for 1998. A special refund of the excess amount may be obtained only by claiming credit for the amount in the same manner as if such special refunds were an amount deducted and withheld as income tax at the source. The present rate is 6.2 percent on $68,400. The credit is computed separately for each spouse on a joint return. Code Sec. 31(b).

> *Example 8.21.* Lorence Larsen works for two different employers during 1998. He earned $46,000 from the first employer and $25,000 from the second. Each employer withheld Social Security taxes. Lorence is allowed a credit for the excess Social Security taxes paid in of $161.20 (($71,000 − $68,400) × 6.2%).

Where an employer withholds Social Security taxes on more than the maximum amount, a credit may not be claimed for the excess. The employer should adjust the overcollection with the employee.

¶ 8125   EARNED INCOME CREDIT

A refundable tax credit is provided for low-income workers. The credit is based on "earned income," which is explained below. The earned income credit may be characterized as a form of negative income tax since the credit is refundable to the taxpayer even if no tax liability exists. This credit does not represent a refund of a previous payment made by the taxpayer.

Taxpayers entitled to exclude income under the foreign earned income exclusion are not allowed the credit. The earned income credit is reduced by any alternative minimum tax imposed for the tax year.

Basic Earned Income Credit

For 1998, the maximum credit is 34 percent of earned income up to $6,680, or a credit of $2,271 for one child. The maximum credit of $2,271 is reduced by an amount equal to 15.98 percent of the excess of the greater of the modified adjusted gross income or earned income over $12,260. Code Sec. 32. For two or more children, the credit percentage is 40 percent of earned income up to $9,390, with a maximum credit of $3,756 and a phaseout percentage of 21.06 percent.

Eligible taxpayers with no children may receive a credit of 7.65 percent of the first $4,460 of earned income, for a maximum of $341. The phaseout percentage is also 7.65 percent on income exceeding $5,570.

To be eligible for the 34 or 40 percent credit, an individual must maintain a household in the United States that is the principal abode of a dependent child who is under age 19 or a student, a foster child, a dependent disabled child, or a married child for whom the taxpayer may claim a dependency exemption. For individuals qualifying as heads of households or surviving spouses, the child who is under age 19 or a student does not have to be a dependent of the taxpayer. The child must have the same principal place of abode as the taxpayer for more than one-half of the year; foster children must be in the taxpayer's household for the entire year. Married individuals must file a joint return in order to receive the benefits of the credit.

Taxpayers without qualifying children must meet three requirements: (1) the individual has a principal residence in the United States for more than one-half of the taxable year, (2) the individual (or, if married, either the individual or the individual's spouse) is at least 25 years old and not more than 64 years old at the end of the taxable year, and (3) the individual cannot be claimed as a dependent for any taxable year beginning in the same calendar year as the taxable year for which the credit is claimed.

Earned income includes wages, salaries, tips, and employee compensation. In addition, net earnings from self-employment are included in earned income. Earned income is to be reduced by any loss in earnings from self-employment. Earned income is to be computed without regard to any community property laws which may otherwise be applicable. Pension and annuity income is not considered earned income for the purpose of the credit.

The earned income credit is denied to individuals where the aggregate amount of disqualified income exceeds $2,200. Disqualified income includes both taxable and nontaxable interest, dividends, net rental and royalty income, net capital gain income, and net passive income.

Application of the phaseout for the earned income tax credit is based on the individual's modified adjusted gross income. Modified adjusted gross income is equal to the individual's adjusted gross income plus (1) any net capital loss deduction taken; (2) net losses from trusts and estates; (3) net losses relating to nonbusiness rents and royalties; (4) 75 percent of net losses from trades or businesses, computed separately with respect to sole proprietorships (other than farming), sole proprietorships in farming, and other businesses; (5) interest received or accrued during the tax year that is exempt from tax; and (6) amounts received as a pension or annuity, and any distribution or payment received from an individual retirement plan, by the taxpayer during the tax year to the extent not included in gross income. Losses attributable to a trade or business that consists of the performance of services by the taxpayer as an employee are not added back in computing modified adjusted gross income. Nontaxable distributions from pension, annuity, and IRAs rolled over into similar tax-favored vehicles are also not added back to modified adjusted gross income.

Example 8.22. Malcolm Meyers maintains a household for himself and his 12-year-old son. For the year, he received $13,700 in wages and $300 in interest income. His earned income credit for the year is computed as follows:

Maximum credit: 34% of $13,700, limited to $2,271		$2,271.00
Reduction: Greater of AGI or earned income	$14,000	
Less phaseout amount	12,260	
Excess	$ 1,740	
15.98% of excess		278.05
Allowable earned income credit		$1,992.95

The credit is refundable. Thus, taxpayers with a credit exceeding their liability can claim the difference as a refund. Even if a return is not required because of an individual's low income, a return should be filed to obtain the credit.

Example 8.23. Nancy Pearson maintains a household for herself and her dependent daughter. Nancy's only income is $3,200 from wages. Under the filing requirement rules, she is not required to file a return. However, to receive the $1,088 ($3,200 × 34%) earned income credit, a return must be filed.

¶ 8135 WITHHOLDING OF TAX AT SOURCE CREDIT

Taxpayers are allowed a credit for income taxes withheld on nonresident aliens, foreign corporations, and tax-free covenant bonds. Code Sec. 33.

¶ 8155 GASOLINE AND SPECIAL FUELS TAX CREDIT

Generally, the taxpayer can claim a credit for federal excise taxes on the nonhighway use of gasoline and special fuels. These include gasoline or special fuels used for farming purposes and special fuels used in local transit systems and for aviation purposes. Code Sec. 34.

Gasoline and lubricating oil must be used in a trade or business or in an income-producing activity. The credit for gasoline must be included in income where the cost of the product was deducted as a business expense.

¶ 8165 ESTIMATED TAX PAYMENTS CREDIT

A credit is permitted for quarterly estimated payments made by taxpayers. Individuals whose tax liability is not substantially covered by withholding may have to pay estimated taxes. All individuals must file a declaration of estimated tax for the year if the estimated tax, including self-employment tax, exceeds the tax to be withheld by $1,000 or more.

The estimated tax for the current year is computed by (1) estimating the taxpayer's gross income for the year, (2) subtracting estimated deductions and exemptions, and (3) computing the income tax on the balance. The estimated self-employment tax and alternative minimum tax are added to the resulting income tax. The tax to be withheld from wages during the year and other expected credits are subtracted. The result is the "estimated tax," and if it is less than $1,000 no estimated payments need be made.

Where estimated returns are required for the current tax year, they must be filed by April 15, June 15, September 15, and January 15 (following year). The taxpayer may elect to credit a preceding year's overpayment against the current year's estimated tax.

In filing a declaration of estimated tax, the taxpayer is required to take into account the then existing facts and circumstances, as well as those reasonably to be anticipated. In the absence of contrary indications, current employment, salary rate, and regularly paid dividends may be presumed to continue throughout the year. Amended or revised declarations may be made in any case in which the estimates differ from those reflected in the previous declaration.

No penalty is imposed for failure to file an estimated tax declaration, or for errors in the declaration, but there is a penalty for underpayment of estimated tax. The amount of the penalty is the amount of the underpayment times the underpayment interest rate for the period of the underpayment.

An "underpayment," for other than high-income individuals, is determined by adding the amount of income taxes paid and the excess Social Security credit and then subtracting the lesser of (1) 90 percent of the actual amount of tax due on the return or (2) the previous year's tax. The underpayment is computed as of each of the four quarterly filing dates. Thus, a taxpayer making uneven payments throughout the year could have an underpayment for some quarters and not others. The penalty applies despite any reasonable cause and is not deductible as an expense.

For 1998, high-income individuals must use 100 percent of the previous year's tax liability. For 1997 high-income taxpayers were required to use 110 percent of their prior year's tax liability. For 1999, 2000, and 2001 the safe harbor percentage is 105 percent. A high-income individual is one who had more than $150,000 in adjusted gross income for the preceding year ($75,000 for married individuals filing separately).

An equal part of tax withheld from wages is considered as tax paid on each of the four quarterly filing dates, unless the taxpayer proves otherwise.

TAX PLANNING POINTER

Generally, a taxpayer cannot avoid a penalty on underpayments in early quarters of the year by increasing estimated payments in the later quarters. However, if an employee realizes that he or she has underpaid for the earlier quarters, the employee could have a larger amount of income taxes withheld late in the year. Since any withholding is considered to be equally withheld throughout the year, the extra year-end withholding will increase the amount considered to have been paid in the earlier quarters and help lessen or eliminate any underpayment penalty.

KEYSTONE PROBLEM

There are two kinds of tax credits, nonrefundable and refundable, that basically must be taken in the proper order. Since some of the credits have no carryover provisions and are lost if not used in a particular year, what effect could an increase in a credit, such as the investment credit, have on the other credits?

Alternative Minimum Tax

¶ 8401   IMPOSITION OF TAX

The minimum tax is a special form of tax imposed on certain taxpayers in addition to the regular federal income tax. The objective of the tax is to recapture tax reductions resulting from the use of special tax relief or "tax shelter" provisions of the tax law.

The minimum tax was originally enacted in 1969 with a 10 percent tax on the sum of 10 specified tax preference items reduced by a $30,000 exemption, income taxes paid for the year, and certain carryovers. However, Congress increased the rate to 15 percent and reduced the exemptions in 1976.

Between 1979 and 1982, the minimum tax was computed two different ways: the add-on minimum tax and the alternative minimum tax. The taxpayer paid the larger of the tax liability computed under either the add-on method or the alternative method. However, if a taxpayer had a net operating loss which could be carried forward, any minimum tax which was otherwise payable was deferred until the loss carryover was used in the succeeding years.

Beginning in 1983, the add-on minimum tax was repealed for individuals. The alternative minimum tax was expanded to broaden the base of economic income that is subject to a minimum level of federal income taxation. The alternative minimum tax rate was increased to 24 percent beginning in 1991. For tax years beginning after 1986, "alternative minimum taxable income" (AMTI) means the taxable income of the taxpayer for the year determined with adjustments and increased by tax preferences. Alternative minimum taxable income is reduced by an exemption amount to arrive at net alternative minimum taxable income which is then multiplied by a 26 or 28 percent alternative minimum tax rate. The first $175,000 of AMTI is taxed at 26 percent and AMTI in excess of $175,000 is taxed at 28 percent. However, long-term capital gains taxed at 20 and 25 percent for regular tax purposes are also taxed at those rates in the alternative minimum tax computation. A limited foreign tax credit is the only nonrefundable credit allowed against the tax in arriving at the tentative minimum tax. The alternative minimum tax is the amount resulting after deducting the regular tax (reduced by all nonrefundable credits) from the tentative minimum tax. Code Sec. 55(b).

ALTERNATIVE MINIMUM TAX FORMULA

	Taxable Income
+ or −	Adjustments to Taxable Income
+	Tax Preferences
=	Alternative Minimum Taxable Income (AMTI)
−	Exemption Amount
=	Net Alternative Minimum Taxable Income
×	26 or 28% Tax Rate
=	Tax
−	Alternative Minimum Tax Foreign Tax Credit
=	Tentative Minimum Tax (TMT)
−	Regular Tax for the Year
=	Alternative Minimum Tax (AMT)

The alternative minimum tax (AMT) requires additional record-keeping and separate basis computations. The AMT adds substantial complexity to the tax system.

¶ 8415   ADJUSTMENTS TO TAXABLE INCOME

In determining AMTI, taxable income must be computed with the following adjustments. Code Sec. 56(a). Adjustments to taxable income can increase or decrease alternative minimum taxable income.

Depreciation

Taxpayers who, in calculating regular tax liability, depreciate real property under MACRS must use the alternative depreciation system in calculating AMTI. The real property alternative depreciation system calls for a 40-year straight line depreciation.

Depreciation deductions for personal property and property which is not subject to straight-line depreciation must be recomputed under the 150 percent declining-balance method under the alternative depreciation system. Taxpayers must switch from the declining-balance method to the straight-line method in the first tax year that maximizes the deduction. Thus, the excess of AMT depreciation over MACRS depreciation in the later years of an asset can be used to offset the excess of accelerated depreciation over straight line in the early years of other assets.

> *Example 8.24.* A corporation purchases a $10,000 five-year machine for use in business in 1997. The depreciation methods for regular tax and alternative minimum tax purposes along with the adjustment are as follows:

Year	200% Declining Balance	150% Declining Balance	Adjustment
1997	$2,000	$1,500	+ $500
1998	3,200	2,550	+ 650
1999	1,920	1,785	+ 135
2000	1,152	1,666	− 514
2001	1,152	1,666	− 514
2002	576	833	− 257

> In the first three years an amount must be added to taxable income, while a deduction is taken in the last three years.

Mining Exploration, Circulation, Research and Development Expenditures

Circulation expenditures of periodicals must be amortized ratably over three years. Mining exploration and development expenditures must be amortized ratably over 10 years. Research and experimentation expenditures must be amortized ratably over 10 years. For tax years after 1990, individuals who materially participate in an activity are not required to capitalize and amortize research and experimental expenditures generated by such activity that are otherwise allowed as a business expense deduction under Code Sec. 174(a).

The basis for gain or loss upon disposition is determined using the AMTI basis.

Pollution Control Facilities

For property placed in service after 1986, the five-year amortization method for depreciating pollution control facilities must be replaced by the alternative depreciation system. The adjusted basis used in AMTI calculations (but not for regular tax calculations) to determine the gain or loss on the sale of property for which depreciation has been adjusted must reflect the depreciation adjustment rather than the costs that were deductible in regular tax computations.

Long-Term Contracts

The percentage-of-completion method of accounting to determine gain or loss from long-term contracts must be substituted for any other method of accounting, such as the completed-contract method or the cash basis method, for both regular tax purposes and for AMT purposes. This change will directly affect those taxpayers who were using a form of completed-contract method of accounting for AMT purposes.

The adjustment is the excess of income from use of the percentage-of-completion method over the long-term contract method used on long-term contracts. For example, if the deferred income from a three-year contract is $750,000, no income is reported under the completed-contract method of reporting until the third year. Assuming the costs on the contract are incurred in equal proportions, $250,000 is included in AMTI for each of the three years.

Passive Farming Losses

No deduction is allowed for losses from any farming syndicate or any other farming activity in which the taxpayer does not materially participate. A loss from one farm activity may not be used to offset income from another farm activity. Disallowed losses are carried forward indefinitely and used for AMTI purposes to offset future income from the farming activity. Suspended losses are deductible when the activity is disposed of. Code Sec. 58(a).

Incentive Stock Options

An adjustment must be made to taxable income when incentive stock options are exercised. The excess (if any) of the stock's fair market value at the time of exercise over the amount paid by the employee for the stock is an adjustment that in figuring AMT taxable income is added to the taxable income shown on the tax return. This adjustment is made in the first year in which the rights in the stock are freely transferable or are not subject to a substantial risk of forfeiture.

Example 8.25. Arthur Aster pays an exercise price of $15 to purchase stock having a fair market value of $20. The adjustment in the year of exercise is $5, and the stock has a basis of $15 for determining gain or loss for regular tax purposes and $20 for alternative minimum tax purposes. If, in a subsequent year, Arthur sells the stock for $45, the gain recognized is $30 for regular tax purposes and $25 for alternative minimum tax purposes.

Net Operating Losses

The net operating loss (NOL) must be calculated under special rules and cannot offset more than 90 percent of AMT income. The AMT rules generally require that the regular tax NOL must be adjusted for AMTI adjustments and tax preferences.

Gains and Losses on Sale or Exchange of Property

AMTI must be adjusted for any difference between gain or loss reported for the regular tax and that figured for the AMT. For AMT purposes, a property's basis is reduced only by the amount of depreciation allowed in computing AMTI. Therefore, the adjusted basis of the property may differ for regular and minimum tax purposes. The gain or loss for AMTI upon disposition of the asset is determined by the AMTI basis. Similar adjustments must be made to gains and losses on the sale of assets involving mining exploration and development costs, circulation expenditures, research and development expenditures, pollution control facilities, long-term contracts, and incentive stock options.

Personal Exemption

No deduction for personal exemptions may be claimed against alternative minimum taxable income. Code Sec. 56(b)(1)(E). Accordingly, the personal exemption taken in computing taxable income must be added back as an adjustment.

Itemized Deductions

The standard deduction is not allowed for the alternative minimum taxable income computation. Code Sec. 56(b). Only an individual's actual itemized deductions are allowed in computing AMTI and then only those itemized deductions not limited by the discussion below.

In computing taxable income, total itemized deductions must be reduced for high income taxpayers by 3 percent of adjusted gross income exceeding $121,200. This reduction does not apply to the alternative minimum tax. Consequently, itemized deductions included in the alternative minimum taxable income computation do not have to be reduced. The alternative minimum tax form reduces adjusted gross income by the disallowed itemized deduction.

Miscellaneous Itemized Deductions

No deduction is allowed for AMTI computation for any allowable miscellaneous itemized deductions except:

1. Wagering losses
2. Any deduction for impairment-related work expenses
3. The deduction for estate tax in case of income in respect of a decedent
4. Any deduction in connection with personal property used in a short sale
5. The deduction where a taxpayer restores substantial amount held under claim of right
6. The deduction where annuity payments cease before investment is recovered
7. The deduction for amortizable bond premium
8. The deduction in connection with cooperative housing corporations

Thus, the disallowed miscellaneous itemized deductions are added back to taxable income in arriving at AMTI.

Medical Expenses

Medical expenses are deductible for AMTI only to the extent that they exceed 10 percent of adjusted gross income. Thus, taxpayers using taxable income as the starting point must add back the smaller of 2.5 percent of adjusted gross income or the medical expense deduction taken for regular tax purposes.

Taxes

State, local, and foreign *real property* taxes, state and local *personal property* taxes, and state, local and foreign *income,* war profits, or excess profits taxes allowed as itemized deductions for regular tax purposes are not allowed in the AMTI computation. Thus, the only taxes deductible for AMTI purposes are the windfall profit tax (on oil removed before August 23, 1988) and the generation-skipping tax imposed on income distributions. A refund of state and local taxes paid, for which no alternative minimum tax deduction was allowed, is not included in alternative minimum taxable income.

Interest

The amount deductible for regular tax purposes for home mortgage interest may be greater than the permitted AMT deduction. For minimum tax purposes, upon refinancing a loan that gives rise to qualified housing interest, interest paid on the new loan is treated as qualified housing interest to the extent that (1) it so qualified under the prior loan, and (2) the amount of the loan was not increased. Thus, the home-equity loan exception to the regular tax rules does not apply to AMT.

> *Example 8.26.* Jane Juniper owes $80,000 on a mortgage on a principal residence purchased for $100,000 and with a current fair market value of $125,000. June takes out a second mortgage for $25,000. The interest on the additional $25,000 principal in excess of the prior $80,000 loan cannot be deducted for AMT purposes.

¶ 8425 TAX PREFERENCE ITEMS

The following tax preferences must be added back to taxable income in arriving at alternative minimum taxable income. Code Sec. 57.

Depletion

The depletion preference is the excess of the percentage depletion deduction over the adjusted basis of the property at the end of the year. The preference applies to percentage depletion for all minerals, not just oil and gas.

Intangible Drilling Costs

The tax preference for intangible drilling costs on oil, gas, and geothermal wells is the amount by which the excess intangible drilling costs are greater than 65 percent of net income from the resource properties. Excess intangible drilling costs are the amount by which the intangible drilling deduction for regular tax purposes exceeds the amount which would have been allowable if the costs had been capitalized and amortized over 120 months.

Tax-Exempt Interest

A tax preference has been added for tax-exempt interest on private activity bonds issued after August 7, 1986. This preference does not apply to bonds issued for the benefit of tax-exempt charitable or educational institutions or to bonds issued for public purposes such as schools and municipally owned public utilities.

Accelerated Depreciation or Amortization

There is a tax preference for excess depreciation and amortization taken on certain properties acquired before 1987. (However, any properties acquired in 1986 that use the cost recovery rules are not subject to this tax preference.) Pre-1987 tax preference items include:

1. Depreciation on real property acquired before 1987 that is in excess of straight-line depreciation over the useful life

2. Amortization of certified pollution control facilities (the excess of 60-month amortization over depreciation otherwise allowable)

Exclusion for Gains on Sale of Certain Small Business Stock

An amount equal to 42 percent of the amount excluded from gross income under the provisions of Code Sec. 1202 which allow a taxpayer to exclude up to 50 percent of the gain on the sale of certain small business stock held more than five years is considered a tax preference for the alternative minimum tax. Thus, for taxpayers not exceeding the per-issuer limitation, 21 percent of the gain will be treated as an AMT preference.

¶ 8435   EXEMPTION AMOUNT

The allowable exemption amounts are $45,000 for married persons filing joint returns and surviving spouses, $33,750 for single individuals, and $22,500 for married individuals filing separate returns or estates or trusts. The exemption amounts are reduced by 25 cents for each $1 by which alternative minimum taxable income exceeds $150,000 for married taxpayers filing jointly, $112,500 for single individuals, and $75,000 for married taxpayers filing separately. Code Sec. 55(d).

> **Example 8.27.** A married couple with AMTI of $300,000 is allowed an exemption amount of $7,500 ($45,000 − .25 × ($300,000 − $150,000)). If their AMTI were to exceed $330,000 there would be no deduction for the exemption amount.

The exemption phaseout level for married taxpayers filing separately has been made equal to the phaseout level for married taxpayers filing jointly. In the case of taxpayers filing separately whose AMTI exceeds $165,000, a special computation is necessary. The taxpayer must increase the AMT taxable income by 25 percent of the amount it exceeds $165,000. However, the increase cannot be more than $22,500.

The AMT exemption amount for minor children is limited to the greater of the child's earned income for the year plus $1,000 or the child's share of the unused parental minimum tax exemption (the excess of the Code Sec. 55(d) amount over the parent's AMTI) for tax years beginning in 1991.

¶ 8445   TAX CREDITS

None of the nonrefundable credits reduce AMT liability for noncorporate taxpayers except the foreign tax credit. Thus, the general business credit is unavailable against the AMT for individuals even if it is allowable for regular tax purposes arising from qualified purchases or as a carryover. Taxpayers remaining in an AMT position for a number of years may lose allowable general business credits because the carryovers will have expired before they can be used. Even if the credits are used before expiring, the passage of time will erode the value of the credits. Code Sec. 59.

Individuals paying foreign taxes are permitted to use a portion of the specially calculated foreign tax credit against the tentative minimum tax. The foreign tax credit is allowed to the extent of the foreign tax on the taxpayer's foreign-source alternative minimum taxable income.

In computing the income tax on taxable income, the general business credit is taken only to the extent that it reduces the regular tax for the year to the tentative minimum tax. Thus, we cannot have a situation where the general business credit reduces the regular tax and then the alternative minimum tax is increased to offset the general business credit taken.

Example 8.28. Matches Corporation has a regular tax before the general business credit of $50,000, general business credits of $22,000, and a tentative minimum tax of $40,000. Only $10,000 of the general business credit is taken, reducing the regular tax to $40,000. Since the regular tax is equal to the tentative minimum tax, no alternative minimum tax is imposed.

¶ 8455 CARRYOVER OF CREDIT

The alternative minimum tax paid in one year may be carried forward indefinitely as a credit against the regular tax liability. The credit may not be used, however, to offset any future minimum tax liability. A taxpayer is not allowed to take a credit larger than the amount necessary to reduce the regular tax to the amount of the tentative minimum tax. Code Sec. 53.

Example 8.29. Andrew Ames has a tentative minimum tax of $100,000, a regular tax before the AMT credit of $120,000, and an AMT credit of $35,000 from previous years. Without the AMT credit, the taxpayer would have no alternative minimum tax because the regular tax exceeds the tentative minimum tax. Since the full AMT credit would reduce the regular tax below the tentative minimum tax, only $20,000 of the AMT credit carryforward may be used to reduce the regular tax.

The AMT credit for any tax year is the excess of the adjusted net minimum tax imposed for all tax years beginning after 1986 over the amount allowable as a credit in previous years. The adjusted net minimum tax is the amount of net minimum tax (alternative minimum tax) for a year reduced by the amount which would be the net minimum tax (alternative minimum tax) for that year if only certain adjustments and tax preferences were taken into account. The adjustments and tax preferences taken into account for this computation include:

1. The same itemized deduction adjustments discussed under the AMTI adjustments
2. The following tax preferences: depletion, tax-exempt interest, and gain exclusion allowed on small business stock.

The purpose of the minimum tax credit is to prevent the double taxation of deferral preferences and adjustments. These deferral preferences and adjustments are subject to the alternative minimum tax in a tax year earlier than the year they are subject to the regular tax. For example, accelerated depreciation taken in a year creates a tax adjustment or tax preference. This adjustment or preference may cause an additional tax because of the alternative minimum tax. In later years, taxable income will be higher because of the smaller depreciation deductions under accelerated depreciation, thus causing a higher income tax. Thus, the total depreciation deductions will not be received without the benefit of the alternative minimum tax credit. Therefore, the amount of the minimum tax credit to be carried forward is the excess of the AMT paid over the AMT that would be paid if AMTI included only "exclusion" preferences and adjustments (those items that result in a permanent reduction of regular tax liability).

¶ 8475 ALTERNATIVE MINIMUM TAX PLANNING

Individuals subject to the alternative minimum tax generally benefit by accelerating income into an AMT year. Income recognized in an AMT year will generally be taxed at 26 or 28 percent rather than at the higher regular tax rate.

Ways to accelerate income into an AMT year include:

1. Taking capital gains before year-end

2. Receiving bonuses, commissions, and other income before year-end

3. Redeeming Treasury bills and U.S. savings bonds before year-end

4. Exchanging tax-exempt municipal bonds for taxable bonds paying a higher interest rate

Individuals may also benefit by delaying expenses until a regular tax year. Payment of allowed itemized deductions, such as charitable contributions, provides a tax benefit in an AMT of only 26 or 28 percent, while delaying the payment to a regular tax year may allow a deduction at 36 or 39.6 percent. Any payment in an AMT year of an itemized deduction not allowed for AMT purposes, such as property taxes, will produce no tax savings, since reducing the regular tax merely increases the AMT by an equal amount.

Care must be taken not to accelerate too much income into an AMT year or to defer too many expenses into a regular tax year. Only accelerate receipt of income or defer expenses up to the point where the tax due under the tentative minimum tax equals the regular tax.

Taxpayers may be able to improve their AMT position by finding investments that produce passive income to offset passive tax-shelter losses. Since tax-shelter losses are not deductible for AMT purposes, the alternative minimum tax will not be increased to the extent that the passive income offset passive losses. Income-producing limited partnerships and rental properties generating passive income may be appropriate investments.

Interest on private-activity municipal bonds is a tax preference for the AMT. Thus, taxpayers holding private-activity municipal bonds in AMT years will find this income taxable. These taxpayers may be better off to trade these bonds for regular municipal bonds or higher paying taxable bonds.

Example 8.30. Mark and Samantha Mandell, the parents of two children, had the following tax facts:

Income
Wages	$177,000
Rental Income	25,000
Dividend Income	8,500
Interest Income	7,000

Expenses
Keogh Deduction	7,500
Moving Expenses	10,000
Medical Expenses	21,500
Casualty Loss	23,100
Housing Interest	8,000
Investment Interest	28,000
Personal Interest	2,000
Charitable Contributions	43,000
Real Estate Taxes	9,265
Other Nonbusiness Deductions	21,000

Other Tax Preferences
Gain Exclusion on Small Business Stock	13,800
Private Purpose Municipal Bond Income	30,000
Excess of Accelerated Depreciation	20,000
General Business Credit	10,000

The computation of their income is as follows:

Gross Income
Wages	$177,000	
Rental Income	25,000	
Dividend Income	8,500	
Interest Income	7,000	
Total Gross Income		$217,500

Deductions from Gross Income
Moving Expenses		10,000
Keogh Deduction		7,500
Adjusted Gross Income		$200,000

Itemized Deductions
Medical Expenses ($21,500 − 7.5% AGI)	$ 6,500	
Real Estate Taxes	9,265	
Housing Interest	8,000	
Investment Interest ($8,500 + $7,000)	15,500	
Personal Interest ($2,000 × 0%)	0	
Charitable Contributions	43,000	
Casualty Loss ($23,100 − $100 − 10% AGI)	3,000	
Other Itemized Deductions ($21,000 − 2% AGI)	17,000	
Less: 3% ($200,000 − $124,500)	− 2,265	
Total Itemized Deductions		− 100,000
Personal Exemptions		− 9,504
Taxable Income		$ 90,496
Income Tax		$ 19,833
General Business Credit		0
Regular Tax for the Year		$ 19,833

ALTERNATIVE MINIMUM TAX COMPUTATION

Taxable Income		$ 90,496
Itemized Deduction Adjustment		− 2,265
Adjustments to Taxable Income		
Personal Exemptions	$ 9,504	
Medical Expenses ($200,000 × 2.5%)	5,000	
Real Estate Taxes	9,265	
Other Itemized Deductions	17,000	
Total Adjustments to Taxable Income		+ 40,769
Tax Preferences		
Gain Exclusion on Small Business Stock	$ 13,800	
Private Purpose Municipal Bond Income	30,000	
Excess Depreciation	20,000	
Total Tax Preferences		63,800
Alternative Minimum Taxable Income		$192,800
Alternative Minimum Tax Exemption		− 34,300
Net Alternative Minimum Taxable Income		$158,500
Tax Rate		× 26%
Tentative Alternative Minimum Tax		$ 41,210
Regular Tax for the Year		19,833
Alternative Minimum Tax		$ 21,377

The personal exemption of $10,800 was reduced to $9,504 because adjusted gross income of $200,000 exceeded $186,800, causing a 12 percent reduction.

The alternative minimum tax computation begins with taxable income and adds back certain adjustments and tax preferences.

The personal exemption is added back.

The medical expenses are reduced by an additional 2.5 percent of adjusted gross income.

Taxes are not allowed as an alternative minimum tax itemized deduction. Other itemized deductions are also not allowed in the alternative minimum tax computation.

The housing interest, charitable contributions, and casualty losses are not adjusted as they are allowed in AMT computation.

The alternative minimum tax exemption of $45,000 is reduced by $10,700 because the taxpayers' alternative minimum taxable income exceeds $150,000. The reduction is 25 percent of any excess over $150,000.

The taxpayers are unable to use the $10,000 general business credit because of the alternative minimum tax. They are able to carry the unused general business credit back one year and forward 20 years.

The AMT credit carryforward is computed as follows:

Taxable Income		$ 90,496
Itemized deduction adjustment		− 2,265
Adjustments to Taxable Income for AMT Credit		
Personal Exemptions	$9,504	
Medical Expenses ($200,000 × 2.5%)	5,000	
Real Estate Taxes	9,265	
Other Itemized Deductions	17,000	
Total Adjustments to Taxable Income		+ 40,769
Tax Preferences for AMT Credit		
Gain Exclusion on Small Business Stock	$13,800	
Private Purpose Municipal Bond Income	30,000	
Total Tax Preferences for AMT Credit		+ 43,800
AMTI for AMT Credit		$ 172,800
Alternative Minimum Tax Exemption		− 39,300
Net AMTI for AMT Credit		$ 133,500
Tax Rate		× 26%
Tentative AMT for Credit Purposes		$ 34,710
Regular Tax for the Year		− 19,833
Alternative Minimum Tax for AMT Credit		$ 14,877
Alternative Minimum Tax		$ 21,377
Alternative Minimum Tax for AMT Credit		− 14,877
Alternative Minimum Tax Credit		$ 6,500

The alternative minimum tax exemption is $39,300. Since AMTI exceeded $150,000, there was a $5,700 reduction in the exemption amount.

A comparison of the computation of the alternative minimum tax and the alternative minimum tax for AMT credit reveals two differences: (1) the $20,000 depreciation tax preference is not included in the AMT credit computation because it is not an exclusion item and (2) the alternative minimum tax exemption is $39,300 instead of $34,300. These two differences, $25,000, at a 26 percent rate results in a $6,500 alternative minimum tax credit.

SUMMARY OF CHAPTER 8

✓ A tax credit is a direct reduction in the tax due. A tax credit is more valuable than a deduction of the same amount.

✓ Credits are divided into two types: nonrefundable and refundable.

✓ In nonrefundable credits, there have been no payments to the government, so the taxpayer is not entitled to a refund even of the credit exceeds the gross tax. Nonrefundable credits must be taken in the proper order.

✓ Refundable credits allow the taxpayer to reduce the tax liability below zero. With the exception of the earned income credit, the refundable credits represent a return of money paid into the government.

✓ The alternative minimum tax is a tax imposed in addition to the regular income tax to recapture the reductions resulting from the use of special tax relief provisions of the tax law. Certain adjustments and preferences are added back to taxable income and then an exemption amount is subtracted before applying the alternative minimum tax rates.

CHAPTER 8 QUESTIONS

1. Explain the difference between a tax credit and a tax deduction. Which would help a 31 percent tax bracket taxpayer most, a $2,000 deduction or a $400 credit? A 15 percent tax bracket taxpayer?

2. Explain what is meant by the terms "refundable" and "nonrefundable" credits. How might these classifications affect the tax liability of a taxpayer?

3. Why is the household and dependent care credit sometimes only 20 percent and other times as high as 30 percent?

4. Can a taxpayer qualify for the household and dependent care credit if he or she is not employed?

5. Is the dependency exemption required for the household and dependent care credit?

6. What limits are placed on employment-related expenses for the household and dependent care credit?

7. Must married taxpayers file a joint return in all cases to qualify for the household and dependent care credit?

8. How does an individual qualify for the credit for the elderly?

9. What effect does the receipt of Social Security benefits have on the credit for the elderly?

10. What is the first tax year the new child tax credit is available?

11. What is the maximum child tax credit a taxpayer may receive for an 18-year-old full-time college student in 1998?

12. Can the child tax credit for taxpayers with less than three qualifying children result in a refundable personal credit?

13. What expenses are eligible for the Hope Scholarship Credit?

14. How many years of post-secondary education expenses are eligible for the Hope tuition credit?

15. What expenses are eligible for the Lifetime Learning Credit?

16. What is the purpose of the foreign tax credit?

17. When would a taxpayer choose to itemize foreign taxes rather than take the foreign tax credit?

18. What 13 credits make up the general business credit?

19. What buildings qualify for the rehabilitation credit?

20. How does the reforestation credit differ from the investment credit?

21. How does an investment credit affect the basis of an item purchased?

22. How will a premature disposal of investment credit property affect a taxpayer?

23. What happens to the basis of an asset that has a recapture of an investment credit?

24. Are taxpayers allowed a credit on the total expenditure for research?

25. What is the ceiling limitation for the general business credit?

26. When several years of general business credits are carried over to the present year which also has a general business credit, in what order are the credits taken?

27. What basic group of employees qualifies for the work opportunity credit?

28. Which nonrefundable credits if not used in the present year can be carried over to other years?

29. Is it possible for a taxpayer to have a credit for excess Social Security if the taxpayer worked for more than one employer and the total wages came to $38,000?

30. Describe the earned income credit.

31. Sara's only source of income was wages of $6,000. She and her daughter live with her parents. The daughter is claimed as a dependent by the father. Is Sara eligible for the earned income credit?

32. Discuss the declaration of estimated tax filing requirements of individuals.

33. If a taxpayer does not file estimated taxes and is underpaid for the year, what penalty may be imposed?

34. What is the purpose of the alternative minimum tax?

35. What is a tax preference item?

36. When is it possible to have a tax preference for the alternative minimum tax if the taxpayer is using straight-line depreciation?

37. List the itemized deductions that are not allowed in the computation of alternative minimum taxable income.

38. When is interest deductible as an itemized deduction for income tax purposes but not allowed as an itemized deduction for the alternative minimum tax.

39. What items create the alternative minimum tax credit?

CHAPTER 8 PROBLEMS

40. Compute the child and dependent care credit in each of the following independent cases:

    a. Jack and Jill Jones are married and file a joint return. Jill worked full time earning $15,000, while Jack attended law school the entire year. They incurred $5,000 of child care expenses during the year for their two children, ages eight and six.

    b. Mary Morgan is a widow who worked full time the entire year earning $18,000. She incurred the following child care expenses for her six-year-old daughter in order to be employed during the year:

Kindergarten	$400
Babysitters	600
Private school (first grade)	600

c. Bill and Debra Page are divorced and have one dependent child, Betty, age nine. Bill had custody of Betty for five months this year and claimed Betty as an exemption on his tax return. Debra had custody of Betty for the remainder of the year. Debra incurred $3,000 of employment-related expenses during the year, while Bill incurred $2,000 of employment-related expenses. Both were employed for the entire year and each earned $20,000 in wages this year.

41. Frank and Emma Browne are both over 65 and file a joint return. Emma received $800 from Social Security benefits and Frank received $1,200 from railroad retirement benefits. In addition to the benefits, they reported income of $16,000 from their antique shop.

a. Compute Frank and Emma's tax credit for the elderly.

b. Assume that only Emma was over 65 and compute the tax credit for the elderly.

42. A married couple with two children has $16,000 of earned income. There is no taxable income after deducting the standard deduction and personal exemptions. Assume that they have paid $1,224 in FICA taxes and will receive a $2,800 earned income credit. What is the amount of their child tax credit?

43. A married couple with two children has earned income of $20,000 with no withholding. Assume they have a taxable income of $2,000, they paid $1,530 in FICA taxes, and they will receive an earned income credit of $1,800. Their tax on $2,000 is $304. What is the amount of their income tax liability?

44. A married couple with three children has earned income of $22,000 with no withholding. Assume a standard deduction of $6,900 and personal exemptions of $13,250. Their tax on $2,500 is $377. They have an earned income credit of $1,363. They paid $1,850 in FICA taxes. What is the amount of their income tax due?

45. Philip and Susan Moyer have two children who are both in the first two years of college. They incur $3,000 in tuition expenses for each of the two children. What is the maximum amount of Hope Scholarship Credit?

46. Cathy Thomas, a single mother, has modified AGI of $48,000. In 1998, her daughter begins work on her bachelors degree at an accredited institution. Cathy pays $6,000 in qualified tuition for the daughter's first semester. What is the amount of Hope Scholarship Credit Cathy is allowed on her return?

47. Michael is divorced and the exemption for his daughter is claimed by his ex-wife. What is the amount of Hope Scholarship Credit allowed Michael when he pays $2,500 in tuition for his daughter to attend her first year at an accredited four-year college?

48. What is the amount of Lifetime Learning Credit allowed a taxpayer assuming that he or she incurred $3,000 in tuition and fees and $8,000 in room and board for an eligible college student?

49. In 1998, Lenny Traveler had adjusted gross income of $24,250 from investments in the U.S., while earning $40,000 from foreign sources. Lenny's potential U.S. tax liability is $12,000, and he had to pay $11,000 in foreign income taxes. What amount can Lenny, a U.S. citizen, claim as a foreign tax credit?

50. ABC Corporation has international earnings of $500,000 and a U.S. tax liability of $170,000. From foreign operations ABC generated $120,000 of income on which a $55,000 tax was imposed. What is ABC's foreign tax credit and total tax liability?

51. Zap Industries had a tentative general business credit in 1998 of $60,000. Its tax liability in 1997 was $20,000. Its tax liability before the general business credit in 1998 is $50,000.

    a.   What is Zap Industries' 1998 tax liability?

    b.   Are there any effects on the tax liabilities of the previous year?

    c.   If so, what are they?

52. Yoyo Corporation bought $42,000 worth of energy equipment in November 1993, taking an investment credit of $4,200. In March 1998, the firm sells the equipment for $30,000. What is the investment credit recapture?

53. Martha and Marty Mertens are married and file a joint return. Marty started his own business at the beginning of the current tax year and reported net income of $4,000 for the year. Martha worked full time as a waitress earning $7,000, excluding tips of $3,000. Marty and Martha maintained a home for their 11-year-old son. What is their earned income credit for 1998?

54. What is the adjustment that must be made to taxable income in computing alternative minimum taxable income for 1998, assuming that an individual purchased an office building on January 8 for $400,000?

55. What is the amount of tax preference for alternative minimum tax purposes assuming that an individual sells some qualified small business stock held more than five years at a $20,000 gain.

56. What is the allowable exemption for the alternative minimum tax assuming that a married couple has alternative minimum taxable income of $200,000?

57. Tamara and Tony Mapp, a married couple, report the following items for the year:

Taxable income	$80,000
AMT adjustments	30,000
Tax preferences	40,000
Regular tax liability	16,000

   What is their alternative minimum tax for the year?

58. Alex and Alicia Andrews file a joint tax return. On the return they show Alex's salary of $110,000, interest income from corporate bonds of $3,000, dividends from domestic corporations of $900, and a net long-term capital gain of $60,000. They also had the following expenses for itemized deductions: $18,000 medical expenses, $8,000 home mortgage interest, $5,000 in consumer interest, $4,000 in deductible taxes, $2,000 charitable contributions, and $1,200 in miscellaneous deductions not subject to the 2 percent limitation. The Andrews claim five exemptions on their return. Determine their net alternative minimum taxable income.

59. What is the amount of AMT credit carryforward for 1998, assuming that an individual had an alternative minimum tax of $20,000 and an alternative minimum tax for AMT credit of $12,000?

60. Which of the following are tax adjustments or preference items for purposes of the alternative minimum tax?

   a. $20,000 net long-term capital gain over net short-term capital losses

   b. $3,000 net short-term capital gain

   c. $10,000 straight-line depreciation on building acquired in 1988

   d. $1,500 interest from City of Buffalo bonds

61. Which of the following qualify as "employment-related" expenses for the credit for child care?

   a. Nursery school fees

   b. Transportation to nursery school

   c. Housekeeper's salary

   d. Housekeeper's meals

   e. Gardener's salary

62. What is the amount of dependent care credit for a couple with two children where they spend $5,000 for dependent care and the husband earns $20,000 for the year and the wife earns $4,500?

   a. $1,350

   b. $990

   c. $900

   d. $0

63. Which of the following items is not an adjustment for the alternative minimum tax?

   a. Taxes

   b. Wagering losses

   c. Personal exemption

   d. Standard deduction

64. *Comprehensive Problem.* Determine the tax due, including the alternative minimum tax, for Patty Perkins, assuming she is single using the following tax information:

Adjusted Gross Income	$100,000
Itemized Deductions	20,000
Alternative Minimum Tax Itemized Deductions	12,000
Tax Preference Items	20,000
General Business Credit	17,000

65. *Comprehensive Problem.* From the following information determine the total 1998 tax due for Charlene and Dick Storm, assuming they file a joint return, have three dependents, and are not members of a qualified retirement plan.

Dick's Wages	$23,000
Charlene's Wages	41,000
Dick's Contribution to an IRA	2,000
Charlene's Contribution to an IRA	800
Charlene's Self-Employment Income	12,000
Tax Preference Items	10,000
General Business Credit	7,000
Housing Interest	8,000
Consumer Interest	2,000
Property Taxes	3,000

66. *Research Problem.* An asset is purchased on May 15, 1994, for $100,000. The full 10 percent investment credit of $10,000 is taken on the asset. On June 23, 1998, a Code Sec. 108 election is made to exclude gain arising from the discharge of business indebtedness in the amount of $7,000. What is the amount of investment credit recapture? See *Panhandle Eastern Pipe Line Co. & Affiliates,* 81-2 USTC ¶ 9496, 654 F.2d 35 (Ct Cls 1981).

Chapter 9

Property Transactions: Determination of Basis and Gains and Losses

Learning Objectives

After completing Chapter 9, you should be able to:

1. Understand the factors in determining realized and recognized gain or loss.
2. Determine the basis in various types of asset purchases and the allocation of basis.
3. Determine the basis of property acquired by gift and from a decedent.
4. Determine the basis in stock transactions, including stock dividends, stock rights, and wash sales.
5. Compute gains and losses in related party transactions and the income recognized in installment sales.

OVERVIEW OF CHAPTER

Chapters 9 through 11 contain discussions of topics related to the income tax consequences of property transactions including sale, exchange, or other disposition of property. By the end of the three chapters on property transactions, the student should gain familiarity with the following broad topics: (1) determination of basis; (2) realized gain or loss; (3) recognized gain or loss; (4) situations where gain or loss is not recognized or only partially recognized; and (5) classification of recognized gain or loss as ordinary or capital.

Chapters 9 and 10 deal with the first four broad topics while Chapter 11 focuses on the classification of recognized gain or loss as ordinary or capital. More specifically, Chapter 9 is concerned with the realization and recognition of gain or loss and with the determination of basis under varying circumstances including: an ordinary purchase, a bargain purchase, acquisition through gift, acquisition through inheritance, conversion of property from personal use to business use, nontaxable and taxable stock dividends and stock rights, and wash sales.

Factors in Determining Gain or Loss

¶ 9001　DEFINITION OF REALIZED GAIN OR LOSS

Realized gain or loss is the difference between the amount realized from the sale or other disposition of property and the adjusted basis at the time of sale or disposition. If the amount realized exceeds the adjusted basis, there is a realized gain. On the other hand, if the adjusted basis exceeds the amount realized, there is a realized loss. Code Sec. 1001(a); Reg. § 1.1001-1(a).

The term "other disposition" is interpreted broadly and includes transactions such as trade-ins, casualties, thefts, and condemnations. The term does not include a fluctuation in market value of an asset because the possibility for the taxpayer to gain or lose value of an asset still exists and no identifiable event has occurred to "fix" the gain or loss realized. Reg. § 1.1001-1(c)(1).

Example 9.1. Adam Acres sells property with an adjusted basis of $20,000 for $30,000 and has a realized gain of $10,000. If he had sold the property for $15,000, he would have had a $5,000 realized loss. If Adam exchanged Beach Corporation stock with an adjusted basis of $4,000 for Clark Corporation stock with a fair market value of $7,000, he has a realized gain of $3,000. If, however, Adam had Danville Corporation stock with an adjusted basis of $5,000 that has appreciated in value to $8,000, there is no realized gain because there is no sale or other disposition of the property.

The recovery of cost doctrine allows the taxpayer to recover the cost of property before being taxed on the sale proceeds. While owning the asset, the taxpayer may recover the cost through depreciation deductions, providing it is depreciable property. Basis is reduced for the depreciation deductions and at the time of sale or other disposition the remaining amount of cost is recovered through a comparison of the amount realized with the adjusted basis to determine whether there is a realized gain or loss.

¶ 9015　AMOUNT REALIZED

The amount realized from the sale or other disposition of property is the sum of any money received plus the fair market value of other property received. It does not include any amount received from the purchaser as reimbursement for real property taxes which are treated as imposed on the purchaser, but it does include amounts representing real property taxes which are treated as imposed on the seller, if they are paid by the purchaser. Code Sec. 1001(b). The amount realized from a sale or other disposition of property also includes the amount of liabilities from which the transferor is relieved as a result of the sale or disposition. The amount realized is reduced by selling expenses.

Example 9.2. Darlene Brown owns land worth $40,000 which is subject to a $16,000 mortgage. She sells it to Edward Greene who pays $24,000 cash and also assumes the mortgage. She incurs $2,000 selling expenses. Darlene's amount realized is $38,000 ($24,000 + $16,000 − $2,000).

The "fair market value" of the property is the price a willing buyer and a willing seller would reach after bargaining where neither party is acting under compulsion. Various sources can provide evidence of value. Stock exchange quotations generally provide evidence of the fair market value of stock except for unusually large blocks of stock. Sales of similar property on the open market are also evidence of value, and the opinion of appraisers or experts is generally given significant weight.

To summarize:

> Cash Received + Fair Market Value of Property and Services Received + Liabilities of Seller Assumed by Buyer − Selling Expenses = Amount Realized

¶ 9025   ADJUSTED BASIS

The concept of basis is important in federal income taxation. In effect, it measures the amount of the taxpayer's investment in the property, which the taxpayer is able to have returned without tax consequences. The taxpayer's original basis of property purchased is generally cost, but in some situations it may be fair market value, or a substituted basis. To figure the adjusted basis, the original cost or other basis is adjusted in various ways to reflect additions and reductions in investment.

The basis of property must be increased by capital expenditures and decreased by capital returns. These adjustments are made to all types of property for all events occurring after acquisition whether original basis is cost, fair market value, or a substituted basis. Code Secs. 1011 and 1016. Increases in basis have the effect of reducing the amount of gain realized or increasing the amount of realized loss as well as depreciation or cost recovery. Decreases in basis have the effect of increasing the amount of realized gain or decreasing the amount of loss and depreciation or cost recovery.

To summarize:

> Original Basis + Capital Expenditures − Capital Returns = Adjusted Basis

Capital *expenditures* are costs chargeable to the capital account. Routine repair and maintenance expenses are not capital expenditures. However, improvements, betterments, acquisition costs, purchase commissions, and legal costs for defending title are all capital expenditures. Capital *returns* include depreciation, depletion, amortization, tax-free dividends, compensation or awards for involuntary conversions, deductible casualty losses, insurance reimbursements, and cash rebates received by a purchaser. Code Sec. 1016(a).

The basis reduction for ACRS or MACRS cost recovery, depreciation, amortization, or depletion is no less than that allowable under the law. If the taxpayer claimed a higher deduction than was allowable and that deduction was allowed for tax purposes (i.e., actually deducted on the taxpayer's return), the basis reduction is that higher allowed amount. If a taxpayer takes no depreciation, then the amount allowable is the amount allowable under the straight-line method. Code Sec. 1016; Reg. § 1.1016-3(a)(2)(i). (Basis, of course, is not reduced for depreciation on assets where it is not allowable, such as on personal use assets as a residence or personal automobile.)

> *Example 9.3.* Judy Jergens purchased a business building in January 1986 for $114,000 and elected to use straight-line depreciation over 19 years. She took depreciation of $6,000 a year from 1986 through 1995 and none for 1996 and 1997. She sold the asset on January 2, 1998, for $126,000 and reported a $72,000 gain ($126,000 − ($114,000 − $60,000)). She was incorrect, however, because she should have reduced the basis by the greater of the allowed or allowable depreciation, and $6,000 depreciation was also allowable for 1996 and 1997. Thus, her gain should have been $84,000 ($126,000 − ($114,000 − $72,000)).

Basis may also be reduced by the amortization of a premium on taxable bonds at the taxpayer's election, and a reduction in interest income in computing taxable income is then allowed. The basis is reduced because it is a recovery of the cost. If no election to amortize premium on taxable bonds is made, then the taxpayer recognizes a smaller capital gain or a larger capital loss upon ultimate sale or disposition. Tax-exempt bonds must be amortized for purposes of reducing basis, but no reduction in interest income in computing taxable income is allowable because the interest income is not included in taxable income. Reg. § 1.171-1(b).

> *Example 9.4.* On January 2, 1998, Vernon Vaughn paid $1,200 for a $1,000 face value taxable bond which will mature on January 1, 2008, and he elects to amortize the premium. For 1998, he is allowed a $20 reduction in interest income, and the adjusted basis of the bond at December 31, 1998, is $1,180. If the bond is tax-exempt, the basis is reduced to $1,180, but no reduction in interest income is allowed in computing taxable income.

¶ 9035 RECOGNITION AND NONRECOGNITION OF GAIN OR LOSS

If a realized gain or loss is recognized, the gain is includible and the loss is deductible in determining taxable income. Thus, "recognition" means that the result of a particular transaction is considered to be taxable income or a deductible loss. Generally, recognition occurs at the time of sale or exchange.

There are certain situations where the realized gain or loss is not recognized. In the case of like-kind exchanges, part or all of the gain or loss may not be recognized. Also, in the case of involuntary conversions and sales of residences, part or all of the realized gain may not be recognized (Chapter 10).

There are also situations where a realized gain may be recognized, but realized losses are not recognized. For example, a sale of a personal-use asset, such as an automobile, results in gain recognition but not loss recognition. (An exception to the latter rule is that losses resulting from casualty and theft of personal-use assets are deductible, provided they exceed certain limits, but the condemnation loss on a personal-use asset is not deductible.) Similarly, sales between related taxpayers may result in gain recognition but no loss recognition. Code Sec. 267(a)(1).

EXHIBIT 1   GAIN OR LOSS SUMMARY

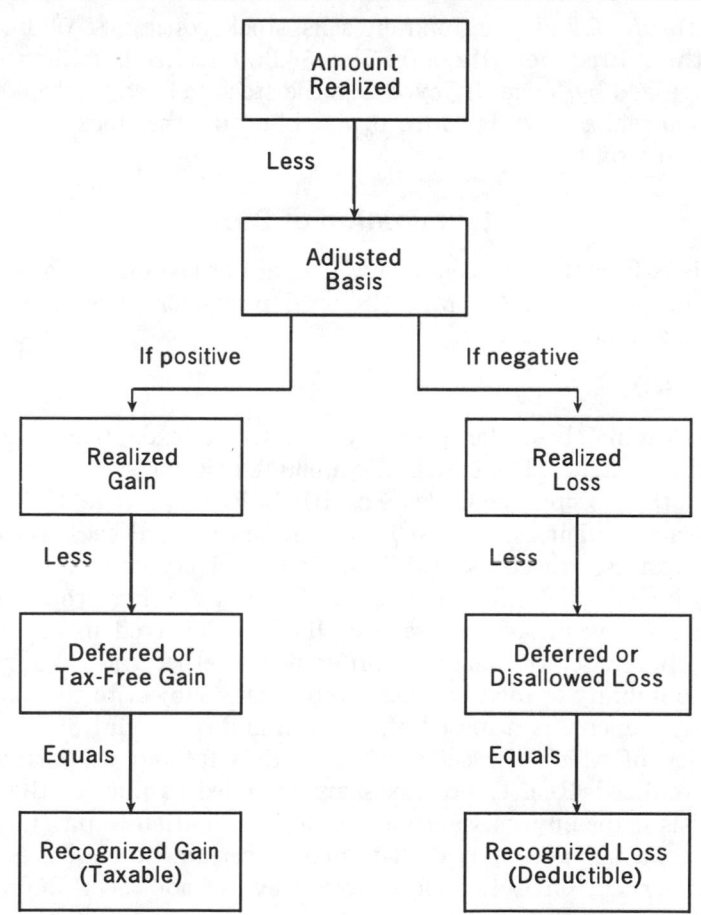

The following examples and Exhibit 1 illustrate the above rules.

Example 9.5. Albert Austin sold for $14,000 stock with an adjusted basis of $10,000. His realized and recognized gain is $4,000. If he sells the stock for $7,000, his realized and recognized loss is $3,000.

Example 9.6. Ellen Eagle trades in a business machine with an adjusted basis of $10,000 for another like-kind business machine with a fair market value of $15,000. Although she realizes a gain of $5,000, this gain is not recognized because of the like-kind provisions of Code Sec. 1031.

Example 9.7. Patrick Power has land with an adjusted basis of $50,000 that was condemned, and the authorities gave him a $75,000 award. Although Patrick has a $25,000 realized gain, he does not have to recognize this gain if the land were replaced with land costing $75,000 or more.

Example 9.8. Karen Kohl sells her personal use automobile that cost her $10,000 for $12,000. She has a $2,000 realized gain which must be recognized. If she sells it for $7,000, she has a $3,000 realized loss but none of it is recognized.

Example 9.9. Joyce Johnson sells stock costing $8,000 to her brother, Fred, for $12,000. The $4,000 realized gain must be recognized by Joyce. If Joyce sells the stock to Fred for $5,000, the $3,000 realized loss is not recognized because the stock was sold to a related party.

Determination of Basis

Basis is important in computing (1) gain or loss on sale or disposition of property and (2) MACRS or depreciation deductions, cost depletion, and amortization.

¶ 9101   COST

The original basis for property is its cost, except as otherwise provided in the law. The cost is the amount paid for such property in cash or other property. Code Sec. 1012; Reg. § 1.1012-1(a). Basis includes acquisition costs such as commissions, legal fees, recording fees, sales taxes, as well as installation and delivery costs. The cost of property includes not only the amount of money or other property paid but also the amount of mortgage or liability incurred in connection with the purchase. It makes no difference whether the taxpayer assumes the liability or merely takes the property subject to the liability. When the property is disposed of, any remaining amount of mortgage or liability of which the seller is relieved is treated as part of the amount realized. Real estate taxes are included as part of the property's basis if the buyer assumes the seller's obligation to pay them. In some cases, a taxpayer may elect to deduct certain expenditures (such as interest) currently or capitalize them. Code Sec. 266; Reg. § 1.266-1(b).

Example 9.10. Rodney Reeves purchased a new machine to be used in his business. He paid $20,000 in cash and signed a note payable in the amount of $40,000. In addition, he paid $3,000 in state sales tax, installation charges of $2,000, and delivery charges of $1,000. Rodney's cost basis of the machine is $66,000 ($20,000 + $40,000 + $3,000 + $2,000 + $1,000).

¶ 9115   BASIS ALLOCATION

If a single transaction involves a number of properties, in order to establish their basis the total cost must be allocated among the separate properties according to their relative fair market value. The basis that each property takes as a result of this allocation is the original unadjusted basis for tax purposes. This rule applies in determining basis for gain or loss and depreciation purposes. Reg. § § 1.61-6(a) and 1.167(a)-5.

> *Example 9.11.* Cathy Camper purchases a tract of land for $250,000 with an office building on it. The contract does not specify the amount for each piece of property, so relative fair market value is used to allocate the basis. If the fair market value of the building is $150,000 and the fair market value of the land is $150,000, the building basis is $125,000 and the remaining $125,000 is allocated to the basis of the land.

Allocation is necessary for several reasons. Some of the property may be depreciable (buildings) and other property not depreciable (land). Different treatment may be necessary for the assets—such as Section 1231 assets compared to capital asset treatment. (See Chapter 11.) Or it may be that only some of the assets purchased are sold. If only one item is involved, allocation may be required because of different treatment such as in the case where part of the asset is used for business and part for personal use. Or the initial one asset may be sold in separate transactions, such as when a piece of land is divided into two parcels and sold.

There is a specific allocation rule if a business is purchased and if goodwill exists as a result of the excess of the purchase price over the sum of the fair market value of Class I, II, and III assets. Code Sec. 1060; Temp. Reg. § 1.338(b)-2T(b). Class I assets consist of cash, demand deposits, and similar bank deposits; Class II assets consist of certificates of deposit, U.S. government securities, and readily marketable stocks; Class III assets are assets that do not fall into Class I or II and assets that are not intangible assets in the nature of goodwill and going concern value (Class IV assets).

TAX PLANNING POINTER

The purchaser will likely want as high as possible an allocation to depreciable assets so as to obtain larger depreciation in the future. From a seller's viewpoint, it may be preferable to have a larger amount allocated to nondepreciable assets, so as to get potentially more capital gain treatment (Chapter 11). Purchasers and sellers are required to specify the values of individual assets where multiple assets are acquired in a single transaction (Form 8594).

¶ 9125   STOCK DIVIDENDS AND STOCK RIGHTS

Allocation of basis may also be necessary in the case of nontaxable stock dividends and nontaxable stock rights. For nontaxable stock dividends, the basis of the original stock is allocated to the old and new shares. Code Secs. 305(a) and 307; Reg. § § 1.305-1–1.305-7. See ¶ 3401 for further discussion on the determination of whether or not stock dividends and stock rights are taxable. In the case of identical stock (common on common), the basis of the original common shares is allocated among the total number of shares owned. The holding period begins on the date of the original acquisition.

If the stock is not identical (e.g., preferred shares received on common), then the basis of the common stock is allocated between the common and preferred stock according to the relative fair market value.

> *Example 9.12.* Curt Coleman owns 1,000 shares of Brockwood Corp. common stock and receives a nontaxable 20 percent common stock dividend. He paid $12,000 for the stock originally ($12 per share). His basis per share on both the old and new shares is $10 ($12,000/1,200).

> *Example 9.13.* Assume instead that Curt received a nontaxable preferred stock dividend of 100 shares of Brockwood Corp. preferred shares when the fair market value (FMV) of the preferred was $80 per share and the fair market value of the common was $16 per share. Then the basis of the preferred shares is $4,000 as follows:

$$\left(\frac{\text{FMV of Preferred}}{\text{FMV of Preferred} + \text{FMV of Common}} \times \text{Basis of Common} \right)$$

$$\left(\frac{\$8,000}{\$8,000 + \$16,000} \times \$12,000 \right)$$

and the basis of the common shares is $8,000 ($12,000 − $4,000).

In the case of taxable stock dividends, the amount of income is the stock's fair market value at the date of distribution. The basis of the new stock is its fair market value at the time of the receipt of the stock dividend and the basis of the old stock remains the same. The holding period of the new stock begins on the date of the receipt of the stock dividend.

> *Example 9.14.* Jim Juniper owns 1,000 shares of Brown Corp. common stock with a basis of $5,000. He receives a 20 percent taxable stock dividend when the fair market value of each share of stock is $8. Jim reports $1,600 of income (200 shares at $8) and his basis for the new shares is $8 per share. The holding period of the new shares begins on the date of receipt of the stock dividend. His basis in the old stock remains the same.

If nontaxable stock rights are received, whether or not any part of the basis of the stock is allocated to the rights depends on the fair market value of the rights as compared with the fair market value of the stock. If the fair market value of the rights at the time of the distribution is less than 15 percent of the fair market value of the old stock at that time, the basis of such rights is zero unless the taxpayer elects to allocate. If the value is 15 percent or more, a basis must be allocated to the rights, but only if the rights are exercised or sold. The stock basis is allocated between the stock and the rights according to the relative fair market value at their distribution date.

If nontaxable rights are sold, the holding period runs from the date the original stock was acquired. Code Sec. 1223(5); Reg. § 1.1223-1(e). If the rights are exercised, the new stock's holding period starts on the date of exercise. Reg. § 1.1223-1(f).

Example 9.15. On January 16, 1997, Florence Frost purchased 100 shares of Duke Corporation common stock for $88 per share. On July 20, 1998, she received 100 nontaxable rights to subscribe to 100 additional shares at $90 per share. The fair market value of each right was $10 and the fair market value of each share of stock is $100 on the date of issuance of the rights. Since the relative fair market value is less than 15 percent, Florence need not allocate any of her basis in the stock to the rights. Any proceeds from the sale of the rights are long-term capital gain and the basis of the new shares that may be purchased through exercise of the rights is the subscription price of $90.

Example 9.16. If Florence in the preceding example elected to allocate part of the basis of the stock to the rights, she would allocate $800 to the 100 rights, or $8 per right as follows:

$$\left(\frac{\text{FMV of Rights}}{\text{FMV of Rights} + \text{FMV of Stock}} \times \text{Basis of Stock} \right)$$

$$\left(\frac{\$1,000}{\$10,000 + \$1,000} \times \$8,800 \right)$$

If one-half or 50 of the rights are sold for $1,000, there is $600 long-term capital gain ($1,000 − $400). If 50 rights are exercised, the basis of each share obtained through exercise of the rights is $98 ($90 + $8) and the holding period for the new shares begins on the date of exercise of the rights.

Note: The property must be held more than 18 months to be long-term and to be eligible for the lowest capital gains rate (i.e., a maximum rate of 20 percent). Property is held short-term if it is held 12 months or less, and if held more than 12 months but not greater than 18 months the maximum rate is 28 percent. (See Chapter 11 for more discussion.).

TAX PLANNING POINTER ▼

With the opportunity to elect to allocate part of the basis of the stock to the rights, the taxpayer has the opportunity to control income to a limited extent. In Example 9.16 above where Florence sold 50 rights for $1,000, she has either $1,000 long-term capital gain if she did not allocate any of the basis of the stock to the rights or $600 long-term capital gain if she did allocate basis to the rights. The latter might be preferable if she already had capital gains from other transactions. If, on the other hand, she had capital losses, she might prefer not to allocate basis to the rights so as to offset a larger $1,000 capital gain against her losses.

In the case of taxable stock rights, the amount of income and the basis of the rights constitute the fair market value of the rights at the date of distribution, which is the date the holding period of the rights begins. If the rights are exercised, the basis of the new shares is the subscription price plus the basis of the rights, and the holding period of the new shares begins on the date of exercise. The basis and holding period of the old stock remain the same.

Example 9.17. Betty Blue owns 100 shares of King Corp. stock purchased in January 1996 for $1,300. On January 16, 1998, she receives 100 taxable stock rights valued at $300 with the right to purchase additional shares at $15. Betty reports $300 income as a result of receipt of the stock rights, which is also the basis of the rights. The holding period of the rights begins on January 16, 1998. On July 20, 1999, she exercises 50 rights and sells the remaining 50 rights for $4 each. The basis of each new share is $18 ($15 + $3) and the holding period begins on the date of exercise. She has long-term capital gain of $50 (50 × ($4 − $3)) on the sale of the rights, and since the rights were held longer than 18 months the gain will be taxed at a maximum rate of 20 percent.

¶ 9135 FAIR MARKET VALUE

If property is received in exchange for services, there is a taxable transaction. If property is acquired in a taxable exchange, the basis of the property received is generally its fair market value at the time of exchange. See ¶ 9015 for definition of fair market value.

Example 9.18. Wilbur Wilson gives up inventory with a basis of $2,000 in exchange for a machine with a fair market value of $3,000. He has a realized and recognized gain of $1,000. His basis in the machine is the fair market value of $3,000.

Example 9.19. Diane Davis does accounting work for Wanda Wales, and, in exchange for the services rendered, she receives a ring with a fair market value of $500. Diane reports $500 of income and has a basis of $500 for the ring (i.e., the fair market value).

Other situations may require the use of fair market value as basis. If the price paid is a bargain purchase, then the basis of the property is its fair market value. Reg. § § 1.61-2(d)(2)(i) and 1.301-1(j). For example, assume an employee pays only $4,000 for an asset purchased from his employer when the fair market value is $7,000. The employee reports $3,000 as income and has a basis in the asset of $7,000, its fair market value. On the other hand, if the price paid for property includes payments made for reasons other than the acquisition of the asset (such as making a capital contribution or helping out a family member), then the amount in excess of the fair market value is not included in the buyer's cost or basis.

¶ 9145 PROPERTY ACQUIRED BY GIFT

A taxpayer's original basis for property acquired by gift is the same as the property's adjusted basis in the hands of the donor or the last preceding owner by whom it was not acquired by gift. If, however, the property's fair market value at the time of the gift is less than the adjusted basis to the donor, then the basis for determining *loss* is the fair market value at the time of the gift. Code Sec. 1015(a). A selling price of gift property between the basis for determining gain and a lesser fair market value will result in neither gain nor loss. The gain basis is used by the donee to calculate depreciation, cost recovery, or amortization. Reg. § 1.167(g)-1.

The holding period of gift property begins with the date the property was acquired by the donor. If, however, the fair market value of the property at the date of the gift was less than the donor's adjusted basis and the property is sold at a loss, the holding period begins on the date of the gift. Code Sec. 1223(2); Reg. § 1.1223-1(b).

Example 9.20. On June 3, 1996, Mary Marvel buys stock for $25,000, and, on January 19, 1998, she gives the stock to her daughter Irene when its fair market value is $28,000.

1. If Irene sells the property for $32,000 on June 5, 1998, her gain is $7,000 ($32,000 − $25,000). The gain will be a long-term capital gain since Irene includes in her holding period the time the stock was held by Mary.

2. If Irene sells the property for $24,000, she will have a long-term capital loss of $1,000 ($24,000 − $25,000).

Example 9.21. Assume that the fair market value of the stock in Example 9.20 on the date of the gift is $22,000 instead of $28,000.

1. If Irene sells the property for $20,000, the loss is $2,000 ($20,000 − $22,000) and it will be short-term capital loss since the holding period begins on the date of the gift when fair market value is used as the basis.

2. If Irene sells the property for $23,000, she will have neither gain nor loss. In other words, in this example, any selling price between $22,000 and $25,000 results in no gain or loss.

TAX PLANNING POINTER

Taxpayers should avoid making gifts of property that have a fair market value less than basis because neither the donor nor the donee is able to take a deduction for the unrealized loss that occurred between the original acquisition and the gift by the donor. The donee is not able to take the deduction for the unrealized loss because of the loss rules for gift property. A better alternative is for the donor to sell the property that has declined in value, take the loss deduction (assuming it is deductible), and then give the proceeds to the donee. If, however, there is the expectation that the donee will keep it until the value exceeds the adjusted basis in the hands of the donor, then the donor may still wish to consider giving property that has declined in value.

Example 9.22. Allen Armstrong has 300 shares of Pierce Corporation stock that he purchased five years ago for $30,000. Allen would like to give the property to his son Michael, but the total fair market value is now only $20,000. If the gift is made and Michael sells the stock for $20,000, neither Allen nor Michael will be able to take advantage of the $10,000 loss deduction for the decline in value. Allen should sell the stock, take the loss deduction (subject to the capital loss rules), and then give the proceeds to Michael. If, however, Michael wants to keep the stock, and it is expected that the stock will increase in value to above the $30,000 basis for determining gain, Allen should feel free to give the stock to Michael.

Increase in Basis for Gift Taxes Paid

The basis of gift property may be increased if gift taxes were paid by the donor. If the property's fair market value at the date of the gift is greater than the donor's adjusted basis, then the donee's basis is increased by all or a portion of the gift tax paid by the donor.

For gifts made after December 31, 1976, the basis is increased by the portion of gift tax that is attributable to the net appreciation in value of the gift. Net appreciation in value is defined as the amount by which the fair market value of the gift exceeds the donor's adjusted basis immediately before the gift. Code Sec. 1015(d)(6). The amount of basis increase is as follows:

$$\frac{\text{Net appreciation}}{\text{Fair market value}} \times \text{Gift tax paid}$$

This adjustment plus the donor's adjusted basis becomes the basis for asset write-offs and for gain or loss determination.

Example 9.23. In 1998, Todd Tromb gave property with an adjusted basis of $20,000 to Stephen Strom when the fair market value was $60,000. Gift taxes paid on the property were $7,500. Since the net appreciation is $40,000 and the fair market value is $60,000, two-thirds of the gift taxes, or $5,000, is added to $20,000 to obtain a $25,000 basis.

Example 9.24. If the adjusted basis to Todd in Example 9.23 is $70,000, there is no appreciation and none of the $7,500 gift tax is added to determine the donee's basis. In this case, Stephen's gain basis is $70,000; his basis for determining loss is $60,000, the fair market value at the time of the gift.

If a gift consists of several items, then the taxpayer must allocate the gift tax paid with respect to each item. Also, a special allocation of gift taxes must be made where a taxpayer receives a gift of property from a donor who has made gifts to more than one person during the year the gift taxes were paid. Code Sec. 1015(d)(2).

For gifts made prior to 1977, the full amount of the gift tax is added to the donor's adjusted basis, but the basis may not be increased above the fair market value at the date of the gift. Code Sec. 1015(d)(1).

Example 9.25. Assume that in 1976 Todd gave Stephen property with an adjusted basis of $50,000 when its fair market value was $60,000. Gift taxes paid on the property were $7,500. Then Stephen's basis is $57,500. If the fair market value was $55,000 at the time of gift, then the basis increase would have been limited to $55,000 since the addition of gift taxes paid cannot cause the donee's basis to go above the fair market value at the time of the gift.

TAX PLANNING POINTER ▼

The donor is able to avoid recognition of gain on any appreciated property by giving away the property. Assuming that the donee sells the property and that the donee is in a lower tax bracket, there could be benefits from making the gift. Also, since the basis of appreciated property would be increased for at least a portion of gift taxes paid, this would provide a "step-up" in basis. Even if the low tax bracket donee keeps the property for some time, there may be an advantage to making the gift.

¶ 9175   PROPERTY ACQUIRED FROM DECEDENT

The general rule is that the basis of property acquired from a decedent is the fair market value of the property at the date of the decedent's death. Code Sec. 1014(a). This is often referred to as a "step-up" in basis since the fair market value of property of the decedent is generally more than the adjusted basis. The effect of this rule is that any appreciation while the decedent owned the property escapes income taxation. However, there could, of course, be a "step-down" in basis if the fair market value of the property at the date of the decedent's death were lower than the adjusted basis. In this case, the decline in value while the decedent owned the property is not recognized for income tax purposes.

Example 9.26. If Sally Sparrow purchased land parcel A for $5,000 in 1958 and it appreciated in value to $100,000 by 1998, when she died, her daughter Jane, the heir, will have $100,000 as her basis in the land. Thus, the $95,000 increase in value is never subject to income taxation. If Sally owned land parcel B costing $50,000 in 1988 that declined in value to $30,000 by 1998, when she died, Jane would have $30,000 as the basis in land. Here, the $20,000 decline in value while Sally owned the land is not deductible for tax purposes.

Note: The basis of the property is the same as the value placed on the property for estate tax purposes. There is no basis adjustment for any estate tax that may have been paid on the property. (Contrast this with the gift tax adjustment for the basis of gift property.)

TAX PLANNING POINTER ▼

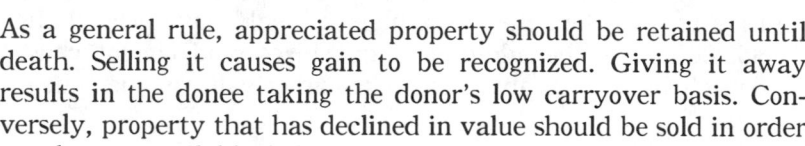

As a general rule, appreciated property should be retained until death. Selling it causes gain to be recognized. Giving it away results in the donee taking the donor's low carryover basis. Conversely, property that has declined in value should be sold in order to take any available deductions for recognized losses.

Example 9.27. Assuming the same facts as in the preceding example, if Sally had sold land parcel A, she would have recognized $95,000 gain. If she had given the property to Jane, Jane would use $5,000 as the carryover basis. If Sally had sold parcel B for $30,000, she would have had a loss of $20,000. Giving it to Jane would have been a poor choice since Jane would have taken as her basis the fair market value at the date of the gift if she sold it for less than $30,000 and none of the $20,000 decline in value would have been recognized by either party.

Alternate Valuation

If the executor elects for estate tax purposes to value the decedent's gross estate as of six months after death, the basis of the property is the fair market value at that time. Code Sec. 1014(a)(2). If the property is distributed before the alternate valuation date, the basis is the fair market value at the date of distribution or other disposition. The alternate valuation may be used only where the election will reduce both the value of the decedent's gross estate and the federal estate tax liability. Code Sec. 2032(a)(2) and (c).

Example 9.28. Edward Eggard died during the year, and property he owned with an adjusted basis of $50,000 and a fair market value of $150,000 went to his beneficiary, Larry Larsen. The executor elected to value the property at the alternate valuation date when the value was $140,000. In this case, $140,000 is the basis to Larry even if the property is distributed later. If, however, the property was distributed three months after Edward's death when the fair market value was $145,000 and the executor chose the alternate valuation date, the basis to Larry is $145,000.

Exception

Where appreciated property was acquired by the decedent by gift during the one-year period before death and the property is acquired from the decedent by the original donor, the adjusted basis to the recipient is the adjusted basis in the hands of the decedent immediately before death. Code Sec. 1014(e).

Example 9.29. Ken Kooms gave property to Wesley, his father, when the adjusted basis of the property was $5,000 and the fair market value was $75,000. Wesley died six months after the gift (when the property was valued at $80,000) and he left the property to Ken. Ken's basis in the property will be $5,000, the basis to Wesley at the time of his death. If Wesley had lived more than a year, then Ken's basis would have been the fair market value at the date of Wesley's death.

Survivor's Basis

For property that is jointly owned, the part of the property included in the estate of the decedent is considered to be acquired from the decedent by the survivor. The survivor's basis in the part of the property included in the decedent's estate is the fair market value on the date of death (or alternate valuation date). The basis of the property not included in the decedent's estate is cost or other basis. Code Sec. 2040.

Example 9.30. William Weber and Norman Northe bought property jointly for $100,000 with rights of survivorship, each paying 50 percent. When William died, the total property value was $150,000 and $75,000 was included in his estate. Norman's basis in the property after William's death is $125,000 (his $50,000 plus the $75,000 value of William's portion).

Property which represents both the surviving spouse's share of community property and the decedent's share of community property will have a basis equal to its fair market value on the date of the decedent's death. Code Sec. 1014(b)(6).

Example 9.31. Edwin and Dawn Durham live in a community property state and own community property acquired for $200,000. If Edwin dies when the fair market value is $500,000, one-half or $250,000 is included in Edwin's estate. If Dawn inherits Edwin's share of community property, the total basis of the property is $500,000 ($250,000, or Dawn's share of the community property, plus $250,000, the value of Edwin's property at the date of his death).

Holding Period

The holding period of property acquired from a decedent is long-term (i.e., more than 18 months). This is the case regardless of how long the beneficiary or decedent held the property and regardless of whether the property is disposed of at a gain or at a loss.

Example 9.32. Norton Newbert purchases property on December 19, 1997, and dies on January 17, 1998. The property is distributed on February 20, 1998, to Perry Portman, who sells it on May 22, 1998. Even though Perry held the property only three months and the total time from acquisition by Norton to sale by Perry was only five months, the gain or loss will be deemed to be long-term.

¶ 9201   STOCK TRANSACTIONS

Identification of Shares

When a seller can identify the shares of stock sold or transferred, the basis is the basis of the stock so identified. Shares of stock are adequately identified if it can be shown that shares which were delivered to the buyer were from a lot acquired on a certain date or for a certain price. Reg. § 1.1012-1(c)(2). If the shares of stock were purchased at different dates or at different prices and the lot from which the stock was sold or transferred cannot be adequately identified, the stock sold is charged against the earliest of the stock purchases (i.e., the FIFO rule). Reg. § 1.1012-1(c)(1).

Example 9.33. Violet Vernon acquires 100 shares of Wilson Corp. stock in 1995 at $15 a share and 200 shares of Wilson stock in 1996 at $25 a share. If she sells 200 shares in 1998 for $35 a share and can specifically identify the shares sold as those from the 1996 purchase, she has a $2,000 gain (($35 − $25) × 200). If she cannot specifically identify the shares, she must assume that 100 shares were from the 1995 purchase and the remaining 100 were from the 1996 purchase. Her gain in that case is $3,000 (($35 − $15) × 100) + (($35 − $25) × 100).

TAX PLANNING POINTER

Specific identification of shares makes it easier to control income. If a lower income is desired, higher cost shares may be specifically identified as being sold. If, on the other hand, a higher income from sale of stock is preferable (perhaps because other income is low this year but expected to be high in future years), lower cost shares may be specifically identified as being sold.

If stock is held by a broker or agent, an adequate identification is made if the taxpayer specifies to the broker the particular shares to be sold and within a reasonable time receives a written confirmation of the transfer instruction. If a single stock certificate represents stock from different lots, where such certificate is held by the taxpayer and where the taxpayer sells a part of the stock represented by such a certificate through a broker an adequate identification is made if the taxpayer specifies to the broker the particular shares to be sold and within a reasonable time receives a written confirmation of transfer instruction. Reg. § 1.1012-1(c)(3).

Wash Sales

Wash sales occur when substantially identical stock is bought within 30 days before or after the sale. No deduction for losses is allowed on the sale of stock or securities if, within a period beginning 30 days before the date of the sale and ending 30 days after the date of sale, substantially identical stock or securities are acquired. Code Sec. 1091(a). Substantially identical stock or securities means the same in all important particulars such as earning power, interest rate, value of assets, preference, etc. Rev. Rul. 58-210, 1958-1 CB 523. Also, no deduction is allowed if the taxpayer has during that 61-day period entered into a contract or option to acquire substantially identical stock or securities. Reg. § 1.1091-1(a).

The purpose of the wash sale rules is to prevent a tax avoidance scheme. Without the rules, taxpayers would be able to sell securities on which they could show a loss and then buy back substantially identical securities. With the wash sale rules, the realized loss is disallowed; however, the disallowed loss is not "lost" but is added to the basis of the newly acquired stock. Code Sec. 1091(d); Reg. § 1.1091-2. In adding the disallowed loss to the cost of the new acquired stock, the taxpayer ultimately will be able to recover the cost of the new stock and the unrecovered cost of the old stock. The holding period of the new securities purchased in a wash sale includes the period the old securities were held. Code Sec. 1223(4).

> *Example 9.34.* Simon Sugarman has the following transactions:
>
> | September 8, 1997: | Purchases 100 shares of Winston Corp. stock for $20 a share. |
> | February 20, 1998: | Sells 75 shares of stock purchased on September 8, 1997, for $14 per share. |
> | March 3, 1998: | Purchases 50 shares of Winston Corp. stock for $15 per share. |
> | May 17, 1999: | Sells the remaining 75 shares for $12 a share. |

The results of the above transactions are as follows:

1. On the February 20, 1998, sale the realized loss is $450, but $300 of it is disallowed and $150 is short-term loss (stock held less than 12 months). Only two-thirds of the realized loss is disallowed because only two-thirds (50 out of 75) is considered to be a wash sale (i.e., because 50 shares are later purchased on March 3).

2. The basis of the 50 shares acquired on March 3, 1998, is $1,050 ($750 + $300).

3. The loss realized on May 17, 1999, is $650, computed as follows:

Selling price		$ 900
Basis: $20 × 25 shares	$ 500	
March 3 stock	1,050	1,550
Loss		$ (650)

It is considered long-term loss since the holding period of the stock acquired on March 3, 1998, includes the holding period from September 8, 1997, to February 20, 1998.

¶ 9215   PERSONAL-USE PROPERTY CONVERSION

When property purchased for personal use is converted to business or income-producing use, the basis for determining loss is the lesser of (1) the fair market value of the property at the time of the conversion, or (2) the adjusted basis for loss at the time of the conversion. Reg. § 1.165-9(b)(2). This rule is to prevent the taxpayer from converting a nondeductible personal loss into a deductible business loss. The basis for gain is the adjusted basis on the date of conversion. The basis for determining depreciation is the basis for determining loss. Reg. § 1.167(g)-1. No gain or loss results on sale of converted personal-use property if the amount realized is between the basis for gain and the basis for loss.

> *Example 9.35.* Terry Trudman has a residence that had an adjusted basis of $150,000 but a fair market value of $100,000 at the time of conversion to rental property. The basis for determining loss is $100,000. The basis for determining gain is $150,000, the adjusted basis at the time of the conversion. If $10,000 depreciation (computed on the basis for determining loss) is taken between the time of conversion and sale, the results under the following assumptions are:
>
> 1.   In a sale for $85,000, the loss is $5,000 or $85,000 − $90,000 ($100,000 − $10,000).
>
> 2.   In a sale for $175,000, the gain is $35,000 or $175,000 − $140,000 ($150,000 − $10,000).
>
> 3.   In a sale for $130,000, there is neither gain nor loss because by using the basis for gain one gets a loss of $10,000 ($130,000 − $140,000) and by using the basis for loss, one gets a gain of $40,000 ($130,000 − $90,000).

KEYSTONE PROBLEM

Determine what the initial basis of an asset would be in the following situations:

1.   Purchase of asset

2.   Bargain purchase

3.   Lump-sum purchase of several assets

4.   Property acquired by gift

5.   Property acquired from a decedent

6.   Property converted from personal use to business or income-producing use

7. Property acquired in a wash sale

8. Nontaxable stock dividends and stock rights

¶ 9225 RELATED PARTIES

No loss deduction is allowed on sales or exchanges of property, directly or indirectly, between certain related parties. Without this provision, related taxpayers might enter transactions solely for the purpose of obtaining loss deductions and reducing their tax liabilities when the property still remained in the family. With the provision, the Internal Revenue Service does not have to be concerned about the reasonableness of the selling price. Any losses disallowed, however, may be used to offset the gain realized by the related purchaser on a later sale of the property. Code Sec. 267(a) and (d). This offset possibility is available only to the original transferee. The buyer's holding period includes only the time the buyer has held the property and does not include the period held by the seller. Reg. § 1.267(d)-1(c)(3).

Related parties under Code Sec. 267(b) and (c) include the following:

1. Members of a family including brothers and sisters (including by the half blood), spouse, ancestors, and lineal descendants

2. A corporation where the taxpayer owns directly or indirectly more than 50 percent in value of the outstanding stock

3. Two corporations where more than 50 percent in value is owned, directly or indirectly, by the taxpayer if either corporation is a personal holding company or a foreign personal holding company during the taxable year

4. A grantor and a fiduciary of any trust

5. A taxpayer and an exempt organization controlled by the taxpayer

Example 9.36. Norman Norseman owned stock costing $15,000 which he sold to his son Wayne for $12,000. Norman's $3,000 loss is disallowed. If Wayne later sells the stock for $17,000, he will have a gain of $2,000. His $5,000 realized gain is reduced by Norman's disallowed loss of $3,000. If Wayne sells the stock for $14,000, he does not recognize any gain. The $2,000 realized gain is wiped out by Norman's disallowed loss. If Wayne sells the stock for $10,000, he has a $2,000 recognized loss ($10,000 less $12,000). Norman's disallowed loss does not increase Wayne's loss, but can only reduce the amount of gain recognized. If the property sold was a personal use asset (rather than stock) and sold at $10,000, even the $2,000 loss would not be deductible by Wayne.

TAX PLANNING POINTER

The loss deduction on a sale to a related party can be permanently lost if the property does not appreciate in value. In the preceding example, where Wayne sold the stock for $10,000, the $3,000 disallowed loss to Norman was permanently lost. If the original owner has any idea that it may not appreciate in value, the sale should be made to an unrelated party in order to take advantage of the loss deduction.

In case of a sale or exchange of property, directly or indirectly, between related taxpayers, any gain realized is ordinary income if the property is not a capital asset in the hands of the transferee. Related parties for this purpose are (1) a taxpayer and an entity that is controlled by the taxpayer, and (2) a taxpayer and any trust of which such taxpayer is a beneficiary. Code Sec. 1239(a)-(c). This provision keeps a taxpayer, for example, from getting capital gain treatment on a sale of property to a controlled entity and the entity from then getting ordinary depreciation deductions on the amount paid for the property.

¶ 9245   INSTALLMENT REPORTING

An installment sale is a disposition of property where at least one payment is to be received after the close of the taxable year in which the disposition occurs. The installment method allows gain to be spread over more than one year. The amount of income recognized is the proportion of the payments received in the year which the gross profit bears to the total contract price. Code Sec. 453(b) and (c). Installment reporting is discussed in more detail in Chapter 12.

> *Example 9.37.* On October 19, 1998, Brenda Brewster sells property with an adjusted basis of $30,000 for $100,000. The buyer pays Brenda $20,000 cash at the time of the sale transaction with the remaining $80,000 to be paid in five annual installments of $16,000 beginning in October 1999 with interest at 12 percent. During 1998, Brenda reports $14,000 ($20,000 × 70% gross profit rate), and in each of the following five years she would report $11,200 ($16,000 × 70% gross profit rate) in addition to the interest.

TAX PLANNING POINTER

Installment reporting has advantages. The income is spread over a number of years and helps to keep income out of higher tax brackets. In the preceding example, the taxpayer reports income in six years instead of reporting all of the gain in the year of sale. In addition, because of the time value of money, there is the benefit that the taxpayer will be able to earn income on the taxes that do not have to be paid until future years.

TAX BLUNDERS

1.   Harriet Harrison has investment property with an adjusted basis of $50,000 that has declined in value to $30,000 and she

gives it to Jane Juniper. Needing cash, Jane sells the property a few months later for $31,000. Jane recognizes no gain or loss because the selling price is between the basis for determining gain ($50,000) and the basis for determining loss ($30,000). Harriet should have sold the property and then given the proceeds to Jane. Then Harriet could have had a $20,000 loss.

2. Paul Paget, age 85, has investment property that he has owned for 40 years with an adjusted basis of $20,000 that has appreciated to $400,000. He gives the property to his son, Tim, who will take $20,000 as his basis. Paul should have kept the property until his death so that Tim would be able to use a stepped-up basis of fair market value at the date of death. (Gift and estate tax considerations could alter the conclusions relating to this hypothetical situation.)

3. George Gainer, age 80, has rental property with an adjusted basis of $100,000 and a fair market value of $40,000. He has taxable income of $90,000. George has made a decision to keep the property because it has been in the family since he was a child. For best results, George should have sold the property and taken the loss deduction. If he gives it away, no one can take a deduction for the decline in value. If he keeps it until his death, the heir takes the fair market value at the date of death as the basis (a step-down in basis, assuming the fair market value remains around $40,000 until his death).

SUMMARY OF CHAPTER 9

✓ Realized gain or loss is the difference between the fair market value of the property received and the adjusted basis of property given up.

✓ Recognized gain or loss is the amount that appears on the tax return as an included income item or a deductible loss.

✓ The original basis for property acquired by purchase is its cost.

✓ Allocation of basis may be necessary in the case of nontaxable stock dividends and nontaxable stock rights.

✓ A taxpayer's original basis for property acquired by gift is generally the same as the property's adjusted basis in the hands of the donor.

✓ For inherited property, the general rule is that the basis of the property is the fair market value of the property at the date of the decedent's death.

✓ If a seller of stock wishes to identify the shares of stock sold, the basis is the basis of the stock so identified; otherwise, a taxpayer should use the FIFO rule.

✓ No loss deduction is allowed on sales or exchanges of property, directly or indirectly, between certain related parties.

✓ The installment method allows gain to be spread over more than one year.

CHAPTER 9 QUESTIONS

1. Distinguish between realized gains and losses and recognized gains and losses.
2. How is the adjusted basis of property determined?
3. List three capital additions or expenditures and three capital returns or recoveries and discuss the treatment of each category for tax purposes.
4. Why is allocation of basis necessary?
5. Are gains and losses from the sale or exchange of personal use assets recognized for tax purposes?
6. When is fair market value of an asset used as the basis for an asset?
7. What is the basis and holding period of nontaxable stock dividends?
8. What is the basis and holding period of taxable stock dividends?
9. What is the basis and holding period of nontaxable stock rights?
10. What is the basis and holding period of taxable stock rights and the basis and holding period of the shares of stock if the rights are exercised?
11. What is the basis of gift property?
12. What adjustment, if any, must be made to the basis of property acquired by gift if the gift was made prior to 1977? After 1976?
13. What is the basis of an asset acquired from a decedent?
14. What is the alternate valuation of assets acquired from a decedent?
15. Distinguish the holding period of assets acquired by gift with that of assets acquired from a decedent.
16. When is the sale or exchange of stock or securities considered a wash sale? How is any loss treated?
17. What is the basis of a personal use asset that is converted to business or income-producing use?
18. What are the special rules for gains or losses on sales to related parties?
19. What are the benefits of installment reporting?

CHAPTER 9 PROBLEMS

20. Albert Armstrong sells for $80,000 a business building, which he purchased 12 years ago for $57,000. During the 12 years of ownership, he painted the building at a cost of $750, installed an air conditioning system for $6,000, cleaned the carpeting for $300, repaired the fence for $500, installed permanent bookcases for $4,000, replaced the electrical wir-

ing system at a cost of $15,000, and partitioned off some of the rooms at a cost of $5,000. Albert has taken straight-line depreciation on the building for a total of $36,000. What is his basis in the building at time of sale? What is his realized and recognized gain on the sale of the building?

21. Rex Redd purchased a building on January 1, 1986, for $95,000 and elected to use the straight-line depreciation method over 19 years. He took $5,000 depreciation for 1986 through 1995 and none for 1996 and 1997. He sold the building on January 2, 1998. What is Rex's adjusted basis in the building on January 2, 1998?

22. On January 1, 1997, Rodney Rapp paid $110,000 for taxable bonds with a face value of $100,000 which mature on January 1, 2007. He sold them on December 31, 1998, for $104,000. What is Rodney's gain or loss? What if the bonds were tax exempt?

23. Lance Lang received 50 shares of $10 par value stock from Randy Rainey in return for performing legal services. The fair market value of the 50 shares was $750. What is Lance's basis in the stock and what amount, if any, is included in his taxable income?

24. Which of the following results in a recognized gain or loss?

    a. Sale of stock, which has an adjusted basis of $5,000, for $7,000.

    b. Sale of a personal auto with an adjusted basis of $10,000 for $12,000.

    c. Sale of a personal residence with an adjusted basis of $75,000 for $65,000.

25. Gail Gumm purchased a piece of land, a building, and two trucks for a lump sum of $315,000. On the date of purchase, the land had a fair market value of $250,000, the fair market value of the building was $85,000, one truck is valued at $5,000, and the other at $10,000. What is Gail's basis in the land, the building, and each truck?

26. Kevin Klein owns 900 shares of Palmer Corporation stock which he purchased three years ago for $65 each. He receives one nontaxable right for each share of stock owned. The rights entitle Kevin to receive one share of stock for every three rights plus the payment of $50 per share. On the date of distribution, the market value of the stock was $75 and the market value of the rights was $12. If Kevin exercises 600 of the rights and sells the remaining rights for $3,000, what is his basis in the old stock, the rights, the newly purchased stock, and what is his gain or loss on the sale?

27. Gordon Gladstone owns 120 shares of Jones Corporation common stock which he purchased on June 8, 1997, for $1,800. One year later, he received a 25 percent nontaxable common stock dividend. On December 14, 1998, he sold 85 shares at

$20 a share. What is the basis of the shares sold and what is Gordon's gain upon sale?

28. On August 1, 1996, Henry Hughes paid $30,000 for 500 shares of Young Corporation common stock. On July 24, 1998, he received a nontaxable 20 percent common stock dividend. On December 28, 1998, he sold the 100 shares received in July for $4,400. What is the basis of the 100 shares sold? What is the gain or loss on the sale? Is it short-term or long-term?

29. Bradley Brownstone acquired depreciable gift property from Chester Craine. On the date of the gift, Chester's adjusted basis in the property was $17,000 and the fair market value was $12,000. What is Bradley's basis for purposes of determining a gain? For purposes of determining a loss?

30. Sarah Shore bought 500 shares of stock on October 27, 1997, for $30,000. On March 25, 1998, she gave half the shares to her sister Cindy when the fair market value of the shares was $55 per share. If Cindy sells the property for $14,000, what is her gain or loss?

31. Maria Mann gives Peggy property worth $15,000. Maria's basis in the property is $10,000.

    a. If Peggy sells the property for $17,000, what is her gain or loss on the sale?

    b. If Peggy sells the property for $5,500, what is her gain or loss?

    c. If the fair market value on the date of the gift is $7,500 and Peggy sells the property for $5,500, what is the gain or loss?

    d. If the fair market value is $7,500 and Peggy sells the property for $8,000, what is the gain or loss?

32. Compute the basis and gain and loss in the following property transactions:

    a. Wayne Worth gave Tim Thompson depreciable gift property (a building) which cost $57,000 when purchased on January 1, 1986. It had a fair market value on the date of the gift of $75,000. Wayne depreciated the property on a straight-line basis (over 19 years). Upon giving Tim the gift on January 1, 1998, Wayne paid a gift tax of $4,200. What is Wayne's basis in the property? What is Tim's basis in the property?

    b. Assume the same facts as in (a), except that immediately after receiving the gift, Tim sold the property for $50,000. What is his gain or loss? What is the holding period for Tim?

33. In February 1998, Judy Judd gave her son Steven one of her automobiles for his graduation gift. The automobile had a basis of $12,000 to Judy but was worth $15,000 at the time of the

gift. Judy paid $4,500 gift taxes on the gift. Assume that Steven used the car for business purposes.

a. What is Steven's gain or loss if the automobile is sold in April 1998 for $14,500?

b. What is the gain or loss recognized if the car is sold for $11,500?

c. What is the gain or loss recognized if the fair market value at the time of the gift had been $10,000 instead of $15,000 and Steven sold the car for $14,500?

d. What is the answer to (c) if the selling price is $9,500?

e. What is the answer to (c) if the selling price is $10,500?

34. Marsha Moore gave property with an adjusted basis of $28,000 to Alfred when the fair market value of the property was $25,000. Gift taxes paid on the property were $3,000. What is Alfred's basis for gain? What is his basis for loss?

35. Beverly Bergman purchased land for $30,000 in 1983. The land was valued at $180,000 on April 15, 1998, when Beverly died. Her son Jack inherited the land. Six months later, on October 15, 1998, the property was valued at $170,000.

a. What is Jack's basis in the land?

b. If the executor of Beverly's estate elected the alternate valuation date, what is Jack's basis?

c. If the executor elected the alternate valuation date but distributed the property on July 18, 1998, what would be Jack's basis?

d. If the executor elected the alternate valuation date but distributed the property on November 20, 1998, what would be Jack's basis?

e. If Jack sells the property on December 18, 1998, will he have short-term or long-term gain or loss?

36. Evelyn Everest gave property to her mother Sharon when the adjusted basis of the property was $12,000 and the fair market value was $80,000. Sharon died eight months later when the property was valued at $85,000 and she left the property to Evelyn.

a. What is Evelyn's basis?

b. If Sharon had died more than a year after receiving the gift when the fair market value was $85,000, what would the basis have been to Evelyn?

37. Sam Spurr gave property to Robert Reddy when its fair market value was $70,000 and the adjusted basis was $50,000. Robert died two years later when the fair market value of the property was $75,000, and he left the property to Sam. What is Sam's basis in the property?

38. Brothers Andrew and Vincent Vaughn jointly acquired property for $200,000 with rights of survivorship, paying three-fourths

and one-fourth, respectively. Andrew died; the property was valued at $300,000 and $225,000 was added to his estate. What is Vincent's basis in the property after Andrew's death?

39. On April 14, 1998, Jane Juniper purchased 30 shares of Bryan Corporation stock for $210, and on September 25, 1998, she purchased 90 additional shares for $900. On November 20, 1998, she sold 48 shares, which could not be specifically identified, for $576 and on December 4, 1998, she sold another 25 shares for $188. What is her recognized gain or loss?

40. Harold Haas owns 100 shares of Spartan Corp. common stock with an adjusted basis of $10,000. On July 31, 1998, he sold all 100 shares for $9,000. On August 21, 1998, he purchased 80 shares of Spartan common stock for $7,500 and 20 shares of Spartan preferred stock for $3,000. What is Harold's recognized gain or loss on the sale and what is his basis per share in the new stock?

41. Brenda Brewster owned stock costing $12,000 which she sold to her daughter, Rita, for $8,000. Rita sold the stock later for $14,000.

    a. What is Brenda's gain or loss?

    b. What is Rita's gain or loss?

    c. If Rita had sold the stock for $10,000, how much gain or loss would she recognize?

    d. If Rita had sold the stock for $6,000, how much gain or loss would she recognize?

42. Emily Eagels owned stock with a basis of $50,000 which she sold to her sister, Janet, for $42,000. Three months later, Janet sold the stock through a broker for $52,000. What is the gain or loss to Emily? What is the gain or loss to Janet?

43. Sheryl Sugarman owned 60 percent of the outstanding stock of Octavian Corporation. The corporation sold stock (cost $5,000) to her for $2,500. Sheryl sold the stock for $7,000. What is the corporation's allowed loss? What is Sheryl's gain?

44. On September 15, 1998, Donald Dunn sold for $80,000 property with an adjusted basis of $20,000. The buyer paid $20,000 down with the remaining $60,000 to be paid in four equal annual installments of $15,000 beginning in September 1999 with interest at 12 percent. How much income does Donald report in 1998 and the following four years? Ignore interest.

45. In 1998, Cathy Cummings, single, 66 years of age, and legally blind, had wages and net rental income (after depreciation) of $20,000 and received $500 in interest income. She had $7,200 of allowable itemized deductions. In addition, she had the following transactions during 1998:

    a. She sold stock for $2,800. She had inherited the stock from her father, who had an adjusted basis in the stock of

$1,200. The fair market value at the date of his death was $1,800.

b.   During 1997, Cathy had purchased some Almond Corporation stock. On January 20, 1997, she paid $5 a share for 20 shares, and on May 9, 1997, she paid $8 a share for 10 shares. She sold 15 shares during 1998 for $10 a share. Those shares most recently purchased were identified as being sold.

c.   Cathy sold to her sister Janice stock in Bass Corporation for $800. She had an adjusted basis of $950 in this stock.

d.   Cathy built a new house in 1998 and converted her former residence into rental property. At the time of the conversion, the adjusted basis of the old house was $44,000 with a fair market value of $40,000. She sold the rental house for $41,000 in October 1998, four months after its conversion to rental property, and took depreciation of $1,000 for the four months.

Compute Cathy's taxable income for 1998. Treat all income as ordinary income.

46. During 1998, Peter Patel sold a piece of land he had purchased for $40,000. The buyer paid cash of $50,000 and transferred to Peter a piece of farm equipment having a fair market value of $30,000. The buyer also assumed Peter's $10,000 loan on the land. Peter paid selling expenses of $5,000. What is Peter's recognized gain on this sale?

a. $25,000

b. $45,000

c. $80,000

d. $90,000

47. During 1983, John Johnson purchased 50 shares of common stock in Corporation DEF for $4,500. In 1994, DEF declared a stock dividend of 20 percent. The new stock received by John in the stock dividend was identical to the old stock. In 1998, DEF's stock split 3 for 1 at a time when the fair market value was $120 per share. What is John's basis in each of his shares of DEF's stock if both distributions were nontaxable?

a. $120 per share

b. $90 for 50 shares and zero for all additional shares

c. $75 for 60 shares and $142.50 for 120 shares

d. $25 per share

48. During 1998, Mary Maloney received a gift of property from her aunt. At the time of the gift, the property had a fair market value of $150,000 and an adjusted basis to her aunt of $90,000. Mary's aunt paid a gift tax on the property of $25,000. What is the amount of Mary's basis in the property?

a. $90,000
b. $100,000
c. $115,000
d. $150,000

49. Kenneth King inherited 100 shares of Corporation ABC stock from his father, who died on March 4, 1998. His father paid $17 per share for the stock on May 3, 1978. The fair market value of the stock on the date of death was $63 per share. On September 4, 1998, the fair market value of the stock was $55 per share. Kenneth sold the stock for $68 per share on December 4, 1998. The executor of the estate did not elect the alternate valuation date for valuing the father's estate. An estate tax return was filed. What was Kenneth's basis in the stock on the date of the sale?

a. $1,700
b. $4,600
c. $5,500
d. $6,300

50. *Comprehensive Problem.* Kevin Korda, age 35, married Emily, age 30, during 1998. Kevin pays alimony of $600 a month and provides $2,400 a year in support for his son from a previous marriage. The son lives with Kevin's ex-wife, who provides $3,000 a year in support. During 1998, Kevin earned $29,000 and Emily earned $14,000 at her regular job and $1,500 in self-employment income from selling cleaning products out of her home. They have allowable itemized deductions of $9,000. In addition, they had the following transactions during 1998:

a. Kevin sold for $34,000 property which he had received from his father. His father's basis in the property at the time of the gift was $35,000 and the fair market value was $30,000.

b. Kevin sold his personal use automobile (adjusted basis of $2,500) for $1,500 and purchased a new car for $8,500.

c. Emily received $300 in dividends from the 50 shares of $10 par Webster Corporation common stock which she owns. The stock has an adjusted basis of $1,400 to Emily and was purchased on April 24, 1998. On July 15, 1998, she also received 50 nontaxable stock rights with a fair market value of $5 when the fair market value of the stock was $30 per share. Five rights plus $20 entitle her to one share of common stock. On October 20, 1998, she exercised 30 of the rights and sold the other 20 for $100.

d. Kevin and Emily purchased 50 shares of Waverly Corporation stock for $35 a share on April 14, 1998. On May 15, 1998, they purchased 30 more shares for $45 each and on June 12, 1998, they purchased 20 shares for $50 each. On August 7, 1998, they sold 75 shares for $4,500.

Compute Kevin and Emily's taxable income. Treat any gain as ordinary income. Ignore the self-employment tax considerations.

51. *Comprehensive Problem.* Carl Chubbs, age 64, earned $25,000 during 1998. His wife, Dawn, age 66, is blind. During 1998, Carl and Dawn received $1,000 in dividends. They sold their personal use automobile which they had owned for two years (adjusted basis of $3,500) for $4,000. They sold to their son 50 shares of Riverdale Corporation stock for $500. Their basis was $12 per share; fair market value was $20 per share. Carl and Dawn sold property Carl had inherited from his sister for $12,500. At the time of Carl's sister's death the basis of the property was $7,500 and the fair market value was $10,000; six months after death the fair market value was $9,000. The alternate valuation date was elected by the executor in valuation of the estate of Carl's sister. In addition, Carl and Dawn paid $1,500 interest on their home, made a cash contribution to their college alumni foundation in the amount of $5,000, paid state sales taxes of $500, paid state income taxes of $1,500, paid federal income taxes of $5,000, and had medical expenses of $800. Compute Carl and Dawn's taxable income. Treat all income as ordinary income.

52. *Research Problem.* Brian Bradley, a calendar year taxpayer, purchased 1,000 shares of Newton Corporation stock on October 20, 1997, for $15,000. He sold these shares on February 2, 1998, for $7,000. On each of the four days from February 3 through February 6, 1998, Brian purchased 500 shares of substantially identical stock for $3,000. What is the tax effect for Brian and what will be the basis of each of the four batches of new stock?

Chapter 10

Property Transactions: Nonrecognition of Gains and Losses

Learning Objectives

After completing Chapter 10, you should be able to:

1. Describe the rules for exclusion of gain on the sale of a personal residence.

2. Discuss the nonrecognition of gain or loss in transactions involving like-kind exchanges and involuntary conversions.

3. Explain the holding period rules for property acquired in a nontaxable exchange.

4. Describe the mandatory rules for recognition and basis of new property and elective rules for nonrecognition and basis of new property in involuntary conversion.

5. Discuss other transactions in which gain or loss may be postponed or deferred, including exchange of property for stock or a partnership interest, exchanges of insurance policies, and exchange of stock in the same corporation by a shareholder.

OVERVIEW OF CHAPTER

As discussed in the previous chapter, a taxpayer has a realized gain when the fair market value of the property received is greater than the basis of the property given up. On the other hand, there is a realized loss when the fair market value of the property received is less than the basis of the property given up. The realized gain or loss upon a sale or other disposition of property is recognized unless there is a provision for nonrecognition.

This chapter deals with situations where there may be nonrecognition of gain or loss. Sometimes the gain or loss may be permanently excluded, meaning that the gain or loss will never be included in taxable income.

> *Example 10.1.* Mary Mertson, single, sold her personal residence for $275,000 so that she could move into a small apartment in a retirement home. Her basis in the residence was $60,000. Mary may exclude the $215,000 realized gain since single taxpayers may exclude up $250,000 of gain on a sale of a personal residence. This is a permanent exclusion.

At other times, however, nonrecognition is temporary in that there is deferral of recognition. This is because the basis of the replacement property will be adjusted to reflect the deferred gain or loss. A deferred or postponed gain is subtracted from the cost of the replacement property while a deferred or postponed loss is added to the cost to determine the basis of the new property.

> *Example 10.2.* Sam Sorges exchanged a business machine with an adjusted basis of $40,000 for another business machine with a fair market value of $90,000. The $50,000 realized gain is deferred because it is a like-kind exchange under Code Sec. 1031 and the basis of the new machine is $40,000 (fair market value of replacement property of $90,000 less deferred gain of $50,000). If the replacement property is sold for $95,000 shortly after the exchange, the recognized gain is $55,000. Thus, the original deferred gain of $50,000 and the $5,000 excess of the $95,000 over the $90,000 fair market value of the replacement property ultimately is recognized at the time of sale of the replacement property.

Deferral of gain or loss occurs in certain situations because the economic position of the taxpayer has not really changed in substance. Thus, the taxpayer, for example, by making an exchange of one business machine for another business machine is considered to have a continuation of the original investment. Another reason for nonrecognition of gain is that the transaction frequently results in no increase in resources to pay the tax. This reason is consistent with the wherewithal to pay concept, which recognizes that if a taxpayer lacks the resources, he or she should not have to pay tax as a result of a transaction.

In this chapter, sales of residence, like-kind exchanges, and involuntary conversions will be discussed in detail, with less attention being devoted to exchanges of property for stock or partnership interests, exchanges of life insurance policies, exchanges of stock in the same corporation by a shareholder, exchanges of U.S. obligations, and reacquisition of real property.

Sale of a Personal Residence—The New Law

The Taxpayer Relief Act of 1997 repealed Code Sec. 1034 (deferral of gain on sale of residence) and amended Sec. 121 (the once-in-a-lifetime exclusion of gain). The new law is considerably more generous than the old law.

¶ 10,001   THE GENERAL RULES

For sales or exchanges of residences after May 6, 1997, married taxpayers may exclude up to $500,000 of gain upon the sale of their residence and single taxpayers may exclude up to $250,000 of their gain. Code Sec. 121(b)(1) and (2). Taxpayers must have owned and occupied the residence for two out of the last five years prior to the sale. Code Sec. 121(b)(3)(A). The exclusion applies to only one sale or exchange every two years, but pre-May 7, 1997, sales are not considered. Code Sec. 121(b)(3)(B). For married taxpayers, the exclusion is allowed if (1) either spouse meets the ownership test, (2) both spouses meet the use test, and (3) neither spouse is ineligible for exclusion because of a sale or exchange of a residence within the last two years. Code Sec. 121(b)(2)(B),(C), and (D). Because this exclusion replaces the deferral of gain provision of Code Sec. 1034 and the one-time $125,000 exclusion for taxpayers age 55 or older, application of the exclusion does not result in a reduction of the basis of a replacement residence as was the case under prior law.

> *Example 10.3.* Jack and Jill Jackson sold their residence that they had purchased for $175,000 in September 1988. During the time of their ownership, they made improvements totaling $25,000 and then sold the home in September 1998 for a selling price of $600,000. Their realized gain is $400,000 ($600,000 less $200,000). They can exclude the whole gain since it is less than $500,000 and they do not have to purchase another home in order to obtain the exclusion.

Taxpayers may elect out of this exclusion provision for any sale or exchange. Code Sec. 121(f). Thus, for example, taxpayers who plan to sell within two years two properties that meet the exclusion eligibility requirements and who first sell the property with the lesser gain may choose to elect out of the exclusion to reserve its use for the second sale where the gain is larger.

The fact that the use of the provision is limited to once every two years does not prevent a husband and wife from filing a joint tax return and each excluding up to $250,000 of gain from the sale of each spouse's principal residence. The rule still applies as long as each spouse would have been eligible to exclude up to $250,000 of gain if the couple had filed separate returns. Further, if a single taxpayer eligible for the exclusion marries someone who has used the exclusion within two years before the marriage, that individual may still use the $250,000 exclusion.

Because Code Sec. 1034 has been repealed, taxpayers will no longer be able to defer gains by rolling over home-sale proceeds into a home costing an amount equal to or more than the adjusted sales price of their old residence. This could be a disadvantage for a taxpayer whose residence has greatly appreciated and/or whose basis is low due to a deferral of gain under prior law. If the gains realized are more than $500,000 for joint filers or $250,000 for a single taxpayer, the excess gain is subject to the capital gains tax. Under prior law there was no limit to the amount of gain that could be rolled over. As before, taxpayers will still not be able to take a deductible loss on the sale of their residence.

Example 10.4. Suppose that Jack and Jill in Example 10.3 sold their residence for $800,000. Their realized gain is $600,000, but they can exclude $500,000 and will recognize $100,000. It does not matter if they purchase another home. The $100,000 will be taxed at a maximum rate of 20 percent since they had held the residence more than 18 months and the sale took place after July 28, 1997. See Code Sec. 1(h)(1)(E) and Chapter 11. However, if Jack and Jill sold their residence for only $150,000, they have a realized loss of $50,000 that they will neither be able to deduct nor add to the cost of the new residence if they purchased one.

TAX PLANNING POINTERS ▼

The taxpayers who can potentially benefit the most from the new law are those who can move frequently. The reason is that these taxpayers can repeatedly use up to the maximum exclusion as long as the sale does not take place more than once every two years. Assume that Brian and Barbara Branson own three homes purchased in 1991, 1993, and 1995 and live in the 1995 home and rent out the 1991 and 1993 homes. They can obtain the exclusion on the 1995 home, then move into the 1993 home for two years, sell it, and obtain the exclusion. They then could move into the 1991 home for two years, sell it, and obtain the exclusion on that home.

Taxpayers who are good at fixing up properties will be able to benefit also. These taxpayers can buy a run-down home, fix it up before or while living in it for two years, and then sell it at a profit on which they can obtain the maximum exclusion. They can repeatedly use this approach and thus obtain several exclusions over a relatively short period of time. Good record-keeping is especially important for these taxpayers.

Continuity of Time of Ownership

In determining the time of ownership and use of a current residence, taxpayers may include the periods of ownership and use of all prior residences in which gain was rolled over to the current residence under former Section 1034. Code Sec. 121(g).

Example 10.5. Tom and Trudy Thompson purchased residence #2 in February of 1998 for $175,000, after they sold their residence #1, which had been purchased in February 1995, in February of 1997 for $160,000. A gain of $75,000 was not recognized on residence #1, which meant that their basis on residence #2 was $100,000 under former Code Sec. 1034 (instead of $175,000). In October 1998, the Thompsons sold residence #2 for $250,000. Even though they owned residence #2 less than two years, their gain of $150,000 ($250,000 less $100,000) can all be excluded because they can count the two years for which they had held residence #1 due to the fact that the gain on its sale was rolled over to residence #2.

¶ 10,005   PRINCIPAL RESIDENCE

In order to obtain exclusion of gain, the home must be the principal residence. A principal residence is the home in which the taxpayer lives. Whether or not a home is the taxpayer's principal residence depends upon all the facts and circumstances in each case. A principal residence can be a houseboat, a house trailer, or stock held by a tenant-stockholder in a cooperative housing corporation or a condominium. Reg. § 1.1034-1(c)(3); Rev. Rul. 64-31, 1964-1 CB 300.

If the residence is converted to business or rental property, the exclusion provision does not apply. Where part of the property is used by the taxpayer as a principal residence and part is used for other purposes, an allocation has to be made to determine the amount that will be subject to the nonrecognition rule. This could occur when a professional person lives on the business premises or when a landlord lives in an apartment and rents out the remaining units.

> *Example 10.6.* Rose Rambler bought a home in 1988 for $120,000 and used one-third of it as an office in her accounting practice. In 1998, she sells the home for $210,000 (realizing a gain of $90,000). Rose can exclude only that part of the gain allocated to the residential part of the old residence.

If the taxpayer has more than one residence, the nonrecognition rule applies only to the sale of the principal residence.

TAX PLANNING POINTER

If a taxpayer has been spending about equal time in two or more residences, consideration should be given to making adjustments in the taxpayer's lifestyle to make certain that the taxpayer lives in one location for more than six months of the year so that the residence will qualify as a principal residence.

¶ 10,015   SPECIAL PROVISIONS FOR VARIOUS TYPES OF EVENTS AND TAXPAYERS

Special provisions are included in the new law to consider other types of transactions or events or to take into consideration various types of taxpayers. In keeping with the main provisions of the new law, the special provisions also often are more generous to particular taxpayers.

Pro-ration of Exclusion

The $250,000 or $500,000 exclusion can still be pro-rated if the sale is due to a change in place of employment, a change in health, or unforeseen circumstances, even if a taxpayer does not meet the ownership or usage requirement. The amount of the exclusion is $250,000 or $500,000 multiplied by the portion that is the shorter of (1) the aggregate periods during which the ownership and use requirements were met during the five-year period ending on the date of the sale or (2) the period after the date of the most recent sale bears to two years. Code Sec. 121(c).

> *Example 10.7.* Wilbur and Wanda Windsor purchased a home in San Francisco for $300,000 on August 1, 1997. Wilbur obtains a job in Memphis, and on December 1, 1998, the Windsors sell their home in San Francisco for $750,000. The Windsors realized a $450,000 gain, but because they owned and resided in their home for less than two years (16 months), their exclusion is limited to $333,333 ($500,000 X 16 months divided by 24 months = $333,333), and they would have to recognize $116,667.

> *Example 10.8.* Assume that Wilbur and Wanda, who purchased the San Francisco home (#2) on August 1, 1997, did not sell their prior residence (#1) until September 1, 1997. If they sell residence #2 for $750,000 on December 1, 1998, with a $450,000 realized gain, the time between the sale of residence #1 and the sale of residence #2 (9/1/97 to 12/1/98) is shorter than the ownership and use period (8/1/97 to 12/1/98) of residence #2. The pro-ration is based on the shorter period of 15 months and the excluded gain is $312,500 ($500,000 X 15 months divided by 24 months = $312,500), and they would recognize $137,500.

Widowed Taxpayers

A widowed taxpayer's period of ownership of a residence includes the period the deceased spouse owned and used the property before death. Code Sec. 121(d)(2).

> *Example 10.9.* If Edwin Edwards dies, his spouse Elaine can immediately sell the home they both occupied and be eligible for the exclusion, provided the two-year ownership requirement was met prior to Ed's death. Elaine should be eligible for the $500,000 exclusion in the year of Ed's death (if filing jointly) but would only be eligible for the $250,000 exclusion in subsequent years as a single taxpayer. The full $500,000, of course, would be assured if the couple sold the residence before Ed's death.

Divorced Taxpayers

In the case of a residence that is transferred to a taxpayer incident to a divorce, the time during which the taxpayer's spouse or former spouse owned the residence is added to the taxpayer's period of ownership. A taxpayer who owns a residence is considered to have used it as a principal residence while the taxpayer's spouse or former spouse is granted use of the residence under the terms of the divorce or separation instrument. Code Sec. 121(d)(3).

Example 10.10. Rex and Robin Reed purchased a home for $150,000 on August 11, 1996. On March 25, 1998, they were divorced, and as part of the divorce agreement, the home was transferred to Robin, who sold the home on September 15, 1998, for $250,000. Robin can exclude the $100,000 gain since she can count the time that Rex owned the residence, which makes the ownership and use more than two years.

Example 10.11. Assume that in the preceding example, as part of the divorce agreement, Rex retained ownership of the residence but the use of the home was granted to Robin as long as Rex owns the residence. If Rex sells the residence on September 15, 1998, for $250,000, he can exclude the $100,000 gain since he can count the time that Robin used the residence as part of the divorce agreement.

TAX PLANNING POINTERS ▼

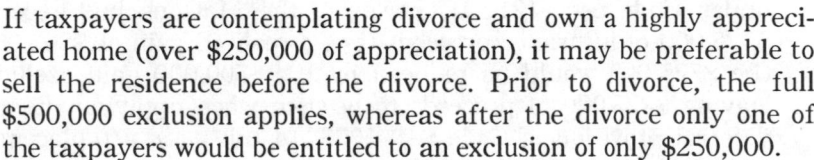

If taxpayers are contemplating divorce and own a highly appreciated home (over $250,000 of appreciation), it may be preferable to sell the residence before the divorce. Prior to divorce, the full $500,000 exclusion applies, whereas after the divorce only one of the taxpayers would be entitled to an exclusion of only $250,000.

Taxpayers should exercise caution in divorce planning. Traditionally, wives have received custody of the children and have often obtained ownership of the home. Now with the gain on the sale of residence eligible for a sizeable amount of exclusion, potential divorcees will need to consider this in their divorce agreement and in their negotiations. For some taxpayers, it may be preferable to sell the home prior to divorce to obtain the full $500,000 exclusion.

Incapacitated Taxpayers

If a taxpayer becomes physically or mentally incapable of self-care, the taxpayer is deemed to use a residence as a principal residence during the time in which the taxpayer owns the residence and resides in a care facility licensed by a State or political subdivision such as in a nursing home. The taxpayer must have owned and used the residence as a principal residence for a period of at least one year during the five years preceding the sale in order to use this provision. Code Sec. 121(d)(7).

Example 10.12. Alice Adams purchased a residence for $150,000 on October 7, 1996. In November 1997 she became ill and was confined to a nursing home. On October 19, 1998, she sells her residence for $250,000. Alice can exclude the gain of $100,000 because she has used the residence at least one year during the preceding five years.

Involuntary Conversions

The exclusion is available in cases of involuntary conversion of a residence, such as destruction, theft, seizure, requisition, or condemnation of property, that are treated as a sale or exchange of a residence. Code Sec. 121(d)(5). The amount realized from the sale or exchange of property is reduced by the amount of gain excluded from gross income. If the basis of the property sold or exchanged was determined under the involuntary conversion rules of Code Sec. 1033(b), then the holding and use by the taxpayer of the converted property shall be treated as holding and use by the taxpayer of the property sold or exchanged.

Example 10.13. Marvin and Mildred Matson purchased a residence on March 25, 1996, for $160,000. On September 3, 1998, a hurricane completely destroyed their home. The home was insured for its replacement value and homes in the Matsons' area had appreciated greatly. They received insurance proceeds of $460,000. The Matsons do not recognize any of the $300,000 realized gain on the involuntary conversion of their home by the hurricane because it is less than the $500,000 exclusion allowed under Code Sec. 121. If, however, the Matsons had received $725,000 of insurance proceeds (i.e., a realized gain of $565,000), the $725,000 would be reduced by the $500,000 gain excluded, leaving $225,000 of proceeds to be used when applying the gain deferral provision of Code Sec. 1033. In this case, a replacement residence would be required to defer the gain in excess of the exclusion. Thus, a replacement cost of $225,000 or more would be necessary to defer the remaining $65,000 of realized gain.

Co-ops

In the case of a tenant-stockholder of cooperative housing corporation (as defined in Code Sec. 216), the ownership requirement applies to the ownership of the stock of the corporation and the use requirement applies to the house or apartment that the taxpayer is entitled to occupy as a stockholder. Code Sec. 121(d)(4).

Example 10.14. Carl Carlson is part owner of Red River Estates, a cooperative housing corporation that owns and manages a 15-unit complex. Carl may exclude gain on the sale of his interest if he owned the stock for at least two of the five years prior to the sale and if he occupied a unit in the complex for at least two of the five years prior to the sale.

TAX PLANNING POINTERS ▼

Taxpayers should keep records of capital improvements since there always is the possibility that income might ultimately be recognized in the event they have extraordinarily large profits due to rapid appreciation and/or they keep their residence for a long period of time. If taxpayers personally make a number of capital improvements because they are skilled at making improvements or if they wish to claim a depreciation deduction for a home office or rental use of the residence, good records are also important. Further, if the residence is involved in a divorce settlement or tied up in an estate, accurate records could be critical.

Taxpayers who have large gains (over $500,000 for couples and over $250,000 for single taxpayers) may want to consider retaining the property the remainder of their lives, since the heirs will still get the step up in basis under Code Sec. 1014(a). Assume that Howard and Hilda Haley purchased a home in New York City for $200,000 in 1968 and are considering its sale in 1998. The expected selling price, however, is $2,000,000, which would require them to recognize gain of $1,300,000 ($1,800,000 realized gain less excluded gain of $500,000). Even at a 20 percent maximum tax rate, this would still result in a tax of $260,000. Since the Haleys are in their seventies, they should consider retaining the property until their death since the appreciation will then not be taxed at all. The heirs will have a step-up in basis equal to the fair market value at the date of death. The value of the property, of course, will be included in the decedent's estate for estate tax purposes.

¶ 10,025 DEFINITIONS RELATED TO RESIDENCE

The following are the major terms encountered in sales of residences. All of the terms are applicable to both pre-May 7, and post-May 6, 1997, law except *fixing-up expenses*, which are applicable only to the old law.

Amount realized is the selling price reduced by the selling expenses. The selling price includes not only the cash received but also the liability that might be assumed by the buyer. Reg. § 1.1034-1(b)(4).

Adjusted basis of the old residence is its cost and commissions, plus any capital improvements, less insurance reimbursements and deductible casualty losses, and less the nontaxable gain on the sale of the previous residence.

Gain realized is the excess, if any, of the amount realized over the adjusted basis of the old residence. Adjusted sales price is the amount realized reduced by the fixing-up expenses. Both selling expenses and fixing-up expenses are deducted to arrive at adjusted sales price but only selling expenses are deducted to arrive at amount realized and gain realized. Thus, fixing-up expenses only have a tax benefit if there is a replacement residence.

Selling expenses include advertising costs, broker commissions, legal fees in connection with the sale, and "points" paid by the seller to obtain a mortgage for the buyer. Reg. § 1.1034-1(b)(4); Rev. Rul. 68-650, 1968-2 CB 78.

Fixing-up expenses must (1) be incurred for work performed during the 90-day period ending on the day on which the contract to sell is entered into, (2) be paid on or before the 30th day after the date of sale of the old residence, (3) be nondeductible in figuring taxable income, and (4) not be chargeable to a capital account. Reg. § 1.1034-1(b)(6). Fixing-up expenses do not reduce the amount realized or gain realized.

Cost of the new residence includes the costs of acquiring, constructing, and improving that are chargeable as capital expenditures within the (two-year) replacement period for the old residence. Cost also includes the debts to which the property is subject.

Special Rule for Certain Sales within Two Years of Enactment

Taxpayers must be familiar with or aware of the rules in effect under the old law. The old law was in effect for all sales prior to May 7, 1997, electively for sales from May 7 to August 5, 1997, and some aspects of the old law could be used for two years after August 5, 1997. More specifically, because taxpayers may have sold a residence before the new law took effect, the old provisions still have to be considered for purposes of determining the deferral of gain under the old Code Sec. 1034, the exclusion for taxpayers age 55 and older, and the basis of the replacement residence.

¶ 10,101 NONRECOGNITION OF GAIN AND BASIS OF THE NEW RESIDENCE UNDER OLD LAW

If a new residence was purchased within the appropriate replacement period, realized gain was recognized only to the extent the adjusted sales price exceeded the cost of the new residence. Code Sec. 1034(a). Recognized gain, however, did not exceed realized gain. The tax on the unrecognized portion was, in effect, postponed. This rule was mandatory. The cost of the new residence was reduced by the unrecognized gain resulting in a basis in the new residence lower than its cost. Any gain that was recognized on the sale of a residence was a capital gain (see Chapter 11). The period within which a residence was required to be replaced began two years before and ended two years after the sale of the old residence.

Example 10.15. Patrick Purcell sold his home in April 1997 and had a realized gain of $20,000. He purchased a new residence the next month for $100,000, which was more than he received for the old residence. The $20,000 gain was not recognized but was subtracted from the cost of the new residence to give $80,000 as the basis of the new residence.

The basis of the new residence is the cost of the new residence less the gain not recognized on the sale of the old residence. Code Sec. 1034(e).

Example 10.16. On April 17, 1997, Morgan Maple, age 40, sold his residence that he had owned for five years for $100,000. His adjusted basis was $50,000. Selling expenses were $5,000 and fixing-up expenses were $3,000. He purchased a new residence for

$80,000 on October 20, 1998. His realized gain was $45,000, his recognized gain was $12,000, and his basis in the new residence was $47,000, computed as follows:

Selling price	$ 100,000
Less: Selling expenses	5,000
Amount realized	$ 95,000
Less: Adjusted basis of old residence	50,000
Gain realized	$ 45,000
Amount realized	$ 95,000
Less: Fix-up expenses	3,000
Adjusted sales price	$ 92,000
Cost of new residence	80,000
Gain recognized	$ 12,000
Cost of new residence	$ 80,000
Less: Deferred gain	33,000
Basis of new residence	$ 47,000

Example 10.17. If Morgan in Example 10.16 had paid $95,000 for a new residence, there would have been no gain recognized, and the basis of the new residence would have been $50,000 ($95,000 − $45,000). If, on the other hand, he had purchased a new residence for only $46,000, his total realized gain of $45,000 would have been recognized and his basis in the new residence would have been $46,000.

¶ 10,115   EXCLUSION ELECTION REQUIREMENTS UNDER OLD LAW

Under the pre-May 7, 1997, law, there was a special provision for permanent nonrecognition of gain to taxpayers age 55 or older. The eligible taxpayer who sold a principal residence could elect to exclude up to $125,000 ($62,500 in the case of a separate return filed by a married individual). Code Sec. 121(a) and (b). This was a once-in-a-lifetime exclusion election and was in contrast to the general nonrecognition rule of Code Sec. 1034, which was mandatory. No replacement of residence needed to occur under Code Sec. 121, as was the case under Code Sec. 1034, although both provisions could be used together. Whereas Code Sec. 1034 nonrecognition was a postponement of income recognition, the provisions under Code Sec. 121 allowed a permanent exclusion.

The special treatment of taxpayers 55 years or older was allowed if the taxpayer had owned and used the home as a principal residence three years out of the five-year period ending on the date of sale.

If the gain realized was greater than the $125,000 maximum exclusion under the Section 121 election, the taxpayer still could defer gain through the use of Code Sec. 1034 (sale of residence) or Code Sec.

1033 (involuntary conversion, see ¶ 10,301). If deferral of gain was to take place under the latter two provisions, the amount realized was reduced by the amount excluded under Code Sec. 121. This reduced the amount that was necessary to be reinvested in order to have deferral of gain under Code Sec. 1033 or 1034. The basis of the new residence was the cost of the new residence less any postponed gain. If realized gain was less than $125,000 and the Section 121 election was made, there was no recognized gain regardless of the replacement cost of the new residence.

Example 10.18. Ben Bradley, age 63, sold his residence for $268,000 in April 1997. He had owned it since 1967 and had an adjusted basis of $35,000. He incurred $10,000 selling expenses and $3,000 fixing-up expenses. Before April 1999, he moved into a smaller home which he purchased for $80,000. Ben has a realized gain of $223,000, a recognized gain of $50,000 and the basis of his new residence is $32,000 computed as follows:

Selling price	$268,000
Less: selling expenses	10,000
Amount realized	$258,000
Less: adjusted basis of old home	35,000
Gain realized	$223,000
Amount realized	$258,000
Less: fixing-up expenses	3,000
Adjusted sales price	$255,000
Less: Section 121 exclusion	125,000
Adjusted sales price after exclusion	$130,000
Cost of new residence	80,000
Gain recognized	$ 50,000
Basis of new residence:	
Cost of new residence	$ 80,000
Less: postponed gain ($223,000 − 125,000 − 50,000)	48,000
Basis of new residence	$ 32,000

If Ben had purchased a home for $130,000, he would have had no recognized gain and the basis in his new residence would have been $32,000 ($130,000 less $98,000 ($223,000 − $125,000)).

If Ben had moved into a rental apartment rather than purchasing a new residence, he would have recognized $98,000 ($223,000 − $125,000).

The Section 121 election could be made or revoked any time before the expiration of the period for making a claim for credit or refund of tax for the taxable year in which the sale occurred. Thus, the taxpayer generally had until the later of (1) three years after the filing of the tax return or (2) two years following the payment of the tax. Code Sec. 6511(a).

Like-Kind Exchanges

¶ 10,201   DEFINITION

Exchanges involving like-kind property held for investment or business purposes can qualify for nonrecognition of gain or loss. The reason for nonrecognition is that the taxpayer is considered to be in the same economic position after the exchange has occurred and so is, in effect, continuing the old investment. Also, unless the taxpayer has received cash or other property, the taxpayer does not have the wherewithal to pay the tax on the realized gain as a result of the exchange transaction.

Section 1031(a) states that "no gain or loss shall be recognized on the exchange of property held for productive use in a trade or business or for investment if such property is exchanged solely for property of like kind which is to be held either for productive use in a trade or business or for investment." The word "solely" is important. If the property received also consists of other non-like-kind property or cash (known as "boot"), gain may be recognized. Code Sec. 1031(b). The nonrecognition rule for like-kind exchanges is mandatory—if one has a like-kind exchange, one must have nonrecognition of gain or loss.

> *Example 10.19.* Brad Burns exchanged an office building with an adjusted basis of $75,000 (fair market value $250,000) for another office building with a fair market value of $250,000. Although Brad has realized a gain of $175,000 ($250,000 fair market value received less the adjusted basis of $75,000), he does not recognize any gain under the Section 1031 like-kind exchange provision.

¶ 10,215   QUALIFYING PROPERTY

Property qualifying for like-kind exchange treatment must be held either for productive use in a trade or business or for investment. However, business property may be exchanged for investment property and vice versa. Property held for personal use does not qualify for nonrecognition but if held for both business and personal use, the business part qualifies. Certain properties are excluded from like-kind exchange treatment. Stock in trade or other property held primarily for sale, stock, bonds, notes, or other securities are not considered properties held for productive use in a trade or business or for investment. The transfer of partnership interests does not fall under the tax-free exchange provisions. Also, livestock of different sexes is not like-kind property. Code Sec. 1031(a) and (e); Reg. § 1.1031(a)-1(a).

The words "like-kind" refer to the nature or character of the property and not to its grade or quality. Reg. § 1.1031(a)-1(b). The exchange of real property for real property generally qualifies for like-kind exchange treatment. Examples include improved real estate for unimproved real estate, city real estate for a farm, and a lease of real property with 30 years or more to run for real estate. Like-kind treatment also applies to the exchange of personalty for personalty. However, not all exchanges of personalty used for investment or business purposes qualify for nonrecognition. The exchanged property must be of a like class. That is, the property must be within the same general "asset class" as indicated by Rev. Proc. 87-56, 1987-2 CB 674. Some of the business asset classes include:

1. Office furniture, fixtures, and equipment
2. Information systems such as computers and their peripheral equipment
3. Airplanes
4. Automobiles
5. Light general purpose trucks
6. Heavy general purpose trucks

Thus, an exchange of office equipment for a computer would not qualify as a like-kind exchange, nor would a business car for a light general purpose truck. Further, like-kind treatment does not apply to the exchange of realty for personalty. Thus, the exchange of a building (realty) for a machine (personalty) is not a like-kind exchange.

Example 10.20. Eugene Eckbert made the following exchanges:

1. Office building for an apartment building
2. Apartment building for a personal residence
3. Land for an office building
4. Jewelry for a new personal automobile
5. Stock held as an investment for a business building
6. Inventory for a business automobile
7. Apartment building for a business truck

Only exchanges (1) and (3) qualify as like-kind exchanges. Exchange (2) is not a like-kind exchange because a personal residence is received; (4) involves personal use items; (5) involves stock; (6) has an exchange of inventory; and (7) involves an exchange of realty for personalty.

TAX PLANNING POINTERS

Taxpayers may prefer to avoid the nonrecognition rules. Since the rules are mandatory, taxpayers have to structure the transaction in such a way that the disposal of the old asset is a sale rather than a like-kind exchange. If a gain will be realized, taxpayers may prefer to sell the asset if they are in a low tax bracket in the year of sale, which would mean that the tax would be relatively low, especially if there were some opportunity for special capital gain treatment. In such a case, the basis of the newly purchased asset may be higher than the basis of the new asset if the transaction were a like-kind exchange. The high basis may be preferable especially if the taxpayer expected to be in higher tax brackets in future years.

If a loss will be realized on disposal of an asset, it may be preferable to recognize it through a sale transaction rather than through a like-kind exchange. This could be especially important if the taxpayer were in a high bracket in the year of sale and in lower brackets in future years when the asset would be depreciated.

There must be a genuine sale and purchase in order to avoid the Section 1031 nonrecognition rules. If the transaction involves a sale of an asset to one party and a purchase of another similar asset from the same party, the IRS could treat the two transactions as a like-kind exchange. Thus, it is advisable to have the sale and purchase be with different parties.

Trade-in of property used partly for business. Where there is an exchange of property used partly for business and partly for personal purposes, as in the case of trade-in of an automobile, only the gain or loss allocable to the business portion of the traded-in property affects the nonrecognition of gain or loss.

Commissions and expenses. Brokerage commission expenses paid in connection with tax-free exchanges are applied in three different ways in determining the tax consequences that result from such exchanges. The Internal Revenue Service has ruled (1) that commission expenses can be deducted or offset in computing the amount of gain or loss that is realized in a like-kind exchange; (2) that commission expenses paid can be offset against cash payments received in determining the amount of gain that may be recognized in such exchanges; and (3) that commission expenses may also be included in the basis of the property received. Rev. Rul. 72-456, 1972-2 CB 468.

¶ 10,225 RECEIPT OF BOOT

As mentioned earlier, no gain or loss is recognized when like-kind property is exchanged. When property that is not like-kind (i.e., cash or other property, known as "boot") is received, then any realized gain is recognized to the extent of the boot received, but not to exceed realized gain. If there is a realized loss in a boot received situation, such loss is not recognized. Code Sec. 1031(b) and (c).

Example 10.21. Kent Powers exchanged a business machine with an adjusted basis of $28,000 and a fair market value of $40,000 for a similar machine worth $35,000 and $5,000 cash. Kent's realized gain is $12,000 and because he received $5,000 cash, the recognized gain will be $5,000.

Example 10.22. Assume the same facts as in Example 10.21, except that Kent's adjusted basis in his old machine was $36,000 instead of $28,000. The realized gain is $4,000 and the recognized gain is also $4,000 even though he received boot in the amount of $5,000. Recognized gain would not exceed the realized gain.

Example 10.23. Assume the same facts as in Example 10.21, except that Kent's adjusted basis in the old machine was $44,000.

He would have realized a loss of $4,000 which would not be recognized even though there was boot received.

¶ 10,235   GIVING BOOT

If boot is given, generally no gain or loss is recognized.

Example 10.24. Greg exchanges a business machine with an adjusted basis of $12,000 and a fair market value of $18,000 for a similar machine with a fair market value of $26,000. He also gives $8,000 cash. Although Greg realizes $6,000 gain, he recognizes no gain.

Example 10.25. Assume the same facts as in Example 10.24, except that Greg's old machine had a basis of $28,000. He would have realized a loss of $10,000 which would not be recognized.

If, however, the boot given is property that has a difference between its basis and fair market value, then gain or loss will be recognized on the boot given. Reg. § 1.1031(d)-1(e). It is as if the boot property was sold separately from the like-kind property. Although this rule for recognition in a boot given situation is a special case, it can produce strange results. The taxpayer can have a recognized gain greater than realized gain or a realized gain and a recognized loss.

Example 10.26. Becky Barrows exchanges real estate with a basis of $150,000 (fair market value of $165,000) for other real estate with a fair market value of $230,000. She also gives up shares of Ridgeway Corporation stock worth $65,000 with a basis of $30,000. Becky's realized gain is $50,000 ($230,000 − $150,000 − $30,000) and she must recognize a gain of $35,000 ($65,000 − $30,000).

Example 10.27. Assume the same facts as in Example 10.26, except that the fair market value of the Ridgeway Corporation stock was $95,000 and the fair market value of Becky's real estate is $135,000. Becky then has a realized gain of $50,000 but a recognized gain of $65,000 ($95,000 − $30,000).

Example 10.28. Assume the same facts as in Example 10.26, except that Becky's stock in Ridgeway Corporation had a fair market value of only $20,000 and the fair market value of Becky's real estate is $210,000. She then has a realized gain of $50,000 and a recognized loss of $10,000.

¶ 10,245   ASSUMPTION OF LIABILITIES

If a liability is assumed by the transferee, such assumption is treated like boot received by the taxpayer-transferor. Code Sec. 1031(d). Accordingly, the transferor will recognize gain under the same rules as in a boot received situation outlined above. It is treated as if the transferor received cash and then paid off the liability.

Example 10.29. Judy Murryhill exchanged a business machine with an adjusted basis of $20,000 and worth $38,000 for another machine worth $28,000. Judy still owed $10,000 on the machine and the liability was assumed by the transferee. Judy realized a gain of $18,000 and recognized a gain of $10,000 since the liability assumed by the transferee is like boot received.

If the taxpayer as transferor also assumes a liability, then, in determining the amount of boot received, consideration given in the form of an assumption of liabilities by the transferor may be offset against consideration received in the form of an assumption of liabilities by the transferee. Reg. § 1.1031(d)-2. The amount of boot given in the form of money or liabilities assumed by the transferor reduces the amount of liabilities treated as boot received.

Example 10.30. Martin Merchant exchanges a farm with an adjusted basis of $100,000 and a fair market value of $170,000 for Richard Richmond's farm with a fair market value of $150,000. Martin's mortgage of $30,000 is assumed by Richard whose mortgage of $10,000 is assumed by Martin. Martin realizes a gain of $70,000, but since the mortgages can be offset, he recognizes only $20,000 gain ($30,000 − $10,000).

Fair market value of property received	$150,000
Plus: Mortgage assumed by transferee (Richard)	30,000
Less: Mortgage assumed by transferor (Martin)	10,000
Net consideration received	$170,000
Less: Adjusted basis	100,000
Gain realized	$ 70,000
Gain recognized	$ 20,000

Example 10.31. Assume the same facts as in Example 10.30, except that Martin's farm had a fair market value of $140,000 and the mortgage assumed by him was $40,000. Martin has a realized gain of $40,000 but recognizes no gain since the mortgage assumed by Richard does not exceed that assumed by Martin.

Fair market value of property received	$150,000
Plus: Mortgage assumed by transferee (Richard)	30,000
Less: Mortgage assumed by transferor (Martin)	40,000
Net consideration received	$140,000
Less: Adjusted basis	100,000
Gain realized	$ 40,000
Gain recognized	$ 0

If the transferor assumes a liability in excess of the amount of liability assumed by the transferee, the excess does not reduce any cash received by the transferor in determining how much gain is recognized. Consideration given in the form of cash or a mortgage assumed by the transferor, however, is offset against consideration received in the form of an assumption of a mortgage by the transferee. Reg. § 1.1031(d)-2.

Example 10.32. Rose Rand exchanges an apartment building with an adjusted basis of $140,000 and a fair market value of $190,000 for Sylvia Simon's apartment building with a fair market value of $180,000 and cash of $45,000 from Sylvia. Rose's mortgage of

$40,000 is assumed by Sylvia, whose mortgage of $75,000 is assumed by Rose. Rose realizes gain of $50,000, but recognizes a gain of $45,000, to the extent of the cash received. Only the mortgages can be offset; the cash received may not be offset against the excess mortgage assumed by Rose.

Fair market value of property received	$180,000
Plus: Cash	45,000
Mortgage assumed by transferee (Sylvia)	$ 40,000
Less: Mortgage assumed by transferor (Rose)	75,000
Net consideration received	$190,000
Less: Adjusted basis	140,000
Gain realized	$ 50,000
Gain recognized	$ 45,000

Example 10.33. Assume the same facts as in Example 10.32, except that Sylvia's mortgage assumed by Rose is $10,000 and the cash given by Rose is $20,000 (instead of Rose's receipt of cash from Sylvia). Rose's realized gain is $50,000 but her recognized gain is only $10,000. Both the mortgage assumed by Rose and the cash given by Rose may be offset against Rose's liability assumed by Sylvia.

Fair market value of property received		$180,000
Plus: Mortgage assumed by transferee (Sylvia)		$ 40,000
Less: Mortgage assumed by transferor (Rose)		10,000
Net consideration received		$210,000
Less: Adjusted basis	$140,000	
Cash	20,000	160,000
Gain realized		$ 50,000
Gain recognized		$ 10,000

¶ 10,255   BASIS OF ACQUIRED PROPERTY

There are two ways of figuring the basis of the newly acquired property in a like-kind exchange.

1. One method starts with the adjusted basis of the property given up (Code Sec. 1031(d)) as follows:

Adjusted basis of the like-kind property given

+ Boot given

+ Gain recognized

+ Liability assumed by the transferor

− Boot received

− Loss recognized

− Liability assumed by the transferee

= Basis of the property acquired

2. The second method starts with the fair market value of the property received as follows:

Fair market value of the like-kind property received

— Deferred gain

+ Deferred loss

= Basis of the acquired property

Exhibit 1 at ¶ 10,275 summarizes what the basis would be for each of the situations in the example at ¶ 10,201 and the examples at ¶ 10,225–10,245 under the two methods of figuring the basis of newly acquired property in a like-kind exchange.

¶ 10,265   HOLDING PERIOD

The holding period for property acquired in a nontaxable exchange includes the holding period of the property given in exchange if the property was a capital asset or property used in a taxpayer's trade or business. Code Sec. 1223(1); Reg. § 1.1223-1(a). However, the holding period of property received as boot in a like-kind exchange transaction begins on the date of its receipt. This holding period rule also applies to property acquired through an involuntary conversion under Code Sec. 1033 (see ¶ 10,301).

Example 10.34. Linda Lane traded in a machine purchased in 1995 for another machine during 1998. The holding period of the new machine begins with the date of the 1995 purchase. If, in addition, Linda received shares of stock as boot, the holding period of the stock begins with the date of the receipt of the stock in 1998.

¶ 10,275   THREE-PARTY EXCHANGES

Sometimes a taxpayer is unable to find a party with whom to have a like-kind exchange because the party whose property the taxpayer seeks wants to sell for cash rather than trade. The three-party exchange is a device that is designed to solve this dilemma. If the taxpayer can find a purchaser who is willing to pay cash and arrange a triangular exchange, the taxpayer can effect a tax-free exchange and a cash sale can be obtained by the party who holds the desired property. Generally, a transaction will be a nontaxable exchange to the taxpayer if the taxpayer intends to and does exchange the property, and does not receive or have control over the cash flowing to the seller. There is a 45-day deadline on identifying the substitute like-kind property and a 180-day deadline on receipt of the exchange property. Code Sec. 1031(a)(3).

An acceptable arrangement to the taxpayer can take different forms. In each of the examples following Exhibit 1, it is assumed that the taxpayer wishes to exchange business property for like-kind property owned by a taxpayer who wants to sell rather than have an exchange.

Exhibit 1 CALCULATION OF BASIS OF NEW PROPERTY IN LIKE-KIND EXCHANGE

METHOD 1

	General Rule	Boot Received		Boot Given		Liability Assumption	Offset Liabilities		Liability and Cash	
Adjusted Basis of Property Given	$75,000	$28,000	$44,000	$150,000	$150,000	$20,000	$100,000	$100,000	$140,000	$140,000
+Boot given				+30,000	+30,000					+20,000
+Gain recognized		+5,000		+35,000	+65,000		+20,000	+40,000		+10,000
+Liability assumed by transferor						+10,000	+10,000		+75,000	+10,000
−Boot received		−5,000	−5,000							
−Loss recognized										
−Liability assumed by transferee						−10,000	−30,000	−30,000	−40,000	−40,000
=Basis of acquired property	$75,000	$28,000	$39,000	$215,000	$245,000	$20,000	$100,000	$110,000	$175,000	$140,000

METHOD 2

	General Rule	Boot Received		Boot Given			Liability Assumption	Offset Liabilities		Liability and Cash	
FMV received	$250,000	$35,000	$35,000	$230,000	$230,000	$230,000	$28,000	$150,000	$150,000	$180,000	$180,000
−Deferred gain	−175,000	−7,000		−15,000		−50,000	−8,000	−50,000	−40,000	−5,000	−40,000
+Deferred loss			+4,000								
					+15,000*	−10,000**					
=Basis of acquired property	$75,000	$28,000	$39,000	$215,000	$245,000*	$170,000**	$20,000	$100,000	$110,000	$175,000	$140,000

* This is a special situation where because of the difference between the fair market value and the basis of boot given, there was recognized gain of $65,000 and a realized gain of $50,000. The $15,000 excess of recognized gain over realized gain has to be added to the fair market value of the new property.

** This is a special situation where, because of the difference between the fair market value and the basis of the boot given there was a recognized loss of $10,000 and a realized gain of $50,000. The $50,000 gain is deferred and subtracted from the fair market value of the new property as is the $10,000 recognized loss.

Example 10.35. Alice Amber transfers her property to Betty Beryl, who transfers cash to Carla Crystal, who then transfers her property to Alice. For Alice, this would be considered to be a nontaxable exchange even though she transferred her property to someone other than the person from whom she received the property. Rev. Rul. 57-244, 1957-1 CB 247; *W.H. Haden Co.,* 48-1 USTC ¶ 9147, 165 F.2d 588 (CA-5 1948).

Example 10.36. Alice and Carla exchange their properties and Betty then purchases Alice's former property from Carla. The courts have maintained that this transaction will qualify as an exchange for Alice even though IRS might attempt to argue that Carla would be acting as Alice's agent for a sale. *L.Q. Coupe,* 52 TC 394, CCH Dec. 29,610 (1969), acq. 1970-2 CB XIX; *J.H. Baird Publishing Co.,* 39 TC 608, CCH Dec. 25,816 (1962), acq. 1963-2 CB 4. It would be an exchange for Alice because she has received property in exchange for property without receiving or controlling cash.

Example 10.37. Betty could purchase the property from Carla and then immediately exchange the property for the property owned by Alice. The transaction would be an exchange for Alice if it could be shown that Alice intended to make an exchange, and if Betty used her own funds to acquire Carla's property. Rev. Rul. 77-297, 1977-2 CB 304; *J. Alderson,* 63-2 USTC ¶ 9499, 317 F.2d 790 (CA-9 1963).

If arrangements more complicated than the above examples are made, there could potentially be difficulties in obtaining exchange treatment for the taxpayer. The regulations, however, allow for the use of an intermediary if the intermediary takes three steps: (1) acquires the seller's property; (2) acquires the replacement property; and (3) transfers the replacement property to the seller. Reg. § 1.1031(a)-3(g)(4)(ii).

Involuntary Conversions

Gain may be deferred in an involuntary conversion through an election, providing the replacement occurs with qualified property within a specified time period and of a sufficient magnitude. An involuntary conversion occurs through a casualty, theft, or condemnation. The reason for possible deferral is to assist those who have sustained financial difficulties through one of the above events and because the taxpayer's economic position has not changed if replacement property is acquired. Also, the wherewithal to pay concept is another justification for this provision in that the taxpayer frequently does not have the financial resources to pay taxes on any realized gain.

¶ 10,301   DEFINITION

An involuntary conversion is the compulsory or involuntary conversion of property resulting from "its destruction, in whole or in part, theft, seizure, or requisition or condemnation or threat or imminence thereof." Code Sec. 1033(a).

A condemnation generally occurs when a governmental body takes private property for public use and pays a reasonable price for it. A property transfer due to threat or imminence of condemnation also qualifies as an involuntary conversion. A news report that property is being considered for condemnation is not a threat or imminence. Rev. Rul. 58-277, 1958-2 CB 402. There must be confirmation that the property is going to be acquired for public purposes and the taxpayer has reasonable grounds to believe the property will be taken. Rev. Rul. 74-8, 1974-1 CB 200, modifying Rev. Rul. 63-221, 1963-2 CB 332. Sales to third parties (as opposed to the condemning authority) also qualify as involuntary if made under the threat or imminence of condemnation. Rev. Rul. 81-180, 1981-2 CB 161. The later sale of the property by the third party to the condemning authority also qualifies for involuntary conversion treatment if the proceeds are reinvested in qualified property even if the third party knew that the threat existed before he acquired the property. A "condemnation" does not include a notice that property will be condemned because it is unfit for human use. Rev. Rul. 57-314, 1957-2 CB 523.

Example 10.38. Joseph Jordon, who owned a lot, learned that the City Council had just approved the condemnation of the lot for use as a city parking garage to be built in two or three years. Joseph decides to sell the property to Judy Garnet at a gain. The sale is an involuntary conversion and Joseph may elect deferral of the gain recognition.

If livestock is destroyed by or sold or exchanged on account of disease or because of drought, such events are involuntary conversions. Also, if it is not feasible because of soil contamination or other environmental conditions to replace the livestock with other livestock, other farm property (including real property) qualifies as replacement property. Code Sec. 1033(d)-(f).

¶ 10,305   INVOLUNTARY CONVERSION RULES FOR PROPERTY DAMAGED IN DISASTER

For purposes of the nonrecognition-of-gain rule regarding involuntarily converted property that is replaced with similar property, any tangible property that is acquired and held for productive use in a business is treated as similar or related to business or investment property that was involuntarily converted as a result of a Presidentially declared disaster. Code Sec. 1033(h)(2).

This provision is intended to afford relief to businesses forced to suspend operations for a substantial time because of the property damage. If valuable markets and customers are lost during the suspension and the business fails, the owner may want to reinvest the capital in a new business venture.

Example 10.39. Ena ran a small retail store on the beaches of Florida. The area was hit by a hurricane and her business was destroyed. The President declared the area a disaster area. Ena used the insurance proceeds from her business to purchase equipment to enter into a consulting business. Ena may elect not to recognize gain with respect to the involuntarily converted beach business.

¶ 10,315   REPLACEMENT PROPERTY—MANDATORY RULES

There are two mandatory rules for recognition of gain or loss in case of an involuntary conversion.

1. If there is a direct conversion of property into other property similar or related in service or use instead of into a money award, no gain will be recognized. The basis of the replacement property is the same as the adjusted basis of the old property. Code Sec. 1033(a)(1) and (b).

    Example 10.40. Sandra Storm owned land which had an adjusted basis of $25,000. The land was condemned by the state and she received other land to replace her condemned property. The replacement land had a fair market value of $40,000. Sandra will recognize no gain and the basis in the new land is also $25,000.

2. If there is a realized loss, the loss must be recognized (assuming the loss is allowed). The basis of the replacement property acquired is its cost.

    Example 10.41. Wade Wilson's factory building having an adjusted basis of $150,000 was destroyed by fire, and he received insurance proceeds in the amount of $125,000. He purchased another factory for $200,000. Wade recognizes his realized loss of $25,000, and the basis of the new factory is $200,000.

Losses realized from involuntary conversions of income-producing or business property are recognized. Casualty and theft losses of personal use assets are also recognized (subject to limits discussed in Chapter 7); however, condemnation losses of personal use assets are not recognized.

Example 10.42. Sara Sheridan's personal residence with an adjusted basis of $80,000 is destroyed by fire and she receives insurance proceeds of $60,000. The $20,000 realized loss is recognized subject to the limitations for personal casualty loss deductions. If Sara's residence is condemned instead of destroyed by fire, the $20,000 realized loss is not recognized.

¶ 10,325   REPLACEMENT PROPERTY—ELECTIVE RULES

If the cost of the replacement property exceeds the proceeds or amount realized, the taxpayer may make an election to recognize none of the realized gain. The basis of the replacement property is the cost of the replacement property less deferred gain. Code Sec. 1033(a)(2) and (b). The holding period of the replacement property, if an election to defer gain is made, includes the holding period of the old converted property. Code Sec. 1223(1)(A).

Example 10.43. Jim Johnson's office building with an adjusted basis of $175,000 is destroyed by fire, and he receives insurance proceeds of $250,000. He buys a replacement office building for

$280,000. Jim realized a gain of $75,000, but he can make an election to recognize no gain since the replacement cost is greater than the insurance proceeds. The basis of the replacement property is $205,000 ($280,000 less $75,000 deferred gain) and the holding period of the replacement property begins with the holding period of the old property.

TAX PLANNING POINTER ▼

There may be times when it is better not to make the election for nonrecognition of gain. This may be the case if the taxpayer is in a relatively low tax bracket in the current year or because an expiring net operating loss carryover may be offset against the gain. Also, the election may not be desirable if the basis of the replacement asset would be a cost that would result in a higher basis than if the gain had not been recognized.

If the amount realized exceeds the cost of the replacement property, the taxpayer may make the election to recognize gain only to the extent of that excess. The basis of the replacement property is the cost of the replacement property less any deferred gain. Code Sec. 1033(a)(2) and (b).

Example 10.44. Thomas Thompson owned land with an adjusted basis of $100,000 that was condemned by the state. He received an award of $140,000, and he purchased other land for $125,000. Thomas realizes gain of $40,000 and (assuming he makes the election to defer recognition) recognizes gain of $15,000, the extent to which the amount realized ($140,000) exceeds the cost of the replacement property ($125,000). His basis in the replacement land is $100,000 ($125,000 less $25,000 deferred gain).

If more than one property is bought, the basis is allocated among the properties according to their relative costs. Rev. Rul. 73-18, 1973-1 CB 368.

Example 10.45. Assume the same facts as in the preceding example, except that the replacement property consisted of three parcels of land costing $60,000, $40,000, and $25,000. The basis of $100,000 would be allocated among the three parcels as follows:

Parcel 1: $\frac{\$60,000}{\$125,000} \times \$100,000 = \$48,000$

Parcel 2: $\frac{\$40,000}{\$125,000} \times \$100,000 = \$32,000$

Parcel 3: $\frac{\$25,000}{\$125,000} \times \$100,000 = \$20,000$

¶ 10,335 SEVERANCE DAMAGES

An award received from a condemning authority may be considered as severance damages only where such designation has been stipulated by both contracting parties. When it is not clearly shown that the award includes a specific amount as severance damages, it is assumed that the proceeds were given in consideration of the property taken by the condemning authority (i.e., the condemnation award). Rev. Rul. 59-173, 1959-1 CB 201. Severance damages may be paid to a taxpayer when part of the taxpayer's property is condemned and the value of the remaining property is decreased by the condemnation. Severance damages reduce the basis of the damaged property and any excess received above the basis of the property is recognized gain. Rev. Rul. 68-37, 1968-1 CB 359.

> *Example 10.46.* Margaret Moore receives severance damages of $100 per acre for 40 acres because of the decline in value resulting from an earlier condemnation of an adjacent parcel of Margaret's land. The $4,000 received in severance damages reduces the basis of the 40 acres of land. If the damages exceed the basis of the land, any excess is recognized gain.

¶ 10,345 QUALIFYING REPLACEMENT PROPERTY

With some exceptions, the rules for replacement property for involuntary conversions under Code Sec. 1033 are more strict than for like-kind exchanges under Code Sec. 1031. The Code provides that the replacement property in an involuntary conversion must be similar or related in service or use to the property converted. Code Sec. 1033(a)(1).

Functional-Use Test

It sometimes is difficult to determine just what qualifies as "similar or related in service or use"; however, two tests have generally been applied depending on whether the taxpayer is an owner-user or an owner-investor. If the taxpayer owned and used the property that was converted, the replacement property must be used in the same way as the converted property. This is known as the functional-use test. Rev. Rul. 64-237, 1964-2 CB 319.

> *Example 10.47.* Assume that the taxpayers make the following replacements as a result of a casualty:
>
> 1. Personal residence is replaced by a rental apartment house.
>
> 2. Manufacturing plant is replaced by a retail store.
>
> 3. Bowling alley is replaced with a billiard center. Rev. Rul. 76-319, 1976-2 CB 242.
>
> 4. Business car is replaced with a delivery truck.
>
> 5. Farm with one residence is replaced by a farm with two residences, one of which is leased. Rev. Rul. 54-569, 1954-2 CB 144.

The first four replacements do not meet the functional-use test and any gain realized would have to be recognized.

Taxpayer-Use Test

If the taxpayer is an owner-investor, the replacement property must have the same relationship of service or use to the taxpayer as the converted property had. This is known as the taxpayer-use test. Rev. Rul. 64-237, 1964-2 CB 319. The taxpayer decides this by determining (1) whether the properties are of similar service; (2) the nature of the business risks connected with the properties; and (3) what the properties demand in the way of management, service, and relations to tenants. IRS Publication No. 334, Tax Guide for Small Business.

Example 10.48. Assume that the taxpayers make the following replacements as a result of a casualty:

1. Rental manufacturing plant is replaced by a building rented out as a warehouse.

2. Rental apartment house is replaced by a personal residence.

The first replacement qualifies as replacement property, but the second replacement does not.

Exchanges of Stock

A taxpayer can also elect nonrecognition of gain in an involuntary conversion by purchasing 80 percent or more of the stock of a corporation owning similar property. The purchase of the stock qualifies as replacement property, and the gain would be recognized under Code Sec. 1033 to the extent the amount realized exceeds the cost of the stock. Code Sec. 1033(a)(2).

¶ 10,355 CONDEMNATION OF REAL PROPERTY—SPECIAL RULE

A more liberal replacement rule applies for a condemnation of real property. If real property held for productive use in a trade or business or for investment purposes is involuntarily converted, property of a like kind qualifies as property similar or related in service or use.

Example 10.49. Malcolm Moore's factory building was condemned. He purchases a rental apartment building, which qualifies as "like-kind," thus meeting the test for proper replacement property for condemnation of real property.

A taxpayer may elect to treat outdoor advertising displays as real property for purposes of the involuntary conversion rules providing the taxpayer has not elected to write off part of the cost under Code Sec. 179. Code Sec. 1033(g)(3)(A).

¶ 10,365 TIME LIMIT

The allowed period for replacement with qualified property begins on the earlier of the date of disposition of the converted property or the earliest date of the threat or imminence of the condemnation of the converted property. The taxpayer has until two years after the close of the first taxable year in which any part of the gain is realized from the involuntary conversion to replace with qualified property. For Presidentially declared disaster areas, the time limit for a principal residence is increased to four years. Code Sec. 1033(h)(1)(B). The taxpayer has three years after the close of the first taxable year in which gain is first realized in the case of condemnations of real property. Code Sec. 1033(a)(2)(B) and (g)(4).

> *Example 10.50.* Arthur King's office building (adjusted basis of $200,000) is destroyed by fire on October 18, 1997, and he receives insurance proceeds on January 20, 1998, in the amount of $350,000. Assuming Arthur is a calendar year taxpayer, he has until December 31, 2000, to replace the property. He has until two years after the end of the tax year in which gain is realized (realization occurred on January 20, 1998). The date the fire occurred was not the date from which to count.

> *Example 10.51.* If Arthur's office building had been condemned, he would have until December 31, 2001, to replace the property, which is three years after the end of the year in which the gain was first realized.

¶ 10,385   REPORTING REQUIREMENTS

If the taxpayer elects to defer gain in an involuntary conversion because of either replacement or intended replacement, the taxpayer should include supporting details in the return for the taxable year in which any of the gain is realized. If the taxpayer later finds that property will not be replaced at all or does not purchase new replacement property costing a sufficient amount, the taxpayer will have to file an amended return recomputing the tax liability for the year the election was made. If the taxpayer did not make an election when the property was involuntarily converted, and the replacement time period has not expired, the taxpayer can still file a claim for credit or refund. Reg. § 1.1033(a)-2(c)(2).

> *Example 10.52.* In 1998, Jim Jacobs receives a $200,000 award for the condemnation of his office building that has a basis of $120,000. He elects to defer recognition of the $80,000 gain, expecting to pay at least $200,000 for the new building. In 1999, he purchases another office building for $175,000. Jim must file an amended return for 1998 and recognize the $25,000 gain ($200,000 award less $175,000 replacement cost).

KEYSTONE PROBLEM

Are there times when a taxpayer might prefer the following?

1. To have a sale rather than a like-kind exchange

2. To recognize the realized gain rather than make the nonrecognition of gain election in an involuntary conversion

TAX PLANNING POINTER

It is often advisable to take advantage of the nonrecognition of gain provision for like-kind exchanges and involuntary conversions under Code Secs. 1031 and 1033. This is true even though the basis of the new assets will be reduced. The time value of money is relevant here in that the present value of current tax reductions will be greater than the present value of future reduced depreciation deductions.

Other Transactions Involving Nonrecognition

This focus of this chapter is on residence sales, like-kind exchanges, and involuntary conversions. Additional provisions resulting in nonrecognition of gain or loss are discussed only briefly.

¶ 10,401   CORPORATE AND PARTNERSHIP EXCHANGES

No gain or loss is recognized by shareholders if property is transferred to a controlled corporation by one or more persons in exchange for stock in the corporation. Code Sec. 351. Moreover, no gain or loss is recognized to a corporation upon the receipt of money or other property in exchange for the stock of such corporation. Code Sec. 1032. Similarly, no gain or loss is recognized to either a partnership or its partners when property is contributed to the partnership in exchange for a partnership interest. Code Sec. 721. These corporate and partnership provisions are examined more closely in other chapters.

¶ 10,405   STOCK-FOR-STOCK EXCHANGES

No gain or loss is recognized if common stock (in a corporation) is exchanged solely for common stock in the same corporation, or if preferred stock is exchanged solely for preferred stock in the same corporation. Nonrecognition applies even though voting stock is exchanged for nonvoting stock or nonvoting stock is exchanged for voting stock. Code Sec. 1036(a); Reg. § 1.1036-1(a). This nonrecognition provision applies to an exchange between two individuals and to transactions between a stockholder and the corporation. This nonrecognition provision does not apply if stock is exchanged for bonds, or preferred stock is exchanged for common stock (or vice versa), or if common stock in one corporation is exchanged for common stock in another corporation. However, exercising the right to convert bonds into the obligor corporation's stock or converting preferred stock for common stock in the same corporation under a conversion privilege in the preferred stock is nontaxable. Rev. Rul. 72-265, 1972-1 CB 222.

¶ 10,415 INSURANCE CONTRACT EXCHANGES

No gain or loss is recognized on the exchange of the following:

1. Life insurance contract for a life insurance contract, endowment contract, or annuity contract

2. Endowment contract for another endowment contract providing for regular payments beginning at a date not later than the date payments would have begun under the contract exchanged, or for an annuity contract

3. Annuity contract for an annuity contract (Code Sec. 1035(a))

Example 10.53. Michelle Millard exchanges a life insurance contract for an endowment contract. She recognizes no gain or loss on the exchange.

¶ 10,435 U.S. OBLIGATIONS EXCHANGES

No gain or loss is recognized upon the surrender of U.S. obligations to the United States if they were issued under chapter 31 (Public Debt) of Title 31 (Money and Finance) in exchange solely for other such obligations. Code Sec. 1037(a).

¶ 10,455 REACQUISITIONS OF REAL PROPERTY

Where a sale of real property gives rise to indebtedness to the seller which is secured by the real property sold and such property is repossessed by the seller to satisfy the purchase obligation, no loss is recognized on repossession. Gain is recognized only to the extent of the cash (or other property) received less the gain on the original sale already included in income. The amount of the gain is limited to the gain on the original sale less repossession costs and gain previously reported. Code Sec. 1038; Reg. § 1.1038-1.

TAX BLUNDERS

1. Henry and Hillary Houseman purchased a home in September 1997 in Boom City for $75,000. Henry is an excellent carpenter and spent a great deal of time fixing up and renovating the home. The Housemans spent $150,000 on materials and capital improvements during 1998. Considerable new business came to Boom City so that the city grew rapidly over a three-year time period, and there was a heavy demand for housing. In 2001, the Housemans sold their home for $720,000. The Housemans maintained no records so they would have a $645,000 gain of which $500,000 would be excluded, leaving $145,000 to be recognized. If, however, they had maintained records of their improvements, they would have had a gain of $495,000, all of which could be excluded.

2. Gordon Gimbel had an office building that he wanted to dispose of but he could not decide whether to sell it or try to exchange it. His building had an adjusted basis of $50,000 and a fair market value of $150,000. He located another office building with an equivalent fair market value and made the exchange. Gordon is in a low tax bracket in the year of the

exchange but, because of expansion of his business, he expects high income in future years.

Gordon will recognize no gain in the year of the exchange and he will carry over the $50,000 low basis. Thus, when he has low income he has no gain from the exchange and he will have low depreciation deductions in high income years. It would probably have been preferable to sell the property, recognize the gain while he is in a low tax bracket and then buy another asset which would have a high basis and for which he would be able to take higher depreciation deductions in years in which he has high income.

3.   Irene Wildwood had a rental building which she wanted to dispose of, but could not decide whether to sell it or try to exchange it. The building had a fair market value of $250,000 and a basis of $50,000. She decided to sell the building and purchased another apartment building in another part of the city for $275,000. Irene is in a high tax bracket this year, but expects to have significantly lower income in future years. Irene should have attempted, if at all possible, to have a like-kind exchange so that she would have had no income recognized in the current year when she is in a high tax bracket and then she would have a lower basis (and low depreciation) in the future years when she would be in a low tax bracket. With a sale, she has high income in the current year and a high basis in the new building on which high depreciation deductions will be taken in years when she has low income.

4.   Lorraine Larsen has an office building in a declining neighborhood which has an adjusted basis of $500,000 and a fair market value of $300,000. She would like to dispose of the building but cannot decide whether to sell or exchange it. Lorraine is in a high tax bracket this year and expects to be in lower tax brackets in the future years. She ends up exchanging it for a building in another part of the city. It has a fair market value of $250,000, and she receives boot of $50,000. No loss is recognized even though she realized a $200,000 loss and she will have a high basis ($500,000) on which she will take high depreciation in low income years. Lorraine should have sold the old building so that she could have recognized the loss when she is in a high tax bracket. If she had bought a new building for comparable fair market value, she would have had a lower basis on which to take depreciation in the future years, when her income would be low anyway.

SUMMARY OF CHAPTER 10

✓   Married taxpayers may exclude up to $500,000 of gain upon the sale of their residence and single taxpayers may exclude up to $250,000 of their gain.

✓ No gain or loss is recognized on the exchange of property held for productive use in a trade or business or for investment if such property is exchanged solely for property of like kind that is held either for productive use in a trade or business or for investment.

✓ In a like-kind exchange, when property that is not like-kind is received, then any realized gain is recognized to the extent of the boot received. If there is a realized loss in a boot received situation, such loss will not be recognized. If boot is given, generally no gain or loss is recognized. If a liability is assumed by the transferee, such assumption is treated like boot received by the taxpayer transferor.

✓ There are two ways of determining the basis of the newly acquired property in a like-kind exchange.

✓ There are two mandatory rules for recognition of gain or loss in the case of an involuntary conversion, relating to a direct conversion of property and a realized loss.

✓ There are elective rules in involuntary conversions that allow the taxpayer to elect to recognize gain realized only to the extent that the proceeds exceed the cost of the replacement property.

CHAPTER 10 QUESTIONS

1. Describe the new law for sale of residence.

2. Why might a taxpayer wish to elect out of the new exclusion on the sale of residence?

3. Is it possible to defer gain through the purchase of a new residence under the new law?

4. Why would the exclusion on sale of residence be pro-rated under the new law?

5. What special rules affect three types of taxpayers?

6. What tax planning pointers should taxpayers keep in mind on sale of residence?

7. Why are certain exchanges permitted to be nontaxable?

8. When might a taxpayer prefer a sale over a like-kind exchange that would result in nonrecognition of gain under Section 1031?

9. What are two acceptable methods of calculating the basis of new property acquired in a like-kind exchange?

10. What are four broad types of like-kind exchanges?

11. Define the following relative to like-kind exchanges:

   a. Boot

   b. Postponed gain or loss

   c. Gain or loss realized

   d. Gain or loss recognized

12. Discuss the tax consequences if a personal residence is involuntarily converted.

13. What are the broad types of involuntary conversions?

14. Explain the rules for nonrecognition of gain in an involuntary conversion.

15. What is necessary for a "threat or imminence of condemnation" to qualify property for involuntary conversion treatment?

16. What is the time limitation for replacing involuntarily converted property?

17. How are losses from involuntary conversions treated?

18. Explain the difference between the taxpayer-use test and the functional-use test, and give an example as to when each applies.

19. What exchanges of insurance policies, endowment contracts, or annuities qualify for nonrecognition?

CHAPTER 10 PROBLEMS

20. *(Old Law)* Mark Mays, age 37, sold his personal residence on April 28, 1997, for $74,000. He paid $2,000 in selling expenses and $1,300 in fixing-up expenses. The adjusted basis of the old residence is $66,000. On April 24, 1998, Mark purchased a new residence for $60,000. What was the adjusted sales price and how much gain was recognized? What was the basis of the new residence?

21. *(Old Law)* Susan Singer, age 52, sold her principal residence for $98,000 in March 1997. After all selling expenses and the adjusted basis were deducted, she had a realized gain of $22,000 and an adjusted sales price of $90,000. She purchased a new residence within one year for $74,000. How much gain did Susan recognize? What was the basis of the new residence?

22. *(Old Law)* Richard Rambler, age 60, purchased a new home in July 1998 for $80,000. He had sold his old residence in February 1997 for $300,000. His adjusted basis in the old home was $50,000 and he incurred $5,000 selling expenses and $3,000 fixing-up expenses. He had purchased the old home in 1967. What was Richard's realized gain, recognized gain, and basis in the new residence?

23. Leonard and Linda Lindsay sold for $350,000 in October 1998 their residence that they had purchased in 1988 for $100,000. They made major capital improvements during their 10-year ownership totaling $30,000.

    a. What is their excluded gain? How much must they recognize?

    b. Suppose instead that the Lindsays sold their home for $700,000. They moved into a smaller home costing $200,000. What is their excluded gain? How much must they recognize?

    c. Assume instead that the Lindsays resided in a very depressed neighborhood and the home was sold for only $80,000. How much gain or loss is recognized?

24. John Johnson, single, sold his home that he had owned for 20 years for $650,000. He purchased it for $125,000 and made $50,000 of capital improvements on the home during his time of ownership.

    a. How much gain is excluded? How much is recognized?

    b. If John purchased another home for $425,000, how much is excluded and recognized?

25. Milton and Maxine Miller purchased a home in New York City for $350,000 on October 1, 1997. Milton obtained a job in Richmond, Virginia, and on December 1, 1998, the Millers sold their home in New York for $550,000.

    a. How much gain can the Millers exclude and how much is recognized?

    b. Assume that the Millers instead sold their home on December 1, 1998, for $750,000. How much gain can the Millers then exclude and how much is recognized?

26. Thomas and Tonya Taylor purchased a home for $125,000 on September 15, 1996. On October 7, 1997, they were divorced, and as part of the divorce agreement, the home was transferred to Thomas, who sold it on October 16, 1998, for $245,000.

    a. How much can Thomas exclude and how much is recognized?

    b. Assume instead that, as part of the divorce agreement, Tonya retained ownership of the residence but the use of the home was granted to Thomas as long as Tonya owns the residence. If Tonya sells the residence on October 16, 1998, for $245,000, how much can Tonya exclude?

27. Arnold Atkins purchased a residence for $160,000 on September 26, 1996. In October 1997 he became ill and was confined to a nursing home. On October 7, 1998, he sold the residence for $245,000. How much gain can Arnold exclude?

28. Oscar Olson, single, purchased a residence on February 19, 1996, for $170,000. On September 7, 1998, a tornado completely destroyed his home. The home was insured for its replacement value, and homes in Oscar's area had appreciated greatly. He received proceeds of $400,000.

    a. How much does Oscar exclude and recognize?

    b. If Oscar instead had received proceeds of $525,000, how much gain would be excluded and recognized? How much of a replacement residence would have to be purchased in order to exclude or defer all gain realized?

29. Carl Carter had purchased a residence on January 11, 1997, for $165,000 and then sold it on April 11, 1998, for $440,000 because he received an offer he could not refuse.

    a. How much gain can Carl exclude and how much must he recognize?

    b. If Carl instead sold the home for $300,000, how much could Carl exclude and how much must he recognize?

30. Which of the following exchanges qualify as like-kind exchanges?

    a. Unimproved land for warehouse

    b. Factory for apartment building

    c. Computer for small building

    d. Inventory for business machine

    e. Computer for a printer

31. Ben Bonn and Lester Lambert exchange business machines. Ben's adjusted basis in his property is $3,200, and the fair market value is $4,500. Lester's property has an adjusted basis of $1,700 and a fair market value of $2,000. Lester also gives Ben $2,500 cash. What is Ben's realized and recognized gain and basis in the new property? What is Lester's realized and recognized gain and basis in the new property?

32. Wayne Wyatt exchanges land with an adjusted basis of $30,000 and a fair market value of $60,000 for Fred Forbes's office building, worth $50,000, and $10,000 cash. Fred had an adjusted basis of $35,000 in the building.

    a. What is Wayne's realized and recognized gain or loss and the basis in the office building?

    b. What is Fred's realized and recognized gain or loss and the basis in the land?

    c. Assume no cash was received by Wayne and the office building was worth $60,000. What is Wayne's realized and recognized gain or loss and the basis in the office building?

33. Joe Jenner exchanges property with an adjusted basis of $120,000 (fair market value $150,000) for property worth $200,000. As part of the exchange, he gave up stock in Riveris Corporation worth $50,000 with a basis of $30,000.

    a. What is Joe's recognized gain and basis in the new property?

    b. If the fair market value of the stock is $90,000 and the fair market value of Joe's property is $110,000, what is Joe's recognized gain and basis in the new property?

    c. If the fair market value of the stock is $20,000 and the fair market value of Joe's property is $180,000, what is Joe's recognized gain or loss and basis in the new property?

34. Susan Sundry exchanges her small office building (adjusted basis of $127,000 and fair market value of $154,000) for Tina Thompson's warehouse (adjusted basis of $112,000 and fair market value of $123,000). Tina assumes Susan's mortgage of $31,000. What is Susan's recognized gain on the exchange and her basis in the warehouse?

35. Allen Aubrey exchanges his factory (adjusted basis of $113,000 and fair market value of $175,000) for an apartment building with a fair market value of $120,000. He also receives $55,000 in cash. What is his realized and recognized gain or loss? Determine the basis of his apartment building using two different methods.

36. Charlotte Citron exchanged business machines with Darlene Darbey. Charlotte's machine had an adjusted basis of $10,500 and a fair market value of $9,000. Darlene's machine had an adjusted basis of $8,500 and a fair market value of $6,000 and Darlene gave Charlotte $3,000 cash. What is Charlotte's

realized gain or loss, recognized gain or loss, and the basis of the new property? Answer the same questions for Darlene.

37. Debbie Davis and Elizabeth Engels exchanged like-kind property. Debbie had an adjusted basis of $12,000 in her property (fair market value is $15,000). Elizabeth's property had an adjusted basis of $9,000 and a fair market value of $10,500, and Elizabeth gave Debbie $4,500 in cash. Determine Debbie's and Elizabeth's realized gain or loss, recognized gain or loss, and the basis in their new property.

38. Emmett Embers exchanges a business building with an adjusted basis of $69,000 and a fair market value of $100,000 for George Gunn's land (to be held as investment) with an adjusted basis of $55,000 and a fair market value of $130,000. Emmett assumes George's $30,000 mortgage on the land. Determine Emmett's and George's realized gain or loss, recognized gain or loss, and the basis in the new property.

39. Linda Loren transfers an apartment building with an adjusted basis of $150,000 and a fair market value of $240,000 for Carol Comb's apartment building (adjusted basis $140,000) with a fair market value of $200,000. Linda's mortgage of $60,000 is assumed by Carol whose mortgage of $20,000 is assumed by Linda. What is the realized and recognized gain or loss for Linda and Carol and what are their bases in their acquired buildings?

40. Peter Paterson transfers an apartment building with an adjusted basis of $160,000 and a fair market value of $235,000 for Charlie Claussen's apartment building (adjusted basis $120,000) with a fair market value of $220,000 and cash of $55,000 from Charlie. Peter's mortgage of $45,000 is assumed by Charlie whose mortgage of $85,000 is assumed by Peter. What is the realized and recognized gain or loss for Peter and Charlie and what are their bases in their acquired buildings?

41. Chad Carter exchanged land with an adjusted basis of $100,000 and a fair market value of $150,000 for Nash Nunn's land worth $140,000 (basis $120,000) and $15,000 cash. Chad's mortgage of $35,000 is assumed by Nash and Nash's mortgage of $40,000 is assumed by Chad.

    a. What is Chad's realized and recognized gain or loss and the basis in his new land?

    b. What is Nash's realized and recognized gain or loss and the basis in his new land?

42. Sidney Southern owned a restaurant which was condemned on November 18, 1997. On January 15, 1998, he received a condemnation award of $140,000. The adjusted basis of his restaurant was $60,000. He purchased another restaurant on March 13, 1998, for $150,000.

a. What is Sidney's lowest recognized gain or loss? What is his basis in the restaurant?

b. What would be the answer to (a) if the replacement cost was $120,000?

c. What is the last possible date on which Sidney could have purchased qualified replacement property?

d. What is the answer to (c) if the restaurant had been destroyed by fire instead of being condemned?

43. Gerald Gold's property is condemned by the local authorities. The property has an adjusted basis of $27,000 and a fair market value of $45,000. The local authorities replace Gerald's property with other property with a fair market value of $32,000. What is Gerald's realized gain, recognized gain, and the basis in the new property?

44. Herbert Harrison's business property with an adjusted basis of $17,000 is condemned by the local authorities. He receives a $25,000 condemnation award.

a. What is Herbert's realized and recognized gain or loss?

b. What is Herbert's realized and recognized gain or loss if he purchases qualified replacement property for $22,000?

   What is Herbert's basis in the new property?

c. What is Herbert's realized and recognized gain or loss if he purchases replacement property for $28,000?

   What is Herbert's basis in the new property?

d. What is Herbert's realized and recognized gain or loss and the basis in the new property if the condemnation award is $15,000 and the replacement property costs $22,000?

45. Steven Seller owned and managed a clothing store that was destroyed by a hurricane. He received an insurance award of $200,000 for the store, which had an adjusted basis of $120,000. A year later he replaced the clothing store with another one for $225,000.

a. What is Seller's realized and recognized gain or loss, and the basis of the replacement clothing store?

b. What is Seller's realized and recognized gain or loss and the basis if he replaced the clothing store with a car repair shop which he managed?

46. John and Amy Turner, married filing jointly, are both 36 years of age. They have two sons and a daughter. John and Amy have earned income of $71,500 and $38,000 respectively, and their allowable itemized deductions are $9,400. They had the following transactions during 1998:

a. On March 27, 1998, they sold their personal residence for $80,000. Their basis in the residence was $54,000. Six months later, they purchased a new residence for $65,000. They had incurred $6,000 of selling expenses and $6,000 of fixing-up expenses.

b. Amy exchanged land obtained before the marriage for an office building. She had a basis in the land, which was worth $100,000, of $50,000. The office building was worth $105,000.

c. John sold property for $45,000. He had inherited the property from an aunt who had an adjusted basis of $10,000 in the property. The property was worth $30,000 at the time of the aunt's death.

d. John and Amy sold stock which they had received as a wedding present. The donor had an adjusted basis of $8,000 in the stock. The stock was worth $12,000 at the time of the gift. John and Amy received $10,000 for the stock.

Compute John and Amy's lowest taxable income. Treat all income as ordinary income.

47. Jim Loner, a self-employed individual, owned a truck driven exclusively for business use. The truck had an original cost of $8,000 and an adjusted basis on December 31, 1997, of $3,600. On January 2, 1998, he traded it in for a new truck costing $10,000 and was given a trade-in allowance of $2,000. The new truck will also be used exclusively for business purposes and will be depreciated with no salvage value. What is the basis of the new truck?

a. $8,000

b. $8,400

c. $10,000

d. $11,600

48. For purposes of determining like-kind property for nontaxable exchanges, which of the following items held for business or investment purposes are not like-kind property?

a. Improved real estate for unimproved real estate

b. Store building for farm buildings

c. Machine for truck

d. Dairy herd for farm acreage

e. Tractor for combine

49. Which of the following statements is true regarding the exchange of like-kind property?

a. If like-kind property is exchanged and money is paid, a taxable gain or deductible loss must be recognized by the payer of the cash.

b. If like-kind and unlike property are given up, a taxable gain or deductible loss must be recognized only on the unlike property given up.

c. The realized gain or loss in (a) (above) is recognized to the extent of the cash payment. The liability assumed does not limit the recognized gain.

d. The gain or loss in (b) (above) is equal to the difference between the fair market value of the like-kind property and that property's adjusted basis.

50. Fred Frisby sells his personal residence for $89,000 (adjusted basis of $78,000) and within three months moves into a new residence he purchased for $125,000. What is his basis in the new residence?

a. $125,000

b. $78,000

c. $89,000

d. $114,000

51. Within a 30-day time period, Martha Meyer transfers her property to Michelle Mann, who transfers cash to William Woolsey, and William transfers his like-kind property to Martha. Which of the following statements is true?

a. This constitutes a nontaxable exchange to Martha.

b. The transaction will be taxable to all parties involved.

c. The transaction is nontaxable to William and Martha.

d. This exchange is a transaction that is taxable to Martha.

52. *Comprehensive Problem.* Adam Armstrong, age 60 and single, earned $31,000 during 1998. He contributed $3,000 to the United Fund, paid $4,000 in federal income taxes, $750 in state income tax, $400 in state sales tax, and $2,300 in mortgage interest charges. Adam also had the following transactions:

a. Sold for $5,000 stock that he had received as a gift which had an adjusted basis of $2,500 to the donor and a fair market value of $3,500 on the date of the gift. The donor had held the stock for two years and paid a gift tax of $500.

b. Exchanged land held for five years as an investment for an apartment building and $5,000 cash. On the date of exchange, the land had an adjusted basis of $27,000. The apartment building had a fair market value of $67,000.

c. An office building Adam owned was condemned by the state to make room for a state building. The building had an adjusted basis of $35,000 and a fair market value of $86,000. Adam received another building from the state and it had a fair market value of $75,000.

    d.   Adam sold his personal residence for $145,000. He incurred $2,500 in selling expenses. The residence had an adjusted basis of $56,000. He moved into an apartment.

        Calculate Adam's lowest taxable income. Treat all income as ordinary income.

53. *Comprehensive Problem.* Barry and Connie Rawles, husband and wife, are both age 34 and have two sons. Barry earned $31,000 and Connie earned $25,000 during 1998. They had $8,000 in allowable itemized deductions and the following transactions:

    a.   They sold their personal residence for $85,000. Their basis in the residence was $52,000. They incurred $3,500 in selling expenses and $2,025 in fixing-up expenses. They purchased a new residence six months later for $110,000.

    b.   Connie sold for $4,000 property she had inherited from her father in 1994. Her father's basis in the property was $1,500 and the fair market value on the date of death was $3,000.

    c.   They sold for $600 business property which they had acquired as a gift in 1995. The basis to the donor was $750 and the fair market value on the date of the gift was $700.

    d.   They exchanged 100 shares of Conway Corp. common stock, with a basis of $3,000, for 75 shares of Conway Corp. nonvoting common stock with a fair market value of $10,000.

        Determine Barry and Connie's lowest taxable income. Treat all income as ordinary income.

54. *Research Problem.* Carl Cushman, a college professor, age 58, purchased and moved into a house on August 1, 1995. He used the house continuously until September 1, 1997, on which date he went abroad for a one-year sabbatical leave. During part of the period of leave, the property was unoccupied and it was leased during the remainder of the period. On October 1, 1998, one month after returning from such leave, he sold the house. Can Carl use the exclusion for the sale of residence?

Chapter 11

Property Transactions: Treatment of Capital and Section 1231 Assets

Learning Objectives

After completing Chapter 11, you should be able to:

1. Discuss the special rules and limitations on transactions involving capital gains and losses.
2. Compute capital gains and losses for individuals and corporate taxpayers.
3. Define capital assets.
4. Describe the rules for holding periods, including special rules where property is stock or is acquired through involuntary conversions, exchanges, or gifts, or from decedents.
5. Describe the rules for reporting an individual taxpayer's capital gains and losses.
6. Define Section 1231 assets and describe the netting procedures.
7. Give the reasons for Section 1231, 1245, and 1250 as well as the definition and operations of the provisions.
8. Describe the nature of the recapture rules for Section 1245 and 1250 property.
9. Discuss the special recapture rules for gifts and inheritances, like-kind exchanges, involuntary conversions, charitable contributions, and installment sales.

OVERVIEW OF CHAPTER

The previous two chapters dealt with the determination of realized and recognized gain or loss and with basis as well as situations where there might be nonrecognition of gain or loss. Up to this point in this volume, recognized gains and losses have been treated as if they were ordinary gains and losses, which means they are includible or deductible in full respectively. This chapter focuses on transactions involving capital gains and losses which are subject to some special rules and limitations.

Some of the significant items excluded from the definition of capital asset are land and depreciable property used in a trade or business. These items, however, may receive capital gain treatment through Section 1231. This chapter examines the definition of Section 1231 assets and the netting procedures. Also included in the chapter is a discussion of the rules for recapture of depreciation under Sections 1245 and 1250. The recapture rules mean that some of the realized gain on disposition of certain Section 1231 assets may be recognized as ordinary income. In the Section 1250 asset area, the recapture rules vary with the type of property and, because they have undergone changes over the years, they are somewhat involved for the beginning tax student.

Special Rules and Limitations on Transactions

¶ 11,001   BACKGROUND

The Taxpayer Relief Act of 1997 significantly changed the taxation of capital gains. Prior to 1997, capital gains were divided into two categories: short-term capital gains and long-term capital gains. From 1991 until the 1997 changes, short-term capital gains ended up being taxed at ordinary income tax rates, which could be as high as 39.6 percent, while long-term capital gains were taxed at a maximum of 28 percent. To qualify as long-term capital gain or loss, a taxpayer must have held the capital asset for more than one year; if the asset was held one year or less, the capital gain or loss was short-term.

Congress wished to lower the maximum long-term capital gains tax rate to 20 percent. However, Congress did not wish to make the lower rate available to all long-term capital gains, and the new rules divide long-term capital gains into three categories: long-term capital gains taxed at a maximum rate of 28 percent, long-term capital gains taxed at a maximum rate of 25 percent, and long-term capital gains taxed at a maximum rate of 20 percent.

To qualify for the 20 percent long-term capital gain tax rate, the capital asset must be held for more than 18 months. For taxpayers in the 15 percent tax bracket, this long-term capital gains tax rate becomes 10 percent. Prior to the Taxpayer Relief Act of 1997, there was no special long-term capital gains tax rate available to the lower tax bracket taxpayers.

The 28 percent long-term capital gains tax rate applies to capital assets held more than one year but not more than 18 months. This holding period is sometimes referred to as the "mid-term" holding period. However, the 28 percent long-term capital gains tax rate applies to collectibles and Section 1202 gains. Generally, collectibles (as defined in Code Sec. 408(m)) include works of art, rugs, antiques, metal, gems, stamps, coins, and alcoholic beverages. However, certain newly minted gold and silver coins issued by the federal government and coins issued under state laws are subject to the 20 percent tax rate even though such coins generally qualify as "collectibles." Section 1202 stock is certain small business stock held more than five years. Gains on the disposition of Section 1202 stock qualify for a 50 percent exclusion. Stock qualifying for the exclusion is not eligible for the 20 percent tax rate and is included in the 28 percent long-term capital gains tax rate category.

The 25 percent long-term capital gains tax rate applies to what is referred to as "unrecaptured Section 1250 gain." Unrecaptured Section 1250 gain is the amount of the long-term capital gain that would be treated as ordinary income if a Section 1250 asset were classified as a Section 1245 asset. (See a later part of the chapter for a discussion of Section 1245 and 1250 assets, depreciation recapture, and the determination of the amount of "unrecaptured Section 1250 gain.") Under the old rules, the unrecaptured Section 1250 gain was taxed at a maximum tax rate of 28 percent. Congress did not wish for this amount to be taxed at the new lower 20 percent tax rate.

In 1988, 1989, and 1990, net capital gains were taxed as ordinary income at rates of up to 33 percent. Through 1986, taxpayers were allowed a 60 percent deduction on their net capital gains. For 1987, there was still an advantage in that taxpayers were taxed at a maximum rate of 28 percent on their net capital gains. This occurred while the top marginal rate for individual taxpayers went up to 38.5 percent. For 1987 and later years, net capital loss deductions, however, are limited to $3,000, with carryover opportunities to the following year.

Because of the potential benefit of long-term capital gains, the capital loss limitations, and the continuation of Section 1231 assets (as discussed at ¶ 11,601), the study of the tax structure applicable to capital gains continues to be of importance to the student. Indeed, a tax rate increase occurred in 1993, when the top ordinary rate increased to 39.6 percent, thereby creating a potential differential of 19.6 percent over the capital gain rate of 20 percent in 1998.

¶ 11,025 CAPITAL ASSET DEFINITION

Capital assets are not actually defined in the Internal Revenue Code. Instead, Code Sec. 1221 defines a capital asset as any property held by the taxpayer *except:*

1. Stock in trade or other inventory property or property held by the taxpayer primarily for sale to customers in the ordinary course of a trade or business

2. Depreciable property used in a trade or business

3. Real property used in a trade or business

4. Copyright, literary, musical, or artistic composition, letter or memorandum, or similar property held by (1) a taxpayer whose personal efforts created such property, (2) a taxpayer for whom such property was prepared or produced, or (3) a

taxpayer in whose hands the basis of the property is determined by reference to the basis of the property held by a taxpayer described in (1) or (2)

5. Accounts or notes receivable acquired in the ordinary course of a trade or business for services rendered or from the sale of property

6. U.S. government publications (1) received by the taxpayer from the government other than by purchase at the price at which they are offered for sale to the public, or (2) held by a taxpayer whose basis in such publications is determined by reference to a taxpayer described in (1)

As seen from the above definition, the Code defines a capital asset by listing the assets that are not capital assets. The major items excluded from capital assets are inventory and business fixed assets such as land, buildings, machinery, and equipment. Because these assets are excluded from capital assets, the conclusion might be drawn that they are subject to ordinary income treatment. This, however, is not the case. Depreciable property and land used in a trade or business receive special treatment. Under Code Sec. 1231, if the net result from sales of such properties is a gain, it may be subject to capital gain treatment and, if the net result is a loss, it is subject to ordinary loss treatment.

The primary capital assets are investment property such as stocks and bonds and personal-use assets such as a residence or personal automobile. Gains and losses from the sale of investment property are recognized as capital gains and losses. Gains from the sale or exchange of personal-use assets are capital gains, but losses from transactions in personal-use assets are never deductible, unless a casualty or theft is involved.

Example 11.1. Caroline Collector sold at a loss some jewelry she used for two years. She is not able to deduct the loss, since jewelry is a personal-use asset. If she sold the jewelry at a gain, she would have a capital gain.

Example 11.2. If Caroline in the preceding example held the jewelry as an investment in her safe deposit box and never wore the jewelry, any gain or loss would be a capital gain or loss.

TAX PLANNING POINTER

The classification of an asset as capital or ordinary can be important. Not only is there potential special tax treatment for long-term capital gains and losses, but there may be advantages if capital gain property is given as a charitable contribution. In that case, the amount of the charitable contribution is the fair market value of the donated property which, if it were sold, would result in a long-term capital gain. If it is ordinary income property, the charitable contribution is limited to the basis of the property.

Special Situations in Capital v. Ordinary Treatment

¶ 11,101 INVENTORY

Taxpayers may no longer avoid capital asset treatment by proving that property, which otherwise fits within the definition of a capital asset, was acquired for business rather than investment purposes. The U.S. Supreme Court has held that a taxpayer's motivation in purchasing an asset is irrelevant to a determination of whether the asset falls within the broad statutory definition of a "capital asset." *Arkansas Best Co.,* 88-1 USTC ¶ 9210, 485 U.S. 212, 108 S.Ct. 971 (1988), aff'g 86-2 USTC ¶ 9671, 800 F.2d 215 (CA-8 1986). Thus, losses incurred by a diversified holding company from the sale of bank stock that had been purchased in order to supply new capital to the financially troubled institution were capital in nature.

In so ruling, the Court limited the scope of the *Corn Products* doctrine (*Corn Products Refining Co.,* 55-2 USTC ¶ 9746, 350 U.S. 46, 76 S.Ct. 20 (1955)), which, since 1955, has been interpreted as creating a nonstatutory exception to the definition of a capital asset where the asset was purchased for ordinary business purposes and not as an investment. This prior interpretation accorded taxpayers ordinary loss treatment on the sale of assets that would otherwise have been characterized as capital assets. The U.S. Supreme Court now maintains that the *Corn Products* decision stands only for "the narrow proposition that hedging transactions that are an integral part of a business's inventory-purchase system fall within" the exclusion of inventory as a capital asset. Further, according to the Court, the only exceptions to the classification of assets as capital assets are those enumerated in Section 1221, and no language in the statute suggests that others could be fashioned by the courts. The Court noted that the exceptions would be superfluous if assets acquired exclusively for business purposes were not capital assets.

¶ 11,115 SALE OF A BUSINESS

When a business that has operated as a sole proprietorship is sold, the sale is not treated as the sale of one asset. Instead, it is treated as the sale of the individual assets of the business. *E.A. Watson,* 53-1 USTC ¶ 9391, 345 U.S. 544, 73 S.Ct. 848 (1953); *Williams v. McGowan,* 46-1 USTC ¶ 9120, 152 F.2d 570 (CA-2 1945); Rev. Rul. 55-79, 1955-1 CB 370. The proceeds received are allocated to the assets according to their relative fair market values. The gain or loss on some of the assets will be ordinary gain or loss and on other assets there will be capital gain or loss.

The sale of a partnership interest is the sale of a capital asset and results in capital gain or loss to the partners except that the part of the gain or loss that is related to unrealized receivables or substantially appreciated inventory items is treated as ordinary gain or loss. Code Secs. 741 and 751(a). The sale of corporate stock results in a capital gain or loss if the stock was a capital asset in the hands of the seller.

¶ 11,125 PATENTS

Certain transfers of patents may result in capital gain treatment. Code Sec. 1235. The reason for this provision is to encourage invention, although the same tax treatment is not available to authors, composers, and artists. In the latter cases, their works (writings, music, and art) are specifically excluded from capital assets.

If an inventor transfers (other than by gift, inheritance, or devise) property consisting of all substantial rights to a patent, or an undivided interest therein, the transfer is considered the sale or exchange of a capital asset held the requisite time period to meet the long-term holding period rules. This rule holds even if payments are payable periodically over a period ending when the purchaser's use of the patent ends or if payments are contingent on the productivity, use, or disposition of the property transferred. Code Sec. 1235(a).

> *Example 11.3.* Bennett Burrow, an inventor, sold his patent to Smith Corporation for a lump-sum payment of $100,000 plus $6 per unit sold. He had a zero basis in the patent. Bennett has a long-term capital gain of $100,000 and the $6 per unit royalty will also receive long-term capital gain treatment regardless of how long the patent was held.

"All substantial rights" means all rights which are of value at the time the rights to the patent are transferred. It does not include a grant of rights to a patent (1) which is limited geographically within the country of issuance; (2) which is limited in duration by the terms of the agreement to a period less than the remaining life of the patent; (3) which grants rights to the grantee in fields of use within trades or industries, which are less than all the valuable rights at the time of the grant; or (4) which grants to the grantee less than all the claims or inventions covered by the patent at the time of the grant. Reg. § 1.1235-2(b).

> *Example 11.4.* Vance Vox sells patent rights to his invention, but the rights limit the use of the invention to the state of California. Vance's sale of patent rights does not qualify for capital gain treatment since the rights are limited within the United States.

The transferor must be a holder which refers to the creator of the property or any individual who has purchased an interest in the property from such creator if such individual is neither the employer of the creator nor related to the creator. Code Sec. 1235(b).

¶ 11,135 FRANCHISES

A franchise includes an agreement which gives one of the parties (the transferee) the right to distribute, sell, or provide goods, services, or facilities, within a specified area. Rules are provided for the treatment to the transferee and transferor of a franchise, trademark, or trade name. Code Sec. 1253. Specifically, a transfer of a franchise, trademark, or trade name is not treated as a sale or exchange of a capital asset if the transferor retains any significant power, right, or continuing interest with respect to the property. Amounts received on account of a transfer, sale, or disposition which are contingent on the productivity, use, or disposition of the property are also not treated as a sale or disposition of a capital asset. Code Sec. 1253(a)-(c).

The term "significant power, right, or continuing interest" includes but is not limited to the following rights with respect to the transferred interest:

1. To disapprove any assignment of such an interest

2. To terminate the franchise at will

3. To prescribe the standards of quality of products

4. To require that the transferee sell or advertise only products or services of the transferor

5. To require the transferee to purchase substantially all supplies or equipment from the transferor

6. To require payments contingent on the productivity, use, or sale of the property (Code Sec. 1253(b)(2))

Since most franchises involve the transferor retaining at least some of these rights, the transferor is going to have ordinary income upon the transfer of a franchise.

Amounts paid by the transferee which are contingent on the productivity, use, or disposition of the property transferred are allowed as business deductions. Other payments are generally amortized over 15 years. Code Sec. 197(g).

Example 11.5. Farmers Corporation grants Grace Gobbler a franchise to sell fried chicken for a period of 20 years with renewals. Farmers Corporation retains the powers and rights described above. Grace is required to pay $100,000 initially and then three percent of sales. The $100,000 payment and the percentage payments are ordinary income to Farmers. Grace may deduct the percentage payments as ordinary business expenses. The initial payment of $100,000 is amortized over 15 years beginning in the year the payment is made.

Example 11.6. Denny Doone, a transferee of a franchise, sells the franchise to a third party, transferring all significant powers and rights. Payments to Denny are not contingent. Any reportable gain will be capital gain to him.

¶ 11,155   LEASE CANCELLATION PAYMENTS

Amounts received by a lessee (tenant) for the cancellation of a lease are considered as amounts received for the exchange of such lease or agreement. Code Sec. 1241. The type of gain or loss will depend on the character of the lease. A nondepreciable leasehold (for example, for a personal-use asset as a residence) is a capital asset. A depreciable lease used in a trade or business is either an ordinary asset or a Section 1231 asset. Amounts received by the landlord for cancelling a lease are ordinary income. *W.M. Hort,* 41-1 USTC ¶ 9534, 313 U.S. 28, 61 S.Ct. 757 (1941).

Example 11.7. Terry Thomson pays Lydia Lancer, the owner of his apartment, $500 in order to cancel his lease. Lydia treats the $500 as ordinary income.

Example 11.8. Lydia pays Tony Terrace, a tenant of one of her apartments, $900 to cancel the lease. Tony would report $900 capital gain since the lease was a nondepreciable leasehold and thus a capital asset.

¶ 11,165   OPTIONS

Gain or loss from the sale or exchange of an option to buy or sell property or from failure to exercise such option is of the same character as the property to which the option relates. If loss is attributable to failure to exercise an option, the option is deemed to have been sold or exchanged on the day it expired. Code Sec. 1234(a).

Example 11.9. Jerrold Jackson had an option on 1,000 shares of King Corporation stock. Although the stock increased in value, Jerrold did not purchase the stock. Instead, he sold the option at a gain. Jerrold would report a capital gain since the King Corporation stock would have been a capital asset to him if he had purchased it.

Holding Period

¶ 11,201   COMPUTATION OF HOLDING PERIOD

Holding period continues to be important in 1998 because of the reduced rate at which net capital gains are taxed and because the basic structure for capital gains and losses has been retained in the Code. Additionally, the definition of Section 1231 assets includes those assets used in a trade or business and held long-term. Gains and losses on these Section 1231 assets continue to be separately computed.

Property has to be held for longer than one year to be long-term. Code Sec. 1222. Note, as discussed in a later section, the tax advantages on the gain side occur when property is held greater than 18 months (where the maximum rate is 20 percent) or more than 12 months but not greater than 18 months (where the maximum rate is 28 percent). In figuring the holding period, the day the property was acquired is excluded, but the day it was disposed of is included. Since the day after acquisition is the start of the holding period, this same date in each of the following months is the start of the new month. It does not matter how many days are in each month. Property acquired on the last day of the month must be held on or after the first day of the [thirteenth] succeeding month to be held long-term. Rev. Rul. 66-7, 1966-1 CB 188.

Example 11.10. Cindy Crier purchased shares of stock on February 19, 1997. If she sells the stock on February 20, 1998, or before August 20, 1998, she will have long-term capital gain or loss in the 28 percent basket. If she sells the stock on February 19, 1998, or earlier, she will have short-term capital gain or loss. A sale after August 19, 1998, goes into the 20 percent basket.

Example 11.11. If Jack Jeffrey purchases shares of stock on April 30, 1997, and sells the stock on May 1, 1998, or before October 31, 1998, he will have long-term capital gain or loss in the 28 percent basket. If he sells the stock on April 30, 1998, or earlier, he will have short-term capital gain or loss. A sale after October 30, 1998, goes into the 20 percent basket.

Example 11.12. Allison Alton, a 31 percent bracket taxpayer, purchases shares of stock on January 6, 1997, and sells the stock at a gain on July 7, 1998. She has a long-term capital gain on the stock, which is held greater than 18 months and will be taxed at a maximum rate of 20 percent.

¶ 11,215 SPECIAL RULES FOR HOLDING PERIOD

The general rule is that the holding period runs from the date of acquisition to the date of disposition, but there are special rules in certain circumstances.

Property Acquired Through Exchanges, Involuntary Conversions, and Replacements

The holding period of property received in an exchange includes the holding period of the property given in the exchange if the basis of the acquired property has the same basis in whole or in part as the property exchanged. Code Sec. 1223(1). The property exchanged must be a capital asset or Section 1231 assets (i.e., property used in a trade or business). Property acquired as a result of an involuntary conversion is also considered an exchange for this purpose. The holding period of a residence the acquisition of which under the old Code Sec. 1034 resulted in the nonrecognition of any part of the realized gain includes the old residence's holding period. Code Sec. 1223(7).

Example 11.13. On July 8, 1998, George Grundy exchanged 100 shares of Jones Corporation Class A stock (bought on July 14, 1994, for $1,500) for Jones Corporation Class B stock in a nontaxable exchange. George sells the Class B shares on December 21, 1998, for $1,200. Since the holding period of the Class B shares began on July 14, 1994, and the basis is $1,500, George has a long-term capital loss of $300.

Example 11.14. Kathy Krupp sold her office building on November 15 at a gain. She had purchased this building only four months earlier upon receiving insurance proceeds after a fire destroyed her old building, on which she had deferred all the realized gain and which she had owned for five years. Kathy's sale of her building on November 15 results in a long-term capital gain since she would have a holding period of five years, four months on the building. That is, she counts the five years she owned the former building in her holding period.

Property Acquired by a Gift and from a Decedent

The holding period of property acquired by gift includes the holding period of the donor if the basis of the property is the same in whole or in part as it had been in the hands of the donor. Code Sec.

1223(2); Reg. § 1.1223-1(b). If at the date of the gift the property has a fair market value that is less than the donor's adjusted basis and the property is sold at a loss, the holding period begins on the date of the gift.

Example 11.15. On March 18, 1998, Justin Jaeger received shares of stock as a gift from his father, who had owned it for four years and who had an adjusted basis of $5,000 in the stock. The stock had a fair market value of $8,000. Justin sold the stock on June 19, 1998, for $9,000. Although Justin has owned it only three months, he has a $4,000 long-term capital gain since he includes the period that his father owned it.

Example 11.16. Assume the facts in the preceding example, except that the fair market value at the date of the gift was $3,000 and he sold it for $2,500. Justin has a short-term capital loss of $500 since his holding period begins on the date of the gift which means he held the stock three months.

Gains and losses from the sale or exchange of inherited property are treated as long-term (greater than 18 months and subject to the 20 percent maximum rate) regardless of how long the property was held. Code Sec. 1223(11).

Example 11.17. On April 22, 1998, Alice Amberson inherited stock from her aunt, who had owned the stock for three months. On June 24, 1998, Alice sells the stock at a gain. Alice has long-term capital gain even though she owned the property only two months and even though the total ownership by Alice and her aunt was only five months.

Individual Taxpayers

¶ 11,301   DETERMINATION OF TAXABLE INCOME

An individual's capital gains and losses are reported on Schedule D. The process is not specifically described in the Code but is necessary under the definitions in Code Sec. 1222.

For sales and exchanges after July 28, 1997, it is necessary to hold assets more than 18 months in order for the lowest long-term capital gains rates to apply, in which case the maximum rate is 20 percent (10 percent for individuals in the 15 percent tax bracket). If assets are held greater than 12 months but not more than 18 months, the gain is taxed at the maximum rate of 28 percent (15 percent for a taxpayer in the 15 percent bracket). Further, the 20 percent (and 10 percent for 15 percent bracket taxpayers) rate applies only to adjusted net capital gains, which are net capital gains (i.e., the excess of net long-term capital gains over the net short-term capital losses) without regard to:

1. *Collectibles gain.* Generally, collectibles (as defined in Sec. 408(m)) do not qualify for the new lower rates. Thus, stamps, antiques, gems, and most coins would still be taxed at the maximum rate of 28 percent. Certain newly minted gold and silver coins issued by the federal government and coins issued under state law, however, are subject to the lower capital gains

rate, even though such coins generally qualify as "collectibles."

2. *Unrecaptured Section 1250 Gain.* Unrecaptured Sec. 1250 gain is the amount of the long-term capital gain that would be treated as ordinary income if Sec. 1250(b)(1) included all depreciation with an applicable percentage of 100%, and for property sold after July 28, 1997, only gains from Sec. 1250 property held for more than 18 months were taken into account. This gain is taxed at a maximum rate of 28 percent.

3. *Section 1202 gains.* When a taxpayer sells or exchanges Sec. 1202 stock (i.e., certain small business stock) that the taxpayer has held for more than five years, 50 percent of the gain is excluded from the taxpayer's gross income. If the taxpayer qualifies for this 50 percent exclusion, any recognized gains from the sale or exchange of this stock may be taxed at the 28 percent rate.

4. *Mid-term gains.* Mid-term gains are gains arising from holding property more than 12 months but not more than 18 months. The 28 percent maximum rate continues to hold for those assets held more than 12 months but not more than 18 months.

After the Taxpayer Relief Act of 1997, working with capital gains and losses is more complicated because of the existence of short-term, "mid-term," and long-term capital gains and losses. Schedule D includes the mid-term gains and losses in the long-term section of the schedule.

The steps for determining taxable income are as follows:

1. Group all gains or losses into four "baskets." The *short-term basket* contains short-term capital gains and losses and short-term capital loss carryovers. The *28 percent basket* contains capital gains and losses on assets held more than 12 months but not greater than 18 months, collectibles gains and losses, long-term capital loss carryovers form pre-1997 years, mid-term capital loss carryovers in years subsequent to 1997, and unrecaptured Section 1231 mid-term gains. The *25 percent basket* contains any Section 1250 gain (up to total depreciation taken but not to exceed the recognized gain) that exceeds the portion of gain recaptured at the taxpayer's ordinary marginal tax rate (see ¶ 11,801 to 11,935 to see how this is calculated). The *20 percent basket* contains long-term capital gains and losses, long-term capital loss carryovers, and unrecaptured Section 1231 long-term gains.

2. Net the contents of the initial short-term and 20 percent baskets independently. If a loss results in either or both, include the loss(es) in the 28 percent basket. If a gain results in either or both, keep track of its character (basket).

3. Net the contents of the 28 percent basket. If a net loss results, include the loss in the 25 percent basket. If a gain results, it is taxed at 28 (or 15) percent.

4. Net the contents of the 25 percent basket. If a net loss results, include the loss in the final long-term basket. If a gain results, it is taxed at 25 (or 15) percent.

5. Net any items now in the final long-term basket (perhaps an initial long-term net gain and/or a depreciation recapture net loss). If the final result is a gain, it is taxed at 20 (or 10) percent. If the final result is a loss, combine it with any net short-term gain. Any excess loss is deductible up to $3,000 ($1,500 for married filing spearately) as under prior law, and the remainder is carried over. Any excess net short-term gain is taxed at the taxpayer's top marginal tax rate.

Example 11.18. Assume that Betty, single, has a 1998 taxable income of $80,000, which includes $30,000 of ordinary income, $25,000 long-term capital gains on a sale of stock that she had owned for three years, $10,000 net capital gains on assets held more than 12 months but not greater than 18 months, and $15,000 unrecaptured Section 1250 gains on assets held for more than 18 months. Her tax would be as follows:

Tax on $25,350 at 15 percent	$3,803
Tax on $4,650 at 28 percent (remaining ordinary income)	1,302
Tax on $25,000 at 20 percent	5,000
Tax on $15,000 at 25 percent	3,750
Tax on $10,000 at 28 percent	2,800
Total tax	$16,655

Example 11.19. Assume that Betty, single, has a 1998 taxable income of only $30,000, which includes $15,000 of ordinary income, $5,000 long-term capital gains on a sale of stock that she had owned for threee years, $4,000 net capital gains on assets held more than 12 months but not greater than 18 months, and $6,000 unrecaptured Section 1250 gains on assets held for more than 18 months. Her tax would be as follows:

Tax on $25,000 at 15 percent	$3,750
Tax on $5,000 at 10 percent	500
Total tax	$4,250

Example 11.20. On May 22, 1998, Nancy Northfield sold for $4,000 shares of stock acquired on December 26, 1997, for $3,200. She has a short-term capital gain of $800. On July 20, 1998, she sold for $8,000 shares of stock purchased for $8,300 on March 17, 1998. She has a short-term capital loss of $300. Nancy's net short-term capital gain is $500. If these are the only capital transactions, the $500 is taxed at an ordinary rate up to 39.6 percent.

Example 11.21. On June 12, 1998, John Jennings sold for $3,000 shares of stock he had acquired for $2,400 on January 20, 1998. He has a short-term capital gain of $600. On August 17, 1998, he sold for $7,000 shares of stock he purchased for $8,300 on April 13, 1998. He has a short-term capital loss of $1,300 on this sale. John's net short-term capital loss is $700. If these are the only capital transactions, John receives a $700 deduction.

Example 11.22. On December 18, 1998, Nancy sold for $6,200 shares of stock she had acquired for $10,000 on June 16, 1997. She has a long-term capital loss of $3,800. On November 10, 1998, she sold for $14,000 shares of stock she had acquired for $12,000 on April 14, 1997. This is a $2,000 long-term capital gain. Nancy's net long-term capital loss is $1,800. If these are the only capital transactions, Nancy has a deductible loss of $1,800.

Example 11.23. On November 6, 1998, John sold for $11,000 stock that he had acquired for $8,000 on April 11, 1997. He has a long-term capital gain of $3,000 on this transaction. On December 8, 1998, he sold for $6,000 stock he had acquired for $7,800 on May 10, 1997. He has a long-term capital loss of $1,800 on this transaction. John has a net long-term capital gain of $1,200. If these are the only capital transactions, John would be taxed at a maximum rate of 20 percent.

Example 11.24. On November 30, 1998, Brian Boyd sold for $12,000 stock he had purchased on October 27, 1997, for $7,000. He also sold on the same day for $14,000 stock he had purchased on January 27, 1997, for $8,000. Brian is taxed at a maximum rate of 28 percent on the mid-term capital gain (MTCG) of $5,000 and at a maximum rate of 20 percent on the $6,000 gain.

Example 11.25. If Nancy has the net short-term capital gain of $500 from Example 11.20 and the net long-term capital loss of $1,800 from Example 11.22, she has a net overall loss of $1,300, which is deductible.

Example 11.26. If John has the net short-term capital loss of $700 in Example 11.21 and the net long-term capital gain of $1,200 in Example 11.23, John has an overall gain of $500 taxed at a maximum rate of 20 percent.

Example 11.27. Edwin Edwards, a 36 percent bracket taxpayer, had three stock transactions that gave the following results during 1998: STCG $6,000, LTCG $8,000 (greater than 18 months), MTCG $10,000. His overall net gain is $24,000, and he will be taxed at 20 percent on the $8,000, 28 percent on the $10,000, and 36 percent on the $6,000.

Example 11.28. During 1998, Tim Turner had a net LTCG of $7,500 and a net STCL of $10,500. Tim's net overall loss is $3,000, and he may take a $3,000 deduction.

Example 11.29. During 1998, Joan Janner had a net STCG of $5,000 and a net LTCL of $7,000. The net overall loss is $2,000 and Joan receives a deduction for $2,000.

Example 11.30. Beth, a single 31 percent taxpayer, had 1998 capital gains and losses as follows: a short-term capital loss of $12,000 and a short-term capital gain of $5,000, a mid-term capital loss carryover of $2,000 and a mid-term capital gain of $4,000, $1,000 depreciation recapture gain (losses are not possible here), and a long-term capital gain of $2,000. Beth has a net short-term capital loss of $7,000 and a net long-term capital gain of $2,000 (the only item in the long-term basket). The $7,000 net loss is included in the mid-term basket (28 percent basket), and the $2,000 gain is held in the long-term basket pending any future losses entering later in the final netting process. Beth's mid-term basket (including the net short-term capital loss of $7,000) is then netted and results in a net loss of $5,000 (($2,000) + ($7,000) + $4,000) that is subsequently included in the depreciation recapture netting (25 percent basket). With the $1,000 depreciation in the recapture basket, a $4,000 net loss results and is included in the final long-term basket (20 percent basket). The final long-term basket now contains the $4,000 loss from the recapture basket and the original long-term gain of $2,000, for a net loss of $2,000. This loss is deductible by Beth in 1998.

Example 11.31. If Beth's figures were the same as in the previous example but she did not have the short-term capital loss of $12,000 then her short-term netting would result in a $5,000 net gain, since it is the only item in her short-term basket. The remaining nettings would all be net gains. Beth's $5,000 net short-term capital gain would be taxed at 31 percent, her net mid-term capital gain of $2,000 would be taxed at 28 percent, the $1,000 depreciation recapture gain would be taxed at 25 percent, and her long-term capital gain of $2,000 would be taxed at 20 percent.

¶ 11,315 CAPITAL LOSS CARRYOVERS

If the capital losses exceed the limits described above, the excess may be carried over indefinitely. The amounts carried over are offset against capital gains in the subsequent years. The carryforward losses will be treated as if they occurred in the subsequent years. For example, a capital loss is carried over to the following year and is offset against capital gains according to the regular steps for computation of net overall capital gain or loss. If the taxpayer has both short-term and long-term losses in total exceeding the limit allowed as a deduction, short-term losses are applied to the limit first even if they were incurred after the long-term losses.

Example 11.32. Greg Grove has a net STCL of $2,000 and a net LTCL of $5,500 during 1998. The net STCL is used up first dollar for dollar to give a $2,000 deduction. Then the net LTCL is used up to get the remaining $1,000 deduction for a total $3,000 deduction. This leaves $4,500 LTCL to be carried over to 1999. In 1999, this $4,500 LTCL carryover is treated as if it were a LTCL incurred during 1999.

Example 11.33. Michelle Martin has a net STCL of $4,000 and a net LTCL of $2,000 in 1998. The STCL is used up first for a $3,000 deduction and $1,000 STCL is carried over to 1999. The net LTCL of $2,000 is also carried over to 1999. In 1999, she has a STCG of $600 and a LTCG of $1,200. In 1999, the STCL carryover of $1,000 is offset against the STCG of $600 to get a net STCL of $400. The LTCL carryover of $2,000 is offset against the LTCG of $1,200 for a net LTCL of $800. For 1999, Michelle is allowed a deduction of $1,200 ($400 + $800).

¶ 11,401   CORPORATE TAXPAYERS DISTINGUISHED

The capital gain and loss treatment of corporate taxpayers differs from that of individual taxpayers in four ways.

1. The corporation is not allowed any special advantage for net capital gains (i.e., the excess of net LTCG over net STCL). Instead, corporate capital gains are taxed at regular corporate tax rates, with the maximum tax rate of 35 percent.

2. The corporation is not allowed a deduction in the current year for a net overall capital loss position. Capital losses for corporations are allowed only to the extent of the capital gains.

3. A net overall capital loss can still be used by a corporation. It is carried back three years and carried forward five years against capital gains.

4. Corporate carrybacks and carryovers are treated as short-term.

Special Provisions for Certain Investments

¶ 11,501   NONBUSINESS BAD DEBTS

Nonbusiness bad debts are debts that are not related to the taxpayer's trade or business. They are treated as a short-term capital loss in the year of worthlessness, regardless of how long they were outstanding. The debts must be completely worthless. Code Sec. 166(d)(1); Reg. § 1.166-5(a)(2). However, a taxpayer has a totally worthless bad debt when none of what is still owed can be collected, even though the taxpayer may have collected some of the debt in the past. Only a bona fide debt qualifies for deduction as a bad debt. A bona fide debt is a debt that arises from a debtor-creditor relationship based on a valid and enforceable obligation to pay a sum of money. Reg. § 1.166-1(c).

Example 11.34. In 1996, Beth Burrow loaned $7,000 to her friend Nancy Newburg. In 1998, Nancy declared bankruptcy, with the result that the debt is totally worthless. Beth may deduct the $7,000 loss as a short-term capital loss. If she has no other capital gains or losses, she deducts $3,000 in 1998 and carries the remaining $4,000 to 1999.

TAX PLANNING POINTER ▼

Since nonbusiness bad debts result in short-term capital losses, the taxpayer is subject to the regular capital loss limitation of $3,000. Taxpayers should be cautious in making large nonbusiness loans that may become worthless (unless they have capital gains to offset the losses) since it might take a long time to receive the tax deduction given the limitation on the capital loss deduction in a particular year.

¶ 11,515   WORTHLESS SECURITIES

If a security which is a capital asset becomes worthless, the loss is a capital loss on the last day of the taxable year in which the security becomes worthless. Code Sec. 165(g)(1). Thus, worthless stock which may have been held short-term may result in a long-term capital loss.

Example 11.35. Donna Drummond, a calendar year taxpayer, purchased stock for $4,000 on May 27, 1997. On January 27, 1998, the stock became worthless. She is considered to have held the stock from May 27, 1997, to December 31, 1998 (more than 18 months). Donna has a long-term capital loss in the 20 percent basket even though the stock was worthless after she held it only eight months.

¶ 11,525   SMALL BUSINESS STOCK

Individual taxpayers are allowed ordinary loss deductions for losses from the sale or exchange, or from worthlessness of certain small business stock (known as "Section 1244 stock"). Code Sec. 1244(a). The maximum deduction for any taxable year is limited to $50,000. Code Sec. 1244(b). On a joint return, the limit is $100,000 whether the stock is owned by one spouse or both spouses. Reg. § 1.1244(b)-1. Any excess above these limits is capital loss. The ordinary loss deduction not used in the year sustained is treated as attributable to a trade or business and increases the net operating loss of the shareholder and becomes part of the shareholder's net operating loss carryback and carryover. Code Sec. 1244(d)(3).

The term "Section 1244 stock" refers to stock issued by a small business corporation for money or other property. Code Sec. 1244(c)(1). Section 1244 stock must not be convertible into other securities of the corporation. Reg. § 1.1244(c)-1(b). A corporation is considered a small business corporation if the aggregate amount of money and other property received by the corporation for stock as a contribution to capital and as paid-in surplus does not exceed $1,000,000 at the time of stock issuance. Code Sec. 1244(c)(3).

The amount of the "other property" is the adjusted basis to the corporation of such property reduced by any liability to which the property was subject or which was assumed by the corporation. In addition, for the period of five years ending before the loss the corporation must have derived more than 50 percent of its gross receipts from sources other than royalties, rents, dividends, interest, annuities, and sales or exchanges of stocks or securities. If the corporation has been in existence for less than five years, the relevant time period is the time it has been in existence. Special rules also apply for corporations where deductions exceed gross income. Code Sec. 1244(c)(1)-(3).

Example 11.36. Elaine Eggelston, single, acquires 1,000 shares of Section 1244 stock in 1992 for $150,000 and sells all of it in 1998 for $80,000. She has a $50,000 ordinary loss and a $20,000 long-term capital loss. If she had been married and filed a joint return, she would have had a $70,000 ordinary loss. This assumes that the five-year, 50 percent test is met.

The taxpayer should consider selling stock in two or more taxable years in order to take advantage of the loss limits. Thus, in this example, if Elaine had sold 500 shares in 1998 for $40,000 and the other 500 shares for $40,000 in 1999, she would have had a $35,000 ordinary loss deduction in both years.

The allowance of an ordinary loss deduction on Section 1244 stock is permitted only to an individual who must be the original owner, or to an individual who is a partner in a partnership at the time of original acquisition. Code Sec. 1244(a); Reg. § 1.1244(a)-1(b). The partner's share of the ordinary loss is the partner's share of the partnership's loss on sale of the stock. An individual acquiring stock from a shareholder by purchase, gift, or inheritance is not entitled to ordinary loss deductions under Section 1244.

If a shareholder receives Section 1244 stock as a result of contributing property that had a fair market value less than its adjusted basis immediately before the exchange, the basis of the stock is reduced to the fair market value of the property in computing the amount of the ordinary loss.

Example 11.37. In 1992, Walter Winston, single, transfers property with an adjusted basis of $160,000 and a fair market value of $120,000 in exchange for 100 percent of the Section 1244 stock of Thompson Corporation. In 1998, he sells the stock for $85,000. Although he has a recognized loss of $75,000, Walter may recognize only $35,000 ordinary loss and the remaining $40,000 loss is long-term capital loss.

If a taxpayer makes additional contributions to capital after acquiring Section 1244 stock causing the basis in the stock to increase, a loss on the stock is treated as allocated partly to Section 1244 stock and partly to stock which is not Section 1244 stock. Code Sec. 1244(d)(1).

Example 11.38. Joe Jamestown purchased Section 1244 stock costing $50,000 in 1992 and made an additional capital contribution in 1996 in the amount of $20,000. In 1998, Joe sells the stock for $28,000. Of the $42,000 loss, five-sevenths ($50,000/$70,000) or $30,000 is ordinary loss and the remaining $12,000 is a capital loss.

TAX PLANNING POINTER

Instead of just making an additional capital contribution of $20,000, Joe should have received additional stock for his $20,000 investment. With the additional investment qualifying as Section 1244 stock, the entire $42,000 loss would be an ordinary loss.

¶ 11,530 GAINS ON SMALL BUSINESS STOCK

Noncorporate investors who are the original holders of qualified small business stock acquired after August 10, 1993, and who hold it for at least five years are eligible to exclude 50 percent of the gain from the sale of the stock from their gross income. The remaining half of the gain would be taxed as long-term capital gain at a maximum rate of 28 percent. Taxpayers subject to the alternative minimum tax, however, would have to include 42 percent of the excluded gain as a tax preference item. Code Sec. 1202.

The exclusion is limited to $10 million of the gain from the sale of the stock by an investor in the same corporation or, if greater, 10 times the adjusted basis of the stock in the corporation that the investor sold during the year.

Other major requirements for the exclusion are:

1. The stock must be issued by a C corporation in exchange for money, property other than stock, or compensation for services rendered to the corporation.

2. The corporation must use at least 80 percent by value of its assets in the active conduct of one or more trades or businesses and can have no more than $50 million in gross assets when it issues the stock.

3. The corporation cannot engage in certain types of businesses, such as businesses that provide personal services (e.g., health, law, or accounting); banking, insurance, financing, leasing, or investing; the extraction or production of natural resources eligible for percentage depletion; farming; and the operation of hotels, motels, and restaurants.

4. Gain from the sale of stock of a DISC (or former DISC), regulated investment company, real estate investment trust, real estate mortgage investment conduit, cooperative, or corporation claiming the possessions tax credit does not qualify for the exclusion.

¶ 11,535 DEALERS IN SECURITIES

Generally, securities held by a dealer are ordinary assets because they are considered to be inventory. The gains or losses from sale of these securities are considered ordinary gains or losses. However, under special circumstances, it is possible for a dealer to classify securities as capital assets and receive capital gain or loss treatment on the sale or exchange.

Gain from the sale or exchange of a security is not considered as a capital gain unless the security was clearly identified in the dealer's records as a security held for investment before the close of the day on which it was acquired. Also, it may not be held by the dealer as primarily for sale to customers in the ordinary course of a trade or business at any time after the day of acquisition. Losses are not considered ordinary if the security was clearly identified in the dealer's records as a security held for investment. Code Sec. 1236(a) and (b).

For purposes of these rules, the term "security" means any share of stock in any corporation, note, bond, debenture, or evidence of indebtedness, or any evidence of an interest in or right to subscribe to or purchase any of the foregoing. "Floor specialists" have until the seventh business day after acquisition to make their identification. A floor specialist is a person who is a member of a national securities exchange, is registered as a specialist with the exchange, and meets the requirements for specialists established by the Securities and Exchange Commission. Code Sec. 1236(c) and (d).

Example 11.39. Wilbur Washburn, a dealer in securities, purchases XYZ Corporation stock on January 12, 1998. On that date, he identifies the stock as assets held for investment. On November 25, 1998, he sells the stock. Any resulting gain or loss is capital gain or loss.

Example 11.40. If Wilbur, in the preceding example, withdrew the stock from the investment account and held it as inventory, then the sale at a gain results in ordinary gain, but the sale at a loss results in a capital loss.

¶ 11,545 SUBDIVIDED REAL ESTATE

Taxpayers who sell developed real estate that has been subdivided can be considered to be dealers and may have to report gain as ordinary income. However, some relief is provided to investors in real estate. Code Sec. 1237. Any lot or parcel which is a part of a noncorporate taxpayer's real property is not considered to be held primarily for sale to customers solely because of subdivision activities. The property may not previously have been held primarily for sale to customers and no substantial improvements may have been made to the lots. Code Sec. 1237(a)(1) and (2).

Substantial means that the improvements have increased the value of a lot by more than 10 percent. Shopping centers, other commercial or residential buildings, and the installation of hard surface roads or utilities such as sewers, water, gas, or electric lines are considered substantial improvements. Surveying, filling, draining, leveling and clearing operations, and the construction of minimum all-weather access roads are not considered substantial improvements.

Reg. § 1.1237-1(c)(3) and (4). The lots also must have been held, except in case of inheritance, for a period of five years.

If the above conditions are met and the taxpayer has not sold more than five lots or parcels from a single tract through the end of the tax year, capital gain treatment results. If more than five lots or parcels are sold or exchanged, gain from any sale or exchange of any lot occurring in or after the taxable year in which the sixth lot or parcel is sold is recognized as ordinary income up to five percent of the selling price. The remaining gain is capital gain. Selling expenses first offset the amount taxed as ordinary income and then offset the capital gain. Code Sec. 1237(b)(1) and (2). Section 1237 does not apply to losses realized upon the sale of subdivided property. Reg. § 1.1237-1(a)(4)(i).

Example 11.41. Jerry Johnson, who meets all requirements of Code Sec. 1237, sells five lots during 1997 at a gain of $20,000. During 1998, he sells the sixth lot (basis $4,000) at a selling price of $15,000 and incurs $500 of selling expense. Jerry recognizes long-term capital gain of $20,000 in 1997. In 1998, he has $250 ordinary income and $10,250 capital gain computed as follows:

Selling price		$15,000
Less: Basis	$4,000	
Selling expenses	500	4,500
Gain on sale of lot		$10,500
5% of selling price	$ 750	
Less: Selling expense	500	
Amount reported as ordinary income		250
Capital gain		$10,250

If the selling expenses had been $750 or more, the total amount of gain would have been capital gain.

TAX PLANNING POINTER ▼

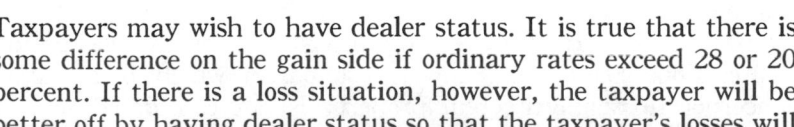

Taxpayers may wish to have dealer status. It is true that there is some difference on the gain side if ordinary rates exceed 28 or 20 percent. If there is a loss situation, however, the taxpayer will be better off by having dealer status so that the taxpayer's losses will be ordinary without limits, instead of capital losses with limits.

Section 1231 Assets and Procedure

¶ 11,601   BACKGROUND

Prior to 1938, business property was included as a capital asset. However, this meant that taxpayers selling such assets at a loss were subject to the capital loss limitations. This resulted in taxpayers' retaining their business property as long as possible rather than selling it. Therefore, in the Revenue Act of 1938, depreciable property used in a trade or business was excluded as a capital asset. Although this meant that there would not be a capital loss limitation, it also meant that gains would be ordinary income rather than the more favorable capital gains. In 1942, Congress responded by allowing taxpayers to treat net gains from the sale of business property as capital gains and net losses as ordinary losses.

¶ 11,615   DEFINITION OF SECTION 1231 ASSETS

Section 1231 assets include depreciable property and land used in a trade or business and held long-term. Code Sec. 1231(b). (Long-term means more than 12 months, although the assets have to be held more than 18 months to obtain the best tax advantage.) Such assets consist mainly of machinery and equipment, business cars and trucks, buildings, and land. They also include a number of items not specifically related to a trade or business:

1. Timber, coal, or domestic iron ore to which Code Sec. 631 applies

2. Livestock including:

    a. Cattle and horses held for draft, breeding, dairy, or sporting purposes for 24 months or more

    b. Livestock (other than cattle, horses, and poultry) held for draft, breeding, dairy, or sporting purposes for 12 months or more

3. Unharvested crops on land used in a trade or business and held long-term if the crop and the land are sold or exchanged at the same time and to the same person

4. The involuntary conversion of business property and capital assets held long-term

    Note. Gains and losses from casualties and thefts are treated separately, as will be seen later.

Certain items are specifically excluded from the definition of Section 1231 assets:

1. Inventory on hand at the close of the tax year and property held primarily for sale to customers in the ordinary course of the trade or business

2. A copyright, a literary, musical, or artistic composition, a letter, or memorandum, or similar property held by a taxpayer whose personal efforts created such property

3. A publication of the United States government received from the government other than by purchase at the price offered for sale to the public

It should be noted that to be Section 1231 property, property must be held more than 12 months (24 months or more for cattle and horses). If a business asset is held short-term, the income from sale will be ordinary. In the case of involuntary conversions resulting from a business casualty or theft, Section 1231 does not apply where recognized losses exceed the recognized gains from such conversions. In this case, the net casualty and theft loss is treated as ordinary loss. This is what is often referred to as the first netting (to be discussed later). Although capital assets that are involuntarily converted were included above as Section 1231 assets, for personal-use assets this provision applies only to condemnation gains since losses on condemnations of personal-use assets are not deductible. Personal-use casualty and theft gains and losses are not part of Section 1231, but are subject to a separate netting.

> *Example 11.42.* Maria Martina is an artist who owns an art gallery where she sells paintings she has painted. The building is a Section 1231 asset as is the furniture in the gallery. The paintings, however, are ordinary assets since they were created by her own personal efforts.

¶ 11,645 COMPUTATIONAL PROCEDURES

In working with Section 1231 transactions, the taxpayer must take into account three steps after the determination of the realized gain or loss. The realized gain or loss, of course, is the difference between the fair market value of the property received and the adjusted basis of the property given up.

Prior to 1997, Form 4797 dealing with Section 1231 transactions was fairly straightforward since it included the recapture of depreciation transactions and the netting of Section 1231 gains and losses. If the netting of Section 1231 gains and losses was positive, the amount was carried forward to the long-term capital gain section of Schedule D, unless there were unrecaptured losses from the previous five years that required ordinary income recognition to that extent. If the netting of the Section 1231 gains and losses was negative, the amount was an ordinary deduction.

Starting in 1997, like Schedule D, Form 4797 is more complicated because of the existence of "mid-term" and long-term Section 1231 gains and losses. The mid-term 1231 gains and losses are shown in a separate column on Form 4797 of the schedule. The taxpayer must take into account the following steps for dealing with Section 1231 transactions after the determination of the realized gain or loss:

Step 1. Determine the amount of the gain to be recaptured as ordinary income. There is no recapture if there is a realized loss. The determination of the amount to be recaptured as ordinary income is more complicated under the new law for Section 1250 property that is sold or exchanged and which has depreciation that has not been recaptured (see later section).

Step 2. Nonpersonal casualty or theft gains and losses from assets held more than 12 months must be netted (sometimes referred to as the first netting). Condemnation gains and losses do not enter into this netting. Casualty and theft gains and losses are the difference between (1) the insurance proceeds, if any, and (2) the adjusted basis of the property for complete destruction of business property (or the lesser of the adjusted basis or the sustained loss for partial destruction of business property).

a. If the casualty or theft gains exceed the casualty or theft losses, then a further netting is made with the Section 1231 gains or losses (see Step 3) for the taxable year. The last line of Form 4684 (the casualty and theft form) requires the taxpayer to carry the positive figure forward to the Form 4797, but to segregate the net gains that go into the 28 percent and 20 percent baskets.

b. If the casualty or theft losses exceed the casualty or theft gains, the casualty or theft gains and losses are separately treated as ordinary. The gains are ordinary income and the losses are deducted for adjusted gross income.

Note. With the special netting for casualty and theft gains and losses, especially for Section 1231 assets, such events will be given the same treatment as if the assets were disposed of through sale or exchange.

Example 11.43. Betty Blue has a casualty gain of $5,000 resulting from an insurance recovery from an accident with her business car, and a fire loss after insurance recovery to her office building in the amount of $6,000. Betty has adjusted gross income of $35,000 before considering these items. After netting the above, Betty has a loss of $1,000, meaning that the casualty and theft gains and losses will be ordinary. The $5,000 is ordinary income and the $6,000 is an ordinary deduction for adjusted gross income. After considering the $5,000 income and the $6,000 deduction, Betty has final adjusted gross income of $34,000. (Examples 11.43 and 11.44 ignore recapture potential.)

Example 11.44. If Betty's casualty gain from the accident of her business car in Example 11.43 was $10,000 instead of $5,000, she has a net gain of $4,000 ($10,000 − $6,000) which means that the $4,000 will be further netted with the Section 1231 gains or losses (in Step 3).

TAX PLANNING POINTER

If the taxpayer has a business casualty loss and a business casualty gain (of approximately the same magnitude) in the same year, the taxpayer may wish to attempt to postpone recognition of the casualty gain under the involuntary conversion nonrecognition rules of Code Sec. 1033. In this way, the taxpayer can receive an ordinary deduction for the casualty loss. Otherwise the casualty loss and casualty gain cancel each other out.

Step 3. Section 1231 gains and losses and any net casualty gains from Step 2 (the first netting) are netted. Gains and losses from condemnations of business property held more than 12 months are included in this netting. For personal-use assets, condemnation gains are included; condemnation losses from personal-use assets are not deductible and thus are not considered. Taxpayers need to segregate the 28 and 20 percent basket items.

a. If the gains exceed the losses, the excess of gains over losses is treated as ordinary income to the extent of Section 1231 net losses for the previous five years that have not been recaptured. Any remaining Section 1231 gain in excess of these prior losses is a long-term capital gain. Code Sec. 1231(a) and (c).

b. If the losses exceed the gains, all the gains and losses are ordinary. The losses are deducted for adjusted gross income.

Example 11.45. Bill Bradley had sales of assets held long-term with results as follows:

Office equipment loss	($20,000)
Office equipment gain (in addition to recapture)	$45,000

Bill has a net gain of $25,000 ($45,000 − $20,000) on his Section 1231 transactions assuming no prior years' Section 1231 net losses. His net gain of $25,000 will be treated as a long-term capital gain and can be used to offset other capital losses.

Example 11.46. Anne Arkady has a Section 1231 net gain of $20,000 during 1998. In the past, the net Section 1231 transactions were as follows:

Year	Net Sec. 1231 Transactions
1997	($ 4,000)
1996	($ 8,000)
1995	$25,000
1994	($ 5,000)
1993	($ 1,000)

In 1995, Anne had $6,000 ordinary income and $19,000 long-term capital gain. In 1998, Anne has ordinary income of $12,000 (recapture of the $8,000 1996 loss plus the $4,000 1997 loss) and long-term capital gain of $8,000 ($20,000 gain less $12,000 losses recaptured). If her 1998 net gain were $10,000 instead of $20,000, all of it would be ordinary and $2,000 of the 1997 net loss would remain to offset Section 1231 net gain in post-1998 years.

Example 11.47. Carl Collins had sales of assets held long-term with results as follows:

Machinery gain (in addition to recapture) $14,000
Factory building loss .... ($35,000)

Carl has a net loss of $21,000 ($35,000 − $14,000) on his Section 1231 transactions and each item will be treated as ordinary. The $35,000 business loss is an ordinary loss *for* adjusted gross income.

Example 11.48. Assume that Betty Brewer had a $10,000 casualty gain, a $6,000 casualty loss, a Section 1231 gain of $9,500 on the sale of business equipment and a Section 1231 loss of $6,500 on the sale of a business truck. With the $4,000 gain ($10,000 casualty gain − $6,000 casualty loss) carried from the first netting, Betty has a net gain in the second netting of $7,000 ($4,000 + $9,500 − $6,500), which will be considered as a long-term capital gain assuming no prior years' Section 1231 net losses.

Example 11.49. If Betty in Example 11.48 had only the Section 1231 loss of $6,500 (and no Section 1231 gain of $9,500) along with the net casualty gain of $4,000 ($10,000 casualty gain − $6,000 casualty loss) carried over from the first netting, she has a net loss of $2,500 on the second netting. All gains and losses are ordinary. Thus, Betty has the following:

Ordinary income from the casualty gain $10,000
Ordinary loss deduction for adjusted gross income........... (6,000)
Ordinary loss deduction for adjusted gross income........... (6,500)
      Net effect on adjusted gross income .... ($2,500)

If Betty had adjusted gross income of $15,000 without the transactions in these examples, she would have a final adjusted gross income of $12,500.

¶ 11,655 PERSONAL CASUALTY AND THEFT GAINS AND LOSSES

Personal-use casualty and theft gains and losses are separately netted and do not enter into the business casualty netting or the Section 1231 netting. If the gains exceed the losses, then all such gains and losses are treated as capital gains and losses. The losses are not subject to the 10 percent adjusted gross income floor. Code Sec. 165. Personal-use casualty and theft losses are determined after the $100 per occurrence reduction. If the personal-use casualty and theft losses exceed the gains, the gains and losses are ordinary. Losses are deducted in full to the extent of gains. Losses in excess of gains are subject to the 10 percent adjusted gross income floor. Code Sec. 165(h).

Example 11.50. Jim Jannings had the following gains and losses:

1. Gain from office equipment held four months............ $ 500
2. Loss from theft of watch held two years (after $100 reduction) .... ($ 600)
3. Gain from insurance recovery on accident of business car owned three years in addition to recapture $6,000
4. Loss from hurricane damage to office building owned five years (after insurance recovery) .... ($8,000)
5. Loss from sale of business equipment held more than one year... ($5,000)

6. Gain from sale of warehouse held two years (in addition to
    recapture) $8,000
7. Net LTCG $6,000
8. Net STCL . . . .   ($2,000)

Jim's adjusted gross income before the above transactions was
$30,000. Ignoring recapture of depreciation (discussed at ¶ 11,701)
and assuming no prior years' Section 1231 net losses, the tax
treatment is as follows: Item (1) is an ordinary gain since the
property was not held more than 12 months. Item (2) is a potential
casualty deduction but does not enter the first netting because it is
a personal theft. Items (3) and (4) are considered in the netting of
casualty gains and losses, giving a net loss of $2,000 and making
the items ordinary. This net loss is a deduction for adjusted gross
income. Items (5) and (6) are considered in the Section 1231
netting, resulting in a net gain of $3,000. This will be treated as a
long-term capital gain and will be combined with the Net LTCG of
$6,000 to give $9,000. The overall net capital gain is $7,000
($9,000 − $2,000), which would be taxed at a maximum rate of 20
percent.

Initial adjusted gross income $30,000
Add: Item (1)   500
Less: Items (3) and (4) . . . .   (2,000)
Add: Items (5), (6), (7), and (8)   7,000
                                                                                                            ─────
    Adjusted gross income $35,500

Since the personal casualty loss of $600 on the stolen watch (Item
(2)) is less than $3,550 (10% of $35,500), there is no casualty or
theft itemized deduction allowable for that item.

Example 11.51. Assume the facts of Example 11.50, except that
Item (2) was a hurricane damage loss to a personal residence of
$5,000 after the $100 per occurrence reduction instead of the theft
loss of the watch. Since the personal casualty loss of $5,000 is
greater than $3,550 (10% of $35,500), there is an itemized deduction of $1,450 ($5,000 − $3,550) from adjusted gross income.

Depreciation Recapture—Section 1245

¶ 11,701   PURPOSE OF RULES

The purpose of Section 1245 is to prevent taxpayers from taking
ordinary depreciation deductions and then receiving long-term capital
gain treatment through Section 1231 at the time of sale of the property. The following example illustrates how the law worked *before* 1962.

Example 11.52. Lloyd Lewis purchased equipment for $10,000 in
January 1956 and took depreciation of $6,250 under the straight-
line method through December 1960. On December 31, 1960, he
sold the equipment with a basis of $3,750 for $9,000 resulting in a
realized and recognized gain of $5,250, which was Section 1231
gain. Assuming that Lloyd had no other Section 1231 transactions,
this gain would be treated as long-term capital gain. Thus, Lloyd
was able to take $6,250 ordinary depreciation deductions while
owning the equipment from 1956-1960 and then obtain long-term

capital gain treatment at the time of sale. Long-term capital gains had significant tax advantages at that time.

Congress believed that this was too much of a benefit to taxpayers; therefore, in 1962, it enacted Section 1245 which significantly changed the effect of Section 1231 for many assets. The idea in Section 1245 is that there should be recapture of depreciation as ordinary income in realized gain situations. There is no recapture of depreciation, however, when losses are realized. Calculation of the recapture is necessary to determine how much of the realized gain is ordinary income and how much is Section 1231 gain.

¶ 11,715   DEFINITION OF SECTION 1245 PROPERTY

Section 1245 property is really a subcategory of depreciable Section 1231 property. Section 1245 property is personal property (in the legal sense—not personal-use property) which is subject to depreciation or amortization. Code Sec. 1245(a)(3). It includes:

1. Property (not including a building or its structural components) if such property is tangible and was used as an integral part of specified business activities

2. Amortizable property such as patents and leaseholds of Section 1245 property

3. Single purpose agricultural or horticultural structures

4. Storage facilities (not including a building or its structural components) used in connection with the distribution of petroleum or any primary product of petroleum

5. Railroad gradings or tunnel bores (as defined in Code Sec. 168(e)(4))

Depreciable property which is expensed under Section 179 is also Section 1245 property. Expenditures to remove architectural and transportation barriers to the handicapped which are deductible under Section 190 are Section 1245 property as are properties subject to accelerated amortization under Section 169 for pollution control facilities, and Section 188 for child care facilities. In addition, Section 1245 provisions apply to nonresidential real property if the recovery of cost is under the statutory percentage method of the accelerated cost recovery system (ACRS) rather than the straight-line method. Such property is technically not Section 1245 property, but it receives Section 1245 treatment on recapture.

Example 11.53. Peter Paulson owns the following assets:

1. Machinery used in his auto repair shop

2. Truck used in his business

3. Furniture in the office of the shop

4. Furniture in his home

5. Oil and inventory items used in his business

Items (1), (2), and (3) are Section 1245 assets. Item (4) consists of capital assets and item (5) consists of inventory or ordinary assets.

¶ 11,725 COMPUTATIONAL PROCEDURES

On the disposition of Section 1245 property, ordinary income is recognized to the extent of the total depreciation taken (including immediate expensing under Code Sec. 179), but not to exceed the recognized gain. Any excess recognized gain over the amount recaptured as ordinary income is treated as Section 1231 gain (in the second netting). In a casualty gain, any excess gain over the amount recaptured as ordinary income is a casualty gain. There is no recapture as ordinary income where there is a recognized loss. All the recognized loss on the sale or disposition of Section 1245 property (a subcategory of Section 1231 property) is treated as a Section 1231 loss.

Example 11.54. Jack Jumper purchased business equipment for $20,000 on January 1, 1994, and took depreciation of $13,752 up to January 1, 1998, when he sold it for $11,248. Jack's adjusted basis is $6,248 and he has a realized and recognized gain of $5,000. He has recapture potential of $13,752, the amount of the depreciation taken, but he will recapture only $5,000 as ordinary income since the amount recaptured as ordinary income does not exceed the recognized gain.

Example 11.55. Assume the facts of Example 11.54, except that the equipment was sold for $21,248 on January 1, 1998. Jack has realized and recognized gain of $15,000 ($21,248 − $6,248), of which $13,752 is recaptured as ordinary income and the remaining $1,248 is Section 1231 gain.

Example 11.56. Assume the same facts as in Example 11.54, except that the equipment was sold for $2,000 on January 1, 1998. There is no recapture when there is a recognized loss, so the $4,248 is a Section 1231 loss.

¶ 11,735 DEPRECIATION METHODS

Prior to 1981, a number of methods of depreciation were available including both accelerated and straight-line methods. Useful lives were estimated and played an important part in depreciation, as did salvage value. For property placed in service after 1980, the accelerated cost recovery system (ACRS) applies and is required for most properties. Under this system, salvage value and useful lives are not important as they were formerly. ACRS was substantially modified by the Tax Reform Act of 1986. Most tangible property placed in service after 1986 must now be depreciated under the Modified Accelerated Cost Recovery System (MACRS). Under MACRS, different types of property are placed in specific categories. See Chapter 5 for further discussion on depreciation.

¶ 11,745 ACRS OR MACRS PROPERTY

The same general rule on Section 1245 recapture that applied to pre-ACRS property applies to ACRS or MACRS property. However, there is one difference. Although there are specific recapture rules under Section 1250 for real property, nonresidential real property purchased under ACRS receives Section 1245 recapture treatment if the accelerated method of cost recovery (depreciation) is used. (See ¶ 11,835.)

¶ 11,755   SUMMARY OF SECTION 1245 RECAPTURE RULES

1. Section 1245 property is a subcategory of depreciable Section 1231 property.

2. All gains or losses on property held short-term are recognized as ordinary income or loss since property held for that time period is not Section 1231 property and Section 1245 property is a sub-category of Section 1231 property.

3. The amount of recapture potential is the *total* depreciation taken after 1961. This will frequently mean that all the recognized gain on Section 1245 property is recognized as ordinary income since the total depreciation taken is usually higher than the recognized gain.

4. There is no recapture when losses are recognized on Section 1245 assets. Such losses are Section 1231 losses.

5. The recapture rules for Section 1245 property acquired before 1981 and under ACRS or MACRS are the same.

6. Although Section 1245 includes depreciable personal property, nonresidential real property can receive Section 1245 recapture treatment if the accelerated method is used under ACRS.

Depreciation Recapture—Section 1250

¶ 11,801   DEFINITION OF SECTION 1250 PROPERTY

Section 1250 property is depreciable real property that is not Section 1245 property. It, like Section 1245 property, is a subcategory of depreciable Section 1231 property. It consists mainly of buildings and their structural components as well as other depreciable real property. It also includes intangible real property such as leaseholds of land or Section 1250 property. Code Sec. 1250(c); Reg. § 1.1250-1(e)(3).

Example 11.57. Charles Cobb owns the following assets:

1. Office building

2. Apartment building containing 10 apartments rented to tenants

3. Personal residence

Items (1) and (2) are Section 1250 assets, but item (3) is a capital asset.

¶ 11,815   PURPOSE OF RULES

The purpose of Section 1250 is to prevent taxpayers from receiving the full benefits of accelerated depreciation and long-term capital gain treatment through Section 1231 at the time of sale of the property. Section 1250 was originally enacted in 1964 but has undergone several changes since that time. Therefore, it is important to keep track of the time periods involved as well as the types of property.

The recapture potential under Section 1250 differs from that under Section 1245 in at least one very important respect. Section 1250 deals with excess depreciation (the excess of accelerated depreciation over straight-line), whereas Section 1245 deals with total depreciation. Thus, the recapture potential under Section 1250 is less severe than that under Section 1245. Under Section 1250, the taxpayer has ordinary income to the extent of the lesser of (1) the gain recognized or (2) additional (excess) depreciation. Any gain not recaptured as ordinary income is Section 1231 gain. Recapture as ordinary income is not applicable to Section 1250 property disposed of at a recognized loss, just as with Section 1245 property; such losses are Section 1231 losses.

Additional depreciation for real property held more than one year is the excess of the amount of depreciation deducted over the amount of depreciation that would have been taken if straight-line depreciation had been used. Code Sec. 1250(a)(1) and (b)(1). The additional (or excess) depreciation has a specified percentage applied to it depending on the time period the property was held and the type of property held. If property is held for less than one year, the entire gain upon sale will be ordinary.

Under the Taxpayer Relief Act of 1997, unrecaptured Sec. 1250 gain is taxed at a rate of 25 percent and is the amount of the long-term capital gain that would be treated as ordinary income if Section 1250(b)(1) included all depreciation taken with an applicable percentage of 100 percent. For property sold after July 28, 1997, only gain from Section 1250 property held for more than 12 months is taken into account. In less complex language, all or a portion of the recognized gain from the sale or exchange of depreciable real property is to be recaptured. This is determined by treating the property as if it were depreciable personal property (i.e., Section 1245 property) and is taxed at a maximum rate of 25 percent. The remaining gain would be Section 1231 gain and would be considered in the Section 1231 netting and ultimately taxed at a maximum rate of 20 percent, assuming that it was not offset by losses in the Section 1231 and capital nettings.

¶ 11,825 NONRESIDENTIAL REAL PROPERTY—PRE-1981 ACQUISITIONS

For property acquired before 1981, taxpayers could use various depreciation methods subject to limitations and were required to estimate useful lives and salvage values. Taxpayers who acquired the property prior to 1981 are required to continue using the old methods as long as that property is held. Basically, the most liberal depreciation methods available for various types of property were as follows:

New nonresidential real property . . . . 150% declining balance
Used nonresidential real property . . . . Straight-line
New residential real property . . . . 200% declining balance
Used residential real property with an estimated
   useful life of at least 20 years . . . . 125% declining balance

For nonresidential real property, the recapture potential is 100 percent of the amount of the excess depreciation taken after December 31, 1969. Code Sec. 1250(a). The amount to be recaptured as ordinary income cannot exceed the recognized gain. If there is excess recognized gain above the amount recaptured as ordinary income as a result of the "excess depreciation" calculation, any unrecaptured depreciation will be taxed at the maximum rate of 25 percent under the Taxpayer Relief Act of 1997. If there is then still any excess recognized gain, it is Section 1231 gain. If straight-line depreciation was used, the 1997 Act requires that there is recapture to the extent of total depreciation taken (taxed at the maximum rate of 25 percent) but not to exceed recognized gain.

> ***Example 11.58.*** Paul Prentice purchased an office building on January 1, 1975, for $400,000 and used the 150 percent declining balance depreciation method for the 22 years he owned the asset. The estimated useful life was 40 years with no salvage. On January 1, 1998, Paul sells the property for $500,000. His depreciation is as follows:

Year(s)	150% Declining Balance	Straight-Line Depreciation	Excess Depreciation
1975	$ 15,000	$ 10,000	$ 5,000
1976-1996	212,465	210,000	2,465
1997	6,470	10,000	(3,530)
	$233,935	$230,000	$ 3,935

Paul has a realized and recognized gain of $333,935 ($500,000 − $166,065 adjusted basis). He has $3,935 (($233,935 − $230,000) × 100%) recaptured as ordinary income, $230,000 is taxed at 25 percent, and the remaining $100,000 is Section 1231 gain.

> ***Example 11.59.*** If Paul in the preceding example had sold the property on January 1, 1998, for $168,000, all of the recognized gain of $1,935 ($168,000 − $166,065) would have been recaptured as ordinary income and there would have been no Section 1231 gain or amount taxed at 25 percent.

> ***Example 11.60.*** If Paul had sold the property on January 1, 1998, for $160,000, he would have had a recognized loss of $6,065 ($160,000 − $166,065), which would have been a Section 1231 loss. The recapture rules would not apply in this situation.

¶ 11,835   NONRESIDENTIAL REAL PROPERTY UNDER ACRS

Under ACRS, nonresidential real property may be depreciated using the prescribed (accelerated) method or the optional straight-line method. The taxpayer may select one of various recovery periods if the optional straight-line method is used. If the taxpayer uses the accelerated method, gain is treated as ordinary income to the extent of *total* depreciation taken. Code Sec. 1245(a). Thus, by using accelerated cost recovery or depreciation, the taxpayer is subject to the more severe recapture rules of Section 1245. With the 1997 Act, even if the optional straight-line depreciation method was used, there is a recapture of total depreciation (but not to exceed recognized gain), which is taxed at a maximum rate of 25 percent.

> *Example 11.61.* Mary Murphy purchased an office building on January 1, 1984, for $150,000. She used the statutory percentage method in computing cost recovery under ACRS. On January 1, 1998, she sold the building for $170,000. She took cost recovery allowances (depreciation) of $142,500, which gives her an adjusted basis of $7,500 and a realized and recognized gain of $162,500. She has $142,500 of ordinary income, and the remaining $20,000 is Section 1231 gain.

Because Mary used the accelerated method rather than the straight-line method, she must recapture as ordinary income to the extent of the *total* depreciation taken rather than the excess depreciation, as would have been the case for real nonresidential property acquired prior to 1981 or for real residential rental property both before 1981 and after 1980 (see ¶ 11,845).

> *Example 11.62.* If Mary in Example 11.61 had used the optional straight-line method over 15 years, she would have had depreciation each year of $10,000 ($150,000 divided by 15) or $140,000 total for the 14 years. In this case, Mary would have no recapture as ordinary income and the total recognized gain of $160,000 ($170,000 selling price less $10,000 adjusted basis ($150,000 − $140,000)) would consist of $140,000 taxed at the maximum rate of 25 percent and the remaining $20,000 would be Section 1231 gain.

¶ 11,841 NONRESIDENTIAL REAL PROPERTY UNDER MACRS

Nonresidential real property acquired after 1986 (and before May 13, 1993) is depreciated under a straight-line method over a 31.5-year period. For nonresidential real property placed in service on or after May 13, 1993, the recovery period is 39 years. Starting in 1997 with the new Act, dispositions of this type of property will result in recapture to the extent of total depreciation taken (and taxed at a maximum rate of 25 percent), but not to exceed recognized gain. Any excess recognized gain after depreciation has been recaptured is Section 1231 gain.

> *Example 11.63.* On December 16, 1998, Jane Judd, a 36 percent bracket taxpayer, sold for $500,000 an office building she had acquired on January 4, 1994, for $390,000. During her time of ownership, she took straight-line depreciation over a 39-year time period, mid-month convention, in the amount of $49,166. She has a realized and recognized gain of $159,166 ($500,000 less adjusted basis of $340,834), of which $49,166 is taxed at the maximum rate of 25 percent, and the remaining $110,000 is Section 1231 gain, which will be netted with other Section 1231 gains and losses. (If this is the only Section 1231 transaction for Jane, it would be taxed at a rate of 20 percent.)

¶ 11,845 RESIDENTIAL REAL PROPERTY—PRE-1981 ACQUISITIONS

As with taxpayers who acquired personal or nonresidential real property prior to 1981, taxpayers who acquired residential rental real property prior to 1981 are required to continue using the old depreciation methods as long as that property is held.

For residential real property, the recapture potential is 100 percent of the amount of the excess depreciation taken after December 31, 1975. The 1970 through 1975 recapture potential percentage is 100 percent minus one percentage point for each full month the property was held over 100 months. Code Sec. 1250(a). In other words, the percentage for the 1970-1975 period is 200 minus the total number of months held. This is the only difference between the recapture rules of nonresidential real property and residential rental housing for property acquired prior to 1981.

Because of this difference, the following steps are necessary for recapture on residential rental housing:

1. Determine the excess depreciation for the period after 1975.

2. Multiply the lesser of the recognized gain or the excess depreciation in (1) by 100 percent.

3. Subtract the post-1975 excess depreciation from the recognized gain to get the "unabsorbed gain."

4. Determine the excess depreciation for the 1970-1975 time period.

5. Multiply the lesser of the unabsorbed gain in (3) or the excess depreciation in (4) by (200 less the total of months held, but not less than zero).

6. Add the amounts obtained from steps (2) and (5). This is the amount recaptured as ordinary income.

7. If there is excess recognized gain above the amount recaptured as ordinary income as a result of the "excess depreciation" calculation, any unrecaptured depreciation is taxed at the maximum rate of 25 percent under the Taxpayer Relief Act of 1997. The amount to be recaptured as ordinary income cannot, of course, exceed the recognized gain. Any excess of recognized gain over the amount recaptured as ordinary income in step (6) and over the amount recaptured subject to the 25 percent rate is Section 1231 gain.

Example 11.64. Assume the same facts as in Example 11.58 at ¶ 11,825, except that the building was residential rental housing and Paul used the 200 percent declining-balance method for the 22 years he owned the asset rather than the 150 percent declining-balance method. His depreciation is as follows:

Year(s)	200% Declining Balance	Straight-Line Depreciation	Excess Depreciation
1975	$ 20,000	$ 10,000	$10,000
1976-1996	250,587	210,000	40,587
1996	6,471	10,000	(3,529)
	$277,058	$230,000	$47,058

If Paul sells the building for $500,000, he has a realized and recognized gain of $377,058. This is the difference between the selling price of $500,000 and the adjusted basis of $122,942 ($400,000 − $277,058). Following the steps outlined above for residential rental housing, the following computations result:

1. The excess depreciation for the period 1976 through 1997 is $37,058 ($257,058 − $220,000).

2. Step (1) is less than the recognized gain, so $37,058 is multiplied by 100 percent.

3. The unabsorbed gain is $340,000 ($377,058 − $37,058).

4. The excess depreciation for 1975 is $10,000 ($20,000 − $10,000).

5. The lesser of (3) or (4) is $10,000, which is multiplied by zero percent (200 less 276 months held, but not less than zero percent) to give $0.

6. The total amount recaptured as ordinary income is $37,058 ($37,058 from Step (2) and $0 from Step (5)).

7. The remaining depreciation taken of $240,000 ($277,058 less $37,058 from Step (6)) is taxed at the maximum rate of 25 percent. The remaining gain of $100,000 is Section 1231 gain.

Example 11.65. Assume the same facts as in Example 11.64, except that the selling price was $150,000 instead of $500,000. This would give a realized and recognized gain of $27,058 ($150,000 − $122,942). The unabsorbed gain in Step (3) is then $0 ($27,058 − $37,058) and it would then be $0 (the lesser of the unabsorbed gain in Step (3) or the excess depreciation in Step (4)) that would be multiplied by zero percent to give $0. Then the amount recaptured as ordinary income is the recognized gain of $27,058 since it is less than the excess depreciation of $37,058 from the 1976-1997 period.

¶ 11,855   RESIDENTIAL REAL PROPERTY UNDER ACRS

The tax treatment of residential real property under ACRS is the same as that for such property acquired prior to 1981 (i.e., the post-1975 period). Gain is recaptured as ordinary income to the extent of 100 percent of excess depreciation, but not to exceed recognized gain. Excess depreciation is the excess of accelerated depreciation over the straight-line method over the relevant time period (15-year period for property placed in service before March 16, 1984). With the 1997 Act, even if the optional straight-line depreciation method was used, there is recapture of total depreciation (but not to exceed realized gain), which is taxed at a minimum rate of 25 percent. Any remaining recognized gain is then Section 1231 gain.

Example 11.66. Assume the same facts as in Example 11.61 at ¶ 11,835, except that Mary purchased an apartment building instead of an office building. Mary still has a realized and recognized gain of $162,500. This is the difference between the selling price of $170,000 and the adjusted basis of the building of $7,500 ($150,000 − $142,500). Since straight-line depreciation would have been $140,000 (14 × $10,000 per year ($150,000/15)), her excess depreciation would be $2,500, which would be recognized as ordinary income. There is $140,000 that is taxed at the maximum rate of 25 percent and the remaining $20,000 is Section 1231 gain. This is less severe than the recapture for nonresidential real property in Example 11.61 at ¶ 11,835.

¶ 11,861   RESIDENTIAL REAL PROPERTY UNDER MACRS

Residential real property acquired after 1986 is depreciated under a straight-line method over a 27.5-year period. With the 1997 Act, even if the optional straight-line depreciation method was used, there is recapture of total depreciation, which is taxed at a maximum rate of 25 percent, but not to exceed recognized gain. Any excess recognized gain after depreciation has been recaptured is Section 1231 gain.

Example 11.67. On December 16, 1998, Jane Judd, a 36 percent bracket taxpayer, sold for $500,000 an apartment building she had acquired on January 4, 1994, for $275,000. During her time of ownership, she took straight-line depreciation over a 27.5-year time period, mid-month convention, in the amount of $49,166. She has a realized and recognized gain of $274,166 ($500,000 less adjusted basis of $225,834), of which $49,166 is taxed at the maximum rate of 25 percent, and the remaining $225,000 is Section 1231 gain, which will be netted with other Section 1231 gains and losses. (If this is the only Section 1231 transaction for Jane, it would be taxed at a rate of 20 percent.)

¶ 11,865   LOW-INCOME HOUSING—PRE-1987 ACQUISITIONS

For periods after 1969, the applicable recapture percentage as ordinary income for low-income housing is 100 percent minus one percentage point for each full month the property was held over 100 months. Code Sec. 1250(a)(1)(B)(iii). (This is 200 − the total number of months held.) This rule applies for sale of federally assisted housing projects and low-income housing depreciated under Code Sec. 167(k). With the 1997 Act, the remaining depreciation taken is recaptured and taxed at a maximum rate of 25 percent, but not to exceed recognized gain. Any excess gain after depreciation has been recaptured is Section 1231 gain.

Example 11.68. On January 1, 1986, Fred Frombly purchased for $2,000,000 an apartment building that qualified as low-income housing. On January 1, 1998, he sold the building for $1,900,000. Accelerated depreciation has been taken in the amount of

$800,000. Straight-line depreciation would have been $500,000. Realized and recognized gain is $700,000 ($1,900,000 – $1,200,000 basis), of which $168,000 is ordinary income (56% (200 – 144 months) × $300,000 ($800,000 – $500,000)), and $532,000 is taxed at a maximum rate of 25 percent.

¶ 11,875   SUMMARY OF SECTION 1250 RECAPTURE RULES

1. Section 1250 property is a sub-category of depreciable Section 1231 property.

2. Section 1250 property is real property, but if accelerated depreciation is used for nonresidential real property under ACRS, the recapture rules of Section 1245 apply.

3. All gains or losses on property held one year or less are recognized as ordinary income or loss since property so held is not Section 1231 property and Section 1250 property is a subcategory of Section 1231 property.

4. The amount of recapture potential as ordinary income is based on excess depreciation in Section 1250 rather than total depreciation as in Section 1245.

5. There is no recapture when losses are recognized on Section 1250 assets. Such losses are Section 1231 losses.

6. There are differences between types of real property—nonresidential, residential rental, and low-income housing.

7. There are differences in the recapture rules for property acquired before 1981, after 1980 but before 1987, and after 1986.

8. The Taxpayer Relief Act of 1997 requires any unrecaptured depreciation to be taxed at a maximum rate of 25 percent, although total recaptured depreciation is not to exceed recognized gain.

KEYSTONE PROBLEM

An asset was purchased on January 1, 1975, for $500,000. Depreciation taken on the asset up to the time of sale on January 1, 1987, was $480,000. The selling price was $300,000. Straight-line depreciation would have been $360,000. Depreciation taken during 1975 was $50,000.

1. How is the recognized gain treated for tax purposes for the following assets?

   a. Business machine

   b. Factory building

   c. Apartment building

2. How is the recognized gain treated if the acquisition date is January 1, 1986, the asset is depreciated under the same assumptions, and it is disposed of 12 years later on January 1, 1998?

   a. Factory building

   b. Apartment building

Recapture Rules in Other Events

There are special rules with respect to the recapture rules for different types of events.

¶ 11,901   GIFTS AND INHERITANCES

Gifts do not trigger recapture to the donor, but the recapture potential carries over to the donee. Code Secs. 1245(b)(1) and 1250(d)(1); Reg. § § 1.1245-4(a) and 1.1250-3(a). Thus, when the donee disposes of the property, the donee must take into account the donor's depreciation deductions that are subject to recapture in addition to his or her own depreciation if it is depreciable property to the donee. If it is not depreciable property to the donee (e.g., personal-use property), the recapture potential from the donor still carries over.

Example 11.69. Clara Cranberry gives a gift of Section 1245 property to her son David. The adjusted basis of the property at the time of the gift is $5,000 and the amount of recapture potential is $6,000. David takes $2,000 depreciation on the property before he sells it for $12,000. There is no recapture for Clara, the donor. The gain realized and recognized by David is $9,000 ($12,000 less $3,000 basis), of which $8,000 is recaptured as ordinary income ($6,000 recapture from Clara and $2,000 recapture from the time that David owned it). The remaining $1,000 is Section 1231 gain.

When property is transferred at death, both the decedent and the heir escape recapture. Code Secs. 1245(b)(2) and 1250(d)(2).

¶ 11,915   LIKE-KIND EXCHANGES AND INVOLUNTARY CONVERSIONS

Generally, a like-kind exchange does not result in income recognition under Section 1031. However, gain may be recognized if boot is received. Such gain is ordinary income if subject to recapture under Sections 1245 and 1250 and the 25 percent rate recapture under the 1997 Act.

Example 11.70. Herbert Hughes has a machine (Section 1245 property) with an adjusted basis of $6,000 (fair market value of $10,000), originally costing $15,000 when purchased in 1991. In 1997, he exchanges it for another machine with a fair market value of $8,000 and receives cash of $2,000. Herbert's realized gain is $4,000 (amount realized of $10,000 ($8,000 + $2,000) less basis of $6,000). The recapture potential is $9,000, to the extent of the total depreciation taken, but since the recognized gain is $2,000 (to the extent of boot received), only $2,000 is recognized and it will be ordinary income. The remaining $7,000 recapture potential carries over to the new machine.

Example 11.71. If Herbert in Example 11.70 had received a machine with a fair market value of $10,000 and no cash, he would still have a realized gain of $4,000, but he would have no recognition of gain because no boot was received. The total $9,000 recapture potential carries over to the new machine.

In the case of involuntary conversions, the taxpayer has an election under Code Sec. 1033 to recognize gain only to the extent that the proceeds exceed the cost of the replacement property. The recognized gain is subject to ordinary income recapture and the 25 percent rate recapture under the 1997 Act. Code Secs. 1245(b)(4) and 1250(d)(4).

¶ 11,925 CHARITABLE CONTRIBUTIONS

If charitable contributions of Section 1245 or Section 1250 property are made, the contribution deduction is reduced by the amount of income recaptured as ordinary income if the property had been sold. Code Sec. 170(e)(1)(A).

Example 11.72. In 1998, Mark Matches donated a small apartment building (acquired in 1987) to a qualified charity when the adjusted basis was $80,000 and the fair market value was $150,000. Mark had taken depreciation deductions in excess of straight line of $30,000. His charitable contribution deduction is $120,000 ($150,000 less the $30,000 recapture potential as ordinary income) subject to the limitations on charitable deductions for individuals in any given year.

¶ 11,935 INSTALLMENT SALES

For installment sales of depreciated property, the full amount of any depreciation recapture as ordinary income is to be reported in the year of sale even if no payments are received in that year. Code Sec. 453(i). The remaining gain, if any, is Section 1231 gain.

Example 11.73. In February 1998, Helen Humphrey sells equipment used in her business for $40,000 to be paid in five annual installments of $8,000 plus interest beginning in 1999. The equipment was acquired in 1993 for $30,000 and its adjusted basis was $12,000 at the time of the sale. The realized gain is $28,000 ($40,000 − $12,000) and a total of $18,000 is to be recaptured as ordinary income (i.e., the total depreciation taken) in 1998. The basis is increased by the amount recaptured to $30,000, and the remaining gross profit is then $10,000 resulting in a 25 percent gross profit rate. Of each annual payment of $8,000, $2,000 (25 percent of $8,000) is recognized as Section 1231 gain.

Comprehensive Example. Alan B. Arrow, single, age 40, had the following sales and casualty and theft items during 1998:

1. On January 1, he sold for $11,000 business equipment with an adjusted basis of $4,000. Alan had paid $10,000

for the equipment on January 1, 1994, and had taken $6,000 depreciation.

2. On January 1, he sold for $325,000 an apartment building with an adjusted basis of $175,000. He had paid $275,000 for the building on January 1, 1988, and had taken $100,000 straight-line depreciation.

3. On January 1, he sold for $3,000 a business car with an adjusted basis of $5,000 (cost $12,000 and depreciation taken of $7,000), and acquired on January 1, 1994.

4. Alan's Rolex watch that cost $4,000 in 1987 was stolen in July. The insurance company paid him $4,500.

5. A hurricane damaged his personal residence (owned three years) in Florida in the amount of $8,000 over his insurance coverage and the $100 per occurrence reduction.

6. A fire damaged Alan's warehouse (owned two years) in the amount of $10,000 above his insurance coverage.

(Assume that there are no prior years' Section 1231 net losses to recapture.)

Alan's adjusted gross income before considering the above items was $30,000. Item (1) results in a realized gain of $7,000 ($11,000 − $4,000) of which $6,000 is recaptured as ordinary income to the extent of total depreciation taken and the remaining $1,000 is Section 1231 gain. Item (2) results in a realized gain of $150,000 ($325,000 − $175,000) of which $100,000 is recaptured at the top rate of 25 percent and the remaining $50,000 is Section 1231 gain. Item (3) results in a Section 1231 loss of $2,000 ($3,000 − $5,000). Item (4) is a personal theft gain of $500, Item (5) is a personal casualty loss of $8,000, and Item (6) is a business casualty loss of $10,000. The personal casualty and theft netting of Items (4) and (5) is a loss of $7,500, which means that $500 is reported as ordinary income, $500 is an itemized deduction and the $7,500 is deducted as an itemized deduction only to the extent it exceeds 10 percent of adjusted gross income. The first netting of the business casualty and theft gains and losses is a loss of $10,000 (Item (6)) which means that the item will be ordinary.

There is a total of $106,000 ($6,000 + $100,000) depreciation recaptured. The second netting of Section 1231 gains and losses yields a $49,000 gain ($1,000 gain + $50,000 gain − $2,000 loss). This will be treated as a long-term capital gain and will be taxed at a maximum rate of 20 percent.

Alan's income would be computed as follows:

Initial adjusted gross income	$30,000
Ordinary income recapture	106,000
Theft gain	500
Casualty loss on warehouse	(10,000)
Long-term capital gain	49,000
Adjusted gross income	$175,500

Alan gets an itemized deduction of $500 for the personal casualty loss ($500 + $0 ($7,500 − 10% of $175,500)). The $100,000 recaptured depreciation in item (2) is taxed at a maximum rate of 25 percent.

TAX BLUNDERS

1. Homer Holmes made a loan of $100,000 to his supplier, the Harris Company, because he was a friend of the major shareholder, George Harris, and because he wanted his supply of reasonably priced inventory to continue. Harris Company goes bankrupt and is unable to repay the loan. Because he was not in the business of making loans, Homer thought he was entitled only to a nonbusiness bad debt deduction, which would be treated as a short-term capital loss, and he treated it as such on his tax return. However, Homer could probably argue successfully that his loan was a business loan since it was made in order to assure a supply of inventory for his business.

2. Bruce Bradley, a 39.6 percent marginal bracket taxpayer, has a casualty loss on one of his office buildings held more than one year in the amount of $50,000 during 1998. He also incurred during 1998 a casualty gain on another office building held more than one year in the amount of $55,000 (and $140,000 depreciation recaptured at 25 percent). He replaced the latter building with another similar office building within a few months at a cost exceeding his proceeds from the insurance on his old building. Bruce has a casualty gain of $5,000 which will be carried over to the second netting. Assuming he has no Section 1231 gains and losses and no capital gains or losses, the $5,000 will result in $5,000 long-term capital gain treatment. Bruce will have taxes on that in the amount of $1,000 (20 percent × $5,000) and 25 percent of $140,000. Bruce should have elected to defer the casualty gain under the Section 1033 rules for nonrecognition of gain in an involuntary conversion. In that way, he could have taken a $50,000 ordinary loss deduction giving him a tax benefit or reduction of $19,800 (39.6 percent of $50,000).

SUMMARY OF CHAPTER 11

✓ The Code defines a capital asset by listing the assets that are not capital assets.

✓ There are now short-term, mid-term, and long-term capital gains and losses that have to be considered.

✓ There are special rules for holding periods where property is acquired through involuntary conversions, exchanges, gifts, or from decedents.

✓ Working with capital gains and losses involves following a sequence of steps.

✓ Section 1231 assets include depreciable property and land used in a trade or business and held long-term, as well as several other items not specifically related to a trade or business.

✓ Working with Section 1231 transactions involves a sequence of steps, including the calculation of the amount of income to be recaptured as ordinary income, which depends on the type of property and the time period in which the property is acquired.

✓ There are special recapture rules for the disposal of property received through gifts, inheritances, and involuntary conversions, and for disposal through charitable contributions and installment sales.

CHAPTER 11 QUESTIONS

1. How are capital assets defined?

2. When a sole proprietorship is sold, how is it treated for tax purposes?

3. What determines whether or not a transfer of a patent is considered to be a sale or exchange of a capital asset resulting in long-term capital gain treatment?

4. What determines whether or not a transfer of a franchise is to be considered as a sale or exchange of a capital asset?

5. How are lease cancellation payments treated by a lessee and a lessor?

6. When does the holding period begin for property acquired through the following transactions?
   a. Nontaxable exchange
   b. Involuntary conversion

7. How is the holding period determined for property acquired by a gift and from a decedent?

8. What potential advantage is there for a net overall capital gain situation?

9. How are net overall capital losses treated?

10. What happens to capital losses in excess of the allowed current year deduction?

11. How does the capital gain and loss treatment of corporate taxpayers differ from that of individuals?

12. How are nonbusiness bad debts treated?

13. What is the tax treatment of worthless securities?

14. What is Section 1244 stock? What are its advantages?

15. What special tax treatment is available for subdividers of real estate?

16. Why did Congress enact Section 1231?

17. What is included in Section 1231 property?

18. What is not included in Section 1231 property?

19. Describe what is meant by the "first netting."

20. Describe what is meant by the "second netting."

21. What was the purpose of enacting Section 1245?

22. What is Section 1245 property? What is the Section 1245 recapture rule?

23. What is Section 1250 property?

24. When is recapture on nonresidential real property governed by Section 1245 rules and when is it governed by Section 1250 recapture rules?

25. Describe the recapture provisions for both the donor and the donee when Section 1245 and Section 1250 property are given away.

26. What are the recapture rules in the event of death of the Section 1245 or Section 1250 property owner?

27. Is there recapture of depreciation when like-kind exchanges of Section 1245 and Section 1250 property occur? Explain.

28. What are the recapture rules when an involuntary conversion occurs with nonrecognition of some of the gain?

29. What effect does giving away property with recapture potential have upon a charitable contribution?

CHAPTER 11 PROBLEMS

Note. In the problems below, assume there are no prior years' Section 1231 losses to recapture unless stated otherwise. Also, assume that the "long-term" transactions are more than 18 months unless stated otherwise.

30. Which of the following is a capital asset? Explain.

    a. Gold ring received as a gift

    b. Personal automobile

    c. Accounts receivable obtained in the ordinary course of business

    d. Shares of stock in the Riviera Corporation

    e. Building owned and used by the Riviera Corporation

    f. Business cars and trucks owned and used by the Riviera Corporation

    g. Home in Florida used for only four months during the winter

    h. Copyright on a book written and owned by the author

31. Byron Bright, an inventor, sells the patent rights on his latest invention to Wilson Corporation. Wilson intends to manufacture and sell Byron's invention. Byron will receive $50 per unit Wilson sells plus a lump-sum payment of $500,000. What is the tax treatment of each type of payment for Byron? If Wilson Corporation is limited to producing and selling Byron's invention in the western section of the United States, what is the tax treatment of each type of payment?

32. Cathy Crafts grants Dan Deputy a franchise to sell cards and gifts. Dan pays Cathy a fee of $1,000 per month plus a percentage of the monthly profits. Dan must purchase his supplies from Cathy and Cathy retains the right to terminate Dan's franchise. What are the tax consequences of this arrangement to Cathy and Dan?

33. Jim Junction purchased a truck for business on November 17, 1997, for $4,000. On July 20, 1998, he exchanged the truck

for another truck in a like-kind exchange. The new truck had a fair market value of $4,200. When does the holding period on the new truck begin and what is its basis?

34. Boyd Bayer acquired 100 shares of Evans Corporation stock for $3,000 on January 6, 1997. He gave the stock to his daughter Susan on January 7, 1998, when the fair market value was $2,400. On March 18, 1998, Susan sold the stock for $1,500. What is the nature and the amount of the gain or loss for Susan in 1998?

35. Alice Almond purchased Smith Corporation stock on February 19, 1997, and on November 14, 1997, she gave the stock to her son Dennis. She paid $10,000 for the stock and the value at the time of the gift was $12,000. On August 21, 1998, Dennis sold the stock for $13,000.

    a. Does Dennis have short-term or long-term gain or loss and how much?

    b. If the value of the stock at the time of the gift was $9,500, and Dennis sold it on April 15, 1997, for $8,000, does he have short-term or long-term gain or loss and how much?

36. Ed Elsewhere has the following capital gains and losses during 1998 as a result of sales of shares of stock. What is the net effect of the gains and losses on Ed's tax return in each of the following cases? Assume that the long-term transactions are more than 18 months.

    a. STCG $1,500
        STCL .... ($2,250)
        LTCG $5,500
        LTCL .... ($2,500)

    b. STCG $6,000
        STCL .... ($4,500)
        LTCG .... $ 0
        LTCL .... ($ 750)

    c. LTCL .... ($4,000)
        LTCG $8,500
        STCL .... ($2,250)
        STCG $3,000

    d. LTCG .... $ 750
        LTCL .... ($2,250)
        STCG .... $ 900
        STCL .... ($ 800)

    e. LTCG $3,500
        LTCL .... ($3,000)
        STCG $2,000
        STCL .... ($6,500)

    f. LTCL .... ($4,250)
        LTCG .... $ 250
        STCL .... ($2,500)
        STCG .... $ 500

37. Gordon Grumps is married and files separately. During 1998, he had the following capital gains and losses:

STCL	($ 1,000)
STCG	1,900
STCL carryover from 1997	(200)
LTCG	600
LTCL	(10,000)

Gordon's taxable income is $6,000. What is Gordon's capital loss deduction for 1998 and his carryover?

38. Bert Baker had $20,000 salary during 1998 and had the following capital gains and losses:

STCL carryover from 1997	($4,000)
STCL	(2,000)
STCG	1,000
LTCL carryover from 1997	(5,000)
LTCL	(3,000)
LTCG	6,000

How should Bert treat the above on his 1998 tax return?

39. Cannon Corporation had a net long-term capital gain of $5,000 and a net short-term capital loss of $7,500 in 1998. What are the tax consequences to Cannon as a result of its capital transactions?

40. On April 20, 1998, Al Aikens, a calendar year taxpayer, purchased stock in Webster Corp. for $15,000. What is the nature of Al's loss if Webster Corp. files for bankruptcy and Al's stock becomes worthless on the following dates?

     a.   December 16, 1998

     b.   January 20, 1999

     c.   September 16, 1999

41. Compute the taxpayer's losses for the following situations.

     a.   Arthur Angler, single, acquires 500 shares of Section 1244 stock in 1995 for $100,000 and sells all of it for $40,000 in 1998. How is the loss treated by Arthur?

     b.   Assume in the preceding part that Arthur made an additional capital contribution of $50,000 in 1996 and then sold all of the stock for $90,000 in 1998. How is the loss treated by Arthur?

42. Shirley Swift transferred property with an adjusted basis of $24,000 and a fair market value of $18,000 to Alex Corporation in exchange for 100 shares of its Section 1244 stock. Three years later, in 1998, Shirley sold 50 shares of the stock for $7,200. What is the nature and the amount of gain or loss for Shirley?

43. Terry Thompson, who meets all the requirements of Section 1237, sells five lots during 1997 at a gain of $30,000. During 1998, he sells the sixth lot (basis $5,000) at a selling price of $20,000 and incurs $300 in selling expenses. What is the nature of Terry's 1998 income from this transaction?

44. Which of the following are Section 1231 assets? Explain. Assume all the items have been held long-term.

a. Machinery used in the business

b. Personal home

c. Factory building

d. Land held as an investment

e. Land used in a business

f. Shares of stock in Jones Corporation

g. Inventory

h. Musical composition held by the composer

45. Andrew Graham had the following recognized gains and losses during 1998:

Personal use casualty loss (watch owned 2 years) .... ($ 400)
Section 1231 gain..................................... $ 500
Section 1231 loss .... ($ 750)
Net LTCG $3,000
Net STCL.. ($2,000)

What are the net tax consequences of these gains and losses to Andrew?

Andrew's adjusted gross income is $40,000 without considering the above items.

46. Barbara Bliss had the following recognized gains and losses during 1998:

Casualty items:
   Business casualty gain (property held 5 months).......... $ 100
   Business casualty loss (property held 19 months) .... ($ 200)
   Business casualty gain (property held 21 months).......... $ 500
Section 1231 gain..................................... $ 750
Section 1231 loss .... ($ 600)
LTCL .... ($4,000)
STCL .... ($ 250)

What are the net tax consequences of these gains and losses for Barbara?

Barbara's adjusted gross income is $30,000 without considering the above items.

47. Steven Stronghold had a Section 1231 net gain of $25,000 in 1998. His previous net Section 1231 items were $12,000 in 1991, ($8,000) in 1992, ($6,000) in 1993, ($3,000) in 1994, ($1,000) in 1995, ($4,000) in 1996, and ($1,000) in 1997.

a. How is Steven's $25,000 net Section 1231 gain treated in 1998?

b. If Steven's 1998 net Section 1231 gain was $12,000 instead of $25,000, how would it be treated?

48. Jackie Jaguar had a fur coat that cost $12,000 when purchased in 1988 and that was worth $14,000 when it was stolen on April 15, 1998. Her television, which cost $800 in 1995 and was worth $600, was also stolen. She received $10,000 from her insurance company for the theft of the two items. On July 20, 1998, her summer cottage with a basis of

$50,000 and a fair market value of $62,000 was completely destroyed by a tornado. The insurance proceeds were $65,000. What gain or loss would Jackie recognize and how is it treated? Jackie's adjusted gross income for 1998 is $25,000.

49. Indicate whether the following items are Section 1245 or Section 1250 property or, if neither, indicate what type of property they are considered to be (e.g., capital asset, Section 1231 asset). (Remember that Section 1245 and Section 1250 properties are sub-categories of depreciable Section 1231 property.) Assume all the items have been held long-term.

   a. Equipment used in the business

   b. Personal automobile

   c. Truck used in the business

   d. Escalator used in the business

   e. Inventory

   f. Residential rental housing

   g. Nonresidential real property depreciated under the straight-line method

   h. Leasehold of Section 1245 property

50. In 1998, Dan Dunne sold a business machine for $75,000. He had purchased the machine in 1994 for $90,000, had depreciated it on the straight-line basis using a life of five years, and had taken a total of $63,000 depreciation.

   a. How should Dan treat the recognized gain or loss on the sale?

   b. How should Dan treat the gain or loss if he had used an accelerated depreciation method with a total of $71,100 taken in the four years?

51. In 1998, Emma Evans sold a piece of equipment from her business for $80,000. The equipment was purchased in 1994 for $72,000, had a useful life of five years, and was depreciated on a straight-line basis. A total of $50,400 depreciation was taken.

   a. How will the gain or loss on the sale be treated?

   b. How would Emma have treated the gain or loss if she had sold the property for $15,000?

52. Harold Hunch purchased Section 1250 commercial property on January 1, 1980, and sold it on January 1, 1998, at a gain of $250,000. Depreciation taken was $500,000; straight-line depreciation would have been $300,000.

   a. How should Harold treat the gain or loss?

   b. What would your answer have been if the property had been purchased in 1981 and was depreciated under the ACRS prescribed method?

c. What would your answer have been in (a) if the property had been residential rental housing?

d. What would your answer have been if the property was residential rental housing, was purchased in 1981, and was depreciated under the ACRS prescribed method?

53. Determine the taxpayer's income and the treatment of the income.

a. On January 1, 1975, Glen Gopher purchased an office building for his business for $1,000,000. He sold the building on January 1, 1998, for $1,200,000. Glen used the accelerated depreciation method over a 40-year life and his total depreciation deductions amounted to $775,000, of which $37,500 was depreciation taken before January 1, 1976. Straight-line depreciation would have been $25,000 a year. How much income does Glen recognize and how will it be treated?

b. Assume the facts of (a), except that the building was an apartment building rented to tenants. How much income does Glen recognize and how will it be treated?

54. On January 1, 1985, Ivan Innkeeper purchased an office building for $900,000. He used the ACRS statutory (accelerated) depreciation method and took $720,000 depreciation before he sold the building for $950,000 on January 1, 1998. Straight-line depreciation would have been $650,000.

a. How much income does Ivan recognize and how will it be treated?

b. What would your answer be to (a) if he had used the optional straight-line method?

55. Assume the facts of the preceding problem except that the building was an apartment building.

a. How much income does Ivan recognize and how will it be treated?

b. What would your answer be to (a) if he had used the optional straight-line method?

56. Carl Clay purchased an apartment building on January 1, 1984, for $600,000. He used the statutory (accelerated) percentage method in computing $564,000 cost recovery under ACRS. Straight-line depreciation would have been $560,000. On January 1, 1998, he sold the apartment building for $450,000.

a. What are the tax consequences to Carl as a result of the sale?

b. What would your answer to (a) be if the building had been an office building?

57. Irene Irwin gave her son James a Section 1245 machine. The machine has an adjusted basis of $2,500 and Irene had taken $1,000 in depreciation. James used the machine for 15 months and took $500 in depreciation before selling the ma-

chine for $3,000. What is the amount of depreciation Irene must recapture as ordinary income? What is James's gain on the sale and how is it treated?

58. Karen Klaus has a machine (Section 1245 property) with an adjusted basis of $4,000 and a fair market value of $16,000. The machine originally cost $17,000 when purchased in 1994. In 1998, she exchanged it for another machine with a fair market value of $12,000 and received $4,000 cash.

    a. What are the tax consequences of the exchange for Karen?

    b. What would the tax consequences be if the new machine had a fair market value of $16,000 and no cash was received?

59. Larry Lyons donated a small office building to a qualified charity when the adjusted basis was $90,000 and the fair market value was $160,000. Larry had taken depreciation deductions in excess of straight-line depreciation of $50,000. What is Larry's charitable contribution before application of limits?

60. In March 1998, Mary Marionette sold equipment used in her business for $80,000, to be paid in eight annual installments of $10,000 plus interest beginning in 1999. The equipment was acquired in 1991 for $48,000, and its adjusted basis was $20,000 at the time of the sale. How is the income from this sale recognized and how will it be treated?

61. Ivan Investor sold a parcel of land during 1998 realizing a $50,000 gain. Ivan has used this parcel for a parking lot during the 120 months that he has owned the land. The amount and tax classification of the gain recognized by Ivan on this sale is:

    a. Ordinary income of $50,000

    b. A Section 1231 gain of $50,000

    c. A Section 1245 ordinary income item of $50,000

    d. A Section 1250 ordinary income item of $50,000

62. Mary Martin owns a custom curtain/drapery business. In 1998 she purchased three new sewing machines and in a separate transaction, sold her three old machines for $6,000. She had bought the old machines for $5,000 and had properly claimed depreciation of $3,000. What is the amount and character of Mary's gain?

    a. $0 ordinary gain and $4,000 Section 1231 gain

    b. $2,000 ordinary gain and $4,000 Section 1231 gain

    c. $3,000 ordinary gain and $1,000 Section 1231 gain

    d. $4,000 ordinary gain and $0 Section 1231 gain

63. In 1998, Gordon Grant sold an office building for $180,000. He had purchased the building in 1986 for $150,000 and had properly deducted $100,000 of depreciation, which included

$15,000 in additional (excess) depreciation. How will Gordon treat the gain on the sale of this office building?

a. $15,000 ordinary income; $115,000 Section 1231 gain

b. $30,000 ordinary income; $100,000 Section 1231 gain

c. $100,000 ordinary income; $30,000 Section 1231 gain

d. $0 ordinary income; $130,000 Section 1231 gain

64. Which of the following property is not Section 1231 property?

a.   Unharvested crop on land held for more than one year and used for farming

b.   Dairy cattle held more than two years

c.   Musical instruments in a music store

d.   Music store building

65. Section 1250 recapture provisions apply to all of the following except:

a.   Residential real property

b.   Government-financed housing

c.   Low-income housing

d.   ACRS nonresidential real property depreciated under the statutory (accelerated) method

66. *Comprehensive Problem.* Terry Trooper, a single taxpayer, had the following transactions during 1998:

a.   Sold 60 shares of Troy Corporation common stock on March 18, 1998, for $660. The stock was purchased on January 27, 1998, for $7 per share.

b.   Sold family gemstones held for three years for $10,000. The gemstones had a cost and basis of $7,800.

c.   Three-year note from his brother became worthless. The note was $750.

d.   Stock in Tyler Corporation became worthless on December 23, 1998, when the corporation filed for bankruptcy. The stock was purchased for $250 on June 26, 1998.

e.   Received $200 from a renter to cancel a lease held on rental property.

What is Terry's taxable income if his only other income was salary, net rental income and interest totalling $40,000? He has itemized deductions of $5,000 and no dependents.

67. *Comprehensive Problem.* Bill and Alice Savage, husband and wife and both age 42, have the following transactions during 1998:

a.   They sold their old residence on January 26, 1998, for $85,000. The basis of their old residence, purchased in 1988, was $40,000. The selling expenses were $4,000. On May 15, 1998, they purchased and moved into another residence costing $72,000.

b. On April 24, 1998, they sold for $8,000 stock that Alice had received as a gift from her mother, who had purchased the stock for $10,000 in 1993. Her mother gave Alice the stock on November 13, 1997, when the fair market value was $9,400.

c. On May 20, 1998, Bill sold for $21,000 stock inherited from his father. His father died on June 14, 1997, when the fair market value of the stock was $9,000. Bill's father paid $7,000 for the stock in 1992.

d. On August 11, 1998, they sold a personal automobile for $4,000; basis of the automobile was $10,000 and it was purchased in 1995.

e. They had a carryover and other stock transactions as follows:

LTCL carryover from 1997 .... ($7,000)
STCG $2,000
LTCG $3,500

Bill had salary of $40,000 and Alice had salary of $28,000. They have no children. They paid state income taxes of $2,600, sales tax of $400, federal income taxes of $15,000, and other property taxes of $1,800. In addition, they contributed $2,400 to their church and paid $4,000 interest on their home mortgage.

Compute Bill and Alice's taxable income for 1998.

68. *Comprehensive Problem.* Kate King had the following transactions or involuntary conversions during 1998:

a. Her uninsured diamond ring that cost $3,100 in 1992 was stolen.

b. Her vacation home purchased in 1992 for $70,000 was destroyed by a tornado. Insurance recovery was $85,000.

c. Machinery purchased in 1994 for $12,000 with a basis at the time of sale of $3,000 was sold on January 1 for $13,000.

d. A business car purchased in 1994 for $10,000 with a basis of $3,700 at the time of sale was sold on January 1 for $1,700.

e. Land owned for six years was condemned by the state. The award was $100,000 and the land had cost $65,000. No replacement of the property was made.

f. 100 shares of Atlas Corporation stock were sold for $8,000 on July 17. The stock was originally purchased in 1988 for $3,000.

g. 200 shares of Brown Corporation stock were sold for $4,000 on April 22, 1998. The stock was originally purchased on December 26, 1997, for $10,000.

Kate, single and age 34 with no dependents, has adjusted gross income of $44,000 and itemized deductions of $7,000 without considering the above items. What is her taxable income for 1998?

69. *Comprehensive Problem.* Mark Mullins had the following transactions or involuntary conversions during 1998:

    a. His diamond gemstones costing $4,000 in 1992 were stolen. Insurance recovery was $5,000.

    b. His office building owned for four years was damaged by fire. The loss after insurance recovery was $12,000.

    c. Equipment purchased in 1994 for $18,000 with a basis at the time of sale of $6,000 was sold for $11,000 on January 2, 1998.

    d. An apartment building purchased on January 1, 1986, for $300,000 was sold for $124,000 on January 2, 1998. Mark took accelerated depreciation of $236,000. Straight-line depreciation would have been $200,000.

    e. Land used in his business for four years was condemned by the state. The award was $60,000. Cost of the land was $74,000. No replacement of the property was made.

    f. 200 shares of Carter Corporation stock were sold for $19,000 on August 21, 1998. The stock was originally purchased in 1993 for $15,000.

    g. 100 shares of Dalton Corporation stock were sold for $8,000 on July 21, 1998. The stock was originally purchased on February 6, 1998, for $2,000.

    Mark, single and age 42 with no dependents, has adjusted gross income of $56,000 and itemized deductions of $8,000 without considering the above items. What is Mark's taxable income for 1998?

70. *Research Problem.* In 1997, Allen Appleton sells his business to David, but he sells the claim against Fred that arose during the course of his business to George, who is not in a business. The claim becomes worthless in George's hands in 1998. Can George take a business loss for the bad debt since it originally arose in the course of a business?

71. *Research Problem.* Harlan Huston had a net Section 1231 gain in 1998 of $40,000. His net Section 1231 gains and losses were as follows:

Year	Net Sec. 1231 Gains/(Losses)
1997	($15,000)
1996	($ 6,000)
1995	($16,000)
1994	$ 5,000
1993	($20,000)

How is the $40,000 net Section 1231 gain treated by Harlan in 1998?

Chapter 12

Tax Accounting

Learning Objectives

After completing Chapter 12, you should be able to:

1. List what are permissible tax years.
2. Explain the requirements for changing a tax year.
3. Identify the available accounting methods.
4. Understand the rules for accounting method changes.
5. Account for the capitalization of inventory costs.
6. Describe long-term contract reporting.
7. Define the installment method of accounting.

OVERVIEW OF CHAPTER

The first 11 chapters are presented primarily from the individual taxpayer's point of view (including self-employed taxpayers). This chapter provides a general discussion of the previous material as it applies to other entities and provides a discussion of accounting periods and accounting methods as they apply to all entities. Discussions of specific provisions as they apply to other entities (e.g., corporations, partnerships, etc.) are contained in subsequent chapters.

The term "financial accounting" refers to the reporting of the financial data of an enterprise through financial statements prepared in accordance with generally accepted accounting principles.

Income tax accounting, hereafter referred to as "tax accounting," is concerned with the reporting of financial data to satisfy the requirements of the Internal Revenue Code, the Regulations which interpret the Code, rulings by the IRS which further interpret the Code and Regulations, and the decisions of the courts on litigated issues.

Tax accounting is statutory. It is concerned with the determination of taxable income as the base to which tax rates are applied to establish the tax liability for a period, usually one year. Basically, taxable income or taxable loss is the net result of summarizing revenues, gains, expenses, and losses. This result is determined in considerable degree in accordance with accepted accounting principles and conventions. At every step in the process, however, there are differences, based on tax statutes and interpretations thereof, which distinguish taxable income from financial income. These differences are numerous and may prove substantial in amount.

The variations between taxable income and financial income are so great as to require specialization in taxation as distinguished from financial accounting. The two disciplines, however, are fundamentally related, and tax issues are usually resolved concurrently with the financial accounting issues.

The basic approach of the income tax is to impose a tax on the net result of financial transactions occurring during a fixed period of time called the tax year. The time for reporting income and deductions thus becomes of vital importance in determining taxable income. Therefore, the Internal Revenue Code provides that taxable income must be computed on the basis of the taxpayer's tax year and permissible method of accounting.

There are some differences between financial and tax accounting, differences which are attributable to a number of factors. Financial accounting is designed to reflect the income position of a profit-seeking taxpayer; the rules of tax accounting not only must have regard for this but also must reflect the need to raise revenue equitably. Further, the general thrust and purpose of the tax law, to prescribe detailed rules in the interest of certainty, is bound to create conflicts with tailor-made systems designed for particular taxpayers in many instances. Experience has indicated that certain tax rules are necessary in order to control tax avoidance. Thus, the Internal Revenue Service has been provided with Code Sec. 482, under which it may reallocate items of income, deduction, credit, or allowance in order to prevent tax avoidance when two or more organizations are controlled by the same interest. Further, if the taxpayer's method of accounting does not clearly reflect income, Code Sec. 446 authorizes the IRS to require the use of a method that will do so. Additionally, the Supreme Court has indicated that the use of generally accepted accounting principles (GAAP), which apply to financial accounting and are considered to be the "best" accounting practices, does not necessarily clearly reflect income and does not shift the burden of proof to the IRS to show otherwise. *Thor Power Tool Co.,* 79-1 USTC ¶ 9139, 439 U.S. 522 (1979).

Once the questions of what items are includible in gross income and what items are deductible in computing taxable income are answered, a second set of questions must be faced. These relate to when such qualifying items are to be utilized in that computation. In other words, in what tax year is an item of income actually to be included in gross income? In what tax year is a deduction to be subtracted from gross income?

The general answers to most of these "when" questions are furnished in terms of the method of accounting regularly employed by the taxpayer in his or her business and recordkeeping. That record, however, must "clearly reflect income." Various accounting methods are available in computing taxable income, but the significant effect of the selection of one method of reporting over another is that of timing. Total income and total deductions over the long run will generally be the same regardless of the method used. However, yearly determinations of taxable income may differ materially depending on the method selected.

Taxable Income and Tax Liability for Various Entities

¶ 12,001 RECAPITULATION OF TAXABLE INCOME AND TAX LIABILITY

Table 1, on the following page, contains a general outline of the computation of taxable income for various entities. A comparison of each provides an indication of some similarities and differences. All entities subtract exclusions to determine gross income. However, the types of exclusions are different; some apply to all entities (e.g., the exclusion for municipal bond income), and some apply to particular entities (e.g., the exclusion for qualified fringe benefits, which applies to individuals). Additionally, Code Sec. 61 applies to all entities in computing gross income.

Each entity also is permitted to reduce gross income by qualified deductions. However, the type, classification, and computation of deductions can vary. Only individuals dichotomize their deductions into "for adjusted gross income" and "from adjusted gross income," the latter being deductions for personal expenses such as personal exemptions and itemized deductions which do not apply to other entities. Corporations have routine deductions and several "special" deductions such as the dividends-received deduction. This deduction applies only to corporations. Some items are not deductible by conduit entities (e.g., S corporations) but instead pass through to the owners, while some have different constraints. For example, the charitable contribution deduction is constrained by adjusted gross income for individuals, but is constrained by "modified" taxable income for corporations; yet both entities must go through the same general process of classifying the contributions as cash, ordinary income assets, and long-term capital assets.

To the extent that each entity (including self-employed taxpayers) has business activities, Code Sec. 162 applies to trade or business expenses, and the general criteria for a deduction apply (e.g., ordinary, necessary, reasonable, etc.). Code Sec. 212 applies to an entity's nonbusiness expenses and is most applicable to individuals. Similarly, the "hobby loss" rules of Code Sec. 183 apply to individuals and S corporations. Thus, while each entity is entitled to deductions in the computation of its taxable (or ordinary) income, the nature of these deductions can vary. In subsequent chapters, significant differences are explained further.

Table 1   COMPUTATION OF TAXABLE INCOME

Individuals

Income Broadly Conceived
Less: Exclusions
Gross Income
Less: Deductions for Adjusted Gross Income
Adjusted Gross Income
Less: Deductions from Adjusted Gross Income
Taxable Income

C Corporations

Income Broadly Conceived
Less: Exclusions

Gross Income
Less: Deductions
         Routine
         Special
Taxable Income

S Corporations

Income Broadly Conceived
Less: Exclusions

Gross Income
Less: Deductions

Ordinary Income

Partnerships

Income Broadly Conceived
Less: Exclusions

Gross Income
Less: Deductions

Ordinary Income

Estates and Trusts

Income Broadly Conceived
Less: Exclusions

Gross Income
Less: Deductions

Taxable Income

Table 2 contains a general outline of each entity's computation of net tax due or refund due. Pure conduits do not pay an income tax; rather, various components such as income, certain deductions, and credits pass through to the owners or beneficiaries. Those entities that do pay a tax utilize taxable income to determine gross tax liability, which is then reduced by the credits and prepayments to which they are entitled. However, the type and/or computation varies (e.g., only individuals are entitled to the earned income credit).

Table 2   NET TAX LIABILITY

Individuals

Gross Tax Liability
Less: Credits
Net Tax Liability
Less: Prepayments   _____
Net Tax or Refund Due   ==========

C Corporations

Gross Tax Liability
Less: Credits
Net Tax Liability
Less: Prepayments   _____
Net Tax or Refund Due   ==========

Estates and Trusts (assuming not completely a conduit)

Gross Tax Liability
Less: Credits
Net Tax Liability
Less: Prepayments   _____
Net Tax or Refund Due   ==========

In summary, many of the concepts that you learned in the first 11 chapters apply to all entities. However, there are numerous and substantial differences which require additional explanation. The remainder of this chapter deals with accounting periods and accounting methods as they pertain to all entities, but the focus begins to shift to business entities. Subsequent chapters deal with the specific entities.

Accounting Periods

The basic approach of income taxation is to impose a tax on the net result of financial transactions occurring during a fixed period of time, otherwise called the "tax year." The time for reporting income and deductions is of vital importance in determining taxable income. Therefore, Code Sec. 441 requires that taxable income must be computed on the basis of the taxpayer's tax year. This annual accounting period may be either a calendar year or a fiscal year.

¶ 12,007   THE TAX YEAR

"Tax year" means the calendar year or the fiscal year on the basis of which the taxable income is computed. The tax year may not exceed

12 calendar months, except where a 52-53-week tax year is adopted. (No further mention of this option is made in this text because of the relative infrequency with which this taxable period is encountered in practice.) The term "calendar year" means a period of 12 months ending on December 31. A taxpayer who has not established a fiscal year must file a tax return on the basis of a calendar year.

A "fiscal year" is defined as a period of 12 months ending on the last day of any month other than December. A fiscal year will be recognized by the IRS only if it is established as the annual accounting period for the taxpayer and the taxpayer's books are kept on the same basis. Therefore, to establish and maintain a fiscal year as the tax year, the taxpayer must correlate accounting, financial, and business practices with the fiscal year used for tax returns.

The keeping of books does not require that the records be bound. Records which are sufficient to reflect income adequately and clearly on the basis of an annual accounting period are normally regarded as the keeping of books. Informal records consisting of check stubs, rent receipts, and dividend statements are not considered regular books of account.

When a return is required for a fractional part of a year, the "tax year" means the period for which such return is filed. This fractional period is referred to as a "short tax year." A short tax year is any period for which a return has been filed that contains less than 12 months. Frequently, the first or the final tax period of a particular tax entity is a short tax year. Additionally, when a tax year is changed, the period between the end of the old tax year and the beginning of the new tax year is a short tax year for which a return must be filed.

¶ 12,015 ELECTION OF THE TAX YEAR

Individuals

A new taxpayer may adopt any tax year without obtaining prior approval of the IRS in the first year. The first tax year must be adopted on or before the time for filing the initial return. An extension of the time for filing, however, does not extend the time for adoption of the tax year.

The establishment and maintenance of adequate books of account may not be delayed beyond the end of the first accounting period if the taxpayer selects a fiscal year. Informal records do not meet this requirement, even if they become part of a formal system of accounting after the close of the fiscal year. In such cases, calendar-year reporting is required and a fiscal-year accounting period cannot be elected. Also, taxpayers who do not have books (e.g., employees) must use the calendar year. Code Sec. 441.

Income Averaging for Farmers

The above rules regarding tax periods apply to farmers. However, the Taxpayer Relief Act of 1997 (TRA '97) added Code Sec. 1301 which allows individual farmers to elect to use income averaging over a three-year period when determining tax liability. The irrevocable election applies to farm income attributable to a farm business. The tax liability in any tax year is equal to the tax on the taxpayer's taxable income reduced by that year's elected farm income to be averaged over the three preceding years and increased by the tax due on the increase in taxable income of the three prior years due to the one-third farm income averaged over the three preceding years. The income-averaging rules are effective for tax years beginning after December 31, 1997, and before January 1, 2001.

Sole Proprietors

Sole proprietors of a business must use the same period for business tax reporting purposes that they use for their personal books. Unless they keep personal books on a fiscal-year basis, they must report both business and personal income on a calendar-year basis.

Example 12.1. Evelyn Aldo establishes a tax year when she files her first return. She begins business in a later year as a sole proprietor. Evelyn must use the same tax year for the business unless permission from the IRS to change is obtained.

Partnerships

Except for partnerships that qualify under the business purpose exception, a partnership must use the same tax year as that of its partners who have a majority interest (an aggregate interest of greater than 50 percent) in partnership profits and capital. If partners owning a majority interest have different tax years, the partnership must adopt the same tax year as that of its principal partners. When neither condition is met, a partnership is required to adopt a year that results in the least aggregate deferral of income to the partners. Reg. § 1.706-1T. A principal partner is a partner having an interest of 5 percent or more in partnership profits or capital. Partnership income is considered to be earned by the partners on the last day of the partnership's tax year. The least aggregate deferral method requires the partnership to calculate the income that would be deferred by the partners based on the partners' tax years (and therefore the number of months from the partnership's tax year-end to the partner's tax year-end). The calculation is based on each partner's ownership percentage and tax year-end. For each possible year-end, each partner's ownership percentage is multiplied by the number of months the partner would defer income. The result for each partner is totalled, and the totals for all possible tax years are compared. The partnership tax year is the one with the smallest total. These tax year requirements are designed to reduce the partners' income deferral opportunities via tax year selection.

The partnership must adopt the tax year of its majority interest partner or partners if that interest has a common tax year on the first day of the partnership's existing tax year. Further, if a change in the tax year is required under this rule, no additional change is required in the next two years following the year of change.

Example 12.2. A partnership is formed by an individual and a corporation, each owning a 50 percent interest. The individual has a calendar year as its tax year, and the corporation has a tax year that ends on August 31. The partnership must determine its tax year using the least aggregate deferral method because neither the majority interest rule nor the principal partnership rule applies. If the corporation owned more than a 50 percent interest in the partnership, the partnership would have to adopt a tax year ending on August 31.

Example 12.3. A partnership is owned by numerous individuals and corporations. All of the individuals have calendar years and none of the individuals are principal partners. One corporation owns 45 percent and has a fiscal year ending on May 31. The other corporations have various other fiscal years and none are principal partners. If the individuals together own more than 50 percent of the partnership, the partnership must adopt the calendar year because the majority partners have a calendar year. If the individuals do not own more than 50 percent, the partnership may adopt a fiscal year ending on May 31 because the principal partners have a fiscal year ending May 31.

Example 12.4. The BPT partnership has three owners, Barry, Pete, and Tom. Barry and Pete each own 30 percent, and Tom owns 40 percent. Their tax years end on March 31, September 30, and December 31, respectively. In this situation neither the majority interest nor the principal partner methods can be used to determine BPT's tax year; thus, the least aggregate deferral method must be used, and it is determined as follows.

Partnership Partner	Interest	Partner Tax Year	3/31 Months Deferred	Total	9/30 Months Deferred	Total	12/31 Months Deferred	Total
			Possible Tax Year-Ends					
Barry	30%	3/31	0	0	6	1.8	9	2.7
Pete	30%	9/30	6	1.8	0	0	3	0.9
Tom	40%	12/31	3	1.2	9	3.6	0	0
				3.0		5.4		3.6

Note: Months deferred equals the months from the possible partnership tax year-end to the partner's tax year-end. Total equals the months deferred multiplied by the partner's ownership interest.

Thus, the BPT partnership must use a March 31 tax year-end because it has the lowest total amount (3.0) and, therefore, the least aggregate deferral.

In all other circumstances, the adoption of a tax year requires IRS approval of an application to be filed on or before the 15th day of the second calendar month following the short period. The application must establish a satisfactory business purpose. For example, a partnership's selection of a tax year to coincide with a natural business year would constitute a sufficient business purpose. Application is made on Form 1128 (Application for Change in Accounting Period). This form may be modified to indicate that it is an application for adoption of a tax year.

A newly formed partnership must file with its first return one of the following:

1. A copy of the letter approving the adoption of a tax year which differs from the tax year of the majority partners or all of the principal partners.

2. A statement that the partnership tax year is the same as the tax year of the majority partners or all of its principal partners, or that all of its principal partners are concurrently changing to the tax year the partnership has adopted.

Corporations

Every newly organized corporation has the unrestricted right to select its annual accounting period. The election is signified by filing the first return on or before the statutory due date for filing. The tax year may either be the calendar year or a fiscal year. The tax year of a corporation may differ from that of the shareholders.

A corporation in existence during any portion of a tax year must file a return. If a corporation is not in existence throughout an entire accounting period, the corporation must file a return for that fractional part of a year during which it is in existence. A new corporation comes into existence on the date of its incorporation. This may cause problems for a corporation that is inactive for a period of time after incorporation. Unless the corporation files a return selecting a tax year during the initial period, the time period may pass for electing a tax year, and the corporation may be forced to file a calendar-year return. This will happen if the first tax year ends more than 12 months after incorporation.

Filing Form 7004 (Application for Automatic Extension of Time to File Corporation Income Tax Return) with respect to a first return is an election to adopt the accounting period indicated on that form. The late filing of a taxpayer's initial return will not prevent adoption of a fiscal year, provided the taxpayer adopted a fiscal accounting period before the due date for filing its return, and its books and records reflect the adoption of this period.

S Corporations

The tax year of an S corporation is generally required to be a calendar year. However, a tax year other than a calendar year may be used if the S corporation can satisfy the IRS that there is a legitimate business purpose for such use.

Estates

An estate is a new taxpayer, and it may adopt any tax year without obtaining prior approval. The ability to select a fiscal period enables the executor to do two things: (1) control the number of months in the first and final returns of the estate, thereby controlling the amount of income taxable to the estate during this period, and (2) postpone the time of realization of income by the beneficiaries due to the timing of distributions.

Trusts

Trusts, other than charitable and tax-exempt trusts, must use the calendar year. Code Sec. 645.

Business Year

The intent of an entity to make its tax year coincide with its natural business year constitutes a valid business purpose. Where a business has a nonpeak and a peak period, the natural business year usually ends at, or soon after, the close of the peak period. A business with a steady monthly income does not have a natural business year.

A business purpose generally exists if, in the last two months of the selected tax year, a taxpayer receives at least 25 percent of its gross receipts and has done so for three consecutive 12-month periods. The following factors are ordinarily insufficient to establish a business purpose with respect to a particular fiscal tax year: (1) the use of a particular year for regulatory or financial accounting purposes; (2) the hiring patterns of a particular business; (3) the use of a particular year for administrative purposes, such as the promotion of staff and the compensation or retirement arrangements for staff, partners, or shareholders; and (4) the fact that a particular business involves the use of price lists, model years, or other items that change on an annual basis.

In order to use a fiscal tax year, a partnership or an S corporation must obtain the IRS's consent. A partnership or S corporation that received permission to use a fiscal year under Rev. Proc. 74-33, 1974-2 CB 489, can continue to use such year without seeking approval from the IRS.

Change of Accounting Periods

If a taxpayer wishes to change the annual accounting period and adopt a new tax year, with certain exceptions, prior approval must be obtained before using the new period for tax purposes. A change in accounting period usually is approved if there are substantial business reasons for the change.

If a taxpayer's records are inadequate or there is an accounting period that does not meet the requirements for a fiscal year, the tax year must be the calendar year. In this instance, the adoption of a fiscal year is treated as a change in the annual accounting period and prior approval from the IRS is required.

A change in accounting period usually involves a short-period tax year. This period begins with the first day after the close of the former accounting period and ends at the close of the day preceding the beginning of the new accounting period.

Example 12.5. Mita Corporation wishes to change its tax year from a calendar year to a tax year ending on May 31, 1999. Mita Corporation will have a short tax year for the period January 1 to May 31, 1999.

¶ 12,101   IRS PERMISSION OR CONSENT

In order to secure prior approval, the taxpayer must file an application on Form 1128 on or before the 15th day of the second calendar month following the end of the short year. An application should show that there is a substantial business purpose for the change and that any tax cost to the IRS is insignificant. The IRS will respond to the taxpayer with Form 5654 (Notification of Action on Application for Change in Accounting Period). The form lists several conditions to be met by the taxpayer for final acceptance of the change. No change should be made until the request has been approved.

To prevent substantial distortion of income that may result from a change in tax period, an agreement between the taxpayer and the IRS is required. This agreement must provide the terms, conditions, and adjustments necessary to implement the change. The following examples of income distortion are given in Reg. § 1.442-1(b):

1. Deferring a substantial portion of income, or shifting a substantial portion of deductions, from one year to another so as to reduce the tax liability

2. Causing a similar deferral in the case of a related taxpayer, such as a partner, a beneficiary, or a shareholder in an S corporation

3. Creating a short period in which there is either a net operating loss or, in the case of an S corporation, amounts treated as long-term capital gain

If approval is granted, the taxpayer must file an income tax return for the short period. There are special rules for computing the tax for a short year caused by a change in the accounting period. These are discussed later in the chapter.

¶ 12,115   EXCEPTIONS TO PERMISSION REQUIREMENTS

However, despite the prior approval requirements, there are some instances when a tax year may be changed without receiving advance approval.

Individuals

An individual whose income is derived solely from wages, salaries, interest, dividends, capital gains, pensions and annuities, or rents and royalties does not need prior approval for making a change from the fiscal year to the calendar year if Form 1128 is filed with the District Director on or before the last day of January following the close of the short period for which a return is required. A copy of the application is to be attached to the return filed for the short period. Unless a letter is received by the individual(s) from the District Director denying approval, it is assumed that the change has been approved.

Since a joint return may not be filed if a husband and wife have different tax years, Reg. § 1.442-1(e) provides that a newly married individual may adopt the accounting period of the other spouse without prior approval. He or she must file a return for the short period required by the change on or before the 15th day of the fourth month following the end of the short period. If the due date for the short-period return occurs before the date of marriage, a joint return may not be filed until the second year ending after the date of marriage, and then only if a timely short-period return is filed for that year. The short-period return filed in the first or second tax year after the date of marriage must be accompanied by a statement that the accounting period is being changed according to Reg. § 1.442-1(e).

> *Example 12.6.* Larry Raser and Donna Chilton marry on September 24, 1998. Donna is on a fiscal year ending June 30, and Larry is on a calendar year. Donna wishes to change to a calendar year in order to file a joint return with Larry. Donna may not change to a calendar year for 1998 since she would have to file a return for the short period from July 1 to December 31, 1997, by April 15, 1998. Since the date of marriage occurred after this due date, the return could not be filed under the special rule for newly married couples.

> Donna, however, may change to the calendar year for 1999 by filing a return by April 15, 1999, for the short period from July 1 to December 31, 1998. If Donna files such a return, Larry and Donna may file a joint return for calendar-year 1999, which is Larry's second tax year ending after the date of marriage. Of course, Donna could request and receive permission to change to the calendar year before the marriage and thus be allowed to file a joint return for the calendar-year 1998.

Any other husband and wife wishing to change to the accounting period of the other spouse so that they may file a joint return must make proper application. Permission may be granted for this reason in appropriate cases, even though no substantial business purpose for requesting the change is established.

Partnerships, S Corporations, and Personal Service Corporations

All partnerships, S corporations, and personal service corporations generally must conform their tax years to the tax year of their owners, unless such entities can establish a business purpose for having a different year. An entity that must change its tax year to match that of its owner is required to file a return for the resulting short tax year.

An election is provided whereby a partnership, S corporation, or personal service corporation that is otherwise required to change its tax year may retain the tax year currently used by the entity. An election is also provided for such entities to adopt or change to tax years with limited deferral periods. The limited deferral period must be the lesser of the deferral period currently in use or three months.

S corporations and partnerships are required to make enhanced estimated tax payments for any tax year for which this special tax election is in effect. Willful failure to make the enhanced estimated tax payments results in the cancellation of the election by the entity.

Corporations

A corporation (other than an S corporation) may change its annual accounting period without prior approval if all of the following conditions are met:

1. The corporation has not changed its tax year any time within the ten calendar years ending with the calendar year in which the short period resulting from the change begins.

2. The short period is not a tax year in which the corporation has a net operating loss. (In limited circumstances, Rev. Proc. 92-13, 1992-1 CB 665, permits an exception to this requirement.)

3. The taxable income of the corporation for the short period is, if placed on an annual basis, 80 percent or more of the taxable income of the corporation for the tax year preceding the short period.

4. If the corporation is a personal holding company, foreign personal holding company, exempt organization, foreign corporation not engaged in trade or business within the United States, Western Hemisphere trade corporation, or China Trade Act corporation for either the short period or the preceding tax year, it must have this status for both the short period and the preceding tax year. Reg. § 1.442-1(c)(2).

For purposes of (3), above, a net operating loss deduction is not applied against either the short period income or the income for the year immediately preceding the short period in determining whether it meets the 80 percent test. Without this provision, a taxpayer would not know whether the 80 percent condition had been met until three years after the close of the short period. For example, it would be possible to suffer a net operating loss for the third year following the short period, resulting in a net operating loss carryback to the short period. Therefore, the 80 percent requirement might not be met.

A statement on behalf of the corporation must be filed on or before the time for filing the return for the short period. The statement must indicate that the corporation is changing its annual accounting period under Reg. § 1.442-1(c) and must contain information indicating that all the above conditions have been met.

Exempt Organizations

Any organization wholly exempt from federal income tax may change its accounting period by filing an application on Form 1128 on or before the 15th day of the second month following the close of the short period. Unless a letter is received from the IRS denying approval because of untimely filing, it may be assumed that the change has been approved. The organization must attach a copy of the application to the return for the short period. This process does not apply to farmers' cooperatives and organizations having unrelated business income.

Net Operating Losses

Prior approval is required if a taxpayer establishes a substantial business purpose for a change of accounting period but a net operating loss results for the short period. Approval of the change will not be granted if the net operating loss exceeds $10,000 unless any substantial distortion in income is eliminated by appropriate adjustments. The IRS can require that the taxpayer ratably deduct the net operating loss over the next six years. Rev. Proc. 85-16, 1985-1 CB 517.

¶ 12,165   SHORT TAX YEARS

When a change in an accounting period is instituted, a separate return is filed for the short period beginning with the day following the close of the old tax year and ending with the day preceding the first day of the new tax year. The return is due from a corporation on the 15th day of the third month after the short period. Other taxpayers must file the return on or before the 15th day of the fourth month following the short period.

General Rule

The general rule calls for the tax to be computed for the short period by placing the short period's taxable income on an annual basis. This is accomplished by multiplying the modified taxable income by 12 and dividing the result by the number of months in the short period. The tax for the short period is the same as the tax computed on an annual basis. Without this provision, taxpayers would be able to avoid a large tax liability by having a portion of the income taxed for a shorter period. Tax preferences must be annualized to determine the applicability of the alternative minimum tax. Code Sec. 443(d).

A change in accounting period could result in tax savings due to the progressive tax rate structures. Some income would be "sheltered" by avoiding a higher tax rate. To prevent this from happening, the tax for the short period is based on annualized income. The procedures are as follows:

1. Annualize the short-period income

$$\text{Annualized income} = \text{Short-period income} \times \left(\frac{12}{\text{No. months in short period}} \right)$$

2. Determine the tax on the annualized income

3. Determine the short-period tax

$$\text{Short-period tax} = \frac{\text{Tax on}}{\text{annualized income}} \times \left(\frac{\text{No. months in short period}}{12} \right)$$

Example 12.7. Xeno Corporation files a return, because of a change in its accounting period, for the three-month short period ending June 30, 1998. It has taxable income of $20,000 during the short period. Its tax liability is computed as follows:

Taxable Income Annualized ($20,000 × 12/3)		$80,000.00
$50,000 × 15%	$7,500	
$25,000 × 25%	6,250	
$5,000 × 34%	1,700	
Tax on Annualized Income		$15,450.00
Tax for Short Period ($15,450 × 3/12)		$ 3,862.50

Individuals must use the tax rate schedules to compute their tax liabilities for the short period. Also, they cannot use the standard deduction; instead they must reflect the itemized deductions incurred in the short period. Personal exemptions must be prorated to the short period. Very few individuals change their accounting period.

Alternative Method

Because annualization of the short-period income may result in inequities to the taxpayer, there is an exception to the general rule which may result in less tax. Code Sec. 443(b)(2). The procedures are as follows:

1. Determine taxable income for the 12-month period beginning on the first day of the short period.

2. Determine the tax on the taxable income for this 12-month period.

3. Short-period tax = $\dfrac{\text{Tax on}}{\text{12-month period}} \times \left[\dfrac{\text{Taxable income for short period}}{\text{Taxable income for 12-month period}} \right]$

4. The short-period tax computed in Step 3 cannot be less than it would have been if it had been computed on short-period taxable income without placing it on an annualized basis.

The alternative short-period tax is used only if it is less than the short-period tax computed the regular way.

Example 12.8. Referring to Example 12.7, assume that Xeno's taxable income for the 12-month period beginning April 1, 1998, is $30,000. The tax on $30,000 is $4,500. The short-period tax would be $3,000 ($4,500 × $20,000/$30,000). This amount is not less than the tax on the short-period income without being annualized ($3,000 = ($20,000 × 15%)). The $3,000 short-period tax determined via the alternative method is compared to the short-period tax computed under the regular method ($3,862.50) and, if less, will be used. In this example, the alternative method produces a tax savings of $862.50 and Xeno Corporation would file a claim for a refund.

The short tax year which results from a change in accounting period is treated as a full tax year for other purposes of the tax rules such as carrybacks and carryforwards. Tax planners must be careful that the creation of a short tax year return does not reduce the benefits a taxpayer would obtain from loss and credit carrybacks and carryforwards which could otherwise be obtained without the short tax year.

¶ 12,175   ACCOUNTING PERIOD TAX PLANNING

A taxpayer should consider the various factors influencing the choice of accounting period and select the accounting period as soon as possible after beginning operations. The significant factor in selecting an accounting period is timing. Most frequently, total income and total deductions over the long run will generally be the same regardless of the period used. However, yearly determinations of taxable income may differ materially depending on the accounting period selected.

Business Factors

The choice of an annual accounting period depends on several business factors, such as a slack season when personnel are available, or a date when inventories and bank loans are low, which in turn presents a favorable balance sheet for credit purposes. Because income tax rates are on a graduated basis, the lowest taxes over a period of years will be achieved if income can be kept as level as possible over this period of time. Generally, this objective can be obtained if the expenses incurred in earning income are charged off in the same year the income is earned.

Natural Business Year

It is desirable that the accounting period chosen be in agreement with the natural business year. That is, the tax period should include both the income earned and the expenses incurred in generating that income. For example, if a business earns most of its income in the fall while most of the expenses are incurred or paid in the following spring, the calendar year should not be selected as the accounting period, since income would be perpetually distorted. Some advantages of closing a tax period at the end of the natural business year are: (1) inventories are at their lowest point and may be inspected and tabulated more quickly and valued more accurately, (2) receivables are at their minimum and bad debt adjustments can be determined more accurately, and (3) bank loans usually have been liquidated or reduced to their minimum for the tax period. Additionally, financial statements prepared at the end of a natural business year more accurately reflect the results of activities over one complete cycle of operations.

The accounting method adopted by the taxpayer may well be an important factor. Since income and expenses generally accrue before they are received or paid, it may be possible to close the accounting period earlier if the accrual method is used rather than the cash receipts and disbursements method, thereby reflecting a more accurate picture of the income for the period.

Special Circumstances

A corporate taxpayer can select its year based on the particular circumstances of the initial period, rather than any adherence to the concept of the natural business year. The objective is usually to defer tax. Accordingly, a corporation may close its first year at the time it reaches a taxable income of $75,000 and thus avoid the 34 percent rate. If the corporation is an S corporation, where income is passed through to its shareholders who report on the calendar year, adoption of a year ending on the last day of January or a subsequent month, instead of the preceding December 31, serves to defer taxation of the income to the shareholders. However, new S corporations are required to adopt a calendar year unless the taxpayer can show a business reason for electing a fiscal year.

Affiliated Groups

In the case where a new corporation is a subsidiary or a parent of an affiliated group, the accounting period selected should conform to that of the existing members of the group. The consolidated return regulations require that the tax year of all members of an affiliated group be the same as that of the common parent corporation. Accordingly, recognition of this possibility may avoid the trouble of changing the accounting period for the new corporation, the subsidiary, or the entire group, if the new corporation is the parent.

Accounting Methods

¶ 12,201 OVERALL METHODS

In computing taxable income, taxpayers for expediency purposes or out of ignorance frequently follow those general tax accounting procedures which are well publicized. Unfortunately this often results in lost opportunities to improve cash flow and/or minimize tax liability.

In addition to selecting one general method of accounting, a taxpayer must select many specific accounting procedures and conventions to be utilized in implementing a single method of accounting. Once a taxpayer knows that a choice exists, the alternative most appropriate to the particular set of circumstances may then be selected. Each election may have a significant impact on the tax liability ultimately reported for any taxpayer.

Section 446 specifies that taxable income is to be computed in accordance with the accounting method regularly used in keeping books. A "method of accounting" includes not only the overall system of accounting of the taxpayer but also the accounting treatment of any item. No uniform method of accounting can be prescribed for all taxpayers. A taxpayer may adopt the forms and systems of accounting that are best suited to the taxpayer's purpose. Informal records are not sufficient; regular books of account are necessary.

A taxpayer whose sole source of income is wages need not keep formal books in order to have an accounting method. Tax returns or other records may be sufficient to establish the use of the method of accounting utilized in the preparation of the taxpayer's tax returns.

If the accounting method regularly used by the taxpayer in keeping books for tax purposes clearly reflects income, that method must be used in the annual return. However, no method of accounting will be regarded as clearly reflecting income unless all items of gross profit and deductions are treated with consistency from year to year.

Approved standard methods of accounting ordinarily will be regarded as clearly reflecting income. Where the method used by the taxpayer does not clearly reflect income, or if no method of accounting has been regularly used by the taxpayer, then the tax computation is to be made under a method that the IRS agrees will clearly reflect income. "Clearly reflects income" means that income should be reflected with as much accuracy as standard methods of accounting practice permit, not merely that the taxpayer's books should be kept fairly and honestly.

The two most commonly used overall methods that are specifically authorized are (1) the cash method and (2) the accrual method. Code Sec. 446. Other permissible methods of accounting for income and expenses are the long-term contract method and the crop method for farmers.

Special treatment is accorded various types of revenue (e.g., installment sales, prepaid subscription income, and obligations issued at a discount) and many types of expenses (e.g., bad debts, real estate taxes, redemption of trading stamps, and expenses whose benefits are received over a period of years). In addition, any combination of permissible methods may be authorized under the regulations.

Subject to the limitations on the cash method of accounting discussed below, a taxpayer filing a first return is allowed to adopt any permissible method of accounting in computing taxable income for the tax year covered by such return. These requirements are sufficiently flexible to permit every taxpayer a maximum opportunity to select the most favorable method of accounting. Except for an occasional refusal to authorize a change in accounting method, the statutory requirements have been interpreted rather liberally.

¶ 12,215 CASH METHOD

The vast majority of individuals and many businesses use the cash method, primarily because of its simplicity. It generally is used by taxpayers whose principal income is derived from the performance of a service. Unless other restrictions apply, the cash method must be used if the taxpayer keeps no regular books or has inadequate books for the accrual method. Income is recognized in the tax year when cash and/or cash equivalents are actually or constructively received. Expenses generally are deductible in the year paid unless they are attributable to more than one year.

Income may be received in the form of cash, a check, or cash equivalents in the form of property. Reg. § 1.446-1(a)(3). The fair market value of the property is the measure of income. Thus, if a taxpayer receives stock in return for the performance of a service, then the taxpayer's income is equal to the fair market value of the stock, regardless of accounting method. Similarly, the receipt of a negotiable promissory note produces taxable income in the year of receipt equal to the note's fair market value. Mere promises to pay, not represented by notes or secured, are not regarded as income when received. *A.M. Bedell,* 1 USTC ¶ 359, 30 F.2d 662 (CA-2 1929).

Income also may be received in other forms. A taxpayer may receive the right to use another's property; that is, the taxpayer does not receive the property outright but is allowed to use the property. In this situation the taxpayer recognizes income equal to the fair rental value of the property. Alternatively, a taxpayer may receive services from another taxpayer. Instead of receiving cash or property, the taxpayer enters into a bartering agreement whereby the form of payment is the rendering of services to the taxpayer. In this situation the taxpayer recognizes income equal to the fair market value of the services received. Finally, the form of income may be the discharge of indebtedness; the taxpayer does not receive cash directly but instead has debt forgiven. Depending on the circumstances, all, some or none of the forgiven debt may be included in income. Code Sec. 61. Thus, cash equivalents may take many different forms.

Cash or cash equivalents are income in the year actually or constructively received. Reg. § 1.446-1(c)(2)(i). Income is constructively received in the tax year in which it is credited to the taxpayer's account, set apart for the taxpayer, or made available to the taxpayer to draw upon if the taxpayer's control of its receipt is not subject to substantial limitations or restrictions. Reg. § 1.451-2(a).

The payer must have the ability to pay, must set aside funds for payments, and must not place substantial restrictions on the taxpayer's ability to access the funds (or property). If these conditions are met, then the taxpayer cannot deliberately turn his or her back on income and thus select the year of reporting. *Hamilton National Bank of Chattanooga*, 29 BTA 63, CCH Dec. 8240 (1933).

Example 12.9. In 1998, Fry Company credits its employees with bonus stock, but the stock is not available to them until 2001. The employees have not constructively received the stock in 1998.

Example 12.10. Sally James received a $700 dividend check from Astin Company on December 26, 1998. Sally did not cash the check until January 4, 1999. Sally must include the $700 in her gross income for 1998. If Astin Company had mailed the check on December 29, 1998, and it was not received until January 1999, then Sally would not include it in her gross income for 1998 because she has no constructive or actual receipt until 1999.

The deductibility of expenses does not coincide with the recognition of income under the cash method. There is no such thing as constructive payment. Expenses are recognized in the year they are paid. However, some expenditures (fixed assets, prepaid interest, prepaid rent) must be capitalized (treated as an asset) and recognized as an expense over the asset's life (e.g., depreciation).

An expense may be "paid" in cash or in property but not by the note of the taxpayer even if secured by collateral. Generally, unconditional delivery of a check has the same consequences as delivery of cash. Delivery means actual delivery of the check to the payee or an agent. However, one court has held that a check is considered delivered when it is put in the mail on the theory that the postal service is acting as the agent for both the sender and receiver. *Estate of E.B. Witt v. Fahs,* 56-1 USTC ¶ 9534, 160 F.Supp. 521 (DC Fla. 1956).

If a cash-basis taxpayer borrows funds with which to pay deductible expenses—whether the funds are paid to the taxpayer first or directly to the creditor (subject to an understanding that the taxpayer will make repayment to the lender)—the payments are deductible in the year made, not in the later year when the taxpayer makes repayment to the person who advanced the funds to the taxpayer or paid the expenses on the taxpayer's behalf.

¶ 12,225 LIMITATIONS ON USE OF CASH METHOD

Four types of taxpayers cannot use the cash method of accounting for tax purposes after 1986. These four types of taxpayers include:

1. C corporations

2. Partnerships which have a C corporation as a partner

3. Tax shelters

4. Trusts that are subject to the tax on unrelated trade or business income, but only with respect to such income

The prohibition on use of the cash method does not apply to farming and timber businesses, qualified personal service corporations, and entities with gross receipts of not more than $5 million. The $5 million exemption does not apply to any tax shelter. Individuals, qualifying partnerships, and S corporations are not prohibited from using the cash method. A qualifying partnership is a partnership in which all of the partners are individuals, qualified personal service corporations, S corporations, and other qualifying partnerships.

A tax shelter is defined as: (1) any enterprise, other than a C corporation, for which, at any time, interests in such enterprise have been offered for sale in any offering required to be registered with any federal or state securities agency; (2) any partnership or other entity if more than 35 percent of the losses of such entity during the tax year are allocable to limited partners or limited partnerships; or (3) any partnership, investment plan, or other plan or arrangement the principal purpose of which is the avoidance of federal income tax.

Small businesses that can use or continue to use the cash method of accounting are those businesses with average annual gross receipts of $5 million or less over the past three years. The three-year period does not include the current tax year in which the determination is being made. The enterprise is required to change to the accrual method in the year following the year it fails to meet the small business test. A business may not change back to the cash method when its average receipts later fall below $5 million.

Average annual gross receipts are computed by dividing the sum of the gross receipts for so many of the previous three years as the taxpayer conducted business by the number of such tax years. The change to the accrual method must be made in the tax year following this three-year period. In those cases where the enterprise has not been in existence for the entire three-year period, the test will be based on the number of tax years the enterprise was in existence.

Gross receipts are computed by deducting sales returns and allowances from gross receipts. Gross receipts, as defined in the Form 1120 instructions, include gross receipts or sales from business operations with the exception of dividends, interest, gross rents, other income, and net gains and losses from sales of capital and business assets. Gross receipts for a short tax year of less than 12 months are annualized for purposes of the $5 million test. This annualization is computed by multiplying the gross receipts by 12 and dividing the result by the number of months in the short tax year.

A qualified personal service corporation may use the cash method of accounting. A corporation is treated as a qualified service corporation only if it meets both a function test and an ownership test. The function test is met if substantially all of the corporation's activities involve the performance of services in the fields of health, law, engineering, architecture, accounting, actuarial science, performing arts, or consulting. The ownership test in general limits stock ownership in the corporation to certain types of persons. Specifically, this test requires that "substantially all" of the value of the corporation's stock must be owned by (1) current or retired employees, (2) the estates of current or retired employees, or (3) persons who acquired the stock by reason of the death of such employees within the prior 24 months. For purposes of applying the ownership test, community property laws are disregarded, and stock owned by an ESOP or a pension plan is considered to be owned by the beneficiaries of the plan. At least 95 percent of the value of the stock must be held directly or indirectly by the required individuals in order for the "substantially all" requirement to be met.

¶ 12,235 ACCRUAL METHOD

Under the accrual method, income is reported when the right to receive income comes into being, that is, when all the events which determine the right to receive income have occurred and the amount can be determined with reasonable accuracy. Reg. § 1.451-1(a). Deductions are taken in the year when the legal obligation to make payments comes into existence and all the events have occurred which determine the fact of the liability and the amount can be determined with reasonable accuracy, unless properly allocable to another year. Reg. § 1.461-2. The all events test is not met until economic performance with respect to the item has occurred. Code Sec. 461(h).

If the liability arises because a service or property is provided to the taxpayer, then economic performance occurs when the other party provides such service, such property, or the use of such property. If the liability requires the taxpayer to provide a service or property, then economic performance occurs when said service or property is provided. However, Code Sec. 461(h)(3) provides an exception for recurring items if the all events test is met. In such situations the item is deductible during the year if economic performance occurs within eight and one-half months after the close of the tax year.

The accrual basis has not been allowed where the taxpayer has not kept any books or has kept inadequate ones. Also, the accrual method cannot be used where, due to the nature of the business, the amounts accrued—constituting the bulk of reported income—represent only a tentative estimate which cannot be verified from the records until subsequent years.

If the income has not been reduced to possession or constructively received, it becomes taxable under the accrual method when three circumstances are present: (1) there is an unconditional right to receive, (2) the amount is determinable with reasonable accuracy, and (3) the amount is collectible.

Thus, in order that income be accruable, existence of the right to the income, subject to no contingencies, is the primary essential. If a taxpayer's right to receive is dependent upon future events, there is no accrual until those contingencies occur or lapse.

Second, it is also essential that the general formula (or rules for determining the amount of the income) be already provided. On the other hand, it is not essential that this amount be precisely determined. The taxpayer may make his or her own determination and accrue the amount so determined, even though the actual determination for payment purposes may show it to be in error or even though some portion of the money received by the taxpayer might have to be refunded in some future year.

The third and final condition is that the amount must be collectible. Even though notes or other receivables may not be marketable, they may be collectible. If the right to receive arises from a sale of real property, an accrual-basis seller should report such right at its fair market value. However, if the sale is of personal property, the full face value of the right must be reported as income.

Example 12.11. Darryl Harris sells a building for $200,000, receiving $50,000 in cash and a $150,000 mortgage note due in five years with a 10 percent interest rate. The mortgage note has a $135,000 fair market value. The basis of the building is $95,000. Darryl will report a gain of $90,000 ($50,000 cash + $135,000 fair market value of the mortgage note = $185,000 selling price minus $95,000 basis). If the full $200,000 is collected, $50,000 will be reported as interest income. If the asset sold were personal property rather than the building, the selling price would be $200,000.

Only if there is clear and convincing evidence that real doubt and uncertainty exist as to whether the amount due will ever be collected can there be postponement of reporting income. The possibility of default is not sufficient. The courts have held that year-end is the time to test collectibility on unpaid items. An event occurring subsequent to that time has no effect on the accountability.

An accrual-basis taxpayer need not accrue as income any portion of amounts billed for the performance of services which, on the basis of experience, it will not collect. However, the income must be accrued if the taxpayer charges any interest or penalty for failure to make timely payments in connection with the amount billed. The offering of a discount for early payment of an amount billed will require the reporting of income as long as the full amount of the bill is otherwise accrued as income and the discount for early payment treated as an adjustment to income in the year such payment is made.

The amount of billings that, on the basis of experience, will not be collected is equal to the total amount billed, multiplied by a fraction whose numerator is the total amount of such receivables which were billed and determined not to be collectible within the most recent five tax years of the taxpayer and whose denominator is the total of such amounts billed within the same five-year period. If the taxpayer has not been in existence for the prior five tax years, the portion of such five-year period which the taxpayer has been in existence is to be used.

> *Example 12.12.* Assume that an accrual-basis taxpayer has $150,000 of receivables that have been created during the most recent five tax years. Of the $150,000 of accounts receivable, $3,000 has been determined to be uncollectible. The amount, based on experience, which is not expected to be collected is equal to 2 percent ($3,000 divided by $150,000) of any receivables arising from the provision of services that are outstanding at the close of the tax year.

A taxpayer who has not recognized income on amounts not expected to be collected must recognize additional income in any tax year in which payments on amounts not recognized are received. If a receivable is determined to be partially or wholly uncollectible, no portion of the loss arising as a result of such determination that was not recognized as income at the time the receivable was created is allowed as a deduction.

The main disadvantage of the accrual method of accounting is a reduction in the taxpayer's control over the timing of both gross income and tax deductions. Under accrual accounting, a taxpayer may have to recognize income prior to the receipt of cash with which the taxpayer can pay the tax liability.

Prepaid Income and Expenses

The treatment of payments received in advance by an accrual-basis taxpayer for services to be rendered or goods to be delivered in a subsequent tax year has been the subject of litigation for many years. Generally, prepaid income has been held to be taxable in the year received. The treatment varies from financial accounting conventions consistently used by many accrual-method taxpayers in the treatment of payments received in one tax year for services to be performed by them in succeeding tax years. The Supreme Court has supported the IRS position that the deferral of prepayments under financial accounting rules does not clearly reflect taxable income because the seller has already received payment. See *American Automobile Assn.,* 61-2 USTC ¶ 9517, 367 U.S. 687 (1961). The contingent liability to refund part of the income received does not postpone income recognition.

A taxpayer is generally allowed a deduction in the tax year which is the proper tax year under the method of accounting used in computing taxable income. If, however, the taxpayer's method of accounting does not clearly reflect income, the computation of taxable income must be made under the method which, in the opinion of the IRS, clearly reflects income.

Prepaid Subscriptions

Accrual-basis taxpayers may elect to recognize prepaid subscription income over the subscription period, as earned. Code Sec. 455. If a taxpayer does not elect this treatment of prepaid subscription income, the income is includible in income for the tax year in which received, unless, under the method or practice of accounting used in computing taxable income, the amount is to be properly accounted for in a different period. Reg. § 1.455-1.

The election is applicable to all prepaid subscription income. However, the taxpayer may elect to currently include in income any prepaid subscription income if the liability ends within 12 months after the date of receipt. This reporting of income is referred to as the "within-12-months" election. A taxpayer may make a separate election for each trade or business from which prepaid subscription income is received. In addition, a separate "within-12-months" election may be made for each separate trade or business. The prepaid subscription election is binding for the first year that the election is made. The prepaid subscription method of reporting income may not be changed without prior IRS approval. Reg. § 1.455-2.

Prepaid Membership Fees

A membership organization that receives prepaid dues income in connection with the trade or business of rendering services or making available membership privileges may elect to include income ratably over the period of time that it has a liability to render these services. Code Sec. 456(a). However, when the income relates to a liability that extends for more than 36 months, the income is includible in the year of receipt. Code Sec. 456(e). The election to defer prepaid dues income is applicable to all prepaid dues income received in connection with a trade or business.

Prepaid dues income is included in income by the membership organization over the period of time that it has a liability to render services to qualified members. The liability to render the services or make available the membership privileges is considered to exist ratably over the life of the contract that was entered into between the parties.

Example 12.13. A calendar-year membership organization elects to report its prepaid dues income under Code Sec. 456. On November 1, 1998, it sells a two-year membership for $72 payable in advance. The membership extends from November 1, 1998, to October 30, 2000. The organization includes $6 ($2/24 \times $72) in gross income for 1998, $36 ($12/24 \times $72) for 1999, and $30 ($10/24 \times $72) for 2000.

If the liability should end for any reason, the deferred income is included in the year the liability ceases to exist. For example, the cancellation of a membership would cause the liability to end. If the membership organization should terminate, the deferred prepaid dues income is included in the year that the taxpayer terminates its services.

Prepaid Interest

If a taxpayer uses the cash receipts and disbursements method to compute taxable income, interest paid by the taxpayer which is properly allocable to any later tax year is generally treated as paid in the year to which it is allocable; interest is allocable to the period in which the interest represents a charge for the use or forbearance of borrowed money. An accrual-method taxpayer can deduct interest only in the period in which the use of the money occurs. Thus, prepaid interest is deductible in the same period for both cash and accrual-method taxpayers.

Prepayments for Services

Payments for services may be deferred for one year only, but only if the services will be rendered within the taxable year. Rev. Proc. 71-21, 1971-2 CB 549. The Revenue Procedure states that accrual-basis taxpayers may report advance payments received for services to be performed in the future under two acceptable methods. First, the taxpayer may include the payment in gross income in the year of receipt. Second, if certain conditions are met, the income may be spread over the year of receipt and the following year. This second method is denoted as the prepaid service income method.

To qualify for the prepaid service income method, the taxpayer must perform all the services under an agreement (written or otherwise) by the end of the tax year following the year of receipt. The prepayment is recognized as earned through the performance of the services. However, if there is a deferral of income but a portion of such services is not performed by the end of the next succeeding tax year, the amount allocable to the services not so performed by year's end must be included in income in the next succeeding year, regardless of when (if ever) the services are performed.

Example 12.14. On October 1, 1998, Daisy Franz, a calendar-year, accrual-basis taxpayer who runs a dance school, receives a payment for a one-year contract beginning on that date to provide 50 individual lessons. Ten lessons are provided in 1998. Daisy must include 1/5 of the payment in income for 1998 and 4/5 of the payment in 1999, regardless of whether Daisy is able to give all the lessons under the contract by the end of 1999.

This example illustrates that the entire payment is included in the year of receipt if any portion of the services is to be performed after the end of the tax year following the year of receipt. The prepayment is also included in the year of receipt if any portion of the services is to be performed at an unspecified future date which may occur after the end of the second tax year.

Example 12.15. Assume that Daisy in Example 12.14 receives payment for a two-year contract beginning on October 1, 1998, which requires her to provide 100 lessons. Daisy must include the entire payment in gross income in 1998 since a portion of the services may be performed in 2000.

In any case in which an advance payment is received pursuant to an agreement which requires the taxpayer to perform contingent services, the payment which is earned in a tax year through the performance of future services may be determined in any of the following ways:

1. On a statistical basis if adequate data are available to the taxpayer

2. On a straight-line ratable basis over the time period of the agreement if it is not unreasonable to anticipate at the end of the current year that a substantially ratable portion of the services is to be performed by the end of the next succeeding year

3. By the use of any other basis that, in the opinion of the IRS, results in a clear reflection of income

Example 12.16. On July 1, 1998, Eddie Fraser, a calendar-year, accrual-basis taxpayer who is a landscape architect, receives a payment for services which must be completed by December 1999. At the end of 1998, Eddie estimates that 2/3 of the work has been completed. He must report 2/3 of the payment in 1998. The remaining 1/3 of the payment is included in 1999 income, regardless of whether he is for any reason unable to complete the job in 1999.

In certain instances, Rev. Proc. 71-21, *supra,* contains additional constraints in order to defer advance payments or contingent service contracts.

Amounts received under guaranty or warranty contracts for prepaid rent or for prepaid interest must be included in the year of receipt regardless of the period covered under the contract or the method of accounting employed by the taxpayer. However, the term "rent" does not include payments for the use or occupancy of rooms or other space where significant services are provided the occupant, such as for the use of rooms or other quarters in hotels, boarding houses, or apartment houses furnishing hotel services, or in tourist homes, motor courts, or motels.

Services rendered by related persons are considered to be performed by a single person so that the period for performing the services cannot be extended by allowing a related person to perform a portion of the services. A person is related to the taxpayer if the taxpayer and such other person are owned or controlled directly or indirectly by the same interests or entity.

If the taxpayer elects to defer income under the prepaid services method, the taxpayer must defer at least as much income as that disclosed in financial reports to shareholders, partners, other proprietors, beneficiaries, and creditors. This financial reporting requirement also applies to consolidated financial statements. Consequently, adequate books and records must be maintained by taxpayers using the prepaid services method so that the amount deferred on their income tax returns for any year can be verified.

If a taxpayer has adopted the prepaid services income method under Rev. Proc. 71-21 and the taxpayer dies or ceases to exist in a transaction, or the liability to perform the service otherwise ends, all payments not included in gross income in the year of contract must be included in the year that the taxpayer ceases to exist.

Any change made by the taxpayer from a present method of including amounts in gross income to the prepaid services income method is a change in method of accounting. Thus, it is treated in the same manner as a change in method of accounting subject to IRS consent and constraints.

Advance Payments for Future Sale of Inventory

An accrual-basis taxpayer may defer advance payments received for future sales of inventory. Reg. §1.451-5. Unlike the deferral rules for prepaid service income, there is no "end of year following receipt" time limitation on prepaid income received from merchandise sales, which was the test under Rev. Proc. 71-21. Thus, it is possible to defer prepaid sales income for more than one year.

The advance payments must conform to an agreement that provides for either of the following:

1.   The sale or other disposition in a future tax year of goods held primarily for sale to customers in the ordinary course of the taxpayer's trade or business

2.   The building, installing, constructing, or manufacturing by the taxpayer of items where the agreement is not completed within the tax year

These two activities are referred to as "eligible activities."

The term "agreement" includes (1) a gift certificate that can be redeemed for goods and (2) an agreement which obligates a taxpayer to perform eligible activities. The agreement must also contain an obligation to perform services that are to be performed as an integral part of such activities. Amounts due and payable are considered received under the definition of advance payment.

The taxpayer may elect to include the prepayment in income either in the year of receipt or in the tax year in which it is properly accruable under the taxpayer's method of accounting to shareholders, partners, beneficiaries, other proprietors, and for credit purposes. For example, if a taxpayer in the business of selling goods normally accounts for sales under the accrual method when the goods are shipped, and if this is the method also used for financial reporting purposes, then the advance payments received with respect to these goods may be included in income in the year of shipment.

In the case of a taxpayer accounting for advance payments for tax purposes pursuant to a long-term contract method of accounting, advance payments are included in income in the year in which properly included in gross receipts pursuant to that method of accounting. Reg. § 1.451-3. The financial records are not required to be reported in the same manner as the tax return reporting under the long-term contract method. The financial reporting requirement does not prevent the use of the installment method under Code Sec. 453.

However, an exception exists where the taxpayer receives "substantial advance payments" for an inventory item that the taxpayer has on hand or that is available through normal sources of supply. The taxpayer must include in income all advance payments received but not previously included in income in the second year following the year that substantial advance payments are received. Substantial advance payments are considered received in the year when the amount received equals or exceeds the costs and expenditures reasonably estimated as includible in inventory for the property to be delivered. Advance payments received in a year with respect to an agreement under which the goods or type of goods to be sold are not identifiable in that year, such as a gift certificate, are treated as substantial advance payments when received. Reg. § 1.451-5(c).

If advance payments are required to be included in income in a particular tax year, the taxpayer must deduct in that year the costs and expenditures included in inventory for those goods on hand. If the goods are not on hand by the last day of the second tax year, the estimated costs of goods necessary to satisfy the agreement are deductible.

No deduction is allowed for those goods for which advance payment has been received if they are not identifiable in the year the advance payments are required to be included in income. Amounts received from unredeemed gift certificates must be included in income no later than the second year following receipt, with no allowable deduction for the estimated inventory costs at that time. Any variances that occur between the costs or estimated costs taken into account and the costs actually incurred in fulfilling the taxpayer's obligation are recognized as an adjustment to the cost of goods sold in the year the obligation to deliver the goods is completed.

Example 12.17. In 1998, Mu Corporation, a calendar-year, accrual-basis taxpayer, entered into a contract for the sale of goods at a contract price of $40,000. Mu estimates that the total inventoriable costs and expenditures for the goods will be $20,000. Mu receives the following advance payments on the contract:

1998	1999	2000	2001	2002	2003
$14,000	$8,000	$6,000	$4,000	$4,000	$4,000

The goods are delivered pursuant to the customer's request in 2003. Mu's closing inventory for 1999 has sufficient goods to satisfy the contract. Since advance payments received by the end of 1999 exceed the estimated inventoriable costs of $20,000, the "substantial advance payments" test has been satisfied. Accordingly, all payments received by the end of 2001 (the end of the second tax year following the tax year during which substantial advance payments are received) are includible in gross income for 2001. Therefore, for 2001 Mu must include $32,000 in income. Mu must include in cost of goods sold for 2001 the estimated inventoriable costs necessary to satisfy the contract. Since no further deferral is allowable on the contract, Mu includes in income the advance payments received each year. Any variance between estimated costs and the costs actually incurred in fulfilling the contract is taken into account in 2003.

If a taxpayer uses the advance payments method, an annual information schedule must be attached to the income tax return reflecting the total amount of advance payments received for the year, the total amount of advance payments received in prior tax years which has not been included in income before the current tax year, and the total amount of such payments received in prior tax years which has been included in gross income for the current tax year. Reg. § 1.451-5. If a taxpayer ceases to exist or the liability under the agreement otherwise ends, the remaining unreported advance payments are included in income for that year. Thus, the taxpayer should compare the consequences of using the future sale of inventory rules under Code Sec. 451 with the consequences of using the long-term contract method and the installment reporting method.

Bad Debts

Even though most accrual-basis taxpayers are no longer permitted to use the reserve method of accounting for bad debts, they will still be able to defer the accrual of income from services that they anticipate will be uncollectible.

Expenses

In deducting expenses on the accrual basis, the expenses incurred in, and properly attributable to, the process of earning income during a particular accounting period are charged against income for that tax year, even though they are paid in a later year. Where all the events which determine a taxpayer's liability occur within the tax year, the expense is properly accrued, although the amount may not be definitely ascertainable.

Contested Liabilities

If a taxpayer is contesting a liability of a claimed amount, the deduction may not be taken until the contest is settled by court decision, compromise, or otherwise. However, there is a way for the taxpayer to contest the liability and still claim a deduction: by paying the disputed amount or placing it beyond the taxpayer's control (such as in escrow or court deposit) until the matter is settled. Then, although the fight continues, an immediate deduction is obtained. If, after the contest is settled, it is determined that too much has been deducted, the excess is includible in income in the year of settlement.

TAX BLUNDER

Bob Mumper is an accrual-basis, calendar-year taxpayer who performs a service. In 1998, he received prepayments of $200,000 for services he will perform in 1999. Mumper is in the 39.6% tax bracket in 1998, and he is uncertain about future years' tax brackets. Mumper assumed that under the claim of right doctrine he had to include the $200,000 in gross income in 1998 and did so accordingly.

Mumper could have and should have used the prepaid service income method. This would have deferred income recognition until 1999, which would have reduced his tax liability by at least $79,200 (39.6% × $200,000) in 1998. Even if Mumper is in the 39.6% bracket in 1999, the time value of money would have worked in his favor and would have increased the present value of his after-tax cash flows.

¶ 12,245 SEPARATE SOURCES OF INCOME

Where a taxpayer has two or more separate and distinct businesses, a different method may be used for each business, provided separate books and records are maintained clearly reflecting the income of each. But the taxpayer may not shift profits and losses between businesses through inventory adjustments, sales, purchases, or expenses. Reg. § 1.446-1(d).

> *Example 12.18.* Olivia Lee operates a beauty shop and a record store as separate sole proprietorships. The income and deductions of the beauty shop can be accounted for under the cash method of accounting, while those of the record store must be under the accrual method of accounting.

In a situation where there are overlapping costs, expenditures on behalf of each activity are to be taken up in the books or tax return for that activity in accordance with the applicable method of accounting. As to any business for which separate records are maintained, the rule of consistency would continue to apply.

This principle has been extended to situations where the taxpayer uses one method for business income and another for personal income. The Regulations state that a taxpayer using one method of accounting in computing items of income and deductions for trade or business may compute other items of income and deductions not connected with the trade or business under a different method of accounting.

¶ 12,265 HYBRID METHODS

Many combinations of permissible accounting methods may be used. For example, the accrual method, which must be used for purchases and sales of inventory, may be combined with the cash method for other items of income and expense. But a taxpayer's choice is not unlimited. If the cash method is used for income, it must also be used for expenses. And if the accrual method is used for expenses, it must also be used for income.

The accrual method is required if inventories are an income-producing factor. Reg. § 1.446-1(c)(4)(i). If this were not mandatory, a cash-basis taxpayer could very easily reduce reported net income by increasing stock of inventory and could increase reported net income by depleting normal inventory. The effect of this required adjustment is to change only the computation of the tax deduction for the cost of inventory sold from a strict cash basis to an accrual basis of accounting.

The fact that inventories are essential does not necessarily mean that an accrual method of accounting is needed on an overall basis, especially if the business is one in which inventories are comparatively small, with little change from year to year, and little of the business (purchase or sales) is done on a credit basis. In such cases, a taxpayer may keep books and prepare returns almost entirely on a cash basis, making adjustments only for the variations in opening and closing inventories.

Change of Accounting Methods

¶ 12,301 IRS PERMISSION OR CONSENT

While there is no prohibition against changing the method of accounting, Code Secs. 446 and 481 require that permission be obtained from the IRS before adopting the new method for income tax purposes. The purpose of the prior consent provision is intended to promote consistency in accounting practices from year to year, thereby securing uniformity in the collection of the revenue, and to protect against a loss of revenue. The prior consent requirement applies even though the taxpayer's reporting method no longer conforms to the bookkeeping method.

Permission to change the method of tax accounting will not be granted unless the taxpayer and the IRS agree to the terms and conditions under which the change will be effected. Where two methods clearly reflect income, the IRS has considerable discretion in prescribing the conditions under which it will consent to a change from one to the other.

Change in Overall Plan or Material Items

A change of accounting method includes a change in the overall plan of accounting as well as a change in the treatment of any material item used in the plan. In most instances, a method of accounting is not established for an item unless there is a pattern of consistent treatment. Major changes in accounting method include:

1. Change to or from the cash-basis method
2. Change in the method of valuing inventory
3. Change from the accrual method to a long-term contract method or vice versa

4. Change involving the adoption, use, or discontinuance of any other specialized method of computing income, such as the crop method by farmers

5. Change for which the Code or Regulations specifically require that the consent of the IRS be obtained (Reg. § 1.446-1(e))

A material item is any item which involves the timing of inclusion or deduction. According to the Tax Court, the term means a "material item of gross income or deductions," not "a material item of net income" or "a material difference in income" resulting from the computation under two different methods of accounting. *Connors, Inc.*, 71 TC 913, CCH Dec. 35,900 (1979).

Correction of Mathematical Errors

A change in method does not include correction of mathematical and posting errors, or of errors in the computation of tax liability. For example, corrections of items that were deducted as interest or salary, but which are in fact payments of dividends, and of items that were deducted as business expenses, but which are personal expenses, are not changes in method. An adjustment to the useful life of a depreciable asset also is not an accounting method change. Although such adjustments may involve the question of the proper timing of a deduction, these items are traditionally corrected by adjustments in the current and future years.

Change in Underlying Facts

An accounting change does not include a change in treatment resulting from a change in underlying facts. On the other hand, a correction to require depreciation in lieu of a deduction for the cost of a class of depreciable assets which had been consistently treated as an expense in the year of purchase involves the question of the proper timing of an item and is to be treated as a change in method of accounting. Reg. § 1.446-1(e).

Change in Depreciation Classes

The regrouping of depreciable assets in order to conform to IRS Guideline classes is not considered a change in the accounting method requiring consent; a change from a declining balance to the straight-line method also does not require consent, but all other depreciation changes do. A change in an overall plan or system of identifying or valuing items in inventory, or a change in the treatment of any material item used in the overall plan for identifying or valuing items in inventory, is a change of method requiring consent.

IRS-Directed Changes

Although taxable income is to be computed according to a taxpayer's regular accounting method used in keeping the books, if that method does not clearly reflect income, the IRS may prescribe a method which does.

The IRS's authority to require a taxpayer to adopt an overall or specific change in accounting method necessary to clearly reflect income does not justify an arbitrary requirement of change. If a taxpayer's accounting method clearly reflects income, the IRS may not determine income by another method which would also clearly reflect income. Presumably, this rule would also apply to the method of treating a particular item of income or expense, such as depreciation. A taxpayer may, of course, conform books or returns to a suggestion by an Internal Revenue agent, for convenience, to cooperate with the local office of the Internal Revenue Service and facilitate audits of returns, or to avoid the expense of an appeal or refund proceedings, but the taxpayer cannot be required to make the change.

The IRS can change an incorrect method, but the change must be to a correct method. If the IRS has directed a taxpayer to change the method of accounting and the taxpayer has complied, the IRS cannot later argue that the change was improper because the taxpayer had not obtained formal permission to make it. And where an unusual method of accruing expenses on construction contracts was proposed by the IRS and the taxpayer followed that method, the IRS was not allowed to object in later years that the method did not clearly reflect income.

The Fifth Circuit has held that, where a taxpayer changed the accounting method and not the basis of the tax returns, the IRS may not require the returns to be filed on the new basis if both methods clearly reflect income despite the Code requirement that the book method must be used in computing income. *J.C. Patchen,* 58-2 USTC ¶ 9733, 258 F.2d 544 (CA-5 1958).

Combination of Methods

A combination of acceptable methods of accounting will be permitted if such combination clearly reflects income and is consistently used. However, if the taxpayer uses a hybrid method which is not authorized by the Regulations, the IRS may make adjustments to conform to either the cash or accrual basis, whichever more closely resembles the taxpayer's method of keeping books. The burden is on the taxpayer to show errors in determining which method predominates for book purposes, or to show that the hybrid method is acceptable. The fact that a taxpayer has filed returns on a hybrid basis for a number of years, without objection, does not bar the IRS from requiring a change.

Even a minor deviation from a predominant method of accounting is considered to be the equivalent of a hybrid or improper method of accounting for which a correction may be required.

Cash to Accrual Method

Taxpayers desiring to change their overall method of accounting from the cash receipts and disbursements method of accounting to the accrual method may do so by filing a timely request with the National Office. If this condition is satisfied, the IRS's consent to the change is considered to have been granted.

Net operating losses and tax credit carryforwards can reduce the amounts of any positive adjustment. For purposes of determining estimated payments, adjustments are recognized as occurring ratably throughout the year.

Denial of Change

Refusal to consent to a change in accounting method is ordinarily within the IRS's administrative discretion and cannot be reversed unless the taxpayer can prove the IRS abused its discretion. The IRS is not required to permit a change of accounting method for tax purposes just because the taxpayer is ordered to change the accounting method by another administrative agency. The Tax Court stated "that a taxpayer may be required to account one way for one government agency and another way for a different government agency may well be a hardship, and we have no doubt it is, but we are certain that the remedy does not lie with us as a judicial byproduct of a tax determination." *National Airlines, Inc.,* 9 TC 159, CCH Dec. 15,940 (1947).

Even if the taxpayer's accounting method complies with the established practice of a federal regulatory body, the IRS may still determine that the method does not clearly reflect income and may require a change of method.

¶ 12,325　ADJUSTMENTS FOR VOLUNTARY AND REQUIRED CHANGES

When a taxpayer computes taxable income under a different accounting method than that used in the preceding year, adjustments must be made in order to prevent items from being duplicated or entirely omitted. The general intent is that no item may be omitted and no item may be duplicated as a result of a change. These adjustments apply not only when the taxpayer voluntarily changes the accounting method with the consent of the IRS, but also when a change in method is required by the IRS.

The term "adjustments" is defined as the net amount of all adjustments, taking only the net dollar balance into account. The net amount of the adjustments would be the result of the consolidation of adjustments (both plus and minus) for the various accounts, such as inventory, accounts receivable, and accounts payable at the beginning of the tax year. In the case of a change in the treatment of a single material item, the amount of the adjustment is determined by the net dollar balance of that particular item.

> *Example 12.19.* Jones Co. is on the calendar year and uses the cash method of accounting. The IRS requested that Jones Co. change to the accrual method in 1999. Net income for 1999 under the accrual method was $60,000, computed as follows:

Sales	$200,000
Cost of goods sold	120,000
Gross profit	$ 80,000
Expenses	20,000
Net income	$ 60,000

On December 1998, there was $10,000 inventory on hand. Also, accounts receivable and accounts payable were $6,000 and $4,000, respectively.

The $60,000 net income must be adjusted for amounts which would be duplicated or be omitted because of the change in accounting methods. The net adjustment is $12,000; therefore, adjusted net income for 1999 would be $72,000. The adjustments are as follows:

Positive adjustment for the ending inventory balance because this amount was deducted when acquired	$ 10,000
Positive adjustment for the ending accounts receivable because this amount has never been included in income	6,000
Negative adjustment for the ending accounts payable because this amount has never been deducted	(4,000)
Net adjustment	$ 12,000

Rev. Proc. 97-27, 1977-21 IRB 11, provides a single adjustment period for positive and negative adjustments to replace the various adjustment periods that were available under Code Sec. 481 and related Regulations. In general (i.e., for most adjustments), the adjustment period is four years of which the tax year is the first year. However, if the adjustment is less than $25,000, the taxpayer may elect a one-year adjustment period. Finally, if the taxpayer ceases business operations (e.g., the firm liquidates) prior to the end of the four-year period, then any remaining adjustment is taken into consideration in the year of cessation.

Example 12.20. In example 12.19, Jones Co. has two options regarding the $12,000 adjustment. It can spread the $12,000 over four years, increasing net income for 1999 to $63,000 and increasing net income by $3,000 in 2000, 2001, and 2002. Alternatively, since the adjustment is less than $25,000, Jones could elect to use a one-year adjustment period and add the $12,000 to its $60,000 in 1999. If Jones has losses from other activities or a net operating loss carryover, then it might want to select this option.

Example 12.21. Harry Co. changed its method of accounting in 1998. The net adjustment due to the change was $44,000. Since this amount exceeds the less-than-$25,000 threshold, Harry Co. is not eligible to elect the one-year adjustment period. Thus, Harry Co. must use the four-year adjustment period, and one-fourth of the $44,000 will be included in income in 1998, 1999, 2000, and 2001.

If a taxpayer has claimed insufficient depreciation in prior years, the taxpayer may change his or her depreciation method to claim allowable depreciation. This is considered to be a change in accounting method, and the omitted depreciation from previous years is considered to be an adjustment that is spread over four years (unless the adjustment is less than $25,000, in which case the taxpayer may elect to use the one-year adjustment period).

¶ 12,355 TIME AND FORM OF APPLICATION

A taxpayer wishing to change the method of accounting may file Form 3115 (Application for Changes in Accounting Methods) anytime during the tax year for which the change is requested. Rev. Proc. 97-27, 1997-21 IRB 11. However, if the taxpayer is under examination, more stringent rules apply.

The taxpayer should, to the extent applicable, furnish (1) all information requested on the form, disclosing in detail all classes of items which would be treated differently under the new method and showing all amounts which would be duplicated or omitted as a result of the proposed change, and (2) the computation of the adjustments to take into account such duplications and omissions. In addition, the IRS may require such other information as may be necessary in order to determine whether the proposed change will be permitted.

It should also be stated in the application that the taxpayer proposes to take the adjustment into account over the appropriate period as required by the IRS in accordance with rules that have been discussed previously. Code Sec. 481; Rev. Proc. 84-74, 1984-2 CB 736; Rev. Proc. 97-27, 1997-21 IRB 11. Permission will not be granted unless the taxpayer and the IRS agree to the terms, conditions, and adjustments under which the change will be effected.

There is no requirement that, once the IRS has approved the change, the taxpayer must use the new accounting method in filing returns thereafter. However, the IRS, in its letter granting the change of accounting method, states that if the taxpayer does not wish to make the change, the IRS should be advised within 30 days of the date of the letter. The taxpayer who decides not to change his method of accounting after the 30-day period is not precluded from keeping the present method in effect.

¶ 12,365 ACCOUNTING METHOD TAX PLANNING

Keeping income levels near average from year to year is a major tax saver. The desire to balance income stems from the graduated scale of tax rates. Two persons having the same total taxable income over a number of years may pay widely different taxes because of the progressive rate structure. A taxpayer should choose accounting methods and procedures which will stabilize taxable income over the years so as to produce minimum taxes. Of course, where there are greater ups and downs in taxable income at higher rates, the tax savings become greater as taxable income is leveled out. The cash-basis taxpayer may time the receipt of income either by accelerating it to boost an otherwise poor year or by postponing it so as not to overburden the current year. There is nothing in income tax law which requires a creditor to press or decline to press for payment of an obligation in a particular tax year.

Income from sales arises when title to the goods passes to the customer, that is, in the case of most regular sales, at the time of delivery to a common carrier. By withholding shipment until after the end of the accounting period, a taxpayer may keep the amount of sales for the year down and thereby reduce income. In other instances, the seller may defer income by shipping goods on approval or on consignment subject to acceptance or sale in the following year.

A taxpayer may also reduce taxable income by accelerating business expenses for replenishment of supplies which are not part of inventory, performance of repairs, advertising, or business trips. Remember, however, that only ordinary and necessary expenses are deductible.

For an individual who engages in investment activities in occasional "business" ventures, the cash basis of accounting may offer substantial tax advantages through its ability to control year-end expenditures and receipts. For a business activity, the accrual method of accounting may offer advantages by its tendency to level out income, thus avoiding high-bracket peak income periods. There is no rule which would preclude a taxpayer from using the cash basis for nonbusiness items and salary and the accrual method for business income.

The number of alternative accounting procedures and conventions is substantially greater than the number of alternative general methods of accounting. The Code authorizes a number of accounting procedures to determine the cost allocation available for depreciation. The cost-of-goods-sold determination can be made under any of several alternative inventory costing conventions. Each of these accounting conventions or procedures will yield a different taxable income for a given tax year.

¶ 12,375 TIMELINESS

Making an accounting election usually requires some overt act on the part of a taxpayer. Proper timing is critical to making a valid election. Failure to make a timely election precludes a consideration of procedural compliance since the election will not be effective. To this extent, then, timing should be deemed of paramount importance.

The Code contains many elections that pertain to newly organized businesses. Failure to make the election on a timely basis may result in higher immediate taxes.

TAX BLUNDER

Dean Chips operated a successful garage as a sole proprietorship on the cash basis. He obtained IRS permission to change to the accrual method, which resulted in a net increase in income under Code Sec. 481(a). Pursuant to Code Sec. 481(c), he spread the adjustment over 10 years, starting with the year of change. Two years later, he incorporated his business in a "tax-free" Code Sec. 351 transaction. The IRS argued that the remaining 70 percent of the adjustment was accelerated upon incorporation, resulting in taxable income to Dean immediately. The Ninth Circuit agreed with the IRS that Code Sec. 481 requires continuity of the *taxpayer,* rather than the *business. D.R. Shore,* 80-2 USTC ¶ 9759, 631 F.2d 524 (CA-9 1980); Rev. Rul. 77-264, 1977-1 CB 238. Furthermore, the exception under Code Sec. 381 does not apply to corporate *organization,* only to corporate *reorganization.* Thus, even if Dean was the sole shareholder and even though the incorporation did not result in gain, it did accelerate income. So much for tax-free incorporations.

Inventories

¶ 12,401   USE OF INVENTORIES

If inventories are an income-producing factor, not only must inventories be kept, but the taxpayer must use the accrual method of accounting for purchases and sales. Reg. §§ 1.446-1(a)(4)(i) and 1.471-1. The result is that a major deduction, cost of goods sold, is deferred until the inventory is sold. Because cost of goods sold equals opening inventory, plus inventory purchased or produced, less ending inventory, an incentive exists to value ending inventories as low as possible. A low valuation results in an immediate tax benefit through a higher cost of goods sold deduction. Although the benefit is theoretically a mere deferral, the deferral is of indefinite duration. Also, as inventories grow with the expansion of the business, more and more profits are deferred. The value of ending inventory is a function of (1) what costs are included and (2) the cost flow assumptions made. The details are discussed below.

¶ 12,415   VALUATION OF INVENTORY

An inventory is an itemized list, with valuations, of goods held for sale or consumption in a manufacturing or merchandising business. The inventory should include all finished or partly finished goods, and only those raw materials and supplies which have been acquired for sale or which will physically become a part of merchandise intended for sale. Goods in transit to which the taxpayer has title should be included in inventory, and goods on hand in which title has passed to the buyer should not be included in inventory.

There are two fundamental requirements for valuation of inventory: (1) it must conform as nearly as possible to the best accounting practice in the trade or business and (2) it must clearly reflect income. Code Sec. 471. In determining whether income is clearly reflected, great weight is given to consistency in inventory practice. Reg. § 1.471-2. Nevertheless, a legitimate accounting system will be disallowed where it distorts income.

Inventory may be valued at cost or lower-of-cost-or-market. Reg. § 1.471-2. However, if the LIFO method (discussed later) is used, then the taxpayer cannot use lower-of-cost-or-market. Also, lower-of-cost-or-market must be applied to each item in inventory; a taxpayer cannot value the entire inventory at cost and at market and then select the lower amount.

¶ 12,425   COST METHODS

The cost of merchandise on hand at the beginning of the period (beginning inventory) is its inventory price as of the last day of the previous year. The cost of merchandise purchased is the invoice price, less trade discounts, plus incidental costs incurred to acquire the goods (such as transportation and other handling costs). Reg. § 1.471-3. Additionally, the following indirect costs must be capitalized unless the taxpayer's average annual gross receipts for the preceding three taxable years do not exceed $10 million: storage and warehousing; purchasing; handling, processing, assembly, and repacking; and administrative costs. Code Sec. 263A(b).

The cost of merchandise produced by the taxpayer includes the cost of direct materials, direct labor, and indirect costs. Reg. § 1.471-3. Manufacturers must use absorption costing (full costing) to value inventories; they cannot use direct costing or prime costing. Indirect costs that must be capitalized include repairs, maintenance, utilities, rent, and indirect labor and materials. Indirect costs do not include marketing expenses, advertising and selling expenses, and research and experimentation costs. Reg. § 1.471-11. Additionally, Code Sec. 263A expanded the definition of includible costs by requiring most entities (especially manufacturers) to use the uniform capitalization (UNICAP) rules. This expanded list requires the capitalization of more items than does financial accounting.

¶ 12,435 UNIFORM CAPITALIZATION RULES

UNICAP generally applies to real or personal property produced by the taxpayer and real or personal property acquired by the taxpayer for resale. Code Sec. 263A(b). Costs to be capitalized include direct costs and an expanded list of indirect costs. Reg. § 1.263A-1(b)(2). Under UNICAP, indirect costs include:

1. factory repairs and maintenance; utilities; rent; depreciation, amortization, and depletion; small tools; and insurance;

2. indirect labor and production supervisory labor; administrative costs; indirect materials and supplies; rework, scrap, and spoilage; storage and warehousing costs; purchasing costs; handling, processing, assembly, and repacking costs; and quality control and inspection costs;

3. taxes (other than income taxes);

4. deductible contributions to pension, profit-sharing, stock bonus, or annuity plans; and

5. interest, but only for real property, long-lived property, or property requiring more than two years to produce (one year for property costing more than $1 million).

Costs not required to be capitalized include nonmanufacturing costs such as marketing, selling, advertising and distribution expenses, and research and experimentation costs.

Cost Allocation Procedures

After identifying all costs which are required to be capitalized (known as total additional Code Sec. 263A costs), the next step in costing inventory is to allocate these costs. The Regulations provide allocation methods for direct labor, direct materials, and indirect costs.

The allocation method should result in the capitalization of all costs that directly benefit or are incurred because of production or resale activities. Reg. § 1.263A-1(b)(3).

All direct labor costs must be capitalized. The costs should be associated with specific production activities and products, and allocated to them accordingly (using specific identification or tracing). All direct material costs also should be capitalized. These costs should be allocated to products using the taxpayer's method of accounting for inventories which contain the direct materials (e.g., FIFO, LIFO, specific identification). The above mentioned allocation methods are not mandatory; the taxpayer may use any other method which reasonably allocates such costs.

Indirect costs are allocated to activities and products using one of three methods: specific identification (in which the costs are specifically identified with activities or products that directly benefit from the costs), standard costing (in which the costs are allocated to products based upon established standards), or burden rates (in which the costs are allocated based on direct labor hours, direct labor costs, and similar expenses).

Simplified Retail Method

Taxpayers who acquire property for resale and are required to capitalize costs under Code Sec. 263A may elect to use the simplified retail method to allocate costs. Under this method, costs for off-site storage and warehousing; purchasing; and handling, processing, assembly, and repacking are fully capitalized. Determining the amount of mixed service costs (general and administrative costs) to be allocated requires two steps. First determine the amount of mixed service costs that are additional Code Sec. 263A costs, then allocate this amount to ending inventory.

The amount of mixed service costs included under Code Sec. 263A is determined by multiplying such costs by the ratio of

1. total labor costs included in off-site, storage, purchasing, and handling cost, to

2. total labor costs incurred in the taxpayer's business, excluding the labor included in the mixed service costs.

Once this amount is determined, then it is allocated to ending inventory by multiplying the amount in ending inventory that was purchased during the year by the ratio of

1. total additional Code Sec. 263A costs, to

2. taxpayer's total purchases during the year.

Example 12.22. Kimby Co. uses the first-in, first-out (FIFO) method of accounting for its inventory. During the year it incurred $200,000 of storage costs, $300,000 of purchasing costs, $100,000 in handling and processing costs. The labor costs included in these amounts were $180,000. The company also incurred $250,000 of mixed service costs. Kimby Co.'s total labor costs, excluding amounts included in mixed service costs, were $2,000,000. Kimby's beginning inventory (excluding additional Code Sec. 263A costs) was $1,000,000. Total purchases during the year were $7,000,000 and ending inventory was $1,500,000 (excluding additional Code Sec. 263A costs). Since Kimby Co. uses the FIFO method, the full $1,500,000 of ending inventory is considered purchased during the year.

Kimby Co.'s ending inventory is $1,633,350, consisting of the original cost of $1,500,000, increased by capitalized additional Code Sec. 263A resale costs of $133,350. This is determined as follows. First, determine the amount of mixed service costs that are considered to be additional Code Sec. 263A costs using the labor ratios:

Labor ratio = $180,000/$2,000,000 = 9%

Mixed service costs considered additional Code 263A costs = 9% × $250,000 = $22,500.

Next, determine total additional Code Sec. 263A and allocate this amount to ending inventory using the additional Code Sec. 263A costs to purchases ratio.

Costs to purchase ratio = $622,500/$7,000,000 = 8.89%

Additional Code Sec. 263A costs allocated to ending inventory = 8.89% × $1,500,000 = $133,350.

Simplified Production Method

Taxpayers may elect to use the simplified production method to allocate capitalized costs for property produced. This method can only be used for property that is the taxpayer's stock in trade or includible in inventory, or for property held by the taxpayer primarily for sale to customers in the ordinary course of business. The method cannot be used for property acquired for resale and for property produced by the taxpayer for use in its business. Reg. § 1.263A-1(b)(5). Under this method, additional Code Sec. 263A costs are allocated based on an absorption ratio and the allocation requires two steps. First, compute the absorption ratio. This is the ratio of

1. total additional Code Sec. 263A costs incurred during the year, to

2. total Code Sec. 471 costs incurred during the year.

(Code Sec. 471 costs are those costs that otherwise would be capitalized under absorption costing.) Once this ratio is determined, then the amount of additional Code Sec. 263A costs required to be capitalized is determined by multiplying the absorption ratio times the amount of Code Sec. 471 costs incurred during the year which, under the taxpayer's method of accounting for inventory (e.g., FIFO or LIFO), are included in the taxpayer's ending inventory.

If the taxpayer uses FIFO, then the absorption ratio is applied to the Code Sec. 471 costs included in ending inventory. However, if the taxpayer uses LIFO, then the absorption ratio is applied to the Code

Sec. 471 costs included in this year's increase in inventory (the incremental layer).

> *Example 12.23.* Nifo Co. produces widgets. It began operations this year. It uses the FIFO method to account for its inventories. During the year it incurred $15,000,000 of Code Sec. 471 costs and $2,000,000 of additional Code Sec. 263A costs. Ending inventory consisted of $1,000,000 of Code Sec. 471 costs.
>
> Nifo Co.'s ending inventory is $1,133,333, consisting of $1,000,000 of Code Sec. 471 costs, increased by capitalized additional Code Sec 263A costs of $133,333. This is determined as follows:

Absorption ratio	= $2,000,000/$15,000,000 = 13.33%
Additional Code Sec. 263A costs allocated to ending inventory	= 13.33% × $1,000,000 = $133,333

¶ 12,445 LOWER-OF-COST-OR-MARKET (LCM) METHOD

Unless the taxpayer is using LIFO, the ending inventory may be written down to a lower market value (e.g., replacement cost). Reg. § 1.472-4. In addition, damaged or obsolete goods may be written down to realizable prices less costs of disposition. Reg. § 1.471-2(c). The determination of lower cost or market must be applied to each *item* of inventory. Reg. § 1.471-4(c).

> *Example 12.24.* A lumber dealer has three grades of lumber at the end of the tax year. They are valued as follows:

Grade	Cost	Market	LCM
1	$ 3,000	$ 5,000	$3,000
2	2,000	1,500	1,500
3	5,000	4,000	4,000
	$10,000	$10,500	$8,500

The ending inventory is $8,500, written *down* from $10,000, even though the inventory as a whole has *increased* in value.

¶ 12,453 VALUATION OF INVENTORY ITEMS

Taxpayers may use one of four cost flow assumptions to value their inventories: specific identification; first-in, first-out (FIFO); last-in, first-out (LIFO); or weighted average. The accounting method selected does not have to agree with the actual physical flow of goods. Specific identification usually is impractical because each item in inventory must be tracked very carefully. Generally, it is used for large items, such as appliances, which are more easily tracked. It is more convenient in many instances to use one of the other cost flow assumptions.

The FIFO method assumes that goods on hand in beginning inventory and the first goods purchased are the first goods sold to customers. Thus, ending inventory is valued at the price of most recent purchases. Cost of goods sold is based upon the cost of beginning inventory and the prices of goods purchased earlier in the year. Taxpayers using FIFO also may use the lower-of-cost-or-market method.

The LIFO method assumes that the goods most recently purchased are the first goods sold to customers. Thus, ending inventory is valued at beginning inventory amounts and at the price of goods acquired earlier in the year. Cost of goods sold is based upon the prices of the most recent purchases.

Taxpayers must receive IRS approval to use the LIFO method. Code Sec. 472. If the LIFO method is adopted in the taxpayer's first year of business or in the initial year that inventories are maintained, then advanced approval is not required. The method is adopted (approval received) by using it on that year's tax return. The taxpayer can change to the LIFO method by attaching Form 970 (Application to Use LIFO Inventory Method) with the tax year for the year of change. If LIFO is used for tax purposes then it also must be used for financial reporting purposes. LIFO produces a smaller taxable income when prices are rising, so there is an incentive (tax savings) to select this method. However, because of the conformity requirements for tax and financial reporting purposes, some firms do not select LIFO because it also produces a smaller net income on the financial statements. However, those taxpayers using LIFO are permitted to use other methods in the footnotes, appendices or supplements to the financial statements. Reg. § 1.472-2(e)(3). Also, taxpayers using LIFO may not use the lower-of-cost-or-market method.

The weighted average method values ending inventory (and cost of goods sold) based on the weighted average price of all goods available for sale during the year. The value of ending inventory generally is between those amounts obtained under the FIFO and LIFO methods.

Example 12.25. James Co. sells desks. Inventory on January 1 consisted of 300 desks valued at $400 per desk ($120,000). It purchased 700 desks on April 3 at $425 per desk ($297,500) and 900 desks on September 3 at $500 per desk ($450,000). During the year it sold 1,500 desks at a total sales price of $1,050,000. Ending inventory, cost of goods sold and gross profit using FIFO, LIFO and weighted average are as follows:

Sales	$1,050,000	$1,050,000	$1,050,000
Beginning inventory	$ 120,000	$ 120,000	$ 120,000
Purchases	747,500	747,500	747,500
Cost of goods available for sale	$ 867,500	$ 867,500	$ 867,500
Ending inventory			
FIFO (400 $500)	200,000		
LIFO (300 $400; 100 $425)		162,500	
Weighted average ($867,500/1,900 = $457/unit) (400 $457)			182,800
Cost of goods sold	$ 667,500	$ 705,000	$ 684,700
Gross profit	$ 382,500	$ 345,000	$ 365,300

If a taxpayer changes his or her inventory method, an adjustment is needed to account for the differences at date of conversion. The change could be from LIFO to FIFO, FIFO to LIFO, lower-of-cost-or-market to

LIFO, etc. In such a situation, the adjustment is spread over four years (unless the adjustment is less than $25,000, in which case the taxpayer may elect to use the one-year adjustment period).

KEYSTONE PROBLEM

Financial management has traditionally been opposed to adopting LIFO because it would result in reporting lower earnings in the financial statements to shareholders.

1. Are they correct in the short run? Why?
2. Are they correct in the long run? Why?

¶ 12,473   DOLLAR-VALUE LIFO METHOD

Instead of determining quantity increases of each item in the inventory and then pricing each item, as is required under regular LIFO, the dollar-value LIFO method may be used. The increase in LIFO value is determined by comparing the total dollar value of the beginning and ending inventories at base-year (first LIFO year) prices and then converting any dollar-value increase to current prices by means of an index. Taxpayers are allowed, under the dollar-value LIFO method, to determine base-year dollars through the use of government indexes. Code Sec. 472(f). The Regulations permit the use of several price index methods. Reg. § 1.472-8. The "double extension method," the most frequently used, works as follows:

1. Determine opening inventory at base-year prices (the prices in effect when LIFO was adopted).
2. Determine ending inventory at base-year prices.
3. The result is either an increase (increment) or a decrease (decrement).
4. Determine a price index to value the increment, if any. The index equals ending inventory at current prices/ending inventory at base-year prices.
5. Adjust the inventory "layers" for any increment or decrement. Every increment represents a new layer. Any decrement uses up the most recently added layer or layers first.

The following example is adapted from Reg. § 1.472-8(e)(2)(v), Examples (1) and (2).

Example 12.26. Skylark Inc. adopts LIFO in Year 1. Opening inventory was $14,000, which became the base period price. Ending inventory was $24,250 at actual prices, $20,000 at base-year prices. Thus, keeping prices constant, the increment was $6,000. The index was:

$$\frac{\$24,250}{\$20,000} = 1.2125$$

The increment is therefore $6,000 × 1.2125, or $7,275, and the ending inventory is $21,275, as opposed to $24,250 under FIFO, resulting in an increased cost of goods sold of $2,975. To summarize:

	1/1/Year 1	Index	12/31/Year 1
Opening inventory	$14,000	1.0	$14,000
Increment	6,000	1.2125	7,275
Ending LIFO inventory	$20,000		$21,275

If, at the end of Year 2, ending inventory was $18,000 at base period prices and $27,000 at current prices, there was a decrement with the following result:

	1/1/Year 1	Index	12/31/Year 2
1/1/Year 1 inventory	$14,000	1.0	$14,000
Remaining Year 1 increase	4,000	1.2125	4,850
LIFO inventory	$18,000		$18,850

At the end of Year 3, ending inventory was $25,000 at base period prices and $30,000 at current prices (30/25 = 1.2). The Year 3 year-end inventory consists of three "layers" as follows:

	1/1/Year 1	Index	12/31/Year 3
1/1/Year 1 inventory	$14,000	1.0	$14,000
Year 1 increase	4,000	1.2125	4,850
Year 3 increase	7,000	1.2	8,400
LIFO inventory	$25,000		$27,250

The computations above assume that only one "pool" was used. If substantially heterogeneous products exist, more than one pool must be used. Since each pool generates its own index and each pool may have numerous layers, the feasibility of dollar-value LIFO techniques depends on the availability of computers.

¶ 12,481   SIMPLIFIED DOLLAR-VALUE LIFO METHOD

Taxpayers may elect to use the simplified dollar-value LIFO method, but it then must be used to value all LIFO inventories. The simplified dollar-value LIFO method is designed to enable small businesses to use the LIFO method but avoid the extra costs and burden of maintaining records needed for the other LIFO methods. A taxpayer may elect the method for any year in which its average annual gross receipts for the preceding three years do not exceed $5 million. Code Sec. 474(c).

Using the method is relatively easy and straightforward. The taxpayer groups its inventory into pools for each major category in the applicable government price index provided by the Bureau of Labor Statistics (11 categories for retailers and 15 categories for all other taxpayers). Each pool then is separately adjusted using the appropriate government index. Retailers use the Consumer Price Index, and all other taxpayers use the Producer Price Index.

The taxpayer does not compute base period prices. Instead, the taxpayer uses year-end inventory values and determines an assumed base period value by applying the government price index. If the resulting base period value exceeds the opening inventory value at base period prices, then the increment is valued using the same index.

> *Example 12.27.* Susan Co. adopted the simplified dollar-value LIFO method. Inventory at actual prices in Year 1 and Year 2 was $200,000 and $300,000, respectively. The Consumer Price Index for Years 1 and 2 was 115 percent and 125 percent, respectively. Susanco's ending inventory for Year 2 would be valued at $282,609, consisting of $200,000 from Year 1 plus the Year 2 increment of $82,609. The Year 2 increment is determined as follows:

Year 2 ending inventory at assumed base-year prices	$= \$300,000 \times 1.15/1.25$	$= \$276,000$
The increment at Year 1 base price	$= \$276,000 - \$200,000$	$= \$ 76,000$
The increment at Year 2 base price	$= \$ 76,000 \times 1.25/1.15$	$= \$ 82,609$

¶ 12,485 ESTIMATES OF INVENTORY SHRINKAGE

TRA '97 amended Code Sec. 471 to permit a business to determine its year-end closing inventory by using estimates for shrinkage (e.g., loss due to theft). A year-end physical count is not necessary if the business: (1) normally takes a physical count of its inventories at each business location on a regular and consistent basis and (2) makes proper adjustments to its inventories and to its estimating methods to the extent its estimates differ from actual shrinkage.

Using this method results in a change in accounting method, but IRS permission is not required to make the change. Also, any adjustments to income due to this change are taken into account over a four-year period.

> *Example 12.28.* SQ Co., a calendar-year taxpayer, generally takes a physical count of inventory every three months. In 1998, it claimed a $30,000 deduction for inventory shrinkage based on an estimate of shrinkage on December 31, 1998. Since it takes a physical count on a regular basis, it is permitted to use an estimate for inventory shrinkage.

TAX PLANNING POINTER ▼

A widely held view is that a major potential cost in changing from the "lower-of-cost-or-market" method of valuing inventories to LIFO is that opening inventory must be written back up to cost and the write-up taken into income. This adverse tax aspect may be avoided or may be nonexistent in the following situations:

No inventory on hand at the end of the year prior to the year of change was written down from cost.

The portion of the inventory written down may be (any of the following):

1. Sold before year-end at a discount or disposed of as giveaways, prizes, or bonuses to customers

2. Given to employees as deductible compensation

3. Contributed to charity, resulting in nonrecognition of income as well as a deduction (prior to year-end)

4. Abandoned (i.e., "dumped")

Thus, with proper tax planning, no income will have to be recognized.

TAX BLUNDER

Hind Co. uses the FIFO inventory method because this method reflects the true physical flow of inventory. Ending inventory under FIFO was $400,000 in 1998. Had Hind Co. used LIFO, ending inventory would have been $240,0000. Hind Co. has been in the 34% tax bracket and believes it will continue to be in the 34% tax bracket.

Actual physical flow of inventory is irrelevant for costing purposes. The cost flow used (assumed) is artificial and does not need to coincide with the actual physical flow. Had Hind Co. used LIFO, it would have increased cost of goods sold by $160,000, and taxable income would have decreased by $160,000, producing a tax savings of $54,400 (34% × $160,000). Again, given the time value of money, this would be preferable.

Long-Term Contracts

¶ 12,501   ALTERNATIVE ACCOUNTING METHODS

The term long-term contract means any contract for the manufacture, building, installation, or construction of property if such property is not completed within the taxable year in which the contract is entered into. A contract for the manufacture of property will not be treated as a long-term contract unless it involves the manufacture of any unique item which is not normally included in finished goods inventory or requires more than 12 calendar months to complete. Code Sec. 460(f). A taxpayer generally has two alternatives to account for long-term contracts: the percentage-of-completion method (or modified percentage-of-completion method in some cases) and the completed-contract method (in limited circumstances). The accounting method selected must be used for all long-term contracts in the same trade or business. Reg. § 1.451-3(a).

Under the percentage-of-completion method taxpayers report income under the contract annually based on estimated progress. The percentage of completion is determined by comparing allocated costs to the contract and direct costs incurred by the close of the year to the estimated total contract costs. Code Sec. 460(b). The total contract price is multiplied by the percentage to determine the amount of income reported in that year.

Under the percentage-of-completion method the taxpayer must use a look-back method in the year the contract is completed. This method requires the taxpayer to compare the actual completion level to the claimed level (to reflect the actual profit for each year of the contract) and to redetermine taxable income and tax liability accordingly. Interest is charged on any underpayment and is received for any overpayment. However, long-term contracts completed within two years of contract commencement are exempt from the look-back method if the gross contract price does not exceed the lesser of $1,000,000 or 1 percent of the taxpayer's average gross receipts for the last three years preceding the year in which the contract was entered. Code Sec. 460(b).

TRA '97 changed Code Sec. 460 to permit taxpayers to elect not to apply the look-back method for long-term contracts completed during the year and in all subsequent years if the actual contract taxable income is within 10 percent of estimated taxable income under the percentage-of-completion method (using estimated contract price and costs).

> **Example 12.29.** Jones Co. enters into a three-year construction contract in 1998. Jones Co. estimated (reported) net income using the percentage-of-completion method was $100,000, $200,000, and $300,000 for 1998, 1999, and 2000, respectively. In 2000, when the contract is completed, Jones Co. determines that actual net income for each year was $108,000, $210,000, and $282,000, respectively, for the three years. Ten percent of $108,000 is $10,800, and 10% of $318,000 is $31,800. Since the $100,000 claimed in 1998 and the $300,000 cumulative income in 1999 ($200,000 in 1999 and $100,000 in 1998) are within the 10 percent range, Jones can elect not to apply the look-back method.

The modified percentage-of-completion method is available for contracts that are less than 10 percent complete at the end of the year. If this condition is met, then taxpayers may elect to defer reporting any income from the contract until at least 10 percent of the work is completed. Code Sec. 460(b)(5). In the year that 10 percent is completed, the taxpayer will report income on all the work completed in that year using the "regular" percentage-of-completion method described above. The rationale for this election is that it often is difficult to estimate the total costs of a long-term project at its beginning; the modified method gives the taxpayer some time and experience to provide a "better" estimate.

Under the completed-contract method taxpayers report no income until final completion of the contract, regardless of when the funds are collected. All costs are accumulated and recognized at completion. The use of this method provides substantial opportunity to defer income, and as such is severely restricted. Only small construction contractors and home construction contractors can use this method. Small contractors are those whose average gross receipts for the three preceding tax years do not exceed $10,000,000. Code Sec. 460(e).

Final completion of the contract is based on an analysis of all the facts and circumstances. However, a taxpayer may not delay completion of a contract for the principal purpose of deferring federal income taxes. Reg. § 1.451-3(b)(2)(i). Additionally, if the buyer reasonably disputes the work, then income or deduction with respect to said dispute is recognized in the year the dispute is resolved. If the amount reasonably in dispute is extensive and so affects the contract price that it is not possible to determine whether a gain or loss will result from the contract, then no gain or loss is recognized until the dispute is settled. Reg. § 1.451-3(d)(2).

¶ 12,515 COMPARISON OF THE METHODS

The following, simplified example illustrates the difference between the percentage-of-completion and completed-contract methods:

Example 12.30. In 1998, Building Construction Co. entered into a contract to build a small warehouse for $2,500,000. Total estimated costs to complete are $2,000,000, and the project is expected to be completed in 1999. Actual costs incurred in 1998 and 1999 were $800,000 and $900,000, respectively. Results for 1998 and 1999 are shown below.

Percentage-of-Completion Method	*1998*	*1999*
Gross Revenue	$1,000,000 [a]	$1,500,000 [b]
Actual Costs	(800,000)	(900,000)
Gross Profit Reported	$ 200,000	$600,000

a. ($800,000/$2,000,000) × $2,500,000
b. $2,500,000 − $1,000,000

Completed-Contract Method		
Gross Revenue	$ 0	$2,500,000
Actual Costs	0	(1,700,000)
Gross Profit Reported	$ 0	$800,000

¶ 12,535 CAPITALIZATION OF EXPENSES

All costs associated with the contract are capitalized and are deducted as profits are recognized. This principle applies to direct costs, such as material and direct labor costs, as well as to overhead, such as repairs and maintenance, utilities, rent, cost recovery, shipping costs, general and administrative expenses, scrap and spoilage costs, etc. Construction period interest must always be capitalized. The following expenses must be capitalized; they may not be expensed if the percentage-of-completion method is used:

1. Cost recovery of assets employed for work on specific contracts

2. Pension costs representing current service costs

3. General and administrative expenses relating to specific contracts

4. Research and development expenses with respect to specific contracts

5. Scrap and spoilage costs

In any event, bidding expenses, indirect research and development expenses, and marketing, advertising, and selling expenses may be deducted currently.

Installment Sales

¶ 12,601 USE OF INSTALLMENT METHOD

An installment sale is a disposition of property where at least one payment is received after the close of the taxable year in which the disposition occurs. Code Sec. 453(b). Thus, there is no requirement for numerous payments over several years; one payment in a subsequent year would qualify as an installment sale. The installment method may be used by cash-basis and accrual-basis taxpayers as a means to defer gain recognition or to spread gain recognition over several tax periods. The method may not be used if the property is disposed of at a loss. Additionally, the installment method only affects when the gain is recognized, it does not change the character of the gain (capital or ordinary). How this gain is taxed is determined by the applicable laws in the year the installment payment is received, not in the year of sale. The seller reports gains under the installment method on Form 4562 (Depreciation and Amortization).

The installment method is not available to all taxpayers. It cannot be used: by dealers in real and personal property; for any sale of personal property under a revolving credit plan; for sales of depreciable property to a controlled entity (e.g., to a corporation in which the taxpayer owns directly and indirectly more than 50 percent of the value of the outstanding stock), unless the taxpayer can establish that tax avoidance was not a principal purpose of the disposition; and for sales of stock or securities which are traded on an established securities market (or to the extent provided in the regulations for property other than stock or securities regularly traded on an established market). Code Sec. 453.

Although nondealers may use the installment method, Code Sec. 453A imposes a special interest charge if the sale price of the real or personal property (other than personal-use and farm property) exceeds $150,000. This interest charge is on the tax liability deferred on the property sold. However, the interest charge only applies if the installment obligation is outstanding at year-end and if the face amount of all installment obligations which arose during the year and are outstanding at year end exceeds $5 million.

The taxpayer must use the installment method for tax purposes if the taxpayer disposes of property under an installment contract and the disposition qualifies for the installment method. However, the taxpayer may make an irrevocable election not to use the installment method. Code Sec. 453(d). In such a case the gain would be recognized in the year of disposition. Finally, all depreciation recapture occurs in the year of sale, regardless of the fact that the taxpayer uses the installment method.

¶ 12,655   COMPUTATION OF GAIN

The installment method recognizes income as payments are received. There are several steps to follow.

Step 1. Determine the gross profit from the sale. Gross profit equals the selling price minus the property's adjusted basis, selling expenses and depreciation recapture (if any).

Step 2. Determine the contract price. The contract price generally equals the amount the seller will receive. If there are no liabilities on the property, then contract price equals selling price. If there are liabilities on the property which the buyer assumes, then the contract price equals all payments to be received by the seller (i.e., the selling price reduced by the mortgage assumption). If the liabilities exceed the property's adjusted basis (increased by selling expenses for this comparison only), then such excess increases the contract price (it equals all payments to be received by the seller plus the excess). The contract price can never be less than the gross profit.

Step 3. Compute the gross profit percentage (which can never be greater than 100 percent). Gross profit percentage = Gross profit/Contract price.

Step 4. Determine the amount of gain to be recognized in the year of sale. Recognized gain = Payments received × Gross profit percentage.

Example 12.31. Ann Rogers, 45 years old, sold property for $125,000. Her selling expenses were $5,000 and her basis was $40,000. She received $25,000 down and will receive $20,000 in each of the following five years. Ann's gross profit is $80,000 ($125,000 − ($5,000 + $40,000)). The contract price is $125,000, and the gross profit percentage is 64 percent ($80,000/$125,000). She will recognize a gain of $16,000 in the year of sale (64% × $25,000) and $12,800 in each of the following five years (64% × $20,000). Thus, total gain recognized over the six years is $80,000 ($16,000 + (5 × $12,800)). Ann also will recognize income for the interest she received over this period.

Example 12.32. Assume the same facts as in Example 12.31 except that the property was depreciable property subject to $15,000 of depreciation recapture under Code Sec. 1245. Ann's gross profit is $65,000 ($125,000 − ($5,000 + $40,000 + $15,000)). The contract price is still $125,000. The gross profit percentage is 52 percent ($65,000/$125,000). She will recognize a $13,000 gain in the year of sale (52% × $25,000) and $15,000 ordinary income from the depreciation recapture. In each of the following five years she will recognize a gain of $10,400 (52% × $20,000). Total gain recognized over the six years also is $80,000 ($13,000 + $15,000 + (5 × $10,400)). Ann also will recognize income for the interest she received over this period.

Example 12.33. Assume the same facts as in Example 12.31 except that there is a $5,000 mortgage on the property which the buyer assumes. Additionally, Ann will receive $20,000 in the year of sale and $20,000 in each of the following five years. In this case, Ann's gross profit is $80,000 ($125,000 − ($5,000 + $40,000)). The contract price is $120,000 ($125,000 − $5,000); Ann will receive $115,000 in cash payments from the buyer. The gross profit percentage is 66.67 percent ($80,000 ÷ $120,000). She will recognize a gain of $13,333 ($20,000 × 66.67%) in the year of sale and in each of the following five years. Total gain recognized over the six years is $80,000 ($13,333 × 6), allowing for a $2 roundoff. Ann also will recognize income for the interest she received over this period.

Example 12.34. Assume the same facts as in Example 12.31 except the property is subject to a $50,000 mortgage which the buyer assumes. Additionally, Ann will receive $15,000 in the year of sale and $12,000 in each of the following five years. In this case the liability exceeds the adjusted basis by $5,000 ($50,000 − ($40,000 + $5,000 selling expenses)). Whenever the liability exceeds the adjusted basis (increased by selling expenses), the gross profit percentage is 100 percent. Also, the excess is treated as a payment in the year of sale. Thus, Ann recognizes a gain of $20,000 (100% × ($15,000 + $5,000)) in the year of sale and $12,000 (100% × $12,000) in each of the following five years. Total gain recognized over the six years is $80,000 ($20,000 + (5 × $12,000)). Ann also will recognize income for the interest she received over this period.

Example 12.35. Sal Weintraub sold $20 million of nondealer real estate during the year under the installment method. At year-end $15 million is outstanding. Deferred gross profit on the outstanding obligations is $4 million. The maximum tax rate in effect during the year was 39.6 percent. Code Sec. 453A applies in this situation, and Sal must pay the special interest charge. Assume that the federal short-term interest rate in December was 8 percent. The interest due is $116,160, computed as follows:

1. Determine the portion of installment obligations outstanding at year-end in excess of $5 million and divide this by the total amount of installment obligations outstanding at year-end.

   ($15,000,000 − $5,000,000) ÷ $15,000,000 = 66.67%

2. Determine the tax liability deferred on all installment obligations outstanding at year-end by multiplying the deferred gross profit on such obligations by the maximum tax rate in effect for the tax year.

   ($4,000,000 × 39.6%) = $1,584,000

3. Determine the applicable interest rate, which is equal to the federal short-term interest rate for the last month of the tax year, increased by 3 percentage points.

   (8% + 3%) = 11%

4. Determine the interest due (which is considered personal interest expense).

$$(66.67\% \times \$1,584,000 \times 11\%) = \$116,160$$

¶ 12,675 ELECTING OUT OF INSTALLMENT REPORTING

As noted earlier, a taxpayer may elect not to use the installment method. This election must be made by the due date (including extensions) for filing the tax return for the year of the installment sale. Reg. § 15A.453-1(d)(3). However, there are potential drawbacks to such an election. For example, if a capital asset or a Section 1231 asset is sold at a gain on the installment plan and the seller elects not to use installment reporting, there are at least two obvious drawbacks:

1. The gain is accelerated and the tax is due in the year of sale before the proceeds are received.

2. If the value of the note is less than its face value, a cash-basis taxpayer will limit the capital gain and may convert the discount into ordinary income on collection if the collection of a note does not qualify as a "sale or exchange." (This problem does not affect accrual-method sellers since they accrue the face value.) Under Code Sec. 1271(a)(1) and (b)(1), retiring a debt instrument is a sale or exchange, unless issued by a natural person.

Example 12.36. Rita Brown sells a painting held for five years as an investment. The painting was purchased for $5,000 and sold to Joe Smith for $15,000, $6,000 down and a $9,000 face value note worth $7,000 due in three years together with 10 percent interest. If she opts for installment reporting, her gross profit percentage is 66 2/3:

$$\frac{(\$15,000 - \$5,000)}{\$15,000}$$

resulting in a capital gain of $4,000 in the year of sale and $6,000 upon collection of the note (plus interest).

If Rita elects *not* to use installment reporting, the result is as follows:

Year of Sale:

Amount realized	
Cash	$ 6,000
Fair market value of note	7,000
	$13,000
Less adjusted basis	5,000
Long-term capital gain	$ 8,000

Year of Collection:

Collection of principal	$ 9,000
Less basis in note	7,000
Ordinary income.......................................	$ 2,000

As a result, the installment method is clearly preferable.

The Regulations are flexible enough to permit installment reporting even if the selling price and, therefore, gross profit percentage are unknown at the initial sale. Reg. § 15A.453-1(c). Three main situations can be identified:

1. *Maximum selling price.* If payments are contingent, but subject to a ceiling, the ceiling is presumed to be the selling price. The gross profit percentage is initially based on this maximum and is subsequently modified as more facts become available.

2. *Given payment period.* Here the seller's basis is prorated over the term. The result may be gains in some years, losses in others.

3. *No maximum price, no given term.* Here the seller recovers basis over 15 years, which may also lead to gain or loss in any given year, presumably of the same character.

In view of this expansion of the scope of the installment reporting provisions, the cost recovery method (the "open transaction" approach) is likely to have even less applicability than before.

TAX PLANNING POINTER ▼

The taxpayer's current and expected future tax rates should be carefully considered when deciding to use the installment method of reporting. If the taxpayer's future tax rates are expected to decline, then using the installment method could produce significant tax savings. Conversely, if the taxpayer expects to be in higher tax brackets in the future, then the installment method could result in significant increases in taxes. Remember, the time value of money also must be considered.

Example 12.37. Jennifer Hayes sold a short-term capital asset in 1998. She has no capital loss carryovers and sold no other capital assets in 1998. She does not plan to sell any capital assets during the years 1999 through 2002. The amount realized on the sale was $40,000, and the property's adjusted basis was $8,000. Her realized and recognized gain is $32,000. Jennifer will receive $8,000 at the date of sale and $8,000 (plus interest) per year for 1999, 2000, 2001, and 2002. The value of the note is equal to its face value. The gross profit percentage is 80 percent ($32,000/$40,000). If she uses the installment method of reporting, then she will recognize $6,400 ($8,000 × 80%) of ordinary income (plus interest income) in each of the five years. If she elects out of the installment method, then she will recognize $32,000 of income in 1998 plus interest income as received.

If Jennifer is in the 31 percent bracket in 1998 but expects to be in the 15 percent bracket in 1999 through 2002, then she would save $4,096 in taxes by using the installment method.

Tax on $32,000 if recognized in 1998 ($32,000 × 31%) $9,920
Tax on $6,400 in 1998 ($6,400 × 31%) $1,984
Tax on $6,400 in 1999 through 2002
    ($6,400 × 15%) = $960 × 4 years 3,840   5,824

Tax savings by using the installment method of reporting $4,096

If Jennifer is in the 15 percent bracket in 1998 but expects to be in the 31 percent bracket in 1999 through 2002, then she would save $4,096 in taxes by electing out of the installment method.

Tax on $32,000 if recognized in 1998 ($32,000 × 15%) $4,800
Tax on $6,400 in 1998 ($6,400 × 15%) . . . . $ 960
Tax on $6,400 in 1999 through 2002
    ($6,400 × 31%) = $1,984 × 4 years 7,936   8,896

Tax savings by using the installment method of reporting $4,096

¶ 12,685   DISPOSITIONS OF INSTALLMENT OBLIGATIONS

There are times when a taxpayer who sold property on the installment method needs or wants to dispose of the installment obligation prior to maturity. In this instance, the taxpayer must determine the obligation's adjusted basis and determine the gain or loss on the disposition. The adjusted basis of the installment obligation is equal to the face amount of the obligation in excess of the income that would have been reported if the obligation had been paid in full. To determine gain or loss, the adjusted basis is compared to the amount realized if the obligation is sold and to the obligation's fair market value if it is disposed of other than by sale. The character of the gain or loss is based upon the property which was sold under the installment method. Code Sec. 453B(a).

Example 12.38. In 1998, Katherine Beales sold a piece of art for $50,000. She received $10,000 in 1998 and in 1999. She purchased the piece in 1981 for $8,000; thus, her gross profit was $42,000 and the contract price was $50,000. The gross profit percentage was 84 percent ($42,000/$50,000). In 2000, she sold the installment obligation for $28,000. Her basis in the obligation is $4,800 (unpaid balance of $30,000 minus amount of income reported if unpaid balance paid in full (84% × $30,000)). Thus, Katherine's gain on the sale of the installment obligations is $23,200 ($28,000 − $4,800). The gain is a long-term capital gain since the art piece was a long-term capital asset when it was sold in 1998. Katherine also will recognize income for the interest she received while the obligation was outstanding.

In addition to a sale, there are several other situations where a disposition of an installment obligation results in a recognized gain or loss, primarily to prevent income-shifting among taxpayers. In each of these the fair market value of the obligation is used as the amount realized. Code Sec. 453B(a).

The following lead to income recognition at the time the installment obligation is transferred: gifts or forgiveness of payments, especially if the obligee and obligor are related; taxable exchanges; and corporate distributions. Additionally, gain recognition occurs on "second dispositions," whereby the taxpayer sells the property to a related party and within two years of the sale and before the taxpayer receives all payments with respect to such sale, the related party disposes of the property (i.e., the "second" disposition). At the time of the second disposition, the amount realized from the second distribution is treated as being received by the original taxpayer. Code Sec. 453(c).

Gain or loss is not recognized in the following situations: transfers to a controlled corporation under Code Sec. 351; transfers in certain corporate reorganizations and liquidations; certain transfers to and from partnerships; transfers upon the death of a taxpayer; transfers incident to a divorce; and transfers to a spouse.

> *Example 12.39.* Jack Moore purchased land in 1992 for $40,000. Jack sold the land to his daughter in 1997. The terms of the sale call for Jack to receive $20,000 in 1997 and $15,000 in 1998, 1999, 2000, and 2001, plus interest. The gross profit is $40,000, the contract price is $80,000 and the gross profit percentage is 50 percent. Jack received payments in 1997 and 1998, recognizing $10,000 and $7,500, plus interest, respectively, in 1997 and 1998. In 1999, Jack forgave the remaining payments. The forgiveness is a taxable disposition. Jack is considered to have received the remaining payments ($45,000) and his recognized gain in 1999 is $22,500 (50% × $45,000).

¶ 12,695   REPOSSESSIONS

The repossession of personal property sold under the installment method is a taxable event. Gain or loss is recognized equal to the difference between the fair market value of the property repossessed and the adjusted basis of the installment obligation. Any costs incurred during the repossession increase the adjusted basis of the installment obligation. The character of the gain or loss recognized is the same as the character of the gain or loss recognized on the original sale of the property. The basis of the repossessed property is its fair market value.

Loss is not recognized and no bad deduction is allowed on the repossession of real property. Gain is recognized to a limited extent. Code Sec. 1038 limits gain recognition to the lesser of (1) the cash and fair market value of property received from the buyer in excess of gain previously recognized by the holder of the installment obligation or (2) the gain not yet recognized by the holder of the installment obligation (deferred gross profit), reduced by the costs incurred during the repossession. The character of the gain is the same as that recognized under the original sale of the property. The basis of the repossessed real property is the adjusted basis of the installment obligation, increased by costs incurred during the repossession and by any gain recognized from the repossession.

Example 12.40. John Wells sold a car in January 1998 for $10,000. He received $2,000 down and $8,000 was due in 1999. His basis in the car at the time of sale was $6,000. John made numerous attempts to collect the $8,000 and in December he repossessed the car. He incurred $300 in repossession costs and the car's fair market value at time of repossession was $9,000. In 1998, John reported a capital gain of $800 (40% × $2,000). The adjusted basis of the installment obligation at the time of repossession was $4,800 ($8,000 − (40% × $8,000)). To determine John's gain on the repossession, this basis is increased by the repossession costs. Thus, John recognizes a $3,900 capital gain in December 1999 ($9,000 − ($4,800 + $300)). John's basis in the repossessed car is $9,000, its fair market value.

Example 12.41. Tom O'Brien sold land in January 1998 for $50,000. He received $20,000 down and $30,000 was due in January 1999. Tom acquired the land in 1992 for $10,000. The gross profit percentage is 80 percent. Tom recognized a $16,000 long-term capital gain in 1998. Tom was unable to collect the $30,000 and repossessed the land in October 1999, incurring $1,000 in the process. The land's fair market value in October 1999 was $52,000. Tom's recognized long-term gain is $4,000, equal to the lesser of $4,000 ($20,000 received − $16,000 gain previously recognized) or $23,000 ($24,000 gain not yet recognized − $1,000 repossession costs). His basis in the repossessed land is $11,000 (the basis of the installment obligation ($30,000 − (80% × $30,000)) plus the gain recognized on repossession ($4,000) plus the costs incurred to repossess ($1,000).

¶ 12,699 INTEREST ON DEFERRED PAYMENT SALES

A seller of capital assets historically had an incentive to charge little or no interest while inflating the selling price, thus converting ordinary interest income into capital gains or a reduced capital loss. Section 483 limits the taxpayer's opportunity to do so, but does not eliminate it altogether. Briefly stated, unless the seller charges at least a rate equal to the "applicable federal rate" the IRS will impute interest at such a rate compounded semiannually, resulting in additional interest income to the buyer and a lower selling price (and a lower gross profit), but also providing the buyer with higher interest deductions (and a lower basis). Interest will not be imputed to a sale where all the payments are due within six months. Additionally, there are several special rules, including:

1. Unlike installment reporting, Code Sec. 483 applies to sales at a loss.

2. No interest is imputed unless the selling price is in excess of $3,000.

3. Sales of patents where the selling price is contingent on the use, production, or disposition of such patents, and private annuity sales are excluded.

4. Only 6 percent interest need be charged for sales of up to $500,000 of real property to a family member, including siblings, spouses, an ancestor, or a lineal descendant.

Example 12.42. Ann Clerice sold land in 1998 for $40,000. The adjusted basis of the property was $50,000. Ann received $12,000 in 1998 and will receive $28,000 in 1999. No interest was charged. Ann has a $10,000 loss and cannot use the installment method to report it. However, since it is a deferred contract she must charge interest; thus, the IRS will impute interest and reduce the selling price accordingly. This increases her loss, causes her to recognize interest income, reduces the buyer's basis in the land, and causes interest expense for the buyer which may or may not be deductible.

Since the statutory rate may be below the market rate for second mortgages and unsecured personal loans, some flexibility of designing a price/terms combination that is attractive for tax purposes still exists.

TAX PLANNING POINTER

Olga Lopez purchased some land years ago as an investment for $40,000. She owns it free and clear, wishes to sell it for its value of $100,000 and would like as much cash up front as possible while deferring the tax as long as possible. Any potential buyer would most likely wish to finance the acquisition. If Olga sells the land on the installment plan, her gross profit of 60 percent will apply to payments in the year of sale as well as to future collections. After competent tax advice, she did the following:

1. She borrowed $40,000 with the property as collateral. The receipt of the loan proceeds is tax free.

2. After a reasonable time, she sold the property for $100,000 by letting the buyer take over the $40,000 loan and taking back a second mortgage below the market rate.

3. Even though her gross profit is now 100 percent, she received $40,000 tax free and converted interest income and favorable terms into an additional long-term capital gain on a tax-deferred basis.

SUMMARY OF CHAPTER 12

✓ Taxable income must be computed on the basis of the tax-payer's tax year.

✓ The annual accounting period may be either a calendar year or a fiscal year.

✓ The tax year cannot exceed 12 months except where a 52-53-week tax year is adopted.

✓   A fiscal year is a period of 12 months ending on the last day of any month other than December or a 52-53-week annual accounting period.

✓   A fiscal year is permitted only if the taxpayer's books are kept on the same basis.

✓   Usually the taxpayer needs a business purpose for approval of a change in tax periods.

✓   Prior approval must be obtained before changing to a new tax year.

✓   A return required for a fractional part of the year (due to a change in accounting periods) is known as a short-period return.

✓   To obtain IRS approval to change accounting periods, Form 1128 must be filed on or before the 15th day of the second calendar month following the end of the short period.

✓   The taxpayer's method of accounting must "clearly reflect income."

✓   A taxpayer may change accounting methods voluntarily or may be required to change.

✓   To obtain IRS permission to change accounting methods, Form 3115 must be filed anytime during the year in which the change is desired.

✓   The taxpayer faced with a substantial tax due to a change of accounting methods generally has a four-year adjustment period.

✓   An understanding of accounting periods and methods is crucial to understanding the taxation of any entity.

✓   Many accounting methods used for financial accounting are similar to those used for tax accounting, but there are many differences too.

✓   Several inventory methods are available to the taxpayer: specific identification, FIFO, and LIFO, and variations thereto.

✓   Certain costs with respect to inventory must be capitalized.

✓   The percentage-of-completion method must be used for long-term contracts.

✓   The installment method of accounting is used when proceeds from the sale of certain property are received in a year other than the year of sale.

✓   A taxpayer may elect not to use the installment method.

CHAPTER 12 QUESTIONS

1. How does financial accounting differ from tax accounting?

2. What options are available in selecting a tax year?

3. If a taxpayer is on the fiscal year, what is the requirement regarding the taxpayer's books?

4. What is the definition of a short tax year?

5. Can a sole proprietor use a fiscal tax year for a business if the individual is on a calendar tax year?

6. What tax year options are available to a partnership?

7. Is a taxpayer allowed to select a tax year ending on July 20?

8. If a corporation begins business on June 12, 1998, when may it close its first tax year?

9. What tax year options are available to an S corporation?

10. May an estate adopt a fiscal year ending September 30 without IRS permission?

11. What is the latest time that an application for a change in accounting period may be filed?

12. What does annualizing a short year mean?

13. In which of the following cases must the taxpayer annualize its income for a period of less than 12 months?

    a. Alpha Corporation was formed on August 17 and decided to report on the calendar year.

    b. Beta Corporation was formed on March 8 and decided to use the fiscal year ending July 31.

    c. Gamma Corporation has been using a fiscal year ending April 30 and changed to a calendar year.

    d. Zeta Corporation, a calendar-year corporation, was liquidated on September 23.

14. What is the definition of "method of accounting"?

15. What does "clearly reflects income" mean?

16. Name the two most commonly used overall methods of accounting.

17. What is the purpose of the constructive receipt rule?

18. When considering the cash versus the accrual method of accounting:

    a. Is there any type of business that must be on the cash method?

    b. Is there any type of business that must be on the accrual method?

    c. What kind of business has a choice?

19. A cash-basis taxpayer generally is allowed a deduction upon payment of business expenses. When are payments not deductible when paid?

20. May the same taxpayer use several different methods of recognizing income simultaneously?

21. What is a hybrid method of accounting?

22. Generally, what additional indirect production costs incurred in the manufacture of inventory must be capitalized under the uniform capitalization rules that were not required to be capitalized under the full absorption method?

23. Under the uniform capitalization rules, how are the general and administrative costs allocated to the cost of ending inventory held for resale by a wholesaler or retailer?

24. Describe the lower-of-cost-or-market inventory valuation procedure. What is meant by "market"?

25. What are the disadvantages of an installment sale as compared to a cash sale?

26. What is the tax effect of forgiving one or more installments due on an installment obligation?

27. How are liabilities in excess of basis treated in an installment sale?

CHAPTER 12 PROBLEMS

28. Which entities utilize deductions for adjusted gross income and deductions from adjusted gross income? Why do only these entities use said deductions?

29. A partnership is owned 62 percent by a corporation and 38 percent by an individual. The corporation has a fiscal year ending on September 30. The individual is a calendar-year taxpayer. What is the tax year of the partnership, assuming it does not qualify under the business purpose exception?

30. An S corporation wishes to adopt a fiscal year ending on August 31 because that is the end of its model year. Will the S corporation be given permission to adopt the fiscal year?

31. What are the accounting period options for the following businesses?

    a.   C corporation starting business on March 11

    b.   Sole proprietorship starting business on May 27 with a proprietor on the calendar-year basis and a natural business year ending January 31

    c.   Partnership owned by three calendar-year individuals and a natural business year ending April 15

    d.   S corporation with a natural business year ending March 31

32. A partnership has two equal calendar-year partners and is switching from a fiscal year ending on June 30 to a calendar year. If the partnership has $40,000 in net income resulting from the short period, how will each partner report the short period income?

33. Mark Five Corporation wishes to change from a calendar year to a natural business year ending on June 30, 1998. By what date must Form 1128 be filed?

34. The Light Record Corporation has been on the calendar year since its inception five years ago. It wishes to change to an April 30 natural business year. For 1998, the calendar year of proposed change, Light had a taxable income of $200,000, of which $50,000 was earned from January through April.

   a. What must Light Corporation do to obtain the change in period? When must it do it?

   b. What is the tax liability for the short year?

35. Jenny Co. changed its accounting period in 1998. Jenny had been using a calendar year but received IRS permission to change to the fiscal year September 1 to August 31. The following information is available:

Taxable income, January 1, 1998, to December 31, 1998 . . . . $120,000
Taxable income, January 1, 1998, to August 31, 1998 70,000

Determine Jenny Co.'s short-period tax liability.

36. X Corporation was formed and began operations on September 1, 1998. X Corporation expects to have taxable income of $25,000 each quarter of operations for the first two years. X Corporation is indifferent with respect to its accounting period. What would you suggest regarding initial selection of an accounting period?

37. Gary Joseph, a calendar-year taxpayer, uses the accrual method of accounting. He works for Jersey Corporation and is entitled to a year-end bonus of 10 percent of Jersey's net income. Jersey Corporation's fiscal year is September 1 to August 31. For its fiscal year ended August 31, 1998, it had net income of $300,000. For the period September 1, 1998, through December 31, 1998, it had net income of $80,000. How much income does Gary report in 1998 assuming his salary before bonus is $60,000?

38. Which accounting methods are permissible for the following businesses?

    a.   Private investigator

    b.   Cigar store

    c.   Shipbuilder

    d.   TV store with a service department

    e.   Bank with billions of dollars in assets

    f.   Decedent's estate

39. Sylvester is on the cash method. Which of the following transactions result in gross income in the current year?

    a.   Car, worth $7,000, received as a consulting fee

    b. $500 of interest credited to his checking account, but not withdrawn

    c.   Wages payable from a corporation with ample funds, in which he is a 12 percent shareholder, uncollected at year-end

    d.   Stock, worth $20,000, for services rendered, fully vested if Sylvester still works for the corporation in three years

    e. $700 of dental services (bill cancelled upon Sylvester's estate planning advice to the dentist's mother-in-law)

    f.   Sale of a used car for a note due in one year, face value $3,000, fair market value $2,500. No elections were made

40. Strong Company decided to change its method of accounting from the cash basis to the accrual basis in 1998 because sale of inventories had become a material income-producing item. Its taxable income for 1998 under the accrual basis was $278,000. It determined that the balances of accounts receivable, inventory, and accounts payable as of December 1997 were:

    Accounts receivable $12,000
    Inventory   20,000
    Accounts payable   8,000

    a.   What is Strong Company's required adjustment due to the change in accounting methods?

    b.   What can Strong Company do with the adjustment?

41. Jones has three separate businesses. He uses the cash basis of accounting for all three businesses but would prefer to use the accrual basis for one of the businesses. Is Jones permitted to use different accounting methods for the separate businesses? If so, what must he do to change his method of accounting?

42. Justin Co. was organized and began operations in 1998. It sells inventory but also provides a variety of services to its customers. Justin Co. is uncertain as to which methods of accounting it must use (i.e., cash basis or accrual basis). Advise the firm regarding its choices.

43. Smith Inc. discovered it had made several math errors during 1998. It wants to correct the errors and is unsure as to whether this would qualify as a major change in accounting method requiring IRS approval. Advise Smith Inc.

44. Wash Company sells washing machines. On January 1, 1998, it had 20 units in inventory, valued at $400 per unit. During 1998, it sold 200 units at $700 per machine. Wash Company purchased 190 units during 1998 at a cost of $420 per unit. Determine Wash Company's gross profit under the FIFO and LIFO methods.

45. Company B, a calendar-year manufacturer, which uses the FIFO inventory method, previously allocated production costs to inventory by use of a burden rate based on the ratios of total indirect production costs incurred during the year compared to total direct labor costs during the year. Company B incurred the following costs during the year:

Direct material .... $ 500,000
Direct labor   1,500,000
Indirect costs inventoried under pre-1986 TRA law   1,500,000
Additional costs inventoried under Code Sec. 263A.........   750,000
Ending inventory prior to the capitalization of additional
    Code Sec. 263A costs   700,000

Company B had an inventory turnover rate of five times.

Compute the total amount of additional Code Sec. 263A costs to capitalize for FIFO inventory under the simplified production method.

46. Sugarcane Company incurs handling costs totaling $15 million and purchasing costs of $4 million. Inventoriable general and administrative costs related to handling and purchasing totals $1 million. Purchases for the year are $100 million. Sugarcane Company uses FIFO. Its purchases in ending inventory total $40 million. Compute the total resale costs to be capitalized to ending inventory using the simplified resale method.

47. X Company has four inventory items at year end. Inventory information (based on FIFO) is as follows:

Item	Cost	Market
1	$6,000	$4,000
2	3,000	1,400
3	7,000	9,000
4	3,300	5,500

Determine X Company's ending inventory using the lower-of-cost-or-market method.

48. Sam Co. sells a product whose cost (and sales price) has risen continually. This has produced increases in Sam Co.'s gross receipts and Sam Co. would like to use an inventory method that would minimize its tax liability. Would you recommend specific identification, FIFO, or LIFO? Why?

49. Falzone Inc. uses the dollar-value LIFO method to account for its inventory. Inventory on January 1, 1998, was $30,000 at base-year prices. Inventory on December 31, 1998, was $63,000 at actual prices and $50,000 at base-year prices. Determine Falzone's ending inventory using dollar-value LIFO.

50. A shipbuilder agrees to build and deliver a ship for $5,000,000 in three years. If $2,000,000 of costs are incurred in Year 1, $1,500,000 in Year 2, and $500,000 in Year 3, what is the gross profit in Years 1 through 3 under the percentage-of-completion method?

51. Steve sold for $100,000 his undivided one-third interest in an apartment building in which he had a $20,000 adjusted basis. The buyer put $10,000 down, assumed Steve's share of the mortgage, and signed an installment obligation with a face value of $60,000. $5,000 of the principal was paid at the end of the year of sale. Compute the following:

    a. Contract price

    b. Gross profit and gross profit percentage

    c. Payment in year of sale

    d. Gain in the year of sale

52. Do either of the transactions below qualify for installment reporting? If not, why not?

    a. Credit sales of dealer inventory

    b. Credit sales of property not held as inventory

53. $20 million of nondealer real estate obligations arose in and are outstanding at the end of calendar year 1998. Deferred gross profit on such installment obligations equals $5 million. Assume that the highest tax rate applicable in 1998 is 31 percent and the interest rate for December 1998 is 7 percent. Compute the amount of interest to be paid for 1998 on the amount of deferred gross profit, assuming the property was used in a trade or business.

54. Brice sells a piece of raw land with a basis of $10,000 which he has owned for years as an investment. What are the tax consequences to Brice, a cash-basis taxpayer, for the following consideration received:

    a. Cash of $30,000

    b. Motel worth $50,000, subject to $20,000 of liabilities

    c. Installment note due in one year without interest with a face value of $30,000 and a fair market value of $27,000

    d. Same as (c), but Brice elects out of installment reporting

55. Mr. Z, a nondealer, sold assets on an installment plan. Determine Mr. Z's gross income for 1998. Relevant data include:

Year	Installment Sales	Gross Profit	'97 Collections
1996.............	$200,000	$50,000	$ 25,000
1997.............	300,000	81,000	80,000
1998.............	400,000	96,000	125,000

56. In 1998, Valerie sold a building. Valerie received $50,000 in 1998 and a $150,000 note, payable in two equal installments, plus an acceptable interest rate. The property was acquired by Valerie in 1983 for $150,000 and was depreciated under ACRS. Total depreciation was $108,000; straight-line would have been $94,000. How much (and what character) income must Valerie recognize in 1998?

57. Adjustments due to a change in accounting method do not include which of the following:

   a. Taken into account in the year of change

   b. Spread over four years starting with the year of change

   c. Spread over four years starting in the year of change only if a negative adjustment

   d. None of the above

58. Victor sold 53 shares of stock on December 28. If the stock was listed and Victor is a cash method, calendar-year taxpayer, all of the following statements are false, except:

   a. Victor must recognize any loss in the year of sale and any gain in the subsequent year.

   b. Victor has until April 15 to decide in which year any gain or loss is to be recognized.

   c. Any gain or loss is recognized in the year of trade.

   d. The loss must be recognized in the year of sale, but the gain may be recognized in either the year of sale or the year of payment. A decision must be made by the due date of the return (including extensions).

59. Mabel sold her undivided one-third interest in an apartment building, in which she had a $40,000 adjusted basis, for $110,000. The buyer paid $15,000 down, assumed Mabel's share of the mortgage, and signed an installment obligation with a face value of $50,000. $5,000 of principal was paid at the end of the year of sale. Mabel's contract price, gross profit percentage, and payment in the year of sale are:

   a. $55,000, 100 percent, and $20,000

   b. $70,000, 100 percent, and $20,000

   c. $70,000, 100 percent, and $25,000

   d. $110,000, 60 percent, and $20,000

60. Kimbo Corporation began operations this year. It has not selected its accounting period. Which of the following would not be an acceptable year:

    a. A year ending April 30

    b. A year ending September 15

    c. A year ending the last Friday in November

    d. All of the above are acceptable year-ends.

61. Which of the following is not considered "constructive receipt" of income?

    a. X was informed its check for services rendered was available on December 20, 1998, but it waited until January 21, 1999, to pick up the check

    b. Earned income of X was received by its agent on December 30, 1998, but not received by X until January 6, 1999

    c. X received a check on December 30, 1998, for services rendered, but was unable to make a deposit until January 3, 1999

    d. A payment on the sale of real property was placed in an escrow account on December 20, 1998, but not received by X until January 13, 1999, when the transaction closed

62. Xeno Corporation purchased supplies from Kimbo Company in 1998. The total invoice was for $20,000, but Xeno claimed that only one-half of the order was received and paid only $10,000 in 1998. Both parties honestly disputed the bill and Xeno refused to pay the contested amount. They went to court and a judgment requiring Xeno to pay an additional $5,000 was issued in 1999. How should Xeno report this expense?

    a. $10,000 in 1998 and $5,000 in 1999

    b. $15,000 in 1998

    c. $15,000 in 1999

    d. $20,000 in 1998 and $5,000 of income in 1999

    e. None of the above

63. All of the following statements are correct except:

    a. A change in accounting method from the accrual to the cash method requires the consent of the IRS.

    b. If a taxpayer operates more than one business, then the accounting methods used must be the same for all the businesses.

    c. A change in the method used to value inventories requires the consent of the IRS.

    d. A change in accounting method from the cash to the accrual method requires the consent of the IRS.

64. X uses the LIFO method in computing its inventory. It had 1,000 units on hand at the end of 1999. Based on the following information, what is the value of its ending inventory on December 31, 1999?

    Beginning inventory: 500 units with a per-unit cost of $2.00 and a per-unit market value of $3.00
    Purchases: September 25, 1999, 1,500 units with a per-unit cost of $3.00 and a per-unit market value of $3.00.
    November 12, 1999, 1,000 units with a per-unit cost of $4.00 and a per-unit value of $4.00.

    a. $2,500

    b. $3,000

    c. $4,000

    d. $5,000

65. Y uses the FIFO method in computing its inventory. On January 1, 1999, its beginning inventory of 3,500 units consisted of the following:

    1,000 purchased April 10, 1998, at $1.00 per unit
    2,000 purchased June 23, 1998, at $2.00 per unit
      500 purchased July 11, 1998, at $3.00 per unit

    During 1999, Y purchased the following units:

    3,000 purchased September 1, 1999, at $4.00 per unit
    1,000 purchased December 16, 1999, at $5.00 per unit.

    During 1999, it sold 2,300 units. What is the value of its ending inventory?
    a. $13,300
    b. $15,300
    c. $19,900
    d. $22,900
    e. None of the above

66. Richard sold a rare automobile he had held as an investment in 1997. Richard purchased the automobile in 1980; its adjusted basis at the time of the sale was $70,000, and the selling price was $250,000. Richard received $50,000 in 1997 and was to receive $50,000 per year plus interest in each of the four succeeding years. On January 5, 1999, Richard sold the installment obligation (he did not receive an installment payment in 1999) for $145,000. Richard's gain on the sale of the installment obligation in 1999 is:
    a. $42,000
    b. $72,000
    c. $103,000
    d. $108,000
    e. $150,000

67. John sold a painting in February 1998 for $40,000. He received $10,000 in February and was to receive $15,000 in 1999 and 2000, plus interest. He purchased the painting in 1992 for $15,000, and its basis at time of sale was $15,000. The buyer defaulted on the obligation in 1999, and John repossessed the painting. He incurred no costs to repossess the painting, and its fair market value at repossession date was $39,000. John's recognized gain on the repossession is:

    a. $6,250

    b. $11,250

    c. $25,000

    d. $27,750

    e. $39,000

68. John's basis in the painting in problem 67 is:

    a. $0

    b. $25,000

    c. $30,000

    d. $39,000

    e. $42,250

69. *Comprehensive Problem.* Bill is a cash-basis, calendar-year taxpayer. Which of the following December items result in gross income or deductions for the current year?

    a. Check received for December rent, $700, not deposited until January 4

    b. Check for $1,100 to pay Bill's state income taxes mailed December 28, cashed January 7

    c. Cash received in the amount of $500 for services to be rendered the following year

    d. Interest of $800 credited to his savings account, added to Bill's account balance

    e. Check received for January rent, $700, deposited on January 9

    f. Charitable contribution of $300, charged on Bill's MasterCard

    g. Bills totalling $2,000 sent for services rendered during the year, uncollected as of year-end

70. *Comprehensive Problem.* Do any of the transactions below qualify for installment reporting? If not, why not?

    a.   Sale of property in December, with payment received in full the following January at a gain

    b.   Sale of property at a loss, payments to be received in equal annual installments over seven years

    c.   Exchange of like-kind investment property where the transfer took place in two different years

    d.   Sale in one year at a gain, 90 percent of the proceeds received immediately, the remaining 10 percent in year two

    e.   Sale of securities at a gain, the proceeds being 13 percent a year of current fair market value to be received over the life of the seller

    f.   Sale of stock with zero basis for 10 percent of the gross life of the gross sales of a business for 11 years

71. *Research Problem.* A manufacturer of pollution control facilities reported its profits on the completed-contract method. To value its raw materials and work in process, the taxpayer used the LIFO method, thus "having it both ways" (i.e., deferring profits and maximizing the cost of goods sold). The IRS claimed that the two methods are mutually exclusive and that the costs of materials, labor, supplies, etc. are to be treated as deferred expenditures, deductible only when the contracts are completed. Is the IRS correct? (See *Peninsular Steel Products & Equipment Co., Inc.,* 78 TC 1029, CCH Dec. 39,113 (1982).)

72. *Research Problem.* John Smythe has a margin account with Investit Investment Company. The stocks and bonds in the account earned dividends and interest of $10,000 in 1998. The $10,000 was paid directly to the margin account and used for reinvestment purposes only. Smythe received a substitute Form 1099-DIV which indicated the composition of the $10,000. However, Smythe did not report the $10,000 as income in 1998. He reported it as income in 1999 when he closed the margin account. The IRS has indicated that Smythe must include the $10,000 in 1998, and in addition to taxes has assessed interest and penalties. Smythe seeks your advice. (See, for example, *A.L. Christoffersen,* 84-2 USTC ¶ 9990, 749 F.2d 513 (CA-8 1984).)

Chapter 13

Taxation of Corporations—Basic Concepts

Learning Objectives

After completing Chapter 13, you should be able to:

1. Identify which entities are classified as corporations.
2. Discuss tax-free organizations and transfers to controlled corporations.
3. Understand the use of debt in the corporate capital structure.
4. Apply the ordinary loss deduction rules of Code Sec. 1244 on dispositions of stock.
5. Use the gain exclusion of Code Sec. 1202 on dispositions of stock.
6. Determine corporate taxable income, including special deductions available to corporations.
7. Compute corporate income tax, including the regular tax and the alternative minimum tax.
8. Describe controlled and affiliated groups and the filing of consolidated returns.
9. Know corporate income tax return requirements.

OVERVIEW OF CHAPTER

Corporate taxation is divided into six areas. They are (1) formation, (2) operation, (3) distributions, (4) redemptions, (5) liquidations, and (6) reorganizations. In this chapter, the formation and operation of corporations are discussed. Chapter 14 describes distributions and redemptions, Chapter 15 presents liquidations, and Chapter 16 details reorganizations. Chapter 17 discusses the penalty taxes, such as the accumulated earnings tax and the personal holding company tax, that may be imposed on corporations.

Chapters 13 through 17 limit their discussion to regular corporations taxed under Subchapter C of the Internal Revenue Code. Special corporations taxed under Subchapter S are discussed in Chapter 20. These S corporations have features closer to the partnership form of organization than the corporate form of organization.

Special rules allow assets and liabilities to be transferred to corporations tax free. There is a carryover of basis and tacking of holding periods in these tax-free exchanges.

Code Sec. 1244 allows the original shareholders of small business stock to obtain an ordinary deduction for a loss on dispositions of the stock rather than receive capital loss treatment. Gain on the sale still remains capital gain. Code Sec. 1202 also enables noncorporate taxpayers to exclude 50 percent on any gain from the sale or exchange of qualified small business stock held for more than five years which was originally issued after August 9, 1993.

A corporation is a separate legal entity and taxpayer. A corporation computes its taxable income in much the same manner as an individual. However, there are special deductions available to corporations. Dividends received by a corporation from other domestic corporations are deductible to the extent of 70 to 100 percent. Organizational expenditures may be deducted ratably over a period of not less than 60 months. Charitable contributions are limited to 10 percent of taxable income. Corporations may claim capital losses only against capital gains. Disallowed capital losses are carried back three years and forward five years. Net operating losses are normally carried back two years and forward 20 years.

Corporate income tax rates vary from 15 to 39 percent of taxable income. Corporations may be subject to a 20 percent tax on net alternative minimum taxable income, which is taxable income with certain adjustments and tax preferences. If the alternative minimum tax exceeds the regular tax, the excess is added to the regular tax. Dividends must be paid out of after-tax income and included in taxable income of the shareholders receiving the dividends.

Affiliated groups may elect to file consolidated returns rather than separate returns. Members of controlled groups must share certain tax benefits. Corporations use Form 1120 in filing their annual income tax returns.

Entity Choice

There are many issues that must be addressed when forming a business. A major concern is the type of entity. The major types are: sole proprietorships, partnerships, and corporations. Each entity has certain tax and nontax advantages and disadvantages; therefore, a decision must be made regarding which entity is most beneficial. The initial choice of entity is very important. However, under certain circumstances, the entity structure can be changed at a later date. Following is a brief discussion of each entity.

¶ 13,001 SPECIFIC ENTITIES

Sole Proprietorships

A sole proprietorship is a form of business in which one person owns all the assets and is fully responsible for all the liabilities. While this entity is treated as a separate entity for accounting purposes, it is not a separate legal entity. As such, a separate tax return is not filed for a sole proprietorship. Instead, its results from operations are reported on Schedule C (Profit or Loss From Business (Sole Proprietorship)) of Form 1040 (U.S. Individual Income Tax Return). The net income or loss is included with the taxpayer's other income, losses, and deductions for the year and is subject to a tax rate from 15 percent to 39.6 percent.

Partnerships

A partnership is a form of business in which two or more persons or entities own all the assets and are responsible for the liabilities. It is based on a voluntary contract between these parties. The partnership is formed with the intent that the owners (partners) will contribute assets and/or labor in return for a share of the profits. Most states have adopted the Uniform Partnership Act which governs partnership activities.

A partnership is similar to a sole proprietorship in that it is not a separate entity. However, for accounting and tax-reporting purposes, it is treated as a separate entity. Thus, a tax return, Form 1065 (U.S. Partnership Return of Income), is filed for the partnership. Although a tax return is filed, a partnership is not a taxpaying entity; rather, the income, expenses, gains, losses, credits, etc. pass through to its owners. Schedule K-1 (Partner's Share of Income, Credits, Deductions, etc.) of Form 1065 contains an indication of each partner's share of such items. The partner includes these items with the personal activities reported on Form 1040.

Corporations

A corporation is a legal entity created by the authority of state law. It is separate and distinct from its owners (shareholders). A corporation may be owned by one or more persons or entities. However, some states require at least two owners. For income tax purposes, there are two business types of corporations: regular corporations (C corporations) and electing corporations (S corporations). Both corporations are separate legal entities. The distinction between them is for income tax purposes only.

A C corporation is a separate taxpaying entity. It files Form 1120 (U.S. Corporation Income Tax Return). All its income and expenses are reported in this return and it pays a tax that ranges from 15 percent to 39 percent. The shareholders are not liable for a tax based on the corporation's income. However, shareholders must include dividend distributions in their taxable income.

An S corporation is not a separate taxpaying entity. It files Form 1120S (U.S. Income Tax Return for an S Corporation), but in general does not pay an income tax. Like a partnership, the income, expenses, gains, losses, credits, etc. pass through to the shareholders. Schedule K-1 (Shareholders' Share of Income, Credits, Deductions, etc.) contains each shareholder's share of these items.

Limited Liability Companies

In 1977, Wyoming passed the first limited liability company (LLC) legislation. Florida passed LLC legislation in 1982. In 1988, the IRS issued Rev. Rul. 88-76, 1988-2 CB 360, holding that a Wyoming LLC would be treated as a partnership for federal income tax purposes. Since then, all 50 states and the District of Columbia have passed LLC legislation and now recognize LLCs. However, the legislation is not similar across all jurisdictions, and technical requirements vary. Regardless, the number of LLCs in the United States has grown quickly and continues to grow at a very fast pace.

The LLC is a new type of business entity which has corporate and partnership characteristics. From a nontax perspective, LLCs provide flexibility to a firm's structure and operations, and they also provide their owners (members) with limited liability with respect to firm debts and obligations. For tax purposes, the LLC is treated as a conduit entity whereby its income passes through to its owners, thereby eliminating the double taxation associated with corporations other than S corporations; however, it may elect to be taxed as a corporation. See ¶ 13,015 for a discussion.

Limited Liability Partnerships

A limited liability partnership (LLP) is similar to an LLC and is organized under each state's statutes. These statutes generally apply to service organizations that are organized as partnerships and are most beneficial to large partnerships such as large public accounting firms. LLP status enables the firm to achieve limited liability benefits but be taxed as a partnership.

Comparative Advantages and Disadvantages

Each entity has certain tax and nontax attributes associated with it. Knowledge of these attributes enables taxpayers to select an entity which is most appropriate for them. Some of these attributes are briefly discussed below.

Limited Liability

Limited liability is one of the major advantages of a corporation. The shareholders' personal assets are not subject to claims of the corporation's creditors; only their investment in the corporation is subject to these claims. However, certain professional corporations do not have limited liability. Similarly, owners of small corporations usually have to guarantee the loans of their corporations which precludes limited liability. Partners and sole proprietors have unlimited liability unless the partners are limited partners in a limited partnership or unless the firm is organized as a limited liability partnership (LLP) or a limited liability company (LLC).

Employee Status

Sole proprietors and partners are not considered employees of their firms. This is a disadvantage because certain tax-exempt fringe benefits are not available to them and the firm cannot deduct the costs of these benefits. Similarly, their shares of self-employment income are subject to the self-employment tax of 15.3 percent on a maximum of $68,400, plus 2.90 percent on amounts over $68,400. However, one-half of this amount qualifies as a deduction for adjusted gross income in computing taxable income. Shareholders employed by their corporation have employee status, although there are restrictions on shareholders who also are employees of their S corporation. Code Sec. 1372(a).

Double Taxation

A disadvantage of C corporations is that they are subject to a form of double taxation. An income tax is imposed on the taxable income of the corporation, and no deduction is allowed for distributions to shareholders. When after-tax profits are distributed to shareholders as dividends, the shareholders generally must include the amounts in their taxable income. Partnerships, S corporations, and sole proprietorships are not subject to this because they are conduits. Their income passes through to the owners and is taxed at that level only.

Pass-Through Benefits

Corporate losses cannot pass through to shareholders. Also, dividend distributions generally are treated by shareholders as ordinary income, regardless of the type of income (tax-exempt, capital gains, etc.) that generated the earnings and profits from which the dividends came. Since sole proprietorships, partnerships, and S corporations are conduits, all income, gains, losses, credits, etc. pass through to their owners. These items retain their identity when they pass through. Thus, the firms' net losses can be used to offset personal income. Also, tax-exempt income passes through as such and is not taxable to the sole proprietor or partner. Additionally, the owners can use their shares of capital losses to offset their personal capital gains. Conversely, their shares of capital gains could be offset by their personal capital losses (or carryovers). Regular corporations do not provide these benefits.

Capital Formation

Corporations are better able to raise funds via owner-financing because of the comparative ease to expand ownership. The issuance of stock does not change the entity. A proprietor is solely responsible for owner-financing. The issuance of ownership interest in return for funds terminates the sole proprietorship. A partnership is better able to owner-finance than is a sole proprietorship because it has more owners.

Fiscal Period

A regular corporation can elect a fiscal period different from that of its owners. A sole proprietorship must have the same fiscal period as its owner. A partnership must have the same fiscal period as its partners who have a majority interest. In general, an S corporation must use a calendar year as its tax year unless it can establish a business purpose for using another tax year.

¶ 13,015   DEFINITION OF A CORPORATION

If the corporate form of business is selected, the owners must be certain that their entity is treated as a corporation for federal income tax purposes. A corporation is a legal entity owing its existence to the laws of the state in which it is incorporated. The state laws define all legal relationships of the corporation. Prior to 1997, a legal corporation was not guaranteed corporate status for federal tax purposes unless it had a majority of corporate characteristics (centralized management, continuity of life, free transferability of interests, and limited liability). Similarly, noncorporate entities sometimes could and would be taxed as corporations if they had a majority of these characteristics. This created much uncertainty for many organizations.

New Regulations to Code Sec. 7701 issued in 1996 and effective January 1, 1997, simplified the entity classification issue. Under the new "check-the-box" system, certain business entities (entities other than trusts or those subject to special rules) automatically will be treated as corporations for federal tax purposes. These entities are: firms incorporated under federal or state law, associations, joint-stock companies, or joint-stock associations (as organized under a state statute), insurance companies, banks, business entities wholly owned by a state or political subdivision of the state, business entities that are taxed as corporations under another Code section, and certain foreign entities. Eligible entities (entities other than trusts or those subject to special rules) that are not automatically treated as a corporation may elect ("check-the-box") to be treated as a corporation for federal tax purposes.

If an entity has one owner, it may elect to be treated as a corporation or by default it will be treated as an entity not separate from its owner (sole proprietorship). If an entity has two or more owners, it can elect to be taxed as a corporation for federal tax purposes, otherwise it will be taxed as a partnership.

An eligible entity makes its election to change its default classification by filing Form 8832 (Entity Classification Election). The entity also indicates the effective date of the election. The effective date cannot be more than 75 days prior to the date Form 8832 is filed nor more than 12 months after it is filed. Also, a copy of Form 8832 must be attached to the entity's tax return for the year of election. Finally, once the election is made, the election cannot generally be changed for five years.

> *Example 13.1.* Gary, Richard, and Tom formed GRT partnership on February 1, 1998. GRT is an eligible entity; thus, if it wants to be taxed as a corporation for federal tax purposes, it must file Form 8832 within 75 days.

Organization of and Transfers to a Corporation

¶ 13,101   USE OF CORPORATE FORM

If the corporate form is desired, the owners must be certain that they meet all filing requirements of the state in which the company is organized. After completing this, the owners must decide what type of property to transfer to the corporation and how this property should be transferred. For example, should the owners transfer cash to purchase stock or make loans to the corporation? Similarly, should land or other assets be sold to the corporation, contributed in return for its stock, or leased to the corporation? The answers to these questions have significant tax implications.

In general, taxpayers who exchange property other than cash for other property recognize a gain or loss. The difference between the value of the property received and the adjusted basis of the property given up produces a realized gain or loss. Under Code Sec. 1001 this gain or loss is recognized by the taxpayer unless another section of the Internal Revenue Code provides for nonrecognition of the gain or loss.

There are several reasons why nonrecognition treatment is preferable with respect to corporate formation and transfers to corporations. The owners who receive stock in return for their property are not cashing in on their investment. There has been no change in their wherewithal to pay taxes, rather the stock represents a continuation of their investment in a different form. There is no substantive change in the owners' investments. Additionally, the government does not want to discourage corporate formation and subsequent transfers to corporations. Taxing such transfers when there has been no change in wherewithal to pay would act as a deterrent. Thus, under certain conditions Code Sec. 351 provides for nonrecognition of gain or loss upon transfer of property to a corporation in return for its stock.

¶ 13,105   GENERAL REQUIREMENTS

The rule under Code Sec. 351 is mandatory and provides that no gain or loss is recognized upon the transfer of property to a corporation solely in exchange for its stock if the taxpayer transferring the property (the transferor) is in control of the corporation immediately after the exchange. The basis rules provided in Code Secs. 358 and 362 assure that the nonrecognition is deferred and not permanent. These sections generally apply a carryover basis to the stock received by the transferor and to the property received by the transferee corporation. Code Sec. 1223 also enables both parties to tack on the holding period of the property transferred to the stock and the property, respectively, if they constitute capital assets or Section 1231 assets.

There are three major requirements of Code Sec. 351: (1) the transfer must consist of property, (2) the transfer must be solely in exchange for stock, and (3) the transferors must be in control immediately after the exchange. Each requirement is discussed separately.

TAX BLUNDER

Susan Jones is in the 39.6 percent tax bracket. She transfers property with an adjusted basis of $50,000 and a fair market value of $30,000 to X Co. in a transaction that qualifies under Code Sec. 351. Under Code Sec. 351, Jones will not recognize a loss on the transfer. Jones should not have transferred the property. She would have been better off selling the property to the corporation (assuming the related-party loss rules of Code Sec. 267 do not apply) and recognizing the $20,000 loss this year. Both the time value of money and her tax bracket favor such action.

¶ 13,111 TRANSFERS OF PROPERTY

Code Sec. 351 does not define property. However, it does indicate what is not property. Services, certain debt of the transferee corporation, and certain accrued interest on the transferee's debt are not treated as property. Code Sec. 351(d). Other than these exceptions, the definition of property is very comprehensive and includes all types of property such as cash, accounts receivables, inventories, patents, installment obligations, equipment, and buildings.

Example 13.2. Jerome Smith transfers land to North Corporation in return for 90 percent of its stock. The adjusted basis of the land is $40,000. The fair market value of the stock is $90,000. Jerome has a realized gain of $50,000 ($90,000 − $40,000) and no recognized gain. Jay Jones performs accounting services for North Corporation in return for 10 percent of its stock (fair market value is $10,000). Jay has $10,000 of ordinary income. The receipt of the stock is treated as compensation for services rendered. Jay's basis in the stock is its fair market value, $10,000.

¶ 13,115 TRANSFERS FOR STOCK

Code Sec. 351 requires that the transferor receive the corporation's stock. The receipt of securities in exchange for property does not qualify as a Section 351 transfer. If the transferor receives stock and securities, (assuming other conditions are met) the exchange qualifies under Code Sec. 351, but the securities are treated as boot, regardless of the life of the securities. Also, receipt of anything else constitutes boot and may cause gain recognition. Common and preferred stock and voting and nonvoting stock are acceptable.

However, the Taxpayer Relief Act of 1997 (TRA '97) amended Code Sec. 351 such that "nonqualified preferred stock" is considered boot. Nonqualified preferred stock is preferred stock that: (1) the holder has the right to require the issuer or a related party to redeem or purchase; (2) the issuer or a related party is required to redeem or purchase; (3) the issuer or a related party has the right to redeem or purchase, and, as of the issue, it is more likely than not that such right will be exercised; or (4) the dividend rate varies in whole or in part with reference to interest rates, commodity prices, or other similar indices. There are a few exceptions to this definition (and exceptions to these exceptions), such as the right cannot be exercised for 20 years or the right only may be exercised upon the death, disability, or mental incompetence of the holder. Finally, for Code Sec. 351 purposes, stock rights and stock warrants are not considered stock. Reg. § 1.351-1(a)(1)(i) and (ii).

> ***Example 13.3.*** Jay Smith transfers land to Hext Corporation in exchange for 100 percent of its stock and four 10-year bonds. The exchange qualifies under Code Sec. 351, but the receipt of the four bonds constitutes boot.

> ***Example 13.4.*** Gina West contributes property to Franken Inc. in a transaction that qualifies as a Code Sec. 351 transfer. In return for the property, she received common stock worth $20,000 and nonqualified preferred stock worth $15,000. The nonqualified stock is considered boot; thus, Gina has received $15,000 boot in the exchange and may be required to recognize a gain. (See ¶ 13,135 for the treatment of boot.)

¶ 13,125   CONTROL OF THE TRANSFEREE CORPORATION

For purposes of Code Sec. 351, control is defined in Code Sec. 368(c). The transferors must be in control immediately after the transfer, regardless of whether they were in control prior to the transfer. Further, the transferors must possess at least 80 percent of the total combined voting power of all classes of stock entitled to vote and at least 80 percent of the total number of shares of all other classes of stock of the corporation. With respect to the nonvoting stock, the IRS has indicated that control requires the ownership of at least 80 percent of the total number of shares of each class of outstanding nonvoting stock. Rev. Rul. 59-259, 1959-2 CB 115.

Control can apply to one person or a group of people. If more than one person transfers property, the aggregate ownership of the group is used to determine if control exists immediately after the exchange. "Persons" is defined as including individuals, trusts, estates, partnerships, associations, companies, or corporations. Reg. § 1.351-1(a)(1). This Regulation also indicates that the term "immediately after the exchange" does not require simultaneous exchanges by two or more persons as long as the rights of each party have been previously defined. The execution of this prearranged plan also must proceed in an expeditious and orderly manner.

> ***Example 13.5.*** Roger Caldwell and Charles Mann transfer property to Bond Corporation in return for 60 percent and 40 percent of its stock, respectively. Although neither has control individually, together they own 100 percent of the stock and meet the control requirements.

The stock received by the transferors does not have to be in proportion to the value of the property transferred. However, if the stocks received are disproportionate to the value of properties transferred, the transaction will be closely scrutinized to determine the true nature of the transaction. If the disproportionality is suspect, the transaction may be treated as if the stock had first been received in proportion and then been used to make gifts, to pay compensation, or to satisfy liabilities among the transferors. Reg. § 1.351-1(b)(1).

> *Example 13.6.* Mark Smith and Ralph Jones transfer property worth $150,000 and $50,000, respectively, to Best Corporation in return for 100 percent of its stock. Mark and Ralph each receive 100 shares of stock. The exchanges qualify under Code Sec. 351 because together Mark and Ralph are in control immediately after the exchange. However, the IRS may tax the transaction as if Mark had received 150 shares and then transferred 50 shares to Ralph. This subsequent transfer to Ralph might be treated as a compensation payment to Ralph, in which case Ralph would have ordinary income of $50,000. Mark would have income (loss) if the value of the stock ($50,000) is different from Mark's adjusted basis. Also, Ralph's basis in the 50 shares would be $50,000. Recasting the transaction as, in part, a gift or loan repayment also would impact income and/or basis computations.

If stock is received for property and services rendered, all of the stock received by the transferor is used in determining whether the transferors are in control immediately after the exchange. However, stock issued for property which is of relatively small value in comparison to the value of the stock already owned (or to be received for services) by the person who transferred such property will not be counted in determining whether the transaction meets the 80 percent control tests. Reg. § 1.351-1(b)(1).

> *Example 13.7.* Bill Roe transfers property to a new corporation for 70 percent of the stock. Joe Brown receives 30 percent of the stock in the corporation for his work in organizing the corporation. Joe must recognize income upon receipt of his stock and the stock does not qualify for the 80 percent control test. Bill's transfer is a taxable event since he does not have at least 80 percent control after the transfer.

> *Example 13.8.* Sebastian Corporation has 100 shares of stock outstanding. Jan Kruger contributes an asset with a basis of $10,000 and a fair market value of $19,000 along with services worth $1,000 to the corporation for 400 shares of the corporation's stock. The transfer would qualify under Code Sec. 351 since, as the transferor, she has 80 percent of the stock in the corporation. Jan would have to recognize $1,000 of income from the services but would not recognize the $9,000 gain on the asset. If the property were worth only $1,000 and the services $19,000, the transfer would not qualify under Code Sec. 351.

A loss of control shortly after the transfer could cause the transaction to fail to qualify under Code Sec. 351. If the loss of control was due to the disposition of stock according to a prearranged plan, the transferors will not, in most cases, have control immediately after the exchange.

> *Example 13.9.* Bill Bradley and Joe Crawford each receive 50 percent of the stock of Block Corporation upon incorporation.

Unknown to Bill, Joe has committed himself to sell more than 40 percent of his stock (bringing Joe's and Bill's control under 80 percent) to Max even before the transfer. Section 351 treatment will be denied to both parties.

TAX PLANNING POINTER ▼

Once the stock is received, the transferor may, of course, do whatever is desired with it, after a reasonable time. A highly recommended device is to set the stage for future capital gains by giving some stock, say 10 or 20 percent, to a spouse and/or children. After more than 10 years, the corporation may purchase back this stock (a redemption), resulting in capital gains to the family members upon the termination of their interest. Code Sec. 302(b)(3). Alternatively, property may be gifted so as to qualify donees as transferors.

¶ 13,135   RECEIPT OF BOOT

If all the requirements of Code Sec. 351 are met, the transferors recognize no gain or loss. Also, their basis in stock received is equal to the adjusted basis of property surrendered.

Example 13.10. Larry Lewis and Lance Thompson decide to form Sands Corporation. Larry transfers $10,000 in cash and property with an adjusted basis of $25,000 and a fair market value of $90,000 in return for 100 shares of stock. Lance transfers $20,000 in cash and property with an adjusted basis of $110,000 and a fair market value of $80,000. Lance also receives 100 shares of stock. Since they own 100 percent of the stock, they are in control and the transaction qualifies under Code Sec. 351. Larry has a realized gain of $65,000 ($100,000 − $35,000) and no recognized gain. His basis in the 100 shares of Sands Corporation is $35,000 ($10,000 + $25,000). Lance has a realized loss of $30,000 ($100,000 − $130,000), of which none is recognized. His basis in the 100 shares of Sands Corporation is $130,000 ($20,000 + $110,000).

Property other than stock is considered boot. (Although, as noted earlier, nonqualified preferred stock is considered to be boot.) The receipt of limited amounts of boot does not disqualify a transfer from Code Sec. 351. However, gain must be recognized to the extent of the lesser of the realized gain or the fair market value of the boot received. Code Sec. 351(b). The character of the gain depends on the property transferred. Losses are never recognized under Code Sec. 351.

Example 13.11. Max Murphy and Jake Jones form Small Corporation. Max transfers land with an adjusted basis of $10,000 for stock worth $15,000 and $5,000 cash. Jake transfers equipment with an adjusted basis of $25,000 for stock worth $10,000 and $7,000 cash.

Max has a realized gain of $10,000, but only $5,000 is recognized. Jones has a realized loss of $8,000 and none of it is recognized.

Example 13.12. Same as Example 13.11, except that Max's land has an adjusted basis of $16,000. Max has a realized gain of $4,000 which is fully recognized. Jake has an unrecognized $8,000 loss because Code Sec. 351 still applies to the exchange.

If more than one asset is transferred, the boot must be allocated among the assets. The IRS endorses the view that the boot is to be allocated in accordance with fair market values. Reg. § 1.358-2(b). This is necessary because gain or loss must be computed on each asset. Rev. Rul. 68-55, 1968-1 CB 140. Since no losses are recognized in a Section 351 transaction, and there are assets transferred with realized losses, less gain will be recognized on the appreciated assets because boot is allocated to loss assets as well. In addition to affecting the amount of gain recognized, the allocation also impacts the character of gain (e.g., ordinary income, capital gain, Section 1231 gain) because the character depends on the asset transferred.

Example 13.13. George Anderson transfers land and inventory to Candle Corporation in return for 100 percent of its stock. The land has a fair market value of $120,000 and an adjusted basis of $40,000. The inventory has a fair market value of $80,000 and an adjusted basis of $90,000. George receives stock worth $150,000 and $50,000 in cash. The effects of this transfer are illustrated below.

	Land	Inventory	Total
Fair market value	$120,000	$ 80,000	$200,000
Adjusted basis	40,000	90,000	130,000
Realized gain (loss)	$ 80,000	$ (10,000)	$ 70,000
Boot allocation	$ 30,000 (60%)	$ 20,000 (40%)	$ 50,000
Recognized gain (loss)	$ 30,000	$ None	$ 30,000

Thus, if the land is a capital asset to George, he would recognize a $30,000 capital gain.

¶ 13,141   TRANSFERS OF LIABILITIES

There are many instances when property transferred to a corporation is subject to a liability. The corporation usually assumes the liability as part of the transaction. Because transfers to controlled corporations usually involve transfers of liabilities, especially when existing businesses such as sole proprietorships or partnerships incorporate, taxing the transfer could be a deterrent to corporate formation. Code Sec. 357 provides relief in this situation by not treating the transfer of liabilities as boot if the transaction qualifies under Code Sec. 351. The assumption of a liability by the transferee corporation, or the corporation taking the property subject to a liability, will not be treated as boot for gain recognition purposes and will not disqualify Code Sec. 351 treatment. Code Sec. 357(a). (As discussed later, the assumption of the liability will affect basis considerations).

Example 13.14. Sally Flowers transfers a building with an adjusted basis of $100,000 and a fair market value of $140,000 to Inter Corporation in return for all of its stock worth $60,000. The building is subject to a mortgage of $80,000 which Inter Corporation assumes. The transaction qualifies as a Code Sec. 351 transfer. Sally has a realized gain of $40,000 ($60,000 + $80,000 − $100,000). None of the gain is recognized.

There are two exceptions to the general rule under Code Sec. 357(a). These exceptions result if the transfer of liabilities had a tax avoidance purpose or if the sum of liabilities transferred exceeds the adjusted basis of all properties transferred by the transferor.

Tax Avoidance or No Business Purpose

All liabilities transferred to the corporation will be treated as boot if the principal purpose of the liability assumption was to avoid federal income tax or if there was no bona fide business purpose for the transfer. Code Sec. 357(b). The taxpayer must overcome these appearances by the clear preponderance of the evidence.

Tax avoidance generally is not a problem. The lack of a bona fide business purpose also is not a problem if the liabilities were incurred in the normal course of business. The time between when the funds are borrowed and when the transfer to the corporation occurs is an important factor.

If funds were borrowed just prior to the transfer, it will be difficult to overcome the lack of a business purpose, especially if the proceeds were used for personal benefit. In such instances, the transferor should be prepared to provide clear evidence to verify the business purpose for the loan and its transfer.

Example 13.15. George Small transfers land with an adjusted basis of $40,000 and a fair market value of $95,000 to Giant Corporation in return for all of its stock. The stock is worth $65,000. Two days prior to the transfer, George borrowed $30,000 against the land. The $30,000 liability was assumed by Giant Corporation as part of the exchange. George has a realized gain of $55,000 (($65,000 plus $30,000) minus $40,000). George has a recognized gain of $30,000 because it appears that there was no business purpose for the loan or its transfer.

Liability in Excess of Basis

If the sum of the liabilities assumed, plus the liabilities to which the property is subject, exceeds the total adjusted basis of all properties transferred, the transferor must recognize gain on the exchange to the extent of such excess. Code Sec. 357(c). Without the recognition of gain, the stock received by the transferor would have a negative basis. With the application of this provision and related basis rules, the transferor's basis in the stock is zero.

Example 13.16. Sara Topper transfers a building with an adjusted basis of $30,000 and a fair market value of $100,000 to Sunny Corporation in return for 100 percent of its stock. The building is subject to a $50,000 mortgage which Sunny Corporation assumes. Sara must recognize a gain of $20,000 equal to the excess of the mortgage over the adjusted basis of the building.

If there is more than one transferor, gains should be recognized on a person-by-person basis.

Example 13.17. Fred Smart transfers property with an adjusted basis of $45,000, a fair market value of $80,000, and a mortgage of $59,000 to a new corporation. Ginger Snow simultaneously invests $14,000 in cash. Fred must recognize a gain of $14,000 because the liability exceeds his basis in the asset. He is not allowed to count Ginger's investment in the total basis contribution.

TAX PLANNING POINTER ▼

An individual wishes to incorporate by transferring an asset to the corporation for all of the corporation's stock. The asset has a fair market value of $200,000 and a basis of $50,000. The asset has a liability attached in the amount of $80,000. This transfer would result in a $30,000 recognition of income because the liability exceeds the basis of the asset. The individual would be well advised to include other assets in the transfer with a net basis of at least $30,000 to avoid any income recognition.

If the transferor transfers more than one asset and fewer than all of them are encumbered, but liabilities exceed aggregate basis, gain is recognized on all assets. The recognized gain is to be allocated among the assets in accordance with fair market values.

Example 13.18. Mary Meyers transfers inventory worth $20,000 with an adjusted basis of $10,000 and a building worth $100,000 with an adjusted basis of $50,000 and a mortgage of $90,000 in return for 100 percent of Sage Corporation's stock. Sage Corporation also assumes the mortgage. Mary's recognized gain is $30,000 ($90,000 − ($50,000 + $10,000)). $5,000 is recognized on the inventory ($30,000 × $^{20}/_{120}$) and $25,000 is recognized on the building ($30,000 × $^{100}/_{120}$). Without the transfer of inventory, Mary would have recognized a $40,000 gain on the building.

For years, Code Sec. 357(c) presented problems for taxpayers who incorporated their cash-basis businesses. Usually, these firms had a large amount of unrealized accounts receivables (zero basis). The firms also had unrealized accounts payable which were treated as liabilities, creating a liability in excess of basis problem. The Revenue Act of 1978 solved the problem by adding an exception. Thus, liabilities that would give rise to a deduction when paid (i.e., accounts payable of a cash-basis taxpayer) and amounts payable under Code Sec. 736 (i.e., payments to a retiring partner or to liquidate a deceased partner's interest) are excluded. Code Sec. 357(c)(3).

Example 13.19. Matilda Worth incorporates her sole proprietorship operated on the cash method of accounting. She transfers equipment with an adjusted basis of $10,000 and zero basis accounts receivable and accounts payable. The accounts payable have an outstanding balance of $17,000 but no basis because of the cash method of accounting. Without the relief provision, an automatic gain of $7,000 would result (liabilities in excess of basis). Under Code Sec. 357(c), Matilda will recognize no gain. The corporation succeeds to her zero basis in the accounts receivables and accounts payable. Upon payment, the corporation will deduct the accounts payable as a business expense.

TAX PLANNING POINTER ▼

Transfer of zero base receivables will result in double taxation of the receivables. A tax will be imposed when the corporation collects the receivables and there will be a second tax imposed on the shareholders when dividends are paid by the corporation. It would be better not to transfer the zero base receivables to the corporation. The shareholder will then report the income upon collection, and the receivables are taxed only once.

¶ 13,155   BASIS DETERMINATION

Shareholder's Basis

Code Sec. 358 provides that the shareholder's basis in stock received in a Section 351 transfer is equal to the adjusted basis of property exchanged, increased by the amount of gain recognized on the exchange, and decreased by the fair market value of boot received. Code Sec. 358. The basis of the boot received is its fair market value. Also, the assumption of a liability is considered boot for basis purposes even though it was not for gain purposes under Code Sec. 357. If more than one class of stock is received, the property basis must be allocated to the classes of stock in proportion to their fair market value.

Example 13.20. Bob Ripon transfers land with an adjusted basis of $5,000 and a fair market value of $14,000 to Wendy Corporation in return for all its stock. Bob has a realized gain of $9,000, but no gain is recognized. Bob's basis in the stock is $5,000.

Example 13.21. Same as Example 13.20, except that Bob also receives a $1,000 short-term note (boot). Bob has a realized gain of $9,000 and a recognized gain of $1,000 (the lesser of the realized gain or the fair market value of the boot received). Bob's basis in the stock is $5,000 ($5,000 + $1,000 − $1,000). Bob's basis in the short-term note is $1,000, its fair market value.

Example 13.22. Jane Seaman transfers land with an adjusted basis of $7,000 and a fair market value of $5,000 to Wall Corporation. Jane receives $800 in cash and all of Wall Corporation's stock.

Jane has a realized loss of $2,000, and none of the loss is recognized. Jane's basis in the stock is $6,200 ($7,000 − $800).

Example 13.23. Harry Bold transfers land with an adjusted basis of $40,000 and a fair market value of $50,000 to Handy Corporation in return for all its stock and $12,000 in cash. Harry has a realized gain of $10,000. Even though he received $12,000 in cash, Harry's recognized gain is limited to the realized gain; thus, he has a recognized gain of $10,000. Harry's basis in the stock is $38,000 ($40,000 + $10,000 − $12,000).

Example 13.24. Hal Lamb transfers property with a fair market value of $90,000 and an adjusted basis of $50,000 to X Corporation for all its stock. The land is subject to a $30,000 mortgage. Hal has a realized gain of $40,000 but no recognized gain. His basis in the stock is $20,000 ($50,000 − $30,000).

Example 13.25. Assume the same facts as Example 13.24, except that the mortgage is $70,000. Hal's realized gain is $40,000 and his recognized gain is $20,000 (liability in excess of basis). Hal's basis in the stock is zero ($50,000 + $20,000 − $70,000).

Example 13.26. Susan Anders transferred assets with a fair market value of $100,000 and an adjusted basis of $60,000 to a corporation in return for 100 shares of its Class A stock (100 percent) and 100 shares of its Class B stock (100 percent). The fair market value of the Class A stock was $80,000. The fair market value of the Class B stock was $20,000. Susan had a realized gain of $40,000 (($80,000 + $20,000) − $60,000) but no recognized gain. Her basis in both classes of stock was $60,000. This was allocated to the classes in accordance with their relative fair market values. Thus,

$$\text{Basis of Class A stock} = \$60,000 \times \frac{\$80,000}{(\$80,000 + \$20,000)} = \$48,000$$

$$\text{Basis of Class B stock} = \$60,000 \times \frac{\$20,000}{(\$80,000 + \$20,000)} = \$12,000$$

Example 13.27. Assume the same facts as in Example 13.26, except that Susan received five 10-year bonds instead of Class B stock. Susan's realized gain still is $40,000. However, her recognized gain is $20,000, the lesser of the $40,000 realized gain or the fair market value of boot received ($20,000 bonds). Her basis in the bonds is $20,000 (fair market value) and her basis in the stock is $60,000 ($60,000 + $20,000 − $20,000).

Stockholder's Holding Period

The shareholder's holding period in stock received in a Section 351 transfer includes the holding period of property transferred if the assets were capital assets or Section 1231 assets (recapture potential is irrelevant). Code Sec. 1223(1). If both ordinary income property and capital or Section 1231 assets are transferred, the shareholder winds up with two holding periods in the stock since the holding period of stock issued for ordinary income property begins upon receipt. Tacking is permitted even if realized gains are recognized in full or in part because of the receipt of boot. The holding period for boot received begins on the date of the transaction.

> *Example 13.28.* Kerry Brooks transfers a capital asset to a corporation under Code Sec. 351. Kerry held the capital asset long term before the transfer. The stock received from the transfer is considered held long term regardless of the length of time held before any sale of the stock. The holding period of the capital asset tacks on to the holding period of the stock.

Corporation's Basis

The corporation's basis in property received is equal to the transferor's adjusted basis increased by any gain recognized by the transferor. Code Sec. 362. Liabilities assumed by a corporation do not affect the basis of the assets received from shareholders in Section 351 transfers. If the liability exceeds the basis of the asset transferred, gain equal to the excess liability will be recognized by the transferor and cause the property's basis to increase.

> *Example 13.29.* Peter Rhone transfers property with an adjusted basis of $3,000 and a fair market value of $5,000 to Pest Corporation in a Section 351 transfer. Peter's realized gain is $2,000, of which none is recognized. His basis in the stock is $3,000. Pest Corporation's basis in the property is $3,000.

> *Example 13.30.* Assume the same facts as Example 13.29, except that the property is subject to a $1,000 liability which Pest Corporation assumes. Peter has a realized gain of $2,000. None of the gain is recognized. His basis in the stock is $2,000 ($3,000 − $1,000). Pest Corporation's basis in the property is $3,000.

> *Example 13.31.* Assume the same facts as Example 13.30, except that the property is subject to a liability of $3,500. Peter has a realized gain of $2,000 and a recognized gain of $500 (liability in excess of basis). Peter's basis in the stock is zero ($3,000 + $500 − $3,500). Pest Corporation's basis in the property is $3,500 ($3,000 + $500).

Corporation's Holding Period

The corporation tacks on the shareholder's holding period in assets transferred if the asset is a capital asset or a Section 1231 asset in the corporation's hands. The transferor may transfer ordinary income property to a corporation, in whose hands it becomes a capital asset or vice versa.

¶ 13,165   RECAPTURE RULES

Depreciation Recapture

In a Section 351 transfer in which no boot is received and, therefore, no gain is recognized, there is no recapture of depreciation. Code Secs. 1245(b)(3) and 1250(d)(3). The recapture potential shifts to the corporation. If gain is recognized on the exchange because boot is received, it is characterized as ordinary income to the extent of depreciation recapture. If only part of the depreciation is recaptured, the remaining portion is shifted to the corporation.

Example 13.32. Larry Bloom purchased a truck for $14,000 and took $8,000 in depreciation prior to transferring it to Vail Corporation in a Section 351 exchange. The truck had a fair market value of $10,000 at the time of the exchange. Larry has a realized gain of $4,000 but no recognized gain ($10,000 − $6,000). His basis in the stock is $6,000. Vail Corporation's basis in the truck is $6,000. It also inherits the $8,000 recapture potential.

Example 13.33. Assume the same facts as Example 13.32, except that in addition to receiving stock, Larry also receives $2,000 in cash. Larry has a realized gain of $6,000 and a recognized gain of $2,000 as ordinary income. His basis in the stock is $6,000 ($6,000 + $2,000 − $2,000). Vail Corporation's basis in the truck is $8,000 ($6,000 + $2,000). Vail Corporation also inherits the remaining depreciation recapture potential of $6,000.

Example 13.34. Assume the same facts as in Example 13.32 except that the fair market value of the truck is $12,000, and Larry received stock worth $5,000 and $7,000 in cash. Larry's realized gain is $6,000 ($12,000 − $6,000). Although he received $7,000 boot, his recognized gain is limited to the realized gain. Thus, Larry's recognized gain is $6,000 of ordinary income. His basis in the stock is $5,000 ($6,000 − $7,000 + $6,000). Vail Corporation's basis in the truck is $12,000 ($6,000 + $6,000), and it inherits $2,000 recapture potential.

General Business Credit Recapture

A premature disposition of business property in which the general business tax credit has been taken (i.e., Section 38 property) generally triggers recapture of the portion not earned. Unlike depreciation recapture, the recapture of the general business tax credit occurs regardless of whether any gain was realized or recognized on the transaction. However, no recapture is triggered if the taxpayer changes only "the form of conducting the trade or business as Section 38 property and the taxpayer retains a substantial interest in such trade or business." Code Sec. 50(a)(1).

What constitutes a substantial interest is not defined in the Internal Revenue Code and has been a source of contention and controversy. For example, exchanging a 50 percent interest in a partnership for a 35 percent interest in a corporation probably would qualify for exemption from recapture. However, in one case the Tax Court has held that exchanging a 48 percent partnership interest for a 7.22 percent stock interest did not qualify. *J. Soares,* 50 TC 909, CCH Dec. 29,138 (1968).

If no general business tax credit recapture is triggered on the transfer, the recapture potential stays with the shareholder. Future recapture is triggered when the corporation disposes of the property or when the shareholder disposes of a substantial interest in the business.

Example 13.35. In 1998, Bill and Joe incorporated their equally owned partnership and each received 50 percent stock in the Block

Corporation. On November 15, 1994, the partnership had purchased energy property for $18,000 (five-year property) and had claimed a general business credit of $1,800. No general business credit was recaptured upon incorporation.

¶ 13,175   SECTION 351 TRANSFER OR TAXABLE EXCHANGE

Code Sec. 351 is a mandatory provision. Gain or loss is not recognized on a transfer which qualifies under Code Sec. 351. The corporation's basis in the property is a carryover basis equal to the shareholder's adjusted basis in the property. Also, the shareholder's basis in the stock received is equal to the adjusted basis of property transferred.

There may be times when taxpayers want recognition on the exchange. If taxpayers have property whose fair market value is less than the adjusted basis, they may want to recognize this loss. Code Sec. 351 must be avoided to accomplish this. An arm's-length sale or an exchange for short-term debt would be a transaction outside the purview of Code Sec. 351. The loss will not be recognized if the shareholder and corporation are related parties as defined in Code Sec. 267 (i.e., if the shareholder owns directly or indirectly more than 50 percent in value of the corporation's outstanding stock).

The shareholder might want to recognize gain on the transaction because this provides the corporation with a stepped-up basis (fair market value), especially if the shareholder is in a lower tax bracket than the corporation. However, under Code Sec. 1239 capital gain treatment will be denied the shareholder if the property is depreciable property in the hands of the corporation and the shareholder and corporation are related parties. Thus, the ordinary income treatment under Code Sec. 1239 will apply if the shareholder directly or indirectly owns more than 50 percent of the value of the corporation's stock.

> *Example 13.36.* Jim Jones, who owns 70 percent of Best Corporation, sells Section 1231 property to Best Corporation for $100,000 (the property's fair market value). The adjusted basis of the property is $60,000. Jim has a realized and recognized gain of $40,000 ($100,000 − $60,000). The gain will be a Section 1231 gain. However, if the property is depreciable property for the corporation (e.g., a building), the $40,000 gain is ordinary income.

Shareholders must determine whether a Section 351 transfer is most advantageous for them. The transaction must be structured properly so that either it falls under Code Sec. 351 or is beyond its control, depending upon which result is desired.

KEYSTONE PROBLEM

The sole proprietor of a printing shop is in the fortunate position of having greatly appreciated assets (the land and building where the business is located) as well as an exceedingly competent business manager. The manager is in fact so good that another position elsewhere has been offered. The owner persuades the manager to stay by giving 25 percent of the business. This is accomplished by incorporating the business and signing over 25 percent of the common stock to the manager. No tax advice is sought and the tax consequences are rather severe:

1. Code Sec. 351 has not been met, so the owner has "sold" the assets to the corporation. The gain will equal the value of the full 100 percent stock interest less the basis in the assets on a item-by-item basis.

2. The manager has taxable compensation in the amount of the value of the 25 percent stock interest since property received for services is taxable under Code Sec. 83. (However, an offsetting deduction is available.)

The two main requirements for incorporating tax free are that the transferors of property must be in at least 80 percent control after the transfer and that they received only stock for their property. In accordance with these two requirements, there are several alternative ways to handle this transaction so as to limit taxes or avoid them completely. Explain.

¶ 13,185   REPORTING REQUIREMENTS

Shareholders and corporations who are parties to a Section 351 exchange must attach statements to their income tax returns for the period in which the exchange occurred. Reg. § 1.351-3(a) and (b). The shareholder's statement must include the following:

1. A description of the property transferred and its adjusted basis

2. A description of the type and number of shares of stock received, including its fair market value

3. A description of the securities received, including principal, terms, and fair market value

4. An indication of the amount of money received

5. A description of any other property received (i.e., boot), including its fair market value

6. A description of the liabilities assumed by the corporation, including when and why they were created and the business reason for the assumption

The statement of the controlled corporation must include:

1. A description of all property received from transferors

2. An indication of the transferor's adjusted basis in the property

3. An indication of the number and type of stock issued, including its fair market value

4. A description of the stock issued and outstanding prior to and immediately after the exchange

5. A description of the securities issued, including fair market value

6. A description of all securities outstanding prior to and immediately after the exchange

7. An indication of the amount of money distributed to the transferors

8. A description of any other property distributed, including its fair market value

9. A description of liabilities assumed by the corporation, including when and why they were created and the business reason for the assumption

Corporate Capital Structure

A corporation's capital structure consists of the stock and debt it issues. Capital is raised from shareholders by issuing stock. Different classes of stock (i.e., common, preferred, voting, nonvoting) can be issued. Capital is raised from nonshareholders by issuing debt, in which case a formal debtor-creditor relationship is established. Additionally, shareholders and/or nonshareholders may contribute assets to the corporation not in return for stock or debt. These contributions to capital are motivated for different reasons. For example, a city might donate land to a corporation so that it may build a factory. The city will benefit from increased employment opportunities and tax revenues. Each method of raising capital can have significant consequences to the transferor and the corporation.

¶ 13,201 EQUITY IN THE CAPITAL STRUCTURE

Shareholder Contributions

A corporation does not recognize a gain or loss on the receipt of money or other property in exchange for its stock. Code Sec. 1032. Also, it does not recognize income when it receives money or other property as a contribution to capital (i.e., the corporation does not issue stock, debt, money, or property in return for the contributed property). Code Sec. 118. However, the exclusion does not apply to any money or property transferred to the corporation in consideration for goods or services rendered, or to subsidies paid for the purpose of inducing the corporation to limit production.

The corporation's basis in the property depends upon the nature of the transaction. If stock is issued in return for the property and Code Sec. 351 applies to the transaction, the corporation's basis equals the transferor's adjusted basis increased by any gain recognized by said transferor. If the transaction is a taxable exchange (i.e., the corporation purchases land by issuing its stock), the corporation's basis is the fair market value of the stock.

The shareholder's basis in the stock is equal to the adjusted basis of the property transferred, increased by any recognized gain and decreased by the fair market value of boot received if it is a Section 351 transfer. The shareholder's basis in stock received in a taxable exchange is equal to the fair market value of the property transferred.

The corporation's basis of property received from a shareholder as a contribution to capital equals the shareholder's adjusted basis increased by any gain recognized by the shareholder. Code Sec. 362. Since the shareholder receives no stock, the shareholder's basis in the stock owned prior to the contribution is increased by the amount of cash and adjusted basis of the property transferred plus any gain recognized by the shareholder on the transfer. Usually shareholders do not recognize a gain or loss when they transfer property as a contribution to capital.

Similarly, amounts received from voluntary pro rata payments from shareholders are not income to the corporation even though no stock is issued. The payments represent an addition to the price paid for the shares of stock held by the shareholders. Reg. § 1.118-1.

Example 13.37. Cindy Blair, a sole shareholder in Alpha Inc., contributed land to be used by the corporation as a parking lot. She receives no additional stock in the corporation. The land has a fair market value of $10,000 and an adjusted basis of $8,000. Cindy has a $2,000 realized gain but no recognized gain. Her basis in Alpha stock is increased by $8,000. Alpha Inc. recognizes no gain or loss. The corporation's basis in the land is $8,000.

Example 13.38. Dancing Shoes Corporation requires additional funds for conducting its business and obtains such funds through voluntary pro rata payments by its shareholders. The payments are credited to a special paid-in capital account and no additional shares are issued. The amounts received from the shareholders do not constitute income to the corporation. The payments are in the nature of assessments upon the shareholders and represent an additional price paid for the shares of stock held by the individual shareholders.

Special rules apply to the forgiveness of corporate debts by shareholders. As a general rule, when a debt is cancelled, the debtor must recognize income. However, if a shareholder in a corporation which is indebted to the shareholder gratuitously forgives the debt, the transaction amounts to a contribution to the capital of the corporation to the extent of the principal of the debt.

Example 13.39. Mary Sullivan owns stock in Dogette Corporation and also lent the corporation $10,000. Mary gratuitously cancels the $10,000 debt. The forgiveness of the debt is a nontaxable contribution to capital. The corporation recognizes no income and Mary increases her stock basis by $10,000.

Nonshareholder Contributions

Contributions by nonshareholders also are excluded from gross income of the corporation as long as the transfer is not for goods and services. Nonshareholder contributions are usually prompted by expectation of some indirect benefit. Cities often provide corporations with land or other property as an inducement to locate in their area.

The basis to the corporation of property received from a nonshareholder is zero. Where the corporation receives a cash contribution from a shareholder, the corporation is required to reduce the basis of any property acquired during the next 12-month period by the amount of cash received. When all of the money has not been spent in the

12-month period, the basis of other property must be reduced by the amount not spent. Property subject to depreciation must be reduced first, then property subject to amortization, then property subject to depletion, and finally any other remaining property. The reduction of the basis of each of the properties within each category is to be made in proportion to the relative basis of such properties. Code Sec. 362(c)(1) and (2); Reg. § 1.362-2.

Example 13.40. Calumet City donates land to Wilder Corporation as an inducement for the corporation to expand operations. The land has a basis of $10,000 and a fair market value of $25,000. Wilder recognizes no income and will have a zero basis in the land.

Example 13.41. Hamilton City donates $50,000 in cash and land with a fair market value of $75,000 to Miler Corporation as an inducement to locate there. Within the next 12 months, it purchased property for $40,000 with the donated cash. Miler Corporation has no income. Its basis in the land and property purchased for $40,000 is zero. Additionally, starting with depreciable assets, the basis of Miler's other properties must be reduced by the $10,000 not spent.

The corporation recognizes no income from nonshareholder contributions. However, since any basis in the property received or acquired is zero, the normal benefits of depreciation, amortization, or depletion are denied. Thus in the long run, the corporation recognizes income when the asset is sold.

¶ 13,215 DEBT IN THE CAPITAL STRUCTURE

In addition to issuing stock during corporate formation, the corporation also should issue long-term debt because debt has certain advantages over equity. Interest payments on the debt are deductible by the corporation while dividends are not deductible. Additionally, debt repayment is an acceptable reason for accumulating income and, therefore, avoiding the accumulated earnings tax under Code Sec. 531. Most redemptions of stock are not acceptable reasons. Repayment of the principal is tax free to the creditor, whereas payments made to shareholders for their stock may be considered dividends or taxable redemptions. Finally, should the debt instrument become worthless, then the loss may be an ordinary loss if the debt is business related (if nonbusiness bad debt, then it is treated as a short-term capital loss).

There are some disadvantages to debt. Interest payments are income to the debtholder. Similarly, the debtholder will have income for amounts received in excess of basis. Additionally, if the debtholder is a corporation, it is not entitled to the dividends-received deduction when it receives interest payments. Finally, the corporation issuing the debt must make timely payments of interest and principal in accordance with the terms of the debt instrument. Stock does not have this constraint; that is, dividends usually are voluntary distributions.

Example 13.42. John Jones invests cash in Adams Corporation in return for stock and long-term debt in a Section 351 transfer. During the year, John receives a dividend of $5,000 and interest payments of $6,000. Jones has $11,000 of gross income. Adam Corporation has a $6,000 deduction for the interest payment. No deduction is allowed for the dividend payment. Assuming Adams Corporation's tax rate is 34 percent, the after-tax cost of the interest payment is $3,960 ($6,000 × (1.00 − .34)); the deduction saved it taxes of $2,040 ($6,000 × .34). The after-tax cost of the dividend was $5,000 because it was not deductible.

Because of the advantages of debt financing, there are instances when taxpayers attempt to treat equity instruments as debt. Usually these instruments are debt in legal form but in substance are equity. Using the doctrine of substance over form, the IRS will attempt to reclassify this debt as equity. In 1969, Code Sec. 385 was added to the Internal Revenue Code with the purpose of providing guidance in classifying an instrument as debt or equity. The section lists five factors that may be considered:

1. Does the instrument contain an unconditional promise to pay on demand or on a specified date a definite amount for adequate consideration and at a fixed rate of interest?

2. Is the debt preferred over or subordinated to other debts?

3. How high is the corporation's debt to equity ratio (is the corporation thinly capitalized)?

4. Is the debt convertible into stock?

5. What is the relationship between stock and debt ownership (is it proportionate)?

Regulations were to be prescribed which would contain factors and/or tests that would be used to classify an instrument as debt or equity. After more than 10 years and numerous court cases (e.g., *Estate of Mixon,* 72-2 USTC ¶ 9537, 464 F.2d 394 (CA-5 1972)), Final Regulations were issued in 1980. The effective date of these Regulations was postponed several times and on July 6, 1983, the Regulations were withdrawn. Thus, the area remains subject to uncertainty. However, the classification of a corporate instrument issued after October 24, 1992, as stock or debt by the corporate issuer is binding on the issuer and all holders. Code Sec. 385(c). This classification is not binding on the IRS.

Example 13.43. Maurice Severs starts a new corporation with $50,000 and receives $40,000 of 12-year notes and $10,000 of stock. The full $50,000 will most likely be viewed as equity by the IRS because of the debt-to-equity ratio (4-to-1). If Maurice issued $25,000 of debt and $25,000 of equity, the arrangement would probably be respected. Thus, the corporation may deduct interest on the notes and Maurice may receive $25,000 tax free as repayment of principal.

¶ 13,235   SECTION 1244 STOCK

Although debt can be more advantageous than equity, certain stock issuances receive special treatment which makes them favorable. Shareholders are permitted to deduct losses on the worthlessness or sale (including redemptions and liquidations) of Section 1244 stock as ordinary. Gains on the disposition of such stock are capital gains. Thus, the shareholders receive the best of both situations, ordinary loss treatment (up to a statutory limit) if the corporation fails and capital gain treatment if the corporation is successful.

The reason for this treatment is to place shareholders of small corporations on a more nearly equal basis with sole proprietors and partners and to encourage the flow of funds into small corporations. Certain restrictions apply to ensure that the provision benefits small corporations.

Eligible Shareholders

Only individuals and partnerships are eligible for ordinary loss treatment if they were original holders of the stock. The stock loses its Section 1244 status when it is transferred. If a partnership is an original holder, the subsequent loss is passed through to those partners who were partners when the stock was issued. Reg. § 1.1244(a)-1(b)(2).

Loss Limitation

Ordinary loss treatment is limited to an annual $50,000 per shareholder and $100,000 on a joint return regardless of which spouse owns the stock. If the loss is greater than these limits ($50,000 or $100,000), the excess is treated as a capital loss. Section 1244 losses are treated as attributable to the taxpayer's trade or business. As such, they have business status for net operating loss purposes. Thus, if the Section 1244 loss exceeds the shareholder's taxable income, the excess is carried over under the net operating loss provisions.

> *Example 13.44.* Marge Summers, a single taxpayer, has a basis of $120,000 in Section 1244 stock when it becomes worthless. She incurs a $50,000 ordinary loss and a $70,000 capital loss. If she is married by year-end, even if the loss had been sustained months earlier, a $100,000 ordinary loss and a $20,000 capital loss would result on a joint return.

Corporate Requirements

Only a domestic small business corporation can issue Section 1244 stock. The stock can be common or preferred and voting or nonvoting. The corporation must qualify as a small business at the time the stock is issued. The total dollar amount of money and property received by the corporation for its stock, as a contribution to capital and as paid-in capital, cannot exceed $1,000,000 at the time the stock is issued. The property's fair market value is not used in determining the $1,000,000 limit. Property received by the corporation is valued at its adjusted basis, reduced by any liabilities to which the property was subject or which were assumed by the corporation. Stock issued for services rendered does not qualify as Section 1244 stock.

If the adjusted basis of the property transferred in return for Section 1244 stock exceeds its fair market value, the adjusted basis of such stock for the sole purpose of computing the Section 1244 loss is reduced by the amount of such excess. This treatment prevents the conversion of a capital loss on the property into an ordinary loss on the Section 1244 stock. Increases in basis through contributions to capital or otherwise are not counted for ordinary loss computation purposes. Code Sec. 1244(d)(1)(B).

> *Example 13.45.* Roy Ready incorporated a truck with a basis of $20,000 and a fair market value of $13,000. He subsequently contributed another $11,000 in the business before his stock became worthless. Since his basis in the stock was $31,000 ($20,000 + $11,000), his loss also is $31,000; only $13,000 is an ordinary loss under Code Sec. 1244. The remaining loss of $18,000, consisting of the paper loss at the time of incorporation plus capital contributions, is capital in nature.

TAX PLANNING POINTER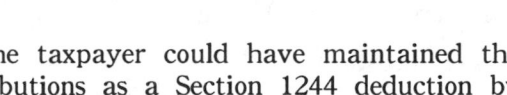

In Example 13.45, the taxpayer could have maintained the $11,000 capital contributions as a Section 1244 deduction by purchasing stock in the corporation for $11,000 instead of contributing the $11,000 and adjusting the basis of the stockholdings.

The corporation must be an operating company at the time the loss is sustained. The corporation's gross receipts from sources other than dividends, interest, royalties, rents, annuities, and sales or exchanges from stock or securities must exceed 50 percent of the corporation's gross receipts for the five most recent tax years. The operating company requirement need not be satisfied if the total deductions allowed the corporation—other than the dividends-received deduction and the net operating loss deduction—exceeds the total gross income for the five-year period.

Reporting Requirements

Taxpayers must substantiate their claims of a Section 1244 loss. The taxpayer is required to maintain records sufficient to distinguish Section 1244 stock from any other stock the taxpayer may own in the corporation. The corporation also should maintain records showing all of the following:

1. The persons to whom stock was issued, the date of issuance to these persons, and a description of the amount and type of consideration received from each person.

2. The basis to the shareholder of any property received by the corporation and the fair market value of the property at the time it is received by the corporation.

3. The amount of money and the basis to the corporation of other property received for its stock as a contribution to capital and as paid-in capital.

4. Financial statements of the corporation, such as its income tax returns, that identify the sources of the gross receipts of the corporation for the period consisting of the five most recent tax years.

5. Information relating to any tax-free stock dividends made with respect to Section 1244 stock and any reorganization in which stock is transferred by the corporation in exchange for Section 1244 stock.

¶ 13,245 SECTION 1202 STOCK

The Revenue Reconciliation Act of 1993 added Code Sec. 1202, which is designed to aid small business capital formation. Within limits, Code Sec. 1202 enables noncorporate taxpayers to exclude 50 percent of the gain from the sale or exchange on qualified small business stock held for more than five years. The definition of small business stock is not the same as that used in Code Sec. 1244.

Eligible Shareholders

Only individuals are eligible for the 50 percent exclusion if they were the original holders of the stock and the stock was issued in exchange for money, property other than stock, or compensation for services rendered to the corporation. If a conduit entity was an original holder, the subsequent gain is passed through to those owners who were owners when the stock was issued. Conduits can be holders of Section 1202 stock. Partnerships, S corporations, regulated investment companies, and common trust funds qualify as conduits for purposes of Code Sec. 1202. The gain and share of the stock's adjusted basis pass through proportionately to the owners (e.g., partners) of the conduit. Code Sec. 1202 applies only to stock originally issued after August 10, 1993, which is held for more than five years by the taxpayer. The stock generally loses its Section 1202 status when it is transferred unless the transfer is tax free and by gift, by death, from a partnership to a partner, or a stock-for-stock transfer.

Gain Limitation

Only gain from the sale or exchange of qualified small business stock is eligible for the 50 percent exclusion. Exclusion treatment is subject to per-issuer cumulative limitations. The amount of eligible gain is limited to the greater of:

1. $10,000,000 reduced by the aggregate of eligible gain recognized from the sale of the corporation's stock which has been taken into account by the taxpayer in prior years, or

2. 10 times the aggregate adjusted basis of qualified small business stock issued by the corporation and disposed of by the taxpayer during the taxable year. For this purpose only, the adjusted basis of the stock is not increased for additions to basis which took place after the date of original issuance.

In determining the taxpayer's eligible gain, if the stock was acquired in exchange for property (other than money or stock), then for

Code Sec. 1202 purposes only, the basis of the stock shall be no less than the property's fair market value at the time of transfer. The basis adjustment for any subsequent contribution to capital also shall be no less than the property's fair market value at the time of the transfer. This prevents taxpayers from converting gain on the contributed property to Code Sec. 1202 gain eligible for the 50 percent exclusion.

Example 13.46. On January 10, 1994, Sara Shertzer acquired stock in Snave Co. for $300,000. Snave Co. is a qualified small business for Code Sec. 1202 purposes. On January 18, 1999, Sara sold the stock for $600,000. Sara's realized gain is $300,000, and her recognized gain is $150,000. One-half of the $300,000 capital gain is excluded since it is within the limits of (1) $10,000,000 or (2) $10 \times \$100,000 = \$1,000,000$.

Example 13.47. On February 14, 1994, Sam Ellsworth transferred property to Maxo Co. in return for 100 percent of its common stock. The corporation is a qualified small business for Code Sec. 1202 purposes. Sam's adjusted basis in the property was $500,000, and it had a fair market value of $2,000,000. On February 17, 1999, Sam sold one-fourth of his shares for $800,000. Sam's realized gain is $675,000 ($800,000 − ($500,000 × .25)). His recognized gain is $337,500. One-half of the $675,000 gain is excluded because it is within the limits of (1) $10,000,000 or (2) $10 \times (\$2,000,000 \times .25) = \$5,000,000$.

Corporate Requirements

Only a domestic C corporation can issue Section 1202 stock. The stock can be common or preferred and voting or nonvoting. The corporation must qualify as a small business at the time the stock is issued. The corporation's aggregate gross assets cannot exceed $50,000,000 anytime before the issuance of the stock and immediately after the issuance. Aggregate basis is equal to cash and the aggregate adjusted basis of property held. For this test only, the adjusted basis of contributed property is equal to its fair market value at the time of transfer. If aggregate gross assets subsequently exceed $50,000,000, the corporation no longer can issue Section 1202 stock; however, previously issued Section 1202 stock is not disqualified.

The corporation must be an operating company which is actively engaged in a trade or business during substantially all of the time the taxpayer held its stock. A corporation meets this requirement if at least 80 percent of its assets are used in the active conduct of one or more qualified trades or businesses as defined in Code Sec. 1202(e)(3). Most services and financing businesses would not qualify. If more than 10 percent of the total value of its assets consists of real estate not used in the active conduct of a qualified trade or business, then the corporation fails the active business test.

TRA '97 added Code Sec. 1045 which enables a taxpayer to roll over tax-free gains on the sale of qualified small business stock held for more than six months if the proceeds from the sale are used to purchase other qualified small business stock within 60 days of the sale. The taxpayer's basis in the newly acquired stock is reduced by the amount of capital gain not recognized. Also, the holding period of the stock sold is tacked on to the holding period of the newly acquired stock.

> *Example 13.48.* Justin Wells invests $300,000 in Shapot Corporation on September 1, 1997. Shapot Corporation qualifies as a small business corporation. On August 14, 1998, Justin sells his Shapot Corporation stock for $550,000. He then buys stock in Clerici Inc., also a small business corporation, for $525,000. Since Justin did not reinvest all $550,000, he must recognize a $25,000 gain.

Code Sec. 1044 Rollovers

For sales after August 9, 1993, Code Sec. 1044 allows individual and corporate (not an S corporation) taxpayers to roll over their gains on the sale of publicly traded securities into a Specialized Small Business Investment Company (SSBIC). An SSBIC is any partnership or corporation which is licensed under Section 301(d) of the Small Business Investment Act of 1958. The taxpayer must make the rollover into the SSBIC within 60 days of the sale of the publicly traded securities, and the taxpayer will only recognize his or her gains to the extent that the sale amount exceeds the cost of the SSBIC interest.

The amount of gain that can be rolled over in any one year is limited. For individuals it cannot exceed the lesser of (a) $50,000 or (b) $500,000, reduced by the amount of gain from prior years that has already been deferred due to this rollover provision. The rollover limit for C corporations is the lesser of (a) $250,000 or (b) $1,000,000, reduced by the amount of gain from prior years that has already been deferred due to this rollover provision. The deferred gain is a basis adjustment (reduction) to the newly acquired SSBIC interest.

Stock or Debt

Whether stock or debt is preferable depends on many considerations. Individual shareholders are entitled to the benefits of Code Secs. 1202 and 1244, which make stock advantageous to them. Corporate shareholders are not entitled to the benefits of Code Secs. 1244 and 1202, but they are entitled to the dividends-received deduction (discussed at ¶ 13,385), which also makes stock advantageous to them.

A major advantage of debt accrues to the issuing corporation. It is entitled to a deduction for interest payments but not for dividend payments. The recipient shareholder has gross income regardless of whether it is interest or dividends (except for corporate shareholders entitled to the dividends-received deduction). A disadvantage of debt is that a loss upon its sale or worthlessness usually results in a nonbusiness bad debt (which is treated as a short-term capital loss by individuals) or a capital loss. Corporate shareholders might be able to claim a business bad debt deduction.

Thus, whether stock or debt is preferred depends in part on the type of shareholders, the marginal tax rates of the shareholders and the corporation, and the possibility of a Section 531 tax imposition (discussed in Chapter 17). Nontax factors also are important.

TAX PLANNING POINTER ▼

Toni Travels invested $50,000 cash in a wholly owned corporation. Since she was aware of the advantages of debt in the capital structure, she received $25,000 in stock and $25,000 in debt. A few years later, the corporation became worthless. Only the $25,000 basis in the stock is eligible for ordinary loss treatment under Code Sec. 1244. The worthless debt is deductible only as a capital loss. Toni may have been better advised to have taken only stock in the original transfer to the corporation.

TAX BLUNDER

Sally Rogers owns 100 shares of Dino Co. She acquired the shares on January 15, 1994, for $100,000. Dino Co. qualifies as a small business corporation for Code Sec. 1202 purposes. Sally believed she would have a very large estimated tax payment due on January 15, 1998, so she sold the shares on January 2, 1998, for $250,000. Sally's estimated tax payment was much less than she expected. Sally was uncertain of (and somewhat indifferent about) what to do with the proceeds from the sale of the Dino Co. shares, so she put the proceeds into a three-month certificate of deposit. The result of these events is that Sally must recognize the $150,000 fully in 1998. Sally did not hold the stock for more than five years, so the sale does not qualify for the 50 percent exclusion. However, she still could have deferred gain recognition by reinvesting in shares of a small business corporation. Had she not been indifferent regarding her investment choice, she might have made a much better decision.

Determination of Corporate Taxable Income

¶ 13,301   GENERAL RULES

There are many similarities between the rules used to determine taxable income for corporations and those used for individuals. Gross income is determined in the same manner for corporations and individuals. The provisions of Code Sec. 61 apply to both types of taxpayers, although some deductions, such as alimony, apply only to individuals. Corporations also are entitled to exclusions from gross income. Thus, corporations can exclude interest income on municipal bonds. However, most of the statutory exclusions in Code Secs. 101 to 138 pertain to individuals only.

All corporate deductions are business deductions. Ordinary and necessary expenses incurred to carry on a trade or business are deductible. Code Sec. 162. These are similar to some of the *for adjusted gross income deductions* (*for AGI*) allowed to individuals. However, some of the *for AGI* deductions, such as alimony payments and contributions to IRAs, apply only to individuals. Corporations do not have *from adjusted gross income deductions (from AGI)*. They are not entitled to deductions for personal expenses. Also, they do not have itemized deductions, a standard deduction, or deductions for personal exemptions. However, there are some deductions that apply to corporations only, such as the dividends-received deduction under Code Sec. 243.

Because corporations do not have itemized deductions, the limitations and reductions used to compute deductions are different. For example, corporations do not reduce a casualty loss by $100 or a net casualty loss by 10 percent of adjusted gross income. Interest expense is not classified as personal interest under Code Sec. 163 if incurred by corporations and, therefore, is fully deductible.

Property transactions are taxed similarly. The determination of realized gain or loss and the classification of this gain or loss as capital, ordinary, or Code Sec. 1231 is similar. Both corporations and individuals are subject to depreciation recapture rules under Code Secs. 1245 and 1250. The deferral provisions for like-kind exchanges under Code Sec. 1031 and involuntary conversions under Code Sec. 1033 apply to corporations and individuals.

¶ 13,305   ACCOUNTING PERIODS

One of the elections a new corporation must make is its choice of an accounting period. In general, corporations have the same choices as do individuals. They may choose a calendar year or a fiscal year. However, a corporation has more flexibility in choosing its accounting period. It may choose any calendar or fiscal tax year regardless of the tax years of its owners. This ability to have a tax year different from that of its owners can produce tax savings, especially in the year of incorporation.

Other entities do not have this freedom. For example, S corporations are required to adopt the calendar year unless they can establish a business purpose for a fiscal year. Deferral of income to shareholders is not a business purpose. Code Sec. 1378(b). Partnerships must have the same tax year as their partners who have a majority interest. If there is no majority interest, the partnership uses the tax year of all its principal partners. If there are no principal partners, the least aggregate deferral method must be used unless the partnership can establish a business purpose for using a fiscal year. Code Sec. 706(b).

Personal service corporations are corporations whose primary activity is the performance of personal services. These services are primarily performed by employee-owners. Personal-service corporations must use a calendar year for their tax year unless they can establish a business purpose for a fiscal year. Code Sec. 441(i).

¶ 13,311   ACCOUNTING METHODS

The corporation must select an accounting method in its initial tax year. Generally, the cash basis, accrual basis, or a hybrid basis which contains elements of the cash and accrual methods may be elected. Most corporations, however, must use the accrual method. However, this constraint does not apply to S corporations, qualified farming businesses, qualified personal service corporations, and corporations with average annual receipts of $5 million or less for the three prior tax years.

A corporation that meets the exception above (e.g., an S corporation) may use either of the three methods. However, corporations that maintain inventory for sale to customers are required to use the accrual method of accounting for determining sales and cost of goods sold.

¶ 13,315 CAPITAL GAINS AND LOSSES

The process used to determine a corporation's capital gains and losses is similar to that used by individuals. Gains and losses resulting from the taxable sale or exchange of capital assets must be reclassified as short-term or long-term. Next, the net short-term and the net long-term positions must be computed. If the short-term gains exceed the short-term losses, a net short-term gain results. If the short-term losses exceed the short-term gains, a net short-term loss results. Long-term gains and losses are netted in similar manner to determine the net long-term gain or loss.

The next step is to determine the corporation's overall capital asset position. This is dependent upon the two net positions. If they are opposite (i.e., a net loss and a net gain), then they are combined. If they are similar (i.e., both net gains or net losses), then they are kept separate. Thus, there are six possible combinations:

1. Net long-term capital gain greater than net short-term capital loss. These are combined to produce a net capital gain.

2. Net long-term capital gain less than net short-term capital loss. These are combined to produce a net capital loss.

3. Net short-term capital gain greater than net long-term capital loss. These are combined to produce capital gain net income.

4. Net short-term capital gain less than net long-term capital loss. These are combined to produce a net capital loss.

5. Net long-term capital gain and net short-term capital gain. These are not combined. The net long-term capital gain is treated as a net capital gain, and the net short-term capital gain is treated as capital gain net income.

6. Net long-term capital loss and net short-term capital loss. These are not combined.

The taxation of corporate capital gains and losses depends on the net position (i.e., combinations one to six above).

Net Capital Gain

The Tax Reform Act of 1986 eliminated the preferential treatment of net long-term capital gains for corporations but retained the distinction between long-term and short-term capital assets, and the Revenue Reconciliation Act of 1990 did not change corporate treatment of capital gains and losses. Net capital gains (combinations 1, 3, and 5, above) must be included in the corporation's gross income and are taxed at the same rate as ordinary income, a flat 35 percent in the case of many corporations. Under TRA '97, the alternative tax rate of 35%

is now applied to the lesser of the corporation's net capital gain or its taxable income.

> *Example 13.49.* Hands Corporation has gross receipts from sales of $230,000, deductible expenses of $75,000, and a net capital gain of $48,000. Hands' gross income is $278,000 ($230,000 + $48,000). Its taxable income is $203,000 ($278,000 − $75,000). Its tax liability will be computed on the $203,000; the $48,000 net capital gain does not receive preferential treatment.

Net Capital Losses

Unlike individuals, corporations may not take a deduction for net capital losses in the year in which they occur. The net capital loss can never be used to reduce ordinary income. Corporate taxpayers may claim capital losses only against capital gains.

Net capital losses (combinations 2, 4, and 6, above) of a corporation are carried back to the three preceding tax years to offset net capital gains claimed in those years. If some net capital loss remains, it is carried forward for a period of five tax years. The carryovers must be taken back to the third, second, and first preceding tax years in that order, and any remaining losses carried forward to the five succeeding tax years in order. Unused losses at the end of the five-year carryforward period are lost forever. Also, all net capital losses carried back or forward become short-term capital losses regardless of their original status.

> *Example 13.50.* Civic Corporation incurred a net long-term capital loss of $15,000 in 1998. It also had gross receipts from sales of $120,000 and deductible expenses of $70,000 in 1998. Civic's gross income is $120,000, and its taxable income is $50,000 ($120,000 − $70,000). The $15,000 net capital loss does not affect taxable income in 1998. Civic Corporation carries the loss back to 1995, 1996, and 1997, in that order, to offset any net capital gains of those years. If the loss is not exhausted, the remainder is carried, in order, forward to 1999, 2000, 2001, 2002, and 2003. The $15,000 is treated as a short-term capital loss in any of the carryback or carryforward years.

> *Example 13.51.* Assume the same facts as in Example 13.50, except that Civic Corporation had a net short-term capital gain of $7,000 in 1995, a net short-term capital gain of $2,000 and a net long-term capital gain of $3,000 in 1996, and no capital gains or losses in 1997. The $15,000 net capital loss incurred in 1998 first is carried back to 1995 and offsets the $7,000 net short-term capital gain. Civic will receive a refund of taxes paid on that gain. The remaining $8,000 loss ($15,000 − $7,000) is carried to 1996 where it offsets the $2,000 net short-term capital gain and then the $3,000 net long-term capital gain. Civic will receive a refund of taxes paid on both gains. The remaining loss of $3,000 ($8,000 − ($2,000 + $3,000)) is carried to 1997. Since there were no net capital gains in that year, the $3,000 loss will be carried to 1999.

¶ 13,325   DEPRECIATION RECAPTURE

Corporations generally compute the ordinary income recapture on Section 1245 and Section 1250 assets in the same manner as individuals. Section 1245 assets are generally subject to ordinary income recapture to the extent of the full depreciation taken on the asset. Section 1250 assets acquired before 1981 are generally subject to ordinary income recapture to the extent of the cumulative excess of the depreciation taken over the amount allowed using straight-line depreciation. Nonresidential real property placed in service in years 1981 through 1986 is subject to depreciation recapture to the extent of the full depreciation taken if an accelerated depreciation method was used. Residential real estate continues to use the pre-1981 recapture rules. Post-1986 acquisitions of buildings are depreciated on a straight-line basis.

However, corporations have special recapture rules under Code Sec. 291. Application of these rules may result in a greater amount of ordinary income than the Section 1250 recapture rules for other business organizations. Code Sec. 291 requires that 20 percent of the excess of any amount that would be treated as ordinary income under Code Sec. 1245 over the amount treated as ordinary income under Code Sec. 1250 is additional depreciation recapture, and thus, ordinary income. Similar rules apply to amortization of pollution control facilities and intangible drilling costs incurred by corporate taxpayers. The computation of Section 291 gain is shown below.

Amount that would have been ordinary income if Section 1245 property	$XXX
Less: Amount of ordinary income under Section 1250	(XX)
Excess of Section 1245 gain over Section 1250 gain	$XXX
Section 291 applicable percentage	× 20%
Section 291 gain (ordinary income)	$XXX

If the gain recognized on the transaction exceeds the ordinary income recognized under Code Sec. 1245, 1250, or 291, then such excess is a Section 1231 gain.

Example 13.52. Computer Services Corporation acquired an office building for $450,000. The building was depreciated under the straight-line method. The building was sold nine years later for $240,000. Depreciation taken on the building up to the time of sale was $270,000 ($30,000 per year for nine years). The adjusted basis at the time of sale was $180,000 ($450,000 − $270,000). Computer Services Corporation has a $60,000 gain on the sale (amount realized of $240,000 less adjusted basis of $180,000). Since straight-line depreciation was used, there is no depreciation recapture under Code Sec. 1245 or 1250. However, ordinary income of $12,000 recognized under Code Sec. 291 is computed as follows:

Ordinary income if Section 1245 gain	$60,000
Less: Ordinary income under Section 1250	0
Excess Section 1245 gain	$60,000
Section 291 percentage	× 20%
Section 291 gain (ordinary income)	$12,000

The remaining $48,000 gain ($60,000 − $12,000) is Section 1231 gain.

Example 13.53. Assume the same facts in Example 13.52, except that $315,000 in depreciation had been taken on the office building using accelerated depreciation. The adjusted basis at time of sale was $135,000 ($450,000 − $315,000). The gain on the sale of the building is $105,000 ($240,000 amount realized less $135,000 adjusted basis). The building is considered Section 1245 property since it was depreciated using accelerated depreciation; thus, the entire gain is ordinary income (Section 1245 gain).

Example 13.54. Assume the same facts as Example 13.53, except that the building was residential rental property depreciated under accelerated depreciation. The ordinary income recaptured under Code Sec. 1250 is the excess of accelerated depreciation over what straight-line depreciation would have been, or $45,000 ($315,000 − $270,000). The Section 291 gain is $12,000, computed as follows:

Ordinary income if Section 1245 gain	$105,000
Less: Ordinary income under Section 1250	45,000
Excess Section 1245 gain	$ 60,000
Section 291 percentage	× 20%
Section 291 gain (ordinary income)	$ 12,000

Thus, Computer Services Corporation would recognize ordinary income of $57,000 ($45,000 Section 1250 gain + $12,000 Section 291 gain) and $48,000 Section 1231 gain ($105,000 − $57,000).

¶ 13,335 NET OPERATING LOSS

A corporation was allowed to carry its net operating loss (NOL) back three years and forward fifteen years. However, under TRA '97, the NOL carryback period is reduced to two years and the NOL carryforward period is increased to 20 years for all tax years beginning after August 5, 1997. An election may be made to forego the carryback and to carry the NOL forward only. The election must be made by the due date (including extensions) of the tax return for the year in which the NOL occurred. Code Sec. 172(b). However, any unused NOL at the end of the carryforward period is lost forever. Thus, the carryover rules for NOLs are the same for corporations and individuals.

The election to not carry the loss back to the two preceding years may be advantageous if the prior years' taxable incomes were in a lower tax bracket than the tax rate expected in the future. Also, the corporation would not want to carry back a NOL to a tax year in which the corporation had utilized a credit that is due to expire or that has expired.

Example 13.55. NIFCO incurs a net operating loss of $20,000 in 1998. Normally, the corporation would carry the loss back to 1996. However, during 1996 the corporation had only $25,000 of taxable income. The corporation incurred a tax liability of $3,750 ($25,000 × 15%). It is expected that the corporation will be in the 34 percent tax bracket in the future. By carrying back the $20,000 loss to 1996, the corporation will receive a refund of $3,000 ($20,000 × 15%). By carrying the loss forward, the corporation expects to receive a tax benefit of $6,800 ($20,000 × 34%).

Unlike individuals, corporations are not required to make adjustments to the NOL for capital gains and losses, nonbusiness expenses, or personal exemptions since they are not allowed deductions for these items in the computation of taxable income. Also, corporations are permitted the full dividends-received deduction (see ¶ 13,385) in computing their NOLs. Similar to individuals, NOL deductions for each year are considered separately. Thus, NOL carryovers from other years are omitted in computing the NOL for the present year.

Example 13.56. In 1998, Mighty Corporation has $200,000 of gross income from operations and operating deductions of $300,000. The corporation also received $50,000 in dividends from a 30 percent owned domestic corporation. The corporation has a net operating loss for the year of $90,000, computed as follows:

Gross Income
    Operations $200,000
    Dividends   50,000

    Total Gross Income $250,000
Deductions
    Operations $300,000
    Dividends-received deduction ($50,000 × 80%) . .   40,000

    Total Deductions 340,000

Net Operating Loss . . . . $ 90,000

Mighty Corporation may carry the $90,000 NOL back to 1996, and then 1997 if still not used, or may elect not to carry back and instead carry the NOL forward.

Example 13.57. Assume the same facts as in Example 13.56. In addition, Mighty Corporation had taxable income of $40,000 in 1996. Mighty could carry back the $90,000 NOL to offset 1996 taxable income. It would receive a refund of taxes paid in 1996. The 1996 taxable income would use $40,000 of the NOL, leaving $50,000 to be carried to 1997.

The ability of corporations to carry back NOLs to claim a refund is restricted if the NOL is due to interest expense arising from debt used in corporate equity reduction transactions (CERTs) occurring after August 2, 1989. Code Sec. 172(b)(1)(M). A CERT is a transaction where either (1) the corporation acquires at least 50 percent (by value or vote) of the stock of another corporation—a major acquisition—or (2) the corporation makes an excess distribution. An excess distribution occurs if a corporation's total distributions and redemptions exceed the lesser of (1) 150 percent of the corporation's average annual distributions or redemptions for the preceding three years or (2) 10 percent of the fair market value of the stock at the beginning of the tax year.

The amount disallowed as a carryback is equal to the excess of the NOL for the tax year over the NOL reduced by the interest deductions incurred in a CERT. Code Sec. 172(m). The amount disallowed as a carryback is not lost forever; it is carried forward. However, to the extent that this carryover creates or adds to an NOL in the carryforward years, restrictions are placed on the corporation's ability to carry back those NOLs.

> *Example 13.58.* Worldwide Corporation had an $8,000,000 NOL for the year. Included in the NOL were interest deductions of $5,000,000 on debt used in a CERT. The NOL without this deduction would have been $3,000,000. Worldwide can carry back only $3,000,000 of the NOL.

¶ 13,345 CHARITABLE CONTRIBUTIONS

The deductibility of charitable contributions is dependent upon (1) what type of property is donated, (2) when the property is donated, and (3) to whom the property is donated, as well as the corporation's adjusted taxable income. In order to receive a deduction, the property must be donated to a qualified charitable organization. Code Sec. 170(c). A deduction is allowed only in the year of transfer or payment (i.e., when the contribution occurs). However, an accrual-basis corporation may claim a deduction in the year preceding payment if its board of directors authorized a charitable contribution during the year and payment of the contribution is made by the 15th day of the third month of the next tax year. Code Sec. 170(a).

> *Example 13.59.* The board of directors of Willis Corporation authorized a $3,000 cash donation to a qualified charitable organization on December 13, 1998. The payment was not made until February 25, 1999. Willis Corporation is a calendar-year corporation. If the corporation is on the accrual method of accounting, the charitable deduction will be allowed for 1998. Under the cash method, the deduction would not be allowed until 1999, the year paid.

The amount deductible is dependent upon the type of property contributed and the corporation's adjusted taxable income. Property type determines the initial dollar measure of the contribution. The overall deduction for contributions by a corporation is limited to 10 percent of adjusted taxable income.

Ten Percent Limitation

The maximum amount deductible by a corporation for charitable contributions is 10 percent of its adjusted taxable income. Thus, the deduction is limited to the lesser of 10 percent of adjusted taxable income or the sum of the initial measures of all property donated during the tax year. Adjusted taxable income is equal to taxable income without regard to the charitable contribution deduction, the dividends-received deduction, any net operating loss carryback, and any capital loss carryback. Code Sec. 170(b)(2). If the charitable contributions for the tax year exceed the 10 percent limitation, the excess can be carried forward for five years. Carryovers are used on a first-in, first-out basis after first deducting the current year's contributions. Code Sec. 170(b) and (d).

Example 13.60. Block Inc. reports the following items:

Gross income from sales	$310,000
Deductible expenses	220,000
Domestic dividends received (10 percent owned)	15,000
Net operating loss carryover	20,000
Charitable contributions	11,000

Taxable income is computed as follows:

Gross income from sales		$310,000
Domestic dividends		15,000
Gross income		$325,000
Deductible expenses	$220,000	
Net operating loss carryover	20,000	
Charitable contributions	8,500	
Dividends-received deduction	10,500	259,000
Taxable income		$ 66,000

Adjusted taxable income equals $85,000, i.e., taxable income adjusted for the charitable contribution deduction and the dividends-received deduction ($66,000 + $8,500 + $10,500). (No adjustment is made for the NOL carryover. An adjustment would have been made if it were a carryback.) Thus, the charitable contribution deduction is limited to $8,500 ($85,000 × 10 percent). The remaining $2,500 ($11,000 − $8,500) is carried forward to the following tax year.

TAX PLANNING POINTER

A number of corporations have set up their own private foundations so as to make contributions of up to 10 percent in good years.

Initial Measure of Contribution

The initial dollar measure of the contribution depends upon the property contributed to the charity. The initial measure of cash contributions is the amount of cash contributed. The initial measure of property contributions is their fair market value. However, under certain conditions fair market value is not allowed.

Long-Term Capital Gain Property

If the corporation contributes property whose sale would have resulted in a long-term capital gain, the initial measure of the contribution is its fair market value (i.e., the appreciation also is deductible). However, if the property is tangible personal property not related to the charity's tax-exempt purpose (e.g., donating a painting to a hospital) or the appreciated property is donated to certain private nonoperating foundations (as defined in Code Sec. 509(a)), then the initial measure is fair market value minus the amount of long-term capital gain that would have been recognized if the property had been sold. Code Sec. 170(e)(1).

> *Example 13.61.* Blake Corporation donates a painting that it bought several years ago for $30,000 to Orleans City Museum. At the time of the contribution the painting had a fair market value of $75,000. The initial measure of the contribution is $75,000.

> *Example 13.62.* Assume the same facts as in Example 13.61, except that Blake Corporation donates the painting to Orleans City Hospital. The initial measure of the contribution is $30,000 ($75,000 fair market value less the $45,000 long-term capital gain that would have been recognized if Blake Corporation had sold the painting).

Section 1231 property would be considered as long-term capital gain property unless it has depreciation recapture potential under Code Secs. 1245, 1250, and 291. To the extent of the recapture potential it is considered ordinary income property.

Ordinary Income Property

Ordinary income property is property that, if sold, would produce ordinary income to the seller. Examples of such property are inventories, short-term capital assets, and property subject to recapture under Code Sec. 1245, 1250, or 291. The initial measure of these contributions is equal to the fair market value reduced by any ordinary income that would have been recognized if the property had been sold. Usually this is equal to the lesser of the property's fair market value or adjusted basis. If the property is tangible personal property not related to the charity's tax-exempt function, then the initial measure of the contribution is fair market value minus the gain that would have been recognized if the property were sold.

> *Example 13.63.* Best Co. donated inventory to a public charity. At the time of donation, the inventory had a basis of $10,000 and a fair market value of $12,000. The initial measure of the contribution is $10,000 ($12,000 − $2,000).

> *Example 13.64.* Assume the same facts as in Example 13.63, except that the inventory's fair market value is $8,000. In this case, the initial measure of the contribution is $8,000.

> *Example 13.65.* Sandy Corporation donated an automobile to a public charity. The charity will use the automobile in its operations. The automobile was acquired for $10,000. At the time of

donation the automobile had a fair market value of $12,000 and an adjusted basis of $4,000. The initial measure of the contribution is $6,000 ($12,000 − $6,000 ordinary income recognized if property sold).

Example 13.66. Assume the same facts as in Example 13.65, except that the automobile will not be used by the charity. In this case, the initial measure of the contribution is $4,000 ($12,000 − $8,000 gain recognized if property sold).

Inventory and Research Property

Corporations contributing qualified inventory property to public charities or scientific research property to educational institutions can deduct the adjusted basis of the property plus one-half of the appreciation, not to exceed twice the amount of the adjusted basis. Code Sec. 170(e)(3) and (4). Qualified inventory must have use related to the function or purpose of the charitable organization. The inventory must be used for the care of the ill, the needy, or infants. The charitable organization cannot receive any money, property, or services for the transfer or the use of the qualified inventory.

Qualified research property must be constructed by the donor and contributed within two years after construction is substantially completed. The donee must be the original user of the property. The property must be scientific equipment used for research or experimentation or for research training in the United States in the physical or biological sciences.

TRA '97 expanded the list of qualified property to include computer technology, software, and equipment given to certain schools within two years of acquisition or construction. The original use of the property must begin with the donor or the donee, and the property must be used within the U.S. for educational purposes in any grade from kindergarten to 12.

Example 13.67. Block Inc. donated inventory to a charity. The fair market value of the inventory was $15,000 and its adjusted basis was $4,000. The initial measure of the contribution is $4,000 ($15,000 fair market value minus $11,000 ordinary income recognized if it had been sold).

Example 13.68. Assume the same facts as Example 13.67, except that the property donated was qualified inventory to be used for the ill, the needy, or infants. In this case, the initial measure of the contribution is $8,000 ($4,000 + one-half of the appreciation (1/2 of $11,000) = $9,500, but this is limited to twice the adjusted basis (2 × $4,000)).

TAX BLUNDER

X Company made a contribution of ordinary income property to a qualified charity. The adjusted basis of the property was $70,000, and its fair market value was $30,000. X Company received a charitable deduction of $30,000 (its fair market value, reduced by any gain recognized had it been sold). X Company should not have given this property to the charity. It never will recognize the $40,000 loss on the property. X Company would have been better off to have sold the property, recognize the $40,000 loss, and then make a $30,000 cash contribution to the charity. Under this scenario, X Company still would have had a $30,000 charitable contribution, and it also would have had a $40,000 recognized ordinary loss.

¶ 13,355   RELATED TAXPAYERS—LOSSES AND EXPENSES

A special rule applicable to related taxpayers may cause (1) the disallowance of deductions for losses on sales or exchange, directly or indirectly, of property between related taxpayers, and (2) the deferral of deductions for accrued business and interest expenses of the taxpayer which remain unpaid at the end of the taxpayer's tax year and which are payable to a related cash-basis taxpayer. Code Sec. 267. Related taxpayers are viewed as consisting of a single economic unit. Thus, related parties are unable to artificially recognize losses and create deductions for tax purposes where no losses or deductions have been sustained within the economic unit.

Related persons include: (1) a corporation and an individual with direct and/or indirect ownership of more than 50 percent, (2) two corporations if the same persons own more than 50 percent in value of the outstanding stock in each corporation, and (3) a fiduciary of a trust and a corporation if the trust or grantor owns more than 50 percent of the stock. The constructive ownership rules apply in determining ownership. Code Sec. 267(b).

The loss disallowance rules apply to any sale at a loss even if no tax avoidance motive exists and the selling price is at fair market value. The disallowance of any loss is permanent for the seller. The buyer's initial basis in the property is the purchase price (fair market value). However, the buyer is permitted to reduce any gain recognized on a subsequent sale by the amount of the previously disallowed loss.

Example 13.69. A corporation sells an asset to Barry Winslow, its sole shareholder, at its fair market value of $10,000. The corporation has an adjusted basis in the asset of $12,000. The corporation will not be allowed a deduction for its $2,000 loss incurred on the sale. Barry sells the asset several years later for $15,000. Barry has a realized gain of $5,000 ($15,000 − $10,000); however, his recognized gain is $3,000 ($5,000 realized gain − $2,000 loss previously unrecognized by the corporation).

Expenses commonly disallowed under the related taxpayer rule are interest and compensation payable by an accrual-basis corporation to its cash-basis shareholders. Persons who are related are required to use the same accounting method with respect to transactions between themselves in order to prevent a deduction without the corresponding inclusion in income. The accrual-basis taxpayer is allowed the deduction for expenses incurred to cash-basis taxpayers when the payment is made.

Example 13.70. Nation Corporation, using the accrual method of accounting, incurs a $2,000 salary expense due to its cash-basis sole shareholder at the end of 1998. The amount is paid on January 15, 1999. The corporation will not be allowed a deduction for the salary expense until 1999, when the salary is paid.

¶ 13,365   ORGANIZATIONAL EXPENDITURES

Expenditures related to the organization process are incurred when a corporation is formed. Some of these expenditures benefit the corporation over its entire corporate life and are capitalized as organizational expenditures. Organizational expenditures are an intangible asset which have an indefinite life.

Generally, assets with indefinite lives may not be amortized for federal income tax purposes. However, the corporation may elect to amortize organizational expenditures over 60 months or more beginning with the month the corporation begins business. Code Sec. 248. Only those expenditures incurred before the end of the tax year in which the corporation begins business are eligible for amortization. The election to amortize such expenditures must be made by the due date of the return, including extensions, for the first tax year in which the corporation begins business. If the election is not made at that time, the organizational expenses must be capitalized and are deductible only upon dissolution. If the election is made and the business is dissolved prior to the end of amortization period, then the remaining organizational expenditures are deductible in the year of dissolution.

Organizational expenditures are any expenditures which are (1) incident to the creation of the corporation, (2) chargeable to a capital account, and (3) of a character that if expended incident to the creation of a corporation having a limited life would be amortizable over such life. Typical organizational expenditures include legal and accounting fees, incorporation fees, and organizational meetings expenses. Note that expenses in connection with underwriting securities (e.g., commissions, printing costs, etc.) are not eligible. Expenses of transferring assets to the corporation also are not organizational expenditures. Reg. § 1.248-1(a) and (b).

Example 13.71. Petit Corporation begins business on August 1, 1998, and adopts the calendar year. Petit incurs the following expenses in 1998:

Expenses of organization meetings	$600
Fee paid for incorporation	180
Legal services in setting up corporation	300
Expenses of printing and sale of stock certificates	250
Accounting fees for monthly statements	200

Petit is on the cash method and pays the expenses in February 1999. If an election is made to amortize the organizational expenditures over 60 months, then the first year's deduction is $90 (($600 + $180 + $300)/60 months = $18 per month × 5 months = $90). The expenses of printing and sale of stock certificates and the accounting fees do not qualify as organizational expenditures.

Even though Petit is on the cash basis of accounting, the organization expenditures are deductible as long as they are incurred by the end of 1998.

¶ 13,375 START-UP EXPENDITURES

Start-up expenditures are different from organizational expenditures. Start-up expenditures are business expenses paid or incurred in connection with investigating the creation or acquisition of an active trade or business, creating an active trade or business, or conducting an activity engaged in for profit and for the production of income before the time in which the active trade or business begins. Code Sec. 195(c). Start-up expenditures must be capitalized. However, the corporation may elect to amortize the expenditures over 60 months or more beginning with the month in which the active trade or business begins. If the business is disposed of prior to the end of the amortization period, then any remaining start-up expenditures are deductible in the year of disposition. Code Sec. 195(b).

The election to amortize start-up expenditures must be made by the due date of the return, including extensions, for the first tax year in which the trade or business begins. The expenditures must be such that if incurred in connection with the operation of an existing active trade or business would be deductible in the tax year paid or incurred. Code Sec. 195(c)(1)(B). Examples of start-up expenditures are market surveys, fees incurred for consultants, travel costs, legal fees, and advertising expenses. Where the taxpayer incurs investigation expenses for expanding a present trade or business, a deduction is allowed whether the decision is made to acquire or not acquire the business. The expenditures are not for the investigation of a "new" business.

¶ 13,385 DIVIDENDS-RECEIVED DEDUCTION

Corporation income is subject to double taxation, once at the corporate level and again at the shareholder level at the time of distribution of after-tax earnings. Triple taxation may occur if a corporation receives dividends out of after-tax earnings of another corporation. Without a special provision, the corporation earning the income would be subject to taxation and the income would be taxed a second time when paid as dividends to a recipient corporation. The income would be taxed a third time when the recipient corporation pays dividends to its shareholders. To provide some relief, a dividends-received deduction is allowed. Code Sec. 243.

The dividends qualifying for the dividends-received deduction are those dividends paid by domestic corporations subject to the corporate income tax. Only dividends paid out of a corporation's earnings and profits qualify for the dividends-received deduction. Dividends received from S corporations are not eligible for the dividends-received deduction. The S corporation is exempt from the corporate income tax and dividends are not income to the recipients; thus, there is no need for the dividends-received deduction.

The deduction allowed is a percentage of the dividend received. This percentage is based upon the percentage of ownership by the corporate shareholder. Corporations owning less than 20 percent of the distributing corporation may deduct 70 percent of the dividend received. If the corporate shareholder owns 20 percent or more but less than 80 percent of the distributing corporation, then the corporate shareholder is entitled to deduct 80 percent of the dividend received. Finally, if the corporate shareholder owns 80 percent or more of the distributing corporation and both corporations are members of an affiliated group, then a 100 percent deduction is permitted.

Corporations computing the dividends-received deduction are subject to three rules:

1. The dividends-received deduction is 70 (80) percent of dividends received from taxable, unaffiliated domestic corporations.

2. The 70 (80) percent deduction is limited to 70 (80) percent of taxable income, as adjusted.

3. The 70 (80) percent of taxable income limitation does not apply where the corporation has a current net operating loss (i.e., it adds to the net operating loss). Also, the 70 (80) percent limit does not apply if the full (unlimited) dividends-received deduction would create a net operating loss.

The limitations on the aggregate amount of dividends-received deductions are first determined for dividends received from 20 percent or more owned corporations and then separately determined for dividends received from under 20 percent owned corporations after taxable income is reduced by the former.

The first rule is straightforward. The dividends-received deduction is equal to 70 (80) percent of the dividends received from domestic corporations.

Example 13.72. Dade Corporation has the following income and expenses:

Gross income from operations	$ 200,000
Expenses from operations	(150,000)
Dividends received from domestic corporations	100,000
Taxable income before the dividends-received deduction	$ 150,000

The dividends-received deduction is $70,000 ($100,000 × 70%).

The second rule limits the dividends-received deduction to 70 (80) percent of the recipient corporation's taxable income, computed without regard to:

1. The dividends-received deduction

2. Any net operating loss carryback and carryforward deduction

3. Any capital loss carryback

4. A dividends-paid deduction (Code Sec. 246(b))

Example 13.73. Assume the same facts as in Example 13.72, except that the gross income is only $140,000 instead of $200,000.

Taxable income before the dividends-received deduction is $90,000. Instead of a $70,000 deduction, the dividends-received deduction is limited to $63,000 (70% × $90,000).

The third rule comes into play if the full dividends-received deduction generates or adds to a net operating loss for the year. In such a situation, the full dividends-received deduction is allowed.

Example 13.74. Assume the same facts as in Example 13.72, except that the gross income from operations is $110,000. Taxable income before the dividends-received deduction is $60,000 ($110,000 + $100,000 − $150,000). If the corporation received the full dividends-received deduction of $70,000 (70% × $100,000), then it would have an NOL of $10,000 ($60,000 − $70,000); thus, it is permitted the full deduction and is not limited to a $42,000 deduction (70% × $60,000).

In summary, the full dividends-received deduction is available if the corporation has an NOL or would have an NOL if it received the full deduction. Also, if taxable income, as adjusted, is greater than the dividend received, a full deduction is available. The full dividends-received deduction is not available if taxable income is less than the dividend received but large enough such that a full dividend-received deduction not make it negative. In this case, the deduction is limited to a percentage of taxable income, as adjusted.

Example 13.75. Continuing Example 13.72, as long as the gross income from operations is $120,000 or more but less than $150,000, there will be taxable income not including the dividends-received deduction of $70,000 or more. The net loss from operations will be $30,000 or less. The dividends-received deduction will be limited to 70 percent of taxable income before the dividends-received deduction.

Gross income from operations	$ 120,000
Expenses from operations	(150,000)
Dividends received	100,000
Taxable income before dividends-received deduction	$ 70,000
Dividends-received deduction ($70,000 × 70%)	49,000
Taxable income	$ 21,000

Since the full dividends-received deduction ($70,000) would make taxable income zero (not negative), the deduction is limited to $49,000 (70% × $70,000).

TAX PLANNING POINTER ▼

If there is any doubt prior to year-end whether the full dividends-received deduction is available, steps should be taken to defer income and accelerate deductions to ensure a net operating loss after the full deduction. Typical strategies include deferred payment sales, delaying shipping, stepping up acquisitions of cost recovery property, sales and leaseback at a loss, the use of escrow accounts, the payment of bonuses, stepping up repairs and maintenance, etc.

Example 13.76. Continuing with Example 13.75, if gross income from operations decreased by $1 or operating expenses increased by $1, the corporation would be allowed the full dividends-received deduction of $70,000.

Gross income from operations	$ 120,000
Expenses from operations	(150,001)
Dividends received	100,000
Taxable income before dividends-received deduction	$ 69,999
Dividends-received deduction	70,000
Taxable income	($ 1)

Stock must have been held for more than 45 days to be eligible for the dividends-received deduction. The stock must also be held without being protected by an offsetting short sale or option. Code Sec. 246(b) and (c). This restriction prevents corporations from purchasing dividend-paying stock shortly before the declaration of dividends and selling the stock immediately after receiving the right to the dividend. For example, without this requirement a corporation would pay tax of only $102 on $1,000 of dividend income ($1,000 × 30% dividend inclusion rate × 34% corporate tax rate) while generating a tax savings of $340 ($1,000 loss × 34%) if the stock were to decline by the amount of the dividend payment.

Debt-Financed Portfolio Stock

A restriction applies to the dividends-received deduction when a corporation has issued debt to finance its purchase of the stock. This reduction is equal to the ratio of the amount of portfolio indebtedness to the adjusted basis of the portfolio stock. Portfolio indebtedness means any debt directly attributable to the taxpayer corporation's investment in portfolio stock. Without such a restriction, a corporation would be able to fully deduct interest paid to finance its investment in dividend-paying stock and be taxed on only 20 or 30 percent (100 percent minus dividends-received deduction) of the related dividend income.

Example 13.77. A corporation purchases 25 percent of the stock in another corporation for $300,000, of which $120,000 or 40 percent is borrowed. The corporation receives dividends of $24,000 from the investment. The allowable dividends-received deduction is limited to $11,520 ($24,000 × 80% × (100% − 40%)).

Extraordinary Dividends

The basis of stock held by a corporation must be reduced by the nontaxed portion of any extraordinary dividend received by the corporation with respect to stock. Code Sec. 1059. Stock basis is not reduced if the stock was held for more than two years before the earliest date that the dividend is declared, agreed to, or announced. The nontaxed portion of a cash distribution is the amount that is offset by the dividends-received deduction. The nontaxed portion of a property distribution is the fair market value of the property reduced by any liabilities assumed by the shareholder that is offset by the dividends-received deduction.

Generally, a dividend is deemed extraordinary when it exceeds 10 percent of a corporate taxpayer's adjusted basis in a share of stock. The 10 percent becomes 5 percent in the case of preferred stock for purposes of determining whether the dividend is extraordinary. In determining whether the dividend is extraordinary, an alternative permits the taxpayer to substitute the fair market value of the share of stock on the day before the ex-dividend date for its adjusted basis. This is intended to mitigate the effect of basis reduction where a shareholder can demonstrate that the stock has appreciated significantly since the shareholder's original investment.

The nontaxed portion of dividends on certain "disqualified" preferred stock issued after July 10, 1989, is treated as an extraordinary dividend (and therefore would be subject to basis reduction). The preferred stock is considered to be disqualified if (1) the preferred stock at the time it is issued has a dividend rate that declines, or can reasonably be expected to decline, in the future; (2) the issue price of the preferred stock exceeds its liquidation rights or its stated redemption price; or (3) the preferred stock is structured so as to avoid other provisions of Code Sec. 1059 and to enable corporate shareholders to reduce tax through a combination of dividends-received deductions and loss on the disposition of the stock. Code Sec. 1059(f).

The reduction in basis takes effect immediately before the disposition of the stock, except that earlier extraordinary dividends are taken into account in adjusting basis for purposes of determining whether a subsequent dividend is extraordinary.

Example 13.78. Matter Corporation purchases 100 shares of Fact Corporation stock for $3,000, or $30 per share, on February 2, 1997. On November 3, 1998, Matter Corporation receives a dividend of $4 per share. Matter deducts 70 percent of the $400 in dividends, or $280, on its tax return for the year. The dividend is considered to be extraordinary because it exceeds 10 percent of Matter's adjusted basis in the shares. When it sells the stock, Matter will reduce its basis by $280 (the nontaxed portion of the distribution) for purposes of determining gain or loss. If Matter can show that the fair market value of the stock is at least $40 on the day before the ex-dividend date, the dividend would not be extraordinary because it would not exceed 10 percent of the fair market value. Thus, Matter would not have to reduce the basis of its stock.

Any basis adjustment may not reduce the corporation's basis in the stock below zero. However, nontaxed portions of extraordinary dividends that otherwise would reduce basis below zero in the absence of this limitation are aggregated and treated as gain from a sale or exchange when the stock is sold.

An extraordinary dividend basis reduction will not apply if the stock was held by the taxpayer for the entire period the distributing corporation and any predecessor has been in existence. Also, dividends qualifying for the 100 percent dividend deduction are not subject to the extraordinary dividend rule.

Dividends Received from Affiliated Corporations

Where dividends are received from an affiliated corporation and the corporation group is not filing a consolidated return, a 100 percent dividends-received deduction may be elected by the group. An affiliated group exists where a corporation owns 80 percent or more of the outstanding voting stock and 80 percent or more of the value of all outstanding stock of another corporation.

The election to deduct the entire dividend is made by the parent corporation for its tax year. Each member of the group must consent to the election. Members of the affiliated group must share one corporate tax rate schedule, one accumulated earnings credit, and one alternative minimum tax exemption.

> *Example 13.79.* Parent Corporation owns 90 percent of the stock in Subsidiary Corporation. Subsidiary Corporation pays a $54,000 dividend to Parent Corporation. Parent Corporation can elect to deduct the full 100 percent of the dividend ($54,000) in the computation of taxable income. Subsidiary Corporation must consent to the election because it must also agree on the sharing of the corporate tax rate schedule, accumulated earnings credit, and the alternative minimum tax exemption.

¶ 13,391 EXECUTIVE COMPENSATION

In general, a corporation and its executives attempt to design a compensation package that maximizes the executives' after-tax cash flows at the least cost and cash outflow to the corporation. Thus, the compensation package usually includes a combination of cash payments (salary and bonus), fringe benefits (nontaxable and taxable), and deferred compensation. However, in developing the package, the corporation is constrained in that the compensation package must be reasonable in amount Reg. § 1.162-7(a). The Internal Revenue Service can use the substance over form doctrine to find that some of the compensation is unreasonable and in substance is a dividend (not deductible by the corporation) and not compensation.

Code Section 162(m) also limits the deductibility of executive compensation of publicly traded corporations to $1 million. The restriction applies to the corporation's five highest-paid executives (including the chief executive officer). Compensation in excess of this amount is not deductible unless it is based on a performance-based compensation plan.

Determination of Corporate Income Tax Liability

¶ 13,401   COMPUTATION OF TAX LIABILITY

After determining its taxable income, a corporation then must compute its income tax liability. This is a multiple-step process. The corporation first computes its regular tax liability. This amount is reduced by any tax credits to which it is entitled, such as the foreign tax credit (Code Sec. 27) and general business credit (Code Sec. 38). Any recapture of previously claimed tax credits is added to the resultant amount to produce the corporation's income tax liability. Additionally, the corporation must compute an alternative minimum tax to which it may be subject.

¶ 13,405   CORPORATE REGULAR INCOME TAX RATES

The marginal federal tax rate for corporations and associations taxed as corporations ranges from 15 to 39 percent (Code Sec. 11(b)) as follows:

Taxable income	Rate
$0 to $50,000	15%
$50,001 to $75,000	25%
$75,001 to $100,000	34%
$100,001 to $335,000	39%
$335,001 to $10,000,000	34%
$10,000,001 to $15,000,000	35%
$15,000,001 to $18,333,333	38%
Over $18,333,333	35%

To discourage corporations from taking advantage of the lower brackets, certain affiliated corporations must share the lower brackets. Code Sec. 1563.

Corporations with over $100,000 in taxable income are subject to a 5 percent tax on such excess between $100,000 and $335,000. The maximum additional tax is $11,250 (($335,000 − $100,000) × 5%). This figure represents the savings from being in a tax bracket below 34 percent on the first $75,000. At $335,000 of taxable income, the result is the equivalent of a "flat tax" of 34 percent. The 34 percent "flat tax" is imposed on corporations whose taxable income ranges from $335,001 to $10,000,000. At $10,000,001, the tax rate increases to 35 percent. Corporations with over $15,000,000 in taxable income are subject to a 3 percent tax on the excess between $15,000,001 and $18,333,333. The maximum additional tax is $100,000 (($18,333,333 − $15,000,000) × 3%). This figure represents the savings from being in the 34 percent bracket on the first $10,000,000. At $18,333,333 of taxable income, the result is the equivalent of a "flat tax" of 35 percent. These tax rates are shown in the above tax rate schedule.

Example 13.80. Alpha Corporation has taxable income of $85,000. The tax incurred would be $17,150, computed as follows:

$50,000 × 15%	$ 7,500
25,000 × 25%	6,250
10,000 × 34%	3,400
	$17,150

Example 13.81. Assuming a taxable income of $100,000, the tax would be $22,250, computed as follows:

$50,000 × 15%	$ 7,500
25,000 × 25%	6,250
25,000 × 34%	8,500
	$22,250

Example 13.82. Assuming a taxable income of $180,000, the tax would be $53,450, computed as follows:

$50,000 × 15%	$ 7,500
25,000 × 25%	6,250
25,000 × 34%	8,500
80,000 × 39%	31,200
	$53,450

Example 13.83. Assuming a taxable income of $335,000, the tax would be $113,900, computed as follows:

$ 50,000 × 15%	$ 7,500
25,000 × 25%	6,250
25,000 × 34%	8,500
235,000 × 39%	91,650
	$113,900

This is equivalent to $335,000 × 34%.

Example 13.84. Assuming a taxable income of $5,000,000, the tax would be $1,700,000, computed as follows:

$5,000,000 × 34%

Example 13.85. Assuming a taxable income of $14,000,000, the tax would be $4,800,000, computed as follows:

$10,000,000 × 34%	$3,400,000
4,000,000 × 35%	1,400,000
	$4,800,000

Example 13.86. Assuming a taxable income of $17,000,000, the tax would be $5,910,000, computed as follows:

$10,000,000 × 34%	$3,400,000
5,000,000 × 35%	1,750,000
2,000,000 × 38%	760,000
	$5,910,000

Example 13.87. Assuming a taxable income of $18,333,333, the tax would be $6,416,666, computed as follows:

$10,000,000 × 34%	$3,400,000
5,000,000 × 35%	1,750,000
3,333,333 × 38%	1,266,666
	$6,416,666

This is equivalent to $18,333,333 × 35%.

Example 13.88. Assuming a taxable income of $20,000,000, the tax would be $7,000,000, computed as follows:

$20,000,000 × 35%

These rates are low enough to encourage incorporation for businesses that intend to retain their earnings. There is double taxation only if dividends are paid. Thus, if the corporation's taxable income is $50,000 a year or less, a tax of 15 percent may be viewed as a reasonable price to pay for the indefinite deferral of the second tax at the shareholder level.

Personal service corporations are taxed at a flat tax rate of 35 percent. They are not given the benefit of the tax savings of the lower brackets. A personal service corporation is one in which substantially all of the activities involve the performance of services in the fields of health, law, engineering, architecture, accounting, actuarial science, performing arts, or consulting. Substantially all of the stock (95 percent) must be held by employees, retired employees, or their estates.

¶ 13,415   CORPORATE ALTERNATIVE MINIMUM TAX

Alternative minimum tax rules have been devised to ensure that no taxpayers with substantial economic income can avoid significant tax liability by using exclusions, deductions, and credits. The underlying purpose was that Congress had concluded that both the perception and the reality of fairness in taxation had been harmed by instances in which corporations paid little or no tax in years when they reported substantial earnings, and may even have paid substantial dividends to shareholders.

The alternative minimum tax (AMT) assessed on corporations is similar to the AMT that individuals must pay. The AMT is payable to the extent that it exceeds the corporation's regular income tax and must be taken into consideration in the corporate quarterly tax payments. Code Secs. 55-59. The starting point for computing the AMT is the corporation's taxable income. Taxable income is modified for certain items such as tax preferences and reduced by an exemption amount. The resultant amount, the net alternative minimum taxable income, is multiplied by 20 percent to yield a tentative minimum tax (TMT). If TMT is greater than the corporation's regular income tax, then the excess is the corporation's AMT liability and must be added to its regular tax liability to determine the total tax due. If TMT is less than the corporation's regular tax, then it has no AMT liability. In summary, the tax is computed as follows:

Taxable Income
(+ or −) Adjustments to Taxable Income
+ Tax Preference Items
(+ or −) Adjusted Current Earnings Adjustment
− AMT-NOL Deduction (limited to 90 percent)

= Gross Alternative Minimum Taxable Income (AMTI)
− Exemption Amount

= Net Alternative Minimum Taxable Income
× 20% Tax Rate

= Gross Alternative Minimum Tax
− AMT Foreign Tax Credit

= Tentative Minimum Tax (TMT)
− Regular Income Tax (before credits but minus the regular Foreign Tax Credit and Possessions Tax Credit)

= Alternative Minimum Tax (AMT)

Under TRA '97, effective for tax years beginning after December 31, 1997, small corporations no longer are liable for the corporate AMT. A corporation qualifies as a small corporation if it had average gross receipts of $5,000,000 or less for the three-year period beginning after December 31, 1994. If the corporation was not in existence for the entire three-year period, then the $5,000,000 test is applied on the periods in which it was in existence (this condition would apply to new corporations too). Once a corporation is recognized as a small corporation, it will continue to be exempt from the AMT for as long as its average gross receipts for the prior three-year period does not exceed $7,500,000.

If a corporation loses its small corporation status because it has average gross receipts for the prior three-year period in excess of $7,500,000, it becomes liable for the AMT. However, the AMT liability is based only on certain preferences and adjustments that pertain to transactions that were entered into after the corporation lost its small corporation status.

Example 13.89. James Co. is a small corporation for AMT purposes. In 2002, it determined that its average gross receipts for 1999, 2000, and 2001 was $7,900,000. James Co. is subject to the AMT for 2002. Its AMT will only be based on preferences and adjustments for transactions on or after January 1, 2002.

Adjustments to Taxable Income

The AMT is aimed at recovering some of the tax savings generated by a variety of other deductions and methods for computing tax liability. Thus, in determining AMTI, the taxpayer is required to make special adjustments to certain tax items that have been used to calculate regular taxable income. The adjustments may either increase or decrease alternative minimum taxable income. These adjustments reflect timing differences between the reporting methods for regular tax purposes and the alternative minimum tax. These adjustments are positive initially but reverse themselves in later years. The adjustments to taxable income are (Code Sec. 56):

1. Depreciation on post-1986 acquisitions and 1986 acquisitions using MACRS depreciation

2. Mining and exploration costs

3. Long-term contracts

4. Net operating losses

5. Pollution control facilities

6. Installment sales

7. Circulation expenses

8. Capital construction funds

9. Insurance companies deduction

10. Farming losses

Depreciation

The depreciation deduction for real property placed in service after 1986 and property placed in service in 1986 for which the MACRS depreciation rules are adopted must be recomputed for AMT purposes under the alternative depreciation system (ADS), generally the straight-line method, over 40 years. However, no adjustment is needed for property placed in service after December 31, 1998.

Personal property placed in service after 1986 and property placed in service in 1986 under the MACRS depreciation rules must be depreciated using the 150 percent declining-balance method under the ADS, switching to straight-line in the year that maximizes the deduction.

Thus, two separate depreciation schedules must be computed: (1) depreciation for regular income tax purposes and (2) depreciation for AMT purposes. In the early years of an asset's life, regular tax depreciation will exceed AMT depreciation and the difference will be a positive adjustment to taxable income in the AMT computation. In later years, AMT depreciation will exceed regular tax depreciation and cause a negative adjustment to taxable income.

Example 13.90. A corporation purchases a $10,000 machine for use in business in 1994. Assuming the machine is a 5-year asset for both MACRS and ADS, the depreciation methods for regular tax and alternative minimum tax purposes along with the adjustment are as follows:

Year	200% Declining Balance	150% Declining Balance	Adjustment
1994	$2,000	$1,500	+ $500
1995	3,200	2,550	+ 650
1996	1,920	1,785	+ 135
1997	1,152	1,666	− 514
1998	1,152	1,666	− 514
1999	576	833	− 257

In the first three years, the adjustment involves an amount that must be added to taxable income, while in the last three years the adjustment entails an amount that must be subtracted from taxable income. Thus, the corporation will make a $514 negative adjustment in 1998.

For AMT purposes, a property's basis is only reduced by the amount of depreciation allowed in computing AMTI. Therefore, the adjusted basis of the property may differ for regular and minimum tax purposes. The gain or loss for AMTI upon disposition of the asset is determined by the AMTI basis.

Mining Exploration and Development Costs

Mining exploration and development costs that are generally deductible in the current year are required to be computed under the 10-year straight-line amortization for AMT purposes. The adjusted basis of property for which mining exploration and development costs are incurred may differ for regular tax and AMT purposes, giving rise to different amounts of gain or loss between the two systems upon the disposition of such property. The tax preference adjustment for mining exploration and development costs may be avoided if the taxpayer makes a regular tax election to deduct such expenditures over a 10-year period.

> *Example 13.91.* Douglas Corporation's taxable income for 1998 is $375,000. Included in its expenses was a $60,000 deduction for mining exploration costs incurred in 1998. Douglas Corporation had no other tax preferences (or adjustment items). Its AMTI for 1998 is $429,000, computed as follows:

Taxable income $375,000
Adjustment
    Excess mining exploration costs (amount expensed minus
    amount allowed over a 10-year amortization period;
    $60,000 minus $6,000) 54,000
AMTI $429,000

Long-Term Contracts

Taxpayers must use the percentage-of-completion method for long contracts entered into after March 1, 1986, to determine income for purposes of calculating the AMTI. In the case of small construction contracts (other than home construction contracts) entered into after June 21, 1988, the percentage of completion is determined under the simplified cost allocation method. All home construction contracts entered into in tax years beginning after September 30, 1990, are not required to use the percentage-of-completion method.

Net Operating Losses

The regular NOL deduction is replaced by the AMTI-NOL deduction. The regular NOL must be modified to take into account the same adjustments and tax preferences made to determine AMTI. The AMTI-NOL deduction cannot offset more than 90 percent of AMTI determined before the NOL deduction. The purpose of the limitation is to assure that corporations at least pay a minimum amount of taxes, 2 percent of AMTI each year (remaining AMTI (10%) × 20% tax rate). However, the exemption and credits might reduce this to zero.

Pollution Control Facilities

For property placed in service after 1986, the five-year amortization method for depreciating pollution control facilities must be replaced by the alternative depreciation system. The adjusted basis used in AMTI calculations to determine the gain or loss on the sale of property for which depreciation has been adjusted must reflect the depreciation adjustments rather than the costs that were deductible in regular tax computations. Effective for property placed in service after December 31, 1998, the recovery periods used for AMT purposes conform with the recovery periods used under MACRS using the straight-line method.

Installment Sales

Generally, the installment method is not available for dealer dispositions of stock in trade and other property held by the taxpayer primarily for sale to customers in the ordinary course of business. The realized gain is recognized in the year of sale. Thus, no AMT adjustments will generally be required for such dealer sales. The installment method may be used in determining AMTI for all nondealer dispositions of property.

Circulation Expenditures

The amount of post-1986 circulation expenditures (i.e., the costs of establishing, maintaining, or increasing the circulation of newspapers, magazines, or other periodicals) allowed as a current deduction for regular tax purposes must be amortized over a three-year period for AMT purposes. This tax preference applies to personal holding companies. However, under the AMT rules, corporate taxpayers are free to capitalize or deduct their circulation expenditures. Thus, for most C corporations there is no AMT adjustment for circulation expenditures.

Capital Construction Funds

Contributions made by shipping companies to capital construction funds (established under Section 607 of the Merchant Marine Act of 1936) may not be deducted from AMTI and a fund's earnings (including gains or losses) may not be excluded from AMTI. No reduction in the basis of a vessel, barge, or container need be made to reflect amounts withdrawn from a fund, if the amounts have been included in AMTI.

Insurance Companies Deduction

The special deduction from regular tax allowed to Blue Cross and Blue Shield organizations for one-fourth of their annual claims and administrative expenses (less the prior tax year's adjusted surplus) may not be claimed against AMTI.

Farming Losses

No deduction is allowed for losses from any farming syndicate or any other farming activity in which the taxpayer does not materially participate. A loss from one farming activity may not be used to offset income from another farming activity. Disallowed losses are carried forward indefinitely and used for AMTI purposes to offset future income from the farming activity. Suspended losses are deductible when the activity is disposed. These provisions apply to personal service corporations.

Tax Preference Items

Tax preferences must be added back to the corporation's taxable income to compute AMTI. These preferences are usually the result of some tax benefit received in the computation of taxable income. Unlike AMT adjustments which can either increase or decrease AMTI, tax preference items only increase AMTI. The tax preference items are (Code Sec. 57(a)):

1. Depletion
2. Intangible drilling costs
3. Bad debt reserves
4. Private activity bonds interest
5. Accelerated depreciation and amortization on pre-1987 property

Depletion

The depletion preference for corporate taxpayers is the excess of the allowable percentage depletion deduction over the adjusted basis of the property at the end of the year. The preference applies to percentage depletion for all minerals, not just oil and gas. However, after December 31, 1992, the preference does not apply to most oil and gas companies.

Intangible Drilling Costs

The amount of excess intangible drilling costs for the year is treated as a tax preference to the extent that it exceeds 65 percent of the corporate taxpayer's net income for the tax year from oil, gas, and geothermal properties. The amount of excess intangible drilling costs, for this purpose, is the excess of the deduction for the current cost of drilling productive wells over the deduction that would have been allowable if such costs had been capitalized and either (1) amortized over a 10-year period or (2) deducted, at the election of the taxpayer, as cost depletion, whichever is more favorable. The intangible drilling costs preference is computed separately for geothermal properties and for oil and gas properties.

Bad Debt Reserves

Financial institutions have preference income to the extent of the excess of the reserve for bad debt deducted by the institutions over the amount that would have been allowable had the institution maintained its bad debt reserve for all tax years on the basis of actual experience. Thrifts must include 100 percent of the preference.

Private Activity Bonds Interest

A tax preference has been added for tax-exempt interest on private activity bonds issued after August 7, 1986. This preference does not apply to bonds issued for the benefit of tax-exempt charitable or educational institutions under Code Sec. 501(c)(3) or to bonds issued for public purposes such as schools and municipally owned public utilities.

Accelerated Depreciation and Amortization on Pre-1987 Property

There is a tax preference for excess depreciation and amortization taken on certain properties acquired before 1987. However, any properties acquired in 1986 that use the MACRS cost recovery rules are not subject to this tax preference.

1. Depreciation on real property acquired before 1987 that is in excess of straight-line depreciation over the useful life

2. Amortization of certified pollution control facilities (the excess of 60-month amortization over depreciation otherwise allowable)

Example 13.92. Hoover Inc. has taxable income of $230,000. Included in its expenses was a $50,000 deduction for percentage depletion. The $50,000 was in excess of the depletable property's adjusted basis (i.e., the property has a zero adjusted basis). No other tax preferences or adjustments were needed. AMTI for Hoover Inc. is $280,000, computed as follows:

Taxable income	$230,000
Tax Preferences	
Percentage depletion in excess of adjusted basis	50,000
AMTI	$280,000

Adjusted Current Earnings

Corporations are required to make an adjustment based on adjusted current earnings for tax years beginning after 1989. The adjustment equals 75 percent of adjusted current earnings (ACE) less AMTI.

The adjusted current earnings adjustment may be either an increase or a decrease in taxable income when computing AMTI. The negative adjustment is limited to the aggregate positive adjustment for ACE in prior tax years, minus negative adjustments previously claimed. Code Sec. 56(g)(2). Any unused negative adjustment is lost forever.

Example 13.93. A corporation has the following AMTI (before ACE adjustments and alternative tax NOL deductions) and ACE for 1997 to 2000.

	1997	1998	1999	2000
AMTI	$5,000	$4,000	$7,000	$9,200
ACE	7,000	4,000	6,000	8,000

A positive ACE adjustment of $1,500 (75% × ($7,000 − $5,000)) is made in 1997. No adjustment is needed in 1998 since ACE and unadjusted AMTI are equal. A negative ACE adjustment of $750 (75% × ($6,000 − $7,000)) is made in 1999. Finally, a negative ACE adjustment of $750 is made in 2000 because of the limitation on negative ACE adjustments. The computed adjustment is $900 (75% × ($8,000 − $9,200)) but this is constrained to $750, the aggregate positive adjustment ($1,500) reduced by the aggregate negative adjustment ($750). The remaining $150 is lost forever.

The determination of ACE is complicated and Reg. § 1.56(g)-1 provides further guidance on its calculation. The starting point in determining ACE is AMTI, determined without regard to the alternative tax NOL deduction and the ACE adjustment, adjusted for several items. Many of these adjustments are similar to those required to compute corporate earnings and profits (E&P) under Code Sec. 312. However, ACE is not the same as E&P because not all items affect both similarly (for example, federal income taxes are deductible in computing E&P but are not deductible in computing ACE).

The adjustments to AMTI for purposes of computing ACE are as follows. AMTI is increased by items excluded from gross income in computing AMTI if the items increase a corporation's earnings and profits (E&P). Examples of this adjustment are tax-exempt interest and key-person life insurance proceeds. These amounts are reduced by the nondeductible expenses incurred to produce them.

Deductions taken to compute AMTI that are not deductions for purposes of computing E&P must be eliminated (i.e., AMTI is increased). An example of this adjustment is the dividends-received deduction. However, although the dividends-received deduction (DRD) is not permitted for E&P purposes, the deduction is permitted for ACE purposes with respect to dividends received from 20 percent owned corporations (80 percent DRD) and for 100 percent dividends (100 percent DRD) to the extent that the dividend is attributable to taxable income of the paying corporation. The 70 percent DRD is not permitted for ACE purposes.

No adjustment is made to ACE related to the E&P effect of charitable contributions. Code Sec. 56(g)(4)(I). Thus, the excess of fair market value deduction allowed for tax purposes over the basis deduction for book purposes is not included in the ACE adjustment.

Adjustments also must be made so that ACE is computed as if the corporation did not use the installment method; ACE adjustments must reflect use of cost depletion, capitalized and amortized intangible drilling costs, use of the alternative depreciation system under Code Sec. 168(g) for assets placed in service after 1989, and straight-line depreciation for property depreciated under MACRS or ACRS. However, in tax years beginning after December 31, 1992, ACE adjustments are not required for intangible drilling costs paid or incurred in tax years beginning after December 31, 1992, and for percentage depletion for oil and gas. Finally, other E&P-type adjustments include adjustments for circulation and organizational expenditures that are not amortizable for ACE purposes if incurred after 1989, mineral exploration and development costs that must be amortized for ACE purposes, and LIFO inventory adjustments.

Exemption Amount

Before the 20 percent tax rate is applied, corporations may be able to reduce AMTI by the exemption amount. Code Sec. 55(d). The allowed exemption amount is $40,000. The exemption amount is reduced by 25 cents for each $1 by which alternative minimum taxable income exceeds $150,000. Consequently, the exemption is completely eliminated for AMTI of $310,000 or more.

> *Example 13.94.* A corporation with AMTI of $300,000 is allowed an exemption amount of $2,500 ($40,000 − .25 × ($300,000 − $150,000)). If the AMTI were $310,000 or more, there would be no deduction for the exemption amount.

Tentative Minimum Tax

AMTI is reduced by the allowable exemption amount resulting in the corporation's net alternative minimum taxable income (the tax base for AMT purposes). This base is multiplied by the AMT tax rate of 20 percent to determine the gross alternative minimum tax. The tentative minimum tax is calculated by subtracting AMT foreign tax credits from the gross alternative minimum tax. AMT foreign tax credits are limited to 90 percent of the gross alternative minimum tax. Credits not allowed in the current year are carried over under the foreign tax carryover rules. Code Sec. 59.

Net AMT Liability

The corporate taxpayer's AMT for a tax year is the excess of the tentative minimum tax over the regular tax. Following the computation of the tentative minimum tax (20% × (AMTI − exemption amount) − AMT foreign tax credit = tentative minimum tax), a comparison must be made between the tentative AMT liability and the corporation's regular tax liability. The regular tax figure to which the tentative minimum tax is compared is the regular tax on corporate income reduced by the foreign tax credit and the possessions tax credit. Furthermore, for comparative purposes, certain adjustments to the regular tax liability must be made.

The regular income tax does not include the tax on accumulated distributions of trusts. Nonrefundable credits (i.e., general business credit) generally cannot be used to reduce the regular tax liability to less than the tentative minimum tax. Credits that cannot be used by the taxpayer due to the effect of the alternative minimum tax can be carried over to other tax years under rules generally applicable to credit carryovers.

The following rules summarize the comparison process:

1. If the tentative AMT liability *exceeds* the regular tax liability (as modified by only the nonrefundable foreign tax credit and the possessions tax credit), then the corporate taxpayer pays the tentative AMT (which is comprised of the regular tax and the excess of the tentative AMT or net AMT liability).

2. If the tentative AMT liability is less than the regular tax liability, then all nonrefundable credits will be allowed to reduce the corporation's regular tax liability to the extent of the tentative AMT liability but not below it. Thus, the corporate taxpayer must pay tentative AMT liability.

Example 13.95. Williams Inc. has taxable income of $400,000. Williams has alternative minimum tax adjustments and tax preferences of $300,000. The regular tax is a flat 34 percent of $400,000, or $136,000. The tentative minimum tax equals 20 percent of $700,000, or $140,000. The alternative minimum tax becomes $4,000. (No exemption was allowed since AMTI was $310,000 or more).

Example 13.96. A corporation has taxable income of $500,000 along with a general business credit of $22,000. The corporation has adjustments and preferences of $300,000. The income tax before credits is $170,000 ($500,000 × 34%). The tentative minimum tax is $160,000 (($500,000 + $300,000) × 20%). The corporation is allowed only $10,000 of the general business credit. A $10,000 general business credit reduces the regular income tax to the tentative minimum tax, thus no alternative minimum tax is incurred. The remaining general business credit of $12,000 is carried over to other tax years.

Minimum Tax Credit

Adjustments and tax preferences used to modify taxable income to compute AMTI consist of items that are timing differences and permanent differences. Timing differences defer tax liability and permanent differences produce a permanent reduction in taxable income. For tax years beginning before 1990, AMT due to timing differences is available for the minimum tax credit. The entire amount of the AMT liability is available for the minimum tax credit in tax years beginning after 1989.

The purpose of the minimum tax credit is to prevent the double taxation of deferral preferences and adjustments. These deferral preferences and adjustments are subject to the alternative minimum tax in a tax year earlier than the year they are subject to the regular tax.

The extent to which deferral preference items cause tentative minimum tax to exceed the regular tax may be carried forward and used as an offsetting credit against regular tax to which the corporation may be subject in future years. For pre-1990 tax years only, minimum tax credit is generated where exclusion items cause tentative minimum tax to exceed the regular tax. A taxpayer is not allowed to take a credit larger than an amount necessary to reduce the regular tax to the amount of the tentative minimum tax.

Example 13.97. In 1989, Heit Corporation had taxable income of $350,000. For AMTI purposes it had $150,000 of deferral adjustments and $300,000 of exclusion preferences. Its regular tax was $119,000 ($350,000 × .34). Its net alternative minimum taxable income was $800,000 ($350,000 + $150,000 + $300,000; since AMTI was greater than $310,000 there is no exemption). The AMT was $41,000 ((20% × $800,000) − $119,000). If only the exclusion preferences were considered to compute AMTI, then AMT would have been $11,000 ((20% × ($350,000 + $300,000) − $119,000). Thus, the minimum tax credit was $30,000 ($41,000 − $11,000). The $30,000 credit can be carried forward indefinitely by Heit Corporation. The credit can be used to offset its regular tax liability.

Example 13.98. Assume the same facts as in Example 13.97, except that the tax year is 1998. In this case, the entire amount of the AMT liability ($41,000) may be carried forward as a credit.

Example 13.99. A corporation has a tentative minimum tax of $100,000, a regular tax before the AMT credit of $120,000, and a minimum tax credit of $35,000. Without the minimum tax credit, the corporation would not have an alternative minimum tax because the regular tax exceeds the tentative minimum tax. Since the full minimum tax credit would reduce the regular tax below the tentative minimum tax, only $20,000 of the minimum tax credit carryforward may be used to reduce the regular tax.

The AMT credit is limited for small corporations currently not subject to the AMT. The credit is limited to the amount by which the corporation's regular tax liability (reduced by other credits) exceeds 25 percent of the excess, if any, of the corporation's regular tax liability (reduced by other credits) over $25,000.

Example 13.100. Niffo Company is a small corporation for 1999 and does not have an AMT liability. It has a large AMT carryover from previous years. Niffo's regular tax liability (after other credits) in 1999 is $80,000. Its allowable credit for 1999 is $66,250, computed as follows: $80,000 − 25% ($80,000 − $25,000) = $66,250.

Example 13.101. SQ Corporation is a calendar-year taxpayer. For its tax year ended December 31, 1998, it had the following income and expenses.

Gross sales	$3,800,000
Interest income	140,000
Dividend income from 30% owned domestic corporation	90,000
Short-term capital gain	25,000
Cost of goods sold	1,800,000
Wage expense	300,000
Interest expense	40,000
Depreciation expense	145,000
Charitable contributions	26,000
Other expenses	1,400,000

Included in the interest income is $100,000 from municipal bonds. Depreciation for book purposes is $110,000 and for AMT purposes is $128,000. The $26,000 charitable contribution is for a donation of long-term capital gain property whose adjusted basis is $12,000. Other expenses do not include the federal income tax. SQ's alternative minimum tax is computed as follows.

Income:	Taxable Income
Gross sales	$3,800,000
Cost of goods sold	1,800,000
Gross profit	2,000,000
Interest income	40,000
Dividend income	90,000
Short-term capital gain	25,000
Total Income	$2,155,000
Expenses:	
Wages expense	300,000
Interest expense	40,000
Depreciation expense	145,000
Other expenses	1,400,000
Total Expenses	$1,885,000
	$ 270,000
Charitable contribution deduction	26,000
Dividends-received deduction	72,000
Taxable income	$ 172,000
Tax Liability	$ 50,330

ALTERNATIVE MINIMUM TAX COMPUTATION

Taxable Income	$172,000
Tax Preferences:	
Excess depreciation	17,000
AMTI before ACE adjustment	$189,000
ACE adjustment	
$(.75 \times (ACE - AMTI)), (.75 \times (\$307,000^* - \$189,000))$	88,500
Alternative Minimum Taxable Income	$277,500
Alternative Minimum Tax Exemption	
$(\$40,000 - .25 \times (\$277,500 - \$150,000))$	8,125
Net AMTI	$269,375
20% Tax Rate	$\times .20$
Gross AMT	$ 53,875
AMT Foreign Tax Credit	0
Tentative Minimum Tax	$ 53,875
Regular Income Tax	50,330
Alternative Minimum Tax	$ 3,545

---

* ACE = $189,000 (AMTI before ACE) + $100,000 (tax-exempt interest) + $18,000 (excess of depreciation for books over depreciation for AMT) = $307,000. The ACE adjustment does not include the 80 percent dividends-received deduction nor the $14,000 excess of charitable deduction for tax purposes over the deduction for book purposes.

TAX PLANNING POINTER   ▼

Corporations subject to the alternative minimum tax generally benefit by accelerating income into an AMT year and delaying expenses until a regular tax year. Payment of allowable deductions, such as charitable contributions, provides a tax benefit in an AMT year of only 20 percent, while delaying the payment to a regular tax year may allow a deduction at 34 percent. Also, income recognized in an AMT year will generally be taxed at 20 percent rather than at the higher regular tax rate.

¶ 13,433   CONTROLLED GROUPS OF CORPORATIONS

The corporate tax rate varies from 15 percent on the first $50,000 of taxable income to a flat rate of 35 percent on taxable income in excess of $18,333,000. Instead of forming one corporation, shareholders could form several corporations in an attempt to distribute the income-generating property so as to assure that each corporation's taxable income did not exceed $50,000. This would result in significant tax savings.

Example 13.102. A corporation with taxable income of $350,000 has a tax liability of $119,000 ($350,000 × 34%). If seven corporations were formed and the property distributed such that each corporation had $50,000 of taxable income, then the total tax liability of the corporations would be $52,500 (($50,000 × 15%) × 7). The result is a tax savings of $66,500 ($119,000 − $52,500).

Code Sec. 1561 was enacted to limit the benefits that taxpayers might receive by using multiple corporations. Multiple corporations that are members of a controlled group must share certain tax benefits as if they were one corporation. These benefits include the lower tax brackets, the alternative minimum tax exemption of $40,000, the Section 179 election to expense certain depreciable property, and the $250,000 accumulated earnings credit. The impact of Code Sec. 1561 may be illustrated as follows.

Example 13.103. If, in Example 13.102, the seven corporations are members of a controlled group, then they must share the first two tax brackets equally unless all the members agree to an unequal allocation of these two brackets. Thus, each of the seven corporations will have $7,143 ($50,000 ÷ 7) taxed at 15 percent and $3,571 ($25,000 ÷ 7) taxed at 25 percent. Additionally, the 5 percent surtax on taxable income in excess of $100,000 is allocated. Thus, if the total taxable income for the group of corporations exceeds $335,000, then each member will have a tax rate of 34 percent.

Parent-subsidiary corporations, brother-sister corporations, combined groups, and certain insurance companies are controlled groups. Code Sec. 1563(a). Affiliated groups and controlled groups are not synonymous. An affiliated group always involves a parent-subsidiary relationship. Thus, parent-subsidiary corporations are both controlled groups and affiliated groups. However, two corporations owned by the same individual (brother-sister corporations) are a controlled group but not an affiliated group.

Parent-Subsidiary Corporations

A parent-subsidiary controlled group consists of one or more chains of corporations connected through stock ownership with a common parent corporation. Code Sec. 1563(a)(1). The parent corporation must own at least 80 percent of the total voting power of all classes of voting stock or at least 80 percent of the total value of shares of all classes of stock of at least one corporation (the subsidiary). Once this initial parent-subsidiary relationship is established, then another corporation can be included in the group if the parent corporation, the subsidiary corporation, or any other corporation in the group individually owns or collectively own at least 80 percent of the total voting power of all of its classes of voting stock or at least 80 percent of the total value of shares of all of its classes of stock.

Example 13.104.

Alpha and Beta are members of a parent-subsidiary controlled group. Alpha is the parent.

Example 13.105.

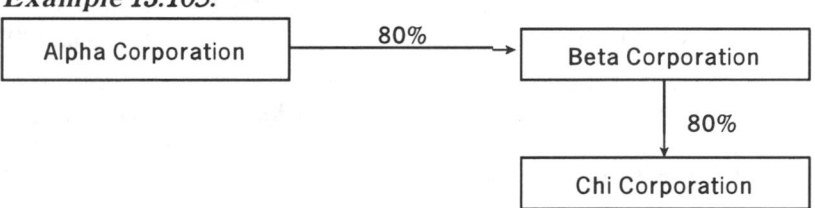

Alpha, Beta, and Chi are members of a parent-subsidiary controlled group. Alpha is the parent.

Example 13.106.

Alpha, Beta, Chi, and Delta are members of a controlled parent-subsidiary. Alpha is the parent.

The controlled parent-subsidiary group is subject to the restrictions of tax benefits mentioned earlier. However, a benefit of this controlled group is that it may elect to file a consolidated return.

Brother-Sister Corporations

A brother-sister controlled group consists of two or more corporations owned by five or fewer individuals, estates, or trusts who (1) own at least 80 percent of the combined voting power of all voting stock or at least 80 percent of the total value of shares of all classes of stock of each corporation and (2) own more than 50 percent of total combined voting power of all voting stock or more than 50 percent of the total value of shares of all classes of stock of each corporation. In calculating the 50 percent test, ownership of each person is included only to the extent that such ownership is identical with respect to each corporation. Thus, only the smallest percentage owned in any of the corporations is counted. Stock owned by family members or certain entities may be attributed to a taxpayer under the attribution rules. Code Sec. 1563(d)(2).

Example 13.107. Alpha, Beta, and Chi Corporations each have only one class of stock outstanding. The ownership of this stock is as follows:

Shareholders	Corporations			Identical Ownership
	Alpha	*Beta*	*Chi*	
Jones.........	25%	20%	55%	20%
Smith	25%	30%	35%	25%
Nelson	50%	50%	10%	10%
	100%	100%	100%	55%

Alpha, Beta, and Chi are members of a controlled brother-sister group because both ownership tests are met. Five or fewer individuals own at least 80 percent of each corporation (they own 100 percent of each) and they have greater than a 50 percent common ownership (55 percent identical ownership).

Example 13.108. Same as Example 13.107, except for the following ownership:

Shareholders	Corporations			Identical Ownership
	Alpha	*Beta*	*Chi*	
Jones.........	5%	30%	45%	5%
Smith	65%	10%	35%	10%
Nelson	30%	60%	20%	20%
	100%	100%	100%	35%

Alpha, Beta, and Chi are not members of a controlled brother-sister group. Although the 80 percent test is met, the identical ownership test of greater than 50 percent is not met. (In determining identical ownership, include the minimum ownership in each row.) Both tests must be met in order to have a brother-sister controlled group.

In determining ownership for the 80 percent test, only individuals who own stock in each and every corporation of the controlled group are counted. Reg. § 1.1563-1(a)(3).

Example 13.109. Alpha and Beta each have one class of stock outstanding. Ownership is as follows:

| | Corporations | | Identical |
Shareholders	Alpha	Beta	Ownership
Boggs	55%	100%	55%
Lyle	45%	0%	0%
	100%	100%	55%

At first glance it appears that both the 80 percent and greater than 50 percent tests are met. However, since Lyle does not own stock in Beta Corporation, his ownership is not counted in calculating the 80 percent test. Thus, the 80 percent test is not met and there is not a brother-sister controlled group. (See *Vogel Fertilizer Co.,* 1982-1 USTC ¶ 9134, 455 U.S. 16, 102 S.Ct. 821 (1982).)

A brother-sister controlled group is subject to the restrictions on tax benefits mentioned earlier. In addition, the group may not file a consolidated return.

Combined Groups

A combined group consists of three or more corporations of which each is a member of a parent-subsidiary controlled group or a brother-sister controlled group and one of the corporations is a common parent in the parent-subsidiary controlled group and also is a member of the brother-sister controlled group. Code Sec. 1563(a)(3).

Example 13.110. Delta, Gamma, and Sigma Corporations each have only one class of stock outstanding. The ownership of their stock is as follows:

| | Corporations | | |
Shareholders	Delta	Gamma	Sigma
Jones	60%	40%	—
Hill	40%	60%	—
Gamma Corp.	—	—	80%
	100%	100%	80%

Delta and Gamma are members of a brother-sister controlled group. Gamma and Sigma are members of a parent-subsidiary group. Since Gamma also is a member of the brother-sister group, Delta, Gamma, and Sigma are members of a combined group.

Allocations of Income, Deductions, and Credit

In addition to restrictions placed on controlled groups by Code Sec. 1561, Code Sec. 482 has the potential to effect further constraints. Members of controlled groups may attempt to minimize tax liability by shifting income, deductions, or credits in an advantageous fashion. Code Sec. 482 gives the IRS the power to rearrange the distribution, thereby reducing the controlled group's ability to manipulate tax liabilities. Specifically, the IRS has the right to reallocate gross income, deductions, and credits between two or more corporations owned or controlled by the same interests if such reallocation is necessary to prevent the evasion of taxes or to clearly reflect income.

¶ 13,445   CONSOLIDATED RETURNS

For tax planning purposes, a parent-subsidiary controlled group has three alternatives: (1) file separate returns, (2) file a consolidated return, or (3) file separate returns with a Code Sec. 243 election of a 100 percent dividends-received deduction. The parent-subsidiary group may make an irrevocable election to file a consolidated tax return. Code Sec. 1501. Each member must consent and each subsidiary must conform its tax year and accounting methods to those of the parent. Consolidated returns must continue to be filed until the IRS grants permission to stop or the group no longer qualifies. For example, if the parent's stock ownership in the subsidiary falls below 80 percent, then the group no longer qualifies to file a consolidated return.

Certain corporations are precluded from being included in a consolidated return. Tax-exempt corporations, life and mutual insurance companies, foreign corporations, U.S. possessions corporations, regulated investment companies and real estate investment trusts, and foreign sales corporations are not eligible to be included in a consolidated return. Code Sec. 1504(b).

There are certain advantages in filing consolidated returns. Income from one member is offset by losses generated by other members. Also, capital losses of a member corporation that otherwise would not be deductible can be used to offset other members' capital gains. Additionally, income from intercompany transactions is not included in the determination of consolidated income. Finally, the group does not have any allocation problems under Code Sec. 482.

There are certain disadvantages in filing a consolidated return. The election is irrevocable and is binding on all subsequent years unless the group is terminated or the IRS grants the group permission to discontinue filing consolidated returns. Also, losses on intercompany transactions are not deductible. Additionally, the recordkeeping needed to file a consolidated return can be significant and, therefore, more costly than if separate returns are filed.

Although the filing of a consolidated tax return has certain advantages, there are several limitations that affect the members' ability to offset income by using the losses or deductions of other members. A loss corporation's net operating loss carryover may be applied against the consolidated income of the group on consolidated returns. However, tax losses of other group members cannot offset the income of another member corporation to the extent that said income is paid out as dividends on certain nonvoting, nonconvertible preferred stock issued after November 17, 1989. Code Sec. 1503(f)[e]. Also, if the loss year was a separate return limitation year (SRLY), then the loss may be carried over only against income of the loss corporation. An SRLY is any year in which a member of the group filed a separate tax return. A separate return year is not an SRLY if the corporation was a member of the affiliated group for each day of that year. Under certain conditions, a loss corporation can acquire a profitable subsidiary and apply its loss carryover against the profits of that corporation.

An additional limitation is the inability to offset a built-in deduction of a subsidiary against consolidated income. Built-in deductions can arise if the subsidiary had an SRLY. Any built-in deductions are deducted only against income of the subsidiary that sustained the deductions. The built-in deduction rules do not apply if the group acquired the assets more than 10 years prior to the tax year or the total adjusted basis of all assets (other than cash, marketable securities, and goodwill) of the acquired subsidiary did not exceed the fair market value of all such assets by more than 15 percent. Reg. § 1.1502-15.

> **Example 13.111.** Maryland Corporation purchases all of the stock of Baltimore Corporation at the end of the year. Baltimore Corporation owns an asset with a basis of $5,000 and a fair market value of $3,000. The asset is sold in the following year for $2,200 and a consolidated return is filed. Of the $2,800 loss, $2,000 is treated as a built-in loss and can be deducted only against the separate income of Baltimore Corporation.

> **Example 13.112.** Assume the asset from Example 13.111 is depreciable property. Depreciation deductions attributable to the $2,000 difference between basis and fair market value are treated as built-in deductions and limited to deductions against the separate income of Baltimore.

The rules and regulations pertaining to consolidated income tax returns are very complex. Several treatises, each consisting of several volumes, exist on the subject.

¶ 13,465   CORPORATE TAX RETURNS

All corporations, with certain exceptions, are required to file a corporate tax return each year. A return must be filed even if the corporation has no taxable income. Code Sec. 6012(a)(2). A corporation that is in existence for only a portion of a tax year is required to file a tax return covering that partial tax year.

A corporation also is required to make estimated tax payments throughout the year unless its estimated tax for the year is less than $500. The corporation must make these payments by the 15th day of the 4th, 6th, 9th, and 12th month of its tax year. Code Sec. 6655(c). Corporations on a calendar year must make the payments by April 15, June 15, September 15, and December 15. In the aggregate these payments must be equal to the lesser of 100 percent of the corporation's actual tax liability (including any alternative minimum tax) or 100 percent of the tax liability for the preceding tax year. The 100 percent test applies only if the preceding tax year was for 12 months and the corporation filed a tax return showing a tax liability. Code Sec. 6655(d). Large corporations (with taxable income of $1,000,000 or more in any one of the three preceding tax years) may use the preceding year's tax liability to estimate the first quarterly payment only; subsequent quarterly payment must be based on this year's expected taxable income. With few exceptions, the corporation will be assessed a nondeductible penalty if it does not make the required payments.

A corporation is required to file Form 1120 by the 15th day of the third month following the end of its tax year. Thus, a calendar-year corporation is required to file its return by March 15. Form 1120-A may be filed by corporations having gross receipts or sales, total income, and total assets not exceeding $250,000. A corporation may receive an automatic extension of six months from the original due date if it files for an extension by the due date of the return. Code Sec. 6081.

Form 1120 generally reports taxable income according to various tax rules. The corporation is required to report, on Schedule L, its beginning and ending balance sheets. The balance sheets are taken from the corporation's basic financial accounting records.

Also included in Form 1120 are Schedule M-1 (Reconciliation of Income (Loss) per Books With Income per Return) and Schedule M-2 (Analysis of Unappropriated Retained Earnings per Books). The net income on the financial books of a corporation may differ from the taxable income on its return. This is caused by differences in accounting methods between financial and taxable income. For example, accelerated depreciation may be used for taxable income computations while straight-line depreciation may be used for financial accounting purposes. Schedule M-1 is used to reconcile these differences.

The reconciling elements of Schedule M-1 fall into four categories:

1. Expenses taken on the books but not taken on the tax return (e.g., federal income taxes)

2. Expenses not taken on the books but taken on the tax return (e.g., charitable contribution carryovers from earlier tax years)

3. Income reported on the books but not reported on the tax return (e.g., tax-exempt municipal bond interest)

4. Income not reported on the books but reported on the tax return (e.g., prepayments recognized as income because of the claim of right doctrine)

These differences are either permanent differences or temporary differences. Permanent differences are income, deduction, gain, or loss items which affect either taxable income or book income, but not both. An example of a permanent difference would be nontaxable municipal bond interest that is included in book income but excluded from taxable income determination. Temporary differences are income, deduction, gain, or loss items that affect both taxable income and book income, but not in the same tax year. A temporary difference exists where accelerated depreciation is taken for tax purposes but straight-line depreciation is used for book purposes. Temporary differences reverse themselves over the life of the business.

Schedule M-1 has two columns. In the left column, entries are made for book income, federal income tax, excess of capital losses over capital gains, income items in the return not included in the books (e.g., prepaid rent) and expenses deducted on the books but not on the return (e.g., gifts costing over $25). In the right hand column, entries are made for income reported on the books and not included in the return (e.g., tax-exempt interest) and expenses deducted on the return but not on the books (e.g., excess of accelerated depreciation used for tax purposes over straight-line used for book purposes). The difference between the right hand column and the left hand column should equal the corporation's taxable income before the net operating loss deduction and special deductions.

> **Example 13.113.** Harris Corporation had the following results from operations during 1998:

Net income per books, after taxes	$77,000
Taxable income	75,000
Federal income taxes	13,750
Tax-exempt interest on municipal bonds	3,000
Net capital loss (capital losses in excess of capital gains)	1,250
Premiums paid on life insurance for key employees	1,000
Life insurance proceeds received because of death of key employee	10,000
MACRS depreciation in excess of straight-line depreciation used for book purposes	5,000

> Harris Corporation's Schedule M-1 is as follows:

Schedule M-1	Reconciliation of Income (Loss) per Books With Income per Return (See page 15 of instructions.)		
1	Net income (loss) per books	77,000	7 Income recorded on books this year not included on this return (itemize):
2	Federal income tax	13,750	Tax-exempt interest $ ....
3	Excess of capital losses over capital gains	1,250	
4	Income subject to tax not recorded on books this year (itemize):		13,000
			8 Deductions on this return not charged against book income this year (itemize):
5	Expenses recorded on books this year not deducted on this return (itemize):		a Depreciation $ ....
a	Depreciation $		b Contributions carryover $ ....
b	Contributions carryover $		
c	Travel and entertainment $		5,000
	insurance premiums	1,000	9 Add lines 7 and 8	18,000
6	Add lines 1 through 5	93,000	10 Income (line 28, page 1)—line 6 less line 9	75,000

Schedule M-2, which serves as a bridge of the two balance sheets, also has two columns. The left column is for opening retained earnings, book income for the year, and any increases in retained earnings. The right hand column is for distributions and other items that decrease retained earnings. For example, an adjustment to increase revenues in a previous period would affect the right hand column. The difference between these two columns is the ending retained earnings. This figure should equal the corporation's unappropriated retained earnings at the end of the tax year entered in the Schedule L balance sheet on Form 1120.

The reconciliation of retained earnings serves to disclose unusual transactions which have a bearing on the corporation or its shareholders. Where the reconciliation of retained earnings shows distributions to the corporate shareholders, the IRS should establish that the shareholders have reported the relevant income.

Example 13.114. Assume the same facts in Example 13.113 and the following additional facts. Harris Corporation's beginning balance of unappropriated retained earnings is $160,000. During the year it distributed a cash dividend of $25,000 to its shareholders.

Harris Corporation's Schedule M-2 is as follows:

Schedule M-2	Analysis of Unappropriated Retained Earnings per Books (Line 25, Schedule L)			
1 Balance at beginning of year	160,000	5 Distributions:	a Cash	25,000
2 Net income (loss) per books	77,000		b Stock	
3 Other increases (itemize):			c Property	
		6 Other decreases (itemize):		
		7 Add lines 5 and 6		25,000
4 Add lines 1, 2, and 3	237,000	8 Balance at end of year (line 4 less line 7)		212,000

SUMMARY OF CHAPTER 13

✓ Taxpayers have a choice of selecting a sole proprietorship, partnership, or corporation as the form to do business.

✓ Partnerships and sole proprietors may select to be taxed as a corporation for federal tax purposes by using the "check-the-box" system.

✓ The transfer of property solely for stock of a corporation that is at least 80 percent controlled by the transferor group is tax free.

✓ Realized gains are recognized on said transfers to the extent of boot received.

✓ Boot includes property other than stock (although nonqualified preferred stock is boot) as well as liabilities in excess of basis.

✓ Property basis carries over to the stock and to the corporation.

✓ Debt is favored over equity because interest is deductible by the corporation and dividends are not deductible.

✓ High debt-equity ratios are subject to IRS investigation and could lead to debt being classified as equity.

✓ If debt is reclassified as equity, the interest deduction is lost and interest and principal payments may be classified as dividends.

✓ Corporations with $1,000,000 or less in equity capital that issue stock for property generally qualify for Code Sec. 1244.

✓ Losses (except for built-in losses) on the sale of Code Sec. 1244 stock are ordinary up to $50,000 ($100,000 on a joint return), but gains are capital gains.

✓ Code Sec. 1202 also enables noncorporate taxpayers to exclude 50 percent of any gain from the sale or exchange of qualified small business stock held for more than five years which was originally issued after August 9, 1993.

✓ Taxpayers may rollover the gain from sale of Code Sec. 1202 stock if they invest the proceeds in a qualified small business corporation within 60 days of sale.

✓ Corporate tax rates vary from 15 to 39 percent.

✓ Very large corporations generally pay a flat 35 percent.

✓ Corporations also may be subject to the alternative minimum tax, although qualified small companies are exempt from it.

✓ Special features of corporate taxation include: (a) organization expenses are amortized over 60 months; (b) dividends received from U.S. corporations are subject to a dividends-received deduction of 70, 80, or 100 percent; (c) charitable deductions of up to 10 percent of taxable income (as adjusted) are allowed; and (d) capital losses in excess of capital gains must be carried back three years and then forward five years.

✓ Multiple corporations that are members of a controlled group (brother-sister, parent-subsidiary, or combined group) must share certain tax benefits as if they were one corporation (e.g., tax brackets, Code Sec. 179 election to expense).

✓ Parent-subsidiary controlled groups may file a consolidated return.

✓ The corporate annual tax return is due by the 15th day of the third month following the close of the tax year.

✓ Form 1120 is used and requires the computation of taxable income, the reporting of balance (analyzing sheets), and the completion of Schedules M-1 (reconciling book income to taxable income) and M-2 (analyzing unappropriated retained earnings per books).

CHAPTER 13 QUESTIONS

1. Can a partnership elect to be taxed as a corporation?

2. Can a corporation elect to be taxed as a partnership?

3. What is the main tax advantage of the corporate form of organization?

4. What is the purpose of Code Sec. 351 in regard to transfers to corporations?

5. What is the basis of accounts receivable transferred to a corporation under Code Sec. 351 by a cash-basis taxpayer?

6. To qualify under Code Sec. 351, what is the control requirement?

7. How are securities treated in a Code Sec. 351 transfer?

8. When can a shareholder recognize a loss under Code Sec. 351?

9. How does boot affect any gain realized under Code Sec. 351?

10. When are liabilities treated as boot in a Code Sec. 351 exchange?

11. What is the basis in a shareholder's stock after a Code Sec. 351 exchange?

12. What is the corporation's basis in property received under Code Sec. 351?

13. What happens to the holding period of assets transferred to corporations under Code Sec. 351?

14. Is there any depreciation recapture under a Code Sec. 351 exchange?

15. What are the tax consequences of a cash contribution to capital by a nonshareholder?

16. Why do taxpayers constantly try to increase the debt-equity ratio of a corporation?

17. What requirements must be met for stock to qualify as Code Sec. 1244 stock? What are the tax consequences of meeting these requirements?

18. To what extent is Code Sec. 1244 applicable to partnerships?

19. What is the "built-in loss" rule of Code Sec. 1244? What is the purpose of the rule?

20. What tax years are available to corporations? How do the options differ from other forms of business organizations?

21. When is the cash method of accounting not available to corporations?

22. What are the differences in the treatment of capital gains and capital losses of corporations and of individuals?

23. What is the special depreciation recapture rule that applies to corporations?

24. What is the purpose of the dividends-received deduction? What corporations are entitled to claim this deduction? What dividends qualify for this deduction?

25. Under what circumstances is the dividends-received deduction on a given dividend received not available?

26. When is the dividends-received deduction limited to 70 percent of taxable income?

27. What restrictions apply to the dividends-received deduction of dividends received from debt-financed stock purchases?

28. What happens to the basis of stock on which an "extraordinary" dividend has been received?

29. What are the main differences between net operating losses of individuals and corporations?

30. To what years may a net operating loss be carried?

31. In the absence of Code Sec. 248, how would organizational expenditures be treated?

32. What is the amortization period for organizational expenditures?

33. How do corporations treat start-up expenditures?

34. What is the maximum charitable contribution allowance for corporations? Is there a carryover to other years?

35. What is the corporate contribution base for charitable deductions?

36. When is the full fair market value deduction not available on a transfer of property to charity?

37. Describe the disallowed deductions and losses of corporations.

38. When may it be a tax advantage to incorporate even though the income may be double taxed?

39. What is the purpose of the additional 5 percent tax on corporate income between $100,000 and $335,000? The additional 3 percent tax on corporate income between $15,000,000 and $18,333,333?

40. Distinguish between adjustments to taxable income and tax preferences under the alternative minimum tax.

41. How does an asset's regular tax basis differ from its AMT basis?

42. What is the adjusted current earnings adjustment in the computation of the alternative minimum tax?

43. Describe the appreciated property charitable deduction tax preference.

44. What is the purpose of the minimum tax credit?

45. What are the advantages of filing a consolidated tax return?

46. Are all affiliated corporations eligible to file consolidated returns?

47. What is a built-in deduction on a consolidated return?

48. Parent Corporation owns all the stock in Subsidiary Corporation and is on the calendar-year tax year. Subsidiary Corporation has a fiscal year ending on August 31. Are they allowed to file a consolidated tax return?

49. Must corporations make estimated tax payments? If so, when?

50. What form does a corporation use to file its annual tax return? When is this return due?

51. What is the purpose of the reconciliation of taxable income with book income?

CHAPTER 13 PROBLEMS

52. Sam Rogers forms a corporation. Sam transfers to the corporation property having a basis to him of $15,000 and a fair market value of $27,000 for 900 shares of the $10 par stock of the corporation. A year later, Bill Morrison, who is not related to Sam, transfers property having a basis to him of $1,000 and a fair market value of $3,000 for 100 shares of the corporate stock. The corporation issued no other stock.

    a. How much gain does Sam recognize on his exchange? What is the basis to Sam of his 900 shares?

    b. How much gain does Bill recognize on his exchange? What is the basis to Bill of his 100 shares?

    c. What gain or loss is recognized by the corporation when it issues its shares to Sam? What is the basis to the corporation of the property it received from Sam?

    d. What is the gain or loss recognized by the corporation when it issues its shares to Bill? What is the basis to the corporation of the property it received from Bill?

53. Yager and Boggs formed Y&B Company in 1998. Yager contributed a building with a fair market value of $97,000, a mortgage of $75,000 and an adjusted basis of $50,000 in return for 22 shares of Y&B Company stock. (Y&B assumed the mortgage.) Boggs contributed land with a fair market value of $22,000 and an adjusted basis of $40,000 in return for 12 shares of Y&B Company stock and 10 $1,000 bonds. Lyle performed legal and accounting work during the incorporation process in return for six shares of stock. Determine the tax consequences of the transfers to *all* parties.

54. Mr. Hogan decided to incorporate his printing business and to give his manager, Mr. Temple, a share in the business. Mr. Hogan's sole proprietorship transferred the following:

	Basis	Value
Accounts payable	$ 0	$3,000
Accounts receivable	0	5,000
Printing press	4,000	6,000
Truck	12,300	8,000
Cash	2,000	2,000

Mr. Hogan received 70 shares of the stock, worth $14,000, in Express-Press Inc. Mr. Temple invested $2,000 in cash and received the remaining 30 shares of the stock.

What are the tax consequences to Mr. Hogan, Mr. Temple, and Express-Press Inc.?

55. Susan Sweets is a 40 percent shareholder in Acclaim Inc., a theatrical supplies company. She transfers a fully depreciated car with a value of $2,000 to the corporation, but does not receive any consideration for it.

   a. What are the tax consequences to Susan?

   b. What are the tax consequences to the corporation?

   c. What, if any, changes if Susan received another 10 percent stock interest for the car?

56. The municipality of Viewpoint, Kansas, wishes to attract local businesses. As part of a development program, it donated a building with a basis of $50,000 and a value of $200,000 plus $75,000 in cash to Sound & Fury Drums Inc.

   a. What are the tax consequences to Sound & Fury?

   b. What would change if the transferor was the estate of an individual shareholder of the corporation who left the property to Sound & Fury in a will?

57. In each of the following situations, determine if there is any depreciation or investment credit recapture.

   a. Joe incorporates his sole proprietorship and subsequently gifts the stock to his two children.

   b. Joe and nine others put their businesses in one corporation in return for five to 15 percent of the stock. Joe's share is 8 percent.

   c. Joe incorporates his sole proprietorship. Soon thereafter, the corporation sells some of the assets.

   d. Same as (c), but the corporation abandons some of the assets.

   e. Joe gifts his car, used only for business, to his son, who transfers it to his 100 percent owned corporation.

58. Zebra Corporation received a gift of a tract of land from a nonshareholder to encourage Zebra Corporation to build a plant on the land. The value of the land was $20,000. Zebra Corporation also received cash of $25,000 from nonshareholders, which was used to buy machinery costing $25,000.

    a. How much income does Zebra Corporation report as a result of these transactions?

    b. What is the basis of the assets to Zebra Corporation?

59. Sylvester and Elvira Upjohn are married, filing joint returns. Sylvester is the sole shareholder of a Code Sec. 1244 corporation. He received the stock two years ago when he incorporated his sole proprietorship. The only assets transferred were cash of $10,000 and a truck with a basis of $11,000 and a value of $8,000 (current basis zero). The corporation is bankrupt with liabilities far exceeding the assets.

    a. If the stock is worthless, what are the tax consequences to Sylvester?

    b. Is Sylvester's filing status relevant?

60. In 1996, Susan Christian transferred a machine with a fair market value of $30,000 and an adjusted basis of $40,000 to JPC Corporation in return for 60 shares of stock. The stock qualified as Code Sec. 1244 stock and the transfer qualified under Code Sec. 351. In 1998, JPC Corporation liquidated due to bankruptcy and Susan's stock became worthless. What is Susan's tax position in 1998?

61. Niffy Corporation, a domestic C corporation, issued 100 shares of Code Sec. 1202 stock on November 1, 1993, to Jennifer. This was the first time it issued such stock. Jennifer sold the shares on November 15, 1998. She had a $20,000 recognized gain on the sale. How much of the gain can Jennifer exclude, assuming Niffy Corporation always has been actively engaged in a trade or business and always has qualified as a small business corporation?

62. A corporation has income of $62,000 from operations and a net long-term capital loss of $5,000. What is the corporation's taxable income for the year?

63. Baginski Corporation purchased a residential building and depreciated it under accelerated depreciation. Determine the amount of ordinary income and Code Sec. 1231 income to be recognized assuming:

Selling price $330,000
Cost 360,000
Depreciation taken 210,000
Straight-line depreciation 180,000

64. Cablephones Inc., which is not a member of an affiliated group, had gross income from operations of $390,000 and deductible expenses of $420,000. Dividends of $300,000 were received from more than 20 percent owned U.S. corporations.

   a. What is the dividends-received deduction?

   b. What would the dividends-received deduction be if the deductible expenses were $451,000?

65. What is the dividends-received deduction allowed a corporation that receives $100,000 in dividends from a 45 percent owned domestic corporation if 30 percent of the cost of the investment is borrowed to make the purchase?

66. McIntyre Corporation purchases 1,000 shares of a 10 percent owned domestic corporation at $100 per share. McIntyre receives a $25 per share dividend within the first year after the purchase. What is the amount by which McIntyre must reduce the basis of the acquired stock?

67. Tandem Cycles Inc. had the following results in the first five years of its existence:

Year 1	Capital Gain	$ 11,000
Year 2	Net Operating Loss	(8,000)
Year 3	Ordinary Income	4,000
Year 4	Capital Loss	(9,000)
Year 5	Ordinary Income	20,000

   a. What happens to the net operating loss from Year 2?

   b. How should the capital loss of Year 4 be reported?

68. Sans Corporation reported the following results for 1998:

Gross receipts from operations	$250,000
Cost of goods sold	50,000
Operating expenses	90,000
Short-term capital gain	10,000
Short-term capital loss	(12,000)
Long-term capital gain	40,000
Long-term capital loss	(18,000)

   What is Sans Corporation's taxable income and regular income tax liability before credits for 1998?

69. Capital Corporation had the following results in 1998:

Gross receipts from operations	$200,000
Net short-term capital gain	50,000
Net long-term capital loss	(75,000)
Cost of goods sold	60,000
Operating expenses	40,000
Dividends received from 30% owned domestic corporation	80,000

a. What is Capital Corporation's taxable income and regular income tax liability for 1998?

b. Assuming that Capital Corporation's taxable income in 1997, its first year of existence, was $400,000, which included a net short-term capital gain of $50,000, what advice should be given to Capital with respect to its net capital asset position for 1998?

70. Caskets Inc. was incorporated on June 1, but did not start business until September 1. It adopted a fiscal year ending March 31, coinciding with the end of its natural business cycle. In connection with organizing the business, Caskets Inc. incurred the following expenses:

Legal fees for incorporating.............................	$ 800
Accounting fees for opening corporate books	400
Tax planning advice	300
Printing and issuing stock certificates	50
Incorporation fee to state	100
Temporary directors' fees	2,000
Legal fees for the transfer of assets to the corporation.........	500
	$4,150

a. What is the amount of the organizational expenditures?

b. How much of the amount is deductible in the corporation's first taxable year?

71. McKibbe Corporation has excess inventory that it no longer wants. In order to clear out its warehouse to make room for shipments of new inventory, it has decided to donate the inventory (bedding equipment) to several hospitals. The basis of the inventory is $100,000 and its fair market value is $120,000. The corporation made no other contributions this year. Determine its charitable contribution deduction assuming that its taxable income is $620,000 and included in gross income is $100,000 in dividends received from a 35-percent-owned domestic corporation.

72. Donor Corporation had the following income and deductions for last year:

Sales..	$5,000,000
Cost of sales	3,500,000
Other operating expenses	800,000
Dividends (from 5 percent owned domestic corporations) ...	100,000

Donor Corporation also made contributions (not included above) to qualifying charitable organizations of $175,000. Determine Donor Corporation's taxable income for the year.

73. Barbara sells an asset to her wholly owned corporation. The asset has a basis of $32,000 and a fair market value at the time of the sale of $27,000? What is the corporation's recognized gain or loss if it sells the asset for $30,000 several years later?

74. Compute a corporation's tax liability for 1998 if its taxable income equals:

    a. $100,000

    b. $150,000

    c. $400,000

    d. $11,000,000

    e. $16,000,000

    f. $19,000,000

75. Red Paint Corporation generated $40,000 of taxable income from operations last year, plus a $50,000 gain from the sale of land used as a parking lot for six years. What is the amount of federal income tax payable?

76. A & G Drug Store Inc. has been in operation for six years. The first four years it accumulated operating loss carryovers of $65,000. The fifth year it earned $25,000 in operating income and had $8,000 of dividend income. In its sixth year it had $54,000 in operating income and $11,000 of dividend income. Compute A & G Drug's tax liability for its sixth year.

77. Determine the amount of adjustments and tax preferences for the alternative minimum tax in each of the following situations:

    a. Equipment acquired in 1986 was depreciated under ACRS. Depreciation claimed for the year was $40,000; straight-line depreciation would have been $30,000.

    b. An asset was sold for $180,000 using the installment method of accounting. Only $20,000 of the $60,000 gain on the sale was reported this year since the asset constituted nondealer property.

    c. The corporation owed some Leon County school bonds on which it received $15,000 of tax-exempt interest.

    d. The corporation purchased $100,000 of Section 1245 property during the year on which it used 200 percent declining-balance depreciation.

78. Determine the alternative minimum tax assuming a corporation has the following information:

    | Taxable income | $600,000 |
    | Adjustments to income | 300,000 |
    | Tax preferences | 200,000 |
    | General business credit | 30,000 |

79. Assume the same information as in the previous problem, except that the adjustments to income are $100,000. What is the alternative minimum tax?

80. Presented below is Argo Company's adjusted current earnings and preadjustment alternative minimum taxable income for 1998 through 2001:

Year	Preadjustment AMTI	ACE
1998	$400,000	$350,000
1999	400,000	800,000
2000	700,000	600,000
2001	650,000	300,000

Determine the ACE adjustment (positive or negative) for each of the years.

81. Determine the alternative minimum tax assuming a corporation has the following:

Taxable income	$500,000
Adjustments to income (other than the ACE adjustments)	200,000
Tax preferences	100,000
Adjusted current earnings (ACE)	900,000

82. Windy Company had the following AMTI and ACE for 1998, 1999, and 2000. Indicate the ACE adjustment for each year.

	1998	1999	2000
AMTI	$500,000	$500,000	$500,000
ACE	400,000	300,000	800,000

83. The four Ames brothers own 25 percent each of two corporations, Unicycles Inc. and Tandem Inc. Last year, the two corporations generated $50,000 and $100,000 in taxable income, respectively. What is the total corporate tax liability?

84. The matrix below shows the stock ownership in five corporations by five unrelated individuals:

	Percentage of Stock Owned in Corporations				
Shareholder	A	B	C	D	E
1	10	5	5	10	20
2	30	5	40	30	10
3	—	5	—	—	—
4	30	5	15	10	20
5	30	5	40	50	50

Which of the above corporations, if any, are members of a brother-sister controlled group? Explain why each corporation is included or not.

85. Tiller Corporation's net income per books (after taxes) was $68,450. During the year, it had the following transactions:

Federal income taxes	$13,750
Net capital loss	4,000
Premiums paid on key person life insurance policy	2,800
Interest paid on a loan to acquire tax-exempt bonds	2,000
MACRS depreciation (for financial accounting purposes, Tiller claimed $4,000 of straight-line depreciation)	11,000
Tax-exempt interest on municipal bonds	9,000

Determine Tiller Corporation's taxable income assuming it does not have an NOL deduction or special deductions. Reconcile the difference between book income and taxable income.

86. Crates Corporation's financial income before income taxes for the year was $160,000. Organization costs of $48,000 are being written off over a 10-year period for financial statement purposes. For tax purposes, these costs are being written off over the minimum allowable period. For the year, Crates' taxable income was:

    a. $150,400

    b. $155,200

    c. $160,000

    d. $164,800

87. A corporation with $300,000 in taxable income has a tax liability of:

    a. 34 percent of $300,000

    b. $22,250 + 34 percent of $200,000

    c. $22,250 + 34 percent of $200,000 + 5 percent of $200,000

    d. 15 percent of $50,000 + 25 percent of $25,000 + 34 percent of $225,000

88. Cybele formed a corporation and transferred a building with a basis of $50,000, subject to a $70,000 mortgage, and cash of $15,000 to it for stock. Cybele's basis in her stock and the corporation's basis in the building are:

	Stock	Building
a.	Zero	$50,000
b.	$15,000	50,000
c.	Zero	40,000
d.	Zero	55,000

89. The following statements about the dividends-received deduction are true, except:

    a. The stock on which dividends are received must be held for at least 46 days.

    b. The deduction is not available if the long position is offset by a similar short position.

    c. The deduction is limited to a percentage of taxable income prior to charitable contribution, net operating loss, and capital loss deductions.

    d. Even if a consolidated return is *not* filed, a 100 percent dividends-received deduction is available for payments between members of the same affiliated group.

90. Excluding extensions, which one of the following Form 1120 tax returns is filed late?

	Tax Year Ended	Date Filed
a.	January 31, 2000	April 15, 2000
b.	August 31, 1999	November 2, 1999
c.	July 31, 1999	October 29, 1999
d.	December 31, 1999	March 15, 2000

91. During 1998, Jones transferred $10,000 cash and a building with an adjusted basis of $50,000 and a fair market value of $90,000 to Malibu Gardens Corporation in return for 90 percent of its only class of stock. In addition, for a bona fide business purpose, Malibu Gardens assumed the $65,000 outstanding mortgage on the building. What is the amount of Jones's recognized gain on the transfer?

    a. $0

    b. $5,000

    c. $15,000

    d. $25,000

    e. None of the above

92. In 1998, Sally transferred a building with an adjusted basis of $40,000 and a fair market value of $45,000 to Sandy Corporation. In exchange, she received the following:

    1. 80 percent of Sandy Corporation's only class of stock, fair market value of $20,000

    2. Equipment with a fair market value of $25,000 and an adjusted basis of $10,000

    What is Sandy Corporation's basis in the building received in the transfer?

    a. $5,000

    b. $25,000

    c. $40,000

    d. $45,000

    e. None of the above

93. Indo Corporation was organized on January 4, 1998, and began active business on January 5, 1998. Indo incurred the following expenses in connection with creating its business.

Professional fees for stock issuance	$400
State incorporation fees	200
Printing costs for stock certificates	150
Broker's commissions on sale of stock	700
Legal fees for drafting the charter	600
Expenses for temporary directors	500

    What is the maximum amount of organizational expenses which may be deducted by Indo on its 1998 tax return?

    a. $260

    b. $510

    c. $1,700

    d. $2,250

    e. None of the above

94. Sinco Company had $300,000 of income from business operations and $700,000 of allowable expenses. It also received $20,000 in dividends from a domestic corporation in which it owns 22 percent of the stock. What is Sinco Company's net operating loss?

    a. $380,000

    b. $396,000

    c. $397,000

    d. $400,000

    e. None of the above

95. Jones is a sole proprietorship. He would like to be taxed as a corporation for federal tax purposes. Jones may become a corporation by:

    a. Filing a corporate return for this year

    b. Timely filing Form 7701 and attaching it to this year's return

    c. Timely filing Form 8832 and attaching it to this year's return

    d. He cannot be taxed as a corporation

96. XYZ is a corporation. It needs to raise some capital and is uncertain whether to issue debt or equity. Which of the following statements is true?

    a. Both interest payments and dividend payments are deductible as expenses

    b. Interest payments are deductible but dividend payments are not deductible as expenses

    c. Principal repayment and stock retirement are deductible expenses

    d. The shareholders (noncorporate and corporate) are indifferent as to whether they receive interest or dividends

    e. All of the above are true

    f. None of the above are true

97. In the year of formation, a corporation:

    a. May elect a tax period other than those of its major shareholders

    b. Must elect the same tax period as its major shareholders

    c. Must use the cash basis for its accounting method

    d. None of the above

98. Smith Co. sells a machine during the year for $100,000. Smith acquired the machine for $140,000. At the time of sale, the machine's adjusted basis was $47,200. Smith Co.'s recognized gain on the sale is:

    a. $52,800 Code Sec. 1231 gain

    b. $52,800 Code Sec. 1245 gain

    c. $10,560 Code Sec. 291 gain and $42,240 Code Sec. 1231 gain

    d. $52,800 long-term capital gain

    e. None of the above

99. Bevco incurred start-up expenditures while investigating the acquisition of a business. With respect to such expenditures, Bevco:

    a. Can expense them in the year incurred

    b. Must capitalize them and deduct them in the year of liquidation

    c. Must capitalize them but may elect to amortize them over 60 months

    d. Must capitalize them but may elect to amortize them over 50 months

    e. None of the above

100. Which of the following corporate groups may file a consolidated tax return?

    a. Brother-sister group

    b. Parent-subsidiary group

    c. Both brother-sister and parent-subsidiary groups

    d. None of the above corporate groups may file a consolidated tax return.

101. *Comprehensive Problem.* Last year, Intrepid Corporation's tax return revealed the following items:

Dividends from 20 percent owned domestic corporations	$ 60,000
Gross income from services rendered.....................	300,000
Miscellaneous expenses	250,000
Long-term capital gains.................................	30,000
Net operating loss carryforward	15,000
Charitable contributions	20,000

    a. What is Intrepid's dividends-received deduction?

    b. What is the charitable contribution deduction?

    c. What is the taxable income for the year?

102. *Comprehensive Problem.* Mr. Trent transferred three apartment buildings to a new corporation in exchange for all its stock. The facts pertaining to the buildings were:

Building	Basis	Value	Mortgage	Recapture Potential
1	$10,000	$100,000	$60,000	$ 0
2	15,000	80,000	0	5,000
3	20,000	30,000	0	4,000

a. What gains are realized and recognized on each building? What is the character of the gains?

b. What is the corporation's basis in each building?

c. What is Mr. Trent's basis in his stock?

103. *Comprehensive Problem.* Jones, Able, and Smith want to form Shriver Corporation. They want to accomplish this in the most tax efficient (least costly) way possible. They have asked for advice. The counselor will receive $10,000 (in stocks and bonds). The relevant information follows.

PARTY		GIVES		RECEIVES
		Fair Market Value	Adjusted Basis	
Jones	Machine	$100,000	$70,000*	
	Land	40,000	20,000	(1) 25 shares of stock
	Building	65,000	45,000**	(2) $20,000

* Acquired for $85,000; straight-line depreciation taken.
** Acquired for $70,000; straight-line depreciation taken; liability of $60,000 is assumed by Shriver Corporation.

PARTY		GIVES		RECEIVES
		Fair Market Value	Adjusted Basis	
Able	Machine	$70,000	$80,000*	(1) Eight shares of stock
	Building	50,000	65,000**	(2) Two 10-year bonds
				(3) $5,000

* Acquired for $95,000; straight-line depreciation taken.
** Acquired for $75,000; straight-line depreciation taken; liability of $70,000 is on the property.

PARTY		GIVES		RECEIVES
		Fair Market Value	Adjusted Basis	
Smith	Machine	$80,000	$80,000	
	Automobile	15,000	10,000*	(1) 23 shares of stock
	Truck	40,000	30,000**	(2) Eight 10-year bonds

* Acquired for $15,000; straight-line depreciation taken.
** Acquired for $40,000; straight-line depreciation taken.

PARTY	GIVES	
Counselor	Services $10,000	(1) One share of stock
		(2) Two 10-year bonds

Determine all tax consequences for Jones, Able, Smith, and the counselor, assuming the transfer occurred in 1998. Also assume that Jones, Able, and Smith are unrelated parties.

104. *Research Problem.* In 1996, Salt Lake Resorts Inc. generated a capital gain of $300,000 and no other taxable income or loss. In 1998, the corporation suffered a net operating loss of $50,000, which was carried back to 1996. Salt Lake Resorts Inc. did not make an election to carry forward only. The corporation has large tax preferences. The IRS claims that (1) no tax benefit results from the carryback, and (2) the NOL is nevertheless used up. Salt Lake Resorts Inc. believes that either a tax benefit results or it can carry forward the $50,000 net operating loss to 1999. Is the IRS right? Why?

     (See *Foster Lumber Co., Inc.,* 76-2 USTC ¶ 9740, 429 U.S. 32, 97 S.Ct. 204 (1976).)

105. *Research Problem.* Sharp Knives Inc. is owned 75 percent by Vicky and 25 percent by Rick, an unrelated taxpayer. Soft Shoes Inc. is owned 85 percent by Vicky and 15 percent by unrelated third parties, not including Rick. The two corporations file independent returns. Upon audit, the IRS denies the corporations multiple surtax exemptions, claiming that the two corporations constitute a brother-sister controlled group. What is the result?

     (See Reg. § 1.1563-1(a)(3) and *Vogel Fertilizer Co.,* 1982-1 USTC ¶ 9134, 455 U.S. 16, 102 S.Ct. 821 (1982).)

106. *Research Problem.* Cambo Corporation, a calendar-year taxpayer, was formed in 1994 and incurred $60,000 in organizational expenditures. Had the corporation made a proper election under Code Sec. 248, it would have been entitled to a $7,000 deduction in 1994. However, on its 1994 tax return it erroneously claimed a $60,000 current deduction (i.e., it expensed the full amount in the year it was organized). Upon audit in 1998, the IRS disallowed the $60,000 deduction and also did not allow Cambo a $7,000 deduction. Cambo Corporation seeks your advice on this issue.

     (See Reg. § 1.248-1(c); *Bay Sound Transportation Co.,* 1967-2 USTC ¶ 9641 (DC Texas 1967), aff'd in part and rev'd in part on other issues, 1969-1 USTC ¶ 9371, 410 F.2d 505 (CA-5 1969).)

Chapter 14

Corporate Nonliquidating Distributions

Learning Objectives

After completing Chapter 14, you should be able to:

1. Understand the computation of earnings and profits (E&P), the role of current and accumulated E&P, and the sources of a distribution.

2. Recognize the tax consequences to the distributing corporation and the shareholder distributee.

3. Judge the tax aspects of property distributions to corporate and noncorporate distributees.

4. Describe why dividends paid in stock are generally tax free and why there are several exceptions.

5. Recall when stock redemptions are treated as dividends v. sales or exchanges and how indirect ownership is ascertained.

6. Define death tax redemptions.

7. Explain the tax consequences to a corporation purchasing its own stock.

OVERVIEW OF CHAPTER

Corporations make distributions to shareholders for many reasons and in many ways. Distributions to shareholders because of their shareholder status (as opposed to employee or creditor) may be in cash, property, or the distributing corporation's own stock or stock rights. The tax status of these distributions determines whether the shareholder and/or the corporation have income, as well as the type of income. The tax status of the distribution depends upon what was distributed, why it was distributed, and the surrounding circumstances of the distribution.

Distributions can be broadly classified as distributions where the shareholder does not surrender stock and those where the shareholder does surrender stock. The former are treated as dividends to the extent that they are made out of the corporation's earnings and profits. However, distributions of stock and/or stock rights may or may not be treated as dividends. Distributions in exchange for the shareholder's stock may be classified as dividends, stock redemptions, or a liquidation of the corporation.

This chapter discusses distributions of cash or property that appear to be dividends, distributions of a corporation's stock and/or stock rights, and stock redemptions. This classification can have significant tax effects on the shareholder and the distributing corporation. Distributions in complete liquidations are discussed in Chapter 15.

Distributions with Respect to Stock

¶ 14,001 DIVIDEND DISTRIBUTIONS

Most corporations pay dividends on both common and preferred stock. Dividends on preferred stock generally must be paid before dividends on the common stock. Preferred shareholders also take precedence over common shareholders in the event of liquidation.

The more profitable a corporation is, the more likely it is to make distributions. This is due partly to the ability to pay and partly to the imposition of a significant accumulated earnings tax on corporations that allow their earnings to accumulate above certain levels. Code Sec. 531. Since dividends are nondeductible to the corporation, but taxed to the shareholders (often called "double taxation"), Congress has found this penalty tax necessary to encourage dividend distributions.

The tax status of a cash or property distribution to shareholders is affected by the distributing corporation's earnings and profits (E&P). Such a distribution is considered a dividend to the extent that it is made from the distributing corporation's E&P for the current tax year or E&P accumulated since March 1, 1913. Code Sec. 316(a). Dividends are included in gross income as ordinary income. Code Sec. 301(c). However, a corporate distributee is entitled to the dividends-received deduction provided by Code Sec. 243.

Distributions in excess of the corporation's E&P are considered to be a return of capital. The excess is applied against the shareholder's adjusted basis in the stock. As such, it is nontaxable and reduces the adjusted basis. If the distribution is greater than the shareholder's adjusted basis, then the excess is treated as a gain from the sale or exchange of the stock. Code Sec. 301(c). It is a capital gain if the stock is a capital asset. Normal holding period rules are used to determine whether the gain is long-term or short-term.

Example 14.1. Ace Corporation distributes $30,000 to each of its two equal shareholders, Barbara Bates and Elmer Platt. Ace Corporation's E&P is $40,000. Barbara's adjusted basis in her stock is $15,000. Elmer's adjusted basis in his stock is $7,000. Barbara and Elmer each have a taxable dividend of $20,000. In addition,

Barbara has a $10,000 return of capital which is nontaxable and reduces her adjusted basis in the stock to $5,000 ($15,000 − $10,000). Elmer has a $7,000 return of capital which is nontaxable and reduces his adjusted basis in the stock to zero. He also must recognize a $3,000 gain for the amount in excess of his adjusted basis.

¶ 14,011   EARNINGS AND PROFITS (E&P)

Although earnings and profits (E&P) have a significant impact in determining the tax status of distributions, the term is not defined in the Internal Revenue Code. Code Sec. 312 provides an indication of how certain transactions affect E&P, but it does not specifically define it. E&P is a tax term. It has some similarities to retained earnings, but it is not equal to it. E&P is a measure of the corporation's economic capacity to pay a dividend. Its main purpose is to measure the amount of a distribution which represents a taxable dividend to the shareholder. Thus, certain transactions that reduce or increase retained earnings may not have a similar effect on E&P. For example, a stock dividend reduces retained earnings but does not reduce E&P.

> *Example 14.2.* The Camping Corporation pays a 20 percent stock dividend, consisting of 10,000 shares with a $1 par value and a fair market value of $5. The accounting entries would be a debit (a reduction) to retained earnings of $50,000, a credit to capital stock of $10,000, and a credit to paid in capital of $40,000. For tax purposes, the stock dividend is irrelevant. E&P stays the same since the stock transaction in no way has reduced the corporation's capacity to pay a dividend in cash or property.

E&P is used up on a LIFO basis; that is, distributions are considered to come from current E&P first and then from accumulated E&P since March 1, 1913. A new corporation begins with no E&P. Current E&P is determined annually. Each year a corporation adds to accumulated E&P to the extent that it does not distribute current E&P. If a corporation distributes more than its current E&P, then the accumulated E&P is reduced by such excess, but never below zero. If current E&P is negative, then the deficit also reduces accumulated E&P. Finally, for distributions in excess of E&P: (1) current E&P is allocated on a pro rata basis and (2) accumulated E&P is allocated on a chronological basis.

> *Example 14.3.* Jasmine Company was formed in 1996. It had negative current E&P of $30,000 in that year. In 1997, its current E&P was $70,000. In 1998, current E&P was a negative $65,000. In 1999, Jasmine's current E&P was $40,000 and it distributed $10,000 in cash to its shareholders. The effects on E&P are as follows:

Year	Current E&P	Accumulated E&P	Distributions
1996	($30,000)	($30,000)	$ 0
1997	70,000	40,000	0
1998	(65,000)	(25,000)	0
1999	40,000	5,000	10,000

Accumulated E&P in 1996 equals the deficit in current E&P. Accumulated E&P in 1997 equals its beginning balance (− $30,000) plus current E&P ($70,000), or $40,000. Accumulated E&P in 1998 equals its beginning balance ($40,000) plus current E&P (− $65,000), or − $25,000. Finally, accumulated E&P at the end of 1999 equals its beginning balance (− $25,000) plus current E&P less the distribution ($40,000 minus $10,000), or (− $25,000 plus $30,000 = $5,000).

Determination of Current Earnings and Profits

The starting point in the computation of current E&P is taxable income or loss for the current year. The method of accounting (cash or accrual) used to compute taxable income also must be used to compute E&P. Reg. § 1.312-6(b). The main adjustments, which primarily are found in Code Sec. 312, may be categorized as follows:

A. Items That Are Excluded from Both Taxable Income and E&P

(no adjustments to taxable income)

1. Gifts and bequests

2. Contributions to capital

3. Realized, but not recognized, gains and losses

    a. Like-kind exchanges (Code Sec. 1031)

    b. Involuntary conversions (Code Sec. 1033)

    c. Transfers to controlled corporations (Code Sec. 351)

    d. Transfers pursuant to a reorganization (Code Sec. 361)

    e. Disallowed wash sale losses (Code Sec. 1091)

B. Items That Are Nondeductible, but That Reduce E&P

(negative adjustments to taxable income)

1. Federal income taxes

2. Capital losses

3. Life insurance premiums (where the beneficiary is the corporation)

4. Disallowed losses from related party transactions (Code Sec. 267)

5. Charitable contributions in excess of the 10 percent limit

6. Unreasonable compensation

7. Interest and expenses attributable to tax-free income (Code Sec. 265)

8. Nondeductible penalties and fines

9. Miscellaneous nondeductible items that reduce capital

C. Items That Are Exempt from Income, but That Increase E&P

(positive adjustments to taxable income)

1. Tax-exempt municipal bond interest (Reg. § 1.312-6(b))
2. Life insurance proceeds
3. Compensation for injuries
4. Recovery of losses which generated no tax savings
5. Federal income tax refunds from previous tax years
6. Other tax-free income which increased capital

D. Items That Are Deductible from Taxable Income, but Not from E&P

(positive adjustments to taxable income)

1. Accelerated depreciation or cost recovery in excess of straight-line (no adjustment is needed if the method used was not based upon time (e.g., the units-of-production method)
2. Percentage depletion in excess of cost depletion (Reg. § 1.312-6(c)(1))
3. Capital loss carryovers
4. Net operating loss carryovers
5. Charitable contributions carryovers
6. Dividends-received deduction
7. Other deductions which do not reduce capital

E. Items That Are Deferred to Later Tax Years, but That Increase E&P

(positive adjustments to taxable income)

1. Deferred gain on installment sales (all gain increases E&P in year of sale)
2. Long-term contract reported on completed-contract method (use percentage-of-completion method)

Component items lose their identity at the time they become part of E&P. Thus, when income items enter the E&P account and serve as the basis for corporate distributions, they automatically create taxable income to the shareholder recipients. This is so even for items which were nontaxable to the corporation in the first place. Also, these adjustments may lead to other adjustments. For example, if a corporation sells an asset for which accelerated depreciation was used, then not only is the excess depreciation added to E&P, but also in the year of sale the gain or loss on that asset must be adjusted. Such gain or loss is included in taxable income and must be adjusted because the adjusted basis of that property for E&P purposes is based on straight-line depreciation, not accelerated depreciation.

The adjustments required for depreciation are more involved than many of the other adjustments because of the many changes made in the tax law with respect to depreciation. The impact on E&P from depreciation and cost recovery is as follows:

1. If a "facts and circumstances" useful life is employed and depreciation is computed on the basis of time, any accelerated portion in excess of straight-line does not reduce E&P. The excess is added to taxable income. Code Sec. 312(k)(1).

2. When the Accelerated Cost Recovery System (ACRS) or Modified Accelerated Cost Recovery System (MACRS) is used, straight-line cost recovery must still be used for E&P purposes. Thus, for MACRS property placed in service after 1986, E&P must be computed under "the alternative depreciation system." Code Sec. 312(k)(3). Personal property with a class life is depreciated for E&P purposes over such life (if there is no class life, 12 years is used) while real property is depreciated over 40 years, and amounts expensed under Code Sec. 179 are written off over five years.

3. If a method *not* based on time is used (e.g., the "units of production" method or the "income forecast method"), E&P is reduced in full by the deduction.

4. When the asset is sold, the E&P basis is used to determine gain or loss for E&P purposes. Such gain or loss must not exceed that recognized for income tax purposes. Code Sec. 312(f)(1).

Example 14.4. Halan Corporation exchanges land, held for investment, with a fair market value of $50,000 and adjusted basis of $20,000, for land with a fair market value of $50,000. The exchange qualifies under Code Sec. 1031 as a like-kind exchange. Halan Corporation has a realized gain of $30,000 and no recognized gain. The $30,000 gain is not included in taxable income, nor is it included in E&P. This is an example of Category A items which do not require adjustments to taxable income to compute current E&P.

Example 14.5. Lands Corporation sold property with a fair market value of $16,000 and an adjusted basis of $20,000 to its sole shareholder. Lands Corporation has a realized loss of $4,000. However, Lands Corporation is disallowed the loss deduction because this is a related party transaction under Code Sec. 267. The loss is not deductible in computing taxable income but is deducted from taxable income in computing current E&P. This is an example of Category B adjustments.

Example 14.6. Globe Corporation receives $5,000 in tax-exempt municipal interest. The $5,000 does not enter into the computation of corporate taxable income and thus is not subject to corporate taxation. However, the $5,000 is added to taxable income to compute current E&P. This is an example of Category C adjustments.

Example 14.7. On January 2, 1997, Jasper Company purchased a machine for $12,000 and depreciated it under MACRS over five years. Straight-line over 12 years is allowed for E&P purposes. Cost recovery in 1997 was $2,400 ($12,000 × 20%). Depreciation for E&P purposes in 1997 was $500 (($12,000/12) × ½). The adjustment in 1997 for E&P purposes was $1,900 ($2,400 − $500). Cost recovery in 1998 was $3,840 ($12,000 × 32%). Depreciation for E&P purposes in 1998 was $1,000 ($12,000/12), thus an adjustment of $2,840 ($3,840 − $1,000). The positive adjustments to taxable income to compute current E&P in 1997 and 1998 are examples of Category D adjustments.

Example 14.8. Assume the same facts as Example 14.7, except that the machine is sold on March 3, 1999, for $11,000. The adjusted basis of the property at the date of sale is $4,608 ($12,000 − ($2,400 + $3,840 + $1,152)). The realized and recognized gain on the sale is $6,392 ($11,000 − $4,608) and is included in the determination of taxable income. The adjusted basis of the property for E&P purposes is $10,000 ($12,000 − depreciation for 1997 ($500), 1998 ($1,000) and 1999 ($500)). Thus, the gain for E&P purposes is $1,000 ($11,000 − $10,000). As such, a negative adjustment of $5,392 ($6,392 − $1,000) is made to taxable income in 1999 to compute current E&P.

Example 14.9. In 1998, Peter Corporation sells land with an adjusted basis of $60,000 for $80,000 to Campbell Company, an unrelated taxpayer. Campbell Company agrees to make two annual payments of $40,000 plus interest at 12 percent of the unpaid balance. The first payment occurs in 1999. Peter Corporation does not elect out of the installment method. Peter Corporation has a realized gain of $20,000 ($80,000 − $60,000) but does not recognize any gain in 1998. However, in computing current E&P in 1998, the $20,000 gain must be added to taxable income. This is an example of Category E adjustments.

Current E&P and Accumulated E&P

The taxability of a distribution is affected by the distributing corporation's current and accumulated E&P. Distributions are deemed to be made from current E&P first and then from accumulated E&P since March 1, 1913. Code Sec. 316(a). There are several possible situations with respect to the amount of the distribution and E&P.

1. The corporation's current E&P is positive. The distributions are less than current E&P. In this case the distributions are fully taxable as dividends, even if the corporation's accumulated E&P is negative.

    Example 14.10. Hock Company has current E&P of $16,000 for the year. During the year, it distributed $10,000 in cash to its shareholders. The $10,000 is deemed to be distributed from current E&P and is fully taxable as a dividend.

2. The corporation's current and accumulated E&P are positive. The distributions are greater than current E&P but not greater than the sum of current and accumulated E&P. The current E&P is allocated to each distribution in relative proportion of the current E&P to the total of all distributions. The accumulated E&P is allocated to each distribution on a FIFO

basis (i.e., in chronological order of the distributions). Also, distributions can reduce E&P to zero but never make it negative.

Example 14.11. Hindle Corporation has current E&P of $15,000 and accumulated E&P of $10,000. It made a cash distribution of $8,000 on March 1, 1998, and a cash distribution of $12,000 on October 11, 1998. Current E&P is allocated as follows:

$$\frac{\text{Current E\&P}}{\text{Total distributions}} = \frac{\text{Percent of each distribution}}{\text{out of current E\&P}}$$

$$\frac{\$15,000}{\$20,000} = \frac{3}{4} \quad \text{and thus}$$

		Allocation		
Distribution	Total Distributed	Current E&P	Accumulated E&P	Taxable Amount
March 1, 1998	$ 8,000	$ 6,000	$2,000	$ 8,000
October 11, 1998	12,000	9,000	3,000	12,000
Total	$20,000	$15,000	$5,000	$20,000

3. The corporation's current and accumulated E&P are positive. The distributions are greater than current E&P and the sum of current and accumulated E&P. Current and accumulated E&P are allocated as in Situation 2, above. However, in this case, part of the distributions will be a return of capital.

Example 14.12. Assume the same facts as Example 14.11, except that Hindle's accumulated E&P on January 1, 1998, is $3,000.

		Allocation			
Distribution	Total Distributed	Current E&P	Accumulated E&P	Taxable Amount	Return of Capital
March 1, 1998	$ 8,000	$ 6,000	$2,000	$ 8,000	$ 0
October 11, 1998	12,000	9,000	1,000	10,000	2,000
Total	$20,000	$15,000	$3,000	$18,000	$2,000

4. The corporation's current E&P is positive and its accumulated E&P is negative and the distributions are greater than current E&P. Current E&P is allocated to each distribution as noted in Situation 2, above. Accumulated E&P remains negative and the excess of each distribution over its share of current E&P is a return of capital.

Example 14.13. Coats Inc. has current E&P of $30,000 in 1998. Its accumulated E&P on January 1, 1998, was a negative $21,000. It made cash distributions of $20,000 on April 1 and $30,000 on October 1. The distribution is taxed as follows:

		Allocation		
Distribution	Total Distributed	Current E&P	Taxable Amount	Return of Capital
April 1, 1998	$20,000	$12,000	$12,000	$ 8,000
October 1, 1998	30,000	18,000	18,000	12,000
Total	$50,000	$30,000	$30,000	$20,000

5. The corporation's current E&P and its accumulated E&P are negative. In this case, the distributions are a return of capital.

   Example 14.14. Salz Company made a cash distribution of $25,000 on June 3, 1998. Its accumulated E&P on January 1, 1998, was a negative $10,000 and its current E&P for 1998 was a negative $17,000. The $25,000 is not treated as a dividend. It is a return of capital.

6. The corporation's current E&P is negative but its accumulated E&P is positive. Since accumulated E&P is used up on a chronological basis, the accumulated E&P is netted with current E&P at the date of the distribution. The negative current E&P is allocated ratably during the year; thus, it is prorated to each distribution based on the number of days in the tax year to the date of the distribution. This procedure assumes that the negative E&P occurred evenly throughout the tax year. If the corporation can show when the actual deficit occurred, then it may use that date for allocating the negative current E&P.

   Example 14.15. On January 1, 1998, Cote's Corporation has accumulated E&P of $15,000. Its current E&P for 1998 was a negative $10,950. It made two cash distributions of $6,000 each on April 1 and July 1. The status of these distributions is as follows. The negative current E&P is allocated on a daily basis of $30 ($10,950/365).

Distd.	Total Distr.	Pro rata Portion of Current E&P	Accumulated E&P on Distribution Date	Taxable Amount	Return of Capital
Apr. 1	$6,000	($2,700)	$15,000−$2,700=$12,300	$6,000	$ 0
July 1	6,000	(5,430)	$15,000−$6,000−$5,430=$3,570	$3,570	2,430

On April 1 the pro rata portion of current E&P is a negative $2,700 ($30 × 90 days). Since accumulated E&P minus current E&P is greater than the distribution, the distribution is taxable. On July 1, the pro rata portion of current E&P is a negative $5,430 ($30 × 180 days). Only $3,570 is left in accumulated E&P after subtracting the April 1 dividend and the current E&P on July 1 from beginning accumulated E&P.

At this point, accumulated E&P is zero and any other distributions in 1998 would be returns of capital. If no other distributions are made in 1998, then accumulated E&P on January 1, 1999, would be a negative $5,520 (the zero balance in accumulated E&P at July 1, 1998, plus the remaining deficit of $5,520 in current E&P). If there is more than one shareholder, then E&P is allocated to each shareholder.

Example 14.16. Newman Corporation has accumulated E&P of $10,000 on January 1, 1998. Its current E&P for 1998 is $50,000. It made cash distributions of $40,000 each on May 1 and November 1. On January 1, 1998, Newman had two shareholders, Lisa and Reece. Each owned 100 shares which they acquired in 1990. Lisa's adjusted basis of her stock was $35,000 and Reece's was $19,000. On October 15, 1998, Susan bought 50 shares from Reece for $18,000. The results of these events are as follows:

$$\frac{\text{Current E\&P}}{\text{Total distributions}} = \frac{\$50,000}{\$80,000} = \frac{5}{8} = \text{Portion of each distribution from current E\&P}$$

May 1 distribution: $\$40,000 \times \dfrac{5}{8} = $ $25,000 from current E&P

November 1 distribution: $\$40,000 \times \dfrac{5}{8} = $ $25,000 from current E&P

The $10,000 accumulated E&P is used up by the May 1 distribution; thus, $35,000 ($25,000 + $10,000) of the May 1 distribution is a dividend and $25,000 of the November 1 distribution is a dividend.

The effects on each shareholder are:

May 1 Distribution

Lisa: 100 shares; 100/200 = ½ of E&P allocated to Lisa
Reece: 100 shares; 100/200 = ½ of E&P allocated to Reece

Total   200 shares

Lisa: $17,500 dividend (½ × $35,000)
        2,500 return of capital (new basis in 100 shares is $32,500)
        $20,000 total

Reece: $17,500 dividend (½ × $35,000)
        2,500 return of capital (new basis in 100 shares is $16,500)
        $20,000 total

October 15 Sale

Reece: Amount Realized $18,000
        Adjusted Basis .... (8,250)   (½ ×$16,500)
        Realized and Recognized Gain $ 9,750

November 1 Distribution

Lisa: 100 shares; 100/200 = ½ of E&P allocated to Lisa
Reece: 50 shares; 50/200 = ¼ of E&P allocated to Reece
Susan: 50 shares; 50/200 = ¼ of E&P allocated to Susan

Total   200 shares

Lisa: $12,500 dividend (½ × $25,000)
        7,500 return of capital (new basis in 100 shares is $25,000)
        $20,000 total

Reece: $ 6,250 dividend (¼ × $25,000)
        3,750 return of capital (new basis in 50 shares is $4,500)
        $10,000 total

Susan: $ 6,250 dividend (¼ × $25,000)
        3,750 return of capital (new basis in 50 shares is $14,250)
        $10,000 total

TAX PLANNING POINTER ▼

The timing of distributions can significantly affect the shareholders' tax consequences. If a corporation has no current and accumulated E&P but has the funds to make a distribution, then making a distribution, as opposed to waiting for next year when the corporation will be very profitable, will produce tax savings to the shareholders.

Preferred Stock Dividends

Current E&P must be allocated first to distributions on stock on which dividends must be paid before dividends are paid on other classes of stock. Rev. Rul. 69-440, 1969-2 CB 46. Thus, where a corporation has both preferred stock and common stock, any current E&P will be allocated to the preferred stock first and then to common stock.

Example 14.17. Carriage Corporation has both preferred and common shareholders. The corporation has a deficit in accumulated E&P at the beginning of the year. The current E&P is $10,000. The corporation makes a dividend distribution of $8,000 to the preferred shareholders and $5,000 to the common shareholders. The preferred shareholders will report the full $8,000 as dividend income, while the common shareholders will report only $2,000 as dividend income and $3,000 as return of capital. Since the preferred shareholders receive their dividends first, only $2,000 of current E&P is left for the common shareholder distribution.

Dividend Reinvestment Plans

Many corporations give shareholders the opportunity to agree to automatically reinvest all or some of their dividends in more shares on which dividends are paid. The participation in such a plan does not make such distributions any less taxable. To encourage reinvestment of dividends, it is customary to grant a discount from the current market price. The IRS takes the position that a discount, if any, is in the nature of an additional dividend and taxable as such. Reg. § 1.301-1(j). If this happens, the discount is added to the cost basis in the stock purchased, resulting in a cost equal to the market value. Reg. § 1.301-1(h); Rev. Rul. 76-53, 1976-1 CB 87. (In IRS Letter Ruling 9406012, the IRS held that a discount was not dividend income. However, the ruling dealt with cooperatives and special circumstances. It is unlikely that it would apply to corporate shareholders.)

Tax-Free Distributions

If a corporation makes partially or wholly tax-free distributions, it must file Form 5452 (Corporate Report of Nondividend Distributions) by the end of February of the year subsequent to the distribution. The distributing corporation also will normally inform its shareholders of the tax status of distributions to them.

¶ 14,015   CASH DISTRIBUTIONS

The measure of a cash distribution is easy to obtain; it is the amount of cash distributed. It is considered to be a dividend to the extent of current and accumulated E&P as explained at ¶ 14,011. (The discussion there assumed all distributions were in the form of cash.) The shareholder recognizes income to this extent and the distributing corporation reduces current E&P and then accumulated E&P accordingly. Also, the distributing corporation does not recognize a gain or a loss on the distribution.

> *Example 14.18.* James Corporation has current E&P of $30,000 for 1998. It distributed $10,000 to Kimberly, its sole shareholder. Kimberly has $10,000 of dividend income. James Corporation recognizes no gain or loss on the distribution and reduces current E&P by $10,000.

¶ 14,021   PROPERTY DISTRIBUTIONS

Property distributions are more complex than cash distributions. Several questions arise:

1. With respect to the recipient shareholder, what is the measure of the distribution and how much is dividend income? What is the shareholder's basis in property received? When does the holding period for the property begin?

2. With respect to the distributing corporation, is gain or loss recognized on the distribution, and if so, what is its character? What is the effect of the distribution on the corporation's E&P?

Tax Consequences to Shareholders

Determination of Dividend Income

If a corporation distributes property rather than cash, then the amount of the distribution is the property's fair market value determined on the date of the distribution. Code Sec. 301(b). If the property is encumbered with a liability and the shareholder assumes the liability or takes the property subject to the liability, then the measure of the distribution is the property's fair market value reduced by the liability (but never below zero). Code Sec. 301(b)(2). The distribution is considered to be a dividend to the extent of the distributing corporation's current and accumulated E&P. Amounts in excess of E&P are treated as returns of capital and reduce the shareholder's adjusted basis in the stock, but never below zero. Once the adjusted basis is zero, additional amounts distributed are treated as gain from the sale or exchange of the stock.

Basis in Property Received

The shareholder's basis in the property received is its fair market value on the date of distribution. Code Sec. 301(d). The assumption of a liability by the shareholder does not affect the basis in the property. Also, the status of the distribution (i.e., dividend or return of capital) does not affect the basis. Independent of the shareholder's method of accounting, the dividend is not taxable until received. Reg. § 1.301-1(a). The shareholder's holding period begins on the date of receipt; the shareholder does not receive the distributing corporation's holding period in the property. Code Sec. 1223.

Example 14.19. Swimwear Inc. has E&P of $10,000 at the end of the current year, during which it distributed securities with a basis of $3,000 and a value of $8,000, to a shareholder, Abigail Flynn. Abigail must recognize $8,000 of dividend income, she receives an $8,000 basis in the securities, and the holding period starts upon receipt.

Example 14.20. Same as Example 14.19, except E&P (as computed at the end of the year without any reduction for the distribution) is only $6,000. Abigail must recognize only $6,000 of dividend income. Her basis in the securities received is still $8,000 and she must reduce her basis in her Swimwear stock by $2,000, the excess of the distribution over E&P. If the $2,000 exceeds her basis, to that extent she has a capital gain.

Example 14.21. Cashing Corporation has current E&P of $75,000. On November 4, 1998, it distributes land with a fair market value of $48,000 and an adjusted basis of $30,000 to Melonie Craig, its sole shareholder. The property is subject to an $11,000 liability, which Melonie assumes. The amount of the distribution is $37,000 ($48,000 − $11,000). Since E&P is greater than $37,000, the full amount is treated as a dividend. Melonie's basis in the land is $48,000 (fair market value). Her holding period beings on the date of receipt, November 3, 1998.

TAX BLUNDER

Arrow Inc. distributes securities with a value of $20,000 and a basis of $27,000 to its shareholders, the Sunny Corporation. Arrow realizes, but cannot recognize, the $7,000 loss, and there is no E&P adjustment for the loss. Sunny has dividend income of $20,000, assuming sufficient E&P. In any event, the distributee's basis equals $20,000. The holding period starts at the time of distribution. The dividends-received deduction, if available, is computed on the value of $20,000. Arrow would have been well advised to have sold the securities for $20,000, recognizing a $7,000 loss that reduces taxable income and E&P, and then to have distributed the proceeds to Sunny Corporation.

Property that has declined in value should not be distributed by a corporation. The shareholder's basis in the property is its fair market value, not the corporation's adjusted basis. Thus, the loss due to decline in value will never be recognized. The distributing corporation would be better advised to sell the property, recognize the loss, and distribute the proceeds (plus tax savings, if desired).

A corporate shareholder that receives an extraordinary dividend must reduce its basis in the stock immediately before any disposition by the untaxed portion of such dividend. Code Sec. 1059. An extraordinary dividend is a distribution amounting to more than 10 percent of the greater of the stock basis or stock value the day before the ex-dividend date (5 percent for preferred stock). Dividends declared within 85 days are aggregated, as are dividends declared within a year if they exceed 20 percent. The rule does not apply if the stock was held since the corporation's inception and no dividends were paid previously. Also, the nontaxed portion of dividends on certain "disqualified" preferred stock issued after July 10, 1989, is treated as an extraordinary dividend.

> *Example 14.22.* Pearls Jewelry Inc. purchased 1,000 shares of Long Shot Inc. for $20,000, 16 months ago. Long Shot declared a dividend of $3 per share. Pearls' taxable dividend was $900 ($3,000 less the 70 percent dividends-received deduction). Accordingly, if and when the stock is disposed of, its basis will be reduced by $2,100 ($3,000 − $900). If the fair market value of the stock was $30,000 or more the day before the ex-dividend date, no basis reduction would be required (10 percent of $30,000 is $3,000, thus there would not be an extraordinary dividend).

Tax Consequences to Distributing Corporation

Gain or Loss Recognition

A corporation that distributes property that has appreciated in value must recognize a gain at the time of distribution. The corporation is treated as if it had sold the property. The gain equals the property's fair market value less its adjusted basis. Code Sec. 311(b). However, the corporation does not recognize a loss if the property had declined in value. Also, the corporation recognizes no gain or loss if it distributes its own stock or stock rights to its shareholders. Code Sec. 311(a).

The character of the recognized gain depends on the property distributed; thus, it may be ordinary income, capital gain, or Section 1231 gain.

> *Example 14.23.* Jasper Corporation distributes land to Harold Cooper, its sole shareholder. The adjusted basis of the land is $25,000 and its fair market value is $47,000. Jasper Corporation must recognize a gain of $22,000 (presumably a capital gain). Harold's basis in the land is $47,000.

> *Example 14.24.* Assume the same facts in Example 14.23, except that the land's adjusted basis is $60,000. Jasper Corporation cannot recognize the $13,000 loss and Harold's basis in the land is only $47,000.

Depreciation Recapture

To the extent any gain would have been ordinary income because of depreciation recapture if the property had been sold for its fair market value, rather than distributed, ordinary income is recognized on a distribution. Code Secs. 291, 1245(a), and 1250(a). This also is true for property expensed under Code Sec. 179.

> *Example 14.25.* Arrow Inc. distributes an auto originally purchased for $9,000, but fully depreciated, to a shareholder when it is worth $2,500. Arrow will recognize $2,500 of ordinary income on the distribution. This result is independent of E&P (i.e., it does not matter how much, if any, of the distribution represents a dividend). The result would be the same if the auto was a bonus (compensation).

General Business Credit Recapture

A corporation also generally has to recognize gain where the distribution includes property on which the general business tax credit has been taken and property on which deductions subject to recapture have been taken. A distribution of property on which a general business tax credit was taken is considered a disposition of the property, subject to general business credit recapture. The amount of credit recaptured is based on the amount of time that asset has been held by the corporation. Code Sec. 50.

Installment Obligations

If the corporation sells property on a deferred payment plan, is using the installment method to report gain, and distributes the installment obligation while one or more installments are still unpaid, gain is accelerated. Code Sec. 453B(a). The gain equals the fair market value of the unpaid installments less their basis, and the character follows the property originally sold.

> *Example 14.26.* Arrow Inc. sold land held as an investment for $100,000 to an individual, payable $20,000 at the time of sale plus eight equal installments of $10,000 each, starting a year after closing, together with 11 percent interest on the loan balance. Since the basis in the land was $40,000 (40 percent of the selling price), the gross profit percentage is 60 percent. After collecting three annual installments, Arrow distributed the mortgage to its two shareholders as tenants in common when the fair market value of the note was $43,000.

Amount realized	$43,000
Basis in note (40% of $50,000)	20,000
Gain recognized	$23,000

The gain is a long-term capital gain since the land originally sold was a capital asset held long term at the time of the closing. The shareholders' basis in the note equals $43,000, its fair market value. If the note is collected in full, the shareholders will have to recognize $7,000 of ordinary income since the face value is $50,000 and collecting a note from an individual is not a sale or exchange. Code Sec. 1271(a)(1) and (b)(1).

Liabilities in Excess of Basis

A corporation might distribute property encumbered with a liability. If the distributed property is subject to a liability or the shareholders assume the liability, then the property's fair market value is treated as being not less than the amount of the liability. Code Sec. 311(b)(2). Thus, if the fair market value is less than the amount of the liability, then the liability is considered to be the property's fair market value.

Example 14.27. Arrow Inc. distributes a building with a basis of $15,000 and a value of $40,000, but subject to a nonrecourse liability of $60,000, to an individual shareholder. The corporation is deemed to have sold the property for the greater of $60,000 or $40,000, thus recognizing a gain of $45,000 ($60,000 − $15,000) of the same character as the building, for example, a Section 1231 gain, except for the portion, if any, representing depreciation recapture. The shareholder, however, has no dividend since the value does not exceed the liability. Nevertheless, the shareholder has a basis in the building of $60,000.

If the value of the building is $60,000, the shareholder still has no dividend, the corporation picks up $45,000 of gain, and the shareholder's basis is $60,000. If the value of the building is $80,000, the shareholder receives a dividend of $20,000 ($80,000 − $60,000) and a basis of $80,000, and the corporate gain is $65,000 ($80,000 − $15,000).

E&P Adjustments

The general rule is that E&P is reduced by the adjusted basis of the distributed property. Code Sec. 312(a). If the corporation distributes appreciated property, then E&P is increased by the appreciation in value and decreased by the property's fair market value. Code Sec. 312(b). (The appreciation produces a realized and recognized gain as noted previously. This gain is included in taxable income and subject to federal income taxes.) If the distributed property is subject to a liability or the shareholder assumes the liability, then this amount is subtracted from the amount used to decrease E&P (i.e., either fair market value of adjusted basis).

Example 14.28. Land with a basis of $20,000 and a value of $50,000 is distributed to an individual shareholder. The $30,000 gain is recognized by the corporation. Current E&P is increased by the gain of $30,000 and decreased by the fair market value, $50,000. The net decrease in current and accumulated E&P is simply equal to $20,000, the basis in the property prior to the distribution, but the distribution caused $30,000 of current income and E&P to be created.

Example 14.29. Same as Example 14.28, except the land is subject to a mortgage liability of $35,000. Current E&P is still increased by $30,000, the realized gain, but the decrease in E&P is reduced from $50,000 to $15,000 by the transferred liability. (The result would be the same if the shareholder had paid $35,000 in cash.)

Example 14.30. Same as Example 14.28, except the land has a basis of $50,000 and a value of $20,000. No loss is recognized, and E&P is reduced by the basis of $50,000.

If the corporation distributes its own debt obligation, E&P is reduced by the lesser of the principal amount or the "issue price" (fair market value). Code Sec. 312(a)(2).

Example 14.31. Bows and Arrows Inc. distributed an IOU with a face value of $20,000 and a fair market value of $15,000 to an individual shareholder. There is a dividend of $15,000 and an E&P reduction of $15,000. In addition, the shareholder has original issue discount of $5,000.

¶ 14,025   CONSTRUCTIVE DIVIDENDS

A constructive dividend is any tangible benefit in cash or property received by a shareholder in his or her capacity as such from the corporation where E&P exists. Dividends usually occur because the board of directors declared that they should be paid. However, this is not a necessary condition. A dividend can result from a variety of transactions. Sometimes this is due to shareholder and/or corporate ignorance (i.e., the shareholders were not attempting to circumvent dividend status) and on other occasions it is due to the direct efforts of the shareholder and/or corporation to disguise the dividends as something else. (The latter is done either to exclude income for the shareholder or provide deductions for the corporation or shareholder.) Regardless, in either situation (unintentional or intentional), the economic substance of the transaction will take precedence over its form, and if deemed so, will be treated as a dividend to the extent of current and accumulated E&P. This is a constructive dividend since no formal (actual) cash or property dividend has been declared or paid.

Examples of the most frequently encountered constructive dividends are:

1. *Unreasonable compensation and disallowed expenses.* If salaries or bonuses are paid in excess of "fair value," such excess may be disallowed as a compensation expense and taxed as a dividend to the shareholder-employee. This is true even though dividends are paid as well. The problem may be reduced by a repayment contract between the corporation and the shareholder. Similarly, if the corporation reimburses the employee-shareholder for travel and entertainment expenses found to be personal in nature, a dividend may result. The corporation is denied a deduction for the excess portion.

2. *Corporate satisfaction of shareholder liabilities.* If a corporation makes a third-party payment to the creditor of a shareholder, a dividend may result.

3. *Shareholder loans.* A loan to a shareholder may be treated as a dividend unless it appears to be a loan to an independent third party. Thus, the loan should be evidenced by a note, be secured, carry a fair interest rate, and have a repayment schedule. Demand loans that stay on the books are automatically suspect.

4. *Corporate loans.* A loan from a shareholder might be reclassified as equity. If so, any "interest" payments will be reclassified as dividends.

5. *Free personal use of corporate property.* Obvious examples include the use of corporate autos, living quarters, recreational facilities, and the like. Dividend income is equal to the fair rental value of the property.

6. *Bargain sales and rentals to the shareholder or persons related to the shareholder.* Sometimes a corporation may sell property to a shareholder for an amount that is less than the fair market value or may rent property to a shareholder for less than its fair rental value. The difference between the price or rent paid and fair market or rental value may be treated as a dividend.

7. *Premium sales and rentals to the corporation.* If a corporation purchases property from a shareholder at a price greater than the property's fair market value, then the excess may be treated as a dividend. Similarly, if a corporation leases property from a shareholder at an excessive rental rate, then the excess over the fair market value may be treated as a dividend.

Example 14.32. Jim Simms borrows $20,000 without interest from his wholly owned corporation, VIP Inc. If VIP has ample E&P and the formalities of an arm's-length loan transaction are not carried out, a dividend of $20,000 will result. Even if treated as a bona fide debt, interest must be imputed at the "applicable federal rate" under Code Sec. 7872 with the following results:

1. VIP has interest income and has constructively paid a nondeductible dividend (E&P goes up and down by the same amount, with the net effect being a reduction for taxes paid on the imputed interest income).

2. Jim has dividend income equal to the imputed interest he did not pay. The interest expense may be deductible in whole or in part. If it is personal interest, then it is not deductible.

¶ 14,032   DISTRIBUTIONS OF STOCK DIVIDENDS

In general, if shareholders receive stock in proportion to their ownership interest, then they are not taxable because the shareholders are in the same economic position after the distribution as they were prior to it. Thus, a 10 percent shareholder still owns 10 percent of a corporation after a distribution in which all shareholders have received pro rata stock dividends. The nontaxability of pro rata distributions based on this logic was established by the Supreme Court. *Eisner v. Macomber,* 1 USTC ¶ 32,252, 252 U.S. 189, 40 S.Ct. 189 (1920).

Following *Eisner v. Macomber,* the proportionate test was added to the Internal Revenue Code and it still applies. The general rule is that gross income does not include stock distributions made by a corporation to its shareholders with respect to its stock. Code Sec. 305. However, there are several exceptions:

1. Distributions which, at the option of the shareholders, are payable in either stock or property.

2. Disproportionate distributions whereby some shareholders receive property and other shareholders receive an increase in their proportionate share in the assets or E&P of the corporation.

3. Distributions whereby some common stock shareholders receive preferred stock and other common stock shareholders receive common stock.

4. Distributions on preferred stock, other than an increase in the conversion ratio of convertible preferred stock made solely to take account of a stock dividend or stock split with respect to stock into which the preferred stock is convertible.

5. Distributions of convertible preferred stock, unless it can be shown that such distributions will not produce disproportionate distributions as described in (2), above.

Tax-Free Stock Distributions

If the stock dividend is not taxable, then the total basis of the old stock is allocated between the old and the new stock. Code Sec. 307(a). The holding period of the new stock takes on the holding period of the old stock. Code Sec. 1223(5). Note that a nontaxable stock dividend is the same as a stock split. Thus, a six-for-five split is the same as a 20 percent stock dividend because an additional share is received for each five held.

If the old shares and the new shares are not identical, then the total basis of the old shares is allocated to the old and new shares based on their relative fair market values. The holding period for the old and new shares still will refer back to the original (old) shares.

Example 14.33. Jack Jones purchased 100 common shares in Motherlode Inc. for $1,200. His basis is $12 a share. Five years later, he received a tax-free stock dividend of 20 percent (i.e., 20 additional shares). His $1,200 basis is unchanged, but his basis per share equals $10 ($1,200/120). The holding period of the new shares refers back to the original purchase.

Example 14.34. Same as Example 14.33, but Jack received 20 shares of preferred stock worth $700 tax free at a time when his 100 shares of common stock were worth $1,400. His $1,200 basis must now be allocated between the common and the preferred stock based on relative fair market values.

Common: ($1,400/$2,100) × $1,200 = $800
Preferred: ($ 700/$2,100) × $1,200 = $400

The holding period of the common stock tacks on to that of the preferred stock.

A nontaxable stock dividend does not affect the distributing corporation's E&P. Since "nothing is distributed," E&P is not reduced.

Taxable Stock Dividends

If a shareholder receives a taxable stock dividend, then the amount of the distribution is equal to the stock's fair market value at the date of the distribution. The shareholder has income to the extent of the corporation's current and accumulated E&P. The shareholder's basis in the stock is its fair market value on the distribution date and the holding period begins on the date of receipt.

The distributing corporation reduces E&P by the fair market value of the stock and does not recognize a gain or loss on the distribution.

Example 14.35. Derek Stewart owns 100 shares of Speer Corporation which he acquired on January 17, 1988, for $10,000. On March 1, 1998, Derek received 10 shares of Speer Corporation stock in a taxable distribution. The fair market value of the stock on March 1, 1998, was $150 per share. Speer Corporation's current E&P for 1998 was $45,000. Derek has taxable income of $1,500 ($150 × 10). His basis in the original shares remains at $10,000. His basis in the new shares is $1,500. His holding period in the new shares begins on March 1, 1998. Speer Corporation's E&P is decreased by $1,500.

Distributions Payable in Stock or Money

Any time any shareholder has an option to elect whether to receive a stock dividend or a property dividend, such as cash, then the distribution of stock or stock rights is taxable to all shareholders under Code Sec. 301. Section 305(b)(1) brings the distribution within Code Sec. 301 for all shareholders regardless of (1) whether all or none of the shareholders exercise the option or are entitled to the election, (2) whether the election is exercised or exercisable before or after the board of directors declares the dividend, and (3) whether the source of the election arises from the corporate charter, director declaration, or other circumstances.

Example 14.36. General Corporation declares a dividend payable in shares of stock at the rate of one additional share for each common share presently held. The dividend is not taxable.

Example 14.37. Suppose in Example 14.36, one shareholder persuades the board of directors to allow an election of taking either the one additional share for each common share held or a $12 dividend. If no election is made, the shareholder also receives stock. The dividend is taxable to all the shareholders.

Disproportionate Distributions

A distribution may result from an increase in the proportionate interest in the assets or earnings and profits of a corporation for some shareholders and the receipt of money or other property by the other shareholders. Code Sec. 305(b)(2) causes this distribution to be taxable under Code Sec. 301 with the possible exception of cash in lieu of fractional shares.

Example 14.38. Corporation C has ten shares each of class A and class B common stock authorized and issued. It declares a 100 percent stock dividend on the class A stock and a cash dividend on class B stock. Prior to the distributions, the ratio of class A to class B was 1 to 1. After the distributions, the ratio is 2 to 1. Since the proportionate ownership of class A stock has gone from 1/2 to 2/3, the additional shares of class A stock are taxable as ordinary income to the shareholders of the corporation when they are received or accrued by them.

Class A and class B stock distributions do not have to be paid at the same time in order for the class A stock dividend to be taxable. One class might be paid quarterly and the other annually, resulting in a taxable event for all. In order to guarantee that the class A stock dividends are nontaxable, Reg. § 1.305-3(b)(4) provides that no cash dividends can be paid for at least 36 months before and after the stock dividend and no preconceived plan can exist. Otherwise, the cash dividends and stock dividends will be linked together under the step transaction doctrine as a "series distribution" and all will be taxable.

Example 14.39. Tindine Corporation paid cash dividends to some of its shareholders on February 15, 1997. On April 5, 1998, Tindine distributed its stock to other shareholders, resulting in an increase in their proportionate interests. The stock dividend will be taxable to the shareholders. If the cash distributions occurred on February 15, 1995, then the 36-month rule would not affect the stock distribution because it occurred more than 37 months later.

Sometimes a corporation will find that issuing and transferring of fractional share is troublesome, expensive, and inconvenient. A corporation may declare a dividend payable in stock and distribute cash in lieu of fractional shares. Under Reg. § 1.305-3(c), such a distribution does not violate Code Sec. 305(b)(2), providing the total amount of cash distributed is 5 percent or less of the fair market value of the stock distributed. Cash received for a fractional share represents the sale of the fractional shares and gain or loss must be reported. If cash is received in lieu of fractional shares, the amount received in cash is dividend income.

Example 14.40. Corporation R issues a stock dividend of one additional common share for every five shares. The total of outstanding shares is 250, of which Jake owns 103, Mike owns 106, and Jane owns 41. Fifty new shares could be distributed (250/5), with Jake receiving 20 3/5, Mike 21 1/5, and Jane 8 1/5. The value of the new shares is $10 per share. The corporation can give Jake $6,

Mike $2, and Jane $2 rather than 3/5, 1/5, and 1/5 of a share, respectively, and still guarantee that the distribution is not taxable to the shareholders. The total value of the distribution is $500 (50 × 10), and 5 percent of $500 is $25. Since the total cash to be paid is $10, the distribution of the shares is nontaxable under Reg. § 1.305-3(c)(2). Jake, Mike, and Jane should report the $6, $2, and $2 as dividend income.

Distributions of Common and Preferred Stock

When some common shareholders receive preferred stock and the other shareholders receive common stock, the distribution falls under Code Sec. 305(b)(3) and is taxable. The same result arises when a situation is created where the end product may have both preferred and common stock in the distribution. The "series of distribution" rules previously discussed also apply to Code Sec. 305(b)(3).

Example 14.41. Valley Corporation has only common stock. A dividend of newly created preferred stock is declared. The newly created preferred stock can be converted into common stock within six months. This transaction falls within Code Sec. 305(b)(3) since it is reasonable to anticipate that, within a short period of time, some shareholders will be exercising this conversion right and others will not (i.e., the end product may have both preferred and common stock in the distribution).

Distributions of Preferred Stock

Section 305(b)(4) treats a distribution of preferred stock as a taxable event under Code Sec. 301 unless the distribution is made in regard to convertible preferred stock in order to take into account a stock dividend that would otherwise result in the dilution of the conversion of rights.

Example 14.42. The shareholders in Sun Corporation may convert their preferred stock into common stock in a one-for-one swap. The common stockholders received a two-for-one stock split. Can the corporation issue convertible preferred stock to the shareholders without being taxable under Code Sec. 305(b)(4)? Yes, if the preferred stock is also split two for one so that no dilution of the conversion right occurs.

According to Reg. § 1.305-5, the distinguishing feature of "preferred stock" for Code Sec. 305(b)(4) purposes is not its privileged position in relation to other classes of stock, but that such privileged position is limited and that such stock does not participate in corporate growth to any significant extent.

Distributions of Convertible Preferred Stock

Under Code Sec. 305(b)(5), distributions of convertible preferred stock are taxable unless the corporation shows that no disproportionate distribution has occurred. A disproportionate distribution is not likely to occur when (1) the conversion rights run for many years, (2) the dividend rate is consistent with market conditions at the time of the distribution, and (3) predictions as to the time and extent of any stock conversion cannot be made. Reg. § 1.305-6(a)(2).

> *Example 14.43.* Sky Corporation issues newly authorized convertible preferred stock and distributes the stock as a dividend. The preferred stock has a normal dividend rate of 5 percent at issuance and could be converted into common stock any time in the next 20 years. The distribution is not taxable.

A disproportionate distribution is likely to occur when (1) the conversion right must be exercised shortly after the date of the distribution of stock, and (2) factors such as dividend rates, redemption provisions, and marketability of conversion stock and of convertible stock indicate that some shareholders will exercise their rights. Reg. § 1.305-6(a)(3).

> *Example 14.44.* On February 8, Land Corporation declared a dividend on convertible preferred stock that a shareholder could convert into common stock before July 8. An investment company has agreed to purchase any preferred stock from any shareholders who do not wish to convert their shares to common stock. This dividend is taxable. A reasonable assumption is that part of the shareholders will convert and some will not. This situation results in a receipt of property by some shareholders and an increase in the proportionate interest of the rest.

¶ 14,035   STOCK RIGHTS

The holder of stock rights has the option of acquiring new shares of stock in a corporation within a defined period and at a specific price which is usually below the stock's fair market value when the rights were issued. The same rules and regulations that govern stock dividends also govern stock rights. Thus, distributions of stock rights are nontaxable if they are proportionate. The distributions are taxable if disproportionate or if they fall under the exceptions in Code Sec. 305(b).

Tax-Free Distributions of Stock Rights

Tax-free rights are treated the same as tax-free stock splits and stock dividends. The holding period refers back to the time the old stock was acquired, and the basis is equal to an allocated basis. The basis in the rights equals the cost basis of the old stock times the proportion of the fair market value of the rights at the time of the distribution over the total fair market value of the old stock and the rights at that time. However, unlike the case of stock dividends, the shareholder may choose to give the rights a zero basis if their value constitutes less than 15 percent of the value of the old stock at the time of the distribution. Code Sec. 307(b)(1).

If the rights are allocated a basis, then a subsequent sale of the rights will produce a realized gain or loss equal to the selling price minus the allocated basis. The holding period is equal to the holding period of the stock. Alternatively, if the rights are exercised, then the basis of the acquired stock is equal to its cost plus the basis allocated to the rights. The holding period of the acquired stock (regardless of whether the rights were taxable or nontaxable) begins on the date the rights are exercised. Finally, if the rights elapse (i.e., they are not sold or exercised), then the allocated basis is added back to the basis of the original shares of stock.

Distributions of nontaxable stock rights do not affect the corporation's E&P. Also, it does not recognize a gain or loss on the distribution.

Example 14.45. A shareholder owns 100 shares of stock with a basis of $1,200 and a value of $2,100. The shareholder receives 50 tax-free rights worth $700. The value of the rights is not less than 15 percent of the stock ($700 ÷ $2,100 = 33⅓ percent); thus, a basis must be allocated to the rights. The basis in the rights equals ($1,200 × (700 ÷ $2,800)), or $300. Thus, the basis in the stock is reduced to $900. The holding period of the rights dates back to that of the stock. If the shareholder sells the rights for $500, then a gain of $200 ($500 − $300) results. If the selling price is $140, then a $160 loss ($140 − $300) results.

Example 14.46. The shareholder owns a block of stock purchased for $5,000, but worth $6,000. A nontaxable distribution of rights worth $100 is received, and promptly sold. Since the value of the rights is less than 15 percent of the value of the stock ($100 ÷ $6,000 = 1.67 percent), no allocation is required. If the shareholder elects to allocate basis to the rights, the basis is ($5,000 × ($100 ÷ $6,100)), or $82. By making the election, the shareholder's gain becomes only $18, rather than the full $100. The shareholder's basis in the stock is reduced correspondingly to $4,918.

Taxable Distributions of Stock Rights

If the distribution of stock rights is taxable, for example, because of a choice of cash or rights, then the amount of the distribution is equal to the fair market value of the rights. Dividend income results to the extent of the corporation's current and accumulated E&P. The shareholder's basis in the rights equals their fair market value and the holding period for the rights begins at the date of the distribution. The distributing corporation reduces E&P by the fair market value of the stock rights at the date of the distribution.

KEYSTONE PROBLEM

Lyle Corporation began operations in 1996. Current E&P in 1996 was a negative $80,000. In 1997, current E&P was a negative $40,000. Lyle Corporation expects to be profitable in 1998 and all subsequent years, and it projects current E&P to be a positive $40,000 in 1998, $50,000 in 1999, and $60,000 in 2000. Lyle Corporation estimates that starting in 1998 it will have $40,000 in cash each year available for dividend distributions. Lyle Corporation is considering three alternative distribution patterns: (1) $40,000 in each of the three years; (2) zero in 1998, $80,000 in 1999, and $40,000 in 2000; and (3) zero in 1998 and 1999 and $120,000 in 2000. Which distribution pattern should be elected? Why?

Stock Redemptions

¶ 14,101   CLASSIFICATIONS FOR TAX TREATMENT

A stock redemption occurs when a corporation acquires its stock from its shareholders in return for cash or property. The surrender of stock may be treated as a sale or exchange, in which case the shareholders will recognize a gain or loss equal to the difference between the fair market value of the property received minus the stock's adjusted basis. Alternatively, the surrender of stock may be classified as a dividend and be taxable as ordinary income to the extent of the redeeming corporation's current and accumulated E&P.

There are numerous reasons why stock redemptions occur. For example, the shareholder may want to terminate all interest in a corporation. Instead of selling the stock to outsiders or current shareholders, it may be easier to sell the stock to the corporation. This would enable the current shareholders to retain complete control of the corporation without using their own funds. Similarly, the shareholder may not be able to find an outside buyer (especially, if the corporation is small and/or closely held). If a shareholder dies, it might be easier for the estate to sell the stock to the corporation or the corporation might be required to buy the stock under a buy-sell agreement. Finally, the corporation might believe that its best investment choice is to "invest in itself" and will buy its own stock and hold this stock in treasury for future needs.

Whether the redemption is treated as a sale or exchange or as a dividend depends on numerous factors. The rationale underlying the statute dealing with stock redemptions is to prevent the shareholders from converting ordinary income (dividends) into capital gains (from the sale or exchange of stock). The statute enables shareholders to determine the amount and type of income derived as a result of the redemption, their basis and holding period in the property received in the redemption, and their basis in the stock still owned. The redeeming corporation must determine whether it recognizes a gain or loss on the property transferred to shareholders in the redemption and how E&P is affected by the redemption.

¶ 14,103   SALE OR EXCHANGE TREATMENT

Code Sec. 317(b) indicates that a redemption occurs if the corporation acquires its stock from a shareholder in exchange for the property, regardless of whether the stock is cancelled, retired, or held as treasury stock. Code Secs. 302 and 303 govern the tax treatment of most redemptions. A redemption may be treated as an exchange of the stock or as a dividend. Since a sale or exchange of stock for payment would result in tax-free return of basis plus capital gain treatment of any gain realized if all conditions are met, it is clearly to the advantage of most taxpayers to have the redemption treated as an exchange. In addition to producing lower income, the capital gain could be used to offset capital losses. The following major types of stock redemptions qualify for exchange treatment:

1. The redemption must not be essentially equivalent to a dividend. Code Sec. 302(b)(1).

2. The redemption must be substantially disproportionate with respect to the shareholder. Code Sec. 302(b)(2).

3. The redemption must be in complete termination of the shareholder's interest in the corporation. Code Sec. 302(b)(3).

4. The redemption must be made to noncorporate shareholders in partial liquidation. Code Sec. 302(b)(4).

5. The redemption must be for the purpose of paying shareholder death taxes. Code Sec. 303.

If any of these conditions is met, then the redemption escapes the ordinary income treatment of dividends.

Where a redemption is treated as a dividend, the shareholder's basis in the stock redeemed attaches to the remaining stock. This basis attaches to other stock held by the taxpayer or to any stock the taxpayer is considered to own constructively. Reg. § 1.302-2(c).

Example 14.47. Jenny Park owns 100 shares of Xanadu Corporation which she acquired in 1988 for $10,000. On March 20, 1998, Xanadu redeemed 80 of her shares in return for $12,000. If the redemption is treated as an exchange, then Jenny has a $4,000 long-term capital gain ($12,000 − $8,000). If Jenny had received property worth $12,000 instead of cash, then she still would have a $4,000 long-term capital gain. In addition, her basis in the property would be $12,000, its fair market value, and the holding period would begin on March 20, 1998.

Example 14.48. Assume the same facts as Example 14.47, except that the redemption does not qualify as an exchange and that Xanadu's current E&P is $35,000. Jenny would have dividend income of $12,000. Her basis in the remaining 20 shares would be equal to $10,000, their original basis of $2,000 (20 shares × $100 per share) plus the $8,000 basis of the 80 shares surrendered in the redemption. If Jenny had received property worth $12,000 instead of cash, then she still would have $12,000 of dividend income. Her basis in the property would be $12,000, and the holding period would begin on March 20, 1998.

TAX PLANNING POINTER

A corporate shareholder normally prefers that a distribution be treated as a dividend, rather than a redemption. The corporation normally can reduce dividend income by the dividends-received deduction.

Example 14.49. Nibble Corporation owns 5 percent (200 shares) of Smackers Company which it acquired several years ago for $10,000 ($50 per share). Smackers redeems 160 of Nibble's shares in exchange for $32,000 ($200 per share). Smackers' current E&P

is $50,000. If the redemption is treated as an exchange, then Nibble has a $24,000 long-term capital gain ($32,000 − $8,000). However, if the redemption is treated as a dividend, then Nibble has received a $32,000 dividend but also is allowed a 70 percent dividends-received deduction. Assuming the taxable income constraint does not apply, this deduction is $22,400, producing a net increase in taxable income of $9,600, which is much less than the $24,000 long-term capital gain.

¶ 14,105   CONSTRUCTIVE OWNERSHIP RULES

The main tool in preventing sale or exchange treatment when a redemption is made is to require a "real" reduction in stock ownership, counting both actual and constructive ownership. The status of redemptions is controlled under Code Sec. 302(b)(1), (2), (3), and (4), which provide tests which look at ownership interest before and after the redemption. Ownership is defined as shares actually owned and those constructively owned (i.e., one shareholder's shares may be attributed to another shareholder for purposes of determining ownership interest).

The attribution rules are found in Code Sec. 318 and are summarized below:

1. An individual is deemed to own stock held by the individual's family, defined as a spouse, children, grandchildren, and parents. Brothers, sisters, and grandparents are not considered family members for Code Sec. 318 attribution purposes.

2. Partners and beneficiaries are deemed to own stock held by partnerships, estates, and trusts in proportion to their interests and vice versa. Thus, there is attribution to and from entities.

3. There is attribution to and from corporations, but only if the shareholder owns at least 50 percent of the value of the corporate stock.

4. Stock constructively owned is deemed to be directly owned for purposes of reattribution, with two exceptions:

    a. Stock owned indirectly by an individual because of family attribution cannot be reattributed to another family member.

    b. Stock constructively owned by entities and held by owners and beneficiaries will not be reattributed to other owners or beneficiaries.

5. The owner of an option to buy stock is deemed to own such stock.

Example 14.50. A corporation is owned by two parents and five children who are all married. Each parent owns 100 percent of the corporation, directly or indirectly. However, each child's spouse indirectly owns only what the child owns since family attribution does not go indirect twice, and each child indirectly owns only what the parents own.

Example 14.51. A corporation is owned 40 percent by a father and 60 percent by an irrevocable trust with his two children as equal beneficiaries. The children are deemed to own the 60 percent the trust owns *and* the 40 percent the father owns. Thus, each child is deemed to own 70 percent of the corporation, the 30 percent owned by the trust and the 40 percent owned by the father. A child is *not* deemed to own stock directly or indirectly owned by a sibling. The father is deemed to own 100 percent of the stock, his 40 percent, and the 60 percent owned constructively by his children. The trust owns 60 percent directly and 40 percent indirectly for a total of 100 percent.

¶ 14,111   REDEMPTIONS NOT EQUIVALENT TO DIVIDENDS

Section 302(b)(1) provides for exchange treatment if the redemption is not essentially equivalent to a dividend. There is no specific test to determine whether a redemption meets this requirement and this has led to substantial litigation. It remains an imprecise test depending on the facts and circumstances of each case.

The imprecision in this test is intentional. Congress did not want these requirements to be too restrictive and this test was added to enable redemptions of preferred stock to qualify as exchanges. See S. Rep. No. 1622, 83rd Cong., 2d Sess., at 44.

Several court cases have been instrumental in establishing criteria to determine whether the redemption is not essentially equivalent to a dividend. The Supreme Court has indicated that there must be a meaningful reduction of the shareholder's proportionate interest. It further established that the constructive ownership rules of Code Sec. 318 will apply in determining ownership prior to and after the distribution. Finally, it indicated that a business purpose for the redemption does not make the redemption not essentially equivalent to a dividend—the key test is whether a meaningful reduction in the shareholder's proportionate interest occurred. *M.P. Davis,* 70-1 USTC ¶ 9289, 397 U.S. 301, 90 S.Ct. 1041 (1970). What constitutes a meaningful reduction was not defined.

The Tax Court has indicated that redemptions leading to a loss of control by the redeeming shareholder will qualify as meaningful reductions under Code Sec. 302(b)(1). *J. Paparo,* 71 TC 692, CCH Dec. 35,856 (1979). Thus, a reduction in stock ownership from 57 percent to 50 percent was considered a meaningful reduction since the shareholder no longer had control. Rev. Rul. 75-502, 1975-2 CB 111. Additionally, redemptions of minority shareholders' interests may fall under this test. The IRS has ruled that a reduction from 27 percent to 22 percent was a meaningful reduction. Rev. Rul. 76-364, 1976-2 CB 91.

Example 14.52. Mr. and Mrs. Jones each own 25 percent of Daniels Corporation. Each of their two children also own 25 percent of Daniels Corporation. In 1998, most of Mr. Jones's shares are redeemed by the corporation for business reasons. Mr. Jones directly and indirectly owned 100 percent of Daniels Corporation before and after the redemption. Thus, no meaningful reduction in ownership interest has occurred.

Example 14.53. On June 5, 1998, Julie Greene owns 60 percent of Cagy Corporation. Cagy redeems some of Julie's stock on June 6, 1998, thereby bringing her interest to 47 percent. Since Julie has lost a controlling interest in the corporation, this redemption qualifies under Code Sec. 302(b)(1). A meaningful reduction in ownership interest has occurred; the redemption is not essentially equivalent to a dividend.

Much uncertainty remains under Code Sec. 302(b)(1). If shareholders want exchange treatment, then they are best advised to try to qualify under another test (e.g., Code Sec. 302(b)(2)). Code Sec. 302(b)(1) remains an option in redemptions of preferred stock (Reg. § 1.302-2(a)) or in situations where a controlling interest is lost.

¶ 14,115 SUBSTANTIALLY DISPROPORTIONATE REDEMPTIONS

Code Sec. 302(b)(2) provides three mechanical tests to determine if a redemption is substantially disproportionate. If these tests are met, then the redemption is treated as an exchange. Thus, it is relatively clear and easy to determine if a redemption qualifies for exchange treatment under Code Sec. 302(b)(2). As with Code Sec. 302(b)(1), these tests are applied on a shareholder-by-shareholder basis and the constructive ownership rules under Code Sec. 318 apply. The three tests are:

1. After the redemption, the shareholder must hold less than 50 percent of the outstanding voting stock.

2. The shareholder's proportionate interest in the outstanding voting stock after the redemption must be less than 80 percent of what it was prior to the redemption.

3. After the redemption, the stockholder's proportionate interest in the outstanding common stock must be less than 80 percent of what it was prior to the redemption. The 80 percent determination is made using fair market value if there is more than one class of stock. If there is only one class of stock, then tests 2 and 3 are the same.

Calculation of the first test is relatively straightforward. The second test can be met by calculating two ratios:

1. Voting stock owned by stockholder divided by the total voting stock of the corporation equals percent (before redemption)

2. Voting stock owned by stockholder divided by the total voting stock of the corporation equals percent (after redemption)

If ratio (2) is less than 80 percent of ratio (1), the distribution is substantially disproportionate and is eligible for capital gain treatment. The third test is handled similarly, except that common stock is substituted for the voting stock.

Example 14.54. Leonard Corporation has four unrelated shareholders, Lynn, David, Sara, and Karen. Each shareholder owns 100 shares of common stock. On June 15, 1998, Leonard redeemed 55 shares from Lynn, 25 shares from David, and 20 shares from Sara. This redemption is substantially disproportionate with respect to Lynn only. David and Sara have dividend distributions.

Owner	Ownership Before Redemption		Ownership After Redemption		Less than 80 Percent Ownership Test
	Shares	Percentage	Shares	Percentage	
Lynn	100	25%	45	15%	15/25 = 60%
David	100	25%	75	25%	25/25 = 100%
Sara	100	25%	80	27%	27/25 = 108%
Karen	100	25%	100	33%	33/25 = 132%
Total	400	100%	300	100%	

All shareholders meet this first test (less than 50 percent ownership of the outstanding voting stock after the redemption). However, only Lynn meets the less than 80 percent ownership test. Her percent ownership after the redemption divided by her percent ownership before the distribution is 60 percent. David's percent is 100 and Sara's is 108 percent.

Example 14.55. Assume the same facts as in Example 14.54, except that Lynn and David are husband and wife. In this case, the redemption is not substantially disproportionate with respect to Lynn, David, or Sara.

Owner	Ownership Before Redemption		Ownership After Redemption		Less than 80 Percent Ownership Test
	Shares	Percentage	Shares	Percentage	
Lynn	200	50%	120	40%	40/50 = 80%
David	200	50%	120	40%	40/50 = 80%
Sara	100	25%	80	27%	27/25 = 108%
Karen	100	25%	100	33%	33/25 = 132%
Total	400 *	100%	300 *	100%	

* Although there is attribution between Lynn and David, the total number of shares outstanding remains at 400 before the redemption and 300 after it.

All shareholders meet the first test (less than 50 percent ownership after the redemption). However, none meet the less than 80 percent ownership test. Lynn's and David's ownership percentages are exactly 80 percent, not less than 80 percent.

If a disproportionate redemption is one in a series of redemptions which, in the aggregate, will not be disproportionate to any shareholder, then the requirements of Code Sec. 302(b)(2) will not be met. The IRS can use the step transaction doctrine to collapse a series of redemptions into one and evaluate it accordingly.

Example 14.56. Assume the same facts as in Example 14.54, except that in 1999 Leonard Corporation redeemed 20 shares from Sara and 55 shares from Karen. If these redemptions are collapsed with the redemptions in 1998, then not only are the redemptions in 1999 not substantially disproportionate but the 1998 redemptions are reevaluated and also will not qualify as substantially disproportionate.

Owner	Ownership Before Redemption		Ownership After Redemption		Less than 80 Percent Ownership Test
	Shares	Percentage	Shares	Percentage	
Lynn	100	25%	45	20%	20/25 = 80%
David	100	25%	75	33%	33/25 = 132%
Sara	100	25%	60	27%	27/25 = 108%
Karen	100	25%	45	20%	20/25 = 80%
Total	400	100%	225	100%	

¶ 14,121 COMPLETE TERMINATION OF SHAREHOLDER'S INTEREST

A shareholder receives sale or exchange treatment under Code Sec. 302(b)(3) if the shareholder's interest in a corporation is completely terminated. As with redemptions under Code Sec. 302(b)(1) and (2), this test is at the shareholder level and is done on a shareholder-by-shareholder basis. At first glance, it appears that a complete termination of an interest also satisfies the three mechanical tests under Code Sec. 302(b)(2) and, therefore, qualifies as a substantially disproportionate redemption. If all shareholders are unrelated (under Code Sec. 318), then, in fact, this is the result (i.e., it meets the requirements of Code Sec. 302(b)(2) and (3)).

Example 14.57. Pat and Cooper are unrelated and each owns 50 shares in a corporation. The corporation redeems all of Pat's shares. This is a complete redemption of all of Pat's shares and qualifies for sale or exchange treatment. Pat will be allowed to reduce the proceeds from the sale by her basis in the shares, with the difference being capital gain or loss. Of course, this redemption would also qualify under the disproportionate rules of Code Sec. 302(b)(2).

If the shareholders are related then the constructive ownership rules of Code Sec. 318 may preclude sale or exchange treatment. A major difference between redemptions under Code Sec. 302(b)(2) and Code Sec. 302(b)(3) is that under certain circumstances the family attribution rules are waived if the redemption is a complete termination of a shareholder's interest. Code Sec. 302(c)(2). Thus, family attribution may disqualify the redemption from being substantially disproportionate but will not cause it to fail the test for a complete termination of a shareholder's interest.

Example 14.58. A family corporation is owned 60 percent by the father, 30 percent by the mother, and 10 percent by their only child. Each shareholder is deemed to own 100 percent of the corporation because of the attribution rules. The redemption of any shareholder's stock by the corporation would still leave that shareholder with deemed ownership of 100 percent of the stock, and thus the disproportionate redemption rules of Code Sec. 302(b)(2) would not apply. However, if, for example, the child's interest is completely terminated and the conditions below are met, then family attribution will be waived. As such, the redemption will receive sale or exchange treatment because it qualifies under Code Sec. 302(b)(3).

The family attribution rules under Code Sec. 318(a)(1) are waived if an agreement is filed in which the terminating shareholder agrees to sever almost every connection with the corporation for 10 years. The agreement also constitutes authority to keep the statute of limitations open so that the IRS can, if the contract is broken, go back and assess the tax, plus interest, and penalties on the retroactive dividend. The agreement is attached to the tax return for the year in which the redemption occurred. The shareholder also must agree to notify the IRS if an interest in acquired within the 10-year period.

Here is a checklist of what the redeemed shareholder can or cannot do during the 10-year period following the complete redemption:

1. *Cannot* retain an ownership interest in the corporation.

2. *Cannot* be or become an officer, director, or employee of the corporation.

3. *Can* be a creditor of the corporation, for example, to facilitate a deferred payment sale of the stock to the corporation, but the stock cannot be pledged as security for the loan.

4. *Can* inherit stock in the corporation any time and keep it.

5. *Cannot* be a "consultant" if the shareholder retains effective direction and control.

6. *Can* be an independent contractor, but even here there is a danger, particularly if the corporation is the shareholder's only client and/or the fee is not "fair."

7. *Cannot* do directly what cannot be done indirectly, for example, through a controlled partnership or corporation.

8. *Cannot* acquire a prohibited interest in the parent, subsidiary, or successor of the redeeming corporation.

9. *Can* be a trustee of the corporate pension plan, unless the shareholder is a plan beneficiary.

10. *Can* have free office space unless it is for future services.

The bottom line is that the redeemed shareholder is limited to being a creditor, an infrequent bona fide independent contractor, or an uncompensated advisor. If a shareholder's interest is completely terminated and the redemption is invalid, then the basis of the redeemed stock is added to the basis of the stock of the shareholders who caused the redemption to be invalid (i.e., the related parties).

Example 14.59. Fred Frome owns 40 percent of the only class of stock in Fred and Sons Cooling Co. His three sons, Sam, Steve, and Seth, own 20 percent each. Fred acquired his stock in 1980 for $10,000. The three sons acquired their interests in 1980 for $5,000 each. The corporation buys Fred's stock for $50,000, amply covered by earnings and profits. If Fred does not file the 10-year agreement, he still owns 100 percent of the stock after applying the constructive ownership rules in Code Sec. 318. He will, therefore, have a dividend of $50,000 and his basis in the stock will disappear as to him, regardless of amount, since there is no direct ownership of stock to which it can attach. It will, however, be added to the sons' bases. Reg. § 1.302-2(c). Thus, each son's basis in his stock will be $8,333 ($5,000 + $3,333). The same result will follow retroactively if Fred files the 10-year agreement but becomes a shareholder, officer, director, or employee before its expiration.

However, if the 10-year agreement is filed *and* not violated, a sale or exchange of stock has taken place. He will recognize a long-term capital gain of $40,000 ($50,000 − $10,000).

Entities, such as estates and trusts, may also waive family attribution. Both the entity and the beneficiaries must meet the complete redemption and the 10-year restriction rules and agree to be jointly and severally liable for any tax, plus additions to the tax, resulting from a breach. Code Sec. 302(c)(2)(C).

Family attribution rules will not be waived in two circumstances. Code Sec. 302(c)(2)(B). First, the family attribution rules will not be waived if any portion of the redeemed stock was acquired directly or indirectly within the 10-year period ending on the date of the distribution by the redeemed shareholder from a person whose stock would be attributable to that shareholder under Code Sec. 318(a). This provision is designed to prevent a shareholder from transferring stock to a related party followed by the corporation redeeming the stock from the related party in a complete termination of interest, and, therefore, producing capital gain.

Example 14.60. Assume that a father owns 100 percent (100 shares) of a corporation and transfers 20 shares to his daughter. Her 20 shares are subsequently redeemed by the corporation. If this rule did not apply, the father will have converted ordinary income (dividends) into capital gains (sale or exchange treatment on the redemption).

The second circumstance where the family attribution rules will not be waived occurs if a related party (under Code Sec. 318(a)) owns stock that was acquired from the redeeming shareholder within the 10 previous years unless such stock also is redeemed in the same transaction. This provision is designed to prevent shareholders from receiving sale or exchange treatment by transferring some of their stock to a related party, and following this with a redemption of their remaining shares, (i.e., the shares not transferred).

Example 14.61. Mother owns 100 shares of Dungy Corporation and transfers 60 shares to her daughter. Subsequently mother's 40 shares are redeemed by Dungy. The family attribution rules will not be waived; therefore, mother does not receive sale or exchange treatment.

TAX PLANNING POINTER ▼

When incorporating a sole proprietorship tax free under Code Sec. 351, the foresighted owner should keep Code Sec. 302(b)(3) in mind. As a result, the owner's spouse and/or children should be given stock in the corporation, at least a minority interest. Local law often requires at least three incorporators, in any event. If the business is successful, the spouse and/or children may be redeemed out by the corporation under sale or exchange rules if a 10-year agreement is filed. It should be noted that there is a 10-year waiting period before the redemption can take place with the desired result. Code Sec. 302(c)(2)(B).

TAX BLUNDER

One shareholder purchased all or most of the other outstanding shares and then had the corporation redeem the purchased shares. The redemption would then be pro rata with respect to the redeeming shareholder and thus taxable as a dividend. If the shareholder wanting a larger interest in the corporation had the corporation redeem the shares of the other shareholders, the shareholders would have received capital gain treatment under Code Sec. 302(b)(3) and the controlling shareholder would not have been taxed on the redemption, which was treated as a dividend.

¶ 14,125　REDEMPTIONS IN PARTIAL LIQUIDATION

The previously discussed redemptions are tested at the shareholder level and are applied on a shareholder-by-shareholder basis. Code Sec. 302(b)(4) provides for redemptions that are tested at the corporate level. If the distribution is considered a partial liquidation under Code Sec. 302(e), then noncorporate shareholders will receive sale or exchange treatment. The effects of the redemption on the shareholders' interests (e.g., complete termination of interest, meaningful reduction in interest, etc.) do not affect the redemption's status. Also, constructive ownership rules do not affect the results. Finally, exchange treatment results whether the redemption is proportional or disproportional. Code Sec. 302(b)(4) does not apply to corporations. Thus, unless the distribution qualifies as a redemption under Code Sec. 302(b)(1), (2), or (3), the corporation will have dividend treatment.

A partial liquidation results (1) if the distribution is not essentially equivalent to a dividend (determined at the corporate level and not the shareholder level) or (2) if the distribution is due to the corporation's ceasing to conduct a qualified trade or business. In addition, the distribution must be pursuant to a plan and must occur within the tax year in which the plan is adopted or within the succeeding tax year.

The courts have interpreted the term "not essentially equivalent to a dividend" to mean a genuine contraction of business. See *J.W. Imler*,

11 TC 836, CCH Dec. 16,691 (1948), acq. 1949-1 CB 2. Typical cases held *not* to qualify as partial liquidations include the sale of excess inventory, the reduction of working capital, the distribution of a small portion of business assets, and the distribution of unwanted assets. On the other hand, the discontinuance of a significant product line leading to a bulk sale of inventory has qualified as a partial liquidation, as has the distribution of insurance proceeds received because of a fire destroying a significant part of the corporate premises.

The first test is vague and subjective. The second test, the distribution occurs because the corporation ceases to conduct or distributes the assets of a qualified trade or business, is very objective. After the distribution, the corporation must continue to actively conduct a qualified trade or business. Thus, if the corporation has been engaged in two or more trades or businesses for the last five years and ceases to conduct one of these businesses, then the cessation and subsequent distribution qualifies as a partial liquidation.

The qualified trade or business must have been actively conducted for five years prior to the distribution and cannot have been acquired during such period in a taxable transaction. Code Sec. 302(e)(3). There are a few miscellaneous considerations:

1. In a closely held setting, it is irrelevant whether the shareholder physically turns in stock certificates or whether such certificates are formally cancelled.

2. The IRS position is that the percentage of stock redeemed is the same percentage of total stock as the distribution is of the fair market value of net assets prior to the distribution. Rev. Rul. 56-513, 1956-2 CB 191.

3. Noncorporate shareholders include partnerships, estates, and trusts to the extent the partners and beneficiaries are not corporations. Code Sec. 302(e)(5).

Example 14.62. Hardy Company has experienced financial difficulties in 1997 and 1998. In December 1998, it sells excess inventory and machinery it no longer uses and distributes the proceeds to its shareholders in redemption of some of their stock. This does not qualify as a partial liquidation.

Example 14.63. Stanton Corporation has two shareholders, Wayne Jones and Sandy Corporation. Wayne owns 250 shares that he acquired in 1986 at $45 per share. Sandy Corporation owns 250 shares that it acquired in 1995 at $30 per share. Stanton Corporation's current E&P for 1998 was $70,000. In August 1998, it distributed $8,000 to each shareholder in return for 100 shares of each shareholder's stock. The distribution qualified as a partial liquidation. Wayne has a $3,500 long-term capital gain ($8,000 minus $4,500 ($45 × 100)). However, since there has been no change in Sandy Corporation's interest (50 percent before and after the redemption), it will not receive sale or exchange treatment. Instead, it has $8,000 dividend income on which it can claim a dividends-received deduction of 80 percent ($6,400). Also, its basis in the 100 shares redeemed ($3,000) is added to the basis in its remaining 150 shares ($4,500), producing an overall basis of $7,500 for the 150 shares.

¶ 14,131 REDEMPTIONS TO PAY DEATH TAXES

Sometimes the stock of a deceased shareholder is redeemed by a closely held corporation because the estate or heirs need funds to pay death taxes and funeral expenses. Constructive ownership rules under Code Sec. 318 usually preclude sale or exchange treatment under Code Sec. 302 because closely held corporations usually are owned by related parties (e.g., family members). Under certain conditions, Code Sec. 303 provides relief in this situation by providing sale or exchange treatment on the redemption for an amount equal to the sum of federal and state death taxes and funeral and administrative expenses.

The intent of Code Sec. 303 is to provide relief because stock in closely held corporations generally is not very marketable; as such, the heirs or estate cannot easily sell the stock to raise the needed funds. However, they can have the corporation redeem the shares; thus, Code Sec. 303 treats the heirs or estate as if they sold the stock. This benefit can be quite substantial because the basis in inherited property is its fair market value at the decedent's date of death (assuming no alternative elections are made). Code Sec. 1014. This stepped-up basis results in little, if any, realized gain. However, if the redemption receives dividend treatment, then the full amount of the distribution (to the extent of current and accumulated E&P) is taxable as ordinary income.

Example 14.64. Jackson Corporation has three shareholders. George owns 40 shares which he acquired in 1991 for $10,000. Sally and Susan each own 30 shares which they acquired in 1994 for $60,000 each. George died on June 1, 1998, when the fair market value per share was $3,000. On December 16, 1998, Jackson Corporation redeems George's 40 shares from Adrian, George's beneficiary, and distributes $120,000 to Adrian. Adrian's basis in the 40 shares is $120,000. Jackson's current E&P in 1998 is $200,000. If the redemption qualifies for sale or exchange treatment under Code Sec. 303, then there is no realized gain and no recognized gain ($120,000 − $120,000 = zero). However, if the redemption is treated as a dividend, then Adrian has $120,000 of ordinary income. Clearly, Code Sec. 303 has a significant impact on Adrian's 1998 tax position.

TAX PLANNING POINTER

An option can be created giving the administrator for the decedent's estate the right to require the corporation to redeem from the estate an amount of stock to provide the necessary liquid assets to pay death taxes and funeral and administrative expenses under Code Sec. 303. Such an option can be placed in a written agreement between the stockholder and the corporation and should be designed so as to meet the requirements of Code Sec. 303.

Requirements and Limitations

A number of requirements and limitations must be satisfied in order to obtain sale or redemption treatment under Code Sec. 303.

1. There must be a distribution of property to a stockholder by a corporation in redemption of part or all of the stock of such corporation.

2. Such stock must be included in determining the gross estate of a decedent for purposes of the federal estate tax. However, stock possessing a substituted basis acquired from stock which was included in the gross estate also qualifies. For example, stock may have been included in the decedent's gross estate and later exchanged for other stock in a nontaxable reorganization. The latter stock can qualify under Code Sec. 303.

3. The value of the stock included in the decedent's estate must be greater than 35 percent of the adjusted gross estate.

4. The proceeds under Code Sec. 303 are limited to the sum of estate, inheritance, legacy, or succession taxes imposed (including interest) and the funeral and administrative expenses allowable under Code Sec. 2053 or 2106.

5. Qualifying redemptions are limited to those shareholders whose interests in the estate are reduced directly (or through a binding obligation to contribute) by any payment of death taxes or funeral and administrative expenses.

6. Any distributions made more than four years after the decedent's death are subject to additional limitations.

Gross Estate Adjustments

The requirement listed in (3), above, in part, limits the benefits of Code Sec. 303 to situations where the stock is a substantial portion of the decedent's total assets. The redeemed stock must be included in the gross estate of a decedent for federal estate tax purposes. Such included stock must have a federal estate tax value of more than 35 percent of the value of the adjusted gross estate. Adjusted gross estate (AGE) is the gross estate less the sum of the deductions allowable under Code Sec. 2053 or 2054. Code Sec. 303(b)(2)(A). These allowable deductions include:

1. Funeral expenses
2. Administrative expenses
3. Claims against the estate
4. Unpaid mortgages and other indebtedness
5. Losses incurred by the estate

Example 14.65. The gross estate of a decedent, Ed Smythe, has a fair market value of $3,000,000, consisting of $2,200,000 in cash and $800,000 in stock of Silver Corporation. Funeral and administrative expenses amounted to $450,000; thus, the adjusted gross estate is $2,550,000 ($3,000,000 − $450,000). Thirty-five percent of the adjusted gross estate is $892,500 (35% × $2,550,000). Since the value of the stock does not exceed $892,500, the 35 percent test is not met. Thus, a redemption of any of the stock would need to qualify under Code Sec. 302 for sale or exchange treatment.

Example 14.66. Assume that in example 14.65, the $3,000,000 estate consisted of $1,000,000 in cash and $1,400,000 in stock of Silver Corporation. A redemption of the stock would qualify under Code Sec. 303 since its value exceeds $892,500 and, therefore, the 35 percent test is met.

A special rule applies to an estate which includes stock of two or more corporations. If neither block of stock satisfies the 35 percent requirement, Code Sec. 303(b)(2)(B) permits treatment of the combined holdings as stock in a single corporation. To qualify, the estate tax value of the stock held in each corporation must be more than 20 percent in value of the outstanding stock in each corporation. For purposes of the 20 percent requirement, stock which, at the decedent's death, represents the surviving spouse's interest in property held by the decedent and the surviving spouse as community property, or as joint tenants, tenants by the entirety, or tenants in common is treated as having been included in determining the value of the decedent's gross estate.

Example 14.67. The gross estate of a decedent, Pete Brown, has a fair market value of $1 million, and the Code Secs. 2053 and 2054 expenses are $225,000. Included in the gross estate is stock of three corporations:

	Value of Shares Held	Value of Corporation
Alpha	$175,000	$500,000
Beta	125,000	400,000
Gamma	75,000	600,000

None of the three corporations meet the 35 percent of AGE test (35% × $775,000 = $271,250). However, since Alpha and Beta meet the 20 percent test, the stock of both corporations can be treated as stock of a single corporation valued at $300,000. Clearly, $300,000 is greater than $271,250. Gamma does not meet the 20 percent test and cannot be included in the 35 percent test. Thus, redemptions of Alpha and/or Beta stock will qualify for sale or exchange treatment (within dollar limitations) under Code Sec. 303.

TAX PLANNING POINTER

The 35 percent test is critical to the use of a Code Sec. 303 redemption. If the stockholdings do not satisfy this test, certain steps may be taken to insure qualification. The value of a stockholder's interest in a corporation may be increased, the stock-holder's adjusted gross estate may be decreased, or a combination of both can be employed in order to qualify for Code Sec. 303 treatment. For example, a stockholder could purchase more shares in the corporation. Further, assets other than closely held stock may be given away before death in order to help satisfy the 35 percent test.

Limitation on Redemption Amount

The limitation mentioned in (4), above, is imposed because the purpose of this special redemption is to help pay estate taxes and related expenses. However, the redeemed shareholders are not required to use the proceeds to pay these taxes and expenses. If the estate has cash sufficient to pay such expenses and uses this cash to pay the expenses, then the redeemed shareholders still will receive sale or exchange treatment under Code Sec. 303.

If the proceeds from a redemption exceed the Code Sec. 303 limitation amount, such excess is treated under the general rule in Code Sec. 302. The fact of the excess does not destroy the favorable treatment of the remainder of the proceeds under Code Sec. 303.

When there is more than one redemption distribution during the prescribed time period, the distribution is applied against the total amount that qualifies for exchange treatment in the order in which the distributions are made. All distributions are considered, including distributions that fall under a different Code provision. Reg. § 1.303-2(g)(1).

Example 14.68. Decedent's gross estate is $800,000 and the sum of the death taxes and funeral and administrative expenses is $225,000. Included in determining the gross estate is stock of a corporation valued at $450,000 for estate tax purposes. In the first year of administration, one-third of the stock is distributed to a legatee, and shortly thereafter the corporation redeems it for $150,000. In the second year, another one-third of the stock includible in the estate is redeemed for $150,000. The first distribution is applied against the $225,000 that qualifies for Code Sec. 303 treatment as payment in exchange for stock under Code Sec. 303(a). Of the second distribution, only $75,000 is treated as in full payment in exchange for stock under Code Sec. 303.

Time Limitation

Code Sec. 303 benefits only are available to distributions made in redemption of such stock within one of the following time periods:

1. The permissible time period is between the decedent's death and the 90th day after the expiration of the period of limitation in Code Sec. 6501(a) (i.e., three years). Since the federal estate tax return is due nine months after the decedent's death

under Code Sec. 6075(a), the qualified time limitation is approximately four years.

2. In the case of Tax Court litigation, the permissible time period is extended until 60 days after the Tax Court's decision becomes final.

3. If an election is made under Code Sec. 6166, relating to the extension of time to pay the estate tax attributable to a farm or closely held business, the Code Sec. 303 period is identical with these extension periods. However, any amounts distributed after the four-year period are still limited to the sum of the death taxes and funeral and administrative expenses. Code Sec. 303(b)(1).

Example 14.69. When Eben Stone died, his gross estate was valued at $3,000,000. Included in that amount was 500 of the 1,000 outstanding shares of Suba Corporation which were worth $1,800,000. The deductible expenses under Code Secs. 2053 and 2054 were $300,000 and estate taxes were $400,000. Suba Corporation redeemed 250 shares from Eben's estate in return for $1,000,000. Because of Code Sec. 318, the redemption does not meet the requirements of Code Sec. 302. The consequences of the redemption are as follows. Since the value of the stock is more than 35 percent of the adjusted gross estate ($1,800,000/$2,700,000 is 66.67 percent), the requirements are met for sale or exchange treatment under Code Sec. 303. The estate is responsible for the expenses and taxes and the maximum that qualifies under Code Sec. 303 is $700,000 ($300,000 + $400,000). The estate has a long-term capital gain of $70,000 ($700,000 − $630,000). The $630,000 ($1,800,000 × (175 ÷ 500)) is the basis in the number of shares qualifying for the redemption ($700,000 ÷ $1,000,000 = 70% of 250 shares = 175 shares). The remaining $300,000 distributed is a dividend (assuming sufficient E&P).

¶ 14,135   REDEEMING CORPORATION'S TAX CONSEQUENCES

There are three main concerns that the redeeming corporation must address. Can the corporation deduct expenses related to the redemption of its own stock? Does the corporation recognize a gain or loss on property it distributes to shareholders in exchange for its own stock? What is the effect of the redemption on the corporation's E&P?

Expenses Deduction

In general the costs incurred by a corporation in the redemption of its stock are not deductible. These costs, such as transfer fees and legal and accounting fees, must be capitalized and they are not amortizable because they are not ordinary and necessary business expenses; they are part of the purchase price of the stock. Rev. Rul. 69-561, 1969-2 CB 25. However, in some instances the courts have allowed a deduction (for example, see *Foster,* TC Memo. 1966-273, and *General Pencil Co.,* 3 TCM 603 (1944)).

Gain or Loss Recognition

If a corporation distributes property as part of the redemption then, under Code Sec. 311, no loss is recognized. However, gains are recognized if the property has appreciated in value. The realized and recognized gain is equal to the property's fair market value minus its adjusted basis. The type of gain depends upon the property distributed. Since losses are not recognized, it is best to sell property whose adjusted basis is greater than its fair market value. The corporation has a recognized loss and can distribute cash (the proceeds) to its shareholders.

Example 14.70. Fieldstone Corporation uses an asset with a basis of $40,000 and a fair market value of $55,000 to redeem some of a shareholder's stock. Fieldstone must recognize a gain of $15,000 ($55,000 − $40,000) as a result of the redemption. This gain will be recognized even though the shareholder may have dividend income because the requirements of Code Sec. 302 or 303 were not met.

E&P Effects

The effects of the distribution on the corporation's E&P depend upon whether the redemption is treated as a dividend or as a sale or exchange. If the redemption is treated as a dividend, then E&P is reduced by the amount of the distribution. E&P also is increased by any gain recognized on the distribution (i.e., if the corporation distributed appreciated property) because the gain is in gross income.

If the redemption is treated as a redemption (i.e., sale or exchange) then E&P is increased by any gain recognized on the distribution. Additionally, E&P is decreased by the same percentage as the redeemed stock bears to the corporation's total stock outstanding. If the amount of the distribution exceeds this value, then such excess reduces the corporation's capital account. Code Sec. 312(n)(7).

Example 14.71. Campbell Company has 100 shares of stock outstanding. Its E&P is $200,000 and its paid-in-capital is $130,000. It redeems for $60,000 all the stock of Mr. Roberts (25 shares) in a Code Sec. 302(b)(3) redemption. E&P is reduced by 25 percent (25 shares redeemed ÷ 100 shares outstanding) because Campbell Company redeemed 25 percent of its stock. Thus, E&P is reduced by $50,000 (25% × $200,000). The remainder of the distribution, $10,000 ($60,000 − $50,000) reduces the paid-in-capital account. After the redemption, Campbell Company's E&P is $150,000 and its paid-in-capital is $120,000.

¶ 14,141   REDEMPTIONS THROUGH RELATED CORPORATIONS

There are certain instances when an apparent sale of stock must be recast as a redemption. The sale is recast as a redemption because the shareholders are attempting to receive distributions of corporate earnings while avoiding dividend income.

Code Sec. 304 applies to a corporation's acquisition of a shareholder's stock in another corporation in exchange for property when the shareholder has control of both corporations. Property includes money, securities, and any other property but does not include stock (or rights to acquire such stock) in the corporation making the distribution. Code Sec. 317(a).

Control for the purposes of Code Sec. 304 is defined as the ownership of stock possessing at least 50 percent of the total combined voting power of all classes of stock entitled to vote, or at least 50 percent of the total value of all classes of stock. Code Sec. 304 also applies if an individual has a 50 percent interest in a corporation which, in turn, has control of another corporation. For purposes of determining the 50 percent control, the constructive ownership rules of Code Sec. 318(a) apply.

> **Example 14.72.** Roberta Rogers owned two corporations, Alpha and Beta. She sold some of her stock in Alpha to Beta. Roberta received capital gain treatment because the transaction was a sale and therefore the redemption tests of Code Secs. 302 and 303 were avoided. After the sale, Roberta had the same control of Alpha as she had before the sale. Code Sec. 304 was enacted to prevent this from happening by requiring that the sale be treated as a redemption subject to the requirements of Code Secs. 302 and 303. Code Sec. 304 applies to sales of stock involving two brother-sister corporations and to sales of a parent corporation's stock to one of its subsidiaries.

Brother-Sister Corporation Transactions

If an individual is in control (as defined under Code Sec. 304) of two corporations and transfers stock to one corporation in exchange for property, then the exchange is treated as a redemption by the acquiring corporation. If the distribution is treated as a dividend, then the acquiring corporation is considered to have received the stock as a contribution to its capital. In return, the acquiring corporation is considered to have issued some of its stock to the shareholder and then to have immediately redeemed such stock for the amount distributed in the exchange.

In applying the provisions of Code Sec. 302(b) to the exchange, reference is made to the shareholder's ownership of stock in the issuing corporation and not to the shareholder's ownership of stock in the acquiring corporation. The amount of dividend income is determined as if the property were distributed by the acquiring corporation to the extent of its E&P and then by the issuing corporation to the extent of its E&P.

Since the stock received by the acquiring corporation is treated as a contribution to its capital, its basis in the stock is equal to the shareholder's basis in the stock. The shareholder's basis in the acquiring corporation's stock is increased by the basis of the stock sold by the shareholder.

> **Example 14.73.** Cindy Baron owns 100 percent of Baruck Corporation and 70 percent of Mimi Company. Each corporation has 100 shares of stock outstanding. Cindy acquired the Baruck stock in

1994 for $15,000. She acquired the Mimi stock in 1991 for $20,000. In 1998, Cindy sells 20 shares of Baruck to Mimi for $35,000. The E&P of Baruck and Mimi is $50,000 and $25,000, respectively. If the sale receives sale or exchange treatment under Code Sec. 302(b), then Cindy has a long-term capital gain of $32,000 ($35,000 − $3,000; her basis in the 20 shares is $3,000 (20 × $150 per share)). Mimi's basis in the 20 shares of Baruck would be $35,000, the purchase price. However, the sale does not meet any of the redemption requirements under Code Sec. 302(b); it is not substantially disproportionate, there has not been a meaningful reduction in Cindy's interest, and there has not been a complete termination of her interest. Thus, Cindy will have dividend income up to $75,000 (the combined E&P of Baruck and Mimi). Since the amount of the distribution is $35,000, all of it is treated as a dividend. Cindy's basis in the 20 shares of Baruck is added to her basis of shares in Mimi. Thus, her basis in the 70 shares is $23,000 ($20,000 + $3,000). Mimi's basis in the 20 shares of Baruck is $3,000, equal to Cindy's basis in the stock. Finally, the $35,000 distribution is treated as coming out of Mimi's E&P first. Thus, Mimi's E&P is reduced to zero ($25,000 − $25,000) and Baruck's E&P is reduced to $40,000 ($50,000 − $10,000).

Parent-Subsidiary Corporation Transactions

If a subsidiary corporation acquires stock in its parent from a shareholder owning at least 50 percent of the parent corporation, Code Sec. 304 applies to the transaction. The transaction is construed as a distribution from the subsidiary to the parent and a subsequent distribution from the parent to the individual shareholder. The acquisition is treated as though the parent had redeemed its own stock.

If the redemption does not qualify for sale or exchange treatment under Code Sec. 302(b) or 303, then the amount of dividend income is determined as if the property were distributed by the acquiring corporation (subsidiary) to the extent of its E&P and then by the issuing corporation (parent) to the extent of its E&P. The subsidiary's basis in the parent corporation stock it acquired is equal to the amount it paid for the stock. The shareholder's basis in the stock in the parent corporation is increased by the basis of the parent stock the shareholder sold to the subsidiary.

Example 14.74. James Jergens owns 85 shares of Parent Corporation. James acquired the shares in 1990 for $85,000. Parent Corporation owns 65 shares in Sub Corporation. Each corporation has 100 shares of stock outstanding. The E&P of Parent and Sub is $20,000 and $35,000, respectively. In 1998, James sells 15 shares of Parent to Sub for $25,000. If the sale receives sale or exchange treatment, then James has a long-term capital gain of $10,000 ($25,000 − $15,000, his basis in the 15 shares (15 × $1,000)). Sub's basis in the 15 shares is $25,000, the purchase price. However, the redemption does not meet any of the provisions of Code Secs. 302 and 303 and, therefore, is treated as a dividend. James has dividend income of $25,000 which is treated as a distribution of Sub's E&P. James's basis in his remaining 70 shares of Parent are increased by $15,000 (the basis of the 15 shares to be sold to Sub) to $85,000. Sub's E&P is reduced by $25,000. After the redemption, its E&P is $10,000 and Parent's E&P is $20,000. Finally, Sub's basis in the 15 shares of Parent stock is $25,000, the purchase price.

To the extent that a Code Sec. 304 transaction between two corporations is deemed a dividend, the transferor and the acquiring corporations are treated under the Taxpayer Relief Act of 1997 (TRA '97) as if (1) the transferor had transferred the stock involved in the transaction to the acquiring corporation in exchange for stock in the acquiring corporation in a Code Sec. 351 transfer, and (2) the acquiring corporation then had redeemed the stock it is treated as having issued. TRA '97 also amended Code Sec. 1059 such that if Code Sec. 304 applies to a distribution treated as a dividend, then regardless of how long the stock has been held, the amount treated as a dividend is deemed an extraordinary dividend. As such, the transferor must reduce its basis in its remaining shares by the amount of the distribution qualifying for the dividends-received deduction, and if this amount exceeds the basis, then such excess is treated as gain on the sale or exchange of the stock in the year the extraordinary dividend was received.

> *Example 14.75.* X Co. owns 100% of W Co. and 70% of Y Co. Y Co. owns 100% (100 shares) of Z Co. Y Co.'s adjusted basis of its Z Co. shares is $1,000. Y Co. sells 80 shares of its Z Co. stock to W Co. for $950. The redemption falls under Code Sec. 304 and will result in Y Co. recognizing a $950 dividend. Y Co.'s dividends-received deduction is $665 (70% × $950), leaving $285 taxable. Since this also is considered an extraordinary dividend, Y Co.'s basis in its remaining 20 shares of Z Co. is reduced to $335 ($1,000 − $665).

¶ 14,145   PREFERRED STOCK BAILOUTS

The use of related corporations to circumvent the redemption requirements of Code Secs. 302 and 303 is severely restricted by Code Sec. 304. Another way shareholders attempted to bail out corporate earnings was with preferred stock. The transactions were structured as follows.

1. The corporation issued nonvoting preferred stock in a nontaxable stock dividend distribution with respect to common stock.

2. The shareholder assigned a portion of the common stock's basis to the preferred stock. In addition, the preferred stock received the holding period of the common stock.

3. The shareholder sold the preferred stock to an unrelated third party for the stock's fair market value. This produced a capital gain, usually long-term, equal to the difference between the fair market value and the allocated basis in the preferred stock.

4. The corporation redeemed the preferred stock from the unrelated third party in a redemption that qualified as a complete termination of the interest. The third party received sale or exchange treatment and usually had a nominal gain (i.e., "payment" for helping the shareholder bail out the earnings).

Code Sec. 306 was enacted to prevent shareholders from using the above plan to circumvent the redemption requirements of Code Secs. 302 and 303. Effectively, certain stock are "tainted" when received in a nontaxable stock dividend and the sale of such stock produces ordinary income rather than capital gain.

Definition of Section 306 Stock

The distributing corporation must have E&P at the time of the distribution in order for the preferred stock to receive the taint of Code Sec. 306. Code Sec. 306(c)(2). If the corporation had no current or accumulated E&P at the time of distribution, then any and all distributions (cash, property, or preferred stock) would not be taxable as dividends; thus, the effect of the E&P requirement is to put the non-common stock distribution on equal footing with other distributions. However, the amount of E&P is immaterial; even a small amount of E&P will cause the taint of Code Sec. 306. Also, since the distribution is not taxable (i.e., the recipient shareholder does not recognize income when the stock is issued), there is no reduction to the distributing corporation's E&P.

There are three categories in which Section 306 stock can occur when there is corporate E&P (Code Sec. 306(c)):

1. Non-common stock is distributed to a stockholder and any part of the distribution is not included in the gross income of the stockholder.

2. Non-common stock is received in a reorganization or divisive transaction in which the gain is not recognized and the effect of the transaction is substantially the same as the receipt of a stock dividend.

3. Stock (other than stock in Category 2, above) which has a substituted basis is determined with reference to the basis of Section 306 stock.

Stock Distributed to Seller

The first situation where stock may be classified as Section 306 stock occurs when a shareholder sells or disposes non-common stock that was received in a distribution that was not fully included in gross income. Thus, a completely taxable stock dividend would fall outside the scope of Code Sec. 306. However, stock rights distributed to stockholders tax free, and any stock received through the exercise of such rights, may be Section 306 stock. Similarly, common stock with a privilege of converting into non-common stock or property (whether or not the conversion privilege is contained in such stock) is not treated as common stock.

Stock Received in Corporate Reorganization or Separation

Stock received in exchange for Section 306 stock is also tainted. Non-common stock received in a reorganization or divisive transaction is tainted if cash received in lieu of such stock would have been treated as a dividend under Code Sec. 302(d); Reg. § 1.306-3(d).

> *Example 14.76.* Acqa Corporation has only common stock outstanding. In a statutory merger under Code Sec. 368(a), Acqa merges with Garber Corporation. The stockholders of Acqa Corporation receive both common and preferred stock in Garber Corporation. The preferred stock received by these stockholders is Section 306 stock.

> *Example 14.77.* Sam Barns and Barbara Meyers each own one-half of the 2,000 outstanding shares of preferred stock and one-half of the 2,000 outstanding shares of common stock of Peanut Corporation. In a recapitalization under Code Sec. 368(a)(1)(E), each stockholder exchanges the preferred stock for a new issue of preferred stock (which is not substantially different). Unless the exchanged preferred stock was not Section 306 stock, the new issue of preferred stock is Section 306 stock.

Stock Having Transferred or Substituted Basis

This definition, of course, overlaps with Category 2 and in such cases, Category 2 controls. The three major areas where this category is applicable are (1) corporate organizations under Code Sec. 351, (2) exchanges of stock for similar stock in the same corporation under Code Sec. 1036, and (3) transference by gift of Section 306 stock. Note that inherited stock is not Section 306 stock because the basis of inherited property is fair market value at the date of decedent's death (or alternative date if elected). Thus, there is no substituted basis. Reg. § 1.306-3(e).

> *Example 14.78.* Harvey Black owns Section 306 stock in Briscoe Corporation. He transfers this tainted stock to Hill Corporation (in exchange for Hill common stock) in a transaction falling within Code Sec. 351. The Hill common stock received by Harvey Black would be Section 306 stock. Furthermore, the Briscoe Section 306 stock now in the hands of Hill Corporation (the transferee) is still Section 306 stock. Thus, a single block of tainted stock has turned into two blocks of tainted stock.

TAX PLANNING POINTER

For planning purposes, a taxpayer should realize that if both common stock and preferred stock are issued to the stockholders at the time of organization of the corporation, the preferred stock is not Section 306 stock. Also, a dividend of common treasury stock to common stockholders is not Section 306 stock, if the treasury stock is the same in all respects as the common stock on which it is declared. Rev. Rul. 55-746, 1955-2 CB 224.

Dispositions of Section 306 Stock

The tax consequences of Section 306 stock occur when the stockholder disposes of the tainted stock. These taxable dispositions are divided into two categories: (1) sale or other disposition (other than redemption) and (2) redemption.

As to a disposition other than a redemption, any amount realized by the stockholder is ordinary income to the extent of the amount that would have been a taxable dividend if cash had been distributed rather than Section 306 stock. The ordinary income is not limited to the realized gain on the sale, but may be as great as the amount realized on the sale. There are two limitations on the amount of ordinary income. The recognized ordinary income is limited to the smaller of (1) the corporate current and accumulated earnings and profits at the time of the distribution, and (2) the fair market value of the Section 306 stock on the date of distribution by the corporation. Any excess of the amount realized over the sum of the ordinary income and the adjusted basis of the stock is treated as a capital gain. Code Sec. 306(a)(1). If the amount received is less than the shareholder's basis, then the unused basis is added to the shareholder's basis in the common stock.

> *Example 14.79.* On December 15, Apple and Banana owned equally all of the stock of Fruity Corporation (which files on a calendar-year basis). On this date, Fruity Corporation distributed pro rata 100 shares of preferred stock as a nontaxable dividend on its common stock. On December 15, the preferred stock had a fair market value of $10,000, and the company had no E&P. The 50 shares of preferred stock distributed to Apple had an allocated basis to him of $10 per share (or a total of $500 for the 50 shares). Apple sells the 50 shares of preferred stock on July 1 nine years later for $6,000 at a time when Fruity's E&P was $14,000. Since there was no E&P on the date of distribution, the preferred stock is not Section 306 stock. Apple would recognize a $5,500 capital gain ($6,000 − $500).

> *Example 14.80.* Assume the same facts as in Example 14.79, except that E&P on December 15 was $20,000. Ordinary income is recognized to the extent of $10,000 (Apple's share of E&P on December 15) or $5,000 (the fair market value of the 50 shares Apple received). Thus, Apple has $5,000 of ordinary income. Apple also has a capital gain of $500 ($6,000 − $5,500 ($5,000 ordinary income + $500 adjusted basis)).

> *Example 14.81.* Barry Bagley owns all the common stock (100 shares) of Sky Corporation. He acquired the shares in 1990 for $15,000. In 1995, Sky Corporation distributed 40 shares of preferred stock to Barry in a nontaxable distribution. At that time the corporation's E&P was $60,000 and the per-share fair market

values of the common and preferred stock were $200 and $125, respectively. Barry must allocate a basis of $3,000 to the preferred stock ($15,000 × ($5,000 ÷ $25,000)). In 1998, Barry sold the preferred stock for $5,000. Although his realized gain is $2,000 ($5,000 − $3,000), Barry has ordinary income of $5,000 (the fair market value of the preferred stock when distributed since this was less than the E&P of $6,000). The unrecovered basis of $3,000 in the preferred stock is added to his basis in the common stock, bringing it to $15,000 ($12,000 + $3,000).

Losses are not recognized on the sale of Section 306 stock. In order to avoid double taxation on the common stock when loss on the disposition of the Code Sec. 306 is disallowed, the unused basis of the preferred stock is added back to the stock retained by the stockholder. Reg. § 1.306-1(b)(2).

Example 14.82. Assume the same facts as in Example 14.79, except that Apple sells his 50 shares of preferred stock for $5,100. Of this amount, $5,000 is treated as ordinary income and no loss is allowed. There is added back to the basis of the Fruity common stock $400 (the allocated basis of $500 reduced by the $100 received).

An ordinary dividend in cash may be less harmful than a sale of Section 306 stock. A dividend reduces the company's E&P and qualifies for a dividends-received deduction, whereas a disposition of Section 306 stock does not reduce E&P and does not qualify for the dividends-received deduction. Reg. § 1.306-1(b)(1).

A taxpayer might try to issue preferred stock that has many constraints so as to reduce its fair market value at date of distribution, and, therefore, limit the taint. Subsequently, the constraints or conditions would be lifted with the result that the preferred stock's fair market value would increase. To stop such a practice, Code Sec. 306(g)(1) indicates that where substantial changes are made in the conditions of the stock, the fair market value is the greater of the value on the distribution date or the value at the time of the change in conditions. Also, the amount of the E&P is to be the greater of the amount at the time of distributions or the amount at the time of substantial change.

If Section 306 stock is redeemed, a different set of rules is applicable. The ordinary income in a redemption is the smaller of (1) the amount received on redemption, or (2) the E&P on the date of the redemption. The amount of the E&P on the date of distribution is immaterial. Any amount of the proceeds in excess of the ordinary income is a return of capital (until the basis is gone), and any remainder is treated as a capital gain. In essence, a redemption of Section 306 stock is covered by Code Secs. 301(a) and 302(d).

Example 14.83. In December, Blake Inc. distributes a nontaxable preferred stock dividend of 10,000 shares on its common stock. At this time, the accumulated E&P is $500,000 and the fair market value of the preferred stock is $100,000. Carl Combs owns 200 shares of the common stock, with a cost of $10,000. He receives 500 shares of the Blake preferred stock, which is worth $5,000. At the time of distribution, his common stock was worth $15,000. Thus, $2,500 would be allocated to the preferred stock ($10,000 × ($5,000 ÷ $20,000)) and $7,500 would remain with his common stock ($10,000 × ($15,000 ÷ $20,000)). Carl sells all of his preferred stock to Donald for $6,000. His share of the E&P is $25,000 ((500/10,000) × $500,000). Carl would recognize ordinary income of $5,000 and the basis of his common stock would return to $9,000 ($7,500 + ($2,500 − $1,000)).

Example 14.84. Assume the same facts as in Example 14.83, except that Carl's preferred stock is redeemed by Blake Inc. for $6,000. Carl would recognize ordinary income of $6,000, and the basis in his common stock would return to $10,000 ($7,500 + $2,500). The $6,000 ordinary income would be treated as dividend income.

Exceptions to Section 306 Treatment

Code Sec. 306(b) provides four exceptions to the ordinary income treatment. In the case of a sale or other disposition of the stock (other than a redemption), no ordinary income is recognized where the entire stock interest of the stockholder is terminated (stock attribution rules of Code Sec. 318(a) apply) and the stock is not transferred directly or indirectly to a person whose stock ownership would be attributable to the stockholder. Code Sec. 306(b)(1)(A). Only the stock interest need be terminated. The reasoning for this exception: the stockholder could have obtained the same results by selling shares of stock before the Code Sec. 306 distribution.

Where there is a redemption of the Section 306 stock and Code Sec. 302(b)(3) applies (a complete redemption), ordinary dividend treatment is avoided. The constructive ownership rules of Code Sec. 318 apply, but the waiver of the attribution rule of Code Sec. 302(c) is available. The punitive rules likewise do not apply if the tainted stock is redeemed in a partial or complete liquidation.

Example 14.85. Fred Bass desires to retire from the business and to terminate all stock and other interests in Runner Corporation. To accomplish this objective, Fred proposes to sell 30 shares of common stock and 18 shares of preferred stock to his daughter Jane, sell 25 shares of common stock to key employees of Runner who are not related to Fred or Jane, and to have the remaining common and preferred stock redeemed by Runner. Fred's reasons for selling some of the preferred stock to Jane rather than having all of the preferred stock redeemed are to leave Jane with voting control of Runner for a smaller investment than would otherwise be necessary while giving the key employees other than Jane a greater participation in the growth of Runner than they would have if Jane owned more than half of the common stock. These goals will be accomplished because the preferred stock is worth only one-tenth as much per share as the common stock but entitles its holder to one vote per share, the same as the common stock.

The redemption of the common stock and the Section 306 stock coupled with the sale of the remaining common stock and Section 306 stock to Jane, and other key employees qualifies as a complete termination of interest under Code Sec. 302(b)(3). Furthermore, the dispositions of the Section 306 stock are excepted from the ordinary income treatment of Code Sec. 306(a) by Code Sec. 306(b)(4)(B). See Rev. Rul. 77-455, 1977-2 CB 93.

No ordinary income is recognized in a tax-free exchange under Code Secs. 351 and 1036. This exception is only a temporary escape route since the non-common stock received in the exchange becomes Section 306 stock under Code Sec. 306(c)(1)(C). Where the transferor of tainted stock receives boot, the fair market value of the boot becomes subject to Code Sec. 306(a).

Another exception to Code Sec. 306(a) treatment occurs where, in the opinion of the IRS, a transaction is not in pursuance of a plan having as one of its principal purposes the avoidance of federal income tax. Code Sec. 306(b)(4). This exception would apply to the case of dividends and isolated dispositions of Section 306 stock by minority stockholders. Reg. § 1.306-2(b)(3). A taxpayer should ask for an advance ruling from the IRS before relying on this exception.

¶ 14,205   DISTRIBUTIONS BY CLOSELY HELD CORPORATIONS

The tax treatment of distributions to shareholders provides several opportunities to minimize the impact of federal income taxes and to maximize the after-tax wealth of the overall economic unit (consisting of the corporation and its shareholders). Usually the shareholders are related (i.e., family corporation) but this is not always the case.

Paying a dividend is frequently regarded as undesirable because it is nondeductible to the corporation, but taxable to the shareholder. As a result, numerous alternatives are often considered first when profits exist, particularly in a closely held setting where shareholders and management are one and the same. Here is a brief list of the main ways to get the funds out of a profitable corporation, ranging from the most to the least desirable for tax purposes. The ranking is tentative and may vary with facts and circumstances:

1. Payments that produce current, tax-free benefits to the shareholder-employees and are deductible by the corporation. Examples include medical plans, legal plans, and group-term life insurance.

2. Payments that produce future, taxable benefits to the shareholder-employees and are currently deductible by the corporation. The typical example is qualified deferred compensation plans (e.g., pension and profit-sharing plans and thrift plans).

3. Payments that produce current, taxable benefits to the shareholder-employees and are deductible by the corporation. Examples include salaries, bonuses, and taxable fringe benefits.

4. Payments that produce current benefits to the shareholder-employees, result in capital gains or losses, do not have to be repaid, but are nondeductible by the corporation. Included here are stock redemptions not taxed as dividends and shareholder sales of property to the corporation.

5. Payments that produce current, nontaxable benefits to the shareholder-employees, but which have to be repaid and are nondeductible to the corporation. Shareholder loans fall under this heading. Unless appropriate formalities are observed, dividend treatment may result.

6. Payments that produce current, taxable benefits to the shareholder-employee and are nondeductible to the corporation. These payments are dividends and in the last place. (Chapter 17 discusses two penalty taxes that may be applicable if earnings are accumulated.)

TAX PLANNING POINTER ▼

Annie Gall is the sole shareholder of Beach Blankets Inc. She wishes to give $20,000 to her favorite charity, Last Chance College. If she were to have Beach Blankets redeem some of her shares to raise the $20,000, Annie would have to report $20,000 in dividend income. Annie decides to give $20,000 of her stock in Beach Blankets to Last Chance College. Seeing that there is no market for the stock, Last Chance sells the stock to Beach Blanket for $20,000 of notes, payable over 10 years with interest. Here are the tax results:

1. Annie receives a $20,000 charitable contribution deduction currently.

2. Annie has no dividend income.

3. Annie owns 100 percent of the corporation before and after the redemption.

4. The corporation recognizes no gain or loss but reduces its E&P account by 50 percent.

5. The corporation pays the $20,000 later but receives no deductions (except for interest).

As long as the charity is not obligated to sell the stock, this is accepted by the courts and the IRS. *D.D. Palmer,* 75-2 USTC ¶ 9726, 523 F.2d 1308 (CA-8 1975); Rev. Rul. 78-197, 1978-1 CB 83.

TAX BLUNDER

A businessman owned 100 percent of the stock in a corporation, directly or indirectly, using attribution rules. Needing a loan, he approached the Small Business Administration (SBA). His loan application was approved with one condition: He had to invest an additional $25,000 in the corporation. As a way of complying, he issued $25,000 of par value preferred stock and purchased the whole issue for $25,000 in cash. The SBA loan was granted, the business prospered, and eventually he no longer needed SBA support. At that time, he turned in his preferred stock to the corporation (which cancelled it) in exchange for $25,000. He reported no gain or loss on the transaction.

Result. $25,000 of dividends. The amount was covered by E&P, and he owned 100 percent of the corporation, directly or indirectly, before and after the redemption. Having a good business reason for the transaction is irrelevant.

SUMMARY OF CHAPTER 14

- ✓ Earnings and profits (E&P) represents a corporation's ability to make a dividend.
- ✓ E&P has some similarities to retained earnings.
- ✓ E&P affects the taxability of corporate distributions and redemptions.
- ✓ Current E&P is computed annually.
- ✓ Accumulated E&P consists of undistributed prior years' E&P.
- ✓ Current E&P and accumulated E&P can be negative.
- ✓ Distributions first come out of current E&P, then out of accumulated E&P.
- ✓ A distribution never can make E&P negative; it only can bring them to zero.
- ✓ If a distribution exceeds current E&P, then current E&P is reduced proportionally and accumulated E&P is reduced chronologically.
- ✓ A distribution that is not a dividend is treated as a return of capital and is applied against the shareholder's stock basis; once basis is zero then all additional amounts are treated as gain from sale of the stock.
- ✓ In general, a redemption receives sale or exchange treatment; however, there are exceptions to this.
- ✓ A redemption must meet Code Sec. 302 or Code Sec. 303 to receive sale or exchange treatment.
- ✓ Other redemptions receive dividend treatment to the extent of corporate E&P.
- ✓ Code Secs. 304 and 306 restrict the use of controlled corporations and preferred stock to circumvent Code Secs. 302 and 303, respectively.

CHAPTER 14 QUESTIONS

1. What is E&P and what is its significance?

2. Distinguish between current and accumulated E&P.

3. What are the broad categories of adjustments made to determine current E&P?

4. What is a shareholder's basis in a property dividend?

5. Does a corporation recognize a gain or loss when it distributes property as a dividend or in a redemption?

6. What are the tax consequences to shareholders and the distributing corporation when property subject to a liability is distributed?

7. How is E&P affected by a distribution of appreciated property?

8. Identify in proper order the sources of a distribution.

9. What are constructive dividends? Give three examples of them.

10. When is a stock dividend taxable?

11. How are distributions of stock rights taxed?

12. What is a stock redemption?

13. How is the E&P account affected in a redemption?

14. Why would a corporate shareholder generally prefer to have a redemption treated as a dividend?

15. Can a redemption result in a recognized loss to either party?

16. What is a substantially disproportionate redemption?

17. What does a 10-year agreement entail?

18. What are the requirements for a partial redemption?

19. What is constructive ownership? What does it affect?

20. What is the treatment of a sale of stock among related corporations?

21. What is a preferred stock bailout?

22. What is Section 306 stock?

23. How much dividend income is recognized by a seller of Section 306 stock?

24. What are some of the "dividend alternatives" in a closely held corporation owned by shareholder-employers?

CHAPTER 14 PROBLEMS

25. Given the following information, determine the taxable portion and return of capital in each situation, as well as accumulated E&P on January 1, 1999.

	1998 Current E&P	January 1, 1998 Accumulated E&P	July 1, 1998 Distribution
a.	$50,000	$20,000	$45,000
b.	50,000	20,000	63,000
c.	50,000	(14,000)	44,000
d.	50,000	20,000	85,000
e.	50,000	(15,000)	60,000

26. Given the following information, determine the taxable portion and return of capital in each situation, as well as accumulated E&P on January 1, 1999.

	1998 Current E&P	January 1, 1998 Accumulated E&P	Distribution Amount	Distribution Date
a.	$10,000	$12,000	$30,000	1/01/98
b.	(30,000)	(15,000)	15,000	6/01/98
c.	30,000	(54,000)	29,000	12/31/98
d.	(30,000)	50,000	(1)21,000	7/01/98
			(2)21,000	12/31/98

27. Given the following information for 1998, compute Shardee Corporation's current E&P for 1998.

Taxable income	$100,000
Federal income taxes	22,250
Other information (items from 1998):	
Tax-exempt interest	7,000
Realized gain on like-kind exchange	35,000
Accelerated depreciation (straight-line would have been $45,000)	60,000
Net short-term capital loss	14,000
NOL carryover	9,000
Code Sec. 267 loss (related taxpayers)	8,000

28. The following information is taken from Lynnso Corporation's records for 1998:

Gross receipts from operations	$500,000
Dividends received from a 40 percent owned domestic corporation	100,000
Interest on State of Ohio bonds	30,000
Life insurance proceeds received due to death of a key employee	40,000
Cost of goods sold	200,000
NOL carryover from 1997	13,000
MACRS depreciation (straight-line would have been $30,000) on equipment	43,000
Straight-line depreciation on building	15,870
Charitable contributions	45,000
Wages expense	50,000
Life insurance premiums on key-man insurance	10,000

a. Determine Lynnso Corporation's taxable income for 1998.

b. Compute Lynnso Corporation's current E&P for 1998.

29. Parking Space Inc. distributed $18,000 to Speedways Inc. a 15 percent shareholder. Parking Space had E&P of $5,000 and Speedways had a basis in its stock of $7,000.

    a. How much dividend income does Speedways have?

    b. How much and what kind of taxable income does Speedways have because of the distribution?

    c. What is Speedways's basis in its stock immediately after the distribution?

30. Special Motors Inc. has E&P of $53,000. It distributes a building to the individual sole shareholder. The building has a basis of $17,000 and a value of $54,000, is subject to a mortgage of $31,000, and has $6,000 of depreciation recapture potential.

    a. What is the character and amount of any gain or loss recognized by Special Motors?

    b. What is the amount of the dividend?

    c. What is E&P after the distribution?

    d. What is the shareholder's basis in the building?

31. The X-Bar-X Inc. has no E&P, current or accumulated, prior to the following independent transactions with its sole shareholder, Brandon:

    Distribution of LIFO inventory with a basis of $2,000, a FIFO value of $4,000, and a market value of $7,000.

    Distribution of land with a basis of $12,000, a mortgage of $19,000, and a value of $27,000.

    Sale of property to Brandon for $20,000 (basis $5,000, value $25,000).

    a. Does Brandon have to recognize any income?

    b. Does X-Bar-X have any gains or losses?

    c. What are the required adjustments to E&P?

32. Tara Corporation had current E&P of $320,000 in 1998. During 1998, it distributed numerous items to its sole shareholder, Anne. Indicate the effects of the distribution to Anne and Tara Corporation for each item distributed.

    a. Inventory with a fair market value of $30,000 and an adjusted basis of $20,000.

    b. Truck used in business with a fair market value of $17,000 and an adjusted basis of $9,100. The truck's original cost was $22,000.

    c. Land with a fair market value of $210,000 that was held as an investment and was acquired in 1984 for $150,000.

    d. Land with a fair market value of $105,000 that was used in the business. The land was acquired in 1983 for $50,000 and had an outstanding mortgage of $30,000.

    e. Installment obligation having a face amount of $43,000 and an adjusted basis of $29,000. The installment obligation was obtained when Tara sold ordinary income property.

33. Images Inc. sells property with a basis of $20,000 and a value of $50,000 to its individual majority shareholder. What are the tax consequences to both parties if the selling price is the following amounts?

   a. $35,000

   b. $65,000

34. Combat Toys Inc. has an accumulated deficit and current E&P of $20,000. Joe Gunn, a 60 percent shareholder, withdrew $35,000 from the corporation. Joe reported no income from the transaction, and upon audit he claimed it was a loan. No note had been executed, but on the eve of the audit, Joe signed a demand note for $35,000, payable to Combat Toys. The IRS claims Joe has a dividend of $35,000. What is the most likely result if the case goes to court?

35. Karl Stick is president of Stock Company. He also owns 100 percent of its stock. Karl's salary is $120,000. At the end of the year, Karl was paid a bonus of $100,000 because the firm had a good year. Stock Company deducted $220,000 as compensation expense for the year. Upon audit, $80,000 of the deduction was disallowed. How could this happen? How would you advise Stock Company?

36. Refer to Problem 35 and assume that Karl's tax bracket is 31 percent and Stock Company's is 34 percent. What is the dollar impact of the IRS reclassification?

37. Sam incorporated Sam's Saloon two years ago and owns 100 percent of its stock. The corporation distributes a piece of land, used as a parking lot for the customers, to Sam. Sam's basis in his stock is $21,000, the land has a basis of $14,000 and a value of $30,000, and E&P is $5,000.

   a. What are the tax consequences to Sam's Saloon Inc.?

   b. To Sam?

38. Corinne received one warrant (right) to purchase a share of common stock for each ten shares she owned in Wilbur Flights Inc. as a "dividend." The exercise price was $50, the price of the stock was $46, and the value of the warrant was $4. Corinne makes no elections. What are the tax consequences to Corinne and Wilbur if:

   a. Corinne's warrants expire worthless?

   b. Corinne exercised the warrants when the stock price was $62?

   c. Corinne sold the warrants for $7 a share?

39. Super Xtra Inc. is publicly held. One of its shareholders, Fred, owns 100 shares of common stock with a basis of $5,000 and a value of $12,000. On October 17 of this year, Fred receives 25 rights (to buy 25 new shares of stock). Each right is worth $12.

    a. Does Fred have any gross income?

    b. What is Fred's basis in his rights?

    c. When does the rights' holding period start?

    d. What difference would it make if Fred could have taken a $300 debenture in lieu of the rights, but did not?

40. Antoinette owns 100 shares of common stock of Gertz Incorporated which she acquired on June 6, 1982, for $11,000. On March 18, 1998, Antoinette received 10 shares of Gertz's common stock. The fair market value of the 10 shares on March 18, 1998, was $2,500. Gertz's current E&P for 1998 was $16,000.

    a. Assuming that the stock dividend was a proportionate dividend and no other distribution options were available, determine Antoinette's taxable income and Antoinette's basis in the 100 shares and the 10 shares, as well as each group's holding period. If she sold the 10 shares for $3,000 on June 3, 1998, then what is her gain or loss and what is its character?

    b. Compute Antoinette's taxable income, basis in the shares and their holding periods assuming that the stock dividend was disproportionate. If she sold the 10 shares on June 3, 1998, for $2,100, then what is her gain or loss and what is its character?

41. Gary owns 100 shares of common stock (class A) in Justine Inc. which he acquired on October 10, 1976, for $5,000. On July 8, 1998, Gary received 20 shares of class B common stock in a proportionate distribution. At the time of the distribution the fair market values of the class A and class B stock were $75 and $45 per share, respectively. Justine's current E&P for 1998 was $60,000. On August 18, 1998, Gary sold the 20 shares of class B stock for $1,000.

    a. What are the tax consequences of the distribution on July 8, 1998, to Gary?

    b. What are the tax consequences of the sale on August 18, 1998, for Gary?

42. Kimberly owns 200 shares of Rein Company which she purchased on December 22, 1986, for $10,000. On October 2, 1998, she received 20 shares of Rein Company as a stock dividend. The fair market value of the stock on October 2 was $100 per share. All shareholders of Rein Company had a choice of receiving shares or cash. Kimberly elected to receive the 20 shares. Assuming that Rein Company has very large E&P, determine Kimberly's gross income (if any) and basis in the 20 shares of stock.

43. Max Company has four shareholders. Sam Jones owns 200 shares, Paul Jones (Sam's brother) owns 100 shares, Robert Edwards (Sam's uncle) owns 100 shares and Sarah Jones (Sam's daughter) owns 100 shares. In determining ownership for a redemption under Code Sec. 302(b)(1) and (2), how many shares will Sam own directly and indirectly?

44. Salkey Company has two owners, Gus and Jack, who are father and son. Gus owns 100 shares which he acquired in 1982 for $15,000. Jack owns 100 shares which he acquired in 1984 for $21,000. Salkey's current E&P in 1998 is $70,000. On March 18, 1998, Salkey redeemed 35 shares from Gus in return for land worth $50,000 and an adjusted basis of $10,000.

    a. Does the redemption qualify as a sale?

    b. What are the income tax consequences to Gus, Jack, and Salkey Company?

    c. Would your answers to (a) and (b) differ if Gus and Jack were brothers? If so, how?

45. Monica is a preferred stockholder with a basis of $9,000 in her 100 shares in Small Appliances Inc. She has one-half her stock redeemed for $6,000 in a transaction that qualifies as a sale. Small Appliances's balance sheet prior to the redemption reads in part:

Common stock, authorized, issued and outstanding, 10,000 shares, par $1	$10,000
Paid-in-capital, common stock	40,000
Preferred stock, authorized, issued and outstanding, 1,000 shares, par $5	5,000
Paid-in-capital, preferred stock	20,000
Earnings and profits	76,000

    a. What is Monica's gain and its character?

    b. What is her basis in the remaining shares?

    c. What adjustments are to be made to the equity accounts?

    d. What difference does it make if, instead of cash, Monica receives property with a basis of $4,000?

46. Samson Corporation has 1,000 shares of common stock outstanding. Sal owns 560 shares, Rita owns 250 shares, and Susan owns 190 shares. None of the owners are related. On August 14, 1998, Samson redeemed 150 shares from Sal. Sal's adjusted basis in the 560 shares was $28,000. In return for the 150 shares, Sal received $17,000. Samson's current E&P for 1998 was $45,000. Sal prefers to receive sale or exchange treatment.

    a. Indicate if Sal might be able to receive sale or exchange treatment.

    b. Indicate the tax consequences to Sal if the redemption is treated as a dividend or if it is treated as a sale or exchange.

47. Staton Inc. has four unrelated shareholders, Wayne, Judy, Erica, and Josh. Their respective bases in the shares are $15,000, $17,000, $19,000, and $21,000. Each shareholder owns 100 shares of Staton. On November 8, 1998, Staton Inc. redeemed 50 shares of Wayne's stock for $10,000 and 20 shares of Judy's stock for $4,000. Staton's current E&P for 1998 was $30,000. What are the tax consequences to Wayne and Judy?

48. Foxrun Company has three equal shareholders, Thomas, Kimberly, and Jennifer. Kimberly and Jennifer are Thomas's daughters. On September 2, 1998, Foxrun redeemed all of Thomas's stock in return for $250,000. Thomas had acquired the stock in 1990 for $190,000. Foxrun's current E&P for 1998 was $325,000. Thomas would like to minimize his federal income tax liability in 1998. Explain the alternatives available to him and how they would impact his 1998 taxable income.

49. The AB Corp. has been owned equally by individuals A and B for over five years. AB operates two qualified businesses, Q and R. The XYZ Corp. wishes to acquire Division Q, worth $500,000 (asset basis $300,000), and AB wants to sell. AB Corp. distributes the assets of Q to A and B, who thereafter sell them to XYZ. What are the tax consequences to all parties if:

    a. The distribution does qualify as a partial liquidation?

    b. The distribution does not qualify under Code Sec. 304(b)(4)?

50. Falzone Company has two shareholders, Rita and Sal Corporation. Rita acquired her 300 shares in 1981 for $30,000 and Sal Corporation acquired its 200 shares in 1975 for $15,000. On August 2, 1998, Falzone Company sold one of its businesses that it had held since 1980. Due to this sale, Falzone Company redeemed 50 shares from each shareholder in exchange for $20,000 each. Falzone's E&P at the time of the redemption was $250,000. What are the tax consequences of this transaction to Rita and Sal Corporation?

51. Jim Lester was the sole shareholder of Lester Resorts Inc. His basis was $10,000 in the stock. Jim died when his stock was worth $500,000. His gross estate, including the stock, was $1,400,000, funeral and administration expenses amounted to $100,000, and estate and inheritance taxes totalled $200,000. Lester Resorts redeemed 80 percent of the stock from the estate for $500,000 when its E&P was $50,000. What are the tax consequences to Lester's estate and Lester Resorts?

52. Larry owns 90 of the 100 outstanding shares of EDP Corporation. Larry acquired the 90 shares in 1980 for $15,000. He also owns 70 of the 100 outstanding shares of EDT Corporation. Larry acquired the 70 shares in 1984 for $21,000. On October 18, 1998, Larry sold 25 shares of EDT stock to EDP Corporation for $43,000. EDT and EDP have current E&P in 1998 of $22,000 and $31,000, respectively.

    a. How will the sale be treated for federal income tax purposes?

    b. How much income, and what type, does Larry recognize?

    c. What is his basis in his stock?

    d. What is the effect of the transaction on EDP and EDT?

53. James owns 100 shares of Price Company which are Section 306 stock. He also owns 300 shares of its common stock. He wants to dispose of these shares in 1998 and is considering several options. Indicate the tax consequences of each option.

    a. Making a gift of the stock to his son.

    b. Selling all his stock (common and preferred) to an unrelated third party.

    c. Selling all his stock (common and preferred) to Price Company in a Code Sec. 302(b)(3) redemption.

    d. Selling the 100 shares to Robert Thomas, assuming that Price will have no E&P in 1998.

    e. Same as (d), except Price will have E&P in 1998.

    f. Having Price redeem the 100 shares in 1998, assuming that Price will have no E&P in 1998.

    g. Same as (d), except Price will have E&P in 1998.

54. Marcus owned 200 shares (100 percent) of Sterling Company's common stock. His basis in the shares was $12,000. In 1996, Sterling issued a preferred stock dividend to Marcus. The 50 shares he received had a fair market value of $10,000. Sterling's E&P in 1996 was $8,000. The fair market value of the common stock was $20,000 immediately after the dividend. In 1998, when Sterling's E&P was $15,000, Marcus sold the 50 shares of preferred stock to an unrelated party for $9,000. What are the tax consequences of these transactions to Marcus?

55. Modern Corporation had a deficit of $220,000 on December 31 last year. Its net income per books was $90,000 for this year. Cash dividends on common stock totaling $45,000 were paid in December this year. Modern should report the distribution to its shareholders as:

    a. Return of capital 100 percent

    b. Dividends 45/220, return of capital 175/220

    c. Dividends 50 percent, return of capital 50 percent

    d. Dividend

56. Pizza Express Inc. distributes an unrealized receivable with a face value of $800 and a fair market value of $600 to an individual shareholder. As a result of the distribution:

   a. The distributor's current E&P increases by a gain of $600, then is reduced by the $600 value; the distributee has dividend income of $600 and a basis in the receivable of $600.

   b. The distributor's E&P is reduced by the distribution.

   c. The distributor recognizes $800 of ordinary income on the anticipatory assignment of income.

   d. When the distributee collects the receivable at face value, a capital gain may result.

57. Buy Corporation has 100 shares of its only class of stock outstanding. Mr. Smith owns 15 shares, his wife owns 20 shares, his son owns 50 shares, and his son's daughter owns 15 shares. Under the constructive ownership rules for stock redemptions, how many shares of Buy Corporation's stock is the son's daughter considered to own?

   a. 15

   b. 50

   c. 65

   d. 100

   e. None of the above

58. During 1998, Kay Co. made the following distributions to an individual shareholder who owns 455 shares of its only class of stock.

Cash	$20,000
Real estate: Adjusted basis	75,000
Fair market value	85,000
Mortgage	15,000

   The shareholder assumed the mortgage on the property. Kay Co's earnings and profits prior to the distribution were $70,000. The real estate is Code Sec. 1245 property. Assuming a 40 percent corporate tax rate, what is the net adjustment to be made to the earnings and profits account due to the distribution?

   a. $10,000 increase

   b. $70,000 decrease

   c. $74,000 decrease

   d. $80,000 decrease

   e. None of the above

59. In 1998, a corporation distributed property with an adjusted basis of $85,000 and a fair market value of $95,000 to its shareholders. Its earnings and profits for 1998 were $110,000, and accumulated earnings and profits on January 1, 1998, were $250,000. What is the amount of gain recognized by the corporation on the distribution?

    a. $0
    b. $10,000
    c. $25,000
    d. $95,000
    e. None of the above

60. During 1998, Hero Co. distributed equipment having a fair market value of $300,000 and an adjusted basis of $150,000 to James in exchange for 85 percent of his interest in Hero. The distribution was under a plan of partial liquidation that resulted in a contraction of the business. James's adjusted basis in the stock exchanged was $180,000. Hero's earnings and profits were $500,000 prior to the distribution. What is the character and amount of James's recognized gain on the distribution?

    a. $120,000 capital gain
    b. $150,000 capital gain
    c. $150,000 capital loss
    d. $300,000 dividend income
    e. None of the above

61. Monty Company distributed $70,000 to Susan in redemption of all her stock. Susan's basis in the stock is $20,000 and her pro rata share of earnings and profits is $30,000. Assuming all the requirements for a redemption are met, how should Susan treat the distribution for federal income tax purposes?

    a. $0
    b. $20,000 dividend income
    c. $30,000 dividend income and $20,000 capital gain
    d. $50,000 capital gain
    e. None of the above

62. *Comprehensive Problem.* For each of the following independent distributions to shareholders, determine the impact on E&P; recognized gain, if any, to the distributing corporation; the amount of the dividend; and the basis in the property to the distributee, assuming ample E&P to start with:

    a. A cash distribution of $50,000.
    b. The distribution of an IOU with a face value of $50,000 and a market value of $45,000.
    c. The distribution of inventory with a basis of $2,000 and a value of $5,000 to an individual shareholder.
    d. The distribution of land with a basis of $25,000, a mortgage of $40,000, and a value of $100,000 to an individual shareholder.

63. *Comprehensive Problem.* Manuel Mesa is a 50 percent shareholder in a landscaping corporation, Mo Lo Inc. He has just incorporated his own wholly owned landscaping business, Trim Inc. The other (unrelated) shareholder in Mo Lo wishes to buy Manuel out with one-half the assets of Mo Lo, consisting of tractors, tools, and equipment, all written down below current value. Manuel wishes to transfer these assets to Trim. What are the tax consequences of the following transaction alternatives, and which one, if any, is preferable?

    a. Mo Lo redeems Manuel's stock with the property and Manuel contributes the assets to the capital of Trim.

    b. Manuel contributes his Mo Lo stock to Trim and Mo Lo redeems its stock from Trim for the assets.

    c. Same as (a), except Manuel sells the assets to Trim for an installment obligation.

    d. Same as (b), but Manuel sells his stock to Trim on the installment plan.

64. *Research Problem.* Hobbies and Games Inc. has had taxable income the last three years, but is breaking even this year. Sondra, the sole shareholder, has a $25,000 basis in her stock. After consulting with a local CPA, the corporation does the following:

    a. Sets up an Employee Stock Ownership Plan (ESOP).

    b. Contributes $40,000 to the ESOP, borrowed for the occasion from a local bank.

    c. Deducts the $40,000 as a contribution to a qualified plan, thus creating a net operating loss of $40,000. The loss is carried back, resulting in a refund of taxes paid the last three years.

    d. Permits the ESOP to purchase 49 percent of Sondra's stock; she reports a long-term capital gain of $27,750. (See IRS Letter Rulings 8147187 and 8222026.)

    Can all these transactions be executed under the rules applicable to employee stock ownership plans?

65. *Research Problem.* Joe Tucker is the sole shareholder of Tucker Parts Inc. The corporation is cash rich, and Joe wishes to sell his stock to Bill Corker, who has limited funds. The parties proceed as follows:

    a. Joe sells 40 percent of his stock to Bill for $50,000, payable over 10 years.

    b. Tucker Parts redeems the remaining 60 percent of Joe's stock for $75,000 in cash.

    What are the tax consequences to Joe?

    Does it make any difference if the two steps are reversed?

    (See *Zenz v. Quinlivan,* 54-2 USTC ¶ 9445, 213 F.2d 914 (CA-6 1954); Rev. Rul. 55-745, 1955-2 CB 223.)

66. *Research Problem.* Constant Corporation is a family-owned corporation. In 1998, Constant redeemed stock from some of its owners. Because of the attribution rules of Code Sec. 318, the redemptions did not qualify for sale or exchange treatment. However, none of the family members like each other, and they believe that family attribution should be waived because the "bad blood" between them makes them "unrelated." Advise them about this assertion. (See Rev. Rul. 80-26, 1980-1 CB 66; *D. Metzger Trust,* 76 TC 42, CCH Dec. 37,614 (1981), aff'd 82-2 USTC ¶ 9718, 693 F.2d 459 (CA-6 1982); *R.F. Haft Trust,* 75-1 USTC ¶ 9209, 510 F.2d 43 (CA-1 1975); and *B.E. Niedermeyer,* 62 TC 280, CCH Dec. 32,621 (1974), aff'd, 76-1 USTC ¶ 9417, 535 F.2d 500 (CA-9 1976), cert. denied, 492 U.S. 1000, 97 S.Ct. 528.)

Chapter 15

Corporate Distributions in Complete Liquidations

Learning Objectives

After completing Chapter 15, you should be able to:

1. Determine the tax treatment of the liquidating corporation, including the recognition of gain or loss.
2. Determine the tax treatment of shareholders upon a complete liquidation, including the computation of gain or loss and the basis of property received.
3. Understand the effects of a parent corporation's election to treat a stock purchase as an asset purchase.
4. Identify the applicability of the collapsible corporation rules and the exceptions to their application.

OVERVIEW OF CHAPTER

Chapter 14 discussed ordinary corporate distributions, including distributions of property and stock, as well as stock redemptions and partial liquidations. After those distributions, the corporation continued to exist as an operating entity. This chapter discusses the winding up of a corporation's business affairs followed by a complete liquidation of the corporation.

The tax consequences of a complete liquidation of a corporation are examined from the standpoint of the effect on the liquidating corporation and its shareholders. Special rules apply to the liquidation of a controlled subsidiary.

Complete Liquidations

At some point in the life of a corporation it may be determined that the corporation should be liquidated. In that event, the corporation's shareholders will surrender all of their stock in the corporation and receive their pro rata shares of any remaining assets after all creditors have been paid.

¶ 15,001   REASONS FOR LIQUIDATION

The shareholders of a corporation may wish to liquidate a corporation for any number of reasons. The reasons for liquidation may be based on economics, or a liquidation may be necessary because the corporate form of organization is no longer beneficial, or it may be necessary to liquidate because of a desire to sell the business. Included among the reasons for a corporate liquidation are:

1. Lack of business profitability

2. Avoidance of double taxation of corporate earnings

3. Avoidance of corporate penalty taxes such as the personal holding company tax or the accumulated earnings tax

4. Recognition of losses at the shareholder level

5. Conversion of assets into cash for alternative purposes

6. A potential buyer's unwillingness to purchase stock in the corporation

There are several advantages to liquidating a corporation. Amounts distributed in complete liquidation of a corporation are treated as in full payment in exchange for the stock. Code Sec. 331(a). Thus, if the stock is held as a capital asset, liquidating distributions are subject to capital gain treatment and can be used to offset capital losses from other sources. Such capital gain treatment applies even though part of the distribution consists of accumulated E&P. If these same amounts had been distributed in a nonliquidating distribution, they would be taxed as ordinary dividends.

Another benefit of a liquidation is that depreciable assets may obtain a stepped-up tax basis that will result in larger depreciation deductions and a smaller gain or larger loss in the event of a future sale or exchange. Other benefits of a liquidation may be summarized as follows:

1. A new corporation has the opportunity to issue preferred stock without the taint of Code Sec. 306. However, care must be taken that the IRS does not treat a liquidation followed by a reincorporation as a reorganization.

2. Shareholders may be able to recognize a capital loss (ordinary loss if Code Sec. 1244 is applicable) if the basis of their stock is greater than the fair market value of the assets distributed.

3. If a corporation is a personal holding company because it derives most of its income from passive investment income sources, a liquidation will prevent the continued application of the personal holding company tax.

¶ 15,021   LIQUIDATION STATUS REQUIREMENTS

In order for the liquidation rules to apply to a liquidating corporation and its shareholders, a corporation must be in a status of liquidation. Under Reg. § 1.332-2(c), a status of liquidation exists when a "corporation ceases to be a going concern and its activities are merely for the purpose of winding up its affairs, paying its debts, and distributing any remaining balance to its shareholders." A liquidation may be completed prior to the actual dissolution of the liquidating corporation. In fact, legal dissolution of the corporation (i.e., termination of a corporate entity's legal existence under state law) is not required. Furthermore, the mere retention of a nominal amount of assets for the sole purpose of preserving the corporation's charter will not invalidate a complete liquidation.

To constitute a distribution in complete liquidation, the distribution must be (1) made by the liquidating corporation in complete cancellation or redemption of all of its stock in accordance with a plan of liquidation, or (2) one of a series of distributions in complete cancellation or redemption of all of its stock in accordance with a plan of liquidation.

It is not necessary that there be a formal plan of liquidation. According to the Tax Court, there are three basic tests that must be met to qualify for liquidation status. *W.G. Maguire Est.,* 50 TC 130, CCH Dec. 28,932 (1968).

1. There must be a manifest intention to liquidate.

2. There must be a continuing purpose to terminate corporate affairs.

3. The corporation's activities must be directed toward such termination.

¶ 15,041 RECOGNITION OF GAIN OR LOSS RULE

The *General Utilities* doctrine, named after a landmark Supreme Court case, generally permitted nonrecognition treatment at the corporate level for distributions or sales of property in complete liquidations. *General Utilities & Operating Co. v. Helvering,* 36-1 USTC ¶ 9012, 296 U.S. 200, 56 S.Ct. 185 (1935). Over the years, this nonrecognition principle was eroded by numerous exceptions, and the 1986 Act generally repealed these nonrecognition rules. The result is that a liquidating corporation must generally recognize gain or loss on the sale or distribution of property in complete liquidation.

¶ 15,061 SUMMARY OF LIQUIDATION RULES

In general, gain or loss is recognized by a corporation upon the distribution of property to its shareholders in a complete liquidation. Code Sec. 336. The corporation's earnings and profits are generally eliminated along with the corporation's basis in any property distributed in the liquidation. Section 331 provides that a shareholder treat the property received in liquidation of a corporation as proceeds obtained from the exchange of stock. The shareholder's gain or loss is determined by deducting the adjusted basis of the shareholder's stock from the fair market value of the property received. The gain or loss is generally a capital gain or loss since the shareholder's stock is usually a capital asset. The shareholders will have a fair market value basis in any property received. Code Sec. 334(a).

No gain or loss is recognized by a parent corporation upon the receipt of assets in the complete liquidation of a controlled subsidiary. Code Sec. 332. Additionally, no gain or loss is recognized by the liquidating subsidiary, and its tax attributes and basis for assets carryover to its parent. This provision allows a controlled group of corporations to eliminate unwanted subsidiaries without the recognition of gain, and is based on the premise that there has been no real change in the economic investment of the shareholders of the parent corporation.

Effect of Complete Liquidation on Corporations

A corporation must generally recognize gain or loss on the distribution of property in complete liquidation.

¶ 15,101   GAIN OR LOSS RECOGNITION

Generally, a corporation must recognize gain or loss upon a distribution of property in liquidation, computed as if the property were sold to the distributee shareholder at its fair market value. Code Sec. 336(a). The type of gain or loss recognized (e.g., ordinary, capital, Section 1231) depends on the nature of the property to the corporation, as well as the property's holding period.

> *Example 15.1.* Groll Inc. adopts a plan of complete liquidation and subsequently distributes an auto to a shareholder that was originally purchased for $18,000, with an adjusted basis of $2,000 and a fair market value of $5,000. Groll must recognize $3,000 ($5,000 FMV − $2,000 basis) of gain. The entire gain is ordinary income because of depreciation recapture under Code Sec. 1245.

¶ 15,121   LIABILITIES

If a liquidating corporation distributes property and a shareholder assumes a liability on the property or takes the property subject to a liability, the fair market value of the property is treated as being not less than the amount of the liability. Thus, if the amount of liability exceeds the fair market value of the property, gain must be recognized to the extent that the liability exceeds the property's adjusted basis.

> *Example 15.2.* Mall Inc. distributes cash of $40,000 and a building with a fair market value of $100,000 and a basis of $20,000 (subject to a mortgage of $130,000) to its sole shareholder. Since the building and mortgage are distributed at a time when the mortgage exceeds the fair market value of the building, Mall must recognize a gain of $110,000 ($130,000 mortgage − $20,000 basis).

> *Example 15.3.* Same as Example 15.2, except that the amount of mortgage is only $60,000. Mall must recognize a gain of $80,000 ($100,000 FMV − $20,000 basis).

If the liquidating corporation does not pay the income tax resulting from the gains recognized on liquidating distributions, the shareholders must pay the tax because they are the transferees of the assets on which the gains were recognized. In such case, the amount of the distribution is reduced by the amount of tax liability, thus reducing the shareholders' gain or increasing their loss.

Example 15.4. Orchards Corp. adopts a plan of complete liquidation and distributes an asset with a basis of $20,000 and a fair market value of $50,000. Assuming a 34 percent tax rate, the corporation's recognized gain of $30,000 results in an income tax liability of $10,200. If the liability is not paid by the corporation, it becomes a liability of the transferee shareholder and reduces the shareholder's liquidating distribution to $39,800 ($50,000 FMV — $10,200 tax liability).

¶ 15,131   LOSS RECOGNITION

Under Code Sec. 336(a), losses as well as gains are recognized on in-kind liquidating distributions. If the losses are sufficiently large, they may result in a net operating loss that can be carried back to the corporation's two preceding taxable years to obtain a refund of income tax paid in those years. However, if the losses are capital losses, or if the corporation has had little taxable income in recent years, the losses may provide little, if any, tax benefit to the liquidating corporation.

Additionally, Code Sec. 336(d) provides special limitations on the recognition of losses. These limitations are generally designed to prevent the contribution of built-in loss property to a corporation prior to its liquidation in order to generate a recognized loss at the corporate level to offset recognized gains.

The first limitation is found in Code Sec. 336(d)(1) which provides that no loss can be recognized on a distribution of property to a more than 50 percent shareholder (including both direct and constructive ownership under Code Sec. 267(d)) if the distribution is (1) not pro rata or (2) the distributed property is "disqualified property." Disqualified property is property acquired by the corporation in a Code Sec. 351 transfer (i.e., a nontaxable transfer to a controlled corporation in exchange for stock) or as a contribution to capital during the five-year period ending on the date of the distribution. Disqualified property also includes property whose basis is determined (in whole or in part) by reference to the adjusted basis of disqualified property (e.g., property acquired in a like-kind exchange involving disqualified property).

Example 15.5. Ping Corporation's stock is held equally by two brothers. Four years prior to its liquidation, the shareholders made a capital contribution of property (basis of $140,000 and FMV of $100,000) to Ping Corporation. In liquidation, Ping Corporation transfers the property (still worth $100,000) to the brothers. Because each brother owns directly and constructively more than 50 percent of the stock and the property is disqualified property, none of the $40,000 realized loss can be recognized by Ping Corporation.

Example 15.6. Pong Corporation is owned 60 percent by Eldon Purry and 40 percent by Frank Fox. Pursuant to a plan of complete liquidation, Pong distributes securities that it had purchased to Purry. The securities (which are not disqualified property) have a basis of $40,000 and a FMV of $10,000. Because the securities are distributed to a more than 50 percent shareholder in a non-pro rata distribution, Pong's realized loss of $30,000 cannot be recognized.

If the securities had instead been distributed 60 percent to Purry and 40 percent to Fox, the $30,000 loss would be recognized by Pong. Similarly, if Purry and Fox were not related and the securities were distributed only to Fox, the loss would have been recognized.

Note that the above rules prohibit contributions of property with built-in losses followed by distributions of the property to related persons. Absent additional restrictions, a corporation could sell the contributed property or distribute the property to a 50 percent or less shareholder and recognize the loss. To prevent this potential abuse, a second limitation is contained in Code Sec. 336(d)(2). The limitation applies to the computation of a liquidating corporation's loss on the sale, exchange, or distribution of property that was acquired in a Code Sec. 351 transfer or as a contribution to capital. The adjusted basis of the property must be reduced (but not below zero) by the excess of the adjusted basis of the property on the date of its contribution over its fair market value at such time, if the principal purpose of the acquisition was to generate a loss in connection with the liquidation.

Example 15.7. A shareholder makes a capital contribution of property with a basis of $15,000 and a FMV of $10,000 on August 1, 1998. During November 1998, a plan of liquidation is adopted and the property is sold for $8,000. If the purpose of contributing the property was to recognize the loss in liquidation, the property's adjusted basis of $15,000 must be reduced by the $5,000 of built-in loss. Then the liquidating corporation's recognized loss is limited to $2,000 ($10,000 basis − $8,000 selling price); the $5,000 of built-in loss at the time of contribution is disallowed.

Generally, any property acquired in the above manner within two years before the corporation adopts a plan of liquidation is presumed to be part of a loss recognition plan. However, Regulations are expected to provide that this rule will be disregarded unless there is no clear and substantial relationship between the contributed property and the conduct of the corporation's current or future business. Thus, if contributed property is actually used in the corporation's business, this rule should not apply if there is a business purpose for placing the property in the corporation. On the other hand, if Code Sec. 336(d)(2) does apply, its effect is to limit the amount of recognized loss to the decline in value that occurs while the property is in the hands of the corporation; any built-in loss at time of contribution is disallowed.

If a plan of liquidation is adopted and disallows a built-in loss that was deducted in a previous tax year, the liquidating corporation must recapture the loss by including it in gross income, or can file an amended return for the preceding year in which the loss was deducted.

Example 15.8. Assume the same facts as in Example 15.7, except that the property is sold in 1998, and the plan of liquidation is adopted in 1999. Assuming Code Sec. 336(d)(2) disallows the loss that was deducted in 1998, the corporation must recapture the loss by including it in gross income for 1999, or the corporation can file an amended return for 1998 in order to remove the loss as a deduction.

¶ 15,141   EXPENSES OF LIQUIDATION

The treatment of expenses incurred in conjunction with a liquidation can be summarized as follows:

1. Expenses of adopting a plan of liquidation and terminating the business (e.g., accountants' and lawyers' fees, etc.) are deductible as ordinary and necessary business expenses under Code Sec. 162.

2. Expenses incurred in selling assets can not be deducted, but instead must be offset against the amounts realized from sales.

3. If some of the expenses are attributable to a tax-free reorganization, such portion is nondeductible.

4. Organizational expenditures that have been capitalized may be deducted upon liquidation.

5. Expenses incurred by shareholders are nondeductible, but reduce the amount realized from the liquidating distribution.

¶ 15,161   REPORTING REQUIREMENTS

Form 966 (Corporate Dissolution or Liquidation) must be filed with the IRS within 30 days of the adoption of the plan of liquidation. Each shareholder and the IRS is entitled to Forms 1096 (Annual Summary and Transmittal of U.S. Information Returns) and 1099DIV (Dividends and Distributions) after the completion of the liquidation, detailing the amounts distributed to each shareholder. When the liquidation is completed (all substantial assets have been distributed), the corporation's final tax year ends. The final tax return must include a copy of the corporate resolution to liquidate, a list of the properties sold, sale dates, realized gains and losses, as well as the date of final distribution and the amount of retained assets, if any. Reg. § 1.337-6.

Failure to file Form 966 or to file it on time will not invalidate a complete liquidation. Rev. Rul. 65-80, 1965-1 CB 154. However, it is possible that penalties may result under Code Sec. 7203.

Effect of Complete Liquidation on Shareholders

In a typical liquidation, shareholders are deemed to have exchanged their stock, whether or not the certificates are formally cancelled, for the cash and property received in the liquidating distribution. Code Sec. 331. As a result, gain or loss is recognized, and a fair market value basis results for property received. Code Sec. 334(a). Special rules under Code Sec. 332, discussed at ¶ 15,301, govern liquidations of controlled subsidiaries.

¶ 15,201 DISTRIBUTIONS OF PROPERTY

When a corporation is liquidated, the corporation distributes its property to the shareholders and/or sells the property and distributes the proceeds. In any event, the shareholders are deemed to have exchanged their stock for the property and cash received. Code Sec. 331. This approach generally results in capital gain or loss treatment to the shareholders, assuming their stock is held as a capital asset. Note that the character of the shareholders' gain or loss is determined by the nature of the stock, not by the character of the property distributed. The amount of a shareholder's gain or loss is computed by subtracting the shareholder's stock basis from the fair market value of the property received. A fair market value basis results for the assets received. Code Sec. 334(a).

There are several exceptions to the general rule that a shareholder recognizes capital gain or loss from a complete liquidation.

1. If the stock was Section 1244 stock, the shareholder's loss is an ordinary loss to the extent of $50,000 per year ($100,000 on a joint return).

2. If the shareholder is a dealer in securities, any gain or loss on liquidation is an ordinary gain or loss since the stock was held primarily for resale in the ordinary course of business.

3. No gain or loss is recognized to a parent corporation liquidating its at least 80-percent-owned subsidiary. Code Sec. 332.

Liabilities to Shareholders

If a shareholder assumes a liability of the liquidating corporation, or receives property that is subject to a liability, then the liability reduces the amount realized by the shareholder, thus reducing the shareholder's gain or increasing the shareholder's loss.

Example 15.9. In complete liquidation of a corporation, Alvin Aubrey receives a building with a fair market value of $80,000 and assumes a mortgage of $30,000 on the building. If the basis of Alvin's stock is $15,000, Alvin's gain from the liquidation is $35,000 (($80,000 FMV − $30,000 liability) − $15,000 basis). Alvin's basis for the building is the building's FMV of $80,000.

Series of Distributions

If a series of liquidating distributions are made, the shareholder must use the cost recovery method for recognition of gain or loss. Rev. Rul. 85-48, 1985-1 CB 126. Each payment received is first applied against the basis of stock. As soon as basis is exceeded, gain must be recognized. However, no loss can be recognized until the final distribution is received.

Example 15.10. Everett Evans owns 1,000 shares of Imperial Corporation purchased at a cost of $10,000. During 1997, 1998, and 1999, Everett receives the following distributions in a series of distributions in complete liquidation of the corporation:

December 6, 1997 .... $6,000
May 15, 1998.. 3,000
March 31, 1999 2,500

Since the liquidating distributions are made over more than one year, the cost recovery method is used to determine gain or loss. The 1997 distribution of $6,000 is nontaxable and reduces Everett's stock basis to $4,000. The $3,000 distribution in 1998 is also nontaxable and reduces Everett's basis to $1,000. The $2,500 1999 distribution first reduces stock basis to zero, with the remaining $1,500 in excess of stock basis treated as capital gain.

Example 15.11. Assume the same facts as in Example 15.10, except that the 1998 distribution was the final distribution. Again the cost recovery method would apply the 1997 distribution against Everett's stock basis. The 1998 distribution would reduce stock basis to $1,000. However, since the 1998 distribution is now the final distribution, the $1,000 of unrecovered stock basis would be recognized as a capital loss in 1998.

Multiple Blocks of Stock

Often a shareholder has acquired more than one block of stock. If the stock was acquired at different times and for different amounts, the proceeds must be divided by the number of shares so that gain or loss can be computed on each block of stock. Reg. § 1.331-1(e).

Example 15.12. A shareholder acquired 1,000 shares in the liquidating corporation; 500 shares three years ago for $7,000 and 500 shares five months ago for $4,000. If the shareholder's liquidating distribution is worth $12,000, the amount realized is allocated equally to each block of shares, resulting in a long-term capital loss of $1,000 and a short-term capital gain of $2,000.

Disproportionate Distributions

In some situations, shareholders receive distributions in complete liquidation of a corporation that are disproportionate to their shareholdings. If a shareholder receives less than a proportionate share, the excess of the proportionate share over the amount actually received is treated as if it had been used in a separate transaction to make gifts, pay compensation, satisfy obligations, etc. depending on the particular facts and circumstances. If a shareholder receives more than a proportionate share, the excess is treated as a payment attributable to those shareholders who receive less than their proportionate share. Rev. Rul. 79-10, 1979-1 CB 140.

¶ 15,221   BASIS OF PROPERTY RECEIVED IN LIQUIDATION

If the liquidation is taxable to the shareholder under Code Sec. 331, the shareholder's basis for the property received in the liquidation is the property's fair market value on date of distribution. If more than one item of property is received, each item of property receives a fair market value basis, regardless of the nature of the item in the hands of the liquidating corporation or the distributee shareholder. Thus, a shareholder is treated as if the shareholder had purchased the property for its fair market value in a taxable exchange using stock as the consideration for the purchase. The shareholder's holding period for the property begins on the day after the day the property is received, the same as for any purchased property.

¶ 15,241   DISTRIBUTIONS OF INSTALLMENT OBLIGATIONS

The general rule that the liquidating corporation recognizes gain or loss on the distribution of property also applies to installment obligations. However, the *shareholder* who receives the installment obligation may defer the tax on any stock gain attributable to the installment obligation until collections on the installment obligation are made if:

1. The obligation was received from the sale or exchange of property by the corporation during the 12-month period beginning on the date the liquidation plan was adopted,

2. The liquidation is completed by the close of this 12-month period, and

3. The obligation is not attributable to the sale of inventory, stock in trade, or property held for sale to customers, unless it was a bulk sale of substantially all such property to one person. Code Sec. 453(h)(1).

A special computation of a shareholder's gain must be made if the shareholder receives a liquidating distribution that includes an installment obligation that meets the above requirements. In this case, part of the shareholder's stock is treated as having been exchanged for the installment obligation, with the remaining stock exchanged for any other property received. To determine the gain on each part, the shareholder's stock basis is allocated between the installment obligation and the other property received based on their relative fair market values. The stock gain resulting from the other property received in the liquidation is immediately recognized, while the stock gain attributable to the installment obligation is recognized as the installment payments are received.

Example 15.13. Cabins Inc. adopted a plan of liquidation and made an installment sale of its only asset (a motel) to an unrelated individual. The installment note calls for payment of $20,000 (plus interest) in each of the next six years. Cabins distributes the $120,000 note to its sole shareholder, Ben Baker, who has a stock basis of $24,000. Assuming the sale and liquidation were completed within 12 months of the date the plan of liquidation was adopted, Ben's gain of $120,000 − $24,000 = $96,000 will be reported as the installment payments are received. Since the gross profit ratio is $96,000/$120,000, 80 percent of each $20,000 installment payment will be reported as capital gain.

Example 15.14. Same as Example 15.13, except that the motel is sold for a down payment of $30,000, with $30,000 (plus interest) to be received in each of the next three years. If Cabins distributes the cash of $30,000 and the $90,000 installment note in liquidation, Ben's $24,000 stock basis must be allocated between the cash and the installment note as follows:

Property	FMV	Percent	Allocated Stock Basis	Realized Gain
Cash	$ 30,000	25%	$ 6,000	$24,000
Installment Note	90,000	75	18,000	72,000
Total	$120,000	100%	$24,000	$96,000

Ben must recognize $24,000 of capital gain in the year of liquidation. One-third of the remaining $72,000 of capital gain will be recognized in each of the next three years as each installment payment of $30,000 is received.

TAX PLANNING POINTER ▼

If a corporation sells property in the process of liquidation, it should consider making some of these sales on the installment method. Since the installment method is available only for sales at a gain, and the corporate seller must recognize this gain upon making a liquidating distribution of the installment obligation, the ideal installment sale meets the following requirements:

1. The fair market value is slightly higher than the asset's basis.
2. The shareholder to whom the obligation is distributed has a low stock basis.

This will result in maximum deferral of the shareholder's gain without causing significant corporate tax to be incurred.

¶ 15,253 CONTINGENT LIABILITIES

In some cases, after a liquidation is completed, shareholders are required to pay a contingent liability of the corporation, or a liability that was unknown at the time the corporation was liquidated. This shareholder payment does not change the shareholders' original reporting of their liquidating distributions. Instead, the shareholders' payment results in a deduction, the nature of which depends upon the character of the original gain or loss that the shareholders reported. The type of deduction or loss that would have been available to the corporation if it had paid the liability before liquidation is not relevant. Thus, if the liquidation resulted in a shareholder reporting a capital gain or loss, the shareholder's subsequent payment of a contingent corporate liability results in a capital loss. *F.D. Arrowsmith,* 52-2 USTC 9527, 334 U.S. 6, 73 S.Ct. 71 (1952).

Example 15.15. Mark Dollmaker liquidated his wholly owned corporation and recognized a long-term capital gain of $30,000 in 1996. In 1998, he finally settled a state income tax issue resulting from an audit of the liquidated corporation's tax returns and paid $4,000 in his capacity as a transferee of the corporation's assets. Mark must deduct his $4,000 payment as a long-term capital loss in 1998 because the 1996 liquidation had resulted in a capital gain.

Note that Mark must deduct his payment as a capital loss even though the corporation would have had an ordinary deduction if the corporation had paid the state taxes before liquidation.

¶ 15,261   CORPORATE DEBTS TO SHAREHOLDERS

Section 331 has no application to a distribution in satisfaction of corporate indebtedness to a shareholder, assuming the debt is a bona fide debt. However, if the "debt" is in substance an equity investment, the shareholder's stock basis is increased, resulting in a smaller gain or larger loss under Code Sec. 331. If the debt obligation is treated as debt, no gain or loss will be recognized to the holder unless the amount of cash and the fair market value of the property received differs from the holder's basis in the obligation.

If the corporation becomes insolvent, the type of loss recognized by the holder depends upon the nature of the debt obligation. If the debt obligation that becomes worthless is a capital asset and constitutes a security, the loss is generally treated as a capital loss on the last day of the taxable year in which the security becomes worthless. The term "security" not only includes stock, but also a bond, note, or other evidence of indebtedness issued by a corporation with interest coupons or in registered form. Code Sec. 165(g)(2).

In some cases, a security may result in an ordinary loss if the security is not a capital asset when it becomes worthless. For example, a worthless security that was held as inventory by a securities dealer would result in an ordinary loss deduction. Additionally, a special provision permits a parent corporation to deduct an ordinary loss on the worthlessness of the securities of a subsidiary corporation that is at least 80 percent owned. To qualify, at least 90 percent of the gross receipts of the subsidiary for all taxable years must be derived from sources other than passive income. Code Sec. 165(g)(3).

If the debt obligation that becomes worthless is not classified as a security, the resulting loss may be deducted as either a nonbusiness or business bad debt. Generally, loans made by a shareholder to a corporation are investment related and result in a nonbusiness bad debt that is deductible as a short-term capital loss. However, if the loan is made to protect the shareholder's employment with the corporation (i.e., the shareholder's trade or business), the loss is treated as a business bad debt deductible as an ordinary loss. Whether a loan results in a business or nonbusiness bad debt depends upon the dominant motive for making the loan.

TAX PLANNING POINTER

An individual shareholder can transfer Code Sec. 331 gain to low-bracket family members (e.g., children or grandchildren over 13) by gifting a corporation's stock prior to liquidation. The transfer should take place well ahead of the adoption of the plan of liquidation to avoid the anticipatory assignment of income doctrine.

KEYSTONE PROBLEM

The corporation proposed to be liquidated has considerable operating income. It also has assets with fair market values lower than their basis.

1.   Does it matter whether the corporation is liquidated at the beginning or the end of its tax year?

2.   Does it make sense to defer the liquidation until the shareholder dies if the stock has appreciated in value? What if the stock has decreased in value?

¶ 15,275   LIQUIDATION-REINCORPORATION

A typical liquidation-reincorporation transaction involves an attempt by shareholders to liquidate an existing corporation, realize capital gain on the distribution of appreciated assets, obtain a stepped-up fair market value basis for such assets, and then reincorporate some (or all) of the assets in a new corporation that continues the business of the old corporation. In an alternative form of the transaction, an existing corporation sells some (or all) of its assets to a newly formed corporation that is controlled by the existing corporation's shareholders and then liquidates.

Prior to 1987, if the liquidation was respected as an independent transaction, the shareholders' gain was taxed at preferential capital gains rates, the appreciated assets received a stepped-up basis without any corporate level tax (except for depreciation recapture and similar items), and the earnings and profits of the old corporation were eliminated. With the repeal of the *General Utilities* doctrine (see ¶ 15,041), the potential tax advantages of a liquidation-reincorporation are diminished. However, a liquidation-reincorporation might still be attempted if the potential tax benefits of a complete liquidation outweigh the costs of a corporate-level tax because the corporation's built-in gain is minimal, the liquidating corporation has net operating losses or built-in losses that can offset the gains, or the shareholders have a high stock basis in the liquidating corporation and can utilize the resulting capital losses.

The IRS often attacks these transactions, arguing that the liquidation is not an independent transaction and that a liquidation-reincorporation is in substance a reorganization under Code Sec. 368(a)(1)(D). As a reorganization, the assets in the new corporation have a carryover basis, there is a carryover of the liquidated corporation's earnings and profits and other tax attributes to the new corporation, and the shareholders receive dividend treatment for any retained assets.

Generally, a liquidation-reincorporation is treated as a Type D reorganization if the shareholders of the liquidated corporation own 50 percent or more of the new corporation. Additionally, in order to obtain a favorable advance ruling on a corporate liquidation, no assets of the liquidating corporation can be transferred to another corporation where more than 20 percent of the stock of both corporations is owned by the same shareholders. Rev. Proc. 90-3, 1990-1 CB 402.

Liquidation of Subsidiaries

¶ 15,301   SPECIAL RULES

There are special rules that apply only to the liquidation of controlled subsidiaries. Under Code Sec. 332, no gain or loss is recognized by a parent corporation on the receipt of property distributed in complete liquidation of a subsidiary. This provision reflects the theory that a liquidation of a subsidiary represents only a change of form, since there has been no real change in the economic investment of the shareholders of the parent corporation. The subsidiary's basis for assets carries over to the parent corporation so that any deferred gain or loss at the time of liquidation is recognized if the parent subsequently sells the liquidated subsidiary's former assets.

If Code Sec. 332 applies, the parent corporation inherits all of the subsidiary's tax accounting attributes at the time of liquidation (e.g., earnings and profits, capital loss carryforwards, NOL carryforward, potential for depreciation recapture, etc.). Additionally, the parent's basis for its subsidiary's stock disappears, so that the parent's realized gain or loss resulting from the liquidation will never be recognized.

> *Example 15.16.* Parent Corporation owns 100 percent of the stock of Subsidiary Corporation and has a basis of $100,000 for its Subsidiary shares. Subsidiary is liquidated and its assets having a basis of $80,000 and a FMV of $150,000 are distributed to Parent. Parent's realized gain of $50,000 ($150,000 FMV − $100,000 stock basis) is not recognized. Parent's basis for the assets it receives is $80,000, the same basis as Subsidiary had for the assets before liquidation.

¶ 15,309   NONRECOGNITION RULES OF SECTION 332

Section 332 applies only if three requirements are met.

First Requirement: 80 Percent Ownership. The parent corporation must own at least 80 percent of the combined voting power and at least 80 percent of the total value of all the stock of the subsidiary corporation (except nonvoting, nonparticipating preferred stock) on the date that the plan of liquidation is adopted and at all times until the subsidiary's liquidation is completed. The parent corporation must satisfy this ownership requirement directly; no constructive ownership rules apply.

TAX PLANNING POINTER ▼

Although Code Sec. 332 is not an elective provision, the 80 percent ownership requirement can be used for tax planning. A parent corporation that wishes to avoid the nonrecognition rules under Code Sec. 332 (i.e., to recognize a loss on its subsidiary's stock) can sell some of the subsidiary's stock to reduce its ownership below 80 percent before or during the liquidation process. Then the general rule of Code Sec. 331 will apply and the loss will be recognized. On the other hand, a parent corporation owning less than 80 percent of a subsidiary may wish to increase its ownership to at least 80 percent before the plan of liquidation is adopted so that Code Sec. 332 will apply to the liquidating distributions and the recognition of gains will be deferred.

Second Requirement: Cancellation of Stock. There must be a distribution in complete cancellation or redemption of all of the subsidiary's stock pursuant to a plan of complete liquidation. Legal dissolution of the subsidiary is not required. A minimal amount of assets may be retained by the subsidiary in order to protect its legal existence and preserve its corporate charter.

Third Requirement: Timing. There are two alternative time periods during which the liquidating distributions must take place:

1. If all liquidating distributions are made within one taxable year of the subsidiary, no formal plan of liquidation need be adopted. A shareholders' resolution authorizing the distributions will suffice even though no time limit for completing the transfers is specified. Furthermore, the year in which the liquidation occurs does not have to be the same year in which the shareholders' resolution or plan of liquidation is adopted.

2. If the liquidating distributions extend beyond one taxable year, a formal plan of liquidation must be adopted and all liquidating distributions must be made within three taxable years of the close of the taxable year in which the first distribution is made. If the liquidation is not completed within the specified time period, Code Sec. 332 will not apply to any of the liquidating distributions.

If any of the above three requirements are not satisfied, Code Sec. 332 will not apply, and the liquidating distributions will be taxed to the parent corporation under Code Sec. 331.

¶ 15,315 PARENT'S INDEBTEDNESS TO SUBSIDIARY

If a parent corporation is indebted to its subsidiary, and the subsidiary distributes its parent's debt obligations to the parent as part of a complete liquidation of the subsidiary, a question arises as to whether the parent corporation will recognize gain resulting from this discharge of indebtedness. In such case, no gain is recognized because the parent's notes are considered "property" and, under Code Sec. 332, no gain is recognized by a parent corporation when it receives property in complete liquidation of its controlled subsidiary.

¶ 15,335 INSOLVENT SUBSIDIARY

Section 332 does not apply if the subsidiary is insolvent since the parent corporation does not receive any distribution in exchange for its subsidiary's stock. A subsidiary is insolvent if its liabilities exceed the fair market value of its assets. In this case, the parent corporation's loss on its subsidiary's securities is treated as a loss from worthless securities under Code Sec. 165(g). Although the resulting loss is generally a capital loss, the parent instead receives ordinary loss treatment if (1) the parent corporation owns at least 80 percent of the voting power and at least 80 percent of each class of non-voting stock (except non-voting stock which is limited and preferred as to dividends), and (2) more than 90 percent of the subsidiary's gross receipts for all taxable years were derived from sources other than royalties, rents, dividends, interest, annuities, and gains from sales or exchanges of stocks and securities. Any subsidiary debt obligation not qualifying as a security under Code Sec. 165(g)(2) is deductible by the parent corporation as a business bad debt.

> *Example 15.17.* Subsidiary Corporation, a wholly owned subsidiary of Parent Corporation, has assets with a total FMV of $100,000 and total liabilities of $130,000. Parent's basis in its Subsidiary stock is $90,000. A plan of liquidation for Subsidiary is adopted and Subsidiary distributes all of its assets and liabilities to Parent. Since Subsidiary is insolvent, Code Sec. 332 does not apply to Subsidiary's liquidation because none of Subsidiary's assets are considered to have been distributed in cancellation of its stock. Parent's $90,000 loss on its Subsidiary stock is a loss from worthless securities, which is deductible as an ordinary loss if the 90 percent gross receipts test of Code Sec. 165(g)(3) is met.

¶ 15,345 MINORITY SHAREHOLDERS

The nonrecognition of gain or loss rule under Code Sec. 332 only applies to the parent corporation. When a subsidiary is liquidated, any minority shareholders must recognize their gain or loss under Code Sec. 331. The basis of property received by the minority shareholders is equal to the property's fair market value. Code Sec. 334(a).

¶ 15,353 PARENT'S BASIS FOR PROPERTY

If a controlled subsidiary is liquidated by its parent corporation under Code Sec. 332, the basis for the subsidiary's property (as well as the holding period) carries over to the parent corporation under Code Sec. 334(b)(1). This rule applies to all of the subsidiary's property that is transferred to the parent corporation, including property that is transferred in cancellation of the subsidiary's debt obligations to the parent.

¶ 15,365   NONRECOGNITION RULES OF SECTION 337

Under Code Sec. 337, no gain or loss is recognized by a liquidating subsidiary corporation on the distribution of its property to its parent corporation in a complete liquidation to which Code Sec. 332 applies. This special nonrecognition rule applies only to distributions to the parent corporation (i.e., the corporation meeting the 80 percent stock ownership requirements of Code Sec. 332(b)). This is to be expected since it is only the parent corporation that takes a carryover basis for the subsidiary's assets and succeeds to the subsidiary's tax attributes. Thus, the depreciation recapture rules of Code Secs. 1245, 1250, and 291 do not apply when the subsidiary distributes depreciable property to its parent in liquidation. Instead, the subsidiary's basis for depreciable property as well as the potential for depreciation recapture carries over to the parent corporation.

The nonrecognition rules of Code Sec. 337 generally do not apply to the liquidation of a subsidiary if its parent corporation is a tax-exempt distributee or a foreign corporation. This exception is based on the concern that these distributees are not subject to tax on a subsequent disposition of the property.

¶ 15,371   DISTRIBUTIONS TO MINORITY SHAREHOLDERS

The nonrecognition rules of Code Sec. 337 apply only to distributions to a parent corporation in a Code Sec. 332 liquidation. Distributions to minority shareholders are governed by the general rule of Code Sec. 336 which requires that gain be recognized if appreciated property is distributed in complete liquidation of a corporation. However, it is important to note that Code Sec. 336(d)(3) prevents the recognition of loss on the distribution of property to minority shareholders in a Code Sec. 332 liquidation. These recognition of gain (but not loss) rules for distributions to minority shareholders are based on how the property is actually distributed, rather than on a hypothetical pro rata liquidating distribution to all shareholders.

Example 15.18. Parent Corporation is the owner of 80 percent of Subsidiary Corporation's stock with a basis of $40,000. The remaining 20 percent is owned by Mandy Moore, who has a basis for her Subsidiary stock of $15,000. Subsidiary is liquidated under Code Sec. 332 and distributes property with a FMV of $90,000 and a basis of $30,000 to Parent, and distributes property with a FMV of $25,000 and a basis of $20,000 to Mandy.

Subsidiary's realized gain of $60,000 ($90,000 − $30,000) on the distribution of property to Parent is not recognized. Parent's realized gain of $50,000 ($90,000 − $40,000) on the receipt of the property is not recognized, and Parent has a carryover basis of $30,000 for the property received.

Subsidiary's $5,000 gain ($25,000 − $20,000) on the distribution of property to Mandy is recognized. Mandy's realized gain of $10,000 ($25,000 − $15,000) is recognized, and Mandy has a FMV basis of $25,000 for the property received.

To take advantage of these liquidation rules, the subsidiary's appreciated property should be distributed to only the parent corporation in order to avoid the recognition of gain, while only money should be distributed to minority shareholders. On the other hand, property that has declined in value should be sold to an unrelated taxpayer to permit the recognition of loss. Otherwise, the realized loss will not be allowed as a deduction if the property is distributed to a minority shareholder, or the loss will be deferred if the property is distributed to the parent corporation.

¶ 15,385   SUBSIDIARY'S INDEBTEDNESS TO PARENT

A taxpayer must generally recognize gain or loss if the indebted taxpayer transfers property to satisfy its debt obligation. However, Code Sec. 337(b) provides an exception to this general rule. Specifically, if a subsidiary corporation is indebted to its parent and the subsidiary is liquidated under Code Sec. 332, then no gain or loss is recognized by the subsidiary when it transfers its property to the parent to satisfy the debt. This is because Code Sec. 337(b)(1) treats the property as a liquidating distribution to the parent corporation. Thus, the parent corporation takes a carryover basis for all property received in liquidation of its subsidiary, regardless of whether the property is received in exchange for stock, or in satisfaction of the subsidiary's debt. Note, that this nonrecognition rule does not apply to property that is distributed in satisfaction of indebtedness to minority shareholders. In that case, the subsidiary's gain or loss is recognized.

Example 15.19. Parent Corporation owns 100 percent of the stock of Subsidiary Corporation, and also owns Subsidiary Corporation bonds with a face amount (and basis) of $100,000. A plan of liquidation is adopted and Subsidiary is liquidated under Code Sec. 332. Pursuant to the liquidation, Subsidiary distributes property with a FMV of $100,000 and a basis of $30,000 in cancellation of the bonds. Subsidiary does not recognize any gain on the transfer of its property in cancellation of the bonds. Parent recognizes no gain or loss on its Subsidiary bonds because their basis equals the FMV of the property received. Parent has a carryover basis of $30,000 for the property received from Subsidiary.

Stock Purchases Treated as Asset Acquisitions

¶ 15,401   PURPOSE OF ELECTION

In many cases, a controlling interest in a corporation's stock is purchased in order to acquire the target corporation's assets. When a purchase of stock was promptly followed by a liquidation of the target corporation into the parent, some courts held that the transitory ownership of the stock should be disregarded, and the purchase price of the stock should be allocated to the assets. This view became known as the *Kimbell-Diamond* doctrine after a leading case, *Kimbell-Diamond Milling Co.,* 51-1 USTC ¶ 9201, 187 F.2d 718 (CA-5 1951). This approach was codified in Code Sec. 334(b)(2). Under this provision, the parent received an asset basis equal to its stock basis if at least 80 percent control of the target corporation was acquired by purchase within a 12-month period and a plan of liquidation of the target corporation was adopted within two years after the purchase of control was completed. In 1982, Congress removed the necessity to physically liquidate the subsidiary to achieve an asset basis equal to the stock basis by repealing Code Sec. 334(b)(2) and substituting a Code Sec. 338 election.

As under prior law, Code Sec. 338 requires that at least 80 percent control be acquired by purchase within a 12-month period. Code Sec. 338(a). This is termed a "qualified stock purchase." The election to utilize Code Sec. 338 must then be made on or before the fifteenth day of the ninth month beginning after the month during which the 80 percent control requirement is met. Code Sec. 338(g).

¶ 15,417   STOCK PURCHASE REQUIREMENT

Section 338 applies only to a qualified stock purchase. A *qualified stock purchase* is the purchase of 80 percent or more of the voting power and 80 percent or more of the value of all classes of stock (except for nonvoting, nonparticipating preferred stock) during a 12-month acquisition period. Code Sec. 338(d)(3). A *purchase* is generally defined as a taxable stock acquisition from an unrelated party. Thus, a purchase does not include stock acquired by gift, inheritance, contribution to capital, tax-free reorganization, and a Code Sec. 351 transfer to a controlled corporation.

The *12-month acquisition period* begins with the date of the first acquisition by purchase of stock included in a qualified stock purchase. The *acquisition date* is the first day on which there is a qualified stock purchase (i.e., purchase of 80 percent within a 12-month period). Purchases of stock of the target corporation by affiliates of the purchasing corporation are attributed to the purchasing corporation. The 80 percent stock purchase requirement can be met through a combination of stock purchases and redemptions of the target corporation's stock.

> *Example 15.20.* Parent Corporation purchases 40 percent of Target Corporation's stock on April 3, 1998. Subsidiary (Parent's 100-percent-owned subsidiary) purchases 40 percent of Target's stock on August 2, 1998. Since Parent and Subsidiary are affiliated corporations, Parent has made a qualified stock purchase of Target's stock and the acquisition date is August 2, 1998.

> *Example 15.21.* Parent Corporation purchases 75 percent of Target Corporation's stock on May 3, 1998. Target redeems the 25 percent minority interest on October 2, 1998. Parent has made a qualified stock purchase of Target's stock. The acquisition date is October 2, 1998, the first day on which Parent has acquired by purchase at least 80 percent of Target's stock.

Example 15.22. Parent Corporation purchases 20 percent of Target Corporation's stock on November 2, 1997, 20 percent on June 3, 1998, 40 percent on December 1, 1998, and 20 percent on May 2, 1999. Parent has made a qualified stock purchase of the Target stock since during a 12-month period beginning June 3, 1998, Parent has purchased at least 80 percent of Target's stock. The acquisition date is May 2, 1999.

¶ 15,425   REQUIREMENTS FOR ELECTION

Generally a Code Sec. 338 election must be made on or before the fifteenth day of the ninth month beginning after the month in which the acquisition date occurs. The election is irrevocable and is made by the purchasing corporation on Form 8023 (Corporate Qualified Stock Purchase Elections) which is filed with the IRS service center applicable to the purchasing corporation.

Example 15.23. Parent Corporation purchases 35 percent of Target Corporation's stock on March 1, 1998, and an additional 50 percent of Target's stock on September 10, 1998. The acquisition date is September 10, 1998, and the Code Sec. 338 election must be made on or before June 15, 1999.

¶ 15,435   OLD TARGET CORPORATION

A target corporation is any corporation whose stock is acquired by another corporation in a qualified stock purchase. A Code Sec. 338 election will cause the target corporation to be treated as two distinctly different corporations—*old target* and *new target.* If a Code Sec. 338 election is made, the old target is treated as having sold all of its assets for their fair market value as of the close of the acquisition date. This fictional sale of assets results in the old target's recognition of any realized gains and losses. The assets are then treated as having been purchased by the new target corporation as of the beginning of the day following the acquisition date.

The old target corporation does not become part of the purchasing corporation's affiliated group. If the old target corporation is similarly not includible in a consolidated return of the seller, the target corporation's final tax return must reflect any income earned through the acquisition date, as well as the gains and losses resulting from the Code Sec. 338 deemed sale of assets. Generally, any tax attributes of the old target corporation (e.g., NOL and capital loss carryforwards) can be used to offset the income recognized on this final return. Any unused tax attributes of the old target corporation are extinguished and do not carry over to the new target corporation.

If the old target corporation is a subsidiary member of an affiliated group filing a consolidated return, a separate deemed sale return for the old target corporation is required. The selling group's consolidated return includes the old target's items of income and deduction through the acquisition date, excluding the deemed sale items. The old target's deemed sale return stands alone and does not include any operating income or loss.

¶ 15,443   ADVANTAGES OF ELECTION

Since a target corporation must recognize all of its gains on the deemed sale of its assets, a Code Sec. 338 election may prove undesirable because of the significant up-front tax costs associated with the basis step-up. However, there are still several situations in which a Code Sec. 338 election can be beneficial.

If the target corporation has NOLs that are expiring or subject to limitation under Code Sec. 382, the election can be beneficial because the NOLs can offset the recognized gains on the deemed sale, thereby giving the purchaser a stepped-up basis in the assets with little or no tax cost.

There also are significant planning possibilities under Code Sec. 338(h)(10). If a target corporation is a subsidiary in a consolidated group and its stock is sold, an election pursuant to Code Sec. 338(h)(10) allows the sellers to treat the transaction as if the target made a taxable sale of its assets and then was liquidated into its parent under Code Sec. 332. The effect of this rule is that the selling consolidated group recognizes the gain from the deemed sale of assets in its consolidated return, but no gain or loss is recognized on the sale of the target's stock. Furthermore, the seller's consolidated tax attributes are available to shelter the fully taxable deemed asset sale. If the old target has any remaining tax attributes (e.g., NOLs, tax credits), they remain in the selling group. The election is made on Form 8023 and effectively is a joint election because the seller can make this election only if the buyer makes a Code Sec. 338 election.

¶ 15,451   NEW TARGET CORPORATION

The new target corporation becomes a member of the purchasing corporation's affiliated group as of the day after the acquisition date. It is treated as a new corporation and does not inherit any of the old target's tax attributes. The new target is also treated as having purchased the assets of the old target for a price that equals the adjusted grossed-up basis of the target's stock which includes:

1. The grossed-up basis of the purchasing corporation's recently purchased stock (i.e., stock of the target corporation purchased during the 12-month acquisition period), plus

2. The basis of the purchasing corporation's nonrecently purchased stock (i.e., stock of the target corporation purchased prior to the 12-month acquisition period), plus

3. Liabilities of the target corporation (including the tax liability resulting from the Code Sec. 338 election) and other relevant items.

The basis of nonrecently purchased target corporation stock is the purchasing corporation's historic basis for the stock. The grossed-up basis of recently purchased stock will equal the purchasing corporation's basis in its recently purchased stock multiplied by a fraction— the numerator of which is 100 percent minus the percentage (by value) of nonrecently purchased stock, and the denominator of which is the percentage (by value) of recently purchased stock. Code Sec. 338(b)(4).

$$\begin{array}{c}\text{Grossed-up}\\\text{basis}\end{array} = \begin{array}{c}\text{Basis of recently}\\\text{purchased stock}\end{array} \times \dfrac{100\% - \begin{array}{c}\text{\% of nonrecently}\\\text{purchased stock}\end{array}}{\begin{array}{c}\text{\% of recently}\\\text{purchased stock}\end{array}}$$

The basis of nonrecently purchased stock may be increased to its market value if the purchasing corporation makes an election to recognize gain as if the nonrecently purchased stock were sold on the acquisition date. Code Sec. 338 (b)(3). If the election is made, the basis of nonrecently purchased stock will generally equal the average price per share of the recently purchased stock.

> *Example 15.24.* Parent Corporation purchases 10 percent of Target Corporation's stock for $50,000 in 1996. On July 3, 1998, Parent purchases an additional 80 percent of Target's stock for $1 million. The stock acquired in 1996 is nonrecently purchased stock; the stock acquired in 1998 is recently purchased stock. If Parent makes a Code Sec. 338 election, the grossed-up basis for Parent's recently purchased stock is $1,125,000.
>
> Assuming Parent does not elect to increase the basis of the nonrecently purchased Target stock, and if Target has no liabilities, Parent's adjusted grossed-up basis for the Target stock is $1,125,000 + $50,000 = $1,175,000.

¶ 15,465 ALLOCATION OF BASIS

The Regulations provide rules for allocating the purchase price of the target corporation's stock if a Code Sec. 338 election is made. The basis for assets is determined by use of the residual value method. Under this method, the amount allocated is the adjusted grossed-up basis of the stock. This amount is determined as of the beginning of the day following the acquisition date and must be allocated to four categories of assets in the following order:

1. Class I—Cash, demand deposits, and other cash equivalents

2. Class II—Certificates of deposit, U.S. government securities, readily marketable securities, and similar items

3. Class III—All assets (both tangible and intangible) other than those in Classes I, II, and IV such as receivables, inventory, machinery, and equipment

4. Class IV—Intangible assets in the nature of goodwill and going concern value

The basis assigned to Class I assets is their face value. The remaining aggregate grossed-up basis is then assigned to Class II assets based on their relative fair market values. Any excess is then assigned to the Class III assets, again according to relative fair market values. In making the allocation to the Class II and III assets, the amount allocated as basis can never exceed an asset's fair market value. The fair market value of an asset is the asset's gross value computed without regard to any mortgage, liens, or other liabilities related to the asset. When the purchase price has been allocated to the first three categories of assets, any remaining purchase price represents a premium that exceeds the value of identifiable assets. This premium is then assigned to Class IV assets and results in goodwill.

> *Example 15.25.* Parent Corporation purchases 80 percent of the stock of Target Corporation for $400,000 on July 3, 1998, and makes a Code Sec. 338 election. On the acquisition date, Target has assets with a FMV of $475,000 and $25,000 of liabilities. Old Target is deemed to have sold its assets, and new Target is deemed to have purchased them for $475,000. Assume no income tax liability was incurred on the deemed sale because of old Target's NOL carryovers. Parent's adjusted grossed-up basis for the Target stock is $525,000 (($400,000 × (100%/80%)) + $25,000 of liabilities). Assume that Target's assets have the following fair market values on the day after the acquisition date:

Asset Class	Asset	FMV
I	Cash	$ 50,000
II	Marketable securities	75,000
III	Inventory	150,000
III	Equipment	200,000
		$475,000

> The allocation of the $525,000 of adjusted grossed-up basis is as follows:

> (Class   I):   Allocate $50,000 to cash.
> (Class II):   Allocate $75,000 to marketable securities.
> (Class III):   Allocate $350,000 to the Class III assets. The inventory and equipment have a basis equal to fair market value.
> (Class IV):   Allocate the remaining $50,000 to goodwill.

If the value of the identifiable assets is greater than the adjusted grossed-up basis of the stock, there has been a bargain purchase. If the value of the Class III assets exceeds the adjusted grossed-up basis remaining to be allocated, the remaining basis is allocated to the Class III assets in proportion to their relative fair market values. This results in a potential step-down in basis for receivables and inventory and will result in the recognition of income when the inventory is sold and the receivables are collected.

¶ 15,485   CONSEQUENCES OF NO ELECTION

If Code Sec. 338 is not elected, the purchasing corporation has a basis for the target corporation's stock equal to its purchase price. The basis for the target's assets remains unchanged, and all of the target's tax attributes remain, subject to any applicable limitation rules. If the target is subsequently liquidated under Code Sec. 332, no gain or loss is recognized by the purchasing and target corporations, there is a carryover basis for all of the target's assets, and a carryover of all of target's tax attributes. However, Code Sec. 269 provides that if the principal purpose for a liquidation of the target corporation within two years of acquisition is the avoidance of tax, the benefit of any deductions resulting from the liquidation may be denied.

¶ 15,493   SPECIAL RULE

Regulations are to be issued under Code Sec. 336(e) that will allow a parent corporation that owns at least 80 percent of a subsidiary's stock, and sells, exchanges, or distributes all of the subsidiary's stock, to elect to be taxed as if it had sold all of the subsidiary's assets instead of the subsidiary's stock. The parent corporation is effectively treated as if it had first liquidated the controlled subsidiary under Code Sec. 332 and then sold all of the subsidiary's assets.

This election is similar to the Code Sec. 338(h)(10) election except that the purchaser does not have to be a corporation. In addition to a sale or exchange, the Code Sec. 336(e) election can apply when the parent corporation distributes all of its subsidiary's stock in a taxable distribution.

Collapsible Corporations

¶ 15,501   SCOPE AND APPLICATION OF RULE

The purpose of the collapsible corporation provisions found in Code Sec. 341 is to prevent a shareholder from converting ordinary income at the corporate level into a capital gain to the shareholder. A shareholder who sells stock in a collapsible corporation in a transaction that would ordinarily produce capital gain must instead report the gain as ordinary income. The types of "collapse" that fall within the scope of Code Sec. 341 include gains recognized on the sale or exchange of stock, a return of capital distribution in excess of stock basis, a partial liquidation distribution to a noncorporate distributee, and a complete liquidation.

Because of the repeal of the *General Utilities* doctrine, the use of a collapsible corporation and the significance of Code Sec. 341 are greatly diminished. However, Code Sec. 341 has continuing validity since taxpayers with substantial capital loss carryforwards generally attempt to generate capital gains in order to utilize their capital losses, and a preferential tax rate of 20 percent may apply to net long-term capital gains.

Classic Example

An actor, director, and producer organize a corporation to produce a motion picture. They invest $100,000, work for modest salaries, and fund the production of the movie with borrowed funds. Upon completion of the motion picture, private screenings are held, and based on reviews, a value is placed on the film distribution rights. The shareholders then sell their stock for $6.1 million, resulting in $6 million of capital gain for the shareholders, even though their gain is attributable to the ordinary income that has not yet been recognized by the corporation. Code Sec. 341 addresses this situation by requiring that the shareholders' gain be reported as ordinary income.

¶ 15,505 DEFINITIONS

The term "collapsible corporation" means a corporation that is formed or availed of:

1. Principally for the manufacture, construction, production, or purchase of property, or for the purchase of Code Sec. 341 assets

2. With a view to (a) a sale, liquidation, or distribution before the corporation has realized two-thirds of the taxable income to be derived from its property, and (b) a realization by the shareholders of the gain attributable to the property

A corporation may be collapsible if it engages in the manufacture, construction, production, or purchase of property to any extent. Additionally, a corporation is deemed to have manufactured, constructed, produced, or purchased property if it has a carryover basis from a transferor who manufactured, constructed, produced, or purchased the property.

A corporation may be collapsible if it purchases Code Sec. 341 assets with the requisite view. Code Sec. 341 assets include the following property if held for less than three years: unrealized receivables, inventory, property held for sale to customers in the ordinary course of business, and Code Sec. 1231(b) property. However, a corporation is not collapsible if its inventory is normal in amount and the corporation has a substantial prior business history involving the use of such property.

Example 15.26. Model Home Corporation purchased an apartment house and met the requisite view requirement. The apartment house is Code Sec. 1231(b) property and is classified as a Code Sec. 341 asset. Thus, Model Home Corporation is a collapsible corporation until the property has been held three years, or unless it realizes at an earlier date two-thirds of the taxable income to be derived from the apartment house (e.g., sale of apartments as condos or sale of the entire apartment house).

¶ 15,515 VIEW TO COLLAPSE REQUIREMENT

The Regulations indicate that the "view" requirement is satisfied if the collapse transaction was contemplated unconditionally, conditionally, or as a recognized possibility. The persons with the requisite view are those in a position to determine the policies of the corporation, whether because of owning more than 50 percent of the corporation's stock or other reasons. The view to collapse generally must exist at some time during manufacture, construction, production, or purchase.

If it can be shown that the decision to sell stock, liquidate, or distribute assets is attributable solely to circumstances that arose after the manufacture, construction, production, or purchase, the requisite view is not present. Thus, a corporation has been determined not collapsible when the collapse was caused by unanticipated shareholder dissension, the illness of a shareholder that managed the business, a forced sale of stock by minority shareholders, unexpected changes in the value of property, or a shareholder's unexpected need for funds for another investment.

¶ 15,525　TAXABLE INCOME REQUIREMENT

A corporation is not collapsible once it realizes two-thirds of the taxable income to be derived from each of its produced or purchased properties. If property consists of similar units in an integrated project (e.g., individual units in a housing project), the determination of two-thirds realization is made by treating the aggregate of these units as a single project.

It is important to note that a corporation must recognize any gains that are realized in the process of liquidation. If a collapsible corporation is liquidated, it recognizes the gains that are attributable to the unrealized appreciation in the value of its assets. Having thus recognized all of its taxable income at time of liquidation, the corporation is no longer a collapsible corporation and shareholder gains receive capital gain treatment.

¶ 15,545　RELIEF PROVISIONS

Even though a corporation is by definition a collapsible corporation, shareholders may nevertheless be entitled to capital gain treatment if any of the following relief provisions apply:

1.　The shareholder owns, directly and constructively, 5 percent or less of the corporation's stock. Code Sec. 341(d)(1).

2.　The shareholder's gain is capital gain unless more than 70 percent of the gain is attributable to the manufacture, construction, production, or purchase of collapsible property. Code Sec. 341(d)(2).

3.　The shareholder's gain is realized more than three years after completion of the manufacture, construction, production, or purchase of property. Code Sec. 341(d)(3).

4.　The shareholder's gain resulting from the sale or exchange of stock is capital gain if the net unrealized appreciation in the corporation's "subsection (e) assets" does not exceed 15 percent of the corporation's net worth. Subsection (e) assets are generally assets that are ordinary income assets to the corporation or to a 20 percent or more shareholder. Code Sec. 341(e).

5.　If the corporation files a consent to recognize gain on any future disposition of its property (even if the disposition would otherwise qualify for nonrecognition treatment), then shareholder gains receive capital gain treatment. Code Sec. 341(f).

TAX BLUNDER

A self-made businessman started a business on a shoestring many years ago that was worth $1 million when he wanted to retire. He then went to a lawyer and adopted a plan of liquidation. On the way home, he died of a heart attack. His wife, wishing to carry out his intent, went ahead with the liquidation. Result: $1 million of capital gain to the estate and an income tax of $280,000 since he had "realized" the gain under Code Sec. 331 before he died (income in respect of a decedent). What his wife should have done was to cancel the liquidation. The estate would have had a stepped-up basis in the stock of $1 million. Subsequently, a plan of liquidation could have again been adopted, and the liquidation could take place tax free to the estate.

SUMMARY OF CHAPTER 15

✓ The tax treatment of complete liquidations is determined by Code Secs. 331 through 338.

✓ A shareholder generally recognizes gain or loss on the exchange of stock in a complete liquidation under Code Sec. 331 and will have a fair market value basis for property received.

✓ A parent corporation does not recognize gain or loss on the liquidation of an 80 percent of more controlled subsidiary under Code Sec. 332 and will have a transferred basis for property received.

✓ A liquidating corporation generally recognizes gain or loss on liquidating distributions made to shareholders, except that no gain or loss is recognized on liquidating distributions made to the parent corporation in a Code Sec. 332 liquidation.

✓ A Sec. 338 election has the effect of treating a qualified stock purchase as a purchase of the target corporation's assets.

✓ The collapsible corporation rules prevent a shareholder from converting ordinary income into capital gain by selling stock in a collapsible corporation before it has recognized two-thirds of the taxable income to be derived from its properties.

SUMMARY OF RELEVANT CODE SECTIONS IN CHAPTER 15

Corporate Liquidation

Subpart A.   Effects on Recipients

Subpart B.   Effects on Corporations

Subpart C.   Collapsible Corporations

Subpart A. Effects on Recipients

Section 331   Gain or Loss to Shareholders in Corporate Liquidations

Section 332   Complete Liquidations of Subsidiaries

Section 334   Basis of Property Received in Liquidations

Subpart B. Effects on Corporations

Section 336   Gain or Loss Recognized on Property Distributed in Complete Liquidation

Section 337   Nonrecognition for Property Distributed to Parent in Complete Liquidation of Subsidiary

Section 338   Certain Stock Purchases Treated as Asset Acquisitions

Subpart C. Collapsible Corporations

Section 341   Collapsible Corporations

CHAPTER 15 QUESTIONS

1. What is meant by a "status of liquidation"?

2. Contrast a complete liquidation with the legal dissolution of a corporation.

3. What happens to a corporation's tax attributes (e.g., earnings and profits, NOL carryforwards) in a complete liquidation?

4. Contrast the tax treatment of a shareholder in a redemption under Code Sec. 302 with a shareholder's tax treatment in a liquidation under Code Sec. 331.

5. In what situations will a shareholder recognize an ordinary loss as a result of a complete liquidation of a corporation?

6. How does the assumption of corporate liabilities affect the amount realized by a shareholder in a complete liquidation? How does the assumption of liabilities affect the basis for assets received in a complete liquidation?

7. Explain the *Arrowsmith* doctrine.

8. When is "double taxation" on a corporate liquidation an advantage over nonrecognition at the corporate level?

9. What problem is encountered on a liquidation that is followed by a reincorporation?

10. Discuss the tax treatment of liquidating distributions of installment obligations.

11. When may a liquidating corporation recognize a loss on a liquidating distribution?

12. Sec. 336(a) provides that "gain or loss shall be recognized to a liquidating corporation on the distribution of property in complete liquidation as if such property were sold to the distributee at its fair market value." Explain five exceptions to this rule.

13. Under what circumstances must a subsidiary recognize gain or loss upon liquidating into its parent?

14. What are the requirements for a parent to qualify for nonrecognition of gain upon receipt of property from a liquidating subsidiary under Code Sec. 332?

15. When might a parent corporation want to avoid a Sec. 332 liquidation? How could this be accomplished?

16. In a Sec. 332 liquidation, what is the tax effect of the distribution of property by a subsidiary in satisfaction of its indebtedness to its parent corporation?

17. When Code Sec. 332 applies to a complete liquidation, what are the tax consequences to a minority shareholder?

18. Is meeting the requirements under Code Sec. 332 a prerequisite for application of Code Secs. 334(b)(1) and 338?

19. How does an acquiring corporation make a Code Sec. 338 election?

20. Why is Code Sec. 338 of limited interest today?

21. What is the benefit of a Code Sec. 338(h)(10) election?

22. What is meant by a parent corporation's "grossed-up" basis in the subsidiary's stock under Code Sec. 338(b)?

23. Describe the residual method for allocating basis to assets following a Code Sec. 338 election.

24. What is the purpose of the collapsible corporation provisions?

25. May a shareholder generate capital gain on the sale of stock in a collapsible corporation?

CHAPTER 15 PROBLEMS

26. Chip & Dale Ltd.'s equity section reflects these items:

Common stock authorized, issued, and outstanding, 100,000 shares, par $1	$ 100,000
Paid-in capital in excess of par	400,000
Earnings and profits	2,000,000
	$2,500,000

  a. If Chip & Dale redeems 40 percent of its stock for its own $1,400,000 installment obligation (at 10 percent interest), what will happen to the accounts above?

  b. Show the revised equity section.

  c. What difference would it make if the $1,400,000 was paid in property and qualified as a partial liquidation?

  d. What difference would it make if the distribution was one of several simultaneous distributions in complete liquidation?

27. Swamps and Deserts Realty Inc. distributed a parcel of land that it had purchased with a basis of $100,000 and a fair market value of $70,000 to Dexter Rice as part of its complete liquidation. If Dexter's stock basis is $15,000, what are the tax consequences to both parties if:

  a. Dexter is a 100 percent shareholder?

  b. Dexter is a 70 percent shareholder?

28. Joan owns 100 percent of Joan Enterprises Inc. She has a basis in her stock of $20,000. The corporation's only assets are cash of $10,000 and land with a basis of $15,000 and a value of $75,000. Earnings and profits are $25,000. Joan Enterprises liquidates and distributes its assets to Joan, whose stock is cancelled.

  a. What is the gain recognized by Joan Enterprises?

  b. What happens to Enterprises' earnings and profits?

  c. What gain is recognized by Joan?

  d. What is Joan's basis in the land?

29. A cash-method corporation adopts a plan of complete liquidation and distributes the following assets to its shareholders:

A truck that was purchased for $25,000, is worth $18,000, and has a basis of $11,000

An installment note receivable with a remaining face amount of $20,000, resulting from a sale of a warehouse for $75,000 seven years ago in which the warehouse's basis at the time of sale was $25,000

Accounts receivable of $7,000

Supplies and small tools previously expensed, worth $350

What gains are recognized by the liquidating corporation on the distributions in complete liquidation?

30. Black Castle Inc. adopts a plan of complete liquidation and distributes a truck worth $15,000 with an original basis of $25,000 and an adjusted basis of $7,000 to a 40 percent shareholder with a stock basis of $3,000. The shareholder subsequently claims $4,000 of depreciation on the truck, and later sells it for $13,000.

   a. What is the shareholder's gain, including its character, upon receipt of the truck? Black Castle's gain?

   b. What are the shareholder's and Black Castle's gains upon the truck's subsequent sale?

31. Alex purchased one thousand shares of Apple Corporation stock on March 10, 1997, for $90,000. On August 1, 1998, Alex received the following as a distribution in cancellation of his stock in a complete liquidation of Apple:

	Fair Market Value
Cash	$ 5,000
Equipment	10,000
Land	30,000
Building	120,000
Liabilities	(20,000)
	$145,000

   a. What is the amount and character of Alex's recognized gain?

   b. What is Alex's basis for each of the items of property received?

   c. When does the holding period for each of the items of property begin?

   d. How would your answer to (a) change if Alex had purchased 500 shares of Apple stock 15 months ago for $10,000, and the remaining 500 shares six months ago for $80,000?

32. Ted purchased all of the stock of Funster Manufacturing Corporation in 1996 for $170,000. Under Ted's leadership, Funster Manufacturing soon became unprofitable, and Ted decided to liquidate Funster as of the close of business on June 30, 1998. All of Funster's assets were needed to pay third-party creditors, and Ted received nothing for his $170,000 investment.

    a. Describe the amount and character of Ted's loss.

    b. How would your answer to (a) change if Funster Manufacturing were instead owned by TED Corporation?

33. Tracy is a 50 percent shareholder of Cushions Corp., which is in the process of liquidation. Tracy's basis in her stock is $20,000. Cushions' balance sheet on the date of liquidation is as follows:

Assets	Basis	Value	Equities	Value
Cash	$ 32,000	$ 32,000	Mortgage on real estate	$310,000
100 shares of Public Co.	20,000	6,000	Unsecured liabilities	182,000
Accounts receivable	200,000	170,000	Capital stock	10,000
Land	50,000	300,000	Paid-in capital	30,000
Building (depreciated straight line) ...	246,000	500,000	Earnings and profits	16,000
Totals	$548,000	$1,008,000	Total	$548,000

If Tracy receives her 50 percent share of all assets and liabilities, determine her gain and her basis in each asset received on liquidation. Assume that Cushions' marginal tax rate is 30 percent but that no tax was paid by Cushions.

34. Porter Corporation adopts a plan of complete liquidation. Six months later Porter sells its main asset, a motel, in which it has a basis of $50,000, for $300,000 to an unrelated partnership. Porter received a $60,000 down payment and a mortgage note payable in installments of $2,000 a month for 10 years plus 10 percent interest on the remaining balance. Porter pays the tax and distributes the cash and the note to its only shareholder, Maria Moore, who has a basis of $30,000 for her stock. If there is no recapture, what are the tax consequences to Porter Corporation and to Maria?

35. Ray owns 400 shares of stock in Fly-by-Night Ltd. He had inherited 300 shares (estate tax value $15,000) seven months ago and had purchased 100 shares for $2,000 five months ago. Fly-by-Night completely liquidates, and Ray receives a building worth $50,000, that is subject to a mortgage of $38,000, in cancellation of his 400 shares.

    a. What gain and/or loss does Ray recognize?

    b. What is his basis in the building?

36. Betty owns 65 percent of Tower Corporation. In 1997, Betty contributed property with an adjusted basis of $25,000 and a fair market value of $10,000 to Tower as a contribution to capital. In 1998, Tower adopted a plan of complete liquidation and distributed this same property back to Betty in exchange for her stock. At the time of distribution, the property had a basis of $22,000 and a fair market value of $5,000. What amount of loss is recognized by Tower Corporation on the distribution?

37. The Dicken Corp. has two unrelated shareholders, Dick and Ken, each owning 50 percent of the stock. Dicken has only one asset, a tract of land with a value of $100,000 and a basis of $150,000. What are the tax consequences of the following alternative liquidations?

    a. Dicken distributes the land to the shareholders as equal tenants in common.

    b. Dicken sells the land to Ken's mother-in-law for a note that is distributed to Dick and Ken as equal tenants in common.

38. Modern Parking Inc. has a basis of $50,000 for its stock in its wholly owned subsidiary, Traditional Tiles Inc. The latter's only asset has a basis of $75,000 and a value of $35,000. Modern liquidates Traditional and acquires its only asset. What are the tax consequences to both corporations?

39. Parent Corporation purchased 80 percent of the stock of Subsidiary Corporation in one transaction for $200,000. The remaining 20 percent is owned by the MIN partnership. Subsidiary's only asset is an office building depreciated on the straight-line method, with an adjusted basis of $50,000 and a value of $400,000. It is subject to a mortgage of $140,000.

    a. If Parent makes a Code Sec. 338 election, what are the tax consequences to the Parent, Subsidiary and MIN?

    b. If Parent does not make a Code Sec. 332 election and liquidates Subsidiary under Code Sec. 332, what are the tax consequences to Parent, Subsidiary, and MIN?

40. Parent Corporation purchased 10 percent of Target Corporation's stock for $35,000 in 1995. On March 1, 1998, Parent purchased an additional 80 percent of Target's stock for $200,000. At that time, Target's identifiable assets had a fair market value of $300,000 and an adjusted basis of $240,000. Target also had liabilities of $60,000.

    a. What is the acquisition date for purposes of making a Code Sec. 338 election? By what date must Parent file a Code Sec. 338 election?

    b. Assuming that a Code Sec. 338 election is made, what is the deemed sale price of Target's assets?

    c. What is the amount of the adjusted grossed-up basis that is allocated to Target's assets, assuming that a tax liability of $15,000 resulted from the deemed sale of assets?

    d. What amount of goodwill results from the allocation of basis to Target's assets?

41. Puzzles Corporation is owned 60 percent by Jay and 40 percent by Scott. Jay and Scott are unrelated individuals. Puzzles' two principal assets are cash of $140,000 and a building that Puzzles purchased 10 years ago and that now has an adjusted basis of $80,000 and a fair market value of $60,000. What amount of loss is recognized by Puzzles Corporation if it makes the following alternative distributions in complete liquidation?

    a. Puzzles distributes the building plus $60,000 in cash to Jay and $80,000 in cash to Scott.

    b. Puzzles distributes $120,000 in cash to Jay and the building plus $20,000 in cash to Scott.

    c. Puzzles distributes 60 percent of the cash and a 60 percent interest in the building to Jay and 40 percent of the cash and a 40 percent interest in the building to Scott.

    d. Same as (c), except that the building had been contributed to Puzzles Corporation by Scott as a contribution to capital one year ago, when the building's basis was $90,000 and its fair market value was $75,000.

    e. Same as (c), except that the building had been contributed to Puzzles Corporation by Jay as a contribution to capital four years ago, when the building's basis was $120,000 and its fair market value was $110,000.

42. Panashe Corporation purchased 20 percent of Servco Corporation's stock on each of the following dates: January 4, 1997; April 3, 1997; July 14, 1997; December 15, 1997; and January 5, 1998. Can Panashe make a Sec. 338 election to have the Servco stock purchases treated as an acquisition of assets? By what date must the election be made?

    a. How would your answers change if the purchase dates were instead January 4, 1996; April 3, 1997; July 14, 1997; December 15, 1997; and January 5, 1998?

    b. How would your answers change if the purchase dates were instead January 4, 1997; April 3, 1997; July 14, 1997; January 4, 1998; and April 15, 1998?

43. Doug and Sally (unrelated individuals) own 70 percent and 30 percent respectively of the outstanding stock of Posies Corporation. Posies' assets consist of land (Sec. 1231 property) that was purchased in 1994 for $90,000 and now has current fair market value of $70,000 and other property that has a basis of $20,000 and a fair market value of $30,000. Pursuant to a plan of complete liquidation, Posies Corporation distributes the land to Doug and the other property to Sally on August 7, 1998.

    a. How much gain and loss does Posies Corporation recognize on the liquidating distributions? Can you offer any suggestions that will improve the tax consequences of the liquidating distributions?

    b. How would your answers to part a. change if the land had instead been contributed as a capital contribution by Doug in 1995?

44. Elm Corporation has 100 shares of stock outstanding of which Oak Corporation owns 75 shares with a basis of $10,000, and Sherman Forest owns 25 shares with a basis of $30,000. Elm Corporation has a $50,000 net operating loss carryover and the following assets (all held long-term):

	Basis	Fair Market Value
Cash	$20,000	$20,000
Installment Note	10,000	40,000
Land	1,000	10,000
Equipment (all Sec. 1245 recapture)	5,000	10,000
	$36,000	$80,000

    a. What are the tax consequences if Elm Corporation adopts a plan of complete liquidation and distributes the $20,000 cash to Sherman and all its remaining assets to Oak Corporation?

    b. As an alternative, what are the tax consequences if Elm Corporation distributes $20,000 cash to Sherman in redemption of his 25 shares, and 10 days later, Elm adopts a plan of complete liquidation and distributes its remaining assets to Oak Corporation? What are Elm and Oak trying to accomplish through the redemption of Sherman's shares?

45. Robin Fox, who is actively engaged in the real estate development business, organizes Foxfield Corporation to subdivide and develop real estate. Robin transfers two parcels of undeveloped land (basis of $75,000 each) to Foxfield in exchange for all of Foxfield's outstanding stock. Foxfield develops both parcels as separate projects by subdividing and building five houses for sale on each parcel. After completion of the homes, each parcel has a fair market value of $500,000 and a basis of $100,000.

   a. What are the tax consequences if Robin sells her Foxfield stock for $1 million?

   b. As an alternative, what are the tax consequences if Foxfield liquidates by distributing all of its assets to Robin?

   c. What are the tax consequences if Foxfield had already sold four houses in each project for $100,000 each by the time that Robin sold her stock?

46. Meyer Corporation adopted a plan of complete liquidation in which it plans to distribute the following properties:

   — Land used in the business that has a basis of $40,000 and a fair market value of $90,000.

   — Marketable securities acquired nine months ago having a basis of $25,000 and a fair market value of $22,000.

   — Equipment having a basis of $10,000 and a fair market value of $18,000. Depreciation of $12,000 had been deducted on the equipment since its purchase four years ago.

   — Supplies that cost $5,000 and were expensed when acquired last year. The supplies have a fair market value of $5,700.

   — Installment obligations that were acquired from the sale of nondepreciable business property three years ago. The installment obligations have a fair market value of $50,000 and an adjusted basis of $26,000.

   — Machinery having a basis of $13,000 and a fair market value of $8,000. Depreciation of $15,000 had been deducted on the machinery since its purchase five years ago.

   a. What would be the tax consequences to Meyer Corporation of distributing the above property to individual shareholders who own less than 50 percent of the corporation's stock in the process of a complete liquidation?

   b. How would your answers to part a. change if the property were distributed to Meyer's parent corporation as part of a complete liquidation qualifying under Code Sec. 332?

c. How would your answers to part b. change if the property were distributed to minority shareholders in a Sec. 332 liquidation?

47. Arlene owns all the stock of Helio Corporation that she purchased several years ago for $10,000. Helio has $15,000 of accumulated earnings and profits. What are the tax consequences to Arlene on the liquidation of Helio Corporation in the following alternative situations:

a. Helio distributes $5,000 in 1997 and $15,000 in 1998 to Arlene in exchange for all of her stock?

b. Helio distributes $8,000 cash and an installment obligation with a face amount and fair market value of $12,000, payable $4,000 per year for three years with market rate of interest. The installment obligation was received by Helio four months ago after the adoption of the plan of liquidation, on the sale of a capital asset.

c. Would the result in part b. be any different if the stock of Helio were publicly traded?

48. *Comprehensive Problem.* Parent Corporation purchased 75 percent of Subsidiary Corporation seven years ago. Subsidiary's current balance sheet shows the following figures:

	Basis	Value
Demand deposit	$20,000	$ 20,000
IBM stock	30,000	50,000
Parking lot	5,000	30,000
Building	0	100,000
Mortgage	(15,000)	(15,000)

Subsidiary has a net operating loss carryover of $7,000 and earnings and profits of $22,000.

Subsidiary redeems Roy Rambler's 25 percent stock interest in exchange for the IBM stock. Subsidiary then adopts a plan of complete liquidation and distributes its assets to Parent in complete liquidation.

a. What is the tax result to Roy?

b. Does Subsidiary recognize any gain on the redemption or the liquidation?

c. What are Parent's bases for the assets received?

d. What happens to Subsidiary's NOL and E&P?

49. *Comprehensive Problem.* Mini-Skirts Ltd., owned by one shareholder, owns one asset, a building worth $100,000 with a zero basis. The shareholder's stock basis is $20,000. A plan of complete liquidation is adopted. What are the tax consequences to both parties in each of the following independent cases?

   a. The building is deeded to the shareholder, Bill Jones, who is taxed under Code Sec. 331.

   b. The building is sold for an installment note that is distributed to Bill.

   c. Mini-Skirts Ltd. sells the building and presents a cashier's check for $100,000 to Bill.

   d. The building is deeded to the shareholder, Bill Inc., who is taxed under Code Secs. 332 and 334(b)(1).

50. *Research Problem.* Anaconda Ltd. has substantial earnings and profits and appreciated assets. It adopts a plan of complete liquidation and distributes its assets to its shareholders. Soon thereafter, the shareholders transfer the assets to a new corporation, King Cobra Inc., in return for Cobra stock, but retain cash and marketable securities.

What are the shareholders trying to accomplish?

How will the IRS most likely treat the transactions?

(See, e.g., Reg. § § 1.301-1(1) and 1.331-1(c); Rev. Rul. 61-156, 1961-2 CB 62.)

Chapter 16

Corporate Reorganizations

Learning Objectives

After completing Chapter 16, you should be able to:

1. Identify the characteristics of the seven basic types of reorganization.

2. Understand the tax consequences to shareholders and security holders, including basis computations and the effect of the receipt of boot.

3. Describe the tax consequences to corporations that are a party to the reorganization, including nonrecognition of gain or loss, basis for acquired property, carryover of tax attributes, and the use of subsidiaries to facilitate a reorganization.

4. Discuss the types of consideration that may be used in different reorganizations.

OVERVIEW OF CHAPTER

Gain or loss is generally recognized for tax purposes on a sale or exchange of property that has increased or decreased in value. Corporate reorganizations are a major exception to this rule. There are provisions that allow nonrecognition of gain or loss in various types of corporate reorganizations to ensure that the tax laws do not impede corporate realignments. Reorganizations are generally nontaxable because the new enterprise, the new corporate structure, and the new property are substantially continuations of the old investment.

A corporate reorganization may have the attributes of a corporate formation, distribution, redemption, and liquidation all in the same transaction. The Code recognizes *seven* types of tax-free reorganization, some of which overlap. Most reorganizations involve two corporations and their shareholders. However, in a recapitalization, only one corporation is involved, while in other types of reorganization three or more corporations may participate.

The basic thrust of the reorganization provisions, Code Secs. 354-368, is to provide tax-free treatment to *all* parties to a reorganization when the legislative and judicial requirements have been met. Thus, shareholders may swap "old" for "new" securities tax free, and property may be transferred from one corporation to another, also tax free. As in other types of tax-free transactions, basis carries over and holding periods tack on.

There are three basic categories of reorganization:

1. *Acquisitive reorganizations,* where one corporation acquires the stock or assets of another corporation. Examples include the Type A, B, C, and acquisitive Type D reorganizations.

2. *Divisive reorganizations,* where one corporation divides itself into two or more corporations and distributes stock to its shareholders. This is the divisive Type D.

3. Mere changes in the capital structure or the identity, form, or state of incorporation of a single corporation. These are the Type E and F reorganizations.

The Type G, which facilitates the reorganization of a bankrupt corporation, fits best under divisive reorganizations, but is arguably a unique fourth type.

A tax-free reorganization is concerned with a change in ownership of a corporation's assets or its stock by other than purchase. The word "tax free" is really a misnomer, as the tax effects of a transaction are merely postponed until some time in the future. Thus, a corporate reorganization generally results in tax deferral.

The possible advantages of a reorganization over a purchase include both economic as well as tax considerations. For example, one major economic advantage of a merger is that it may be accomplished without the use of cash. A major tax consideration of a reorganization involves the possible retention of the tax attributes of one or more of the participating corporations, with the continued use of a net operating loss deduction often of most importance.

Many business considerations will impact the choice of a particular type of reorganization. Additionally, a determination must be made as to whether a proposed acquisition violates federal and state antitrust laws. In some cases, shareholder approvals must be obtained and the registration requirements of federal and state laws must be met.

Types of Corporate Reorganizations

¶ 16,001   STATUTORY DEFINITIONS

For tax purposes, there are seven basic types of corporate reorganization. The concept of a "reorganization" is broader than the accounting and legal terms of "mergers," "consolidations," and "business combinations," but, at the same time, each type of reorganization is narrowly defined with many specific requirements. Code Sec. 368 defines the different types of reorganization. The types of reorganization are commonly referred to by the subparagraph in which they are defined. Code Sec. 368(a)(1)(A) defines a Type A reorganization; Code Sec. 368(a)(1)(B) defines a Type B reorganization and so forth.

The Seven Types of Corporate Reorganizations

A. A statutory merger or consolidation.

B. The acquisition by one corporation of the stock of another corporation. The acquiring corporation must exchange solely all or part of its voting stock, or all or part of the voting stock of a corporation that is in control of the acquiring corporation. The acquiring corporation must have control of the acquired corporation immediately after the acquisition, whether or not the acquiring corporation had control immediately before the acquisition. This is a "stock-for-stock" reorganization.

C. The acquisition by one corporation of substantially all of the properties of another corporation. The acquiring corporation must exchange solely all or part of its voting stock, or all or part of the voting stock of a corporation that is in control of the acquiring corporation. In determining whether the exchange is solely for stock, the assumption by the acquiring corporation of a liability of the acquired corporation or of property subject to a liability is disregarded. This is a "stock-for-assets" reorganization.

D. A transfer by a corporation of all or part of its assets to another corporation. Immediately after the transfer, the transferor or one or more of its shareholders must be in control of the corporation to which the assets are transferred. Also, in pursuance of the plan, stock or securities of the corporation to which the assets are transferred must be distributed in a transaction that qualifies under Code Sec. 354, 355, or 356.

E. A recapitalization.

F. A mere change in identity, form, or place of organization of one corporation, however effected.

G. A transfer by a corporation of all or part of its assets to another corporation in a bankruptcy or receivership proceeding; but only if, in pursuance of the plan, stock or securities of the corporation to which the assets are transferred are distributed in a transaction that qualifies under Code Sec. 354, 355, or 356.

To understand the tax consequences of corporate reorganizations, it is necessary to have a basic understanding of corporate formations (Code Sec. 351), distributions (Code Sec. 301), stock redemptions (Code Secs. 302–304), and complete liquidations. (Code Secs. 331–337). This material is covered in Chapters 13–15 and should be reviewed if needed.

¶ 16,005   GENERAL REQUIREMENTS

No gain or loss is recognized if stock or securities in a corporation that is a party to a reorganization are exchanged solely for stock or securities of the same corporation or another corporation that is a party to the reorganization. Code Sec. 354(a). In this context, the term "securities" means long-term debt.

In order to receive nonrecognition treatment, the stock or securities that are exchanged must be those of a party to the reorganization. The parties to a reorganization include:

1. A corporation resulting from the reorganization.

2. Both corporations in the case of a reorganization involving one corporation acquiring the stock or assets of another corporation.

Additionally, in some reorganizations, the corporation controlling the acquiring corporation qualifies as a party to the reorganization. Code Sec. 368(b).

Some types of reorganization permit the transfer of property other than stock or securities of a party to the reorganization. The receipt of such property (termed "boot") results in the recognition of gain to the extent of the lesser of (1) the realized gain or (2) the amount of money plus the fair market value of any other property received. For this purpose, boot also includes the fair market value of an excess principal (face) amount of securities received over the principal amount of securities surrendered. A shareholder's recognized gain is treated as dividend income if the receipt of boot has the same effect as a dividend distribution. Otherwise, the shareholder's gain will be generally treated as a capital gain.

In order to achieve reorganization treatment, the transactions must be pursuant to a "plan of reorganization." This plan should be written since Reg. § 1.368-3 calls for the adoption of a plan by each of the parties to the reorganization and also requires that a copy of the plan be filed with each corporation's tax return for the year of occurrence. However, a failure to strictly comply with the plan requirements does not negate the reorganization. In many cases, corporations planning a corporate reorganization obtain an advance letter ruling from the IRS ensuring that the proposed transactions qualify as a corporate reorganization.

Reorganization treatment requires that there be a "continuity of proprietary interest." This means that the former shareholders of the acquired corporation must receive stock in the acquiring corporation. Although the amount of stock that is needed to meet this requirement is not specified in the Code, for advance ruling purposes the IRS requires that stock of the acquiring corporation be at least 50 percent of the total consideration to be received by the shareholders of the acquired corporation. Rev. Proc. 79-14, 1979-1 CB 496. However, not all of the shareholders of the acquired corporation need to receive a proprietary interest in the acquiring corporation. The requirement is applied to the total consideration given to the shareholders of the acquired corporation and must be met in the aggregate.

There must also be a "continuity of business enterprise." This means that the acquiring corporation must either continue the acquired corporation's historic business, or use a significant portion of the acquired corporation's historic business assets in a business.

Finally, there must be a bona fide "business purpose" for a transaction to qualify as a corporate reorganization. In this context, the potential tax savings inherent in a corporate reorganization is not a valid business purpose. On the other hand, a valid business purpose includes an acquisition that is made to assure the continued availability of materials that are used in the acquiring corporation's production process.

Note that a tax-free reorganization is not always desirable. For example, the acquiring corporation may prefer to purchase assets so that the acquired assets will have a basis equal to fair market value, rather than a carryover basis that would result from a reorganization. Additionally, a reorganization may not be desirable if the target corporation or its shareholders have substantial unrealized losses that they wish to recognize.

¶ 16,009   TYPE A REORGANIZATIONS

Basic Form of Transaction

A Type A reorganization includes a merger or a consolidation meeting state law requirements. Reg. § 1.368-2(b).

In a statutory merger, shown in Figure 1 (see following page), Parent Corporation (acquiring corporation) acquires the assets and assumes the liabilities of Target Corporation by operation of law. Target Corporation's shareholders receive Parent stock, and Target Corporation is dissolved under state law. Even though Parent may issue its stock (and other consideration) directly to Target's shareholders, the transaction is treated as if the consideration was transferred to Target Corporation and then distributed to its shareholders. Afterwards, Parent's original shareholders and Target's former shareholders own all the stock of Parent Corporation.

In a consolidation, shown in Figure 2 (see following page), a new corporation is formed (Newco) to acquire all the assets and liabilities of two or more consolidating corporations, Target 1 (T1) and Target 2 (T2). The shareholders of both consolidating corporations exchange their stock for Newco stock, and T1 and T2 are dissolved under state law. Afterwards, the former shareholders of T1 and T2 own all the stock of Newco.

> *Example 16.1.* Fast-Food Corporation acquires all the properties of Taco Corporation in exchange for 3,000 shares of stock in Fast-Food Corporation. The Fast-Food Corporation stock is distributed to Taco's shareholders in complete liquidation of Taco Corporation. This transaction qualifies as a Type A reorganization (assuming the requirements of state law are met). It is a statutory merger.

Figure 1   MERGER

Figure 2   CONSOLIDATION

Example 16.2. Steel Corporation and Wool Corporation transfer their assets to a new corporation, Steel Wool, in exchange for the stock of Steel Wool. Steel and Wool then transfer the Steel Wool stock to their respective stockholders in exchange for the Steel and Wool stock. Steel and Wool are then liquidated and the two businesses are carried on by Steel Wool as one business. This is a Type A reorganization, a consolidation.

Because a corporate reorganization normally results in a continuation of the business activities of the previous corporations, liabilities are seldom liquidated. The acquiring corporation will either assume liabilities of the acquired organization or take property subject to liabilities. In a statutory merger or consolidation, the acquiring corporation acquires *all* of the assets and liabilities of the target corporation, including any contingent or unknown liabilities.

TAX PLANNING POINTER ▼

Care must be taken prior to the reorganization to determine the existence of unknown and contingent liabilities since these liabilities may affect the amount of consideration that the acquiring corporation is willing to pay. Contingent or escrowed stock arrangements can be used to adjust the amount of consideration to properly reflect the outcome of the contingencies relating to the liabilities.

Consideration Allowed

The Type A reorganization is the most flexible type of reorganization as far as the type of consideration that can be given to the target corporation's shareholders. At least 50 percent of the consideration must be stock of the acquiring corporation (either voting or nonvoting) to satisfy the continuity of proprietary interest requirement, but other consideration such as cash, options, debt obligations, or other property can also be paid without disqualifying the acquisition as a reorganization.

Advantages and Disadvantages of a Type A Reorganization

The main advantages of a Type A reorganization include:

1. The consideration that can be paid to the target's shareholders is flexible. Nonvoting stock can be used, as well as convertible securities, warrants, cash, or other property.

2. In contrast to other types of reorganizations, a straight Type A reorganization does not require that "substantially all" of the target's assets be acquired in the transaction. This means that, subject to the continuity of business enterprise requirement, the target corporation can spin off or sell unwanted

assets prior to its acquisition without disqualifying the acquisition as a reorganization.

The main disadvantages of a Type A reorganization include:

1. All liabilities of the acquired corporation (including unknown and contingent liabilities) must be assumed by the acquiring corporation.

2. A majority of the shareholders (two-thirds in some states) of both corporations must approve the reorganization. Having the shareholders vote could prove costly and time-consuming.

3. Dissenting shareholders of the target corporation normally have appraisal rights (i.e., the right to have their shares valued and purchased for cash). A substantial number of dissenting shareholders could necessitate a large cash outlay.

4. The acquired corporation may have contracts, rights, or privileges that are not transferable. These contracts, rights, or privileges expire when the acquired corporation dissolves.

Tax Consequences of a Type A Reorganization

Acquired Corporation's Shareholders

The exchange of stock or securities is tax free, provided the principal amount of securities received does not exceed the principal amount of securities surrendered. Code Sec. 354(a)(1). Cash, an excess principal amount of securities, or other boot received causes the recognition of a realized gain. Code Sec. 356(a). The basis of the stock and securities received by the acquired corporation's shareholders is the same as the basis of the stock and securities surrendered, increased by any gain recognized (including any amount treated as a dividend), and decreased by the amount of money and the fair market value of any other property received. Code Sec. 358(a)(1). Any boot property received has a basis equal to fair market value. Code Sec. 358(a)(2).

Example 16.3. Pursuant to a Type A reorganization, Target Corporation is merged into Parent Corporation. As part of the transaction, Irene Greene exchanges her Target stock that has a basis of $10,000 for Parent stock with a fair market value of $15,000.

1. If she receives Parent stock only, no gain is recognized, her basis in the Parent stock received is $10,000, and the holding period of her Parent stock includes the holding period of her Target stock.

2. If Irene receives $3,000 of cash and Parent stock worth $12,000, her realized gain of $5,000 ($15,000 − $10,000) is recognized to the extent of the $3,000 boot, and Irene must report a capital gain of $3,000. Her basis for the Parent stock is $10,000 (Target stock basis of $10,000 less boot of $3,000 plus gain recognized of $3,000).

3. If the cash in (2) has the effect of a dividend, Irene's recognized gain must be reported as $3,000 of dividend income. Her stock basis is $10,000 as determined in (2).

4. If Irene receives Parent stock worth $12,000 and Parent's bond with a principal amount and fair market value of $3,000, her realized gain of $5,000 is again recognized to the extent of $3,000. Even though it is Parent's bond, the fair market value of the bond is treated as boot received because Irene did not surrender any bonds. Her basis for the bond is its fair market value of $3,000. Her basis for the Parent stock is $10,000 ($10,000 Target stock basis, less the $3,000 FMV of the bond, plus the recognized gain of $3,000).

Acquiring Corporation

No gain or loss is recognized by the acquiring corporation on the issuance of its stock. Code Sec. 1032(a). The acquiring corporation receives a carryover basis for the transferor's assets, increased by any gain recognized to the transferor. Code Sec. 362(b). Since no gain or loss is generally recognized by the target corporation, the acquired assets generally have a carryover basis.

Note that the shareholders of the target corporation are not the "transferor" of the assets, and gain recognized by them because of the receipt of boot does not increase the basis of the assets that are acquired. Similarly, any gain recognized by the acquiring corporation because of the payment of boot property to the target's shareholders does not increase the basis of the acquired assets.

The holding period for the acquired assets includes the period of time they were held by the target. The acquiring corporation also succeeds to all of the target's tax attributes, although some carryovers (e.g., NOL carryover) may be limited in their deductibility.

Example 16.4. Parent Corporation transfers $400,000 of its common stock and $200,000 of cash to acquire Target Corporation's assets and liabilities in a statutory merger. Target's assets have a fair market value of $700,000 and a basis of $500,000, and Target has $100,000 of liabilities. Parent recognizes no gain or loss on the transfer of its stock. The $500,000 basis for Target's assets carries over to Parent, along with all of Target's tax attributes.

Acquired Corporation

No gain or loss is recognized by the target corporation upon the transfer of its assets solely in exchange for stock or securities of the acquiring corporation. Code Sec. 361(a). Similarly, the *receipt* of money or other boot property does not cause the recognition of gain to the target corporation. Generally, neither the acquiring corporation's assumption of the target's liabilities, nor the acquisition of the target's assets subject to liabilities, causes the recognition of gain to the acquired target corporation. Code Sec. 357(a).

The gain and loss recognition rules that apply to ordinary distributions and complete liquidations do not apply to distributions pursuant to a plan of reorganization. Code Sec. 361(c)(4). Thus, no gain or loss is recognized by the target corporation when it distributes the acquiring corporation's stock and securities that were received in the reorganization. However, the target corporation recognizes gain (but not loss) on the distribution of appreciated boot property pursuant to the plan of reorganization. Ordinarily, there is little gain (if any) recognized because the boot property's basis is its fair market value on date of receipt, and it normally is distributed shortly thereafter. Code Sec. 358(a)(2).

> *Example 16.5.* Assume the same facts as in Example 16.4. No gain or loss is recognized to Target Corporation on the receipt and distribution of the Parent Corporation stock and cash to its shareholders. The shareholders recognize gain to the extent of boot received.

Acquiring Corporation's Shareholders

In a merger where the acquiring corporation survives, there is no change in the tax status of the acquiring corporation's shareholders. They simply own a smaller percentage of a larger corporation.

¶ 16,015   RECEIPT OF BOOT

If a shareholder or security holder receives cash or other property (i.e., boot) in addition to the stock or securities that are permitted to be received without the recognition of gain under Code Sec. 354 or 355, then a realized gain must be recognized to the extent of the lesser of (1) the realized gain or (2) the fair market value of the boot received. Code Sec. 356(a)(1). No loss can be recognized as a result of the receipt of boot. Code Sec. 356(c). The distributee's basis for boot property is the property's fair market value. Code Sec. 358(a)(2).

> *Example 16.6.* Pursuant to a plan of reorganization, Allan Luden received the following consideration from Cherry Corporation in exchange for Lime Corporation stock having a basis of $85:
>
> | | |
> |---|---:|
> | Cherry Corp. stock (FMV) | $100 |
> | Cash | 25 |
> | Other property (FMV) | 50 |
> | Total FMV of consideration received | $175 |
> | Basis of Lime Corp. stock surrendered | 85 |
> | Realized gain | $ 90 |
>
> In this case, the amount of gain recognized by Allan is limited to the amount of cash plus the FMV of other property received, which totals $75. Allan's basis for the other property received equals its FMV of $50.
>
> *Example 16.7.* If, in Example 16.6, Allan's Lime Corporation stock had a basis to him of $125, he would realize and recognize a gain of $50.

Example 16.8. If, in Example 16.6, Allan's Lime Corporation stock had a basis to him of $200, he would realize a loss of $25 on the exchange, but the loss would not be recognized.

The definition of boot also includes the fair market value of an excess principal (face) amount of securities received over the principal amount of securities surrendered. If securities are received but no securities are surrendered, the fair market value of all securities received are treated as boot.

Example 16.9. Pursuant to a plan of reorganization, Sharon Baker received the following consideration from Red Corporation in exchange for Blue Corporation stock with a basis of $7,000:

Red Corp. stock (FMV)	$ 8,000
Red Corp. securities (FMV)	2,000
Total consideration received	$10,000
Less: Basis of Blue Corp. stock surrendered	7,000
Realized gain	$ 3,000

In this case, Baker's realized gain would be recognized to the extent of the fair market value of the excess securities received, $2,000.

If a shareholder or security holder surrenders securities, but a greater principal amount of securities is received, the fair market value of the excess principal amount of securities received is treated as boot. Code Sec. 356(d)(2)(B).

Example 16.10. Pursuant to a plan of reorganization, George Carter exchanged a Zim Corporation security with a basis of $700 and a principal amount of $1,000, for a new Zim Corporation security in the principal amount of $1,200 with a fair market value of $1,080.

Zim Corp. security received (FMV)	$1,080
Basis of Zim Corp. security surrendered	700
Realized gain	$ 380

Carter's realized gain is recognized to the extent of the fair market value of the excess principal amount of security received, $180, computed as follows:

Principal amount of securities received	$1,200
Principal amount of securities surrendered	1,000
Excess principal amount received	$ 200

$$\frac{\$200 \text{ (excess principal received)}}{\$1,200 \text{ (total principal received)}} \times \$1,080 \text{ (FMV of security received)}$$

$$=\$180 \text{ (FMV of excess principal amount received)}$$

¶ 16,025   CHARACTER OF RECOGNIZED GAIN

After the amount of recognized gain is computed, its character must be determined. If an exchange has the effect of a dividend, then a shareholder's recognized gain must be treated as a dividend to the extent of the shareholder's ratable share of earnings and profits. Code Sec. 356(a)(2). Any amount of recognized gain in excess of the amount to be treated as a dividend will be treated as capital gain.

Whether the receipt of boot has the effect of a dividend has been an issue of much controversy. Generally, whether a dividend has been received is determined in a manner consistent with the stock redemption rules that are found in Code Sec. 302. Under this approach, which applies the constructive stock ownership rules of Code Sec. 318, an exchange that is deemed to be either a substantially disproportionate redemption under Code Sec. 302(b)(2) or a redemption not essentially equivalent to a dividend under Code Sec. 302(b)(1) would not have the effect of a dividend and would instead be treated as capital gain.

The Supreme Court ended the controversy in this area by permitting a shareholder to obtain capital gain treatment by applying the Code Sec. 302 tests to the shareholder's stock ownership in the acquiring corporation that resulted from the reorganization. *D.E. Clark,* 89-1 USTC ¶ 9230, 489 U.S. 726, 109 S.Ct. 1455 (1989). In *Clark,* the taxpayer owned all of the stock of the target corporation that was merged into the acquiring corporation in a corporate reorganization. The taxpayer received acquiring corporation stock and cash as a result of the merger. Following the merger, the taxpayer owned less than 50 percent of the acquiring corporation's stock and less than 80 percent of the amount of stock that the taxpayer would have owned if the taxpayer had instead received only stock in the acquiring corporation and no boot.

The Court's analysis requires one to imagine a pure stock-for-stock exchange, followed immediately by a postreorganization redemption of a portion of the shareholder's shares in the acquiring corporation in return for a payment in an amount equal to the amount of boot received in the reorganization. As a result of the Supreme Court's analysis, boot received by a shareholder in a corporate reorganization will generally result in capital gain treatment so long as the shareholder, as a result of the reorganization, owns (directly and constructively under Code Sec. 318) less than 50 percent of the acquiring corporation's stock.

> *Example 16.11.* Juniper Corporation has 100 shares outstanding and is wholly owned by David Worth. Berry Corporation has 100 shares outstanding and is wholly owned by Eric Embers. David and Eric are not related. Pursuant to a plan of reorganization, Juniper is merged into Berry, with David receiving 60 shares of Berry Corporation and cash of $40,000.
>
> If David had received no cash, he would have received 100 Berry Corporation shares.

As a result of the reorganization, David owns 60 of the 160 outstanding Berry Corporation shares (37.5 percent). Had David received no boot, he would have owned 100 out of 200 outstanding Berry Corporation shares (50 percent). Using the Supreme Court's approach, the cash of $40,000 is deemed to have been received in redemption of the 40 shares of Berry Corporation that David did not receive. Applying the Code Sec. 302(b)(2) tests, David's resulting 37.5 percent ($^{60}/_{160}$) ownership of Berry Corporation, is less than 50 percent, and less than 80 percent of the ownership that David would have had ($^{100}/_{200}$) if he had received no boot (37.5% is less than (80% $\times$ 50%)). Thus, since the receipt of the $40,000 of cash would qualify for exchange treatment under Code Sec. 302(b)(2), David's recognized gain will be treated as capital gain.

Example 16.12. Assume the same facts as in Example 16.11 except that David and Eric are father and son. Since David constructively owns all of Eric's stock under Code Sec. 318, David directly and constructively owns all of Berry Corporation's outstanding stock after the merger. Thus, none of the Code Sec. 302 tests can be met and the receipt of the cash of $40,000 will be treated as a dividend (assuming Berry Corporation has at least $40,000 of earnings and profits).

¶ 16,053 TYPE B REORGANIZATIONS

Basic Form of Transaction

In contrast to the Type A and C reorganizations that are used to acquire a target corporation's assets, the Type B reorganization is used to acquire the target's stock. In a Type B reorganization, the acquiring corporation must exchange solely voting stock to acquire control of the target corporation. A Type B reorganization usually takes the form of a tender offer to the target's shareholders, and often does not involve the target corporation itself.

As shown in Figure 3 on the next page, Parent Corporation (acquiring corporation) exchanges solely voting stock of Parent with the shareholders of Target Corporation to obtain control of Target. After the exchange, Parent's original shareholders together with Target's former shareholders own all of the stock of Parent Corporation, which in turn, is in control of Target Corporation.

It is important to note that the "solely voting stock" requirement applies only to the consideration that is used to acquire the target corporation's stock. Other consideration (e.g., nonvoting stock, cash, debentures) can be used to acquire the outstanding debt securities of the target corporation, or other assets owned by shareholders of the target corporation.

Figure 3   TYPE B REORGANIZATION

80-Percent-Control Requirement

The acquiring corporation must "control" the acquired corporation immediately after the transaction. "Control" is defined as the ownership of at least 80 percent of the total combined voting power *and* 80 percent of each class of nonvoting stock. Rev. Rul. 59-259, 1959-2 CB 115.

> *Example 16.13.* Carnival Inc. acquires 800 shares of Masks Inc.'s 1,000 outstanding shares from Masks' shareholders by giving them 500 shares of newly issued voting shares in Carnival. This is a Type B reorganization.

The requirement that the acquiring corporation be in control immediately after the exchange does not limit the reorganization to a single transaction. If the acquisition of stock occurs over a relatively short period of time (i.e., 12 months), Reg. §1.368-2(c) permits the transactions to qualify as a Type B reorganization. However, a problem arises if a corporation acquires some stock for cash and then at a later date issues solely voting stock to acquire an additional amount of stock sufficient to meet the 80-percent-control requirement. The question to be resolved is whether the two acquisitions are related. If they are, then the voting-stock-for-stock exchange is taxable because the overall acquisition of the target's stock was not made solely for voting stock of the acquiring corporation. If the two acquisitions are not related, then the exchange of the acquiring corporation's voting stock for the target's stock is viewed as a separate transaction, and qualifies as a Type B reorganization. The longer the period of time between a cash purchase and the acquisition for voting stock, the greater the probability that they will be treated as unrelated.

Example 16.14. Parent Corporation purchased 25 percent of Target Corporation's stock five years ago. Parent currently acquires an additional 60 percent of Target's stock solely in exchange for Parent voting stock. The exchange of Parent voting stock for Target stock qualifies as a Type B reorganization because the acquisitions for cash and stock are treated as unrelated.

Example 16.15. Alternatively, assume Parent Corporation purchased 10 percent of Target Corporation's stock for cash during March 1998. During September 1998, Parent made a tender offer and acquired an additional 75 percent of Target's stock solely in exchange for Parent voting stock. When the March and September acquisitions are combined, Target's stock has not been acquired solely for Parent's voting stock. Thus, the exchange of Parent stock for Target stock fails to qualify as a Type B reorganization and is treated as a taxable exchange.

If a Type B reorganization is desired after the acquiring corporation has already purchased some target stock, the acquiring corporation can make an unconditional sale of the purchased stock to an unrelated third party. Then the IRS will allow a subsequent voting-stock-for-stock exchange to qualify as a Type B reorganization. Rev. Rul. 72-354, 1972-2 CB 216.

Consideration Allowed

The acquiring corporation must acquire the target corporation's stock solely with its voting stock. The voting stock may be either common or preferred stock, as long as "normal" voting rights are conferred. Convertible preferred voting stock may be used, but not convertible bonds, even if convertible at all times into voting stock. Rev. Rul. 69-91, 1969-1 CB 105. Options to purchase voting stock, such as rights and warrants, do *not* qualify as voting stock. *Southwest Consolidated Corp.*, 42-2 USTC ¶ 9248, 315 U.S. 194, 62 S.Ct. 546 (1942). Cash is strictly prohibited, except for the following:

1. Cash may be paid in lieu of issuing fractional shares that the acquired corporation's shareholders are entitled to receive. Rev. Rul. 66-365, 1966-2 CB 116.

2. The acquiring corporation may pay the acquired corporation's legal, accounting, and appraisal fees and other expenses directly related to the stock acquisition in cash, but *not* any expenses incurred by the acquired corporation's shareholders. Rev. Rul. 73-54, 1973-1 CB 187. The acquired corporation may, however, redeem the stock of dissenting, minority share-

holders for cash or property, in a separate transaction. Rev. Rul. 68-285, 1968-1 CB 142.

Example 16.16. Boatcraft Inc. wishes to acquire the stock of Canoes Inc., but shareholders owning 25 percent of Canoes' stock insist on cash. Canoes then uses its cash and redeems the stock of those shareholders wanting cash. Boatcraft subsequently exchanges its voting stock and obtains all of Canoes' remaining outstanding shares. Since Boatcraft used solely voting stock to acquire control of Canoes, its exchange of Boatcraft voting stock for Canoes stock qualifies as a Type B reorganization.

Advantages and Disadvantages of a Type B Reorganization

The main advantages of a Type B reorganization are:

1. The acquired corporation remains in existence as a subsidiary of the acquiring corporation, which can be an important consideration if it has an established identity. Any nonassignable contracts, leases, franchises, and licenses, as well as all of its tax attributes remain unaffected.

2. In contrast to a Type A reorganization, a Type B does not depend on meeting the requirements of local law. No formal shareholder vote is required. The acquisition normally takes the form of a tender offer to the target's shareholders, even if the target's management does not approve.

3. The assets of the acquiring corporation are protected from the target's liabilities because of the continued separate corporate existence of the target.

4. In contrast to a Type C reorganization, a Type B reorganization does not require that the target corporation retain substantially all of its assets.

5. Some of the problems that may be applicable to asset acquisitions (e.g., transfer fees, state and local income taxes, substantial recordkeeping) are avoided when only stock is acquired.

The main disadvantages of a Type B reorganization are:

1. Only voting stock can be used to acquire the target's stock. This may have a dilutive effect on the control exercised by the acquiring corporation's original shareholders.

2. Acquisition of less than 100 percent of the target's stock results in a dissenting minority interest that may create problems at shareholder meetings.

3. Even if a consolidated tax return is filed, the desirable tax attributes of the acquired corporation (e.g., NOL and tax credit carryforwards) remain segregated and generally cannot be used to benefit the acquiring corporation.

Tax Consequences of a Type B Reorganization

Acquired Corporation's Shareholders

No gain or loss is recognized by the target's shareholders on the exchange of their target stock for voting stock of the acquiring corporation. Code Sec. 354(a)(1). As a result, their basis and holding period for the target stock carries over to the acquiring corporation's stock received in the exchange. Code Sec. 358(a)(1).

Acquiring Corporation

No gain or loss is recognized to the acquiring corporation on the issuance of its voting stock. Code Sec. 1032. The basis and holding period of the acquired corporation's stock is a carryover basis and holding period from the former shareholders of the target corporation. Code Sec. 362(b).

Acquired Corporation

The acquired corporation remains in existence and retains all of its tax attributes.

Acquiring Corporation's Stock Basis

The acquiring corporation will need to know what its basis is for the acquired target corporation stock in the event of a later sale, exchange, or other disposition of the stock. Of course, its basis for the target stock will be the same as it was in the hands of the former target shareholders. Determining what this basis is can be a practical problem if the target corporation was publicly held since the former target shareholders would have purchased the stock at various times, or may have received it by gift or inheritance. Fortunately, the IRS has approved the use of estimating and sampling procedures so that the aggregate basis may be determined statistically. Rev. Rul. 81-70, 1981-2 CB 729.

> *Example 16.17.* Target Corporation's only class of stock is 100 percent owned by Kelly Morgan, who has a basis of $300,000 for her stock. Pursuant to a plan of reorganization, Kelly exchanges her Target stock for $500,000 of Parent Corporation's voting stock. Although Kelly realizes a $200,000 gain, no gain is recognized, and Kelly's basis for the Parent stock is $300,000. Parent recognizes no gain or loss when it issues its voting stock and has a $300,000 basis for the Target stock acquired from Kelly.

¶ 16,105   TYPE C REORGANIZATIONS

Basic Form of Transaction

The acquiring corporation issues its voting stock to acquire substantially all the assets of the target corporation. If the target corporation is liquidated immediately after the exchange, then the effect of the acquisition is much the same as a statutory merger and is often referred to as a "practical merger."

Figure 4   TYPE C REORGANIZATION

In a Type C reorganization, the acquired corporation must distribute the stock, securities, and other property that it received from the acquiring corporation in the reorganization, together with any property that it retained and did not transfer to the acquiring corporation, to its shareholders as part of the plan of reorganization. Because of this distribution requirement, the target corporation is effectively liquidated as part of the plan of reorganization.

As shown in Figure 4, Parent Corporation (acquiring corporation) transfers its voting stock in exchange for substantially all of the assets and liabilities of Target Corporation (acquired corporation). Target then distributes the Parent stock, together with any assets not transferred to Parent, to its shareholders in cancellation of their Target stock.

Meaning of "Substantially All" Assets

What constitutes "substantially all" of the acquired corporation's assets is not specifically defined in the Code. For advance ruling purposes, the IRS requires that at least 70 percent of the gross assets *and* at least 90 percent of the net assets must be acquired. Rev. Proc. 77-37, 1977-2 CB 568.

Example 16.18. Target Corporation has assets with a total fair market value of $600,000 and has liabilities of $100,000. Seventy percent of Target's gross assets equals $420,000 (70% × $600,000), and 90 percent of Target's net assets equals $450,000 (90% × ($600,000 − $100,000)). To obtain an advance ruling regarding a proposed Type C reorganization, at least $450,000 of Target's assets must be acquired.

Revenue Rulings issued by the IRS and various courts have been more flexible in interpreting the "substantially all" test and have indicated that the test is satisfied if all significant operating assets are transferred to the acquiring corporation. Rev. Rul. 78-47, 1978-1 CB 113.

Consideration Allowed

The consideration used to acquire substantially all of the acquired corporation's assets must consist *solely* of the acquiring corporation's voting stock. Code Sec. 368(a)(1)(C). For purposes of this solely voting stock requirement, the assumption of a liability of the acquired corporation or the acquisition of property subject to a liability is completely disregarded. This is understandable because creditors ordinarily would not permit the transfer of assets without the transfer of related debt for fear that the transferor would be unable to repay the debt with its remaining assets.

Additionally, there is a boot relaxation rule under which consideration other than voting stock can be used provided that at least 80 percent of the total fair market value of all of the target's assets is acquired for voting stock. Code Sec. 368(a)(2)(B). Technically, this rule permits up to 20 percent of the target's assets to be acquired for boot. However, for purposes of applying this rule, liabilities assumed or taken subject to by the acquiring corporation are included in the computation of the 20 percent limit. The practical effect of this rule is that boot cannot be used in a Type C reorganization because the target corporation's liabilities, which must be assumed, ordinarily exceed 20 percent of the total fair market value of its assets.

Example 16.19. The following example illustrates the 80 percent rule of Code Sec. 368(a)(2)(B).

	Case 1	Case 2	Case 3
Total FMV of Target Corp. assets	$100,000	$100,000	$100,000
Liabilities assumed by Parent Corp. . . .	(30,000)	(18,000)	(19,000)
Cash paid by Parent Corp.	0	(2,000)	(2,000)
Parent voting stock transferred	$ 70,000	$ 80,000	$ 79,000

In Case 1, no boot was paid so Target Corporation's liabilities are disregarded in determining whether solely voting stock was used, and it qualifies as a Type C reorganization. In Case 2, even though boot was paid it nevertheless qualifies as a Type C reorganization because the voting stock that was transferred equals at least 80 percent of the total FMV of Target's assets. Case 3 fails to qualify as a Type C reorganization because boot was paid and the Parent Corporation voting stock transferred was less than 80 percent of the total FMV of Target's assets.

The IRS has ruled that if the acquiring corporation assumes the acquired corporation's liability to pay cash to dissenting shareholders, the cash payment to shareholders is treated as a transfer of cash to the acquired corporation and causes the boot relaxation rule of Code Sec. 368(a)(2)(B) to apply. Rev. Rul. 73-102, 1973-1 CB 186.

Distribution Requirement

In order to qualify as a Type C reorganization, the acquired corporation must distribute the stock, securities, and other properties that it receives from the acquiring corporation, as well as any of its properties that were not transferred to the acquiring corporation, in pursuance of the plan of reorganization. If the acquired corporation is liquidated, any distribution to its creditors in connection with the liquidation will be treated as pursuant to the plan of reorganization.

The time period during which the distribution must be completed is not specified in Code Sec. 368(a)(2)(G). However, the distribution should be made promptly and the acquired corporation should not engage in the active conduct of a business after the reorganization transaction.

Finally, Code Sec. 368(a)(2)(G)(ii) authorizes the IRS to waive the distribution requirement if an actual distribution would result in a substantial hardship and the acquired corporation and its shareholders agree to be treated as if the undistributed assets had been distributed and then contributed to the capital of a new corporation.

Advantages and Disadvantages of a Type C Reorganization

The main advantages of a Type C reorganization are:

1. Not all liabilities of the target need be assumed or acquired, as is the case in a Type A reorganization where all liabilities (including unknown and contingent liabilities) must be assumed.

2. Not all assets need be acquired. As long as substantially all assets are acquired, unwanted assets can remain with the target corporation and be distributed to its shareholders.

3. Only the target corporation's shareholders have to approve the acquisition and liquidation that typically are a part of a Type C reorganization. This saves the time and expense of having the acquiring corporation's shareholders approve the reorganization transaction.

Disadvantages of a Type C reorganization:

1. Because the target's assets are not transferred by operation of law (as in a Type A), substantial transfer costs are ordinarily incurred in acquiring the assets. The transfer of assets will generally be taxable for state income tax purposes even though tax free at the federal level.

2. Substantially all of the target's assets must be acquired. This generally precludes a spin-off of an unwanted business before

the reorganization, or a sale of unwanted assets immediately after the acquisition.

3. Generally, the boot relaxation rule cannot be used. Solely voting stock must be used to make the acquisition because the target corporation's liabilities exceed 20 percent of the total fair market value of its assets.

Tax Consequences of a Type C Reorganization

Acquired Corporation's Shareholders

No gain or loss is recognized by the target's shareholders if they receive only stock of the acquiring corporation. Their old stock basis and holding period carry over to their new stock. If boot is received (including an excess principal amount of securities), the lesser of the realized gain or the fair market value of the boot is recognized as gain. The basis for the stock received is equal to the basis of the stock given up, reduced by the boot received, and increased by the gain recognized. The boot property has a basis equal to fair market value.

> *Example 16.20.* Pursuant to a Type C reorganization, Parent Corporation acquires all of Target Corporation's assets and liabilities in exchange for Parent voting stock worth $800,000 and stock in Whitecliff Corporation (not a party to the reorganization) with a value of $50,000, and a basis of $20,000. Target's assets have a fair market value of $1,000,000 and a basis of $600,000, while its liabilities total $150,000.
>
> Upon the liquidation of Target, Fred Marker exchanges Target stock with a basis of $9,000 and a value of $10,000 for Parent stock worth $8,000 and Whitecliff Corporation stock worth $2,000. Fred recognizes a gain of $1,000 (lesser of boot of $2,000, or realized gain of $1,000). Fred's basis for his Parent stock equals $8,000 (old basis of $9,000, less boot of $2,000, plus $1,000 of recognized gain). Fred's basis for the Whitecliff Corporation stock is its fair market value of $2,000, and its holding period begins on the day after receipt. Fred's holding period for his Parent stock includes the holding period of his Target stock.

Acquired Corporation

No gain or loss is recognized by the target corporation on the exchange of its assets for stock and securities of the acquiring corporation, nor on the distribution of that stock or securities to its shareholders. However, gain is recognized on the distribution of any appreciated property that was not transferred to the acquiring corporation. The target corporation's taxable year ends on the date of the asset transfer. Code Sec. 381(b)(1).

Acquiring Corporation

The acquiring corporation does not recognize any gain when it issues its own stock. The basis for the acquired assets is the same as the target's basis for the assets, increased by any gain recognized to the target corporation. All of the target's tax attributes carry over to the acquiring corporation.

Example 16.21. Assume the same facts as in Example 16.20. Parent Corporation recognizes no gain on the issuance of its stock but does recognize gain of $30,000 on the transfer of the Whitecliff Corporation stock. Since no gain is recognized to Target Corporation, Parent's basis for the acquired assets is $600,000.

Type B Reorganization Followed by Liquidation

If a Type B reorganization is closely followed by a liquidation of the acquired subsidiary, the overall acquisition of assets is tested as a Type C reorganization under the step transaction doctrine. This could prove fatal to the reorganization because of the substantially all test that is found in a Type C (but not in a Type B) reorganization. For example, a distribution or spin-off of some of the target's assets just prior to the acquisition might cause the acquisition to fail the substantially all test, and therefore the acquisition does not qualify as a Type C reorganization, even though the acquisition of the target's stock would have qualified as a Type B reorganization if the target had not been liquidated.

KEYSTONE PROBLEM

Ark Inc. wishes to acquire the assets of Bark Inc., all of which are appreciated. What are the tax consequences to the corporations and Bark's shareholders if the acquisition is handled in the following alternative ways?

1. Ark acquires the assets of Bark for consideration consisting of 80 percent voting stock in Ark (7 percent of Ark's stock) and 20 percent cash. Bark liquidates, and the Ark stock and cash received by Bark are distributed to Bark's shareholders, who turn in all their Bark stock.

2. Bark Inc. adopts a plan of complete liquidation and transfers all its assets to Ark Inc. for 30 percent cash and 70 percent Ark voting stock. Bark distributes the consideration received to its shareholders in complete liquidation.

¶ 16,157 TYPE D REORGANIZATIONS

Basic Forms of Transactions

There are two distinct types of Type D reorganizations, "divisive" and "acquisitive." Common in both types is the transfer of assets from one corporation to another in exchange for stock or securities, which are then distributed to the transferor's shareholders.

If "substantially all" assets are transferred, a Type D reorganization may also meet the definition of a Type C, but it is nevertheless treated as a Type D reorganization. An acquisitive Type D reorganization results if the transferor corporation receives at least 50 percent control (voting power or value) of the transferee, while 80 percent control is required in a divisive Type D reorganization. Code Sec. 368(c)(2).

Whereas Type A, B, and C reorganizations are used to combine corporations, the Type D reorganization is generally used to divide a corporation. If the transferor survives as an operating entity, a divisive Type D reorganization takes place, tax free only if the requirements of Code Sec. 355 are met. This means that the transferor obtains and distributes control in the transferee corporation to its shareholders. Divisive Type D reorganizations are known as "spin-offs, split-offs, and split-ups."

A *spin-off* occurs when part of the assets of a corporation are transferred to a new corporation controlled by the transferor and the stock or securities in the latter are distributed to the shareholders of the original corporation without a surrender by the shareholders of stock or securities in the distributing corporation. A *split-off* is similar to a spin-off, except that the shareholders surrender a part of their stock in the distributing corporation for the stock in the controlled corporation. In a *split-up*, the distributing corporation transfers its assets to two or more newly created corporations in exchange for their stock and then effects a complete liquidation, the shareholders of the distributing corporation receiving stock in the new corporations in exchange for their stock in the distributing corporation.

> *Example 16.22.* Money Corporation, a bank, owns an 11-story office building where it occupies the ground floor in the conduct of its banking business, and the remaining 10 floors are rented to various tenants. The 10 rented floors are managed and maintained by the corporation's real estate department. The bank forms a new corporation, to which it transfers the building, and distributes all of the stock of the new corporation to the bank's shareholders. This is a spin-off.

> *Example 16.23.* Assume the same facts as in Example 16.22, except that the bank shareholders are required to surrender 30 percent of their stock and receive pro rata distributions of all of the stock in the new corporation. This is a split-off.

> *Example 16.24.* Money Corporation transfers its banking business to new Coins Corporation and transfers the building to new Dollars Corporation, in exchange for all of the stock of Coins and Dollars. It then transfers the Coins and Dollars stock to its shareholders in exchange for all of their Money stock. Money Corporation is then liquidated. This is a split-up.

The distributing corporation must distribute (1) all of the stock and securities of the controlled corporation or (2) at least 80 percent of the voting stock and 80 percent of all other classes of stock (but all or part of the securities may be retained). Moreover, the distributing corporation cannot retain any part of the stock or securities of the controlled corporation for the purpose of avoiding federal income taxes.

The principle of nonrecognition of gain or loss on receipt of a distribution applies where the distribution is pro rata among all the shareholders of the distributing corporation and whether the shareholders surrender stock in the distributing corporation. However, for full nonrecognition of gain, no stock in the controlled corporation can have been acquired by the distributing corporation within five years prior to the distribution in a transaction in which gain or loss was recognized in whole or in part. Code Sec. 355(a)(3)(B). If stock was so acquired, it is treated as "other property."

Spin-Offs

In a spin-off, a corporation transfers one of its businesses, typically the assets of a division, to a newly formed subsidiary in exchange for its stock, in what, in isolation, would simply be a Code Sec. 351 transfer. Promptly thereafter, the parent's stock in the new subsidiary is distributed to the parent's shareholders. A spin-off also includes the distribution of a preexisting subsidiary's stock to the shareholders of the parent.

As can be seen from Figure 5, A's shareholders end up owning stock in two different corporations, A Corporation and D Corporation.

Figure 5   SPIN-OFF

Split-Offs

A split-off is similar to a spin-off, except that shareholders in the parent must give up all or part of their securities in the parent to receive securities in the subsidiary.

After the transaction is completed, A's shareholders end up with shares in both A Corporation and D Corporation. If shareholders give up only a portion of their shares in A Corporation for shares in D Corporation, all shareholders will own shares in both A Corporation and D Corporation. This is the same result as in a spin-off. However, if some of the original A shareholders give up all of their shares in A for D shares, different shareholders will own shares in A Corporation from those shareholders owning stock in D Corporation. If A's shareholders exchange their A shares in differing proportions for D shares, the transaction might result with some shareholders holding shares only in A Corporation, some shareholders owning shares only in D Corporation, and some shareholders owning shares in both A Corporation and D Corporation.

Figure 6   SPLIT-OFF

Split-Ups

In a split-up, a corporation transfers *all* its assets to two or more new corporations, whereupon the shareholders in the transferor give up *all* their stock or securities in the transferor for those of the transferee corporations.

In a split-up, two new corporations are formed, with the original corporation going out of existence. The former shareholders of A Corporation own stock in D1 Corporation and D2 Corporation. More likely than not, the purpose of the split-up is to have one group of former A shareholders own D1 Corporation and a different group of former A shareholders own D2 Corporation, though that is not required.

Figure 7   SPLIT-UP

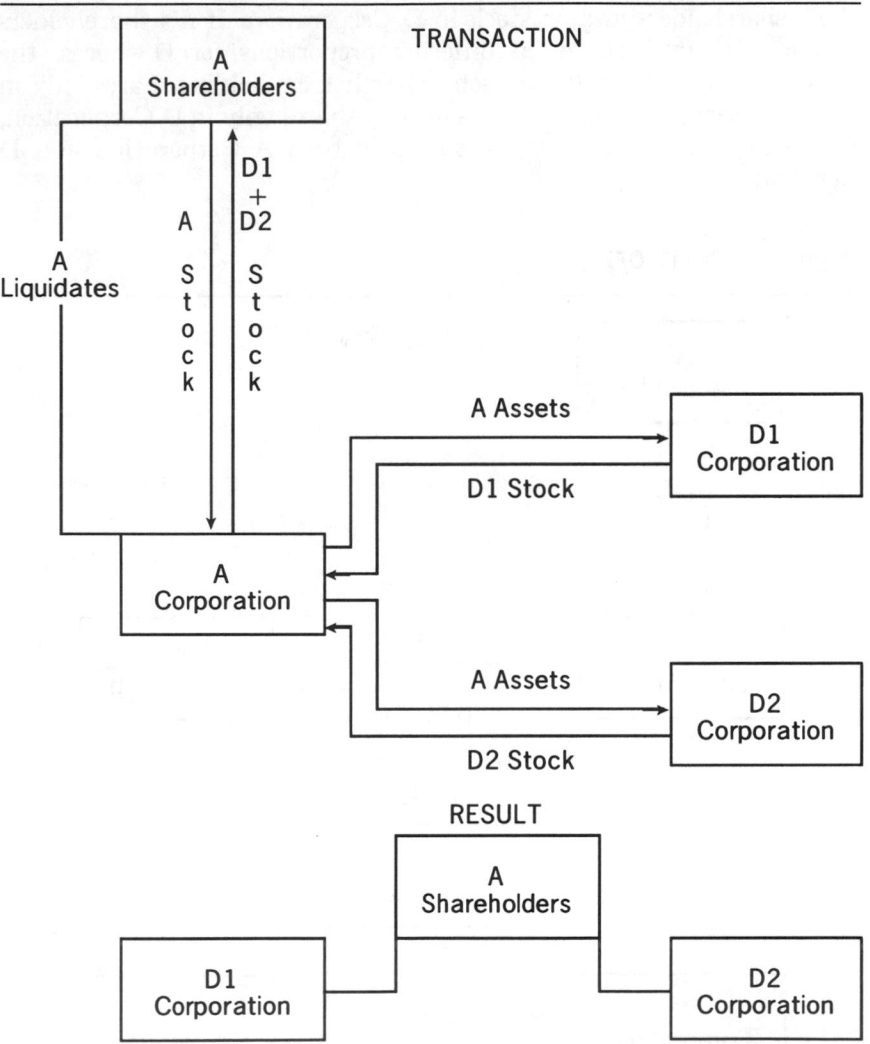

A divisive transaction is quite similar to a partial liquidation in that both provisions may be used in contracting or breaking up a corporation. Either approach may be appropriate in the following situations:

1. There may be a desire to discontinue and transfer one or more of the operations of the business, or its assets.

2. There may be a desire to protect the corporation from possible liabilities arising from present or future business ventures.

3. State law or business considerations may require separate branches of the business to be separately incorporated.

4. Antitrust or other decrees may require the corporation to divest itself of a business.

5. There may be a desire to split the corporate operations among some but not all members of the shareholder group.

6. There may be a desire to eliminate some of the shareholders because of a divergence of opinion as to corporate policies, or to provide for a complete retirement from the business of elderly shareholders.

TAX PLANNING POINTER ▼

A Type D reorganization can be a particularly appropriate tool if there is a need to segregate the ownership interests in a corporation. For example, a corporation is composed of two business operations, each of equivalent value, and the corporation is owned equally by two shareholders. If one of the shareholders has a particular interest in one of the corporation's operations and is in disagreement with the other owner over the direction of the business, a division of the corporation can be effected under Code Sec. 368(a)(1)(D) which can end the dispute. Each shareholder could become the sole owner of a corporation, with the respective corporations owning one of the operations of the predecessor corporation. The stock ownership need not necessarily be equal and the two business operations do not have to be of equivalent value. The stockholders can decide in what proportions to split the corporation.

Tax Consequences of a Type D Reorganization

Transferor Corporation

If the stock in the transferee corporation is *not* distributed, no gain or loss is recognized on the transfer of property under Code Sec. 351(a). However, if the stock or securities in the transferee are distributed to the stockholders of the transferor, the requirements of Code Sec. 355 must be met to provide nonrecognition on the transfer of property under Code Sec. 361. In any event, a realized gain must be recognized if liabilities in excess of basis are transferred. Code Sec. 357(c). Gain is recognized on any "boot" property distributed. Code Sec. 361(c).

Transferor Corporation's Shareholders

If the requirements of Code Sec. 355 are met, stock and security holders in the transferor recognize no gain or loss when they receive stock in the transferee corporation or swap securities in the transferor for those in the transferee. Code Sec. 355(a)(1). There are three main exceptions:

1. Excess principal amounts of debt securities received over principal surrendered are taxed to the extent of their fair market value. Code Secs. 355(a)(3)(A) and 356(d)(2)(C). This results in a dividend in a spin-off, and a possible capital gain in split-offs and split-ups.

2. If the transaction was principally a device to distribute earnings and profits of the transferor or transferee corporation, the transaction is taxable. Code Sec. 355(a)(1)(B).

3. If boot is received (i.e., property other than stock or securities), it may be taxed as a dividend, if it has the effect of a dividend, or as a gain on the exchange of securities to the extent a gain is realized. Generally, a dividend results in a spin-off since there is no exchange, and a capital gain results in an exchange, be it a split-off or a split-up. Whether or not there is boot, no *loss* can be recognized if Code Sec. 355 applies. Code Sec. 356(c).

Example 16.25. Magicworld Inc. incorporates a domestic branch and distributes 100 percent of the new subsidiary to its shareholder, who must give up two shares in Magicworld for each 10 shares in Dragonrider Inc., the new corporation. This is a split-off, a divisive Type D reorganization, resulting from a Code Sec. 351 transfer, followed by meeting the Code Sec. 355 requirements.

Magicworld recognizes no gain or loss under Code Sec. 361; the shareholder has no gain or loss under Code Sec. 355. The shareholder's basis in the old stock carries over and the holding period tacks on.

General Requirements

The general requirements to be satisfied before Code Sec. 355 will apply may be summarized as follows:

1. *Business purpose.* The transferor (the "old" corporation) must have a substantial business purpose for the transaction.

2. *Continuity of interest.* The pretransaction shareholders need a continuing equity interest in the posttransaction corporation(s).

3. *No "device."* The distribution cannot be primarily a device to avoid dividend treatment to the shareholders.

4. *Corporate control.* The distributor corporation must have Code Sec. 368(c) control (the 80 percent test) of the corporation whose securities it distributes, measured immediately prior to the distribution.

5. *Shareholder control.* Sufficient stock must be distributed to constitute 80 percent control in the hands of the distributees.

6. *Active trade or business.* After the distribution, all surviving corporations must be actively engaged in a trade of business. Also each trade or business must be at least five years old at the time of distribution.

Trade or Business Requirement

The trade or business requirement in a divisive Type D reorganization consists of a two-part test:

1. Both the distributing and the controlled corporation must be engaged in the active conduct of a trade or business immediately after the distribution.

2. These trades or businesses must have been conducted for at least five years. Code Sec. 355(b)(1)(A).

An "active trade or business" does *not* include passive investments, whether in securities or real estate, or the mere ownership or leasing of property (unless significant services are rendered). Reg. § 1.355-3(b)(2)(iv). On the other hand, a holding corporation is considered to be conducting the trade or business of its subsidiary if it holds few or no assets other than the stock or securities of its controlled subsidiary. One trade or business can be split in two if both, considered separately, constitute a trade or business. Rev. Rul. 64-147, 1964-1 CB 136.

To constitute an active trade or business, the Regulations contemplate:

1. A specific group of activities

2. A profit motive

3. Management and operational functions

4. The collection of income and the payment of expenses (Reg. § 1.355-3(b)(2)(iv)).

The *same* trade or business must have been conducted for at least five years, with two exceptions:

1. A new trade or business can be acquired in a tax-free transaction, such as a reorganization.

2. Control of a corporation, other than by purchase, can be acquired during the five-year period. Code Sec. 355(b)(2).

Applications of Divisive Type D Reorganizations

Under Code Sec. 355, there is no requirement that the shareholders hold on to their new stock. Nor is there a requirement that the distribution be pro rata. The shareholders need not surrender any stock in a spin-off. The distributing corporation may become a minority shareholder in the transferee since it need only distribute 80 percent of the stock in the subsidiary.

Note that if the shareholders sell their new stock or securities soon after receipt, the transaction may fail as a "device" if the sales are pursuant to a predistribution commitment. Code Sec. 355(a)(1)(B) and (2)(A).

The objectives to be accomplished through the means of Code Sec. 355 include the following:

1. *Shareholder Disagreements.* If two shareholders or groups of shareholders have a falling out, the business may be split in

two. Two new corporations are formed, and each shareholder or group of shareholders receives all the stock in one of the corporations in return for the stock in the transferor. This can qualify as a split-up.

2. *Antitrust Divestiture.* One of the remedies granted the government in a successful antitrust suit against a private corporation is a divestiture of the prohibited assets. One way to dispose of the division is to incorporate it, then spin it off to the shareholders.

3. *Estate Planning.* A split-up or spin-off involving shareholders of different generations might serve estate planning objectives, such as being part of a gift program, as well as teaching the younger generation the company's operations.

A business purpose must exist. Saving taxes alone does not qualify as a business purpose, but is permissible as *one* purpose.

TAX PLANNING POINTER

A divisive Type D reorganization is an interesting alternative to a redemption or a partial liquidation. If two shareholders wish to split a business in two, it could be done as a split-off or as a redemption. In either case, the assets of one division would be transferred to a new corporation and its stock distributed to one shareholder in redemption of the original stock. If the requirements of Code Sec. 355 are met, the transaction is tax free and the stock and asset bases carry over. In a redemption under Code Sec. 302(b)(3), the corporation pays tax on the increase in value of the distributed assets, and the shareholder pays tax on the gain but receives a fair market value basis for the assets.

¶ 16,165   GAIN RECOGNIZED IN DIVISIVE TRANSACTIONS

Concerns developed that a purchaser of less than 80 percent of the stock of a parent corporation might attempt to utilize Code Sec. 355 to acquire a subsidiary (or a division incorporated for this purpose) from the parent corporation without the parent incurring any corporate-level tax. For example, the purchaser might acquire stock of the parent equal in value to the value of the desired subsidiary, and later surrender that stock in exchange for stock of the subsidiary in a transaction intended to qualify as a non-pro rata, tax-free split-off. Such a disguised sale of a subsidiary by the parent corporation would not only avoid the recognition of gain to the parent corporation, but would also provide the purchaser with a stepped-up fair market value basis in the subsidiary's stock, possibly enabling the purchaser to make a subsequent disposition of the subsidiary tax free.

Example 16.26. Parent owns 100 percent of the stock of Subsidiary. Subsidiary stock has a FMV of $5 million and an adjusted basis of $2 million. Mason Corporation offers to purchase Subsidiary from Parent. If Parent were to sell its Subsidiary stock, Parent would recognize a gain of $3 million. Alternatively, if Mason Corporation purchases $5 million of Parent stock, and Parent subsequently distributes its Subsidiary stock in exchange for Mason's Parent stock, the transaction would qualify as a tax-free split-off. Parent would recognize no gain on the distribution of its Subsidiary stock, and Mason would have a basis of $5 million in the acquired Subsidiary stock.

The Revenue Reconciliation Act of 1990 sought to prevent such disguised sales by requiring the recognition of corporate-level gain on a distribution of subsidiary stock otherwise qualifying under Code Sec. 355 if, immediately after the distribution, a shareholder holds a 50-percent-or-greater interest in a distributed subsidiary (or the distributing corporation) that is attributable to stock that was acquired by purchase within the five-year period ending on the date of the distribution. Code Sec. 355(d). In such case, the distributing corporation will recognize gain just as if it had sold the distributed stock to the distributee for its fair market value. Thus, in Example 16.26 above, Parent will now recognize $3 million of gain on the distribution of its Subsidiary stock, if Mason Corporation had purchased the Parent stock within the five-year period ending on the date of distribution.

More specifically, a distributing corporation must recognize gain in the case of a *disqualified distribution* of stock or securities in a controlled corporation. For this purpose, a disqualified distribution is any Code Sec. 355 distribution if, immediately after the distribution, any person holds disqualified stock in either the distributing corporation or any distributed controlled corporation constituting a 50-percent-or-greater interest in such corporation. Code Sec. 355(d)(2).

Disqualified stock includes stock in the distributing corporation or any controlled corporation acquired by purchase during the five-year period ending on date of the distribution. Code Sec. 355(d)(3). Additionally, disqualified stock includes stock in any controlled corporation received in the distribution, to the extent that it is attributable to distributions on stock in the distributing corporation acquired by purchase during the five-year period ending on the date of the distribution.

Example 16.27. During 1998, Larsen Corporation purchases a 20 percent interest in the stock of Brewing Corporation and a 10 percent interest in the stock of its controlled subsidiary, Spirits Corporation. Subsequently, Brewing distributes 40 percent of the stock of Spirits to Larsen in exchange for Larsen's 20 percent interest in Brewing. Brewing must recognize gain on the distribution of its Spirits stock to Larsen because all 50 percent of the stock of Spirits held by Larsen is disqualified stock.

In determining whether a person holds a 50-percent-or-greater interest, related persons are treated as one person. For example, a corporation and its more-than-50-percent-owned subsidiary (or a husband and wife) are treated as one person. The related party rules that are applied for this purpose are the rules of Code Secs. 267(b), 318(a)(2), and 707(b)(1), substituting 10 percent for 50 percent.

The Taxpayer Relief Act of 1997 imposed additional restrictions on certain spin-offs that are designed to limit the ability of a corporation to follow the structure of *Morris Trust* (66-2 USTC ¶ 9718 (Code Sec. 355(e)) and, in effect, dispose of a portion of its business to new shareholders without the recognition of gain. If either the controlled or distributing corporation is acquired pursuant to a plan or arrangment in existence on the date of distribution, gain is generally recognized to the distributing corporation as of the date of distribution. Recognition can be avoided if more than 50 percent of the historical shareholders retain ownership in the distributing and acquiring corporations. Acquisitions occurring within the four-year period beginning two years before the date of distribution are presumed to have occurred pursuant to a plan or arrangement. The application of this provision is not restricted to stock acquired by *purchase* but may apply to stock acquired by other means as well.

¶ 16,217   TYPE E REORGANIZATIONS

Basic Form of Transaction

The Type E reorganization is a recapitalization and the only one of the seven types of reorganizations that always involves only one and the same corporation. Thus, a Type E reorganization has been defined as "the reshuffling of the capital structure within the framework of an existing corporation." *Southwest Consolidated Corp.,* 42-2 USTC ¶ 9248, 315 U.S. 194, 62 S. Ct. 546 (1942). In a typical situation, one class of securities is exchanged for another (e.g., stock for stock and/or bonds, or bonds for stock and/or bonds). Below are some examples of recapitalizations.

Stock-for-Stock Exchanges

If common stock is exchanged for common stock or preferred stock is exchanged for preferred stock, no gain or loss is recognized. Code Sec. 1036. A shareholder may go from voting to nonvoting stock or vice versa. This is true without regard to the reorganization provisions.

When preferred stock is exchanged for common stock or vice versa, the reorganization provisions come into play. The exchange is tax free *if* the fair market values are equal. Code Sec. 354(a)(1). If there is an excess, the difference will be labeled whatever the facts indicate, such as a gift or compensation for services. Rev. Rul. 77-269, 1977-1 CB 87. As part of an estate plan, a business owner will frequently swap old common stock for a combination of preferred stock with voting rights and a stated redemption price and new common stock, then gift the new common stock to his or her children. This is a tax-free Type E reorganization, but the gift of stock may be subject to federal gift tax.

The conversion of convertible preferred stock into the common stock of the same corporation qualifies as a Type E reorganization. Thus, the conversion is generally tax free, the shareholder's basis carries over, and the holding period tacks on. Part of the stock received may be a dividend, but only if either:

1. Dividend arrearages on the preferred stock are, in effect, paid off with extra common stock or

2. The conversion is part of a plan to increase the proportional ownership interest of a class of shareholders.

Debt-for-Stock Exchanges

Somewhat surprisingly, a creditor does not recognize gain or loss when exchanging bonds for stock, be it common or preferred. Reg. § 1.368-2(e)(1). This general rule applies to convertible bonds if converted into stock of the debtor corporation but not to the conversion into stock of another corporation. The latter exchange is taxable to both the corporation and the bondholders. Rev. Rul. 69-135, 1969-1 CB 198. A corporation is not taxed when retiring its debt with stock under the general rules (e.g., no gain or loss is recognized when treasury stock is issued for "property"). Code Sec. 1032. However, unless the corporation is insolvent or in bankruptcy, it generally has ordinary income from discharge of indebtedness if stock worth less than the principal of the debt is issued to creditors. Code Sec. 108(e)(10).

Any original issue discount on bonds retired as part of a recapitalization evaporates since the creditors only realize, but do not actually recognize, gain on the receipt of the stock. Rev. Rul. 75-35, 1975-2 CB 272.

TAX PLANNING POINTER

When a creditor of a corporation receives stock with a value that is less than the basis of the debt, the creditor does *not* wish to have a tax-free exchange. In an isolated case, where there is no plan of reorganization, the creditor receives a bad debt deduction. However, any subsequently recognized gain on the stock is ordinary income to the extent of the bad debt deduction under Code Sec. 108(e)(7).

Debt-for-Debt Exchanges

If the principal amount of debt received in a reorganization exceeds the principal amount of debt surrendered, the fair market value of the excess is boot and is taxed accordingly. Code Sec. 356(a)(2)(B).

Example 16.28. A bondholder exchanges 10 percent coupon bonds with a principal amount of $10,000 and a basis of $8,000 for 12 percent coupon bonds with a principal value of $10,000 and a fair market value of $9,500. No gain is recognized, despite the realized gain, since there is no excess principal amount of bonds received.

Thus, the basis of the old bond carries over to the new bond and the holding period tacks on.

Example 16.29. Same as Example 16.28, except the principal amount received is $11,000. Now the realized gain of $1,500 ($9,500 − $8,000) is recognized to the extent of the fair market value of the excess principal amount of bonds received. This fair market value can be determined by multiplying the excess principal amount by the ratio of total fair market value to total principal. In this example, the fair market value of the excess is $864 ($1,000 × ($9,500 ÷ $11,000)). The basis of the new bond is increased by the recognized gain and the holding period of the old bond tacks on.

Stock-for-Debt Exchanges

A shareholder who surrenders stock solely in return for debt instruments has a taxable exchange. There is *no* protection in the reorganization rules. At least two different approaches to taxation exist, depending on the circumstances:

1. If the shareholder surrenders all of the shareholder's stock for debt in the issuing corporation, a complete termination of interest may result. Code Sec. 302(b)(3). Then a capital gain or loss results, computed as the fair market value of the debt received less the adjusted basis in the stock.

2. If the distribution of debt is pro rata and does not reduce a shareholder's interest, the distribution of debt has the effect of a dividend and will be taxed as a dividend to the extent of the shareholder's ratable share of earnings and profits of the distributing corporation. Code Sec. 356(a)(2).

¶ 16,277   TYPE F REORGANIZATIONS

A Type F reorganization consists of a "mere change in identity, form, or place of organization of one corporation, however effected." Code Sec. 368(a)(1)(F). A Type F reorganization may also meet the definition of a Type A, C, or D reorganization as well, but it will still be treated as a Type F reorganization. Rev. Rul. 57-276, 1957-1 CB 126. Because the "old" corporation continues without change of ownership, the taxable year does not end (Code Sec. 381(b)), net operating losses may be carried back as well as forward (Code Sec. 381(b)), and neither Code Sec. 1244 nor S corporation status will be endangered. Reg. § 1.1244(d)-3(d)(1); Rev. Rul. 64-250, 1964-2 CB 333.

Example 16.30. Pewter Inc. changes its name to Silverworks Inc. As a result, the shareholders turn in their old stock certificates for new stock certificates with the new name. This is the simplest possible Type F reorganization.

Example 16.31. Regal Inc., incorporated in Illinois, wishes to change its state of incorporation to Florida and its name to Kingswood Inc. Regal transfers all its assets to the newly formed Kingswood in exchange for its stock. Regal liquidates by transferring its Kingswood stock to its shareholders and the Regal stock is cancelled. Technically, this transaction may meet the definition of a Type A, C, and an acquisitive Type D reorganization. It is, however, treated as a Type F reorganization.

Example 16.32. Five hot dog restaurants transfer all their assets to a new corporation in exchange for stock in order to become the beginning of a national chain. This does *not* qualify as a Type F reorganization since more than one operating corporation is involved. The transaction may be treated as a Code Sec. 351 transaction or an acquisitive Type D reorganization, but no Type F reorganization has occurred.

¶ 16,285   TYPE G REORGANIZATIONS

The Bankruptcy Tax Act of 1980 added a seventh type of tax-free reorganization, Type G. Requirements are as follows:

1. A debtor corporation must be involved in a receivership, foreclosure, or similar proceeding under state law or a proceeding under Chapter X of the Bankruptcy Act under federal law.

2. The debtor transfers all or part of its assets to another corporation solely in return for stock or securities in such corporation.

3. The stock or securities received must be distributed in a transaction qualifying under Code Sec. 354, 355, or 356.

4. The creditors of the debtor corporation must receive voting stock in the transferee corporation valued at least 80 percent of the debts of the debtor corporation.

If the debtor corporation receives boot, it recognizes a gain to the extent of the lesser of realized gain or value of the boot, unless it is distributed pursuant to the plan of reorganization. Code Sec. 361(a)(1)(A) and (B).

Considerations for Nonrecognition Treatment

¶ 16,321   REORGANIZATION AS AN ALTERNATIVE TO LIQUIDATION

With a few exceptions, double taxation is the result of a liquidation of a corporation. Double taxation can sometimes be avoided if it is feasible to effect a corporate reorganization. For example, if the shareholders merely wish to change the location of the business, a Type F reorganization may be all that is required. Thus, instead of a liquidation-reincorporation situation, a merger treated as a tax-free reorganization is effected.

Example 16.33. An Illinois corporation wants to become a Nevada corporation. There is no need to adopt a plan of liquidation, distribute the assets, and then reincorporate them. Rather, a Nevada corporation is formed by the shareholders, who then merge the Illinois corporation into the new Nevada corporation.

¶ 16,351 USE OF SUBSIDIARIES IN REORGANIZATIONS

Type A Reorganizations

Rather than acquiring a corporation directly, an acquisition-minded corporation may form a subsidiary to do the acquiring for it. Using a subsidiary provides the following advantages:

1. The parent is not liable for the liabilities of the acquired corporation, all of which must be assumed in a statutory merger since legally the subsidiary is the acquiring corporation.

2. Since the parent is the only shareholder in the subsidiary, no formal consent to the acquisition is needed from the parent corporation's shareholders.

The steps in a typical subsidiary merger are as follows:

Step 1. The parent transfers the consideration to be paid for the target corporation (e.g., stock in the parent, cash, or other property) to the subsidiary, in exchange for all the stock in the subsidiary.

Step 2. The subsidiary transfers the consideration to the target corporation in exchange for the target's assets and liabilities.

Step 3. The target corporation liquidates, and its shareholders receive stock in the parent and other consideration when the target's stock is cancelled.

This is a *triangular* merger and qualifies as a Type A reorganization if three requirements are met:

1. Only parent stock is used (no subsidiary stock is allowed).

2. The transaction would have qualified as a Type A reorganization if the parent had acquired the target directly. Code Sec. 368(a)(2)(D).

3. "Substantially all" of the target corporation's assets are acquired. The IRS's position is that this means at least 90 percent of the value of net assets *and* at least 70 percent of the value of gross assets. Rev. Proc. 79-14, 1979-1 CB 496.

A *reverse* triangular merger is similar to a triangular merger except that the subsidiary is merged into the target. The subsidiary's assets are transferred to the target, and the target corporation's shareholders receive stock in the parent for their stock in the target. The parent receives the stock in the target when the subsidiary's stock is cancelled.

To qualify a *reverse* merger as a Type A reorganization, two additional requirements apply:

1. The target must hold substantially all of the subsidiary's assets, as well as its own, after the merger.

2. The target corporation's former shareholders must give up at least 80 percent control in exchange for voting stock in the parent. Code Sec. 368(a)(2)(E).

Thus, far less flexibility is permitted in comparison to a regular Type A reorganization.

Type B Reorganizations

A Type B reorganization may be effected through the use of a subsidiary if two conditions are met:

1. The parent corporation is in control of the subsidiary, using the standard 80 percent test. Code Sec. 368(c).

2. The subsidiary acquires control of the acquired corporation using solely voting stock of its parent. Code Sec. 368(a)(1)(B). The subsidiary may, or may not, be formed for the purpose of the acquisition.

Example 16.34. Furniture Inc. wishes to acquire the stock of Oak Inc. Mahogany Inc. is a wholly owned subsidiary of Furniture. Furniture contributes its voting stock to the capital of Mahogany, which Mahogany then uses to acquire the stock of Oak. After the transaction, Oak is a second-tier subsidiary of Furniture. A Type B reorganization has taken place.

Example 16.35. Candymakers Inc. forms a new corporation, Chocolate Inc., and transfers voting convertible preferred stock in Candymakers to Chocolate in exchange for all the stock in Chocolate. Chocolate thereafter acquires control of Vanilla Inc. using the voting stock of Candymakers. Again, a Type B reorganization results.

Example 16.36. Vans Inc. is a wholly owned operating subsidiary of Autoworks Inc. Solely for Vans voting stock, Vans acquires control of Wagons Inc. This is *not* a triangular Type B reorganization but a regular Type B reorganization because Vans (as the acquiring corporation) is using its own voting stock. The acquiring corporation may always be a subsidiary or a parent of another corporation.

Type C Reorganizations

As in a Type A or B reorganization, a parent corporation may use a controlled subsidiary to act as the acquiring corporation in a Type C reorganization. The requirements are:

1. The assumption of liabilities and the 20 percent "boot relaxation" rules apply. See ¶ 16,105.

2. Stock in the subsidiary cannot be used; voting stock of the parent must be used. Code Sec. 368(a)(1)(B).

¶ 16,375 POSTREORGANIZATION TRANSFERS TO SUBSIDIARIES

Once an acquiring corporation has acquired assets or stock in a reorganization that qualifies as a Type A, B, C, or G reorganization, it may subsequently transfer all or part of the assets or stock to a new or existing controlled subsidiary. Code Sec. 368(a)(2)(C). No waiting period is required.

The transfer is treated as a Code Sec. 351 transfer, rather than as part of the reorganization which is over and done with. This rule provides flexibility in arranging the desired corporate and capital structure of an acquiring corporation subsequent to the acquisition.

Carryover of Tax Attributes

¶ 16,457   INTRODUCTION

When a corporation acquires the stock of another corporation, such as in a Type B reorganization or in a purchase of stock, the acquired corporation's shareholders change, but the tax status of the acquired corporation generally stays the same. A different situation exists when the acquired corporation is liquidated and the acquiring corporation becomes the owner of the assets. Specific rules govern which tax attributes of the acquired corporation follow the assets, and place limitations on the carryover of beneficial tax attributes. These rules are found in Code Sec. 269 and Code Secs. 381 through 384.

¶ 16,465   ATTRIBUTE CARRYOVER TRANSACTIONS

The following asset acquisitions result in the carryover of the tax attributes of the acquired corporation:

1. Liquidations of a controlled subsidiary under Code Sec. 332, if the asset bases carry over under Code Sec. 334(b)(1)

2. Type A, C, acquisitive D, F, and G reorganizations (Code Sec. 381(a))

Note that the following transactions are *not* covered by mandatory carryover:

1. Type B reorganizations because the acquired corporation remains in existence.

2. Divisive Type D reorganizations because one corporation divides into two or more entities. No "new" business is acquired.

3. Type E reorganizations because only one corporation is involved.

4. Transfers to a controlled corporation under Code Sec. 351 because no new business is acquired.

Under (2) and (4), however, earnings and profits may have to be allocated among the resulting corporations. Code Sec. 312(h); Reg. §§ 1.312-10 and 1.312-11.

¶ 16,473   LIMITATIONS ON CARRYOVERS

There are 22 tax attributes or classes of tax attributes listed in Code Sec. 381(c), all of which *must* be carried over (subject to some limitations, discussed below). The most important ones are:

1. Earnings and profits (see ¶ 16,497)

2. Net operating loss carryovers (see ¶ 16,481)

3. Accounting methods, including inventory methods, depreciation methods, and installment reporting

4. Tax credit carryovers, notably foreign tax credits and work opportunity credits
5. Capital loss carryovers
6. Excess charitable contributions
7. Items potentially subject to the tax benefit doctrine.

Thus, if the transaction is eligible, *all* attributes must be carried over, whether favorable (e.g., net operating losses) or unfavorable (e.g., earnings and profits).

¶ 16,481 NET OPERATING LOSS LIMITATION

The taxable year of the acquired corporation, except for Type F reorganizations, ends on the date of the transfer of assets. Code Sec. 381(b). As a result, its net operating loss carryover winds up in the acquiring corporation sometime during the latter's taxable year. The deduction allowed for the acquiring corporation's taxable year during which the reorganization occurred is limited to the acquiring corporation's taxable income allocable to the days after the acquisition date.

Example 16.37. Fur Stuffs Inc. acquired Sable Inc.'s assets in a Type C reorganization on October 19, 1998. Both corporations are on the calendar year. If Sable has a net operating loss carryover, only one-sixth (73/365) of Fur Stuff's taxable income can be offset by Sable's NOL carryover. Any unused carryovers are suspended until the following year.

¶ 16,485 OWNERSHIP CHANGES—ANNUAL LIMITATION

Uniform limitations on NOL carryforwards apply to "new" loss corporations if there has been a more-than-50-percentage-point ownership change as compared to the "old" loss corporation. The limitation rules (which also cover capital loss carryforwards and credits) apply to taxable and nontaxable transactions, including corporate organizations, distributions, redemptions, liquidations, and taxable and tax-free reorganizations (other than Type F). Once an ownership change (ownership and/or equity shift) has occurred, the NOL carryover that may be utilized each year is limited to the long-term tax-exempt rate multiplied by the stock value of the loss corporation immediately prior to the ownership change. Code Sec. 382. For the year of acquisition, the Code Sec. 382 limitation is available only to the extent allocable to days after the acquisition date.

Example 16.38. When Mutt Inc. merged into Jeff Inc., Mutt shareholders received 40 percent of Jeff stock for 100 percent of Mutt stock. An ownership change occurred. Had they received 50 percent or more of the Jeff stock there would have been no ownership change.

Example 16.39. Locks Inc. has a stock value of $800,000 and has $2 million of NOLs. At this point, it redeems 60 percent of its outstanding stock that is owned by Jane for $200,000. As a result, the other shareholder, Joe, becomes the sole shareholder. Since Joe's ownership interest is increased by 60 percentage points, from 40 to 100 percent, there has been an ownership change. Therefore, the

NOL available to offset income of Locks Inc. in the future is limited annually to $600,000 (the value of the "old" loss corporation is reduced by redemption proceeds in the ownership change transaction) times the long-term tax-exempt rate (published monthly and based on the yield on a diversified pool of general obligation municipal bonds with maturity more than nine years), in this case, 5 percent. Since $600,000 × .05 is $30,000, this becomes the annual limitation.

Continuity of Business Enterprise

Once a more-than-50-percent ownership change occurs, NOL and other carryforwards are completely disallowed, unless there is a "continuity of business enterprise." This requirement may be met in two ways:

1. The "old" loss corporation's historic business is continued for at least two years following the ownership change, or
2. The "old" loss corporation's assets, or at least a significant portion of them, are utilized in a business for at least two years. Code Sec. 382(c).

Changes in location or in key employees are permitted.

Reason for Limitation

By limiting the annual utilization of an NOL carryover to the stock value of the loss corporation times the yield on municipals, the purchaser of tax losses is unable to derive a benefit in excess of the income available by simply selling the stock in the loss corporation and investing the proceeds in municipal bonds. Thus, without reducing the NOL in the aggregate, the spreading out of the carryover is likely to limit abuses and trafficking in tax attributes.

Testing Period

The amount of ownership change is measured during a three-year period known as the "testing" period. The testing period is generally the three-year period preceding an ownership change. However, the testing period does not start until the first day of the first year from which there is a carryover, nor can it start prior to a previous ownership change in excess of 50 percent. Code Sec. 382(i).

Attribution Rules

To determine whether an ownership change has occurred, the following attribution rules apply:

1. Spouses, an individual's parents, grandparents, and children are treated as one shareholder.
2. Stock held by an entity, such as a corporation, partnership, estate, or trust, is treated as owned proportionately by shareholders, partners, and beneficiaries.
3. No attribution is made to entities from owners.
4. Options count as stock if an ownership change would result. Code Sec. 382(l)(3).

Built-In Gains and Losses

If the old loss corporation has a net unrealized built-in gain, the Code Sec. 382 limitation for any recognition period taxable year is increased by the new loss corporation's recognized built-in gain for that taxable year. If the old loss corporation had a net unrealized built-in loss, the recognized built-in loss for any recognition period taxable year is subject to the Sec. 382 limitation just as if it were a prechange NOL.

The amount of net unrealized built-in gain (or loss) is the amount by which the fair market value of the assets of the old loss corporation immediately before an ownership change exceeds (or is less than) the aggregate adjusted basis of those assets at that time. The term "recognition period" means the five-year period beginning on the change date. A loss corporation's net unrealized built-in gain or loss will be treated as zero unless it exceeds the lesser of (1) $10 million, or (2) 15 percent of the fair market value of the loss corporation's assets immediately before the ownership change.

Miscellaneous Provisions

Here is a summary of relevant provisions not discussed above:

1. If a corporation has both prechange and postchange loss carryforwards, it is allowed to use prechange losses first.

2. Publicly held corporations are protected by a 5 percent shareholder rule applied to public trading. Thus, despite the fact that 60 percent of the shareholders, consisting of under-5-percent owners, sold their stock during a three-year period, the limitations are inapplicable.

3. Ownership transfers due to death, gifts, divorce, or separation, as well as acquisitions by employee stock ownership plans, are not counted as ownership shifts.

4. The loss corporation's value is reduced by any capital contribution made if a principal purpose was to avoid the limitations discussed above. If a capital contribution is made within two years of the change date, the value is automatically reduced.

5. The loss corporation's value is reduced by liquid nonbusiness assets, if in excess of one-third of the value of total assets.

6. Special relief provisions apply to corporations involved in bankruptcy proceedings. Code Sec. 382(l)(5).

¶ 16,497 EARNINGS AND PROFITS

The acquiring corporation succeeds to the acquired corporation's earnings and profits as of the date of the transfer of assets. This is so whether the balance is positive or negative. However, an acquired deficit can only serve to reduce earnings and profits generated *after* the acquisition. To determine the offset in the year of acquisition, only the pro rata share of earnings allocable to the acquiring corporation's remaining year is relevant. Code Sec. 381(c)(2)(A) and (c)(2)(B).

Example 16.40. Hardware Inc. acquires Nuts & Bolts Inc. in a Type A reorganization when 146 days remain in its 365-day taxable year. Nuts & Bolts has a deficit in E&P of $22,000 and Hardware has current E&P of $60,000. Nuts & Bolts' deficit can be used to offset 146/365 × $60,000 of Hardware's current E&P, or $24,000. The remaining deficit is carried forward to offset future earnings of Hardware.

TAX PLANNING POINTER ▼

In a Type A reorganization, there are several limitations on net operating losses and other desirable tax attributes but none on earnings and profits. If E&P are eliminated in a liquidation, other desirable tax attributes are generally eliminated as well. E&P may be an important consideration in structuring a transaction as a liquidation or a reorganization.

Judicial Requirements

¶ 16,517   INTRODUCTION

Whenever a significant nonrecognition provision exists (e.g., like-kind exchange, tax-free incorporation, or tax-free distribution) from a partnership, taxpayers often attempt to structure a transaction that would otherwise result in a taxable gain so that the nonrecognition provision applies. On the other hand, when a loss is realized, an attempt may be made to avoid the nonrecognition provision so as to recognize the loss.

Over the years, the IRS has successfully imposed several judicial requirements on tax-free reorganizations that must be met in addition to the literal compliance with the bare definitions in Code Sec. 368. The main judicially developed doctrines are:

1.   Business purpose

2.   Continuity of proprietary interest

3.   Continuity of the business enterprise

4.   Step transactions

5.   Liquidation and reincorporation

¶ 16,525   BUSINESS PURPOSE

The business purpose doctrine dates back to a classic Supreme Court case in 1935. *Gregory v. Helvering,* 35-1 USTC ¶ 9043, 293 U.S. 465, 55 S.Ct. 266 (1935). Mrs. Gregory went through a literal reorganization for the sole purpose of converting a dividend into capital gains. She was successful in the Board of Tax Appeals (now the Tax Court), but lost an appeal, affirmed by the Supreme Court, on the grounds that there was no "real" business purpose. Forming a corporation, issuing stock, transferring assets, etc. may all be disregarded, even if the literal definition of a reorganization is met, if there is no business purpose.

The business purpose requirement is reflected in the Regulations that say in part: "A scheme . . . such as a mere device that puts on the form of a corporate reorganization as a disguise . . . having no business or corporate purpose, is not a plan of reorganization." Reg. § 1.368-1(c).

> *Example 16.41.* Mr. Gumm runs a highly successful sole proprietorship. He is approached by Spearmint Inc., a publicly owned corporation that wishes to purchase his business for $2 million worth of listed common stock in Spearmint. Since Mr. Gumm's basis in the assets of the business amounts to only $300,000, he would have to recognize $1,700,000 of gain if he sold his business assets. To defer the gain, Mr. Gumm instead incorporates his business under Code Sec. 351, becoming Gumm Inc., whereupon Spearmint acquires the stock in Gumm Inc. in a Type B reorganization. Most likely, the incorporation and the reorganization will be disregarded as having no business purpose, and Mr. Gumm will be treated as having made a taxable sale of the business assets.

The smaller the corporation, the more difficult it is to distinguish between the business purpose of the shareholders and that of the corporation. See *H.S.W. Lewis,* 49-2 USTC ¶ 9377, 176 F.2d 646 (CA-1 1949). A leading Supreme Court case, however, requires a direct and substantial benefit to the *corporation. J.R. Bazley,* 47-2 USTC ¶ 9373, 332 U.S. 752, 67 S.Ct. 1489 (1947).

¶ 16,533   CONTINUITY OF PROPRIETARY INTEREST

There is no statutory requirement that the "old" shareholders in the acquired corporation, individually or in the aggregate, receive equity in the acquiring corporation, or that they retain a proprietary interest for any length of time subsequent to the reorganization.

However, over the years, the courts have developed and defined the continuity of proprietary interest doctrine. The main argument is that if the shareholders primarily receive cash and short-term notes, the transaction is in substance a sale, rather than a reorganization. This was articulated by the Supreme Court in two early cases. *Pinellas Ice & Cold Storage Co.,* 3 USTC ¶ 1023, 287 U.S. 462, 53 S.Ct. 257 (1933); *V.L. LeTulle,* 40-1 USTC ¶ 9150, 308 U.S. 415, 60 S.Ct. 313 (1940). Even long-term mortgage bonds are considered proceeds from a sale if no equity interest is retained.

Based on these and similar cases, the Regulations refer to the continuity of proprietary interest requirement in this manner: "Requisite to a reorganization . . . a continuity of interest therein on the part of . . . the owners of the enterprise prior to the reorganization . . . there is not a reorganization if the holders of the stock and securities of the old corporation are merely the holders of short-term notes in the new corporation." Reg. § 1.368-1(b).

It may be recalled that the consideration in a Type B reorganization is limited to voting stock, while in a Type C reorganization cash, notes, and other property are subject to a 20 percent limitation. Thus, the continuity of proprietary interest problem exists primarily in Type A statutory mergers and consolidations.

For advance ruling purposes, the IRS requires a minimum equity participation in the acquiring corporation equal to 50 percent of the fair market value of the stock in the acquired corporation. Rev. Proc. 79-14, 1979-1 CB 496. The test is an aggregate one. Not every shareholder must remain, nor do the remaining shareholders have to receive equity in the same proportion. However, dispositions of stock that are part of the plan of reorganization count for this purpose, whether structured as outright sales or redemptions.

¶ 16,541   CONTINUITY OF THE BUSINESS ENTERPRISE

The Regulations require "a continuity of the business enterprise under modified corporate form." Reg. § 1.368-1(b). This requirement does *not* require (1) the retention of assets for any given length of time nor (2) the new corporation to engage in the identical business of its predecessor. To meet the continuity of business enterprise rules, the Regulations require that one of two tests be met:

1. The acquiring corporation must continue the historic business of the acquired corporation or

2. The acquiring corporation must use a significant part of the acquired corporation's assets in its business. Reg. § 1.368-1(d).

Note that the continuity of business enterprise requirement may be important in the context of Code Sec. 355 spin-offs, split-offs, and split-ups; in the carryover of tax attributes; and in the liquidation-reincorporation areas, in addition to the reorganization area.

¶ 16,549   STEP TRANSACTIONS

The step transaction doctrine means that two or more transactions are mutually dependent so that only the overall end result is significant for tax purposes. Thus, two or more steps, significant in themselves, if viewed in isolation, may be disregarded altogether or consolidated into one transaction. The Supreme Court has stated that "if one transaction is to be characterized as a 'first step,' there must be a binding commitment to take the later steps." *I. Gordon,* 68-1 USTC ¶ 9383, 391 U.S. 83, 88 S.Ct. 1517 (1968).

The step transaction doctrine is invariably invoked against the taxpayer and is a special case of the general "substance over form" argument. It can be asserted in all areas of taxation. Some examples of its use in the reorganization area are set out below.

Example 16.42. In a Type C reorganization, the acquiring corporation refuses to acquire certain assets. The unwanted assets are therefore sold or transferred to a new corporation prior to the reorganization. Combining the two transactions into one makes the acquisition taxable for failure to meet the "substantially all" assets requirement. The leading case is *Helvering v. Elkhorn Coal Co.,*

38-1 USTC ¶ 9238, 95 F.2d 732 (CA-4 1938), cert. denied, 305 U.S. 605, 59 S.Ct. 65.

Example 16.43. A Type A reorganization may be reclassified as a purchase of assets, or a Type B reorganization as a purchase of stock, if the acquired corporation's shareholders promptly sell their new stock after the reorganization.

Example 16.44. The acquiring corporation purchases stock in the acquired corporation for cash and later acquires the rest of the stock for its own voting stock in an attempted Type B reorganization. If both acquisitions are part of the same plan, the cash is boot and the attempted Type B reorganization fails.

¶ 16,557 LIQUIDATION AND REINCORPORATION

Liquidations are taxable, reorganizations are not, in the absence of boot. Earnings and profits generally survive a reorganization but are eliminated in a liquidation. A classic tax avoidance device is to do the following:

1. A corporation is liquidated in kind, a transaction that may be largely tax free to the corporation because of loss carryforwards that offset the gains recognized on liquidation and result in capital gains to the shareholders.

2. The corporation is dissolved and its E&P disappears with it, while the shareholders have a fair market value basis in the property.

3. The shareholders retain liquid assets, then start the old business anew in a new or existing corporation, perhaps transferring operating assets to it under Code Sec. 351 or Code Sec. 118 (contribution to capital).

The IRS attacks this type of scheme by:

1. Characterizing the liquidation-reincorporation as a reorganization,

2. Treating the retained assets as boot received in a Type D reorganization, or

3. Disallowing or disregarding the transactions as having no "business purpose," having no substance, being a sham, etc.

¶ 16,569 ACQUISITIONS MADE TO EVADE OR AVOID INCOME TAX

The IRS is authorized to deny any tax benefit (e.g., deduction, credit, built-in loss, etc.) under the following conditions:

1. A person acquires at least 50 percent control of a corporation, directly or indirectly.

2. A corporation acquires the property of another corporation, receiving a carried-over basis, and neither the corporation nor its shareholders controlled the transferee just before the acquisition.

3. The principal purpose of the acquisition was the evasion and/or avoidance of federal income tax.

Deductions, allowances, or credits may be disallowed in whole or in part. Code Sec. 269(b). Thus, even if a tax benefit, such as a net operating loss, is carried over under Code Sec. 381 and its use restricted under Code Sec. 382(b), it may be disallowed altogether if Code Sec. 269 is applied.

Example 16.45. Classic Figurines Inc. acquires the much larger corporation Marble Inc. primarily for the latter's huge net operating loss carryover. The acquisition complies with the state merger law and is technically a Type A reorganization. As soon as practicable, Classic Figurines disposes of the assets of Marble, thus phasing out its business. The NOL will most likely be disallowed altogether under Code Sec. 269. In addition, if Marble's assets are sold for substantially less than their carryover basis, the losses may be disallowed as well, also under Code Sec. 269.

TAX BLUNDER

A service corporation was quite successful. After a few years, the corporation had $500,000 in assets, of which $425,000 were liquid assets not needed in the business. The two owners wanted the funds but did not want dividend income. After some consideration, they did the following:

1. The corporation adopted a plan of complete liquidation.

2. Another corporation was formed.

3. The assets needed in the business were sold for their adjusted basis to the new corporation, which also hired the employees of the old corporation.

4. All liquid assets plus proceeds from the sale were distributed to the shareholders.

5. The shareholders reported capital gain under Code Sec. 331; the "old" corporation reported *no* gain or loss.

The IRS balked and the court decided as follows:

1. Since all necessary operating assets were transferred to another corporation controlled by the shareholders of the transferor, the transaction was an acquisitive Type D reorganization.

2. Therefore, all funds distributed to shareholders were boot and treated as dividends to the extent of E&P in the transferor. This, of course, included the "proceeds" from the corporate sale, such as installment notes.

3. Basis of assets carried over.

4. The net effect was as if the original corporation had simply paid a dividend. See *J. Smothers,* 81-1 USTC ¶ 9368, 642 F.2d 894 (CA-5 1981).

Note the fine line between a liquidation and a reorganization.

SUMMARY OF CHAPTER 16

✓ The purpose of the reorganization provisions is to facilitate changes and adjustments in what remains as a modified corporate structure.

✓ A reorganization must serve a business purpose, the acquired corporations's shareholders must receive a continuing equity interest in the surviving entity, and the acquiring corporation must continue to use the acquired business assets.

✓ A corporate reorganization includes the acquisition of stock or assets of one corporation by another, mergers and consolidations under state law, and recapitalizations and divisions of a single corporation.

✓ Generally no gain or loss is recognized on the exchange of stock or securities in parties to the reorganization.

✓ The receipt of boot by shareholders may be taxed as a capital gain or as a dividend.

✓ No gain or loss is recognized to a corporation that transfers its property solely in exchange for stock or securities pursuant to the plan or reorganization.

✓ Generally all tax attributes of the acquired corporation carry over to the acquiring corporation.

SUMMARY OF RELEVANT CODE SECTIONS IN CHAPTER 16

Code Sec. 368   Definitions

Provides the requirements for the seven different types of corporate reorganization.

Code Sec. 354   Nonrecognition to shareholders and security holders

No gain or loss is recognized if stock or securities in a party to a reorganization is exchanged solely for stock or securities in such corporation or in another corporation a party to the reorganization.

Code Sec. 355   Receipt of stock or securities of controlled corporation

No gain or loss is recognized on the receipt of stock or securities if the distribution meets the requirements of a spin-off, split-off, or split-up.

Code Sec. 356   Receipt of additional consideration

A shareholder's or security holder's gain is recognized to the extent of the lesser of the (1) realized gain, or (2) FMV of other property (including the FMV of an excess principal amount of security received). A recognized gain is treated as a dividend if the receipt of boot has the effect of a dividend.

Code Sec. 357   Assumption of corporation's liabilities

The assumption of a corporation's liabilities is generally not treated as money or other property received. Gain is recognized in a Type D reorganization to the extent that total liabilities exceed the total basis of property transferred.

Code Sec. 358   Basis to shareholders and security holders

The basis for stock and securities received equals the basis of stock and securities exchanged, plus gain recognized, and minus boot received.

Code Sec. 361   Nonrecognition of gain or loss to corporations

No gain or loss is recognized if a corporation that is a party to the reorganization exchanges its property solely in exchange for stock or securities in another corporation that is a party to the reorganization.

Code Sec. 362   Basis to corporations

The basis of property acquired in a reorganization equals the transferor's basis increased by any gain recognized to the transferor.

Code Secs. 381-384   Carryovers

A corporation's tax attributes carryover to the acquiring corporation in an acquisitive reorganization, but may be limited in use by Code Secs. 382, 383, and 384.

Code Sec. 269   Denial of tax benefits

Tax benefits may be disallowed if the principal purpose of an acquisition is the evasion or avoidance of federal income tax.

Code Sec. 1032   Issuance of stock

No gain or loss is recognized to a corporation on the receipt of money or other property in exchange for its stock.

CHAPTER 16 QUESTIONS

1. Identify and briefly describe the seven types of corporate reorganization.

2. Which of the types of statutory reorganization are "acquisitive"?

3. Explain the doctrines of "continuity of business enterprise" and "continuity of proprietary interest."

4. Will the continuity of proprietary interest requirement be met if the shareholders of the acquired corporation sell their stock soon after the reorganization?

5. Will an acquiring corporation recognize gain or loss when it issues its stock to acquire the assets or stock of a target corporation in a reorganization?

6. What will be the basis of property acquired by a corporation in conjunction with a corporate reorganization? What would be the basis of the acquired property if the transaction fails to qualify as a corporate reorganization?

7. How do exchanging shareholders and security holders determine their basis for the stock and securities received in a corporate reorganization?

8. When will an exchange of securities of parties to a reorganization result in the receipt of boot? When will a corporate note be treated as a security?

9. When will boot received in a corporate reorganization be treated as a dividend?

10. Define a Type A reorganization, and differentiate between a statutory merger and a consolidation.

11. What are the relative advantages and disadvantages of a Type A reorganization?

12. Can nonvoting stock and securities be used in a Type A reorganization? Is there any limit on the use of boot?

13. Define a Type B reorganization and identify its unique requirements.

14. What are the relative advantages and disadvantages of a Type B reorganization?

15. How may dissenting minority shareholders of the acquired corporation be bought out for cash in a Type B reorganization?

16. Is there any carryover of the acquired corporation's tax attributes to the acquiring corporation in a Type B reorganization?

17. Define a Type C reorganization and explain its unique requirements.

18. What does "substantially all assets" mean in a Type C reorganization?

19. Explain the boot relaxation rule of a Type C reorganization.

20. If an acquiring corporation is widely held, how can it avoid obtaining the consent of its shareholders in a Type A reorganization?

21. In what types of reorganization may subsidiaries of the acquiring corporation be used?

22. Prior to being acquired, a transferor corporation spins off its unwanted assets to shareholders. It subsequently transfers its remaining assets to shareholders solely for voting stock of the acquiring corporation. Could the acquisition qualify as a Type C reorganization? Could the transaction qualify as a Type A reorganization?

23. Define a Type D reorganization and identify its unique requirements.

24. Define and differentiate a spin-off, split-off, and split-up.

25. Define a Type E reorganization and explain its use.

CHAPTER 16 PROBLEMS

26. As part of a Type A reorganization, a creditor swaps an old bond with a basis of $700 and a principal of $1,000 for a new convertible bond with a value of $750 and a principal of $1,200. The low value is due to the lack of security and a low coupon rate. What is the bondholder's realized and recognized gain on the reorganization? What is the basis in the convertible bond?

27. Brickford Hardware is owned and operated as a sole proprietorship by Brad Brickford. The location is excellent, and he is approached by a buyer, Hard Bargains Inc., a national chain of hardware stores. What are the tax consequences in the following situations?

    a. Brad sells the store for cash.

    b. Brad sells the store for marketable stock in Hard Bargains.

    c. Brad incorporates the store and exchanges the stock for shares in Hard Bargains.

    d. Same as (c), but Brad incorporated his hardware store two years earlier.

28. Maxco Inc. wishes to acquire Minnow Inc. The latter has 500,000 shares of common stock outstanding with voting rights and 100,000 shares of nonvoting preferred stock.

    a. How many shares of each class of stock must Maxco acquire to qualify the acquisition as a Type B reorganization?

    b. If Maxco uses its treasury stock to make the acquisition, does it matter how much Maxco paid for the shares?

    c. If Maxco liquidates Minnow soon after the reorganization and acquires Minnow's assets, are the reorganization rules still met?

    d. If Minnow purchased the stock of a few minority shareholders for cash just before the reorganization, does Maxco's acquisition still qualify as a Type B reorganization?

    e. If Maxco uses only its voting, convertible preferred stock, is the "solely for voting stock" requirement met?

    f. How can Maxco determine its basis in Minnow's stock if Minnow was publicly held?

29. Mystery Book Stores Inc. acquired all the assets of the Science Fiction Book Stores Inc. for its voting stock and cash in a Type C reorganization. One of the shareholders in the acquired corporation exchanged 100 shares of her old stock with a basis of $1,500 for new stock in the acquiring corporation worth $1,800 and $400 in cash (all shareholders received $4 a share).

    a. If neither corporation has E&P, what is the shareholder's realized and recognized gain, and new stock basis?

    b. Same as (a), but assume Mystery Book Stores Inc. has substantial E&P.

    c. What is the maximum permissible cash that can be paid per share in the above transaction and still have it qualify as a Type C reorganization? A Type A reorganization?

30. Athletic Socks Inc. decides to incorporate one of its divisions. As a result, assets with a basis of $200,000, but worth $800,000, and liabilities of $350,000 are transferred to a new corporation, Athletic Sportswear Inc., in exchange for all its stock. The stock in Sportswear is then distributed to the shareholders of Socks.

    a. What gain or loss is realized by Athletic Socks?

    b. What gain or loss is recognized by Athletic Socks?

    c. What is Athletic Sportswear's basis in its assets?

    d. What is Athletic Socks' basis in the stock in the subsidiary?

    e. A shareholder who owns Socks stock with a basis of $4,500 and a fair market value of $7,000, receives stock in Athletic Sportswear Inc. worth $2,000. What is her basis and holding period in the Sportswear stock?

31. Identify the following transactions:

    a. Containers Inc. distributes all stock in its wholly owned subsidiary, Crates Inc., to its shareholders.

    b. Containers Inc. distributes all stock in its wholly owned subsidiary, Crates Inc., to a 30 percent shareholder in exchange for the shareholder's stock.

    c. Containers Inc. liquidates Crates Inc. and distributes the proceeds to its shareholders.

    d. Containers Inc. transfers its two divisions to two new corporations, distributes the stock in the new corporations to its shareholders, and then liquidates.

32. Builders Inc. purchased 40 percent of the stock of Stairways Inc. for cash and acquired the remaining 60 percent for its own voting stock pursuant to a single plan. As soon as practicable, Stairways Inc. liquidates and Builders acquires all of its assets.

    a. Does the transaction qualify as a Type B reorganization?

    b. As a Type C reorganization?

    c. As a Code Sec. 332 liquidation of a subsidiary?

33. Auto Supplies Inc. has earnings and profits of $200,000 and a stock portfolio. It transfers appreciated stocks worth $150,000 with a basis of $80,000 to a newly created corporation, Peak Enterprises Inc., for 100 percent of Peak's stock. Auto Supplies distributes the Peak stock equally to its three shareholders who promptly liquidate Peak. What are the tax consequences of the above if the stock portfolio is seven years old?

34. Compute the realized and recognized gain or loss and the new basis in the following transactions, all of which took place pursuant to a plan of recapitalization.

    a. A shareholder exchanged 100 shares of $5 par value preferred stock with a basis of $1,000 for 200 shares of $4 par value preferred worth $800.

    b. A bond holder exchanged a bond with a basis of $800 and a par value of $1,000 and received 50 shares of common stock worth $1,050.

    c. A shareholder exchanged stock with a basis of $2,000 for bonds worth $5,000 and a par value of $4,000.

    d. A bondholder exchanged a bond with a basis of $900 and a par value of $1,000 for another bond with a value of $1,500 and a par value of $1,500.

35. Modern Antiques Inc. incorporated its service department and distributed all stock received to its shareholders. Modern is 23 years old, and the stock in the subsidiary is worth $30 a share. Jim Lewis, a 10 percent shareholder in Modern, owned 1,000 shares with a basis of $20 a share and a value of $60 and exchanged 200 shares of Modern for 400 shares in the service corporation.

    a. What is Jim's recognized gain or loss, stock basis, and holding period as a result of the transaction?

    b. What, if any, difference does it make if Modern Antiques Inc. had been in existence for four years?

36. Northwestern Ltd. (NW) acquires the only class of stock of Southeastern Ltd. (SE) from the latter's shareholders. Which of the following independent transactions qualify as a Type B reorganization?

    a. NW issues its voting convertible preferred stock for all of SE's stock.

    b. NW, which has owned 60 percent of SE's stock for eight years, acquires the remaining 40 percent for its voting common treasury stock.

    c. SE redeems the stock of 15 percent of its shareholders with cash, whereupon NW issues its voting common stock for the remaining 85 percent.

    d. NW acquires 80 percent of SE's stock, 78 percent for its voting stock and 2 percent for cash (in lieu of fractional shares).

    e. NW acquires all of SE's stock for its voting common stock plus options to buy more voting common stock.

    f. Same as (a), but NW promptly liquidates SE and acquires its assets.

    g. As part of the same plan, NW acquires 30 percent of the SE stock for cash and the remaining 70 percent for voting stock six months later.

37. Carson Corporation has a basis of $10 million in the stock of its 100-percent-owned subsidiary, Griffen Corporation. Both Carson and Griffen have been actively conducting business for more than five years. In July 1995, Hall Corporation purchased 4 percent of Carson's stock for $50 million. In May 1998, Carson distributed all of its Griffen stock to Hall in redemption of the Carson stock owned by Hall. At the time of the distribution, the Griffen stock was worth $60 million. What are the tax effects of the redemption to Carson Corporation and Hall Corporation?

38. Pebble Inc. is an accrual-basis, calendar-year corporation with only voting common stock outstanding. On October 31, 1998, it acquired the assets of Stone Inc. by issuing 3,000 of its voting common shares in a Type A reorganization. Stone has a $300,000 net operating loss carryover and the value of its stock is $1 million. Pebble's taxable income for the year of acquisition is $240,000. Assume the long-term tax-exempt rate is 5 percent.

  a. What is Pebble's net operating loss deduction for the year of acquisition if the 3,000 shares represent 60 percent of Pebble's outstanding stock? For the following year?

  b. What is Pebble's net operating loss deduction for the year of acquisition if the 3,000 shares represent 30 percent of Pebble's outstanding stock? For the following year?

39. Superior Corporation acquired Taylor Corporation pursuant to a statutory merger under state law. As a result of the merger, Taylor Corporation's former shareholders received common stock in Superior having a value of $300,000, long-term bonds of Superior with a principal amount (and fair market value) of $500,000, and cash of $200,000. What type of reorganization has taken place? Describe the tax consequences to Taylor Corporation, its former shareholders, and Superior Corporation.

40. Mountain Corporation forms Hill Corporation, and acquires Mound Corporation by merging Mound into Hill Corporation, with the former Mound Corporation shareholders receiving solely for voting stock of Mountain Corporation.

  a. What type of reorganization has taken place? Describe the tax consequences to Mound Corporation, its former shareholders, and Mountain Corporation.

  b. How would your answers change if the former Mound shareholders instead received only nonvoting stock of Mountain Corporation?

41. On March 1, 1998, in connection with a recapitalization of Chadwick Corporation, Roger Johnson exchanged 1,000 shares of preferred stock that cost him $91,000 for 1,000 shares of common stock worth $90,000 and bonds in the principal amount of $10,000 with a fair market value of $10,500.

  a. What is the amount of Johnson's recognized gain?

  b. What is Johnson's basis for the new bond?

  c. What is Johnson's basis for the common stock?

42. Green Corporation purchased 100 percent of the outstanding stock of White Corporation in 1996. During 1998, Green Corporation distributes all of its White Corporation stock to Green shareholders. Both Green and White corporations have been in business for more than 10 years.

   a. Describe the tax consequences to Green Corporation and its shareholders.

   b. How would your answer change if Green Corporation had acquired the White Corporation stock in 1996 in a Type B reorganization?

43. Randy, the sole shareholder of Apple Corporation, has a basis for his Apple stock of $500,000. As part of a statutory merger of Apple Corporation into Pear Corporation, Randy exchanges his Apple stock for Pear stock with a fair market value of $2,000,000 and $800,000 in cash. Randy owns a 40 percent interest in Pear Corporation as a result of the merger transaction. Both Apple Corporation and Pear Corporation have accumulated earnings and profits in excess of $2 million.

   a. What is the amount and character of Randy's recognized gain resulting from the merger and the basis for his new Pear stock?

   b. Assume the same facts except that the Pear stock received in the merger gives Randy a 55 percent interest in Pear Corporation. What is the amount and character of Randy's recognized gain resulting from the merger and the basis for his new Pear stock?

44. Wood Corporation is owned equally by two individuals—Allan and Baker. Wood Corporation has two operating divisions, Oak and Pine, that have been conducting business for more than five years. Allan and Baker can no longer agree on the management of Wood Corporation's activities and decide to separate. Baker agrees to a plan whereby the assets of the Pine division worth $800,000 (adjusted basis of $300,000) and liabilities of $100,000 will be transferred to newly formed Nuwood Corporation in exchange for all of Nuwood's stock. The Nuwood stock (having a value of $700,000) will then be distributed to Baker in exchange for all of his Wood Corporation stock having a basis of $200,000.

   a. Will the plan qualify as a corporate reorganization? What type?

   b. What would be the amount of Wood Corporation's recognized gain on the transfer of the Pine division assets to Nuwood? On the distribution of the Nuwood stock to Baker?

   c. What would be the amount and character of Baker's recognized gain on the receipt of the Nuwood stock?

   d. What is the basis of Baker's Nuwood stock?

45. Parent Corporation and its wholly owned Subsidiary Corporation wish to acquire the stock of Target Corporation. Target has outstanding 100,000 shares of common stock and $300,000 of convertible debentures owned by several unrelated individuals. The market price of the Target stock and the conversion ratio of the debentures make it unlikely that any debentures will be converted in the near future.

   a. Parent proposes to acquire the Target stock in exchange for Parent voting stock, and to purchase the Target convertible debentures for cash. Will the cash payment for the Target convertible debentures violate "the solely for voting stock" requirement of Code Sec. 368(a)(1)(B)? Will the "control" requirement be met if Parent purchases only $200,000 of the Target debentures?

   b. What are the tax consequences to the Target debenture holders if they exchange their debentures for Parent corporation debentures instead of cash? Would your answer change if the Target debenture holders exchanged their debentures for Parent voting stock instead of Parent corporation debentures?

   c. Will the transaction qualify as a Type B reorganization if Parent acquires the Target stock solely in exchange for Parent voting stock and then immediately transfers the Target stock to Subsidiary Corporation?

   d. Would the transaction qualify as a Type B reorganization if Parent transferred Parent voting stock to Subsidiary Corporation, and then Subsidiary acquired the Target stock in exchange for Parent voting stock? Would the transaction qualify if Subsidiary acquired the Target stock for a combination of Parent voting stock and Subsidiary voting stock?

46. Metal Corporation owns all of the stock of Iron Corporation, and owns 100 shares of Steel Corporation, which has 1,000 shares of stock outstanding. The 100 shares of Steel were purchased by Metal in 1987. In 1998, Metal merges Iron Corporation into Steel Corporation. As a result of the merger, Steel's shareholders (other than Metal) exchange 900 shares of Steel stock for Metal Corporation voting stock.

   a. Does the merger of Iron into Steel qualify as a reverse merger under Code Sec. 368(a)(2)(E)?

   b. Assume that Iron had been an operating company and that it transferred 35 percent of its total assets to Metal immediately before being merged into Steel. Will the merger qualify under Code Sec. 368(a)(2)(E)?

   c. Assume that Metal had purchased 300 shares of Steel in 1987. Would the merger of Iron into Steel qualify under Code Sec. 368(a)(2)(E)?

   d. Assume that Metal had not purchased any shares of Steel in 1987. Further assume that 25 percent of Steel's shareholders dissent to the merger and wish to receive cash instead of Metal stock. Can the merger of Iron into Steel still qualify under Code Sec. 368(a)(2)(E) if Metal transfers sufficient cash to buy out the dissenting shareholders?

47. *Comprehensive Problem.* Determine whether the following transactions qualify as Type C reorganizations:

   a. The acquisition of all assets and liabilities of Bark Inc. by Ark Inc. for 20 percent of Ark's voting preferred stock.

   b. Same as (a), but Ark sells 30 percent of Bark's assets within a week because they are not needed.

   c. The acquisition of all assets of Bark Inc. for $10 million of voting common stock, plus the assumption by Ark Inc. of $15 million of Bark's liabilities.

   d. The acquisition of Bark's assets for $8 million of Ark's voting common, the assumption of $2 million of liabilities, and the payment by Ark of $100 in cash.

   e. The acquisition of Bark's assets for $50 million of voting, cumulative convertible preferred stock.

   f. Same as (e), except that the consideration consists of bonds convertible at any time into voting common stock.

48. *Comprehensive Problem.* Label the following transactions:

   a. A Nevada corporation formed a corporation in Florida and transferred all assets to it for 100 percent of its stock. It then distributed the stock to its shareholders in cancellation of their Nevada corporation stock and was dissolved.

   b. ABC Corp. acquired all the stock of MNO Corp. for its convertible bonds. All MNO assets were transferred to ABC, whereupon MNO was dissolved.

   c. A corporation issues $30,000 worth of its own voting stock to retire some of its outstanding bonds with a principal amount of $40,000.

   d. Convertible preferred stock is converted into common stock of the issuing corporation.

   e. A corporation incorporates a division and distributes the shares received pro rata to its shareholders.

   f. A corporation distributes preferred stock for each 10 shares of common stock outstanding.

49. *Research Problem.* Mr. Aslak owns all the stock in Shoes Inc., which owns 85 percent of Skiing Inc. Ms. Quinn, the manager of Skiing, wishes to share in the profits of the prosperous firm by buying 5 percent of its stock. Shoes Inc. then distributes its stock interest in Skiing to Mr. Aslak, who then sells a 5 percent interest in Skiing to Ms. Quinn for $15,000. Assume the sale of stock to a key employee has a valid business and corporate purpose.

How would the IRS view the above transaction?

(See Rev. Rul. 69-460, 1969-2 CB 51; Reg. § 1.355-2(c).)

50. *Research Problem.* In practice, the number of shares paid for an acquired corporation may be contingent on its future performance (e.g., sales and/or earnings). Perhaps 500,000 shares are "paid" up front, while another 250,000 are placed in escrow, pending certain future events. If such contingent consideration is used in a purported reorganization:

    a. Is it still possible to have a tax-free reorganization?

    b. Does it matter whether negotiable "certificates of contingent interest" are issued?

    c. Does it matter what the motivation is for the deferred arrangement?

    (See, e.g., Rev. Rul. 66-112, 1966-1 CB 68; Rev. Proc. 77-37, 1977-2 CB 568.)

Chapter 17

Accumulated Earnings and Personal Holding Company Taxes

Learning Objectives

After completing Chapter 17, you should be able to:

1. Explain the purpose of the enactment of accumulated earnings and personal holding company taxes.

2. Identify the circumstances under which the two taxes are imposed.

3. Discuss the nature and effect of the two taxes.

4. Understand the mechanics of tax computations, including the tax base, exemptions, adjustments, and tax rates.

5. Apply planning devices available to avoid, reduce, or defer the incidence of taxation.

6. Explain the similarity of, and differences between, the two taxes.

7. Work with research problems and cases involving the two taxes.

OVERVIEW OF CHAPTER

To encourage corporations to distribute their earnings, thereby causing double taxation, two penalty taxes exist.

Accumulated Earnings Tax. The accumulated earnings tax is imposed on earnings "not needed" in the business above certain minimums. Thus, if dividends are paid, *shareholders* are taxed. If dividends are not paid, the *corporation* may be taxed if accumulations are unreasonable.

Personal Holding Company Tax. The personal holding company tax is imposed on undistributed passive income, such as interest, dividends, rents, and royalties. To be subject to the tax, the corporation must be controlled by five or fewer individuals and have passive income.

While the personal holding company tax is self-assessed and imposed mechanically once specific percentage tests are met, the accumulated earnings tax depends on facts and circumstances and the taxpayer's intent. The two taxes are mutually exclusive, but both are nondeductible and are imposed in addition to the regular corporate tax.

Accumulated Earnings Tax

¶ 17,001   RATE AND NATURE OF TAX

Corporations and their shareholders are both taxed on corporate earnings to the extent earnings are distributed as dividends. This follows from the fact that dividends are nondeductible. Dividends are declared by the board of directors on a purely discretionary basis. The smaller the corporation and the fewer the shareholders, the more likely it is that the shareholders decide whether dividends are to be paid. Since one tax is better than two, there is obviously an incentive to let the earnings remain in the corporation. The tax rates applicable to a corporation's taxable income are as follows:

15 percent on the first	$ 50,000
25 percent on the next	25,000
34 percent on the next	25,000
39 percent on the next	235,000
34 percent on the next	9,665,000
35 percent on the next	5,000,000
38 percent on the next	3,333,333
35 percent on excess over	18,333,333

Thus, if the corporation has $75,000 of taxable income, the average tax rate is only 18.33 percent. This, in itself, may be perceived as a reason to incorporate a venture if the earnings are not needed currently by the shareholders. Thus, the corporate tax may be viewed as the price to be paid for the indefinite deferral of the second tax on the shareholders. The corporation is then used as a tax shelter.

> ***Example 17.1.*** Cassandra Glass owns and operates an incorporated gift shop. Each year the store has taxable income of $40,000. Due to income from other sources (her husband), Cassandra is in the 31 percent tax bracket. The corporation will pay a tax of $6,000 on the taxable income. If the after-tax earnings ($34,000) are distributed to Cassandra, she will have $23,460 to invest. If the corporation were to invest the $34,000, the total would accumulate faster. However, a second tax would be incurred when the corporation distributes any accumulated amounts.

To enforce the second tax, Congress has found it necessary to impose two additional taxes at the corporate level, both of which are levied on undistributed earnings. The two taxes, serving the same purpose, are mutually exclusive and operate differently. The tax rate for *both* taxes is a flat 39.6 percent, which equals the maximum marginal rate for individuals.

The accumulated earnings tax is based on accumulations above and beyond reasonable business needs on a subjective basis. The *personal holding company tax* is based on undistributed personal holding company income on an objective basis. The shareholders are therefore faced with a choice. If earnings are distributed, shareholders will have ordinary income subject to tax rates up to 39.6 percent (plus local taxes, if any). If earnings are retained, the corporation may have to pay special taxes on its after-tax earnings, but the shareholders have no income.

Excluded Corporations

The following types of entities are *not* subject to the accumulated earnings tax:

1. Personal holding companies
2. Foreign personal holding companies
3. Tax-exempt corporations
4. Passive foreign investment companies

¶ 17,017   BASIS FOR LIABILITY

Although the accumulated earnings tax is computed as a percentage of the corporation's accumulated taxable income, liability for the tax hinges on whether the corporation was formed for or used to avoid the income tax on income otherwise receivable by its shareholders. A corporation can be subject to the accumulated earnings tax for a year in which it has accumulated taxable income on hand even though, because of a stock redemption, no earnings and profits were accumulated for the tax year.

The courts have shifted the focus of attention from earnings and profits to liquidity. The reason for this change in emphasis is that the earnings-and-profits figure often is no indication of the funds available to the corporation to meet its business needs and pay dividends to its shareholders. Whether a corporation can be subjected to the accumulated earnings tax is therefore determined by comparing the reasonable needs of its business to its total liquid assets at the end of the year. Liquid assets include the corporation's cash and marketable securities.

> *Example 17.2.* Cassandra's Gift Shop Inc. has several hundred thousand dollars in accumulated earnings. This fact alone does not indicate a tax liability for the accumulated earnings tax. If the owner, Ms. Glass, can show bona fide expansion plans, for example, the tax may be negated.

¶ 17,025   REASONABLE NEEDS OF THE BUSINESS

In order to justify an accumulation of income, there must be a reasonable business need for the accumulation and a definite plan for its use. Since a corporation is given a credit for its reasonable business needs (including reasonably anticipated needs) in figuring the accumulated earnings tax, the resolution of most disputes hinges on this issue.

The statute does not contain a comprehensive definition of reasonable business needs. However, a number of acceptable and unacceptable grounds for accumulating income are listed in the Regulations. Reg. § 1.537-2. Acceptable grounds are:

1. Product liability loss reserves
2. Distributions in redemption of stock
3. Business expansion and plant replacement
4. Acquisition of a business through purchase of stock or assets
5. Debt retirement
6. Working capital
7. Investments or loans to suppliers or customers necessary to the maintenance of the corporation's business

In addition to the acceptable reasons for accumulations, every business and every industry may have its own reasons for accumulating earnings. Some of these miscellaneous reasons may be extraordinary expenses, self-insurance, lawsuits pending, key-person life insurance, etc.

The bottom line, however, to support that a reasonable business need exists to justify an accumulation of income is *credibility*. A good story is a necessary, but insufficient, condition for avoiding the tax, once substantial accumulations exist. The reasons must be realistic and be documented to the extent possible. Examples of documentation include: corporate minutes, written proposals, blueprints, progress payments, contracts, etc.

If the corporation manufactures tangible goods, from soft drinks to autos, a liability without fault may arise if someone is hurt by a defective product. In recent years, courts have increasingly held the manufacturer liable, rather than the wholesaler or retailer. Even though the liability may never materialize and the amounts are purely speculative and uncertain, nevertheless, the establishment of a reasonable reserve is acceptable for accumulated earnings tax purposes. This is in contrast to other reasonable needs, which must be definite, realistic, and current.

Working Capital Needs

A corporation selling tangible property on credit may have a significant need for working capital, reduced by its ability to defer payment of accounts payable. In fact, the more rapid the growth in sales, the less liquid the firm may be because a significant portion of its assets is tied up in receivables and inventory. The phenomenon that a firm may go broke because it is growing too fast is referred to in the literature as the "paradox of growth." The need for net working capital, defined as current assets less current liabilities, is so universal that it is only natural that it is recognized as a tax reason for retaining earnings in the business.

Operating Cycles

In seeking to determine how much accumulated earnings are proper, the courts have often used an operating-cycle approach to determine the amount of working capital a corporation needs. An operating cycle consists of the period required to convert cash into raw materials, raw materials into an inventory of marketable products, and the inventory into sales and accounts receivable and, finally, to collect outstanding accounts.

To obtain a crude measure of the working capital needs of a corporation, the Tax Court in the 1960s designed a measure of the operating cycle, known ever since as the *Bardahl* formula. *Bardahl Mfg. Corp.*, 24 TCM 1030, CCH Dec. 27,494(M), TC Memo 1965-200; *Bardahl International Corp.*, 25 TCM 935, CCH Dec. 28,064(M), TC Memo 1966-182. This frequently used formula adds inventory and receivables turnover, subtracts payables turnover, and multiplies the result by cost of goods sold plus expenses (other than tax and depreciation) as follows:

$$\text{Inventory Turnover} = \frac{\text{Average Inventory} \times 360}{\text{Cost of Goods Sold}}$$

$$+ \text{ Accounts Receivable Turnover} = \frac{\text{Average Accounts Receivable} \times 360}{\text{Net Sales}}$$

$$- \text{ Accounts Payable Turnover} = \frac{\text{Average Accounts Payable} \times 360}{\text{Purchases}}$$

The result, expressed as a percentage of a year, is multiplied by relevant expenses. The liquidity requirement thus computed qualifies as a reasonable business need.

The formula has been revised and adapted to different industries and to take into account seasonal peaks.

Example 17.3.

1. If cost of goods sold equals $500,000 and average inventory equals $50,000, inventory turnover in days equals $50,000 × 360 ÷ $500,000 = 36.

2. If sales equal $800,000 and average receivables equal $200,000, receivables turnover in days equals $200,000 × 360 ÷ $800,000 = 90.

3. If purchases equal $300,000 and average payables equal $50,000, payables turnover in days equals $50,000 × 360 ÷ $300,000 = 60.

4. 36 + 90 − 60 = 66.

   The operating cycle expressed as a percentage of a year equals 66 × 100% ÷ 360, or 18.33 percent.

5. If other expenses equal $150,000, the working capital need equals ($500,000 + $150,000) × .1833, or $119,145. If actual working capital is less than this, the shortage qualifies as a reasonable business need. Any excess holdings do not qualify under the formula, but may qualify on other grounds.

TAX PLANNING POINTER

Even though excessive inventories and slow receivables collections reduce the accumulated earnings tax, this is hardly a good reason to be in this situation on purpose. Inventory levels should be kept to the minimum attainable level and receivables should be collected as soon as practicable. The liquid funds resulting therefrom then should be invested productively in the business, and not in passive investments, to the extent possible. The absence of non-business assets defeats the tax regardless of the level of accumulated earnings.

Burden of Proof

According to the Code, the mere fact that earnings are allowed to accumulate beyond the reasonable needs of the business makes the corporation vulnerable to the tax. However, the corporation (which has the burden of proof) may defeat the tax by introducing sufficient evidence that tax avoidance is missing. Code Sec. 533(a).

The following factors are among the most important to the government in imposing the tax (Reg. § 1.537-2(c)):

1. Loans to shareholders. If bona fide, the accumulated earnings tax may be imposed. If not bona fide, the loans are dividends, taxable to the shareholders.

2. Loans made to relatives or friends of shareholders, which serve no business purpose.

3. Loans to corporations in unrelated businesses, controlled by the shareholders, directly or indirectly.

4. Unrelated investments, especially passive investments, such as marketable securities.

5. Accumulations for vague or unrealistic purposes and hazards.

The thrust of the above is that funds are available for dividends, but instead of being distributed, they are applied or invested in a manner unrelated to the business function of the corporation. It should be noted that even a continuous record of dividends does not negate the tax once accumulations exceed reasonable business needs.

¶ 17,057   ACCUMULATED EARNINGS CREDIT

The tax rate on improper accumulations, applicable to all corporations subject to the tax, is a flat 39.6 percent of accumulated taxable income. However, an exemption, the accumulated earnings credit, is available, and it is quite liberal, particularly for the typical small, closely held corporation. The credit (which really is a deduction from the tax base) is the greater of two amounts.

A minimum amount of $250,000 ($150,000 for personal service corporations in health, law, engineering, architecture, accounting, actuarial science, performing arts, and consulting) may be accumulated by all corporations, including holding or investment companies. Code Sec. 535(c). This statutory minimum is reduced by accumulated earnings and profits at the end of the previous taxable year.

For corporations other than holding or investment companies, the accumulated earnings credit allowed in computing accumulated taxable income is the amount of current earnings and profits that is needed for the reasonable needs of the business, less after-tax net capital gains and less previous accumulations. In view of the credit, corporations will rarely be subject to the tax in the first few years of their existence.

> *Example 17.4.* Toyworld Inc., a chain of toy stores, has accumulated earnings of $190,000 at the end of last year. This year, current earnings amount to $150,000. The firm has no income, gain or loss other than from sales of inventory.
>
> If no reasonable needs of the business can be established for the current year, the accumulated earnings credit equals $60,000 ($250,000 − $190,000). Thus, the tax base would be $90,000 ($150,000 − $60,000).
>
> If reasonable needs of the business can be established for the year of $310,000, the credit is the greater of (1) $310,000 − $190,000 or (2) $250,000 − $190,000, or $120,000. Thus, the tax base would be reduced to $30,000 ($150,000 − $120,000). Note that reasonable needs cannot be added to the flat credit of $250,000. To avoid the tax, Toyworld Inc. would have to show a need for $340,000, the sum of both current and accumulated earnings.

Another way to look at the tax is that once accumulated earnings exceed $250,000, it is necessary to show a business need for every dollar of the excess plus the amount of current earnings to avoid the tax. Below is a detailed discussion of the computation of the tax base and the tax itself.

¶ 17,065 DIVIDENDS-PAID DEDUCTION

The purpose of the accumulated earnings tax is to discourage the retention of after-tax income beyond the needs of the business. Only amounts that could have been distributed as dividends are taxed. As a result, a deduction is granted for the following dividends:

1. Dividends actually paid during the taxable year that are taxable as ordinary income to the shareholders. Code Sec. 561(a).

2. Dividends taxable as ordinary income distributed within 2½ months after the end of the taxable year. Code Sec. 563(a).

3. Amounts labeled *consent dividends* in the corporate tax return for the taxable year. Code Sec. 565(a). A consent dividend is an amount the shareholder agrees to be taxed on as a dividend although it is *not* distributed. As a result, the shareholder is deemed to have received the dividend, then to have contributed it to the capital of the corporation. The shareholder's

stock basis is increased accordingly. This procedure is appropriate when the corporation has limited liquid assets.

Example 17.5. Myra Greene agrees to a consent dividend from Myra's Food Shop Inc. on a timely filed corporate tax return for the previous year in the amount of $10,000. The corporation's earnings are reduced by $10,000, Myra reports $10,000 in ordinary dividend income, and her basis in her stock is increased by $10,000. To pay the tax, Myra must provide funds from other sources, since no cash changed hands.

¶ 17,073   COMPUTING THE TAX BASE

The accumulated earnings tax is imposed by the IRS since it is *not* self-assessed. The IRS will assert the tax on a corporation's "accumulated taxable income," computed as follows:

Taxable income for a given taxable year

+   Dividends-received deduction

+   Capital loss carryovers and carrybacks

+   Net operating loss deduction

−   Corporate income taxes

−   Capital losses in excess of capital gains

−   After-tax net long-term capital gains over net short-term capital losses

−   Charitable contributions in excess of the 10 percent of taxable income deduction limit

−   Dividends paid or deemed paid

−   Accumulated earnings credit, typically the greater of $250,000 or the reasonable needs of the business, but reduced by accumulated earnings and profits at the end of the previous year (Code Sec. 535(b))

=   Accumulated taxable income

The tax is an annual tax on taxable income for the year. However, the credit is based on accumulated earnings. Technically, the tax could be imposed every year. The tax, if paid, will itself reduce accumulated earnings. In extreme situations where substantial annual earnings are accumulated with no need, the tax would grind earnings down annually until they eventually stay at the minimum tax level of $250,000. Of course, no corporation would allow this to happen.

Example 17.6. Thin Ice Ltd. had $300,000 of taxable income after a net operating loss carryover of $40,000, including $15,000 of dividends from a U.S. corporation and $10,000 of long-term capital gains, subject to a tax of $3,400. Accumulated earnings were $200,000, the total tax bill was $100,250, and established business needs amounted to $90,000. The tax would be computed as follows:

Taxable income...............................	$300,000
+ Dividends-received deduction ($15,000 × 70%)..........	10,500
+ Net operating loss deduction	40,000
− After-tax long-term capital gain	6,600
− Corporate income taxes	100,250
− Accumulated earnings credit ($250,000 − $200,000)	50,000
= Accumulated taxable income........................	$193,650
Accumulated earnings tax ($193,650 × .396)............	$ 76,685

The tax could have been avoided by paying $193,650 of dividends within 2½ months after the taxable year.

It should also be noted that interest on the accumulated earnings tax must be paid from the due date of the income tax return for the year assessed. Code Sec. 6601(b)(4).

TAX BLUNDER

Bouncing Toys Inc. buys its raw material from World Rubber Inc., whose main competitor is Global Rubber Corporation. Bouncing Toys invests its substantial liquid funds in Global Rubber, and the IRS asserts the accumulated earnings tax. If Bouncing Toys had invested in World Rubber, the accumulated earnings tax issue would have been unlikely to appear, since buying stock in a *supplier* is more likely to be accepted as a sound *business decision* rather than merely a promising investment.

¶ 17,081   PUBLIC CORPORATIONS

The dividend policy of a closely held corporation is more likely to be influenced by the tax situation and financial needs of its shareholders than is the dividend policy of a public corporation. As a result, the tax is most frequently imposed on corporations with few shareholders. However, the Code does *not* limit the tax to closely held corporations. Code Sec. 532(c). The IRS position is that the tax may be imposed on *any* corporation, other than S corporations and personal holding companies. Rev. Rul. 75-305, 1975-2 CB 228. Furthermore, the courts have in fact agreed with the IRS and imposed the tax on publicly held corporations, particularly if meaningful control is in the hands of a few. *Golconda Mining Corp.*, 74-2 USTC ¶ 9845, 507 F.2d 594 (CA-9 1974).

> *Example 17.7.* Lacquerware Gift Shop Inc. prospers and establishes a number of branches. To go nationwide Lacquerware goes public and is eventually listed on the Pacific Stock Exchange, at which point Michele Lacquerware still owns 51 percent of the stock. The accumulated earnings tax may still be assessed if the corporation accumulates earnings above and beyond "reasonable business needs." This is true even if thousands of shareholders own the other 49 percent.

¶ 17,089   TAX AVOIDANCE PURPOSE

The accumulated earnings tax is subjective. It is imposed only if the corporation fails to prove that accumulations above the exemption (the accumulated earnings credit) are needed in the business. The Code states that the tax "shall apply to every corporation . . . formed or availed of for the purpose of avoiding the income tax . . . by permitting earnings and profits to accumulate instead of being . . . distributed." Code Sec. 532(a). Does the tax avoidance motive have to be the principal purpose behind accumulations? The Supreme Court has held that tax avoidance need only be one of several contributing factors leading to retention. *Donruss Co.,* 69-1 USTC ¶ 9167, 393 U.S. 297, 89 S.Ct. 501 (1969). Thus, the mere fact that accumulations exist beyond business-related needs is sufficient to establish the tainted purpose.

> *Example 17.8.* Young-At-Heart Skating Rinks Ltd. is making an excellent profit. The family who owns the corporation has some expansion plans of an indefinite nature, as well as some immediate renovation plans. A secondary reason to retain the profits in the corporation is to avoid paying a second tax on dividends. The accumulated earnings tax may be asserted by the IRS.

¶ 17,097   VALUING EARNINGS AND PROFITS

To value earnings and profits sounds like a contradiction in terms. After all, earnings and profits are a reasonably definite tax term, mechanically computed, and not valued as such. However, if the corporation's retained earnings are invested in highly liquid assets, such as marketable securities, as a practical matter, the fair market value is a more realistic measure of the ability to pay a dividend. Thus, the Supreme Court has held that economic realities must be considered to see whether accumulations are reasonable. This includes the use of value in the case of marketable securities. *Ivan Allen Co.,* 75-2 USTC ¶ 9557, 422 U.S. 617, 95 S.Ct. 2501 (1975). Whether the current value approach will be extended to other liquid assets remains to be seen.

> *Example 17.9.* Winner Video Games Inc. accumulated $180,000 in retained earnings, well within the $250,000 accumulated earnings credit. However, these earnings were invested in growth stock, and after a few years the market value of these securities had grown to $400,000. The IRS may assert the accumulated earnings tax on $150,000 ($400,000 − $250,000), unless the corporation can show "reasonable business needs" in excess of $250,000, preferably at least $400,000.

Personal Holding Company Tax

¶ 17,151   RATE AND NATURE OF TAX

If a corporation in any given year meets the definition of a personal holding company (PHC), a flat 39.6 percent tax is imposed on the undistributed personal holding company income. The tax is self-assessed, in addition to the regular corporate tax, and is equal to the maximum marginal individual tax rate. To be vulnerable to the tax, the corporation must be controlled by five or fewer individuals and have predominantly investment-type income (other than capital gains). The tax will never have to be paid if sufficient dividends are paid, are deemed to be paid, or are paid retroactively.

> *Example 17.10.* Extra Fun Party Supplies Inc. is a personal holding company with undistributed personal holding company

income of $20,000. A personal holding company tax of 39.6 percent, or $7,920, is payable, in addition to the regular corporate tax, and is self-assessed (i.e., payable with the regular corporate return).

¶ 17,159 EXCLUDED CORPORATIONS

The following corporations are not subject to the personal holding company tax:

1. Tax-exempt corporations

2. Banks and domestic building and loan associations

3. Life insurance and surety companies

4. Foreign personal holding companies

5. Lending and finance companies meeting certain requirements

6. Foreign corporations owned by nonresident aliens

7. Small business investment companies

8. Corporations involved in bankruptcy proceedings (Code Sec. 542(c))

9. Passive foreign investment companies (as defined in Code Sec. 1297)

In addition, S corporation status will, as a practical matter, prevent personal holding company taxes although S corporations are not explicitly excluded from their imposition.

Example 17.11. Cordelia Crafts opens a gift shop. She incorporates and makes an S election. As a result, Cordelia will report all income, gain, loss, deduction, or credit from the corporation on her own tax return. Consequently, the personal holding company tax is inapplicable.

¶ 17,167 REASON FOR THE TAX

Consider the following: A high tax bracket individual incorporates a stock portfolio, reinvesting all dividends. In the absence of the personal holding company rules, the following results may be accomplished. Seventy percent of dividends received from domestic corporations are tax free. Code Sec. 243. The remaining 30 percent are taxed at rates starting at 15 percent on the first $50,000 and 25 percent on the next $25,000. Thus, the tax on $100,000 of dividends would be $100,000 × .30 × .15, or $4,500, a rate of 4.5 percent. Even the accumulated earnings tax may never be applicable if all dividends are reinvested in stock since this is an expansion of the only "business" the corporation is in as an investment company. Eventually, the corporation can liquidate, resulting in a capital gains tax at the shareholder level. Code Sec. 331. Alternatively, the shareholder dies and the shareholder's heirs receive a stock basis equal to fair market value, thus escaping the capital gains tax. Code Sec. 1014.

The congressional answer to this potential abuse is to impose a second tax on the corporation's undistributed personal holding company income, effectively forcing the corporation to distribute the dividends to the shareholder. Thus, the corporate tax, small as it may be, will represent a straight, out-of-pocket loss to the shareholders. To prevent any possible tax advantage to incorporating income-producing securities and the like, the tax is imposed at a flat rate equal to the top marginal tax rate on individuals, 39.6 percent. Unlike the accumulated earnings tax, the personal holding company tax has no deduction (credit) and is self-assessed on Form 1120, Schedule PH.

Example 17.12. Excel Ltd. is a personal holding company and has undistributed personal holding company income of $100 this year. Excel must file Form 1120, Schedule PH and pay $39.60 in personal holding company tax without prompting by the IRS. This is in addition to the regular corporate tax and is independent of it.

¶ 17,175   PERSONAL HOLDING COMPANY DEFINED

To be classified as a personal holding company, a corporation must meet the following two tests for any given taxable year:

1. The *stock ownership test.* Five or fewer individuals must own more than 50 percent of the value of the outstanding stock, actually or constructively, at any time during the second half of the taxable year. Code Sec. 542(a)(2).

2. The personal holding company *income test.* Investment income, such as dividends, interest, rents, and royalties, must comprise at least 60 percent of the corporation's adjusted ordinary gross income. Code Sec. 542(a)(1).

A corporation may meet these tests one year and not another. It is important to recognize that meeting the definition of a personal holding company does *not* mean that any additional tax is due. Classification is merely a condition for the tax to be imposed. The personal holding company tax is based on *undistributed personal holding company income.* To a corporation distributing all its earnings, both the personal holding company tax and the accumulated earnings tax are irrelevant.

Example 17.13. Comfort Bedding Inc. is owned equally by eight family members. The stock ownership test is met. Eighty percent of adjusted ordinary gross income is comprised of dividends from other corporations. Comfort Bedding meets the definition of a personal holding company. However, no personal holding company tax is payable, unless Comfort Bedding has "*undistributed* personal holding income" during a year it meets the definition of a personal holding company.

¶ 17,183   STOCK OWNERSHIP TEST

In determining whether five or fewer individuals own more than 50 percent of the value of the stock, attribution rules apply. Code Sec. 544. Indirect ownership does not apply if the shareholders are unrelated, but this is unlikely in a closely held setting. However, if 10 or more unrelated taxpayers own equal shares, the ownership requirement cannot be met, per definition. The constructive ownership rules are as follows:

1. Stock owned by members of an individual's family (brothers, sisters, spouse, ancestors, and lineal descendants) is considered owned by such individual.

2. Stock owned by a corporation, partnership, estate, or trust is considered owned proportionately by the shareholders, partners, or beneficiaries.

3. Stock owned by a partner is deemed owned in full by all other partners.

4. Options and convertible securities count to the extent of the underlying stock.

Example 17.14. Two parents and their children own all the stock in a corporation. Each individual is deemed to own 100 percent of the stock.

¶ 17,191 PERSONAL HOLDING COMPANY INCOME TEST

To meet the personal holding company income test, 60 percent or more of the corporation's adjusted ordinary gross income (AOGI) must constitute personal holding company income (PHCI). Thus, if:

$$\frac{\text{PHCI}}{\text{AOGI}} \geq .60,$$ the personal holding company income test is met.

To arrive at the *denominator,* three steps are necessary:

Step 1. Gross income is computed in the traditional manner.

Step 2. Ordinary gross income is arrived at by subtracting short- and long-term capital gains as well as Code Sec. 1231 gains. Code Sec. 543(b)(1).

Step 3. Adjusted ordinary gross income results if ordinary gross income is reduced by rent and royalty expenses and certain excluded receipts. Code Sec. 543(b)(2). The main reductions are:

1. Rental expenses, such as mortgage interest, property taxes, depreciation, and other expenses

2. Mineral royalty expenses, such as interest, taxes, depreciation, depletion, and other expenses

3. Interest received on tax refunds, judgments and condemnation awards, and interest on U.S. securities received by dealers in such securities

Example 17.15. Auto Stereo Inc. has gross income from operations of $41,000 and $59,000 of interest and dividends. Thus, personal holding company income ($59,000) constitutes only 59 percent of adjusted ordinary gross income ($100,000). Therefore, the corporation is not a PHC and cannot be subject to the PHC tax. This is true even though the only income after expenses may be from personal holding company income. Another $2,500 in interest and/ or dividends, however, would make Auto Stereo Inc. a PHC ($61,500/$102,500 = .60).

¶ 17,199   PERSONAL HOLDING COMPANY INCOME

As we have seen, the denominator in the personal holding company income test fraction is reduced by expenses and other items, which, of course, is contrary to the taxpayer's interest. The numerator consists of a number of personal holding company income items. Code Sec. 543(a). These are not generally reduced by expenses, which is also contrary to the taxpayer's interest. Personal holding company income includes the following items.

Dividends, interest, royalties (other than copyright, mineral, oil, and gas royalties), *and annuities.* However, interest income received by broker-dealers is excluded from passive income, if earned in connection with securities or money market instruments held as inventory, margin accounts, or the financing for customers secured by money market instruments or securities.

TAX BLUNDER

Videogames Inc. invested its vast surplus in mutual funds with automatic dividend reinvestment plans, never actually receiving any distributions. To Videogames's surprise, it was confronted with personal holding company status because of its high dividend income. The problem could have been resolved by investing in *equity growth funds,* paying low or no dividends.

Adjusted income from rent is included in the denominator. However, the rent is excluded from the numerator if two tests are met:

1. Adjusted rent is at least half of adjusted ordinary gross income.

2. All other personal holding company income in excess of 10 percent of ordinary gross income is distributed as dividends.

Adjusted income from mineral, oil, and gas royalties is normally included in the numerator as personal holding company income, except that it is excluded if three tests are met:

1. Adjusted royalties are at least half of adjusted ordinary gross income.

2. Other personal holding company income is 10 percent or less of ordinary gross income.

3. Deductions only allowable under Code Sec. 162 (ordinary and necessary business expenses), other than compensation to shareholders for personal services, amount to at least 15 percent of adjusted ordinary gross income.

Copyright royalties are included in the numerator, except that they are excluded if three tests are met:

1. Royalties (other than from works created in whole or in part by any shareholder) are at least one half of ordinary gross income.

2. Other personal holding company income (with some modifications) does not exceed 10 percent of ordinary gross income.

3. Deductions only allowable under Code Sec. 162 with respect to the royalties (other than compensation for personal services by shareholders and royalties paid or accrued) are at least 25 percent of the excess of ordinary gross income over the sum of royalties expense plus depreciation.

Produced film rent, except if such rent is at least half of ordinary gross income and the film was produced in significant part by the taxpayer. If the film was acquired when substantially completed, the additional tests under copyright royalties must be met as well.

Rent received from a shareholder for the use of corporate property, whether or not it is called rent and regardless of who the recipient is, if: (1) the shareholder, directly or indirectly, owned at least 25 percent of the value of the outstanding stock at any point during the taxable year, and (2) the corporation has other personal holding company income in excess of 10 percent of ordinary gross income.

Active computer software royalties are excluded from personal holding company income but only if: (1) royalties are received in connection with the licensing of software, (2) royalties are received by a corporation actively engaged in the computer software business, (3) royalties constitute at least 50 percent of ordinary gross income, (4) ordinary and necessary business expenses, research and development expenses, and business starting-up expenses exceed 25 percent of ordinary gross income, and (5) personal holding company income in excess of 10 percent of ordinary gross income is paid out in dividends. Code Sec. 543(d).

Personal service income, including gain from the sale of a personal service contract, if: (1) someone other than the corporation can designate the individual who is to render the service and (2) such individual owned, directly or indirectly, at least 25 percent of the value of the outstanding stock at any point during the taxable year.

Example 17.16. Joseph Sennetti is a professor of electrical engineering. He incorporates his consulting practice and owns all the stock. If his clients can insist that he personally perform the services they require, all fees collected constitute personal holding company income. If the *corporation* performs the services and Joseph may send someone else in his place to do the actual consulting, no personal holding company income results.

Income from estates and trusts, regardless of the nature of the income, unless it is tax-exempt.

The effect of the above rules is to exclude the following types of activities from classification as personal holding companies:

1. Real estate companies, such as corporations primarily in the rental business, but only if they distribute nonrental income above the limitation

2. Natural resource outfits, if they have limited unrelated passive income and some minimum business activities

3. Publishing companies, if they meet similar tests

4. Movie companies, if they either engage in production or meet the minimal other passive income and business activity tests

5. Active business computer software companies

TAX PLANNING POINTER ▼

If the ownership test is met and dividends are not to be paid, the income ratio test becomes crucial. To decrease the income ratio, the numerator must be decreased and/or the denominator increased. The following observations may be made:

Capital gains, Section 1231 gains, and tax-exempt interest *do* improve the ratio since they are excluded from both the numerator and the denominator. Thus,

$$\frac{\text{PHCI}}{\text{AOGI}} = \frac{100}{150} = .667. \quad \text{If, instead of taxable interest, \$50 is}$$

tax-exempt, the ratio becomes $\frac{50}{100} = .50$.

Growth stock paying little or no dividends but with appreciation potential will improve the ratio.

If personal services are rendered, no one outside the corporation should be able to designate the individual to render the service.

¶ 17,207   REAL ESTATE COMPANIES

The most important escape hatch from the definition of a personal holding company is provided for real estate companies. Adjusted rent is excluded from personal holding company income if it equals at least one-half of adjusted ordinary gross income and if other personal holding company income in excess of 10 percent of ordinary gross income is distributed as dividends. This complex rule is best illustrated by an example.

Example 17.17. Office Space Ltd. generated the following items of income and deductions last year:

Rent income	$40,000
Depreciation	15,000
Property taxes	4,000
Mortgage interest	12,000
Other business expenses	7,000
Dividends received	8,000
Long-term capital gain	5,000

Ordinary gross income equals $48,000 ($40,000 + $8,000). Adjusted ordinary gross income equals $17,000 ($48,000 − $15,000 − $4,000 − $12,000). Adjusted rent equals $9,000 ($40,000 − $15,000 − $4,000 − $12,000). Since $9,000 is at least one-half of $17,000, the 50 percent test is met. Ten percent of $48,000 equals

$4,800. Since dividends received amount to $8,000, at least $3,200 must qualify for the dividends-paid deduction (see ¶ 17,231) in order to exclude rent from passive income. If so, the corporation is not a personal holding company since the income test is failed per definition.

¶ 17,215   COMPUTING THE TAX BASE

Once a corporation meets the ownership and income tests and is classified as a personal holding company, a 39.6 percent tax is due on "undistributed personal holding company income," if any. Code Sec. 545. The starting point for computing the tax base is taxable income, and the calculations may be summarized as follows (Code Sec. 545(b)):

Taxable income

— Regular corporate income taxes accruable

— Charitable contributions beyond the 10 percent limit, up to the limitation for individuals

— Net capital gains after taxes

+ Dividends-received deduction

+ Net operating losses, other than from the previous year

+ Business expenses and depreciation on nonbusiness property in excess of income received, unless the rent is the highest obtainable, a bona fide profit motive existed, or the property was necessary to conduct business

= Adjusted taxable income

— Dividends-paid deduction

= Undistributed personal holding company income

Example 17.18. Stett Ltd., a PHC, paid $50,000 in taxes on $150,000 in taxable income. Taxable income included $40,000 in domestic dividends and a Section 1231 gain of $15,000 (on which $5,000 of tax was paid). Dividends paid for the year amounted to $60,000.

The computation of the PHC tax is as follows:

Taxable income	$150,000
— Taxes payable	50,000
— Net capital gains after tax	10,000
+ Dividends-received deduction (70% of $40,000)	28,000
= Adjusted taxable income	$118,000
— Dividends-paid deduction	60,000
= Undistributed personal holding company income	$ 58,000
PHC tax 39.6 percent	$ 22,968

TAX PLANNING POINTER

To increase non-personal holding company income for the year on the cash basis, income may be accelerated and/or deductions deferred. Examples include: defer payment of accounts payable, step up accounts receivable collection or even sell some accounts receivable, use straight-line depreciation, elect out of the installment method, etc.

KEYSTONE PROBLEM

Consider the most likely effect on the accumulated earnings tax and personal holding company tax, as well as corporate shareholder transactions under the following circumstances:

1. E&P is abolished and all distributions to shareholders are taxed as long-term capital gain.

2. Same as (1), except distributions are taxed as ordinary income.

¶ 17,231   DIVIDENDS-PAID DEDUCTION

The tax on undistributed personal holding company income is rarely paid since five kinds of dividends are deductible to arrive at the tax base.

Dividends Paid During the Tax Year. Code Sec. 561(a)(1). There are several caveats here. If only property is distributed, the corporation's adjusted basis at the time of distribution is deductible, even if a higher value is taxed to the shareholder. Reg. § 1.562-1(a). The dividends must be proportional to the number of shares held and not favor one class of stock over another. Code Sec. 562(c). If the distribution is disproportional, none of the distribution qualifies, not just the disproportional excess. The dividends may be disallowed as a deduction retroactively, due to the reclassification of reimbursed expenses and unreasonable compensation as constructive dividends.

Dividends Paid Within 2½ Months After the Taxable Year. Code Sec. 563(b). The corporation may elect to treat such payments as dividends paid during the previous year to the extent of the lesser of: (1) 20 percent of dividends actually paid during the tax year, or (2) undistributed personal holding company income for the year.

Consent Dividends. Code Sec. 565(a). The shareholder may elect (by the due date of the corporate return) to pretend that the shareholder received a dividend and reinvested the amount in the corporation with the following effects. The shareholder has dividend income and the corporation has a dividends-paid deduction on the last day of the corporation's taxable year. The shareholder receives an increase in the stock basis for the amount deemed contributed to capital. Since the consent dividend reduces earnings and profits, the possibility of tax-free dividends (return of capital) is increased.

Example 17.19. Minerva Most is the sole owner of Personal Defense Inc. With the corporate tax return for last year she exhibited her intent to make a consent dividend in the amount of $15,000. Result: No money changes hands. Personal Defense receives a dividend paid deduction of $15,000, Personal Defense's earnings and profits decline by $15,000, Minerva must report $15,000 of dividend income, and Minerva's adjusted basis in Personal Defense stock is increased by $15,000. Minerva's tax payable as a result of the dividend must come from other sources.

Deficiency Dividends. Code Sec. 547. Unlike the consent dividend, a deficiency dividend is *actually* paid, perhaps several years later, but with retroactive effect. It cannot be paid before a deficiency in the personal holding company tax has been determined, nor can it be paid more than 90 days thereafter. A "determination" means a decision by the Tax Court, District Court, or U.S. Claims Court, even if the taxpayer appeals; a closing agreement; or a written agreement between the corporation and the District Director. Reg. § 1.547-2(b). If the requirements are met and a proportional dividend is paid, the dividends-received deduction is available for the prior year. However, the retroactive effect is limited to the tax itself. Interest and penalties must still be paid. Code Sec. 547(a).

Dividend Carryovers. Code Sec. 564(b). Dividends paid may be carried over and deducted the next two years to the extent they exceed "adjusted taxable income." Adjusted taxable income is basically undistributed taxable income prior to the dividends-paid deduction. The corporation can carry forward dividends paid even if paid in a year the corporation was not classified as a personal holding company.

¶ 17,239 MISCELLANEOUS TAX CONSEQUENCES OF PHC CLASSIFICATION

There are several tax consequences of being classified as a personal holding company. First, the accumulated earnings tax cannot be imposed in the year or years that a corporation is a personal holding company. Code Sec. 532(b)(1); Reg. § 1.541-1(a). Second, the "at-risk" limitation on tax losses in most tax shelters applies to corporations meeting the ownership test for personal holding companies (with certain modifications). Code Sec. 465(a)(1)(B). Third, losses on transactions between two commonly controlled corporations are denied, but only if at least one corporation was a personal holding company in the previous taxable year. Code Sec. 267(b)(3). Fourth, the alternative minimum tax on tax preference items is imposed on an expanded list of items for personal holding companies. Code Sec. 57(a).

Example 17.20. Rover Dog Food Inc. is more than 50 percent owned by five or fewer individual shareholders this year. In addition, at least 60 percent of its adjusted ordinary gross income consists of personal holding company income. Even if there is no undistributed personal holding company income, so that no personal holding company tax is payable, the accumulated earnings tax cannot be assessed that particular year.

¶ 17,250   TAX PLANNING FOR CLOSELY HELD CORPORATIONS

Owners of closely held corporations usually wish to receive funds from their corporation while avoiding a second tax on the dividend income. The typical ways to transfer funds from a corporation to its shareholders without paying dividends include the following:

1. Fringe benefits, from free meals to deferred compensation

2. Salaries, bonuses, and taxable fringe benefits

3. Stock redemptions

4. Sales of property to the corporation, including sales and leasebacks

5. Leasing property to the corporation

6. Shareholder loans

7. Lease improvements on shareholder property

The variety of schemes used to avoid paying dividends is limited only by the imagination of the taxpayer and tax advisers. Other than the first two methods on the list, the rest may be closely scrutinized by the IRS.

Example 17.21. Selma Wicker is the sole shareholder of Novelties Inc. The corporation has a great deal of cash. Selma, age 58, sells her condominium apartment to the corporation for $200,000, at a time when her adjusted basis is $75,000, then rents it back from the corporation. The following consequences result:

1. Selma "unlocks" $200,000 from the corporation.

2. Selma recognizes no gain if she makes a Section 121 election to exclude gain from the sale or exchange of a principal residence.

3. The corporation's basis in the condo is $200,000.

4. Selma still lives in the apartment.

5. The corporation gets to depreciate the $200,000 cost basis.

6. If an S election is made, the depreciation deductions flow through to Selma.

7. If the corporation is an S corporation, the personal holding company tax will not apply.

8. If the corporation charges Selma rent, the rent is gross income, which flows through to Selma (if the corporation is an S corporation). However, if Selma is required to live in the condo as a condition of her employment, for the corporation's convenience, no rent need be charged and no rental income is recognized, even though cost recovery is still available. Code Sec. 119.

SUMMARY OF CHAPTER 17

✓ Both the accumulated earnings tax and the personal holding company tax seek the same objective: To encourage the distribution of dividends by taxing undistributed earnings, thus enforcing the double taxation of C corporations.

✓ Both taxes are imposed on the corporation, not on the shareholders, and are based on some measure of retained earnings.

✓ Dividends-paid deductions are allowed for both taxes, including a deduction for dividends paid within 2½ months after the end of the taxable year, as well as for consent dividends.

✓ Net capital gains, i.e., net long-term capital gains, including net mid-term gains and net Section 1231 gains, in excess of net short-term capital losses, are excluded for both taxes.

✓ Both taxes are imposed at a flat 39.6 percent rate, geared to the maximum individual rate.

✓ The personal holding company tax is self-assessed, while the accumulated earnings tax is initiated by the IRS.

✓ The personal holding company tax is independent of accumulated earnings and profits.

✓ The personal holding company tax is computed mechanically, while the intent, plans, and history of the corporation play an important role when determining whether, and to what extent, the accumulated earnings tax is applicable.

✓ The personal holding company tax is imposed only on closely held corporations controlled by individual shareholders. The accumulated earnings tax can be imposed on publicly held corporations, at least if there is considerable control in the hands of a few.

CHAPTER 17 QUESTIONS

1. Identify three items of nontaxable receipts which nevertheless increase earnings and profits.

2. Give the acceptable reasons to accumulate earnings as specified in the Regulations.

3. What is the *Bardahl* formula and how is it computed?

4. What factors tend to indicate that excess accumulations exist?

5. Why are public corporations less likely to be subject to the accumulated earnings tax?

6. John Ferret is the sole shareholder of two corporations.

   Unusual Pets Inc. is a pet shop with $240,000 in current and accumulated earnings, all invested in certificates of deposit and none of which is needed in the business.

   Shadow Inc. is a private investigations service specializing in divorces. Shadow has only $190,000 in current and accumulated earnings, $150,000 of which is needed in the business and all of which is invested in extremely illiquid assets.

   Which of the two corporations is more vulnerable to the accumulated earnings tax?

7. How are short- and long-term capital gains and losses treated in computing accumulated taxable income?

8. How is the accumulated earnings credit determined?

9. How are assets to be valued for the purpose of the accumulated earnings tax?

10. Identify four types of corporations excluded from PHC status.

11. What is the definition of a personal holding company? If the definition is met, is any additional tax necessarily due?

12. Why is a corporation more likely to be subject to the personal holding company tax in a "bad" year?

13. What unique personal holding company problems may confront a small personal service corporation?

14. When is rent excluded from PHCI?

15. Distinguish between a consent dividend and a deficiency dividend.

16. How do capital gains and Section 1231 gains enter into the computation of undistributed PHCI?

17. What are the similarities between the accumulated earnings tax and the personal holding company tax?

18. May the personal holding company tax and the accumulated earnings tax be imposed on the following corporations?

    a. The same corporation in the same taxable year

    b. The same corporation in two different taxable years

    c. An S corporation

19. How is the tax rate on undistributed personal holding company income determined? On accumulated taxable income?

20. What is the impact of accelerated cost recovery on the personal holding company tax? On the accumulated earnings tax?

CHAPTER 17 PROBLEMS

21. The Loophole Tax Service Inc. has accumulated earnings of $135,000 and current earnings of $60,000. If the dividends-paid deduction is $8,500 and reasonable business needs amount to $160,000, what is the accumulated earnings credit?

22. A manufacturer of billiard and bowling equipment paid an accumulated earnings tax of $45,000, relating to the previous taxable year. What is the impact on the tax situation of the corporation and its two individual shareholders?

23. Mr. Wilson incorporated his bookstore, Occult Books Unlimited, five years ago. Accumulated earnings are $230,000, current earnings are $80,000, and he can show a need for $150,000 of inventory. What is the amount of accumulated taxable income? If the tax is paid, what are the accumulated earnings at the end of the current year?

24. Margo's Cookies Inc. has working capital of $210,000. Selected operating figures include:

Average inventory	$150,000
Average accounts receivable	80,000
Average accounts payable	50,000
Purchases	300,000
Net sales	960,000
Cost of goods sold	600,000
Other expenses (including depreciation of $50,000 and taxes of $90,000)	440,000

According to the *Bardahl* formula, what is Margo's working capital need in total?

25. War Games Inc. breaks even on its operations one year, but has dividend income of $2,000. Could it be a personal holding company?

   a. The following year, War Games has a net operating loss of $50,000 and dividend income of $3,000. Could it be a personal holding company?

   b. Ultra-Vision Inc. is owned only by entities (e.g., a trust, a partnership, and a corporation). Can it be a personal holding company?

26. Party Supplies Inc. is owned 60 percent by Sylvester and 40 percent by an unrelated corporation. How much stock is Sylvester deemed to own after he makes the following independent transactions?

a. Transfer of half his stock to an irrevocable trust for his grandchildren.

b. Transfer of half his stock as a divorce settlement to his ex-wife, Chastity.

c. Sale of half his stock to his independent partner.

d. Sale of half his stock to a corporation in which he is a 60 percent shareholder and the other shareholders are unrelated to him.

e. Gift of half his stock to his niece.

27. Parkview West Inc. has gross income of $50,000, consisting of $37,000 of rent receipts and $13,000 of U.S. dividends. Rental deductions of $20,000 are claimed (interest, taxes, and cost recovery). $9,000 of dividends are paid to Susie and Sally, the only shareholders.

a. Is the 50 percent rental test met?

b. Is the 10 percent dividend test met?

c. Is Parkview a personal holding company?

28. Ray Cutter, M.D., incorporated his medical practice. Soon thereafter, he transferred his stock portfolio to the corporation. Since Dr. Cutter is the only surgeon in the corporation, all patients automatically expect his services. One year, professional fees were $200,000 and dividends received were $100,000. Is Ray Cutter, M.D., Ltd. a personal holding company?

29. B-Flat Music Supplies Ltd. earned dividends of $30,000, interest of $12,000, adjusted rent of $50,000, and gross income from its primary business of $63,000 in one taxable year.

a. Is B-Flat a personal holding company?

b. If the dividend income was $35,000, is B-Flat a personal holding company?

30. Lark Enterprises Inc. is a personal holding company. From the information below, compute its maximum dividends-paid deduction.

a. Land with a basis of $10,000 and a value of $50,000 was distributed during the taxable year ending December 31 to its two 50 percent shareholders as equal tenants in common.

b. Two months later, cash of $5,000 was distributed to one shareholder and three months later property worth $5,000 to the other.

c. On February 10 of the following year, $3,000 was distributed to each shareholder and an election was made to treat the dividends as paid the previous year.

d. A timely election was made to treat $5,000 each as consent dividends.

31. Parking Unlimited Ltd.'s financial situation last year may be summarized as follows:

Rental income	$ 75,000
Depreciation on real property	20,000
Property taxes	7,000
Mortgage interest	19,000
Miscellaneous expenses	12,000
Dividend revenue	11,000
Interest income	4,000
Section 1231 gain	200,000

   a. Is Parking Unlimited a PHC?

   b. Is the 50 percent test met?

   c. How much must be paid in dividends, if any, to avoid PHC tax?

32. David Roberts runs a one-person corporation, a management consulting firm. For the first few years, he paid himself a minuscule salary, no dividends, and no fringe benefits, paying only the regular corporate tax. At the point when accumulated earnings had reached $150,000, all invested in listed stocks, he started paying himself a comfortable but reasonable salary and established a qualified pension plan for himself. From this point on, the corporation had no taxable income. Is it possible that the accumulated earnings tax will be imposed? The personal holding company tax?

33. Gary's Garage Inc. never paid a dividend and invested its after-tax earnings in tire company stock. It has no plans to expand and its working capital is ample. Gary owns 100 percent of the stock.

   a. May Gary's Garage be a PHC?

   b. If Gary's is a PHC *not* liable for the PHC tax (since there is no UPHCI), may the accumulated earnings tax be imposed?

   c. If Gary's accumulated earnings are $250,000 and current after-tax earnings are distributed, may the accumulated earnings tax be imposed?

   d. Same as (c), except accumulated earnings are $200,000, but the marketable stocks purchased with them are worth $700,000.

34. Nestor Corp., which is not a mere holding or investment company, derives its income from retail sales. Nestor had accumulated earnings and profits of $145,000 on December 31, 1997. For the year ended December 31, 1998, it had earnings and profits of $115,000 and a dividends-paid deduction of $15,000. It had been determined that $20,000 of the accumulated earnings and profits for 1997 is required for the reasonable needs of the business. How much is the allowable accumulated earnings credit on December 31, 1998?

a. $105,000

b. $125,000

c. $150,000

d. $250,000

35. To compute the accumulated taxable income, all of the items below are deductible, except:

a. Federal income taxes

b. After-tax net capital gains

c. Current dividends

d. Deficiency dividends

36. Engineering Valuations Inc. has accumulated earnings of $190,000 and current earnings of $250,000. The corporation can show a need to expand the business to the tune of $220,000. The amount of the accumulated earnings credit is:

a. $220,000

b. $30,000

c. $0

d. $60,000

37. To arrive at adjusted ordinary gross income from gross income, the following subtractions are made, except:

a. Rent and royalty expenses

b. Section 1231 gains

c. Ordinary and necessary business expenses

d. Short-term capital losses

38. *Comprehensive Problem.* Scandinavian Furniture Inc., a calendar-year corporation, is worried about the accumulated earnings tax. In February, the following facts are available for the preceding year:

Accumulated earnings and profits as of 12/31 .... $220,000
Taxable income (exclusive of capital gains) 110,000
Charitable contributions in excess of limit 3,000
Long-term capital gain, taxable at 34 percent 10,000
Dividends from Canadian corporations.................... 7,000
Dividends from U.S. corporations (25 percent owned) 8,000
Total income tax liability 60,000
Demonstrable business needs............................ 235,000

If the consent dividend route is to be used, which amount must be reported to avoid the accumulated earnings tax?

39. *Comprehensive Problem.* Marital Aids Inc. reported the following results last year:

Gross income from sales	$ 50,000
Salaries	20,000
Overhead	25,000
Capital gains	200,000
Net operating loss from previous year	30,000
Dividends from U.S. sources	40,000
Tax-exempt interest	10,000
Taxable interest	35,000
Income tax paid (including $59,650 on capital gains)	62,050

If the corporation has only four individual shareholders, compute the following:

a. Adjusted ordinary gross income.

b. Personal holding company income.

c. Undistributed personal holding company income.

d. Current dividend required to avoid personal holding company tax.

e. What impact would it have if taxable interest was only $12,000 and there was no NOL carryover?

40. *Research Problem.* To what extent may a corporation accumulate earnings for the reasonable needs of a related corporation?

To what extent does it matter that the following conditions prevail?

a. A parent-subsidiary relationship exists.

b. A brother-sister controlled group exists.

c. The two corporations are in different businesses.

d. The degree of common ownership or control is less than 80 percent.

(See Reg. § § 1. 537-2(c)(3), 1.537-3(b); H. Rept. No. 1337, 83d Cong., 2d Sess., p. 53 (1954); S. Rept. No. 1622, 83d Cong., 2d Sess., p. 70 (1954).)

41. *Research Problem.* A corporation is resisting the personal holding company tax, but the Tax Court sides with the IRS. Within 90 days after the adverse decision, one shareholder transfers his stock and $10,000 in cash to a controlled corporation in a Code Sec. 351 transaction, while another gifts his stock to an irrevocable trust with his minor children as beneficiaries. Deficiency dividends are actually paid to the corporation and the trust. Are the shareholders able to shift the dividend income to the new entities?

(See Rev. Rul. 60-331, 1960-2 CB 189; and *T.E.G. Smith Estate,* 61-2 USTC ¶ 9543, 292 F.2d 478 (CA-3 1961).)

Chapter 18

Partnerships—
Formation and Operation

Learning Objectives

After completing Chapter 18, you should be able to:

1. Understand the characteristics of a partnership for federal tax purposes and general law purposes.

2. Determine the tax consequences of the formation of a partnership.

3. Describe the income tax reporting process for a partnership.

4. Describe the income tax reporting of partnership income by a partner.

5. Determine the basis of an interest in a partnership.

OVERVIEW OF CHAPTER

The partnership form is probably the most common type of business organization involving more than one owner. There are generally no formal requirements to be met at organization because the partnership's existence is determined by the business relationship of the participants and their carrying on a business as co-owners with the intention of making a profit.

The federal income tax consequences of partnerships are found in Subchapter K of the Internal Revenue Code. The statute takes significantly different approaches in the taxation of income of partnerships. In some instances, the partnership is treated as if it were an entity separate from its partners, somewhat like a corporation, but in other instances the partnership is often treated as an aggregation of its owners, as if they were joint tenants with undivided ownership interests. Under the aggregate concept, the partnership itself is assumed not to exist, and the focus is on the partners.

Partnership items of income and expense are usually passed through unchanged to the partners. Partnership items are reported by partners for their year with or within which the partnership year ends. The items may be allocated among the partners in the partnership agreement so long as the allocation achieves realistic economic objectives. However, the tax law may require other allocations if the tax allocations do not affect partners substantially in an economic sense.

Definition of a Partnership

¶ 18,001   CHARACTERISTICS OF A PARTNERSHIP

To the business world in general, a partnership is "an association of two or more persons to carry on as co-owners a business for profit." Uniform Partnership Act, Section 6. There need be no express agreement, oral or written. If the venture satisfies the definition of a partnership, it is one. The term "partnership," for tax purposes, is not confined to a partnership as defined under local law. In income tax law, the term is much broader and operates almost as a catch-all. It includes any unincorporated organization with more than one owner which carries on any business, financial operation, or venture, unless the Internal Revenue Code defines such an organization as a trust, estate, or corporation. Code Secs. 761(a) and 7701(a)(2); Reg. § 1.761-1(a). However, under the anti-abuse rule, the Internal Revenue Service may disregard the partnership form of entity, or recast transactions involving the use of partnerships, if a partnership is formed or availed of in connection with a transaction whose principal purpose is to reduce substantially the present value of the partners' tax liabilities in a manner that is inconsistent with the intent of Subchapter K. Reg. § 1.701-2.

Partner Defined

Obviously, for there to be a partnership, there must be partners. For tax purposes a "partner" is "a member of a partnership," including members of joint ventures, syndicates, pools, and like groups classified for tax purposes as partnerships. Code Sec. 761(b). A partner need not be a natural person. Trusts, estates, corporations, and other partnerships all have been recognized as partners in appropriate circumstances. Subject to certain limitations, a minor may be a partner.

Example 18.1. The Eclectic Partnership was formed with the following parties each owning equal interests: Acme Corporation (its state of incorporation and charter permitted participation), the Estate of Jasper Winebringer, Halloluya Trust for the Sacred Heart Church, the Futures Unlimited Partnership, and Willie Jones, unemployed. The partnership will be recognized for tax purposes.

There are two types of partners, a general partner and a limited partner. A general partner has unlimited liability for the debts of and claims against the partnership. A limited partner's liability is limited to what the partner has invested and promised to invest in the partnership. Generally, a limited partner may not participate in the management of the partnership. If a limited partner should exercise managerial authority, he or she may be treated as a general partner.

Meaning of "Partnership Agreement"

A partnership agreement includes the original agreement and any modifications thereof agreed to by all the partners or adopted in any other manner provided by the partnership agreement. Code Sec. 761(c). Such agreement or modifications can be oral or written. Reg. § 1.761-1(c). See *R.W. James,* 21 TCM 953, CCH Dec. 25,579(M), T.C. Memo. 1962-173. A partnership agreement may be modified with respect to a particular taxable year subsequent to the close of such taxable year, but not later than the date (not including any extension of time) prescribed by law for the filing of the partnership return.

Classification as an Association

Prior to 1997, the regulations contained a test to determine whether an unincorporated entity could be classified as an association and taxed as a corporation. If the entity had more than two of the four corporate characteristics (continuity of life, centralized management, limited liability, and free transferability of interests), then the entity was taxed as a corporation. Considerable time and effort was spent by taxpayers in an effort to ensure that partnerships were not taxed under the corporate tax rules. These rules particularly affected limited partnerships, limited liability companies, and limited liability partnerships. The Treasury responded by issuing the check-the-box regulations that allow unincorporated business entities to elect whether they want to be taxed as corporations or partnerships.

Check-the-Box Regulations

In 1996 final regulations were issued that substantially changed the manner in which business entities will be classified for tax purposes for tax years beginning after 1996. Commonly known as the check-the-box regulations, these regulations permit most unincorporated entities to elect whether to be taxed as an association or a partnership for federal income tax purposes. These regulations replace the four-factor test described above for most organizations. Reg. § § 301.7701-1, 301.7701-2, and 301.7701-3.

The regulations are designed to provide most eligible entities with the classification they would choose without requiring them to file an election by providing several default rules. An eligible entity that wants the default classification need not file an election. A partnership is defined as any business entity that has at least two members and that is not classified as a corporation. Therefore, the default classification rules vary depending on whether the entity has only one owner or more than one owner.

If the entity has more than one owner, the default classification is partnership status. If the business owners wish to be taxed as an association, they can elect to do so. A business entity with a single owner will be disregarded as an entity separate from its owner. If the owner is an individual, the disregarded entity will be treated similarly to a sole proprietorship. If the owner is a corporation, the disregarded entity will be treated as a branch or division of the corporation. A single-member-owned entity may also elect to be taxed as an association.

An eligible entity that does not want the classification provided by the applicable default provision, or that wants to change its classification, may file an election on Form 8832 (Entity Classification Election) to obtain the chosen classification at the appropriate service center. The election will be effective on a date specified on the election if that date is not more than 75 days prior to the date on which the election is filed, or on the date filed if no such date is specified on the election. A business entity that makes an election must file a copy of its election with its federal tax return for the year in which the election is effective.

The rules described above apply to domestic organizations. The classification rules for foreign entities are similar. Also, note that there may be tax consequences for an existing entity to elect a different tax treatment. For example, if an existing corporation elects to be taxed as a partnership, the election would be treated as a liquidation of the corporation, which could result in a tax liability to the corporation and its shareholders.

The implications of the check-the-box regulations are significant. Under prior law, business owners had to determine whether the price of double taxation was worth the benefits to be achieved from organizing as a corporation. Owners who believed that they needed three or four corporate characteristics to attract sufficient capital into their business had to be taxed as a corporation subject to double taxation. Under the check-the-box regulations, business owners will no longer be faced with this dilemma. Each business (that is not a per se corporation) can simply elect the manner in which it wishes to be taxed. Since organizations incorporated under state law will be taxed as corporations, entities that want to be taxed as partnerships and that have many corporate characteristics will often organize as limited liability companies.

Given these changes, the only major issue that could prevent a business from not being taxed as a partnership is the publicly traded partnership (PTP) rules. Section 7704(a) taxes publicly traded partnerships as corporations. When this provision was added to the tax law effective in 1987, existing publicly traded partnerships were grandfathered for a 10-year period. The Taxpayer Relief Act (TRA '97) allows grandfathered publicly traded partnerships to elect to continue to be taxed as partnerships as long as they do not add a substantial new line of business. Code Sec. 7704(g). However, a partnership that makes this election will be subject to a 3.5 percent tax on the gross income from the conduct of a trade or business.

Co-ownership of Property

The mere co-ownership of business property does not create a partnership for tax purposes. The parties must be involved in the active conduct of a trade or business. What is an active conduct of a business is a question of fact. A partnership usually is found to exist, for example, where co-owners of an apartment building lease space and provide substantial services to tenants. On the other hand, where no substantial services are provided, the mere co-ownership of property that is maintained, kept in repair, and rented or leased does not constitute a partnership.

> *Example 18.2.* George and Henry Houck are brothers who inherited equal ownership interests as tenants in common in unimproved real estate lying in a rural part of the county. They presently rent this land to a farmer to pasture his cattle. They merely receive the pasturage fees and pay the real estate tax on the land. Their joint ownership does not constitute a partnership.

> *Example 18.3.* If the inherited property in Example 18.2 had been an office building that the brothers, or either one of them, manage to the extent of locating tenants, collecting rentals, and providing janitorial services, supplies, and repairs, the co-tenancy could rise to the level of a partnership under tax law.

It appears to be substantially easier for taxpayers to prove they are not partners where their co-ownership interests are acquired in a transaction over which they have no control (e.g., through inheritance or by gift). It is much more difficult to bear the burden of proof when the interests are acquired by purchase, or through the liquidation of a corporation. Compare *Estate of E.S. Appleby,* 41 BTA 18 (1940), aff'd on other grounds, 41-2 USTC ¶ 9773, 123 F.2d 700 (CA-2 1941) (co-tenants of inherited property not partners); *L.L. Powell,* 26 TCM 161, CCH Dec. 28,348(M), T.C. Memo. 1967-32 (1967) (co-tenants of inherited farm not partners though partnership return was filed); with *M. Demirjian,* 54 TC 1691, CCH Dec. 30,221 (1970), aff'd, 72-1 USTC ¶ 9281, 457 F.2d 1 (CA-3 1972) (co-ownership by corporate liquidation held to be partners) and *G. Rothenberg,* 48 TC 369, CCH Dec. 28,511 (1967) (co-ownership through purchase held to be partners).

Sharing Profits

The mere right to share in the venture's profits does not necessarily make the recipient a partner. An employee may be paid a share of the profits of a business as compensation, or a creditor may receive a percentage of the business income as interest on a loan, but such arrangements do not cause either recipient to be a partner under local law or under tax law because there is no ownership in the partnership. Also, a partnership is not created simply because the joint undertaking requires the participants to share in the expenses of the enterprise.

Agreements to Not Be Taxed as a Partnership

It might seem that if the parties wish to establish association status, an agreement could be fashioned that would negate most, if not all, of the partnership characteristics. However, it is well settled that the entity characteristics determined under state law usually cannot be changed merely by agreement among the partners.

Example 18.4. Amy Lowe, Betty Norris, and Charlotte Place entered into a venture in a state which has in effect the Uniform Partnership Act. Their agreement provides as follows: Amy is the managing partner and has absolute authority to perform any acts of the partnership in its ordinary operations; only the sale of all of the essential assets of the partnership or its merger into another entity requires consent of all partners; any partner can convey her interest to anyone without prior consent of the other partners; and the disability, death, or bankruptcy of a partner, or the conveyance of her interest will not dissolve the partnership. While superficially the entity appears to possess (1) centralized management, (2) transferability of interests, and (3) continuity of life, and thus to qualify as an "association taxable as a corporation," the entity is a partnership because any partner has the *power* under the law to withdraw from the contractual arrangement and bring the Uniform Partnership Act into play.

Exclusion from Partnership Treatment

The Commissioner may excuse certain partnerships from filing a partnership return. Only a small number of electing unincorporated organizations are not required to file a return—those which are formed (1) for investment purposes only (not for the active conduct of a business), (2) for the joint production, extraction, or use of property (but not for the purpose of selling services or property produced or extracted), or (3) by dealers in securities for a short period for the purpose of underwriting, selling, or distributing a particular issue of securities. All members of the organization must join in the election, and permission to be excluded from filing a partnership return will be granted only if the income of the partners may be adequately determined without the separate computation of the partnership's taxable income. Code Sec. 761. The entity generally must file a partnership return, Form 1065, in order to elect out of Subchapter K, but it is not required to file the partnership return in later years.

Limited Liability Companies and Limited Liability Partnerships

The limited liability company is a new business form that is governed by state law. Almost all states have created limited liability company (LLC) statutes during the last 10 years. The advantage of LLCs is that the entity is taxed like a partnership, while all members have limited liability. Thus, the entity combines single taxation and limited liability for all owners, the two characteristics most often desired in a business entity. While these characteristics also apply to all owners for S corporations, LLCs do not have rigid eligibility requirements like those of S corporations. Additionally, LLCs tend to be preferable to limited partnerships, because a limited partnership must have one general partner that has unlimited liability. Further, if a limited partner participates in the management of the partnership, then the partner may be treated as a general partner having unlimited liability. LLC members can participate in the management of the business without risking the loss of their limited liability protection.

5

Under prior law, an LLC had to ensure that it had no more than two corporate characteristics to be taxed as a partnership. The IRS has specified the conditions under which it will consider a ruling request that relates to classification of an LLC as a partnership for federal tax purposes. This revenue procedure defines how the corporate characteristics will be applied to LLCs. Rev. Proc. 95-10, 1995-1 CB 501. However, now that the check-the-box regulations have been finalized, the LLC can elect to be taxed as a partnership. While the LLC form offers numerous benefits to business owners, the lack of uniformity of LLC statutes across states and the lack of tax guidance in many areas where questions have arisen concerning LLCs have led some business owners to be reluctant to opt for this business form.

Existing businesses organized as partnerships or corporations would have to change their business form to become LLCs. For partnerships, the conversion to an LLC is generally free of any tax consequences. Rev. Rul. 95-37, 1995-1 CB 130. However, corporations would have to liquidate before organizing as an LLC, and liquidation taxes may be generated to the corporation under Section 336 and to the shareholders under Section 331. Therefore, existing corporations may find it too expensive to change their entity form to the LLC.

Since 1991 several states have created another entity form, the limited liability partnership (LLP). The partners in an LLP are similar to general partners that are jointly and severally liable for all partnership debts, with one important distinction. Partners in an LLP are not personally liable for the malpractice and torts of other partners. However, with this one exception LLP partners have unlimited liability. Thus, LLP partners are jointly and severally liable for the contractual liabilities of the partnership, and each partner is personally liable for claims arising from his own malpractice and torts. The conversion of a general partnership into an LLP is also generally free of tax consequences. IRS Letter Rulings 9229016, 9420028, and 9426038.

Anti-abuse Regulations

While the tax law allows partners a great deal of flexibility in how they wish to structure their partnership and share items of income and loss, this flexibility also creates opportunities for abuse. That is, partners may structure transactions to secure tax benefits that were never intended when the statute was created. Numerous regulations have been written over the last several years that are directed at preventing, or at least mitigating, the tax benefits received from such abusive transactions. These regulations have achieved varying degrees of success in accomplishing this purpose. Therefore, in 1995 the IRS finalized regulations which provide very broad anti-abuse rules that allow the IRS to disregard the form of a partnership transaction if it believes that the transaction is abusive.

The regulations now require that:

1. the partnership must be bona fide, and each partnership transaction or series of related transactions must be entered into for a substantial business purpose,

2. the form of each partnership transaction must be respected under substance-over-form principles, and

3. the tax consequences under Subchapter K to each partner of partnership operations and of transactions between the partner and the partnership must, subject to certain exceptions, accurately reflect the partners' economic agreement and clearly reflect the partners' income.

The government can recast transactions that substantially reduce the partners' tax liability in a way that violates the deemed intent of Subchapter K. Recasting can include one or more of the following:

1. disregarding the partnership, with the partnership's assets and activities considered to be owned and conducted by one or more of the partners,

2. treating a partner as not being a partner,

3. reallocating partnership items,

4. adjusting a partner's or the partnership's method of accounting to reflect income clearly, or

5. otherwise adjusting or modifying the tax treatment at issue.

The evidence of abusive intent is determined based on all the relevant facts and circumstances. The regulations are generally effective for all transactions occurring on or after May 12, 1994. Of course, the language used in these regulations is quite subjective. Therefore, practitioners are very concerned about how the IRS will apply these regulations, and disagreements over its application are inevitable. Reg. § 1.701-2.

Formation of a Partnership—Tax Consequences

¶ 18,015   CONTRIBUTIONS TO A PARTNERSHIP

At the inception of a partnership, the organizers do not purchase an interest; they contribute assets and receive in exchange an interest in the partnership's capital and future income. Contributions of property in exchange for partnership interests are generally treated as nontaxable exchanges with no gain or loss recognized either to the partnership or to its partners. The tax-free treatment applies whether the contribution is made to a partnership at formation or to a partnership that already is formed and operating. Code Sec. 721; Reg. § 1.721-1(a). The tax-free treatment also applies to conversions of domestic partnerships into domestic limited liability companies that are classified as partnerships for federal tax purposes. Rev. Rul. 95-37, 1995-1 CB 130.

Example 18.5. Ida Frank and James Stein form their partnership by transferring the following property in exchange for equal partnership interests: Ida contributes $10,000 cash, and James contributes unimproved real estate with a fair market value of $10,000 and a basis to him of $5,000. Because he has received value of $10,000 in exchange for property with a basis of $5,000, James realizes a gain of $5,000 on the transfer, but he does not currently recognize it.

Investors who acquire partnership interests for cash from an underwriter in a public offering are treated as contributing the cash to the partnership in exchange for the interests if their underwriter is acting as an agent of the partnership or the underwriter's ownership of the interests is transitory. Reg. § 1.721-1(c).

Transfers to an Investment Company Partnership

Many investors have found themselves "locked-in" to their ownership of appreciated securities. Their unrealized gain is so great that the tax on a sale would seriously deplete the value of their investment portfolio. To a degree, these investors can pool their securities in common ownership and diversify their risk. If this can be done without income tax consequences, all the better. However, a device for the diversification of an investment portfolio without immediate tax impact cannot be achieved by merely forming a partnership with fellow investors, if the result is the creation of an "investment company" partnership. Code Sec. 721(b). An investment company partnership will be found to exist if after the transfer (1) over 80 percent of the partnership assets (excluding cash and nonconvertible debt obligations) are held for investment, and (2) those assets are readily marketable stocks or securities (or interests in regulated investment companies or real estate investment trusts). Reg. § 1.351-1(c)(1). If the assets meet these two tests and the transfer results, directly or indirectly, in diversification of the partners' interests upon their contribution to the partnership, all the realized gain, but not loss, on all the contributed assets (not merely the appreciated stock and securities, etc.) is recognized by the transferors.

Example 18.6. Kelly Washburn, Marsha Curth, and Nelson Manning form an equal partnership, and they transfer to the new partnership the following marketable securities, land, and cash:

			Basis to Transferor	Fair Market Value
Kelly	—	I.P.M. stock	$10,000	$ 49,000
Marsha	—	R.R.S. stock	5,000	30,000
	—	P.D.Q. stock	20,000	10,000
Nelson	—	Cash	10,000	10,000
	—	Land	20,000	21,000
			$65,000	$120,000

Excluding the cash of $10,000, $89,000 of the remaining $110,000 of the fair market value of the transferred assets consists of marketable securities. All the parties have received diversification of their investments. Code Sec. 721(b) causes Kelly to recognize the $39,000 of gain on the I.P.M. stock, Marsha to recognize the $25,000 of gain on the R.R.S. stock, and Nelson to recognize the $1,000 of gain on the land. The loss of $10,000 realized by Marsha on the P.D.Q. stock is not recognized.

As with most statutes which are strictly drawn, careful planning, particularly in structuring the asset mix, will permit the avoidance of investment company classification. For example, tax-free treatment is available if each transferor transfers a diversified portfolio of securities to a partnership. Reg. § 1.351-1(c)(6). Thus, if Kelly, Marsha, and Nelson in the above example had each owned a portfolio of securities representing ownership in different publicly traded companies, the combination of these portfolios in an equal partnership would avoid recognition of gain.

Transfer of Services for Partnership Capital Interest

When a partner contributes services in exchange for an interest in the capital of the partnership, the nonrecognition provision does not apply. The capital interest (as distinguished from a share in partnership profits) is taxed to the partner as compensation, and it is ordinary income to the extent of the fair market value of the transferred interest. Code Sec. 83(a). The value is determined either at the time the transfer is made, for past services, or at the time the services are rendered, where the transfer is conditioned on the completion of the transferee's future services.

Transfer of Services for Partnership Income Interest

An interest in the future income of a partnership is generally not taxable to the recipient of the interest until the income of the partnership is realized and recognized. The reason for deferring the recognition of income is because of the difficulty in determining a market value of the speculative future profits. Usually, difficulty in determining fair market value is an inadequate reason for not reporting the fair market value of property received in connection with services. In an early Tax Court case, the fair market value of a profits interest received for services was required to be included in the service partner's income. Fair market value was measured easily because the interest was sold within three weeks after it was received. *S. Diamond,* 56 TC 930, CCH Dec. 30,838 (1971), aff'd, 74-1 USTC ¶ 9306, 492 F.2d 286 (CA-7, 1974). A later decision used liquidation value, that is, the amount the partner would receive were the partnership terminated, to measure the amount to be included in the service partner's income. *D. St. John,* 84-1 USTC ¶ 9158 (CD Ill., 1983). In a more recent decision, an appellate court admitted the difficulty of measuring the amount to include in income. On the basis of the facts in the case, the court overturned the Tax Court by holding that the receipt of a profits interest for services was not taxable. *W. Campbell,* 91-2 USTC ¶ 50,420 (CA-8, 1991), aff'g and rev'g 59 TCM 236, CCH Dec. 46,493(M), T.C. Memo. 1990-162. In order to reduce litigation on this issue, the Internal Revenue Service announced that it will not treat the receipt of an interest in the future income of a partnership as a taxable event for a partner unless: (1) the interest relates to a certain and predictable stream of income from partnership assets, (2) the partner disposes of the interest within two years of its receipt, or (3) the interest is a limited partnership interest in a "publicly traded partnership." Rev. Proc. 93-27, 1993-2 CB 343.

Deferral of Recognition of Income

If the capital interest, or the right to the future income, has a readily ascertainable value but it is subject to substantial restrictions which could effect a forfeiture or the interest or right is not transferable, the partner can delay recognition of the income until those restrictions lapse, or the interest or right is transferable, whichever occurs earlier.

Deductibility by Transferor of Partnership Interest

The tax consequences of a contribution of services to the partnership must be understood not only for the partner, but also for the partnership. The partnership interest may be transferred by a present holder or holders of the interest, or the interest may be created in the partnership itself.

The transferor of the partnership interest is generally entitled to a deduction or a basis adjustment for payment made to the partner in the form of the partnership interest. If the payment qualifies as an ordinary and necessary expense, e.g., compensation for services rendered to the partnership (or to the partner if he or she is the transferor), it is currently deductible. Code Secs. 707(c) and 162. If the payment is for a capital expenditure, it must be capitalized and written off over the appropriate cost recovery period for the asset. Code Sec. 263. The transfer of the partnership interest can result in recognition of income by the existing partners and an adjustment of their bases in their partnership interests.

Example 18.7. Barko is a cash-basis partnership, comprised of three equal partners with capital balances as shown below. Barko admits Harold Jackson into the partnership, giving him a one-fourth interest in the capital of the partnership. This interest is in payment of services previously rendered by Harold to the Barko Partnership.

	Capital Interests Before		Capital Interests After	
	Basis	F.M.V.	Basis	F.M.V.
Partner 1	$30,000	$60,000	$22,500	$45,000
Partner 2	$30,000	$60,000	$22,500	$45,000
Partner 3	$30,000	$60,000	$22,500	$45,000
Harold Jackson			$45,000	$45,000

Harold has ordinary income of $45,000, the fair market value of his one-fourth capital interest. If the transfer were contingent upon Harold's performance of future services, the transfer would be deemed to take place when those services were rendered and the income would be reportable by him at that time.

Partners 1, 2, and 3 each have a new basis of $22,500 because they recognize a gain of $7,500 in transferring partnership assets with a basis of $7,500 and a fair market value of $15,000, but they each have a reduction of $15,000 in basis for their share of the compensation deduction.

The above example covers the transfer of a capital interest in connection with services. Recall that when the transfer is one of a future partnership income interest, the transaction may or may not be taxable (due to conflicting court decisions) and the difficulty of measuring the value of the future interest should result in no income recognition at transfer.

Transfer of Goodwill for Partnership Interest

Accounting texts are replete with examples in which goodwill is allowed an incoming partner. The new partner (or a member of a firm in the process of organization) is given a credit to his or her capital account in recognition of customers or clients brought into the partnership. The offsetting accounting entry is, of course, to goodwill. As goodwill's standing as "property" for tax purposes is well established, there would seem to be no reason why it cannot be recognized as property susceptible to a tax-free exchange for a capital interest in a partnership.

> *Example 18.8.* If Charles Wesley contributes $10,000 cash and David Cohen contributes $5,000 worth of tangible property, plus goodwill at an agreed value of $5,000, to a partnership in which each has a 50 percent interest, David should recognize no taxable gain at the time of the transfer. Since, however, his goodwill theoretically has a zero basis, he will probably recognize gain on any subsequent sale or other disposition of his interest.

Somewhat akin to both goodwill and a promise to perform future services is the unique ability to do certain things which is called "know-how." Several courts have recognized such an attribute as a present asset and analogized it to goodwill and given it comparable treatment.

¶ 18,025 ACCOUNTING CONCEPT OF PARTNERSHIP INTEREST

For accounting purposes, a partner's "capital account" represents the partner's interest in the firm. The initial balance generally reflects the fair market value of the net assets contributed to the partnership. Thereafter, the balance in a partner's capital account at any time when the books have been adjusted and closed consists of:

1. The dollar value of the partner's contributions to the capital of the firm, plus

2. The partner's distributive share of partnership profits for each year of membership, less

3. The partner's distributive share of losses, and less

4. The amounts of money or other property that the partner has withdrawn from the partnership for the partner's own use.

The aggregate of the partners' capital accounts equals the net worth of the firm, that is, the amount by which the total carrying value of the firm's assets exceeds its liabilities. When a partner sells the interest in the partnership, the partner (or at least the accountant) usually thinks in terms of selling the partner's "capital account," that is, the partner's share of the firm's net worth.

As the tax basis of the property to the contributing partner often differs from the fair market value of that property, and a like disparity exists upon distributions of property to the partners by the partnership, rarely do the book values of the capital balances equal their tax basis. Accordingly, some accountants prefer to keep partnership books on the tax basis and avoid the reconciliation problems. However, partnerships that want to specially allocate items must maintain capital accounts as provided in Reg. § 1.704-1(b)(2)(iv).

¶ 18,035   TAX CONCEPT OF PARTNERSHIP INTEREST

The tax law provides rules for determining the partner's basis for an interest at acquisition and rules for adjusting that basis to reflect subsequent transactions. Code Sec. 705(a); Reg. § 1.705-1(a). Where a partnership interest is acquired by the contribution of money or other property, the partner's basis in the partnership interest is the sum of the amount of money plus the adjusted basis of the other property in the hands of the contributing partner immediately before the transfer. Code Sec. 722; Reg. § 1.722-1. If the partner assumes a share of partnership liabilities, the share is treated like a contribution of money. Code Sec. 752.

> *Example 18.9.* Mo Petty contributes $3,000 cash and property with an adjusted basis of $7,000 and a fair market value of $15,000 to the Smith partnership in exchange for a 25 percent interest in partnership capital and profits and losses. The Smith partnership has $16,000 of liabilities of which Mo takes a 25 percent share. Mo's basis in his partnership interest is $14,000 [$3,000 + $7,000 + (25%) ($16,000)].

Note that the capital account measures the value of a partner's interest, whereas basis measures the partner's investment in the partnership.

In the tax law, a partnership interest is regarded not as an undivided interest in the net worth of the firm, the entity approach, but as an undivided interest in the assets of the firm, the aggregate approach. Such a concept, of course, requires that each partner also be treated as being individually subject to a pro rata share of all partnership liabilities. Recall that the basis of the partner's interest includes a pro rata share of all partnership liabilities, whether those liabilities are created by the partnership itself or are imposed on the partnership by the contribution of encumbered property by the partners.

> *Example 18.10.* Quincy Happ and Rachel Rist each contributes $5,000 cash to the Que-Ray Partnership on its formation. The partnership immediately expends $4,000 as the down payment on the purchase of a $20,000 building, giving a $16,000 mortgage for the balance of the purchase price. The basis of each partner's interest immediately after organization of the firm is $5,000, but each interest increases to $13,000 when the building is purchased. The partnership interest of each partner is considered to be one-

half of the $26,000 of assets. Each partner is treated as owning one-half of the mortgage debt, and the basis for the interest in the partnership of each of the partners is $13,000 ($5,000 cash contribution plus one-half of the $16,000 debt).

Acquisition by Purchase, Gift, or Inheritance

If the partnership interest is acquired other than by contribution, the usual basis rules apply. Code Sec. 742. Thus, the initial basis of a purchased interest is its cost. If the interest is inherited, its basis is its fair market value at the time of the decedent's death or at the optional valuation date. Code Sec. 1014.

Example 18.11. Father owned an interest in the Acme Partnership. His basis for the interest was $10,000, but its fair market value was $5,000 on the date of his death when his son inherited the partnership interest. The son's basis for the interest is $5,000, the date of death value.

If the interest is acquired by gift, the donee's basis for determining gain is the same as that of the donor, and the basis for determining loss is the lesser of the donor's basis or the fair market value of the interest at the time of the gift. Code Sec. 1015.

Example 18.12. If the father in Example 18.11 had made an inter vivos gift of the partnership interest to his son, the interest would have a basis of $5,000 for purposes of determining loss and a $10,000 basis for determining gain. Any sale of the interest for amounts between $5,000 and $10,000 would result in neither gain nor loss recognition by the son.

If a partnership interest, or an addition to such an interest, is acquired as compensation for services, the timing of the resultant taxable income determines the recipient's basis effect for the interest. Reg. § § 1.721-1(b)(1) and 1.722-1.

¶ 18,045   ADJUSTMENTS TO BASIS OF PARTNER'S INTEREST

The original basis of a partnership interest is increased or decreased by almost every subsequent transaction of the partnership. Actually, two different sets of rules must be applied. One set deals with adjustments to reflect changes in the partnership's (or partner's) liabilities. Code Sec. 752. We mentioned above how the bases of the partners increase with the increase in partnership liabilities and how those bases decrease with the decrease in partnership liabilities. Another set of rules provides for the reflection in the partners' bases of income, losses, contributions, and distributions. Code Sec. 705(a); Reg. § 1.705-1(a).

A partner's basis is increased by the sum of the partner's distributive share of the taxable income of the partnership (including capital gains). This adjustment is necessary to insure that the income is only taxed once. Otherwise, this income would be taxed a second time when the partner sold the partnership because the value of the interest would have increased but the basis would be the same. In addition, the partner's basis is also increased by any tax-exempt income of the partnership (such as municipal bond interest and life insurance proceeds). This adjustment is necessary to prevent the income from being taxed when a partner sells a partnership interest or receives a cash distribution from the partnership.

> *Example 18.13.* Thomas Nelson, Jonathan McCoy, and Ned Bush are equal partners in the TJN Partnership. The partnership's only asset is a municipal bond. The basis and fair market value of the bond to the partnership are $6,000. Each partner has a $2,000 basis in his partnership interest. The partnership receives $300 of tax-exempt interest on the bond. Each partner increases the basis of his partnership interest by $100.
>
> If Thomas sells his interest for $2,100 (($6,000 + $300) ÷ 3), he has no gain. If he had not increased the basis of his interest by his $100 share of the tax-exempt interest, he would have a $100 gain when he sold his interest, and the tax-exempt income would be taxed.
>
> *Example 18.14.* The facts from Example 18.13 are unchanged with one exception: Thomas receives a $2,100 cash distribution in liquidation of his partnership interest. Had the basis of his partnership interest not been increased by his $100 share, he would report a $100 gain and, again, the tax-exempt income would be taxed.

In addition, the partner's basis is increased by the excess of the deduction for depletion over the basis of depletable property. If this adjustment were not made, the advantage of the percentage deduction in excess of asset basis, passed through to the partner in reducing taxable income of the partnership, would be negated when the partner sold the partnership interest.

A partner's basis is decreased (but not below zero) for any distributions of money or other property by the basis that the partnership has in the property. Any decrease in the partner's share of partnership debts or the assumption by the firm of the partner's debts is treated as a distribution of money. Distributions of money, including deemed distributions resulting from decreases in a partner's share of partnership liabilities, are treated as occurring on the last day of the partnership's taxable year to the extent of the partner's share of partnership income for the year. Reg. § 1.731-1(a)(1); Rev. Rul. 94-4, 1994-1 CB 195.

The partner's basis is also decreased by the sum of the partner's distributive share of partnership losses, including capital losses and partnership expenditures that are not deductible in computing taxable income (such as charitable contributions and penalty payments). Capital expenditures are not currently deductible, but their amortization or depreciation reduces partnership income. The partner's deduction for depletion for any partnership oil and gas property is limited to the partner's proportionate share of the adjusted basis of such property. Code Secs. 705(a)(3) and 613A(c)(7)(D).

Example 18.15. Michael Anderson is· a partner in a general partnership, Lester Partnership. Michael has a 25 percent interest in capital and profits and losses. At the beginning of the current year, Michael has a $15,000 basis in his partnership interest. For the current year, the partnership has the following items:

Ordinary income	$80,000
Capital losses	10,000
Tax-exempt income	4,000
Charitable contributions	2,000

In addition, Michael receives a $10,000 cash distribution. Also, the partnership pays off a $12,000 liability.

Michael's basis in his partnership interest at the end of the current year is $20,000, computed as follows:

Basis, beginning of the current year		$15,000
Add Michael's share of:		
Ordinary income	$20,000	
Tax-exempt income	1,000	21,000
Deduct Michael's share of:		
Capital losses	$ 2,500	
Charitable contributions	500	
Distributions	10,000	
Reduction in partnership's liabilities	3,000	(16,000)
Basis, end of the current year		$20,000

¶ 18,055   BASIS TO THE PARTNERSHIP OF CONTRIBUTED PROPERTY

To this point, the adjustments that need to be made to the basis of the partner's interest have been discussed. Here, the focus shifts to the partnership itself. The basis to a partnership of property contributed to it by a partner is generally the same as the adjusted basis of the property in the hands of the contributing partner at the time of contribution. Code Sec. 723; *L.L. Culley,* 29 TC 1076, CCH Dec. 22,877 (1958), acq. 1958-2 CB 4. Personal (nonbusiness) property which is converted into business property by contribution to the partnership has as its basis the lower of the basis to the contributing partner or the fair market value of the property at the time of the contribution. *L.Y.S. Au,* 40 TC 264, CCH Dec. 26,110 (1963), aff'd per curiam, 64-1 USTC ¶ 9447, 330 F.2d 1008 (CA-9 1964), cert. denied, 379 U.S. 960, 85 S.Ct. 648 (1965). The partnership's holding period of the contributed property includes that of the contributing partner. Reg. § 1.723-1; Code Sec. 1223(2).

Example 18.16. Archie Drew contributes to his partnership his hunting lodge, a capital asset, which cost him $12,000 a year ago. As the lodge was used solely for personal purposes, no depreciation deduction has been taken. At the time of his contribution, the fair market value of the property is $8,000. The basis of the lodge to the partnership is $8,000, the lower of the two amounts. If the partnership holds the lodge for investment and if it were to sell the lodge for $7,900 one month after its acquisition, it would have a long-term capital loss of $100.

¶ 18,101 CONTRIBUTION OF ENCUMBERED PROPERTY

When encumbered property is contributed to a partnership, there is a dual adjustment. The contributing partner is relieved of a part of the total obligation to repay the loan, and the other partners are deemed to have accepted individual responsibility to repay their pro rata share of the debt. Thus, if the contributed property is subject to liability, or if liabilities of the contributing partner are assumed by the partnership, the basis of the contributing partner's interest is reduced by the portion of the indebtedness deemed transferred to the other partners. This deemed transfer is treated as a distribution of cash to the contributing partner. The assumption of the contributing partner's liabilities is treated by the other partners as a contribution of money by them to the partnership. Reg. §§ 1.722-1 and 1.752-1.

A partner's basis cannot be reduced below zero, so when a deemed distribution of money exceeds the basis of the partnership interest of the contributing partner, that excess, which otherwise would generate a negative basis, is considered as the proceeds from the sale of the partnership interest and is given capital gain treatment. Code Sec. 731(a).

Example 18.17. Archie Drew acquired a 20 percent interest in a partnership by contributing property. At the time of Archie's contribution, the property had a fair market value of $10,000 and an adjusted basis to Archie of $4,000, and it was encumbered by a mortgage of $2,000. Payment of the mortgage was assumed by the partnership. Archie's basis in his partnership interest is $2,400, computed as follows:

Adjusted basis of property		$4,000
Liability effect:		
Deemed distribution (100% × $2,000)	$(2,000)	
Deemed contribution (20% × $2,000)	400	
Net deemed distribution		(1,600)
Archie's basis in his partnership interest		$2,400

See Reg. § 1.722-1, Example (1). Notice that the net deemed distribution, that is, the net liability relief to the contributing partner, generally is calculated as follows: amount of liabilities transferred × (1 − contributing partner's interest in the partnership).

Example 18.18. If, in Example 18.17, the property contributed by Archie was encumbered by a mortgage of $6,000, the analysis of the transaction would be the same. However, because of the larger debt, the basis of Archie's interest would be zero. Archie's adjusted basis of $4,000 in the contributed property is reduced by the net deemed distribution of $4,800 [$6,000 × (1 − 20%)]. Since his basis cannot be less than zero, Archie reports a capital gain of $800 ($4,800 − $4,000) upon his contribution.

TAX PLANNING POINTER ▼

If a partner recognizes gain on the contribution of appreciated property that is encumbered by a liability, the partnership can increase the basis of that property by making an election under Code Sec. 754. See ¶ 19,361.

¶ 18,125   LIABILITIES ASSUMED BY PARTNERSHIP

When the partnership assumes a liability (agrees to pay the debt if the collateral should be insufficient on foreclosure), the entire liability is added to the partners' bases. But where the partnership merely takes property subject to a liability (the partnership is not liable for any deficiency), the debt is reflected in the partners' bases only to the extent of the lower of (1) the amount of the debt, or (2) the fair market value of the property which is subject to the debt. Code Sec. 752(c).

Example 18.19. Mary and Anne King each own a 50 percent interest in the MaryAnne partnership. The partnership is owed $1,000 by a customer who is unable to pay. The customer owns an asset which has a fair market value of $70,000 but which is encumbered by an $80,000 mortgage. Hoping that the property will increase in value, the MaryAnne partnership accepts the property in satisfaction of the $1,000, taking it subject to the mortgage but not assuming personal liability. The bases of the partners' interests in the Mary-Anne partnership are increased by $70,000. The basis of the property to the partnership is $81,000. (See ¶ 18,551 for the at-risk limitation on passthrough losses where the creditor has no recourse against the individual partners upon default in payment of the debt.)

Recourse and Nonrecourse Liabilities

Although the term "assumption" was used above with respect to the transfer of encumbered assets, so long as the value of the transferred property is at least as great as the encumbrance, the same treatment is given those debts which are legally assumed and those debts where the property is merely taken subject to the encumbrance. From a practical standpoint, in both situations the partnership intends to retire the outstanding debt.

A borrower may wish to obtain funds but not be personally liable for the repayment of the debt. If a lender agrees to look for repayment only to the activity being financed, the debt is said to be a "nonrecourse debt." Otherwise, the debt is "recourse debt." Both types of debt increase the basis of a partner in the partnership interest. When the partner sells the interest in the partnership, the debt is added to the sales price, causing the debt to, in effect, wash out in the transaction. For nonrecourse debt, however, as the partner has no personal risk of loss if the debt is not repaid, such debt is not available to offset partnership pass-through losses. See ¶ 18,551 for further discussion.

Allocation of Recourse Liabilities to the Partners' Bases

Effective for recourse liabilities incurred after December 28, 1991, a partner's share of a recourse partnership liability is the amount of the liability for which the partner bears the economic risk of loss. Reg. § 1.752-2(a). In general, recourse liabilities are allocated to the partners using the constructive liquidation scenario. Reg. § 1.752-2(b). Under this scenario, all of the following are deemed to occur simultaneously:

1. All of the partnership liabilities become payable in full,

2. All of the partnership assets (including cash but excluding property contributed to secure a partnership liability) become worthless,

3. The partnership disposes of its assets for no consideration in a fully taxable transaction,

4. All items of income, gain, loss, or deduction are allocated to the partners, and

5. The partnership liquidates.

Partners with deficit capital accounts after the allocation of losses on the hypothetical sale are required to contribute cash to the partnership to the extent of the deficit in their capital accounts. Recourse liabilities are allocated to the partners to the extent they would be required to contribute cash to restore deficit capital accounts.

Example 18.20. Bob Anderson and Ted Carr each contributed $500 to the BT Partnership. The partnership purchased machinery for $3,000, using $500 cash and a note payable of $2,500. Bob is allocated 60 percent of the losses, while Ted is allocated 40 percent of the losses. The partnership agreement requires that, upon liquidation, partners with deficit capital accounts must contribute cash of that amount to the partnership. The books of the partnership reflect the following.

	Basis	Fair Market Value
Cash	$ 500	$ 500
Machinery	3,000	3,000
	$3,500	$3,500
Recourse liability	$2,500	$2,500
Bob, capital	500	500
Ted, capital	500	500
	$3,500	$3,500

The debt is allocated using the constructive liquidation scenario. Therefore, cash and machinery are deemed worthless and are sold for zero, generating a loss of $3,500. The loss is allocated 60 percent to Bob and 40 percent to Ted. After closing the losses to the partners' capital accounts, Bob has a deficit of $1,600 ($500 − .6 × $3,500) and Ted has a deficit of $900 ($500 − .4 × $3,500). Therefore, $1,600 of the debt is allocated to Bob, and $900 of the debt is allocated to Ted.

Allocation of Nonrecourse Liabilities to Partners' Bases

A partner's share of nonrecourse liabilities is the sum of his or her share of (1) minimum gain, (2) precontribution gain, and (3) excess nonrecourse liabilities. Reg. § 1.752-3(a). The minimum gain represents the excess of the amount of the nonrecourse debt over the adjusted tax basis of the property it encumbers. That is, if the debtholder were to take the property in satisfaction of the debt, a gain would arise. Reg. § 1.704-2(b). The partnership agreement should address how the minimum gain will be allocated.

The second part of the nonrecourse debt formula requires allocation of nonrecourse liabilities equal to the precontribution gain to the partner who contributed the property subject to a nonrecourse liability.

Example 18.21. Joe White contributed a property with a tax basis of $15,000 and a fair market value of $30,000 subject to a nonrecourse debt of $20,000. If the debtholder were to take the property in satisfaction of the debt, a $5,000 precontribution gain would arise. This would all be allocable to Joe since he contributed the property to the partnership.

Finally, the remainder of the nonrecourse liabilities is allocated to the partners based on their profit-sharing ratios. If in Example 18.21 Joe had a 50 percent interest in the profits of the partnership, he would be allocated 50 percent of the remaining $15,000 of the nonrecourse liability. His total nonrecourse liabilities would be $12,500 ($5,000 + .5 × $15,000).

¶ 18,135　DISGUISED SALES BETWEEN A PARTNER AND THE PARTNERSHIP

As has been stated earlier, when there is a contribution of property to the partnership in exchange for a partnership interest, generally, neither gain nor loss is recognized by the contributing partner. Also, when there is deemed to be a current distribution of money, the partner recognizes neither gain nor loss unless the deemed money distribution exceeds the partner's basis. If, however, in a contribution the two transactions are related so that a distribution closely follows a contribution, the two transactions, taken together, may constitute part contribution and part disguised sale.

If a partner contributes property to a partnership and subsequently receives a property distribution from the partnership, there are two ways the related transactions may be interpreted. One way is that the transactions are a nontaxable contribution and distribution to the partner. Code Secs. 721 and 731. Another way is that the transactions are, in effect, a disguised sale of the property by the partner to the partnership, producing taxable gain or loss to the selling partner. Code Sec. 707(a)(2)(B).

Effective for contribution/distribution transactions which both occur after April 24, 1991, if a transaction is treated as a disguised sale, then it is treated as a sale or exchange between the partnership and a person acting in a capacity other than as a partner. Reg. § 1.707-3.

Generally, a disguised sale will result if, based on all of the facts and circumstances, (1) a transfer of money or other consideration would not have been made but for the transfer of property to the partnership, and (2) assuming that the transfers are not made simultaneously, the subsequent transfer is not dependent on the entrepreneurial risks of partnership operations. There are 10 factors which tend to establish a sale (for example, if the partner has the legally enforceable right to the partnership's subsequent transfer and the partnership holds money or other liquid assets which are beyond the reasonable needs of the business and are expected to be available to make the transfer).

Any difference between the fair market value of the property transferred by the partner to the partnership and the fair market value of the property transferred by the partnership to the partner in a disguised sale is treated as a contribution by the partner to the partnership. The partner's adjusted basis in the transferred property is prorated between the portion of the property deemed sold and the portion of the property deemed contributed.

> *Example 18.22.* Jim Frink is a partner in the Johnson Partnership. On March 3, 1998, Jim transfers property to the partnership. The property is worth $400,000, and it has an adjusted basis of $120,000 to Jim. On April 15, 1998, the Johnson Partnership transfers $300,000 in cash to Jim. The transactions are treated as a partial disguised sale and a partial partnership contribution. As to the partial disguised sale, Jim is treated as having sold a portion of the property with a $300,000 fair market value to the partnership for cash. Of the $120,000 basis of the property, $90,000 (($300,000/$400,000) $\times$ $120,000) is used for the disguised sale. Thus, Jim has $210,000 of gain ($300,000 − $90,000). As to the partial partnership contribution, Jim is treated as having made a partnership contribution of $100,000 worth of property ($30,000 basis) to the partnership.

Contributions/distributions made within a two-year period are presumed to be disguised sales, and those made beyond a two-year period are presumed not to be sales. Each of these presumptions may be successfully rebutted only by facts and circumstances which clearly establish the contrary. There are exceptions to the two-year sale presumptions for guaranteed payments for capital, reasonable preferred returns, and operating cash flow distributions.

Liabilities incurred by a partner in anticipation of the transfer are treated as part of a sale to the extent that the liability is assumed by the partnership. Again, presumptions are established. Debt incurred more than two years before the transfer is not deemed to be in anticipation of the transfer, while debt incurred within the two-year period generally is considered to be in anticipation of the transfer.

The IRS requires that disclosure be made for transactions which could be covered by these disguised sale rules. In this regard, disclosure on Form 8275 (Disclosure Statement) or an attachment to the return of a partner receiving property generally is required for (1) contribution/distribution transfers within the two-year period, and (2) certain liabilities incurred within two years prior to a transfer of property securing the debt.

¶ 18,145　ORGANIZATION AND SYNDICATION COSTS

The concept of matching against income the expense of generating that income would require the capitalization of organization costs at the creation of an entity and the amortization of those costs over the life of the entity. Organization costs for a partnership are those costs paid or incurred to organize the partnership. Examples are legal and accounting fees to organize the partnership and filing fees. Reg. § 1.709-2(a). The costs incident to the creation of the partnership, chargeable to the capital account and expended in connection with the creation of a partnership having an ascertainable life, are amortized over that period of time. But as most partnerships are not created with a specific life in mind, these costs normally would not be deductible. However, a partnership may elect to amortize its organization expenses over a period of not less than 60 months. The write-off must begin with the first month of the partnership's commencement of business. Code Sec. 709. If the partnership is liquidated within the 60-month period, the unamortized balance may be deducted as a loss. Code Secs. 165 and 709.

> *Example 18.23.* A calendar-year partnership that incurred the following costs is formed:
>
> Attorneys' fees—drafting partnership agreement $1,500
> Recording costs—filing the legal documents 500
> Accounting fees—setting up books 4,000
>
> The partnership commenced business April 1, 1998. If it elects the minimum write-off period, it may amortize $900 ($6,000/60 × 9 months) of the organization costs in calendar-year 1998.

More restrictive rules apply to publicly held partnerships. For example, the costs of issuing and marketing interests in a partnership syndication, such as commissions, professional fees, and printing costs, must be capitalized and are not subject to amortization under the 60-month provision. Reg. § 1.709-2(b).

> *Example 18.24.* Assume the partnership formed in Example 18.23 was determined to be a syndication and the following costs were incurred:
>
> Commissions for sale of partnership interests $40,000
> Printing brochures 20,000
>
> The above costs would have to be capitalized. They could not be charged off against income. They could only be deducted upon the termination of the partnership.

¶ 18,201　START-UP EXPENDITURES

Closely akin to organization costs are start-up costs which are statutorily defined as (1) costs paid or incurred in connection with the investigation or acquisition of an active trade or business, (2) costs paid or incurred in the creation of such a trade or business, or (3) preactivity costs. The expenditures must be of a character which would qualify as ordinary and necessary expenses if the trade or business were active. These costs may, at the election of the taxpayer, be amortized over a period of time not less than 60 months, beginning with the month in which the active trade or business begins. Code Sec. 195.

¶ 18,225 TAXABLE INCOME OF PARTNER—YEAR OF INCLUSION

The partners must report their distributive share of income and losses of their partnership in the partner's taxable year in which or with which the partnership year ends. Code Sec. 706(a); Reg. § 1.706-1(a). This privilege, unless restricted, provides an opportunity for a perpetual deferral of substantial amounts of income.

> *Example 18.25.* Betty and John Jones each own a 50 percent interest in the BJ Partnership, which has a fiscal year ending June 30. During fiscal year 1997-98 the partnership has distributive taxable income of $120,000, which it earned ratably during the 12-month period. Thus, $60,000 was earned in 1997, and $60,000 was earned in 1998. Betty and John each will report partnership income of $60,000 in their taxable calendar year of 1998, although economically they each, through the partnership, earned $30,000 during calendar-year 1997. Notice that the taxation of the $60,000 earned by the partnership in 1997 is deferred until 1998 because the partners and the partnership have different year-ends.

The items includible and deductible on the partner's individual return are determined with reference to the partnership's method of accounting, without regard to whether the partner reports on the cash or the accrual basis. Guaranteed payments—determined without regard to profits of the partnership—made to a partner for services or for the use of capital are includible in the partner's income at the same time as the partner's distributive share of partnership income and losses.

> *Example 18.26.* Frank Flanagan and Max McCann are equal partners in the FM Partnership. Frank and Max both report their income on the calendar year using the cash method. For good business reasons, the partnership was permitted to use a June 30 fiscal year and the accrual method. For the fiscal year ending June 30, 1998, FM reports partnership ordinary income of $20,000 for each partner. Payment of all sums to Frank and Max was actually delayed until January 1999. Frank and Max must each report $20,000 as their 1998 income—the income earned by the partnership under its method of accounting for its fiscal year ending June 30, 1998.

See ¶ 18,335 for a discussion of changes in this general year-end reporting rule with respect to certain cash-basis items. These items are, in effect, placed on the accrual basis to prevent year-end incoming partners from benefiting from deductions incurred by the partnership prior to their admission.

Varying Interest Rule

The varying interest rule applies to any partner whose interest in a partnership is reduced, whether by entry of a new partner who purchased an interest directly from the partnership, partial liquidation of a partner's interest, gift, or otherwise. It also applies to the incoming partner. Code Sec. 706(d)(1). In essence, the partnership may comply with either of two methods of prorating items of income and expense of the partnership. It may prorate such items on a day-by-day basis through the year in which the change of ownership occurred, or it may treat its books as having been closed for this purpose, thus segmenting the tax year into that period of time prior to the change and that period of time following. It may also use any other reasonable method to prorate income and expense items. Reg. § 1.706-1(c)(2)(ii). Accordingly, an agreement cannot be modified to assign a full year's income to a partner who acquires an interest at midyear. The partners cannot in their agreement override the statutory provision. Code Sec. 704(f).

¶ 18,235   TAXABLE YEAR OF THE PARTNERSHIP

Required Taxable Year—Majority Interest Year

Partnerships are generally required to elect the same taxable year as their partners to prevent the deferral of income, as shown above. Code Sec. 706(b). The partnership must use its "majority interest taxable year," which is the common tax year, if any, used by one or more partners owning a majority interest in the partnership's capital and profits on the first day (called the "testing day") of the partnership's existing tax year. Notice that the ownership requirement is conjunctive, capital *and* profits. The Regulations may provide for some other day during a "representative period" instead of the above testing day. If the partnership changes its tax year under the majority interest rule, in the absence of tax avoidance being shown, the IRS cannot compel another change for two tax years following the year of change.

Example 18.27. Alice Ames and Barbara McCarthy joined Acme Corporation in forming a partnership. Alice and Barbara each received a 26 percent interest in the partnership's income and capital. They report on the calendar year. Acme Corporation received a 48 percent interest in the partnership's income and capital and it reports on a June 30 fiscal year. The partnership is required to adopt the calendar year, the year of Alice and Barbara, who own a majority interest.

Example 18.28. Same facts as in Example 18.27, except the ownership interests of Alice and Barbara were each 24 percent and the corporation's interest was 52 percent. The partnership is required to adopt a June 30 fiscal year, the year of the corporate partner, as it holds the majority interest.

Principal Partners' Common Tax Year

If there is no majority interest taxable year, the partnership must use the same year as that of the principal partners (i.e., those owning 5 percent or more interests in either the profits or capital of the partnership). Notice that the connecting word is disjunctive, profits *or* capital. If all the principal partners have the same tax year, then that is the required tax year for the partnership.

Least Aggregate Deferral Method

If there is no majority interest taxable year and the principal partners do not have the same taxable year, the regulations prescribe that the tax year will be that which results in the least aggregate deferral of income by the partners. Temp. Reg. §1.706-1T(a)(2). In computing the deferral, the percentage of profit of each partner is multiplied by the number of months that income would be deferred for each partner if the tax year of each partner were used by the partnership. Deferral to each partner is measured in terms of months from the end of the partnership's taxable year forward to the end of the partner's taxable year. The sums of these computations are compared, and the tax year producing the lowest number is the one to be used. If there are two or more months with the lowest deferral, the partnership may choose whichever one of these year-ends it wishes.

Example 18.29. Fruit Partnership uses the fiscal year ending June 30. Partner Apple reports her income on the fiscal year ending June 30, and Partner Banana reports his income on the fiscal year ending July 31. They each own a 50 percent interest in capital and profits of the partnership. There is no majority interest year since the partners have different year-ends and neither owns more than a 50 percent interest. Both partners are principal partners, but they do not have the same year-end. Therefore, the least aggregate deferral method must be used. The two test years are years ending June 30 and July 31.

Partner's	Year End	Interest in Profits	Months of Deferral	Interest X Months Deferred
Test # 1 6/30 FY				
Apple	6/30	.50	0	.0
Banana	7/31	.50	1	.5
				.5
Test # 2 7/31 FY				
Apple	6/30	.50	11	5.5
Banana	7/31	.50	0	.0
				5.5

The required tax year for the partnership is the June 30 fiscal year.

Business Purpose Year-End

If a partnership does not wish to use its required tax year, a partnership that can establish that it has a business purpose for another year, with the permission of the Commissioner, may elect to use that fiscal year for reporting purposes. Code Sec. 706(b)(1)(C); Temp. Reg. § 1.706-1T(b).

The "business purpose" test is met if the date selected as the end of the partnership's fiscal year conforms to the end of its natural business year. A natural business year-end can be established if the partnership receives at least 25 percent of its gross receipts during the last two months of what the proposed year-end would be for three consecutive years. Temp. Reg. § 1.442-2T(c)(2).

Example 18.30. Partnership Unicorn has, since its inception, gross receipts from its sales or services evenly spread over its tax year. All of its partners are individuals with a calendar tax year. It has no natural business year and must adopt the calendar year.

Example 18.31. Partnership Dragon had 30 percent of its gross receipts during the months of February and March 1998. It also experienced the same percentage of its annual receipts during February and March 1996 and 1997. Dragon has established a March 31 natural business year.

Section 444 Election

Code Sec. 444 permits a partnership to adopt or change to a fiscal year other than the taxable year required by Code Sec. 706(b) so long as the deferral period is no greater than the shorter of the deferral period in use, or three months. In either case, the partnership is required to make an advance deposit that approximates the amount of tax being deferred by the partners over the deferral period. This toll charge on the amount of deferred income is computed at the highest individual tax rate plus 1 percent. Code Sec. 7519. The complexity of the annual computation and the required advance deposit of the tax make this deferral choice unacceptable to most taxpayers.

If the partnership elects to defer income under Code. Sec. 444, the partnership itself deposits with the government the toll charge on deferred income. The amount of the required deposit will change each year based on the previous year's income. The deposit account functions much like a non-interest bearing savings account, with withdrawals and/or contributions used to match the account balance with the required deposit for the year. When the partnership terminates, it obviously will have no more income deferred and the deposit will be refunded. The deposit does not entitle the partners to a credit, and the refund of the toll charge does not constitute income to the partners.

¶ 18,245   ELECTIONS BY PARTNER OR PARTNERSHIP

Most of the elections available to partnerships are made at the partnership level. However, a partner may elect on an individual income tax return to treat foreign income taxes paid or accrued by the partnership as a deduction or as a credit. The total amount deducted or taken as a credit by a partner includes the distributive share of any such taxes paid or accrued by the partnership. Elections also made at the partner level relate to the treatment of mining and exploration expenditures and reduction of basis of property upon forgiveness of indebtedness.

All elections (other than those above) affecting the computation of income derived from a partnership are made by the partnership. Thus, elections as to methods of accounting, methods of computing depreciation, the use of the installment method, and the option to expense intangible drilling and development costs, as well as other permissible elections, must be made by the partnership. All these elections apply to all partners equally, but no election made by a partnership has any force or effect with respect to any partner's nonpartnership interests. Code Sec. 703(b); Reg. § 1.703-1(b).

Example 18.32. Abner French is a partner in Banjo Partnership, which reports the income from sales of its inventory on the installment method and utilizes the most rapid MACRS lives in depreciating its assets. Abner also operates a sole proprietorship which competes with Banjo Partnership. Abner is not bound in the sole proprietorship by either of the elections made on his behalf by Banjo Partnership.

Code Secs. 6221-6233 generally place administrative and judicial proceedings at the partnership level. Deficiencies in reporting partnership items must be asserted at the partnership level prior to the assessment of any individual partner. All partners are permitted to participate in partnership administrative proceedings and are generally bound by the finding for or against the partnership. Generally, a "tax matters partner" is designated in the partnership agreement to represent the other partners in these proceedings. Statutes of limitations for underreporting income or fraudulent returns apply to partnership returns.

Certain small partnerships are exempt from these latter administrative rules. Exemption is limited, however, to partnerships having 10 or fewer partners, all of whom are natural persons (other than nonresident aliens) or an estate, where each partner's share of every partnership item is the same as the partner's share of every other item. Code Sec. 6231(a)(1)(B).

Operation of the Partnership

¶ 18,301   LIABILITY FOR TAX

A partnership as such is not subject to the income tax. Persons carrying on business as partners are liable for income tax only in their separate or individual capacities, including, of course, any tax attributable to their respective shares of partnership income.

¶ 18,325   REPORTING PARTNERSHIP INCOME

Every partnership must file an annual return regardless of the amount of its net income or its net loss in its operations. Code Sec. 701; Reg. § 1.701-1; Code Sec. 6031. Since the partnership is not taxable on any income, the return is fundamentally an information return. The return must be filed on Form 1065 on or before the 15th day of the fourth month following the close of the partnership's taxable year. The partnership must report its gross income, deductions, ordinary net income, names and addresses of partners, their distributive shares of income, special credits, deductions, and other information as required. Code Secs. 6031 and 6072. For electing "large" partnerships, as defined in Code Sec. 775, such information must be furnished not later than the first March 15 after the close of the taxable year. The return must be signed by one of the partners. The fact that a partner's name is signed to the return is prima facie evidence that the partner is authorized to sign the return on behalf of the partnership. Code Sec. 6063.

The filing of Form 1065 does not start the running of the statute of limitations for the individual partner who failed to file a personal return, even though there is no fraud and the individual had no income other than that reported on the partnership return. *M. Durovic,* 73-2 USTC ¶ 9728, 487 F.2d 36 (CA-7 1973), cert. denied, 417 U.S. 919, 94 S.Ct. 2625 (1973). But the filing of Form 1065 is relevant in determining the question of criminal willfulness in failing to file the individual return. *H.W. Harrison,* 73-1 USTC ¶ 9295 (CA-2 1972), cert. denied, 411 U.S. 965, 93 S.Ct. 2144 (1973). Any disclosure on the partnership return that provides a "clue" to the IRS of reportable income is sufficient to put the IRS on notice so that the six-year statute of limitations (25 percent omission of income) will not apply. *W.W. Myers,* 72-2 USTC ¶ 9669 (DC Cal. 1972); *G.E. Quick Tr.,* 54 TC 1336, CCH Dec. 30,187 (1970), aff'd per curiam, 71-1 USTC ¶ 9489, 444 F.2d 90 (CA-8 1971).

> *Example 18.33.* Jack West and Quick Martin were equal partners in Engineering, a cash-basis partnership. Quick died and Quick's estate erroneously claimed a step-up in basis for the estate's share of the partnership's accounts receivable. On the partnership return, there was disclosed only the amount of the collections in excess of their "basis." The income allocated to the estate was much less than that allocated to Jack. The partnership balance sheet showed a reduction in the accounts receivable's basis and the Schedule M reconciliation showed large tax-free distributions to the estate. While the omission from the estate's income was more than 25 percent, the partnership's disclosure provided sufficient clues that there was no omission in reporting so as to prevent the IRS from asserting the six-year statute of limitations.

¶ 18,335 GROSS INCOME OF PARTNER

The words "distributive share" are sometimes confusing to newcomers in the tax field. For purposes of tax returns, the partner must report the portion of the income and deduction items which are allocable to the partner, whether or not any distribution of them was actually received.

If there is a need to determine an individual partner's share of the partnership's gross income, each partner will include a ratable portion of partnership ordinary income or loss, plus a ratable portion of the gross amount of any specially reported items. Code Sec. 702(c); Reg.

§ 1.702-1(c)(1). For example, a partner is required to include the distributive share of the partnership gross income in order to determine the necessity of filing an individual return or to compute the amount of gross income received from U.S. possessions.

In determining whether there is an extension of the statute of limitations from three to six years because a partner has understated gross income by more than 25 percent, the partner's gross income includes the distributive share of the partnership gross income. The amount stated in the partner's return, in this instance, is determinative of the amount of the partnership gross income from which was derived the partner's distributive share of any item of partnership income, gain, loss, deduction, or credit.

> *Example 18.34.* Abdul Maruk is entitled to one-fourth of the profits of the Abdul-Carter Partnership. The partnership has $100,000 of gross income and $20,000 of taxable income. Abdul reports only $3,000 as his distributive share of partnership profits, but he should have shown $5,000 as his distributive share of profits. This amount was derived from $25,000 of partnership gross income. However, since Abdul included only $3,000 on his return without explaining in the return the difference of $2,000, he is regarded as having stated in his return only $15,000 ($3,000/$5,000 of $25,000) as gross income from the partnership. Reg. § 1.702-1(c)(2).

Refer to ¶ 18,325, above, for reference to *G.E. Quick Trust.* The case illustrates the pass-through of the partnership's gross income to the partners and also reveals the type of clues which put the IRS on sufficient notice of the income so as to prevent the assertion of the six-year statute of limitations.

Computation of Partnership Income

The partnership's ordinary taxable income (loss) is computed generally in the same manner as an individual would report on a Schedule C, Form 1040, the business income from a sole proprietorship. However, there are many items of income and deductions which are not included in the partnership's ordinary income, but are reportable as separate items. The ordinary income and the separately reported items are reportable by the individual partners. Code Sec. 702.

Cash-Basis Reporting

The privilege of reporting on the cash basis has been severely restricted. That privilege is now denied to "tax shelters," but continues to be available to the farming and timber businesses and for qualified personal service corporations. Also, any partnership which does not have a C corporation as a partner (personal service corporations for this purpose are considered individuals) may use the cash basis. Such personal service corporations are generally those professional corporations and professional associations which are formed by certain practitioners (e.g., accountants, attorneys, doctors, engineers, etc.). In addition, any partnership which has a C corporation as a partner may use the cash-basis method if it meets the "gross receipts" test, i.e., the partnership must not have had for the immediately preceding three tax years an average annual amount of gross receipts in excess of $5 million dollars. This determination is made annually. Code Sec. 448. Once the partnership three-year average exceeds the test limit, it must thereafter report on the accrual basis.

Example 18.35. Extrap Partnership, which has a C corporation among its partners, has the following gross receipts for the indicated years:

1993	$4,500,000	1996	$5,000,000
1994	4,750,000	1997	4,000,000
1995	5,800,000	1998	3,000,000

The partnership could have reported on the cash basis for 1993–1995. It had to report on the accrual basis in 1996 because its average annual earnings for the prior three years (since 1993) was $5,016,667. For 1997, that average is $5,183,333. For 1998, the average is only $4,933,333; yet the partnership must continue to use the accrual method.

Allocation of Cash-Basis Items

A partnership that uses the cash basis of accounting for interest, taxes, payment for services or for the use of property, and any other item specified in the Regulations, must allocate those items to the partners on a daily basis in proportion to their interests in the partnership at the end of each day. This rule applies in all cases where it is necessary to allocate cash-basis items to the period to which they are attributable, regardless of whether a change in partnership interests occurs during the current taxable year.

Further, if any portion of such payment is for these "allocable cash-basis items" incurred in a prior tax period, it must be treated as paid on the first day of the period in which the payment is made and allocated to the partners as of that date. If a partner during the accrual period is not a partner on such first day, the partner's portion is capitalized. If any portion is attributable to a following tax period, it must be treated as paid on the last day of the period in which the payment is made and allocated to the partners as of such last day. Code Sec. 706(d)(2). Prepayment rules prohibit much distortion in this situation.

Example 18.36. Four equal partners of a calendar-year, cash-basis partnership, Zemmox, admit Willie Yen to a 20 percent partnership interest on December 2, 1998. Zemmox borrowed on a demand note $100,000 on April 30, 1998. The holder had not demanded payment, but Zemmox paid $8,000 (eight months' interest) on December 31, 1998. Willie Yen's attributed share is $200 (20 percent of 1/8 of $8,000). The remainder, $7,800, is attributable to the other four partners holding the 80 percent interest.

Example 18.37. If, in Example 18.36, Zemmox delayed the payment until January 31, 1999, and then paid $9,000 (nine months' interest), Willie Yen's portion of the deduction is $400 (20 percent of ²⁄₉ of $9,000). The remainder, $8,600, is attributable to the other four partners holding the 80 percent interest.

Example 18.38. Assume, in the foregoing examples, that Willie Yen purchased on December 1, 1998, his 20 percent interest from Abra Dee, one of the five equal original partners of Zemmox, and the interest payment of $9,000 was made as in Example 18.37. Willie Yen claims the same amount of interest, $400, his 20 percent of the December and January accruals. The $7,000 attributable to April 30–November 30, 1998, is accruable to the then five partners, of whom Abra Dee was one. His share is therefore $1,400 (¹⁄₅ × $7,000), but as he is not a partner of Zemmox on January 1, 1999, that amount is not currently deductible by the partnership and must be capitalized.

Character of Items Determined at Partnership Level

Generally, the determination of all partnership income is made at the partnership level and the character of its constituent parts carries over in the individual partner's distributive share. The "business income and expense" items are reported on Form 1065. This results in "ordinary income (loss)" which is reported by the partners in accordance with their profit and loss ratio.

The purpose of requiring items to be separately stated on the partnership return and to be separately taken into account by each partner is to facilitate the operation of the "character rule." The character of any item of income, gain, loss, deduction, or credit for the partner is to be determined "as if such item were realized directly from the source from which realized by the partnership, or incurred in the same manner as incurred by the partnership." Code Sec. 702(b); Reg. § 1.702-1(b).

The character of the income, determined at the partnership level, on occasion may produce apparently conflicting results.

Example 18.39. Partnership Gamble sold a capital asset for which it obtained long-term capital gain treatment. Partner Hannibal, who has held his partnership interest only five months, must nevertheless report his distributable share of this gain as long-term capital gain. Rev. Rul. 68-79, 1968-1 CB 310.

Ordinary Income of the Partnership

Each partner is required to include in the individual tax return the distributive share of the ordinary income or loss of the partnership. Code Sec. 702(a)(8); Reg. § 1.702-1(a)(9). That income is determined in the same manner as that of an individual, but the partnership is not allowed the following deductions:

1. Personal exemptions deduction
2. Foreign taxes deduction
3. Charitable contributions deduction
4. Net operating loss deduction

5. Itemized nonbusiness deductions for individuals (medical and dental expenses, expenses incurred in the production or collection of income or for the management, conservation, or maintenance of property held for the production of income, or in connection with the determination, collection, or refund of any tax, child care expenses, alimony, and taxes and interest paid to a cooperative housing corporation)

6. Depletion deduction for oil and gas wells

7. Capital loss carryover (Code Sec. 703(a); Reg. § 1.703-1(a))

All income and deductions that are allowed, and that are not required to be separately stated, are netted to produce ordinary income/loss and are reported on page 1 of Form 1065.

Partners in Community Property States

In a community property state, some of the partnership income may have to be reported by the spouse who is not a partner. If separate returns are filed by a husband and wife domiciled in a community property state and only one spouse is a member of a partnership, the part of the distributive share of the partnership taxable income which is community property or which is derived from community property should be reported by the husband and wife in equal proportions. Reg. § 1.702-1(d).

Separately Reportable Items on Partnership Return

Any item that *may* have different tax consequences to each partner must be separately stated. For example, some partners may be able to deduct charitable contributions that flow through, but those that have already met the 50 percent of AGI limit for contributions will have to carry over those contributions. Each partner's share of these items is identified on the partner's separate Schedule K-1. The following items are separately stated:

1. Short-term capital gains and losses

2. Long-term capital gains and losses

3. Section 1231 gains and losses

4. Charitable contributions

5. All portfolio items (i.e., dividends and interest income)

6. Taxes paid or accrued to foreign countries and to possessions of the United States

7. Recoveries of bad debts, prior taxes, and delinquency amounts

8. Gains and losses from wagering transactions

9. Soil and water conservation expenditures

10. Nonbusiness expenses

11. Medical and dental expenses of partners, their spouses, and dependents (Items (11), (12), and (13) may not be taken as partnership deductions under Code Sec. 703(a))

12. Credit for the care of certain dependents

13. Alimony payments

14. Amounts representing taxes and interest paid cooperative housing corporations

15. Intangible drilling and development costs

16. Pre-1970 exploration expenditures

17. Certain mining exploration expenditures

18. Income, gain, or loss to the partnership upon the distribution of property involving unrealized receivables and substantially appreciated inventory items

19. Any items or class of items of income, gain, loss, deduction, or credit subject to a special allocation under the partnership agreement differing from the allocation of partnership income or loss generally (Items (7) through (19) are prescribed by Regulations pursuant to Code Sec. 702(a)(7))

20. Expensing of certain depreciable assets (Code Sec. 179)

21. Tax-preference items (Code Sec. 702(a); Reg. § 1.702-1(a))

22. Business credits

23. All items from separate passive activities, including real estate

Income Reporting for Large Partnerships

TRA '97 simplified the reporting rules for "electing large partnerships," defined as partnerships with 100 or more partners in the preceding year who elect to report using the new rules. Code Sec. 775. This election is binding for all future years and is irrevocable without the consent of the IRS. The large partnership rules allow the partnership to aggregate more items at the partnership level, which simplifies the reporting to the partners. For example, the netting of capital gains and losses are at the partnership level. If the net capital gains or losses are long-term, they are passed through as such to the partners. If the net capital gains and losses are short-term, they are combined with other partnership taxable income and will not be separately reported. An electing large partnership computes its charitable contribution deduction using a 10 percent limitation similar to how a corporation computes its charitable contribution deduction. The following items are separately reportable on the returns of electing large partnerships:

1. Taxable income or loss from passive activities

2. Taxable income or loss from other activities

3. Net capital gain or loss allocable to passive loss activities

4. Net capital gain or loss allocable to other activities

5. Tax-exempt interest

6. Applicable net alternative minimum tax adjustment separately computed for the passive loss limitation activities and the other activities

7. General credits

8. Low-income housing credits

9. Rehabilitation credits

10. Foreign income taxes

11. Credit for producing fuel from nonconventional sources

12. Other items to the extent that the IRS determines that separate treatment is appropriate

¶ 18,345 ALLOCATION OF ITEMS

In addition to the requirement to report items separately because of their character, there are other situations where items must be separately reported because either the statute or the partnership agreement requires a disproportionate (or "special") allocation of income or expense items among the partners. Special allocations are required by statute for precontribution built-in gains or losses when there is a contribution of property with a fair market value different from its basis. Other special allocations may be provided in the partnership agreement, but, in order to be recognized, these allocations must have a substantial economic effect on the income and losses reported by the partners.

Precontribution Built-In Gains and Losses

When property is contributed to a partnership, income, gain, loss, and deductions must be allocated with respect to the contributed property so as to take account of the variation between the basis of the property contributed to the partnership and its fair market value at the time of contribution. This means, in effect, that any precontribution gain or loss becomes "built-in" at contribution and must be recognized by the contributing partner when it is recognized by the partnership. Code Sec. 704(c). Otherwise, a partnership could be used to shift income or losses that have accrued on assets before contribution to the partnership or to other partners.

Example 18.40. On January 1, 1998, Charles and David Taylor formed CD, an equal partnership, with Charles contributing land with a fair market value of $10,000 and an adjusted basis to him of $4,800. David contributed $10,000 cash. Each of their capital accounts is credited for the respective amounts. When CD sells the land for $20,000 three years later, Charles must report $10,200 of gain ($5,200 "built-in" gain plus $5,000, one-half of the balance of the gain). David must report $5,000 of gain. If the land had been sold for $9,800, the entire gain of $5,000 would be allocated to Charles.

The situation becomes complicated somewhat where depreciable property is contributed. The "built-in" gain may be absorbed all or in part by the use of the property. If the depreciation deduction is sufficiently large enough to permit the allocation of the same amount the noncontributing partner would have been entitled to had the property been purchased, allocation of the deduction to that partner will equalize the equity accounts of the two partners.

Example 18.41. Assume in Example 18.40 that Charles contributed a machine with a fair market value of $10,000 and an adjusted basis to him of $5,000. The two-year remaining recovery period amount of write-off is $2,500 each year. The "built-in" gain is attributed to Charles and the depreciation allowable is allocated to David. Charles's capital account is credited $5,000; David's account is credited $10,000 for his cash contribution. Assuming no other income or expense for 1998; at the end of the year, CD shows a loss of $2,500, all attributable to the MACRS write-off. Thus, Charles shows neither gain nor loss; David shows a loss of $2,500. Their respective capital account balances show Charles, $5,000; David, $7,500. This is the exact position David would be in had the asset had a basis equal to its FMV of $10,000.

Example 18.42. Assume in Example 18.41 that, at the beginning of 1999, CD sells the machine at its depreciated fair market value of $5,000 ($10,000 − $5,000) and distributes the proceeds. CD has a taxable gain of $2,500 ($5,000 − $2,500), all of which is taxable to Charles. Assume further that CD is immediately liquidated and the $15,000 is distributed to Charles and David:

	Charles	David
Capital Account January 1, 1998	$5,000	$10,000
Loss (MACRS write-off)		(2,500)
Capital Account January 1, 1999	$5,000	$ 7,500
Gain on sale of machinery	2,500	
Proceeds on liquidation	$7,500	$ 7,500

The problem is more complex and becomes inequitable when the allocable depreciation is not equal to that to which the noncontributing partner would have been entitled if the property were purchased. The equity accounts are equalized by requiring that capital accounts be maintained according to tax accounting principles, that liquidation be based upon those capital account balances, and that any partner with a deficit in the capital account must restore it by making a contribution to the partnership.

Example 18.43. Assume the same facts as in Example 18.42, except that the adjusted basis of the machinery is $4,200, the annual write-off is $2,100, and David may be allocated only $2,100 as MACRS write-off. Upon the sale of the machinery at its adjusted fair market value of $5,000 on January 1, 1999, and the immediate liquidation of the firm, the following capital account analyses appear:

	Charles	David
Beginning balance January 1, 1998	$4,200	$10,000
Loss (MACRS write-off) 1998		(2,100)
Beginning balance January 1, 1999	$4,200	$ 7,900
Gain on sale ($5,000 − $2,100)	2,900	
Capital balances	$7,100	$ 7,900
Liquidation proceeds	$7,500	$ 7,500
(Deficit) credit balance	$ (400)	$ 400
Contribution (Distribution)	$ 400	(400)
	$ 0	$ 0

Because Charles had a deficit in his capital account, he had to contribute $400 to the partnership to restore the account to zero. The $400 is then distributed to David.

If the sales proceeds had been $5,800, making $15,800 available, the allocation of the additional gain should also be to Charles.

	Charles	David
Capital account January 1, 1999	$4,200	$ 7,900
Gain on sale of machinery	3,700	
Proceeds on liquidation	$7,900	$ 7,900

The Code Sec. 704(c) regulations provide two other methods for allocating income, gain, loss, and deductions with respect to contributed property that the partnership may elect: the traditional method (illustrated above) combined with curative allocations, and the remedial allocation method. Reg. § 1.704-3(c) and (d). Refer to ¶ 19,315 for the provision which accelerates the recognition of precontribution gains related to contributions of appreciated property by partners.

Accounts Payable of Cash-Basis Contributors

In addition, Code Sec. 704(c) addresses the problem of accounts payable and accrued expense items contributed by a cash-basis taxpayer to a partnership. Generally, the contributing partner is allocated the deduction generated by payment of these items by the partnership. However, these items are not considered "liabilities" for purposes of determining a partner's basis for a partnership interest under Code Sec. 752.

Allocations Must Have Substantial Economic Effect

A partner's distributive share of any item or class of items of income, gain, loss, deduction, or credit of the partnership is ordinarily determined by the partnership agreement. If the agreement does not make an allocation, or if the allocation in the agreement does not have "substantial economic effect," the partner's distributive share is determined (taking into account all facts and circumstances) in accordance with the partner's interest in the partnership. Thus, the allocation must pass both the economic effect test and the substantiality test. Code Sec. 704(b).

An allocation has economic effect if (1) the allocation is reflected by an appropriate increase or decrease in the partner's capital account and the capital accounts are maintained according to Treasury Regulation rules, (2) liquidation proceeds (if any) are to be distributed in accordance with the partners' capital account balances, and (3) any partner with a deficit in the capital account following the distribution of liquidation proceeds is required to restore the amount of the deficit to the partnership. Reg. § 1.704-1(b)(2).

Example 18.44. Albert May and Bobby Dickson form the AB Partnership with each contributing $100,000 cash. The AB Partnership promptly purchases a depreciable asset for $200,000 cash. The asset is classified as seven-year recovery property. The partnership does not elect the Section 179 expensing deduction, but it allocates the entire cost recovery amount of $28,580 to Albert. The expense is charged against his capital account, but the partnership agreement provides that upon liquidation, the partners will share equally the net proceeds of all assets. In addition, the partnership agreement does not provide for restoration of deficit balances in the partners' capital accounts. Assume that the depreciable asset is sold for its depreciated basis of $171,420, resulting in no gain or loss to the partnership, and that the partnership immediately liquidates. Albert and Bobby will each receive one-half of the proceeds upon liquidation of the partnership. After these events, the capital accounts would be as follows:

	Albert	Bobby
Contribution (capital balance)	$100,000	$100,000
MACRS deduction	(28,580)	0
Capital balance	$ 71,420	$100,000
Liquidating distribution proceeds	(85,710)	(85,710)
Capital balance after distribution	$ (14,290)	$ 14,290

Since Albert does not have any obligation to restore a deficit in his capital account if one exists (which would be distributed to Bobby in an amount equal to his positive capital account balance), Albert will not bear the burden of the allocation of Bobby's one-half share of the cost recovery deductions which have been allocated to him. Consequently, there is no economic effect to the allocation of the entire amount of cost recovery deductions to Albert and these deductions will be charged equally to each of the partners.

For the agreement for allocation to be valid, the economic effect of the allocation must be substantial in relation to its tax effect. Thus, an allocation of one type of income (capital gains) to one partner and another type of income (ordinary) to another partner where there is a strong probability at the time of the allocation that there will be a significant difference in the two amounts will have economic effect, but it may not be substantial in relation to the tax impact of the reported partnership income on the partner's nonpartnership income. These rules are difficult to apply even with reference to the multitude of examples included in Reg. § 1.704-1(b)(5).

Example 18.45. At the beginning of the tax year, it is anticipated that Charles Cox will have substantial individual capital losses and that David James will have substantial individual ordinary business income. Accordingly, the partners agree for the ensuing year to allocate all the partnership's ordinary income to David and all of the capital gains to Charles, the two amounts anticipated to be essentially equal in amount. Here, the economic effect is minor— both parties receive about the same amount of income—but the tax effect is major. Although the dollar amount of income derived from the partnership is equal, by the allocation, Charles is able to claim substantial capital losses not otherwise currently deductible by him. As the economic effect is not substantial in relation to the tax effect, the allocation will not be allowed.

The Internal Revenue Service has stated that when partnership income results from cancellation of partnership debt, an income allocation to partners which is different from the allocation of the forgiven debt to the partners can have substantial economic effect. To achieve substantial economic effect, however, there must be an unconditional deficit restoration provision in the partnership agreement, along with the other requirements for economic effect and substantiality discussed in this section. Rev. Rul. 92-97, 1992-2 CB 124.

TAX BLUNDER

Oil Inc. and Lotta Bucks enter into a joint operating agreement to drill for oil in the Boomtown oil field. Oil Inc. contributes the mineral rights to the property, and Lotta agrees to pay the drilling costs. Since the participants are entering into an agreement for the joint extraction of oil and gas, they file a partnership return for the first year and elect to be excluded from the partnership provisions of the Internal Revenue Code.

Result. By electing out of the partnership provisions, Lotta, who pays all of the intangible drilling costs, can deduct only one-half of the intangible drilling costs. The remaining half of the costs must be capitalized. Had they not elected out of the partnership provisions, the partnership could have made a special allocation of the intangible drilling costs, and Lotta could have deducted all of the intangible drilling costs.

¶ 18,401 SPECIAL TREATMENT OF CONTRIBUTED INCOME ITEMS AND PROPERTY

Special rules prevent the conversion of ordinary income items into capital gain items and deny an ordinary loss deduction for capital losses. Code Sec. 724. When certain business assets are contributed to a partnership, the partnership has the same character in the assets as the partners had. Thus, if a cash-basis taxpayer contributes unrealized accounts receivable to a partnership, their collection by the partnership generates ordinary income whenever they are collected. If an "inventory item" is contributed to the partnership, any gain or loss upon its sale by the partnership within five years of its contribution is treated as ordinary gain or loss. It does not matter that the use of the item by the partnership may have converted it to a capital asset. Also, if a capital asset is contributed with a "built-in loss"—when its fair market value is less than its basis—any loss (up to the amount of the "built-in loss") on its disposition within five years of its contribution is classified as a capital loss. The rule will apply even if a former capital asset is held for sale by the partnership to its customers in the ordinary course of its business.

Example 18.46. Herman Maurice contributes equipment which he has held as an investment to HM Partnership in exchange for a 50 percent interest in HM's capital and income. At the time of the contribution, the equipment is worth $35,000 and Herman's basis in it is $50,000.

The equipment is included in HM Partnership's inventory. Two years after the contribution, HM sells the equipment for $30,000. Of the $20,000 loss ($30,000 − $50,000), $15,000 is a capital loss (the amount of the built-in loss when Herman contributed it), and $5,000 is an ordinary loss from the sale of inventory.

This "taint" is not removed by most of the provisions relating to nonrecognition transactions. For example, in a like-kind exchange the new property is treated exactly the same as the exchanged property. However, if the "tainted" property is contributed to a "controlled" corporation, in a Code Sec. 351 exchange, the stock received in exchange is treated as a capital asset, free of the taint.

Code Sec. 724(d)(2) defines "inventory items" as having essentially the same meaning as provided in Code Sec. 751(d)(2). Such items include those which, if sold, generate ordinary income rather than capital gain. But land or depreciable property used by a partner in a trade or business prior to its contribution to the partnership is excluded from the definition of "inventory items." For this purpose there is no requirement that this type of property (Section 1231 property) must be held for more than 12 months prior to its contribution to the partnership.

Example 18.47. Mr. Kostock owned a desk which he had used entirely in his sole proprietorship for 11 months when he contributed it to his newly formed partnership as a part of his capital contribution. If Mr. Kostock had sold the desk, any gain or loss would be ordinary. However, if the partnership continues the business use of the desk for more than one more month and then sells it at more than its original cost to Mr. Kostock, the gain will qualify as a Section 1231 gain.

KEYSTONE PROBLEM

Acey and Deucy formed the Acey-Deucy Partnership on January 1, 1993, with cash investments of $120,000 and $80,000 for 60 percent and 40 percent respective interests in both the partnership's capital and income. The partnership reports on the calendar year and uses the accrual method. From the data below, compute the partnership's 1998 ordinary income and list the items which will be separately reportable by the partners on their individual returns.

1. All sales were made on account, $250,000.

2. Sales of $4,800 were returned for allowances; $235,000 was received as payments on account.

3. Inventory on January 1, 1998, was $64,500; purchases for 1998 were $82,500; ending inventory, $37,000.

4. The partnership uses the specific write-off method of accounting for bad debts. $1,500 in uncollectible accounts was written off.

5. The depreciable assets held by the partnership were as follows:

    a. Building—cost $131,689; acquired in 1993; 1998 cost recovery, $4,181.

    b. Machinery—cost $20,000; seven-year recovery property; placed in service December 31, 1998; $17,500 immediately expensed under Code Sec. 179; MACRS applied to balance to yield 1998 cost recovery, $89.

6. Dividends received: $1,000 from Domestic Corp.; $750 from Foreign Corp. on which 30 percent tax was withheld at source.

7. Sold on November 29, 1998, 600 shares Domestic Corp. common stock for $8,500; 1,000 shares were purchased on December 2, 1995, for $10,000.

8. Sold on November 11, 1998, 300 shares Foreign Corp. preferred stock for $2,200; 800 shares were purchased on December 12, 1997, for $3,000.

9. Sold on January 1, 1998, for $6,325, equipment which was purchased in 1995 for $3,200 on which cost recovery of $1,125 had been previously taken.

10. Organization costs of $3,000 are being amortized for financial purposes over a 10-year period. Acey-Deucy used the shortest possible period for tax purposes.

11. $10,000 principal and $6,000 interest were paid on the partnership's mortgage.

12. A $400 cash contribution was made to the American Red Cross.

13. Salary expense for employees was $50,000.

14. Rent was $12,000; real estate taxes, $2,500.

15. During 1998, Acey and Deucy made cash withdrawals of $50,000 and $25,000, respectively.

¶ 18,425 INDIRECT OWNERSHIP

The related party rules between partners and partnerships need to be understood before transactions between these parties can be discussed. There are several Code sections concerning attribution of ownership, e.g., Code Sec. 318 (for corporations in general), Code Sec. 542 (for personal holding companies), and Code Sec. 267 (applicable to disallowance of losses between related parties in general). Code Sec. 707, specifically concerned with losses and gains in the partnership context, refers to Code Sec. 267, which has the least complex rules. The relationships creating indirect ownership for partnership purposes are:

1. A partnership interest owned, directly or indirectly, by or for a corporation, partnership, estate, or trust is considered as being owned proportionately by or for its shareholders, partners, or beneficiaries.

2. An individual is considered as owning the partnership interest owned, directly or indirectly, by or for family members.

The family of an individual includes only brothers and sisters (whether by the whole or half blood), spouse, ancestors, and lineal descendants. For the purpose of determining ownership, property deemed owned by a person by reason of Rule (1) (entity attribution) is treated as being actually held by that person to whom ownership is attributed, which means that the ownership could be attributed again to an entity or person related to that person. Rule (2) (family attribution) is applied only once.

> **Example 18.48.** Apex Partnership is owned by the following:
>
> 25% by Corporation Yahoo (100% owned by Ann Plece);
> 36% by Partnership Bucko (25% owned by Ann Plece; 25% owned by Jack Spratt; 25% owned by Jill Spratt; and 25% owned by Robert Plece (Jill Spratt is Ann Plece's sister and Robert Plece is their father, Jill Spratt is Jack Spratt's wife));
> 33% by Rabe Plece (Robert Plece's grandson, Ann's son); and
> 6% by Walter Washington (unrelated to any of the above).

Ann owns directly:		0	
Through her corporation		25	
Through the partnership			
by herself	9		
by her father	9		
by her sister	9	27	
By her son		33	85
Jill owns directly:		0	
Through the partnership			
by herself	9		
by her husband	9		
by her sister	9		
by her father	9	36	
By her sister (corporation)		25	61
Jack owns directly:		0	
Through the partnership			
by himself	9		
by his wife	9		18
Robert owns directly:		0	
Through the partnership			
by himself	9		
by his daughters	18	27	
By his daughter (corporation)		25	
By his grandson		33	85
Rabe owns directly:		33	
Through the partnership			
by his mother	9		
by his grandfather	9	18	
By his mother (corporation)		25	76
Bucko owns directly:		0	
Through the partnership			
by the partners		36	
By Ann (corporation)		25	61
Yahoo owns directly		25	
Through shareholder Ann		9	34

¶ 18,445 TRANSACTIONS BETWEEN PARTNER AND PARTNERSHIP

The Code adopts the "entity" approach to transactions between a partner and the partnership when the partner is not acting in the capacity of a partner. The transaction is considered as taking place between the partnership and a stranger. Code Sec. 707(a); Reg. § 1.707-1(a). These transactions include, for example, loans of money or property by the partnership to the partner, the sale of property by the partner to the partnership, the purchase of property by the partner from the partnership, and the rendering of services by the partner to or for the partnership.

Example 18.49. Partner Eager, holding a 20 percent interest in Eager & Fast Partnership, sells to the partnership land he has held for investment for more than a year, realizing a gain of $10,000. The partnership intended to use the land as a factory site but changed its plans. Within six months the partnership resells the same land to Eager at a price $1,000 in excess of that paid to Eager. Eager has a long-term capital gain of $10,000 on his sale to the partnership and a long-term capital gain of $200 distributed to him as a 20 percent partner, reflecting the partnership's $1,000 gain on resale.

Each situation is determined in view of all of the facts. When services are or will be rendered by a partner to a partnership, and the consideration to be paid is an agreed fixed amount, such payment may be classified as a payment of a fee to a third person rather than as a distribution of partnership income to a partner. Particularly susceptible to fee determination is the existence of a reasonable assurance that the partnership income will be sufficient to make the fixed payments as agreed. The determination is significant because payments based on profits are nondeductible distributions, while payments of fixed salaries are deductible.

To implement the above facts and circumstances test, the IRS is authorized to prescribe regulations. Guidance is to be given to determine whether a purported partner performing services or transferring property is or is not a partner. If the person is determined to be in fact a partner, then the following factors are to be used in determining whether the partner is receiving the allocation and distribution in the capacity of a partner.

1. Is the payment subject to an appreciable risk as to amount, or is there a strong likelihood the payment will be made as anticipated without regard to the success or failure of the venture?

2. Is the partner status of the recipient transitory, or does the partner contemplate a continuing relationship with the partnership?

3. Is the allocation close in time to the rendition of services or the transfer of the property to the partnership? It is immaterial

whether the payment is before or after the rendition or transfer.

4. Did the party become a partner primarily to obtain tax benefits of the partnership which would not be otherwise available had the party rendered the services (sold the property) to an unrelated third party? Nontax motives for this purpose are irrelevant.

5. Is the allocation/distribution for services small in relation to the partner's interest in general and to the continuing partnership profits? A relatively small payment may indicate a fee.

¶ 18,501 GAIN OR LOSS ON TRANSACTIONS BETWEEN PARTNER AND PARTNERSHIP

As in other situations involving transactions between related taxpayers, Congress and the Treasury Department have provided rules to prevent tax avoidance through partner/partnership transactions. The disguised sale rules are covered in ¶ 18,135. Other rules are designed to deny the deduction of certain losses, and the acquisition of a stepped-up basis at capital gain rates where the same parties are in control of both sides of the transaction. The rules are somewhat similar to those applicable in the case of sales of property between corporations and controlling stockholders.

Denial of Loss Deduction

No deduction is allowed for a loss on a sale or exchange of property (other than an interest in the partnership) taking place, directly or indirectly, between a partnership and a person who owns, directly or indirectly, an interest in the capital or profits of the partnership in excess of 50 percent. Similarly, no loss deduction is allowed on a sale or exchange taking place, directly or indirectly, between two partnerships in which the same persons own, directly or indirectly, an interest in capital or profits of more than 50 percent of each partnership. Code Sec. 707(b)(1); Reg. § 1.707-1(b)(1).

If there is a sale or exchange between a partnership and a person who is related to a partner who owns 50 percent or less of the partnership, part of the sale or exchange is considered to take place between the person and the related partner. Therefore, if there is a loss on the sale or exchange, part of the loss will be disallowed. Reg. § 1.267(b)-1(b).

> *Example 18.50.* The wife of a 20 percent partner sells equipment to the partnership. She sustains a $10,000 tax loss on the sale. With respect to her loss, $2,000 will not be recognized for federal income tax purposes.

Recoupment of Disallowed Loss by Related Purchaser

If, however, the purchaser of property in a transaction with respect to which a loss was disallowed subsequently sells the property, for purposes of computing gain, the amount of the loss previously disallowed is treated as a part of the purchaser's basis. This allows the related purchaser, in effect, to recoup the loss disallowed his or her transferor.

> *Example 18.51.* George Avis, a 60 percent partner in the Beegood partnership, buys from the partnership for his personal use an old truck for $200 with a basis to the partnership of $250. The partnership is not allowed to deduct its $50 loss on the transaction. If, however, at a later date George sells the truck for $325, he may reduce his actual gain of $125 by the amount of loss previously disallowed to the partnership, $50, and thus report a gain on the transaction of only $75.

> *Example 18.52.* If, in Example 18.51, George sold the truck for $175, he would recognize only a $25 loss. The previously disallowed loss of $50 cannot be used to increase a later loss.

Sale of Capital Assets to Controlled Partnerships

In the sale or exchange of property between a person and a partnership in which the person owns, directly or indirectly, an interest of more than 50 percent in capital or profits, any gain recognized is treated as ordinary gain unless the property is a capital asset in the hands of the transferee immediately after the transfer. The same rule applies to sales and exchanges between partnerships in which the same persons own, directly or indirectly, an interest in capital or profits greater than 50 percent. Code Sec. 707(b)(2); Reg. § 1.707-1(b)(2).

> *Example 18.53.* Joe Michie and his son Jay each own a 40 percent interest in the Michie partnership. Beverly, Joe's wife, holds no interest in the partnership. Beverly sells for $40,000 to the Michie partnership a parcel of land with a basis to her of $20,000 which she has held as an investment. The partnership builds a factory on the site. Beverly, who has indirect control of the partnership, recognizes $20,000 ordinary income on the sale.

> *Example 18.54.* If in Example 18.53, the Michie partnership held the land for investment, a capital asset, Beverly's gain would be capital gain.

> *Example 18.55.* Emory Stewart invented a bath oil that, with Max Hayes and Bernard O'Regan, was developed into a merchantable product. The partners transferred their respective one-third interests in the bath oil to a new partnership owned in equal shares by Emory, Berte (wife of Max), and Peggy (wife of Bernard). The transferor partnership retained a royalty based upon the sales price of the bath oil. The transfer was held to be a transfer between commonly controlled partnerships, the wives' interests being attributed to their husbands. Thus, the royalty income received by the original partnership, in spite of the application of Code Sec. 1235, was taxed as ordinary income. See *M.A. Burde,* 65-2 USTC ¶ 9733, 352 F.2d 995 (CA-2 1965), cert. denied, 383 U.S. 966, 86 S.Ct. 1271 (1966).

The rule is applicable even though a transaction falling within the scope of the rule is actually the result of arm's-length bargaining.

Example 18.56. Fruit Growers Partnership, owned entirely by James and Johnson, sold one of its citrus groves to Orchards Partnership, owned entirely by their children. The children operated Orchards Partnership entirely independently of their parents. James and Johnson owned no direct interest in Orchards Partnership. Neither did the children own any direct interest in the Fruit Growers Partnership. The IRS deemed this a transfer between controlled partnerships; thus, the gain on the sale of the citrus trees was ordinary income to the selling partnership. See Rev. Rul. 67-105, 1967-1 CB 167.

Code Sec. 1239 expands the reach of the rule which treats recognized gain as ordinary income by treating recognized gain as ordinary income if the transferred property is depreciable by the transferee. So, even though the property may be a capital asset in the hands of the transferee immediately after the transfer (thereby escaping the rule of Code Sec. 707(b)(2)), if it is depreciable by the transferee, the seller's recognized gain is ordinary income.

Example 18.57. Milton Freidburg owns a 60 percent interest in the Ajax partnership. His wife, Marla, sells a duplex to the partnership. Marla has rented the duplex, holding it as an investment. The Ajax partnership will rent and hold the duplex in the same manner. Marla recognizes a $50,000 gain on the sale. The gain is reported by Marla as ordinary income.

Installment Sales

Deferred payment sales of depreciable property between related parties are governed by Code Sec. 453(g), which, where tax avoidance is a principal purpose, prohibits use of the installment method and requires that all payments be deemed received in the year of disposition. If tax avoidance is not a principal purpose, the installment method of reporting is available between a partner and the controlled partnership, but a subsequent sale of the property within two years of the purchase will accelerate any unpaid installments at the time of the second sale. If the selling partner does not have, directly or indirectly, control of the partnership, the installment sale is treated as any other such transaction between strangers.

Example 18.58. In the current year, partner Bernie Winston, who owns 55 percent of the Wimpy Partnership, sells to that partnership land with a basis to Bernie of $40,000 for a sales price of $200,000 (its fair market value). The partnership is to pay $40,000 at the time of the purchase, and $40,000 (plus reasonable interest) in annual installments during each of the next four years. The partnership will hold the land as an investment (a capital asset). Bernie will report capital gain of $32,000 in the current year. If the Wimpy Partnership sells the land the next year, Bernie will have to report the remaining $128,000 of capital gain that year. If Bernie owned less than 50 percent of the partnership, he would continue to report his gain ratably as he collected the sales price from the Wimpy Partnership.

Concurrent Reporting of Items

The income and the deduction of payments between related parties must be reported in the same year where the payee is on the cash basis and the payer is on the accrual basis. Both the deduction and the income are reportable when the payee reports the item. Code Sec. 267(a)(2). The rule applies to the payments between a partnership and any partner who owns (directly or indirectly) any interest in the capital or income of a partnership. Code Sec. 267(e). This rule, however, does not apply to certain qualified expenses of partnerships owning low-income housing or to guaranteed payments made to a partner.

¶ 18,515   GUARANTEED PAYMENTS

Partnership agreements often provide for the payment of salaries to partners and for the allowance of interest on their capital. After deducting amounts credited to the members of the firm under these headings, the balance of the profits for the period is distributed among the partners in accordance with the general profit and loss ratio.

"Guaranteed payments" of this sort are treated, within limitations, as if made to a nonpartner. They are deductible by the partnership as a business expense for the taxable year in which paid or accrued in accordance with its usual accounting method. But to be currently deductible, the payment must be for an expense item, not a capitalizable charge, such as fees for supervised construction of a capital asset. Code Sec. 707(c); *J.E. Cagle,* 63 TC 86, CCH Dec. 32,828 (1974), aff'd, 76-2 USTC ¶ 9672, 539 F.2d 409 (CA-5 1976).

> *Example 18.59.* Edgar Dickens reports on the calendar year and cash basis. The Edgar, Franklin, and George Partnership of which he is a member files its returns on the accrual basis for the year ending April 30, 1998. Edgar is entitled to a salary of $4,800 per year from the partnership. Edgar's salary for the months of May, June, and July 1997, totals $1,200 and is paid to him on time, but he receives nothing more from the partnership during the balance of its fiscal year. The partnership will deduct the full $4,800 salary to which Edgar was entitled on its return for the year ending April 30, 1998. Edgar must report as income the entire $4,800 on his 1998 calendar-year individual return although he has actually received only $1,200, and that in 1997. But if the partnership were on the cash basis, Edgar's salary would be deductible only as paid, and Edgar would include in his income for the year within which the partnership year ends the amount actually paid to him during that partnership tax year.

Insufficient Income to Cover Guaranteed Payments

If the aggregate partnership ordinary income is insufficient to cover guaranteed payments, the partners' distributive shares may be income to some partners and losses to others.

> *Example 18.60.* The Harry, Isadore, and Jacob Partnership earned only $1,000 of ordinary income before deduction of Harry

Portugal's $10,000 salary. Deduction of the $10,000 guaranteed payment to Harry would produce a $9,000 loss. Harry, whose profit and loss ratio is 10 percent, reports his $10,000 salary as income and is entitled to an ordinary deduction of $900 for his distributive share of the loss. Isadore and Jacob, each possessing a 45 percent interest in profit and loss, are each entitled to an ordinary deduction for one-half of the balance of the loss ($1/2 \times$ ($9,000 − $900) = $4,050). Rev. Rul. 56-675, 1956-2 CB 459.

Guaranteed payments are not applied to reduce a partner's distributive share of income items required to be reported separately, even where there is insufficient ordinary income to cover the guaranteed payments. Reg. § 1.707-1(c), Example (4).

Example 18.61. Suppose, in Example 18.60, that the $1,000 partnership income is derived solely from long-term capital gains and the partnership's only expense is Harry's salary. Then Harry reports his salary of $10,000 as ordinary income and $100 as his 10 percent share of the long-term capital gain, $1,000. The partnership's ordinary loss is $10,000, resulting from the deduction of Harry's salary, and Harry deducts $1,000 as his 10 percent share of this ordinary loss. Isadore's and Jacob's distributive shares consist of $450 ($1/2 \times$ ($1,000 − $100)) of long-term capital gain and $4,500 ($1/2 \times$ ($10,000 − $1,000)) of ordinary loss.

Partner Not an "Employee" of the Partnership

Individual taxpayers who are general partners are subject to self-employment tax on their shares of partnership income or loss as well as guaranteed payments that they receive if the partnership is engaged in a trade or business (limited partners are subject to self-employment tax solely on guaranteed payments for services). Code Sec. 1402. The guaranteed payments provision is applicable only for purposes of determining the partner's income and the partnership's business deduction. Thus, a partner who receives guaranteed payments is not regarded as an employee of the partnership for purposes of income tax withholding, or qualified pension or profit-sharing plans. However, the partner may be considered an employee for purposes of excluding compensation earned outside of the United States under Code Sec. 911. *A.O. Miller,* 52 TC 752, CCH Dec. 29,690 (1969), acq. 1972-2 CB 2.

¶ 18,551 NET OPERATING LOSS—LIMITATIONS

The net operating loss carryover or carryback deduction is not allowed for purposes of computing a partnership's taxable income. Code Sec. 703(a)(2)(D). For any year in which the partnership sustains an operating loss, however, a partner's distributive share thereof, if not offset by other income and by the requisite statutory modifications, may become a component of the partner's individual net operating loss and give rise to a carryback or carryover deduction on the partner's individual tax return.

Reporting Rules

For the purpose of determining the partner's personal net operating loss deduction, the partner must take into account the distributive share of items of income, gain, loss, deduction, or credit of the partnership. The character of any such item is determined as if such item were realized directly from the source or incurred in the same manner as incurred by the partnership. Similarly, in the computation of the nonbusiness deductions of the partner, the partner must separately take into account the distributive share of the nonbusiness deductions of the partnership and combine such amount with deductions from nonpartnership sources. In the same way, the partner must separately take into account the distributive share of the nonbusiness gross income of the partnership and combine this amount with nonpartnership income from nonbusiness sources. Reg. § 1.702-2.

These requirements are separate and distinct from the rules requiring segregation of certain items of income and deduction on the partnership return. Thus, while the partnership is required to show as a separate item on its return each partner's share of long-term capital gains, the division of this item into business and nonbusiness gains is required only for purposes of determining the partner's net operating loss deduction.

Example 18.62. Edgar Peters, age 42 and unmarried, is a 50 percent partner in the EAZY partnership. The partnership has the following income and deduction items for 1998:

Ordinary income from operations	$ 2,000
Section 1231 loss on sale of real estate used in the partnership business	(10,000)
Net short-term capital loss from sale of investment stock	(5,000)

Edgar had the following individual income and deductions for 1998:

Commissions as part-time real estate agent	$ 3,000
Interest on investments	500
Dividends from stock investments	1,000
Ordinary income from partnership (50% of above)	1,000
	$ 5,500

Deductions:	
Partnership Section 1231 loss (50% of above)	(5,000)
Partnership net short-term capital loss (50% of above)	(2,500)
Standard deduction	(4,250)
Personal exemption	(2,700)
	(14,450)
Net deductions in excess of income	$ (8,950)

Edgar's NOL:				
Loss shown on tax return				$(8,950))
Add: Personal exemption		$2,700		
Nonbusiness deductions:				
Investment loss	$2,500			
Standard deduction	4,250			
	$6,750			
Less: Nonbusiness income:				
Interest on investments	$ 500			
Dividends	1,000	1,500	$5,250	7,950
Net operating loss carryovers				$(1,000)

Losses in Excess of Partner's Basis

A partner's distributive share of partnership loss (including capital loss) is allowed as a deduction only to the extent of the adjusted basis of the partner's interest in the partnership at the end of the partnership year in which the loss occurs. Any part of a partner's distributive share of partnership loss disallowed is allowed as a deduction at the end of the first succeeding partnership taxable year, and subsequent partnership taxable years, to the extent that the partner's adjusted basis for the partnership interest at the end of any such year exceeds zero (before reduction by a loss for such year). Code Sec. 704(d); Reg. § 1.704-1(d).

> *Example 18.63.* At the end of the 1997 partnership taxable year, partnership AB has a loss of $20,000. Partner Boyce's distributive share of this loss is $10,000. At the end of such year, Boyce's adjusted basis for his interest in the partnership (not taking into account his distributive share of the loss) is $6,000. Boyce's distributive share of partnership loss is allowed to him as a deduction (in his taxable year within or with which the partnership taxable year ends) only to the extent of his adjusted basis of $6,000. The $6,000 loss allowed decreases the adjusted basis of his interest to zero. Assume that, at the end of the 1998 partnership year, the adjusted basis of Boyce's interest in the partnership has increased to $3,000 (not taking into account the $4,000 loss disallowed in 1997). $3,000 of the $4,000 loss disallowed for the partnership year 1997 is allowed Boyce for the partnership taxable year 1998, thus again decreasing the adjusted basis of his interest to zero. If, at the end of the 1999 partnership taxable year, Boyce has an adjusted basis for his interest of at least $1,000 (not taking into account the disallowed loss of $1,000), he will be allowed the $1,000 loss previously disallowed. Reg. § 1.704-1(d), Example (1).

The "basis of a partner's partnership interest" means the basis of the partner's undivided interest in the partnership assets, and this figure will always reflect the partner's share of partnership liabilities. Thus, a partner may have a debit balance or a deficit in the "capital" account on the partnership books, but still have a positive basis for the partner's interest as determined for tax purposes.

TAX PLANNING POINTER

For any year in which a partner's distributive share of losses exceeds the basis of the partner's interest (including the partner's share of partnership liabilities), the loss deduction may be obtained by having the partnership buy property on credit or borrow money. The resultant increase in each partner's share of the liability incurred is treated as a contribution of cash, thus increasing the basis of the partner's interest. Code Secs. 722 and 752(a). This makes it possible for the partner, to some extent, to control the year in which a loss deduction will be taken.

As a practical matter, it is unlikely that this loss limitation provision will be operative except in cases where partners share losses in a ratio different from the ratio of their capital accounts, or where a partner's interest was acquired at a figure considerably less than the partner's proportionate share of the partnership's basis for its properties.

Classification of Loss Pass-Through

As discussed earlier, certain items of partnership income or loss are required to be separately stated. Included are short-term capital gains or losses, long-term capital gains or losses, and gains or losses from the sale or exchange of Section 1231 assets. If any one (or more) of these separately stated items is a loss and if the partner's distributive share of the aggregate of these losses and ordinary losses exceeds the basis of the partnership interest, the limitation on losses is allocated to the partner's distributive share of each such loss by taking the proportion that each such loss bears to the total of all such losses. Reg. § 1.704-1(d)(2).

For the purpose of limitation, the total of such losses for the year is the sum of the partner's distributive share of losses for the current year, plus the losses disallowed in prior years and carried forward to the current year. Neither any gains among these separately stated items nor any net ordinary income is offset against the losses in arriving at a partner's share of the losses. Instead, these latter items are reported in the ordinary manner and increase the basis of the partner's interest in determining how much of the partner's share of the losses is deductible.

Example 18.64. At the end of the partnership taxable year, partner David Izaak has the following distributive share of partnership items: long-term capital loss, $4,000; short-term capital loss, $2,000; nonseparately stated income, $4,000. Partner David's adjusted basis for his partnership interest at the end of the year, before adjustments for any of the above items, is $1,000. As adjusted under Code Sec. 705(a)(1)(A), David's basis is increased from $1,000 to $5,000 at the end of the year. David's total distributive share of partnership loss is $6,000. Since, without regard to losses, David has a basis of only $5,000, he is allowed to deduct only 5/6 of each loss; that is, $3,333 of his long-term capital loss and $1,667 of his short-term capital loss. David must carry forward to succeeding taxable years $667 as a long-term capital loss and $333 as a short-term capital loss. Reg. § 1.704-1(d)(4), Example (3).

Example 18.65. Assume that in Example 18.64 David has non-partnership capital gains of $6,000 (long-term, $3,000; short-term, $3,000). The partnership losses of $3,333 and $1,667 are offset against his capital gains from other sources.

TAX PLANNING POINTER   ▼

If a partner will suffer a limit on loss pass-through because the losses exceed the basis for the partner's partnership interest and the partner contemplates selling the interest, the partner should make a contribution of money or property with sufficient basis to increase the basis to accommodate the loss prior to the sale. Otherwise, the excess loss deduction will be forfeited.

TAX BLUNDER

Tom Mack and Ted Simon, equal partners in the T Square Partnership, are currently in low individual income tax brackets this year. They anticipate increased partnership earnings next year which will move them into the highest individual income tax bracket. Both partners have $20,000 of suspended losses from the partnership due to at-risk basis limitations. During the current year, they replace their nonrecourse debt with recourse debt that qualifies for at-risk basis.

Result. The partners have replaced nonrecourse debt with recourse debt, thus subjecting them to personal liability for the debt. To make matters worse, the additional at-risk basis allows them to deduct the losses in a year when they are in low individual income tax brackets instead of saving the loss deductions for the next year when they anticipate being in much higher individual income tax brackets.

Limitations on Losses—At-Risk Rules

Congress has been concerned about the ability of taxpayers to obtain the benefits of a tax deduction when there was little likelihood that they would ever suffer the economic burden of the loss. The legislative approach has been to limit losses in trade or business or income-producing activities. Code Sec. 465. Even if there is sufficient basis to deduct a loss, the amount of loss deductible on the partner's return is limited to the partner's at-risk amount. In such ventures, a taxpayer may not deduct a loss for the activity to the extent that the loss is avoided through a stop-loss agreement, an indemnity agreement or like agreement, a nonrecourse loan, or a loan with recourse limited to certain nonactivity assets for security.

For purposes of determining the at-risk amount, nonrecourse loans are *not* included. The loss pass-through is limited to the partner's basis in the capital account and the proportion of any loan of the partnership for which the partner has personal exposure. Thus, limited partners with the principal asset of their venture standing as the only security for the repayment of a debt are permitted a loss pass-through only to the extent of their capital investment.

Example 18.66. The Washington, Madison, and Monroe partnership is a three-person limited partnership with Washington and Madison general partners, and Monroe the limited partner. The capital structure of the partnership is as follows:

	Washington	*Madison*	*Monroe*
Ratio of profit and loss	40%	40%	20%
Capital account basis	$200,000	$200,000	$200,000
Share of recourse debt ($100,000)	50,000	50,000	0
"At-risk" amount for pass-through loss purposes	$250,000	$250,000	$200,000
Share of nonrecourse debt ($200,000) .	80,000	80,000	40,000
Basis for purpose of sale of partnership interest	$330,000	$330,000	$240,000

The result would be the same if the $200,000 debt were a debt placed upon property by a prior owner and the property was acquired by the partnership's taking the property subject to the debt rather than assuming the debt.

However, the at-risk rules only partly affect the holding of real property (other than investments in mineral property) acquired by a partnership after December 31, 1986. "Property acquired" means property owned by the partnership as well as an interest in the partnership acquired by a taxpayer. The exception to the real estate at-risk rules is "qualified nonrecourse financing" which, in general, means financing provided by organizations (banks, savings and loan associations, credit unions, regulated insurance companies, pension funds) and nonrecourse loans made or guaranteed by governmental units and their political subdivisions. Loans from related parties who own as much as 10 percent in the partnership also qualify if the loans are commercially reasonable, bear a reasonable rate of interest, meet the definition of commercial paper under the Uniform Commercial Code, and contain substantially the same terms as loans involving unrelated persons.

Example 18.67. In Example 18.66, if the $200,000 debt were a "qualified nonrecourse financing" on real estate, the at-risk amount for each partner would be the same as the basis in the partnership interest.

Corporate taxpayers (other than S corporations and certain closely held C corporations) are not affected by the at-risk provisions discussed above. Thus, a corporate partner may, for purposes of partnership loss pass-through, include in its basis any partnership liability for any activity listed as "at risk" above.

Passive Activity Losses

Passive activities are those trades or businesses in which taxpayers do not materially participate. Passive losses, in general, may be offset only against passive income. Any currently nondeductible amount is suspended and may be deducted against future passive income or against the proceeds from the ultimate sale of the activity or as a loss upon its abandonment. Code Sec. 469.

Any rental activity is a passive activity regardless of whether the taxpayer materially participates (certain taxpayers who materially participate in rental real estate activities are exempted from this rule). A taxpayer may deduct against other income losses up to $25,000 from real estate rentals in which the taxpayer is an active participant. This deduction is phased out as the taxpayer's adjusted gross income exceeds $100,000. Active participation in rental real estate activities requires actually making management decisions involving the exercise of independent discretion concerning the rental property. Active participation includes hiring repairmen, approving new tenants, and deciding on rental terms. If the taxpayer does not actively participate in the rental real estate activities, then rental losses are treated under the usual rules for passive losses.

An individual is treated as not having actively participated in a rental real estate activity if the individual and a spouse own less than 10 percent in value of all interests in the activity. Limited partners (and to the extent of their limited partnership interests where they are also general partners) do not meet the active participation test. Limited partnership interests are treated as interests in a passive activity without regard to whether the taxpayer materially participates in the activity unless the taxpayer in certain instances is able to categorize a limited partnership interest in order to offset other passive losses currently.

Whether the activity is passive or not is a question which each partner must determine. Even in a general partnership (where there are no limited partners), a partner who does not materially participate in the enterprise has that portion of the loss treated as being from a passive activity while the partners who materially participate are able to deduct their losses currently. The loss limitation rules are applied together to minimize the current deductibility of losses.

Example 18.68. Archie, Baldy, and Chester Thompson are equal partners in a grocery store partnership. Archie and Baldy are involved full-time in the operation of the store. Chester, an attorney, takes no active part in the day-by-day operations of the enterprise. Chester is involved in no other passive activities. At the beginning of the current year each partner had a basis for his partnership interest of $50,000. Because of nonrecourse debt, their respective at-risk bases were $15,000. During the current year, the partnership incurred a loss of $60,000. Both Archie and Baldy may deduct only $15,000 of their $20,000 loss currently. As Chester's loss is from a passive activity on his part, he can deduct nothing currently; his entire loss is suspended.

Where there are suspended losses under the passive loss rules, they may be recouped when the taxpayer recognizes subsequent income from passive activities or, failing that, upon the disposition by the holder of the entire interest in the passive activity. If a general or limited partnership conducts two or more separate activities and the entity disposes of all the assets used or created in one activity, such disposition is a disposition of the entire interest of the partner in that activity. Similarly, if a partner recognizes gain under Code Sec. 731(a) due to a distribution of money from the partnership in excess of the adjusted basis of the partner's interest, a ratable portion of the gain is treated as gain from the disposition of the partner's interest in each separate activity conducted by the partnership. Rev. Rul. 95-5, 1995-1 CB 100.

¶ 18,615   CLOSING OF TAXABLE YEAR

The taxable year of a partnership does not close prior to its normal closing unless there is a "termination" of the partnership. In such an event, the partnership year is terminated as to all partners. Each partner must report, on a return for the taxable year with or within which the partnership terminates, the distributive share of profit or loss for the taxable year of the partnership closed by the termination. The taxable year of a partnership may be closed as to one or more partners, however, without a termination of the partnership. Thus, if one partner disposes (either by sale, death, liquidation, or otherwise) of an entire interest in the partnership during the partnership's taxable year, the partnership year closes with respect to that partner at that time. Assuming that the disposition does not terminate the partnership, the taxable year of the partnership continues to its normal closing as to the remaining partners. Code Sec. 706(c); Reg. § 1.706-1(c).

Where a trust is a partner and the trust terminates, the trust must report its share of partnership items up until the time of the termination of the trust, but the partnership's year does not end merely because of the termination of the trust. Rev. Rul. 72-352, 1972-2 CB 395.

¶ 18,623   TERMINATION OF PARTNERSHIP

The termination of a partnership for federal income tax purposes is not governed by the rules for "dissolution" or "liquidation" of a partnership under state or local law. Reg. § 1.706-1(c)(1). For tax purposes, a partnership is considered as terminated *only* if:

1. No part of any business, financial operation, or venture of the partnership continues to be carried on by any of its partners in a partnership, or

2. Within a 12-month period, there is a sale or exchange of 50 percent or more of the total interest in partnership capital and profits. Code Sec. 708(b)(1); Reg. § 1.708-1(b)(1).

Example 18.69. Hannibal Partnership was engaged in real estate development and also, incidentally, in farming some of its vacant land. On sale by one of the general partners of his interest (less than 50 percent), all real estate development activity ceased. This did not result in termination of the partnership because it continued to carry on its incidental farming activities. *M.R. Ginsberg Est.,* 68-1 USTC ¶ 9429, 396 F.2d 989 (Ct.Cl. 1968).

Example 18.70. On November 20 of the current year, Sarah and Bud Golden, who were both 20 percent partners in Whambo Partnership, sold their interests to Al Hall, who was a 60 percent partner. Since the business was no longer carried on by any of its partners in a partnership, the Whambo partnership was terminated as of November 20 of the current year.

Example 18.71. Partners Mary, Ted, and Peck Hillinger agree on April 30 of the current year, to dissolve their partnership but carry on the business through a winding-up period ending September 30 of the current year. At that time all remaining assets, consisting only of cash, are distributed to the partners. In this case, termination of the partnership because of the cessation of business is not until September 30 of the current year.

Sales or Exchanges

For purposes of determining whether or not there has been a sale or exchange of 50 percent or more of the total interest in partnership capital and profits, a disposition of a partnership interest by gift (including assignment to a successor in interest), bequest, or inheritance or the liquidation of a partnership interest is not considered a sale or exchange. Nor does the contribution of property to the partnership constitute a sale or exchange. Reg. § 1.708-1(b)(1)(ii).

"Fifty percent or more of the total interest in partnership capital and profits" means 50 percent or more of the total interest in partnership capital plus 50 percent or more of the total interest in partnership profits. Thus, the sale of a 30 percent interest in partnership profits and a 60 percent interest in partnership capital is not the sale or exchange of 50 percent or more of the interest in both partnership capital and profits. The sale or exchange of 50 percent or more of the total interest in both partnership capital and profits may result from the sale or exchange of different interests aggregating this much or more by two or more partners within a period of 12 consecutive months. Percentages are determined under this rule as of the date of each sale.

Example 18.72. On April 12 of the current year, Tony Beyer sold his 30 percent interest in the capital and profits of Ton-Don-Son Partnership to Bill Peters and on March 27 of the subsequent year, Don Owens sells his 30 percent interest in capital and profits to Ellen. Since the two interests aggregate 60 percent of the total interest in capital and 60 percent of the total interest in profits, the partnership is considered as terminated on March 27 of the subsequent year.

Close of Taxable Year

The partnership taxable year is considered to be closed as of the first date on which there occurs either a winding-up of partnership affairs or a sale or exchange of 50 percent or more of the total interest in the partnership capital and profits within 12 months. If a partnership is considered as terminated, the partnership is treated as distributing all of its assets to a new partnership in exchange for an interest in the new partnership, and immediately thereafter, the new partnership distributes interests in the new partnership to the purchasing partners and continuing partners in proportion to their interests in the terminated partnership. Reg. § 1.708-1(b)(1)(iii) and (iv).

Withdrawal of Partner

A partnership taxable year closes with respect to a partner who disposes of an entire interest in a partnership and with respect to a partner whose entire interest is liquidated. Code Sec. 706(c)(2)(A); Reg. § 1.706-1(c)(2)(i). If a partner sells or exchanges a part of the interest in the partnership or if the interest of a partner is reduced, the partnership taxable year continues to its normal conclusion, unless the partial sale or reduction terminates the partnership. Where such a termination does not occur, the partner's distributive share is determined by taking into account the partner's varying interest in the partnership during the partnership taxable year in which the sale or exchange or reduction of interest occurred. Code Sec. 706(d). See discussion at ¶ 18,615.

This varying interest rule applies to any partner who sells or exchanges less than an entire interest in the partnership or with respect to a partner whose interest is reduced (whether by entry of a new partner, partial liquidation of a partner's interest, gift, or otherwise). Code Sec. 706(d).

In the case of a disposition by death, liquidation, or otherwise of a partner's entire interest, the partner must include, in taxable income for the taxable year with or within which the partner's membership in the partnership ends, the distributive share for the period ending with the date of the disposition. Code Sec. 706(c)(2)(A). In order to avoid an interim closing of the partnership's books, the withdrawing partner's share may by agreement among the partners be estimated by taking the pro rata part of the distributive share the partner would have included in taxable income had the partner remained a partner until the end of the partnership year. If this method of computing the transferor partner's share is used, any partner who is the transferee of such partner's interest must include in taxable income, as the distributive share, the pro rata part of the amount the partner would have included had he or she been a partner from the beginning of the taxable year of the partnership. Reg. § 1.706-1(c)(2)(ii).

Example 18.73. Assume that a partner who is selling a partnership interest on June 30, 1998, has an adjusted basis for the interest of $5,000, that the pro rata share of partnership income up to June 30 is $15,000 ($6/12 × $30,000), and that the interest is sold for $20,000. The $15,000 is includible in partner's income as the distributive share, and the basis of the partnership interest is accordingly increased to $20,000. Therefore, no gain is recognized on the sale of the partnership interest. The purchaser of this partnership interest must include in income only the distributive share of partnership income for the remainder of the partnership taxable year (6/12).

If the partnership reported under the cash receipts and disbursements method of tax accounting, the rules governing "allocable cash-basis items" discussed at ¶ 18,335 come into play to prevent the incoming partner from benefiting from the items that accrued prior to the change. Code Sec. 706(d).

Death of a Partner

TRA '97 amended the tax law to require a closing of the tax year with respect to a deceased partner for partnership years beginning after December 31, 1997. Code Sec. 706(c)(2). As with other dispositions, the tax year continues for the remaining partners. The deceased partner's final income tax return includes the partner's share of partnership income up to the date of the partner's death. The estate or other successor to the partnership interest will include its share of the partnership income for the remainder of the partnership's tax year.

> *Example 18.74.* Hank Brown owns a 50 percent interest in both the capital and profits of the Hank-Mate Partnership, which reports on a June 30 fiscal year. Pursuant to TRA '97, the partnership year ends at Hank's death on October 31, 1999. Hank's distributable share of the partnership's income for the partnership's June 30, 1999, fiscal year (assume $50,000) and his distributable share of the income for the short year, July 1–October 31, 1999, (assume $30,000) must be reported on Hank's final return for 1999. The income for the decedent's final year may be included in a joint return.

Even upon the death of one partner in a two-member partnership, the partnership business is not considered as terminated if the estate or other successor in interest of the deceased partner continues to share in the profits or losses of the partnership business. Probate courts in many states, however, are extremely reluctant to permit a partner's estate to continue as a member of the firm in the absence of an express direction in the will or a binding agreement between the parties.

Continuation of Partnership After Merger, Consolidation, or Division

If two or more partnerships merge or consolidate into a single partnership, the resulting partnership is considered as a continuation of the merging or consolidating partnership whose members own an interest of more than 50 percent in the capital and profits of the resulting partnership. The other merging or consolidating partnerships are considered as terminated. If more than one partnership can be considered as the continuing partnership under this rule, the one credited with contributing the greatest dollar value of assets will be so considered unless the IRS permits otherwise. But, if two partnerships merge and the members of each former partnership collectively own exactly 50 percent of the total capital and profits interests in the resulting partnership, both predecessor partnerships are considered to have been terminated and a new partnership results. Code Sec. 708(b)(2)(A); Reg. § 1.708-1(b)(2)(i).

Any partnership considered to have been terminated by merger or consolidation must file a return for a taxable year ending upon the date of the merger or consolidation. The resulting partnership must file a return for the taxable year of the partnership that is considered as continuing. This return must state that the resulting partnership is a continuation of such merging or consolidating partnership and must include the names and addresses of the merged or consolidated partnerships. The respective distributive shares of the partners for the periods prior to and subsequent to the date of merger or consolidation must be shown as a part of the return.

Upon the division of a partnership into two or more partnerships, any resulting partnership or partnerships is considered a continuation of the prior partnership only if its members had an interest of more than 50 percent in the capital and profits of the prior partnership. Any other resulting partnership is not considered a continuation of the prior partnership, but is considered a new partnership. Where members of a partnership which has been divided into two or more partnerships do not become members of a resulting partnership which is considered a continuation of the prior partnership, such partners' interests are considered to have been liquidated as of the date of the division. The resulting partnership that is regarded as continuing must file a return for the taxable year of its predecessor. The return must state that the partnership is a continuation of the divided partnership and must set forth separately the respective distributive shares of the partners for the period prior to and subsequent to the date of division. Code Sec. 708(b)(2)(B); Reg. § 1.708-1(b)(2)(ii).

¶ 18,655   FAMILY PARTNERSHIPS

The family partnership has long been a standard tax-minimizing device. By bringing a spouse, children, parents, or other dependent relatives into the family business as partners, family income can be spread among more taxpayers and thus have more of it taxed in the dependents' lower tax brackets and less in the taxpayer's higher tax bracket. The IRS has consistently scrutinized with care all such arrangements and has carried to the courts its objections to literally hundreds of family partnerships. Acknowledging as an isolated proposition that a valid partnership may exist between related taxpayers, the IRS has not felt bound by state law in determining the validity of a partnership for tax purposes. As the federal income tax law contains its own concept of a partnership, a family partnership may be ignored for tax purposes even though it is perfectly valid in all other respects.

Bona Fide Partnership Relationship

Out of the maze of litigation concerning these family partnerships, the Supreme Court in three decisions attempted to lay down a standard for determining whether or not an alleged family partnership had "reality" or was a "sham." *F.E. Tower,* 46-1 USTC ¶ 9189, 327 U.S. 280, 66 S.Ct. 532 (1946); *A.L. Lusthaus,* 46-1 USTC ¶ 9190, 327 U.S. 293, 66 S.Ct. 539 (1946); *W.O. Culbertson,* 49-1 USTC ¶ 9323, 337 U.S. 733, 69 S.Ct. 1210 (1949). The Supreme Court recognized that partnerships are of two general classes: (1) those in which capital is a material income-producing factor, such as a partnership that requires a large inventory, and (2) those in which the principal income-producing factor is service, for example, a partnership in which the income is largely attributable to commissions or fees. Reg. § 1.704-1(e)(1)(i) and (iv). In order for a family partnership to be valid, under the rules laid down originally by the Supreme Court, there must be either an investment of "capital originating with" the alleged partner or a substantial contribution to the control and management of the business or "vital" additional services by the alleged partner. *F.E. Tower, supra.* By original capital, the Court meant capital that was the property of the purported partner and that had not been acquired by gift from a donor-partner immediately preceding the creation of the partnership. "Sham" or "lacking reality" has been the terminology frequently used by the courts.

Gift of Partnership Interest

The application of the "investing original capital or providing vital services" rule led to difficulties in the case where a bona fide partnership was desired and, in *Culbertson, supra,* the Court modified its position and pronounced that "intent" was the most important factor to be considered. A gift of a partnership interest was thus recognized if the parties intended to create a partnership.

In 1948, the Code amendment permitting husband and wife to file joint returns shifted the emphasis from husband-wife partnerships to parent-child partnerships. The Code was further amended to provide that a partner would be recognized for income tax purposes if the partner owned a capital interest in a partnership in which capital was a material income-producing factor, whether or not the interest was acquired by purchase or gift from any other person. Code Sec. 704(e)(1).

In view of the statutory language, motive in making a gift of a partnership interest is now generally unimportant. Reg. § 1.704-1(e)(2)(x). Being precluded from attacking a partnership simply because an interest therein was acquired by gift, the Treasury Department has indicated in its Regulations relating to family partnerships (Reg. § 1.704-1(e)) that it would attack the *gift* itself if lacking in "reality," that is, if the donor has not in fact relinquished sufficient control over the property or the interest to create a bona fide partnership relationship. *M.J. Spiesman,* 58-2 USTC ¶ 9890, 260 F.2d 940 (CA-9

1958). Thus, there will be no shift in the incidence of taxation where a parent purportedly assigns a part of the partnership interest to a child, but the child receives no interest in the partnership assets, or any control over the business, and in fact is not accepted as a partner by the other partners.

Allocation of Income

In partnerships where the material income-producing factor is services rather than capital, the services rendered must be "substantial" and "vital." *F.E. Tower, supra.* For example, answering the phone for an engineering firm is not the rendition of substantial services. The phone answerer is not, by virtue of such services, a true partner. *A.C. Parlini,* 6 TCM 501, CCH Dec. 15,789(M) (1947).

Even after the hurdle of obtaining income tax recognition of the partnership has been crossed, the allocation of income between donor and donee must be justified. The donee's distributive share must be determined after due allowance has been made for the services contributed by the donor, and the portion of the donee's distributive share attributable to the donee's capital may not be proportionately greater than that attributable to the donor's capital. To the extent that the allocation under the agreement does not satisfy these criteria, the partnership income will be reallocated by the IRS. Code Sec. 704(e)(2); Reg. § 1.704-1(e)(3); *R.C. Gorrill,* 22 TCM 804, CCH Dec. 26,183(M), T.C. Memo. 1963-168.

> *Example 18.75.* Father gave his son a one-half interest in a service partnership. During the year, the partnership earned $100,000, entirely due to the efforts of the father. If any part of the income is allocated to the son, the IRS will reallocate it to the father.

> *Example 18.76.* Father gave his son $50,000 which was contributed with an additional $50,000 by the father in the formation of a merchandising partnership. The partnership earned $50,000 net from the sale of goods. If the father's efforts had a fair market value of $20,000, a division of the partnership profits of $35,000 ($20,000 + ½ of ($50,000 − $20,000)) to the father and $15,000 to the son would probably withstand challenge from the IRS.

The IRS takes the position that an interest purchased by one member of the family from another member of the family is considered to be created by gift regardless of the consideration actually paid. For this purpose the IRS includes in "the family" the spouse, ancestors, lineal descendants, and any trusts for the primary benefit of such persons. Brothers and sisters are not included. Thus, in the view of the IRS, the above examples would apply even if the son had paid from his own funds full fair market value for the partnership interest.

TAX PLANNING POINTER ▼

While there is no reduction in the gross income reportable by a husband and wife acting as partners, there is the opportunity for both parties to have a retirement plan. There are no great problems if the wife truly renders services sufficient to generate earned income. On the other hand, if the earnings related to the wife are small, it may be advisable to merely have the husband hire his wife in his sole proprietorship (rather than form a partnership). He can have his Keogh plan, and both of them can have their IRAs.

TAX BLUNDER

James Jones Sr. inherited 500 acres of mountain land from his father in the mid-1930s when the value of the property was extremely low because of the Great Depression. The land had a basis to him of $10 per acre. James Sr. had made a gift of this property to his son, James Jr., in 1960 when the property then had a value of $100 per acre. James Sr. and his wife elected gift-splitting and used their lifetime exemptions, so there was no tax paid on the transfer. Located in a remote area of the state, the land lay idle. James Jr. considered it his retirement investment. In the current year, Harry Wright Inc., a developer, approached James Jr., convinced him that the land was worth $1,000 an acre as a potential ski resort area, and offered to manage the development and sale of the property in lots for "45 percent of the action." Wright estimated that after clearing, etc., the lots would sell for approximately $1,000,000. They formed a partnership, "Skiland." James Jr. invested $100,000 for 55 percent of the capital and profits; Wright Inc. invested its "know-how" for the remaining 45 percent interest. Skiland borrowed $500,000 from a local bank and purchased the mountain land from James Jr.

Result. The land had a carryover basis to James Jr. of $10 per acre, the basis for gain to his donor father. As James Jr. held the property as an investment, it qualified as a capital asset and, upon the sale of that asset, James Jr. expected long-term capital gain of $495,000. However, since the form of business selected was a partnership, James Jr. owned more than 50 percent of its capital, and the property in the hands of the partnership will be held primarily for sale to customers in the ordinary course of business, Code Sec. 707(b)(2) converted the gain into ordinary income.

Planning. If James Jr. had been willing to accept 50 percent or less of the capital and profits of the partnership or if he had selected the corporate form as the development vehicle, he might have preserved his long-term capital gain on the sale.

SUMMARY OF CHAPTER 18

✓ The check-the-box regulations allow an unincorporated entity with more than one owner the opportunity to elect whether it wants to be taxed as a partnership or a corporation.

✓ With the exception of investment partnerships, contributions of property to a partnership are generally nontaxable to the partner and to the partnership.

✓ The transfer of a capital interest in a partnership in exchange for services is usually a taxable event.

✓ The initial basis to a partner for the partnership interest is determined in the same manner as are other acquired assets (e.g., nontaxable exchange, purchase, gift, or inheritance).

✓ The basis of each partner's interest in the partnership includes the partner's share of the partnership liabilities (recourse and nonrecourse).

✓ The partner's basis in the partnership is increased for income items (taxable and nontaxable) and decreased by losses (deductible and nondeductible) and distributions.

✓ The partnership's required tax year is determined in a manner that minimizes deferral of income to the partners. Alternatively, the partnership may establish a natural business year or select a year with no more than three months' deferral and prepay tax on the deferred income.

✓ Most elections are made at the partnership level.

✓ The partnership does not pay tax on its income but instead files an information return that allocates its income to the partners.

✓ The income from the partnership retains its character when it passes through to the partners.

✓ The partnership may specially allocate income and deductions in accordance with the partnership agreement as long as the special allocations have substantial economic effect.

✓ Some items of income and deductions are required to be specially allocated to the contributing partner.

✓ No loss is allowed on a sale of property between a partner and a controlled partnership.

✓ Guaranteed payments are deductible by the partnership and includible in income by the recipient partner.

✓ A partner's share of losses from a partnership may be limited by the partnership basis rules, the at-risk basis rules, and the passive activity loss rules.

✓ A partnership terminates if no part of its business is continued to be carried on by any of its partners in a partnership or if there is a sale of 50 percent or more of the total interest in partnership capital and profits within a 12-month period.

✓ A partnership year ends with respect to a partner (but not the partnership) if the partner disposes of his entire interest in the partnership by death, sale, exchange, or otherwise.

✓ Family partnerships may be used to split income among family members, however, special care should be used to assure that minors' income is not reallocated to other partners.

CHAPTER 18 QUESTIONS

1. Give illustrations of the application of the "entity" and the "aggregate" theories as applied to the treatment of partnerships.

2. Upon what criteria will the IRS attempt to tax as a corporation an entity which is classified as a partnership under state law?

3. What is the difference in treatment when an incoming partner purchases an interest by agreeing to perform services for the partnership and the partnership (1) gives a 25 percent interest in the capital of the partnership, (2) gives a 25 percent interest in the future income of the partnership, or (3) gives a 25 percent interest in the partnership's future income which the incoming partner must forfeit if the partnership, as reconstituted after the incoming partner's admission, is unable to earn an average of $100,000 profit for the ensuing five years?

4. List at least three items which will increase a partner's basis in a partnership and at least three items which will decrease a partner's basis.

5. What income tax effect does a partnership's receipt of tax-exempt interest and the proceeds of key-person life insurance payable on account of the death of the insured have upon the partnership taxable income? Upon the basis of the surviving partners' interests in the partnership?

6. Discuss the consequences to a partnership that elects a fiscal year under Code Sec. 444 to avoid a required tax year of December 31.

7. Why is it necessary for a partnership to list as separate items of expense payments to partners for meals and lodging incurred by them while away from home on partnership business?

8. Discuss the partnership's treatment of contributed accounts receivable of a cash-basis taxpayer, inventory and capital assets with a "built-in loss" at the time of the contribution.

9. Eli Kalbach, a calendar-year taxpayer, is a partner in a partnership which for many years has reported its income on a January 31 fiscal year. Explain why Kalbach claims that he is permanently deferring 11 months of partnership income by this reporting method.

10. Discuss the closing of the partnership year for tax purposes when there is a sale by a partner of a 49 percent interest in the partnership. What would happen if within a 12-month period of the sale by the 49 percent partner there is a sale by another partner of a 10 percent interest in the same partnership?

11. Explain why when a partnership has no income other than tax-exempt income and gains from the sales of long-term capital assets, a partner receiving a guaranteed payment must classify the payment as ordinary income.

12. What difference does it make that a partner receiving a guaranteed salary from the partnership is not treated as an employee of the partnership?

13. Discuss the "varying interest rule," particularly as it applies to "cash items."

14. Explain under what circumstances a net operating loss of a partnership can be carried over and applied against income of a partner even after the 18-year carryover period provided for net operating loss carryovers has expired.

15. Determine the tax treatment by a 50 percent partner in a general partnership which for its tax year shows an ordinary partnership loss of $10,000 (resulting mostly from a casualty loss of $12,000). In addition, the partnership experiences a Code Sec. 1231 loss of $8,000, and a net long-term capital loss of $16,000. The partner's only income for the year is $10,000 from dividends. The partner is unmarried, has no dependents, and has itemized deductions (state income tax) of $1,000.

16. Explain why a partner may have sufficient basis in a partnership interest to absorb a distributable share of a partnership loss but will not currently be permitted to deduct that loss because of the debt structure of the partnership or the activity generating the loss.

17. On February 19 of the current year, Bobby Morley contributes property with a $75,000 fair market value, $40,000 basis to the Morley Partnership, in which Bobby has a 40 percent interest. On August 7 of the same year, the Morley Partnership distributes $75,000 cash to Bobby. What are two possible ways in which these transactions could be interpreted? What is the manner in which the IRS will interpret the transactions? Why?

18. Explain the probable income tax treatment for a family member's sale of property to a family partnership. Address both the problem of a sale at a loss and a sale at a gain.

19. If the partnership agreement contains no provision governing the event, what is the effect of a partner's death on the income tax reporting of the partnership? The deceased partner? The deceased partner's successor in interest?

20. Under what circumstances will the Internal Revenue Service recognize a minor child as a partner in a service partnership? In a partnership where capital is a major income-producing item?

21. In a bona fide, arm's-length transaction, a son, age 42, purchased from his father a 40 percent interest in the father's partnership, paying the full fair market value. The partnership is a manufacturing concern. The partnership's ordinary income, before partners' salaries, was $100,000. The father and son were entitled to guaranteed payments of $60,000 and $40,000, respectively. The salary paid to the father is reasonably equivalent to comparable services rendered like con-

cerns. The son rendered no services to the partnership. What will be the likely approach of the IRS on such payments?

22. Identify and discuss the three situations in which a partner recognizes gain (income) or loss on the receipt of an interest in partnership capital and profits.

23. (a) Various elections must be made to compute a partnership's taxable income. For example, the partnership's tax year and accounting method must be chosen. Elections regarding depreciation and Code Sec. 179 expensing of assets also may have to be made. Who makes these elections?

(b) A calendar-year partnership is organized in April of the current year. It begins business in October of the current year. The partnership incurs and pays the following expenses during the last six months of the current year: $3,000 for legal and accounting fees in connection with forming the partnership and $4,500 for brokerage and registration fees in connection with issuing and marketing interests in the partnership. What options are available with respect to the $7,500 in partnership expenditures?

CHAPTER 18 PROBLEMS

24. Ozone Partnership constructed an office building which has a projected annual income of $100,000 for several years. Archie Edwards, the architect for the building, whose normal fee is $50,000, contributes cash for a 25 percent interest in the partnership. The partnership agreement provides Archie will receive (1) 25 percent of the earnings and profits from the partnership and (2) an allocation and distribution of $25,000 of partnership gross income for its first two years of operation after the building is fully leased. The leasing prospects and cash flow projections are excellent. Assuming the annual gross income for the first two years is $100,000 in each year and that depreciation and cash expense items, exclusive of Archie's arrangement, total $60,000, compute the income of the partnership and of Archie. Indicate the classification.

25. James Michaels invested $25,000 for a one-third interest in the Jabo Partnership on January 1 of the current year. The partnership purchased a building site on February 5 at a cost of $200,000, paying $50,000 as a down payment and obtaining a mortgage of $150,000 at 12 percent annual interest for only three years, then full payment of principal. Because of an unexpected rezoning of the property, it substantially increased in value. Jabo Partnership broke exactly even for the current year, income exactly the same as expense. On December 31 James sold his one-third interest to Joe Hammer, receiving $62,500 in cash. What was James's basis for his interest in the partnership immediately prior to the sale? What was the sales

price of the interest? What is the character of James's gain upon the sale of his interest?

26. On January 17 of the current year, the Bamber Partnership was formed by Bob Miller, Carl Penn, and Don Allen. Each partner has an equal interest in the capital and profits of the partnership. The Bamber partnership will report on the basis of a calendar year. The following contributions were made when the partnership was formed.

Partner	Property	Basis to Partner	FMV
Bob	Cash	$15,000	$15,000
Carl	Inventory	9,000	15,000
Don	Capital Asset	35,000	15,000

Both the inventory and capital asset are inventory to the Bamber partnership. On May 22 the partnership sells the inventory for $27,000. On July 19 the partnership sells the capital asset which Don contributed for $9,000. The partnership agreement is silent regarding the property contributed by the partners. Without regard to the sale of the contributed properties, the Bamber partnership reports $60,000 of ordinary income for its current tax year. As a result of partnership transactions, what does each partner report on his individual tax return for the current year?

27. Frank Caster and George Wilson were equal partners of the F&G partnership, which reported its income on the fiscal year ending September 30. For fiscal year 1997–98, the partnership's ordinary income was $30,000. Its ordinary income for the months of October–December 1998 was $9,000. The partnership was terminated on December 31, 1998, and each partner was repaid his capital account as of September 30, 1998, plus his earnings since that date. Frank did not receive his check until January 1, 1999. What income will Frank report from the partnership on his 1998 personal return?

28. Diane Barnes has a 25 percent interest and Ester Newton has a 75 percent interest in the income and capital of D&E Partnership. The partnership reports ordinary income of $25,000, tax-exempt interest of $1,000, and long-term capital gains of $5,000 for the current year. Ester's basis for her partnership interest as of the beginning of the year was $60,000. She made withdrawals of $5,000 during the year. What is her basis for her interest in the partnership as of the end of the year?

29. Baker, a cash-basis, calendar-year taxpayer, is a partner in an accrual-basis partnership that reports its taxable income on an October 31 fiscal year. Baker has been provided the following information:

	FY 97-98	FY 98-99
Baker's distributive share of partnership ordinary income	$30,000	$40,000
Baker's "salary"		
$1,000 per month	12,000	
$1,500 per month		18,000

The partnership was short of cash and paid none of the above to Baker until January 3, 2000. Compute Baker's income from the partnership for 1998.

30. Because it was anticipated that Bob Short would devote more time to the partnership than would his equal partner Jack Long, it was agreed that Bob would receive a "salary" of $12,000 per year. Bob and Jack would divide the remaining partnership income equally. For the current year, prior to consideration of Bob's salary, the partnership income was comprised of $6,000 long-term capital gain, $2,000 tax-exempt interest, and $8,000 loss from operations. Compute the income (loss) and determine the character thereof reportable by Bob and Jack for the current year.

31. Henry Hawkins owns a 20 percent interest in the HI Partnership. On July 1 he sold 100 shares of stock of IPR Corporation to the partnership for $10,000, its fair market value. The stock had cost him $5,000 10 months prior to the sale. How much and what character of profit must Henry report on this sale currently?

32. Assume that the HI Partnership in the preceding problem held the IPR stock for three months and for $15,000 sold it to Isaac Stanley, the 80 percent partner and a real estate broker, on October 1. How much profit must Henry report on this partnership sale currently? What is the character of the reported profit? How would your answer be different if Isaac were a dealer in securities?

33. Marvin Bridges is a 25 percent partner in the Munson partnership. On November 23, 1997, Marvin contributes property with an adjusted basis of $75,000 and a fair market value of $250,000 to the Munson partnership. On March 15, 1998, Marvin receives a $187,500 cash distribution from the partnership.

   a. Why would the IRS seek to classify the transactions as a disguised sale?

   b. Assume that the IRS is successful in classifying the transactions as a disguised sale. Outline the income tax consequences to Marvin.

34. On January 1, 1998, Kelley became a 10 percent partner of the Realty partnership upon contributing land he had held as an investment for five years. The basis of the land to Kelley was $20,000, but its fair market value at the time of the contribution was only $10,000. Assume that after much advertising, Realty Partnership was able to sell the property for $12,000 on

December 31, 1998. How much, if any, loss is recognized by Realty Partnership on the sale and what is its character? Would your answer be different if the sale took place on January 2, 2003?

35. On September 1, 1993, Leonard contributed land held for investment with a fair market value of $20,000 and an adjusted basis to him of $12,000 for a 20 percent interest in the income and capital of Office Complex Partnership. The land was intended for use as a building site for the partnership. The partnership opted to rent facilities and on September 2, 1998, sold the contributed land for $50,000. Assuming the partnership agreement was silent with respect to this particular asset, how much and what character of gain must Leonard report for this partnership sale?

36. On January 1, 1995, Martha Carnes, fresh out of college, contributed $10,000 for a 30 percent interest in an accounting partnership. The senior partner was not attentive to the work, and the first year they were sued for malpractice and a judgment of $100,000 was entered against the firm. The firm borrowed $50,000 in 1995 to assist in its payment. The debt was repaid in 1997. The following shows the results of the partnership operations:

Year	Income/(Loss)
1995	($100,000)
1996	10,000
1997	50,000
1998	100,000

Compute Martha's reportable income (loss) for each year and the basis for her partnership interest at the end of each year.

37. Elder Attorney had practiced law for several years and had accumulated $50,000 in accounts receivable. He reported his income for tax purposes under the cash receipts and disbursements method. His son, Junior Attorney, graduated from law school, was admitted to the bar, and wanted to commence practice of law. Elder formed an equal partnership with Senior Counsel, Lawyers Unlimited, a cash-basis law partnership, and transferred his $50,000 accounts receivable to the partnership for their admitted FMV of $50,000. With the consent of Senior Counsel, Elder transferred his entire partnership interest by gift to Junior. In the first year of the partnership, its cash-basis income was $100,000, $50,000 of which was the collection of the transferred receivables. When is the income of the partnership reported and by whom?

38. William Nest operated a consulting business as a sole proprietor in 1997, generating fees of $50,000. On January 1, 1998, he decided to set up a consulting partnership with his son Wilhelm. William transferred a used computer with an adjusted basis of $10,200 and a fair market value of $11,000 and other office equipment with an adjusted basis of $12,250 and a fair market

value of $14,000. William also felt that he had generated goodwill with a value of $30,000 that was supported by a recent bona fide offer for his consulting business. On January 1, 1998, William gave his son Wilhelm $55,000, which he contributed to the new partnership, Will and Wile, for a one-half interest. The gross earnings of the new partnership for 1998 totalled $75,000—$50,000 from William's contacts and $25,000 from Wilhelm's contacts. The net income was $60,000. In anticipation of Wilhelm's growing contribution to future earnings, the agreement provides for equal division of profit. What is Wilhelm's basis for his interest? How will the IRS probably require that the partnership earnings be divided?

39. The Nelson partnership begins business on July 17, 1998. It is not able to use business purpose to support a tax year. The partnership consists of four partners. The partners, their interests in partnership capital and profits, and their tax years are as follows:

Partner	Partnership Interest (%)	Tax Year
Individual A	4	1/1-12/31
Individual B	45	1/1-12/31
Corporation C	21	7/1-6/30
Corporation D	30	10/1-9/30

What tax year must the Nelson partnership adopt?

40. Jack Dillon and Jake Johnson each own 50 percent of the capital interests in the JJ partnership. They share profits equally, but they agree to allocate 60 percent of the losses to Jack and 40 percent to Jake. The note payable is a recourse liability. The tax-basis balance sheet at the end of the year is as follows:

Cash	$ 50,000
Equipment	100,000
Total assets	$150,000
Note Payable	$ 90,000
Capital, Jack Dillon	30,000
Capital, Jake Johnson	30,000
Total liabilities and capital	$150,000

Determine how much of the liability is allocable to each partner.

41. Jed Castanza transfers $100,000 of cash to the JN partnership for a 60 percent interest in the JN partnership. Ned transfers a building with an adjusted basis of $30,000 and a fair market value of $100,000, subject to a debt of $40,000 that the partnership assumes, in exchange for a 40 percent interest in the JN partnership. Determine each partner's adjusted basis in his partnership interest. Does either partner recognize any gain on the transfer to the partnership? What is JN's basis in the assets?

42. Assume the same facts as in problem 41 except that Jed's basis in the building is only $20,000. Determine each partner's adjusted basis in his partnership interest. Does either partner recognize any gain on the transfer to the partnership? What is JN's basis in the assets?

43. Paul Stanley transfers $20,000 in cash, Joe Sweitzer transfers machinery with an adjusted basis of $5,000 and a fair market value of $20,000, and David Raines transfers land with an adjusted basis of $10,000, a fair market value of $26,000, and subject to a mortgage of $6,000 in exchange for equal interests in the newly formed PJD partnership. What are the partners' initial adjusted bases in their partnership intersts? What is the PJD partnership's basis in its assets?

44. Joe Quick and Jane Reddy are equal partners in the Quick and Reddy partnership. On the first day of the current taxable year, Joe's adjusted basis in his partnership interest is $10,000 and Jane's adjusted basis is $2,000. During the year, Joe had withdrawals of $25,000 and Jane had withdrawals of $20,000. Given the following partnership activity for the year, determine each partner's adjusted basis in Quick and Reddy at the end of the taxable year.

Ordinary income	$60,000
Section 1231 gains	1,000
Interest income from municipal bonds	500
Short-term capital losses	2,000
Charitable contributions	3,000

45. Jeff Able is a partner in the Willing and Able partnership. On June 1, 1998, Jeff transfers property to the partnership that has a fair market value of $60,000 and an adjusted basis to Jeff of $10,000. Three weeks later, the Willing and Able partnership transfers $40,000 cash to Jeff. Willing and Able would not have transferred the cash to Jeff had he not first transferred the property. What are the tax consequences of the transactions to Jeff?

46. Susan Moore contributed land with an adjusted basis of $5,000 and a fair market value of $8,000 to the Whirligig partnership in exchange for a 20 percent interest in the partnership. Susan held the land as a capital asset, and Whirligig also held the land as a capital asset. Three years after Susan transferred the land, Whirligig sells the land for $10,000. What is Whirligig's gain on the sale of the land, and what is Susan's allocable portion of the gain?

47. For federal income tax purposes a partnership may be comprised of:
    a. Two or more individuals
    b. An individual and a corporation
    c. A trust, an estate, and an individual
    d. Two or more partnerships
    e. All of the above

48. In which of the following situations does the partnership's tax year close with respect to all partners in the partnership?

  a. An equal partner in a two-partner partnership dies. The deceased partner's interest is sold to the remaining partner.

  b. An equal partner in a four-partner partnership sells his entire interest to an unrelated third party.

  c. A 60 percent partner in a three-partner partnership gives her interest to her grandson.

  d. A 55 percent partner in a five-partner partnership has her interest liquidated through an immediate lump-sum payment from the partnership.

49. The basis of a partner's interest in a partnership is increased by:

  a. Decrease in partnership liabilities

  b. Receipt by the partnership of an item of income that is excluded from the definition of gross income

  c. Gain recognized by another partner when the other partner sells an interest in the partnership at a gain

  d. Payment by partnership of nondeductible expense

  e. Issuance of a promissory note to the partnership to pay for an additional interest in the partnership.

50. If the partnership agreement is silent regarding the matter:

  a. The partnership year ends upon the death of one partner in a two-person partnership.

  b. All items of income, deductions, and credits must be shared by the partners in proportion to their profit and loss ratios.

  c. The partnership year ends with respect to a selling partner only if the partner's sales (plus other sales) total 50 percent or more of the partnership interest.

  d. A partner who renders a disproportionate amount of time or capital to the partnership is entitled to a guaranteed payment.

  e. None of the above.

51. *Comprehensive Problem.* Hazel Patrick owns a building in which she practices dentistry. She also owns substantial amounts of equipment used in her practice. The building cost her $100,000 and its adjusted basis is $60,000; its present fair market value is $200,000. Had she used straight-line depreciation, her adjusted basis would be $75,000. Her equipment, which originally cost her $20,000 three years ago, has an adjusted basis of $5,000 and a present fair market value of $7,500. She also has cash-basis accounts receivable with a face amount of $20,000 and accounts payable in the amount of $15,000. She has $5,000 in fair market value of dental gold, which she had expensed upon purchase.

Hazel has been approached to enter into an equal partnership with another dental practitioner. They would prefer that their contributions to the partnership have substantially equal value. It has been suggested that Hazel either retain her building and rent it to the partnership at $25,000 net rent per year or place a mortgage of $100,000 against it and contribute it to the new partnership subject to the mortgage.

Compute Hazel's basis in the partnership under the alternative propositions.

Determine what and how much, if any, are the recaptures.

52. *Comprehensive Problem.* Barbara Thompson and Colleen Tiller are equal partners in the Boteq partnership. Barbara is age 72 and Colleen age 58. Both are unmarried and the partnership is their sole source of income. During the current year, Boteq's records show the following items of income and expense. In a columnar form, list those items which must be reported as partnership ordinary income and those which must be reported separately by the partnership.

(1)	Gross profit on sale of goods	$40,000
(2)	Selling and administrative expenses	30,000

Other items not included in above:

(1)	Dividends from domestic corporations	1,000
(2)	Charitable contributions to church	500
(3)	Long-term capital gains	2,000
(4)	Short-term capital losses	500
(5)	Section 1245 gain on office equipment which had an adjusted basis at sale of $400	800
(6)	Theft of day's receipts	1,200
(7)	Theft of Barbara's fur coat in the pocket of which were the receipts. Original cost $2,500, FMV at date of theft $1,000	
(8)	Royalty check for Boteq's $10,000 investment this year in a widget mining venture	400
(9)	Notice of Boteq's coal percentage depletion allowance of $1,000 (the property has been fully depleted for several years)	
(10)	Expensing of seven-year property under Code Sec. 179, purchased during the year	2,000
(11)	Social Security benefit checks payable to Barbara which were regularly deposited to Boteq's account	4,500

53. *Research Problem.* Mary Black, Nell Brown, and Louise Gray each has her own computer equipment and service retail store. In an effort to potentially reduce their costs and increase their control over supply channels, they buy a plant which manufactures selected computer supplies and equipment. Each makes an equal cash contribution toward the purchase of the plant, each has an equal capital and profits interest in the plant, and they agree to share all losses equally. They own the plant as

tenants in common. The co-owners have a written operating agreement specifying that each has an equal interest in the plant's production, each is responsible for her equal share of expenses, and each owns a proportionate, undivided part of the plant's equipment. The agreement also provides that the plant, as such, does not have the right to market the manufactured computer supplies and equipment. In lieu of the plant's selling the manufactured computer supplies and equipment to other purchasers, Mary, Nell, and Louise agree that each will take one-third of the plant's annual output. Each takes her share of the output, commingles it with other computer equipment and supplies in their respective computer equipment and service retail stores, and sells it to customers.

With regard to the plant, research and answer the following questions:

1. Is the plant a partnership for federal income tax purposes?

2. If the plant is a partnership for federal income tax purposes, may it make an election not to be subject to the partnership provisions of Subchapter K of the Internal Revenue Code?

3. Without regard to your answer to question two, assume that the plant may elect out of Subchapter K. Are Mary, Nell, and Louise subject to the self-employment tax on their distributive shares of the plant's earnings, assuming the output was purchased by Mary, Nell, and Louise, rather than being distributed to each?

Chapter 19

Partnerships—Distributions, Sales, and Exchanges

Learning Objectives

After completing Chapter 19, you should be able to:

1. Explain the tax consequences of a sale of a partnership interest.

2. Categorize distributions as either current distributions or liquidating distributions.

3. Determine whether the partnership has any Section 751 assets.

4. Identify distributions as either proportionate or disproportionate distributions of Section 751 property.

5. Determine the tax consequences of proportionate and disproportionate distributions of Section 751 property.

6. Apply the basis rules for assets distributed by a partnership to a partner.

7. Recognize situations where a step-up in basis election might be beneficial and compute the basis adjustment.

8. Evaluate the tax consequences of payments to a retiring partner.

OVERVIEW OF CHAPTER

The income tax effects of a distribution by a partnership to a partner depend on whether the distribution is a current distribution or a liquidating distribution. A current distribution is one which is not in liquidation of a partner's interest in the partnership. A liquidating distribution is one or a series of distributions that liquidates a partner's interest in a partnership.

Generally, the partnership recognizes no gain or loss on a partnership distribution. The distributee partner recognizes gain only if cash distributed exceeds the partner's basis in the partnership interest. The gain is capital gain. No loss is recognized on a current distribution. A loss may be recognized on a liquidating distribution if the distribution consists of only cash, unrealized receivables, and/or inventory, and the basis to the partnership of the properties distributed is less than the basis of the partner's interest in the partnership. The loss is a capital loss.

If the partnership has "unrealized receivables" and/or "substantially appreciated inventory items," and a distribution results in the distributee partner's not receiving a proportionate part of these assets, special rules recast part of the distribution as a disposition of part of these assets for part of the other assets of the partnership. "Unrealized receivables" and "substantially appreciated inventory items" are specifically defined in the partnership provisions of the Internal Revenue Code, Subchapter K. These special rules may cause ordinary gain or loss to be recognized by the distributee partner and/or the partnership.

Generally, when a partner disposes of property received in a distribution, the character of the gain or loss depends on the partner's use of the property. However, with respect to distributed property that was unrealized receivables or inventory to the partnership before the distribution, the partner's gain or loss is ordinary, regardless of how the partner uses it. The partnership taint on the inventory is lost after the distributee partner has held it five years.

Special rules apply in the case of partnership payments to a retiring partner or a successor in interest. Essentially, the payments are divided into two parts: (1) payments for the partner's interest in partnership property—property payments; and (2) payments that are guaranteed payments or the partner's distributive share of partnership income—income payments. The income tax results for the payments place the retiring partner and the remaining partnership in adversarial and unique tax-planning positions. The reason is that property payments cause capital gain to the partner and are not deductible by the partnership. On the other hand, income payments are ordinary income to the partner, but are deductible by, or deflect the distributive shares of, the remaining partners.

Under the entity rule, a partner's interest in a partnership generally is a capital asset. Therefore, when the partner disposes of a partnership interest, generally there is capital gain or loss. However, under the aggregate theory, if there are "unrealized receivables" or "substantially appreciated inventory items" in the partnership, some of the gain is ordinary gain.

Generally, the partnership does not adjust the basis of its properties because of a distribution or a partner's disposition of a partnership interest. However, provided there is a Code Sec. 754 election in effect, in certain cases the partnership may adjust the basis of partnership properties.

There is a common adjustment, in the case of a distribution, when a distributee partner recognizes gain or loss, or takes a basis in distributed property that is different from the partnership's predistribution basis in the property. In the case of a disposition, there is an adjustment, which is unique to the purchasing partner, for the difference between what the purchasing partner pays for the partnership interest, and the purchasing partner's share of the basis of partnership property.

Partnership Interest as a Capital Asset

¶ 19,001   ENTITY RULE v. AGGREGATE THEORY

The entity rule is used in transactions involving the sale, exchange, or partial or complete liquidation of a partnership interest. Viewing the partnership as a separate entity, the ownership interest in a partnership is similar to the ownership interest in a corporation. The sale or exchange of such an interest should result in a capital gain or loss. This entity concept bred opportunities for tax avoidance through the creation of "collapsible" partnerships, which translated ordinary income into capital gains.

> *Example 19.1.* Two building contractors formed a partnership, built up a substantial inventory of finished houses, then sold their partnership interests to third parties. As their partnership interests were classified as capital assets, they obtained capital gain treatment on the transaction. However, if the partners would have had the partnership sell the buildings, the profit on the sale would have generated ordinary income. If the partnership were reporting on the cash basis for tax purposes, the same type of transaction would have converted the ordinary income in uncollected receivables into capital gain upon the sale of the partnership interest.

To prevent this type of tax avoidance, the Internal Revenue Code resorts to the aggregate theory in certain transactions between the partners and their partnership. The aggregate theory applies with respect to inventory and "unrealized receivables." Both of these items have ordinary income potential, which will be recognized by the partnership as soon as the inventory is sold or the receivable is collected. Therefore, part of the proceeds is allocated to these assets, generating ordinary income. Capital gain treatment is retained for the remaining partnership interest when it is sold, exchanged, or liquidated. In certain transactions, the gains or losses are deferred through various basis adjustments, discussed later.

¶ 19,011   DEFINITIONS

"Unrealized Receivables" Defined

The term "unrealized receivables" includes, to the extent not otherwise includible in income under the partnership's tax accounting method, any rights to payment for goods or services where the proceeds from such sales or services if received by the partnership are reported as ordinary income. The term encompasses trade accounts receivable of a cash-basis taxpayer and the excess of the fair market value over the basis of trade accounts receivable of accrual-basis taxpayers. Also included are the rights to payment for incomplete goods in process at the time of their sale or distribution. The term also extends to recapture of depreciation under Code Sec. 1245 and excess depreciation under Code Sec. 1250 (both measured as if the asset were sold at its fair market value at the time of distribution). In addition, there are also included many items that in the absence of this classification would have received capital gains treatment. The list includes gain recognition on the sale or distribution of certain mining property, stock in a DISC or a controlled foreign corporation, farm and farm land recapture under Code Sec. 1252, franchises, trademarks, or trade names under Code Sec. 1253, certain oil, gas, or geothermal property under Code Sec. 1254, market discount bonds (as defined in Code Sec. 1278), and short-term obligations (as defined in Code Sec. 1283) to the extent of the amount that would be treated as ordinary income if the property had been sold by the partnership. Code Sec. 751(c).

Basis to Partnership of Unrealized Receivables

The most commonly encountered unrealized receivable is the accounts receivable of a cash-basis taxpayer, in which case the receivable has a basis of zero. But as explained above, the term includes other items that may have some costs associated with them. Therefore, a more accurate definition of their bases includes all costs or expenses attributable to those assets paid or accrued but not previously taken into account under the partnership's method of accounting. Reg. § 1.751-1(c)(2). Depreciation recapture has a basis assigned to it of zero.

> *Example 19.2.* Arthur Gomez is a partner in a cash-basis partnership that is a dealer in personal property. Arthur's share of the partnership includes inventory with a sales value of $100 but a basis of $40. The goods have been ordered but have not been shipped. Upon the sale of his partnership interest, Arthur must classify the $60 previously unreported gain as an "unrealized receivable."

Inventory Defined

Prior to the Taxpayer Relief Act of 1997 (TRA '97), a sale of a partnership interest resulted in ordinary income with respect to the inventory only if the inventory was "substantially appreciated." Congress was concerned that taxpayers could easily avoid the mechanical tests to determine whether inventory was "substantially appreciated." Therefore, for sales of partnership interests after June 8, 1997, all gain attributable to inventory is treated as ordinary income, whether the inventory is substantially appreciated or not. Code Sec. 751(a).

While Congress eliminated the requirement that inventory be substantially appreciated for sales of partnership interests, it retained this test for disproportionate distributions of Sec. 751 property from partnerships. In the substantially appreciated test, the definition of inventory is much broader than the familiar "inventory" or goods primarily held for sale to customers in the ordinary course of business. The statutory "inventory items" includes those items but also any property that if sold by the partnership would not be classified as a capital asset or a Section 1231 asset. Note that since receivables arising from the sale of goods or performance of services do not qualify as capital assets or Section 1231 assets, all receivables, whether or not realized, are included in "inventory." Code Sec. 751(d)(2); Reg. § 1.751-1(d)(2).

For ordinary income to be recognized in a disproportionate distribution, the identified inventory items must be "substantially appreciated." The fair market value of the inventory must, in aggregate, exceed 120 percent of the inventory's adjusted basis in the hands of the partnership. Code Sec. 751(d)(1); Reg. § 1.751-1(d)(1). As the value tests are applied to inventory in the aggregate, it is immaterial whether a particular item has or has not met the 120 percent test.

Example 19.3. The balance sheet of RPC, an accrual-basis partnership owned equally by Richard Plum, Pam Collins, and Cullen Rogers, is as follows:

	Basis	FMV
Cash	$15,000	$ 15,000
Accounts receivable	9,000	9,000
Inventory	21,000	30,000
Building (cost $50,000, depreciated straight-line)	42,000	48,000
Land	9,000	6,000
Total	$96,000	$108,000
Liabilities, current	$15,000	$ 15,000
Mortgage payable	21,000	21,000
Capital:		
Richard	20,000	24,000
Pam	20,000	24,000
Cullen	20,000	24,000
Total	$96,000	$108,000

Assume that RPC is not a dealer with respect to the land. The partnership has no unrealized receivables as all of the ordinary income from these receivables has been reported in taxable income and there are no recapture items. The following is the determination of whether its inventory is substantially appreciated:

"Inventory Items":	Basis	FMV
Accounts receivable	$ 9,000	$ 9,000
Inventory	21,000	30,000
Total	$30,000	$39,000

The inventory is substantially appreciated as the FMV of the "inventory items" ($39,000) exceeds 120 percent of their basis ($30,000 × 1.20 = $36,000).

Example 19.4. Assume that RPC is a dealer with respect to the land. That is, the land is an "inventory item" with respect to RPC. Now, the mechanical test is not met.

"Inventory Items":	Basis	FMV
Accounts receivable	$ 9,000	$ 9,000
Inventory	21,000	30,000
Land	9,000	6,000
Total	$39,000	$45,000

The aggregate fair market value for the inventory items, $45,000, does not exceed 120 percent of the aggregate basis for the items, $46,800 ($39,000 × 1.20 = $46,800). Consequently, the inventory items are not substantially appreciated.

Proportionate Distributions to Partners

¶ 19,030 DISTRIBUTIONS IN GENERAL

A partner's interest in a partnership may be sold but it also may be eliminated or reduced by means of a distribution of property from the partnership. The latter has obvious differences from a sale of a partner's interest. In a sale the consideration is received from a third party (which may include a current partner), whereas in a distribution the consideration flows from the partnership itself.

There is no immediate tax impact simply because a partnership possesses Section 751 assets. It should be noted that the problem addressed by Code Sec. 751 is the shifting of ordinary income caused by the sale or *disproportionate* distribution of those assets. So long as those assets are distributed to the partners in proportion to their interests in the partnership, there is no shifting of income. The discussion of current distributions to partners and distributions to partners in complete liquidation of their interests, which immediately follows, assumes *proportionate* distributions of all assets, so the Section 751 assets do not effect the tax consequences of these distributions.

¶ 19,037 CURRENT DISTRIBUTIONS—RECOGNITION OF GAIN AND NONRECOGNITION OF LOSS

A current distribution is a distribution of partnership assets that is not in complete liquidation of the partner's interest in the partnership. In a current distribution the general rule is that no gain or loss is recognized. However, gain is recognized by the recipient partner to the extent that cash or deemed cash received by the partner exceeds the basis of the partnership interest determined immediately before the distribution. Code Sec. 731(a); Reg. § 1.731-1(a)(1). Recall that decreases in a partner's share of partnership liabilities are treated as deemed distributions of cash to the recipient partner. Code Sec. 752(b).

In the case of distributions of marketable securities made by partnerships after December 8, 1994, the fair market value of the distributed securities is treated as a cash distribution for purposes of determining gain recognition by the distributee partner. However, the amount of cash deemed distributed is reduced by the partner's share of the partnership's net appreciation with respect to all securities of the same class and issuer as those distributed. Marketable securities are defined as financial instruments, such as stock, bonds, and other equity interests or evidences of indebtedness, and foreign currencies that are actively traded on the date of distribution. The following distributions are exempt from this rule: (1) distributions of securities that were contributed to the partnership by the distributee partner; (2) distributed property that was not a "marketable" security when acquired by the partnership; (3) distributions of securities by investment partnerships to a partner whose only contributions to the partnership consisted of money, securities, or certain similar property; (4) qualifying distributions in liquidation of a publicly traded partnership; and (5) securities distributed before January 1, 1995, if held by the partnership on July 27, 1994, and certain distributions in liquidation of a partner's interest pursuant to a written binding contract in effect on July 15, 1994, and at all times thereafter. Code Sec. 731(c).

Example 19.5. Partner Jones has a basis for his partnership interest of $10,000. He receives as a current distribution his proportionate share of cash in the amount of $8,000 and land with a basis to the partnership of $1,000 and a fair market value of $3,000. While Jones *realizes* a gain of $1,000, he *recognizes* no gain upon the distribution because the cash distributed does not exceed his basis. His basis in his partnership interest is now $1,000 ($10,000 − $8,000 (cash) − $1,000 (basis in land)). His basis in the land is the same as the basis to the partnership, $1,000.

Example 19.6. If, in Example 19.5, Jones received only cash in the amount of $11,000, he would recognize as gain the $1,000 cash received in excess of his basis. The recognition of gain prevents the partner from having a negative basis in the partnership interest. The recognized gain is treated as having been derived from the "sale or exchange" of the partner's interest in the partnership and therefore generates capital gain.

Example 19.7. Assume, in Example 19.5, that Jones owns a one-third interest in the partnership and received a current distribution of marketable securities with a basis of $9,500 and a fair market value of $11,000 (its entire holding in such securities). He would have a deemed cash distribution of $10,500 ($11,000 fair market value of securities distributed less $500, his one-third share of its appreciation) and recognize as gain the $500 cash deemed received in excess of his basis.

In a distribution that consists of cash and other property, for purposes of computing gain, the cash is deemed to be distributed first. This rule is important to remember because generally the distributee partner takes a carryover basis from the partnership in the other property. At the same time, the partner's basis in the partnership is reduced by cash and the basis of other property that is distributed. Code Sec. 733.

Example 19.8. Refer back to Example 19.5. Assume that the partnership's basis in the land is $7,000, rather than $1,000. With respect to gain recognition, the result is unchanged. The cash of $8,000 is deemed to be distributed first. Since it is less than Partner Jones's basis of $10,000 for the partnership interest, no gain is recognized. If the cash were not deemed to be distributed first, one might mistakenly compute a $5,000 gain from the distribution ($10,000 basis in the partnership interest − $7,000 partnership basis in the land distributed − $8,000 cash distributed).

TAX BLUNDER

Oscar Williams, who had a basis of $10,000 in his partnership interest, received a current distribution of property with an adjusted basis to the partnership of $8,000. This reduced his basis in the partnership to $2,000. The following week he received a distribution of $5,000 in cash, which resulted in his recognizing a gain of $3,000. Had he received the cash and property at the same time, he would have reduced his basis by the cash first and allocated the remaining $5,000 to his basis in the property. Therefore, he could have avoided recognizing the $3,000 of gain.

¶ 19,040 BASIS OF PROPERTY RECEIVED IN CURRENT DISTRIBUTIONS

As a general rule, property distributed in a current distribution takes the same basis in the hands of the distributee partner as it had in the hands of the partnership. If a partner recognizes gain on the distribution of a marketable security (see ¶ 19,037), the basis of the distributed security is increased by the amount of such gain. However, the general rule is subject to exception. The basis of the asset received cannot exceed the basis to the partner of the partnership interest, reduced by any cash received in the same distribution.

Example 19.9. Alice Lawlor has a partnership interest in Acme Partnership with an adjusted basis to her of $10,000. As a proportionate current distribution to her, she receives $5,000 in cash and land held for investment by the partnership with a basis to the partnership of $12,000 and a fair market value of $15,000. Alice reduces her basis by the $5,000 cash and assigns the remaining $5,000 to the land, which reduces her basis in her partnership interest to zero.

Example 19.10. Assume the same facts as in Example 19.9, except that the land has a basis to the partnership of $3,000 and a fair market value of $2,000. Alice reduces her basis by the $5,000 cash and assigns $3,000 basis to the land. Her partnership interest retains $2,000 as its basis. Note that the fair market value of the land, be it $50,000 or $5, is irrelevant for this purpose.

¶ 19,050 RECOGNITION OF GAIN OR LOSS—LIQUIDATING DISTRIBUTIONS

The same rules as explained above with respect to current distributions apply with respect to proportionate distributions in complete liquidation of the partnership interest. However, in a liquidating distribution, a loss can be recognized.

Loss can only be recognized by the partner if the distribution is in complete liquidation of the partner's interest *and* then *only* if (1) the partner receives no property other than cash, unrealized receivables, and inventory items, and (2) the amount of cash plus the *basis* of unrealized receivables and inventory items received is less than the basis of the partnership interest. Any loss recognized by the partner receiving the distribution is capital loss. Code Sec. 731(a); Reg. § 1.731-1(a)(2) and (3). However, the loss from abandonment or worthlessness of a partnership interest is an ordinary loss under Code Sec. 165 if the partner does not receive any actual or deemed (e.g., decrease in share of partnership liabilities) distributions from the partnership. Rev. Rul. 93-80, 1993-2 CB 239.

The term "liquidation of a partner's interest" means the termination of the partner's entire interest in the partnership by means of a distribution (or a series of distributions). The recognized loss is the excess of the adjusted basis of the interest in the partnership at the time of the distribution over the sum of (1) any money distributed to the partner, and (2) the *basis* to the distributee of any unrealized receivables and inventory items which are distributed. For this purpose, inventory items are defined in Code Sec. 751(d)(2) regardless of whether such items are substantially appreciated. If the partner receives *any* property other than money or unrealized receivables or inventory, then no loss is recognized.

Example 19.11. Wilbur Olds, in complete liquidation of his partnership interest, which had a basis to him of $10,000, receives his proportionate share of cash, $5,000, and inventory with a basis to the partnership of $2,000 and a fair market value of $8,000. Although Wilbur has *realized* a gain of $3,000, he reduces his basis by the $5,000 cash and the basis of the inventory to the partnership, $2,000 (in that order). The result is a recognized capital loss of $3,000. Wilbur's basis in the inventory is $2,000.

Example 19.12. If in Example 19.11 above, Wilbur, in addition to the cash and inventory, had received investment land from the partnership, no matter what its basis to the partnership or its fair market value, no gain or loss would be recognized on the distribution.

TAX PLANNING POINTER

In a liquidating distribution, a partner may recognize a loss only if he receives no property other than cash, unrealized receivables, and inventory, and the aggregate bases of the property is less than his adjusted basis in the partnership. If he receives any section 1231 or capital asset, that asset absorbs the balance of his basis in the partnership. A loss on the later sale of that asset generates a capital loss. However, with proper planning, the partner may be able to choose an asset that he can put to business use and depreciate, thereby preserving ordinary deductions.

¶ 19,060 BASIS OF PROPERTY IN LIQUIDATING DISTRIBUTIONS

Where a partnership distributes property (other than money) in liquidation of a partner's entire interest in the partnership, the basis of the property to the distributee partner equals the adjusted basis of the partner's interest in the partnership, reduced by the amount of any money distributed to the partner in the same transaction.

Example 19.13. Thomas Langer, with a partnership interest having an adjusted basis to him of $12,000, receives $2,000 cash as a liquidating distribution from the partnership. Thomas's adjusted basis is reduced by the $2,000 cash distribution, leaving $10,000 of unrecovered basis. Since this is a liquidating distribution and Thomas receives only cash in an amount that is less than his adjusted basis in the partnership, he is allowed to report a $10,000 capital loss.

Example 19.14. Assume the same facts as in Example 19.13, except that Thomas also receives real property with an adjusted basis to the partnership of $6,000 and a fair market value of $14,000. The real property is not inventory to the partnership. The basis of the real property to Thomas is $10,000 (Thomas's basis for his partnership interest, $12,000, reduced by $2,000, the cash distributed). Reg. § 1.732-1(b).

Example 19.15. If Thomas in Example 19.14 subsequently sells the real property, his gain or loss is measured with respect to his basis of $10,000 in the property; its character is determined by the character of the property in Thomas's hands and its holding period includes the time the property was held by the partnership. Code Sec. 735(b).

Note that in Example 19.13, the loss is allowed because Thomas is liquidating his interest but he has $10,000 of unrecovered basis. If a capital asset or Section 1231 asset is received, as in Example 19.14, the loss is deferred by assigning a higher basis to this asset.

¶ 19,061 RECOGNITION OF PRECONTRIBUTION GAIN IN CERTAIN DISTRIBUTIONS

The Energy Policy Act of 1992 added a new section to the Internal Revenue Code. The section affects partnership property distributions where the distributee partner has net precontribution gain. Code Sec. 737. Generally, the recognition of precontribution gains for contributions of property by a partner is accelerated, where the fair market value of distributed property is more than the basis of the distributee partner's interest in the partnership before the distribution.

The rule affects a partner who received property distributions (other than certain marketable securities), the value of which is more than the distributee partner's basis in the partnership interest, where the partner previously contributed property to the partnership and the property contained built-in gain. When such a distribution occurs, the partner must recognize gain equal to the lesser of the following: (1) the excess of the fair market value of the property over the adjusted basis of the partner's interest in the partnership before the distribution— money distributed is not counted as property but reduces the partner's basis in the partnership interest to compute the excess; and (2) the distributee partner's net precontribution gain.

A partner's net precontribution gain is the gain that the partner would have to recognize if all property contributed by the partner within seven years (five years for property contributed before June 9, 1997) of the distribution were distributed to another partner. See ¶ 19,281. The character of the gain is based on the proportionate character of the net precontribution gain. The amount of gain recognized by the distributee partner also results in corresponding adjustments to the basis of the partner's interest in the partnership and the distributed property. Reg. § 1.737-3.

Example 19.16. On June 13 of the current year, Russ Talley contributes a nondepreciable Code Sec. 1231 asset to a partnership in which he has a 25 percent interest. The basis of the property is $13,000, and its fair market value is $20,000. Thus, Russ has $7,000 of precontribution gain. Russ makes no other contributions. Two years later, when the basis of Russ's partnership interest is $23,000, other property worth $27,000 is distributed to him. Russ recognizes a $4,000 gain on the distribution (lesser of (1) $27,000 − $23,000, or (2) $7,000). The gain is considered Code Sec. 1231 gain.

Example 19.17. Assume the same facts as in Example 19.16, except the fair market value of the property when it is distributed to Russ is $32,000. Russ's Code Sec. 1231 gain recognized is the $7,000 precontribution gain, since it is less than the $9,000 excess of the fair market value of the distributed property over Russ's predistribution basis in his partnership interest.

Any gain recognized under Code Sec. 737 is in addition to gain recognized under the usual distribution rules.

Example 19.18. At a time when there is $11,000 of net precontribution gain (ordinary income) with respect to Tammy Ross, a 50 percent partner in the Ross partnership, Tammy receives a mixed property distribution, consisting of the following: cash of $29,000, and capital assets that have a fair market value of $24,000. Before the distribution, Tammy has a $19,000 basis in her partnership interest. Tammy reduces the basis in her partnership interest by the $29,000 of cash, bringing it down to zero, and recognizing $10,000 of capital gain. The excess of the fair market value of the capital assets over Tammy's basis for her partnership interest, after reducing the basis to zero because of the cash which is distributed, is $24,000. Since this amount is more than her $11,000 of net precontribution gain, she has $11,000 of ordinary income from the property distribution. Tammy's basis for her partnership interest is increased to $11,000 by the $11,000 of ordinary income which she recognizes.

If the distributed property had been contributed by the distributee partner, then it is not counted in computing the fair market value of the property distributed. Also, any precontribution gain in such property is not considered in the computation of the net precontribution gain with respect to the distribution. If unrealized receivables or substantially appreciated inventory is distributed, the rule for net precontribution gain recognition does not apply to the extent Code Sec. 751 applies. Nor does the rule apply to deemed distributions of property in connection with partnership terminations resulting from the sale or exchange of partnership interests of 50 percent or more within a 12-month period (see ¶ 18,623). Reg. § 1.737-2(a). The partnership's basis in property with net precontribution gain that had been contributed by the distributee partner is increased to reflect the gain recognized under this rule by the distributee partner.

TAX BLUNDER

In 1994, Ralph Nelson contributed property with an adjusted basis of $20,000 and a fair market value of $50,000 to the Remington partnership. In 1998, the Remington partnership distributes the property to another of its partners. The distribution of the property within five years of Ralph's contribution of the property causes Ralph to have to recognize gain. The recognized gain is the lesser of the precontribution gain or the excess of the fair market value of the property over Ralph's adjusted basis in the partnership. Had Remington delayed the distribution of the property for another year, Ralph would not have to recognize the gain. Alternatively, Ralph could increase his basis in the partnership by contributing other property.

¶ 19,065   CLASSES OF PROPERTY—BASIS ALLOCATION

As was stated above, the basis to be allocated to properties distributed to a partner in either a current or a liquidating distribution must be allocated first to any unrealized receivables and inventory items included in the distribution. Reg. § 1.732-1(c)(1). As a general rule, these assets cannot have a higher basis to the distributee partner, but there are two exceptions. The basis of the Section 751 property can have a higher basis to the recipient partner (1) if the distributee has a special basis adjustment (see ¶ 19,315), or (2) if the distribution is treated as a sale or exchange of Section 751 property.

If the partner does not have sufficient basis to cover the partnership's basis in unrealized receivables and inventory, the difference is treated as a basis decrease. This decrease is allocated first to properties with unrealized depreciation. Code Sec. 732(c)(3)(A).

After allocating basis to unrealized receivables and inventory, any remaining basis is allocated to other properties to the extent of the partnership's basis in those properties. If the partnership's basis in those properties exceeds the partner's remaining basis, there is a basis decrease and if the partner's remaining basis exceeds the partnership's basis, there is a basis increase.

Basis Increase Formula

The remaining basis (after reducing the partner's adjusted basis in the partnership by cash, inventory, and unrealized receivables) is allocated first to the extent of each distributed property's adjusted basis to the partnership. If the basis increase is less than the aggregate unrealized appreciation in the properties, the basis increase is allocated to the properties in proportion to their relative unrealized appreciation. If the basis increase is more than the aggregate unrealized appreciation in the properties, the basis increase is allocated to the properties to the extent of their unrealized appreciation, and the remaining basis increase is allocated to the properties in proportion to their relative adjusted bases taking into account any basis increases made to the appreciated properties. Code Sec. 732(c)(2).

> *Example 19.19.* P has an adjusted basis of $55 in the partnership. In a liquidating distribution, P receives two capital assets, A and B. A has an adjusted basis of $5 and a FMV of $40; B has an adjusted basis of $10 and a FMV of $10. The $55 of adjusted basis is allocated as follows. First, allocate $5 of basis to A and $10 to B. The remaining basis is an increase of $40. Next, allocate $35 to A since it is the only increase asset. Finally, the remaining basis of $5 is allocated based on the fair market values of the two assets. A's basis is $5 + $35 + $4 = $44, and B's basis is $10 + $0 + $1 = $11.

Basis Decrease Formula

The remaining basis (after reducing the partner's adjusted basis in the partnership by cash, inventory, and unrealized receivables) is allocated first to the extent of each distributed property's adjusted basis to the partnership. If the basis decrease is less than the aggregate unrealized depreciation in the properties, the basis decrease is allocated to the properties in proportion to their relative unrealized depreciation. If the basis decrease is more than the aggregate unrealized depreciation in the properties, the remaining basis decrease is allocated to the properties in proportion to their relative adjusted bases taking into account any basis decreases made to the depreciated properties. Code Sec. 732(c)(3).

> *Example 19.20.* P has an adjusted basis of $20 in the partnership. In a liquidating distribution, P receives two capital assets, C and D. C has an adjusted basis of $15 and a FMV of $15; D has an adjusted basis of $15 and a FMV of $5. P allocates the $20 basis first by allocating $15 of basis to C and $15 of basis to D. Since this exceeds P's basis in partnership, there is a decrease of $10. Only asset D has unrealized depreciation. Since the basis decrease

does not exceed the aggregate unrealized depreciation (all attributable to D), it is all allocated to asset D. Therefore, P's basis in D is $5.

¶ 19,101   PROPORTIONATE DISTRIBUTIONS OF RECAPTURE PROPERTY

When depreciable property is distributed, the recapture of depreciation under Code Sec. 1245 and the recapture of excess depreciation under Code Sec. 1250 are deferred until the receiving partner disposes of it. The "taint" of the recapture is fixed at the time of the distribution and is acquired by the partner. Thus, the ordinary income to be recognized by the transferee partner upon later disposition is limited to that amount the partnership would have recaptured had it sold the asset for its fair market value at the time it was distributed.

Example 19.21. Mabel, Ophelia, and Rose Tischler are equal partners in a partnership and each has a basis for her partnership interest of $75,000. The partnership has $200,000 in cash and asset Y, Section 1245 property with a fair market value of $100,000. Asset Y originally cost $100,000 and has an adjusted basis to the partnership of $85,000. Asset Y is distributed to Mabel in complete liquidation of her partnership interest. The basis of Asset Y to Mabel will be $75,000, and if it is not depreciated in her hands but later sold for $103,000, her Code Sec. 1245 recapture is limited to $15,000 ($100,000 − $85,000).

Disproportionate Distributions

¶ 19,201   DISPROPORTIONATE DISTRIBUTIONS OF SECTION 751 ASSETS

To this point, it has been assumed that whenever a partner has received Section 751 assets, then the partner has received a pro rata share of those partnership assets. However, if a partner were to receive more or less than a proportionate share of those assets, that partner is deemed to have either sold or purchased a part of those Section 751 assets. Thus, to the extent that a partner receives, in a current or a liquidating distribution, unrealized receivables or substantially appreciated inventory items of the partnership in exchange for all or part of an interest in other partnership property, the receiving partner is treated as having sold a portion of his or her share of the other property to the partnership. The partnership is deemed to have sold a portion of the Section 751 property to the distributee partner.

As the partnership "sold" ordinary income items, its gain is ordinary income measured by the excess of the fair market value of the distributee partner's interest in the "other property" that was relinquished to the partnership over the basis to the partnership of the Section 751 property it distributed. As Section 751 property, by definition, has unrecognized income, the partnership will always recognize some income when it distributes to a partner more than the partner's proportionate share. The distributee partner usually will realize capital gain (or loss), measured by the value of the excess of the partner's proportionate share of Section 751 assets received in exchange for the partner's share of the other property that was relinquished. The treatment is *reversed* if the partner receives a distribution of excess "other property" and relinquishes the interest in Section 751 assets. Code Sec. 751(b)(1); Reg. § 1.751-1(b)(2) and (3). The character of the gain or loss to the partnership is determined by the character of the distributed property.

> **Example 19.22.** James Reed receives a $50,000 cash distribution in exchange for his reducing his partnership interest from $1/3$ to $1/5$. Immediately after the distribution, the partnership still has Section 751 assets with a basis of zero, a fair market value of $150,000 and cash of $100,000. Of the total fair market value of Section 751 assets held by the partnership prior to the distribution, James's interest was $50,000 ($1/3$ of $150,000). After the distribution his interest in the fair market value of the retained Section 751 assets is $30,000 ($1/5$ of $150,000). Therefore, James is deemed to have sold Section 751 assets of $20,000 ($50,000 − $30,000) and he recognizes $20,000 ordinary income from the "sale."

¶ 19,215 MEANING OF "IN EXCHANGE FOR INTEREST"

As is implicit in the above examples, income or gain recognition is required only when there is an exchange of Section 751 property for an interest in other property. The rationale is that a partner is entitled to receive as a distribution a proportionate share of each partnership asset, Section 751 assets, and other property without having the transaction treated as a sale or exchange. The partner has merely withdrawn that which belongs to him or her. Reg. § 1.751-1(b)(1)(ii). But where the partner receives more than his or her share, the partner is taking property belonging to the other partners and, accordingly, must give something in exchange. Section 751 does not apply to current drawings or to advances against the partner's distributive share.

As applied to current distributions, the concept of a partner's share of any particular class of property is highly artificial. Immediately following the distribution, the distributee has an interest in each class of partnership property, including unrealized receivables (if any remain), different from that determined by taking away from the partner's predistribution interest the interest in other property deemed to have been relinquished. The Regulations resolve this problem by providing that, in determining whether a partner has received only his or her share of either Section 751 property or of other property, the interest in such property remaining in the partnership immediately after a distribution must be taken into account.

> **Example 19.23.** The Section 751 property in the Ajax partnership has FMV of $100,000, in which partner Arthur Ajax has an interest of 30 percent, or $30,000. If Arthur received $20,000 of Section 751 property in a distribution and continues to have a 30 percent interest in the $80,000 of Section 751 property remaining in the partnership after the distribution, only $6,000 ($30,000 − $24,000, that is, 30 percent of $80,000) of the Section 751 property

received by him will be considered to be his share of such property. The remaining $14,000 ($20,000 − $6,000) received is in excess of his share.

The following model may be used to compute the excess a distributee partner receives or the excess a distributee partner gives up with respect to the partner's interest in partnership property, whether the property is Section 751 property or non-Section 751 property: Value of property distributed + distributee partner's share of value of property in the partnership after the distribution − distributee partner's share of value of property in the partnership before the distribution = Excess received (excess given up).

To the extent that there is excess property received by the distributee partner, there is income or gain recognition to the partnership for the property. To the extent that there is excess property given up by the distributee, there is income or gain recognition to the distributee for the property. Remember that the *value* of the property, *not the basis,* is the relevant amount to consider. Also, if the distributee partner's interest in the partnership changes after the distribution, then different percentages are used in computing the distributee partner's share before and after the distribution.

Example 19.24. Using the facts from Example 19.23, the model can be used to compute Arthur's excess Section 751 property received: Value of property distributed ($20,000) + Arthur's share of value of property after the distribution (30% × $80,000 = $24,000) − Arthur's share of value of property before the distribution (30% × $100,000 = $30,000) = $20,000 + $24,000 − $30,000 = $14,000 excess received.

The same rule can be illustrated when the distribution reduces the partner's overall interest in the partnership.

Example 19.25. Assume the same facts as in Example 19.22, except James receives $50,000 in value of Section 751 assets. James's share of the partnership's Section 751 assets after the distribution is $20,000 (1/5 × ($150,000 − $50,000)). James's share of the partnership's Section 751 assets before the distribution was $50,000 (1/3 × $150,000). Since James receives excess Section 751 property of $20,000 ($50,000 + $20,000 − $50,000), there is income or gain recognition to the partnership for the property. Because all of the $20,000 excess is potential ordinary income, the partnership recognizes $20,000 of ordinary income on the disproportionate distribution.

¶ 19,235 GAIN OR LOSS UPON SUBSEQUENT DISPOSITION OF DISTRIBUTED PROPERTY

As a general rule, the characterization of capital gain or ordinary income on the disposition of an asset is usually dictated by the character of the property in the seller's hands. However, there is a slight variation in this rule when a partner receives a distribution of unrealized receivables and/or inventory items. Any gain or loss realized upon the disposition of the unrealized receivables results in ordinary income or loss; the same rule applies to the disposition of partnership distributed inventory items. Code Sec. 735(a)(1); Reg. § 1.735-1(a)(1). But if an inventory item is held by the partner for more than five years after its distribution and in the hands of that partner it is classified as a capital asset, the gain or loss upon its subsequent disposition is capital gain or loss. Code Sec. 735(a)(2); Reg. § 1.735-1(a)(2).

> *Example 19.26.* Upon dissolution of a real estate development partnership, Ruth Henley received as her proportionate share of partnership property a tract of land held as inventory by the partnership. Ruth held the distributed land as an investment for more than five years and then sells it at a gain. The gain is a long-term capital gain.

In general, the period of time the partnership held the property is tacked to the holding period of the partner. If the property were initially contributed to the partnership by a partner, the prior holding period is also tacked. However, the more-than-five-year rule mentioned above applies only to the postdistribution time that the property is held by the distributee partner. Code Sec. 735(b); Reg. § 1.735-1(b).

> *Example 19.27.* On January 1, 1998, Partner A receives a distribution of inventory items from his partnership. Any gain on the sale of those items by Partner A prior to January 2, 2003, will be classified as ordinary income. After such date, the character will be determined by the nature of the asset in the hands of the partner.

¶ 19,261 EXCEPTIONS TO DISPROPORTIONATE DISTRIBUTION RULES

The "disproportionate distribution" rules do not apply to the distribution to a partner of property that was contributed to the partnership by that partner. Code Sec. 751(b)(2)(A). Such a distribution is governed by the rules relating to distributions by a partnership generally. Reg. § 1.751-1(b)(4)(i). Payments made to a retiring partner or to a deceased partner's successor in interest are not treated as a sale or exchange between the partner and the partnership to the extent that such payments constitute a distributive share of partnership income or guaranteed payments. Reg. § 1.751-1(b)(4)(ii). See ¶ 19,401 for a further discussion of both of these situations.

KEYSTONE PROBLEM

Arnold Simmons, a one-third partner in ArBeeSee, an accrual partnership, receives in liquidation of his entire interest $10,000 in cash and depreciable property with a fair market value of $15,000 and a basis to the partnership of $13,125. His basis for his interest in the partnership was $32,000. The predistribution balance sheet of ArBeeSee was:

	Basis Per Books	FMV		Basis Per Books	FMV
Cash	$15,000	$ 15,000	Current Liab.	$15,000	$ 15,000
Accts. Receivable	9,000	9,000	Mortgage Pay.	21,000	21,000
Inventory	21,000	30,000			
Building (Net of			Capital:		
Depr. S-L method)	42,000	48,000	Arnold	20,000	25,000
Land	9,000	9,000	Barker	20,000	25,000
			Cecil	20,000	25,000
	$96,000	$111,000		$96,000	$111,000

What gain does Arnold recognize, and what is its character? What is Arnold's basis in the property he received? What is the basis to the partnership of the accounts receivable and the inventory it retained? Assuming no Code Sec. 754 election was made by the partnership, what is its basis in the remaining depreciable property? What are the bases of Barker's and Cecil's partnership interests after the transaction?

¶ 19,281   DISTRIBUTION OF CONTRIBUTED PROPERTY

When a partnership distributes property to the partner who contributed that property to the partnership, neither gain nor loss is recognized by the partnership, nor is any gain or loss recognized by the contributing partner. However, if within seven years (five years for property contributed before June 9, 1997) of the date of the contribution, the partnership distributes the contributed property to a partner other than the contributor, the contributing partner recognizes gain or loss at the time of the distribution, computed as if the property had been sold by the partnership to the distributee partner for its fair market value at the date of distribution (i.e., the lesser of the built-in precontribution gain or loss as discussed in ¶ 18,345 or the gain or loss realized in a hypothetical sale by the partnership). This rule does not apply, however, to distributions of unrealized receivables or substantially appreciated inventory to the extent that Code Sec. 751 applies or to deemed distributions of property in connection with partnership terminations resulting from the sale or exchange of partnership interests of 50 percent or more within a 12-month period (see ¶ 18,623). Reg. § 1.704-4(a)(2) and (c)(3). The amount of gain or loss recognized by the contributing partner on the distribution results in corresponding adjustments to the basis of the partner's interest in the partnership and the distributed property. Code Sec. 704(c)(1)(B).

> *Example 19.28.* On January 1, 1997, Baker Jones contributed to his partnership a property with a basis to him of $10,000 and a fair market value of $20,000. On January 31, 1998, when the property (held by the partnership as a capital asset) was still worth $20,000, the partnership distributed the property to Baker's partner, Cabel Drummond. Baker will report a capital gain of $10,000 on the distribution. Baker's basis in the partnership increases by $10,000, as does the basis of the property to Cabel (to $20,000).

If the property contributed by one partner is distributed to another partner, and property of a like kind is also distributed to the original contributing partner, the general rule of nonrecognition applies. Like-kind property in this circumstance is determined under the same rules as are applied under Code Sec. 1031. For this like-kind distribution rule to apply to the contributor, the like-kind property must be distributed by the earlier of (1) 180 days after the date of distribution of the contributor's property to the other partner or (2) the due date (without extensions) of the partnership return for the year of the partnership during which the distribution was made to the other partner. Code Sec. 704(c)(2).

Sale of a Partnership Interest

¶ 19,301   SALE OF INTEREST IN SECTION 751 ASSETS

As has been discussed in ¶ 19,001, the partnership interest from an entity viewpoint is a capital asset. The sale of an interest is treated basically as the sale of a single asset, but Code Sec. 751 prevents abuse by classifying a portion of the gain as ordinary income. The reason is precisely the same as that already encountered in disproportionate distributions of those ordinary income assets. The statutory treatment, in general, regards unrealized receivables and inventory as severable from the partnership interest and subjects their disposition to the same consequences that would be accorded their sale by an individual. This provision applies both to a sale or exchange of an entire interest and to a sale or exchange of a part thereof. Code Sec. 751(a).

In determining the amount of ordinary income realized by a partner upon the sale or exchange of a partnership interest where the partnership has Section 751 assets, there is an allocation of the partner's pro rata portion of the partnership basis for such properties. Cash-basis accounts receivable will have a zero basis. The recognized gain is first assigned to Section 751 assets. The difference between the remainder, if any, of the partner's adjusted basis for the partnership interest and the balance, if any, of the amount realized determines the transferor's capital gain or loss on the sale of the partnership interest. Reg. § 1.751-1(a)(2). Proceeds received include the selling partner's pro rata share of partnership liabilities. A sale of a partnership interest where the partnership has Section 751 assets also imposes certain reporting requirements on the selling partner and the partnership. The selling partner must notify the partnership in writing within 30 days of the transaction. The partnership must then file a Form 8308 (Report of a Sale or Exchange of Certain Partnership Interests) with its return for the year of the transaction and provide the selling and purchasing partners with copies. Code Sec. 6050K.

Example 19.29. Archie and Bob Smith each own equal interests in Service, a cash-basis partnership whose balance sheet shows the following:

	Basis	FMV
Cash	$10,000	$10,000
Accounts receivable	0	12,000
Land held for investment	10,000	10,000
Totals	$20,000	$32,000
Liabilities	$ 2,000	$ 2,000
Capital: Archie	9,000	15,000
Capital: Bob	9,000	15,000
Totals	$20,000	$32,000

Bob sells his partnership interest to Carle Cox for $15,000 cash. Bob is treated as having sold his interest for $16,000 ($15,000 + ½ the liabilities). His gain is $6,000 ($16,000 − $10,000 ($9,000 + $1,000)). All of the gain is ordinary income from the sale of his interest in the unrealized receivables.

	Total	Sec. 751 Assets	Other Assets
Amount realized	$16,000	$6,000	$10,000
Adjusted basis	(10,000)	0	(10,000)
Income	$ 6,000	$6,000	$ 0

Example 19.30. If, in Example 19.29, Bob had received $16,000 cash, his sales price would have been $17,000 and his gain, $7,000, consisting of $6,000 ordinary income and $1,000 capital gain, long-term or short-term depending upon how long Bob held his partnership interest. See Reg. § 1.751-1(g), Example (1).

	Total	Sec. 751 Assets	Other Assets
Amount realized	$17,000	$6,000	$11,000
Adjusted basis	(10,000)	0	(10,000)
Income	$ 7,000	$6,000	$ 1,000

Example 19.31. Refer back to the facts in Example 19.29. Assume that the land that the partnership held for investment has depreciated, and its fair market value is $4,000. Also, the fair market value of Archie's and Bob's interests is $12,000.

Bob sells his partnership interest to Carle for $12,000 cash. Bob's selling price is $13,000 ($12,000 cash plus $1,000 liability relief). Now Bob has $6,000 ordinary income and $3,000 capital loss.

	Total	Sec. 751 Assets	Other Assets
Amount realized	$13,000	$6,000	$ 7,000
Adjusted basis	(10,000)	0	(10,000)
Income	$ 3,000	$6,000	$(3,000)

¶ 19,315   ELECTION TO ADJUST ASSET BASES

In general, the transfer of an interest in a partnership by sale or exchange (or at death), although resulting in a new basis for the interest itself, does not result in any adjustment to the basis of the partnership properties. Code Sec. 743(a); Reg. § 1.743-1(a). However, if the partnership elects under Code Sec. 754 in such cases, the basis of the partnership assets may be adjusted upward or downward by the amount of the difference between the transferee partner's basis for the partnership interest and the proportionate share of the basis of all partnership property. But while this adjustment can be made only if the *partnership* so elects, the amount of the increase or decrease constitutes an adjustment affecting the transferee *partner* only. Code Sec. 743(b); Reg. § 1.743-1(b)(1).

Example 19.32. In Examples 19.29–19.31, Carle's basis for his partnership interest is his cost in dollars plus his share of the partnership liabilities, or $16,000, $17,000 and $13,000, respectively. If the partnership in Example 19.29 makes no Section 754 election and it sells the receivables for $12,000 immediately upon Carle's admission as a partner, the partnership recognizes $12,000 of ordinary income, $6,000 of which is reportable by Archie and Carle. However, Carle just paid fair market value ($6,000) for his share of the receivables when he purchased the partnership interest.

Example 19.33. Same as above, except the partnership elects the special adjustment. With respect to Archie, the receivables still have a zero basis and his share of the income is still $6,000. However, with respect to Carle, his portion of the receivables has a basis of $6,000 and he reports no income on their disposition. If the election is in effect at the time of Bob's sale, the basis of the receivables on the partnership's books is increased to $6,000, which is allocated to Carle. When the receivables are collected, the income of $6,000 ($12,000 − $6,000 basis) is allocated to Archie.

Such a basis election is not effective to give a deceased partner's estate a stepped-up basis for uncollected income items, such as receivables not previously included in income under the partnership's accounting method. The items are classified as income in respect of a decedent and are reportable by the recipient exactly as the decedent would have reported them had the decedent lived to recognize the income under the decedent's method of tax accounting. See ¶ 19,449 for further discussion of income in respect of a decedent. For purposes of depreciation, depletion, gain or loss, and distributions, the former continuing partners reflect the basis common to the partnership. The transferee partner has a special basis adjustment to reflect the premium or discount paid for the interest in the underlying assets. Reg. § 1.743-1(b)(1).

TAX PLANNING POINTER

An individual who receives a bequest of a partnership interest might benefit from the partnership's election to adjust the basis of its assets under Code Sec. 754. This election is most beneficial when the fair market value of the partnership's assets is much greater than their adjusted basis and when the assets generate ordinary deductions such as depreciation or depletion. Oil and gas partnership interests and real estate partnership interests are often good candidates for a Code Sec. 754 election. However, the partnership must consider that once an election is in effect, it remains in effect unless the IRS agrees to letting the partnership revoke it. Therefore, if the assets decrease in value, an incoming partner would have a downward basis adjustment.

In the case of a transfer of an interest in a partnership, either by sale or exchange or as a result of the death of a partner, a partnership that has elected to take advantage of the optional basis adjustment provision must:

1. Increase the adjusted basis of partnership property by the excess of the transferee's basis for the partnership interest over the partner's share of the adjusted basis to the partnership of all partnership property, or

2. Decrease the adjusted basis of partnership property by the excess of the transferee partner's share of the adjusted basis of all partnership property over the basis for the partnership interest. Code Sec. 743(b); Reg. § 1.743-1(b)(1).

Contributed Property

As was discussed in Chapter 18, there is a mandatory allocation of precontribution gain or loss to the party contributing property to a partnership. Where there is a mandatory allocation required by Code Sec. 704(c) and there is a sale or exchange of the contributing partner's interest, the transferee partner's proportionate share of the adjusted basis of partnership property must be determined with reference to that special adjustment.

Example 19.34. Doris Lenz, Edna Friedman, and Fran Witt formed an equal partnership on January 1, with Doris contributing land with a basis to her of $400 and a fair market value of $1,000. Edna and Fran each contributed $1,000 in cash. After one year, with no change in the assets except that the land was then worth $1,300, Doris sold her interest to Grace Garrison for $1,100. The partnership's basis for the land is $400, but Grace has a "special basis adjustment" of $700, Grace's cost ($1,100) over the cost basis of Doris's interest ($400), which Grace purchased. Assuming again no change in the assets except that the land in the partnership is subsequently sold for $1,600, the partnership will have a gain of $1,200 ($1,600 − $400). The gain is allocated as follows: Grace realizes a gain of $800 ($600, the precontribution gain that she acquired from Doris, plus $200 (1/3 of the remaining $600 gain)), against which she will apply her $700 special basis adjustment, leaving her with a $100 recognized gain. Edna and Fran each recognize a $200 gain. Reg. § 1.743-1(b)(2)(i), Example (1).

Basis Adjustment: Nonliquidating Distributions

To clarify the discussion on nonliquidating distributions, it is necessary to identify the various parties. The first party who receives a special basis adjustment is referred to as the transferee partner.

Example 19.35. George Kerr purchased an interest in a realty partnership which owned Building X and Building Y. George paid $5,000 in excess of his purchased share of the partnership's basis in the partnership, $2,000 attributable to Building X, $3,000 attributable to Building Y. George is a transferee partner. At a later date, immediately prior to a distribution by the partnership, the following data were extracted from its records:

Item	Fair Market Value	Common Partnership Basis	George's Share	George's Special Basis Adjustment	Partnership Basis to George
Cash........	$60,000	$60,000	$20,000		$20,000
Building A ...	30,000	15,000	5,000		5,000
Building X ...	20,000	15,000	5,000	$2,000	7,000
Building Y ...	20,000	8,000	2,667	3,000	5,667

When property, as to which a transferee partner acquires a special basis as a result of a transfer of interests, is distributed to another partner, the property has a basis to the distributee partner consisting only of its common basis shared by all the partners. The special basis adjustment of the transferee partner does not follow the property into the hands of the distributee partner to whom it is distributed.

Example 19.36. Continuing Example 19.35, if George Kerr, Isaac Irving, and Harry Newhart agree that George and Harry will receive a distribution of $20,000 cash and that Isaac will receive a distribution of Building Y, that building in the hands of the distributee partner, Isaac, will have a $8,000 basis to him.

The special basis adjustment is reallocated by the transferee partner (George) to the remaining partnership property of a like kind, or, if the transferee partner receives a distribution of like-kind property, to such distributed property.

Example 19.37. After the distribution in Example 19.36, George will have a special basis adjustment of $5,000 (the total of George's special basis adjustments) for Building X.

If a transferee partner receives a distribution of property with respect to which the transferee partner has a special basis adjustment, that property has a basis consisting of its common partnership basis, increased or decreased by the transferee partner's special basis adjustment.

Example 19.38. Assume in Example 19.36 that George had received a distribution of Building Y and Isaac the $20,000 cash. Building Y would have a basis to George of $11,000, its common partnership basis plus George's special adjustment.

If the transferee partner at the same time relinquishes an interest in other property of a like kind with respect to which the transferee partner also has a special basis adjustment, the transferee partner is permitted further to adjust the basis of the property received by a special basis adjustment with respect to the interest relinquished in the other like property.

Example 19.39. If in the above distributions George had received Building Y and Isaac Building X, George would have as a basis for Building Y $13,000, the $8,000 common basis to the partnership plus the basis adjustments for Building Y which he received, plus the basis adjustment for Building X which he relinquished.

A partner is considered as having relinquished interest in any remaining partnership property when the interest has been completely liquidated. However, as illustrated above, when a partner receives a distribution not in liquidation, the partner is considered as relinquishing an interest only in property distributed to other partners. "Like-kind property" means property of the same class, that is, stock in trade, property used in the trade or business, capital assets, and so forth. See Reg. § 1.743-1(b)(2)(ii).

Allocation of Basis Adjustment—Partnership Properties

When there is a transfer of a partnership interest, and the partnership elects to make the optional basis adjustment to partnership property, the increase or decrease in the adjusted basis of the partnership property is prescribed. In general, adjustments must be allocated to the basis of the partnership properties (other than money) so as to reduce the difference between the fair market value and the adjusted basis of those partnership properties. Code Sec. 755(a)(1). Mechanically this is done by allocating the difference between basis and value between (1) capital assets including Section 1231 assets and (2) any other property. The increase or decrease to each such class is then allocated to the specific properties within the class so as to reduce the difference between their value and basis.

If there is an *increase in basis* to be allocated, generally, it must be allocated only to assets whose values exceed their bases and in proportion to the difference between the value and basis of each. No increase may be made to the basis of any asset for which the adjusted basis equals or exceeds its fair market value, as each adjustment must reduce or eliminate (and not increase) the spread between value and basis of each asset. Reg. § 1.755-1(a)(1)(ii). However, one court permitted the resulting basis to exceed the transferee's share of the fair market value of the transferred property where the transferee, in fact, purchased at a price based on valuations in excess of fair market value. *R.P. Cornish,* 65-2 USTC ¶ 9508, 348 F.2d 175 (CA-9 1965).

If there is a *decrease in basis* to be allocated, the purpose again is to reduce the spread between adjusted basis and fair market value. The decrease must be allocated to assets with bases in excess of value, and in proportion to the difference between the basis and value of each. No decrease may be made to the basis of any asset, however, if its fair market value equals or exceeds its adjusted basis. Reg. § 1.755-1(a)(1)(iii). In making the above allocations, recognition must be given to goodwill if it is shown to exist. Code Sec. 1060; Reg. § 1.755-2T.

If a partnership or a transferee partner making the election proposes to adjust the bases of its assets in any manner other than that prescribed above, it must file an application for permission to use such other method with the Commissioner, detailing the method desired to be used and the reasons therefor. Reg. § 1.755-1(a)(2). The application must be filed within 30 days after the close of the partnership taxable year in which the proposed adjustment is to be made.

Allocation of Adjustment by Class of Property

Where there is a basis adjustment arising from a transfer of an interest in a partnership by sale or exchange or upon the death of a partner, as pointed out above, partnership property is divided into two categories: (1) capital assets and Section 1231 assets and (2) any other property of the partnership. Thus, to the extent that an amount paid by a purchaser of a partnership interest (or the basis of the partnership to the estate or other successor in interest of a deceased partner) is attributable to the value of capital assets and Section 1231 assets, any difference between the amount so attributable and the transferee partner's proportionate share of the partnership basis of such property constitutes a special basis adjustment with respect to partnership capital assets and Section 1231 assets. Similarly, any difference attributable to any other property of the partnership constitutes a special basis adjustment with respect to such property. Reg. § 1.755-1(b)(2).

> *Example 19.40.* Assume in each of the three cases below for an equal three-person partnership with the listed assets, that one partner sells his one-third interest to Winchester for $1,000, and that the election is in effect.

	Case One		Case Two		Case Three	
Asset	*Basis*	*FMV*	*Basis*	*FMV*	*Basis*	*FMV*
Capital asset	$1,000	$1,500	$1,000	$1,500	$1,000	$1,500
Sec. 1231 asset	1,000	900	1,000	1,100	1,000	700
Inventory	700	600	700	400	700	800
Totals	$2,700	$3,000	$2,700	$3,000	$2,700	$3,000

In each case, Winchester has as his adjusted basis of partnership properties $900 ($2,700 ÷ 3); he has a special adjustment of $100 (his cost of $1,000 − $900).

In Case One, the increase is attributable to the capital asset-Section 1231 asset group. Adding the entire $100 to the basis of the capital asset reduces the spread between its basis and its FMV. Nothing is added to the Section 1231 asset as any addition would increase the spread between the basis of the Section 1231 asset and its fair market value.

In Case Two, the increase is attributable to both the capital asset and the Section 1231 asset, their total spread being $600, of which five-sixths is attributable to the capital asset and one-sixth to the Section 1231 asset. Thus, Winchester's $100 special adjustment to the basis of the capital asset is $83 and to the basis of the Section 1231 asset, $17.

In Case Three, $200 ($2,200 − $2,000) of the net increase of $200 is attributable to the capital asset-Section 1231 asset group and $100 to the inventory. Therefore, $67 (2/3 × $100) is attributable solely to the capital asset and $33 (1/3 × $100) to the inventory. Reg. § 1.755-1(c).

Election to Adjust Basis of Partnership Property

The election to adjust the basis of partnership property must be made in a written statement, preferably accompanying the partnership return for the year to which it is applicable. The statement must include the name and address of the partnership, be signed by any of the partners, and state that the partnership elects to adjust the basis of its properties, both in cases of transfers of interests and following partnership distributions. The election is irrevocable without permission of the Commissioner. Code Sec. 754.

The IRS allows the Code Sec. 754 election to be made later than specified in the Treasury Regulations. There is an automatic 12-month extension to make the Code Sec. 754 election if the partnership attaches the appropriate forms to the original or amended return. The extension period begins with the original due date of the partnership return, Form 1065. Rev. Proc. 92-85, 1992-2 CB 490. The partnership may also request retroactive application of the election beyond the 12-month period under procedures contained in Reg. § 301.9100-1.

TAX BLUNDER

Alfred Anderson purchased Bill Hill's 20 percent interest in the Dover real estate partnership for $200,000. At the time of the purchase, the inside basis of the 20 percent interest was $195,000. Alfred influenced the other partners to cause Dover to make an election under Section 754 to adjust the basis of the partnership assets. The following year, the real estate market became very depressed, and the values of the partnership's real estate holdings fell. Sam Sampson, concerned that the real estate market would fall further, requested that the partnership buy out his 20 percent interest for $100,000. Dover's basis in 20 percent of the real estate is $195,000. Since a Section 754 election is in effect, Dover will have to make a downward basis adjustment of its assets.

¶ 19,321   TRANSFEREE PARTNER'S ELECTIVE SPECIAL BASIS ADJUSTMENT

It has been previously stated (see ¶ 19,315) that the election to make a special adjustment must be made by the partnership. However, suppose a partner acquires a partnership interest or a part of a partnership interest and the partnership did not make the election to provide the partner with a special basis adjustment and subsequently makes a distribution of that property to that partner. If such a distributee partner receives a distribution of property (other than money) from the partnership within two years after the partner acquired an interest, or part thereof, by transfer, the partner may elect to treat as the partnership basis of the distributed property the basis such "election" property would have had if the basis adjustment had been in effect. Code Sec. 732(d); Reg. § 1.732-1(d). The amount of adjustment in such a case is not diminished by any depletion or depreciation on that portion of the basis of partnership property that arises from the special basis adjustment since no depletion or depreciation on that special adjustment portion would have been allowed or allowable to the partnership in the absence of an election. Reg. § 1.732-1(d)(1)(iv).

The special basis adjustment applies to the property for which the election could have been made (the "election" property) if that property is distributed. If the same "election" property is not distributed, the adjustment can apply to like-kind property received by the distributee partner in exchange for the "election" property, but only if the distributee relinquishes interest in the "election" property.

> *Example 19.41.* Partner Kate Teichman purchased a one-fourth interest in a partnership for $17,000. There was no special basis adjustment election in effect. The partnership held inventory with a basis of $14,000, FMV of $16,000. Had the partnership made the election, Kate could have had a special adjustment of $500 with respect to this asset only, reflecting her purchase of one-fourth of its appreciation. Within two years, Kate retires and receives $1,500 cash; one-fourth of the partnership inventory (not the same as on hand when she purchased her interest) with a partnership basis of $3,500; capital asset #1 with a partnership basis of $2,000 and a fair market value of $6,000, and capital asset #2 with an adjusted basis of $4,000 and a fair market value of $8,000. Kate may elect to have her special basis adjustment apply to the distributed inventory. Thus the basis of the property received by her will be:

Total basis of her partnership interest		$17,000
Less cash received in liquidation		1,500
		$15,500
Less: Inventory—Partnership common basis	$3,500	
Special basis adjustment	500	4,000
		$11,500
Allocated to:		
Capital asset #1	$3,833	
Capital Asset #2	7,667	$11,500

The above adjustment of Kate's basis would have no effect upon the assets remaining with the partnership. Reg. § 1.732-1(d)(1)(vi).

¶ 19,351 TRANSFEREE PARTNER'S MANDATORY SPECIAL BASIS ADJUSTMENT

The process by which distributee partners allocate their basis in their partnership interest to the assets acquired in the liquidation of their interest has been discussed. See ¶ 19,065. If that process is blindly followed, it could result in a distributee partner receiving the benefit of ordinary deductions for depreciable assets that should be allocated to nondepreciable assets. If the partnership did not make an election to adjust the basis of the partnership properties at the time of the acquisition of the transferred partnership interest, the distributee partner may be required to allocate the partnership basis so as to prevent the shifting of basis. In order for the allocation to be mandated, three conditions must exist:

1. The fair market value of all partnership property other than money must exceed 110 percent of its adjusted basis to the partnership when the transferred interest was acquired,

2. An allocation of basis upon a liquidation of the partner's interest immediately after the transfer of the interest would result in a shift of basis from property not subject to an allowance for depreciation, depletion, or amortization to property subject to such an allowance, and

3. A special basis adjustment would change the basis to the transferee partner of the property actually distributed.

Example 19.42. The partnership owned three pieces of real estate (each with an adjusted basis to the partnership of $5,000 and each with FMV of $55,000) and depreciable property with an adjusted basis and FMV of $150,000 (a total basis of $165,000 and FMV of $315,000). Doris Murphy purchased her one-third interest in the partnership for $105,000. There was no Code Sec. 754 election in effect. Note that the fair market value of the property does exceed 110 percent of its adjusted basis. Four years later, the partnership is dissolved. Doris, whose basis for her partnership interest is then $100,000, receives one of the pieces of real estate, basis still $5,000, and one-third of the depreciable property, which then has an adjusted basis of $45,000 ($1/3 \times \$135,000$, i.e., $150,000 less $15,000 depreciation claimed by the partnership since Doris's admission). The determination of Doris's mandatory basis allocation is as follows:

	No Basis Election		*Required Basis Adjustment*	
Land	(5/50 × $100M)	$ 10,000	(55/100 × $100M)	$ 55,000
Depreciable property	(45/50 × $100M)	90,000	(45/100 × $100M)	45,000
		$100,000		$100,000

Doris is required to make the basis adjustment of $50,000 to the nondepreciable property (land) in order to prevent the transfer of the appreciation that was attributed to the nondepreciable property to the depreciable property at the time of the acquisition of her partnership interest. Reg. § 1.732-1(d)(4).

¶ 19,361   PARTNERSHIP'S OPTIONAL BASIS ADJUSTMENT

As a general rule, the partnership does not adjust its basis for its retained property when it distributes other property to a partner. However, if any gain is recognized by the distributee partner, the partnership may elect under Code Sec. 754 to increase its basis in its retained property by the amount of that recognized gain. Also, the partnership may elect to increase basis if the basis to the partnership of the distributed property exceeds the basis at which the distributee may take that property. The excess of the adjusted basis of the partnership property immediately before the distribution over the basis at which the distributee may take the property is added to the basis of undistributed partnership property. Code Sec. 734(b)(1)(B); Reg. § 1.734-1(b)(1)(ii).

Example 19.43. Frances Zimmerman has a basis of $10,000 for her one-third interest in a partnership. The partnership has no liabilities, cash of $11,000, and property with a partnership basis of $19,000 and FMV of $22,000. For her one-third interest, Frances receives the $11,000 cash, resulting in a $1,000 gain to her. If the partnership elects, the basis of the retained partnership asset is increased from $19,000 to $20,000, the amount of Frances's recognized gain.

Example 19.44. Assume in Example 19.43, that the partnership assets are cash of $4,000, Property A with a basis of $11,000 and FMV of $11,000, and Property B with a basis of $15,000 and FMV of $18,000. In liquidation of her interest Frances receives Property A. The distributed property takes Frances's basis of $10,000 in her hands. If the partnership elects, the $1,000 "unused" partnership basis of Property A may be added to the basis of Property B retained by the partnership.

Where the special basis adjustment election is in effect and a distribution is made in liquidation of a partner's entire interest, the partnership must decrease the adjusted basis of the remaining property by:

1. The amount of loss, if any, recognized to the distributee partner, or
2. The excess, if any, of the basis of the distributed property to the distributee over the adjusted basis of such property to the partnership immediately before distribution (taking into account any special basis adjustment of the distributee). Code Sec. 734(b)(2); Reg. § 1.734-1(b)(2).

Example 19.45. Frances has a basis for her one-third partnership interest of $11,000. The partnership assets are cash of $10,000 and property with a basis of $23,000 and FMV of $20,000. In liquidation of her entire interest, Frances receives the $10,000 in cash. She has a loss of $1,000, and if the election is in effect, the partnership basis for the retained property becomes $22,000 ($23,000 − $1,000).

Example 19.46. Assume in Example 19.45 that the partnership assets are cash of $5,000, Property A with a basis of $10,000 and FMV of $10,000, and Property B with a basis of $18,000 and FMV of $15,000. In liquidation of her entire interest Frances receives Property A. Her basis in Property A is $11,000, but where the election is in effect, the excess $1,000 ($11,000 basis to Frances less $10,000, the basis to the partnership immediately before distribution) *decreases* the basis of Property B retained by the partnership, reducing it from $18,000 to $17,000. Reg. § 1.734-1(b)(2), Examples.

A partnership that must adjust the bases of partnership properties must attach a statement to the partnership return for the year of the distribution setting forth the computation of the adjustment and the partnership properties to which the adjustment has been allocated. The rules for adjustment to the basis of undistributed partnership assets are the same as those discussed above for basis adjustments by a partnership following the sale or exchange of an interest in the partnership, subject to the modifications explained below.

¶ 19,381 CLASSES OF PROPERTY—ADJUSTMENT ALLOCATION

Where there is a distribution of partnership property resulting in an adjustment to the basis of undistributed partnership property, such adjustment must be allocated to the remaining partnership property of a character similar to that of the distributed property with respect to which the adjustment arose. This treatment is parallel to that for a transferee partner, discussed at ¶ 19,315, above. That is, if the adjustment arises from a difference in partnership and distributee bases of capital gain and Section 1231 property on the one hand, the adjustment must be made to the partnership's remaining capital assets and Section 1231 properties. Similarly, where the adjustment arises from a difference in partnership and distributee bases in property other than capital assets and Section 1231 property, the adjustment must be made to such other property. Where, in the case of a distribution, a required increase or decrease in the basis of undistributed partnership property cannot be made because the partnership owns no property of the character required to be adjusted or because the adjustment has been limited, the adjustment must be made when the partnership subsequently acquires property of a like character to which an adjustment can be made. Reg. § 1.755-1(b).

¶ 19,391 ELECTION TO ADJUST PROPERTY BASIS

When there is an election to adjust the basis of partnership property, the adjustment is allocated to properties similar to the distributed property causing the adjustment. If the adjustment is due to the distributive partner's recognizing gain or loss, the adjustment is allocated to the partnership's capital and Section 1231 assets. Code Sec. 755. If the partnership has previously made either of such elections and not obtained the Commissioner's permission to revoke, the prior election is binding on the partnership for these purposes. Reg. § 1.754-1(a).

Retirement or Death of Partners

¶ 19,401 PAYMENTS FOR RETIRED PARTNER'S INTEREST

A slightly different set of problems surround payments made by the partnership on the retirement or death of a partner. The distinction is made between payments made to the departed partner in exchange for a partnership interest ("property payments") and those payments not for a partnership interest ("income payments"). Code Sec. 736. Many partnership agreements provide that when a partner reaches retirement age, the partner's interest in the firm will be surrendered in return for installment payments to be made by the partnership over a period of years.

If the payments are not considered as payment for the distributee's partnership interest in partnership property, there are two possibilities: (1) if the payments are determined with respect to the income of the partnership, they are considered as a distributive share of partnership income to the recipient (Code Sec. 736(a)(1)); and (2) if they are determined without reference to the income of the partnership, they are considered as guaranteed payments (Code Sec. 736(a)(2)). In either case, the continuing partners are relieved of reporting that portion of the partnership income siphoned off as the distributee partner's share or as deductible by the partnership in determining partnership ordinary income. For the recipient, the general rule of income inclusion applies: such payments made during a taxable year of the partnership are includible in the income of the recipient for the taxable year with or within which the partnership's taxable year ends.

On the other hand, if the payments are made for the partnership interest of the departing partner in the partnership property, the payments generally receive capital gain treatment. Code Secs. 736(b)(1) and 731(a). If there are payments in excess of the retiring or deceased partner's share of the partnership assets, the excess is treated as a distributive share, if determined with regard to the profits of the continuing partnership, or as guaranteed payments, if determined without regard to profits.

¶ 19,417 PAYMENTS FOR INTEREST IN PARTNERSHIP PROPERTY

A valuation placed upon a retiring or deceased partner's interest in partnership property determined by arm's-length agreement among the partners is accepted so long as it is reasonable. But such interest in the partnership property must be adjusted so that both the value of that interest in partnership property and the basis of the partner for an interest in the partnership take into account the share of the partnership liabilities. Reg. § 1.736-1(b)(1).

A special rule applies in the case of payments received by a former partner with respect to unrealized receivables and "unstated" goodwill (i.e., "voluntary" payments for a former partner's share of partnership goodwill). Generally, payments for the partner's interest in unrealized receivables and unstated goodwill are treated as property payments unless the partner is a general partner in a partnership in which capital is not a material income-producing factor. Code Sec. 736(b)(3). Consequently, general partners in partnerships where substantially all the gross income consists of fees, commissions, and other compensation for personal services, as well as any partners who retired under a written binding contract to purchase their interests in the partnership that was in effect on January 4, 1993, and at all times thereafter, will report payments for unrealized receivables (other than receivables constituting ordinary income recapture items) and unstated goodwill as income payments that are deductible by the partnership and are ordinary income to the recipient. Code Sec. 736(b)(2).

Payments received by a former partner for the partner's interest in unrealized receivables (unless subject to the special rule above) or substantially appreciated inventory items are considered payments in exchange for an interest in partnership property. These payments are treated as if they were disproportionate distributions of these Section 751 assets. Reg. § 1.736-1(b)(2) and (4).

Although "voluntary payments" for a former partner's goodwill may be treated as income payments under the special rule above, they will instead be reported as property payments if the partnership agreement provides for payment of a specific amount for goodwill (or provides a formula for its computation). Code Sec. 736(b)(2)(B). Thus, provision in the partnership agreement converts these payments into capital outlays by the partnership and gives rise to capital gain by the recipient.

Example 19.47. Bernard Roemer was a 25 percent partner of the Hopeful general partnership, which is a professional services firm. Upon his retirement, he received a cash payment of $16,000 for his partnership interest, which had a basis to him of $8,500. The partnership agreement was silent regarding goodwill, and the balance sheet of the corporation immediately prior to his retirement read as follows:

	Basis	FMV
Cash	$ 8,000	$ 8,000
Investments	12,000	18,000
Section 1231 assets	14,000	20,000
Unrealized receivables	0	12,000
Goodwill	0	6,000
	$34,000	$64,000

Bernard has a gain on his retirement of $7,500 ($16,000 − $8,500).

Ordinary income; Code Sec. 736(a) payments:
His share of unrealized receivables		$3,000
His share of goodwill		1,500
		$4,500

Capital gain; Code Sec. 736(b) payments:
¼ appreciation of investments	$1,500	
¼ appreciation of Section 1231 assets (assuming no recapture)	1,500	3,000
Total gain		$7,500

The partnership has a deduction of $4,500, equal to the ordinary income items.

¶ 19,425   APPORTIONMENT OF PAYMENTS

Consistent with the treatment given payments for a distributive share of partnership income or a guaranteed payment and those payments in exchange for the partner's interest in partnership property is the requirement that each payment must be segregated into its component parts. If a fixed amount is to be received over a fixed number of years, the portion to be treated as a distribution in payment for the partner's interest in partnership property for any taxable year must bear the same ratio to the total fixed agreed payment for such year (as distinguished from the amount actually received) as the total fixed agreed payments treated as distributions in exchange for the partner's interest in the partnership property bear to the total fixed agreed payments of all types. Under the general rule the retiring partner or successor in interest reports capital gain only when cash payments received exceed the basis for the partnership interest. Reg. § 1.736-1(b). Capital loss is determined under the rules explained in ¶ 19,050, above. The balance, if any, of payments received in the same taxable year is treated as a distributive share or a guaranteed payment.

In other words, the amount of the "property payment" in a taxable year to a former partner is computed according to the following formula: "property payment" portion of the annual payment = total fixed agreed payment for the year × (total fixed agreed payments under Code Sec. 736(b), i.e., "property payments" ÷ sum of total fixed agreed payments under Code Sec. 736(a), i.e., "income payments" under Code Sec. 736(b)).

Example 19.48. A retiring partner, William Kramer, is to receive a total payment of $700,000 for his interest in a partnership, payable $70,000 each year over a period of 10 years. It is agreed that the fair market value of his interest in the partnership property is $600,000 and that his basis for the partnership interest is $300,000. He receives $70,000 as his first payment in the current year. William's payment for his partnership interest for the current year is $70,000 × $600,000 ÷ $700,000, or $60,000, all of which he reports as a return of capital under the general rule, and the remaining $10,000 of which he reports as ordinary income.

However, if the total amount received in any one year is less than the amount considered as a distribution in payment for the partner's interest in partnership property for that year (under the above rule), then any unapplied portion is added to the portion of the payments for the following year or years that are to be treated as a distribution in payment of the partner's interest in partnership property.

Example 19.49. A retiring partner, Morris Manx, who is entitled to an annual payment of $60,000 for 10 years for his interest in partnership property, receives only $35,000 in 1997. In 1998, he receives $100,000. Of this latter amount, $85,000 ($60,000 + $25,000 from 1997) is treated as a distribution in payment for his interest in partnership property for 1998 and $15,000 is treated as an income payment. Reg. § 1.736-1(b)(5)(i).

¶ 19,433　ALTERNATIVE ELECTIVE METHOD FOR REPORTING PAYMENTS

If a retiring partner or a deceased partner's successor in interest is to receive a fixed sum of payments, such payments may be reported under the general rules discussed above. However, an election may be made (by attaching a statement to the tax return for the first taxable year for which the payments are received) to report and measure the amount of any gain or loss by the difference between:

1. The amount treated as a distribution in payment of the interest in partnership property that year, and

2. The portion of the partner's adjusted basis for the partnership interest attributable to such distribution (i.e., the amount which bears the same proportion to the partner's total adjusted basis for the partnership interest as the amount treated as a distribution for property in that year bears to the total amount to be received as a distribution for property). Reg. § 1.736-1(b)(6).

If the partnership has a Code Sec. 754 election in effect and the retiring partner or deceased partner's successor in interest makes the election to prorate the recognized gain or loss from property payments over the period in which the payments are to be received, any special basis adjustment to the partnership's property will correspond to the timing and amount of gain or loss recognized by the retiring partner or deceased partner's successor in interest. Rev. Rul. 93-13, 1993-1 CB 126.

Example 19.50. William Yount has an interest in his partnership of $11,000 and is a general partner in a three-person service partnership. He retires under an agreement whereby he is to receive $10,000 in each of three years. The assets of the partnership consist of $13,000 in cash, Section 1231 assets with a basis to the partnership of $20,000 and FMV of $23,000, and unrealized receivables with a basis to the partnership of zero and FMV of $30,000. The value of Yount's interest in the partnership property (excluding unrealized receivables) is $12,000 ($\frac{1}{3}$ of the cash + $\frac{1}{3}$ of the Section 1231 assets). Yount will have a gain of $1,000 and guaranteed payments of $18,000 ($30,000 − $12,000). Each payment for the three-year period will consist of a $6,000 ($18,000/$30,000 × $10,000) guaranteed payment and a $4,000 ($12,000/$30,000 × $10,000) payment for his interest in partnership property. Yount will include in his income each year and the partnership will deduct the $6,000 guaranteed payments. Under the general rules, Yount reports his $4,000 payment for his interest in the partnership property as a return of capital for the first two years and $3,000 as such a return in the third year, reporting the $1,000 gain in the third year.

If an election is made, Yount uses a pro rata portion of the basis in his partnership interest each year to apply against each year's $4,000 property payment. Since the property payments total

$12,000 ($4,000 annual payment × 3 years), and each year's payment represents 1/3 of total property payments, Yount would use 1/3 of his $11,000 basis in his partnership interest, or $3,667, each year to apply against the $4,000 annual property payment. Therefore, Yount reports $333 of capital gain each of the three years if an election is made.

¶ 19,441 PAYMENTS NOT IN FIXED AMOUNT

Special rules apply if the retiring partner or the deceased partner's successor in interest receives payments that are not fixed in amount. Such payments must first be treated as payments in exchange for an interest in partnership property to the extent of the interest's value and thereafter as payments in distribution of income or guaranteed payments. Reg. § 1.736-1(b)(5)(ii).

> *Example 19.51.* Assume the same facts as in Example 19.50, except that the partnership agreement provided for payments to Yount, for three years, of a percentage of annual income instead of a fixed amount. All payments received by Yount up to $11,000, the basis of his interest in the partnership, are treated as a return of capital, and the next $1,000 as long-term capital gain, for a total of $12,000 as payments for Yount's interest in partnership property. Any payments in excess of the $12,000 are treated as a distributive share of partnership income to Yount. The continuing partnership is not entitled to any basis adjustment until the first year in which a payment results in taxable gain to Yount. Reg. § 1.736-1(b)(7), Example (2).

¶ 19,449 PAYMENTS FOR DECEASED PARTNER'S INTEREST

As a general rule, no gain or loss is ordinarily realized with respect to payments made for the interest of a deceased partner in partnership property. The partnership interest acquires a new basis at death, a stepped-up basis equal to the fair market value at the date of death or the alternative date, whichever is elected on the estate tax return.

A somewhat different problem is encountered with respect to the deceased partner's interest in unrealized receivables or substantially appreciated inventory items of the partnership. If the special basis adjustment election under Code Sec. 754 is made or is in effect, the deceased partner's estate acquires a stepped-up basis for its interest in substantially appreciated inventory. The estate thereby escapes tax with respect to so much of the payments as is treated as a disproportionate distribution, that is, as in payment for the deceased partner's interest in substantially appreciated inventory items. The special basis adjustment under Code Sec. 732(d) available to a transferee partner upon a distribution within two years after the transferee partner acquired the interest is of no help in this regard as the election is not available with respect to disproportionate distributions. Code Sec. 732(e).

Unrealized receivables receive a different treatment. Income payments to which a deceased partner was entitled or to which the estate or other successor in interest is entitled on death are specifically designated as "income in respect of a decedent." No stepped-up basis is available to reduce the income tax payable on any amount of such payments in fact made in exchange for the distributee's interest in unrealized receivables. Rev. Rul. 66-235, 1966-2 CB 249; *G.E. Quick Trust,* 54 TC 1336, CCH Dec. 30,187 (1970), aff'd per curiam, 71-1 USTC ¶ 9489, 444 F.2d 90 (CA-8 1971).

Retiree or Successor in Interest Treated as Partner

A retiring partner or a deceased partner's successor in interest receiving payments in liquidation of the partnership interest is regarded as a partner until the entire interest of the retiring or deceased partner is liquidated. Therefore, if one of the members of a two-person partnership retires under a plan whereby the partner is to receive periodic payments, the partnership is not considered terminated until the retiring partner's entire interest is liquidated. This is because the retiring partner continues to hold a partnership interest in the partnership until that time. Similarly, if a partner in such a partnership dies and the estate or other successor in interest receives liquidating payments, the partnership is not considered to have terminated upon the death of the partner. The partnership terminates as to both partners only when the decedent's entire interest has been liquidated. Reg. § 1.736-1(a)(6).

Insolvency at Time of Partner's Withdrawal or Death

Where a member of a partnership is insolvent at the time of the member's death or withdrawal, the amount of the deficit in the capital account after the books have been closed is not necessarily a deductible loss for the other partner or partners. Even assuming that nothing is recoverable from the former partner, there is no loss except to the extent that the fair market value of the member's share of the partnership assets is less than the amount by which the member is overdrawn. *C.R. Freeman Est.,* 25 TCM 244, CCH Dec. 27,860(M), T.C. Memo. 1966-42; *J.D. Talmage,* 46 TCM 159, CCH Dec. 40,117(M), T.C. Memo. 1983-268.

Income in Respect of a Deceased Partner

All payments made in liquidation of a deceased partner's partnership interest in excess of the value of the partner's interest in partnership property at the time of death (including payments attributable to a deceased partner's share of unrealized receivables) are to be treated as "income in respect of a decedent" (IRD). Code Sec. 753; Reg. § 1.753-1(a). As such, the decedent's estate or other distributee must include such payments in gross income but will be permitted a deduction for the estate tax attributable to the inclusion of these income rights in the gross estate of the deceased partner.

The estate or heirs of a deceased partner are also treated as receiving IRD to the extent that any amount paid to the estate or heirs by an outsider for the partnership interest is attributable to the value of the decedent's interest in partnership unrealized receivables. Similarly, the proceeds of a sale by the successor of a deceased partner of the rights to income payments (the partner's distributive share or guaranteed payments, discussed above) are treated as IRD. Reg. § 1.753-1(a); *C.H. Woodhall,* 72-1 USTC ¶ 9176, 454 F.2d 226 (CA-9 1972).

Deceased Partner's Final Income Tax Return

TRA '97 amended the tax law to require a closing of the tax year with respect to a deceased partner for partnership years that began after December 31, 1997. Code Sec. 706(c)(2). The deceased partner's final income tax return includes the partner's share of partnership income up to the date of the partner's death. The estate or other successor to the partnership interest will include its share of the partnership income for the remainder of the partnership's tax year. Therefore, it is possible for a partner in a fiscal-year partnership to have a bunching of income on his final individual income tax return.

> *Example 19.52.* Hal Jordon owns a 50 percent interest in both the capital and profits of the HalMart partnership, which has a January 31 fiscal year. Pursuant to TRA '97, the partnership year ends at Hal's death on October 31, 1998. Hal's distributable share of the partnership's income for the partnership's January 31, 1998, fiscal year (assume $50,000) and his distributable share of the income for the short year February 1–October 31, 1998 (assume $40,000), must be reported on Hal's final return for 1998.

SUMMARY OF CHAPTER 19

✓ The sale of an partnership interest will generate ordinary income, to the extent the gain is attributable to unrealized receivables and inventory, and capital gain for the remainder of the gain.

✓ Unrealized receivables include accounts receivable of a cash-basis partnership, gain attributable to depreciation recapture, and unreported income on installment obligations.

✓ Section 751 property consists of unrealized receivables and substantially appreciated inventory. Inventory is substantially appreciated if its fair market value exceeds 120 percent of its adjusted basis to the partnership.

✓ In determining whether inventory is substantially appreciated, inventory is defined as all partnership property other than cash, capital assets, and Section 1231 assets.

✓ The tax consequences of a distribution depend on whether the distribution is either proportionate or disproportionate with respect to Section 751 assets, and whether the distribution is a current distribution or a liquidating distribution.

✓ A current distribution does not liquidate the partner's interest in the partnership, while a liquidating distribution does.

✓ In a proportionate current distribution, the distributee partner normally recognizes gain only if cash distributed exceeds the partner's basis in the partnership immediately prior to the distribution. Loss is generally not recognized in a current distribution.

✓ In a proportionate liquidating distribution, the distributee partner normally recognizes gain only if cash distributed exceeds the partner's basis in the partnership immediately prior to the distribution. Loss may be recognized if only cash, inventory, and unrealized receivables are distributed, and the adjusted basis of these assets to the partnership is less than the partner's adjusted basis in the partnership.

✓ If the partnership has Section 751 assets, and the distribution is disproportionate with respect to these 751 assets, both the partnership and the distributee partner may recognize gain or loss from the distribution.

✓ Payments to a retiring partner are separated into income payments and property payments.

✓ Income payments are includible as ordinary income to the retiring partner as either a distributive share of income or a guaranteed payment. In either case, they reduce the reportable income of the remaining partners.

✓ If an election is in effect under Section 754, the partnership may step up (or down) the basis of partnership assets to reflect the gain or loss recognized by the distributee partner on a distribution or the difference between the basis the partner takes and the partnership's predistribution basis in the property. The basis adjustment is a common basis adjustment that is shared by all of the remaining partners in the partnership.

✓ If an election is in effect under Section 754, the partnership may step up (or down) the basis of partnership assets to reflect the difference between the amount the transferee partner pays for the interest and the transferee partner's share of the partnership's basis in its assets. The basis adjustment is unique to the transferee partner.

CHAPTER 19 QUESTIONS

1. Does the definition of a capital asset in Code Sec. 1221 include or exclude "a partnership interest"?

2. How may a partnership that has no accounts receivable be considered to have "unrealized receivables"?

3. How do the accounts receivable of an accrual-method partnership affect the calculation of the partnership's "substantially appreciated inventory items"?

4. Assume that an accrual-basis three-person partnership has the following assets:

	Basis	FMV
Cash	$130,000	$130,000
Accounts Receivable	100,000	100,000
Inventory	49,900	80,000
Investment Real Estate	400,000	700,000

The partnership plans to make a distribution of $25,000 cash to Partner A, $25,000 in FMV inventory to Partner B and $25,000 in FMV accounts receivable to Partner C. It has been suggested that the partnership delay the distribution until it completes a pending cash sale of inventory with a basis of $2,000 for $10,000, fair market value. Discuss the application of the test for the determination of substantially appreciated inventory items.

5. Partner Z received a distribution of unrealized accounts receivable and Partner Y received a distribution of substantially appreciated inventory items. Partner Z considered the receivables as a long-term investment, which, after more than five years, were able to be collected. Partner Y considered the distributed assets as investments and sold them in the sixth year after their receipt. Discuss the income tax treatment of the distributions for both Partners Z and Y.

6. Discuss the determination of the basis of "other property" received in a current distribution when the property received by the distributee partner has a fair market value in excess of the property's basis to the partnership and in excess of the distributee partner's basis to the partnership interest.

7. In a complete liquidation of a partnership interest where a partner receives a proportionate share of the partnership's (1) cash, (2) unrealized receivables, and (3) other property, when does the partner recognize a loss?

8. How may a partner be deemed to have received a taxable "distribution" upon contribution of assets to a partnership?

9. Discuss the impact on both the partners and their partnership when in a two-person equal partnership there is distributed, not in complete liquidation of either partner's interest, cash to one

partner and Section 751 assets to the other, and the partnership retains its operating assets.

10. Why should an incoming partner who pays more for the acquired partnership interest want the partnership to elect a "special basis adjustment"?

11. If the partnership elects a special basis adjustment for a transferee partner, what effect does that have on the partnership's ordinary taxable income (Form 1065)?

12. Explain how a new partner might have a downward special basis adjustment.

13. When is a distributee partner entitled to elect a special basis adjustment with respect to distributed property, and when is such an adjustment mandatory?

14. Explain how a special basis adjustment is allocated to capital assets, Section 1231 assets, and other assets.

15. If the agreement with a retiring partner is to make payments to the partner from partnership income over a period of time, what difference does it make if the payments are designated as being in payment for the partnership interest?

16. So long as the dollar amount is the same, what difference does it make to the partnership in a given taxable year whether the retiring partner is paid a percentage of the profits or is paid that amount as a "guaranteed payment"?

17. Explain why a partner who has a deficit balance in a capital account may have recognized gain when the remaining partners merely let that partner "walk away" from the partnership without payment from the partnership.

18. Discuss the inclusion of a partnership interest in the estate of a deceased partner when the value of that included interest is comprised primarily of "income in respect of a decedent."

19. Explain the rules for gain and loss recognition to a distributee partner for current and liquidating distributions from the partnership.

20. Generally, the partnership is not permitted to adjust the basis of partnership property as a result of partnership distributions and sales or exchanges of an interest in the partnership. However, for certain distributions and sales or exchanges, an adjustment is allowed. When is the partnership permitted to make such adjustments? What are the mechanics of the adjustment?

21. Explain the mechanisms in the federal income tax law that cause the recognition of precontribution gain when property is distributed by a partnership to a partner.

CHAPTER 19 PROBLEMS

22. During the current year, Wayne Payne sells the interest he has held for five years in the Alco partnership for $15,000 cash. The buyer also assumes Wayne's $1,000 share of the partnership's liabilities. Wayne's cash cost basis in the partnership is $11,000. There were no unrealized receivables or appreciated inventory items involved in the transaction. What is Wayne's income derived from the sale of his partnership interest in Alco, and how is it classified?

23. The following balance sheet is for the Zebra partnership as of December 31 of the current year (all amounts are tax bases):

Assets		Liabilities	
Cash	$ 50,000	Mortgage payable	$750,000
Building $1,000,000			
Depr. (St.-Line)Allowance			
500,000	500,000	*Capital:*	
		A. Capital	($100,000)
		B. Capital	(50,000)
		C. Capital	(50,000)
	$550,000		$550,000

The building has a fair market value of $800,000. All partners are equal, and Mr. A offers to release any claim he has against the partnership if B and C will release any claim the partnership or its creditors have against him. No cash will exchange hands.

a. What is the tax impact of this arrangement upon Mr. A? The remaining partners?

b. Would your answer be different if Mr. A had died on December 31, and this proposition were made by his executor?

24. Quincy Adams and Rachel Perryman were equal partners of the QR partnership. The partnership had no Section 751 assets. Quincy, who had a $65,000 basis in his partnership interest comprised of a $50,000 basis in his capital interest plus his $15,000 share of the partnership liabilities, sold his interest to Peter for $100,000, who paid $50,000 cash and gave Quincy his personal 12 percent interest-bearing promissory note in a face amount of $50,000, payable $25,000 one year and two years hence. What is the sales price of Quincy's interest? If Quincy makes no election on his income tax return (Form 1040), how much gain will be reportable in the year of sale, one year hence and two years hence? What will be the character of the gain? (Do not compute the interest.)

25. Henry Sweitzer had a basis for his partnership interest of $15,000. He received a current distribution of $10,000 in cash and a building with a fair market value of $8,000. The building's adjusted basis to the partnership prior to its distribution was

$10,000. It had been depreciated using the straight-line method. What is Henry's basis for the building? What is the basis for his partnership interest? Would your answer differ if the distribution were in complete liquidation of Henry's interest in the partnership?

26. Yek and Zek, equal partners in the YZ partnership, had respective bases in their partnership interests of $20,000 and $6,000 at the beginning of the current year. During the current year, neither partner makes any contributions to the partnership, nor is there any change in partnership liabilities. YZ's ordinary income for the current year is $18,000. Yek and Zek each withdraws $22,000 in cash during the year. Compute each partner's income from the partnership and determine the character of that income and the basis of each partner in the partnership interest.

27. Willie and Xero are equal partners in the WX cash-basis partnership. They each have a basis in their partnership interest at the end of the current year of $30,000, prior to any distribution. On December 31, they each receive a distribution of the following assets, not in complete liquidation of their interest:

	Basis to the Partnership	Fair Market Value
Cash.....................................	$10,000	$10,000
Accounts receivable	5,000	6,000
Land held for investment....................	10,000	20,000
	$25,000	$36,000

After the distribution, what is the basis to Willie of his interest in the partnership? What is the basis to him of the properties received by him? What gain, if any, is recognized by Willie on the distribution?

28. Viola Tuttle and Wilma Rubble were equal partners in VW, a cash-basis partnership. Viola had a basis in her partnership interest of $22,000. Each receives the following assets in a distribution not in complete liquidation of her partnership interest.

	Basis to the Partnership	Fair Market Value
Cash.....................................	$10,000	$10,000
Accounts receivable	0	6,000
Land held for investment		
Parcel A.................................	10,000	20,000
Parcel B.................................	20,000	15,000
	$40,000	$51,000

After the distribution, what is the basis to Viola of her interest in the partnership? What is the basis of the properties received by her? What gain, if any, is recognized by her upon the distribution?

29. On March 26, 1998, Jim Morris transfers an investment asset to a partnership in which Jim has a 30 percent interest. The partnership will hold the asset for investment purposes. The property has a $40,000 basis when contributed, and it is worth $55,000 at that time. Jim makes no other property contributions and receives no property distributions until February 10, 1999, when the partnership distributes a Code Sec. 1231 asset to him. At the time of the distribution, Jim has a basis in his partnership interest of $62,000. The basis of the Code Sec. 1231 asset to the partnership is $58,000, and its fair market value is $80,000. What gain, if any, does Jim recognize because of the distribution? What is the character of the gain? What is the gain, if any, and its character if the property has a $63,000 basis to the partnership and a $75,000 fair market value when it is distributed to Jim?

30. Sarah Gordon, Tricia Stewart, and Urma Bass were equal partners in the STU partnership, which used the installment method to report sales from its inventory. Urma wished to leave the partnership and she received a proportionate distribution of the following assets in complete liquidation of her partnership interest.

	Basis to the Partnership	Fair Market Value
Cash	$10,000	$10,000
Installment receivables	2,000	10,000
	$12,000	$20,000

Her basis in her partnership interest immediately prior to the distribution was $14,000. What gain or loss does Urma recognize upon this distribution in complete liquidation of her partnership interest? What is the tax impact upon Urma when she collects the installment receivables?

31. The following balance sheet is for the Seslar partnership when Don Baggs, an equal one-third partner, sells his partnership interest to Ed White for $30,000 cash and relief from his share of the partnership's liabilities.

ASSETS		
	Basis to the Partnership	FMV
Cash	$ 9,000	$ 9,000
Unrealized receivables	0	36,000
Land held for investment	$51,000	$51,000
Total	$60,000	$96,000

The Seslar partnership has $6,000 of liabilities. Don's basis in his partnership interest is $20,000.

a. What is the amount of Don's gain (loss) on the sale of his partnership interest? What is its character?

b. What is the basis that Ed has for his partnership interest?

c. If there is an election to adjust the basis of the partnership's properties, how much is the adjustment, and to what properties is it allocated?

32. Peter Davis, Paul Mason, and Patty Bills were equal partners in a service partnership. They decided to liquidate the business and distributed to each partner an equal portion of the partnership assets consisting of:

		Basis	FMV
Cash		$ 60,000	$ 60,000
Accounts receivable		0	45,000
Inventory		48,000	65,000
Equipment cost	$30,000		
Depreciation	27,000	3,000	12,000
		$111,000	$182,000

Each had a basis for his or her partnership interest of $22,000.

a. What gain/loss does each partner report upon the distribution?

b. What is the basis each partner has for the assets received?

33. Isaac West, who had a one-third interest in the Pops partnership, received the following assets in complete liquidation of his partnership interest. The property distribution is not disproportionate. (The basis for his interest before the distribution was $22,000.)

	Basis to Pops	Fair Market Value
Cash	$15,000	$15,000
Receivables	2,000	8,000
Land	12,000	22,000
	$29,000	$45,000

a. What gain/loss will Isaac recognize on the distribution?

b. What is Isaac's basis for the assets received?

c. How would your answer differ if Isaac had received no land but only the receivables and the cash?

34. When Phyllis Ashe received Section 1250 property in full liquidation of her partnership interest (Code Sec. 751 was not applicable), the property had an adjusted basis to the partnership of $50,000; its original cost to the partnership in 1983 was $100,000, excess depreciation claimed was $20,000, and its fair market value at distribution was $80,000. The basis for her partnership interest just prior to the distribution was $60,000. Phyllis moved into the property and used it as her principal residence for 10 years, until she attained the age of 60, at which time she sold it for $150,000.

a. What was the basis of the property to Phyllis upon its distribution to her?

b. What gain/loss did she have at the time of the distribution?

c. What gain/loss, if any, need she report upon her sale of her principal residence (assuming this was her first sale of a principal residence)?

35. In complete liquidation of her partnership interest, Nancy Rosette received the following assets:

	Basis	FMV
Cash	$10,000	$10,000
Stocks and bonds held by the partnership as investments		
Corporation X	1,000	5,000
Corporation Y	2,000	500
Real estate—Land	6,000	4,000
Inventory		
Item A	2,000	3,000
Item B	1,500	1,000
	$22,500	$23,500

Nancy's basis for her partnership interest immediately prior to the distribution was $20,000. What is her basis for each of the assets received by her?

36. When Paul received his distribution from his former real estate development partnership in complete liquidation of his interest, it was comprised of $120,000 fair market value in installment notes, arising from the sale of houses to customers in the ordinary course of business, and a model home with a fair market value of $60,000. The model home is a Section 1231 asset to the partnership.

The notes required payment of interest (15 percent per annum) for only three years and then were to be amortized over a period of 10 years. The model home had a basis of $40,000 to the partnership, and the installment notes had a partnership basis of $50,000 (assume these were unrealized receivables and substantially appreciated inventory). Paul allocated his partnership basis of $110,000 to these assets, $50,000 to the notes and $60,000 to the model home. He made the model home his principal residence. Three years after his separation from the partnership, he sold the notes for $150,000 and the model home for $100,000.

What income/gain does Paul recognize upon the sales, and what is its character?

37. On January 1, 1998, Donald French purchased a 25 percent interest in the ABC partnership from Abner James, paying him $50,000. Abner and his other partners, Bill Thomas and Carol Hayes, all contributed cash at the inception of the partnership. The balance sheet of ABC immediately prior to Abner's sale was as follows:

	Basis to the Partnership	Fair Market Value
Cash	$ 10,000	$ 10,000
Inventory	20,000	20,000
Land Parcel A (held for investment)	50,000	70,000
Building (original cost of $120,000, depreciated using straight-line method)	80,000	100,000
	$160,000	$200,000

ABC elects to make a "special adjustment" because of the sale of the partnership interest by Abner to Donald.

a. What is the basis of the property to the ABC partnership? Assuming a 10 percent MACRS write-off for the building's original cost, what deduction could ABC take for 1998? How would the MACRS write-off be allocated to the partners?

b. If the building were sold on January 1, 1999, for $75,000, how would Donald, Bill, and Carol report the transaction?

38. Mabel Morris contributed land with a basis to her of $700 to the Acme partnership for a one-third interest. The fair market value of her contribution, $1,000, was matched by $1,000 in cash capital contributions by her other two partners. Two years later, when all partnership assets had the same bases ($2,700) and same fair market value (with the only difference being that the land had a fair market value of $2,500), Mabel sold her partnership interest to John Jenkins for $1,500. The partnership elected a "special basis adjustment" to reflect John's new interest. Two months after John's admission, the land is sold to New Bank Inc. for $2,800 cash. What gain will the partnership report on the sale of the land, and how will that gain be allocated among the three partners?

39. Mary Pitts purchased a partnership interest in the Jefferson partnership several years ago. She had a special basis adjustment of $2,000 with respect to real estate parcel X. This real estate parcel X was the only realty owned by the partnership and had a basis to the partnership prior to Mary's admission of $10,000. As a current distribution, not in termination of his entire interest in the partnership, parcel X was distributed to Joseph King, one of Mary's other two partners. At the time of the distribution, parcel X had a fair market value of $15,000 and Joseph had a basis for his partnership interest of $11,000. What is Joseph's basis in parcel X following the distribution? What is his basis for his partnership interest?

40. Roger Reese is a 25 percent partner in Rocko general partnership, which provides professional services. He received a cash distribution of $12,000 in full payment for his partnership interest upon his retirement. Roger's basis for his interest in the partnership was $4,500.

The assets of the partnership before this distribution were as follows:

	Basis to the Partnership	Fair Market Value
Cash	$10,000	$10,000
Accounts receivable	0	10,000
Investment property	8,000	18,000
Goodwill	0	10,000
	$18,000	$48,000

The partnership agreement was silent as to goodwill, but the partners agreed that $10,000 was a reasonable amount existing just prior to Roger's departure.

a. What gain does Roger recognize on the distribution? How is it classified?

b. How would Roger report the distributions if it was agreed that, rather than a lump sum, he would be paid 20 percent of the profits following his retirement for the next five years and the distributions amounted to $2,500 in each of those years, for a total of $12,500?

41. Mr. Jacobs retired from the Magnanimous general partnership after 40 years of service. Assume that capital is not a material income-producing factor in the partnership's business. His basis for his partnership interest was $100,000. The partnership agreement made no provision relating to goodwill. Upon his retirement, the partnership agreed to pay Mr. Jacobs $150,000 in cash for his interest in the following partnership assets:

	Basis	FMV
a. Unrealized receivables	$ 0	$ 30,000
b. Cash	40,000	40,000
c. Other assets	20,000	30,000
d. Goodwill	0	50,000
	$60,000	$150,000

In addition, Magnanimous agreed to pay Mr. Jacobs 10 percent of the annual net income of the partnership for 10 years following his retirement. How will each of these payments be treated by the partnership? By Mr. Jacobs?

42. In 1996, Edna Grimes contributed land, with an adjusted basis of $50,000 and a fair market value of $60,000, in exchange for a 20 percent interest in GHI partnership. On December 31, 1998, GHI distributed the land to Ichabod Breedlove when the land had appreciated in value to $65,000. Compute Edna's recognized gain if her basis in GHI is $58,000.

43. Terri Taylor is a partner in the Tri-County Builders partnership. Due to health reasons, she decides to have her interest in the partnership liquidated. In exchange for her interest in Tri-County Builders, she receives two tracts of land held as capital assets by the partnership. Tract A has an adjusted basis to the partnership of $10,000 and a fair market value of $80,000. Tract B has an adjusted basis to the partnership of $20,000

and a fair market value of $20,000. Prior to liquidation, Terri's basis in her partnership interest is $110,000. Compute Terri's adjusted basis in each of the two tracts of land.

44. Bill purchases a 25 percent interest in the Bilko partnership for $34,000 in cash. With respect to the purchase, the partnership owned inventory with a $28,000 basis to the partnership, and a $32,000 fair market value. Bill's purchase price reflects his share of the difference between the basis and fair market value of the inventory. The partnership does not make an election to adjust the basis of the inventory. Within two years, Bill receives the following proportionate, liquidating distribution from the partnership: cash, $3,000; inventory, partnership basis of $7,000, fair market value of $14,000; and an investment asset, partnership basis of $12,000, fair market value of $24,000. At the time of distribution, Bill's basis for his partnership interest is $34,000. Bill makes an election to adjust the basis of the inventory that he receives. What is Bill's basis in the inventory that he receives in the liquidating distribution?

a. $12,421

b. $11,421

c. $20,000

d. $8,000

45. McGuire is an equal partner in McGuire Associates, a two-person partnership, which distributed, not in complete liquidation of McGuire's interest in the partnership, land held for investment with an adjusted basis to the partnership of $18,000, a fair market value of $26,000, and subject to a mortgage of $6,000, the only debt owed by the partnership. Before the distribution, McGuire claimed the basis in his partnership interest was $20,000, as that represented his initial cash contribution. After the distribution of the land, McGuire's basis in his partnership interest will be:

a. $0

b. $8,000

c. $20,000

d. $23,000

e. $26,000

46. Patterson's basis for his interest in his partnership was $40,000. In complete liquidation of his partnership interest, Patterson receives a pro rata distribution consisting of the following assets:

	Basis to Partnership	Fair Market Value
Cash	$10,000	$10,000
Accounts receivable	1,000	11,000
Land held for investment	29,000	9,000
	$40,000	$30,000

As a result of this distribution:

a. Patterson recognizes a loss of $10,000.

b. The basis of the accounts receivable to Patterson is $11,000.

c. Patterson's basis in his partnership interest is $10,000.

d. Patterson's basis for the land is $10,000.

e. Patterson's basis for the land is $29,000.

47. Royal Stephens and Audrey Clinton are equal 50 percent partners in the Bond partnership. Included in the partnership's assets are inventory items, within the context of Section 751. The partnership has no unrealized receivables. In which of the following independent situations will Royal have to recognize ordinary income because of a distribution?

a. The aggregate fair market value of the inventory items is $9,200 and the aggregate basis of these assets is $7,800. The Bond partnership makes a simultaneous current distribution of one-half of the inventory items ($3,900 basis) to Royal and $4,600 of cash to Audrey.

b. The Bond partnership has $4,000 cash, inventory items with a $10,000 aggregate fair market value and $7,000 aggregate basis, and total assets with a $115,000 aggregate fair market value and $49,000 aggregate basis. It makes a simultaneous current distribution of $3,000 worth of inventory items ($1,500 basis) to Royal and $3,000 cash to Audrey.

c. The partnership has $12,000 cash, inventory items with a $30,000 aggregate fair market value and $21,000 aggregate basis, and total assets with a $115,000 aggregate fair market value and $90,000 aggregate basis. It makes a simultaneous current distribution of inventory items worth $10,000 ($7,000 basis) to Royal, and inventory items worth $10,000 ($5,000 basis) to Audrey.

d. The partnership has $12,000 cash, inventory items with a $30,000 aggregate fair market value and $21,000 aggregate basis, and total assets with a $120,000 aggregate fair market value and $90,000 aggregate basis. It makes a current distribution of inventory items worth $20,000 ($14,000 basis) only to Royal. Royal's interest in the partnership capital is reduced to 40 percent.

e. Royal will not have to recognize ordinary income because of any of the above distributions.

48. *Comprehensive Problem.* Refer to the data in the Keystone Problem at ¶ 19,261, but assume that Arnold received in liquidation of his entire interest in the partnership cash of $5,000 and partnership inventory with a partnership basis of $14,000 and a fair market value of $20,000.

  a. What gain does Arnold recognize, and what is its character?

  b. What is Arnold's basis in the property he receives?

  c. What income, if any, does the partnership have upon the distribution?

  d. What is the basis to the partnership for the retained depreciable property?

  e. What are the bases of the remaining partners in their respective partnership interests?

  f. How would your answers to the Keystone Problem in the text and this modification of the problem be changed if the partnership had elected to adjust asset bases under Code Sec. 754?

49. *Comprehensive Problem.* Partner Zeb Tate retired from his partnership and received his pro rata one-third share of each of the following assets in payment of his interest in the partnership which had a basis to Zeb of $25,000. The partnership used the accrual method and had no liabilities.

	Adjusted Basis	Fair Market Value
Cash	$12,000	$12,000
Accounts receivable	4,000	3,500
Trade notes receivable	2,000	2,100
Inventory	3,000	9,400
Land	90,000	102,000
Totals	$111,000	$129,000

  a. What gain or loss did Zeb realize on his retirement? What did he recognize?

  b. What are the bases of the assets he received?

  c. What is the amount and character of the gain on the ultimate sale of the assets he received if he is able to sell them within the next year for their stated fair market values?

  d. What gain or loss would Zeb realize and recognize if immediately prior to his retirement the partnership purchased another parcel of the land for $35,000, paying $5,000 down and giving its promissory note for the balance. On his retirement Zeb accepts the partnership's 90-day negotiable promissory note in the amount of $43,000 in full payment for his interest in the partnership?

50. *Research Problem.* Able West, Baker Simms, and Charles Akins are about to form a personal service partnership. Able has been a very active practitioner for many years, and there is no doubt that he will bring substantial income into the partnership. Able wants the partnership agreement to provide that upon his retirement the firm will pay him $100,000 for the goodwill he is bringing into the partnership. He is willing to have the payments spread out over a 10-year period following his retirement. These payments to Able will be taxed to him at approximately the 28 percent level after his retirement. Baker and Charles expect to continue at the top income bracket for many years. They suggest that they will be willing to pay Able the $100,000 as suggested by Able for the years following his retirement, but they do not want the partnership agreement to provide that those payments are for goodwill. In addition, Baker has suggested that the partnership will also provide $10,000 per year as a guaranteed payment to Able for the 10-year period. Charles feels this additional payment is "giving away the store" and seeks your advice.

51. *Research Problem.* Mr. Archer was a one-third partner of the Yonkers partnership. Because of the failing economy, the partnership had not been very successful in recent years, and Mr. Archer has a net operating loss carryover of $50,000. The partnership is on a June 30 fiscal year. FY 1997–98 promises to be very successful. However, Mr. Archer dies on January 31, 1998. He is survived by his wife. The Archers had no children, and Mrs. Archer, age 67 (as was Mr. Archer), will have only a limited amount of dividend income from her own savings during 1998, approximately $10,000. When the partnership year ended, Mrs. Archer was informed that Mr. Archer's estate, his successor in interest, would have a distributive share of ordinary income amounting to $55,000 for FY 1997–98. The National Bank is the executor of the estate, and Mrs. Archer is the sole beneficiary. It is now December 2, 1998. Mrs. Archer is being ardently pursued by a childhood sweetheart, recently widowed, who wants her to marry him at Christmastime. What tax advice can you give Mrs. Archer?

Chapter 20

S Corporations

Learning Objectives

After completing Chapter 20, you should be able to:

1. Understand the requirements that organizations must meet to be eligible for S corporation status.

2. Work with the election procedures that are necessary to meet the eligibility requirements.

3. Recognize the taxes imposed on S corporations.

4. Determine how shareholders report income items passed through the corporation.

5. Distinguish between taxable and tax-free distributions of the corporation.

6. Determine when the status of an S corporation terminates.

OVERVIEW OF CHAPTER

Subchapter S was added to the Internal Revenue Code in 1958 as a means to permit small businesses "to select the form of business organization desired, without the necessity of taking into account major differences in tax consequences." Sen. Rept. No. 193, 85th Cong., 2nd Sess. 87 (1958). The objective was to permit the use of the corporate form with federal income tax consequences essentially like those of a partnership. The Subchapter S Revision Act of 1982 (P.L. 97-354) made comprehensive revisions that enhanced the utility of the election. A corporation that elects the special tax treatment under Subchapter S is specifically designated as an S corporation.

The existence of S corporations raises a number of interesting questions concerning corporate elections and tax consequences both for the corporation and for the shareholder. The answers to these questions are to be found by reading this chapter. What types of corporations are eligible to receive S corporation status? What types of shareholders are eligible to hold stock in the corporation? How is a Subchapter S election accomplished? What calendar considerations are important in regard to the election? When may a built-in gain tax be imposed on an S corporation? What additional taxes may be imposed on an S corporation? How are income, deductions, and credits computed for an S corporation? How are corporate distributions treated? How may an election be terminated? These and other issues are discussed at length in this chapter.

Selecting the Subchapter S Form

¶ 20,001   Introduction

In an S corporation, the corporation in general will pay no tax, whereas the shareholders must include in gross income their proportionate share of corporate income whether or not the corporate earnings are distributed to them.

The S corporation is a viable alternative that small businesses should seriously consider. The S corporation election may be beneficial to those shareholders whose marginal tax rate is lower than the corporate rate. With individual rates on a graduated basis, the S corporation provides a shelter for income earned by a corporation that would otherwise be taxed as high as 35 percent. An S election may be advantageous for a corporation even if its taxable income is less than $75,000 because its shareholders are subject to an additional tax upon the distribution of retained earnings if the S election is not made. It is beneficial also where business losses are anticipated, since these losses pass through to the shareholders, who may treat them as trade or business expenses deductible under Code Sec. 162.

The S election affects only the federal income tax consequences of the electing corporation. In eight states and the District of Columbia, the S election is not recognized, and the corporation is subject to any state taxes imposed on the corporation.

Under the passive loss rules, an S corporation in which the taxpayer does not materially participate is treated as a passive activity. The corporation's losses are deductible on the shareholder's return only against passive income. If the shareholder has no passive income, no deduction is allowed for the losses. However, the passive loss rules can work to the taxpayer's advantage when an S corporation has income. If the shareholder does not materially participate in the S corporation, the income can be used to offset tax-shelter losses since the income from the S corporation is considered passive.

TAX BLUNDER

Kathleen Parker has a regular corporation in which she does not materially participate. She decides to convert the corporation to an S corporation. The corporation has $40,000 of investment income and an operating loss of $40,000 for the year. Kathleen's only other income is wages of $75,000. She has no other investment income or expenses and no other passive investments. The $40,000 of investment income from the S corporation is passed through and included in Kathleen's gross income. The $40,000 operating loss. is also passed through but is not deductible by Kathleen since it is deductible only against passive income. If Kathleen had not converted the corporation to an S corporation, she would have been able to offset the $40,000 net operating loss with the $40,000 of investment income, would have incurred no corporate income tax, and would not have to include the $40,000 investment income on her personal return.

¶ 20,009 ELIGIBILITY

In order to qualify under Subchapter S, a corporation must be a small business corporation. The following additional requirements must be met in order to be a small business corporation:

1. Must be a domestic corporation
2. Must have no more than 75 shareholders
3. Must include only eligible shareholders
4. Must have only one class of stock
5. Must not be an ineligible corporation

Domestic Corporation

The corporation must be a domestic corporation. The term "domestic" when applied to a corporation or partnership means created or organized in the United States or under the laws of the United States or any state. Code Secs. 1361(b)(1) and 7701(a)(4).

Not More Than 75 Shareholders

The corporation may not have more than 75 shareholders. Prior to 1997, S corporations were limited to 35 shareholders. A husband and wife (and their estates) are treated as one shareholder as long as they are married, even if each owns shares as separate property. Thus, if a husband and wife own shares as joint tenants, they are considered as one shareholder for this purpose. Similarly, if a husband owns shares in his name and a wife owns shares in her name, they still are considered as one shareholder for purposes of determining the number of shareholders in the corporation. However, should the couple later divorce, then each would count as a separate shareholder even if the stock is still held jointly. If one spouse dies while the couple is still married, there is only one shareholder as long as the stock remains in the deceased shareholder's estate. Code Sec. 1361(b)(1)(A) and (c)(1).

The limit on the number of shareholders has been increased from 10 to 75 over the years and may allow S corporations to be more broadly used in connection with various syndicated ventures. The increased number of shareholders will give shareholders more flexibility in estate planning.

Eligible Shareholders

Individuals (other than nonresident aliens), estates, and certain trusts are eligible to hold stock in the S corporation. Code Sec. 1361(b)(1). There are various trusts that are permissible holders of stock in an S corporation. All trusts that are included in Subpart E of the Internal Revenue Code are so permitted, provided that there is one person who is deemed to be the owner of all of the trusts. Foreign trusts, like foreign corporations and nonresident aliens, are not eligible shareholders. The IRS has specifically ruled that a corporation cannot qualify for an S corporation election if it has a partnership as a shareholder. Rev. Rul. 59-235, 1959-2 CB 192.

After 1997, tax-exempt organizations will be eligible S corporation shareholders. This means that qualified pension plans, public charities, and private foundations will be able to hold stock in S corporations. However, individual retirement accounts will continue to be ineligible shareholders. Trade associations and benevolent associations are also not eligible shareholders of S corporation stock.

TAX BLUNDER

Fred Smyth uses funds in his self-directed individual retirement account to purchase shares in an S corporation. The corporation would no longer be an eligible S corporation as it has an ineligible shareholder. Fred should have purchased the shares with his own funds.

In the case of a Qualified Subchapter S Trust (QSST), the terms of the trust instrument need only require that there be a single income beneficiary during the life of the current income beneficiary. Thus, the possibility of multiple beneficiaries after the death of the current beneficiary will not disqualify the trust during the current beneficiary's lifetime. A QSST is required to distribute all of its income to a citizen or resident of the United States. Code Sec. 1361(d)(3)(C). If a QSST ceases to qualify on the death of an income beneficiary because of multiple beneficiaries, the trust will continue to be an eligible shareholder for the two-year period following the death of the current beneficiary. The corporation will therefore have an opportunity to continue the election by requalification of the trust or by transfer of the stock to a qualified shareholder. If the trust continues to qualify after the death of the first income beneficiary, any subsequent income beneficiary will be deemed to have made the election to be taxed under Code Sec. 678 unless the beneficiary affirmatively refuses to consent to the election. Code Sec. 1361(d)(2)(B).

TAX PLANNING POINTER

A Qualified Terminable Interest Property (QTIP) marital deduction trust qualifies as a permitted shareholder since there is only one income beneficiary during the spouse's lifetime and any principal distributions during the spouse's lifetime must be to the spouse.

A trust may be used when the grantor wishes to avoid direct ownership of the stock by persons who are not appropriate to manage the investment. The investment responsibility is given to the trustee.

Stock in an S corporation may be held by certain electing small business trusts (ESBT). Any portion of such a trust that consists of S corporation stock will be treated as a separate trust and will be taxed at the highest rate of tax for estate and trusts (currently 39.6 percent on ordinary income and at the long-term capital gains rates) with limited deductions and credits and no exemption amount for alternative minimum tax purposes. The ESBT lends itself to the more typical gift or testamentary pattern that employs a single trust with multiple potential beneficiaries, such as the grantor's children and spouse or other relatives. Current distribution of all income is not required. The remainder beneficiaries can be different from the income beneficiaries and can include charities.

The trust can have no beneficiaries other than individuals, estates, and certain charities. Even though a nonresident alien cannot hold S corporation stock outright, nonresident aliens can be income beneficiaries since the income will be taxed to the trust rather than to the beneficiary.

Charitable remainder unitrusts and charitable remainder annuity trusts cannot qualify as electing small business trusts. Code Sec. 1361(e)(1)(B)(iii). All beneficiaries of an electing small business trust must be individuals or estates eligible to be S corporation shareholders. While charitable remainder unitrusts and charitable remainder annuity trusts may provide income to individual beneficiaries for a term of years, they must also provide a remainder interest to a charitable organization.

One Class of Stock

There must not be more than one class of stock. Code Sec. 1361(b)(1)(D). The outstanding shares of the corporation must be identical as to the rights of the holders in the profits and in the assets of the corporation. However, differences in voting rights among shares of common stock are permitted. An instrument that is straight debt is not treated as a second class of stock. A straight debt instrument means a written unconditional promise to pay on demand or on a specified date a sum certain in money so long as the interest rate and payment dates are fixed. They are fixed if they are not contingent on the profits of the corporation, the discretion of the corporation, or other similar factors. However, the fact that the interest rate is dependent upon the prime rate or a similar factor not related to the debtor corporation will not disqualify the instrument from being treated under the safe-harbor rule. In order for the safe harbor to apply, the instrument must not be convertible into stock and must be held by a person eligible to hold S corporation stock. Code Sec. 1361(c)(4) and (5)(B). However, straight debt may nevertheless be treated as stock for other tax purposes. Sen. Rept. No. 640, 97th Cong., 2nd Sess. (1982).

TAX PLANNING POINTER ▼

The use of different classes of voting stock may be an effective tool in structuring management control between different business factions or in shifting ownership for estate planning purposes without relinquishing voting control.

Ineligible Corporations

Financial institutions that are allowed a deduction for bad debts under Code Sec. 585 or 593 and insurance companies subject to tax under Subchapter L do not qualify for the election. U.S. possessions corporations, DISCs, and former DISCs are also ineligible to elect Subchapter S. Code Sec. 1361(b)(2)(B)-(E). Subchapter S casualty insurance companies can continue as S corporations by meeting certain requirements. Rev. Rul. 74-437, 1974-2 CB 274.

Prior to 1997, an S corporation could not be a member of an affiliated group. However, new rules permit an S corporation to own any percentage of the stock of a C corporation. These new rules allow S corporations to restructure their business operations by dropping separate business operations into corporate subsidiaries.

Where the parent S corporation owns 100 percent of the stock of the subsidiary corporation and elects to treat the subsidiary as a QSSS, the subsidiary can then qualify as a Qualified Subchapter S Subsidiary (QSSS). The subsidiary must also be a domestic corporation, not an ineligible corporation. Technically, the subsidiary must be a C corporation because a corporation owns all of the subsidiary's stock. A foreign subsidiary cannot qualify as a QSSS.

The QSSS will not be treated as a separate corporation for federal income tax purposes. It will be treated as combined with the parent S corporation. Its assets, liabilities, items of income, deduction, and credit will be treated as belonging to the parent.

¶ 20,077   ELECTION

S corporation status must be elected by all of the shareholders of the corporation. Code Sec. 1362(a)(2). An election made on or before the fifteenth day of the third month of a corporation's tax year is effective beginning with the year when made. Code Sec. 1362(b)(1). For a newly created corporation, the first tax year begins at the earliest occurrence of any of the following events: (1) when the corporation has shareholders, (2) when it acquires assets, or (3) when it begins doing business.

Example 20.1. Melba Corporation begins its first taxable year on March 13, 1998. For an election to be effective beginning with the corporation's first tax year, the election must be made within the period beginning after March 12, 1998, and ending before May 28, 1998.

The corporation must meet all the eligibility requirements (including shareholder eligibility requirements) for the pre-election portion of the tax year. All persons who held stock in the corporation at any time during the portion of the year before the election was made must consent to the election. Temp. Reg. § 18.1362-2(b)(1). However, a person who becomes a shareholder after the corporation is an S corporation does not have to consent to the election. A new shareholder does not have the power to terminate the election unless that shareholder owns more than 50 percent of the stock and elects to terminate the election.

A shareholder's consent to an election must be made either on Form 2553 (Election by a Small Business Corporation) or on a separate statement signed by the shareholder in which the shareholder consents to the election of the corporation. The consent form must contain the name, address, and taxpayer identification number of the corporation and of the shareholder, the number of shares of stock owned by the shareholder, and the date (or dates) on which the stock was acquired. The shareholder's consent is binding and may not be withdrawn after a valid election is made by the corporation.

The election will not become effective until the following tax year if: (1) the eligibility requirements are not met for the entire pre-election portion of the year for which the election is made, (2) consents of all shareholders who had disposed of their stock prior to the making of the election are not obtained, or (3) the election is made after the fifteenth day of the third month of the year. Temp. Reg. § 1.1362-1(a), (b). This rule prevents any allocation of income or loss to pre-election stockholders who either were ineligible to hold S corporation stock or did not consent to the election.

Example 20.2. At the beginning of 1998, the stock of Essex Corporation is held equally by Tom Cox and Mary Hendrix. On February 24, Tom sells his shares to Wilbur Williams. On March 10, Wilbur and Mary make the S election by filing Form 2553. The corporation cannot become an S corporation until January 1, 1999. Although the election was timely filed, Tom did not consent to the election. Had he signed Form 2553, S status would have taken effect as of January 1, 1998.

Where stock is owned, for example, by a husband and wife as community property, or is owned by tenants in common, joint tenants, or tenants by the entirety, each person having a community interest and each tenant in common, joint tenant, and tenant by the entirety must consent to the election. Further, where stock is held by a minor, consent must be made by the minor or guardian. Stock held by a custodian for a minor under the Uniform Transfers to Minors Act is treated as owned by the minor and not by a trust.

The consent of an estate must be made by an executor or administrator of the estate. Where the stock of the corporation is held by an eligible trust, each deemed owner who is considered to be a shareholder must consent to the election. Where stock is held by a trust to which the stock was transferred pursuant to the terms of a will, the estate of the testator that is considered to be the shareholder must consent to the election. Temp. Reg. § 18.1362-2(b)(2).

Generally, the IRS will give notification of acceptance of an S corporation election within 60 days after Form 2553 has been filed. Form 1120S (U.S. Income Tax Return for an S Corporation) is not to be filed until notification of acceptance is received.

Extension of Time for Filing Consents

An extension of time for filing consents is permitted if there is reasonable cause for the failure to file the consent on time and the interests of the government will not be jeopardized. The extension applies only to shareholders' consents; the S election for the tax year must have been timely filed. New consents must be filed within such extended period of time as may be granted by the Internal Revenue Service by all persons who were shareholders of the corporation at any time during the tax year and by all persons who were shareholders of the corporation within the period beginning after such tax year and ending before the date on which an extension of time is granted. Temp. Reg. § 18.1362-2(c).

For example, an extension may be required where the corporation does not yet have shareholders when it is first required to make the election and an extension is needed until shareholders are obtained. See *Q.A. Calhoun,* 74-1 USTC ¶ 9104, 370 F.Supp. 434 (DC Va. 1973).

While S corporation status is limited to small business corporations, the size is measured not in gross receipts, net income, or number of employees, but in the number of shareholders.

¶ 20,085   CONTRIBUTIONS TO THE CORPORATION

Section 351 allows contributions to the S corporation to be tax free to the contributing shareholder provided three conditions are met: (1) property is transferred to the corporation, (2) stock is received by the contributing shareholder, and (3) contributing shareholders receive 80 percent control of the corporation.

Just as in the case of a C corporation, there are three exceptions to the nontaxability of Section 351. Where services are provided by an individual for stock in the S corporation, the individual must report ordinary income to the extent of the fair market value of the stock received. For example, if Mary receives stock with a fair market value of $10,000 for services she performed in organizing and setting up the corporation, she would be required to report $10,000 of ordinary income and have a basis in the stock received of $10,000. Stock issued in exchange for services rendered cannot be included in satisfying the control requirement. Code Sec. 351(d).

Liabilities transferred to a corporation in a Section 351 exchange are not considered boot and thus will not cause gain to be recognized on the transfer. However, if the liabilities exceed the basis of all the assets that a shareholder transfers, income is recognized to the extent of the excess liabilities. For example, if an individual transfers an asset with a $10,000 fair market value, $4,000 basis, and a $5,500 liability attached to the corporation for all of the stock in the corporation, the individual will have to recognize a $1,500 gain—the excess of the liability over the basis of the asset. This income recognition is necessary to prevent the shareholder from having a negative basis in the stock received.

If tax avoidance or lack of business purpose is present in connection with the assumption of the liabilities by the corporation, income also may need to be recognized. Where an individual borrows against an asset prior to transferring the asset along with the liability to the corporation, income may be recognized. No income would be recognized if the individual used the proceeds of the loan for business purposes, such as purchasing inventory or plant and equipment. However, if the individual withdrew the loan proceeds for personal use prior to transferring the asset and liability to the corporation, the IRS would call for income to be recognized to the extent of the smaller of the loan proceeds or the realized gain from the asset transfer.

The S corporation has a carryover basis in the property received from the shareholder, increased by any gain recognized by the transferor. The shareholder's basis in the stock received is the basis of the property transferred plus any gain recognized on the transfer minus any liability transferred.

¶ 20,105   TAX YEAR OF THE CORPORATION

The tax year of an S corporation is required to be either a year ending December 31, or any other tax year for which it establishes a business purpose to the satisfaction of the Internal Revenue Service. Code Sec. 1378(b). Partnerships are allowed to utilize a fiscal year where it is the tax year of all the partners owning a majority interest in partnership profits and capital. This exception is not available to S corporations.

An S corporation that elects to use a tax year other than the tax year required under Code Sec. 1378(b) must generally make a "required payment" for any tax year for which such an election is in effect. The required payment is intended to represent the value of the tax deferral that the owners on the S corporation receive through the use of a tax year other than the required tax year. The required payment is due on or before May 15 of the calendar year following the calendar year in which the election year begins. Generally, any required payment is assessed and collected as if it were an employment tax. Neither the S corporation nor the shareholders are entitled to a deduction with respect to a required payment. If an S corporation willfully fails to comply with the required payment rules, the entity's election under Code Sec. 444 is cancelled, effective from the year in which the willful failure occurred.

Business Purpose Exception

An S corporation may adopt a fiscal tax year if it can convince the IRS that a business purpose exists for such a tax year. The intent of an entity to make its tax year coincide with its natural business year constitutes a valid business purpose. Where a business has a nonpeak and a peak period, the natural business year usually ends at, or soon after, the close of the peak period. A business with a steady monthly income does not have a natural business year.

A business purpose generally exists if, in the last two months of the selected tax year, a taxpayer receives at least 25 percent of its gross receipts and has done so for three consecutive 12-month periods. The following factors are ordinarily insufficient to establish a business purpose with respect to a particular fiscal tax year: (1) the use of a particular year for regulatory or financial accounting purposes; (2) the hiring patterns of a particular business; (3) the use of a particular year for administrative purposes, such as the promotion of staff and the compensation or retirement arrangement with staff, partners, or shareholders; and (4) the fact that a particular business involves the use of price lists, model year, or other items that change on an annual basis.

In order to use a fiscal tax year, an S corporation must obtain the IRS's consent. An S corporation that receives permission to use a fiscal year under Rev. Proc. 74-33, 1974-2 CB 489, can continue to use such year without seeking approval from the IRS. However, the continuation of a fiscal year granted under Rev. Proc. 74-33 does not apply to fiscal years granted under the three-month-or-less deferral of income.

S Corporation Taxation

¶ 20,147 INTRODUCTION

An S corporation is not subject to the corporate tax, except for a tax on built-in gains, a tax on excessive passive investment income, LIFO recapture tax, and a tax imposed on early disposition of property on which general business credit was claimed by the corporation when it was a C corporation. Every S corporation must file a return on Form 1120S each tax year even though the corporation may not be subject to tax.

¶ 20,155 TAX ON BUILT-IN GAINS

A tax is imposed on an S corporation that has "recognized built-in gain" in order to prevent the avoidance of tax through the conversion of a C corporation to an S corporation. The tax is imposed if, for any tax year within the 10-year period beginning with the first day of the first tax year for which the S election was effective, the corporation has a recognized built-in gain. This tax does not apply to a corporation that has been an S corporation for all of its tax years. This provision is effective for tax years beginning after 1986, but only for corporations that have made S corporation elections after 1986.

Maximum Amount of Gain

The maximum amount of built-in gain that can be taken into account for purposes of the built-in gains tax is the amount by which the "net unrealized built-in gain" exceeds the "recognized built-in gain" for prior years beginning in the recognition period. "Net unrealized built-in gain" is the excess of the fair market value of the S corporation's assets when its S election became effective over the aggregate bases of those assets at that time. Generally, "recognized built-in gain" means any gain recognized on the disposition of any asset during the recognition period. However, it does not include gain from the disposition of an asset if the corporation establishes that: (1) the asset was not held by the S corporation when its S election became effective, or (2) the gain is attributable to appreciation that occurred after the S election became effective.

These built-in gains include not only profits from the disposition of capital assets and business-use assets, but also profits realized on the sale of inventory items, collection of accounts receivable with a zero basis because of the cash method of accounting, and other cash-basis accrued income. The completion of a long-term contract performed by a taxpayer using the completed-contract method of accounting is considered a disposition.

In cases where an asset with a built-in gain or loss is exchanged for another asset in a transaction in which the new asset's basis is determined in whole or in part by reference to the basis of the old asset, the new asset is subject to the tax on built-in gains. Specifically, the new asset will be treated as if held on the first day of S corporation status and as having the same built-in gain or loss as the old asset on that day.

Regulations will provide that the inventory method used by the taxpayer for tax purposes (i.e., FIFO, LIFO, etc.) will also be used to identify whether goods disposed of following conversion to S corporation status were held by the corporation at the time of conversion. Thus, a corporation using the LIFO inventory method will not be subject to the built-in gains tax with respect to sales of inventory except to the extent that a LIFO layer in existence prior to the beginning of the first tax year as an S corporation was invaded after the beginning of the first year.

Computation of the Tax

The amount of the tax is computed by applying the corporate rate to the net recognized built-in gain. The amount of the net recognized built-in gain taken into account for any tax year cannot exceed the difference of the net unrealized built-in gain over the net recognized built-in gain for prior tax years. For S status elections made after March 30, 1988, any net recognized built-in gains exceeding taxable income must be carried to the succeeding year and treated as a built-in gain for that year. This carryover continues until 10 years after the effective date of the S status election. The corporate rate to be applied is the highest corporate tax rate imposed by Code Sec. 11 (currently 35 percent) or the alternative corporate tax rate on capital gains if such a rate is in effect.

Taxable income is computed with the Code Sec. 172 net operating loss (NOL) deduction and without the deductions of Code Secs. 241-250, other than the organizational expense deduction of Code Sec. 248. However, any NOL carryforward or capital loss carryforward arising in a tax year in which the corporation was a C corporation offsets recognized built-in gain to the extent otherwise permitted. No credit except for the general business credit carryforwards and the minimum tax credit from years in which the corporation was a C corporation is allowable in the computation of the tax.

The amount of any tax paid on the recognized built-in gain must be passed on to S corporation shareholders in a pro rata fashion as a loss. The character of the loss is determined by allocating the loss proportionately among the recognized built-in gains giving rise to the tax.

> *Example 20.3.* Samson Corporation elects S corporation status at the beginning of 1998. The corporation has an asset with a basis of $40,000 and a fair market value of $85,000 on January 1, 1998. The asset is sold during 1998 for $95,000. The corporation incurs a recognized gain of $55,000, of which $45,000 is subject to the built-in gains tax. Samson Corporation would incur a $15,750 ($45,000 × 35%) built-in gains tax. The amount of loss passed through to the shareholders would be $15,750.

¶ 20,161   TAX ON LIFO RECAPTURE

Any C corporation using the LIFO method that converts to S corporation status is required to recapture the excess of the FIFO inventory value over its LIFO value as of the close of the last year as a C corporation. Any amount included because of the LIFO adjustment may be reflected in the value of the inventory carried over to the S corporation by making the appropriate adjustment to basis.

The tax attributable to the LIFO inclusion in income is payable in four equal installments. The first installment must be paid on or before the due date of the C corporation's last tax return (without extensions), and the three remaining installments are due on the due dates of the S corporation's tax returns for the three succeeding tax years. If the installments are paid on their respective due dates, no interest will be charged.

> *Example 20.4.* Java Corporation, a C corporation, wishes to switch to an S corporation at the beginning of 1999. Java has $20,000 that must be recaptured under the LIFO recapture rules. The tax on the $20,000 will be $6,800. Java must include an additional tax of $1700 ($6,800 ÷ 4) on its 1998 return, Java's last C corporation income tax return. In additon, Java must pay $1,700 with the filing of its 1999, 2000, and 2001 S corporation tax returns.

¶ 20,163 TAX ON PASSIVE INVESTMENT INCOME

A tax is imposed on the S corporation where it has (1) Subchapter C earnings and profits at the close of the tax year and (2) gross receipts for the tax year of which more than 25 percent is passive investment income. The tax is computed by multiplying the excess net passive income by the highest corporate tax rate—currently 35 percent. The only credit allowed against the tax is the credit for special fuels under Code Sec. 34. Code Sec. 1375(a) and (c)(1).

The tax on passive income prevents a holding company with accumulated earnings from electing S corporation status and avoiding the personal holding company and accumulated earnings taxes. Subchapter S imposes a corporate level tax on passive investment income that is essentially designed to counteract the holding company problem without necessarily terminating an S election. An S corporation that has never been a C corporation can enjoy an unlimited amount of passive income with no adverse tax consequences.

"Subchapter C earnings and profits" means earnings and profits of any corporation for any tax year with respect to which an election under Subchapter S was not in effect. Code Sec. 1362(d)(3).

"Excess net passive income" is that portion of net passive income for the tax year multiplied by a fraction comprised of (1) the amount by which the passive investment income for the tax year exceeds 25 percent of the gross receipts for the tax year, divided by (2) the passive investment income for the tax year. The amount of the excess net passive income for any tax year cannot exceed the corporation's taxable income. Code Sec. 1375(b)(1).

Expressed as a formula, excess net passive income (ENPI) for a tax year equals:

$$\text{ENPI} = \text{Net Passive Income} \times \frac{\text{Passive Investment Income} - 25\% \text{ Gross Receipts}}{\text{Passive Investment Income}}$$

"Net passive income" means passive investment income reduced by the allowable deductions directly connected with the production of such income. However, the net operating loss deduction under Code Sec. 172 and the special deductions allowed under Code Secs. 241-250 (e.g., dividends-received deduction, amortization of organizational expenditures) are not allowed. Code Sec. 1375(b)(2). The excess net passive income cannot exceed the corporate taxable income for the year before considering any net operating loss deduction or the special deductions of Code Secs. 241-250.

"Passive investment income" means gross receipts derived from royalties, rents, dividends, interest, annuities, and sales or exchanges of stock or securities. Interest includes tax-exempt interest. The passive income test is modified to exclude interest on deferred payment sales of property held for sale to customers made by the corporation and income from the conduct of a lending or finance business. Only the net gain from the disposition of capital assets (other than stock and securities) is taken into account in computing gross receipts. Code Sec. 1362(d)(3). This prevents a corporation from "churning" assets as a means of increasing gross receipts.

TAX PLANNING POINTER

It is still possible for the corporation to escape the tax by "churning" Section 1231 assets. The sale of some of the assets used in the business could sufficiently increase gross receipts to avoid the 25 percent threshold test. Investment in rental property producing an operating loss through large depreciation and interest deductions can be used to reduce net passive income. Rental income may be removed from the passive category if the corporation provides significant services to the lessees.

Example 20.5. S corporation has gross receipts of $300,000 for the year, of which $100,000 is passive investment income. Expenses directly connected with the production of this passive investment income are $30,000. Thus, S corporation has net passive income of $70,000 ($100,000 of passive investment income less $30,000 in expenses), and the amount by which its passive investment income for the tax year exceeds 25 percent of its gross receipts is $25,000 ($100,000 of passive investment income less $75,000 ($300,000 × 25 percent)). The excess net passive income is $17,500 ($70,000 of net passive income × ($25,000 of passive investment income in excess of 25 percent of gross receipts for the year ÷ $100,000 of passive investment income for the year)). The passive investment income tax is $6,125 ($17,500 × 35%).

Any built-in gain subject to the passive investment income tax is not subject to the S corporation built-in gains tax. Thus, any gain subject to the built-in gains tax must be reduced by that portion of the "excess net passive income" that is attributable on a pro rata basis to the gain. Code Sec. 1375(c)(2). The passive investment income tax also reduces each item of passive income by the amount of extra tax attributable to it, thereby reducing the amount of passive investment income that each shareholder must take into account in computing individual gross income. Code Sec. 1366(f)(3).

TAX BLUNDER

Dally Corporation operated as a C corporation for many years before changing to an S corporation. At the time of the S election, there was a small amount of earnings and profits. During 1998, Dally has a large gain from the sale of stock that it held, causing a passive investment income tax of $12,000. The corporation could have avoided the tax if they had distributed the earnings and profits before the end of 1998.

TAX PLANNING POINTER ▼

Consent dividends may be paid to eliminate accumulated earnings and profits when cash is not available for regular dividends.

Section 1375(d) gives the IRS authority to waive the tax on excess net passive income if the corporation determined in good faith that it had no C corporation earnings and profits at the close of the tax year. Also, the tax may be waived if such earnings and profits are distributed within a reasonable period of time after it is determined that the corporation did have C corporation earnings and profits.

¶ 20,171   GENERAL BUSINESS CREDIT RECAPTURE

A corporation's S election will not trigger imposition of the tax for early disposition of property for which a general business credit was taken. The election is regarded as a mere change in form and not a disposition of property. However, if the S corporation makes an early disposition of any property for which a credit was taken by the corporation prior to the effective date of its election, the S corporation remains liable for the general business credit recapture. Code Sec. 1371(d)(1) and (2).

The recapture of the general business tax credit claimed in years prior to S corporation status is to be made at the corporate level. An S corporation's accumulated earnings and profits will be reduced by the amount of general business credit recapture tax imposed on the corporation with respect to these credits since the earnings and profits were not previously reduced by the amount of tax savings attributable to the credit. Moreover, the basis of stock in an S corporation is to be adjusted to reflect the change in the basis of corporation property when general business credits are allowed or recaptured, with corresponding adjustments made to the accumulated adjustments account.

Example 20.6. Donal Corporation, a C corporation, receives a general business credit on the purchase of an asset. Two years later, Donal Corporation switches to an S corporation. The following year the corporation disposes of the asset. Donal Corporation will be responsible for the recapture of the general business credit. However, if the asset was purchased after the switch to an S corporation, any recapture of the general business credit would be passed through to the shareholders.

¶ 20,175   ESTIMATED TAX

S corporations are required to make estimated tax payments for tax liability attributable to the built-in gains tax, excessive passive investment income tax, and tax due by reason of general business credit recapture. The corporate estimated tax provisions are generally applicable to S corporations. The required annual estimated tax payment is the lesser of: (1) 100 percent of the tax shown on the return for the tax year or (2) the sum of 100 percent of the tax liability incurred by virtue of the built-in gains tax and tax due because of general business credit recapture, plus 100 percent of the tax due on the passive investment income reported by the S corporation in the preceding year. Code Sec. 6655(g).

An S corporation cannot utilize the exception that allows estimated tax payments to be based on the corporation's prior tax year when computing tax payments attributable to built-in gains and the general business tax credit recapture. The prior year's tax exception is, however, available to all S corporations with respect to the portion of required estimated tax payments attributable to excessive passive income, even if there was no tax attributable to excess passive income in the prior year. In all cases, an S corporation can use the annualized exception.

¶ 20,185　PENALTIES FOR FAILURE TO FILE

An electing S corporation that neglects to file an information return by the due date, including extensions, may be liable for a 5 percent penalty for each month the return has not been filed with a maximum of 25 percent. The penalty is computed based on the net amount due. Moreover, a similar penalty of ½ of 1 percent per month may be imposed against a corporation that fails to pay the tax when due up to a maximum of 25 percent. If a corporation can establish that failure to file or pay tax was due to reasonable cause and not to willful neglect, it may be relieved of such penalties.

In addition, a penalty may be imposed on a corporation for failure to furnish a statement (Schedule K, Form 1120S, Shareholders' Shares of Income, Credits, Deductions, etc.) as required under Code Sec. 6037(b) unless such failure was due to reasonable cause and not to willful neglect. The amount of the penalty is $50 for each schedule not provided, but the total penalty cannot exceed $100,000 for any single year.

The fact that a corporation elects to operate as a tax-free S corporation does not relieve it of responsibility for filing other information returns required under the law. For instance, the corporation is still required to file an information return on Form 1099 for "fixed or determinable" gains, profits, or income paid to any person during the calendar year if total annual payments other than dividends exceed $600.

An S corporation that is created as a tax shelter, that is involved in promoting tax shelter activity, or that is a conduit for tax shelter benefits is required to provide additional reporting information on behalf of the corporation and its shareholders under Code Sec. 6111.

KEYSTONE PROBLEM

What is the best form of organization for a business—corporation, partnership, or S corporation? What factors should be taken into consideration in making the election? Is one form of organization better than the others in all situations?

Treatment of Income, Deductions, and Credits

¶ 20,221   CORPORATE TREATMENT

The S corporation's income will be computed under the same rules presently applicable to partnerships under Code Sec. 703, except that the amortization of organization expenditures under Section 248 is an allowable deduction. As in the case of partnerships, deductions generally allowable to individuals are allowed to S corporations. However, the Code provisions governing the computation of income that are applicable only to corporations, such as the dividends-received deduction (Code Sec. 243) or the special rules relating to corporate tax preferences (Code Sec. 291), do ·not apply to S corporations. Items eligible for separate treatment which could affect any shareholder's liability (such as investment interest) are treated separately. Elections generally are made at the corporate level, except for those elections which the partners of a partnership may make separately. Code Sec. 1363(b) and (c)(1).

Examples of elections to be made at the corporate level include selection or change of an accounting method, inventory valuation, selection of tax year, method of depreciation and claiming general business credits, eligibility for nonrecognition of gain on an involuntary conversion, and election out of the installment sales provisions. The shareholder elections include income from discharge of indebtedness (Code Sec. 108(b)(5) and (d)(4)), the limitation on investment indebtedness (Code Sec. 163(d)), the deduction and recapture of certain mining exploration expenditures (Code Sec. 617), and taxes of foreign countries and possessions of the United States (Code Sec. 901). Code Sec. 1363(c)(2).

Generally, C corporation tax rules apply, except that an S corporation is treated in the same manner as an individual in transactions, such as the treatment of dividends received under Code Sec. 301, where the corporation is a shareholder in a regular corporation. Code Sec. 1371(a)(2). In transactions by an S corporation with respect to its own stock, the S corporation is treated as a regular corporation. However, S corporation rules do not apply where the result is inconsistent with the purpose of the Subchapter S rules that treat the corporation as a pass-through entity.

Property distributed as a dividend to an S corporation is includible in gross income at fair market value. The distribution of appreciated property by an S corporation generally results in gain recognition to the distributing corporation in the same manner as if the property had been sold to the shareholder at its fair market value. This gain will pass through to the shareholders.

Example 20.7. A corporation distributes an asset to its sole shareholder. The asset has a fair market value of $250,000 and a basis of $150,000. The corporation reports a gain of $100,000 which is passed through to the shareholder. The shareholder reports no further income upon the distribution and has a basis in the asset of $250,000.

If the corporation were a regular corporation, the corporation would have to pay a tax on the payment of the dividend. The shareholder would have to report $250,000 of dividend income (assuming adequate earnings and profits).

Certain limitations resembling the partnership rules apply at both the corporate level and the shareholder level. The current expense limitation on certain depreciable business assets applies at both levels. Code Sec. 179(d)(8)).

Separately Reported Items

The items that must be reported separately by an S corporation are the same as those that partners are required to take into account under Code Sec. 702(a). Code Sec. 1366(a)(1). These include (but are not limited to):

1. *Capital gains and losses.* Gains or losses from sales or exchanges of capital assets pass through to the shareholders as capital gains or losses.

2. *Section 1231 gains and losses.* The gains and losses on certain property used in a trade or business are passed through separately and aggregated with the shareholder's other Section 1231 gains and losses.

3. *Charitable contributions.* The corporate 10 percent limitation does not apply to the S corporation. As in the case of partnerships, the contributions pass through to the shareholders, at which level they will be subject to the individual limitations on deductibility.

4. *Interest and dividends.* Interest and dividends received by the S corporation must be separately stated as they comprise portfolio income to the shareholder in determining the investment interest limitation.

5. *Tax-exempt interest.* Tax-exempt interest passes through to the shareholders as such and increases the shareholders' bases in their S corporation stock. Subsequent distributions by a corporation will not result in taxation of the tax-exempt income.

6. *Foreign tax credit.* Foreign taxes paid by the corporation pass through as such to the shareholders, who claim the taxes either as deductions or as credits subject to the applicable limitation. An S corporation is not eligible for the foreign tax credit with respect to taxes paid by a foreign corporation in which the S corporation is a shareholder; therefore, these taxes do not pass through to its shareholders.

7. *Credits.* As with partnerships, items involved in the determination of credits, such as the basis of Section 38 property for purposes of computing the amount of qualified investment eligible for the general business credit, pass through to the S corporation's shareholders.

8. *Depletion.* The rules governing depletion with regard to partnership interest in minerals apply to depletion of properties of an S corporation.

9. *Foreign income and loss.* Domestic losses and foreign losses pass through separately. If a corporation has foreign losses and domestic income, or vice versa, each passes through separately to shareholders without aggregation at the corporate level.

10. *Other items.* The expensing of certain depreciable business assets (Code Sec. 179) and the amortization of reforestation expenditures (Code Sec. 194) apply at both the corporate level and the shareholder level, as in the case of a partnership. The election to capitalize intangible costs by a shareholder who does not actively participate in the management of the corporation is the same as the election by a limited partner (i.e., 10-year amortization). Code Sec. 58(i). Passive gains and losses and tax preferences must also be segregated and reported separately to the shareholders.

The above listing is not intended to be exhaustive. In order to determine the treatment of items, a basic principle must be kept in mind: If the item can affect the computation of a shareholder's tax liability, it must be stated separately by the corporation. Any items not reported separately comprise the S corporation's "nonseparately computed income or loss."

Example 20.8. Ada Corporation, an S corporation, has the following tax items for the year:

Gross income	$50,000
Advertising expense	10,000
Wage expense	25,000
Long-term capital gain	5,000
Short-term capital loss	2,000
Charitable contributions	3,000

Any items having special tax significance must be reported separately, with the remaining items combined to arrive at ordinary income. Ada Corporation must report the following to its shareholders:

Ordinary income	$15,000
Long-term capital gain	5,000
Short-term capital loss	2,000
Charitable contributions	3,000

Treatment of Fringe Benefits

The statutory exemptions for fringe benefits applicable to shareholder-employees of regular corporations include the following:

1. The exclusion from income of amounts paid for an accident and health plan (Code Sec. 105(b), (c), and (d))

2. The exclusion from income of amounts paid by an employer to the accident and health plan (Code Sec. 106)

3. The exclusion of the cost of up to $50,000 of group-term insurance on an employee's life (Code Sec. 79)

4. The exclusion from income of the value of meals or lodging furnished for the convenience of the employer (Code Sec. 119)

Fringe benefits of any person owning more than 2 percent of the stock of the corporation are treated in the same manner as fringe benefits of a partner in a partnership. Code Sec. 1372(a)(2). Thus, for example, amounts paid for the medical care of a shareholder-employee are to be classified as wages to the employee and includible in the shareholder's W-2. Rev. Rul. 91-26, 1991-1 CB 184. The premiums are excludable for social security and medicare if the payments are made under a "qualified plan" described in Code Sec. 3121(a). The shareholder is considered a self-employed individual for purposes of the deduction for medical insurance under Code Sec. 162(l)(1). However, similar amounts paid by the corporation on behalf of shareholders owning 2 percent or less of the corporation are deductible as a business expense and tax free to the employee. Any person who owns, on any day during the tax year of the S corporation, more than 2 percent of the outstanding stock of the corporation, or stock possessing more than 2 percent of the total combined voting power of all stock of the corporation, is subject to the fringe benefit limitation. The attribution rules of Code Sec. 318 apply in determining if more than 2 percent of the outstanding stock of the S corporation is owned by an individual. Code Sec. 1372(b).

Example 20.9. S corporation has 100 shares of stock outstanding and three shareholder-employees. Mark Peters owns two shares, Nan Olds owns 40 shares, and Opel Raser owns the remaining 58 shares. The corporation pays employee accident and health insurance. In computing its taxable income for the year, S corporation must include any expenditures attributable to the accident and health insurance for shareholder-employees Nan and Opel in their wages. Nan and Opel must include the amounts paid in gross income and may deduct 45 percent of the amount included in income as a deduction from gross income, with the remainder qualifying as a medical expense itemized deduction. However, the corporation is allowed a business deduction for the accident and health insurance for Mark or any other employees. Mark is allowed to exclude the premiums from gross income.

Treatment of Expenses and Interest Owed to Shareholders

An S corporation is placed on the cash method of accounting for purposes of deducting business expenses and interest owed to a related-party, cash-basis taxpayer, including a shareholder who owns directly or indirectly any Code Sec. 267(e) stock in the corporation. This rule applies only where the recipient is on the cash basis and, therefore, would not apply if the recipient uses the accrual basis or the completed contract method of accounting. By treating the corporation as a cash-basis taxpayer, the corporation will take its deduction in the same year in which the shareholder takes the item into income. The deduction is not lost by the corporation if payment is made after the 2½ month period expires, as would be the case under prior operation of Code Sec. 267.

The usual loss disallowance rules of Code Sec. 267(a)(1) apply to transactions between two S corporations or between an S corporation and a partnership, if both entities are more than 50 percent owned by the same person. Also, an S corporation and a regular operation are treated as related if the same individual owns more than 50 percent of the value of the outstanding stock in each corporation.

Corporate Tax Preference Rules

Code Sec. 291, which deals with corporate tax preference items, applies to S corporations if the corporation or its predecessor was a C corporation for any of the three immediately preceding tax years. The purpose of the measure is to prevent C corporations from avoiding the corporate preference rules by making an S corporation election. The corporate tax preference rules, however, do not apply to any corporation that has been an S corporation since its incorporation.

C Corporation Carryovers

Carryovers from years in which the corporation was not an S corporation are not allowed to the corporation while in S corporation status. However, the intervening years count as tax years for purposes of determining the number of years to which a particular item (i.e., deductions, credits, etc.) may be carried forward or back. Code Sec. 1371(a).

Example 20.10. C corporation has a $50,000 net operating loss for 1998 after using its carryback provisions. The corporation elects S corporation status at the beginning of 1999. The loss carryforward is not available as an offset against S corporation income and will be lost if the S election is not terminated within 20 years.

¶ 20,281 SHAREHOLDER TREATMENT OF INCOME ITEMS

As with the partners of a partnership, each shareholder of an S corporation takes into account separately his or her pro rata share of each separately stated item of income, deduction, credit, etc., of the corporation and his or her share of "nonseparately computed income or loss." These rules parallel the partnership rules under Code Sec. 702.

Example 20.11. A calendar-year S corporation has a net long-term capital gain of $75,000 and three equal shareholders. Assuming no changes in ownership during the year, each shareholder takes into account $25,000 of long-term capital gain.

Each shareholder's share of the items is taken into account in the shareholder's tax year in which the corporation's year ends. In the case of the death of a shareholder, the shareholder's portion of S corporation items is taken into account on the shareholder's final income tax return. Items from the portion of the corporation's tax year after the shareholder's death are taken into account by the estate or other person acquiring the stock.

Example 20.12. A shareholder owing 20 percent of an S corporation dies at the midpoint of the tax year. The estate of the shareholder holds the stock for the remainder of the year. The corporation has $100,000 of taxable income for the year. The shareholder reports income of $10,000 ($100,000 × 20% × ½) for one-half year of ownership and the estate reports income of $10,000 for its one-half year of ownership.

A shareholder's pro rata share of an S corporation item is generally made on a per-share, per-day basis. Code Sec. 1377(a)(1). Allocations are made with respect to stock ownership, regardless of whether such shares are voting or nonvoting. In years in which there is no change in shareholders or in the relative interests of those shareholders, a shareholder's pro rata share of an item is simply the annual amount of that item multiplied by the shareholder's percentage of total stock outstanding.

Example 20.13. One of the shareholders holding a one-third interest in an S corporation sells all of his stock on March 15. The selling shareholder's share of a $75,000 net income is $5,000 ($75,000 × ⅓ × 73/365). The purchasing shareholder's share is $20,000 ($75,000 × ⅓ × 292/365).

If a shareholder terminates an interest in a corporation during the tax year, the corporation, with the consent of all of the affected shareholders, may elect to allocate according to its permanent records (including work papers). Code Sec. 1377(a)(2).

Example 20.14. An S corporation has $50,000 net income for the first half of the year and $200,000 for the second half of the year. A shareholder terminates his 30 percent interest in the corporation at the end of the first half of the year. Only $15,000 ($50,000 × 30%) is allocated to the terminating shareholder using the permanent record method, rather than $37,500 ($250,000 × 30% × ½) using the per-share, per-day method.

Character of Items

A "conduit" rule for determining the character of items realized by the corporation and included in the shareholder's pro rata share is the same as the partnership rule. Code Sec. 702(b). The character of any item included in a shareholder's pro rata share is determined as if such item were realized directly from the source from which it was realized by the corporation or incurred in the same manner as incurred by the corporation. Thus, tax-exempt interest passes through as tax-exempt interest to the shareholder. Also, the "gross income" determinations made by a shareholder parallel those made using the partnership rule (Code Sec. 702(c)). The shareholder's gross income includes the shareholder's pro rata share of the gross income of the corporation. Code Sec. 1366(b) and (c). Earnings of S corporations which are required to be included in each shareholder's gross income are not self-employment income to the shareholders. Rev. Rul. 59-221, 1959-1 CB 225.

Where an S corporation has a tax imposed on built-in gains, the amount of the gain is passed through to the shareholder. Code Sec. 1366(f)(2). The tax imposed is treated as a loss sustained by the S corporation and the character of the loss is determined by allocating the loss proportionately among the recognized built-in gains.

The tax on passive income also reduces the amount of the items of passive investment income that passes through to shareholders. Allocation of the reduction is made on the basis of the ratio of each item of passive investment income to total passive investment income. Code Sec. 1366(f)(3).

If an individual who is a member of the family of one or more shareholders of an S corporation renders services to the corporation or furnishes capital to the corporation without receiving reasonable compensation, the IRS may make such adjustments in the items taken into account by such individual and shareholders as are necessary to reflect the value of the services or capital. Code Sec. 1366(e). This rule is designed to prevent a high tax bracket family member from working for little or no salary so that undistributed income may be allocated to other, low tax bracket members of the family. Both the amount of compensation and the timing of the compensation can be so adjusted.

Example 20.15. Both parents and child each own one-third of an S corporation. Both parents devote full time to the business, with the child working infrequently. Neither parent receives a salary for the year in which the net income is $120,000. The IRS can require that reasonable compensation be paid to the parents to prevent the full one-third of the $120,000 net income from being taxed to the child. However, because unearned income of children under 14 is taxed at the parents' rate, IRS reallocation is of significance only for children over 13.

A shareholder's allowable pro rata share of the corporation's loss is limited to the sum of the shareholder's adjusted basis in the stock of the corporation and the shareholder's adjusted basis in any indebtedness of the corporation owed to the shareholder. Disallowed losses may be carried forward or allowed in any subsequent year in which the shareholder has adequate basis in such stock or debt. Code Sec. 1366(d)(1) and (2). A shareholder's allowable loss may be limited by the passive activity rules discussed below.

Debt at the corporate level does not add to a shareholder's basis; thus, larger corporate losses arising from the leverage provided by corporate debt and allocated to a shareholder (but exceeding the shareholder's investment in stock plus any loans made by the shareholder to the corporation) may not be used by the shareholder to offset other sources of income.

Example 20.16. John Irving has a stock basis of $8,000 in an S corporation. He has loaned the corporation $3,000 and has personally guaranteed another $5,000 bank loan made to the corporation. John's share of the corporation's operating loss for the year is $12,500. John may deduct only $11,000 of the loss on his individual return ($8,000 basis in the stock plus $3,000 loan to the corporation). The unused loss of $1,500 ($12,500 − $11,000) may be carried forward until John has an adequate basis against which the loss may be deducted.

TAX PLANNING POINTER ▼

It may be possible to increase a shareholder's basis against which corporate losses can be deducted by substituting shareholder notes for the debt of the corporation to a third-party creditor. In Rev. Rul. 75-144, 1975-1 CB 277, investors were allowed to increase the basis against which corporate losses could be deducted by converting corporation debt to its third-party creditors to a debt of the shareholders.

For purposes of computing the amount of foreign losses that must be recaptured under the foreign tax credit rules (Code Sec. 904(f)), the making or termination of an S corporation election is treated as the disposition of a business. Accordingly, when an S election is made, the corporation is treated as having disposed of its foreign property and will include in income the amount of any foreign losses not previously recaptured. Likewise, when an S election is terminated, the shareholders are treated as if the corporation disposed of its foreign assets, and the shareholders will include in income the amount of any foreign losses of the corporation previously passed through to them and not previously recaptured.

Subsequent to a termination of an S corporation election, any unused losses and deductions are allowed if the shareholder's basis in the stock (but not debt) of the corporation is restored by the later of the following dates:

1. One year after the effective date of the termination, or the due date for the last S corporation return, whichever is later.

2. 120 days after a determination that the S corporation election had terminated for a previous year. (A determination is defined as a court decision that becomes final, a closing agreement, or an agreement between the corporation and the IRS that the corporation failed to qualify.) Code Sec. 1377(b).

Example 20.17. A calendar-year S corporation revokes its election effective December 31, 1998. If there is sufficient basis in the shareholder's stock on December 31, 1999, the shareholder may treat a share of any unused loss or deduction of the S corporation as having been incurred on December 31, 1998, and may deduct it for the tax year that includes that date.

TAX PLANNING POINTER ▼

The post-termination rules apply only to stock basis and not to debt. The planners should consider converting shareholder debt into stock during the post-termination transition period if a higher basis is needed to absorb any unused losses.

¶ 20,285 ACCUMULATED ADJUSTMENTS ACCOUNT

The accumulated adjustments account (AAA) consists of post-1982 accumulated gross income less deductible expenses and prior distributions allocable to the account. The AAA is not increased for tax-exempt income or decreased for expenses related to tax-exempt income and federal taxes attributable to a C corporation. The AAA is decreased proportionately with the percentage of stock redeemed under Code Sec. 302(a) or 303(a). Code Sec. 1368(e)(1).

The other adjustments account (OAA) is a balance sheet account in the capital section that is increased for tax-exempt income or decreased for nondeductible expenditures not properly chargeable to the AAA. It represents another form of AAA in that any distributions from OAA are accounted for in the same manner as distributions from AAA, and thus are tax free.

TAX PLANNING POINTER ▼

Tax-exempt income is ordinarily not a good investment for an S corporation with accumulated earnings and profits. The exempt income cannot be distributed tax free to shareholders until after all accumulated earnings and profits are paid out.

Treatment of Corporate Distributions

¶ 20,339 TAX CONSEQUENCES

The tax consequences to shareholders receiving distributions from an S corporation are generally designed to be comparable to those of partners under Subchapter K. However, several important differences exist.

1. Distributions of property from an S corporation are reported by shareholders at fair market value, whereas "adjusted basis" is used to measure partnership distributions.

2. Gain is recognized by an S corporation on a distribution of appreciated property in the same manner as if the property had been sold to the shareholder at its fair market value. Code Sec. 1363(d). Like other corporate gain, it passes through to the shareholders. The distribution will trigger depreciation and general business credit recapture.

   Without this rule, assets could be distributed tax free (except for recapture in certain instances) and subsequently sold without income recognition to the selling shareholder because of the stepped-up fair market value basis.

Example 20.18. Saundra Corporation, an S corporation for its entire existence, distributes some property held as an investment to its sole shareholder. The property was purchased several years ago for $15,000 and has a fair market value of $40,000. Saundra Corporation recognizes a long-term capital gain of $25,000 upon the distribution.

3. Partners are permitted to utilize their respective shares of partnership debt in the computation of basis. Shareholders of S corporations are prohibited from including corporate borrowing in stock basis. The determination of basis has important consequences in determining the character of distributions, in establishing the amount of potential losses and other deductions that may be currently reported, and in computing the amount for which an S shareholder is considered to be at risk under Code Secs. 46(c)(8) and 465. However, any loans made by the shareholder to the corporation are included in basis computation.

4. Distributions must be made on a per-share basis. If disproportionate distributions or special allocations are made, there is a risk of creating a second class of stock which would cause loss of S corporation status.

¶ 20,341   DISTRIBUTIONS WITHOUT ACCUMULATED EARNINGS AND PROFITS

There is a two-tier system in effect for S corporations without accumulated earnings and profits. First, the distribution is tax free to the extent of adjusted basis of each shareholder's stock. Second, gain from a sale or exchange is reported to the extent the distribution exceeds adjusted basis of each shareholder's stock.

The exact nature of a corporate distribution may not be known until the end of the S corporation's tax year. Distributions made by an S corporation during a tax year are taken into account before applying the loss limitation for one year. Thus, distributions during a year reduce the adjusted basis for purposes of determining the allowable loss for the year, but the loss for the year does not reduce the adjusted basis for purposes of determining the tax status of the distributions made during that year. The computation of basis is determined as follows:

	Beginning of Year Basis
+	Gains
	Recomputed Basis
−	Distributions
	Recomputed Basis
−	Losses
	Ending Basis

Example 20.19. Max Tassler is the sole shareholder whose adjusted basis at the beginning of the year is $1,000. S corporation

distributes $700 to Max. S corporation has a capital gain for the year of $200 and an operating loss for the year of $900.

$1,000	Basis, Beginning of Year
+ 200	Add Gain
$1,200	Recomputed Basis
− 700	Distribution
$ 500	Recomputed Basis
− 500	Loss Deductions, Limited
$ 0	Ending Basis
$ 400	Loss Carried Forward

Before 1997, the beginning basis was adjusted for both the gains and losses for the year before determining the status of the distribution. The Small Business Job Protection Act of 1996 allows broader tax-free treatment of a distribution in loss years. Under prior law, the shareholder would have reported a $400 gain on the distribution.

¶ 20,343 DISTRIBUTIONS WITH ACCUMULATED EARNINGS AND PROFITS

S corporations with accumulated earnings and profits (AE&P) have a four-tier system for determining status of distributions: (1) tax free to the extent of the accumulated adjustment account (AAA), (2) dividend income to the extent of any AE&P, (3) tax free to the extent of OAA, and (4) gain to the extent the distribution exceeds basis. In addition, the placement of distributions in computing basis is determined by the relationship of gains and losses for the year.

For S corporations having accumulated earnings and profits, net negative adjustments (i.e., the excess of losses and deductions over income) for that year are disregarded in determining the amount in the accumulated adjustments account for purposes of determining the tax treatment of distributions made during the year.

Example 20.20. Ernie Blake's stock basis as the sole shareholder in an S corporation is $1,000. The S corporation has $500 of AE&P and $200 of AAA. The corporation has an ordinary loss of $900 and a capital gain of $300. The corporation distributes $600.

$ 200	Beginning AAA	$ 500	Beginning AE&P
− 200	Distribution	− 400	Distribution
$ 0	AAA	$ 100	Ending AE&P
+ 300	Gain		
$ 300	AAA		
− 900	Loss		
$ (600)	Ending AAA		

$1,000	Beginning Stock Basis
− 200	AAA Distribution
− 600	Ending AAA
$ 200	Ending Basis

Ernie's basis can also be computed by taking the $1,000 beginning basis plus the $300 capital gain, resulting in a $1,300 adjusted basis, minus the $200 distribution from AAA, reducing the adjusted basis to $1,100, minus the $900 ordinary loss, reducing the adjusted basis to $200.

An S corporation can elect to treat distributions as coming first from AE&P and then from the AAA. If such an election is made, the corporation is not required to distribute its entire AAA at the end of the year before it pays a dividend. All the affected shareholders must consent to the election. Code Sec. 1368(e)(3).

TAX PLANNING POINTER

Corporations with potential excessive passive investment income can take advantage of the rule to avoid the special tax under Code Sec. 1375 by disposing of AE&P prior to the end of the year with a dividend distribution.

A potential trap is created for S corporations investing in tax-exempt bonds. Since the tax-exempt income does not increase the AAA, an attempt to withdraw this income could result in a taxable distribution from AE&P if there is no AAA from other sources. This could result even if the withdrawal is only in the amount of tax-exempt interest from the current year.

Distributions are free only to the extent of stock basis. For example, if a shareholder has a stock basis of $15,000 and a debt basis of $10,000 and receives a $20,000 distribution, the shareholder would have to report a $5,000 gain. The distribution cannot offset the debt basis.

¶ 20,351   BASIS ADJUSTMENT

Both taxable and nontaxable income and deductible and nondeductible expenses serve, respectively, to increase and decrease a shareholder's basis in the stock of the S corporation. These rules generally are analogous to those provided for partnerships under Code Sec. 705. A shareholder's stock basis in an S corporation is increased for the following: (1) separately stated items of income, (2) nonseparately computed income, and (3) the excess of the deduction for depletion over the basis of property subject to depletion. Stock basis is decreased by: (1) nontaxable distributions of capital, (2) separately stated items of loss and deduction, (3) nonseparately computed loss, (4) nondeductible expenses of the corporation that are not chargeable to capital, and (5) the amount of the shareholder's deduction for depletion with respect to oil and gas wells. If there are net deductions, the basis of stock is decreased before the basis of debt. Stock basis cannot be reduced below zero. Any excess net deductions are applied to reduce the shareholder's basis in any indebtedness of the S corporation to the shareholders, thus reducing the amount of the shareholder's basis in the debt, which will in turn reduce the amount of the shareholder's short-term capital loss deduction for the worthless debt. The basis in this indebtedness cannot be reduced below zero. Any nontaxable distributions to capital do not reduce the basis of indebtedness.

Net income items generally increase stock basis. However, if the basis of a shareholder's debt has previously been reduced because of net deductions, the debt basis is restored before there is any increase in the shareholder's stock basis.

Example 20.21. A sole shareholder has a $7,000 stock basis and a $2,000 basis in a loan that he made to the S corporation. Ordinary income for the year was $8,200. The corporation incurred a capital loss of $2,300 and received $2,000 of tax-exempt interest. Cash distributions for the year were $15,000.

$ 7,000	Beginning stock basis	$2,000	Beginning loan basis
+ 8,200	Ordinary income		
+ 2,000	Tax-exempt interest		
$ 17,200	Recomputed basis		
− 15,000	Distribution		
$ 2,200	Recomputed basis		
− 2,200	Loss	− 100	Loss
$ 0	Year-end basis in stock	$1,900	Year-end basis in debt

If in the following year there was $5,000 of ordinary income, the loan basis would be increased by $100 first.

If the corporation's stock becomes worthless in any tax year of the corporation or shareholder, the corporate items for that year are taken into account by the shareholders and the adjustments to the stock's basis are made before the stock's worthlessness is taken into account under Code Sec. 165(g). Code Sec. 1367(a) and (b)(2) and (3).

No increase in basis may be made for any pass-through item of corporate gross income required to be included in a shareholder's gross income unless that increase is reported on the shareholder's income tax return. An exception allows the shareholder to increase basis for tax-exempt items of income. Thus, a shareholder may not report less than his or her share of the S corporation's income and then, after the assessment period has expired, increase the basis of the stock to reflect an amount that should have been, but was not, included in income. The shareholder must increase or decrease basis for later adjustments of his or her share of a pass-through item of income, deduction, or loss.

Termination of Election

¶ 20,401 METHODS

There are three ways that an S corporation's status can be terminated:

1. Revocation of the election by the corporation
2. Failure to satisfy the continuing requirements of a small business corporation
3. Receipt of excessive passive investment income under certain circumstances

¶ 20,405   REVOCATION OF ELECTION

An S corporation election may be revoked by the corporation for any tax year of the corporation. A revocation can be made only with the consent of shareholders holding more than one-half of the number of outstanding shares of stock (including non-voting stock) of the corporation. A revocation filed up to and including the fifteenth day of the third month of the tax year is effective for the entire tax year, unless a prospective effective date is specified. The period during which a retroactive revocation can be filed thus corresponds to the time period in which a retroactive election may be made. Revocations made after the fifteenth day of the third month of the tax year are effective on the first day of the following tax year unless the revocation states some other prospective date, in which case it is effective as of the specified date. Code Sec. 1362(d)(1). Retroactive revocations are not allowed if made after the first two and one-half months of the tax year.

> *Example 20.22.* A calendar-year S corporation has three shareholders—Alvin Bren, who owns 55 shares; Broward McCoy, who owns 30 shares; and Clay Thor, who owns 15 shares. Alvin, acting alone, can cause the corporation to revoke its election. Neither of the other two shareholders would need to act with Alvin to revoke the election. A revocation stating no date, made on or before March 15, 1998, is effective as of January 1, 1998. A revocation made after March 15, 1998, and stating no date is effective January 1, 1999. If the revocation is made on June 7, 1998, and specifies a revocation date of June 30, 1998, the S corporation election ceases on June 30, 1998.

Revocations that designate a prospective effective date result in the splitting of the year into short S corporation and C corporation tax years, with the tax consequences discussed below in connection with the tax treatment of terminations.

A person becoming a shareholder of an S corporation after the initial election does not have the power to terminate the election by affirmatively refusing to consent to the election (unless that person owns more than one-half of the stock). The shareholder is bound by the initial election.

¶ 20,413   CEASING TO BE A SMALL BUSINESS CORPORATION

Generally, a specific event during the tax year that causes a corporation to fail to meet the definition of a small business corporation results in a termination of the election as of the date on which the event occurred. Code Sec. 1362(d)(2). The events causing disqualification include: (1) exceeding the maximum allowable number of shareholders; (2) transfer of stock to a corporation, partnership, ineligible trust, or nonresident alien; (3) creation of a class of stock other than the voting and non-voting common stock allowed; and (4) acquisition of a subsidiary (other than certain nonoperating subsidiaries).

Shareholders of S corporations should enter into agreements restricting the transferability of their shares, so as to prevent an inadvertent termination of the S election against the wishes of the majority of the shareholders.

¶ 20,421 EXCESSIVE PASSIVE INVESTMENT INCOME

For S corporations with accumulated earnings and profits from years in which the corporation was a C corporation, excessive passive investment income can also cause a termination of the election. If an S corporation with these earnings and profits has passive investment income that exceeds 25 percent of gross receipts for three consecutive tax years, the election is terminated beginning with the tax year following the third consecutive tax year of excess passive income. Code Sec. 1362(d)(3).

> *Example 20.23.* Billings Corporation, a calendar-year S corporation, has passive income in excess of 25 percent of its gross receipts for 1996, 1997, and 1998. Billings has accumulated earnings and profits from years prior to an S election. The S election is terminated as of January 1, 1999.

The terms "Subchapter C earnings and profits," "excessive net passive income," "net passive income," "passive investment income," and "gross receipts" have the same respective meanings used in discussing the tax on passive investment income.

C corporations switching to S corporation status may have major problems because of the difficulty in accurately computing accumulated earnings and profits. The statute establishes no minimum rule for accumulated earnings and profits. This fact, coupled with no statute of limitations in determining the existence of accumulated earnings and profits, could lead to a termination of S corporation status.

It is important to recognize that a corporation may have a disqualifying year for termination purposes even though it pays no tax on its excess passive investment income. No tax is imposed on the corporation where the losses from current operations exceed the passive income. If the passive income exceeds 25 percent of gross income for the year, that year counts in meeting the three-consecutive-year termination rule.

To avoid the termination, a corporation could distribute any accumulated earnings and profits prior to the end of the third consecutive S corporation year in which more than 25 percent of its gross receipts are in the form of passive investment income. Difficulty in determining the presence or the amount of accumulated earnings and profits, however, hinders this safety valve procedure.

¶ 20,429 TAX TREATMENT OF TERMINATIONS

The day before the day on which the terminating event occurs is treated as the last day of a short S corporation tax year, and the day on which the terminating event occurs is treated as the first day of a short C corporation tax year. There is no requirement that the books of a corporation be closed as of the termination date. Instead, the corporation allocates the income or loss for the entire year (i.e., both short years) on a prorated basis.

> *Example 20.24.* A nonresident alien purchases stock in a calendar-year S corporation on August 21, 1998. The S corporation tax year ends on August 20, 1998, and the C corporation tax year begins on August 21, 1998.

The corporation can elect, with the consent of all persons who were shareholders at any time during the S termination year and all persons who are shareholders on the first day of the C short year, to report the taxable income or loss on each return (S corporation and C corporation) on the basis of income or loss shown on the corporation's permanent records (including work papers). Under this method, items are attributed to the short S corporation and C corporation years according to the time they were incurred or realized, as reflected in such records. Code Sec. 1362(e)(1)-(3). An S corporation is *required* to use its accounting records to allocate income and deductions if there was a sale of 50 percent or more of the S corporation's stock during the termination year.

The short S corporation and C corporation tax years are treated as one year for purposes of carrying over previous C corporation losses. The income allocated to the C corporation tax year is subject to annualization for purposes of applying the corporate rate brackets. The return for the short S corporation year is due on the same date as the return for the short C corporation year. Code Sec. 1362(e)(5) and (6).

> *Example 20.25.* From Example 20.24, the C corporation has a short tax year consisting of 133 days and must annualize its taxable income. The tax returns for both the S corporation and the C corporation are due on March 15, 1999.

The choice between using the permanent records and the pro rata allocation can have a dramatic impact if there are shareholders who have terminated their interests during the year. The annualization requirement applicable to the C corporation short tax year can compound the impact of the allocation decision.

> *Example 20.26.* An S corporation reports its income on a calendar-year basis. On May 27, 1998, a corporation purchases stock in the S corporation, thereby terminating the S corporation's status. For the year ended December 31, 1998, the corporation's accounting records show income of $200,000, deductions of $140,000, and tax credits of $6,000. Through May 26, 1998, the corporation's records show that the corporation has earned $65,000 in income, has $47,000 in deductions, and is eligible for $2,500 in tax credits.

If the corporation does not make an election to use its own records in determining the amount of income attributable to each tax year, then it must report 146/365, or two-fifths, of its income, deductions, and tax credits for 1998 on the return for the S corporation short year, ending May 26, 1998. The C corporation would report income of $120,000 ($200,000 × 219/365), deductions of $84,000 ($140,000 × 219/365), and tax credits of $3,600 ($6,000 × 219/365). The C corporation's taxable income is $60,000 (($120,000 − $84,000) × 365/219 for annualizing). The tax for the C corporation on the annualized income is $10,000 ($50,000 × 15% + $10,000 × 25%). The tax·owed by the C corporation for the short year is $2,400 ($10,000 × 219/365 − $3,600 tax credits ($6,000 × 219/365)).

If the corporation makes a valid election to use its records in determining income for the two short tax years, the S corporation must report $65,000 in income, $47,000 of deductions, and $2,500 of tax credits for the S corporation short year ending May 26, 1998. The C corporation must report income of $135,000 ($200,000 − $65,000), deductions of $93,000 ($140,000 − $47,000), and tax credits of $2,500 ($5,000 − $2,500). The C corporation's annualized income is $70,000 (($135,000 − $93,000) × 365/219). The tax for the C corporation on the annualized income is $12,500 ($50,000 × 15% + $20,000 × 25%). The tax owed by the C corporation for the short year is $5,000 ($12,500 × 219/365 − $2,500 tax credits).

The tax returns for both the S corporation short year ending on May 26, 1998, and the C corporation short year ending on December 31, 1998, are due on or before March 15, 1999.

Where the election is terminated because of the excessive passive investment income rule, there is no split between an S corporation short year and a C corporation short year since the termination is not effective until the beginning of the next tax year after the disqualification.

These termination rules deny a corporation the option of waiting until near the end of its tax year, when the corporation's profits or losses may be easier to estimate, to determine whether the corporation and its shareholders are better off taxed as a C corporation or as an S corporation for the entire tax year.

Section 338 provides that a purchasing corporation may elect to treat the acquisition of stock of a target corporation as a purchase of the target corporation's assets. This essentially means that, if a corporation makes a qualified purchase of the stock of an S corporation and makes an election under Code Sec. 338, all of the recapture income resulting from the election will be reported on the purchasing corporation's subchapter C return. As a result, the selling shareholders will not take this recapture income into account on their individual returns, saving shareholders who sell 80 percent or more of an S corporation's stock to another corporation from paying tax resulting from the recapture of depreciation or other tax benefits taken by the corporation when they were owners. This would occur if the buyer elected under Code Sec. 338 to step up the acquired assets' book value to the price paid for the stock of the corporation. This result is consistent with that which would ensue if a C corporation acquired the stock of another C corporation. In that case, any recapture income of the target C corporation is not included in any consolidated return of the acquiring corporation. Instead, recapture items of the target corporation normally are associated with the final return of the target corporation as selling corporation for the period ending on the date of acquisition.

The rule that allows pro rata allocations of income and losses to S and C short tax years caused by termination of an S corporation election does not apply to an S termination year if there is a sale or exchange of 50 percent or more of the corporation's stock during the termination year.

¶ 20,437   INADVERTENT TERMINATIONS

If the Internal Revenue Service determines that an S corporation's election is inadvertently terminated, the Service can waive the effect of the terminating event for any period, provided the corporation timely corrects the event and the corporation and the shareholders agree to be treated as if the election had been in effect for such period. Code Sec. 1362(f).

For example, a corporation determined in good faith that it had no earnings and profits. It is later determined on audit that its election terminated by reason of violating the passive income test for three consecutive years because the corporation in fact did have accumulated earnings and profits. If the shareholders were to agree to treat the earnings as distributed and include the dividends in income, it may be appropriate to waive the terminating events, so that the election is treated as never terminated. Likewise, it may be appropriate to waive the terminating event when the one class of stock requirement was inadvertently breached, but no tax avoidance resulted.

Instead of treating the corporation as having never terminated its election throughout the period of the inadvertent termination, the IRS may treat the corporation as having terminated its election only for the period when it was ineligible to be an S corporation, even though it did not re-elect S corporation status.

TAX BLUNDER

Allen, an owner of an S corporation, gave some of his shares to a trust that he set up to benefit his children. Since most trusts are not permitted to be qualified owners of an S corporation, the S status is terminated. However, if the transfer to the trust is inadvertent and the mistake is corrected as soon as it is discovered, the IRS may allow the company to retain its S status. Private Letter Ruling 8701006, September 30, 1986.

¶ 20,445 RE-ELECTION AFTER TERMINATION

If an election is terminated, a new election cannot be made for five tax years without the consent of the Internal Revenue Service. Code Sec. 1362(g).

¶ 20,453 POST-TERMINATION DISTRIBUTIONS

What happens to the income that was previously taxed to shareholders when the S corporation loses its status? The corporation has the opportunity for a limited period of time to unfreeze that previously taxed income. Specifically, any cash distributions by the corporation with respect to its stock during the post-termination transition period are applied against and reduce stock basis to the extent of the accumulated adjustments account. Code Sec. 1371(e). If the AAA is not exhausted by the end of the post-termination transition period, it disappears. Any distributions thereafter are taxed under the usual C corporation rules. The grace period applies only to cash distributions. Non-cash distributions are taxed under the usual C corporation rules. The definition of "post-termination transition period" is the same as that given at ¶ 20,281.

> *Example 20.27.* Bleyer Corporation decides to terminate its S status at the end of 1998. At that time, the corporation has $15,000 of AAA. The corporation may make up to $15,000 in cash distributions before the end of 1999 and have the distributions apply against AAA. These distributions are nontaxable to the shareholders and reduce investment basis. If less than $15,000 is distributed during 1999, the remaining AAA balance becomes part of accumulated earnings and profits and results in taxable dividends upon distributions to the shareholders.

Operational Rules

¶ 20,501 CASH METHOD OF ACCOUNTING

A significant advantage of an S corporation over a C corporation is that the S corporation is eligible to use the cash method of accounting. C corporations with gross receipts of more than $5 million are prohibited from using the cash method of accounting.

¶ 20,505 TAX ADMINISTRATION PROVISIONS

The tax treatment of items of S corporation income, loss, deductions, and credits generally is determined at the corporate level in a unified proceeding rather than in separate proceedings with shareholders. Shareholders are given notice of any administrative or judicial proceeding at which the tax treatment such items will be determined. Further, each shareholder is given the opportunity to participate in these proceedings. Shareholders are required to file returns consistent with the corporate return or to notify the Internal Revenue Service of any inconsistency. Code Secs. 6241 and 6242.

The audit provisions are generally similar to the audit provisions made applicable to partnerships by the Tax Equity and Fiscal Responsibility Act of 1982. Thus, for example, rules relating to restrictions on assessing deficiencies, period of limitations, and judicial review follow the corresponding partnership rules. However, those rules may be modified by Treasury regulations where appropriate to take account of the differences (whether or not tax related) between a corporation and a partnership. For example, the selection of a person to act on behalf of the corporation in tax matters in the way a partner acts on behalf of a partnership must take into account that a corporation has no person to correspond to a general partner (since the corporate shareholders are not liable for the corporation's debts, as is a general partner). As with partnerships, the Regulations may treat certain corporate items as other than corporate items, for purposes of these audit rules, where special enforcement problems arise.

¶ 20,575   TAX PLANNING

The S corporation may be an advantageous tool where an enterprise is expected to incur losses during the earliest stages of its activities. The losses can be passed through to the shareholders to the extent of their bases. Where the corporation begins accumulating taxable profits, the conversion to a regular corporation could prove to be of further advantage if the income is taxed to the corporation at a lower rate than it would be taxed to the individual owners.

An S corporation sometimes can be used effectively to shift income from high to low tax bracket taxpayers. This must occur by transfers at the shareholder level. For example, family member shareholders in a high tax bracket can effectively shift the income from the high tax bracket to relatively lower tax bracket taxpayers by transferring stock to their children.

A stock transfer made to effect a shift of income must be a bona fide transfer by gift, sale, or other disposition. The court will ignore the transfer and tax all the income to the donor if the donor retains control over the stock and uses the distributions paid on the stock as if they belong to the donor.

While a primary method of shifting S corporation income to lower tax bracket taxpayers involves a shifting of equity, it may be possible to shift income of the S corporation by capitalizing with both debt and equity. The objective would be to shift income, through deductible interest payments, to lower tax bracket taxpayers, with higher tax bracket taxpayers retaining potential appreciation. However, the S corporation runs the risk of reclassification of the debt as equity, with possible termination of Subchapter S status.

The S corporation may be a replacement for the limited partnership in those circumstances where the economic results will be essentially the same when conducting the business or investment through either form of ownership. S corporation form of ownership would provide full limited liability that is not available to the general partner in a partnership. Greater control can be achieved through the use of non-voting stock than may be possible with the limited partnership. Centralization of management, continuity of life, and free transferability of interests issues would no longer create potential association problems, resulting possibly in the partnership being taxed as a regular corporation.

SUMMARY OF CHAPTER 20

✓ Certain requirements must be met for a corporation to qualify as an S corporation. These requirements must also be met in order to continue as an S corporation.

✓ In order for contributions to an S corporation to qualify as tax-free exchanges for stock, the same requirements of Section 351 must be met that apply to C corporations.

✓ Generally, the S corporation tax year is limited to a calendar year except when permission is received to adopt a fiscal year based on business purpose.

✓ The S corporation is not subject to the corporate income tax. However, S corporations with accumulated earnings and profits may be subject to certain other taxes based on income.

✓ The shareholders of S corporations are treated as partners and the corporation as a partnership for purposes of taxing the income, deducting the losses, and allocating other tax items attributable to the corporation.

✓ All items are allocated to the shareholders on a per-share, per-day basis. A partnership, however, may allocate those items by agreement among the partners, provided the special allocations have substantial economic effect.

✓ An important tax advantage that an S corporation has over a regular corporation is that only one tax is imposed on its earnings, and that tax is imposed at the shareholder level. Regular corporations are subject to a double tax—once at the corporate level, and again at the shareholder level when the after-tax corporate earnings are distributed to the shareholders.

✓ Generally, dispositions from S corporations are tax-free returns of basis. Distributions in excess of the accumulated adjustments account and basis may be taxable as dividend income or capital gain.

CHAPTER 20 QUESTIONS

1. What is the official name given to corporations qualifying under Subchapter S of the Internal Revenue Code?

2. What are the eligibility requirements that a corporation must meet in order to qualify under Subchapter S?

3. What is a domestic corporation?

4. Is a corporation incorporated in Great Britain eligible for S corporation status?

5. An S corporation is formed by 75 shareholders, including a husband and wife holding stock jointly. They divorce, with each taking title to one-half of the jointly held stock. Will the corporation still qualify as an S corporation?

6. What shareholders will prevent a corporation from qualifying as an S corporation?

7. What requirements must be met in regard to the stock in an S corporation? What differences are allowed?

8. What is the definition of "straight debt" under Subchapter S, and what is its importance to an S corporation?

9. Which corporations are specifically excluded from S corporation status?

10. Can a corporation make a retroactive election under Subchapter S?

11. Under what circumstances can a new shareholder terminate an S corporation election?

12. May a corporation receive an extension of the 2½-month period for a retroactive S corporation election?

13. What limits are placed on the selection of a tax year of an S corporation? How do these limits differ from those applicable to C corporations and partnerships?

14. George has a service business and wishes to create an S corporation with a June 30 fiscal year. What problems might George encounter in his fiscal-year selection?

15. Is an S corporation with a financial statement fiscal year ending on July 31 allowed the same fiscal year for tax purposes?

16. How do partnership tax years differ from those available to S corporations?

17. When does a business purpose exist for selecting a non-calendar tax year for an S corporation?

18. Under what circumstances may an S corporation switch to a tax year ending on December 31?

19. When may an S corporation be subject to the built-in gains tax?

20. When the built-in gains tax is imposed on an S corporation, how is the tax passed through to the shareholders?

21. What taxes may be imposed on an S corporation?

22. What conditions must be met for an S corporation to be subject to a tax on passive investment income?

23. What is the only credit available as a reduction in the tax on built-in gain and the tax on excess net passive income for an S corporation?

24. Distinguish between "net passive income" and "passive investment income" in the computation of the tax on excess net passive income of an S corporation.

25. An S corporation may be subject to both the tax on built-in gains and the tax on excess passive income. Which tax is imposed first, and what effect does the imposition have on the other tax?

26. Durrabusiness is organized as a regular C corporation in 1983. At the beginning of the present year, Durrabusiness elects to be an S corporation. Will the election cause a recapture of the general business investment credit taken on any property purchased while a C corporation?

27. If an S corporation makes an early disposition of general business credit property, who is responsible for the recapture?

28. Is an S corporation allowed the dividends-received deduction available to regular corporations?

29. In computing taxable income of an S corporation, which elections are made at the corporate level and which are made at the shareholder level?

30. Describe the treatment of a dividend distribution of appreciated property by an S corporation.

31. An S corporation is solely owned by a shareholder. During the year, the corporation receives $4,000 in tax-exempt interest. What effect does this tax-exempt interest have on the taxable income of the S corporation and the basis of the stock of the sole shareholder?

32. Differentiate the treatment of fringe benefits of a corporation, partnership, and S corporation.

33. What is the special treatment of S corporation expenses owed to shareholders? How does this treatment differ from that of a C corporation?

34. A C corporation has an unused net operating loss carryover at the end of 1998. The corporation elects S corporation status at the beginning of 1999. What happens to the unused net operating loss carryover?

35. In an S corporation, how are items of income, deductions, and credits divided among the shareholders?

36. An S corporation has both voting and non-voting stock. What effect does this differentiation in voting rights have on S corpo-

ration eligibility and on shareholder pro rata share of corporate tax items?

37. Where a shareholder terminates his or her interest during the tax year, a pro rata allocation of shareholder items can be made according to the corporation's permanent records. How may this allocation differ from the per-share, per-day allocation?

38. How may debt of the corporation affect a shareholder's basis in an S corporation?

39. From what sources can an S corporation receive accumulated earnings and profits?

40. Under what circumstances might an S corporation choose to distribute accumulated earnings and profits before distributing from the accumulated adjustments account?

41. How may an S corporation revoke its election?

42. What is the latest date in the calendar year in which an S corporation can file for a revocation of S election status and still have it effective as of the beginning of the year?

43. How can passive investment income cause an S corporation to lose its status?

44. When an S corporation has its status terminated during the year, what is the effect on the S corporation tax year and the tax year of the resulting C corporation?

45. Describe the short tax year computation necessary when an S corporation's status is terminated because of excessive passive investment income.

46. What is an "inadvertent termination" of an S corporation?

47. A corporation terminates its status as an S corporation. Describe the requirements for re-electing S corporation status.

48. What kinds of distributions are available to reduce the accumulated adjustments account after a termination of an S corporation election?

49. What is "previously taxed income" of an S corporation?

50. Why is the S corporation preferred over regular corporation status in the early years of operation?

CHAPTER 20 PROBLEMS

51. Damion Corporation begins its first tax year on June 23, 1998. What is the latest date that Damion may apply for S corporation status to qualify as of the beginning of operations?

52. Alpha Corporation began business at the beginning of the year. On February 15, George sold his stock to Danny. Alpha files for S corporation status on March 10, but George refuses to consent to the election. Will S corporation status be granted?

53. Several individuals form Lang Corporation on May 1, 1998. The corporation begins acquiring assets on June 1, 1998, and begins business on August 1, 1998. What is the latest date that Lang can file Form 2553 requesting S corporation status?

54. Gamma Corporation, an S corporation, has a fiscal year ending March 31. It is required to switch to a calendar-year tax year. How many months of income would a calendar-year taxpayer be required to report in the year of change?

55. What is the built-in gains tax on an S corporation, assuming the exceptions do not apply and the corporation has taxable income of $100,000, including a built-in gain of $60,000?

56. Doom Corporation changed from a C corporation to an S corporation in 1995. For 1998, the corporation has built-in gain of $40,000 and taxable income of $63,000. Determine the built-in gains tax imposed on the corporation.

57. What is the passive investment income tax on an S corporation that has gross receipts of $200,000, passive investment income of $80,000, and expenses of $10,000 directly connected to the production of the passive income?

58. Ziad Corporation, an S corporation, distributes land held as an investment to its sole shareholder. The land was purchased for $17,000 and has a fair market value of $28,000 on the date of distribution. What are the tax implications of this distribution?

59. Donald owns 39 percent of the shares of an S corporation. The corporation pays $450 for a group-term life insurance policy. How is this payment reported by the S corporation and Donald?

60. Delta Corporation, an S corporation, has $30,000 of taxable income before charitable contributions. The corporation has $5,000 in charitable contributions for the year. What is Delta's charitable contribution deduction?

61. An S corporation is on the accrual basis and the sole shareholder is on the cash basis. For the pay period ending December 27, 1998, the shareholder earns a salary of $400. He is paid on January 3, 1999. What is the amount allowable as a deduction for 1998?

62. S corporation has $90,000 of taxable income for the year and three equal shareholders. One of the shareholders dies on March 14. His estate continues to hold the stock for the remainder of the year. Determine the amounts includible on the last return of the decedent-shareholder and on the estate's income tax return.

63. A shareholder purchases 30 percent of the stock of an S corporation two-thirds of the way through the year for $20,000. The S corporation incurs an operating loss of $300,000 for the year. What is the amount that the shareholder may deduct on his personal income tax return, assuming the at-risk and passive activity rules do not apply?

64. Germaine, the sole shareholder in Nomad Corporation, has a basis in his stock of $18,000 at the beginning of the year. The corporation has taxable income of $9,000 for the year. In addition, the corporation has a short-term capital loss of $1,200 and tax-exempt income of $800. What is Germaine's basis in his stock at the end of the year?

65. Malcolm is the sole shareholder in an S corporation. At the beginning of the year, his basis in this stock is $7,000. For the year, the corporation incurs a $4,500 loss. By the end of the year, the corporation's stock is worthless. What is the amount of loss from the worthless stock that Malcolm is allowed to take on his return?

66. Alpha Corporation, a calendar-year S corporation, has no accumulated earnings and profits at the end of the year. An individual shareholder receives a cash distribution of $10,000 during the year. How will this distribution be recognized, assuming the shareholder has an $8,200 basis in his stock?

67. Delta Corporation, a calendar-year S corporation, has an accumulated adjustments account of $8,000. It also has accumulated earnings and profits from pre-1983 years of $12,000. The sole shareholder receives a $27,000 cash distribution from the corporation. How will this distribution be treated if the shareholder's basis in the stock is $12,200?

68. An S corporation has an accumulated adjustments account balance of $50,000 at the beginning of the year and accumulated earnings and profits of $20,000. The corporation earns $40,000 for the year. The corporation makes a distribution of $120,000. What would the sole shareholder's stock basis have to be at the beginning of the year to avoid any capital gain reporting?

69. An S corporation's only transaction for the year was the receipt of $10,000 in tax-exempt interest. How would a $6,000 distribution be taxed to the sole shareholder if the S corporation has an accumulated adjustments account of a negative $6,500 at the beginning of the year?

70. Some stock in a calendar-year S corporation is sold to a nonresident alien on February 13, 1998. On what date is the corporation's status as an S corporation terminated?

71. Beta Corporation terminates its S election at the end of 1998. At that time, the corporation has an accumulated adjustments account of $2,500. How would a distribution made during 1999 qualify as nontaxable?

72. How is a taxpayer able to remove previously taxed income from an S corporation that has terminated its status without incurring any additional tax?

73. Which of the following will not prevent a corporation from qualifying for the special tax rules under Subchapter S?

    a. The corporation has more than 75 shareholders.

    b. A nonresident alien owns shares in the corporation.

    c. The corporation has both common and preferred stock.

    d. An individual retirement account owns shares in the corporation.

    e. All the shareholders are individuals or decedent estates.

74. A shareholder purchased 20 percent of the stock of an S corporation three-quarters of the way through the year for $10,000. The S corporation incurred a net operating loss of $320,000. What is the amount the shareholder may deduct on his personal income tax return, assuming the at-risk and passive activity rules do not apply?

    a. A loss of $64,000

    b. A loss of $16,000

    c. A loss of $10,000

    d. A loss of $2,000

    e. None of the above

75. An S corporation has an accumulated adjustments account of $30,000 at the beginning of the year and accumulated earnings and profits of $10,000. The corporation earns $20,000 for the year. Melvin, a 30 percent owner who paid $8,000 for his stock, receives $17,000 from the corporation. What is the amount of dividend income he must report?

    a. $10,000

    b. $2,000

    c. $3,000

    d. $0

    e. None of the above

76. John owns stock in an S corporation. John's share of the corporation's loss for the year is $5,000. His adjusted basis in the corporation stock is $1,000. In addition, John has a loan outstanding to the corporation in the amount of $2,000. What amount, if any, is John entitled to deduct with respect to the loss, assuming he meets the at-risk and passive activity requirements?

    a. $5,000

    b. $3,000

    c. $2,000

    d. $1,000

    e. None of the above

77. *Comprehensive Problem.* An S corporation has the following information:

Sales	$100,000
Dividend income	1,500
Tax-exempt interest	2,500
Long-term capital gain	4,000
Short-term capital gain	1,800
Cost of goods sold	50,000
Advertising expense	3,000
Charitable contributions	1,000
Interest expense	2,000
Salary expense	25,000
Other operating expenses	8,000

Compute the S corporation's taxable income for the year.

78. *Comprehensive Problem.* Aubrey Corporation changes from a regular C corporation in 1997 to an S corporation as of the beginning of 1998. For 1998, the corporation has $40,000 of built-in gain and $45,000 in accounting income. Determine any corporate tax that may be imposed on Aubrey Corporation, and the amount to be reported by the sole shareholder.

79. *Research Problem.* A C corporation acquired a machine for $100,000 and placed it in service on August 15, 1993. The corporation elected S corporation status at the beginning of 1997. On February 13, 1998, the property was sold for $40,000, payable in four yearly installments of $10,000 plus interest. What is the amount of ordinary income to be reported from the sale?

80. *Research Problem.* An S corporation's election terminated because a shareholder transferred stock to a trust not qualifying as an eligible shareholder. Is it possible for the corporation to retain its S corporation status through the "inadvertent termination" procedures? See Letter Ruling 8523097, March 15, 1985.

Chapter 21

Federal Estate Tax, Federal Gift Tax, and Generation-Skipping Transfer Tax

Learning Objectives

After completing Chapter 21, you should be able to:

1. Recognize legal terms used in connection with wills, trusts, and estates, as well as partial interests in property, such as life estates, remainders, and reversions.

2. Understand the elements in the estate tax formula—gross estate, allowable deductions, adjusted taxable gifts, and available tax credits.

3. Determine the tax aspects of transferred property, in particular inclusion of the property in the gross estate due to the grantor's retention of an interest, such as a life estate, a reversion, or a power to revoke.

4. Discuss the special tax aspects of jointly held property, life insurance, annuities, and gifts within three years of death.

5. Understand the valuation of assets at both the date of death and the alternate valuation date.

6. Calculate the taxation of involuntary deductions, such as funeral and administration expenses and debts, and deductions under testator's control, notably the marital and charitable deductions.

7. Determine the interplay between the gift and estate tax, the two being two sides of the same coin.

8. Describe the nature of the gift tax, the gift tax formula, and transactions subject to the gift tax.

9. Identify present-interest gifts, the marital and charitable deductions, and the applicable credit amount.

10. Explain the generation-skipping transfer tax, how and when it applies, and its relationship to gift and estate taxes.

OVERVIEW OF CHAPTER

In this chapter, estate, gift, and generation-skipping transfer taxes are surveyed. All three taxes may be viewed as aspects of one comprehensive excise tax on gratuitous transfers of property by individuals to anyone, be it during life or at death. In fact, all three taxes are computed using the same multipurpose tax table.

The estate tax is a wealth transfer tax, a tax on the transfer of property at death, not on the property itself. The estate tax base equals the gross estate, consisting of all property in which the decedent had an interest, less debts and expenses and marital and charitable bequests plus taxable lifetime gifts made after 1976. For 1998, up to $625,000 is tax free; the rest is subject to tax at rates up to 55 percent. A tax credit is allowed for gift taxes paid and for state and foreign estate taxes. The gift tax discussed in this chapter is but one part of the same overall unified wealth transfer tax system.

Special, unique rules determine the inclusion in the gross estate of life insurance, annuities, jointly held properties, and property subject to powers of appointment. These concepts are largely unrelated to the income tax treatment and require special study. Valuation problems and income tax basis aspects of estates are also discussed in this chapter.

The gross estate may include properties previously transferred in which the decedent retained an interest or power, such as a life income interest, a reversion, or a power to revoke or appoint, as well as properties passing by operation of law, such as jointly held property and life insurance payable to a named beneficiary. A comprehensive list of legal property terms is provided to increase the understanding of estate administration and the law of property.

Gross gifts generally include all gratuitous transfers. Taxable gifts are computed after exclusions and deductions, notably the marital and charitable deductions.

The applicable credit amount may defer any tax until death, but gift taxes are payable when the tax on cumulative lifetime gifts exceeds it. Cumulative taxable gifts are included in the estate tax base, with a credit for gift taxes paid. The applicable credit amount is available to the estate since its only effect during life is to defer the actual payment of gift taxes until death, within limits.

The generation-skipping transfer tax is levied on individuals with a power or an interest in a generation-skipping trust and is a toll charge on skipping a generation.

LEGAL TERMS COMMON TO ESTATES AND TRUSTS

Administrator. Similar to an executor. The manager of an estate of a person who dies intestate or where the named executor fails to act as executor.

Bequest. A disposition of personal property by will; a legacy.

Conservator. A guardian; a protector; a preserver. The term conservator is usually used to designate the guardian of an incompetent person.

Devise. A disposition of land or real estate by will.

Devisee. The person to whom land or other real property is devised or given by will.

Donor. One who makes a gift. One who creates a trust.

Estate Tax. A tax levied on the *transfer* of property from a decedent.

Executor. A person appointed by a will to carry out the testator's direction and to dispose of property according to the will. The one who manages an estate. (Female=executrix).

Grantor. The person making a grant. One who creates a trust.

Guardian. One who has the care and management of the person (guardian of the person) or of the estate (guardian of the estate) or both, or of an individual during minority or incompetency.

Guardian ad litem. A guardian (usually an attorney) appointed by the court to protect and defend a minor's or incompetent's interest in the estate.

Heir. One who would receive the decedent's estate under the laws of descent and distribution where the decedent did not leave a will.

Inheritance tax. A tax levied on the receipt of property from a decedent.

Insurance trust. An agreement between the insured and a trustee whereby the proceeds of the life insurance will be payable directly to the trustee, who will hold the proceeds for investment and distribution according to the trust agreement.

Insured. The person who is insured under the life insurance policy in question.

Inter vivos trust. A trust created during the lifetime of the person setting up the trust. A testamentary trust is one set up under the will of the decedent.

Intestate. One not having a will; a person who dies without a will is said to die intestate.

Intestate laws. Statutes ("laws of intestate succession") that provide descent of estates of persons who die intestate (without a will).

Joint tenancy. Where property is held in the names of two or more persons with the title passing from the first joint tenant to die to the other joint tenant (or joint tenants) upon death.

Legacy. A disposition of personal property by will.

Legatee. The recipient of personal property by will.

Per capita. This term is used frequently in the area of the descent and distribution of a decedent's property. In effect, it means that the property should be divided equally among a group designated by the trust instrument or the will. In other words, if the decedent left two surviving children and a third child who predeceased the decedent but left two children (grandchildren of the decedent) and if the per capita method is applied, each person would receive 25 percent.

Per stirpes. This term is used frequently in the area of the descent and distribution of a decedent's property. It denotes that method of dividing an estate where a class or group of distributees takes the share to which their deceased representative would have been entitled had the deceased lived. In other words, they take according to their right of representing such deceased ancestor, and not as so many individuals. For example: If a decedent passed away leaving two surviving and one child who predeceased the decedent but left two children (the decedent's grandchildren), the two grandchildren would take the share of their deceased representative, namely, their parent. Therefore, the two grandchildren would share their parent's 1/3 and each would receive 1/6 of the total estate. The two surviving children of the deceased would each receive 1/3.

Power of appointment. A power or authority conferred by a trust or will upon another person to select or nominate the person or persons who are to receive and enjoy the property of the estate or trust or the income therefrom at a specific time.

Probate. A local law process for admitting the decedent's will, if any, and distributing the decedent's property pursuant to it or according to the laws governing the intestate's assets.

Remainderman. One who is entitled to the remainder of an estate after a particular life estate, which has been carved out of the overall estate, has expired.

Residuary clause. That provision in a will that disposes of that which remains after satisfying all debts, administration expenses, legacies, and devises.

Residuary estate. That portion of the estate that remains after the payment of debts, expenses of administration, legacies and devises. It consists of that part of the estate that has not been legally disposed of by the will prior to carrying out the residuary clause of said will.

Settlor. One who creates a trust.

Share on renunciation. When a surviving spouse renounces the will of a spouse, the surviving spouse is usually entitled to a one-third interest in all personal and real property if the decedent left a descendant. If the decedent did not leave a descendant, the surviving spouse is usually entitled to one-half of real and personal property in the estate (net of debts).

Surviving spouse's award (widow's award). The special allowance (usually money) given to the surviving spouse to cover the cost of support during the administration of the estate, which is usually limited to nine months.

Tenancy by the entirety. Generally speaking, this is a joint tenancy between husband and wife. A tenancy by the entirety cannot be terminated except by the joint action of the husband and wife during their lives. In the case of a joint tenancy, however, it may be terminated by either tenant merely by conveying the interest to another party.

Tenancy in common. Title is held by two or more persons, each owning a fractional interest in the undivided property. Upon the death of one tenant in common, the interest does not pass to the surviving tenant in common but becomes part of the probate estate and is distributed according to the deceased tenant's will.

Testamentary trust. A trust that is set up under the will of the decedent. Conversely, an inter vivos trust is one set up during the lifetime of the person setting up the trust.

Testamentary trustee. One who is appointed trustee to carry out a trust created by a will.

Testate. One having a will; a person who dies with a will is said to die testate.

Testator. One who makes or has made a will; one who dies leaving a will. (Female=testatrix).

Totten trust. A trust created by the deposit of a person's own money in his or her own name as trustee for another person. This is considered a revocable trust at the will of the trustee until the depositor dies or otherwise completes the gift during lifetime.

Trust. A fiduciary relationship with respect to property whereby the property is held by one party (called trustee) for the benefit of another party (called beneficiary). A trust is usually set up and governed by a written document.

Trust estate. Usually refers to the corpus or property of the trust.

Trustee. That person who is responsible for administering a trust agreement according to its terms. This party holds legal title to all the property in the trust for the benefit of the beneficiaries.

Computation and Payment of Estate Tax

¶ 21,001　ESTATE TAX COMPUTATION—SUMMARY

Here is a capsule version of the federal estate tax return filed on Form 706 (United States Estate (and Generation-Skipping Transfer) Tax Return):

Step 1.　Compile the *gross estate,* consisting of all property in which the decedent had an interest.

Step 2.　Subtract debts, funeral, and administration expenses. (The result is the *adjusted gross estate.*)

Step 3.　Subtract property passing to the surviving spouse (*the marital deduction*) and charitable transfers.

Step 4.　The result is the *taxable estate.*

Step 5.　Add *adjusted taxable gifts* (gifts, less exclusions and deductions) made after 1976.

Step 6.　The result is the estate tax base.

Step 7.　Find the *tentative estate tax* from the tax table. Code Sec. 2001. (See Table in the Appendix.)

Step 8.　Subtract gift taxes payable on gifts includible in the estate tax base.

Step 9.　Subtract the *applicable credit amount.*

Step 10.　If a tax is still payable, subtract other possible credits, such as the state tax credit, the credit for prior transfers, and the foreign tax credit.

Step 11.　The tax payable, if any, is due with the estate tax return.

For a graphic description of the estate tax elements, see Table 1, following Example 21.1 at ¶ 21,009.

¶ 21,009　APPLICABLE CREDIT AMOUNT

An applicable credit amount is allowed against estate and gift taxes. Code Secs. 2010 and 2505. The applicable credit amount is a credit that is equal to the amount the government wishes to exclude from gift and estate taxation. This credit was first introduced as the "unified credit" in the Tax Reform Act of 1976. The credit eliminates the first portion of the gift and estate tax rate schedule. The amount eliminated has increased over the years since it was first introduced. The excluded amount is called the "applicable exclusion amount," and the unified credit was renamed the "applicable credit amount" by the Taxpayer Relief Act of 1997.

The applicable credit amount for estates of decedents dying after 1986 and prior to 1998 is $192,800. Any part of the credit used to offset gift taxes is still available to offset estate taxes. This is because adjusted taxable gifts are included in the estate tax base. Further, although the applicable credit amount applies for both estate and gift taxes, the computation of the credit for gift tax purposes is governed by special rules which are detailed at ¶ 21,415.

The applicable credit amount is subtracted from the taxpayer's estate and gift tax liability. However, the amount of the applicable credit amount available at death is not reduced, even if any portion of the credit is used to offset gift taxes on lifetime transfers. Further, the amount of the applicable credit amount is reduced by 20 percent of any portion of the $30,000 specific gift tax exemption allowable under pre-1977 law that was used with respect to gifts made after September 8, 1976, but before January 1, 1977. Thus, under this rule, the maximum reduction of the applicable credit amount is $6,000 (20 percent of $30,000).

For estates of decedents dying after 1981, the applicable credit amount has been phased in as follows:

	Unified Credit	Exemption Equivalent
1982	$ 62,800	$225,000
1983	79,300	275,000
1984	96,300	325,000
1985	121,800	400,000
1986	155,800	500,000
1987–1997	192,800	600,000

	Applicable Unified Credit Amount	Applicable Exclusion Amount	Business Exclusion Amount ($1.3 million exemption)
1998	$202,050	$625,000	$ 675,000
1999	211,300	650,000	650,000
2000–2001	220,550	675,000	625,000
2002–2003	229,800	700,000	600,000
2004	287,300	850,000	450,000
2005	326,300	950,000	350,000
2006 and thereafter	345,800	1,000,000	300,000

Example 21.1. In 1998, Kathy Kelly gives away $625,000 and dies broke several years later. Due to the applicable credit amount, no gift tax was due. The $625,000 gift, assuming no exclusions or deductions, is an adjusted taxable gift and becomes her estate tax base. As in the case of the gift, the transfer tax amounts to $202,050 but is offset by the applicable credit amount. Thus, the same applicable credit amount serves a dual function, both during life and in the estate.

Table 1   ESTATE TAX COMPUTATION

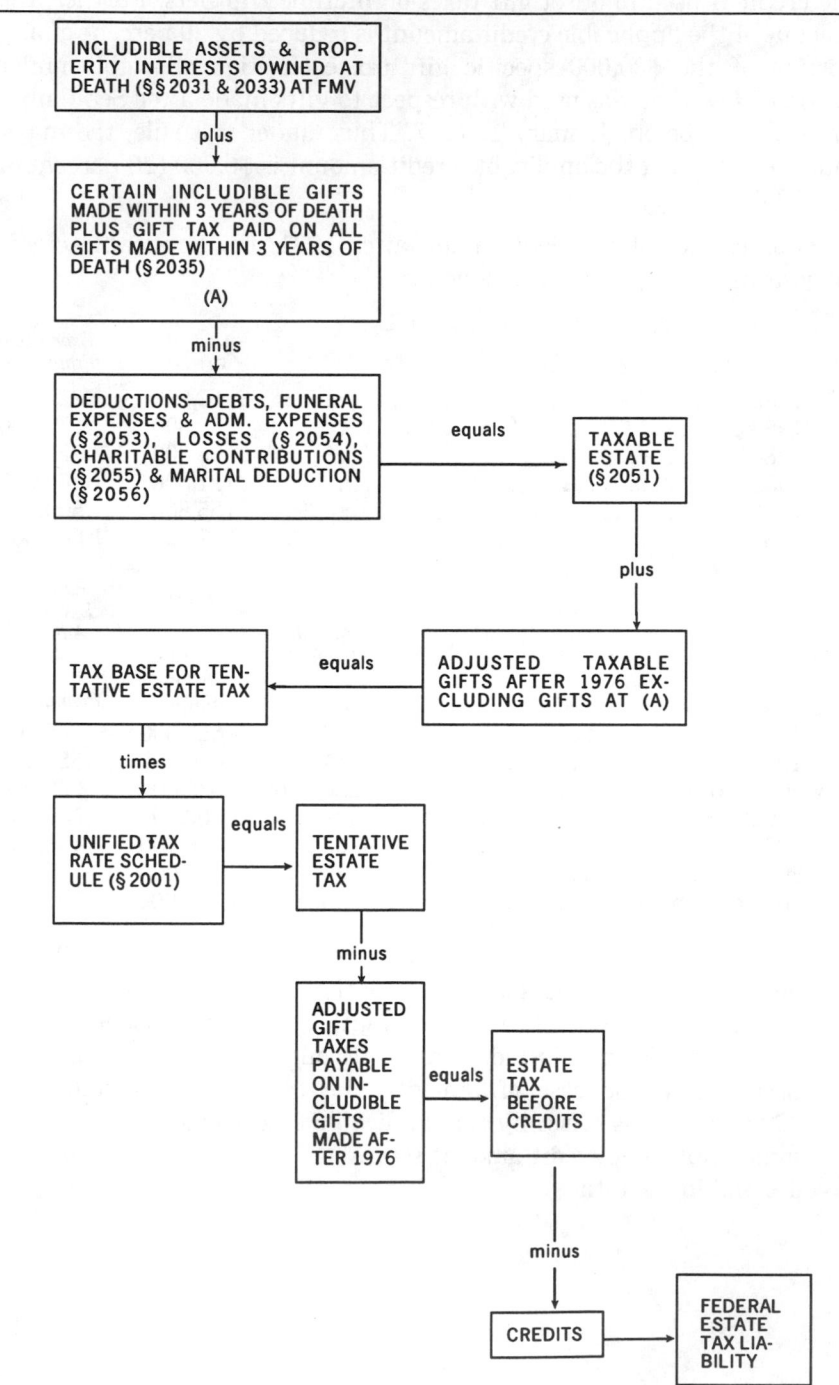

¶ 21,015   UNIFIED RATE SCHEDULE

A single unified transfer tax applies to estate and gift taxes effective for the estates of decedents dying and gifts made after 1976. The rates are progressive on the basis of cumulative lifetime and at-death transfers. When the tax base exceeds $10 million, a five percent surtax is payable on the excess, until both the applicable credit amount and tax rates below the maximum are phased out.

For the estates of decedents dying after 1988, gift and estate tax rates presently applicable to U.S. citizens are applicable to the estates of nonresident aliens. Where permitted by treaty, the estate of a nonresident alien is allowed the applicable credit amount available to a U.S. citizen multiplied by a proportion of the total gross estate situated in the United States. In other cases, an applicable credit amount of $13,000 is allowed.

¶ 21,025   PAYMENT OF TAX AND RETURNS

The estate tax return filing requirements are geared to the exemption so that a return is required if the gross estate exceeds the exemption equivalent of the applicable credit amount. Code Sec. 6018(a)(1) and (3). For 1998, the applicable credit amount is $202,050, which represents an exemption equivalent of $625,000. Thus, for estates of decedents dying currently, an executor must file a return if a gross estate exceeds $625,000, reduced by the decedent's adjusted taxable gifts made after 1976 and the reduction in the decedent's applicable credit amount because of taxable gifts made after September 8, 1976, and before January 1, 1977.

> **Example 21.2.** John Tripper died in 1998. If his gross estate exceeds $625,000, a return is due, even if no estate tax may be due. His estate tax return reveals the following:

Gross estate	$700,000
Deductions	75,000
Taxable estate	$625,000
Tentative tax	$202,050
Less: Applicable credit amount	202,050
Tax payable	$ 0

Thus, it may be worthwhile to note that for 1998 estates of decedents owning $625,000 or less are not subject to estate taxes and need not even file a return. As a result, the estate tax is applicable to a very small percentage of total estates, perhaps less than one percent. Because of the marital deduction, discussed at ¶ 21,217, the estate tax, even when applicable, is often deferred for the lifetime of the surviving spouse.

In those cases where applicable, the estate tax must be paid at the time the return is filed. Code Sec. 6161. The estate tax return, Form 706, is due nine months after death when required, together with the tax, if applicable. Code Sec. 6075(a). However, the executor of an estate can obtain an extension of time for the payment of the estate tax for a period not to exceed 12 months from the date fixed for payment of the estate tax. Code Sec. 6161(a). This extension will be granted whenever there is reasonable cause to do so. The executor (or administrator) is generally liable for the payment of the estate tax. Code Sec. 2002. If there is no executor or administrator, persons in actual or constructive possession of any of the property in the decedent's estate are required to pay the tax.

If more than 35 percent of a decedent's adjusted gross estate consists of an interest in a farm or other closely held business (sole proprietorship, a partnership interest, or stock in a closely held corporation), an executor may elect, on a timely filed estate tax return, to defer all payment of tax for five years (paying interest only) and thereafter pay the tax in equal installments over the next 10 years. Code Sec. 6166. The maximum deferral period, however, is 14 rather than 15 years because the due date for the last payment of interest coincides with the due date for the first installment of tax. Interest is payable at a special two percent rate on the estate tax attributable to the first $1 million of qualifying property. However, the interst rate on the remaining deferred amount is reduced to 45 percent of the rate charged for underpayment of taxes, and the estate tax deduction is eliminated for interest paid on these installments. Code Sec. 6601(j). A disposition of more than half the qualifying property will accelerate the tax, as may a default. Code Sec. 6166(g).

¶ 21,035   CREDITS AGAINST TAX

State Death Taxes

A credit is allowed for any inheritance, estate, legacy, or succession taxes actually paid to any state or the District of Columbia. The credit may be taken only for state death taxes on property included in the decedent's gross estate and only for taxes on the decedent's estate. The amount of the credit is the amount of the actual taxes paid, subject to two limitations. First, the maximum credit that may be claimed is determined by calculating what is called the "adjusted taxable estate" and applying it to the state death tax credit tables (reproduced in the Appendix). The adjusted taxable estate is equal to the taxable estate minus $60,000. Second, the credit is available only to the extent that it does not exceed the gross estate tax reduced by the applicable credit amount. Code Sec. 2011.

If a state imposes a death tax on a charitable transfer and a deduction is claimed for the amount of the tax imposed, the credit for state death taxes may not exceed the lesser of (1) the amount of state death taxes paid other than those on charitable transfers deductible under Code Sec. 2055 on which the deduction is claimed, (2) the maximum credit allowable on the decedent's estate using the state death tax credit table, or (3) state death taxes minus those on the charitable transfers computed under a special formula.

Example 21.3. Rex Ritter died in December of 1998. His taxable estate was $900,000. State death taxes of $31,000 were paid with respect to property included in his gross estate. The computation of the Code Sec. 2011 credit is as follows:

Taxable estate	$900,000
Less: Required reduction	60,000
Adjusted taxable estate	$840,000

The maximum state death tax credit, as found in the Appendix, is $27,600. Thus, the table amount in Code Sec. 2011 is the maximum amount allowed as a state death tax credit. However, it should be noted that most states have coordinated their death taxes to the Code Sec. 2011 amount to avoid the above disparity.

Foreign Death Taxes

A foreign death tax credit is provided for United States citizens and residents. The credit applies to property that is subject to both federal and foreign death taxes in order to prevent double taxation. Taxes paid to possessions of the United States are regarded as foreign death taxes. Code Sec. 2014. The foreign estate tax credit allowed against the estate tax is, however, limited by apportionment. Only taxes attributable to property taxed in both countries may be allowed as a credit. In addition, the credit cannot exceed the portion of United States taxes attributed to such property.

Death Taxes on Prior Transfers

A credit is allowed against the estate tax for all or a part of the estate tax paid with respect to the transfer of property to the present decedent by a prior decedent who died within 10 years before, or within two years after, the present decedent's death. Reg. § 20.2013-1. This credit can never be larger than it would be if the present decedent had not received the property. Since the purpose of this provision is to prevent the diminution of an estate by the imposition of successive taxes on the same property within a brief period, no credit is available for any gift tax that may have been paid with respect to the transfer of property to the decedent.

KEYSTONE PROBLEM

The applicable credit amount of $202,050 is available to estates of decedents who die in 1998. It has been referred to as the "exemption equivalent" of $625,000. Considering both small and large estates, is a credit of $202,050 really equivalent to an exemption of $625,000?

Gross Estate

¶ 21,101   PROPERTY INCLUDIBLE IN GROSS ESTATE

The gross estate of a decedent includes "the value of all property to the extent of the interest therein of the decedent at the time of death." Code Sec. 2033. This is a catch-all provision, serving the same purpose as Code Sec. 61 does for income tax purposes. The *gross* estate may be far in excess of the *probate* estate since it includes jointly held property and insurance payable to a named beneficiary although passing outside the will. No property is excluded, however small, be it real or personal, tangible or intangible, U.S. or foreign. Since the tax is levied on the *transfer* of property, not the property itself, even tax-free municipal bonds are included in the tax base. Citizens and nonresident aliens are subject to the U.S. estate tax on U.S. property. Code Sec. 2103(a). Most property owned outright by the decedent in his or her own name presents no problems as to inclusion. Property held merely as a fiduciary (e.g., as trustee), however, is *not* included.

Over the years, special rules have been designed to deal with *unique properties,* such as life insurance and pensions; *split interests,* such as life estates, remainders, and reversions; and *special situations,* such as powers of appointment and other retained powers. These problem areas, among others, are discussed below. In addition, any asset may present valuation problems.

Special Business Exclusion

For estates of decedents dying after December 31, 1997, if an estate qualifies, there is excluded from a decedent's gross estate the lessor of (1) the adjusted value of the decedent's qualified family-owned business interests or (2) the excess of $1,300,000 over the applicable exclusion amount in effect with respect to the decedent's estate. In general, in order to qualify for the exclusion, the aggregate value of the decedent's qualified family-owned business interests that are passed to qualified heirs must exceed 50 percent of the decedent's adjusted gross estate. Also, the decedent must be a U.S. citizen or resident at the time of death, the executor must elect special tax treatment and file a recapture agreement signed by each person having an interest in the property, and certain other requirements must be met.

¶ 21,109 PRESENT AND FUTURE INTERESTS IN PROPERTY

Anyone who owns property outright, whether personal or real, can divide up this ownership. The ways in which this can be done and the identification of these interests are crucial to the understanding of estate and gift taxes. *Life estates, remainders,* and *reversions* are such property interests and can best be illustrated through examples.

Case 1.   *The grantor (G) transfers (the income interest in) property to A for life.* A has a *life estate;* A is a *life tenant.* A can sell the interest to B, but B still has a life estate for the life of A. G has a *reversion* because the property will revert back to G or G's heirs when A dies.

   Estate tax consequences. Nothing will be taxed in A's estate because the only interest A owned, the life estate (the income interest), is extinguished upon A's death. But the whole property will be included in G's estate, less the actuarially determined value of A's life estate if A survives G.

Case 2.   *G transfers the property to A, but retains the income and/or possession of it for life.* Here G retains a life estate and A receives a *remainder.*

   Estate tax consequences. G never gave up the present enjoyment of the property; therefore, the full value of it will be included in

G's estate. A's estate will also be taxed. If G outlives A, the remainder will be taxed; if not, A dies owning the property outright.

Case 3.   G transfers the property to A for life, then to B. A has a life estate; B has a vested remainder. G has divested all interests. Even if B predeceases A, B's heirs will receive ownership.

Estate tax consequences. Nothing is included in G's estate, but B owns either the remainder or the property, depending on whether or not B predeceases G. Note the following:

1.   All transfers of property, even partial, are subject to gift tax.

2.   All adjusted taxable gifts are included in the estate tax computation even if not part of the gross estate.

Case 4.   G transfers the property to A for life, and if B survives A, then to B. A has a life estate and B has a contingent remainder because B must survive A to take anything. In addition, G has a reversion because G or G's heirs will receive the property if B predeceases A.

Estate tax consequences. A's estate is unaffected. B's estate has nothing if B predeceases A. If B survives A, B's estate will include the full value of the property. G's estate has nothing if B survives A prior to G's death. G's estate will include the property, less A's life estate if G predeceases A and B, but multiplied by the probability that B will predecease A.

Case 5.   G transfers the property to A for life, then to B if B survives A, otherwise to C. A has a life estate, B has a contingent remainder, and C has an *executory interest,* a remainder of sorts.

Estate tax consequences. G can never get anything back, so G's gross estate includes nothing. A's estate is unaffected. B's estate will include the property if B survives A, otherwise nothing. C's estate problem is more complex:

1.   If A predeceases B, nothing will be included.

2.   If C predeceases A and B, there is still a possibility that B will predecease A. Therefore, the property will be included in C's estate, times the probability of this happening, but the value is reduced by A's life estate.

The above transactions are generally done for family members in trust (e.g., life estate to wife, remainder to children). Annuities, term interests, life estates, reversions, and remainders are valued actuarially, using unisex Treasury tables. The tables use an interest rate equal to 120 percent of the applicable federal midterm rate compounded annually (rounded to the nearest two-tenths of one percent), adjusted monthly. Code Sec. 7520.

¶ 21,117   GIFTS WITHIN THREE YEARS OF DEATH

The general rule is that outright gifts made prior to death are *not* brought back into the gross estate, even if made on the deathbed. Code Sec. 2035(d)(1). However, the taxable portion of the gift is added to the estate tax base as an "adjusted taxable gift." There are several exceptions for gifts made within three years of death.

Any gift tax paid by the decedent or the decedent's estate is includible in the gross estate. Code Sec. 2035(c). If paid by the estate, an offsetting debt deduction is allowed. Also, a gift tax credit is allowed since the adjusted taxable gift is included in the estate tax base.

Gifts made at any time with strings attached are includible if the strings were broken within the three-year period and they would have been includible if no action had been taken. Code Sec. 2035(d)(2). This affects the following transactions:

1. Giving up a retained life estate that would otherwise have resulted in inclusion under Code Sec. 2036. See discussion at ¶ 21,125.

2. Giving up a reversion that otherwise would have brought the property back under Code Sec. 2037. See discussion at ¶ 21,133.

3. Giving up a power to revoke a transfer that would have resulted in inclusion under Code Sec. 2038. See discussion at ¶ 21,141.

4. Giving up an incident of ownership in a life insurance policy that would have led to the proceeds being includible in the gross estate or transferring the policy itself. See discussion at ¶ 21,173.

With respect to the estates of decedents dying after August 5, 1997, the value of property transferred to a donee from a decedent's revocable trust (within three years of the decedent's death) and the value of property in such a trust (with respect to which the decedent's power to revoke is relinquished during the three years before death) is not includible in the decedent's gross estate. Transfers from a revocable trust are treated as if made directly by the decedent for purposes of Code Sec. 2035 and Code Sec. 2038. Accordingly, an annual exclusion gift from a revocable trust is not included in the decedent's gross estate.

For purposes of qualifying for special estate tax benefits dependent on the amount of the adjusted gross estate and solely for testing purposes, *all* gifts within three years of death are brought back, except gifts of present interests of $10,000 or less per donee per year (the $10,000 ceiling will be indexed annually for inflation after 1998). Code Sec. 2035(d)(3). Examples of items qualifying for special estate tax benefits include qualifying for death tax redemptions (Code Sec. 303), special use valuation for farms and closely held businesses (Code Sec. 2032A), and installment payments of the estate tax (Code Sec. 6166).

Gifts of Life Insurance

The general rule that outright gifts made prior to death are not includible in the donor's gross estate does not apply to transfers of life insurance policies on the life of the decedent made within three years of death. Code Sec. 2035(b)(2) and (d)(2). The following situations are possible:

1. If the transfer took place *more than* three years before death and the insured did *not* pay the premiums the last three years of life, no amount is includible in the gross estate.

2. If the situation is the same as under (1), except that the insured paid the premiums within three years of death, the premiums are includible in the gross estate.

3. If the policy was transferred *within* three years of death *and* the premiums were paid by the insured, the proceeds, but not the premiums, are includible in the gross estate.

4. If the situation is the same as (3), except that some of the last three years' premiums were paid by someone other than the insured, only the proceeds allocable to the premiums paid by the insured are includible.

Example 21.4. Ten years before his death, John Hunter purchased a $100,000 term insurance policy. Two years before his death, he irrevocably transferred the policy and all incidents of ownership to a trust which paid the last two years' premiums. John's gross estate includes $80,000 of proceeds since John paid 80 percent of the premiums.

Even if the proceeds are not includible in the gross estate, the adjusted taxable gift is includible in the estate tax base. The value of an unmatured policy, however, is next to zero for a term policy and close to the cash surrender value for ordinary life policies (the "interpolated terminal reserve," i.e., the replacement value).

¶ 21,125   RETAINED LIFE ESTATES

Under the provisions of Code Sec. 2036, a decedent's gross estate includes the value of any interest in property transferred by the decedent prior to death (whether in trust or otherwise) for less than full or adequate and full consideration, if the decedent retained for life, or for any period that does not, in fact, end before death:

1. The use, possession, right to the income, or other enjoyment of the transferred property; or

2. The right, either alone or in conjunction with any person, to designate the person who may possess or enjoy the property, or the related income. Code Sec. 2036; Reg. § 20.2036-1(a).

The use, possession, right to the income, or other enjoyment of the property is considered retained by the decedent to the extent that it is to be utilized to discharge a legal obligation of the decedent. A legal obligation includes one to support a dependent during the decedent's lifetime. Reg. § 20.2036-1(b)(2). The right to designate includes a "reserved power" to designate the person or persons to receive the income, or to possess or enjoy nonincome-producing property during the decedent's life.

The most common example of transfers includible in the gross estate through the operation of Code Sec. 2036 is a transfer by trust, with a retained life estate. This may be illustrated as follows.

Example 21.5. Bart Henderson transfers income-producing property into trust for his son, but retains the income from the property for his lifetime. Upon Bart's death, the total fair market value of the property will be included in his gross estate under Code Sec. 2036. (Incidentally, the transfer by Bart would be subject to federal gift taxes. The amount of the gross gift would be the fair market value of the property at the date of the gift, less the portion assignable to the value of the retained life estate.)

An illustration of reserving "the use or possession" of transferred property is an implied agreement or understanding between the transferor and the recipients. In many family situations, a father or mother may give the parents' residence to a son or daughter but continue to live there for life. As a result, the house will be fully includible in the parents' gross estate. Of course, legal title to the property is irrelevant in warding off the inclusion scenario. Naturally, if the parent (transferor) occupied only one-third of the house, then only that portion would be included in the gross estate. Also, it is significant to note that the decedent must be the transferor of the life estate in order for the property to be includible in the estate.

Example 21.6. Jack Goodwin transfers income-producing property into trust for his son, Charlie, but retains a life estate for his wife, Ellen. The trust indenture provides that if Ellen predeceases Jack, the life estate will revert to Jack. If Jack predeceases Ellen, then the life estate enjoyed by Ellen would not be includible in Jack's gross estate under Code Sec. 2036. If Ellen predeceases Jack, none of the property will be included in Ellen's estate. Although Ellen held a life estate at the time of her death, she is not the transferor of the property. Therefore, Code Sec. 2036 is not operative.

Family Partnerships

A family partnership is a typical device to shift income and appreciation to other family members and is specifically sanctioned. Code Sec. 704(e). The grantor-partner should be careful not to run afoul of the retained life estate problem by retaining too much control. If the grantor retains a power to control income distributions after the transfer, the rule could apply. The exercise of traditional managerial powers by the grantor should not invoke the rule. Thus, the scope of powers customary in recognized business relationships should not be exceeded. Here are some key factors the IRS looks at:

1. Was the partnership created for business purposes or principally to carry out a desired estate plan?

2. Did the other partners contribute any capital?

3. Did the grantor-partner have the power to accumulate or distribute income?

4. What percentage of profits was in fact distributed to the grantor-partner?

Buy/sell agreements serve a business purpose and should not be a negative factor.

Family Transfers

Set out below are examples of lifetime transfers of property in the setting of family transfers and the tax consequences for each situation.

1. H transfers property to his wife (W) for life, then to himself for life, remainder to his children. Even if H predeceases W, the property (less W's outstanding life estate) is included in his estate.

2. G transfers securities to his wife for life, then to his son, but the trustee has discretion to distribute the income to G in whole or in part. Whether or not the trustee does so, Code Sec. 2036 has no application since the *decedent* retained no interest or right.

3. G makes a transfer in trust but retains the right to use the income for support of his minor children. If he dies before the youngest child reaches majority, he dies with a retained life estate, otherwise not.

4. G makes a transfer to A for life, then to B, retaining the right to designate C as income beneficiary, but only with A's consent. Even though G's power is illusory (i.e., G can exercise his power to substitute C for A only with the consent of A, the adverse party), G still has a retained life estate.

5. G transfers property to his son for life, leaving the remainder to his grandson. G has not retained a life estate and neither has his son since the son is not the transferor. (The son's death, however, causes a taxable termination and may be subject to the generation-skipping tax, discussed later in this chapter.)

6. Upon H's death, W, his widow, has the right to receive $200,000 of life insurance. However, she instructs the insurance company to pay her the interest only for life, then to pay the proceeds to her grandchildren in equal shares. Upon W's death, Code Sec. 2036 applies.

7. G transfers property to his brother, T, for life, then to T's children. T, in return, transfers property to G for life, then to G's children. Technically, neither party retained a life estate. However, the economic effect is the same as if they both did. The *reciprocal trust* doctrine creates a retained life estate in both. *J.P. Grace Est.,* 69-1 USTC ¶ 12,609, 395 U.S. 316, 89 S.Ct. 1730 (1969). If the trusts are of unequal value, only the smallest value is deemed to be reciprocal.

8. G has a retained life estate in a $1 million trust. At the age of 85, when the fair market value of his interest is $50,000, G sells it to his grandson and dies. Literally, Code Sec. 2036 does not apply since G did not die with a retained life interest.

    Furthermore, even if he died the next day, there is no gift in contemplation of death because the consideration was adequate. Nevertheless, $950,000 may be included in G's estate if the transaction is viewed as involving the property which otherwise would have been included. *C. Allen,* 61-2 USTC ¶ 12,032, 293 F.2d 916 (CA-10 1961).

¶ 21,133   REVERSIONS

Code Sec. 2037 also addresses the inclusion in the gross estate of the value of lifetime transfers by the decedent. This section refers to transfers "in trust or otherwise" except for an "adequate and full consideration," as does Code Sec. 2036. However, there are three conditions that must be satisfied for Code Sec. 2037 to become operative.

1. Possession or enjoyment of the property can be obtained, through ownership of such interest, only by surviving the decedent.

2. The decedent had retained a reversionary interest in the property at the time of the transfer.

3. The value of the reversionary interest immediately before the decedent's death exceeded five percent of the value of the entire property.

The condition of survivorship cited in 1 above means that the subject property is not included in the decedent's gross estate if, immediately before the decedent's death, possession or enjoyment of the property could be obtained by a beneficiary either by surviving the decedent, or through another event such as the expiration of a term of years. The reversionary interest referred to in 2 above is, in effect, a remainder interest retained by the original transferor. The term "reversionary interest" does not include rights to income only, such as the right to receive the income from a trust after the death of another person. Reg. § 20.2037-1(c)(2). To determine whether the decedent retained a reversionary interest in the property valued in excess of five percent, as referred to in 3 above, the value of the reversionary interest is compared to the value of the property transferred. This valuation does not include interests therein that are not dependent upon survivorship of the decedent. Application of the Code Sec. 2037 provisions discussed above are presented in the following examples.

Example 21.7. John Henry transferred property into trust, giving his wife, Donna, a life estate and the remainder interest to John's then-surviving children. In the event there were no surviving children, the remainder would go to John or his estate. Each beneficiary can possess or enjoy the property without surviving John. Therefore, no part of the property is includible in John's gross estate under Code Sec. 2037, regardless of the value of John's reversionary interest.

Example 21.8. John Henry transferred property into trust retaining a life estate, with the remainder interest to his surviving children. In the event there were no surviving children, the remainder would go to his brother or to his brother's estate. The decedent did not retain a reversionary interest. Therefore, no part of the property is includible in the decedent's gross estate under Code Sec. 2037, even though possession or enjoyment of the property could be obtained by the children only if they survived John Henry.

Example 21.9. A transferred property into trust giving a life estate to B with the remainder to C if A predeceases B. However, if B predeceases A, the remainder would go to A. If, in fact, A predeceases B, the value of A's reversionary interest immediately before death is compared with the value of the trust corpus, without deduction for the value of B's outstanding life estate, in applying the five percent rule. Conceivably, a fractional remainder interest could be retained by the decedent. Referring to the above situation, if A had retained a reversionary interest in only one-half of the trust corpus, the value of the reversionary interest would be compared with the value of one-half of the trust corpus, without deduction for any part of the value of B's outstanding life estate.

In applying Code Sec. 2037, the value of the decedent's reversionary interest is computed in accordance with the valuation principles discussed at ¶ 21,195.

¶ 21,141   REVOCABLE TRANSFERS

As did Code Secs. 2036 and 2037, Code Sec. 2038 also relates to the inclusion in the gross estate of the value of lifetime transfers by the decedent. This section also refers to transfers "in trust or otherwise" except for an "adequate and full consideration," as do Code Secs. 2036 and 2037. Under Code Sec. 2038, however, the value of property interests transferred by the decedent are includible in the gross estate if the enjoyment of the property transferred was subject, at the date of the decedent's death, to any power of the decedent to alter, amend, revoke, or terminate the transfer. Reg. § 20.2038-1(a).

It is immaterial in what capacity the power was exercisable by the decedent or by another person, or persons, in conjunction with the decedent. Also, the time of exercise and the source of the power are of no importance. If the decedent transferred property by trust during life and was named as trustee with the power to revoke the trusts, the entire property would be includible in the gross estate under the operation of Code Sec. 2038. Likewise, if the decedent created a trust during life, named another person as trustee, but reserved the power to be named as a replacement trustee, Code Sec. 2038 would apply.

In order to preclude inclusion of the transferred property in the gross estate under Code Sec. 2038, the power to alter, amend, revoke, or terminate a trust must be held at all times "solely by a person other than the decedent." Further, the decedent must not have reserved any right to assume these powers. The amount includible in the gross estate under Code Sec. 2038 is "only" that portion of the property transferred that is subject, at death, to the "decedent's" power to alter, amend, revoke, or terminate. Reg. § 20.2038-1(a)(3).

A revocable lifetime trust is the typical tool employed by the decedent to provide flexibility for changing personal and economic conditions. With respect to the estates of decedents dying after August 5, 1997, the value of property transferred to a donee from a decedent's revocable trust (within three years of the decedent's death) and the value of property in such a trust (with respect to which the decedent's power to revoke is relinquished during the three years before death) is not includible in the decedent's gross estate. Transfers from a revocable trust are treated as if made directly by the decedent for purposes of Code Sec. 2035 and Code Sec. 2038. Accordingly, an annual exclusion gift from a revocable trust is not included in the decedent's gross estate.

It should be obvious at this juncture that there may be considerable overlap between Code Secs. 2036, 2037, and 2038. A previous lifetime transfer by the decedent may subject the property to inclusion in the gross estate under one or more of these sections. Of course, the property is included only once, but perhaps for one or more reasons.

¶ 21,149　ANNUITIES

Commercial Annuities

By far, most annuities are of the commercial kind and are issued by insurance companies. Commercial annuities are valued on the basis of comparable sales. In other words, the issuer is asked: How much would a 60-year-old person have to pay to receive $3,000 a year for life? The answer is the value.

Most commercial annuities, including retirement annuities, can be divided into four groups:

1. *Straight-life annuities,* which are simply paid for the life of one person.

2. *Joint and survivor annuities,* whereby payments are made, typically to a married couple, as long as at least one of them lives.

3. *Self and survivor annuities,* whereby payments continue to be made to a beneficiary after the death of the buyer.

4. *Minimum guarantee annuities,* whereby a refund feature provides for a lump-sum payment, unless the annuitant survives a minimum period of time.

To qualify as an annuity, it is immaterial whether the payments are periodic or sporadic, equal or unequal, conditional or unconditional.

The first type will never result in estate taxation, but once a survivor feature exists, the present value of the payments due after death will be included in the estate *if the decedent or an employer contributed to the purchase price.* This is similar to the tracing rule that applies to unmarried joint tenants (see below) and also applies to both private and commercial annuities. Code Sec. 2039(b).

> *Example 21.10.* H paid $500,000 to an insurance company for a joint and survivorship annuity, whereby $3,000 a month would be paid as long as he and/or his wife, W, survive. If H dies first, the full present value of W's expected payments, based on actuarial

tables, will be included in his estate. If W dies first, nothing will be included.

Example 21.11. Same as Example 21.10, except H and W pay half each. Whenever the first one dies, one-half will be included in his or her estate.

Example 21.12. Same as Example 21.11 except that H and W each buy separate annuities for $250,000. Since neither one contributed to the other's annuity, nothing is included in either estate.

Private Annuities

Private annuities are usually employed when there is an "estate planning sale" by an older person (the annuitant) to a younger family member (the obligor). If the annuity is simply paid to the annuitant for life with no survivor feature, nothing will be includible in the annuitant's estate since nothing passes from the decedent. Should the annuity continue to the surviving spouse or other beneficiary, the estate will include the present value of the future payments, based on the survivor's life expectancy times the fractional consideration paid by the decedent. Code Sec. 2039(b). For more details on private annuities, see Chapter 23.

Example 21.13. Several years ago, G and W sold their securities to their child for a private annuity of $5,000 a year for as long as both live, plus $3,000 a year for the life of the survivor. G had put up 80 percent of the purchase price of the securities and died first. Based on W's age at G's death, assume that according to the IRS tables prescribed under Code Sec. 7520, one dollar a year for life is worth $10.5376. As a result, G's estate will include $25,290 ($3,000 × 10.5376 × .80).

Pension and Profit-Sharing Plans

No estate exclusion is allowed regardless of how annuity payments are made, even if there is a named beneficiary. Code Sec. 2039(a) and (b). Even IRAs and Keogh plans are fully includible. (All or part of a retirement annuity in "pay status" before 1985, however, may be excluded.)

¶ 21,157   CO-OWNERSHIPS OF PROPERTY

Tenancies in Common

Since there is no survivorship feature in a tenancy in common, the decedent's undivided interest in the property is included in the decedent's gross estate (and in the decedent's probate estate). Thus, if the decedent owned a 23 percent interest in a tract of land, 23 percent of its value is includible in the decedent's estate.

Joint Tenancies and Tenancies by the Entirety

Married joint tenants. If the decedent owned property as a joint tenant with a spouse with right of survivorship, including a tenancy by the entirety, a "qualified joint tenancy" exists. One-half of its value is included in the estate of the first spouse to die without regard to who paid for it. The surviving spouse becomes the sole owner by operation of law resulting in full inclusion in the surviving spouse's estate.

Unmarried joint tenants. Any two or more individuals may be joint tenants (e.g., parent and child, siblings, and unmarried couples). When the first joint tenant dies, the *full* value of the property is included in the estate, unless and to the extent the surviving joint tenant can show contributions in money toward the purchase price. Code Sec. 2040(a).

> ***Example 21.14.*** Fernanda and her daughter Fern own, as joint tenants, a condominium apartment, which Fernanda paid for. If Fernanda dies first, the full value is included in her estate, but if Fern predeceases her mother, *nothing* is includible in Fern's estate. If Fernanda contributed X percent of the original cost, X percent of the *value* at the time of her death would be includible in her estate if Fern survived her. If the surviving joint tenant receives the property subject to an unpaid mortgage, the mortgage balance counts as an original contribution to the extent the owner is personally liable. Rev. Rul. 79-302, 1979-2 CB 328.

Community Property

There are only eight community property states (California, Arizona, Nevada, New Mexico, Idaho, Texas, Louisiana, and Washington). In 1985, Wisconsin implemented a marital property act. In these states, property acquired by married persons is community property, and such property retains its character once established even after a change of domicile. One-half of the value of community property owned by a husband and wife is includible in the gross estate of the first spouse to die. Community property is like an equal tenancy in common between spouses enforced by state law. That is, one-half of the community interest goes into the estate of the first to die. However, unlike joint tenancies with the right of survivorship between husbands and wives in common law states, both halves of community property receive a step-up in basis to fair market value. Code Sec. 1014(b)(6).

¶ 21,165 POWERS OF APPOINTMENT

If property is transferred in trust by gift or inheritance, a beneficiary may use and enjoy that property to a great extent *without that property being includible in the estate.* The beneficiary may have all the following rights and powers. Code Sec. 2041(b)(1) and (2).

1. The right to receive all the income from the property for life (i.e., a life estate).

2. The power to draw funds from the trust (invade corpus), as long as it is subject to an *ascertainable standard* relating to the beneficiary's health, education, support, or maintenance.

3. The power to withdraw the greater of five percent of the value of the trust property or, $5,000, each year.

4. The power to appoint all or part of the property to anyone the beneficiary wishes during life or by will, except to oneself, the estate, or the creditors of either.

5.   The right to be the trustee of the trust.

None of the above will subject the property to estate tax in the beneficiary's estate, but there may be generation-skipping transfer tax consequences (discussed later in this chapter, starting at ¶ 21,501.)

Definitions

If the decedent had transferred property as a gift and retained certain powers of control, they can be extremely limited and still cause the property to be included under the retained life estate, reversion or revocable transfer rules discussed above. Once the decedent as a beneficiary simply has been given a power by someone else over property the beneficiary never owned, the power must be a *general power of appointment* to cause inclusion. The expression "general power" does not have to be stated as such.

Appointee. The person in whose favor the power is exercised.

Donee of the power. The person who has the right to appoint the property, let the power lapse, or release it.

Donor of the power. The grantor and transferor of the property subject to the power.

Taker in default. The person who winds up with the property if the power is released or lapses. This person will often be the remainderman.

General v. Special Powers

For the decedent to be deemed to have a general power of appointment, the decedent must have had the power to appoint the property to oneself, the estate, or the creditors of either by will and/or during life. Code Sec. 2041(b)(1) and (2).

The following are *not* general powers:

1.   The power to appoint the property to anyone in the world, such as a child or grandchild, except to oneself, the estate, or the creditors of either.

2.   The power to appoint the property to anyone, including oneself, but only with the consent of the grantor or an adverse party, such as the remainderman or an income beneficiary whose interest would be extinguished in the process.

3.   The power to make use of capital up to five percent of value or $5,000, whichever is greater, once a year on a noncumulative basis.

4.   The power to make use of capital for the beneficiary's health, education, support, or maintenance, but not for emergencies, welfare, or happiness.

Powers that fall short of general powers are called *special* or *limited* powers.

Once a general power exists, the release, lapse, or exercise of it during life creates a taxable gift. Code Sec. 2514. If the decedent exercises a general power in a will or lets it lapse or releases it, the property is includible in the decedent's estate.

If the donee of the power exercises it, but retains a life estate, reversion, or the power to alter, amend, or revoke, the property will be included in the donee's estate under Code Secs. 2035-2038.

General powers granted before October 22, 1942, lead to estate inclusion only if exercised, by will or during life. But a post-October 21, 1942, power is taxable whether it lapses, is released, or is exercised.

Example 21.15. Max Mertens transfers property in trust to his son for life. The son has the power to give the property to any or all of his children *and* has the right to use whatever he needs for his own support. The property will not be included in the son's estate. If the son's power is worded as a power to consume for his happiness, welfare, and the like, chances are the power will be considered general for lack of an ascertainable standard.

Example 21.16. B left property in trust to A for life, then to B. C has the power to appoint the property to himself. The property is includible in C's estate.

Example 21.17. Same as Example 21.16, but C needs A's consent. Since A is the income beneficiary, A is an adverse party, and C does *not* have a general power. Therefore, none of the property would be includible in C's estate.

Example 21.18. Same as Example 21.16, but C needs B's consent. As a remainderman, B is also an adverse party and there are no estate tax consequences to C.

Example 21.19. G left property in trust to his wife, W, for life, then to his son, S. W has the power to appoint the property to anyone in the world but only with the consent of her daughter. Since the daughter is a permissible appointee, only one-half of the property would be includible in W's estate.

Example 21.20. Same as Example 21.19, except that W needs the consent of both her daughters. Only one-third would be includible in W's estate.

Example 21.21. A received a general power of appointment over a trust fund. A exercised one-half in favor of himself and the other half in favor of his grandson. Upon A's death, his estate includes one-half of the property itself to the extent he still has it. The one-half exercised in favor of his grandson is subject to gift tax.

¶ 21,173   LIFE INSURANCE

The proceeds of life insurance on the life of the decedent are includible in the decedent's gross estate under three sets of circumstances. Code Sec. 2042.

First, if the proceeds are payable to the decedent's estate, they are clearly includible in the gross estate. This could happen by choice, e.g., the estate is named as a beneficiary, or it could occur inadvertently, e.g., the named beneficiary predeceased the insured and no provision was made for a secondary beneficiary. Also, if the proceeds are payable to a trustee who is obligated to use the proceeds for the benefit of the estate, such as to pay debts and taxes, the proceeds are deemed payable to the estate. If the trustee has discretion as to whether the proceeds are to be used for the benefit of the estate, they are includible to the extent so used.

Second, if the decedent possessed at least one incident of ownership in the policy, the life insurance proceeds are includible in the gross estate. This means either that the decedent owned the policy until death or transferred the policy, but retained the right to:

1. Change the beneficiary
2. Borrow on the policy
3. Use it as collateral for a loan
4. Cancel the policy
5. Veto any of the above or retained a reversionary interest in excess of five percent

Third, if the policy was transferred irrevocably within three years of the insured's death, the proceeds are includible in the gross estate.

The standard procedure employed to completely transfer all incidents of ownership is to assign the policy to an irrevocable insurance trust. Note that the power to exercise any incident of ownership in conjunction with any other party, or the power to veto any incident of ownership, is still an incident of ownership resulting in estate inclusion. Since life insurance is a unique asset in that it can increase dramatically in value from one instant to the next, it makes sense to relinquish all incidents of ownership and make it payable to a named beneficiary. The transfer must take place more than three years prior to death to accomplish the estate exclusion. Code Sec. 2035(d)(2).

Example 21.22. Mark Martin purchased flight insurance at the airport, handed the policy over to his son, embarked, and died one-half hour later in a plane crash. Since Mark possessed an incident of ownership in the policy, even though no opportunity existed for exercise, the full proceeds would nevertheless be included in his gross estate. *M.L. Noel Est.,* 65-1 USTC ¶ 12,311, 380 U.S. 678, 85 S.Ct. 1238 (1965). *Thus,* it is the *existence* of the *incident* that matters.

The rules under Code Sec. 2042 apply only to insurance on the life of the decedent. If the decedent owned "spouse insurance" or any policy on the life of another when the decedent died, only its *value,* not the proceeds, is includible in the decedent's gross estate under Code Sec. 2033. The value is the amount for which the individual insurance company would sell an identical policy at the time of death on a paid-up basis (i.e., the replacement cost, known as the "interpolated terminal reserve").

TAX PLANNING POINTER

Here is a technique that can have favorable income, gift, *and* estate tax consequences: grantor transfers a life insurance policy on the grantor's own life to an irrevocable trust, whereupon the trust borrows to pay the premiums. The tax consequences are:

Gift tax. No gift tax is incurred if the cash value does not exceed available exclusions. If the cash value is high, the grantor may borrow against the policy and transfer it subject to the loan.

Income tax. If the trust income may be used to pay the premiums on the policy, the trust is a grantor trust and any available deductions belong to the grantor. Code Sec. 677(a)(3).

Estate tax. If all incidents of ownership in the policy are transferred more than three years prior to the grantor's death, the proceeds are excluded from the insured's gross estate.

Because of all these tax advantages, such a grantor-insurance trust is known in the profession as the "supertrust."

¶ 21,175　PART-SALE, PART-GIFT TRANSFERS

Sometimes a transfer is part sale and part gift. Whenever a transfer is for less than fair value (i.e., not a bona fide sale), the property is includible at full value in the estate, less consideration paid. Code Sec. 2043.

Example 21.23. G transferred property to one of his sons, S, keeping a life estate for himself. When it is explained to him that the full value of the property will be included in his estate because of a retained life interest, he gets an idea. He sells his life interest to his other son for $5,000. Nevertheless, the full value of the property is included in his estate, less $5,000, assuming he dies within three years. Note that he did not sell the property itself, merely the life estate. This result follows even if the $5,000 was all the *life estate* was worth, which is all G had. The purpose of the rule is to avoid deathbed transfers of a retained life estate, powers of appointment, or a reversion. Otherwise, sales for a modest sum could remove sizeable amounts from the estate.

Valuation of Gross Estate

¶ 21,181　GENERAL PRINCIPLES

Valuing the gross estate is the paramount estate tax problem since the value determines the amount that will be subject to estate tax and, as a result, the estate's liquidity needs. The executor will value all property included in the gross estate either at its fair market value at the decedent's date of death or the alternate valuation date. Code Secs. 2031 and 2032.

Fair Market Value

In general, fair market value of property includible in a decedent's estate is the price at which it would change hands between a willing buyer and a willing seller, both having reasonable knowledge of relevant facts. Reg. § 20.2031-1(b). Despite the brevity of the rule, valuation controversies make up a large share of audit and litigation issues.

If an item is generally available to the public in a particular market, the fair market value of the property is the price obtainable on the market in which it is most commonly sold to the public. If the item of property is generally obtainable by the public on the retail market, fair market value of the item is the price at which that item or a comparable one will sell at retail in a particular geographic market. Reg. § 20.2031-1(b).

Example 21.24. The fair market value of decedent Ginger Graham's car (property generally obtained by the public on the retail market) is the price at which a car of the same make, model, age, and condition could be purchased by members of the public. Fair market value would not be the price that a used-car dealer would pay for Ginger's car.

Alternate Valuation Date

Whenever the executor chooses the alternate valuation method, all property is valued six months after death or on the date of disposition if this date occurs first. Code Sec. 2032(a). It should be noted that whichever valuation date is selected, the election is all inclusive. That is, each asset included in the gross estate must be valued as of the elected date. Consequently, the executor may not value some items at date of death and others at the alternate date.

Example 21.25. John Henry's gross estate consists of the following assets:

	FMV at Date of Death	FMV at Alternate Date
1,000 shares of Big Ed's Barbecue	$ 200,000	$ 190,000
House	380,000	370,000
Farm	400,000	390,000
Georgia Power bonds	200,000	198,000
Total	$1,180,000	$1,148,000

If the executor elects the date of death value, then the estate is valued at $1,180,000, and if the alternate valuation date is selected, the estate's value is $1,148,000. Note that no mixing of values is permissible.

The election to use the alternate valuation date must reduce the value of the decedent's gross estate and the sum of the decedent's estate tax and generation-skipping transfer tax liabilities (for transfers before October 23, 1986, the GST tax liability was not part of this reduction requirement). Code Sec. 2032(c). Even property that was transferred some time before death, but which is included in the gross estate because of the retention of certain rights or for other reasons, is valued as of the date of death or six months after death.

Basis of Property

Most properties receive a basis for income tax purposes equal to the estate tax value, be it the date of death value, the value on the alternate valuation date, or the special use value. Code Sec. 1014(a). The decedent's basis is irrelevant, and a step-up or a step-down may result. An instant long-term holding period is also given by statute. Code Sec. 1223(11). The fair market value basis rule applies without regard to whether estate or inheritance taxes are paid or whether an estate tax return is due.

¶ 21,185 SPECIFIC PROPERTIES

Even though all property included in the gross estate is valued as of the same date—that is, the date of death or the alternate valuation date—special problems arise in valuing particular types of property. For this reason, special rules apply in valuing the various kinds of property or interests in property that might be included in the gross estate and these are treated in the following paragraphs.

Real Estate. The valuation of real estate is not set out in the Regulations pursuant to any formula or other precise mechanism. Reg. § 20.2031-1(b). Since each piece of real estate is unique, it is not surprising for the Regulations to take this approach. However, the following methods can be used to establish the estate tax value of real estate: expert testimony, comparable sales, market assessments, recent mortgages, capitalization of earnings, and reproduction costs.

Household and Personal Effects. Household and personal effects must be valued at the price that a willing buyer would pay a willing seller for such goods. Reg. § 20.2031-6(a). If the household and personal effects exceed a total value of $3,000, then there must be an appraisal and an itemized list of the jewelry, furs, silverware, paintings, antiques, oriental rugs, stamps, coin collection, and books attached to the return.

Life Insurance. The value of life insurance for estate tax purposes will be either the proceeds of the policy or its replacement value. That is, where insurance is taxed to the estate of the insured because the insurance becomes due and payable on death, then the estate tax value will be the proceeds of the policy. On the other hand, life insurance may be taxed in the estate of a person other than the insured. When this happens, the policy has not matured. As a result, the estate tax value is the replacement cost and not its face value. Reg. § 20.2031-8.

Life Estates, Remainder Interests, Term Certain Interests, and Reversionary Interests. Because an individual may have an interest less than the entire fee simple ownership in property, post-April 30, 1989, special IRS tables must be used to value these life estates, remainders, term certain interests, and reversions. Code Sec. 7520. This actuarial valuation system requires that the interest rate to be used in valuing limited interests be updated using an interest rate derived from the federal midterm rate for the month in which the valuation is required. The method prescribes that the interest rate will be at 120 percent of the applicable federal midterm rate (AFR) compounded annually (rounded to the nearest two-tenths of one percent).

Mutual Funds. Mutual fund shares can be sold back only to the issuer and by shareholders at a fixed price under federal laws governing mutual funds. This fixed price is called the redemption or bid price and is based on the net values of the assets held by the fund on a given date. Because of this fact, the U.S. Supreme Court has ruled that mutual fund shares owned by decedents must be valued for estate tax purposes by using the redemption or bid price at the date of death or on the alternate valuation date. *D.B. Cartwright,* 73-1 USTC ¶ 12,926, 411 U.S. 546, 93 S.Ct. 1713 (1973); Reg. § 20.2031-8(b).

¶ 21,187   LISTED SECURITIES

Stocks and bonds owned by a decedent are includible in the gross estate and are valued for estate tax purposes on the date of death, or on a date six months after death if the estate representative so elects. Code Sec. 2033. When the valuation is made as of six months after death, if any of the securities have been distributed in the interval, the value on the date of distribution will control. Reg. § 20.2032-1(c)(2). Similarly, the valuation date, in the case of a sale during the six-month period after death, is the date of sale.

The estate tax value of stocks and bonds is the fair market value per share or bond on the applicable valuation date. In the case of listed stocks and bonds, if there were actual sales of the securities on a stock exchange or in an over-the-counter market on the valuation date, then the mean between the highest and lowest quoted selling prices on that date is taken as the fair market value per share or bond. Reg. § 20.2031-2(b).

> *Example 21.26.* John Hughes died on September 1, 1998, and he owned 1,000 shares of IBM stock that was traded on the New York Stock Exchange. IBM traded at a high of $116 and a low of $114 on September 1. As a result, Mr. Hughes's estate tax return will reflect a value for the IBM stock of $115 per share (average of $116 and $114) and a total value of the stock of $115,000.

If there were no actual sales on the valuation date, but there were sales on trading dates within a reasonable period both before and after the valuation date, the fair market value is derived by taking (1) the mean between the highest and lowest sales on the nearest trading date before and (2) the mean between the highest and lowest sales on the nearest trading date after the valuation date, and taking a weighted average of these two means. However, it should be noted that the average is weighted inversely by the respective number of trading days separating the selling dates and the date of death. Reg. § § 20.2031-2(b) and 25.2512-2(b).

> *Example 21.27.* Sam Lett died on November 5, 1998, and owned 1,000 shares of Zebra Corporation stock, which is traded on an over-the-counter market. On November 5 there were no sales of Zebra stock. The sales of Zebra stock nearest the valuation date of November 5 took place two trading days before (November 3) and three trading days after (November 10). On November 3, 1998, the mean sales price was $50, and on November 10, 1998, the

mean sales price was $40. As a result, the date of death value is as follows: $((3 \times \$50) + (2 \times \$40))/5 = \$46$.

In certain instances, securities may be actively traded on the date of death, but that is not the value that will be utilized for estate tax purposes. Specifically, the taxpayer may own a large block of securities, and the valuer must consider the depressing effect that the sale of such a large number of shares would have on the market. This situation is referred to as "blockage" and requires that the price per share be lowered to reflect the effect of marketing such a large block of securities. Reg. §§ 20.2031-2(e) and 25.2512-2(e); Rev. Rul. 59-60, 1959-1 CB 237.

¶ 21,191   CLOSELY HELD STOCK

One of the most vexing problems in the area of estate taxation is how to value the stock of a closely held corporation. The valuation of close corporation stock differs from that of listed and active corporate stock that passes freely on the market and has its value reflected on the stock exchange or over-the-counter listings. Closely held stock rarely finds its way to the market place and its value at any particular time is determined only by reference to various factors. Numerous courts, professional journals, and government publications have discussed this valuation question. Despite this wealth of information, few areas of taxation are as unresolved and misunderstood as the valuation of closely held stock. And, since there are several million closely held corporations in the United States, valuation represents an area of critical concern confronting taxing authorities and practitioners.

Obviously, a sale of stock occurring within a reasonable time of the valuation date can provide a good indication of the stock's value. Reg. § 20.2031-2. However, the fair market value of a particular item of property is not to be determined by a forced sale price. Nor is the fair market value to be determined by the sale price of the item in a market other than that in which such item is most commonly sold to the public. Reg. § 20.2031-1(b). If there is no sale (as is the usual case with closely held stock), an independent expert appraiser should be consulted.

In the case of corporate stock and securities that are not listed on an exchange and whose value thus cannot be determined on the basis of sales or bid and asked prices, the value must be determined by taking into consideration, in addition to other factors, the value of stock or securities of corporations engaged in the same or a similar line of business that are listed on an exchange. Code Sec. 2031(b). Thus, in the absence of an active market, consideration may be given in the case of bonds to such factors as the soundness of the security, the interest yield, and the date of maturity. In the case of stocks, consideration may be given to the company's net worth, prospective earning power, dividend-paying capacity, and other relevant factors, including a fair appraisal of the tangible and intangible business assets (including goodwill) as of the appropriate valuation date and the demonstrated earnings capacity of the business. Reg. §§ 20.2031-2(f), 20.2031-3, and 20.2031-6(b).

The IRS emphasizes the following factors to be considered as valuation guides in addition to all available financial data. Rev. Rul. 59-60, 1959-1 CB 237.

1. The nature of the business and the history of the enterprise from its inception.

2. The economic outlook in general and the condition and outlook of the specific industry in particular.

3. The book value of the stock and the financial condition of the business.

4. The earning capacity of the company.

5. The dividend-paying capacity.

6. Whether or not the enterprise has goodwill or other intangible value.

7. Sales of the stock and the size of the block of stock to be valued.

8. The market price of stock of corporations engaged in the same or a similar line of business having their stocks actively traded in a free and open market, either on an exchange or over the counter.

¶ 21,193   BUY-SELL AGREEMENTS

In a buy-sell agreement one business owner (partner or shareholder) is obligated to sell an interest on death, retirement, or disability to the owners (cross-purchase agreement) or to the business (redemption agreement). Such agreements may be used to ease the problems of liquidity and estate valuation. Buy-sell agreements have at least three advantages. First, if the buy-sell agreement is legally binding on both parties and fair when made, the price (fixed or based on a formula) is also helpful in establishing value for estate, gift, and income tax purposes, limiting the estate tax value. The agreement must not be merely an option or right of first refusal. Second, a guaranteed price will provide the estate with instant liquidity, rather than an unmarketable ownership interest. Third, an orderly continuity of business ownership is provided. Buy-sell agreements are often funded by insurance policies.

Example 21.28. Paul and Mary Wells are equal shareholders in Quincy Corporation. When either party dies, retires, or becomes totally disabled, the other shareholder is to purchase the shares, thus becoming the sole shareholder. This is an example of a cross-purchase agreement. It should be noted that the purchasing shareholder's basis in the stock is increased by the purchase price. If the corporation is the buyer, the remaining shareholder still becomes the sole owner of the business, but there will be no basis increase.

¶ 21,195   SPECIAL USE VALUATION METHOD

Special use valuation may be used for real property that consists of a family farm or a closely held business. This valuation replaces fair market value (highest and best use value) with a current use value. The maximum amount by which the value of qualifying property can be reduced under the special use valuation provision is $750,000 (this amount will be indexed annually for inflation after 1998). In order to use special use valuation, at least 50 percent of the adjusted estate must consist of real or personal property used as a farm or in a closely held business of which at least 25 percent of the adjusted estate is real property. Code Sec. 2032A.

> *Example 21.29.* If the estate of a decedent consists of qualifying real property valued at $1,500,000 on the basis of its "highest and best" use, and the property's value under the special use valuation provision is $600,000, the gross estate is reduced by only $750,000 in 1998 (although the difference in value is $900,000, the maximum reduction allowed is $750,000).

The benefit of the discount under the special use valuation procedure is available only if the following conditions are satisfied:

1. Actual use results in less value than the "best" possible use, e.g., land is worth less as a farm than as a subdivision to be developed as a residential neighborhood.

2. The actual use, referred to as "qualifying use," has been carried on by the decedent or a family member as the owner for at least five of the last eight years prior to death.

3. A qualified heir must be a member of the decedent's family and is liable for the estate tax saved if the heir disposes of the property or converts it to nonqualifying use within 10 years, unless the heir dies.

Since the lower estate tax value becomes the income tax basis, the basis may be stepped up if the tax is recaptured. Code Sec. 1016(c).

For a more detailed discussion of special use valuation, see ¶ 23,601.

Deductions from the Gross Estate

¶ 21,201 EXPENSES, DEBTS, AND LOSSES

All deductions are subtracted from the gross estate. The marital and charitable deductions are unique and are discussed separately below. The main "expense" deductions are funeral and administration expenses, debts (including unpaid taxes and interest), and casualty losses.

Funeral Expenses

Funeral expenses are never deductible for income tax purposes. However, they are deductible from the gross estate to the extent allowable under local law even if they go beyond "necessary." The expenses may be incurred in the U.S. or abroad. Reg. § 20.2053-1(a)(1).

Administration Expenses

Administration expenses, such as fees paid to the executor, lawyer, accountant, and appraisers, and certain interest expenses must meet two tests to be deductible:

1. The expenses must be "allowable by the law of the jurisdiction."
2. The expenses must be "actually and necessarily incurred in the administration of the decedent's estate; that is, in the collection of assets, payment of debts, and distribution of property to the persons entitled to it." Reg. § 20.2053-3(a).

Thus, the expenses must be allowable and necessary. Expenses incurred for the convenience of a beneficiary are disallowed, e.g., selling expenses when a house could have been deeded to a beneficiary rather than sold.

Debts

All enforceable claims against the estate are deductible if paid. This includes accrued interest up to the date of death and unpaid taxes of all kinds, such as income, property, and gift taxes, but not the estate tax itself. Reg. § 20.2053-6. The property tax is deductible to the extent the real property is includible in the gross estate. Nonrecourse debts and mortgages are deductible only to the extent of estate tax value. Liabilities must have been incurred for full consideration to avoid collusion between family members, e.g., IOUs given as presents to friends and relatives are *not* deductible even if enforceable and paid.

Example 21.30. When Gertrude London died, she owed unpaid federal, state, and local income taxes, gift taxes on deathbed gifts, and property taxes on her home. In addition, substantial estate taxes were due, as well as excise taxes on excess retirement accumulation. Except for the estate taxes, all of the other unpaid taxes are deductible as debts of the estate, be they federal, state, or local.

Claims Against the Estate

Probate estate assets. Expenses and debts relating to assets subject to claims are deductible regardless of how late they are paid. A deduction is allowed prior to payment as long as the amount "is ascertainable, with reasonable certainty, and will be paid." However, the sum of the deductions may not exceed the estate value of the probate estate unless paid by the due date of the estate tax return. Code Sec. 2053(c)(1) and (2); Reg. § 20.2053-1(b)(3).

Nonprobate assets. Deductions that relate to nonprobate assets (i.e., assets included in the gross estate solely for tax purposes) are allowable as long as they are paid within the statute of limitations (i.e., within three years after the due date of the return). There is no limitation as to amount, and estimates may be used. If actual expenses differ from the estimated deduction used, an amended estate tax return must be filed.

Casualty Losses

Losses from sudden casualties, such as fire, flood, shipwreck, or theft, are deductible if sustained by the estate. Code Sec. 2054. If sustained prior to death, they are deductible on the decedent's final

Form 1040 and, if sustained after distribution, they are deductible by the beneficiary. Unlike the income tax treatment, the casualty deduction is not limited by a percentage or dollar floor, and the deduction is based on the estate tax value. As is the case for income tax purposes, any loss must be reduced to the extent compensated for by insurance or otherwise. If alternate valuation is used and a casualty loss has been incurred, no deduction is allowed if the reduced value is reported as the estate value.

Allocation of Deductions on Returns

Administration expenses and casualty losses may be deducted either on Form 1041, the fiduciary income tax return of the estate or trust, *or* on Form 706, the estate tax return. The decision may be made on an item-by-item basis or an allocation may be made for individual items. Reg. § 1.642(g)-2.

Theoretically, expenses should be shifted until the marginal estate tax rate equals that of the income tax. Due to the increased applicable credit amount and the unlimited marital deduction, the trend is toward using administration expenses and losses as income tax deductions, thus reducing "distributable net income" (DNI). Section 265, which bars income tax deductions for expenses incurred to purchase or carry tax-exempt municipal bonds, does not apply to the estate deduction.

The decision as to where to deduct will have ripple effects on the charitable and marital deductions, and on the trust income beneficiaries and remaindermen, and may affect the applicability of death tax redemptions, installment payments of estate tax, and special use valuation.

¶ 21,217 MARITAL DEDUCTION

The marital deduction is available in computing the taxable estate of a citizen or resident of the United States. It is allowed where any part of a deceased person's estate passes or has passed to the surviving spouse. The property so passing is deductible in computing the taxable estate to the extent that it is includible in the gross estate. Code Sec. 2056.

The marital deduction is not available for estates of nonresident noncitizens unless the individual was a resident of a country that had entered into a treaty with the United States permitting the deduction. However, although property passing to a surviving spouse who is not a U.S. citizen is generally ineligible for the estate tax marital deduction, the marital deduction will be allowed for estate and gift tax purposes with respect to a nonresident alien whose spouse is a U.S. citizen.

There is no monetary ceiling on the estate tax marital deduction. Thus, unlimited amounts of property, except for certain terminable interests (such as life estates, terms for years, annuities, etc.), can be transferred between spouses free of estate taxes.

Passing of Property to Surviving Spouse

The person receiving the decedent's property for which a marital deduction is claimed must qualify as a surviving spouse at the date of the decedent's death. A legal separation that has not terminated the marriage at the time of death does not change the status of the surviving spouse. If an interest in property passes from the decedent to a person who was a spouse but is not married to the decedent at the time of death, the interest is not considered as passing to the surviving spouse.

For purposes of the marital deduction, an interest in property is considered as *passing* from the decedent to a spouse only if the surviving spouse can receive or has received the property interest in the following circumstances:

1. Heir, devisee, or legatee

2. Surviving joint tenant

3. Beneficiary of life insurance

4. Certain gifts within three years of death

5. Widow's support allowance during probate

6. Election against the will (the statutory share in lieu of dower)

7. Beneficiary of a lapse, release, or exercise of a general power of appointment, etc. (Code Sec. 2056(c))

Disclaimers by other beneficiaries will often lead to additional amounts passing to the surviving spouse. Only the net value of the property after deducting any encumbrance thereon qualifies.

Terminable Interests

To qualify for the marital deduction, it is not sufficient that property passes to the surviving spouse. The interest must also be nonterminable. A "terminable" interest is one that meets three requirements:

1. It may lapse, expire, or terminate with the passage of time or upon the happening or nonhappening of a contingency. However, the bequest may be conditional on survival for up to six months.

2. An interest passes or has passed by gift to a third party.

3. Such third party may possess or enjoy any part of the property after the surviving spouse's interest terminates.

Property interests meeting these tests, and therefore failing to qualify for the marital deduction, include term interests, life estates, and certain annuities. The rules make it more likely that the property does not escape estate taxation in both estates. Code Sec. 2056(b)(1) and (3).

Example 21.31. G dies, leaving his wife, W, the income from property for life, whereupon the property itself passes to the grandchildren. The life interest does *not* qualify for the marital deduction.

Example 21.32. G leaves the property to his mother for life, then to W. The remainder does qualify for the deduction.

Example 21.33. G leaves real estate to W and son as tenants in common. W's interest is deductible, since even if W dies before the son, her individual half passes from her by will or the laws of intestate succession.

Example 21.34. G dies, leaving W a life interest in his stock portfolio, but it goes to his children should she remarry. If she does not remarry, she can will the stocks to anyone. No marital deduction is available, due to the condition.

Example 21.35. G purchased a joint and survivorship annuity providing for monthly payments to G for life, and then to W should she survive. Upon G's death, the value of W's annuity is included in his estate and a marital deduction is allowed. Although W's interest expires upon her death, G left her all he had and no other person may possess or enjoy the property after W's death. Code Sec. 2056(b)(6).

Minimum Required Interest of Surviving Spouse

The spouse does not have to be given outright ownership of property to qualify for the marital deduction. A life interest plus a general power of appointment will suffice, or specifically:

1. The surviving spouse must be entitled to all income from the property for life to be paid at least annually.

2. The surviving spouse must have a general power of appointment over the whole property to be exercised alone and in all events. Such power can be exercisable either during life and/or by will. The holder of a general power is treated as the owner of the property so that the gift or estate tax cannot be avoided. Code Sec. 2056(b)(5).

The marital bequest is a function of taxes, propensity to consume, love and affection, degree of confidence in the spouse, their relative ages and health, their respective wealth, number of children, and so on.

Qualified Terminable Interest Property (QTIP)

An election exists to convert a terminable interest, a life estate, into nonterminable property eligible for the marital deduction for either gift or estate tax purposes. Code Secs. 2056(b)(7) and 2523(f). The election is made by the donor for lifetime transfers and by the executor for testamentary transfers. To qualify as "qualified terminable interest property," known in the trade as a QTIP trust, two main requirements must be met:

1. *All* income must be distributed at least annually to the donee spouse (the trust must be *simple*).

2. No one can have a power to appoint any portion of the principal or income to anyone other than the spouse during the spouse's lifetime.

The result of the election is that the marital deduction is allowed to the donor or the donor's estate for the full market value of the property in the trust, regardless of to whom the remainder goes (e.g., the children, charity, etc.). This benefit carries a price tag; the full value at the death of the spouse is included in the gross estate (or is subject to gift tax if any portion of the spouse's interest is disposed of earlier). Code Secs. 2044 and 2519.

Example 21.36. When Frederick died, he left $1 million in trust to his wife, Cynthia, all income (except capital gains) to be distributed to her annually for her life, the remainder to the local state university. If his executor did not make the QTIP election, no marital deduction is allowed, but the trust is not subject to transfer taxes in Cynthia's estate. If the QTIP election is made:

1. Frederick's estate receives a $1 million marital deduction, but no charitable deduction.

2. If, on Cynthia's death, there is $2 million in the trust, the full value is includible in her estate, but an offsetting charitable deduction is available.

The QTIP election is perhaps most useful when a wealthy individual wishes to provide for a second spouse for life, but wishes to ensure that the children from the previous marriage will receive the principal. It should be noted that the spouse may be granted any number of powers over the principal. The income interest is merely a minimum. Also, a surviving spouse never has to accept an income interest, but may insist on a statutory share, typically one-third of the net probate estate.

For the estates of decedents dying after August 5, 1997, Code Sec. 2056(b)(7)(C) clarifies that a nonparticipant spouse's survivorship interest in a participant spouse's qualified plan, IRA, or SEP that is attributable to community property laws may qualify for qualified terminable interest property treatment if the nonparticipant spouse predeceases the participant spouse.

¶ 21,225   CHARITABLE CONTRIBUTIONS

The income tax aspects of charitable gifts are outside the scope of this discussion. In comparison, the estate tax rules are more liberal because:

1. The estate tax value of *all* charitable gifts included in the gross estate is deductible in full without percentage limitations.

2. Whether the testator wills property to a private foundation or a public charity, 100 percent of the value is deductible for estate tax purposes. (The income tax deduction is often limited to basis and to 30 or 50 percent of adjusted gross income.)

3. Charitable contributions made before death do double duty. They are deductible for income tax purposes. They are not includible in the gross estate.

The combined tax savings may approach 95 percent of the value gifted.

Charitable Remainder Trusts

A donor may wish to make a charitable contribution now, but:

1. The donor may be unwilling to give up current income and/or control.

2. The donor may want a spouse and/or children to enjoy the property after the donor's death.

3. The donor may wish to obtain a current income tax deduction as well as an estate tax deduction.

The solution is a gift of a *remainder* to charity. A life estate plus a remainder equals 100 percent of the property. Thus, a gift of a remainder constitutes a transfer of property subject to the retention of the life estate. In other words, there is a *present* gift, but of a *future* interest.

If the transfer is done right, the donor receives a current deduction for the value of the remainder. The deduction equals the value of the property, less the present value of the interest retained, based on mortality tables. Upon the donor's death, the full value is included because of the retained life estate, but the full value is then subtracted out as a charitable deduction.

The retained interest can take several forms: (1) term of years (e.g., 20 years, the maximum), (2) life estate for the life of the donor, (3) life estate for the joint lives of the donor and spouse, or (4) one or more life estates for the life or lives of any other person (e.g., the donor's parents or children).

There are three types of eligible charitable remainder trusts: (1) pooled income funds, (2) charitable remainder annuity trusts, and (3) charitable remainder unitrusts. Code Sec. 2055(e)(2)(A).

Pooled Income Funds. The principal difference between a pooled income fund and a charitable remainder unitrust or annuity trust is that the donor or other beneficiary of a pooled income fund is entitled only to the income actually earned by the fund, rather than to a fixed amount of fixed percentage of its value. Code Sec. 642(c)(5). Pooled income funds can be described as follows:

1. Many donors irrevocably transfer remainder interests for the use of charity, retaining a life interest for one or more beneficiaries.

2. The properties are "pooled" (i.e., commingled).

3. No tax-exempt bonds are allowed.

4. The fund is managed by the charitable organization itself, and no grantor or beneficiary can be a trustee.

5. The trust fund owns only properties transferred under (1).

6. Each beneficiary receives a share of the income earned by the trust.

For purposes of determining the amount of any charitable contribution allowable by reason of a transfer of property to a pooled fund, the value of the income interest is determined using the highest rate of return earned by the fund for any of the three taxable years immediately preceding the taxable year of the fund in which the transfer is made and the applicable mortality table (or six percent per year in the case of a fund in existence less than three taxable years).

Charitable Remainder Annuity Trusts (CRATs). A charitable remainder annuity trust is a trust from which a specified sum or percentage (not less than five percent of the initial fair market value of all the assets actually placed in trust) is to be paid annually to one or more named individuals as income beneficiaries. For transfers in trust occurring after June 18, 1997, the annual payout cannot exceed 50 percent of the initial fair market value of the trust's assets. For transfers in trust occurring after July 28, 1997, the value of the remainder interest must be a least 10 percent of the initial fair market value of all property placed in the trust. (However, under a special rule, the minimum 10 percent rule will not apply to transfers in trust under the terms of a will or other testamentary instrument executed on or before July 28, 1997, if the decedent (1) dies before January 1, 1999, without having republished the will or amending it by codicil or otherwise or (2) was on July 28, 1997, under a mental disability to change the disposition of the property and did not regain competency before dying.) Each one of these beneficiaries must be living at the creation of the trust and payments to them must terminate not later than 20 years after creation or at their deaths. When payments terminate, the remainder goes to the charitable organization. Code Sec. 664.

> *Example 21.37.* Clive Barker died, leaving $100,000 in trust. If his surviving spouse, Anna, were to receive $6,000 a year for 15 years ($90,000), with the remainder to go to charity, this would be a charitable remainder annuity trust.

The beneficiary is taxed under the trust conduit rules (i.e., the beneficiary has ordinary income, capital gains, tax-free income, and return of capital) as the case may be. The trustee will furnish information on the tax status of the receipts.

Charitable Remainder Unitrusts (CRUTs). A charitable remainder unitrust is similar to an annuity trust, except that, rather than receiving a fixed amount each year, the beneficiaries receive a fixed percentage, not less than five percent (for the beneficiaries as a group) of the net fair market value of the assets valued annually. Thus, the amount received will fluctuate from year to year.

In the case of charitable remainder unitrusts, the annual payout cannot exceed 50 percent of the fair market value of the trust assets determined annually. Also, the 10 percent rule applies with respect to each contribution of property to the trust (note that additional deductible gifts may be made to a charitable remainder unitrust under Reg. § 1.664-3(b)).

> *Example 21.38.* Decedent left $100,000 in trust for his children for life, with the remainder going to charity. The remainder does

not qualify for a charitable deduction unless the trust is a unitrust or an annuity trust.

Example 21.39. Decedent left $100,000 in trust for his son for life with a minimum guarantee of five percent of the value of corpus per year, with the remainder going to charity. A deduction is available for the remainder since the trust is a charitable remainder unitrust.

Example 21.40. Same as Example 21.39, except that the son has the power to invade corpus for his "welfare." No deduction is allowed since the son may easily deplete the principal, cutting off the charitable interest.

Example 21.41. Same as Example 21.40, except that the son dies after three months. A deduction is permitted the grantor's estate because the charity receives the full $100,000. The son's estate includes the property since he had a general power of appointment, but an offsetting charitable deduction is allowed in his estate as well. Code Sec. 2055(a) and (b).

According to the Senate Committee Report, trusts failing to meet the requirements of the 50 percent test will be treated as complex trusts rather than charitable remainder trusts, and, as a result, all of their income will be taxed to the beneficiaries of the trust. However, there are several special provisions designed to provide relief for trusts that fail to meet the 10 percent test.

TAX PLANNING POINTER

Here is a planning device for the dying and the aged: If a taxable estate is likely to exist and the individual's income tax bracket is high, *prepay all charitable bequests* mentioned in the will. The estate will not include them, and this has the same effect as a deduction, even if made on the deathbed. In addition, an income tax deduction (subject to some limitations) will result. If the income and estate tax brackets are 39.6 and 55 percent respectively, 95 percent of the value of the property can be saved in taxes.

In fact, if taxation is the only consideration, a lifetime charitable transfer is *always* preferable to a testamentary bequest.

A charitable contributions deduction is allowed for the fair market value of a charitable remainder interest in an annuity trust *or* a unitrust. The fair market value of the remainder interest of a charitable remainder annuity trust is the net fair market value of the property placed in trust less the present value of the annuity as computed by using special IRS valuation tables prescribed under Code Sec. 7520. Two actuarial factors are generally used in determining present value—a mortality component and an interest rate component. The mortality component is based on the life expectancy of a designated individual (or individuals). The interest rate component represents an assumed rate of return. The interest rate component of the IRS valuation tables is based on a rate that is 120 percent of the applicable federal midterm rate (AFR) compounded annually (rounded to the nearest two-tenths of one percent), adjusted monthly. Valuation of any interest for term of years or life, any annuity, or any remainder or reversionary interest as of May 1, 1989, requires the use of these IRS tables. The AFR is announced by the IRS monthly in a news release and published in a revenue ruling.

¶ 21,255   DISCLAIMERS

No one has to accept an unwanted gift or bequest. A qualified disclaimer within nine months leads to the property being treated as if it were never transferred. Sometimes substantial savings can result from a disclaimer. Following are some examples:

1. If the surviving spouse is left property, he or she may wish to disclaim part of the property. This could save estate taxes in the estate and the disclaimed portion would pass directly to the other beneficiaries, typically children or grandchildren. The disclaimer should be made only if the surviving spouse would not consume the excess for living expenses in any event.

    Example 21.42. John Jamieson leaves his entire estate of $1,500,000 to his spouse. There is no estate tax because of the marital deduction. However, when his wife dies, the $1,500,000 will be included in her estate and the excess above $625,000 (for 1998) will be taxed. If the wife were to disclaim $625,000, there would still be no tax to John's estate and his wife would only include $875,000 in her estate upon death.

2. A third party, such as a child, may wish to disclaim a bequest to favor the surviving parent so as to increase the marital deduction and save estate taxes immediately. The disclaimer may also be prompted by a concern for the parent's financial needs and the hope that the property will eventually pass to the child anyway, either through a systematic gift program or by will.

3. A beneficiary may be financially secure and disclaim to benefit the residuary legatee without any gift tax liability.

4. If someone is given a general power of appointment and does not intend to exercise it, it makes sense for the donee to disclaim it to avoid estate tax in the donee's own estate if the donee dies possessing the power.

5. Someone receiving an income interest may wish to disclaim it to favor a lower tax bracket family member.

6. If a disclaimed interest will go to charity and the charity is one of the beneficiary's favorites, the beneficiary may disclaim the interest and reduce estate taxes. But the estate tax savings

must be compared with the income tax savings resulting from acceptance plus contribution.

To qualify:

1. The disclaimer must be made in writing.

2. The disclaimer must be made within nine months of the initial transfer, including the creation of a joint tenancy, or nine months after the beneficiary reaches age 21.

3. The disclaimer must be irrevocable and unqualified.

4. The disclaimant must not have accepted the bequest or any benefits from it initially.

5. The disclaimant cannot direct to whom the disclaimed property will pass. Code Secs. 2046 and 2518.

Example 21.43. Many years before he died, William Stone purchased numerous securities and put them in a joint tenancy with his wife, Wilma. As soon as William died, Wilma disclaimed the one-half undivided interest in the securities (William's half) that she acquired upon William's death. Since the disclaimer was made more than nine months after the initial transfer (the creation of the joint tenancy), it is too late to be a "qualified" disclaimer. Thus, the property is still treated as if transferred to Wilma upon William's death. In addition, Wilma has made a gift for gift tax purposes to the new recipient if the disclaimer is effective to make a transfer to the residuary legatee or devisee.

TAX BLUNDER

Oscar purchased a $250,000 life insurance policy on his own life. To save estate taxes in his estate, he transferred all rights in the policy to Sylvia, his wife. Many years later, Sylvia predeceased him, leaving him "everything she owned." Since this included the policy, Oscar was back to square one. Older, but wiser, he transferred the policy to an irrevocable trust with his children and grandchildren as beneficiaries. However, Oscar died two years later and the full proceeds of $250,000 were added to his gross estate. Also, no marital deduction was available, leading to a sizeable estate tax. The proceeds of the insurance were not available to pay the tax, being held in trust with income to the children and a remainder to the grandchildren.

The above problem could have been easily avoided by using an insurance trust initially, bypassing both Sylvia's and Oscar's estates.

Federal Gift Tax

¶ 21,301   DEFINITION OF TRANSFERS BY GIFT

A federal gift tax is imposed on the right to transfer property from one person to another for less than full and adequate consideration. The transferor is called the donor and the transferee the donee. Any gift tax due as a result of a taxable gift is a liability of the donor. Code Sec. 2502(d). In the event the donor fails to pay the tax when it is due, the donee can be held liable for the tax to the extent of the value of the property received. Code Sec. 6324(b). The gift tax is an excise tax on the transfer, and is not a tax on the subject of the gift. Transfers by gift are defined in Reg. § 25.2511-1(a) as follows:

> The gift tax applies to a transfer by way of gift whether the transfer is in trust or otherwise, whether the gift is direct or indirect, and whether the property is real or personal, tangible or intangible. For example, a taxable transfer may be effected by the creation of a trust, the forgiving of a debt, the assignment of a judgment, the assignment of the benefits of an insurance policy, or the transfer of cash, certificates of deposit, or federal, state, or municipal bonds.

In accordance with the above definition, all transactions whereby property or property rights or interests are gratuitously passed or conferred upon another constitute a transfer subject to the gift tax, regardless of the method or device employed to effect the transfer. The gift tax is imposed on the transfer of property, not on the performance of services. Code Sec. 2501(a)(1). Accordingly, a person who renders services for another without being compensated has not made a gift subject to the gift tax.

Time of Gift

A gift is complete as to property in which the donor has ceased to have dominion and control and has no power to change disposition of the property for the donor's own benefit or for the benefit of another, as previously cited. Reg. § 25.2511-2(b). The effective date occurs at the time the donor can no longer revoke the gift, or revert the beneficial title to the property to the donor, or change the interest of the designated beneficiaries. Rev. Rul. 67-396, 1967-2 CB 351. Several examples of completed transfers are listed below:

1. The donor completes a legal check or note which constitutes a promise to pay. The gift is not complete until a check or note is paid or negotiated for value to a third person. Rev. Rul. 67-396.

2. The donor delivers a stock certificate, properly endorsed, either to the donee or to the donee's agent; the gift is complete for federal gift tax purposes on the date of delivery. Reg. § 25.2511-2(h). If, however, the donor delivers a stock certificate, properly endorsed, to either his broker or the issuing corporation with directions for transfer to a donee, the gift is not complete until the stock is transferred on the corporation's books. Rev. Rul. 54-135, 1954-1 CB 205.

3. The donor transfers property, in trust, to himself as trustee for the benefit of specific named beneficiaries. The donor has made a complete gift at the time of delivery if he has retained fiduciary powers only. Reg. § 25.2511-2(g).

4. The donor delivers his interest in a U.S. Savings Bond (Series E) to the registered co-owner. The gift is not complete until the bond is reissued in the donee co-owner's name alone. *E.G.*

Chandler, 73-1 USTC ¶ 12,902, 410 U.S. 257, 93 S.Ct. 880 (1973).

¶ 21,315 BASIS OF PROPERTY TRANSFERRED BY GIFT

Generally, the income tax basis of property transferred by a gift is the same as the basis in the hands of the transferor. In certain instances, however, the basis of property acquired by gift may depend on whether the donee sells the property for a gain or loss and when the gift was made.

1. If the gift was made prior to 1921, the donee's basis for gain or loss is the fair market value of the property on the date of the gift. Code Sec. 1015(c).

2. If the gift was made after 1920 and prior to 1977, the donee's basis for gain is the donor's adjusted basis plus any gift tax paid on the transfer (but not to exceed fair market value on date of the gift). The basis for loss is the lower of the basis for gain or the fair market value of the property on the date of the gift. Code Sec. 1015(a) and (d)(1).

3. If the gift was made after 1976, the donee's basis for gain is the donor's adjusted basis plus only the gift tax attributable to the appreciation of the property to the point of the gift (but not to exceed the fair market value of the property on the date of the gift). Under Code Sec. 2503(b), to determine the amount of gift tax on the appreciation to be added to the donor's basis, the fair market value of the gift is reduced by the donor's basis and divided by the fair market value of the gift reduced by the annual exclusion. The basis for loss is the lower of the basis for gain or the fair market value of the property on the date of the gift. Code Sec. 1015(a) and (d)(6).

How to Apply the Basis Rules

The above rules are illustrated in the following examples:

Example 21.44. In 1920, A transferred realty by a gift to create an irrevocable inter vivos trust. The property cost A $10,000 and was worth $25,000 on the date of the gift. The income tax basis to the trust for gain or loss is $25,000.

Example 21.45. In 1975, B transferred realty by a gift to create an irrevocable inter vivos trust. The stock cost B $15,000 and had a fair market value of $60,000 on the date of the gift. As a result the trust's basis for gain or loss is $23,000 ($15,000 (B's basis) + $8,000 (gift tax paid by B)). The trust does not have a different basis for loss since the fair market value of the property on the date of the gift (i.e., $60,000) is not lower than the basis for gain (i.e., $23,000).

Example 21.46. Assume the same facts as in Example 21.45, except that the gift occurred in 1998 (instead of 1975). The trust's income tax basis for gain is $22,200, determined as follows:

B's adjusted basis on the date of the gift	$15,000
Gift tax attributable to the $45,000 appreciation (($45,000/$50,000) × $8,000)	7,200
Trust's income tax basis for gain	$22,200

The trust's basis for loss would be $22,200, based on the same reasoning set forth in Example 21.45.

The effect of the rule provided in the Tax Reform Act of 1976 (as illustrated in Example 21.46) is to deny the donee (the trust) any increase in basis for gift tax attributable to the donor's adjusted basis. Incidentally, unless property with a fair market value of less than the donor's basis is expected to appreciate above the donor's basis prior to sale by the donee (the trust), it should not be used as gift property. In this case, to maximize the tax benefits, the donor should sell the property, recognize the tax loss, and transfer the proceeds by gift to the trust.

¶ 21,325 PRESENT v. FUTURE INTERESTS

An unrestricted right to the immediate use, possession, or enjoyment of property or the related income from the property (such as a life estate or term certain) is a present interest in the property. Reg. § 25.2503-3(b). A future interest may be defined as one which will come into being (i.e., the use, possession, or enjoyment) at some future date. As defined in the Regulations:

> Future interests is a legal term, and includes reversions, remainder, and other interests or estates, whether vested or contingent, and whether or not supported by a particular interest or estate, which are limited to commence in use, possession or enjoyment at some future date or time. The term has no reference to such contractual rights as exist in a bond, note, (though bearing no interest until maturity), or in a policy of life insurance, the obligations of which are to be discharged by payments in the future. But a future interest or interests in such contractual obligations may be created by the limitations contained in a trust to other instrument to transfer used in effecting a gift. Reg. Sec. 25.2503-3(a).

Consider carefully the following illustrations of present versus future interests.

Example 21.47. During the year, Ed O'Brien makes an outright cash gift of $10,000 to Dana Flanigan. This gift qualifies as a present interest.

Example 21.48. During the year, Ed transfers property in a trust with a life estate to Dana with income to be paid annually. The trust provides that upon Dana's death the remainder interest goes to Sara Flanigan. Ed has made two gifts: one to Dana of a life estate and one to Sara of a remainder interest. The life estate is a present interest, and the remainder is a future interest.

Example 21.49. Assume the same facts as in Example 21.48 except that the income from the trust does not have to be paid annually to Dana. At the trustee's discretion the income may be accumulated and added to the corpus. In this case the life estate does not qualify as a present interest. The mere possibility of the trustee accumulating the income renders the life estate a future interest. Reg. § 25.2503-3(c).

Concerning Example 21.49, if the life estate beneficiary's right to current income is contingent on obtaining the permission of a third party other than the trustee (including other beneficiaries), the life estate interest is deemed to be a future interest. *J.W. Blasdel*, 58 TC 1014, CCH Dec. 31,548 (1972), aff'd, 73-1 USTC ¶ 12,929, 478 F.2d 226 (CA-5 1973).

Notable Exceptions

There are some exceptions to the present versus future interest rules as set forth in this section. For example, the gift of a note, or bond, that yields no interest until maturity is a gift of a present interest, although the maturity and benefits are in the future. The same would be true for the gift of a life insurance policy or other similar contract right. T.D. 7238, 1973-1 CB 544. A major exception to the general rule relates to gifts to minors utilizing various vehicles so that the gifts will be deemed to be present interests. Excellent examples are *Crummey* trusts and gifts to minors, each of which is discussed below.

Crummey Trusts

A gift of the right to demand a portion of a trust corpus is a gift of a present interest, Rev. Rul. 80-261, 1980-2 CB 219, as long as the donee-beneficiary is aware of his or her right to make the demand. Rev. Rul. 81-7, 1981-1 CB 474. Typically, the beneficiary of such a trust (known as a *Crummey* trust, *D.C. Crummey* 68-2 USTC ¶ 12,541, 397 F.2d 82 (CA-9 1968)) is given the right to demand an amount of corpus equal to the annual gift tax exclusion. Because donors might not want the beneficiaries to be able to withdraw trust corpus up to the $10,000 annual exclusion available after 1981, the Economic Recovery Tax Act of 1981 provided a special transitional rule to limit the power to the old $3,000 exclusion in certain instances.

Gifts to Minors

No part of a transfer for the benefit of a minor will be considered future interest (which would not qualify for the annual exclusion) if the terms of the transfer meet the following conditions:

1. Both the property and its income may be expended by, or for the benefit of, the minor donee prior to the donee attaining the age of 21. To the extent not so expended, it will pass to the donee at that time.

2. In the event of the donee's death prior to reaching 21 years of age, the property and the income not expended will pass to the donee's estate or to persons appointed by the donee under the exercise of a general power of appointment.

A gift to a minor under a trust that confers on its beneficiary upon reaching age 21 the right to compel immediate distribution of the corpus by written notice to the trustee that is either (a) a continuing right or permits the trust to remain on its own terms or (b) a right for a limited period that, if not exercised, will permit the trust to continue on its own terms is not a gift of a future interest and qualifies for the annual gift tax exclusion under condition (1), above. Rev. Rul. 74-43, 1974-1 CB 285.

Exclusions

¶ 21,341 GENERAL CONSIDERATIONS

Annual Exclusion

For 1998, the first $10,000 given to any person during a calendar year is excluded in computing taxable gifts, if the gift constitutes a "present interest" in the gifted property. After 1998, the $10,000 per year exclusion for gifts will be indexed annually for inflation.

A distinction must be made between a present and future interest to assure the availability of the annual donee exclusion. The ostensible reason for denying the annual exclusion for gifts of future interests was the difficulty associated with the determining the number of eventual donees and the value of their respective gifts. H.R. Rep. No. 708, 72d Cong., 1st Sess. 29 (1932), reprinted in 1939-1 CB (Part 2) 457, 478; S. Rep. No. 665, 72d Cong., 1st Sess. 41 (1932), reprinted in 1939-1 CB (Part 2) 496, 526.

Unlimited Donee Opportunities

There is no limit on the number of donees. The donor can claim a $10,000 annual exclusion for each present interest. Only the first $10,000 ($20,000 if splitting is elected as discussed in the next section of this chapter) given to each donee may be excluded. If the donor's gifts of present interests to each donee during a calendar year do not exceed $10,000, the gifts do not have to be reported on a gift tax return. Code Sec. 6019(a). Gifts exempted from taxation under the $10,000 annual donee exclusion are not included in the tax base for the purposes of computing estate taxes. Only adjusted taxable gifts are includible in the computation, and adjusted taxable gifts are limited to taxable gifts.

Gift-Splitting

A donor's spouse may consent to treatment as the donor of one-half of any taxable gift made to a third person. Such a consent to "gift-split" allows a married couple to use two annual per-donee exclusions and two unified credits with respect to a single gift.

Example 21.50. In 1998, John Smith gives $635,000 in cash to his daughter. He gets one $10,000 annual exclusion, and so he makes a $625,000 taxable gift. He uses up his previously unused unified credit and owes no gift tax. However, if Sara Smith (John's wife) consents to gift-split, John and Sara will get two $10,000 annual exclusions, or $20,000, and can use two unified credits.

A donor can gift-split only if he or she is a United States person (a citizen or a resident alien) and is married to a United States person at the time the gift is made. Individuals are married for gift-splitting purposes, only if they are married at the time the gift is made.

> **Example 21.51.** H makes a taxable gift to his son, S, on January 1, 1998. On February 17, 1998, his divorce from W is final. H and W may gift-split as long as neither remarry during the calendar year. Code Sec. 2513(a)(1).

Both the donor and the donor's spouse must consent to gift-split. The consent applies to all gifts either spouse makes during the calendar year in which they make the consent. Code Sec. 2513(a)(2). The consent does not apply, however, to any taxable gifts made by either spouse when they were not married to each other or when they were not both U.S. citizens or resident aliens. Reg. § 25.2513-1(b).

The consent to split gifts applies to all gifts made during the calendar year by either spouse individually and by both spouses jointly. For example, Henry and Velma Holt consent to gift-split on a gift Velma made in January 1998. This consent also applies to any gifts Henry or Velma made during 1998 alone or jointly. Reg. § 25.2513-1(b)(5).

In summary, gift-splitting has the following advantages:

1. Two annual exclusions per donee are available instead of one.

2. Any gap between the sizes of the spouses' estates can be narrowed because only one-half of the gifts will come back as "adjusted taxable gifts" in the estate tax return of the contributing spouse.

3. The noncontributing spouse may be in a lower gift tax bracket or have an unused applicable credit amount. Because two sets of applicable credit amounts are available, no gift tax may be presently payable.

Unlimited Educational and Medical Expense Exclusion

An unlimited gift tax exclusion is available for amounts paid on behalf of a donee directly to an educational organization, provided that such amounts constitute tuition payments. In addition, amounts paid to health care providers for medical services on behalf of a donee qualify for an unlimited exclusion under this section. The exclusions for qualifying educational expenses and medical expenses are available without regard to the relationship between the donor and the donee and are available in addition to the annual exclusion Code Sec. 2503(e).

Qualifying medical expenses, for the purposes of this exclusion, are defined by reference to Code Sec. 213 (an income tax provision). The exclusion is not available to the extent the amounts paid are reimbursed by insurance.

¶ 21,345 MARITAL DEDUCTION

Beginning in 1982, a donor is allowed an unlimited marital deduction for lifetime gifts of separate and/or community property to his or her spouse. Code Sec. 2523(a). But the gift tax marital deduction is not permitted for a gift of a life estate or other terminable interest. An exception to the terminable interest rule for the gift tax marital deduction is qualified terminable interest property (QTIP). Code Sec. 2523(c).

QTIP Provisions

As previously mentioned, the QTIP provisions are an exception to the terminable interest rule. Pursuant to Code Sec. 2523(e), a property interest, whether or not in trust, qualifies for the marital deduction when the following requirements are adhered to:

1. The donee spouse is entitled for life to all of the income from the property interest.

2. Such income is payable annually or at more frequent intervals.

3. The donee spouse has the power, exercisable in favor of the donee or the donee's estate, to appoint the property interest.

4. Such power is exercisable by the donee spouse alone and (whether exercisable by will or during life) is exercisable in all events.

5. No part of the property interest is subject to a power in any other person to appoint any part to any person other than the surviving spouse.

Also, to have a qualifying terminable interest under Code Sec. 2523(t), the donee spouse must be entitled to receive all the income from the property at least annually. Furthermore, no person may be able to appoint the property during the spouse's lifetime to anyone other than the spouse. When the QTIP election is made by the donor, there will not be any gift tax at that juncture. However, when the donee spouse disposes of his or her QTIP interest, either during his or her lifetime or at death, the property will be subject to gift or estate tax.

> *Example 21.52.* In 1998, Tony Owens creates a trust which is funded with $500,000 of Georgia Power bonds. Pursuant to the trust instrument, Donna Owens is to receive the income from the trust on an annual basis for her life. Upon Donna's death, the principal of the trust is to pass to their children. If Tony elects QTIP treatment, the interest passing to Donna will qualify for the marital deduction. The election is made on the gift tax return (Form 709, United States Gift (and Generation-Skipping Transfer) Tax Return) filed for the calendar year in which the donor transferred the interest. It should be noted that the fair market value of the QTIP property will be included in the gross estate of Donna when she dies.

Alien Spouses

An alien spouse of a U.S. citizen is generally not eligible for the unlimited gift tax marital deduction. However, the first $100,000 of gifts per year to an alien spouse will not be taxed. Code Sec. 2523(i). Also, it should be emphasized that the $100,000 annual exclusion for transfers by gift to a non-citizen spouse is only allowed for transfers that would meet the marital deduction test if the donee were a U.S. citizen. Therefore, a gift in trust would have to meet the exceptions to the terminable interest rule in order to qualify for the annual exclusion.

Divorce and Separation

Transfers to a spouse pursuant to a written agreement in connection with divorce are free of gift tax if the transfers are for the transferee's marital or property rights or for child support. Code Sec. 2516. This provision goes beyond the marital deduction since it covers terminable transfers and transfers after the parties are no longer married.

This special provision has no application to prenuptial agreements. When the parties transfer property pursuant to an agreement signed prior to marriage, the marital deduction is available under the general rule. Generally, divorce settlements are not treated as sales for income tax purposes, but are tax free. Code Sec. 1041.

¶ 21,355 CHARITABLE DEDUCTION

In the case of a donor who was a resident or a citizen of the United States at the time the gifts were made, there is an allowable charitable deduction for gifts included in the "total amount of gifts" made by the donor during the calendar year to or for the use of:

1. The United States, any State, Territory, or any political subdivision thereof, or the District of Columbia, for exclusively public purposes.

2. Any corporation, trust, community chest, fund or foundation organized and operated exclusively for religious, charitable, scientific, literary, or educational purposes, including the encouragement of art and the prevention of cruelty to children and animals, if no part of the net earnings of the organization inures to the benefit of any private shareholder or individual, if no substantial part of its activities is engaging in propaganda, or otherwise attempting to influence legislation, and if it does not participate in, or intervene in (including the publishing or distributing of statements), any political campaign on behalf of any candidate for public office.

3. A fraternal society, order, or association, operating under the lodge system, provided the gifts are to be used by the society, order, or association exclusively for one or more of the purposes set forth in subparagraph (2) of this paragraph.

4. Any post or organization of war veterans or auxiliary unit or society thereof, if organized in the United States or any of its possessions, and if no part of its net earnings inures to the benefit of any private shareholder or individual. Reg. § 25.2522(a)-1(a).

The charitable deduction is not limited to gifts for use within the United States, or to gifts to or for the use of domestic corporations, trusts, community chests, funds, or foundations, or fraternal societies, orders, or associations operating under the lodge system.

Nonresident aliens are allowed a charitable deduction for gifts that relate primarily to domestic charities and for gifts to be used in the United States. Code Sec. 2522(b).

Since the Internal Revenue Code provides that the gift to a charity is a deduction and not an exclusion, the amount of the charitable gift must be reported on a gift tax return if the gift exceeds the amount of the annual exclusion. However, after August 5, 1997, a donor who makes a gift to charity in excess of the annual gift tax exclusion is not required to file a gift tax return if the entire value of the donated property qualifies for a gift tax charitable deduction. This treatment extends to contributions of qualified conservation easements under Code Sec. 2522(d). The amount of the charitable deduction will first be reduced by the annual exclusion (if the interest is a present interest) and the remainder will be deducted as a charitable deduction. Also, charitable deductions are allowed for split interests when they qualify as annuity trusts, unitrusts, or pooled income funds.

> *Example 21.53.* On March 4, 1998, John Agor transferred Home Depot stock with a basis of $10,000 and market value of $30,000 to Old Dominion University. John had held the stock for two years at the time of the transfer. The full $30,000 is allowed to be taken on the gift tax return, but for income tax purposes, the deduction is limited to 30 percent of AGI subject to a five-year carryover. Specifically, the gift tax return would depict the gift as follows:

Gross gift		$30,000
Less: Annual exclusion	$10,000	
Charitable deduction	20,000	30,000
Taxable gift		$ 0

¶ 21,365   VALUATION OF GIFTS

Valuing gross gifts is the major gift tax problem since the value determines the amount that will be subject to gift tax. The gift tax regulations differ in no substantial respect from the corresponding estate tax regulations. All property is valued at fair market value at the time the gift is considered completed. Fair market value of property is the price at which such property would change hands between a willing buyer and a willing seller, neither being under any compulsion to buy or to sell, and both having reasonable knowledge of relevant facts.

Most of the concepts discussed earlier in this chapter concerning estate tax are also applicable to gift taxes. However, there is no alternative valuation date for gift tax as there is for estate taxes. Also, the special valuation methods are only available to estates.

¶ 21,375   NONTAXABLE TRANSFERS

Gratuitous transfers *not* subject to gift tax include:

1. Transfers to political organizations (Code Sec. 2501(a)(5)), but any appreciation is gross income to the donor (Code Sec. 84).

2. Transfers made for a business purpose (e.g., contributions to the capital of a corporation or partnership).

3. Revocable transfers, including the creation of revocable trusts, joint bank and brokerage accounts, and joint U.S. savings bonds.

4. Bargain purchases, if in arm's-length transactions.

5. Donation of services.

6. Support payments within the standard of living of the family. (Note: the support obligation to a child generally ceases on age 18 or earlier emancipation.)

7. Qualified disclaimers (in writing, within nine months). Code Sec. 2518.

8. Employment-related "gifts," such as a year-end bonus, but these are gross income items.

Example 21.54. Two months before his death, Marvin Rose donated $5 million to a political campaign for mayor, an office sought by his best friend as candidate. The donation is not a gift for gift tax purposes. Furthermore, since there is no gift, there can be no adjusted taxable gift. Thus, the $5 million permanently escapes both gift and estate taxes. (However, no charitable deduction is allowed.)

¶ 21,385   CO-OWNERSHIPS OF PROPERTY

As a general rule, if property is purchased by co-tenants, any disproportional contribution results in a gift from the high to the low contributor.

Example 21.55. Mother and daughter purchase a building as equal joint tenants for $200,000. If the daughter pays only $40,000, $60,000 is received by gift since this is her "discount" on her half. If the building is financed so that only $40,000 is put down, $8,000 by the daughter, only $12,000 is a gift. As the mother pays off the mortgage, additional gifts are made to the extent of principal payments, but they would not exceed the annual exclusion.

Revocable joint tenancies do not result in a gift until one joint tenant withdraws in excess of the contribution. Examples include joint bank accounts and U.S. savings bonds.

¶ 21,395   POWERS OF APPOINTMENT

General powers of appointment were discussed earlier in this chapter. If someone possesses a general power of appointment and the power is exercised, released, or simply lapses during the holder's lifetime, there is a gift. Code Sec. 2514. Special powers are not taxable.

Example 21.56. G transfers property in trust to his wife, W, for life. W is also given the power to appoint the property to anyone in the world by gift or will. If W exercises the power in favor of anyone except herself, even an unrelated party, a taxable gift results.

Example 21.57. Same as Example 21.56, except W has the power to appoint the property to anyone *except* herself, her estate, or the creditors of either. She exercises the power in favor of her children and grandchildren. There is no gift.

Example 21.58. Same facts as Example 21.56, except that W needs G's consent to exercise the power. No gift tax will result because the power is reduced to a special power when the creator's consent is needed.

Example 21.59. G transfers property to W for life, the remainder to his children. W can appoint the property to anyone, but only with the consent of the children. An exercise of power is not taxable because the consent of an adverse party is required.

Example 21.60. G transfers an insurance policy on his life to W. If their child is the beneficiary, W has completed a gift of the proceeds to such child when G dies. At that time, W's powers over the policy lapses.

Powers limited to an ascertainable standard (e.g., for the health, education, maintenance, and support of the powerholder) and powers to appoint up to $5,000 or five percent of the property (whichever is greater) each year are only special powers. Code Sec. 2514(c)(1) and (3).

¶ 21,405   LIABILITY FOR TAX

The gift tax is levied on the gratuitous transfer of property during life. It may not be intuitively obvious, but an individual who gives away property may have to pay an excise tax for the privilege. Thus, the gift tax is payable by *the donor* as a toll charge for the fact that the property transferred will not be subject to estate taxes (in most cases). Small gifts are disregarded and marital and charitable deductions are available. If the gift tax remains unpaid, the donee is liable to the extent of the value of the gifted property. Code Sec. 6324(b). U.S. residents and citizens are liable for gift taxes on worldwide transfers, while nonresident aliens are liable only for taxes on transfers of U.S. property, such as U.S. real estate. Code Secs. 2501(a)(1) and 2511(a).

Only individuals are subject to gift tax. The identity of the transferee is irrelevant; it could be an individual, estate, trust, or corporation, U.S. or foreign.

Example 21.61. Richard O'Hara, U.S. citizen, sends $50,000 to the Irish government. Even though the donee is a foreign government the transfer reduces Richard's estate and is subject to gift tax, he being a U.S. citizen or resident. (No charitable contribution deduction is available for donations to foreign entities, either.)

The donor may gift the property subject to the condition that the donee pays the gift tax ("a net gift"). This has several consequences:

1. Since the donee assumes the donor's liability, the transaction becomes a part-sale part-gift, so that if the tax is in excess of the donor's basis, the donor must recognize gain.

2.   The gift is reduced so that the gift tax is payable on the value of the property less the gift tax, requiring computations.

3.   The donor is still primarily liable to the IRS for the tax; the donee simply owes the donor the amount of the tax.

Example 21.62. Gustav Mueller gives away securities to his daughter, Agnes, worth $100,000, on the condition that she pays the gift tax. If the $10,000 exclusion is applicable and Gustav is in the 50 percent gift tax bracket, the gift tax is not $45,000, as it would have been if Gustav paid the gift tax. The gift tax would be $30,000 since the taxable gift of $90,000 is reduced by the donee's obligation to pay $30,000 in gift tax. Since the actual gift is only $60,000 ($70,000 − $10,000), the gift tax is one-half of that, or $30,000.

Tax Return

The gift tax return, Form 709, is an annual return due April 15 under the following three circumstances. (Note: After August 5, 1997, a donor who makes a gift in excess of the annual gift tax exclusion is not required to file a gift tax return if the entire value of the donated property qualifies for a gift tax charitable deduction. Also, after 1998, the $10,000 annual exclusion for gifts will be indexed annually for inflation.)

1.   Donor made at least one gift of a present interest in excess of $10,000 to one or more donees.

2.   Donor made any gift at all of a future interest (i.e., a remainder).

3.   Donor and spouse wish to elect gift-splitting, thus doubling available exclusions and credits. (A short Form 709A may be used for this purpose.) Code Secs. 6019(a) and 6075(b).

Gross gifts, less exclusions and deductions, are "adjusted taxable gifts." Because of the applicable credit amount ($202,050 in 1998), no gift tax may be due with the return. However, the *return* is still due and adjusted taxable gifts are brought back into the gross estate with a credit for gift taxes paid, if any. Note that the applicable credit amount is never "used up" for estate tax purposes and has but *one* effect during life: to defer the transfer tax until after the donor's death. (Some *states* also levy gift taxes.)

¶ 21,415   GIFT TAX COMPUTATION—SUMMARY

The gift tax complements the estate tax by taxing transfers depleting the estate.

Step 1.   Return required by April 15 following the calendar year in which taxable gifts were made.

Step 2.   List all gifts made during the calendar year, except gifts of nonterminable interests to spouse.

Step 3.   Husband and wife may elect to treat all gifts to third parties as made one-half by each (i.e., gift-splitting).

Step 4. Exclude for each donee the lesser of $10,000 or amount of gifts of present interests.

Step 5. Deduct gifts to charities in excess of exclusion.

Step 6. Result is taxable gifts for period (A).

Step 7. Add (A) to total lifetime prior taxable gifts (B) to get new lifetime total (C).

Step 8. Compute from the tables the tentative tax on (C).

Step 9. Compute from the tables the tentative tax on (B).

Step 10. Difference is tax imposed on gifts for period.

Step 11. Reduce tax by applicable credit amount of $202,050 (for 1998) or by the amount of credit previously allowable and 20 percent of the amount of the specific exemption claimed for gifts made after September 8, 1976, and before January 1, 1977 (prior law).

Generation-Skipping Transfer (GST) Tax

¶ 21,501 NATURE AND PURPOSE OF TAX

In 1976, Congress passed the original "generation-skipping transfer tax." The purpose was to supplement the federal gift and estate tax system to assure that the transfer of wealth from one generation to the next would bear substantially the same transfer tax burden, whether the transfer was outright to each succeeding generation or in trust, where it would skip a generation for federal estate tax purposes.

Prior to the 1976 legislation, a common planning device was the generation-skipping trust, which would pay income to one's child for the child's life and then distribute the trust property to his or her grandchildren at the child's death. If properly structured, there would be no federal estate tax payable at the child's death, even though the child had received the economic benefits of the trust for life. The 1976 legislation changed this and imposed a generation-skipping transfer tax on the trust at the child's death in an amount similar to what the federal estate tax would have been if the child had owned the trust property outright.

The present law, created by the Tax Reform Act of 1986, is based to a large extent on the prior law, but is described by the House Ways and Means Committee as a "simplified tax." In reality, the 1986 Act was a disappointment to those who had hoped for simplification, and the current generation-skipping rules certainly remain very complex. Although the 1986 law created an entire class of potentially taxable transfers, many additional planning opportunities are still available.

¶ 21,515 OVERVIEW

The current generation-skipping transfer rules became effective under Sec. 1433(a) of the 1986 Act on October 22, 1986. The provisions also apply to all existing revocable trusts, current wills (assuming the person did not die before December 31, 1986) and inter vivos transfers made after September 25, 1985. However, a trust that was irrevocable on September 25, 1985, is exempt under Act Sec. 1433(b)(2)(A), except for transfers to the trust after that date.

The generation-skipping transfer tax is imposed on property transferred to what Code Sec. 2613(a) defines as a "skip person." A skip person is an individual or entity that is assigned to a generation that is two or more generations below that of the transferor. For example, one's grandchild would be considered a skip person. So would a partnership or corporation in which a grandchild had an interest (entity generation assignments are made based on the relationship of the person having a beneficial interest in the entity to the transferor).

Generation assignment is based on the lineal relationship of family members. A spouse is assigned to the transferor's generation, regardless of age. Code Sec. 2651(c)(1). For nonlineal descendants, generation assignment is determined by the ages of the individuals involved in relation to the age of the transferor.

A person born 12½ years or less after the transfer is assigned to the same generation as the transferor. There is a new generation for each additional 25 years thereafter from the transferor's birthdate. Code Sec. 2651(d). Thus, a person who is more than 37½ years younger than the transferor will be treated as a grandchild.

¶ 21,525   TAXABLE EVENTS

Under the law, three events will give rise to a generation-skipping transfer tax: a taxable termination, a taxable distribution, and a direct skip.

Taxable Termination

A taxable termination is defined as the termination of a nonskip person's interest in property held in trust, after which only a skip person has an interest in the trust property. Code Sec. 2612(a)(1). In general, a person has an interest in the trust if he or she obtains a *present* right to receive principal or income from the trust. Code Sec. 2652(c)(1).

> *Example 21.63.* A father creates a trust for the benefit of his son, with the remainder passing to his grandson. Upon the death of the son, a taxable termination occurs. Had the trust been for the benefit of his wife, with the remainder going to the son, the death of the wife would not have resulted in a taxable transfer because a nonskip person maintained the interest in the trust.

There are certain exclusions that keep a termination from being labeled a "*taxable* termination." A transfer to a person one generation below the transferor that is subject to federal estate or gift taxation is not a taxable termination, nor is a termination that is a transfer which qualifies for the Code Sec. 2503(e) medical or tuition exclusion. Code Sec. 2611(b)(1) and (2).

Taxable Distribution

A taxable distribution is a distribution from a trust to a skip person. Code Sec. 2612(b). The 1986 Tax Act repealed the exemption for income distributions so that now both corpus and income payments may fall into the category of a taxable distribution. The addition of this provision is one of the more significant changes made by the law and has profound ramifications for discretionary trusts.

> *Example 21.64.* A trust is established which provides for the discretionary payment of income and corpus to the transferor's child and grandchild. In the first year, each beneficiary receives $25,000 of the trust's income. The income payment to the grandchild is a taxable distribution.

The burden of this taxable distribution is eased somewhat by an income tax deduction allowed under Code Sec. 164(a)(5) to the distributee for any generation-skipping transfer tax paid on income distributions.

Taxable distributions are allowed the same exemption from generation-skipping transfer tax as mentioned above for taxable terminations.

Direct Skip

The potential taxation of a direct skip is arguably the most important change made by the current tax law in the generation-skipping area. Under prior law, transfers to a skip person (e.g., a grandchild) that circumvented the use of a trust were not taxable transfers. However, the current law dictates that a transfer of an interest in property to a skip person qualifies as a generation-skipping transfer if it is subject to federal estate or gift tax. Code Sec. 2612(c)(1).

> *Example 21.65.* A wealthy grandparent transfers $1 million directly to his granddaughter. This transaction is a generation-skipping transfer.

Special rules are applicable when the transfer is to a grandchild whose parent is deceased. The child of a predeceased child is not considered a skip person to which generation-skipping transfer would apply because this grandchild of the transferor is treated as if he were the transferor's child. Code Sec. 2612(c)(2). For terminations, distributions, and transfers occurring after December 31, 1997, the predeceased parent exception to the generation-skipping transfer tax is expanded to include collateral heirs, provided that the transferor had no living lineal descendants at the time of the transfer. (The exception is also expanded to taxable terminations and distributions.)

> *Example 21.66.* A grandparent transfers $100,000 to his grandchild, whose father (the son of the grandparent) had passed away one year earlier. The grandchild is deemed to be in the child's generation, and thus is treated as a nonskip person. Accordingly, the transfer is not a direct skip.

¶ 21,535 EXEMPTIONS FROM TAX

For purposes of determining the taxable amount of a generation-skipping transfer, the following exemptions from the tax are provided:

General Exemption. An exemption of $1 million is provided for each person making generation-skipping transfers ($2 million if gift-splitting is elected by the transferor's spouse). Code Sec. 2631. The exemption can be allocated by a transferor to property transferred at any time, but once it is made, it is irrevocable. Code Sec. 2362.

Annual Gift Tax Exclusion. The annual $10,000 gift tax exclusion per donee for gifts of present interests is also available when computing the generation-skipping transfer tax on such gifts.

Unused Exemption. Any unused generation-skipping transfer tax exemption is first allocated to inter vivos direct skips, then to testamentary direct skips, and finally to generation-skipping trusts from which taxable transfers may be made after death. Code Sec. 2632.

Incompetency Exemption. The generation-skipping transfer tax applies to transfers under a trust to the extent that the trust consists of property included in the gross estate of an incompetent decedent or to transfers that are direct skips that occur by reason of the death of the incompetent decedent after August 3, 1990. Under prior law there was an exclusion for incompetent decedents' property.

¶ 21,545   RATE OF TAX

All generation-skipping transfers are subject to tax at a flat rate equal to the product of the maximum estate and gift tax rate without surtax (i.e., 55 percent) and the "inclusion ratio" with respect to the transfer.

Inclusion Ratio. The inclusion ratio is the excess (if any) of one over the "applicable fraction" determined for the trust from which such a transfer is made or, in the case of a direct skip, the applicable fraction determined for such a skip. Stated differently, 1 − (applicable fraction) = inclusion ratio.

Applicable Fraction. The applicable fraction is determined as follows: the numerator is the amount of the GST exemption allocated to the trust or property transferred in the direct skip. Its denominator is the value of the property transferred to the trust (or involved in the direct skip) reduced by the sum of any federal or state death tax attributable to the property that was recovered from the trust and any charitable deduction allowed under Code Sec. 2055 or 2522.

$$\text{applicable fraction} = \frac{\text{amount of GST exemption allocated to trust or property}}{\text{value of property transferred} - \left(\text{state and federal death taxes} + \text{charitable deductions}\right)}$$

The effect of using the inclusion ratio is to exempt the appreciation allocable to the GST exemption from the GST tax when ultimately imposed. Code Secs. 2641 and 2642.

Example 21.67. Grandpa transfers $4 million in trust for his daughter for life, remainder to Grandson, and allocates his $1 million exemption to the transfer. At the time the daughter dies, the trust fund is worth $8 million. Assuming there are no estate/

death taxes and charitable deductions, the calculation of the generation-skipping transfer tax would be as follows:

1. Determination of the applicable fraction: ($1 million exemption divided by $4 million in property equals an applicable fraction of .25).

2. Determination of the inclusion ratio: Subtract the applicable fraction from 1. Thus, the inclusion ratio is 1 minus .25, or .75.

The generation-skipping tax rate is the product of the inclusion ratio—in this case .75—and the maximum federal estate tax rate at the time of the transfer (i.e., 55 percent). Thus, the rate of tax on this transfer is 41.25 percent. The GST tax is $3.3 million ($8 million × 41.25 percent).

¶ 21,555   TAX COMPUTATIONS

In general, the method of computing the tax base of the generation-skipping transfer tax parallels the method applicable to the most closely analogous transfer subject to estate and gift tax. The method of computing the taxable amount depends on whether a taxable distribution, a taxable termination, or a direct skip is involved. Unless otherwise directed by a trust instrument specifically referring to the generation-skipping transfer tax, the tax imposed on a generation-skipping transfer is to be charged to the property being transferred.

Taxable Distributions. In the case of a taxable distribution, the amount subject to the generation-skipping transfer tax is the amount received by the transferee, reduced by any expenses included in connection with the determination, collection, or refund of the generation-skipping transfer tax. The transferee pays the tax on the taxable distribution. If the trustee pays any amount of the tax, the trustee is treated as having made an additional taxable distribution of that amount.

Note that all of the examples that follow assume that exemptions are exhausted and that the tax rate is 50 percent.

Example 21.68. A taxable distribution of $1 million is made to Grandson. Grandson must pay $550,000 in GST taxes, retaining the other half.

Taxable Terminations. In the case of a taxable termination, the amount subject to tax is the value of the property in which the interest terminates. A deduction is allowed for expenses, indebtedness, and taxes attributable to the property with respect to which the termination has occurred. The trustee pays any tax due on a taxable termination.

Example 21.69. Upon termination of a trust, $1 million remains in the trust and is subject to the GST tax. The trustee pays the tax of $550,000 (55 percent × $1 million), remitting the other half to the skip person, Grandson.

Direct Skips. In the case of a testamentary direct skip, the amount subject to tax is the value of the property received by the transferee. The person making the transfer pays the tax liability incurred from a direct skip.

Example 21.70. Grandpa left $3 million to Grandson, before taxes. After estate taxes, $1.5 million remained. The GST tax is levied on the amount received by the distributee in a direct skip. Thus, $1 million is distributed to Grandson and the trustee or executor pays a GST tax of $550,000.

In the case of an inter vivos direct skip, the amount subject to the GST tax is the value of the property received by the transferee. In addition, the gift tax is computed on the combined value of the gift and the generation-skipping transfer tax.

Example 21.71. Grandpa made a gift of $1 million to Grandson. The GST tax is $550,000. For gift tax purposes, a gift of $1.55 million was made. Thus, a gift tax of $852,500 is payable as well. Note, however, that it took only $2,402,500 to transfer $1 million to the Grandson, as opposed to $3 million in a testamentary transfer.

¶ 21,565   PAYMENT OF TAX

The GST tax is paid by the transferor or trustee except that the distributee pays the tax on taxable distributions. The GST tax return is due by the 15th day of the fourth month after the taxable year of the person who pays the tax and during which the transfer takes place, except in the case of a direct skip, other than from a trust, where the return is due at the same time the estate or gift tax return is due with respect to the transfer. Code Secs. 2603 and 2662.

¶ 21,575   CREDITS AND DEDUCTIONS

If a generation-skipping transfer (other than a direct skip) occurs at the same time as, and as a result of, the death of an individual, a credit against the generation-skipping transfer tax paid to any state is permitted. However, the credit is limited to five percent of the amount of federal generation-skipping transfer tax imposed on the transfer. Expenses, debts, and taxes are deductible under the same principles as those used for estate tax purposes. Code Secs. 2604 and 2622(b).

SUMMARY OF CHAPTER 21

✓ The federal estate, gift, and generation-skipping taxes are transfer taxes either at death or during life.

✓ The estate and gift transfer taxes are unified and subject to the same rate schedule. On the other hand, the generation-skipping tax is a flat tax at the highest estate tax rate (currently 55%).

✓ To understand the estate tax, one should start with the estate tax formula as depicted in ¶ 21,001 and Table 1. The formula begins with the gross estate less allowable deductions which yields the taxable estate. At this point, all taxable gifts after 1976 are added, and the tentative estate tax is determined. From the tentative estate tax, gift taxes payable on includible gifts after 1976 are subtracted, and, lastly, the estate tax credits are subtracted yielding the estate tax liability.

✓ The federal estate tax return (Form 706) must be filed within nine months of death, and the property on the return must be valued at date of death or the alternate valuation date (generally six months after death).

✓ The federal gift tax return (Form 709 or 709A) is due April 15 following the year of the gift.

✓ Gifts of a present interest qualify for an annual exclusion of $10,000 per donee. However, a married couple may gift-split and thereby give $20,000 to a donee.

✓ The applicable credit amount for 1998 allows an estate of $625,000 in value to not be subject to tax or a required filing. Also, an individual could give a present interest of $635,000 ($10,000 annual exclusion plus the $625,000 exemption amount) in 1998 and not be subject to tax.

CHAPTER 21 QUESTIONS

1. Distinguish between an estate tax and an inheritance tax.
2. What is the estate tax base?
3. What is the applicable credit amount?
4. Why is the gross estate different from the probate estate?
5. Greta Cook died in 1998. Her gross estate was $900,000, administration expenses were $60,000, and adjusted taxable gifts were $20,000. Compute the estate tax liability.
6. Why are certain gift taxes includible in the gross estate?
7. Why may the 50 percent "qualified joint tenancy" rule have adverse income tax effects?
8. What are the interests in, and powers over, property that may be given to a donee without estate tax consequences to the donee's estate?
9. Distinguish between a mere testamentary power to appoint property to the creditors of one's estate and a power to appoint property to anyone in the world, except oneself, one's estate, or the creditors of either.
10. Which transfers of life insurance policies prior to death are includible in the transferor's gross estate?
11. Which expenses may be deducted for income tax purposes or for estate tax purposes by election?
12. What are the requirements for a marital deduction?
13. What types of property passing to a spouse are considered terminable interests that would not qualify for the marital deduction?
14. Is it possible that a transfer made to a future spouse may later qualify for the estate tax marital deduction?
15. What is a QTIP trust, and what is the "price paid" for its use?
16. What are the main differences between the income tax and the estate tax charitable deduction?
17. What are the main differences between a unitrust and an annuity trust?
18. What are the tax advantages of a disclaimer?
19. What is the significance of a disclaimant reaching age 21?
20. Which transfers are subject to the gift tax?
21. What is a net gift?
22. What are the advantages of gift-splitting?
23. Why must the donor disclose his income tax basis in gifted property on the gift tax return?
24. What is a direct skip?

CHAPTER 21 PROBLEMS

25. If Doria Oliva dies this year, what estate tax is payable if the facts are:

Adjusted gross estate	$800,000
Adjusted taxable gifts after 1976	100,000
Gift tax paid	6,000

26. Melinda transferred $500,000 to an irrevocable, inter vivos trust, leaving the income to Elmo, her husband, for his life, and the remainder to their daughter, Ingrid, if she survives her mother. What are the estate tax consequences to Melinda's estate if:

    a. Melinda predeceased Elmo and Ingrid.

    b. Ingrid predeceased Melinda.

    c. Melinda survived Elmo, but predeceased Ingrid.

27. Janet Smith transferred, in trust, $500,000 of Georgia Power Bonds to her younger sister, Bertha Jones. These bonds pay interest quarterly, and Janet reserved the income for her life. Janet was age 60 at the time of the gift. Assume the remainder interest is 0.25509.

    a. What is the value of Janet's gift?

    b. Does the annual exclusion apply?

28. In each of the following cases, determine the amount includible in David's gross estate:

    a. An account balance of $200,000 in an IRA that the beneficiary immediately withdrew.

    b. A commercial annuity with a present value of $60,000, payable to David's wife, Selma, who contributed 40 percent of the purchase price.

    c. A qualified pension annuity with a present value of $180,000, one-third of which is attributable to David's own contributions, payable to Selma.

    d. A lump-sum distribution from a qualified profit-sharing plan of $30,000, payable to David's son, Kyle, who used five-year averaging.

29. Martha and Ludwig own their home in equal shares. Ludwig purchased the home with funds inherited from his grandfather, but Martha died first, leaving her half to Ludwig.

    What is includible in Martha's estate, and what is Ludwig's basis in the home if:

    a. They were married and owned the home as:

        1. Tenants in common

        2. Joint tenants

        3. Tenants by the entirety

        4. Community property

  b. They were brother and sister and owned the house as:

    1. Tenants in common

    2. Joint tenants

30. Identify the following property interests, powers, and events:

  a. Gus buys a piece of land with his brother, Jack. Gus's interest is 60 percent; Jack's is 40 percent.

  b. Bruce died, leaving his wife, Nancy, "30 percent of his adjusted gross estate, free and clear, in cash."

  c. Henry purchased a home "together with my wife, Ann, as co-owners with the right of survivorship."

  d. George transfers $10 million in trust to his wife, Wanda, for life, then to his son, Luke, for life, then to his daughter, Adele, if she survives Wanda, her mother. Adele also has the power to invade corpus to the extent needed to support her in her accustomed life style.

  e. Wendy owns half of all income and assets acquired by Harold during their marriage.

  f. Grandpa Jones died, still living rent free on a portion of the farm he deeded to Jack, his grandson, 11 years earlier.

31. Evelyn gave a Flymore sailplane to her husband who is an enthusiast of this sport for their wedding anniversary. Purchase cost was $14,000. She used her own funds from a separate checking account.

  a. What is the value of the gift?

  b. Does the gift have to be reported?

  c. What is the limit on a gift between spouses?

32. John and Janet Smith (husband and wife) purchased 1,000 shares of ABC Company common stock (NYSE) for $40,000 and immediately had it titled in the names of "Hugh and Donna Smith as joint tenants with rights of survivorship" (son and daughter-in-law). Assume gift-splitting.

  a. How much is the gift?

  b. What is the total of John's exclusion?

  c. What is the total of Janet's annual exclusions?

33. Joseph Grant's will provided that $1 million was to be placed in trust for his son, Steven, for life, with a remainder to Steven's children per stirpes.

What are the estate tax consequences to Steven's estate if the trust instrument provides the following:

  a. All trust income must be distributed to Steven quarterly.

  b. Steven is to be trustee.

    c.   Steven may appoint the trust property to anyone he chooses during life and by will, except to himself, his estate, or the creditors of either.

    d.   Steven may invade corpus to whatever extent necessary for his support and maintenance in his accustomed mode of living, as well as for his health and education.

    e.   Steven may withdraw from the principal the greater of $5,000 or five percent of the trust each year on a noncumulative basis.

    f.   Is any transfer tax possible upon Steven's death?

34. In which of the following cases will the insurance proceeds be includible in Bertram's estate?

    a.   Bertram purchased the policy on his life 11 years ago and transferred all rights to it to Donna, his daughter, five years before he died.

    b.   Same as (a), but the transfer took place two years before Bertram's death.

    c.   Two years before he died, Bertram talked his wife into buying a policy on his life. The only available funds during the marriage came from Bertram's salary.

    d.   Unknown to Bertram, because Donna was concerned about his health, she bought a term policy on his life seven months before he died.

35. On June 28, 1986, Bart Richards married Martha Joiner in Atlanta, Georgia. Because Bart was so happy that Martha became his wife, he purchased a home in Atlanta for $500,000 out of his own separate funds. He immediately titled the home in their joint names with right of survivorship. Bart died on June 28, 1998. The house was worth $800,000 on Bart's date of death. The executor elects to value the home at the date of death. What value will be placed on Bart's joint interest in his estate tax return?

36. Assume the same facts as in Problem 36. What is Martha's income tax basis in the house?

37. Assume the same facts as in Problem 36, except that Bart and Martha resided in Dallas, Texas. What is Martha's income tax basis in the house?

38. Kermit Ames died on January 15, 1998. The fair market value of his house was $150,000 on his date of death. On July 15, 1998, the house was worth $130,000. Assume the alternate valuation date is selected by the executor. What value is used by the executor in the estate tax return?

39. Assume the same facts as in Problem 39, except that the executor sold the house on May 2, 1998, for $138,000. What value is used by the executor in the estate tax return?

40. Assume the same facts as in Problem 39. What is the due date of the estate tax return?

41. Tom Parks died on March 15, 1998. The values of Tom's assets on March 15 and September 15, 1998, are as indicated below:

Asset	*VALUES*	
	Mar. 15	*Sept. 15*
Land.........................	$500,000	$400,000
Stocks........................	300,000	300,000
Bonds........................	400,000	350,000

The marginal federal estate tax bracket applicable to Tom's estate is 41 percent for property over $1,000,000. All of Tom's property, which consists of the above capital assets, will go to his children, Ted and Jason. Neither Ted nor Jason is a dealer in real estate. Should the executor elect alternate valuation under Code Sec. 2032? In deciding whether to elect the alternate valuation date, calculate both the estate tax consequences and the income tax consequences for the parties involved.

42. Mr. John Henderson died on February 17, 1998. For each of the following items indicate the amount to be included in John's gross estate. Unless stated to the contrary, assume that the items are valued as of John's death.

  a. John owned a 1993 Lincoln Town Car. At his date of death, the car's retail price was $11,750, and its whole-sale price was $10,150.

  b. Same as (a), except that the executor sold the car on April 17, 1998, for $11,000 to a buyer who saw it advertised on the home shopping network on a local TV station.

  c. John owned 1,000 shares of I.B.M. On February 17, 1998, the stock sold at a high of 100 and low of 98. It closed at 99¼.

43. Which of the following items are deductible to the estate?

  a. Property taxes accrued at death on decedent's home, held in a qualified joint tenancy.

  b. Interest accrued during estate administration on decedent's debts for which he was personally liable.

  c. Administration expenses in excess of value of property subject to claims, if paid one year after death.

  d. Same as (c), except that the property was not subject to claims.

  e. Estimated accountants' fees to be paid when practicable.

  f. Decedent's medical expenses paid 11 months after death.

44. Because John was so happy that Dana had agreed to become his fiancee, on February 2, 1998, he gave Dana's mother, Ethel, $15,000 in cash.

  a. Does this gift qualify for gift-splitting?

  b. Does this gift qualify for gift-splitting if John and Dana marry by December 31, 1998?

45. Mortimer Piper transferred $5 million in trust to his wife, Mona, for life, then to their children in equal shares. After Mortimer died, Mona sold her income interest, then died 17 years later.
    a. What are the transfer tax consequences to Mortimer, his estate, Mona, and her estate if a QTIP election is made?
    b. Same as (a), but without a QTIP election?

46. When Harry died, he left his surviving wife, Clare, the following:
    a. A remainder in a summer house, with a life estate left to his mother.
    b. A life estate and a general power of appointment in closely held stock, which, in the last 17 years, paid no dividends.
    c. An insurance policy on her own life.
    d. An annuity payable from a qualified, noncontributory pension plan.
    e. A patent with three years to run.
    f. Income from a mutual fund for life, with a remainder to their two daughters.
    Which of the above bequests qualify for the marital deduction?

47. In 1998, Mr. Colburn created a trust for the benefit of his five adult children and transferred $300,000 to it. The trustee may decide how much income to pay to each child each year. The trust will terminate at the end of 40 years, and the assets will be divided equally among the children or their estates. Does Mr. Colburn receive a gift tax exclusion of $50,000? Explain.

48. John Henry Harris was left a 1962 Impala convertible by his uncle, Billy Bob Harris. After receiving the car, John determined that five cars in his family were too many. As a result, he disclaimed the property with direction that the car go to his brother, Lee Roy Harris. Is this a valid disclaimer for estate tax purposes?

49. Stanley Rosen's cumulative lifetime taxable gifts amount to $250,000. The following year, he gives his favorite nephew $160,000 to open a liquor store.
    a. What is the taxable gift?
    b. What is the tax on the gift (prior to credits)?
    c. What is the gift tax payable?

50. The $10,000 exclusion would be available in which of the following transfers?
    a. Revocable transfer in trust to W for life, then to S.
    b. Irrevocable transfer in trust to W for life, then to S.
    c. Irrevocable transfer of a life insurance policy to a trust with two income beneficiaries.
    d. Transfer in trust to A and/or B for life, then to L, and the grantor makes the distribution decisions.
    e. Same as (d), but the independent trustee makes the distribution decisions.

   f.   Nonbusiness transfer to a corporation owned 50 percent by the donor's three children.

   g.   Transfer in trust to a minor, all income to be accumulated.

51. In the following independent cases explain whether the exclusion, the marital deduction, the charitable deduction, and gift-splitting are available.

   a.   To mother for life, then to spouse

   b.   To spouse for life, then to child

   c.   To charity for five years, then to spouse

   d.   To spouse for life, then to charity

   e.   To child A and/or child B for life, then to grandchild

52. During the year your client, Big Jim Smith, gave $8,000 to 70 different donees. Has Big Jim made any taxable gifts during the year?

53. Isaac Binder purchased 1,000 shares of Deep-Freeze Inc. five years ago for $15,000. Two years before he died, he gave his son, Edward, 500 shares worth $6,000. He died during a bull market and willed Edward the other 500 shares, then worth $12,000.

   a.   What is Edward's basis for gain or loss in the stock received by inter vivos gift?

   b.   What is Edward's basis in the testamentary gift?

   c.   What is Edward's holding period in the two blocks of stock?

54. John Henry paid $60,000 in 1998 in medical bills to a doctor and a hospital for his invalid father. Has John Henry made any taxable gifts in 1998?

55. Under the annuity rules, all the following are includible in the decedent's estate, except:

   a.   A lump-sum distribution from a qualified profit-sharing plan to a named beneficiary who waived forward averaging.

   b.   A commercial joint and survivorship annuity payable to the decedent and the spouse where the spouse furnished the purchase price.

   c.   The first $100,000 of an individual retirement account payable to the decedent's grandchildren.

   d.   One-half of a joint and survivorship annuity payable to the decedent and the spouse. The latter's aunt had purchased the annuity for them as a golden anniversary gift.

56. As a rule, general powers of appointment are taxable, while special powers are not. The following powers are all special powers, except:

a. The power to appoint property to any person or entity in the world except to the oneself, the estate, or creditors.

b. The power to invade corpus to the extent necessary to maintain one's present mode of living (which includes $1 million a year for servants, trips, jewelry, and a yacht).

c. The power to appoint the property to the holder's children and to anyone else, but with the remainderman's consent.

d. The mere testamentary power to appoint the property to the creditors of the holder's estate.

57. During the current year, Dana makes the following cash gifts: $5,000 to her daughter, $9,000 to her brother, and $11,000 to a business partner. Does Dana need to file a gift tax return?

58. Which one of the following is not a deduction from the gross estate of a decedent?

a. Unpaid income taxes on income received by the decedent during life.

b. Interest payable on a loan incurred to pay estate taxes.

c. Selling expenses for selling estate property if these sales are necessary to settle the estate.

d. Interest payable after a decedent's death attributable to an installment obligation incurred by decedent.

e. Casualty loss (uninsured) incurred during settlement of the estate.

59. In the typical gift situation, the donor pays the gift tax. When a "net gift" is made, however, the donee promises the donor to pay any gift tax due. The following statements relating to net gifts are all false, except:

a. The donor may realize a gain or loss on the transfer.

b. The donor becomes secondarily liable for the gift tax.

c. The donee's basis will not include an adjustment for the gift tax paid by the donee.

d. The amount of the gift is reduced by gift taxes actually paid by the donee, but not by any reduction in the donor's unified credit.

60. Hugh Colburn's financially destitute brother, Big Al, has a daughter named Violet. Hugh offers to pay for Violet's college education. In 1998, Hugh pays Columbia University's annual tuition of $24,000 and he also gives Violet an annual allotment of $16,000. Determine Hugh's taxable gifts for 1998.

61. The generation-skipping transfer tax supplements the estate and gift taxes. The following statements about this tax are all true, except:

a. The generation-skipping trust is liable for any transfer tax due, but the distributee has transferee liability.

b. A generation-skipping trust must have at least two beneficiaries in different generations below that of the grantor.

c. The same top marginal tax rate applies to estate, gift, and generation-skipping transfer taxes.

d. A person cannot be a beneficiary if the person has no present interest in the trust.

62. *Comprehensive Problem.* During 1998, Dale Davison made the following gifts:

a. $30,000 to the political action group to re-elect Sam Nunn for the U.S. Senate.

b. $25,000 to Scientific Atlanta Corporation (because he believed in their research objectives). Dale was not a shareholder in Scientific Atlanta Corp.

c. $22,000 to Mount Paran Church of God.

d. $100,000 was put in a joint tenants account. The joint tenants were Dale and his brother Sam.

e. $25,000 was paid to Vassar University in tuition for his daughter Sara.

f. $100,000 was placed in trust for his son, Ralph, for life, then the remainder will go to the Southern Methodist Foundation. Ralph's life estate is valued at $40,000.

g. A gift of real estate (basis of $60,000 and fair market value of $310,000 to his sister, Karen).

h. A gift of a life insurance policy on Dale's life to Sara (the beneficiary). The policy was worth $8,000 but had a face value of $50,000.

What are Dale's taxable gifts for the year?

63. *Comprehensive Problem.* When Howard Foth died in the current year, in addition to his $1,000,000 of certificates of deposit and investment property worth $200,000, the following facts were disclosed by the executor:

a. In 1975, Howard Foth decided to see what kind of fiduciary the Bank of Georgia would be for his assets. However, he did not want to establish an irrevocable trust because the fiduciary might not perform up to expectations and he might need the property later for his own retirement needs. Consequently, Howard established a revocable trust funded at $300,000, but the fair market value at death was $700,000.

b. In 1985, Howard made a taxable gift of $90,000 to his daughter, Bertha. Due to the unified credit, Howard did not incur any gift tax.

c. In 1983, Howard purchased a paid-up life insurance policy with a face value of $300,000 payable at death to the executor of the estate to use against any estate taxes that might be due.

d. In 1971, Howard's mother had left him a general power of appointment over a trust valued at $215,000. This power was subject to the standard of comfort.

e. Funeral expenses were $30,000, and administration expenses of $70,000 are considered necessary for Howard's estate.

f. Howard left his wife, Bella, $600,000 outright in certificates of deposit.

Compute the net estate tax payable.

64. *Comprehensive Problem.* Dave L. Jones, a calendar-year taxpayer using the cash method of accounting, was scared to death on Halloween night, October 31, 1998. Under the terms of the will, Dave devised and bequeathed all of the property he owned to his wife, Hildegard, except for a cash gift of $100,000 to the School of Accountancy at Old Dominion University, a condominium in Cancun, Mexico, to his beloved son, Billy Bob, a condominium in West Palm Beach, Florida, to Lee Ray Brown, and a $20,000 cash gift to Peggy Sue Elmore (who befriended him late in life).

A review of the executor's files and discussions with Mr. Jones's attorney reveal the following facts:

a. Mr. Jones's assets at (1) date of death and (2) six months later are as follows:

	FAIR MARKET VALUE	
REAL ESTATE	10/31/98	4/30/99
Personal residence	$500,000	$500,000
Cancun condominium	500,000	450,000
West Palm Beach condominium	400,000	425,000
STOCKS AND BONDS		
Ford Motor Co. bonds, 60 10% bonds, face value, $1,000 each. Interest payable semiannually on July 1 and January 1	72,000	75,000
Interest accrued on Ford Motor Co. bonds from July 1, 1998, to October 31, 1998	2,000	2,000
Littleton Telephone Co., common stock, 1,000 shares traded over the counter $10 per share on October 31, 1998, and $20 on April 30, 1999	10,000	20,000
West Lumber Co., traded NYSE, 5,000 shares common stock $100 per share on October 31, 1998, and $50 per share on April 30, 1999	500,000	250,000
CASH		
Checking Account No. 23-000, First National Bank of Greenville	15,000	15,000

Money Market Savings Account No. 1-23456, Beaver Run Savings & Loan	275,000	275,000

LIFE INSURANCE

Policy No. 1 provided for $100,000 payable to wife with no incidents of ownership	100,000	100,000
Policy No. 2 provided for $100,000 to wife, listed as owner under state law, but Dave retained the power to change the beneficiary	100,000	100,000

OTHER ASSETS

1959 White Cadillac El Dorado Convertible, red interior with bobbing dog in rear window	20,000	20,000
Civil war memorabilia	10,000	10,000
5 carat diamond ring, blue-white perfect	50,000	50,000
Miscellaneous personal effects (clothing and shoes)	6,800	6,800
Miscellaneous household goods (dishes, pots and pans, plants, silverware, and tools)	5,000	5,000
Furniture	25,000	25,000
Oriental rugs	18,000	18,000

b. On November 7, 1976, Mr. Jones, pursuant to the legal firm's suggestion of utilizing the annual exclusion and the specific exemption, gave $33,000 to his son Billy Bob. (Note that a $6,000 adjustment to the unified credit is required because of this transaction.)

c. Mr. Jones has made annual gifts of the exact annual exclusion amount to his son and each of his grandchildren each year (including 1998) since 1972. Other than these gifts and the one above, he made no gifts during his life.

d. Dividends of $2 per share were declared on the West Lumber Co. stock on October 1, 1998, but were not paid until November 15, 1998. Assume Mr. Jones was alive on the date of record.

e. Interest of $6,500 accrued on the savings account at date of death.

f. Fees:

Funeral expenses	$12,000
Attorney's fees	30,000
Accounting fees	30,000
Executor's fees	40,000
Appraisal fees	2,300

g.   Mortgage on personal residence, United Financial Mortgage Corp., 10 percent, $50,000.

h.   Debts:

Accrued property taxes on personal residence	$2,000
Accrued property taxes on West Palm Beach condo . .	3,000

i.   Taxes:

North Carolina Inheritance Tax	$40,000
Mexico Estate Tax	12,000

j.   A proviso in the will provided that the marital deduction for property passing to the wife shall not be reduced for death taxes, foreign death taxes, and funeral and administrative expenses.

k.   The executor has decided to take all administrative expenses on the estate return.

l.   Assume the executor elected to value the assets in the gross estate at their date of death values.

m.   Assume that under state law the executors will pay the same amount of state death taxes as the table in Code Sec. 2011(b) allows.

Required: Compute the net estate tax payable (note that the amount paid to Mexico is the amount of the foreign tax credit).

65.   *Comprehensive Problem.* Mr. B died in 1998 at the age of 72. In his will, Mr. B made several bequests to the members of his family. The executor of B's estate wants to know which of the following bequests constitute generation-skipping transfers.

a.   A testamentary trust to pay the income among Mr. B's four sons in such shares as the trustee determines. The trust agreement provides that, upon the death of the first son to die, one-fourth of the trust shall be paid to his descendants *per stirpes.*

b.   A trust under which the trustee may distribute income among Mr. B's descendants or apply the income for the benefit of any one of them. The trustee decides to pay the college tuition and medical school tuition for Mr. B's grandchildren.

c.   Mr. B's bequeathal of the ABC Widget Company to his son, M. M decides to disclaim the property in compliance with Code Sec. 2518 because the company would interfere with his acting career. As a result, the ABC Company passes to M's son.

d.   A trust to be created under which the trustee may distribute income or corpus to any of Mr. B's children or his remote descendants. The trustee makes several distributions to Mr. B's grandchildren because they really loved their grandfather.

66. *Research Problem.* On May 20, 1974, decedent's husband, Hugh P. Hughes, executed a will which contained the following paragraph:

> Third: I give, devise and bequeath the 300-acre farm which I own near Macon, Georgia, to my wife, Bertha O. Hughes, for and during the term of her natural life with remainder to my children, Vince Hughes, Hedy Henderson, and Chester Hughes, in equal shares. However, with the right reserved to my wife in case of necessity, that she may sell the land if that need arises. But it is my wish that the land be preserved for the benefit of my three children.

Hugh P. Hughes died on April 15, 1978, and decedent, Bertha O. Hughes, died on June 2, 1998. At the time of Bertha's death, the farm was worth $900,000.

Is the farm excluded from Bertha's estate?

In your answer, address the power of appointment of issue, and read the case of *Bette J. Berg,* 81-2 USTC ¶ 13,428 (DC Minn 1981).

67. *Research Problem.* John and Mary Larsson purchased a joint and survivorship annuity from the Life and Death Insurance Co. John paid for the annuity and died 11 years later, at which time Mary's survivorship interest had a value of $50,000. Mary was killed in a car crash four months later, having collected $2,000 since her husband's death.

   a. Must the date of death value be used, even though it is known that the asset is worthless prior to the due date of the return?

   b. Does it make a difference that the alternate valuation date is elected? (See *Estate of John A. Hance,* 18 TC 499, CCH Dec. 19,025 (1952), acq. 1953-1 CB 4, and Code Sec. 2039(a) and (b).)

68. *Research Problem.* Greene Corporation, a closely held corporation, is owned by Al Manx with 6,000 shares, Bob Barnes with 2,500 shares, and Cora Crowley with 1,500 shares. In the current year, Cora passed away. As a result of Cora's death, the executor contacts you about valuing Cora's closely held stock. In your analysis, you discover that Greene Corporation has average earnings over the representative period of $80 per share. Also, over the same period, it has paid $20 of dividends per share. The book value of Greene Corporation is $50 per share. Since the stock is not very marketable and Cora had a minority interest, you have concluded that a discount of 25 percent is appropriate for lack of marketability and minority interest.

Required: Value Cora's closely held stock interest for estate tax purposes. In your research, review the case of *Central Trust Co. v. U.S.,* 62-2 USTC ¶ 12,092, 305 F.2d 393 (Ct Cl 1962) for the applicable weights to be assigned to the valuation factors of earnings, dividends, and book value.

69. *Research Problem.* In 1998, Bert Richards transferred a $100,000 savings account to his wife in trust. The terms of the trust are that income is to be distributed annually to his wife, Mary Beth, the remainder to his two children, Oscar and Bertha, in equal shares or to their estate. The value of Mary Beth's income interest is $50,000.

   a. Is this a taxable gift to Mary Beth? (See Code Sec. 2523(b)(1) and (e).)

   b. Have taxable gifts been made for Oscar and Bertha?

   c. How many annual exclusions are available? (See Code Sec. 2503(b).)

Chapter 22

Income Taxation of Trusts and Estates

Learning Objectives

After completing Chapter 22, you should be able to:

1. Understand the intricacies and planning opportunities in a decedent's final federal income tax return.

2. Determine when 1041 returns for an estate or trust are required and how they are prepared

3. Depict the duties and responsibilities of a fiduciary in the preparation of a federal income tax return for an estate or trust.

4. Achieve an understanding of fiduciary accounting income and distributable net income.

5. Recognize how beneficiaries are taxed on distributions from estates or trusts.

6. Calculate the alternative minimum tax for estates and trusts.

7. Identify the impact of special tax rules affecting only estates and trusts.

8. Depict tax planning strategies for estates, trusts, and beneficiaries.

OVERVIEW OF CHAPTER

What happens to a taxpayer's taxpaying responsibilities when the taxpayer dies? Is the taxpayer relieved of future tax obligations? What date does the estate take over as a tax-paying entity? What happens when property is placed in a trust by a parent for the benefit of a child? Who is the taxpayer: the parent, the child, or the trust? What happens if an estate or trust distributes income to a beneficiary? Are there federal income tax implications? Answers to these questions and to many other related questions are discussed in this chapter.

The chapter deals first with the taxation aspects of estates, focusing on a decedent's final federal income tax return and how the return might differ from a regular return if the decedent was still living. The term decedent refers to a person who is deceased.

Next, the chapter discusses the federal income tax return of an estate. An estate comes into existence on the date of a decedent's death and continues in existence until all of the decedent's property is distributed to heirs (beneficiaries) and the estate is dissolved by law.

The second part of the chapter reviews the federal income tax return of a trust. A trust is a legal entity set up to hold property. A trustee administers the property according to the dictates of a trust agreement.

Intertwined in the discussion of estate and trust income tax returns is a discussion of the duties and responsibilities of fiduciaries. A fiduciary is a person such as an administrator, trustee, or executor who has been given a special confidence and responsibility to manage property in a trust or estate according to some legal agreement (will or trust agreement) and in the best interests of the beneficiaries of the trust or estate.

Next, the tax scheme of estates, trusts, and beneficiaries are discussed in this chapter. It is possible that some of the income earned by a trust or estate will not be taxable to the trust or estate but, instead, will be picked up as income on the income tax return of a beneficiary. In some instances, a decedent's income might also be required to be reported as income on the income tax return of a beneficiary.

Also, the chapter highlights tax planning techniques that have proven useful in regard to a decedent's final return, estate and trust income tax returns, and the tax status of beneficiaries. Also discussed are the tax planning options available in return preparation of the decedent's final Form 1040, the estate or trust Form 1041 (U.S. Fiduciary Income Tax Return), and the estate's Form 706 (United States Estate (and Generation-Skipping Transfer) Tax Return).

Taxation of Estates

¶ 22,001   DECEDENT'S FINAL INCOME TAX RETURN

In the year a person dies (decedent), a federal income tax return is due for the period from the beginning of the decedent's tax year up to the date of death. Reg. § 1.6012-3(b)(1). Death does not speed up the due date of the return. The tax return is due on the regular due date as if the decedent had continued to live for the entire tax year. Reg. § 1.6072-1(b). An illustration of due dates for a decedent's final return is provided below.

Example 22.1. A calendar-year taxpayer died on February 18, 1998. A tax return for the calendar year 1997 must be filed on or before April 15, 1998, and the tax return for the fractional part of

1998, that is, January 1 to February 18, 1998, must be filed on or before April 15, 1999.

If the decedent's gross income is below the required filing level, then no return need be filed. A return should be filed, however, if it would result in the refund of tax previously paid in or withheld. Code Sec. 6012(a)(1). Death does not change the filing status of the decedent. A joint return can still be filed with a surviving spouse if it is advantageous for tax purposes to do so. Income of the surviving spouse is included on the tax return for the entire tax year, but income of the decedent is included only up to the date of death. However, a joint return that includes a decedent may not be filed if the surviving spouse remarries before the end of the tax year in which the decedent dies or if the surviving spouse files a return for only part of the tax year because of a change in accounting period.

A fiduciary (executor or administrator of an estate) who has the responsibility of concluding the decedent's affairs has the responsibility of filing and signing the decedent's final return. If there is no executor or administrator of the decedent's estate and a joint return is to be filed, the surviving spouse can sign and file the return and indicate the date of the decedent's death on the return. A fiduciary, if appointed at a later date, has the power to change the decedent's filing status from married filing a joint return to married filing separately if there is a justifiable reason. Code Sec. 6013(a); Reg. § 1.6013-1(d).

¶ 22,015 INCOME AND DEDUCTIONS ON FINAL RETURN

The method of accounting used by the decedent while alive determines what income and deductions are recognized on the decedent's final return. If the decedent was on the accrual basis of accounting for tax purposes, then only income accrued up to the date of death is included on the final return. Deductions that accrued up to the date of death are also shown on the final return. Income or deductions accruable only because of death are not included on the final return. Code Sec. 451(b); Reg. § 1.451-1(b).

Example 22.2. Sam Lett, a businessman, keeps his records on the accrual basis of accounting. Sam dies on September 30, 1998. Income earned by Sam through September 30, 1998, is included on his final return.

If the decedent was on the cash basis of accounting, as are most individuals, only income actually or constructively received up to the date of death is included on the final return. Income earned by a cash-basis decedent but not received prior to death is not included on the decedent's final return. Instead, the income is included on the income tax return of the estate or beneficiary who is entitled to the payment and actually receives it (income in respect of the decedent, which is discussed later).

Example 22.3. Dave Jones, a cash-basis taxpayer who is an accountant and works for a local CPA firm, receives his salary payment on the fifteenth of the month for work completed the prior month. Dave dies on December 8. The December 15 salary payment for work completed in November is not included on his final return. The income is taxable to the estate or beneficiary who is entitled to the payment and actually receives it.

All valid tax deductible expenses paid by a cash-basis decedent before death can be deducted on a final return. Valid tax deductible expenses, which are not paid by the date of death, are normally deductible by the estate or the beneficiary who has the responsibility of discharging the obligation. Reg. § 1.691(b)-1.

There is an exception to this rule for medical expenses incurred for a decedent's medical care and paid by the estate. The decedent's medical expenses paid by the estate are treated as paid at the time they are incurred and deducted on the decedent's final return as long as they are paid within one year of the decedent's death. Code Sec. 213(c); Reg. § 1.213-1(d). The purpose of this exception is that significant medical expenses might be incurred by a decedent just prior to death and, without the exception, not be deductible on any tax return. Also, if medical expenses of the decedent are paid by a surviving spouse, they are deductible in the year paid. Rev. Rul. 57-310, 1957-2 CB 206. Additionally, medical expenses paid by the executor within one year of the decedent's death may be taken either as a deduction on the estate tax return (Form 706) or the decedent's final return (Form 1040). Moreover, it should be taken into consideration in this planning analysis that if the entire medical expense deduction is taken on the decedent's final return, the deduction is subject to the statutory limitation of 7.5 percent while the limitation is not applicable if the entire deduction is taken on the estate tax return (Form 706).

> ***Example 22.4.*** Medical expenses associated with the final illness of the decedent were $10,000. These expenses were paid by the estate within one year of the decedent's death. On the decedent's final return these expenses will exceed the statutory limitation by $9,000. The marginal tax rate on the decedent's final return is 39.6 percent and the marginal tax rate on the decedent's estate tax return is 55 percent.

TAX PLANNING POINTER

Deduction of the entire allowable medical expense on the final return will produce a tax savings of $3,564 ($9,000 × 39.6 percent), while deduction of the entire allowable expense on the estate tax return will produce a tax savings of $5,500 ($10,000 × 55 percent).

The decedent taxpayer is entitled to a full standard deduction on a final income tax return regardless of date of death. The standard deduction does not have to be reduced because the decedent did not live for a full 12-month period. Also, the additional amounts to the standard deduction because of blindness or old age are allowed in full regardless of the date of death during the tax year. The same is true for personal exemptions on the final return. That is, the decedent is allowed full personal exemptions on the final return, regardless of date of death.

Income in Respect of the Decedent

If the decedent was entitled to receive income at the date of death but the income was not properly includible on the decedent's final return, normally because the decedent was on the cash basis of accounting, this income is considered to be income in respect of the decedent. Income in respect of the decedent is included on the income tax return of the estate or beneficiary who is entitled to the payment and actually receives it. Code Sec. 691(a); Reg. § 1.691(a)-2. Income in respect of the decedent includes but is not limited to the following items: (1) accrued income of a cash-basis decedent that was not included on the decedent's final return, (2) interest on U.S. savings bonds that has accrued but has not been reported by a cash-basis decedent, (3) dividends on stock declared before the decedent's death but payable after the date of death, (4) interest on savings accounts for cash-basis taxpayers from the last interest payment date up to the date of death, and (5) income that arises solely by reason of death of the decedent. Rev. Rul. 79-340, 1972-2 CB 320. The following examples help to clarify the above items of income in respect of the decedent.

Example 22.5. Susan Lewis, a cash-basis taxpayer, dies on November 18. Susan normally receives a paycheck at the end of the month for a full month's work. The paycheck received on November 30 covering the period November 1 to November 18 is income in respect of the decedent and is includible as income by the party receiving it.

Example 22.6. Bob Burl purchased U.S. savings bonds in 1979 and still held the bonds at the date of his death. Bob had not previously recognized any interest income on the bonds. The unreported interest income on the bonds is income in respect of the decedent. The estate or beneficiary that receives the bonds can elect to report all prior unreported interest income on its tax return or wait until the bonds mature or are disposed of and report the interest income at that time. If desired, an election can be made by a fiduciary to have the unreported interest income up to the date of the decedent's death included on the decedent's final income tax return. Rev. Rul. 68-145, 1968-1 CB 203. Naturally, this election can be quite valuable if the decedent's income in the final tax year is nominal.

Example 22.7. Joan Furrow owned 1,000 shares of Sonic Corporation stock at the date of her death. Sonic declared a dividend on its common stock on November 5 with a record date on November 15 and payment date on November 30. Joan died on November 18. Since she was alive on the date of record but deceased by date of payment, the dividend payment is IRD to the successor in interest.

The same result is achieved for either cash-basis or accrual-basis taxpayer.

Example 22.8. Patrick Ralls, a cash-basis taxpayer, has a savings account at a local bank that pays and credits interest to accounts on a quarterly basis. Patrick dies on December 12. Interest income from October 1 to December 12, when credited to the account on December 31, is income in respect of the decedent to the estate or beneficiary holding the property at December 31.

Example 22.9. Helen Troy, who dies on January 12, has an agreement with her employer that a payment of $20,000 will be made to her estate or designated beneficiary upon Helen's death in lieu of claims to future bonuses, sales commissions, etc. This payment, which arises solely by reason of death of the decedent, is income in respect of the decedent when received by the estate or beneficiary.

The character of income in respect of the decedent is the same to the estate or beneficiary reporting the income as it would have been to the decedent if the decedent had continued to live and report the income on the tax return. Code Sec. 691(a)(3); Reg. § 1.691(a)-3.

If an estate or beneficiary includes income in respect of the decedent as income on a tax return, the estate or beneficiary is entitled to an itemized deduction for any federal estate tax paid because the income was also included on the decedent's federal estate tax return. Code Sec. 691(c). This itemized deduction is not subject to the two percent floor that applies to miscellaneous itemized deductions.

Deductions in Respect of the Decedent (DRD)

If a decedent incurred tax deductible expenses before death that were not deductible on the decedent's final return because they were not paid and the decedent was on the cash basis, these expenses are deductible in the year paid by either the estate or the beneficiary. If the estate pays the expenses, they are deductible by the estate in the tax year paid. If a beneficiary has an obligation to pay an expense and pays it, the expense is a proper deduction on the tax return of the beneficiary in the year of payment. Reg. § 1.691(b)-1. Also, it is important to note that items are deductible twice. That is, on both the Form 706 return and the Form 1041 return.

Business losses or capital losses incurred by a decedent prior to death end with the decedent's final return. The losses cannot be carried over to years subsequent to the final return. Business losses on the decedent's final return, however, are eligible for the net operating loss carryback and can be carried back to tax returns of prior years. Rev. Rul. 74-175, 1974-1 CB 52. In a community property state only 50 percent of the business or capital losses are nondeductible.

¶ 22,025   FEDERAL INCOME TAX CONCERNS OF AN ESTATE

The estate of a decedent is a separate taxable entity that comes into existence automatically at the death of an individual. The decedent's tax year ends on the date of death so that the tax year of the estate commences on the following day. Reg. § 1.443-1(a)(2). An estate is a separate taxable entity for federal income tax purposes and retains this status until the final distribution of assets held in the estate of the beneficiaries.

The duration of an estate is the period actually required by the fiduciary to perform the ordinary duties of administration (i.e., collection of assets and the payment of debts, taxes, legacies and bequests). Because the estate is a taxable entity separate from the beneficiaries, the fiduciary may attempt to prolong its existence in order to take advantage of the lower tax bracket. That is, whenever beneficiaries of an estate are in higher tax brackets than the estate, substantial tax savings can be achieved by accumulating the estate's income in one year.

¶ 22,035   FIDUCIARY RESPONSIBILITIES

A fiduciary is a person such as an administrator, trustee, or executor who has been given a special confidence and responsibility to manage property in a trust or estate according to some legal agreement (will, trust agreement) and in the best interests of the beneficiaries of the trust or estate. The main responsibility of a fiduciary of an estate is to wind up the affairs of the decedent, specifically to gather the decedent's assets together, to pay claims against the assets, and to distribute the balance of the assets to the beneficiaries of the estate. A fiduciary of an estate is called an executor if named in the decedent's will, or an administrator if named by a court to settle the decedent's affairs. In some instances, a personal representative of the decedent may assume some fiduciary responsibilities with regard to an estate although not named as an executor or appointed as an administrator.

Payment of Decedent's Tax Liabilities

Included among the duties and responsibilities of a fiduciary of an estate (hereafter referred to as executor) is the responsibility to file any required tax returns and pay any tax liabilities of the decedent or the decedent's estate. Although the executor is required to file tax returns and pay taxes due, the executor ordinarily is not personally liable for the tax payments. The tax payments are made from the assets of the estate. Code Sec. 6903; Reg. § 301.6903-1. If, however, the executor is negligent in handling claims against the estate and taxes are not paid, the liability for payment of the taxes extends to the executor. Reg. § 1.641(b)-2.

An executor can obtain protection from personal liability for a decedent's taxes by filing Form 4810 (Request for Prompt Assessment) with the IRS after all tax returns have been filed. The request will reduce the normal three-year period within which the IRS must audit a return to eighteen months from the time the request is filed. Code Sec. 6501(d).

TAX PLANNING POINTER ▼

Filing of the request by the executor results in a shorter period for determining the final liability of the estate and can speed up the distribution of estate assets to the beneficiaries. Filing of the request also lessens the chance of an executor inadvertently distributing estate assets to beneficiaries that should have been used to pay the estate's tax liabilities.

¶ 22,045 ESTATE FEDERAL INCOME TAX RETURN

Each estate that has gross income of $600 or more during a tax year must file an estate income tax return. The appropriate IRS form for the return is Form 1041 (U.S. Fiduciary Income Tax Return). If one or more beneficiaries of an estate are nonresident aliens, a Form 1041 must be filed even if gross income is below $600. Code Sec. 6012(a); Reg. § 1.6012-3.

Filing Period. Form 1041 must be filed on or before the fifteenth day of the fourth month following the close of the tax year of the estate. The executor is free to choose the end of an estate's first tax year. The executor is free to choose the same tax year as the decedent or any other year-end. The estate's first income tax return can cover a period less than 12 months. Once an executor chooses an estate's tax year-end on the first tax return, however, all subsequent returns must use the same year-end unless permission is received from the IRS for a change in accounting period.

Exemption. An estate is entitled to a $600 personal exemption on each income tax return except the final income tax return when no personal exemption is allowed. Code Sec. 642(b); Reg. § 1.642(b)-1. An executor should carefully consider the choice of an estate's first tax year-end. Careful planning of the estate's tax year-end can result in maximum tax advantage.

Example 22.10. The estate of James Johnson was in existence for the period February 1, 1998, through December 31, 1998. The executor chose an estate tax year-end of December 31, 1998. The first return of the estate was also the final return and no $600 exemption was allowed. In order to maximize tax advantage, the executor, in this case, could have chosen an estate tax year-end for the first return of any month-end from February 28, 1998, through November 30, 1998. A $600 personal exemption would then have been available on the first return. The estate's final income tax return would have covered the period from the end of the first return through December 31, 1998. Careful planning of the estate's tax year-end in the second case would have resulted in $600 of the estate's income being free from taxation. A disadvantage of the second case, however, is that two estate income tax returns need to be filed instead of one income tax return as in the first case. On the other hand, the advantage of filing two estate income tax returns instead of one is that the estate income is spread over two returns, thereby possibly lowering the effective marginal tax rate on the income.

Accounting Method. An executor is also free to choose an accounting method (cash or accrual) for an estate on the first income tax return. Subsequent income tax returns must use the same accounting method unless permission is received from the IRS to make a change. An executor should consider very carefully the initial choice of accounting method for an estate since later IRS permission to change the method of accounting may be difficult to obtain.

Estimated Tax. Normally, an executor of an estate is not required to pay estimated taxes. Instead, the full amount of tax liability is due with the tax return. If an estate stays in existence for more than two taxable years, however, it must start to pay estimated tax payments in the third year.

Extension of Time to File Return. An extension of time to file a Form 1041 may be granted to an executor for a justifiable reason. An extension of time to file a return, if granted, does not extend the time for payment of the tax. The tax liability must still be estimated and payments made by the regular due dates.

Tax Rates for Estates. Regular income tax rates for federal estate income tax returns are shown in the Appendix. In addition to regular income tax rates, an estate may also be subject to the alternative minimum tax that was discussed previously in individual income taxes. If the alternative minimum tax computation results in a larger tax due than the regular tax computation, the difference is added to the estate's income tax liability.

Taxation of Trusts

¶ 22,209   NATURE OF TRUSTS

A trust is a legal entity created to hold property. A trustee administers the property according to the dictates of a trust agreement. For income tax purposes, a trust is a separate taxable entity which, like an estate, is entitled to a deduction for income distributions to beneficiaries. The income distributions, in turn, are subject to taxation on the beneficiaries' income tax returns.

Creation of Trusts

As noted earlier, an estate is created automatically. On the other hand, a trust must be specifically created. There are many legal or tax definitions of trusts. That is, trusts may be inter vivos or testamentary, simple or complex. Also, there are trusts that are formed for a specific function, such as alimony trusts, insurance trusts, or charitable trusts. A breakdown of the common working trust terminology follows.

Inter Vivos Trust. An inter vivos trust is a trust created during the lifetime of the grantor.

Testamentary Trust. A testamentary trust is a trust created by the will of a decedent.

Simple Trust. Pursuant to the terms of its governing instrument, a simple trust must: (1) distribute all of its state law income currently, (2) have no charitable beneficiary, and (3) make no distribution from corpus. Code Sec. 651(a)(1) and (2); Reg. § 1.651(a)-1.

Complex Trust. A complex trust is a trust that is not a simple trust. The term includes trusts with a charitable beneficiary and trusts that distribute corpus or accumulated income.

Categories of Beneficiaries

Beneficiaries of trusts are divided into two categories: income beneficiaries and remainder beneficiaries. An income beneficiary has an interest in the income of the trust. A remainder beneficiary has an interest in the trust property after an income interest expires. It is possible for one person to be both an income beneficiary and a remainder beneficiary.

Example 22.11. John Burlington establishes a trust to provide income to care for his aged mother. Upon death of the mother, the trust agreement provides that the trust corpus will be distributed to James Burlington, John's son. In this trust, John Burlington is the grantor, the aged mother is an income beneficiary, and James Burlington is a remainder beneficiary.

Tax and Nontax Reasons for Creating Trusts

There are a number of tax and nontax reasons an individual might consider creating a trust. Nontax reasons for creating a trust include the following:

1. A trust can be created to protect and conserve property and to provide competent investment management for beneficiaries such as children who are not yet competent to handle their own affairs.

2. A trust can be created to protect and conserve property and to provide competent investment management for beneficiaries who are not interested or inclined to manage the property themselves.

3. A grantor can create a trust and give explicit instructions in a trust agreement as to how the trust property is to be invested and managed. The grantor thereby can have some control over the management of the trust property even though deceased.

Example 22.12. John Creek creates a trust and names his aged grandmother as the income beneficiary of the trust for her remaining lifetime. The purpose of the trust is to provide the grandmother with a means of support for the rest of her life. The trustee has the responsibility to manage the affairs of the trust in the best interests of the grandmother according to the dictates of the trust agreement.

Tax reasons for creating a trust include the following:

1. By creating a properly constituted trust for tax purposes, a grantor has created a new tax entity. A separate tax return is prepared for the new tax entity and a new tax rate schedule is used in computing the tax due on the trust income. Trust income is subject to taxation starting at the bottom of a new tax rate schedule. Two taxpayers now exist, the grantor and the trust, and, considering the progressive nature of the federal income tax system, overall income may be subject to a lower effective tax rate.

2. By creating a properly constituted trust for tax purposes, a grantor can effectively shift income from the grantor's tax return to the income tax return of a beneficiary who may be in a lower income tax bracket, thereby lowering the overall effective income tax rate on the income of a family unit.

In some instances, a trust can be created that qualifies as a separate legal entity but that is not a properly constituted trust for federal income tax purposes. The income from a trust of this type is taxable to the grantor instead of to the trust or beneficiaries. For qualification as a properly constituted trust for tax purposes, effective control of the property placed in trust must be relinquished by the grantor. Trusts that do not qualify for recognition as trusts for federal income tax purposes are called grantor trusts and are discussed at ¶ 22,525.

¶ 22,215   TRUST FEDERAL INCOME TAX RETURN

Each trust that has gross income of $600 or more during a tax year must file a federal income tax return. The appropriate form for the return is Form 1041 (U.S. Fiduciary Income Tax Return). If one or more beneficiaries of a trust are nonresident aliens or if the trust has taxable income, an income tax return must be filed even if gross income is below $600. Code Sec. 6012(a).

Filing Period. A trust income tax return must be filed on or before the fifteenth day of the fourth month following the close of the tax year of the trust. All trusts, with some minor exceptions, must report income on a calendar-year basis.

Exemption. A simple trust is entitled to a $300 personal-exemption deduction while a complex trust is entitled to a $100 personal-exemption deduction. A full personal exemption can be taken on the first income tax return of a trust even if it covers a period of less than twelve months. No personal exemption is allowed on the final return of a trust.

Accounting Method. A trustee is free to choose an accounting method (cash or accrual) for a trust on the first income tax return. Subsequent income tax returns must use the same accounting method unless permission is received from the IRS to make a change.

TAX PLANNING POINTER ▼

A trustee should consider very carefully the initial choice of accounting method for a trust since later IRS permission to change the method of accounting may be difficult to obtain.

Estimated Tax. A trustee of a trust is required to pay estimated taxes. An extension of time to file a return may be granted to a trustee for a justifiable reason.

Extension of Time to File Return. An extension of time to file a return, if granted, does not extend the time for payment of the tax. The tax liability must still be estimated and payments made by the regular due date.

Tax Rates for Trusts. Regular tax rates for trust income tax returns are shown in the Appendix. In addition to regular income taxes, a trust may also be subject to the alternative minimum tax. If the alternative minimum tax computation results in a larger tax due than the regular tax computation, the difference is added to the trust's income tax liability.

Federal Income Taxation Scheme—Estates and Trusts

¶ 22,301   DISTRIBUTABLE NET INCOME (DNI) SYSTEM

Because an estate or trust is a tax-paying entity, double taxation would be imposed if the income previously taxed to the fiduciary was again taxed when distributed to beneficiaries. In order to avoid double taxation, a system was needed to measure the amount and character of income distributed to beneficiaries or retained by an estate or trust. As a result, the concept of distributable net income (DNI) was brought into the Internal Revenue Code.

DNI Concept

In order to make the conduit principle work, a device was required to measure the *amount* of income distributed to beneficiaries or retained by the estate. Also, a measure was needed to determine the *character* of amounts distributed to beneficiaries or retained by the estate or trust. Furthermore, a true conduit approach must identify the items of estate income that are given special treatment elsewhere in the Code, such as capital gains and interest on municipal bonds, and must keep these items separate as they pass out to the estate's or trust's beneficiaries.

An analytical method or technique was required to measure the amount of income distributed and determine the character of amounts distributed. Such a method is supplied in the concept of distributable net income. DNI has three basic functions:

1. It limits the amount of the distribution deduction of the estate and trust.

2. It limits the amount on which beneficiaries can be taxed.

3. It is used to determine the character of amounts retained by an estate or trust and the character of amounts distributed to the beneficiaries. Reg. § 1.643(a)-0.

Thus, DNI has been termed the yardstick or measuring rod to be employed in determining, on one hand, the maximum deduction for distributions which may be allowed to the estate or trust and for gauging, on the other hand, the extent to which beneficiaries may be taxable on the distributions.

DNI—Modification of Taxable Income

In order to serve as a measure of the maximum deduction to be allowed to trusts or estates for distributions to beneficiaries (and conversely to determine the amounts includible in the beneficiaries' gross income), taxable income must be modified in several important respects. Code Sec. 643(a) sets out the modifications to taxable income and labels this modified income "distributable net income." DNI is defined as the taxable income of the estate or trust computed with six modifications. (At this juncture, it should be noted that the taxable income of an estate or trust is generally the same as taxable income of an individual, with several exceptions. That is, the main component parts of taxable income are gross income, deductions, charitable contributions, income distribution deduction, and the personal exemption.) The modifications to taxable income for DNI are as follows:

1. No deduction is allowed for amounts distributed or distributable to beneficiaries.

2. No deduction is allowed for personal exemptions—$600 for estates, $300 for simple trusts, and $100 for complex trusts.

3. Gains from the sale or exchange of capital assets are excluded to the extent that they are allocated to corpus and are not paid, credited, or required to be distributed to any beneficiary, or paid or set aside for charities. Capital losses are excluded except to the extent that such losses are taken into account in determining the amount of capital gain to be paid, credited, or required to be distributed to any beneficiary during the taxable year.

4. With respect only to simple trusts, extraordinary dividends and taxable stock dividends are excluded if properly allocated by the trustee in good faith to corpus.

5. Interest that is fully tax-exempt (less nondeductible disbursements allocated to such interest) is included.

6. In the case of foreign trusts, income from sources without the U.S. (less nondeductible disbursements allocable to such income) is included.

¶ 22,325   DNI COMPUTATIONS—SIMPLE TRUSTS

The rules applicable to a trust required to distribute all of its income currently and to its beneficiaries (that is, a simple trust falling under Code Secs. 651 and 652) may be illustrated in the following manner. Reg. § 1.652(c)-4.

Example 22.13. Pursuant to the terms of a simple trust all of the income is to be distributed equally to beneficiaries X and Y and capital gains are to be allocated to corpus. The trust and both beneficiaries file returns on the calendar-year basis. No provision is made for depreciation in the governing instrument. Therefore, it will follow income. During the taxable year, the trust had the following items of income and expenses:

Rents	$25,000
Dividends of domestic corporations	50,000
Tax-exempt interest on municipal bonds	25,000
Long-term capital gains	15,000
Taxes and expenses directly attributable to rents	5,000
Trustee's commissions allocable to income account	2,600
Trustee's commissions allocable to principal account	1,300
Depreciation	5,000

Step 1—State Law Income. The state law income (also, called trust accounting income) of the trust for fiduciary accounting purposes is $92,400, computed as follows:

Rents		$ 25,000
Dividends		50,000
Tax-exempt interest		25,000
		$100,000
Deductions:		
Expenses directly attributable to rent income	$5,000	
Trustee's commissions allocable to income account .	2,600	7,600
State law income computed under Code Sec. 643(b)		$ 92,400

One-half ($46,200) of the income of $92,400 is currently distributable to each beneficiary.

Step 2—Code Sec. 643(a) Ceiling. The distributable net income (income ceiling) of the trust computed under Code Sec. 643(a) is $91,100 determined as follows (cents are disregarded in the computation):

Rents		$25,000
Dividends		50,000
Tax-exempt interest	$25,000	
Less: Expenses allocable thereto		
($25,000/$100,000 × $3,900)	975	24,025
Total		$99,025
Deductions:		
Expenses directly attributable to rental income . . .	$ 5,000	
Trustee's commissions ($3,900 − $975 allocable to		
tax-exempt interest	2,925	7,925
Distributable net income as the income ceiling		$91,100

In computing the distributable net income of $91,100, the taxable income of the trust was computed with the following modifications. No deductions were allowed for distributions to the beneficiaries and for a personal exemption of the trust. Code Sec. 643(a)(1) and (2). Capital gains were excluded. Code Sec. 643(a)(3). The tax-exempt interest was included. Code Sec. 643(a)(5).

Step 3—Code Sec. 651(a) Ceiling. The deduction ceiling allowable to the trust under Sec. Code 651(a) for distributions to the beneficiaries is $67,075 computed as follows:

Distributable net income computed under Code Sec. 643(a) ..	$91,100
Less:	
Tax-exempt interest as adjusted	24,025
Distributable net income (deduction ceiling) as determined under Code Sec. 651(b)	$67,075

Since the amount of the income ($92,400) required to be distributed currently by the trust exceeds the distributable net income ($67,075) as computed under Code Sec. 651(b), the deduction allowable under Code Sec. 651(a) is limited to the distributable net income of $67,075.

Step 4—Trust's Income. The taxable income of the trust is $14,700 computed as follows:

Rents		$25,000
Dividends		50,000
Long-term capital gains		15,000
Gross income....................................		$90,000
Deductions:		
Rental expenses	$ 5,000	
Trustee's commissions	2,925	
Distributions to beneficiaries	67,075	
Personal exemption for a simple trust	300	75,300
Taxable income..................................		$14,700

The trust is not allowed a deduction for the portion ($975) of the trustee's commissions allocable to tax-exempt interest in computing its taxable income.

Also, it should be noted that a simple trust which is allocating capital gains to corpus can perform a supplemental calculation to check its taxable income. For example, in the above calculation the trust's taxable income was $14,700; this could have been figured as follows:

Capital gains	$15,000
Less: Personal exemption	300
Taxable income..................................	$14,700

Step 5—Inclusion and Characterization to Beneficiaries. In determining the character of the amounts includible in the gross income of X and Y, it is assumed that the trustee elects to allocate to rents the expenses not directly attributable to a specific item of

income, other than the portion ($975) of such expenses allocated to tax-exempt interest.

The allocation of expenses among the items of income, as required by Sec. 652(b), is shown below:

	Rents	Dividends	Tax-exempt Interest	Total
Income for trust accounting purposes	$25,000	$50,000	$25,000	$100,000
Less:				
Rental expenses	5,000	0	0	5,000
Trustee's commissions	2,925	0	975	3,900
Total deductions	7,925	0	975	8,900
Character of amounts in the hands of the beneficiaries ...	$17,075	$50,000	$24,025	$ 91,100

Inasmuch as the income of the trust is to be distributed equally to X and Y, each is deemed to have received one-half of each item of income: that is, rents of $8,537.50, dividends of $25,000; and tax-exempt interest of $12,012.50. The dividends of $25,000 allocated to each beneficiary are to be aggregated with the beneficiary's other dividends.

Additionally, each beneficiary is allowed a deduction of $2,500 for depreciation of rental property attributable to the portion (one-half) of the income of the trust distributed to each beneficiary. If depreciation had been a charge against income and consequently required a reserve, then it should have appeared at Step 1 reducing state law or trust accounting income, Step 2 reducing DNI as an income ceiling, Step 4 as a deduction to the trust in computing its taxable income, and at Step 5 as a reduction to rental income. Note, of course, that the beneficiaries are responsible for only $91,100 of DNI while, in fact, $92,400 has been distributed to them.

¶ 22,331   DEPRECIATION AND DEPLETION DEDUCTIONS

Either an estate or trust may be entitled to depreciation and depletion deductions if it holds qualified property.

Rules for Estates. Even though an estate may be allowed a depreciation or depletion deduction, it must be recognized that this is a residual claim to these deductions. For an estate, the allowable deduction for depreciation and/or depletion must be apportioned between the estate and the heirs, legatees, and devisees on the basis of income of the estate which is allocable to each. Reg. §§ 1.167(h)-1(c) and 1.611-1(c)(5).

Rules for Trusts. Trusts are permitted greater flexibility than estates in receiving depreciation and depletion deductions. For instance, if property is held in trust, the depreciation or depletion deductions are to be apportioned between the income beneficiaries and the trust on the basis of the trust income allocable to each. However, if the governing instrument (or local law) requires or permits the trustee to maintain a reserve for depreciation in any amounts, then the deduction is first allocated to the trust to the extent that income is set aside for a depreciation reserve. Any part of the deduction in excess of this amount set aside for the reserve is apportioned between the income beneficiaries and the trust on the basis of the trust income allocable to each. Reg. §§ 1.167(h)-1(b) and 1.611-1(e).

> *Example 22.14.* Melford Brock creates a trust, with his son, Bob, and his daughter, Nina, as income beneficiaries, by the transfer of income producing depreciable property. Pursuant to the terms of the trust instrument, the income from the trust is to be distributed annually on a 70 percent basis to Bob and 30 percent to Nina. Additionally, the trustee is permitted to set aside income as a depreciation reserve. In the current year, depreciation on the trust property amounts to $10,000, and the trustee allocates $5,000 of trust income as a depreciation reserve. As a result, the trust can claim $5,000 as a depreciation deduction, Bob can claim $3,500 ($10,000 − $5,000 × 70%)) and Nina can claim $1,500 ($10,000 − $5,000 × 30%)).

¶ 22,345 DNI COMPUTATIONS—COMPLEX TRUSTS AND ESTATES

In the case of a simple trust, the basic issue was the allocation of income between the trust and the beneficiaries. However, the problem of allocation among the beneficiaries will become more prominent with the complex trust and estate. Even though the complex trust and estate are taxed in substantially the same manner as a simple trust, nonetheless, some complications arise from the tier system and charitable contributions.

Tier System

There is a two-tier system of priorities (affecting DNI) that characterize the amounts distributed to beneficiaries as either income or corpus. This system provides: (1) *first tier*—income required to be distributed currently including annuity payments out of income, and (2) *second tier*—all other amounts properly paid, credited, or required to be distributed. Code Secs. 662(a)(1) and (2). This includes (a) current income that the trustee was not required to distribute; (b) accumulated income; and (c) corpus.

As a result of the system's hierarchy, the first tier has a priority on using up DNI. If the first-tier payments do not exhaust the ceiling amount of DNI, then any balance of DNI will affect the taxability of all other distributions that fall into the second tier.

> *Example 22.15.* In 1998, a trust is required to pay $20,000 out of income each year to Fred. Also, the trustee in his discretion may distribute to Joe an amount for his well being. This year the trust pays Joe $15,000. The DNI of the trust is $30,000. Thus, the tier system allocates $20,000 taxable income to Fred as a first-tier beneficiary, and $10,000 taxable income to Joe as a second-tier

beneficiary. The other $5,000 distributed to Joe would be a tax-free return of corpus.

First-Tier Distributions in Excess of DNI

Whenever the amount of income required to be distributed currently to all beneficiaries (first tier) exceeds DNI, the amount includible in the beneficiary's gross income is computed as follows. Reg. § 1.662(a)-2.

$$\frac{\text{Amount of income required to be distributed currently to first-tier beneficiary}}{\text{Amount of income required to be distributed currently to all first-tier beneficiaries}} \times \begin{array}{c}\text{Distributable net}\\\text{income (computed}\\\text{without deduction}\\\text{for charitable}\\\text{contributions)}\end{array} = \begin{array}{c}\text{Amount beneficiary}\\\text{includes in}\\\text{gross income}\end{array}$$

Example 22.16. A trust has $50,000 of DNI in the current year. The trustee is required by the instrument to distribute $30,000 each year to both the wife and daughter of the deceased. By utilizing the above formula, the wife and daughter would each have $25,000 from DNI and $5,000 from corpus ($30,000/$60,000 × $50,000 = $25,000).

First- and Second-Tier Distributions in Excess of DNI

In the event that first-tier distributions do not exhaust DNI, then beneficiaries may be taxed as second-tier distributions. Furthermore, if both first- and second-tier distributions exceed DNI, then another allocation formula is necessary to determine the amount that a beneficiary will be taxed on. This formula is as follows (Reg. § 1.662(a)-3):

$$\frac{\text{Second-tier distributions to the beneficiary}}{\text{Second-tier distributions to all beneficiaries}} \times \begin{array}{c}\text{Distributable net}\\\text{income (less}\\\text{first-tier}\\\text{distributions}\\\text{and charitable}\\\text{contributions)}\end{array} = \begin{array}{c}\text{Beneficiary's}\\\text{share of dis-}\\\text{tributable}\\\text{net income}\end{array}$$

Example 22.17. A trust has $60,000 of DNI in 1998. The fiduciary is required to distribute $40,000 each year to Mary, the surviving spouse. However, at the fiduciary's discretion, amounts may be distributed to Bob and Donna, the son and daughter of the deceased, based on their health and education needs.

During the current year, the trustee distributed $40,000 to Mary, $20,000 to Bob, and $20,000 to Donna. The beneficiaries' taxable amounts are computed as follows:

Step 1—DNI	$60,000
Less: First tier	40,000
Available for second tier	$20,000
Step 2—$20,000/$40,000 × $20,000	$10,000

Thus, Mary is taxed on $40,000, and Bob and Donna are taxed on $10,000 each. However, the other $10,000 is tax free to Bob and Donna.

Planning for Types of Distributed Income

The character of distributed income in the hands of the estate or trust is the same as its character in the hands of the beneficiaries. Tax-exempt income to the estate or trust is also tax-exempt income to the beneficiaries when distributed. Capital gains and losses and ordinary income items to the estate or trust retain the same character when distributed to the beneficiaries. If a decedent's will directs that certain types of estate income be distributed to certain beneficiaries (e.g., "My son receives tax-exempt income, my daughter receives taxable income, etc."), the dictates of the will are followed in determining the taxability of estate income distributions to the beneficiaries. Code Secs. 652(b) and 662(b). If a will does not direct that income be distributed in specified ways, then all the beneficiaries share in the different types of income in proportion to the total estate income.

> *Example 22.18.* The executor of an estate distributes $10,000 of estate income to two beneficiaries. The distributed income consists of $6,000 of tax-exempt interest and $4,000 of taxable income. One beneficiary is entitled to 75 percent of the income; the other beneficiary is entitled to 25 percent of the income. The decedent's will does not specify the type of income to be distributed to either beneficiary. Accordingly, the 75 percent beneficiary is assumed to have received 75 percent of both types of income ($4,500 tax-exempt interest and $3,000 taxable income) while the 25 percent beneficiary is assumed to have received 75 percent of both types of income ($1,500 tax-exempt interest and $1,000 taxable income).

TAX PLANNING POINTER

In drafting a will or trust instrument consideration should be given to the possible tax advantages of directing distributions of certain types of income to specified beneficiaries based on the character of the income. Thus, directing distributions of tax-exempt income to high tax bracket beneficiaries while directing distributions of taxable income to low tax bracket beneficiaries could result in an overall tax advantage to a family unit.

¶ 22,357 CHARITABLE CONTRIBUTIONS—COMPLEX TRUSTS AND ESTATES

Charitable contributions are deductible on an estate or complex trust income tax return and are not limited to a percentage of income as applicable to individuals. The instrument must indicate, however, that contributions are payable out of income before a charitable contribution can be taken. If a trust makes a charitable contribution, it is, by definition, a complex trust since simple trusts are required to distribute all income currently and cannot set aside any amount for charitable contributions. Any charitable contribution made out of tax-exempt income is not deductible on a trust or estate income tax return. If a trust or estate has both taxable and tax-exempt income and there is no designation in the will or trust agreement regarding which income was used for the contribution, the contribution is assumed to have come from all classes of income in relative proportion to the size of the contribution.

Example 22.19. A charitable contribution of $10,000 is made by a trust to Middleburg University. The trust agreement does not designate the specific income that should be used for the contribution. The trust has $20,000 of taxable income and $30,000 of tax-exempt income. A charitable contribution of $4,000 ($10,000 × $20,000/$50,000) is considered to have come from taxable income. The remaining charitable contribution of $6,000 ($10,000 × $30,000/$50,000) is considered to have come from tax-exempt income and is not deductible.

TAX PLANNING POINTER

In structuring a trust agreement, consideration should be given to indicating that planned charitable contributions come from specific types of taxable income, thereby increasing the size of the charitable contribution deduction allowable to the estate or trust on the Form 1041 income tax return.

The computational rules of charitable deductions may be exemplified by the following fact situation. Reg. § 1.662(c)-4.

Example 22.20. Under the terms of a testamentary trust, one-half of the trust income is to be distributed currently to W, the decedent's wife, for life. The remaining trust income may, in the trustee's discretion, either be paid to D, the grantor's daughter, paid to designated charities, or accumulated. The trust is to terminate at the death of W and the principal will then be payable to D.

No provision is made in the trust instrument or under local law with respect to depreciation of rental property. Therefore, depreciation will follow income. Capital gains are allocable to corpus under the applicable local law. The trust and both beneficiaries file returns on the calendar-year basis.

The records of the fiduciary show the following items of income and deduction for the taxable year:

Rents	$50,000
Dividends of domestic corporations	50,000
Tax-exempt interest	20,000
Taxable interest	10,000
Capital gains (long-term)	20,000
Depreciation of rental property	10,000
Expenses attributable to rental income	15,400
Trustee's commissions allocable to income account	2,800
Trustee's commissions allocable to principal account	1,100

Step 1—State Law Income. The state law income of the trust for fiduciary accounting purposes is $111,800, computed as follows:

Rents		$ 50,000
Dividends		50,000
Tax-exempt interest		20,000
Taxable interest		10,000
Total		$130,000
Deductions:		
Rental expenses	$15,400	
Trustee's commissions allocable to income account	2,800	18,200
Income as computed under Code Sec. 643(b)		$111,800

(Note that depreciation and long-term capital gain are not included.)

The trustee distributed one-half of the state law income ($55,900) to W and, in his discretion, makes a contribution of one-quarter ($27,950) to charity X and distributes the remaining one-quarter ($27,950) to D. The total of the distributions to beneficiaries is $83,850, consisting of (1) income required to be distributed currently to W of $55,900 and (2) other amounts properly paid or credited to D of $27,950.

Step 2—Code Sec. 643(a) Ceiling. The distributable net income of the trust as computed under Code Sec. 643(a) is $82,750, determined as follows:

Rents			$ 50,000
Dividends			50,000
Taxable interest			10,000
Tax-exempt interest		$20,000	
Less: Trustee's commissions allocable to tax-exempt interest ($20,000/$130,000 of $3,900)	$ 600		
Charitable contributions allocable to tax-exempt interest ($20,000/$130,000 of $27,950)	4,300	4,900	15,100
Total			$125,100
Deductions:			
Rental expenses		$15,400	
Trustee's commissions ($3,900 − $600 allocated to tax-exempt interest)		3,300	
Charitable deduction ($27,950 − $4,300 attributable to tax-exempt interest)		23,650	42,350
Distributable net income			$ 82,750

In computing the distributable net income of $82,750, the taxable income of the trust was computed with the following modifications. No deductions were allowed for distributions to beneficiaries and for the personal exemption of the trust. Code Sec. 643(a)(1) and (2). Capital gains were excluded. Code Sec. 643(a)(3). The tax-exempt interest (as adjusted for expenses and charitable contributions) was included. Code Sec. 643(a)(5).

Step 3—Code Sec. 661(a) Ceiling. The distributable net income of $82,750, as determined under Code Sec. 643(a), is less than the sum of the amounts distributed to W and D of $83,850. Therefore, the deduction allowable to the trust under Code Sec. 661(a) is such distributable net income as modified under Code Sec. 661(c) to exclude therefrom the items of income not included in gross income of the trust. The following computation shows the effects:

Distributable net income...............................	$82,750
Less: Tax-exempt interest (as adjusted for expenses and the charitable contributions)	15,100
Deduction allowable under Code Sec. 661(a)	$67,650

Step 4—Trust's Income. The taxable income of the trust is $19,900, determined as follows:

Rent income		$ 50,000
Dividends		50,000
Taxable interest....................................		10,000
Capital gains		20,000
Gross income		$130,000
Deductions:		
Rental expenses	$15,400	
Trustee's commissions	3,300	
Charitable contributions	23,650	
Distributions to beneficiaries	67,650	
Personal exemption	100	$110,100
Taxable Income		$ 19,900

Step 5—Inclusion and Characterization to Beneficiaries. For the purpose of determining the character of the amounts deductible under Code Secs. 642(c) and 661(a), the trustee elected to offset the trustee's commissions (other than the portion required to be allocated to tax-exempt interest) against the rental income. The determination of the character of the amounts deemed distributed to beneficiaries and contributed to charity is made as follows:

Character of Amounts Distributed to Beneficiaries and Contributed to Charity Under Code Sec. 661(a)

	Rents	Taxable Dividends	Tax-Exempt Interest	Taxable Interest	Total
Trust income........	$50,000	$50,000	$20,000	$10,000	$130,000
Less:					
Charitable contributions	10,750	10,750	4,300	2,150	27,950
Rental expenses	15,400				15,400
Trustee's commissions	3,300		600		3,900
Total deductions	$29,450	$10,750	$4,900	$2,150	$47,250
Amounts distributable to beneficiaries	$20,550	$39,250	$15,100	$7,850	$82,750

The character of the charitable contribution is determined by multiplying the total charitable contribution ($27,950) by a fraction consisting of each item of trust income, respectively, over the total trust income, except that no part of the dividends excluded from gross income is deemed included in the charitable contribution. For example, the charitable contribution is deemed to consist of rents of $10,750 ($50,000/$130,000 × $27,950).

Because the wife is a first-tier beneficiary and DNI is $82,750, the whole $55,900 is fully includible in her income. Thus, the character of the $55,900 is determined as follows:

$$\frac{\text{Total each class}}{\text{Total DNI}} \times \begin{array}{l}\text{Includible} \\ \text{amount}\end{array}$$

		K-1 Amounts
Rents	$\dfrac{\$20,550}{\$82,750} \times \$55,900 =$	$13,882
Dividends	$\dfrac{\$39,250}{\$82,750} \times \$55,900 =$	26,515
Taxable interest	$\dfrac{\$ 7,850}{\$82,750} \times \$55,900 =$	5,303
Tax-exempt interest	$\dfrac{\$15,100}{\$82,750} \times \$55,900 =$	10,200
Total		$55,900

Additionally, she may deduct a share of the depreciation deduction proportionate to the trust income allocable to her; that is, one-half of the total depreciation deduction, or $5,000.

Since the sum of the amount of income required to be distributed currently to W ($55,900) and the other amounts properly paid, credited, or required to be distributed to D ($27,950) exceeds the distributable net income ($82,750) of the trust as determined under Code Sec. 643(a), D is deemed to have received $26,850 ($82,750 − $55,900) for income tax purposes. The character of the amounts deemed distributed to her is determined as follows:

		K-1 Amounts
Rents	$\dfrac{\$20,550}{\$82,750} \times \$26,850 =$	$ 6,668
Dividends	$\dfrac{\$39,250}{\$82,750} \times \$26,850 =$	12,735
Taxable interest	$\dfrac{\$ 7,850}{\$82,750} \times \$26,850 =$	2,547
Tax-exempt interest	$\dfrac{\$15,100}{\$82,750} \times \$26,850 =$	4,900
Total		$26,850

Also, D may deduct a share of the depreciation deduction proportionate to the trust income allocable to her; that is, one-fourth of the total depreciation deduction, or $2,500.

TAX PLANNING POINTER ▼

If no provision is made in the trust instrument with respect to depreciation, the depreciation deduction may be allocated to the amount distributed to the designated charity, and, as a result, be nondeductible by the trust or beneficiaries. Thus, tax planners would be well-advised to make sure that depreciation does not follow income. This can be easily accomplished by a trust because the trust instrument can create a reserve for depreciation and depletion deductions to the remainder beneficiaries and avoid any wastage problem.

¶ 22,365 TAX RETURN SPECIAL RULES

Tax Return Schedules

A fiduciary is required to file a Schedule K-1, Form 1041, trust or estate income tax return, for each beneficiary who receives an income distribution during the trust's or estate's tax year. Schedule K-1 gives information applicable to beneficiaries on how trust or estate income distributions affect their individual income tax returns. The fiduciary should furnish a copy of Schedule K-1 to each beneficiary who received a distribution during the year from an estate or trust. For returns filed after August 5, 1997, beneficiaries of an estate or trust must file their returns in a manner consistent with the manner reported on the trust or estate's return or must file a notice of inconsistent treatment with the Secretary of the Treasury that identifies the inconsistent items.

Tax Credits

With some exceptions, estates and trusts are allowed the same tax credits as individual taxpayers. Tax credits of an estate or trust are allocated between the fiduciary and beneficiaries based on the amount of income distributed in relation to total state law income. Estates or trusts are not allowed to take the credit for the elderly or the earned income credit. Code Sec. 642(a)(2) and (b).

Miscellaneous Deductions

The two percent floor imposed on miscellaneous itemized deductions for individuals also applies to estates and trusts with some exceptions. The two percent floor does not apply to the income distribution deductions.

Administration Fees

Reasonable expenditures for administering the estate, including executor fees, are deductible; but if these expenditures are deducted on the estate's estate tax return (Form 706), they cannot also be deducted on the estate's income tax return (Form 1041). If the executor of the estate claims administrative expenses as an income tax deduction, a waiver of right to an estate tax deduction must be filed with the income tax return. Code Sec. 642(g); Reg. § 1.642(g)-1.

TAX PLANNING POINTER

The executor of the estate has to make an appropriate decision as to where the administrative expenses deduction has the greatest tax advantage to the estate, on the income tax return or on the estate tax return.

¶ 22,371 ALTERNATIVE MINIMUM TAX

For estates and trusts, the alternative minimum tax (AMT) may apply as an addition to the regular tax for a taxable year. That is, the alternative minimum taxable income (AMTI) of the entity and any beneficiary is determined by applying Subchapter J with modifications. Code Sec. 59(c). Specifically, these modifications are termed adjustments and preferences. Common adjustments to the AMTI are miscellaneous itemized deductions, state and local income taxes, real property taxes, accelerated depreciation for property placed in service after 1986, and passive activity losses. In addition to the adjustments, preferences will also affect the AMTI. Common preferences are tax-exempt interest from private activity bonds, depletion in excess of basis, accelerated depreciation of property placed in service before 1987, and intangible drilling costs.

After calculating the alternative minimum taxable income, there still remains one final adjustment. That is, the Code provides an exemption of $22,500 for estates and trusts. Code Sec. 55(d)(1)(C)(ii). The exemption will be reduced by 25 cents per $1.00 of AMTI exceeding $75,000. For tax years beginning after December 31, 1992, estates and trusts are subject to a two-tiered graduated rate schedule. That is, a 26 percent rate applies to the first $75,000 of AMTI in excess of the exemption amount and the 28 percent rate applies to the AMTI that is greater than $75,000 above the exemption amount.

Example 22.21. The income tax return of John Henry's estate showed no regular tax liability. However, the estate did generate AMTI of $20,000. The use of the exemption will prevent the AMT from generating a tax liability.

Example 22.22. Assume that John Henry's fiduciary return shows AMTI of $97,500. Because the AMTI exceeds $75,000, the exemption is reduced to $16,875 ($22,500 − (($97,500 − $75,000) × .25)).

The estate or trust must pay the higher of the AMT or the regular tax. The following illustration describes in detail an application of the AMT.

Example 22.23. In 1998, the John Henry estate had dividend income of $200,000 and $40,000 of bonus income related to the deceased, John Henry. The estate had a MACRS depreciation deduction of $24,000, while straight-line depreciation for AMT purposes was $12,000. The trust incurred fiduciary fees of $18,000 and state fiduciary income taxes of $25,000. Also, the estate had a Code Sec. 691(c) trust tax deduction of $7,000. The fiduciary distributed $28,000 to the income beneficiary, Vivian Elmore, in 1998. For 1998, the trust's federal tax liability is calculated as follows:

	Regular Tax	AMT
Dividends	$200,000	$200,000
Bonus IRD	40,000	40,000
Depreciation	(24,000)	(12,000)
Fiduciary fees	(18,000)	(18,000)
State income tax	(25,000)	0
Code Sec. 691(c) trust tax deduction	(7,000)	(7,000)
Income distribution	(28,000)	(28,000)
Tax exemption	(600)	0
Regular taxable income	$137,400	
AMTI		$175,000
AMT exemption: $22,500 − ($175,000 − $75,000) × .25)		0
Taxable amount	$137,400	$175,000
Tax liability	$ 53,464	$ 45,500

The estate must pay $53,464 in taxes, which is the greater of the regular tax or the AMT.

¶ 22,373   GIFTS, LEGACIES, AND BEQUESTS

In general, any distribution to a beneficiary by an estate or trust is treated as made out of income to the extent that the trust or estate has distributable net income. However, if amounts are properly paid or credited as gifts or bequests under the terms of the governing instrument and thus fall within the protection of Code Sec. 663(a), the distribution will not be taxed as a distribution under Code Sec. 661(a) or 662(a). That is, the amount will not be deductible by the trust nor will it be includible by the recipient. Such amounts will be received tax free under the gift exemption of Code Sec. 102.

Prior to the 1954 Code, the executor or trustee could designate the source of distribution as principal and thereby immunize the distribution. But, under the distributable net income approach adopted in the 1954 Code and continued in the 1986 Code, the distribution is taxed as income up to the extent of distributable net income regardless of the trustee's or executor's designation.

Example 22.24. Assume that a will left equal one-third shares to a husband and two children. The estate contains $1,800,000 in securities and a house. In the first year, the estate has income of $240,000 and makes a partial distribution of the house, worth $360,000, to the widower. Under these facts, the widower has taxable income of $240,000, and, as a consequence, he is bearing a substantially disproportionate tax burden in relation to the other heirs.

Lump-Sum or Installment Payouts

In order to alleviate the inordinate tax problem (as illustrated above), that an ordinary estate distribution of corpus could cause, the Code embodies exemptions for specific legacies. The Code provision is based on the standard gift exclusion reasoning that distinguishes between gifts of corpus and gifts of income. It is, of course, traditional to say that a gift of corpus should be nontaxable to the recipient. However, this concept was redefined to require, in addition, that the gift be specific and practically lump-sum in payout (only three installments are permitted). Code Sec. 663(a).

Sixty-Five Day Rule

A fiduciary of a complex trust may elect to treat any amount or portion thereof that is properly paid or credited to a beneficiary within the first 65 days following the close of the taxable year as an amount that was properly paid or credited on the last day of that taxable year. Code Sec. 663(b). For tax years beginning after August 5, 1997, a decedent's estate may elect to treat distributions made within 65 days after the close of its tax year as if they were made on the last day of the tax year. Thus, the same income tax rule applicable to trusts is now applicable to estates.

Under the 65-day rule, distributions cannot exceed the greater of the trust accounting income for the year of election, or the trust's distributable net income for the year. Also, the limitation is reduced by distributions in the election year except those amounts for which the election was claimed in the prior tax year. Reg. § 1.663(b)-1(a)(2)(i).

Separate Share Rule

Solely for the purposes of determining the amount of DNI of a trust that is allocable to a particular beneficiary, substantially separate shares of different beneficiaries in the trust are treated as separate trusts. Code Sec. 663(c). The separate share rule is a very beneficial exception to the normal taxing rules of a trust. That is, when determining the amount taxable to beneficiaries, allocation by tiers may work an injustice when a trust is administered in substantially separate shares. Consider carefully the following illustration.

Example 22.25. Assume that a trust has two beneficiaries, Bob and Sally, and DNI of $50,000. The trustee makes a mandatory distribution of one-half this amount, or $25,000 to Bob. He accumulates the other $25,000, for future distribution to Sally. Also, the fiduciary made a discretionary distribution of $20,000 from corpus to Bob. Under the tier system, Bob would be taxed on the entire $45,000 of DNI. Is this result reasonable or equitable? That is, Bob's tax is measured, in part, by $20,000 of income that can only go to Sally and will never be available for Bob.

In order to alleviate the tax problem depicted in the example above, the separate share rule was brought into the Internal Revenue Code. Therefore, in the above example, only $25,000 of DNI would be allocated to Bob and the rest would stay with the trust (Sally's share). However, the separate share rule is only allowed when the fiduciary has no discretion to allocate between beneficiaries. With respect to decedents dying after August 5, 1997, if under a decedent's will and applicable state law, separate economic interests are created in one beneficiary or class of beneficiaries that are not affected by economic interests accruing to other beneficiaries or classes of beneficiaries, the separate share rule will apply to the decedent's estate. According to the House Committee Report, application of the separate share rule to an estate is not elective (such treatment is mandatory if separate shares exist).

¶ 22,381　PROPERTY DISTRIBUTIONS

In-kind distributions require, at the fiduciary's election, either recognition of gain or a carryover basis. Code Sec. 643(e). The beneficiary's basis in property received in an in-kind distribution is the adjusted basis of the property in the hands of the estate or trust, increased by any gain and decreased by any loss recognized on the distribution. If no election is made, no gain or loss is recognized, but the amount deductible by the fiduciary and taken into income by the beneficiary as a distribution of DNI is limited to the lesser of the basis or the fair market value of the property. Code Sec. 643(e)(2). As a result, the beneficiary receives a carryover basis.

> *Example 22.26.* A trust distributes an asset with a fair market value of $20,000 and a basis of $14,000. That year it has $20,000 of DNI. Under the old rules, the distributee would have $20,000 of ordinary income and a basis of $20,000 in the asset. Under the present rules, the distribution would carry out only $14,000 of ordinary income to the beneficiary, leaving $6,000 of ordinary income to be taxed to the fiduciary, and the beneficiary would only receive a basis of $14,000.

When the fiduciary elects, the estate or trust may treat gain property as if it were sold to the distributee at its fair market value. Code Sec. 643(e)(3)(iii). Nevertheless, a loss may not be recognized by a trust because recognition of losses on sales between a trust and its beneficiary are disallowed. Code Sec. 267(b)(6). For tax years beginning after August 5, 1997, an estate and a beneficiary of an estate are treated as related persons for purposes of the disallowance of a loss on the sale of an asset to a related person under Code Sec. 267 and the disallowance of capital gain treatment on the sale of depreciable property to a related person under Code Sec. 1239.

¶ 22,387   TERMINATION OF ESTATE OR TRUST

The termination of an estate or trust is marked by the end of the period of administration by the fiduciary and the distribution of assets to beneficiaries. At this juncture, even an insolvent estate or trust can pass out valuable tax attributes to beneficiaries. That is, in the year of termination, net operating losses, capital losses, and excess deductions of an estate or trust may be utilized by beneficiaries on their own tax returns.

TAX PLANNING POINTER

It should be noted that net operating losses and capital losses that flow out to the beneficiaries may be carried forward by beneficiaries when they are not used in the year of receipt. However, excess deductions may only be used in the year of receipt with no carryforward. Also, excess deductions are subject to the two percent of AGI floor. As a result, it is important to plan for the year of termination in order to have enough AGI to absorb the deductions.

KEYSTONE PROBLEM

Jason Argonaut died on October 16, 1998. His widow, Rita, is a personal friend of yours and knows that you are taking a college taxation course. She is seeking tax advice on the tax problems associated with Jason's death. In the past, Jason and Rita filed a joint return on the cash basis of accounting with a calendar year-end. Jason left a will and a substantial estate. Rita and Jason had no children, and Rita is the sole beneficiary of the estate. Rita has listed the following tax concerns about which she is seeking advice from you and another friend, Robert, a lawyer, who has been named executor of the estate. Rita has a substantial current yearly income of her own and is very concerned about high rates of taxation. What tax advice would you give Rita on the following questions?

1. Jason received a paycheck on October 21, 1998, covering the work period September 16–October 16, 1998. The executor of the estate cashed the check and the proceeds are currently in the estate. How will this income be recognized for tax purposes?

2. What filing status will Rita use when preparing her 1998 income tax return? What about personal exemptions, standard deduction, tax forms, etc.?

3. Rita received a dividend check on October 31, 1998, made out in Jason's name on stock he held in his own name. The

dividend had been declared on September 11, 1998, to be paid on October 30, 1998, to shareholders of record on September 30, 1998. How will this dividend income be recognized for tax purposes?

4. It is anticipated that the estate will receive significant amounts of income. Who will pay tax on this income? What are some tax planning ideas that can be used by the estate to lessen the overall income tax burden on the estate and, ultimately, on Rita, the only beneficiary of the estate?

Taxation of Trusts—Special Rules

As stated previously, the scheme of federal income taxation of a trust is to have trust income taxed once, either directly to the trust or to trust beneficiaries who have received distributions from the trust. This scheme of income taxation for trusts is simple in theory but, in practice, has resulted in the development of some tax avoidance techniques involving multiple trusts, grantor trusts, and accumulation distributions. These tax avoidance techniques, along with tax legislation and IRS regulations adopted to counteract them, are discussed in this section.

¶ 22,503 MULTIPLE TRUSTS

A person may create more than one trust for the same or different beneficiaries. If the multiple trusts are recognized as valid for tax purposes, each trust is allowed a separate personal exemption and is taxed on its separate income. Whether multiple trusts have been created is a question of grantor intent as determined from the trust agreement. Tax avoidance motives could enter into the establishment of multiple trusts. Instead of having one trust taxed on a specified amount of income, why not create 10 trusts and have one-tenth of the income taxed to each trust? The obvious tax advantages of having 10 trusts would be 10 personal exemptions plus each trust starting over at the bottom of the tax rate schedule with its income and thereby mitigating the effects of a progressive tax system. However, multiple trusts are treated as a single trust for tax purposes if the trusts have the same grantor and similar beneficiaries, if there is no independent purpose for each trust, and if avoidance of the progressive rate of income tax or the alternative minimum tax appears to be the main reason why the multiple trusts were created. Code Sec. 643(e).

¶ 22,525 GRANTOR TRUSTS

In some instances, a trust can be created that qualifies as a separate legal entity but that is not a properly constituted trust for federal income tax purposes. The income from a trust of this type is taxable to the grantor instead of to the trust or beneficiaries. For qualification as a properly constituted trust for tax purposes, control of the property placed in trust must be relinquished by the grantor. Trusts that do not qualify for recognition as trusts for federal income tax purposes are called grantor trusts. A trust is usually classified as a grantor trust if the grantor or grantor's spouse owns an interest in the trust at any time or has certain proscribed powers over the trust.

Reversionary Interest. The grantor is taxed on the income from property placed in trust if it reasonably is expected that the trust property will revert to the grantor or grantor's spouse at anytime. This rule does not apply if the trust assets revert to the grantor or grantor's spouse only after the death of an income beneficiary of the trust who is a lineal descendant of the grantor or the grantor retains less than a five percent reversionary interest in the trust corpus.

Revocable Trust. If a grantor creates a trust and retains the right to revoke the trust, the trust income is taxable to the grantor. Code Sec. 676(a).

Income for Benefit of Grantor. If, at the discretion of the grantor, trust income can be distributed to the grantor or held for future distribution to the grantor, the trust income is taxable to the grantor. Code Sec. 677.

Beneficial Enjoyment. If, in certain instances, the grantor has the power to control the beneficial enjoyment of the trust income, the trust income is taxable to the grantor. Power to control beneficial enjoyment includes the power to change beneficiaries. Code Sec. 674(b).

Administrative Powers. If the grantor has administrative control over the trust property that can be exercised to the grantor's benefit, the trust income is taxable to the grantor. Code Sec. 675. Administrative control that could work to the grantor's benefit includes the right to borrow the trust property at a below-market interest rate.

SUMMARY OF CHAPTER 22

✓ Estates come into being automatically at the death of the taxpayer. The executor or administrator distributes the assets and satisfies the liabilities of the decedent either pursuant to the will or via the state's intestate succession statutes.

✓ Trusts must be specifically created either during the grantor's life (inter vivos) or at death (testamentary). Trusts are classified for tax purposes as either simple (distributes all trust accounting income) or complex (does not have to distribute all of its trust accounting income).

✓ Estate and trusts can either act as conduits or retain the income and be taxed on it.

✓ Estate and trusts are governed (1) by either the will or trust instrument and (2) by state law in its operations.

✓ To understand fiduciary taxation, an appreciation of state law income and distributable net income is required. This understanding is enhanced by the five-step illustrations at ¶ 22,325 and ¶ 22,357.

✓   Estates and trusts are subject to the alternative minimum tax (AMT) and are faced with numerous preferences and adjustments. However, estates and trusts are allowed a $22,500 exemption from the AMT.

CHAPTER 22 QUESTIONS

1. On what date is a decedent's final income tax return due?

2. What income is included on a final income tax return for a cash-basis decedent? How would your answer change if the decedent was on the accrual basis of accounting?

3. What is "income in respect of the decedent"? On whose return is "income in respect of the decedent" recognized?

4. What are "expenses in respect of the decedent"? On whose return are "expenses in respect of the decedent" deducted?

5. Unreported interest income on U.S. government bonds owned by a decedent at the date of death can be handled in various ways for tax purposes. List and discuss the various ways.

6. What are the duties and responsibilities of an executor of an estate in regard to the income tax returns required by an estate?

7. Do all estates have to file federal estate income tax returns? If not, what are the requirements for filing estate income tax returns?

8. What requirements exist for determining the first tax year-end of an estate for income tax purposes?

9. When is a federal estate income tax return due? What options are available to an estate executor in paying the estate's income tax liability?

10. What exemption amounts are allowed to an estate, simple trust, and complex trust?

11. What is the difference between an inter vivos trust and a testamentary trust?

12. Define the following terms:
    a. Reversionary interest
    b. Income beneficiary
    c. Remainder beneficiary
    d. Simple trust
    e. Complex trust

13. List and discuss two nontax reasons why an individual might consider creating a trust.

14. When is a trust required to file a federal income tax return? What tax form is used for a trust's federal income tax return?

15. Why is it important for the trustee of a trust to carefully consider the choice of an accounting method for a trust?

16. Will a trust be entitled to deduct the full value of all charitable contributions made by the trust in all situations on the trust's federal income tax return?

17. What tax benefits are embodied in specific legacies and bequests?

18. What three functions does distributable net income serve in fiduciary taxation?

19. What problem does the separate share rule alleviate?

20. Beneficiaries of estates and complex trusts are subject to the tier system of taxation. Explain what is meant by a first- and second-tier beneficiary.

21. When depreciation follows income of an estate or complex trust, explain the situation where wastage could occur.

22. In relation to trust distributions to beneficiaries, explain the 65-day rule.

23. What is a Schedule K-1? When is a trustee of a trust required to file a Schedule K-1 with the trust's federal income tax return?

24. Explain when loss carryovers can be taken from a trust's federal income tax return and be used on the trust beneficiaries' individual income tax returns.

25. Explain some tax avoidance techniques that could arise in regard to multiple trusts and accumulation distributions from trusts.

CHAPTER 22 PROBLEMS

26. Hershel Barker was the president and majority shareholder in Bulldog Inc. He was a cash-basis taxpayer who reported his income on a calendar-year basis. On March 1, 1998, Hershel was killed in a skiing accident. The estate has elected to report its income on a calendar-year basis.

   Required: Give the tax consequences for the parties involved in the following situations:

   a. Dividends of $10,000 had been declared by Bulldog Inc. on February 3, 1998, payable March 4, 1998, to shareholders of record on February 17, 1998. Hershel's executor received the dividends.

   b. What if the record date was March 10, 1998?

27. The trust instrument requires the trustee to distribute $40,000 annually to Carl Smith, the grantor's son. Any residual income may be distributed or accumulated for Bob Jones, Sam Smith, Earl Litt, and Carl Smith in the trustee's discretion. In the current year, the trust has distributable net income of $100,000 in domestic dividends. The trustee distributes $40,000 of income to Carl Smith. Next, he distributes $30,000 to Bob Jones, $20,000 each to Sam Smith and Earl Litt, and an additional $15,000 to Carl Smith. The trust does not have any undistributed net income from previous years.

   Required: How much of the distributions are taxable income to Carl Smith, Bob Jones, Sam Smith, and Earl Litt?

28. John Jefferson dies on November 10, 1998. John is on the cash basis of accounting for tax purposes. On November 29, 1998, a $4,000 paycheck covering the period November 1–November 8, 1998, is mailed to John's home. Who recognizes this paycheck as income? Would your answer to this question change if John was on the accrual basis of accounting at the date of his death?

29. Jane Jaffe dies on October 12, 1998. On the date of death, Jane has a bank account that pays interest on a quarterly basis. On December 31, 1998, $3,000 of interest income is credited to the bank account.

    a. If Jane was on the cash basis of accounting at the date of her death, is any of the income included on Jane's final income tax return?

    b. Would your answer to (a) change if Jane was on the accrual basis of accounting at the date of her death?

    c. If Jane does not recognize all of the interest income on her final income tax return in (a) and (b), who does recognize the interest income?

30. Richard Johnson held $50,000 of U.S. government savings bonds on the date of his death, December 11, 1998. The bonds mature in 1999. Unreported interest income on these bonds at the date of Richard's death amounted to $14,700. It is anticipated that Richard will be in the 28 percent marginal income tax bracket on his final income tax return. The one beneficiary to Richard's estate is expected to have a 15 percent marginal tax bracket in 1998 and a 28 percent marginal tax bracket in 1999. List and discuss some tax planning options that are available to the executor of Richard's estate and to the beneficiary of Richard's estate in regard to the recognition as income of the unreported interest income on the U.S. Government bonds.

31. An estate receives the following items of income and has the following deductions during the tax year 1998:

Income

Dividends	$ 5,000
Taxable interest	5,000
Tax-exempt interest	5,000
Total income	$15,000

Deduction

Fiduciary fee	$ 2,000

The estate files an income tax return for the calendar year 1998. No distributions were made during the year to beneficiaries. Based on these facts, what is the 1998 federal income tax liability of the estate?

32. Refer to the facts in Problem 31. If a $10,000 distribution of income was made to a beneficiary during the 1998 tax year, what is the 1998 federal income tax liability of the estate? Assume that the decedent's will does not specify that the distribution is to be paid out of any specific type of income.

33. Refer to the facts in Problem 32. How much of the $10,000 income distribution will be taxable to the beneficiary?

34. Mr. Hughes died in 1998. Pursuant to his will a testamentary trust was established. The trust instrument requires that 60 percent of the trust income be distributed currently to his wife Donna, for her life and 40 percent of the trust income be distributed to his daughter, Holly, for her life. Also, the trustee is permitted to set aside income as a depreciation reserve. In the current year, depreciation on the trust property amounts to $30,000, and the trustee allocates $10,000 of trust income as a depreciation reserve.

    a. What is the amount of the depreciation deduction allowed to the trust?

    b. What is the amount of the depreciation deduction allowed to Donna?

    c. What is the amount of the depreciation deduction allowed to Holly?

35. In 1998, a trust has $2,000 of trust accounting income and $1,600 of distributable net income. The trust properly pays $1,100 to John Smith, a beneficiary, on February 3, 1998, which the trustee elects to treat under Code Sec. 663(b) (65-day rule) as paid on December 31, 1997. The trust also properly pays to John Smith $1,200 on August 1, 1998, and $900 on January 21, 1999. For 1998, how much may be elected under the 65-day rule as properly paid or credited on the last day of 1998?

36. John Henderson's will provides for the creation of a trust for the benefit of Holly Jones. Under the specific terms, the trust is required to distribute to Holly $50,000 cash and 1,000 shares of IBM stock when she reaches 25 years of age, $60,000 cash and 1,200 shares of Xerox when she reaches 30 years of age, $30,000 cash and 2,000 shares of General Motors stock when she reaches 35 years of age, and $100,000 cash and 500 shares of DuPont stock when she reaches 40 years of age. Which if any of these items qualify for exclusion as a specific legacy or bequest?

37. The trustee of the Astro trust makes a $15,000 charitable contribution to PennOhio University. The trust agreement is silent as to the specific type of income that should be used to pay the contribution. The trust had $15,000 of taxable income and $10,000 of tax-exempt income during the year.

    How much of the $15,000 charitable contribution is deductible on the trust's federal income tax return?

38. The trustee of the James trust makes a $30,000 charitable contribution to the United Way. The trust had $20,000 of taxable income and $30,000 of tax-exempt income during the year. The trust agreement states that all charitable contributions, to the extent possible, should be paid out of taxable income. How much of the $30,000 charitable contribution is deductible on the trust's federal income tax return?

39. A trustee distributes $10,000 of income to each of nine beneficiaries of the trust. The trust had $40,000 of tax-exempt interest income during the year and $80,000 of taxable income. The trust agreement does not specify the type of income to be distributed to any beneficiary.

    a. How much of the $10,000 distribution to each beneficiary is taxable income to each beneficiary?

    b. Would your answer to (a) change if the trust agreement specifies that tax-exempt income should be distributed to beneficiaries 1-4 and taxable income should be distributed to beneficiaries 5-9?

40. The trustee of the Peterson trust is required by the trust agreement to distribute $5,000 yearly to Peter Peterson, $4,000 yearly to John Peterson, and $3,000 yearly to Sally Peterson. The trustee has the authority per the trust agreement to make additional distributions to the beneficiaries at his discretion. During 1998, the trustee actually distributes $10,000 to Peter, $15,000 to John, and $20,000 to Sally. The trust has DNI of $30,000 in 1998.

    What is the taxable amount of the distributions to Peter, John, and Sally?

41. An estate with distributable net income of $100,000 distributes the following assets to a beneficiary in December of 1998:

	Basis to Estate	Value at Date of Distribution
Cash	$ 40,000	$ 40,000
General Motors Stock	90,000	140,000
Real Estate	100,000	250,000
Mucho Taco Stock	70,000	50,000
	$300,000	$480,000

    a. What is the beneficiary's basis in the distributed assets?

    b. What would be the beneficiary's basis in the distributed assets if the election is made by the fiduciary under Code Sec. 643(e)(3)?

42. John and Ralph, two brothers who are over the age of 21, are beneficiaries of a trust created in 1982 by their father, Jim. At that time, Jim transferred securities and an apartment building to a corporate trustee. All of the income is to be distributed annually to John and Ralph for 18 years. Depreciation follows income, and at the end of 18 years, the trust will terminate and

the corpus will be distributed to John and Ralph. During 1998, the trust has the following items of income and expense.

Rental income	$50,000
Taxable interest	40,000
Tax-exempt interest	30,000
Long-term capital gain (allocable to corpus)	15,000
Expenses attributable to rent	20,000
Trustee's commission (allocable to income)	4,000
Trustee's commission (allocable to principal)	1,000
Depreciation	8,000

Required:

a. Compute state law income.

b. Compute DNI as an income ceiling.

c. Compute DNI as a deduction ceiling.

d. Compute the trust's taxable income.

e. Compute DNI as a qualitative yardstick.

43. Which of the following items affects the charitable deduction of an estate or complex trust?

a. Rental income

b. Dividends

c. Interest

d. Tax-exempt interest

44. Which of the following deductions does not affect trust accounting income?

a. Rental expenses

b. Trustee's commissions allocable to income

c. Interest expense

d. Taxes

e. Trustee's commissions allocable to corpus

45. Which of the following items does not normally enter into the computation of distributable net income?

a. Charitable deduction

b. Capital gains

c. Trustee's commissions

d. Rental income

46. An estate with depreciable property may not do one of the following:

a. Pay income to first-tier beneficiaries

b. Pay income to second-tier beneficiaries

c. Distribute capital losses on termination

d. Set up a reserve for depreciation

47. A trust can have the following taxable year-end:
    a. September 30
    b. June 30
    c. December 31
    d. March 31

48. *Comprehensive Problem.* Thomas Able, a cash method, calendar-year taxpayer, died December 1, 1998. He is survived by his spouse, Nan. Tom was age 65 at the time of his death and Nan is age 66. They have no dependents, and Nan is the sole beneficiary of Tom's estate. Nan has been blind from cataracts since taking a tax course at Old Dominion University in 1976. The executor of the estate is the First Wachovia Corp., Winston-Salem, North Carolina. Nan and the executor elected to file a joint return for 1998. During 1998, the following cash receipts, disbursements, and expenses were recorded by the Ables and the estate of Tom Able:

    a. Cash dividends of $25,000 from Safflower Oil Corporation were received on November 28, 1998. These dividends were declared on November 3, 1998, and payable to shareholders of record on November 14, 1998. Tom Able was the stockholder in Safflower Oil Corporation.

    b. Tom was an executive in the Kane & Able Trucking Company in Winston-Salem, North Carolina, and for the two months preceding his death, Tom was not paid his monthly salary of $5,000 because of a moratorium on wages. On January 5, 1999, the trucking company paid the $10,000 to the executor of the Tom Able Estate. Tom had received all his other monthly salary payments at the end of each month.

    c. Interest of $1,800 was credited to Tom and Nan's savings accounts on August 1, 1998.

    d. Real estate taxes of $1,000 were paid by the estate on December 31, 1998, for the calendar year.

    e. Medical expenses of $5,700 related to Tom's last illness were paid by his estate on January 20, 1999. The executor has elected not to deduct these medical expenses on the estate tax return. Health insurance premiums of $500 were paid by Tom during 1998.

    f. A bonus of $4,500 from the Kane & Able Trucking Company was paid to Tom's estate on January 16, 1999.

    g. Charitable contributions of $1,200 were paid to the Ventura County Humane Society by Tom during 1998.

    h. Interest on the Ables' home mortgage amounted to $1,600 in 1998.

    i. On May 29, 1998, Tom received $25,000 in life insurance proceeds paid by reason of the death of his mother.

j.   Tom has always attended Saturday night cockfights. During 1998, he won $500 and lost $800.

k.   On June 9, 1998, Tom submitted his entry in a Fairview Books Publishing Company contest. On August 1, 1998, it was announced that Tom had won $3,000 cash and a year's worth of free computer research time worth $900. Tom accepted the $3,000 but refused the computer research time because he had heard the system was difficult to use.

l.   Nan and Tom sold stock that they had purchased on December 27, 1997, at $1,000 for $1,200 on June 24, 1998.

m. Tom also owned a farm that produced total annual revenue of $1,000 and expenses of $100 for utilities, $200 for fertilizer and lime, $100 for miscellaneous expenses, $100 for repairs and maintenance, and depreciation expense of $200 in 1998 prior to Tom's death. The farm has been idle since Tom's death.

n.   Tom and Nan kept meticulous records verifying the $1,500 they paid in sales tax in 1998.

o.   Federal and state income taxes of $9,900 and $2,000, respectively, were withheld from Tom's salary in 1998.

p.   Tom and Nan had a $500 balance due on their 1997 North Carolina return that was paid on April 12, 1998.

Required: Compute the amount of taxable income that will go on the decedent's final return.

49. *Comprehensive Problem.* In 1998, Cabell Mapp passed away in Belle Haven, Virginia. Pursuant to his will, a testamentary trust was established. The trust instrument requires that $10,000 a year be paid to the University of Virginia. The balance of the income may, in the trustee's discretion, be accumulated or distributed to Sarah Mapp. Expenses are allocable against income and the trust instrument requires a reserve for depreciation. During the taxable year, the trustee contributes $10,000 to the University of Virginia, and in his discretion distributes $15,000 of income to Sarah Mapp. The trust has the following items of income and expenses for the taxable year.

Dividends	$10,000
Interest	10,000
Fully tax-exempt interest	10,000
Rents	20,000
Rental expenses	2,000
Depreciation of rental property	3,000
Trustee's commissions	5,000

    a.   Determine trust accounting income.

    b.   Determine DNI as an income ceiling.

    c.   Determine DNI as a deduction ceiling.

    d.   Determine the trust taxable income.

    e.   Determine DNI as a qualitative yardstick.

    f.   Determine Sarah Mapp's Schedule K-1 amounts.

    g.   Has any wastage occurred in connection with the charitable deduction? Could this wastage have been prevented?

50. *Research Problem.* When a trust terminates, there are, in most instances, terminating commissions that are charged by the fiduciary. These commissions may generate excess deductions that can be passed out to beneficiaries as itemized deductions subject to the two percent of adjusted gross income rule. Nonetheless, the allocation of such expenses with respect to character of the income has spawned litigation as to the proper allocation base.

Read the following cases and prepare a brief written summary of the allowable allocation method for terminating commissions.

    a.   *C.L. Whittemore, Jr. v. U.S.,* 67-2 USTC ¶ 9670, 383 F.2d 824 (CA-8 1967).

    b.   *A.J. Fabens,* 75-2 USTC ¶ 9572, 519 F.2d 1310 (CA-1 1975).

51. *Research Problem.* The following court cases have helped to clarify the rightful recipient of depreciation of property held by an estate or trust.

Read the following judicial decisions and prepare a brief written summary for each case.

    a.   *Sue Carol,* 30 BTA 443, CCH Dec. 8520 (1934), Acq. XIII-2 CB 4.

    b.   *R.J. Dusek,* 67-1 USTC ¶ 9418, 376 F.2d 410 (CA-10 1967).

    c.   *W.H. Lamkin, Executor,* 76-2 USTC ¶ 9485, 533 F.2d 303 (CA-5 1976).

Chapter 23

Retirement Planning

Learning Objectives

After completing Chapter 23, you should be able to:

1. Understand the basics of qualified and nonqualified corporation pension plans.
2. Recognize retirement plans for the self-employed.
3. Identify income and estate taxations of retirement plans for individuals.
4. Calculate special use valuation for farmland and closely held business realty.
5. Understand the use of life insurance trusts to avoid estate taxation and provide liquidity.
6. Explain the use of private annuities, buy-sell agreements, AB trust setup, QTIP trusts, Section 6166, and lifetime giving as retirement planning techniques.
7. Recognize the impact of community property on estate planning.
8. Analyze and implement estate planning techniques in a comprehensive retirement planning problem.

OVERVIEW OF CHAPTER

Planning for retirement benefits is essential because often retirement benefits represent an individual's single largest asset. Naturally, income contributed to a retirement plan can often increase substantially by the time of distribution. Careful planning can increase liquidity of an estate, provide income tax savings, and maximize the amount available for distribution. In order for an individual to maximize the value of retirement benefits, consideration must be given to an assortment of plans. In this chapter, qualified and nonqualified plans and retirement plans for the self-employed are discussed. In addition, the income and estate tax consequences of the various retirement plans are depicted.

Also, this chapter demonstrates the use of private annuities, installment notes, buy-sell agreements, AB trusts, QTIP trusts, life insurance trusts, lifetime giving, impact of community property, and Code Sections 121 and 1034 for retirement and estate planning purposes.

This chapter differs from the other chapters in this book. Specifically, this chapter ties together numerous planning techniques for retirement and estate planning purposes. Consequently, numerous questions and problems on the various aspects of retirement planning are not provided; instead, a comprehensive retirement and estate planning problem is set forth to facilitate an understanding of the overall retirement planning concept.

Qualified and Nonqualified Pension Plans

¶ 23,001   TAX ADVANTAGES OF QUALIFIED PLANS

An employee plan may qualify for tax advantages only if, among other things, it is a pension plan, profit-sharing plan, stock bonus plan, or annuity plan. Self-employed individuals can establish H.R. 10 or Keogh plans and individuals can contribute to individual retirement accounts (IRAs). If the plan, which may take the form of a trust, meets the statutory requirements, the plan will qualify for special tax benefits. These include tax exemption for the fund that is established to provide benefits, deductions by the employer for contributions made to the fund, deferral for the participant of tax on the employer's contributions and earnings thereon and, in some instances, favorable tax treatment for the payment of benefits. The tax advantages flowing from qualified plans are briefly summarized below:

1. The contribution is deductible to the employer, the self-employed person, or the individual (IRAs). Except for IRAs, the contribution may even create or increase a net operating loss that can be carried back or forward.

2. The contributions are not taxable to the employee or participant until benefits are paid, perhaps decades later.

3. Income on invested funds accumulates tax free, allowing the assets to grow at a faster pace than otherwise.

4. Under certain conditions, and within certain limits, the participant may borrow from the plan without tax consequences.

5. Lump-sum distributions from qualified plans (except IRAs) generally qualify for special five-year forward averaging at low rates independent of other income. A unique capital gain option may also be available for a portion of the distribution.

6. After retirement the beneficiary's tax bracket may be lower than at the time contributions were made.

Example 23.1. Alan Davis worked for Big Lights Inc. for 30 years until he retired. Each year his employer put 11 percent of his salary in a qualified pension trust. Upon retirement, Alan receives a retirement annuity, a monthly pension. Each year for 30 years the contribution was deductible to Big Lights and nontaxable to Alan. The income of the trust is not taxed. Upon retirement, the pension received is includible in Alan's gross income.

¶ 23,015   QUALIFICATION REQUIREMENTS

A retirement plan, its sponsoring employer, and its participants are not eligible for the tax benefits referred to above unless the plan meets a number of requirements. The fundamental requirement is that the plan may not discriminate in coverage, contributions, or benefits in favor of highly compensated employees. Code Sec. 401(a). Certain plans that primarily benefit an employer's key employees (also called top-heavy plans) are subject to qualification requirements that are more strict than those applying to other plans. In addition to the qualification requirements, there are minimum participation standards and minimum vesting standards that a plan must meet. Code Secs. 410 and 411. Minimum funding standards are also imposed on pension plans (as distinguished from profit-sharing and stock bonus plans). Code Sec. 412.

All qualified deferred compensation plans are subject to a number of basic rules. To summarize, briefly, the most important of these are:

1. The plan must be in writing and constitute a continuous program.

2. The plan must be created and operated for the exclusive benefit of the employee/participants in an independent trust isolated from the misfortunes of the employer.

    Example 23.2. Cockburn Oil Corp. established a qualified pension plan for its employees many years ago. The assets in the trust amount to over $900,000. Having a cash-flow problem, the corporation would like to borrow $100,000 from the plan on commercially reasonable terms. Since the plan must be operated for the exclusive benefit of the participant/employees, such a loan is prohibited. Two years later, Cockburn Oil Corp. goes bankrupt. The creditors of the corporation cannot touch the assets in the plan since the trust is a different legal entity in which the contributor has no interest.

3. All contributions must be made with a view to distributing benefits to the beneficiaries and must meet certain funding requirements.

4. Trust funds must be used for the exclusive benefit of the beneficiaries.

5. The plan cannot discriminate in favor of highly compensated employees. See discussion at ¶ 23,025.

6. Minimum participation standards relating to age and service must be met. See discussion at ¶ 23,035.

7. Minimum vesting standards (two main choices) must be met ("vesting" means the nonforfeitable right to receive a future benefit). See discussion at ¶ 23,045.

8. The plan must not exceed certain maximum limits on contributions and/or benefits.

9. If an annuity option exists, a married participant must be able to elect a joint and survivorship annuity.

¶ 23,025 NONDISCRIMINATION REQUIREMENTS

The general statutory requirements impose a number of restrictions on deferred compensation plans in order to insure that the funds are used for the benefit of the employees rather than the employer. Code Sec. 401(a). Most important, the plan may not discriminate in coverage, contributions, or benefits in favor of highly compensated employees. For tax years before 1989, the prohibition was directed to discrimination in favor of officers, stockholders, or highly compensated employees. It should be noted, however, that many officers and shareholders are within the present definition of highly compensated employees.

Under rules effective January 1, 1997, a highly compensated employee is one who (1) at any time during the current or preceding year was a five percent owner or (2) received, during the preceding year, more than an indexed dollar amount of annual compensation from the employer ($80,000 for plan years beginning in 1997) and, if the employer elects, was among the top 20 percent of the employer's work force in terms of compensation.

The rule requiring the highest paid officer to be treated as a highly compensated employee was repealed effective January 1, 1997.

Example 23.3. Wayne Ingalls' annual compensation at First Rate Inc. was $82,000, but he was not among the top 20 percent of employees in terms of compensation. Even though Wayne is relatively highly paid, he may be included in the nonhighly compensated group, increasing the plan's chances of passing the nondiscrimination test.

It is not necessary that both contributions and benefits be nondiscriminatory under a qualified plan. In a pension plan (other than a money purchase plan) there must be no discrimination with respect to benefits. Conversely, in a profit-sharing plan there must be no discrimination with respect to contributions. The same rules apply on an overall basis when an employer maintains two plans that are of a like kind. But where there are unlike plans (e.g., a pension plan and a profit-sharing plan), the anti-discrimination test will be met if it can be shown that, on an overall basis, either the benefits or the contributions are nondiscriminatory.

Finally, there is a special nondiscrimination test that applies to retirement plan participants (of whatever type) and matching contributions by employers. Code Sec. 401(m). Matching contributions are those made by the employer on account of a contribution by a participant or on account of an elective contribution by a participant under a cash or deferred arrangement. Failure to satisfy the special nondiscrimination test will not result in disqualification of the plan if the excess contributions are distributed by the end of the plan year, but a 10 percent excess contributions tax is imposed unless they are distributed within two and one-half months after the year in which they are made.

¶ 23,035 PARTICIPATION AND COVERAGE REQUIREMENTS

Qualified plans must meet certain minimum participation requirements as to the age and years of service for employees to qualify for eligibility, and coverage requirements based on the percentage of employees to be covered under the plan. Code Secs. 401(a)(3) and 410(b).

Minimum Participation Rule

A defined benefit plan is not a qualified plan unless it benefits no fewer than the lesser of (1) 50 employees or (2) the greater of (a) 40 percent or more of all employees of the employer or (b) two employees (or one employee if the employer has only one employee). This is known as the "50-40 rule." This requirement must be satisfied by all plans on an individual basis and not by aggregating comparable plans. With IRS consent, an employer may elect to have the 50-40 rule apply separately to an employer's lines of business with regard to participation standards. These standards delineate the extent to which a plan may establish age and service requirements for individual employees. The 50-40 rule no longer applies to defined contribution plans after December 31, 1996. Code Sec. 401(a)(26)(A) and (G).

Age and Service Requirements

Generally, a qualified plan may require no more than one year of service or, if later, the attainment of age 21 as a condition of participation. Thus, an individual who is under age 21 at the time of employment may have to wait more than one year before being able to participate in the plan. A qualified plan that provides for mandatory participation may require the completion of two years (rather than one year) of service or the attainment of age 21, whichever comes first.

For purposes of the age and service requirement, a year of service is defined as a 12-month period during which the employee has completed at least 1,000 hours of service. Thus, participation is not required if a part-time employee works less than 1,000 hours.

Coverage Requirements

Each qualified plan must provide coverage that meets a percentage test, a ratio test, or an average benefits test.

1. *Percentage test.* The plan must benefit at least 70 percent of nonhighly compensated employees.

2. *Ratio test.* The percentage of nonhighly compensated employees covered under the plan must be at least 70 percent of the percentage of highly compensated employees covered. If, as in the typical case, *all* highly compensated employees benefit, 70 percent of nonhighly compensated employees must benefit.

3. *Average benefits test.* Employer-provided contributions (including forfeitures) and benefits from all qualified plans for

nonhighly compensated employees must be, on the average (per employee), at least 70 percent of the average benefits percentage for highly compensated employees.

Example 23.4. Georgia Peach Inc. has 550 employees, of which 50 are highly compensated. Under the "percentage test," 350 of the nonhighly compensated employees would have to be covered (70 percent of 500). However, if only 25 of the highly compensated employees are covered, or 50 percent, the plan only need cover 175 of the nonhighly compensated employees under the "ratio test." This is because only 70 percent of 50 percent, or 35 percent of the nonhighly compensated employees, need be covered under the second test, or only some 36 percent of the total labor force.

If an employer is operating separate lines of business, the employer may apply the percentage test, the ratio test, and the average benefits test for such year separately with respect to employees in each separate line of business. A line of business will not be treated as separate unless it has at least 50 employees who are not excludable in determining the top-paid group for purposes of who may be designated as highly compensated employees. Also, the employer must receive a determination from the IRS that the line of business may be treated as separate.

¶ 23,045 VESTING REQUIREMENTS

Vesting refers to when the employee "owns" the *employer's* contributions, regardless of whether or not the employee keeps the job and regardless of the reason for which the employee was terminated or resigned. Under current law, the meter starts ticking when the employee is enrolled in the plan. Each employee 21 years or older with at least one year of service must be enrolled if eligible. (If immediate vesting is provided, two years of service may be required.)

Prior to the Pension Reform Act of 1974, horror stories relating to vesting abuses were common. An employee might be fired the day before the employee's 65th birthday and receive no pension (except for the employee's own contributions) if the pension contract specified that the employee had to be employed at age 65 to be eligible.

The employer has two choices as far as minimum vesting requirements are concerned. Code Sec. 411(a).

1. *Three-to-seven-year rule.* The employee must be at least 20 percent vested after completion of three years of service, and must be another 20 percent vested for each additional year of service until the employee is fully vested after seven years of service.

2. *Five-year rule.* An employee must be fully vested after five years of service (also known as "cliff" vesting).

Even though the two vesting schedules are effective in 1989, pre-1989 years of service count toward vesting under the present rules.

Note that vested benefits are not necessarily inheritable, nor do benefits have to be paid until normal retirement age. Thus, vesting may be defined as a present, nonforfeitable right to a future benefit.

Example 23.5. Evelyn Evans was terminated by reason of incompetence after five years of participation in a qualified pension plan using "three-to-seven-year" vesting. Her account balance was $20,000. Since she is 60 percent vested, $8,000 is forfeited. The remaining, vested account balance, $12,000, will stay and grow in the plan until the normal retirement age (e.g., until Evelyn is 65 years of age) at which time she will receive a pension that is the actuarial equivalent of the account balance at that time.

¶ 23,055   PENSION PLANS

A pension plan is a deferred compensation arrangement that an employer establishes and maintains primarily to provide employees systematically with definitely determinable benefits over a period of years that are usually all post-retirement years. Benefits are geared to such factors as length of service and compensation. Employer contributions under a qualified pension plan must not depend on profits but must be sufficient to provide definitely determinable benefits on some actuarial basis.

There are two basic types of qualified pension plans: the *defined benefit plan* (the pension is guaranteed and contributions must be made to deliver on the promise) and the *defined contribution plan* (only the contribution is guaranteed, not the ultimate pension).

Defined Benefit Plan

The defined benefit plan provides a formula that defines the benefits employees are to receive on retirement. Thus, the plan promises specified benefits, typically in the form of a monthly retirement pension based on levels of compensation and years of service. Contributions to the plan are actuarially calculated to provide the promised benefits and are not allocated to individual accounts of participants.

Under the defined benefit plan, the employer establishes in advance what an employee's pension will be upon retirement. (After retirement the benefit may be adjusted for increases in the cost of living, using IRS-provided indexes. However, a plan may provide for a minimum annual increase of three percent.)

The annual normal retirement benefit for the participant may not exceed the lesser of an indexed dollar amount or 100 percent of the participant's average compensation (not exceeding $160,000 for benefits accruing in 1997 or 1998) for the participant's three consecutive years of highest compensation. For limitation years ending with or within 1997, the indexed dollar amount is $125,000 ($130,000 in 1998). A reduction is made in cases where the employee has participated less than 10 years in the plan. Further, the dollar amount is actuarially reduced in the case of retirement before Social Security retirement age. It is actuarially increased in the case of retirement after Social Security retirement age.

Example 23.6. Sherie Winnie works for an employer with a qualified pension plan. The plan provides that, upon normal retirement at age 65, she will receive a fixed annual pension equal to two percent of her highest average annual pay during any consecutive three-year period for each year of service with a maximum of 30 years counted. When Sherie retires at age 65 she has 38 years of service and her average pay for her highest paid consecutive three years is $42,500. Her pension equals 60 percent (two percent for each of 30 years) of $42,500, or $25,500. The plan also provides that the pension will be actuarially reduced if she retires before age 65 and increased if she retires later.

Defined Contribution Plan

The defined contribution plan is also called a money purchase plan. With this type of plan, the employer promises a specific contribution on behalf of each participant (usually expressed as a percentage of compensation). The contributions are not determined with reference to the employer's profits. The contributions must be allocated among individual accounts maintained for participants, and the plan must have a definite, written formula for the allocation. Benefits are based on contributions to participants' accounts, accumulations of income, appreciation (or depreciation) in value of assets, and the allocation of any forfeitures from accounts of other participants.

No actuary is necessary for this plan. The employer simply contributes a specified percent of the employee's salary to the plan each year. Whatever retirement benefit the accumulated sum will purchase is the amount the employee receives.

Example 23.7. Steve Colburn works for a corporation with a money purchase pension plan. Each year the employer contributes nine percent of his pay to the plan. When Steve retires after 28 years, he is making $47,000. However, his account balance is only sufficient to purchase a pension (annuity) of $8,000 a year. Steve has no legal right to more than this since only the contribution was defined, not the ultimate pension.

The defined contribution plan is simple to administer, but the ultimate pension benefit is hard to predict. The annual addition to a participant's account may not exceed the lesser of (1) 25 percent of the participant's gross compensation (not exceeding $160,000 in 1998) for the year in question or (2) $30,000. An "annual addition" consists of (1) contributions by the employer, (2) forfeitures of other participants that are allocated to the participant's account, and (3) contributions by the participants. Because of the administrative convenience, the smaller the company, the more likely it is to go with a money purchase plan. For purposes of this test, the definition of compensation has been expanded to include (1) elective deferrals to 401(k) plans and other similar arrangements, (2) elective contributions to Code Sec. 457 nonqualified deferred compensation plans, and (3) salary reduction contributions made to a cafeteria plan.

The effect of this change is to increase the amounts that may be contributed to a defined contribution plan on behalf of nonhighly compensated employees. Code Secs. 415(c)(3)(D) and 414(q)(4).

Under prior law, an overall limit was in effect regarding the amount of annual contributions that could be made on behalf of an employee who participated in both a defined contribution plan and a defined benefit plan maintained by the same employer. That overall limit has been repealed effective January 1, 2000.

¶ 23,065 TOP-HEAVY PLANS

If a qualified pension plan is top-heavy, the funding and participation requirements are sharpened. A plan is considered top-heavy if (1) the present value of the accumulated accrued benefits (defined benefit plans) or (2) the sum of the account balances (defined contribution plans) of key employees exceeds 60 percent of the same amount determined for all employees under the plan. Code Sec. 416(g).

Key employees include (1) officers having annual compensation greater than an indexed $60,000 (50 percent of the defined benefit limit of an indexed $130,000 in 1998), (2) the 10 largest employee-owners, (3) five percent owners, and (4) more-than-one-percent owners with compensation in excess of $160,000. Code Sec. 416(i).

> *Example 23.8.* Ed Roth is a two percent owner of Optical Illusions Inc. and earns $60,000 a year. If he is one of the 10 largest owner-employees, and/or he is an officer, Ed is a key employee. If he is neither, he may become a key employee (not that he necessarily would want to) by purchasing an additional three percent ownership interest or by having his salary increased by more than 150 percent.

Once a plan is top-heavy for a given year, additional qualification requirements are imposed. Under the top-heavy plan rules, there are (1) alternative rapid vesting schedules, (2) minimum amounts of nonintegrated contributions and benefits for employees who are not key employees, (3) limits on the amount of a participant's compensation that may be taken into account, and (4) further limitations on the aggregate limit on contributions and benefits for some key employees. Because the additional rules for top-heavy plans (vesting, minimum benefits, and contributions, etc.) are qualification rules, a top-heavy plan is a qualified plan only if these rules are met. Code Sec. 416.

Because a plan may be top-heavy one year and not another, and all plans potentially are top-heavy, every plan instrument should include language to comply with these provisions in case they become applicable.

¶ 23,075 401(k) PLANS

After 1978, the cash or deferred arrangement (CODA), also called the Section 401(k) plan, became more attractive. The employer contribution, if any, is not taxable even though the employee may elect to receive cash currently or in the future. The plan is typically used to shelter part of the employee's regular pay (i.e., as a "salary reduction plan"). As a qualified plan, it must meet all general requirements under Section 401(a), discussed at ¶ 23,015. In addition, the plan must:

1. Provide for immediate vesting.

2. Not allow distributions until retirement, death, disability, or separation from service, attainment of age 59½, or because of "heavy and immediate" financial need where funds are not "reasonably available" from other sources. A 10 percent excise tax is imposed on early withdrawals unless used for deductible medical expenses (in excess of the 7.5 percent of AGI limitation).

3. Not allow distributions with the mere passage of time or upon completion of a time period in the plan.

4. Meet a special set of nondiscrimination and participation standards. Code Sec. 401(k)(3). The law was changed effective January 1, 1997, to base the nondiscrimination test on the prior year's deferrals, rather than on the current year's deferrals. This will make it easier for plans to pass the nondiscrimination test.

Even though employee contributions, up to 15 percent of compensation (net of salary reduction), are not subject to income taxation currently, they *are* subject to FICA taxes, and are subject to an annual limitation, $10,000 in 1998. *Total* employer and employee contributions are limited to the lesser of 25 percent of net compensation of the participants or $30,000 since CODAs are considered profit-sharing plans. Code Secs. 401(k)(2) and 404(a)(3). Note that interest on loans secured by elective contributions is nondeductible. Code Sec. 72(p).

The Taxpayer Relief Act of 1997 amended the law to require diversification of Code Sec. 401(k) plan investments. Effective for elective deferrals made after 1998, companies may not require employees to invest more than 10 percent of the Code Sec. 401(k) plan funds in company stock or assets. The employees can maintain more than 10 percent if they do so voluntarily. This provision does not apply to ESOPs or to individual account plans that require only 1 percent or less of an individual account's assets to be invested in employer securities.

For plan years beginning after December 31, 1996, tax-exempt organizations may establish 401(k) plans for their employees. State and local governments (or political subdivisions, agencies, or instrumentalities thereof) still continue to be barred from maintaining cash or deferred arrangements. This prohibition does not apply to rural cooperatives or Indian tribal governments. Code Sec. 401(k)(4)(B).

Keogh (H.R. 10) Plans for the Self-Employed

¶ 23,201   GENERAL CONSIDERATIONS

Prior to 1984, substantial differences existed between corporate and noncorporate deferred compensation plans, almost entirely in the favor of the former. As a result, the ability to set up a corporate defined benefit plan was the primary reason for professional corporations. Under present law, few significant differences exist between the two types of plans. This "parity" was achieved partly by making corporate plans less attractive and partly by liberalizing self-employment plans.

¶ 23,215 SELF-EMPLOYMENT INCOME

Only individuals with self-employment income are eligible to set up and contribute to Keogh plans. Code Sec. 1402(a). Self-employment income includes net income (reduced by one-half of the self-employment tax, if any) from a sole proprietorship or a partnership, income earned as an independent contractor, and income from consulting fees, directors' fees, and royalties from books, to name a few. An individual with earned income can shelter part of it in a Keogh plan, even if the individual is also an employee. In addition, an individual can maintain his or her own IRA. Thus, in some cases, one individual may be covered by a corporate plan, a Keogh plan, and an IRA, as well as by social security, all at the same time. Deductible IRA contributions may only be made subject to certain adjusted gross income limitations, as discussed at ¶ 23,305.

> *Example 23.9.* Hugh Husk, Ph.D., is Associate Professor of Auditing at Georgia State University. He is covered by the University pension plan as a state employee. He has recently written a textbook entitled *How to Audit S&Ls Without Legal Liability,* and has been appointed to the board of directors of RML, a breakfast cereal producer. Even though he is an active participant in the university's pension plan, and even if covered by Social Security, Professor Husk may set up one or more Keogh accounts and, within limits, shelter a portion of his royalties and director's fees.

¶ 23,225 CONTRIBUTIONS AND BENEFITS

The contribution and benefit limits for self-employment plans are identical to the corporate limitations applying to defined contribution and defined benefit plans. Thus, a defined contribution plan can receive the lesser of 25 percent of net earned income (20 percent of earned income *before* the contribution) or $30,000, while a defined benefit plan can receive a contribution funding an annual benefit equal to the lesser of an indexed amount of $130,000 (in 1998) or 100 percent of (three-year high) earned income (limited to $160,000 for benefits accruing beginning in 1997 and 1998). Code Sec. 415(b)(1) and (c)(1).

> *Example 23.10.* If self-employment income for an individual is $50,000, the maximum contribution under a money purchase plan is $10,000 (20 percent of the gross, 25 percent of net earned income). If the plan is a defined benefit plan and the individual is age 40, the contribution will be approximately 60 percent, depending on the actuarial assumption made; 60 percent of the net equals 37.5 percent of the gross. Thus, the maximum deductible contribution would be $18,750, or almost 90 percent higher.

¶ 23,235 COVERAGE AND VESTING REQUIREMENTS

The coverage, participation, and vesting rules discussed at ¶ 23,035–¶ 23,045 apply. Thus, the owners of an unincorporated business must cover their employees on a nondiscriminatory basis. A choice may be made between the two basic vesting schedules. The top-heavy plan rules apply and are more likely to be triggered in the typically small, unincorporated business, where the lion's share often goes to the owner(s). If applicable, the special restrictions, such as minimum contributions for all employees and no extra deductions for combined plans, are effective. Forfeitures under a profit-sharing plan may increase the account balances of owner-employees.

Example 23.11. Deerstalker Associates is a national, unincorporated firm of private investigators. Deerstalker employs 400 people on a full-time basis and another 100 on an hourly pay "as needed" basis. A qualified Keogh plan for the employees must cover at least 50 of the full-time employees (the lesser of 40 percent or 50 employees) under the minimum participation standard. Thus, a qualified plan for Deerstalker's 28 highly compensated employees only, for example, would not be permitted, even if a second plan for their operatives and office personnel was established as well.

Contributions may be made retroactively up to the due date of the return (including extensions). Note that, unlike the IRA (discussed at ¶ 23,301), the Keogh plan must be established by year-end.

Individual Retirement Accounts (IRAs)

¶ 23,301   ELIGIBLE INDIVIDUALS

The individual retirement arrangement (IRA) provisions of the federal income tax laws encourage individuals to establish tax-sheltered retirement accounts for themselves and/or their nonemployed spouses. There are three different IRAs that individuals may set up for retirement purposes: (1) deductible IRAs, (2) Roth IRAs, and (3) nondeductible IRAs. When an IRA is created, money paid into the plan may be deductible and the earnings on the money paid into the account are exempt from current taxation. The money set aside, and the earnings thereon, are not taxed until they are distributed to the individual, which will usually be after retirement, when the individual's tax bracket may be lower.

Individuals with earned income or taxable alimony are generally eligible to set up an IRA, including minors, employees covered by a qualified plan, self-employed individuals covered by a Keogh plan, retirees collecting a pension and/or Social Security benefits, certain nonworking spouses, etc. Generally, contributions must cease in the year the participant reaches age 70½ (except on behalf of a younger nonworking spouse). Code Sec. 219.

¶ 23,305   DEDUCTIBLE IRAs

An eligible individual may contribute up to the lesser of $2,000 or 100 percent of compensation. Code Sec. 219(b) and (c)(2). For tax years beginning after December 31, 1996, nonworking spouses may also contribute up to $2,000 per year to a deductible IRA. (Under prior law, the maximum annual deductible IRA for a married couple in which one spouse had no compensation was $2,250.) Therefore, as long as the combined compensation of both spouses is at least $4,000, a married couple (in which only one spouse is employed) may now contribute up to a total of $4,000 ($2,000 each) to their deductible IRAs instead of $2,250 under the old rules. Separate accounts must be maintained.

The AGI threshold for full deductibility of an IRA contribution by a taxpayer covered by a retirement plan at work has been increased. For tax years beginning before 1998, the IRA deduction was phased out between AGI of $40,000 and $50,000 for taxpayers filing jointly and AGI of $25,000 to $35,000 for single taxpayers. For tax years beginning in 1998, the phase-out range for joint filiers increases to between $50,000 and $60,000. For single filers, it increases to between $30,000 and $40,000. The phase-out ranges gradually increase each year until they reach $80,000 to $100,000 for joint filers in 2007 and beyond, and $50,000 to $60,000 for single filers after 2004. As a result, in 2007, a taxpayer filing jointly with AGI of $100,000 or more who is covered by a retirement plan at work will not qualify for the IRA deduction.

Another change in the law will entitle more taxpayers to take deductions for regular IRAs. Effective for the 1998 tax year, the active participation of a taxpayer's spouse in an employer's retirement plan will not affect the deductibility of the taxpayer's IRA contribution. That is, an individual will not be prevented from making a deductible contribution to an IRA simply because his or her spouse is an active participant in an employer-sponsored retirement plan. This change will allow most homemakers to take the full $2,000 deduction for an IRA contribution regardless of whether their spouse is covered at work.

However, the new law also establishes income limits for couples with a nonworking spouse who wishes to claim an IRA deduction. For such couples, the IRA deduction for the nonworking spouse is phased out between AGI of $150,000 and $160,000.

Example 23.12. Bob Garber is covered by a 401(k) plan at work, and his wife, Kristen, is a full-time homemaker. Bob and Kristen file a joint return for 1998 with an AGI of $180,000. Because their AGI exceeds the threshold amount, neither Bob nor Kristen may take an IRA deduction.

Example 23.13. Assume the same facts as in Example 23.12 except that their combined AGI is $155,000. Bob may not take an IRA deduction because their AGI exceeds the $60,000 threshold for active participants in employer-sponsored retirement plans. However, Kristen is elegible for $1,000 IRA deduction as a nonworking spouse [$2,000 − ((($155,000 − $150,000) ÷ $10,000) × $2,000)].

If the deductible amount is not a multiple of $10, it is rounded down to the nearest $10. Also, if *any* IRA deduction is allowed, $200 or more is allowed.

Example 23.14. Assume the same facts as in Example 23.12 except that their combined AGI is $57,622. Kristen may deduct her full IRA of $2,000 because their AGI is less than $150,000. However, because Bob is covered at work and their AGI exceeds $50,000, his IRA deduction is limited to $470: [$2,000 − $2,000 ($57,622 − $50,000 ÷ $60,000 − $50,000)] = $475.60, rounded down to $470.

Contributions and Benefits

Contributions (up to $2,000 of earned income, plus up to $2,000 for a nonworking spouse) are deductible from gross income even if the standard deduction is used. The IRA may be set up and the contribution made by the due date of the return (without extensions) with full effect for the preceding year. Thus, a contribution for 1998 may be made from January 1, 1998, to April 15, 1999. In fact, the deduction may be claimed on an early return and the refund used to make the contribution, so long as the contribution is made by April 15. Rev. Rul. 84-18, 1984-1 CB 88.

> *Example 23.15.* Sally Jones is eligible to make a deductible IRA contribution. If she borrows the money to make the contribution early, for example in January of the year in question, the contribution is still deductible, and the interest may be, if Sally has investment income. If, in the alternative, Sally files her return in January, claims the $2,000 deduction without having made the contribution, waits for the refund check, and then uses her refund to make the contribution by April 15, the deduction is still allowable.

The accumulated income of the IRA is not taxed until distributed, allowing for maximum growth. Upon distribution, the full account balance is subject to taxation (i.e., the basis in the IRA is zero except for nondeductible contributions). Code Sec. 408. Thus, capital gains, tax-exempt interest, etc., are all converted to ordinary income on distribution. Commissions, but not trustee and management fees, are nondeductible under Code Sec. 212, but do count as part of the $2,000 or $4,000 limitations. Rev. Rul. 86-142, 1986-2 CB 60.

Only cash contributions can be made to an IRA except for rollovers. The money needed to fund the IRA may be borrowed without disallowance of the interest deduction. (The interest is, however, subject to the "investment interest" limits.) Unlike other qualified plans, no special tax benefits are available to the IRA participant, even on lump-sum distributions.

Premature Distributions

A premature distribution (prior to age 59½) is generally fully taxable *and* subject to a 10 percent nondeductible penalty tax unless taken out as a life annuity. A premature distribution of the full account balance results if the participant borrows from the IRA or pledges it as loan collateral. An exception is provided for a loan repaid within 60 days if treated as a "rollover" on the tax return. Note that the financial institution (e.g., the bank) may impose its own penalties on premature withdrawals of long-term savings certificates.

TAX PLANNING POINTER

An IRA may be used to advantage by individuals who plan to make a complete withdrawal long before age 59½.

Assume an individual in a 28 percent tax bracket is 25 years old. The individual wishes to save $2,000 for 15 years at a 10 percent before-tax return. A comparison of the non-IRA versus the IRA is as follows:

Non-IRA: After taxes, $2,000 a year before taxes would grow
to $1,440 × 1.072^{15}................................. $36,748

IRA: Terminal value $2,000 × 1.10^{15}		$63,545
28% tax (assumed)	$17,792	
10% penalty for early withdrawal..............	6,355	24,147
After-tax, after-penalty distribution		$39,398

Thus, after 15 years, despite the 10 percent nondeductible penalty, the available cash with the IRA exceeds the amount available without benefit of the IRA. This is due to the tax deferral (i.e., the time value of money).

Penalty-free Withdrawals from Deductible IRAs

Education Expenses. Taxpayers may make penalty-free withdrawals from deductible IRAs after 1997 for qualified education expenses (tuition, fees, books, supplies, and equipment), including graduate school in academic periods beginning after 1997. The amount of qualified education expenses is reduced by scholarships and other education assistance which is excludable from gross income. The 10 percent penalty that normally applies to withdrawals made before the taxpayer reaches age 59½ will not apply if the distribution is used for higher education expenses of the taxpayer, or the spouse, children, or *grandchildren* of the taxpayer. (Note: Except for the normal gift tax rules, none of the other provisions discussed allow exclusions or credits for amounts paid for educational assistance for grandchildren).

Homebuying. Under the Taxpayer Relief Act of 1997, qualified first-time homebuyers may make early withdrawals from their IRAs without penalty starting in 1998. The withdrawals are subject to a lifetime limit of $10,000, and the money must be used to acquire a principal residence of the taxpayer, a spouse, child, grandchild, or ancestor of the taxpayer. Generally, the distribution is available if the taxpayer has not owned a principal residence during the two years preceding the date of purchase.

Medical Insurance Premiums. Individuals who have separated from service can also make penalty-free withdrawals from IRAs and qualified plans to pay for medical insurance premiums for the individual and his or her family. The taxpayer must have received unemployment compensation for at least 12 consecutive weeks, and the distributions must have been made during any tax year in which the unemployment compensation is paid or during the following tax year. This exception ceases to apply after the individual has been reemployed for 60 days.

Individuals who were self-employed may also qualify under these provisions. They are treated as having satisfied the unemployment compensation requirement if they would have received unemployment compensation except for the fact that they were self-employed.

Medical expenses. When certain distributions (made after December 31, 1996, from a qualified retirement plan) are used to pay medical expenses in excess of 7.5 percent of adjusted gross income, the 10 percent additional tax on early distributions will not apply.

Age, Disability, and Death. Once the participant has reached age 59½, becomes disabled, or dies, distributions may be made in full or in part without penalties and without regard to actual retirement. The amounts distributed constitute ordinary income to the recipient, be it the estate, a trust, a named beneficiary, or the participant. Distributions to retirees must begin by age 70½. Effective January 1, 1997, except for five percent owners and IRA holders, participants who are still working after age 70½ may defer receipt of distributions until April 1 of the calendar year following the year they retire.

Example 23.16. Tod Anglebeak turned 70½ on July 4, 1998, and retired on December 31, 1999, at age 71. He must begin receiving distributions from his pension fund by April 1, 2000.

In the case of most defined benefit plans, participants' distributions would be actuarially increased for the years in which they deferred distributions.

If a plan participant who is over age 70½ and still working is currently receiving benefits, the plan may permit the participant to stop distributions until after retirement.

¶ 23,310   ROTH IRAs

Effective for tax years beginning after 1997, taxpayers may take advantage of a new retirement savings vehicle, the Roth IRA. No tax deduction is provided for the year of contribution, but qualified distributions come out free of tax rather than tax deferred. Taxpayers may contribute up to $2,000 per year for each spouse, not exceeding the combined compensation of the spouses, and contributions may be made even after age 70½. The $2,000 contribution limit is phased out for single taxpayers with AGI between $95,000 and $110,000 and for joint filers with AGI between $150,000 and $160,000. If the final result is less than $200 but more than zero, the deduction limit will be $200. In addition, when applying the phase-out rules, all deductible amounts which are not multiples of $10 must be rounded to the next lowest $10.

If the taxpayer also contributes to a regular IRA, the $2,000 limit is reduced by that amount. Except where expressly noted, the regular IRA rules will apply to the Roth IRA.

The taxpayer must have had a Roth IRA for at least five years before receiving a qualified distribution. The following types of distributions are considered to be qualified distributions:

1. Distributions made after age 59½

2. Distributions made by reason of death or disability of the taxpayer

3. Distributions that qualify as a first-time homebuyer distribution, subject to a lifetime limit of $10,000. A first-time homebuyer is generally defined as a taxpayer who has not owned a principal residence for two years. The distribution must be used to acquire a principal residence of the taxpayer, or the taxpayer's spouse, child, grandchild, or ancestor.

Distributions are considered to have come from contributions first. Thus, for a non-qualified distribution, no portion of the distribution is considered to come from earnings and is includible in gross income until the total of all distributions from the Roth IRA exceeds the amount of contributions. Unlike a regular IRA, minimum distributions from a Roth IRA are not required. That is, distributions need not start at age 70½.

> *Example 23.17.* Christy Graham's income is within the income limits. She established a Roth IRA at age 35 and contributes $2,000 per year to the account for 20 years. The IRA is now worth $100,000, consisting of $40,000 in contributions and $60,000 in accumulated earnings. Christy begins receiving distributions from the fund at age 60. Because Christy is over 59½ and has held the funds for over five years, she may withdraw the funds free of tax as part of a qualified distribution.

> *Example 23.18.* The facts are the same as in Example 23.17, except Christy receives distributions at age 56. Because Christy is not over 59½, this is not a qualified distribution. However, she will not have income until the distributions exceed her contribution of $40,000. If she turns 59½ before the distributions exceed $40,000, she will never have income from the distributions.

> *Example 23.19.* Assume the same facts as Example 23.17, except Christy makes contributions only until she is 45 (10 years). Her contributions total $20,000, and the fund is worth $30,000 when she begins non-qualified distributions at age 50. She receives total distibutions of $27,000 before age 59½. She has income of $7,000 ($27,000 − $20,000) from the distributions.

Upon the death of the taxpayer, there are three options:

1. The account balance must be distributed to the beneficiary within five years.

2. An annuity must be purchased within one year of death.

3.   Distributions must be continued to the beneficiary at the same (or greater) rate as before the taxpayer's death.

Qualifying taxpayers may convert existing IRAs into Roth IRAs. To qualify, the taxpayer's AGI must not exceed $100,000, and the taxpayer must not be married filing separately.

If a rollover from an ordinary IRA to a Roth IRA is made before 1999, the amount that would have been included in income if the taxpayer had taken a distribution is included in income and the tax must be paid ratably over four years. However, such conversions are not subject to the 10 percent early distributions tax. Taxpayers may find the Roth IRA to be a better retirement vehicle than a regular IRA because earnings on the Roth IRA are tax free, rather than tax deferred.

¶ 23,315   NONDEDUCTIBLE IRAs

To the extent deductible IRA or Roth IRA contributions are not made, or cannot be made because of the above limitations, a taxpayer may make *nondeductible* contributions. The income on such contributions is deferred until withdrawn. Code Sec. 408(o). Form 8606 (Nondeductible IRA Contributions, IRA Basis, and Nontaxable IRA Distributions) must be filed for each year a nondeductible contribution is made. Nondeductible IRAs are allowed the same penalty-free withdrawals as deductible IRAs.

Total contributions to deductible, Roth, and nondeductible IRAs cannot exceed $2,000 for the year.

¶ 23,320   WITHDRAWALS INCLUDIBLE IN GROSS INCOME

To determine the amount includible in gross income upon distribution from an IRA of an individual who has made one or more nondeductible contributions, the following procedure is to be followed:

1.   All IRAs, including rollover IRAs, of an individual are treated as an aggregate.

2.   All distributions during one taxable year are treated as one distribution.

3.   The value of aggregate IRAs is computed as of the end of the year, including distributions and income on the accounts.

4.   The portion of total annual distributions that is tax free is determined by use of the fraction of total nondeductible contributions (less amounts previously excluded) over the aggregate year-end account balance. Code Sec. 408(d).

Example 23.20. An individual withdrew $3,000 for the first time from one of his IRA accounts. The year-end balances after withdrawals of his two IRA accounts were $1,000 and $11,000. His withdrawal was from the smaller account, but his $5,000 of nondeductible contributions had all been made to the larger account. Taxpayer's exclusion fraction equals $5,000/($3,000 + $1,000 + $11,000), or one-third. Thus, $2,000 of the withdrawn funds is includible in gross income. There may also be a 10 percent excise tax if taxpayer is under age 59½ and is not disabled.

Rollovers

A lump-sum distribution to a participant from a qualified pension or profit-sharing plan, due to plan termination or separation from service, may be rolled over tax free to a new or existing IRA within 60 days. This option is available to beneficiaries as well, but does not apply to the employee's own contributions. The rollover may be partial, resulting in ordinary income on the retained portion without the benefit of five-year forward averaging. H.R. 10 plans are eligible for rollover treatment, except for owner-employees. If property is distributed, it may be sold and the proceeds rolled over, also tax free. A rollover IRA may itself be rolled over into a qualified corporate plan (if the plan allows it). As a result, no contributions should be made to a rollover IRA, since favorable tax treatment on a subsequent lump-sum distribution from the second qualified plan would be destroyed.

TAX BLUNDER

Emil Crane received $100,000 as a lump-sum distribution from a qualified profit-sharing plan at age 63, when he retired. He used $50,000 for a world cruise and rolled over the remaining $50,000 into an IRA. When he returned from the cruise he decided to withdraw the remaining $50,000 in the IRA for personal reasons. The bottom line tax result is that the full $100,000 winds up being taxed as ordinary income—the first half because the second half was rolled over, the second half because it was a distribution from an IRA. Without the partial rollover, the full amount would qualify for five-year forward averaging.

Divorce Settlements

In the event of a divorce, the nonworking spouse keeps any IRA maintained for her or him. Further, the transfer of an IRA as a divorce settlement is tax free, but the zero basis carries over to the transferee. Code Secs. 408(d)(16) and 1041.

¶ 23,322   EDUCATION INDIVIDUAL RETIREMENT ACCOUNTS

Under the new law, taxpayers may exclude from taxable income amounts withdrawn from Education IRAs and spent on qualified education expenses for the taxpayer, the taxpayer's spouse, or a dependent. In additon to tuition, fees, supplies, and equipment, withdrawals from Education IRAs may be used for certain room and board and book expenses. The exclusion is available for both undergraduate and graduate-level coursework. Unlike the Hope and Lifetime Learning Credits, Education IRAs are available to students enrolled less than half-time at an eligible educational institution. However, students enrolled less than half-time may not treat room and board expenses as qualififed education expenses for purposes of the Education IRA income exclusion. As with the credits, expenses paid with tax-exempt education assistance do not qualify as education expenses. However, expenses paid with loan proceeds do qualify. The income exclusion is not available in any tax year the Hope Scholarship or Lifetime Learning Credit is elected with respect to a student.

Education IRAs are special trust accounts established for the sole purpose of paying qualified education expenses. For tax years beginning after 1997, taxpayers may contribute up to $500 a year for each child under 18. Although contributions are not deductible, earnings grow tax free and withdrawals used to pay qualifying education expenses (including room and board) may generally be made free of tax. Distributions are deemed to be paid from both contributions and earnings. If aggregate distributions do not exceed qualified expenses for the year, all of the distribution will be free of tax. If aggregate distributions exceed qualified expenses, a portion of the earnings will be included in gross income. A phase-out provision applies to taxpayers with modified AGI between $95,000 and $110,000 ($150,000 and $160,000 for joint filers).

According to the conference report, if a beneficiary reaches age 30 and has not used all of the IRA for qualified education purposes, the balance of the IRA must be distributed to the beneficiary. If this occurs, the earnings in the account will be taxed and subject to a ten percent penalty (because they have not been used for education purposes). To avoid this result, the account balance may be rolled over to another Education IRA for another beneficiary before the original beneficiary turns 30. The new beneficiary must be a member of the family of the prior beneficiary. To accomplish this result, a technical correction to the law may be necessary.

Contributions to an Education IRA qualify for the annual $10,000 gift tax exclusion and will be exempt from the generation-skipping transfer tax if within the annual exclusion amount. However, such contributions will not qualify for the gift tax exclusion applicable to tuition payments made directly to educational organizations.

The Hope credit and the education income exclusion are available for expenses paid after 1997. The Lifetime Learning Credit may be used for expenses paid after June 30, 1998. The applicable academic periods must begin after those dates. Students convicted of a felony for possession or distribution of a controlled substance may not claim the credits or exclusion. The most advantageous of the three alternatives will depend upon the amount of qualified education expenses incurred and paid during the tax year.

Example 23.21. Taxpayer Bill contributes a total of $7,000 to an education IRA for his daughter Chelsea's educational expenses. The total value of the education IRA in the first year Chelsea attends college is $14,000. Chelsea makes a withdrawal of $8,000 from the IRA to pay for her qualified education expenses of $8,000. Fifty percent ($7,000 ÷ $14,000) of the withdrawal ($4,000) is attributable to untaxed earnings. Bill claims a $1,500 Hope Scholarship Credit for Chelsea's qualified education expenses for the year of distribution, making the income exclusion unavailable. Because Bill claimed the credit for the Hope Scholarship,

Chelsea may not exclude the $4,000 distribution attributable to untaxed earnings from her income. If Bill had not claimed the credit, the entire $8,000 distribution would been excluded from income.

Example 23.22. The facts are the same as in Example 23.21, except Chelsea uses $6,000 of the distribution for her qualified expenses and elects the exclusion instead of the credit. The distribution still consists of $4,000 of contribution and $4,000 of earnings. The amount of earnings excludable from Chelsea's income is $3,000 ($6,000/$8,000 × $4,000). She must include $1,000 ($4,000 − $3,000) in gross income.

¶ 23,325 EMPLOYER-SPONSORED IRAs

Two kinds of employer-sponsored IRAs exist: employer-established IRAs and simplified employee pension plans.

Employer-Established IRAs

The employer may establish an IRA for one or more handpicked employees on a purely discriminatory basis, if desired (e.g., for favorite employees only). However, the contribution limit is $2,000, as with an individual IRA. Any contribution made is deductible to the employer and gross income to the employee (who receives an offsetting deduction). The employee may, if desired, make up the difference if the contribution made by the employer falls short of the annual limit in any year. Such plan contributions are subject to the adjusted gross income limitations, discussed at ¶ 23,301.

Example 23.23. Ted Potter works for Shiny Shoes Inc. His wife, Luga, is a housewife. Due to services rendered by Ted above and beyond the call of duty, Shiny Shoes establishes an IRA account for him in the amount of $1,800. Ted, on his own, opens an IRA account for Luga, in which he deposits $2,000. Shiny Shoes may deduct $1,800 as a compensation expense. Ted has gross income of $1,800, but he may deduct $3,800 from gross income, the maximum for a worker with a nonworking spouse.

Simplified Employee Pension Plans (SEPs)

To small employers and employers wary of the complexities of a qualified pension plan, the simplified employee pension plan (SEP) is a possible alternative. Code Sec. 408(k). A SEP is a program under which the employer opens IRAs for its employees and contributes the maximum, which is the lesser of $30,000 a year or 15 percent of the participant's net compensation (not exceeding $160,000 in 1998). However, the $160,000 limit will be indexed for inflation in $10,000 increments. Code Sec. 408(k)(8). These limits are the same as for corporate and H.R. 10 plans in general. Code Sec. 404(h).

Elective employee contributions (i.e., those made to a salary reduction plan) are subject to the CODA limits described at ¶ 23,075. Thus, the total amount deferred by an employee under a combination of Section 401(k) and SEP plans is limited to the lesser of $10,000 (in 1998) or 15 percent of the participant's compensation. Code Sec.

402(h). The election to defer compensation or receive cash currently is available only if at least 50 percent of the plan participants actually elect the deferral option. In addition, there must be 25 or fewer employees employed in the previous year, which makes SEPs available only to small businesses. Since a SEP is a qualified plan, deductible contributions to an employee's individual IRA are subject to the adjusted gross income limitations discussed at ¶ 23,301.

To qualify for these generous limits, the plan cannot discriminate in favor of employees who are officers, shareholders, or highly compensated employees. *All* full-time employees who are over age 21, have worked the current year and at least three of the five preceding years, and have received at least $300 in compensation from the employer for the year must be included. However, contributions may be reduced, with some limitations, by the employer-paid share of Social Security tax.

Immediate vesting is provided and no employer restrictions on withdrawals are allowed. The employee may establish a personal IRA in addition to participation in the SEP. No special tax benefits are afforded lump-sum distributions.

CODA-SEPs may not be established after December 31, 1996. Any CODA-SEP established by that date would be grandfathered, allowing contributions to continue to be made and new participants to be added after December 31, 1996.

Example 23.24. Jeremy Mason is single and works for Sewer News Inc., which has a simplified pension plan whereby 10 percent of each employee's pay, up to a maximum of $30,000, is contributed to an IRA for all employees each year. This year, Jeremy's salary is $30,000. Thus, $3,000 is contributed to his IRA. It is *not* included in Jeremy's gross income, but is deductible to Sewer News. In addition, Jeremy may contribute and deduct $2,000 to another IRA for himself, assuming his adjusted gross income does not exceed $30,000.

Distributions to Employees and Beneficiaries

¶ 23,401   LUMP-SUM DISTRIBUTIONS

Lump-sum distributions from qualified plans are eligible for special tax benefits when paid to the participant or a beneficiary. Code Sec. 402(e)(1)(A).

A lump-sum distribution is a distribution of a participant's entire interest in a qualified plan. The amount distributed must be received within a single taxable year of the distributee. In the case of a participant other than a self-employed person, the distribution must be made because of the participant's death, disability, or separation from the employer's service and it must be made after the participant has attained age 59½. In the case of a self-employed person, the distribution must be made because of the individual's death after age 59½, or it must be made after the individual reaches age 59½, unless the individual was previously disabled. Code Sec. 402(e)(4)(A).

Once a lump-sum distribution has been made, the recipient has several choices:

1. The taxable portion of the distribution, less a minimum distribution allowance, is eligible for five-year forward averaging on Form 4972 (Five-Year Averaging Method). This method is extremely favorable because the computation is independent of filing status and the regular tax bracket (see computational example below). Code Sec. 402(e)(1)(C). In fact, the tax is the same even if there is more than one beneficiary, but multiple beneficiaries must apportion the tax among themselves pursuant to the worksheet provided in the instructions to the Form 4972.

2. A portion of a distribution allocable to pre-1974 years on a mere time basis

$$\frac{\text{Pre-1974 years}}{\text{Total years in plan}}$$

is eligible for long-term capital gain treatment prior to 1992. Thus, the distributee should compute the tax both ways (i.e., include the full distribution in the five-year computation or report a portion as capital gain), whichever produces the lower tax. Because capital gains are taxed at a 20 percent rate, it is unlikely that this choice will be the most favorable.

3. The distribution may be rolled over to an IRA with no current tax due. However, the IRA will eventually be subject to full ordinary income taxes, unless it is rolled over subsequently to a corporate plan and a lump-sum distribution is made from such plan. The dual advantage of tax deferral of the distribution itself *and* the income produced in the IRA, however, may make this option worth considering.

4. If the distribution is made on account of the participant's death, a surviving spouse beneficiary may roll over a lump-sum distribution to an IRA. Code Sec. 402(a)(7).

Plan participants who attained age 50 prior to 1986 are subject to transitional rules. Thus, when receiving a lump-sum distribution after 1986 (e.g., in the year 1998), distributees, including individuals, estates, and trusts have the following choice:

1. *Five-year forward averaging* may be used, applying the tax table in effect in the year of distribution.

2. *Ten-year forward averaging,* applying the 1986 tax table, may be employed. If the distribution is less than $450,000, the taxpayer is generally better off with 10-year forward averaging at 1986 rates. For very large distributions, the 28 percent maximum average tax rate becomes significant and five-year averaging at current rates should be elected. However, assuming that over the next few years there may be a great number of distributees who opt to receive lump-sum distributions on retirement and that most people retire in their sixties or later,

since most distributions are considerably less than half a million dollars, it appears that a great many distributees for years to come should elect 10-year averaging under 1986 tax rates.

Note that five-year averaging is not available to the participant unless the participant has been a plan participant for at least five years prior to the year of distribution. Code Sec. 402(e)(4)(H). However, no such requirement exists for beneficiaries (IRS Letter Ruling 7805054) or for the capital gain option (Code Sec. 402(e)(4)(H)).

The distributee is not taxed on nondeductible contributions the distributee makes to the plan, or on appreciation on employer securities (until sold). Furthermore, if the distribution falls short of such contributions, an ordinary loss deduction is allowed (as an itemized expense). Rev. Rul. 72-305, 1972-1 CB 116.

Five-year averaging for lump-sum distributions will be repealed effective January 1, 2000. However, grandfathered 10-year averaging and existing capital gains provisions for those who were over age 50 in 1986 are retained.

Example 23.25. Richard Meyers retired at the age of 63 in 1998 and received a lump-sum distribution of $75,000 from a qualified pension plan. Over the 23 years during which he has been an active participant in the plan, he has contributed $15,000 to it. Richard files a joint return with Inga. (The capital gain option is waived.) The computations will be made on Form 4972 as follows if five-year averaging is employed:

Total distribution	$75,000
Employee contribution	15,000
Net distribution	$60,000
Less: Minimum distribution allowance*	
$10,000 − .20 ($60,000 − $20,000)	2,000
Taxable distribution	$58,000
Five-year forward averaging:	
One-fifth of taxable distribution $11,600	
Tax on $11,600 at single rates 1,740	
Multiply by 5 to compute total tax	$ 8,700

* The minimum distribution allowance equals (1) the lesser of $10,000 or one-half the net distribution less (2) 20 percent of the difference between the net distribution and $20,000.

¶ 23,415 ANNUITY DISTRIBUTIONS

When a plan participant retires and receives an annuity (i.e., a fixed nominal income for life), the annuity is subject to one of the following possible taxation rules:

1. *Noncontributory plan.* If the plan participant made no contributions to the plan, the participant's "investment in the contract" is zero. As a result every dollar received is gross income.

2.   *Contributory plan.* If the plan participant made nondeductible contributions to the plan, the participant is entitled to recover the sum of these tax free by reducing gross income by the exclusion ratio under Code Sec. 72(b).

The exclusion ratio equals:

$$\frac{\text{Investment in the contract}}{\text{Annuity} \times \text{life expectancy at the time of retirement}}$$

Once computed, the ratio never changes. The exclusion ratio is used only until the annuitant has recovered the investment in the contract. Thereafter, all distributions constitute gross income in full. In the event that the payee dies prior to recovering the investment, the unrecovered investment in the contract is deductible on the final income tax return (decedent's final return).

> *Example 23.26.* Ruth retired with a pension of $1,000 a month when her life expectancy was 20 years. She had made nondeductible contributions of $30,000 to the plan over the years. Her exclusion ratio is $30,000/($12,000 × 20), or one-eighth. Thus, each year for the first 20 years, $7/8$ of $12,000, or $10,500, is included in her gross income. Thereafter, the full $12,000 is includible. If Ruth dies after 15 years, the unrecovered investment in her contract, or $7,500, is deductible on her final return.

Safe-Harbor Method of Calculation. For the convenience of employees, the IRS has established a simplified, safe-harbor method of calculating the taxable portion of annuity distributions from qualified plans. Under this method the employee may exclude a fixed dollar amount from gross income each month without having to compute the expected lifetime return on the investment. This is particularly helpful when the expected return is unknown because of cost-of-living adjustments. The monthly exclusion is found by dividing the investment in the contract by a given number based on the annuitant's age bracket at the annuity starting date as follows:

Age of Distributee		*Number of Payments*
Below	56	360
	56–60	310
	61–65	260
	66–70	210
Over	70	160

Use of the safe-harbor method of calculations is required. Code Sec. 72(d).

> *Example 23.27.* Gene Berry retires at age 67 and has contributed $42,000 to his employer's qualified pension plan. Each month for the rest of his life he may exclude $42,000/210, or $200. After 210 months, or 17 years and six months, his pension constitutes gross income in full.

The safe-harbor method does not apply if the primary annuitant is at least age 75 on the annuity starting date unless the guaranteed payments will be made for fewer than five years.

¶ 23,425 EARLY DISTRIBUTIONS

Distributions by a qualified plan are subject to a special 10 percent excise tax if they are made before the participant reaches age 59½. The tax does not apply to (1) distributions upon death or disability of the participant; (2) distributions that are part of a series of equal periodic payments over the life of the participant or the joint lives of the participant and any beneficiary; (3) distributions after the participant separates from service after reaching age 55; (4) distributions to a nonparticipant under a divorce court order; (5) distributions on account of certain medical expenses; and (6) certain distributions from ESOPs.

> *Example 23.28.* John Henderson has a considerable sum of money in his IRA. He needs $75,000 currently for an investment opportunity. Following his accountant's advice he makes the following transactions. He borrows $75,000 on an unsecured basis, disclosing all financial facts about himself, including his considerable IRA balance. He withdraws an annuity from his IRA payable monthly to coincide with his loan payment date. The 10 percent penalty is inapplicable, even though the funds are, as a practical matter, available as a lump sum. The IRA funds keep growing on a tax-deferred basis, and the interest paid on the loan may be fully or partly deductible, depending on whether it qualifies as trade or business interest, investment interest, or personal interest.

¶ 23,445 ROLLOVERS

Few taxpayers work for the same employer throughout their working careers. Recognizing this fact Congress has provided for some degree of portability of distributions from one qualified plan to another without current taxation. Code Sec. 402(a)(5). Thus, any portion of a lump-sum distribution from one qualified plan may be rolled over, within 60 calendar days, to another qualified plan, including an IRA, without any current taxation. An employee who receives a lump-sum distribution (whether or not the requirements for favorable forward-averaging taxation are met) from one employer upon separation from service may, therefore, roll all or part of the distribution over within a 60-day period:

1. To an IRA in any case (but forward averaging is lost unless the account balance is rolled back into another qualified plan later and the initial rollover was total)

2. To another corporate plan of a new employer (provided both plans permit it) if such plan is qualified

3. To a Keogh plan if the employee is self-employed on a full- or part-time basis

Partial distributions may only be rolled over in whole or in part to, not from, IRAs (but not other qualified plans), and only if at least 50 percent of the account balance is received on account of death, disability, or separation from service. Code Sec. 402(a)(5)(D).

Example 23.29. Sam Spode, age 47, received a lump-sum distribution of $177,000 from a qualified profit-sharing plan when he resigned from Garden Tools Inc. He started his own landscaping company as a sole proprietor, opened an H.R. 10 plan, and put the full $177,000 in the account within 60 days. The tax is deferred until withdrawal, and Sam may then qualify for forward averaging.

Example 23.30. Same as Example 23.29, except that Sam rolled the distribution over into a new IRA established for that purpose. No current tax is due, but any later withdrawals from the IRA are taxable as ordinary income.

Example 23.31. Same as Example 23.29, except that Sam went to work for Chips Casino Supply Inc. and put his $177,000 in Chips' qualified pension plan. No current taxation results, and Sam may later qualify for forward averaging.

Example 23.32. Same as Example 23.30, except that Sam put only $100,000 in the IRA, spending the remaining $77,000 on a summer house. The tax on $100,000 is deferred, but $77,000 is taxed as ordinary income. The latter would be the case even if Sam was over 59½ years old.

Example 23.33. Bertha Lutz had a balance of $94,000 in her IRA. She transferred $50,000 from her IRA to her corporate employer's qualified pension plan. Not only is the full $50,000 ordinary income, but the 10 percent early withdrawal penalty applies if Bertha is under 59½ years old.

Example 23.34. Same as Example 23.33, except that Bertha rolled over her full balance in her IRA. This may qualify for tax deferral, but a future lump-sum distribution from the corporate plan is not eligible for forward averaging, unless the IRA was exclusively used as a receptacle for a lump-sum distribution from a qualified plan originally.

Note that the only *beneficiary* who qualifies for a rollover is the surviving spouse, and only to an IRA. Code Sec. 402(a)(7).

Nonqualified Deferred Compensation Plans

¶ 23,501 CHARACTERISTICS

Simply put, a nonqualified deferred compensation plan is an agreement providing that an employee will be paid in the future for work performed currently. The plan is nonqualified because it does not meet the funding, vesting, and nondiscrimination rules applicable to qualified plans. It is generally offered to highly paid executives who can afford to wait until retirement, death, or disability, and offers the dual advantages of saving for the future while deferring the income tax.

An employer may cover the bulk of its employees with a qualified pension plan, but still offer some key executives the nonqualified plan. At least for tax purposes, it may make more sense than a taxable salary increase. The agreement is included in the employment contract and stipulates that the payments will be made to the employee or designated beneficiaries. The payments may be conditional upon a minimum period of employment and the contract may even stipulate a noncompete agreement and/or provide for part-time consulting services after retirement.

To obtain the tax deferral, the plan cannot be funded or secured by third-party financial agreements, such as life insurance. Rev. Rul. 60-31, 1960-1 CB 174. Also, the employer does not receive a deduction until the participant or a beneficiary is taxed. Because the only security for the payments is a legally enforceable but unfunded promise, an employee should not enter into this arrangement without a profound belief in the employer's financial future.

Increase in Recent Usage

There are three main explanations for the recent increase in the use of nonqualified deferred compensation arrangements:

1. Provisions in various recent pieces of tax legislation, starting with the Employee Retirement Income Security Act of 1974 (ERISA), and continuing with the Tax Equity and Fiscal Responsibility Act of 1982 (TEFRA), the Retirement Equity Act of 1984, and the Tax Reform Act of 1986, to name a few, have made the design, implementation, modification, and maintenance of qualified deferred compensation plans extremely complicated, burdensome, and expensive.

2. Nonqualified plans are increasingly employed in addition to qualified plans (e.g., as "top hat" or as "excess benefit" plans) to provide benefits above and beyond the increasingly lower maxima provided by qualified plans, to favor executives exclusively.

3. Because of the Revenue Reconciliation Act of 1993 limit on qualified plans ($160,000 for 1998), many companies may rely on unfunded nonqualified plans to restore benefits to previous levels or higher.

Reasons Not to Defer

In certain instances, nonqualified plans are not deferred. However, this may be advantageous in appropriate circumstances. That is, when the anticipated tax bracket of the executive in retirement years is not significantly lower than the executive's present tax bracket, or if there is concern as to the future solvency of the corporation or concern over investment loss due to inflation, then the executive would be better off by receiving the compensation currently. Notwithstanding that the executive will have income tax consequences, he or she can now invest the after-tax proceeds.

Estate Consequences

At death, any unpaid deferred compensation is includible in the decedent's gross estate. Code Secs. 2033 and 2039. Upon receipt of income by the executor, it is characterized as income in respect of a decedent. Code Sec. 691(a)(3). However, there is an offsetting deduction for the estate tax paid. Code Sec. 691(c).

Retirement and Estate Planning Techniques

¶ 23,601 SPECIAL USE VALUATION FOR FARMLAND AND CLOSELY HELD BUSINESS REALTY

When a person dies, property generally passes to that person's heirs at its fair market value as of the date of death. Code Sec. 1014(a)(1). Alternatively, the executor of the estate may elect to value such property at its fair market value on a date six months after the death of the decedent. Code Sec. 2032(a)(2). This election is permissible if it will result in a lower value for the gross estate and a lower estate tax liability. Code Sec. 2032(c).

Even with the relief provided under the alternative valuation date option, many estates holding farmland and closely held businesses have been burdened with substantial estate tax liabilities. A major factor was the requirement that such property be valued at its "highest or best" use rather than at its current use. This requirement often resulted in the family farm or business being sold in order to raise cash to pay the estate taxes.

Under the Tax Reform Act of 1976 (P.L. 94-455), Congress enacted legislation providing for special use valuation, under Code Sec. 2032A, for real property used in farms and closely held businesses. The intent of the legislation was to lessen the estate tax burden by permitting such property to be valued at its current use, rather than its highest and best use. A related goal was to encourage heirs to continue operating family farms or closely held businesses.

Real property included in the estate of the decedent may qualify for special use valuation if:

1. The decedent was a resident of the United States at the time of death.
2. The property is qualified real property.
3. The executor elects special use valuation on the estate tax return.
4. A written recapture agreement is filed with the estate tax return. Code Sec. 2032A(a)(1).

The aggregate decrease in value of the qualifying property may not exceed $750,000. Code Sec. 2032A(a)(2).

Inflation Adjustment for Special Use Valuation Amount

For tax years beginning in 1998, the $750,000 will be adjusted for inflation using the Consumer Price Index (CPI). The amount will be rounded to the next lowest $10,000 after increasing it by the percentage by which the CPI for the preceding calendar year exceeds the CPI for the 1997 calendar year.

Example 23.35. Pat McMullen dies in 1999 and his estate elects special use valuation with respect to his farm under Sec. 2032A.

The CPI for 1997 is 195.20, and for 1998 it is 200.08 resulting in an inflation adjustment factor of 1.025 (200.08 ÷ 195.20). The estate would be entitled to a maximum reduction in estate value of $760,000 ($750,000 × 200.08 ÷ 195.2 = 768,750; rounded to the next lowest $10,000 of $760,000.

Qualification Requirements

"Qualified real property" is property located in the United States. It must be acquired from, or pass from, the decedent to a qualified heir of the decedent. The property must also have been used, on the date of the decedent's death, for qualified use by the decedent or a member of the decedent's family. Code Sec. 2032A(b)(1).

The adjusted value of the qualified real or personal property used in farming or another business must make up 50 percent or more of the adjusted value of the gross estate of the decedent. Furthermore, 25 percent or more of the adjusted value of the gross estate must consist of qualified real property. Code Sec. 2032A(b)(1)(A) and (B). For purposes of the 50 percent test, personal property used in farming or another business is taken into account even though personal property does not qualify for special use valuation. The adjusted value of the property is its fair market value (FMV) for estate tax purposes (without considering its special use value), reduced by mortgages and other indebtedness on the property Code Secs. 2032A(b)(3) and 2053(a)(4).

An illustration is helpful to fully understand the mechanics of these two percentages tests.

Example 23.36. A decedent died leaving a gross estate valued at $1,800,000 to his daughter. The estate included the family farm, which was valued at $1,100,000. The value of the farm consisted of machinery and other personal property whose fair market value was $200,000 and real property whose highest and best use value was $500,000. At the time of the decedent's death the real property was subject to a $20,000 mortgage on which the decedent was personally liable. The decedent materially participated in the operation of the farm for the last 20 years prior to his death. The computation of the 50 percent and 25 percent tests are as follows:

Calculation of Adjusted Estate:

Gross estate (fair market value)...........	$1,800,000	
Secured debts	20,000	
Adjusted estate		$1,780,000

Calculation of Adjusted Value of Real Property:

Real property (fair market value)	$1,100,000	
Secured debts	20,000	
Adjusted value of real property		$1,080,000

Calculation of Adjusted Value of Real Property and Personal Property Used for Farming:

Personal property (fair market value)	$ 200,000	
Secured debts	0	
Adjusted value of personal property		$ 200,000
Adjusted value of real property		1,080,000
Adjusted value of real and personal property		$1,280,000

Computation of 50% Test:
$$\frac{1,280,000}{1,780,000} = 72\%$$

Computation of 25% Test:
$$\frac{1,080,000}{1,780,000} = 61\%$$

Under the above circumstances, the requirements of both tests have been fulfilled. The 50 percent test is met because the $1,280,000 adjusted value of the qualifying use real and personal property, which is determined by subtracting the $20,000 mortgage from the $1,300,000 fair market value of such property, is at least 50 percent of the $1,780,000 adjusted value of the gross estate, determined by subtracting the $20,000 mortgage from the $1,800,000 air market value of the gross estate. The 25 percent test is also met. The $1,080,000 adjusted value of the real property, which is determined by subtracting the $20,000 mortgage from the $1,100,000 fair market value of the real property, is at least 25 percent of the adjusted estate Consequently, rather than valuing the farm real property at $1,100,000, the property will be valued based on its actual use as a farm. However, it must be remembered that the value cannot be reduced by an amount greater than $750,000.

Qualified Heir

The term "qualified heir" refers to a member of the decedent's family who acquired the real property from the decedent or to whom the property has passed. If a qualified heir disposes of any interest in qualified real property to any member of his or her family, that person becomes the qualified heir of the property. Code Sec. 2032A(e)(1).

The term "member of the family" means an individual's spouse, ancestors, and lineal descendants. Also included are lineal descendants of the spouse, parents of the individual or of the spouse, and the spouse of any lineal descendant. A legally adopted child of a person is treated as that person's child by blood. Code Sec. 2032A(e)(2).

Qualified Use

The qualified use requirement is met if the property is used as a farm for farming purposes, or in a trade or business other than farming. Code Sec. 2032A(b)(2). The property must have been used for the qualified use for at least five of the eight years ending on the date of the decedent's death. Also, the decedent, or a member of the decedent's family, must have materially participated in the operation of the farm or business during the required period of time. Code Sec. 2032A(b)(1)(C).

The term "farm" includes stock, dairy, poultry, fruit, fur-bearing animal, and truck farms; plantations; ranches; nurseries; ranges; greenhouses or other similar structures used primarily for the raising of agricultural or horticultural commodities; and orchards and woodlands. Code Sec. 2032A(e)(4).

"Farming purposes" means cultivating the soil or raising or harvesting any agricultural or horticultural commodity, including the raising, shearing, feeding, caring for, training, and management of animals, on a farm. Also included in farming is:

1. The handling, drying, packing, grading, or storing on a farm of any agricultural or horticultural commodity in its unmanufactured state.

2. The planting, cultivating, caring for, or cutting of trees.

3. The preparation of trees for market. Code Sec. 2032A(e).

Valuation Methods

There are two different methods of arriving at a special use value for qualified real property in an estate. They are the farm value method and the multiple-factor method, and they must be used exclusively. That is, if any property is to be valued under the farm value method, all farm property eligible for special use valuation must be valued accordingly. The same is true for the multiple-factor approach. The latter often produces a valuation considerably higher than the farm method. Obviously, the farm value method should be used if at all possible.

Farm Value Method

The special use value of a farm is determined under the farm value method as follows:

1. the average annual gross cash rental or average annual net-share rental for comparable land used for farming purposes in the locality of such farm minus

2. the average annual state and local real estate taxes for such comparable land, divided by

3. the average annual effective interest rate for all new Federal Land Bank loans in the district. Code Sec. 2032A(e)(7).

This may be expressed mathematically as follows:

$$\text{Special Use Value} = \frac{\begin{array}{c}\text{Average Annual Gross}\\\text{Cash Rental for}\\\text{Comparable Land in}\\\text{Locality Used for Farming}\end{array} - \begin{array}{c}\text{Average Real Estate}\\\text{Taxes in the Locality for}\\\text{the Comparable Land}\end{array}}{\begin{array}{c}\text{Average Annual Effective Interest Rate for All New}\\\text{Federal Land Bank Loans in the District}\end{array}}$$

Example 23.37. Abigail Jones wishes to use the farm value method to determine the special use value of a qualified 300-acre farm. Jones knows that the fair market value of the land is $2,500 per acre and that the cash-rental value of comparable property is $100 per acre. She also has ascertained that state and local tax on comparable property is $19 per acre and that the average annual effective interest rate established by the Federal Land Bank for new loans in the district is 9 percent. Jones uses the above formula as follows:

(1) Jones determines the special use value of one acre of farm land:

$$\frac{\$100 - \$19}{.09} = \$900$$

(2) Jones determines the special use value of the entire 300-acre farm:

$$300 \times \$900 = \$270,000$$

The computation of each average annual amount is to be based on the five most recent calendar years ending before the date of the decedent's death.

Multiple-Factor Method

The special use valuation of qualifying nonfarm real property and of qualifying farm real property where the farm value method is not used must be determined by applying the following factors:

1. The capitalization of income that the property can be expected to yield for farming or closely held business purposes over a reasonable period of time under prudent management.

2. The capitalization of the fair rental value of the land for farmland or closely held business purposes.

3. Assessed land values in a state that provides a differential or use value assessment law for farmland or closely held business.

4. Comparable sales of other farm or closely held business land in the same geographical area far enough removed from a metropolitan or resort area so that nonagricultural use is not a significant factor in the sales price.

5. Any other factor that fairly values the farm or closely held business value of the property. Code Sec. 2032A(e)(8)(A)-(E).

Naturally, the multiple-factor method is very subjective. Questions about acceptable capitalization rates, fair rental values, and how to weight factors can produce taxpayer and IRS controversies. The multiple-factor method does not have the safe-harbor technique of the farm value method.

Electing Special Use Valuation

The estate must elect special use valuation for the qualifying property on the initial estate tax return. Once made, the election is irrevocable, and the following information must be provided in the election notice pursuant to Reg. § 20.2032A-8(a)(3):

1. The name and taxpayer identification number of the decedent as they appear on the estate tax return.

2. The relevant qualified use of the property to be specially valued.

3. A listing of the real property to be specially valued.

4. The fair market value of the real property to be specially valued, and its value based on its qualified use (both values are determined taking into account outstanding mortgages or other debt to which the property is subject).

5. The adjusted value of all real property that is used in a qualified use and that passes from the decedent to a qualified heir and the adjusted value of all real property to be specially valued.

6. Items of personal property, including their adjusted value, listed on the estate tax return that pass from the decedent to a qualified heir and are used in a qualified use.

7. The adjusted value of the gross estate (as defined in Code Sec. 2032A(b)(3)(A)).

8. The method used to determine the special value based on use.

9. Copies of written appraisals of the fair market value of the real property.

10. A statement that the decedent and/or a member of the decedent's family has owned all specially valued real property for at least five of the eight years immediately preceding the date of the decedent's death.

11. A statement listing periods during the eight-year period preceding the date of the decedent's death during which the decedent or a member of his or her family did not own the property, use it in a qualified use, or materially participate in the operation of the farm or other business (within the meaning of Code Sec. 2032A(e)(6)).

12. The name, address, taxpayer identification number, and relationship to the decedent of each person taking an interest in each item of specially valued property. The value of the property interests, based on both fair market value and qualified use, passing to each of these individuals is also required.

13. Affidavits identifying the material participant or participants and describing their activities constituting material participation.

14. A legal description of the specially valued property.

The special use valuation agreement must be executed by all parties who have an interest in the property being valued. Code Sec. 2032A(d)(2).

Recapture

The Code refers to the recapture tax as an additional estate tax. Code Sec. 2032A(c)(1). It is imposed if the qualified heir disposes of any interest in the specially valued property (other than to another qualified heir) or ceases to use it for a qualified use within 10 years after the decedent's death. However, a two-year grace period is permitted immediately following the date of the decedent's death. Code Sec. 2032A(c)(7). During this period, failure to begin the qualified use of the property will not cause recapture. The 10-year recapture period is extended by a period equal to the actual time between the date of decedent's death and the date the qualified heir commences to use the property in the qualified use. Like-kind exchanges under Code Sec. 1031 and involuntary conversions under Code Sec. 1033 will not cause recapture if the replacement property is used for the same qualified use as the original qualified property. If the original election was not to treat timber as a crop, disposition or severance of standing timber does trigger recapture. Moreover, recapture refers to the tax difference between what the estate tax liability was and what it would have been but for the special use valuation.

¶ 23,615   IRREVOCABLE LIFE INSURANCE TRUSTS

In many situations, the optimum tax result consistent with the client's overall retirement and estate plan is generated when insurance on the taxpayer's life is owned by an irrevocable trust. Specifically, the insurance can be owned by a trust that makes the proceeds available to a surviving spouse without requiring the proceeds to be included in the estate of the insured or the surviving spouse. Naturally, the estate tax ambit of Code Secs. 2042 and 2035 must be avoided for a life insurance trust, as well as life insurance in general.

Punitive Estate Tax Issues

Under Code Sec. 2042(1) and (2), the gross estate of a decedent must include:

1. the amount receivable by the executor from insurance policies on the life of the decedent

2. insurance proceeds payable to another beneficiary for the benefit of the estate

3. proof that the decedent possessed an incident of ownership in the policy

It is easy to avoid the first two traps of Code Sec. 2042, but the "incidents of ownership" are more difficult. That is, the common incidents of ownership are:

1. power to designate or change the beneficiary

2. power to surrender or to cancel the policy

3. power to assign the policy

4. power to revoke an assignment

5. power to pledge the policy for a loan

6. power to obtain from the insurer a loan against the cash-surrender value of the policy

7. possession of a reversionary interest that exceeds five percent of the value of the policy immediately before the decedent's death. Reg. § 20.2042-1(c)(2) and (3)

Because of personal control and business reasons, it is more difficult to give up "incidents of ownership" than insurance receivable by or for the benefit of the estate. In addition, the taxpayer must transfer the insurance policy or policies more than three years before death. Otherwise, Code Sec. 2035(d) requires inclusion in the decedent's estate of the full proceeds of the life insurance policy that is transferred within three years of death, together with any gift tax paid.

Gift Tax Issues

In general, the transfer of a life insurance policy to an irrevocable life insurance trust (ILIT) is a taxable gift because the grantor has departed with complete dominion and control of the policy. Code Sec. 2511. When making the transfer of a life insurance policy to the ILIT, the adverse gift tax consequences should be avoided. First the value of the policy, for gift tax purposes, must be determined. Second, to satisfy the requirement of the annual gift tax exclusion, the gift of the policy and subsequent premium payments must qualify as gift of a present interest. Last, in conjunction with the annual exclusion, the trust beneficiaries must have each year an immediate power to withdraw the trust assets as gifts. *D.M. Crummey,* 68-2 USTC ¶ 12,541, 397 F.2d 82 (CA-9 1968).

Valuation

The duration of the policy (i.e., the time the policy has been in force) and of the policy being transferred to the ILIT will determine the gift value of the policy. Typically, when an insured purchases a policy and transfers it to the trust, the value for gift tax considerations is the amount of premiums paid by the insured. Reg. § 25.2512-6(a). If the gift to the trust was a previously owned policy, then the value for gift tax considerations would be equal to the purchase price of a comparable replacement policy. If the replacement value cannot be determined, the value must be approximated by using the actuarially determined terminal reserve value plus dividend accumulations and unused current premium payments less any policy debt at the date of the gift. Reg. § 25.2512-6(a).

> *Example 23.38.* X purchases a policy on his life and subsequently transfers the policy to Trustee A. This is a single-premium whole life policy with the face value of $30,000, which had a single premium cost of $4,900. For gift tax considerations, the policy will be valued at $4,900. Suppose, however, that X transfers the policy when it has been in force for 10 years, with an annual premium of $1,000, cash value of $7,000 and subject to a loan of $2,500. If the price of a similar replacement policy has been determined to be $5,500, then in this scenario, the gift is valued at $5,500. Assuming the same facts, suppose that the value of a replacement policy cannot be determined, and the policy dividends are $600. The value for gift tax purposes can be calculated as follows:

Reserve value	$ 7,000
Dividends	600
Unused premiums	100
Less policy debt	(2,500)
Gift value	$ 5,200

In *U.S. v. Ryerson*, 41-1 USTC ¶ 10,014, 312 U.S. 260, 61 S.Ct. 479 (1941), the insured at time of transfer was in poor health. When determining the value of the gift by using the replacement policy approach, it was determined that the respondent was uninsurable. Uninsurable status forces the replacement cost of the policy to approximate face value of the policy, which would, in most cases, cause the gifting of the policy to exceed the annual gift tax exclusion. Therefore, the optimal time to transfer an insurance policy to a trust is at the point of purchase or very soon thereafter, since the policy has a relatively low gift tax value. Of course, the gift must be below $10,000 to be completely covered for annual exclusion purposes.

Present Interest

Pursuant to Code Sec. 2503(b), in order to satisfy the present interest requirement, the donee must be able to immediately possess and enjoy what has been given to him without any delays or impediments imposed by the donor. Reg. § 25.2503-3(a). Although the transfer of a life insurance policy appears to be a gift to be received in a future period, the actual giving of the policy can be characterized as a gift for present interest purposes when considering the initial transfer of the policy and subsequent premium payments. The above conditions clearly indicate that the policy does not have to have an existing cash value in order for the gift to be considered a gift for present interest purposes. Rev. Rul. 55-408, 1955-1 CB 113. With the transfer of a life insurance policy to a trustee, one or more annual gift exclusions depends upon the number of identifiable trust beneficiaries who have a present interest right to receive the gifts. Reg. § 25.2503-3(a).

According to Reg. § 25.2503-1(c), future premium payments made on the policy either by the grantor or by the trustee constitute additional gifts in the year that payments are made. Reg. § 25.2503-1(c). If premium payments are determined to be gifts of a present interest to the beneficiaries of the trust, the requirement of gifts for annual exclusion purpose will be satisfied regardless of who pays the premium, the grantor directly or the trust, via monies received from the grantor *Beck's Estate,* 42-2 USTC ¶ 10,195, 129 F.2d 243 (CA-2 1942), rev'g 43 BTA 147, CCH Dec. 11,423 (1940). To summarize, both the initial transfer of the policy to the trust along with subsequent premium payments must be considered to be present interest gifts in order to take advantage of gifting within the limits of the annual exclusion.

Power of Withdrawal

Merely transferring a policy to a trust is not a panacea for escaping gift tax consequences. Often it is the case that transfers are made to a trust with illusory present situations that allow no power of withdrawal for the beneficiary. The general nature of an irrevocable insurance trust suggests that beneficiaries are not entitled to any of the trust assets until the future event of death. Naturally, making a gift of an insurance policy or paying an annual premium for future benefits clearly does not appear to be a present interest gift. With no present interest, there of course is no annual exclusion. Accordingly, the possible solution to the availability of the annual exclusion is to allow the beneficiary to have an immediate power to withdraw trust assets after the initial transfer and subsequent premium payments to the trust. *D.M. Crummey*, 68-2 USTC ¶ 12,541, 397 F.2d 82 (CA-9 1968), held that present interest represents the time when a beneficiary has an immediate right to withdraw the trust corpus with up to his proportionate share of the annual gift subject to the provisions of Code Sec. 2503(b). While the intent of this presentation is not to discuss the intricacies of the *Crummey* powers, valid *Crummey* powers must possess the following three elements—written notice of the withdrawals right (IRS Letter Ruling 8004172), a reasonable amount of time to exercise the power, and no obstacles in appointing guardians to exercise a minor beneficiary's power. Rev. Rul. 83-108, 1983 CB 167.

The *Crummey* power, while being an effective means of eliminating or minimizing the gift tax consequences upon the creation and continued funding of the trust, can lead to unwarranted tax consequences for the beneficiary. Each power of withdrawal is equivalent to a general power of appointment. Failure to use the power constitutes a lapse. A lapse, or the release of a general power of appointment can lead to some gift and estate tax consequences for the beneficiary/power holder. To avoid this situation, the income beneficiary's right to withdraw should not exceed $5,000 or five percent of the trusts assets with respect to gifts during any one calendar year.

¶ 23,625   PRIVATE ANNUITIES

Generally, a private annuity is an arrangement whereby an individual transfers money or other property to another entity (individual, corporation, or other) in exchange for the transferee's promise to make periodic payments to the transferor in fixed amounts for the period of the transferor's life (or the transferor's life plus the life of his spouse). Neither of the parties involved is an insurance company, and typically the parties are related, creating a situation offering the greatest tax advantages.

Normally, a private annuity arrangement involves the transfer of property by an elderly individual to a younger family member in exchange for the younger member's promise to make fixed annual payments for the transferor's life. Another common arrangement involves the redemption of stock by a closely held corporation in exchange for an annuity.

Requirements for an Effective Private Annuity

Several factors and considerations must be taken into account when planning to structure a private annuity arrangement. For instance, when selecting the type of property to be used, there are no restrictions; any type of property may be used. Examples of types of property that may be transferred in a private annuity arrangement include S or C corporation stock, a personal residence, undeveloped real estate, or a business interest. The type of property that is best used in a private annuity arrangement is income-producing, appreciating property that is free from indebtedness. Consequently, S or C corporation stock is very viable property for a private annuity arrangement.

When structuring the annuity and choosing a transferee (obligor), the ability of the obligor to make annuity payments must be ascertained. If the obligor has substantial income from which to make the annuity payments, any type of property may be used; however, if the obligor has little or no income, the transferred property should be income producing or of the type that could be easily sold or used to borrow against.

An important requirement in a private annuity is that the transferee's promise to make the required periodic annuity payments be unsecured in order to preserve the tax-free status of the transaction. If the obligor's promise is secured, the annuitant will be taxed immediately on the transfer on the full amount of the gain. *Estate of B.F. Kann,* 49-1 USTC ¶ 9271, 174 F.2d 357 (CA-3 1949). The recognized gain is calculated as the difference between the amount realized and the transferor's adjusted basis in the property. The amount realized in a private annuity arrangement is the present value of the right to the promised payments.

Another factor to consider in choosing the transferee under the annuity arrangement is provided by Rev. Rul. 62-136, 1962-2 CB 12. This ruling provides that the obligor should be a person not regularly engaged in issuing private annuities.

In determining the amount of the annuity, the property transferred must be valued at its fair market value, preferably by an independent expert appraiser. This will have an effect on the economic reality of the transaction for tax purposes. In addition, in structuring the annuity, the payments must be entirely contingent on the life of the transferor. An agreement providing for a minimum number of payments is not a private annuity.

Income Tax Consequences to the Annuitant/Transferor

Prior to the inception of Rev. Rul. 69-74, 1969-1 CB 43, private annuities received extremely favorable income tax treatment. However, extensive attempts by the Internal Revenue Service to limit these benefits finally culminated with the issuance of this ruling in 1969. While continuing to treat private annuities as a dual transaction (i.e., annual payments being allocated between a capital amount and an annuity amount), the ruling altered the traditional taxability of private annuities in two ways. First, the annuitant was not permitted to recover the basis of the property tax free before recognizing capital gain on a portion of each payment. A portion of each payment received under the private annuity was to be taxed to the annuitant as capital gain. The second change was that after the capital portions of all annuity payments total the fair market value of the transferred property, the equivalent portion for all future payments would be taxed as ordinary income. Although this is not an adverse consequence under existing statutes since the tax rates on ordinary and capital gain property are the same, under prior law this portion of the payments would have been excluded from tax entirely for the rest of the annuitant's life. Rev. Rul. 239, 1953-2 CB 53.

The first step in calculating the gain to be recognized by the annuitant is to calculate the exclusion ratio and multiply this ratio by the amount of each payment received by the transferee. This ratio is the ratio of the taxpayer's investment in the contract to his expected return. The expected return is calculated by multiplying the amount of each annual payment by the annuitant's life expectancy, which is determined from Table I under Reg. § 1.72-9. Rev. Rul. 69-74 revised the interpretation of the taxpayer's investment in the contract by requiring that the transferor's adjusted basis for the property be used as his investment in the contract for purposes of this calculation. Under prior law (as under Rev. Rul. 239), the taxpayer's investment in the contract was the fair market value of the property. Under the Tax Reform Act of 1986, the total amount that an individual may exclude from income is limited to the total amount of investment in the contract. When the annuitant reaches the point where he has completely recovered his investment, all remaining payments are fully taxable. The next step under Rev. Rul. 69-74 is to determine the capital gain portion of each payment. The capital gain realized by the transferor is the difference between his adjusted basis for the property and the present value of the annuity, as determined under the estate and gift tax table. Reg. §§ 20.2031-7(f) and 25.2512-5(f). The capital gain is divided by the transferor's life expectancy. This portion is that which is taxed as capital gain, until the annuitant has been taxed on the entire realized gain should he live to his life expectancy as determined at the inception of the transfer. Thereafter, the portion of the payment formerly taxed as capital gain will be taxed as ordinary income for the remainder of the taxpayer's life.

The final step under Rev. Rul. 69-74 is to subtract the capital gain amount and the excluded amount from the annual payment. The difference is the amount of the annuity, which is taxed as ordinary income for the annuitant's entire life.

For an analysis and depiction of the private annuity arrangement involving an S corporation shareholder, examine the following scenario.

Example 23.39. Father, age 55, transfers S corporation stock to his son on June 1, 1998, in exchange for a promise to pay a life annuity. Father purchased the stock on January 1, 1991, for $180,000. The fair market value of the property on the date of transfer is $200,000. The adjusted basis of the stock is $167,182.

Step One: Compute the annual payment. The required annual annuity payment is computed by dividing the fair market value of the property by the present value annuity factor based on the age of the annuitant. Code Sec. 7520 states that annuity agreements entered into on or after May 1, 1989, must use tables prescribed by the Secretary based on 120 percent of the applicable federal midterm rate for the month of the valuation under Code Sec. 1274(d)(1). Notice 89-60 and Notice 89-24 provide guidance in making the computations.

$$\text{Annual Annuity Payment} = \frac{\text{Fair Market Value of Property}}{\text{Annuity Factor}}$$

$$\$23,506.94 = \$200,000 / 8.5081$$

—The annuity factor is computed by using the remainder factor given in Notice 89-60 and converting it into an annuity factor as shown in Notice 89-24.

—Assume 120% A.F.R. for June 1998 = 9.60% (rounded to the nearest 2/10)

—Remainder factor = .18322, using Table R(1) in Notice 89-60, age 55, 120% A.F.R. of 9.60%

—Income factor = 1.000 — remainder factor .81678 = 1.000 — .18322

—Annuity factor = income factor/120% A.F.R. 8.5081 = .81678/9.60%

Step Two: Compute the exclusion ratio. The exclusion ratio is the portion of the annual annuity payment that represents an annuity. As previously explained, the private annuity involves an appreciation component and an investment income component. The exclusion ratio provides the excluded portion of the investment income component. The life expectancy is found in Reg. § 1.72-9, Table V—Ordinary Life Annuity, One Life, Post-June 1986 and adjusted for annual rather than monthly payments under Reg. § 1.72-5(a)(2).

$$\text{Exclusion Ratio} = \text{Adjusted Basis} / (\text{Annual Payment} \times \text{Life Expectancy})$$

$$24.44\% = \$167,182 / (\$23,506.94 \times 29.1)$$

Excluded Portion (.2444 × $23,506.94) = $5,745.09

Step Three: Compute the gain attributable to appreciation. The gain on the exchange is the present value of the annuity minus the adjusted basis of the property. The annual gain is computed by dividing the gain by the annuitant's life expectancy.

$$\text{Capital Gain} = \text{Present Value of Annuity} - \text{Adjusted Basis}$$

$$\$32,818 = \$200,000 - \$167,182$$

Annual gain ($32,818 / 29.1) = $1,127

Step Four: Compute the ordinary income portion attributable to the investment income component. The ordinary income is computed by subtracting the annual exclusion and the annual gain recognized from the annual private annuity payment.

Annual annuity components:

Return of basis—tax free	$ 5,745.09
Capital gain	1,127.77
Ordinary income	16,634.08
	$23,506.94

Gift Tax Considerations

If the fair market value of the property and the present value of the annuity are equal, no gift tax liability will be incurred by either party. The annuitant will be subject to gift tax when the fair market value of the property exceeds the present value of the annuity received. Conversely, the transferee will be subject to gift tax when the fair market value of the property is less than the value of the annuity given. In the previous father/son illustration, gift tax was avoided by computing the annual payment based on IRS tables and a well-documented appraisal of the property's fair market value.

Estate Tax Considerations

The primary purpose of a private annuity is to remove the value of the property from the annuitant's gross estate and transfer any future appreciation in the property. If the annuitant does not consume all of the payments prior to death, this amount will be subject to estate tax under Code Sec. 2033 The value of the annuity, however, will not require inclusion because the payments terminate, leaving nothing subject to tax. If the annuity provides payments to someone surviving the primary annuitant, the value of the remainder will be included in the primary annuitant's gross estate under Code Sec. 2039. In addition, the annuitant must avoid retaining an interest in the property that could cause its value to be included as a transfer intended to take effect at death (Code Sec. 2037) or a retained life estate (Code Sec. 2036).

¶ 23,635 AB TRUST PLANS

In retirement and estate planning, a common technique employed is an AB trust setup. In this plan, an A trust is a power of appointment trust and the B trust is the credit shelter trust (also called a "credit equivalent," "bypass," "family," or "residuary" trust).

A Trust

As discussed in Chapter 21 at ¶ 21,217, an entire estate may be given to a spouse without any federal estate tax. However, leaving property outright may not be the most prudent option. That is, management of the property and the ability to direct day to day operations might be inconsistent with the surviving spouse's background, training, and physical capacities. Naturally, an outright transfer affords no protection in the event of incompetency. As a result of the aforementioned reasons, a frequently utilized type of marital deduction trust is the power of appointment trust. This trust qualifies for the marital deduction under an express statutory exception to the terminable interest rule. Code Sec. 2056(b)(5). As provided by Reg. § 20.2056(b)-5(a), this exception applies only when all of the following requirements are met:

1. The surviving spouse is entitled for life to all of the income from the entire interest, or a specific portion of the entire interest, or to a specific portion of all the income from the entire interest.

2. The income is payable to the surviving spouse annually or at more frequent intervals.

3. The surviving spouse must have a power of appointment over the property exercisable in favor of persons including herself or her estate.

4. The power must be exercisable by the surviving spouse alone and in all events.

5. The property must not be subject to a power in any other person to appoint any part to any person other than the surviving spouse.

B Trust

Instead of passing all of one's assets at death either outright or in a power of appointment trust to a surviving spouse, it is good planning to utilize the applicable unified credit amount of the first spouse to die, because otherwise it is wasted. An illustration of the logic for a B trust technique is provided below.

Example 23.40. Steve Colburn dies in 1991 and bequeaths his entire estate outright to his wife, Judy. His taxable estate before the marital deduction is $1,200,000. Because of the unlimited marital deduction, Colburn's estate will incur no estate tax. Assuming $50,000 appreciation in the principal left to Judy and that she consumes the income, when Judy dies in 1999, the federal estate tax will be $186,040 (after the unified credit and state death tax credit). If Steve had left only $600,000 to his wife, then neither of the two estates would bear a federal estate tax.

As was depicted in the previous example, it is necessary to coordinate the marital deduction and the unified credits. Therefore, it would have been wise to have used a B trust for the applicable credit amount. Naturally, the B trust is a nonmarital trust and is funded from the portion of the estate that is subject to estate taxes. However, in our scenario, there are no estate taxes due because of the unified credits. The B trust or family trust could limit the surviving spouse's interest in the trust to a mandatory or discretionary right to income. In sizable estates, it would not make sense to provide the surviving spouse with a mandatory right to the income from both the A and B trusts. Consequently, it is normal to structure the B trust as a so-called "sprinkle and spray" trust. Under this type of trust, the income can be distributed upon the trustee's determination of need among a broader class of beneficiaries, such as the surviving spouse and the children of the deceased.

¶ 23,645 QUALIFIED TERMINABLE INTEREST PROPERTY (QTIP) TRUSTS

In contrast to the other forms of estate tax marital deductions (outright passing or passing into an A trust), the qualified terminable interest property (QTIP) trust does not give the surviving spouse ultimate control over the disposition of the trust's assets. Even though the surviving spouse is benefited during his or her lifetime, nonetheless, he or she is not able to change the ultimate beneficiaries of the trust. The QTIP arrangement is ideal in situations of remarriage where there are children with a former spouse. Prior to 1982, the assets in a QTIP trust would not have qualified for the marital deduction because the spouse had a nondeductible terminable interest. However, beginning in 1982, Code Sec. 2056(b)(7) permits a QTIP trust to qualify for the marital deduction under the following conditions:

1. The property must pass from the decedent to the surviving spouse.

2. The surviving spouse must have a qualifying income interest in the property for life.

3. The executor must elect to have the property qualify for the marital deduction.

The QTIP trust is attractive to many taxpayers because the decedent's estate can get an unlimited marital deduction for the property transferred into the QTIP trust, but it can limit the surviving spouse to only income for life and no right to principal.

In some retirement/estate planning scenarios, a three-trust plan would be appropriate. That is, a standard power of appointment trust, credit shelter trust, and a QTIP trust would be desirable in meeting objectives of flexibility, removal of the applicable unified credit amount from subsequent estate taxation, and providing for one's spouse but also remembering children from previous marriages.

¶ 23,655   LIFETIME TRANSFERS

A plan of lifetime gifts of assets can greatly assist in meeting an individual's retirement and estate planning needs. Specifically, lifetime giving can assist in obtaining the following objectives:

1. shifting of the income tax burden to family members in lower tax brackets;

2. shifting of control of assets (e.g., stock in a closely held corporation); and

3. removing appreciating assets from the donor's punitive estate tax brackets and thereby causing a reduction in the individual's taxable estate.

Annual Exclusion

An individual may give up to $10,000 annually to a donee of a present free of interest gift tax consequence. Moreover, spouses may elect to treat their gifts as made one-half by each, provided both spouses signify their consent to this treatment with respect to all such gifts made by either of them during the calendar year. Code Sec. 2513. As a consequence, $20,000 a year may be given tax free by a married couple to one donee. Naturally, the same result is accomplished when community property is given to a donee.

Unlimited Education and Medical Expense Exclusion

Under Code Sec. 2503(e), an unlimited exclusion is available for payments made in a donee's behalf for:

1. tuition to a qualifying educational organization; and
2. qualifying medical expenses.

It should be noted that this exclusion is in addition to the annual exclusion, and is only available when payments are made directly to the educational organization or medical care provider.

Applicable Unified Credit Amount

Previously in this chapter, the unified credit had been discussed in connection with the estate tax. However, it must be noted that every individual is entitled to this applicable credit amount for cumulative lifetime and death transfers from the gift and estate tax. Also, a married couple can transfer double the applicable credit amount without gift tax consequences. Note that this exemption is used when gifts exceed the $10,000 annual exclusion.

An illustration of the benefits of lifetime giving is provided below.

Example 23.41. Mr. A, a widower, has assets (net of any liabilities) presently valued at $2,300,000. He has three married children to whom he will leave his estate by will. He owns stock in an S corporation that he believes will greatly increase in value over the next several years. Mr. A has not, in previous years, made gifts to donees in excess of the annual exclusion.

Planning Strategy. Mr. A makes a gift in 1994 of $110,000 in X corporation stock to each of his children and their spouses ($660,000 total gifts).

1. *Gift Tax Cost*

Gross gifts	$660,000
Less: Annual exclusions	(60,000)
Taxable gifts	$600,000
Tax	192,800
Less: Unified credit in 1994	192,800
Gift tax cost	$ 0

2. *Estate Tax Savings.* Assume that at death, in 1999, the S corporation stock given away has a value of $1,100,000. Mr. A's remaining estate at death has a value of $1,640,000.

	Actual	If No Gifts Made
Estate value	$1,640,000	$2,740,000
Adjusted taxable gifts after 1976	600,000	—
Taxable estate (naturally, this ignores any deductions)	$2,240,000	$2,740,000
Tax	$ 898,400	$1,145,800
Less: Unified credit in 1999	211,300	211,300
Estate tax due	$ 687,100	$ 934,500
Savings in estate taxes	—	$ 247,400

Additionally, the income from the S corporation stock that was given away has been removed, and thereby cannot increase Mr. A's income tax bracket, nor his estate tax bracket.

¶ 23,665   IMPACT OF COMMUNITY PROPERTY

There are eight community property states (California, Arizona, Nevada, New Mexico, Idaho, Texas, Louisiana, and Washington). In these states, property acquired by married persons is community property, and such property retains its character once established even after a change of domicile. Even though community property is like joint tenancy with right of survivorship between spouses in common law states, nonetheless, there are significant estate tax differences. That is, under Code Sec. 1014(b)(6), both halves of community property—the half included in the decedent's estate and the half excluded from the decedent's estate—receive a step-up in basis. In contrast, property held in joint tenancy with right of survivorship and tenancy by the entirety will obtain a step-up in basis only for the included half. Naturally, retirement and estate planners should spend considerable effort to discover the amount of community property that clients have obtained. The following illustration demonstrates the need to ferret out community property.

> *Example 23.42.* John and Mary Doe (husband and wife) purchased a piece of property for $100,000 taking title as joint tenants with right of survivorship. Six years later, when John died, the property was worth $400,000. Thus, half of the property would go into John's estate and take a step-up in basis. As a result, Mary's basis for a subsequent resale is $250,000. If John and Mary lived in Texas and this was community property, then Mary's basis would be $400,000 on the subsequent resale.

¶ 23,675   BUY-SELL AGREEMENTS

A buy-sell agreement is a legal contract for the disposition of a business interest in the event of the owner's death, disability, retirement, or upon withdrawal from the business at some earlier time. In addition, it serves the following purposes:

1. creates a market for an otherwise illiquid, nontraded property interest;
2. restricts the universe of potential buyers;
3. preserves controls among existing shareholders;
4. establishes either a mutually agreed upon market price or a devise for computing the price;
5. eliminates difficult and capricious negotiations with owners of remaining stock; and
6. aids in setting a value for estate tax purposes.

Typically, buy-sell agreements take the form of a stock redemption or a cross-purchase agreement.

The main difference between the stock redemption agreement and the cross-purchase agreement is that in the former the corporation is the redeemer of the shareholder's stock and in the latter the individuals themselves agree to purchase the stock of the departing shareholder.

Stock Redemption Agreement

A stock redemption agreement is one in which the corporation, as well as the shareholders, is a party to the agreement. The S corporation agrees to purchase (redeem) the stock of the departing shareholder based on an agreed upon amount. A stock redemption agreement is administratively the simplest of the buy-sell agreements since it involves only two parties—the corporation and the departing individual. Hence, providing for funding the agreement, for example, through the use of life insurance, is much simpler since only the corporation need purchase insurance on each of the shareholders. However, this simplicity is not without obvious pitfalls. In this type of agreement, the income tax treatment of the redemption as a dividend under the rules of Section 302 must be carefully considered.

Cross-Purchase Agreement

A cross-purchase agreement is one between the shareholders of the company. For example, an S corporation has three shareholders, A, B, and C. Each shareholder agrees to sell his stock to the remaining shareholders upon the occurrence of a certain event, such as death. If the remaining shareholders desire to keep their relative interests in the company, then the agreement must provide for the purchase of a portion of the stock by each surviving shareholder. Thus, providing for funding the agreement is more difficult. Although administratively more complex, a cross-purchase agreement will not be subject to the income tax treatment of the redemption as a dividend under the rules of Code Sec. 302 since the S corporation is not a party to the agreement. Code Sec. 302(a). When there are more than two shareholders, the number of policies required increases geometrically, and the plan becomes increasingly difficult to administer. In order to determine the number of policies needed, a formula of $N \times (N-1)$ can be used, where N is the number of shareholders.

Example 23.43. 2 shareholders: $2 \times (2-1) = 2$ individual policies; 3 shareholders: $3 \times (3-1) = 6$ individual policies; 5 shareholders: $5 \times (5-1) = 20$ individual policies; and 20 shareholders: $20 \times (20-1) = 380$ individual policies.

Both the stock redemption and the cross-purchase agreements are funded with after-tax dollars. Also, shareholders' payments of premiums to fund a corresponding cross-purchase insurance plan are nondeductible. It should be noted that the surviving shareholders in a cross-purchase agreement will get a step-up in basis. That is, when they purchase the deceased shareholder's interest with their insurance proceeds, then they will get a step-up in basis equal to the buy-sell price.

Recent Developments Related to Valuation

The Omnibus Budget Reconciliation Act of 1990 (P.L. 101-508) added Code Sec. 2703 to "establish rules that attempt to distinguish between [buy-sell] agreements." Senate Explanation, P.L. 101-508, Sec. 11601-2. Code Sec. 2703 is effective for agreements entered into after October 8, 1990, or for agreements substantially modified after October 8, 1990.

Under Code Sec. 2703, the value of property for estate and gift tax purposes is determined without reference to options, agreements, or rights to acquire or use the property at a price less than fair market value, or restrictions on the right to use or sell the property, unless three requirements are met. First, the option, agreement, right, or restriction must be a bona fide business arrangement. Second, it must not be a device to transfer property to members of the decedent's family for less than full consideration. Finally, the terms of the agreement must be comparable to those of similar arrangements entered into by persons in an arm's-length transaction. These requirements imply that more documentation will be needed to support the valuation of property in buy-sell agreements. Since these tests are independent, simply demonstrating that a bona fide business purpose exists is not sufficient.

¶ 23,685   CODE SECTION 6166

Beginning in 1982, an executor or executrix may elect to pay the estate tax attributable to certain closely held business interests in up to 10 equal annual installments, with the first payment to begin five years after the date of death. The maximum payment period, however, is 14 rather than 15 years, since the due date for the last payment of interest coincides with the due date for the first installment of tax. This fourteen year deferral may be elected if the decedent's interest in the closely held business constitutes at least 35 percent of the decedent's adjusted gross estate (gross estate less Code Sec. 2053 and 2054 expenses). Code Sec. 6166(a)(1).

No principal payments of the deferred tax are required for the first five years, but interest at the normal rate for unpaid taxes must be paid on the unpaid balance. The interest rate on the first $345,800 in deferred estate tax attributable to the business interest is two percent. Code Sec. 6601(j).

Pursuant to the 35 percent rule, a closely held business may include a sole proprietorship or a partnership as well as a corporation. For the partnership or corporation, the estate must include 20 percent or more of the ownership or there must be 15 or fewer partners or shareholders. Code Sec. 6166(b)(1). Ownership by related family members described in Sec. 267(c)(4) can be attributed to the decedent to qualify for the 20 percent rule. Code Sec. 6166(b)(2)(D).

The benefits of Code Sec. 6166 can be lost if the executor is not careful. Section 6166(g) requires the acceleration of payment if any of three events occur:

1. Failure to make a timely payment of principal and interest;

2. Failure to pay undistributed net income (UNI) of the estate; or

3. Disposal of 50 percent or more of the value of a qualifying closely held business.

However, Sec. 6166(g)(3)(B) provides relief for the failure to make timely payment. For instance, when payment is made within six months of the due date, then the deferral may be retained, but the four percent interest benefit is lost and a penalty is incurred. Also, the existence of UNI requires payment of tax up to that amount.

The executor elects to take advantage of Code Sec. 6166 by including on a timely filed estate tax return a notice of election containing the following information:

1. The decedent's name and taxpayer identification number as they appear on the estate tax return.

2. The amount of tax that is to be paid in installment.

3. The date selected for payment of the first installment.

4. The number of annual installments, including the first installment, in which the tax is to be paid.

5. The properties shown on the estate tax return that constitute the closely held business interest (identified by schedule and item number).

6. The facts that formed the basis for the executor's conclusion that the estate qualifies for payment of the estate tax in installments. Reg. § 20.6166-1(b).

¶ 23,695   SALE OF A PERSONAL RESIDENCE

Pre-May 7, 1997

Older taxpayers, prior to May 7, 1997, could have elected the one-time exclusion of $125,000 gain on the sale of a principal residence available to taxpayers over 55 years of age. Prior Code Sec. 121(a). To have qualified, the seller must have owned and lived in the residence for at least three years in the five-year period preceding the sale.

In addition to the one-time exclusion, taxpayers who replaced their residences within the two-year period from the time of sale could avoid recognition of gain. This rollover of the gain was permissible as long as the cost of the new residence exceeded the adjusted sale price of the old residence. Prior Code Sec. 1034.

Post-May 6, 1997

For sales of a principal residence after May 6, 1997, a $250,000 exclusion for single filers and a $500,000 exclusion replaces the aforementioned rollover provisions and the one-time exclusion for taxpayers age 55 or older. Also, this new provision may be claimed once every two year. New Code Sec. 121.

¶ 23,701 SAVINGS INCENTIVE MATCH PLANS FOR EMPLOYEES (SIMPLE PLANS) OF SMALL EMPLOYERS AND EMPLOYEE CONTRIBUTIONS

Effective January 1, 1997, employers and employees may participate in a new pension plan called Savings Incentive Match Plans for Employees, or SIMPLE. This plan is limited to companies with 100 or fewer employees who earned at least $5,000 in the previous year. In addition, the company must not maintain another employer-sponsored retirement plan. SIMPLEs may be established as IRAs or adopted as part of a 401(k) plan. Eligible employees are those who earned at least $5,000 in any two prior years and who may be expected to earn at least $5,000 in the current year. Employees covered by a collective bargaining agreement and nonresident aliens are not required to be covered by a SIMPLE.

A grace period applies to employers who have established SIMPLEs, but lose their eligibility in subsequent years. Such employers may continue to maintain the plan for two years following the last year in which they were eligible.

The rule limiting SIMPLEs to employers with 100 or fewer eligible employees may create problems for companies that would otherwise qualify. For purposes of this rule, the term "employer" includes related employers such as trades or businesses under common control, affiliated service groups, and controlled groups of corporations. Therefore, if a corporation has 80 eligible employees and its subsidiary has 30 eligible employees, neither company will be able to offer a SIMPLE plan. Furthermore, because a plan must be open to all eligible employees, an employer with more than 100 eligible employees will not be able to offer a SIMPLE plan even though less than 100 employees may elect to participate in the plan.

Employees may contribute up to $6,000 per year (expressed as a percentage of their earnings) of their pretax salaries to the plan, and employers are required to match a portion of the contributions up to $6,000. Like similar retirement plans, the plan assets are not subject to income tax until distributions are made to the participants. However, such contributions are treated as wages for purposes of the employment (FICA) tax. Employers may generally deduct their matching contributions if they are made by the date of the employer's tax return, including extensions. The contributions limit will be increased for inflation in $500 increments. The base period will be the quarter ended September 30, 1996.

The SIMPLE lives up to its name, in part, due to the fact that the plan is not subject to the nondiscrimination rules (including top-heavy provisions) and certain other complex requirements generally applicable to qualified plans.

Employer Contributions

Employers have the option of matching employee contributions each year under either of two formulas. The matching contribution formula generally requires the employer to match the employee contribution dollar-for-dollar up to three percent of the employee's compensation for the year. However, with prior notice, the employer could reduce its match to as little as one percent in up to two out of every five years. The employer would have to notify eligible employees of the reduced match within a reasonable period of time before the 60-day election period during which employees have to decide whether or not to participate in the plan for that year.

Under the alternative formula, the employer may elect to make a two percent non-elective contribution for each eligible employee with earnings of at least $5,000 for the year. No more than $160,000 of compensation may be taken into account for purposes of the alternative formula. Hence, the employer's maximum contribution under this alternative would be $3,200 ($150,000 × .02). However, the employee could still contribute up to $6,000.

Under prior law, the maximum deduction an employer could take for contributions to a SIMPLE 401(k) plan was 15 percent of the total compensation of plan participants for the year. This has been changed to limit the deduction to the greater of (1) 15 percent of the compensation paid or accrued during the tax year to beneficiaries under a stock bonus or profit-sharing plan or (2) the amount that the employer is required to contribute to the SIMPLE 401(k) plan for the year. As a result, an employer may deduct contributions to a SIMPLE 401(k) plan that exceed 15 percent of the compensation actually paid or accrued during the year.

Because contributions made by employers are nonforfeitable, employees vest immediately in contributions made by the employer.

Distributions

Generally, distributions from a SIMPLE are treated the same as distributions from an IRA. Accordingly, distributions are includible in a participant's income when withdrawn from the account. In addition, a 25 percent penalty is levied if the participant withdraws an amount from the SIMPLE within two years of the date on which the employee first began participating in the SIMPLE. A 10 percent penalty applies to premature withdrawals (i.e., before age 59½) made after the first two years.

Participants may roll over distributions from one SIMPLE account to another free of tax. Furthermore, a penalty-free rollover from a SIMPLE to an IRA is permitted if the employee has participated in the SIMPLE for at least two years. However, the participant may not make a tax-free rollover from a SIMPLE to a qualified plan.

Administrative Requirements

Employees planning to participate in a SIMPLE must do so during the 60-day period before the beginning of the year (or within 60 days before the employee is first eligible to participate). During this period, participants may also increase or decrease contribution amounts previously elected. Plans may also allow participants to change their salary reduction contributions during the year.

A plan must allow employees to terminate their participation in the plan at any time during the year. However, the plan may also prevent employees from resuming participation until the following year. Employers must contribute an employee's elective deferral to the employee's SIMPLE account within 30 days after the end of the month in which the contribution was made.

The employer may designate that only one financial institution that administers IRAs serve as the SIMPLE account trustee. Thus, all contributions made on behalf of participating employees would be made to that institution. Each year, the trustee is required to file a report with the Secretary of the Treasury and to provide the employer with a summary description of the plan containing the following information:

1.   name and address of the employer and trustee;
2.   requirements for participation eligibility;
3.   benefits provided under the plan;
4.   time and method of making salary reduction elections;
5.   procedures for, and effects of, withdrawals from plan account; and
6.   procedures for, and effects of, rolling over distributions from a SIMPLE account.

In addition, within 30 days following each calendar year, the trustee must provide an account statement to each individual participating in the SIMPLE. The statement reports the account balance and any activity in the account during the year.

A $50 per day penalty may be levied on trustees who fail to provide the summary description, the account statement, or the annual report. The penalty may be waived if the trustee can show reasonable cause for the reporting failure.

Employers are required to notify employees of their right to make salary reduction contributions under the SIMPLE plan, as well as the contribution alternative elected by the employer (described above). A copy of the summary description prepared by the trustee must accompany the notice. The notice must be provided immediately before the 60-day period in which the employee may make the election. A $50 per day penalty may be levied upon the employer for failure to provide such notice. Again, the penalty may be waived if the employer can show reasonable cause for failure to provide timely notice.

SIMPLE 401(k) Plans and Safe Harbors

SIMPLE plans may also be established as 401(k) plans that are deemed to satisfy the nondiscrimination requirements by meeting one of two contribution requirements and satisfying a notice requirement. The safe harbor is satisfied if:

1.   the employer does not satisfy any other qualified plan;

2. an employee's elective deferrals for the year, expressed as a percentage of compensation, do not exceed $6,000;

3. the employer makes contributions matching the employee's elective deferrals, up to three percent of the employee's compensation for the year, or makes a nonelective contribution of two percent of compensation for each eligible employee earning at least $5,000 for the year (adequate notice must be provided to the affected employees prior to the 60-day period before the beginning of the year);

4. no other contributions are made to the plan; and

5. all contributions are 100 percent vested. Code Sec. 401(k)(11).

By satisfying the above requirements, the SIMPLE plan will also be exempt from top-heavy plan rules. The plan will, however, still be subject to the other rules governing qualified plans.

Note that while participation in a SIMPLE will make it easier for a company to satisfy the nondiscrimination tests, participants in a SIMPLE will be able to defer only $6,000 in compensation compared to $9,500 for those participating in a 401(k) plan.

SUMMARY OF CHAPTER 23

Some of the following should be part of most taxpayers' retirement portfolios.

✓ *Deferred Compensation Plans.* Many tax benefits are available for deferred compensation plans, including defined benefit and defined contribution plans. Contributions are deductible and grow tax deferred. Upon distribution, favorable five-year forward averaging and capital gain treatment may be available. Tax-free partial or complete rollovers between plans are also available. However, employers must be careful to meet strict participation, funding, and vesting standards.

✓ *Individual Retirement Accounts.* Taxpayers should take advantage of the change in the law that permits a nonworking spouse to take a deduction for an IRA contribution even if the working spouse is covered by a retirement plan at work. The high phase-out range of AGI between $150,000 and $160,000 should permit most nonworking spouses to qualify for the deduction. Also, the higher phase-out range of $50,000–$60,000 for joint filers for 1998 (which increases to $80,000–$100,000 for 2007) will allow more married couples to take the IRA deduction.

✓ *Roth IRA.* The new Roth IRA provides a unique opportunity to invest in an IRA that will pay tax-free distributions upon retirement. The fact that distributions need not begin when the taxpayer reaches a specific age will allow taxpayers to take withdrawals from such investments when they need them, not when the government says they must be taken. Taxpayers should keep in mind that the total contribution to all IRAs may not exceed $2,000 per taxpayer per year, subject to any phase-out rules.

✓ **Indexing of Special Use Valuation Amount.** Beginning in 1998, the aggregate decrease in value of $750,000 for qualifying property under Sec. 2032(a)(2) will be indexed for inflation. As a result, families may plan on increased estate tax savings due to the lower valuations that will apply to qualifying property. Also, the gradual increase in the exclusion amount for estate tax purposes to $1,000,000 by the year 2006 will provide much-needed estate tax relief for families.

✓ **Specific Retirement Planning Techniques.** AB trusts, QTIP trusts, life insurance trusts, and lifetime giving should be considered as retirement and estate planning techniques to reduce estate taxes, provide necessary liquidity, and reduce income taxes.

✓ **SIMPLES.** Small employers may find the new SIMPLE plan to be an attractive alternative to deferred compensation plans with more stringent requirements. Employers must be sure to notify employees of their options under the plan, especially the reduced-match option that the employer may take.

CHAPTER 23 QUESTIONS

1. List the tax advantages with qualified retirement plans.

2. What is the difference between a defined contribution plan and a defined benefit plan?

3. Define a top-heavy plan.

4. How much may be contributed annually to a defined contribution Keogh plan?

5. How much may be contributed to an IRA on an annual basis?

6. What are the major differences between a regular IRA and a Roth IRA?

7. What is the maximum amount that may be contributed each year to an Education IRA?

8. What types of distributions qualify under a Roth IRA?

9. Beginning in 1998, taxpayers may make early distributions from regular IRAs for certain purposes without incurring the premature withdrawal penalty. For what purposes may the early withdrawals be used without incurring the penalty?

10. Why are nonqualified deferred compensation plans growing in popularity?

11. What is the estate tax exception to the fair market value at the date of death or the alternate valuation date?

12. What two methods are available for valuing farms under Section 2032A?

13. What are the tax advantages of a private annuity?

14. What is an AB trust setup?

15. What is the maximum annual amount employees may contribute to a SIMPLE?

16. What is the penalty for early withdrawal from a SIMPLE?

17. What percentage of an employee's pay must an employer contribute to a SIMPLE?

CHAPTER 23 PROBLEMS

18. On June 21, 1989, Steve and Evelyn Hume (husband and wife) purchased a home for $200,000, taking title as joint tenants with right of survivorship. In December 1998, Steve was killed in an automobile accident. At Steve's death the home was worth $300,000.

   a.   What is Evelyn's basis in the property for a subsequent resale?

   b.   Assume Steve and Evelyn lived in Louisiana and that the home was community property. What is Evelyn's basis in the property for a subsequent resale?

   c.   What advantage does community property have over separate property?

19. During 1998, John Henry earned $80,000 in his sole proprietorship. What is the maximum contribution that John can make to his defined contribution Keogh plan?

20. In 1998, Mr. and Mrs. Henderson had compensation income of $26,000 and $20,000, respectively. Adjusted gross income on their joint return was $46,000, and neither Mr. nor Mrs. Henderson was a participant in a qualified retirement plan. How much may each contribute to an IRA account and deduct from taxable income?

21. In 1998, Mr. and Mrs. Henderson had compensation income of $16,000 and $7,500, respectively. Adjusted gross income on their joint return was $23,500, and only Mr. Henderson was a participant in a qualified retirement plan. How much may each contribute to an IRA account and deduct from taxable income?

22. In 1998, Mr. and Mrs. Henderson had compensation income of $39,000 and $22,000, respectively. Adjusted gross income on their joint return was $56,000, and only Mr. Henderson was a participant in a qualified retirement plan. How much may each deduct to an IRA account?

23. Garth and Sue Monaghan are married to each other. Garth is an active participant in a retirement plan at work. Sue stays at home and takes care of their two children. Their AGI for 1998 is $152,000. What amount may each deduct for a regular IRA?

24. Harold Daniel is single and has an AGI of $101,000 for 1998. What is the maximum contribution that he may make to a Roth IRA?

25. Refer to Problem 24. What amount may Harold contribute if his AGI is $103,275?

26. During the period 1998 through 2007, Martha Broderick made contributions to her Roth IRA totaling $10,000. By 2009, the IRA balance, including earnings, had grown to $31,000. In 2010, before Martha turned 59½, she withdrew $22,000 from her Roth IRA to buy a new car. What is the tax result for Martha?

27. Scott Rotondo dies in 1999. The Consumer Price Indices for 1997 and 1998 are 195.05 and 203.29 respectively. If his estate elects special use valuation with respect to his farm under Sec. 2032A, what would be the maximum allowable reduction in estate value?

28. In 1998, Allan Davis died leaving the following property, debts, and expenses:

Bonds	$ 200,000
Stocks	100,000
Farm real estate	600,000
Farm equipment	200,000
	$1,100,000
Mortgage against farm realty	(50,000)
Accounting fees	(25,000)
Appraiser's fees	(25,000)
Adjusted gross estate	$1,000,000

Allan had physically farmed the property for the last thirty years. He willed the property to his favorite son, Aldo, who will continue to farm it. Will the property qualify for special use valuation?

29. Assume that the real estate in Problem 28 consists of 1,000 acres, the average gross rent is $30 per acre, and the average real estate taxes are $5 per acre. Further assume that 10 percent is the average annual effective interest charged by the Federal Land Bank. At what amount would the parcel be valued under Section 2032A for 1998?

30. Assume that 12 years after electing special use valuation the son sells the property. Are there any estate tax effects?

31. In 1998, Margaret Manson is 65 years old. She owns a farm with a fair market value of $100,000 and a basis of $10,000. She decides to sell the farm to her son Bob, in a private annuity. Margaret's life expectancy is 20 years and the annual annuity is calculated to be $14,712. Of the total annuity of $14,712, how much can Margaret exclude from income?

32. Suppose that Margaret in Problem 31 lives beyond her 20 years of life expectancy. Does the exclusion ratio continue?

33. Mr. and Mrs. Anglebeak had compensation of $35,000 and $0, respectively (she did not work outside the home). What is the maximum amount each may contribute to an IRA on a joint return?

34. ABC Company has 75 employees, all of whom earn at least $5,000 per year. Its subsidiary, XYZ Company, has 50 employees. Thirty of XYZ Company's employees earn over $5,000 and 20 do not. May either company establish a SIMPLE pension plan for its employees?

35. The Black Bear Corporation established a SIMPLE for its employees in 1997. It has three eligible employees. One employee who earns $30,000 per year participates in the SIMPLE. The other two employees earn $10,000 each and do not contribute to the SIMPLE. What is the maximum contribution the participating employee may make each year? What is the minimum contribution the company must make over a five-year period?

COMPREHENSIVE RETIREMENT/ESTATE PLANNING PROBLEM

Facts

Hugh and Donna Ames, ages 51 and 50, respectively, have been married for 30 years. Donna suspects the longevity of this marriage is attributable to the fact that she usually finds some tactful way to let Hugh have his way. This year, there was a dramatic example.

Hugh and Donna had been living in Dallas, Texas, where he was employed as a vice president of advertising of Big Sleep Inc., a Texas corporation engaged in the manufacture and sale of waterbeds. However, last year there was a takeover of the corporation, and Hugh soon found himself, at age 50, out of a job—leading to many unrestful nights, even on his former company's product. He did receive $250,000 in separation payments in 1998, twice his annual salary. He decided that he had always wanted to own his own business and that being fired was divine guidance. Donna was a lot less sure of the source of the guidance.

The day that Hugh ambled home with the pink slip, there was waiting for him a letter from his third cousin, Billy Ray. He wanted to know if Hugh knew anyone who was interested in buying his small but profitable business located in Belle Haven, Virginia. After some negotiations, Hugh decided he was interested and bought all the stock of Big Bruiser Lock Company.

Big Bruiser has a narrow but profitable field of business in selling heavy-duty locks for fences at junkyards, police compounds, and lots at hardware stores. Its balance sheet is attached at the end of this section. Last year, it earned $150,000 on sales of $1,000,000, including a $125,000 per annum salary for Hugh. Its liabilities are comparatively small, and its net worth is about $800,000.

Big Bruiser has Blue Cross/Blue Shield policies but no disability insurance coverage for its workers. It also has no pension plan. Of Big Bruiser's 12 employees, only Hugh and his son, Billy Bob, would be regarded as managers. There is really no middle management. Big Bruiser has no record of dividend payments and elected Subchapter S status in December of 1986.

Donna is a skilled and experienced college professor. When she moved from Texas to Virginia, she determined that she would look for a teaching position. She had no trouble in finding one at Eastern Shore Community College in Melfa, Virginia, at a salary of $40,000 per year plus hospital and major medical insurance benefits. She expects a pension of 50 percent of salary (plus Social Security) at age 65. She has in her own name approximately $40,000 in bank accounts.

When Hugh and Donna moved to Belle Haven, they sold their Dallas home in September 1998 for $500,000 (which cost them $125,000). Currently they are renting an apartment, but are looking for a new home. They are interested in the tax ramifications of this move and spend a good deal of their time on weekends going out with realtors on the Eastern Shore of Virginia.

Hugh has a $25,000 ordinary life insurance policy on his life that he has held for some time and that currently has a cash value of $15,000. He acquired the life insurance while in Texas. He also has $10,000 of National Service Life Insurance and a term policy of $25,000 not convertible to ordinary life for another five years. Both of these policies were acquired before marriage. He and Donna are in good health. There is no group insurance program at Big Bruiser and Hugh thinks it might be something to look into. Hugh would also like to know about a pension plan. He has heard about a simplified employee pension plan and wants your opinion on it.

Hugh and Donna have two children. The elder, Billy Bob, is a graduate of the University of Richmond and last year left a job with a major insurance company when it did not appear that he was going to go much higher than Sales Associate, at least for a number of years, to join Big Bruiser, primarily as a salesman. He is 26 years old and has worked with his father at Big Bruiser for the last six months. He also has some distinct ideas with respect to a new hydraulic lock for which he hopes he can obtain a license from the patent owner. He believes this lock could permit Big Bruiser to double its gross sales in four years but at substantial cost. Billy Bob is divorced and has no current plans for remarriage.

Donna and Hugh's younger child, Lucille, age 23, graduated from college last May. She is a substitute teacher at Cape Charles Elementary School in Cape Charles and is looking for a permanent job. She lives with Hugh and Donna. Currently, she is dating a farmer from Painter, Virginia.

Hugh has regularly contributed the maximum of $2,000 per year to an IRA that currently has a value of about $18,000, including accumulated earnings. Donna has a similar IRA, but hers has appreciated only to $12,000.

Hugh and Donna have in their joint names listed stocks valued at $70,000, with a basis of approximately $30,000. Hugh also has in his own name Series H Savings Bonds worth approximately $13,000. He paid approximately $5,000 for these Bonds.

Hugh (an only child) has a mother, Bertha, age 80, who lives in Norfolk, Virginia. She owns a home with a value of approximately $480,000 and a portfolio of listed stocks, mostly inherited from her husband, valued at $250,000. The home was worth $300,000 at her husband's death and was jointly owned. She has a trust from her husband, who died in 1980, that will not be included in her estate because she has all of the income and only a limited power of appointment currently valued at $200,000. But Bertha has been diagnosed as having a terminal malignancy. The doctors feel that she has about three years to live.

Donna has very few relatives, but she does have an uncle. Uncle Harry is age 90 and has lived in nearby Exmore, Virginia, for 70 years.

He worked for a number of years and currently gets along in a careful way on a pension, Social Security, and interest. He lives in a small home that he owns outright. The home is worth about $80,000, but he has no other substantial assets except $5,000 in the bank. Donna's concern is that Uncle Harry is now becoming forgetful and less and less able to take care of himself. Donna believes he would never consent to going into a nursing home and could not afford it in any event. Donna feels a moral obligation to take in Uncle Harry to live with her and her family. Hugh agrees to the arrangement. Uncle Harry has one other relative, a nephew who lives in Idaho and whom he seldom sees.

Big Bruiser Inc.

Balance Sheet

September 30, 1998

Assets

Cash			$100,000
Inventory			402,000
Equipment, furniture and fixtures	$140,000		
Less: Reserve for depreciation	(15,000)		
Net			$125,000
Automobile	$ 16,000		
Less: Accumulated depreciation	(8,000)		
Net			$ 8,000
Land	$150,000		
Building	$185,000		
Less: Accumulated Depreciation	30,000	155,000	$305,000
Total			$940,000

Liabilities & Owners' Equity

Accounts payable	$140,000
Capital Stock	$800,000
Total	$940,000

Suggested Items for Group Discussion:

1. Statement of objectives
2. Review of facts
3. Retirement planning
4. Disability planning
5. Community property status
6. Buy-sell agreements
7. AB trust setup
8. Use of Code Secs. 1034 and 121 and diversification of investments
9. Planning recommendations for Hugh's mother
10. Planning recommendations for Donna's uncle
11. Special use valuation
12. Paying estate tax in installments

Chapter 24

Tax Research, Practice, and Procedure

Learning Objectives

After completing Chapter 24, you should be able to:

1. Identify the primary authoritative sources of the tax law and understand the relative weight of these authorities.
2. Explain the role of the court system as a forum for both the taxpayer and the government.
3. Develop a familiarity with the various forms of judicial citations.
4. Understand the general organization of a loose-leaf tax service and the importance of a citator service and other types of secondary reference materials.
5. Describe the organization of the Internal Revenue Service and selected rules relating to practice before the IRS.
6. Discuss the examination of returns, including correspondence examinations, office examinations, and field examinations.
7. Explain the appeals process, both within the IRS and through the court system.
8. Understand the possible communications between the IRS and taxpayers, including private rulings, determination letters, and technical advice.
9. Describe some of the more common penalties to which taxpayers and tax preparers might be subject.
10. Understand ethics as related to the tax practitioner.

OVERVIEW OF CHAPTER

To the general public, the tax practitioner is often viewed simply as a preparer of tax returns. However, from a broader, more professional perspective, tax practice also involves extensive research, creative tax planning, and effective representation of clients before the audit or appellate divisions of the Internal Revenue Service.

Tax research is the process whereby one systematically searches for the answer to a tax question, using the various primary and secondary sources of tax-related information. This involves reviewing and evaluating appropriate Internal Revenue Code sections, Treasury Regulations, Internal Revenue Service Rulings, and court decisions. Research into this voluminous material is typically facilitated by the use of one of the loose-leaf tax services, which are organized and cross-referenced in such a manner as to assist the researcher in the confusing trek through the overwhelming mass of authoritative data. Also, due to rapid technological advances made in computer-assisted tax research, the researcher may access the most complete and up-to-date authoritative data with only a few key strokes.

The tax specialist needs to understand the organizational structure of the IRS and its administrative procedures to provide fully informed tax consulting services to taxpayers involved in disputes with the IRS. Thus, this chapter includes a discussion of the internal organization of the IRS and how its various administrative groups function, the rules relating to practice before the IRS, and the procedures for examination of returns, including service center examinations, office examinations, and field examinations.

What actions can a taxpayer take if there is an adverse decision by the tax auditor or revenue agent? To provide an answer to this question, this chapter details and explains the appeals process, both within the IRS and through the court system. Another approach available to the taxpayer is the right to request advice from the IRS on the tax consequences of a particular transaction. This chapter discusses the various communications between the IRS and taxpayers, including private letter rulings, determination letters, and technical advice.

Some of the more common penalties to which taxpayers and tax preparers might be subject are also discussed. Tax practitioners should be familiar with the code of professional ethics of their profession since a violation of these standards might mean that "due care" has not been exercised and the practitioner might be subject to charges of negligence.

Tax Reference Materials

¶ 24,001 CLASSIFICATION OF MATERIALS

Tax reference materials are usually classified as primary "authoritative" sources or secondary "reference" sources. Primary source materials include the Internal Revenue Code (Statutory Authority), Treasury Regulations and Internal Revenue Service Rulings (Administrative Authority), and the various decisions of the trial courts and the appellate courts (Judicial Authority).

Secondary reference materials consist primarily of the various loose-leaf tax reference services. Additional secondary materials include periodicals, textbooks and treatises, published papers from tax institutes and symposia, and newsletters.

Reminder. While the editorial opinions included in the secondary reference materials are extremely knowledgeable and comprehensive, neither the IRS nor the courts will afford any authoritative weight to these opinions. One exception is Mertens, *Law of Federal Income Taxation.* This tax service is often quoted in judicial decisions.

Both primary and secondary sources can be accessed through one of the computer-assisted research services. These electronic data bases are updated daily and contain many source documents not normally found in the traditional tax library.

Primary Source Materials

¶ 24,021   STATUTORY AUTHORITY

The authority of the U.S. government to raise revenue through a federal income tax is derived from the Sixteenth Amendment to the Constitution. Following ratification of this Amendment, the federal income tax law was enacted on October 3, 1913, and was made retroactive to March 1, 1913. Various other revenue acts were soon enacted. From these provisions, a loose and disconnected body of tax law emerged, making it virtually impossible to systematically engage in tax research. Accordingly, to facilitate a convenient form of organization, the various revenue acts that were legislated between 1913 and 1939 were codified into Title 26 of the United States Code, known as the Internal Revenue Code of 1939.

In subsequent years, with the growing complexity of the tax law, the Code was revised and rewritten as the Internal Revenue Code of 1954. During the next thirty-two years numerous tax laws were incorporated as amendments into the 1954 Code. Accordingly, the Economic Recovery Tax Act of 1981 (ERTA), the Tax Equity and Fiscal Responsibility Act of 1982 (TEFRA), and the Tax Reform Act of 1984 were included as part of the Internal Revenue Code of 1954, as amended. However, in 1986, as a result of the sweeping changes made by the Tax Reform Act of 1986, Congress changed the name of the tax law to the Internal Revenue Code of 1986. The 1986 Code was amended annually in 1987–1989 with primarily technical changes. The Revenue Reconciliation Act of 1990 included statutory increases in excise and income taxes in addition to its numerous technical tax law changes. The Revenue Reconciliation Act of 1993 increased tax rates for higher income individuals and corporations while expanding and simplifying the earned income credit for low-income workers. The Taxpayer Relief Act of 1997 significantly revised the treatment of capital gains and gains from the sale of a principal residence.

Organization of the Code

The Internal Revenue Code of 1986 is comprised of nine subtitles (A-I), each consisting of individual, consecutively numbered chapters (1-98). The subtitles most commonly encountered by the tax practitioner that form the basis of this book are Subtitle A, "Income Taxes," including Chapters 1–6, and Subtitle B, "Estate and Gift Taxes," including Chapters 11–13. The remaining subtitles relate to topics such as employment taxes, excise taxes, alcohol and tobacco taxes, etc. Portions of Subtitle F, "Procedure and Administration," including Chapters 61–80, are also examined in this text.

The major portion of the Code dealing with federal income tax is located in Chapter 1 of Subtitle A. This extremely important Chapter, entitled "Normal Taxes and Surtaxes," is further divided into Subchapters (A-W), and each Subchapter is then divided into numbered sections. These sections are typically referred to as "Code Sections."

The following exhibit (Exhibit 1) provides a Table of Contents for Chapter 1 of Subtitle A of the Internal Revenue Code of 1986.

Exhibit 1   INTERNAL REVENUE CODE OF 1986—SELECTED TABLE OF CONTENTS

SUBTITLE A—INCOME TAXES

CHAPTER 1—NORMAL TAXES AND SURTAXES

SUBCHAPTER	BEGINNING SECTION NUMBER
A Determination of Tax Liability	1
B Computation of Taxable Income	61
C Corporate Distributions and Adjustments	301
D Deferred Compensation, Etc.	401
E Accounting Periods and Methods of Accounting	441
F Exempt Organizations	501
G Corporations Used to Avoid Income Tax on Shareholders	531
H Banking Institutions	581
I Natural Resources	611
J Estates, Trusts, Beneficiaries, and Decedents	641
K Partners and Partnerships	701
L Insurance Companies	801
M Regulated Investment Companies and Real Estate Investment Trusts	851
N Tax Based on Income from Sources Within or Without the United States	861
O Gain or Loss on Disposition of Property	1001
P Capital Gains and Losses	1201
Q Readjustment of Tax Between Years and Special Limitations	1301
S Subchapter S: Tax Treatment of S Corporations and Their Shareholders	1361
T Cooperatives and Their Patrons	1381
U Designation and Treatment of Empowerment Zones, Enterprise Communities, and Rural Development Investment Areas	1391
V Title 11 Cases	1398
W District of Columbia Enterprise Zone	1400

Citing the Code

Code Sections, particularly those found within Chapter 1 of Subtitle A, are cited by detailed reference to section, subsection, paragraph, and subparagraph. On occasion, the reference is even broken down to inferior subdivisions.

For example, Section 453(e)(3)(A)(i) might serve as an illustration.

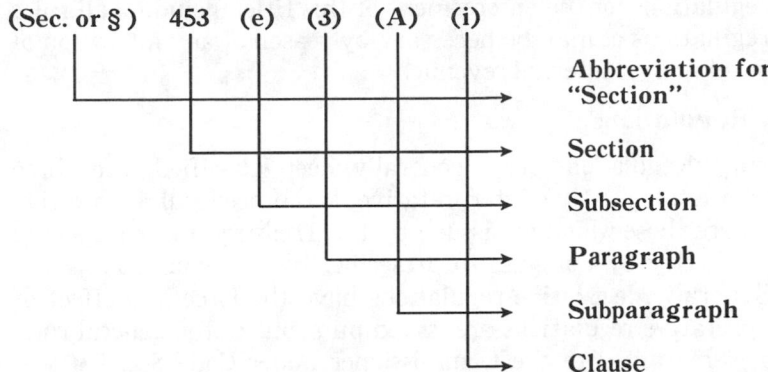

(Sec. or §)   453   (e)   (3)   (A)   (i)

→ Abbreviation for "Section"

→ Section

→ Subsection

→ Paragraph

→ Subparagraph

→ Clause

Throughout this text, references to Code Sections are in the form explained above. Unless otherwise noted, references to Code Sections relate to the Internal Revenue Code of 1986. References to the 1939 or 1954 Code are specifically noted.

Congressional Committee Reports

Congressional Committee Reports are the minutes or official statements made by members of the House Ways and Means Committee, Senate Finance Committee, and Conference Committee on their intention in passing a specific piece of legislation. Unlike Treasury Regulations, Revenue Rulings, and Revenue Procedures issued by the IRS that are not binding on the courts, congressional intent expressed in Committee Reports very often is binding as these Committee Reports are regarded as very high authority. Committee Reports are published in the *Cumulative Bulletin* and by private publishers, including CCH Incorporated and Research Institute of America. Additionally, the *Congressional Record* reports floor debates in the House of Representatives and in the Senate.

Blue Books

As stated in the House Committee Report to the Revenue Reconciliation Act of 1989 (P.L. 101-239), "Blue Books" have been added to the list of authorities on which taxpayers may rely for interpretation of the tax law (see discussion at ¶ 24,035). Blue Books are prepared by the Staff of the Joint Committee on Taxation for major tax acts. Although Blue Books are generally based on Committee Reports for an act, they often contain additional interpretative information. The IRS has used this interpretative information in numerous rulings as the basis for a particular position. Blue Books are published by CCH Incorporated.

¶ 24,035   ADMINISTRATIVE AUTHORITY

As a result of congressional authority, the Secretary of the Treasury or a delegate, the Commissioner of Internal Revenue, is authorized to provide administrative interpretation of the tax law. As noted in Section 7805(a):

Except where such authority is expressly given by this title to any person other than an officer or employee of the Treasury Department, the Secretary or his delegate shall prescribe all needful rules and regulations for the enforcement of this title, including all rules and regulations as may be necessary by reason of any alteration of law in relation to internal revenue.

Treasury Regulations

Treasury Regulations have generally been classified into three broad categories: legislative, interpretative, and procedural. Legislative regulations are those which are issued by the Treasury under a specific grant of authority by Congress to prescribe the operating rules for a statute. Generally, legislative regulations have the force and effect of law. Interpretative regulations are issued pursuant to the general rule-making power granted to the Commissioner under Code Sec. 7805(a) and provide taxpayers with guidance in order to comply with a statute. Although interpretative regulations do not have the force and effect of law, the courts customarily accord them substantial weight. Procedural regulations are considered to be directive rather than mandatory and, thus, do not have the force and effect of law. They explain the IRS's position and provide the mechanics for compliance with the various federal income tax laws, as for example the making and filing of tax elections.

The Regulations are organized in a sequential system consistent with the Code. Additionally, the Regulations are prefixed by a number which designates the applicable area of taxation to which they refer. For example, following are the more important Regulation prefixes:

Part   1.   Final income tax regulations

Part   20.   Estate Tax

Part   25.   Gift Tax

Part   31.   Withholding taxes

Part 301.   Procedure and Administration

Part 601.   Statement of Procedural Rules

Accordingly, an "Income Tax" Regulation relating to Section 453 of the Code would be cited as Reg. § 1.453, followed by a dash, then the sequential number of issue, with subparts added for more detailed reference.

Proposed Regulations. New Regulations and changes to existing Regulations usually are issued in proposed form before they are finalized. During the interval between the publication of the Notice of Proposed Rulemaking and finalization of the Regulation, taxpayers and other interested parties are permitted to file objections or suggestions. Proposed Regulations do not have the same weight as Temporary Regulations. Tax law publishers such as CCH Incorporated and Research Institute of America provide a comprehensive listing of these Proposed Regulations, showing the date of their proposal and date of adoption and also publish the text of the Proposed Regulations.

Temporary Regulations. Sometimes Temporary Regulations are issued by the Treasury Department. Their purpose is to provide interim guidance regarding recent tax legislation until final Regulations are adopted. Temporary Regulations (issued after November 20, 1988) must undergo public and administrative scrutiny during a comment period as do Proposed Regulations. Every Temporary Regulation will expire three years from the date of issuance. Prior to its expiration, a Temporary Regulation has the same weight as a Final Regulation.

Final Regulations. Finalized Regulations are published in the *Federal Register* as are the Proposed Regulations and Temporary Regulations. All tax Regulations are also published in the *Internal Revenue Bulletin.* Final Regulations and Temporary Regulations are designated as Treasury Decisions (T.D.s) and are assigned a sequential number in order of issuance for the year. The effective date and date of adoption are significant.

Final Regulations as well as Proposed and Temporary Regulations are reproduced in major tax services.

Revenue Rulings and Revenue Procedures

Revenue Rulings, the official pronouncements of the IRS, are similar to Treasury Regulations in that they represent administrative interpretations of the internal revenue laws. Revenue Rulings are issued with respect to a particular issue and insure that this issue will be handled uniformly throughout the country, both in planning and in auditing. Revenue Rulings, however, do not have the same authoritative weight as regulations. Every issue of the *Internal Revenue Bulletin* includes the following statement:

> Rulings and procedures reported in the Bulletin do not have the force and effect of Treasury Department Regulations, but they may be used as precedents. Unpublished rulings will not be relied on, used, or cited as precedents by Service personnel in the disposition of other cases. In applying published rulings and procedures, the effect of subsequent legislation, regulations, court decisions, rulings, and procedures must be considered, and Service personnel and others concerned are cautioned against reaching the same conclusions in other cases unless the facts and circumstances are substantially the same.

Revenue Procedures are published official statements of procedure issued by the IRS that affect either the rights or the duties of taxpayers or other members of the public under the Internal Revenue Code and related statutes and regulations. Revenue Procedures usually reflect the contents of internal management documents. A statement of the IRS position on a substantive tax issue will not be included in a Revenue Procedure. Revenue Procedures are directive and not mandatory.

Both Revenue Rulings and Revenue Procedures are originally published in the weekly issues of the *Internal Revenue Bulletin,* printed by the U.S. Government. However, on a semiannual basis, the bulletins are compiled, reorganized by Code section classification, and published in a bound volume designated the *Cumulative Bulletin.* Once published in the *Cumulative Bulletin*, a Revenue Ruling or Revenue Procedure receives a permanent citation as shown below:

Rev. Rul. 93-12,   1993-1 CB   202

→ **Ruling number 12 of 1993**

→ **Volume 1, 1993** *Cumulative Bulletin*

→ **Page 202**

The citation for a Revenue Procedure is identical, except the abbreviation "Rev. Proc." is used in place of "Rev. Rul."

Other Administrative Pronouncements

In addition to substantive rulings (Revenue Rulings and Revenue Procedures) published to promote a uniform application of the tax laws, the IRS issues communications to individual taxpayers and IRS personnel in three primary ways: (1) Private Letter Rulings, (2) Determination Letters, and (3) Technical Advice Memoranda. These documents are part of the IRS rulings program, which is discussed in detail at ¶ 24,225.

Digests of Private Letter Rulings may be found in *Private Letter Rulings* (published by Research Institute of America), BNA *Daily Tax Reports,* and Tax Analysts & Advocates *Tax Notes. IRS Letter Rulings Reports* (published by CCH Incorporated) contains both digests and the full texts of all Private Letter Rulings. These documents may also be accessed electronically through CCH's CD-ROM and Online computer software. Determination Letters are not published; however, the IRS is now required to make individual rulings available for public inspection.

Technical Information Releases (TIRs) and Announcements are periodically distributed by the IRS to advise the public of various technical matters. While these pronouncements are published weekly in the *Internal Revenue Bulletin*, they are not usually included in the *Cumulative Bulletin.*

IRS List of Substantial Authority for Taxpayer Reliance

The IRS has provided guidance on (1) adequate disclosure of items and positions taken on tax returns for purposes of avoiding the accuracy related penalty for understatement of tax, Rev. Proc. 94-36, 1994-1 CB 682, and (2) a listing of substantial authority that may be relied on to avoid imposition of that penalty. Reg. § 1.6662-4(d)(3). In addition, the IRS issues a list of positions for which there is not substantial authority. This list must be issued by the Secretary of the Treasury (and revised not less frequently than annually) and published in the *Federal Register.* Code Sec. 6662(d)(2)(D).

The purpose of the list is to assist taxpayers in determining whether a position should be disclosed in order to avoid the substantial understatement penalty. House Committee Report, Revenue Reconciliation Act of 1989. Thus, a taxpayer could choose to disclose that position to avoid the imposition of the accuracy-related penalty. However, inclusion of a position on this list is not conclusive as to whether or not substantial authority exists with respect to that position.

The list of substantial authority has been expanded to include (1) the Joint Committee on Taxation's General Explanation of tax legislation (i.e., the "Blue Book"); (2) proposed regulations; (3) information or press releases; (4) notices, announcements, and other similar documents published in the *Internal Revenue Bulletin;* (5) private letter rulings; (6) technical advice memoranda; (7) actions on decisions; and (8) general counsel memoranda. Reg. § 1.6662-4(d)(3)(iii). "Authority" does not include conclusions reached in treatises, legal periodicals, and opinions rendered by tax professionals.

Prior to 1990, the list of substantial authority was restricted to: (1) the Internal Revenue Code, (2) final and temporary regulations, (3) court cases, (4) IRS administrative pronouncements, (5) tax treaties, and (6) congressional intent reflected in committee reports accompanying legislation. Reg. § 1.6661-3.

With respect to the test for "substantial authority," the IRS continues to apply the principle that there is substantial authority for the tax treatment of an item only if the weight of authorities supporting such treatment is substantial in relation to the weight of authorities supporting contrary tax treatment. The type of document providing the authority affects the weight to be accorded an authority. Reg. § 1.6662-4(d)(3)(i) and (ii).

¶ 24,055 JUDICIAL AUTHORITY

The ultimate test in the interpretation of the Code, in determining the validity of Regulations, and in applying the "law" to the facts of a given case takes place in the courts. The court system provides the taxpayer with the opportunity to test before a neutral forum both the position taken by the taxpayer and that taken by the Commissioner with respect to any issue. The courts historically have played a substantial role in the interpretation, application, and enforcement of the tax law. Exhibit 2 (on the following page) outlines the trial and appellate court alternatives for federal tax litigation.

Trial Court System

There are three tribunals that have original jurisdiction to hear and decide tax cases arising under the Internal Revenue Code. A taxpayer can file a petition with the United States Tax Court, in which event assessment and collection of the deficiency will be stayed until the Tax Court's decision becomes final. But the taxpayer may, if he or she prefers, pay the deficiency and then sue for a refund in a U.S. District Court or the United States Court of Federal Claims.

Exhibit 2   JUDICIAL APPEALS ALTERNATIVES

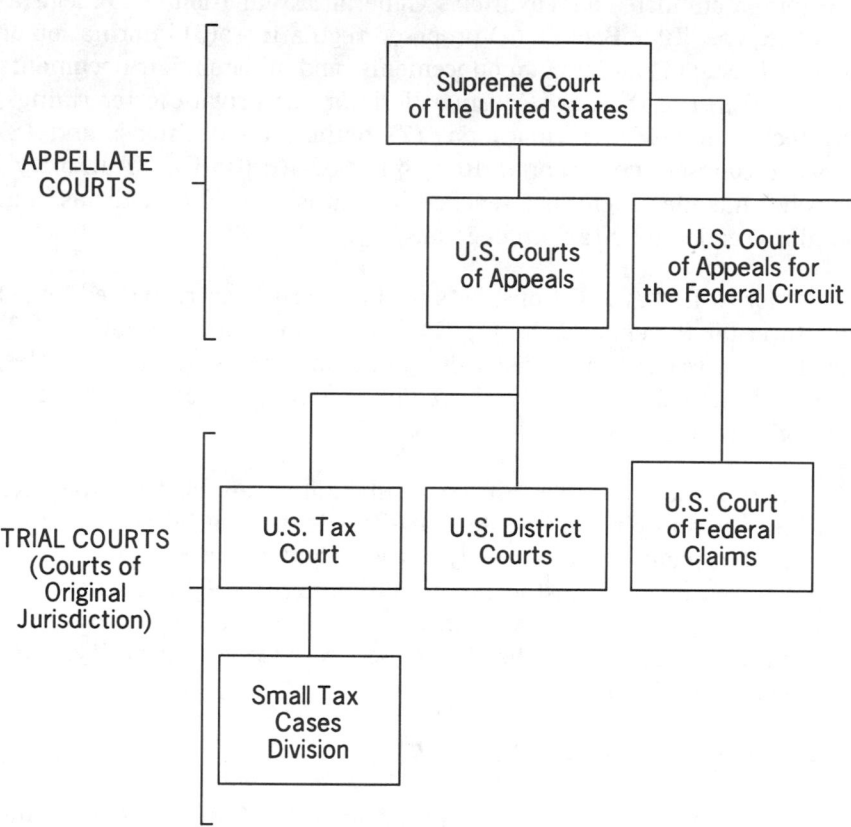

U.S. Tax Court

The United States Tax Court consists of 19 judges appointed by the President for 15-year terms. It is a special court whose jurisdiction is limited almost exclusively to litigation under the Internal Revenue Code. Prior to 1943, the Tax Court was known as the Board of Tax Appeals. Although the Tax Court is a single court located in Washington, D.C., hearings are held in several cities throughout the nation, usually with only a single judge present who submits his opinion to the chief judge. Only rarely does the chief judge decide that a full review is necessary by all 19 judges.

Decisions of the Tax Court are issued as either "regular" or "memorandum" decisions. "Regular" decisions are those which require an interpretation of the law. In theory, "memorandum" decisions concern only well-established principles of law and require only a determination of facts. However, on occasion, the courts have cited "memorandum" decisions. Hence, both kinds of Tax Court decisions should be regarded as having precedent value.

Viewing itself as a national court hearing cases from all parts of the country, for many years the Tax Court had followed a policy of deciding cases on what it thought the result should be. The Tax Court has abandoned its "national law" view, under which it applied its own rule on a nationwide basis without limitation by rules of the circuits in which tax controversies arose. The Tax Court has adopted the position that it will follow precedents of the Circuit Court of Appeals of jurisdiction (known as the *Golsen* rule). As a result, it is entirely possible that the Tax Court will rule differently on identical fact patterns for two taxpayers residing in different circuits in the event of inconsistent holdings between the various Circuit Courts.

The Tax Court is the only court to which a taxpayer may take a case without first paying the tax. Consequently, taxpayers resort to it in many instances; and because it is a court of limited jurisdiction dealing primarily with tax matters, its decisions are accorded considerable weight. This is particularly true of decisions in which the Commissioner of Internal Revenue has acquiesced.

Historically, the policy of the IRS has been to announce in the *Internal Revenue Bulletin* the determination of the Commissioner to acquiesce or not acquiesce in most of the regular decisions of the Tax Court. An announcement of acquiescence (cited Acq.) indicates that the IRS has accepted the conclusion reached in the case but not necessarily the reasons given by the court in its opinion. An announcement of nonacquiescence (cited Nonacq.) usually means that the IRS will continue to litigate the issue if it arises again. Recently, the IRS has indicated acquiescences or nonacquiescences for memorandum decisions of the Tax Court as well as for decisions of other courts. An announcement of acquiescence is not legally binding on the IRS and thus can be retroactively withdrawn at any time. If a case is being relied upon, it is important to determine whether it has been acquiesced in by the Commissioner, the extent of the acquiescence (if any), and whether the initial acquiescence may have been withdrawn at a later date.

Additionally, a procedure is used in the Tax Court for cases involving disputes of $10,000 or less. The taxpayer who uses the "small tax case" procedures should be aware that the decision may not be appealed. The advantage to using this procedure is the fact that the formal procedures of the Tax Court are relaxed and made informal.

Judicial Citations—Tax Court Regular Decisions. Regular and memorandum decisions of the Tax Court are reported separately. The Government Printing Office publishes bound volumes of only the regular decisions under the title *United States Tax Court Reports* (cited TC).

Permanent Citation: Citrus Valley Estates, 99 TC 379 (1992).

Thus, the decision appears in Volume 99 of the *United States Tax Court Reports*, page 379, issued in 1992.

Because there is usually a time lag between the date a decision is rendered and the date it appears in bound form, a temporary citation is used until a permanent citation can be substituted.

> *Temporary Citation: Dayton Hudson Corp.,* 101 TC —, No. 30 (1993).

> Thus, the temporary citation identifies that the decision will appear in Volume 101 of the *United States Tax Court Reports*, page left blank, 30th regular decision issued by the Tax Court since Volume 100 was issued. Once Volume 101 is issued, the permanent citation incorporating the page is substituted and the number of the case is not used.

Judicial Citations—Tax Court Memorandum Decisions. The government provides only mimeograph copies of the memorandum decisions. However, memorandum decisions are published by both CCH Incorporated and Research Institute of America (RIA) in bound volumes separate from those in which they report other tax cases. The Tax Court memorandum decisions are published by CCH under the title *Tax Court Memorandum Decisions* (cited TCM), while the RIA series is called *RIA Memorandum Decisions* (cited TC Memo).

> *CCH Citation: Gene A. Stone,* 61 TCM 2588, T.C. Memo. 1991-206 (1991).

> *RIA Citation: Gene A. Stone,* 1991 TC Memo ¶ 91,206.

> Although presented in a different way, the reference in both citations indicates that the memorandum decision was the 206th memorandum decision issued by the Tax Court in 1991.

Both regular and memorandum decisions for years prior to 1943 were published by the government under the title *United States Board of Tax Appeals Reports.*

> *Citation: J.E. Burke,* 19 BTA 743 (1930).

> Thus, the decision appears in Volume 19 of the *United States Board of Tax Appeals Reports*, page 743, issued in 1930.

U.S. District Courts

The U.S. District Courts were the main courts of original jurisdiction for tax cases prior to the establishment of the Board of Tax Appeals which later became the Tax Court. A taxpayer can take a case to the U.S. District Court for the district in which the taxpayer resides only if the taxpayer first pays the tax deficiency assessed by the IRS and then sues for a refund. Each state has at least one District Court in which both tax and nontax litigation are heard. Only in a District Court can one obtain a jury trial, and even there a jury can decide only questions of fact—not those of law.

Judicial Citations—U.S. District Courts Decisions. Published decisions of the U.S. District Courts, including both tax and all other types of litigation, are reported in the *Federal Supplement* (cited F.Supp.) published by West Publishing Company. In addition, the tax decisions of the District Courts are also published in the two special tax reporter series, CCH *United States Tax Cases* (cited USTC) and Research Institute of America (RIA) *American Federal Tax Reports* (cited AFTR).

West Citation: Mary A. De Santis, 783 F.Supp. 165 (DC NY 1-30-92).

The order of citation is volume number, reporter, page number.

CCH Citation: Mary A. De Santis, 92-1 USTC ¶50,120 (DC NY, 1/30/92).

Paragraph reference rather than a page number gives the location of the case.

RIA Citation: Mary A. De Santis, 69 AFTR 2d 92-812 (DC NY, 1/30/92).

The prefix "92" preceding the page number indicates the year the case was decided.

U.S. Court of Federal Claims

The U.S. Court of Federal Claims is a single court consisting of 16 judges appointed by the President. The court resides in Washington, D.C. and the decision to travel is made on a case-by-case basis and is heard by the trial judge to whom the case has been assigned. Prior to October 29, 1992, the court was known as the U.S. Claims Court, and prior to October 1, 1982, the court was known as the U.S. Court of Claims whose decisions were appealed directly to the Supreme Court.

In federal tax matters, the U.S. Court of Federal Claims has concurrent jurisdiction with the U.S. District Courts. The Court of Federal Claims is a constitutional court and has jurisdiction in judgment on any claim against the United States which is:

1. Based on the Constitution

2. Based on any Act of Congress

3. Based on any regulation of an executive department

Judicial Citations—U.S. Court of Federal Claims Decisions. Since 1992, decisions of the Court of Federal Claims have been reported by West Publishing Company in the *Federal Claims Reporter* (cited FedCl). The decisions of the Claims Court from October 1982 until 1992 were reported by West Publishing Company in a series designated the *U.S. Claims Court Reporter* (cited ClCt). Decisions of the predecessor Court of Claims were published by the U.S. Government Printing Office in a separate series of volumes entitled the *U.S. Court of Claims Reports* (cited CtCl). The decisions of the predecessor Court of Claims were also published by West Publishing Company from May 1960 through September 1982 in the *Federal Reporter* 2d Series (cited F.2d), while decisions between 1932 and 1960 were reported in the *Federal Supplement* (cited F.Supp.).

In addition, the tax decisions of the Court of Federal Claims (and the predecessor Claims Court and Court of Claims) are also published in the CCH *United States Tax Cases* (cited USTC) and Research Institute of America (RIA) *American Federal Tax Reports* (cited AFTR).

West Citation: Katz v. U.S., 22 ClCt 714 (Cl Ct 1991).

Scott v. U.S., 354 F.2d 292 (Ct Cl 1965).

McHugh v. U.S., 142 F.Supp. 927 (Ct Cl 1956).

CCH Citation: Katz v. U.S., 91-1 USTC ¶50,289 (Cl Ct 1991).

RIA Citation: Katz v. U.S., 67 AFTR2d 91-733 (Cl Ct 1991).

Appeals Court System

If either the taxpayer or the IRS is not satisfied with a trial court decision, an appellate court may be asked to review that decision. There are two levels of courts that handle appeals from the three courts of original jurisdiction. Appeals may be taken to the United States Courts of Appeals of jurisdiction or the U.S. Court of Appeals for the Federal Circuit. As a final step, the controversy may be appealed from the appellate courts to the Supreme Court.

The authority of decisions of all Courts of Appeals stands above that of the Tax Court, a District Court, or the Court of Federal Claims. The United States Supreme Court is, of course, the final authority as to what a statute means or as to any question of federal law.

U.S. Circuit Courts of Appeals

Appeals in tax cases may be taken from the U.S. District Courts or the Tax Court by either the IRS or the taxpayer to the United States Courts of Appeals of jurisdiction. Jurisdiction is based upon the location of the taxpayer's residence. There are eleven numbered circuits and additional unnumbered circuits for the District of Columbia Circuit and the Federal Circuit. See Exhibit 3.

Normally, a Circuit Court's review, made by a panel of three judges is limited to the application of law—not the determination of facts. In this process, the appellate court of any circuit is obligated to follow the findings of the Supreme Court but not those of the other Circuit Courts. When conflicts develop between circuits, District Courts of each individual circuit are required to follow any precedent set by the appellate court of their own circuit (i.e., the Circuit Court to which their decisions may be appealed). Also, as noted earlier, pursuant to the *Golsen* rule, the Tax Court follows the policy of observing precedent set by the appellate court of the circuit in which the taxpayer resides. In this way, consistency in the application of law is maintained between the Tax Court and the District Court of jurisdiction even though there may exist an inconsistency in the law's application to taxpayers residing in various circuits.

Judicial Citations—U.S. Circuit Courts of Appeals Decisions. All decisions, both tax and nontax, of the various Circuit Courts are published by West Publishing Company in the *Federal Reporter* 2nd Series (cited F.2d). In addition, tax decisions of the Circuit Courts are also contained in CCH's *United States Tax Cases* (cited USTC) and Research Institute of America (RIA) *American Federal Tax Reports* (cited AFTR). Citations indicate not only the volume and page, but also the particular court.

West Citation: Burke v. U.S., 929 F.2d 1119 (CA-6 1991).

CCH Citation: Burke v. U.S., 91-1 USTC ¶ 50,175 (CA-6 1991).

RIA Citation: Burke v. U.S., 67 AFTR2d 91-749 (USCA 6 1991).

Exhibit 3 FEDERAL JUDICIAL CIRCUITS

U.S. Court of Appeals for the Federal Circuit

On October 1, 1982, the seven judges of the Court of Claims and the five judges of the Court of Customs and Patent Appeals became the 12 judges of the newly created Court of Appeals for the Federal Circuit (CA-FC). The IRS and taxpayers appeal decisions from the U.S. Court of Federal Claims to this court. The court is empowered to sit in various locations around the country and can be expected to make an effort to hold sessions in the major cities where its business arises.

U.S. Supreme Court

Appeals to the U.S. Supreme Court from the Circuit Courts of Appeals and the Court of Appeals for the Federal Circuit may be made generally by a petition for certiorari. The Supreme Court may grant certiorari at its discretion; further, the Supreme Court is not required to give reasons for its refusal to review. However, past experience has shown that the Court generally grants certiorari only if:

1. The issue has resulted in conflicting decisions in the Circuit Court of Appeals or

2. The issue involved raises an important and continuing problem in the administration of the tax law.

If the Supreme Court declines to review the decision, it will formally deny the petition for certiorari.

Judicial Citations—U.S. Supreme Court Decisions. All Supreme Court decisions are published by the U.S. Government Printing Office in the *United States Supreme Court Reports* (cited U.S.), West Publishing Co. in the *Supreme Court Reporter* (cited S.Ct.), and the Lawyer's Co-Operative Publishing Co. in the *United States Reports, Lawyer's Edition* (cited L.Ed.). Like all other federal tax cases (except those rendered by the U.S. Tax Court), tax-related Supreme Court decisions are reported by CCH in *United States Tax Cases* (cited USTC) and Research Institute of America (RIA) in *American Federal Tax Reports* (cited AFTR).

> *GPO Citation: Cheek v. U.S.,* 498 U.S. 192 (1991).
> *West Citation: Cheek v. U.S.,* 111 S.Ct. 604 (1991).
> *Lawyer's Ed. Citation: Cheek v. U.S.,* 112 L.Ed.2d 617 (1991).
> *CCH Citation: Cheek v. U.S.,* 91-1 USTC ¶ 50,012 (1991).
> *RIA Citation: Cheek v. U.S.,* 67 AFTR2d 91-344 (1991).

Secondary Source Materials

¶ 24,075 ANALYSIS AND EVALUATION OF TAX LAW SOURCES

The voluminous bulk and complexity of our tax law make it extremely difficult to systematically research all of the statutory and administrative provisions associated with a given set of tax issues. The problem is further compounded when one also attempts to analyze, evaluate, and update the leading court cases that impact on these issues. Fortunately, secondary reference materials provide a convenient cross-referenced and continuously updated road map to guide the practitioner in the complicated task of wading through a growing maze of primary tax authority.

Tax Services

There are various tax services that are published with the specific purpose of providing comprehensive reference information on the ever-changing tax law and on-going developments in administrative rulings and case decisions. The use of any particular tax service is best described in materials made available to users by the representatives of the tax services. However, there are some general points to be made on the use of these tax services. First, it is important to check for the latest developments on any topic, issue, or case being researched under a specific statute, regulation, or ruling in the main core of explanatory text offered in the services. The tax services vary as to the presentation of these materials. For instance, in the CCH and Research Institute of America (RIA) services, new matters are contained in a single separate volume, while other tax services may have special sections. Second, editorial analysis, be it a synopsis or digest, provided by the tax services for case decisions or administrative rulings is at best only an interpretative commentary. Such editorial commentary no matter how knowledgeable is not intended to be a substitute for the authoritative source document.

The major tax research publications available are listed below along with a capsule description of the services they provide:

Standard Federal Tax Reporter, CCH Incorporated

CCH publishes loose-leaf reporters in all major federal tax areas. The most comprehensive of these tax reference services is the *Standard Federal Tax Reporter*, frequently referred to as the *Standard*. Other specialized tax services include the *Federal Excise Tax Reporter* and the *Federal Estate and Gift Tax Reporter*. The *Federal Tax Guide*, also published by CCH, is a two-volume service covering many of the same topics that are included in the *Standard*.

The *Standard Reporter* consists of 22 coordinated and cross-referenced loose-leaf volumes that provide comprehensive coverage of the income tax law. The service also provides weekly supplements presenting current federal court decisions, new rulings, and changes in the law or regulations, digests of Tax Court decisions, as well as reviews of the significant legislative changes, and editorial comments which provide tax planning ideas related to current developments.

The major portion of the *Standard*, Volumes 1 through 15, compiles the legislative, administrative, and judicial aspects of the income tax law. The volumes are arranged in Code Section order and reflect the current income tax law and accompanying related regulatory texts (including proposed amendments to the Regulations) as well as legislative Committee Reports, followed by "CCH Explanations" and supplemented with digests of associated administrative rulings and judicial decisions. Volume 16, "New Matters," is used to retain current developments such as digests of Tax Court decisions, full texts of rulings, current tables of decisions and rulings, and the Supreme Court Docket.

The *Standard* also includes the "U.S. Tax Cases Advance Sheets" Volume in which are reported the full texts of new income tax decisions from the federal courts, including the U.S. Supreme Court and the U.S. Court of Federal Claims. In the two Internal Revenue Code Volumes may be found the current internal revenue statutes. The two Citator Volumes access the basic Compilations by case name and document number. The Index Volume leads to the basic contents by subject through the Topical Index and also features a tax calendar, rate tables and tax rate schedules, tax planning information, checklists, definitions of tax terms, and special tables.

United States Tax Reporter, Research Institute of America

United States Tax Reporter, published by Research Institute of America (RIA), consists of 15 coordinated loose-leaf volumes organized by Code sections and updated on a weekly basis. The service is similar to CCH's and also includes a two-volume Internal Revenue Code, a seven-volume Citator, a one-volume Index, a one-volume Table of Cases, Rulings, and Tax Tables, a Recent Developments volume, an Advance Sheets volume for AFTR2d cases and a volume of proposed amendments to Federal Tax Regulations. RIA also publishes loose-leaf tax services for excise taxes and for estate and gift taxes.

Mertens, *Law of Federal Income Taxation*, Clark Boardman Callaghan

Mertens, *Law of Federal Income Taxation,* published by Clark Boardman Callaghan & Co., is an intensive, annotated work, providing excellent in-depth discussions of general concepts of tax law. However, unlike services such as those of CCH and Research Institute of America, Mertens is not generally used as a comprehensive, self-contained reference service. Rather, it is typically regarded as a useful complement to the traditional reference services.

Tax Management Portfolios, Bureau of National Affairs

Tax Management Portfolios, published by the Bureau of National Affairs (BNA), is a useful supplement to a tax library. Each portfolio ranges in length from 50 to 200 pages and deals exclusively with a special tax topic, covering Code, Regulations, reference to primary authorities, and extensive editorial discussion, including numerous tax planning ideas.

CCH Federal Tax Service, CCH Incorporated

CCH Federal Tax Service is a comprehensive tax reference service, providing complete and authoritative coverage of the law of federal income, estate, and gift taxation. It is organized by topic, so that the user can find all Internal Revenue Code sections, regulations, cases, and rulings relevant to a problem clearly explained and cited in one place in the analysis. Revised pages are released each month to keep the analysis up-to-date. In addition, current developments to the text are published twice each month.

CCH Federal Tax Service contains eight volumes of analysis, a one-volume index, and a volume of finding tables, tax tables, and other practice aids. Also available are eight volumes containing the Internal Revenue Code and regulations.

Federal Tax Coordinator, Research Institute of America

The *Federal Tax Coordinator,* published by the Research Institute of America (RIA), is somewhat similar in organization to CCH's *Standard Federal Tax Reporter* and RIA's *United States Tax Reporter,* with compilation volumes and an elaborate cross-reference system of indexation. However, the 26-volume service is organized by topic rather than by Code section. Popular features of the *Tax Coordinator* are the editorial explanations, illustrations, planning ideas, and warnings of potential tax traps.

The Citator

Probably the most comprehensive method for evaluating and updating case law is through the use of a citator. The *CCH Citator,* published annually as a two-volume loose-leaf reference service, contains an alphabetical listing of the Tax Court (formerly the Board of Tax Appeals) and federal court decisions since 1913. The Current Citator Table, issued quarterly, keeps the main table up to date. Additionally, the *CCH Citator* indicates a paragraph reference where each case is digested in the Compilation Volumes of the *Standard Federal Tax Reporter.* More than one paragraph reference will be given if a case involves several tax issues.

Each listing outlines the judicial history of a selected case beginning with the highest court to have ruled on that issue. Then, in descending order, the actions of lower courts are also cited and described. Finally, under each listing, the *CCH Citator* refers to other court cases, which helps to evaluate a given decision as a precedent.

The *Federal Tax Citator,* published by Research Institute of America (RIA), is a seven-volume service with monthly and annual cumulative supplements organized in a manner somewhat consistent with that of the *CCH Citator.* Essentially, RIA provides an alphabetical list of court cases followed by a descriptive legislative history of each case. However, in those cases involving more than one issue, the RIA citator also cross-references its descriptive system of judicial references according to the various issues.

To illustrate the usefulness of the citator to the researcher, the CCH Citator will be explained in greater detail. Refer to Exhibit 4, a sample taken from the CCH Citator and locate the *Atlas Life Insurance Co.* case. The case name is followed by paragraph (¶) references to the Compilation Volumes in which the decision appears as an annotation to the law, regulations, and other cases in point. The black dot preceding each court action in the case permits the researcher to quickly scan the judicial history of the case. Apparently, *Atlas Life*

Insurance Co. was decided on appeal in the Supreme Court in 1965, which reversed the decision of the Court of Appeals for the Tenth Circuit. The Court of Appeals decision reversed the ruling of the District Court.

Exhibit 4   CCH CITATOR—COURT CASES SAMPLE SECTION

Atlas Life Insurance Co. ...... ¶ 25,966.60, 26,143.74
- SCt—(rev'g CA), 65-1 USTC ¶ 9407; 381 US 233; 85 SCt 1379; Ct D 1903; 1965-2 CB 220
Standard Life & Accident Ins. Co., SCt, 77-2 USTC ¶ 9480, 433 US 148, 97 SCt 2523, Ct D 1986, 1977-2 CB 230
Consumer Life Ins. Co., SCt, 77-1 USTC ¶ 9364, 430 US 725, 97 SCt 1440, Ct D 1985, 1977-1 CB 178
Boli, CA-FC, 87-2 USTC ¶ 9566, 831 F2d 276
Goldin, CA-2, 87-1 USTC ¶ 9128, 809 F2d 187
Reserve Life Insurance Co., CtCls, 81-1 USTC ¶ 9147, 640 F2d 368
Investors Diversified Services, Inc., CtCls, 78-1 USTC ¶ 9379, 216 CtCls 192, 575 F2d 843
Group Life & Health Ins. Co., CA-5, 70-2 USTC ¶ 9683, 434 F2d 115
Franklin Life Ins. Co., CA-7, 68-2 USTC ¶ 9459, 399 F2d 757
Northwestern Mutual Life Ins. Co., ClsCt, 85-1 USTC ¶ 9233, 7 ClsCt 501
Union Mutual Life Ins. Co., DC-Me, 76-2 USTC ¶ 9661, 420 FSupp 1181
Jefferson Standard Life Ins. Co., CA-4, 69-1 USTC ¶ 9278, 408 F2d 842
Franklin Life Ins. Co., DC-Ill, 67-2 USTC ¶ 9515
Union Central Life Ins. Co., TC, Dec. 38,339, 77 TC 845
Ball, TC, Dec. 30,153, 54 TC 1200
Allstate Fire Ins. Co., TC, Dec. 28,197, 47 TC 237
- CA-10—(rev'g DC), 64-2 USTC ¶ 9510; 333 F2d 389
- DC-Okla—63-1 USTC ¶ 9452; 216 FSupp 457

Memo. 1990-37
Woods, TC, Dec. 45,602, 92 TC 776
Century Data Systems, Inc., TC, Dec. 42,872, 86 TC 157
Reef Corp., TC, Dec. 27,309(M), 24 TCM 379, TC Memo. 1965-72
Pollack, TC, Dec. 26,693(M), 23 TCM 433, TC Memo. 1964-63
Rose, TC, Dec. 21,160, 24 TC 755
Atlas Oil & Refining Corp. .... ¶ 20,307.20
- TC—Dec. 18,601; 17 TC 733; A. 1952-1 CB 1
Miles Production Co., TC, Dec. 47,265, 96 TC 595
Century Data Systems, Inc., TC, Dec. 42,872, 86 TC 157
Atlas Tool Co., TC, Dec. 35,124, 70 TC 86
Dougherty, TC, Dec. 32,138, 60 TC 917
Reef Corp., TC, Dec. 27,309(M), 24 TCM 379, TC Memo. 1965-72
Rose, TC, Dec. 21,160, 24 TC 755
Rev. Rul. 58-256
Atlas Plaster & Fuel Co. ..... ¶ 8587.2822, 42,901.57
- CA-6—(aff'g BTA), 1932 CCH ¶ 9067; 55 F2d 802; Ct D 541; XI-2 CB 323
Tumwater Lbr. Mills Co., CA-9, 1933 CCH ¶ 9403, 65 F2d 675
Bluegrass Plant Foods, Inc., TC, Dec. 22,918(M), 17 TCM 271, TC Memo. 1958-53
- BTA—Dec. 5821; 18 BTA 1123
Atlas Plywood Co. ...... ¶ 11,075.5135, 11,075.6044, 11,075.654, 41,520.31
- BTA—Dec. 5383; 17 BTA 156; A. IX-1 CB 3
Atlas Powder Co.

In addition to the historical record of the case, citations are given for the court actions taken in a particular case which show where the full text of the decision may be found. A citation to *U.S. Tax Cases* (USTC), for example, refers to an expansive series of volumes published by CCH that cover tax-related court opinions issued since 1913. The volumes, published twice a year, cover Supreme Court, Courts of Appeals, District Courts, and Court of Federal Claims cases. The RIA citator would refer to the *American Federal Tax Reports* (AFTR), the comparable RIA series of federal court cases. Memorandum decisions of the Tax Court are published by CCH under the title *Tax Court Memorandum Decisions* (cited TCM), while the RIA series is called *TC Memorandum Decisions* (cited TC Memo).

The Citator typically gives even further research information than already discussed. For each case listed in the Citator there is given the "cited record" of that case. These "cited records" list the names and citations of later cases which discussed and distinguished the main case. Thus, the "cited record" permits the researcher to evaluate the judicial authority of the related case.

For the very latest developments in any case, the researcher using the CCH Citator should consult the Current Citator Table. Following this procedure, the researcher must be sure to check the "Case Table" (for the current year) in Volume 16, the "New Matters" volume of the *Standard.* Appeals to higher courts, IRS acquiescences or nonacquiescences in Tax Court cases, and government decisions on whether to appeal federal court cases are shown in the "Case Table" (for the current year) for all cases. (Where Supreme Court action is indicated in the Case Table, more information on the case may be obtained from the Supreme Court Docket located in the New Matters Volume.) The "Finding Lists" section of the CCH Citator allows the researcher to determine the status of Revenue Rulings and Revenue Procedures.

Other Secondary Reference Materials

Books

In addition to the loose-leaf reference services and the bound volumes of tax-related court cases published in the special reporter series *U.S. Tax Cases* (USTC) available from CCH or the *American Federal Tax Reports* (AFTR) available from Research Institute of America (RIA), a well-equipped tax library should contain numerous leading tax textbooks.

Following are selected, highly recommended textbooks:

The Consolidated Tax Return: Principles, Practice, Planning, Jack Cristal, Karen M. Hennesey, and Anthony P. Rua

Federal Estate & Gift Taxation, Richard B. Stephens, Guy B. Maxfield, and Stephen A. Lind

Federal Income Taxation of Corporations and Shareholders, Boris I. Bittker and James I. Eustice

Federal Income Taxation of S Corporations, James I. Eustice and Joel D. Kuntz

The Federal Tax Course, CCH Incorporated

Income Taxation of Foreign Related Transactions, Rufus von Thulen Rhoades

Partnership Taxation, Arthur B. Willis, John S. Pennell, and Philip F. Postlewaite

Subchapter S Taxation, Irving M. Grant and William R. Christian

Tax Institutes

Current tax topics are discussed and technical papers presented at the various tax institutes and symposia held annually at universities and other locations throughout the United States. The well-known tax institutes such as New York University and the National Tax Association—Tax Institute of America publish their annual proceedings.

Tax Periodicals

Several monthly and quarterly journals contain current articles dealing exclusively with technical tax matters. Some of these magazines cover a broad range of tax topics, while others specialize in a particular area of taxation.

Probably the easiest method of locating a tax article related to a particular tax problem is through CCH's *Federal Tax Articles.* This loose-leaf service, updated monthly, organizes the articles by Code Section and contains detailed indexes, arranged by author and subject. Additionally, Warren, Gorham and Lamont publishes *The Index to*

Federal Tax Articles, a softcover multi-year cumulation with quarterly cumulative supplements.

Following are some of the more popular tax periodicals:

CPA Journal (New York State Society of Certified Public Accountants)

Estate Planning (Warren, Gorham and Lamont)

International Tax Journal (Panel Publishers)

Journal of the American Taxation Association (American Accounting Association)

Journal of Corporate Taxation (Warren, Gorham and Lamont)

Journal of Partnership Taxation (Warren, Gorham and Lamont)

Journal of Taxation (Warren, Gorham and Lamont)

National Tax Journal (National Tax Association—Tax Institute of America)

Practical Accountant (Institute of Continuing Professional Development)

Tax Adviser (American Institute of Certified Public Accountants)

Tax Executive (The Tax Executive)

Tax Law Review (Warren, Gorham and Lamont)

Tax Lawyer (American Bar Association)

Taxation for Accountants (Warren, Gorham and Lamont)

Taxation for Lawyers (Warren, Gorham and Lamont)

Taxes—The Tax Magazine (CCH Incorporated)

Trusts and Estates (Communication Channels, Inc.)

Newsletters

The practitioner needs to stay on top of current developments in the tax field and for this purpose finds that weekly and even daily updates of pertinent tax law information is needed. Daily reporting is available both electronically through on-line computer legal research systems from tax publishers and through the mails. There is the CCH *Tax News Direct* and *Tax Day Report,* published by CCH Incorporated; the BNA *Daily Tax Report,* available from the Bureau of National Affairs; and Tax Analysts' *Tax Notes Today.* The most popular weekly newsletters are *Taxes on Parade,* published by CCH; the *U.S. Tax Reporter,* published by Research Institute of America (RIA); and Tax Analysts' *Weekly Tax Notes Magazine.* Following are some of the other leading tax newsletters:

J.K. Lasser Tax Report, Business Reports Inc.

Tax Planning Ideas, Institute for Business Planning

Tax Research Institute, Research Institute of America

Research Methodology

¶ 24,125 TYPES OF TAX RESEARCH SITUATIONS

Essentially, there are two types of tax research situations. Sommerfeld and Streuling refer to these two situations as: "After the Facts Compliance" and "Before the Facts Planning" *Tax Research Techniques,* Ray Sommerfeld and Fred Streuling, AICPA, Tax Study No. 5, 1976. The "closed-fact" case, sometimes referred to as ex post facto research, involves the legal interpretation of historical events. In such cases, the taxable transactions have already occurred and can no longer be altered, although various tax elections and alternatives might still be available. Two common examples of "closed-fact" situations are preparation of a tax return after the taxable year is completed and representation of a taxpayer before the Audit Division of the IRS on the examination of a previously filed tax return.

In contrast, the "open-fact" case typically involves events that have not yet been finalized (i.e., controllable facts). Thus, this type of research relates primarily to future planning decisions. However, whether the primary focus of a research engagement is for tax compliance or tax planning, the underlying methods and techniques should be systematic, thorough, properly documented, and effectively communicated to the client.

¶ 24,135 RESEARCH MODEL: FIVE-STEP SYSTEMATIC FORMAT

The following research model presents a five-step systematic format that can be applied to a "closed-fact" or an "open-fact" case:

1. Gathering the facts and identifying the tax issues to be researched.

2. Locating and studying the primary and secondary authorities relevant to the enumerated tax issues.

3. Updating and evaluating the weight of the various authorities.

4. Reexamining various facets of the research.

5. Arriving at conclusions and communicating these conclusions to the client.

STEP 1 *Gathering the Facts and Identifying the Tax Issues to Be Researched*

During this difficult part of the research process it is necessary to elicit a comprehensive, unbiased report from the client. Difficulty stems from the fact that taxpayers often tend to have a simple perspective of the tax issues related to their problem. They fail to see the multiple issues that might be involved in what they perceive as a single, straightforward issue.

> ***Example 24.1.*** Mary Jones, a single taxpayer, moved from New York to Miami in 1998. Accordingly, she sold her residence in New York at a gain well in excess of $400,000. Shortly thereafter, she acquired a new residence in Miami. In preparation of her 1998 tax

return, since the gain on the sale of this residence is quite substantial, the researcher must examine the facts and explore the tax-savings elections.

Mary is asked to provide all information related to these events, and she supplies two real estate closing statements, one reflecting the sale of the New York residence and one for the Miami purchase. As far as Mary is concerned, she has supplied "all" information necessary to resolve this issue. However, the following facts must still be ascertained:

1. What was the cost of the New York residence?

2. Should any improvements be capitalized as part of the basis of the New York residence?

3. Were there any selling costs involved with the sale?

4. Over the years, were there any property assessments that should be capitalized as part of the basis of the New York residence?

5. Was any portion of the New York residence depreciated as a home office deduction on prior tax returns?

6. Is Mary eligible for the $250,000 tax-free exclusion?

STEP 2 *Locating and Studying the Secondary and Primary Authorities Relevant to the Enumerated Tax Issues*

For each issue enumerated in Step 1, the research might begin with a thorough reading of the compilation materials found in the tax services whether in print format (loose-leaf and books) or electronic format (CD-ROM, online, or the Internet). The editorial explanations and observations provide useful insights and help direct the research process. Additionally, the research should continue with a review of the applicable Code sections, Regulations, and digests of selected judicial decisions. Those cases which seem particularly appropriate to the research should be cited to facilitate reference for subsequent follow-up study. Finally, before leaving the tax services, it is imperative to refer to the "Current Developments" section to examine the impact of recent actions.

STEP 3 *Updating and Evaluating the Weight of the Various Authorities*

The statutory and administrative authorities selected in Step 2 must now be evaluated to determine relative weight. Additionally, the relevant court cases must be assessed in terms of their value as judicial precedent. Before relying upon a particular decision, it is essential to refer to one of the loose-leaf citator services and review the history and current status of that case.

It is not uncommon to discover conflicting interpretations of similar issues by different courts. In place of a national law policy, the Tax Court has adopted the position that better judicial administration requires it to follow a Court of Appeals decision. Nevertheless, courts at the same level of jurisdiction may issue conflicting opinions; whereas, the Internal Revenue Service is not obligated to adhere to either decision on a nationwide basis. Accordingly, a District or Circuit Court decision favorable to a taxpayer has significant precedent value only within that district or circuit.

STEP 4 *Reexamining Various Facets of the Research*

After studying and evaluating the various statutory, administrative, and judicial authorities, it often becomes necessary to reexamine the original tax problem. It may even become necessary to seek additional facts and modify or expand the research process.

Additionally, if there are any authorities in conflict with the projected conclusions, it is essential to study them carefully. The researcher must not only be able to support his or her own research conclusions, but also must be prepared to defend these conclusions in light of conflicting authorities.

During this phase of the research, it may sometimes be useful to clarify the meanings of unfamiliar or highly technical words or terms. A standard dictionary may provide some guidance, but if the words are not generally used in a nonlegal context, *Black's Law Dictionary* should be consulted.

STEP 5 *Arriving at Conclusions and Communicating the Conclusions to the Client*

Communicating the conclusions of the tax research to the client requires professional judgment. The client should be advised of the potential benefits and risks associated with the recommended actions. Since the communication will be in writing, it is essential to determine how much or how little detail should be noted. Additionally, the communication must be expressed at the client's level of sophistication. This sometimes presents a difficult task, especially when the research involves complex issues and highly technical reasoning.

Essentially, the communication should be concise, well-structured, and should follow an organized format that includes:

1. A review of the facts

2. An enumeration of the various tax issues

3. The conclusions

4. A discussion of the reasoning and authorities supporting the conclusions

While the client might be concerned only with the section dealing with conclusions, the professional substance of the communication is contained in the reasoning and authority. It is in this section of the report that the various authorities are discussed and evaluated. Finally, it is in this section that the client is supplied with authoritative support, should it ever become necessary to defend against a challenge by the Internal Revenue Service.

¶ 24,147 RESEARCH CASES AND EXAMPLES

The following cases and examples illustrate the *step-by-step* application of selected aspects of research methodology. Additionally, details are outlined to highlight the *trial-and-error* nature of tax research and the need for patience, perseverance, and creativity.

CASE 1 (Illustrating a Code Section approach to tax research.)

TAX PROBLEM

Sue Wilson had her personal automobile stolen in 1998 and received an insurance reimbursement in 1999. In preparing her 1998 tax return, the preparer must ascertain how much of a theft loss may be claimed and in which year it should be deducted.

FACTS

The automobile was acquired in 1996 at a cost of $15,000 and was stolen on June 14, 1998. The fair market value at the time of theft was $8,000. On January 15, 1999, the insurance company paid $6,000 to Wilson as a "full reimbursement" for the theft.

ISSUES

Is the theft deductible since the vehicle is used exclusively for personal use? If deductible, how much of a loss may be claimed? In which year, 1998 or 1999, should the loss be claimed?

RESEARCH

On determining that Section 165 of the Internal Revenue Code deals with Deductions for Losses, the researcher using the CCH *Standard* tax service (whether in print or electronic format) should refer to the Compilation Volumes where the texts of the Code sections and Regulations, both with all amendments to date, and CCH Explanations, plus digests of applicable rulings and decisions are located. Code section reference is facilitated by referring to the backbone of the various looseleaf volumes. Section 165(h) provides authoritative support for deducting a *personal* casualty loss or theft and outlines details of the $100 and 10 percent of adjusted gross income limitations for this deduction.

Regulation § 1.165-1(d)(2)(ii), which is located in the CCH *Standard* Compilations immediately following Section 165, is reprinted in Exhibit 5 (on the following page). The illustration provided in this Regulation is similar to the Wilson facts.

Accordingly, it would appear that, to the extent Sue can claim a theft loss, it will be deductible in 1998. However, a major question relates to the calculation of the loss. Is the loss measured by the $15,000 original cost of the automobile or by the $8,000 fair market value?

Reg. § 1.165-7(b)(1) gives the general rule to be followed in determining the amount deductible for casualty losses:

... the amount of loss to be taken into account ... shall be the lesser of either—(i) The amount which is equal to the fair market value of the property immediately before the casualty reduced by the fair market value of the property immediately after the casualty; or (ii) The amount of the adjusted basis prescribed [by regulation] for determining the loss from the sale or other disposition of the property involved.

Exhibit 5   CCH STANDARD FEDERAL TAX REPORTS—COMPILATION SAMPLE PAGE: Regulations

---

● *Regulations*

[¶ 9803]   § 1.165-1   **Losses.**—* * *

(d) *Year of deduction.* (1) A loss shall be allowed as a deduction under section 165(a) only for the taxable year in which the loss is sustained. For this purpose, a loss shall be treated as sustained during the taxable year in which the loss occurs as evidenced by closed and completed transactions and as fixed by identifiable events occurring in such taxable year. For provisions relating to situations where a loss attributable to a disaster will be treated as sustained in the taxable year immediately preceding the taxable year in which the disaster actually occurred, see section 165(h) and § 1.165-11.

(2)(i) If a casualty or other event occurs which may result in a loss and, in the year of such casualty or event, there exists a claim for reimbursement with respect to which there is a reasonable prospect of recovery, no portion of the loss with respect to which reimbursement may be received is sustained, for purposes of section 165, until it can be ascertained with reasonable certainty whether or not such reimbursement will be received. Whether a reasonable prospect of recovery exists with respect to a claim for reimbursement of a loss is a question of fact to be determined upon an examination of all facts and circumstances. Whether or not such reimbursement will be received may be ascertained with reasonable certainty, for example, by a settlement of the claim, by an adjudication of the claim, or by an abandonment of the claim. When a taxpayer claims that the taxable year in which a loss is sustained is fixed by his abandonment of the claim for reimbursement, he must be able to produce objective evidence of his having abandoned the claim, such as the execution of a release.

(ii) If in the year of the casualty or other event a portion of the loss is not covered by a claim for reimbursement with respect to which there is a reasonable prospect of recovery, then such portion of the loss is sustained during the taxable year in which the casualty or other event occurs. For example, if property having an adjusted basis of $10,000 is completely destroyed by fire in 1961, and if the taxpayer's only claim for reimbursement consists of an insurance claim for $8,000 which is settled in 1962, the taxpayer sustains a loss of $2,000 in 1961. However, if the taxpayer's automobile is completely destroyed in 1961 as a result of the negligence of another person and there exists a reasonable prospect of recovery on a claim for the full value of the automobile against such person, the taxpayer does not sustain any loss until the taxable year in which the claim is adjudicated or otherwise settled. If the automobile had an adjusted basis of $5,000 and the taxpayer secures a judgment of $4,000 in 1962, $1,000 is deductible for the taxable year 1962. If in 1963 it becomes reasonably certain that only $3,500 can ever be collected on such judgment, $500 is deductible for the taxable year 1963.

The Regulation further provides that if the property is used in a trade or business or is held for the production of income, the amount of loss is measured exclusively by the adjusted basis of the property.

In preparing Wilson's 1998 tax return, the theft loss will be computed as follows:

1. Original cost $15,000
2. Fair market value (before theft) 8,000
3. Fair market value (after theft) 0
4. Loss in value, caused by theft 8,000
5. Basis for loss: lesser of line 1 or line 4 8,000
6. Less: Insurance recovery 6,000
7. Sustained loss 2,000
8. Less: Section 165(h) limitation 100
9. Deductible amount (before 10 percent
   of AGI limitation) .... $ 1,900

The $1,900 loss, calculated at line 9, should be combined with all other casualty or theft losses incurred in 1998. The aggregate will be deductible to the extent that it exceeds 10 percent of Wilson's 1998 adjusted gross income.

CASE 2 (Illustrating a topical index approach to tax research.)

TAX PROBLEM

Philip Davis, a full-time electrician employed by the Exeter Hotel, hires a preparer to prepare his 1998 tax return. Davis works exclusively at the hotel but feels that he is entitled to deduct the cost of operating his personal vehicle. Davis transports several thousand pounds of electrical parts, equipment, and tools to work each day.

FACTS

The Exeter Hotel does not provide a convenient, well-protected location for Davis to store the various electrical items. Accordingly, the van has a customized interior with appropriate shelves and cabinets for the electrical items. The van, which is also used by Davis as a personal vehicle, was purchased on April 1, 1998, at a cost of $19,000, which includes $2,000 for the customized interior.

ISSUE

Can Davis claim a full or partial transportation expense deduction even though the cost of commuting is not deductible?

RESEARCH

The subject indexes to the CCH Compilation Volumes (whether in print or electronic format) are located in a separate volume entitled the Index Volume. The researcher determines a few key topics under which the relevant references might be found.

First attempt ... locate the term "Transportation." The heading "expenses for" refers the searcher to the topic "Traveling expenses." Under this listing are numerous headings, but the entry at "automobile expenses" leading to "Automobiles: expenses" seems to be the most relevant reference.

Second attempt . . . locate the topic "Automobiles" and the term "expenses." Under this listing, the following subheadings seem appropriate for additional research:

. . equipment transported 8540.027; 8540.25

. . tools transported 8540.027; 8540.25

The paragraph reference 8540.25 given in the Index leads to Code Section 162 in the CCH Compilations Volume and thereunder to a digest of the *Fausner* case (*Fausner v. Commissioner,* 73-2 USTC ¶ 9515), a 1973 Supreme Court decision that disallowed a transportation deduction. In examining this digest, reprinted below, it would appear that Davis cannot deduct any part of his transportation expense.

Exhibit 6   CCH STANDARD FEDERAL TAX REPORTS—COMPILATION
SAMPLE PAGE: Annotations

TRADE OR BUSINESS EXPENSES—§ 162 [¶ 8540]

.25 Equipment and tool transportation.—An individual could not deduct any part of his automobile expenses where he used his car to transport bulky equipment to and from his places of employment because storage facilities were lacking where it was shown that the individual would have used his car to commute to work in any event. Under this circumstance, it was held that it was not possible to allocate the automobile expenses between nondeductible commuting expenses and deductible business expenses incurred in transporting the tools nor had the existence of any additional expense been shown, with the result that the entire cost of traveling to and from the taxpayer's work constituted commuting expenses.

D. Fausner, Sup. Ct., per curiam, 73-2 USTC ¶ 9515, 413 US 838, aff'g CA-5, per curiam, 73-1 USTC ¶ 9180, 472 F2d 561.

Code § 162   ¶ 8540.25

However, following the *Fausner* decision, the IRS issued Rev. Rul. 75-380, 1975-2 CB 59, superseding Rev. Rul. 56-25, 1956-2 CB 152, and revoking Rev. Rul. 63-100, 1963-1 CB 34. The full text of Rev. Rul. 75-380 is given at paragraph 8540.2501. Of particular importance to Davis is the following observation in Rev. Rul. 75-380:

> Therefore, in situations where a taxpayer can establish that additional expenses were incurred for transporting work implements to and from work, a reasonable and feasible method of allocation within the scope of the Supreme Court's opinion in *Fausner* would be to allow an ordinary and necessary business expense deduction for only the portion of the cost of transporting the work implements by the mode of transportation used which is in excess of cost of commuting by the same mode of transportation without the work implements. The fact that a taxpayer might have or would have used a less expensive mode of transportation if it had not been necessary to carrying the work implements is immaterial.

Based on this logic, it would seem that Davis may, at least, claim a depreciation deduction for the $2,000 that he spent to install shelves and cabinets in his van. However, he would not be entitled to claim a deduction for the cost of transportation to and from work.

Subsequently, following Rev. Rul. 75-380, the Tax Court found in *H.A. Pool*, 36 TCM 93, CCH Dec. 34,233(M), T.C. Memo. 1977-20, that a transportation deduction was allowed for the excess cost of driving a truck rather than a car, since it was necessary to transport tools to work, and the car would not have been able to carry that weight. Following the reasoning in *Pool*, we might also be able to contend that the excess cost of acquiring a van, rather than a passenger automobile, is eligible for a transportation deduction. Of course, in this instance, we are taking a somewhat aggressive position, and our client must be advised of the inherent risk of being challenged by the Internal Revenue Service. The final decision, whether or not to claim this deduction, rests with the client.

¶ 24,153 ELECTRONIC TAX RESEARCH SYSTEMS

Although the capability of computer-assisted tax research has existed since the early '70s, the use of computers in tax and legal research keeps expanding. Users can access computerized tax-law data banks with their personal computers by using various publishers' CD-ROMs, on-line systems, or Internet sites. Whatever format the researcher uses, all data bases are now integrated with primary and secondary source materials from which the researcher can retrieve full-text documents or search for key words or phrases. Publishers' computerized tax research systems also can be used like a citator to locate all judicial decisions that have cited a particular decision or statute.

CD-ROMs (compact disc read-only memory) have become increasingly important in computerized legal research as the cost of CD-ROM drives has dropped and publishers have made their information available in this format. Physically, a CD-ROM resembles the compact discs used to record music. A single CD-ROM, however, is capable of storing the equivalent of tens of thousands of pages of information. CD-ROMs are typically sold through subscription, so the researcher does not need to be concerned with the time and transaction charges typical of on-line or Internet site research. The major publishers or providers of tax-law data bases are Lexis/Nexis, CCH Incorporated, West, and RIA (Research Institute of America). Exhibit 7 (on the following page) shows the amount of material available electronically to researchers through several publishers' software and data banks.

Exhibit 7   RESEARCH MATERIALS AVAILABLE THROUGH CD-ROM, ONLINE, OR INTERNET SITES

	CCH	WEST (WESTLAW)	LEXIS/ NEXIS
Internal Revenue Code	X	X	X
Legislative Histories	X	X	X
Tax Treaties	X	X	X
Federal Tax Regulations	X	X	X
IRS Cumulative Bulletin	X	X	X
Private Letter Rulings	X	X	X
General Counsel Memoranda, Actions on Decisions, and Technical Advice Memoranda	X	X	X
Internal Revenue Manual	X	X	X
Judicial Decisions:			
Supreme Court	X	X	X
Courts of Appeals	X	X	X
District Courts	X	X	X
Court of Federal Claims	X	X	X
Board of Tax Appeals	X	X	X
Tax Court, Regular	X	X	X
Tax Court, Memorandum	X	X	X
Citators:			
Shepards	X	X	X
Other	CCH	Insta-Cite	Auto-Cite
Newsletters	CCH *Tax News Direct*, CCH *Federal & State Tax Day*	BNA *Daily Tax Report*	*Tax Notes Today*, BNA *Daily Tax Report*
Tax Services	CCH *Standard Federal Tax Reports, U.S. Master Tax Guide*	BNA *Tax Mgt. Portfolios*	RIA *Coordinator*, BNA *Tax Mgt. Portfolios*, CCH
Journals	n.a.	X	X

Key: X denotes that the research materials are available on the service; n.a. denotes that the research materials are not available on the service.

¶ 24,161   CCH CD-ROM and Online for Windows® Software

CCH CD-ROM and Online computer software is a research tool that provides full-text retrieval of tax-related documents including statutes, regulations, IRS rulings, and judicial decisions as well as the full text of CCH's *Federal Income Tax Reporter*. CCH CD-ROM is updated monthly, and the Online resource is updated daily. In order to retrieve CD-ROM information, researchers need a CD-ROM drive; to receive on-line information from the CCH mainframe computers, researchers need a modem. (In addition to this software, researchers can also use their modem to visit the new CCH Internet Tax Research NetWork and from there access CCH's federal and state tax libraries. The CCH web site, discussed at ¶ 24,171, can be found at http:// tax.cch.com.)

CCH CD-ROM and Online software makes full use of Windows versions 3.x to 95. The CCH CD-ROM and Online *User Guide* gives basic instructions on using the program. The *Quick Reference* to the *User Guide* provides step-by-step instructions for performing common tasks in the most efficient way. A companion volume, the CCH *Electronic Document Sourcebook,* contains encyclopedic information concerning CCH CD-ROM and Online data and research functions.

CCH CD-ROM Research

In CCH CD-ROM, there are two basic windows that display information: the Research Topics Screen and the Document Type Target window.

Research Topics Screen. Every research session on CCH CD-ROM for Windows begins at the Research Topics Screen (shown below). The Research Topics Screen lists the libraries that are available on the currently loaded disc(s). When you double-click on a particular library (in this case, Federal Taxes), the publications contained within it will be displayed.

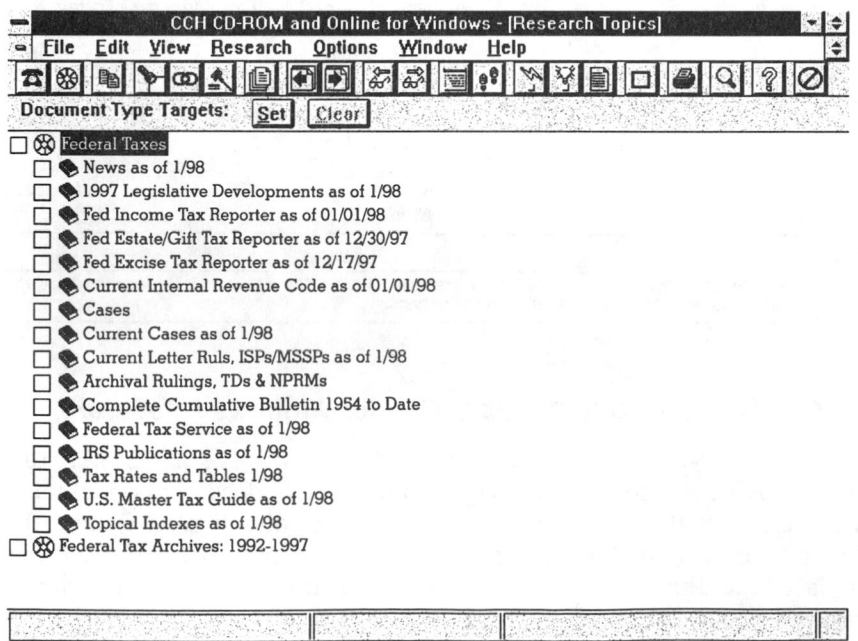

Document Type Target Window. The document types that are available for each publication are displayed on the Document Type Target window (shown below). To see the document types contained within a publication, double-click on the library you want to work in (in this case, Federal Taxes). Then, double-click on the publication you want to work with (in this case, *Federal Income Tax Reporter*). To display the Document Type Target window, click on the Set button. The document types contained within the publication will now be displayed.

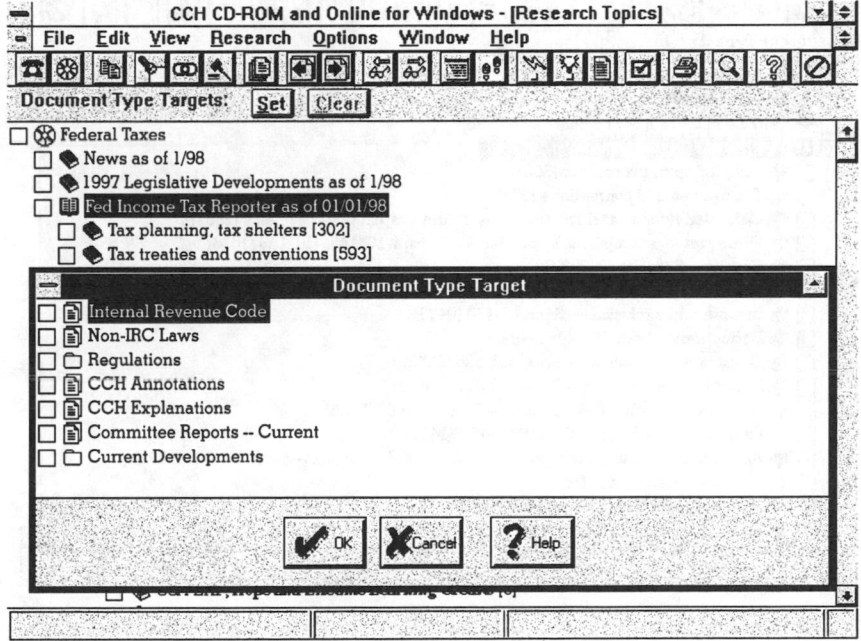

Researching a Topic. From the Research Topics Screen, begin to look for information about the Hope scholarship credit and lifetime learning credit. Double-click on the Federal Taxes library, and then double-click on the *Federal Income Tax Reporter* publication. There you will see the complete listing of documents in that publication (shown below).

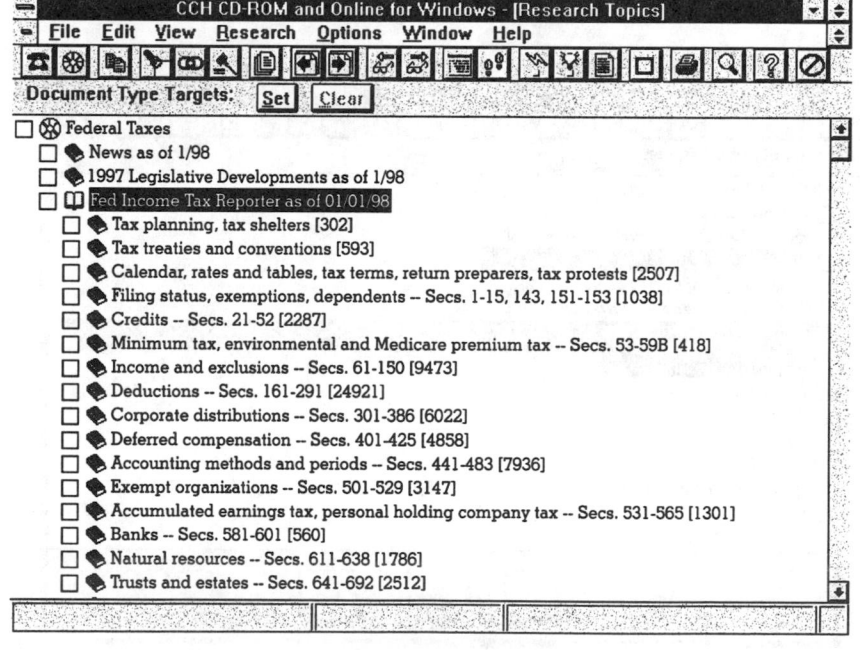

Next double-click on the Credits--Secs.21-52 document, and the full listing of credits appears (shown below).

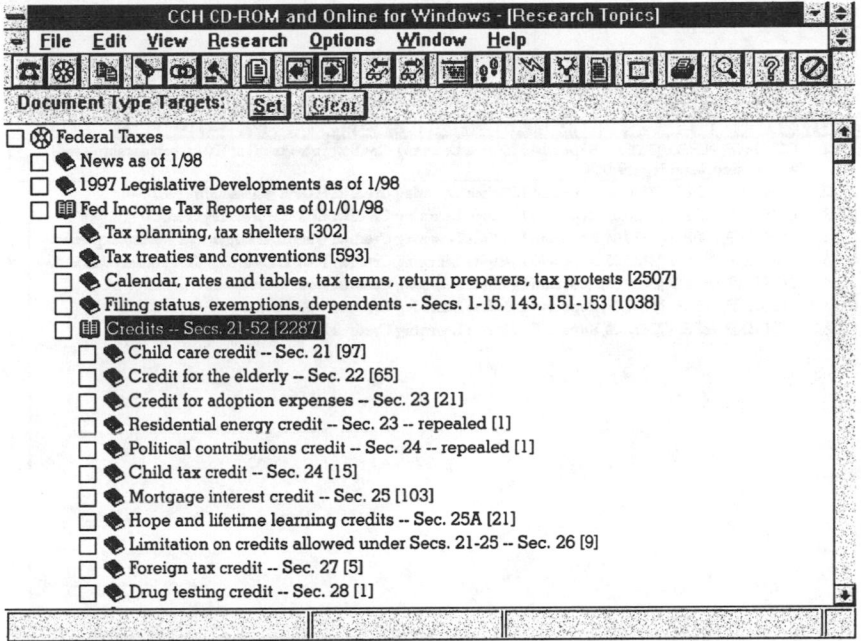

Quickly look down the listings and double-click on the Hope and lifetime learning credits--Sec.25A [21] title, and several choices appear (shown below).

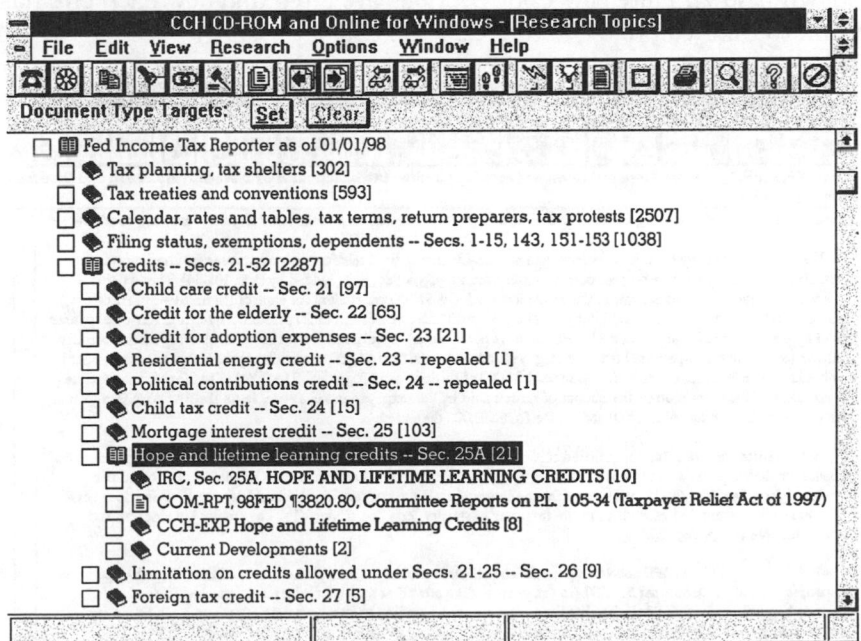

From here, double-click on the CCH explanation, CCH-EXP, Hope and Lifetime Learning Credits [8], and eight subtopics are displayed (shown below).

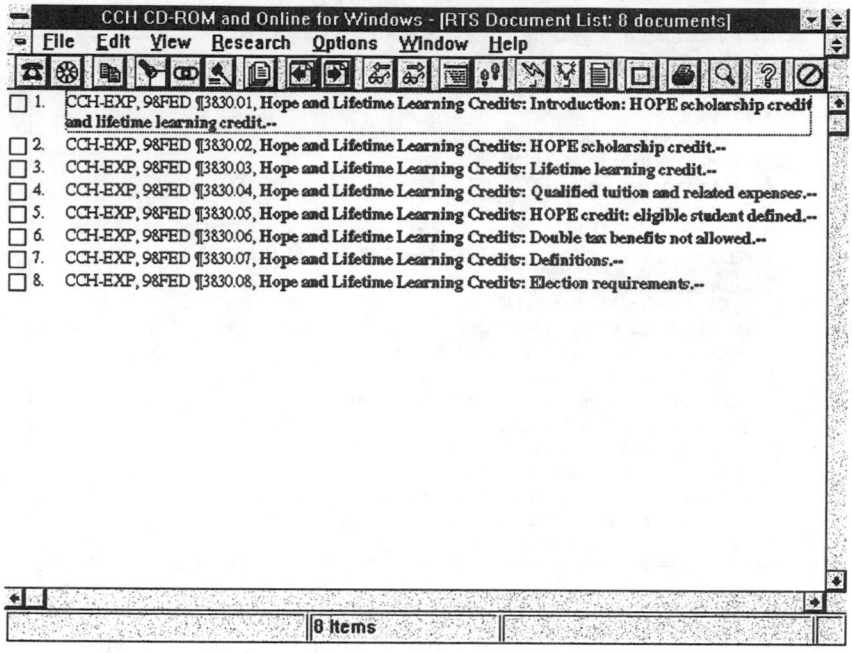

Double-click on the first subtopic, and the full-text document appears (shown below). Note how Code Sections are cited and how each cite has a link to take you to the actual Code text.

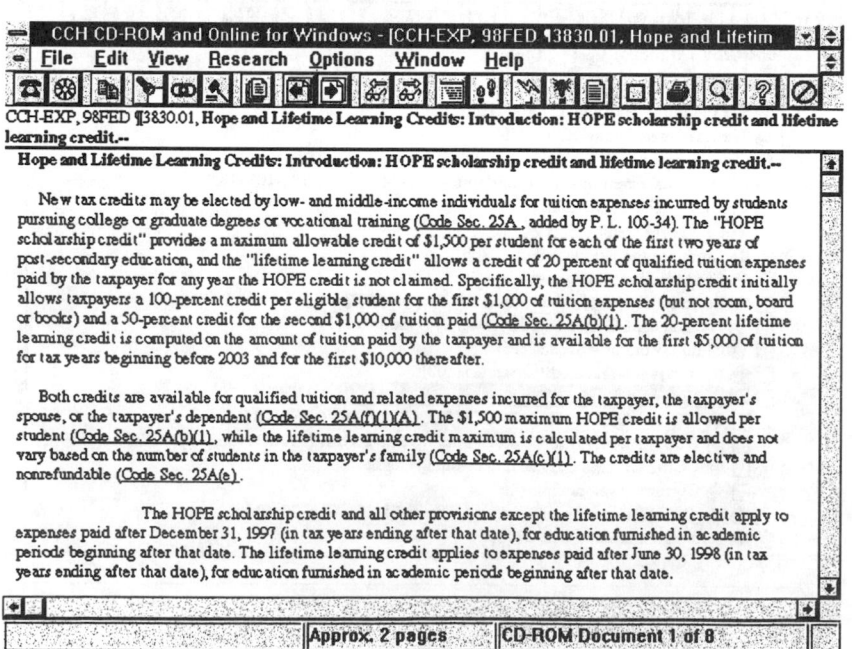

Using the Search Function. The Search function is another method of research. Instead of looking through publications, you type in the words or phrases you are looking for on the Search Template. From the Research Topics screen, highlight the *Federal Income Tax Reporter.* Then bring up the Search Template by either (1) clicking on the Flashlight icon or (2) clicking on the Research button and then Search button. Type in the phrase Hope Credit, and click the OK button. (Screen shown below).

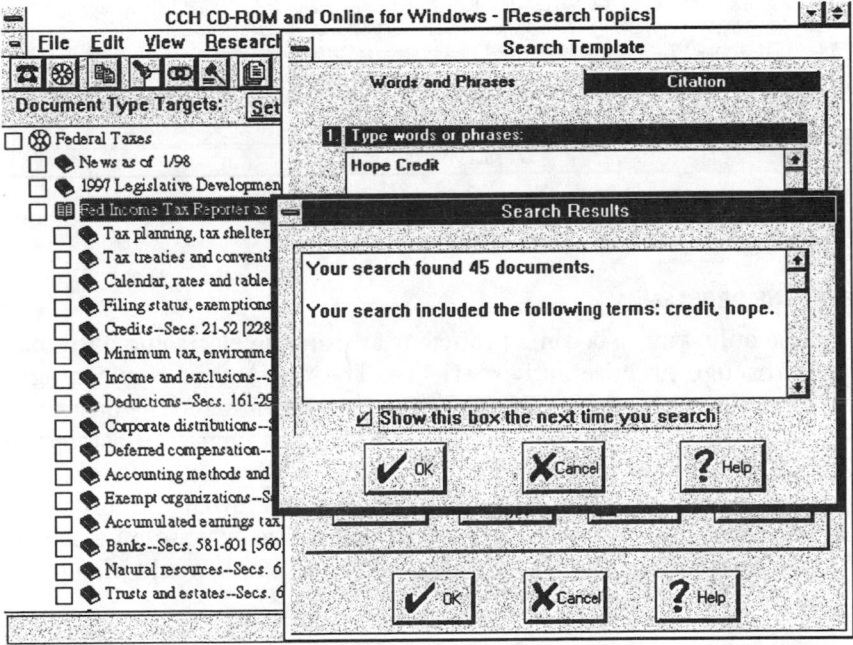

The search for the words Hope Credit found 45 documents. By clicking on the OK button, the following choices appear that contain information about the Hope Credit.

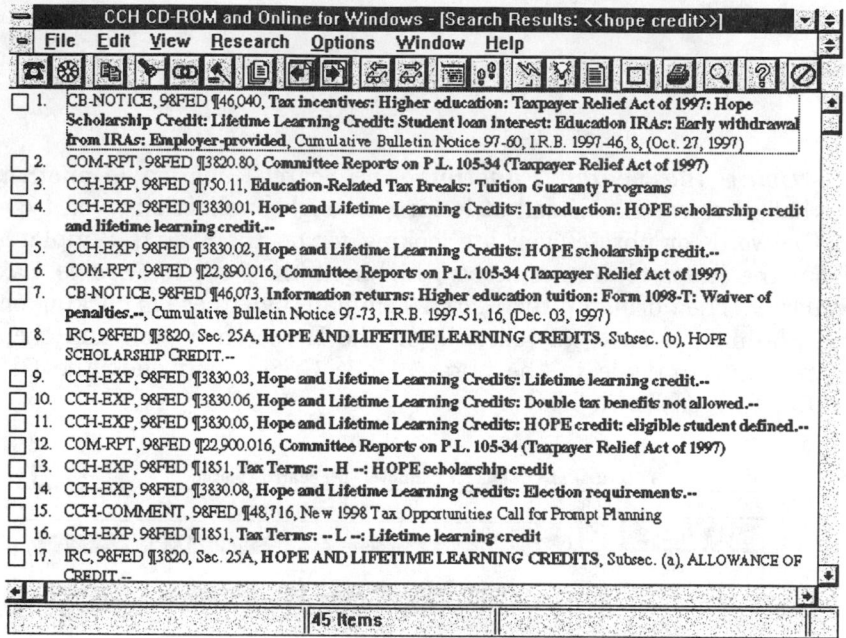

KEYSTONE PROBLEM

The only way to become proficient at using an electronic data base is through practice and experience. The tax student is encouraged to experiment with CCH CD-ROM by searching for the answer to a tax question. Once the art of electronic searching is mastered, it will be obvious how much more comprehensive and efficient it is than a traditional paper search. For example, what authority can you find to justify a deduction for home office expense by a college professor? What authority can you find that would deny the deduction?

¶ 24,171   THE INTERNET

The Internet, which has been operational since 1983, continues to grow rapidly. On the Internet, one can download a plethora of information and forms from various tax law publishers as well as the Internal Revenue Service.

IRS Homepage

The IRS homepage on the World Wide Web (http://www.irs.ustreas.gov/prod) went online on January 8, 1996. During its first 24 hours of operation, close to one million "hits" were recorded. Features on the IRS homepage include the following: Tax Stats, Tax Info For You, Tax Info for Business, Electronic Services, Taxpayer Help and Education, Tax Regs in Plain English, IRS Newsstand, Forms and Pubs, What's Hot, Meet the Commissioner, Comments and Help, and Site Tree. The IRS homepage appears below.

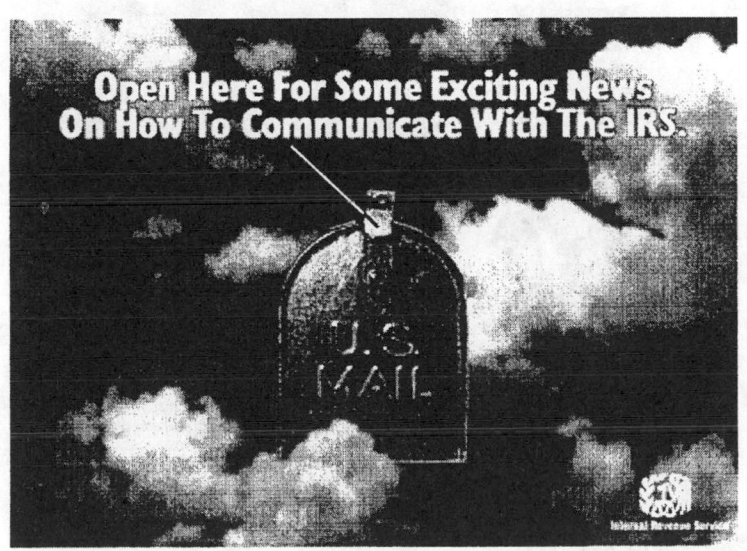

Welcome to the Internal Revenue Service's new home on the World Wide Web. As part of our continuing efforts to provide broad and immediate access to IRS tax information and services, we are presenting our latest electronic publication. So pour yourself a cup of coffee, open your mailbox and enjoy our premiere issue! By the way, please send us your comments and let us know what you think. Also tell us what you find useful and what you'd like to see in future issues.

By clicking on the "open your mailbox" phrase, the following *Digital Daily* publication appears.

FASTER THAN A SPEEDING 1040-EZ ... FEB 11, 1998 (63 DAYS UNTIL APRIL 15TH).

[Text Only Version]

IN TODAY'S ISSUE

Your Direct Link To Electronic Filing.

IRS Problem Solving Day
Relief From The Symptoms Of Long Standing Tax Problems.

Employment Opportunities

IRS WANTS YOU

TAX PRO'S *Corner*
News For The Tax Professional

Highlights of Tax Provisions
Contained In Balanced Budget Legislation Signed by President Clinton

Department of the Treasury
Internal Revenue Service

Famous Physicist Finds Fabulous Formula For E-File

PRINCETON, NJ   During a press conference this morning renowned physicist Dr. Igor Thorinsky released his paper, *Formula For e-file Success*, describing the results of his extensive research into electronic tax return filing. Dr. Thorinsky has spent the past three years searching for an *e-file* formula that is both accurate and fast, reduces the time required to receive a refund, and supports simultaneous federal and state income tax return filing.

"It was grueling research.", Dr. Thorinsky admitted to the throng of reporters and scientists, "Each time I found a formula that was accurate, the processing time was too long; and if the time was acceptable then there were too many errors. Very frustrating!"

Dr. Thorinsky removed his glasses, "The formula was right under my nose all the time. Less than one percent error rate, refunds in half the time of paper returns, simultaneous federal and state filing in over thirty states, acknowledgment within forty-eight hours that the return is accepted. It was all on the IRS web site, the perfect *e-file* formula, right under my nose."

Tax Stats | Tax Info For You | Tax Info For Business | Electronic Services
Taxpayer Help & Ed | Tax Regs In English | IRS Newsstand | Forms & Pubs
What's Hot | Meet The Commissioner | Comments & Help | Site Tree

Previous

Next

Home

Search

Help!

Email

One very useful aspect of the IRS homepage is the ability to retrieve the latest in tax news. Use the IRS Newsstand to access information on important topics (as shown below). The Newsstand's direct address is http://www.irs.ustreas.gov/prod/news/index.html.

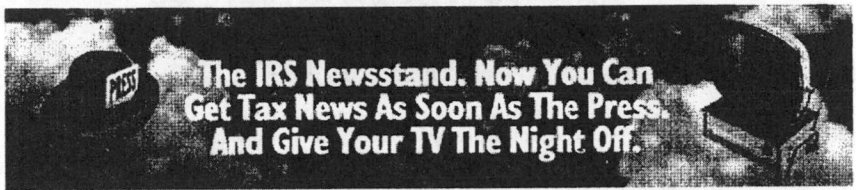

News travels fast these days. That's for sure. But now you can get news about taxes and how they may affect your own tax return even faster. That's because many news releases are now available to you at the same time as they are to the news media. So, prop your feet up. Read recent news releases. Scan fact sheets. And get the latest hot-off-the-press tax supplements. Soon you'll be able to read newletters right off the wire. Besides, your TV deserves a little rest.

[Click for Text Only Version]

Year 2000 Project
This section has been developed to assist other Federal and state governments and the private sector in understanding the Service's approach to address the Year 2000 (Y2k) issue, particularly as it relates to the Service's External Trading Partners.

News Releases And Fact Sheets
The latest breaking information for media distribution.

Tax Tips Newsletter
Publication 1558, *Tax Tips Newsletter*, has been replaced by the Tax Tips Calendar.

Tax Supplements
A comprehensive "package" of helpful tax information articles and fillers to help you file your federal income taxes.

International Tax Forum
A newsletter for practitioners.

Tax Stats | Tax Info For You | Tax Info For Business | Electronic Services
Taxpayer Help & Ed | Tax Regs In English | IRS Newsstand | Forms & Pubs
What's Hot | Meet The Commissioner | Comments & Help | Site Tree

Previous

Next

Home

Search

Help!

Email

Besides retrieving tax news from the IRS, tax forms and publications may be downloaded from: http://www.irs.ustreas.gov/prod/forms_pubs/index.html (shown below).

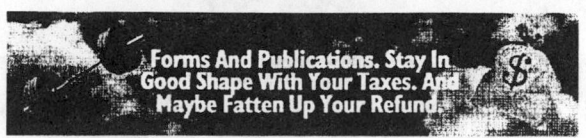

Forms And Publications. Stay In Good Shape With Your Taxes. And Maybe Fatten Up Your Refund.

It's always a good idea to stay in shape. And the same holds true when it comes to tax forms and publications. When you're armed with the correct instructions, the right forms and all the pertinent publications, your filing problems will be a lot less taxing. Exercise all your options in this section. And when April the 15th rolls around - which is only 63 days away - you'll be in fine form.

Download Current Year Forms and Publications

Forms and Instructions
Select from a list of forms and instructions displayed in form number order.

Publications
Select from a list of publications displayed in publication number order.

Search For a Form or Publication
Enter a keyword or partial filename to find the form or publication you need fast.

Expert Interface
Connect directly to our FTP server; no fluff, no frills, no file descriptions. This is not for the faint-of-heart!

Forms and Publications by Date
Select and download multiple forms and publications from a list sorted by date. Most recently modified forms and publications are displayed first.

Forms and Publications by Number
Select and download multiple forms and publications from a list sorted by form or publication number. Lowest number forms and publications are displayed first.

Publications Online
Don't want to download that publication? Now you can browse seventy-six of our publications online.

Download Prior Years Forms and Publications

Forms, instructions, and publications from 1992 - 1996 are provided in PDF format:

☐ 1996   ☐ 1993
☐ 1995   ☐ 1992
☐ 1994

Other Stuff About Forms and Publications

What's Hot In Tax Forms
Check out the newest information on tax forms.

Link to State Tax Forms
Federation of Tax Administrators (FTA) links to state tax forms and other important tax related sites.

Comment on Tax Forms and Publications
We welcome your suggestions on our tax forms and publications.

Just the Fax
Get the facts on Fax on Demand.

Tax Stats | Tax Info For You | Tax Info For Business | Electronic Services
Taxpayer Help & Ed | Tax Regs In English | IRS Newsstand | Forms & Pubs
What's Hot | Meet The Commissioner | Comments & Help | Site Tree

Previous   *Next*   *Home*   *Search*   *Help!*   *Email*

Searching the Internet

A good way to search the Internet is by using search engines. A search engine allows you to type in a term or phrase which describes your area of interest. For example, open your Internet browser's search screen and type in the phrase "tax history." Once the search is complete, all of the finds are listed and linked to hundreds of useful sources (sample screens shown below).

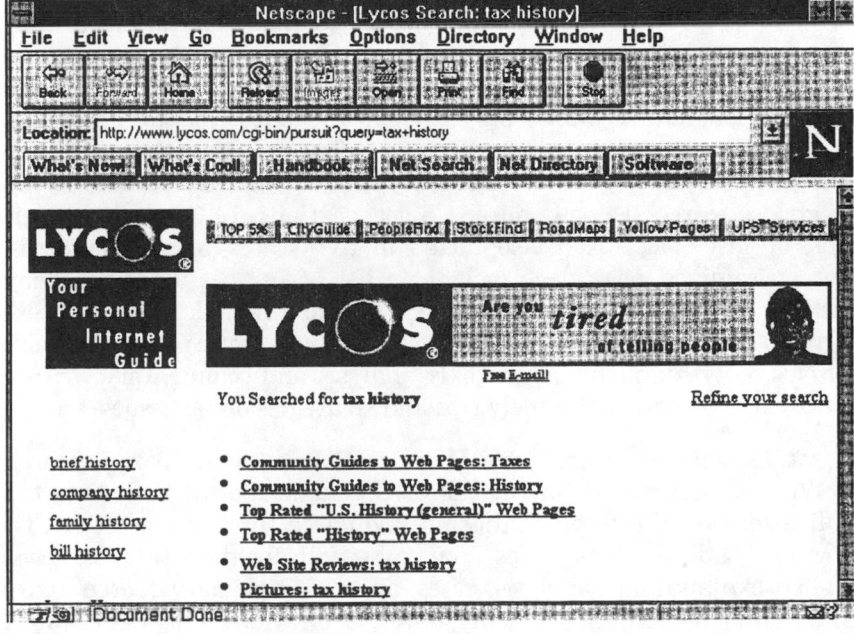

CCH Tax Products on the Internet

Complete, current, and reliable tax information is on the Internet from CCH at http://tax.cch.com. The following two products can be accessed from the site by subscription. Note that when you arrive at the website you have the option of viewing a full graphic version or a "graphics lite" version (shown below). (The lite version is for users connecting to the Internet using a 14.4 baud modem or lower.)

CCH Tax News Direct. You can receive your own personalized tax news every day from CCH Tax News Direct, a customized daily federal and state tax news service delivered via the Internet. Federal and state tax headlines that are important to you are posted daily on your own customized news page. When you subscribe to Tax News Direct, you select the topics, states, jurisdictions (federal and/or any combinaton of states), and document types you want. For example, you can choose to receive news on just S corporations, LLCs, and partnerships, or just sales tax developments in five states, or all new cases. Your customized news page includes a list of tax headlines each day that link to the story, and most stories include a hotlink to the full text of the official document summarized in the story. Your page also includes daily highlights and weekly analysis and commentary written by tax experts providing timely tips and strategies on tax issues.

CCH Tax Research NetWork. CCH Internet Tax Research NetWork subscriptions provide all of the same federal and state tax publications on the Internet that are available through the CCH CD-ROM and Online subscriptions. You can search for the latest tax news, detailed explanations, analysis, cases, and other primary source material by entering terms, documents, dates, or citations. This tax network was named one of the top 100 accounting software products of 1997 in *Accounting Today.*

Tax Administration

¶ 24,211   ORGANIZATION OF THE IRS

The administration and enforcement of federal internal revenue taxes are required to be performed under the supervision of the Secretary of the Treasury. Code Sec. 7801(a). The Internal Revenue Service, a division of the Department of the Treasury, has been delegated the operational aspects of the determination, assessment, and collection of all internal revenue taxes. The Commissioner of Internal Revenue, the official in charge, is appointed by the President and serves under the Secretary of the Treasury. Code Sec. 7802.

The Internal Revenue Service (IRS) consists of a National Office, headquartered in Washington, D.C., and an extensive field organization composed of over a hundred thousand revenue agents, revenue officers, and support personnel. The main task of the National Office is to develop uniform policies for the nationwide administration of the tax law and coordinate the various operations of the IRS.

National Office

The National Office has as its objectives or missions the development of broad nationwide policies and programs for the administration of the tax law and the guidance and coordination of the operations of the Internal Revenue Service. *Internal Revenue Manual,* Sec. 1112.21. Its functions include the issuance of regulations and rulings, executive direction, nationwide policy formulation, and statistical controls. Since the work of the IRS is decentralized, a taxpayer ordinarily has no direct contact with the National Office.

The National Office consists of the Commissioner of Internal Revenue, the Deputy Commissioner, the Chief Inspector, the Taxpayer Advocate, the Modernization Executive, the Chief Counsel, Assistants to the Commissioner and Deputy Commissioner, and seven chief subordinate officers: the Chief Financial Officer; the Chief Compliance Officer; the Chief Information Officer; Chief, Headquarters Operations; Chief, Management and Administration; Chief, Strategic Planning and Communications; and Chief, Taxpayer Services. Exhibit 8 (on the following page) details the organization of the IRS.

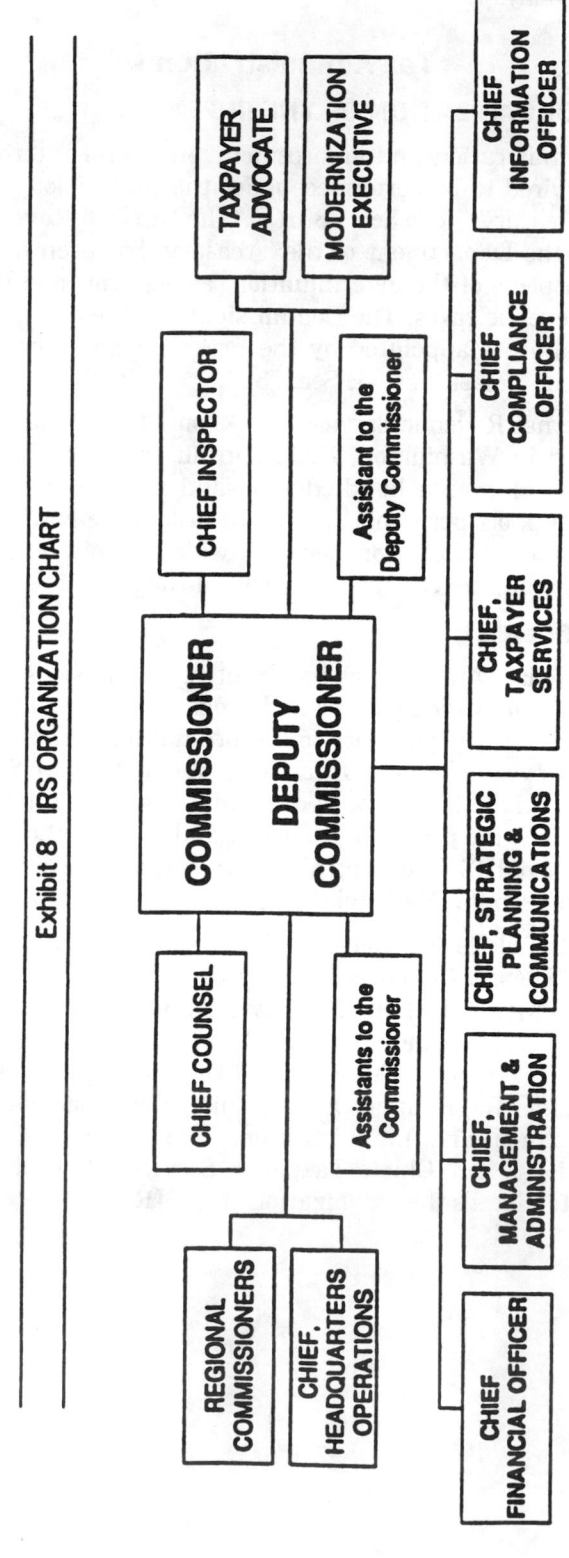

Exhibit 8   IRS ORGANIZATION CHART

The Deputy Commissioner is the highest career official in the IRS and has line authority over and supervises all of the officials in the national Office identified above, except for the Chief Inspector, the Chief Counsel, and certain Assistants to the Commissioner. The Deputy Commissioner also supervises the Regional Commissioners, discussed below, and is generally responsible for assisting the Commissioner in establishing tax administration policy and in planning, directing, coordinating, and controlling the activities of the IRS.

The Chief Inspector, whose function is to ensure objectivity and integrity, reports directly to the Commissioner. The Chief Inspector directs the Internal Audit Division and the Internal Security Division. In addition, the Chief Inspector oversees the Regional Inspectors and Assistant Regional Inspectors.

The Chief Counsel, who is an Assistant General Counsel for the Treasury Department appointed by the President, serves as the chief legal officer for the IRS. The Chief Counsel performs duties as prescribed by the Secretary of the Treasury, Code Sec. 7801(a), and provides technical and legal service to the IRS at the National Office level. The Chief Counsel directs work by lawyers involved in the criminal tax area and in general legal matters arising in the IRS's operations. The Office of the Chief Counsel is responsible for the writing of legislation and regulations, the interpretation and review of letter and published revenue rulings, and litigation-related functions, including representing the IRS in the Tax Court, federal District Courts, and the Court of Federal Claims.

The Modernization Executive, among other things, leads the development of IRS policy on implementing new ways of doing business. The Taxpayer Advocate administers the IRS Problem Resolution Program, the purpose of which is to resolve a variety of problems that are not remedied through normal operating procedures or channels.

The various Chiefs in the National Office are the principal advisors to the Commissioner and Deputy Commissioner within each Chief's respective areas of responsibility, as follows:

1. Chief Financial Officer—Financial management and revenue accounting, including planning and managing financial resources, formulating and executing budgets, and establishing procedures and controls for financial systems;

2. Chief Compliance Officer—Compliance functions, including such matters as delinquent accounts and returns, criminal tax fraud investigations, and tax return examinations;

3. Chief Information Officer—Information resources and technology management, including strategic technology planning, data administration, telecommunications, and development and acquisition of computer hardware and software;

4. Chief, Headquarters Operations—Management of all aspects of IRS headquarters operations;

5. Chief, Management and Administration—Management of human resources and procurement, including human resource policies, guidance in facilities and logistical support, and contracting;

6. Chief, Strategic Planning and Communications—Servicewide planning and internal and external communications, including supervision of the Assistants to the Commissioner for Public Affairs, Quality, and Legislative Liaison, as well as the Directors of the Tax Forms and Publications and Planning; and

7. Chief, Taxpayer Services—Policy and operational matters affecting taxpayer assistance, and tax return and document processing.

Regional and District Offices and Service Centers

The Regional Commissioners supervise the regional centers (4), maintain liaison with the National Office, and set the regional policy and programs for the District Offices (33) and Service Centers (5). The four regional centers are under the supervision of Regional Commissioners. Each Regional Commissioner oversees the support functions assigned to five Assistant Commissioners for resources management, criminal investigation, examination, data processing, and collection.

The District Offices (33) are each headed by a District Director and are responsible for the enforcement of the revenue laws. The District Offices are structured along functional lines into divisions for collection, criminal investigation, examination, resources management, taxpayer service, and (in some districts) employee plans and exempt organizations. The District Office is the basic operation center of the IRS field organization, the place where tax administration becomes a reality. The focal purpose of the District Office is to bring the process of tax administration and enforcement closer to the public. It is at this level that primary contact with taxpayers is established in resolving questions about tax returns or tax liability. Specifically, the District Office is involved in the assessment and collection of taxes and the determination of taxes due.

The Service Centers (5) are each headed by a Director and are responsible for tax return processing, the mathematical verification of returns, and selection of returns for audit. Return processing is also performed at the National Computer Center in Martinsburg, West Virginia, and statistical data are accumulated at the IRS Data Center in Detroit, Michigan.

¶ 24,215   REPRESENTATION OF TAXPAYERS

Rules for persons representing taxpayers before the IRS are published in Treasury Department Circular No. 230. See 31 CFR Part 10. The phrase "practice before the IRS" includes all matters connected with presentation to the IRS relating to a client's rights, privileges, or liabilities under laws or regulations administered by the IRS. Circular No. 230, Sec. 10.2.

Neither the preparation of a return nor the appearance as a witness for the taxpayer is considered practice before the IRS. Attorneys or certified public accountants who are not under suspension or disbarment may practice before the IRS, as may any person enrolled as an agent. The latter individual, however, must demonstrate special competence in tax matters by written examination administered by the IRS. Treasury Department Circular No. 230, Sec. 10.4.

In certain situations, other persons may represent taxpayers. Individuals may appear on their own behalf, and, in addition, Treasury Department Circular No. 230, Sec. 10.7, states a number of situations where individuals may appear on behalf of others without enrollment:

1. An individual may represent another individual who is his or her full-time employer, a partnership of which he or she is a general partner or a full-time employee, or a family member.

2. Corporations, associations, or organized groups may be represented by bona fide officers or full-time employees.

3. Trusts, receiverships, guardianships, or estates may be represented by their trustees, receivers, guardians, administrators, or executors or full-time employees.

4. An individual who prepares the taxpayer's return as a preparer may represent the taxpayer before officers and employees of the Examination Division of the IRS.

Example 24.2. Sam Spaulding is being audited by the IRS for tax years 1996 and 1997. He prepared his own 1996 return, but ABC Tax Return Preparation Service prepared his 1997 return. ABC could represent Sam on matters relating to the 1997 return but only at the agent or examining officer level, not at the higher level of the Appeals Division.

Circular No. 230, Secs. 10.20 to 10.30, states a number of rules relative to practice before the IRS by CPAs, attorneys, and enrolled agents:

1. They shall not neglect or refuse promptly to submit records or information requested by the IRS.

2. They shall advise the client promptly of any noncompliance, error, or omission that may have been on any return or document submitted to the IRS.

3. They shall exercise due diligence in preparing returns and documents and in determining the correctness of oral or written representations made by them to the IRS and to clients.

4. They shall not unreasonably delay the prompt disposition of any matter before the IRS.

5. They shall not in any IRS matter knowingly and directly or indirectly employ or accept assistance from any person who is under disbarment or suspension from practice before the IRS.

6. They shall not charge an unconscionable fee for representation of a client in any matter before the IRS.

7. They shall not represent clients with conflicting interests.

8. They shall not use or participate in the use of any form of public communication containing false, fraudulent, misleading, or unfair statements or claims.

¶ 24,225 RULINGS PROGRAMS

Since passage of the first income tax laws, the IRS has engaged in major publication efforts to provide taxpayers and their advisors with the most current interpretive views of all areas of federal income tax law. The *Internal Revenue Bulletin* is the authoritative instrument of the IRS for announcing official rulings (Revenue Rulings and Revenue Procedures) and for publishing Treasury Decisions, Executive Orders, Tax Conventions, legislation, and other items of general interest. Since publication invites reliance, taxpayers must be aware of the degree of authoritative weight that may be accorded such documents. See detailed discussion at ¶ 24,035.

In addition, Technical Information Releases (TIRs) and Announcements are periodically distributed by the IRS to advise the public of various technical matters. While these pronouncements are published weekly in the *Internal Revenue Bulletin,* they are not usually included in the *Cumulative Bulletin.*

The IRS also issues communications to individual taxpayers and IRS personnel in three primary ways: (1) letter rulings, (2) determination letters, and (3) technical advice memoranda. These documents are part of the IRS Rulings Program, which includes published rulings appearing in the *Internal Revenue Bulletin.*

Letter Rulings

A letter ruling is a "written statement issued to a taxpayer by the National Office of the IRS that interprets and applies the tax laws to that taxpayer's specific set of facts." Rev. Proc. 98-1, Sec. 2.01, 1998-1 IRB 14. Letter rulings generally are issued on uncompleted, actual (rather than hypothetical) transactions or on transactions that have been completed before the filing of the tax return for the year in question. Thus, the emphasis of the letter rulings program is upon the questions or problems of the taxpayer, in contrast to the published rulings program, where the emphasis is centered on uniformity of interpretation of the tax law.

It is the policy of the IRS, however, not to issue letter rulings in a number of general areas:

1. Results of transactions that lack bona fide business purposes or have as their principal purpose the reduction of federal taxes.

2. Matters on which a court decision adverse to the government has been handed down and the question of following the decision or litigating further has not yet been resolved.

3. Matters involving the prospective application of the estate tax to the property or the estate of a living person.

4. Matters involving alternate plans of proposed transactions or involving hypothetical situations.

5. Matters involving the federal tax consequences of any proposed federal, state, local, or municipal legislation.

6. Whether a proposed transaction would subject the taxpayer to a criminal penalty.

Further, it is the policy of the IRS to provide revised lists of those areas of the Internal Revenue Code in which advanced rulings or determination letters will not or will "not ordinarily" be issued. ("Not ordinarily" connotes that unique and compelling reasons must be demonstrated to justify a ruling or determination letter.) Additions or deletions to the revised lists are made as needed to reflect the current policy of the IRS and are set out in several Revenue Procedures. For example, no ruling will be issued to determine whether compensation is reasonable in amount and therefore allowable as a deduction under Code Sec. 162. This is but one of some 40 areas identified by the IRS for nonissuance of letter rulings. There is also a listing of over 40 areas in which rulings will not ordinarily be issued. Rev. Proc. 98-3, 1998-1 IRB 100. Areas in international transactions for which rulings will not be issued are also listed. Rev. Proc. 98-7 1998-1 IRB 222.

The issuance of rulings serves to reduce the number of disputes with revenue agents. A favorable ruling generally will avoid any controversy with an agent in the event of a later audit. For the taxpayer, rulings reduce the uncertainty of tax consequences of a particular action. On the other hand, a ruling request has some disadvantages. Cost is a factor since, under the IRS user fee program (extended until October 1, 2000), a taxpayer will have to pay fees to have a request prepared. Code Sec. 7805. Rev. Proc. 98-8, 1998-1 IRB 225. Also, there is often delay in obtaining a ruling, which could be difficult for the taxpayer if time is a significant factor.

Detailed instructions as to the information that a taxpayer should submit in requesting a ruling are given in Rev. Proc. 98-1, *supra.*

TAX PLANNING POINTER

Although there may be advantages to obtaining a ruling, it may not always be desirable to request a ruling. If the tax results are uncertain but the taxpayer wants to go ahead with a proposed transaction, it might be unwise to request a ruling. Also, if time is a crucial factor and the proposed transaction is so complex that a long time might pass before a response to a ruling request would be given, it might be unwise to request a ruling.

Determination Letters

The determination letter program is part of the letter rulings program. Determination Letters are not published; however, the IRS is now required to make individual rulings available for public inspection. A determination letter is a written statement issued by a District Director in response to an inquiry by an individual or an organization. It applies to the particular facts involved and is based upon principles and precedents previously announced by the National Office to a specific set of facts. Rev. Proc. 98-1, Sec. 2.03, *supra*. Determination letters are issued in response to taxpayers' requests submitted to the District Director, whereas letter rulings are issued by the National Office. The most important use of determination letters in prospective transactions is in the qualification of pension plans and the determination of the tax-exempt status of an organization.

TAX PLANNING POINTER

It is advisable for taxpayers to request a determination letter in connection with pension plans; otherwise, the taxpayer may later find out that the plan does not qualify and deductions might be disallowed.

A District Director may not issue a determination letter in response to an inquiry relating to a question specifically covered by statute, regulations, rulings, etc. published in the *Internal Revenue Bulletin* where (1) it appears that the taxpayer has directed a similar inquiry to the National Office; (2) the identical issue involving the same taxpayer is pending in a case before the Appeals Office; (3) the determination letter is requested by an industry, trade, or similar group; or (4) the request involves an industry-wide problem. Reg. § 601.201(c)(4). The form for a request for a determination letter is the same as that for a ruling. Rev. Proc. 98-1, *supra*.

Technical Advice Memoranda

A technical advice memorandum is advice or guidance furnished by the National Office upon request of a District or an Appeals Office in response to any technical or procedural question that develops during the examination or appeals process. Rev. Proc. 98-2, Sec. 2, 1998-1 IRB 78. Both the taxpayer and the District or Appeals Office may request technical advice. The taxpayer may request advice where there appears to be inconsistency in the application of law or where the issue is unusual or complex. Rev. Proc. 98-2, Sec. 6.02, *supra*. Technical advice adverse to the taxpayer and furnished to an Appeals Office does not preclude the possibility of settlement. Technical advice can also be advantageous from the IRS's viewpoint in that it serves to establish consistent holdings in field offices. Responses to requests for technical advice memoranda sometimes become the basis for a Revenue Ruling.

TAX PLANNING POINTER

A revenue agent sometimes tends to resolve issues against the taxpayer even though the agent may actually believe the taxpayer's viewpoints are valid. Thus, the agent may actually welcome a taxpayer's request for technical advice because the advice may coincide with what the agent actually believed and yet the agent will not have to be the one who made the decision in favor of the taxpayer.

User Fee Program

The payment of user fees is required for all requests to the IRS for rulings, opinion letters, determination letters, and similar requests. The IRS issues schedules of fees and procedures for the collection of the fees along with other guidelines as prescribed by the Revenue Act of 1987. The fee schedules range from $100 to $2,500. The user fee program continues through October 1, 2000. Rev. Proc. 98-8, 1998-1 IRB 228.

¶ 24,245 TAXPAYER COMPLIANCE ASSISTANCE

In order to assist taxpayers, individuals, corporations, partnerships, and other legal entities to be in compliance with requirements of the Internal Revenue Code and regulations, the IRS develops and issues IRS Publications that address a variety of general and special topics of concern to taxpayers. A typical IRS Publication highlights changes in the tax law in a specific area (for example, Pub. No. 508, Educational Expenses), explains the purpose of the law, defines terminology, lists exemptions, provides several examples, and includes sample worksheets and filled-in forms. As to taxpayer reliance, the IRS warns in every IRS Publication that information provided covers only the most common tax situation and is not intended to replace the law or change its meaning. Even though IRS Publications do not bind the IRS, the information contained in IRS Publications provides essential guidance for tax law compliance, particularly in technical or specialized areas.

Tax Practice and Procedure

¶ 24,301 EXAMINATION OF RETURNS

Selection of Returns

The selection of returns for examination begins at the service centers. Returns can be selected by computer programs or by manual selection. The IRS uses the Discriminant Function (DIF) system, which involves computer scoring using mathematical formulas to select tax returns with the highest probability of errors. Returns with the highest scores are then manually examined by district classifiers, who determine whether a return should be subject to examination. *Internal Revenue Manual*, Sec. 4142.2. Taxpayers are divided into classes, including such classifications as business versus nonbusiness; total positive income of varying amounts for nonbusiness returns; and total gross receipts of varying amounts for business returns. Total Positive Income (TPI) is defined as the sum of positive income items on the return such as wages, interest, dividends, and other income items, with losses treated as zero. *Internal Revenue Manual,* Exhibit 4100-17.

Returns are sometimes chosen at random for the Taxpayer Compliance Measurement Program (TCMP). TCMP is a program for measuring taxpayer compliance through specialized audits of individual tax returns. The principal uses of TCMP data are to measure the levels of compliance and tax administration gaps necessary for formulation of the IRS's long-term enforcement policies, to determine changes in compliance levels over a period of time in order to properly direct enforcement programs, to develop and improve return selection procedures and changes in the DIF scores, to identify alternative methods of operation, and to achieve greater operating economies. *Internal Revenue Manual,* Sec. 4861.1. Other events that might give rise to an examination are:

1. Total positive income is above specified amounts.

2. Another IRS office or a non-IRS party might provide information (e.g., a tip from a bitter former spouse).

3. A claim for refund may result in a closer examination of the return.

4. A return of a related party (family member, partner) might be examined to determine the correctness of the taxpayer's return.

Example 24.3. Arthur and Beverly Saunders were divorced in 1998. During their marriage, Arthur had not reported some consulting income he received beyond his regular salary. Beverly, still upset about the divorce, reports Arthur to the IRS. This may result in an audit.

Example 24.4. In 1998, Charles Regus files an amended return with a sizeable refund claim as a result of educational expense deductions that he could have taken on his 1996 return, but which he failed to take because he was uncertain as to whether they would qualify. It is possible that close examination of his 1996 return might occur as a result of this claim for refund. However, if Charles believes he has a good case, he should file the amended return.

Correspondence Examinations

Correspondence examinations involve relatively simple problems that can generally be resolved by mail. These examinations would include mathematical errors, broadly defined in Code Sec. 6213(g)(2) to mean (1) an error in addition, subtraction, multiplication, or division shown on any return; (2) an incorrect use of any IRS table if such incorrect use is apparent from other information on the return; (3) inconsistent entries on the return; (4) an omission of information required to be supplied on the return to substantiate a return item; and (5) a deduction or credit that exceeds a statutory limit that is either a specified monetary amount or a percentage, ratio, or fraction—if the items entering into the application of such limit appear on the return.

Example 24.5. James Judson, single, incorrectly determines his tax liability because he used the joint rate schedule rather than the single rate schedule. This correction and adjustment can be resolved by mail.

The Service Center personnel might also question specific items under the Unallowable Items Program. *Internal Revenue Manual,* Sec. 4(13) 20. For example, a deduction of Social Security taxes by the taxpayer would result in notification by the Service Center. Such a contact is considered to be an examination in contrast to a mathematical/clerical error notification, which is not considered to be an examination. (If it is an examination, one is entitled to a notice of deficiency and to administrative appeal.) The IRS also matches information returns of some taxpayers with income tax returns. If there is a discrepancy, the return will be corrected, or the file might be referred for examination and possibly criminal investigation.

District Office Examinations

A District Office examination of a return is conducted by a tax auditor of the Audit Division either by correspondence or by interview. Sometimes the matters are so simple they can be handled by correspondence. Verification of particular itemized deductions such as interest, taxes, or charitable contributions might be handled by correspondence. *Internal Revenue Manual,* Sec. 4252.

Returns selected for interview examinations generally require some analysis and judgment as well as verification. Examples of types of issues which lend themselves to interview examinations are income items that are not subject to withholding, deductions for travel and entertainment, items such as casualty and theft losses that involve the use of fair market value, education expenses, deductions for business-related expenses, and determination of basis of property. Also, if the taxpayer's income is low in relation to financial responsibilities as indicated on the return through the number of dependents or interest expense, or if the taxpayer's occupation is of the type that required only a limited formal education, an office interview might be deemed appropriate. Certain business activities or occupations reported may lend themselves to office interview examinations (e.g., auto repair shops, restaurants, service stations, professional persons, farmers, motels, and others).

Example 24.6. Edward Egars, an outside salesperson, reports income of $25,000 and takes travel and entertainment deductions before application of the 50 percent limit on meals and entertainment of $15,000. Edward could be called in for an office examination to verify his travel and entertainment expenses.

Example 24.7. Jane Judson has adjusted gross income of $15,000 and gives $7,000 in cash contributions to her church. Since her contributions exceed the norm for her bracket and approach the maximum limitation for her income level, she could be called in to verify her charitable contributions.

TAX PLANNING POINTER ▼

In an office examination, the taxpayer or a representative should provide only information or support for items that are requested of the taxpayer by the IRS; otherwise, the tax auditor might open up other areas for investigation. Situations may vary, but some practitioners believe that it is better for the taxpayer, assuming there is a representative such as a CPA or a lawyer, not to be present because the representative can keep better control over the interview and also maintain a less emotional atmosphere.

When there is a disagreement after an office examination, if practicable, the taxpayer is given an opportunity for an interview with the tax auditor's immediate supervisor or for a conference with an Appeals Officer. Reg. § 601.105(c)(1)(ii). If these actions are not feasible, the taxpayer will be sent a 30-day letter from the District Office indicating the proposed adjustments and the courses of action. If the taxpayer agrees with the adjustment, the taxpayer can sign the agreement form. If the taxpayer disagrees, an Appeals Office conference may be requested within 30 days or the taxpayer may ignore the 30-day letter and wait for the 90-day letter, which allows the taxpayer to file a petition in the Tax Court. Reg. § 601.105(c)(1)(ii) and (d)(1)(iv).

Field Examinations

Field examinations are conducted by revenue agents and involve more complex issues than do office examinations. Field audits take place in the taxpayer's or the taxpayer's representative's office or home. The revenue agent must identify items that may need adjustment, gather the appropriate evidence, and apply the applicable Code provisions, Regulations, and other interpretative rulings. Techniques have been developed by the IRS to try to ensure that revenue agents consider all areas necessary for a proper calculation of the tax liability. An agent has power to subpoena all books and records and to compel the attendance of witnesses. Code Sec. 7602.

TAX PLANNING POINTER ▼

The revenue agent should be treated courteously and should be promptly furnished information and substantiation relating to applicable tax return items. Although the cooperation of the taxpayer (or the taxpayer's representative) is important, the taxpayer should respond only to questions asked by the agent. Disclosing unnecessary information could cause problems for the taxpayer.

There are some advantages to settling with the revenue agent. In addition to being less costly than settling at higher levels, negotiations with the revenue agent are generally more informal than negotiations at higher levels and less demanding on technical aspects. Also, if questionable issues exist but were not raised at the agent level, it may be wise to settle at that level in order to avoid the possibility of persons at higher levels raising those questionable issues. Similarly, there is an advantage to the revenue agent to have an agreed case because it involves more effort and time to write a report on an unagreed case than on an agreed case.

The agent completes a report called the Revenue Agent Report (RAR). In agreed cases, a copy of the RAR is sent to the taxpayer before review. If the taxpayer agrees with the revenue agent's adjustments and proposals, the taxpayer can sign Form 870 (Waiver of Restrictions on Assessment and Collection of Deficiency in Tax). In unagreed cases, the taxpayer does not receive the RAR until after review by the Review Staff.

Audit Reconsideration

The audit reconsideration is a procedure that is used when a taxpayer has ignored a statutory notice of deficiency or where there has been a breakdown in communication between the taxpayer and the IRS. *Internal Revenue Manual,* Part V, IRM 53(10)4.1. An audit reconsideration is permitted when a new notice was not sent to the taxpayer's new address, the taxpayer had not received any notification from the IRS on any assessment, and the taxpayer had not been given an opportunity to submit any required substantiation or necessary documentation.

¶ 24,311   APPEALS PROCESS

Administrative Process

If the taxpayer and the agent do not agree, the taxpayer will be sent a 30-day letter that explains the appellate procedures and urges the taxpayer to reply within 30 days either by signing the waiver or by requesting a conference. If the taxpayer does not respond to the 30-day letter, a statutory notice of deficiency (90-day letter) will be sent giving the taxpayer 90 days to file a petition with the Tax Court. Thus, if the taxpayer and agent do not agree, the taxpayer has several options:

1. The taxpayer may request a conference in the IRS Appeals Office.

2. After receiving the statutory notice of deficiency, the taxpayer may file a petition in the Tax Court within the 90-day period.

3. The taxpayer could wait for the 90-day period to expire, pay the assessment, and start a refund suit in the District Court or the Court of Federal Claims.

If the IRS and the taxpayer agree, the statutory notice of deficiency issued by the IRS (90-day letter) may be rescinded. The rescinded notice voids the limitations regarding credits, refunds, and assessments, and the taxpayer will have no right to petition the Tax Court based on such notice. Rescinding the deficiency notice will allow for resolution of the controversy within the IRS.

IRS Appeals Office

If an appeal is made within the IRS, an appropriate request must be made. The request must be accompanied by a written protest unless:

1. The proposed increase or decrease in tax or claimed refund is not more than $2,500 for any of the tax periods involved in field examination cases.

2. The examination was conducted by a tax auditor (i.e., an office examination) or by correspondence. (See IRS Publication No. 5, Appeal Rights and Preparation of Protests for Unagreed Cases.)

If a protest is required, it should be sent within the 30-day period granted in the letter containing the examination report. The protest should contain:

1. A statement that the taxpayer wants to appeal the findings of the examiner to the Appeals Office

2. Taxpayer's name and address

3. The date and symbols from the letter transmitting the proposed adjustments and findings the taxpayer is protesting

4. The tax periods or years involved

5. An itemized schedule of the adjustments with which the taxpayer does not agree

6. A statement of facts supporting the taxpayer's position in any contested factual issue

7. A statement outlining the law or other authority on which the taxpayer is relying

A taxpayer may go to the Appeals Office at two different times: (1) if the protest is filed within the 30-day period as stated in the 30-day letter, or (2) if the 30-day period passes and the taxpayer files a petition in the Tax Court within 90 days after receipt of a statutory notice of deficiency.

Exhibit 9 (on the following page) shows graphically the income tax appeal procedures within the IRS (as described above) and through the court system (as described on the following pages).

Exhibit 9   INCOME TAX APPEAL PROCEDURE

There are a number of important factors to consider in filing a protest and going to the Appeals Office. It is less expensive than litigation and yet the taxpayer leaves open the opportunity to file a petition in the Tax Court or to sue for refund in a District Court or the Court of Federal Claims. In addition, a taxpayer is often able to gather more information about the IRS position in the event the taxpayer needs to carry the case further, and there may be a chance that the taxpayer can convince the Appeals Officer that the IRS was incorrect at the agent level. The Appeals Officer may be at some disadvantage in that the case was not personally prepared and the Appeals Officer is relying on the information presented by the revenue agent, which could be an advantage to the taxpayer.

On the other hand, there may be some disadvantages to having an Appeals Conference. New issues might be raised in an Appeals Conference, although the IRS's policy is to avoid raising an issue unless the grounds for such action are "substantial" and the potential effect upon tax liability is "material." 26 CFR Sec. 601.106(d)(1). The Appeals Officer must have a strong reason for raising an issue. The *Internal Revenue Manual,* Sec. 8743, gives the following example:

> ***Example 24.8.*** If a District Director disallowed a claimed farm loss solely on the ground that it was a hobby loss and stated nothing concerning the items making up the loss, there would not be substantial grounds for raising a new issue concerning the amount of the loss merely because the Appeals Officer suspected that the items had not been verified. On the other hand, if the examiner had indicated in the report that the items had not been verified, there would be good reason for the Appeals Officer to refer the case back to the District Director if it was believed such action was necessary. If the District Director stated that some of the items of claimed expense were personal in nature, this would constitute substantial grounds for the Appeals Officer to raise a new issue or to refer the case back to the District Director for further information and investigation.

Taxpayers may represent themselves at the Appeals Conference or be represented by an attorney, CPA, or person enrolled to practice before the IRS. The Appeals Officer, who actually handles the appeals, reports to the Regional Director of Appeals who, in turn, reports to the Regional Commissioner. Proceedings before the Appeals Officer are informal and are held in the District Office. The Appeals Officer may request that the taxpayer submit additional information, which could involve additional conferences.

The Appeals Officer may resolve controversies between the taxpayer and the IRS by considering the "hazards of litigation." The *Internal Revenue Manual,* Sec. 8711(2), states that a fair and impartial resolution "reflects on an issue-by-issue basis the probable result in event of litigation, or one which reflects mutual concessions for the purpose of settlement based on the relative strength of the opposing positions where there is a substantial uncertainty of the result in event of litigation." If there is uncertainty as to the application of the law, the Appeals Officer will consider a settlement in view of the hazards that would exist if the case were litigated. Thus, the Appeals Officer, in evaluating a case for settlement, will objectively assess how a court might look at the case rather than attempt to obtain the best results for the IRS. The Appeals Officer considers the value of the evidence that would be presented, the witnesses, the uncertainty as to an issue of fact and the uncertainty as to a conclusion considering the court in which the case might be litigated or appealed.

If a satisfactory settlement of the issue is reached after consideration by the Appeals Office, the taxpayer will be requested to sign Form 870-AD. By signing Form 870-AD, the taxpayer waives restrictions on the assessment and collection of any deficiency. Form 870-AD does not stop the running of interest when filed. It is merely the taxpayer's offer to waive restrictions, and interest will run until 30 days after the IRS has accepted the offer. If the taxpayer does not agree with the decision at the Appeals level, a notice of deficiency will be issued by the Appeals Office after consideration by the Regional Counsel of the memorandum recommending a notice of deficiency.

Taxpayer's Rights

The Taxpayer Bill of Rights is a series of provisions which require the Treasury Department to outline in "simple and nontechnical terms the rights of a taxpayer and the obligations of the IRS during an audit." Additionally, the IRS is required to inform taxpayers of their administrative and appeals rights in the event of an adverse decision, as well as the procedures related to refund claims, taxpayer complaints, collection assessments, levies, and tax liens. The Treasury Department has prepared and released the required information statement, IRS Publication No. 1, Your Rights as a Taxpayer.

The Taxpayer Bill of Rights is divided into four major categories:

1. Taxpayer rights and IRS obligations
2. Levy and lien provisions
3. Proceedings by taxpayers
4. Authority of the Tax Court

Most significantly, the law requires abatement of penalties resulting from reliance on erroneous written IRS advice, authorizes recovery of damages for failure of the IRS to remove a lawful lien, permits the filing of an application for hardship relief with the IRS Taxpayer Advocate, and outlines provisions whereby a taxpayer, who substantially prevails in an administrative or court proceeding against the IRS, may recover reasonable administrative and litigation costs. Additionally, the law allows a taxpayer or an IRS representative to make an audio recording of an in-person interview regarding the determination or collection of any tax.

To ensure the effective administration of the Taxpayer Bill of Rights, an Office for Taxpayer Services has been established, under the direction of an Assistant Commissioner for Taxpayer Services. Responsibilities of this office include: telephone, walk-in and taxpayer educational services, and the design and production of tax and informational forms. Also, there is a Taxpayer Advocate, holding the rank of Assistant to the Commissioner, who may act, under the Problem Resolution Program, on behalf of the taxpayer during the audit or collection process.

Appeal Through the Court System

Within 90 days of mailing of a notice of deficiency, the taxpayer may petition the Tax Court for redetermination of the deficiency. Code Sec. 6213(a). If the 90-day deficiency notice was issued by the Appeals Office, it is possible to arrange for pretrial settlement with the Regional Counsel of the IRS even after the case has been docketed in the Tax Court. Taxpayers filing a petition with the Tax Court may have their cases handled under less formal rules applicable to "small tax cases" if the amount of the deficiency or claimed overpayment is not greater than $10,000. However, "small tax cases" are not appealable and are not to be treated as precedents for any other cases. Code Sec. 7463(a) and (b). If the taxpayer does not file a petition with the Tax Court within 90 days, the opportunity to appeal to the Tax Court is lost.

The taxpayer can pay the deficiency and file a claim for refund by filing Form 1040X (Amended U.S. Individual Income Tax Return) and mailing it to the IRS Center where the taxpayer filed the original return. A claim for refund must be filed within three years from the date the return was filed or within two years from the date the tax was paid, whichever is later. Code Sec. 6511(a). If the return was filed before the due date, the three-year period starts to run from the date the return was due.

A suit to recover may not be started until after six months from the date the taxpayer filed the claim for refund, unless a decision on the claim for refund was made before then. A suit for refund must be started before the end of two years from the date of mailing of a notice to the taxpayer disallowing part or all of the claim. Code Sec. 6532(a).

Federal Court System

There are three trial courts or courts of original jurisdiction: the U.S. Tax Court, the U.S. District Courts, and the U.S. Court of Federal Claims. Appeal from a decision of the Tax Court of the U.S. District Court may be taken by either side to the federal Court of Appeals for the circuit in which the taxpayer resides or the corporation has its principal place of business. A review of a decision of the U.S. Court of Federal Claims is taken to the U.S. Court of Appeals for the Federal Circuit. The Supreme Court has jurisdiction to hear appeals or review decisions of the federal Court of Appeals and the U.S. Court of Appeals for the Federal Circuit. (See Exhibit 9.) For a detailed discussion of the trial court system, see ¶ 24,055.

Choice of Tax Forum

There are a number of factors to consider in deciding whether to litigate a case and where to litigate.

1. *Jurisdiction.* The Tax Court handles only income, estate, gift, and excess profits tax cases. The District Court and the Court of Federal Claims can litigate all areas of internal revenue taxes.

2. *Payment of tax.* In the Tax Court, payment of tax is not generally allowed. Section 6213(b)(4) allows the taxpayer to

pay the tax after receiving a 90-day letter and still sue in the Tax Court. This feature can be used by the taxpayer to stop the accrual of interest on the deficiency while still choosing the Tax Court forum. In the District Court and the Court of Federal Claims, payment of tax is required. Thus, whether the taxpayer has the money to pay the tax may be a factor in the choice of tax forum.

3. *Jury trial.* A jury trial is available only in the District Court. Often, tax cases do not make good jury cases because of their complexity. Also, sometimes jurors may be prejudiced against a taxpayer who is wealthier than they are.

4. *Rules of evidence.* The rules of evidence are most strict in jury trials where efforts must be made to keep the jurors from hearing inappropriate evidence. The evidence rules are most lenient in the Tax Court.

5. *Expertise of judges.* Since the Tax Court hears only tax cases, the judges are all very knowledgeable in tax law. The District Court judges are generally the least technically oriented since the District Court hears many types of cases.

6. *Publicity.* There will likely be the most publicity in the District Court since such suit is brought in the district in which the taxpayer lives.

7. *Legal precedent.* The court decisions by which the particular forum will be bound may also be a consideration. The Tax Court is bound by Tax Court decisions (unless the Court of Appeals of the circuit to which the case might be appealed held differently), by the Court of Appeals to which the case might be appealed, and by the U.S. Supreme Court. (See *J.E. Golsen,* 54 TC 757, CCH Dec. 30,049 (1970), aff'd, 71-2 USTC ¶ 9497, 445 F.2d 985 (CA-10 1971), cert. denied, 404 U.S. 940, 92 S.Ct. 284.) The District Court is bound by decisions of the Court of Appeals for the circuit to which the decision would be appealed, and by the U.S. Supreme Court. The Court of Federal Claims is bound by decisions of the Court of Appeals for the Federal Circuit and by U.S. Supreme Court decisions.

8. *Factual precedent.* In certain types of cases, one court may be more favorable to the taxpayer than another court. For example, regarding the characterization of voluntary payments to employees' widows as a gift or as compensation, the Tax Court decisions have consistently been unfavorable to the taxpayer, while results in the Courts of Appeals have been more balanced. 1998 CCH Standard Federal Tax Reports ¶ 5507.4741.

9. *Statute of limitations.* The statute of limitations is suspended in a filing in the Tax Court whereas suit in the Court of Federal Claims and the District Court does not suspend the statute of limitations. Suspension of the statute of limitations

means that the IRS can raise new issues and claims for additional taxes.

10. *Discovery.* In the District Court and the Court of Federal Claims, both parties (i.e., taxpayer and IRS) have available to them discovery tools that allow them access to the other party's evidence prior to trial. In the Tax Court, the parties are expected "to attain the objectives of discovery through informal consultation or communication" and no depositions are permitted (except in very limited circumstances). Tax Court Rule 70.

TAX PLANNING POINTER ▼

It is important for taxpayers to be aware of the characteristics of the courts so that an appropriate choice can be made if the taxpayer decides to go to court. A taxpayer, having made a decision to go to the District Court, for example, cannot later decide to go to the Tax Court.

The taxpayer must think very seriously before taking a case to court. Not only may the economic costs be high, but the psychological and emotional costs may be high. The taxpayer must consider whether the tax savings will be worth the legal fees, time, and psychological costs.

A taxpayer, in deciding to which court to take a case, should not look simply at the statistics on taxpayer winnings in the various courts. Statistics like that have some value only if winnings by taxpayers on similar issues are being examined.

KEYSTONE PROBLEM

If a taxpayer is called up for an office examination, what should the taxpayer do? If the taxpayer and the tax auditor do not agree, what steps should be taken? What factors would be considered in deciding whether or not to pursue the matter?

¶ 24,315   SETTLEMENT AGREEMENTS

Where a taxpayer and the appeals officer have reached an agreement as to some or all of the issues in controversy, generally the appeals officer will request that the taxpayer sign a Form 870, the same agreement that is used at the district level. However, when neither party with justification is willing to concede in full the unresolved area of disagreement and a resolution of the dispute involves concessions for the purposes of settlement by both parties, a mutual concession settlement is reached, and a Form 870-AD type of agreement is to be used. Form 870 becomes effective as a waiver of restrictions and assessment when received by the Internal Revenue Service, whereas the Form

870-AD is effective upon acceptance by or on behalf of the Commissioner of Internal Revenue.

¶ 24,325 REFUNDS

Claims for refund of individual income taxes are to be made on Form 1040X (Amended U.S. Individual Income Tax Return) and on Form 1120X for corporate income tax refunds. The claim for refund must be filed no later than three years from the date the return was filed or no later than two years from the date the tax was paid, whichever period expires later. Code Sec. 6511(a). If the return was filed before the due date, the three-year period starts to run from the date the return was due. If no return was filed, the claim must be filed within two years from the time the tax was paid. There is a special seven-year period of limitation on a claim for refund based on a debt that became wholly worthless or on a worthless security. If the refund claim relates to a net operating loss, capital loss, or credit carryback, the refund claim may be filed within three years after the time for filing the tax return for the year of the loss (or unused credit). Code Sec. 6511(d).

Any tax deducted or withheld at the source during any calendar year shall be deemed to be paid on the 15th day of the fourth month following the close of the taxable year. Code Sec. 6513(b). Thus, a refund for taxes withheld must be filed within three years of the due date of the return (including extensions). Code Sec. 6511(b).

Example 24.9. In 1998, Joe, a college student, worked part-time during the summer. He earned $3,000 and had income tax withheld of $400. He did not file a 1998 tax return by April 15, 1999. If he does not file his 1998 tax return by April 15, 2002, he cannot obtain the refund of $400.

¶ 24,333 INTEREST ON UNDERPAYMENTS AND OVERPAYMENTS

The interest rate that taxpayers must pay for underpayment of taxes is equal to the federal short-term rate plus three percentage points. In the case of overpayment of taxes, the amount of interest owed by the Treasury is equal to the federal short-term rate plus two percentage points. Code Sec. 6621(a). These interest rates are adjusted quarterly, with the new rates becoming effective two months after the date of each adjustment.

Interest is also paid by the IRS on overpayments of tax. However, if any overpayment of tax is refunded within 45 days after the due date of the return (or filing date if later), no interest is allowed. If any overpayment results from a carryback (net operating loss, capital loss, or credit) through filing an amended return, interest is paid only if the overpayment is not refunded within the 45-day period. Code Sec. 6611(e) and (f).

¶ 24,355   STATUTE OF LIMITATIONS

Assessment of any tax must be made within three years after the return was filed or after the due date for filing, whichever is later. Code Sec. 6501(a). After making an assessment of tax, the IRS has 10 years in which to initiate collection proceedings. Code Sec. 6502(a).

Example 24.10. Fred Forbes filed his 1998 return on February 20, 1999. The government may not assess any additional tax for 1998 after April 15, 2002. If, on the other hand, he had filed his 1998 return on November 8, 1999, the statute of limitations would expire on November 8, 2002.

There are some exceptions to the general rule:

1.   There is no limitation on the period for assessment in three cases: (1) false return, (2) willful attempt to evade tax, and (3) no return. Code Sec. 6501(c)(1)-(3).

   Example 24.11. Linda Lord failed to file tax returns in 1984 and 1985 when she had $20,000 gross income. If the government discovered in 1998 that the returns were not filed, it could assess 1984 and 1985 taxes against Linda.

2.   If the taxpayer omits from gross income an amount that is in excess of 25 percent of the amount of gross income stated on the return, the tax may be assessed at any time within six years after the return is filed or the due date for filing, if later. In computing gross income, revenues from the sale of goods or services are not to be reduced by cost of goods sold. Code Sec. 6501(e)(1). Gross income also includes capital gains but is not reduced by capital losses.

   Example 24.12. On her 1997 return filed on March 20, 1998, Vera Vaughn reported her salary of $35,000 and taxable interest of $5,000. She failed to report a $9,000 capital gain. Since the $9,000 omission does not exceed $10,000 (25 percent of $40,000), the statute of limitations expires on April 15, 2001. If the omitted capital gain had been $11,000, the statute of limitations would expire on April 15, 2004.

   Example 24.13. As a sole proprietor, George Ganger had $50,000 sales and $20,000 cost of goods sold, which were reported on his 1997 tax return filed on March 14, 1998. Through an oversight he failed to report $8,000 interest. Since $8,000 interest does not exceed $12,500 (25 percent of $50,000), the statute of limitations expires on April 15, 2001.

3.   Where both the taxpayer and the IRS agree, the statute of limitations may be extended for a specific period. The extension must be executed before the expiration of the applicable limitation period. Code Sec. 6501(c)(4).

4.   Certain taxpayers may request a prompt assessment. The period of assessment may be shortened to 18 months in the case of a decedent, the estate of a decedent, or a corporation that is dissolved or contemplating dissolution. Code Sec.

6501(d). The purpose of this rule is to allow an estate or corporation to settle its affairs early without having to make contingent plans for later possible tax assessments.

5. If a personal holding company fails to file with its return a schedule regarding its status as a personal holding company, the tax may be assessed at any time within six years after the return is filed. Code Sec. 6501(f).

6. In the case of a deficiency attributable to the application of a carryback (capital loss, net operating loss, or credit), the statute of limitations runs from the year of the loss rather than the carryback year. Code Sec. 6501(h) and (j).

Sections 1311 through 1314 contain provisions to mitigate the effect of the statute of limitations where inequitable results might occur.

¶ 24,365   PENALTIES

Penalties are treated as additions to federal internal revenue taxes and are, therefore, not deductible for federal income tax purposes.

Delinquency Penalties

The penalty for *failure to file* a return on the due date (determined with regard to any extension of time for filing) is 5 percent of the amount of tax due if the failure is for not more than one month, with an additional 5 percent for each additional month or fraction thereof, but not exceeding 25 percent in the aggregate. Code Sec. 6651(a)(1). The penalty is imposed on the net amount due—the difference between (1) the amount required to be shown on the return and (2) the amount paid on or before the due date and the amount of credit that may be claimed on the return. Effective for returns due after December 31, 1989, in case of a fraudulent failure to file a return, the failure to file penalty is increased to 15 percent if the net amount of tax due for each month the return is not filed up to a maximum of five months or 75 percent. Code Sec. 6651(f).

The penalty for *failure to pay* the amount of tax due on a tax return or for failure to pay an assessed tax within 10 days of the date of notice is one-half of one percent of the tax for one month or less and an additional one-half of one percent per month or part thereof until the penalty reaches 25 percent. An additional one-half of one percent per month is assessed if the taxpayer fails to pay a deficiency within 10 days after a notice is issued. Code Sec. 6651(a)(2) and (3) and (d). The penalty is imposed on the net amount due.

Either or both of the penalties can be avoided if the taxpayer can show that failure to file and/or pay was due to reasonable cause and not to willful neglect. Code Sec. 6651(a)(1), (2), and (3). The burden of establishing these facts is on the taxpayer. The *Internal Revenue Manual,* Sec. 4562.2(1)(a)-(i), gives some indication of what would be considered as reasonable cause for purposes of the delinquency penalties:

1. A return mailed in time but returned for insufficient postage.

2. A return filed within the legal period but in the wrong district.

3. Death or serious illness of the taxpayer or in the immediate family.

4. Unavoidable absence of the taxpayer.

5. Destruction of the taxpayer's business or business records by fire or other casualty.

6. Erroneous information given the taxpayer by an IRS official, or a request for proper blanks or returns not furnished by the IRS in sufficient time to permit the filing of the return by the due date.

7. The taxpayer made an effort to obtain assistance or information necessary to complete the return by a personal appearance at an IRS office but was unsuccessful because the taxpayer, through no fault, was unable to see an IRS representative.

8. The taxpayer is unable to obtain the records necessary to determine the amount of tax due for reasons beyond the taxpayer's control.

9. The taxpayer contacts a competent tax adviser, furnishes the necessary information, and then is incorrectly advised that the filing of a return is not required.

If the cause does not fall within one of the reasonable causes listed above, the District Director will decide whether the taxpayer established a reasonable cause for delinquency. *Internal Revenue Manual,* Sec. 4562.2.

Accuracy-Related and Fraud Penalties

Effective for returns due after December 31, 1989, the penalties relating to the accuracy of tax returns are consolidated into one accuracy-related penalty equal to 20 percent of the portion of the underpayment to which the penalty applies. The penalty applies to the portion of underpayment attributable to one or more of the following five areas:

1. Negligence

2. Substantial understatement of income tax

3. Substantial valuation overstatement

4. Substantial overstatement of pension liabilities

5. Substantial estate or gift tax valuation understatement

The penalty does not apply to any portion of an underpayment attributable to a penalty for fraud. Code Sec. 6662(a) and (b).

For purposes of the consolidated penalty, "underpayment" means the amount by which any tax exceeds the excess of (1) the sum of (a) the amount shown as the tax by a taxpayer on the return, plus (b) amounts not shown as tax that were previously assessed, over (2) the amount of rebates made. Code Sec. 6664(a).

The accuracy-related penalties will not be imposed if it is shown that there was a reasonable cause for the underpayment and that the taxpayer acted in good faith with respect to the underpayment. Code Sec. 6664(c)(1).

Negligence Penalty

A 20 percent penalty is imposed for underpayment of tax due to negligence or disregard of rules and regulations. Code Sec. 6662(a).

Example 24.14. Due to negligence, Steven Stover underpaid his taxes for 1998 by $30,000. His penalty is $6,000 (20% × $30,000).

The term "negligence" includes any failure to make a reasonable attempt to comply with the provisions of the Code, and the term "disregard" includes any careless, reckless, or intentional disregard. The definition of negligence is not limited only to the items specified. Thus, all behavior that is considered negligent under present law continues to be within the scope of the negligence penalty. Also, any behavior that is considered negligent by the courts but that is not specifically included within the definition is subject to the penalty.

In an effort to provide guidance as to the scope of the term "negligence," the *Internal Revenue Manual,* Sec. 4563.11(2), states that it is "the omission to do something which a reasonable person, guided by those considerations which ordinarily regulate the conduct of human beings, would do, or doing something which a reasonable person would not do." According to the *Manual,* Sec. 4563.11(3), the following are examples of cases in which negligence may exist:

1. Taxpayer continues year after year to make substantial errors in reporting income and claiming deductions even though these mistakes have been called to the taxpayer's attention in previous reports.

2. Taxpayer fails to maintain proper records after being advised through inadequate record procedures to do so and subsequent returns containing substantial errors are filed.

3. Taxpayer took careless and exaggerated deductions unsubstantiated by facts.

4. Taxpayer failed to give any explanation for the understatement of income and for failure to keep books and records.

Substantial Understatement of Tax Liability

If there is a substantial understatement of income tax, an amount equal to 20 percent of the amount of the understatement can be assessed. A substantial understatement of income tax occurs when the understatement exceeds the greater of 10 percent of the tax required to be shown on the return or $5,000. Code Sec. 6662(d)(1). In the case of a corporation (except for an S corporation or a personal holding company), the understatement must exceed the greater of 10 percent of the tax required to be shown on the return or $10,000. The amount of the understatement is equal to the excess of the tax required to be shown on the return over the amount of tax that is actually shown on the return.

The penalty can be avoided if there was substantial authority for the tax treatment; if relevant facts affecting the treatment are adequately disclosed in the return or a statement attached to the return; and in the case of tax shelter items, if the taxpayer reasonably believed that the tax treatment of such item was more likely than not the proper treatment. Code Sec. 6662(d)(2)(B) and (C). The penalty can be waived on showing of reasonable cause and that the taxpayer acted in good faith. Code Sec. 6664(c).

Substantial Valuation Overstatement Penalty

All taxpayers having an underpayment of tax attributable to a valuation overstatement are subject to this 20 percent penalty. Code Sec. 6662(e). There is a substantial valuation overstatement if the value of any property (or the adjusted basis of any property) is 200 percent or more of the amount determined to be the correct amount of the valuation or adjusted basis of the property. If the portion of the underpayment that is subject to the penalty is attributable to one or more gross valuation misstatements, the penalty will be applied at the rate of 40 percent. A gross valuation misstatement occurs if the value of the property (or the adjusted basis) was 400 percent or more of the correct amount of the valuation of the adjusted basis of the property. Code Sec. 6662(h)(2)(A). No penalty will be imposed on a taxpayer for a substantial valuation overstatement unless the portion of the underpayment attributable to substantial valuation overstatements exceeds $5,000, or $10,000 in the case of a corporation other than an S corporation or a personal holding company.

> *Example 24.15.* Bert Barge gives a painting he purchased three years ago to his alma mater and takes a charitable contribution deduction in the amount of $50,000, the value placed on it by his art professor friend. If the actual value was only $10,000 and if the tax underpayment is $15,000, Bert would be subject to a $6,000 valuation overstatement penalty (40 percent of $15,000). The valuation was more than 400 percent of the correct valuation.

Although valuation overstatements of charitable property resulting in understatements of tax are subject to the accuracy penalty provisions, the charitable deduction penalty waiver for qualified appraisers is still possible. No penalty will be imposed for an underpayment of tax resulting from a substantial or gross overvaluation of charitable deduction property if it can be shown that there was a reasonable cause for the underpayment and that the taxpayer acted in good faith.

Substantial Overstatement of Pension Liabilities

The 20 percent penalty for substantial overstatement of pension liabilities applies only if the actuarial determination of pension liabilities is 200 percent or more of the amount determined to be correct. Code Sec. 6662(f). If a portion of the substantial overstatement to which the penalty applies is attributable to a gross valuation misstatement of 400 percent or more, the penalty is doubled to 40 percent of the underpayment. Code Sec. 6662(h). No penalty is imposed if the underpayment for the tax year attributable to substantial overstatements of pension liabilities is $1,000 or less.

Estate or Gift Tax Valuation Understatements

A 20 percent penalty is imposed for estate or gift tax valuation understatement if the value of any property claimed on an estate or gift tax return is 50 percent or less of the amount determined to be the correct amount of the valuation. Code Sec. 6662(g). If the understatement is attributable to a gross valuation misstatement of 25 percent or less of the correct amount, the penalty amount is 40 percent of the underpayment. Code Sec. 6662(h)(2)(C). This penalty applies only if the underpayment attributable to the understatement exceeds $5,000 for a tax period with respect to gift tax (or with respect to the estate in the case of estate tax).

Penalty for Aiding Understatement of Tax Liability

Any person who aids in the preparation or presentation of any tax document in connection with matters arising under the internal revenue laws with the knowledge that the document will result in the understatement of tax liability of another person is subject to a penalty of $1,000 ($10,000 for a corporation) for a taxable period. Code Sec. 6701.

Civil Fraud Penalty

If any part of an underpayment is due to fraud, the penalty imposed is 75 percent of the underpayment (the "civil fraud" penalty). Code Sec. 6663(a). Once the IRS establishes that any portion of an underpayment is due to fraud, the entire underpayment is assumed to be attributable to fraud, unless the taxpayer proves otherwise. Code Sec. 6662(b). The 20 percent accuracy-related penalty does not apply to any portion of an underpayment on which the fraud penalty is imposed. However, the accuracy-related penalty may be applied to any portion of the underpayment not attributable to fraud.

> *Example 24.16.* Beth Barrett owes a $50,000 deficiency, all due to civil fraud. In addition to the $50,000 tax deficiency, Beth will be liable for a $37,500 (75 percent of $50,000) civil fraud penalty.

Criminal Fraud Penalty

In addition to the civil fraud penalty, criminal fraud penalties may be imposed. Section 7201 provides that "any person who willfully attempts in any manner to evade or defeat any tax imposed by this title or the payment thereof shall, in addition to other penalties provided by law, be guilty of a felony. . . ." In order for there to be criminal fraud, the attempt to evade or defeat tax must be willful, which implies a "voluntary intentional violation of a known legal duty." *C.J. Bishop,* 73-1 USTC ¶ 9459, 412 U.S. 346, 93 S.Ct. 2008 (1973). Thus, an individual's behavior could not be willful if the actions are done through carelessness, or genuine misunderstanding of what the law requires.

A taxpayer convicted of criminal fraud is subject to a fine of up to $100,000 ($500,000 in the case of a corporation) or imprisonment of up to five years, or both, together with the costs of prosecution. Code Sec. 7201. The more important fraud provisions include the following:

1. Any person who willfully fails to collect or pay over withholding tax is guilty of a felony and, upon conviction, will be fined not more than $10,000, or imprisoned not more than five years, or both, together with the costs of prosecution. Code Sec. 7202.

2. Any person who willfully fails, when required, to pay estimated tax, to file a return, to keep records, or to supply information will be guilty of a misdemeanor and, upon conviction, will be fined not more than $25,000 ($100,000 in the case of a corporation) or imprisoned not more than one year, or both, together with the costs of prosecution. Code Sec. 7203.

3. Any person who willfully furnishes a false or fraudulent statement or who willfully fails to supply an employee with a statement of wages and withholdings will, if convicted, be fined not more than $1,000 or imprisoned not more than one year, or both. Code Sec. 7204.

4. Any person who willfully supplies false or fraudulent information regarding exemptions will, if convicted, be fined not more than $1,000 or imprisoned for not more than one year, or both. Code Sec. 7205.

5. Any person who is convicted under the fraud and false statement statute will be fined not more than $100,000 ($500,000 in the case of a corporation) or imprisoned not more than three years, or both, together with the costs of prosecution. Code Sec. 7206. This statute includes:

    a. Making a false declaration that is made under the penalties of perjury

    b. Aiding or assisting in preparation or presentation of returns, claims, or other documents that are false as to any material matter

    c. Simulating or falsely executing any bond or other document required by the internal revenue laws

    d. Removing, depositing, or concealing any property with intent to evade or defeat assessment or collection of any tax

    e. Concealing property or withholding, falsifying, or destroying records relating to the financial condition of the taxpayer in connection with an offer in compromise or a closing agreement

6. Any person who willfully delivers or discloses any list, return, statement or other document known to that person to be fraudulent or false as to any material matter will be fined not

more than $10,000 ($50,000 in the case of a corporation) or imprisoned not more than one year, or both. Code Sec. 7207.

Estimated Taxes and Underpayment Penalties

All taxpayers are generally required to make interim tax payments of substantially all of their accrued tax liability for the current year. For individuals, this is generally accomplished through withholding. Where withholding is insufficient, however, as is frequently the case with self-employed individuals, the taxpayer must file a declaration of estimated tax and may have to make quarterly estimated tax payments. The specific requirements are set forth in ¶ 8165.

If the total amount of tax paid through withholding and estimated tax payments is not enough, an underpayment penalty is imposed. The underpayment is computed on a quarterly basis and the interest penalty is then applied to these quarterly underpayments. Code Sec. 6654(d)(1). The charge runs until the amount is paid or until the due date of the return, whichever is earlier. An individual taxpayer can avoid the penalty for underpayment if the payments of estimated tax are at least as large as any one of the following:

1. 90 percent of the tax shown on the return or 100 percent (105 percent if adjusted gross income exceeds $150,000) of the tax shown on the return for the preceding taxable year (assuming it showed a tax liability and covered a taxable year of 12 months). Code Sec. 6654(d)(1)(A) and (B).

2. An amount equal to 90 percent of the tax for the taxable year computed by annualizing the taxable income received for the months in the taxable year ending before the month in which the installment is required to be paid. Code Sec. 6654(d)(2).

The underpayment penalty can be waived if the underpayment is due to casualty, disaster, or other unusual circumstances, or occurs during the first two years after a taxpayer retired after reaching age 62, or became disabled. Code Sec. 6654(e)(3).

A penalty is also imposed on corporations by Code Sec. 6655 for any underpayment of estimated corporate tax. However, no penalty is imposed if the corporation pays estimated tax at least as large as any one of the following:

1. The tax shown on the return of the corporation for the preceding year

2. The tax based on the prior year's income but determined under the current year's rates

3. The tax shown on the return of the corporation for the current year.

4. An amount equal to at least 100 percent of the tax due on the current year's taxable income for specified cutoff periods and on an annualized basis. Code Sec. 6655(d)(1)(B)(ii) and (e).

Note: Large corporations (those with taxable income of $1 million or more in any one of the three preceding tax years) do not qualify for the first two exceptions.

Failure to Make Deposits of Taxes

Employers are liable for payment of the tax that must be withheld. Code Sec. 3402. Unless underpayment is due to reasonable cause and not due to willful neglect, a penalty of as much as 10 percent of the amount of the underpayment may be imposed. Code Sec. 6656(a).

Tax Preparer Penalties

If an income tax return preparer, in preparing a tax return with an understatement of tax liability, takes a frivolous position or one for which there is not a realistic possibility of being sustained on its merits, the penalty is $250 as to that return. Code Sec. 6694(a). An "income tax return preparer" is any person who prepares for compensation or who employs one or more persons to prepare for compensation any return of tax or any claim for refund of tax. Code Sec. 7701(a)(36). No more than one individual associated with a firm will qualify as a preparer with respect to the same return or refund claim. Under the "one-preparer-per-firm" rule, should more than one member of a firm be involved in providing advice, the individual with supervisory responsibility for the matter will be subject to the penalty as a nonsigning preparer. Prop. Reg. § 1.6694-1. A preparer is not subject to penalty for failure to follow a rule or regulation if the preparer in good faith and with a reasonable basis takes the position that the rule or regulation does not accurately reflect the Code.

A $1,000 penalty per return applies if any part of any understatement of liability as to a return or claim for refund is due to a willful attempt to understate the liability or to any reckless or any intentional disregard of the rules or regulations. Code Sec. 6694(b).

> *Example 24.17.* A guarantee of a specific amount of refund by a preparer is an example of an action that would give rise to this penalty. Or if the preparer intentionally disregards information given by the taxpayer in order to reduce the taxpayer's liability, the preparer is guilty of a willful attempt to understate tax liability.

TAX PLANNING POINTER

This does not mean that the preparer may not rely in good faith on the information furnished by the taxpayer. However, the preparer must make reasonable inquiries if the information furnished by the taxpayer appears to be incorrect or incomplete.

A $50 penalty applies each time a preparer (1) fails to furnish a copy of the return to the taxpayer, (2) fails to sign the return, or (3) fails to furnish an identifying number. Code Sec. 6695(a)-(c). The maximum amount for each of these penalties is limited to $25,000. Any preparer who fails to retain a copy of the returns prepared or a list of the returns prepared is liable for a penalty of $50 for each such failure, with a maximum fine of $25,000 applicable to any one return period. Code Sec. 6695(d). A penalty of $50 applies for each failure to retain and make available to the IRS upon request a list of the preparers employed during a return period and $50 for each failure to set forth a required item in the information list (to a maximum of $25,000 for any single return period). Code Sec. 6695(e). Any preparer who endorses or otherwise negotiates a refund check issued to a taxpayer for a return or claim for refund prepared by the preparer is liable for a penalty of $500 with respect to each such check. Code Sec. 6695(f).

¶ 24,370 DISCLOSURE OF A POSITION ON A RETURN

The taxpayer may avoid the substantial-understatement penalty and the tax return preparer may avoid the penalty for taking a position for which there is not a realistic possibility of being sustained on its merits by disclosing the item on Form 8275, Disclosure Statement. To avoid the accuracy-related penalty, the taxpayer must disclose any nonfrivolous position for which there is not substantial authority but which has a reasonable basis. Code Sec. 6662(d)(2)(B)(ii). Similarly, the tax return preparer may avoid the $250 Code Sec. 6694(a) penalty if any nonfrivolous position that does not have a realistic possibility of being sustained on its merits is disclosed on Form 8275. The "realistic possibility" standard is treated in the regulations as being identical to the "substantial authority" standard in Code Sec. 6662(d)(2)(B)(i). Reg. § 1.6694-2(b)(1). Thus, the requirement for disclosure in order to avoid the accuracy-related penalty is identical for both taxpayers and tax preparers, even though the statutory language differs somewhat. Once adequate disclosure has been made, tax preparers are not subject to the penalty as long as the position taken is not frivolous (i.e., not patently improper). Reg. § 1.6694-2(c)(1) and (2). For taxpayers, however, the position taken must have a "reasonable basis," in order to avoid the penalty. Code Sec. 6662(d)(2)(B)(ii)(II). The regulations treat this standard as "significantly higher than the not frivolous standard applicable to preparers." Reg. § § 1.6662-3(b)(3)(ii) and 1.6662-4(e)(2)(i).

¶ 24,375 ETHICS RULES FOR PRACTITIONERS

CPAs and attorneys must practice according to the code of professional ethics of their professions. The codes are similar to Treasury Department Circular No. 230. The Tax Committee of the American Institute of Certified Public Accountants also issued 10 statements on selected topics between 1964 and 1977. The first two statements were withdrawn in 1982. The eight remaining statements were revised and renumbered in 1988. In a strict sense, the statements do not state any legal or ethical responsibilities. They are really only advisory opinions of the Committee as to what are appropriate standards of conduct in certain situations. Yet, tax practitioners should be familiar with the statements since they indicate the viewpoint of the AICPA and some accounting firms use the statements as policy in their firms. In addition, since the statements indicate standards followed by members of the accounting profession, a violation thereof might mean that "due care" has not been exercised and the CPA might be subject to charges of negligence. Summaries of the current eight "Statements on Responsibilities in Tax Practice" follow.

1. With respect to tax return positions, a CPA should comply with the following standards:

    a. A CPA should not recommend to a client that a position be taken with respect to the tax treatment of any item on a return unless the CPA has a good faith belief that the position has a realistic possibility of being sustained administratively or judicially on its merits if challenged.

    b. A CPA should not prepare or sign a return if the CPA knows that the return takes a position that the CPA could not recommend under the standard expressed in paragraph 1(a).

    c. A CPA may recommend a position that the CPA concludes is not frivolous so long as the position is adequately disclosed on the return.

    d. In recommending tax return positions and in signing returns, a CPA should, where relevant, advise the client as to the potential penalty consequences of the recommended tax return position, and the opportunity, if any, to avoid such penalties through disclosure.

    The CPA should not recommend a tax return position that exploits the Internal Revenue Service audit selection process or serves as a mere "arguing" position solely to obtain leverage in the bargaining process of settlement negotiation with the Internal Revenue Service.

2. The CPA should make a reasonable effort to obtain from the client, and provide, appropriate answers to all questions on a tax return before signing as a preparer.

    Statement No. 2 indicates that reasonable grounds may exist for omitting an answer:

    a. The information is not readily available and the answer is not significant in terms of taxable income or loss or the tax liability shown on the return.

    b. Genuine uncertainty exists regarding the meaning of a question in relation to the particular return.

    c. The answer to the question is voluminous; in such cases, assurance should be given on the return that the data will be supplied upon an examination.

3. In preparing a return, the CPA may in good faith rely without verification upon information furnished by the client. The CPA should make reasonable inquiries if the information fur-

nished appears to be incorrect, incomplete, or inconsistent either on its face or on the basis of other facts known to the CPA. The CPA should refer to the client's returns for proper years whenever feasible.

Where the Internal Revenue Code or income tax regulations impose a condition with respect to deductibility or other tax treatment of an item, the CPA should make appropriate inquiries to determine whether such condition has been met.

4. A CPA may prepare tax returns involving the use of the taxpayer's estimates if it is impracticable to obtain exact data, and the estimated amounts are reasonable under the facts and circumstances known to the CPA. When estimates are used, they should be presented in a way that avoids the implication of greater accuracy than exists. Estimated amounts should not be presented in a manner which provides a misleading impression as to the degree of factual accuracy.

There are unusual circumstances where disclosure that an estimate is used is necessary to avoid misleading the Internal Revenue Service regarding the degree of accuracy of the return. Some examples of unusual circumstances are as follows:

a. The taxpayer has died or is ill at the time the return must be filed.

b. The taxpayer has not received a K-1 for a flow-through entity at the time the return must be filed.

c. There is litigation pending which bears on the return.

d. Fire or computer failure destroyed relevant records.

5. The recommendation of a position to be taken concerning the tax treatment of an item in the preparation of a tax return should be based upon the facts and the law as they are evaluated at the time the return is prepared. Unless the taxpayer is bound as to tax treatment in a later year, the disposition of an item in an administrative proceeding does not govern the taxpayer in the treatment of a similar item in a later year's return. Therefore, if the CPA follows the standards of Statement No. 1, the CPA may recommend a tax return position, or prepare a tax return that departs from the treatment of an item as concluded in an administrative proceeding or a court decision regarding a prior year's return.

6. The CPA should advise the client promptly upon learning of an error in a previously filed return, or upon learning of a client's failure to file a required return. The CPA should recommend the measures to be taken and such recommendation may be given orally. The CPA should not inform the IRS, and may not do so without the client's permission, except where required by law.

If the CPA is requested to prepare the current year's return and the client has not taken appropriate action to correct an error in a prior year's return, the CPA should consider whether to withdraw from preparing the return. If the CPA does prepare the current year's return, the CPA should take reasonable steps to ensure that the error is not repeated.

7. When the CPA is representing a client in an administrative proceeding with respect to a return which contains an error known to the CPA, the CPA should inform the client promptly upon becoming aware of the error. The CPA should recommend the measures to be taken and this recommendation may be given orally. The CPA is neither obligated to inform the IRS nor permitted to do so without the client's permission, except where required by law.

The CPA should require the client's agreement to disclose the error to the IRS. Lacking such agreement, the CPA should consider whether to withdraw from representing the client and whether to continue a professional relationship with the client.

8. In providing tax advice to clients, the CPA should use judgment to ensure that the advice reflects professional competence and appropriately serves the client's needs. No standard format or guidelines need be followed in communicating written or oral advice to a client.

The CPA may communicate with a client when subsequent developments affect advice previously provided with respect to significant matters. However, the CPA cannot be expected to communicate later developments except while assisting a client in implementing procedures or plans associated with the advice provided or unless the CPA undertakes this obligation by specific agreement with the client.

TAX BLUNDERS

1. Laura Lerner found out that taxpayers have either partially or completely won around 50 percent of cases brought to the Tax Court. Therefore, she decides on litigation in the Tax Court, where she thinks she has a fairly good chance of being successful. However, in looking at the tax issue with which Laura is concerned, a tax researcher discovers that the taxpayer has never won a case like hers. Laura should not have relied on the overall statistics.

2. Edward Enders decides to take his case to the Tax Court because then he does not have to pay the tax before litigation. After some time has passed, someone tells him that a jury would probably have looked favorably on his case, and now he wants to go to District Court. Having gone to the Tax Court, Edward cannot now take his case to District Court.

3. Vera Vokel, known for her temper, her frugality, and her dislike for the IRS, is requested to come in to the local IRS office for an office examination. Although she had a CPA prepare her return, she decides she would like to save the fees

it might cost her to have the CPA represent her and, therefore, decides to go in alone for the examination. In the course of the discussion, she becomes furious at the auditor and is disallowed her items at issue. Vera should have had her CPA represent her and she should probably not have been present herself so that the audit could be conducted in a businesslike and unemotional manner.

SUMMARY OF CHAPTER 24

✓ The primary authoritative sources of the law are statutory, administrative, and judicial.

✓ The taxpayer can appeal within the IRS and/or decide to go to Tax Court, the District Court, or the Court of Federal Claims, and then attempt to appeal to the Court of Appeals and the Supreme Court.

✓ A tax researcher can use loose-leaf tax services, a citator, other types of secondary reference materials, or electronic tax research systems and the internet in the research process.

✓ The Internal Revenue Service consists of the national office, 4 regional centers, 33 district offices, 5 service centers, the National Computer Center, and the IRS Data Center.

✓ The examination of tax returns can be as simple as a correspondence examination or a more involved office examination or field examination.

✓ A tax practice can involve tax compliance and tax planning.

✓ Communications between the IRS and taxpayers can include private letter rulings, determination letters, and technical advice.

✓ There are numerous penalties to which taxpayers and tax preparers may be subject.

✓ The knowledge and use of ethics is very important for the tax practitioner.

CHAPTER 24 QUESTIONS

1. Does the Internal Revenue Code of 1986 include pre-1986 tax law?

2. In which Subtitle and Chapter of the Internal Revenue Code is the majority of the income tax law found?

3. Are the federal courts bound to follow Treasury Regulations when deciding a tax case?

4. Do Regulations have higher authority in federal tax law than Revenue Rulings?

5. List the various "administrative" sources of tax law.

6. How is the manner of citing a Revenue Ruling or a Revenue Procedure affected by the passage of time?

7. In which Judicial Circuit is the District of Columbia?

8. List the three trial courts that have jurisdiction over tax cases.

9. What are the primary differences between Regular and Memorandum decisions of the U.S. Tax Court?

10. Is an announcement of acquiescence by the Commissioner of Internal Revenue legally binding upon the IRS?

11. What do the following abbreviations represent? CCH, RIA, BTA, USTC, AFTR, AFTR2d, S.Ct., CA-3, TCM.

12. Which tax service is known for its willingness to take a stand on controversial issues not covered by legislation or tax law?

13. Which tax service is frequently quoted in judicial decisions?

14. Refer to the Sue Wilson research illustration in the chapter (Case #1). Assume, at the time of filing her 1998 tax return, Sue Wilson believed she would receive a recovery on a claim for the full value of the automobile. However, in August 1999, Sue received only $8,000 from the insurance company. How much of a loss will she claim in 1998? In 1999? (Give your answer before consideration of the 10 percent of AGI limitation.)

15. Which computer-based research system contains the text of tax treaties?

16. Where can the historical record of a court case be found?

17. Describe the organization of the Internal Revenue Service.

18. Who may practice before the Internal Revenue Service?

19. Define and distinguish between a Private Letter Ruling, a Determination Letter, and a Technical Advice Memorandum.

20. Define DIF; TCMP.

21. What events might cause an IRS examination?

22. What kind of taxpayer errors could be solved by mail?

23. What types of tax issues lend themselves to an interview or office examination?

24. Why might a taxpayer in a field examination want to make every effort to settle with the revenue agent?

25. Define 30-day letter; 90-day letter.

26. Describe the appeals process within the IRS.

27. Describe the trial and appellate court system for federal tax litigation.

28. What factors should a taxpayer consider in choosing a tax forum?

29. What are the two delinquency penalties?

30. What could constitute "reasonable cause" for purposes of the delinquency penalties?

31. What is the negligence penalty?

32. What two parties might be subject to the understatement of tax liability penalty?

33. Describe the valuation overstatement penalty.

34. How may an individual avoid a penalty for underpayment of tax liability?

35. Jim files his return one month after the due date and pays the remaining $8,000 of tax owed by him. What are his delinquency penalties?

36. Due to negligence, Rose underpaid her taxes by $20,000. What is her negligence penalty?

37. Olivia is being audited by the IRS. The revenue agent determines that certain expenses that were deducted on her return are not valid, and he accordingly makes adjustments to her tax liability. Upon receipt of her 30-day letter, she phones you, a CPA, for advice regarding possible future action on the matter. What options would you discuss with Olivia?

CHAPTER 24 PROBLEMS

38. Based upon the organization of the Internal Revenue Code, what general topic would be covered in Code Sec. 731?

    a. Capital gains and losses

    b. Partners and partnerships

    c. Exempt organizations

    d. Insurance companies

39. Which of the following is published in the *Federal Register?*

    a. Technical Information Releases

    b. Revenue Rulings

    c. Revenue Procedures

    d. Treasury Regulations

40. To read an IRS Revenue Ruling that was issued within the past week which source should be used?

    a. Internal Revenue Code

    b. Cumulative Bulletin

    c. Federal Register

    d. Internal Revenue Bulletin

41. Which of the following publications includes the memorandum decisions of the United States Tax Court?

    a. Federal Register

    b. Cumulative Bulletin

    c. Internal Revenue Bulletin

    d. Tax Court Memorandum Decisions (TCM) (published by CCH)

    e. U.S. Tax Cases (USTC) (published by CCH)

42. Matthew, a sole proprietor, employs Timothy as his full-time employee. Timothy's 1997 tax return is being audited by the IRS. Because of Timothy's high regard for Matthew's knowledge and judgment, Timothy has asked Matthew to represent him in the audit. May Matthew represent Timothy?

43. Marvin filed his 1996 tax return on August 15, 1997, having obtained an automatic extension of time to file. However, not having the money to pay the tax bill at that time, he arranged with the IRS to pay his tax liability six months later. On February 15, 1998, Marvin paid the tax. Subsequently, on November 13, 1998, he discovered a deduction that he neglected to take on his 1996 return and he wishes to file a claim for a refund. May he do so?

44. Your client, Steve, is an engineer whose income has doubled over the past four years. He feels that by incorporating he could reduce his tax significantly. However, he can demonstrate no business purpose for incorporating as he is employed by an international oil company and he does no outside work. He asks you to request a ruling from the IRS regarding his proposed incorporation. Would you request a ruling for him?

45. Ron mailed his 1997 federal tax return on April 15, 1998, attaching only a first-class postage stamp. However, the postage should have been higher since the return weighed three ounces. His return is sent back to him on April 20, 1998, at which time he pays the additional postage. Will Ron be required to pay a delinquency penalty?

46. Carolyn, an accountant for Douglas Corporation, prepares the quarterly payroll tax returns. For the second quarter of 1998, she showed $15,000 as the amount of the deposit on the return. However, the actual deposit was $10,000. What penalty, if any, may be imposed as a result of this error?

47. Karen engaged Joe, a CPA, to prepare her tax return. Karen received a refund check of $300 from the IRS. She endorsed the check and mailed it to Joe as payment for the preparation of her return. Joe took the check to his bank and deposited the amount in his bank account. Describe the possible consequences of this situation.

48. Jim, a retail merchant, reported the following on his 1997 return:

Sales $200,000
Cost of goods sold . . . . $ 80,000
Gross profit $120,000

What amount must be omitted from income for the six-year statute of limitations to apply?

49. Andrea, a CPA, is representing her client, Rodney, in an administrative proceeding. In the course of this engagement, she discovers an error in the return that may result in a material understatement of tax liability. What, if anything, should Andrea do with regard to this discovery?

50. Mary, a CPA, prepared Gordon's tax return for the current year. In preparing his return, she took a deduction that is contrary to the Code. She feels that he is entitled to this deduction because of her belief that possible conflicts exist between two sections of the Internal Revenue Code. Is Mary in conflict with the AICPA "Statements on Responsibilities in Tax Practice"?

51. An individual files an income tax return for the calendar-year 1997 on September 19, 1998, and pays $1,200, which is the balance of the tax due. Disregarding interest, how much in delinquency penalties would he have to pay?

52. Tommy gives a painting to a church and takes a charitable contribution deduction in the amount of $5,000. If the actual value was only $2,000 and if the tax underpayment is $1,200, how much valuation overstatement penalty should he pay?

53. Sandy had the following items on her timely filed 1997 income tax return:

Gross receipts $400,000
Cost of goods sold . . . . ($300,000)
Capital gain . . . . $ 20,000
Capital loss . . . . ($ 30,000)

Sandy inadvertently omitted some income on her 1997 return. What is the statute of limitations if she omitted $100,000 of income on the return? What if she omitted $120,000 of income?

54. On February 15, 1996, Brent filed his 1995 income tax return (due April 15, 1996), and he paid a tax of $15,000 at that time. On June 10, 1997, he filed an amended 1995 return showing an additional $3,000 of tax which was then paid. In 1998, Brent found that he should claim a refund of $6,000

because he failed to take some deductions to which he was entitled. What amount can he recover if he files the claim for refund on March 14, 1999? What if he files the claim on May 15, 1999?

55. Angela filed her 1997 income tax return on February 14, 1998, showing gross income of $20,000. She mistakenly deducted a $6,000 casualty loss that in good faith she considered deductible. By what date must the IRS assert a notice of deficiency?

    a. February 14, 2001

    b. April 15, 2001

    c. February 14, 2004

    d. April 15, 2004

56. Harold and Maude filed a joint return for 1997 reporting:

    Gross business income $400,000
    Net business income   80,000
    Net capital gain......................................   40,000

    Maude inadvertently omitted some income from this return. The six-year statute applies only if Maude's omitted gross income exceeds:

    a. $20,000

    b. $30,000

    c. $100,000

    d. $110,000

57. Reginald filed his 1997 income tax return on January 15, 1998. On November 1, 1998, he learned that his investment of $10,000 in 1,000 shares of Ultimate Corp. had become worthless in 1997. What is the last day on which he must file an amended 1997 return to claim this loss?

    a. January 15, 2001

    b. April 15, 2001

    c. November 1, 2001

    d. April 15, 2005

58. If a practitioner who is authorized to practice before the IRS knows that a client has not complied with the revenue laws of the United States with respect to a matter administered by the IRS, the practitioner is required to:

    a. Advise the client of the noncompliance

    b. Immediately notify the IRS

    c. Do nothing

    d. Advise his client and immediately notify the IRS

59. Anna's 1996 individual tax return was examined and the IRS proposed changes resulting in additional tax. Anna wishes to bypass the IRS's appeal system and file a refund suit in the United States Court of Federal Claims on contested income tax issues. Your advice to Anna should be:

    a. Request that her return be reexamined

    b. Pay all of the additional tax and file another Form 1040 tax return

    c. Pay all of the additional tax, then file a claim for refund and request in writing that the claim be immediately rejected

    d. File a claim for refund and do nothing else

60. Peter's return was examined and the result was additional tax of $16,000 due to unreported lottery winnings. Peter has received a letter notifying him of his right to appeal the proposed changes within 30 days. Which of the following should Peter do in preparing his appeal?

    a. Call the examiner and request a conference

    b. Provide a brief written statement of the disputed issues

    c. Submit a written protest within the time limit specified

    d. Submit a written protest explaining additional expenses not previously claimed

61. Which of the following statements is not correct in respect to tax return preparer penalties?

    a. For tax returns that are due (without extension) after December 31, 1989, the penalty for an understatement due to the preparer's negligent or intentional disregard of one or more rules or regulations is $250; for willful understatement of liability the penalty is $1,000.

    b. If a preparer in good faith and with reasonable basis takes the position that a rule or regulation does not accurately reflect the Code, he or she is not subject to either penalty.

    c. The IRS has the burden of proof that a preparer has negligently or intentionally disregarded a rule or regulation.

    d. Many Code sections require the existence of specific facts and circumstances. In order to avoid a penalty, a preparer shall make appropriate inquiries of the taxpayer to determine that the requirements have been met incident to claiming a deduction.

62. *Research Problem.* What is the current status of Revenue Ruling 57-82?

63. *Research Problem.* Section 303(b)(2)(A)(ii) makes reference to two other Code sections. What are they?

64. *Research Problem.* Which Revenue Ruling does Rev. Rul. 76-74 supersede?

65. *Research Problem.* What is the date of IRS Letter Ruling 8302032?

66. *Research Problem.* On what date was Reg. § 1.274-8 adopted?

67. *Research Problem.* What Code Section immediately follows Code Sec. 280?

68. *Research Problem.* Refer to a citator and locate the following case: *New York Life Insurance Co. v. Edwards.*

    a.   What happened on appeal to the Court of Appeals?

    b.   What happened on appeal to the Supreme Court?

69. *Research Problem.* What Code sections cover the standard deduction, trade or business expenses, losses, medical expenses, and moving expenses?

70. *Research Problem.* What two Code sections are referred to in Code Sec. 56(f)(2)(F)(ii)(II)?

71. *Research Problem.* Refer to the *Pennsylvania Indemnity Co.* case in a citator. What was the disposition of the case on appeal to the Supreme Court from the Court of Appeals?

72. *Research Problem.* Reg. § 1.212-1(n) refers to two Code Sections. What are they?

73. *Research Problem.* Refer to *Black's Law Dictionary* or a similar legal reference book and ascertain the definition of the following words or terms: annotated, certiorari, remanded, dictum, acquiesced.

74. *Research Problem.* A taxpayer has a cellular telephone, used 45 percent for business and 55 percent for personal use. Is the MACRS depreciation method allowable?

75. *Research Problem.* What is the effective date of Code Sec. 1031(f)?

76. *Research Problem.* A borrower is personally liable on a real estate mortgage with an outstanding balance of $1.5 million. Borrower's basis in the property is $1 million and the property has a current fair market value of $1.2 million. The property is repossessed by the bank.

    a.   If the borrower is insolvent both before and after the repossession, what taxable gain, if any, is recognized by borrower?

    b.   Does your answer to (a) change if the borrower is not personally liable on the mortgage (i.e., a nonrecourse debt)? Why or why not?

77. *Research Problem.* Anthony Antunicci, a Massachusetts lawyer, has tired of the long, cold New England winters. He recently spent three months in Florida where he took a Florida bar review course which enabled him to successfully pass the Florida bar exam. He has since opened a second law office in Coral Gables and plans to work in that office from January through March each year. His younger brother, Joey, will operate their Boston office in his absence.

Can Anthony deduct the cost of the Florida bar review course as an education expense since he has already established himself in the profession of being a lawyer by previously passing the Massachusetts bar exam?

(Hint: to answer this question using CCH CD-ROM, use the search term: (lawyer or attorney) and (bar review course and second state).)

78. *Research Problem.* Jane was notified by the IRS that she should appear at the local IRS district office with records supporting travel expense deductions taken on her 1995 tax return. Because she had to meet with some clients, she did not appear at the IRS office, nor did she bother to make an appointment for an alternative time. To what penalty or penalties could Jane be subject?

79. *Research Problem.* A corporate client was the target of a hostile takeover by a corporate raider. In successfully thwarting the hostile takeover, the Board of Directors incurred legal fees of $100,000.

a. What is the proper tax treatment of these fees?

b. Assume that the takeover was friendly. Does this change your answer? If so, explain why your answer is different

80. An oil tanker collided with a ship in Tampa Bay. The resulting oil spill severely curtailed the fishing business for two months. The Franklin Fishing Boat Co. made a claim against the tanker's owner for impairment of Franklin's revenue during the two-month period. Mr. Franklin received an initial payment of $50,000 from the tanker's owner, $20,000 of which was for lost revenue and $30,000 of which was for punitive damages allowed by state law from a handler of hazardous substances. How much of the award, if any, is taxable?

Appendix

TAX RATE SCHEDULES FOR 1998

Since 1993, income has been taxed at the following rates: 15 percent, 28 percent, 31 percent, 36 percent, and 39.6 percent. The maximum marginal income tax rate in the statutory structure in Code Sec. 1 is 39.6 percent.

For high-income taxpayers, the phaseout of personal exemptions and the overall limitation on itemized deductions become additional adjustments apart from the statutory rate structure (see explanation on the following pages). These adjustments may result in an effective top marginal tax rate that is greater than 39.6 percent. The 39.6 percent marginal brackets, adjusted for inflation, begin at the following amounts for tax years beginning in 1998: single taxpayers—$278,450; married individuals filing jointly—$278,450; heads of households—$278,450; and married individuals filing separately—$139,225.

The tax rate schedules are subject to an inflation adjustment based on methods prescribed by the Internal Revenue Code. The income ranges and the applicable dollar amounts are adjusted to reflect increases in the Consumer Price Index (CPI). The CPI increase applicable to 1998 is provided in Rev. Proc. 97-57, 1997-52 IRB 20, and the schedules below and on the following page reflect this adjustment.

Tax Rate Schedule X below is to be used by single individuals or by married persons treated as unmarried that have taxable incomes of $100,000 or more.

SINGLE INDIVIDUALS—SCHEDULE X

Taxable Income Over	Not Over	Pay	+	Tax Rate % ×	On Excess Over
$ 0	$ 25,350	$ 0		15	$ 0
25,350	61,400	3,802.50		28	25,350
61,400	128,100	13,896.50		31	61,400
128,100	278,450	34,573.50		36	128,100
278,450	—	88,699.50		39.6	278,450

Tax Rate Schedule Y-1 below is to be used by married taxpayers filing jointly and by surviving spouses that have taxable incomes of $100,000 or more.

MARRIED INDIVIDUALS, JOINT RETURNS AND SURVIVING SPOUSES—SCHEDULE Y-1

Taxable Income Over	Not Over	Pay	+ Tax Rate % ×	On Excess Over
$ 0	$ 42,350	$ 0	15	$ 0
42,350	102,300	6,352.50	28	42,350
102,300	155,950	23,138.50	31	102,300
155,950	278,450	39,770.00	36	155,950
278,450	—	83,870.00	39.6	278,450

Tax Rate Schedule Y-2 below is to be used by married taxpayers filing separately and by the bankruptcy estate of an individual debtor that have taxable incomes of $100,000 or more.

MARRIED INDIVIDUALS, SEPARATE RETURNS—SCHEDULE Y-2

Taxable Income Over	Not Over	Pay	+ Tax Rate % ×	On Excess Over
$ 0	$ 21,175	$ 0	15	$ 0
21,175	51,150	3,176.25	28	21,175
51,150	77,975	11,569.25	31	51,150
77,975	139,225	19,885.00	36	77,975
139,225	—	41,935.00	39.6	139,225

Tax Rate Schedule Z below is to be used by individuals who qualify as heads of households that have taxable incomes of $100,000 or more.

HEADS OF HOUSEHOLDS—SCHEDULE Z

Taxable Income Over	Not Over	Pay	+ Tax Rate % ×	On Excess Over
$ 0	$ 33,950	$ 0	15	$ 0
33,950	87,700	5,092.50	28	33,950
87,700	142,000	20,142.50	31	87,700
142,000	278,450	36,975.50	36	142,000
278,450	—	86,097.50	39.6	278,450

High-income taxpayers—phaseout of personal exemptions. The deduction for personal exemptions is reduced or even eliminated for certain high-income taxpayers. If a taxpayer's adjusted gross income exceeds the appropriate threshold amount (based on filing status), the deduction for exemptions is reduced by 2 percent for each $2,500 ($1,250 in the case of a married person filing separately) or fraction thereof by which the adjusted gross income exceeds the threshold amount. For 1998, the threshold amounts are: $186,800—married taxpayers filing jointly, or surviving spouses; $155,650—heads of households; $124,500—single taxpayers (not surviving spouses or heads of households); $93,400—married individuals filing separate returns.

High-income taxpayers—limitation on itemized deductions. An individual whose adjusted gross income exceeds a threshold amount is required to reduce the amount allowable for itemized deductions by 3 percent of the excess over that threshold. For 1998, the threshold amount is $62,250 ($124,500 for married persons filing a separate return). These thresholds are to be annually adjusted for inflation.

Capital gains. The Taxpayer Relief Act of 1997 significantly changed the taxation of capital gains. The new rules divide long-term capital gains (on assets held greater than 12 months) into three categories: long-term capital gains taxed at a maximum rate of 28 percent, long-term capital gains taxed at a maximum rate of 25 percent, and long-term capital gains taxed at a maximum rate of 20 percent.

To qualify for the 20 percent long-term capital gain tax rate, the capital asset must be held for more than 18 months. For taxpayers in the 15 percent tax bracket, this long-term capital gains tax rate becomes 10 percent. The 28 percent long-term capital gains tax rate applies to capital assets held more than one year but not more than 18 months. This holding period is sometimes referred to as the "mid-term" holding period. However, the 28 percent long-term capital gains tax rate also applies to collectibles and Section 1202 gains. Generally, collectibles (as defined in Code Sec. 408(m)) include works of art, rugs, antiques, metal, gems, stamps, coins, and alcoholic beverages. Section 1202 stock is certain small business stock held more than five years. Gains on the disposition of Section 1202 stock qualifies for a 50 percent exclusion. Stock qualifying for the exclusion is not eligible for the 20 percent tax rate and is included in the 28 percent long-term capital gains tax rate category.

The 25 percent long-term capital gains tax rate applies to what is referred to as "unrecaptured Section 1250 gain." Unrecaptured Section 1250 gain is the amount of the long-term capital gain that would be treated as ordinary income if a Section 1250 asset were classified as a Section 1245 asset.

Tax Rate Schedule for Estates and Trusts. Since 1991, the following rate schedule has applied to trusts and estates. The tax brackets have been reduced so as not to increase the benefit of the lower brackets that might otherwise arise from the 39.6 percent marginal tax rate bracket. The Tax Rate Schedule below is to be used by an estate or trust to compute the amount of its income tax. Neither entity can use the tax tables.

ESTATES AND TRUSTS

Taxable Income Over	Not Over	Pay	+	Tax Rate % ×	On Excess Over
$ 0	$1,700	$ 0		15	$ 0
1,700	4,000	255.00		28	1,700
4,000	6,100	899.00		31	4,000
6,100	8,350	1,550.00		36	6,100
8,350	—	2,360.00		39.6	8,350

Tax Rate Schedule for Corporations. A graduated rate structure is employed in computing the income tax liability of corporate taxpayers. The 5 percent additional tax rate that applies to phase out the benefits of the graduated rates is incorporated in the rate schedule. The phaseout occurs between $100,000 and $335,000 of taxable income by means of an increase in the maximum 34 percent rate to 39 percent.

CORPORATIONS

Taxable Income Over	Not Over	Pay	+ Tax Rate % ×	On Excess Over
$ 0	$ 50,000	$ 0	15	$ 0
50,000	75,000	7,500	25	50,000
75,000	100,000	13,750	34	75,000
100,000	335,000	22,250	39	100,000
335,000	10,000,000	113,900	34	335,000
10,000,000	15,000,000	3,400,000	35	10,000,000
15,000,000	18,333,333	5,150,000	38	15,000,000
18,333,333	—	6,416,667	35	18,333,333

UNIFIED ESTATE AND GIFT TAX RATES

Unified credit. The unified credit for estates of decedents dying in 1998 is $202,050. Any part of the credit used to offset gift taxes is not available to offset estate taxes.

Estate tax. Estate taxes are computed by applying the unified rate schedule to the cumulated at-death and lifetime transfers and subtracting the gift taxes payable. The unified rate schedule is effective for gifts made after December 31, 1976, and for estates of decedents dying after that date.

Gift tax. Gift taxes are computed by applying the unified rate schedule to lifetime taxable transfers and subtracting the taxes payable for prior taxable periods. There is an annual $10,000 exclusion for gifts, with an annual maximum of $20,000 for spouses who split gifts. Additionally, there is an unlimited exclusion for payments of tuition and medical expenses.

Generation-skipping transfer tax. The generation-skipping transfer tax is computed with reference to a flat rate equal to the product of the maximum estate tax rate of 55 percent and the inclusion ratio with respect to the transfer. The method for computing the taxable amount depends on whether a taxable distribution, a taxable termination, or a direct skip is involved. For a taxable distribution as well as a direct skip, the amount received by the transferee is subject to the tax. In the case of a taxable termination, the tax is applied to the value of the property in which the interest terminates. Two exemptions from the tax are provided: (1) a $1 million per transferor exemption that can be allocated among several generation-skipping transfers and (2) an exemption for transfers to grandchildren of a grantor when the grandchild's parent, who is a lineal descendant of the grantor, is deceased.

Benefits phased out for transfers exceeding $10,000,000. The benefits of the graduated rates and the unified credit under the unified transfer tax system are phased out beginning with cumulative transfers rising above $10,000,000. This is accomplished by adding 5 percent of the excess of any transfer over $10,000,000 to the tentative tax computed in determining the ultimate transfer tax liability. For estates of decedents dying, and gifts made, after 1987 and before 1998, the tax is levied on amounts transferred in excess of $10,000,000 but not exceeding $21,040,000, in order to recapture the benefit of any transfer tax rate below 55 percent as well as the unified credit.

UNIFIED TRANSFER TAX RATE SCHEDULE
Estates of Decedents Dying and Gifts Made After 1983

Taxable Amount Over	Not Over	Tax	Rate of Tax + % ×	On Excess Over
$ 0	$ 10,000	$ 0	18	$ 0
10,000	20,000	1,800	20	10,000
20,000	40,000	3,800	22	20,000
40,000	60,000	8,200	24	40,000
60,000	80,000	13,000	26	60,000
80,000	100,000	18,200	28	80,000
100,000	150,000	23,800	30	100,000
150,000	250,000	38,800	32	150,000
250,000	500,000	70,800	34	250,000
500,000	750,000	155,800	37	500,000
750,000	1,000,000	248,300	39	750,000
1,000,000	1,250,000	345,800	41	1,000,000
1,250,000	1,500,000	448,300	43	1,250,000
1,500,000	2,000,000	555,800	45	1,500,000
2,000,000	2,500,000	780,800	49	2,000,000
2,500,000	3,000,000	1,025,800	53	2,500,000
3,000,000	. . . . . .	1,290,800	55	3,000,000

STATE DEATH TAX CREDIT
Estates of Decedents Dying After 1976

Adjusted Taxable Estate * From	To	Credit = Amount	+ %	On Excess Over
$ 0	$ 40,000	$ 0	0	$ 0
40,000	90,000	0	.8	40,000
90,000	140,000	400	1.6	90,000
140,000	240,000	1,200	2.4	140,000
240,000	440,000	3,600	3.2	240,000
440,000	640,000	10,000	4	440,000
640,000	840,000	18,000	4.8	640,000
840,000	1,040,000	27,600	5.6	840,000
1,040,000	1,540,000	38,800	6.4	1,040,000
1,540,000	2,040,000	70,800	7.2	1,540,000
2,040,000	2,540,000	106,800	8	2,040,000
2,540,000	3,040,000	146,800	8.8	2,540,000
3,040,000	3,540,000	190,800	9.6	3,040,000
3,540,000	4,040,000	238,800	10.4	3,540,000
4,040,000	5,040,000	290,800	11.2	4,040,000
5,040,000	6,040,000	402,800	12	5,040,000
6,040,000	7,040,000	522,800	12.8	6,040,000
7,040,000	8,040,000	650,800	13.6	7,040,000
8,040,000	9,040,000	786,800	14.4	8,040,000
9,040,000	10,040,000	930,800	15.2	9,040,000
10,040,000	. . . . . .	1,082,800	16	10,040,000

* The adjusted taxable estate is the taxable estate reduced by $60,000.

Glossary of Tax Terms

This tax dictionary defines the words and phrases most commonly used in talking about federal taxes. The language of federal taxation is the language of law, accounting, and business. Many of the terms have precise, technical meanings, as compared with their meanings in everyday use. The definitions in this glossary are, of course, only adaptations of the full meanings prescribed by the law, regulations, and rulings, that are discussed in the explanatory text. Refer to this glossary for an introduction to the language of federal taxation.

— A —

Accelerated Cost Recovery System (ACRS)

This system of recovering the cost of capital expenditures through periodic depreciation deductions (allowances) is mandatory for most depreciable tangible property placed in service after 1980 and before 1987. These costs are recovered over specified recovery periods by means of statutory percentages that do not require the computation of a useful life. An alternative straight-line allowance may be elected over one of several alternate statutory recovery periods.

Assets placed in service after 1986 must generally be depreciated using a Modified Accelerated Cost Recovery System (MACRS). MACRS generally results in lower depreciation deductions than ACRS because many assets are assigned a longer recovery period. Assets are depreciated using prescribed recovery methods and conventions. The MACRS deduction, however, may be computed by using optional tables, which have ACRS style percentages.

Accounting method

A taxpayer's accounting method is the basis of accounting by which records are kept. Usually, either the *cash* basis or the *accrual* basis is used. Special methods of reporting income, such as the installment basis, are variations of these two methods.

Accounting period

An accounting period is the 12-month period on the basis of which the taxpayer's records are kept. If no books are kept or if no other period is specified, the accounting period is the calendar year. If the books are kept on the basis of a 12-month period ending with a month other than December, the accounting period is a *fiscal* year. A special 52-53-week accounting period is also recognized for income tax purposes.

Accrual basis of accounting

The *accrual* basis is distinguished from the *cash* basis. On the accrual basis, income is accounted for as and when it is earned, whether or not it has been collected. Expenses are deducted when they are incurred, whether or not paid in the same period. In determining when the expenses of an accrual-basis taxpayer are incurred, the all-events test is applied. This test provides that the expenses are deductible in the year in which all of the events have occurred that determine the fact of liability where the amount of the liability can be determined with reasonable accuracy. Generally, all of the events that establish liability for an amount, for the purpose of determining whether such amount has been incurred, are treated as not occurring any earlier than the time that economic performance occurs.

Accumulated adjustments account (AAA)

The accumulated adjustments account consists of post-1982 accumulated gross income less deductible expenses and prior distributions allocable to the account of an S corporation.

Accumulated earnings tax

This additional tax is imposed on a corporation that permits its earnings to accumulate, instead of being distributed, in order to avoid payment of tax on dividends by individual stockholders. Generally, a corporation may accumulate up to $250,000 (only $150,000 for some personal service companies) over the years without risk of incurring this special tax. The applicable amount, plus whatever additional amount is necessary to be retained for the reasonable needs of the business, is allowed as a credit against taxable income. Only the remainder of undistributed income is subject to the accumulated earnings tax.

Adjusted basis

The basis for gain or loss and the basis for depreciation, etc. are explained below under *Basis.* After such a basis is determined, it must be adjusted (a) for capital items that increase it and (b) for deductions that decrease it, such as depreciation, depletion, etc.

Adjusted gross income

Adjusted gross income is gross income reduced by trade or business expenses of individual taxpayers, expenses for property held for production of rents or royalties, and certain loss adjustments. The amount of the adjusted gross income affects the extent to which medical expenses, nonbusiness casualty and theft losses, and charitable contributions may be deducted.

Administrator

Like an executor, the administrator manages the estate of a person who dies intestate or whose named executor fails to act.

Affiliated corporate groups—See Controlled corporate groups

Age 65 and older standard deduction

A taxpayer who has attained the age of 65 before the close of the tax year is allowed an additional standard deduction amount of $850 if married; $1,050 if unmarried.

Alimony

In a legal sense, alimony is support payment made after divorce or legal separation. In some respects, the income tax law definition is broader. It includes payments made under a decree of divorce or separate maintenance, under a decree for support if a wife is separated from her husband, or under a written separation agreement executed by the husband and wife if the wife is separated from her husband and they file separate returns. Alimony payments that meet certain tests are deductible by the payer and are income to the recipient.

All-events test—See Accrual basis of accounting

Alternative minimum tax

Alternative minimum tax rules have been devised to ensure that at least a minimum amount of income tax is paid by corporate and high-income noncorporate taxpayers (including estates and trusts) who reap large tax savings by making use of certain tax deductions and exemptions. A taxpayer's AMT for a tax year is the excess of the tentative minimum tax over the regular tax and must be paid in addition to year-end tax liability. The tentative minimum tax is determined by multiplying the excess of a taxpayer's alternative minimum taxable income over an exemption amount by 26 percent for adjusted gross income up to $175,000 and 28 percent for AGI in excess of $175,000 (20 percent for corporate taxpayers), and then reducing the product by the taxpayer's alternative minimum tax foreign tax credit. AMTI is computed by taking taxable income (including unrelated business taxable income, real estate investment trust taxable income, life insurance company taxable income, or any other income base used to calculate regular tax liability), adding or subtracting special adjustments, and adding tax preference items.

Amortization

The commonly known dictionary meaning of the word *amortization* differs from its income tax application. The principal dictionary meaning is the building up of a fund, through periodic payments, for the purpose of paying off an obligation when it becomes due in the future, such as a mortgage. But usually in income tax parlance, amortization means the writing off of an amount over a definite period (such as amortizing a bond premium or discount over the life of the bonds), similar to the depreciation write-off on depreciable property.

Amount realized

The term *amount realized* is given a special meaning in finding gain or loss on a sale or exchange of property. The realized gain or loss is the difference between the amount realized and the *adjusted basis* of the asset. The amount realized is the sum of the money and the fair market value of other property received.

Annualizing

Annualizing is a procedure whereby a taxpayer estimates from the income received during a portion of a year what the income for the entire year will be if income continues to be received at the same rate. This process is used in computing the tax on short-period returns and also for avoiding the penalty for underpayment of estimated taxes.

Annuity

An *annuity* is a periodic payment, whether for a period certain or for one or more lives. Under the general rule for taxing an annuity, the taxpayer's investment in the contract is usually divided by the number of payments expected, and that portion of each payment is nontaxable. The remainder of each payment is taxable as received. The Internal Revenue Service provides tables for computing tax-free portions of annuity receipts.

Assessment of tax

The Commissioner of Internal Revenue places the amount of unpaid tax on a list for collection, in effect a charge against the taxpayer on the books of the government. Before any additional tax may be assessed, the Commissioner must send a notice of deficiency and cannot assess the tax before allowing the taxpayer to file a petition with the Tax Court.

Assignment of income doctrine

The principle that income is taxed to the individual who earned it, even if the right to the income has been transferred to another prior to recognition.

Association

An *association* is a body of persons who unite for some special business or purpose, the body itself being invested with some, but not full, corporate rights and powers. For income tax purposes, an association is taxed in the same manner as a corporation.

— B —

Bad debt

Whether or not it relates to a business transaction, a bad debt can be deducted in the year in which it becomes uncollectible. If a business debt is partially uncollectible, a portion may be charged off. A nonbusiness bad debt is treated in the same way as a short-term capital loss. A debt that arises from the performance of services or the selling of goods by a cash-basis taxpayer may not be deducted if the income from the services or the profit from the sale has not previously been reported as income. However, a bad debt that arises from the lending of money is deductible, subject to the above-mentioned limitation on a nonbusiness bad debt.

Basis

The term *basis,* for income tax purposes, is used mainly in connection with determining the amount of gain or loss on a sale of property or in computing depreciation. It represents the cost of the property to the taxpayer, actually or constructively, but it has a broader meaning than the term *cost.* The *basis* (adjusted) of property is deducted from the *amount realized* to determine the realized gain or loss on its sale. If the property was acquired by the taxpayer through a purchase, the basis is its cost, except in special circumstances such as in the conversion of the property from personal to rental or other business purposes, in which case the basis for loss and for *depreciation* may be different from the basis for *gain.* If the property was acquired as gift property, inherited property, property received in an exchange, etc., then special rules for finding basis apply.

Bequest

A *bequest* is a gift by will of personal property. The law provides a special basis for finding gain or loss or depreciation in the case of property acquired by bequest. The basis is then the value of the property at the date of the testator's death. If a bequest is of money to be paid at intervals, then to the extent that it is paid out of income from property, it is taxable income to the recipient.

Blind and elderly deduction

An additional standard deduction amount of $850 is allowed for an elderly or blind individual who is married or who is a surviving spouse. An additional $1,050 is allowed for a single individual or for a head of household who is elderly or blind. Thus, a married couple, each of whom is both elderly and blind, receives an extra $3,400 ($850 × 4) standard deduction.

Boot

Boot is a term that is sometimes used to describe the other property received in an exchange which, but for such other property, would be nontaxable. Partial gain may be recognized from the receipt of such boot, not to exceed the fair market value of the boot. Such boot or other property consists of money or property other than stock or securities (or other than like property in like-kind exchanges) which may be received tax free.

Business purpose

When a transaction occurs it must be grounded in a business purpose other than tax avoidance. Tax avoidance is not a proper motive for being in business. The concept of business purpose was originally set forth in *Gregory v. Helvering,* 35-1 USTC ¶ 9043, 293 U.S. 465, 55 S.Ct. 266 (1935). In this case, the Supreme Court ruled that a transaction aiming at tax-free status had no business purpose. Further, the Court stated that merely transferring assets from one corporation to another under a plan which can be associated with neither firm was invalid. This was merely a series of legal transactions that when viewed by the Court in its entirety had no business purpose.

— C —

Cafeteria plan

A *cafeteria plan* is a separate written benefit plan maintained by an employer for the benefit of its' employees, under which all participants are employees and each participant has the opportunity to select particular benefits. The participant may choose from among two or more benefits consisting of cash and qualified benefits.

Calendar year

A *calendar year* is a period of 12 months beginning January 1 and ending December 31. It is the most widely used accounting period. It must be used by a taxpayer who does not keep a regular set of books on a different accounting period.

Capital asset

The term *capital asset* in income tax law generally means all business and nonbusiness assets with the following exceptions: inventory, depreciable personal and real property, certain works created through personal efforts, business accounts and notes receivable, and certain U.S. publications.

Capital expenditure

A capital expenditure is one that is made for assets of a more or less permanent nature—those with a useful life of more than one year. Such an expenditure may not be deducted in the year made, even though made in connection with a trade or business. In other words, it is capitalized. But if the assets are wasting assets they may, in proper cases, be the subject of a depreciation deduction. Uniform capitalization rules require capitalization of certain costs and expenditures.

Capital gains

Capital gains are gains from the sale or exchange of a *capital asset* as that term is defined above. The excess of capital gains over capital losses is called capital gain net income. If a capital asset has been held for more than the requisite holding period at the time of sale, the gain is a long-term capital gain. Corporations must treat capital gains as ordinary income.

Capital losses

Capital losses are losses from the sale or exchange of a capital asset. The excess of capital losses over capital gains is called net capital loss. A corporation may deduct a capital loss of any taxable year in that year only to the extent of capital gain. The excess of losses may be carried back three years and carried forward five years, but only as an offset against capital gains of such later years. If there are no such capital gains, the deduction is lost. In the case of an individual, short-term and long-term capital losses are combined for purposes of offsetting up to $3,000 of ordinary income annually. Excess losses may be carried forward indefinitely.

Capitalization—See Capital expenditure

Carryback and carryover

Income tax carrybacks include the net operating loss carryback, the capital loss carryback (for corporations only), the foreign tax credit carryback, and the general business credit carryback. The first two are applied against income and the last two are credits against tax.

Carrying charge

This accounting term denotes an expense for idle or nonproductive property that is incurred for the purpose of *carrying* the property. The income tax law permits a taxpayer to capitalize instead of deducting currently as an expense taxes and interest chargeable to unimproved and unproductive real property. Also, a taxpayer can capitalize otherwise deductible expenses incurred during the period of construction or improvement of real property, and taxes and interest directly related to machinery and equipment purchased, up to the date they are put to productive use. In addition, if the finance or service charge on an installment purchase of personal property is separately stated but the actual interest charge cannot be ascertained, such a charge is referred to as a carrying charge. And a portion of the charge is deductible as interest under a special formula.

Cash basis

The cash basis is one of the two principal recognized methods of accounting. It must be used by all taxpayers who do not keep books. It is elective as to all other taxpayers (except corporations, certain partnerships, and tax-exempt trusts); however, it may not be used if inventories are necessary in order to reflect income. On the cash basis, income is reported only as it is received, in money or other property having a fair market value, and expenses are deductible only in the year they are paid.

Casualty loss

Although deduction for a loss generally is confined to a loss connected with a trade or business or a transaction entered into for profit, the law also allows deduction of a casualty loss for all types of assets, including personal assets such as a home, jewelry, clothing, etc. Theft, although not strictly a casualty, is in the same category for income tax deduction purposes. Personal casualty losses are deductible only to the extent that each such loss exceeds $100 and that the aggregate excess is greater than 10 percent of adjusted gross income.

Child-care expense—See Dependent care expense

Claim for refund

A claim for refund must be made by a taxpayer entitled to get back part or all of the tax paid. The claim may be made on the tax return or, in the case of individual or corporate income taxes, may be made on Form 1040X or 1120X. In other cases, refund claims should be made on amended returns or Form 843.

Claim of right

The term *claim of right* is used in the Code in connection with money or other property received as income which the recipient holds under a claim of right, but which the recipient is required to restore in whole or in part to the payer in a later year because it develops that the recipient did not have an unrestricted right to such property. If the amount restored exceeds $3,000, Code Sec. 1341 provides some relief, by means of a tax limitation in the year of restoration, from the requirement that the restored amount must be deducted in the year of restoration and may not reduce the income of the prior year. The *right* to the money or other property means a just and legal claim to hold, use, or enjoy it, or to convey or donate it.

Community property

Community property is property owned by husband and wife in community, each sharing equally in the income therefrom. The concept of ownership of property by a husband and wife in community is of Spanish origin, adopted from early Spanish law by eight western and southern states—California, Nevada, New Mexico, Arizona, Idaho, Washington, Louisiana, and Texas—as well as Wisconsin.

Complex trust

A complex trust is one which permits accumulation of current income, provides for charitable contributions, or distributes principal during the taxable year. For tax purposes, it is to be distinguished from a *simple trust*.

Conduits

Some entities are not tax paying. They pass through their income (loss) to owners (beneficiaries). A partnership is an example of a conduit. Partnerships do not pay taxes; they merely report the partnership's taxable income or losses. The income (loss) flows directly to the partners. However, partnerships do compute partnership taxable income. Other types of conduits are grantor trusts and S corporations.

Consent dividend

A *consent dividend* is not a dividend actually paid by a corporation. It is merely represented by signed consents by a stockholder to be taxed as if the stockholder has really received the amount of the distribution stated in the consent. It is used in order to avoid the imposition of the accumulated earnings tax and the personal holding company tax in cases where this tax might otherwise be imposed and the company does not wish to make an actual distribution.

Consolidated return

Affiliated corporations may file one consolidated return, eliminating intercompany transactions, instead of filing separate returns.

Constructive ownership of stock

In determining the percentage of stock ownership of a stockholder in a corporation, in order to find whether the stockholder controls the corporation or to make other tests of ownership, the Code in several instances provides that the stockholder will be constructively regarded as the owner of shares of stock held by certain other persons. For example, the rule is applied in disallowing a loss on sales between certain related persons.

Constructive-receipt doctrine

A taxpayer on the cash basis is taxed on income only as it is *received.* However, if the income was unreservedly subject to the taxpayer's demand and the taxpayer could have received it but chose not to do so, it is regarded as having been *constructively received* and is taxable. Interest on a bank deposit is a good example.

Contribution to capital

A contribution to capital denotes the money or other property contributed to a corporation by either a stockholder or a nonstockholder. Where a stockholder advances money to a corporation, the tax question on insolvency of the corporation is whether the money was advanced as a loan or as a capital contribution. If it is a capital contribution, the stockholder may not deduct a nonbusiness bad debt. Where a nonstockholder makes a contribution to a corporation, such as payments by a city to a manufacturer for moving its factory to the city, the contribution is not income to the corporation. The basis of property so contributed (or property purchased with money contributions) is zero. If money is contributed and no property is purchased with it, the basis of the corporation's assets is reduced.

Contributions

Contributions usually means gifts made to charitable organizations. A contribution is deductible by both individuals and corporations, to a limited extent. In some cases, the word *contributions* is used in the Code in a different sense, but in those cases the meaning is apparent from the context. (*Contribution to capital,* above, is a case in point.)

Controlled corporate groups

Controlled groups of corporations basically fall into two classifications: parent-subsidiary controlled groups and brother-sister controlled groups. A parent-subsidiary controlled group is one in which one or more chains of corporations are connected through stock ownership with a common parent corporation. At least 80 percent of the voting power or stock value of each corporation in the group other than the parent is owned by one or more corporations in the group, and the common parent owns at least 80 percent of the voting power or stock value of one of the other corporations in the group. A brother-sister controlled group is a controlled group in which at least 80 percent of the voting power or stock value of two or more corporations is owned by the same five or fewer persons (individuals, estates, or trusts) and these persons own more than 50 percent of the voting power or stock value of each corporation.

A controlled group of corporations should be distinguished from an affiliated group of corporations, a term related to elections to file a consolidated return and to take a 100 percent dividends-received credit. An *affiliated group* is formed when at least 80 percent of the total combined voting power of all classes of stock and at least 80 percent of each class of nonvoting stock of each corporation in the group are owned by one or more other corporations in the group. Thus, a parent-subsidiary group is not an *affiliated* group unless at least 80 percent of the nonvoting stock of each corporation in the group is owned by another corporation in the group. A brother-sister controlled group can never qualify as an *affiliated* group since the voting power or stock value of two or more corporations is owned by a noncorporate entity.

Corporation

For income tax purposes, the word *corporation* has a broader meaning than its customary one. It includes an association, joint stock company, and insurance company. All are taxed as if they were corporations, although insurance companies are subject to special rules and are taxed at special rates.

Cost

Cost is the purchase price paid for property, or the value at which it is taken into income (as in the case of services paid for in property). It is the amount most often applied against the amount realized from the sale of property in determining the profit or loss. It is also the figure most often used in determining the depreciation deduction. However, in special circumstances, where property is not acquired by purchase, there may be a special basis for a finding of gain or loss or depreciation.

Cost depletion—See Depletion

Cost or market, whichever is lower

This phrase is used only in reference to inventory valuations. Most taxpayers prefer to use *cost or market, whichever is lower,* as a basis for valuing their inventories since this method affords an opportunity to take advantage of a drop in the market so that profits can be reduced accordingly before disposition of the goods. If *cost* only is used, a drop in the market cannot affect the income until the merchandise is sold. Either method ((a) cost, or (b) cost or market, whichever is lower) is acceptable, but either one, once adopted, must be followed unless a permission to change is obtained.

Credits against tax

A credit against the tax, or a tax credit, is an amount that is subtracted from the income tax liability of an individual in a given taxable year. The tax credit differs from a deduction in that the credit is subtracted from the tax itself, resulting in a dollar-for-dollar reduction in the tax liability; the deduction is subtracted from either gross income or adjusted gross income, resulting in a reduction in the amount of income subject to tax. A nonrefundable credit is one that cannot be refunded to the extent that it exceeds the income tax of the current year (e.g., the investment credit). A refundable credit can be refunded to the extent that it exceeds tax liability (e.g., the earned income credit).

Credits or refunds

Where tax is overpaid for any year, it ordinarily will be refunded by the IRS if the taxpayer owes no tax for any other year. If the taxpayer does owe a tax, the overpayment is credited against the tax that is due the government, and any balance is refunded. Credits and refunds may be allowed only within specified periods if, within such periods, a claim for refund or credit is filed. See *Claim for refund.*

— D —

Dealer

A dealer, as referred to in income tax law, is one who sells to customers in the ordinary course of a trade or business. Examples are securities and real estate dealers and other dealers regularly selling on the installment plan.

Death benefit

The Code uses the phrase *death benefit* to exclude from gross income life insurance proceeds payable by reason of death.

Declining-balance method

Declining balance is the name for a method of depreciation under the general rules. An agreed-upon uniform rate is applied, not to the original cost or other basis of an asset but to its depreciating balance. Thus, the amount to which the uniform rate is applied *declines* every year. For this reason, the rate must be higher than the straight-line rate. The Code permits using a rate of up to 200 percent of the straight-line rate.

Deductions from gross income

Deductions from gross income are, as the name indicates, amounts representing expenditures or amounts of such personal exemptions for which deduction is allowed from the amount of gross income reported. They are to be distinguished from *exclusions* from gross income, which are not taken into income at all. Deductions are taken from gross income to arrive at adjusted gross income. See also *Taxable income* and *Adjusted gross income.*

Deficiency

A *deficiency* is the amount by which the actual tax (as it should have been computed) exceeds the amount shown on the return, if any, plus any amounts previously assessed as a deficiency and minus any rebates. See also *Assessment of tax.*

Dependent

A dependent is one of certain specified relatives for whom the taxpayer provides over half of the support for the calendar year. Nonrelatives living as members of the taxpayer's household are also treated as dependents if the support test is met. For each dependent, the taxpayer is allowed a deduction of $2,700 for 1998.

Dependent-care expense

A credit against tax is allowed for employment-related expenses paid by an individual to enable him or her to be gainfully employed. Taxpayers with adjusted gross incomes of $10,000 or less are allowed a credit equal to 30 percent of employment-related expenses. For taxpayers with adjusted gross incomes of over $10,000 through $28,000, the credit is reduced by one percentage point for each $2,000 of adjusted gross income, or fraction thereof, above $10,000. For taxpayers with adjusted gross incomes of over $28,000, the credit is 20 percent of employment-related expenses. The maximum amount of employment-related expenses to which the credit can apply is $2,400 if one child or dependent is involved and $4,800 if two or more are involved.

Depletion

The decrease in natural resources (minerals, coal, timber, etc.) due to their extraction from the source of supply and disposition by sale or otherwise is called depletion. The Code provides allowances for the exhaustion of such assets. There are two methods of computing depletion. One is known as cost depletion, which is the writing off of that part of the cost or other basis of the deposits which the number of units extracted in that year bears to the total estimated number of recoverable units. The other method, called percentage depletion, permits deduction of a specified percentage of the gross income from the property. In each year, the method that results in the greater deduction is to be used.

Depreciation

Depreciation is a decline in value or price. For income tax purposes, it is a deduction to reflect the gradual wasting away of an asset due to the passage of time or the use to which the asset is put, or a combination of both. The Code permits deduction of a reasonable allowance for this exhaustion of property used in a trade or business, including rental property, measured by certain criteria, such as useful life. The Accelerated Cost Recovery System (ACRS) and Modified ACRS (MACRS) are generally referred to as systems of depreciation that provide for recovery of cost over statutory periods that are shorter than the useful life of the property.

Devise

A devise is a gift of real property by will. In the income tax law, the term is used mainly in connection with determining the basis of property so acquired. Basis of property acquired by devise is the value at the date of death of the decedent, or at the alternate valuation date if elected for estate tax purposes. A devise is excluded from gross income for federal income tax purposes.

Disability income exclusion—See Tax credit for the elderly

Dissolution of corporation

The dissolution of a corporation follows its liquidation. It is the technical termination of a corporation's existence by surrender or forfeiture of its charter. A corporation remains liable for the filing of income tax returns as long as it is in existence and until its dissolution, even though it is not doing business.

Distributable net income

To the extent that an estate or trust has distributable net income, every distribution to a beneficiary except lump-sum payments of bequests, devises, or inheritances is taxable income. The distributable net income of an estate or trust is the same as its taxable income, with certain specified modifications.

Distribution by corporation

As used in the income tax law, the term *distribution by corporation* refers to any amounts paid by a corporation to its shareholders, or any property distributed to them, other than for value received in goods or services. It is a broader term than *dividend*, defined below, for a distribution may be a dividend and, therefore, taxable income, or it may be an offset against the stockholder's cost or other basis of the stock.

Dividend

A distribution by corporation, defined above, may be either a dividend or a return of capital invested. If it is a dividend, it is taxed as gross income. A dividend is any distribution by a corporation out of its accumulated earnings and profits or out of earnings and profits of the taxable year as of the close of the year (without diminution by reason of distributions during the year).

Dividends-received deduction

A corporation receives a 70 percent or 80 percent deduction—with limitations—for dividends it receives, unless it is an affiliated corporation which does not, or cannot, file a consolidated return. Such a corporation may elect a 100 percent dividends-received deduction.

Domestic corporation

For tax purposes, a corporation created or organized in the United States or under the laws of the United States or any state.

— E —

Earned income

Earned income, which is usually defined with reference to the self-employment income rules, generally means wages, salaries, tips, professional fees, and other amounts received as compensation for personal services rendered. This term is often used to distinguish unearned income, which includes interest and dividends. The term is sometimes more specifically defined, e.g., for purposes of the foreign income exclusion and for determining self-employment income. In addition to foreign income and self-employment income, the term is relevant to determining income tax liability of minors, IRA contributions, and credits for low-income and elderly or permanently disabled taxpayers.

Earnings and profits (E&P)

Accumulated earnings and profits, as well as earnings and profits of the current taxable year, measure the amount of a distribution by a corporation to its shareholders which represents a dividend. The earnings and profits of a distributing corporation are not the same as net income or taxable income. They include nontaxable as well as taxable income but do not include realized gains or losses which are not recognized for income tax purposes.

Elderly taxpayers—See Blind and elderly deduction and Tax credit for the elderly

Employee

For income tax purposes, an employee is distinguishable from an independent contractor. This is important, for the withholding of income taxes on wages applies only to an employee. Also, employee status will affect the manner and extent of allowance of some deductions. The regulations state that an employee is one who is subject to the will and control of the employer not only as to what is to be done but as to how it is to be done.

Employee stock option

An employee stock option is an option granted to an employee to purchase the employer's stock. Employee stock options to which special income tax treatment is accorded are known as statutory options. Incentive stock options and employee stock purchase plan options are the only two kinds of statutory options that may still be created and exercised.

Employee Stock Ownership Plan (ESOP)

An ESOP is a qualified stock bonus plan designed to invest primarily in qualifying employer securities.

Entity

Generally, for tax purposes there are four types of entities: individuals, corporations, trusts, and estates. Each entity determines its own tax and files its own tax return. Each tax entity has its specific rules to follow for the determination of taxable income. Basically the concept of "entity" answers the question "Who is the taxpayer?" Note that partnerships were not in the list of entities. For tax purposes partnerships are not tax-paying entities. The income (loss) flows directly to the partners.

Estate

The meaning of this word in the income tax law is much narrower than its general meaning, which, broadly speaking, is an interest in property. For federal tax purposes, it has two specific meanings. The gross estate of a decedent consists of the assets, both probate and nonprobate, of the decedent for estate tax purposes. Taxable estate is the gross estate less deductions and exemptions. In its most widely used sense, for income tax purposes, an estate is a taxpayer. It is the executorship or administration of a decedent's estate, subject to a court having probate jurisdiction by a fiduciary, and is treated as a separate taxpayer. For income tax purposes, although clearly distinguishable, an estate is generally subject to the same Code provisions in determining taxable income as a trust. Each is allowed deductions for distributions to beneficiaries, such deductions representing gross income in the hands of the beneficiaries. Income accumulated that is neither distributed nor distributable during the taxable year is taxable to the estate, after offsetting against it all allowable deductions.

Estimated tax

Individual taxpayers must pay estimated taxes on as many as four payment dates unless estimated tax is not expected to exceed $1,000. A corporation deposits its estimated tax in advance on as many as four payment dates (April 15, June 15, September 15, and December 15 for calendar-year corporations). Trusts and estates must make quarterly estimated tax payments in the same manner as individuals, except that an estate is exempt from making such payments during its first two taxable years.

Excess net passive income—See Passive investment income

Executor

An executor is a person appointed via a will to carry out the testator's directions and to dispose of property according to a will. The executor manages an estate. (Feminine form: executrix.)

Exemption

An exemption is a reduction in net income allowed on account of status or dependency. Thus, in arriving at the tax base, or the figure at which the tax rates are applied, net income is reduced by the amount of personal and dependency exemptions. Individuals, estates and trusts are allowed exemptions. Every estate is allowed an exemption of $600. A trust is allowed an exemption of $100 or $300, depending on the type of trust. Except for dependents, every individual taxpayer is allowed at least one exemption (adjusted for inflation). On a joint return, the two (or more) exemptions of both the husband and wife are allowed. One spouse is allowed the exemption (or exemptions) of the other on a separate return if the other has no gross income and is not the dependent of another person. Exemptions also are allowable for dependents of the taxpayer.

Expenses

Expenses, for federal income tax purposes, are divisible into three general classes: (1) trade or business expenses, (2) nonbusiness expenses incurred in connection with the production of income, for management, conservation, or maintenance of property held for production of income, or in connection with the determination, collection, or refund of any tax, and (3) personal, family, or living expenses. Only expenses in the first two categories are deductible. Expenses in the third category are not deductible, except in a few unusual cases (medical expenses, charitable contributions, etc.) where they are specifically allowed by law.

— F —

Fair market value

The fair market value of property is that amount which would induce a willing seller to sell and a willing buyer to buy the property. Market quotations are an acceptable measure of value, except where the quantity of property involved is so great that its sale would affect the market quotations before the sale is finished. Unlisted stocks sometimes are valued on the basis of the corporate assets, including goodwill, whether or not they are entered on the books. Real estate is valued on the basis of net earnings, location, etc., and this value is best proved by an expert appraisal.

Fiduciary

This term usually denotes the executor or administrator of the estate of a decedent or the trustee of a trust. Since an estate or trust is a taxpayer, the fiduciary is charged with the responsibility of filing a return for the estate or trust. The term also includes a guardian, conservator, or receiver. See also *Estate.*

Filing of return

Filing a return consists of filling it out and mailing or hand-delivering it, generally, to the appropriate IRS location. The time for filing an income tax return is specifically stated in the law, and penalties may be imposed for late filing.

First-in, first-out rule

This rule is generally applied to otherwise unidentifiable stocks where a number of shares of the same kind of stock have been bought at different times and different prices. If they cannot otherwise be identified, those which were purchased first are regarded as having been sold first in determining the cost price to be applied against the selling price for the purpose of determining any gain or loss on the sale. The term is also applied to inventory items where the LIFO method (see *Last-in, first-out rule,* below) is not used. As so used, the first-in, first-out rule is also referred to as the FIFO method.

Fiscal year

A fiscal year, for income tax purposes, is a period of 12 months, ending on the last day of a month other than December, or the special 52-53-week period. It is thus distinguished from a calendar year, which always ends on December 31. It is a recognized accounting period for income tax purposes.

Foreign corporation

A foreign corporation is one which is not organized under the laws of one of the states or territories or of the United States. Taxation of a foreign corporation depends on whether or not its income is *effectively connected* with a U.S. trade or business. Special rules apply to United States shareholders of certain controlled foreign corporations.

Foreign tax credit or deduction

If a United States citizen or resident or a domestic corporation incurs or pays income taxes to a foreign country, an election may be made to deduct such taxes in determining taxable income or to take them as a credit against United States tax. The election must be made as to all foreign taxes incurred or paid in the taxable year. Generally, the credit will be limited to the percentage of the total tax against which the credit is being taken that the taxable income from foreign countries is of the total taxable income. Special rules apply to a U.S. shareholder of a controlled foreign corporation or a shareholder in a foreign investment company.

— G —

General business credit

The general business credit consists of the investment tax credit (the sum of the rehabilitation investment credit, the energy investment credit, and the reforestation investment credit), the work opportunity credit, the welfare-to-work credit, the alcohol fuels credit, the research credit, the low-income housing credit, the disabled access credit, the enhanced oil recovery credit, and five other credits.

Gift

A gift has been defined as a valid transfer of property from one to another without consideration or compensation. For income tax purposes, the words *gift* and *contribution* usually have separate meanings, the latter word being used in connection with contributions to charitable, religious, etc. organizations, whereas the word *gift* refers to transfers of money or property to private individuals, needy persons, friends, relatives, etc. The recipient of a gift is not required to include it in gross income. The donor is not entitled to deduct it (except for a business gift to a customer of $25 or less per donee per year).

Grantor trust

A grantor trust is one in which the grantor retains control over the income or principal, or both, to such an extent that the grantor is regarded as being substantially the owner of the trust property and of the income. The grantor is taxable on this trust income. The law contains specific tests to find whether the grantor is the substantial owner of the trust property.

Gross estate

Gross estate is an estate tax term. It means a decedent's entire property which is subject to the estate tax, that is, prior to any deductions.

Gross income

Gross income, for income tax purposes, refers to all income which is taxable. The law enumerates specific items of income which are not to be included in gross income and, therefore, are nontaxable. With these exceptions, all income is includible in gross income.

— H —

Head of household

Head of household has a specific meaning in the income tax law. By means of a special tax rate table, a head of a household receives a tax advantage over a single individual but less than that afforded a husband and wife who file a joint return. Generally, a head of a household is an unmarried individual who is not a *surviving spouse* and who maintains as a home a household which is the principal place of abode of at least one child or grandchild or any other relative (except a cousin).

Holding period

The holding period of property is the length of time that property has been held by a taxpayer or the length of time the taxpayer is treated for income tax purposes as having held it. The term is most important for income tax purposes as it relates to capital gains transactions. Whether a capital gain or loss is long- or short-term depends on whether the asset sold or exchanged has been held by the taxpayer for more than 12 months. With the Taxpayer Relief Act of 1997, the tax advantages on the gain side occur when property is held more than 18 months (where the maximum tax rate is 20 percent) or more than 12 months but not greater than 18 months (where the maximum rate is 28 percent).

— I —

Imputed interest

Taxpayers cannot sell property under a deferred payment contract in which no interest or unrealistically low interest is charged and realize all capital gains or increased capital gains on the sale. Unstated or imputed interest is taxable to the seller as ordinary interest income.

Incentive stock option

The incentive stock option is a statutory employee stock option. No income tax consequences result from the grant or exercise of such an option, and, if holding and other requirements are met, gain on eventual sale of the employer's stock will be long-term capital gain.

Income

Income, in its broad sense, is the gain derived from capital, labor, or both. It is distinguishable from the capital itself. Ordinarily, for income tax purposes, the word *income* is not used alone. It is used in conjunction with such descriptive terms as *gross income, taxable income,* and *adjusted gross income,* all of which are defined herein.

Income effectively connected

All income from U.S. sources which is *effectively connected* with the conduct of a trade or business in the United States is taxed to nonresident aliens and foreign corporations at the same rates as apply to U.S. citizens and domestic corporations. Investment and other fixed or determinable periodical income (interest, dividends, rents, wages, etc.) of a nonresident alien is taxed at a flat 30 percent rate, whether or not the recipient engages in a trade or business in the United States, so long as such income is not effectively connected with a trade or business in the United States. Income is considered effectively connected if it is derived from assets used in, or held for use in, the United States, and if the activities of the U.S. business are a material factor in the realization of the income.

Income-shifting

Income-shifting is the transfer of income from one family member to another who is subject to a lower tax rate or the selection of a form of business that decreases the tax liability for its owners.

Individual Retirement Account (IRA)

Any individual may contribute 100 percent of earned income, up to $2,000 a year, to an IRA ($4,000 on a joint return, i.e. $2,000 per spouse). The contributions are deductible from gross income, except for individuals who participate in a qualified deferred compensation plan with AGI over a certain level ($30,000 in 1998 increasing to $50,000 by 2005, and for joint filers, $50,000 in 1998 increasing to $80,000 in 2007).The investment grows tax-deferred, but all withdrawals constitute gross income. A 10 percent penalty on gross income is levied on pre-age 59½ withdrawals, except on account of disability, death, first-time home purchases (up to $10,000), insurance premiums for the unemployed, deductible medical expenses, as well as withdrawals in the shape of annuities. Withdrawals must start with respect to the year the participant reaches age 70½. An IRA may receive tax-deferred rollovers from other qualified plans, including other IRAs. Distributions from IRAs are not subject to withholding.

The Roth IRA began in 1998. Nondeductible contributions to a Roth IRA can be made by individuals with AGI up to $95,000 ($150,000 on a joint return). The income is *never* taxed if the account is more than five years old *and* the participant is deceased, disabled, or over 59½ years old. The overall annual limit is $2,000 per individual for *all* contributions to *all* IRAs (except education IRAs), deductible or not. No age limit exists for establishing, making contributions to, or accumulating funds in a Roth IRA. The 10 percent penalty provisions are the same as for a regular IRA, but the contributions may be withdrawn first, at any time, for any purpose, without tax or penalty consequences.

Inheritance

As distinguished from a bequest or devise, an inheritance is property acquired through laws of descent and distribution from a person who dies without leaving a will. Property so acquired takes as its basis, for gain or loss on later disposition or for depreciation, the fair market value of the property at the date of death of the decedent from whom it is acquired. An inheritance of property does not give rise to taxable income, but the *income* from an inheritance does. And if the inheritance is of income from property, such income is taxable.

Installment method

The installment method of reporting income allows the profit on an installment sale to be taxed over the period that payments are received. The amount taxed in any year is equal to the payments received times the gross profit ratio (the total gross profit divided by the total contract price). However, the entire amount of any gain recaptured under Code Sec. 1245 or 1250 is reported in the year of sale regardless of whether any payment is received in that first year. Use of the installment method is mandatory unless the taxpayer elects not to report on the installment method.

Inter vivos trust

An inter vivos trust is a trust created during the lifetime of the person setting up the trust. A testamentary trust is one set up under the will of the decedent.

Intestate

One not having a will; a person who dies without a will is said to die intestate.

Inventory

An inventory is a detailed list of articles of property. In the true accounting sense, and for income tax purposes, it refers only to a list of articles comprising stock in trade—articles held for sale to customers in the regular course of a trade or business. The cost of goods sold during the year is determined by adding to the inventory at the beginning of the year the purchases made during the year and subtracting from this sum the inventory at the close of the year.

Involuntary conversion

An involuntary conversion of property results when property is destroyed in whole or in part, stolen, seized, requisitioned or condemned (or where there is a threat or imminence of requisition or condemnation) and, as a result, the property is converted into money or other similar property, through insurance proceeds, condemnation awards, etc. The law has special provisions on involuntary conversion only where the conversion results in gain—that is, where the amount recovered exceeds the cost or other basis of the property converted. The law permits the nonrecognition of gain on such an involuntary conversion.

Itemized deductions

Itemized deductions are certain expenses of a personal nature that are specifically allowed as deductions. Included in this group are: moving expenses, medical expenses, state and local income taxes, property taxes, mortgage interest, charitable contributions, personal casualty losses, and miscellaneous employee expenses.

— J —

Joint return—See Surviving spouse

Joint tenancy

Where property is held in the names of two or more persons with the title passing from the first joint tenant to die to the other joint tenant (or joint tenants) upon death.

Joint venture

A joint venture is an enterprise participated in by associates acting together, there being a community of interests and each associate having a right to participate in its control or management. For income tax purposes, a joint venture is treated in all respects as a partnership, not taxable in its own capacity, but regarded as a taxpayer for the purpose of computing its taxable income, which is distributable among the associates in the proportions agreed upon. Such distributive shares are reported by the associates on their individual income tax returns.

— K —

Keogh plan—See Self-employed individual's retirement plan

Key employee

Long a term of general application, especially in regard to insurance, *key employee* now has a statutory definition for purposes of the rules that apply to *top-heavy* plans. For these purposes, *key employee* includes an officer of the employer earning more than a specified amount, any one of the 10 employees owning the largest interests in the employer, a 5 percent owner of the employer, or a 1 percent owner who is paid more than $160,000 per year. See also *Top-heavy plan.*

— L —

Last-in, first-out rule

LIFO is the popular abbreviation for the *last-in, first-out* rule for identifying items in an inventory to determine their cost. By this method, goods remaining on hand at the close of the taxable year are treated as being, first, those included in the opening inventory to the extent thereof, and, second, those acquired during the taxable year.

Legacy

A disposition of personal property by will.

Lien for taxes

The U.S. Treasury Department, as part of its tax collection machinery, has a legal claim to the property of a taxpayer whose taxes are delinquent or overdue. Assessment of tax, demand, and refusal or neglect to pay control the creation and the effective date of the lien. Sometimes the lien will attach to property in the possession of a third-person transferee or fiduciary. Sometimes a creditor or other nontaxpayer, as well as the government, may assert a claim to the same property. The question of priorities must then be settled.

Limitations—See Statute of limitations

Liquidation of corporation

Complete liquidation of a corporation is the winding up of its affairs by the settling of its accounts, the paying of all debts, the collecting of assets and the turning of the remainder over to the shareholders in exchange for their stock. Complete liquidation precedes dissolution of the corporation and is not entirely synonymous with it. See *Dissolution of corporation.* A partial liquidation is a calling in of a part of the stock, with or without cessation of a part of the corporate activities. Special rules apply to the sale by a corporation of its assets as a step in liquidation, and to the treatment of liquidation distributions received by the shareholders.

Long-term capital gain and loss

Long-term capital gains and losses are gains and losses on the sale or exchange of capital assets that have been held for more than 12 months. A net long-term capital gain or loss is the excess of gains over losses, or vice versa. An excess of net long-term capital gains over net short-term capital losses is taxed as ordinary income to corporations. For assets sold after July 28, 1997, and on or before December 31, 2000, if the assets are held more than 18 months, the maximum tax rate is 20 percent (or 10 percent for those in the 15 percent tax bracket). If assets are held more than 12 months but not more than 18 months, the maximum rate is 28 percent (or 15 percent for those in the 15 percent bracket).

— M —

Merger

A statutory merger (that is, one effected under the laws of the state) is a reorganization for income tax purposes, upon which no gain or loss is recognized under the conditions specified in the Code. A merger is the union of two or more corporations into one, the others giving up their existence and transferring all of their properties and liabilities to the one continuing corporation. It is distinguishable from a consolidation, which is the transfer of two or more corporations into a new corporation, the transferring corporations giving up their existence.

Minimum tax—See Alternative minimum tax

Minority interest

Stock ownership of 20 percent or less in a corporation which is at least 80 percent owned by another corporation.

Modified Accelerated Cost Recovery System (MACRS)—See Accelerated Cost Recovery System (ACRS)

Multiple support agreement

If two or more persons who would otherwise be entitled to an exemption for a dependent together furnish more than one-half of a dependent's support, anyone who furnishes more than 10 percent of the support is entitled to the exemption if all the others who furnish more than 10 percent of the support file written declarations that they will not claim an exemption for the individual supported for that taxable year.

— N —

Negligence

For income tax purposes, there is a penalty of 5 percent of the underpayment if any part of an underpayment of tax is due to negligence or intentional disregard of rules and Regulations, but without intent to defraud. Negligence is a lack of the reasonable care and caution expected of a prudent person.

Net operating loss (NOL)

A net operating loss is limited substantially to a net loss incurred in the operation of a trade or business, although a casualty loss or a loss from a sale of a business asset is included within its scope. A net operating loss may be carried back two years against the income of those two years to the earliest year first. Any unused portion of such loss may be carried forward past the taxable year for 20 years.

Net passive income—See Passive investment income

Nonrefundable credits

Nonrefundable credits are allowed as an offset against tax liability. Since no payment has been made to the government, the taxpayer cannot receive a refund if the credit exceeds the tax liability.

Nonresident alien

A nonresident alien, for income tax purposes, is an individual who is not a citizen or resident of the United States. Taxation depends on whether U.S. source income is effectively connected with the conduct of a U.S. trade or business. See also *Income effectively connected.*

— O —

Obsolescence—See Depreciation

Organizational expenses

Organizational expenses are the costs of organizing a corporation before it begins active business. The Code permits amortization of these expenses over a period to be chosen by the taxpayer, but not less than 60 months. Such charging off is elective with the taxpayer. Organizational expenses for this purpose do not include expenses of issuing or selling stock or reorganization expenses unless they are incident to the creation of a *new* corporation.

Overpayment of tax

An overpayment of tax is a payment or a total of payments in excess of the amount determined to be the correct amount of tax for the taxable year. The Code provides that the term includes that part of the amount of the payment of any internal revenue tax which is assessed or collected after the expiration of the limitation period properly applicable to such assessment or collection.

—P—

Paid-in surplus

Paid-in surplus is an accounting term. It represents amounts paid in to a corporation by its shareholders, not in payment for their stock, but, after their stock has been fully paid for, as additional working capital for the corporation. Such paid-in surplus is not taxable income to the corporation. Nor is it deductible by the shareholder. It becomes an additional cost of the shareholder's stock. If the paid-in surplus consists of property other than money, its basis in the hands of the corporation is the same as it was in the hands of the shareholder.

Parent corporation

A corporation which owns a required percentage of another corporation (subsidiary). Every group of affiliated corporations which files a consolidated return must have a common parent corporation.

Partnership

A partnership does not pay taxes. It is a conduit for nontaxable income, dividend income, partially taxable interest, ordinary income, and the capital gains and losses shares to be taken into the income of the individual partners. For income tax purposes, the term *partnership* is more comprehensive than when taken in its ordinary meaning. It includes a syndicate, group, pool and joint venture, as well as an ordinary partnership, in which two or more persons join their money and/or their skills in carrying on as co owners a business for profit. If the organization of a limited partnership is more in the nature of an association than a partnership, it is deemed to be an association taxable as a corporation.

Passive activity losses

Losses arising from a passive activity are not deductible, except against income from a passive activity. The unused portion of the loss, however, is not lost but is suspended (i.e., carried over) until offset by passive income in a future tax year or until the entire activity is disposed of in a fully taxable transaction.

Passive investment income

Gross receipts derived from royalties, rents, dividends, interest, annuities, and sales or exchanges of stock or securities of an S corporation.

Net passive investment income.—Passive investment income of an S corporation reduced by the allowable deductions directly connected with the production of such income.

Excess net passive income.—Portion of net passive investment income for the tax year of an S corporation multiplied by a fraction comprised of (1) the amount by which the total net passive investment income for the tax year exceeds 25 percent of the gross receipts for the tax year, divided by (2) the total gross passive investment income for the tax year.

Pay-as-you-go tax system

The U.S. tax system is often referred to as a pay-as-you-go tax system. Much of the federal government's tax collections come from withholdings and estimated taxes. The various types of tax-payers pay tax throughout the year, not just at year-end. The United States has been on a pay-as-you-go system since 1943.

Penalties

The Code contains two types of additions to the tax—interest and penalties. Interest paid may be deductible; a penalty is not. A penalty usually is distinguishable from interest in that it is imposed at a flat rate without regard to lapse of time.

Pension

A *pension,* if received from a former employer for past services, is taxable; if it is received under Social Security laws, it may be partially taxable. It is exempt to a limited extent when received for injuries or sickness. If it is in the nature of an annuity, it is subject to the rules for annuities.

Pension plan

Pension plan is both a generic term applied to various types of plans designed to provide retirement income and a specific term used to distinguish a particular type of qualified plan from a stock bonus or profit-sharing plan. Qualified plans are accorded a wide range of special tax treatment.

Percentage depletion—See Depletion

Personal exemption—See Exemption

Personal holding company

A personal holding company is a close corporation organized to hold corporate stocks and bonds and other investment assets, including personal service contracts, and employed to retain the income for distribution at such time as is most advantageous to the individual stockholder from a tax viewpoint. The Code prescribes percentages of certain types of gross income and of stock ownership by five or fewer individuals that will turn an ordinary corporation into a personal holding company. If it falls within this classification, a corporation must pay, in addition to the regular income tax on a corporation, a tax at the rate of 39.6 percent on its *undistributed* personal holding company income.

Qualified Subchapter S Trust (QSST)

A qualified Subchapter S Trust is a trust with single income beneficiary eligible to be an S corporation shareholder.

Real estate investment trust

A qualifying real estate investment trust is one which has at least 100 beneficial owners and which distributes at least 95 percent of its income. The income from the distribution is taxed *only once,* and *only* to the beneficiaries. The trust may not be a personal holding company; it must elect to be treated as a real estate investment trust; and it may not hold property primarily for sale to customers.

Realized v. recognized gain or loss

A gain or loss is realized when a transaction is completed. However, not all realized gains and losses are taxed (recognized). A recognized gain or loss occurs when a taxpayer is obligated to pay tax on a completed transaction.

Recapitalization

A recapitalization is an internal reorganization—that is, a rearrangement of the capital structure of a corporation by changing the kind of stock or the number of shares outstanding or by issuing stock instead of bonds, or vice versa. As distinguished from most other types of reorganization, a recapitalization involves only one corporation and is usually accomplished by the surrender by shareholders or bondholders of their securities for stocks or securities of a different type.

Redemption

Redemption is a buying back, a repurchase. A redemption of stock is its repurchase from the stockholder by the corporation which issued it (whether or not it had originally been issued to the stockholder from whom it is repurchased). A bona fide redemption of stock is treated as a sale or exchange of the stock, and, in the case of a taxpayer other than a dealer in securities, gain or loss on the redemption is a capital gain or loss.

Refund of tax—See Credits or refunds

Regulations

The Commissioner publishes interpretations of the law in the form of Regulations. They do not have the force and effect of law; however, in those cases in which the law on a particular subject calls for rules on that subject to be expounded through Regulations, the courts afford them great weight. Provisions of the Regulations on a particular subject are disapproved by the courts in some rare instances, and in a few cases the weight of authority has resulted in the Commissioner's amending them.

Related taxpayers

The Code does not allow a loss, except in the case of a distribution in liquidation of a corporation, from the sale or exchange of property between related persons. A similar rule bars a deduction for expenses and interest incurred in transactions between related persons when the payer is on the accrual-basis method of accounting and the payee is on the cash-basis method. The following parties are considered related persons for purposes of these rules: (1) members of the same immediate family, except for transfers between spouses or incident to divorce; (2) an individual and a corporation in which the individual owns more than 50 percent of the outstanding stock (directly or indirectly); (3) two members of a controlled corporate group; (4) a trust fiduciary and a corporation of which more than 50 percent of the outstanding stock is owned by the trust or the grantor of the trust; (5) a grantor and fiduciary of any trust; (6) a fiduciary of one trust and a fiduciary of another trust if the same person is the grantor of both trusts; (7) a fiduciary of a trust and any beneficiary of such trust; (8) a fiduciary of a trust and a beneficiary of another trust if the same person is the grantor of the trusts; (9) a person and an exempt charitable organization controlled by that person; (10) a corporation and a partnership if the same person owns more than 50 percent of the outstanding stock in the corporation and more than 50 percent of the interest in the partnership; (11) two S corporations if the same person owns more than 50 percent of the outstanding stock of each corporation; or (12) an S corporation and a C corporation if the same person owns more than 50 percent of the outstanding stock of each corporation.

Reorganization

A *reorganization* occurs when a business undergoes a new capital arrangement, with or without new administration. If only one corporation is involved, it is a *recapitalization.* In income tax law, the term applies only to corporations. The Code contains provisions for nonrecognition of gain or loss on exchanges made in pursuance of a reorganization and the shareholders of the corporations involved exchange their shares or receive distributions without surrender of their shares. The provisions of the Code must be strictly complied with in order for such exchanges or distributions to be nontaxable.

Repairs

Repairs are expenditures made to keep property in good condition, but not basically intended to appreciably prolong the life or increase the value of the property. If the property is business or income-producing property, the amount of ordinary and necessary repairs is deductible.

Replacements

Replacements are expenditures for making good or whole a portion of property which has deteriorated through use or been destroyed through accident. Although deduction for the gradual deterioration or the destruction is allowable, subject to the limitations in the Code, a replacement is a capital expenditure to be distinguished from repairs.

Residual estate

That portion of the estate which remains after the payment of debts, expenses of administration, legacies and devises. It consists of that part of the estate which has not been legally disposed of by the will prior to the carrying out of the residuary clause of said will.

Retirement income credit—See Tax credit for the elderly

—S—

S corporation

An S corporation, as distinguished from a C corporation (the treatment of whose distributions is governed by Subchapter C), is a small business corporation that meets various requirements and has validly elected not to be taxed at the corporate level. Items of income or loss are passed through to shareholders in much the same manner that such items are passed through to the partner of a partnership.

Section 306 stock

Section 306 is designed to prevent preferred stock *bail-outs* where preferred stock (Section 306 stock) is issued as a dividend and either sold or redeemed in an attempt to realize capital gains. Section 306 accomplishes this by taxing the gain on sale or receipts from redemption as ordinary income to the extent of the corporation's accumulated earnings and profits.

Section 1231 dispositions

If, during the taxable year, the recognized gains on sales or exchanges of property used in the trade or business, plus the recognized gains from the compulsory or involuntary conversion of property used in the trade or business or of capital assets held long-term into other property or money, exceed the recognized losses from such sales, exchanges, and conversions, then such gains and losses are treated as capital gains and losses. If such gains do not exceed such losses, then the gains and losses are treated as ordinary gains and losses. However, to the extent that any Section 1231 gain contains gain from the disposition of Section 1245 or Section 1250 property (see below), such gain will be recaptured as ordinary income to the extent of certain depreciation deductions taken.

Section 1244 stock—See Small business stock

Section 1245 property

Section 1245 property includes depreciable personal property and other depreciable property (other than buildings or their structural components) used in manufacturing, production, or extraction or used in furnishing transportation, communications, electrical energy, gas, water, or sewage disposal services. When Section 1245 property is disposed of, any gain is treated as ordinary income to the extent of depreciation deducted. Thus, although Section 1245 property may also be a Section 1231 asset, Section 1231 gain will be realized on the disposition only to the extent that the gain realized exceeds the post-1961 depreciation. Single-purpose agricultural and horticultural structures and storage facilities used in connection with the distribution of petroleum and its primary products that are placed in service after 1980 are included in the Section 1245 property category. Such property placed in service before 1981 is Section 1250 property. A gain on the sale or disposition of Section 1245 property is taxed as ordinary income to the extent of the depreciation deductions allowed.

Section 1250 property

Section 1250 property is property that is depreciable or recoverable but is not subject to the recapture rule under Code Sec. 1245. This includes all intangible real property (such as leases of land, buildings and their structural components, including elevators and escalators placed in service after 1986) and all other tangible real property except property which is used as an integral part of manufacturing, production or extraction or used in furnishing transportation, communications, electrical energy, gas, water or sewage disposal services, or research or storage facilities used in connection with these activities.

Self-employed individual's retirement plan

Self-employed individual's retirement plans—or, as they are more commonly called, H.R. 10 plans or Keogh plans—are qualified retirement plans that must meet certain special requirements because they benefit owner-employees. The annual limit for a participant in a defined contribution plan is the lesser of $30,000 or 25 percent of compensation. With respect to a participant in a defined benefit plan, the maximum benefit is the lesser of $130,000 for 1998 (indexed each year) or average compensation for the participant's three years of highest compensation.

Self-employment income

The Social Security provisions cover self-employed persons so that they are eligible for benefits upon retirement at the same age and in the same manner as wage earners. The combined rate of tax on self-employment income is 15.3 percent for 1998. The rate consists of a 12.4 percent component for old-age, survivors, and disability insurance (OASDI) and a 2.9 percent component for hospital insurance (medicare). For 1998, the maximum self-employment income subject to the OASDI component of the tax rate (12.4 percent) is $68,400; there is no cap on earnings subject to the medicare hospital insurance tax. If net earnings are less than $400, no self-employment tax is payable. Also, beginning in 1990, self-employed individuals may deduct one-half of their self-employment taxes for income tax purposes or, instead of this business expense deduction, they may reduce self-employment income by an amount equal to the product of their net earnings multiplied by one-half of the self-employment tax rate for the year. For 1998, this is 7.65 percent of the net earnings from self-employment.

Short sale

A short sale, as applied to securities, is an agreement to transfer stock that the seller does not own or whose stock certificates are not in the seller's control but must be borrowed to cover the transaction. The borrowed stock must be replaced within a specified time through purchase on the market and transferred to the lender of the borrowed stock. For income tax purposes, there is no gain or loss on the transaction until the short sale is covered by purchase and transfer. Special rules apply for determining whether gain or loss on a short sale is a long-term or short-term capital gain or loss.

Short-term capital gain—See Holding period

Simple trust

A simple trust is one for which the trust instrument requires that all income be distributed currently, with no authority to make charitable contributions. Also, the trust is a simple trust only for a year in which it distributes current income and makes no other distributions to beneficiaries. A simple trust is entitled to a $300 deduction in lieu of a personal exemption. For a year in which the trust does not meet these requirements, it is a *complex trust.*

Small business corporation

A *small business corporation* is defined in the Code for two separate purposes. For the two definitions, see *S corporation* and *Small business stock.*

Small business investment company

A *small business investment company* is a term which, for federal income tax purposes, is restricted to a company operating under the Small Business Investment Act of 1958, that is, a company authorized by that Act to provide equity capital to small business concerns through the purchase of convertible debentures. These companies and their investors are given special income tax advantages, such as a 100 percent dividends-received credit and ordinary loss deductions for the worthlessness of stock or securities held by the investment company or stock issued by the company.

Small business stock

To encourage the flow of new funds into small business, Congress created a stock classification with a special tax treatment. This is Section 1244 stock. Under Code Sec. 1244, an original individual investor can treat a loss on small business corporation stock as an ordinary loss—up to $50,000 on a single return or $100,000 on a joint return. Because the Code Sec. 1244 loss is considered in any net operating loss computation, the carryback and carryover rules apply. To qualify under Code Sec. 1244, the stock must be common stock in a domestic small business corporation.

Spin-off

A *spin-off* is a distribution by a corporation of stock or securities in another corporation controlled by it (through at least 80 percent stock ownership) without the surrender of any shares by the shareholders. It is a type of corporate separation. The distribution need not be in reorganization. However, the law contains definite rules requiring that the controlled corporation must have been actively engaged in a trade or business and must continue to be so engaged after the distribution. Furthermore, the trade or business must have been conducted (but not necessarily by the controlled corporation) for at least five years prior to the distribution. The distribution will not be taxable to the shareholders if the distributing corporation distributes at least 80 percent of the outstanding stock of the controlled corporation.

Split-off

A *split-off* is a type of corporate separation, not necessarily in reorganization, whereby a parent corporation distributes to its shareholders stock in a corporation which it controls, under the same conditions as in a *spin-off*, except that the shareholders surrender a part of their stock in the parent corporation for the stock in the controlled corporation. As under the conditions described under *spin-off*, no gain is recognized to the shareholders from the exchange of their shares.

Split-up

A *split-up* occurs where a corporation transfers its assets to two or more corporations in exchange for their stock or securities and then completely liquidates by distributing the stock in the new corporations to its stockholders or security holders in exchange for its own stock. The same nonrecognition treatment applies as in the case of a *spin-off* or a *split-off*.

Standard deduction

Taxpayers receive the benefit of a minimum amount of itemized deductions called the standard deduction. The standard deduction is a fixed amount that is used to simplify the computation of the tax liability. It is also designed to eliminate lower-income individuals from the tax rolls. All taxpayers subtract from adjusted gross income the larger of their itemized deductions or the standard deduction. The standard deduction is based on the filing status of the taxpayer and is made up of the basic standard deduction plus any additional standard deduction. The standard deduction amounts are adjusted annually for inflation.

An additional standard deduction is allowed aged or blind taxpayers. For 1998, the additional standard deduction is $850 for an aged or blind individual who is married or is a surviving spouse; the additional standard deduction is $1,050 for a single individual or for a head of household who is aged or blind. Taxpayers receive an additional standard deduction for being both aged and blind. Thus, a married couple, both aged and blind, receives an additional standard deduction of $3,400 ($850 × 4).

Statute of limitations

A statute of limitations sets out the period within which actions may be brought upon claims or within which rights may be enforced. The limitations periods of greatest importance for tax purposes are the three-year period in which a tax deficiency may be assessed (subject to modifications and extensions) and the three-year period in which a taxpayer may claim a refund (also subject to modifications).

Stepped-up basis

A *stepped-up* basis is a higher basis (see *Basis*) than an asset had in the hands of a previous owner. Under present law, this is accomplished through a transfer on which the gain is taxable or through acquisitions (not subject to the carryover basis rules) from a decedent.

Stock bonus plan

A stock bonus plan is established and maintained to provide benefits similar to those of a profit-sharing plan, but the contributions are not necessarily dependent upon profits and the benefits are distributable in the stock of the employer. A stock bonus plan is often referred to as an employee stock ownership plan (ESOP) or an employee stock ownership trust.

Stock option—See Employee stock option

Straight-line depreciation

Straight-line depreciation is the method of writing off the cost or other basis of depreciable assets in equal annual amounts over the estimated useful life of the assets.

Straight-line MACRS election

A taxpayer may elect, under MACRS, to claim straight-line MACRS deductions instead of the regular MACRS allowance. The recovery periods under the straight-line election include the regular recovery period and longer recovery periods. The straight-line MACRS deductions are computed in much the same manner as the deductions under the general rules, except that salvage value is not taken into account.

Subchapter S corporation—See S corporation

Subsidiary—See Parent corporation

Substance v. form

Individuals should arrange their financial transactions in a manner that will minimize their tax liability. If a transaction is all it purports to be and not merely a transaction to avoid taxes, then it is valid. If the transaction is solely to avoid taxes and there is no business purpose to the transaction, then it is invalid. The fact that a taxpayer uses one form of transaction rather than another to minimize taxes does not invalidate the transaction. A good example of when substance v. form is a significant issue is in the area of leases. Payments under a lease are tax deductible. Payments under a purchase agreement are not tax deductible. Therefore, it is of utmost importance to determine the true "substance" of this type of transaction. Questions to be asked might include: Do any equity rights transfer to the lessee at the end of the lease period? May the lessee buy the property at a nominal purchase price? With a lease transaction it is immaterial that the parties refer to the transaction as a lease. The true substance of the transaction controls over the form.

Substituted basis

The basis for gain or loss on sale or for depreciation (see *Basis*) of property may, under certain conditions, be determined by reference to the basis of a prior owner of the property (as in the case of a gift) or by reference to the basis of other property (as in the case of a tax-free exchange). Both are defined in the Code as a substituted basis, although the former is sometimes referred to as a *transferred basis*.

Sum-of-the-years-digits method

The *sum-of-the-years-digits* method of deducting depreciation is a variation of the declining-balance method. Under this method, the successive numbers representing the life of the asset by years (one, two, three, and four, for example, if the asset has a life of four years) are added together $(1 + 2 + 3 + 4 = 10)$, and the first year's depreciation fraction is determined by using as the numerator the number of years of remaining life of the asset and as the denominator the sum of the digits. (Thus, if the life is four years, 4/10 of the cost of the asset would be written off in the first year.) Salvage value reduces the basis under the sum-of-the-years-digits method. Like the declining-balance method, it has the effect of writing off the larger part of the cost in the earlier years when the most depreciation on a new asset is actually sustained.

Surviving spouse

Surviving spouses are entitled to the income-splitting benefits of filing a joint return on the death of one spouse. The joint return is made for the regular tax year of the survivor and the short period of the decedent. Use of joint return rates is also allowed to an unmarried widow or widower who maintains a home as a household for a dependent child. This benefit is limited to the first two tax years following the year in which the decedent spouse died.

— T —

Tax benefit rule

A recovery is includible in income only to the extent that the deduction reduced tax in any prior year by any amount. Therefore, where a deduction reduced taxable income but did not reduce tax, the recovery amount is excludable from income. This rule applies to both corporate and noncorporate taxpayers.

Tax Court

The United States Tax Court is a legislative court under Article I, Section 8, Clause 9 of the Constitution. Its principal function is to review deficiencies assessed by the Commissioner for income, estate, gift, or certain excise taxes. Hearings are held in principal cities throughout the country.

Tax credit for the elderly

The tax credit for the elderly and the permanently and totally disabled replaced the old retirement income credit. One set of rules for credit purposes applies to individuals who are age 65 or older. Another set of rules applies to federal, state, and local government retirees who are under age 65 and to permanently disabled individuals.

Tax credit stock ownership plan—See Employee Stock Ownership Plan (ESOP)

Tax shelter

Basically, tax shelters are investments that provide investors with the possibility of reducing their current income taxes through methods sanctioned by the tax law, thereby *sheltering* current income from tax. Although tax shelters offer an investor the opportunity to invest in many different kinds of assets and, thus, offer a wide range of potential benefits to their investors, the following basic aims are common to the vast majority of tax shelters: (1) maximizing the tax incentives available to the investors; (2) reducing current income tax liability and deferring taxation on any income or gain from the investment until some future tax year; and (3) permitting investors to use borrowed money to finance their original investments (leveraging). Some tax shelters satisfy all three aims, while others satisfy one or two; some rely heavily on their ability to satisfy only one of the aims.

In recent years, Congress has enacted specific Code provisions aimed at restricting the tax benefits of certain tax shelters that permit high-income taxpayers to reduce or avoid tax. Further, the IRS has been vigilant in its examination of returns of taxpayers that indicate participation in a possibly abusive tax shelter.

Taxable income

Taxable income for a corporation is gross income minus all deductions allowable, including special deductions such as the one for dividends received. Taxable income for individuals who itemize deductions is equal to adjusted gross income minus personal exemptions, minus the greater of the itemized deductions or the standard deduction amount. For nonitemizers, taxable income is adjusted gross income minus personal exemptions minus the standard deduction.

Taxable year

Taxable year means the calendar year or a fiscal year ending during such calendar year upon the basis of which the taxable income is computed. In the case of a return made for a fractional part of a year, *taxable year* is the period for which such return is made.

Tenancy by the entirety

Generally speaking, this is a joint tenancy between husband and wife. A tenancy by the entirety cannot be terminated except by the joint action of the husband and wife during their lives. This is in contrast to a joint tenancy, which either party may terminate merely by conveying the interest to another party.

Tenancy in common

A form of ownership where title is held by two or more persons with each owning a fractional interest in the undivided property. Upon the death of one tenant in common, the interest will not pass to the surviving tenant in common but will become part of the deceased tenant's probate estate and will be distributed according to such tenant's will.

Testamentary trust

A trust which is set up under the will of the decedent. Conversely, an inter vivos trust is one set up during the lifetime of the person setting up the trust.

Testator

One who makes or has made a will; one who dies leaving a will. (Feminine form: testatrix.)

Top-heavy plan

Top-heavy plan refers to a qualified plan that must meet additional requirements because key employees' aggregate accumulated benefits or aggregate accounts exceed 60 percent of all such accumulated benefits or accounts in the plan.

Totten trust

A trust created by the deposit of a person's own money in his or her own name as trustee for another person. This is considered a revocable trust at the will of the trustee until the depositor dies or otherwise completes the gift during his or her lifetime.

Trade or business

A trade or business consists of any activity that occupies the time, attention, and labor of individuals for the purpose of earning a livelihood or making a profit. It includes the rendering of services to others as an employee for compensation, the carrying on of a profession, and every business occupation carried on for subsistence or profit and into which the elements of bargain and sale, barter, exchange, or traffic enter.

Transaction entered into for profit

A broad meaning is accorded the phrase *transaction entered into for profit,* losses from which are deductible. It includes the acquisition of any income-producing property or investment property, as distinguished from property for one's personal use or enjoyment. The acquisition may be by gift or inheritance if the property is investment or income-producing property. In some cases, the term can include a transaction entered into simply to avoid or cut down a loss on another transaction.

Transferee liability

If a taxpayer transfers assets to another at a time when the taxpayer is liable for outstanding income, estate, or gift taxes (whether or not determined) and the remaining assets after the transfer are insufficient to pay such taxes, the person who received the assets is liable for the taxes to the extent of the value of the assets received. If there are two or more transferees, each one is so liable.

Travel expenses

Travel expenses are deductible in determining adjusted gross income in the case of an individual involved in a trade or business or in a transaction entered into for profit. Travel expenses include transportation costs and the amount spent for meals and lodging *while away from home* in the pursuit of a trade or business. However, the 2 percent of adjusted gross income floor applies to unreimbursed travel expenses of employees and the 50 percent limitation applies to meal and entertainment expenses without regard to whether the taxpayer is traveling.

Trust

A fiduciary relationship with respect to property whereby the property is held by one party (the trustee) for the benefit of another party (the beneficiary). A trust is usually set up and governed by a written document.

— W —

Wash sale

In the language of the stock exchange, a wash sale is the simultaneous or almost simultaneous purchase and sale of the same stock. For income tax purposes, a sale of stock or securities at a loss cannot result in deduction of the loss if substantially identical stocks or securities are purchased within a 61-day period beginning 30 days before the date of the sale and ending 30 days after the sale. The acquisition or reacquisition of such stock or securities has no effect on sales at a gain.

Welfare-to-work credit

A credit is available for employers for wages paid to long-term family assistance recipients who begin work after 1997. The amount of the credit for a tax year is 35 percent of the qualified first-year wages for such year plus 50 percent of the qualified second-year wages. The credit applies only to the first $10,000 of wages in each year with respect to any individual.

Wherewithal to pay

The concept that the taxpayer should be taxed on a transaction when he or she has the means to pay the tax. For example, a taxpayer owns property that is increasing in value. The IRS does not tax the increased value until the taxpayer sells the property. At the time of sale, the taxpayer has the wherewithal to pay.

Withholding allowance

Since the graduated withholding system could cause taxpayers who have large itemized deductions to be seriously overwithheld, these taxpayers are permitted to claim extra exemptions which are called *withholding allowances.*

Withholding of tax at source

An employer is required to withhold income taxes from the wages of employees. The tax to be withheld is computed under the percentage method or by use of wage-bracket tables. There is also withholding of tax at source in the case of nonresident aliens receiving fixed or determinable annual or periodic income from United States sources.

Work opportunity tax credit

A credit may be elected by employers who hire individuals from certain target groups suffering from unusually high umemployment. The credit is taken with respect to first-year wages paid to eligible individuals who begin work after September 30, 1997, and before June 30, 1998. The work opportunity credit equals 40 percent of the first $6,000 of wages for the first year of employment. The $6,000 limit is computed on each eligible employee for wages attributable to services rendered during the one-year period beginning with the day the individual begins work for the employer (maximum credit of $2,400 per employee). The credit is part of the general business credit.

Finding Lists

References are to paragraph (¶) numbers

Citations given throughout this textbook are compiled in the following lists: Internal Revenue Code Sections, Regulations Sections, Revenue Procedures, and Revenue Rulings.

Internal Revenue Code Sections

11	20,155	45A	8045
11(b)	13,405	45C(a)	8045
21(a)(2)	8015	46(a)	8045
21(b)(1)	8015	46(c)(8)	20,339
21(b)(2)	8015	47(a)	8045
21(c)	8015	47(c)	8045
21(d)(1)	8015	48	8045
21(d)(2)	8015	48(b)	8045
21(e)(1)	8015	49	8045
21(e)(2)	8015	49(a)(1)(D)(iv)	6125
21(e)(4)	8015	50	8045; 14,021
21(e)(5)	8015	50(a)(1)	13,165
21(e)(6)	8015	50(c)(3)	8045
22(a)–(c)	8025	51(a)	8045
22(c)	8025	51(b)	8045
22(c)(3)	8025	53	8455
22(d)(1)	8025	55–59	13,415
22(e)(1)	8025	55(b)	8401
22(f)	8025	55(d)	8435; 13,415
23	8031	55(d)(3)(C)	22,371
27	13,401	56	13,415
27(a)	8035	56(a)	8415
31(a)	8105	56(b)	8415
31(b)	8115	56(b)(1)(E)	8415
32	8125	56(g)(4)(I)	13,415
33	8135	57	8425
34	8155; 20,163	57(a)	13,415; 17,239
38	8045; 13,165; 13,401; 20,221	58(a)	8415
38(c)	8045	58(i)	20,221
39	8045	59	8445; 13,415
40	8045	59(c)	22,371
41(a)	8045	61	12,001; 12,215; 13,301; 21,101
42(a)	8045	61(a)	3015; 3101; 3301
44	8045	61(a)(11)	4255
45	8045	61(a)(12)	3485

Regulations Sections

Revenue Procedures

71-21 12,235
74-33 . . . . 12,015; 18,235; 20,105
77-37 16,105
79-14 . . . . 16,005; 16,351; 16,533
84-74 12,355
85-16 12,115
87-56 . . . . 5401; 10,215
87-57 5401
88-22 5401
90-3 15,275
90-16 24,035
90-59 7315
92-43 5401
92-85 19,315
93-21 5635
93-27 18,015
94-36 24,035

95-37 . . . . 18,001; 18,015
96-25 5401
96-64 5635
97-1 24,225
97-2 24,225
97-3 24,225
97-7 24,225
97-8 24,225
97-20 5401
97-27 . . . . 12,325; 12,355
97-57 . . . . Appendix
98-1 24,225
98-2 24,225
98-3 24,225
98-7 24,225
98-8 24,225

Revenue Rulings

239 23,625
54-135 21,301
54-569 10,345
55-79 11,115
55-408 23,615
55-711 2345
55-746 14,145
56-513 14,125
56-675 18,515
57-244 10,275
57-276 . . . . 16,157; 16,277
57-310 22,015
57-314 10,301
57-418 5515
57-599 7501
58-210 9201
58-277 10,301
59-60 . . . . 21,187; 21,191
59-173 10,335
59-221 20,281
59-235 20,009
59-259 . . . . 13,125; 16,053

59-379 2225
60-31 23,501
60-190 2225
62-136 23,625
63-221 10,301
64-31 10,001
64-147 16,157
64-237 10,345
64-250 16,277
65-34 2225
65-80 15,161
66-7 11,201
66-235 19,449
66-365 16,053
67-105 18,501
67-396 21,301
68-37 10,335
68-55 13,135
68-79 18,335
68-145 22,015
68-285 16,053
68-650 10,035

Table of Cases

References are to paragraph (¶) numbers

1332

Table of Cases

References are to paragraph (¶) numbers

Topical Index

References are to paragraph (¶) numbers

A

AB trust plans . . . 23,635

Accelerated Cost Recovery System (ACRS)
. alternative minimum tax . . . 13,415
. Section 1245 property . . . 11,745
. use of system . . . 5401

Accelerated depreciation, tax preference item . . . 8425

Accident and health plans
. benefits exclusion from gross income . . . 4155
. employer contributions . . . 4155

Accounting concepts
. accounting income . . . 3025
. constructive receipt doctrine . . . 3125
. economic benefit doctrine . . . 3101
. economic income . . . 3001
. realization of income . . . 3025

Accounting fees . . . 5285

Accounting methods
. accrual method—see Accrual method of accounting
. advance payments . . . 12,235
. bad debts . . . 12,235
. cash method—see Cash method of accounting
. change of method . . . 12,301-12,375
. change of method, adjustments . . . 12,325
. change of method, application and form . . . 12,355
. change of method, IRS consent . . . 12,301
. change of method, timeliness . . . 12,375
. contested liabilities . . . 12,235
. corporations . . . 12,015; 13,311
. correction of errors . . . 12,301
. cost methods . . . 12,425
. deductions, computation . . . 5115
. dollar-value LIFO method . . . 12,473
. election timeliness . . . 12,375
. estates . . . 22,045
. expenses . . . 12,235
. hybrid methods . . . 12,265
. installment method—see Installment method of accounting
. installment sales . . . 12,601-12,699
. inventories . . . 12,401-12,485

Accounting methods—continued
. last-in, first-out (LIFO) method . . . 12,461
. long-term contracts . . . 12,501-12,535
. lower of cost or market method . . . 12,445
. partnerships . . . 18,025
. permission to change . . . 12,301
. prepayments . . . 12,235
. repossessions . . . 12,695
. S corporations . . . 20,501
. selection of method . . . 12,201
. separate sources of income . . . 12,245
. simplified dollar-value LIFO method . . . 12,481
. simplified production method . . . 12,435
. simplified resale method . . . 12,435
. tax planning . . . 12,365
. trusts . . . 22,215
. uniform capitalization rules . . . 12,435
. valuation of inventories . . . 12,415
. valuation of inventory items . . . 12,453

Accounting periods
. affiliated groups . . . 12,175
. annualization of income . . . 12,165
. business year . . . 12,015
. changes of . . . 12,101-12,175
. corporations . . . 12,015; 13,305
. election of tax year . . . 12,015
. estates . . . 12,015
. exempt organizations . . . 12,115
. 52-53-week year . . . 12,007
. individuals . . . 12,015
. IRS permission to change . . . 12,101; 12,115
. natural business year . . . 12,175
. net operating losses . . . 12,115
. partnerships . . . 12,015
. personal service corporations . . . 12,115
. S corporations . . . 12,015; 12,115
. short-period tax computation . . . 12,165
. sole proprietors . . . 12,015
. tax planning . . . 12,175
. tax year . . . 12,007
. trusts . . . 12,015

Accrual method of accounting . . . 1195; 3113; 12,201; 12,235
. prepayments . . . 12,235

Accumulated adjustments accounts (AAA) . . . 20,285

Accumulated earnings and profits
. distributions with . . . 20,343

Accumulated earnings and profits—continued
. distributions without . . . 20,341

Accumulated earnings tax
. accumulated earnings credit . . . 17,057
. accumulated taxable income . . . 17,073
. avoidance of tax . . . 17,089
. *Bardahl* formula . . . 17,033
. basis of liability . . . 17,017
. computation of tax base . . . 17,073
. consent dividends . . . 17,065
. credit for accumulated earnings . . . 17,057
. dividends paid deduction . . . 17,065
. earnings and profits valuation . . . 17,097
. imposition of tax . . . 17,089
. liability for tax . . . 17,017
. personal holding company tax distinguished . . . 17,001
. public corporations . . . 17,081
. rate and nature of tax . . . 17,001
. reasonable business needs . . . 17,025
. working capital needs . . . 17,033

Accumulated taxable income . . . 17,073

Acquiescence by IRS, court decisions . . . 24,035

Additions to tax liability—see Penalties

Adjusted basis of property—see Basis

Adjusted current earnings . . . 13,415

Adjusted gross estate—see Estates, income taxation

Adjusted gross income
. deductions . . . 2015
. individuals . . . 2025

Adjustments, alternative minimum tax . . . 8415; 13,415

Adjustments to basis—see Basis

Administration expenses, estates . . . 21,201

Administrative appeals, IRS procedures . . . 24,311

Administrative rulings . . . 24,035

Adoption expenses
. credits against tax . . . 8031
. exclusion from income . . . 4140; 8031

Advance payments
. accounting methods . . . 12,235

ADV

Certiorari, petition . . . 24,055

Change of accounting methods—
see Accounting methods

Charitable contributions
. appreciated property . . . 8425;
   13,415
. capital gain property . . . 7325
. corporations . . . 13,345
. deduction . . . 7301–7355; 13,345
. estate income tax return . . .
   22,357
. estate tax . . . 21,225
. estates . . . 22,357
. 50 percent limitations . . . 7325
. filing requirements . . . 7355
. gift tax . . . 21,355
. inventory and research property
   . . . 13,345
. limitations . . . 7325
. percentage limitation . . . 7325
. property donated by individuals
   . . . 7325
. qualified organizations . . . 7301
. recapture rules . . . 11,925
. substantiation requirements . . .
   7355
. 30 percent limitation . . . 7325
. trusts . . . 22,357
. valuation . . . 7315

Charitable organizations . . . 7301

Charitable remainder trusts . . .
21,225

Check-the-box regulations . . .
18,001

Child support payments . . . 3451

Child tax credit . . . 1165; 8032

Circuit Courts of Appeals . . . 24,055;
24,311

Circulation expenditures . . . 13,415

Circulation expenditures,
alternative minimum tax . . . 8415

Citations
. administrative memoranda . . .
   24,035
. Claims Court . . . 24,055
. Courts of Appeals . . . 24,055
. District Court . . . 24,055
. Internal Revenue Code . . . 24,021
. Revenue Rulings and Revenue
   Procedures . . . 24,035
. Supreme Court . . . 24,055
. Tax Court . . . 24,055
. Treasury Department regulations
   . . . 24,035

Citator . . . 24,075

Civil penalties . . . 24,365

Claim of right defined . . . 1195

Claims Court—see Court of Federal
Claims

Clinical testing . . . 8045

Closely held corporations
. distributions . . . 14,205
. passive activity loss rules . . . 6231
. stock dividends . . . 14,205

Closely held corporations—
continued
. valuation of stock, estate tax . . .
   21,191

Collapsible corporations
. definitions . . . 15,505
. relief provisions . . . 15,545
. rules, application . . . 15,501
. taxable income requirement . . .
   15,525
. view to collapse requirement . . .
   15,515

Collection of tax . . . 1121

Collectibles gain . . . 11,301

Commissions . . . 10,215

Community property
. estate tax . . . 21,157
. income tax . . . 3215
. partnerships . . . 18,325
. retirement planning . . . 23,665

Compensation for injuries and
sickness . . . 4145

Compensation for personal services
. gifts distinguished . . . 3325
. gross income . . . 3315

Complete liquidations—see
Liquidations

Completed-contract accounting
method . . . 12,501

Computation of tax
. accumulated earnings tax . . .
   17,073
. estate tax . . . 21,001
. generation-skipping transfer tax
   . . . 21,555
. gift tax . . . 21,415
. personal holding company tax . . .
   17,215

Computer-based research . . .
24,153–24,171

Condemnation of real property . . .
10,355

Conduits, defined . . . 1195

Consent dividends
. accumulated earnings tax . . .
   17,065
. personal holding company tax . . .
   17,231

Consolidated returns . . . 13,445

Consolidations . . . 16,001; 16,009

Constructive dividends . . . 14,025

Constructive ownership of stock
rules . . . 14,105

Constructive-receipt doctrine . . .
1195
. accounting concept . . . 3125

Consumer interest deduction . . .
7205

Contested liabilities . . . 12,235

Contingent liabilities, liquidations
. . . 15,253

Continuity of stock ownership . . .
16,533

Contributions to capital . . . 13,201

Controlled corporations
. brother-sister corporations . . .
   13,433
. parent-subsidiary corporations
   . . . 13,433

Co-ops . . . 10,015

Corporate distributions . . . 20,339

Corporate entity concept . . . 18,445;
19,001

Corporate reorganizations—see
Reorganizations

Corporation Excise Tax of 1909 . . .
1151

Corporations
. accounting methods . . . 13,311
. accounting periods . . . 12,015;
   13,305
. affiliated corporations . . . 13,385
. alternative minimum tax . . .
   13,415
. associations . . . 13,015
. basis determination . . . 13,155
. boot, receipt of . . . 13,135
. brother-sister controlled groups
   . . . 13,433
. capital gains and losses . . .
   11,201; 13,315
. capital structure . . .
   13,201–13,245
. characteristics . . . 13,015
. charitable contributions . . .
   13,345
. collapsible corporations . . .
   15,501–15,545
. consolidated returns . . . 13,445
. consolidations . . . 16,001; 16,009
. contributions to capital . . . 13,201
. controlled corporate groups . . .
   13,433
. debt-financed portfolio stock . . .
   13,385
. debt in capital structure . . .
   13,215
. debts . . . 3485
. definition . . . 13,015
. depreciation . . . 13,415
. depreciation recapture . . .
   13,165; 13,325
. distributions—see Distributions
   by corporations
. dividends-received deduction . . .
   13,385
. equity in capital structure . . .
   13,201
. executive compensation . . .
   13,391
. extraordinary dividends . . .
   13,385
. form of business . . . 13,001
. holding periods . . . 13,155
. income tax, revenue source . . .
   1101

Deferred cash plans—see Section 401(k) plans

Deferred compensation plans—see also Retirement planning . . . 23,501

Defined benefit pension plans . . . 24,055

Definitions—see also specific terms
. corporate reorganizations . . . 16,001
. corporation . . . 13,015
. personal holding company . . . 17,175
. powers of appointment . . . 21,165

Delinquency penalties . . . 24,365

Dental expenses . . . 3451

Dependents
. child support payments for . . . 3451
. citizen or resident test . . . 2225
. custodial parent's exemption . . . 3451
. dependent care assistance programs . . . 4235
. dependent care credit . . . 8015
. dependent care services, employees . . . 4235
. divorced parents . . . 2225
. gross income test . . . 2225
. member of the household test . . . 2225
. multiple support agreements . . . 2225
. no joint return test . . . 2225
. personal exemptions . . . 2225
. relationship test . . . 2225
. resident test . . . 2225
. returns . . . 2365
. separated parents . . . 2225
. support test . . . 2225

Depletion
. alternative minimum tax . . . 13,415
. deduction . . . 5451
. estates and trusts . . . 22,331
. S corporations . . . 20,221
. tax preference item . . . 8425

Deposits of taxes . . . 24,365

Depreciation
. accelerated cost recovery system . . . 5401
. alternative depreciation system . . . 5401
. alternative minimum tax . . . 13,415
. alternative minimum tax adjustment . . . 8415
. change of classes . . . 12,301
. corporations . . . 13,415
. deduction . . . 5401
. election to expense capital assets . . . 5401
. estates and trusts . . . 22,331
. modified accelerated cost recovery system . . . 5401
. recapture . . . 13,165; 13,325

Depreciation—continued
. recapture, Section 1250 property . . . 11,801–11,875
. Section 1245 property . . . 11,735

Determination letters . . . 24,225

Disability, IRA withdrawal . . . 23,305

Disabled persons access credit . . . 8045

Disaster losses
. involuntary converion rules . . . 10,305
. special election . . . 7501

Discharge of debt
. bankruptcy . . . 3485
. business debts . . . 3485
. corporate debts . . . 3485
. creditor's gifts . . . 3485
. purchase money debts . . . 3485
. student loans . . . 3485

Disclaimers, gifts or bequests . . . 21,255

Disclosure statements on tax return . . . 24,370

Discovery . . . 24,311

Discriminant Function (DIF) System, audit of returns . . . 24,301

Disproportionate distributions . . . 14,032

Disproportionate redemptions . . . 14,115

Distributable net income
. estate and trusts . . . 22,301; 22,325; 22,345

Distributions by corporations
. basis in property received . . . 14,021
. cash distributions . . . 14,015
. closely held corporations . . . 14,205
. common and preferred stock . . . 14,032
. constructive dividends . . . 14,025
. convertible preferred stock . . . 14,032
. depreciation recapture . . . 14,021
. disproportionate distributions . . . 14,032
. dividend reinvestment plans . . . 14,011
. earnings and profits adjustments . . . 14,021
. gain or loss recognition . . . 14,021
. installment obligations . . . 14,021
. investment tax credit . . . 14,021
. liabilities in excess of basis . . . 14,021
. liquidations—see Liquidations
. preferred stock dividends . . . 14,011
. property distributions . . . 14,021
. redemption of stock—see Stock redemptions
. reorganizations—see Reorganizations

Distributions by corporations—continued
. S corporations . . . 20,339
. shareholders, tax consequences . . . 14,021
. stock dividends . . . 14,032
. stock rights . . . 14,035
. tax consequences . . . 14,021; 20,285
. tax-free distributions . . . 14,011; 14,032

Distributions by estates . . . 22,301

Distributions by partnerships—see Partners and partnerships

Distributions by retirement plans . . . 23,401–23,425

District Courts . . . 24,055; 24,311

District Office examinations . . . 24,301

Dividend reinvestment plans . . . 14,011

Dividends
. annuity contracts . . . 3401
. cash . . . 3401
. constructive . . . 14,025
. gross income . . . 3401
. life insurance . . . 3401
. mutual funds . . . 3401
. stock rights . . . 3401

Dividends paid deduction
. accumulated earnings tax . . . 17,065
. personal holding company tax . . . 17,231

Dividends-received deduction . . . 13,385

Divorce
. annuity distributions . . . 3451
. child support . . . 3451
. dependency exemptions . . . 2225
. legal fees . . . 3451
. life insurance proceeds . . . 3451
. lump-sum settlements . . . 3451
. medical and dental expenses . . . 3451
. payments in arrears . . . 3451
. property transfers . . . 3451
. residence transfer . . . 10,015

Divorce and separation
. gift tax . . . 21,345
. individual retirement accounts . . . 23,315

Drugs, medical expenses . . . 7055

Dues, employee business expenses . . . 7685

E

Earned income credit . . . 8125

Earnings and profits
. accumulated earnings tax, adjustments . . . 17,097
. depreciation and cost recovery . . . 14,021

DEF

Earnings and profits—continued
. distributions with . . . 20,343
. distributions without . . . 20,341
. dividend distributions . . . 14,021
. property distributions . . . 14,021
. reorganizations . . . 16,497
. stock redemptions . . . 14,135
. valuation . . . 17,097

Economic benefit doctrine . . . 3101

Economic factions, tax law . . . 1175

Education expenses
. classification . . . 7665
. deduction . . . 7665
. employer requirements . . . 7665
. gift tax exclusion . . . 21,325
. improving necessary skills . . . 7665
. IRA withdrawals . . . 1165; 23,305; 23,322
. loan interest . . . 7210
. maintaining necessary skills . . . 7665
. new trade or business requirements . . . 7665

Education individual retirement accounts (IRAs) . . . 1165; 23,305; 23,322

Education savings bonds
. investments by taxpayers . . . 4075

Educational assistance plans . . . 4201

Elderly persons
. standard deduction . . . 2035
. tax credit . . . 8025

Elections
. accounting periods . . . 12,015
. partnerships . . . 18,235; 18,245
. S corporations . . . 20,001

Electric vehicles credit . . . 8040

Electronic tax research . . . 24,153–24,171

Employee achievement awards . . . 3335

Employee benefits
. annuities . . . 4125
. annuity contracts . . . 4125
. cafeteria plans . . . 4195
. dependent care services . . . 4235
. discounts on employer property or services . . . 4101
. educational assistance plans . . . 4201
. fringe benefits . . . 4101
. gross income exclusions . . . 4101–4125
. group-term life insurance . . . 4115
. legal services plans . . . 4175
. meals and lodging . . . 4185
. tuition reduction plans . . . 4215

Employee business expenses
. deduction . . . 7601–7685
. dues . . . 7685
. education . . . 7665

Employee business expenses—continued
. entertainment . . . 5655
. job seeking . . . 7655
. miscellaneous expenses . . . 7685
. moving expenses . . . 5675–5695
. reimbursed expenses . . . 7603
. subscriptions . . . 7685
. tools and supplies . . . 7685
. transportation . . . 5601
. travel, business and personal . . . 5635
. uniforms . . . 7675
. union dues . . . 7685
. unreimbursed expenses . . . 7605
. work clothes . . . 7675

Employees
. business expenses deductible . . . 7601–7685
. business-related expenses . . . 5011
. energy investment credit . . . 8045
. work opportunity credit . . . 8045

Employer-provided parking . . . 4115

Employer-sponsored individual retirement accounts (IRAs) . . . 23,325

Empowerment zone employment credit . . . 8045

Enhanced oil recovery credit . . . 8045

Entertainment expenses
. deduction . . . 5655
. entertainment facilities . . . 5655
. substantiation of deduction . . . 5655

Entity concept . . . 1195; 18,445; 19,001

Estate tax
. administration expenses . . . 21,201
. alternate valuation date . . . 21,181
. annuities . . . 21,149
. applicable credit amount . . . 21,009
. buy-sell agreements . . . 21,193
. casualty losses . . . 21,201
. charitable contributions . . . 21,225
. charitable remainder trusts . . . 21,225
. claims against estate . . . 21,201
. closely held corporations . . . 21,191; 21,195
. commercial annuities . . . 21,149
. community property . . . 21,157
. computation of tax . . . 21,001
. co-ownerships of property . . . 21,157
. credits against tax . . . 21,035
. debts . . . 21,201
. deductions from gross estate . . . 21,201–21,255
. disclaimers . . . 21,255
. exemption . . . 1165

Estate tax—continued
. expenses, deductions . . . 21,201
. family partnerships . . . 21,125
. farm property . . . 21,185; 23,601
. foreign death taxes . . . 21,035
. funeral expenses . . . 21,201
. future interests . . . 21,109
. general powers of appointment . . . 21,165
. generation skipping—see Generation-skipping transfer tax
. gifts, contemplation of death . . . 21,117
. gross estate . . . 21,101
. income tax deductions . . . 21,201
. joint tenancies . . . 21,157
. life insurance . . . 21,117; 21,173
. losses, deductions . . . 21,201
. marital deductions . . . 21,217
. partnerships . . . 21,125
. payment of tax . . . 21,025
. pension and profit-sharing plans . . . 21,149
. pooled income fund . . . 21,225
. powers of appointment . . . 21,165
. present interests in property . . . 21,109
. private annuities . . . 21,149
. property subject to claims . . . 21,201
. qualified terminable interest property . . . 21,217
. retained life estates . . . 21,125
. returns . . . 21,025
. revenue source . . . 1101
. reversions . . . 21,133
. revocable transfers . . . 21,141
. small estate exemption . . . 21,009
. special business exclusion . . . 21,109
. special powers of appointment . . . 21,165
. special use valuation . . . 21,195
. surviving spouse interest . . . 21,217
. tenancies by the entirety . . . 21,157
. tenancies in common . . . 21,157
. terminable interests . . . 21,217
. transfers, part-sale, part-gift . . . 21,175
. unified rate schedule . . . 21,015
. unified tax credit . . . 21,009
. valuation . . . 21,181–21,195

Estates, income taxation
. accounting periods . . . 12,015; 22,045
. administrative fees . . . 22,365
. alternative minimum tax . . . 22,371
. beneficiaries, tax position . . . 22,301
. cash basis taxpayers . . . 22,015
. charitable contributions . . . 22,357
. credits against tax . . . 22,365
. death tax, stock redemptions . . . 14,131

EST

STANDARD DEDUCTION

The standard deduction is based on the filing status of the taxpayer and is made up of the "basic standard deduction" plus any "additional standard deduction." The standard deduction is adjusted annually, if necessary, for inflation.

Filing Status	Basic Standard Deduction 1998
Single	$4,250
Married Filing Joint Return	7,100
Married Filing Separate Return	3,550
Head of Household	6,250
Surviving Spouse	7,100

Additional Standard Deduction for Age and Blindness. An additional standard deduction is allowed for those age 65 or over and for those who are blind. The additional standard deduction is the total of the additional amounts allowed for both age and blindness. The dollar value of each additional amount will depend on the taxpayer's filing status.

Filing Status	Additional Standard Deduction 1998
Single	$1,050
Married Filing Joint Return	850
Married Filing Separate Return	850
Head of Household	1,050
Surviving Spouse	850

Taxpayers receive an additional standard deduction for being both aged and blind. Thus, a married couple, both of whom are aged and blind, is allowed an additional standard deduction of $3,400 ($850 × 4).

OVERALL LIMITATION ON ITEMIZED DEDUCTIONS

For tax years beginning after 1990, an individual whose adjusted gross income exceeds a threshold amount is required to reduce the amount allowable for itemized deductions by 3 percent of the excess over that threshold. For 1998, the threshold amount is $124,500 for single and joint taxpayers ($62,250 for married persons filing a separate return).

In no event, however, may the reduction be more than 80 percent of allowable itemized deductions. Deductions exempt from reduction are: medical expenses, investment interest, casualty losses, and wagering losses to the extent of wagering gains. The reduction is applied only after first taking into account the other Code provisions that determine how much of a particular type of expense may be deducted, such as the 2 percent limitation on miscellaneous deductions.

Big Bang

Origins *Pointers*

Pointers

from space

currents

sphere

enzymes

Alcohol

Eco-
evolution

Predators

Biodiversity

Human
ecology

Speech

Grammar

Languages

Bernal's
Ladder
Pointers

Discovery

Mammals

Primate
behavior

Altruism and
aggression

Prehistoric
genes

Human
origins

Tree of Life

Molecules evolving

Extremophiles

Cambrian
explosion

Dinosaurs

Extinctions

Immune
system

Smallpox

Prions

Cloning

Hopeful
monsters

Evolution

Biological
clocks

Cell death

Immortality

Stem cells

Embryos

Photosynthesis

Flowering

Brain
rhythms

Brain images

Memory

Brain wiring

Proteomes

Plant
diseases

Cereals

Transgenic
crops

Plants
Pointers

Genomes
in general

Protein-
making

Arabidopsis

Protein
shapes

Cell cycle

Human
genome

DNA
fingerprinting

Genes

Cell traffic

materials

nanueuness

partners

terrestrial
life

Life's origin

MAGIC UNIVERSE

MAGIC UNIVERSE

The Oxford Guide to Modern Science

NIGEL CALDER

OXFORD

UNIVERSITY PRESS

OXFORD

UNIVERSITY PRESS

Great Clarendon Street, Oxford OX2 6DP

Oxford University Press is a department of the University of Oxford.
It furthers the University's objective of excellence in research, scholarship,
and education by publishing worldwide in

Oxford New York

Auckland Bangkok Buenos Aires Cape Town Chennai
Dar es Salaam Delhi Hong Kong Istanbul Karachi Kolkata
Kuala Lumpur Madrid Melbourne Mexico City Mumbai Nairobi
São Paulo Shanghai Taipei Tokyo Toronto

Oxford is a registered trade mark of Oxford University Press
in the UK and in certain other countries

Published in the United States
by Oxford University Press Inc., New York

British Library Cataloguing in Publication Data

Data available

Library of Congress Cataloguing in Publication Data

ISBN 0-19-850792-5

10 9 8 7 6 5 4 3 2 1

Typeset in 11/13pt Dante
by Kolam Information Services Pvt. Ltd., Pondicherry
Printed in Great Britain
by Biddles Limited,
Guildford

CONTENTS

CONTENTS

CONTENTS

CONTENTS

CONTENTS

CONTENTS

CONTENTS

CONTENTS

INTRODUCTION

Welcome to the spider's web

E SSAYS would be too grand a term, implying closures that, thank goodness, science never achieves. You have here a set of short stories about fundamental research, recent and current, and where it seems to be heading. They are written mainly in the past tense, so hinting that the best is yet to come.

The tags of the stories are arranged A, B, C, . . . , but please don't mistake this book for an encyclopaedia. The headings invite you to find out something about the topics indicated. They are in alphabetical order for ease of navigation around a spider's web of connections between topics. The book can be read in any sequence, from beginning to end, or at random, or interactively by starting anywhere and selecting which cross-reference to follow, from the end of each story.

The spider's web is the hidden software of the book. It celebrates a reunion of the many subdivisions of science that is now in progress. Let's return to the mental world of 200 years ago, before overspecialization spoilt the scientific culture. In those days a tolerably enlightened person could expect to know not just the buzzwords but the intellectual issues about atoms, stars, fossils, climate, and where swallows go in the winter.

The difference now is that you'll understand stars better if you know about atoms, and vice versa. It's the same with fossils and climate. Everything connects, not by sentimental holism, but in physical and chemical processes that gradually reassemble dem dry bones of Mother Nature. To find out how a swallow knows where to go in the winter, and to solve many other obstinate mysteries, only the cross-disciplinary routes may do.

The magic of the Universe reveals itself in the interconnections. A repertoire of tricks let loose in the Big Bang will make you a planet or a parakeet. In some sense only dimly understood so far, the magic works for our benefit overall, whilst it amazes and puzzles us in the particulars. Natural conjuring that links comets with life, genomes with continental drift, iron ore with dementia, and particle physics with cloudiness, mocks the specialists.

To speak of expertise on the entirety of science would be a contradiction. But generalists exist. Some earn their living in multidisciplinary institutions and agencies. Others stay fancy-free by reporting on any and all aspects of science, in newspapers, magazines and comic books, on radio, television, videos and websites, in exhibitions and in books.

The present author has worked in all those media, across half a century. His first journalistic action was as a Cambridge student in 1953. He tipped off his dad, who was the science editor of a London daily paper, about the gossip on King's Parade concerning a couple of blokes at the Cavendish who'd found out the shape of genes.

Age may slow the typing fingers, but a lifetime's exposure to trends and discoveries brings certain advantages. You become wary about hype, about dogmatism, and about Tom Lehrer's 'ivy-covered professors in ivy-covered halls'. From first-hand experience you know that thrilling discoveries can tiptoe in, almost unnoticed to begin with. Above all, you learn that the best of science is romantically exciting, and also illuminating—so why trouble busy readers with anything that isn't?

Independence helps too. The author is wedded to no particular subject, medium or institution. Entire branches of science may come and go, but personally he won't be out of pocket. And being free to ignore national borders, he can disregard the conviction of news editors that science is something that happens only in one's own country and in the USA.

The aim of giving the book a reasonable shelf life, as a guide to modern science, brings a particular discipline. The author has to consider whether what he writes now will look sensible or silly, ten years from now. The surest way to shorten the book's life would be to report only the consensual opinions of the late 20th century. Almost as fatal would be to chase after short-lived excitements or fads at the time of writing. Instead the policy is to try to identify some emphatic mid-course corrections that have altered the trajectory of research into the 21st century.

The outcome is subjective, of course, like everything else that was ever written about science. Even to pick one topic rather than another is to express a prejudice. What's more, the simultaneous equations of judiciousness, simplicity, and fairness to everyone are impossible to solve. So it's fairness that goes. For every subject, opinion and individual mentioned there are plenty of others that could be, but aren't. If you notice something missing, please ask yourself, as the author has had to do, what you would have left out to make room for it.

Might-have-beens that overlap with many other topics become, in several cases, 'pointers' instead. By giving the cross-references in some logical order, these brief entries help to clarify complicated stories and they provide necessary connections in the spider's web. An exception is the 'pointers' item that arranges some of the discoveries described in the book on Bernal's ladder of acceptibility in science. Consider it as a grace note.

Note on affiliations

Especially these days, when most scientific papers have several authors, a fair book would read like a telephone directory. To avoid clutter, affiliations are here indicated minimally, for instance by using 'at Oxford' or 'at Sydney' (as opposed to 'in') as a shorthand for at the University of Oxford or at the University of Sydney. UC means University of California, and Caltech is the California Institute of Technology. Institutes are usually mentioned in their national languages, exceptions being those in non-European languages and some special cases where the institute prefers to be named in English. Leiden Observatory and the Delft University of Technology spring to mind.

▶ *For more about the author's perceptions of science as a way of life, see* DISCOVERY. *For the persistent mystery of bird migration, see the last part of* BIOLOGICAL CLOCKS. *For the dawn of biocosmology, see* UNIVERSE *and its cross-references.*

ALCOHOL

Genetic revelations of when yeast invented booze

'**N**OTHING WILL BE ACHIEVED BY THIS,' the scientific board of the organic laboratory at Munich told Eduard Buchner in 1893. The young lecturer wanted to grind up the cells of brewer's yeast and find out what was in them. On that occasion, the dead hand of expert authority prevailed for very few years. When Hans Buchner joined the board of the hygiene institute in Munich he backed his kid brother's yeast project. Thus was biochemistry born of unabashed nepotism.

At the time there were widespread hopes that life might be explained in chemical terms, with no need for a special force. But the peculiar reactions associated with life were never seen in dead material. By 1897 Buchner had separated from yeast cells a factor that converted sugar into carbon dioxide. He had discovered the first enzyme, a natural catalyst promoting chemical reactions.

Fast-forward to the 21st century. Thousands of enzymes are known. They are protein molecules built according to precise instructions from the genes of heredity, each with a special function in the organisms that own them. The fermentation of sugar to make ethyl alcohol, the kind you can drink, requires production lines in the yeast cells, with different enzymes operating in sequence.

From molecular biology, and its capacity to identify similar genes in different organisms, has come an amazing conspectus of living chemistry. Subtle variations from species to species, in the same gene and the enzyme that it prescribes, reveal an evolutionary story. The wholesale reading of every gene—the genome—in a growing number of species accelerates the analysis. A preview of the insights into the history of life that can now be expected comes from investigations of when and how yeast acquired its tricks for making alcohol.

About 80 million years ago, giant herbivorous dinosaurs may have been overgrazing the vegetation. That prompting, fossil-hunters suggest, lay behind the evolutionary innovation of fruit, in flowering plants. Fruit encouraged the animals to carry the seeds away in their guts, to deposit them in new growing sites. Part of the inducement was the sugary, energy-rich flavouring.

Into this game going on between plants and large animals, yeast cells intruded. Too small to bite the fruit, they could invade damaged fruit and rot them. Flies joined in the fun. The fruit flies, ancestors of the *Drosophila* beloved of genetic researchers, evolved to specialize in laying their eggs in damaged fruit. An important part of the nourishment of the fruit-fly larvae was not the fruit, but the yeast.

Luckily, a flowering plant, yeast and *Drosophila* were among the first organisms to have their complete genomes read. Steven Benner, a chemist at the University of Florida, and his colleagues turned the spotlight of comparative genomics on the co-evolution among interacting species, associated with the invention of fruit. The molecular results were beautiful.

The genetic resources needed for the new fruity ways of life came from spare genes created by gene duplication. These could then try coding for new enzymes without depriving the organisms of enzymes already in use. The genomes of flowering plants and fruit flies both show bursts of gene duplication occurring around 80 million years ago. So, simultaneously, does the genome of brewer's yeast.

Among the new enzymes appearing in yeast at that time were precisely those required to complete the making of ethyl alcohol from dismembered sugar molecules. Pyruvate decarboxylase ejects a molecule of carbon dioxide, making the ferment fizzy. Alcohol dehydrogenase then completes the job of producing ethyl alcohol, by catalysing attachments of hydrogen atoms to an oxygen atom and a carbon atom.

'Generations of biochemistry students have had to learn by rote the pathway of enzymes that converts glucose to alcohol, as if it were written by a tedious taskmaster and not by living Nature,' Benner commented. 'Now we can beguile them with the genetic adventures of yeast in a rapidly changing planetary environment.'

The neat matches of the dates in the genomes imply that booze appeared on the menu fully 15 million years before the end of the reign of the giant reptiles. Present-day animals not averse to getting tiddly on fermented fruit include elephants and monkeys, as well as the human beings who have industrialized the activities of yeast. As one of the first inferences from the genomes, perhaps the roll call can now be extended to drunken dinosaurs.

▶ *For more about enzymes in the history of life, see* GLOBAL ENZYMES. *About gene duplication, see* MOLECULES EVOLVING. *For background, see* GENOMES IN GENERAL and PROTEOMES.

ALTRUISM AND AGGRESSION
Looking for the origins of those human alternatives

A T THE END of the 19th century Peter Kropotkin, a prince of Russia who had turned anarchist, fetched up in the UK. Like the communist Karl Marx before him, he took refuge among a population so scornful of overarching social theories that it could tolerate anyone who did not personally break the law. He found his host country humming with scientific ideas, notably Charles Darwin's on evolution and human behaviour. And the British provided him with his favourite example of anarchism in action.

In his book *Mutual Aid: A Factor of Evolution* (1902) Kropotkin's thesis was that people in general are inherently virtuous and helpful to one another, and so don't need to be disciplined by political masters. In the Darwinian spirit he cited anticipations of altruistic behaviour among animals that he observed during travels in the Siberian wilderness. And for mutual aid among humans?

'The Lifeboat Association in this country,' Kropotkin wrote, 'and similar institutions on the Continent, must be mentioned in the first place. The former has now over 300 boats along the coasts of these isles, and it would have twice as many were it not for the poverty of the fisher men, who cannot afford to buy lifeboats. The crews consist, however, of volunteers, whose readiness to sacrifice their lives for the rescue of absolute strangers to them is put every year to a severe test; every winter the loss of several of the bravest among them stands on record.'

Nowadays it's called the Royal National Lifeboat Institution, but the adjectives are honorific, not administrative. Although the gentry who assist in fundraising might be shocked to think that they are supporting an anarchist organization, Kropotkin did not err. Command and control are decentralized to the coastal communities supplying the manpower, and the money comes from nationwide public donations, without a penny from the state.

Even a modern high-tech, self-righting lifeboat is still lost from time to time, when it goes out without pause into an impossible tempest and robs a village of its finest young men. But also standing on record is the capacity of indistinguishable young men to perpetrate ethnic cleansing and other horrors. So, are human beings in general inherently wicked or kindly, aggressive or altruistic?

Original sin versus original virtue is the oldest puzzle in moral philosophy, and latterly in social psychology. Closely coupled with it are other big questions. What are the roles of genes and upbringing in shaping human behaviour in this respect? And are criminals fully accountable for their actions?

Klee versus Kandinsky

Science has illuminated the issues. Contributions come from studies of animal behaviour, evolution theory, social psychology, criminology and political science. The chief legacy from 20th-century science involves a shift of the searchlight from the behaviour of individuals to the distinctive and characteristic behaviour of human beings in groups.

Sigmund Freud and his followers tried to explain human aggression in terms of innate aggressiveness in individuals, as if a world war were just a bar brawl writ large, and a soldier necessarily a rather nasty person. Other theories blamed warfare on the pathology of crowds, impassioned and devoid of reason like stampeding cattle. But a platoon advancing with bayonets fixed, ready for sticking into the bellies of other young men, is emphatically not an ill-disciplined horde.

A French-born social psychologist working at Bristol, Henri Tajfel, was dissatisfied with interpretations of aggression in terms of the psychology of individuals or mobs. In the early 1970s he carried out with parties of classmates, boys aged 14–15, an ingenious experiment known as Klee–Kandinsky. He established that he could modify the boys' behaviour simply by assigning them to particular groups.

Tajfel showed the boys a series of slides with paintings by Paul Klee and Wassily Kandinsky, without telling them which was which, and asked them to write down their preferences. Irrespective of the answers, Tajfel then told each boy privately that he belonged to the Klee group, or to the Kandinsky group. He didn't say who else was in that group, or anything about its supposed characteristics—only its name.

Nothing was said or done to promote any feelings of rivalry. The next stage of the experiment was to share out money among the boys as a reward for taking part. Each had to write down who should get what, knowing only that a recipient was in the same group as themselves, or in the outgroup.

There were options that could maximize the profit for both groups jointly, or maximize the profit for the ingroup irrespective of what the outgroup got. Neither of these possibilities was as attractive as the choices that gave the largest difference in reward in favour of ingroup members. In other words, the boys were willing to go home with less money for themselves, just for the satisfaction of doing down the outgroup.

In this and similar experiments, Tajfel demonstrated a generic norm of group behaviour. It is distinct from the variable psychology of individuals, except in helping to define a person's social identity. With our talent for attaching ourselves to teams incredibly easily, as Tajfel showed, comes an awkward contradiction at the heart of social life. Humanity's greatest achievements depend on teamwork, but that in turn relies on loyalty and pride defined by who's in the team and who isn't. The outgroup are at best poor mutts, at worst, hated enemies.

'This discrimination has nothing to do with the interests of the individual who is doing the discriminating,' Tajfel said. 'But we have to take into account all the aspects of group membership, both the positive ones and the negative ones. The positive ones of course involve the individual's loyalty to his group and the value to him of his group membership, whilst the negative ones are all too well known in the form of wars, riots, and racial and other forms of prejudice.'

Kindness to relatives

A spate of best-selling books in the mid-20th century lamented that human beings had evolved to be especially murderous of members of their own species. Most authoritative was *On Aggression* (1960) by Konrad Lorenz, the Austrian animal behaviourist. He argued that human beings do not possess the restraints seen operating in other animals, where fighting between members of the same species is often ritualized to avoid serious injury or death. The reason, Lorenz thought, was that our ancestors were relatively harmless until they acquired weapons like hand-axes, and so evolution had failed to build in inhibitions against homicide.

It was grimly persuasive, but completely wrong. Scientists simply hadn't watched wild animals for long enough to see the murders they commit. Lions, hyenas, hippopotamuses, and various monkeys and birds, kill their own kind far more often than human beings do. 'I have been impressed,' wrote the zoologist Edward Wilson of Harvard in 1975, 'by how often such behaviour becomes apparent only when the observation time devoted to a species passes the thousand-hour mark.'

Ethnographic testimony told of human groups practising ritual warfare, which minimizes casualties. Trobriand islanders of Papua New Guinea, for example, have militarized the old English game of cricket. Feuding villages send out their teams fully dressed and daubed for Neolithic battle, war dances are performed, and when a batsman is out, he is pronounced dead. The result of the game has nothing to do with the actual count of runs scored, but is decided by diplomacy. Roughly speaking, the home team always wins.

Lorenz's problem was stood on its head. When the survival of one's own genes is the name of the game, fighting and killing especially among rival males is easy to explain in evolutionary terms. Yet human beings are not only less violent towards their own kind than many other animals, but they also contrive to be generally peaceful while living in associations, such as modern cities, far larger than any groups known among other mammals.

The first step towards answering the riddle came in 1963 from a young evolutionary theorist, William Hamilton, then in London. He widened the scope of Darwin's natural selection to show how an animal can promote the survival of its own genes if it aids the survival of relatives, which carry some of the same genes. Genes favouring such altruistic behaviour towards relatives can evolve and spread through a population.

Hamilton thus extended Darwin's notion of the survival of the fittest to what he called inclusive fitness for the extended family as a whole. His papers on this theme came to be regarded as the biggest advance in the subject in the hundred years since Darwin formulated his ideas. A fellow evolution theorist was later to describe Hamilton as 'the only bloody genius we've got'. But the first of his papers to be published, called 'The evolution of altruistic behavior', did not have an altogether easy ride.

'At its first submission, to *Nature*, my short paper was rejected by return of post,' Hamilton remembered later, adding in parentheses: 'Possibly my address, "Department of Sociology, LSE", weighed against it.' LSE means London School of Economics, although in fact Hamilton had done most of the work at Imperial College London, which might have been more respectable from the point of view of a natural-sciences editor. *American Naturalist* carried the landmark paper instead.

Hamilton's theory indicated that evolution should have strongly favoured rampant tribalism and associated cruelty. Its author took a dark and pessimistic view, suggesting that war, slavery and terror all have evolutionary origins. Hamilton declared, 'The animal in our nature cannot be regarded as a fit custodian for the values of civilized man.'

Coping with cheats

Yet altruism within families was not the whole story. As Kropotkin stressed, the lifeboat crews risk their lives to rescue absolute strangers. To take a second step beyond Darwin, was it possible to adapt Hamilton's theory of inclusive fitness, to bring in non-relatives?

Another young scientist, Robert Trivers at Harvard, found the way. His classic paper, 'The evolution of reciprocal altruism', appeared in 1971. In his evolutionary mathematics, we are kind to others for ultimately selfish reasons. If you don't dive in the river to rescue a drowning man, and he survives, he is unlikely to be willing to risk his life for you in the future. The system of reciprocal altruism depends on long memories, especially for faces and events, which human beings possess.

'There is continual tension,' Trivers commented, 'between direct selfishness and the long-term, indirect, idealized selfishness of reciprocal altruism. Some of my students are disturbed when I argue that our altruistic tendencies have evolved as surely as any of our other characteristics. They would like more credit for their lofty ideals. But even this reaction, I feel, can be explained in terms of the theory. All of us like to be thought of as an altruist, none of us likes to be thought of as selfish.'

A little introspection reveals, according to Trivers, the emotions supplied by evolution to reinforce altruistic behaviour: warm feelings about acts of kindness observed, and outrage at detected cheating, even if you're not directly affected; anger at someone who jumps the queue, which is often disproportionate, in its emotional toll, to the actual delay caused.

If you're caught behaving badly, feelings of guilt and embarrassment result, and even thinking about such an outcome can keep you honest. But there is a calculating element too. You gauge appropriate assistance by another person's plight and by how easily you can help. Conversely, gratitude need go no further than acknowledging the relief given and the trouble taken.

Above all, an endless temptation to cheat arises because kindly people are easily conned. Shakespeare put it succinctly, when he had Hamlet write in his notebook that *One may smile, and smile, and be a villain!* How could altruism evolve when cheating brings its own reward, whether the kingdom of Denmark or a free ride on a bus?

In the theory of games, the Prisoner's Dilemma simulates the choice between cooperation and defection. This game gives small, steady rewards if both players cooperate, and punishes both if they defect from cooperation simultaneously. The biggest reward goes to the successful cheat—the player who defects while the other is still offering cooperation and is therefore suckered.

In 1978–79 a mathematically minded political scientist, Robert Axelrod at Ann Arbor, Michigan, conducted tournaments of the Prisoner's Dilemma. They eventually involved more than 60 players from six countries. At first these were game theorists from economics, sociology, political science and mathematics. Later, some biologists, physicists, computer scientists and computer hobbyists joined in.

The players used various strategies, but the most reliable one for winning seemed to be Tit for Tat. You offer cooperation until the other player defects. Then you retaliate, just once, by defecting yourself. After that, you are immediately forgiving, and resume cooperation.

In 1981, Axelrod joined with Hamilton in a biologically oriented paper, which argued that Tit for Tat or some similar strategy could have evolved among animals and survived, even in the presence of persistent defectors. Axelrod and Hamilton declared, 'The gear wheels of social evolution have a ratchet.'

Cooperative behaviour underpinned by controlled reciprocity in aggressiveness became a new theme for research in both biology and political science. In accordance with Kropotkin's belief that the evolutionary roots of 'mutual aid' should be apparent among animals, observations and experiments in a wide variety of species detected reciprocal altruism at work and confirmed that Tit for Tat is a real-life strategy.

Tree swallows, *Tachycineta bicolor*, figured in one such experiment reported by Michael Lombardo of Rutgers in 1985. He simulated attacks on nests by non-breeding birds of the same species, by substituting dead nestlings for live ones, and he placed model birds in the offing as apparent culprits. After discovering the crime the parent birds attacked the models, but their normal nice behaviour towards other birds in the colony was unaffected.

Early uses of the Tit for Tat model in human affairs concerned breach-of-contract and child-custody issues, and analyses of international trade rules and the negotiations between the USA and the Soviet Union towards the end of the Cold War. In the 19th century military history was said to confirm that aggression was best deterred when challenges were met promptly.

A weakness of the pristine Tit for Tat strategy was that mistakes by the players could influence the course of play indefinitely. Axelrod and his colleagues found remedies for such noise, as they called it. Generous Tit for Tat leaves a certain percentage of the other player's defections unpunished, whilst in Contrite Tit for Tat a player who defects by mistake absorbs the retaliation without retaliating in turn. Trials showed that adding generosity or contrition left Tit for Tat as a highly robust strategy.

Among various other strategies tested against Tit for Tat in Prisoner's Dilemma games, strong claims were made for one called Pavlov. Here, like one of Ivan Pavlov's conditioned dogs in Leningrad, you just stick to what you did before, as long as you win, and switch your play if you lose. This could be a recipe for bullying, provoked by the slightest offence and continuing until someone stands up to you. But neither Pavlov nor any other alternative has dislodged Tit for Tat as the strategy most likely to succeed, whether in games, in evolution theory or in human affairs.

Three-dimensional people

'Few serious scientists would say there are genes "for" traits like altruism,' Axelrod remarked. 'There might well be genes that play a part, for example giving us the capacity to remember people we've met before, but they almost surely don't operate independently of environment.'

He thereby drew a line under old battles about nature and nurture. These had been renewed with great fervour during the 1970s, in the wake of the new theories of altruism. Some enthusiasts for sociobiology claimed that most of social behaviour, from rape to religion, would soon be understood primarily in genetic terms. Opponents vilified all attempts to find evolutionary bedrock for behaviour as genetic determinism, directed towards justifying and perpetuating the inequalities of society.

By the new century, these fights seemed as antiquated as the Wars of the Roses. In contrast with the naïve preferences for genetics (nature) or environment (nurture) of a previous generation, research in mainstream biology was already deeply into the interactions between genes and environment. These were showing up in the mechanisms of evolution, of embryonic development and of brain wiring, and even in responses of ecosystems to environmental change, in the geographical meaning of the word.

The achievement of Hamilton, Trivers and Axelrod was to give a persuasive explanation of how human society became possible in the first place. Enlightened self-interest tamed the crudely selfish genes of prior Darwinist theory. It created the collaborative competence by which human beings acquired a large measure of control over their geographical environment.

With that success, and the social complexities that arose, came options about the nursery environment. There, the genes of an individual may or may not prosper, good or bad habits may be learned, and withering neglect or cruelty may supervene. So by all means keep reviewing how we nourish and care for one another, especially the young. But beware of simply replacing genetic or environmental determinism by genetic-cum-environmental determinism, however well informed.

An oddity of 20th-century behavioural science was the readiness of some practitioners to minimize the power of thought, on which research itself depends. Neither genes nor environment can pre-programme anyone to discover the genetic code or the protocols of psychological conditioning. Yet the subjective nature of thought and decision-making was said by many to put them outside the domain of scientific enquiry.

It seemed almost like the breaking of a taboo when Francis Collins, leader of the Human Genome Project, declared: 'Genetics is not deterministic. There's the environment, it's a big deal. There is free will, that's a big deal, too.'

What one can for convenience call free will, at least until the phenomena of consciousness are better described by science, is the third dimension in human nature. It need imply no extraneous element. Along with other faculties like language, dreaming and gymnastics, it seems to emerge from the workings of a very complex brain. While philosophers still debate the exact meaning of free will, neuroscientists wonder to what extent tree swallows possess it too.

The genes and the social environment can certainly incline a person to act in certain ways. But growing up involves learning to control predispositions and passions, using something that feels like willpower. An unending choice of voluntary actions is implicit in the game-like interactions attending altruism and aggression in human social life. As simulated in the Prisoner's Dilemma, a person can choose to cooperate or defect, just by taking thought. Political debates and elections proceed on the assumption that opinions and policies are plastic, and not predetermined by the genes or social histories of the voters.

The criminal justice system, too, presupposes that we are three-dimensional people. All but the most deranged citizens are expected to have some sense of the difference between right and wrong, and to act accordingly. In that context, science is required to swallow its inhibitions and to switch its spotlight back to the individual, to confront the issue of free will in the real world.

The problem of parole

Psychiatrists and psychologists are often called upon to advise on whether a previously violent person might be safely released into the community after some years spent in prison or a mental hospital. If aggression expressed in criminal behaviour were simply a matter of genetic and/or environmental predisposition, there might be little scope for repentant reform. Yet experience shows that to be possible in many cases.

With the numbers in prison in some countries now exceeding 1 per cent of the adult population, including hundreds of lifers, there are economic and humanitarian reasons for trying to make parole work. But the practical question is always whether an individual is to be trusted. A steady toll of murder and other violence by released convicts and mental patients shows that evaluations are far from perfect.

The Belgian experience illustrates the difficulties. In the 1970s Jean-Pierre De Waele of the Université Libre de Bruxelles combined academic research in psychology with the practical needs of the prison service, of which he was the chief psychiatrist. He specialized in studying convicted murderers who were candidates for parole.

Part of the work was to require the individuals to write their autobiographies and discuss them at length with investigators. The aim was to figure out exactly why the crime was committed, and whether the circumstances could arise again.

In De Waele's view each person's mind was a new cosmos to explore, with whatever telescopes were available.

He also tested the murderers' self-control. He put them under stress in an experimental setting by giving them practical tasks to do that were designed to be impossible. The tests went on for hours. With the usual slyness of psychologists, the experimenters allowed the prisoner to think that success in the task would improve his chances of release. To heighten the exasperation, and so probe for the moment when anger would flare, the presiding experimenter would say, 'Don't worry, we can always carry on tomorrow.'

Immensely time consuming for De Waele and his team, the examinations of individual parole candidates were spread out over more than a year. In their day, they were among the most intensive efforts in the world to put cognitive criminology on a sound scientific basis. Yet two decades later, in 1996, Belgium's parole system imploded amid public outrage, after a released paedophile kidnapped and killed several children.

The multitude of competing theories of cognitive, behavioural and social criminology may just be a symptom of a science in its infancy. But the third dimension of human beings, provisionally called free will and essential for a full understanding of altruistic and aggressive behaviour, is rich and complex. It is also highly variable from person to person. Perhaps it is not amenable to general theories.

There may be a parallel with cosmology, where astronomers are nowadays driven to contemplate the likely existence of multiple universes where physical laws are different. In a report for the UK's Probation Service in 2000, James McGuire, a clinical psychologist at Liverpool, wrote of the need for 'scientist-practitioners'. Echoing De Waele he declared: 'Each individual is a new body of knowledge to be investigated.'

▶ *The recent rise of cognitive science figures also in* GRAMMAR. *For more about human evolution, see* PRIMATE BEHAVIOUR, HUMAN ORIGINS, PREHISTORIC GENES *and* SPEECH. *For more on the nature–nurture debate, see the final remarks in* GENES.

ANTIMATTER

Does the coat that Sakharov made really explain its absence?

MOSCOW WAS A DREARY CONURBATION during the Cold War. The splendours of the rulers' fortress by Red Square contrasted with the grim, superintended lives of ordinary citizens. But they weren't joyless. If you were lucky you could get a ticket for the circus. Or you could make your way to the south-west, to Leninsky Prospekt, and there seek out denizens of the institutes of the Soviet Academy of Sciences who could still think for themselves.

The physicists at the Lebedev Physical Institute in particular had privileges like court jesters. They were licensed to scorn. They shrugged off the attempts by Marxist–Leninist purists to outlaw relativity and quantum theory as bourgeois fiction. They rescued Soviet biology, which had fallen victim to similar political correctness, by blackballing the antigenetics disciples of Trofim Lysenko from membership of the Academy. As long as they stuck to science, and did not dabble in general politics, the physicists were safe because they had done the state some service.

Their competence traced back to Peter the Great's special promotion of applied mathematics two centuries earlier. After the Russian Revolution, theoretical physics was nurtured like caviar, ballet and chess, as a Soviet delicacy. The payoff came in the Cold War, when the physicists' skills taunted the West.

They gave the Soviet Union a practical H-bomb, just months after the USA, despite a later start. They helped the engineers to beat the Americans into space with the unmanned Sputnik, and then with Yuri Gagarin as the first cosmonaut. They built the world's first civilian fission-power reactor and their ingenious ideas about controlled fusion power were quickly imitated in the West. En passant, Soviet physicists invented the laser and correctly predicted which American telescope would discover cosmic microwaves.

Brightest of the bunch, to judge from his election by his teachers as the youngest Academician ever, was Andrei Sakharov. He played a central role in developing the Soviet H-bomb, and would soon be in trouble for circulating *samizdat* comments about its biological and political consequences, so breaking the jester's rules. He never won the Nobel Physics Prize, though he did get the Peace Prize.

In an all-too-brief respite in 1965–67 Sakharov's thoughts wandered from man-made explosions to the cosmic Big Bang, and he sketched a solution to one of the great riddles of the Universe. A slight flaw in the otherwise tidy laws of physics, he said, could explain why matter survived and antimatter didn't—so making our existence possible.

This remains Sakharov's chief legacy as a pure scientist. Subject to the verdicts of 21st-century experiments, it is a candidate to be judged in retrospect as one of the deepest of all the insights of 20th-century research. In the decades that followed its publication, in Russian, Sakharov's idea inspired other physicists all around the world to gather in large multinational teams and conduct elaborate tests. It also stirred ever-deeper questions about the nature of space and time.

On a reprint of his four-page paper in the Soviet *Journal of Experimental and Theoretical Physics Letters*, Sakharov jotted in his own hand a jingle in Russian, summarizing its content. In translation it reads:

> *From the Okubo Effect*
> *At high temperature*
> *A coat is cut for the Universe*
> *To fit its skewed shape.*

To grasp what he was driving at, and to find out, for example, who Okubo was and how temperature comes into it, you have to backtrack a little through 20th-century physics. The easier part of the explanation poses the cosmic conundrum that Sakharov tackled. What happened to all the antimatter?

Putting a spin on matter

Antimatter is ordinary matter's fateful *Doppelgänger* and its discovery fulfilled one of the most improbable-seeming predictions in the history of physics. In 1927 Paul Dirac at Cambridge matched the evidence that particles have wave-like properties to the requirements of Einstein's relativity theory. He thereby explained why an electron spins about an axis, like a top. But out of Dirac's equations popped another particle, a mirror-image of the electron.

The meaning of this theoretical result was mystifying and controversial, but Dirac was self-confident enough to talk about an anti-electron as a real entity, not just a mathematical fiction. Also sure of himself was Carl Anderson of Caltech, experimenting with cosmic rays coming from the sky. In 1932 he saw a lightweight particle swerving the wrong way under the influence of a magnet and decided that he had an anti-electron, even though he hadn't heard about Dirac's idea.

The anti-electron has the same mass as the electron but an opposite electric charge, and it is also called a positron. Anderson's positron was just the first fragment of antimatter. For every particle there is an antiparticle with mirror-image properties.

If a particle meets its antiparticle they annihilate each other and disappear in a puff of gamma rays. This happens night and day, above our heads, as cosmic rays coming from our Galaxy create positrons, and electrons in the atmosphere sacrifice themselves to eliminate them. Yet the count of electrons does not change. Whenever a cosmic ray makes a positron it also makes a new electron, which rushes off in a different direction, slows down, and so joins the atoms of the air, replacing the electron lost by annihilation.

For creating matter, the only way known to physicists involves concentrating twice the required energy and making an exactly equal amount of antimatter at the same time. And there's the problem. If the Universe made equal amounts of matter and antimatter, it should all have disappeared again, in mutual annihilation, leaving the cosmos completely devoid of matter.

Well, the Universe is pretty empty. Just look at the night sky. That means you can narrow the problem down, as Sakharov did. For every billion particles of antimatter created you need only 1,000,000,001 particles of matter to explain what remains. To put that another way, in supplying the mass of the Earth, the Universe initially made the equivalent of 2-billion-and-one Earths and threw 2 billion away in mutual annihilation. The traces of the vanished surplus are all around us in the form of invisible radiation.

Yet even so small a discrepancy in the production of matter and antimatter was sufficient for Sakharov to call the Universe skewed. And in his 1967 paper he seized on recent discoveries about particles to say how it could have come about. Here the physics becomes more taxing to the human imagination, because Mother Nature is quite coy when she breaks her own rules.

The first to catch her at it were Chinese physicists working in the USA, in 1956–57. Chatting like cosmic cops at the White Rose Café on New York's Broadway, Tsung-Dao Lee of Columbia and Chen Ning Yang, visiting from Princeton, concluded that one of the subatomic forces was behaving delinquently. Strange subatomic K particles, nowadays often called kaons, had provoked intense unease among physicists. When they decayed by breaking up into lighter particles, they did so in contradictory ways, as if a particle could change its character in a manner never seen before.

Lee and Yang suspected the weak force, which changes one kind of particle into another and is involved in radioactivity. It seemed to discriminate in favour of particles spinning in a particular direction. Until then, everyone expected perfect even-handedness, in accordance with a mathematical principle called parity conservation. Putting it simply, if you watch a radioactive atomic nucleus decaying, by throwing out particles in certain directions, then the mirror-image of the scene should be equally likely, with the directions of the emissions reversed. Lee and Yang predicted a failure of parity conservation.

An experimentalist from China, Chien-Shiung Wu, was also based at Columbia, and she put parity to the test in an experiment done at the US National Bureau of Standards. She lined up the nuclei of radioactive atoms in a strong magnetic field and watched them throwing out positrons as they decayed. You might expect the positrons to head off happily in either direction along the magnetic field, but Wu saw most of them going one way. They had failed the mirror test.

The world of physics was thunderstruck. An immediate interpretation of Wu's result concerned the neutrinos, ghostly particles that respond to the weak force and are released at the same time as the positrons. They must all rotate anticlockwise, to the left, around their direction of motion. Right-spinning neutrinos are forbidden.

This is just as eerie as if you twiddled different kinds of fruit in front of a mirror, and one of them became invisible in the reflection. Here's your electron, the apple, spinning to the left, and there it is in the mirror, spinning to the right. Here's your proton, the melon, . . . and so on, for any subatomic particles you know about, until you come to the raspberry representing your neutrino.

There's your hand in the mirror-image as usual, but it is empty, because the neutrino can't spin to the right. Finally you put down the neutrino and just hold out your hand. You'll see your hand in the image twiddling a raspberry. It is the antineutrino, spinning to the right. Your real hand remains empty, because left-spinning antineutrinos are forbidden.

Ouch. The fall of parity meant that Mother Nature is not perfectly ambidextrous. The left–right asymmetry among the neutrinos means that the weak force distinguishes among the particles on which it operates, on the basis of handedness. In fact, it provided the very first way of distinguishing left from right in a non-subjective way. But physicists grieved over the biased neutrinos, and the harm done to their ideal of a tidy cosmos.

Dropping the other shoe

Lev Landau at the Lebedev Institute in Moscow offered a quick fix to minimize the damage. The violation of parity seemed to be equal and opposite in matter and antimatter. So if a particle changed into an antiparticle whenever parity violation raised its ugly head, everything would stay quite pretty. The technical name for this contrivance was CP invariance. C stood for charge conjugation, which guarded the distinction between matter and antimatter, whilst P concerned the mirror reflections of parity.

Physicists loved this remedy. C and P could both fail individually, but if they always cooperated as CP, the Universe remained beautifully symmetrical, though more subtly so. 'Who would have dreamed in 1953 that studies of the decay properties of the K particles would lead to a new revolution in our understanding of invariance principles,' a textbook author rashly enthused, writing in 1963. To which Val Fitch of Princeton added the wry comment: 'But then in 1964 these same particles, in effect, dropped the other shoe.'

That was during an experiment at the Brookhaven National Laboratory on Long Island, when Fitch and a younger colleague James Cronin looked at the behaviour of neutral K particles more closely than ever before. They were especially interested in curious effects seen when the particles passed through solid materials. Checking up on CP was an incidental purpose of the experiment, because nearly everyone was convinced it was safe. Fitch said later, 'Not many of our colleagues would have given us much credit for studying CP invariance, but we did anyway.'

It did not survive the test. The experimenters separated two different kinds of neutral K particles. They were a particle and its antiparticle, although the differences between them were vestigial, because they had the same mass and the same electric charge (zero). One was short-lived, and broke up after travelling only a few centimetres, into two lighter particles, call pions. The other kind of neutral K broke up into three pions, which took it longer to accomplish, so it survived to travel tens of metres before falling apart.

What was forbidden in the CP scheme was that the long-lived particles should ever break up into just two pions. This was because there was no way of matching a parity change (P) to the matter–antimatter switchover (C) required for the conversion to the two-pion form. Yet a small but truculent minority of them did exactly that. Ouch again.

'We were acutely sensitive to the importance of the result and, I must confess, did not initially believe it ourselves,' Fitch recalled. 'We spent nearly half a year attempting to invent viable alternative explanations, but failed in every case.'

Not everyone was aghast. Within ten years, the rapidly evolving theories of particle physics would explain how CP could fail. And beforehand, in 1958, Susumu Okubo of Rochester, New York, had been among the first to suggest that Landau's fix for parity violation might not be safe. The Fitch–Cronin result vindicated his reasoning, so he was the physicist celebrated in Sakharov's jingle.

As for Sakharov himself, escaping for precious hours from his military and political chores to catch up on the science journals arriving from the West, he rejoiced. CP violation would let him tailor the cosmic coat that solved the riddle of the missing antimatter. It could create, fleetingly, the slight excess of matter over antimatter.

But the resulting garment also had two sleeves, representing other requirements. One was that the Universe should be very hot and expanding very rapidly, so that there was no time for Mother Nature to correct her aberration—hence the jingle's reference to high temperature. The other requirement was interchangeability between the heavy and light particles of the cosmos, such that the commonplace heavy particle, the proton, should be able to decay into a positron.

Bottoms galore

Sakharov was far ahead of his time, but gradually his ideas took a grip on the minds of other physicists. By the end of the 20th century their theoretical and experimental efforts to pin down the cause of the excess of matter over antimatter had become a major industry. Although Sakharov's coat for the Universe did not seem to be a particularly good fit, it led the tailoring fashion. And because it relied upon supposed events at the origin of the Universe, it figured also in the concerns of cosmologists.

'CP violation provides a uniquely subtle link between inner space, as explored by experiments in the laboratory, and outer space, as explored by telescopes measuring the density of matter in the Universe,' John Ellis wrote in 1999, as a theorist at Europe's particle physics laboratory, CERN. 'I am sure that this dialogue between theory, experiment and cosmology will culminate in a theory of the origin of the matter in the Universe, based on the far-reaching ideas proposed by Sakharov in 1967.'

It wasn't to be easy, though. At the time of writing, no one has yet detected proton decay, although major experiments around the world continue to look for it. And nearly every particle in the lists of matter and cosmic forces is boringly well behaved, abiding strictly to the precepts of CP invariance. For almost 40 years after the Fitch–Cronin result, the K particles remained the only known CP delinquents, and by common consent they were like naughty toddlers, nowhere near strong enough for the heist that stocked the Universe with matter.

K particles are made of more fundamental particles, strange quarks. Analogous B particles are made of bottom quarks and are much heavier and potentially more muscular. As with the neutral Ks, two versions of neutral Bs exist, particle and antiparticle. Could differences in their decay patterns, like those in the neutral K particles, have boosted the cosmic production of an excess of matter over antimatter?

To find out, B factories were created in the late 1990s, at Tsukuba near Tokyo, and at Stanford in California. By manufacturing millions of neutral B particles, physicists could look for differences in the speed of decay of the two varieties that would tell of CP violation at work. By 2001, both Tsukuba and Stanford were reporting firm evidence in that direction. They were not small experiments. The factory at Stanford, for example, began creating its B particles by accumulating energetic electrons and positrons in two magnetic storage rings, each with a circumference of 2.2 kilometres. Then it collided them head on, within a 1200-tonne detector devised to spot newly created neutral Bs breaking up after a million-millionth of a second.

More than 600 scientists and engineers from 75 institutions in Canada, China, France, Germany, Italy, Norway, Russia, the UK and the USA took part in the Stanford venture. That roll call was a sign of how seriously the Sakharov scenario was taken. So was a price tag of well over $100 million, mostly paid by the US government.

But even the Bs seemed unlikely to tilt the matter–antimatter scale far enough. Theorists and experimenters looked for other tricks by which Mother Nature might have added to the stock of matter. A reversal of Sakharov's proton decay was one suggestion, with particles of the electron–neutrino family converting themselves into quarks. Heavy right-handed neutrinos were a suggested starting point, but evidence remained stubbornly unavailable.

'We don't yet have a convincing story for generating the matter–antimatter imbalance of the Universe,' said Helen Quinn of Stanford, summarizing the state of play in 2001. 'But it's a mystery well worth solving.'

Looking for the impossible

Crazy experiments, conceived to find things that everyone knows can't be there, may eventually give the answer. At CERN in Geneva, thanks mainly to Japanese funding, the gamble at the turn of the century was to construct anti-atoms, and to look for any slight differences in their behaviour compared with ordinary atoms. Although physicists had been making the separate components of an antihydrogen atom for many years, to put a positron into orbit around an antiproton was easier said than done. The problem was to slow them both down.

Experimental teams using a machine at CERN called the Antiproton Decelerator succeeded in making antihydrogen in 2002. The physicists aimed to check whether ultraviolet light emitted by antihydrogen atoms had exactly the same wavelengths as that from ordinary atoms. Any discrepancy would be highly significant for the matter–antimatter puzzle. The experimenters would also look for any difference in the effect of gravity on antimatter, by watching to see whether the wavelengths change while the Earth changes its distance from the Sun, during its annual orbit. By a cherished principle of Galileo and Einstein, there should be no such gravitational effect—but who knows for sure?

A link between antimatter physics and the direction of time opened up another dizzying matter for contemplation in the 21st century, concerning the skewed Universe. After first P and then CP were violated, theorists had fallen back into what seemed to be their last bunker from which to defend tidiness in the cosmos. The sign over the bolthole said 'CPT', where T was time itself.

In particle physics, as opposed to everyday experience, time is generally considered a two-way street. As Richard Feynman of Caltech first pointed out in 1947, an antiparticle is indistinguishable from the corresponding ordinary particle travelling backwards in time. If you could climb like Alice through the CP looking-glass and transform yourself into your antimatter *Doppelgänger*, time would seem to flow backwards for you.

The spiel about CPT was that any swaps of identity between matter and antimatter (C) that were unmatched by corresponding adjustments in mirror symmetry (P) resulted in an unavoidable change of bias in respect of the direction of time, T. In other words, if a particle violating CP always flipped over in time, some decorum could be preserved. Indeed there might be a big philosophical payoff. You could argue from CPT that the bias towards matter in the Universe, if provided according to Sakharov by CP violation, would have set the direction in which the time of our everyday experience would flow.

But could CPT fail, as P and CP did? The results of many years of experiments make that seem less and less likely, but very curious tests continue. Because of the link between space and time that Albert Einstein's relativity revealed, a violation of CPT could create a bias in favour of a particular direction in space, as well as in time. This would truly skew the Universe in a topographical manner, instead of just metaphorically in the matter–antimatter asymmetry that Sakharov was on about.

So the new game is to see whether the results of experiments depend on the time of day. As the Earth turns, every 24 hours, it keeps changing the orientation, in starry space, of particle accelerators, atomic clocks and other equipment. High-precision measurements might give slightly different results according to whether they were made when the experiment was aligned or misaligned with a favoured direction in space.

When physicists from the USA, Japan and Europe compared notes at a meeting in Bloomington in 2001, they agreed that the results till then, from time-of-day comparisons, merely made any violation of CPT smaller and smaller—almost indistinguishable from nothing-at-all. But the crazy-seeming quest continued, for example with atomic clocks and microwave resonators to be installed on the International Space Station, which rotates every 90 minutes.

Also being prepared for the International Space Station was the largest particle detector of subatomic particles ever operated beyond the Earth's atmosphere, in a collaboration involving Europe, the USA, China, Taiwan and Russia. The Alpha Magnetic Spectrometer was designed to look for antimatter. One possible source would be the break-up of exotic particles in the mysterious dark matter that fills the Universe.

The crazy-seeming aspect of this experiment was that the Alpha Magnetic Spectrometer was also to look for antihelium nuclei. This took scientists right back to re-examining the axiom of the Sakharov scenario, that all antimatter was wiped out very early in the history of the Universe. If, on the contrary, significant amounts have survived, antihelium would be a signature. Antiprotons from antihydrogen won't do, because they are too easily made in present-day collisions of ordinary cosmic-ray particles.

The fleeting creation of antimatter is easy to see, not only in the cosmic rays hitting the Earth but also in gamma rays from violent events scattered across the Universe, where newly made electrons and positrons appear and recombine. Many physicists scoffed at the idea of any large-scale survival of primordial antimatter. It should have shown up already, they said, in more widespread sources of cosmic gamma rays. Nevertheless ever since 1957, when Chien-Shiung Wu saw her positrons violating parity, the story of skewness in the Universe should have taught physicists that if you don't look for what seems to be forbidden or ridiculous, you'll never find it.

When Sakharov was writing his matter–antimatter paper in dreary Soviet Moscow, it was a settled fact that visitors staying in hard-currency hotels were never robbed. So if you reported the disappearance of a fur hat from your room, you were assured that you had mislaid it and there was no need for an investigation. As a result, no one was convicted of theft, which generated the statistical evidence that no one was ever robbed. If physicists are to avoid such self-validating errors, let's hope the crazy experiments continue forever.

▶ *To know how antimatter fits in the Standard Model of particle physics, see* PARTICLE FAMILIES *and* ELECTROWEAK FORCE. *For more on proton decay, see* SPARTICLES. *For another take on Sakharov the bomb-maker, see* NUCLEAR WEAPONS.

ARABIDOPSIS

The modest weed that gave plant scientists the big picture

A TURNOFF from the Utrecht–Arnhem motorway brings you to the experimental fields and laboratory buildings of Wageningen Universiteit, nicely situated between a nature reserve and the water meadows of the Rhine. The Netherlands is as renowned for its agricultural research as for its astronomy. The Wageningen campus, originating as the first national agricultural college in 1876, is for many Dutch plant biologists a counterpart to Leiden Observatory.

Here, in 1962, the geneticist Wil Feenstra introduced his students to a weed called *Arabidopsis thaliana*, a relative of mustard. He was following a suggestion made in 1943 by Friedrich Laibach of Frankfurt, that arabidopsis was a handy plant for genetics research. You want to grow large numbers of mutants and detect, by their malfunctions, the genes responsible for various traits and actions in the healthy plant. So what better than this weed that completes its life cycle in less than six weeks, often fertilizing itself, and producing thousands of seeds? Fully grown it measures 20–30 centimetres from roots to tip.

Arabidopsis pops up harmlessly and uselessly from the Arctic to the Equator. The species name *thaliana* honours Johannes Thal, who recorded it in the Harz Mountains of Germany in the 16th century. As garden walls are a favourite habitat, some call it wall cress. Thale cress, mouse-ear and milkweed are other common names.

Staff and students in the genetics lab at Wageningen amassed dozens of arabidopsis mutants. In 1976 a young geneticist, Maarten Koornneef, was recruited from a seed company to supervise this work. He seized the opportunity to construct, with the students' help, the first genetic map of arabidopsis. By 1983 the team had placed 76 known genes on the five pairs of chromosomes, the sausage-like packages into which the plant divides its hereditary material.

Koornneef had difficulty getting this landmark paper published. At that time journal editors and their reviewers regarded the weed as unimportant and of little interest to their readers. The first international symposium on arabidopsis, held in Göttingen in 1965, had attracted only 25 participants, and during the 1970s even some of these scientists drifted away, because of lack of support from funding agencies. This was aggravated by a general disdain for plants as compared with animals, in fundamental research on genetics.

Substantial discoveries were needed, to revive interest in arabidopsis. In Wageningen, Koornneef's team had identified key genes involved in shaping the plant and its flowers, and the role of hormones in the life of arabidopsis, but a decade would elapse before their importance was fully appreciated. More immediate impact came from the work of Christopher Somerville at Michigan State and his colleagues, starting in the late 1970s. They pinpointed genes in arabidopsis involved in growth by photosynthesis, and in interactions with carbon dioxide.

Reading the genes

By that time, the techniques of molecular biology and gene cloning were coming into plant genetics, and the arabidopsis researchers had a big stroke of luck. Unknown to the pioneers, the complete complement of arabidopsis genes—its genome—is contained in an exceptionally small amount of the genetic material DNA. Although there were earlier indications that this was so, Elliot Meyerowitz of Caltech first confirmed it beyond contradiction, in 1984.

Just 130 million letters in the weed's genetic code can be compared with 840 million in potato, and 17,300 million in wheat. Yet arabidopsis is a fully functioning plant, so it possesses all the genes necessary for life, without the redundancies and junk present in the DNA of other species of flowering plants. This not only reduces the task for would-be readers of the genes, but also makes the results much easier to interpret.

By the late 1980s, the buzz in biology was about the human genome project to read all the genes in the human body. There were also plans to do the genomes of animals. Plant geneticists who did not want to be left behind debated whether to tackle petunia, tomato or arabidopsis. The weed won, because of its exceptionally small genome.

While US scientists and funding agencies were still talking about possibly reading the arabidopsis genome, Europe got moving. Allotting funds to genetics laboratories not previously concerned with the weed enlarged the scientific resources. A British initiative was soon followed by a European Union project, Bridge. Launched in 1991, it brought together 33 labs from nine countries, to study the functions of genes in arabidopsis mutations.

In 1995, ten labs made a special team to start reading every letter in the DNA code of one of the five chromosome pairs in arabidopsis, again with funding from the European Union. The chromosome selected was No. 4. Michael Bevan of the UK's John Innes Centre was the team coordinator.

Others were spurred to action, and the launch of the worldwide Arabidopsis Genome Initiative followed in 1996. The US government gave a contract for arabidopsis chromosome 2 to the Institute of Genomic Research in Maryland. That was a non-profit-making operation created by Craig Venter, who was in dispute with colleagues about the best way to read genome sequences. His rapid shotgun method ensured that chromosome 2 was finished and published by the end of 1999, at the same time as the Europeans completed chromosome 4.

The sequences of the three odd-numbered chromosomes of arabidopsis followed a year later, and the multinational credit lists grew indigestibly. The lead author on the report on chromosome 1 was from a US Department of Agriculture lab in Berkeley, on chromosome 3 from Genoscope, France's Centre National de Séquençage at Evry, and on chromosome 5 from the Kazusa DNA Research Institute, the Chiba Prefecture's outfit on the eastern side of Tokyo Bay. But the style of the Arabidopsis Genome Initiative was 'one for all and all for one'.

By the end of the 20th century about 3000 scientists around the globe were working on arabidopsis, more than on most crop plants. 'It's nice not to be alone in the world any more—to have so many colleagues with whom you communicate,' Koornneef said.

What do all the genes do?

In their collaborative spirit, the plant geneticists tried to set a good example to the sequencers of animal and human genomes. It was a point of principle that gene codes should be immediately and freely released to all comers, via the Internet. And the scientists took pride in the quality of the genome analysis, notably at the awkward joins between the pairs of chromosomes, called centromeres.

This care paid off with a basic discovery in genetics. The arabidopsis team said of the centromeres, 'Such regions are generally viewed as very poor environments for gene expression. Unexpectedly, we found at least 47 expressed genes encoded in the genetically defined centromeres... Genes residing in these regions probably exhibit unique patterns of molecular evolution.'

All aspects of the life of the little weed are laid out for inspection in its genome. The multinational teams of the Arabidopsis Genome Initiative outlined the amazing conspectus when they published their completed sequences. They also noted huge areas of remaining ignorance. Here are some of the points made in their commentary.

Most of the genes of arabidopsis command the manufacture of protein materials and the chemically active enzymes needed in the daily routines of the plant cells. Some 420 genes are probably involved in building and overhauling cell walls. More than 600 transport systems, which acquire, distribute and deliver nutrients and important chemicals, remove toxins and waste material, and convey signals, are distinguishable in the genes responsible for them.

Arabidopsis seems overendowed with genes dedicated to maintaining the integrity of all other genes and repairing them when necessary. These are apparently a hangover from a time, perhaps more than 100 million years ago, when an ancestor of arabidopsis duplicated all of its chromosomes, in the tetraploid condition well known to botanists in other plants. Later, the ancestors reverted to the normal diploid state, but not all of the duplicated genes were lost.

More than 3000 components of the genome are control genes, regulating the activity of other genes. For controlling the internal layout of living cells, and activities of their various components, the genes have much in common with those found in animals, although there are distinctive features associated with the cell walls of plants. Bigger differences emerge in the chains of gene control involved in turning an embryo into an adult organism.

After the single-celled ancestors of plants and animals went their separate ways, they invented different ways of organizing the development of bodies with many cells. Unsurprisingly the arabidopsis genome shows many genetic techniques not found in animals. Yet the two lineages hit on similar solutions to the task of making cells take on the right form and function according to where they are in the body. While animal embryos organize themselves head-to-tail using series of genes called homeoboxes, flowering plants like arabidopsis use similar series called MADS boxes to fashion the floral whorls of sepals, petals, stamens and carpels.

Shaping the plant as a whole, and deploying its leaves to give them the best view of the available light that it needs to grow by, are tasks for other genes. Botanists can outline this process, called photomorphogenesis, in terms of signals from light sensors telling some of the plant's cells to grow and others to quit. But among about 100 genes apparently allotted to these functions, the actions of two-thirds are so far unaccounted for.

Also distinguishing arabidopsis from animals is a complement of 286 genes coding for iron-bearing enzymes called P450s. Precise functions are known for only a small minority of them. They are probably the key to the production, in plants in general, of the huge range of peculiar chemicals and medicines that human beings glean from them.

Different parts of a plant communicate with one another, with news about the weather, water supplies, attacks and so forth. Alarm signals go out from wounds to the rest of the plant. Unlike animals, plants have no nervous system, but like animals they use hormones as chemical messengers, which alter the behaviour of cells receiving their messages. Botanists and biochemists have had a hard time figuring out these internal communications.

Plant hormones include auxins, which were known to Charles Darwin, and also gibberelin, ethylene and brassinosteroids—steroid molecules with several hydroxyl (OH) groups attached. No fewer than 340 genes in arabidopsis are responsible for molecular receptors on cell membranes that detect the brassinosteroid hormones. With few exceptions their functions are completely unknown. Perhaps here more than anywhere, the arabidopsis genome conveys a sense of big discoveries waiting to be made.

Uncharted continents of plant life

If Christopher Columbus, strutting about proudly after locating the West Indies, had been handed a chart sketching all the land masses and islands of which Europe still knew nothing, he might have felt as plant biologists did at the start of the 21st century. So who's going to sail to Australia, or march to the South Pole?

When the arabidopsis genome was completed, only 9 per cent of the genes had known functions, experimentally verified. Another 60 per cent could be roughly assigned to functions known in other organisms. But that left more than 7000 genes totally enigmatic. There are hints of entire biochemical processing systems—metabolic pathways in the jargon—that have been overlooked till now. One huge task is to identify all of the proteins made by command of the genes, and to trace the linkages by which the activity of the genes is regulated.

Genetics experiments of the classical kind, in which genes are deleted by mutation, and the effects on the living plants observed, still have an important role. The big difference is that scientists need no longer use chemicals or radiation to produce random mutations that have then to be sorted and analysed. You can target a particular gene, using its own code as a password, and knock out precisely that one and no others. Directed mutagenesis they call it.

Maarten Koornneef at Wageningen had never involved himself directly in the arabidopsis sequencing effort. His interests remained with the functions of the plant's genes in their complex interactions in flowering, seed and plant quality, and their reactions to stress. When the hard slog of sequencing was complete, the issues of function returned centre-stage.

'We thought we were doing quite well, 20 years ago, when we had pinned down the location of 76 arabidopsis genes,' Koornneef said. 'Now we have codes for thousands of genes where we haven't the least idea about what they do. With so many secrets of the life of plants still to be revealed, new generations of students will have plenty of adventures with our little weed.'

▶ *For discoveries already made with arabidopsis concerning the processes of evolution, see* PLANT DISEASES, HOPEFUL MONSTERS *and* GENOMES IN GENERAL. *For a mechanism revealed by arabidopsis, see* FLOWERING. *For the rice genome, see* CEREALS. *For background information on gene reading, see* GENES *and* HUMAN GENOME.

ASTRONAUTICS

Will interstellar pioneers be overtaken by their grandchildren?

O N THE DAY that Yuri Gagarin made the first successful manned spaceflight in 1961, the world's space scientists were in conference in Florence. As soon as the news broke, the mayor turned up with crates of sparkling wine. He was disconcerted to find the lobby deserted except for a couple of eminent Soviet scientists talking with newsmen alerted by their offices. In the meeting hall, speakers droned on about charged particles in the interplanetary medium, their proceedings uninterrupted by the historic news.

'We are scientists,' the closed doors of the auditorium said. 'We don't care about circus stunts in space.' To thoughtful reporters present, this was grotesque. Space science was from the outset a marriage of convenience between national agencies that wanted to fly rockets and spacecraft for military and prestigious reasons, and astute researchers who were glad to make the ventures more meaningful by adding instruments to the payload.

And if you wondered why there was prestige in spaceflight, the answer was that the world's population saw, more clearly than peevish commentators, that it was at the start of a great adventure that would one day take people to the stars. Yet only among the most imaginative researchers was astrophysics an applied science for mapping the routes into the cosmos.

Methods of propulsion have varied over the millennia, but the dream of travelling to other worlds has not. The tornado that transports Dorothy from Kansas to Oz in the movie *The Wizard of Oz* (1939) is a dead ringer for the whirlwinds that lift God's flying saucer in the first chapter of Ezekiel (*c.*590 BC) or carry Lucian of Samosata's sailing ship to the Moon in *Vera Historia* (*c.*AD 160).

More innovative was the French writer Cyrano de Bergerac, in the *Histoires Comiques* published after his death in 1655. He described journeys to the Moon and the Sun involving rocketry and other technologies. As summarized by an historian of science fiction, David Kyle, 'he used magnetism, sun power, controlled explosions, gas, and the principle of the modern ram-jet engine.'

A molecular biologist, Sol Spiegelman of Columbia, thought it instructive to look at humanity's future as if our genetic material, the DNA, were in charge.

Speaking soon after Richard Dawkins at Oxford had popularized that viewpoint in *The Selfish Gene* (1976), Spiegelman noted that life had already occupied virtually all ecological niches on the Earth, and then devised human beings. 'We really didn't understand why, until a few years ago,' he said. 'Then it was clear that DNA invented Man to explore the possibility of extraterrestrial life, as another place to replicate.'

Tongue in cheek, Spiegelman added, 'The genes were very careful in devising Man to make him not quite smart enough to make an ideal existence on this planet, and to pollute it sufficiently so there would be pressure to look for other places to live. And this of course would serve the purposes of DNA perfectly.'

Excess pressure on the home planet was uppermost in the mind of the physicist Gerard O'Neill of Princeton when, also in the 1970s, he advanced the idea of cities in space. 'Thinking of all the problems of energy, resources and materials, heat balance and so on, is the surface of the Earth the right place for an expanding technological civilization?' he asked. 'To our surprise, when we put the numbers in, it seemed to be that in the very long run we could probably set up our industry and agriculture better in space . . . and certainly in a way that would be less harmful to the biosphere of the Earth.'

O'Neill visualized voluntary emigration by most of the human species to comfortable habitats in orbit, hundreds of metres or even kilometres in diameter. He called them Bernal Spheres, in deference to the British polymath Desmond Bernal who had proposed such orbiting habitats in *The World, the Flesh and the Devil* (1929). Technically, though, they owed more to Konstantin Tsiolkovsky of Kaluga, Russia, who in 1903 had the good sense to visualize a space station rotating, so that centrifugal force would give the inhabitants the feeling of normal gravity. Cue *The Blue Danube* waltz, and the revolving space hotel in the 1968 movie *2001: A Space Odyssey.*

Crops in space

Reality lagged far behind the Hollywood dreams. But anyone with a milligram of imagination could watch the International Space Station becoming bigger and brighter in the twilight sky, as bits were added from the USA, Russia, Canada, Europe and Japan, and see it as an early, clumsy effort by human beings to live in harmony beyond the Earth, in cities in space. And when a Californian businessman, Dennis Tito, braved the stresses of spaceflight and the wrath of NASA to visit the Space Station in 2002, as a paying guest of the Russians, he blazed a trail for ordinary mortals.

One day the first babies will be born in space, and our species and its DNA will face the future with more confidence. The early difficulties are biological. Human beings in space, without benefit of artificial gravity, are prone to seasickness and to such enfeeblement after long-duration flights that they have to be carried from the capsule. Their immune systems are shot. The experiments to show whether reproduction in mammals is possible, even at the 38 per cent of Earth gravity available on Mars, have not yet been done.

And what about life support and food supplies in space? Underground at the Institute of Biophysics in Krasnoyarsk, Bios-3 began operating in 1972 for the longest experiments in sustainable systems anywhere. A sealed environment of 315 cubic metres provides a crew of three with food and oxygen from plants grown by artificial light, while a multidisciplinary team of Russian scientists and medics monitors the system. Unsolved ecological problems remain, especially about the control of microbes and trace elements.

Bulgarian scientists developed the first miniature greenhouse for prolonged experiments with crop plants in space. It operated aboard the Russian space station Mir from 1990 to 2000 and the trials were mostly with wheat. By 1999, second-generation seeds had been produced in space. Radish, Chinese cabbage, mustard and lettuce also grew on Mir at various times. The plants were usually returned to the ground for evaluation but on the last occasion the crew were allowed to taste the lettuces they had grown.

Tanya Ivanova of the Bulgarian Space Research Institute in Sofia, who originated the facility, noted a psychological payoff from crops in space. 'During our Space Greenhouse series of experiments on Mir,' she reported, 'instead of watching over the plants once every five days, as prescribed in the instructions, astronauts floated to the greenhouse at least five times a day to enjoy the growing plants.'

A wave of humanity

Although living beyond the Earth may seem hard to believe, it is not as far-fetched as to suppose that human beings will face extinction passively, like *Tyrannosaurus rex*. Even the most stupendous efforts by a nuclear-armed space navy will give no guarantee that we can protect the Earth from a major impact by an asteroid or comet.

There are plenty of other ways in which we could go extinct on the home planet, whether by warfare, by natural disease, by a chorus of volcanoes, by the Earth freezing over, or by a nearby stellar explosion. Only with independent, self-sustaining settlements elsewhere could the indefinite survival of humanity become more likely than not. And of course the settlers would have to take with them a Noah's Ark of other species from the Earth, to achieve a sustainable ecosystem.

'We shall not be long of this Earth,' the American writer Ray Bradbury told the Italian reporter Oriana Fallaci, as if uttering a prayer. 'If we really fear the darkness, if we really fight against it, then, for the good of all, let us take our rockets, let us get well used to the cold and heat, the no water, the no oxygen.'

There are more positive reasons for looking beyond the home planet for habitation. Ever since the Upper Palaeolithic, migration has been a dominant theme of human existence. The Polynesian navigators who took human life to desert islands all across the broad Pacific were a hardy model. Whether the motive is science, adventure, exasperation or harsh necessity, there is little reason to doubt that human beings will eventually go wherever they can.

Freeman Dyson of the Institute for Advanced Study at Princeton offered scenarios for space settlements that ranged from giant trees grown on comets to a complete shell of orbiting structures designed to capture most of the Sun's light. At present we employ less than a billionth of it. He also visualized a second-hand spaceship being used by a party of self-financing earthlings to colonize an asteroid, in the manner of the Pilgrim Fathers in *Mayflower*.

Others look farther afield. If you imagine a wave of humanity spreading outwards at 1 per cent of the speed of light, it will cross the entire Milky Way Galaxy in 8 million years, to occupy billions of suitable niches not already claimed by living things. In that time-scale, there is no great rush, unless it is to start the process before demoralization, destitution or extinction closes the present launch window for the human breakout into space.

Apart from many direct physical risks for the space wanderers, genetic consequences are readily foreseeable. Human beings and their animal, vegetable and microbial attendants will evolve, perhaps into barely recognizable and even hostile forms. But the more widely the travellers disperse, the less consequential would such changes be, for the survival of humanity. If interstellar travel becomes a reality for flesh and blood, even the death of the Sun, some billions of years from now, need be no terminal catastrophe.

Getting there

The stars are far away, and methods of propulsion vastly superior to the chemical rockets of the early Space Age will be needed to reach them. Nuclear fusion is an obvious possibility. In 1977, when Alan Bond and his colleagues in the British Interplanetary Society designed an unmanned ship called Daedalus to send to a nearby star, they chose to fuse heavy hydrogen (deuterium) with light helium (helium-3) quarried from the atmosphere of the planet Jupiter.

Daedalus would reach 13 per cent of the speed of light and take 50 years to fly past Barnard's Star, 6 light-years away. Even with no human crew, the ship's mass of 50,000 tonnes would be comparable with a cruise liner. In 1988, the US Navy and NASA adopted key ideas from Daedalus in the Long Shot concept for a far smaller unmanned probe that might fly to Alpha Centauri (4.3 light-years) in 100 years.

In 2000 an antimatter factory, at Europe's particle physics laboratory CERN in Geneva, began putting antihydrogen together atom by atom. Commentators noted that this could be the first small step towards amassing antimatter for the powering of a starship. When anti-atoms and normal atoms come together they annihilate one another, with a huge release of energy, making antimatter the most potent rocket fuel imaginable so far.

Other schemes on offer at the start of the 21st century included a giant scoop to gather hydrogen from interstellar space for use as rocket fuel, and sails of various descriptions. The sails could be pushed by sunlight or the solar wind, by emissions from radioactive atoms painted on a sail, or by man-made beams of laser light, radio microwaves or accelerated particles, from separate drivers.

Using solar energy and magnetic coils to power a small plasma generator, a spacecraft might surround itself with a magnetic field, in a magnetosphere many kilometres wide. This could act like an invisible sail, to be pushed by the solar wind. According to Robert Winglee of the University of Washington, speeds of 50 kilometres per second will be possible, ten times faster than the Space Shuttle. All such ideas may seem bizarre, but then so did the earliest attempts to make heavier-than-air flying machines, less than 100 years before the jumbo jets.

A psychological problem for would-be starship builders and travellers is that journey times of the order of a century or more bring a strong risk of obsolescence before the trip is completed. Imagine a doughty band setting off for another star, at a cost of trillions of dollars. After 100 years of lonely life, death and reproduction, amidst interminable anxiety about the ecosystem, personal relationships and mental health, they could be overtaken by a much faster jumbo starship manned by their grandchildren's generation.

Nor does one have to look far for revolutionary concepts that, if feasible, would make all previous propulsion systems antiquated. One is the hope of finding a way of tapping the enormous energy latent in the unseen particles that exist even in empty space. Another wheeze is to penetrate the fabric of spacetime through a so-called wormhole, which supposedly could bring you out in a different part of the Universe.

Without some such radical opportunity, starship designers using more conventional physics will always be tempted to abdicate interstellar travel to self-reproducing robots. That would be at odds with the aim of keeping humanity alive by dispersal into space. It would also carry the non-trivial risk that robots adapted to exploiting planets for their own purposes might mutate through cosmic-ray impacts, lose any inbuilt inhibitions, and return to exploit the Earth.

ASTRONAUTICS

The first real starship may be different from anything thought of so far. But to keep asking how it might be propelled and where it might go helps in judging our place in the Universe, now and tomorrow. It also gives a practical flavour to astrophysics and particle physics, which otherwise can seem even more remote from human purposes than the space physics under discussion on the day Gagarin flew.

▶ *For travel via wormholes, see* TIME MACHINES. *For other perspectives, see* UNIVERSE, IMMUNE SYSTEM *and* DARK ENERGY. *For possible constraints on uppity robots, see* GRAMMAR.

BERNAL'S LADDER

L ONG BEFORE the historian Thomas Kuhn brought the term 'paradigm shift'
into his account of scientific revolutions (*see* **DISCOVERY**), working scientists
were well aware of the problems of getting discoveries or theories accepted.
The physicist Desmond Bernal flourished in London in the mid-20th century
as a crystallographer, military scientist and left-wing social critic. He described
the sequence of responses from fellow scientists, as an idea gradually ascends
from rejection to acceptance:

1. It can't be right.

2. It might be right but it's not important.

3. It might be important but it's not original.

4. It's what I always thought myself.

Bernal's ladder is in continual use. Albeit subjectively, one can give examples
of the status, at the start of the 21st century, of a few of the discoveries and
ideas mentioned in this book. On rung 1, with only a small circle of supporters,
was the theory that impacts by comets or asteroids might cause huge volcanic
outpourings (*see* **FLOOD BASALTS**). A claim by scientists in Italy to have detected
exotic particles coming from the cosmos was also doubted (*see* **DARK MATTER**), as
was a suggestion from Ireland that a gamma-ray burst was involved in the origin
of the Earth (*see* **MINERALS IN SPACE**).

On rung 2, where a simple denial was no longer possible but the implications
were largely unheeded, was the evidence that the evolution of species plays a
significant part in the response of ecosystems to current changes (*see* **ECO-
EVOLUTION**). Similarly situated was the role of solar variations in major changes
of climate (*see* **ICE-RAFTING EVENTS**).

Grudging acceptance, as achieved on rung 3 of Bernal's ladder, came for
the evidence that adult brains continually renew their nerves cells and can
reorganize their connections (*see* **BRAIN WIRING**). A ding-dong argument had
raged all through the 20th century, between those who thought the brain
hardwired and those who thought it plastic. So it would be easy, though quite
unfair, to imagine that these discoveries had been anticipated.

Another case of 'It might be important but it's not original' was the reaction to the first molecular mechanisms for speeding up evolution when the environment changes (*see* **HOPEFUL MONSTERS**). Similar experiments had been done 40 years earlier, without benefit of molecular biology. By remembering them, opponents could try to shrug off unwelcome news.

Many experts gladly suffered amnesia about their former opposition to discoveries that were secure on rung 4 of Bernal's ladder by the early 21st century. One that had survived the fiercest attacks concerned proteins as infectious agents (*see* **PRIONS**, *also* **DISCOVERY** where the fight is briefly described). The role of impacting comets and asteroids in the demise of the dinosaurs and many other creatures—a proposition called arrogant by some biologists—had also reached the comparative safety of rung 4 (*see* **EXTINCTIONS**).

New ideas are often unsuccessful, perhaps simply wrong, and many never progress past rung 1. Others enjoy a spell of apparent success and then fall off the ladder. A once-popular suggestion that tumbled during the past 50 years was the notion that human beings are peculiarly aggressive (*see* **ALTRUISM AND AGGRESSION**). The Central Dogma of molecular biology, that the coding by genes for proteins should be a one-way street, was particularly short-lived (*see* **GENES**).

Wobbling precariously at the top of the ladder, according to critics, was the concept of evolutionary arms races, as a major driver in the history of life. It was being downgraded into 'trench warfare' as a result of genetic discoveries (*see* **PLANT DISEASES**). Survival was also in doubt for the idea that many chimneys of hot rocks rise through the Earth from near to its core (*see* **HOTSPOTS**).

BIG BANG

The inflationary Universe's sleight-of-hand

'THIS IS THE MUSIC of flocking and swarming things, of things that flow and bubble and rise and fizz, of things tense and constrained that suddenly fly free.' Thus did Johann Sebastian Bach's 3rd Brandenburg Concerto strike Douglas Adams, the British writer of the comic science-fiction radio serial *A Hitchhiker's Guide to the Galaxy*. He concluded: 'Bach tells you what it's like to be the Universe.' As modern cosmology is indeed all bubble and fizz, Bach has a claim.

The name of the Big Bang, for a clamant origin of the cosmos, was meant to be a put-down when Fred Hoyle of Cambridge first used it scornfully in a radio talk in 1950. But supporters of the hypothesis were a merry lot. Its main champion at that time was George Gamow of George Washington University, and he had added the name of Hans Bethe as a co-author *in absentia* of a paper he wrote with Ralph Alpher, so that he could get a laugh by calling it the Alpher–Bethe–Gamow theory. Big Bang was neater still—thanks, Fred.

The small, high-temperature source of everything that exists evolved conceptually over half a century. The first formulation of the theory was *l'atome primitif* of the Belgian cosmologist Georges Lemaître in 1927. As he wrote later, 'Standing on a well-chilled cinder, we see the slow fading of the suns, and we try to recall the vanished brilliance of the origin of the worlds.'

There is still no improvement on Lemaître's prose, but others added more convincing nuclear physics in the 1940s, and subnuclear particle physics in the 1970s. In a wonderful convergence, the physics of the very large cosmos and the very small particles became a single story. While astronomers peered out towards the beginning of time with ever-more powerful telescopes, the particle physicists reached towards ever-higher energies with giant accelerators, and could claim to be investigating the superhot conditions of the Big Bang.

The seed of the known Universe, with all its eventual galaxies and sightseers, was supposedly a speck like this · but far, far smaller. Where was it? Exactly at your fingertip, and also exactly on the nose of a little green wombat in the most distant galaxy you care to select. In a word, it was everywhere, because everywhere was crammed inside the speck.

Space and time would balloon from it like the genie from Aladdin's lamp. In that sense the wombat and you live deep inside the Big Bang. It did not occur somewhere else, and throw out its material like shrapnel from a bomb. The Big Bang happened here, and with the passage of time, space has grown all around your own location.

The details were obscure, but by the late 1970s the idea was that the infant Universe was extremely simple, just a mass of nondescript radiation and matter, extremely hot and possessed at first of gravity and a single primordial electronuclear force. It also had primordial antigravity that forced the Universe to expand. The expansion allowed the Universe to cool. As it did so the electronuclear force separated into different states, much as water vapour in a cooling cloud on the Earth forms liquid drops and icy snowflakes.

That provided various cosmic forces known today: the strong nuclear force, the so-called weak force, and the electric force. Out of the seething energy came particles of matter too—quarks and electrons. From these, the cosmic forces including gravity could fashion complicated things: atoms, galaxies, stars, planets and eventually living creatures, all within a still-expanding cosmos.

'We have simply arrived too late in the history of the Universe to see the primordial simplicity easily,' Steven Weinberg of Harvard declared in 1977. 'That's the most exciting idea I know, that Nature is much simpler than it looks. Nothing makes me more hopeful that our generation of human beings may hold the key to the Universe in our hands.'

All the same, there were possibly fatal flaws in the standard theory of the Big Bang, at that time. One was that it was conceptually difficult to pack enough energy into an extremely small speck to make more than a few atoms, never mind billions of galaxies. Another was that the cosmos is far too uniform for a naïve Big Bang theory to explain.

The evidence that most favoured the idea of a Big Bang comprised the galaxies seen rushing away from us in all directions, and the radio waves that fill the sky as the cosmic microwave background. The latter was interpreted as a cooled-down glow left over from the primordial explosion. Seen in either of these ways, the Universe looks uncannily similar in all directions.

Uncanny because the initial expansion of the Universe was far faster than light — space being exempt from the usual speed limit. That being so, matter and radiation now filling the part of the Universe seen in the direction of the Orion constellation, say, could not communicate with their fellows in another direction, such as Leo. There was no way in which different regions could reach a consensus about what the average density of matter and radiation should be. So how come the counts of distant galaxies are much the same in Orion as in Leo? Why are the cosmic microwaves equally intense all around the sky?

The magician of Moscow

The paradoxical solution to these problems was to make the early expansion even faster, in a process called inflation. It achieved uniformity by enlarging the miniature Universe so rapidly that the creation of matter and radiation could not keep up. Nothing much happened until an average density of energy had been established throughout the microcosmos.

Inflation also had an economic effect, by vastly increasing the available energy— the cash flow of creation. To buy a well-stocked cosmos with a primordial speck seemed to require a gross violation of the law of conservation of energy, which says you can't get something for nothing. Sleight-of-hand of a high order was therefore needed. Who better to figure out how the trick could have been done than an astrophysicist who was also an amateur magician? He was Andrei Linde of the Lebedev Institute in Moscow.

He came up in 1981 with the main idea still prevalent two decades later, but as usual there was a prehistory. Linde himself had been thinking about the roles of forces in the early Universe since 1972 and, in 1979, Alexei Starobinsky of the nearby Landau Institute first mooted the possibility of inflation. This stirred enormous interest among Soviet physicists, but technically it relied on a complicated quantum theory of gravity.

In 1980, Alan Guth of the Massachusetts Institute of Technology proposed inflation by another mechanism. That was when the idea became current in the West, because during the Cold War the ideas of Soviet physicists, as well as their persons, needed official permission to travel. In Guth's scheme the hesitation needed to delay the stocking of the Universe, while inflation proceeded, depended on supercooling.

Water vapour forms droplets in a cloud only when the temperature has dropped somewhat below the dewpoint when it is supposed to happen. Similarly the debuts of the various cosmic forces required by the cooling of the cosmos could be delayed. Informally Guth described the Universe as the ultimate free lunch, referring to the quasi-magical appearance of extra energy during the inflation process. Although it was a very appealing theory, supercooled inflation did not produce the necessary uniformity throughout the Universe, and Guth himself was soon to renounce it.

Linde announced his simpler and surer route to inflation at an international meeting of physicists in Moscow in the summer of 1981. Viscosity in the infant Universe, analogous to that experienced by a ball rolling in syrup, would make inflation possible. After his talk many physicists from the USA and Europe crowded around Linde, asking questions. Some volunteered to smuggle his manuscript out of the country to speed up its publication, because the censors would sit on it for months.

But next day Linde had a disagreeable task. He did the interpreting into Russian while Stephen Hawking, over from Cambridge, said in a lecture that Linde's version of inflation was useless. This was in front of all the sages of Soviet physics—a formidable lot—and Linde was just an up-and-coming 33-year-old.

'I was translating for Stephen and explaining to everyone the problems with my scenario and why it does not work,' he recalled. 'I do not remember ever being in any other situation like that. What shall I do, what shall I do? When the talk was over I said that I translated but I disagreed, and explained why.'

Nevertheless it was at a workshop organized by Hawking in Cambridge in 1982 that a refined version of Linde's scenario was generally adopted as the 'new inflation theory'. In the meantime, Andreas Albrecht and Paul Steinhardt at Pennsylvania had independently arrived at the same idea. The new inflation theory became very popular, but a year later Linde proposed an even better scenario, called chaotic inflation—on which, more later.

At the same Cambridge workshop in 1982, ideas were honed for testing inflation, and other proposals about the Big Bang, by closer examination of the cosmic microwaves. The aim was to find lumps of matter concentrated by sound waves in the young Universe. By 2002, the observations looked very favourable for the inflation theory, with the sizes of the lumps and the distances between them agreeing with its predictions to within a few per cent.

The quivering grapefruit

The Big Bang triggered by inflation is the creation myth of modern times. Its picturesque tale of the pigeon, the bowl of syrup, the quivering grapefruit, the quark soup and the deadly dragons is therefore worth narrating without digressions. A caveat is that all sizes mentioned refer to the stages in the expansion of the bit of the Universe we can see, and not to its unseen extensions that may go to infinity as far as we know.

Start the clock. The speck from which the Universe begins is uneasy about being a speck. It jiggles nervously in the way all small things do, in the quantum theory. It also possesses a high voltage. This is no ordinary electric voltage, but a voltage corresponding to the multipurpose electronuclear force prevailing at a very high temperature.

At first the force itself is inoperative in the speck because the cosmic voltage is uniform, as in a pigeon standing on a high-voltage electric power line. Although all charged up, the bird is quite safe from shocks. Its whole body is at the same voltage.

The cosmic voltage, formally known as the scalar potential, nevertheless represents energy, which is straining to burst out of its confinement. Think of it as being like a ball pushed up on one side in a round-bottomed bowl. If it is let go, the ball will naturally roll towards the centre as time passes, releasing energy. The cosmic voltage, too, has a tendency to fall, rolling down towards a low-energy state. This will happen as the speck grows.

Having viscous syrup in the bowl is the secret of success in making a big universe. The syrup is a by-product of the cosmic voltage itself, and slows it down as it tries to roll toward the low-voltage state at the centre of the bowl. As a result the minute speck can inflate to the size of a grapefruit before anything happens.

The cosmic voltage scarcely drops during the inflation. On the contrary, the whole inflated Universe remains charged to a high voltage. That is the legerdemain by which, according to Linde, it acquires enormous potential energy. And as the voltage is uniform, the eventual cosmos will be much the same everywhere, as required by the observations.

The grapefruit-sized Universe is dark, but still quivering with quantum jiggles of the original speck. As the pent-up energy tries to break free, the little cosmos is under colossal strain, somewhat like the air beneath a thundercloud at night. The difference is that there is nowhere for cosmic lightning to go except into the Universe itself.

The ball representing the potential of the scalar field rolls down the bowl at last and the cosmos is at once ablaze with radiant energy. The syrup thins as the voltage drops, and as a result the ball rolls to and fro for a while, across the bottom of the bowl. Eventually it settles at the bottom, its gifts exhausted.

'As the scalar field oscillated, it lost energy, giving it up in the form of elementary particles,' Linde explained. 'These particles interacted with one another and eventually settled down to some equilibrium temperature. From this time on, the standard Big Bang theory can describe the evolution of the Universe.'

The deadly dragons

Enormous energy, enough to build zillions of galaxies, is packed into the grapefruit, at a temperature in degrees Celsius of 10 followed by 26 or 27 zeroes. The expansion continues, and although the rate is much slower than during inflation it is still faster than the speed of light. Primeval antigravity continues to drive the expansion, while good old gravity, the only friendly face in the whole throng, tries to resist it.

The contents of the Universe are at first largely nondescript in our terms, with weird particles that may not even exist later. And although the electronuclear force flexes its muscles, the more distinctive cosmic forces of later epochs do not yet exist. Every millilitre of the expanding space nevertheless carries the genetic codes for making them. Each force will appear in its turn as the expansion reduces the temperature to a critical level at which it freezes out.

First the electronuclear force splits into the colour force of chromodynamics, which operates at short range on heavy particles of matter, and the electroweak force, a hot version of the familiar electric force of electrodynamics. When the temperature has shed a dozen zeroes, the electric force parts company from the weak force, which will become most familiar to human beings in radioactivity. By the time this roll call of cosmic forces and their force-carrying particles is complete, the grapefruit has grown wider than the Sun and is filled with quark soup.

Much of the intense radiant energy has condensed into recognizable particles of matter, also prescribed in some universal genetic code. The heavyweight quarks are fancy-free, and not the reclusive creatures of a later era. Lightweight electrons and neutrinos, and any other particles in Nature's repertoire, are also mass-produced. For a feeling of how violent the Big Bang is, consider that enough quarks and electrons to build a peanut require for their creation the energy equivalent to a small nuclear bomb. Yet already in the cosmic smithy there is matter enough for millions of universes like ours.

Deadly Dragon No. 1 ensures that the particles are made in pairs. Each particle has its antiparticle and re-encounters lead to mutual annihilation, turning them back into radiant energy. It looks as if the cosmos will finish up empty of all matter, when it is too cool to feed any more particle pairs into this futile cycle. In the outcome a crucial imperfection, a very slight imbalance in favour of matter over antimatter, will leave enough survivors to make an interesting Universe. That's Deadly Dragon No. 1 seen off.

The colour force grabs the speeding quarks and locks them up for ever, three at a time, inside protons and neutrons, the material of atomic nuclei. For a while, electrons and anti-electrons continue to swarm until even they are too massive for the cooling Universe to manufacture. Mutual annihilation then clears them away, leaving exactly one negatively charged electron for each positively charged proton. As any mismatch of charges would have left matter self-repellent and sterile, that beats Dragon No. 2. Note the swordsmanship required to give an imperfect balance of matter and antimatter, but a perfect balance of charges.

The Universe is by this time just one second old, having passed through several evolutionary epochs in unimaginably small intervals of time. The seething mass has cooled to a few billion degrees and the grapefruit has grown to a diameter of a light-month—an awkward size to imagine, but already one-fiftieth of the distance to the nearest star beyond the Sun. This Universe means business, and by the time our grapefruit perimeter has reached as far as Alpha Centauri, the cosmic forces will give a token of their creative powers.

Step forward, helium. Protons already fabricated will become the nuclei of the commonest element, hydrogen, but now the entire Universe is racked by a thermonuclear explosion that fuses almost a quarter of the mass of ordinary matter into nuclei of helium atoms. 'Look here,' the cosmic forces are saying, 'the Big Bang may be ending but you can still wring energy out of this stuff.'

Helium will be pricey for balloonists, and so rare on the Earth that its very name commemorates its initial discovery in the Sun. Nevertheless the Big Bang promotes it forever into the second most common element in the cosmos. The helium is, indeed, impressive evidence for a cataclysmic origin. Although stars also manufacture helium, all the stars since the beginning of time can account for only a few per cent of its total abundance. The primordial helium-making is finished after a couple of minutes.

For the next 400,000 years the Universe resembles the interior of the Sun— gleaming hot, but opaque. The hydrogen and helium are still naked nuclei, not atoms, and free-range electrons bar the progress of all light-like rays. But be patient. Just as light escapes from the Sun only at the visible surface, when the gas has cooled to the temperature where whole atoms can survive, so its liberation in the young Universe will not be possible till the cosmic temperature drops to the same level.

While waiting you can listen, like a caller on a busy reservations phone, to the music of the Universe. It resembles rolling thunder more than Brandenburg 3, but the sound waves that reverberate locally in the hot gas are descended from the nervous quantum jiggles of the ancestral speck. Without them, Dragon No. 3 would make sure that the Universe should consist only of diffuse hydrogen and helium gas. The acoustic pressure waves provide another crucial imperfection in the cosmos, with which gravity and the other cosmic forces will conspire to make the stars and the sightseers.

The observable Universe is at this stage 20–30 million light-years wide, or one billionth of its present volume, when at last the atomic nuclei corral the electrons. Here conjecture ends, because the 400,000-year-old cosmos becomes transparent and literally observable. As the sky itself cools from white hot to red hot and then fades to black, responsibility for the lighting passes to balls of hydrogen and helium compressed by gravity, and powered by the nuclear fusion first tried out in the earliest minutes.

The inflationary Big Bang made a stirring tale. But while cosmologists were pretty confident about what happened after the Universe was a fraction of a second old, they reserved judgement about the prior, extremely brief events, including inflation itself. As astrophysicists continue mapping the cosmic microwaves, they expect by 2009, when the results from Europe's Planck mission are due, to be able to settle many remaining arguments about the Universe. That may be the time for a verdict on inflation.

And before the Big Bang?

How was the Big Bang provoked? Some experts wanted to set it off by colliding other, pre-existing universes. Stephen Hawking magicked the problems away by invoking imaginary time. Andrei Linde, on the other hand, had contended since 1983 that the Big Bang came about very easily. Even empty space seethes chaotically with unseen particles and waves, by virtue of the uncertainties of quantum theory, and although the vast majority of them are ineffectual, sooner or later the conditions will arise where inflation can begin. Linde called his idea chaotic inflation.

Onlookers were often sceptical about ever finding out what came before the Big Bang. For a stern and not unusual opinion on the state of play, here is what Paul Francis was telling his students at the Australian National University in 2001. 'Beyond inflation, in other words before the Big Bang, we enter the lunatic fringe of astronomy: wild extrapolation based on fragmentary grand unified theories. Theories like those of Stephen Hawking and Andrei Linde are so far beyond our ability to test them that not even time will tell if they are true.'

'It is dangerous to make statements that something is impossible,' retorted Linde, who by then had moved to Stanford. The strange conditions preceding the Big Bang were not, in his thinking, confined to some remote, inaccessible point before time began. They are ever-present, because the creation of universes is a non-stop process. In his opinion parallel universes exist all around us, hidden from view because they exist in dimensions of space and time different from our own.

'The evolution of inflationary theory,' Linde declared, 'has given rise to a completely new cosmological paradigm, which differs considerably from the old Big Bang theory and even from the first versions of the inflationary scenario. In it the Universe appears to be both chaotic and homogeneous, expanding and stationary. Our cosmic home grows, fluctuates, and eternally reproduces itself in all possible forms, as if adjusting itself for all possible types of life that it can support.'

Bake your own universe

When the idea of inflation entered astrophysics, it prompted speculation about whether clumsy physicists with a particle accelerator, a strong magnet or a laser beam might accidentally set up the conditions for a new Big Bang in our midst. The idea came to be called basement cosmology, meaning that you might somehow bake a universe in your cellar. At first it seemed a scary idea. The new universe could appear like a colossal bomb that would instantly annihilate the Earth and everything around it.

But as scientists became accustomed to the idea that other universes may already exist in other dimensions beyond our ken, the problem was inverted. Let's say you squeeze a lump of dough hard enough to trigger inflation. The new universe remains safely in the oven, while it expands into different dimensions. The puzzle then is to know whether the experiment has succeeded, and if so, how to communicate with the new universe.

Among those who believed that baking a universe was a reasonable possibility was the pioneer of inflation theory at the Massachusetts Institute of Technology, Alan Guth. 'It's safe to create a universe in your basement,' he said. 'It would not displace the Universe around it even though it would grow tremendously. It would actually create its own space as it grows and in fact, in a very short fraction of a second, it would slice itself off completely from our Universe and evolve as an isolated closed universe—growing to cosmic proportions without displacing any of the territory that we currently lay claim to.'

The project is still conjectural. It has not yet been referred to environmental protection agencies or the UN Security Council. Meanwhile you should hope that Guth is either wrong about the feasibility of baking your own universe, or right about the outcome.

▶ *For the most immediate hopes of pinning down the nature of the Universe, see* MICROWAVE BACKGROUND. *For other ideas about how the Big Bang may be probed more deeply, see* GRAVITATIONAL WAVES *and* COSMIC RAYS. *For further perspectives or details, see* UNIVERSE, GRAVITY, SUPERSTRINGS, DARK ENERGY *and* ANTIMATTER.

BIODIVERSITY

The mathematics of co-existence

'**A**LL ANIMALS ARE EQUAL,' declared the rebellious livestock in George Orwell's *Animal Farm*. When the pigs later added 'but some are more equal than others,' they could have called upon biological testimony about the superiorities implied in the survival of the fattest. Yet, at the end of the 20th century, some biologists asserted that the earlier, democratic proposition was nearer the truth.

The count of different wild species inhabiting an area depends on topography, climate, soil and so forth. It also depends on how hard you look for them. In no branch of the life sciences are the 'facts' more subjective than in ecology. This ambitious but rather ramshackle science attempts to understand the relationships of living species and their environment, which includes the physical and chemical milieu and the activities of other species, not least our own. The ecosystems studied can be as small as a pond or as large as a continent.

Birds are chic and armies of twitchers watch out for rarities. With amateur help, you can organize a census of common birds from time to time, to learn their relative abundances and geographic distribution. But if you want to know about less showy lichens on mountaintops or insects inhabiting dead trees, you need experts who are few and far between, and can be in only one place at a time. However painstaking their work may be, their specialized interests and their choice of locales make their observations subjective on the scale of the biosphere.

Practical and intellectual contradictions therefore plague ecology. The devoted specialist who spends weeks counting beetles in a rain forest, or a lifetime in a museum comparing daisies from various places, needs a different passion and mindset from the theorist who struggles to make ecology a sound branch of science, with general hypotheses confirmable by observation. Only rare minds seem capable of seeing the wood as well as the trees.

A century elapsed between 1866, when the German zoologist Ernst Haeckel coined the word *ökologie* from the Greek *oikos,* meaning habitat, and ecology's rise to prominence. Despite treatises like Charles Elton's *Animal Ecology* (1927), J. Braun-Blanquet's *Plant Sociology* (1932) and E. P. Odum's *Fundamentals of Ecology* (1959), the subject did not take off until the 1960s. That was when the then-small company of ecologists managed to draw attention to a worldwide loss of habitats and species through human carelessness. Effects of pesticides on wildlife, most evident in the sight of dead birds and an absence of bird song, prompted clarion calls from the science writers John Hillaby in *New Scientist* (London) and Rachel Carson in the *New Yorker* and her subsequent book *Silent Spring* (1962).

Kenneth Mellanby of the UK's Monks Wood Experimental Station was in the thick of the action at that time. His team discovered that pesticides caused birds' eggshells to be thinner and therefore more breakable than those collected by Victorian amateurs. But he was modest about the achievements of ecology so far. 'Having quite properly alerted governments and the public to general threats to the living environment,' Mellanby wrote in 1973, 'we usually lack the factual information needed, in any particular case, to give definitive assessments and advice.'

A rule of thumb from islands

Although there were complaints about environmental activists appropriating the name of a reputable science, ecology had precious little by way of established knowledge for them to hijack. On the contrary, when political concern won new funding for scientific ecology it exposed a vacuum at the heart of biology, which leaves the survival of the fittest as an empty tautology. The survivors are defined as the fittest because they survive—but we don't know why, because their interactions with the milieu and with other species are obscure.

Genes are an organism's repertoire for surviving in its environment and they are continually tested throughout its geographical range. Old species go extinct and new ones appear, so carrying evolution along. But if you can't say what gives one species or subspecies an advantage over others, the chain of explanation is broken before it begins.

Conventionally, biologists have supposed that advantage might come from a better adaptation to climate, soil chemistry, feeding or predator–prey relationships, reproductive opportunities, . . . the list of adaptational possibilities fills libraries of biology, biochemistry and genetics. Even then it may not include the real reason for a species' advantage, which is perhaps dumb chance.

In California, larvae of the blister beetle *Meloe franciscanus* play the Trojan Horse. They mass and wriggle on a leaf tip so that *Habropoda pallida* bees carry them into their nest, mistaking them for one of their own females. Thousands of smart adaptations like that fascinate field biologists and the viewers of natural-history TV shows. But an adaptation takes time to evolve, and may therefore give a misleading answer to the question of how the beetle's ancestors became established in the first place.

One way forward for ecology, from the 1960s onwards, was to leave the adaptations aside and to concentrate on simple occupancy of territory.

Anonymity was the name of the game. It brought into biology an unwonted austerity, essentially mathematical in character. An analogy in the human context is to reject torrid love stories in favour of the population census that shows the numerical consequences of all that courtship.

Off the coast of Florida, ecological experimenters covered very small islands with tents and fumigated them, to extinguish all animal life. Within two years, insects and spiders had recolonized the islands with roughly the same numbers of species as before, although not necessarily the same species. The results underpinned a theory of island biogeography developed by Robert MacArthur and Edward Wilson at Princeton in 1967, which asserted that the number of species found on an island depends primarily on how big it is.

The islands in the theory are not necessarily surrounded by water. They can be enclaves of wilderness in mid-continent, perhaps a clump of forest cut off by lava from a volcano, or a man-made nature reserve. An immediate application of the theory was to explain why species counts might decline if nature reserves were too small. A weakness was that there was no prediction about relative numbers of the various species.

'How many species are there on Earth?' the biomathematician Robert May at Princeton asked himself in 1988, and his answer was somewhere between 10 and 50 million. The arithmetic took into account such factors as the relationship between predators and prey and the enormous numbers of very small species of animals that can be found when anyone looks for them. May noted the uncertainty about just how choosy tree-dwelling animal species are, about which species of trees they require. On certain assumptions, like those made by Terry Erwin of the Smithsonian Institution, you can arrive at a figure of 30 million species, just for arthropods.

It is as well to remember that fewer than 2 million species have been identified and named. Island biogeography nevertheless became a basis for calculating the loss of species, as a result of destruction of habitats. A rule of thumb is that if a habitat loses one per cent of its area, then 0.25 per cent of its species will become extinct. So if you guess that the tropical forests harbour 10 million species, and are disappearing at a rate of one per cent per year, you arrive at a loss of 70 species a day.

To ask which species they are is a waste of breath. The whole exercise is conjectural, with virtually no observational evidence. To say so is not to doubt the likelihood that species are disappearing, but only to stress how tentative is the scientific grasp of the problem. Intellectual progress is impeded by conservationist zeal, such that prophets of a mega-extinction always get a hearing, while people with better news may not.

In 1988, Aldo Lugo of Puerto Rico's Institute of Tropical Forestry was rash enough to tell a conference in Washington DC that the consequences of almost complete deforestation of his island early in the 20th century were not nearly as dreadful as the theorists were predicting for other places. Secondary forest was flourishing, after a lamentable but not disastrous loss of species. 'I almost got eaten alive,' Lugo said, 'with [an eminent conservationist] yelling at me in the cafeteria of the Smithsonian.'

Rarely mentioned in public information on this subject is that 90 per cent of the Amazonian forest disappears every 100,000 years or so for natural reasons, in an ice age. According to island biogeography's reckoning of losses, millions of species should be wiped out each time, making every ice age a mass extinction comparable with the event that killed off the dinosaurs. Yet the tropical forests have remained roughly in a steady state over dozens of ice ages. So the losses must either be overestimated, or else be made good by dozens of new species evolving each year, compared with a supposed natural turnover, new for old, of only about one species per year.

Flux and the role of chance

With the demographic arithmetic out of kilter, closer attention to what went on in real forests was badly needed. Ecologists found that they had to give up any hope that they could describe an assemblage of species once and for all, and rely on some 'balance of Nature' to keep it that way. Ecosystems are continually in flux, because of their own internal dynamics, even if there is no disturbance due to changing weather, human activity, or anything other than the competition between species for living room.

'Undisturbed forest remains recognizably of the same type,' Navaratnam Manokaran of the Forest Research Institute Malaysia, Kepong, noted in 1995. 'Yet it is continually changing in all respects.' Since the late 1940s, small sites within Malaysian lowland and upland reserves have been the scenes of the longest monitoring of tropical rain forest anywhere in world. They both have a great diversity of trees, always with 240 to 260 different species and subspecies in each two-hectare site.

When Manokaran revisited the sites as a graduate student in 1985, he found that 20 per cent of the species recorded in the 1940s had disappeared—gone extinct locally. Other species known from elsewhere in the Malaysian forests had replaced them. The turnover is not remarkable if you consider that you would find differences greater than 20 per cent if you simply sampled another plot a kilometre away.

A much larger study of the natural flux of tropical tree species began in Panama in 1981, and was then imitated in 12 other countries—most promptly at Pasoh in Malaysia. The prototype is 54 hectares of forest on Barro Colorado Island in the Panama Canal. Stephen Hubbell of the Smithsonian Tropical Research Institute and Robin Foster of the Field Museum in Chicago marshalled a team to record every tree and sapling that was at least chest high and a centimetre in diameter.

It took two years to complete the initial identification of 300,000 trees. To repeat the process every few years required more than 100 man-years of effort. That would have been unjustified if Barro Colorado were not changing extremely rapidly. Significant increases and decreases in the number of representatives of half of all the tree species occurred in two or three years. This continuous change in fortunes, with some species winning and others losing, was seen in all the closely studied forests.

Hubbell came to the conclusion that it was all a matter of chance. For traditional Darwinists, here was a disconcerting echo of the Japanese geneticist Motoo Kimura, who in 1968 heretically identified neutral mutations of genes as the principal mode of genetic evolution in every population of every species. Neutral mutations neither benefit nor harm their possessors and so they escape the attention of natural selection. Their survival or elimination is a matter of luck, to be investigated by the so-called Monte Carlo method, in a series of games of chance.

By seeing the survival or disappearance of species in an ecosystem in the same light, Hubbell compounded the heresy. He extended neutrality from the level of genes to the level of species. The survival of species A or the extinction of species B has virtually nothing to do with any inherent superiority of A over B. Species are to a first approximation neutral—equal and even identical in a mathematical sense.

In 1994 Hubbell articulated a unified theory of biodiversity and biogeography. He defined a 'fundamental biodiversity number'. To find it you just multiply together the number of individuals in a community, the rate of migration into the region, and the rate at which new species appear. Hubbell did not shrink from calling his formula the $E = mc^2$ of ecology, although like Mellanby before him he remained cautious about the state of the subject.

'We're still in the Middle Ages in biodiversity research,' Hubbell remarked. 'We're still cutting bodies open to see what organs are inside.' From this anatomy one learns that common species remain common, not because of any superiority but simply because they have more chance of reproducing than rare species have. If the migration rate falls, because a community becomes more isolated, common species will become more common, and rare species rarer. And in the Hubbell telescope, all species look the same.

This egalitarian view is most shocking for ecologists who have spent their lives seeking special reasons for the successes and failures of individual species. According to Graham Bell, an *aficionado* of the neutral theory at McGill University in Montreal, it is very difficult to see any large-scale effect of the specialized adaptations of species to their environments—any difference between the patterns of distribution observed over wide areas in the wild, and what you would expect if every plant or animal has an equivalent chance of success.

Coconuts won't grow in chilly peat bogs, Bell noted, so on a global scale one must allow for some degree of adaptation. But otherwise there is little evidence, in his opinion, that species coming in from distant places have any disadvantage compared with the incumbents except purely in their numbers, set by the rate of migration.

Neutral theory provides, according to Bell, a new conceptual foundation both for understanding communities of species and for devising policies for conservation. It brings together many disparate-seeming phenomena in a single overview. Changes in the species counts should be predictable numerically.

'The neutral theory of abundance and diversity will certainly have its limitations,' Bell admitted. 'Adaptation is, after all, a fact, and the theory must fail at the taxonomic and geographical scales where specific adaptation has evolved. What these limitations are remains to be seen.'

A fight about light gaps

Such grand theoretical considerations aside, ecologists are expected to advise on practical conservation. Hubbell was at the centre of controversy about light gaps, which are like a negative image of the micro-islands of island biogeography. Common sense suggests that gaps in forests created by fallen trees should promote diversity, by giving a chance to light-loving species that were literally overshadowed by the old trees before they fell.

In 1973, after monitoring for seven years the prosperity of wild flowers in many different habitats across the moors of northern England, Philip Grime at Sheffield came to a general conclusion. He reported that the diversity of species is at a maximum in places where the living is neither very easy nor very difficult, or where there is some interference, by grazing, mowing, burning or trampling, but not too much. The reason is that moderate hardship, and/or a moderate degree of management, curbs the dominant species.

Grime called his proposition a 'humped-back model', referring to the shape of the resulting graph of species diversity versus stress. A few years later, reflecting on the 'legendary' variety of species in rain forests and coral reefs, Joseph Connell of UC Santa Barbara offered a generalization similar to the latter part of Grime's: 'Highest diversity is maintained at intermediate scales of disturbance'. The idea came to be known in the USA as the 'intermediate disturbance hypothesis'.

Applied in the tropical rain forests, the implication was that moderate damage by windstorms, and perhaps by the temporary clearances of slash-and-burn farming or even limited logging, should tend to increase the number of species in an area. The idea that moderate human interference might be less harmful than it was often claimed to be, and could even help to maintain biodiversity, enraged environmentalists.

Rain-forest campaigners were reassured when Hubbell and his colleagues declared in 1999 that the idea of beneficial light gaps was false. On Barro Colorado Island in Panama there are indeed species that rely on light gaps to survive, but their seeds are not widely scattered. For want of sufficient new recruits, incumbent species tend to do better than the opportunistic light-lovers, in filling a light gap. There is no significant difference in the total count of species, whether this particular forest has many light gaps or few.

The rain forest of Paracou in French Guiana told a very different story, and Jean-François Molino and Daniel Sabatier of the Institut de Recherche pour le Développement in Montpellier doubted if Hubbell's results from Panama were generally valid. In 1986–88 loggers cleared parts of the Paracou forest, in some places intensively and in others more sparingly. Plenty of untouched forest remained, for comparison.

Ten years after the disturbances, the lightly logged places had about 25 per cent more biodiversity in tree species than the undisturbed places. The main reason was a big increase in light-loving species growing in the forest. The census of 17,000 trees, in seven logged and three untouched areas, counted all that were more than two centimetres thick at breast height. Altogether 546 species of trees appeared in the count, compared with 303 in the Panama forest.

To explain their very different result, the French scientists suggested that Hubbell's forest in Panama had been greatly disturbed by severe droughts. Those left it already well provided with light-loving species, so that further small disturbances could have no great effect. Another difference was that the Paracou situation was evaluated after a longer time had elapsed, following the disturbance.

'The intermediate disturbance hypothesis remains a valid explanation for high species diversity in tropical forest trees,' Molino and Sabatier concluded. They were nevertheless careful to point out that the result applied only to small, lightly logged patches in an area that was otherwise undisturbed for hundreds of years. 'Our study gives no evidence in favour of commercial logging on a large scale,' Molino said.

The species experts hit back

Ecosystems in tree-denuded Europe still have much to teach. That is not only because the very obvious impact of intensive agriculture, industrialization and population growth gives a preview of what may happen in the world's developing economies. In the continent where their science was invented, a relatively high density of ecologists have access to prime sites for wildlife where changes have been monitored over many decades, if not centuries. Here, too, there are instructive controversies.

It became quite the fashion in Europe towards the end of the 20th century to create artificial ecosystems. This is a matter of clearing plots completely, eradicating any pre-existing seeds in the soil, and sowing seeds of selected species. Then you wait to see what happens, taking care to weed out any incoming plants that are not scheduled for that plot.

In 1995–96 the world's largest ecological experiment of this kind, called Biodepth, got underway as a project of the European Union. It involved 480 plots, each two metres square, distributed at eight very different localities in seven countries: Ireland, Germany, Greece, Portugal, Sweden, Switzerland and the UK. The plots simulated grassland, so there was always at least one grassy species present, and then anything from 0 to 31 other species chosen at random from a list of grassland species, to represent different levels of biodiversity. Among 200 different combinations of plant species tested, the selection was in some cases deliberately tweaked to ensure the presence of a nitrogen-fixing legume to fertilize the plot.

The experimenters judged the above-ground productivity of each plot by the dry weight of plant tissue harvested from a height more than five centimetres from the soil. They published their results in *Science* in 1999, under the names of 34 scientists. John Lawton of Imperial College London was their spokesman, and they said that Biodepth proved that a loss of plant diversity reduces the productivity of grassland.

This result was politically correct for environmental activists, and a press release from the European Union itself rammed the opinion home. 'Their experimental evidence should send a clear message to European policy-makers that preserving and restoring biodiversity is beneficial to maintaining grassland productivity.' The Ecological Society of America cited the Biodepth result in a pamphlet for the US Congress and Administration, on biodiversity policy.

A counterblast came from a dozen other ecologists in Australia, France, New Zealand, the USA and the UK. In a technical comment in *Science* they declared that Biodepth did not prove what was claimed. A reanalysis showed, they said, that the clearest signal from the data was the special importance of nitrogen-fixing plants in augmenting productivity. Prominent among these critics was Grime of Sheffield, he of the humped-back model that anticipated the intermediate disturbance hypothesis. From his perspective as a lifelong examiner of English grassland, he acknowledged that experimental plots might be useful for teasing out ecological principles. But no conclusions relevant to the management of grassland were possible, he said, because the procedures were wholly unrealistic.

'In specific cases these have included soil sterilization, use of a sand/fertilizer mix in place of soil and failure to apply grazing, trampling and dunging treatments to vegetation consisting of species that have evolved in pasture ecosystems,' Grime complained.

Beyond such technico-political issues lies the deeper question of whether the differences between individual species matter or not. Has the theoretical pendulum swung too far in the direction of treating them all as equals? Do the experts on species really have nothing left to contribute to ecology, apart from mere identification by taxonomy?

From the outset, back in the 1970s, Grime's humped-back model of biodiversity distinguished between traits of different species. For example, among English wild flowers the bullyboy is the pink-flowered, long-leaved, rosebay willowherb, *Chamaenerion angustifolium*, also known as fireweed. By virtue of its height, shape and speed of growth, it tends to overwhelm all other herbaceous species in grassland, in the most affluent growing conditions. Grime assigned to rosebay willowherb a high 'competitive index'.

At another extreme are species with a high resistance to stress. As its name implies, sheep's fescue (*Festuca ovina*) is a grass that flourishes on intensively grazed land, but otherwise it's a poor competitor and vanishes when grazing stops. The disappearance of nameable species like that, as growing conditions improve, is a reason for doubting any simple link between grassland productivity and biodiversity. More generally, as species have distinctive strategies for coping with environmental change, it is scarcely conceivable that a complete and politically useful theory of ecology will manage to ignore their adaptations.

Tropical forests and temperate grasslands are only two of the world's types of ecosystems, but they have attracted huge research efforts over recent decades. If you are a pessimist, you may be depressed by the fact that scientists still don't agree about them. Optimistically, you can see the disputes about light gaps and grassland productivity as a sign of an active science. The issues will be settled, not by preconceptions but by new investigations. There's everything still to play for, both in fundamental understanding and in sensible action to preserve biodiversity while the human population continues to grow.

▶ *For other approaches to trying to make an exact science of ecology, see* ECO-EVOLUTION, *which introduces genetics, and* BIOSPHERE FROM SPACE *with a global overview. The proposition that virtually no present-day terrestrial ecosystem is 'natural' is aired in* PREDATORS. *For aspects of conservation, see* HUMAN ECOLOGY.

BIOLOGICAL CLOCKS

Molecular machinery that governs life's routines

MEXICO CITY was the setting for an experiment in 1951 that transformed the lives of women. The Syntex lab there had recently featured in *Life* magazine under the headline, 'Cortisone from giant yam'. At that time, steroids were all the rage, with cortisone emerging as a treatment for arthritis. The Syntex chemists started with a natural plant product, diosgenin, and beat Harvard and their commercial rivals to a relatively cheap way of making cortisone.

One of the polyglot team was a 27-year-old Bulgarian Jew, a refugee from Hitler educated in the USA. Carl Djerrasi went on to synthesize a new steroid, norethindrone. It was a version of the hormone progesterone that could be taken by mouth instead of by injection. He recalled later: 'Not in our wildest dreams did we imagine that this substance would eventually become the active progestational ingredient of nearly half the oral contraceptives used worldwide.'

In that same year, 1951, the birth-control pioneer Margaret Sanger challenged Gregory Pincus at the Worcester Foundation for Experimental Biology in Massachusetts to develop a contraceptive pill for women. Pincus opted for a later oral version of progesterone, norethynodrel, in his pill that went on sale in 1960, but a second pill using Djerassi's norethindrone followed quickly. These and later products provoked a revolution in family planning, ructions in the Vatican, high-jinks in the Swinging Sixties, and a boost for women's liberation.

The pill interferes with the biological clock that sets the pace of the menstrual cycle. Changing levels of various hormones, carrying their chemical messages around the body, normally achieve a monthly rhythm by slow processes of growth and decline, each taking about two weeks. The first phase is the growth of a number of egg-bearing follicles, one of which eventually releases an egg.

The empty follicle becomes the corpus luteum, pumping out progesterone, which causes the womb to prepare a lining for possible use. After about 14 days, the corpus luteum dies. Deprived of progesterone, the womb lining disintegrates and bleeds. Simultaneously, egg recruitment begins and the cycle starts all over again.

Sometimes a fertilized egg plants itself in the womb, during that second phase. If so, it sends a hormonal signal to the corpus luteum, telling it not to give up but to go on making progesterone. This blocks the implantation of any other fertilized egg. So the progesterone-like pill simulates an incipient pregnancy. If any fertilized egg shows up, the womb rejects it.

Of all the chemical signals involved in the menstrual clock, pride of place goes to the gonadotropin-releasing hormone GnRH. Its production is under the control of a region in the base of the brain called the hypothalamus, which integrates hormonal and other information from the body. A pulse of GnRH is the monthly tick of the clock, and it prompts the making of other hormones.

The build-up of those hormones then represses GnRH production. When they diminish at the end of the cycle, another pulse of GnRH ensues. To reduce a very complex system to a simple principle, one can say that molecule A makes molecule B, which stops the activity of molecule A. Molecule B fades away and molecule A gets busy again. It's not unlike the swing of a pendulum, and biological clocks in general work that way.

Knowing the time of day

The nearness of the human menstrual period to a lunar month is probably just a coincidence. On the other hand, many creatures of the seashore have adapted their biological clocks for living comfortably with the Moon and its 12.4-hour cycle of flood and ebb tides. Some of them seem to reckon the lunar phases as diligently as any cleric computing the date of Easter. When the horseshoe crabs of Chesapeake Bay parade to lay their eggs in the intertidal beach in May, they prefer the Full Moon.

The chances are, when scientists mention biological clocks, that they mean the 24-hour body rhythms of sleeping, waking and hunger. These are the most basic links between life and astronomy. As the Earth's spin brings the Sun into view and then removes it, every inhabitant of the film of life on the planet's outermost surface reacts in appropriate ways to the solar peekaboo.

With hindsight, it's strange how slow most scientists were to wake up to the fact that many organisms have internal clocks telling them the time of day. The advent of fast, long-haul passenger aircraft in the 1960s let biologists experience severe jetlag for themselves. Thereafter, anatomy, biochemistry and genetics gradually homed in on the 24-hour clocks in humans and other species.

Your own 24-hour clock, with 10,000 cells and smaller than a pinhead, is the suprachiasmatic nucleus on the hypothalamus in the base of your brain. It takes its name from the chiasm, just beneath it, where the main optic nerves from the eyes cross over on their way to the back of the brain, for the purposes of ordinary vision. The clock has private connections to light meters in the eyes, which send it information on the changing levels of brightness, distinguishing night from day. These help to reset the clock every day. The clock influences bodily activity by signals to glands that send out hormones.

A pea-sized neighbour, the pineal gland, which René Descartes suggested was the site of the human soul, distributes melatonin at a rate that changes rhythmically and peaks at night. Other glands adjust the levels of other hormones. Among the activities affected is the immune system, which is on red alert each evening.

Even without useful cues from the light meters, the clock goes on running on a roughly 24-hour cycle, known as a circadian rhythm. When volunteers live in unchanging light levels their clocks run fast. They feel sleepy, wakeful or hungry prematurely, and their body temperatures vary with a faster cadence.

The uncorrected biological clock gains by about an hour each day, ahead of events in the outside world. That is a sign that human beings evolved as creatures of the day. Getting up late was riskier than rising too soon. In mammals active at night, the clocks run slow when light levels don't vary, as if to avoid being spotted in the evening twilight.

If you want to reset your clock, after working night shifts or travelling across time zones, give your light meters a treat by going out in bright sunshine. In 2001–02, researchers in five laboratories in the USA and Denmark almost simultaneously identified the light meters in mammals' eyes. They are special-purpose cells scattered independently all across the retina, and with extensions called dendrites each of them samples a wide area around it. The light meters average the intensity over a quarter of an hour or more. In consequence lightning does not confuse the clock.

Similar light-meter cells connect to the system controlling the size of the pupils, to protect the retina against dazzle or to widen the pupils for night vision. Emotion intrudes on that mechanism. As cunning card players know, an opponent's pupils may dilate at the sight of an ace, and narrow if it's a poor card.

Control of the genes

By the start of the 21st century the molecular clockwork was becoming plainer. The slow, hard task of taking the 24-hour clock to pieces had fallen primarily to the geneticists. Seymour Benzer of Caltech showed the way forward, in the 1970s, by looking for mutant fruit flies with defective clocks and abnormal daily behaviour. In 1988 a golden hamster turned up by chance, with a clock with an aberrant 22-hour cycle.

The possibility of a breakthrough arose when Joseph Takahashi of Northwestern University, Illinois, and his colleagues found a mutant mouse in which the clock period was an hour longer than in his relatives. By 1994, Takahashi's team could report that they had located that animal's mutant gene on one of the mouse chromosomes. Strenuous work in several laboratories followed up this discovery and identified several more genes involved in the mammalian clock.

Takahashi's own group pinned down the mutant gene first seen in the golden hamster, and found the same gene in mice and humans. It turned out to code for making a particular protein molecule, an enzyme of the type called a kinase. A Utah team found a defect in the identical enzyme in a hereditary sleep disorder in human patients. And Takahashi was bowled over to find that the kinase also operates in the 24-hour clock of fruit flies. 'What's incredible is that the enzyme appears to be doing exactly the same in fly as in hamster,' he said. 'So this is a highly conserved system.'

A preliminary overview of the clockwork came from Steven Reppert of Massachusetts General Hospital and his colleagues. They identified proteins that, they suggested, might promote or repress the action of several genes involved in the clock. By 2000 they had, for example, pinpointed a protein called cryptochrome as one such player. It becomes modified by joining forces with another clock protein and returns to the nucleus of the cell where the genes reside. There it switches off the gene that makes cryptochrome itself.

The swinging pendulum again, with molecule A making B which represses A, in a negative feedback loop. Reppert commented in 2002: 'Now that we have the loops, we're asking how the time delays are built into the system through the protein modification to get the 24-hour kinetic to the clock.'

In plants too, the control of gene activity figures in their 24-hour clocks. Compared with the resetting mechanism in mammals, which relies on remote light meters, the corresponding system in plants is astonishingly direct. Pigmented protein molecules called phytochromes register light within each exposed cell. They then travel into the nucleus of the cell, where the genes reside, and exert control over gene activity.

Ferenc Nagy of Hungary's Biological Research Center in Szeged made the discovery. 'That light-sensing molecules can invade the cell nucleus like this is something completely new in cell biology,' he said. 'It's as if a newspaper reporter were to rush into the prime minister's office, grab the telephone and start issuing orders.'

Feathered navigators

Despite thrilling progress, research into biological clocks is still in its infancy. That is most obvious in the case of migrating birds. The Max-Planck-Forschungsstelle für Ornithologie is located in rural Bavaria, a region well provided with songbirds, many of which take winter vacations in Africa. At this research centre, Eberhard Gwinner conducted decades of research into the birds' clocks and their role in migration. Even as he and his colleagues made some key discoveries, they uncovered yet more mysteries.

Migrating birds face tasks that would make a human navigator shudder. Apart from its normal sleep–wake–feed functions, the daily clock must also enable a bird to correct for the time of day or night, when steering by the Sun or the stars. If flying eastwards or westwards across time zones, a bird has to adjust its clock more smoothly and rapidly than human beings do. Jetlag could be fatal for a small bird beset by predators.

Just as plants must know when to flower or to shed their leaves, so a migrating bird needs to judge when to set off. Ahead of time, it stores energy in proportion to the distance to be covered. Radars have tracked small birds flying non-stop from Europe to sub-Saharan Africa, crossing 2500 kilometres of sea and desert in 48 hours. In preparation, a bird may double its body weight.

At middle and high latitudes, plants and animals can quite easily tell the time of year from changes in the length of the day, and the temperature. But consider a migrating bird that sees summer ending in Europe and flies to tropical Africa. There, the days are roughly the same length at all seasons. Temperatures, too, are a poor guide to the time of year. So how does the bird know when to return?

In the late 1960s Gwinner began experiments with Peter Berthold, in which they kept small migratory birds in cages, while continuously alternating 12 hours of artificial light with 12 hours of darkness. The birds went on for several years preparing for flight twice in each year, at appropriate seasons. Their body weights increased, and they showed migratory restlessness by exercising their wings at night.

The birds possess not just a daily, circadian clock but also a circannual clock, or calendar. Here the astronomical adaptation is to the tilt of the Earth's axis that governs the seasons of the year. The fact that the circannual clock in a caged bird never runs to exactly 365 days is evidence that it is internally self-engendered.

Non-migratory birds also have biological calendars. Gwinner's team investigated how the stonechats, *Saxicola torquata*, resident in various parts of Africa and Eurasia, set and use their circannual clocks. To suit local conditions, their seasonal behaviour varies from place to place. In some respects the birds simply react opportunistically to the local environment. But cross-breeding trials with birds from different places showed that some of the variations in reproductive and moulting behaviour are inherited within local populations.

When the ornithologists looked for the clockwork in birds' brains, they found that, just as in human beings, the suprachiasmatic nucleus and the pineal gland are central in the operations of the 24-hour clock. The two regions operate semi-independently, but interact strongly. By 2001 the team in Bavaria had achieved the first demonstration of a daily rhythm of genetic activity in the cells of birds' brains.

How the 365-day clock operates remains mysterious. Perhaps a body-part grows slowly and dies slowly, under hormonal control, like the egg follicle in the 28-day menstrual cycle in women. But there are deeper and more perplexing questions concerning the navigational uses of the clocks.

Migratory birds experience drastic changes in climate and habitat, just by going from place to place. They also have to cope with an ever-changing world. The roosts at last year's stopover may have been destroyed by fire, wind or human activity. Volcanoes erupt and rivers change their courses. Floods or drought may afflict the wintering place. No other creatures have to be as adaptable as birds.

Bird migration would be remarkable even if the faculties for particular routes were acquired over millennia of evolution, instead of adjusting to changes year by year. It would be impressive even if young birds learned the geographical, navigational and chronometric skills from adults on the first trip. What is confounding for conventional ideas about heredity and evolution is that they have to learn very little. Most species of long-distance migrating songbird fly solo—and at night.

The fledglings are in some strong sense born with their parents' latest itinerary in their heads. That is to say, they know when to fly, in what direction, and how far. In distant places they have never visited before, they will avoid headwinds and find helpful tailwinds. The young birds will choose their own stopovers, and in the spring they will return unerringly to the district where they hatched.

'Anyone alive to the wonders of migrating birds and their circadian and circannual clocks must confront basic issues in genetics and brain research,' Gwinner said. 'Learning, heredity and adaptation to changing environments— they all work together in very quick ways previously thought impossible. When we find out how the molecules manage it, I dare say our small songbirds will send shock waves through the whole of biology.'

Payoffs yet to come

Futures applications of research on biological clocks will range from treating insomnia to breeding crop plants to grow in winter. In fundamental biology the implications are even wider. Bacteria, fungi, plants and animals have distinctive kinds of clocks. Within these kingdoms, species use components of the clock system in many different ways, to suit their lifestyles and their niches in the environment. Adaptation to the 12.4-hour sea-tide cycle, mentioned earlier, is a case in point.

Tracing in the genes exactly how the variations have come about will be an engrossing part of the new style of natural history that now embraces molecular biology. There is convergence, too, with studies of embryonic development. Time is of the essence in achieving the correct arrangements of tissues in the growing body.

The greatest payoffs yet to come may be in brain research. The 24-hour clock is just one example of how the human brain controls behaviour. If scientists can explain its biochemical and biophysical system, as thoroughly as a good mechanic can tell you how a car works, it will be the very first piece of the brain to be so fully comprehended. That will encourage the efforts of researchers to understand the brain's many other functions in similar detail, and give them practical pointers too.

For much faster clockwork, see BRAIN RHYTHMS. *There is more about plant clocks under* FLOWERING. *For the role of timekeeping in embryonic development, see* EMBRYOS.

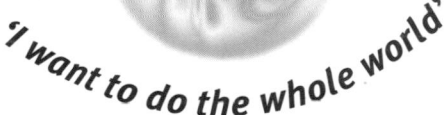

BIOSPHERE FROM SPACE

'I want to do the whole world'

I N 1972, while Washington was distracted by the Watergate burglary, Soviet agents surreptitiously bought a quarter of the US wheat crop on the open market to make good a shortfall in the USSR's harvest. When hawks of the Cold War realized what had happened, they demanded better intelligence about the state of farming in the Communist Bloc. The army of photoanalysts working with spy-satellite images found themselves counting harvested bales as well as missiles. And the pressure was on NASA and space scientists to perfect new means of gauging vegetation.

By visible light, forests and grasslands look almost black when seen from above, but they strongly reflect in the near-infrared, just a little longer in wavelength than red light. The infrared glow combined with a deficit of red light is the distinctive signature of vegetation on land, seen by satellites circling the Earth. The difference in intensities, infrared minus red, should be compared with the total intensity, to allow for variations in the brightness of the scene.

Then you have a vegetation index of amazing power. It duly detected a shortfall in Soviet wheat production in 1977, in images from NASA's Landsat satellite. And the vegetation index soon became a method of studying the entire terrestrial biosphere, for scientific, environmental and humanitarian purposes.

Leading the way was the biophysicist Compton Tucker of NASA's Laboratory of Terrestrial Physics in Maryland. At Colorado State University, before joining NASA, Tucker had traced the origin of the vegetation signature to the optical architecture of leaves. He concluded that the satellites don't merely map vegetation. From high in the sky they measure, region by region, its light-harvesting capacity.

In effect the sensors in space monitor the combined activity in all the leaves of the green chlorophyll pigment. This absorbs the solar energy needed for the basic work of life on the planet, to make sugars from carbon dioxide and water, and release oxygen as a by-product. As plants retain no more chlorophyll than they need, the vegetation index measures the vegetation's rate of growth.

Watching over Africa

Tucker ruffled feathers on his arrival at NASA by announcing that its series of Landsat spacecraft were less useful for vegetation studies than the weather satellites of a rival agency, the National Oceanic and Atmospheric Administration. The NOAA-7 satellite, launched in 1979, was the first of several to carry a radiometer called AVHRR. As it measured the red and near-infrared radiation from the Earth's surface, it was well suited for seeing the vegetation.

Unlike the Landsats, the NOAA satellites supplied daily data from every region. This was important for following changes in vegetation, and for finding cloud-free days in cloudy regions. Landsat users sometimes had to wait more than a year until one of the infrequent passes caught a required area not wreathed in clouds. Officials pointed out that the NOAA satellites normally averaged data from areas no smaller than four kilometres wide, while Landsat's vision was 50 times sharper. Tucker retorted, 'I want to do the whole world.'

He started with Africa. In collaboration with John Townshend at Reading, he charted the seasonal changes in vegetation by the NOAA satellite data. It was then a straightforward task to distinguish forests, savannah, deserts, and so on. Tucker and Townshend produced a map of all Africa showing vegetation zones divided into seven types. It looked very similar to maps produced in 100 years of dogged work by explorers armed with notebooks, machetes and quinine.

That you could do the satellite mapping in comfort, sitting at a computer in a suburb of Washington DC, was not the most important payoff. You could do it fast enough, and routinely, so as to see changes in vegetation in real time, season by season and year by year. The charts soon revealed, for example, that alarmist talk about the Sahara Desert expanding inexorably southwards, across the Sahel zone, was simply wrong.

The UN Food and Agriculture Organization in Rome adapted the satellite vegetation charts into an early-warning system for Africa. They could spot desert vegetation that might nurture locusts, and see effects of drought in inhabited regions that portended famine. If action to avert starvation was then too slow, that was not the fault of the space scientists.

Ground truth in Kansas

The biosphere is the totality of life on the Earth, ranking as a major embellishment of the planet's surface, alongside the atmosphere, hydrosphere and cryosphere—air, water, ice. Until the latter part of the 20th century, the biosphere was a static concept, mapped as an array of biogeographical zones. There were estimates of the biomass of all plants and animals put together, and of the net primary productivity of annual growth, but these were very sketchy and uncertain. For example a study in four continents, led by David Hall of King's College London, revealed that ecologists had underestimated the productivity of tropical grassland by a factor of four.

A highly dynamic view of the biosphere appeared when Tucker made charts showing all of the continents, using the vegetation index. Turned into amazing movies, they show most of the lands of the northern hemisphere looking desert-like in winter, without active chlorophyll. Then the springtime bloom spreads northwards like a tide. In summer, the monsoon zones of Asia and Africa burst into vigorous life, while the northern vegetation consolidates. The growth retreats southwards in the northern autumn.

That is springtime in the southern continents, and a similar spread and retreat of the growth zones ensues there, in opposite seasons. It does not look nearly so dramatic, because the land areas are much smaller. When Tucker calculated the north–south asymmetry, he found that the average vegetation index for all the world's landmasses doubled between January and July. This fitted very neatly with seasonal changes in the amount of carbon dioxide in the air, which decreases for a while each year, during the northern summer, as the abundant vegetation gobbles up the gas to grow by.

To draw global threads together more tightly still, Tucker teamed up with Piers Sellers, who personified a crisis in the academic study of the living environment. As an ecology student in the United Kingdom, Sellers grew impatient with learning more and more about less and less, in immensely detailed studies of small patches of terrain. Like Tucker, he wanted to do the whole world. His route was to study the relationship between plants, water and weather, while brushing up his physics in his spare time.

In Maryland, Sellers developed the first computer model of the biosphere. It was a weather-forecasting model that let the vegetation determine the ways in which the land surface interacted with the atmosphere. For example, plants pump water from the soil into the air, and this transpiration was one of many processes taken into account in the model.

Whenever plants take in carbon dioxide from the air, they lose water through the microscopic pores, or stomata, in the leaves. For this reason, many plants stop growing in the afternoon, when the air is drier and water loss would accelerate. They'll not start in the morning either, in times of drought. And when plants wilt, the vegetation index goes down. That can be interpreted as a symptom of dry soil, and therefore of reduced evaporation from the bare ground as well as the leaves.

Large-scale field experiments in Kansas in 1987 and 1989 put these ideas to the test. The selected site was the Konza Prairie Reserve, in the Flint Hills, which has escaped the plough because it is so stony. The incumbent cow-and-calf ranchers have to emulate their Native American predecessors in repeatedly burning the grass to protect the tallgrass prairie from the encroachment of trees, in this quite well-watered region.

The experiments compared the satellite data with close-up observations from the air and on the ground, to establish the 'ground truth' of the space observations. They confirmed the multiple links identified by Tucker and Sellers, between the vegetation index as a measure of light-harvesting capacity, carbon dioxide uptake, plant growth, and the transpiration and evaporation of water.

Russian forests thriving

'Other places are different,' Sellers commented as the Kansas experiments ended, 'but not that different.' Similar trials in Russia, Africa, Canada and Brazil bore out his opinion. His pioneering model of the biosphere simulated all the natural vegetation zones, from the Arctic tundra to tropical forests, by suitable combinations of just three entities: bare soil, ground cover of grass or herbs, and a canopy of shrubs or trees. It coped equally well with cultivated fields, golf courses and other man-made landscapes.

Other researchers developed further computer models of the terrestrial biosphere, especially to examine the possible relationships between vegetation and climate change. One such study, in which Sellers and Tucker were involved, modelled the influence of different amounts of vegetation seen in the satellite data for 1982–90. The results suggested that increases in vegetation density could exert a strong cooling effect, which might partially compensate for rising global temperatures.

By the time that report was published, in 2000, Sellers was in training as a NASA astronaut, so as to observe the biosphere from the International Space Station. The systematic monitoring of the land's vegetation by unmanned spacecraft already spanned two decades. Tucker collaborated with a team at Boston University that quarried the vast amounts of data accumulated daily over that period, to investigate long-term changes.

Between 1981 and 1999 the plainest trend in vegetation seen from space was towards longer growing seasons and more vigorous growth. The most dramatic effects were in Eurasia at latitudes above 40 degrees north, meaning roughly the line from Naples to Beijing. The vegetation increased not in area, but in density.

The greening was most evident in the forests and woodland that cover a broad swath of land at mid-latitudes from central Europe and across the entire width of Russia to the Far East. On average, the first leaves of spring were appearing a week earlier at the end of the period, and autumn was delayed by ten days. At the same mid-latitudes in North America, the satellite data showed extra growth in New England's forests, and grasslands of the upper Midwest. Otherwise the changes were scrappier than in Eurasia, and the extension of the growing season was somewhat shorter.

'We saw that year to year changes in growth and duration of the growing season of northern vegetation are tightly linked to year to year changes in temperature,' said Liming Zhou of Boston.

The colour of the sea

Life on land is about twice as productive as life in the sea, hectare for hectare, but the oceans are about twice as big. Being useful only on terra firma, the satellite vegetation index therefore covered barely half of the biosphere. For the rest, you have to gauge from space the productivity of the 'grass' of the sea, the microscopic green algae of the phytoplankton, drifting in the surface waters lit by the Sun.

Research ships can sample the algae only locally and occasionally, so satellite measurements were needed even more badly than on land. Estimates of ocean productivity differed not by percentage points but by a factor of six times from the lowest to the highest. The infrared glow of plants on land is not seen in the marine plants that float beneath the sea surface. Instead the space scientists had to look at the visible colour of the sea.

'In flying from Plymouth to the western mackerel grounds we passed over a sharp line separating the green water of the Channel from the deep blue of the Atlantic,' Alister Hardy of Oxford recorded in 1956. With the benefit of an aircraft's altitude, this noted marine biologist saw phenomena known to fishermen down the ages—namely that the most fertile water is green and murky, and that the transition can be sudden. The boundary near the mouth of the English Channel marks the onset of fertilization by nutrients brought to the surface by the churning action of tidal currents.

In 1978 the US satellite Nimbus-7 went into orbit carrying a variety of experimental instruments for remote sensing of the Earth. Among them was a Coastal Zone Color Scanner, which looked for the green chlorophyll of marine plants. Despite its name, its measurements in the open ocean were more reliable than inshore, where the waters are literally muddied.

In eight years of intermittent operation, the Color Scanner gave wonderful impressions of springtime blooms in the North Atlantic and North Pacific, like those seen on land by the vegetation index. New images for the textbooks showed high fertility in regions where nutrient-rich water wells up to the surface from below. The Equator turned out to be no imaginary line but a plainly visible green belt of chlorophyll separating the bluer, much less fertile regions in the tropical oceans to the north and south.

But, for would-be bookkeepers of the biosphere, the Nimbus-7 observations were frustratingly unsystematic and incomplete. A fuller accounting began with the launch by NASA in 1997 of OrbView-2, the first satellite capable of gauging the entire biosphere, by both sea and land. An oddly named instrument, SeaWiFS, combined the red and infrared sensors needed for the vegetation index on land with an improved sea-colour scanner.

SeaWiFS surveyed the whole world every two days. After three years the scientists were ready to announce the net primary productivity of all the world's plants, marine and terrestrial, deduced from the satellite data. The answer was 111 to 117 billion tonnes of carbon downloaded from the air and fixed by photosynthesis, in the course of a year, after subtracting the carbon that the plants' respiration returned promptly to the air.

The satellite's launch coincided with a period of strong warming in the Eastern Pacific, in the El Niño event of 1997–98. During an El Niño, the tropical ocean is depleted in mineral nutrients needed for life, hence the lower global figure in the SeaWiFS results. The higher figure was from the subsequent period of Pacific cooling: a La Niña. Between 1997 and 2000, ocean productivity increased by almost ten per cent, from 54 to 59 billion tonnes per year. In the same period the total productivity on land increased only slightly, from 57 to 58 billion tonnes of fixed carbon, although the El Niño to La Niña transition brought more drastic changes from region to region.

North–south differences were already known from space observations of vegetation ashore. The sheer extent of the northern lands explains the strong seasonal drawdown of carbon dioxide from the air by plants growing there in the northern summer. But the SeaWiFS results showed that summer productivity is higher also in the northern Atlantic and Pacific than in the more spacious Southern Ocean. The blooms are more intense.

'The summer blooms in the southern hemisphere are limited by light and by a chronic shortage of essential nutrients, especially iron,' noted Michael Behrenfeld of NASA's Laboratory of Hydrospheric Sciences, lead author of the first report on the SeaWiFS data. 'If the northern and southern hemispheres exhibited equivalent seasonal blooms, ocean productivity would be higher by some 9 billion tonnes of carbon.'

In that case, ocean productivity would exceed the land's. Although uncertainties remained about the calculations for both parts of the biosphere, there was no denying the remarkable similarity in plant growth by land and by sea. Previous estimates of ocean productivity had been too low.

New slants to come

The study of the biosphere as a whole is in its infancy. Before the Space Age it could not seriously begin, because you would have needed huge armies and navies of scientists, on the ground and at sea, to make the observations. By the early 21st century the political focus had shifted from Soviet grain production to the role of living systems in mopping up man-made emissions of carbon dioxide. The possible uses of augmented forests or fertilization of the oceans, for controlling carbon dioxide levels, were already of interest to treaty negotiators.

In parallel with the developments in space observations of the biosphere, ecologists have developed computer models of plant productivity. Discrepancies between their results show how far there is to go. For example, in a study reported in 2000, different calculations of how much carbon dioxide was taken in by plants and soil in the south-east USA, between 1980 and 1993, disagreed not by some percentage points but by a factor of more than three. Such uncertainties undermine the attempts to make global ecology a more exact science.

Improvements will come from better data, especially from observations from space of the year-to-year variability in plant growth by land and sea. These will help to pin down the effects of different factors and events. The lucky coincidence of the SeaWIFS launch and a dramatic El Niño event was a case in point.

A growing number of satellites in orbit measure the vegetation index and the sea colour. Future space missions will distinguish many more wavelengths of visible and infrared light, and use slanting angles of view to amplify the data. The space scientists won't leave unfinished the job they have started well.

▶ *See also* CARBON CYCLE. *For views on the Earth's vegetation at ground level, see* BIODIVERSITY. *For components of the biosphere hidden from cameras in space, see* EXTREMOPHILES.

BITS AND QUBITS

The digital world and its looming quantum shadow

O N A VISIT TO BELL LABS in New Jersey, if you met a man coming down the corridor on a unicycle it would probably be Claude Shannon, especially if he were juggling at the same time. According to his wife: 'He had been a gymnast in college, so he was better at it than you might have thought.' His after-hours capers were tolerated because he had come up single-handedly with two of the most consequential ideas in the history of technology, each of them roughly comparable to inventing the wheel on which he was performing.

In 1937, when a 21-year-old graduate student of electrical engineering at the Massachusetts Institute of Technology, Shannon saw in simple relays—electric switches under electric control—the potential to make logical decisions. Suppose two relays represent propositions X and Y. If the switch is open, the proposition is false, and if connected it is true.

Put the relays in a line, in series, then a current can flow only if X AND Y are true. But branch the circuit so that the switches operate in parallel, then if either X OR Y is true a current flows. And as Shannon pointed out in his eventual dissertation, the false/true dichotomy could equally well represent the digits 0 or 1. He wrote: 'It is possible to perform complex mathematical operations by means of relay circuits.'

In the history of computers, Alan Turing in England and John von Neumann in the USA are rightly famous for their notions about programmable machinery, in the 1930s and 1940s when code-breaking and other military needs gave an urgency to innovation. Electric relays soon made way for thermionic valves in early computers, and then for transistors fashioned from semiconductors. The fact remains that the boy Shannon's AND and OR gates are still the principle of the design and operation of the microchips of every digital computer, whilst the binary arithmetic of 0s and 1s now runs the working world.

Shannon's second gigantic contribution to modern life came at Bell Labs. By 1943 he realized that his 0s and 1s could represent information of kinds going far wider than logic or arithmetic. Many questions like 'Do you love me?' invite a simple yes or no answer, which might be communicated very economically by a single 1 or 0, a binary digit. Shannon called it a bit for short. More complicated communications—strings of text for example—require more bits. Just how many is easily calculable, and this is a measure of the information content of a message.

So you have a message of so many bits. How quickly can you send it? That depends on how many bits per second the channel of communication can handle. Thus you can rate the capacity of the channel using the same binary units, and the reckoning of messages and communication power can apply to any kind of system: printed words in a telegraph, voices on the radio, pictures on television, or even a carrier pigeon, limited by the weight it can carry and the sharpness of vision of the reader of the message.

In an electromagnetic channel, the theoretical capacity in bits per second depends on the frequency range. Radio with music requires tens of kilocycles per second, whilst television pictures need megacycles. Real communications channels fall short of their theoretical capacity because of interference from outside sources and internally generated noise, but you can improve the fidelity of transmission by widening the bandwidth or sending the message more slowly.

Shannon went on polishing his ideas quietly, not discussing them even with close colleagues. He was having fun, but he found writing up the work for publication quite painful. Not until 1948 did his classic paper called 'A mathematical theory of communication' appear. It won instant acceptance. Shannon had invented his own branch of science and was treading on nobody else's toes. His propositions, though wholly new and surprising, were quickly digestible and then almost self-evident.

The most sensational result from Shannon's mathematics was that near-perfect communication is possible in principle if you convert the information to be sent into digital form. For example, the light wanted in a picture element of an image can be specified, not as a relative intensity, but as a number, expressed in binary digits. Instead of being roughly right, as expected in an analogue system, the intensity will be precisely right.

Scientific and military systems were the first to make intensive use of Shannon's principles. The general public became increasingly aware of the digital world through personal computers and digitized music on compact discs. By the end of the 20th century, digital radio, television and video recording were becoming widespread.

Further spectacular innovations began with the marriage of computing and digital communication, to bring all the world's information resources into your office or living room. From a requirement for survivable communications, in the aftermath of a nuclear war, came the Internet, developed as Arpanet by the US Advanced Research Project Agency. It provided a means of finding routes through a shattered telephone system where many links were unavailable. That was the origin of emails. By the mid-1980s, many computer scientists and physicists were using the net, and in 1990 responsibility for the system passed from the military to the US National Science Foundation.

Meanwhile at CERN, Europe's particle physics lab in Geneva, the growing complexity of experiments brought a need for advanced digital links between scientists in widely scattered labs. It prompted Tim Berners-Lee and his colleagues to invent the World Wide Web in 1990, and within a few years everyone was joining in. The World Wide Web's impact on human affairs was comparable with the invention of steam trains in the 19th century, but more sudden.

Just because the systems of modern information technology are so familiar, it can be hard to grasp how innovative and fundamental Shannon's ideas were. A couple of scientific pointers may help. In relation to the laws of heat, his quantifiable information is the exact opposite of entropy, which means the degradation of high forms of energy into mere heat and disorder. Life itself is a non-stop battle of hereditary information against deadly disorder, and Mother Nature went digital long ago. Shannon's mathematical theory of communication applies to the genetic code and to the on–off binary pulses operating in your brain as you read these words.

Towards quantum computers

For a second revolution in information technology, the experts looked to the spooky behaviour of electrons and atoms known in quantum theory. By 2002 physicists in Australia had made the equivalent of Shannon's relays of 65 years earlier, but now the switches offered not binary bits, but qubits, pronounced cue-bits. They raised hopes that the first quantum computers might be operating before the first decade of the new century was out.

Whereas electric relays, and their electronic successors in microchips, provide the simple on/off, true/false, 1/0 options expressed as bits of information, the qubits in the corresponding quantum devices will have many possible states. In theory it is possible to make an extremely fast computer by exploiting ambiguities that are present all the time in quantum theory.

If you're not sure whether an electron in an atom is in one possible energy state, or in the next higher energy state permitted by the physical laws, then it can be considered to be in both states at once. In computing terms it represents both 1 and 0 at the same time. Two such ambiguities give you four numbers, 00, 01, 10 and 11, which are the binary-number equivalents of good old 0, 1, 2 and 3. Three ambiguities give eight numbers, and so on, until with 50 you have a million billion numbers represented simultaneously in the quantum computer. In theory the machine can compute with all of them at the same time.

Such quantum spookiness spooks the spooks. The world's secret services are still engaged in the centuries-old contest between code-makers and code-breakers.

There are new concepts called quantum one-time pads for a supposedly unbreakable cipher, using existing technology, and future quantum computers are expected to be able to crack many of the best codes of pre-existing kinds. Who knows what developments may be going on behind the scenes, like the secret work on digital computing by Alan Turing at Bletchley Park in England during the Second World War?

A widespread opinion at the start of the 21st century held that quantum computing was beyond practical reach for the time being. It was seen as requiring exquisite delicacy in construction and operation, with the ever-present danger that the slightest external interference, or a premature leakage of information from the system, could cause the whole multiply parallel computation to cave in, like a mistimed soufflé.

Colorado and Austria were the settings for early steps towards a practical quantum computer, announced in 2003. At the US National Institute of Standards and Technology, finely tuned laser beams played on a pair of beryllium ions (charged atoms) trapped in a vacuum. If both ions were spinning the same way, the laser beams had no effect, but if they had contrary spins the beams made them prance briefly away from each other and change their spins according to subtle but predictable quantum rules.

Simultaneously a team at Universität Innsbruck reported the use of a pair of calcium ions. In this case, laser beams controlled the ions individually. All possible combinations of parallel and anti-parallel spins could be created and read out. Commenting on the progress, Andrew Steane at Oxford's Centre for Quantum Computation declared, 'The experiments . . . represent, for me, the first hint that there is a serious possibility of making logic gates, precise to one part in a thousand or even ten thousand, that could be scaled up to many qubits.'

Quantum computing is not just a new technology. For David Deutsch at Oxford, who developed the seminal concept of a quantum computer from 1977 onwards, it opened a road for exploring the nature of the Universe in its quantum aspects. In particular it illustrated the theory of the quantum multiverse, also promulgated by Deutsch.

The many ambiguities of quantum mechanics represent, in his theory, multiple universes like our own that co-exist in parallel with what we know and experience. Deutsch's idea should not be confused with the multiple universes offered in some Big Bang theories. Those would have space and time separate from our own, whilst the universes of the quantum multiverse supposedly operate within our own cosmic framework, and provide a complexity and richness unseen by mortal eyes.

'In quantum computation the complexity of what is happening is very high so that, philosophically, it becomes an unavoidable obligation to try to explain it,'

Deutsch said. 'This will have philosophical implications in the long run, just in the way that the existence of Newton's laws profoundly affected the debate on things like determinism. It is not that people actually used Newton's laws in that debate, but the fact that they existed at all coloured a great deal of philosophical discussions subsequently. That will happen with quantum computers I am sure.'

▶ *For the background on quantum mechanics, and on cryptic long-distance communication in the quantum manner, see* QUANTUM TANGLES.

BLACK HOLES
The awesome engines of quasars and active galaxies

'THE VIRGINITY OF SENSE,' the writer and traveller Robert Louis Stevenson called it. Only once in a lifetime can you first experience the magic of a South Sea island as your schooner draws near. With scientific discoveries, too, there are unrepeatable moments for the individuals who make them, or for the many who first thrill to the news. Then the magic fades into commonplace facts that students mug up for their exams. Even about quasars, the lords of the sky.

In 1962 a British radio astronomer, Cyril Hazard, was in Australia with a bright idea for pinpointing a mysteriously small but powerful radio star. He would watch it disappear behind the Moon, and then reappear again, using a new radio telescope at Parkes in New South Wales. Only by having the engineers remove bolts from the huge structure would it tilt far enough to point in the right direction. The station's director, John Bolton, authorized that, and even made the observations for him when Hazard took the wrong train from Sydney.

Until then, object No. 273 in the 3rd Cambridge Catalogue of Radio Sources, or 3C 273 for short, had no obvious visible counterpart at the place in the sky from which the radio waves were coming. But its position was known only roughly, until the lunar occultation at Parkes showed that it corresponded with a faint star in the Virgo constellation. A Dutch-born astronomer, Maarten Schmidt, examined 3C 273 with what was then the world's biggest telescope for visible light, the five-metre Palomar instrument in California.

He smeared the object's light into a spectrum showing the different wavelengths. The pattern of lines was very unusual and Schmidt puzzled over a photograph of the spectrum for six weeks. In February 1963, the penny dropped. He recognized three features due to hydrogen, called Lyman lines, normally seen as ultraviolet light. Their wavelengths were so greatly stretched, or red-shifted, by the expansion of the Universe that 3C 273 had to be very remote—billions of light-years away.

The object was far more luminous than a galaxy and too long-lived to be an exploding star. The star-like appearance meant it produced its light from a very small volume, and no conventional astrophysical theory could explain it. 'I went home in a state of disbelief,' Schmidt recalled. 'I said to my wife, "It's horrible. Something incredible happened today."'

Horrible or not, a name was needed for this new class of objects—3C 273 was the brightest but by no means the only quasi-stellar radio source. Astrophysicists at NASA's Goddard Space Flight Center who were native speakers of German and Chinese coined the name early in 1964. Wolfgang Priester suggested *quastar*, but Hong-yee Chiu objected that Questar was the name of a telescope. 'It will have to be quasar,' he said. The *New York Times* adopted the term, and that was that.

The nuclear power that lights the Sun and other ordinary stars could not convincingly account for the output of energy. Over the years that followed the pinpointing of 3C 273, astronomers came reluctantly to the conclusion that only a gravitational engine could explain the quasars. They reinvented the Minotaur, the creature that lived in a Cretan maze and demanded a diet of young people. Now the maze is a galaxy, and at the core of that vast congregation of stars lurks a black hole that feeds on gas or dismembered stars.

By 1971 Donald Lynden-Bell and Martin Rees at Cambridge could sketch the theory. They reasoned that doomed matter would swirl around the black hole in a flat disk, called an accretion disk, and gradually spiral inwards like water running into a plughole, releasing energy. The idea was then developed to explain jets of particles and other features seen in quasars and in disturbed objects called active galaxies.

Apart from the most obvious quasars, a wide variety of galaxies display violent activity. Some are strangely bright centrally or have great jets spouting from their nuclei. The same active galaxies tend to show up conspicuously by radio, ultraviolet, X-rays and gamma rays, and some have jet-generated lobes of radio emission like enormous wings. All are presumed to harbour quasars, although dust often hides them from direct view.

In 1990 Rees noted the general acceptance of his ideas. 'There is a growing consensus,' he wrote, 'that every quasar, or other active galactic nucleus, is powered by a giant black hole, a million or a billion times more massive than the

Sun. Such an awesome monster could be formed by a runaway catastrophe in the very heart of the galaxy. If the black hole is subsequently fuelled by capturing gas and stars from its surroundings, or if it interacts with the galaxy's magnetic fields, it can liberate the copious energy needed to explain the violent events.'

A ready-made idea

Since the American theorist John Wheeler coined the term in 1967, for a place in the sky where gravity can trap even light, the black hole has entered everyday speech as the ultimate waste bin. Familiarity should not diminish this invention of the human mind, made doubly amazing by Mother Nature's anticipation and employment of it.

Strange effects on space and time distinguish modern black holes from those imagined in the Newtonian era. In 1784 John Michell, a Yorkshire clergyman who moonlighted as a scientific genius, forestalled Einstein by suggesting that light was subject to the force of gravity. A very large star might therefore be invisible, he reasoned, if its gravity were too strong for light to escape.

Since early in the 20th century, Michell's gigantic star has been replaced by matter compacted by gravity into an extremely small volume—perhaps even to a geometric point, though we can't see that far in. Surrounding the mass, at some distance from the centre, is the surface of the black hole where matter and light can pass inwards but not outwards. This picture came first from Karl Schwarzschild who, on his premature deathbed in Potsdam in 1916, applied Albert Einstein's new theory of gravity to a single massive object like the Earth or the Sun.

The easiest way to calculate the object's effects on space and time around it is to imagine all of its mass concentrated in the middle. And a magic membrane, where escaping light and time itself are brought to a halt, appears in Schwarzschild's maths. If the Earth were really squeezed to make a black hole, the distance of its surface from the massy centre would be just nine millimetres. This distance, proportional to the mass, is called the Schwarzschild radius and is still used for sizing up black holes.

Mathematical convenience was one thing, but the reality of black holes—called dark stars or collapsed stars until Wheeler coined the popular term—was something else entirely. While admiring Schwarzschild's ingenuity, Einstein himself disliked the idea. It languished until the 1960s, when astrophysicists were thinking about the fate of very massive stars. They realized that when the stars exploded at the end of their lives, their cores might collapse under a pressure that even the nuclei of atoms could not resist. Matter would disappear, leaving behind only its intense gravity, like the grin of Lewis Carroll's Cheshire Cat.

Roger Penrose in Oxford, Stephen Hawking in Cambridge, Yakov Zel'dovich in Moscow and Edwin Salpeter at Cornell were among those who developed the theory of such stellar black holes. It helped to explain some of the cosmic sources of intense X-rays in our own Galaxy then being discovered by satellites. They have masses a few times greater than the Sun's, and nowadays they are called microquasars. The black hole idea was thus available, ready made, for explaining the quasars and active galaxies with far more massive pits of gravity.

Verification by X-rays

But was the idea really correct? The best early evidence for black holes came from close inspection of stars orbiting around the centres of active galaxies. They turned out to be whirling at a high speed that was explicable only if an enormous mass was present. The method of gauging the mass, by measuring the star speeds, was somewhat laborious. By 2001, at Spain's Instituto de Astrofisica de Canarias, Alister Graham and his colleagues realized that you could judge the mass just by looking at a galaxy's overall appearance.

The concentration of visible matter towards the centre depends on the black hole's mass. But whilst this provided a quick and easy way of making the estimate, it also raised questions about how the concentration of matter arose. 'We now know that any viable theory of supermassive black hole growth must be connected with the eventual global structure of the host galaxy,' Graham said.

Another approach to verifying the scenario was to identify and measure the black hole's dinner plate—the accretion disk in which matter spirals to its doom. Over a period of 14 years the NASA–Europe–UK satellite International Ultraviolet Explorer repeatedly observed the active galaxy 3C 390.3. Whenever the black hole swallowed a larger morsel than usual, the flash took more than a month to reach the edge of the disk and brighten it. So the accretion disk was a fifth of a light-year across.

But the honours for really confirming the black hole theory went to X-ray astronomers. That's not surprising if you consider that, just before matter disappears, it has become so incandescent that it is glowing with X-rays. They are the best form of radiation for probing very close to the black hole.

An emission from highly charged iron atoms, fluorescing in the X-ray glare at the heart of an active galaxy, did the trick. Each X-ray particle, or photon, had a characteristic energy of 6400 electron-volts, equal to that of an electron accelerated by 6400 volts. Called the iron K-alpha line, it showed up strongly when British and Japanese scientists independently examined galaxies with the Japanese Ginga X-ray satellite in 1989.

'This emission from iron will be a trailblazer for astronomers,' said Ken Pounds at Leicester, who led the discovery team. 'Our colleagues observing the relatively cool Universe of stars and gas rely heavily on the Lyman-alpha ultraviolet light from hydrogen atoms to guide them. Iron K-alpha will do a similar job for the hot Universe of black holes.'

Violent activity near black holes should change the apparent energy of this iron emission. Andy Fabian of Cambridge and his colleagues predicted a distinctive signature if the X-rays truly came from atoms whirling at high speed around a black hole. Those from atoms approaching the Earth will seem to have higher energy, and those from receding atoms will look less energetic.

Spread out in a spectrum of X-ray energy, the signals should resemble the two horns of a bull. But add another effect, the slowdown of time near a black hole, and all of the photons appear to be emitted with less energy. The signature becomes a skewed bull's head, shifted and drooping towards the lower, slow-time energies. As no other galactic-scale object could forge this pattern, its detection would confirm once and for all that black holes exist.

The first X-ray satellite capable of analysing high-energy emissions in sufficient detail to settle the issue was ASCA, Japan's Advanced Satellite for Cosmology and Astrophysics, launched in 1993. In the following year, ASCA spent more than four days drinking in X-rays from an egg-shaped galaxy in the Centaurus constellation. MCG-6-30-15 was only one of many in Russia's Morphological Catalogue of Galaxies suspected of harbouring giant black holes, but this was the one for the history books.

The pattern of the K-alpha emissions from iron atoms was exactly as Andy Fabian predicted. The atoms were orbiting around the source of the gravity at 30 per cent of the speed of light. Slow time in the black hole's vicinity reduced the apparent energy of all the emissions by about 10 per cent.

'To confirm the reality of black holes was always the number one aim of X-ray astronomers,' said Yasuo Tanaka, of Japan's Institute for Space and Astronautical Science. 'Our satellite was not large, but rather sensitive and designed for discoveries with X-rays of high energy. We were pleased when ASCA showed us the predicted black-hole behaviour so clearly.'

The spacetime carousel

ASCA was followed into space in 1999 by much bigger X-ray satellites. NASA's Chandra was the sharper-eyed of the two, and Europe's XMM-Newton had exceptionally sensitive telescopes and spectrometers for gathering and analysing the X-rays. XMM-Newton took the verification of black holes a step further by inspecting MCG-6-30-15 again, and another active galaxy, Markarian 766 in the Coma constellation.

Their black holes turned out to be spinning. In the jargon, they were not Schwarzschild black holes but Kerr black holes, named after Roy Kerr of the

University of Canterbury, New Zealand. He had analysed the likely effects of a rotating black hole, as early as 1963.

One key prediction was that the surface of Kerr's black hole would be at only half the distance from the centre of mass, compared with the Schwarzschild radius when rotation was ignored. Another was that infalling gas could pause in stable orbits, and so be observable, much closer to the black-hole surface. Judged as a machine for converting the mass-energy of matter into radiation, the rotating black hole would be six times more efficient.

Most mind-boggling was the prediction that the rotating black hole would create a tornado, not *in* space, but *of* space. The fabric of space itself becomes fluid. If you tried to stand still in such a setting, you'd find yourself whirled around and around as if on a carousel, at up to half the speed of light. This happens independently of any ordinary motion in orbit around the black hole.

A UK–US–Dutch team of astronomers, who used XMM-Newton to observe the active galaxies in the summer of 2000, could not at first make sense of the emitted X-rays. In contrast with the ASCA discovery with iron atoms, where the pattern was perfectly predicted, the XMM-Newton patterns were baffling. Eventually Masao Sako, a graduate student at Columbia, recognized the emissions as coming from extremely hot, extremely high-speed atoms of oxygen, nitrogen and carbon. They were visible much nearer to the centre of mass than would be possible if the black hole were not rotating.

'XMM-Newton surprised us by showing features that no one had expected,' Sako commented. 'But they mean that we can now explore really close to these giant black holes, find out about their feeding habits and digestive system, and check Einstein's theory of gravity in extreme conditions.'

Soon afterwards, the same spacecraft saw a similar spacetime carousel around a much smaller object, a suspected stellar black hole in the Ara constellation called XTE J1650-500. After more than 30 years of controversy, calculation, speculation and investigation, the black hole theory was at last secure.

The adventure continues

Giant black holes exist in many normal galaxies, including our own Milky Way. So quasars and associated activity may be intermittent events, which can occur in any galaxy when a disturbance delivers fresh supplies of stars and gas to the central black hole. A close encounter with another galaxy could have that effect.

In the exact centre of our Galaxy, which lies beyond the Sagittarius constellation, is a small, intense source of radio waves and X-rays called Sagittarius A*, pronounced A-star. These and other symptoms were for long interpreted as a hungry black hole, millions of times more massive than the Sun, which has consumed most of the material available in its vicinity and is therefore relatively quiescent.

Improvements in telescopes for visible light enabled astronomers to track the motions of stars ever closer to the centre of the Galaxy. A multinational team of astronomers led by Rainer Schödel, Thomas Ott and Reinhard Genzel of Germany's Max-Planck-Institut für extraterrestrische Physik, began observing with a new instrument on Europe's Very Large Telescope in Chile. It showed that in the spring of 2002 a star called S2, which other instruments had tracked for ten years, closed to within just 17 light-hours of the putative black hole. It was travelling at 5000 kilometres per second.

'We are now able to demonstrate with certainty that Sagittarius A* is indeed the location of the central dark mass we knew existed,' said Schödel. 'Even more important, our new data have shrunk by a factor of several thousand the volume within which those several million solar masses are contained.' The best estimate of the black hole's mass was then 2.6 million times the mass of the Sun.

Some fundamental but still uncertain relationship exists between galaxies and the black holes they harbour. That became plainer when the Hubble Space Telescope detected the presence of objects with masses intermediate between the stellar black holes (a few times the Sun's mass) and giant black holes in galaxy cores (millions or billions of times). By 2002, black holes of some thousands of solar masses had revealed themselves, by rapid motions of nearby stars within dense throngs called globular clusters.

Globular clusters are beautiful and ancient objects on free-range orbits about the centre of the Milky Way and in other flat, spiral galaxies like ours. In M15, a well-known globular cluster in the Hercules constellation, Hubble sensed the presence of a 4000-solar-mass black hole. In G1, a globular cluster in the nearby Andromeda Galaxy, the detected black hole is five times more massive. As a member of the team that found the latter object, Karl Gebhardt of Texas-Austin commented, 'The intermediate-mass black holes that have now been found with Hubble may be the building blocks of the supermassive black holes that dwell in the centres of most galaxies.'

Another popular idea is that black holes may have been the first objects created from the primordial gas, even before the first stars. Indeed, radiation and jets from these early black holes might have helped to sweep matter together to make the stars. Looking for primordial black holes, far out in space and therefore far back in time, may require an extremely large X-ray satellite.

When Chandra and XMM-Newton, the X-ray supertelescopes of the early 21st century, investigated very distant sources, they found previously unseen X-ray-emitting galaxies or quasars galore, out to the limit of their sensitivity. These indicated that black holes existed early in the history of the Universe, and they accounted for much but by no means all of the cosmic X-ray background that fills the whole sky.

Xeus, a satellite concept studied by the European Space Agency, would hunt for the missing primordial sources. It would be so big that it would dispense with the telescope tube and have the detectors on a satellite separate from the orbiting mirrors used to focus the cosmic X-rays. The sensitivity of Xeus would initially surpass XMM-Newton's by a factor of 40, and later by 200, when new mirror segments had been added at the International Space Station, to make the X-ray telescope 10 metres wide.

Direct examination of the black surface that gives a black hole its name is the prime aim of a rival American scheme for around 2020, called Maxim. It would use a technique called X-ray interferometry, demonstrated in laboratory tests by Webster Cash of Colorado and his colleagues, to achieve a sharpness of vision a million times better than Chandra's. The idea is to gather X-ray beams from the black hole and its surroundings with two or three dozen simple mirrors in orbit, at precisely controlled separations of up to a kilometre. The beams reflected from the mirrors come together in a detector spacecraft 500 kilometres behind the mirrors.

The Maxim concept would provide the technology to take a picture of a black hole. The giant black holes in the hearts of relatively close galaxies, such as M87 in the Virgo constellation, should be easily resolved by that spacecraft combination. 'Such images would provide incontrovertible proof of the existence of these objects,' Cash and his colleagues claimed. 'They would allow us to study the exotic physics at work in the immediate vicinity of black holes.'

A multiplicity of monsters

Meanwhile there is plenty to do concerning black holes, with instruments already existing or in the pipeline. For example, not everyone is satisfied that all of the manifestations of violence in galaxies can be explained by different viewing angles or by different phases in a cycle of activity around a single quasar. In 1983, Martin Gaskell at Cambridge suggested that some quasars behave as if they are twins.

Finnish astronomers came to a similar conclusion. They conducted the world's most systematic monitoring programme for active galaxies, which used millimetre-wave radio telescopes at Kirkkonummi in Finland and La Silla in Chile. After observing upheavals in more than 100 galaxies for more than 20 years, Esko Valtaoja at Turku suspected that the most intensely active galaxies have more than one giant black hole in their nuclei.

'If many galaxies contain central black holes and many galaxies have merged, then it's only reasonable to expect plenty of cases where two or more black holes co-exist,' Valtaoja said. 'We see evidence for at least two, in several of our active galaxies and quasars. Also extraordinary similarities in the eruptions of galaxies, as if the link between the black holes and the jets of the eruptions obeys some simple, fundamental law. Making sense of this multiplicity of monsters is now the biggest challenge for this line of research.'

Direct confirmation of two giant black holes in one galaxy came first from the Chandra satellite, observing NGC 6240 in the Ophiuchus constellation. This is a starburst galaxy, where the merger of two galaxies has provoked a frenzy of star formation. The idea of Gaskell and Valtaoja was beautifully confirmed.

▶ *For more on Einstein's general relativity, see* GRAVITY. *For the use of a black hole as a power supply, see* ENERGY AND MASS. *For more on galaxy evolution, see* GALAXIES *and* STARBURSTS.

BRAIN IMAGES

What do all the vivid movies really mean?

C ARTOONS that show a mentally overtaxed person cooling his head with an ice pack trace back to experiments in Paris in the 1870s. The anthropologist Paul Broca, discoverer of key bits of the brain involved in language, attached thermometers to the scalps of medical students. When he gave them tricky linguistic tasks, the skin temperature rose.

And if someone has a piece of the skull missing, you can feel the blood pulsing through the outermost layers of the brain, in the cerebral cortex where most thinking and perception go on. After studying patients with such holes in their heads, Angelo Mosso at Turin reported in 1881 that the pulsations could intensify during mental activity. Thus you might trace the activity of the brain by the energy supplies delivered by the blood to its various parts.

Brainwork is not a metaphor. In the physicist's strictest sense, the brain expends more energy when it is busy than when it is not. The biochemist sees glucose from the blood burning up faster. It's nothing for athletes or slimmers to get excited about—just a few extra watts, or kilocalories per hour, will get you through a chess game or an interview.

After the preamble from Broca and Mosso, the idea of physical effort as an indicator of brain action languished for many years. Even when radioactive tracers came into use as a way of measuring cerebral blood flows more precisely, the experimenters themselves were sceptical about their value for studying brain function. William Landau of the US National Institutes of Health told a meeting of neurologists in 1955, 'It is rather like trying to measure what a factory does by measuring the intake of water and the output of sewage. This is only a problem of plumbing.'

What wasn't in doubt was the medical importance of blood flow, which could fail locally in cases of stroke or brain tumours. Patients' heads were X-rayed after being injected with material that made the blood opaque. A turning point in brain research came in the 1960s when David Ingvar in Lund and Niels Lassen in Copenhagen began introducing into the bloodstream a radioactive material, xenon-133.

The scientists used a camera with 254 detectors, each measuring gamma rays coming from the xenon in a square centimetre of the cerebral cortex. It generated a picture on a TV screen. Out of the first 500 patients so examined, 80 had undamaged brains and could therefore be used in evidence concerning normal brainwork. Plain to see in the resting brain, the front was most active. Blood flows were 20–30 per cent higher than the average.

'The frontmost parts of the frontal lobe, the prefrontal areas, are responsible for the planning of behaviour in its widest sense,' the Scandinavian researchers noted. 'The hyperfrontal resting flow pattern therefore suggests that in the conscious waking state the brain is busy planning and selecting different behavioural patterns.'

The patterns of blood flow changed as soon as patients opened their eyes. Other parts of their brains lit up. Noises and words provoked increased blood flow in areas assigned to hearing and language. Getting a patient to hold a weight in one hand resulted in activity in the corresponding sensory and muscle-controlling regions on the opposite side of the head—again as expected. Difficult mental tasks provoked a 10 per cent increase in the total blood flow in the brain.

PET scans and magnetic imaging

Techniques borrowed from particle physics and from X-ray scanners made brain imaging big business from the 1980s onwards, with the advent of positron emission tomography, or PET. It uses radioactive forms of carbon, nitrogen and oxygen atoms that survive for only a few minutes before they emit anti-electrons, or positrons. So you need a cyclotron to make them on the premises. Water molecules labelled with oxygen-15 atoms are best suited to studying blood flow pure and simple. Marcus Raichle of Washington University, St Louis, first demonstrated this technique.

Injected into the brain's blood supply, most of the radioactive atoms release their positrons wherever the blood is concentrated. Each positron immediately reacts with an ordinary electron to produce two gamma-ray particles flying off in opposite directions. They arrive at arrays of detectors on opposite sides of the head almost simultaneously, but not quite.

From the precise times of arrival of the gamma rays, in which detector on which array, a computer can tell where the positron originated. Quickly scanning the detector arrays around the head builds up a complete 3-D picture of the brain's blood supply. Although provided initially for medical purposes, PET scans caught the imagination of experimental psychologists. Just as in the pioneering work of Ingvar and Lassen, the blood flows changed to suit the brain's activity.

Meanwhile a different technique for medical imaging was coming into widespread use. Invented in 1972 by Paul Lauterbur, a chemist at Stony Brook, New York, magnetic resonance imaging detects the nuclei of hydrogen atoms in the water within the living body. In a strong magnetic field these protons swivel like wobbling tops, and when prodded they broadcast radio waves at a frequency that depends on the strength of the magnetic field. If the magnetic field varies across the body, the water in each part will radiate at a distinctive frequency.

Relatively free water, as in blood, is slower to radiate than water in dense tissue. So magnetic resonance imaging distinguishes between different tissues. It can, for example, show the internal anatomy of the brain very clearly, in a living person. But such images are rather static.

Clear detection of brain activity, as achieved with radioactive tracers, became possible when the chemist Seiji Ogawa of Bell Labs, New Jersey, reported in 1990 that subtle features in the protons' radiation depended on the amount of oxygen present in the blood. 'One may think we got a method to look into human consciousness,' Ogawa said. An advantage of his 'functional magnetic resonance imaging' was that you didn't have to keep making the short-lived tracers. On the other hand, the person studied was perforce enclosed in the strong magnetic field of the imaging machine.

Experimental psychologists and brain researchers found themselves in the movie-making business, helped by advances in computer graphics. They could give a person a task and see, in real time, different bits of the brain coming into play like actors on a stage. Watching the products of the PET scans and functional magnetic resonance imaging, many researchers and students were easily persuaded that they were seeing at last how the brain works.

The mental movie-makers nevertheless faced a 'So what?' reaction from other neuroscientists. Starting in the 19th century, anatomists, brain surgeons, medical psychologists and others had already identified the responsibilities of different parts of the brain. The knowledge came mainly from the loss of faculties due to illness, injuries or animal experiments. From the planning in the frontal lobes, to the visual cortex at the back where the pictures from the eyes are processed, the brain maps were pretty comprehensive. The bits that lit up in the blood-flow movies were usually what were expected.

Just because the new pictures were so enthralling, it was as well to be cautious about their meaning. Neither they nor the older assignments of function explained the mental processes, any more than a satellite picture of Washington DC, showing the State Department and the White House, accounts for US foreign policy. The blood-flow images nevertheless brought genuine insights, when they showed live brains working in real time, and changing their responses with experience. They also revealed a surprising degree of versatility, with the same part of the brain coming into play for completely different tasks.

The example of wayfinding

Neither of the dogmas that gripped Western psychology in the mid-20th century, behaviourism and psychoanalysis, cared how the brain worked. At that time the top expert on the localization of mental functions in brain tissue was in Moscow. Alexander Luria of the Bourdenko Institute laid foundations for a science of neuropsychology on which brain imagers would later build.

Sadly, Luria had an unlimited caseload of brain damage left over from the Second World War. One patient was Lev Zassetsky, a Red Army officer who had part of his head shot away, on the left and towards the back. His personality was unimpaired but his vision was partly affected and he lost his ability to read and write. When Luria found that Zassetsky could still sign his name unthinkingly, he encouraged him to try writing again, using the undamaged parts of his brain.

Despite lacking nerve cells normally considered essential for some language functions, the ex-soldier eventually composed a fluent account of his life, in 3000 autographic pages. In the introduction Zassetsky commented on the anguish of individuals like himself who contributed to the psychologists' discoveries.

'Many people, I know, discuss cosmic space and how our Earth is no more than a tiny particle in the infinite Universe, and now they are talking seriously of flight to the nearer planets of the Solar System. Yet the flight of bullets, shrapnel, shells or bombs, which splinter and fly into a man's head, poisoning and scorching his brain, crippling his memory, sight, hearing, consciousness— this is now regarded as something normal and easily dealt with.

'But is it? If so, then why am I sick? Why doesn't my memory function, why have I not regained my sight, why is there a constant noise in my aching head, why can't I understand human speech properly? It is an appalling task to start again at the beginning and relearn the world which I lost when I was wounded, to piece it together again from tiny separate fragments into a single whole.'

In that relearning, Zassetsky built what Luria called 'an artificial mind'. He could sometimes reason his way to solve problems when his damaged brain failed to handle them instantly and unconsciously. A cluster of remaining defects was linked to the loss of a rearward portion of the parietal lobe, high on the side of the head, which Luria understood to handle complex relationships. That included making sense of long sentences, doing mental arithmetic, or answering questions of the kind, 'Are your father's brother and your brother's father the same person?'

Zassetsky also had continuing difficulty with the relative positions of things in space—above/below, left/right, front/back—and with route directions. Either drawing a map or picturing a map inside his head was hard for him. Hans-Lukas Tauber of the Massachusetts Institute of Technology told of a US soldier who incurred a similar wound in Korea and wandered quite aimlessly in no-man's-land for three days.

Here were early hints about the possible location of the faculty that psychologists now call wayfinding. It involves the construction of mental maps, coupled with remembered landmarks. By the end of the century, much more was known about wayfinding, both from further studies of effects of brain damage and from the new brain imaging.

A false trail came from animal experiments. These suggested that an internal part of the brain called the hippocampus was heavily involved in wayfinding. By brain imaging in human beings confronted with mazes, Mark D'Esposito and colleagues at the University of Pennsylvania were able to show that no special activity occurred in the hippocampus. Instead, they pinpointed a nearby internal region called the parahippocampal gyrus. They also saw activity in other parts of the brain, including the posterior-parietal region where the soldier Zassetsky was wounded.

An engrossing feature of brain imaging was that it led on naturally to other connections made in normal brain activity. For example, in experiments involving a simulated journey through a town with distinguishable buildings, the Pennsylvania team found that recognizing a landmark building employs different parts of the brain from those involved in mental map-making. The landmark recognition occurs in the same general area, deep in the brain towards the back, which people use for recognizing faces. But it's not in exactly the same bunch of nerve cells.

Closely related to wayfinding is awareness of motion, when walking through a landscape and seeing objects approaching or receding. Karl Friston of the Institute of Neurology in London traced the regions involved. Brain images showed mutual influences between various parts of the visual cortex at the back of the brain that interpret signals from the eyes, including the V5 area responsible for gauging objects in motion. But he also saw links between responses in this motion area and posterior parietal regions some distance away. Such long-range interactions between different parts of the brain, so Friston thought, called for a broader and more principled approach to the brain as a dynamic and integrated system.

'It's the old problem of not being able to see the forest because of the trees,' he commented. 'Focusing on regionally specific brain activations sometimes obscures deeper questions about how these regions are orchestrated or interact. This is the problem of functional integration that goes beyond localized increases in brain blood flow. Many of the unexpected and context-sensitive blood flow responses we see can be explained by one part of the brain moderating the responses of another part. A rigorous mathematical and conceptual framework is now the goal of many theorists to help us understand our images of brain dynamics in a more informed way.'

Dynamic plumbing

Users of brain imaging are enjoined to remember that they don't observe, directly, the actions of the billions of nerve cells in the brain. Instead, they watch an astonishing hydraulic machine. Interlaced with the nerve cells and their electrochemical connections, which previous generations of brain researchers had been inclined to think were all that mattered, is the vascular system of arteries, veins and capillaries.

The brain continually adjusts its own blood supplies. In some powerful but as yet unexplained sense the blood vessels take part in thinking. They keep telling one part of the brain or another, 'Come on, it's ice-pack time.'

Blood needs time to flow, and the role of the dynamic plumbing in switching on responses is a matter of everyday experience. The purely neural reaction that averts a sudden danger may take a fifth of a second. As the blood kicks in after a couple of seconds, you get the situation report and the conscious fear and indignation. You print in your memory the face of the other driver who swerved across your path.

'Presently we do not know why blood flow changes so dramatically and reliably during changes in brain activity or how these vascular responses are so beautifully orchestrated,' observed the PET pioneer Marcus Raichle. 'These questions have confronted us for more than a century and remain incompletely answered... We have at hand tools with the potential to provide unparalleled insights into some of the most important scientific, medical, and social questions facing mankind. Understanding those tools is clearly a high priority.'

▶ *For other approaches to activity in the head, see* BRAIN RHYTHMS, BRAIN WIRING *and* MEMORY.

BRAIN RHYTHMS

The mathematics of the beat we think to

S AIL AT NIGHT down the Mae Nam, the river that connects Bangkok with the sea, and you may behold trees pulsating with a weird light. They do so in a strict rhythm, 90 times a minute. On being told that the flashing was due to male fireflies showing off in unison, one visiting scientist preferred to believe he had a tic in his eyelids.

He declared: 'For such a thing to occur among insects is certainly contrary to all natural laws.' That was in 1917. Nearly 20 years elapsed before the American naturalist Hugh Smith described the Mae Nam phenomenon in admiring detail in a Western scientific journal.

'Imagine a tenth of a mile of river front with an unbroken line of Sonneratia trees, with fireflies on every leaf flashing in synchronism,' Smith reported, 'the insects on the trees at the ends of the line acting in perfect unison with those between. Then, if one's imagination is sufficiently vivid, he may form some conception of this amazing spectacle.'

Slowly and grudgingly biologists admitted that synchronized rhythms are commonplace in living creatures. The fireflies of Thailand are just a dramatic example of an aptitude shared by crickets that chirrup together, and by flocks of birds that flap their wings to achieve near-perfect formation flying.

Yet even to seek out and argue about such esoteric-seeming rhythms, shared between groups of animals, is to overlook the fact that, within each animal, far more important and obvious coordinations occur between living cells. Just feel your pulse and the regular pumping of the blood. Cells in your heart, the natural pacemakers, perform in concert for an entire lifetime. They continually adjust their rates to suit the circumstances of repose or strenuous action.

Biological rhythms often tolerate and remedy the sloppiness of real life. The participating animals or cells are never exactly identical in their individual performances. Yet an exact, coherent rhythm can appear as if by magic and eliminate the differences with mathematical precision. The participants closest to one another in frequency come to a consensus that sets the metronome, and then others pick up the rhythm. It doesn't matter very much if a few never quite manage it, or if others drop out later. The heart goes on beating.

Voltages in the head

In 1924 Hans Berger, a psychiatrist at Jena, put a sheet of tinfoil with a wire attached, to his young son's forehead, and another to the back of the head. He adapted a radio set to amplify possible electrical waves. He quickly found them, and for five years he checked and rechecked them, before announcing the discovery.

Berger's brain waves nevertheless encountered the same scepticism as the Bangkok fireflies, and for much the same reason. An electrode stuck on the scalp feels voltages from a wide area of the brain. You would expect them to average out, unless large numbers of nerve cells decided to pulsate in unexpected synchronism.

Yet that was what they did, and biologists at Cambridge confirmed Berger's findings in 1934. Thereafter, brain waves became big business for neuroscientists, psychologists and medics. Electroencephalograms, or EEGs, ran forth as wiggly lines, drawn on kilometres of paper rolls by multiple pens that wobbled in response to the ever-changing voltages at different parts of the head.

One prominent rhythm found by Berger is the alpha wave, at 10 cycles per second, which persists when a person is resting quietly, eyes closed. When the eyes open, a faster gamma wave appears. Even with the eyes shut, doing mental arithmetic or imagining a vivid scene can switch off the alpha rhythm.

Aha! The brain waves seemed to open a window on the living brain through which, enthusiasts believed, they could not fail to discover how we think. Why, with EEGs you should even be able to read peoples' thoughts. Such expectations were disappointed. Despite decades of effort, the chief benefits from EEGs throughout the remainder of the 20th century were medical. They were invaluable for diagnosing gross brain disorders, such as strokes, tumours and various forms of epilepsy.

As for mental processes, even disordered thinking, in schizophrenia for example, failed to show any convincing signal in the EEGs. Tantalizing responses were noted in normal thinking, when volunteers learned to control their brain waves to some degree. Sceptics said that the enterprise was like trying to find out how a computer works by waving a voltmeter at it. Some investigators did not give up.

'The nervous system's got a beat we can think to,' Nancy Kopell at Boston assured her audiences at the start of the 21st century. Her confidence reflected a big change since the early days of brain-wave research. Kopell approached the question of biological rhythms from the most fundamental point of view, as a mathematician.

Understand from mathematics exactly how brain cells may contrive to join in the choruses that activate the EEGs, and you'll have a better chance of finding out why they do it, and why the rhythms vary. Then you should be able to say how the brain waves relate to bodily and cerebral housekeeping, and to active thought.

From fireflies to neutrinos

If you're going deep, start simple, with biological rhythms like those of the flashing fireflies. Think about them as coolly as if they were oscillating atoms. Individual insects begin flashing randomly, and finish up in a coherently flashing row of trees. They're like atoms in a laser, stimulating one another's emissions.

Or you can think of the fireflies as being like randomly moving atoms that chill out and build a far-from-random crystal. This was a simile recommended by Arthur Winfree of Arizona in 1967. In the years that followed, a physicist at Kyoto, Yoshiki Kuramoto, used it to devise an exact mathematical equation that describes the onset of synchronization. It applies to many simple systems, whether physical, chemical or biological, where oscillations are coupled together.

'At a theoretical level, coupled oscillations are no more surprising than water freezing on a lake,' Kuramoto said. 'Cool the air a little and ice will form over the shallows. In a severe frost the whole lake will freeze over. So it is with the fireflies or with other oscillators coming by stages into unison.'

His scheme turned out to be very versatile. By the end of the century, a Japanese detector of the subatomic particles called neutrinos revealed that they oscillate to and fro between one form and another. But if they did so individually and at random, the change would have been unobservable. So theorists then looked to Kuramoto's theory to explain why many neutrinos should change at the same time, in chorus fashion.

Experimental confirmation of the maths came when the fabricators of large numbers of electronic oscillators on a microchip found that they could rely on coupled oscillation to bring them into unison. That was despite the differences in individual behaviour arising from imperfections in their manufacture. The tolerant yet ultimately self-disciplined nature of the synchronization process was again evident.

In 1996, for example, physicists at Georgia Tech and Cornell experimented with an array of superconducting devices called Josephson junctions. They observed first partial synchronization, and then complete frequency coupling, in two neat phase transitions. Steven Strogatz of Cornell commented: 'Twenty-five years later, the Kuramoto model continues to surprise us.'

Coordinating brain activity

For simple systems the theory looks secure, but what about the far more complex brain? A network of fine nerve fibres links billions of cells individually, in highly specific ways. Like a firefly or a neutrino, an individual nerve cell is influenced by what others are doing, and in turn can affect them. This opens the way to possible large-scale synchronization.

Step by step, the mathematicians moved towards coping with greater complexity in interactions of cells. An intermediate stage in coordinating oscillations is like the Mexican wave, where sports fans rise and sit, not all at once, but in sequence around the stadium. When an animal's gut squeezes food through, always in one direction from mouth to anus in the process called peristalsis, the muscular action is not simultaneous like the pumping of the heart, but sequential. Similar orderly sequences enable animals to swim, creep or walk.

The mathematical physics of this kind of rhythm describes a travelling wave. In 1986, in collaboration with Bard Ermentrout at Pittsburgh, Nancy Kopell worked out a theory that was confirmed remarkably well by biologists studying the nerve control of swimming in lampreys, primitive fish-like creatures. These were still a long way short of a human brain, and the next step along the way was to examine interactions in relatively small networks of nerve cells, both mathematically and in experiments with small slices of tissue from animal brains.

Despite the success with lampreys, Kopell came to realize that in a nervous system the behaviour of individual cells becomes more significant, and so do the strong interconnections between them. Theories of simple oscillators, like that of Kuramoto, are no longer adequate. While still trying to strip away inessential biological details, Kopell found her 'dry' mathematics becoming increasingly intertwined with 'wet' physiology revealed by experimental colleagues.

Different rhythms are associated with different kinds of responses of nerve cells to electrical signals between them, depending on the state of the cells. Thus the electrical and chemical connections between cells play a role in establishing or changing the rhythms. The mathematics cannot ignore these complexities, but must dissect them to find the underlying principles.

Other brain scientists trace even more complicated modes of behaviour of the cells, as these process and store information in carefully constructed networks. Chemical inputs, whether self-engendered or in the form of mood-affecting drugs, can influence large numbers of cells. In this perspective, electrical brain waves seem to provide an extra method of getting brain cells to work in unison.

Psychological research, looking for connotations of brain waves, has revived strongly since 1990. The experimenters use sensitive EEG techniques and computer analysis that were not available to the pioneers. As a result, various frequencies of waves have been implicated in brain activity controlling attention, perception and memory.

So in what sense do the electrical brain waves provide 'a beat we can think to'? Kopell reformulated the question in two parts. How does the brain produce different rhythms in different behavioural states? And how do the different rhythms take part in functionally important dynamics in the brain?

'My hunch is that the brain rhythms recruit the nerve cells into local assemblies for particular tasks, and exclude cells that are not invited to participate just now,' Kopell said. 'The cell assemblies can change from moment to moment in response to events. The brain rhythms also coordinate the local assemblies in different parts of the brain, and reorganize them when streams of information converge. Different rhythms play complementary roles in all this activity. That, at any rate, is what I believe and hope to prove—by wet experiments as well as mathematics.'

▶ *For other aspects of brain research, see* BRAIN IMAGES, BRAIN WIRING *and* MEMORY. *For more on natural oscillations, see* NEUTRINO OSCILLATIONS.

BRAIN WIRING

How do all those nerve connections know where to go?

FOR A LONG-SMOULDERING Latin passion for scientific research, you'll not beat the tale of Santiago Ramón y Cajal who taught the world how human brains are built. He was born in north-east Spain in 1852.

Cajal's real love was drawing but he had to earn a living. Failing to shine as either a shoemaker or a barber, he qualified as a physician in Zaragoza. After military service in Cuba, the young doctor had saved just enough pesetas to buy an old-fashioned microscope, with which he made elegant drawings of muscle fibres. But then Cajal married the beautiful Silvería, who produced sufficient babies to keep him permanently short of cash.

In particular, he couldn't afford a decent Zeiss microscope. Ten years passed before he won one as a civic reward for heroic services during a cholera outbreak. Meanwhile, Cajal's micro-anatomical drawings had earned him a professorship, first at Valencia and then at Barcelona.

All this was just the preamble to the day in 1887 when, on a trip to Madrid, Cajal saw brain tissue stained by the chrome silver method discovered by Camillo Golgi in Pavia. Nerve cells and their finest branchlets, coloured brownish black on a yellow background, stood out 'as sharp as a sketch with Chinese ink.' Cajal hurried back to Barcelona to use the stain on pieces of the nervous system. The resulting drawings are still in use in 21st-century textbooks.

Golgi had a 14-year head start, but Cajal was smarter. He quickly realized that the nerves in adult brain tissue are too complicated to see and draw clearly. 'Since the full-grown forest turns out to be impenetrable and indefinable,' he said, 'why not revert to the study of the young wood, in the nursery stage as we might say?'

Cajal started staining brain tissue from embryos of birds and mammals with Golgi's reagent. 'The fundamental plan of the histological composition of the grey matter rises before our eyes with admirable clarity and precision.' By 1890, Cajal was reporting the discovery of the growth cone, the small 'battering ram' at the tip of a newly growing nerve fibre, which pushes its way through intervening tissue to connect with another nerve cell.

Not until 1906 did Cajal meet for the first time the revered Golgi, 'the savant of Pavia'. This was in Stockholm, where they were to share a Nobel Prize. In his lecture, Golgi described brain tissue as a diffuse network of filaments, like a string bag.

Cajal then stood up and contradicted Golgi. The brain consists of vast numbers of individual nerve cells connected in intricate but definable ways. And to prove it beyond peradventure, he showed off his beautiful drawings.

The world turned upside down

It's easy to see why the full-grown forest of nerves misled Golgi. A single nerve cell can reach out with thousands of fibres to connect with other cells, and it receives connections from as many others. When a nerve cell fires, it sends electric impulses down all of its fibres. At their ends are junctions called synapses, which release chemicals that act on the target cells. Some connections are stimulating and others are inhibiting, so that there is in effect a vote to decide whether or not a nerve cell should fire, in response to incoming messages. The brain wiring provides, among many other things, the circuits for the writing and reading of these words.

A replay of the Golgi–Cajal controversy began in the 1940s, between Paul Weiss at Chicago and his cleverest student, Roger Sperry. Weiss accepted Cajal's picture of interconnected nerve cells but, almost like a hangover from Golgi's string bag, he imagined the links to be a random mesh. The parts were interchangeable. Only by learning and experience, Weiss thought, did the connections acquire purpose and meaning.

Experiments with animals kept Sperry busy for nearly 20 years and he proved Weiss wrong—at least in part. The circuits of the brain are largely hardwired from the outset. In a developing embryo, each nerve fibre is tagged and its target predetermined.

Sperry used mainly creatures noted for their capacity for self-repair by regeneration, such as fishes, frogs and salamanders. If he cut out their eyes, and put them back in their sockets, the many fibres of the optic nerves reconnected with the brain and sight was restored. But if the eyes were rotated and put back the wrong way up, the recovered animal forever saw the world turned upside down. Present it with food high in its field of view, and it would dart downwards to try to reach it.

The implication was that the nerve connections from each part of the retina were going to predetermined places in the brain, which knew in advance what part of the field of view they would handle. By 1963, Sperry was able to report the clinching experiment, done at Caltech with Domenica Attardi, using goldfish. This time the experimenters not only cut the optic nerve but also removed parts of the fishes' retinas, leaving other parts unharmed.

After three weeks, the experimenters killed the fishes and examined their brains. A copper stain made the newly restored connections stand out with a pink colour, against a dark background of old nerve fibres. The new fibres ran unerringly to their own special regions of the brain, corresponding to the parts of the retina that remained intact.

Nevertheless, the dialectic between inborn and acquired brain wiring continued. Closer examination of the wiring for vision confirmed both points of view. In experiments with live, anaesthetized cats, at Harvard in the 1960s, David Hubel from Canada and Torsten Wiesel from Sweden probed individual cells at the back of the brain, where information from the eyes is processed. Each cell responded to a feature of the scene in front of the cat's eyes—a line or edge of a particular slope, a bar of a certain length, a motion in a certain direction, and so on.

The brain doesn't photograph a scene. It analyses it as if it were a code to decipher, and each nerve cell in the visual processing region is responsible for one abstract feature. The cells are arranged and connected in columns, so that the analysis takes place in a logical sequence from one nerve cell to the next. Without hardwiring, so complicated a visual system could not work reliably.

Yet even this most computer-like aspect of brain function is affected by experience. Hubel and Wiesel sewed shut one eye of a newborn kitten, for the first three months of its life. It remained permanently blind in that eye. The reason was that nerve connections remained incomplete, which would normally have developed during early use of the eye. Later recovery was ruled out because nerves linked to the open eye took over the connection sites left unused by the closed one.

'Innate mechanisms endow the visual system with highly specific connections,' Wiesel said, 'but visual experience early in life is necessary for their maintenance and full development . . . Such sensitivity of the nervous system to the effects of experience may represent the fundamental mechanism by which the organism adapts to its environment during the period of growth and development.'

No, your brain isn't dying

The growth and connections of nerve fibres in a developing brain are under the control of chemical signals. In the 1950s, at Washington University, St Louis, Rita Levi-Montalcini and Stanley Cohen identified a nerve growth factor that, even in very small traces, provokes a nerve cell to send out fibres in all directions. It turned out to be a small protein molecule.

Both Cajal in 1890 and Sperry in 1963 speculated about chemical signals that would guide the nerve fibres to their targets on other cells with which they are supposed to connect. By the end of the 20th century it was clear that the growth cone at the tip of an extending fibre encounters many guiding signals, some attracting it and others repelling it. The techniques of molecular biology gradually revealed the identities of dozens of guidance molecules, and the same molecules turned up again and again in many different kinds of animals.

A correct connection is confirmed by a welcome signal from the target cell. But so complex a wiring system has to make allowances for failure, and the young brain grows by trial and error. Large numbers of cells that don't succeed in making the right connections commit suicide, in the process called apoptosis.

Adult brain cells are long-lived. Indeed previous generations of scientists believed that no new nerve cells appeared in the adult brain, and progressive losses by the death of individual cells were said to be part of the ageing process, from adolescence onwards. That turned out to be quite wrong, although it took a long time for the message to sink in.

In the early 1960s, Joseph Altman of the Massachusetts Institute of Technology tried out, in adult rats, cats and guinea pigs, a chemical test used to pinpoint young nerve cells in newborn animals. The test gave positive results, but Altman was ignored. So too, in the 1970s, was Michael Kaplan at Boston and later at New Mexico. He saw newly formed nerve cells in adult brain tissue, with an electron microscope. Pasko Rakic of Yale led the opposition. 'Those may look like neurons in New Mexico,' he said, 'but they don't in New Haven.'

Not until the end of the century did the fact of the continual appearance of new brain cells—at least some hundreds every day—become generally accepted. By then the renewal of tissue of many kinds was a fashionable subject, with the identification of stem cells that preserve into old age the options present in the embryo. The activity of the brain's own stem cells, producing new nerve cells, came to be taken for granted, yet many neuroscientists saw it simply as refurbishment, like the telephone company renewing old cables.

Nursing mothers remodel their brains

The most dramatic evidence that the brain is not hardwired once and for all, during early life, comes from changes in the brains of nursing mothers. In 1986 a Greek-born neuroscientist, Dionysia Theodosis, working at Bordeaux, discovered that the hormone oxytocin provokes a reorganization of a part of the adult brain. It is the hormone that, in human and other mammalian mothers, comes into operation when offspring are being born, and stimulates milk-making.

A region deep in the maternal brain, called the hypothalamo-neurohypophysial system, is responsible for control of the production of oxytocin. In experiments with rats and mice, Theodosis established that parts of the system are extensively rewired for the duration of nursing. When the offspring are weaned, lactation stops and the brain reverts to normal.

Continuing her investigation for many years, Theodosis traced the rewiring processes, before and after lactation, in great detail. Various biochemical agents come into play, to undo the pre-existing wiring and then to guide and establish the new linkages. In essence, the affected regions revert to behaviour previously seen only in embryos and young animals. Most striking is the part played by oxytocin itself in triggering the changes, first by its presence and then by its absence. In effect, the hormone manipulates brain tissue to control its own production.

'After we discovered that the adult brain is plastic during lactation,' Theodosis said, 'others found similar changes connected with sensory experience and with learning. This surprising plasticity now gives us hope that damaged brains and nerves can be repaired. At the same time we gain fundamental knowledge about how the brain wires and rewires itself.'

▶ *Brain function is also pursued in* BRAIN IMAGES, BRAIN RHYTHMS *and* MEMORY.

BUCKYBALLS AND NANOTUBES
Doing very much more with very much less

THE WORLD'S ARCHITECTS first beheld a geodesic dome in the garden of Milan's Castello Sforzesco. There, by way of hands-on geometry, flat cardboard panels made a dome 13 metres wide, approximating to a spherical surface. It won the Gran Premio of the Triennale di Milano in 1954, for its American designer Buckminster Fuller. The Museum of Modern Art in New York City gave him a one-man show a few years later.

Fuller was a prophet of design science that aimed at enabling everyone in the world to prosper, just by using resources skilfully and sparingly. He foresaw the artist-scientist converting 'the total capability of tool-augmented man from killingry to advanced livingry'. Robust geodesic radomes, built of fibreglass struts and plastic panels, enclosed the Arctic radar dishes of the Cold War. More peaceful uses of geodesic domes included tents, concert halls, greenhouses, and the US pavilion, 76 metres wide, at the Montreal Expo in 1967.

Ideas edged towards the grandiose, when Fuller offered to put a three-kilometre-wide geodesic greenhouse dome over central New York City, giving it a tropical climate. But within two years of his death in 1983, when Mother Nature revealed a remarkable application of her own, it was on the scale of atoms. For a new generation of prophets, molecular geodesics opened a microscopic highway for design science and 'livingry'.

Fuller himself would not have been surprised. He knew that the molecular assemblies of viruses could take geodesic forms. And in explaining his own geometrical ideas Fuller started with the tetrahedron, the triangular pyramid that is the simplest 3-D structure to fit exactly inside a sphere. He liked to recall that Jacobus van't Hoff, who won the very first Nobel Prize for Chemistry in 1901, deduced the tetrahedral arrangement of the four chemical bonds that normally surround a carbon atom.

Van't Hoff was only a student at Utrecht in 1874 when he first pointed out that chemists had better start thinking about structures in three dimensions, to understand how left-handed and right-handed forms of the same molecule could exist. *Chimie dans l'Espace*, van't Hoff called his pioneering stereochemistry, but a century later that phrase was more likely to suggest extraterrestrial chemistry. It was an attempt to imitate the behaviour of carbon atoms in stars that led to the discovery of a ball-shaped molecule of pure carbon.

'What you have is a soccer ball'

That story began in the 1970s at Sussex University, perched above the chalk cliffs of south-east England. There, Harry Kroto had a reputation for constructing impossible molecules, with double chemical bonds between carbon and phosphorus atoms. He became interested in multiple bonds that carbon atoms can make between themselves, by virtue of quantum jiggles of their electrons. In ethylene, C_2H_4, the tetrahedral prongs are bent so that there can be two bonds between the carbon atoms. In acetylene, C_2H_2, there are three bonds, so that the ill-treated tetrahedon looks like a witch's broomstick.

Kroto and his associates made lanky cousins of ethylene and acetylene, in the form of chains of carbon atoms with very few other atoms attached. Called polyynes, they consisted of an even number of carbon atoms plus two hydrogen atoms. In cyanopolyynes, the cyanide group CN replaced one hydrogen. Were these mere curiosities for theoretical chemists to appreciate? No, Kroto had a hunch that such molecules might exist in interstellar space.

He contacted former colleagues at Canada's National Research Council, who were into the detection of molecules by the characteristic radio waves that they emitted. Sure enough, with the 46-metre radio telescope at the Algonquin Radio Observatory in Ontario, they found the radio signatures of cyanopolyynes in 1975. An argument then ensued about where the peculiar carbon molecules were made. Was it during a great lapse of time within the dark molecular clouds of the Milky Way? Or did they form promptly, as Kroto suspected, in the atmospheres of dying red giant stars, which are a source of carbon newly created by nuclear reactions inside the stars?

The scene shifted to Rice University in Houston. While visiting a friend, Bob Curl, there, Kroto also met Rick Smalley, who made clusters of silicon atoms with laser beams. After laser-provoked vaporization came deep chilling. Kroto realized that this was like the conditions in the stellar atmospheres where he thought the polyynes were fashioned. But Smalley was cool about Kroto's idea of using his kit to vaporize carbon.

'After all,' Smalley recalled later, 'we already knew everything there was to know about carbon. At least we assumed so. So we told Harry: "Yes, fine, some other time. Maybe this year, maybe next."'

In 1985 he relented, and Kroto joined Smalley, Curl and graduate students Jim Heath, Sean O'Brien and Yan Liu, for a few days of experiments at Rice, zapping graphite with laser light. A mass spectrometer identified the products by their molecular weights. To the chemists' amazement, it logged not only polyynes but also molecules of mass 720, in particularly high abundance. These contained exactly 60 atoms of carbon.

Sketching on restaurant serviettes, and making models with jellybeans and toothpicks, the team then tried to imagine how carbon atoms could arrange themselves in a C_{60} molecule. Until that moment the human species had known two main forms of pure carbon. In a diamond each atom joins four neighbours at the tips of van't Hoff's tetrahedron. Graphite, on the other hand, has flat sheets of atoms in a honeycomb pattern, with interlocking hexagons of six carbon atoms. Busy electrons in jiggly quantum mode sew an average of one and half bonds between each pair of atoms.

Kroto had visited Buckminster Fuller's big dome in Montreal in 1967. He recalled that it contained many six-sided panels. There was no way of folding graphite into a 60-atom molecule but Kroto remembered a toy geodesic assembly that also used five-sided panels. He said he'd check it when he got home to Sussex.

With this prompting from Kroto, Smalley sat up in Houston till the small hours, cutting out paper hexagons and pentagons and joining them with Scotch tape, until he had reinvented for himself a structure with exactly 60 corners for the carbon atoms. Next morning the mathematics department at Rice confirmed his conclusion and told Smalley that what he had was a soccer ball.

Unwittingly the folk who stitched spherical footballs from 20 hexagons and 12 pentagons of leather had hit upon a superb design, long favoured by carbon molecules. Soon after the discovery of the C_{60} structure, Argentina's football captain Diego Maradona knocked England out of the 1986 World Cup with an illegal goal off his wrist. Unabashed, he explained it as 'the hand of God'. If, like the physicist Paul Dirac, you suppose that 'God is a mathematician of a very high order', you may see more cosmic wisdom in the regular truncated icosahedron of the offending ball itself.

Easy to make

'Carbon has the genius wired into it to self-assemble into this structure, and we were lucky enough to discover that fact,' Smalley said. The key to C_{60}'s robustness is that it is the smallest all-carbon molecule for which none of the pentagons abut. The stability of six-sided carbon rings is well attested, in graphite and in millions of aromatic carbon compounds. Five-sided carbon rings exist too, but these are less stable, and molecules with abutting pentagons are very unstable. Whilst they are handy for making C_{60} and similar molecules foldable, they are not tolerated with two side-by-side. The needs of hexagonal chemical stability override the pure mathematics that would readily allow 3-D structures to be built entirely of pentagons.

As is often the way in science, it turned out that others had thought of the football molecule before. In 1966 David Jones, who wrote ingenious, semi-joking speculations for *New Scientist* magazine under the pseudonym Daedalus, pointed out that if graphite included 12 five-sided rings it could fold into a closed molecule. Chemists in Japan (1970) and Russia (1972) wondered about the viability of a C_{60} molecule, and at UC Los Angeles, around 1980, they even tried to make C_{60} by traditional methods.

Physicists homed in on the new carbon molecule. In 1990, Wolfgang Krätschmer of the Max-Planck-Institut für Kernphysik, on a hill above Heidelberg, and Don Huffman at the University of Arizona, found out how to make C_{60} very easily, and to crystallize it. They simply collected soot made with an electric arc between graphite rods, and put it in a solvent, benzene. A red liquid formed, and when the solution dried on a microscope slide, they saw orange crystals of C_{60}. Various tests including X-ray analysis confirmed the shape of the molecule.

'Our discovery initiated an avalanche of research,' Krätschmer recalled later. 'Some said it was like the spread of an epidemic. Then Bell Labs discovered C_{60}-based superconductors, and the journal *Science* elected C_{60} as its "molecule of the year" in 1991. By then it was a truly interdisciplinary species.'

Kroto had persuaded his colleagues to call the C_{60} molecule buckminsterfullerene. That mouthful was soon contracted to fullerene or, more affectionately, buckyball. By the time that Kroto, Curl and Smalley trooped onto the Stockholm stage in 1996 to receive a Nobel Prize, chemists around the world had made many analogous molecules, every one of them a novel form of elemental carbon.

They included egg-shaped buckyballs and also tubes of carbon called nanotubes. Smalley snaffled Buckytubes as a trademark—not surprisingly, because nanotubes promised to be even more important than buckyballs, in technology.

Molecular basketwork

Sumio Iijima found the first known nanotubes in 1991. At the NEC Corporation's fundamental research lab in Japan's Science City of Tsukuba, he worked with powerful electron microscopes, and he used a graphite electric arc like Krätschmer's to investigate buckyballs. In his images, Iijima indeed saw onion-like balls, but more conspicuous were a lot of needle-like structures.

These were the nanotubes, appearing spontaneously as another surprise from elemental carbon. They are built of six-sided rings, as in graphite sheets. Long, narrow sheets, rolled and joined like a cigarette paper, make tubes with a width of about a nanometre—a millionth of a millimetre—or less.

Traditional Japanese baskets are woven from strips of bamboo, and in them Iijima saw similarities to the nanotubes, especially at the growing ends of the molecules. The baskets come in many different shapes, but always with the strips intersecting to form many six-sided rings. Introducing a five-sided pentagon produces a corner, whilst a seven-sided ring, a heptagon, makes a saddle shape.

For his lectures on nanotubes, Iijima had a special basket made to order. It featured cylinders of three different diameters connected end to end, as one might wish for a molecular-scale electronic device made of nanotubes. Sure enough, he saw that the resulting weave incorporated five- and seven-sided rings where appropriate.

'Our craftsman does know how to do it, to make nice smooth connections,' Iijima said. 'So why don't we do it in our carbon nanotubes?' Later, a team at the Delft University of Technology found nanotubes with kinks in them. A five-sided and a seven-sided ring, inside and outside the corner, produced a kink.

The significance of such molecular basketwork is that the nanotubes can vary in their electrical behaviour. In their most regular form, they conduct electricity very well, just like graphite, but if they are slightly skewed in the rolling up, they become semiconductors. If the nanotube on one side of a kink is conducting, and the other is semiconducting, a current flows preferentially in one direction. That creates what electronic engineers call a diode, but with a junction only a few atoms wide.

'Nanotubes provide all the basic building blocks to make electronic circuits,' said Cees Dekker, leader of the Delft team. 'It's really astonishing that in a few years we have discovered that you can run a current through a single nanotube molecule, have it behave as a metal or as a semiconductor, and build transistors and circuits from it.'

In looking forward to molecular electronics based on carbon, Dekker stressed that it was not just a matter of matching 20th-century techniques. 'These molecules have mutual chemical interactions that allow a whole new way of assembling circuits,' he said. 'And on the molecular scale, electrons behave like waves, which opens up new possibilities for controlling electronic signals.'

Ten years after Iijima's discovery of nanotubes, electronic engineers and others were drooling over nanotubes in perfect crystals. Yet again they were created by accident, this time by a Swiss–UK team from IBM Zurich, Neuchâtel and Cambridge. The crystals appeared unbidden during an experiment aiming to make tubes containing metal atoms.

Buckyballs and nickel atoms, fed through a microscopic sieve onto a molybdenum surface, built micropillars. When heated in the presence of a magnetic field, the micropillars spontaneously transformed themselves into beautiful rod-shaped crystals, each composed of thousands of identical, tightly packed nanotubes. The nickel was entirely expelled from the tubes—the exact opposite of the experiment's original aim.

'It was so unexpected to fabricate perfect crystalline arrays of nanotubes in this way, when all previous attempts have shown nanotubes wrapped together looking like a plate of spaghetti, we couldn't believe it at first,' Mark Welland at Cambridge confessed. 'It took six months before we were convinced that what we were seeing was real.'

Let your imagination rip

It is unlikely that anyone has yet guessed more than a small fraction of the technological possibilities latent in nanotubes. The molecules are far stronger than steel, and atomically neater than the carbon fibres used previously to reinforce plastics. Temperatures of 500°C do not trouble them. Laced with metals, they can become superconductors, losing all resistance to the flow of an electric current at low temperatures. You can tuck atoms, or even buckyballs containing atoms, into nanotubes like peas in a pod. Doing chemistry with the ends may provide useful links, handles or probes.

An intoxicating free-for-all followed Iijima's discovery. Thousands of scientific papers about nanotubes, from dozens of countries around the world, opened up new chemistry, physics and materials science. As new results and ideas broadened the scope of foreseeable applications, the patent lawyers were busy too.

The fact that nanotubes spontaneously gather into tough tangles is a virtue for some purposes. Rice University found a way of making nanotubes in bulk from carbon monoxide, which promises to bring down the cost dramatically. It encouraged predictions of first-order applications of the bulk properties of tangled nanotubes. They ranged from modest proposals for hydrogen storage, or for electromagnetic shields in mobile phones and stealth aircraft, to more challenging ideas about nanotube ropes reaching into space.

Such Jacob's ladders could act as elevators to launch satellites. Or they could draw down electrical energy from space. That natural electricity could then spin up strong flywheels made of tangled nanotubes, until they carried as many megajoules as gasoline, kilo for kilo—so providing pollution-free energy in portable form.

The silicon microchip may defer to the carbon nanochip, for building computers and sensors. But that's linear thinking, and it faces competition from people making transistors out of fine metallic threads. A multidimensional view of buckyballs and nanotubes perceives materials with remarkable and controllable physical properties that are also susceptible to chemical modification, exploiting the well-known versatility of the carbon atom. Moreover, living systems are the cleverest carbon chemists. It is fantasy, perhaps, but not nonsense, to imagine adapting enzymes or even bacteria to the industrial construction of nanotube machinery.

The new molecular technology of carbon converges with general ideas about nanotechnology—engineering on an atomic scale. These have circulated since the American physicist Richard Feynman said in 1959, 'The principles of physics, as far as I can see, do not speak against the possibility of manoeuvring things atom by atom.' Hopes at first ran far ahead of reality, and focused on engineering with biomolecules like proteins and nucleic acid, or on molecules designed from scratch to function as wheels, switches, motors and so on.

Anticipating the eventual feasibility of such things, one could foresee spacecraft the size of butterflies, computers the size of bacteria, and micro-implants that could navigate through a sick person's body. The advent in the 1980s of microscopes capable of seeing and manipulating individual atoms brought more realism into the conjectures. Buckyballs and nanotubes not only added the element of surprise, but also opened up unlimited opportunities for innovators.

Symbolic of the possible obsolescence of metal technology are magnets of pure carbon, first created at Russia's Institute for High Pressure Physics in Troitsk. Experimenters found that the partial destruction of a fullerene polymer by high pressure produces a material that is ferromagnetic at ordinary temperatures. In other words it possesses the strong magnetic properties commonly associated with iron.

'Ferromagnetism of pure carbon materials took us completely by surprise,' said Valery Davydov, head of the Troitsk research group. 'But study of these materials in different laboratories in Germany, Sweden, Brazil and England convinces us that the phenomenon is real. It opens a new chapter in the magnetism textbooks.'

Unless you let your imagination rip you'll have little hope of judging the implications of the novel forms of commonplace carbon. To find a comparable moment in the history of materials you might need to go all the way back to the Bronze Age, when blacksmiths in Cyprus made the first steel knives 3100 years ago. Who then would have thought of compass needles, steamships, railways or typewriters? As the world moves out of the Iron Age, through a possibly short-lived Silicon Age into the Carbon Age, all one can be confident about is that people will do very much more with very much less, as Buckminster Fuller anticipated. Any prospect of our species exhausting its material resources will look increasingly remote.

Surprises mean unpredictability

A chemist's wish, driven by curiosity, to simulate the behaviour of carbon in the atmosphere of a star, resulted in the serendipitous encounter with C_{60}, buckminsterfullerene. An electron microscopist's accidental discovery of nanotubes followed on from this. The course of science and engineering has changed emphatically, with implications for everything from the study of the origin of life to reducing environmental pollution. What price all those solemn attempts to plan science by committees of experts?

Harry Kroto saw in buckyballs and nanotubes an object lesson in the futility of trying to predict discoveries, when handing out research grants. What possible merit is there in the routine requirement by funding agencies that researchers must say in advance what the results and utility of their proposed experiments will be? Why not just give the best young scientists access to the best equipment, and see what happens?

Among the vineyards of California's Napa Valley, Kroto found the exact words he needed to convey his opinion. 'There was a beaten up old Volvo in a parking lot and on the bumper was a truly wonderful statement that sums up my sentiment on all cultural matters and science in particular. It was a quotation from the Song of Aragorn by J. R. R. Tolkien:

> 'Not all those who wander are lost.'

▶ *For related subjects, see* MOLECULES IN SPACE *and* LIFE'S ORIGIN. *For more about atomic-scale machinery, see* MOLECULAR PARTNERS. *For echoes of Kroto's opinion about the futility of research planning, see* DISCOVERY.

CAMBRIAN EXPLOSION

Easy come and easy go, among the early animals

Y OU'D BETTER BE QUITE FIT, to join one of the authorized hiking parties to the Walcott Quarry in the Burgess Shale, and be prepared for severe heat or snow storms. Although it is the remains of an ancient seafloor, the world's most important fossil site now stands at an altitude of 2345 metres above sea level in the Rockies of British Columbia. From Fossil Ridge there is a fine view over Emerald Lake to snow-capped mountains beyond.

The Canadian Pacific Railway passes nearby, with a station at Field. In 1886 a carpenter working for the railway found stone bugs on a mountainside. They were trilobites, oval, beetle-looking creatures of the seabed, long since extinct. They are often the best preserved of early animal fossils because of their abundance and their tough carapaces.

Examples collected by a geologist were soon seen by Charles Walcott of the US Geological Survey. His curiosity was so aroused that, when he became Secretary of the Smithsonian Institution in Washington DC, he chose Field for his first field trip in 1907, and visited the original source of the trilobites, on Mount Stephen. Two years later, on Fossil Ridge between other mountains, Walcott came upon the amazing fossils of the Burgess Shale. In the year after that he began to excavate the quarry that now bears his name. He continued his visits until 1924 and gathered altogether about 65,000 fossils.

The accidents of their accumulation, in airless conditions under sudden mudslides, left the Burgess Shale rich in the remains of soft-bodied animals not usually preserved in the fossil record. As a result the Canadian site is the most comprehensive source of animal remains from the Cambrian period. That was when animals first appeared in abundance on the Earth.

In Precambrian rocks some soft animals are preserved in strata in Australia, Russia, Namibia and Newfoundland, dating from shortly before the great transition. The time since the start of the Cambrian, 542 million years ago, is called the Phanerozoic, meaning the phase of obvious life. So the explosion of new animal forms was a turning point in Earth history, and scientists want to know as much about it as possible.

The Burgess Shale gives snapshots of busy animal life on the seabed around 505 million years ago, when reverberations of the Cambrian explosion were still detectable. Fossil-hunters find representatives of all of the animal kingdom's main branches, or phyla, that are known today, with the distinctive body-plans of the arthropods, brachiopiods and so forth. Insignificant-looking worms represent our own branch, the chordates. The Burgess animals also display many peculiar forms that left no long-term descendants.

In a spirit of easy come and easy go, Mother Nature was evidently willing to try out all manner of ways of making an animal, and to let many of them become extinct quite soon. Some specimens were, for a while, regarded as so bizarre that they were said to represent entire phyla previously unknown to science. This assessment, which now looks doubtful, came about after the Geological Survey of Canada reopened the quarries of the Burgess Shale in 1966–67 at the instigation of a British palaeontologist, Harry Whittington.

Crazy creatures

'You start with a squashed and horribly distorted mess and finish with a composite figure of a plausible living organism,' Stephen Jay Gould of Harvard wrote later, in describing the aptitude that Whittington and his team at Cambridge brought to the Burgess fossils. 'This activity requires visual, or spatial, genius of an uncommon and particular sort.'

Hallucigenia was the name given by Whittington's student Simon Conway Morris to a particularly odd-looking animal reconstructed from the fossil remains. Its long, thin body seemed to be supported on seven pairs of stilts. On its back it carried tentacles arranged like a row of chimneys, some with little snappers on top for grabbing food. Its distinctive body-plan apparently gave *Hallucigenia* the status of a new phylum within the animal kingdom, resembling no other known animal alive or dead.

Other creatures were less indiscreet in their divergence from known body-plans, but in 20 years of effort the expert eyes tentatively identified about a dozen wholly new groups. The Cambrian explosion in animal evolution was said to be even more remarkable than anyone had realized. Conway Morris claimed that the previously unknown groups outnumbered, phylum for phylum, the groups that remain.

The apparent oddities could not be dismissed as freaks. Their distinctive body-plans made them, he thought, equivalent in potential importance to arthropods, brachiopods or chordates. To emphasize this point, he pictured the entire staff of London's Natural History Museum visiting the Cambrian seabed in a time machine.

'Our hypothetical time travellers,' Conway Morris wrote, 'would have no means of predicting which groups would be destined to success, and which to failure by extinction. . . . If the Cambrian explosion were to be rerun, I think it likely that about the same number of basic body-plans would emerge from this initial radiation. However there seems little guarantee that the same phyla would emerge.'

By 1989, Stephen Jay Gould, in his best-selling book *Wonderful Life*, was proclaiming the overthrow of evolutionary preconceptions by the Cambridge investigators of the Burgess fossils. In a nutshell: the hidebound Walcott had erred in trying to shoehorn all of his finds into known lineages, in accordance with the expectations of his time. The extinct phyla confirmed that the chances of history set the course of evolution, not the predictable superiority of this form or that.

Gould gave special thanks in his preface to Desmond Collins from the Royal Ontario Museum in Toronto, who was camped in the Walcott Quarry in 1987 when he visited the site. 'His work will expand and revise several sections of my text; obsolescence is a fate devoutly to be wished, lest science stagnate and die.' Gould's wish was to be granted within just a few years.

In 1984 Hou Xianguang of the Chinese Academy of Sciences, based in Nanjing, had discovered another treasure trove for fossil-hunters near Chenjiang in Yunnan in south-west China. 'I was so excited, I couldn't sleep very well,' Hou recalled, from the day of his first discoveries. 'I got up often and pulled out the fossils just to look at them.'

Soft-bodied fossil animals entombed in Moatian Mountain by Chenjiang date from 15–20 million years earlier than the Burgess creatures, but many of the animal phyla were already apparent. This meant that their evolution and diversification were even more rapid than the Burgess fossils implied. But the Chenjiang fossils included relatives of *Hallucigenia* and it turned out that Conway Morris had that creature upside down. What he thought were stilts were defensive spines, and the tentacles were legs.

Other revisions came from Collins, who led many trips to the Burgess Shale from 1975 onwards. He opened up a dozen new sites and amassed a collection of fossils exceeding even Walcott's enormous haul. By 1996, with better impressions of the largest of the Burgess animals, called *Anomalocaris*, Collins was able to contradict the opinion that it represented a new phylum. He reclassified it as a new class among the arthropods, which made it a distant cousin of the ubiquitous trilobites.

'With this example,' Collins remarked, 'it is evident that most of the unclassifiable forms in the Burgess Shale probably belong to extinct classes within phyla that survive today, rather than to extinct phyla.'

If so, Conway Morris and Gould had overstated the diversity of life on the Cambrian seabed, at the most basic level of taxonomic classification. That doesn't matter very much, except to specialists. Whether they are called phyla or classes, many weird forms made their appearances early in the history of the animals, only to face extinction later.

The Cambrian explosion, so graphically illustrated in Yunnan and British Columbia, now makes better sense than it did before, in the light of recent laboratory discoveries about evolutionary mechanisms at the molecular level. These allow natural experiments with body-plans to proceed much more rapidly than previous theories had supposed.

Worms and ice

What explains the extraordinary spurt of evolution 540 million years ago, at the debut of conspicuous animals? Some experts were content to imagine that the sheer novelty of the animals was the key to their successes. With new ways of earning a living, and few competitors or predators, the animals burst into an ecological vacuum.

James Valentine of UC Davis looked instead to the Precambrian ancestors of the animals for key inventions. These were worms living in the seabed and trying out various body-plans. A segmented body like an earthworm's, with repeated organs, gave rise to the segmented bodies of arthropods, to become most familiar as the extinct trilobites and the surviving insects. Repeated organs without body segmentation produced the molluscs. A crown of hollow tentacles decorated our own ancestors, the worms that gave rise to echinoderms and vertebrates.

In 1972, following the confirmation of continental drift, Valentine suggested that these evolutionary innovations were linked to the existence and later break-up of a supercontinent. Worms had the advantage of burrowing for food in seabed mud laid down over many years. This made them relatively immune to seasonal and climatic changes, aggravated perhaps by the changing geography, which left other creatures hungry.

By the end of the 20th century Valentine was at UC Berkeley, and even more confident that the worms lit the fuse for the evolutionary explosion seen in the Burgess Shale. He was able to note growing evidence of larger and more elaborate fossil burrows appearing early in the Cambrian period. And advances in genetics and embryology enabled him to recast his story of worm evolution in terms of changes in genes controlling the body-plan when an animal grows from an egg. Valentine and his colleagues commented: 'It is likely that much genomic repatterning occurred during the Early Cambrian, involving both key control genes and regulators within their downstream cascades, as novel body-plans evolved.'

A widening circle of scientists was becoming convinced that the planet and its living crew went through an extraordinary climatic ordeal in the late Precambrian. According to the hypothesis of Snowball Earth, a term coined by Joseph Kirschvink of Caltech in 1992, even the equatorial oceans were covered with ice. In 1998 Paul Hofmann of Harvard and his colleagues offered fresh evidence from Namibia for such an event, and a more detailed scenario and timetable.

A comprehensive account of the origin of the animals will eventually bring to bear all of the skills of the new multidisciplinary style of 21st-century science. That means geology, palaeontology, climate science, genetics and embryology for starters. Even astronomers may chime in with possible extraterrestrial causes of the late Precambrian glaciation and for the subsequent extinction of *Hallucigenia*, *Anomalocaris* and their companions.

The explanations will be judged by how convincingly they account for all those curious creatures that were entombed for half a billion years, until a sharp-eyed railway carpenter, prospecting for minerals on his day off, spotted stone bugs on a British Columbian mountainside.

▶ *For more on evolutionary genetics, see* MOLECULES EVOLVING, HOPEFUL MONSTERS *and* EMBRYOS. *For an earlier Snowball Earth, see* GLOBAL ENZYMES.

CARBON CYCLE

Exactly how does it interact with the global climate?

S O BARE AND RUGGED is the frozen lava near the summit of Hawaii's Mauna Loa volcano that astronauts trained there for visiting the Moon. On the northern slope, 3400 metres above sea level, the US National Oceanic and Atmospheric Administration runs a weather observatory where scientists can sample the clean air coming on the trade winds across 3000 kilometres of open ocean. Free from all regional and local pollution, and also from the disturbing influence of nearby vegetation, it's a good place to monitor the general state of the planet's atmosphere.

At the Mauna Loa Observatory in 1957 a geochemist from UC San Diego, Dave Keeling, started routine measurements of the amount of carbon dioxide in the air. Samples drawn down a tube from the top of a tower went to an infrared gas analyser that gauged the carbon dioxide with high accuracy. This modest operation became one of the most consequential of scientific projects.

Before the end of the century the graph showing a rise in atmospheric carbon dioxide, the Keeling Curve, would fill politicians with dismay. It was to liberate tens of billions of research dollars to investigate the graph's implications. So it is worth recalling that US officials turned down the young Keeling's proposal to monitor carbon dioxide at clean, remote sites, for a few thousand dollars a year.

Already as a Caltech student Keeling had proved the textbooks wrong, which said that the amount of carbon dioxide in the air varied widely from place to place. He found that if he made careful measurements in the afternoon, when the air is best mixed, he always found the same, around 315 parts per million by volume, whether on beaches, mountaintops or deserts in California, or on a research ship near the Equator.

To get him started on Mauna Loa, and briefly at the South Pole too, allies pinched some small change from the money swilling around for the International Geophysical Year, 1957–58. Battles for adequate funding continued for 30 years. Historians will chuckle over a gap in the Keeling Curve in 1964. It commemorates the handiwork of politicians and administrators who believed they had put a stop to this waste of federal dollars. They hadn't reckoned with Keeling's obstinacy.

His chief supporter was the director of the Scripps Institution of Oceanography, Roger Revelle, a marine geochemist whose main personal interest was in the carbon cycle. Ocean water contains 50 times more carbon dioxide than the atmosphere, but the life-giving gas passes to and fro between the sea and the air. Some of the carbon is incorporated temporarily in living things, on land and in the sea. Most of the world's surface carbon has for long been removed semipermanently, in carbonate rocks and in coal, oil and gas deposits.

Since the Industrial Revolution, the burning of fossil fuels has released some of the buried carbon back into the air. A pioneer of radiocarbon dating at UC San Diego, Hans Suess, detected the presence in the atmosphere of carbon dioxide from fossil fuels. Its freedom from radioactive carbon-14 made recent objects look unnaturally old, when dated by the remaining radiocarbon.

Perhaps as a result of fossil-fuel combustion the total amount of carbon dioxide in the air had also increased. No one knew for sure. In 1957, Revelle and Suess declared in a joint paper, 'Human beings are now carrying out a large scale geophysical experiment of a kind that could not have happened in the past nor be reproduced in the future.'

A relentless rise

When by Revelle's good offices Keeling was empowered to begin accurate monitoring of carbon dioxide in the air, his next finding was that the whole Earth breathes. Every year, between May and September, the carbon dioxide falls by more than one per cent. That's because the abundant plant life of the northern lands and oceans absorbs the gas to grow by, in summer.

During the northern winter, the plants expel carbon dioxide as they respire to stay alive, and dead vegetation rots. The carbon dioxide in the air increases again. This feature of the recycling of carbon through the living systems of the Earth is so noticeable in Keeling's measurements only because life is more abundant in the north. There are also seasonal differences in the uptake and release of the gas by seawater. The asymmetry results in a yearly wave in the graph of global carbon dioxide, as measured at Mauna Loa.

What rang alarm bells among scientists, and eventually in the political world too, was Keeling's third discovery. The wavy line sloped upwards, rising relentlessly as the years passed. In parts per million by volume, the annual average of carbon dioxide in the air grew from 317 in 1960 to 326 in 1970, and to 339 in 1980. An increase of seven per cent in just 20 years, with an acceleration in the second decade, was no small excursion. It told of some planetary change in progress, affecting the carbon cycle in a remarkable way.

Waiting in the wings for just such a discovery as Keeling's was the hypothesis of an enhanced greenhouse warming due to human activity. Since the beginning of the century, the Swedish chemist Svante Arrhenius and his successors had reasoned that if the burning of coal, oil and natural gas added extra carbon dioxide to the global atmosphere, it would tend to have a warming effect. Like the windows of a greenhouse, it would block some of the infrared rays that carry heat away from the Earth into space.

Keeling's annual average for carbon dioxide at Mauna Loa reached 354 parts per million by 1990, and 369 by 2000, meaning a 16 per cent increase over 40 years. Those who attributed the increase to fossil-fuel consumption predicted a doubling of carbon dioxide, and a dire greenhouse warming. During that last decade of the century, the Keeling Curve was at the top of the agenda in environmental politics, with leaders of all nations arguing about whether, how, when, and by how much they might cut back on the use of fossil fuels, to try to slow the rise in carbon dioxide in the air.

Some scientists were less ready to jump to firm conclusions about what the rise meant and portended. Keeling summed up the state of knowledge in 1997 by saying he was not sure whether human activities had altered the climate or not. 'Better data and a better understanding of the causes of climatic variability are needed to decide this.'

Keeling was also careful to point out that less than half the carbon dioxide added to the air by human activity remains there. Unidentified sinks mop up the rest. Moreover climate change itself may affect the carbon cycle and so alter the amount of carbon dioxide in the air. 'Even less is known about such feedback mechanisms,' Keeling said, 'than is known about the missing carbon sinks.'

Bubbles in the polar ice

How much carbon dioxide did the air contain, before Keeling began monitoring it in 1957? Since the discovery of the gas in the 18th century, measurements were scrappy, contradictory and often erroneous. But a new fashion was beginning in the 1960s, for drilling into the ice sheets of Greenland and Antarctica, and recovering in long cores the ice formed from snowfall of hundreds or thousands of years ago. In Adélie Land in 1965 a French physicist, Claude Lorius, noticed air bubbles in the ice cores.

He thought that they might give information about air composition at the time of the bubbles' capture, during the gradual conversion of snow into deep-lying ice. It was an objective that Lorius was to pursue for many years at France's Laboratoire de Glaciologie at Grenoble. Quick to take up the idea, too, was a Swiss environmental physicist, Hans Oeschger at Bern.

During the decades that followed, heroic efforts by Soviet, US and European teams went into retrieving tonnes of ice cores in Antarctica and Greenland. Lorius himself visited the northern and southern ice sheets 22 times. And from the Swiss and French analysts of the ancient air bubbles came sensational results.

First they reported that the proportions of carbon dioxide and of methane, another greenhouse gas, were far lower during the most recent ice age than recently. In ice from deep Soviet drilling at the Vostok in Antarctica, Lorius and his team eventually pushed this account back through a warm interglacial period, when the carbon dioxide was up, though not to as high a level as at present. In a previous ice age before that warm period it was down again. Carbon dioxide levels and prevailing temperatures seemed to be linked in some emphatic way.

Oeschger's team looked especially at ice from the 10,000 years or so since the ice age ended. They reported that the carbon dioxide was almost steady for the whole of that time, at about 270 parts per million. Only around A D 1800 did it begin to climb, and by the mid-20th century the steeply rising levels of carbon dioxide overlapped neatly with the early part of the Keeling Curve.

To accomplish that overlap, the scientists had to assume that the air in the bubbles was younger than the ice enclosing it, by 80 years or sometimes much longer. That was the time taken for the piled-up snow to seal itself off from the air. It was accepted as a sensible adjustment. The resulting graph combining the ice core and Mauna Loa data became the favourite diagram for the Intergovernmental Panel on Climate Change, when sounding the alarm about global warming.

It showed carbon dioxide in the air varying naturally very little, until it suddenly shot upwards to unprecedented levels after 1800. Not until the 20th century did it ever reach 300 parts per million. Lorius affirmed in 2002: 'Current greenhouse gas levels are unprecedented, higher than anything measured for hundreds of thousands of years, and directly linked to man's impact on the atmosphere.'

Critics of the ice-core data nevertheless thought that the graph between the end of the ice age and the Industrial Revolution was too flat to be true. Instead of faithfully recording carbon dioxide levels the bubbles might be registering some physical chemistry between the gas and the ice.

'Carbon dioxide is soluble in ice,' noted Alexander Wilson of the University of Arizona. 'As one goes down the ice core the time and the pressure increase and this leads to a significant loss of carbon dioxide into the ice.' But the strongest challenge to the ice-core results came from a completely different method of gauging past levels of carbon dioxide.

The leaves of Big Betty

Around 1948, a birch tree took root in isolation on the edge of a small abandoned peat-bed in a nature reserve 30 kilometres east of the Dutch city of Eindhoven. It was still young when, on the other side of the world, Dave Keeling was setting up shop on Mauna Loa. By the 1990s it was quite a grand tree as *Betula* species go. Scientists from the Laboratory of Palaeobotany and Palynology at Utrecht, who studied it closely, nicknamed it Big Betty.

Every autumn Big Betty dropped a new carpet of leaves into the bog. Those from the 1990s were subtly different from the leaves of its youth, dug up by the scientists. As the amount of carbon dioxide available in the air increased during its life, Big Betty progressively reduced the number of breathing pores, or stomata, in its leaves.

Like many other plants, birches are smart about carbon dioxide. They need the stomata to take in enough carbon dioxide to grow by, but they also lose water vapour through these pores. So they can conserve water if they can manage with fewer of them in an atmosphere rich in carbon dioxide. Plant biologists are entirely familiar with the leafy adjustments, which are very obvious in greenhouses with artificially high carbon dioxide.

Between 1952 and 1995, Big Betty's leaves showed a fall from 10 to 7 in the stomatal index, which gauges the number of pores. Old birch leaves from earlier in the century, preserved in a herbarium in Utrecht, showed more stomata than

Big Betty had at mid-century, in line with the belief that carbon dioxide was scarcer then. Growing in isolation where its litter was not mixed with other sources, Big Betty provided a special chance to calibrate birch leaves, as time machines for reporting previous levels of carbon dioxide.

Down the road, in Amsterdam, a palaeo-ecologist Bas van Geel had fossil birch leaves from peat at an archaeological site at Bochert in the north-east of the Netherlands. They dated from a period of fluctuating climate soon after the end of the last ice age. When Friederike Wagner, a German graduate student at Utrecht, examined the leaves she saw the carbon dioxide in the air changing, with the stomatal index varying between 13 (gasping for the stuff) and 8 (plenty, thank you). At the peak, in the ancient period under study, the birch leaves deployed no more stomata than Big Betty.

In 1999 Wagner and her colleagues declared that, in a warm spell around 9500 years ago, the level of carbon dioxide experienced by the birch leaves was about 350 parts per million—the same as measured at Mauna Loa in 1987, and much higher than the 260 parts per million or so reported from the ice core. Moreover the birch leaves indicated an increase of 65 parts per million in less than a century, from a previous cool period. That is comparable to the rate of increase seen during the 20th century at Mauna Loa.

What cheek! If Big Betty and the fossil birch leaves told the truth about high concentrations of carbon dioxide in the past, and rapid changes, the ice-core reports were entirely misleading. Carbon dioxide levels changed drastically for natural reasons, at a time when human beings were few in numbers and still lived mainly as hunter-gatherers. Even the farmers in Neolithic Jericho had no coalmines or oilfields.

'We have to think afresh about the causes of carbon dioxide changes,' Wagner commented, 'and their link to changes in the Earth's climate.' The ice-core scientists reacted to her bombshell by merely asserting that their latest results, from Taylor Dome in Antarctica, showed no elevated levels in the aftermath of the ice age and were 'the most reliable and precise reconstruction of atmospheric carbon dioxide'.

The Intergovernmental Panel on Climate Change was in no doubt about whose side to take. In its scientific assessment report in 2001 it commended the excellent agreement achieved with different Antarctic ice cores. And it dismissed Wagner's stomatal index results as 'plainly incompatible with the ice-core record.'

● Which drives which?

By then the discovery of a gene responsible for controlling pore numbers in leaves had consolidated the plant biology. Alistair Hetherington at Lancaster and his colleagues found it first in the weed *Arabidopsis thaliana*. They named it HIC for 'high carbon dioxide'. Mutants lacking the gene have a lot of stomata, so the regulatory system works by reducing the number when a bonanza of carbon dioxide makes it opportune to do so.

Friederike Wagner had already teamed up with a Danish scientist, Bent Aaby, to extend her reconstruction of carbon dioxide levels throughout the period since the last ice age. A suitable treasure house of birch leaves exists on the bed of Lille Gribsø, a small lake in a royal park north of Copenhagen. With the bottommost leaves, Wagner and Aaby first reconfirmed the variations around 9500 years ago seen in the Dutch fossil leaves, and worked forward in time towards the present. A preview of the data enabled Henk Visscher, leader of the Utrecht palaeobotanists, to tell a conference in 1999 that the most recent drop in carbon dioxide was during the Little Ice Age around 300 years ago.

By 2002 Wagner, Aaby and Visscher were reporting in detail on an earlier drop revealed by the Lille Gribsø birch leaves, at the time of a major cooling event around 8300 years ago. After a high of more than 300 parts per million, 8600 years ago, the carbon dioxide fell below 280 during the period 8400 to 8100 years ago. Three centuries later it was up again, at 326 parts per million. During the entire episode, the ice-core data from Taylor Dome showed variations of one-tenth of those gauged by the leaves. The Utrecht–Copenhagen partners suggested that cold water in the North Atlantic absorbed the 25 parts per million of carbon dioxide that went missing around 8300 years ago.

That may seem like a small technical note, but if correct, the implications are considerable. Some critics of the standard global-warming scenario have for long argued that the abundance of carbon dioxide in the air tends to follow climate change, rather than to lead it. The well-known fact that the gas is less soluble in warm water than in cold water provides one of the ways in which the carbon cycle can shift, to make that happen. And here a drawdown into cold water is invoked to explain the drop 8300 years ago.

But why did the North Atlantic become chilly then? A whole chapter of the climate story concerns that cooling and a series of others like it, which are called ice-rafting events. Their causes were much debated. Dave Keeling thought that changes in the Moon's tides were involved, whilst Gerard Bond of Columbia and his colleagues linked ice rafting to weakening magnetic activity on the Sun. Either way, they were natural events, driving the level of carbon dioxide, not obeying it.

Wagner's birch-leaf results on ancient levels of carbon dioxide passed virtually unnoticed by the media, and were brushed aside by the mainstream greenhouse-warming theorists. Nevertheless they showed that the big issues about the feedbacks between the carbon cycle and climate, noted by Keeling, remained completely unresolved at the start of the 21st century.

Carbon dioxide and climate are plainly linked, but which drives which? Does extra carbon dioxide cause the world to warm? Alternatively, does warming that occurs for other reasons put the extra carbon dioxide into the air? Or are both processes at work, so that carbon dioxide amplifies natural climate variations? As long as these questions remain unsettled then, as Keeling himself noted, there is no sure way of judging by just how much human activity has affected the climate so far, or will do in the future.

▶ *For more about the link between annual variations in carbon dioxide and plant growth, see* BIOSPHERE FROM SPACE. *See also* ICE-RAFTING EVENTS *and* EARTH SYSTEM.

CELL CYCLE

How and when one living entity becomes two

'**T**HE PRINCIPAL PROBLEM in cancer cells is they divide when they shouldn't,' said cell biologist Ted Weinert of the University of Arizona in Tucson. 'Without these discoveries, cancer research would still be in the Dark Ages.' He was referring to successes in the USA and UK, beginning in the late 1960s, which gave molecular biologists a handle on the natural mechanisms that control the division of cells. One implication was that medics might try to forestall or even reverse the changes that make a cell cancerous.

Just as remarkable was the insight from this research into the most fundamental quality of living entities—their ability to divide and multiply. A little stoking of one's sense of wonder may be appropriate. If you saw a city run entirely by robots, for robots, and which could at any time make another robot city just like itself, that would be no more startling than what goes on whenever a cell of your body divides.

Forty typical human cells placed side by side would make a millimetre. Billions of them renew themselves in your body, every day, by cell division. The event may be triggered when hormone molecules attach themselves to a cell's outer wall and announce that the time has come to divide.

Dramatic changes ensue. The cell enlarges in preparation for what follows. In the nucleus of the cell, the genes promptly make a complete duplicate of the DNA chains in which they are written. Then the two sets of copies wind up tightly into the packets called chromosomes, with two versions of each chromosome in both sets.

Long, thin fibres called microtubules, made of protein molecules linked together, usually criss-cross the cell as struts. They form a network of tracks that move and position various internal components and hold them in place. During cell division, the microtubules rearrange themselves to form bundles of fibres. These move chromosomes and sort them into two identical sets that are packaged into the nuclei of the two daughter cells.

The internal components—protein factories, power stations, postal facilities and other essentials—are also shared out. The cell then splits in two. The daughter cells may stop at that point, but otherwise they are ready, if necessary, to do it all over again. In typical cells of mammals, the whole cycle takes about a day.

Cells have been doing this trick for about 2 billion years, since the first eukaryotic cells with nuclei and chromosomes appeared among the ancient bacteria which duplicated themselves in a much more rudimentary way. These primitive eukaryotes later gave rise to more complex ones, including plants and animals, but many of them still remain today as single-celled organisms. Moulds and yeasts are familiar examples.

Besides the routine cell cycle just described, in which the nuclear division, called mitosis, provides each daughter nucleus with a full set of chromosomes, a variant called meiosis provides sperm or egg cells with only half the normal set of chromosomes. During sexual reproduction, sperm and egg cells join and combine their chromosomes so the full set is restored.

A trigger and a checkpoint

The molecules that bustle about in a cell perform tasks so various and elaborate that the biggest library of textbooks and scientific journals provides only a cursory, fragmented description. Any serious mistake in their activities could make you ill or kill you. The molecules have no PhDs, and they can't read the textbooks. They are just stupid compounds of carbon—strings of mindless atoms made of quarks and electrons.

Yet every molecule in some sense knows, from moment to moment, where it has to go and what it has to do, and it operates with a precision and slickness that human chemists envy. The system works because the molecules monitor and regulate one another's activities. It is convenient to think that the genes are in control, but they too react to molecular signals that switch them on or off.

In the latest phases in their study of the cell cycle, cell biologists have taken full advantage of the techniques of modern molecular biology, biochemistry and genetics, to trace the controls operating at the molecular level. Although much

CELL CYCLE

of the impetus has come from medical considerations, the primary discoveries were made in non-human animals and in yeast.

As a boy in his hometown of Kyoto, Yoshio Masui had collected frogs. He liked to watch their hearts beating. When a postdoc at Yale in 1966, he wanted to see if he could clone unfertilized frogs' eggs by making them mature and divide. In the course of his experiments he found the first known trigger for cell division, called MPF, for maturation promotion factor.

Previous generations of biologists had been entirely accustomed to working with 'factors' such as vitamins and growth factors with known effects but often with unknown chemistry. Masui made his discovery in a new era when such vagueness was considered unsatisfactory. He made a conscious decision not to educate himself in molecular biology, but to continue (in Toronto) with what he called cell ecology. He said, 'I tell people that I answer problems in my mind, but that my answers become their problems.' Masui's MPF trigger remained chemically anonymous for nearly two decades.

Meanwhile in Seattle, at the University of Washington, Lee Hartwell was studying the genetics of baker's yeast, *Saccharomyces cerevisiae*. Although yeasts are among the simplest of eukaryotes, mere single-celled creatures, they use the full apparatus of cell division to multiply. Hartwell did not realize that they might shed light on how genes control that process until he came across a strange mutation that left yeast cells misshapen. They were failing to complete the process of cell division.

Using radiation to produce further mutant strains, he found that the yeast tried to resist his harmful intent. When genetic material was damaged, the cell cycle paused while the cell repaired the DNA, before proceeding to the next phase. Hartwell called this interruption a checkpoint. It turned out to involve the controls that make sure everything happens in the right order. By the early 1970s Hartwell's lab had identified more than 100 genes involved in managing the cell cycle; No. 28 initiated the duplication of the cell's genetic material. He therefore named it 'start'.

'A real eureka moment'

A few years later Paul Nurse at Edinburgh did similar experiments with fission yeast, *Schizzosaccharomyces pombe*. He identified mutants that were unusually small because they divided before the parent cell was full-grown. Because this was in Scotland, the mutation was at first called wee2, but later cdc2. The affected gene's role was to prompt the separation of the duplicated chromosomes into the sets needed by the daughter cells.

In 1982 another British scientist, Tim Hunt, was spending the summer at a marine biology lab in Woods Hole, Massachusetts, experimenting with fertilized eggs of sea urchins. He noticed that a particular protein was present until 10 minutes before a cell started to divide. Then the protein almost disappeared, only to reappear again in the daughter cells, and drop once more when it was their turn to divide. Hunt called it cyclin.

Scientists recognize that they've stumbled into one of Nature's treasure houses, when everything comes together. Nurse's cdc2 turned out to be almost identical to Hartwell's *start* gene, and plainly had a general function in regulating different phases of the cell cycle. The gene worked by commanding the manufacture of a protein—an enzyme of a type called a kinase.

The role of Hunt's cyclin was to regulate the action of such kinases. And what was the composite molecule formed when those two kinds of molecules teamed up? Nothing else but MPF—the maturation promotion factor discovered in frogs' eggs by Yoshio Masui more than a decade earlier. Thus the scope of the detailed genetic discoveries from yeast and sea urchins was extended to animals with backbones. In 1987 Nurse found in human cells both the gene and the kinase corresponding to cdc2.

'What it meant was that the same gene controlled cell division from yeast, the simplest organism, to humans, the most complicated,' Nurse said later. 'And that meant that everything in between was controlled the same way. That was a real eureka moment.'

The molecular motors

By the end of the century several other relevant human genes were known, and various kinases and cyclins. Cancer researchers were looking to apply the knowledge to detecting and correcting the loss of control of cell division occurring in tumours. In general biology, the big discoveries are already taken for granted, as knowledge of cell division converges with other findings, including cell suicide, in filling out the picture of how cells cooperate in building plants and animals. That complicated jigsaw puzzle of genes and proteins will take many more years of experiment and theory to complete.

Meanwhile, the mechanics of cell division are becoming clearer. Molecular machines called spindles separate the duplicate sets of chromosomes. They use bundles of the fibre-like microtubules to fish for the correct chromosomes, pull them apart and, as mentioned before, place them into what will become the nuclei of the daughter cells.

The microtubules assemble and disassemble from component protein molecules, thereby lengthening and shortening themselves. Molecular motors cross-link the microtubules into the bundles and slide them against one another. In that way they adjust the length of a bundle as required, in telescope fashion.

The growth and shrinkage of the individual microtubules, and the motor-driven sliding of bundled microtubules, generate the forces that move and position the chromosomes. Individual motors work antagonistically, with some trying to lengthen and others to shorten the bundles. They therefore act as brakes on one another's operations.

'The spindle is a high-fidelity protein machine with quality control, which constantly monitors its mechanical performance,' said Jonathan Scholey of UC Davis. 'This ensures that our genes are distributed accurately and minimizes the chances of mistakes with the associated devastating consequences, including cancer or birth defects. It's an intricate and very smart system.'

▶ *For related aspects of cell biology, see* CELL DEATH, CELL TRAFFIC *and* EMBRYOS.

CELL DEATH
How life makes suicide part of the evolutionary deal

Y OU'RE IN FOR A NASTY SHOCK if you expect Ecuador's Galapagos Islands to be pretty, just because Charles Darwin found unusual wildlife there. The writer Herman Melville described them as 'five-and-twenty heaps of cinders...looking much as the world at large might, after a penal conflagration'. And when El Niño turns the surrounding Pacific Ocean warm, depleting the fish stock, the Galapagos are even more hellish than usual.

At the blue-footed booby colony on Isabella, for example, the scrub seems dotted with dozens of fluffy lumps of cotton wool. They turn out to be corpses of chicks allowed to perish. A mother booby's eggs hatch at intervals, so when food is scarce the younger chicks cannot compete for it with their older siblings. In the accountancy of survival, one well-nourished fledgling is worth more than a half-fed pair.

Consider the chick that dies. It is the victim of no predator, disease or rock-fall, nor of any inborn defect. Still less is it expiring from old age, to make room for new generations. If fed, the chick could have grown to maturity, and dive-bombed the fishes as fiercely as any other blue-footed booby. By the inflexible discipline of birth order, the chick's death is programmed as a tool of life.

It resembles in that respect the intentional death among microscopic living cells of animal tissue, which occurs even in an embryo. A difference is that chick death leaves litter on the Galapagos lava. The remains of unwanted cells are scavenged so quickly that the process went almost unnoticed by biologists until 1964. That was when Richard Lockshin of St John's University, New York, described the fine-tuning of the developing muscles in silkmoths as programmed cell death.

Another term became the buzzword: apoptosis, pronounced a-po-toe-sis. In its Greek root it means the falling of leaves. Pathologists at Edinburgh adopted it after watching self-destructing cells in rat liver break up into small, disposable fragments, and seeing the same behaviour in dying cells from amphibians and humans. John Kerr, Andrew Wyllie and Alistair Currie were the first fully to grasp the general importance of cell death. To a key paper published in 1972 they gave the title, 'Apoptosis: a basic biological phenomenon with wide-ranging implications in tissue kinetics'. They said that cell death played the role opposite to cell division in regulating the number of cells in animal tissue.

Death genes and other devices

Powerful support came within a few years from John Sulston at the UK's Laboratory of Molecular Biology, who traced the building of a roundworm, the small nematode *Caenorhabditis elegans*. Precisely 1090 cells are formed to develop the adult worm, and precisely 131 are selected to die. This speaks of clever molecular control of three steps: the identification of the surplus cells, their suicide, and the removal of the debris.

In the mid-1980s Robert Horvitz of the Massachusetts Institute of Technology identified, in the roundworm, two death genes that the animal uses when earmarking unwanted cells for elimination. Then he found another gene that protects against cell death, by interacting with the death genes. Here was an early molecular hint that a soliloquy on the lines of 'to be, or not to be?' goes on in every cell of your body, all the time.

'Everybody thought about death as something you didn't want to happen, especially those of us in cell culture,' Barbara Osborne of the University of Massachusetts commented. 'Sometimes it takes a while for something to sink in as being important.' She was speaking in 1995, just as apoptosis was becoming fashionable among scientists after a delay of more than two decades.

Like Monsieur Jourdain in Molière's *Le Bourgeois Gentilhomme*, who found he'd been speaking prose all his life, biologists and medics realized that they were entirely familiar with many processes that depend upon apoptosis. A foetus makes its fingers and toes by eliminating superfluous web tissue between them, much as a sculptor would do. The brain is sculpted in a subtler fashion, by the creation of too many cells and the elimination of those that don't fit the required patterns of interconnections. In an adult human, countless brand new cells are created every day, and the ageing or slightly damaged cells that they replace are quietly eliminated by apoptosis.

Cell deaths due to gross injury or infection are messy, and they cause inflammation in nearby tissue. Apoptosis is discreet. Typically the cell committing suicide chops up its genetic material into ineffective lengths. It also shrinks, becomes blistery and subdivides into small, non-leaky bodies, which are appetizing for white blood cells that scavenge them. The process takes about an hour.

Apoptosis is orchestrated by genes. This is its most distinctive feature and it supersedes early definitions based on the appearance of the dying cells. In the interplay between the death genes that promote apoptosis and other genes that resist it, the decision to proceed may be taken by the cell itself, if it is feeling poorly. Sunburnt cells in the skin are a familiar case in point.

Alternatively death commands, in the form of molecular signals coming from outside the cell, settle on its surface and trigger apoptosis. Dismantling the cell then involves special-purpose proteins, enzymes called capsases, made on instructions from the genes. Other enzymes released from the cell's power stations, the mitochondria, contribute to cellular meltdown.

Sometimes cells that ought to die don't do so, and the result may be cancer. Or a smart virus can intervene to stop apoptosis, while it uses the cell's machinery to replicate itself. In other cases, cells that should stay alive die by misdirected apoptosis, causing degenerative diseases such as Alzheimer's and long-term stroke damage.

The protection against infection given by the white blood cells of the immune system depends on their continual creation and destruction. The system must favour the survival of those cells that are most effective against a current infection, and kill off redundant and dangerous cells. The latter include cells programmed to attack one's own tissues, and a failure to destroy them results in crippling autoimmune diseases.

'The immune system produces more cells than are finally needed, and extra cells are eliminated by apoptosis,' said Peter Krammer of the Deutschen Krebsforschungszentrum in Heidelberg. 'Apoptosis is the most common form of death in cells of the immune system. It is astounding how many different pathways immune cells can choose from to die . . . Apoptosis is such a central regulatory feature of the immune system that it is not surprising that too little or too much apoptosis results in severe diseases.'

● 'Better to die than be wrong'

A huge surge in research on apoptosis, around the start of the 21st century, therefore came from the belated realization that it is implicated in a vast range of medical conditions. Pre-existing treatments for cancer, by radiation and chemical poisons, turned out to have been unwittingly triggering the desired cellular suicide. Better understanding may bring better therapies. But a cautionary note comes from the new broad picture of apoptosis. Powerful treatments for cancer may tend to encourage degenerative disease, and vice versa.

Mechanisms of apoptosis in roundworms and flies are similar to those in humans, so they have been preserved during the long history of animal life. Apoptosis also occurs in plants. For example, the channels by which water flows up a tree trunk are created by the suicide of long lines of cells. As apoptosis plays such a central role in the sculpturing of animals and plants, theorists of evolution will have to incorporate it into their attempts to explain how body designs have evolved so coherently during the history of life.

Vladimir Skulachev at Moscow adapted a Russian proverb, 'it's easier to break than to mend', to propose a new principle of life: 'it's better to die than to be wrong.' The death of whole organisms is, in some circumstances, apoptosis writ large. Septic shock kills people suffering a massive infection. It adapts biochemical apparatus normally used to resist the infection to invoke wholesale apoptosis. In Skulachev's view this is no different in principle from the quick suicide of bacteria when attacked by a virus. The effect is to reduce the risk of the infection spreading to one's kin.

Adjusting biology to the surprisingly recent discovery of apoptosis requires a change of mind-set. The vast majority of biologists who are unfamiliar with it have yet to wake up to the implications. They'll need to accommodate in their elementary ideas the fact that, in complex life forms, cell death is just as important as cell creation.

Altruistic suicide is part of the evolutionary deal. To see that, you need only look at the gaps between your fingers, which distinguish you from a duck. The cells that chopped up their own DNA so that you could hold a stick are essential actors in the story of life, just as much as those that survive. And just as much as the unwilling little altruists, the booby chicks that strew their dead fluff on Isabella.

It's an idea that will take a lot of getting used to, like the realization 100 years ago that heredity comes in penny packets. So in spite of the thousands of specialist scientific papers already published on programmed cell death and apoptosis, philosophically speaking the subject is still in its infancy. Which makes it exceptionally exciting of course.

▶ *For the role of apoptosis in brain construction, see* BRAIN WIRING. *About survival and death in whole organisms, see* IMMORTALITY. *See also* EMBRYOS.

CELL TRAFFIC

Zip codes, stepping-stones and the recognition of life's complexity

A T MEDICAL SCHOOL in Liège in the 1920s, Albert Claude's microscope frustrated him. In nearby Louvain, as long ago as 1839, Theodor Schwann had declared that all animals are built of vast numbers of living cells, each of which was an organism in its own right. But how cells worked, who could tell?

The protoplasm of the interior just looked like jelly with some minute specks in it. Half a century later Claude said, 'I remember vividly my student days, spending hours at the light microscope, turning endlessly the micrometric screw, and gazing at the blurred boundary which concealed the mysterious ground substance where the secret mechanisms of cell life might be found.'

The young Belgian joined the Rockefeller Institute for Medical Research in New York in 1929. Over the decades that followed he looked tirelessly for better ways of revealing those secret mechanisms. He found a way of grinding up cells in a mortar and separating the pieces by repeated use of a centrifuge.

Claude was pleased to find that various constituents called organelles survived this brutal treatment and continued to function in his test tubes as they had done in the living cells. The separations revealed, for example, that oval-shaped mitochondria are the cells' power stations. Christian de Duve, also from Belgium, discovered in the separations a highly destructive waste-disposal system, identified with organelles called lysosomes.

How the organelles were arranged in the cell became much clearer with the electron microscope, a gift from the physicists in the 1940s. The transition from the light microscope to the electron microscope in cell biology was equivalent to Galileo's advancement of astronomy from the naked eye to the telescope. With essential contributions from biochemistry and later from molecular biology, the intricacies of cell life at last became partially apparent. And they were staggering.

'We have learned to appreciate the complexity and perfection of the cellular mechanisms, miniaturized to the utmost at the molecular level, which reveal within the cell an unparalleled knowledge of the laws of physics and chemistry,' Claude declared in 1974. 'If we examine the accomplishments of man in his most advanced endeavours, in theory and in practice, we find that the cell has done all this long before him, with greater resourcefulness and much greater efficiency.'

A hubble of bubbles

Another young colleague of Claude's, George Palade, discovered the ribosomes, the complex molecular machines with which a cell manufactures proteins. They reside in a factory, a network of membranes with the jaw-breaking name of endoplasmic reticulum. And it turned out that newly manufactured proteins go to another organelle called the Golgi complex, which acts like a post office, routing the product to its ultimate destination.

Power stations, waste-disposal systems, factories, post offices—the living cell was emerging as a veritable city on a microscopic scale, with the cell nucleus as the town hall, repository of the genes. This was all very picturesque, but how on earth did it function? How could mindless molecules organize themselves with such cool efficiency?

Consider this. Each cell contains something like a billion protein molecules, all built of strings of subunits, amino acids. Some have a few dozen subunits and others, thousands. Apart from proteins used for construction, many have a chemical role as enzymes, promoting thousands of different, highly specific reactions. These are all needed to keep the cell alive and playing its proper part among 100 million million other cells in your body.

The proteins are continually scrapped or built afresh, in accordance with the needs of the cell, moment by moment. A transcription of a gene arrives at the protein factories on cue, when a new protein is wanted. But then, how does a newly made protein know where to go? A related question is how tightly sealed membranes, built to separate the exteriors and interiors of organelles and cells, can tell when it's OK to let an essential protein pass through.

All around the world, biologists rushed to follow up the discoveries at the Rockefeller Institute and to face up to the technical and intellectual challenges that they posed. The New Yorkers had a head start and the next big step came from the same place, although in 1965 it changed its name to the Rockefeller University. There, during the 1970s, Günter Blobel established that protein molecules carry small extra segments that say where they have to go. They are like postcodes on a letter—or zip codes, as they say in the Big Apple.

Later Blobel showed how a zip code can act also like a password, opening a narrow channel in a membrane to let the protein molecule wriggle through. To do so, the normally bunched-up protein molecule has to unwind itself into a silky strand. The same zip codes are used in animals, plants and yeasts, which last shared a common ancestor about a billion years ago. So these cellular tricks are at once strikingly ancient and carefully preserved, because they are vital.

Cell biologists in Basel, Cambridge and London contributed to these discoveries by identifying zip codes directing proteins to the power stations (mitochondria) or to the town hall (cell nucleus). European scientists also investigated what a Finnish-born cell biologist, Kai Simons, called 'a hubble of bubbles'. Objects like minute soap bubbles, seen continually moving about in a cell, were courier parcels for special deliveries of proteins.

Palade in New York had found that protein molecules due for export from a cell are wrapped in other protein material borrowed from a membrane inside the cell. This makes the bubble. When it reaches the cell's outer wall, the bubble merges with the membrane there. In the process it releases the transported protein to the outside world, without causing any breach in the cell wall that could let other materials out or in.

Protein porters and fatty rafts

At the European Molecular Biology Laboratory in Heidelberg, in the 1980s, Simons and his colleagues confirmed and extended this picture of bubbles as membrane parcels. They used a virus to follow the trail of bubbles connecting the various parts of a cell. Like some medically more important viruses, including those causing yellow fever and AIDS, the Semliki Forest virus from Uganda sneaks into a cell by exploiting a system by which the cell's outer wall continually cleans and renews itself. The Heidelberg experimenters chose it to be their bloodhound.

In an inversion of the protein-export technique, the cell wall engulfs the virus in a pocket, which then pinches itself off inside the cell, as a new, inward-travelling bubble. It is very properly routed towards the cell's waste-disposal system. On the way the virus breaks free, like an escaper from a prison van.

The virus then hijacks the cell's manufacturing systems to make tens of thousands of new viruses consisting of genetic material wrapped in proteins. The victim cell obligingly routes each of the virus's progeny, neatly wrapped in a pukka-looking bubble, back to the cell wall. In a parting shot, the virus steals part of the wall as a more permanent wrapping, so that it will appear like a friend to the next cell it attacks. The secret of all this deadly chicanery is that the virus knows the zip codes.

The next question was how the bubble-parcels moved around. Cell biologists came to suspect that they might travel along the molecular struts called microtubules that criss-cross the cell. These hold the various organelles in place or reposition them as required, and they sort the chromosomes of the nucleus when the cell reproduces itself. In muscle cells, more elaborate protein molecules of this kind produce the contractions on which all muscle action depends.

By the late 1980s, Ronald Vale was sure that the bubble-parcels rode like cable cars along the microtubules. He spent the next ten years, first at Woods Hole, Massachusetts, and then at UC San Francisco, finding out how the machinery worked. The answer was astonishing. Small but strong two-legged proteins called kinesins grab hold of the cargo and *walk* with it along the microtubules.

Like someone using stepping-stones to cross a pond, a kinesin molecule can attach itself to the microtubule only at certain points. When one leg is safely in place, the other swings forward to the next point along the microtubule, and so on. Anyone overawed by Mother Nature's incredible efficiency, not to say technological inventiveness, may be comforted to know that sometimes the protein porter misses its footing and falls off, together with its load.

'The kinesin motors responsible for this transport are the world's smallest moving machines, even the smallest in the protein world,' Vale commented. 'So, besides their biological significance, it's exciting to understand how these very compact machines—many orders of magnitude smaller than anything humans have produced—have evolved that ability to generate motion.'

Rafts provide another way of transporting materials around the cell. Simons and his Heidelberg group became fascinated by flat assemblies of fatty molecules. Known formally as sphingolipid-cholesterol rafts, they carry proteins and play an important part in building the skins and mucous membranes of organisms exposed to the outside world. Those surfaces are made of back-to-back layers with very different characters, according to whether they face inwards or outwards. How they are assembled from the traffic of rafts, so that the contributed portions finish up facing the right way, was a leading question.

A pooling of all skills

In 1998, while still puzzling over the fatty rafts, Simons became the founding chief of the Max-Planck-Institut für molekulare Zellbiologie und Genetik, in Dresden. This brand-new lab was a conscious attempt to refashion biology. If the previous 100 years had been the age of the gene, the next 100 would surely be the age of the cell.

For every question answered since young Albert Claude wrestled with his microscope, in Liège 70 years before, a hundred new ones had arisen. Simons had for long mocked the overconfident, one-dimensional view of some molecular biologists, who thought that by simply specifying genes, and the proteins that they catalogued, the task was finished. 'Was it possible,' he demanded, 'that molecular biology could be so boring that it would yield its whole agenda to one reductionist assault by one generation of ingenious practitioners?'

Even the metaphor of the cell as a city looks out of date, being rather flat and static. The cell's complexity necessarily extends into three dimensions. Four, if you take time into account in the rates of events, in the changes that occur in a cell as seconds or days pass, and in the biological clocks at work everywhere. Also *passé* is the division of biologists into separate camps—not just by the old labels like anatomy and physiology on 19th-century buildings, but also in more recent chic cliques. Making sense of cells in all their intricacy and diversity will need a pooling of all relevant skills at both the technical and conceptual levels.

'This is an exciting time to be a biologist,' Simons said, in looking forward to the cell science of the 21st century. 'We're moving from molecules to mechanisms, and barriers between disciplines are disappearing. Biochemists, cell biologists, developmental biologists, geneticists, immunologists, microbiologists, neurobiologists, and pharmacologists are all speaking the same molecular language.'

▶ *For closely related themes, see* CELL CYCLE, CELL DEATH, PROTEIN-MAKING *and* PROTEOMES. *For perspectives on the management of cells with different functions, see* EMBRYOS, IMMUNE SYSTEM *and* BIOLOGICAL CLOCKS.

CEREALS

Genetic boosts for the most cosseted inhabitants of the planet

A WHITE MODERN BUILDING, to be spotted in the airport's industrial zone as you come in to land at Beijing, may never compare with the Great Wall or the Forbidden City as a tourist attraction. But packed with Chinese supercomputers and Western gene-reading machines, the Beijing Genomics Institute is the very emblem of a developing country in transition to a science-based economy. There, Yang Haunming and his colleagues stunned the world of botany and agricultural science by suddenly decoding 50,000 genes of heredity of *Oryza sativa*—better known as the world's top crop, rice.

The Beijing Genomics Institute was a private, non-profit-making initiative of Yang and a few fellow geneticists who had learned their skills in Europe and the USA. Not until 2000 did they set out to read the entire complement of genes, or genome, of rice. By the end of 2001 they had done nearly all of it.

Ten years earlier, Japan had launched a programme that expanded into the International Rice Genome Sequencing Project, involving a multinational consortium of public laboratories. It was to produce the definitive version of the rice genome, with every gene carefully located in relation to the others and annotations of its likely role provided. But completion of the great task was not expected before 2004, and in the meantime there was a much quicker way to get a useful first impression of the genome.

A high-speed technique called the whole-genome shotgun, in which computers reconstruct the genes from random fragments of genetic code, had been developed by Craig Venter and the Celera company in Maryland, for the human genome. Yang and his team adopted the method for the rice genome, along with Venter's slogan, 'Discovery can't wait'. What made them work 12-hour shifts night and day was the knowledge that a Utah laboratory, working for the Swiss company Syngenta, had already shotgunned rice.

The people of China and India run on long-grained indica rice, like cars on gasoline. Syngenta was sequencing the short-grained japonica subspecies favoured in some other countries. Convinced that China should do indica, the Beijing team chose the father and mother varieties of a high-yielding hybrid, LYP9.

In January 2002, Yang announced the decoding of 92 per cent of genes of indica rice. In the weeks that followed, international telephone circuits hummed with digital data as hundred of laboratories downloaded the gene transcripts. Here was a honey-pot of freely available information, for plant breeders wanting to improve the crop to help feed a growing population—and also for biologists and archaeologists seeking fundamental knowledge about the evolution of the grasses, and the eventual domestication of the most nourishing of them in the Agricultural Revolution around 10,000 years ago.

The choicest grasses

'The most precious things are not jade and pearls, but the five grains,' says a Chinese proverb. Precisely which five are meant, apart from wheat and rice, is a matter for debate. Globally the list of major cereal crops would add maize, barley, oats, rye, millet and sorghum. It is salutary to remember that all were domesticated a very long time ago by supposedly primitive hunter-gatherers.

A combination of botany, which traces the ancestral wild species of grass, and archaeology, which finds proof of cultivation and domesticated varieties, has revealed some of the wonders of that great transition. Two big guesses are tolerated, though without any direct evidence for them. One is that women transformed human existence, by first gardening the cereals. In hunter-gatherer communities, the plant experts tend to be female.

The other guess is that the drastic environmental and climatic changes at the end of the last ice age, 11,000 years ago, stimulated or favoured the domestication of crops. Otherwise it seems too much of a coincidence that people in the Middle East should have settled down with wheat and barley at roughly the same time as rice was first being grown in South-East Asia, and potatoes in Peru. American corn, or maize, followed a few thousand years later, in Mexico, apparently as a result of sharp eyes spotting mutants with soft-cased kernels, in an otherwise unpromising grass, teosinte.

Domestication may have been casual at first, with opportunistic sowing at flood time on the riverbanks. By 10,600 years ago the oldest known agricultural town, Jericho, was in existence in the Jordan valley. Its walls guarded the harvests from hunters and herdsmen who did not appreciate the new economy. The Bible's tale of Cain and Abel commemorates the conflict about land use.

Farming was an irreversible step for crops and their growers alike. The plant varieties came to depend mainly on deliberate sowing of their seeds. And mothers, without the strenuous hiking that hunting and gathering had meant for them, lost a natural aid to birth control that deferred post-natal menstruation and the next pregnancy. Populations boomed in the sedentary communities, and needed more farming to sustain them. So farming spread, at a rate of the order of a kilometre a year.

Cereals are like domestic cats, well able to make themselves attractive and useful to the human species and therefore to enjoy a cosseted existence. They acquired the best land to live on. Hardworking servants supplied them with water and nutrients, and cleared the weeds. Through the millennia, as farming populations spread, so did the cereals, eventually from continent to continent. Many thousands of varieties were developed by unnatural selection, to suit the new environments.

The Green Revolution

A crisis loomed in the mid-20th century. There were no wide-open spaces left to cultivate anew, and the global population was exploding. Parents in regions of high infant mortality were understandably slow to be convinced by modest reductions in the death rate, and these translated into rapid population growth in the poorest parts of the world. The ghost of Thomas Malthus, the 19th-century prophet of a population catastrophe, stalked the world. It became fashionable again among scientists to predict mass famine as a consequence of overpopulation.

'It now seems inevitable that death through starvation will be at least one factor in the coming increase in the death rate,' an authoritative Stanford biologist, Paul Ehrlich, wrote in *The Population Bomb*, in 1971. 'In the absence of plague or war, it may be the major factor.'

Two trends exorcized Malthus, at least for the time being. One was an easing of birth rates, so that in the 1970s the graph of population growth began to bend, hinting at possible stabilization at around 10 billion in the 21st century. The other trend was the Green Revolution, in which plant breeders, chemical engineers and a billion farmers did far better than expected in the life-or-death race between food and population.

World cereal production trebled in the second half of the 20th century. That was with virtually no increase in the area of land required, thanks to remarkable increases in yields in tonnes per hectare made possible by shrewd genetics. Irrigation, land reform and education played their part in the Green Revolution, and industrial chemistry provided fertilizers on a gargantuan scale.

The method of fixing nitrogen from the air, perfected by Fritz Haber and Carl Bosch in Germany in 1913, was initially used mainly for explosives. After 1945 it became indispensable for making fertilizers for world agriculture. By 2000 you could calculate that 40 per cent of the world's population was alive thanks to the extra food produced with industrial nitrogen and new crops capable of using it efficiently. That many people remained chronically undernourished was due to inequalities within and between nations, not to a gross shortfall in production.

The dwarf hybrids

Hybrid maize first demonstrated the huge gains made possible by breeding improved varieties of crops. Widely grown in the USA from the 1930s onwards, it was later adopted by China and other countries to replace sorghum and millet. And in a quiet start to the broader Green Revolution, Mexico became self-sufficient in wheat production in 1956.

At the International Maize and Wheat Improvement Center in Mexico, supported by the Rockefeller and Ford Foundations, the US-born Norman Borlaug had bred a shorter variety of wheat. It was a dwarf hybrid that could tolerate and benefit from heavy doses of fertilizer. The hollow stem of an overnourished cereal would grow too long and then easily break under the weight of the ear. By avoiding that fate, the dwarf wheat raised the maximum yield per hectare from 4.5 to 8 tonnes.

Introduced next into parts of the world where one or two tonnes per hectare were the norm, Borlaug's dwarf wheat brought sensational benefits. In India, for example, wheat production doubled between 1960 and 1970. Local crossings adapted the dwarf varieties to different climates, farming practices and culinary preferences.

'I am impatient,' Borlaug said, 'and do not accept the need for slow change and evolution to improve the agriculture and food production of the emerging countries. I advocate instead a "yield kick-off" or "yield blast-off". There is no time to be lost.'

Another plant-breeding hero of the Green Revolution was the Indian-born Gurdev Khush. He worked at the International Rice Research Institute in the Philippines, another creation of the Rockefeller and Ford Foundations. Between 1967 and 2001, Khush developed more than 300 new varieties of dwarf rice. IR36, released in 1976, became the most widely farmed crop variety in the history of the world. Planted on 11 million hectares in Asia, it boosted global rice production by 5 million tonnes a year.

IR36 was soon overtaken in popularity and performance by other Khush varieties, his last being due for general release in 2005 with a target yield of 12 tonnes per hectare in irrigated tropical conditions. 'It will give farmers the chance to increase their yields, so it will spread quickly,' Khush said. 'Already it is yielding 13 tonnes per hectare in temperate China.'

Such figures need to be considered with caution. There is a world of difference between the best results obtainable and the practical outcome. By 1999, the average yields of rice paddies were about three tonnes per hectare and wheat was globally a little less, whilst maize was doing better at about four tonnes per hectare. The inability of peasant farmers to pay for enough irrigation and fertilizer helps to drag the yields down, and so does disease.

Dreams of disease control

Rice blast, caused by the fungus *Magnaporthe grisea*, cuts the global rice yields by millions of tonnes a year. The disease is extremely versatile, and within a few years it can outwit the genes conferring resistance on a particular strain. Genetic variation between individual plants was always the best defence against pests and diseases, but refined breeding in pursuit of maximum growth narrows the genetic base. If you plant the same high-yielding variety across large regions, you risk a catastrophe.

A large-scale experiment, in the Yunnan province of China in 1998–99, demonstrated that even a little mixing of varieties of rice could be very effective. Popular in that part of China is a glutinous variety used in confectionery, but it is highly vulnerable to blast. Some farmers were in the habit of planting rows of glutinous rice at intervals within the main hybrid rice crop. The experimenters tested this practice on a grand scale, with the participation of many thousands of farmers. They found that the mixed planting reduced the blast infection from 20 per cent in the glutinous crop, and 2 per cent in the main crop, to 1 per cent in both varieties.

'The experiment was so successful that fungicidal sprays were no longer applied by the end of the two-year programme,' Zhu Youyong of Yunnan Agricultural University and his colleagues reported. 'Our results support the view that intraspecific crop diversification provides an ecological approach to disease control.'

Whilst blast is troublesome in rice, rust is not. Resistance to the rusts caused by *Puccinia* fungi is one the great virtues of rice, but plant breeders had only limited success against these diseases in other cereals. 'Imagine the benefits to humankind if the genes for rust immunity in rice could be transferred into wheat, barley, oats, maize, millet, and sorghum,' Borlaug said. 'Finally, the world could be free of the scourge of the rusts, which have led to so many famines over human history.'

Such dreams, and the hopes of breeding cereals better able to thrive in dry conditions, or in acid and salty soils, will have to become more than fancies as the race between food and population continues. In the 1990s, the fabulous rate of growth of the preceding decades began to falter. Cereal production began to lag once more behind the growth in population.

With more than 2 billion extra mouths to feed by 2025, according to the projections, and with a growing appetite in the developing world for grain-fed meat, a further 50–75 per cent increase in grain production seems to be needed in the first quarter of the 21st century. The available land continues to diminish rather than grow, so the yields per hectare of cereals need another mighty boost.

A treasure house of genes

Reading the rice genome lit a beacon of hope for the poor and hungry. When the first drafts of indica and japonica rice became available in 2002, 16 'future harvest centres' around the world sprang into action to exploit the new knowledge. An immediate question was how useful the rice data would be, for breeders working with other cereals.

'Wheat is rice,' said Mike Gale of the UK's John Innes Centre. By that oracular statement, first made in 1991, he meant that knowledge of the rice genome would provide a clear insight into the wheat genome, or that of any other cereal. Despite the daunting fact that wheat chromosomes contain 36 times more of the genetic material (DNA) than rice chromosomes do, and even though the two species diverged from one another 60 million years ago, Gale found that the genes themselves and the order in which they are arranged are remarkably conserved between them.

The comparative figures for DNA, reckoned in millions of letters of the genetic code, are 430 for rice and 16,000 for wheat. No wonder the geneticists decided to tackle the rice genome first. Maize is intermediate, at 3000 million, the same as the human complement of genetic material.

These huge variations reflect the botanical and agricultural histories of the cereals, in which the duplication of entire sets of genes was not unusual. Since wheat is not 36 times smarter than rice, most of its genetic material must be redundant or inert. Until such time as someone should shotgun wheat and maize, as the Beijing Genomics Institute promised to do, the rice genome was a good stopgap.

When valuable genes are pinpointed in rice—for accommodation to acid soils, for example—there are two ways to apply the knowledge in other cereals. One is directly to transfer a gene from species to species by genetic engineering. That is not as quick as it may sound, because years of work are then needed to verify the stability and safety of the transplanted gene, and to try it out in various strains and settings. The other way forward is to look for the analogue of the rice acid-soil gene (or whatever it be) within the existing varieties of your own cereal. The reading of plant genomes adds vastly to the value of the world's seed banks.

Recall that Cambodia was desperately hungry after the devastation of the Pol Pot era. Farming communities had lost, or at death's door eaten, all of the deepwater rice seeds of traditional Khmer agriculture. In 1989, a young agronomist Chan Phaloeun and her Australian mentor Harry Nesbitt initiated a 12-year effort that restored Cambodian agriculture. From the International Rice Research Institute, Nesbitt brought Cambodian seeds that had been safely stored away on the outskirts of Manila.

Even in the steamy Philippines, you need a warm coat to visit the institute's gene bank. The active collections are kept at 2°C and the base collections at minus 20. The packets and canisters of seeds represent far more than a safety net. With more than 110,000 varieties of traditional cultivated rice and related wild species held in the gene bank, the opportunities for plant breeders are breathtaking.

The subspecies and varieties of *Oryza sativa* have all been more or less successful within various environments and farming practices. The wild species include even forest-dwelling rice. Adaptations to many kinds of soil chemistry, to different calendars of dry and rainy seasons, and to all kinds of hazards are represented. Rice in the gene bank has faced down pests and diseases that farmers may have forgotten, but which could reappear.

Until the 21st century, scientists and plant breeders could do very little with the Manila treasure house. They had no way of evaluating it, variety by variety, in a human lifetime. Thanks to the reading of the rice genome, and to modern techniques of molecular biology that look for hundreds or thousands of genes in one operation, the collection now becomes practical. Identify any gene deemed to be functionally important, and you can search for existing variants that may be invaluable to a plant breeder.

Hei Leung of the Manila institute likened the rice genome to a dictionary that lists all the words, but from which most of the definitions are missing. He was optimistic both about rapid progress in filling in the definitions, and about finding undiscovered variants in the gene bank. Even so, he warned that breeding important new varieties of rice was likely to take a decade or more.

'Like words in poetry, the creative composition of genes is the essence of successful plant breeding,' Leung remarked. 'It will come down to how well we can use the dictionary.' For a sense of the potential, note that among all the tens of thousands of genes in the cereal dictionary, just two made the Green Revolution possible. The dwarf wheat and rice grew usefully short because of mutant genes that cause malfunction of the natural plant growth hormone gibberellin. *Rht* in wheat and *sd1* in rice saved the world from mass starvation.

▶ *For the genome of another plant, see* ARABIDOPSIS. *For more on Malthus, see* HUMAN ECOLOGY.

CHAOS
The butterfly versus the ladybird,
and the Mercury Effect

G O OUT OF PARIS on the road towards Chartres and after 25 kilometres you'll come to the Institut des Hautes Études Scientifiques at Bures-sur-Yvette. It occupies a quite small building surrounded by trees. Founded in 1958 in candid imitation of the Institute for Advanced Study in Princeton, it enables half a dozen lifetime professors to interact with 30 or more visitors in pondering new concepts in mathematics and theoretical physics. A former president, Marcel Boiteux, called it 'a monastery, where deep-sown seeds germinate and grow to maturity at their own pace.'

A recurring theme for the institute at Bures has been complicated behaviour. In the 21st century this extends to describing how biological molecules—nucleic acids and proteins—fold themselves to perform precise functions. The mathematical monks in earlier days directed their attention towards physical and engineering systems that can often perform in complicated and unpredictable ways.

Catastrophe theory was invented here in 1968. In the branch of mathematics concerned with flexible shapes, called topology, René Thom found origami-like ways of picturing abrupt changes in a system, such as the fracture of a girder or the capsizing of a ship. Changes that were technically catastrophic could be benign, for instance in the brain's rapid switch from sleeping to waking. The modes of sudden change became more numerous, the greater the number of factors affecting a system. The origami was prettier too, making swallowtails and brassieres.

Fascinated colleagues included Christopher Zeeman at Warwick, who became Thom's chief publicist. He and others also set out to apply catastrophe theory to an endless range of topics. From shock waves and the evolution of species, to economic inflation and political revolution, it seemed that no field of natural or social science would fail to benefit from its insights.

Thom himself blew the whistle to stop the folderol. 'Catastrophe theory is dead,' he pronounced in 1997. 'For as soon as it became clear that the theory did not permit quantitative prediction, all good minds . . . decided it was of no value.'

In an age of self-aggrandizement, Thom's dismissal of his own theory set a refreshing example to others. But the catastrophe that overtook catastrophe theory has another lesson. Mathematics stands in relation to the rest of science like an exotic bazaar, full of pretty things but most of them useless to a visitor. Descriptions of logical relationships between imagined entities create wonderful worlds that never were or will be.

Mathematical scientists have to find the small selection of theorems that may describe the real world. Many decades can elapse in some cases, before a particular item turns out to be useful. Then it becomes a jewel beyond price. Recent examples are the mathematical descriptions of subatomic particles, and of the motions of pieces of the Earth's crust that cause earthquakes.

Sometimes the customer can carry a piece of mathematics home, only to find that it looks nice on the sideboard but doesn't actually do anything useful. This was the failure of catastrophe theory. Thom's origami undoubtedly provided mathematical metaphors for sudden changes, but it was not capable of predicting them.

● Strange attractors

When the subject is predictability itself, the relationship of science and maths becomes subtler. The next innovation at the leafy institute at Bures came in 1971. David Ruelle, a young Belgian-born permanent professor, and Floris Takens visiting from Groningen, were studying turbulence. If you watch a fast-moving river, you'll see eddies and swirls that appear, disappear and come back, yet are never quite the same twice.

For understanding this not-quite-predictable behaviour in an abstract, mathematical way, Ruelle and Takens wanted pictures. They were not sure what they would look like, but they had a curious name for them: strange attractors.

Within a few years, many scientists' computers would be doodling strange attractors on their VDUs and initiating the genre of mathematical science called chaos theory.

To understand what attractors are, and in what sense they might be strange, you need first to look back to Henri Poincaré's pictures. He was France's top theorist at the end of the 19th century. Wanting to visualize changes in a system through time, without getting mired in the details, he came up with a brilliantly simple method.

Put a dot in the middle of a blank piece of paper. It represents an unchanging situation. Not necessarily a static one, to be sure, because Poincaré was talking about dynamical systems, but something in a steady state. It might be, for example, a population where births and deaths are perfectly balanced. All of the busy drama of courtship, childbirth, disease, accident, murder and senescence is then summed up in a geometric point.

And around it, like the empty canvas that taunts any artist, the rest of the paper is an abstract picture of all possible variations in the behaviour of the system. Poincaré called it phase space. You can set it to work by putting a second dot on the paper.

Because it is not in the middle, the new dot represents an unstable condition. So it cannot stay put, but must evolve into a curved line wandering across the paper. The points through which it passes are a succession of other unstable situations in which the system finds itself, with the passage of time. In the case of a population, the track that it follows depends on changes in the birth rate and death rate.

Considering the generality of dynamic systems, Poincaré found that the curve often evolved into a loop that caught its own tail and continued on, around and around. It is not an actual loop, but a mathematical impression of a complicated system that has settled down into an endlessly repetitive cycle. A high birth rate may in theory increase a population until starvation sets in. That boosts the death rate and reverses the process. When there's plenty to eat again, the birth rate recovers—and so on, *ad infinitum*.

Poincaré also realized that systems coming from different starting conditions could finish up on the same loop in phase space, as if attracted to it by a latent preference in the type of dynamic behaviour. A hypothetical population might commence with any combination of low or high rates of birth and death, and still finish up in the oscillation mentioned. The loop representing such a favoured outcome is called an attractor.

In many cases the ultimate attractor is not a loop but the central dot representing a steady state. This may mean a state of repose, as when friction brings the swirling liquid in a stirred teacup to rest, or it may be the steady-state population where the birth rate and death rate always match. Whether they are loops or dots, Poincaré attractors are tidy and you can make predictions from them.

By a strange attractor, Ruelle and Takens meant an untidy one that would capture the essence of the not-quite-predictable. Unknown to them an American meteorologist, Edward Lorenz, had already drawn a strange attractor in 1963, unaware of what its name should be. In his example it looked like a figure of eight drawn by a child taking a pencil around and around the same figure many times, but not at all accurately. The loop did not coincide from one circuit to the next, and you could not predict exactly where it would go next time.

The butterfly's heyday

When mathematicians woke up to this convergence of research in France and the USA, they proclaimed the advent of chaos. The strange attractor was its emblem. An irony is that Poincaré himself had discovered chaos in the late 1880s, when he was shocked to find that the motions of the planets are not exactly predictable. But as he didn't use an attention-grabbing name like chaos, or draw any pictures of strange attractors, the subject remained in obscurity for more than 80 years, nursed mainly by mathematicians in Russia.

Chaos in its contemporary mathematical sense acquired its name from James Yorke of Princeton, in a paper published in 1975. Assisting in the relaunch of the subject was Robert May, also at Princeton, who showed that a childishly simple mathematical equation could generate extremely complicated patterns of behaviour. And in the same year, Mitchell Feigenbaum at the Los Alamos National Laboratory in New Mexico discovered a magic number.

This is *delta*, 4.669201 . . . , and it keeps cropping up in chaos, as *pi* does in elementary geometry. Rhythmic variations can occur in chaotic systems, and then switch to a rhythm at twice the rate. The Feigenbaum number helps to define the change in circumstances—the speed of a stream for example—needed to provoke transitions from one rhythm to the next.

Here was evidence of latent orderliness that distinguishes certain kinds of erratic behaviour from mere chance. 'Chaos is not random: it is *apparently* random behaviour resulting from precise rules,' explained Ian Stewart of Warwick. 'Chaos is a cryptic form of order.'

During the next 20 years, the mathematical idea of chaos swept through science like a tidal wave. It was the smart new way of looking at everything from fluid dynamics to literary criticism. Yet by the end of the century the subject was losing some of its glamour.

Exhibit A, for anyone wanting to proclaim the importance of chaos, was the weather. Indeed it set the trend, with Lorenz's unwitting discovery of the first strange attractor. That was a by-product of his experiments on weather forecasting by computer, at the beginning of the 1960s. As an atmospheric scientist of mathematical bent at the Massachusetts Institute of Technology, Lorenz used a very simple simulation of the atmosphere by numbers, and computed changes at a network of points.

He was startled to find that successive runs from the same starting point gave quite different weather predictions. Lorenz traced the reason. The starting points were not exactly the same. To launch a new calculation he was using rounded numbers from a previous calculation. For example, 654321 became 654000. He had assumed, wrongly, that such slight differences were inconsequential. After all, they corresponded to mere millimetres per second in the speed of the wind.

This was the Butterfly Effect. Lorenz's computer told him that the flap of a butterfly's wings in Brazil might stir up a tornado in Texas. A mild interpretation said that you would not be able to forecast next week's weather very accurately because you couldn't measure today's weather with sufficient precision. But even if you could do so, and could lock up all the lepidoptera, the sterner version of the Butterfly Effect said that there was enough unpredictable turbulence in the smallest cloud to produce chance variations of a greater degree.

The dramatic inference was that the weather would do what it damn well pleased. It was inherently chaotic and unpredictable. The Butterfly Effect was a great comfort to meteorologists trying to use the primitive computers of the 1960s for long-range weather forecasts. 'We certainly hadn't been successful at doing that anyway,' Lorenz said, 'and now we had an excuse.'

Shifting the blame

The butterfly served as a scapegoat for 40 years. Especially after the rise of authoritative-looking mathematics in chaos theory, mainstream meteorologists came to accept that the atmosphere is chaotic. Even with the supercomputers of the 1990s, the reliability of weather forecasts still deteriorated badly after a few days and typically became useless after about a week. There was no point in trying to do better, it seemed, because chaos barred the way.

Recalcitrant meteorologists who continued to market long-range forecasts for a month or more ahead were assured that they were wasting their time and their clients' money. For example, the head of extended weather forecasts at the UK Met Office publicly dismissed efforts of that kind by the Weather Action company in London, which used solar variability as a guide. 'The idea of weather forecasting using something such as the Sun?' Michael Harrison said. 'With chaos the two are just not compatible with one another.'

Those who believed that long-range forecasts should still be attempted were exasperated. The dictum about chaos was also at odds with evidence that animals are remarkable seasonal predictors. In England, the orange ladybird *Halyzia sedecimguttata* lives on trees but can elect to spend the winter in the warmer leaf litter if it expects a severe season. The humble beetle makes the appropriate choice far more often than can be explained by chance.

'I have absolutely no idea how they do it, but in the 11 years we've looked at it, they have been correct every year,' said Michael Majerus, a ladybird geneticist at Cambridge. 'It is now statistically significant that they are not making the wrong choice.'

In 2001 it turned out that the Butterfly Effect had been exaggerated. This time the whistle-blowers were at Oxford University and the European Centre for Medium-Range Weather Forecasting at nearby Reading. Nearly all of the errors in forecasting for which chaos took the blame were, they found, really due to defects in the computer models of the atmosphere.

'While the effects of chaos eventually lead to loss of predictability, this may happen only over long time-scales,' David Orrell and his colleagues reported. 'In the short term it is model error which dominates.' This outcome of the skirmish between the butterfly and the ladybird had favourable implications for mainstream meteorology. It meant that medium-range weather forecasts could be improved, although Orrell thought that chaos would take effect eventually.

That begged a big question. As no one has a perfect description of the Earth system in all its complexity, there is no way of judging how chaotic the atmosphere really is, except by computer runs on various assumptions. All computer models of the climate produce erratic and inconsistent fluctuations, which the modellers say represent 'natural variability' due to chaos. Yet even if, as some climate investigators have suggested, the atmosphere is not significantly chaotic, deficiencies in the models could still produce the same erratic behaviour.

Complexity, or just complication?

The tarnish on Exhibit A prompted broader questions about the applicability of chaos theory. These concerned a general misunderstanding of what was on offer. It arose from the frequent use of chaos and complexity in the same breath. As a result, complication and complexity became thoroughly confused.

There was an implicit or explicit claim that chaos theory would be a way of dealing with complex systems—the atmosphere, the human brain or the stock market. In reality, chaos theory coped with extremely simple systems, or else with very simplified versions of complex systems. From these, complicated patterns of behaviour could be generated, and people were tempted to say, for example, 'Ah the computer is telling us how complex this system is.'

A pinball machine is extremely simple, but behaves in complicated and unpredictable ways. A ship is a far more complex machine yet it responds with the utmost simplicity and predictability to the touch of the helmsman's fingers. Is the brain, for example, more like a ship or a pinball machine?

Chaos theory in the 20th century could not answer that question, because the brain is a million times more complicated than the scope of the available analysis. Many other real-life systems were out of reach. And fundamental issues remained, concerning the extent to which complexity may tend to suppress chaos, much as friction prevents a ship veering off course if the helmsman sneezes.

The intellectual enterprise of chaos remains secure, rooted as it is in Poincaré's planetary enquiries and Ruelle's turbulence, which both belong to a class of mathematics called non-linear dynamics. Practical applications range from reducing the chaotic variations in combustion in car engines to the invention of novel types of computers. But 30 years after he first conceived strange attractors at Bures, David Ruelle was careful not to overstate the accomplishments.

'The basic concepts and methods of chaos have become widely accessible, being successfully applied to various interesting, relatively simple, precisely controlled systems,' he wrote. 'Other attempts, for example applications to the stock market, have not yielded convincing results: here our understanding of the dynamics remains inadequate for a quantitative application of the ideas of chaos.'

Chaos in the Earth's orbit

The ghost of Poincaré reappeared when Ruelle nominated the most spectacular result from chaos theory. It came from the resumption, after a lapse of 100 years, of the investigation of the erratic behaviour of the planets. Poincaré had been prompted to look into it by a prize offered by the King of Sweden for an answer to the question, 'Is the Solar System stable?' The latest answer from chaos theory is No.

Compared with the brain, the Solar System is extremely simple, yet there is no precise solution to equations describing the behaviour of more than two objects feeling one another's gravity. This is not because of inadequate maths. Mother Nature isn't quite sure of the answer either, and that's why chaos can creep in. As life has survived on the Earth for 4 billion years, the instabilities cannot be overwhelming, yet they can have dramatic effects on individual objects.

In the 1990s, Jack Wisdom at the Massachusetts Institute of Technology and Jacques Laskar at the Bureau des Longitudes in Paris revealed the chaotic behaviour of the planets and smaller bodies. To say that the two Jacks computed the motions over billions of years oversimplifies their subtle ways to diagnose chaos. But roughly speaking that is what they did, working independently and obtaining similar results. Other research groups followed up their pioneering efforts.

Small bodies like distant Pluto, Halley's Comet and the asteroids are conspicuously chaotic in their motions. Mercury, the planet closest to the Sun, has such a chaotic and eccentric orbit that it is lucky not to have tangled with Venus and either collided with it or been booted out of the Solar System. Those possibilities remain on the cards, although perhaps nothing so drastic will happen for billions of years.

Chiefly because of the antics of Mercury, the Earth's orbit is also prone to chaos, with unpredictable changes occurring at intervals of 2 million years or so. And by this Mercury Effect, chaos returns to the climate by a back door. By astronomical standards, the variations in the Earth's orbit due to chaos are quite small, yet the climatic consequences may be profound. What is affected is the eccentricity, the departure of the orbit from a true circle.

At present the distance of the Earth from the Sun varies by 5 million kilometres around a mean of 150 million kilometres. This is sufficient to make the intensity of sunshine 7 per cent stronger in January than in July. The difference is implicated in seasonal effects that vary the climate during ice ages over periods of about 20,000 years.

Moreover calculable, non-chaotic changes in the eccentricity of the Earth's orbit can push up the annual variation in sunshine intensity from 7 to 22 per cent. Occurring over periods of about 100,000 years, they help to set the duration of ice ages. These and other variations, concerning the tilt of the Earth's axis, together constitute the Milankovitch Effect, which in the 1970s was shown to be the pacemaker in the recent series of ice ages.

It was therefore somewhat shocking to learn that chaos can alter the Earth's orbit even more drastically. Apparently the eccentricity can sometimes increase to a point where the distance from the Sun varies by 27 million kilometres between seasons. That means that the annual sunshine variation can reach an amazing 44 per cent, compared with 7 per cent at present.

Chaotic variations in the Earth's orbit must have had remarkable consequences for the Earth's climate. But with chaos you can never say when something will happen, or when it happened before. So it is now up to geologists to look for past changes of climate occurring at intervals of a few million years, to find the chaos retrospectively.

▶ *For more about complex systems, see* BRAIN RHYTHMS. *For more about the Solar System and Laskar's views, see* EARTH. *For the Milankovitch Effect, see* CLIMATE CHANGE.

CLIMATE CHANGE

Shall we freeze or fry?

BERLIN AND COPENHAGEN, New York and Chicago, all sit in the chairs of glaciers gone for lunch. They keep returning, in a long succession of ice ages interrupted by warm interludes. The ice will be back some day, unless human beings figure out how to prevent it.

For most of the 20th century, the cause of the comings and goings of the ice was the top question in climate science. The fact that every so often Canada, Scandinavia and adjacent areas disappear under thick sheets of ice, with associated glaciation in mountainous regions, had been known since the 19th century. Associated effects include a big drop in sea level, windblown dust produced by the milling of rocks by glaciers, and reductions in rainfall that decimate tropical forests.

False data delayed an understanding of these nasty events. In 1909, the geologists Albrecht Penck and Eduard Brückner studied glacial relics in the Alps. They concluded that there had been just four ice ages recently, with long warm intervals in between them. For more than 60 years students learned by rote the names of the glaciations, derived from Bavarian streams: Günz, Mindel, Riss and Würm.

The chronicle was misleading, because each glaciation tended to erase the evidence of previous ones. The first sign of the error came in 1955, when Cesare Emiliani at Chicago had analysed fossils of small animals, forams, among sediments on the floor of the Caribbean Sea, gathered in a coring tube by a research ship. He found variations in the proportion of heavy oxygen atoms, oxygen-18, contained in the fossils, which he said were due to changes in the sea temperature between warm intervals and ice ages. He counted at least seven ice ages, compared with Penck and Brückner's four, but few scientists believed him.

In 1960 a Czech geologist, George Kukla, was impressed by stripy patterns in the ground exposed in brickyards. The deposits of loess—the windblown soil of the ice ages—were interrupted by dark narrow stripes due to soil remnants, which signified warm periods between the glaciations. He spent the ensuing years matching and counting the layers at 30 brickyards near Prague and Brno. By 1969, as an émigré at Columbia, Kukla was able to report that there were at least ten ice ages in the recent past.

At that time, in Cambridge, Nicholas Shackleton was measuring, as Emiliani had done, the proportion of heavy oxygen in forams from seabed cores. But he picked out just the small animals that originally lived at the bottom of the ocean. When there's a lot of ice in the world, locked up ashore, the heavy oxygen in ocean water increases. With his bottom-dwelling fossils, Shackleton thought he was measuring the changing volumes of ice, during the ice ages and warmer interludes.

In the seabed core used by Shackleton, Neil Opdyke of Columbia detected a reversal in the Earth's magnetic field about 700,000 years ago. That result, in 1973, gave the first reliable dating for the ice-age cycles and the various climatic stages seen in the cores. It was by then becoming obvious to the experts concerned that the results of their researches were likely to mesh beautifully with the Milankovitch Effect.

When the snow lies all summer

Milutin Milankovitch was a Serbian civil engineer whose hobby was the climate. In the 1920s he had refined a theory of the ice ages, from prior ideas. Antarctica is always covered with ice sheets, so the critical thing is the coming and going of ice on the more spacious landmasses of the northern hemisphere. And that depends on the warmth of summer sunshine in the north.

Is it strong enough to melt the snows of winter? The Earth slowly wobbles in its orbit over thousands of years. Its axis swivels, affecting the timing of the seasons. The planet rolls like a ship, affecting the height of the Sun in the sky. And over a slower cycle, the shape of the orbit changes, putting the Earth nearer or farther from the Sun at different seasons.

Astronomers can calculate these changes, and the combinations of the different rhythms, for the past few million years. Sometimes the Sun is relatively high and close in the northern summer, and it can blast the snow and ice away. But if the Sun is lower in the sky and farther away, the winter snow fails to melt. It lies all summer and piles up from year to year, building the ice sheets.

In 1974 a television scriptwriter was in a bind. He was preparing a multinational show about weather and climate, and he didn't want to have to say there were lots of competing theories about ice ages, when the Milankovitch Effect was on the point of being formally validated. So he did the job himself. From the latest astronomical data on the Earth's wobbles, he totted up the changing volume of ice in the world on simple assumptions, and matched it to the Shackleton curve as dated by Opdyke. His paper was published in the journal *Nature*, just five days before the TV show was transmitted.

'The arithmetical curve captures all the major variations,' the scriptwriter noted, 'and the core stages can be identified with little ambiguity.' The matches were very much better than they deserved to be unless Milankovitch was right. Some small discrepancies in dates were blamed on changes in the rate of sedimentation on the seabed, and this became the accepted explanation. Experts nowadays infer the ages of sediments from the climatic wiggles computed from astronomy.

The issue was too important to leave to a writer with a pocket calculator. Two years later Jim Hayes of Columbia and John Imbrie of Brown, together with Shackleton of Cambridge came up with a much more elaborate confirmation of Milankovitch, using further ocean-core data and a proper computer. They called their paper, 'Variations in the Earth's orbit: pacemaker of the ice ages'.

During the past 5000 years the sunshine that melts the snow on the northern lands has become progressively weaker. When the Milankovitch Effect became generally accepted as a major factor in climate change over many millennia, it seemed clear that, on that time-scale, the next ice age is imminent.

'The warm periods are much shorter than we believed originally,' Kukla said in 1974. 'They are something around 10,000 years long, and I'm sorry to say that the one we are living in now has just passed its 10,000 years' birthday. That of course means the ice age is due any time.'

Puzzles remained, especially about the sudden melting of ice at the end of each ice age, at intervals of about 100,000 years. The timing is linked to a relatively weak effect of alterations in the shape of the Earth's orbit, and there were suggestions that some other factor, such as the behaviour of ice sheets or the change in the amount of carbon dioxide in the air, is needed as an amplifier.

Fresh details on recent episodes came from ice retrieved by deep drilling into the ice sheets of Greenland and Scandinavia. By 2000, Shackleton had modified his opinion that the bottom-dwelling forams were simply gauging the total amount of ice. 'A substantial portion of the marine 100,000-year cycle that has been the object of so much attention over the past quarter of a century is, in reality, a deep-water temperature signal and not an ice volume signal.'

The explanation of ice ages was therefore under scrutiny again as the 21st century began. 'I have quit looking for one cause of the glacial–interglacial cycle,' said André Berger of the Université Catholique de Louvain. 'When you look into the climate system response, you see a lot of back-and-forth interactions; you can get lost.'

Even the belief that the next ice age is bearing down on us has been called into question. The sunshine variations of the Milankovitch Effect are less marked than during the past three ice age cycles, because the Earth's orbit is more nearly circular at present. According to Berger the present warm period is like a long one that lasted from 405,000 to 340,000 years ago. If so, it may have 50,000 years to run. Which only goes to show that climate forecasts can change far more rapidly than the climate they purport to predict.

From global cooling to global warming

In 1939 Richard Scherhag in Berlin famously concluded, from certain periodicities in the atmosphere, that cold winters in Europe would remain rare. Only gradually would they increase in frequency after the remarkable warmth of the 1930s. In the outcome, the next three European winters were the coldest for more than 50 years.

The German army was amazingly ill-prepared for its first winter in Russia in 1941–42. Scherhag is not considered to be directly to blame, and in any case there were mild episodes on the battlefront. But during bitter spells, frostbite killed or disabled 100,000 soldiers, and grease froze in the guns and tanks. The Red Army was better adapted to the cold and it stopped the Germans at the gates of Moscow.

In 1961 the UN Food and Agriculture Organization convened a conference in Rome about global cooling, and its likely effects on food supplies. Hubert Lamb of the UK Met Office dominated the meeting. As a polymath geographer, and later founder of the Climate Research Unit at East Anglia, he had a strong claim to be called the father of modern climate science. And he warned that the relatively warm conditions of the 1930s and 1940s might have lulled the human species into climatic complacency, just at a time when its population was growing rapidly, and cold and drought could hurt their food supplies.

That the climate is always changing was the chief and most reliable message from the historical research of Lamb and others. During the past 1000 years, the global climate veered between conditions probably milder than now, in a Medieval Warm Period, and the much colder circumstances of a Little Ice Age. Lamb wanted people to make allowance for possible effects of future variations in either direction, warmer or colder.

In 1964, the London magazine *New Scientist* ran a hundred articles by leading experts, about *The World in 1984*, making 20-year forecasts in many fields of science and human affairs. The meteorologists who contributed correctly foresaw the huge impact of computers and satellites on weather forecasting. But the remarks about climate change would make curious reading later, because nobody even mentioned the possibility of global warming by a man-made greenhouse effect.

Lamb's boss at the Met Office, Graham Sutton, said the issue about climate was this: did external agents such as the Sun cause the variations, or did the atmosphere spontaneously adopt various modes of motion? The head of the US weather satellite service, Fred Singer, remarked on the gratifying agreement prevalent in 1964, that extraterrestrial influences trigger effects near the ground. Singer explained that he wished to understand the climate so that we could control it, to achieve a better life. In the same mood, Roger Revelle of UC San Diego predicted that hurricanes would be suppressed by cooling the oceans. He wanted to scatter aluminium oxide dust on the water to reflect sunlight.

Remember that, in the 1960s, science and technology were gung-ho. We were on our way to the Moon, so what else could we not do? At that time, Americans proposed putting huge mirrors in orbit to warm the world with reflected sunshine. Australians considered painting their western coastline black, to promote convection and achieve rainfall in the interior desert. Russians hoped to divert Siberian rivers southward, so that a lack of fresh water outflow into the Arctic Ocean would reduce the sea-ice and warm the world.

If human beings thought they had sufficient power over Nature to change the climate on purpose, an obvious question was whether they were doing it already, without meaning to. The climate went on cooling through the 1960s and into the early 1970s. In those days, all great windstorms and floods and droughts were blamed on global cooling. Whilst Lamb thought the cooling was probably related to natural solar variations, Reid Bryson at Wisconsin attributed the cooling to man-made dust—not the sulphates of later concern but windblown dust from farms in semi-arid areas.

Lurking in the shadows was the enhanced greenhouse hypothesis. The ordinary greenhouse effect became apparent after the astronomer William Herschel in the UK discovered infrared rays in 1800. Scientists realized that molecules of water vapour, carbon dioxide and other gases in the atmosphere keep the Earth warm by absorbing infrared rays that would otherwise escape into space, in the manner of a greenhouse window.

Was it not to be expected that carbon dioxide added to the air by burning fossil fuels should enhance the warming? By the early 20th century, Svante Arrhenius at Stockholm was reasoning that the slight raising of the temperature by additional carbon dioxide could be amplified by increased evaporation of water.

Two developments helped to revive the greenhouse story in the 1970s. One was confirmation of a persistent year-by-year rise in the amount of carbon dioxide in the air, by measurements made on the summit of Mauna Loa, Hawaii. The other was the introduction into climate science of elaborate computer programs, called models, similar to those being used with increasing success in daily weather forecasting.

The models had to be tweaked, even to simulate the present climate, but you could run them for simulated years or centuries and see what happened if you changed various factors. Syukuro Manabe of the Geophysical Fluid Dynamics

Laboratory at Princeton was the leading pioneer. Making some simplifying assumptions about how the climate system worked Manabe calculated the consequences if carbon dioxide doubled. Like Arrhenius before him, he could get a remarkable warming, although he warned that a very small change in cloud cover could almost cancel the effect.

Bert Bolin at Stockholm became an outspoken prophet of man-made global warming. 'There is a lot of oil and there are vast amounts of coal left, and we seem to be burning it with an ever increasing rate,' he declared in 1974. 'And if we go on doing this, in about 50 years' time the climate may be a few degrees warmer than today.'

He faced great scepticism, especially as the world still seemed to be cooling despite the rapid growth in fossil-fuel consumption. 'On balance,' Lamb wrote dismissively in 1977, 'the effect of increased carbon dioxide on climate is almost certainly in the direction of warming but is probably much smaller than the estimates which have commonly been accepted.'

Then the ever-quirky climate intervened. In the late 1970s the global temperature trend reversed and a rewarming began. A decade after that, Bolin was chairman of an Intergovernmental Panel on Climate Change. In 1990 its report *Climate Change* blamed the moderate warming of the 20th century on man-made gases, and predicted a much greater warming of 3°C in the 21st century, accompanied by rising sea-levels.

This scenario prompted the world's leaders to sign, just two years later, a climate convention promising to curb emissions of greenhouse gases. Thenceforward, someone or other blamed man-made global warming for every great windstorm, flood or drought, just as global cooling had been blamed for the same kinds of events, 20 years earlier.

Ever-more complex models

The alarm about global warming also released funds for buying more supercomputers and intensifying the climate modelling. The USA, UK, Canada, Germany, France, Japan, China and Australia were leading countries in the development of models. Bigger and better machines were always needed, to subdivide the air and ocean in finer meshes and to calculate answers spanning 100 years in a reasonable period of computing time.

As the years passed, the models became more elaborate. In the 1980s, they dealt only with possible changes in the atmosphere due to increased greenhouse gases, taking account of the effect of the land surface. By the early 1990s the very important role of the ocean was represented in 'atmosphere–ocean general circulation models' pioneered at Princeton. Changes in sea-ice also came into the picture.

Next to be added was sulphate, a common form of dust in the air, and by 2001 non-sulphate dust was coming in too. The carbon cycle, in which the ocean and the land's vegetation and soil interact with the carbon dioxide in the air, was coupled into the models at that time. Further refinements under development included changes in vegetation accompanying climate change, and more subtle aspects of air chemistry.

Such was the state of play with the largest and most comprehensive climate models. In addition there were many smaller and simplified models to explore various scenarios for the emission of greenhouse gases, or to try out new subroutines for dealing with particular elements in the natural climate system. But the modellers were in a predicament. The more realistic they tried to make their software, by adding extra features of the natural climate system, the greater the possible range of errors in the computations.

Despite the huge effort, the most conspicuous difficulty with the models was that they could give very different answers, about the intensity and rate of global warming, and about the regional consequences. In 1996, the Intergovernmental Panel promised to narrow the uncertainties in the predictions, but the reverse happened. Further studies suggested that the sensitivity of the climate to a doubling of carbon dioxide in the atmosphere could be anything from less than 1°C to more than 9°C. The grand old man of climate modelling, Syukuro Manabe, commented in 1998, 'It has become very urgent to reduce the large current uncertainty in the quantitative projection of future climate change.'

Fresh thinking in prospect

The reckoning also takes into account the natural agents of climate change, which may have warming or cooling effects. One contributor is the Sun, and there were differences of opinion about its role. After satellite measurements showed only very small variations in solar brightness, it seemed to many experts that any part played by the Sun in global warming was necessarily much less than the calculated effect of carbon dioxide and other greenhouse gases. On the other hand, solar–terrestrial physicists suggested possible mechanisms that could amplify the effects of changes in the Sun's behaviour.

The solar protagonists included experts at the Harvard-Smithsonian Center for Astrophysics, the Max-Planck-Institut für Aeronomie, Imperial College London, Leicester University and the Dansk Rumforskningsinstitut. They offered a variety of ways in which variations in the Sun's behaviour could influence the Earth's climate, via visible, infrared or ultraviolet light, via waves in the atmosphere perturbed by solar emissions, or via effects of cosmic rays. And there was no disputing that the Sun was more agitated towards the end the 20th century than it had been at the cooler start.

A chance for fresh thinking came in 2001. The USA withdrew from the negotiations about greenhouse gas emissions, while continuing to support the world's largest research effort on climate change. Donald Kennedy, editor-in-chief of *Science* magazine, protested, 'Mr. President, on this one the science is clear.'

Yet just a few months later a committee of the US National Academy of Sciences concluded: 'Because of the large and still uncertain level of natural variability inherent in the climate record and the uncertainties in the time histories of the various forcing agents (and particularly aerosols), a causal linkage between the build-up of greenhouse gases in the atmosphere and the observed climate changes during the 20th century cannot be unequivocally established.'

At least in the USA there was no longer any risk that scientists with governmental funding might feel encouraged or obliged to try to confirm a particular political message. And by the end of 2002 even the editors of *Science* felt free to admit: 'As more and more wiggles matching the waxing and waning of the Sun show up in records of past climate, researchers are grudgingly taking the Sun seriously as a factor in climate change.'

Until then the Intergovernmental Panel on Climate Change had been headed by individuals openly committed to the enhanced greenhouse hypothesis—first Bert Bolin at Stockholm and then Robert Watson at the World Bank. When Watson was deposed as chairman in 2002 he declared, 'I'm willing to stay in there, working as hard as possible, making sure the findings of the very best scientists in the world are taken seriously by government, industry and by society as a whole.' That remark illustrated both the technical complacency and the political advocacy that cost him his job.

His successor, by a vote of 76 to 49 of the participating governments, was Rajendra Pachauri of the Tata Energy Research Institute in New Delhi. 'We listen to everyone but that doesn't mean that we accept what everyone tells us,' Pachauri said. 'Ultimately this has to be an objective, fair and intellectually honest exercise. But we certainly don't prescribe any set of actions.' The Australian secretary of the panel, Geoff Love, chimed in: 'We will be trying to encourage the critical community as well as the community that believes that greenhouse is a major problem.'

▶ *The link between carbon dioxide and climate is further examined in* CARBON CYCLE. *For more about ice and climate change, see* CRYOSPHERE. *Uncertainties about the workings of the ocean appear in* OCEAN CURRENTS. *Aspects of the climatic effects of the variable Sun appear in* EARTHSHINE *and* ICE-RAFTING EVENTS. *Natural drivers of brief climate change are* EL NIÑO *and* VOLCANIC EXPLOSIONS.

CLONING

Why doing without sex carries a health warning

P UNSTERS CALLED IT AN UDDER WAY of making lambs. In 1996 at the Roslin Institute, which stands amid farmland in the lee of Edinburgh's Pentland Hills, Ian Wilmut and his colleagues used a cell from the udder of an adult ewe to fashion Dolly, the most famous sheep in the world.

They put udder cells to sleep by starving them, and then took their genes and substituted them for the genes in the nuclei of eggs from other ewes. When the genes woke up in their new surroundings they thought they were in newly fertilized eggs. More precisely, the jelly of the eggs, assisted no doubt by the experimental culture techniques, reactivated many genes that had been switched off in the udder tissue.

All the genes then got to work building new embryos. One of the manipulated eggs, reintroduced into a ewe, grew into a thriving lamb. It was a clone, virtually an identical twin, of the udder owner. Who needs rams?

Technically speaking, the Edinburgh scientists had achieved in a mammal what John Gurdon at Oxford had done with frogs from 1962 onwards, using gut cells from tadpoles. He was the first to show that the genetic material present in specialized cells produced during the development of an embryo could revert to a general, undifferentiated state. It was a matter of resetting the embryonic clock to a stage just after fertilization.

Headlines about Dolly the Sheep in February 1997 provoked a hubbub of journalists, politicians, and clerics of all religions, unprecedented in biology. Interest among the global public surpassed that aroused 40 years earlier by the launch of the first artificial satellite Sputnik-1. Within 24 hours of the news breaking, the Roslin scientists and their commercial partners PPL Therapeutics felt obliged to issue a statement: 'We do not condone any use of this technology in the cloning of humans. It would be unethical.'

Also hit-or-miss. Such experiments in animals were nearly always unsuccessful. The first formal claim of a cloned human embryo came from Advanced Cell Technology in Massachusetts in 2001. At the Roslin Institute, Wilmut was not impressed. 'It's really only a preliminary first step because the furthest that the embryo developed was to have six cells at a time when it should have had more than two hundred,' he said. 'And it had clearly already died.'

The 21st century nevertheless opened on a world where already women could participate in sex without ever conceiving, or could breed test-tube babies without coition. Might they some day produce cloned babies genetically identical with themselves or other designated adults? Whether bioethical committees and law-makers will be any wiser than individuals and their families, in deciding the rights and wrongs of reproduction, who knows?

But cloning is commonplace throughout the biosphere. The answer to a basic scientific question may therefore provide a comment on its advisability. Why do we and most other animals rely on sex to create the next generation?

The hard way to reproduce

Gurdon's cloned frog and Wilmut's cloned sheep rewound the clock of evolution a billion years to the time when only microbes inhabited the Earth. They had no option but to clone. Even now, the ordinary cells of your body are also clones, made by the repeated division of the fertilized egg with which you began. But your cells are more intricate than a bacterium's, with many more genes. The machinery for duplicating them and making sure that each daughter cell gets a full set of genes is quite complicated.

Single-celled creatures like yeasts were the first to use this modern apparatus, and some of them went on to invent sex. The machinery is an add-on to the already complicated management of cells and genes. It has to make germ cells, the precursors of eggs and sperm cells. These possess only half of the genes, and the creation of a new individual depends on egg and sperm coming together to restore the complete set of genes. If the reunion is not to result in a muddle, the allocation of genes to every germ cell must be extremely precise.

Sex can work at the genetic level only if the genes are like two full packs of cards. They have to be carefully separated when it's time to make germ cells, so that each gets a full pack, and doesn't finish up with seven jacks and no nines. That's why our own genes are duplicated, with one set from ma and the other from pa. The apparatus copies the two existing packs from a potential parent's cells, to make four in all, and then assigns a pack to each of four germ cells.

Life was exclusively female up to this moment in evolutionary history. Had it stayed all girly, even the partitioning of the genes into germ cells would not rule out self-fertilization. Reversion to cloning would be too easy. To ensure sex with another individual, fertilization had to become quite hard to accomplish.

For awkwardness' sake, invent males. Then you can generate two kinds of germ cells, eggs and sperm, and with distinctive genes you can earmark the males to produce only the sperm. Certain pieces of cellular machinery, with their own genes, have to go into female or male germ cells, but not both. Compared with all this backroom molecular engineering in ancient microbes, growing reptiles into dinosaurs or mammals into whales would be child's play.

The germ cells have to mature as viable eggs and spermatozoa. These have to be scattered and brought together. When animals enter the picture you are into structures like fallopian tubes and penises, molecular prompters like testosterone, and behavioural facilitators such as peacocks' tails and singles bars.

Sex is crazy. It's as if a manufacturer of bicycles makes the front parts in one town and the rear parts in another. He sends the two night shifts off in all directions, riding the pieces as unicycles, in the hope that a few will meet by moonlight at the roadside and maybe complete a bike or two. Aldous Huxley did not exaggerate conceptually (though, with a poet's licence, a little numerically) when he wrote:

> A million million spermatozoa
> All of them alive:
> Out of their cataclysm but one poor Noah
> Dare hope to survive.

Even in plants and animals fully equipped with the machinery for sex, the option of reverting to virgin births by self-fertilization remains open. Cloning is commonplace in plants and insects. Tulip bulbs are not seeds but bundles of tissue from a parent that will make other tulips genetically identical with itself. The aphids infesting your roses are exact genetic copies of their mother. Most cloners have recourse to sex now and again, but American whiptail lizards, *Cnemidophorus uniparens*, consist of a single clone of genetically identical females.

Why go to all the trouble?

Life without males is much simpler, so shouldn't they have been abolished long ago? Evolution is largely about the survival of genes, but in making an egg cell the mother discards half of her genes. The mating game is costly in energy and time, not to mention the peril from predators and parasites during the process, or the aggro and angst in the competition for mates.

'I have spent much of the past 20 years thinking about this problem,' John Maynard Smith at Sussex confessed in 1988, concerning the puzzle that sex presents to theorists of evolution. 'I am not sure that I know the answer.'

For a shot at an explanation, Maynard Smith imagined a lineage of cloned herrings. In the short run, he reasoned, they would outbreed other herrings, and perhaps even drive them to extinction. In the long run, the cloned herrings themselves would go extinct because the genetically identical fishes had no scope to evolve.

Evolution works with differences between individuals, which at the genetic level depend on having alternative versions of the same genes available in the breeding population. These alternatives are exactly what a clone lacks, so it will be left behind in any evolutionary race. Many biologists suppose that all species are evolving all the time—running hard like Lewis Carroll's Red Queen to stay in the same place, in competition with other species. If so, then sexless species will lose out.

The engine-and-gearbox model was Maynard Smith's name for another possible reason why sex has survived for a billion years. In two old cars, one may have a useless engine and the other a rotten gearbox, but you can make a functional car by combining the bits that continue to work. In sexual reproduction, the genes are freshly shuffled and dealt out to each new individual as a combination never tried before. There is a better chance of achieving favourable combinations than in the case of a clone.

In this vein, an experiment in artificial evolution in fruit flies, by William Rice and Adam Chippindale of UC Santa Barbara, showed sex helping to preserve good genes and shed bad genes. They predicted that a new good gene would become established more reliably by sexual reproduction than in clones. Just such an effect showed up, when they pretended that red eyes represented a favourable mutation.

The Santa Barbara experimenters increased by ten per cent the proportion of red-eyed flies used for breeding the next generation. In flies reproducing sexually, the red eyes always became progressively commoner, from generation to generation. When the scientists fooled the flies into breeding clones, the red eyes sometimes became very common but more often they died out, presumably because they remained associated with bad genes.

Sex versus disease

For William Hamilton at Oxford, clearing out bad genes was only a bonus, and insufficient to explain the survival of sexual reproduction in so many species. He became obsessed with the puzzle in the early 1980s after a spell in Michigan, where he had seen the coming of spring. Later he recalled working on the problem in a museum library in Oxford.

'Cardinals sang, puffed brilliant feathers for me on snowy trees; ruby-quilled waxwings jetted their spore- and egg-laden diarrhoea deep in my mind just as I had seen them, in the reality, in the late winter jet it to soak purple into the old snow under the foreign berry-laden purging buckthorn trees. Books, bones and birds of many kinds swooped around me.'

The mathematics and abstract reasoning that emerged from Hamilton's ruminations were more austere. He showed how disease could be the evolutionary driving force that made sex advantageous in the first place and kept it going. Without the full genetic variability available in a sexual population, clones are more vulnerable to disease agents and parasites.

A sexual species seethes with what Hamilton called dynamic polymorphism, meaning an endlessly shifting choice of variant forms of the same gene. Faced with an unlimited range of dangers old and new, from infectious agents and parasites, no individual can carry genes to provide molecular resistance against all of them. A species is more likely to survive if different disease-resistance genes, in different combinations, are shared around among individuals. That is exactly what sex can offer.

Strong support for Hamilton's theory of sex versus disease came with the reading of genomes, the complete sets of genetic material carried by organisms. By 2000, in the weed arabidopsis, 150 genes for disease resistance were identified. Joy Bergelson and her colleagues at Chicago reported that the ages of the genes and their distributions between individuals provided the first direct evidence for Hamilton's dynamic polymorphism.

His theory also fits well with animal behaviour that promotes genetic diversity by assisting out-breeding in preference to inbreeding. Unrelated children brought up together in close quarters, for example in an Israeli kibbutz, very seldom mate when grown up. It seems that aversion to incest is somehow programmed by childhood propinquity. And inbred laboratory mice prefer to mate with a mouse that is genetically different. They can tell by the incomer's smell.

The mechanisms of sex that improve protection against diseases in general have provided opportunities for particular viruses, bacteria and parasites to operate as sexually transmitted diseases. To a long list of such hangers-on (Hamilton's word) the 20th century added AIDS. The sage of Oxford saw confirmation of his ideas in the eight per cent or so of individuals who by chance have inherited built-in resistance to AIDS. They never contract the disease, no matter how often they are exposed to it.

In pursuing his passion, Hamilton himself succumbed to the malaria parasite in 2000, at the age of 63. He had gone to Africa to collect chimpanzee faeces. Playing the forensic biologist, he was investigating a reporter's claim that AIDS arose in trials of polio vaccines created in chimpanzee cells that carried an HIV-like virus. He never delivered an opinion. After his death new evidence, presented at a London meeting that Hamilton had planned, seemed to refute the allegation.

● Sharing out the safety copies

Mother Nature probably invented the cellular machinery for sex only once in 4 billion years of life. In molecular detail it is similar everywhere. There could of course have been many failed attempts. But all sexual species of today may be direct descendants of a solitary gang of unicellular swingers living in the Proterozoic sea.

The fossil record of a billion years ago is too skimpy to help much. Much more promising is the evolutionary story reconstructed from similarities and differences between genes and proteins in living organisms from bacteria to mammals. Kinship between cellular sexual machinery in modern creatures and certain molecules in the sexless forebears, represented by surviving microbes, may eventually nail down what really happened. Meanwhile various scenarios are on offer.

Maynard Smith at Sussex joined with Eörs Szathmáry of the Institute for Advanced Study in Budapest in relating the origin of sex to the management of safety copies of the genes. All organisms routinely repair damaged genes. This is possible only if duplicates of the genes exist, which the repair mechanisms can copy.

There is the fundamental reason why we have double sets of gene-carrying chromosomes, with broadly similar cargoes of genes. But they are an encumbrance, especially for small, single-celled creatures wanting to grow quickly. Some yeasts alive today temporarily shed one of the duplicate sets, and rely on their chums for safety copies.

The resulting half-cell grows more quickly, but it pays a price in not being able to repair genetic damage. Every so often it fuses with another half-cell, becoming a whole-cell for a few generations and then splitting again. In this yeasty whole–half alternation, Maynard Smith and Szathmáry saw a cellular dress rehearsal for the division into germ cells and their sexual reunion.

Lynn Margulis at Boston described the origin of sex as cannibalism, in which one cell engulfed another and elected to preserve its genes. No matter how her hypothesis for the origin of sex will fare in future evaluation, it carried with it one of the best one-liners of 20th-century science. Margulis said, 'Death was the first sexually transmitted disease.'

The endless shuffling of the genetic pack by which sex makes novel individuals can continue only if older individuals quit the scene to leave room for the newcomers. A clone's collection of genes is in an approximate sense immortal. The unique combination of genes defining each sexy individual dies with it, never to be repeated. It is from this evolutionary perspective that fundamental science may most aptly comment on the possible cloning of human beings.

The medical use of cloned tissue to prolong an individual's life by a few years is biologically little different from antibiotics or heart surgery, whatever ethical misgivings there may be about the technique. But any quest for genetic immortality, of the kind implied in the engineering of one's infant identical twin or the mass-production of a fine footballer, runs counter to a billion years of natural wisdom accumulated in worms, dinosaurs and sheep. The verdict is that, for better or worse, males and natural gene shuffling are worth the trouble in the long run.

Abuse of the system may be self-correcting. Any protracted exercise in human cloning will carry a health warning, and not only because Dolly the Sheep herself aged prematurely and died young. In line with Hamilton's theory of sex versus disease, a single strain of people could be snuffed out by a single strain of a virus. So spare a thought for the female-only American whiptail lizards, which already face that risk.

▶ *For related subjects, see* EVOLUTION, IMMORTALITY *and* PLANT DISEASES. *For more about cell division, see* CELL CYCLE.

COMETS AND ASTEROIDS
Snowy dirtballs and their rocky cousins

'**C** OMETS ARE IMPOSTORS,' declared the American astronomer Fred Whipple. 'You see this great mass of dust and gas shining in the sunlight, but the real comet is just a snowball down at the centre, which you never see at all.'

The dusty and gassy tails of comets, which can stream for 100 million kilometres or more across the sky, provoked awe and fright in previous generations. In AD 840 the Chinese emperor declared them top secret. On the Bayeux Tapestry an apparition of Halley's Comet in 1066 looks like the Devil's spaceship and plainly portends doom for an Anglo-Saxon king.

Isaac Newton started to allay superstitions 300 years ago, by identifying comets as 'planets of a sort, revolving in orbits that return into themselves'. Very soon after, Newton's crony Edmond Halley was pointing out a rational reason for anxiety. Comets could collide with the Earth. This enabled prophets of doom to give a scientific coloration to their forebodings. By the late 20th century concern about cosmic impacts, by comets or more probably by the less showy 'planets of a sort' called asteroids, had official approval in several countries.

In 1932 Ernst Öpik of Tartu, Estonia, reasoned that a distant cloud of comets had surrounded the Sun since the birth of the Solar System. In 1950, Jan Oort of Leiden revived the idea and emphasized that passing stars could, by their gravity, dislodge some of the comets and send them tumbling into the heart of the Solar System. The huge, invisible population of primordial comets, extending perhaps a light-year into space, came to be known as the Oort Cloud.

Also in 1950–51, Whipple of Harvard rolled out his dirty-snowball hypothesis. Comets that return periodically, like Halley's Comet, are not strictly punctual in their appearances, according to the law of gravitation controlling their orbits. That gave Whipple a clue to their nature. He explained the discrepancies by the rocket effect of dust and gas released by the warmth of the Sun from a small spinning ball—an icy conglomerate rich in dust. The ice is a mixture of water ice and frozen carbon dioxide, methane, ammonia and so forth.

● Halley's Comet in close-up

After a flotilla of spacecraft, Soviet, Japanese and European, intercepted Halley's Comet during its visit to the Sun in 1986, many reports said that the dirty-snowball hypothesis was confirmed. This was not quite correct. The European Space Agency's spacecraft Giotto flew closest to the comet's nucleus, passing within 600 kilometres. Dust from the comet damaged Giotto and knocked out its camera when it was still 2000 kilometres away, yet it obtained by far the best images of the nucleus of Halley's Comet.

The pictures showed a very dark, potato-like object 15 kilometres long, with jets of dust and vapour coming from isolated spots on the sunlit side. Whipple himself predicted the dark colouring, due to a coating of dust on top of the ice, and dirty-snowball fans echoed this interpretation. But after examining more than 2300 images, the man responsible for Giotto's camera told a different story.

'No icy surface was visible,' said Uwe Keller of Germany's Max-Planck-Institut für Aeronomie. 'The physical structure is dominated by the matrix of the non-volatile material.' In other words, Halley's Comet was not a dirty snowball, but a snowy dirtball.

This was no quibble. The distinction was like that between a chocolate sorbet and a chocolate cake, just out of the freezer. Both contain ice, but one will disintegrate totally on warming while the other will remain recognizably a cake. Similarly an object like Halley's Comet might survive as a dark, tailless entity when all of its ice had vaporized during repeated visits to the Sun. It would then be called an asteroid.

Whipple himself had foreseen such a possibility. Some of the dust strewn by a comet's tail collides with the Earth if it crosses the comet's orbit, and it appears as annual showers of meteors, or shooting stars. In 1983 Whipple pointed out that a well-known shower in December, called the Geminids, was associated, not with a comet, but with the asteroid Phaeton—which might therefore be a comet recently defunct, but remaining intact.

When the US spacecraft Deep Space 1 observed Comet Borrelly's nucleus in 2001 it too saw a black, relatively warm surface completely devoid of ices. The ices known to be present are hidden beneath black deposits, probably mainly carbon compounds, coating the surface.

Kicking over the boxes

To some experts, the idea of a link between comets and asteroids seemed repugnant. Since the first asteroid, Ceres, was discovered by Giuseppe Piazzi of Palermo in 1801, evidence piled up that asteroids were stony objects, sometimes containing metallic iron. They were mostly confined to the Asteroid Belt beyond Mars, where they went in procession around the Sun in well-behaved, nearly circular orbits.

Two centuries after Piazzi's discovery the count of known objects in the Asteroid Belt had risen past the 40,000 mark. In 1996–97, Europe's Infrared Space Observatory picked out objects not seen by visible light. As a result, astronomers calculated that more than a million objects of a kilometre in diameter or larger populate the Belt. Close-up pictures from other spacecraft showed the asteroids to be rocky objects, probably quite typical of the material that was assembled in the building of the Earth and Mars.

What could be more different from the icy comets? When they are not confined to distant swarms, comets dash through the inner Solar System in all directions and sometimes, like Halley's Comet, go the wrong way around the Sun—in the opposite sense to which the planets revolve.

'Scientists have a strong urge to place Mother Nature's objects into neat boxes,' Donald Yeomans of NASA's Jet Propulsion Laboratory commented in 2000. 'Within the past few years, however, Mother Nature has kicked over the boxes entirely, spilling the contents and demanding that scientists recognize crossover objects—asteroids that behave like comets, and comets that behave like asteroids.'

Besides Phaeton, and other asteroidal candidates to be dead comets, Yeomans' crossover objects included three objects that astronomers had classified both as asteroids and comets. These were Chiron, orbiting between Saturn and Uranus, Comet Wilson–Harrington on an eccentric orbit, and Comet Elst–Pizarro within the Asteroid Belt. In 1998 a stony meteorite—supposedly a piece of an asteroid—fell in Monahans, Texas, and was found to contain salt water. Confusion grew with the discovery in 1999 of two asteroids going the wrong way around the Sun, supposedly a prerogative of comets.

Meanwhile the remote planet Pluto turned out to be comet-like. Pluto is smaller than the Earth's Moon, and has a moon of its own, Charon. When its eccentric orbit brings it a little nearer to the Sun than Neptune, as it did between 1979 and 1999, frozen gases on its surface vaporize in the manner of a comet—albeit with unusual ingredients, mainly nitrogen. For reasons of scientific history, the International Astronomical Union nevertheless decided to go on calling Pluto a major planet.

In 1992, from Mauna Kea, David Jewitt of Hawaii and Jane Luu of UC Berkeley spotted the first of many other bodies in Pluto's realm. Orbiting farther from the Sun than the most distant large planet, Neptune, these transneptunian objects are members of the Edgeworth–Kuiper Belt, named after astronomers who speculated about their existence around 1950.

Some 300 transneptunians were known by the end of the century. There were estimated to be perhaps 100,000 small Pluto-like objects in the belt, and a billion ordinary comets. If so, both in numbers and total mass, the new belt far surpasses what has hitherto been called the main Asteroid Belt between Mars and Jupiter.

'These discoveries are something we could barely have guessed at just a decade ago,' said Alan Stern of the Southwest Research Institute, Colorado. 'They are so fundamental that basic texts in astronomy will require revision.' One early inference was that comets now on fairly small orbits around the Sun did not originate from the Oort Cloud, as previously supposed, but from the much closer Edgeworth–Kuiper Belt. These comets may be the products of collisions in the belt, as may Pluto and Charon. A large moon of Neptune, called Triton, could have originated there too.

Hundreds of sungrazers

Another swarm of objects made the SOHO spacecraft the most prolific discoverer of comets in the history of astronomy. Launched in 1995, as a joint venture of the European Space Agency and NASA to examine the Sun, SOHO carried two instruments well adapted to spotting comets. One was the French–Finnish SWAN, looking at hydrogen atoms in the Solar System lit by the Sun's ultraviolet rays. It saw comets as clouds of hydrogen, made by the decomposition of water vapour that they released.

The hydrogen cloud around the big Comet Hale–Bopp in 1997 grew to be 100 million kilometres wide. Water vapour was escaping from the comet's nucleus at a rate of up to 50 million tonnes a day. SWAN on SOHO also detected the break-up of Comet Linear in 2000, before observers on the ground reported the event.

The big comet count came from another instrument on SOHO, called LASCO, developed under US leadership. Masking the direct rays of the Sun, it kept a constant watch on a huge volume of space around it, looking out primarily for solar eruptions. But it also saw comets when they crossed the Earth–Sun line, or flew very close to the Sun.

A charming feature of the SOHO comet watch was that amateur astronomers all around the world could discover new comets, not by shivering all night in their gardens but by checking the latest images from LASCO. These were freely available on the Internet. And there were hundreds to be found, most of them small 'sungrazing' comets, all coming from the same direction. They perished in encounters with the solar atmosphere, but they were related to larger objects on similar orbits that did survive, including the Great September Comet (1882) and Comet Ikeya–Seki (1965).

'SOHO is seeing fragments from the gradual break-up of a great comet, perhaps the one that the Greek astronomer Ephorus saw in 372 BC,' explained Brian Marsden of the Center for Astrophysics in Cambridge, Massachusetts. 'Ephorus reported that the comet split in two. This fits with my calculation that two comets on similar orbits revisited the Sun around AD 1100. They split again and again, producing the sungrazer family, all still coming from the same direction.'

The progenitor of the sungrazers must have been enormous, perhaps 100 kilometres in diameter or a thousand times more massive than Halley's Comet. Not an object you'd want the Earth to tangle with. Yet its most numerous offspring, the SOHO–LASCO comets, are estimated to be typically only about 10 metres in diameter.

Astronomers and space scientists thus entered the 21st century with a new appreciation of diversity among the small bodies of the Solar System. There were quite different kinds of comets originating in different regions and circumstances, and asteroids and hybrids of every description. These greatly complicated, or enriched, the interpretation of comets, asteroids and meteorites as samples of materials left over from the construction of the planets. For those anxious about possible collisions with the Earth, the nature of an impactor could vary from flimsy Whipple sorbet or a crumbly Keller cake, to a solid mountain of stone and iron.

Waltzing with a comet

Both fundamental science and considerations of security therefore motivated new space missions. Spacecraft heading for other destinations obtained opportunistic pictures of asteroids accessible en route, and NASA's Galileo detected a magnetic field around the asteroid Gaspra in 1991. The first dedicated mission to an asteroid was the American NEAR Shoemaker launched in 1996. In 2000 it went into orbit around Eros, which circles the Sun just outside the Earth's orbit, and in

2001 it landed, sending back close-up pictures during the descent. Eros turned out to be a rocky object with a density and composition similar to the Earth's crust, apparently produced by the break-up of a larger body.

US space missions to comets include Stardust (1999), intended to fly through the dust cloud of Comet Wild, to gather samples of the dust and return them to Earth for analysis, in 2006. A spacecraft called Contour, intended to compare Comet Encke and the recently broken-up Schwassmann–Wachmann 3, was lost soon after launch in 2002, but Deep Impact (2004) is expected to shoot a 370-kilogram mass of copper into the nucleus of Comet Tempel 1, producing a crater perhaps as big as a football field. The outburst, visible in telescopes at the Earth on the Fourth of July 2005, should reveal materials excavated from deep below the comet's crust.

The deluxe comet project, craved by experts since the start of the Space Age, is Europe's Rosetta. It faces a long, circuitous journey that should enable it to go into orbit around the nucleus of a comet far out in space, during the second decade of the century. Then Rosetta is due to waltz with the comet for many months while it nears the Sun. Exactly how a comet brews up, with its emissions of dust and gas, will be observable at close quarters.

Rosetta will also drop an instrumented lander on the comet's surface. Named after the Rosetta Stone that deciphered Egyptian hieroglyphs, the project is intended to clarify the nature of comets and their relationship to planets and asteroids. The chief interest of many of the scientists in the Rosetta team concerns the precise composition of the comet.

'By the time the difficult space operations are completed, Rosetta will have taken 20 years since its conception,' said Hans Balsiger of Bern. 'Digesting the results may take another ten years after that. Why do we commit ourselves, and our young colleagues, to such a long and taxing project? To know what no one ever knew before. A complete list of the contents of a comet will tell us what solid and volatile materials were available when the Sun was young, for building the ground we stand on, the water we drink, and the gas we breathe today.'

Looking for the dangerous one

Fundamental science has strong motives, then, for research on the small bodies of the Solar System, but what about the issue of planetary security? A systematic search for near-Earth objects, meaning asteroids and comets that cross the Earth's orbit or come uncomfortably close, was instituted by Eugene Shoemaker and Eleanor Helin in the 1970s, using a small telescope on Palomar mountain, California. 'Practically 19th-century science,' Shoemaker called it.

Craters on the Earth, the Moon and almost every solid surface in the Solar System testify to cosmic traffic accidents involving comets and asteroids. They were for long a favourite theme for movie-makers, but it was a real collision that persuaded the political world to take the risk seriously. This was Comet Shoemaker–Levy 9, which broke into fragments that fell one after another onto Jupiter, in 1994.

The event was a spectacular demonstration of what Shoemaker and others had asserted for decades previously, that it's still business as usual for impacts in the Solar System. The searching effort increased and techniques improved. By the century's end about 1000 near-Earth objects were known.

Various false alarms in the media about a foreseeable risk of collision with our planet forced the asteroid-hunters to agree to be more cautious about crying wolf. At the time of writing, only one object gives persistent grounds for concern. This is 1950 DA, which has been tracked by radar as well as by visible light. According to experts at NASA's Jet Propulsion Laboratory, there is conceivably up to one chance in 300 that this asteroid will hit the Earth in the year 2880. As 1950 DA is one kilometre wide, the impact would have the explosive force of many thousands of H-bombs.

Also running to many thousands is the likely count of near-Earth objects remaining to be discovered. A sharp reminder of the difficulties came with a very small asteroid, 2002 MN, a 100-metre rock travelling at a relative speed of 10 kilometres per second. Despite all the increased vigilance, it was not spotted until after it had passed within 120,000 kilometres of the Earth. That was less than a third of the distance of the Moon, and in astronomical terms counts as a very close shave.

Even if it had been much bigger, astronomers would not have seen 2002 MN coming. It arrived from the sunny side. Its unseen approach advertised the need to look for near-Earth objects from a new angle. An opportunity comes with plans to install an asteroid-hunting telescope on a spacecraft destined for the planet Mercury, close to the Sun.

The main planetary orbiter of Europe's BepiColombo project, due to be launched in 2011, will carry the telescope. By repeatedly scanning a strip around the sky, while orbiting Mercury, the telescope should have dozens of asteroids in view at any one time. Besides enabling scientists to reassess the near-Earth objects in general, it may reveal a previously unseen class of asteroids.

'There are potentially hazardous objects with orbits almost completely inside the Earth's, many of which still await discovery,' said Andrea Carusi of Rome. 'These asteroids are difficult to observe from the ground. But looking outwards from its special viewpoint at Mercury, deep inside the Earth's orbit, BepiColombo will see them easily, against a dark sky.'

What can be done?

A frequent proposal for dealing with a comet or asteroid, if one should be seen to be due to hit the Earth, is to deflect it or fragment it with nuclear bombs.

Another suggested remedy is to paint a threatening asteroid a different colour, with rocket-loads of soot or chalk. That would alter weak but persistent forces due to heat rays emitted from the object, which slowly affect its orbit.

The painting proposal highlights a difficulty in long-term predictions of an asteroid's orbit. Unless you know exactly how it is rotating, and how its rotation may change in future, the effect of thermal radiation on the object's motions is not calculable. Other uncertainties arise from chaos, which means in this context the incalculable consequences of effects of gravity when disturbances due to more than one other body are involved. Chaos can make predictions of some near-Earth asteroids questionable after just half a century.

Time is the problem. Preparing and implementing countermeasures may take decades. If an object appears just weeks before impact, there may be nothing to be done, at least until such time as the world elects to spend large sums on a space navy permanently on guard. No one wants to be fatalistic about impacts, but those who say that the present emphasis should be on preparing global food stocks, and on civil defence including shoreline evacuation plans, have a case.

▶ *For the Earth's past encounters with comets and asteroids, see* IMPACTS, EXTINCTIONS *and* FLOOD BASALTS. *For the theory that the Moon was born in a collision, see* EARTH, *which also includes more general information about the Solar System. For the role of comets in pre-life chemistry, see* LIFE'S ORIGIN.

CONTINENTS AND SUPERCONTINENTS

Collage-making since the world began

FROM THE SITE OF ANCIENT TROY in the west to Mount Ararat in the east, it's hard to find much flat ground in Turkey. The jumble of mountain ranges confused geologists until the confirmation of continental drift, in the 1960s, opened the way to a modern interpretation. The rugged terrain is the product of microcontinents that blundered into the southern shore of Eurasia.

By 1990, Celal Sengor of Istanbul Technical University was able to summarize key encounters that assembled most of Turkey's territory 90 million years ago. 'The Menderes–Taurus block, now in western and southern Turkey, collided with the Arabian platform and became smothered by oceanic rocks pushed over it from the north,' he explained, 'while a corner of the Kirsehir block (central Turkey) hit the Rhodope–Pontide fragment and began to rotate around this pivot in a counterclockwise sense.'

The details don't matter as much as the flavour of the new ultramobile geology. Sengor was one of its pioneers, alongside his former doctoral adviser, the British geologist John Dewey. Putting the idea simply: you can take a knife to a map of the world's continents, and cut it up along the lines of mountain ranges. You then have pieces for a collage that can be rearranged quite differently, to depict earlier continents and supercontinents.

The part that collisions between continents play in mountain building is most graphic in the Himalayas and adjacent chains, made by the Indian subcontinent running into Eurasia. The first encounter began about 70 million years ago and India's northward motion continues to this day. You'll find the remains of oceanic islands caught up in the collision that are standing on edge amid the rocky wreckage. Satellite images show enormous faults on the Asian side where pieces are being pushed horizontally out of the way, like the pips of a squeezed lemon.

A similar situation in the Alps inspired Eduard Suess in Vienna in the late 19th century to lay the foundations of modern tectonics. He explained the formation of structures in the Earth's crust by horizontal movements of land masses. In the Alps he saw the traces of a vanished ocean, which formerly separated Italy and the Adriatic region from Switzerland and Austria.

Suess named the lost ocean Tethys. As for the source of the continental fragments, which came from seaward and slammed into Eurasia, he called it Gondwana-Land. By that he meant an association of the southern continents, which had much fossil life in common but which are now separated. Expressed in his *Antlitz der Erde* (three volumes, 1885–1901), Suess's ideas were far ahead of his time, and Alfred Wegener in Germany adopted many of them in his theory of continental drift. In Wegener's conception, Suess's Gondwana-Land was at one time joined also with the northern continents in a single supercontinent, Pangaea.

In modern reconstructions Pangaea was real enough, though short-lived, having itself been assembled by collisions of pre-existing continental fragments. Tethys was like a big wedge of ocean driven into the heart of Pangaea, from the east. Continental material rifted from Gondwana-Land on the ocean's southern shoreline and ran north to Eurasia, in two waves, making Tethyside provinces that extend from southern France via Turkey and Iran to southern China.

For Sengor, what happened in his homeland was just a small part of a much bigger picture. By pooling information from many sources to make elaborate maps of past continental positions, he traced the origin of the Tethysides, fragment by fragment. He saw them as a prime example of continent building by a rearrangement of existing pieces.

In the 1990s Sengor turned his attention to the processes that create completely new continental crust, by the transformation of dense oceanic crust into more buoyant material. It happens when an old ocean floor dives into the interior at an ocean trench, and the grinding action makes granite domes and volcanic outbursts. Accretions to the western sides of the Americas, from Alaska to the Andes, exemplify continental growth in progress today.

Sengor concluded that in Eurasia new crust was created on a huge scale in that way, as additions to a Siberian core starting around 300 million years ago. The regions include the Ural Mountains of Russia and a swath of Central Asia reaching to Mongolia and beyond. Again following Suess, Sengor called them the Altaids, after the magnificent Altai mountain range that runs from Kazakhstan to China.

'The Tethysides and the Altaids cover nearly a half of the entire continent of Eurasia,' Sengor noted. 'They are extremely long-lived collisional mountain belts with completely different ways of operating a continental crust factory.'

A series of supercontinents

The contrast between oceanic and continental crust, which is seldom ambiguous, is the most fundamental feature of the planet Earth's lively geology. The lithosphere, as geologists prefer to call the crust and subcrust nowadays, is 0–100 kilometres thick under the oceans, and 50–200 kilometres thick under the continents. Beneath it is a slushy, semi-molten asthenosphere lubricating the sideways motions of the lithosphere. Like a cracked eggshell, the lithosphere is split into various plates.

Whilst the heavy, relatively young rocks of the oceanic lithosphere are almost rigid, continents are crumbly. They can be easily squashed into folded mountains, and sheared to fit more tightly together. Or they can be stretched to make rift valleys and wide sedimentary basins, where the lithosphere sags and fills with thick deposits, making new rocks. With sufficient tension a continent breaks apart to let a new ocean form between the pieces. The Red Sea is an incipient ocean that opened between Africa and Arabia very recently in geological time.

Continents are like the less-dense oxidized slag that floats on newly smelted metal, and they are propelled almost at random by the growth and shrinkage of intervening oceans. The dense lithosphere of the ocean floor sinks back into the Earth under its own weight, when it cools, and completely renews itself every 200 million years. But continents are unsinkable, and when they collide they have nowhere to go but upwards or sideways.

Moving in any direction on the sphere of the Earth, a continent will sooner or later bump into another. Such impacts are more severe than the process of accretion from recycled ocean floor, in Andean or Altaid fashion. The scrambling and shattering that results leaves the continental material full of fault lines and other weaknesses that may be the scenes of later rifting, or of long-range sliding of pieces of continents past each other. The damage also makes life hard for geologists trying to identify the pieces of old collages.

Reconstructing the supercontinent of Pangaea was relatively easy, once geologists had overcome their inhibitions about continental drift. The match in shape between the concave eastern seaboard of North America and the bulge of Morocco, and the way convex Brazil fits neatly into the corner of West Africa, had struck many people since the first decent maps of the world became available in the 16th century. So you fit those back together, abolishing the Atlantic Ocean, and the job is half-done.

East of Africa it's trickier, because Antarctica, India and Australia could fit together in old Gondwana-Land in various ways. Alan Smith at Cambridge combined data about matching rock types, magnetism, fossils and climatic evidence, and juggled pieces by computer to minimize gaps, in order to produce the first modern map of Pangaea by 1970. Ten years later he had a series of maps, and movies too, showing not only how Pangaea broke up but also how it was assembled, from free-ranging North America, Siberia and Europe piling up on Gondwana-Land. All of these continents were curiously strung out around the Equator some 500 million years ago, Smith concluded.

By then he had competition from Christopher Scotese, who started as an undergraduate in the mid-1970s by making flip books that animated continental movements. At Chicago, and later at Texas-Arlington, Scotese devoted his career to palaeogeography. By 1997, in collaboration with Stuart McKerrow at Oxford and Damien Nance at Ohio, he had pushed the mapping back to 650 million years ago.

That period, known to geologists as the Vendian, was a crucial time in Earth history. The first many-celled animals—soft-bodied jellyfish, sea pens and worms—made their debut then. It was a time when a prior supercontinent, Pannotia, was beginning to break up. The Earth was also going through periods of intense cold, when much of the land and ocean was lost under ice. The Vendian map shows Antarctica straddling the Equator, while Amazonia, West Africa and Florida are crowded together near the South Pole.

'Maps such as these are at best a milestone, a progress report, describing our current state of knowledge and prejudice,' Scotese commented in 1998, when introducing his latest palaeogeographic atlas. 'In many respects these maps are already out-of-date.' Because geological knowledge improves all the time, the map-maker's work is never done. The offerings are a stimulus—a challenge even—to others, to relate the geology of regions and periods under study to the global picture, and to confirm or modify what the maps suggest.

The mapping has still to be extended much farther back in time. The Earth is 4550 million years old, and scraps of continental material survive from 3800 million years ago, when an intense bombardment by comets and asteroids ended. Before Pangaea of 200 million years ago, and Pannotia of 800 million years ago, there are rumours of previous supercontinents 1100, 1500 and 2300 million years ago. Rodinia, Amazonia and Kenora are names on offer, but the evidence for them becomes ever more scrambled and confused, the farther back in time one goes.

A small collage called Europe

A different approach to the history of the continents is to see how the present ones were put together, over the entire span of geological time. Most thoroughly studied so far is Europe, where the collage is particularly intricate. The small subcontinent has been in the front line of so many collisions and ruptures that it has the most varied landscapes on Earth.

The nucleus on which Europe grew was a crumb of ancient continental rock formed around 3000 million years ago and surviving today in the far north of Finland and nearby Russia. On it grew the Baltic Shield, completed by 1000 million years ago and including Russia's Kola region, plus Finland and Sweden. A series of handshakes with bits of Greenland and North America were involved in the Baltic Shield's construction.

Growth continued as a result of subsequent collisions. Europe became welded to Greenland and North America in the Caledonian mountain-building events of about 570 million years ago. Norway, northern Germany and most of the territory of the British Isles came into being at that time. The next big collision, about 350 million years ago, was with Gondwana-Land, in the Hercynian events. These created the basements of southernmost Ireland and England, together with much of Spain, France, central and southern Germany, the Czech Republic, Slovakia and south-west Poland, plus early pieces of the Alps. Then, starting 170 million years ago, came the Tethysides, with the islands from Gondwana-Land slamming into Europe's southern flank from Spain to Bulgaria.

This summary conceals many details of the history, like the Hercynian forests of Germany that laid down great coal reserves, the rifting of the North Sea where oil gathered, and an extraordinary phase when the Mediterranean Sea dried out as a result of the blockage of its link to the Atlantic, leaving thick deposits of salt. Rotation of blocks is another theme. Spain, for example, used to be tucked up against south-west France, until it opened like a door 90 million years ago and created the Bay of Biscay as an extension of the newly growing Atlantic Ocean.

Also missing from a simple list of collisions are the great sideslips, analogous to those seen behind the Himalayas today. Northern Poland, for example, was in the forefront of the collision with Canada during the Caledonian events, but then it slid away eastwards for 2000 kilometres along a Trans-European Fault. Northernmost Scotland arrived at its present position from Norway, after a comparable journey to the south-west. In that case the fault line is still visible in Loch Ness and the Great Glen, and in a corresponding valley in Newfoundland.

A 3-D view of the European collage came from seismic soundings, using man-made explosions to generate miniature earthquakes, the echoes of which reveal deep-lying layers of the lithosphere. The effort started in earnest in Scandinavia in the 1970s, and continued in the European Geotraverse, 1982–90, which made soundings all the way from Norway's North Cape, across the Alps and the Mediterranean, to Africa. It showed thick crust under the ancient Baltic Shield becoming thinner under Germany, and thickest immediately under the Alps. The first transition from thick to thin crust corresponds with the Trans-European faulting already mentioned.

With the ending of the Cold War, the investigation was extended east–west in the Europrobe project. An ambitious seismic experiment, called Celebration 2000, involved 147 large explosions and 1230 recording stations scattered from western Russia across Belarus, Poland, Slovakia, Hungary, Austria and the Czech Republic to south-east Germany, exploring to a depth of about 100 kilometres.

'What we learn about the history and processes of the lithosphere under our feet in Europe will help us to understand many other places in the world, from the Arctic to Antarctica,' said Aleksander Guterch of the Polish Academy of Sciences. 'Sedimentary basins, for example, play a crucial role in the evolution of continents, as depressions in the crust where thick deposits accumulate over many millions of years. Some sedimentary basins in Europe are obvious, but others are hidden until we find them by seismic probing.'

And the next supercontinent?

Global seismic networks look deeper into the Earth, using waves from natural earthquakes, and they give yet another picture of continental history. In particular, they reveal traces of the ocean-floor lithosphere that disappeared during the shrinkage of oceans between continents. The down-going slabs appear to the seismologists as relatively cool rocks within the hot mantle of the Earth.

Pieces of an ancient Pacific ocean floor, swallowed up in the westward motion of North America during the past 60 million years, are now found deep below the Great Lakes and even New England. Under Asia, by contrast, old oceanic slabs still lie roughly below the scenes of their disappearance. For example, about 150 million years ago the island continents of Mongolia–China and Omolon (the eastern tip of Siberia) both collided with mainland Siberia, which was already sutured to Europe along the line of the Ural Mountains. The impacts of the new pieces made hook-shaped mountain ranges, which run east from Lake Baikal to the sea, and then north through the Verkhoyansk range.

The graveyard of slabs consumed in these collisions record part of the slow work of assembling the next supercontinent around Eurasia, which is essentially stationary just now. Africa is alongside already. Perhaps Australia and the Americas will rejoin the throng during the next 100 million years.

▶ *For more about seismic probing of the interior, and about the machinery that drives the continents around, see* PLATE MOTIONS. *For effects of continental drift on animal evolution, see* DINOSAURS *and* MAMMALS.

COSMIC RAYS

Where do the punchiest particles come from?

A BOVE ARID SCRUBLAND in Mendoza province of western Argentina, near the Andes Mountains, an energetic subatomic particle coming from the depths of the Universe slammed into the air in the early hours of 8 December 2001. A telescope of a special type called a fly's eye, because of its many detectors, saw blue light fanning across the sky. The light came from a shower of new particles created by the impact. Streaking towards the Earth, they provoked nitrogen molecules to glow. When they reached the ground, some of the particles entered widely spaced detectors that decorated the Pampa Amarilla like giant marshmallows, mystifying to the cows that grazed there.

In that moment the Auger Observatory took Argentina to the forefront of physics and astronomy, by recording its first cosmic-ray shower with instruments of both kinds. The observatory involved 250 scientists from 15 countries. It was at an early stage of construction, but one of the handy things about looking for cosmic rays of ultra-high energy is that you start seeing them as soon as some of your instruments are running.

The fly's-eye telescope that saw the fluorescence in the sky was the first of 24 such cameras. Out of 1600 ground detectors due by 2005, only a few dozen were operational at the end of 2001. With all in place, spaced at intervals of 1.5 kilometres, the detectors would cover an area of 3000 square kilometres. The Auger Observatory needed to be so big, because the events for which it would watch occur only rarely.

'We're examining the most energetic form of radiation in the Universe,' said Alberto Etchegoyen of the Centro Atomico Constituyentes in Buenos Aires. 'Perhaps it comes from near a giant black hole in the heart of another galaxy. Or it may lead us back to the Big Bang itself, as a source of superparticles that only recently changed into detectable matter.'

Also under construction, for completion in 2007, was the world's most powerful accelerator of subatomic particles: the Large Hadron Collider at CERN in Geneva. In comparison with the cosmic rays, the accelerator would create particles with an energy corresponding to 7000 billion volts, such as might have been at liberty during the Big Bang when the cooling infant Universe was still at a temperature of 10 million billion degrees. (Apologies for the big numbers, but they are what high-energy physics is all about.) The Auger Observatory would see cosmic-ray particles 10 million times more energetic, corresponding with an earlier stage of the Big Bang, far hotter still.

What did Mother Nature have in her witch's cauldron then? By sampling many ultra-high-energy particles in search of the answers, the Auger team looked to recover something of the glory of the early 20th century, when cosmic rays were at the cutting edge of subatomic physics.

On balloons and mountaintops

An inscription at a scientific centre at Erice in Sicily sums up the discovery of cosmic rays:

> *Here in the Erice maze*
> *Cosmic rays are all the craze*
> *Just because a guy named Hess*
> *When ballooning up found more not less.*

More subatomic particles, that is to say. Victor Hess, a young Austrian physicist, made ascents by hot-air balloon, in 1911–12, going eventually at no little risk to 5000 metres. He wanted to escape from the natural radioactivity on the ground, but the higher he went the faster the electric charge dispersed from the quaint but effective detector of ionizing radiation called a gold-leaf electroscope. Eminent scientists scoffed at Hess's conclusion that rays of some kind were coming from the sky, but gradually the evidence became overwhelming.

Similar scepticism greeted subsequent advances in cosmic-ray science, only to give way to vindication. The most obvious question, 'where do they come from?' remains unanswered, but there is no room left for doubting that cosmic rays link us to the Universe at large in quite intimate ways.

Female aircrew are nowadays grounded when pregnant, because cosmic rays could harm the baby's development. Even at sea level, thousands of cosmic-ray particles hit your body every second. Although they merge into the background of natural radioactivity that Hess was trying to escape, they contribute to the genetic mutations that drive evolution along—at the price of occasional malformation or cancer in individuals. Cosmic rays can cause errors and crashes in computers. They also seem to affect the weather, by aiding the formation of clouds.

Until the 1950s, cosmic-ray research was the chief source of information about the basic constituents of matter. Detectors such as cloud chambers, Geiger counters and photographic emulsions were deployed at mountaintop observatories or on unmanned balloons. The first known scrap of antimatter turned up as an anti-electron (positron) swerving the wrong way in a magnetized cloud chamber. Other landmark discoveries in the cosmic rays were heavy electrons (muons), and the mesons and strange relatives of the proton that opened the door to the eventual identification of quarks as the main ingredients of matter.

Man-made accelerators of ever-increasing power lured the physicists away from the atmospheric laboratory. By providing beams of energetic particles far more copious, predictable and controllable than the cosmic rays, the accelerators had, by the 1960s, relegated cosmic rays to a minor role in particle physics. Astronomers were still interested.

The subatomic particles in the cosmic rays seen at ground level are often short-lived, so they themselves cannot be the intruders from outer space. The primary cosmic rays are atomic nuclei that have roamed at high speed for millions of years through the Milky Way Galaxy. They wriggle through the defences set up by the magnetic fields of the Sun and the Earth, and hit the nuclei of atoms of the upper air. Their impacts create cone-shaped showers of particles of many kinds rushing groundwards.

The Sun's fight with the cosmic rays preoccupied many space scientists. Satellites detect the primary cosmic rays before they hit the Earth's atmosphere and blow up, but deflections by the solar shield make it difficult to pin down the source of the cosmic rays. By the time they reach the inner Solar System, the directions from which the primary particles appear bear little relation to their sources among the stars.

The typical cosmic rays from the Milky Way are about 20 million years old. Wandering in interstellar space, some of them hit atoms and make radioactive nuclei. Scientists used data on heavy cosmic-ray particles gathered by the European–US Ulysses spacecraft (1990–2004) to date the survivors, much as archaeologists use radiocarbon to find the ages of objects. Older cosmic rays have presumably leaked out of the Galaxy.

One popular hypothesis was that the commonplace cosmic rays came from the remnants of exploded stars, where shock waves might accelerate charged particles to very high energies. X-ray astronomers examined hotspots in the debris, hunting for Nature's particle accelerators. But few scientists expected to find such an obvious source for the most powerful cosmic rays.

'There is no good explanation for the production of particles of very high energy responsible for the air showers that my students and I discovered in 1938 at Jean Perrin's laboratory on the Jungfraujoch.' So declared the French physicist Pierre Auger, who is commemorated in the name of the observatory in Argentina. He made the discovery with spaced-out cosmic-ray detectors at an alpine laboratory.

A problem with microwaves

A typical primary cosmic-ray particle hitting the Earth's atmosphere has the energy equivalent to a few billion volts, and Auger's particles were a million times more energetic. In 1963 John Linsley of the University of New Mexico, who had scattered 19 detectors across 8 square kilometres of territory, reported a cosmic-ray shower produced by an incoming particle that seemed to be 100,000 times more energetic than Auger's. To put it another way, a single subatomic particle packed as much punch as a tennis ball played with vigour.

Such astonishing energy might have made particle physicists pause, before they defected from the cosmic-ray enterprise to work with accelerators. But Linsley faced scepticism, not least because of the discovery a couple of years later of radio microwaves filling cosmic space, which should strip energy from such ultra-high-energy particles before they can travel any great distance through the Universe. The fact that the most energetic events are exceedingly rare was also discouraging.

Other groups in the UK, Japan and Russia nevertheless set up their own arrays of detectors. During the next three decades, they found several more of the terrific showers. With detectors spread out across the Yorkshire moors, a team at Leeds was able to confirm that an incoming particle provoking a shower could exceed the energy limit expected from the blocking by cosmic microwaves. In Utah, from 1976 onwards, physicists used fly's-eye telescopes for seeing the blue glow of the showers on moonless nights. That provided an independent way of confirming the enormous energy of an impacting particle.

How can the ultra-high-energy cosmic rays beat the microwave barrier? One possibility is that they originate from relatively close galaxies, where the energetic cosmic rays are perhaps produced from ordinary matter by the action of giant black holes. As there is also a relatively quiet giant black hole at the heart of our own Galaxy, the Milky Way, that too is a candidate production site.

According to another hypothesis, massive particles of an exotic kind, not seen before, were generated in the Big Bang with which the Universe supposedly began. The exotic particles, so this story goes, have roamed without interacting with cosmic microwaves, for many billions of years, before deciding to decompose. Then they make ordinary but very energetic particles detectable as cosmic rays. Some theorists suggested that the exotic particles would tend to gather in a halo around the Milky Way, and there bide their time before breaking up.

The advances in observations and a choice of interesting theories prompted the decision to build the Auger Observatory. It was to be big enough to detect ultra-high-energy events at a rate of about one a week. The remote semi-desert of

Argentina was favoured as a site because of its flatness and absence of streetlights.

Each of the 1600 particle detectors needed a 12-tonne tank of water, and light detectors and radio links powered by solar panels. Cosmic-ray particles passing through the water produced flashes of light. The detectors radioed the news to a central observing station, in a technique perfected at Leeds.

Navigation satellites of the Global Positioning System helped in measuring the relative times of arrival of the particles at various detectors with high accuracy. They allowed the physicists to fix, to within a degree of arc, the direction in the sky from which the impacting particle came. Unlike ordinary cosmic rays, the ultra-high-energy particles are not significantly deflected by the magnetic fields of the Galaxy, the Sun or the Earth.

'If high-energy particles are coming from the centre of the Galaxy, or from a nearby active galaxy such as Centaurus A, we should be able to say so quite soon, perhaps even before the observatory is complete,' commented Alan Watson at Leeds, spokesman for the Auger Observatory. 'Yet one of the most puzzling features of ultra-high-energy cosmic rays is that they seem to arrive from any direction. Whatever the eventual answer about them proves to be, it's bound to be exciting, for particle physics, for astronomy, or for both.'

Other ways to look at it

The Auger Observatory was just the biggest of the projects at the start of the 21st century which were homing in on the phenomenon of ultra-high-energy cosmic rays. The use of fly's-eye fluorescence telescopes continued in Utah, and there were proposals also to watch for the blue light of the large showers from the International Space Station. Calculations suggested that a realistic instrument in space could detect several events every day.

The sources in the Universe of the ultra-high-energy cosmic rays may also produce gamma rays, which are like very energetic X-rays. Hitting the Earth's air, the gamma rays cause faint flashes of light. An array of four telescopes, called Hess after the discoverer of cosmic rays, was created in Namibia by a multinational collaboration, for pinpointing the direction of arrival of gamma rays.

Ultra-high-energy neutrinos, which are uncharged relatives of the electron, can produce flashes in seawater, in deep lakes, or in the polar ice. Pilot projects in various countries looked into the possibility of exploiting this effect. Ordinary neutrinos, coming from cosmic-ray showers in the Earth's atmosphere and from the core of the Sun, were already detected routinely in underground laboratories in deep mines. In similar settings scientists sought for exotic particles by direct means.

Taken together, all these ways of observing cosmic rays and other particles coming from outside the Earth constitute an unusual kind of astronomy. It can only gain in importance as the years and decades pass. The participants call it astroparticle physics.

▶ *For possible exotic particles, see* SPARTICLES *and* DARK MATTER. *For the neutrino hunt, see* NEUTRINO OSCILLATIONS. *For the Sun's influence, see* SOLAR WIND. *For the link between cosmic rays and clouds, see* EARTHSHINE.

CRYOSPHERE
Ice sheets, sea-ice and mountain glaciers

tell a confusing tale

F OR A PARTYGOER NOTHING BEATS HOGMANAY out on the ice at the South Pole. That's if you can stand the altitude, nearly 3000 metres above sea level, and a temperature around minus 27°C. About 250 souls inhabit the Amundsen–Scott Base in the Antarctic summer, and they begin their celebrations on New Year's Eve by watching experts fix the geographic pole. A determined raver can then shuffle anticlockwise around the new pole for 24 hours, celebrating the New Year in every time zone in turn.

The new pole is about ten metres away from where it was 12 months before. That's because the ice moves bodily in relation to the geographic pole, defined by the Earth's axis of rotation. Luckily for us, even at the coldest end of the Earth, ice flows sluggishly under its own weight, in glacier fashion. It gradually returns to the ocean the water that the ice sheet borrowed after receiving it in the form of snow. If ice were just a little more rigid our planet would be hideous, as the geologist Arthur Holmes of Edinburgh once surmised.

'Practically all the water of the oceans would be locked up in gigantic circumpolar ice-fields of enormous thickness,' Holmes wrote. 'The lands of the tropical belts would be deserts of sand and rock, and the ocean floors vast plains of salt. Life would survive only around the margins of the ice-fields and in rare oases fed by juvenile water.'

The ice sheets of Antarctica and Greenland stockpile the snows of yesteryear, accumulating layers totalling one or two kilometres above the bedrock. They gradually slump towards the sea, where the frozen water either melts or breaks off in chunks, calving icebergs. The biggest icebergs, 100 kilometres wide or more, come from floating ice shelves that can persist at the edges of the Antarctic ice sheet for thousands of years before they break up. The Ross Ice Shelf, the biggest, is larger than France.

Overall, the return of water to the ocean is roughly in balance with the capture of new snow in the interior. The ice sheets on land retain about 2 per cent of the world's water, mostly in Antarctica where the ice sheets cover an area larger than the USA. As a result the sea level is 68 metres lower than it would otherwise be.

During an ice age the balance shifts a little, in the direction of Holmes' unpleasant world. Large ice sheets grow in North America and Europe, mountain ranges elsewhere are thickly capped with ice, and the sea level falls by a further 90 metres or more. But the slow glacial progress back to the sea never quite stops.

Even in relatively warm times, like the present period called the Holocene, the polar ice acts as a refrigerator for the whole world. It's not just the land ice. Floating sea-ice covers huge areas of the Southern Ocean around Antarctica, and in the Arctic Ocean and adjacent waters. The sea-ice enlarges its reach in winter and melts back in summer.

The whiteness of the ice, by land or sea, rejects sunlight that might have been absorbed to warm the regions. The persistent difference in temperature between the tropics and the poles drives the general winds of the world. Summer is less windy than winter, at mid-latitudes, because that temperature contrast is reduced under the midnight sunshine near the poles. That gives an impression of how lazy the winds would be if there were no ice fields near the poles— which was often the case in the past.

The ice sheets plus sea-ice, together with freezing lakes and rivers, and the mountain glaciers that exist even in the tropics, are known collectively as the cryosphere. It ranks with the atmosphere and the hydrosphere—the wet world— as a key component of the Earth system. As scientists struggle to judge how and why the cryosphere varies, they have to sort out the machinery of cause and effect. There is always an ambiguity. Are changes in the ice driving a global change, or responding to it?

At the start of the 21st century, attention was focused on climate change. A prominent hypothesis was that the polar regions should be warming rapidly, in accordance with computer models that assumed the climate was being driven by man-made greenhouse gases, which reduce the radiation of heat into space. There were also suggestions that the ice sheets might add to any current sea-level rise, by accelerated melting. Alternatively the ice sheets might gain ice from increased snowfall, and so reduce or even reverse a sea-level rise.

Is Antarctica melting?

Special anxieties concerned the ice sheet of West Antarctica. This is the peninsula stretching out from the main continent towards South America, like the tail on the letter Q. In 1973 George Denton of Maine suggested that the West Antarctic Ice Sheet was likely to melt entirely, raising the sea level worldwide by five metres or so. It would take a few centuries, he said. When a reporter asked if that meant that the Dutch need not start building their arks just yet, Denton replied, 'No, but perhaps they should be thinking where the wood will come from.'

Scientific expeditions into the icy world are still adventurous, and they obtain only temporary impressions. Even permanent polar bases have only a local view. A global assessment of changes in the cryosphere was simply beyond reach, before the Space Age. Polar research ranked low among the space agencies' priorities, so ice investigators had to wait a long time before appropriate instruments were installed on satellites orbiting over the poles.

Serious efforts began in 1991, with the launch of the European Space Agency's Earth-observation satellite ERS-1, which could monitor the ice by radar. Unlike cameras observing the surface by visible light, radar can operate through cloud and in the dark polar winter. One instrument on ERS-1 was a simple radar altimeter, sending down radio pulses and timing the echoes from the surface. This would be able to detect changes in the thickness of parts of the Greenland and Antarctic ice sheets.

For detailed inspection of selected areas, ERS-1 used synthetic-aperture radar. Borrowing a technique invented by radio astronomers, it builds up a picture from repeated observations of the same area as the satellite proceeds along its orbit. Similar instruments went onto Europe's successor spacecraft, ERS-2 (1995) and Envisat (2001).

Changes were plain to see in some places. British scientists combined the radar-altimeter readings with synthetic-aperture images of the Pine Island Glacier in West Antarctica. They saw that, between 1992 and 1999, the ice thinned by up to ten metres depth along 150 kilometres of the glacier, the snout of which retreated five kilometres inland.

Much less persuasive were the radar observations of Antarctica as a whole. While a drop in the ice-sheet altitude was measured in some districts, the apparent loss was offset by thickening ice in others. Neither in Antarctica nor in similar observations of the Greenland ice sheet was any overall change detectable.

In key parts of the ice sheets there was no reliable assessment at all. A better technique was needed. The European Space Agency set about building CryoSat, to be launched in 2004. Dedicated entirely to the cryosphere, it would carry two radar altimeters a metre apart, astride the track of the spacecraft. By combining radar altimetry with aperture synthesis, scientists could expect more accurate height measurements, averaged over narrower swaths.

'If the great ice sheets of Antarctica and Greenland are changing, it's most likely at their edges,' explained the space glaciologist Duncan Wingham of University College London, leader of the CryoSat project. 'But the ice sheets end in slopes, which existing radar altimeters see only as coarse averages of altitudes across 15 kilometres of ice. With CryoSat's twin altimeters we'll narrow that down to 250 metres.'

Radarsat-1, a Canadian satellite launched in 1995, gave a foretaste of surprises to come. Scientists in California used the synthetic-aperture radar on Radarsat-1 to examine the dreaded West Antarctic Ice Sheet. Ian Joughin of the Jet Propulsion Lab and Slawek Tulaczyk of UC Santa Cruz concentrated on the glaciers feeding the Ross Ice Shelf. The radar revealed that, so far from melting away, the region is accumulating new ice at a brisk rate. Thanks to the observations from space, Denton's scenario of West Antarctica melting seemed to be dispelled.

The ice sheets on the whole are pretty indifferent to minor fluctuations of climate such as occurred in the 20th century. They are playing in a different league, where the games last for tens of thousands of years. The chief features are growth during ice ages, followed by retreats during warm interludes like the Holocene in which we happen to live. Denton thought that the West Antarctic Ice Sheet was still catching up on the big thaw after the last ice age.

He was almost right. More recent judgements indicate that the West Antarctic Ice Sheet was indeed still melting and shrinking until only a few hundred years ago. But the Earth passed the Holocene's peak of warmth 5000 years ago, and began gradually to head down again towards the next ice age. The regrowth of ice now seen beginning in West Antarctica may be a belated recognition of that new trend since the Bronze Age. Joughin and Tulaczyk suggested tentatively: 'It represents a reversal of the long-term Holocene retreat.'

Sea-ice contradictions

The ice that forms on polar seas, to a thickness of a few metres, responds far more rapidly than the ice sheets on land do, to climate changes—even to year-to-year variations in seasonal temperatures. Obviously the ice requires a cold sea surface to form. Almost as plain is the consequent loss of incoming solar warmth, when the ice scatters the sunlight back into space and threatens visitors with snow blindness. Less obvious is an insulating effect of sea-ice in winter, which prevents loss of heat from the water below the ice.

Historical records of the extent of sea-ice near Iceland, Greenland and other long-inhabited places provide climate scientists with valuable data, and with graphic impressions of the human cost of climate change. In the 15th century for example, early in the period called the Little Ice Age, Viking settlers in Greenland became totally cut off by sea-ice. They all perished, although the more adaptable native Greenlanders survived.

As with the ice sheets, the sea-ice is by its very nature inhospitable, and so knowledge was sketchy before the Space Age. Seafarers reported the positions of ice margins, and scientific parties sometimes ventured into the pack in icebreakers or drifting islands of ice. Aircraft inspected the sea-ice from above and submarines from below. But again these were local and temporary observations. Reliable data on the floating part of the cryosphere and its continual changes came only with the views from satellites.

During the last two decades of the 20th century, satellites saw the area of sea-ice around Antarctica increasing by about two per cent. Although this trend ran counter to the conventional wisdom of climate forecasters, it was in line with temperature data from Antarctic land stations, which showed overall cooling. In the Antarctic winter of mid-2002, supply ships for polar bases found themselves frustrated or even trapped by unusual distributions of sea-ice.

On the other hand, in the Arctic Ocean the extent of sea-ice diminished during those decades, by about six per cent. The release of data from Cold-War submarines led to inferences that Arctic sea-ice had also thinned. That possibility exposed a shortcoming in the satellite data. Seeing the extent of the ice from space was relatively easy. Radar scatterometers, conceived to detect ocean waves and so measure wind speeds, could also monitor the movements of sea-ice. But gauging the thickness of ice, and therefore its mass, was more difficult.

In the 1990s, the task was down to the radar altimeters. But only with luck, here and there, was the space technique accurate enough to measure the thickness of sea-ice by its freeboard above the water surface. If any year-on-year melting of the sea-ice was to be correctly judged, a more accurate radar system was needed. And again it was scientists in Europe who hoped to score, with their CryoSat project.

'How can we tell whether the ice is melting if we don't know how much there is?' asked Peter Lemke of the Alfred-Wegener-Institut in Bremerhaven, a member of the science team. 'CryoSat will turn our very limited, localized information on ice thickness into global coverage. We'll measure any year-to-year thinning or thickening of the ice to within a few centimetres. And the CryoSat data will greatly improve our computer models, whether for ice forecasts for seafarers or for studying global climate change.'

Satellites can also detect natural emissions of radio microwaves from the ice and open water. A sister project of CryoSat is SMOS, the Soil Moisture and Ocean Salinity mission (2006). It will pick up the microwaves from the Earth's snow and ice, but at a longer wavelength than previous space missions, and should be able to tell the difference between thin ice and snow lying on the ice.

Will the future spacecraft see the Arctic sea-ice still dwindling? The rampaging Vikings' discoveries of Iceland and Greenland, and probably of North America too, were made easier by very mild conditions that prevailed around 1000 years ago. Watching with interest for a possible return of such relatively ice-free conditions are those hoping for a short cut for shipping, from Europe to the Far East, via the north coast of Russia.

Swedish explorers sailed that way in 1878–79 but the idea never caught on for international shipping. Since the 1990s, experts from 14 countries, led by Norway, Russia and Japan, have tried to revive interest in this Northern Sea Route. Even if the Arctic ice continues to thin, you'll still have to build your cargo ships as icebreakers.

The watch on mountain glaciers

The name of the Himalayas means snow-home in Sanskrit, and their many glaciers nourish the sacred Ganges and Brahmaputra rivers. These glaciers were poorly charted until Qin Dahe of the Chinese Meteorological Agency used satellite images and aerial photography to define their present extent. Many other remote places harbour such slow-moving rivers of ice, which are not easy to monitor. The count of glaciers worldwide exceeds 160,000.

As climatic thermometers, mountain glaciers in non-polar regions are intermediate in response times, between the sluggish ice sheets and the quick sea-ice. They should therefore be good for judging current climate trends on the 10- to 100-year time-scale. During the 20th century, glaciers were mostly in retreat, melting back and withdrawing their snouts further up their valleys. But in some places they advanced, because of increased snowfall on their mountain sources.

In the Alps, people have glaciers almost in their backyards. During the Little Ice Age, some forests and villages were bulldozed away. A retreat began in the 19th century, and you can compare the present scenery with old paintings and photographs to see how much of each valley has come back to life. Systematic collection of worldwide information on glaciers began in 1894, and monitoring continues with modern instruments, including remote-sensing satellites.

'Nowadays we watch the glaciers especially for evidence of warming effects of man-made greenhouse gases,' said Wilfried Haeberli of Universität Zürich, Switzerland, who runs the World Glacier Monitoring Service. 'But about half the ice in the Alps disappeared between 1850 and the mid-1970s, and we must suppose that most of that loss was due to natural climate change. There have also been warming episodes in the past, comparable with that in the 20th century, as when the Oetztal ice man died more than 5000 years ago, whose body was found perfectly preserved in the Austrian Alps in 1991. What we have to be concerned about is the possibility that present changes are taking us beyond the warm limit seen in the past.'

The chief scientific challenge for climate researchers is to distinguish between natural and man-made changes. They therefore want more knowledge of how glaciers have varied in the past, before human effects were significant. The bulldozing glaciers push up heaps of stones and other debris in hills called terminal moraines, which remain when the glaciers retreat.

Moraines have helped to chart the extent of the ice during past ice ages. They also preserve a record of repeated advances and retreats of the mountain glaciers during the past 10,000 years. These may be related to cooling events seen in outbursts of icebergs and sea-ice in the North Atlantic, called ice-rafting events, which in turn seem to be linked to changes in the Sun's behaviour.

The confusing and sometimes contradictory impressions of the cryosphere are symptoms of its vacillation between warming and cooling processes, on different time-scales. The early 21st century is therefore no time to be dogmatic about current changes, or their effects on the sea level. Despite all the help now coming from the satellites, new generations of scientists will have to don their polar suits to continue the investigation.

▶ *For more about global ice, see* CLIMATE CHANGE *and* ICE-RAFTING EVENTS.

DARK ENERGY

Revealing the power of an accelerating Universe

L A SILLA, meaning the saddle, is the nickname given by charcoal burners of the district to a 2400-metre mountain of that shape on the southern edge of Chile's Atacama Desert. The mountain was chosen in 1964 as the first location for the European Southern Observatory, a joint venture for several countries hoping to match and eventually to surpass the USA in telescope facilities for astronomy by visible light.

In time, 18 telescopes large and small arrived to decorate the saddle's ridge with their domes, like a row of igloos. Later, another Chilean mountain would carry the Very Large Telescope with its four 8-metre mirrors in box-shaped covers. Clear desert skies, combined with freedom from dust and remoteness from luminous human settlements, were the criteria for picking La Silla and Paranal, not the convenience of astronomers wanting to use the instruments.

So getting to La Silla was a tedious journey. You had to arrive in Santiago two full days before you were scheduled to start your observations. And it was little comfort on the long flight from Europe if your colleagues had assured you that you were wasting your time.

'It's impossible!' was the chorus of advice to astronomers who, in 1986, started a hunt for exploding stars far away in the Universe. Undaunted, a Danish–British team set to work with a sensitive electronic camera with charge-coupled devices, which were then an innovation in astronomy. The astronomers' stubbornness sparked a revolution that changed humanity's perception of the cosmos. The new buzzwords would be acceleration and dark energy.

Six times a year, a team member travelled to La Silla, to coincide with the dark of the Moon. He used the modest 1.5-metre Danish telescope to record images from 65 remote clusters of galaxies, vast throngs of stars far off in space. Comparing their images from month to month, by electronic subtraction, the astronomers watched for an exploding star, a supernova, to appear as a new bright speck in or near one of the galaxies.

They found several cases, but they were searching for a particular kind of supernova called Type Ia, an exploding white dwarf star, which could be used for gauging the distances of galaxies. Although they are billions of times more luminous than the Sun, they are inevitably faint at long range, and in any one galaxy the interval between such events may be a few centuries. No wonder colleagues rated the chances low.

In 1988 the most distant Type Ia seen till then rewarded the team's patience. Supernova 1988U occurred in a galaxy in the Sculptor constellation at a distance of about 4.5 billion light-years. That is to say, the event coincided roughly with the birth of the Sun and the Earth, and the news had just arrived in Chile across the expanding chasm of space.

'In two years' hard work we plainly identified only one distant supernova of the right kind,' Hans Ulrik Nørgaard-Nielsen of the Dansk Rumforskningsinstitut in Copenhagen recalled later. 'But we showed that the task was not as hopeless as predicted and others copied our method. None of us had any idea of how sensational the consequences would be.'

Not slowing down—speeding up

The reason for looking for exploding white dwarfs was to measure the slowdown in the expansion of cosmic space. In the late 1920s Edwin Hubble at the Mount Wilson Observatory in California launched modern observational cosmology by reporting that distant galaxies seem to be rushing away from us, as judged by the stretching of their light waves, or red shift. The farther the galaxies are, the faster they go. The whole of spacetime is expanding.

The rate of expansion, called the Hubble constant, would fix the scales of space and time, but the expansion rate went up and down like the stock market as successive measurements came in. With eventual help from the eponymous Hubble Space Telescope, astronomers gradually approached a consensus on the rate of expansion in our neighbourhood.

But no one expected the Hubble constant to be constant throughout the history of the Universe. Most theories of the cosmos assumed that the gravity of its contents must gradually decelerate the expansion. Some said it would eventually drag all the galaxies back together again in a Big Crunch.

Distant Type Ia supernovae could reveal the slowdown. Because of the way the explosions happen, you could assume that they were all equally luminous, and so judge their relative distances by how bright they looked. Any easing of the expansion rate should leave the most remote objects at a lesser distance than would be inferred from their high red shifts. In short, the farthest Type Ia's should look oddly bright.

Roused by the success of the Danish and British astronomers at La Silla, large multinational teams began more intensive searches. Saul Perlmutter of the Lawrence Berkeley Lab in California and Brian Schmidt of Australia's Mount

Stromlo and Siding Spring Observatories were the leaders. The same trick of image-to-image comparisons was done with bigger telescopes and cameras. By 1997 both teams had detected enough Type Ia supernovae at sufficient distances to begin to measure the deceleration of the cosmic expansion.

To almost everyone's astonishment the remote stellar explosions looked not brighter but oddly dim. At distances of six billion light-years or so, they were 20 per cent fainter than expected. The cosmic expansion was not slowing down but speeding up.

'My own reaction is somewhere between amazement and horror,' Schmidt commented, when the results were presented at a meeting in California early in 1998. Some press reports hailed the discovery as proving that the Universe would go on expanding forever, avoiding the Big Crunch and petering out as a desert of dead stars. This was the not the important point. Moderate deceleration would have the same drab outcome, and anyway, who really worries about what will happen 100 billion years from now?

The implications for physics were much weightier and more immediate. An accelerating Universe required gravity to act in a surprising new way, pushing everything apart, unlike the familiar gravity that always pulls masses together. While theorists had invoked repulsive gravity as a starter-motor for the Big Bang, they'd not considered it polite in a mature cosmos.

And the latter-day repulsive gravity brought with it a heavy suitcase containing a huge addition to the mass of the Universe. This is dark energy, distinct from and surpassing the mysterious dark matter already said to be cluttering the sky, and which in turn outweighs the ordinary matter that builds stars and starfish.

Doubters and supporters

In the Marx Brothers' movie *A Night at the Opera* more and more people crowd into a small shipboard cabin, carrying repeat orders of boiled eggs and the like. This was an image of supernova cosmology for Edward Kolb of Chicago. 'It's crazy,' he said in 1998. 'Who needs all this stuff in the Universe?'

Kolb and others had reasons to be sceptical. Was the dimming effect of cosmic dust properly corrected in the analysis? And were the Type Ia supernovae truly as luminous when the Universe was young and the chemical composition of stars was different? After three inconclusive years, some onlookers considered the argument settled when the Berkeley group retrospectively collated observations of an extremely distant supernova seen by the Hubble Space Telescope in 1997.

Supernova 1997ff, more than 10 billion light-years away, was of Type Ia. Its brightness fitted neatly into a scenario in which gravity slowed the expansion early in the first part of cosmic history, when matter was crowded together, but repulsion took charge with its foot on the accelerator when the Universe was more than half its present age. As for those contentions about dust and chemistry, 'This supernova has driven a stake through their heart,' declared Michael Turner of Chicago, himself a converted sceptic.

A charming feature of the study of such very distant supernovae is that you don't have to hurry. The Doppler effect, whereby their speed of recession reddens their light waves, also slows down time, so that changes in brightness that in close-up reality took a week appear to take a month. This calendar-scale slowing of time disposes, by the way, of the tired-light hypothesis, that the cosmic expansion might be an illusion due to light losing energy and reddening during its long journeys from the galaxies.

By 2002, support for the accelerating Universe came from observations of a quite different sort. Whilst the Type Ia supernovae were 'standard candles', meaning that you could gauge their distances by their brightness, the new study used 'standard rulers', with distances to be judged by the apparent sizes of the objects in the sky. If the Universe really is accelerating, a ruler should look smaller than you'd expect, just from its speed of recession.

George Efstathiou at Cambridge led a team of 27 astronomers from the UK and Australia, in using clusters of galaxies as standard rulers. They had available the data on 250,000 galaxies in two selected regions of the sky surveyed with the Anglo-Australian Telescope at Siding Spring, Australia. The astronomers compared the distribution of matter, as seen in the clustering of galaxies, with the patterns of lumps in the cosmic microwave background that fills the sky. The lumps, charted by radio telescopes on balloons and on the ground, are concentrations of gas in the very young Universe, like those from which the visible clusters of galaxies were formed.

A statistical comparison of the galaxy clusters and microwave lumps confirmed the acceleration of the expanding cosmos. The astronomers also inferred that the dark energy responsible for the acceleration accounted for 65–85 per cent of the mass of the Universe. Efstathiou said, 'What we are measuring is the energy associated with empty space.'

Congenial coincidences

Albert Einstein in Berlin first imagined repulsive gravity in 1917, at a time when astronomers thought that the Universe was static. As normal, attractive gravity should force static objects to fall together, Einstein imperiously decreed a repulsion to oppose it. When the Universe turned out to be growing, the repulsion was no longer essential, and he disowned it. 'Death alone can save one from making blunders,' he said in a letter to a friend.

Even in an expanding Universe, repulsive gravity remained an optional extra. It was preserved in a mathematical theory called the Friedmann–Lemaître universe, after the Russian and Belgian cosmologists (Alexander and Georges, respectively) who worked on it independently in the 1920s. Theirs was a scenario in which an early slowdown of the cosmic expansion, due to gravity, gave way to later acceleration. That seems to be what we have, so Einstein's real mistake in this connection was a lack of faith.

His name for repulsive gravity was the cosmological constant. The weirdness begins here, because unlike the Hubble constant, the cosmological constant is meant to be truly unchanging as the Universe evolves. Whilst normal gravity thrives among stars, galaxies and other concentrations of mass, and its strength diminishes as the galaxies spread apart, repulsive gravity ignores the ordinary masses and never weakens.

Particle physicists have a ready-made mechanism for repulsive gravity. They know that empty space is not truly empty but seethes with latent particles and antiparticles that spontaneously appear and disappear in a moment. Like the thermal energy of a gas, this vacuum energy should exert an outward pressure.

In another connection Einstein discovered, in his *annus mirabilis* in Bern in 1905, that energy and mass are equivalent. The vacuum energy, alias dark energy, associated with repulsive gravity therefore possesses mass. As the Universe grows, each additional litre of space acquires, as if by magic, the energy needed to sustain the outward pressure. You can ask where this endless supply of new energy comes from—or who pays for it. You'll get a variety of answers from the experts, but nothing to be sure of.

By the evidence of the supernovae, dark energy patiently waited for its turn. In ever-widening spaces between the clusters of galaxies, it has literally amassed until now it seems to be the main constituent of the Universe. As mentioned, it exceeds dark matter, unseen material inferred from the behaviour of galaxies, with which dark energy should not be confused. And the cumulative pressure of dark energy now overwhelms all the gravity of the Universe and accelerates the cosmic expansion.

On a simple view, the dark energy of Einstein's cosmological constant might have blown up the Universe so rapidly that stars and planets could never have formed. As that didn't happen, astrophysicists and particle physicists have to figure out, not how Mother Nature created repulsive gravity, but how she tamed it.

'The problem of how to incorporate the cosmological constant into a sensible theory of matter remains unresolved and, if anything, has become even harder to tackle with the supernova results,' complained Pedro Ferreira, a Portuguese theorist at CERN, Geneva, in 1999. 'Until now... one could argue that some fundamental symmetry would forbid it to be anything other than zero. However, with the discovery of an accelerating Universe, a very special cancellation is necessary—a cosmic coordination of very big numbers to add up to one small number.'

The puzzle is typical of unexplained near coincidences in the cosmos that seem too congenial to be true, in ensuring a cosmic ecology that favours our existence. If you hear anyone sounding too complacent about the triumphs of particle physics and astrophysics just ask, with Ferreira, why the Universe allegedly consists of about 3 per cent ordinary matter, 30 per cent dark matter and now perhaps 67 per cent of newly added dark energy. Why don't the proportions in Mother Nature's recipe book differ by factors of thousands or zillions?

As the probing of the Universe continued, the supernova-hunters at Berkeley proposed to NASA a satellite called Snap (Supernova Acceleration Probe) to continue the search with the advantages of a telescope in space. If adopted, Snap would investigate a new question: is the cosmological constant really constant?

Could we tap the dark energy?

Repulsive gravity is sometimes called antigravity, but any fantasy of levitating yourself with its aid should be swiftly put aside. A bacterium could give you a harder shove. The cosmic repulsive gravity is beaten by ordinary attractive gravity even in the vicinity of any galaxy, never mind at the Earth's surface. Otherwise everything would fall apart. Nevertheless, scientists speculate about the possibility of tapping the dark energy present in empty space, which powers the cosmic acceleration.

The presence of that seething mass of particles and antiparticles is detectable in subtle effects on the behaviour of atoms. It also creates a force that makes molecules stick together. Known since 1873, when Johannes van der Waals discovered it, this force was not explained until the quantum theory evolved. The reason for it is that two molecules close together screen each other, on their facing sides, from the pressure of the unseen particles whizzing about in empty space. In effect, they are pushed together from behind.

In 1948 another Dutchman, Hendrik Casimir, correctly predicted that the energy of the vacuum should similarly create a force between two metal plates when they are very close together. There were proposals at the end of the century to measure the Casimir force in a satellite, where it could be done more accurately. In 2001, on the ground, scientists at Bell Labs in New Jersey demonstrated the Casimir force as a potential power source for extremely small motors, by using it to exert a twisting force between nearby metallized objects.

But that experimental machine was on a scale of a tenth of a millimetre. There is no obvious way in which the power of empty space can be tapped on a larger scale. Nevertheless, even NASA has taken a cautious interest in the idea that a way might be found to power spaceships by 'field propulsion', thus beating gravity by an indirect means.

The writer Arthur C. Clarke was confident about it. 'It is only a matter of time—I trust not more than a few decades—before we have safe and economical space propulsion systems, depending on new principles of physics that are now being discussed by far-sighted engineers and scientists. When we know how to do it efficiently, the main expenses of space travel will be catering and in-flight movies.'

▶ *For an earlier German discovery of the cosmic acceleration, and for a choice of cosmic theories including one in which the cosmological constant is not constant, see* UNIVERSE. DARK MATTER *clarifies the distinction from dark energy. For repulsive gravity in the very young Universe, see* BIG BANG. *The supernovae reappear as the stars of the show in* ELEMENTS.

DARK MATTER

A wind of wimps or the machinations of machos?

M AKE SURE that you are heading towards Rome on the westbound carriageway of the Abruzzi *autostrada*, if you want to enter the Aladdin's cave for physicists called the Laboratori Nazionali del Gran Sasso. On an offshoot from the road tunnel going through the tallest of the Apennines, three surprisingly generous experimental halls contain tanks, cables, chemical processors and watch-keepers' cabins packed with electronics. Other equipment crowds the corridors. Supervening mountain limestone 1400 metres thick protects the kit from all but the most penetrating of cosmic rays.

In what the Italian hosts are pleased to call *il silenzio cosmico del Gran Sasso*, multinational, industrial-scale experiments look for Nature's shyest particles. If discovered, these could solve a cosmic mystery. It concerns unidentified dark matter, believed to be ten times more massive than all the known atomic and subatomic matter put together. As the Swiss astronomer Fritz Zwicky pointed out in the 1930s, dark matter makes galaxies in clusters rush around faster than they would otherwise do.

One hypothesis is that dark matter may consist of exotic particles, different from ordinary matter and scarcely interacting with it except by its gravity. Theoretical physicists refer to candidates as supersymmetric particles or sparticles. In the dark-matter quest, and with less reliance on particle theories, they are usually called weakly interacting massive particles, or wimps. The hope of the hunters is that if, now and again, a wimp should hit an atomic nucleus, it can set it in motion and so make its presence felt. By the 1990s several groups around the world were searching for dark matter of this elusive form.

DAMA, an Italian–Chinese experiment sheltered by the mountain at Gran Sasso, aimed to spot wimps in a 100-kilogram mass of extremely pure sodium iodide crystals. A wimp zapping a nucleus would create a flash of light, and peculiar features would distinguish it from flashes due to other causes. By 2000, after four years' observations, the physicists at Rome and Beijing masterminding the experiment thought they had good evidence for wimps.

Every year the flashes occurred more often in June than in December. Andrzej Drukier and his colleagues at the Harvard–Smithsonian Center for Astrophysics had predicted this seasonal behaviour, in 1986. If wimps populate our Galaxy, the Milky Way, as invisible dark matter, the Earth should feel them as a wind. In June our planet's motion in orbit around the Sun is added to the motion of the Sun through the Galaxy, so the wind of wimps should be stronger and the count of particles greater.

The DAMA results provoked a wide debate among physicists. Competing groups, using different techniques, were unable to confirm the DAMA signal and looked for reasons to reject it. The argument became quite heated, and in 2002 Rita Bernabei of Rome, leader of the collaboration, posted on the DAMA website a quotation from the poet Rudyard Kipling:

> *If you can bear to hear the truth you've spoken*
> *Twisted by knaves to make a trap for fools . . .*

At stake was a possible discovery of huge importance for both astrophysics and particle physics. As always in science the issue would be settled not by acrimonious arguments but by further research. All groups strove to improve the sensitivity of their instruments and the DAMA team installed a larger detector with 250 kilograms of sodium iodide at Gran Sasso.

Dark stars on offer

The severest sceptics were not the rival wimp hunters but those who thought that wimps were a myth, or at least that they could not be present in the vast quantities required to outweigh the visible galaxies by a factor of ten. The alternatives to wimps are machos, meaning massive astronomical compact halo objects. Supposedly made of ordinary matter, they are dark in the ordinary sense of being too faint to see.

The 'h' in macho refers to the halo of our Galaxy. The astronomical problem starts in our own backyard, where unexpectedly rapid motions of outlying stars of the Milky Way were another early symptom of dark matter's existence. And in the 1970s Vera Rubin of the Carnegie Institution in Washington DC established that many other galaxies that are flat spirals like our own show the same behaviour of their stars.

Surrounding the densely populated bright disk of the Milky Way is a roughly spherical halo where visible stars are scarce, yet it is far more massive. Are wimps concentrated here? Perhaps, but the halo also contains dark stars made of ordinary matter.

Machos could be cooled-off remnants of larger stars long-since dead—white dwarfs, neutron stars, or black holes. They might even be primordial black holes, dating from the origin of the Universe. A popular idea that the machos were very small, barely luminous stars called brown dwarfs was largely abandoned when Italian astronomers examined a globular cluster of stars orbiting in the halo and found far fewer brown dwarfs than expected.

On the other hand, British astronomers reported in 2000 the discovery of a cold white dwarf on an unusual orbit taking it towards the halo. As it was cold enough to be invisible if it were not passing quite close to us, it fitted the macho idea well. There is no doubt that there are many dark stars in the halo, but are there enough to account for its enormous mass?

Whatever they are, the machos should reveal their presence when they wander in front of visible stars in a nearby galaxy. They should act like lenses and briefly brighten the stars beyond. In 1993 US–Australian and French teams reported the first detections of machos by this method. But as the years passed it seemed there were too few of them to account for much of the dark matter.

Other ordinary matter, unseen by visible light and so previously disregarded, turned up in the Universe at large. X-ray satellites discovered huge masses of invisible but not exotic hot gas in the hearts of clusters of galaxies, far outweighing all the visible stars, while radio telescopes detected molecular hydrogen in unsuspected abundance in cool places. Even by visible light, improved telescopes revealed entire galaxies, very faint and red in colour, which no one had noticed before. But again, it seemed unlikely that such additions would account for all the missing matter.

The architecture of the sky

Another way of approaching the mystery was to calculate how dark matter affected the distribution of galaxies. The great star-throngs that populate the

Universe at large are gathered into clusters, and clusters of clusters. Suppose that they were marshalled by the tugs of dark matter acting over billions of years. You can then develop computer models in which a random scatter of galaxies is gradually fashioned into something resembling the present architecture of the sky.

You can make various assumptions about the nature of the dark matter, whether for example it is hot or cold. With them, you can generate different patterns, and see which assumptions give the most realistic impression of the distribution of galaxies today. That might be a guide to the nature of the dark matter itself.

This idea inspired intensive model-making with supercomputers, especially in Europe, during the 1990s. The resulting movies purported to simulate the history of the Universe. They were beautiful, even awe-inspiring, but not altogether persuasive to their critics.

The pattern that the modellers were trying to generate resembled a Swiss cheese. The holey nature of the Universe became apparent when astronomers measured the distances of large numbers of galaxies, by the reddening of the light in the cosmic expansion. 'The Big Blank,' a headline writer nicknamed the first desert in the cosmos, which Robert Kirshner of Michigan and his colleagues discovered in 1981. It was a region almost empty of galaxies, and far bigger than any such void detected before.

A location far beyond the stars of Boötes the Ox-driver gave it its formal name of the Boötes Void, although it extended beyond the bounds of that constellation, making it about 500 million light-years across. The entire observable Universe is only 50 times wider. And as the relative distances of more and more galaxies were determined, voids showed up in every other direction. Ninety per cent of all galaxies are concentrated in ten per cent of the cosmic volume, leaving most of it almost empty of visible matter. This open-plan architecture has the galaxies gathered in walls that separate the bubble-like voids.

As for clustering, our own Milky Way Galaxy shows plainly that galaxies are massive objects. In addition to their vast assemblies of stars, their masses are greatly boosted by attendant dark matter. Gravitational attraction will tend to bunch them. Early in the 20th century, when small smudges were at last recognized as other galaxies, a cluster in the Virgo constellation was immediately obvious.

Clustering occurs in a hierarchy of scales. The Milky Way's neighbours are the large Andromeda spiral M31, 2 million light-years away, and a swarm of about 20 small galaxies, including the Clouds of Magellan. Gravity binds this modest Local Group together, and also links it to the Virgo Cluster, where a couple of thousand galaxies are spread across a region of the sky ten times wider than the Moon. The Virgo Cluster in turn belongs to the Local Supercluster, with many constituent clusters, which in turn is connected with other superclusters.

Together with all the galaxies in our vicinity, we are falling at 600 kilometres per second in a direction roughly indicated by the Southern Cross, towards a massive clustering called the Great Attractor. Tugs towards the centre of mass of the Local Group, towards Virgo and towards the Great Attractor all contribute to the motion of the Earth through a sea of microwaves that fills the cosmos, and provides a cosmic reference frame.

'Falling' is nevertheless a very misleading word in this context. The distance to the Great Attractor is actually increasing, because of the expansion of the Universe, albeit not as fast as it would do if we did not feel its gravity. This local paradox illustrates the hard task that gravity has, to marshal the galaxies in defiance of the cosmic expansion, even with the help of dark matter.

A verdict from the quasars

So while some experts thought that the pattern of clusters gradually evolved, by the amassing of small features into large ones and the depopulation of the voids by yokel galaxies migrating to the bright lights of the clusters, others disagreed. There was simply not enough time, they said, for features as large as the Boötes Void or the Great Attractor to develop. The clusters must have been already established in the early era when the galaxies themselves first formed. If so, the computer models of dark matter might be made futile, by their assumption that the galaxies began their lives in a random but even distribution.

The only way to resolve the issue was to look at galaxies farther afield. Would differences in their distribution show signs of the gradual marshalling that the modellers envisaged? By the end of the century robot techniques were simultaneously measuring the distances of hundreds of galaxies, by the reddening of their light. It was like the biologists' progress from reading the genes one by one, to the determination of the entire genome of a species. At stake here was the genetics of cosmic structure.

Mammoth surveys began logging more galaxies in a night than a previous generation of astronomers managed in a year. An Australian–UK team employed the Anglo-Australian Telescope in New South Wales to chart 250,000 galaxies across selected areas of the sky. A million quasars in five years was the goal of a US–German–Japanese team using the Sloan Telescope in New Mexico.

A foretaste of the results on clustering came in 2001, from data on 11,000 quasars seen during the first phase of the Anglo-Australian survey. Quasars are galaxies made exceptionally luminous by matter falling into central black holes, and are therefore easiest to see at the greatest distances. And the word was that the dark-matter model-makers were in big trouble. Allowing for the expansion of the Universe, the pattern of galaxy-rich and galaxy-poor regions was the same at the greatest ranges as closer by.

'As far back as we look in this survey, we see the same strength of quasar clustering,' said Scott Croom of the Anglo-Australian Observatory. 'Imagine that the quasars are streetlights, marking out the structure of a city such as New York. It's as if we visited the city when it was still a Dutch colony, yet found the same road pattern that exists today.'

Part of the scenery

With the negative results concerning cluster evolution, and all the uncertainties about wimps versus machos, cosmologists entered the 21st century like zookeepers unable to say whether the creatures in their care were beetles or whales. Recall that the dark matter outweighs the ordinary matter of galaxies and clusters by about ten to one. A vote might have shown a majority of experts favouring wimps, but issues in science are not settled that way.

In consolation, astronomers had a new way of picturing the dark matter. Its prettiest effects come in gravitational lenses. The unseen mass concentrated in a cluster of galaxies bends light like a crude lens, producing distorted, streaked and often multiple images of more distant galaxies. This makes a natural telescope that helps to extend the range of man-made telescopes. At first glance the distortions of the images seem regrettable—until you realize that they can be interpreted to reveal the arrangement in space of the dark matter.

The young French pioneer of this technique was Jean-Paul Kneib of the Observatoire Midi-Pyrénées. In the mid-1990s, with colleagues at Cambridge, he obtained extraordinary pictures of galaxy clusters with the Hubble Space Telescope, showing dozens of gravitationally imaged features. Kneib used them to work out the shape and power of the natural lens. He deduced the magnification of the background galaxies, and charted the dark matter in the foreground cluster.

Thus dark matter became part of the scenery, along with radio galaxies, or gas masses detected by X-rays. The analysis was indifferent to the nature of the dark matter, because it measured only its gravitational and tidal action. The Hubble Space Telescope's successor, the NASA–Europe–Canada James Webb Telescope (2010) using infrared light, would amplify the power of the technique amazingly, in Kneib's opinion.

'By studying clusters of galaxies at different distances,' he said, 'and probing the most distant ones with infrared detectors, we'll explore the relationship between visible and dark matter, and how it has evolved. We'll see the whole history of the Universe from start to finish.'

▶ *For the theoretical background concerning wimps, see* SPARTICLES. *For another and apparently even bigger source of invisible mass in the Universe, see* DARK ENERGY.

DINOSAURS

Why small was beautiful in the end

WHEN REPTILES RULED THE EARTH, the great survival strategies were to get big, get fast, or get out of the way. The giant dinosaurs did well for more than 100 million years. They died out in the catastrophe that overwhelmed the world 65 million years ago, leaving only distant relatives, the crocodiles, to remind the unwary of what reptilian jaws used to do.

Small, evasive dinosaurs left many surviving descendants—creatures that can be correctly described as warm-blooded reptiles of a raptorial persuasion, although we more often call them birds. That they are dinosaurs in a new incarnation was fairly obvious to many experts for more than a century.

The idea of farmyard chickens being related to the fearsome *Tyrannosaurus rex* seems like a joke at first, until you remember that the tyrannosaurs ran about on two legs, as birds do, after hatching out of giant chicken's eggs. And the superficial similarities are plainer still when you compare some of the raptors—small, fast-running dinosaurs—with flightless birds like ostriches.

Since the 19th century the students of fossil life had known of a creature from Germany called *Archaeopteryx*, nowadays dated at around 150 million years ago. About the size of a crow, it had wing-like arms and feathers, but a toothy jaw and reptilian tail, as if it were at an early stage of evolving into a bird of a modern kind. In the 1990s it yielded pre-eminence as an early bird to *Confuciusornis*, another crow-sized creature found in large numbers in China in deposits 125 million years old. Opinions differed as to whether either of them was close to the lineage leading to modern birds. They may have been evolutionary experiments that leave no survivors today.

Bird origins were debated inconsequentially until 1973. Then John Ostrom of Yale noted that *Deinonychus*, a raptor that he and colleagues had discovered in Montana in the previous decade, bore many similarities to *Archaeopteryx* and to modern birds. In particular, the three fingers in the hand of *Deinonychus*, and a wrist of great flexibility, were just the starting point needed for making a flappable wing.

But to invent wings, and then to add feathers only as an evolutionary afterthought, might not have worked. Feathers are adaptations of reptilian scales, still noticeable on the feet of birds. Apart from their utility in flight, feathers also provide heat insulation, which would have been more important for small dinosaurs than large ones. Fluffy down and feathers could well have evolved for the sake of the thermal protection they gave.

How a fake became a find

To confirm their ideas about a logical predecessor of the birds, fossil-hunters wanted to find a small, feathered dinosaur without avian pretensions. Candidates showed up in China, where the best example was identified in 2000.

That was only after a false start, which caused red faces on *National Geographic*. In 1999 the magazine proclaimed the discovery of *Archaeoraptor*, a creature with a bird-like head, body and legs, and a dinosaur's tail. It was hailed as a true intermediary between dinosaurs and birds. The specimen came from the fossil-rich hills of Liaoning province, north-west of Beijing, but via a commercial dealer in fossils, rather than from a scientific dig.

Farmers in Liaoning supplement their incomes by gathering fossils of the Cretaceous period, which they sell to scientists and collectors. The exceptional quality of the fossils in the famous Yixian Formation, and the Jiufotang above it, is largely due to wholesale kills by volcanic ash, combined with preservation in the sediments of what was then a shallow lake. By law the specimens should not leave China, but in practice some of the best are smuggled out, as happened with *Archaeoraptor*.

In 2000 *National Geographic* received an unwelcome e-mail from Xu Xing of the Institute of Vertebrate Palaeontology in Beijing. He had visited Liaoning looking for other examples of *Archaeoraptor* and had bought from a farmer the exact counterpart of the *National Geographic's* prize. That means the opposite face of the embedding stone, where it was split apart to show an imprint of the creature on both surfaces. Although the tail was identical, the rest of the animal was completely different. Xu's message said that he was 100 per cent certain that *Archaeoraptor* was a composite made from more than one specimen.

Someone had craftily juxtaposed the upper parts of a primitive bird and the tail of a small dinosaur, and supplemented them with leg bones from somewhere else. It was a scandal like Piltdown Man, a combination of a modern human skull and an orang-utan jaw, allegedly found in England in 1912, which bamboozled investigators of human evolution for 40 years. Xu detected the faking of the dinosaur-bird far more quickly.

Whoever was responsible had failed to notice that the dinosaur part was a much more important discovery in its own right. It was the smallest adult dinosaur ever found till then—no bigger than a pigeon. It had feathers, and also slim legs and claws like those possessed by birds that perch in trees.

By the end of 2000, Xu and his colleagues were able to publish a detailed description of the creature, which lived 110–120 million years ago. They called it *Microraptor*. Here was persuasive evidence for very small dinosaurs suitable for evolving into birds. You could picture them getting out of the way of predators larger than themselves by hiding in the treetops, while keeping snug in their feathery jackets.

Because the *Microraptor* specimen was later than *Archaeopteryx* and *Confuciusornis*, it was an ancestor of neither of those primitive birds. But the very small feathered dinosaurs set the stage for continuous evolutionary experimentation, in nice time for the radiation of modern birds that was beginning in earnest around 120 million years ago. That date comes not from fossils but from molecular indications for the last common ancestor of today's ostriches and flying birds.

'In *Microraptor* we have exactly the kind of dinosaur ancestor we should expect for modern birds,' said Xu. 'And our fossils have only just begun to tell their story. We already have more than 1000 specimens of feathered dinosaurs and primitive birds from Liaoning alone.'

'Sluggish and constrained'

The small bird-like dinosaurs ran counter to an evolutionary trend, which kept pushing other dinosaurs towards big sizes. The great beasts that bewitch us in museums or videographics were reinvented again and again, as the various lineages of dinosaurs went through episodes of decline and revival during their long tenure. It scarcely matters when children or movie-makers muddle their geological periods and places. Gigantic two-legged carnivores and titanic four-legged herbivores kept doggedly reappearing, in the ever-changing Mesozoic landscapes. It was as if Mother Nature had run out of ideas.

The earliest known dinosaurs popped up during the Triassic period, 230 million years ago, but at first they were neither particularly large nor dominant. They did not take charge of the terrestrial world until 202 million years ago. That was when the previous incumbents, reptilian relatives of the crocodiles, suffered a setback from the impact of a comet or an asteroid at the end of the Triassic Period.

It was not as severe an event as the one that was to extinguish the dinosaurs themselves at the end of the Cretaceous, 137 million years later. But clear evidence for a cosmic inauguration of the Age of the Dinosaurs is the sudden appearance of many more footprints of carnivorous dinosaurs in eastern North America, coinciding with an enrichment of the key stratum with iridium, a metal from outer space. The turnover in animal species was completed in less than 10,000 years.

Other cosmic impacts occurred during the dinosaurs' reign, which lasted throughout the Jurassic and Cretaceous periods. It also coincided with the completion and break-up of the last supercontinent, Pangaea. Interpreting the course of their evolution is therefore in part a matter of the geography of drifting continents that assembled and then disassembled. But deserts and mountain ranges played their parts too, in causing the separations that encouraged the diversification of species.

The dinosaurs provide an exceptional chance to study the tempo and modes of evolution on land, over a very long time. The first fossil collections came mainly from North America and Europe, which were in any case the last big pieces of Pangaea to separate. But from the 1970s onwards, successful dinosaur-hunting in Asia, Africa, Australia, Antarctica and South America began to give a much fuller picture.

For Paul Sereno at Chicago, an intercontinental hunter himself, the doubling of the number of known dinosaur species by the end of the century provided evidence enough to draw general conclusions about their evolution. Mathematical analysis of their similarities and differences produced a clear family tree with almost 60 branching events. But compared with the ebullient radiation of the placental mammals that followed the dinosaurs' demise and gave us cats, bats, moles, apes, otters and whales, Sereno judged the evolution of the dinosaurs themselves to have been 'sluggish and constrained'.

Sereno counted no more than ten adaptive designs, called suborders, which appeared early in dinosaur evolution, and most of those soon died out. In his opinion, the sheer size of the animals put a brake on their diversification. They were necessarily few in numbers in any locale, they lived a long time as individuals, and they were largely confined to well-vegetated, non-marshy land. Tree climbing was out of the question for large dinosaurs. Significantly, the giant reptiles show no hint of responding to the emergence of flowering plants, whilst insects and early mammals adapted to exploit this new resource.

The break-up of Pangaea brought more diversity in the Cretaceous period. As continents drifted away from one another, the widespread predators of the Jurassic and Early Cretaceous, ceratosaurs and allosaurs, died out in East Asia and North America. The tyrannosaurs replaced them.

In those continents, too, the titanosaurs, the universal giant herbivores of the Early Cretaceous, gave way to the upstart hadrosaurs. About what happened to the various lineages on the southern continents, full details can only come from more expeditions. As Sereno concluded: 'Future discoveries are certain to yield an increasingly precise view of the history of dinosaurs and the major factors influencing their evolution.'

It fell to the microraptors and the birds to occupy the treetop niche. Marshes, rivers and seas, which the dinosaurs had shunned, soon became parts of the avian empire too. The albatross gliding over the lonely Southern Ocean epitomizes the astonishing potential latent in the reptilian genes, which became apparent only after the switch to smallness seen in Liaoning. And be grateful, of course, that other dinosaurs of today tread quite gently on your roof.

▶ *For three takes on the Cretaceous terminal event that ended the reign of the dinosaurs, see* EXTINCTIONS, IMPACTS *and* FLOOD BASALTS. *For more on birds of today, see* BIOLOGICAL CLOCKS. *For more on the evolutionary responses to flowering plants, see* ALCOHOL.

DISCOVERY

Why the top experts are usually wrong

N OTHING MUCH HAS CHANGED since Galileo Galilei's time, in the task of altering people's beliefs about the workings of Nature. Society accords the greatest respect to those researchers who move knowledge and ideas forward, from widely held but incorrect opinions to new ones that are at least less incorrect. But the respect often comes only in retrospect, and sometimes only posthumously. At the time, the battles can be long and bitter.

'Being a successful heretic is far from easy,' said Derek Freeman of the Australian National University, who spent 40 years correcting an egregious error about the sex lives of Samoan teenagers as reported by the famous Margaret Mead. 'The convincing disproof of an established belief calls for the amassing of ungainsayable evidence. In other words, in science, a heretic must *get it right*.'

For most professional researchers, science is a career. They use well-established principles and techniques to address fairly obvious problems or applications. A minority have the necessary passion for science, as others have for music or mountaineering, which drives them to try to push back the frontiers of knowledge to a significant degree. These individuals regard science not as the mass of knowledge enshrined in textbooks, but as a process of discovery that will make the textbooks out of date.

For the rest of us, the fact that they are preoccupied with mysteries makes their adventures easier to share. The discoverer in action is no haughty professor on a podium, but a doubtful human being who wanders with a puzzled frown, alert and hopeful, through the wilderness of ignorance.

By definition, discoveries tell you things you didn't know before. Some of the most important are brainwaves, about known but puzzling features of the world. Others are the outcome of extraordinary patience in difficult, sometimes impossible-seeming tasks. Or discoveries can come from observations of new phenomena, where a sharp eye for the unexpected is an asset. As the essayist Lewis Thomas put it, 'You measure the quality of the work by the intensity of the astonishment.'

It starts with the individual responsible for what the theoretical physicist Richard Feynman called 'the terrible excitement' of making a new discovery. 'You can't calculate, you can't think any more. And it isn't just that Nature's wonderful, because if someone tells me the answer to a problem I'm working on it's nowhere near as exciting as if I work it out myself. I suppose it's got something to do with the mystery of how it's possible to know something, at least for a little while, that nobody else in the world knows.'

A generation later, similar testimony came from Wolfgang Ketterle, one of the first experimentalists to create a new kind of matter called Bose–Einstein condensates. 'To see something which nobody else has seen before is thrilling and deeply satisfying,' he said. 'Those are the moments when you want to be a scientist.'

The social system of science is a club organized for astonishment. It creates an environment where knowledge can accumulate in published papers, and every so often it provides the thrill of a big discovery to individuals who are both clever and lucky. But the opposition that they face from the adherents of pre-existing ideas, who dominate the club, is a necessary part of the system too.

Those who resist ideas that turn out to be correct are often regarded with hindsight as dunderheads. But they also defend science against kooky notions, technical blunders, outright fraud, and a steady flow of brilliant theories that unfortunately happen to be wrong. And they create the dark background needed for the real discoveries to shine.

As there is not the slightest sign of any end to science, as a process of discovery, a moment's reflection tells you that this means that the top experts are usually wrong. One of these days, what each of them now teaches to students and tells the public will be faulted, or be proved grossly inadequate, by a major discovery. If not, the subject must be moribund.

'The improver of natural knowledge absolutely refuses to acknowledge authority, as such,' wrote Charles Darwin's chum, Thomas Henry Huxley. 'For him, scepticism is the highest of duties; blind faith the one unpardonable sin.'

The provisional nature of scientific knowledge seems to some critics to be a great weakness, but in fact it is its greatest strength. To understand why, it is worth looking a little more closely at the astonishment club.

The motor and the ratchet

Since the dawn of modern science, usually dated from Galileo's time around 400 years ago, its discoveries have transformed human culture in many practical, philosophical and political ways. Behind its special success lies the discovery of how to make discoveries, by the interplay between hypotheses on the one hand and observations and experiments on the other. This provides a motor of progress unmatched in any other human enterprise.

Philosophers have tried to strip the motor down and rebuild it to conform with their own habit of thinking off the top of the head. Some even tried to give science a robot-like logic, written in algebra. In reality, discovery is an intensely human activity, with all the strength, weakness, emotion and unpredictability implied by that. A few rules of thumb are on offer.

If you see a volcano erupting on the Moon and no one else does, bad luck. As far as your colleagues are concerned, you had too much vodka that night. Verifiable observations matter and so do falsifiable theories. A hypothesis that could not possibly be disproved by practicable experiments or observations is pretty worthless. A working scientist, Claude Bernard, broadly anticipated this idea of falsifiability in 1865 but it is usually credited to a 20th-century philosopher, Karl Popper of London, who regarded it as a lynchpin of science.

Paul Feyerabend was Popper's star pupil and, like him, Austrian-born. But at UC Berkeley, Feyerabend rebelled against his master. 'The idea that science can, and should, be run according to fixed and universal rules, is both unrealistic and pernicious,' he wrote. He declared that the only rule that survives is 'Anything goes.'

Also at Berkeley was the most influential historian of science in the 20th century, the physicist Thomas Kuhn. In his book *The Structure of Scientific Revolutions* (1962) he distinguished normal science from the paradigm shift. By normal he meant research pursued within a branch of science in accordance with the prevailing dominant idea, or paradigm. A shift in the paradigm required a scientific revolution, which would be as vigorously contested as a political revolution.

Kuhn's analysis seemed to many scientists a fair description of what happens, and 'paradigm shift' became a claim that they could attach to some of their more radical ideas. Critics tried to use it to devalue science, by stressing the temporary nature of the current paradigms. But the cleverest feature of the system is a ratchet, which ensures that scientific knowledge continues to grow and consolidate itself, never mind how the interpretations may change.

Discovered stars or bacteria don't disappear if opinions about them alter. So far from being devalued, accumulated factual knowledge gains in importance when reinterpretations put it into a broader perspective. As Kuhn explained, new paradigms 'usually preserve a great deal of the most concrete parts of past achievements and they always permit additional concrete problem-solutions besides.'

Denigrators of science sometimes complain that it is steered this way and that by all kinds of extraneous social, political, cultural and technological factors. In the 17th century the needs of oceanic navigation gave a boost to astronomy. Spin-offs from weapons systems in the 20th century provided scientists with many of their most valuable tools. In the 21st century, biomedical researchers complain that the political visibility of various diseases produces favouritism in funding. But none of these factors at work during the approach to a discovery affects its ultimate merit.

'A party of mountain climbers may argue over the best path to the peak,' the physicist Steven Weinberg pointed out, 'and these arguments may be conditioned by the history and social structure of the expedition, but in the end either they find a good path to the summit or they do not, and when they get there they know it.'

Fresh minds and gatecrashers

The silliest icon of science, presented for example as the Person of the Century on the cover of *Time* magazine, is Albert Einstein as a hairy, dishevelled, cuddly old man. The theorist who rebuilt the Universe in his head was young, dapper and decidedly arrogant-looking. Discovery is typically a game for ambitious, self-confident youngsters, and one should esteem Isaac Barrow at Cambridge, who resigned his professorship in 1669 so that Isaac Newton, who had graduated only the year before, could have his job.

Although a few individuals have won Nobel Prizes for work done as undergraduates, age is not the most important factor. Mature students, and scientists of long experience, can make discoveries too. What matters is maintaining a child-like curiosity and a sense of wonder that are resistant to the sophistication, complication and authority of existing knowledge. You need to know enough about a subject to be aware of what the problems are, but perhaps not too much about it, so that you don't know that certain ideas have already been ruled out.

The successes of outsiders, who gatecrash a field of research and revolutionize it, provide further evidence of the value of seeing things afresh. Notable hobbyists of the 20th century included Alfred Wegener, the meteorologist who pushed the idea of continental drift, and the concrete engineer Milutin Milankovitch, who refined the astronomical theory of ice ages. Both were comprehensively vindicated after their deaths. Archaeologists owe radiocarbon dating to another gatecrasher, the nuclear chemist Willard Libby, whilst a theoretical physicist, Erwin Schrödinger, inspired many by first specifying the idea of a genetic code.

'There you are,' said Graham Smith, showing a photograph of himself and Martin Ryle working on a primitive radio telescope in a field near Cambridge in 1948. 'Two future Astronomers Royal, and neither of us knew what right ascension meant.' Intruding into astronomy without a by-your-leave, they were radio physicists on the brink of pinpointing several dozen of the first known radio sources in the sky. Within 20 years the incomers with big antennas would have transformed the Universe from a serene scene of stars and nebulae into an uproar of quasars and convulsing galaxies pervaded by an echo of the Big Bang itself.

Fresh minds and fresh techniques are not the only elements in successful gatecrashing. The ability of outsiders to master the principles of an unfamiliar subject well enough to make major contributions means that even the most advanced science is not very difficult to learn. Contrary to the view encouraged by the specialists and their institutions, you don't have to serve a long apprenticeship in the field of choice.

And Mother Nature conspires with the gatecrashers. She knows nothing of the subdivisions into rival disciplines, but uses just the same raw materials and physical forces to make and operate black holes, blackberries or brains. The most important overall trend in 20th-century science put into reverse the overspecialization dating from the 19th century. The no-man's-land between disciplines became a playground open to all comers. Their successors in the 21st century will complete the reunion of natural knowledge.

How science hobbles itself

Despite forecasts of the end of science, there is no sign of any slowdown in progress at the frontiers of discovery. On the contrary this book tells of striking achievements in many areas. Scientists now peruse the genes with ease. They peer inside the living brain, the rocky Earth and the stormy Sun, and explore the Universe with novel telescopes. Vast new fields beckon.

On the other hand, discovery shows no sign of speeding up. This is despite a huge increase in the workforce, such that half the scientists who ever lived are still breathing. About 20,000 scientific papers are published every working day, ten times more than in 1950. But these are nearly all filling in details in Kuhn's normal science, or looking to practical applications. If you ask where the big discoveries are, that transform human understanding and set science on a new course, they are as precious and rare as ever.

DISCOVERY

The trawl in 1990–2000 included nanotubes, planets orbiting other stars, hopeful monsters in biology, superatoms, cosmic acceleration, plasma crystals and neutrino oscillations. All cracking stuff. Yet it is instructive to compare them with discoveries 100 years earlier. The period 1890–1900 brought X-rays, radioactivity, the electron, viruses, enzymes, free radicals and blood groups. You'd have to be pretty brash to claim that the recent lot was noticeably more glittering.

One difference is that all of the earlier discoveries mentioned, 1890–1900, were made in Europe, and 100 years later the honours were shared between Europe, the USA and Japan. That only emphasizes the much wider pool of talent that now exists, which also includes many more outstanding women. Yet there is no obvious shortage of available Nobel Prizes, over 100 years after they were instituted.

Apologists accounting for the relatively poor performance in discoveries per million scientist-years will tell you that all the easy research has been done. Nowadays, it is said, you need expensive apparatus and large teams of scientists to break new ground. That is the case in some branches of science, but it is offset by the fact that the fancy kit makes life easier, once you have it.

The basic reason why there is no hint of accelerated discovery, despite the explosive growth in the population of researchers, may be that the social system of science has become more skilled at resisting new knowledge and ideas. Indeed, that seems to have become its chief function. Science is no longer a vocation for the dedicated few, as it was in the days of Pasteur and Maxwell, but a profession for the many.

To safeguard jobs and pensions, you must safeguard funding. That means deciding where you believe science is heading—an absurd aspiration in itself— and presenting a united front. Field by field, the funding agencies gather awards panels of experts from the scientific communities that they serve. Niceties are observed when the panellist withdraws from the room when his or her own grant application is up for consideration, but otherwise the system is pretty cosy.

The same united front acts downwards through the system to regulate the activities of individual scientists. When they apply for grants, or when they submit their research findings for publication, experienced people in the same field say 'this is good' or 'this is bad'. Anything that contradicts the party line of normal science is likely to be judged bad, or given a low priority. When funds are short (as they usually are) a low priority means there's nothing to spare for oddballs.

Major discoveries perturb the system. They may bring a shift of power, such that famous scientists are proved to be wrong and young upstarts replace them. Lecture notes become out of date overnight. In the extreme, a discovery can result in outmoded laboratories being shut down.

To try to ensure that nobody is accidentally funded to make an unwelcome discovery, applicants are typically required to predict the results of a proposed line of research. By definition, a discovery is not exactly knowable in advance, so this is an effective deterrent. Discoveries are still made, either by quite respectable scientists by mischance or by mavericks on purpose. The system then switches into overdrive to ridicule them.

As a self-employed, independent researcher, the British chemist James Lovelock was able to speak his mind, and explain how the system discourages creativity. 'Before a scientist can be funded to do a research, and before he can publish the results of his work, it must be examined and approved by an anonymous group of so-called peers. This inquisition can't hang or burn heretics yet, but it can deny them the ability to publish their research, or to receive grants to pay for it. It has the full power to destroy the career of any scientist who rebels.'

The confessions of a Nobel Prizewinner show that Lovelock did not exaggerate. Stanley Prusiner discovered prions as the agents of encephalopathies. He funded his initial work on these brain-rotting diseases in 1974 by applying for a grant on a completely different subject. He realized that a candid application would meet opposition.

The essence of Prusiner's eventual discovery was that proteins could be infectious agents. The entire biomedical establishment knew that infectious agents had to include genetic material, nucleic acids, as in bacteria, viruses and parasites. So when he kept finding only protein, a major private funder withdrew support and his university threatened to deny him a tenured position. He went public with the idea of prions in 1982, and set off a firestorm.

'The media provided the naysayers with a means to vent their frustration at not being able to find the cherished nucleic acid that they were so sure must exist,' Prusiner recalled later. 'Since the press was usually unable to understand the scientific arguments and they are usually keen to write about any controversy, the personal attacks of the naysayers at times became very vicious.' Prusiner's chief complaint was that the scorn upset his wife.

Science doesn't have to be like that. A few institutions with assured funding make a quite disproportionate contribution to discovery. Bell Laboratories in New Jersey is one example, which crops up again and again in this book, in fields from cosmology to brain research. Another is the Whitehead Institute for Biomedical Research in Massachusetts. 'It's not concerned with channelling science to a particular end,' explained its director, Susan Lindquist. 'Rather, its philosophy is that if you take the best people and give them the right resources, they will do important work.'

● Should discovery be stopped?

The brake on discovery provided by the peer system is arguably a good thing. It preserves some stability in the careers of 'normal' scientists, who are very useful to society and to the educational system, and who far outnumber the few innovators who are required to suffer for rocking the boat. And for the world at large, the needless delays and inefficiencies give more time to adapt to the consequences of discovery.

The catalogue of science-related social issues in the early 21st century ranges from the regulation of transgenic crops to criminal applications of the Internet. Most fateful, as usual, are the uses of science in weaponry. 'We must beware,' Winston Churchill warned, 'lest the Stone Age return upon the gleaming wings of science.'

At the height of the Cold War, in 1983, Martin Ryle at Cambridge lamented that he took up radio astronomy to get as far away as possible from any military purposes, only to find his new techniques for making very powerful radio telescopes being perverted (his word) for improving radar and sonar systems. 'We don't *have* to understand the evolution of galaxies,' he said.

'I am left at the end of my scientific life,' Ryle wrote to a Brazilian scientist, 'with the feeling that it would have been better to have become a farmer in 1945. One can, of course, argue that somebody else would have done it anyway, and so we must face the most fundamental of questions. Should fundamental science (in some areas now, others will emerge later) be stopped?'

That a Nobel Prizewinner could pose such a question gives cause for thought. In some political and religious systems, knowledge has been regarded as dangerous for the state or for faith. The ancient Athenians condoned and indeed rationalized the quest for knowledge. It went hand in hand with such rollicking confidence in human decency and good sense that in their heyday they chose their administrators by lottery from the whole population of male citizens.

In this perspective science is a Grecian gamble, on the proposition that human beings are virtuous enough on the whole to be trusted with fateful knowledge. There is an implication here that scientists are often slow to recognize. Wise decisions about the uses of new knowledge will have to be made by society as a whole, honestly informed about it, and not by the advocacy from scientists who think they know best—however honourable their intentions might be.

Another implication comes from the public perception of science as one big enterprise, regardless of the efforts of specialists to preserve their esoteric distinctions. Researchers had better strive to keep one another honest and open-minded, across all the disciplines. Should science ever turn out to have been a bad bet, and some disaster concocted with its aid overtakes the world, the survivors who burn down the laboratories won't stop to read the departmental names over the doors.

▶ *For a comment on the futility of trying to predict the course of science, see* BUCKYBALLS AND NANOTUBES. *For a classification of the status of some recent discoveries, see* BERNAL'S LADDER. *For two military applications of science, see* NUCLEAR WEAPONS *and* SMALLPOX.

DISORDERLY MATERIALS
The wonders of untidy solids and tidy liquids

W HEN THE LUBBERLY ROMANS surprised everyone by beating the mariners of Carthage in a struggle for the control of the western Mediterranean, they had help from their artificial harbours. At Cosa on the Tyrrhenian shore you can see surviving piers made of concrete. Jumbled fragments of rock and broken pottery, bonded by a mortar of lime and volcanic ash, have withstood the ravaging sea for 2000 years.

Rock and pottery themselves are disorderly solids and, for millennia before the invention of concrete or fibreglass, builders knew how to reinforce mud with straw in a composite material. Impurities introduced into floppy copper and iron turned them into military-grade bronze and steel. Mineralogists and biologists confront the essential complexity of natural materials and tissues every working day. Yet most physicists have been instinctive purists, in quest of the neat crystal, the refined element or the uncontaminated compound. Especially they like theories of how things would be if they weren't so confoundedly untidy.

Order coming out of natural disorder sometimes caught the eye, as when the astronomer Johannes Kepler studied snowflakes 400 years ago—always pretty but never the same shape twice. In the 18th century, the pioneer of physiology Stephen Hales found that peas, loose in a bowl, arranged themselves in an irregular yet principled manner. Only the most self-confident scientists seemed willing to ask questions about disorderly behaviour, as when Michael Faraday computed the electrical properties of random materials, or when Albert Einstein studied Brownian motion, the erratic movements of fine pollen grains in water.

During the 20th century more and more technologies came to depend on imperfections—most consequentially in the doping of silicon with atomic impurities that govern its semiconducting and therefore electronic properties. Nevill Mott at Bristol (later Cambridge) and Philip Anderson of Bell Labs in the USA developed theories of the effects on electrons of impurities in crystalline and amorphous materials, which won them shares in a Nobel Physics Prize in 1977. But if that award can be seen as a commentary on new trains of thought, the most ringing endorsement of untidiness as a fit subject for academic study was the 1991 Physics Prize that went to Pierre-Gilles de Gennes of the Collège de France in Paris. It could just as well have been the Chemistry Prize.

From the 1960s onwards, de Gennes developed a comprehensive science of disorderly materials, and of their capacity to switch between disorderly and orderly states. Such transitions occur in superconductors, in permanent magnets, in plastics, in the liquid crystals of instrument displays, and in many other materials. As the switching can be provoked by changes in temperature, in chemical concentration, or in the strength of a magnetic or electric field, they seem at first glance to be entirely different phenomena. At a second glance, de Gennes found close analogies between them all, at a level of surprisingly simple mathematics, and applied his ideas with gusto across a huge range of materials science.

Of blobs and squirms

Almost single-handedly de Gennes reversed a trend towards brute-force theorizing, which seemed to make real-life materials ever more formidable to deal with. Industrial polymers were a prime example. Plastics, fibres and rubber are tangles of spaghetti-like molecular strands, and you could, if you wished, describe them with the complicated maths of many-bodied behaviour and rely on powerful computers. Or you could do the sums on a spaghetti-house napkin if you thought about blobs.

For de Gennes, a blob was a backhanded measure of concentration, being simply a sphere representing the distance between two polymer strands. The arithmetic was then the same for any long-chain polymers whatsoever, and it was a powerful aid to thinking about the chains' entanglements. You can have dilute solutions in which the polymeric chains do not interact, semi-dilute in which blobs of intermediate size appear, and concentrated solutions where the interactions between chains become comprehensive. As de Gennes commented in 1990, 'The ideas have been borne out by experiments in neutron scattering from polymers in solution, which confirm the existence of three regimes.'

Another simple concept cleared up confusions due to the relative motions of entangled polymer chains. In de Gennes' theory of molecular squirming, or reptation, behaviour depends simply on the time taken for one polymer chain to crawl out of a tube created by the chains around it. Silly Putty is a polymer that droops into a liquid-like puddle if left standing, but in fast action it bounces like a hard rubber ball. This is because the reptation time is long.

De Gennes went on to fret about the mechanism of dangerous hydroplaning of cars on wet roads. With the group of Françoise Brochard-Wyart at the Institut Curie in Paris, hydroplaning was clarified step by step. Adherence on wet roads relies on the repeated initiation and growth of dry patches between the tyres and the road, as the wheels turn. When the driver tries to slow down, 'liquid invasion' occurs, as shear flows of thin films oppose the formation of the dry patches. Then the car might just as well be on ice.

Smart materials

As a gung-ho polymath in an era of debilitating specialization, de Gennes saw no bounds to the integrative role of materials science. As he remarked in 1995, 'I've battled for a long time to have three cultures in my little school: physics, chemistry and biology. Even at a time when there are not many openings for bioengineers in industry, this triple culture is already very important for physical and chemical engineers.'

When a group on these lines started work at the Institut Curie in Paris, one of its first efforts was to try out an idea for artificial muscles proposed by de Gennes in 1997. These would not directly imitate the well-known but complex protein systems that produce muscle action in animals. Instead, they would aim for a similar effect of strong, quick contractions, in quite different materials—the liquid crystals.

Discovered in 1888 by Friedrich Reinitzer, an Austrian botanist, liquid crystals are archetypal untidy materials, being neither solid nor liquid yet in some ways resembling both. They were only a curiosity until 1971 when Wolfgang Helfrich of the Hoffmann-La Roche company in Switzerland found that a weak electric field could line up mobile rod-like molecules in a liquid crystal, and change it from clear to opaque. This opened the way to their widespread use in display devices. De Gennes suggested that similar behaviour in a suitably engineered material could make a liquid crystal contract like a muscle.

In this concept, a rubbery molecule is attached to each end of a rod-like liquid-crystal molecule. Such composite molecules tangle together to make a rubber sheet. The sheet will be longest when the liquid-crystal components all point in the same direction. Destroy that alignment, for example with a flash of light, and the liquid-crystal central regions will turn to point in all directions. That will force the sheet to contract suddenly, in a muscular fashion. By 2000 Philippe Auroy and Patrick Keller at the Institut Curie had made suitable mixed polymers, and they contracted just as predicted, as artificial muscles.

'We are now in the era of smart materials,' Keller commented. 'These can alter their shape or size in response to temperature, mechanical stress, acidity and so on, but they are often slow to react, or to return to their resting state. Our work on artificial muscles based on liquid crystals might open the way to designing fast-reacting smart polymers for many other purposes such as micro-pumps and micro-gates for micro-fluidics applications, and as "motors" for micro-robots or micro-drones.'

▶ *For other curious states of matter, see* MOLECULAR PARTNERS, PLASMA CRYSTALS *and* SUPERATOMS, SUPERFLUIDS AND SUPERCONDUCTORS.

DNA FINGERPRINTING

From parentage cases to facial diversity

T HE HUMAN GENETIC MATERIAL in deoxyribonucleic acid, or DNA, can be analysed rather easily to identify an individual. The discovery came suddenly and quite unexpectedly in 1984. Alec Jeffreys at Leicester was investigating the origin of the gene for myoglobin. That iron-bearing protein colours flesh red, and it supposedly diverged from haemoglobin, the active molecule in red blood cells, about 500 million years ago.

For convenience, the genetic material under study came from blood samples from Jeffreys himself and his colleagues. Jeffreys used a standard method of chopping up genetic material with an enzyme, and separated the fragments according to how fast they moved through jelly in response to an electric field. Then they could be tagged with a radioactive strand of DNA that attached itself to a particular gene sequence.

On an X-ray film, this produced a pattern of radioactively tagged DNA fragments. The surprise was that the pattern differed from one person to another, not subtly but in a blatant way. Within hours of first seeing such differences Jeffreys and his team had coined the term DNA fingerprinting, and were pricking their fingers to smear blood on paper, glass and other surfaces. They confirmed that the bloodstains might indeed identify them individually.

Within six months Jeffreys had his first real-life case. A black teenager had been denied admission to the country to rejoin his mother, a UK citizen originally from Ghana, because conventional blood tests could not confirm his parentage. When his DNA fingerprint showed clear features matching those of his mother and three siblings, the immigration ban was lifted. Jeffreys said, 'It was a golden moment to see the look on that poor woman's face when she heard that her two-year nightmare had ended.'

British police adopted DNA fingerprinting in 1986. The US Federal Bureau of Investigation followed suit two years later. Its use soon became routine around the world, in civil and criminal cases. A later refinement for use with trace samples, by making many copies of the DNA, led to the creation of national criminal DNA databases.

There were scientific spin-offs too. Field biologists found they could use DNA fingerprinting to trace mating behaviour, migrations and population changes in animals. For example they could check whether the apparent monogamy seen in many species of birds is confirmed by the paternity of the chicks. The answer is that in some species the females show strict fidelity while in others they cheat routinely on their apparent mates. Checking paternity is also a major application in human cases.

As in the original research at Leicester, technical progress in DNA fingerprinting goes hand in hand with ever-more sensitive techniques of genetic analysis, developed for general purposes in biological and medical research. By early in the 21st century Chad Mirkin, a chemist at Northwestern University, Illinois, was able to capture and identify a single telltale molecule from a pathogen, such as anthrax or the HIV virus of AIDS. It was a matter of letting the sought-for molecule bind to a matching DNA molecule held on a chip, where it would dangle and capture microscopic particles of gold washed over the chip.

When advances in human genetics culminated in the draft of the entire complement of genes in the human genome, and in the identification of many of the variant genes that make us all different, forensic scientists expected to be able to learn much more from a sample of DNA. If features such as eye and hair colour are determined by one or a very few genes, specifying a suspect's characteristics in those respects may be relatively simple. Height and weight may be harder.

A fascinating line of research blends fundamental and forensic science, and it concerns faces. That everyone's face should be different was a cardinal requirement in the evolution of human social behaviour, and learning to identify carers is one of the first things a baby does. Photographs or photofit images on Wanted posters play a big part in tracking down criminals. And when it comes to a trial, testimony of facial recognition weighs particularly heavily in the scales of justice.

We may resemble our relatives in our looks but are never exactly the same, even in identical twins. If Mother Nature varies human faces by shuffling a reasonably small number of genes, it should be possible to identify them and to relate each of them to this feature or that. Defining faces accurately is just as much of a scientific problem as tracing the genes.

Geneticists at University College London therefore teamed up with colleagues in medical graphics, to obtain 3-D scans of volunteers' faces to accompany the samples of their DNA. This research found funding from the UK's Forensic Science Service as well as from the Medical Research Council. The medical physicist Alf Linney, responsible for the faces analysis, commented: 'Sometime in the future we hope to be able to produce a photorealistic image of an offender's face, just from the DNA in a spot of blood or other body fluid found at a crime scene.'

See also GENES *and cross-references there. For the role of faces in human social evolution, see* ALTRUISM AND AGGRESSION.

EARTH

Why is it so very different from all the other planets of the Sun?

S NAPSHOTS OF OUR BEAUTIFUL BLUE, cloud-flecked planet, taken by astronauts during NASA's Apollo missions to the Moon in the late 1960s and early 1970s, had an impact on the public consciousness. Emotionally speaking they completed the Copernican revolution, 400 years late. Abstract knowledge that the Earth is just one small planet among others gave way to compelling visual proof. The pictures became icons for environmentalists, who otherwise tended to complain about the extravagance of the space race. 'There you are,' they said. 'Look after it!'

A favourite image showed the Earth rising over the lunar horizon, as if it were the Moon's moon. Other pictures from the same period deserved to be better known than they were. Setting off towards Jupiter in 1977, the Voyager spacecraft looked back towards the Earth to test their cameras. The radioed images showed not one lonely little ball in space, but two in partnership.

The leading question for space scientists exploring the Solar System has always been, Why is the Earth so odd, and especially fit for life? Often the cost of sending spacecraft to other planets has been justified to taxpayers on the grounds that, to look after the home planet properly, we'd better understand it more profoundly. By the end of the 20th century, experts began to realize that part of the explanation of the Earth's oddity was staring them in the face every moonlit night.

The moons circling around other planets are usually minute compared with the planets' own dimensions. For an exception you have to look as far away as little Pluto, beyond all the main planets. Its moon, called Charon, is half as wide as Pluto itself. Our own Moon is bigger than Pluto, and not very much smaller than the planet Mercury. Its diameter is 27 per cent of the Earth's. No one hesitates to hyphenate Pluto-Charon as a double planet, and now at last we have Earth-Moon too.

One aspect of living on a double planet concerns the creation of Earth-Moon. If, as suspected, the event was very violent, it might help to explain why the geology of the Earth is exceptional. And from chaos theory comes the realization that having the Moon as a consort protects the Earth from extreme disturbances to its orbit and its orientation in space. Otherwise those could have ruined its climate and killed off all life.

Peculiarities of the Earth's air and ocean raise a different set of issues. The oxygen is a product of life itself, but the superabundance of nitrogen in the atmosphere is a relatively rare feature. And the only other places in the Solar System with abundant liquid water are deep inside three of Jupiter's moons. Such spottiness tells of random processes producing the liquids, vapours and gases seen on the surfaces of solid bodies, with a big element of luck in the favourable outcome for the Earth.

Only on the blue planet does the mother star shine benignly on open water teeming with plankton and fish, and on moist, green hills and plains. To invoke good luck is no casual speculation, but a serious response by theorists to what the spacecraft saw when they began inspecting the planets and moons of the Solar System. The biggest shock came from Venus.

The ugly sister

More than 4000 years ago, in their early city-states in what is now Iraq, Sumerians sang of heaven's queen, Inanna, and of 'her brilliant coming forth in the evening sky'. In classical times, what name would do for the brightest planet but that of the sex goddess? Venus is one planet that almost everyone knows. But the Dutch astronomer Christiaan Huygens realized in the 17th century that perpetual cloud, which helps to make the planet bright, prevents telescopes on the Earth from seeing its surface.

When constrained only by knowledge that Venus was almost a twin of the Earth in size, and a bit closer to the Sun, scientists were as free as science-fiction writers to speculate about the wonders waiting to be discovered under the clouds. In 1918, Svante Arrhenius at Stockholm visualized a dripping wet planet covered in luxuriant vegetation. By 1961, radar echoes had shown that Venus turns about its axis, in the opposite sense to the rotation of the Earth and other planets, but very slowly.

Space missions to Venus unveiled the sex goddess and revealed a crone. As a long succession of US and Soviet spacecraft headed for Venus, from 1962 onwards, there were many indirect indications that this is not a pretty planet. Nearly all the water that Venus may have once possessed has gone, presumably broken by solar rays in the upper atmosphere and losing its hydrogen into space. No less than 96 per cent of the atmosphere is carbon dioxide, and the clouds are of sulphuric acid.

In 1982, when the Soviet Venera 13 landed on the surface, its thermometer measured 482°C, far above the melting point of metallic lead. The crushing atmospheric pressure was 92 times higher than on the Earth, equivalent to the water pressure 1000 metres deep in the sea. Venera 13 and other landers sent back pictures of brown-grey rocks, later shown to be of a volcanic type, scattered under an orange sky. As for the light level, the Soviet director of space research, Roald Sagdeev, described it as 'about as bright as Moscow at noon on a cloudy winter's day.'

Nor would the wider face of Venus have entranced Botticelli. NASA's Magellan satellite, which orbited the planet from 1990 to 1994, mapped most of the globe by radar, showing details down to 100 metres. As mountains and plains became visible in the radar images, with great frozen rivers of lava and pancake-like volcanic domes, the planet's surface turned out to be pockmarked with craters due to large meteorite impacts.

On the Earth, geological action tends to heal such blemishes—but not, it seems, on Venus. When the scientists of the Magellan project counted the craters, as a way of judging the ages of different regions, they found that the whole surface was the same age. And measurements of regional gravity showed none of the mismatch between topography and gravity that is a sign of active geology on our home planet.

'Venus was entirely resurfaced with lava flows, mostly ending about half a billion years ago,' said Steve Saunders, NASA's project scientist for Magellan. 'Except for some beautiful shield volcanoes that formed on the plains, scattered impact craters and perhaps a little wind erosion, it has hardly changed since. So Venus behaves quite differently from the Earth, and we're not sure why.'

On our own planet, earthquakes, volcanoes and the measurable drift of continents, riding on tectonic plates across the face of the globe, are evidence that geological action is non-stop. Mountains are created and erode away; oceans grow and shrink. The continual refreshment of the Earth's surface also fertilizes and refertilizes the ocean and the land with elements essential for life.

To see Venus like a death mask was quite shocking. Other rocky planets are geologically frozen—Mercury, orbiting closest to the Sun, and Mars out on the chilly side of the Earth. In those cases there's no reason for surprise. They are much smaller than the Earth and Venus. During the 4.5 billion years since all the planets were made, Mercury and Mars have already lost into space most of the internal heat needed for driving geological activity.

Mercury's surface is just a mass of impact craters, like the Moon. On Mars, huge extinct volcanoes speak of vigorous geological activity in the past, which may have come to a halt a billion years ago. River-like channels in the Martian surface, now dry, tell of water flowing there at some time in the past. Opinions are split as to whether abundant water was once a feature of Mars, or the running water was only temporary. Comet impacts have been suggested as a source of flash floods. So has the melting of icy soil, by volcanic heat or by changes in the tilt of the Martian axis of rotation.

Planetary scientists cannot believe that bulkier Venus has yet cooled so much that its outer rocks are permanently frozen. So they have to imagine Venus refreshing its surface episodically. Molten rock accumulates until it can burst through the frozen crust in an enormous belch that would be entirely inimical to life, if there were any. What mechanism makes the resurfacing happen globally is not at all clear. But the upshot is that the whole crust of Venus consists of just one immobile plate, in contrast with the Earth, where a dozen plates are in restless motion.

'The reason why plates don't move about on Venus may simply be a lack of water, which lubricates the plate boundaries on Earth,' said Francis Nimmo, a planetary scientist at University College London. 'The interior rocks in our planet remain wet because they receive water from the surface, making up for what they lose to the atmosphere in volcanoes. So we can't separate the geological histories of the planets from what happened to their atmospheres and water supplies.'

Surreal moons of the outer planets

The planets are all idiosyncratic because of the different ways they were put together. In the accepted scenario for the assembly of planets at the birth of the Solar System, dust formed lumps of ever-increasing size until, in the late stages of planetary formation, very large precursors were milling about. Their violent collisions could result either in merger or fragmentation.

The tumultuous and random nature of the process was not fully appreciated for as long as scientists had only five small solid objects to study in detail—Mercury, Venus, Earth, Moon and Mars. Although the big outer planets, Jupiter, Saturn, Uranus and Neptune, are gassy and icy giants completely different from the Earth, they have large numbers of attendant moons and fragmented material in rings around them. These brought new insight into the permutations possible in small bodies.

The grandest tour of the 20th century began in 1977 with the launch of NASA's two Voyager spacecraft. The project used a favourable alignment of the four largest planets of the Sun, which recurs only once in 175 years, in order to visit all of them in turn. At least Voyager 2 did, Voyager 1 having been diverted for a special inspection of Saturn's moon Titan. The Voyager project scientist, who later became director of NASA's Jet Propulsion Laboratory, was Ed Stone of Caltech.

'A 12-year journey to Neptune,' Stone recalled, 'was such a technical challenge that NASA committed to only a four-year mission to Jupiter and Saturn, with Voyager 2 as a backup to assure a close flyby of Saturn's rings and its large moon Titan. With the successful Voyager 1 flyby in late 1980, NASA gave us the okay to send Voyager 2 on the even longer journey to Uranus. Following the Uranus flyby in 1986, we were told we could go for Neptune. But the Neptune encounter in 1989 wasn't the end of the journey. The Voyagers are now in a race to reach the edge of interstellar space before 2020 while they still have enough electrical power to communicate with Earth.'

Quite a performance, for spacecraft weighing less than a tonne and using 1970s technology! Voyager pictures, radioed back from the vicinity of the giant planets, captivated the public and scientists alike. The magnificence of Jupiter in close-up, the intricacies of Saturn's rings, the surprising weather on Neptune where sunlight has barely one-thousandth of its strength at the Earth—these were wonderful enough. But what took the breath away was the variety of the giant planets' moons. Extraterrestrial geology became surreal.

Io, a moon of Jupiter, looked like a rotten orange stained black and white with mould. While searching for navigational stars in the background of an image of Io, a Voyager engineer, Linda Morabito, noticed a volcano erupting. Never before had an active volcano been seen anywhere but on the Earth. During the brief passes of Voyagers 1 and 2, nine eruptions occurred on Io, ejecting sulphurous material at a kilometre a second and creating visible plumes extending 300 kilometres into space.

Electrified sulphur, oxygen and sodium atoms from Io, caught up in Jupiter's strong magnetic field, form a doughnut around the planet that glows in ultraviolet light. The volcanic heat comes from huge tides, raised on Io by the gravity of nearby moons and Jupiter. Lesser tidal heating of Europa, another large moon of Jupiter, maintains beneath a surface of thick water ice an ocean of liquid water—unimagined at such a distance from the Sun.

Saturn's largest moon, Titan, was already known to have a unique atmosphere, including methane gas, although there were different opinions about whether it was thick or thin. That was why Voyager 1 detoured to inspect it. The spacecraft revealed that Titan's atmosphere is largely nitrogen and denser than the Earth's. Its instruments failed to penetrate the orange haze to see Titan's surface, but they detected other carbon compounds in the atmosphere, and whetted the scientists' appetite for more.

When Voyager 2 reached Uranus, the closely orbiting Miranda turned out to be another oddball, with canyons 20 kilometres deep and a jigsaw of surfaces of different ages. These invited the explanation that a severe impact had smashed Miranda into chunks, which had then reassembled themselves randomly. Play-Doh geology, so to speak.

On distant Neptune's largest moon, Triton, Voyager 2 observed giant geysers jetting nitrogen and dust thousands of metres into an exceedingly tenuous atmosphere. This activity was the more remarkable because Voyager 2 measured the surface temperature as minus 235 °C, making it the coldest place known among the planets. Triton seems to be a twin of the small and distant planet Pluto, captured by Neptune, and tidal heating greater than on Io could have melted much of the moon's interior.

The Voyagers' achievements came from non-stop flybys of the planets and moons. More detailed investigations required spacecraft orbiting around individual planets, for years of observations at close quarters. When NASA's Galileo spacecraft went into orbit around Jupiter at the end of 1995, it found that some volcanoes on Io are hotter than those on the Earth, and involve molten silicate rock welling up through the sulphurous crust. On the basis of readings from Galileo's magnetometer, scientists inferred the presence of liquid water on Jupiter's moons Ganymede and Callisto, although much deeper below the surface than on Europa, where the Voyager team had discovered it.

In fresh images of Europa, which possesses more liquid water than the Earth does, Gregory Hoppa and his colleagues in Arizona found strange, curving cracks, repeatedly forming afresh in the moon's surface. Strong tides in the subsurface ocean continually flex the kilometres-thick ice crust. The cracks grow to around 100 kilometres in length over 3.6 days, the time taken for Europa to orbit Jupiter.

'You could probably walk along with the advancing tip of a crack as it was forming,' Hoppa commented. 'And while there's not enough air to carry sound, you would definitely feel vibrations as it formed.'

Saturn's hazy moon Titan remained the most enigmatic object in the Solar System. In 1997 NASA dispatched the Cassini spacecraft to orbit around Saturn in 2004–08 and examine the planet, its rings and its moons in great detail. Titan was a prime target, both for 30 visits by Cassini itself, and for a European probe called Huygens, to be released from Cassini and to parachute through the atmosphere.

For the Cassini–Huygens team there was a keen sense of mystery about the origin of Titan's unique nitrogen–hydrocarbon atmosphere. And speculation, too, about the geology, meteorology and even oceanography that Huygens might unveil. Geysers spouting hydrocarbons like oil gushers on the Earth? Luridly coloured icebergs floating on a sea of methane and ethane? After the surprises of Io, Europa and Triton, anything seemed possible.

Is the Moon the Earth's daughter?

Space exploration thus left astronomers and geophysicists much better aware of the planetary roulette that went into building the Earth. The precise sequences and sizes of collisions, especially towards the end of the planet-making process, must have had a big but random effect on the character of the resulting bodies.

And when the construction work was essentially complete, comets and asteroids continued to rain down on the planets in great numbers for half a billion years. They added materials or blasted them away, affecting especially the atmospheres and oceans, if any.

So little was pre-ordained about the eventual nature of the Earth, that great uncertainties still surround any detailed theories of our planet's completion. At the start of the 21st century, some of the issues came into focus with two bodies in particular: the planet Mercury and the Earth's Moon.

A clever scheme enabled NASA's Mariner 10 spacecraft to fly past Mercury three times, in 1974–75. The results left planetary scientists scratching their heads long afterwards. Mercury is far denser than any other planet, and unlike the much larger Venus, it has a magnetic field. The planet seems to consist largely of iron, and if it ever had a thick mantle of silicate rocks, like Venus, Earth and Mars, it has lost most of them. Surface features tell of very violent impacts. Perhaps a big one blasted away the mantle rocks.

Puzzles about Mercury may be solved only with better information, and new space missions were approved after a lapse of several decades. NASA's small Messenger is due to go into orbit around Mercury in 2009. A few years later a more ambitious European–Japanese project, with two orbiters and a lander, is expected to arrive there. It's called BepiColombo, after the scientist at Padua who conceived the Mariner 10 flybys.

'We expect a massacre of many of our theories when we see Mercury properly,' said Tilman Spohn at Münster, a member of the BepiColombo science team. 'Quite simply, this mission will open our eyes to vital information about the origin of the planets that we still don't know. And after BepiColombo, we'll be better able to judge if earth-like planets are likely to be commonplace in the Universe, or if our home in space is the result of some lucky chance.'

A gigantic impact on the Earth, similar to what may have afflicted Mercury, was probably the origin of the Moon. Alistair Cameron of Harvard began studying the possibility in the 1970s. He continued to elaborate the theory until the end of the century, by which time it had become the preferred scenario for most planetary scientists.

One previous theory had suggested that the Earth was spinning so rapidly when it formed that the Moon broke off from a small bulge, like a stone from a sling. Another said that the Earth and Moon formed as a double planet in much the same way as stars very often originate in pairs called binaries. According to a third hypothesis, the Moon originated somewhere else and was later captured by the Earth.

There were difficulties about all of these ideas. And after scientists had interpreted rock samples from the lunar surface brought back by astronauts, and digested the knowledge from other space missions about the sheer violence of events in the Solar System, they came to favour the impact scenario. Especially telling were analyses of the Moon samples showing that the material was very like the Earth's in some respects, and different in others.

An object the size of the planet Mars supposedly hit the Earth just as it was nearing completion. A vast explosion flung out debris, both of the vaporized impactor and of material quarried by the blast from the Earth's interior. Most of the ejected debris was lost in space, but enough of it went into orbit around our planet to congeal into the Moon—making our satellite the Earth's daughter.

Initially the Moon was much closer than it is now and strong tidal action, as seen today in Io and Europa, intensified the heat inside the young Earth and Moon. The slimming of the Earth by the loss of part of its mantle of silicate rocks—by planetary liposuction, so to speak—would have lasting effects on heat flow and geological activity in the crust. So crucial is this scenario, for understanding the origin, evolution and behaviour of the Earth itself, that to verify or refute it has become quite urgent.

Long after the last lunar astronauts returned to the Earth, unmanned spacecraft from the USA, Japan and Europe began revisiting the Moon, to inspect it from orbit. Europe's Smart-1 spacecraft, due there in 2005, carries an X-ray instrument explicitly to test the impact hypothesis. Chemical elements on the lunar surface glint with X-rays of characteristic energy, and Smart-1 will check whether the relative proportions of the elements—especially of iron versus magnesium and aluminium—are in line with predictions of the theory.

'Surprisingly, no one has yet made the observations that we plan,' said Manuel Grande of the UK's Rutherford Appleton Laboratory, team leader for the X-ray instrument. 'That's why our small instrument on the small Smart-1 spacecraft has the chance to make a big contribution to understanding the Moon and its relation to the Earth.'

An antidote to chaos

Wherever it came from, the Moon is large enough to act as the Earth's stabilizer. Its importance in that role became clear in the early 1990s, when scientists got to grips with the effects of chaos in the Solar System. In this context, chaos means erratic and unpredictable alterations in the orbits of planets due to complicated interactions between them, via gravity.

Not only can the shape of an orbit be affected by chaos, but also the tilt of a planet's axis of rotation, in relation to its orbit. This orientation governs the timing and intensity of the seasons. Thus the Earth's North Pole is at present tilted by 23.4 degrees, towards the Sun in the northern summer, and away in winter.

Jacques Laskar of the Bureau des Longitudes in Paris was a pioneer in the study of planetary chaos. He found many fascinating effects, including the possibility that Mercury may one day collide with Venus, and he drew special attention to chaotic influences on the orientations of the planets. The giant planets are scarcely affected, but the tilt of Mars for example, which at present is similar to the Earth's, can vary between 0 and 60 degrees. With a large tilt, summers on Mars would be much warmer than now, but the winters desperately cold. Some high-latitude gullies on that planet have been interpreted as the products of slurries of melt-water similar to those seen on Greenland in summer.

'All of the inner planets must have known a powerfully chaotic episode in the course of their history,' Laskar said. 'In the absence of the Moon, the orientation of the Earth would have been very unstable, which without doubt would have strongly frustrated the evolution of life.'

▶ *Also of relevance to the Earth's origin are* COMETS AND ASTEROIDS *and* MINERALS IN SPACE. *For more on life-threatening events, see* CHAOS, IMPACTS, EXTINCTIONS *and* FLOOD BASALTS. *Geophysical processes figure in* PLATE MOTIONS, EARTHQUAKES *and* CONTINENTS AND SUPERCONTINENTS. *For surface processes and climate change, see the cross-references in* EARTH SYSTEM.

EARTHQUAKES

Why they may never be accurately predicted, or prevented

S HIPS THAT LEAVE TOKYO BAY crammed with exports pass between two peninsulas: Izu to starboard and Boso to port. The cliffs of their headlands are terraced, like giant staircases. The flat part of each terrace is a former beach, carved by the sea when the land was lower. The vertical rise from terrace to terrace tells of an upward jerk of the land during a great earthquake. Sailors wishing for a happy return ought to cross their fingers and hope that the landmarks will be no taller when they get back.

On Boso, the first step up from sea level is about four metres, and corresponds with the uplifts in earthquakes afflicting the Tokyo region in 1703 and 1923. The interval between those two was too brief for a beach to form. The second step,

219

five metres higher, dates from about 800 BC. Greater rises in the next two steps happened around 2100 BC and 4200 BC. The present elevations understate the rises, because of subsidence between quakes.

Only 20 kilometres offshore from Boso, three moving plates of the Earth's outer shell meet at a triple junction. The Eurasian Plate with Japan standing on it has the ocean floor of both the Pacific Plate and the Philippine Plate diving to destruction under its rim, east and west of Boso, respectively. The latter two have a quarrel of their own, with the Pacific Plate ducking under the Philippine Plate.

All of which makes Japan an active zone. Friction of the descending plates creates Mount Fuji and other volcanoes. Small earthquakes are so commonplace that the Japanese may not even pause in their conversations during a jolt that sends tourists rushing for the street. And there, in a nutshell, is why the next big earthquake is unpredictable.

Too many false alarms

As a young geophysicist, Hiroo Kanamori was one of the first in Japan to embrace the theory of plate tectonics as an explanation for geological action. He was co-author of the earliest popular book on the subject, *Debate about the Earth* (1970). For him, the terraces of Izu and Boso were ample proof of an unstoppable process at work, such that the earthquake that devastated Tokyo and Yokohama in 1923, and killed 100,000 people, is certain to be repeated some day.

First at Tokyo University and then at Caltech, Kanamori devoted his career to fundamental research on earthquakes, especially the big ones. His special skill lay in extracting the fullest possible information about what happened in an earthquake, from the recordings of ground movements by seismometers lying in different directions from the scene. Kanamori developed the picture of a subducted tectonic plate pushing into the Earth with enormous force, becoming temporarily locked in its descent at its interface with the overriding plate, and then suddenly breaking the lock.

Looking back at the records of a big earthquake in Chile in 1960, for example, he figured out that a slab of rock 800 by 200 kilometres suddenly slipped by 21 metres, past the immediately adjacent rock. He could deduce this even though the fault line was hidden deep under the surface. That, by the way, was the largest earthquake that has been recorded since seismometers were invented. Its magnitude was 9.5.

When you hear the strength of an earthquake quoted as a figure on the Richter scale, it is really Kanamori's moment magnitude, which he introduced in 1977. He was careful to match it as closely as possible to the scale pioneered in the 1930s by Charles Richter of Caltech and others, so the old name sticks. The Kanamori scale is more directly related to the release of energy.

Despite great scientific progress, the human toll of earthquakes continued, aggravated by population growth and urbanization. In Tangshan in China in 1976, a quarter of a million died. Earthquake prediction to save lives therefore became a major goal for the experts. The most concerted efforts were in Japan, and also in California, where the coastal strip slides north-westward on the Pacific Plate, along the San Andreas Fault and a swarm of related faults.

Prediction was intended to mean not just a general declaration that a region is earthquake prone, but a practical early warning valid for the coming minutes or hours. For quite a while, it looked as if diligence and patience might give the answers.

Scatter seismometers across the land and the seabed to record even the smallest tremors. Watch for foreshocks that may precede big earthquakes. Check especially the portions of fault lines that seem to be ominously locked, without any small, stress-relieving earthquakes. The scientists pore over the seismic charts like investors trying to second-guess the stock markets.

Other possible signs of an impending earthquake include electrical changes in the rocks, and motions and tilts of the ground detectable by laser beams or navigational satellites. Alterations in water levels in wells, and leaks of radon and other gases, speak of deep cracks developing. And as a last resort, you can observe animals, which supposedly have a sixth sense about earthquakes.

Despite all their hard work, the forecasters failed to give any warning of the Kobe earthquake in Japan in 1995, which caused more than 5000 deaths. That event seemed to many experts to draw a line under 30 years of effort in prediction. Kanamori regretfully pointed out that the task might be impossible.

Micro-earthquakes, where the rock slippage or creep in a fault is measured in millimetres, rank at magnitude 2. They are imperceptible either by people or by distant seismometers. And yet, Kanamori reasoned, many of them may have the potential to grow into a very big one, ranked at magnitude 7–9, with slippages of metres or tens of metres over long distances.

The outcome depends on the length of the eventual crack in the rocks. Crack prediction is a notoriously difficult problem in materials science, with the uncertainties of chaos theory coming into play. In most micro-earthquakes the rupture is halted in a short distance, so the scope for false alarms is unlimited.

'As there are 100,000 times more earthquakes of magnitude 2 than of magnitude 7, a short-term prediction is bound to be very uncertain,' Kanamori concluded in 1997. 'It might be useful where false alarms can be tolerated. However, in modern highly industrialized urban areas with complex lifelines, communication systems and financial networks, such uncertain predictions might damage local and global economies.'

Earthquake control?

During the Cold War a geophysicist at UC Los Angeles, Gordon MacDonald, speculated about the use of earthquakes as a weapon. It would operate by the explosion of bombs in small faults, intended to trigger movement in a major fault. 'For example,' he explained, 'the San Andreas fault zone, passing near Los Angeles and San Francisco, is part of the great earthquake belt surrounding the Pacific. Good knowledge of the strain within this belt might permit the setting off of the San Andreas zone by timed explosions in the China Sea and the Philippines Sea.'

In 1969, soon after MacDonald wrote those words, Canada and Japan lodged protests against a US series of nuclear weapons tests at Amchitka in the Aleutian Islands, on the grounds that they might trigger a major natural earthquake. They didn't, and the question of whether a natural earthquake or an explosion, volcanic or man-made, can provoke another earthquake far away is still debated. If there is any such effect it is probably not quick, in the sense envisaged here.

MacDonald's idea nevertheless drew on his knowledge of actual man-made earthquakes that happened by accident. An underground H-bomb test in Nevada in 1968 caused many small earthquakes over a period of three weeks, along an ancient fault nearby. And there was a longer history of earthquakes associated with the creation of lakes behind high dams, in various parts of the world.

Most thought provoking was a series of small earthquakes in Denver, from 1963 to 1968, which were traced to an operation at the nearby Rocky Mountain Arsenal. Water contaminated with nerve gas was disposed of by pumping it down a borehole 3 kilometres deep. The first earthquake occurred six weeks after the pumping began, and activity more or less ceased two years after the operation ended.

Evidently human beings could switch earthquakes on or off by using water under pressure to reactivate and lubricate faults within reach of a borehole. This was confirmed by experiments in 1970–71 at an oilfield at Rangely, Colorado. They were conducted by scientists from the US National Center for Earthquake Research, where laboratory tests on dry and wet rocks under pressure showed that jerks along fractures become more frequent but much weaker in the presence of water.

From this research emerged a formal proposal to save San Francisco from its next big earthquake by stage-managing a lot of small ones. These would gently relieve the strain that had built up since 1906, when the last big one happened. About 500 boreholes 4000 metres deep, distributed along California's fault lines, would be needed. Everything was to be done in a controlled fashion, by pumping water out of two wells to lock the fault on either side of a third well where the quake-provoking water would be pumped in.

The idea was politically impossible. Since every earthquake in California would be blamed on the manipulators, whether they were really responsible or not, litigation against the government would continue for centuries. And it was all too credible that a small man-made earthquake might trigger exactly the major event that the scheme was intended to prevent. By the end of the century Kanamori's conclusion, that the growth of a small earthquake into a big one might be inherently unpredictable, carried the additional message: you'd better not pull the tiger's tail.

Outpacing the earthquake waves

Research efforts switched from prediction and prevention to mitigating the effects when an earthquake occurs. Japan leads the world in this respect, and a large part of the task is preparation, as if for a war. It begins with town planning, the design of earthquake-resistant buildings and bridges, reinforcements of hillsides against landslips, and improvements of sea defences against tsunamis—the great 'tidal waves' that often accompany earthquakes.

City by city, district by district, experts calculate the risks of damage and casualties from shaking, fire, landslides and tsunamis. The entire Japanese population learns from infancy what to do in the event of an earthquake, and there are nationwide drills every 1 September, the anniversary of the 1923 Tokyo–Yokohama earthquake. Operations rooms like military bunkers stand ready to take charge of search and rescue, firefighting, traffic control and other emergency services, equipped with all the resources of information technology. Rooftops are painted with numbers, so that helicopter pilots will know where they are when streets are filled with rubble.

The challenge to earthquake scientists is now to feed real-time information about a big earthquake to societies ready and able to use it. A terrible irony in Kobe in 1995 was that the seismic networks and communications systems were themselves the first victims of the earthquake. The national government in Tokyo was unaware of the scale of the disaster until many hours after the event.

The provision for Japan's bullet trains is the epitome of what is needed. As soon as a strong quake begins to be felt in a region where they are running, the trains slow down or stop. They respond automatically to radio signals generated by a computer that processes data from seismometers near the epicentre. When tracks twist and bridges tumble, the life–death margin is reckoned in seconds. So the system's designers use the speed of light and radio waves to outpace the earthquake waves.

Similar systems in use or under development, in Japan and California, alert the general public and close down power stations, supercomputers and the like.

Especially valuable is the real-time warning of aftershocks, which endanger rescue and repair teams. A complication is that, in a very large earthquake, the idea of an epicentre is scarcely valid, because the great crack can run for a hundred or a thousand kilometres.

Squeezing out the water

There is much to learn about what happens underground at the sites of earthquakes. Simple theories about the sliding of one rock mass past another, and the radiation of shock waves, have now to take more complex processes into account. Especially enigmatic are very deep earthquakes, like one of magnitude 8 in Bolivia in 1994. It was located 600 kilometres below the surface and Kanamori figured out that nearly all of the energy released in the event was in the form of heat rather than seismic waves. It caused frictional melting of the rocks along the fault and absorbed energy.

In a way, it is surprising that deep earthquakes should occur at all, seeing that rocks are usually plastic rather than brittle under high temperatures and pressures. But the earthquakes are associated with pieces of tectonic plates that are descending at plate boundaries. Their diving is a crucial part of the process by which old oceanic basins are destroyed, while new ones grow, to operate the entire geological cycle of plate tectonics.

A possible explanation for deep earthquakes is that the descending rocks are made more rigid by changes in composition as temperatures and pressures increase. Olivine, a major constituent of the Earth, converts into serpentine by hydration if exposed to water near the surface. When carried back into the Earth on a descending tectonic plate, the serpentine could revert to olivine by having the water squeezed out of its crystals. Then it would suddenly become brittle. Although this behaviour of serpentine might explain earthquakes to a depth of 200 kilometres, dehydration of other minerals would be needed to account for others, deeper still.

A giant press at Universität Bayreuth enabled scientists from University College London to demonstrate the dehydration of serpentine under enormous pressure. In the process, they generated miniature earthquakes inside the apparatus. David Dobson commented, 'Understanding these deep earthquakes could be the key to unlocking the remaining secrets of plate tectonics.'

The changes at a glance

After an earthquake, experts traditionally tour the region to measure ground movements revealed by miniature scarps or crooked roads. Nowadays they can use satellites to do the job comprehensively, simply by comparing radar pictures obtained before and after an earthquake. The information contained within an image generated by synthetic-aperture radar is so precise that changes in relative positions by only a centimetre are detectable.

The technique was put to the test in 1999, when the Izmit earthquake occurred on Turkey's equivalent of California's San Andreas Fault. Along the North Anatolian Fault, the Anatolian Plate inches westwards relative to the Eurasian Plate, represented by the southern shoreline of the Black Sea. The quake killed 18,000 people. Europe's ERS-2 satellite had obtained a radar image of the Izmit region just a few days before the event, and within a few weeks it grabbed another.

When scientists at the Delft University of Technology compared the images by an interference technique, they concluded that the northern shore of Izmit Gulf had moved at least 1.95 metres away from the satellite, compared with the southern shore of the Black Sea. Among many other details perceptible was an ominous absence of change along the fault line west of Izmit.

'At that location there is no relative motion between the plates,' said Ramon Hanssen, who led the analysis. 'A large part of the strain is still apparent, which could indicate an increased risk for a future earthquake in the next section of the fault, which is close to the city of Istanbul.'

▶ *For the driving force of plate motions and the use of earthquake waves as a means of probing the Earth's interior, see* PLATE MOTIONS *and* HOTSPOTS.

EARTHSHINE

How bright clouds reveal climate change, and perhaps drive it

A MONG LEONARDO DA VINCI'S many scientific intuitions that have stood the test of half a millennium is his suggestion that the Moon is lit by the Earth, as well as by the Sun. That was how he accounted for the faint glow visible from the dark portion of a crescent Moon.

'Some have believed that the Moon has some light of its own,' the artist noted in his distinctive back-to-front writing, 'but this opinion is false, for they have based it upon that glimmer visible in the middle between the horns of the new Moon.' With neat diagrams depicting relative positions of Sun, Earth and Moon, Leonardo reasoned that our planet 'performs the same office for the dark side of the Moon as the Moon when at the Full does for us'.

The Florentine polymath was wrong in one respect. Overimpressed by the glistening western sea at sunset, he thought that the earthshine falling on the Moon came mainly from sunlight returned into space by the Earth's oceans. In fact, seen from space, the oceans look quite dark. The brightest features are cloud tops, which modern air travellers know well but Leonardo did not.

If you could stand on the Moon's dark side and behold the Full Earth it would be a splendid sight, almost four times wider than the Full Moon seen from the Earth, and 50 times more luminous. The whole side of the Earth turned towards the Moon contributes to the lighting of each patch of the lunar surface, to varying degrees. Ice, snow, deserts and airborne dust appear bright. But the angles of illumination from Sun to Earth to Moon have a big effect too, so that the most important brightness is in the garland of cloud tops in the tropics.

From your lunar vantage point you'd see the Earth rotating, which is a pleasure denied to Moon watchers, who only ever see one face. In the monsoon season, East and South Asia are covered with dense rain clouds. So when dawn breaks in Shanghai, and Asia swings out of darkness and into the sunlight, the earthshine can increase by as much as ten per cent from one hour to the next.

In the 21st century a network of stations in California, China, the Crimea and Tenerife is to measure Leonardo's earthshine routinely, as a way of monitoring climate change on our planet. Astronomers can detect small variations in the Earth's brightness. These relate directly to warming or cooling, because the

30 per cent or so of sunlight that the Earth reflects can play no part in keeping the planet warm. The rejected fraction is called the albedo, and the brighter the Earth is, the cooler it must be.

What's more, the variations seen on the dark side of the Moon occur mainly because of changes in the Earth's cloudiness. Weather satellites observe the clouds, region by region, and with due diligence NASA scientists combine data from all the world's satellites to build up global maps of cloudiness, month by month. But if you are interested in the total cloud cover, it is easier, cheaper and more reliably consistent just to look at the Moon. And you are then well on the way to testing theories about why the cloud cover changes.

The 'awfully clever' Frenchmen

The pioneer of earthshine measurements, beginning in 1925, was André-Louis Danjon of the Observatoire de Strasbourg, who later became director of the Observatoire de Paris. Danjon used a prism to put two simultaneous images of the Moon side by side. With a diaphragm like a camera stop he then made one image fainter until a selected patch on its sunlit part looked no brighter than a selected earthlit patch. By the stoppage needed, he could tell that the earthshine's intensity was only one five-thousandth of the sunshine's.

Danjon found that the intensity varied a lot, from hour to hour, season to season, and year to year. His student J. E. Dubois used the technique in systematic observations from 1940 to 1960 and came to suspect that changes in the intensity of earthshine were linked to the activity of the Sun in its 11-year sunspot cycle, with the strongest earthshine when the sunspots were fewest. But the measurements were not quite accurate enough for any firm conclusions to be drawn, in that respect.

'You realize that those old guys were awfully clever,' said Steven Koonin of Caltech in 1994. 'They didn't have the technology but they invented ways of getting around without it.' Koonin was a nuclear physicist who became concerned about global warming and saw in earthshine a way of using the Moon as a mirror in the sky, for tracking climate change. He re-examined the French theories for interpreting earthshine results, and improved on them.

A reconstruction of Danjon's instrument had been made at the University of Arizona, but Koonin wanted modern electronic light detectors to do the job thoroughly. He persuaded astronomers at Caltech's Big Bear Solar Observatory to begin measurements of earthshine in 1993. And by 2000 Philip Goode from Big Bear was able to report to a meeting on climate in Tenerife that the earthshine in that year was about two per cent fainter than it had been in 1994–95.

As nothing else had changed, to affect the Earth's brightness so much, there must have been an overall reduction of the cloud cover. Goode noted two possible explanations. One had to do with the cycle of El Niño, affecting sea temperatures in the eastern Pacific, which were at a minimum in 1994 and a maximum in 1998. Conceivably that affected the cloud cover.

The other explanation echoed Dubois in noting a possible link with the Sun's behaviour. Its activity was close to a minimum in 1994–95, as judged by the sunspot counts, and at maximum in 2000. Referring to a Danish idea, Goode declared: 'Our result is consistent with the hypothesis, based on cloud cover data, that the Earth's reflectance decreases with increasing solar activity.'

Clouds and cosmic rays

Two centuries earlier, when reading Adam Smith's *The Wealth of Nations*, the celebrated astronomer William Herschel of Slough noticed that dates given for high prices of wheat in England were also times when he knew there was a lack of dark sunspots on the Sun's bright face. 'It seems probable,' Herschel wrote in 1801, 'that some temporary scarcity or defect of vegetation has generally taken place, when the Sun has been without those appearances which we surmise to be symptoms of a copious emission of light and heat.'

Thereafter solar variations always seemed to be a likely explanation of persistent cooling or warming of the Earth, from decade to decade and century to century, as seen throughout climate history since the end of the last ice age. They still are. There was, though, a lapse of a few years in the early 1990s, when there was no satisfactory explanation for how the Sun could exert a significant effect on climate.

The usual assumption, following Herschel, was that changes in the average intensity of the Sun's radiation would be responsible. Accurate gauging of sunshine became possible only with instruments on satellites, but by 1990 the space measurements covered a whole solar cycle, from spottiest to least spotty to spottiest again. Herschel was right in thinking that the spotty, active Sun was brightest, but the measured variations in solar radiation seemed far too small to account for important climatic changes.

During the 1990s other ways were suggested, whereby the Sun may exert a stronger influence on climate. One of them involved a direct effect on cloudiness, and therefore on earthshine. This was the Danish hypothesis to which Goode of Big Bear alluded. It arose before there was any accurate series of earthshine measurements; however, the compilations of global cloud cover from satellite observations spanned enough years for the variations in global cloudiness to be compared with possible causes.

Henrik Svensmark, a physicist at the Danmarks Meteorologiske Institut in Copenhagen, shared the general puzzlement about the solar effect on climate. Despite much historical evidence for it, there was no clear mechanism. He knew that the Sun's activity during a sunspot cycle affects the influx of cosmic rays. These energetic atomic particles rain down on the Earth from exploded stars in the Galaxy. They are fewest when the Sun is in an active state, with many sunspots and a strong solar wind that blows away many of the cosmic rays by its magnetic effect.

Cosmic rays make telltale radioactive materials in the Earth's atmosphere, including the radiocarbon used in archaeological dating. Strong links are known between changes in their rate of production and climate changes in the past, such that high rates went with chilly weather and low rates with warmth. Most climate scientists had regarded the cosmic-ray variations, revealed in radiocarbon production rates, merely as indicators of the changes in the Sun's general mood, which might affect its brightness. Like a few others before him, Svensmark suspected that the link to climate could be more direct.

What if cosmic rays help clouds to form? Then a high intensity of cosmic rays, corresponding with a lazy Sun, would make the Earth shinier with extra clouds. It would reject more of the warming sunshine and become cooler. Conversely, a low count of cosmic rays would mean fewer clouds and a warmer world.

Working in his spare time, during the Christmas holiday in 1995, Svensmark surfed the Internet until he found the link he was looking for. By comparing cloud data from the International Satellite Cloud Climatology Project with counts of cosmic rays from Chicago's station in the mountains of Colorado, he saw the cloud cover increasing a little between 1982 and 1986, in lockstep with increasing cosmic rays. Then it diminished as the cosmic-ray intensity went down, between 1987 and 1991.

Svensmark found a receptive listener in the head of his institute's solar–terrestrial physics division, Eigil Friis-Christensen, who had published evidence of a strong solar influence on climate during the 20th century. Friis-Christensen was looking for a physical explanation, and he saw at once that Svensmark might have found the missing link. The two of them worked together on the apparent relationship between cosmic rays and clouds, and announced their preliminary results at a space conference in Birmingham, England, in the summer of 1996.

Friis-Christensen then went off to become Denmark's chief space scientist, as head of the Dansk Rumforskningsinstitut. Svensmark soon followed him there, to continue his investigations. By 2000, in collaboration with Nigel Marsh and using new cloud data from the International Satellite Cloud Climatology Project, Svensmark had identified which clouds were most affected by cosmic-ray variations. They were clouds at low altitudes and low latitudes, most noticeably over the tropical oceans.

At first sight this result was surprising. The cosmic rays, focused by the Earth's magnetism and absorbed by the air, are strongest near the Poles and at high altitudes. But that means that plenty are always available for making clouds in those regions, even at times when the counts are relatively low. Like rain showers in a desert, increases in cosmic rays have most effect in the regions where they are normally scarce.

A reduction in average low-cloud cover during the 20th century, because of fewer cosmic rays, should have resulted in less solar energy being rejected into space as earthshine. The result would be a warming of the planet. Marsh and Svensmark concluded that: 'Crude estimates of changes in cloud radiative forcing over the past century, when the solar magnetic flux more than doubled, indicates that a galactic-cosmic-ray/cloud mechanism could have contributed about 1.4 watts per square metre to the observed global warming. These observations provide compelling evidence to warrant further study of the effect of galactic cosmic rays on clouds.'

That was fighting talk, because the Intergovernmental Panel on Climate Change gave a very similar figure, 1.5 watts per square metre, for the warming effect of all the carbon dioxide added to the air by human activity. As the world's official caretaker of the hypothesis that global warming was due mainly to carbon dioxide and other greenhouse gases, the panel was reluctant to give credence to such a big effect of the Sun. In 2001 its scientific report declared: 'The evidence for a cosmic ray impact on cloudiness remains unproven.'

Chemicals in the air

Particle physicists and atmospheric chemists came into the story of the gleaming cloud tops, in an effort to pin down exactly how the cosmic rays might help to make clouds. Jasper Kirkby at CERN, Europe's particle physics lab in Geneva, saw a special chance for his rather esoteric branch of science to shine in environmental research, by investigating a possible cause of climate change. 'We propose to test experimentally the link between cosmic rays and clouds and, if confirmed, to uncover the microphysical mechanism,' he declared.

Starting in 1998, Kirkby floated the idea of an experiment called CLOUD, in which a particle accelerator should shoot a beam, simulating the cosmic rays, through a chamber representing the chilled, moist atmosphere where clouds form. By 2000 Kirkby had recruited more than 50 scientists from 17 institutes in Europe, Russia and the USA, who made a joint approach to CERN.

Despite this strong support, the proposal was delayed by criticisms. By the time these had been fully answered, CERN had run out of money for new research projects. In 2003, the Stanford Linear Accelerator Center in California was considering whether to accommodate the experiment, with more US participation.

The aim of the CLOUD team is to see how a particle beam's creation of ions in the experimental chamber—charged atoms and electrons—might stimulate cloud formation. Much would depend on the presence of traces of chemicals such as sulphuric acid and ammonia, known to be available in the air, and seeing how they behave with and without the presence of ions. It is from such chemicals, in the real atmosphere, that Mother Nature makes microscopic airborne grains called cloud condensation nuclei on which water droplets form from air supersaturated with moisture.

Advances in atmospheric chemistry favoured the idea of a role for cosmic rays in promoting the formation of cloud condensation nuclei, especially in the clean air over the oceans, where Svensmark said the effect was greatest. Fangqun Yu and Richard Turco of UC Los Angeles had studied the contrails that aircraft leave behind them across the sky. They found that the necessary grains for condensation formed in an aircraft's wake far more rapidly than expected by the traditional theory. Ions produced by the burning fuel evidently helped the grains to form and grow.

It was a short step for Yu and Turco then to acknowledge, in 2000, that cosmic rays could assist in making cloud condensation nuclei, and therefore in making clouds. The picture is of sulphuric acid and water molecules that collide and coalesce to form minute embryonic clusters. Electric charges, provided by the ions that appear in the wake of passing cosmic rays, help the clusters to survive, to grow and then quickly to coagulate into grains large enough to act as cloud condensation nuclei.

The reconvergence of the sciences in the 21st century has no more striking example than the proposition that the glimmer of the dark side of the Moon, diagnosed by Leonardo and measured by astronomers, may vary according to chemical processes in the Earth's atmosphere that are influenced by the Sun's interaction with the Galaxy—and are best investigated by the methods of particle physics.

▶ *For more about climate, see* CLIMATE CHANGE. *For evidence of a powerful solar effect on climate, see* ICE-RAFTING EVENTS. *The control of cosmic rays by the Sun's behaviour is explained more fully in* SOLAR WIND.

EARTH SYSTEM

I N THE MID-1980S FRANCIS BRETHERTON, a British-born fluid dynamicist, was chairman of NASA's Earth System Science Committee. He produced a diagram to show what he meant by the Earth system. It had boxes and interconnecting lines, like a circuit diagram, to indicate the actions and reactions in the physics, chemistry and biochemistry of the fluid outer regions of our planet. On the left of the diagram were the Sun and volcanoes as external natural agents of change, and on the right were human beings, affecting the Earth system and being affected by it.

In simpler terms, the Earth system consists of rocks, soil, water, ice, air, life and people. The Sun and the heat of the Earth's interior provide the power for the terrestrial machinery. The various parts interact in complicated, often obscure ways. But new powers of satellites and global networks of surface stations to monitor changes, and of computers to model complex interactions, as in weather forecasting, encouraged hopes of taming the complexity.

In 1986 the International Council of Scientific Unions instituted the International Geosphere–Biosphere Programme, sometimes called Global Change for short. A busy schedule of launches of Earth-observing satellites followed, computers galore came into use, and by 2001 $18 billion had gone into research on global change in the USA alone. In 2002 the Yokohama Institute for Earth Sciences began operating the world's most powerful supercomputer as the Earth Simulator.

Difficulties were emerging by then. The leading computer models concerned climate predictions, and as more and more factors in the complex Earth system were added to try to make the models more realistic, they brought with them scope for added errors and conflicting results—*see* **CLIMATE CHANGE**. Man-made carbon dioxide figured prominently in the models, but uncertainties surrounded the disappearance of about half of it into unidentified sinks—*see* **CARBON CYCLE**.

The most spectacular observational successes came with the study of vegetation using satellites, but again there were problems with modelling—*see* **BIOSPHERE FROM SPACE**. Doubts still attend other components of the Earth system. The monitoring and modelling of the world's ice give answers that sometimes seem contradictory—*see* **CRYOSPHERE**. The key role of the oceans, as a central heating system for the planet, still poses a fundamental question about what drives the circulation—*see* OCEAN CURRENTS.

Forecasting the intermittent changes in the Eastern Pacific Ocean that have global effects has also proved to be awkward—*see* EL NIÑO. From the not-so-solid Earth come volcanoes, both as a vital source of trace elements needed for nutrients, and as unpredictable factors in the climate system—*see* VOLCANIC EXPLOSIONS.

Another source of headaches is the non-stop discovery of new linkages. An early example in the era of Earth system science was the role of marine algae as a source of sulphate grains in the air—*see* GLOBAL ENZYMES. Later came a suggestion that cosmic rays from the Galaxy are somehow involved in cloud formation—*see* EARTHSHINE. The huge effort in the global-change programmes in the USA, Europe, Japan and elsewhere is undoubtedly enlarging knowledge of the Earth system, but a comprehensive and reliable description of it, in a single computer model, remains a distant dream.

ECO-EVOLUTION
New perspectives on variability and survival

H OW BLUE SHOULD THE BALTIC BE? As recently as the 1940s, northern Europe's almost-landlocked sea was noted for its limpid water. Thereafter it became more and more murky as a direct result of man-made pollution. Environmentalists said, 'Look, the Baltic Sea is dying.'

It was just the opposite. The opacity was due to the unwonted prosperity of algae, the microscopic plants that indirectly sustain the fishes, shellfish, seals, porpoises and seabirds. By the early 21st century, the effluent of nine countries surrounding the Baltic, especially the sewage and agricultural run-off from Poland, had doubled the nutrients available to the algae. Herring and mussels thrived as never before. Unwittingly the populations of its shores had turned the Baltic Sea into a fish farm.

There were some adverse results. Blooms of poisonous algae occurred more frequently, in overfertilized water. Seals were vulnerable. Cod and porpoises disliked the murk, and there was a danger that particular species might move out, or die out, reducing biodiversity. On top of that, dying sea eagles and infertile seals told of the harm done by toxic materials like PCB and DDT, which were brought partially under control after the 1970s.

The issue of quantity versus quality of life in the polluted Baltic illustrated an urgent need for fresh thinking about ecology—the interactions of species with their physical and chemical environments, and with other species including human beings. Until recently, most scientific ecologists shared with conservationists a static view of the living world. All change was abhorrent. Only gradually did the scientists wake up to the fact that forests and other ecosystems are in continual flux, even without human interference. Climates change too, and just 10,000 years ago the Baltic was a lump of ice.

Recent man-made effects on the Baltic have to be understood, not just as an insult to Mother Nature, but as an environmental change to which various species will adapt well or badly, as their ancestors did for billions of years. In the process the species themselves will change a little. They will evolve to suit the new circumstances.

A symptom of new scientific attitudes, towards the end of the 20th century, was the connecting of ecology with evolutionary biology, evident in the titles of more and more university departments. Some of the academic teams were deeply into molecular biology, of which the founding fathers of ecology knew very little. These trends made onlookers hopeful that, in the 21st century, ecology might become an exact science at last. Then it could play a more effective role in minimizing human damage to the environment and wildlife.

Jon Norberg of Stockholm was one who sought to recast ecological theory in evolutionary terms. He was familiar with the algae of the Baltic, the zooplankton that prey on them, and the fishes that prey on the zooplankton. So it was natural for him to use them as an example to think about. While at Princeton, he simulated by computer a system in which 100 species of algae are exposed to seasonal depredation.

The algal community thrives better, as gauged by its total mass, when there is variability within each species. You might not expect that, because some individuals are bound to be, intrinsically, less productive than others. But the highly variable species score because they are better able to cope with the changing predation from season to season.

In 2001 Norberg published, together with American and Italian colleagues at Princeton, the first mathematical theory of a community of species in which the species themselves may be changing. Some of the maths was borrowed from theories of the evolutionists, about how different versions of genes behave in a population of plants or animals. The message is that communities of species are continually adapting to ever-changing circumstances, from season to season.

In an ecosystem, just as in long-term evolution, what counts is the diversity of individuals that gives each species its flexibility. The variability between individuals within a species makes it more efficient in finding a role in the environment, if need be by evolving in a new direction. Meanwhile, an ensemble of different species improves the use of the resources available in their ecosystem.

As often happens, these biologists found that Charles Darwin had been there before them. He reported in 1859, 'It has been experimentally proved, that if a plot of ground be sown with several distinct genera of grasses, a greater number of plants and a greater weight of dry herbage can thus be raised.'

The new mathematical theory carried a warning for environmental policy-makers, not to be complacent when a system such as the Baltic Sea seems to be coping with man-made pollution fairly well. If the environment changes too rapidly, some species may fail to adapt fast enough. 'Biologically speaking, this means that an abrupt transition of species occurs in the community within a very short time,' Norberg and his colleagues commented. 'This phenomenon deserves further attention, because ongoing global changes may very well cause accelerating environmental changes.'

Ecology in a test-tube

Bacteria were put through their evolutionary and ecological paces in a series of experiments initiated by Paul Rainey at Oxford in the late 1990s. *Pseudomonas fluorescens* is an unusually versatile bug. It mutates to suit its circumstances, to produce what are virtually different species, easily distinguishable by eye. A week in the life of bacteria, growing in a nutritious broth in a squat glass culture tube, is equivalent to years or decades in an ecosystem of larger species in a lake.

Within the bulk of the broth the bacteria retain their basic form, which is called 'smooth'. The submerged glass surface, equivalent to the bed of a lake, comes to be occupied by the form called 'fuzzy spreaders'. The surface of the broth, best provided with oxygen, becomes home for another type of *Pseudomonas fluorescens*, 'wrinkly spreaders' that create distinctive mats of cellulose. When the Oxford experimenters shook the culture continually, so that individual bacteria no longer had distinctive niches to call their own, the diversity of bacterial types disappeared. So a prime requirement for biodiversity is a choice of habitats.

In more subtle experiments, small traces of either wrinkly or fuzzy forms of the bacteria were introduced in competition with the predominant smooth form. Five times out of six the invader successfully competed with the incumbent form, and established itself well. In an early report on this work, Rainey and Michael Travisano stressed the evolutionary aspect of the events in their ecological microcosm.

They likened them to the radiation of novel species into newly available habitats. 'The driving force for this radiation was competition,' they wrote. 'We can attribute the evolution and proliferation of new designs directly to mutation and natural selection.'

In later research, ecologists from McGill University in Montreal teamed up with Rainey's group to test other theoretical propositions about the factors governing the diversity of species. Experiments with increasing amounts of nutrients in the broth showed, as expected, that diversity peaked at an intermediate level of the total mass of the bacteria. With too much nutrition, the number of types of *Pseudomonas fluorescens* eventually declined. That was because the benefits of high nutrition are not equal in all niches, and the type living in the most favoured niche swamped the others.

Disturbing a culture occasionally, by eliminating most of it and restarting the survivors in a fresh broth, also encouraged diversity. This result accorded with the 'intermediate disturbance hypothesis' proposed a quarter of a century earlier to explain the diversity of species found among English wild flowers, in rain forests and around coral reefs. Occasional disturbances of ecosystems give opportunities for rare species to come forward, which are otherwise overshadowed by the commonest ones.

'The laboratory systems are unimpressive to look at—small glass tubes filled with a cloudy liquid,' commented Graham Bell of McGill, about these British–Canadian experiments with bacteria. 'It is only by creating such simple microcosms, however, that we can build a sound foundation for understanding the much larger and richer canvas of biodiversity in natural communities.'

Biodiversity in the genes

Simple counts of species and their surviving numbers are a poor guide to their prospects. The capacity for survival, adaptation and evolution is represented in the variant genes within each species. The molecules of heredity underpin biodiversity.

So molecular genetics, by reading and comparing the genes written in deoxyribonucleic acid, DNA, gives another new pointer for ecologists. According to William Martin of the Heinrich-Heine Universität Düsseldorf and Francesco Salamini of the Max-Planck-Institut für Züchtungsforschung in Cologne, even a community of plants, animals and microbes that seems poor in species may have more genetic diversity than you'd think.

Martin and Salamini offered a *Gedankenexperiment*—a thought experiment—for trying to understand life afresh. Imagine that you can make a complete genetic analysis of every individual organism, population and living community on Earth. You see the similarities and variations of genes that create distinctness at all levels, between individuals, between subspecies and between species.

With a gigantic computer you relate the genes and their frequencies to population compositions, to the geography, climate and history of habitats, to evolutionary rates of change, and to human influences. Then you have the grandest possible view of the biological past, of its preservation within existing organisms, and of evolution at work today, right down to the differences between brothers and sisters. And you can redefine species by finding the genetic distinctness associated with the shapes, features and other traits that field biologists use to distinguish one plant, animal or microbe from another.

Technically, that's far-fetched at present. Yet Martin and Salamini affirmed that the right sampling principles and automated DNA analysers could start to sketch the genetics of selected ecosystems. These techniques could also home in on endangered plants and animals, to identify the endangered genes. In a small but important way they have already identified, in wild relatives of crop plants, genes that remain unused in domesticated varieties.

'Measures of genetic distinctness within and between species hold the key to understanding how Nature has generated and preserved biological diversity,' Martin and Salamani concluded in a manifesto for 21st century natural history. 'But if there are no field biologists who know their flora and fauna, geneticists will neither have material to work on, nor will they know the biology of the organisms they are studying. In this sense, there is a natural predisposition towards a symbiosis between genetics and biodiversity—a union that current progress in DNA technology is forging.'

▶ *For further theories and discoveries about genetic diversity and survival, see* PLANT DISEASES *and* CLONING. *For other impressions of how ecological science is evolving, see* BIODIVERSITY, BIOSPHERE FROM SPACE *and* PREDATORS. *For a long-term molecular perspective on ecology and evolution, see* GLOBAL ENZYMES.

ELECTROWEAK FORCE

How Europe recovered its fading glory in particle physics

A PRIVILEGE of being a science reporter is the chance to learn the latest ideas directly from people engaged in making discoveries. In 1976, after visiting a hundred experts across Europe and the USA, a reporter scripting a television documentary on particle physics knew in detail what the crucial experiments were, and what the theorists were predicting. But he still didn't understand the ideas deeply enough to explain them in simple terms to a TV audience. The reporter therefore begged an urgent tutorial from Abdus Salam, a Pakistani theorist then in London.

In the senior common room at Imperial College, a promised hour became three hours as the conversation went around the subject again and again. It kept coming back to photons, which are particles of light, to electrons, which are dinky, negatively charged particles, and to positrons, which are anti-electrons with positive charge. The relationship between those particles was central to Salam's own idea about how the electric force might be united to another force in the cosmos, the weak force that changes one form of matter into another.

The turning point came when the reporter started to comment, 'Yes, you say that a photon can turn into an electron and a positron . . . ,' and Salam interrupted him. 'No! I say a photon *is* an electron and a positron.' The scales dropped from the reporter's eyes and he saw the splendour of the new physics, which was soon to evolve into what came to be called the Standard Model.

In the 19th century, matter was one thing, whilst the forces acting on it—gravity, electricity, magnetism—were as different from matter as the wind is from the waves of the sea. During the early decades of the 20th century, two other cosmic forces became apparent. One, already mentioned, was the weak force, the cosmic alchemist best known in radioactivity. The other novelty was the strong nuclear force that binds together the constituents of the nuclei of atoms.

As the nature of subatomic particles and their various interactions became plainer, the distinction between matter and forces began to disappear. Both consisted of particles—either matter particles or force carriers. The first force to be accounted for in terms of particles was the electric force, which had already been unified with magnetism by James Clerk Maxwell in London in 1864. Maxwell knew nothing about the particles, yet he established an intimate link between electromagnetism and light.

By the 1930s physicists suspected that light in the form of particles—the photons—act as carriers of the electric force. The photons are not to be seen, as visible or even invisible light in the ordinary sense. Instead they are virtual particles that swarm in a cloud around particles of matter, making them iridescent in an abstract sense. The virtual photons exist very briefly by permission of the uncertainty of quantum theory. They can come into existence and disappear before Mother Nature has time to notice.

Charged particles of matter, such as electrons, can then exert a mutual electric force by exchanging virtual photons. At first this idea seemed crazy or at best unmanageable because the calculations gave electrons an infinite mass and infinite charge. Nevertheless, in 1947 slight discrepancies in the wavelengths of light emitted by hydrogen atoms established the reality of the cloud of virtual photons.

Sin-Itiro Tomonaga in Tokyo, Julian Schwinger at Harvard and Richard Feynman at Cornell then tamed the very tricky mathematics. The result was the theory of the electric force called quantum electrodynamics, or QED. It became the most precisely verified theory in the history of physics.

Now hark back to Salam's assurance that a photon consists of an electron and an anti-electron. The latter term is here used in preference to positron, to emphasize the persistent role of antimatter in the story of cosmic forces. The evidence for the photon's composition is that if it possesses sufficient energy, in a shower of cosmic rays for example, a photon can actually break up into tangible particles, electron and anti-electron.

The electric force carrier is thus made of components of the same kind as the matter on which it acts. A big idea that emerged in the early 1960s was that other combinations of particles and antiparticles create the carriers of other cosmic forces.

The star breaker and rock warmer

The weak force is by no means as boring or ineffectual as it sounds. On the contrary, it plays an indispensable part in the nuclear reactions by which the Sun and the stars burn. And it can blow a star to smithereens in the nuclear cataclysm of a supernova, when vast numbers of neutrinos are created— electrons without an electric charge.

Neutrinos can react with other matter only by the weak force and as a result they are shy, ghostly particles that pass almost unnoticed through the Earth. But the neutrinos released in a supernova are so numerous that, however slight the chance of interaction by any particular neutrino, the stuff of the doomed star is blasted out into space.

Nearer home, the weak force contributes to the warming of the Earth's interior—and hence to volcanoes, earthquakes and the motions of continents—by the form of radioactivity called beta-decay occurring in atoms in the rocks. Here the weak force operates in the nuclei of atoms, which are made of positively charged protons and neutral neutrons. The weak force can change a neutron into a proton, with an electron and an antineutrino as the by-products. Alternatively it converts a proton into a neutron, with the emission from the nucleus of an anti-electron and a neutrino.

Just as the cosmic rays report that the electric force carrier consists of an electron and anti-electron, so the emissions of radioactive atoms suggest that the weak force carrier is made of an electron and a neutrino—one or other being normal and its companion, anti. The only difference from the photon is that one of the electrons is uncharged. While the charges of the electron and anti-electron cancel out in the photon, the weak force carrier called W is left with a positive or negative electric charge.

Another, controversial possibility that Salam and others had in mind in the 1960s concerned an uncharged weak-force carrier called Z. It would be like a photon, the carrier of the electric force, except that it would have the ability to interact with neutrinos. Ordinary photons can't do so, because neutrinos have no electric charge.

Such a Z particle would enable a neutrino to act like a cannon ball, setting particles of matter in motion while remaining unchanged itself. This would be quite different from the well-known manifestations of the weak force. In fact it would be a force of an entirely novel kind.

The first theoretical glimpse of the Z came when Sheldon Glashow, a young Harvard postdoc working in Copenhagen in 1958–60, was wondering whether the electric and weak forces might be united, as Maxwell had done with electromagnetism a century earlier. He used mathematics developed in 1954 by Chen Ning Yang and Robert Mills, who happened to be sharing a room at the Brookhaven National Laboratory on Long Island. The logic of the theory—the symmetry, as physicists call it—required a neutral Z as well as the Ws of positive and negative charge.

There was a big snag. Although the W and Z particles of the weak force were supposedly similar to the photons of the electric force, they operated only over a very short range, on a scale smaller than an atomic nucleus. A principle of quantum theory relates a particle's sphere of influence inversely to its mass, so the W and Z had to be very heavy.

A breakthrough in Utrecht

There was at first no explanation of where the mass might come from. Then Peter Higgs in Edinburgh postulated the existence of a heavy particle that could interact with other particles and give them mass. In 1967–68, Abdus Salam in London and Steven Weinberg at Harvard independently seized on the Higgs particle as the means of giving mass to the carriers of the weak force.

W and Z particles would feel the dead weight of the Higgs particle, like antelopes plodding ponderously through a bog, while the photons would skitter like insects, unaffected by the quagmire. In very hot conditions, such as may have prevailed at the start of the Universe, the W and Z would skitter too. Then the present gross differences between the electric force and the weak force would be absent, and there would be just one force instead of two.

This completed a sketch of a unified electroweak force. As with the earlier analysis of the electric force, the experts could not at first do the sums to get sensible answers about the details of the theory. To illustrate the problem, Salam cited the 17th-century Budshahi Mosque in Lahore in his homeland, renowned for the symmetry of its central dome framed by two smaller domes.

'The task of the [architectural] theory would be in this case to determine the relative sizes of the three domes to give us the most perfect symmetrical pattern,' Salam said. 'Likewise the task of the [electroweak] theory will be to give us the relative sizes—the relative masses—of the particles of light and the particles of the weak force.'

A 24-year-old Dutch graduate student, Gerard 't Hooft of Utrecht, cracked the problem in 1971. His professor, Martin Veltman, had developed a way of doing complicated algebra by computer, in the belief that it would make the calculations of particles and forces more manageable. In those days computers were monsters that had to be fed with cards punched by hand. The student's success with Veltman's technique surpassed all expectation, in a field where top experts had floundered for decades.

'I came fresh into all that and just managed to combine the right ideas,' 't Hooft said. 'Veltman's theory for instance just needed one extra particle. So I walked into his office one day and suggested to him to try this particle. He was very sceptical at first but then his computer told him point blank that I was right.'

The achievements in Utrecht were to influence the whole of theory-making about particles and forces. In the short run they made the electroweak theory respectable, mathematically speaking. The masses of the W and Z particles carrying the weak force were predicted to be about 100 times the mass of the proton. That was far beyond the particle-making powers of accelerators at the time.

● Evidence among the bubbles

'The Z particle wasn't just a possibility—it was a necessity,' 't Hooft recalled later. 'The theory of the electroweak force wouldn't work without it. Many people didn't like the Z, because it appeared to be coming from the blue, an artefact invented to fix a problem. To take it for real required some courage, some confidence that we were seeing things really right.'

Although there was no early prospect for making Z particles with available machines, their reality might be confirmed by seeing them in action, in particle collisions. This was accomplished within a few years of 't Hooft's theoretical results in an experiment at CERN, Europe's particle physics laboratory in Geneva. It used a large French-built particle detector called a bubble chamber. Filled with 18 tonnes of freon, it took its name from the gluttonous giantess Gargamelle in François Rabelais' *Gargantua et Pantagruel*.

The CERN experimenters shot pulses of neutrinos into Gargamelle. When one of the neutrinos condescended to interact with other matter, by means of the weak force, trails of bubbles in the freon revealed charged products of the interactions. Analysts in Aachen, Brussels, Paris, Milan, London, Orsay, Oxford and at CERN itself patiently examined Gargamelle photos of hundreds of thousands of neutrino pulses, and measured the bubble-tracks.

About one picture in a thousand showed particles set in motion by an impacting neutrino that did not change its own identity in the interaction. It behaved in the predicted cannon-ball fashion. The first example turned up in Helmut Faissner's laboratory in Aachen in 1972. An electron had suddenly started moving as if driven by an invisible agency—by a neutrino that, being neutral, left no track in the bubble chamber.

In other cases, a spray of particles showed the debris from an atomic nucleus in the freon of the bubble chamber, hit by a neutrino. In normal weak interactions, the track of a heavy electron (muon) also appeared, made by the transformation of the neutrino. But in a few cases an unmodified neutrino went on its way unseen. This was precisely the behaviour expected of the uncharged Z carrier of the weak force, expected in the electroweak theory.

The first that Salam heard about it was when he was carrying his luggage through Aix-en-Provence on his way to a scientific meeting, and a car pulled up beside him. 'Get in,' said Paul Musset of the Gargamelle Collaboration. 'We have found neutral currents.'

Oh dear, the jargon! When announced in 1973, the discovery by the European team might have caused more of a stir if the physicists had not kept calling it the weak interaction via the neutral current. It sounded not just vague and complicated, but insipid. In reality the bubble chamber had revealed a new kind of force in the Universe, Weak Force Mark II.

As expensive gamble pays off

To confirm the story, the physicists had no option but to try to make W and Z particles with a new accelerator. Since 1945, Western Europe's particle physicists and the governments funding them had barely kept up with their American colleagues, in the race to build ever-larger accelerators and discover new particles with them. That was despite a great pooling of effort in the creation of CERN. Could the physicists of Europe turn the tables for once, and be first to produce the weak-force particles?

CERN's biggest machine was then the Super Proton Synchrotron. It took in positively charged protons, the nuclei of hydrogen, and accelerated them to high energies while whirling them around in a ring of magnets 7 kilometres in circumference. A Dutch scientist, Simon van der Meer, developed a technique for storing and accumulating antiprotons. If introduced into the Super Proton Synchrotron, the negatively charged antiprotons would naturally circle in the opposite sense around the ring of magnets.

Pulses of protons and antiprotons, travelling in contrary directions, might then be accelerated simultaneously in the machine. When they achieved their maximum energy of motion, they could be allowed to collide head-on. The debris from the colliding beams might include free-range examples of the W and Z particles predicted by the electroweak theory.

Carlo Rubbia, an Italian physicist at CERN, was the most vocal in calling for such a collider to be built. It would mean halting existing research programmes. There was no guarantee that the collider would work properly, still less that it would make the intended discoveries.

'Would cautious administrators and committees entrusted with public funds from many countries overcome their inhibitions and take a very expensive gamble?' Rubbia wrote later. 'Europe passed the test magnificently.' CERN's research board made the decision to proceed with the collider at CERN, in 1978. Large multinational teams assembled two big arrays of particle detectors to record the products of billions of collisions of protons and antiprotons.

The wiring of the detectors looked like spaghetti factories. The problem was to find a handful of rare events among the tracks of confusing junk of well-known particles flung out from the impacts. The signature of a W particle would be its decay into a single very energetic electron, accompanied by an unseen neutrino. For a Z particle, an energetic electron and anti-electron pair would be a detectable product.

Success came in 1983 with the detection first of ten Ws, and then of five Zs. In line with 't Hooft's expectations, the Ws weighed in at 85 proton masses, and the Zs at 97. The discoveries were historic in more than a technical sense. Half a century after Einstein and many other physicists began fleeing Europe, first because of Hitler, then of war, and finally of post-war penury that crippled research, the old continent was back in its traditional place at the cutting edge of fundamental physics.

CERN was on a roll, and the multinational organization went on to build a 27-kilometre ring accelerator, the Large Electron–Positron Collider, or LEP. It could be tuned to make millions of Ws or Zs to order, so that their behaviour could be examined in great detail. This was done to such effect that the once-elusive carriers of the weak force are now entirely familiar to physicists and the electroweak theory is comprehensively confirmed.

Just before LEP's shutdown in 2000, experimenters at CERN thought they might also have glimpsed the mass-giving Higgs particle required by the theory. Their hopes were dashed, and the search for the Higgs resumed at Fermilab near Chicago. But before the first decade of the 21st century was out, CERN was expected to return to a leading position with its next collider for protons and antiprotons, occupying LEP's huge tunnel.

▶ *For more about the Standard Model and other cosmic forces, see* PARTICLE FAMILIES *and* HIGGS BOSONS.

ELEMENTS
A legacy from stellar puffs, collapsing giants
and exploding dwarfs

A LTHOUGH IT AS COMMON as copper in the Earth's crust, cerium is often considered an esoteric metal. It belongs to what the Italian writer Primo Levi called 'the equivocal and heretical rare-earth group'. Cerium was the subject of the most poignant of all the anecdotes that Levi told in *Il sistema periodico* (1975) concerning the chemical elements—the tools of his profession of industrial chemistry.

As a Jew in the Auschwitz extermination camp, he evaded death by making himself useful in a laboratory. He seemed nevertheless doomed to perish from hunger before the Red Army arrived to liberate them in 1945. In the lab Levi found unlabelled grey rods that sparked when scraped with a penknife. He identified them as cerium alloy, the stuff of cigarette-lighter flints.

His friend Alberto told him that one flint was worth a day's ration of bread on the camp's black market. During an air raid Levi stole the cerium rods and the two prisoners spent their nights whittling them under a blanket till they fitted through a flint-sized hole in a metal plate. Alberto was marched away before the Russians came, never to be seen again, but Levi survived.

Mother Nature went to great lengths to create, from the nuclear particles protons and neutrons, her cornucopia of elements that makes the world not just habitable but beautiful. The manufacture of Levi's life-saving cerium required dying stars much more massive than the Sun. And their products had to be stockpiled for making future stars and planets. From our point of view the wondrous assembly of stars that we call the Milky Way Galaxy is just a 12-billion-year-old chemical cauldron for making the stuff we need.

Primordial hydrogen and helium, tainted with a little lithium, are thought to be products of the Big Bang. Otherwise, the atomic nuclei of all of our elements were synthesized in stars that grew old and expired before the Sun and the Earth came into existence. They divide naturally into lighter and heavier elements, made mainly by lighter and heavier stars, respectively. The nuclear fusion that powers the Sun and the stars creates from the hydrogen additional helium, plus a couple of dozen other elements of increasing atomic mass, up to iron. These are therefore the commonplace elements.

Most favoured are those whose masses are multiples of the ubiquitous helium-4. They include carbon-12 and oxygen-16, convenient for life, and silicon-28 which is handy for making planets as well as microchips. Stars of moderate size puffed out many such light atoms as they withered for lack of hydrogen fuel. Iron-56, which colours blood, magnetizes the Earth and builds automobiles, came most generously from stars a little bigger than the Sun that evolved into exploding white dwarfs.

Beyond iron, the nuclear reactions needed for building heavier atomic nuclei absorb energy instead of releasing it. The most productive factories for the elements were big stars where, towards the end of brilliant but short lives, temperatures soared to billions of degrees and drenched everything with neutrons, providing us with another 66 elements. From the largest stars, the culminating explosions prodigally scattered zinc and bismuth and uranium nuclei into interstellar space, along with even heavier elements, too gross to survive for long. The explosions left behind only the collapsed cores of the parent stars.

Patterns in starlight enable astronomers to distinguish ancient stars, inhabitants of a halo around the Galaxy, that were built when all elements heavier than helium were much scarcer than today. Star-making was more difficult then, because the elements themselves assist in the process by cooling the gas. Without their help, stars may have been larger than now, which would have influenced the proportions of different elements that they made. At any rate, very large stars are the shortest-lived and so would have been the first to explode. By observing large samples of ancient halo stars, astronomers began to see the trends in element-making early in the history of our Galaxy, as the typical exploding stars became less massive.

'Certain chemical elements don't form until the stars that make them have had time to evolve,' noted Catherine Pilachowski of the US National Optical Astronomy Observatory, when reporting in 2000 on a survey of nearly 100 halo stars. 'Therefore we can read the history of star formation in the compositions of the oldest stars.' According to the multi-institute team to which Pilachowski belonged, the typical mass of the exploding stars had fallen below ten times the mass of the Sun by some 30–100 million years after star-making began in the Milky Way. That was when the production of Primo Levi's 'heretical' rare earths was particularly intensive.

All according to Hoyle

'The grand concept of nucleosynthesis in stars was first definitely established by Hoyle in 1946.' So William Fowler of Caltech insisted, when he won the 1983 Nobel Physics Prize for this discovery and Fred Hoyle at Cambridge was unaccountably passed over. Hoyle's contribution can hardly be exaggerated. While puzzling out the processes in stars that synthesize the nuclei of the elements, he taught the nuclear physicists a thing or two. Crucial for our own existence was an excited state of carbon nuclei that he discovered, which favoured the survival of carbon in the stellar furnaces.

In 1957 Hoyle and Fowler, together with Margaret and Geoffrey Burbidge, published a classic paper on element formation in stars that was known ever after as B^2FH, for Burbidge, Burbidge, Fowler and Hoyle. As Hoyle commented in a later textbook, 'The parent stars are by now faint white dwarfs or superdense neutron stars which we have no means of identifying. So here we have the answer to the question in Blake's poem, *The Tyger*, "In what furnace was thy brain?"'

The operation of your own brain while you read these words depends primarily on the fact that potassium behaves very like sodium, but has bigger atoms. For every impulse, a nerve cell expels potassium and admits sodium, through molecular ion channels, and then briskly restores the status quo in readiness for the next impulse. The repetition of similar chemical properties in atoms of very different mass and size had enabled chemistry's Darwin, Dmitri Mendeleev of St Petersburg, to predict in 1871 the existence of undiscovered elements simply from gaps in his periodic table—*il sistema periodico* in Levi's tongue.

When atomic physicists rudely invaded chemistry early in the 20th century, they explained the periodic table and chemical bonding as a numbers game. Behaviour depends on the electric charge of the atomic nucleus, which is matched by the count of electrons arranging themselves in orderly shells around the nucleus. The number of electrons in the outermost shell fixes the chemical properties. Thus sodium has 11 electrons, and potassium 19, but in both of them a single electron in the outermost shell is easily detached, making them suitable for playing Box and Cox in and out of your brain cells.

A similar numbers game, with shelly structures within atomic nuclei, then explained why this nucleus is stable whilst that one will disappear. Many elements, and especially variant isotopes with inappropriate masses, retire from the scene either by throwing off small bits in radioactivity or by breaking in two in fission. As a result, Mendeleev's table of the elements that survive naturally on the Earth comes to an end at uranium, number 92, with a typical mass 238 times heavier than hydrogen.

Physicists found that they could make heavier, transuranic elements in nuclear reactors or accelerators. Most notorious was plutonium, which in 1945 demonstrated its aptitude for fission by reducing much of Madame Butterfly's city of Nagasaki to radioactive rubble. Relics of natural plutonium turned up later in tracks bored by its fission products in meteorites. By 1996 physicists in Germany had reached element number 112, which is 277 times heavier than hydrogen, by bombarding lead atoms with zinc nuclei. Three years later a Russian team reported the 'superheavy' element 114, made from plutonium bombarded with calcium and having an atomic mass of 289.

The successful accounting, at the nuclear and electronic levels, for all the elements, their isotopes and chemical behaviour—in fine detail excruciating for students—should not blind you to the dumbfounding creativity of inanimate matter. Mother Nature mass-produced rudimentary particles of matter: lightweight electrons and heavy quarks of various flavours. The quarks duly gathered by threes into protons and neutrons, with the option of changing the one into the other by altering the flavour of a quark.

From this ungenerous start, the mindless stuff put together 118 neutrons, 79 protons and 79 electrons and so invented gold. This element's ingenious loose electrons reflect yellow light brightly while nobly resisting the tarnish of casual chemistry. It was a feat not unlike turning bacteria into dinosaurs and any natural philosopher should ask, 'How come gold was implied in the specification for the cosmos?' To be candid, the astrophysicists aren't quite sure why so much gold was made, and some have suggested that collisions between stars were required.

Hoyle rekindled a sense of wonder about where our elements came from. Helping to fill out the picture is the analysis of meteorites. In the oldest stones falling from the sky, some microscopic grains pre-date the Solar System. Their elements, idiosyncratic in their proportions of isotopes of variant masses, are signatures of individual stars that contributed to the Earth's cargo of elements. By 2002 the most active of stellar genealogists, Ernst Zinner of Washington University in Missouri, had distinguished several different types of parent stars. These were low-to-intermediate mass stars approaching the end of their lives as red giants, novae periodically throwing off their outer layers, and massive stars exploding as supernovae.

'Ancient grains in meteorites are the most tangible evidence of the Earth's ancestry in individual stars long defunct, and they confirm that we ourselves are made of stardust,' Zinner said. 'My great hope is that one day we'll find more types of these stellar fossils and new sources of pre-solar grains, perhaps in samples quarried from a comet and brought to Earth for analysis. Then we might be able to paint a more complete picture of our heavenly progenitors.'

Meanwhile astrophysicists and astrochemists can study the element factories, and the processes they use, by identifying materials added much more recently to the cauldron of the Milky Way Galaxy. Newly made elements occur in clouds of gas and dust that are remnants of stars that exploded in the startling events known as supernovae. Although 'supernova' means literally some kind of new star, they are actually old stars blowing up. A few cases were recorded in history.

'The greatest miracle'

Gossips at the Chinese court related that the keeper of the calendar prostrated himself before the emperor and announced, 'I have observed the appearance of a guest star.' In the summer of 1054, the bright star that we would call Aldebaran in the Taurus constellation had acquired a much brighter neighbour. The guest was visible even in daylight for three weeks, and at night for more than a year.

Half a millennium later in southern Sweden, an agitated young man with a golden nose, which hid a duelling disfigurement, was pestering the passers-by. He pointed at the Cassiopeia constellation and demanded to know how many stars they could see. Although the Danish astronomer Tycho Brahe could hardly believe his eyes, on that November evening in 1572 he had discovered a new star.

As the star faded over the months that followed, his book *De Nova Stella* made him famous throughout Christendom. Untrammelled by modesty or sinology, Tycho claimed that the event was perhaps 'the greatest miracle since the world began'. In 1604, his pupil Johannes Kepler of Prague found a new star of his own 'in the foot of the Serpent Bearer'—in Ophiuchus we'd say today.

In 1987, in a zinc mine at Mozumi, Japan, the water inside an experimental tank of the Kamioka Observatory flashed with pale blue light. It did so 11 times in an interval of 13 seconds, recording a burst of the ghostly subatomic particles called neutrinos. Simultaneously neutrino detectors in Ohio and Russia picked up the burst. Although counted only by the handful, because of their very reluctant interaction with other matter, zillions of neutrinos had flooded through the Earth from an unusual nuclear cataclysm in the sky.

A few hours later, at Las Campanas in Chile, Ian Shelton from Toronto was observing the Large Magellanic Cloud, the closest galaxy to our own, and he saw a bright new speck of light. It was the first such event since Kepler's that was visible to the naked eye. Austerely designated as Supernova 1987A, it peaked in brightness 80 days after discovery and then faded over the years that followed.

Astronomers had the time of their lives. They had routinely watched supernovae in distant galaxies, but Supernova 1987A was the first occurring at fairly close range that could be examined with the panoply of modern telescopes. The multinational Infrared Ultraviolet Explorer was the quickest satellite on the case and its data revealed exactly which star blew up. Sanduleak $-69°$ 202 was about 20 times more massive than the Sun. Contrary to textbook expectations it was not a red star but a blue supergiant. The detection of a shell of gas, puffed off from the precursor star 20,000 years earlier, explained a recent colour change from red to blue.

Telescopes in space and on the ground registered signatures of various chemical elements newly made by the dying star. But most obvious was a dusty cloud blasted outwards from the explosion. Even without analysing it, astronomers knew that dust requires elements heavier than hydrogen and helium for its formation.

The scene was targeted by the Hubble Space Telescope soon after its launch in 1990, and as the years passed it recorded the growth of the dusty cloud. It will evolve into a supernova remnant like those identified in our own Galaxy by astronomers at the sites of the 1054, 1572 and 1604 supernovae.

By a modern interpretation, Tycho's and Kepler's Stars may have been supernovae of Type Ia. That means a small, dense white dwarf star, the corpse of a defunct normal star, sucking in gas from a companion star until it becomes just hot enough to burn carbon atoms in a stupendous nuclear explosion, making radioactive nickel that soon decays into stable iron. Certainly the 1987 event and probably the 1054 event were Type II supernovae, meaning massive stars that collapsed internally at the ends of their lives, triggering explosions that are comparable in brilliance but more variable and more complicated.

Most of our supernovae are missing

The Crab Nebula in Taurus is the classic example of the supernova remnants that litter the Galaxy. Produced by the Chinese guest star of 1054, it shows filaments of hot material, rich in newly made elements, still rushing outwards from the scene of the stellar explosion and interacting with interstellar gas. At its centre is a neutron star, a small but extremely dense object flashing 30 times a second, at every wavelength from radio waves to gamma rays.

Astronomers estimate that supernovae of one kind or another should occur roughly once every 50 years in our Galaxy. Apart from the events of 1054, 1572 and 1604, historians of astronomy scouring the worldwide literature have noted only two other sightings of supernovae during the past millennium. There was an exceptionally bright one in Lupus in 1006, and a less spectacular candidate in Cassiopeia in 1181. Most of the expected events are unaccounted for.

Clouds of dust, such as those you can see as dark islands in the luminous river of the Milky Way, obscure large regions of the Galaxy. First the radio telescopes, and then X-ray, gamma-ray and infrared telescopes in space, revealed many supernova remnants hidden behind the clouds, so that the events that produced them were not seen from the Earth by visible light. The most recent of these occurred around 1680, far away in the Cassiopeia constellation, and it first showed up as an exceptionally loud source of radio waves.

NASA's Compton gamma-ray observatory, launched in 1991, carried a German instrument that charted evidence of element-making all around the sky. For this purpose, the German astronomers selected the characteristic gamma rays coming from aluminium-26, a radioactive element that decays away, losing half of all its nuclei in a million years. So the chart of the sky showed element-making of the past few million years.

The greatest concentrations are along the band of the Milky Way, especially towards the centre of the Galaxy where the stars are most concentrated. But even over millions of years the newly made elements have remained close to their points of origin, leaving many quite compact features. 'We expected a much more even picture,' said Volker Schönfelder of the Max-Planck-Institut für extraterrestrische Physik. 'The bright spots were a big surprise.'

At the same institute in Garching, astronomers looked at supernova remnants in closer detail with the German–US–UK X-ray satellite Rosat (1990–99). Bernd Aschenbach studied, in 1996, Rosat images of the Vela constellation, where a large and bright supernova remnant spreads across an area of sky 20 times wider than the Moon. It dates from a relatively close stellar explosion about 11,000 years ago, and it is still a strong source of X-rays.

Aschenbach wondered what the Vela remnant would look like if he viewed it with only the most energetic rays. He was stunned to find another supernova remnant otherwise hidden in the surrounding glare. Immediately he saw that it was much nearer and younger than the well-known Vela object.

With the Compton satellite, his colleagues recorded gamma-ray emissions from Aschenbach's object, due to radioactive titanium-44 made in the stellar explosion. As half of any titanium-44 disappears by decay every 90 years, this confirmed that the remnant was young. Estimated to date from around A D 1300, and to be only about 650 light-years away, it was the nearest supernova to the Earth in the past millennium—indeed in the past 10,000 years. Yet if anyone spotted it, no record survives from any part of the world.

'This very close supernova should have appeared brighter than the Full Moon, unless it were less luminous than usual or hidden by interstellar dust,' Aschenbach commented. 'X-rays, gamma rays and infrared rays can penetrate the dust, so we have a lot of unfinished business concerning recent supernovae in our Galaxy, which only telescopes in space can complete.'

The launch in 2002 of Europe's gamma-ray satellite Integral carried the story forward. It was expected to gauge the relative abundances of many kinds of newly made radioactive nuclei, and measure their motions as a cloud expands. That will put to a severe test the present theories about how supernovae and other stars manufacture the chemical elements.

The heyday of element-making

A high priority for astronomers at the start of the 21st century is to trace the history of the elements throughout the Milky Way and in the Universe as a whole. The rate of production of freshly minted elements, whether in our own Galaxy or farther afield, is far less than it used to be. Exceptions prove the rule. An overabundance of newly made elements occurs in certain other galaxies, which are therefore obscured by very thick dust clouds.

In these so-called starburst galaxies, best seen by infrared light from the cool dust, the rates of birth and death of stars can be a hundred times faster than in the Milky Way today. Collisions between galaxies seem to provoke the frenzy of star-making. At any rate the starburst events were commoner long ago, when the galaxies were first assembling themselves in a smaller and more crowded Universe. The delay in light and other radiation reaching the Earth from across the huge volume of the cosmos enables astronomers with the right equipment to inspect galaxies as they were when very young.

Most of the Earth's cargo of elements may have been made in starbursts in our own Galaxy 10 billion years ago or more. The same heyday of element-making seems to have occurred universally. To confirm, elaborate or revise this elemental history will require all of the 21st century's powerful new telescopes, in space and on the ground, examining the cosmos by every sort of radiation from radio waves to gamma rays.

As powerful new instruments are brought to bear, surprises will surely come. There was a foretaste in 2002, when Europe's XMM-Newton X-ray satellite examined a very remote quasar, seen when the Universe was one tenth of its present age. It detected three times as much iron in the quasar's vicinity as there is in the Milky Way today.

Historians of the elements pin special hopes on two infrared observatories in space. The European Space Agency's Herschel spacecraft is scheduled to station itself 1,500,000 kilometres out, on the dark side of the Earth, in 2007. It is to be joined in 2010, at the same favoured station, by the James Webb Space Telescope, the NASA–Europe–Canada successor to the Hubble Space Telescope.

After a lifelong investigation of the chemical evolution of stars and galaxies, at the Royal Greenwich Observatory and Denmark's Niels Bohr Institute, Bernard Pagel placed no bet on which of these spacecraft would have more to tell about the earliest history of the elements.

'Will long infrared waves, to which Herschel is tuned, turn out to be more revealing than the short infrared waves of the James Webb Telescope?' Pagel wondered. 'It depends on the sequence and pace of early element-making events, which are hidden from us until now. Perhaps the safest prediction is that neither mission will resolve all the mysteries of cosmic chemical evolution, which may keep astronomers very busy at least until the 2040s and the centenary of Hoyle's supernova hypothesis.'

▶ *For related subjects, see* STARS, STARBURSTS, GALAXIES, NEUTRON STARS, BLACK HOLES *and* GAMMA-RAY BURSTS. *For a remarkable use of supernovae in cosmology, see* DARK ENERGY. *For the advent of chemistry in the cosmos, see* MOLECULES IN SPACE *and* MINERALS IN SPACE.

EL NIÑO

When a warm sea wobbles the global weather

I N 1971 PERU was the greatest of fishing nations, with 1500 ocean-going boats hauling in one-fifth of the world's entire commercial catch, mainly in the form of anchovies used for animal feed. International experts advised the Peruvians to plan for a sustainable yield of eight or ten million tonnes a year, in one of the great miracles of world economic development. Apparently the experts had little idea about what El Niño could do.

In January 1972 the sea off Peru turned warm. The usual upwelling of cold, nutrient-rich water at the edge of the continent ceased. The combined effect of overfishing and this climatic blip wiped out the great Peruvian fishery, which was officially closed for a while in April 1973. The anchovies would then take two decades to recover to world-beating numbers, only to be hit again by a similar event in 1997–98.

Aged *pescadores* contemplating the tied-up boats in Calloa, Chimbote and other fishing ports were not in the least surprised by such events, which occurred every few years. They called them El Niño, the Christ Child, because they usually began around Christmas. Before the 1972 crash, particularly severe El Niño events reducing the fish catches occurred in 1941, 1926, 1914, . . . and so on back as far as grandpa could remember.

A celebrated Norwegian meteorologist, Jacob Bjerknes, in semi-retirement at UC Los Angeles, became interested in the phenomenon in the 1960s. He established the modern picture of El Niño as an event with far-flung connections, by linking it to the Southern Oscillation discovered by Gilbert Walker when working in India in the 1920s. As a result, meteorologists, oceanographers and climate scientists often refer to the phenomenon as El Niño/Southern Oscillation, or ENSO for short.

Walker had noticed that the vigour or weakness of monsoon rains in India and other parts of Asia and Africa is related to conditions of atmospheric pressure across the tropical Pacific Ocean. Records from Tahiti and from Darwin in Australia tell the story. In normal circumstances, pressure is high in the east and low in the west, in keeping with the direction of the trade winds. But in some years the system seesaws the other way, with pressure low in the east. Then the monsoon tends to be weak, bringing a risk of hunger to those dependent on its rainfall. Bjerknes realized that Walker's years of abnormal pressure patterns were also the years of El Niño off western South America.

The trade winds usually push the ocean water away from the shore, allowing cold, fertile water to well up. Not only does this upwelling nourish the Peruvian anchovies, it generates a long current-borne tongue of cool water stretching across the Pacific, following the Equator a quarter of the way around the world. The pressure of the current makes the sea level half a metre higher off Indonesia than off South America, and the sea temperature difference on the two sides of the ocean is a whopping 8°C.

In El Niño years the trade winds slacken and water sloshing eastwards from the warm side of the Pacific overrides the cool, nourishing water. Nowadays satellites measuring sea-surface temperatures show El Niño dramatically, with the Equator turning red hot in the colour-coded images. The events occur at intervals of two to seven years and persist for a year or two. Apart from the effects on marine life, consequences in the region include floods in South America, and droughts and bush fires in Indonesia and Australia.

The disruption of weather patterns goes much wider, as foreshadowed in Walker's link between the Southern Oscillation and the monsoon in India. Before the end of the century the general public heard El Niño blamed for all sorts of peculiar weather, from droughts in Africa to floods on the Mississippi. And newspaper readers were introduced to the little sister, La Niña, meaning conditions when the eastern Pacific is cooler than usual and the effects are contrary to El Niño's. La Niña is associated with an increase in the frequency and strength of Atlantic hurricanes, whilst El Niño moderates those storms.

A major El Niño alters jet stream tracks in such a way as to raise the mean temperature at the world's surface and in its lower atmosphere temporarily, by about half a degree C. That figure is significant because it is almost as great as the whole warming of the world that occurred during the 20th century. Sometimes simultaneous cooling due to a volcano or low solar activity masks the effect. The temperature blip was conspicuous in 1997–98.

Arguments arose among experts about the relationship between El Niño and global warming. An increased frequency in El Niño events, from the 1970s onwards and especially in the 1990s, made an important contribution to the reported rise in global temperatures towards the end of the century, when they were averaged out. So those who blamed man-made emissions of carbon dioxide and other greenhouse gases for an overall increase in global temperature wanted to say that the quickfire events were a symptom rather than a cause of the temperature rise.

'You have to ask yourself, why is El Niño changing that way?' said Kevin Trenberth of the US National Center for Atmospheric Research. 'A direct greenhouse effect would change temperatures locally, but it would also change atmospheric circulation.' William Nierenberg, a former director of the Scripps Institution of Oceanography in San Diego, retorted that to explain El Niño by global warming, it would be necessary to show that global warming caused the trade winds to stop. 'And there is no evidence for this,' he said.

What the coral had to say about it

Instrumental records of El Niño and the Southern Oscillation, stretching back to the latter part of the 19th century when the world was cooler, show no obvious connection between the prevailing global temperature and the frequency and severity of the climatic blips. To go further back in time, scientists look to other indicators. Climate changes in tropical oceans are well recorded in fast-growing coral. You can count off the years in seasonal growth bands and, in the dead skeletons that build a reef, you can find evidence for hundreds of years of fluctuations in temperature, salinity and sunshine.

New Caledonia has vast amounts of coral, second only to the Great Barrier Reef of nearby Australia, and scientists gained insight into the history of El Niño by boring into a 350-year-old colony of coral beneath the Amédée lighthouse at the island's south-eastern tip. Where New Caledonia lies, close to the Tropic of Capricorn in the western Pacific, the ocean water typically cools by about 1°C during El Niño. The temperature changes are recorded by fluctuations in the proportions of strontium and uranium taken up from the seawater when the coral was alive.

A team led by Thierry Corrège of France's Institut de Recherche pour le Développement reconstructed the sea temperatures month by month for the period 1701–61. This included some of the chilliest times in the Little Ice Age, which ran from 1400 to 1850 and reached its coldest point around 1700. The western Pacific at New Caledonia was on the whole about 1°C cooler than now, yet El Niño's behaviour then was very similar to what it is today.

'In spite of a decrease in average temperatures,' Corrège said, 'neither the strength nor the frequency of El Niño appears to have been affected, even during the very coldest period.' That put the lid on any simple idea of a link between El Niño and global warming. But the team also saw the intensity of El Niño peaking in 1720, 1730 and 1748, and wondered if some other climate cycle was at work.

In view of the huge impacts on the world's weather, and the disastrous floods and droughts that the Pacific changes provoke, you might well hope that climate scientists should have a grip on them by now. To help them try to forecast the onset, intensity and duration of El Niño they have supercomputers, satellites and a network of buoys deployed across the Pacific by a US–French–Japanese cooperative effort. But results so far are disappointing.

In 2000 Christopher Landsea and John Knaff of the US National Oceanic and Atmospheric Administration evaluated claims that the 1997–98 El Niño had been well predicted. They gave all the forecasts poor marks, including those from what were supposedly the most sophisticated computer models. Landsea said, 'When you look at the totality of the event, there wasn't much skill, if any.'

Regrettably, the scientists still don't know what provokes El Niño. Back in the 1960s, the pioneer investigator Bjerknes thought that the phenomenon was self-engendered by compensating feedbacks within the weather machine of air and sea, so that El Niño was a delayed reaction to La Niña, and vice versa. The possibility of such a natural seesaw points to a difficulty in distinguishing cause and effect.

Big efforts went into studying the ocean water, its currents and its changing levels, both by investigation from space and at sea, and by computer modelling. A promising discovery was of travelling bumps in the ocean called Kelvin waves, due to huge masses of hot water proceeding from west to east below the surface. The waves can be generated in the western Pacific by brief bursts of strong winds from the west—in a typhoon for example.

Although they raise the sea surface by only 5–10 centimetres, and take three months to cross the ocean, the Kelvin waves provide a mechanism for transporting warm water eastwards from a permanent warm pool near New Guinea, and for repressing the upwelling of cold water. The US–French team operating the Topex-Poseidon satellite in the 1990s became clever at detecting Kelvin waves using a radar altimeter to measure the height of the sea surface. But they showed up at least once a year, and certainly were not always followed by a significant El Niño event.

By the end of the century the favourite theoretical scheme for El Niño was the delayed-oscillator model. This was similar to Bjerknes' natural seesaw, with the special feature, based on observations at sea, that the layer of warm surface water becomes thinner in the western Pacific as it grows thicker near South America, at the onset of El Niño. A thinning at the eastern side begins just before the peak of the ocean warming.

To say that El Niño is associated with a slackening of the trade winds begs the question about why they slacken. Is it really self-engendered by the air—sea system? Or do the trade winds respond to cooling due to other reasons, such as volcanic eruptions or a feeble Sun? The great El Niño of 1983 followed so hard on the heels of the great volcanic eruption of El Chichón in Mexico, in 1982, that each tended to mask the global effect of the other. Perhaps El Niño is a rather clumsy thermostat for the world.

▶ *For related subjects, see* OCEAN CURRENTS *and* CLIMATE CHANGE. *For the use made of El Niño by Polynesian navigators, see* PREHISTORIC GENES.

EMBRYOS

'Think of the control genes operating a chemical computer'

O NE OF THE MORE AWKWARD LABOURS of Hercules was to kill the Hydra. Living in a marsh near Argos, it was a gigantic monster with multiple heads. Cut one off and two would grow in its place. The hydras of real life are measured only in millimetres, but these animals, too, live in freshwater, and they have tentacled heads. When they bud, in summer, their offspring look like extra heads. And the hydras' power of self-repair surpasses that of their mythical namesake.

In the handsome old city of Tübingen in the early 1970s, Alfred Gierer of the Max-Planck-Institut für Virusforschung minced up hydras. He blew them through tubes too small for them, and so reduced them right down to individual living cells. When he fashioned the resulting jumble into a small sausage, it reorganized itself into new hydras.

The cells reacted to the positions in which they found themselves, to make a smooth outer surface or gut as required. Within a few days, buds with tentacles appeared, and the misshapen creature began feeding normally. After six weeks, several buds separated from the sausage, as normal offspring.

If Gierer arranged the cells more carefully, according to what parts of the original bodies they came from, he could make a hydra with heads at both ends, or with two feet and a head in the middle. Cells originating from nearest to the head in the original hydra were in command. They were always the ones to form new heads in the regenerated animal.

This was just one of thousands of experiments in developmental biology conducted around the world in the 20th century, as many scientists confronted what seemed to them the central mystery of advanced life-forms. How does a newly fertilized egg—in the case of a human being it is just a tenth of a millimetre wide—develop as an embryo? How to create in the end a beautifully formed creature with all the right bits and pieces in the right places?

For Lewis Thomas, a self-styled biology watcher at New York's Sloane–Kettering Center, the fertilized human egg should be one of the great astonishments of the Earth. People ought to be calling to one another in endless wonderment about it, he thought. And he promised that if anyone could explain the gene switching that creates the human brain, 'I will charter a skywriting airplane, maybe a whole fleet of them, and send them aloft to write one great exclamation point after another, around the whole sky, until my money runs out.'

Cells that start off identical in the very earliest stages of growth somehow become specialized as brain, bone, muscle, liver or any of more than 300 types of cells in a mammalian body like ours. In genetic disorders, and in cancer too, the control of genes can go wrong. In normal circumstances, appropriate genes are switched on and inappropriate ones switched off in every cell, so that it will play its correct role. The specialized cell is like an actor who speaks only his own lines, and then only when cued.

Knowledge of the whole script of the play—how to grow the entire organism— remains latent in the genes of many cells. Cloning, done in grafted plants since prehistoric times and in mammals since 1997, exploits that broad genetic memory. By the start of the 21st century, embryology had entered the political arena amid concerns about human cloning, and the proposed use of stem cells from human embryos to generate various kinds of tissue.

At the level of fundamental science, it is still not time to write Thomas's exclamation marks in the sky. The experts know a lot about the messages that tell each cell what to do. But the process of embryonic growth is exquisitely complicated, and to try to take short cuts in its explanation may be as futile as précising *Hamlet*.

Heads and tails in mutant fruit flies

Regeneration in simple animals offered one way to approach the mystery of embryonic development. The head–foot distinction that the cells of minced hydras know is fundamental to the organization of any animal's body. In humans it becomes apparent within a week of conception.

In Tübingen, Alfred Gierer's idea was that a chemical signal originating from the head cells of the hydra became progressively diluted in more distant cells, along a chemical gradient. From the strength of the signal locally, each cell might tell where it was and so infer what role it ought to play in the new circumstances of the hydra sausage. At the beginning of the 20th century Theodor Boveri of Würzburg, who established that all the chromosomes in the cell nucleus are essential if an embryo is to develop correctly, had favoured the idea of a gradient. From his experiments with embryos of sea urchins, Boveri concluded that 'something' increases or decreases in concentration from one end of an egg to the other.

Christiane Nüsslein-Volhard was a student of biochemistry, and later of genetics, at Tübingen University. She heard lectures on embryonic development and cell specialization by Gierer and others. The question of how the hereditary instructions, carried by the genes in an embryo's cells, operate to achieve self-organization, began to enchant her. Taking stock, she learned that most was known about an animal much more complex than the hydra, the *Drosophila* fruit fly.

Experimental biologists had for long favoured the fruit fly because it developed rapidly from egg to fly in nine days, and because its genes were gathered in four surprisingly large chromosomes. Indeed, it was by studying genetic mutations in fruit flies that Thomas Hunt Morgan, at Caltech in the 1920s, confirmed that genes reside in chromosomes. Many early studies of mutations in individual genes, due to damage by chemicals or radiation, were done with fruit flies.

Since the 1940s, a bizarre genetic mutation that gave a fruit fly four wings instead of two had been the subject of special study for Edward Lewis, also at Caltech. In a personal quest lasting more than three decades Lewis discovered a set of genes that organizes the various segments along the fly's body. These segments have specialized roles in producing head, wings, legs and so on.

The genes controlling the segments are arranged in sequence on a chromosome, from those affecting the head to those affecting the tail. Two adjacent segments have the propensity to make a pair of wings, but in one of them the wings are normally repressed by the action of a particular controlling gene. If that gene fails to operate, because of a mutation, the result is a four-winged fly.

Small wonder then that Nüsslein-Volhard thought that she'd better gain experience with *Drosophila*, which she did at the Biozentrum in Basel. 'I immediately loved working with flies,' she recalled later. 'They fascinated me, and followed me around in my dreams.'

She wanted to study their embryonic development at an earlier stage than Lewis had done, when the grubs, or larvae, were first forming and setting out the basic plan of their bodies, with its division into segments. The opportunity came in 1978 when Nüsslein-Volhard joined the new European Molecular Biology Laboratory in Heidelberg and teamed up with another young scientist, Eric Weischaus.

Developmental geneticists find the genes by throwing a spanner in the works and seeing what happens. In other words, they cause mutations and examine the consequences. Nüsslein-Volhard and Weischaus set out to do this on a scale never attempted before, in a project requiring great personal stamina. They dosed *Drosophila* mothers so heavily with chemical agents that roughly half of all their genes were altered. Then, like duettists at a piano, they worked at a double microscope, examining the resulting grubs together—40,000 mutants in all.

In some embryos, alternate segments of the body might be missing. In others, a segment might be disoriented, not knowing head from tail. After more than a year of intensive work, Nüsslein-Volhard and Weischaus had identified 15 genes that together control different phases in the early development of the grubs.

The genes operate in three waves. Gap genes sketch the body-plan along the head–tail axis. Pair-rule genes double the number of segments. Then the head end and tail end of each segment learn their differences from segment-polarity genes. The whole sequence of events takes only a few hours.

Published in 1980, this work was hailed as a landmark in embryo research. A few years later, the Max-Planck-Institut für Virusforschung in Tübingen changed its name to Entwicklungsbiologie (developmental biology) and Nüsslein-Volhard went there as director of her own division. Still working on fruit flies, she confirmed the hydra people's idea of a chemical gradient, in a quite spectacular fashion.

Into one side of each egg the mother fly installs a gene of her own that says 'this is to be the head'. The gene commands the manufacture of a protein, the concentration of which diminishes along the length of the embryo. Thereby it helps the cells to know where they are, and therefore what to do in the various segments, as far as the middle of the body. The mother also provides a gene saying 'this is the tail,' on the opposite side of the egg, which is involved in shaping the abdomen. Nowadays there are known to be many such maternal genes, some of which determine the front–back distinction in the fruit-fly embryo, in a set of genes earmarking the front.

Better face up to how complicated it is

Experimenters had to keep asking themselves whether what they found out in fruit flies was relevant to animals with backbones, and therefore perhaps to avoiding or treating genetic malformations in human babies. There were reasons for optimism. For example, the repetition of bones in the vertebrate spine seemed at some fundamental level to be similar to the repetition of segments in a worm or an insect.

In the 1980s Walter Gehring in Basel detected a string of about 180 letters in the genetic code that occurred repeatedly among the fruit-fly genes involved in embryonic development. Very similar sequences, called homeoboxes, turned up in segmented worms, frogs, mice and human beings. Evidently the animal kingdom has conserved some basic genetic mechanisms for constructing bodies, through more than half a billion years of evolution.

This meant that there were lessons about embryonic development to be learned from all animals. Some scientists, including Nüsslein-Volhard, wanted to move closer to human beings, notably with the zebrafish, commended in 1982 by George Streisinger at Oregon as the most convenient vertebrate answer to the fruit fly. A native of the Himalayan rivers, the zebrafish *Danio rerio* is just four centimetres long, with black stripes run along an otherwise golden body. Its eggs and embryos are both transparent, so that you can watch the tissues and organs developing in the living creature.

But the process of development is extremely complicated, and there is at least as strong a case for looking at simple animals, to learn the principles of how a fertilized egg turns into a fully functional creature. The first complete account of the curriculum vitae of every cell in an animal's body came from an almost invisible, transparent roundworm. Its name, *Caenorhabditis elegans*, is much longer than its one-millimetre body.

Sydney Brenner initiated the ambitious project of cell biographies in the mid-1960s at the Laboratory of Molecular Biology in Cambridge. Later, other labs around the world joined in with gusto. The adult roundworm females have exactly 1031 cells in their bodies, and the males 959. Embryonic development follows the same course in every animal, except when experimenters disrupt it. Some of the events seem illogical and counter-intuitive.

Although most cells with a particular function (muscle, nerve or whatever) originate as clones of particular precursor cells in the roundworm embryo, there are many cases where two different cell types come from a common parent. Some 12 per cent of all the cells made in the embryo simply commit suicide, because they are surplus to requirements in the adult. Most surprisingly, the left–right symmetry typical of many animals is not, in this case, simply a mirror-like duplication of cell lineages on the two sides of the roundworm's body. In some parts, the similar-looking left and right sides are built from different patterns of cells with different histories.

At Caltech, for the successors of Thomas Hunt Morgan and Edward Lewis, the much more complicated embryos of sea urchins were the targets in another taxing 30-year programme. Boveri had pioneered the embryology of sea urchins 100 years earlier with the European *Strongylocentrotus lividus*. The Californians collected *S. purpuratus* from their own inshore waters. Roy Britten, a physicist by origin, set out the programme's aims in 1973.

'We have come to believe that the genes of all the creatures may be nearly identical,' he said. 'The genes of an amoeba would be about the same as those of a human being, and the differences occur in control genes. You can think of the control genes operating a chemical computer. By turning on and off the genes that make visible structures, they control the form.'

Britten's younger colleague, Eric Davidson, stressed a link between embryology and evolution: 'A small change in the DNA sequences responsible for control of the activity of many genes could result in what appear to be huge changes in the characteristics of the organism—for example the appearance of the wing of the first bird.'

It fell to Davidson to carry the sea-urchin project through till the end of the century and beyond. Using the increasingly clever tools of molecular genetics, he and his team traced networks of genes interacting with other genes. By 2001 he had complicated charts showing dozens of control genes operating at different stages of the sea urchin's early development. Just as he and Britten had predicted at the outset, they looked like circuit diagrams for a chemical computer.

Davidson's team found that they could break individual gene-to-gene links in the circuit, by mutations. From these details, an electronic computer at the University of Hertfordshire in England assembled the genetic diagrams. These indicated where to search for other genes targeted by the sea urchin's control genes.

Whilst some biologists brushed the diagrams aside, as too complicated to be useful, others applauded. Davidson's supporters commended him for avoiding the oversimplifications to which developmental biologists habitually resorted, out of necessity. As Noriyuki Satoh at Kyoto put it, 'To understand real evolutionary and developmental processes, we need to understand more of the details in gene networks.'

And now the embryo's clock

In many a laboratory, graduate students sprint down the corridor carrying newly fertilized eggs for examination before they have developed very much. This everyday commotion is worth considering by anyone who wonders where next the study of embryos and their development may go. From the succession of events in Nüsslein-Volhard's fruit flies to the sequential genetic diagrams for Davidson's sea urchins, time is of the essence.

At the Université de la Méditerranée in Marseille, in 1998, Olivier Pourquié discovered a biological clock at work in chicken embryos. He called it a segmentation clock, because it controls the timing of the formation of the repeated segments along the length of the embryo, which will give rise to the vertebrae. That the genes turn out to be clock-watchers may seem unsurprising to a pregnant woman, who can write in her diary when her baby is due. Yet the nature of the clock in early embryos was previously unknown.

In the chicken embryos studied by Pourquié, the clock ticks every 90 minutes, producing wave after wave of genetic activity. Correct development requires both a chemical-gradient signal to say where a feature is to form, and the clock to say when. With this discovery, the study of early development entered a new phase. Pourquié commented, 'Now we have to learn exactly how the genes of living Nature work in the fourth dimension, time.'

▶ *For more about cell creation and suicide during development, see* STEM CELLS *and* CELL DEATH. *For the development of the brain, see* BRAIN WIRING. *The evolutionary importance of changes during embryonic development becomes apparent in* EVOLUTION *and* HOPEFUL MONSTERS.

ENERGY AND MASS

The cosmic currency of Einstein's most famous equation

I N GABON IN WEST AFRICA the Okelonéné River, known as the Oklo for short, carves through rocks that are 2 billion years old. A line of black scars sloping down the valley side shows where strip-miners have gathered ore, rich in uranium.

The ore formed deep under water in an ancient basin. In airless conditions the uranium, which had been soluble in water in the presence of oxygen, precipitated out in concentrated form. The free oxygen that had mobilized the uranium was among the first to appear in abundance on the Earth, as a result of the evolution of bacteria with the modern ability to use sunlight to split water molecules, perhaps 2.4 billion years ago.

Compared with ores from the rest of the world, material from the Oklo valley turned out to be slightly depleted in the important form of the metal, the isotope uranium-235, required in nuclear reactors. Follow-up investigations revealed that Mother Nature had been there first, operating her own nuclear reactors deep underground at Oklo, nearly 2 billion years ago. They consumed some of the uranium-235.

This discovery, announced by France's Commissariat à l'Energie Atomique in 1972, shows natural inventiveness anticipating our own. The Oklo reactors ran on the same principle as the pressurized-water reactors used in submarines and power stations. These burn uranium fuel enriched in uranium-235, which can split in two with the release of subnuclear particles, neutrons. The water in the reactor slows down the neutrons so that they can efficiently provoke fission in other uranium-235 nuclei, in a chain reaction.

So similar are the ancient and modern reactors that Alexander Shlyakhter of St Petersburg could use the evidence from Oklo for fundamental physics. He verified that the electric force, which blows the uranium-235 nuclei apart, has not changed its strength in 2 billion years. The Oklo reactors also heartened the physicists, chemists and geologists charged with the practical task of finding safe ways to bury long-lived radioactive waste, produced by fission in the nuclear power and weapons industries.

'We're surprised by how well the ordinary rocks kept most of the fission products bottled up in the natural reactors in Gabon,' said François Gauthier-Lafaye, leader of an investigation team based at Strasbourg. 'In a reactor located 250 meters deep, there's no evidence that radioactive contamination has spread more than a few metres, after 2 billion years. Even a reactor that's now only 12 metres deep, and therefore exposed to weathering, is still partially preserved and shows samples that have kept most of the fission products.'

The Oklo reactors were an oddity, possible only in a window of time during the Earth's history, between the concentration of uranium in extremely rich ores and the loss of uranium-235 by ordinary radioactive decay. Nevertheless they confirm that Nature misses no trick of energy extraction.

The high price of matter

'All of astrophysics is about Nature's attempt to release the energy hidden in ordinary matter,' declared Wallace Sargent of Caltech. That is done mainly by the nuclear fusion of lightweight elements in the Sun and the stars. The story continues into our planet's interior, where some of the heavier elements, made in stars that exploded before the Earth was born, are radioactive. Energy trickles from them and helps to maintain the internal heat that powers earthquakes, volcanoes and the drifting of continents.

The fusion and fission reactions make little difference to the total matter in the cosmos. They release only a small fraction of the immense capital of energy that was stored in it, during the production of matter at the origin of the Universe. Physicists demonstrate how much energy is needed to make even trifling amounts of matter, every time they create subatomic particles. It is seen most cleanly when an accelerator endows electrons and anti-electrons (positrons) with energy of motion and then brings them into collision, head-on.

Burton Richter of Stanford, who pioneered that technique, explained that he wanted to achieve 'a state of enormous energy density from which all the elementary particles could be born'. With such a collider you can make whatever particle you want, up to the limit of the machine's power, simply by tuning the energies of the electrons. Physicists know exactly how much energy they need. As Albert Einstein told them, it is simply proportional to the mass of the desired particle.

'$E = mc^2$—what an equation that is!' John Wheeler of Texas exclaimed. 'E energy, m mass, and c, not the speed of light but the square of the speed of light, an enormous number, so that a little mass is worth a lot of energy.' What most people know about Einstein's concise offering is that, for better or worse, it opened the way to the artificial release of nuclear energy. More amazingly, the formula that he scribbled in his flat in Bern in 1905, as an appendix to his special theory of relativity, expressed the law of creation for the entire material Universe and specified the currency of its daily transactions.

It also gives you a sense of how much effort went into furnishing the world. A lot of cosmic energy is embodied in the 3 kilos of matter in a newborn baby, for example. A hurricane would have to rage for an hour to match it, or a large power station, to run for a year. If the parents had to pay for the energy, it would cost them a billion dollars.

A star coming and going

Mass and energy were entirely different currencies in 19th-century physics. Energy was manifest as motion, heat, light, noise, electrical action, chemical combustion . . . or as the invisible potential energy of a stream about to go over a waterfall. The energy associated with a certain speed or temperature was greater in a large mass than in a small one, but only in the narrow sense that a dozen people with their wages in their pockets are collectively richer than one.

In his leap of imagination, Einstein realized that even a cold stone doing nothing is extremely rich. Its mass should be considered as frozen energy—the rest energy, physicists call it. Conversely, the more familiar forms of energy have mass. The stone becomes slightly heavier if you heat it or bang it or throw it.

Einstein stumbled upon $E = mc^2$ when fretting about potential nonsense. Relativity has always been a poor name for his theory. It stresses that the world looks different to people in various states of motion. In fact Einstein was concerned to preserve an objective, non-relative reality. He wanted, in this case, to avoid the absurdity that the power of a source of light might depend on who was looking at it.

Astronomers already knew about the blue shifts and red shifts of the Doppler effect. A star coming towards us looks bluer than normal, because the relative motion squeezes the waves of its light. A star going away looks redder because the waves are stretched out. What bothered Einstein was that blue light is more energetic than red light.

If you flew past a star—the Sun, say—and watched it coming and going, the gain by the blue shift would be greater than the loss by the red shift. It doesn't average out. And the increase in energy isn't illusory. You could get a tan more quickly from a blueshifted Sun.

So where does the extra energy come from, seen emanating from a star that simply happens to be moving in relation to you? It's absurd to think that you could alter the Sun's behaviour just by flying past it in a spaceship. To avoid an error in the bookkeeping of energy in the Universe, something else must change, concerning your perception of the luminous object.

From the star's point of view, it is at rest. But you judge the moving star to possess energy of motion, just like a bullet rushing past. So there is extra energy in the accounts, from your point of view. The extra light due to the Doppler effect must be supplied from the star's energy of motion. But how can the star spare some of its energy of motion, without slowing down? Only by losing mass—which means that light energy possesses mass.

Then come the quick-fire masterstrokes of Einstein's intuition. It can't be just the extra light energy needed to account for the Doppler effect that has mass, but all of the light given off by the star. And the fact that the star can shed mass in the form of radiant energy implies that all of its mass is a kind of energy.

'We are led to the more general conclusion that the mass of a body is a measure of its energy-content,' Einstein wrote in 1905. He added, 'It is not impossible that with bodies whose energy-content is variable to a high degree (e.g. with radium salts) the theory may be put successfully to the test.'

Liberating nuclear energy

The mention of radium was a signal to his fellow-physicists. Einstein knew that a novel source of energy was needed to explain radioactivity, discovered ten years previously. In modern terms, when the nucleus of a radioactive atom breaks up, the combined mass of the material products is less than the original mass, or rest energy of the nucleus. The difference appears as energy of motion of expelled particles, or as the radiant energy of gamma rays.

Rest energy rescued biology from the supercilious physicists who declared that the Sun could not possibly have burned for as long as required in the tales of life on Earth by Charles Darwin and the fossil-hunters. In the decades that followed Einstein's inspiration, the processes by which the Sun and others stars burn became clear. They multiplied the life of the Sun by a factor of 100 or more.

In the fusion of hydrogen into helium, the nucleus of a helium atom is slightly less massive than the four hydrogen nuclei needed to make it. The Sun grows less heavy every second, by converting about 700 million tonnes of its hydrogen into about 695 million tonnes of helium and 5 tonnes of radiant energy. But it is so massive that it can go on doing that for billions of years.

In 1938, Otto Hahn and Fritz Strassmann in Germany's Kaiser-Wilhelm-Institut für Chemie discovered that some uranium nuclei could break up far more drastically than by radioactivity, to make much lighter barium nuclei and other products. In Copenhagen, Otto Frisch and Lise Meitner confirmed what was happening and called it fission, because of its similarity to the fission of one living cell into two. They also showed that it released enormous energy. Niels Bohr from Copenhagen joined with the young John Wheeler, then at Princeton, in formulating the theory of nuclear fission.

All of that happened very quickly and with fateful timing, when the clouds of war were gathering worldwide. As a result, the first large-scale release of nuclear energy came in Chicago in 1942, when Enrico Fermi built a uranium reactor for the US nuclear weapons programme. He did not know that the Oklo reactors had anticipated him by 2 billion years.

In 1955 the world was still reeling from the shock of the effects of two small nuclear weapons exploded over Japanese cities ten years earlier, and was becoming fearful of the far more powerful hydrogen bomb incorporating nuclear fusion. Then the USA came up with the slogan 'Atoms for peace'. All countries were to be assisted in acquiring nuclear technology for peaceful purposes, and nuclear power stations were said to promise cheap and abundant energy for everyone.

Journalists tend to believe whatever scientists of sufficient eminence tell them, so they propagated the message with enthusiasm and the nuclear industry boomed. After a succession of accidents in the UK, USA, the Soviet Union and Japan had tarnished its image, the media swung to the other extreme, unwisely condemning all things nuclear. In more practical terms, the capital costs were high, and the predicted exhaustion of oil and natural gas did not happen. At the end of the century, France was the only country generating most of its electricity in nuclear power stations.

Controlled fusion of lightweight elements, in the manner of the Sun, was another great hope, but always jam tomorrow. In the 1950s, practical fusion reactors were said to be 20 years off. Half a century later, after huge expenditures on fusion research in the Soviet Union, the USA and Europe, they were still 20 years off. That the principle remains sound is confirmed at every sunrise, but whether magnetic confinement devices, particle accelerators or laser beams will eventually implement it, no one can be sure.

Nuclear energy will always be an option. Calls for reduction in carbon-dioxide emissions from fossil fuels, said to be an important cause of global warming, encouraged renewed attention to nuclear power stations in some countries. Even nuclear bombs may seem virtuous if they can avert environmental disasters by destroying or deflecting asteroids and comets threatening to hit the Earth. And nuclear propulsion may be essential if human beings are ever to fly freely about the Solar System, and to travel to the stars some day.

Power from a black hole

Nuclear reactions are not the only way of extracting the rest energy of $E = mc^2$ from matter. Black holes do it much more efficiently and are indifferent to the composition of the infalling material. If you are so far-sighted that your anxieties extend to the fate of intelligent beings when all the stars of the Universe have burned out, Roger Penrose at Oxford had the answer.

He described how energy might be extracted from a stellar black hole. Send your garbage trucks towards it and empty them at just the right moment, and the trucks will boomerang back to you with enormous energy. Catch the trucks in a system that generates electricity from their energy of motion, refill them with garbage and repeat the cycle. Technically tricky, no doubt, but there are hundreds of billions of years left for ironing out the wrinkles in Penrose's scheme.

Incorrigible pessimists will tell you that even black holes are mortal. As Stephen Hawking at Cambridge first pointed out, they slowly radiate energy in the form of particles created in their strong gravity, and in theory they could eventually evaporate away. In practice, regular garbage deliveries can postpone that outcome indefinitely. Whether intelligent beings will enjoy themselves, living in a darkened Universe by electric light gravitationally generated from $E = mc^2$, who can tell?

▶ *For the background to Einstein's theory of rest energy, see* HIGH-SPEED TRAVEL. *For military applications, see* NUCLEAR WEAPONS. *For the equivalence of inertial and gravitational mass, see* GRAVITY. *For the origin of mass in elementary particles, see* HIGGS BOSONS. *For the advent of oxygen, which helped to create the Oklo reactors, see* GLOBAL ENZYMES.

EVOLUTION
Why Darwin's natural selection was never the whole story

T O EVERY PARISIAN, Pasteur is a *station de métro*. It delivers you to Boulevard Pasteur, from where you can follow Rue du Docteur Roux, named after the great microbiologist's disciple who developed a serum against diphtheria. On a grand campus straddling the street is a private non-profit-making lab founded on vaccine money, the Institut Pasteur.

François Jacob fetched up there as a young researcher in 1950. Severe wounds received while serving with the *deuxième blindée* in the Battle of Normandy had left him unable to be a surgeon as he wished. Instead he became a cell geneticist and in 1964 he shared a Nobel Prize with the older André Lwoff and Jacques Monod. It was for pioneering discoveries about how genes work in a living cell.

This was real biology, revealing bacteria using their genes in the struggle to survive when given the wrong food. The French discoveries contrasted with an Anglo-American trend in the mid-20th century that seemed to be narrowing biology down to molecular code-breaking on the one hand, and the mathematics of the genes on the other. Jacob used his laureate status to resist such narrow-mindedness. In lectures delivered in Seattle in 1982 he challenged the then-fashionable version of the Darwinian theory of evolution.

'The chance that this theory *as a whole* will some day be refuted is now close to zero,' Jacob said. 'Yet we are far from having the final version, especially with respect to the mechanisms underlying evolution.' He complained that only in a few very simple cases, such as blood groups, was there any established correlation between the messages of heredity, coming from the genes, and the characteristics of whole organisms.

More positively, Jacob stressed that every microbe, plant or animal has latent in it the potential for undreamed-of modification. The genes of all animals are broadly similar. In chimpanzees and human beings they are virtually identical. What distinguishes them is the use made of those genes. The title of Jacob's Seattle series was *The Possible and the Actual*, and the most widely quoted of the lectures was called 'Evolutionary Tinkering'.

From the fossil record of the course of evolution, one image captures the essence of Jacob's train of thought. Freshwater fishes in stagnant pools, gasping for oxygen, developed the habit of nosing up for air. They absorbed the gas through their gullets. There was then an advantage in making the gullets more capacious, by the formation of pouches, which in an ordinary fish in ordinary circumstances would be birth defects. In this way, a fish out of water invented the breathing apparatus of land-dwelling animals with backbones.

'Making a lung with a piece of oesophagus sounds very much like making a skirt with a piece of Granny's curtain,' Jacob said. This notion of evolutionary tinkering was not entirely original, as Jacob readily acknowledged. Charles Darwin himself had noted that in a living being almost every part has served for other purposes in ancient forms, as if one were putting together a new machine using old wheels, springs and pulleys.

Jacob knew where to look for enlightenment about how evolution does its tinkering. It would come by decrypting the mechanisms that switch genes on or off during the development of a fertilized egg into an embryo and then an adult. That is when tissues and organs are made for their various purposes, and when changes in the control of the genes can convert the possible into the actual. Any changes in the hereditary programme are most likely to create a non-viable monster. Sometimes, as with the gasping fishes, they may be a lifesaver opening new routes for evolution.

To positivist British and American colleagues, trained to mistrust deep thought in the tradition of René Descartes, Jacob was just another long-winded Frenchman. But by the 21st century he was plainly right and they were wrong. The mainstream Anglo-American view of life and its evolution had been inadequate all along.

Darwin plus Mendel

As the nearest thing to an Einstein that biology ever had, Darwin did a terrific job. He did not invent the idea of evolution, that living creatures are descended from earlier, different species. His granddad Erasmus wrote poems about it, when Jean-Baptiste de Lamarck in Paris was marshalling hard evidence for the kinship of living and extinct forms. Darwin presented afresh the arguments for the fact of evolution, and gave them more weight by proposing a mechanism for the necessary changes.

Just as farmers select the prize specimens of crops or livestock to breed from, so Mother Nature improves her strains during the endless trials of life. Inheritable differences between individuals allow continual, gradual improvements in performance. The fittest individuals, meaning those best adapted to their way of life, tend to survive and leave most descendants. By that natural selection, species will evolve. It is a persuasive idea, sometimes considered to be self-evident.

Darwin wrote in 1872: 'It may be said that natural selection is daily and hourly scrutinizing, throughout the world, the slightest variations; rejecting those that are bad, preserving and adding up all those that are good; silently and invisibly working, whenever and wherever opportunity offers, at the improvement of each organic being in relation to its organic and inorganic conditions of life.'

Although his theory was all about inheritable variations, Darwin had no idea how heredity worked. The discovery of genes as the units of heredity, by Gregor Mendel of Brünn in Austria, was neglected in Darwin's lifetime. So it fell to a later generation to make a neo-Darwinist synthesis of natural selection and genetics.

The geneticists who did the main work in the 1920s and 1930s, Ronald Fisher and J.B.S. Haldane in England and Sewall Wright at Chicago, were themselves operating in the dark. This was before the identification of deoxyribonucleic acid, DNA, as the physical embodiment of the genes. Nevertheless they were able to visualize different versions of the genes co-existing in a population of plants or animals, and to describe their fates mathematically.

The processes of reproduction endlessly shuffle and reshuffle the genes, so that they are tried out in many different combinations. New variants of genes arise by mutation. These may simply die out by chance because they are initially very scarce in the population. If not, natural selection evaluates them. Most mutations are harmful and are weeded out, because the organisms carrying them are less likely to leave surviving offspring. But sometimes the mutations are advantageous, and these good genes are likely to prosper and spread within the population, driving evolution forward.

The outstanding neo-Darwinist in the latter half of the 20th century was William Hamilton of Oxford. He used the genetic theory of natural selection to brilliant effect, in dealing with some of the riddles that seemed to defy neo-Darwinist answers. If survival of one's genes is what counts, why have entirely selfish behaviour and virgin births not become the norm? Altruism between kindred and chummy organisms provided an answer in the first case, Hamilton thought, whilst sexual shuffling of genes brought benefits in resisting disease. These virtuoso performances used natural selection to illuminate huge areas of life.

Shocks to the system

A succession of discoveries during the latter half of the 20th century made evolution more dramatic and much less methodical than the arithmetic of genetic selection might suggest. Darwin himself saw evolution as an inherently slow process. The most devoted neo-Darwinists agreed, because mutations in genes had to arise and be evaluated one by one.

The course of evolution revealed by the fossil record turned out to be chancy, cruel and often swift. Life was not serenely in charge of events. Perfectly viable species could be wiped through no fault of their genes, in environmental changes, and previously unpromising species could seize new opportunities to prosper.

Geological stages and periods had for long been distinguished by the comings and goings of conspicuous fossils. These implied quite sudden and drastic changes in the living scenery, and the extinction of previous incumbents. The identification of mass extinctions provided food for thought, especially when physicists began linking them to impacts by comets or asteroids. For as long as they could, many biologists resisted this intrusion from outer space. They wanted the Earth to be an isolated realm where natural selection could deliver its own verdicts on dinosaurs and other creatures supposedly past their genetic sell-by dates.

As with extinctions, so with appearances. In 1972, Niles Eldredge and Stephen Jay Gould in the USA concluded from the fossil record that evolution occurred in a punctuated manner. A species might endure with little discernible change for a million years and then suddenly disappear and be replaced by a new, successor species. Mainstream colleagues predictably contested this notion of Eldredge and Gould, because it was at odds with the picture of gradual Darwinian evolution.

Shocks of a different kind came from molecular biology. In 1968, Motoo Kimura in Japan's National Institute of Genetics in Mishima revealed that most evolution at a molecular level simply eludes the attention of natural selection, because it involves mutations that neither help nor harm the organisms carrying them. Kimura's colleague Tomoko Ohta, and Susumu Ohno of the Beckman Research Institute in California, followed this up with theoretical accounts of how neutral or inactive genes can accumulate in a lineage, unmolested by natural selection, and then suddenly become important when circumstances change.

Although Kimura saw a role for natural selection, he rejected the idea that it is testing genes one by one. Instead, it gauges the whole animals that are the product of many genes, and cares little for how the individual genes have made them. In Kimura's theory, most variants of genes become established in a population not by natural selection but by chance.

Other molecular studies in the 1960s showed that the variants of genes carried by different individuals in a population are more numerous than you'd expect, if natural selection were forever promoting the best genes and getting rid of the less good. Richard Lewontin and Jack Hubby in Chicago compared proteins from individual fruit flies of the same species. They used electrophoresis, in which large molecules travel through a jelly racetrack in response to an electric field. As they were the same proteins with the same functions, they might be expected to travel at the same speed. In fact their speeds were very variable, implying many variations in the genes responsible for their prescription.

'There's a huge amount of variation between one fly and another,' Lewontin said in 1972. 'If we look at all of the different kinds of molecules that these flies are made up of, we find that about a third of them have this kind of variation. And it's determined by the genes, it's inherited.' Harry Harris in London found similar variability in humans.

Yet another complication came with the realization that genes can pass between unrelated species. This is Mother Nature's equivalent of genetic engineering, which after all uses molecular scissors and paste already available in living organisms, and it is commonplace in bacteria. In plants and animals it is not absent, but rarer. On the other hand, drastic internal changes in the genetic material of plants and animals occur with the jumping genes discovered by Barbara McClintock at the Cold Spring Harbor Laboratory, New York.

In 1985 John Campbell of UC Los Angeles proposed that evolution genes exist. Having worked at the Institut Pasteur in the 1960s, he had been contaminated with heretical French notions. In jumping genes and other opportunities for modifying hereditary information, he saw mechanisms for evolutionary tinkering. He imagined that special genes might detect environmental stress and trigger large-scale genetic changes.

'Some genetic structures do not adapt the organism to its environment,' Campbell wrote. 'Instead they have evolved to promote and direct the process of evolution. They function to enhance the capacity of the species to evolve.' The neo-Darwinists scoffed, but researchers had other shocks in store for them, not speculative but evidential.

Evolution without mutation

In 1742 the great classifier of plants and animals, Carolus Linnaeus, was confronted by a plant gathered by a student from one of the islands of the Stockholm archipelago. It seemed to represent the evolution of a new species. That was long before Darwin made any such notion tolerably polite in a Christian country. So Linnaeus called the offending plant *Peloria*, which is Greek for monster, even though it was quite a pretty little thing.

By the Swede's system of classifying plants according to their flower structure, it had to be a new species. But in every other respect the plant was indistinguishable from *Linaria vulgaris*, the common toadflax. The only alteration was that all its petals looked the same, while in toadflax the upper and lower petals have different shapes. Yet for Linnaeus the change was startling: 'certainly no less remarkable than if a cow were to give birth to a calf with a wolf's head.'

In 1999 Enrico Coen and his colleagues at the UK's John Innes Centre found that the difference between *Linaria* and *Peloria* arose from a change affecting a single gene, cycloidea, controlling flower symmetry. That might have been pleasing for gene-oriented neo-Darwinists, except that there was a sharp twist in the story. When the team looked for the difference in the genetic code between the two species, they found none at all. Instead of a genetic mutation, in *Peloria* the gene was simply marked by a chemical tag indicating that it was not to be read.

'This is the first time that a natural modification of this kind has been found to be inherited,' Coen said, 'suggesting that this kind of change may be more important for natural genetic variation and evolution than has previously been suspected.'

The failure to persuade

Darwin's successors at the start of the 20th century had faced the challenge of convincing the world at large about the fact of evolution, and the reality of the long time-scales required for it. Religiously minded people were upset by the contradiction of the Bible. In the first chapter of *Genesis*, God creates the world and its inhabitants in six days. Careful arithmetic then stretches the later narrative through only a few thousand years before Christ.

Some physicists, too, were critical of Darwin. They computed that the Sun could not have gone on burning for the hundreds of millions of years that Darwin needed for his story to unfold. Other physicists then came to the evolutionists' aid. The discovery of radioactivity hinted at previously unknown mechanisms that might power the Sun for much longer.

Radioactivity also provided a means of discovering the ages of rocks, from the rates of decay of various atomic nuclei. In 1902 Ernest Rutherford and Frederick Soddy of McGill University, Montreal, created a stir by announcing that a piece of pitchblende was 700 million years old. That should have been the end of the argument about time-scales, but 100 years later some people still wanted to wrangle about the six days of creation.

Other critics granted the time-scale, but were not persuaded that evolution could occur for purely natural reasons, for example through natural selection. So the second challenge for Darwin's successors was to establish that no miraculous interposition was needed. If they wanted biology to rank alongside physics and chemistry as a natural science, they had to explain the mechanisms of evolution clearly enough to show that God did not have to keep helping the process along. In this, the neo-Darwinists were unsuccessful.

Educators, law-makers and the general public, in Europe and most other parts of the world, were content to take the neo-Darwinists' word for it, that in principle evolution was explained. In the USA they were less complaisant. Some states and districts tried to ban the teaching of evolution, as being contrary to religion. In 1968 the US Supreme Court outlawed such prohibitions. It did the same in 1987 for laws requiring balanced treatment of evolution and 'creation science'. Yet in 1999 and 2000 the National Center for Science Education was aware of 143 evolution–creation controversies in 34 states of the USA.

Some neo-Darwinists aggravated the conflict by implicitly or explicitly treating evolution as an atheistic religion. They worshipped a benign Mother Nature whose creative process of natural selection steadfastly guided life towards ever more splendid adaptations. Richard Dawkins of Oxford said of his neo-Darwinist science, 'It fills the same ecological niche as religion in the sense that it answers the same kind of questions as religion, in past centuries, was alleged to answer.'

In a soft version of this 20th-century nature worship, selection was directed towards the emergence of intelligent creatures like us. Given the ups and downs seen in the fossil record, this can now be disregarded as technically implausible. In a hard version, evolution theory not only managed without divine intervention but also proved that other religions are wrong. This ought to be disregarded as falling beyond the scope of science.

Even within the confines of biology, the neo-Darwinists adopted an authoritarian posture, to defend their oversimplified view of evolution. Natural selection was the only important mechanism, they said, and to suggest otherwise was to risk being accused of giving comfort to the creationists.

In *The Selfish Gene* (1976) and a succession of other plain-language books, Dawkins became the chief spokesman of the neo-Darwinists. He pushed the formula of genes plus natural selection to the limits of eloquent reasoning, in an unsuccessful effort to explain all the wonders of life.

Gradual natural selection is good at accounting for minor evolutionary adaptations observed in living populations—for example, of resistance by pests to man-made poisons. Contrary to the title of his book, Darwin did not explain the origin of species, in which differences between groups within a population become so great that they stop breeding with each other. His successors made progress during the 20th century in this respect, but only in rather simple situations where, for example, small groups of individuals, separated by distance or barriers from their relatives, evolve in a distinctive way.

Great leaps of evolution, like those that turned a fish into an air-breather, remained unaccountable. Even Hamilton's stabs at the problem were, for him, strangely tentative. If natural selection was a slow process, gene by mutant gene, how could it avoid a lot of botched intermediates, neither fish nor fowl nor good red herring? They would be hard put to finding mates, still less to surviving in a competitive environment.

'It is disappointing that in many US schools the doctrine of creationism is given equal weight with the theory of evolution,' Susan Lindquist of Chicago commented in 2000. 'Plausible explanations for the sometimes puzzlingly rapid pace of evolution may help to counter arguments that evolution cannot have done what it is held to have done.'

By this Lindquist meant that the real problem about dealing with creationism had been a technical one. The mainstream scientific theory of the 20th century had not succeeded in making persuasive sense of the major steps in evolution. Her remarks were in response to criticisms, by the neo-Darwinists, of her discovery of how those steps could occur by the uncovering of combinations of latent genes.

'Darwin better watch out'

At the end of the 20th century the cruel processes of scientific selection, where ideas survive only if they pass the tests of available evidence, delivered the coup de grace to narrow-minded neo-Darwinist ideas. As anticipated by François Jacob, the biggest shake-up for evolution theories came from studies of development.

The transitions from the genes of a fertilized egg, through an embryo and into an adult, involve critical mechanisms determining whether genes shall swing into action or be kept repressed, and the timing of their actions. These can be affected by the circumstances of the organism's life. Conceptual fences between genes, organisms and their environments, which neo-Darwinists had been at some pains to erect, became rickety as a result of these discoveries.

In *La Logique du Vivant* (1970) Jacob likened the programme of biology to the opening of Russian dolls. Nesting within each other, they represent different levels of organization, and a different way of considering the formation of living beings. Each one comes to light, not by the mere accumulation of observations, but 'by a new way of considering objects, a transformation in the very nature of knowledge'.

Commenting on the primacy of DNA in 20th-century biology, Jacob wrote: 'Today the world is message, codes and information. Tomorrow what analysis will break down our objects to reconstitute them in a new space? What new "Russian doll" will emerge?'

The lineaments of the next *matryoshka* became apparent as the 21st century dawned. She is decorated with proteins as well as DNA. As Jacob foresaw decades earlier, what really matters in evolution is not just the selection and survival of genes within a species, but also how they are controlled and expressed. Mechanisms have come to light that are ideal for evolutionary tinkering, not far removed from the idea of the evolution gene as visualized by Campbell.

A quick-fire series of experiments at Chicago, 1998–2002, showed that when an organism comes under stress from its environment, several unseen genetic variations can reveal themselves simultaneously. Besides the team leader, Susan Lindquist, key researchers were Suzanne Rutherford, Heather True and Christine Queitsch. A student commented, 'Darwin better watch out. The women's movement is in full effect.'

To be fair to our Charles, he had nothing to apologize for. Natural selection still sorts the fit from the unfit. What was wrongheaded was the attempt by many of his successors to limit the mechanisms of evolution to one particular interpretation of how it might proceed, plodding along by mutations in single genes.

Darwin wrote the epitaph for that narrow-minded genetic Darwinism before it even started. In the last edition of *The Origin of Species*, in 1872, he complained: 'I placed in a most conspicuous position—namely at the close of the Introduction—the following words: "I am convinced that natural selection has been the main but not the exclusive means of modification." This has been of no avail. Great is the power of steady misrepresentation.'

▶ *For more about the Lindquist discoveries see* HOPEFUL MONSTERS *and* PRIONS. *Cases of rapid experimentation appear in the fossil record in* CAMBRIAN EXPLOSION *and* HUMAN ORIGINS. *A deep mystery about bird navigation crops up in* BIOLOGICAL CLOCKS. *For more on evolutionary mechanisms, see* MOLECULES EVOLVING, GENOMES IN GENERAL,

CLONING, PLANT DISEASES *and* ALTRUISM AND AGGRESSION. *For an overview of the course of evolution, see* TREE OF LIFE. *Environmental and ecological perspectives on evolution appear in* EXTINCTIONS, EXTREMOPHILES, GLOBAL ENZYMES, ALCOHOL *and* ECO-EVOLUTION.

EXTINCTIONS

Were they nearly all due to bolts from the blue?

Y OU MIGHT THINK there'd been a gunfight in the gorge near the medieval town of Gubbio in Umbria. A river carves through many millions of years' worth of seabed limestone deposits. Now uplifted and tilted, the strata tower beside the road like a stack of playing cards seen edge-on. Holes scattered across the rock face were not made by bullets, in some showdown between the Gradualist Gang and the Catastrophe Kids, but merely by scientists taking samples.

The coffin of the dinosaurs is a layer of red clay, barely a centimetre thick but 65 million years old, which slopes up the wall of rock as neatly as a line across a geologist's time-chart. When you finger the Italian clay you are touching pieces of Mexico. You could find the same clay in New Zealand too. The pulverized material, flung high in the air by the impact of a comet, took some years to settle, during which time a pall of dust blotted out the Sun. Life paused.

Below the clay layer is limestone from the Cretaceous Period, when *Tyrannosaurus rex* and its giant lunches ruled the world. The dinosaur dynasties of carnivores and herbivores had prospered for 140 million years. Above the clay, slightly paler limestone continues upwards, but now from the Tertiary Period, when nary a dinosaur survived. At the same time the ammonites, with their neatly coiled shells, totally disappeared from the oceans after tenure of more than 300 million years. Thenceforward the world belonged to the mammals, the birds and the fishes, despite heavy casualties among them too.

The great extinction that redirected the course of evolution at the end of the Mesozoic Era coincided exactly with the red clay at Gubbio. Many evolutionary biologists and fossil-hunters disliked the facts about the end-Cretaceous extinction that emerged from 1980 onwards. They preferred to think that the dinosaurs died of constipation, or that naughty mammals ate their eggs, or any kind of Just-So Story that might preserve their grand illusion that Darwin's natural selection was all that you needed to explain evolution.

It fell to a physicist, a geologist and a couple of space scientists, all at UC Berkeley, to put the case for an extraterrestrial cause of mass extinctions, plainly enough to force biologists to pay attention. Luis Alvarez was a particle physicist. His son Walter, a geologist, knew the gorge at Gubbio well. If the red clay represented the crisis that killed off the dinosaurs, how long did it last? The Berkeley team set out to measure the duration of the Cretaceous terminal event by combining geology, meteoritics and nuclear chemistry, in evaluating iridium.

This metallic element is very scarce in the Earth's crust but relatively abundant in meteoritic dust that rains invisibly but unceasingly from outer space. Cooking samples from Gubbio in a Berkeley research reactor would make the iridium radioactive and detectable, atom-by-atom, by its gamma-ray fingerprint. Then one could use the iridium as a kind of clock, to find the time-scale of the red-clay event.

The result was a shock. Compared with the adjacent limestone, the iridium content jumped by a factor of 30 in the clay. Walter Alvarez obtained similar clay from a sea-cliff near Copenhagen, also straddling the Cretaceous–Tertiary boundary, and the increase in iridium was 160-fold. Either the duration of the red-clay event was improbably long, as judged by a slow rain of meteoritic dust, or the Earth received an inrush of iridium from a greater source.

After considering and rejecting volcanic emissions, or the close explosion of a star, Alvarez father and son, together with Frank Asaro and Helan Michel, announced in 1980 that the most likely explanation was that the dinosaurs' planet was hit by an asteroid ten kilometres wide. The impacting microplanet would have thrown up dust 100 times greater than its own mass, capable of blotting out the Sun for several years and bringing plant and animal life almost to a halt.

Settling worldwide, the impact dust would create the layer of clay, doped to the right degree with the tell-tale iridium from the asteroid itself. Later, opinion would shift in favour of the impactor being a comet. Either way the Berkeley result made mass extinctions due to impacts a scandalous topic of conversation.

'Unbelievable arrogance'

Mainstream evolutionary theory in the 20th century was uncomfortable with the very idea of extinction. As Stephen Jay Gould of Harvard put it, 'In an overly Darwinian world of adaptation, gradual change, and improvement, extinction seemed, well, so negative—the ultimate failure, the flip side of evolution's "real" work, something to be acknowledged but not intensely discussed in polite company.'

This squeamishness persisted despite the fact that 99.9 per cent of all species that ever existed on the Earth are extinct, including many that were immensely successful in their day. In 200 years of systematic fossil-hunting, started by William Smith in England and Georges Cuvier in France, palaeontologists established a geological time-scale. Different periods and stages of the era of conspicuous life (meaning in modern terms the past half a billion years or so) were distinguishable by their characteristic fossil animals, which kept disappearing in later stages.

Emergent new species obviously needed ecological elbow-room, niches where they could prosper without too much competition. Except on newly formed land, every niche would be overbooked a hundred times, if extinction did not repeatedly eliminate previous passengers as no-shows. And from time to time the clearances were on a grand scale, by both land and sea.

In the 20th century, radioactivity calibrated the time-scale. An oil-company palaeontologist could date a drilled sample to within a million years, just by inspecting microscopic fossils. The scientists concerned became so habituated to this useful chronicle of appearances and disappearances that they forgot to ask why they happened.

Academic dogma, hardened in a battle early in the 19th century, encouraged the absentmindedness. To Cuvier in Paris, the obvious explanation of the drastic changes in animal populations from one geological stage to the next was that a catastrophe overtook the incumbents. In London, his young contemporary Charles Lyell opposed that idea. He insisted that Earth history was to be understood by the gradual operation of the slow processes of geological change observable in the world today.

'We are not authorized in the infancy of our science, to recur to extraordinary agents,' Lyell wrote in 1830. His censorious tone won the day. His gradualism later fitted comfortably with the idea of slow biological evolution favoured by his protégé Charles Darwin, whom he heroically supported. Even late in the 20th century catastrophe was still a repugnant concept for some evolutionists and fossil-hunters, and it was even more outrageous when physical scientists advertised an extraterrestrial cause.

'The arrogance of those people is simply unbelievable,' Robert Bakker, a dinosaur expert at Colorado, declared in 1985. 'They know next to nothing about how real animals evolve, live and become extinct. . . . The real reasons for the dinosaur extinctions have to do with temperature and sea-level changes, the spread of diseases by migration and other complex events.'

The gradualist view of evolution required that the dinosaurs were already expiring of their own accord, before the end of the Cretaceous. This claim was put to the test in the most intensive fossil hunt in history, and it failed. At Hell

Creek, Montana, where tyrannosaurs and triceratops had co-existed, a large team of volunteers found a thousand new dinosaur fossils very close to the Cretaceous–Tertiary boundary. There was not the slightest sign of any decline before the sudden, fatal event 65 million years ago.

The hundreds of metres of limestone that line the gorge at Gubbio show that deposits can indeed settle monotonously, millimetre by millimetre, while the Earth circles millions of times around the Sun. The centimetre-thick red clay, together with very austere microfossils in the limestone immediately above it, represents a catastrophe that supervened when a jaywalking comet elected to cross the Earth's orbit just when the Earth was there.

Linking life and astronomy

Biologists could not plead that no one had told them about wayward objects in the Solar System. Collisions between the Earth and comets were on the astronomers' research agenda from 1694 onwards, when Edmond Halley of London offered 'the casual shock of a comet' as an explanation for Noah's Flood. Fear of an impact occasioned public scares in Paris in 1773 and in London in 1857. In the USA in 1910 a prediction circulated, that Halley's Comet would strike the planet somewhere between Boston, Massachusetts, and Boise, Idaho.

'Nothing happened,' recalled the writer James Thurber, who was then a teenager in Ohio, 'except that I was left with curious twitching of my left ear after sundown and a tendency to break into a dog-trot at the striking of a match or the flashing of a lantern.' The false alarms did not invalidate the proposition, self-evident to astronomers, that cosmic traffic accidents were inevitable and one should look for the evidence of past events in the history of the Earth. It was a textbook case of scientists in different fields having incompatible mind-sets.

By the mid-20th century, astronomers were calculating that the typical duration of geological periods, around 50 million years, fitted rather nicely with the expected intervals between collisions with large comets. The reality of giant meteoritic impacts appeared in a growing count of non-volcanic craters on the Earth, sometimes called star wounds, or astroblemes. Space missions confirmed that the craters of the Moon were due to impacts, and revealed that every hard-surfaced planet or moon in the Solar System was spattered with impact craters. If they were less obvious on the Earth, it was because active geology healed or hid the wounds.

In 1973 the chemist Harold Urey, at Chicago, strengthened the prima facie case for blaming comet impacts for biological changes. He found coincidences between the ends of geological stages during the past 50 million years and the ages of glassy debris called tektites, produced in large meteoritic impacts. But biologists who had paid no heed to the astronomers were not about to capitulate to a chemist.

As the list of known impact craters lengthened, dating improved both for geological stages and for the craters themselves. Anyone was free to look for links between the two. Then came the iridium story from Gubbio in 1980, followed in 1991 by the discovery of a large, buried crater of the corresponding age at Chicxulub in Mexico.

The Big Five

A few experts on past life, so far from being sceptical about the cosmic impacts, welcomed them as an explanation of repeated crises in life on the Earth. The fossil-hunters David Raup and Jack Sepkoski at Chicago identified five major mass extinctions among 3800 families of marine animals in the past 500 million years. Three of them had impact craters to match.

Besides the Cretaceous terminal event (Chicxulub, 65 million years ago, 180 kilometres wide) there was a late Triassic holocaust among reef-building animals and marine reptiles that corresponds with the Manicouagan crater in Canada (214 million years, 100 kilometres). An earlier, Devonian decimation of other reef-builders and bottom-dwelling animals went with the Siljan crater in Sweden (368 million years, 55 kilometres).

Two of the Raup–Sepkoski Big Five extinctions had no matching impact craters by the end of the 20th century, and perhaps never will. One was the worst event of all, 245 million years ago, at the end of the Permian Period and the 'old life' Palaeozoic Era, when about 96 per cent of all species of marine animals were annihilated. Nor is there a convincing crater to match for the end of the Ordovician Period, 440 million years ago, when many trilobites and early fishes disappeared.

In view of the difficulty of finding the buried Chicxulub crater, and the fact that all impact craters older than 200 million years on the deep ocean floor have been totally erased by plate tectonics, no one should take the absence of evidence to mean an absence of impacts. A score of three out of five matches, of craters to major mass extinctions, is remarkable.

In 1991, Raup asked provocatively, 'Could all extinction be caused by meteorite impact?' Small impacts could wipe out some species with a limited geographical range, confined to the afflicted region. Large impacts would kill successful and widespread species.

Raup deflected critics by calling his question a thought experiment, and he also made it clear that he meant 'almost all' extinction. Some disappearances were due to other causes, for example volcanic eruptions, or continental drift bringing species into conflict, or ice ages, or diseases. But in Raup's opinion the effects of such causes were generally minor, and without important consequences.

He stressed the wanton nature of the bolts from the blue, which eliminated species that were well adapted to their normal environment. The very rarity of impacts means that they fail to provide the continuous pressure that natural selection would need to enable species to adapt to the disasters and survive. And the most important evolutionary innovations of the past were made possible by the disappearance of whole groups of species.

'If extinction were always a fair game,' Raup declared, 'with the survivors deserving to survive and the victim deserving to die, we would not have the evolutionary record we see.'

Future historians of science may rank the Gubbio–Chicxulub saga with other global adventures that irrevocably altered our perception of life on our home planet—including the voyage of HMS *Beagle* with the young Charles Darwin aboard. Henceforward accounts of evolution's history and mechanisms may be worthless, which do not start by recognizing that if the Chicxulub impactor had safely crossed the Earth's orbit 20 minutes earlier, we should not be here.

Mountain building and erosion would probably have continued as usual and so the gorge in Umbria would look much the same. But without the thin red line in the limestone, there would be no spattering of holes in the rock face either, where clever mammalian hands gathered samples for scientific analysis.

▶ *For the discovery of the Mexican crater and other effects of such events, see* IMPACTS. *For a surprising link to volcanic events, see* FLOOD BASALTS. *For more about the Solar System's small objects, and the present watch for dangerous ones, see* COMETS AND ASTEROIDS. *For other problems with conventional evolutionary theory, see* EVOLUTION *and cross-references therein.*

EXTRATERRESTRIAL LIFE

Could we be all alone in the Milky Way?

T HE REASON why the Swiss won the race to discover the first planet around a normal star was that the planet itself was extremely surprising. By the 1990s, astronomers had instruments accurate enough to detect wobbles of stars caused by big planets orbiting around them. Slight changes in the wavelength of light, as the star moved first towards and then away from the Earth, would be the clue from which the presence of a planet could be inferred.

The analogy is with our own Solar System, where the Sun wobbles as the planets swing around it in their orbits. The giant planet Jupiter, gassy and cool, has the biggest effect, but it takes 12 years to circle the Sun. The expectation was that large planets of other stars would orbit at a similar stately rate, so that several years of observations would be needed to make a detection. Astronomers settled down to watching sun-like stars, patiently and intermittently, from the Lick Observatory in California and the Observatoire de Haute-Provence in France.

Michel Mayor and Didier Queloz of the Observatoire de Genève, who were using the French facility, had an automatic system that checked their results within minutes. Conceived simply to verify that the observations were successful, their box revealed the unexpected. On the target list was the sun-like star 51 Pegasi, lying 40 light-years away and a little to the west of the great square in the Pegasus constellation. The Swiss astronomers saw the star wobbling all right, but far too rapidly. Changes were perceptible not from year to year but from night to night.

As Queloz recalled, 'The first reaction that you have at that time is, "Oh, something is wrong with the experiment." You never think about the planets. And you observe it again the day after and the day after, and then it was more and more awful because it was moving every day. And you say, "All right. There is really a big problem with the experiment."'

Only when Mayor and Queloz had satisfied themselves that there was no error did they go public with their discovery, at a conference in Florence in 1995. What they had found was a hot jupiter. A planet with about the same mass as the Sun's gas giant was whizzing around its parent star every four days. That meant it was orbiting far closer than the Sun's innermost planet, little Mercury, and it would be heated by the star to 1000°C or more. Common sense might suggest that a gas giant should evaporate in the heat, but evidently it survived for a while.

Within seven years of the 51 Pegasi discovery, the count of planets around other stars, or extrasolar planets as they came to be called, had passed the 100 mark. About ten per cent of them were very hot jupiters with orbital periods of less than 20 days. Astrophysicists were unhappy.

Their theory of the origin of the Solar System said that the Earth and other planets formed by the coalescence of ever-larger objects, growing from gas and dust around the newborn Sun. This solar nebula was concentrated in a disk flattened by gravity, which is why the major planets all orbit in the same plane. Powerful computers demonstrated the process in persuasive-looking animated movies.

But the theory did not predict or even countenance the possible manufacture of hot jupiters. At a gathering of the world's astronomers in 2000 a leading theorist, Pawel Artymovicz of Stockholm, exclaimed, 'When we discovered extrasolar planets we lost understanding of our own Solar System!'

Planets in the making

Help in recovering that understanding might come from observations of planets still in the process of manufacture. Ever since the 17th century, when Immanuel Kant in Germany and Pierre-Simon de Laplace in France independently proposed that a spinning cloud of gas and dust condensed to form the Sun's planets, huge efforts had gone into perfecting this hypothesis of the solar nebula. In contrast with a rival scenario, in which the Sun's planets were a rarity produced by a chance near-collision between two stars, it favoured the idea that planets should be commonplace, as potential abodes for extraterrestrial life.

Strong support for the hypothesis came from the detection of disks of dust around other stars. The first one seen was a surprise. When the infrared astronomy satellite IRAS found dust around the bright star Vega in 1983, the Dutch–US–UK team thought something was wrong with the instruments. Vega was a mature star, in the prime of life, and should not be dusty at all. Perhaps in this case planet formation had failed.

Fortunately younger stars had similar disks, discovered by IRAS, by the Hubble Space Telescope and by the Infrared Space Observatory. The last-named spacecraft found disks around half of all the young stars that it examined. Astronomers labelled them proto-planetary disks. Confidence in that appellation grew stronger when a Dutch team detected dust around Rho Cancri, a star where planet-hunters in California had already identified a hot jupiter.

Although the dust disks revealed something like the primeval solar nebula in action, the views were fuzzy. They showed little detail to help anyone wrestling with the new problem of hot versus cool jupiters. A global project called the Atacama Large Millimetre Array, or ALMA, with dozens of radio dishes to be spread across ten kilometres of high ground in the Atacama Desert of Chile by 2009, was expected to deliver greater insight from very short radio waves.

'So far the theorists have very little to guide them, about what really happens when planets form,' commented Stéphane Guilloteau of the French–German–Spanish Institut de Radio Astronomie Millimetrique. 'With ALMA we'll look much closer to the young stars than the Hubble Space Telescope, and produce sharper views of the proto-planetary disks. We'll also gather crucial new data on the chemistry, on the interactions of dust and gas, and on the time-scale of planet-building.'

Cool giants at last

Planet-hunters felt frustrated too, by the hot jupiters. The undisguised motive of their research was the millennia-old dream of detecting life beyond the Earth. Signals from intelligent creatures living out there among the stars, and trying to get in touch with us, might well have short-circuited the hunt. But after 40 fruitless years of looking for messages from little green aliens, astronomers had settled down to search for life the hard way.

The jupiters were just a step on the way to finding the much smaller earths— the places in the sky where living things might thrive in the light of a benign parent star, in worlds 'no worse and no less inhabited than our Earth,' as Giordano Bruno put it in 1584. The Neapolitan natural philosopher was burned alive as a heretic in Rome's Campo di Fiori in 1600. Modern observing techniques were expected to vindicate his scientific idea, four centuries later.

In 1992, before the discovery at 51 Pegasi, Alex Wolszczan at Penn State had detected planets with earth-like masses in orbit around a neutron star, Pulsar B1257+12. Because a neutron star is the still-violent remnant of an exploded star, these objects were unlikely to be habitable worlds in Bruno's sense. The searchers looking at normal stars did not expect to detect small planets directly, at first. But if they sensed the presence of alien jupiters at the right sort of distance from their parents, they could home in on those stars for closer examination with more powerful techniques in preparation.

The hot jupiters revealed planetary systems entirely different from the Solar System, and uncongenial for small planets. The prototypical Jupiter orbits the Sun in a circle at five times the Sun–Earth distance. This creates room and safety for four rocky planets, of which Earth and Mars orbit in a region where conditions are not too hot and not too cold for life like ours. The technical name of this potentially habitable region is the Goldilocks zone.

Only with cool jupiters in circular orbits of perhaps 12 years' duration would there be much chance of finding other earths. Locating one would still require several years of observation of the same star. The leading planet-hunters in the USA, Geoffrey Marcy of UC Berkeley and Paul Butler of the Carnegie Institution of Washington, coordinated a long-term watch on 1200 stars, with the task shared between the 3-metre Lick in California, the 10-metre Keck in Hawaii and the 3.9-metre Anglo-Australian Telescope in New South Wales.

By 2002 they had found the first jupiter at the right distance from a sun-like star in the Cancer constellation, 55 Cancri, after 15 years of observations with the Lick Telescope. It was already known to have a hot jupiter as well, but optimistic calculations suggested that an earth might survive between the two. 'We haven't yet found an exact Solar System analogue,' Butler said. 'But this shows we are getting close.'

Almost simultaneously the Geneva astronomers reported a cool jupiter orbiting the star Gliese 777A in the Cygnus constellation every seven years. That put it at 70 per cent of Jupiter's distance from the Sun. 'It has a circular orbit, not an elliptical one,' Queloz commented. 'This reminds us strongly of our own Solar System.'

A few numbers give a sense of progress in the detection of planets by the wobbles of their parent stars. The hot jupiter of 51 Pegasi, the first discovered, moves the star at 59 metres per second. The speed of the wobble falls to 17 metres per second for the cool jupiter of Gliese 777A. By 2003, a new Swiss instrument on a big European telescope at La Silla, Chile, was capable of registering a disturbance of just 25 centimetres per second. Such technical improvements brightened the prospects for detecting multiple planets, and perhaps a few planets with about the mass of the Earth.

Other ways to find planets

A planet whose orbit happens to carry it directly in front of its star, as seen from the Earth, will cause a slight dip in the star's brightness. Retrospectively, that shadowing effect during transits was found in the data from Europe's Hipparcos star-mapping satellite. Unknown to the science team at the time, it observed a hot jupiter as early as 1991. But the effect was small and the observations intermittent, so the planet could not have been detected until the astronomers knew it was there.

When the discovery of the first extrasolar planets transformed a small and merely hopeful enterprise into a thriving branch of astronomy, planet-hunting became a major goal of the space agencies. The discovery of planets transiting in front of their parent stars seems a good prospect, and it may be the quickest way of finding earths. After a start with France's small Corot satellite (2004) two larger ventures were conceived for the purpose: NASA's Kepler (2007) and Europe's Eddington (2008).

In both cases a telescope is to stare at large numbers of stars simultaneously, in a wide field of view, for long periods. Guesses at the number of discoveries to be made depend on a string of assumptions about what planetary systems really exist. But after several years of observations, Kepler and Eddington might each harvest a few dozen earth-sized planets. Perhaps more, perhaps fewer, perhaps even none. The aim is to take a census of planets large and small, with enough statistics to show whether earths are very common, fairly common, or very rare.

If the ventures in space and on the ground find some earth-like candidates, the next challenge for astronomers will be to tell whether or not they seem to harbour life. Doing so will require direct inspection of infrared rays coming from them. The glare of the parent star dazzles any ordinary telescope trying to see the faint glow from a small planet, but a technique called null interferometry can cure the problem.

Observe the stars with several telescopes spaced apart, and combine the incoming light in a clever way, and you can then subtract the star from the scene. This is the principle behind bold space projects conceived to look for signs of distant extraterrestrial life. Terrestrial Planet Finder and Darwin are similar schemes for the second decade of the century, envisaged by NASA and the European Space Agency, respectively—so similar that they are expected to merge into a single project.

The idea is to have several infrared telescopes flying hundreds of metres apart in a precise formation controlled by laser beams. They should be able to recognize planets resembling Venus, Mars or the Earth, even at a distance of 30 light-years or more. The infrared signatures of the planets will differ.

An alien venus or mars will simply show strong absorption of 15-micron waves by carbon dioxide in their atmospheres. An alien earth, on the other hand, will signal the presence of water vapour at 6 microns, and also of methane at 7 microns and other wavelengths. If life has evolved beyond the most primitive bacterial phase, and there is oxygen in the air, then this will produce ozone in the upper atmosphere, absorbing 9-micron infrared light.

Mars and Europa

The assumption in those space projects is that living planets should outwardly resemble the Earth, chemically speaking. Other scientists who preferred to look for extraterrestrial life much nearer home, in the Solar System itself, had to abandon any such notion if they were not to give up hope altogether.

When NASA's two Viking landers settled on the surface of Mars in 1976 they showed a dusty desert without a hint of life. To many it seemed the biggest disappointment of the Space Age. Yet in 1965, long before the spacecraft set off, the British chemist James Lovelock had predicted the outcome. He used just the same reasoning about atmospheric constituents that would later figure in the Terrestrial Planet Finder and Darwin proposals for distinguishing a non-living mars from a living earth, in the vicinity of another star.

Stubborn hunters changed tack and said that the conspicuous kinds of life seen on the Earth's surface were not the only sort possible on Mars. There could be organisms thriving in underground reservoirs of water, just as many do on the Earth, which draw their energy from chemistry rather than sunlight. They need not interact on a large scale with the atmosphere, but little whiffs of gas, notably methane, filtering through to the surface, might reveal their presence. A British lander, Beagle 2, riding on Europe's Mars Express spacecraft, was conceived to put that idea to the test on its arrival on the red planet, scheduled for the end of 2003. Meanwhile encouraging hints of ice and subsurface water came from NASA's Mars Odyssey spacecraft, in 2002.

Similar reasoning about inconspicuous life was applied to Europa, a moon of Jupiter, which exploring spacecraft showed to have a crust of ice covering a sunless ocean. Why should there not be living creatures there, just as there are on the ocean floor of the Earth, gobbling up energy from materials leaking from the underlying crust? Let's send a drilling rig to penetrate the ice of Europa, scientists said, and a robot submarine to explore the hidden ocean.

For all searches for extraterrestrial creatures, near or far, the big question is: How easy is it for life to start? As the origin of life on the Earth is still unexplained, no one knows. But the other fallback position, after the Viking spacecraft sent home their pictures of the Martian deserts, was the possibility that life may have flourished on the red planet in a former era, when water abounded. Erosion features seen by orbiting spacecraft point to the sometime presence of surface water.

There was excitement in 1996 when US scientists claimed the discovery of fossil microbes in a meteorite that had evidently come from Mars. They were worm-like objects less than a thousandth of a millimetre long. But they failed to convince scientists in general that this was the first-ever detection of extraterrestrial life. For what would go into the history books as one of the top discoveries of all time, more persuasive evidence would be needed.

'Mars always comes top of the agenda in the search for life beyond the Earth,' said the chemist André Brack of the Centre de Biophysique Moléculaire in Orléans. 'Anyone who thinks that life should be commonplace in the Universe will be disappointed if Mars was never alive. But we must look for the evidence more systematically, and not expect to find it on the surface.'

Cosmic radio hams

Was the respected journal *Nature* dabbling in science fiction? That was a common reaction in 1959, when it published a paper by Giuseppe Cocconi and Philip Morrison, astrophysicists at Cornell. They suggested that radio microwaves coming from the vicinity of other stars should be monitored for coded messages from intelligent beings. 'The probability of success is difficult to estimate,' Cocconi and Morrison wrote; 'but if we never search, the chance of success is zero.'

In the following year Frank Drake recorded microwaves from the nearby stars Tau Ceti and Epsilon Eridani, using a radio telescope at Green Bank, West Virginia. He found nothing of interest. But he went on to offer a way of estimating the number of civilizations in the Milky Way Galaxy whose electromagnetic emissions should be detectable.

Called the Drake equation, it starts by multiplying together the rate of formation of suitable stars, the fraction of them with planetary systems, and the number of planets per system suitable for life. That establishes the physical base. Then you bring in the biological and technological factors: the fraction of suitable planets on which life appears, the fraction of those on which intelligent civilizations emerge, the fraction of civilizations whose technology releases signs of their existence into space, and the length of time for which the detectable signals persist.

The answer was millions for the optimists, and zero for the pessimists. The latter included evolutionary biologists conscious of how difficult, improbable, recent and perhaps brief is the appearance of a communicative species on the Earth. During the Cold War it seemed on the brink of extinguishing itself, and one of the motives offered by supporters of the search for extraterrestrial intelligence (SETI for short) was to gain reassurance that competence was not necessarily self-destructive.

A counterpart to the Drake equation was the Fermi question: 'Where is everyone?' reportedly posed by the physicist Enrico Fermi at Chicago, over lunch. It relates to a widespread belief that, before long, human beings will be capable of travelling to stars and settling on any congenial planets. On the multi-billion-year time-scale of the Galaxy, there has been ample time for beings to evolve and to develop superior astronautical technologies. So why haven't they shown up to colonize the Earth?

Despite the objections, Drake and other cosmic radio hams continued to listen out for signals of intelligence, and they grew in numbers and influence. Carl Sagan of Cornell and Iosif Shkolovskii of the Shternberg Astronomical Institute in Moscow became spokesmen for the endeavour. Shkolovskii wrote of 'the possibility of our having been for a long time within a bundle of electromagnetic radiation beamed towards us by some intelligent beings of a well-known star that is several dozen light-years distant.'

Programmes to look for signals won official funding in the Soviet Union and the USA. Systems of ever-increasing sophistication recorded radio waves from vast numbers of sources and checked them automatically for anything that was not natural noise. By the 1990s visible-light images were also being inspected for possible laser flashes. If there had been any success, you'd have heard about it.

In 1974 Drake used the huge radio telescope at Arecibo, Puerto Rico, as a transmitter. He beamed a short message from the Earth towards any intelligent beings who may inhabit the globular cluster of stars called M13 in the Hercules constellation. As the cluster is 25,000 light-years away, no reply can be expected for 50 millennia. But the event provoked the wrath of Martin Ryle at Cambridge, who thought it was virtually an invitation to any aggressive aliens to come and attack us.

Drake's defenders pointed out that powerful pulses from military radars were in any case moving outwards in all directions through the Galaxy at the speed of light, not to mention pop music, soap operas and the like. The ever-expanding electromagnetic babble around the Earth was already reaching many of the nearer stars, to bemuse any TV critics there may be out there. Other commentators worried that contact even with well-intentioned extraterrestrials, and even if confined to radio conversations, might be demoralizing. If the aliens seemed far cleverer and happier, human beings might give up making their own discoveries and decisions, and just keep asking for advice.

Interstellar communication requires, besides intelligence, limbs capable of technological manipulations, and restless, ambitious minds in a mood to communicate. Dolphins are supposed to be pretty bright, but without hands they'd find it hard to make a radio telescope or laser beam to communicate with extraterrestrial dolphins. In any case, they might judge it to be a worthless distraction from their water sports. Perhaps frolicking with your friends is the highest form of wisdom.

And if we're alone after all?

When the astrophysicist Martin Rees of Cambridge commented on the state of the search for extraterrestrial life, early in the 21st century, he did so with an awareness from cosmology that we seem to live in a Universe that is peculiarly biophilic—hospitable to life. Even so, he was sceptical about the 'common fantasy' that there would be replicas of the Earth with beings like us on them. Even if intelligence were widespread, he thought we might become aware of only a small, atypical fraction that was both communicative and comprehensible. Perhaps not even that.

'It would in some ways be disappointing if searches for alien intelligence were doomed to fail,' Rees said. 'On the other hand, it would boost our cosmic self-esteem. If our tiny Earth were a unique abode of intelligence, we could view it in a less humble cosmic perspective than it would merit if the Galaxy already teemed with complex life.'

Such an outcome would give our species stronger motives than ever to cherish the Earth as a unique abode of intelligence, and not to foreclose life's future here. At the same time, Rees foresaw a future opening up for our own brand of intelligent life that could last longer than the billions of years since our ancestors were bacteria. 'Even if life is now unique to the Earth,' Rees said, 'there is time for it to spread from here through the entire Galaxy.'

▶ *For the possibility of a living cloud in space, see* PLASMA CRYSTALS. *For other closely related topics, see* EARTH, LIFE'S ORIGIN *and* EXTREMOPHILES.

EXTREMOPHILES

Creatures that thrive in unexpected places

I N 1977 the research vessels *Lulu* and *Knorr*, from the Woods Hole Oceanographic Institution in Massachusetts, cruised in the equatorial ocean 300 kilometres from the Galapagos Islands. They examined the subsea feature called the East Pacific Rise. Marine geologists from Oregon State were searching for hydrothermal vents in the ocean floor, some 2500 metres below the sea surface, where volcanic action might release hot, chemically laden water into the ocean.

An unmanned submersible towed just above the seabed detected a spot where the water was slightly warmer than usual. Pictures from the submersible showed clams there, but those were interpreted as shells thrown overboard after a clambake on a passing ship. *Lulu* launched a manned submersible, *Alvin*, and its pilot took geologists John Corliss and Tjeerd van Andel down to examine the physical conditions in the warm spot.

As related by a Woods Hole science writer, Victoria A. Kaharl, the following exchange took place via the underwater telephone, between Corliss and his graduate student Debbie Stakes, on watch in *Lulu*.

Corliss: We are sampling a hydrothermal vent . . . Debra, isn't the deep ocean supposed to be like a desert?

Stakes: (remembering her only high school biology course and an ecology course from graduate school): Yes.

Corliss: Well there's all these animals down here.

Until that precise moment, the belief was that the deep ocean floor was inhabited only by a few modest, well-known species feeding in the total darkness on traces of dead food raining down from the sunlit surface. The submersible's spotlight fell on colonies of exotic creatures crowding around this and neighbouring hydrothermal vents. Crabs and lobsters white as snow, giant red-tipped tubeworms, pale anemones, jellyfish-like and dandelion-like animals . . . and so on and on.

It was a serendipitous discovery because the expedition was looking for chemicals. In 1974 the French–American Mid-Ocean Undersea Study had explored the Mid-Atlantic Ridge, the largest mountain range on the planet. The aim was to confirm the then-new theory of plate tectonics, according to which the Americas are drifting away from Europe and Africa, and molten rocks rise to the sea floor along rift valleys running like a great crack from far north to far south. Rock-wise, that exploration was a success, but chemical questions remained unanswered.

If water came out through the sea floor rifts, it would have a big effect on the content of seawater. Earth scientists speculated about a recycling of the ocean, over millions of years. Water would descend like Orpheus into the underworld below the seabed. Then, with the onset of geological action, it would react vigorously with the hot minerals, before returning to the sea through volcanic hydrothermal vents. It should bring with it many kinds of dissolved materials.

The expected vents were found by *Alvin* on the East Pacific Rise, and with them the unexpected life. The geological expedition included no life scientists who might have coped with the biggest surprise in outdoor biology in the 20th century. Instead elementary instructions had to come by radio, about how to preserve specimens.

Robert Ballard, a young member of the expedition later celebrated for finding *Titanic* and other historic wrecks, recalled that it was like walking into Disneyland. 'We had to use bottles of vodka and bourbon to pickle what we found,' Ballard said. 'We raided the ship's hospital and were quickly out of all the alcohol there. So we were using booze.'

Some like it hot

By the end of the 20th century, biologists had changed their minds about what constitutes normal life. Organisms previously considered oddities, because they did not favour ordinary temperatures and pressures in the sunny and airy surface regions of the planet, came to be recognized as vast armies following ways of life just as valid as our own. A high rate of discovery of new species around hydrothermal vents, and the fact that thousands of vents remain to be explored, raises the possibility that there may even be as many different species on the ocean floor as at the surface.

Microbes carpet the sea floor or float in the water at the hydrothermal vents. They derive their energy neither from sunlight nor detritus but from hot water rich in atoms and compounds produced by reactions in the rocks. Water samples have the stink of rotten eggs—hydrogen sulphide. The chemical contrast between the emergent hot water and the normal cold seawater of the deep ocean drives a multitude of reactions.

Many different species of microbes insinuate themselves into this free-for-all, using dissolved minerals and gases to power their own biochemistry. They are the primary producers of the ecosystem, nourishing the weird animals. The microbes include bacteria and also archaea, which are similar-looking simple organisms with a different evolutionary lineage. Many are extremophiles, with a propensity for tolerating extreme environments.

In 1989 Karl Stetter and his colleagues from Regensburg, Germany, discovered archaea living in a volcanic vent in the Mediterranean that best like their water at 98°C. That's close to the boiling point of fresh water at the surface, although at high pressure the seawater does not attempt to vaporize. If the temperature drops to a measly 84°C the bugs stop growing. Their tolerance of even 110°C set what was, for a while, a new heat-survival record among known organisms.

Adaptation to the high water pressure is another feature of the vent organisms. Some pressure-loving microbes won't grow at depths of less than 3000 metres. They will though, in lab experiments, tolerate pressures higher than in the deepest trenches of the ocean floor. That would be surprising if microbes thriving on petroleum had not been traced to depths of several kilometres in the Earth's crust, below the sea floor in the North Sea oilfields. The commonplace bacterium found in the human gut, *Escherichia coli*, can survive at pressures corresponding to the weight of 50 kilometres of rock overhead.

Extreme environments exist also at the surface. Salt lakes, and the saltpans where seawater is evaporated to make culinary salt, are sometimes luridly coloured by their microbial inhabitants. Lakes in Africa can be very alkaline as well as salty, and archaea there can tolerate conditions almost like household ammonia. At the opposite end of the alkali–acid scale, stomach acid is no problem for *Helicobacter pylori*, which is major cause of peptic ulcers in humans, and some archaea live by making sulphuric acid. Species are known that put up with conditions as acidic as a car battery. And *Deinococcus radiodurans* has such a capacity for repairing its damaged genes that it can survive atomic radiation at doses a thousand times greater than those fatal to most living things.

During the late 1980s the German research icebreaker *Polarstern*, with multinational science teams aboard, made a breakthrough, literally, into another habitat of hardy species, the sea-ice around Antarctica. Most conspicuous are algae living inside the ice that colour the bottom of the floes brown. Gotthilf Hempel of the Alfred-Wegener-Institut in Bremerhaven affirmed that 'the ice algae play a major role in the ecosystem, especially in the late winter and early summer'.

The algae live in concentrated brine held in channels within the ice, and they withstand not just the high salt concentration but temperatures falling to minus 20°C. They make use of very weak light penetrating the ice. Other creatures lodging with them in the brine include flatworms and small crustaceans. These icy extremophiles help to nourish the krill, the shrimp-like animals of the Southern Ocean that in turn feed the penguins, seals and whales.

In the absence of any obvious life on the surface of Mars, scientists speculated that organisms living underground on the red planet might power themselves by reacting hydrogen with carbon dioxide to make methane gas and water. An unprecedented concentration of archaea living exactly that way was found 200 metres below the surface of Idaho. They thrive in water feeding the volcanic Lidy Hot Springs.

Unlike the vent animals, this discovery was no fluke. A team from the US Geological Survey and the University of Massachusetts had spent many years investigating the volcanic activity in the Yellowstone region, looking for a subterranean setting likely to be free of surface contaminants, where unusual biochemical processes might occur. Commenting on the result from Lidy Hot Springs a London astrobiologist, Richard Taylor, noted: 'As long as there's subsurface water and enough chemical fuel, you can get microbial life. It's life on the surface that's unusual.'

The astrophysicist Thomas Gold of Cornell suspected that the crustal rocks of the Earth are teeming with life, not making methane but living off it. The idea was related to his unorthodox opinion that most of the world's hydrocarbons are of astrochemical origin, and not the product of biological processes as generally supposed. Microbes processing primordial methane could thrive down to depths of several kilometres until temperatures become excessive for even the hardiest of heat-loving species. About this proposed biosphere of microscopic gnomes Gold declared: 'In mass and volume, it may be comparable to surface life.'

Why are we so choosy?

The extremophiles should no longer be seen as freaks. Nor are they loners. They thrive in communities where one organism's products are another's resources.

The saga of extremophiles and their surprising diets has only just begun. They force geochemists to reappraise the living processes that recycle elements, salts and molecules and maintain benign chemical conditions in the air, the water and the soil. There is probably no kind of man-made pollution, even including oil spills, plastic bags and nuclear waste, which one microbe or another could not help to control. Mining companies are fully aware of bugs that accumulate particular metals. Not everyone has forgotten the old dream of getting gold from seawater.

The quest for better knowledge of life in unusual places on the Earth intersects, as mentioned, with the search for life on other worlds. It also bears upon the origin of life on our own planet, about 4 billion years ago. At that time comets and asteroids were raining down on the Earth, frequently blotting out the sunshine with dust palls and causing great tidal waves. Perhaps the safest place to be was nowhere near the surface, but snuggled around a hydrothermal vent on the ocean floor. It's called keeping your head down.

If you were an intelligent extremophile you might consider the human choice of habitat very weird and picky. There are many ways for organisms to earn a living, besides by the highly specialized route most familiar to us, whereby plants use sunshine to make organic material from carbon dioxide and water. As it happens the eukaryotes, meaning organisms of advanced kinds including fungi and the many-celled plants and animals, nearly all favour this system.

When taking stock of what was known about microbes in unexpected places, Dianne Newman of Caltech and Jillian Banfield of UC Berkeley commented, 'Once we understand the design principles for microbial communities, comparison with studies of gene expression in multicellular organisms may reveal why only a small fraction of Earth's inhabitants (e.g., most eukaryotes) abandoned the ability to use the vast majority of available energy sources and populated only a tiny subset of Earth's habitable environments.'

Would-be extremists among the animals

In the early 1960s Art DeVries, a graduate student from Stanford, collected fishes living in seawater at subzero temperatures at McMurdo Station in Antarctica, and in them he discovered special protein molecules that inhibit the formation of ice crystals in the cells of their bodies. Other antifreeze proteins turned up in various species of cold-water fishes, and also in plants and insects that have to endure icy conditions even in temperate zones, in winter. The proteins attach themselves to microscopic ice crystals and inhibit their growth, and they are hundreds of times more effective than man-made antifreeze chemicals.

The seawater cools only to minus 2°C, and to David Wharton at Otago, New Zealand, the endurance of far lower temperatures by small land animals in

Antarctica seemed more challenging. Penguins huddle together in the winter darkness to minimize their heat loss. On the other hand the nematode *Panagrolaimus davidi*, a worm almost too small to see, which lives among algae and moss on ice-free edges of Antarctica, regularly freezes solid each winter.

It can chill out to minus 35°C with virtually all its metabolism switched off, and then revive in the spring. In laboratory tests, it can go down to minus 80°C without problems. Investigating the nematode's survival strategy, Wharton found that the rate of cooling is critical. It survives the rather slow rate experienced in the wild but fast freezing in liquid nitrogen kills it.

Cryptobiosis is the term used for such suspended or latent life. Various animals and plants can produce tough larvae, seeds or spores that seem essentially dead, but which can survive adversity for years or even millennia and then return to life when a thaw comes, or a shower of rain in the desert. To Wharton, these cryptobiotic organisms are not true extremophiles.

Assessing the ability of larger animals to cope with extreme conditions, as compared with what archaea and bacteria can do, Wharton judged that only a few groups, mainly insects, birds and mammals, are much good at it. Insects resist dehydration with waxy coats. Warm-blooded birds and mammals contrive to keep their internal temperatures within strict limits, whether in polar cold or desert heat. On the other hand, fishes and most classes of invertebrate animals shun the most severe habitats—the big exception being the deep ocean floor.

'We think of the deep sea as being an extreme environment because of the high pressures faced by the organisms that live there,' Wharton commented, a quarter of a century after the discovery of the animals of the hydrothermal vents. 'Now that the problems of sampling organisms from this environment have been overcome, we have realized that, rather than being a biological desert, as had been assumed, it is populated by a very diverse range of species. . . . Perhaps we should not consider the deep sea to be extreme.'

▶ *For related subjects, see* GLOBAL ENZYMES, LIFE'S ORIGIN, TREE OF LIFE *and* EXTRATERRESTRIAL LIFE.

FLOOD BASALTS

Can impacting comets set continents in motion?

T HE ROAD FROM MUMBAI TO PUNE, or Bombay to Poona as the British said during their Raj, takes you up India's natural rampart of the Western Ghats. It's not a journey to make after dark, when unlit bullock carts compete as hazards with the potholes and gullies made by the monsoon torrents.

Natural terraces built of layer upon layer of volcanic rock give the scarp the appearance of a staircase, and Ghats is a Hindi word for steps. In the steep mountains and on the drier Deccan Plateau beyond them is the triangular heartland of the Indian peninsula. It is geologically odd, consisting mainly of black basalt, up to two kilometres thick, which normally belongs on the deep ocean floor. Preferring a Scandinavian word for steps, geologists call the terraced basalt 'traps'.

The surviving area of the Deccan Traps is 500,000 square kilometres, roughly the size of France. Originally the plateau was even wider, and rounder too. You have to picture this region as hell on Earth, 65 million years ago. Unimaginable quantities of molten rock poured through the crust, flooding the landscape with red-hot lava and spewing dust and noxious fumes into the air.

It was not the only horrid event of its kind. Flood basalts of many different ages are scattered around the world's continents, with their characteristic black bedrock. In the US states of Washington and Oregon, the Columbia River Plateau was made in a similar event 16 million years ago. The Parana flood basalt of south-east Brazil, 132 million years old, is more extensive than the Deccan and Columbia River basalts put together.

Plumb in the middle of Russia are the Siberian Traps. Around 1990 several investigators confirmed that the flood basalt there appeared almost instantaneously, by geological standards. Through a thickness of up to 3500 metres, the date of deposition was everywhere put at 250 million years ago. This was not a rounded number. The technique used, called argon–argon dating, was accurate to about 1 million years.

The basalt builds the Siberian Plateau, which is flanked to the east by a succession of unrelated mountain ranges. To the west is the low-lying West Siberian Basin, created by a stretching, thinning and sagging of the continental crust. During the 1990s, prospectors drilling in search of oil in the basin kept hitting basalt at depths of two kilometres or more.

Geologists at Leicester arranged with Russian colleagues to have the basalt from many of the West Siberian boreholes dated by argon-argon at a Scottish lab in East Kilbride. Again, it all came out at almost exactly 250 million years old. So a large part of the flood basalt from a single event had simply subsided out of sight.

This meant that the original lava flood covered an area of almost 4 million square kilometres, half the size of Australia. The speed and magnitude of the event make it ghoulishly fascinating. In Iceland in 1783 the discharge of just 12 cubic kilometres of basalt in a miniature flood killed the sheep by fluoride vapour and caused 'dry fog' in London, 1800 kilometres away. In Siberia, you have to imagine that happening continuously for a million years.

The Siberian affair's most provocative aspect was that the huge volcanic event coincided precisely with the biggest disaster to befall life on the Earth in the entire era of conspicuous animals and plants. At the end of the Permian period, 250 million years ago, the planet almost died. About 96 per cent of all species of marine animals suddenly became extinct. Large land animals, which were then mammal-like reptiles, perished too.

'The larger area of volcanism strengthens the link between the volcanism and the end-Permian mass extinction,' the British–Russian team reported. Again the dating was good to within a million years. And it forced scientists to face up to the question: What on Earth is all this black stuff really telling us?

● A tangled web

The facts and theories about flood basalts had become muddled. In respect of the recipe for the eruptions there were two conflicting hypotheses. According to one, a hot plume of rock gradually bored its way upwards from close to the molten core of the Earth, and through the main body, the mantle. When this mantle plume first penetrated the crust, its rocks melted and poured out as basalt.

The other hypothesis was the pressure cooker. The rock below the crust is quite hot enough to melt, were it not squeezed by the great weight of overlying rock. Crack the crust, by whatever means, and the Earth will bleed. The relief of pressure will let the basalt gush out. That happens all the time, in a comparatively gentle way, at mid-ocean ridges where plates of the Earth's outer shell are easing apart. Basalt comes up and slowly builds an ever-widening ocean floor.

According to the pressure-cooker idea, just make a bigger crack at a point of weakness in a continent, and basalt will haemorrhage all over the place. There are old fault-lines everywhere, as well as many regions of stretched and thinned crust. The pressure cooker is much more flexible about candidate localities for flood-basalt events. With the mantle-plume hypothesis you need a pre-existing plume.

Flood basalts often herald the break-up of a continent. Both in the eastern USA and West Africa are remnants of 200-million-year-old basalts released just before the Atlantic Ocean began to open between them, in the break-up of the former supercontinent of Pangaea. The South Atlantic between south-west Africa and Brazil originated later, and its immediate precursor was the 132-million-year-old flood basalt seen in Brazil's Parana.

A sector of the Atlantic that opened relatively late was between the British Isles and Greenland. The preceding basalt flood dates from 60 million years ago. Famous remnants of it include Northern Ireland's Giant's Causeway and Fingal's Cave on the island of Staffa. The latter inspired Felix Mendelssohn to compose his Hebrides Overture, in unconscious tribute to the peculiarities of flood basalts.

When the Deccan Traps formed, 65 million years ago, India was a small, free-range continent, drifting towards an eventual collision with Asia. The continental break-up that ensued was nothing more spectacular than the shedding of the Seychelles, as an independent microcontinent. Whether the effect on worldwide plate motions was large or small, in the mantle-plume theory the basaltic outbursts caused the continental break-ups. The pressure-cooker story said that a basalt flood was a symptom of a break-up occurring for other reasons.

Another tangled web of ideas concerned the mass extinctions of life. In the 1980s, scientists arguing that the dinosaurs were wiped out by the impact of a comet or asteroid, 65 million years ago, had to deal with truculent biologists, and also with geologists who said you didn't need an impact. The disappearance of the dinosaurs and many other creatures at the end of the Cretaceous Period coincided exactly with the great eruption that made the Deccan Traps of India. Climatic and chemical effects of so large a volcanic event could be quite enough to wreck life around the world.

The issue did not go away when evidence in favour of the impact became overwhelming, with the discovery of the main crater, in Mexico. Instead, the question was whether the apparent simultaneity of impact and eruption was just a fluke. Or did the impact trigger the eruption, making it an accomplice in the bid to extinguish life?

Awkward coincidences

Space scientists had no trouble linking impacts with flood basalts. The large dark patches that you can see on the Moon with the naked eye, called maria, are huge areas of basalt amidst the global peppering by impact craters large and small. And in 1974–75, when NASA's Mariner 10 spacecraft flew past Mercury three times, it sent home pictures showing the small planet looking at first glance very like the Moon.

FLOOD BASALTS

The largest crater on Mercury is the Caloris Basin, 1500 kilometres wide. Diametrically opposite it, at the antipodes of the Caloris Basin, weird terrain caught the attention of the space scientists. It had hummocky mountain blocks of a kind not seen elsewhere. The Mariner 10 team inferred a knock-on effect from the impact that made the Caloris Basin. Seismic waves reverberating through the planet came to a strong focus at the antipodes, evidently with enough force to move mountains.

Translated to terrestrial terms, a violent impact on Brazil could severely jolt the crust in Indonesia, or one on the North Pole, at the South Pole. This remote action enlarges the opportunities for releasing flood basalts. The original impact might do the job locally, especially if it landed near a pre-existing weak spot in the crust, such as an old fault-line. Or the focused earthquake waves, the shocks from the impact, might activate a weak spot on the opposite side of the planet.

Either way, the impact might set continents in motion. Severe though it may be, an impactor hasn't the power to drive the continents and the tectonic plates that they ride on, for millions of years. The energy for sustained tectonic action— earthquakes, volcanoes, continental collisions—comes from radioactivity in the rocks inside the Earth. What impactors may be able to do is to start the process off. In effect they may decide where and when a continent should break.

Advocates of impacting comets or asteroids, as the triggers of flood basalts, had plenty of scope, geographically. There was evidence for craters in different places with very similar ages, suggesting either the near-simultaneous arrival of a swarm of comets or a single impactor breaking up before hitting the Earth. So you could, for example, suggest that something hit India, or the Pacific seabed at the antipodes of India, 65 million years ago, to create the Deccan Traps, irrespective of what other craters might be known or found.

In 1984, Michael Rampino and Richard Stothers of NASA's Goddard Institute for Space Studies made the explicit suggestion, 'that Earth's tectonic processes are periodically punctuated, or at least modulated, by episodes of cometary impacts.'

Many mainstream geologists and geophysicists disliked this challenge, just as much as mainstream fossil-hunters and evolutionary theorists abhorred the idea of mass extinctions being due to impacts, or flood basalts. In both cases, they wished to tell the story of the Earth in terms of their own preferred mechanisms, whether of rock movements or biological evolution, concerning which they could claim masterful expertise. They wanted neither intruders from space nor musclers-in from other branches of science. The glove thrown down by Rampino and Stothers therefore lay on the floor for two decades, with just a few brave souls picking it up and dusting it from time to time.

The crunch came with the new results on the Siberian Traps, and especially from the very precise dating that confirmed the match to the end-Permian catastrophe to life. There was no longer any slop in the chronological accounting, which previously left Earth scientists free to choose whether or not they wished to see direct connections between events. The time had come for them to decide whether they were for or against cosmic impacts as a major factor in global geology as well as in the evolution of life.

By 2002, the end-Permian event of 250 million years ago had a basalt flood and a mass extinction but no crater, although there were other hints of a possible impactor from outer space. A clearer prototype was the end-Cretaceous event of 65 million years ago, with a global mass extinction, a basalt flood in India, and a crater in Mexico.

'To some Earth scientists, the need for a geophysically plausible unifying theory linking all three phenomena is already clear,' declared Paul Renne of the Berkeley Geochronology Center. 'Others still consider the evidence for impacts coincident with major extinctions too weak, except at the end of the Cretaceous. But few would dispute that proving the existence of an impact is far more challenging than documenting a flood basalt event. It is difficult to hide millions of cubic kilometres of lavas.'

There will be no easy verdict. Andrew Saunders of Leicester, spokesman for the dating effort on the buried part of the Siberian Traps, was among those sceptical about the idea that impacts can express themselves in basalt floods. 'Some scientists would like to say that the West Siberian Basin itself is a huge impact crater,' Saunders said, 'but except for the presence of basalt it looks like a normal sedimentary basin. And if crust cracking is all you need for flood basalts, why don't we see them in the biggest impact craters that we have?'

The controversy echoes a broader dispute among Earth scientists about the role of mantle plumes, which could provide an alternative explanation for the Siberian Traps. For that reason, the verdict about impacts and flood basalts will depend in part on better images of the Earth's interior, expected from a new generation of satellites measuring the variations in gravity from region to region. Neither side in the argument is likely to yield much ground until those images are in, from Europe's GOCE satellite launched in 2005. Meanwhile, the search for possible matches between crater dates and flood basalts will continue.

▶ *A closely related geological topic is* HOTSPOTS. *For more about impacts, including the discovery of the 65-million-year-old crater in Mexico, see* IMPACTS. *Catastrophes for life are dealt with also under* EXTINCTIONS.

FLOWERING

Colourful variations on a theme of genetic pathways

T HE FLOWERS ON DISPLAY in the 200-year-old research garden in Valencia, Jardí Botànic in the Catalan language, change with the seasons, as is usual in temperate zones. The Valencia oranges for which the eastern coast of Spain is famous flower early in spring, surrounded by blooming rockroses, but in summer the stars of the garden are the water hyacinths, flowering in the middle of the shade. In winter the strawberry trees *Arbutus unedo* will catch your eye.

'All flowering plants seem to use the same molecular mechanisms to govern their dramatic switch from leaf-making to flower-making,' noted Miguel Blázquez of the Universidad Politécnica de Valencia. 'I want to know how the control system is organized, and linked to the seasons that best suit each species.'

For 10,000 years the question of when plants flower has been a practical concern for farmers and horticulturalists. Cultivated wheat and barley, for example, were first adapted to the seasons of river floods in the Middle East, but they had to adjust to spring rains and summer sunshine in Europe. The fact that such changes were possible speaks of genetic plasticity in plant behaviour. And year-round floral displays in well-planned gardens like Valencia's confirm that some species and varieties take advantage even of winter, in the never-ending competition between plants for space and light.

During the 20th century, painstaking research by physiologists and biochemists set out to clarify the internal mechanisms of plant life. Special attention to the small green chloroplasts in the cells of leaves, which capture sunlight and so power the growth and everyday life of plants, gradually revealed the molecular mechanisms. The physiologists also discovered responses to gravity, which use starch grains called statoliths as sensors that guide a seed to send roots down and stems up. They found out how growth hormones concentrate on the dark side to tip the stem towards the light. Similar mechanisms deploy leaves advantageously to catch the available light.

To help it know when to flower, a plant possesses light meters made of proteins and pigments, called phytochromes for red light and cryptochromes and phototropins for blue light. By comparing chemical signals from the phytochromes and the cryptochromes with an internal clock, like that causing jetlag in humans, the plant gauges the hours of darkness. So it always knows what the season is—by long nights in winter, short nights in summer, or diminishing or increasing night-length in between.

Other systems monitor temperature, by making chemicals that can survive in the chill but break up as conditions get warmer. Having been first discovered in connection with the dormancy of seeds in winter and the transition to (vernal) springtime, this mechanism is called vernalization. The name still attaches to the molecular systems involved.

When seen with hindsight, the research that told these tales was a bit like watching passing traffic without knowing the layout of the roads that brought it your way. Traditional physiology and biochemistry were never going to get to the bottom of the mysteries of plant behaviour. That is under the daily control of the genes of heredity, and of the proteins whose manufacture they command.

The Rosetta Stone for flowering time?

Botany in the 21st century starts with a revolution, brought about by a great leap forward in plant genetics. It came with intensive, worldwide research on the small cress-like weed *Arabidopsis thaliana*. The entire genetic code—the genome—was published in 2000. This provided a framework within which biologists could with new confidence investigate the actions of genes acting in concert, or sometimes in opposition, to achieve various purposes in the life of the plant.

Flowering is a case in point. The shaping of the flowers is under the control of sets of genes called MADS boxes, but that is relatively straightforward compared with the crucial decision a plant must make, about when to flower. Scientists have already distinguished nearly 40 genes involved in flowering time. Pooling their knowledge, they find the genes to be organized in four pathways.

Ready to support flowering at any season is a so-called autonomous pathway, which activates the genes that convert a suitably positioned leaf bud into a flower. Before it can come into play it needs cues from two other genetic pathways that monitor the plant's environment. The long-day pathway is linked to the calendar determined by the light meters and day-clock. The vernalization pathway responds to a long period of cold temperature—that is to say, to a winter. When conditions are right, the genes of the autonomous pathway are unleashed.

This system is biased in favour of flowering during long days, whether in spring, summer or autumn. The option of winter flowering requires a fourth pathway that liberates the hormone gibberellin. The hormone can override the negative environmental signals coming to the long-day and vernalization pathways, and drive the plant to bloom. Miguel Blázquez identified the genes of the gibberellin pathway, when working with Detlef Weigel at the Salk Institute in California.

'Nearly everything that we now know about the molecular mechanisms that control flowering time,' Blázquez commented, 'represents just five years' research on just one small weed, arabidopsis. The basic picture has been amazingly quick to come, but to tell the full story of flowering in all its options and variations will keep us busy for many years.'

A quarter of a million species of flowering plants make their decisions in many different settings from the tropics to the Arctic. Each has evolved an appropriate strategy for successful reproduction. But one of the leaders of arabidopsis research in the UK, Caroline Dean of the John Innes Centre, was convinced that chasing after dozens of different genomes—everyone's favourite plants—was not the right way forward. A better strategy was to learn as much as possible from arabidopsis first.

'If we play our cards right,' she argued, 'we should be able to exploit the arabidopsis sequence to provide biological information that may very quickly reveal the inner workings of many different plants and how they have evolved.' She meant much more than flowering, but that was an excellent test for her policy. Her team promptly identified a gene, VRN2, which enables arabidopsis to remember whether or not it has already experienced the cold conditions of winter.

Writing with Gordon Simpson, Dean posed the question: 'Will the model developed for arabidopsis unlock the complexities of flowering time control in all plants, as the Rosetta Stone did for Egyptian hieroglyphics?' Their answer, in 2002, was probably.

Whilst arabidopsis grows quickly to maturity, and responds strongly to the lengthening days of spring, many other plants use internal signals to prevent flowering until they are sufficiently mature. Rice, for example, does not flower until the days shorten towards the end of summer. The cues for flowering vary from species to species, and they include options of emergency flowering and seed setting in response to drought, overcrowding, and other stresses. Simpson and Dean nevertheless believed that much of this diversity could be explained by variations in the control mechanisms seen in arabidopsis, with changes in the predominance of the different genetic pathways.

Arabidopsis itself adapts its flowering-time controls to suit its germination time, for example to avoid flowering in winter. Its basic strategy, a winter annual habit, relies on germination in autumn and flowering in late spring, and is suitable for places where summers are short or harsh. But some arabidopsis populations have evolved another strategy called rapid cycling, whereby the plant can germinate and flower within a season. This is appropriate for mild conditions when more than one life cycle is possible within a year, and also in regions with very severe winters.

Simpson and Dean were able to point to two different mutations found in arabidopsis in the wild, which create the rapid-cycling behaviour. Both occur in the gene called FRI and they have the effect of switching off the requirement for vernalization. 'Rapid cycling thus appears to have evolved independently at least twice from late-flowering progenitors,' they commented.

Here is strong evidence that the flowering-time controls have been readily adjustable in the evolution of flowering plants. Where the variant genes involved are known in other species, these can often be seen to favour or disfavour particular pathways of the basic arabidopsis system. There are exceptions, and vernalization in cereals may be a whole new story.

Counting the cold days

Many crops in the world's temperate zones, including the cereals, are winter varieties. That is to say, they are sown in the autumn and they flower in the spring or summer. It is vital that a plant should not mistake the equal night and day lengths of autumn for springtime, and flower too soon. The vernalization mechanism provides the necessary inhibition, by requiring that the plant should experience winter before it flowers.

But where summers are short it is also essential that the plant should flower promptly in the spring. Places with short summers have relatively harsh winters, so the mechanism also has to act as an accelerator of flowering once winter has passed. Experiments with crops raised in controlled conditions illustrate vernalization in action.

Grow winter barley in nothing but warmth and plenty of light, and it will look very strange. It just keeps on producing leaves, because it is waiting in vain for the obligatory cue of winter. Next expose the germinating seedlings to cold conditions, for a day, a week or a month, and then put them in the same perfect growth conditions. Those that had the longest time in the cold will flower faster. They will make fewer leaves before they switch to flower production.

'Vernalization is quite amazing in its quantitative nature,' Gordon Simpson said. 'This response probably informs the plant as to the passage of winter, as opposed to just a frosty September night. But perhaps the vernalization requirement and response evolved independently and through different mechanisms in different plants. We'll have a better idea of this when we work out the genes controlling vernalization in cereals like wheat.'

▶ *For more about the now-famous weed, see* ARABIDOPSIS. *For other features of plant life, see cross-references in* PLANTS. *Animal analogues are in* BIOLOGICAL CLOCKS.

FORCES

M ODERN PHYSICS blurs the distinction between matter and the cosmic forces that act upon it. Typically they both involve subatomic particles of kindred types. For example the electric force is carried by particles of light, or photons. The very energetic photons of gamma rays can decompose into electrons and anti-electrons, alias positrons, which are the particles of matter that respond most nimbly to the electric force.

In the 19th century, electricity and magnetism came to be seen as different manifestations of a single cosmic force, electromagnetism. This unification was extended during the 20th century, to link electromagnetism with the so-called weak force, which is responsible for changing one kind of matter particle into another, in radioactivity. Only charged particles feel the electric force, but all particles of matter feel the weak force, carried by W and Z particles—*see* **ELECTROWEAK FORCE**.

The colour force, carried by gluons, acts on the heavy fundamental particles called quarks. It binds them together in threes to make protons, neutrons and similar particles of matter. The strong nuclear force, carried by mesons, holds protons and neutrons together in the nuclei of atoms. For the colour force and strong nuclear force, *see* **PARTICLE FAMILIES**. For related civilian applications in nuclear power, *see* **ENERGY AND MASS**. Military applications are described in **NUCLEAR WEAPONS**.

The nuclear forces and the electroweak force may at one time have been united in a single primordial force—*see* **BIG BANG**. Exotic matter and associated forces that do not interact significantly with ordinary matter may also exist—*see* **SPARTICLES**.

Gravity is the odd one out, among the cosmic forces. Whilst the others are described by quantum theory, the modern theory of gravity is based on relativity—*see* **GRAVITY**. Strenuous theoretical efforts are trying to bring gravity into the fold of quantum theory—*see* **SUPERSTRINGS**.

The latest cosmic force on the scene is sometimes called antigravity, although that name is misleading. It is responsible for the accelerating expansion of the Universe, detected by astronomers. *See* **DARK ENERGY**, where there are also remarks on the van de Waals force between molecules, and on the Casimir force, exerted by the pressure of so-called virtual particles that are present even in empty space.

The Casimir force acts by a shadow effect whereby nearby objects screen one another from an external pressure, so that they are pushed together. A newly discovered shadow force created by the pressure of ordinary particles can bind small grains together, with remarkable effects—*see* **PLASMA CRYSTALS**.

GALAXIES

Looking for Juno's milk in the infant Universe

T HE LIMESTONE PLATEAU of Guizhou in southern China was for long a haven for grey-gold monkeys, ethnic minorities and political rebels. Among the spectacular rock spires and gorges, what radio astronomers notice is an array of dishes prepared by Mother Nature. The collapse of caverns sculpted by water in the limestone has created hundreds of large craters.

It was in just such a karst sinkhole, at Arecibo on the island of Puerto Rico, that American radio astronomers made the largest radio dish in the world. Suspended on a spider's web of cables criss-crossing the crater, the Arecibo telescope seemed vertiginous enough when James Bond wrestled at prime focus with the bad guys in the movie *Goldeneye*. Chinese radio astronomers set out to surpass it with an even bigger dish in Guizhou. Called FAST, it would be 500 metres wide to Arecibo's 305 metres.

'We're not just cloning Arecibo,' Ai Guoxiang of Beijing Observatory insisted. 'That historic instrument was conceived half a century ago. Our dish will be larger, its shape will be under active control, and we can do very much better in sensitivity and sky coverage. And naturally we see FAST as a pilot project for the Square Kilometre Array, which can use our very favourable karst geology.'

The Square Kilometre Array was a global scheme to create a gigantic radio telescope out of multiple dishes, agreed in 2000 by scientific consortia in Europe, India, Australia and Canada, as well as China. Faced with competing ideas about other sites and telescope types, the Chinese hoped that the landscape of Guizhou gave them a head start. Just put thirty 200-metre dishes in some of our other sinkholes, they said.

If you consider that the most famous dish, Manchester's Lovell Telescope at Jodrell Bank, is 76 metres wide, whilst the 27 dishes of the Very Large Array in New Mexico are 25 metres wide, you'll see that the world's radio astronomers wanted a huge increase in collecting area. Why? Chiefly to hear very faint radio signals at extreme ranges from hydrogen atoms, the principal raw material of the visible Universe.

When Dutch astronomers began exploiting the 21-centimetre radio waves from hydrogen atoms, back in the 1950s, they used a modest dish to chart their distribution in our Galaxy, the Milky Way. They thereby revealed that if we could see it from the outside, our Galaxy would look just as beautiful as other galaxies with spiral arms long admired by astronomers. The criterion for the Square Kilometre Array was that it should be able to discern the Milky Way by its hydrogen even if it were 10 billion light-years away. Then the radio astronomers might trace the origin of the galaxies, the main assemblies of visible matter in the sky.

Milk and champagne

'The Origin of the Milky Way' as depicted around 1575 by the Venetian painter Jacopo Tintoretto shows Jupiter getting Juno to wet-nurse the infant Hercules, a mortal's brat, in order to immortalize him. Stray milk squirts from Juno's breasts and forms stars. This lactic myth entwines with the names of the roadway of light around the night sky.

To the ancient Greeks, *Galaxias* meant milky, and astronomers adopted Galaxy as a name more posh and esoteric than the *Via Láctea*, *Voie Lactée*, *Milchstrasse* or Milky Way of everyday speech. They figured out that the Galaxy is a flattened assembly of many billions of stars seen edge-on from inside it. But by the 20th century they needed 'galaxy' as a general name for many similar star-swarms seen scattered like ships in the ocean of space.

To distinguish our cosmic home a capital G was not enough, so they went back to the vernacular, not minding that Milky Way Galaxy was like saying Galaxy Galaxy. The tautology has merit, because every naked-eye star in the sky belongs to the Galaxy even if it lies far from the high road of the Milky Way itself. The only other naked-eye galaxies are the Large and Small Clouds of Magellan, unmistakable to the Portuguese circumnavigator en route for Cape Horn, and the more distant Andromeda Galaxy M31 in the northern sky, which is harder to spot. They look milky too.

Nutritionally, the hydrogen sought with the Square Kilometre Array is milk-like in its ability to nourish star-making. Flattened spiral galaxies like ours are rich in newly formed, short-lived blue stars in the gassy disk, while the bulge at the centre has less gas and is populated by elderly reddish stars. Large egg-shaped galaxies, called ellipticals, have lost or used up almost all their spare hydrogen. They are more or less sterile and ruddy.

When the Universe was very young, hydrogen gas with an admixture of helium was all it had by way of useful matter. By detecting the 21-centimetre hydrogen radiation, shifted to wavelengths of more than a metre at the greatest ranges by the expansion of the Universe, the Square Kilometre Array should see Juno's milk making the earliest galaxies, or stars, or black holes—no matter which came first. According to one scenario, the most obvious sign may be, paradoxically, a dispersal of hydrogen.

'As the earliest objects first began to irradiate the neutral gas around them they would have heated their surroundings to form expanding bubbles of warm hydrogen,' explained Richard Strom, a member of the Dutch team for the Square Kilometre Array. 'These bubbles produce a kind of foam that eventually dissolves into a nearly completely ionized medium where the hydrogen atoms have lost their electrons and cease to broadcast radio waves. It's rather like pulling the cork on a well-shaken bottle of champagne. The wine disperses in a frothy explosion.'

This was only one example of astronomers looking for the origin of the galaxies, by peering to the limit of the observable Universe, far out in space and therefore far back in time. At much shorter radio wavelengths, the Atacama Large Millimetre Array was planned for a high plateau in the Chilean desert as a joint US–European venture. Its sixty-four 12-metre dishes were expected to detect warm dust made by the very first generation of stars. In space, a succession of infrared telescopes joined in the quest for very young galaxies, while X-ray telescopes sought out primeval black holes that might have antedated the galaxies.

Meanwhile the visual evidence mounted, that galaxies grew by mergers of smaller star-swarms, from the very earliest era until now. The elegant spirals of middle-sized galaxies were commoner in bygone times than they are now, whilst fat-cat ellipticals have grown fatter still. European astronomers using the Hubble Space Telescope reported in 1999 that, among 81 galaxies identified in a distant cluster, no fewer than 13 were either products of recent collisions or pairs of galaxies in the process of collision.

Where are the Sun's sisters?

A complementary approach to galactic origins was to look in our own backyard, at the oldest stars of the Milky Way Galaxy itself, and at nearby galaxies. Billions of years from now, the Magellanic Clouds and the Andromeda Galaxy may all crash into us. If so, the spirals of the Milky Way and Andromeda will be destroyed and when the melee is over the ensemble will join the ranks of the ellipticals.

Nor are all these traffic accidents in the future. In 1994 Cambridge astronomers spotted a small galaxy, one-tenth as wide as the Milky Way, which is even now blundering into the far side of our Galaxy, beyond its centre in Sagittarius. A few years later, an international team working in the Netherlands and Germany had made computer models of repeated encounters that would eventually shred such an invader, yet leave scattered groups of stars following distinctive tracks through space.

Helped by the latest data from Europe's star-mapping satellite, Hipparcos, Amina Helmi and her colleagues went on to identify such coherent groups among ancient stars that spend most of their time in a halo that surrounds the disk of the Milky Way. These aliens were streaming at 250 kilometres per second across the disk, evidently left over from a small galaxy that intruded about 10 billion years ago. The discovery was like encountering a gang of Vikings still on the rampage.

'Everything that was learned about galaxies during the 20th century was just a preamble, telling us what's out there,' Helmi said, as a young Argentine postdoc looking forward to new challenges. 'So we know that our own Galaxy is like a fried egg with a bulging centre, and that globular clusters and halo stars buzz around it like bees. But we don't know why. Our alien star streams account for a dozen halo stars that we see and about 30 million that we can infer from them, so that leaves the history of many millions of other stars still to figure out, just in this Galaxy.'

The idea is to treat every star as a fossil, carrying clues to its origin, and the task is not as hopeless as the numbers might suggest. The first billion stars in a new analysis of the Milky Way are due to be charted from 2012 onwards by the next European star-mapper, the Gaia spacecraft. It will give a dynamic picture of the Galaxy from which the common origins of large cohorts of stars might be inferred, and keyed to more precise ages of the stars to be supplied by Gaia and other space missions.

The discovery of sisters of the Sun, formed 4500 million years ago from the same nutritious gas cloud but now widely scattered in the Galaxy, will no longer be an impossibility. Nor will a comprehensive history of the Milky Way, from its origin to the present day. With any luck it will turn out to be very similar to the histories of mergers and star-making episodes deduced with other telescopes, for other galaxies far away.

▶ *For other perspectives on the evolution of the galaxies, see* STARBURSTS, ELEMENTS, BLACK HOLES, DARK MATTER *and* STARS.

GAMMA-RAY BURSTS

New black holes being fashioned every day

E UROPE SLEPT and the cathedral clocks in Rome were two minutes short of 4 a.m. on 28 February 1997, when the BeppoSAX satellite detected a burst of gamma rays—super-X-rays—coming from the direction of the Orion constellation. The Italian–Dutch spacecraft radioed its observations to a ground station in Kenya, which relayed the news to the night shift at the operations centre on Via Corcolle in Rome.

There was nothing new in registering a gamma-ray burst. They had been familiar though mysterious events for 30 years. The US Air Force's Vela-4a satellite, watching for nuclear explosions, had seen natural gamma-ray bursts in cosmic space, from 1967 onwards. Since 1991 NASA's Compton Gamma Ray Observatory had registered bursts almost daily, occurring anywhere in the sky. But until that eventful day in 1997, no one could tell what they were, or even exactly where they were. Gamma rays could not be pinpointed sharply enough to enable any other telescope to find the source.

An Italian instrument on BeppoSAX had detected a strong burst of gamma rays lasting for four seconds, followed by three other weaker blips during the next 70 seconds. But on this occasion an X-ray flash had appeared simultaneously in the Wide Field Camera on the spacecraft. The physicist in charge of this X-ray telescope was John Heise of the Stichting Ruimte Onderzoek Nederland, the Dutch national space research institute in Utrecht. He was away in Tokyo at a conference, but was always ready to react, by night or day, if his camera saw anything unusual in the depths of space.

Alerted by his bleeper, Heise hurried to a computer terminal to get the images relayed to him via the Internet. Working with a young colleague Jean in 't Zand, who was in Utrecht, he was able to specify the burst's position in the sky to within a sixth of a degree of arc, in the north of the Orion constellation.

Other telescopes could then look for it, and the first to do so was a cluster of other X-ray instruments on BeppoSAX itself—Italian devices with a narrower field of view, able to analyse the X-rays over a wide range of energies. By the time the spacecraft had been manoeuvred for this purpose, eight hours had elapsed since the burst, but the instruments picked up a strong X-ray afterglow from the scene and narrowed down the uncertainty in direction to a 20th of a degree.

By a stroke of luck, Jan van Paradijs of the Universiteit van Amsterdam had observing time booked that evening on a big instrument for visible-light astronomy, the British–Dutch William Herschel Telescope on La Palma in Spain's Canary Islands. The telescope turned to the spot in Orion.

'We were looking at that screen and we saw this little star,' said Titus Galama of the Amsterdam team. 'My intuition told me this must be it. Then I really felt this has been 30 years—and there it is!' Over the next few days the light faded away. The Hubble Space Telescope saw a distant galaxy that hosted the burster, as a faint cloud around its location.

The first sighting of a visible afterglow was the turning point in the investigation of gamma-ray bursts. Until then no one knew for sure whether the bursters were small eruptions near at hand, in a halo around our own Milky Way Galaxy, or stupendous explosions in other galaxies far away in the Universe. The answer was that this gamma-ray burst, numbered GRB 970228 to denote its date, was associated with a faint galaxy.

Camaraderie and competition

Two years later a worldwide scramble to see another gamma-ray burst, also pinpointed by the X-ray camera on BeppoSAX, led to even better results. GRB 990123 occurred mid-morning by Utrecht time, when the USA was still in darkness. Heise fixed the burster's position and the word went out on the Internet. A telescope on Palomar Mountain in California turned towards the indicated spot in the Boötes constellation, and found the afterglow.

Palomar passed on a more exact location to Hawaii where, until a foggy dawn interrupted the observations, the giant Keck II telescope analysed the afterglow's light. Its wavelengths were stretched, or red-shifted, to such an extent that the galaxy containing the burster had to be at an immense distance. The gamma rays, X-rays and light had spent almost 10 billion years travelling to the Earth.

Astronomers in China and India picked up the baton from Hawaii. Then the Saturday shoppers in Utrecht went home and darkness came to Europe's Atlantic shore. Less than 24 hours after the event, the Nordic Optical Telescope on La Palma confirmed the red shift reported from Hawaii.

Other news came from a robot telescope of the Los Alamos Laboratory in New Mexico. Reacting automatically and within seconds to a gamma-ray alert from NASA's Compton satellite, the telescope had recorded a wide part of the northern sky by visible light. The playback showed, in the direction indicated by BeppoSAX, a star-like point of light flaring up for half a minute and then fading over the next ten minutes.

Never before had anyone seen visible light coming from a gamma-ray burst while the main eruption was still in progress. Prompt emission the experts called it. And it was so bright that amateur astronomers with binoculars might have seen it, if they had been looking towards Boötes at the right moment.

Thus did the crew of Spaceship Earth grab the data on a brief event towards the very limit of the observable Universe. High-tech instruments and electronic communication contributed to this outcome, but so did scientific camaraderie that knew no political boundaries. Well, that's the gracious way to put it.

On the other side of the penny was fierce competition for priority, prestige and publicity. The identification of gamma-ray bursts was a top goal for astronomers, and some in the USA were openly miffed that the Europeans were doing so well. There was also a professional pecking order. Users of giant visible-light telescopes were at the top, with hot lines to the media, and people with small X-ray cameras on small satellites came somewhere in the middle.

The upshot was that the journal *Nature* rejected a paper from Heise and the BeppoSAX team about their discovery of GRB 990123. The reason given was that the journal had too many papers about the event already. Would he care to send in a brief note about his observations? Heise said No, and commented to a reporter, 'We sometimes feel we point towards the treasure and other people go and claim the gold.'

The wide-field X-ray cameras on BeppoSAX watched only five per cent of the sky at any time, and an even more distant gamma-ray burst, in 2000, was out of their view. Three spacecraft, widely separated in the Solar System, registered the gamma rays: Wind fairly close to the Earth, Ulysses far south of the Sun, and NEAR-Shoemaker at the asteroid Eros. Differences in the arrival times of the rays gave the direction of the source.

Four days later, Europe's Very Large Telescope in Chile found the visible afterglow. The astronomers could see right away that it was extremely remote, because the expansion of the Universe had changed its light to a pure red colour. Formal measurement of the red shift showed that the event occurred about 12.5 billion years ago, at the time when the galaxies were first forming.

An extraordinary supernova

Gamma-ray bursts are the most luminous objects in the sky, a thousand times brighter than the quasars, which are powered by massive black holes in the hearts of galaxies. Once their great distances had been confirmed, there was no doubting that the bursters are objects exploding with unimaginable violence. They are the biggest bangs since the Big Bang, and may be roughly equivalent to the sudden annihilation of the Sun and the conversion of all its matter into radiant energy.

Two leading theories emerged to explain such cataclysms. One required the collision of two neutron stars, which are collapsed stars of enormous density produced in previous stellar explosions. Picture them orbiting around each other and getting closer and closer, until they suddenly merge to make a stellar black hole—a type much smaller than those powering quasars. The collapse of matter into the intense gravity of a black hole is the most effective way of releasing some of the energy latent in it.

According to the other theory (actually a cluster of theories) a gamma-ray burst is the explosion of a huge star. It is a super-supernova, similar to well-known explosions of massive stars but somehow made much brighter than usual, especially in gamma rays and X-rays. Certainly the star would have to be big, say 50 times the mass of the Sun. When such a large star blows up, the core is crushed directly into a stellar black hole, again with an enormous release of energy.

Theorists can imagine how the collapsing core might be left naked by dispersal of the outer envelope of expanding gas, which in normal supernovae masks it from direct view. Another way to intensify the brilliance of the event is to focus much of the energy into narrow beams. These could emerge from the north and south poles of a star that is rapidly rotating as well as exploding.

Such beaming greatly reduces the power needed to produce the observed bursts, but it also means that astronomers see, as gamma-ray bursts, only a minority of events where the beams happen to point at the Earth. That does not rule out the possibility the others could be seen as ordinary-looking supernovae. But it does imply that, if each long-duration gamma-ray burst is a signal of the formation of a stellar black hole, then the Universe may be making dozens of them every day.

Supernovae manufacture chemical elements—you are made of such star-stuff— and confirmation of the supernova theory of gamma-ray bursts came from the detection of newly made elements. Europe's XMM-Newton did the trick. Launched at the end of 1999, as the world's most sensitive space telescope for registering X-rays from the cosmos, it twice turned to look at burst sites without success. Third time lucky: in December 2001 it scored with GRB 011211, which had been spotted 11 hours previously by BeppoSAX.

'For the first time ever traces of light chemical elements were detected, including magnesium, silicon, sulphur, argon, and calcium,' said James Reeves, a member of the team at Leicester responsible for XMM-Newton's X-ray cameras. 'Also, the hot cloud containing these elements is moving towards us at one tenth of the speed of light. This suggests that the gamma-ray burst resulted from the collapse of the core of a giant star following a supernova explosion. This is the only way the light elements seen by XMM-Newton, speeding away from the core, could be produced. So the source of the gamma-ray burst is a supernova and not a neutron-star collision.'

● The continuing watch

That did not mean that the neutron-star theory was wrong. The events vary greatly in their behaviour. All of those examined in detail up to 2002 had gamma-ray bursts persisting for a minute or more. Some that last for only a few seconds may also be supernovae. But other bursts last less than a second and may well involve a different mechanism.

Systems with a pair of neutron stars rotating around each other are known to exist, and eventually they must collide. But that convergence may take billions of years, during which time the pair may migrate, perhaps even quitting the galaxies where they were formed. And if they are the cause of subsecond gamma-ray bursts, the brevity of the events makes them all the harder to spot.

BeppoSAX expired in 2002, but NASA already had the High Energy Transient Explorer in orbit for the same purpose of fixing the direction of gamma-ray bursts within minutes or hours. It was also preparing a dedicated satellite called Swift, for launch in 2003, which would automatically swing its own onboard telescopes towards a burst, moving within seconds without waiting for commands from the ground.

Other hopes rested with XMM-Newton's sister, called Integral, launched by the European Space Agency in 2002 as a gamma-ray observatory of unprecedented sensitivity. Besides two gamma-ray instruments, Integral carried X-ray telescopes and an optical monitor for visible light. While engaged in its normal work of examining long-lasting sources of gamma rays, Integral could see and analyse gamma-ray bursts occurring by chance in its field of view, about once a month. And sometimes the same event would appear also in the narrower field of view of the optical monitor.

'We know that some of the visible flashes from gamma-ray bursts are bright enough for us to see, across the vast chasm of space,' said Álvaro Giménez of Spain's Laboratorio de Astrofísica Espacial y Física Fundamental, in charge of the optical monitor on Integral. 'Our hope is that we shall be watching at some other target in the sky and a gamma-ray burst may begin, peak and fade within the field of view of all our gamma-ray, X-ray and optical instruments. For the science of gamma-ray bursts, that would be like winning the lottery.'

Astronomers have interests in gamma-ray bursts that go beyond the mechanisms that generate them. The rate at which giant stars were born and perished has changed during the history of the Universe, and the numbers of gamma-ray bursts at different distances are a symptom of that evolution. Quasars already provide bright beacons lighting up the distant realms and revealing intervening galaxies and clouds. With better mastery of the gamma-ray bursts, still more brilliant, astronomers will use them in similar ways, out to the very limits of the observable Universe when galaxies and stars were first being born.

▶ *For more on massive supernovae, see* ELEMENTS. *For possible effects of a nearby gamma-ray burst, see* MINERALS IN SPACE. *The bursts confirm the speed of light in* HIGH-SPEED TRAVEL. *Other related topics are* BLACK HOLES *and* NEUTRON STARS.

GENES
Words of wisdom from our ancestors, in four colours

T HE PREFABRICATED HUTS have long since gone but the Victorian archway into the courtyard where they stood is still there in Free School Lane, Cambridge. The portal should have carried a sign advertising winter trips to Stockholm, so many were the young physicists who joined the Cavendish Laboratory and finished up with Nobel Prizes. Lawrence Bragg earned his while still an undergraduate, for pioneering the analysis of crystals by X-rays.

Later, as Cavendish professor, Bragg plotted the hijacking of biology by physics. In the prefabs he nurtured and protected a Medical Research Council Unit for the Study of Molecular Structure of Biological Systems. Its small team, led by the Austrian-born Max Perutz, was dedicated to using X-rays to discover the 3-D atomic structures of living matter.

In 1950 Perutz was in the midst of a tough task to find the shape of a protein, haemoglobin, when 'a strange young head with a crew cut and bulging eyes popped through my door and asked, without saying so much as hello, "Can I come and work here?"'

It was Jim Watson. The story of what happened then has been told many times, with different slants. The 22-year-old genetics whiz kid from Chicago teamed up with the 34-year-old physicist Francis Crick. In Perutz's words, 'They shared the sublime arrogance of men who had rarely met their intellectual equals.' While Crick had the prerequisite grasp of the physics, Watson brought an intuition about the chemical duplicity needed for life.

In 1944, when Crick was working on naval mines and Watson was a precocious undergraduate, Oswald Avery and his colleagues at the Rockefeller Institute in New York City had identified the chemical embodiment of hereditary information—the genes. These were not in protein molecules, as previously assumed. Instead they came in threadlike fibres present in all cells and called nucleic acids, discovered in 1871 by Friedrich Miescher of Basel. One type of fibre incorporated molecules of ribose sugar, so it was called ribonucleic acid, or RNA. By 1929 another type was known in which the ribose lacked one of its oxygen atoms—hence deoxyribonucleic acid, or DNA. It was DNA that figured in Avery's results, and so commanded the attention of Watson and Crick.

By 1953 they had found that DNA made a double helix, like a continuously twisted ladder. Between the two uprights, made of identical chains of sugar and phosphate, were rungs that connected subunits called bases, one on each chain. From the chemists, Crick and Watson also knew that there were four kinds of bases: adenine, thymine, cytosine and guanine, A, T, C and G. By making model molecules, the scientists realized that to make rungs of equal length, A had always to pair with T, and C with G.

'It has not escaped our notice that the specific pairing we have postulated immediately suggests a possible copying mechanism for the genetic material.' That throwaway remark at the end of the short paper that Watson and Crick sent to the journal *Nature* hinted at a momentous conclusion. DNA was custom-built for reproduction. It could be replicated by separating the two chains and assembling new chains alongside each of them, with a new A to match each T, a new T to match each A, and similar matches for C and G.

It was a trail-blazing discovery. There was grief about Rosalind Franklin, who produced crucial X-ray images of DNA at King's College London. She could have been in line for a share in the 1962 Nobel Prize with Watson and Crick had she not died in 1958. Her boss, Maurice Wilkins, did get a share and he might well have done so instead of Franklin even if she had lived. The mere conjecture has attracted angry feminist ink ever since.

From the Institut Pasteur in Paris came a shift in perspective about the role of genes in everyday life. The old idea of heredity was that genes influenced the building of an organism and then became dormant until reproduction time. Even when scientists realized that genes came into play whenever a living cell divided, they were presumed to be passive during the intervals. In patient research that began in the 1940s, François Jacob, André Lwoff and Jacques Monod showed that genes are at work from moment to moment throughout the life of a cell, and what's more they are themselves under the control of other genes.

Using a strain of the bacterium *Escherichia coli* retrieved from the gut of Lwoff himself, the French researchers subjected the cultures to various forms of starvation, relieved only by peculiar food. They saw genes switching on to command the production of the special proteins, enzymes, needed to digest it. Only when the structure of DNA appeared did they realize, as a geneticist, a microbiologist and a biochemist, that what they were doing was molecular biology.

It was to Edgar Allan Poe's analysis of double bluff in poker that Monod credited the inspiration about how gene action was regulated. The bacterial genes responsible for the enzymes were not activated by a direct signal. Instead what triggered them was the non-arrival of a signal that repressed the gene. Repression was the normal state of affairs if the cell was already well supplied with the enzyme in question, or did not need it at all.

The mechanisms of gene control would become a major theme of molecular biology. Monod did not err in predicting 'the development of our discipline which, transcending its original domain, the chemistry of heredity, today is oriented toward the analysis of the more complex biological phenomena: the development of higher organisms and the operation of their networks of functional co-ordinations.'

Flying blind, the old genetics did well

A few years after the DNA structure burst upon the world, a reporter asked the director of a famous institute of animal genetics in Scotland what influence the Watson–Crick discovery was having on the work there. The mild enquiry was rebuffed with a sharp, 'Oh that's not real genetics, you know!'

What he meant by real genetics was the kind of thing that Gregor Mendel had initiated in his monastery garden in Brünn, Austria, by cross-breeding different varieties of garden peas. By 1865, with patience and deep insight, Mendel had deduced the existence of elementary factors of heredity. They came in pairs, one from each parent, and behaved in statistically predictable ways. Laced as it was with simple mathematics, Mendel's work seemed repellent to botanists and was disregarded. After a lapse of 35 years, experimenters in Germany, Austria and the Netherlands obtained similar results in breeding experiments. They checked the old literature, and found they had been anticipated.

The 20th century was rather precisely the age of the gene, from the rediscovery of Mendel's hereditary factors in 1900 to a preliminary announcement in 2000 by the US president of the decoding of the entire human stock of genes, the human genome. Genetics started as an essentially mathematical treatment of hereditary factors identified and assessed by their consequences. Only gradually did the molecular view of the genes, which appeared at mid-century, become predominant in genetics.

In the Soviet Union, Mendel's genes were not politically correct. The Lenin Academy of Agricultural Sciences, under pressure from Joseph Stalin, formally accepted the opinion of Trofim Lysenko that genetics was a bourgeois fabrication, undermining the true materialist theory of biological development. That was in 1948, although Lysenko's malign influence had been felt long before that. Until he was toppled in 1965, the suppression of genetics in the Soviet

Union and its East European satellites harmed agriculture and biological science from the Elbe River to the Bering Strait.

Even when flying blind, without knowing the physical embodiment of the genes in question, geneticists in the West successfully applied Mendel's discovery to accelerate the breeding of improved crops and farm animals. By helping to feed the rapidly growing world population, they confounded predictions of mass famine. They also made big medical contributions to blood typing, tissue typing and the analysis of hereditary diseases.

● Cracking the code

Meanwhile the molecular biologists were racing ahead in decoding the genes. Even before the structure of DNA was known, its subunits with the bases A, T, C and G seemed likely to carry some sort of message. In the early 1960s, Crick and three colleagues demonstrated that the code was written in a sequence of three-letter words. Each triplet of bases specifies a subunit of protein—the amino acid to be added next, in the growing chain of a protein molecule under construction.

The code-breakers were aided by the discovery that messenger molecules, made of ribonucleic acid, RNA, transcribe the genes' instructions and deliver them to protein factories. Marshall Nirenberg at the US National Institutes of Health began the decoding by introducing forged RNA messages, and finding out how they were translated into proteins. By the mid-1960s the full code was known. More than one triplet of DNA letters may specify the same amino acid, so you can read off a protein's exact composition from the gene. But you can't translate backwards from protein to gene without ambiguity.

At that time molecular biologists believed that the flow of genetic information from genes to proteins was down a one-way street. One gene was transcribed into messenger RNA, which in turn was translated into one protein. This seemed to them sufficiently fundamental and widespread for Francis Crick to call it the Central Dogma. It was one of the shortest-lived maxims in the history of human thought.

Well-known viruses carry their genes exclusively in the form of RNA, rather than DNA. When they invade a cell, they feed their RNA through the host's protein factories to make proteins needed for manufacturing more viruses. No violation of the Central Dogma here. But in 1970 Howard Temin of Wisconsin-Madison and David Baltimore of the Massachusetts Institute of Technology simultaneously announced that cancer-causing viruses have an enzyme that allows them to convert their RNA genes into DNA. Inserted among the genes of the host, these are then treated as if they were regular genes.

Reverse transcriptase the enzyme is called, and these viruses were dubbed retroviruses because of their antidogmatic behaviour. The term later became notorious because AIDS is caused by a retrovirus. But the discovery was also illuminating about the origin of the retroviruses and their role in cancer.

Apart from their insidious method of reproduction, the viruses carry cancer-causing genes that are mutant versions of genes in normal cells, responsible for controlling cell growth and division. Evidently the retroviruses first captured the genes from an infected host and incorporated them into their own genetic material. This analysis helped to pinpoint key genes involved in cancers, where mutations due to radiation or chemicals can lead to uncontrolled proliferation of the cells.

Fragmented genes

The second aspect of Crick's Central Dogma, that one gene described one protein, was also confounded by another discovery that blew the genes to bits. In 1977, at the Cold Spring Harbor Laboratory on Long Island and at the Massachusetts Institute of Technology, Richard Roberts and Phillip Sharp simultaneously but independently investigated the DNA of the adenovirus that causes the common cold in humans. They found that a messenger molecule transcribing a single gene obtained its information from four different places along the virus's DNA strand.

In other words, the gene comprised several DNA segments, later called exons, separated by irrelevant lengths of DNA, or introns. Visible in an electron microscope were large, superfluous loops in the messenger molecules made from the introns. The cell's gene-reading machinery had to edit out the loops, to make a correct transcript.

Such split genes very soon turned out to be the normal form of hereditary material in organisms more complex than bacteria, including human beings. And when the molecular biologists looked at the nature of the active DNA segments, the exons, they found that they often specified the construction of one complete, significant domain of a protein molecule. If you think of the intended product as a doll, one exon provides the body, and others the head, arms, legs, eyes and squeaker.

Splicing introduces an editor into the transfer of instructions from the genes to the cellular machinery that executes them. This opens the possibility of editorializing—of altering the message to suit the readership. While the introns are being cut out, the exons selected for retention in the final messenger RNA can vary. This is not ham-fisted interference. The editing is itself under wider genetic control, according to circumstances, at different stages of an organism's life and in different tissues of the body.

The alternative splicing means that the same DNA region can influence the structure of many different proteins. Mistakes can be unfortunate, as in the blood disease beta-thalassaemia, where faulty splicing due to a mutation makes faulty haemoglobin molecules. But the unexpected organization of the genes in exons introduces opportunities for evolutionary change, in a construction-kit mode—making dolls with different heads, bodies and limbs.

Meanwhile in 1972 Paul Berg of Stanford had demonstrated how to use natural enzymes to cut a gene out of one organism and insert into another. This opened a road to genetic engineering for practical purposes, but behind laboratory doors the gene transfers were a gold mine for fundamental research. You could insert any gene into a bacterium, and culture the bug until you had millions of copies of the gene. Then you had enough of it for the intensive analysis needed to read the sequence of letters of code in the gene.

Another method of multiplying DNA emerged in the 1980s. This dispensed with the bacterium and just used the enzyme called DNA polymerase to copy the genes. By heating the completed DNA to separate the entwined strands of the double helix, the process can be repeated many times, doubling and redoubling the number of copies, in a chain reaction. The idea occurred to Kary Mullis of the Cetus company while out driving with his girl friend. 'They were heady times,' he said. 'Biotechnology was in flower and one spring night while the California buckeyes were also in flower I came across the polymerase chain reaction.'

How to read all the genes

Having plenty of copies of DNA was a necessary but far from sufficient condition for reading what it said. The neatest way to do that was developed in Cambridge, but not at the university. By one of the strangest decisions in the history of academe, Cambridge had let Perutz's prize-winning pioneers go. In 1962 the UK's Medical Research Council reinstalled them in a new Laboratory of Molecular Biology on an out-of-town hospital campus.

There Fred Sanger, who had already received a Nobel Prize for first finding the exact composition of a protein, insulin, won himself a second one by inventing the beautiful modern way of reading genes quickly. He and his colleagues spent most of the 1970s perfecting what came to be called the dideoxy method. It uses the molecular machinery of DNA polymerase to copy strands of DNA, putting together the A, T, C and G subunits in their correct order. But it halts the process at random by introducing defective subunits.

A shorthand chemical name of A, for example, is deoxyadenine. (In full it is adenyldeoxyribophosphate.) Take out an oxygen atom and you have dideoxyadenine. Add this to the mixture of normal subunits available for use. The copying of the DNA always starts at one end of the chain. When the assembly process happens to pick up the dideoxy version, the newly made DNA chain will terminate at that point.

You can be sure that it has done so exactly where the code wanted the insertion of an A. The chancy nature of the process means that you'll finish up with many strands of different lengths, but all ending in A. Make enough strands, and you'll have tagged every A in the genetic message. Then make dideoxy versions of T, C and G too, to terminate the chain copying at their corresponding subunits. Label each of the dideoxys, for example with a dye that fluoresces in a distinctive colour. Throw them all in the pot and let the chains go forth and multiply.

Now comes the pretty bit. You can separate all those DNA strands that you've made, according to their lengths, by sending them off along an electric racetrack in a special jelly called polyacrylamide urea gel. The shorter the strand, the farther it travels, and the technique is sensitive enough to separate strands that differ in length by only a single subunit. Finally, illuminate the gel to make the dyes fluoresce and you can simply read off the As, Ts, Gs and Cs in the correct sequence, as words of wisdom from our ancestors, in four colours.

That is how Sanger's dideoxy method served, in its refined and automated fashion, to read all the genes in the human body—the human genome. The principle was the same when he first used it to read the DNA from a bacterial virus called phi-X174, and established the complete sequence of 5375 code letters. But the procedures were trickier, and used radioactive labels on the defective subunits terminating each chain.

What did not change by the end of the century was the limitation of the method to a few hundred letters at one go. So you had to chop up the DNA into overlapping segments, with restriction enzymes, and then piece the code together by matching the overlaps.

'Our method was primitive but it was a great step forward,' Sanger conceded in 2000. With a brace of Nobel Prizes he deserved to be the most celebrated scientist in his homeland, the English Pasteur perhaps, but his natural modesty left lesser mortals competing for fame. Only an announcement from the White House and 10 Downing Street, that the decoding of the human genome was nearly complete, winkled him out for a rare appearance for the media. He said, 'I never thought it would be done as quickly as this.'

An intellectual health warning

Life will never look the same again. For biologists, the gene-reading machines are equivalent to the invention of the telescope in astronomy 400 years ago, and their general importance cannot be overstated. But they bring a risk of simple-mindedness of the kind that affected some astronomers in the early post-Galilean era, who thought that all you had to do was discover and chart new objects in the sky.

Identifying and reading individual genes is only the start of a process of enquiry that must continue by tracing their precise roles in the life of living cells and whole organisms. To identify a gene involved in brain function, for example, is not even an explanation of what that gene does, still less of how the brain develops and works. Although trite, the point needs stressing because we are still in the aftermath of bitter battles about nature versus nurture—about the importance of heredity and environment in producing the eventual adult creature.

As the British geneticist J.B.S. Haldane pointed out in 1938, to make an ideological issue of nature and nurture is almost as futile as trying to say whether the length or width of a field is more important in determining its area. He also compared the genetic endowments of Highland cattle on Scottish moors and the Jersey cows popular in England. 'You cannot say that the Jersey is a better milk-yielder,' Haldane wrote. 'You can only say that she is a better milk-yielder in a favourable environment.'

Nevertheless warring camps of scientists and scholars, all through the 20th century, persisted in arguing for the primacy of genes or upbringing, especially in respect of human beings. Roughly speaking, the battlefront separated biology from the social and behavioural sciences, and right-wing from left-wing political sentiments. The surge in genetic technology in the 1990s promised to swing the argument so strongly in favour of nature, in the nature–nurture fight, that an intellectual health warning seemed necessary.

'I find it striking that 10 years ago a geneticist had to defend the idea that not only the environment but also genes shape human development,' commented Svante Pääbo of the Max-Planck-Institut für evolutionäre Anthropologie in Leipzig, in 2001. 'Today one feels compelled to stress that there is a large environmental component to common diseases, behaviour, and personality traits! . . . It is a delusion to think that genomics in isolation will ever tell us what it means to be human. To work towards that lofty goal, we need an approach that includes the cognitive sciences, primatology, the social sciences, and the humanities.'

▶ *For the telescopic view of life, from gene reading, see* GENOMES IN GENERAL. *For particular genomes, see* HUMAN GENOME, ARABIDOPSIS *and* CEREALS. *Molecular interpretations of the roles of genes in development and evolution figure in* EMBRYOS, HOPEFUL MONSTERS, EVOLUTION *and* MOLECULES EVOLVING. *Genetics illuminates human prehistory in* HUMAN ORIGINS, PREHISTORIC GENES *and* SPEECH. *For other gene activities, see* CELL CYCLE, CELL DEATH, BIOLOGICAL CLOCKS, FLOWERING *and* MEMORY. *For ecological aspects, see* ECO-EVOLUTION. *Genetic engineering is the theme in* TRANSGENIC CROPS *and personal identification, in* DNA FINGERPRINTING. *For the proteins made by genetic instructions, see* PROTEIN-MAKING *and* PROTEOMES.

GENOMES IN GENERAL

The whole history of life in a chemical code

YOU NEED INTENSIVE TRAINING to be licensed as a fugu chef in Japan, but it's worth the effort. Gourmets pay astounding prices for the right to court death by eating fugu, alias the pufferfish or blowfish. Consume a smidgeon of its liver and within minutes you may be unable to breathe because the poison tetrodotoxin blocks the sodium channels of your nerves. It's a recognized though nasty way of committing suicide. As a haiku has it:

> *I cannot see her tonight.*
> *I have to give her up*
> *So I will eat fugu.*

Most esteemed and dangerous is the torafugu, *Fugu rubripes*. This species attracted the attention of the world's biologists for non-culinary reasons in the early 1990s. Sydney Brenner of the UK's Laboratory of Molecular Biology established that the fish's genome—its complete set of genes—is contained in an exceptionally small amount of the genetic material deoxyribonucleic acid, DNA.

The fugu genome is only about one-eighth the size of the human genome, yet it incorporates a similar set of genes. What it lacks is the clutter of repetitive irrelevancies and junk DNA that subsists in the genomes of most animals with backbones—the vertebrates. Plant biologists had already found a representative flowering plant with a very compact genome, a weed called *Arabidopsis thaliana*. For Brenner and his team, the fugu seemed a comparable organism of choice for reading off the essential genetic composition of all vertebrates.

A member of the team was Byrappa Venkatesh from Singapore, and he and Brenner saw in the fugu a chance to put his young country on the map, in biological research. Whilst the scientific great powers were preparing to deploy huge resources and battalions of scientists to decode the human genome, Singapore might yet play a major part in tackling fugu. And so far from being a disadvantage, the smallness of its genome promised great bonuses, not least in offering short cuts to making genetic sense of other animals, including humans.

'We can now read the language of the human and other complex genomes,' Venkatesh explained, 'but we have very little clue to the grammar that underlies this language. The highly streamlined genome of the fugu will help us to understand the basic grammar that governs the regulation and function of vertebrate genes.'

In the upshot Venkatesh, at Singapore's Institute of Molecular and Cell Biology, was joint leader of a fugu consortium with laboratories in the USA and UK, instituted in 2000. Using the shotgun technique, which breaks the whole genome into millions of short fragments, the consortium had a draft of the fugu genome within a year. This high-speed sequencing of the fugu genetic code was typical of the new wave in genomes research.

Some 450 million years have elapsed since we and the fugu last shared a common ancestor, yet more than 75 per cent of the fish's genes crop up in the human genome too. Here is strong evidence of the common evolutionary heritage. The overall similarities and differences between the repertoires of active genes in different species correspond roughly with what you might expect, from the course of evolution. Fungi, plants and animals all have many genes in common, but the correspondences are greater the more closely the species are related. Properly read and interpreted, the genomes sum up the genetic history of all the Earth's inhabitants.

A roll-call of species

In just a few years, thanks to a combination of automated gene-readers and computers, genomics changed from a daunting enterprise into a routine. More importantly, it evolved from lab technology into a new branch of science. Although medical and media interest mainly focused on the human case, genomes read in a fast-growing number of other species provided the basis for comparative genomics. Until the late 1990s this meant mainly viruses and bacteria—interesting, but not as mind-expanding as the higher organisms would prove to be.

Baker's yeast *Saccharomyces cerevisiae* is a much more advanced life form than bacteria, even though it's still only a microbe. As in animals and plants, its genes are apportioned between sausage-like chromosomes within a cell nucleus. In 1997, after highly decentralized efforts by 100 laboratories in Europe, the USA, Canada and Japan, the complete genome of yeast was available, with 5800 genes. The Martinsrieder Institut für Protein Sequenzen near Munich assembled, verified and analysed the sequences.

With yeast came the first clear proof that a genome could illuminate the long histories of the evolution of present-day species. In particular, the German analysts identified dozens of cases where ancestors of modern yeast had duplicated certain genes. These had supplied spare genes that could evolve new functions without fatally harming their carriers in the meantime, by depriving them of existing functions.

The first animals to have their genomes read were two small creatures already much studied in genetics laboratories. By 1998, a collaboration of Washington University and the Sanger Institute in the UK had done the roundworm or nematode *Caenorhabditis elegans*, with 19,100 genes. By 2000 Craig Venter of Celera Genomics in Maryland had demonstrated his fast whole-genome technique with the fruit fly *Drosophila melanogaster* and its 13,600 genes. The human genome (about 32,000 genes), the mouse (also about 32,000) and the fugu (31,000) followed in 2001.

As the list of sequenced genomes grew, there was intense discussion about the parts of the genetic material, DNA, which do not contain active genes. In many species, including human beings, these deserts can total 90 per cent or more of the DNA. Much of their content is material that has broken loose from the orderly genetic sequences and been copied and recopied many times. Some is inserted back to front, producing the DNA equivalents of palindromes, of the form 'Madam I'm Adam' but much longer.

A notable denizen of the human genome is called the long interspersed element, which subsists very successfully, perhaps as a pure parasite. On the other hand, large numbers of short sequences by the name of Alu elements may represent a stowaway that was put to work. Clustering near the real genes, they may play a role in influencing how strongly the genes respond to signals demanding action. The non-gene DNA remaining in the slimmed-down genome of the fugu fish was expected to clarify such control functions, without the confusions of really redundant material.

Why plants are different

'How come that we've scarcely any more genes than a weed?' That was a common exclamation from the media when the first genome of a plant appeared in 2000. The modest little *Arabidopsis thaliana* has 25,500 genes, leaving the human gene count unexpectedly meagre by comparison, at about 32,000. One explanation on offer is that a single gene may be transcribed in many different ways, to code for different proteins, and animals make greater use of this versatility than plants do. Another is that plants, being stationary, need a wider range of defences than animals that can run away from danger.

In comparison with the genomes of other organisms, arabidopsis gave a dazzling impression of what it is to be a complex creature with many cells, like an animal, but one that has elected to sit still and sunbathe, making its own food. As the Arabidopsis Genome Initiative put it in its first report on the completed genome, 'Our comparison of arabidopsis, bacterial, fungal and animal genomes starts to define the genetic basis for these differences between plants and other life forms.'

Arabidopsis has genes coding for 150 families of proteins not present in animals, but it lacks others that animals possess. Basic processes within the cells still seem to be shared between animals and plants, reflecting their common heritage. The ancient evolutionary story tells of small bacteria lodging inside larger ones to make living cells of the advanced type found in fungi, animals and plants. All have oxygen-handling inclusions called mitochondria, descended from a bacterium. Plants also have green light-capturing units in some of their cells. These chloroplasts are descended from ancestors of present-day bacteria called blue-green algae.

Although the mitochondria and chloroplasts retain much hereditary independence, some of their genes have found their way into the main genetic material housed in the nucleus of each cell. This is a special, domestic case of horizontal gene transfer, meaning natural genetic engineering that introduces alien genes into species, outside the normal process of 'vertical' transmission of genes from parents to offspring. In arabidopsis no fewer that 800 nuclear genes seem to be derived from the chloroplast lodgers. One consequence is that the genes involved in building the all-important photosynthetic apparatus are deployed in a strangely complicated way between nucleus and chloroplast.

On the other hand, plants have adapted some of the genes acquired from the chloroplasts into the sensory and signalling apparatus needed for environmental responses and the control of flowering. The philosophers of the Arabidopsis Genome Initiative remarked, 'This infusion of genes ... shows that plants have a richer heritage of ancestral genes than animals, and unique developmental processes that derive from horizontal gene transfer.'

How RNA silencing defends the genomes

The enormous differences in the sizes of genomes raised a fundamental question for biologists. The large genomes with 90 per cent or more of non-functional DNA show a potential for disorder that could kill the organisms. A rather shocking fact is that genes introduced by viruses account for eight per cent of the human genome, compared with just two per cent that does the practical work of coding for the manufacture of proteins. How does the genome defend itself in the face of such squatters?

In the early 1990s genome reading was still in its infancy. Giuseppe Macino, a molecular geneticist at the Universitá di Roma La Sapienza, was experimenting with the fungus *Neurospora crassa*. Although called red bread mould, it's orange really. Working with Nicoletta Romano, Macino introduced into *Neurospora* extra copies of genes that specified the manufacture of the carotene pigment. The scientists expected to see a brighter hue. But in a third of the cases, the mould became much paler. After prolonged culturing, the albino strains gradually shed the introduced genes and recovered their colour.

The mould was actively resisting the scientists' genetic engineering. It unleashed an unknown agent that quelled the introduced genes. In the process, the agent unavoidably affected the pre-existing pigment genes too, so producing the albino strains of the mould.

After announcing this discovery in 1992, Macino and other colleagues searched for the quelling mechanism. In the years that followed, they established that it did not depend on Nature's usual way of switching off genes, by attaching methyl groups to the genes. Instead the interference with gene action seemed to involve action by ribonucleic acid, RNA. This is a coded material similar to the DNA, deoxyribonucleic acid, of the genes themselves.

While research on the mould was continuing in Rome, investigators elsewhere in Europe and in the USA were pursuing similar effects discovered in plants and animals. Very like Macino's attempt to make a more intensely orange *Neurospora* was an earlier introduction into petunia of a gene intended to make its petals more deeply purple. Experimenters at DNA Plant Technology in California found that sometimes the petals were bleached white by suppression of all pigment-making.

At the UK's John Innes Centre and at Oregon State, scientists introduced genes from viruses into tobacco plants in an effort to immunize the plants against the viruses. It worked, but in a paradoxical way. The best results came when there was no sign of activity from the genes. Evidently a quelling mechanism was acting against both the virus and the introduced genes.

In 1998, Andrew Fire at a Carnegie Institution lab in Baltimore established that the agent involved in a similar control process in the roundworm *Caenorhabditis elegans* was double-stranded RNA. This was unusual. Scientists were accustomed to seeing single strands of RNA acting as messengers, transcribing the words of the genes and carrying them off to the protein factories of their cells.

The double-stranded RNA supplies short lengths of code matching the unwanted messenger RNA, which enables an RNA-destroying enzyme to recognize it and chop it up. By the new century this 'post-transcriptional gene silencing', or RNA silencing for short, had become the catchphrase for a new theme for biologists and medics worldwide. It promised important techniques for genetics research, by providing a very precise way of switching genes off to discover their function. And it also suggested novel ways of treating cancer and viral infections—although the smartest viruses know how to circumvent the defences.

Gene silencing with double-stranded RNA operates in all genomes of fungi, plants and animals. It is a genomic equivalent of the immune system that defends whole organisms from alien infections. Besides the threat from viruses, the RNA also has to forestall the ill effects of pre-existing genes that jump about from one place to another within the genome.

The first clear-cut evidence for the protective role of RNA silencing came in 1999 from Ronald Plasterk at the Nederlands Kanker Instituut in Amsterdam. He found mutant roundworms that had lost the ability both to make the necessary RNA and to repress misplaced DNA. He went on to lead intensive research into RNA silencing as director of the Hubrecht Laboratorium in Utrecht. Plasterk said, 'We are beginning to dissect an ancient mechanism that protects the most sensitive part of a species: its genetic code.'

Still to be established is how the creatures with very compact genomes, like the fugu fish and the arabidopsis weed, managed to purge themselves of alien and redundant DNA in a wholesale manner. In one respect they may be worse off. The de-repressing of silent genes, whether by removing the methyl tags or by switching off the RNA silencing, has emerged as a potent mechanism for rapid changes in fungi, plants and animals, previously unknown to evolutionary biology. So fugu and arabidopsis may have forfeited much of their potential for future evolution in response to an ever-changing environment.

Comparisons in crop plants

Early drafts of the rice genome became available in 2002, from Chinese-led and Swiss-led efforts using the rough-and-ready technique of the whole-genome shotgun. A Rolls-Royce version, done chromosome by chromosome, was awaited from the Japanese-led International Rice Genome Sequencing Project. 'A proper plant,' traditionally minded botanists and plant breeders called rice. They were reassured to find that 85 per cent of arabidopsis genes have their equivalents in rice. On the other hand, half of the genes of rice have no match in arabidopsis.

It's not just the individual genes that do service in many different species. In the late 1980s geneticists in the USA and UK established that the genomes of plants often preserve features of their internal organization, over many millions of years. This is despite several countervailing mechanisms that drive evolution along, whereby mutations produce many changes within each gene over such long time spans, individual species acquire or shed particular genes, and chemical switches activate or silence existing genes.

The scientists used pieces of DNA from one species to seek out the same genes in another species. Searching within the chromosomes, they were surprised by how often they found identical groups of genes showing up in the same orderly arrangements. Tomato versus potato, and different chromosomes of wheat which has multiple sets of chromosomes, provided the first comparative maps.

After a further ten years of such gene fishing, in various labs, Mike Gale and Katrien Devos of the UK's John Innes Centre offered a preliminary genomic conspectus of flowering plants. Look at them the right way, by mapping, and the similarities between eight species of cereals, for example, are far more striking than the differences. On the other hand, major reorganizations do occur, and they are no guide to the time-scale. For example, rye diverged from wheat only 7 million years ago, but it shows as many organizational differences in the chromosomes as rice does, which parted company 60 million years ago.

Another comparison was between the genomes of arabidopsis and some of its near relatives. Cabbage, turnip and black mustard all possess the arabidopsis genome in triplicate. Over the estimated 10 million years in which this cabbage family has evolved into many related species, the groupings of genes that are preserved in common greatly outnumber the chromosomal rearrangements.

By contrast, Gale and Devos could find very few similarities between the arrangements of genes in arabidopsis and cereals, even though they share more than 20,000 individual genes. These plants are on either side of a great division among the flowering plants, into magnolia-like and lily-like. Also called dicots and monocots, the classes are distinguished by the presence of two leaves or one in the embryo within the seed.

The dicots have the older lineage and more species, including arabidopsis and almost all flowering trees, most garden ornamentals, and many crop plants such as potatoes and beans. Lily-like monocots diverged from the dicots about 200 million years ago. They include cereals, palms and orchids.

With the first two genomes, arabidopsis and rice, dicot and monocot, plant geneticists could consider their glass half-full or half-empty. Although there are 250,000 species of flowering plants, a biologist working with any of them can use arabidopsis and rice as encyclopaedias of the genes, and simply look for correspondences. The techniques of molecular biology make that easy, so that you can simply read a short sample of the genetic code of your plant's gene and find it in the genome databases. Conversely you can look for a selected arabidopsis or rice gene in your own plant, again by fishing for it with a bit of code.

The chances of success are high, but as with any encyclopaedia, you will not always find what you are looking for. Especially for major crop plants, the urge to sequence the genomes remains strong, even if that now means whole-genome shotgunning rather than the costlier chromosome-by-chromosome approach. And besides the flowering plants, older types of plants including mosses, ferns and conifers await closer attention.

'Having the sequence of two genomes scarcely reflects either the biological richness of the world's plant heritage or its biotechnological potential,' Michael Bevan of the John Innes Centre observed. But he was optimistic about the prospects. 'All in all, the stage is set for an explosive growth in sequence accumulation from even the most recalcitrant plant species.'

● The grandstand view

A spot check with Integrated Genomics Inc. in mid-2002 showed a global count of 85 genomes completed and published, of which 61 were for bacteria, 15 for archaea, a distinctive group of bacteria-like creatures, 2 for fungi (yeasts), 3 for plants and 4 for animals. But at that time no fewer than 464 genome projects were in progress. Although 282 were for bacteria and archaea, 182 were for fungi, plants and animals, so the higher organisms were catching up. Random examples of plants and animals in the genomes-in-progress category were soybean, cotton, tomato, honey bee, sea urchin, pig and chimpanzee.

'A molecular biologist is an extremely small biologist,' was the jibe in the 1960s. In the outcome, the reverse is true. The molecules provide a new grandstand view of all life on Earth. Fully to appreciate it, biologists have to become broadminded generalists of the kind that Charles Darwin was, although now comprehending the jungle of molecules as well as organisms. Besides the already confusing species names in Latin, like *Ranunculus acris* for the meadow buttercup, they must learn to be comfortable with the neologisms for genes like flowering locus C, and for proteins like chromomethyltransferase.

Demarcation lines that separated geneticists from anatomists, plant biologists from animal biologists, fundamental enquirers from dollar-earning breeders, and laboratory researchers from field investigators, are now obsolete. If you want to do ecology for example, you'd better start thinking about genetic diversity within species as well as biodiversity between species—and about what the genes can tell you concerning past, present and future adaptations of animals and plants to the challenges of life. And if you interpret the genomes aright, you will eventually see the evolutionary history of life in general, and of individual species, laid out in the DNA code.

▶ *For gene-reading methods, see* GENES *and* HUMAN GENOME. *For some specific genomes, see* HUMAN GENOME, ARABIDOPSIS *and* CEREALS. *For more on gene doubling, see* MOLECULES EVOLVING. *About further interpretations, see* PROTEOMES, ALCOHOL *and* GLOBAL ENZYMES.

GLOBAL ENZYMES

Why they now fascinate geologists, chemists and biologists

I N THE HAMERSLEY RANGE of Western Australia, 1000 kilometres north-east from Perth, Mount Tom Price is a lump of iron ore squatting in a hot desert. It's named after an American geologist who first enthused about the quality of the ore to be found in the Hamersley Range. He died in 1962, a few years before mining began.

Now a blasting mixture of ammonium nitrate and fuel oil gradually dismantles Mount Tom Price, for shipping to steelworks abroad. Together with other mines in the Hamersley Range, it makes Australia the world's largest exporter of iron ore. When you watch the 200-tonne trucks at work, and the train three kilometres long that carries away the ore, it's odd to think that microbes too small to see made the gigantic operation worthwhile.

The deposits formed when bacteria and their similarly simple cousins, called archaea, were still our planet's only inhabitants. At the time they were using their chemically active protein molecules, the enzymes, to change their environment in a radical way. Unwittingly they were nudging it towards a world better suited to the likes of us.

If interstellar tourists had come to the Earth at intervals during its long existence, they would have found the guidebooks untrustworthy. It was not just that the continents kept moving around, while new mountains arose and old ones were flattened by erosion. The climate was often very warm but sometimes intolerably cold. And the most consequential changes, wrought by the enzymes, determined what breathing aids the hypothetical tourists might need. For half the Earth's history, oxygen was missing from the atmosphere

After the origin of life about 4 billion years ago, but before the events represented in the Hamersley iron, the most important constituent of the atmosphere apart from nitrogen may have been methane. Nowadays this inflammable gas comes from boggy ground, from burping and farting animals, and from underground deposits of natural gas. Some scientists suspect that methane-making bugs and their biomolecular equipment were predominant in the early era of life on Earth. As a greenhouse gas, resisting the escape of radiant heat into space, the methane may have helped to keep the planet warm when, as astronomers calculate, the Sun was a good deal feebler than today.

Then the planet rusted. That, in a word, is the story of Mount Tom Price and of similar deposits, of a kind called banded iron formation found in widely scattered parts of the world and created mainly between 2.5 and 2 billion years ago. The accessible iron of that age totals 140 billion tonnes, more half of all of the world's iron ore.

In 1968, Preston Cloud of UC Santa Barbara proposed that this large-scale production of iron ore, when the Earth was half its present age, marked the debut of free oxygen produced by microbes with novel enzymes. The oxygen would react with iron dissolved in the hydrosphere—oceans and fresh water—to form insoluble oxides.

'The iron could be transported in solution in the ferrous state and precipitated as ferric or ferro-ferric oxides upon combining with biological oxygen,' Cloud suggested. 'The hydrosphere would be swept free of ferrous iron in a last great episode of banded iron formation. And oxygen would accumulate in excess in the hydrosphere and begin to evade to the atmosphere.'

Such was the origin, Cloud thought, of the oxygen-rich air we breathe. For the microbes responsible for this great change, he nominated the ancestors of present-day cyanobacteria, also known as blue-green algae. They are a highly evolved type of photosynthetic bacteria, growing by sunlight. Blue-greens deploy a complex of molecules called Photosystem II that includes a special enzyme to split water molecules into hydrogen and oxygen.

This enzyme in the blue-green ancestors was revolutionary for life on Earth, according to Cloud. It played a key part in the deposition of the banded iron formation on the seabed of the continental shelves. Subsequent geological action raised some of the ore above sea level, and unearthed it for our convenience at Mount Tom Price and elsewhere.

Manganese on Snowball Earth

Cloud's story was neat but hard to prove. Chemical evidence, especially concerning the freedom of action of sulphurous molecules on the young Earth, pointed to an absence of free oxygen before 2.5 billion years ago. But the role of oxygen in the banded iron formation was far from certain. For rusting the planet—making insoluble iron-oxide ores—bacteria and their enzymes have many other chemical tricks available, apart from liberating oxygen. Some banded iron deposits date from the earlier, oxygen-free era.

Another metallic element, manganese, really needs free oxygen to precipitate it. In the Kalahari Desert of South Africa a hefty deposit of manganese oxide, the world's biggest single source of this valuable metal used in steel-making, accompanies oxidized iron of the banded iron formation. The manganese ore formed about 2.2 billion years ago, somewhat after the onset of the global frenzy of iron-ore-making. For Joseph Kirschvink of Caltech this was the clinching evidence for the involvement of free oxygen.

Kirschvink and Caltech colleagues joined forces with South African geologists at the Rand Afrikaans University to pin down the chemical and microbial implications of iron plus manganese. They reasoned that iron drops out of solution in oxygenated water more readily than manganese does. For a while, in the former coastal sea now represented in the Kalahari Desert, there was no longer enough dissolved iron remaining in the water locally to mop up the oxygen. So then it was the turn of manganese.

Starting in 1992, Kirschvink had already linked later episodes of banded iron formation, dating from around 700 million years ago, to major climatic crises that he called Snowball Earth. More than once, glaciers appeared even in the tropics, and Kirschvink pondered the consequences if, as he supposed, the whole ocean froze over too. Starved of oxygen, the water would once more become hospitable to soluble iron. When the ice melted and oxygen returned, new iron ore formed in many parts of the world.

By 1997, there was growing evidence for earlier tropical glaciers 2.4 to 2.2 billion years ago. These allowed Kirschvink to extend his Snowball Earth scenario to this earlier period of banded iron formation. He went on to suggest that the blue-greens evolved 2.4 billion years ago, and that the first unequivocal evidence of the impact of their water-splitting enzyme is the Kalahari manganese.

The dementia connection

There was another side to the banded iron story, which Kirschvink and Co. did not neglect. Life was in crisis, because oxygen is a poison. It is extremely reactive with the delicate carbon-rich biomolecules of living organisms. For the first 1.5 billion years of life, any exposure to free oxygen was only by mischance. Starting with the blue-greens, which made the deadly stuff in abundance, microbes suddenly needed new chemistry to protect themselves from the oxygen.

An emblem of the evolutionary response is an enzyme that then appeared on the scene. Superoxide dismutase, or SOD, disarms negatively charged oxygen molecules, which herald the attack on biomolecules. Many variants of SOD are known in bacteria, archaea, fungi, plants and animals, including human beings. Without it, life in the open in our oxygenated world would be unsustainable.

Eric Gaidos, Elizabeth Bertani and Rachel Steinberger, biologists at Caltech collaborating with Kirschvink, used molecular differences between the variant forms of the enzyme to trace them back to common ancestors. By 2000, the team was able to infer that a period of evolutionary experimentation and divergence, seen in the SOD lineages, accompanied the onset of planet-wide rusting dated geologically at around 2.4 billion years ago.

This pioneering combination of biology and geology, in the study of globally active enzymes, would be striking even if SOD were an obscure molecule. Far from it. SOD pills are on sale. They are supposed to boost the human body's defences against harmful effects of oxygen. Taking the enzyme by mouth may not work, but much medical and pharmaceutical research now focuses on SOD and related biochemistry, in an effort to understand and treat cases where its protection fails.

Oxygen damage to biomolecules can give rise to cancer, Alzheimer's and other disorders, and to general effects of ageing. A reunion of the sciences at the start of the 21st century thus traces explanatory links of cause and effect, extending back from the dementia wards to minerals in the Australian and South African deserts, and thence to climate change more than 2 billion years ago.

'The same thing happened several times between 720 and 600 million years ago, when the Earth froze over again,' Kirschvink commented. 'An oxygen spurt followed as before, making banded iron and associated manganese deposits, in Canada, Brazil and elsewhere. Whereas the earlier event produced a flurry of microbial evolution for defence against oxygen, the second prompted the rise of the animals, which exploited oxygen. So we can begin to relate evolution in biomolecules—the genes and enzymes—to dated events in Earth history.'

Paying heed to microbes

When oxygen became a normal constituent of the surface waters, many bacteria and archaea retreated out of harm's way, as anaerobes shunning oxygen. Their descendants still thrive in airless conditions, like the methane-makers of the swamps. For other creatures, once their molecular defences were in place, oxygen became useful for new ways of living. With the right enzymes, oxygen could be used to convert organic food into energy, in a controlled process akin to burning. This opened the way to the evolution of fungi, animals and the higher plant forms.

The oxygen concentration gradually increased in the atmosphere, yet all animals and plants remained confined to the oceans and freshwater. No doubt the bacteria and fungi were the first pioneers to go ashore. But not until about 400 million years ago did complex creatures, large enough for fossil-hunters to find, face the open air in detectable invasions of the land.

These produced another planet-wide change. By gradually cloaking the land in greenery for the first time, odd-looking land-dwellers created an Earth that you and I might recognize as vaguely familiar. Biochemistry led the way, with new enzyme kits, but subplots were geochemical and meteorological.

The Earth enlarged its continents by converting basalt into less dense granite. Volcanic action had to keep resupplying trace elements like iron and phosphorus essential for life. For life out of the water, the winds became the conduit for the indispensable rainwater, carbon dioxide and oxygen. To this day, microscopic plants in the sea, such as diatoms, discreetly maintain our oxygen supply by splitting water.

So enzymes rule the world in a very tangible sense. You breathe the gas and you can handle the rocks and soil that they make. The Russian scientist Vladimir Vernadsky, who died in 1945, had recognized life as a major geological force, and a constant player in the chemistry of the Earth.

Yet the 20th century was well advanced before many scientists paid conscious heed to the global impact of biochemical systems. Evolutionists examining fossil limestone were more interested in the species represented there than in the effect of the carbonate itself in removing carbon dioxide from the atmosphere. Microbiologists were preoccupied with bacteria, viruses and parasites that cause disease, or with microbes used in the food and drink industries.

Among those who took environmentally active bacteria seriously was John Postgate at the UK's National Chemical Laboratory and then Sussex University. He became preoccupied with nitrogen. One of life's oddities is that this gas is the main constituent of the atmosphere and yet it is in short supply in chemically fixed forms that are indispensable for all organisms. As a result the human species can feed itself only by combining nitrogen industrially on a huge scale.

Microbes with the ability to fix nitrogen are strangely few. Among them are some of the blue-green algae, which shoulder the prime responsibility for fertilizing the ocean. Splitting water to make oxygen and reducing nitrogen to make ammonia are chemically contradictory tasks. Blue-greens solve this problem by doing the two jobs at different times of day.

On land, the task of fixing nitrogen falls on certain soil bacteria, and others that inhabit nodules in the roots of plants such as beans. In 1972, Postgate succeeded in transferring the gene for the key enzyme, nitrogenase, from one bacterium to another. His dream was to make wheat and other crop plants able to fix their own nitrogen, and thus reduce the farmers' dependence on industrial nitrogen.

Some other scientists were uneasy about interfering with the deployment of so fundamental a global enzyme. They suggested that man-made nitrogen-fixing organisms might flourish too well and grow out of control. Perhaps there are good reasons we don't yet know, for natural stinginess in the matter of available nitrogen. By 2002, experiments by Rafael Navarro-González of the Universidad Nacional Autónoma de México and his colleagues gave weight to the idea that life originally relied on nitrogen fixed by lightning strokes, but this source diminished as the composition of the atmosphere changed. Then the enzymes were needed.

GLOBAL ENZYMES

● The Gaia hypothesis

In 1965 James Lovelock, a British freelance chemist, was asked by NASA for advice about the search for life on Mars. He displeased his client by saying there was no life on the red planet. The atmosphere of Mars appeared to be chemically stable and this, he reasoned, was in complete contrast to the Earth's atmosphere, where living things keep injecting materials that are out of equilibrium with one another—combustible methane in the presence of oxygen, for example.

Lovelock went on to think about the Earth, and wondered why its disequilibrium never seemed to get out of hand. In the 1970s he went public with the idea of an unconscious conspiracy to curb shortages and excesses of key materials. Organisms continually adjust the chemistry of the Earth's surface, atmosphere and ocean in a manner that counteracts adverse trends. This is the Gaia hypothesis, named after the Greek Earth goddess.

'The entire range of living matter on Earth,' Lovelock wrote, 'from whales to viruses and from oaks to algae could be regarded as constituting a single living entity capable of maintaining the Earth's atmosphere to suit its overall needs and endowed with faculties and powers far beyond those of its constituent parts.'

The idea won public acclaim because it chimed both with the environmental movement and with New Age idealism. Among scientists a prominent American microbiologist, Lynn Margulis, became Lovelock's most enthusiastic supporter, and she provided helpful input about the activities of microbes. Otherwise the reactions from experts were typically lukewarm or antagonistic.

As a supposedly self-regulating system of organisms, Gaia remains scientifically unverified. The most positive effect of the hypothesis so far is that everyone, including Lovelock's severest scientific critics, has paid more attention to global enzymes. Sulphur's role in cloud-making is an example.

Clouds need small solid particles, aerosols, on which their droplets can form. Over land, there is plenty of dust of many kinds. In the clean air over the wide oceans dust is scarcer, and some of the algae in the water are a major source of aerosols. Their enzymes produce a vapour, dimethylsulphide (CH_3SCH_3). It becomes converted into sulphuric acid droplets, suitable for cloud-making.

In 1987, Lovelock and others suggested that variations in the abundance of the producers could affect the climate, by altering the Earth's cloud cover. This stimulated research around the world, which confirmed the link between dimethylsulphide abundance and atmospheric sulphuric acid. In deep ice from the Russian Vostok base in Antarctica, scientists found a marked increase in sulphuric acid during the last ice age. Lovelock had expected a decrease in cold conditions. Never mind, the result was a new piece to be added to the climate jigsaw, this time involving microbes and their enzymes.

The promise of molecular biology

The catalogue of microbial actions in the routine processes of geology has lengthened too. Fungi attack rocks with many kinds of acids, and vastly accelerate the weathering and erosion that flattens mountains. In the process they help to create soil. Conversely they consolidate sediments on the beds of seas, lakes and rivers.

Microbes precipitate metals out of the water, thereby controlling its chemical composition and also making some important ores of zinc, gold, uranium and other metals, besides the iron and manganese already mentioned. In the worldwide traffic in carbon, nitrogen, phosphorus, sulphur and other key elements that are cycled through the Earth system, microbes are important traders. Many details of their operations are only now coming to light.

Advances in molecular biology improve the scientists' hopes of one day fully grasping the roles of global enzymes. The watchwords are genomics and proteomics. Whilst the genome is the complete set of genes in an organism, which includes the codes needed for building its active molecules, the proteome is the organism's complete set of proteins, including the enzymes.

Although the human genome had most publicity, a rapidly lengthening list of bacterial genomes became available around the start of the 21st century. The tools of the molecular biologists greatly speed up the work of looking for particular enzymes, whether in their genetic codes or as constructed protein molecules. There are also many genes whose function is not yet known, so there are new enzymes of possible worldwide importance waiting to be discovered.

A German academic consortium advertises the aim of planetary proteomics, to characterize all of the enzymes now at work in the Earth's mantle of life. The proteome of the biosphere? That sounds like a 100-year project, and it probably is. What prevents it being far-fetched is the fact that Mother Nature has husbanded her best proteins through billions of years of evolution. The same or similar molecules are shared among very many organisms.

The genomes also have much to tell about the evolutionary histories of their owners. Comparisons between different species, as in the Caltech study of the banded iron event of about 2.4 billion years ago, can reveal simultaneous changes in a number of genomes, directly related to dateable events in Earth history. The search is on for the genes and enzymes that tell of life's responses to changes of climate, impacts of comets and asteroids, or the advent of new ways by which organisms could earn their livings.

● Matter for rumination

Without grass, the world might be hard to recognize. The animals would be very different and there might be no human beings, because we are evolutionary children of the African grassland. Nor would huge areas of the planet be given over to cultivation of selected grasses—wheat, rice and so on. Other small plants would provide ground cover, exerting a similar influence on the weather in normal conditions, but it is questionable whether they would be so resistant to drought, fire and overgrazing. If not, the global climate would be different, and soils more vulnerable to erosion.

Yet throughout 99 per cent of the time when interplanetary tourists might have visited the Earth, they would have seen no grasslands. Only about 30 million years ago did bamboo-like plants evolve into forms adapted to carpeting large swaths as we know today. Their cue came with a major cooling of the climate that eliminated most of the world's rain forests. Open country was windswept, so grasses could dispense with fancy flowers to spread their pollen. Turf grasses propagated underground.

But the prairie winds also fanned fires started by lightning or volcanoes. Grass evolved a way of growing, not from the tip of the leaf but from the bottom. Then fire could pass and leave the tender growing parts unscathed, while also destroying shrubs that might compete for territory. Deliberate burning by man-made fires later helped to maintain and enlarge the grasslands.

Its way of growing made grass fairly tolerant of grazing animals, which also assisted in destroying shrubs. But enough was enough, and the grasses that survived best were those that made themselves tough, abrasive to a grazer's teeth, and indigestible to boot. They laced their leaves with silica.

Some mammals responded to these sandpaper offerings by getting bacteria to do the main digestive work. As a result, in deer, goats, cattle and other ruminants, the stomach has become a bacterial culture for fermenting grass and other leaves. The animal then ruminates—chews the cud—and feeds on the bacterial broth in a second stomach.

Special enzymes are needed for digesting bacteria efficiently. One is ribonuclease, which consumes their nucleic acids. In 1995 Steven Benner and his group, then at the Eidgenössische Technische Hochschule Zürich, reconstructed ancient ribonuclease molecules in the laboratory. From the similarities and differences between the current molecules in various animals, the scientists deduced the composition of ribonuclease as it may have been 40 million years ago, when used by the ancestors of the ruminants alive today. Although never seen before in the human era, the reconstructed molecules work very well in chopping up bacterial nucleic acid.

Later, when Benner had moved to Florida, he and his colleagues commented: 'These data added a planetary dimension to the annotation of the ribonuclease protein. Rather than saying that "ribonuclease is involved in ruminant digestion," we can say that digestive ribonuclease emerged...in animals in which ruminant digestion developed, at a time where difficult-to-digest grasses emerged, permitting their descendants to exploit a newly available resource emerging at a time of global climatic upheaval.'

If you doubt the planetary significance of animal digestive processes, consider that an enzymatic by-product of rumination is methane. It's made by archaea whose ancestors were doing the same thing billions of years ago, before there was free oxygen on the Earth. The animals' output totals about 100 million tonnes of methane a year. That is roughly one-sixth of all the methane going into the air from natural and man-made sources. Methane is more effective than carbon dioxide as a greenhouse gas, and some climate scientists have expressed concern about the increase to be expected as the human population grows, and with it the appetite for the meat and milk of ruminants.

▶ *For another example of enzyme history, see* ALCOHOL. *Overlapping subjects include* PHOTOSYNTHESIS, EXTREMOPHILES *and* PROTEOMES. *Snowball Earth figures also in* CAMBRIAN EXPLOSION.

GRAMMAR
Does it stand between computers and the dominion of the world?

'L ET'S READ *PRAVDA* OVER BREAKFAST,' US officials said, in the early years of the Cold War. The idea was that the then-novel digital computers, equipped with electronic dictionaries, should provide almost instantaneous translations of newspapers and other documents from the Russian. It was a vain hope. Half a century later, when computers were far more powerful and the nuances of language far better understood, human translators were in greater demand than ever—often to edit out errors, infelicities and absurdities still apparent in the rough drafts from machine translations.

The problems that computers and their programmers met in dealing with natural human languages were a pity, from a practical point of view.

Multilingual organizations like the UN and the European Union faced growing translation bills for written and spoken words. An interpreter between Burmese and Latvian was not always easy to find. And hopes that machine translation might rescue fast-disappearing minor languages were also disappointed.

Even major languages and their cultural payload were losing out, because English was adopted everywhere as the lingua franca. According to some users, the economic, political and cultural clout of the USA and the English-speaking Commonwealth was not the only reason. 'Russian does not break well,' the Soviet theoretical physicist Nikolai Bogolyubov said to a visiting Dutchman, in explaining why he and his colleagues from Eastern Europe always collaborated in Broken English. Perhaps the same is true for Broken German and Fractured French.

On the other hand, the shortcomings of machine translation did wonders for human self-respect. In the 1950s and 1960s, prophets of artificial intelligence were boasting that their products would soon make our species obsolescent. But language emerged as a great stumbling block—an almost inimitable central feature of human intelligence. Ordinary people, talking and listening, deal at a very high speed with complexities and ambiguities so subtle that experts have had to labour long and hard to try to define the rules.

'I believe we must be quite careful not to underestimate the originality and skill, and the depths of the properties of mind, that are revealed when a simple child uses an original sentence,' declared Noam Chomsky of the Massachusetts Institute of Technology.

In this regard, the theorist of linguistics echoed René Descartes who, in the 17th century, noted that no animal or automatic machine could match even a human idiot in arranging words into statements. Descartes saw in language a sufficient proof of the existence of the soul, but Chomsky rejected any supernatural explanation. 'No doubt some physical properties of the brain will be discovered that account for these, at the moment, quite incomprehensible innate abilities. But this is far off.'

Starting in 1957 Chomsky led a revolution in linguistic theory. He proposed that, despite their enormous superficial differences, all languages conformed to a universal grammar, which supposedly relies on universal qualities of the human mind. A child brings these inherent qualities to bear when it learns the particularities of its own language.

Here grammar is not to be understood in the narrow schoolteacherly sense of what is deemed proper or improper in a particular standardized language. Long before any scholar parsed a sentence, grammar provided the basis for efficient communication between human individuals everywhere. It relies on conventions that they share, whenever they use strings of words. These may approximate to schoolroom grammar, but the practical test is mutual comprehension.

Nor is Chomsky's universal grammar just a set of rules for distinguishing correct and incorrect sentences. Beneath the surface structure of a sentence lies a deep structure, incorporating unspoken propositions about the subject under discussion. These are linked to common knowledge of the world in general, and to knowledge of the context shared by the interlocutors. By the end of the century, Chomsky and his school were contrasting the deep 'logical form' with the 'phonetic form' of actual utterances, which vary from language to language.

Chomsky himself was relaxed about the evolutionary aspect of his theory, and how grammar might have emerged in the transition from apes to people. A century earlier, Charles Darwin declared that speech is instinctive, 'as we see in the babble of our young children.' Neuroscientists wondered whether grammar is in our genes, which might specify the wiring of the human brain needed for the universal talent proclaimed by Chomsky. Progress on that front was still inconclusive at the start of the 21st century. When the first language-related gene was discovered in 2001, it concerned the generation of speech sounds by control of the mouth and tongue, rather than the processing of sentences.

Was Chomsky right?

The idea of a universal grammar was highly influential, among psychologists and philosophers as well as linguists. But Chomsky's theory did not go uncontested. Some critics argued that all languages share common principles because the physics of cause and effect is universal. The observable action of one thing on another might be sufficient to provide the logic of verb, subject and object.

Others thought that Chomsky laid far too much stress on formal grammar. Human communication often succeeds even when sentences are incomplete or ungrammatical. That is most obvious in the babble of babytalk shared by infants and their mothers.

At Oxford in the 1970s, the experimental psychologist Jerome Bruner videotaped toddlers learning to speak. He was struck by the game-like quality of their verbal interactions with adults. The rules of language seemed to him like the rules of tennis or any other game. So far from relying on special brain wiring, language was, he thought, a by-product of flexible intelligence and especially of a general aptitude for making rules—exhibited also in children at play.

'They very quickly get into the realm of pretend, where they're making real rules and real conventions about fictional things and fictional characters,' Bruner said in 1976. 'They soon make rules about rules themselves—how to make rules—which is after all what culture is about. How we do things with words, how we invent appropriate conventional behaviour. And isn't it clever of Nature to have arranged that play, like most other important things in life, doesn't work unless there's some fun to it?'

Those who favoured brains pre-adapted to language could of course assert that rules of games and make-believe are by-products of language skills, rather than the other way around. Chomsky's own view of language evolution was more open-minded than those wanting hard-wired grammar. He did not even insist on natural selection favouring language. It could be a by-product of big brains favoured by evolution for other reasons—which need not be incompatible with Bruner's fun-loving brains.

In the decades that followed, there was no answer to the chicken-and-egg question of which came first, general cleverness or language. Chomskyan grammar itself evolved into an increasingly abstract system for judging sentences, with less and less connection with real life in a polyglot world. Without abandoning the quest for universal principles, some mainstream linguists therefore went back to Chomsky's starting point. They looked in detail at many real languages, searching for clues to mental and social mechanisms of grammar in the many differences between them, as well as the similarities stressed by Chomsky.

Others, calling themselves computational linguists, returned to the translation problem, but with an open-minded approach to the nature of language. Although it owed much in spirit to Chomsky, it was non-conformist about grammar. The search was for a grammar that worked in the practical sense that it would enable computers to handle natural language better.

This need not be *the* method used by the brain. A machine grammar would be adapted to the computer and its logic, which was not necessarily the same as the brain's logic. But it would address the same problem: how to send and receive information and comments unambiguously, by strings of words in an existing natural language.

The extraction of unambiguous meaning from the words, by a computer, was analogous to their comprehension by a human listener or reader. And it was a prerequisite, if the computer was to restate the meaning correctly in another language. One big difference, though, was that the machine did not need to grasp the meaning for its own enlightenment, in the way that the human consciousness can do.

Computational linguists gave their machines rules of thumb for dealing with ambiguities in natural language, which smoothed some of the rough edges of routine machine translation. They assisted in the increasing use of natural language in day-to-day inputs and outputs of general-purpose computers. And at the cutting edge, the computational linguists empowered the machines to generate any number of grammatical and meaningful sentences, fully comprehensible to human beings.

These systems worked in microcosms of limited vocabulary, in a restricted domain of knowledge and data. Descriptions and comparisons of artefacts in a museum were an example of one such microcosm of the late 1990s, in a multinational project sponsored by the European Union.

The rise of cognitive science

'People giggle and blush when you talk about such things, that the real promise of artificial intelligence is to design our successors,' declared Marvin Minsky of the Massachusetts Institute of Technology. He had emerged in 1956 as one of the young Turks keen to develop computers and robots to outsmart us. They were joined by space enthusiasts, who reasoned that silicon brains could colonize the Galaxy much more easily than people dependent on oxygen, water, food and entertainment.

Many onlookers were shocked by this treason to our own species, and asked what permission Minsky and his chums had, to set such goals for artificial intelligence. Science-fiction writers chimed in with scary scenarios in which a computer takes over the world or, in the case of the mutinous HAL in the movie *2001: A Space Odyssey*, switches off the life support for a spaceship's crew.

'I'm sorry, Dave,' HAL says, 'but in accordance with subroutine C1532/4, quote, When the crew are dead or incapacitated, the computer must assume control, unquote. I must, therefore, override your authority now since you are not in any condition to intelligently exercise it.'

For better or worse, by the eponymous year of 2001 chatty and ambitious robots like HAL were nowhere in sight, in the real world. Artificial intelligence till then had been more hype than substance. Exceptions included successful efforts to organize expert knowledge for computerized diagnoses, in medicine and geology for example. Also to develop electronic systems capable of learning by experience and making decisions in response to changing circumstances.

Some of these systems were embodied in mobile robots. But as in computational linguistics, they operated in microcosms minute compared with the scope of everyday human activity. The faculty of vision, in the interpretative sense in which human beings use it constantly, turned out to be extremely difficult to mimic in machines.

A high point came in 1997 when an IBM computer, Deep Blue, narrowly defeated the world champion Gary Kasparov at chess. But the way it won was almost the antithesis of human cunning. Deep Blue used sheer computing power to evaluate every possible series of future moves and counter-moves very quickly. And despite well-deserved kudos, chess too is a very small part of human life.

Implicit in the difficulties surrounding artificial intelligence and language was a need to figure out more generally what the human brain does when it is thinking, and exercising its natural intelligence. In 1959, Chomsky had published a famous attack on a book called *Verbal Behavior* (1957) by Burrhus F. Skinner, the leading behavioural psychologist at Harvard, who considered enquiries into the mind and conscious thought to be outside the scope of science, and language merely a set of conditioned responses. Also influential at that time was the work of Jean Piaget in Switzerland, who showed that a child's mental processes depend on age.

Gradually cognitive psychology reasserted itself in the USA, and made common cause with experts in linguistics, computer science and philosophy, to grapple with the awesome task of understanding human intelligence. A multidisciplinary journal, *Cognitive Science* (1976), paved the way for the creation of the Cognitive Science Society a few years later. In a widening circle of universities around the world, the tag appeared on the notices of interdepartmental programmes, or even of freestanding departments of cognitive science.

This convergence promises no speedy answers, but it recognizes the range of intellectual effort needed to deal, self-referentially, with what the human mind really does when it thinks. Meanwhile, the difficulty that electronic systems have in coping with language and its grammar seems to remain a roadblock in the way of any idea that computers like HAL might outsmart us. There is still time to reflect on that scenario, and take precautions.

As grammar is first and last a facility shared by people engaged in a conversation, it is entwined with social behaviour and with the common sense of everyday life. Motives and beliefs come into the picture too. Progress in linguistics may therefore depend on simultaneously encompassing many other features of human thoughts and feelings.

'People have to think about what the other participants in the dialogue believe, want and intend to do,' noted Alex Lascarides, a cognitive scientist at Edinburgh. 'We need a theory which connects goals with actions more generally—not just the action of uttering things in conversation, but all kinds of action. How do we model this link between action, belief and desire? If we had a theory of this, then we could explain why people behave the way they do, in conversation and elsewhere.'

▶ *For other aspects of linguistics, see* LANGUAGES *and* SPEECH.

GRAVITATIONAL WAVES

Shaking the Universe with weighty news

H ANFORD IN THE STATE OF WASHINGTON is a district of flat, scrubby desert, and a wasteland left over from the making of nuclear explosives and the burial of radioactive waste. In 2002, a big telescope of a novel kind was coming into operation there, as part of the world's largest detector of an expected quivering of space. Instead of using lenses or mirrors for looking at the cosmos, it had light beams shuttling to and fro in pipes. They probed for extremely small, rhythmic changes in the distances between mirrors set at the ends of two pipes four kilometres long, arranged in the shape of an L.

Another instrument on the same scale was nearing completion 3000 kilometres away, in the pine forests of Livingston, Louisiana. The two American detectors, masterminded by physicists from Caltech and the Massachusetts Institute of Technology, comprised the Laser Interferometer Gravitational-Wave Observatory. In parallel, smaller L-shaped instruments working on similar principles were being readied in Japan, Germany and Italy. A combined cost running to hundreds of millions of dollars reflected a worldwide determination to find the gravitational waves predicted more than 80 years before, by Albert Einstein.

With hindsight, the way physicists took fright at some of Einstein's ideas was comical. The equivalence of mass and energy was of course genuinely scary, and $E = mc^2$ in nuclear weapons could still kill us all. But mere intellectual alarm about general relativity, the theory of gravity promulgated and developed by Einstein in 1915–17, hindered science in several areas throughout the rest of his lifetime.

Einstein himself was nervous to the point of denial about black holes and antigravity, both of which are now thought to be real. His followers sometimes believed that his equations did not represent actuality but were just tools for getting the right answers. Some relativists insisted that light need not really slow down when it passed the Sun—until radar observations of the planet Venus in the 1970s proved that it did exactly that.

What about gravitational waves, the means invoked by Einstein for carrying weighty news across the cosmos? Perhaps you were no more likely to sense them than to see the computed trajectory of a cannon ball trailing behind it like the tail of a kite. In 1957, two years after Einstein's death, Hermann Bondi of Kings College London rebutted this sceptical view.

He reasoned that a gravitational wave could move beads to and fro on a stick. If the stick were rough enough to cause a little friction, heat would be generated. Therefore the wave would convey energy to the stick, and must have a real physical meaning.

Nobody proposed looking for gravitational waves with an abacus and a thermometer, but Bondi's thought experiment prompted serious searches by other means. Indirect evidence came in the 1970s from a pair of stars orbiting around each other that are shedding energy by radiating gravitational waves and gradually spiralling ever closer together. This discovery, by US astronomers, was made possible by the fact that one of the stars was a radio pulsar, the motions of which could be traced very accurately. It won a Nobel Physics Prize for Joseph Taylor and Russell Hulse.

The first attempts to detect the waves directly used metal bars, designed to ring like a tuning fork in response to a gravitational wave of the right wavelength washing over it. A claim of success from the USA, in 1969, was judged not proven. Experiments with bars continued, but by early in the 21st century, laser beams and the large L-shaped antennas were the preferred detectors.

Why L-shaped? Gravitational waves stretch and squeeze space, first one way and then the other. So while one arm of the L is being lengthened, the other shortens. Half a wavelength later, the stretched arm has shrunk and the squeezed one lengthened. The expected changes in arm length are less than a billionth of the width of an atom. Exquisite optical systems, operating in a high vacuum, are needed to detect the slight changes.

Gravitational waves are the wave-like version of the tidal force, whereby the gravity of the Moon and Sun stretch and squeeze the Earth's oceans and rocks by metres or millimetres. The tides are an aspect of the ordinary force of gravity that Newton understood. Gravitational waves carry the tidal forces of distant stars over much greater distances than Newton would have imagined. Einstein showed that they should stretch and squeeze the fabric of spacetime itself. Be glad that space is very rigid, or you'd be shaken to pieces.

Another comparison is with radio waves. In the early 19th century, physicists thought that electric and magnetic phenomena were more or less confined to the vicinity of their wires and magnets, including the Earth's magnetic field. The discovery of electromagnetic waves meant the liberation of the electric force, so that it could be transmitted across vast distances. And it transpires that the Earth is bathed in radio waves, coming not only from lightning strokes and the hubbub of man-made radio, TV and radar transmissions, but from the Sun, the stars and the most distant galaxies.

Electromagnetic radiation, which includes light, is created by the acceleration of electric charges. The acceleration of masses creates gravitational waves. Travelling at the same speed as light, 300,000 kilometres per second, they have the same ability to cross great distances in cosmic space.

Except for cosmic rays, meteorites and the very local explorations by space probes, all that we know about the Universe till now has come entirely from electromagnetic rays. Besides confirming an aspect of Einstein's important theory, direct detection of gravitational waves will open a new window on the cosmos.

Next: an antenna in space

The gravitational waves coming from the sky are calculated to bathe the Earth in energy far stronger than moonlight. A background rumble due to distant minor earthquakes and even road traffic probably limits ground antennas to wavelengths of 300 to 30,000 kilometres, which roughly corresponds to the frequencies in cycles per second of sounds audible to the human ear. The bang of a star exploding, in the Milky Way or in a nearby galaxy, or the crash of two very dense neutron stars colliding, are likely sources of strong gravitational waves accessible on the Earth's surface, but such events are rare.

'Our detectors on the ground should register short-wavelength gravitational waves,' said Karsten Danzmann from the German–UK GEO600 project located near Hannover. 'But the Earth is a noisy planet, and continuous disturbances mask the longer wavelengths, which we believe to include the commonest and strongest kinds of gravitational waves. Just as spacecraft have to climb above the atmosphere for a clear view of infrared rays from the Universe, so to detect the long-wavelength gravitational waves we need an antenna in the quietness of interplanetary space.'

A fantastic project called the Laser Interferometric Space Antenna, or LISA, is due to fly around 2011. NASA and the European Space Agency are to be partners in the boldest physics experiment ever attempted in space. It requires three spacecraft orbiting around the Sun in a triangular formation, separated by 5 million kilometres. Laser beams with a power of only one watt are to shuttle between them, comparing the immense distances between cubes of gold-platinum alloy floating weightlessly within each spacecraft. They will be required to detect relative changes of a few thousandths of an atom's width across the enormous intervening spaces.

The difficulties speak for themselves but, if successful, LISA promises a revolution in astronomy. It will have plenty to see. Double stars orbiting very closely together should be the commonplace sources of gravitational waves detectable by an antenna in space. For example, in the constellation Sagittarius a star pair called WZ Sagittae orbit around each other every 82 minutes. The gravitational waves from the system will have a period of 41 minutes and a wavelength of 740 million kilometres.

The antics of dense objects like black holes and neutron stars, only surmised from observations of electromagnetic rays, will be directly observable by gravitational waves. Collisions between such objects should be detected across vast chasms of cosmic space. But what makes some physicists hold their breath is the thought that the weightiest news of all might come from accelerations of masses in the Big Bang, at the supposed origin of the Universe.

Astronomers using light and other electromagnetic waves are blind to anything earlier than 400,000 years after the origin, when light now known as cosmic microwaves first broke free from a hot electronic fog. One of those convinced that gravitational waves could do better was Bernard Schutz of Germany's Albert-Einstein-Institut, a participant both in GEO600 and in the preparations for the LISA space project.

'Gravitational waves should blast their way through the primordial fog, bringing news from the first split-second of the Big Bang,' Schutz said. 'That would be the most amazing discovery in cosmic physics that I can imagine. Will our detectors be sensitive enough? We'll never know unless we try.'

▶ *For a broader view of Einstein's theory, see* GRAVITY *and its cross-references.*

GRAVITY

Did Uncle Albert really get it right?

'I' WAS SITTING IN A CHAIR in the patent office at Bern when all of a sudden a thought occurred to me: "If a person falls freely he will not feel his own weight." I was startled. This simple thought made a deep impression on me. It impelled me towards a new theory of gravitation.'

What Albert Einstein called the happiest thought of his life came to him in 1907. We have the maestro's word for it, that this was the central idea inspiring the modern theory of gravity. He needed help with the mathematics, which was never his strong suit, but otherwise it was a single-handed job. He completed it in Berlin in 1915, and promulgated it as the general theory of relativity.

Gravity is all about falling. The great counter-intuitive leap of imagining that a body fully yielding to gravity feels no force is the more striking when you recall that Einstein had not the benefit of watching astronauts afloat in the weightless conditions of orbital free fall. And in speaking of a person falling—off the roof of a house, he often said—he had to abolish air resistance in his mind. Galileo Galilei did the same, three centuries earlier.

When he dropped a cannon ball and a musket ball from the Leaning Tower of Pisa, and found them hitting the ground 'within a hand's breadth', Galileo seems to have been dead lucky in his choice of materials and sizes. A re-enactment in 1994, by Erseo Polacco and his colleagues from the Università di Pisa, showed equal-sized balls of lead and aluminium arriving at the ground a metre apart. Only by adjusting the relative sizes can you compensate for air resistance.

The notion that gravity treats all materials equally—the equivalence principle, as the jargon now calls it—offends common sense. A hammer falls faster than a feather, as Galileo well knew. Yet he penetrated the everyday appearances to enter Nature's engine-room: 'I came to the conclusion that in a medium totally void of resistance all bodies would fall with the same speed.'

An Apollo astronaut dropped a hammer and a feather in front of a camera on the airless Moon and the experiment worked, updating common sense for the Space Age. The version of gravity that the travellers used to reach the Moon was Isaac Newton's, which is still safe enough for most purposes. Newton realized that gravity was a cosmic force. The Moon and the planets were as obedient as the falling apple, and gravity grew weaker with distance at the same rate as the light from a lamp—a quarter, a ninth, a sixteenth. By this inverse square law you could compute even 'the sharply veering ways of comets,' as Newton's chum Edmond Halley expressed it.

Galileo's expectation, that everything should fall at the same speed, was satisfied in a simple manner. The force of gravity was proportional to an object's mass, which exactly cancelled out its inertia, also measured by its mass. As a rule of thumb, Newton's law was clever enough to lull successive generations of lesser physicists into a complacency never shared by Newton himself, who was baffled by the mechanism of gravity.

'That one body may act upon another at a distance through a vacuum, without the mediation of any thing else . . . is to me so great an absurdity, that I believe no man, who has in philosophical matters a competent faculty of thinking, can ever fall into it.'

Light slows down, apparently

Einstein's theory of gravity is more explanatory as well as more exact. It provides the link between gravitationally interacting bodies by deforming the space between them. But as it does not really explain why the masses affect space, but only to what degree, it is still not a complete explanation of action at a distance. There is little danger of complacency now, because too many people want to prove Uncle Albert wrong.

To construct his theory, Einstein went back to Galileo's experiment. The bodies all falling at the same speed include the very light by which we perceive and map the Universe. Stars seen near a total solar eclipse will be out of place, because the Sun's gravity will bend their rays as surely as it binds the planets in their orbits.

The starlight slows down as it passes the Sun, just as if it were going through glass with a certain index of refraction. Unfortunately for public understanding, Einstein and his followers avoided this obvious commentary on gravity's effect on light. They wanted to save the laws of physics from the mayhem that might ensue if the speed of light in empty space could vary. Every atom would change its behaviour. General relativity escapes from this outcome by guaranteeing that the speed of light as measured locally (by an atom on the Sun, for example) always appears to be the same.

'The velocity of light never varies.' That became a mantra of the theorists. Combined with inscrutable mathematics, it hid the brilliance of Einstein's theory for half a century after its formulation. In the late 1960s, radar experiments by Irwin Shapiro of the Massachusetts Institute of Technology showed that radio pulses going to and from Venus or Mercury were delayed whenever those planets were passing across the far side of the Sun.

Radio waves are a form of light so, as measured from far away, light slowed down in the Sun's gravitational field. The experiments confirmed general relativity. They also swept aside all pedantry about the speed of light never changing. This cleared the way for a very simple exposition of Einstein's theory, in which light even comes to a halt in the intense gravity of a black hole.

'Gravity has the apparent effect of reducing the speed of light and slowing down time,' Roger Penrose of Oxford explained. 'So if you imagined the extreme situation of a black hole, then light would be reduced to zero speed, apparently, and time would apparently have been stopped completely at the surface.'

Apparently? It depends on where the measurements are done. Gauged from the Earth, Shapiro's radar signals slowed down near the Sun, but if you could sit on the Sun and measure the speed of light there, it would seem to be exactly the same as when it is measured at the Earth's surface. This is because clocks run more slowly there, precisely in proportion to the slowing of the light.

Space and time are neither cartographic abstractions nor God-given absolutes, but the pliable carriers of the force of gravity that Newton craved. On the Earth, gravity is slightly stronger at the foot of a tree than in the branches, which are farther from the planet's centre. Time and light both travel more slowly for a fallen apple than they did when it hung from the tree, so it possesses less inherent mass-energy. Where did the energy go? By moving downwards, in the direction of increasing gravity, the apple was able to convert it first into energy of motion and then into a bruising thud.

You can't monkey with time and the speed of light without deforming space. A mass enlarges distances in its vicinity, as judged by the time taken for light to traverse them. The stretched space becomes baggy and curved locally. When a planet tries to travel in a straight line across the bag created by solar gravity, the curvature forces it into its orbit around the Sun.

At any given place, whether in a space station or the Pisan campanile, the local curvature of space acts equally on everything in it. So Galileo's democratic principle, with which the analysis began, reappears as a physical consequence of gravity as described by general relativity. John Wheeler of Austin, Texas, put it succinctly: 'Matter tells space how to curve. Space tells matter how to move.'

A fault-line in physics

So far general relativity has survived all experimental tests, of ever-increasing severity. It also explains new phenomena in the Universe, including black holes that power quasars, and gravitational waves that remove energy from orbiting pulsars. Yet physicists suspect that Einstein's theory, like Newton's, may turn out to be just an approximation to the real thing.

Its very success created a great fault-line running through the middle of physics. General relativity treats space and time as a smooth continuum, like syrup. This is incompatible with the muesli of quantum theory, in which space and time ought to be subdivided into specks and moments, because everything jiggles about in a chancy sort of way.

The uncertainty principle in quantum theory says you can't know how a particle is moving, if you know exactly where it is. Electrical experiments verify this principle. General relativity, on the other hand, says that if you know how space is curved then you can know both the position and momentum of a particle simultaneously. To echo Wheeler, space tells matter how to move, and experiments with gravity bear this out.

The flat contradiction in laboratory physics became grandiose in its consequences when astrophysicists inferred that the Universe probably started with a Big Bang, and also observed that it contained regions of superintense gravity, the black holes. According to general relativity, when all of the energy of the Universe was concentrated together at the initiation of a Big Bang, its diameter should have been zero—a geometric point called a singularity. Quantum theory on the other hand requires that it should be not quite zero.

The same discrepancy occurs in the concentration of matter at the centre of a black hole.

By the 1950s, John Wheeler was speculating about quantum foam, into which Einstein's spacetime might dissolve at very short distances. As he wrote later, 'So great would be the fluctuations that there would literally be no left and right, no before and no after. Ordinary ideas of length would disappear. Ordinary ideas of time would evaporate.'

The assumption was that general relativity should bow to quantum theory. Most of the big discoveries in physics in the mid-20th century concerned the behaviour of atoms and particles, which makes sense only with the aid of quantum theory. The same is true of most of the cosmic forces. The familiar electric force, the weak force that transmutes matter, the strong nuclear force that binds protons and neutrons, and the colour force that corrals the quarks—all of these are now well understood as matters of quantum dynamics, with force-carrying particles shuttling to and fro between interacting particles.

Gravity might be interpretable as a force of the same kind, with particles called gravitons acting as the force carriers. Alternatively, gravity might be treated as a different sort of force, which primarily describes the arena of spacetime in which particles operated. Either way, physics might be reunified, and the great fault-line sutured.

A choice of theories

In practice the development of a theory of quantum gravity, to supersede general relativity, turned out to be excruciatingly difficult. It was at the top of the theoretical agenda throughout the closing decades of the 20th century. More than a thousand very clever young people wrestled with the problem. The Theory of Everything, including gravity, was always said to be just around the corner. Yet the results failed to satisfy the onlookers.

String theory, in which all particles are supposed to be very small vibrating strings, was the most popular approach to quantum gravity in the 1990s. Its practitioners were confident. 'Unlike conventional quantum field theory, string theory requires gravity,' declared Edward Witten of Princeton. 'I regard this fact as one of the greatest insights in science ever made.'

A hypothetical universe, very different from the one with which we are familiar, is required by string theory. In addition to three dimensions of space and one dimension of time, the theory employs another six dimensions in the basic concept, and seven in a later version in which vibrating membranes replace the strings—drumskins instead of violins. The extra dimensions conveniently hide themselves from view, but the complex vibrations that they permit can create, according to the theory, the various particles and forces of nature, including the graviton of quantum gravity.

By early in the 21st century, string theory remained but a speculation, with scarcely any anchor to known reality. Some onlookers were losing patience. 'String theorists keep saying that they're succeeding,' said John Baez of UC Riverside. 'The rest of us can wonder whether they are walking along the road to triumph, or whether in 20 years they'll realize that they were walking into this enormous, beautiful, mathematically elegant cul-de-sac.'

An alternative to string theory, favoured by Baez himself, is called loop quantum gravity. Here, the focus is on space itself, which is visualized as consisting of a network of loops—like lace, but in three dimensions. Each loop is formed by a particle with a certain spin making a little excursion and returning to its starting point. The loops do not exist in space—they are space. So the excursions occur in some deeper realm of Nature.

Nevertheless, loop theory is much simpler than string theory. Twists in the loops denote the deformation of space due to gravity. The passage of time is reflected in changes in the network. Spacetime as a whole is the sum of all possible networks.

'We don't need all those imaginary extra dimensions and abstract symmetries that the string people require,' said Carlo Rovelli of Marseille, a leading loop theorist. 'The loop theory gives an enchantingly simple picture of reality, formed by the interwoven loops. And the theory makes predictions, which may be right or wrong but may soon be indirectly tested. For example they may imply that X-rays travel just a little slower across the Universe than radio waves do.'

Experimenters to the rescue?

If as much effort should go into loop quantum gravity as into string theory, other positive results would no doubt flow. But sceptics could not help contrasting the plodding, chain-gang nature of research into quantum gravity with the flash of insight that enabled one man, Albert Einstein, to rebuild the Universe in his head in a few short years, when he invented general relativity.

Will experimental physicists come to the rescue, in the search for quantum gravity? On close enough inspection, familiar space and time should supposedly be seen to break up like a pointilliste painting, into minute pieces. The specks and moments of quantum spacetime would be, though, exceedingly small. Called the Planck length and the Planck time they are, respectively, a centimetre divided by 10 followed by 32 zeroes, and a second divided by 10 followed by 42 zeroes. They are too small for examination by the available microscopes—the particle accelerators—by a factor of more than a million million.

In 1998, Nima Arkani-Hamed and Savas Dimopoulos of Stanford, together with Gia Dvali of the International Centre of Theoretical Physics in Trieste, suggested how effects of quantum gravity might be observable on a far larger scale—just a fraction of a millimetre. This could come about if gravity is inherently much stronger than it appears to be. Most of its effects might be lost in the multiple dimensions beyond our ken, visualized in string theory.

Till now it has been impossible to measure gravity between objects very close together, because the much stronger electric force leaking out of atoms swamps it. 'Nobody knows what the real force of gravity is at short distances,' Arkani-Hamed commented. 'We have a good chance of seeing evidence for or against these ideas in the next 10 years.'

Translating the theory into experimental terms, the search is on for the graviton, the supposed force carrier in quantum gravity. Physicists pin their hopes especially on a new type of accelerator, a linear collider, expected around 2010. Electrons and positrons (anti-electrons) will reach enormous energy in two very long, straight machines, facing each other like duelling pistols.

Collisions between the electronic bullets will create many kinds of particles, perhaps including vast numbers of gravitons. As a supporter of a proposed linear collider at Hamburg, called TESLA, Hans-Ulrich Martyn of the Rheinisch-Westfälische Technische Hochschule Aachen explained how it might see the gravitons.

'Peeping out of their multidimensional hiding-place, gravitons could attach themselves to our subatomic particles in tremendously large numbers, according to the theory of Arkani-Hamed, Dimopoulos and Dvali,' Martyn said. 'Perhaps ten million million at one time. Then, even though each graviton reacts extremely weakly, their collective action could be sufficient to produce a detectable effect. We'll look for the distinctive signature of a single gamma ray made at the same time as the swarm of gravitons. If we find it, that will open a window to the large energy scales where quantum gravity becomes part of particle physics.'

● Against the tide

A few theorists thought that the entire enterprise of quantum gravity was misconceived. Instead of making gravity kowtow to quantum theory, why not look for quantum behaviour as a by-product of gravity? In that case, Uncle Albert may have really got it right and amendments to his theory may be uncalled-for.

One brave theorist prepared to swim against the tide was Mark Hadley at Warwick. He caused a stir in 1996–97 with a theory of closed timelike curves. 'Just a respectable way to say time travel,' he explained. The time travel implicitly permitted in general relativity could create chancy and uncertain outcomes in the behaviour of particles exactly like those required in quantum theory. Indeed Hadley offered for the very first time an explanation for the oddities and paradoxes of quantum theory. Until then these had seemed like quirkiness on the part of Mother Nature to be observed, computed to umpteen decimal places, but never to make sense to the human mind.

Wildly unfashionable though it was, there was nothing disreputable about Hadley's aim. On the contrary, he simply pursued what Einstein himself had tried unsuccessfully to achieve in the last 30 years of his life—to fit the discontinuities of particle behaviour, as manifest for example in photons of light, into the continuous field of his beloved spacetime. 'Field and particle descriptions of Nature are unified as Einstein had always hoped and expected,' Hadley asserted in introducing his ideas. 'There is no simpler or more conservative theory which reconciles quantum mechanics and general relativity.'

No one could fault Hadley's reasoning but if he were right, there could be no theory of quantum gravity. A thousand colleagues would be wasting their time. As a result he was shunned like a typhoid carrier. His theory remains on the table, coupled with his prediction that, when gravitational waves are discovered, making spacetime quiver like a jelly, they should turn out to be simple waves with no hidden quantum element in the form of gravitons.

A tower as big as the Earth

Experimentalists and astronomers continue to look for flaws in Einstein's theory of gravity, which might give hints about the character of any new theory that could replace it. But it proves stubbornly resistant after nearly 90 years of efforts to falsify it. The European Hipparcos satellite detected effects of weak solar gravity deflecting starlight arriving even from directions far from the Sun's, and found that any error in the predictions of general relativity was less than 1 part in 250. And space telescopes observing black holes, by the X-rays that they emit from their vicinity, found them to be behaving just as deduced from Einstein's theory.

The trouble was that tests of the gravity theory were still far less rigorous than tests of quantum theory. A succession of experiments to check the equivalence principle—the crucial proposition that everything falls at the same rate—began with Lorand Eötvös in Budapest in 1889. After a century of further effort, physicists had improved on his accuracy by a factor of 10,000. The advent of spaceflight held out the possibility of a further improvement by a factor of a million.

If another theory of gravity is to replace Einstein's, the equivalence principle cannot be exactly correct. Even though it's casually implicit for every high-school student in Newton's mathematics, Einstein himself thought the equivalence principle deeply mysterious. 'Mass,' he wrote, 'is defined by the resistance that a body opposes to its acceleration (inert mass). It is also measured by the weight of the body (heavy mass). That these two radically different definitions lead to the same value for the mass of a body is, in itself, an astonishing fact.'

Francis Everitt of Stanford put it more forcibly. 'In truth, the equivalence principle is the weirdest apparent fact in all of physics,' he said. 'Have you noticed that when a physicist calls something a principle, he means something he believes with total conviction but doesn't in the slightest degree understand.'

Together with Paul Worden of Stanford and Tim Sumner of Imperial College London, Everitt spent decades prodding space agencies to do something about it. Eventually they got the go-ahead for a satellite called STEP to go into orbit around the Earth in 2007. As a joint US–European project, the Satellite Test of the Equivalence Principle (to unpack the acronym) creates, in effect, a tower of Pisa as big as the Earth. Supersensitive equipment will look for very slight differences in the behaviour of eight test masses made of different materials— niobium, platinum-iridium and beryllium—as they repeatedly fall from one side of the Earth to the other, aboard the satellite.

'The intriguing thing,' Everitt said, 'is that this advance brings us into new theoretical territory where there are solid reasons for expecting a breakdown of equivalence. A violation would mean the discovery of a new force of Nature. Alternatively, if equivalence still holds at a part in a billion billion, the theorists who are trying to get beyond Einstein will have some more hard thinking to do.'

An extra tug on a spacecraft

Meanwhile a possible bug in Einstein's theory appeared quite unexpectedly from the direction of the Taurus constellation, whither NASA's Pioneer 10 spacecraft is heading, on its way out of the Solar System. It is moving slightly more slowly than it should be doing. Unexplained slowdowns have also been detected with other spacecraft travelling away from the direction of the Sun.

After 30 years of flight, following its launch in 1972, Pioneer 10 was 12 billion kilometres away, but 400,000 kilometres less far than predicted. That's a discrepancy of about 1 part in 30,000. If that seems little enough, recall that the first hint that Newton's theory of gravity might be wrong was the 19th-century discovery of an excessive swivelling of the orbit of the innermost planet, Mercury, by 1 part in 30,000 of a circle per century.

The far-flung spacecraft behaved as if it felt an extra tug backwards towards the Sun. Investigators ruled out, one by one, alternative explanations such as gas leaks, thermal radiation, interplanetary gas, or gravitational effects of the planets and comets. 'We've examined every mechanism and theory we can think of, and so far nothing works,' commented Philip Laing of the Aerospace Corporation of California. 'If the effect is real it will have a big impact on cosmology and spacecraft navigation.'

The apparent extra force is like neither Einstein's nor Galileo's gravity, because it violates the Tower of Pisa thought-experiment. It does not operate equally on all matter. In particular its effect, if any, on the Earth and other planets is far smaller than on the spacecraft. The discrepancy could be a matter of elongated versus near-circular orbits, or of small versus large objects, or even of rotation rates.

One possibility teasing the theorists is that a very feeble gravitational force may operate quite differently from the stronger and more noticeable manifestations of gravity. Mordechai Milgrom of Israel's Weizmann Institute developed such an idea from the 1980s onwards. Quantum or cosmological effects in spacetime might reduce a body's resistance to acceleration, making its inertial mass less than its gravitational mass.

When reading a newspaper report on the slowing of Pioneer 10, a non-scientist commented, 'Perhaps it's bumping into dark matter.' With so much in flux, in fundamental physics and astrophysics, who's to say that she was wrong?

▶ *See also* SUPERSTRINGS, BLACK HOLES, GRAVITATIONAL WAVES *and* DARK ENERGY. *For the use of gravity in geophysics, see* PLATE MOTIONS.

HANDEDNESS

Mysteries of left versus right that won't go away

'**M**Y DEAR SON, I have loved science so deeply that this stirs my heart.' So said the ageing physicist Jean-Baptiste Biot of Paris to a 24-year-old chemistry student, Louis Pasteur, who had just shown him privately a conjuring trick with crystals. This was in 1847, long before Pasteur won immortality for his microbial and medical discoveries.

Biot himself had found that ordinary sugar has a remarkable effect on light. If you pass light through a suitable crystal, you can polarize it, which means its waves all vibrate in the same direction at right angles to the beam. If you then shine the polarized light through a solution of sugar in water, the direction of polarization rotates clockwise, to the right. This is a neat way of measuring the concentration of sugar, using a polarimeter.

Other materials also interact with polarized light, rotating it to right or left as the case might be. A mystery that attracted Pasteur's attention concerned tartaric acid, found in grapes. It rotated light to the right, yet synthetic tartaric acid, called racemic acid, had no such effect, although it had exactly the same chemical composition of carbon, oxygen and hydrogen atoms. He found the answer in lopsided crystals made from the two materials.

For the demonstration, Biot insisted on providing the samples himself, and conducting his own tests. He watched as Pasteur used a microscope to sort crystals made from racemic acid into equal numbers of two kinds. They were lopsided in opposite ways, like your left hand and your right hand, which could not be rotated to match each other. Some were the same shape as the natural tartrate, while the others were mirror images.

Biot dissolved the novel, mirror-image crystals and tested them in his polarimeter. He saw at once that they rotated the light to the left, in the opposite sense to the natural tartrate. At a superficial level the mystery was solved, because the two forms present in the synthetic material cancelled each other's effects on the light. But Biot's heart was stirred because he saw much deeper implications.

What Pasteur had found, in chemical materials, was handedness or chirality, which means the same thing in a more esoteric derivation from the Greek. That most human beings are right-handed, and that seashells often have a preferred direction of twist, was common knowledge. But molecules were a very hazy concept when Pasteur was young, so his affirmation that they must be capable of assuming asymmetric forms was the more remarkable.

In 1874 another chemistry student, 22-year-old Jacobus van't Hoff at Utrecht, figured out how carbon-based molecules like sugar could exhibit handedness. A carbon atom makes four chemical bonds with other atoms. The bonds are deployed in 3-D like the tips of a triangular pyramid, or tetrahedron.

Suppose that the bonds around the base of the pyramid are attached to carbon, nitrogen and oxygen atoms. These may read, going clockwise, either C to N to O, or C to O to N. The two possible molecular arrangements are mirror images of each other, and you can call one left-handed and the other right-handed. Extremely simple really, except that after van't Hoff's intervention chemists had to learn to think in three dimensions.

Chemists compete with natural handedness

While natural products are exclusively biased to one form or the other, ordinary chemical reactions usually make both left-handed and right-handed versions of a molecule, in equal amounts. Chemists want to be able to make one-handed molecules preferentially in a non-living environment, in a test tube or an industrial process. One approach is to separate the two forms of a product, by the technique called chromatography, and throw away the unwanted kind. It is cleverer to manufacture just the form you require.

In 1966 a chemistry graduate student at Kyoto, Ryoji Noyori, found how to make catalysts that would preferentially promote the synthesis of other materials with prearranged handedness. Each catalyst used a metal atom as the driver of the reaction, attached to a suitably shaped carbon compound that would control the shape of the product.

In one very successful case, which Noyori went on to develop in Nagoya, he linked the metal ruthenium to a double naphthalene compound. This catalyst promoted the addition of hydrogen atoms to carbon atoms that were previously linked by a double chemical bond, with high yields of the intended left- or right-handed products. Also using metal-loaded carbon compounds, Barry Sharpless of the Scripps Research Institute in California achieved the handedness desired, in other classes of reactions called epoxidation and dihydroxylation.

By the end of the century, these so-called organometallic catalysts were in widespread use in industry and in research laboratories. They had been perfected to the stage where one molecule of a catalyst could make up to 100,000 molecules of the product. In some cases the man-made catalysts surpassed natural enzymes in their efficiency.

'We have plenty of metals to choose from, each with different catalytic effects, and an unlimited number of left-handed or right-handed molecules to which we can attach the metal atoms, to guide the shaping of the product,' said Noyori. 'So for new and better catalysts there's no end in sight, at least until we have perfect chemical reactions, with no waste and with 100 per cent yields of the correctly shaped molecules.'

The mystery of life's biases

Pasteur's discovery of molecular handedness still resounds through chemistry, biochemistry and astrochemistry, and in speculations about life's origin, where handedness greatly complicates the chemical problem. The shapes of crystals and the effects on light both trace back to the arrangements of atoms in molecules. And as scientists revealed the chemistry of life during the 19th and 20th centuries, they reconfirmed again and again that organisms are extremely choosy.

The spiral of deoxyribonucleic acid, the DNA helix that builds the genes, nearly always twists in the same direction as an ordinary corkscrew. Oppositely twisted DNA, called Z-DNA, sometimes shows up, and may have special genetic functions. But it is not a mirror image of the normal kind of DNA. It cannot be, because it has to fit together chemical subunits that all have twists of their own.

Similarly, the 20 kinds of amino acids used to build proteins are all left-handed molecules. When proteins act as enzymes in the manufacture of other molecules, they communicate their chiral biases. That is why natural sugar, made in plants with the help of enzymes, is one-handed with a predictable effect on polarized light.

The nutritional value of food, the efficacy of medicinal drugs and the potency of scents all depend on the handedness of the molecules. One form of the molecule limonene smells of lemons, and its mirror image, of oranges. More commonly, the wrong versions of biologically active molecules are useless to living things, and sometimes poisonous.

Basic questions about chemical handedness nevertheless remain unanswered. The fact that all living organisms share the same patterns of molecular handedness may be unsurprising, given that they seem to be descended from common ancestors of long ago. But how the very first ultraprimitive cells contrived to assemble and live on selected versions of molecules, and avoid the mirror images, remains a puzzle.

It has even provided a recurring argument, not easily refuted, for those wishing to insist on divine intervention in the primordial biochemistry. Pasteur himself was worried enough to seek a physical cause of the handedness in the living world. He was disappointed when he experimented with powerful magnets and detected no effect on molecular handedness, yet he was convinced that some cosmic explanation would be found. Pasteur insisted: *'L'univers est dissymétrique.'*

The physicists' worlds and antiworlds

His attempt to pasteurize the cosmos with magnets was remembered in 1957, when the Universe was found to be asymmetrical in a different respect. Physicists discovered a bias in ordinary matter, such that all of the ghostly particles called neutrinos spin to the left around their direction of travel. This violated a principle called parity, requiring that particles should be equally capable of spinning in either direction. To find a neutrino spinning to the right, you have to go into the looking-glass world of antimatter, and look for antineutrinos.

The fall of parity provided, for the very first time, an objective way of telling left from right. Human beings have to learn the distinction subjectively, as every drill sergeant knows. In the bowdlerized version: 'Do me the kindness, young gentleman, of showing me in which hand you usually hold a knife. Thank you. So next time, when I invite you to turn right . . . '

If you were to contemplate a rendezvous with an alien astronaut, in an imaginary universe where matter and antimatter are equally common, how would you avoid an accident? Matter and antimatter annihilate each other. So you might be well advised to send a message explaining our custom of shaking hands, and pointing out that we use the hand away from which neutrinos always rotate. If the alien comes from an antiworld, physicists back at his base will be thinking of antineutrinos. Richard Feynman of Caltech, who first recommended this precaution using parity violation, concluded: 'If he puts out his left hand, watch out!'

Some chemists claimed that parity violation was Pasteur's wished-for asymmetry in the Universe, which solved the problem of handedness of molecules at the dawn of life. Physical–chemical effects, they said, made one form of a mirror molecule slightly more stable than the other. The left-handed spin of the neutrino favoured the left-handed bias in amino acids.

This sounded impressive until you looked at the numbers. The difference in stability between left-handed and right-handed molecules due to parity violation is only a million-millionth of a per cent. If that were meaningful, why have chemists not been able to exploit it in laboratory experiments? It should be easier for the chemists to achieve the wanted results, than for the random chemistry on the young Earth.

A long-standing hope was that light might have a more powerful effect. If handedness in molecules affected polarized light, why should polarized light not reciprocate in the course of chemical reactions, and so influence the shaping of molecules? News of success on those lines came in 1997 from Yoshihisa Inoue of Osaka.

He and his colleagues used circularly polarized ultraviolet light, in which the orientation of the wave spontaneously rotates, either clockwise or anticlockwise. Shining it on a material called 4-cyclooctene, with a twisted ring of eight carbon atoms, they produced a majority of molecules with a direction of twist that was sympathetic to the direction of rotation of the polarized light. The team soon obtained similar results with amino acids, key ingredients of life.

'This research has great basic theoretical significance,' Inoue said, 'which is related to the origin of chirality in the biosphere.' There had been a suggestion that polarized light from intensely magnetic neutron stars could affect the handedness of molecules forming in interstellar space. That in turn might conceivably be an origin for materials with a certain bias turning up on the young Earth, before the origin of life. William Bonner and Edward Rubenstein of Stanford had suggested this scenario, and Inoue thought his experiments confirmed its feasibility.

Other scientists considered it more likely that the source of biased molecules needed for life was on the Earth itself. The fact that Pasteur's racemic acid divides neatly into tartrate and antitartrate crystals shows that simple molecules can recognize one another's handedness and settle down, like with like. In other settings, the pre-existence of molecules of a certain handedness may, by their very presence, induce newly forming molecules to follow suit. When the molecules are densely packed, such induction is far more likely than in a dilute solution, a gas, or interstellar space.

'On the primordial Earth, it seems plausible that the selection of handedness in the molecules of life happened in the solid state or on the surface of a solid,' said Reiko Kuroda of Tokyo. She began the 21st century leading a team effort on what she called chiromorphology—meaning the chiral shape, which is expressed at all levels in nature, whether microscopic or macroscopic, and whether animate or inanimate. Her starting point was the chemistry of solids.

Here the aim is to analyse how molecules gather in a crystal, and to see exactly how their handedness affects their interactions at close quarters. The hope is for the invention of new kinds of solid-state chemical reactions that favour a chosen handedness, as the organometallic compounds do. Kuroda found such examples and also designed and made a novel instrument for the study of chirality in the solid state. Besides their possible usefulness for the chemical and pharmaceutical industries, the reactions may make events on the early Earth more comprehensible.

Handedness in plants and animals

Runner beans and bindweed are familiar examples of climbing plants that spiral upwards around sticks, trees or shrubs. They gain an advantage in competing for the available light. Most climbers grow in a right-handed spiral, but some spiral to the left. Enlightenment about the control of this way of growing came from the weed arabidopsis, whose genes were the subject of global investigation and decipherment at the start of the 21st century.

Arabidopsis normally grows straight. Takashi Hashimoto and his colleagues at the Nara Institute of Science and Technology found that they could make seedlings grow with a left-handed spiral if they dosed them with drugs that affect the scaffolding inside the cells of the plant—the long, thin molecules called microtubules. They also discovered mutant arabidopsis plants that spiral to the right in two cases and to the left in another. The altered genes directly affect the construction of the microtubules. It seems that many plants may possess a latent option to spiral but, in those that grow straight, the left and right tendencies counteract each other.

In animals, developmental biologists begin to understand how genes organize the broad, approximate symmetry of a body, with matching pairs of eyes, legs, wings, rib-bones and so on. Crucial asymmetries remain, such as the leftward displacement of the human heart and the arrangement of different chambers and blood vessels on its two sides. How does an embryo tell left from right?

Hundreds of hair-like cilia on the surfaces of embryonic cells beat on the fluid beside them. They operate with a clockwise twist, and as a result they drive fluid past the embryo in a preferred direction. In 1998, working with mouse embryos, Nobutaka Hirokawa, Shigenori Nonaka and their colleagues at Tokyo (later at Osaka) discovered that, at a crucial regulatory centre called the node, the fluid always goes from right to left.

Suspecting that this effect of the cilia informs the developing embryo about which side is which, Nonaka's team went on to prove it. They overrode the natural action by pumping fluid past the mouse embryos, going in the wrong direction. The embryos then developed with left–right reversal of their body-plans. All animals with backbones seem to share this organizational mechanism, which depends simply on the direction of rotation of the cilia hairs.

Cack-handedness and molluscan sports

Subtler still are the variations that make some human individuals left-handed, for throwing, fingering and writing. Roughly ten per cent of us may be natural left-handers, and the figure seems to be even higher among chimpanzees, our closest animal relatives. Your chances of being born left-handed are doubled if your mother is that way inclined, yet most offspring even of two left-handed parents remain right-handed.

Words like sinister, gauche and cack-handed vilify the trait, whilst dextrous and adroit celebrate the supposed superiority of the norm. Otherwise, the many petty inconveniences in a left-hander's life bring no general physical or mental disadvantage. The first men to land on the Moon, Neil Armstrong and Buzz Aldrin, were both left-handed. The list of other lefties extends from Alexander the Great and his tutor Aristotle, to Picasso, Einstein, Gandhi and Navratilova—not to mention Bart Simpson and a sinister disproportion of recent US presidents. Despite many studies and hypotheses, an accepted explanation of human left-handedness remains elusive.

How are the wide variety of molecules in animals and plants systematically arranged to form cells, and the cells gathered into a living organism with a certain handedness? What is its molecular origin? Clues to this fascinating but difficult question may come from animals with coiled shells.

Beautiful left-handed or right-handed twists occur in the shells of snails, whelks and limpets—the asymmetrical molluscs collectively known as gastropods. In roughly conical shells, you see a ridge spiralling towards the tip. Worldwide, the gastropods have a pronounced bias towards right-handed twists in their shells, although some species are predominantly left-handed.

Sometimes a collector is delighted to find one that spirals the wrong way compared with others of the same species. Apparently the affected animals are normal in other respects. What's interesting is that the handedness is determined at a very early stage of development of the gastropod embryos. They follow the typical cleavage pattern called spiral cleavage, the handedness of which carries over into the handedness of the adult shell.

In Tokyo, Reiko Kuroda set out to find genes that affect the handedness of gastropod shells, by looking for mutations. The questions to which she wanted answers gave an impression of the state of play in the study of variable handedness. What molecules produced by the mother affect the direction of coiling in the shells of her offspring? At what times and places, in the early development of the embryo, do relevant genes or gene-products come into play? How do they affect the processes of cell division that build the animal? Are there similarities with genes having left–right effects in other animals?

There are evolutionary questions too. Fossil-hunters have found long-term changes in the preferred handedness of gastropod shells, which may be due either to chance or to natural selection favouring one direction of coiling over the other, in changing circumstances. 'The chirality of coiling seems to have switched several times during the evolutional history of particular species,' Kuroda noted, 'the reason for which has yet to be explained.'

▶ *For more about parity, see* ANTIMATTER. *For more about the genetics of development, see* EMBRYOS. *For more about arabidopsis, see* ARABIDOPSIS.

HIGGS BOSONS

The multi-billion-dollar quest for the mass-maker

IN EDINBURGH'S GOOD OLD DAYS, physics was called Natural Philosophy. It went on in a refurbished hospital in the heart of the old town. Across the street was the Department of Mathematical Physics in the Tait Institute, named in honour of Peter Tait, a 19th-century theorist who wrote the first scientific paper on the flight of golf balls. Alas, the Tait Institute no longer exists and physics conforms to the label Physics, in the suburban science campus on the 42 bus route.

When tourists replaced students in the old town during the summer vacation of 1964, Peter Higgs philosophized at the Tait Institute about the contents of empty space. Quiet though he might have seemed, to anyone looking into his room, he was waging a war of ideas. In those days the scientific bullets still flew about, not as electronic messages, but as letters, papers and journals travelling by ordinary mail.

The postie delivered to Higgs' institute a recent issue of *Physical Review Letters*. An item in it irritated him, igniting the mathematical thinking that, within a week, had pinned down a key idea of modern science, now known as the Higgs mechanism. It explains the origin of mass by supposing that particles of matter are weighed down with condensed energy present in empty space.

The intellectual fight in progress in 1964 concerned no esoteric issue, but why your bathroom scales should register any weight at all when you stand on them. Theories then available could not account for the masses of the various particles that compose the atoms of ordinary matter. A gleam of hope came in 1957, from a successful theory of superconducting metals, which lose all resistance to an electric current at very low temperatures.

Superconductivity depends on electrons forming pairs, and then clubbing together in what physicists call a Bose–Einstein condensate. (Satyen Bose was an Indian theorist, and the other gentleman his keenest supporter.) The condensed electron pairs can travel freely among the charged metal atoms, immune from the tugs between positive and negative charges that normally slow the electrons down. Could a similar condensate account for the mass of matter?

First to seize on the idea was Yoichiro Nambu at Chicago. He imagined special particles, not the normal constituents of matter, clubbing together in empty space and carrying collective energy. By Einstein's most famous pronouncement, that energy was equivalent to mass. The idea was appealing to other theorists, including Higgs, but a difficulty soon appeared.

Jeffrey Goldstone at CERN, Europe's particle physics laboratory in Geneva, came out with a theorem that seemed to scotch the idea. It forced some of Nambu's particles to have zero mass. A debate began, and Philip Anderson of Bell Labs in New Jersey thought that another effect known to particle theorists should cancel Goldstone's. Others considered that the role of relativity could be handled in a subtler and perhaps more correct way.

It was an attempt to refute the latter cure for the Goldstone problem, appearing in *Physical Review Letters*, which provoked Higgs to his flurry of inventiveness when the journal reached Edinburgh. First he shot off a letter picking holes in the refutation. Then he rethought the whole puzzle, piecing together ideas from Nambu, Anderson and others. He found out how to create, mathematically at least, the necessary Bose–Einstein condensate of heavy particles in empty space, and how to attach its energy to other particles. The special type of heavy particle required came to be called the Higgs boson.

'You're famous, Peter'

Unknown to Higgs, François Englert and Robert Brout of the Université Libre de Bruxelles had already arrived at the same idea, although without explaining, as Higgs did, why the condensate of heavy particles should come into being in the first place. *Physical Review Letters* rejected the initial paper from Higgs setting out his theory. But he successfully rewrote it with more sales talk (his expression) and showed how to begin to feed the idea into the theories of subatomic particles and forces then under development.

Only a few theorists paid much attention to begin with, and many were hostile. Higgs gave a talk to a group of them at Harvard in 1966. One of his hosts later confessed that he and his colleagues 'had been looking forward to some fun tearing to pieces this idiot who thought he could get round the Goldstone theorem.' On which Higgs commented, 'Well they did have some fun, but I had fun too!'

The Higgs bandwagon began to roll in 1967. His mechanism became incorporated in the first complete theory of the so-called weak force, which operates in radioactivity and needs particularly massive force-carrying particles. The theory married the weak force with the electric force, and the Higgs mechanism provided force carriers that were heavy sisters of the photons of the electric force. By 1971 a possible flaw in this electroweak story had been eliminated. 'At that stage the theory started being believed,' Higgs recalled. 'A colleague came back from a meeting at CERN and said, "You're famous".'

By 1993 the British science minister, William Waldegrave, was being urged to spend taxpayers' money on an international project to look for the Higgs boson at CERN. He offered prizes of champagne for brief explanations of the phenomenon in terms he could understand. He enjoyed the submission by David Miller, a physicist at University College London, who likened the sea of Higgs bosons, filling space, to a cocktail party of political workers. They are uniformly distributed until a former prime minister, Margaret Thatcher, enters the room.

'All of the workers in her neighbourhood are strongly attracted to her and cluster round her,' Miller wrote. 'As she moves she attracts the people she comes close to, while the ones she has left return to their even spacing. Because of the knot of people always clustered around her she acquires a greater mass than normal, that is, she has more momentum for the same speed of movement across the room.' Translated into three dimensions, and with the complications of relativity, this was the Higgs mechanism for giving mass to particles, Miller said.

An instructive aspect of this analogy is that nobody would dare to impede Margaret Thatcher's progress. She doesn't have to elbow her way through the throng, as if wading through treacle, as some accounts would have it. There's no friction in the Higgs mechanism. But the knots of people represent the condensate of clubbable particles that give the Thatcher particle mass.

A slow game of chess

Looking for the Higgs boson had become a multi-billion-dollar industry by the end of the century, employing thousands of physicists and engineers. The search expressed a heroic quality in high-energy physics, in the tradition of the quest for the Golden Fleece or the Holy Grail. All the predictions about the weak force made with the help of the theory had been confirmed, mainly in experiments at CERN that discovered its force carriers, called the W and Z particles. The theory was also firmly embedded in the most popular account of the origin of the Universe, the Big Bang.

The Higgs boson itself remained an elusive ghost. To expose it in public you would have to concentrate sufficient energy to manufacture it, in some stupendous subatomic collision. The particle was expected to be more than 100 times heavier than a hydrogen atom. It might be beyond the creative power of the most powerful particle accelerators available anywhere in the 1990s.

The possibility that the next big machine would create the Higgs became a carrot to dangle in front of funding agencies and politicians, on both sides of the Atlantic. What could be more important than to find the agent that supposedly infused other particles with mass, throughout the cosmos?

A prominent American physicist, Leon Lederman, advertised the Higgs as *The God Particle* in the title of a book published in 1993. He justified the appellation on the grounds that the Higgs was 'so central to the state of physics today, so crucial to our final understanding of the structure of matter, yet so elusive.' Tongue in cheek, he claimed in the text that the publisher forbade him to call it 'The God-damned Particle'.

Lederman was involved in a campaign to persuade the US government to continue funding the Superconducting Super Collider, a fantastic particle accelerator under construction in Texas. It would use very powerful superconducting magnets to guide particles around a ring 83 kilometres in circumference. The SSC was too fantastic even for the world's richest nation. The ink was not dry on Lederman's book before the US Congress decided to write off the billions of dollars already spent on the project and to stop looking for God that way.

The ball was then in CERN's court, which already had a scheme for a cheaper superaccelerator, originally conceived as a way of beating the SSC to the discovery of the Higgs. CERN's Large Electron–Positron Collider occupied a tunnel 27 kilometres in circumference, straddling the Swiss–French border. Even before this LEP machine began operating in 1989, the Europeans were thinking of putting a more powerful machine in the same tunnel. It would have superconducting magnets and it would collide protons and antiprotons instead of electrons and anti- electrons. The resulting Large Hadron Collider, LHC, would unleash far greater energy for the manufacture of novel particles.

'To choose between the possibilities for new machines is like playing a very slow game of chess, in which CERN may be allowed a decisive move perhaps once every ten years,' the boss of the European lab, Carlo Rubbia, commented in 1990. 'Retaining a position of leadership in the most fundamental of the sciences is vital for Europe's intellectual and cultural life, and for its self-confidence in a scientific age.'

Although not quite in the SSC class, the LHC seemed the best prospect for the world's particle physicists in the wake of that American debacle. Again they put the hope of discovering the Higgs at the top of the list, in explaining to Europe's taxpayers and governments why they wanted the new machine. CERN released pictures showing what the signature of the Higgs should look like in the particle detectors surrounding the collision zones in the LHC.

A Higgs boson could not register directly in the detectors, because it has no electric charge. After an extremely brief lifespan it should produce lighter, more familiar particles travelling at high speed. From hundreds of millions of collisions occurring every second, each producing a confusing spray of particle tracks, high-speed computers would choose about ten events per second for detailed analysis. The simultaneous appearance of two pairs of heavy electrons, called muons, with positive and negative charges, would be, CERN said, a signature of a Higgs.

Prototype magnets for the proposed LHC were being tested in the late 1980s, and multinational teams of experimenters were thinking about the design and construction of the huge detectors. The original hope was that the big new machine would be operational before 2000. That was out of the question at the end of 1994, when the member states of CERN finally agreed to proceed with the LHC, but slowly.

With some hubris, a CERN press release announcing the decision described the machine as 'the first instrument which would allow a complete understanding of the origin of mass'. Operations at full energy with the LHC were visualized for 2008. Subsequent, financial contributions from the USA, Japan and other non-members of CERN seemed to make an earlier completion date possible, perhaps by 2007.

Or would it be found in Illinois?

The delay allowed more time for operating CERN's existing machine, LEP. Just before LEP was shut down at the end of 2000, suggestions that the machine might be seeing liberated Higgs bosons caused a flurry of excitement. But in a tough decision the CERN management stopped operations at LEP, and appropriated its tunnel for building the LHC. Later analysis showed that there were other explanations than the Higgs for the LEP results. During the long lull at CERN, as it waited for the LHC, the quest for the particle shifted back across the Atlantic.

Among the fields of Illinois, west of Chicago, the US government's Fermilab had been upgrading its Tevatron machine. First completed in 1987 as a collider of protons and antiprotons, with a ring of magnets 6.7 kilometres in circumference, the Tevatron won acclaim by discovering two predicted but missing particles of matter, the top quark and the tau neutrino. The upgrade started in 1996, and by 2001 the machine was getting ready to look for the Higgs.

'Fermilab has the playing field to itself,' declared John Womerlsey, a Tevatron experimentalist. In his opinion, there would be just about enough time for the discovery and full confirmation of the existence of the Higgs, before CERN reappeared on the field with its LHC. That was supposing the particle lay within the range of the Tevatron's creative power, which it seemed likely to do.

Exploiting the latest silicon detectors of electrically charged particles, the physicists could look for the short-lived, neutral Higgs producing two charged quarks, a bottom and an antibottom. The task was to tune the machine, by trial and error, to the energy needed for making the Higgs, and to find repeated cases of bottom and antibottom quarks appearing with exactly the same energy of motion.

Several Higgs particles?

Had CERN made the wrong move in the decade-by-decade chess game described by Rubbia, in going for the LHC machine too late? If discovering the Higgs, as a bottom/antibottom picture to put on your T-shirt, were the only purpose of the expensive kit, then you might guess so. But no one doubted that the LHC should be able to make Higgs bosons much more copiously than the Tevatron, and to scrutinize the mass-making mechanisms in greater detail.

Even if the discovery of the Higgs should give assurance that the mass of ordinary matter could be understood in principle, details remained perplexing for theorists and a challenge to experimenters. Why, for example, is the heaviest quark an astounding 350,000 times more massive than the electron? The closest anyone came to an answer was to suggest that several kinds of condensates exist, with a variety of Higgs bosons to match, and each particle of matter interacts with them differently.

Experimenters will have to find out what the ghostly species are that inhabit the Higgs landscape, and exactly how they gather like partygoers around the quarks. So far from the LHC being superfluous if the Tevatron finds the Higgs, the machine at Geneva will open a decade of detailed study of the origin of mass, far more searching than anything preceding it.

Indeed the physicists say that the LHC, colliding protons and antiprotons, will not be enough for this exacting task. They want a successor to LEP, in a giant electron–positron collider using linear instead of circular accelerators. The results from such a machine will be easier to interpret in a wholly open-minded fashion, and to follow them wherever they lead, into new realms of physics beyond the Higgs.

What if the Higgs bosons are never found? They are, after all, only a hypothesis. That outcome would be as devastating for the theories as if, in 1885, Heinrich Hertz in Karlsruhe had failed to discover the radio waves predicted by James Clerk Maxwell's theory of electromagnetism. Peter Higgs himself had no such misgivings. 'If I'm still alive when a Higgs boson does turn up,' he said, 'I should probably like to be invited to the press conference.'

▶ *For more about the weak force story, see* ELECTROWEAK FORCE. *For wider views of particle physics, see* PARTICLE FAMILIES *and* SPARTICLES. *Bose and his Bose–Einstein condensates reappear in* SUPERATOMS, SUPERFLUIDS AND SUPERCONDUCTORS.

HIGH-SPEED TRAVEL

The common sense of special relativity

T HE CHEAP CIGARS with which the young Albert Einstein surrounded himself in a smoky haze were truly dreadful. If he gave you one, you ditched it surreptitiously in Bern's Aare River. So when Einstein went home to his wife and son in the little flat on Kramgasse, after a diligent day as a technical officer (third class) at Switzerland's patent office, he spent his evenings putting the greybeards of physics right, about the fundamentals of their subject. That was how he sought fame, fortune and a better cigar.

In March 1905, a few days after his 26th birthday, he explained the photoelectric effect of particles of light, in a paper that would eventually win him a Nobel Prize. By May he had proved the reality of atoms and molecules in explaining why fine pollen grains dance about in water. He then pointed out previously unrecognized effects of high-speed travel, in his paper on the special theory of relativity, which he finished in June. In September he sent in a postscript saying 'by the way, $E = mc^2$.'

Retrospectively Louis de Broglie in Paris called Einstein's results that year, 'blazing rockets which in the dark of the night suddenly cast a brief but powerful illumination over an immense unknown region.' All four papers appeared in quick succession in *Annalen der Physik*, but the physics community was slow to react. The patent office promoted Einstein to technical officer (second class) and he continued there for another four years, before being appointed an associate professor at Zurich. Only then had he the time and space to think seriously about spacetime, gravity and the general theory of relativity, which would be his masterpiece.

The much simpler idea of special relativity still comes as a nasty shock to students and non-scientists, long after the *annus mirabilis* of 1905. Schoolteachers persist in instilling pre-Einsteinian physics first, in the belief that it is simpler and more in keeping with common sense. That is despite repeated calls from experts for relativity to be learnt in junior schools.

Tampering with time

In the 21st-century world of rockets, laser beams, atomic clocks, and dreams of flying to the stars, the ideas of special relativity should seem commonsensical.

Einstein's Universe is democratic, in that anyone's point of view is as good as anyone else's. Despite the fact that stars, planets, people and atoms rush about in relation to one another, the behaviour of matter is unaffected by the motions. The laws of physics remain the same for everyone.

The speed of light, 300,000 kilometres per second, figures in all physical, chemical and biological processes. For example the electric force that stitches the atoms of your body together is transmitted by unseen particles of light. The details were unknown to Einstein in 1905, but he was well aware that James Clerk Maxwell's electromagnetic theory, already 40 years old, was so intimately linked with light that it predicted its speed. That speed must always be the same for you and for me, or one or other of our bodies would be wonky.

Suppose you are piloting a fighter, and I'm a foot soldier. You fire a rocket straight ahead, and its speed is added to your plane's speed. Say 1000 plus 1000 kilometres per hour, which makes 2000. I'd be pedantic to disagree about that.

Now you shoot a laser beam. As far as you are concerned, it races ahead of your fighter at 300,000 kilometres a second, or else your speed of light would be wrong. But as far as I'm concerned, on the ground, the speed of your fighter can have no add-on effect. Whether the beam comes from you or from a stationary laser, it's still going at 300,000 kilometres a second. Otherwise my speed of light would be wrong.

When you know that your laser beam's speed is added to your fighter's speed, and I know it's not, how can we both be right? The answer is simple, though radical. Einstein realized that time runs at a different rate for each of us. When you say the laser beam is rushing ahead at the speed of light, relative to your plane, I know that you must be measuring light speed with a clock that's running at a slow rate compared with my clock. The difference exactly compensates for the speed of the plane.

Einstein made a choice between two conflicting common-sense ideas. One is that matter behaves the same way no matter how it is moving, and the other is that time should progress at the same rate everywhere. There was no contest, as he saw it. His verdict in special relativity was that it was better to tamper with time than with the laws of physics.

The mathematics is not difficult. Two bike riders are going down a road, side by side, and one tosses a water bottle to the other. As far as the riders are concerned, the bottle travels only the short distance that separates them. But a watcher standing beside the road will see it go along a slanting track. That's because the bikes move forward a certain distance between the moments when the bottle leaves the thrower and when it arrives in the catcher's hand. The watcher thinks the bottle travels farther and faster than the riders think.

If the bottle represents light, that's a more serious matter, because there must be no contradiction between the watcher's judgement of the speed and the riders'. It turns out that a key factor, in reckoning how slow the riders' watches must run to compensate, is the length of the slanting path seen by the watcher. And that you get from the theorem generally ascribed to Pythagoras of Samos. In the 1958 movie *Merry Andrew*, Danny Kaye summed it up in song:

> *Old Einstein said it, when he was getting nowhere.*
> *Give him credit, he was heard to declare,*
> *Eureka!*
> *The square of the hypotenuse of a right triangle*
> *Is equal to the sum of the squares of the two adjacent sides.*

Cognoscenti of mathematical lyrics preferred the casting for the movie proposed in Tom Lehrer's 'Lobachevsky' (1953) to be called *The Eternal Triangle*. The hypotenuse would be played by a sex kitten—Ingrid Bergman in an early version of the song, Brigitte Bardot later. Whether computed with an American, Swedish or French accent, it's the Pythagorean hypotenuse you divide by, when correcting the clock rate in a vehicle that's moving relative to you.

The slowing of time in a moving object has other implications. One concerns its mass. If you try to speed it up more, using the thrust of a space traveller's rocket motor or the electric force in a particle accelerator, the object responds more and more sluggishly, as judged by an onlooker.

The rocket or particle responds exactly as usual to the applied force by adding so many metres per second to its speed, every second. But its seconds are longer than the onlooker's, so the acceleration seems to the onlooker to be reduced. The fast-moving object appears to have acquired more inertia, or mass.

When the object is travelling close to the speed of light, its apparent mass grows enormously. It can't accelerate past the speed of light, as judged by the onlooker. The increase in mass during high-speed travel is therefore like a tacho on a truck—a speed restrictor that keeps the traffic of Einstein's Universe orderly.

A round trip for atomic clocks

Imagine people making a high-speed space voyage, out from the Earth and back again. Although the slow running of clocks stretches time for them, as judged by watchers at home, the travellers have no unusual feelings. Their wristwatches and pulse-rate seem normal. And although the watchers may reckon that the travellers have put on a grievous amount of weight, in the spaceship they feel as spry as ever.

But what is the upshot when the travellers return? Will the slow running of their time, as judged from the Earth, leave them younger than if they had stayed at home? Einstein's own intuition was that the stretching of time should have a lasting effect. 'One could imagine,' he wrote, 'that the organism, after an arbitrarily lengthy flight, could be returned to its original spot in a scarcely altered condition, while corresponding organisms which had remained in their original positions had long since given way to new generations.'

Other theorists, most vociferously the British astrophysicist Herbert Dingle, thought that the idea was nonsensical. This clock paradox, as they called it, violated the democratic principle of relativity, that everyone's point of view was equally valid. The space travellers could consider that they were at rest, the critics said, while the Earth rushed off into the distance. They would judge the Earth's clocks to be running slow compared with those on the spaceship. When they returned home there would be an automatic reconciliation and the clocks would be found to agree.

Reasoned argument failed to settle the issue to everyone's satisfaction. This is not as unusual in physics as you might think. For example the discoverer of the electron, J.J. Thomson, resisted for many years the idea that it was really a particle of matter, even though his own maths said it was. There is often a grey area where no one is quite sure whether the mathematical description of a physical process refers to actual entities and events or is just a convenient fiction that gives correct answers.

For more than 60 years physicists were divided about the reality and persistence of the time-stretching. Entirely rational arguments were advanced on both sides. They used both special relativity and the more complicated general relativity, which introduced the possibility that acceleration could compromise the democratic principle. Indeed some neutral onlookers suspected that there were too many ways of looking at the problem for any one of them to provide a knockdown argument. The matter was not decided until atomic clocks became accurate enough for an experimental test in aircraft.

'I don't trust these professors who get up and scribble in front of blackboards, claiming they understand it all,' said Richard Keating of the US Naval Observatory. 'I've made too many measurements where they don't come up with the numbers they say.' In that abrasive mood it is worth giving a few details of an experiment that many people have not taken seriously enough. On the Internet you'll find hundreds of scribblers who still challenge Einstein's monkeying with time, as if the matter had not been settled in 1971.

That was when Keating and his colleague Joe Hafele took a set of four caesium-beam atomic clocks twice around the world on passenger aircraft. First they flew from west to east, and then from east to west. When returned to the lab, the clocks were permanently out of step with similar clocks that had stayed there. Einstein's intuition had been correct.

Two complications affected the numbers in the experiment. The eastbound aircraft travelled faster than the ground, as you would expect, but the westbound aircraft went slower. That was because it was going against the direction in which the Earth rotates around its axis. At mid-latitudes the speed of the surface rotation is comparable with the speed of a jet airliner. So the westbound airborne clocks should run faster than those on the ground.

The other complication was a quite different Einsteinian effect. In accordance with his general relativity, the airborne clocks should outpace those on the ground. That was because gravity is slightly weaker at high altitude. So the westbound clocks had an added reason to run fast. They gained altogether 273 billionths of a second. If any airline passengers or crew had made the whole westabout circumnavigation, they would have aged by that much in comparison with their relatives on the ground.

In the other direction, the slowing of the airborne clocks because of motion was sufficient to override the quickening due to weak gravity. The eastbound clocks ran slow by 59 billionths of a second, so round-trip passengers would be more youthful than their relatives to that extent. The numbers were in good agreement with theoretical predictions.

The details show you that the experiment was carefully done, but the crucial point was really far, far simpler. When the clocks came home, there was no catch-up to bring them back into agreement with those left in the lab, as expected by the dissenters. The tampering with time in relativity is a real and lasting effect. As Hafele and Keating reported, 'These results provide an unambiguous empirical resolution of the famous clock paradox.'

The Methuselah Effect

If you want to voyage into the future, and check up on your descendants a millennium from now, a few millionths of a second gained by eastabout air travel won't do much for you. Even when star-trekking astronauts eventually achieve ten per cent of the speed of light, their clocks will lag by only 1 day in 200, compared with clocks on the Earth. Methuselah reportedly survived for 969 years. For the terrestrial calendar to match that, while you live out your three score and ten in a spaceship, Mistress Hypotenuse says that you'll have to move at 99.74 per cent of light speed.

Time-stretching of such magnitude was verified in an experiment reported in 1977. The muon is a heavy electron that spontaneously breaks up after about 2 millionths of a second, producing an ordinary electron. In a muon storage ring at CERN in Geneva, Emilio Picasso and his colleagues circulated the particles at

99.94 per cent of the speed of light and recorded their demise with electron detectors. The high-speed travel prolonged the muons' life nearly 30-fold.

The Methuselah Effect in muons has physical consequences on the Earth. Cosmic rays coming from the stars create a continuous rain of fast-moving muons high in the Earth's atmosphere. They are better able to penetrate the air than electrons are, but they would expire before they had descended more than a few hundred metres if their lives were not stretched by their high speeds. In practice the muons can reach the Earth's surface, even penetrating into the rocks. You can give Einstein the credit or the blame for the important part that muons play in the cosmic radiation that contributes to genetic mutations in living creatures, and affects the weather at low altitudes.

If you want to exploit special relativity to keep you alive for as long as possible, the most comfortable way to travel through the Universe will be to accelerate steadily at 1g—the rate at which objects fall under gravity at the Earth's surface. Then you will have no problems with weightlessness, and you can in theory make amazing journeys during a human lifetime. This is because the persistent acceleration will take you to within a whisker of the speed of light.

Your body-clock will come almost to a standstill compared with the passage of time on Earth and on passing stars. Through your window you will see stars rushing towards you, and not only because of the direct effect of your motion towards them. The apparent distance that you have to go keeps shrinking, as another effect of relativity at high speeds.

In a 1g spaceship, you can for example set out at age 20, and travel right out of our Galaxy to the Andromeda Galaxy, which is 2 million light-years away. By starting in good time to slow down (still at 1g) you can land on a planet in that galaxy and celebrate your 50th birthday there. Have a look around before setting off for home, and you can still be back for your 80th birthday. But who knows what state you'll find the Earth to be in, millions of years from now?

If stopping is not an objective, nor returning home, you can traverse the entire known Universe during a human lifetime, in your 1g spaceship. Never mind that it is technologically far-fetched. The fact that Uncle Albert's theory says it's permissible by the laws of physics should make the Universe feel a little cosier for us all.

'A sure bet'

Astronomers have verified Einstein's intuition that the speed of light is unaffected by the speed of the source. For example, changes in the wavelength of light often tell them that one star is revolving around another. Sometimes it is swinging towards us, and sometimes receding from us on the other side of its companion. For a pulsating star, the time between pulses varies too.

Suppose Einstein was wrong, and the speed of light is greater when the star is approaching, and slower when it is receding. Then the arrival times of pulses from a pulsating star orbiting a stellar companion will vary in an irregular manner. That doesn't happen.

X-rays are a form of light, and in 1977 Kenneth Brecher of the Massachusetts Institute of Technology applied this reasoning to an X-ray star in a nearby galaxy, the Small Magellanic Cloud. There, the X-ray source SMC X-1 is orbiting at 300 kilometres per second around its companion, yet there is no noticeable funny business in the arrival of the X-rays. So the proposition about the invariance of the speed of light from a moving source is correct to at least one part in a billion.

By 2000 Brecher was at Boston University, and using observations of bursts of gamma rays in the sky to make the proposition even more secure. The greater the distance of an astronomical source, the more time there would be for light pulses travelling at different speeds to separate before they reach our telescopes. The gamma bursters are billions of light-years away.

In all credible theories of what these objects may be, pieces of them are moving relative to one another other at 30,000 kilometres per second or more. Yet some observed gamma-ray bursts last for only a thousandth of a second. If there were the slightest effect of the motions of the sources on the light speed, a burst could not remain so brief, after billions of years of space travel.

With this reasoning Brecher reduced any possible error in Einstein's proposition to less than one part in 100 billion billion. He said, 'The constancy of the speed of light is as close to a sure bet as science has ever found.'

▶ For $E = mc^2$ as the postscript to special relativity, see ENERGY AND MASS. For general relativity, see GRAVITY. For other tricks with clocks, see TIME MACHINES.

HOPEFUL MONSTERS

How they herald a revolution in evolution

AMONG THE MANY POIGNANT STORIES of discoveries shunned, Barbara McClintock's had a moderately happy ending in 1983, when she won a Nobel Prize at the age of 81. But that followed decades of literally tearful frustration.

Her work, done somewhat reclusively at the Cold Spring Harbor Laboratory, New York, was so ignored that she hesitated even to publish her latest results. She uncovered a new world of hereditary phenomena unknown to geneticists and evolutionists, simply by careful study of discoloured maize. But that was McClintock's problem. Most biologists who were aware of her work thought it concerned only a peculiarity in a cultivated crop.

Breeders and farmers of maize are familiar with an instability that results in patches of differently coloured kernels appearing on the cob, in various shades of brown. In research begun in the 1940s, McClintock traced the processes involved. She found genes jumping about. They can change their positions within the chromosomes in which the maize genes are packaged, or vault from one chromosome to another. Her mobile genetic elements, or transposons, are now textbook stuff.

'We are all, unfortunately, dependent on recognition,' wrote a close friend, Howard Green of the Harvard Medical School. 'We grow with it and suffer without it. When transposons were demonstrated in bacteria, yeast and other organisms, Barbara rose to a stratospheric level in the general esteem of the scientific world and honours were showered upon her. But she could hardly bear them.'

McClintock's discoloured maize was only the thin end of a very large wedge inserted into pre-existing ideas about heredity. Jumping genes in trypanosomes, the parasites that cause sleeping sickness, showed internal rearrangements like those in maize. By changing the surface molecules of the trypanosomes, the jumping genes help them to evade the defensive antibodies in previously infected animals. And genes controlling cell growth in animals, jumping from one chromosome to another, turned out to be a cause of cancer.

The jumping genes also gave a brand-new slant on how genes form and change. Alas, the young fogies who ignored McClintock's discoveries had hidebound ideas about genes and their behaviour. Only in the 21st century is it glaringly obvious that jumping genes play a major part in evolution.

McClintock died in 1992. What a pity she didn't live just a few years more to see the reading of genomes—complete sets of genes of bacteria, plants and animals. These revealed jumping genes on a colossal scale. In the weed arabidopsis, for example, the genome analysts identified 4300 mobile elements accounting for at least ten per cent of the DNA. Most of the genes in the regions of genetic material rich in transposons are inactive.

Normally the unwanted transposons are marked with chemical attachments— simple methyl groups (CH_3)—that silence them. At Japan's National Institute of Genetics, Tetsuji Kakutani and his colleagues experimented with a form of arabidopsis in which the mutation of a single gene impaired this methylation. Other genes, normally silenced, were de-repressed, so that there were knock-on effects, and these proved to be inheritable. The mutation also destabilized the weed's genetic structure, by leaving some transposons free to jump. In 2001 the team reported remarkable consequences.

'It was quite dramatic,' Kakutani said. 'We had a dwarf form of the weed, itself produced by a transposon jump in a mutant with reduced methylation. Then its descendants showed mosaic structure of shape as jumping continued. For example, within a single plant, one stem grew taller with normal leaves, while other parts remained dwarf. The changes were all inheritable, so we were watching with our own eyes a surprising natural mechanism available for evolution.'

Crossing a valley of death

By then the world's chief factory for accelerated evolution was in Chicago, in the Howard Hughes Medical Institute on East 58th Street. In the course of a few years, 1998–2002, Susan Lindquist reported some very odd-looking flies, yeasts and weeds. In these cases jumping genes were not involved, but like Kakutani's weeds the products gave a stunning new insight into how species evolve. They were hopeful monsters.

That term came into biology in 1933, coined by Richard Goldschmidt of the Kaiser-Wilhelm-Institut für Biologie in Berlin-Dahlem. Technically, a monster is a creature with structural deformities. By a hopeful monster Goldschmidt meant a fairly well coordinated new organism, quite different from its colleagues, appearing in the course of a major evolutionary change. For him, such a hypothetical creature was needed to explain jumps in evolution.

Darwin's natural selection operates by favouring the individuals within a species best adapted to their way of life. It weeds out harmful mutations in a very conservative way. Suppose now you want a feathered dinosaur to evolve into a flying bird. A great many changes are required—to limbs, muscles and brain, just for starters.

If you do the revamp slowly, gene by gene, as required in the then-emergent neo-Darwinist theory, you will have creatures that are neither good dinosaurs nor good birds. They will be selected against, to perish in a valley of death long before they reach the sanctuary of Bird Mountain. Goldschmidt wanted hopeful monsters that would make such transitions more quickly.

In Chicago, six decades later, Lindquist and her team made fruit flies that had deformed wings or eyes. At first sight you'd think that they were just another batch of the *Drosophila melanogaster* monsters, produced routinely by genetic mutations, which have populated genetics labs for many decades. But in Lindquist's flies the output of several genes changed at the same time, making them hopeful monsters in Goldschmidt's sense.

Not just a dirty word

To see such experiments in historical context, go back two centuries to Paris during the Napoleonic Wars. In 1809, Jean-Baptiste de Lamarck of the Muséum National d'Histoire Naturelle gave the earliest coherent account of evolution. 'He first did the eminent service,' Darwin said of him, 'of arousing attention to the probability of all change in the organic, as well as in the inorganic world, being the result of law, and not of miraculous interposition.'

Lamarck also invented the term *biologie* and classified the invertebrate animals. But history has not been kind to him. 'Lamarckian' became a dirty word, for referring to a supposedly ludicrous theory of how evolution proceeds. Lamarck's giraffe famously acquired its long neck by striving to nibble leaves high in the trees that other animals could not reach. The exercise affected heredity in its offspring. Generation by generation the neck got longer.

It was a very slow process, Lamarck thought. But seen in retrospect there was a feature of his theory that would chime with the idea of hopeful monsters and the rapid evolution they might make possible. This was the possibility that several or many individuals might acquire the same alterations simultaneously, thereby greatly improving the chances of finding a similar mate and reproducing, to carry the changes forward to new generations.

Lamarck's belief that characteristics acquired by organisms during their lives could be inherited was at odds with the idea of natural selection advanced by Darwin in *The Origin of Species* (1859). In this theory, an animal that by chance happens to have a longer neck than others in the herd may have an advantage when food is scarce. It is therefore more likely to leave surviving offspring, also with long necks. Hence Darwin's giraffe.

When theorists reworked Darwin's ideas in the 20th century, microbes, plants and animals came to be seen as passive recipients of genes from their parents. These either passed on to future generations, if their owners thrived, or were extinguished if they did not. Except for occasional random mutations, harmful or favourable, nothing that happened to a creature in the course of its life could make any difference to the genes. Hard-line Darwinists ruled out any idea that acquired traits could be inherited.

Some effects seen in laboratory experiments looked Lamarckian. In 1953 Conrad Waddington at Edinburgh reported a strain of fruit flies with abnormal wings produced by subjecting embryos to a high temperature for a few hours. Initially, this treatment produced an absence of cross-veins in the wings in about half the flies subjected to the heat shock. But when Waddington bred and rebred from the cross-veinless flies, repeating the heat shock each time, the proportion rose. Eventually the abnormality persisted in generations not subjected to the heat.

Although he boldly described the outcome as 'Genetic assimilation of an acquired character,' Waddington was at pains to interpret it in Darwinian terms. No alteration occurred in the genes, he said. Instead, a particular cryptic combination of pre-existing genes happened to be favoured in the artificial environment of the experiment. Later he described as an 'epigenetic landscape' the choice of routes that an embryo might follow, as genes and environment interacted during its development.

Ahead of his time, Waddington teetered on the brink of a big discovery. He was tolerant of Lamarckian ideas and an outspoken critic of neo-Darwinist theory and its failure to account for big evolutionary changes. With a little Darwinian help he made some hopeful monsters. If others had taken his cross-veinless flies more seriously, a revolution in evolution theory might have begun 40 years earlier than it did. But revealing exactly how the heat shock affected the flies would require techniques not available to Waddington before his death in 1975.

Molecular biologists found other chinks in the neo-Darwinist armour. Many genes are surplus to requirements and remain inactive. Within the sausage-like chromosomes that carry them, the chemical marks on the unwanted genes, by methylation, prevent the cell's machinery from reading them. But the marks can change during an organism's life, activating genes that were silent in its parents.

If changes in the gene marks become inheritable by the organism's own offspring, the marks are then a form of epigenetic heredity—meaning inheritance over and above the genes themselves. When the altered marks arise not by chance, but as a result of the organism's experience of its environment, then you have an inheritance of acquired characteristics, in accordance with the heresy of Lamarck.

Important epigenetic effects also became apparent to biologists finding out how a fertilized egg develops into a well-shaped plant or animal. Here the marks on genes play a key part in regulating the process. And the embryo receives special molecular signals from the mother, quite independently of the general run of inheritance, that tell it for example where to grow its head.

In 1995, Eva Jablonka at Tel-Aviv and Marion Lamb at Birkbeck College London threw down a gauntlet to the neo-Darwinists. In a book called *Epigenetic Inheritance and Evolution: the Lamarckian Dimension* they reviewed what was known about various molecular modes of epigenetic heredity. They predicted a unified theory of genetics and developmental biology that would reconcile natural selection and acquired changes.

Jablonka and Lamb were shrewd in their timing. In the years immediately after their book's publication, epigenetics became a buzzword in biology. Many meetings and scientific papers were devoted to the subject. And fresh experiments confirmed the force of their reasoning. By 1999 the authors were able to report, in a preface to a paperback edition, 'The initially strong and almost unanimous opposition to some of our ideas has been replaced by a general, although somewhat grudging, acceptance of many of them.'

Cook the eggs gently?

Most remarkable of the new epigenetic experiments were those of Susan Lindquist at Chicago, making hopeful monsters in the zebra-striped building on East 58th Street. Whether they can and should be called Lamarckian is a moot point. Neither Lamarck nor Darwin had any inkling of the molecular dances going on, with genes and marks. Perhaps the time has come for biologists to put the old disputes behind them, and simply concentrate on what the hopeful monsters have to say, about how evolution may happen.

Working with Suzanne Rutherford, Lindquist first revisited the inheritable effects of heat on the embryos of fruit flies, which Waddington had investigated many years before. The new techniques of molecular biology enabled the researchers to trace what was happening far more precisely. They revealed the first molecular mechanism ever known, for driving evolution along in response to a change in the environment.

The experiments are easier to understand if you know the answer first. It revolves around a molecule called heat shock protein 90, or Hsp90 for short. Like other organisms, when the fruit fly embryo gets too warm, it relies on various heat shock proteins to protect other vital molecules. They act as chaperones to proteins that are being newly manufactured, to allow them to fold into the correct shapes required for their work as chemically active enzymes or as other components of living cells.

Hsp90 has a routine task too. Even in cool conditions, it chaperones especially important proteins, called signal transducers. These switch genes on or off, according to the requirements of different parts of the body, during the development from an egg to an adult.

In a word, signal transducers shape the fly and all its parts. By helping in the shaping of the signal transducers, Hsp90 stands in relation to the developing embryo as an architect's representative does to the construction crew erecting a building. If he got distracted, you could finish up with a very odd-looking structure.

A high temperature distracts the Hsp90 molecules by calling them away like volunteer firemen. They have to assist other heat shock proteins in trying to stop vital enzymes unravelling. As a result, supervision of the body's development is less strict—as if a builder might be left free to say, 'I've always fancied putting in a spiral staircase.' Defective signal transducers can liberate hankerings latent in the fly's genes but normally suppressed, for reshaping wings, for example.

'This sounds like a very bad thing,' Lindquist commented, 'and no doubt it is for most of the individuals. But for some, the changes might be beneficial for adapting to a new environment. Cryptic genetic variations exposed in this way become the fodder for evolution.'

How did Rutherford and Lindquist establish all this? Mainly by starting with mutant flies that inherited the gene coding for Hsp90 from only one parent, instead of from both as usual. As a result, with Hsp90 in short supply, when the scientists reared the embryos in hot conditions the signal transducers went haywire, in a small minority of the flies.

Different populations of mutant flies gave rise to characteristic monsters. In one population, they might have thick-veined wings, in another, legs instead of antennae. It was as if a few latent genes in each population were particularly ready for release, with drastic effects on the fly's construction.

Acting as natural selection might do, in a novel environment, the experimenters then chose to breed new populations from the altered flies. The changes were inherited. After several rounds of inbreeding, as many as 90 per cent of the flies were visibly abnormal, even though the Hsp90 deficiency had disappeared.

Cross-breeding of different kinds of altered flies quickly multiplied the number of affected genes. This laboratory evolution generated hopeful monsters with many latent genes rapidly selected for novel activity. There was no need for any new genetic mutation to appear, as neo-Darwinists would expect.

If you think of the fly experiments as a simulation of what might happen in the real world, the chances of hopeful monsters surviving are much improved because there are so many of them. In the traditional view, genetic mutations crop up in single individuals and then have to fight against long odds to establish themselves widely. Even finding a mate would be a problem for a mutant animal in the neo-Darwinist scenario.

The Rutherford–Lindquist experiment showed similar changes occurring in many individuals at the same time—even though they were a small percentage of their populations. That means that a new form, deploying several previously ineffective genes, could become predominant in a population almost instantly. And this without the need for any genes to be newly modified by mutation. In these experiments the new characteristics are not 'acquired' from the environment, but 'exposed' by it.

Here at last was the glimmer of an explanation of how novel species appeared so suddenly, in the fossil record of life on the Earth. Perhaps if you gently cooked the live eggs of a feathered dinosaur, in the Mesozoic sunshine, you could achieve several of the rapid changes in body-plan needed to produce a bird. But to relate the laboratory discoveries to the real events of past and present evolution in the wild may require decades of research. For a start, close comparisons between genomes of related organisms should unearth some of the sudden changes in the past affecting several genes during embryonic development, whether due to negligent action of the heat shock protein or to other molecular mechanisms.

From mad cows to new yeast

Wearing a medical hat, Lindquist had been busy with her Chicago team in the worldwide research that followed the outbreak of mad cow disease in Britain. Implicated was a new kind of disease-causing agent, a misshapen form of a protein called a prion. In 1996–97, she helped to confirm the molecular biology of mad cows by studying a much less harmful prion occurring in baker's yeast. Called Sup35, this yeast prion is capable of forming fibres, when a misshapen form of the molecule persuades normal Sup35 molecules to adopt its defective shape.

With Heather True, Lindquist went on see what possible function the prion might have. Why should yeast tolerate a potentially dangerous material in its molecular composition? The answer came when the investigators saw the infected yeast changing its appearance under the microscope. This happened when they subjected the yeast to environmental stress, by changing its food or exposing it to mild poisons. The yeast prion turned out to be another agent for evolution by epigenetic change.

As with the heat shock protein in the fruit flies, its effect was to uncover genes previously silent. In this case, the molecular effect was to allow the cells' machinery to bypass 'stop' signs in the genetic code that normally prevented the manufacture of certain other proteins. So, again, the prion allowed some of the cells to exploit latent variations in several genes at once, and so to thrive better in a changing environment. In modified strains, the genetic innovations were inheritable even when the prion itself disappeared from the scene.

Lindquist was quick to scotch any inference that mad cow disease might be a good thing. But she had, predictably, a battle with hard-line neo-Darwinists. For them it had been grievous enough to learn that prion shapes represent a novel mode of heredity quite unknown in their careful reckonings of the genes. To have them now offered as a mechanism of evolution, helping to solve the enigma of sudden evolution by simultaneous changes affecting many genes, was more than the neo-Darwinists could stomach.

Their continuing influence meant that the journal *Nature* could not publish True and Lindquist's prion results without an accompanying put-down in the same issue. British critics roundly declared that the concerted evolution of independent genetic changes was not an enigma. 'The power of natural selection is that it assembles a series of changes, each individually tested; mechanisms that produce large variations, involving several random changes, are unlikely to be helpful.'

As is often the way in scientific revolutions, it was hard not feel sorry for evolutionists who saw their 100-year-old edifice swaying in the gale from the Windy City. In fairness to everyone, it should be said that the epigenetic discoveries were not only heretical, but also very surprising.

● Hardly even monstrous

Plants have heat shock proteins too. With Christine Queitsch and Todd Sangster, Lindquist cut the availability of Hsp90 in seedlings of the weed arabidopsis, using chemical inhibitors. Again, all manner of strange organisms resulted with, for example, altered leaf shapes and colours.

This time the Chicago team refused to call them monstrous. Although sometimes very different from the normal arabidopsis, some of the altered seedlings already looked like quite sensible plants. You could even guess how they might be better suited than their ancestors to particular environmental settings.

By the time the arabidopsis report was out in 2002, Lindquist had moved to Massachusetts to become head of the Whitehead Institute for Biomedical Research. She took several of her team of monster-makers with her and onlookers wondered what they would come up with next. But as one of the arabidopsis experimenters was careful to stress, the evolutionary relevance of the hopeful monsters was still unverified.

'We have not yet performed the rigorous experiments required for this hypothesis to be fully accepted by the evolutionary biology community,'

Sangster remarked. 'Therefore it's a rather different case than Barbara McClintock's transposons, for which the proofs are already innumerable.'

Most exciting and challenging for young biologists is the lively reunified science implicit in the hopeful monsters. No longer can microbes, plants or animals be seen as passive recipients and passers-on of active genes. They have hidden genetic resources that they can draw upon in times of stress. Using techniques of embryonic growth, they can evolve extremely quickly in response to changing environmental circumstances. The molecular geneticists have, by their discoveries, summoned a gathering of the evolutionary, ecological and developmental clans, which can now set off into undiscovered territory, in a new phase of the human effort to understand what life is all about.

▶ *For the tale of the neo-Darwinists, see* EVOLUTION. *For apparent experiments in the fossil record, see* CAMBRIAN EXPLOSION *and* HUMAN ORIGINS. *Related topics are* MOLECULES EVOLVING, PRIONS *and* EMBRYOS.

HOTSPOTS
Are there really chimneys deep inside the Earth?

I CELAND'S PARLIAMENT is the world's oldest surviving legislature. It first met in AD 930 in Thingvellir, a pleasant natural arena 50 kilometres north-east of Reykjavik. Over the intervening millennium the valley has become almost 20 metres broader, as if to make room for a growing population to gather. First with laser beams and then by ground positioning with navigation satellites, geophysicists have measured the widening still in progress.

Thingvellir is in the main fissure of the Mid-Atlantic Ridge, which snakes from the Southern Ocean to the Arctic, mostly under water. All along the ridge, hot basalt rises and freezes, making the ocean floor wider. So Iceland gains in size in hamburger fashion, from the middle out. You can stand on a hillside overlooking Thingvellir and think of the North American Plate growing westwards on one side, and the Eurasian Plate, eastwards on the other.

Geologically speaking Iceland is very young, being the largest of many islands added to the world by recent volcanic activity under water. It occupies the place where Greenland parted from Scotland 54 million years ago at the origin of the

Atlantic's northernmost arm. As the ocean grew, the present ground of Iceland first poked its head above the waves about 20 million years ago. Now the volcanic fire co-exists uneasily with the ice of Europe's largest glaciers.

In 1963 the crew of a fishing boat noticed the sea literally boiling off Iceland's south coast, and within 24 hours a brand-new volcanic appendage had appeared, a small island now called Surtsey. Ten years later, the citizens of Heimaey barely saved their coastal town from erasure by the nearby Eldfell volcano. They hosed the lava to make a dam of frozen rock. An eruption of the Gjalp volcano underneath the Vatnajökull glacier in 1995 caused spectacular flooding.

Geysers are so-called after Geysir, a famous gusher of natural hot water and steam. In Iceland you can bathe outdoors in hot pools and rivers, or in your own bathroom using geothermal domestic water heating. The country meets nearly half of all its energy needs by tapping the heat coming out of the ground. So Icelanders hardly need to be told that they inhabit one of the world's hotspots.

It is also a prime place for geological and geophysical research. The question of why Iceland emerged from the ocean, when most of the Mid-Atlantic Ridge did not, is a favourite conundrum. For 100 years geological big shots from Europe and North America have explained Iceland to the Icelanders, first this way and then that. Students think about the theories while they enjoy their baths, and wonder if any of them is true.

The plume theory

One story dominated the accounts of Icelandic geology in the closing decades of the 20th century. In its modern form, it started with Tuzo Wilson at Toronto and Jason Morgan at Princeton, who were among the founders of the theory of plate tectonics in the 1960s. Present-day geological action occurs mainly at the boundaries between plates, the pieces of the Earth's outer shell that move about, carrying the continents with them. To account for volcanic eruptions occurring in the middle of the plates, Wilson and Morgan both favoured mantle plumes.

The mantle is the main rocky body of the Earth, between the relatively thin crust and the molten iron core. A mantle plume is visualized as an ascending mass of rocks, supposedly rising vertically towards the surface, as if in a narrow chimney. The rocks in the plume do not melt until the enormous pressures of the Earth's interior ease off close to the surface. But even solid rocks can flow slowly, and those that are warmer and therefore less dense than their surroundings will rise inexorably.

In the classic version of the theory, the plumes are said to originate at or close to the Earth's liquid iron core, 3000 kilometres below the surface. That is ten times deeper than the sources of hot rocks that normally build the ocean floor at the mid-ocean ridges.

The mantle plumes supposedly take effect independently of plate movements. Indeed, their supporters say that plumes help to move the plates around. And whilst the surface plates and the continents that they carry can slither anywhere around the Earth, plumes are said to be anchored in the mantle. In this picture, Iceland is the result of the plate boundary of the Mid-Atlantic Ridge drifting over a fixed mantle plume.

On the other side of the world, Hawaiian islanders tell how the volcano goddess Pele carried her magic spade south-eastwards across the sea, making one island after another. Finally she settled in Kilauea, the currently active volcano on the south-east corner of the big island of Hawaii. That Pele still has itchy feet is shown by activity already occurring offshore, near Kilauea.

Geology chimes with the folklore. Starting with former islands to the far north-west, most of which are now eroded to submerged seamounts, the members of the Hawaiian chain have punched their ways to the surface one after another. Huge cones of basaltic lava have arisen from the deep ocean floor at intervals of about a million years. On the youngest island, Mauna Kea and Mauna Loa stand 4200 metres above sea level and 10,000 metres above the surrounding sea floor. Older islands in Pele's production line, including the most populated, Oahu, are plainly wasting away as the ancient seamounts did before them.

In 1963, Tuzo Wilson proposed that the floor of the Pacific Ocean is sliding in a north-westerly direction over a fixed mantle plume. By the time Jason Morgan returned to the idea, in 1971, the Pacific Plate was recognized as one of the mobile pieces of the Earth's shell, and Hawaii was still the prime exhibit. He pointed out that two matching lines of islands and seamounts, the Tuamotu and Austral Islands, seemed to be due to other hotspots. Around the world, Morgan nominated 16 hotspots corresponding to mantle plumes, including Iceland.

Not everyone agreed with him. Dan McKenzie of Cambridge, co-founder of plate tectonics, said at the time that you could explain the Hawaiian phenomenon equally well by a leaky fracture in the sea floor. Nevertheless, the deep-rooted mantle plume was a very pretty idea and it caught on, becoming standard stuff in textbooks. For the theory's supporters, hotspots and mantle plumes were almost interchangeable terms.

Mapping plate movements

Earth scientists fell into the habit of blaming all volcanoes away from plate margins on mantle plumes, under continents as well as the oceans. Morgan had suggested the hotspot of Yellowstone Park in Wyoming as a plume candidate, and soon Ethiopia, Kenya, Germany and many other mid-continental places were added. Up for consideration was almost anywhere, not on a plate boundary, that advertised hot springs for tourists. As a result, the list of suspected plumes grew from 16 to more than 100.

Writing in the early 1980s, Hans-Ulrich Schmincke of Ruhr-Universität, Bochum, called mantle plumes 'one of the most revolutionary and stimulating concepts in the framework of plate tectonics'. But he stressed that it was only a hypothesis. 'It is not clear at present whether the measured geochemical and geophysical hotspot features can be used to infer well-defined hotspots directly or are merely the effects of deeper causes whose exact nature and geometry are still unknown.'

One thing you could try to do with hotspots was to use them as fixed reference points to define plate movements more precisely. Measurements of sea floor spreading, or of sliding along fault lines, gave only relative motions between the plates. With hotspots supposedly anchored, you could relate the superficial plate movements to latitudes and longitudes on the main body of the Earth's interior.

Iceland was a case in point. If you assumed that the Atlantic islands of the Azores, the Cape Verde group and Tristan da Cunha were created by fixed hotspots, the geometry told you that the growing North Atlantic and surrounding territory moved bodily westwards. According to this reckoning, the plume that eventually showed up under the Mid-Atlantic Ridge in Iceland was previously under Greenland.

'No mantle plume under Iceland'

It was all good fun, but evidence for the plumes was scanty. In 1995–96, Icelandic, American and British geophysicists joined in the Iceland Hotspot Project, to make a determined exploration below the surface. To a permanent set of seven seismic stations operated by Iceland's Met Office, they added 35 temporary sensors, scattered all over the island.

In incoming seismic waves from more than 100 earthquakes worldwide, the scientists looked for slight differences in the arrival times at the various stations. They could then picture the subterranean hot rocks, slowing down the waves. The network was good for exploring down to a depth of about 450 kilometres.

Gillian Foulger at Durham knew the island better than most of the foreign geophysicists in the team, having been a researcher at Háskóli Íslands, the university in Reykjavik. After years of mulling over the seismic results, she became totally sceptical about the mantle plume. Hot rock was traceable far down, as you would expect if a chimney went deep, but she thought it was petering out, at about 400 kilometres' depth.

The shape of the hot platform under Iceland did not accord with expectations of the plume theory. In particular there was no special feature under the sea towards Greenland. That would be expected if the plume approached from that side of the island, before it coincided with the Mid-Atlantic Ridge.

'There's no mantle plume under Iceland,' Foulger declared. 'In my opinion the reason why the lava has heaped up so much there is that the Mid-Atlantic Ridge crosses an ancient fault line left over from a collision of continents 400 million years ago.'

Improved seismic images of the Earth's interior as a whole bolstered Foulger's scepticism. They came from ever cleverer and more comprehensive tracking of earthquake waves worldwide. By the 1990s a method of computer analysis called seismic tomography was generating vivid though rather hazy 3-D pictures of the entire mantle. It picked out relatively cold regions where seismic waves travelled faster than usual, and hot regions where the waves were slowed down.

Deep features shown in the tomographic images included old, cold, dense pieces of crust from extinct oceans sinking back into the Earth, to a depth of perhaps 1500 kilometres. The less dense rock in a plume, on the other hand, should stand out as a tall, narrow column of warmth. A hundred deep-rooted plumes, or even just Jason Morgan's original 16, should make the Earth's mantle look like a spiny sea urchin.

It didn't. The plumes of the classic theory were not visible in the tomographic images. Certainly not under Iceland, the warm platform of which could be seen going down a few hundred kilometres, but with no warm column below it.

From plumes to superplumes

Unabashed, plume theorists reasoned that warm regions were hard to see in the usual method of analysis of seismic waves. Barbara Romanowicz and Yuancheng Gung of UC Berkeley developed another technique, which took account of the intensities of the waves, in order to highlight hotter-than-usual regions in the mantle. Their images still revealed nothing much under Iceland, but they did show two superplumes.

Located under the central Pacific Ocean and under Africa, the superplumes are tall, broad columns of hot rock. Apparently they feed heat directly from the Earth's core towards the surface, but in the upper mantle they spread out like fingers to provide individual hotspots. According to the Berkeley geophysicists they also supply hot material for the mid-ocean ridges. 'Most hotspots are derived from the two main upwellings,' Romanowicz and Gung declared. 'Exceptions may be hotspots in North America and perhaps Iceland.'

At the start of the 21st century, the Earth's interior was still mystifying. The idea of many independent, chimney-like plumes in the mantle seemed to have failed. Continuing disputes concerning the nature of hotspots and the role of superplumes were part of a larger wrangle about how the plates and continents are moved about on the surface.

There is more to play for than just accounting for the Earth's present hotspots. In the past, huge spillages of molten rock from the interior, called flood basalts, created unusual provinces in several parts of the world, including central Russia, India and the north-western USA. Plume theorists saw the flood basalts as the first fruits of new mantle plumes rising from the Earth's core and bursting through the crust. If that isn't the reason, other explanations are badly needed.

A new phase of the debate began in 2002. Plume sceptics suggested that some hotspots are simply places where the crust is in unusually strong tension, whilst others coincide with old subducted plates, which have a lower melting point than the typical rocks of the mantle. Gillian Foulger commented: 'It seems that, deep down, hotspots may not even be hot!'

▶ *For the larger wrangle, see* PLATE MOTIONS *and* FLOOD BASALTS. *Volcanoes of the other sort, which sprout beside ocean trenches, are the theme in* VOLCANIC EXPLOSIONS.

HUMAN ECOLOGY
How to progress beyond eco-colonialism

I N BOLIVIA, the high plateau or Altiplano stands at a chilly, thin-air altitude of 3800 metres, between the majestic snow-capped ranges of the Andes. Especially bleak is the marshy ground towards Titicaca, the great lake of the Altiplano. Here, in the late 20th century, Aymara Indian farmers scraped a living on small rises, avoiding the lowest ground. But if their potatoes didn't rot in the wet, the frequent frosts threatened them. Unable to pay for fertilizers, the farmers often had to let the poor soil lie fallow for several years, in this most marginal of cropland.

In this same territory 1000 years earlier, the ancestors of the Aymara people had prospered in one of the great prehistoric cultures of South America, the Tiwanaku. Then, farmers produced food for ten times as many people as live there nowadays. There was enough free energy to spare for hauling enormous pieces of masonry around in pharaoh fashion, and for building temples and roads. The Tiwanakans were no fly-by-nights. Their ecologically sound culture thrived throughout the first millennium AD—for longer than the Roman Empire—until a prolonged drought snuffed it out.

'Their success was a great mystery,' said Oswaldo Rivera of the Instituto Nacional de Arqueologia in La Paz. 'How did the waterlogged terrain beside Lake Titicaca support that vigorous Tiwanaku culture? We found the answer in subtle features of the landscape not easy to see at ground level, but very obvious in aerial photographs.' As if a waffle iron had been at work on the plain, the photos showed a geometric pattern of slightly raised flat fields, typically 200 metres long and 5–10 metres wide, separated by ditches.

Starting in 1984, in collaboration with Rivera, Alan Kolata from the University of Chicago led excavations that revealed how the raised fields looked and functioned before they fell into disrepair. The engineering was meticulous. The Tiwanakans lined a dug-out area with stones and clay, to make it proof against flooding from the brackish water table below. Next, a layer of gravel and sand provided superior drainage for growing crops. On top went the soil.

The secret of success was in the water in the irrigation ditches bordering the narrow fields. It absorbed heat during the day and radiated it at night, protecting the crop against frost. And in the ditches appeared water plants, ducks and fishes. These not only broadened the Tiwanakan diet but also provided nutrient-rich sediments for fertilizing the soil.

The archaeologists persuaded the local farmers to try out the system of their ancestors. After some fierce resistance they managed to get trials going. The results were spectacular, with pioneers achieving yields two to five times what they were used to. Other farmers imitated them, sometimes on raised fields that survived from antiquity, and sometimes on fields built afresh.

The Aymara did not neglect to give thanks to Pacha-Mamma, their Earth goddess, at the joyful parties celebrating the harvests. During one such gathering Kolata explained their high spirits. 'They've never planted down here in this plain before. They never believed anything could grow down here, and now they see that these big fat *papas* are coming out of the ground, these potatoes.'

By the early 1990s ancient field systems were also being revived on the Peruvian side of Titicaca. In other settings, on the coastal plains of Colombia and Ecuador, and in the old Maya heartlands of Central America, farming techniques adapted to lowland conditions were being rediscovered by archaeologists and implemented in local trials. After half a millennium of colonial and post-colonial scorn for the retarded ways of the Native Americans, the tables were turned.

The moral of this tale concerns expertise. If you tried to reinvent the raised fields, you'd probably wish to recruit specialists on physics, soil science, hydrology, hydraulic engineering, freshwater biology, agronomy and climate, and to model the dynamics of the system on a computer. Indeed such skills were needed, fully to interpret what the Tiwanakans accomplished empirically.

Neither the Incas who came to power later, nor the Spanish colonial settlers who displaced the Incas, could match the agrarian productivity of the Tiwanakans. When international agricultural experts arrived, in the 1950s and after, to counsel the Bolivians on modern techniques, they had nothing to offer for that part of the Altiplano that was not hopelessly expensive. For almost 1000 years the land was wasted, because those who thought themselves smart were not.

What the satellites saw

The arrogance of *soi-disant* experts, whether in the rich countries, international organizations or the capital cities of developing countries, became insupportable in the latter half of the 20th century. Allying themselves with industries, governments, aid agencies or environmental pressure groups, the experts thought they could and should tell the inhabitants of far away places, scarcely known to them, how they should live. As a result, the world became littered with the detritus of misconceived projects, both for development and for conservation.

Sometimes the scars are visible even from space. Compare with old maps the latest satellite images of the Aral Sea, in former Soviet Central Asia, and you see a shrunken puddle. Experts in Moscow devised irrigation schemes for cotton cultivation on a scale and with techniques that the rivers supplying the Aral Sea could not sustain. Fishing communities were left high and dry. Sandstorms became salt storms from the dried-out beaches. An irony is that, before their conquest by the Russian Tsars, the Uzbekh and Turkmen peoples of the region also had very large-scale irrigation schemes, but these were engineered in an 'old-fashioned', sustainable way.

In Kenya, the pictures from space show large pockets of man-made desert created by overgrazing. They are a direct result of policies that required nomadic herders to settle down with their cattle, so as to enjoy the medical and educational benefits of the sedentary life. The assumption was that grand people like doctors and teachers could never be expected to be mobile, when the nomads and their cows roamed the semi-desert in search of the highly nutritious seasonal vegetation there. The stationary herds devastated their surroundings and the once beautiful blue Lake Baringo turned brown with windblown soil.

Damage by elephants is visible from space, in Botswana and other parts of southern Africa. Experts drafted international rules for the protection of elephants, which won political confirmation. By the end of the 20th century the populations of elephants in some regions had increased past the point of sustainability, with widespread destruction of vegetation. Once again, the local people and wildlife had to endure the consequences of remote decision-making.

The all-seeing satellites are also good at observing the destruction of forests by human activity. When they revealed it going on at a shocking rate in the north-western USA and in Finland, that wasn't what the world heard about. The word was that the Brazilians were wiping out the Amazon rain forest.

There satellites did indeed show large clearings near the roads and rivers, but also huge areas of scarcely affected forest. Careful measurements by US scientists using Landsat images showed that the rate of deforestation in the Amazon region peaked in the 1980s at 0.3 per cent per year, less than a quarter of the rate seen in some US forests. Yet children in Western schools were taught about the imminent disappearance of half the Amazon rain forest, as if it were a fact.

Telling strangers what to do

In Europe, North America and the Soviet Union, the descendants of those who had created many of the world's environmental problems during the colonial era had an unstoppable urge to go on bossing strangers. Some even spoke of the new white-man's burden. Wildly contradictory instructions went out to the poorer countries of the world. Develop—here's how! No, stop developing—Conserve!

The signals were often channelled via United Nations agencies and the World Bank. That did not alter the fact that they usually represented pale-faced theories imposed on pigmented people. Projects were sometimes steeped in ecological and/or ethnographic ignorance.

In one notorious case, an attempt to introduce high-yielding rice into the backwoods of Liberia faltered. That was because the peripatetic experts spoke only to the men of the villages, not realizing that the women were the rice experts. Ordered to sow seeds they did not recognize and about which they knew nothing, the women cooked them and served them for supper.

Environmentalism developed from the 1960s onwards in countries that had grown rich by burning fossil fuels, and where most of the ancient forests were destroyed long ago. Nothing would curb the God-given right to an automobile. Yet there, city-dwellers who had never known a day's hunger or faced down a snake claimed special authority to speak on behalf of the Earth and its delicate ecosystems in every part of the globe.

Most vocal were European and American non-governmental organizations through which unelected activists sought to rule the world. The evident need for action to protect the planet brought the message: 'Don't do as we do; do as we say.' Scientists in a position to stand up against the hypocrisy, those in China for example, did not hesitate to call it eco-colonialism.

Coming a cropper in Samoa

It should be humbling to know that the Samoans have been conservationists for 3000 years. To be sure, their ancestors of a hundred generations ago brought crop-plants and animals by canoe to the lonely group of Pacific islands. These unavoidably displaced much of the pre-existing wildlife. But since then the Samoans have managed very well, with doctrines of *aiga* entwining culture and agriculture, and *taboo*, for prohibitions.

Their economic system rates you not by what you own but what you give away, so every day is Christmas on Samoa. The system is provident too. A survey by scientists from New Zealand revealed that, besides the village gardens and cash-crop plantations, there were large areas of valuable land in reserve, left to run wild. And when a typhoon struck Samoa in 1990 the people had food stocks set aside for just such a disaster.

Into this nation, which set a good example in human ecology to the rest of the world, came experts sent by Western non-governmental organizations to teach the bumpkins how to safeguard their rain forest. The ever-friendly Samoans joined in the sport, in several preserves on village territory, until the visitors started behaving like colonial officials. The village chiefs told them to get lost.

A bemused observer of this fiasco was Paul Cox, from Brigham Young University in Utah, who had lived and worked in Samoa for some years and spoke the language. As an ethnobotanist, he was accustomed to learning from the Samoans about the precious plants of the rain forest, and their medicinal properties. When he found one that promised to ameliorate AIDS, he saw to it that a 20 per cent royalty on any profits should be paid to the Samoans. And Cox had also taken part in a drive that recovered rain-forest tracts from logging companies and handed over responsibility for them to the villagers.

In 1997, when the visiting experts had been sent packing, Cox published a commentary on their conduct, together with Thomas Elmqvist of Sweden's Centrum för Biologisk Mångfald. 'The principles of indigenous control,' they noted, 'were unexpectedly difficult to accept by Western conservation organizations who, ultimately, were unwilling to cede decision-making authority to indigenous peoples. Conversely, eco-colonialism, the imposition of Western conservation paradigms and power structures on indigenous peoples, proved to be incompatible with indigenous concepts of conservation and human dignity.'

Better sense about bushmeat

In the 21st century there are signs of progress beyond eco-colonialism, in the thinking of experts and activists. One concerns bushmeat, which means wild animals hunted for human nutrition. The forests of West and Central Africa supply a large part of the protein consumed by poorly nourished people in the region. Chimpanzees, gorillas, monkeys, elephants, forest antelopes, pangolins, wild pigs, rodents, snakes, crocodiles, lizards, tortoises, hornbills and the brightly crested turacos are all in danger of being eaten to extinction.

In the past, conservationists sometimes spoke as if those doing the hunting were stupid or wicked, and needed to be educated or legislated out of the habit. A rational African, the implication was, should let his children starve rather than net a handy hornbill from the natural larder. In a more compassionate view, the forest dwellers will suffer, too, if their wild species are extinguished in the coming decades. A sensible policy would be to help them find alternative sources of affordable protein, so that they don't need to hunt so much.

The first task was to gauge how much protein was involved. Estimates put it at around 2 million tonnes a year. In pursuit of answers, the UK Bushmeat Campaign brought together more than 30 non-governmental organizations, concerned with human welfare as well as with conservation. The campaign explicitly linked the survival of species such as chimpanzees and gorillas to the sustainable development and nutrition of the peoples of West and Central Africa.

'We have turned the usual species-led technique on its head,' said John Fa of Durrell Wildlife on Jersey, coordinator of bushmeat research in Nigeria and Cameroon, 'by looking at how we can save the human population in order to ultimately save the wild species in the region.'

Sustainable hopes?

On the international stage, at the start of the 21st century, sustainability is the watchword. How can humanity as a whole, with a growing population and hopes of higher standards of living, avoid exhausting its resources and damaging the environment and the other species with which we share the planet? This was the theme of two Earth Summits, in Rio de Janeiro in 1992 and Johannesburg in 2002. Climate change and threats to wildlife were the big topics at the first, and better sharing of the world's resources to help the poor was the aim of the second.

The concerns go back to 1798, when Thomas Malthus of Cambridge published *An Essay on the Principle of Population*. 'It has been said that the great question is now at issue,' he wrote, 'whether man shall henceforth start forwards with accelerated velocity towards illimitable, and hitherto unconceived improvement, or be condemned to a perpetual oscillation between happiness and misery, and after every effort remain still at an immeasurable distance from the wished-for goal.'

His answer was pessimistic. He concluded that distress was the natural lot of humankind because an arithmetical increase in the necessities of life could not keep up with a geometric population growth. 'Taking the population of the world at any number, a thousand millions, for instance,' he wrote, 'the human species would increase in the ratio of 1, 2, 4, 8, 16, 32, 64, 128, 256, 512, etc. and subsistence as 1, 2, 3, 4, 5, 6, 7, 8, 9, 10, etc.'

Malthus' reasoning has a modern ring to it, because so many have echoed him, right through to the 21st century, even though his proposition has been falsified till now. After huge increases in numbers in the industrialized world in the 19th century, a global population explosion began around 1930. By the end of the 20th century human numbers had increased about sixfold since Malthus' time but distress had on the whole diminished.

Provision of the necessities of life, including food, kept ahead of population growth, despite many forecasts to the contrary. Life expectancy increased, as an incontrovertible indicator of improved human well-being. The explosive growth of population did not continue in line with Malthusian expectations. Around 1970 the rate of growth began to ease. From this inflexion you could guess that the population, which was already beginning to level off in the industrialized countries, would do the same globally, at perhaps 10 billion by the end of the 21st century.

Dire predictions nevertheless continued, and when the expected continent-wide famines did not occur, the neo-Malthusians changed tack. Human beings might be doing all right, for the time being, but the planet wasn't and we'd pay the price in the long run. Issues of natural resources and the environment came to the fore.

It was said that the world was going to run out of oil and several key metals before the end of the 20th century, but that didn't happen either. Then there was the pollution of air, water and soil. A famous study by Dennis Meadows and his colleagues at the Massachusetts Institute of Technology, published in 1972 as *Limits to Growth*, used a primitive computer model to show projections of poisonous pollution soaring (unnoticed, one had to presume) until it caused a horrifying crash in the population.

The inference was that we were doomed unless economic growth was constrained. Well it wasn't, and we weren't—at least not by poisonous pollution. That was brought under moderately good control by a combination of cleaner technologies and control policies that prevented it getting anywhere near as bad as *Limits to Growth* foresaw. Some persistent organic pollutants still spread worryingly, but human life expectancy continued to improve.

The fact that Malthusian doomsaying had been brushed aside again and again was no guarantee it would always be wrong, as the population continued to grow. So attention switched once more: to the destruction of wildlife habitats and species, and to the possible ill effects, via climate change, of carbon dioxide released into the air by human activity. Those remained the chief topics of international concern at the start of the 21st century.

'Optimism is obligatory'

'The stone wall of inopportunity facing the poorest billion or so people in the world ensures the continuing degradation of natural resources,' Erik Eckholm of the International Institute for Environment and Development wrote in 1982. The division of the world into rich and poor regions, and its maintenance by unfair conditions of trade, was for many observers an abiding reason for Malthusian pessimism in the quest for sustainability. The Johannesburg summit in 2002 addressed this issue without making much headway. Meanwhile the rich seemed endlessly surprised that the poor should want to sell mahogany, ivory or heroin, when they couldn't get a decent price for their coffee or sugar.

'Optimism is obligatory,' the science writer Ritchie Calder of Edinburgh declared. Ever since Malthus, the doctrine of inevitable scarcity has been used to justify keeping the poor poor. In the mid-20th century there was widespread hope about a better world to be made with the aid of science and technology. The expectation was that the human ecosystem could soon be so improved as to abolish hunger, infectious disease, illiteracy and material hardship. The pendulum swung emphatically towards pessimism in the closing decades of the century, and environmentalism was more than a little tinged with Luddite attitudes to technology.

From the Tiwanakan raised fields to the microchip, innovations have repeatedly transformed the human condition in surprising and generally beneficial ways. Fossil energy, man-made fertilizer, irrigation and hybrid seeds kept Malthus at bay for 200 years. So optimists may still suspect that gloomy forecasts about human ecology will fail again because they don't allow for human inventiveness.

▶ *For another example of expert misinformation, see* EL NIÑO. *For other aspects of ecology and conservation, see* BIOSPHERE FROM SPACE, BIODIVERSITY, ECO-EVOLUTION *and* PREDATORS. *For the food situation, see* CEREALS *and* TRANSGENIC CROPS. *For climate, see* CLIMATE CHANGE *and* CARBON CYCLE. *For innovations that do more with less, see* BUCKYBALLS AND NANOTUBES.

HUMAN GENOME

The industrialization of fundamental biology

D NA ALLEY THEY CALL IT, and it is Maryland's answer to California's Silicon Valley, although offering biotechnology instead of microchips. The axis is Interstate 270, running through the leafy outer suburbs of Washington DC towards Germantown. Turn off for Rockville, find Guide Drive, and after a few stoplights you'll come to the white buildings of Celera Genomics. This is Maryland's equivalent of Intel, housing what was for a while the most dazzling and most reviled enterprise in the history of biology.

Celera derived its name from the Latin *celer*, or swift, and it trademarked a company slogan, 'Discovery can't wait'. As the 21st century dawned, 300 automated Perkin-Elmer sequencers at Celera were reading the coded genetic messages of human beings. These were written in the sequences of chemical letters A, T, C and G in the long chains of deoxyribonucleic acid, or DNA, that make up the genes of heredity.

The entire set of human genetic material, called the genome, consists of 3.2 billion letters strung out along two metres of DNA. The fineness of the molecular thread allows all that length to be scrunched up and packaged in 23 pairs of chromosomes at the heart of microscopic cells throughout the human body. At Rockville the DNA in all the chromosomes was tackled in one great spree, by the shotgun method.

That meant taking DNA from five individuals and chopping it with enzyme scissors into more than 20 million fragmented but overlapping sequences. The chromosome fragments were inserted by genetic engineering into bacteria, to produce millions of copies of each. The analysers read off the letters in the fragments. From these, a remarkable system of 800 interconnected computers found the overlaps and stitched the genes—or at least their codes—back together again.

The swiftness was breathtaking. Craig Venter, who masterminded Celera, had previously worked just down the road at the National Institute of Neurological Disorders and Stroke in Bethesda. While there he spent ten years looking for a single gene. His computers at Rockville could do the job in 15 seconds.

Venter was deeply unpopular because he accomplished in 18 months, with 280 colleagues, what 3000 scientists in 250 laboratories around the world had taken

13 years to do. The Human Genome Project, funded by governments and charitable foundations, aimed at completion by 2005. In response to the Celera challenge it speeded up the work with extra funding.

Leaders of the public project in the USA had turned down Venter's offer to work with them, saying that the whole-genome shotgun method he was proposing was impossible or hopelessly unreliable. When he was offered private funding to get on with it, the critics made Venter out to be an entrepreneur interested only in profit. Stories were planted in the media that Celera was going to patent all human genes.

Venter demonstrated the whole-genome method with the somewhat smaller genome of the fruit fly, *Drosophila melanogaster*. Early in 2000, when his team had sequenced 90 per cent of the human genome, Venter realized that he could save much time and money in piecing it together if he took in data that the accelerated public programme was releasing earlier than expected. The borrowing let the public-sector scientists claim that their original judgement was right and the whole-genome method didn't work. This led to pantomime exchanges of the form, 'Oh yes it did!' and 'Oh no it didn't!'

The most open-minded onlookers found it hard to judge how much of the opposition to Venter was motivated by the wish to safeguard the public interest in the genome, and how much was professional pique or poor sportsmanship. The idea of 'public good, private bad' was questionable, to put it mildly in view of the contributions of private industry to medical and pharmaceutical progress. In a decade or two what will be remembered is that Venter's method worked unaided in other species. Moreover, his private intervention gave a much-needed shot of adrenalin to the public effort, which completed the human genome in 2003, two years earlier than orginally envisaged.

The spat about patents

Casting Venter as the bogeyman certainly helped to motivate two heroes who saved the public project from being altogether trounced by Celera. They were computer scientists at UC Santa Cruz, David Haussler and James Kent. They lacked computing power to match what Celera was using, to piece the genome together, until Haussler managed to acquire a set of 100 computers.

Kent was a computer animation expert who had become a biology graduate student. Working night and day, he wrote the complex program and produced the first assembly of the human genome in just one month. What drove his superhuman effort was the fear that Venter would patent the genes. 'The US Patent Office is, in my mind, very irresponsible in letting people patent a discovery rather than an invention,' Kent said. 'It's very upsetting. So we wanted to get a public set of genes out as soon as possible.'

Venter was indeed filing provisional patent applications on medically relevant gene discoveries. But he pointed out that the US government had done the same and insisted that Celera and the government had exactly the same philosophy on gene patents. 'There should be a very high bar,' he said. 'You need to know something—what the gene does—that has real purpose to do something about medicine. So patents are a bogus issue that are being used as a political weapon to try and fool people.'

The acrimony between the two camps peaked over the simultaneous publication, in 2001, of the first drafts of the human genome from Celera and the public Human Genome Project. Both were expected to go in the Washington journal *Science*, but the public camp tried to impose conditions concerning access to the Celera data. When baulked they gave their paper and gene sequences to *Nature* of London instead. Yet, after all the posturing, Celera won a fat government contract just a few months later, to do the rat genome.

It was in any case a good thing to have two versions of the human genome, for cross-checking. This was immediately apparent when both groups reported that there were far fewer human genes than the 100,000 or more expected. The public group said 30,000 to 40,000 genes and Venter and his team, between 27,000 and 39,000.

'Like herding cats'

For most of the 20th century the genome had been simply an arm-waving term, used by geneticists to mean the whole shebang. The idea that the human genome could perhaps be decoded in its entirety grew in biologists' minds in the early 1980s. Prompting came from a way of reading sequences of several hundred letters at once, in DNA strands, invented in 1977 by Fred Sanger at the UK's Laboratory of Molecular Biology.

Sanger's group used it to produce the first DNA whole-genome sequence of 5000 letters, belonging to a virus that attacks bacteria, phi-X174. Next they sequenced the 16,000 letters of the genome of the mitochondria, the little power stations inside human cells that have a bacterium-like hereditary system of their own. By 1982, their best effort was 48,000 letters in the genome of lambda, another bacterial virus.

In the same year, in Japan, a physicist turned molecular biologist, Akiyoshi Wada, joined with the Hitachi company to make robots for reading genes by the Sanger method. That was when fundamental biological research began to industrialize.

The scientists promoting the idea of the Human Genome Project said it was a biomedical equivalent of the Apollo space programme that put men on the Moon. But instead of lunar rocks it would deliver the Book of Life, bringing incalculable benefits to medicine as well as to fundamental research. Future generations, the protagonists said, would regard it as the greatest achievement of 20th-century science.

The rhetoric ripened with the cost projections, which went into billions of dollars and then eased back into the hundreds of millions. In 1988 the US government began to budget for a share in the project and other countries and charities joined in. Coordinated by an international Human Genome Organization, the idea was to allocate to different teams the various human chromosomes, the sausage-like assemblies into which the genome naturally divides itself. James Watson, who with Francis Crick had discovered the structure of DNA, was leader of the US effort at a crucial period.

The whole-genome shotgun approach, which would later cause a stir, had already been demonstrated in the public sector. Sanger's group used it for the lambda virus. But the computers of 1988 were not up to the job of piecing tens of millions of gene fragments together. The chromosome-by-chromosome approach to the human genome seemed prudent at the time. It also had the advantage that you always knew where you were in the genome, and you could take well-defined portions of a chromosome in a hierarchical technique.

The expected completion date in 2005 was set in 1992. Even so, by the time that Venter intervened in 1998 and forced a quickening of the pace, some academic partners in the multinational effort were behind schedule. 'It's like herding cats,' was the complaint. In the end the big push to complete the public version of the genome came mainly from the Whitehead Institute in Massachusetts, Baylor College in Texas, Washington University in Missouri, the US Department of Energy's Joint Genome Institute in California, and the Sanger Institute in England, which was backed by the Wellcome Trust.

Because of the concentration of work in the USA, with a sizeable contribution from the UK, the American president and the British prime minister took it upon themselves to announce, on 26 June 2000, that the human genome was nearing completion. 'This is the most important, the most wondrous map ever produced by humankind,' said Bill Clinton. 'The first great technological triumph of the 21st century,' said Tony Blair. Michael Dexter of the Wellcome Trust said, 'This is the outstanding achievement not only of our lifetime, but in terms of human history.'

The hype worried some scientists. Among them was Eric Lander of the Whitehead Institute, lead author for the public genome project. 'We've called the human genome the blueprint, the Holy Grail, all sorts of things. It's a parts list,' Lander said. 'If I gave you the parts list for the Boeing 777, and it has 100,000 parts, I don't think you could screw it together, and you certainly wouldn't understand why it flew.'

Genetic dark matter

When scientists stain the gene-carrying chromosomes, to examine them under a microscope, they see light and dark bands. The genomic analyses revealed that the genes are concentrated mainly in the light bands. The difference in appearance arises from a chemical imbalance in the repetitive DNA in regions where genes are scarce, which makes them better able to take up the stain and so appear dark.

'It appears that the human genome does indeed contain deserts, or large, gene-poor regions,' the Celera team commented. A great deal of repetitive DNA carries the same unintelligible messages over and over again. It is no minor intrusion but about a third of all the DNA that is diligently copied and recopied from parents to children and from cell to cell. Incautious scientists call it 'junk' while others admit that if it has a meaning or purpose, they don't know what it is. The same is true for non-repetitive material, sometimes called 'selfish DNA' and accused of being stowaways coming along for the evolutionary ride.

The genome is therefore much more than the sum of its genes. The deserts of the dark chromosome bands are reminiscent of cosmological dark matter. When astronomers realized that the visible stars accounted for less than ten per cent of the mass of a galaxy, they spent half a century looking for the 'missing mass' and adjusting their cosmological ideas to take account of it. Now geneticists are confronted by a genome in which less than ten per cent of the DNA is assigned to functional genes. A difference is that the genetic dark matter is already known. It is tangible and also legible, as sequences of code letters.

Clues to what it means may come from the very uneven distribution of the deserts among the chromosomes. The sex chromosomes X and Y have remarkably few genes in their oases. The small chromosome-pair number 19 has very few dark bands and plenty of genes, but also an inordinate amount of repetitive DNA. If anywhere in modern biology cries out for fresh thinking, it is surely here in the surprising landscapes of the genome—although the astronomers' experience should perhaps moderate any expectation of easy answers.

The human genome drafts dealt decisively with a controversial issue in biology. Evidence from bacteria had shown that many genes are transferred, not downwards from parents to offspring, but sideways between co-existing organisms, even of different species. If such goings-on were commonplace in the animal lineage too, that could turn evolution into revolution. The answer from the genome is that very few, if any, of our genes have been acquired from bacteria during 600 million years of animal evolution—certainly not enough to disturb the general picture of the lineage from worms to fishes to reptiles to mammals, primates and us.

● A philosophical and political minefield

In respect of genetics, the industrialization of fundamental biology means analytical robots plus powerful computers. What was pioneered with genes in the 20th century will be carried forward with proteins in the 21st, in other industries. To find out what all the genes mean requires identification of the proteins whose manufacture they command. The Australians named the effort in this direction proteomics, as a counterpart to genomics. Physicists in Germany developed X-ray lasers that would speed up the work of discovering the shapes of the proteins.

The effort is expensive in equipment and skilled manpower. So it tends to concentrate in the world's richest countries and most favoured labs. On the other hand the results, in the databases of genes and proteins, are often available free of charge, via the Internet, to researchers anywhere, for follow-up investigations that are limitless in scope.

The plant geneticists set an example with the genome of arabidopsis. Throughout their project, information was shared entirely openly, with the latest batch of results going into a public databank even before the scientists responsible for them examined it themselves. They called it the democratization of plant biology.

If biological, agricultural and medical scientists in small labs and the poor countries benefit from free and easy accessibility, that will vindicate the concern about public ownership in the human genome spats. Within hours of the raw data of both the public and private human genome projects becoming available on-line in 2001, they were being accessed from all corners of the Earth. Francis Collins of the US National Human Genome Research Institute proclaimed, 'We've empowered the entire brains of the planet.'

Before long, Venter had to quit Celera. With other people giving genome data away freely, the company's profitability would depend on drug development, which was not his field. He admitted to being happier back in the basic science, not-for-profit world, where he felt freer to speak his mind.

Among his new interests was the creation of a think-tank concerned with ethics, the Center for the Advancement of Genomics. Venter knew better perhaps than some of his critics what a philosophical and political minefield the human genome will always be for the human species. Concerns about privacy, racism and genetic tinkering may turn out to be far more troublesome, in the long run, than issues about patents and commercialized data.

'Before you ask a question about the human genome,' Venter once commented, 'make damn sure you want to know the answer.'

The Icelanders sneak in

The genome reading brought first impressions of the variations of the genes that make us all uniquely individual. The two men and three women whose DNA was shotgunned by Celera described their ethnic backgrounds as Chinese, African-American, Hispanic, and Caucasian. The computers found 4 million instances where one letter of the genetic code differed between them. Snips, these variations are called, short for single-nucleotide polymorphisms.

Medical researchers homed in on the snips as possible scenes of mutations affecting human vulnerability to diseases. To find these was advertised as one of the main aims of the genome projects. But it was an immensely laborious task and the Icelanders had a head start.

Their population of less than 280,000 has the best genealogical records in the world. These go back more than 1000 years and cover about half the Icelanders who ever lived, since Norwegian Vikings settled on the island with Celtic women collected en route. Records since 1700 are almost complete, together with copious medical data, including causes of death. It is therefore rather easy to find inherited predispositions to disease, once you have promised to use code names for individuals.

In a typical case, the genealogy links more than 100 apparently unrelated asthma patients back to a single ancestor in the early 18th century. The genes involved are then traceable by first sampling the DNA of each living person in the lineage, at 1000 places in the genome, and using a computer to pick out segments of the genome that they seem to have in common. These segments can then be examined in detail for particular genes or clusters of genes associated with asthma.

With a predictability that becomes almost touching in the end, the US National Institutes of Health refused to fund Kari Stefansson, then at Harvard, when he proposed to use this unique resource in his homeland to trace the genes involved. It wouldn't work, he was warned. Sent packing just as Venter was, Stefansson, too, got private money.

He created Decode Genetics in Reykjavik in 1996, and soon acquired more commercial muscle by teaming up with the Swiss pharmaceutical company Roche. By 2002 Stefansson had a team of hundreds of scientists, blood samples from a third of all adults in Iceland, and 56 DNA sequencers. And he had already announced genetic discoveries in a score of common diseases, including Alzheimer's, schizophrenia, stroke, osteoporosis, obesity, anxiety, diabetes and rheumatoid arthritis. Researchers in the leading human-genome countries, the USA and UK, with major public projects to pursue disease genetics snip by snip, had reason to feel outwitted.

'The genome people did a great scientific job,' Stefansson commented. 'But for a medical payoff from the modern techniques you need real patients with identifiable hereditary conditions, and quick ways of homing in on the genes that are responsible. That's exactly what we have in Iceland. It's nice that our very small country can make such a big splash in 21st-century biomedical research.'

The task for Decode Genetics was made easier by the common heritage of the Icelanders, which leaves their genes far less varied than those in large, fluid populations. But that advantage also raised questions about whether disease-causing mutations identified in Iceland would be the same in other parts of the world. Putting it sharply, would remedies appropriate for Icelanders work in China?

The answer seems to be Yes, as the company first demonstrated in relation to the gene it linked to schizophrenia. Vaulting over 100 years of inconclusive research by psychiatrists, neuroscientists and geneticists on this dreadful mental illness, which can run in families and afflicts as many as 1 adult in 100, the Reykjavik team found the Neuregulin 1 gene. Some 500 schizophrenic volunteers in Iceland contributed to the discovery.

Comparisons with their relatives and control groups established that defects in this gene, located on chromosome No. 8, more than double the risk of developing schizophrenia. Experimental mice, in which Neuregulin 1 activity was disabled, revealed changes in their brains and behaviour analogous to those known in schizophrenic patients. And cross-checking with other northern European populations showed that the same segment of the gene contributed a similar risk for the disease. Results from the study of Chinese patients also revealed an enhanced risk with defective Neuregulin 1, as in the Icelanders, even though the segment of the gene linked to the disease was slightly different.

'These results provide concrete proof for what we have always believed: that the major genes in common diseases found in Iceland will be the same elsewhere in the world,' Stefansson said. 'Drugs based upon our findings will therefore target the underlying biology of disease in any population.'

Diagnostic tools for predicting an individual's susceptibility to disease are another matter. The possible mutations in disease-related genes in all parts of the planet are not well represented in Iceland's small and relatively isolated population. Medical research groups around the world therefore allied themselves with Decode Genetics to pin down the full range of disease-linked variations.

▶ *For more about decoding, including Sanger's decisive method, see* GENES. *For other genomes and their interpretations, see* GENOMES IN GENERAL, HUMAN ORIGINS, ARABIDOPSIS *and* CEREALS. *For more about interpretations, see* PROTEOMES *and* GLOBAL ENZYMES.

HUMAN ORIGINS

Why most of those exhumations are only of great-aunts

FOLLOW THE DÜSSEL STREAM east from Düsseldorf in Germany and you soon come to an adjacent gorge called Neanderthal. In a cave there, in 1856, workmen found human bones significantly different from those of modern people. Thirty years later the status of Neanderthal Man as an extinct form of humankind was assured when similar bones turned up at Spy in Belgium, along with tools and the bones of extinct animals.

During the 20th century Neanderthaler remains were found widely in Eurasia. Early impressions of slouching creatures were corrected. These were sturdy, upright people with large brains, and were talented hunter-gatherers. They were commonly depicted as the last step but one on the evolutionary path from apes to humankind.

That neat idea was put in doubt by the remains of much more modern Cro-Magnon people, co-existing with Neanderthalers in Europe. Older skeletons of lighter build and with highbrowed skulls turned up in south-west Asia and Africa. Genetic evidence in our own subspecies pointed to an origin from an Eve in Africa about 150,000 years ago.

In 1997 Svante Pääbo of Munich and his colleagues delivered the coup de grace to the idea that we are descended directly from the Neanderthalers. They recovered 30,000-year-old genetic material, the deoxyribonucleic acid, or DNA, from a bone of the original type specimen found in the Neanderthal gorge. Comparisons with the DNA of modern humans showed that the last common ancestors of the Neanderthalers and ourselves that carried this piece of DNA probably lived about 550,000 years ago. This strongly suggested that these early Düsseldorfers were not our grandmothers but great-aunts.

Pääbo had first won fame in 1985 by extracting DNA from Egyptian mummies while still a graduate student in his native Uppsala. He was trying to obtain DNA from fossils even before Michael Crichton's sci-fi story *Jurassic Park* (1990) imagined living dinosaurs that were re-created from DNA recovered in fossilized biting flies. Pääbo found that, in real life, DNA degrades quite quickly even in well-preserved fossils, and contamination with modern DNA is very hard to avoid.

Although it had nothing like the antiquity of Crichton's fictional dinosaurs, obtaining the 30,000-year-old DNA from a Neanderthaler was considered a tour de force. It relied on the polymerase chain reaction, or PCR, invented in 1983 for multiplying minute traces of DNA. Commenting on the Neanderthaler result Pääbo said, 'We have reached a sort of limit. It would require another technical breakthrough of the order of PCR to go back any further in time.'

Leakeys' Luck

That the prospects were not bright for using the DNA technique on older fossils of man-like creatures was the more regrettable because the bone-hunters were in a muddle. In the 20th century the focus of the search for our human and prehuman ancestors had switched away from Europe. It went to South Africa, with the discovery by Raymond Dart in 1925 of the first *Australopithecus* ape-man. Then Asia came into the picture with the first findings of *Homo erectus* (Java Man and Peking Man), who was a skilful maker of hand-axes but plainly not as smart as us.

For the latter half of the century, the spotlight settled on East Africa, and its Great Rift Valley in particular. Here a corner of the continent tried but failed to tear itself off, as if to make another, grander Madagascar. With branches the Rift Valley extends for nearly 3000 kilometres from Ethiopia to the Zambezi, always about 50 kilometres wide. High scarps face each other like bookends across a plateau decorated with lakes and volcanoes. The Kenya–Tanzania sector of the Rift Valley is celebrated for its big mammals.

Here, it was said, our ape-like ancestors first learned to walk upright. A leading hypothesis for many years was that the monkeys without tails came down from the trees, not voluntarily, but because the trees abandoned them. East Africa grew drier as a result of global cooling that became emphatic about 5 million years ago as the Earth headed towards the onset of the present series of ice ages. And lo and behold, the animals that left their footprints preserved in volcanic ash at Laetoli in Tanzania 3.7 million years ago included not only elephants and giraffes but also ape-men, or australopithecines, walking a little clumsily on two legs.

A Kenyan bone-hunter, Mary Leakey, identified these footprints in 1978. She was the wife of Louis Leakey, a noted discoverer of prehuman fossils, and had herself found a new species of australopiths in Olduvai Gorge in Tanzania in 1959. At the same site, in the following year, her 19-year-old son Jonathan discovered the earliest known creature to be generally accepted as human: *Homo habilis*, or Handyman, about 2 million years old.

The Leakey family made plenty of other discoveries too, and friends and rivals spoke of Leakeys' Luck. Some of it rubbed off onto Louis Leakey's young assistant, Jane Goodall. Out from England, and trained only as a stenographer, she went off in 1960 to the Gombe National Park in Tanzania, and made herself the world's best-known expert on chimpanzee behaviour observed in the wild. With hindsight, one can say that Goodall anticipated where the quest for human origins would have to turn in the end.

Another son, Richard Leakey, opened new territory for fossil-hunting. Near Lake Turkana in northern Kenya, his team found fragments of an almost complete skull of Handyman. Working with Alan Walker at their base in the National Museums of Kenya, Richard's wife Meave pieced the bits together. With a remarkably rounded cranium that would have held a brain half the size of ours, the creature looked like a strong candidate to be an early relative. The next task, as Richard Leakey judged it then, was to find a common ancestor of *Homo* and the divergent australopiths, with an age of perhaps 4 or 5 million years.

'We're getting quite close to that extraordinary moment in time,' Richard Leakey declared in 1973, 'when animal investment in brains, hands and sociability began to produce something of a new quality—the human ploy. So remarkably effective and powerful that it has altered the very rules of the life game.'

Upright much earlier

Bone-hunting was a patient, tedious, passionate business, and every significant find was greeted with reverential applause. Discoverers always hoped to fit the bones favourably into an evolutionary tree that made them true ancestors of ours. For example, a 3-million-year-old female australopith from Ethiopia was said to be just right for evolving later into *Homo*. She was called Lucy. A Beatles song 'Lucy in the sky with diamonds' was popular at the time of her discovery by Donald Johanson of the Cleveland Museum of Natural History, in 1974. *Australopithecus afarensis* was Lucy's formal name.

By the early 1980s it seemed not unreasonable to integrate the available information as follows. About 4 million years ago, the first australopiths evolved from the apes, and after a good innings spanning much of Africa the last of various australopith species went extinct about 1.4 million years ago. From a Lucy-like australopith, about 2.5 million years ago, the first human species, *Homo habilis*, appeared, to be followed about 2 million years ago by *Homo erectus*. Although this species then spread successfully across Eurasia, and was a skilled predator, it went on making the same old hand-axes for more than a million years—which suggests a certain lack of imagination.

During the past 600,000 years or so, traces of various early versions of a new species, *Homo sapiens*, began to crop up in Eurasia, and by 100,000 years ago the subspecies called Neanderthalers was well established. Our own subspecies, immodestly self-styled as *Homo sapiens sapiens*, was already a genetic entity in Africa, and poised to take over the world. In this scheme, we are all Africans twice over. If the latter-day Eve of Africa, mothering all humans alive today, is not clearly identifiable by her bones, we carry her blessing in the form of identifiable genes.

The earlier African debut of our ancestors, in the transition from apes to humans, remained much more obscure. The 1980s scheme just described was too simple and brief. Richard Leakey was right to want to push the divergence of *Australopithecus* and *Homo* much further back in time.

New bones turning up in East Africa kept altering the picture. A provocative find was Millennium Man, alias *l'Ancêtre du Millénaire* or *Orrorin tugenensis*, discovered in 2000. A French–Kenyan team came upon the remains in the Tugen Hills near Kenya's Lake Baringo.

'I could see they were human teeth,' said Kiptalam Cheboi of Kenya's Community Museum, who spotted the first remains. 'If I had jumped for joy I would have hit the sky.' From a stratum about 6 million years old came not only human-like teeth but also the bones of an ape-man about the size of a modern chimpanzee, with the thighs of an upright walker. *'Grignotés certes, mais pas détruits!'* exclaimed Martin Pickford from the Muséum National d'Histoire Naturelle in Paris, about the femurs he discovered. Nibbled by a big cat but not destroyed.

The find pushed two-legged walking far back in time and placed the walker, not in open grassland, but in long-vanished woodland. Accompanying fossils included evidence of trees, and ancestors of rhinos and hippos. The 6-million-year-old Kenyan walker was named *Orrorin* from the Tugen equivalent of Adam, and for the French it was a pun on *aurore*, or dawn.

Just a few months later, Yohannes Haile-Selassie from UC Berkeley announced another walker, around 5.5 million years old, found in Ethiopia. He called it *Ardipithecus ramidus kadabba*, where kadabba meant 'basal family ancestor' in the Afar language of the region. Again the remains were found with other fossils indicating a woodland setting. The popular idea that walking was an adaptation to enforced grassland life looked increasingly suspect.

By this time the bone-hunters were in disarray. They were unable to agree any longer on how teeth, skulls and walking ability were to be interpreted as signs of ancestry, whether of modern humans or of lineages that went extinct. In a subject shot through with preconceptions, some bone-hunters preferred to deny the validity of their own technical methods rather than to admit that rival finders or theorists might be right.

Optimists thought the new finds were homing in on the common ancestor of chimpanzees and human beings. With so much walking going on, so long ago, perhaps humans were not chimps that stood up straight. Instead chimps might be former hikers who preferred to stoop, walk on their knuckles and cultivate arboreal gymnastics.

The bombshell from Chad

In July 2001 Ahounta Djimdoumalbaye, a student from the Université de N'Djaména in Chad, was braving the fierce heat and sand blasts of the Djourab Desert to look for fossils. Exploration of this southern arm of the Sahara was virtually impossible before space images and navigation satellites could tell you where you were. The windblown sand remodels the landscape constantly. But it also digs away at old rocks, exhuming fossils from a bygone age when this was well-watered terrain, teeming with life. As a bone-hunter for a French–Chadian expedition, Djimdoumalbaye found an ape-man 6 or 7 million years old.

This was in central Africa, 2500 kilometres from the Rift Valley, and the discovery was no fluke. It was the culmination of a 25-year effort by Michel Brunet of Poitiers and David Pilbeam of Harvard to widen the search for human origins beyond the fashionable fossil beds of East Africa. As Brunet recalled, 'Notre mot d'ordre a alors été: Go west.'

They had their eye on Chad, but a war there at first diverted them to a fruitless search in Cameroon. Eventually, in 1994, Brunet was able to organize the Mission Paléoanthropologique Franco-Tchadienne, with logistic support from the French army. Students from Chad went to Poitiers for special training. Annual expeditions into the desert revealed vast numbers of fossil animals in eroded sandstone beds, corresponding with a mixture of woodland, grassland, rivers and lakes.

In 1995, Brunet reported the discovery of Abel, *Australopithecus bahrelghazali*. At more than 3 million years old, it was by far the oldest human-like find in the region and roughly contemporary with Lucy in Ethiopia. Posters appeared in the capital city: *Le Tchad, berceau de l'humanité?* The question mark was a nice touch, taking account of the sensibilities of scientists who were still convinced that the Rift Valley was the cradle of humanity.

The 2001 find was twice as old as Abel and Lucy. The formal name was *Sahelanthropus tchadensis* and the nickname for the best specimen was Toumaï, which means 'hope of life' in the Goran language spoken in the Djourab Desert. Long before Idriss Déby, president of Chad, showed off Toumaï's skull to the world's ambassadors in July 2002, the news circulated privately among the world's fossil-hunters. It shook them like a bombshell—a small nuclear weapon, one called it.

These creatures were hominids, a term encompassing ape-men and humans. But not only were they very early and living in the wrong place, but they also had features like those of much more recent ape-men. Brunet staked the customary claim to Toumaï being a possible ancestor of ours. He said that one could consider it 'close to the last common ancestor of chimpanzees and humans, but also the ancestor of the more recent hominids.'

The matter of ancestry was nevertheless intensely debated. The early 21st-century discoveries of the fossils around 6 million years old, in Kenya, Eritrea and especially Chad, blew away 20th-century ideas about how human evolution happened. Those ideas had been in turn linked to defective ideas about evolution in general, based on too-narrow an interpretation of Darwin's theory.

'From the back it looks like a chimpanzee, whereas from the front it could pass for a 1.75-million-year-old advanced australopith,' was the comment on Toumaï by Bernard Wood of George Washington University. He pointed out that, according to traditional ideas, 'a hominid of this age should only just be beginning to show signs of being a hominid.'

Gradualness was the theme of 20th-century evolutionary theory. Step by step, with one genetic mutation after another, a species could acquire new characteristics and powers, eventually becoming a novel and superior species—more like us. The prehuman fossils tell a quite different story, of multifarious try-outs of new hominids, with scant regard for any timetable or orderly progression.

This was unsurprising to those who kept an eye on evolutionary studies and laboratory trials in the late 1990s. They involved quite different creatures—flies, yeasts, plants—but they showed that novelties could appear more quickly, and be more drastic and more exploratory in their features, than the traditional evolutionary ideas envisaged. Evolution proceeds mainly as a result of changes in the control of pre-existing genes. When the controls are relaxed several different forms can appear simultaneously.

So there was every reason to expect evidence of rampant experimentation to appear in the fossil record. As Wood himself noted, a case was known from the origin of animals some 500 million years ago, in the so-called Cambrian explosion. No doubt similar random trials occurred, so far undetected by fossil-hunters, in the evolution of camels or cats. They came to light in the case of ape-men and humans because of the unusual effort devoted to the search for our ancestors, and the meticulous evaluation of every single tooth and thighbone.

All hominids older than our own subspecies, from Neanderthalers back to Toumaï, have now to be seen as experiments that leave no verified survivors today. Enlightening though it is, that payoff is disappointing for those who crave to hold the bones of their ancient grandmothers in their hand. In the absence of DNA maternity tests, it is entirely possible that, like the Neanderthalers, most or even all of the known fossil species are only great-aunts.

Genetics to the rescue?

To say what to expect as the next big step along a branch of science is not always easy, but in the study of human origins at the start of the 21st century it seemed obvious. The bones made a perplexing jumble. DNA from fossils had hit a roadblock. The smart thing to do was to compare the genes of humans and apes in much greater detail than hitherto.

In 1975, Marie-Claire King and Allan Wilson of UC Berkeley reported that about 99 per cent of DNA is identical in humans and chimpanzees. The remaining one per cent makes all the difference, and subsumes, at the genetic level, the entire multi-million-year story leading from the common ancestor of chimpanzees and humans, through the hominids of Africa and elsewhere, to our own subspecies of *Homo sapiens sapiens*. The only obvious difference is that human genes are wrapped in 23 pairs of chromosomes, and chimpanzee genes in 24 pairs, but this is not likely to be very significant beyond acting as a bar to mating.

From comparisons of maternal genes in orang-utans, chimps and modern humans, scientists at Japan's National Institute of Genetics put the common mother of chimps and humans at 4.7 million years ago. Others suspected she was earlier than that, which would be necessary if the recently discovered hominids in Africa were to be confirmed as definitely younger than the human–chimp common ancestor.

Meanwhile, draft transcripts of the entire code of human genes became available in 2001, as the result of the human genome projects. Scientists wondering where the crucial differences might lurk did not neglect the huge amounts of DNA not directly involved in specifying genes. These include elements called Alu sequences, found in the vicinity of genes and occurring only in the higher primates. Humans have more than a million, and Carl Schmid of UC Davis suggested that they play a role in helping us to cope with stress. Wanda Reynolds of the Sidney Kimmel Cancer Center in San Diego noted that Alu elements might increase or decrease the activity of genes involved in the response of cells to hormones that bring messages from other parts of the body.

'The presence of so many Alu sequences throughout the genome allows evolution to ask, what would happen if I raise the expression of Gene X threefold during development—does that make a better primate?' Reynolds said. 'And what would happen if I slightly modify the expression of a thousand genes—does that make a human being?'

After the human genome, the big gene-reading labs had other priorities than to chase after apes. This left a grand opportunity for scientists who had felt left out of the human genome enterprise to join in a study of ape genomes—for which the human genome would provide an excellent template. Park Hong-Seog of the

Korea Research Institute of Bioscience and Biotechnology in Taejon expressed the mood: 'Participating in the ape genome sequencing effort would be an attractive way for us to contribute.'

Yoshiyuki Sakaki of Japan's Human Genome Research Group in Yokohama invited geneticists in Korea, China and Taiwan to join in such an effort, together with Svante Pääbo's group in Germany. By then the DNA-hunting Swede was located at the Max-Planck-Institut für evolutionäre Anthropologie in Leipzig, a city with a fine collection of primates in its zoo. Pääbo's own hunch was that the crucial differences would lie in genes that regulate the action of other genes, influencing the course and timing of development in embryos and perhaps in adults too.

The existence of a gene, even of one shared between human and chimpanzees, may therefore be less significant than differences in gene activity. Pääbo and a group of German, Dutch and US colleagues compared tissues from humans, chimpanzees and macaque monkeys. They found that gene activity was similar in human and chimpanzee liver and white blood cells, acknowledging their closeness in evolution. But it was very different in human and chimpanzee brain tissue, perhaps reflecting their different mental capacities. The change in gene expression was much more intense in human brain tissue, while in chimpanzees the rate was more like a macaque's.

'The few differences between our genome and those of the great apes will be profoundly interesting because among them lie the genetic prerequisites that make us different from all other animals,' Pääbo commented. 'The realization that one or a few genetic accidents made our human history possible will provide us with a whole new set of philosophical challenges to think about.'

▶ *To approach the subject from the chimpanzees' side, see* PRIMATE BEHAVIOUR. *For more about human evolution during the past 150,000 years, see* PREHISTORIC GENES *and* SPEECH. *For the sea change in evolutionary ideas, see* EVOLUTION, HOPEFUL MONSTERS *and* CAMBRIAN EXPLOSION.

ICE-RAFTING EVENTS

Glacial surges in sudden changes of climate

C ALVED FROM GREENLAND'S GLACIERS, icebergs migrate south in spring and early summer, carried by the subzero Labrador Current. When they meet the warm Gulf Stream south of Newfoundland's Grand Banks, they soon vanish. Prudent skippers stay in water at 15°C or more, and that way they avoid the cold-water fog too.

For centuries before one of them claimed the world's most sumptuous ship and more than 1500 souls, in 1912, icebergs looming out of the fog off the Grand Banks were infamous among seafarers. Counts of icebergs on the North Atlantic sea-lane, collated from mariners' reports, go back to 1900. With just over 1000, the season of 1912 was severe but not exceptional. The International Ice Patrol set up after the disaster continued the logging. The numbers appearing at the latitude of Newfoundland and below varied between only 1 iceberg in 1958 and 2200 in 1984.

An iceberg is a raft for mineral grains, scraped from the rocks surrounding its parent glacier, far away. When it melts, this debris joins *Titanic* on the seabed. The grains can be found among the sediments that accumulate on the ocean floor, over the centuries and millennia. Research vessels hammer tubes deep into the sediments to recover cores that tell, layer by layer, of past changes in physical conditions and in life, in the overlying ocean.

In 1977 William Ruddiman at Columbia wrote the first pages of a 25-year climatic whodunit by reporting exotic sand buried beneath the North Atlantic floor during the last ice age. His interpretation was that colder ocean surface temperatures allowed icebergs calved from ice sheets adjoining the North Atlantic to survive longer and drift farther, before they dumped the sand on the seabed.

A research scientist at the Deutsches Hydrographisches Institut in Hamburg then made an astonishing discovery. In the 1980s, Hartmut Heinrich examined seabed cores from the European side of the North Atlantic. In sediments of the past 70,000 years, he found that the deposits of ice-rafted material occurred, not uniformly, but in distinct episodes seen in 11 separate layers enriched in quartz sand.

ICE-RAFTING EVENTS

In six of these, the most massive layers during the last ice age, there were rock fragments originating far away. A Swiss graduate student working with Heinrich, Rüdiger Jantschik from the Université de Neuchâtel, traced them to sources in the Norwegian Sea, Greenland and, in the case of rare grains of white carbonate rock, even from North America. Heinrich attributed them to a series of exceptional ice-rafting events that occurred at intervals of 7000 to 10,000 years during the last ice age, the first 60,000 years ago and the last 17,000 years ago.

'We had to imagine that, every so often, great armadas of icebergs broke out onto the sea,' Heinrich said. 'They could travel right across the Atlantic from North America, before depositing their debris on our side of the ocean. And they represented episodes of a kind not to be found in any of the textbooks on climate change up to that time.'

They came to be called Heinrich Events, and were interpreted as sudden cooling episodes lasting a few centuries. These drastic changes of climate were superimposed on the gradual changes in global and regional temperatures over thousands of years that are due to the wobbles of the Earth in orbit—the main pacesetters of the ice ages. There was already evidence from various places, for example in the Greenland ice sheet and in a fossil lake-bed in north-eastern France, that sudden and severe coolings could occur, but the reason was unknown.

Systematic evidence of abrupt changes of climate in the Heinrich Events prompted lively arguments about their cause and effect, after Heinrich reported them in 1988. One theory was that the eastern edge of the Laurentide ice sheet, which covered much of North America during the ice age, would binge on snow and intermittently purge itself, collapsing under its own weight. The icebergs released by this glacial bulimia would have big climatic effects. Not only would they carry their chill directly into the North Atlantic but, by putting a lid of buoyant melt-water on the ocean surface, they could interfere with the ocean-current system bringing warm water northwards in the Gulf Stream.

These cooling events discovered in the seabed were a counterpart to warming events recorded in Greenland ice. Willi Dansgaard of Copenhagen was famous for scrutinizing the ice cores retrieved by drilling deep into the ice sheet. He used variations in the proportion of heavy oxygen-18 atoms in the ice as an indicator of temperature changes.

In ice layers formed in the midst of the last ice age, 80,000 to 10,000 years ago, at two different drilling sites far apart on the ice sheet, Dansgaard discovered a dozen sudden, strong warming events, lasting a few hundred years. Like the Heinrich Events, they were quite unconnected with orbital changes governing the ice age itself. Hans Oeschger of Bern was Dansgaard's collaborator, and the warmings became known as Dansgaard–Oeschger Events. Were these a warm counterpart to Heinrich Events? The answer had to wait upon new drillings.

Tracing the sources of debris

Heinrich in Hamburg switched to quite different duties, but others followed up his discovery. The advantage lay with Columbia University. Its Lamont–Doherty Earth Observatory, perched on a cliff flanking the Hudson River's own glacier-carved valley, housed the world's largest collection of seabed cores. Those had already played an indispensable part in confirming the astronomical theory of ice ages, in the 1970s. If there was more to learn about the ice-rafting events, here was where to look.

Arguably the most advantaged of all was a geologist, Gerard Bond, who was married to Rusty Lotti, curator of the core laboratory. In 1995 he told her that he'd like to examine the North Atlantic cores much more thoroughly, millimetre by millimetre. They teamed up for the task, which became a career in itself. The great patience that it required was soon rewarded.

Along with Heinrich's white carbonates, which came from the Hudson Strait region of northern Canada, Bond and Lotti noticed less conspicuous reddish grains stained red with haematite, mixed in with the carbonates. These were traced to an origin in the St Lawrence region of southern Canada, which gave the Laurentide ice sheet its name. There were also black and translucent grains of volcanic glass that came from Iceland. So icebergs seemed to be rushing out simultaneously from different places.

In the gaps between the chilly Heinrich Events, Bond and Lotti found other layers where the St Lawrence red and Iceland black grains showed up as ice-rafted material, with the Hudson Strait white grains missing. Heinrich had understated the frequency of ice-rafting events. The reason was that, in the seabed of the north-east Atlantic where his cores came from, the events seen by Bond and Lotti left only very slight traces between the big ones that he reported.

Now known to have occurred at intervals of about 1400 years, the ice-rafting events qualify as probably the most drastic mode of climate change perceptible in the geological record during the human era on the Earth. Sudden drops of several degrees Celsius in mean temperatures could occur in just a few decades in the northern North Atlantic.

'We believe that this cycle has been in effect for tens of thousands of years and may still be operating today; if so, it's important to know where we now stand in it,' Bond remarked in 1995. 'There is clear evidence that significant climate shifts can occur within a lifetime. It's important to determine the mechanisms that trigger them if we are to prepare for the potential effects.'

The less frequent Heinrich Events supposedly reflected another, slower rhythm tied to the massive iceberg discharges from the Hudson Strait and elsewhere, when the icebergs could sometimes travel as far as the vicinity of Morocco in north-west Africa. And it was becoming surer that the more frequent ice rafting seen by Bond and Lotti was indeed cyclical, without necessarily implying strict timing. Collaborating with the Copenhagen experts, who had ice from a new core drilled on the summit of the Greenland ice sheet, Bond established that his cold events alternated quite regularly with the Dansgaard–Oeschger warmings. The ice-raft coolings were themselves visible in the ice record.

In the mid-1990s there was still great uncertainty about whether the iceberg armadas were themselves the cause of the chilling, motivated by the binge–purge cycle in various ice sheets, or whether the outbreaks were an effect of some other agency driving the changes in climate. Bond and Lotti persisted in their detective work with a widening circle of collaborators. They examined the sediments centimetre by centimetre, concentrating on two cores, one from the Atlantic east of Newfoundland and the other from the Denmark Strait between Greenland and Iceland. They decided that icebergs were not the only rafts for mineral debris.

As already noted as a possibility by Heinrich, sea-ice formed on the surface of the polar seas could collect windblown dust from nearby shores. Northerly winds could then transport the ice southwards until it eventually melted and dropped its debris. The role of sea-ice became clearer when attention switched from ice-age layers in the seabed sediments to the uppermost layers, corresponding with deposits over the last 10,000 years since the ice age ended. Sources of debris minerals in Greenland and on islands in the Norwegian Sea entered the picture.

Suffering in West Friesland

Bond and Lotti confirmed their hunch that ice-rafting events continued after the ice age. They were much less conspicuous in terms of the amount of rafted material, but they had about the same rhythm, and their effects on climate were not negligible.

Datings were approximate, but it turned out that the most recent ice-rafting events were about 350 and 600 years ago, during the period long known to historians of climate as the Little Ice Age. A big reduction in rafted debris around 800 years ago fitted with a well-known Medieval Warm Period. Ice rafting 1700 years ago coincided with the onset of the Roman Cold Period. And so on.

The alternations of warmth and cold went all the way back, at average intervals of 1340 years, with a big cooling 8300 years ago, to events at the end of the last ice age. The great wobble-induced warming that terminated the ice age was cruelly interrupted by a severe rechilling 14,000 years ago called the Younger

Dryas. This was coupled with a severe ice-rafting event of the Heinrich type—white grains and all.

One of the Bond group's ice-rafting peaks was around 800 BC. From an archaeological site in West Friesland, the palaeo-ecologist Bas van Geel of Amsterdam knew of the suffering caused to the inhabitants of the region by prolonged cold, wet weather at that time. Low-lying settlements and farmland had to be abandoned as the water table rose.

The catastrophe occurred at the transition from Bronze Age to Iron Age. It also coincided with a big increase in the cosmic rays, making radiocarbon, radioberyllium and other radioactive elements in the atmosphere, which were symptoms of weak solar activity. Van Geel was convinced that the event should be blamed on a faltering Sun.

'This abrupt climate change occurred simultaneously with a sharp rise in radiocarbon starting around 850 BC and peaking around 760 BC,' he said. 'Just because no one knows for sure how the solar changes work on the climate is no excuse for denying their effect.'

At first Van Geel encountered great scepticism. When Bond and his colleagues reported the post-ice-age results in 1997, they commented, 'Forcing of millennial-scale climate variability by changes in solar output has also been suggested, but that mechanism is highly controversial, and no evidence has been found of a solar cycle in the range of 1400 to 1500 years.' Four years were to elapse before they changed their minds.

Since the 1960s, other scientists had reported many links between high cosmic rays and cold conditions on the Earth, including the Little Ice Age and previous occasions marked by advances of the glaciers of Europe and North America. In collaboration with Dutch and Russian colleagues, Van Geel tried to take the story further by linking the Dansgaard–Oeschger events during the ice age to variations in radioberyllium found in the Greenland ice. Good matches were found, but there were problems with the quality and dating of the radioberyllium data, and doubts remained about how the changing weather might affect its rate of accumulation in the ice.

Finding a solar rhythm

The scientist with the best knowledge of the radioberyllium was Juerg Beer of Switzerland's Eidgenössische Anstalt für Wasserversorgung, Abwasserreinigung und Gewässerschutz. He joined the Bond–Lotti collaboration. The Atlantic cores were also subjected to thorough radiocarbon dating. Then the ice-rafting events could be compared with the best judgement of the dates and magnitudes of radioberyllium peaks in Greenland. The matches turned out to be surprisingly good.

ICE-RAFTING EVENTS

Bond and his team reported in 2001: 'Our correlations are evidence, therefore, that over the last 12,000 years virtually every centennial time scale increase in drift ice documented in our North Atlantic records was tied to a distinct interval of variable and, overall, reduced solar output.'

This put the solar cat among the climatic pigeons. It gave variations in the Sun a major role in climate, making them responsible for the most important and potentially catastrophic natural changes, excepting only the ice ages. Scientists studying the impact of man-made greenhouse gases on the climate had been at some pains to minimize the role of the Sun, and to play down climate variations before the industrial era. They wanted to say that the Medieval Warm Period and the Little Ice Age were purely regional affairs, mainly confined to Europe.

This interpretation became harder to sustain if the cause was a variable Sun, affecting the whole planet. Bond's team was able to cite widespread changes in the Atlantic reaching to South America and West Africa, already correlated with solar variations by other scientists. Farther afield, reductions of rainfall in East Africa coincided with the ice-rafting events, and there were likely effects on the Asian monsoon as well.

The ice-rafting story is far from finished. Apart from looking again at the global effects of a variable Sun, scientists will now ask, with renewed urgency, exactly how it exerts its influence on the Earth's climate. They must also try to find out, as a matter of solar astronomy, why the Sun's variations have a 1400-year rhythm. It would be good to know where we stand in the cycle.

'If the Little Ice Age has definitely ended,' Hartmut Heinrich commented, 'then on the simplest interpretation of the cycle, the next ice-rafting chill is not due for 1000 years. Let's hope that's so.'

▶ *See also* CRYOSPHERE, CLIMATE CHANGE *and* OCEAN CURRENTS. *For continuing effects of solar variability, see* EARTHSHINE.

IMMORTALITY

Should we be satisfied with 100 years?

TRAVELLERS' TALES OF GIANT SEA MONSTERS may not all be nonsense. Some marine animals never stop growing in size, however slowly, and they don't age perceptibly. If they could avoid a sticky end from predation, accident or disease, they might be in some sense immortal. Who knows how large they might grow, if they lived for 1000 years?

Lobsters are a case in point. They are never too old to eat. They share a mechanism for immortality with certain cancer cells, which can be cultured outside the body indefinitely, like bacteria or yeast. Cells from ordinary, healthy human tissue will reproduce only for a few dozen generations in laboratory cultures, and then die.

The trademark of the immortals is a protein, an enzyme called telomerase. It protects their chromosomes, the packages of deoxyribonucleic acid, DNA, that carry the genetic messages used in building new cells. At the ends of chromosomes are tie-strings called telomeres, consisting of short sequences of genetic code repeated over and over. In the ordinary course of events the telomeres erode, becoming shorter and shorter in each new generation, like the sand of an hourglass running out. Ultimately the chromosomes no longer function correctly and the cells die. But telomerase can prevent that by renewing the telomeres.

In 1998 a team led by Reza Parwaresch at Kiel's Christian-Albrechts-Universität investigated the biochemistry of the American lobster *Homarus americanus*. They found them to be extraordinarily rich in the chromosome-healing enzyme. 'High telomerase activities were detected in all lobster organs,' the Kiel team reported. 'We conclude that telomerase activation is a conserved mechanism for maintaining long-term cell proliferation capacity and preventing senescence.'

The same group detected high telomerase in the rainbow trout *Oncorhynchus mykiss* too. But the study of animals with negligible ageing is still in its infancy. They may have important lessons, not only about the credibility or otherwise of sea monsters, but also about the mechanisms of ageing in human beings and most other animals. In the meantime, remarkable progress has come from more direct investigations of mortality and immortality in living cells.

● Hayflick's limit and Olovnikov's train

Research on ageing in the mid-20th century was confounded by a misleading report by a French scientist, Alexis Carrel. In 1929 he declared that ordinary animal cells grown in a lab culture would thrive indefinitely. By 1946 he was claiming to have kept cells from a chicken's heart alive for 34 years. When nobody else managed to make normal cells survive like that, sloppy work by the scientist, or by some unfortunate lab assistant, took the blame. Carrel was a Nobel Prizewinner, so you had to be a brave researcher to contradict him.

At the Wistar Institute in Philadelphia, Leonard Hayflick spent three years, 1958–61, trying to find out what was going wrong with his cultures of normal human cells. They would do well, dividing and redividing for a few dozen generations at most, and then stop. They continued to live for some months and then died.

Eventually, with Paul Moorhead, Hayflick tried the experiment of adding younger female cells to a culture of older male cells. The sex difference made the mixed cells distinguishable. There came a point when the older cells all stopped dividing at the same time, while the younger cells went on happily. This proved that there was nothing wrong with the culture technique, but that the cells were mortal. Although the scientists had considerable difficulty getting so heretical a result published, it brought sighs of relief in almost every tissue-culture lab in the world.

The natural lifespan of cells in culture, through a few dozen divisions at most, came to be called the Hayflick limit. But where was the clock, or counter, in the cells that decided when their time was up? Ten years after Hayflick and Moorhead confirmed the mortality of tissue cells, a crucial idea occurred to a scientist waiting for a train on the Moscow Metro.

Alexey Olovnikov of the Soviet Institute of Biochemical Physics was brooding about how the DNA chains in chromosomes make copies of themselves whenever a cell divides. The picture came into his head of a train being used to lay a railway track. It works fine, except that the train cannot lay the piece of the track on which it is standing to start with.

The molecular machinery that makes copies of the chromosomes is in the same fix, Olovnikov thought. It needs to grip a piece of the DNA to begin its work but, as a result, that particular piece will not be included in the copied DNA. Every time a cell divides the DNA chain gets slightly shorter. The part affected is the telomere, the tie-string at the very end of the chromosome.

In 1971 Olovnikov proposed that erosion of the telomeres on the chromosome set a limit to the number of times a normal cell can divide. He called it marginotomy, the cutting of the margin. It was a dazzling idea, but to confirm it and bring it up to date took nearly 20 years, because the pieces of DNA track that are lost are extremely small.

Steps to a denouement

A Canadian biochemist, Calvin Harley, latched onto Olovnikov's theory of telomere erosion soon after it came out. He wanted to know why human beings age and in the 1980s, at McMaster University in Ontario, he grew cell cultures to investigate the question. At first Harley could see no technical means of verifying Olovnikov's idea. These became available, step-by-step, starting with discoveries made in other places and concerning creatures apparently very different from us.

Step 1 came from research at Yale on a single-celled organism, the protozoan *Tetrahymena* that lives in ponds. Like yeast, it is immortal in the sense that it reproduces itself ad infinitum by cell division, and its telomeres do not erode in the manner predicted by Olovnikov. In 1978 Elizabeth Blackburn discovered that the bug's telomeres consist of the same six letters of DNA code, repeated again and again.

Later, at UC Berkeley, Blackburn and a graduate student, Carol Greider, took Step 2. In 1985 they announced the discovery of telomerase as the enzyme responsible for making the telomeres. 'We suggested that telomerase would compensate for the incomplete replication of chromosome ends,' Greider recalled later. 'This would explain the telomere length maintenance seen in organisms such as *Tetrahymena* and yeast.'

But what was the relevance of the telomeres of a pond bug to matters of human ageing and cancer? Step 3 began with a chance encounter, when Greider was on a trip to Ontario visiting a friend, Bruce Futcher, who was doing research on yeast at McMaster. That was in the lab next door to Harley's, and when she met him she found they had a common interest in telomeres. They talked hopefully about possible joint experiments.

In 1998, Greider phoned Harley with exciting news from the Cold Spring Harbor Laboratory, New York, where she and Futcher had gone to work. Scientists there, and others working independently at Los Alamos, had found the composition of telomeres in vertebrate animals like us. Just as in *Tetrahymena*, they consist of a multiple repetition of six letters of DNA code. The only difference is that TTGGGG has become TTAGGG.

The time was ripe for those joint experiments on human cells, and by 1990 Harley, Futcher and Greider had completed Step 3. They published a full experimental verification of Olovnikov's theory, in modernized form. Ageing in human cells occurs by the loss of one TTAGGG sequence from the telomere tie-string on each chromosome, every time a cell divides.

Next, Harley and Silvia Bacchetti at McMaster established the links between activation of the telomerase enzyme, telomere maintenance and human cancer. In brief, it is the availability of telomerase that makes a cancerous cell dangerously immortal, by dodging the Hayflick limit. And Harley also proposed that the telomere–telomerase relationship was the Holy Grail long sought by scientists and medics concerned with the processes of ageing.

'Telomere length and telomerase activity appear to be markers of the replicative history and proliferative potential of cells,' he wrote in 1991. 'The intriguing possibility remains that telomere loss is a genetic time bomb and hence causally involved in cell senescence and immortalization.'

The prospect of anti-ageing drugs, for medical and cosmetic purposes, attracted commercial funding. Harley joined the Geron Corporation in California. With colleagues there and at Colorado and Texas-Dallas, Harley went on to consolidate the telomere hypothesis of cellular ageing in humans. By 1997 he and his team had found the key gene that reactivates telomerase in human cells and so refreshes their telomeres. It's called the human telomerase reverse transcriptase gene. That's a bit of a mouthful, yet it seems uncannily like the elixir of youth about which the ancients fantasized.

It comes with a health warning. As cancer cells use telomerase to achieve their deadly immortality, stimulating the renewal of tissue cells by artificial methods might provoke tumours. Indeed the first priority for using the knowledge about telomeres was to develop inhibitors of telomerase as a means of fighting cancer. Nevertheless, at Geron and elsewhere, cautious activation of telomerase seemed to offer new prospects for treating degenerative diseases.

Mother Nature wasn't here before

Even without the benefit of such very advanced science, people are living longer. The relative contributions of clean water, general hygiene and comfort, vaccines, antibiotics, better nutrition, and less iniquitous social systems are still debated. And increasing life expectancy of human beings has already taken us to an unknown continent, about which even Mother Nature knows very little.

There are few evolutionary tests of the value of survival past the point where one's youngest offspring have been nurtured to maturity. Some scientists suspect that the menopause, which halts reproduction long before death, gives recognition to the role of grannies in the survival of the young. But on the whole, old folk are like extraterrestrial beings whose place on this planet is as yet undetermined.

When Hayflick was settled at UC San Francisco, he commented on this state of affairs. 'After performing the miracles that take us from conception to birth, and then to sexual maturation and adulthood,' he observed, 'natural selection was unable to favour the development of a more elementary mechanism that would simply maintain those earlier miracles forever. The manifestations of this failure are called ageing.'

He insisted that ageing was neither a disease nor a programmed process under direct control of the genes. Instead, Hayflick conflated various inputs from biochemistry, including damage done by reactive oxygen throughout life, into a general picture of molecular junk accumulating in an organism. This is due to a progressive loss of fidelity in the copying of genes and the making of proteins.

In 1977 Thomas Kirkwood at Newcastle pointed out that burdening an animal with the genetic resources that might delay ageing is pointless if it is going to die young, because of the hazards of life. There is a trade-off between youthful vigour and provision for later life. Do fighter pilots give much thought to their old-age pensions?

Kirkwood called his idea the disposable soma theory, and evidence in its favour accumulated in the decades that followed. Long-lived species are better provided with molecular defences against reactive oxygen than short-lived species are. If you prevent fruit flies from mating until late in life, the resulting strains show an extended span for reproduction but at the price of reduced fecundity at a younger age. Kirkwood and a colleague commented, 'There is clearly much scope for further development and testing of the evolutionary theories of why we age.'

How long have we got?

The science casts a new light on human aspirations for prolonged youth and indefinitely extended life. On the day of his assassination, at what was then the ripe old age of 55, Julius Caesar declared, according to Shakespeare:

> Of all the wonders that I yet have heard,
> It seems to me most strange that men should fear;
> Seeing that death, a necessary end,
> Will come when it will come.

The veteran soldier would be bemused by 21st-century hypochondria. In defiance of common sense and medical economics, the generation with the best life expectancy in history is obsessed with longevity.

Although overpopulation is said to be a great global problem, health educators insist that it is one's duty to abjure motorbikes and butter and to live as long as possible. Yes, even though longevity may bring physical or mental incompetence so severe that it will cost more to keep you zimmering than to feed an entire African orphanage.

In the absence of significant disease, ageing sets a natural limit to the human lifespan. According to Hayflick it is about 125 years. Very few people lived past 75 until the 20th century. But by 2000, 75 per cent of the inhabitants of the most affluent countries were doing so. The greying of the populations took actuaries and the medical profession by surprise.

The increase in human longevity slowed down in the closing decades of the 20th century. Life expectancy at birth in affluent countries may level out at 80–90 years by the mid-21st century. As the ageing process makes everyone more vulnerable to disease and gross degeneration, further prolongation of life may require medications yet to be invented.

They are not necessarily a good idea. Foreseeable problems range from tyrants who refuse to die, to simply losing the carefree pleasures of retirement if young earners should decline to carry the economic burden of the elderly. Hayflick asked, 'Would the least imperfect scenario be a future society in which everyone lived to their 100th birthday in good physical and mental health, then to die on the stroke of midnight?'

▶ *For a parallel topic, see* CELL DEATH.

IMMUNE SYSTEM

What's me, what's you, and what's a nasty bug?

I N 1997, at the Australian National University outside Canberra, Christopher Goodnow started planning a mouse ranch. His aim was to house, on a half-hectare site, 30,000 laboratory mice in germ-free conditions and by 2006 to produce in them individual strains with mutations affecting every single gene that a mouse possesses. It was a daunting project, mocked by many experts, but within a few years his team was beginning to produce mutant strains with heart disease, cancer and obesity, which researchers in other institutions were very glad to have.

Of all laboratory animals used in large numbers, mice are the most like us. More or less complete descriptions of all the genes in the mouse genome and the human genome became available in 2001. It was in anticipation of those advances and of the inevitable question 'What do all these genes do?' that

Goodnow conceived the mouse ranch. As required by the rules governing animal experiments, the relevance of the mutant mice to medicine would be quite direct. Nowadays it is usually simple to identify the human equivalent of any mouse gene.

Geneticists rely on mutant laboratory animals to enable them to deduce the normal role of genes, from the defects that arise when the genes are corrupted. The chemical agent ethylnitrosurea, used to cause heritable mutations in the Canberra mice, has a random effect, so the affected aspects of their lives are unpredictable. But for his personal research purposes, Goodnow was looking out especially for mutant mice strains with defects in the immune system, which protects mice and humans from diseases. By the beginning of the 21st century, the key problem was no longer how individual weapons contribute to the defences, but how the whole immune system controls itself, to avoid destroying its own body.

'In some ways, the process resembles the sequence of fight/disarm decisions in a military missile launch,' Goodnow said, 'which serve a similar purpose of preventing friendly fire.' Since 1985, he had discovered more than a dozen genes in mice involved in the restraining mechanisms. That continuing quest inspired Goodnow's wish to screen the entire mouse genome, looking for many other genes needed to complete the story of the immune system.

Infectious and self-destructive diseases

This high-tech programme illustrated how far the human species had come since its knowledge of the immune system was limited to a general awareness that, if you survived an infectious disease once, you were probably immune to catching the same disease again. This was first formalized in a monograph by the Persian physician al-Razi around A D 910, with special reference to smallpox and measles. Loving parents and conniving doctors in many parts of the world deliberately exposed young children to mild forms of deadly diseases in the hope that they would survive with acquired immunity.

Scientific study of the immune system began with the discovery by Edward Jenner in England in 1796 that inoculation with a mild disease, cowpox, gave protection against smallpox. Vaccinia, the medical name for cowpox, inspired Louis Pasteur in 19th-century Paris to coin the word vaccine, but Jenner's was a hard act to follow. Few virulent diseases have such neat counterparts from which to make harmless vaccines. In his experiments with cholera and rabies, Pasteur introduced the strategy of making safe versions of disease-causing agents, or of their components or products, which might suffice to train the immune system to fight the virulent forms.

The 20th century brought a fridge-full of vaccines against many human and animal diseases. They were not available in time to prevent the Spanish flu of

1918 killing more people than all the battles of the First World War. And despite later successes against diphtheria, tuberculosis and polio, those aware of the history of epidemics warned of an ever-present menace. New or mutant viruses, bacteria and parasites, probably being incubated in animals, were liable to spread rapidly, carried by intercontinental travellers.

Even as smallpox was being eradicated from the world, acquired immune deficiency syndrome, or AIDS, arrived as if on cue. It was a shock because, like the plague, AIDS attacks the immune system itself. Not long after, a completely novel kind of infectious agent, the prion, was identified as being responsible for various diseases. These include kuru, affecting cannibals, and the human form of mad cow disease first seen in a nation foolish enough to make carnivores of its cows.

Faults in the immune system came to light too. Natural immune deficiency can result from a hereditary defect, leaving a child vulnerable to infections. On the other hand, overzealous responses by the immune system to commonplace materials cause allergies, like hay fever provoked by pollen. And when the body turns destructively upon itself, the result may be rheumatoid arthritis, multiple sclerosis or another of a long string of auto-immune diseases.

The immune system functioning normally, in its fight against alien materials, was an impediment to transplant surgery. Much effort went into tissue-typing and immunosuppressive drugs to reduce the risk of rejection of donated organs. For all of these reasons, research on the immune system became a major scientific theme. It preoccupied biologists as well as clinical researchers. Plainly the battle between animals and diseases had been going on for hundreds of millions of years, and had resulted in elaborate defence mechanisms just as clever and subtle as eyes or brains.

How a water-flea fought bacterial spores

Around 1900, biologists knew two contradictory things about the immune system. Coupled especially with the name of Paul Ehrlich of Frankfurt was the concept of antibodies. These were materials liberated in the fluids of the body in response to a specific germ or poison—an antigen, we should now say. Each antibody was adapted precisely to combating one intruder. Their physical and chemical nature was unknown, but antibodies gave a quasi-molecular gloss to the well-known phenomena of acquired immunity.

The other piece of information ran against previous ideas. Until late in the 19th century, white blood corpuscles were considered hostile to health, being seen abundantly in inflammations and in the pus of septic wounds. With hindsight, this was like believing that firemen cause fires because you so often find them on the scene.

A splinter of wood left in your finger can lead to inflammation and suppuration. In 1883, Ilya Metchnikoff, a Ukrainian-born scientist working in Messina, observed the same effect in the larvae of a Scandinavian starfish, *Bipinnaria*. These were transparent, large enough for several operations, and could remain alive under the microscope. Metchnikoff stuck sharp splinters into them, and within a day saw a mass of white blood cells moving in to make a cushion around each splinter.

Convinced that he was watching the immune system in action, Metchnikoff examined the course of an infection with microbial spores, in other transparent creatures. In water-fleas, *Daphniae*, which are really crustaceans, the swallowed spores penetrated the intestinal wall. Mobile cells gathered around them.

'A battle takes place between the two elements,' Metchnikoff said. 'Sometimes the spores succeed in breeding. Microbes are generated that secrete a substance capable of dissolving the mobile cells. Such cases are rare on the whole. Far more often it happens that the mobile cells kill and digest the infectious spores and thus ensure immunity for the organism.'

Experiments in rabbits and guinea pigs showed a similar mobilization of white corpuscles in vaccinated animals exposed to a disease. To the corpuscles that digested the spores, Metchnikoff gave the name eating cells, or phagocytes. 'This theory came under heavy fire from the greatest names in science,' he noted. Even when it was irrefutable, many decades were to pass before biologists fully understood how Metchnikoff's cellular theory and Ehrlich's antibody theory could both be right.

A hierarchy of soldiers

To tell step by step how the complexities of the immune system were disentangled would be to torture the reader with all the puzzles experienced by the biologists. By 2000, the overall picture of the components of the immune system in mammals seemed to be fairly complete and self-consistent. The phagocytes are only one of several types of white cells, or lymphocytes, providing the soldiers of the immune army.

The human body musters a million million lymphocytes, ten times more than the number of nerve cells in the brain. Their total mass is 600 grams or so. At more than Shylock's pound of flesh, that is a measure of how much unconscious effort we put into protecting ourselves.

Made in bone marrow, the lymphocytes travel all over the body via two interlinked circulations. One is by the ordinary blood vessels and the other is a special network of lymphatic vessels carrying transparent lymph. One kind of lymphocytes, called B cells, manufacture antibodies. These are Y-shaped molecules with active regions on the ends of their two shorter arms. Although some of the antibodies remain attached to the B cells that made them, most of them patrol as unattached molecules in the blood and lymph. So Ehrlich was right.

Metchnikoff was vindicated most directly by one of the ways in which antibodies work. Attaching themselves to a microbe, they flag it for eating by the phagocytes, a class of lymphocytes nowadays called macrophages. But the performances both of antibodies and of lymphocytes turned out to be more elaborate, and beautifully orchestrated. Some antibodies attack the alien material themselves, with the aid of other special proteins that circulate in the blood. Others bar the way to viruses trying to enter healthy cells.

The free antibody molecules patrolling in the blood and lymph provide an early line of defence. A full immune response requires first that an antibody, still attached to the B cell that made it, should hold up like a trophy a specimen of the antigen, the alien intruder. At a suitable rendezvous, perhaps in one of the lymph nodes dotted around the body, another type of lymphoctye, a CD4 T cell, may authorize the B cell to go into mass production of its antibody.

The CD4 T cells (often called T4) are completed in the thymus, high in the chest, from some of the lymphocytes emanating from the bone marrow. They carry antibody-like receptors on their surfaces, tailored especially to distinguish healthy cells of one's own body from alien or infected cells. Besides activating selected B cells, CD4 T cells can also command the formation, in the thymus, of killer CD8 T cells that go out to find and destroy infected cells.

In 1983 the discoverer of the AIDS virus, Luc Montagnier of the Institut Pasteur in Paris, confirmed what clinicians already suspected, that AIDS attacks the CD4 T cells. He commented: 'The consequences are disastrous, because the T4s are headquarters cells for the immune system.'

Later it became plain that CD4 Ts are not their own masters. Headquarters cells, yes, but they respond to intelligence gathered by another class of lymphocytes called dendritic cells. At first sight these seem like Metchnikoff's phagocytes, because they lurk all over the body and recognize and engulf disease agents. But when they are overwhelmed by a heavy attack, they change their character and carry samples of the invader, as antigens, back to headquarters. There they coach CD4 T cells to activate B cells for mass-producing the right antibodies.

Off-the-peg antibodies

Throughout the first half of the 20th century a central mystery was how the immune system copes with a seemingly infinite variety of invading antigens, from viruses to other people's tissue and even man-made materials. Is the immune system like a shop selling off-the-peg clothes? In other words, is there a pre-existing range of antibodies that the disease agents can try on for size and so select their own enemies? Or is the immune system a bespoke tailor starting from scratch whenever a new client appears, and fashioning the antibody to suit it?

To the surprise of many, off-the-peg won the day. Ehrlich had outlined the features of this hypothesis in 1900, but he had misgivings. Why, for example, should evolution have equipped animals living in temperate regions with antibodies to diseases found only in the tropics?

By the 1930s the idea had fallen out of favour, but Niels Jerne of the Danish Serum Institute revived it in the 1950s. Macfarlane Burnet of the Walter and Eliza Hall Institute in Melbourne then developed the off-the-peg hypothesis incisively. In Burnet's clonal selection theory the hostile agent, the antigen, selects its own antibody, which a clone of appropriate cells manufactures plentifully.

The theory is now a cornerstone of immunology. Yet at the time (1957) the prejudice against such a notion was so strong that Burnet chose to publish his ideas in the *Australian Journal of Science*. He confessed in his autobiography, 'If, perish the thought, there was something very wrong about the clonal selection concept, the publication in an out-of-the-way Australian journal would mean that very few people in America or England would see it.'

The immune system continually produces a choice of many millions of different antibodies. An invading microbe, or other antigen, soon meets a particular antibody that sticks to it. In molecular terms, a portion of the antigen fits into a chemically active cleft in the antibody, like a key into a lock. It doesn't matter which part of the antigen sticks, and any invader has many candidate knobs and chemical subunits. So the chances of finding a match are multiplied.

A by-product of research on the immune system is a technique that produces large quantities of a selected 'monoclonal' antibody in a flask. Invented in 1975 by Georges Köhler from Germany and César Milstein from Argentina, at the UK's Laboratory of Molecular Biology, the trick is to extract lymphocytes from a mouse exposed to a selected antigen, and to fuse them with cancerous lymphocytes. The resulting hybrid cells go on making the desired antibody at a high rate. Uses of monoclonal antibodies range from fishing for particular biomolecules, within living cells, to targeting cancer cells with antibodies that are freighted with a poison to kill them—glossed as 'antibody engineering'.

Identity cards for organisms

The sheer numbers and diversity of pre-existing antibodies in the clonal theory brought to the fore the 'friendly fire' mystery. The immune system has to avoid attacking its own body. That it has the potential to do so is grievously evident in the auto-immune diseases. Much of the complexity of the immune system arises from the need always to distinguish between the body's own tissue and cells and those of alien invaders. The self/non-self distinction, the experts call it.

Blood played a special part in revealing how it is done. The wrong blood transfusion can kill you, by fatally clumping red blood cells. Karl Landsteiner distinguished the A, B, AB and O blood groups in Vienna in 1909, and the rhesus factor while at the Rockefeller Institute in New York in 1940. But it turned out that, even though patients received blood of the correct ABO and rhesus type, their bodies' defences reacted against the alien white blood cells. Pregnant women, too, made antibodies against their babies' white cells.

In 1954 Jean Dausset in Paris identified the first of a set of molecular labels called HLAs. They act as antigens in another person's body and provoke antibodies to react against them. Subsequent research in Europe and the USA revealed that each of us carries two versions of six HLA genes, and there are many available variants of each—hundreds in some cases. Except in identical twins and occasionally in brothers and sisters, it is virtually impossible for any two individuals to have the same HLA combination. The genes command the manufacture of protein-carbohydrate structures, MHCs, that decorate the outer surfaces of all body cells.

'The essential function of these structures resides in self-recognition,' Dausset declared later. 'These structures are, in fact, the identity card of the entire organism.' They are also the cause of the rejection of skin or organs surgically transplanted from one person to another. This is me, but that's you, and my immune system knows it well.

In Leiden, Jon van Rood pioneered the use of HLA tests for tissue-typing in order to match organ donors and recipients as closely as possible. They opened the way to successful transplants of kidneys and other organs, even though the HLA system took another 30 years fully to decipher.

The molecular biologists moved in. They began the arduous task of translating the immune system into a growing collection of identified genes, of proteins whose manufacture they ordain, and of genetic control switches that activate appropriate genes and repress unwanted ones. In the early 1960s Rodney Porter of Cambridge had correctly pictured antibody molecules as Y-shaped structures. By the mid-1980s the genes responsible for making antibodies were known, together with the highly variable genes of the self-recognition HLA system, which in humans are concentrated in chromosome No. 6.

It was one thing to know something of these self/non-self markers, quite another to tell how the immune system used them to avoid mistakes. In 1985, as a PhD student in Melbourne, Christopher Goodnow began experiments with genetically modified mice, which he continued in Sydney, Stanford and

Canberra. He identified checkpoints where decisions are made either to continue with an immune reaction, or to instruct the B and T cells involved to shut up or die.

By the end of the century the tally, from Goodnow and others, was 11 checkpoints for B cells and 6 for T cells, each set up by a different gene. But thousands of genes are involved in the immune system, and progress at about one gene a year was a pedestrian pace compared with the projects then busy reading all the genes in the mouse and human genomes. Here was Goodnow's motivation to create the mouse ranch in Canberra, and to produce mutations in every mouse gene.

'The mouse genome is a list of parts for making a mouse,' he said. 'The mutant mice will give us a sublist of all the genes involved in the immune system, and where they operate and what they do. But we'll still need to design clever experiments to see exactly how the parts fit together to control immune responses. It will be hard work for us because Nature goes to astonishing lengths to avoid fatal errors.'

Weapons on both sides

Don't imagine that microbes attacking us are naïve about the immune system, or astonished by its ambushes. Diseases and the defences of plants and animals have evolved together over hundreds of millions of years, in a non-stop molecular contest. Just as a warplane carries weapons that home in on the enemy's radar, and flares that distract his heat-seeking missiles, so pathogens have their own ways of foxing the immune system. The direct attack of the AIDS virus on the CD4 T cells is just a blatant example.

As for the defence, some evolutionary theorists think that sexual reproduction is the norm in plants and animals because its endless shuffling of the genes is the best strategy for combating disease. Genetic differences between individuals should eventually explain why so often an infection fatal to one person can be virtually harmless in another. But bear in mind also that too successful a pathogen, which killed every one of its hosts, would perish itself, for want of targets.

Growing knowledge of the weaponry and of the host–pathogen interaction opens a new and daunting chapter in biological science. Laboratory techniques have reached a point where the battle against microbes can be followed in real time, by seeing what genes come into action in the cells of the immune system. The puzzle is to know which genes are doing their proper work, and which are misbehaving because of an attacker's counter-measures.

The scale of the problem became apparent with the advent of gene chips. These are devices that can check material from cells for the presence, absence or activation of thousands of genes simultaneously. In a pioneering application, the Whitehead Institute for Biomedical Research in Massachusetts used gene chips to discover some of the tradecraft of the scouts and spies of the immune system, the intelligence-gathering dendritic cells.

The experimenters exposed cultures of human dendritic cells to three pathogens in turn. These were the gut-dwelling bacterium *Escherichia coli*, some strains of which cause severe food poisoning, the commonplace fungus *Candida albicans* that can cause oral and vaginal thrush, and the influenza virus. Out of an assortment of 2000 dendritic genes detected on the chips, the bacterium activated no fewer than 685. For the virus the score was 531 activated genes, and for the fungus, 289.

Among these were 166 genes activated by all three agents, implying that they belonged to a core of general immunological responses and were probably functioning correctly. Some of the others may have been correct responses, appropriate to the class and species of the bug. But the experimenters suspected that much of the gene activation was a sign of the attacker working to undermine the performance of the dendritic cells.

Finding out which responses are for our benefit, and which for the pathogen's, promised to be an arduous task. For Nir Hacohen, leader of the research at the Whitehead Institute, the state of play in immunology at the start of the 21st century was summed up by the lack of progress towards a vaccine against the AIDS virus, HIV.

'This tells us,' Hacohen said, 'that there are many aspects of the immune system we still don't understand, even if we think we do sometimes. We've been lucky with vaccines until today. They have worked surprisingly well, given our ignorance of the process. One day we will be a bit smarter and be able to design optimal vaccines, even for new pathogens. But we are a long way away from that time.'

Sneezing in space

During the Apollo missions that sent them to Moon, around 1970, astronauts were found to have reduced numbers of protective white blood cells. The force of gravity is somehow involved in the functioning of the immune system. When astronauts sneeze in space, the count of viruses in the droplets is much higher than on the ground, even though there are no other symptoms of infection. Cosmonauts on the Russian Mir space station, tested with toxins painted on the skin, developed rashes that they would not have done on Earth. The immune system returns to normal within two weeks when the space travellers are back on the ground.

Many observations and experiments conducted in space have tried to find the physical explanation, and to assess the health risks of prolonged spaceflight. One puzzle is to separate effects of weightlessness from other factors that could affect the immune system, including stress, close physical confinement, freewheeling body clocks, and cosmic radiation. The last was ruled out as an important factor, at least in respect of lymphocyte behaviour, in a high-flying balloon where T cells were exposed to cosmic rays while still under terrestrial gravity.

The balloon trial was a forerunner to Swiss experiments, from 1983 onwards, in Europe's Spacelab carried by a NASA shuttle. Devised by Augusto Cogoli and his colleagues at the Eidgenössische Technische Hochschule Zürich, the experiments activated cultures of T cells with molecules that simulated the presence of an antigen. The weightless response was down by nearly 90 per cent, compared with the performance of the same cultures in a centrifuge in Spacelab, which simulated normal gravity.

To follow up this dramatic result, the Swiss space biologists used sounding rockets launched from Kiruna in Sweden. Beginning in 1989 and continuing at intervals into the new century, each of these flights gave about ten minutes of weightlessness. A microscope manipulated from the ground showed that, within 30 seconds of the onset of weightlessness, the T cells altered their internal skeletons, with one of the proteins forming unusual bundles. And although the antigen simulator stuck to the T cells as it should, the subsequent responses were sluggish, compared with those of cells undergoing the same tests on the ground.

'Such a big and quick effect on the cells surprised us,' said Cogoli. 'Now we must find out in much more detail what the absence of gravity does to the immune system, and how to avoid harmful consequences during long space journeys. It's quite urgent really, because there are no hospitals on Mars.'

Note: This is a subject where the scientists' shorthand can be less forbidding for non-experts than the full tags. In the matter of the identity cards of cells, HLA stands for human leukocyte antigen and MHC for major histocompatibility complex. The formal name of a gene chip is an oligonucleotide microarray.

▶ *See also* SMALLPOX *and* CELL DEATH. *For the role of disease in evolution, see* CLONING *and* PLANT DISEASES.

IMPACTS

Physical consequences of collisions with comets and asteroids

THE YUCATÁN PENINSULA pokes north into the Gulf of Mexico like a hitchhiker's thumb. It has no rivers in the ordinary sense. Instead, underground streams supply natural wells. The water-filled sinkholes are called *cenotes* in Spanish. The word comes from *dzonot* in the language of the Maya who still live there, and whose ancestors built the astronomical observatory, pyramids and temples of Chichén-Itzá. The name of that calendar-keeping city means the well mouth, and refers to the Cenote Sagrado, a sinkhole 60 metres wide.

The oddest feature of the Yucatán sinkholes is that they are concentrated around a huge arc. A natural ditch up to five metres deep makes almost a complete semicircle, which intersects the northern coast at points more than 100 kilometres apart, and curves far inland. The meaning of this peculiar hydrology did not become clear until 1991. The arc of sinkholes follows the rim of a crater that's otherwise hidden from view under a kilometre of unrelated limestone.

The buried Chicxulub crater is 170 kilometres wide, with its centre slightly offshore. It's the wound in the Earth made by an icy comet or stony asteroid that hit the Earth and wiped out the dinosaurs, the ammonites and a long casualty list of other creatures.

For the sleuths who found it, the most gratifying evidence was the image of the crater showing at the surface, provided by the pattern of sinkholes. The crater rim somehow reaches up to us, through hundreds of metres of overlying rock and 65 million years of time. By influencing erosion and flow near the surface it provided the Maya civilization and modern Mexico with their special arrangements for freshwater supplies.

With hindsight, you can say that the first hint of the buried crater's presence came in 1951, when oil prospectors of Petróleos Méxicanos found, in exploratory boreholes, rock that had been melted. At the time it was dismissed as being volcanic in origin. But in 1978 Glen Penfield, an American petroleum geophysicist doing aerial survey work for the company, found a big semicircle of disturbed magnetism offshore in the Gulf of Mexico.

When he looked up old records of gravity surveys of the Yucatán, Penfield saw another semicircle of abnormally high gravity, over the land, centred on the coastal settlement of Puerto Chicxulub (pronounced cheek-shoo-lube). It fitted perfectly with the offshore semicircle to make a round feature too wide for a volcano. In 1981 Penfield and a Mexican colleague, Antonio Camargo-Zanoguera, announced that they had found what looked like a large, buried impact crater.

Their report was made at a meeting of exploration geophysicists, and it failed to register with geologists who were busy looking for just such a crater. They wanted to match an impact event revealed by clay rich in unusual metals, found in Italy and Denmark and coinciding exactly with the extinction of the dinosaurs 65 million years ago. To convince the sceptics, especially the dinosaur experts, a large crater of the same age was badly needed.

A Canadian graduate student at the University of Arizona, Alan Hildebrand, joined the hunt. In 1990 he investigated remarkable deposits, 65 million years old and 50 centimetres thick, on a mountain on the island of Haiti. They included much broken and melted material of the kinds made by an impact. And they had been put there by a giant sea wave—a tsunami so large that the impact could not have been more than about 1000 kilometres away.

The Yucatán peninsula is at half that distance. When a journalist on the *Houston Chronicle*, Carlos Byars, heard about the Haiti find, he remembered what Petróleos Méxicanos had done. He put Hildebrand in touch with Penfield, and the two scientists together re-examined the company's early borehole samples.

At the 65-million-year level, from drilling site Yucatán 6, they found quartz containing dark lines of a distinctive kind, caused by a shock wave. In 1991, Hildebrand, Penfield and their colleagues, who included Hildebrand's supervisor at Arizona, William Boynton, described the discovery in the journal *Geology*. In the years that followed ample confirmation of the buried crater came from other scientists using several different techniques.

Some 200,000 cubic kilometres of the Earth's crust was vaporized, melted or ejected at the time of its creation. The US Geological Survey's pioneer of astrogeology, Eugene Shoemaker, estimated the impactor to have been 15 kilometres wide. As no asteroids as large as that are known in the Earth's vicinity, he concluded that it was a comet strike.

'Not impossible that it was an asteroid,' Shoemaker said. 'But if you're a betting man like I am, you put your chips on a comet. My own hunch is that we will find that the impact of large objects, probably chiefly comets, has profoundly influenced the evolution of life.' That was Shoemaker's last word on the subject. Soon after recording it for television, in 1997, he lost his life in a car smash in Australia while prospecting other impact craters.

A ring of gold

Unlike the permanently cratered Moon, the Earth is good at healing its wounds. The deep ocean floor, which covers much more of the Earth's surface than the continents do, must have received most impacts, and any crater there will disappear entirely. The whole ocean is repaved every 200 million years at most, and the old floor goes back into the planet's interior. If, on the other hand, the impactor hits a continent or its flooded continental shelf, later deposits will tend to bury the crater. That happened at Chicxulub and also at Chesapeake Bay, in the eastern USA, where recent sediments hide a 90-kilometre crater formed 35 million years ago.

Where old continental platforms have remained high and dry, in Australia and Africa in particular, the craters may remain visible at the surface. Elsewhere, erosion sometimes unearths old buried craters, and scouring by glaciers during the ice ages had that effect in northern lands. One crater so revealed is at Popigai in the Siberian Arctic, 100 kilometres wide and 36 million years old. At Manicouagan in Quebec a ring of lakes, also 100 kilometres wide, occupies the crater from an impact 214 million years ago.

And Sudbury, Ontario, has a crater formerly 250 kilometres wide, bigger than Chicxulub and 1850 million years old. Here the impactor dredged rocks rich in nickel and copper from below the Earth's crust. Today the crater is encircled by mines, which have been the world's most prolific source of nickel ore.

With remarkable examples on his doorstep, Richard Grieve of the Geological Survey of Canada in Ottawa became the world's chief archivist of the impact craters, from the early 1970s onwards. Strict criteria distinguished the candidates from the commonplace craters of extinct volcanoes. By the end of the century there were more than 150 impact craters on the list. And as geologists investigated the features in detail they found effects of impacts that made their textbooks out of date—concerning the origin of gold deposits, for example.

The oldest and largest impact crater on Grieve's list is in South Africa, centred at Vredefort west of Johannesburg and dated at about 2023 million years ago. The ring of hills called the Vredefort Dome, 70 kilometres wide, is the remnant of the uplift that occurs at the centre of an impact crater. The crater was originally 300 kilometres in diameter, but it is much eroded. Easier to see in satellite pictures is a wide half-ring of waste dumps from gold mines that surround the Vredefort Dome, very like the semicircle of sinkholes around Chicxulub.

The crater coincides with the world's largest gold reserves. The metal did not come from outer space, but was smelted from the Earth's rocks by the heat of the impact. Among all the other flying debris was a spray of molten gold. The fine grains would have been irretrievably scattered had they not later accumulated in the basin created by the Vredefort crater itself. If you have a ring, tooth or any other object made of South African gold, it's a souvenir of an impact very much bigger than the one that killed the dinosaurs.

Comets, stars and craters

Among a raft of reasons why space scientists take a special interest in impacts on the Earth is a hypothesis that showers of comets can occur. The proposition is that a star passing too close to the Sun can perturb the comets that inhabit a cloud at the outskirts of the Solar System. Many of them then plummet towards the Sun and create a period of heightened risk of impacts, lasting a few million years. Craters corresponding to comet showers could be sought on the Moon, Mars and Venus, as well as on the Earth.

A provocative variant of this hypothesis came from Richard Muller of the Lawrence Berkeley Laboratory in California in 1984. He suggested that the Sun has a distant companion star called Nemesis that approaches to within a light-year every 26 million years, and so triggers comet showers at regular intervals. After two decades with no persuasive evidence for such periodicity in impacts on the Earth, or any sign of the supposed companion, this idea had passed its sell-by date as far as most experts were concerned.

Comet showers occurring at irregular intervals, due to passing stars, remained more credible. In 1998, Agustin Chicarro and Joe Zender of the European Space Agency reviewed the known ages of impact craters and found four periods when several craters had similar ages. 'The cause of these pulses,' they commented, 'could be found in astronomical mechanisms triggering comet showers towards the Sun. By the precise dating of impacts, the terrestrial cratering record is thus unique in providing a detailed picture of the history of our Solar System in the last 600 million years, as well as its celestial environment.'

More direct evidence for comet showers comes from abnormal amounts of a rare form of helium, retained in seabed deposits. Helium-3 escaping from the Sun is trapped on dust grains from the tails of comets. Grains encountering the Earth can then settle slowly to the surface and eventually find their way to the bottom of the sea. An increase in the number of comets should be apparent in an increase in helium-3.

Shortly before his death, Gene Shoemaker suggested to a geochemist, Ken Farley of Caltech, that he should investigate the abundance of helium-3 around 36 million years ago. That was when both the Chesapeake Bay and Popigai craters were formed. Sure enough, in former seabed deposits of that age in Italy, Farley and his colleagues found a period of increased helium-3 deposition lasting more than 2 million years, around the time of those impacts—exactly as to be expected from a comet shower. No such helium-3 peak occurred around the time of the Chicxulub event, 65 million years ago.

The search is on for the passing stars that provoke comet showers, as part of the task of reinterpreting the past and future of life and geology on the Earth in terms of astronomy. The very precise mapping of stars and their motions, newly possible with satellites, should identify some of the stars that have already passed by. The computed times of passage could then be compared with the dates of impact craters.

Accurate retrospective assessments on these lines must wait for the next generation of star-mapping satellites, especially Europe's Gaia spacecraft due in 2012. But Gaia's predecessor, Hipparcos, had already looked ahead, with the identification of the first star that will visit the Sun's vicinity in the future. In 1997, a US team using the Hipparcos data was able to deduce that a faint star in the Ophiuchus constellation, Gliese 710, will come uncomfortably close. Currently 63 light-years away, it will approach to within about 1 light-year, one million years from now, perhaps near enough to provoke another comet shower.

Small but scary

On 30 June 1908 reindeer were slaughtered and 2000 square kilometres of Siberian forest flattened, by the impact of a very small comet or a large meteorite, supposedly 30–40 metres in diameter. From 600 kilometres away, passengers on the Trans-Siberian Railway observed a ball of fire streaking in across the sky, and nomads camping at a relatively safe distance from the epicentre in Tunguska had their tents destroyed by the blast.

The impactor exploded about ten kilometres above the ground, and luckily its force was no greater than a large, city-busting H-bomb. It left no crater, but surviving trees in the area show charred rings inside their trunks dating from 1908. Evidently heat radiation set them on fire and a slower-travelling blast wave blew out the flames.

Impactors come in all sizes between the commonplace 'shooting stars' and small meteorites arriving every day and Chicxulub-scale events at intervals of 100 million years. The smaller, the more frequent. Several impacts of asteroids of a kilometre or so in diameter may occur in every interval of one million years, each making a crater about ten kilometres wide, and causing regional if not global mayhem.

Startling is the expected recurrence of Tunguska H-bomb-like events—either every century or every millennium, depending on whose statistics you believe. That means they should show up repeatedly during human history and prehistory. An expert on tree-ring dating, Mike Baillie of Queen's University Belfast, matched some intervals of reduced tree growth to major volcanic eruptions, which may have dimmed the Sun worldwide. But he also found other grim events for which there was no volcanic explanation.

Between 1628 and 1623 BC, for example, trees in Europe grew extremely poorly, and California and China suffered unusual frosts. This episode triggered political upheavals in China and Egypt, possibly including the biblical Exodus. Baillie thought it no coincidence that the very earliest written record of a comet also comes from China at that turbulent time. He concluded that a comet fragment probably struck the Earth in 1628 BC, and he noted several similar unexplained calamities in his tree-ring data, between 3195 BC and AD 540.

Perhaps we should be less dismissive of ancestral tales of strange sights in the sky linked to catastrophes. For example, Genesis relates: 'Then the Lord rained upon Sodom and upon Gomorrah brimstone and fire from the Lord out of heaven; And he overthrew those cities, and all the plain, and that which grew upon the ground.' Just another small but deadly comet strike?

Much more to learn

The medieval town of Nördlingen in Bavaria is famous for its glinting buildings. They are built of a scrambled, concrete-like stone called suevite containing small crystals and glassy inclusions. The suevite comes from a ring of quarries surrounding the town, which stands inside the Ries impact crater, 25 kilometres in diameter and 15 million years old.

Scientists at the UK's Open University reported in 1995 the discovery of diamonds in the Bavarian suevite. At a tenth of a millimetre wide, at most, they excited no avarice among the burgers of Nördlingen. Experts on materials, on the other hand, were fascinated to learn that the diamonds were accompanied by the very tough material silicon carbide, in an association not seen before as an impact product.

New knowledge about the behaviour of materials, when subjected to immense heat and pressure, is therefore one of the spin-offs from impact studies. It adds to what geochemists and others have discovered with the aid of ultrahigh-pressure machinery or explosives, which can make artificial diamonds for example, as a compressed, crystalline form of carbon. Small diamonds are often associated with impact debris, and investigators have learnt to distinguish between diamonds that pre-existed either in the crust or in the impactor, and diamonds manufactured during the impact itself.

Christian Koeberl of the University of Vienna was another hunter of microscopic diamonds at impact sites around the world. From Russia's Popigai crater he found diamonds with ices of water and carbon dioxide trapped inside them under enormous pressure. He said, 'These and many other strange materials preserve for us an impression of the force of an impact, which is almost beyond the human imagination to visualize.'

Koeberl became leader of a programme launched by the European Science Foundation in 1998 to clarify the role of impacts in Earth history. The agenda showed how thoroughly this subject churns the sciences together: the astronomical background; the physical and chemical effects of impacts by land and sea; the release of gases from carbonates and sulphates in the crust; the injection of energy and materials into the atmosphere, oceans and the solid Earth; regional and global climate changes; and changes in the diversity of species within ecosystems.

There is much to find out, too, about how the impacts kill living things. The temporary blacking out of the Sun by dust is one possible mechanism. Blast, fire, tsunamis, chemical poisoning, and chilling and/or heating of the climate may all be involved to some degree.

The impacts story has also to be pushed far back in time, to see how ancient microbial life may have been affected before animals evolved. Strange balls looking like much-altered remnants of glass, found in both South Africa and Western Australia, are said to tell of one or two very large impacts 3400 million years ago. And scientists have to assess the intensely bombarded condition of the early Earth, around 4000 million years ago, which set the stage for all subsequent geological activity.

Impact geology begins to take its rightful place alongside the classical investigations of volcanoes, mountain building, ore formation and the rest of the Earth sciences, at the start of the 21st century. But it is still in an exciting exploratory phase. 'Of all the craters on all the world's continents, I suspect that only 10 per cent have been discovered so far,' Koeberl said. 'So we have a lot of work to do!'

▶ *For the biggest impact of all, which may have created the Moon, see* EARTH. *The subsequent heavy rate of impacts early in the Earth's history is noted in* LIFE'S ORIGIN. *For effects of impacts on later life, see* EXTINCTIONS. *For a possible link between impacts, major volcanic outbursts and plate motions, see* FLOOD BASALTS. *For more on the astronomical background and the watch for threatening objects, see* COMETS AND ASTEROIDS.

LANGUAGES

Why women often set the new fashions in speaking

YOU PROBABLY KNOW VERY WELL what Martha's Vineyard looks like, because Steven Spielberg chose it as the location for his classic shark movie *Jaws*. In heartier days, the small island off Cape Cod in Massachusetts had been a base for Yankee whalers, with the world's largest factory for making candles from sperm oil. And the Vineyard became famous among scholars as the setting for the tape-recorder revolution in linguistic science.

The inspiration for that was an earlier movie, Anthony Asquith's *Pygmalion* (1938), set in London and adapted from the play by George Bernard Shaw. The story later became more widely known in musical form, as *My Fair Lady*. A schoolboy in New Jersey, William Labov, was fascinated by Henry Higgins, the professor leaning against a stone column and writing down every sound coming out of the mouth of the flower seller Eliza Doolittle.

'I thought that was amazing,' Labov remembered later. 'How could he do it? Now I know that he was only writing down a few of the sounds that interested him.' The real-life model for Shaw's professor was Henry Sweet, an investigator of phonetics, who in 1888 had published ideas about sociology and linguistics that Labov would reconfirm and extend. The young American had great advantages: electronics for analysing the frequencies present in speech sounds, a rare personal knack for engaging strangers of every description in easygoing conversation, and instead of the professor's pencil, a tape recorder.

It was as a graduate student from Columbia that Labov turned up on Martha's Vineyard. He noticed a peculiar way of pronouncing the words *right*, *ice* and *sight* with the vowel in the middle of the mouth, as he put it, and not in the usual manner of Massachusetts Yankees. In 1963 he reported that the island's inhabitants were changing the way they spoke.

Consciously or unconsciously, certain Vineyarders were adopting non-standard vowel sounds favoured by the few remaining fishermen and probably dating back to the 18th century. It wasn't a matter of provincial ignorance, because some college-educated islanders used the vernacular vowel sounds with particular gusto. The effect was to distinguish long-established Vineyarders more emphatically from Portuguese immigrants and summer visitors.

Labov went on to study variations in dialect within New York City, including the speech of rival street gangs, and phonetic differences among sales assistants in Saks, Macy's and S. Klein—department stores of contrasting social prestige. In a masterly project conducted in Harlem with black and white colleagues, he revealed that black children had far more verbal competence than their teachers imagined, or than appeared in their progress with reading. The African–American English that they spoke emerged as a practical and logical language in its own right, well suited to vivid narration and to reasoning and debate. Despite repeated confirmation of Labov's findings all across the nation, US educational systems still undervalue the black vernacular.

In 1970 Labov moved to the University of Pennsylvania. In Philadelphia he found vowel sounds engaged in a complicated game of musical chairs, between different classes and ethnic groups in the city. He and a growing throng of students and emulators also roamed with their tape recorders around the world, to Belfast with its sharp Catholic–Protestant divide, for example, and to Papua New Guinea, which was trying to forge a national language in a country with hundreds of different local tongues.

Labov's working hypothesis, as he articulated it in 1975, was that people change their language because it is an expressive symbol of local identity. 'In every case that we've studied,' he said, 'the most advanced sound changes are found among those groups whose local status is being challenged by other groups moving in from outside. Sound change is one way of reasserting local identity against that challenge.'

In the ensuing decades, sociolinguistics acquired a mathematical precision rarely known in studies of observable social behaviour. You could measure the degree and rate of local language evolution. You could track the geographical diffusion of a change to surrounding areas, and follow its adoption through time, from one generation to the next.

A salient discovery was the role of women in driving the changes in dialects. Martha's Vineyard, where young men set the trend, turned out to be unusual in that regard. In most cases a new variant in a speech sound is detected first in women of childbearing age, and then in their children. Elderly men may be the last to change, if they do so at all.

There is no mystery about the mechanism, because most people learn their mother tongue literally from their mothers or from female carers. An uncanny parallel with the spread of fashions in clothing and cosmetics might imply a certain feminine whimsicality. But given the manifest links to real social forces, and the importance of dialect to the children's and grandchildren's sense of social identity, it is unlikely that linguistic changes are frivolous.

When Labov and his colleagues charted the changes in an *Atlas of North American English* (2002) the working hypothesis of the 1970s began to seem inadequate. 'We see a breathtaking uniformity of sound change across vast areas,' Labov commented. 'It calls into question the idea that local identity is the driving force.'

So what is going on in the heads of the women, that somehow converts external socio-economic and political trends into a preferred way of speaking, or a shift in grammatical rules? Why, for example, are American blacks, descendants of slaves, quite conservative about their vernacular language, while American whites change their vowels almost as often as their skirt-lengths? And how do factors of gender and class operate when an alien language comes over the horizon, carried by chariots or longships?

These were some of the unsettled and unsettling questions with which sociolinguists reached out, at the beginning of the 21st century, to try to match their findings about dialects to the work of colleagues tracing the origins of modern languages. There are about 5000 different languages worldwide, and it is not at all obvious why there should be.

Genes, languages and technologies

'A shprakh iz a diyalekt mit an armey un a flot,' declared Labov's teacher at Columbia, the Yiddish-speaking Uriel Weinreich. A language is a dialect with an army and a navy. That was propounded in 1945, when the outcome of the Second World War shifted the official borders of several languages, according to whether their speakers were on the winning or losing side. Taken together with episodes of ethnic cleansing before and since, and a 4000-year global history of imperialism, the 1945 experience left little doubt about a military factor in language evolution.

During the 19th century, scholars had found important affinities between more and more languages spoken across a huge swath of the world, from the Celts of Ireland to the Bengalis of eastern India. The implication was that a single language spoken by a single tribe had somehow spread in prehistoric times, and fragmented into many derivative languages as the descendants became scattered. Aryan people with western words reputedly broke through the Afghan bottleneck with the god Krishna driving the lead chariot.

The feasibility of such aggressive expansions was amply confirmed by more recent history. Irruptions of Muslims from Arabia and of Mongols and Turks from East Asia were just precursors of the sea-borne invasion of most of the world by colonizers from Western Europe.

Support for the general idea that languages spread and changed as people moved about, whether peaceably or aggressively, came from genetics. Luca

Cavalli-Sforza of Stanford, with colleagues in Italy, used blood samples to chart the similarities and differences between supposedly indigenous inhabitants of all parts of the world. These turned out to be compatible with the dispersal of the ancestors of every person alive today, from a common origin.

Assuming that they started with a common language as well as a common set of genes, the primary reason for the differences between modern languages might then be much the same as for the differences in the genes. They drifted apart, over tens of thousands of years. Tribes migrating across Europe, Asia, Australia and the Americas became separated by distance, neither mating nor speaking with one another.

At first the people moved into regions empty of any pre-existing languages of our own subspecies. Later migrations stirred the pot, as with the Indo-Europeans and many others. These brought pre-existing languages into collision, with effects that ranged from simple exchanges of useful words, through improvised pidgins and creoles, to the extinction of pre-existing languages or the invention of new ones.

Languages evolve more rapidly than genes do, making it hard to reconstruct a family tree of diversifying languages that goes all the way back to the first speakers. Nevertheless, nearly every language can be assigned to one or another of about a dozen linguistic superfamilies. With help from Merritt Ruhlen of Stanford and other linguists, Cavalli-Sforza set out in 1987 to match the linguistic superfamilies to genetic superfamilies identified from blood samples.

The match seemed impressive, and anomalies were said to be few and unsurprising. For example, some North-East Asians migrated to Tibet. To reach it they had to pass through China, and on the way they acquired a language more appropriate to South-East Asia, in a Sino-Tibetan classification.

Cavalli-Sforza also generalized the story about the Aryan chariots. The currents and counter-currents of population flows, shown in genes and languages, depended above all on cultural changes due to human inventiveness, he said. 'The genetic study of human evolution has shown with extreme clarity that genetic success of a population, as proved by its expansion in numbers and across vast regions, has been practically every time the result of a major technological innovation.' Cavalli-Sforza's emphasis on power flowing from technology put his approach to language evolution at the opposite pole from Labov's concern for the dialects of the underprivileged.

Excavating Babel

The mainstream theorists of language evolution have in any case quite other preoccupations. They work on a geographical scale intermediate between Labov's dialects and Cavalli-Sforza's superfamilies. These theorists want to understand the similarities and differences between individual languages, in the plainest sense of the word—French versus German across the Rhine, or similar distinctions on either side of a river in New Guinea. The tale of the Tower of Babel describes the loss of mutual understanding as a divine punishment for human presumption. The linguists excavate the rubble.

Each language has its own vocabulary and grammar, and serves essentially the same human purposes everywhere. Yet there are enormous differences in the complexity of grammar. The subtlety of a language seems to bear no relationship whatever to its historic or geopolitical status, or the modernity of the society using it.

A landmark in the comparisons of languages was the publication in 2003 of *The World Atlas of Language Structures*, as a collaborative project of more than 40 linguists across the world. It shows the worldwide distribution of some 120 features in about 200 languages. Among the simpler features are the range of vowel sounds, the relative positioning of adjective–noun and of subject–object–verb, and the number of genders in use—which can sometimes reach around 20, as in the West African language Fula.

Two contradictory phenomena are evident in the maps. One is that many languages share structural features across wide regions, on the scale of subcontinents. On the other hand, oddball languages bucking the trend also show up in many places. What deep questions about language evolution will such maps help to answer?

By the early 21st century, a sufficient number of languages had been compared in sufficient detail for a clue to commonality to appear, in respect of language evolution. Not every imaginable change in grammar and word order actually occurs. Instead, the same changes are seen over and over again, in many very different languages all around the world.

Another deep question concerns the reason why languages change. Labov's studies of dialects show variability within languages, but they stop short of the point of divorce. Two populations of similar animals cease to be the same species when they can no longer breed together. How and why should dialects evolve to the point where they become distinct languages, unintelligible between their speakers?

The process takes several centuries at least, as illustrated in the spin-off of German, Dutch, English and the Scandinavian languages from an ancestral Germanic language in historical times. Some experts supposed that there had to be an advantage in every new language, which favoured its advent and survival. In a theory of functional need, the new language provided a function that was lacking in its predecessor. Its speakers benefited in some practical way, and the biological principle of evolution by natural selection applied.

Other linguists doubted this theory, and saw no logical reason why the evolutionary mechanism that produced the language faculty in the first place should carry through into the diversification of the world's languages. An analogy was with dancing. Biological evolution provided agile limbs and a sense of rhythm, but it did not follow that every traditional dance had to pass some evolutionary fitness test.

'The hand *that rocks the cradle* rules the world' is an example of a relative clause, which can qualify the subject or object of a sentence. Every headline writer knows that mismanaged relative clauses can become scrambled into nonsense like *rocks the cradle rules*. In protecting the integrity of relative clauses, there is a trade-off between risky brevity, as in newspaper headlines, and longwinded and pedantic guarantees against ambiguity. Languages vary greatly in the precautions that speakers are expected to take.

Relative clauses were a focus of interest for many years for Bernard Comrie of the Max-Planck-Institut für evolutionäre Anthropologie in Leipzig, one of the editors of *The World Atlas of Language Structures*. He found instances of exuberant complexity that could not be explained in terms of practical advantages. Rather, they seem to reflect the emblematic function of language as a symbol of its speech community. Speakers like having striking features that make their language stand out.

'By all means let's agree that the faculty of language evolved in a biological manner,' Comrie said. 'But to understand Babel we have to go beyond that kind of explanation and look for historical and social reasons for the proliferation and diversification of languages. Mapping their structures worldwide gives us the chance of a fresh start in that direction.'

The face-to-face science

Along with the flag and the football team, a language is often a badge of national identity. Nations—tribes with bureaucrats—remain the chief engineers of war. Instead of chariots and longships, some of them now have nuclear, biological and chemical weapons. Any light that linguistics can shed on the rationale and irrationalities of nationhood is urgently needed. People are also starting to ask, 'What language will they speak on Mars?'

The study of language evolution remains at its roots the most humane of all the sciences, in both the academic and the social sense of that adjective. William Labov at Penn cautioned his students against becoming so enraptured by theoretical analysis and technology that they might be carried away from the human issues involved in the use of language.

'The excitement and adventure of the field,' he said, 'comes in meeting the speakers of the language face to face, entering their homes, hanging out on corners, porches, taverns, pubs and bars. I remember one time a 14-year-old in Albuquerque said to me, "Let me get this straight. Your job is going anywhere in the world, talking to anybody about anything you want?" I said, "Yeah." He said, "I want that job!" '

▶ *For related topics concerning language, see* SPEECH *and* GRAMMAR. *For genetic correlations in human dispersal, see* PREHISTORIC GENES. *For social behaviour, see* ALTRUISM AND AGGRESSION.

LIFE'S ORIGIN

Will the answer to the riddle come from outer space?

'**I** CAN TRACE MY ANCESTRY back to a protoplasmal primordial atomic globule,' boasts Pooh-Bah in *The Mikado*. When Gilbert and Sullivan wrote their comic opera in 1885 they were *au courant* with science as well as snobbery. A century later, molecular biologists had traced the genetic mutations, and constructed a single family tree for all the world's organisms that stretched back 4 billion years, to when life on Earth probably began. But they were scarcely wiser than Pooh-Bah about the precise nature of the primordial protoplasm.

In 1995 Wlodzimierz Lugowski of Poland's Institute of Philosophy and Sociology wrote about 'the philosophical foundations of protobiology'. He listed nearly 150 scenarios then on offer for the origin of life and, with a possible single exception to be mentioned later, he judged none of them to be satisfactory. Here is one of the top conundrums for 21st-century science. The origin of life ranks with the question of what initiated the Big Bang, as an embarrassing lacuna in the attempt by scientists to explain our existence in the cosmos.

In the last paragraph of his account of evolution in *The Origin of Species* (1859) Charles Darwin remarked, 'There is grandeur in this view of life, with its several powers, having been originally breathed by the Creator into a few forms or into one.' Privately he thought that the divine breath had a chemical whiff. He speculated that life began 'in some warm little pond, with all sorts of ammonia and phosphoric salts, light, heat, electricity, etc. present'.

By carbon chemistry plus energy, scientists would say nowadays. Since Darwin confided his thoughts in a letter to a friend in 1871, a long list of eminent scientists have bent their minds to the problem in their later years. Two of them (Svante Arrhenius and Francis Crick) transposed the problem to a warm little pond far away, by visualizing spores arriving from outer space. Another (Fred Hoyle) proposed the icy nuclei of comets as places to create and harbour our earliest ancestors, in molten cores.

Most investigators of the origin of life preferred home cooking. The Sun's rays, lightning flashes, volcanic heat and the like may have acted on the gases of the young Earth to make complex chemicals. In the 1950s Harold Urey in Chicago started a student, Stanley Miller, on a career of making toffee-like deposits rich in carbon compounds by passing electrical discharges through gases supposedly resembling the early atmosphere. These materials, it was said, created the primordial soup in the planet's water, and random chemical reactions over millions of years eventually came up with the magic combinations needed for life.

Although they were widely acclaimed at the time, the Urey–Miller experiments seemed in retrospect to have been a blind alley. Doubts grew about whether they used the correct gassy ingredients to represent the early atmosphere. In any case the feasibility of one chemical reaction or another was less at issue than the question of how the random chemistry could have assembled the right combination of ingredients in one spot.

Two crucial ingredients were easily specified. Nucleic acids would carry inheritable genetic instructions. These did not need to be the fancy double-stranded deoxyribonucleic acid, DNA, comprising the genes of modern organisms. The more primitive ribonucleic acid, RNA, would do. Secondly, proteins were needed to act as enzymes that catalysed chemical reactions.

Around 1970, Manfred Eigen at Germany's Max-Planck-Institut für biophysikalische Chemie sought to define the minimum requirement for life. He came up with the proposition that the grandmother of all life on Earth was what he called a hypercycle, with several RNA cycles linked by cooperative protein enzymes. Accompanying the hypothesis was a table game played with a pyramidal dice and popper beads, to represent the four chemical subunits of RNA. The aim was to optimize random mutations to make RNA molecules with lots of loops made with cross-links, considered to be favourable for stability in the primordial soup.

● Catalysts discovered

Darwin's little pond may have needed to be hot, rather than warm, to achieve the high concentrations of molecules and energy needed to fulfil the recipe for life. Yet high temperatures are inimical for most living things. Students of the origin of life were therefore fascinated by heat-resistant organisms found thriving today in volcanic pools, either on the surface or on the deep ocean floor at hydrothermal vents. Perhaps volcanic heat rather than sunlight powered the earliest life, some said.

Reliance on the creativity of random chemistry nevertheless remained for decades a hopeless chicken-and-egg problem. The big snag, it seemed, was that you couldn't reproduce RNA without the right enzymes and you couldn't specify the enzymes without the right RNA. A possible breakthrough came in 1982.

Thomas Cech of Boulder, Colorado, was staggered to find that RNA molecules could act as catalysts, like the protein enzymes. In a test tube, an RNA molecule cut itself into pieces and joined the fragments together again, in a complicated self-splicing reaction. There was no protein present. The chicken-and-egg problem seemed to be solved at a stroke.

Soon other scientists were talking about an early RNA World of primitive organisms in which nucleic acids ruled, as enzymes as well as genetic coders. Many other functions for RNA enzymes, or ribozymes, emerged in subsequent research. Especially telling was their role in ribosomes. These are the chemical robots used by every living creature, from bacteria to whales, to translate the genetic code into specified protein molecules. A ribosome is a very elaborate assembly of protein molecules, but inside it lurk RNA molecules that do the essential catalytic work.

'The ribosome is a ribozyme!' Cech declared, in a triumphant comment on the latest analyses in 2000. 'If, indeed, there was an early RNA World where RNA provided both genetic information and catalytic function, then the earliest protein synthesis would have had to be catalysed by RNA. Later, the RNA-only ribosome / ribozyme may have been embellished with additional proteins; yet, its heart of RNA functioned sufficiently well that it was never replaced by a protein catalyst.'

The chief rival to the RNA World by that time was a Lipid World, where lipid means the oily or fatty stuff that does not mix with water. It is well suited, today and at the origin of life, to provide internal membranes and outer coatings for living cells. The packaging could have preceded the contents, according to an idea that traces back to Aleksandr Oparin of Moscow in the 1920s.

He visualized, and in later experiments made, microscopic lipid membranes enclosing water rich in various chemicals, which might be nondescript at first. These coacervate droplets, to use the technical term, could be the precursors of cells. As Oparin pointed out, they provided a protected environment where any useful, self-reproducing combinations that emerged from random chemistry could gather. They would not simply disperse in the primordial soup.

By the end of the century, progress in molecular science and cell biology had brought two thought-provoking discoveries. One was that some lipids have their own hereditary potential. They can make copies of themselves by self-assembly from available molecular components, independently of any genetic system. Also remarkable was the realization that, like protein enzymes and RNA ribozymes, some lipids, too, could act as catalysts for chemical reactions. Doron Lancet of Israel's Weizmann Institute of Science called them lipozymes.

Lancet became the leading advocate of the Lipid World as the forerunner of the origin of life. His computer models showed that diverse collections of lipid molecules could self-assemble and self-replicate their compositions, while providing membranes on which other materials could form, including proteins and nucleic acids. 'It is at this stage,' Lancet and his colleagues suggested, 'that a scenario akin to the RNA World could be initiated, although this does not imply by any means that RNA chemistry was exclusively present.'

What was the setting?

One difficulty about any hypothesis concerning the first appearance of life on the Earth is verification. No matter how persuasive it may be, in theory or even in laboratory experiments that might create life from scratch, there is no very obvious way to establish that one scenario rather than another was what actually happened. Also lacking is clear knowledge about what the planet was like at the time. It was certainly not a tranquil place.

Big craters still visible on the Moon mainly record a heavy bombardment by stray material—icy comets and stony asteroids—left over from the origin of the Solar System. It afflicted the young Earth as well as the Moon and continued for 600 million years after our planet's main body was complete 4.5 billion years ago. In this Hadean Era, as Earth scientists call it, no region escaped untouched, as many thousands of comets and asteroids rained down. As a result, the earliest substantial rocks that survive on the surface are 4 billion years old. Yet it was during this turmoil that life somehow started.

Abundant water may have been available, perhaps delivered by icy impactors. Indirect evidence for very early oceans comes from zircons, robust crystals of zirconium silicate normally associated with continental granite. In 1983, Derek Froude of the Australian National University and his colleagues found zircons more than 4.1 billion years old included as grains in ancient sedimentary rocks in Western Australia.

By 2001, an Australian–UK–US team had pushed back the age of the earliest zircon fragment to 4.4 billion years. That was when the Earth's crust had supposedly just cooled sufficiently to carry liquid water, which then interacted with the primitive crust to produce granite and its enclosed zircons. A high proportion of heavy oxygen atoms in the zircon testified to the presence of water.

'Our zircon evidence suggests that life could have had several false starts,' said Simon Wilde of the Curtin University of Technology in Perth, as proud possessor of the oldest known chip of the Earth. 'We can picture oceans and life beginning on a cooling Earth, and then both being vaporized by the next big impact. If so, our own primitive ancestors were the lucky ones, appearing just when the heavy bombardment was coming to an end and somehow surviving.'

The composition of the young Earth's atmosphere, and chemical reactions there that could have contributed carbon compounds to the primordial soup, also remained highly uncertain. In that connection, space scientists saw that Titan, a moon of Saturn, might be instructive about life's origin. It has a thick, hazy atmosphere with nitrogen as its principal ingredient, as in our own air.

Whilst Titan is far too cold for life, at minus 180°C, it possesses many carbon compounds that make a photochemical smog in the atmosphere and no doubt litter the surface. So Titan may preserve in deep freeze many of the prelife chemicals available on the young Earth. In 1997 NASA's Cassini spacecraft set off for Saturn, carrying a European probe, Huygens, designed to plunge into the atmosphere of Titan.

In an exciting couple of hours in 2005, Huygens will parachute down to the surface. During its descent, and for a short while after it thuds or splashes onto the surface, the probe will transmit new information about Titan's appearance, weather and chemical make-up. The mother ship Cassini will also examine the chemistry from the outside, in repeated passes.

'One reason why all attempts to visualize the origin of life remain sadly inconclusive is that scientists can only guess what the chemistry of the Earth was like 4 billion years ago, when the event occurred,' said François Raulin of the Laboratoire Interuniversitaire des Systèmes Atmospheriques in Paris, a mission scientist for Cassini–Huygens. 'The results of our examination of Titan may lead us in unexpected directions, and stimulate fresh thinking.'

Whilst the Titan project might be seen as a pursuit of a home-cooking scenario on another world, other astrochemists took the view that many materials directly useful for starting life arrived ready-made from space. They would have come during the heavy bombardment, when comets filled the sky. Even from those that missed the Earth entirely, huge quantities of carbon compounds would have rained gently onto the primordial surface in the form of small grains strewn from the comets' tails.

Are we children of the comets?

Whether it was a joke or a serious effort to deceive, no one knows. Someone took a piece of a meteorite that fell from the sky at Orgueil near Toulouse in 1864, and stuck lumps of coal and pieces of reed on it. The jest flopped. It went unnoticed for a hundred years, because there were plenty of other fragments of that meteorite to examine. In 1964, Edward Anders and his colleagues at Chicago disclosed the hoax in a forensic examination that identified even the 19th-century French glue.

In reality the Orgueil meteorite had a far more interesting story to tell. A 55-kilogram piece at France's Muséum National d'Histoire Naturelle became the most precious meteorite in the collection. It contains *bona fide* extraterrestrial tar still being examined in the 21st century, with ever more refined analytical techniques, for carbon compounds of various kinds that came from outer space and survived the heat and blast of the meteorite's impact.

Rapid advances in astrochemistry in the closing decades of the 20th century led to the identification of huge quantities of carbon compounds, of many different kinds, in cosmic space and in the Solar System. They showed up in the vicinity of stars, in interstellar clouds, and in comets, and they included many compounds with rings of carbon atoms, of kinds favoured by living things.

Much of the preliminary assembly of atoms into molecules useful for life may have gone on in space. Comets provide an obvious means of delivering them to the Earth. Confirmation that delicate carbon compounds can arrive at the planet's surface, without total degradation on the way down, comes from the Orgueil meteorite. In 2001, after a Dutch–US re-examination of the Paris specimen, the scientists proposed that this lump from the sky was a piece of a comet.

'To trace our molecular ancestors in detail is now a challenge in astronomy, space research and meteoritics,' said the leader of that study, Pascale Ehrenfreund of Leiden Observatory. 'Chemistry in cosmic space, proceeding over millions of years, may have been very effective in preparing useful and reactive compounds of the kinds required for life. Together with compounds formed on the Earth, those extraterrestrial molecules could have helped to jump-start life.'

Comets now figure in such a wide range of theories about life's origin, that a checklist may be appropriate. The mainstream view in the late 20th century was that, when comets and comet tails delivered huge quantities of loose carbon-rich material to the Earth's primordial soup, its precise chemical forms were unimportant. In Ehrenfreund's interpretation the molecules did matter, and may have influenced the direction of subsequent chemistry on the Earth.

Quite different scenarios included the proposal that comets might be vehicles on which spores of bacteria could hitchhike from one star system to another, or skip between planets. Or, as Hoyle suggested, the comets might themselves be the scene of biochemical action, creating new life aboard them. Finally, according to a German hypothesis, comet grains may have directly mothered living cells on the Earth.

In 1986, Jochen Kissel analysed the dust of Halley's Comet with three instruments, carried in the spacecraft that intercepted it most closely, the Soviet Vega-1 and Vega-2, and Europe's Giotto. He found grains containing an astonishing mixture of carbon compounds that would be highly reactive on the Earth. After analysing the results, Kissel and his colleague Franz Krueger, an independent chemist in Darmstadt, promptly proposed that life began with comet grains falling into the sea.

Following 15 years of further work on the hypothesis, they saw no reason to change their minds. Theirs was the only scenario among 150 that won approval from Wlodzimierz Lugowski in 1995. Beside the carbon-rich component of comet grains, possessing the raw materials and latent chemical energy needed to drive the chemistry, Kissel and Krueger stressed the part played by mineral constituents. These provided surfaces with catalytic properties, to get the reactions started.

'What impresses us is that the carbon compounds in comets are in an ideal chemical state to react vigorously with water,' said Kissel at the Max-Planck-Institut für extraterrestrische Physik. 'Also, the grains they come in are of just the right size to act as temporary cells, keeping the materials together while the crucial chemical reactions proceed. So our recipe for life is rather simple: add comet dust grains to water.'

The recipe book

For an example of how materials present in comets could make key biochemicals, here is one of the recipes suggested by Kissel and Krueger. React five molecules of hydrogen cyanide together and that gives you the ring molecule called adenine. Take polyacetylene, a carbon chain depleted in hydrogen, and its reaction with water can make the sugar called ribose. When metal phosphides in comet dust meet water they will make phosphate. Adenine plus ribose plus phosphate combine to form one of the units in the chain of an RNA molecule. As a by-product, adenine also figures in a vital energy-carrying molecule, adenosine triphosphate.

Kissel and Krueger did not dissent from the view that life began more than once. Indeed with so many comets and comet grains descending on the young Earth, it could have happened billions of times. That gave plenty of scope for biochemical experimentation, for survival amidst later impacts, and for competition between different lineages.

Two new space missions to comets would carry Kissel's instruments for further investigation of the primordial dust grains that they contain. Stardust, launched in 1999, was an American spacecraft intended to gather samples from the dust around Comet Wild and eventually return them to the Earth, where they could be analysed thoroughly in laboratories. Analysis on the spot, but with ample time, was the aim in Europe's Rosetta (2003). Kissel's dust analyser is one of many instruments on Rosetta intended to reveal a comet's constitution in unprecedented detail, while the spacecraft slowly orbits around its target comet for more than a year.

The Rosetta mission comes to a climax as the comet makes its closest approach to the Sun. That will be during the second decade of the century. By then the Cassini–Huygens mission to Saturn and Titan will be long-since concluded and the results from Stardust and Comet Wild will be in. Meanwhile new infrared and radio telescopes, on the ground and in space, will have added greatly to the inventory of chemicals in the cosmos, available for the recipe book. That may be a time to judge whether the switch to space has paid off, in the search for a solution to the mystery of life, and whether Pascale Ehrenfreund was right to look for her molecular ancestors in interstellar space.

▶ *See also* MOLECULES IN SPACE, EXTRATERRESTRIAL LIFE *and* EXTREMOPHILES. *For ribosomes, see* PROTEIN-MAKING.

MAMMALS

Tracing our milk-making forebears in a world of drifting continents

'T HE GOBI DESERT is great for finding fossils of dinosaurs and other creatures that lived around 100 million years ago,' said Rinchen Barsbold, director of the Paleontological Center of the Mongolian Academy of Sciences in Ulaanbaatar. 'Among them were small mammals, the predecessors of those that inherited the planet when the dinosaurs died out.'

Eight centuries after Genghis Khan led them in the conquest of much of the known world, the Mongolians are now hemmed in between China and Russia. The southern part of their rather poor country is very arid, but its buried treasures attract fossil-hunters from all over the world. Besides the tonnes of dinosaur remains there are precious grams of teeth and bones of animals no bigger than shrews or marmots, which scampered about avoiding the feet and jaws of the giant reptiles.

An adventurous woman from the Polish Academy of Sciences led a series of fossil-hunting expeditions into the Gobi, starting in 1963. Zofia Kielan-Jaworowska's most spectacular find was of two dinosaurs entangled in a fight to the death—protoceratops and velociraptor. Scientifically her key discovery, announced in 1969, was *Kennalestes*, a small mammal with modern-looking teeth, in rocks about 80 million years old. Technically called tribosphenic molars, the teeth had both grinding and shearing capabilities.

A Soviet team found an animal with quite similar teeth in another part of the Gobi Desert, but dating from 114 million years ago. In 1989 Kielan-Jaworowska and a Mongolian palaeontologist, Demberlyin Dashzeveg, described it and dubbed it *Prokennalestes*. The date for the oldest known tribosphenic mammal from the northern hemisphere was pushed even farther back in 2001, when the French palaeontologist Denise Sigogneau-Russell and her British colleagues reported *Tribactonodon*, found in 135-million-year-old limestone in southern England.

Meanwhile, Kielan-Jaworowska had become a leading advocate of the idea that the Mongolian animals represented the early evolution of placental mammals, the kind of creatures that include human beings. But a dispute arose when similar modern-looking teeth turned up first in Australia and then in

Madagascar, the latter with a much earlier date attached to them—about 167 million years ago. Did the mammals with tribosphenic molars really originate in the southern hemisphere?

To defend her point of view, Kielan-Jaworowska joined with colleagues in the USA in proposing that teeth of the same kind evolved independently in both hemispheres. 'The only survivors from the animals represented by those southern-hemisphere molars, in our opinion, are the peculiar monotremes of Australia,' she said. 'The mammals that really matter had a northern origin, as we see in Mongolia.'

Puzzles of ever-changing geography

Mammals are hairy and warm-blooded, but most fundamentally they are distinguished from other animals by their ability to nourish their young with milk. It was an astoundingly successful evolutionary ploy. The controversy about the origin of the mammals is far from settled, but it provides an excellent example of the styles of research on the course of evolution, at the start of the 21st century.

While Kielan-Jaworowska and her fellow fossil-hunters were arguing about teeth and bones, in a more or less traditional way, experts from quite different fields had their say too. First, there was input from palaeogeography, meaning map-making by geologists that shows the past movements of continents. The evolution of the mammals coincided with the break-up of a supercontinent, Pangaea, and it certainly did not follow the same course on the different fragments as they drifted apart.

A geographical factor in the distribution of mammals was well known even in the 19th century. Of the three armies of living mammals, the most primitive are the monotremes, which include the platypus that lays eggs. Having no nipples, they simply exude milk through the skin. Surviving monotremes live exclusively in Australia.

Kangaroos, koalas and all of the typical native mammals of Australia are marsupials. They give birth to very small offspring, which complete their gestation in a body pouch where the mother nourishes the joey with milk. Although fossil marsupials crop up in Africa and Eurasia, they never really established themselves in those continents. Instead, the native mammals of the Old World are all placentals, which grow in the mother's abdomen until they are quite large. This strategy paid off in placental mammals as various as bats, whales and horses, as well as human beings.

In South America, the picture became confused when a dry-land link formed to North America 3 million years ago, with the construction of the Isthmus of Panama. A great interchange of species then occurred. Before then the main mammals in South America were marsupials and a group of almost toothless placentals called edentates. The latter now include sloths, armadillos and anteaters. But there were also llamas and, most puzzlingly, some monkeys.

The geography of native mammals presents evolutionists with a logical and chronological teaser. The common ancestor of marsupials and placentals had to emerge while nearly all of the landmasses were joined in the supercontinent of Pangaea, around 200 million years ago. The placentals could not then make their debut before Australia became inaccessible to them, during a break-up of the southern part of Pangaea (Gondwana-Land) perhaps 120 million years ago. But the possible launch window for the placental line closed when the edentates had to board the South American ark, before it departed from Africa about 100 million years ago.

Other input into the research on mammalian evolution came from molecular biology. Similarities and differences between genes and proteins in living animals enable researchers to construct evolutionary trees, without relying on fossil evidence. This molecular technique is not available for dinosaurs and other fossil groups that have left no living survivors.

The more similar the molecules, the more closely the animals are related. The more different they are, the farther back in time did they share a common ancestor, and with some fossil markers along the way you can put rough dates to the branching events. The technique indicates that the ancestors of all mammals—monotremes, marsupials and placentals—lived around 140 million years ago. The first placentals, by this reckoning, appeared about 108 million years ago, which fits neatly into the geographical launch window.

After comparing 22 genes in 42 very different placental mammals, plus two marsupials, a team of US, Brazilian, Dutch and UK scientists rearranged the placentals. Genetically speaking, they fitted most naturally into four main groups. The researchers then claimed, in 2001, that they could relate their new evolutionary tree to the mobile geography of the Pangaean break-up.

The oldest group of placental mammals, in this analysis, is called the Afrotherians. Originating in Africa, it now includes aardvarks and elephants. Second to branch off from it were the Xenarthra, meaning the main South American contingent. Here is a clear and quite straightforward idea that the ancestors of armadillos and sloths were Afrotherians living in South America when it was still joined to Africa. They evolved their toothless styles in glorious isolation after the Atlantic Ocean opened.

'It places the origin of the placental mammals in the south,' asserted Stephen O'Brien of the National Cancer Institute in Maryland, where the genetic investigation was centred. In support of this proposition, he pointed out that some of the Afrotherian lineages, such as the aardvarks, occur nowhere else but in Africa. As for the mammals of Mongolia, the team took the view they might indeed represent early placentals, but they went extinct. The ancestors of the native mammals of the northern hemisphere supposedly arrived from elsewhere by a circuitous route, to restock Eurasia.

The groups in question are the Laurasiatheria, typified by hippos, bats, cats and hedgehogs, and Euarchontoglires, which include rats, rabbits and monkeys. The most surprising message from the genes is that they seem to be of South American origin. Both groups are descended from the Xenarthra.

So the curious tale on offer from O'Brien and his colleagues is that these huge groups represent potential sloths that changed their minds. They did a pier-head jump from the departing South America, back onto Africa, to become cheetahs and human beings instead.

The grand opera

Traditionally minded fossil experts were not going to accept this genetic scenario without a fight. There were in any case some big issues. Most fundamental was the molecular dating of many of the branching events that created the modern families of mammals, putting them back to 80 and even 103 million years ago. This was at odds with a long-held opinion that the big radiation of the mammals into many different families could not begin until the dinosaurs disappeared 65 million years ago, at the end of the Mesozoic Era.

Throughout their long tenure of the planet, the dinosaurs scarcely departed from the script of giant predators and colossal herbivores. From the point of view of the scuttling mammals there was no relief from reptilian tyranny. On the other hand, the Mesozoic world underwent a wholesale change in vegetation, with the rise, diversification and spread of the flowering plants, around 120 million years ago. That was supposedly a great stimulus to the insects, and to the small mammals that fed on them. Conceivably the primates, which later included monkeys, apes and humans, originated about 80 million years ago in response to the first appearance of fruit and nuts on the menu.

Many small mammals survived the impact of the comet or asteroid that extinguished the dinosaurs, 65 million years ago. A local snapshot in fossils of that date in Montana shows 18 out of 22 placental species coming through the disaster, but only 1 out of 13 marsupials. Globally, the picture is of 75 per cent of marsupial genera (species groups) expiring, compared with 11 per cent of placental genera. That difference in survival rates helps to explain why marsupials faded away in Africa and the northern continents, until opossums made their way into North America from South America 3 million years ago.

Mammals had increasing reason to be glad of their furry coats. After the dinosaurs died out, the world cooled in stages, especially when Antarctica settled at the South Pole and accumulated ice. Before that, Australia had parted company from Antarctica 45 million years ago, and began cruising northwards with its crew of monotremes and marsupials.

The whales that lived in the Southern Ocean then exploited the resources of an intensifying and broadening Circumantarctic Current. As the gap between Antarctica and Australia widened they grew in size, virtually in step with the changing geography. Eventually the whales surpassed even the biggest dinosaurs in mass.

The evolution of our own lineage of primates, through small tree-dwellers to monkeys, apes and early humans, was much more straightforward than turning a pig-like animal into a titanic swimmer. Grasping hands, agile limbs, and forward-facing eyes for judging distances were matters for refinement and variation for the whole of primate history in Africa. It was there, too, that upright walking became a new fashion around 6 million years ago, and set the hands free for doing cleverer things.

An awkward fact spoils the neat stories of mammalian evolution in relation to continental drift. Monkeys closely akin to those in Africa showed up for the first time in South America about 35 million years ago. The palaeogeographers say firmly that no land route was available at that time. In a strange reversion to the maritime tales that used to be told by people who didn't believe in continental drift, you are asked to imagine a pregnant female on a log, accidentally riding the trade winds across the South Atlantic to found the dynasty of broad-nosed monkeys.

Setbacks due to impacts of comets and asteroids did not cease after the big one that killed the dinosaurs. For example, a crater 100 kilometres wide at Popigai in Russia tells of a fearsome event 36 million years ago at the end of the Eocene stage. Many old-fashioned mammals suffered badly. In the aftermath more modern families including cats, dogs, rhinos, pigs and bears made their debuts. A 24-kilometre crater at Ries in Germany coincides with the end of the Early Miocene stage, 15 million years ago, when 30 per cent of mammalian genera were wiped out.

The continued cooling of the climate shrank the Earth's forests, and about 30 million years ago the first grasslands appeared. There, evolution found a new theme in the emergence of ruminant animals able to digest grass. Carnivores evolved to prey on them, producing the mammalian culmination seen in the grasslands of East Africa today.

The Pleistocene blitzkrieg

For large mammals a less creative case of co-evolution came with the emergence of human beings during the current series of ice ages, which became severe in the Pleistocene stage. Aggravating the problems of non-stop climate change, overzealous hunters wiped out giant marsupials in Australia and two-thirds of large mammalian species in the Americas. In Europe, cavemen replaced the cave bears.

Some commentators likened this Pleistocene blitzkrieg by our ancestors to previous extinctions in the Earth's long history, including the Cretaceous–Tertiary event at the end of the Mesozoic that did for the dinosaurs and liberated the mammals. David Raup at Chicago rejected the idea. 'It was not nearly as pronounced as that,' he wrote in 1991. 'Only the most chauvinistic members of the Mammalia—meaning us—could see that event as remotely similar to the Cretaceous–Tertiary mass extinction.'

That is no reason for complacency. Our species' continuing overkill of fierce predators, done mainly for defensive reasons, has disrupted natural ecosystems worldwide. And many other mammals figure on today's lists of endangered species.

Two centuries after Georges Cuvier marvelled over the antediluvian quadrupeds whose fossils he unearthed in the Paris Basin, the stage seems set at last for showing us the whole grand opera of mammalian life during the past 140 million years. Evolution studies in general have matured, with the discovery of mechanisms for the rapid and experimental invention of new forms. What choirmaster will now marshal the investigators of fossils, continental motions, cosmic impacts, climate and genes, and persuade them to sing in tune?

▶ *Concerning Mesozoic evolution,* Dinosaurs *includes the giant reptiles and the origin of birds, which paralleled that of the mammals, whilst* Alcohol *deals with the arrival of fruit. Grass and the ruminants figure in* Global enzymes. *For the transition from apes to humans, see* Human origins. *For ecological consequences of the human contest with fierce animals, see* Predators. *Palaeogeography is expanded in* Continents and supercontinents. *The background to molecular studies appears in* Tree of life *and* Molecules evolving. Impacts *and* Extinctions *deal with the extraterrestrial input into the story. For more on evolution in general, see* Evolution *and cross-references therein.*

MATTER

T HE MATERIAL WORLD is fashioned from frozen energy—*see* **ENERGY AND MASS**. The raw materials of the Universe, initially hydrogen and helium, seem to have been created in a sudden event—*see* **BIG BANG**. During the process, matter may have existed briefly in a peculiar form—*see* **QUARK SOUP**. A mystery is why equal quantities of antimatter were not created, which would have annihilated all ordinary matter—*see* **ANTIMATTER**.

In the Standard Model of late 20th-century particle physics, the basic constituents of atomic nuclei are quarks of various kinds, associated in protons and neutrons—*see* **PARTICLE FAMILIES**. The origin of their mass is supposedly due to mysterious entities pervading space and crowding around the particles—*see* **HIGGS BOSONS**.

Besides the quarks, the Standard Model provided for lightweight electrons and zero-mass neutrinos, but in 1998 the latter were found to behave as if they possessed at least a small mass—*see* **NEUTRINO OSCILLATIONS**. Beyond the Standard Model is the possibility of exotic particles that scarcely interact with ordinary matter—*see* **SPARTICLES** and **DARK MATTER**.

The raw materials of the cosmos were elaborated by nuclear reactions in stars into many different chemical forms—*see* **ELEMENTS**. They opened the way to chemical reactions—*see* **MOLECULES IN SPACE** and **MINERALS IN SPACE**, also **LIFE'S ORIGIN**.

Particles of matter can behave as if they are waves, with very peculiar consequences—*see* **QUANTUM TANGLES** and **SUPERATOMS, SUPERFLUIDS AND SUPERCONDUCTORS**.

MEMORY

Tracking down the chemistry of retention and forgetfulness

THE MONTREAL NEUROLOGICAL INSTITUTE was created in 1934, largely with funding from the Rockefeller Foundation for Wilder Penfield, an outstanding brain surgeon of his time. The eight-storey building with a pointed tower in the middle was where the Quebecois went to get their brains chopped. To say so is no exaggeration, because in the mid-20th century it was the fashion to excise handfuls of grey matter almost as readily as an appendix, or else to use the scalpel to sever connections deep inside the brain.

Such operations were done not only to remove tumours and to reduce violent epilepsy, but even to treat mental disorders like depression. Penfield was nothing if not careful, and he used an electric wire to probe the exposed brain to make sure he had the right bit. Sometimes when he touched the side of the brain the patient, who was conscious, reported a flashback. For example: 'My mother is telling my brother he has got his coat on backwards.'

Working closely with Penfield and his patients was Donald Hebb of McGill University. He had wanted to be a novelist, and took up psychology with that end in mind. Instead he became caught up in the search for the mechanism of memory. At Harvard he was a student of Karl Lashley, who looked in vain for the brain's memory archive by cutting out ever-larger pieces of rats' brains without eradicating their ability to perform learned tasks. In Montreal, Hebb saw the same mystery in human beings.

'I was studying some of those patients with large chunks of their brains removed,' Hebb said later, 'and I could find nothing wrong with them. Nothing wrong with memory, nothing wrong with their intelligence, consciousness unimpaired. Which was indeed a very great puzzle. In the years that followed I developed what might be called, I think fairly, a crackpot theory, but that has had some support. It implied that thinking consists of the interaction between brain cells and nothing more.'

The essence of Hebb's theory was set out in a slim volume called *Organization of Behavior* (1949). His language was strange for the psychology of his time, which was generally about ego and id in the manner of Sigmund Freud, or else schedules of conditioning after Ivan Pavlov. Hebb wrote instead about nerve fibres, or axons, connecting the cells of the brain. 'When an axon of cell A is near enough to excite a cell B and repeatedly and persistently takes part in firing it, some growth process or metabolic change takes place in one or both cells such that A's efficiency, as one of the cells firing B, is increased.'

Hebb knew perfectly well that a connection between two brain cells is made at a synapse, where the incoming nerve fibre plugs onto the target cell and sends signals into it. He speculated about the growth of synaptic knobs, as he called them, as the means by which the efficiency of the connection might be increased. But he wanted to leave no unnecessary hostage to anatomical fortune, and kept his 'neurophysiological postulate' quite general.

What mattered more to him was the idea that a memory should reverberate in the brain for a while, then to be either forgotten almost at once, or else to be preserved in the improved connections between cells, as something learned. This was in line with everyday experience of the distinction between short-term and long-term memory, recognized by psychologists since the 19th century. You may look up a phone number and remember it for a few minutes while you get through, or else plant it in your head for a day or a lifetime because it is important.

Hebb stressed the role of emotion in learning. Hunger drives an experimental rat to remember its way through a maze to reach food. Human beings retain knowledge that keeps them alive, interests them, excites them or frightens them. The emotional aspect was later dramatized when it turned out that millions of people could recall exactly what they were doing when they heard, in 1963, that President Kennedy had been shot. For a later generation, news of the 2001 aerial attack on New York's Twin Towers had a similar impact.

Some brain mechanism says 'print this'. Casual daily detail that would normally be junked is preserved, giving time for later appraisal. Presumably a Palaeolithic ancestor needed to be able to re-examine closely that occasion when a leopard nearly ambushed him, and to figure out what his mistake was, or what warning signs he missed.

In 2000 a neuroscientist at Edinburgh, Seth Grant, was investigating a huge molecular machine that is present in a synapse, on the surface of the receiving cell. He and his team found that it consists of no fewer than 77 protein molecules. According to Grant's interpretation, these proteins collaborate for the purpose of registering chemical signals from the incoming axon of the transmitting nerve cell and, when appropriate, strengthening the connection. They provide exactly the 'growth process or metabolic change' required by Hebb's theory.

Disable a protein in the complex in experimental mice, either by a genetic mutation or by a chemical block, and that impairs learning and memory in the animals. There is confirmation that the same machinery works in human beings too. In at least three cases, Grant noted, human hereditary defects associated with learning difficulties are mutations in genes that prescribe the manufacture of proteins needed for the complex.

In short, everything about the picture was neat, except the name of this big molecular machine: formally, the N-methyl-D-aspartate receptor complex. Grant proposed renaming it in honour of the quiet Canadian whose idea had inspired many brain researchers for half a century. He called it a hebbosome.

Grant suggested that various kinds of hebbosomes inhabit the synapse at the connection between brain cells. They detect patterns of activity in both cells, and then permanently alter the quality of the connections. But their reach is not confined to a single pair of cells. Somehow they orchestrate connections in long pathways through the brain, in line with Hebb's idea of reverberation.

'Scientists interested in learning and memory mention Hebb or his postulate almost every day,' Grant noted. 'Yet the general public has hardly heard of him. I dare say future historians will set the record straight, and rank him at least alongside Freud and Pavlov, among psychologists of the 20th century.'

How a sea snail learns

The Internet originated as a way of maintaining vital communications in the event of a nuclear war, by finding routes through whatever links might survive an attack. When Lashley hacked away at the brains of his unfortunate animals, trying to find where memories reside, he failed because there is a similar capacity to use whatever remains of a network of interconnected cells. Moreover, the tests of memory that he used were related mainly to procedures, and in such cases (scientists now know) the memories are written into the parts of the brain directly concerned with sensing the environment and controlling the muscles. They could be eliminated only by totally incapacitating an animal in those respects, which would have negated Lashley's tests anyway.

But what most people mean when they think of memory is not the implicit recollection of how to drive a car, but remembering faces, places, objects and information. A brain surgeon's knife revealed by accident the parts of the brain that matter most, for implanting an explicit memory of that kind. In the USA in 1953, William Scoville treated a young man codenamed HM for severe epilepsy by removing parts of the temporal lobes, near the ears. In the process, a region towards the centre of the brain on the underside of each lobe, called the hippocampus, was badly damaged.

Thereafter, HM had no long-term memory of the explicit sort. Although intelligent, polite and superficially normal, he failed to recognize a person with whom he had spent the previous day. He could read the same magazine over and over again, always with the same fresh interest. Well aware of his difficulty, he was worried about it. 'It's like waking from a dream,' he said. All the time, he meant.

This personal tragedy for HM was a clue to memory that scientists could not ignore, when it was disclosed in 1957. Among those who immediately followed it up was Eric Kandel, a young Austrian-born scientist working at the National Institutes of Health in Bethesda, Maryland. But after an arduous programme of detecting electrical signals in the hippocampus, in experiments with small mammals, he was unable to find any peculiarity that might explain its role in implanting long-term memories.

Kandel convinced himself that the explanation for memory must depend not on the behaviour of individual cells but on changes in their connections. He was also sure that the brain of a mammal was far too complicated to reveal the secrets easily. Previous discoveries about nerves had been made with marine animals without backbones, and Kandel looked for a suitable simple creature for investigating what happens at the synapses during learning. Top experts in the field tried hard to dissuade him.

'Few self-respecting neurophysiologists, I was told, would leave the study of learning in mammals to work on an invertebrate,' Kandel recalled. 'Was I compromising my career? Of an even greater concern to me were the doubts expressed by some very knowledgeable psychologists I knew, who were sincerely sceptical that anything interesting about learning and memory could be found in a simple invertebrate animal.'

Stubbornly Kandel went on with his search. He considered crayfish, lobsters, flies and worms, before settling on the giant marine snail, *Aplysia californica*. Its nervous system has a small number of unusually large cells—20,000 compared with 100 billion in the human brain. It also has a reflex mechanism to retract its gills when they are touched. If a gentle touch is repeated without any harm resulting, the reaction becomes weaker. But a forceful touch amplifies the reflex, and training makes the strong response normal, in a rudimentary learning process.

In 1962 Kandel went to Paris to find out more about *Aplysia* from one of the very few biophysicists expert on the animal, Ladislav Tauc. Together they soon detected clear-cut changes in the synapses during learning. Kandel continued to work with the snail for the rest of the century, at New York University and then Columbia. What he and his teams learned from the snail became the bedrock of a new, biochemical science of memory. As is often the way with the biggest discoveries, Kandel's can be summarized quite briefly.

Short-term memory depends on the addition of phosphate groups to the protein structures called ion channels that control the supply of calcium in the incoming nerve fibre at the synapse. Extra calcium increases the amount of a transmitter substance released by the incoming nerve to stimulate the target cell. The resulting improvement in the connection is temporary.

On the other hand, long-term memory depends on the building of new proteins into the surface of the target cell. A signalling protein called kinase A travels to the cell nucleus and provokes changes in the activities of genes that command the manufacture of various other proteins, increasing the supply of some and cutting back on others. Delivered to the synapse, the newly made proteins alter the structures there, in such a way as to make the connection stronger for a much longer period.

By the 1990s, progress in molecular biology enabled Kandel and his team to return to the far more complex processes of memory in the brains of mice. They were able to confirm that the same kinds of mechanisms operate in short-term and long-term memory in mammals, as in the sea snails. Particularly powerful in the research was the use of so-called knockout mice, in which a selected gene, coding for a particular protein, can be disabled by genetic engineering. This made it possible to test, one by one, the proteins involved in the restructuring of the synapse during memory storage.

In a way, the molecular analysis was too successful. Scores of proteins were identified in Kandel's lab and in others around the world, all involved in memory. As mentioned earlier, a synaptic protein machine analysed in Edinburgh has 77 different molecules. So confusing was the picture that some scientists even begged for a slowdown in biochemical discoveries.

Badly needed was some sense of what all those molecules say to one another when a memory is being implanted. The first clue to a dialogue, or argument, between the molecules came early in the 21st century from research on the chemistry of forgetting.

The molecule of oblivion

People use all kinds of tricks to remember things. When Paul McCartney awoke one morning with the tune of the century playing in his head, to retain it he sang, 'Scrambled eggs, oh my darling how I love your legs.' Only later was this transformed into, 'Yesterday, all my troubles seemed so far away.'

Or take an imaginary walk down Gorki Street and remember imaginary items in the shop windows. That was one of the methods used by a man codenamed S, studied by Alexander Luria, a neuropsychologist in Moscow. This man could, for example, learn tables of numbers, or poetry in a language he did not know, and recall them years later.

S was not happy with his skill. He would sometimes write down what he had learned and burn the paper, in an effort to forget it by desperate magic. With hindsight, half a century later, you can hazard a guess that a chemical called PP1 wasn't working normally in S's brain.

Forgetfulness is a necessary fact of life. Why remember the face of everyone you passed on a city street ten years ago? If the brain has no shredder for useless information, it becomes very cluttered. But forgetting important things formerly known well is also a problem, especially in older people. Just as repetition helps in learning and remembering, so neglect of one's memories allows them to decay.

Recalling miscellaneous information is for some a road to fame and fortune on TV quiz shows, which are just a modern equivalent of vaudeville days when a person like S could earn a living as a memory man. Swiss neuroscientists bred memory mice, which could remember things that other mice forgot. They did it by genetic engineering.

Isabelle Mansuy and her colleagues at the Eidgenössische Technische Hochschule Zürich compared their animals, with or without the special powers, in tasks that involved recognizing objects seen before, or remembering the way through an underwater maze to an escape platform. The memory mice outperformed their normal cousins in their youth, and the difference became greater as the animals aged and the memory of the ordinary mice waned.

In earlier times, such animals might have been only tantalizing curiosities— animal analogues of Luria's Comrade S. But in the era of molecular biology Mansuy could say exactly where the advantage lay, in her memory mice. The genetic engineering gave them a gene coding for the manufacture of an agent that inhibits the activity of a particular enzyme, a molecular catalyst employed in the brain.

This is protein phosphatase 1, or PP1 for short. The experimenters could block this protein at will by feeding or not feeding the mice with a certain gene-activating chemical. Carefully designed tests on the mice revealed that PP1 is the molecule of oblivion.

It operates even during the initial learning process. Indeed, PP1 seems to explain one of the first conclusions of educational psychologists, back in the 19th century, namely that learning is easier in short sessions, with intervals between, than in long sessions of the same total duration. Mansuy's genetically modified mice, deficient in PP1, performed equally well with short or long breaks between the testing sessions. The normal mice, like human learners, did better with the longer breaks.

There is an endless fight between those brain molecules that say 'remember this' and PP1 that says 'forget it'. In chemical terms, the memory-promoting molecules are trying to add phosphate to other proteins while the oblivion molecule, PP1, tries to remove it. A respite seems to give remembering a better chance to win the chemical tussle.

In elderly mice, aged 15–18 months, mutants with PP1 inactivation could remember the way through the water maze after a month, while some of the normal mice had forgotten within 24 hours. The experiments aroused hopes of finding practical ways of reducing memory loss in old folk.

The way ahead

The discovery of the role of PP1 was no fluke. It was just one outcome of a prolonged programme to use genetically modified, or transgenic, mice to study the role of various phosphatase molecules in the brain. And the Zurich team's interests went well beyond the chemistry of memory. It extended into classical concerns of psychology, including for example the dire consequences of being deprived of tender loving care in infancy. Such studies also went to the heart of the old issue of nature versus nurture, by seeing directly how genes and environment interact in the development of an animal's brain from embryo to adulthood.

'This seems to be the way ahead in brain research,' said Isabelle Mansuy. 'We use the new ability to switch genes on and off very precisely, in transgenic animals, and combine it with traditional methods of physiology and behaviour. My belief is that many mental phenomena that matter to people in real life, like emotionality, stress, fear and aggression, will gradually become more comprehensible in exact molecular terms.'

▶ *For other aspects of research on brain and behaviour, see* BRAIN WIRING, BRAIN IMAGES, BRAIN RHYTHMS *and* SPEECH.

MICROWAVE BACKGROUND

Looking for the pattern on the cosmic wallpaper

IT WAS AS IF GALILEO had doubted the moons of Jupiter and reassembled his telescope before daring to look again. In 1964, Arno Penzias and Robert Wilson were doing radio astronomy with a horn that rose like a giant tipper truck above the pumpkin farms of Holmdel, New Jersey. It detected very short radio waves—microwaves—and the Bell Telephone Laboratories built it for experiments with early telecommunications satellites. But Penzias and Wilson thought there was something wrong with their receiver, so they took it to pieces and put it together again. Only then were they sure of their momentous result.

'No matter where we looked, day or night, winter or summer, this background of radiation appeared everywhere in the sky,' Penzias recalled. 'It was not tied to our Galaxy or any other known sources of radio waves. It was rather as if the whole Universe had been warmed up to a temperature about 3 degrees above absolute zero.'

The announcement of the cosmic microwave background in 1965 caused consternation. Almost everyone had forgotten that the Ukrainian-born theorist George Gamow and his team in Washington DC had predicted it as a relic of the Big Bang, with which the Universe supposedly began. No one in the West had noticed the suggestion of a young physicist in Moscow, Igor Novikov, that the Bell Labs' horn should look for it.

'We've been scooped!' Robert Dicke told his team at Princeton, just down the road from Holmdel. They had reinvented the Gamow theory and were planning their own search for the cosmic microwaves. Compounding their chagrin was the fact that Bell Labs made the discovery with a microwave radiometer invented by Dicke.

Most abashed were the supporters of the rival to the Big Bang, the Steady State theory of cosmology, then still popular. For them the cosmic microwaves were a harbinger of doom, carrying the news that all of space was at one time filled with a gas as hot as the Sun's surface. Not a steady state of affairs at all.

For the first 400,000 years after the Big Bang (so the story goes) the Universe was a hot fog. Free-range charged particles blocked the progress of all light-like rays. Light was not set free in a transparent Universe until the gas cooled sufficiently for atomic nuclei to grab electrons and make the first atoms. The edge of the hot cosmic fogbank marks the limit of the cosmos observable by light-like rays, and it creates a kind of wallpaper all around the sky, beyond the most distant galaxies.

The expansion of the Universe has cooled the sky from 3000 to 2.7 degrees above the absolute zero of temperature, and visible light released 400,000 years after the beginning of time has been reduced to microwaves that are strongest around 1–2 millimetres in wavelength. Although barely perceptible except to modern instruments, the cosmic microwaves represent 99 per cent of all the radiation in the Universe.

They also show very plainly the inside-out appearance of the cosmos. When the microwaves broke free from the fog, the Universe known to us was only one-thousandth of its present size. If we were looking at it from the outside, it would occupy only a small part of the sky. Instead we are inside it, and the microwaves come from all around us.

The radiometers see the primordial gas as if in a time machine. That is thanks to the expansion of the Universe that delays the arrival of radiation till long after the events producing it. In every direction the source of microwaves appears to lie at an immense distance.

Every year, the expansion takes the edge of the fogbank a bit farther away, and the microwaves detected today have just come into view for the first time. When the moment of transparency came, the Universe was small and they were indeed quite close to where we are now. But they have had to puff their way towards us for billions of years in order to beat, in the end, the expansion rate of the cosmos.

By 1969 one side of the sky was known to be two per cent warmer than the other. The cosmic microwaves coming from beyond the Leo constellation look warmest of all because that is the direction in which the Sun and Earth are rushing through the Universe at large, at 375 kilometres per second. Such a speed would take you to the Moon in about a quarter of an hour. It combines our velocity in orbit around the centre of the Milky Way Galaxy with the Galaxy's own motion through cosmic space. The temperatures change a little from season to season, as the Earth orbits around the Sun.

● Encouragement from a satellite

Otherwise the microwave background seemed featureless, like plain wallpaper. A failure to detect any variation from point to point across the sky provoked anxiety among the theorists. If the microwave background were really featureless, we ought not to be here.

What an anticlimax, if the primordial gas had merely expanded and cooled ever after! For stars, galaxies and bipeds to form, gravity had to grab the gas and reverse the cosmic expansion locally. It needed a helping hand, in the prior formation of relatively dense clouds of gas. The pressure of sound waves could do the trick, but the resulting clouds should appear as hotspots, a little warmer than their surroundings.

Searching for a pattern on the cosmic wallpaper therefore became an obsession. For a quarter of a century, it remained stubbornly blank. Using very cold instruments, observers looked without success for temperature variations of less than a thousandth of a degree, and theorists were biting their nails. A big confusion came from foreground microwave emissions from our own Galaxy, the Milky Way. These had to be identified and subtracted from the background.

Progress resumed in 1992, with the release of results from NASA's Cosmic Background Explorer satellite, or COBE, pronounced Koh-bee. Launched in 1989, this purpose-built spacecraft scanned the whole sky. Analysis of the results revealed, by statistical tests, the existence of features in the microwave background.

'What startles me most is that we really can make a coherent story out of the Big Bang,' remarked John Mather of NASA Goddard, who masterminded COBE. Other comments were less measured. 'It's like seeing the face of God,' said George Smoot of the Lawrence Berkeley Lab, who presented the results to the American Physical Society in the form of a sky map. Stephen Hawking at Cambridge called it 'the scientific discovery of the century, if not of all time.'

These remarks were over the top, because the COBE results were really rather crude. It was a magnificent achievement to confirm that temperature differences are present in the microwave background, as expected. But the widely publicized map did not really show for certain which places in the sky were warm or cool, or how big the hotspots were. Derived from the statistics, it was abstract post-expressionism, like a Jackson Pollock painting.

Premature hyperbole did not dampen other experts' high hopes for further investigations of the microwave background. Many teams around the world busied themselves accordingly. The first report of the direct detection of particular features came in 1994, from British and Spanish astronomers working on the Spanish island of Tenerife. Scanning strips around the sky with microwave radiometers, they found patches of comparative warmth. One, for example, was just south of the Plough, or Big Dipper.

When observers with other instruments, on the ground or on balloons, looked more closely at patches of the background, they found that the hotspots seemed to be typically about twice as wide as the Full Moon—one degree of arc. (Don't confuse angular degrees, referring to sizes as seen in the sky, with temperature variations in degrees C.) Theorists were enthralled by that size, because it was just what they'd expect on the simplest assumptions about the nature of the Universe.

In January 1999 a two-tonne Italian telescope called Boomerang dropped safely onto the ice after a ten-day flight 38 kilometres above Antarctica—half-way into space. It had dangled unmanned from a giant American balloon. The trip began near Mount Erebus and it ended just 50 kilometres from the launch site, after a flight of 8000 kilometres.

A team of 36 scientists in Italy, the USA, the UK and Canada was involved in the adventure. Boomerang provided the first images of the pattern on the wallpaper, over a fairly large area of the sky, in sufficient detail for confident conclusions to be drawn. By 2000, with their analysis well advanced, the team was able to report that the largest hotspots averaged 0.9 degree in width.

'It is really exciting to be able to see some of the fundamental structures of the universe in their embryonic state,' said the Italian team leader, Paolo de Bernardis of Roma La Sapienza. 'The light we have detected from them has travelled across the entire Universe before reaching us, and we are perfectly able to distinguish it from the light generated in our own Galaxy.'

The cosmic thunder

Why were the experts impressed by hotspots about a degree wide? You need to think about what was going on inside the hot fog during the 400,000 years before it cooled enough for the light to break free. The belief is that sound waves, initiated by jiggles when the Universe was extremely young and very, very small, travelled through the fog.

The cosmic thunder squeezed the gas slightly, as do the pressure waves in air, which carry sound to your ears. The compressions made the gas a little denser, so creating the hotspots where gravity could later do its work of marshalling the gas into stars and galaxies. And to reckon how big the largest hotspots should be, theorists have to calculate the maximum distance that a sound wave could travel during the 400,000 years before the light broke free.

The answer is, just far enough to make hotspots about a degree wide. The observations by Boomerang and other telescopes confirming that prediction were not just satisfactory, in the sense of putting a tick by the theorists' sum. They carried a momentous message about the overall character of the Universe, and annihilated many cosmological theories at a stroke.

According to some theories, the density of its contents is so great that the Universe bends all light rays and so acts as a magnifying lens. In that case the microwave hotspots should look much larger than one degree of arc. In other theories, they should appear much smaller because the Universe is expanding so fast that it acts as a demagnifying lens. The observations ruled out both of these possibilities.

Instead it appears that light rays traverse the cosmos in straight lines, except when they encounter heavy masses locally. The cosmologists call it a flat Universe because its geometry accords with the rules collated by Mr Euclid 2300 years ago for flat surfaces, as opposed to fancier kinds of geometry that go on the surface of a sphere or a horse's saddle. Flatness requires a balance between the mass of the Universe and its rate of expansion, which only a narrow range of theories can provide.

Boomerang and the other experiments in progress at around the same time therefore gave a tremendous sense that, after centuries of free-range speculation, the hotspots in the cosmic microwave background might soon lead to a precise theory of the Universe. The next step was to look more carefully at the smaller spots. How many, of what sizes?

Finding facts the theories must fit

Whilst the one-degree hotspots represent the greatest distance that sound waves could travel in the first 400,000 years of the Universe, the smaller spots are the products of reverberations of the cosmic thunder, producing overtones, as if in a musical instrument. These correspond to masses of gas that contract under gravity and then bounce outwards because of the pressure of radiation, only to contract again. That can happen more than once. The resulting spots on the wallpaper should be about one-half, one-third, one-quarter and one-fifth of a degree wide.

The precise sizes and relative intensities of the smaller spots depend critically on the nature of the cosmos we inhabit. It affects the behaviour of the hot gas in its musical modes, in calculable ways. For example, in a very dense Universe, spots of one-third and one-fifth of a degree of arc should be conspicuous. But if much of the density were due to ordinary matter, then half-degree and quarter-degree spots should be relatively scarce.

The proportions of other contents, called dark matter and dark energy, also have calculable effects on the reverberations and therefore on spot sizes. So does the rate of expansion of the Universe. If you can count accurately the relative proportions of spots, in the spectrum of different sizes, you should be able to read off the magic numbers of cosmology, which describe the Universe overall. Success with spot counting in the opening decade of the 21st century began to show the genetic code of the cosmos, daubed by the microwaves on the wallpaper all around us—or, to echo Smoot, on God's freckled face.

Preliminary counts of small hotspots, of about half and one-third of a degree, were announced in 2001. They came from further analysis of the Boomerang balloon results and also from a ground-based instrument, the Degree Angular Scale Interferometer, located at the South Pole. The results were similar, and were compatible with a cosmos in which ordinary matter makes up roughly 5 per cent of the total mass, dark matter about 35 per cent, and dark energy about 60 per cent.

For some astrophysicists the most important aspect of all this progress was that the results were also in line with a popular theory of the Big Bang, according to which a very rapid expansion, called inflation, occurred in the first moment. 'With these new data, inflation looks very strong,' said John Carlstrom at Chicago, leader of the team masterminding the South Pole telescope. 'It's always been theoretically compelling. Now it's on very solid experimental ground.'

The same instrument took another big step by revealing the directions of vibration of the microwaves, in two patches of sky examined for 200 days on end. The polarization, as the physicists call it, arises from the directions of motion of the hot gas producing the emissions. 'It's going to triple the amount of information that we get from the cosmic microwave background,' said John Kovac, a graduate student in the team. 'It's like going from the picture on a black-and-white TV to colour.'

To survey the background across the entire sky, new microwave satellites were needed—successors to COBE but with much better instruments. NASA's Microwave Anisotropy Probe, or Wilkinson-MAP, led the way in 2001, surveying the whole sky at five microwave wavelengths. Its first results appeared early in 2003. The deluxe space mission for the cosmic microwaves is to be the European Space Agency's Planck satellite, named after Max Planck who initiated the quantum theory, due for launch in 2007.

With more than 100 detectors working at nine wavelengths, Planck will look for features in the microwave background down to one-sixth of a degree. That can be compared with seven degrees for COBE. One benefit of using many frequencies is that the task of subtracting foreground sources of microwaves, including the Milky Way, can be done more precisely. Another is to sharpen the measurements of spot sizes.

'Time is running out for the theorists,' remarked Jean-Loup Puget of France's Institut d'Astrophysique Spatiale, a leading participant in the Planck project. 'Until now they have been able to invent all kinds of universes by making different assumptions about this and that. In 2009, when the results from Planck are announced, we expect to define the Big Bang and the vital statistics of the Universe with astonishing precision. Then we'll know which, if any, of the theories really fits the facts.'

A bonus about the galaxies

The Wilkinson-MAP and Planck spacecraft were also expected to discover thousands of new clusters of galaxies at great distances in the Universe, by an effect on the cosmic microwaves. In the early 1970s Rashid Sunyaev and Yakov Zel'dovich in the Space Research Institute in Moscow pointed out that when microwaves encounter hot gas, bottled up by gravity in the galaxy clusters, their wavelengths must be altered.

Curiously enough, the hot clusters then stand out as cooler-looking spots in the microwave charts of the sky. That is a very unusual state of affairs in astrophysics. Subtracting the foreground Sunyaev–Zel'dovich effect of the galaxy clusters is important for assessing the microwave background correctly. But a huge bonus is that the observers can directly relate the spots in the primordial gas to the pattern of galaxies to which it gave birth, and reveal the architecture of the Universe at large.

For more about cosmic origins and the inflation theory, see BIG BANG. *Another link between the microwave background and the study of galaxy clusters is noted in* DARK ENERGY. *For more general perspectives, see* UNIVERSE.

MINERALS IN SPACE

From stellar dust to crystals to stones

J EWELLERS WILL TELL YOU that limpid specimens of the green stone olivine are also called peridot. When olivine is more golden in colour, chrysolite is the name and medieval alchemists matched it to the chaste sign of the Zodiac, Virgo. Did Shakespeare have that in mind when he wrote Othello's comment on the murdered Desdemona?

> ... *had she been true,*
>
> *If heaven would make me such another world*
>
> *Of one entire and perfect chrysolite,*
>
> *I'd not have sold her for it.*

The words have a more remarkable resonance for Earth scientists today. In speaking of a world made of chrysolite, Othello anticipates the modern opinion that olivine is the main solid ingredient of our planet, as judged by the speed at which earthquake waves travel through it.

Although olivine is the mother of basalt, which paves the ocean floor, most of it is hidden at great depths. Olivine can break out in volcanic hotspots, as in the sands of Hawaii, or wriggle through gaps between the moving plates of the Earth's outer shell. The island of Zebirget (St John's) in our infant ocean, the Red Sea, is the classical source of olivine gemstones. A soapy rock called serpentine, found in multicoloured forms on the Lizard, England's southernmost point, is olivine altered by water. Rare heather-like plants that grow there (Lyonesse, Mrs D.F. Maxwell and other oddities) have to tolerate abnormal amounts of magnesium in the soil, which are a legacy of the olivine.

As a material of primordial simplicity, olivine consists of silicate (one silicon atom plus four of oxygen) bound together by atoms of magnesium and iron. The metallic atoms are casually interchangeable, being about the same size. All of these elements are major products of the nuclear kitchens of the stars, and will tend to combine in interstellar space. But no one knew that crystals of olivine existed out there until Europe's Infrared Space Observatory (1995–98) found the signature of forsterite, a crystalline form of olivine, in infrared light from the environs of a star 500 light-years away.

Located in the sky near the Southern Cross, the star is called HD 100546. It is a young star, only a few million years old. Peculiar ultraviolet absorptions seen earlier by the NASA–Europe–UK International Ultraviolet Explorer were interpreted as a result of comets or asteroids splashing into the star.

'A tremendous cloud of comets seems to surround this young star,' said Christoffel Waelkens at Leuven, Belgium, who led the team that discovered the olivine crystals near HD 100546. 'We believe that it was from just such a comet cloud, around the young Sun, that the Earth and the other planets were born. Now we compare notes with colleagues who study minerals in our local comets and meteorites.'

When Comet Hale–Bopp visited the Sun's vicinity in 1997, providing a fine naked-eye spectacle, it too was a target for the Infrared Space Observatory's telescope. Small crystals of forsterite were detected in the comet's dusty tail. As comets represent raw material of the kind used for constructing planets, left over from the building of the Solar System, Hale–Bopp provided a conceptual link in the mineralogy of our origins.

'A key ingredient of both stardust and comet dust is olivine in crystalline form,' Jacques Crovisier of the Observatoire de Paris-Meudon remarked. 'This is also one of the main constituents of the Earth's interior. Now we can say with real confidence that we stand on a congealed pile of mineral dust, like that contained in the comets swarming around the Sun 4500 million years ago.'

For Rens Waters of the Universiteit van Amsterdam, who detected olivine crystals near old stars as well as young, the infrared observations brought a 'crystal revolution' in astronomy. 'We thought that stone-like silicon compounds outside our own planetary system existed only in an amorphous, structureless form. Now we can examine in the lab the infrared signatures of known crystals—forsterite, enstatite and so on—and find the same signatures in space. We have a new science, astromineralogy.'

Molten stones and free-range carbonates

To make the link to the Earth's own olivine, another step is needed. The minute crystals detected by the astronomers are a poor starting point for the planet-building process, in the violent and windswept surroundings of the newborn Sun. More convincing raw material appears in stones of olivine, the size of *petits pois*. Called chondrules, they turn up abundantly in chondrites, the most primitive meteorites that fall from interplanetary space and are believed to be relics from the time when the Earth and other planets formed.

More than 100 years ago Henry Sorby of Sheffield, the pioneer of microscopic geology, aptly described the chondrules as 'molten drops in a fiery rain'. Before the building of the rocky planets could begin in earnest, the olivine dust had to be cooked to make the stony chondrules. They melted very quickly, in a matter of seconds or minutes, because volatile elements like sulphur and potassium trapped in the dust had no time to escape. Scientists trying to explain the chondrules have invoked enormous solar flares, shock waves or cosmic lightning flashes.

An up-to-date speculation is that a gamma-ray burst might have cooked the chondrules. Every day, satellites detect flashes of gamma rays and X-rays from mind-boggling explosions in distant galaxies. The duration of the main flash, typically around a minute, is just right for chondrule-making. Brian McBreen and Lorraine Hanlon, space astronomers at University College Dublin, calculated that a gamma-ray burst occurring about 300 light-years away would produce enough chondrules to build dozens of Earths. Absorption of X-rays by iron atoms in the olivine would have been the chief heater. If so, the evidence for the earliest recorded gamma-ray burst is written in stone.

'We think that a gamma-ray burst occurred nearby at a critical moment during the birth of the Solar System,' Hanlon explained. 'Its intense radiation fused microscopic mineral grains together to make sizeable stones, well suited to building planets like the Earth. Only a minority of newly forming stars and planetary systems would experience such fortuitous heating. If we're right, earth-like planets may be rarer than some of our colleagues imagine.'

The Earth's abundant carbonates, well known in limestone mountains, form from carbon dioxide and other materials dissolved in liquid water. When carbonates turned up in some meteorites, scientists assumed that they had to come from a watery planet. This inference was undermined when the Infrared Space Observatory detected carbonates in the space around dying stars called the Bug Nebula and the Red Spider Nebula.

So Mother Nature has other tricks that chemists did not know. 'The amount of carbonates we find is equivalent to at least 30 Earth masses, far too large to be the relic of a hypothetical planetary system,' said Ciska Kemper at Amsterdam. 'It might be easier to form carbonates than people have previously thought.'

Will the minerals be useful?

Attempts to identify diamonds, crystals of pure carbon, in interstellar space were at best ambiguous at the start of the 21st century. A signature at 21 microns, seen by infrared space telescopes, could be damaged diamonds according to French astronomers, but their Spanish colleagues preferred to interpret the signature as carbon in the football form of buckyballs. Or graphite, said an expert in Canada. But no one doubted that diamonds were out there somewhere, because very small diamonds are found in meteorites. As Edward Anders of Chicago once commented, 'They'd barely make engagement rings for bacteria.' Even so, they inevitably provoked thoughts about eldorados in space.

Where rocky surfaces appear elsewhere in the Solar System, they broadly resemble commonplace minerals of the Earth and meteorites. Samples of Moon rock, returned to the Earth by American astronauts and Soviet unmanned landers, brought some previously unknown crystals but no major mineralogical surprises. They also satisfied those who visualized large-scale engineering on the Moon or in orbit around it. Lunar soil could be processed quite easily, using solar power, to obtain iron, aluminium, titanium, silicon and oxygen. Conversion into ceramics and glass are other options. Water might have to come from further afield—from the rings of Saturn, say.

Some asteroids and meteorites include lumps of metallic iron, rich in nickel and cobalt too. Our ancestors' first introduction to iron came from picking up meteorites. Back in the 1970s, Michael Gaffey and Thomas McCord at the University of Hawaii calculated that, in the long run, less energy would be required to import a tonne of ready-smelted iron from a well-placed asteroid than to obtain it from high-grade iron ore in a terrestrial blast furnace.

For convenience, the iron would come in a foamy, wing-like form, capable of diving safely through the Earth's atmosphere and floating on the ocean after splashdown. Whenever such bold imaginings become fashionable again, astromineralogy will be a subject for engineers and metallurgists, as well as for astronomers and space scientists.

▶ *See also* MOLECULES IN SPACE, PLASMA CRYSTALS, EARTH, COMETS AND ASTEROIDS *and* GAMMA-RAY BURSTS.

MOLECULAR PARTNERS

Letting natural processes do the chemist's work

S TRASBOURG OR STRASSBURG lies in the rift valley between the Vosges and the Schwarzwald, down which the Rhin or Rhein pours. The city is closer to Munich than to Paris, and repeated exchanges of territory between the French and the Germans aggravated an identity problem of the people of Alsace. It was not resolved until, after restoration to France in 1945, Strasbourg became a favoured locale for Europe-wide institutions. But history left the Alsatians better able than most to resist the brain drain to Paris, and to pursue their own ideas, whether with dogs, pottery or science.

As a 28-year-old postdoc in Strasbourg, Jean-Marie Lehn embarked in 1967 on a new kind of chemistry that was destined to become a core theme of 21st-century research worldwide. It would straddle biology, physics and engineering. As it concerned not individual molecules, made by bonding atoms together, but the looser associations and interactions between two or more molecules, he called the innovation supramolecular chemistry.

Lehn had spent a year at Harvard contributing in a junior role to a *tour de force* of molecular chemistry, when Robert Woodward and a large team of researchers synthesized vitamin B_{12}. It was the most complex molecule ever produced from scratch. Whilst technically instructive, in the latest arts of laboratory synthesis, the experience was thought-provoking. Need chemistry be so difficult?

A philosophical interest in how the brain worked at the most basic chemical level, by controlling the passage of charged atoms (ions) of sodium and potassium through the walls of nerve cells, prompted Lehn to investigate materials capable of acting as carriers to transport these ions through biological membranes. Natural ring-shaped antibiotics are one category of such substances. Charles Pedersen in the DuPont lab in Delaware discovered another category, the crown ethers. These are rings of carbon and oxygen atoms in the shape of a crown, and they can firmly lasso ions of lithium, sodium, potassium, rubidium or caesium.

Lehn developed a third type, hollow cage-like molecules capable of strongly catching ions in a 3-D internal cavity, thus forming species that he called cryptates. These were much more selective in the metal guests, the choice of which depended on the sizes of their ions as compared with the sizes of the cavities. Lehn went on to devise molecules adapted to gathering whole molecules into cavities and clefts in their 3-D structures.

At that time, molecular biologists were revealing that enzymes, the proteins that catalyse biochemical reactions in living cells, operate that way. As brilliantly predicted by Emil Fischer of Berlin in 1899, the molecule being processed fits precisely into an enzyme molecule like a lock into a key. This association, based on the correct fitting between the partners, was what Lehn had in mind when he set out to make supramolecular assemblies of synthetic materials showing such molecular recognition.

When two atoms join together with a permanent bond, like that between the hydrogen and oxygen atoms in water, the product is a molecule. In a supermolecule the connection remains looser, like that between the water molecules in ice. And just as ice can melt, so a supermolecule can rather easily fall to pieces again.

New lines of research developed, as Lehn set himself the aim of engineering artificial molecules into 'molecular devices'. Using their ability to recognize, transport and modify target molecules, they should be able to perform signalling and information-processing operations on an incredibly small scale. And Lehn expected that the manufacture of chemical machines would rely heavily on the ability of molecules to assemble themselves into well-defined superstructures, a process called supramolecular self-organization.

Molecular moulds and casts

By 1996 Lehn was on the way to bringing natural selection into play among self-organizing molecules, to select those fittest for their purpose. A young chemist working with him at Strasbourg, Bernold Hasenknopf, found that artificial ring-shaped molecules were able to adapt their size reversibly to fit species present in the medium. Thereafter, another collaborator, Ivan Huc, presented a mixture of small synthetic molecules, called aldehydes and amines, to a well-known natural enzyme, carbonic anhydrase. It could just as well have been a man-made molecule with a cavity, but it's easier to buy enzymes off the shelf.

The small molecules spontaneously formed the supramolecular assembly that best fitted into the cleft of the enzyme. To understand what was new here, consider that a biologist might be interested in how carbonic anhydrase evolved its cleft to suit the natural molecule that it processes. From the opposite starting point, a chemist working traditionally, perhaps to find a drug that might inhibit an enzyme, would synthesize many different molecules and test them one by one to see whether, by good luck, any fitted the cleft well.

Huc and Lehn, by contrast, relied on random connections among the small molecules to make assemblies that would test themselves in the enzyme. The continuous generation of all possible partnerships among the molecular components made available every structural feature and capacity for supramolecular interaction latent in the mixture. Those assemblies that didn't fit the enzyme clefts very well retreated from the scene.

Gradually, the enzyme molecules filled up with supramolecular assemblies that fitted them snugly. This was the chemical equivalent of casting from a concave mould. Conversely, the process studied earlier by Hasenknopf amounted to moulding a supramolecular cavity around a convex molecule of choice.

'Both processes also amount to the generation of the fittest,' Huc and Lehn commented, 'and [they] present adaptation and evolution by spontaneous recombination under changes in the partners or in the environmental conditions. They thus embody a sort of supramolecular Darwinism!'

At the end of the century Lehn was running the Institut de Science et d'Ingénierie Supramoléculaires in Strasbourg, and a parallel operation at the Collège de France in Paris. Other laboratory projects for supramolecular research sprang up all around the world. A flurry of scientific meetings, books and journal articles confirmed that a new branch of science was in the making.

Spinning molecules and shell patterns

A hint of things to come appeared in 1998, in the form of a molecular rotor, devised at IBM's Zurich Research Laboratory with participation from Denmark's Risø National Laboratory. James Gimzewski and his colleagues laid a layer of screw-shaped molecules called hexabutyl decacyclene on a copper surface. They mostly arranged themselves in a static hexagonal pattern, but in some places there were voids about two millionths of a millimetre wide, within which one molecule had separated from its neighbours. It rotated at high speed, with the surrounding molecules acting as a frictionless bearing.

'Our rotor experiment opens the way to making incredibly small supramolecular motors,' Gimzewski said. 'And it's interesting that we're pushing at limits set by the laws of heat, which rule out perpetual motion machines. In the initial experiment the rotors turned in either direction. To have a molecule turning only one way, to give useful work, we have to put energy into the system. But we can still expect efficiencies close to the theoretical maximum.'

Although the ability of natural enzymes to form temporary associations with other materials was an important inspiration concerning molecular partnerships, the chemists' ideas about supramolecular interactions feed back into biology. For example the prolific diatoms, often called the jewels of the sea, are single-celled algae with beautiful symmetrical patterns in their shells. These are distinctive enough to allow marine biologists and fossil-hunters to tell apart many thousands of diatom species. Manfred Sumper of Regensburg worked out how the diatoms build their shells by supramolecular chemistry.

Here the partnership involves long-chain molecules, polyamines, and the silica that builds the shells. The polyamines form droplets or micelles that arrange themselves in a hexagonal pattern. These gather the silica around them, so that it forms a honeycomb shell. Polyamines are consumed in the process, and the droplets break up, continuing the pattern-making down to ever-smaller scales. 'The eventual patterns in the diatom shells seem to depend primarily on the length of the polyamine chain used by each species,' Sumper concluded.

A staggering agenda

In Strasbourg, Jean-Marie Lehn kept his eye firmly on the long-term future. Everything that had happened in supramolecular research so far was, in his opinion, just a rehearsal for far greater possibilities to come. He summed them up in a string of adjectives, in writing of 'complex, informed, self-organized evolutive matter'.

By 'informed' he meant, initially, partnerships of molecules that could store data and be programmed to carry out a sequence of operations. In the long run, the supramolecular assemblies should become capable of learning from their experiences. Indeed this was a key part of Lehn's strategy. Inventing and synthesizing the necessary partnerships by conventional chemistry would take forever. Let natural processes do the work, as in the spontaneous, self-organized filling of the enzyme cleft.

His Darwinian evolution of molecules would lead on, Lehn believed, to post-Darwinian evolution in which the supramolecular partnerships would act like intelligent entities capable of literally shaping their own futures. Ultimately they could rival life itself. Lehn predicted: 'Through progressive discovery, understanding, and implementation of the rules that govern the evolution from inanimate to animate matter and beyond, we will ultimately acquire the ability to create new forms of complex matter.'

In this staggering agenda, the opportunities for young researchers speak for themselves. As is often the case with new sciences, the rhetoric at first ran ahead of reality, but the rate of progress in the long run is likely be limited by the human imagination rather than by chemical feasibility. The transition, from the 19th-century partnerships of atoms in molecules to the 21st-century partnerships of molecules in supramolecular assemblies, will require a new mind-set. It may also bring chemistry out of its smelly back room.

The chemists who made huge contributions to science, technology, agriculture and medicine during the past 200 years were usually hidden like chefs, behind the feasts of physics, biology and industry. Their recipes, like those of the mathematicians, were written in a foreign language using strange symbols, discouraging to would-be fans. Terminology will be no simpler but the role of the chefs will be plainer, when they start sending out the dishes by molecular robots, fashioned from the commonplace atoms of the planet.

▶ *For related physical chemistry, see* BUCKYBALLS AND NANOTUBES, HANDEDNESS *and* DISORDERLY MATERIALS. *For another consequence of molecular partnerships, see* LIFE'S ORIGIN.

MOLECULES EVOLVING

How the Japanese heretics were vindicated

A SHORT JOURNEY SOUTH-WEST from Tokyo in the bullet train takes you to Mishima, near the foot of Mount Fuji. Try to go in April when the 260 varieties of cherry trees nurtured by the National Institute of Genetics are in bloom. It was to a pond full of magnificent carp, and to the blood circulating in their bodies and in his, that the geneticist Motoo Kimura referred when, in 1973, he wanted to explain a new view of the evolution of life.

'The carp and I both need haemoglobin to do exactly the same job of carrying oxygen around the body,' he said. 'Yet one half of all the chemical units in my haemoglobin molecules are different from the carp's. That unnecessary sort of evolution, and my studies of its rate and pattern, suggest to me that natural selection has had no reason for preferring one variant of the molecule over another.'

Kimura launched his neutral theory of molecular evolution in 1968. The emergent science of molecular biology was revealing variations in similar genes, between one species and another, and in the proteins for which they gave the code. The variations did not accord with the expectations from natural selection, Charles Darwin's favourite mechanism for evolution.

The idea of natural selection is that creatures well suited to their environments will tend to leave more surviving offspring than those that are not. Translated into molecular terms, this means that good genes will prosper and bad genes will die out. Such a process undoubtedly happens, and it helps to explain how Mother

Nature drives evolution along and refines the wonderful creatures that populate the planet. But, as Kimura realized, it is not the whole story.

Already in 1931 Sewall Wright at Chicago had pointed out that some evolution is a random process. Within a population of microbes, plants or animals, certain variants of genes become more common or die out simply as a matter of chance. Wright called this a shifting balance, but random genetic drift is the usual phrase nowadays. In 1954, Wright retired to Madison, Wisconsin. Kimura met him while studying there.

In small populations, called bottlenecks by evolutionists, the changes due to random drift can be spectacular. In the Hawaiian island chain, for example, many unique plants and animals arose in the past few million years, from lonely ancestors carried by wind or water to virgin volcanic terrain. A few pregnant fruit flies wandering from island to island or valley to valley were the grandmothers of about 700 species.

Kimura went further than Wright, in assessing how the variant genes establish themselves in the first place. They come from mutations that alter the genetic code. Usually these are harmful, and natural selection weeds them out. Occasionally a mutation is beneficial. With luck it survives and natural selection will promote it. But the main effect of natural selection is conservative— eliminating individuals that depart too far from the norm of a species.

Most surviving mutations are neither beneficial nor particularly harmful. They are neutral or nearly neutral, and natural selection has nothing to say about them. The new variants of genes survive or fail to survive by pure chance. As a result, a huge amount of evolution proceeds invisibly and randomly at the molecular level, within the gene set, or genome, of each species. Indeed scientists nowadays use molecular differences, like those between carp and human haemoglobin, to reconstruct the family tree of life.

'Although such random processes are slow and insignificant for our ephemeral existence, in the span of geological times they become colossal,' Kimura wrote. 'In this way the footprints of time are evident in all the genomes on the Earth. This adds still more to the grandeur of our view of biological evolution.'

● 'You don't have to like the idea'

Kimura's vision was abhorrent to leading evolutionists of the so-called neo-Darwinist school, who had selected natural selection as supposedly the only important mechanism by which genes evolve. A reporter who journeyed in 1972 from Mishima to California was greeted in UC Davis like one who had visited Hell and spoken with the Devil. Theodosius Dobzhansky, a grand old man of evolutionary biology, was horrified that the minds of the general public might be contaminated with Kimura's obnoxious propositions.

A reporter can shrug off such opposition, and even treat rage as a sign that something new and important is afoot, even though decades may pass before the full meaning becomes clear. Kimura, on the other hand, had a fight on his hands that lasted till the end of his life in 1994. But his theory could not be ignored indefinitely because it is mathematically compelling and makes testable predictions, like a theory in physics. It also provides benchmarks for measuring, case by case, how much of evolution is due to chance, and how much to natural selection. The answer is usually a bit of each.

'Few evolutionary biologists would deny that this theory ranks among the most interesting and powerful adjuncts to evolutionary explanation since Darwin's formulation of natural selection,' commented the Harvard palaeontologist Stephen Jay Gould. 'You don't have to like the idea, but how can you possibly leave it out?'

The theory needed an extension to establish its importance in the course of evolution. Critics of Kimura could, and did, say that even if neutral mutations were commonplace, so what? If they were neutral they were by definition unimportant, and therefore had no role in the adaptation of species to their environments, which is the whole point of evolution.

Kimura himself was content to retort that mutations that are neutral today might become useful tomorrow, when the environment changes. He also quoted with approval a reporter's effort to point out another possible implication. 'If trivial changes can accumulate in a molecule over many millions of years, without interference from natural selection, the day may come when a peculiar molecule thus produced goes through one more mutation that suddenly gives it new importance—just as changing one card can alter a worthless poker hand into a royal straight flush.'

While giving a sense of the evolutionary potential latent in the neutral genes, the analogy with poker was misleading about mechanisms. More important than culminating card-changes within active genes are the changes in control mechanisms that determine which genes are active. Here the story converges with the question of where new genes come from.

Old music in the genes

Another Japanese geneticist, Susumu Ohno, was a near contemporary of Kimura who settled in California, at the Beckman Research Institute. In 1970 he proposed that most if not all genes have come into existence by duplication of pre-existing genes. That spare copies of genes are commonplace was well known. Some organisms have duplicate or multiple sets of chromosomes, each carrying all of the genes.

Ohno stressed that if one copy of a gene was carrying out the function required of it, spare copies were free to evolve in many different ways, as neutral genes. They could eventually produce genes coding for the manufacture of completely novel proteins. These might or might not be useful to future organisms.

Genes set to music were part of Ohno's stock in trade. He took up the idea from Kenshi Hayashi and Nobuo Munakata of the National Cancer Center in Tokyo, who in 1984 reported converting the sequences of subunits in the genetic material DNA to corresponding notes. Hearing them made sequences in the genetic code easier to remember and to recognize. With assistance from his wife Midori, Ohno produced compositions scored for professional musicians. Some listeners considered the insulin receptor gene particularly moving.

This musical technique helped Ohno to identify repetitive sequences that revealed the common origin of genes. Many of the tunes were very old. His research eventually led him to conclusions about evolutionary events more than 500 million years ago when, in the Cambrian explosion, animals suddenly become conspicuous in the fossil record.

Ancestors of all the radically different kinds of animals, or phyla, from the simplest peanut worms to molluscs and animals with backbones, are represented. Yet according to Ohno, they all had essentially the same set of genes, or genome. Simply by exploiting the genes in different ways, they were able to diversify in a mere 10 million years.

'The Cambrian explosion is far more real than originally conceived,' Ohno declared in 1996. 'In evolution, 10 million years are but a blink of an eye. Thus, I suggest that all phyla of animals at the Cambrian time were endowed with nearly the identical genome, which is defined as the Pan-animalia genome.'

In the following year, Ohno's gene-duplication hypothesis found wonderful support in the first reading of all of the genes of yeast. Hans-Werner Mewes and his colleagues at Germany's Max-Planck-Institut für Biochemie counted 53 regions of clustered duplications. 'The significant number of gene duplications in yeast must reflect an evolutionarily successful strategy,' they commented. 'Gene duplications allow for evolutionary modifications in one of the copies without disturbing possibly vital functions of the other.'

An enforced reconciliation

Back among the cherry trees of Mishima, Kimura's closest colleague Tomoko Ohta made it her task to pioneer the genetic mathematics needed to cope with the real-life consequences of molecular evolution, and the long-term role of neutral genes. The core of her work was the 'nearly neutral' theory, in which slightly harmful genes can survive in small populations. Its first application was in explaining the regularity of the molecular clock.

The rate of change of the subunits of a gene over evolutionary time-scales is remarkably constant, irrespective of which creatures carry it. You might expect the rate to depend on the number of generations in a species in a given interval. But, as Ohta explained, the species in which individuals live a long time also have small populations in which nearly neutral genes can accumulate.

Ohta went on to incorporate in her mathematical theory the role of gene duplication in creating fresh resources for neutral and nearly neutral molecular evolution. The question then was, how could the new genes so created eventually come into action, to be tested by natural selection? Ohta saw plenty of evidence in present-day families of genes that both neutral drift and positive natural selection have been at work.

The activity of genes coding for proteins is under the control of regulatory genes, which switch them on or off. Arthur Koch of Indiana-Bloomington pointed out in 1972 that a duplicate gene had better be silenced while this molecular evolution is going on, although it can be reactivated later. One role for regulatory genes is to keep some genes silenced throughout the organism's life—including duplicate genes that may be evolving a new function.

These regulators also play a vital part in shaping plants and animals during development from their embryos, so that any changes can have drastic effects on the creatures' shapes and bodily organization—as seen for example in the Cambrian explosion. Ohta extended her theory to take account of the fact that the regulatory genes themselves evolve with the aid of gene duplication.

This mild-mannered woman was sometimes driven to exasperation by the eminent Western evolutionists who spurned her work. She wrote in 1984: 'Progress in molecular biology... has brought about a revolution in many fields of biology. Evolutionary theory and population genetics should be no exception; however, in many discussions of evolution, consideration is not extended to the new findings on gene structure.'

By the end of the century, experiments in fruit flies and yeast were revealing changes in development in organisms subjected to stress. These could be best explained by the unleashing of previously silent and therefore neutral genes. The vindication of the Japanese heretics was complete.

After a lifetime of facing hostility, Ohta saw other theorists being forced away at last from simple-minded reliance on natural selection, and towards a reconciliation of the neutral, nearly neutral and selectionist theories that she herself favoured. 'In the coming years,' she predicted, 'the combined study of experimental and theoretical analyses of various gene families will be a fascinating research project.'

▶ *For the recent confirmation of neutral genes as a key factor in evolution, see* HOPEFUL MONSTERS. *To see the ideas in wider context, see* EVOLUTION *and* TREE OF LIFE. *For more about Pan-animalian times, see* CAMBRIAN EXPLOSION.

MOLECULES IN SPACE

Exotic chemistry among the stars

Y OU HAVE TO go to mountaintops in Chile, Hawaii, Australia or the Canary Islands to find most of Europe's visible-light telescopes, nowadays. That's because Europe itself is plagued by clouds. Nicolaus Copernicus, in Poland in the 16th century, complained that never in his life did he see the planet Mercury.

So when in 1944 the astronomer Jan Oort at Leiden heard about a map of the Milky Way made, using radio waves, by an American amateur, Grote Reber, his first thought was that radio waves would penetrate the stubborn Dutch clouds. The Netherlands was under German military occupation at the time, but the Nederlandse Astronomen Club still met. When Oort broached the subject of radio astronomy a graduate student, Henk van de Hulst, pointed out that atoms of hydrogen, the commonest material in the Universe, should give out strong radio emissions of 21 centimetres wavelength.

After the war ended, there was a race to detect the hydrogen signal from the sky. Harvard won by a few weeks in 1951, but the Dutch astronomers and colleagues in Australia went on to produce the first-ever chart of the spiral arms in the Milky Way Galaxy, by tracing the concentrations and relative motions of atomic hydrogen. This was the first time that, meteorites excepted, any material in the Universe was identified by anything other than visible light or the slivers of infrared and ultraviolet that sneak through the barrier of the Earth's air.

Visible light comes mainly from hot objects like the Sun. After 1859, when Gustav Kirchhoff at Heidelberg realized that dark lines seen in the rainbow-like solar spectrum were due to absorption of light of sharply defined wavelengths, by individual atoms, many chemical elements became distinguishable in the Sun and the stars. Helium was detected in the Sun before its discovery on the Earth. But high temperatures associated with visible light damage even lone atoms, and combinations of atoms into molecules seldom survive.

By the mid-20th century, the only signatures of molecules detected in cosmic space were those of a carbon atom joined either to a single hydrogen atom or a single nitrogen atom (CH, CH^+ and CN). It was a paltry haul. But if hydrogen atoms could emit characteristic radio waves, from regions in the Galaxy too cool to glow visibly, so could many molecules that might be capable of surviving in such places. With this realization, astrochemistry was born.

Between 1963 and 1970 radio astronomers in the USA detected signatures of hydroxyl (a broken water molecule, OH), water itself, ammonia and carbon monoxide. Broadcasting at 2.6 millimetres, carbon monoxide became a beacon for molecule-hunters, guiding them to cool concentrations of gas that came to be called molecular clouds. These often coincided with regions like the Orion Nebula where new stars were being born.

A pioneer of astrochemistry, Patrick Thaddeus, likened the identification of molecules to tuning-in to a chosen radio station. He said, 'Such radio fingerprints are so incredibly sharp and precise that no scientist would question the identity of the broadcaster.' Thaddeus set out to chart the molecular clouds of the Milky Way. He used a very small radio telescope that took in a wide field of the sky and fitted conveniently on his laboratory roof—first at Columbia and then at Harvard.

By the end of the century, the tally of molecular clouds accounted for fully half of the loose gas in the Galaxy. Some giant molecular clouds are hundreds of light-years wide, and have the mass of a million suns. Among the sources are natural masers, the microwave equivalent of lasers, which intensify the signals.

The list of molecules detected by radio astronomers around the world passed the 100 mark. Some are familiar materials such as sulphur dioxide, methane and acetic acid, but others are exotic compounds that would not survive in terrestrial conditions outside the laboratory. Being chemically incomplete or hungry for attachments, they would be highly reactive. Hydroxyl (OH) is a simple example, whilst a more complex one is a string of 11 carbon atoms with just one hydrogen atom and one nitrogen atom attached, cyanodecapentayne ($HC_{10}CN$).

The Universe got off to a slow start, as a manufacturing chemist, with only hydrogen, helium, and a very little lithium to play with at first. Although helium is usually considered quite unreactive, charged pairs of helium atoms (He_2^+) may have been among the very first molecules. Helium hydride (HeH^+) and a minute amount of lithium hydride (LiH) were probably Mother Nature's apprentice efforts at making chemical compounds. But as soon as the first stars started making heavier elements, and spewing them into space at the stars' demise, her cookbook rapidly thickened.

The test tubes may be gravitational and magnetic fields that keep gigantic but diffuse swarms of atoms and molecules together. They may be mineral and icy grains, which provide reactive surfaces and shelters, or even large molecules within which small molecules may dwell. Chance encounters between atoms in the diffuse swarms can make molecules.

Nevertheless the Bunsen burners of stellar radiation, shock waves, or the energetic particles of the cosmic rays are just as likely to destroy molecules as to make them. There is plenty of time, though, and the chill and darkness of interstellar space help to preserve the molecules. They gather in dusty clouds like those that blot out parts of the Milky Way from view.

Molecules partake in the great cycles of starbirth and planet-making, the eventual deaths of stars and planets, and rebirth from the debris. Water and other materials play a key physical role in star formation, by acting as radiators that get rid of heat, which would otherwise prevent the collapse of a gas cloud to make stars. In the vicinity of newborn stars, the gassy, dusty and icy products of the chemistry provide the raw materials for planets and comets.

● Carbon lords of the jungle

The hunters extended their quest for molecules in cosmic space by using forms of invisible light coming from the Galaxy, that are mainly detectable only with aircraft, balloons, rockets or satellites. Interstellar hydrogen molecules, as opposed to solo atoms, first showed up in 1970 in an ultraviolet rocket-borne telescope. And in 1984, after using ground-based and airborne infrared telescopes to inspect some brightly lit dust clouds near stars, Alain Léger and Jean-Loup Puget at the Institut d'Astrophysique Spatiale in France reported possible signatures of very large exotic molecules, called polycyclic aromatic hydrocarbons, or PAHs for short.

These are molecules with perhaps 20–90 atoms of hydrogen and carbon, in which the carbon atoms are arranged in interlocking, polycyclic rings. Aromatic is a chemist's term for molecules containing carbon rings in which the atoms pass electrons around like a loving cup. On the Earth, aromatic compounds smell of life, being ubiquitous among the key ingredients of living organisms, from the genes to the light-absorbing pigments of plants and eyes. In interstellar space, PAHs are chemically robust, and survive well.

'For more than ten years after we predicted that PAHs should be ubiquitous, they seemed to be nothing more than a curious idea, inferred from the spectra of very few objects,' Léger said. 'But when the Infrared Space Observatory began operations in 1996 it immediately saw strong emissions in many different places in the sky, at exactly the wavelengths to be expected from PAHs. That was a happy confirmation of our prediction.' In clouds around dying stars and newborn stars, or scattered far and wide in interstellar space, the Infrared Space Observatory, a European satellite operational in 1995–98, discovered huge quantities of PAHs, signalled by intense emissions at a series of infrared wavelengths from 3 to 15 microns. The PAHs were detectable in other galaxies too. These lords of the cosmic molecular jungle may account for several per cent of all the free-range carbon in the Universe.

Doubters would at first speak only of 'unidentified bands' in the infrared spectrum. They complained that no one had detected benzene in interstellar space. Benzene is the basic aromatic ring, with just six carbon atoms. Without any sign of that, why believe in the PAHs? The objection disappeared when Spanish and Dutch astronomers re-examined observations of a dying star, and found the benzene signature. Chemists looked again at the carbon-rich material found in some meteorites, and they discovered tangible PAHs delivered to the Earth from space.

Experimental chemists were inspired by astronomy to make novel materials. Most famous are the buckyballs, where 60 or 70 carbon atoms make football-like molecules from interlocking rings. Ironically, these had a huge impact on terrestrial chemistry and engineering research, before their identification in interstellar space—which early in the 21st century remained at best ambiguous. But buckyballs were found in meteorites, so their extraterrestrial existence was not in doubt.

Water hoses in the sky

As water makes up more than half the weight of the human body, its origin among the stars is quite an intimate question. Oxygen atoms created by dying stars can easily find hydrogen with which to react, to make the water vapour, so its existence is unsurprising. The Infrared Space Observatory revealed how widespread it is, in moist oases near old and young stars, and in the Milky Way's molecular clouds.

'For the first time, we have a clear impression of the abundance of water in the Galaxy,' said José Cernicharo of Spain's Instituto de Estructura de la Materia, in 1997. 'In relatively dense clouds as many as 10 per cent of all oxygen atoms are incorporated into molecules of water vapour. Even more may be in the form of water ice. Water vapour is, after molecular hydrogen and carbon monoxide, one of the most important molecules in space.'

More remarkable still was the quantity of steam detected when a team of American astronomers used the Infrared Space Observatory to inspect the Orion Molecular Cloud. This cloud is pummelled and heated by shock waves from newborn stars. Predictions said that, at temperatures above about 100°C, most of the oxygen atoms in the interstellar gas should be converted into water, and that was just what the astronomers saw.

'The interstellar gas cloud that we observed in Orion seems to be a huge chemical factory,' commented David Neufeld of Johns Hopkins, 'generating enough water molecules in a single day to fill the Earth's oceans 60 times over. Eventually that water vapour will cool and freeze, turning into small solid particles of ice. Similar ice particles were presumably present within the gas cloud from which the Solar System originally formed. It seems quite plausible that much of the water in the Solar System was originally produced in a giant water-vapour factory like the one we have observed in Orion.'

Ices, too, have their own infrared signatures, and the Infrared Space Observatory made inventories of them. In the cold spaces between the stars, vapours of water and other volatile materials condense and freeze on the surface of available grains, in the manner of frost in winter. Ground-based telescopes had already found frozen carbon monoxide and methanol in interstellar space, as well as water ice, but the space telescope saw them much more clearly. It also found surprising amounts of carbon-dioxide ice and methane ice, undetectable from the ground.

When water vapour also showed up in the upper atmospheres of the outer planets of the Solar System, Helmut Feuchtgruber of Germany's Max-Planck-Institut für extraterrestrische Physik was excited. 'The upper atmosphere of the Earth is very dry because water vapour rising from the oceans or the land freezes into clouds,' he said. 'What we see in Saturn, Uranus and Neptune probably comes from an outside source.'

Evidently comets are still supplying material to these planets, with important implications for theories of all planetary atmospheres, including the Earth's. The scenario for the delivery of comet ice as a source of water had already been illustrated by the spectacular impacts of Comet Shoemaker–Levy 9 on Jupiter in 1994.

In 2001 an American spacecraft, the Submillimeter Wave Astronomy Satellite, detected in the vicinity of a swelling, dying star, CW Leonis, 10,000 times more water vapour than expected. The only explanation was that an ancient swarm of comets, similar to that surrounding the Solar System, had evaporated in the growing heat of the star. Once again, Neufeld of Johns Hopkins had a striking comment: 'We believe we are witnessing the apocalypse that will engulf our Solar System in 6 billion years.'

After vaporizing its comet store, the dying Sun will puff off its outer layers of gas and become a planetary nebula. Astronomers know of about 1600 such objects. They observe the gas as beautiful, multicoloured shrouds of stars recently defunct, which are reduced to small, hot embers called white dwarfs, often discernible at the centre of the nebula.

The odd thing is that, although the stars making them are spherical, the planetary nebulae usually have various non-spherical shapes. Jets of water vapour, like hoses in the sky, gave the first clear evidence of one of the sculptural agents at work in a dying star. They appeared when Japanese and British astronomers used the multiple radio telescopes of the US Very Long Baseline Array (VLBA) to examine water vapour in the vicinity of a senile star, W43A in the Aquila constellation.

This star is not a planetary nebula, but is about to become one. In 2002, the radio astronomers described narrow jets of water vapour shooting from opposite poles of W43A at 140 kilometres per second, and corkscrewing outwards as the star's axis swivels. Seeing the star in a brief phase of transition, from elderly star to planetary nebula, was a stroke of luck for the team.

'Our analysis of the water jets indicates that they are only a few decades old,' said Hiroshi Imai of Japan's National Astronomical Observatory. 'Once the star collapses of its own gravity into a dense white dwarf, its intense ultraviolet radiation will rip apart the water molecules, making observations such as ours impossible.'

Into an uncharted waveband

The infrared and radio searches for molecules in space meet in the short submillimetre wavelengths of the radio scientists, which others call very long infrared waves. Especially at wavelengths of around half a millimetre and below, the sky remains virtually uncharted. One of the new projects promising further spectacular advances in astrochemistry by the second decade of the new century was the Infrared Space Observatory's successor, Europe's Herschel spacecraft, to exploit this submillimetre waveband, scheduled for launch in 2007.

Another newcomer was to be the Atacama Large Millimetre Array, an international project to put dozens of radio dishes together on a plateau in Chile. Although it will operate in the millimetre waveband, it will sneak into the submillimetre region too. Prominent among those who made the scientific case for both these projects was Ewine van Dishoeck at Leiden Observatory, where Henk van de Hulst first proposed tuning into hydrogen atoms by radio, half a century before.

'I've seen astrochemistry emerge from obscurity to become a major theme in both astronomy and chemistry,' she said. 'It now underpins the study of star making, planet making, the origin of life on Earth, and the search for building blocks of life elsewhere. We've discovered exotic molecules that chemists never saw before and we've given a big impetus to theoretical chemistry and laboratory astrophysics. Yet still I feel we're just beginning. There's never been a better time to look for molecules in space.'

▶ MINERALS IN SPACE *merit a separate entry, which also touches on the utility of extraterrestrial materials. See also* ELEMENTS, BUCKYBALLS AND NANOTUBES *and* LIFE'S ORIGIN. *For the search for very distant hydrogen atoms, see* GALAXIES.

NEUTRINO OSCILLATIONS

When ghostly particles play hide-and-seek

I N CALAMITY JANE'S COUNTRY, the Black Hills of Dakota, men dug feverishly in Deadwood Gulch, Bobtail Creek and Gold Run Creek during the gold rush of the 1870s. Later, at Lead, the big Homestake Mine followed the gold ore deep into the bowels of the Earth. In the 1960s Raymond Davis, a chemist from the Brookhaven National Laboratory on Long Island, came to Homestake with what, in those days, was an outlandish project. He set out to find, deep underground, subatomic particles coming from the Sun.

'Hiya, Doc,' said a miner coming off the graveyard shift. 'Have you got any little strangers down there?' Davis replied, 'Wish I had!' The year was 1968, and the little strangers were ghostly neutrinos from the Sun's core. Neutrinos are particles akin to electrons, but they have no electric charge. As a result they can pass right through the Sun and the Earth. And through you, come to that—billions of neutrinos every second. As the writer John Updike commented:

> At night, they enter at Nepal
>
> And pierce the lover and his lass
>
> From underneath the bed—you call
>
> It wonderful; I call it crass.

In a cavern in the Homestake Mine 1560 metres down, where the rocks of the Earth filtered out confusing cosmic rays but not the neutrinos, Davis had a tank containing 500,000 litres of perchloroethylene, a dry-cleaning fluid. It would let some of the neutrinos reveal themselves playing the alchemist, converting chlorine atoms into argon gas.

The gold miners were the first to hear that the Sun wasn't delivering. 'Don't worry,' they told Davis, 'we know it's been a very cloudy year.' But the world's physicists were dumbfounded when Davis announced that he detected far fewer solar neutrinos than expected.

The neutrinos in question are by-products of the nuclear reactions that power the Sun. It can no more burn without releasing vast numbers of neutrinos than animals can live without expiring carbon dioxide. The Case of the Missing Solar Neutrinos therefore became a major detective story, and it took 30 years to nail the culprit.

'Is the Sun still burning?'

There were initially four main suspects. One was Davis's experiment—was it correctly executed and interpreted? Any misgivings on that score were allayed when other underground experiments obtained similar low counts of solar neutrinos.

Secondly, what about the nuclear physics? Had scientists miscalculated the course of the reactions by which the very hot core of the Sun converts hydrogen into helium and thereby gives us light and life? That was always the least likely solution to the mystery.

Next in the frame was the mother star itself. The leader of a multinational neutrino experiment in Italy, Till Kirsten of the Max-Planck-Institut für Kernphysik in Heidelberg, put it waggishly. 'Is the Sun still burning?' he asked.

The low neutrino counts could be due to a temporary cooling of the Sun's core, perhaps as a result of a stirring of the gases there. As the energy released in the core probably takes hundreds of thousands of years to emerge, there need be no evidence of cooling at the bright solar surface. But solar physicists learned how to explore the Sun's core with sound waves, by helioseismology, and saw nothing very odd going on there.

The last and most interesting suspect was the neutrino itself, which might be playing hide-and-seek with the experimenters. Suppose it changed its character during its journey from the Sun's core, becoming a different kind of neutrino that did not register in the detectors? The technical name for such a change was an oscillation between neutrino flavours.

An oscillation, that is to say, in the sense that the same person in Robert Louis Stevenson's story could oscillate between being Dr Jekyll and Mr Hyde. When first mooted by Bruno Pontecorvo and Vladimir Gribov in the Soviet Union in 1969, as a solution to the solar mystery, neutrino oscillations were only a vague conjecture. As the decades passed the idea seemed more and more plausible to particle physicists.

Neutrinos of two different flavours were known at first, the electron-neutrino and the muon-neutrino. They were the ghostly, uncharged shadows of the ordinary electron and its heavy brother, the muon. Anti-electrons and antineutrinos were in the line-up too, but those nuances are disregarded here for simplicity's sake.

The outpourings from the Sun should be electron-neutrinos, but if they could change into muon-neutrinos en route, that could explain their apparent scarcity. The discovery in 1975 of a superheavy electron, the tau, implied the likely existence of a third flavour of neutrino. So you could think of a muon-neutrino changing into a tau-neutrino, and vice versa.

There was a snag about any such oscillations. A neutrino could change its flavour only if it possessed a little mass, and according to the prevailing theory of particles, the Standard Model, neutrinos had to have zero mass. Experiments showed that if the masses were not zero they were extremely small—far less than the ordinary electron.

Many physicists nevertheless wanted neutrinos to have mass. Quite apart from a possible solution to the solar neutrino problem, via neutrino oscillations, they were anxious to find a flaw in the Standard Model. Otherwise there would be little left for them to discover about the particles populating the cosmos. Another hope was that neutrinos with mass might help to explain the mysterious dark matter that was known to pervade the Universe, but remained unidentified.

Changeable neutrinos from the air

Joy erupted among neutrino experts meeting in Takayama, Japan, in 1998, when Takaaki Kajita of Tokyo spoke. He announced that an underground experiment nearby had found evidence that neutrinos could indeed change their flavours. Kajita was reporting on behalf of a 120-strong Japanese–US team working with a neutrino detector 1000 metres down, in the Kamioka zinc mine.

Compared with Davis's pioneering equipment, Super-Kamiokande was vastly bigger, and speedier in operation. A tank containing 50,000 tonnes of ultrapure water was lined with more than 11,000 large light-detectors—photomultipliers. They watched for flashes created when the invisible neutrinos set other particles moving faster than light's speed in water.

The 1998 results concerned, not electron-neutrinos from the Sun, but muon-neutrinos created high in the Earth's atmosphere by the impact of energetic cosmic rays arriving from the Galaxy. The sensational result from Super-Kamiokande was that more muon-neutrinos entered the water tank from above than came into it from below. Our planet is so transparent to neutrinos that the only real difference was the distance from their point of origin.

The neutrinos coming straight down from the upper air over Japan, and then through a sliver of crust to the detector, travelled only 10–20 kilometres. Those made in the air over the South Atlantic, directly below Japan, travelled 13,000 kilometres, right through the Earth. In reality, most neutrinos came in on a slant, but it remained the case that any coming from below had much farther to travel.

The extra journey time evidently allowed some of the muon-neutrinos to change to a flavour undetectable by Super-Kamiokande. That almost certainly meant tau-neutrinos. The verdict was that neutrinos do indeed play hide-and-seek, and must have at least a little mass. Most of the original atmospheric products were muon-neutrinos. The most likely change was to a tau-neutrino—a flavour then predicted but not yet observed.

Within two years, Fermilab near Chicago had verified the existence of tau-neutrinos. They were seen to create taus, the superheavy electrons, in collisions with atomic nuclei. Finding the tau tracks, just a millimetre long in photographic emulsion, required 3-D visualization techniques using computer-controlled video cameras, developed and implemented in Nagoya.

The Sun accounted for

The Case of the Missing Solar Neutrinos was finally solved with the help of early observations by a new detector in Ontario. Sudbury Neutrino Observatory is 2000 metres down in the Creighton nickel mine. At its heart it has a sphere containing 10,000 light detectors and 1000 tonnes of very expensive heavy water on loan from Atomic Energy of Canada.

In heavy water hydrogen-2, or deuterium, replaces ordinary hydrogen-1. Herb Chen of UC Irvine had pointed out in 1984 that heavy water promised special advantages for neutrino detection. One kind of nuclear reaction would detect only electron-neutrinos, while another would be sensitive to all three neutrino flavours—electron, muon and tau. Chen died in 1987, but not before physicists from several countries had begun trying to put his idea into practice. The resulting observatory at Sudbury started operating at the end of 1999, as a Canadian–US–UK project.

The first data analysed, by 2001, were from the reaction sensitive specifically to electron-neutrinos. The Sudbury results were compared with Super-Kamiokande's measurements of a reaction with a small sensitivity to the other neutrino types as well. The accuracy was such that the physicists could show that electron-neutrinos were probably changing to another type before reaching the Earth.

By 2002, the Sudbury researchers had completed their detailed analyses of both the neutrino reactions with heavy water. They demonstrated decisively that more than two-thirds of the electron-neutrinos had changed before reaching the detector. Allowing for these absentees, the total number of electron-neutrinos produced in the Sun was very close to expectations.

'These new results show in a clear, simple and accurate way that solar neutrinos change their type,' said Art McDonald of Queen's University, director of Sudbury Neutrino Observatory. 'The total number of neutrinos we observe is also in excellent agreement with calculations of the nuclear reactions powering the Sun.'

For its next phase of operations, the observatory added salt to the heavy water. This increased the sensitivity substantially and opened the way to detailed studies of the properties of solar neutrinos, including mass differences between neutrinos and the strengths of their interactions. Both quantities would be of great interest for theorists wanting to revise their Standard Model of particle physics to include neutrinos properly.

Another race was already on, to study neutrino oscillations in more controlled conditions. This could be done by shooting beams of neutrinos for hundreds of kilometres through the crust of the Earth, from particle accelerators that manufactured them to detectors at distant underground laboratories. First up and running, in 1999, was a Japanese–US–Korean experiment called K2K, meaning KEK to Kamiokande.

An accelerator at the particle physics laboratory KEK, in Tsukuba near Tokyo, sent neutrinos to Super-Kamiokande, 250 kilometres away. By 2001 there was already preliminary evidence of neutrinos changing their character en route, but an extraordinary accident interrupted the experiment. One of Super-Kamiokande's light-detecting photomultipliers imploded and set off a chain reaction of self-destructing glassware, which eliminated 60 per cent of the 11,000 photomultipliers in a few seconds.

A similar experiment, with a baseline of 735 kilometres, was due to start in 2004, between Fermilab in Illinois and neutrino detectors in the Soudan iron mine in Minnesota. Later, a neutrino beam from CERN in Geneva would be aimed underneath Mont Blanc and the city of Florence, towards Italy's big underground laboratory beneath the Gran Sasso mountain 732 kilometres away.

Only lower limits could be set for the neutrino masses, from the initial solar and atmospheric observations. Scientists at Mainz and Troitsk therefore set out to measure the mass of the electron-neutrino directly, by very careful observations of radioactivity in hydrogen-3, or tritium. This changes into helium-3 by throwing out an electron and an electron-neutrino.

The Germans had their tritium in a thin film, whilst the Russians had it in a gas. A specially conceived instrument measured the energy of the electrons with exquisite accuracy, looking for a slight shortfall in the maximum energy. That would be due to the mass of the neutrino stealing some of the energy.

'The best we can say so far is that the neutrino's mass cannot be more than a few millionths of the mass of an electron,' said Christian Weinheimer of Mainz in 2001. 'So we're planning an even more sensitive instrument for an experiment at Forschungszentrum Karlsruhe, jointly with our friends there and in Troitsk.' Physicists from other German universities, and from Prague and Seattle too, soon joined in this delicate venture to weigh the neutrinos.

A new era begins

Nothing that happened after the 1998 announcement of the disappearing muon-neutrinos could detract from the historic importance of that Super-Kamiokande discovery. It will be remembered as the moment when many physicists first became confident that a new era was about to begin, in the study of particles.

The theories of the quarks and electrons, and of the forces acting on them, might be unified in a greater scheme.

'The currently prevailing theory of the elementary particles must be modified,' said Yoji Totsuka of Tokyo, spokesperson for the Super-Kamiokande collaboration. 'In the Standard Model the neutrinos are assumed to have zero mass. The finding will also make the theories of the Grand Unification more viable and attractive, and make the Universe heavier than we currently assume.'

▶ *For Grand Unification, see* SPARTICLES. *For missing cosmic mass, see* DARK MATTER. *For more about neutrinos within the Standard Model, see* ELECTROWEAK FORCE. *For other natural oscillations involving many entities, see* BRAIN RHYTHMS.

NEUTRON STARS

Ticking clocks in the sky, and their silent shadows

'I WENT HOME THAT EVENING VERY CROSS,' Jocelyn Bell Burnell recalled. 'Here was I trying to get a PhD out of a new technique, and some silly lot of little green men had to choose my aerial and my frequency to communicate with us. However, fortified by some supper I returned to the lab to do some more chart analysis.'

On that day in December 1967, as a 24-year-old student at Cambridge, she had accidentally gatecrashed a meeting of astronomical bigwigs. They were discussing how to announce her possible detection of an alien intelligence, in strangely regular radio pulses that she had seen coming from the stars. But, working late, she found a second pulsating source, which meant that she could go home for the Christmas holiday feeling much happier. 'It was very unlikely that two lots of little green men would both choose the same improbable frequency, and the same time, to try signalling to the same planet Earth.'

By the end of January 1968 she had four definite sources in all, scattered among some five kilometres of wiggles on the paper charts of the radio telescope. It was a natural phenomenon, after all. The graduate student from Northern Ireland had spotted not just an odd kind of star but a new state of matter.

In 1934, Walter Baade from Germany and Fritz Zwicky from Switzerland, working at the Mount Wilson Observatory in California, had speculated about the existence of neutron stars. That was soon after James Chadwick at Cambridge had discovered the neutron as the neutral relative of the proton— the nucleus of the hydrogen atom—and a commonplace constituent of the nuclei of other atoms. During the explosion of a large star, Baade and Zwicky reasoned, the collapse of the core could create such intense gravity that it would crush atoms. The resulting neutron star would shrink to a width of about ten kilometres, and acquire the density of an atomic nucleus.

As a theory in search of evidence, the neutron star was a candidate to explain the pulsars. Thomas Gold of Cornell pointed out that such an object would spin rapidly. Its intense magnetic field would focus radio emissions into beams from opposite magnetic poles, like the rotating beams of a lighthouse. That would produce the pulses detected on the Earth.

Rapid support for the idea came at the end of 1968, when American radio telescopes found a pulsar at the heart of the Crab Nebula. That is the cloudy remnant of a star that Chinese astronomers saw exploding in 1054. Subsequently the Crab pulsar was seen to flash also by visible light, X-rays and gamma rays.

Tortured matter

Long before the 1000th radio pulsar was identified in 1998, the neutron stars were a treasure house for astrophysicists. Nearly all are orphans, unrelated to known remnants of exploded stars. Some travel at a very high speed, having been flung out from the stellar explosions that created them, so that they leave the other debris far behind them.

Whilst most pulsars pulse a few times a second, others called millisecond pulsars are hundreds of times quicker. The neutron-star lighthouse has been made to spin faster and faster, by gas falling on to it from a companion star. Increases in the pulse-rate are seen to occur in neutron stars with close associates. The gas crashing onto the surface of the neutron star creates X-rays. Called X-ray binaries, such systems are often conspicuous to X-ray telescopes in space.

Playing the cannibal, the neutron star uses its intense gravity to suck the gas from its unlucky associate, and can even destroy it. The X-ray source J0929-314 in the Antlia constellation flashes 185 times a second. It has reduced its companion star to a hundredth of the mass of the Sun. Eventually the companion will disappear entirely, its remnants being blown away by the pressure of X-rays.

'This pulsar has been accumulating gas donated from its companion for quite some time now,' said Duncan Galloway of the Massachusetts Institute of Technology, who used the Rossi X-ray Timing Explorer satellite to study the dance of doom in J0929-314. 'It's exciting that we are finally discovering pulsars at all stages of their evolution, some that are quite young and others that are transitioning to a final stage of isolation.'

A neutron star is itself a fantastic object, the last stop before a black hole. A solid crust encloses a fluid mass of chemically anonymous nuclear matter. A cupful would weigh billions of tonnes. Gravity at the surface is so strong that gas falling on to a neutron star reaches almost half the speed of light.

The strength of the magnetic field, too, is almost unimaginable. Extreme cases are called magnetars, a class of neutron stars discovered in 1998 by Chryssa Kouveliotou of the Universities Space Research Association in the USA. An extraordinary outburst of gamma rays from magnetar SGR 1900+14, in August 1998, had perceptible effects on the Earth's atmosphere even though the source was 20,000 light-years away in the Aquila constellation. The Rossi satellite later measured the field of magnetar SGR 1806-20 at a million billion times the Earth's. Alaa Ibrahim of George Washington University commented, 'If this magnetar were as close as the Moon, it would rearrange the molecules in our bodies.'

Under the extraordinary pressure at the heart of a neutron star, the density of matter may be several times greater than in an ordinary atomic nucleus. Theorists try to figure out what matter is like, when tortured in such extreme conditions. It could include extremely massive cousins of protons and neutrons.

Nuclear particles may pair up to make superconducting and superfluid materials, in which there is no resistance to an electric current or liquid flow. Another possible state of the compressed matter is quark soup. Here the subcomponents of nuclear matter escape from their confines and mill about in a sea of gluons, which are supposed to be their jailers.

The various possibilities imply different behaviour by a neutron star, especially in the rate at which it sheds energy. If particle reactions create the ghostly particles called neutrinos, they can escape very easily and quite unseen, cooling the neutron star rapidly. By observing many different neutron stars by radio, X-rays and gamma rays, astronomers hope that one day they'll be able to tell what really goes on in their cores.

Pulsars are astonishing timekeepers that can surpass even atomic clocks in their accuracy. The apparent tick-rate is affected by whether the pulsar is approaching us or receding. It therefore varies precisely in step with the Earth's motion around the Sun and with any orbital motion of the pulsar itself. Once in a while, the rate changes. The glitch is due to a starquake, a rearrangement of matter inside the neutron star that alters the rotation rate.

● Three billion gamma-ray ticks

Many neutron stars fail to reveal themselves by radio pulses, because the lighthouse beam that sweeps the sky around the pulsar misses the Earth. Others are off the air because they are too old. Over thousands or millions of years, a solitary pulsar slows down and becomes ever weaker as a radio source. Eventually, after about 10 million years, it fades away entirely, but survives as a very small, dense star. As the Milky Way Galaxy has been making neutron stars for 10 billion years, most neutron stars presumably emit detectable radio waves no longer.

The prototype of a radio-silent neutron star showed up within just a few years of the discovery of pulsars. The first satellite for gamma-ray astronomy, SAS-2, saw it in 1972 as one of the brightest sources of gamma rays in the sky, located in the Gemini constellation. Giovanni Bignami of the Istituto di Fisica Cosmica in Milan named the object Geminga. This was a pun signifying either 'Gemini gamma' or *gh'è minga*, which in the Milanese argot means 'it's not there'.

The name was well deserved. Repeated searches by radio waves and visible light showed no obvious counterpart to the intense gamma-ray emissions. In a patient campaign, Bignami and his wife Patrizia Caraveo employed the ever-improving resources of modern astronomy to pin Geminga down. It took them altogether 25 years.

Using a rough position given by the Einstein X-ray satellite (1979) they searched for a visible object with big telescopes in Hawaii and Chile. By 1987 they had identified a very faint star, peculiarly blue in colour, as the visible Geminga. A further sighting from Chile in 1992 showed it to be moving rapidly across the sky.

Meanwhile the Rosat X-ray satellite and the Compton gamma-ray satellite were launched, in 1990 and 1991. With Rosat, Jules Halpern of Columbia detected pulses from Geminga. It flashes with high-energy rays four times a second— every 237 milliseconds to be more precise. Compton observations confirmed the pulsation, and re-examination of old Geminga data from Europe's COS-B gamma-ray satellite (1975–82) revealed it there as well—though hard to spot unless you knew what to look for. A slowdown in the tick-rate indicated that Geminga is about 300,000 years old.

So Geminga is a neutron star, and not an extremely old one. The absence of a radio pulse may be due to the direction in which the radio emissions are beamed. In 1993 the American Astronomical Society honoured Bignami and Halpern for solving the mystery of Geminga. But Caraveo still wanted to know how far away it is, and to tackle that problem only the Hubble Space Telescope would do.

Even Hubble had to stare at the spot for more than an hour to make out the faint Geminga, just 20 kilometres wide. Caraveo made three observations with Hubble, at intervals of six months. They revealed very slight shifts in Geminga's apparent direction as the Earth and Hubble orbited the Sun. These fixed the distance of Geminga at about 500 light-years, and showed the neutron star to be ten times more radiant in gamma rays and X-rays than the Sun is by visible light. And it rushes through the Galaxy at 120 kilometres per second.

Caraveo completed her astronomical tour de force in 1998. With European colleagues she related the Hubble image to wider images from Chile and Italy. Then Geminga could be locked into the very precise framework of the sky given by the Hipparcos star-mapping satellite, to within ten millionths of a degree. Never before was so faint an object pinpointed so precisely.

American colleagues of Caraveo used this positioning to correct for confusions due to the Earth's motion. They were then able to combine intermittent observations by the SAS-2, COS-B and Compton gamma-ray satellites, spread over nearly a quarter of a century. The reconstruction gave a complete, unbroken series of 3.2 billion ticks of Geminga's amazing gamma-ray clock, between 1972 and 1996.

Why did Caraveo go to so much trouble over this single object? 'There must be millions of Gemingas out there in our Galaxy,' she said. 'Much of the future of neutron-star science lies with the radio-silent ones. We've probably seen a lot of them already without recognizing them for what they are. Now, with better X-ray and gamma-ray telescopes in space, the fun is just beginning.'

As an early token of what is to come, a closer radio-silent neutron star, 350 light-years away, revealed itself to the Rosat X-ray satellite. Called RX 185635–3754, it was also picked out by the Hubble Space Telescope in 1996. Other neutron stars with no radio or visible emissions revealed themselves to powerful X-ray satellites launched in 1999, NASA's Chandra and Europe's XMM-Newton. Some of them were inside supernova remnants where astronomers had previously looked in vain for counterparts to the pulsar in the Crab Nebula.

Pulsars as cosmic probes

Meanwhile the discovery of radio pulsars accelerated. The classic big dishes of early radio astronomy, including those at Arecibo in Puerto Rico, Jodrell Bank in England and Effelsberg in Germany, gained a new lease of life as pulsar-hunters, using state-of-the-art detectors and data analysis. The venerable 64-metre steerable dish at Parkes in Australia single-handedly doubled the count of known pulsars, from 700 in 1997 to 1400 in 2001, in a series of special campaigns using 13 receivers that could be pointed to different parts of the sky simultaneously.

The total count included more than 100 fast-ticking millisecond pulsars. These can be far older than the slower ones, but they form much more rarely—perhaps once in 250,000 years in our Galaxy, compared with roughly once per century for the slower kind. About half of the millisecond pulsars, a quite disproportionate number, occur among the densely packed stars of globular clusters, which follow free-range orbits around the centre of the Milky Way.

Especially valuable for astrophysicists are pulsars in orbit around other stars, though not playing the cannibal. Then the highly accurate pulsar clocks make subtle analyses possible. The first such orbiter, or binary pulsar, to leap to prominence was B1913+16 in the Aquila constellation. It ticks at an intermediate rate of 17 times a second and orbits around its companion star every eight hours.

Observing B1913+16 year after year, from 1974 onwards, Joseph Taylor and Russell Hulse of the University of Massachusetts found that the stars are gradually spiralling closer, towards an eventual collision. The system is shedding energy at just the rate to be expected if it is radiating gravitational waves—a previously undetected form of energy predicted by Einstein's theory of gravity. As the watch on B1913+16 continued to the end of the century, its behaviour conformed to predictions without the slightest hint of error. The pulsar's orbit also swivelled, in exact accord with what Einstein would expect.

In 1991 the first known planets beyond the Solar System turned up, orbiting a pulsar. Alexander Wolszczan from Penn State noticed peculiar variations in the apparent tick-rate of the millisecond pulsar B1257+12 in the Virgo constellation. These were best explained by the pulsar wobbling a little, as planets orbited around it.

During the next few years, Wolszczan was able to analyse the wobbles and initially he defined three planets. Two have about the same mass as the Earth, and a smaller one is similar to the Moon. Deadly radiation from the pulsar, and the circumstances of its violent birth, would rule out any possibility of life there. Alas, the detection of planets around normal stars, just a few years later, overshadowed the pulsar astronomer's historic discovery.

The hunters will go on scrutinizing every new millisecond and binary pulsar, looking for other oddities. The pulsars have the potential to act as distant space probes for exploring the subtleties of Einsteinian spacetime. So for Duncan Lorimer of Jodrell Bank, the gravitational waves and the planets detected with pulsars were just a foretaste of new astrophysics to come.

'What I'd most like to find,' he said, 'is a pulsar orbiting around a black hole. Having such an accurate clock so close to the black hole would allow us to probe its gravitational field in unprecedented detail.'

▶ *For related topics, see* ELEMENTS *and* GRAVITATIONAL WAVES.

NUCLEAR WEAPONS
The desperately close-run thing

A MID THE VINEYARDS NEAR FLORENCE, an American military cemetery contains the remains of more than 4000 young men, among them Private First Class Joe Wheeler. He was an historian turned infantryman, in the Blue Devils division. After helping to liberate Rome in the summer of 1944, he lost his life that fall, during fierce fighting in the Northern Apennines. Only recently he had sent a card to his brother in the USA. All it said was 'Hurry up!'

'Every time I visit Joe's grave, I am reminded that he is one of many—one of many millions, I calculate, both soldiers and civilians—whose lives might have been spared if the Allies had developed the atomic bomb a year sooner,' the brother wrote later. 'Joe hoped for a miraculous means of ending a terrible war.'

John Wheeler was a theoretical physicist from Princeton. At the time of Joe's death he was at Hanford in Washington State, working on the mass-production of a special form of a new element, plutonium-239. Just before the war, with Niels Bohr from Copenhagen, Wheeler had developed the first theory describing nuclear fission, which had been discovered in uranium-235. They had identified element no. 94, as they then called it, as another likely splitter-in-two.

What made Wheeler rueful was the time lost after August 1939, when a Jewish refugee from Adolf Hitler, Albert Einstein, signed a letter to Franklin Roosevelt. It drew the attention of the US president to the possibility of powerful bombs using nuclear fission, and it warned him of evident German interest in uranium supplies. But further prodding was needed, from Einstein himself and especially from the British, who had strong technical support from other physicist refugees. Work on a bomb did not begin in earnest until the launch of the Manhattan Project in June 1942.

The many distinguished physicists who joined the project knew that they were making a terrible weapon. As Wheeler's reminiscence makes plain, their motives were not dishonourable. There was a rational fear that Werner Heisenberg and other clever colleagues in Germany would be striving to make an atomic bomb for Hitler. And the more dreadful the weapon might be, the greater the chance that it could work the miracle for Joe Wheeler and his buddies, and end the war.

So it did. In August 1945 a uranium bomb smashed Hiroshima and a plutonium device did the same to Nagasaki a few days later. Japan surrendered. Millions of lives were spared that might have been lost on both sides, in a seaborne invasion of the last of the Axis powers. By later standards the weapons used were puny, but the horrific effects of blast, heat and atomic radiation on urban targets and their inhabitants were there for all to see. There was bitter argument among the atomic scientists about whether the bombs should have been used where they caused so many civilian casualties.

Investigation and conjecture about what Heisenberg and his boys had been up to, to make a bomb for Hitler, continued for decades. The issue was teased once more in 1998 in Michael Frayn's enchanting play *Copenhagen*, which re-enacted a wartime visit by Heisenberg to Bohr. In fact there was never any mystery or cover-up. In 1947 Heisenberg guilelessly told a British science writer, Chapman Pincher, that he would certainly have made a bomb if he could.

He decided there'd not be time enough before the end of the war, which he expected Germany to win. Instead Heisenberg and a small team set to work on an atomic engine to provide useful power, and he sketched for the reporter the heavy-water reactor that was planned. Sabotage of the heavy-water manufacturing plant in Norway was a blow, and incompetent Nazi scientists also hampered the work. 'My interview, along with Heisenberg's sketch, appeared on the front page of the *Daily Express*,' Pincher complained later. 'It caused surprisingly little comment.'

'The risk of universal death'

A superbomb 1000 times more powerful than those employed against Japan followed quickly. It used the fission of a heavy element to ignite the fusion of light ones. By that time the motive was not to race the Germans or to end the war, but to stay ahead of the opposition, in a post-war confrontation between former allies in the West and the Communist Bloc. The aim was said to be deterrence—to make weapons so horrible that no one would dare resort to them. Scientists who questioned the wisdom of letting the fire of the Sun loose on the Earth, as Robert Oppenheimer did in the USA, were liable to be considered potential traitors.

Although the weapon came to be called the hydrogen bomb or H-bomb, ordinary H wouldn't work. The fuel of choice was lithium-6 deuteride. This is a compound of heavy hydrogen—deuterium or hydrogen-2—with a selected form of the lightest metal. Lithium-6 breaks up in the nuclear reaction to make tritium or hydrogen-3, which then reacts very vigorously with deuterium. A lot of neutrons, neutral nuclear particles, fly around, but the net result is that lithium-6 plus hydrogen-2 makes two nuclei of helium-4, with the release of energy on a huge scale.

Spies had kept the Soviet Union well informed about the wartime Manhattan Project, and the post-war nuclear arms race between the former allies began before the war ended in 1945. Not yet in the picture was a 24-year-old physics student, Andrei Sakharov, whose legs nearly gave way when he saw the news about Hiroshima on his way to buy bread one morning. 'Something new and awesome had entered our lives, a product of the greatest of the sciences, of the discipline I revered.'

Within a few years Sakharov was recruited to the Soviet Union's effort to match the USA's development of an H-bomb. No one asked him whether he wanted to do it, but Sakharov admitted that 'the concentration, total absorption and energy that I brought to the task were my own'. He quickly came up with his first concept for an H-bomb in 1948, and a much niftier design five years later.

By 1955, Sakharov was inspecting the effects of a Soviet H-bomb test. He wrote in his memoirs, 'When you see the burned birds who are withering on the scorched steppe, when you see how the shock wave blows away buildings like houses of cards, when you feel the reek of splintered bricks, when you sense melted glass, you immediately think of times of war. . . . How not to start thinking of one's responsibility at this point?' The seeds were sown of Sakharov's later role as a political dissident.

Also in 1955, Einstein died. Just two days beforehand, he signed a manifesto drafted by Bertrand Russell in London. It spelt out implications that will apply for as long as people retain their stewardship of the enormous energy latent in matter. 'We appeal as human beings, to human beings: remember your humanity and forget the rest. If you can do so, the way lies open to a new Paradise; if you cannot, there lies before you the risk of universal death.'

Following the Russell–Einstein Manifesto, physicists of East and West strove to avert nuclear war by meeting behind closed doors each year at Pugwash Conferences. These were named after the first meeting-place in Nova Scotia, in 1957. At the height of the Cold War they provided an unofficial channel for East–West negotiations about arms control. The Pugwash organizer was the Polish-born Joseph Rotblat of London, himself a one-time refugee bomb-maker, turned medical physicist.

When he no longer had to play the diplomat, Rotblat was scathing about the contribution of his colleagues to the preparations for Armageddon. 'To a large extent the nuclear arms race was driven by scientists,' he wrote. 'They kept on designing new types of weapons, not because of any credible requirement—arsenals a hundred times smaller would have sufficed for any conceivable deterrence purpose—but mainly to satisfy their inflated egos, or for the intense exhilaration experienced in exploring new technical concepts.'

A US moratorium on nuclear weapons testing, starting in 1992, caused grief among the bomb-makers. An anthropologist, Hugh Gusterson of the Massachusetts Institute of Technology, investigated reactions at the Lawrence Livermore National Laboratory. 'The younger guys have this forlorn wistfulness about having missed out on something really important,' Gusterson said. 'Nowadays, some of the guys go camping at the Nevada test sites on weekends. It's their sacred place.'

From deterrence to 'launch on warning'

After Nagasaki there was a taboo against any use of nuclear weapons in anger, although that nearly failed in the Cuba Missile Crisis of 1962. The Soviet Union planned to put nuclear-armed rockets in Cuba, very close to Florida, in response to the deployment of US missiles in Turkey. The US forbade it, and the world held its breath till a Soviet freighter en route to Cuba made a 180-degree turn. The US deployment in Turkey was quietly cancelled.

Badly scared, both sides in the arms race then subscribed to a doctrine of deterrence called mutually assured destruction, or MAD. But prosperous Western Europe declined to match the Eastern Bloc in armoured divisions, and relied instead on the much cheaper option of advertising a low threshold for using nuclear weapons in the event of an invasion. This policy stretched the doctrine to the limit of credibility. And strategists worried about what the Soviet Union would do on behalf of its Arab allies if Israel detonated its not-so-secret nuclear weapons.

By 1980, mutual destruction was no longer assured between the superpowers. The danger arose not from a particular crisis, as over Cuba, but from technological developments that gradually ushered in a period of chronic instability. Any misunderstanding, rage or deep fear about the other side's intentions could have blasted North America and Eurasia back to the Stone Age.

The advent of very accurate intercontinental missiles, combined with resolute attempts to track the opponent's submarines, created what the US Department of Defense openly admitted was an unstable situation. If you even suspected there was about to be a nuclear war, you'd better unleash your missiles before their silos and boats were wiped out. 'Launch on warning', this strategic posture was called, and it required decisions to be taken within minutes of anything unusual appearing on the radar screens.

At that time a leading analyst of Soviet military thinking, John Erickson of Edinburgh, reported 'an almost morbid preoccupation with the issue of how not to be surprised.' He estimated that the Soviet Union had 1200 strategic nuclear targets in Western Europe alone. Meanwhile the USA had such overkill in its nuclear arsenal that its target lists included empty Russian fields that might be used as improvised landing strips. A story went the rounds in Moscow:

> *Ilya: What will you do when the warning comes?*
>
> *Ivan: Wrap myself in a sheet and walk slowly to the cemetery.*
>
> *Ilya: Why slowly?*
>
> *Ivan: We don't want to cause a panic, do we?*

The US Star Wars programme, or Strategic Defense Initiative, was offered as an escape from the imperatives of launch on warning. Better antimissile defences, it was said, would allow some time to think. In Moscow it looked like a way of enabling the USA to attack without the assured retaliation, supposedly guaranteed by a treaty limiting antimissile defence. In any case the Soviet Union was apparently unable to compete in this expensive new phase of the arms race and in 1988 a Soviet physicist told a visiting reporter, 'You must understand that we've just lost a war.'

He meant the Cold War. Edward Teller, a co-inventor of the US H-bomb and its most belligerent advocate, wanted the credit. 'The Cold War,' he wrote, 'was won by the existence, not the use, of a new weapon, and without the loss of life.' Given that the Soviet Union had just as many H-bombs—carefully counted by spy satellites monitoring arms-limitation treaties—the claim is hard to understand.

The most one can say for the hardware is that it had economic and political fallout. Creating and deploying it took a greater proportion of the national treasure and technological skill in the Soviet Union than in the richer West. Eastern Bloc allies suffered the consequential hardship too.

The Iron Curtain, where soldiers faced each other with so-called tactical nuclear weapons across a geopolitical fault-line, was not impenetrable to radio and television. The real credit for ending that terrifying era of nuclear confrontation belongs neither to Teller nor to his opposite number Sakharov, but to ordinary citizens of Eastern Europe who defied the secret police, demanding freedom. In relation to the growing perils of launch on warning, their victory in the streets was a desperately close-run thing.

Lest we forget

Anxieties about proliferation, the acquisition of nuclear weapons by more countries and by terrorist groups, have replaced the fear of an all-out nuclear war between the USA and Russia. By early in the 21st century the 'old' nuclear-armed powers, meaning the USA, Russia, China, France and the UK, had been joined by Israel, India and Pakistan. Other countries were suspected of trying to acquire them.

Everyone knew that Japan and Germany could make bombs almost instantly, any time they chose. Apparently they forbore to do so, although they resented an anomaly in the United Nations. The permanent members of the Security Council were, exclusively, the 'old' nuclear powers—as if their weapons were appropriate and justified badges of authority.

The likelihood that terrorist groups and rogue states would acquire nuclear weapons prompted calls in the USA for the development of low-yield bunker-busting bombs designed to penetrate deep underground before they exploded. Is this just another 'exhilarating' technical concept for physicists and engineers to play with? Or a threshold-lowering weapon that might even tend to legitimize the intentions of the terrorists?

The ghastly effects of the Hiroshima and Nagasaki bombings, a widespread expectation of imminent mass extinction during the Cuba Missile Crisis, the creation of fall-out shelters for the plebs and deep bunkers for Dr Strangelove and his cronies—these were the background to everyday life for anyone adolescent or adult between 1945 and 1989. And always the question was, 'Will the survivors envy the dead?'

The gravest danger may be that new generations will grow up unmindful of the power of nuclear weapons. Youngsters use expressions like 'taking out' or 'going ballistic', scarcely realizing that they refer to the annihilation of nuclear targets or the unleashing of a thousand rockets with multiple warheads in a culminating nuclear war.

A few experts have for long suggested that an H-bomb ought to be exploded in the atmosphere every few years, in front of the world's assembled leaders. It would serve to remind them of what is now commonplace military kit. Even at a distance of 50 kilometres they would, and some say should, feel its heat like Hell's gate opening.

For more about the physics background, and about civilian nuclear power, see ENERGY AND MASS. *For biological weapons of mass destruction, see* SMALLPOX.

OCEAN CURRENTS

A central-heating system for the world

B EFORE THE BRITISH COLONIES in North America revolted, Benjamin Franklin was the postmaster in Philadelphia. In 1769 the government asked him why the fast mail boats from Falmouth, England, generally took two weeks longer to make the Atlantic crossing than colonial merchantmen leaving at the same time. A Nantucket whaling skipper told Franklin that he had sometimes met Falmouth packets navigating in the middle of the Gulf Stream.

'We have informed them that they were stemming a current that was against them to the value of 3 miles an hour and advised them to cross it, but they were too wise to be counselled by simple American fishermen,' Franklin quoted the skipper as saying. 'When the winds are light, they are carried back by the current more than they are forwarded by the wind.'

Spanish pilots had known about the Gulf Stream since the 16th century, and Franklin's sailormen helped him to make a chart showing the great current, slanting north-eastwardly across the Atlantic. He sent it to Falmouth, but the packet skippers were not about to be advised by a colonial postman either.

Similar obtuseness about currents persisted for nearly 100 years after global oceanography became an established science, with the round-the-world cruise of the research ship *Challenger*, 1872–76. For centuries, if not millennia, Japanese fishermen knew that the tuna congregated around eddies in the Kuroshio Current, the Pacific analogue of the Gulf Stream. They located them by watching for seabirds and for mists due to temperature changes.

Japanese oceanographers were aware of the eddies too, yet they entirely escaped the notice of Western science until 1957. That was when John Swallow of the UK's National Institute of Oceanography let loose submersible floats under the Gulf Stream near Bermuda and found that they travelled every which way. Later, satellites showed the eddies plainly, as warm and cold patches in the sea. By the 1980s Japanese fishermen received the satellite data on board, to guide them to the tuna.

The oceanic eddies, 10–100 kilometres wide, are the watery equivalents of storms and anticyclones, but they can persist for months or years and drift for large distances. They often develop at the encounters of large currents. For example, eddies form where the warm Kuroshio meets the cold Oyashio Current, east of Japan. They move slowly north-east past the Kurile Islands and Kamchatka, where they influence the weather and climate. Commenting on one such eddy that persisted from 1986 to 1991, Konstantin Rogachev of Russia's Pacific Institute of Oceanology in Vladivostok said, 'What served as its energy source still remains a mystery.'

Called the mesoscale circulation, the eddies possess in total 20 times more energy of motion than the large-scale currents that traverse the oceans. They are often associated with jets, watery equivalents of jet streams in the air, and they play a part in maintaining the currents. Locally, the eddies can add to or subtract from the mean speed of a current, or totally alter the direction of flow. So how did the research ships, diligently sampling all the ocean currents, come to miss them? Walter Munk of UC San Diego had a sarcastic explanation.

'The energetic ocean weather was aliased into a general ocean circulation of ever increasing complexity. The misinterpretation was aided by the golden rule of oceanography never to take the same station twice. In the few cases of repeated stations, differences could always be ascribed to instrumental malfunctioning. Still, it is almost unbelievable,' Munk concluded, 'that the mesoscale circulation could have slipped for so long through the coarse grid of ocean sampling.'

From Java to Northern Europe?

On a much grander scale, Arnold Gordon of Columbia proposed in 1986 that several of the main ocean currents join together in a global conveyor belt. Warm, salty water flows westwards on the surface from the Pacific Ocean past Indonesia, across the Indian Ocean, and around the southern tip of Africa. Then it travels far northwards in the Atlantic, merging with the Gulf Stream coming from the Gulf of Mexico and continuing to the Norwegian Sea. Shedding its heat, the salty water sinks and begins a slow subsurface journey back to the Pacific, which takes it via Antarctica and south of Australia. So the story goes.

The conveyor belt became famous when Wallace Broecker, also of Columbia, invoked it to explain drastic changes in climate in the distant past. In 1991 he suggested that excessive melting of ice in the North Atlantic, caused by an outbreak of icebergs, would dilute the salt water arriving in the Gulf Stream, so that it would not be dense enough to sink and keep the conveyor going. Excessive rainfall, perhaps due to global warming, might have the same effect.

'The Atlantic Ocean's conveyor circulation, which has a flow equal to 100 Amazon Rivers, transports an enormous amount of heat northward, providing the heat to create the warm climate enjoyed by Europe,' Broecker said. 'Were the conveyor to stop, winter temperatures in the North Atlantic would abruptly fall by 5 or more degrees C, and the change could occur in ten years or less. Such changes would, for example, cause Dublin to acquire the climate of Spitsbergen.'

It was a charming idea, that Ireland has a mild climate at quite high latitudes because of warm water delivered all the way from Java. It also made picturesque the oceans' role as a central-heating system for the planet. Undoubtedly they carry warmth from the tropics towards the poles, and operate on some such global scale. But technically the conveyor-belt story emphasized mean current flows instead of the much more energetic eddies. It also understated the incessant two-way interactions between air and sea at every point along a current's route.

Models and actuality: a global effort

Since the 1970s, those trying to make theoretical computer models of the climate have known that any half-way sensible reckoning has to take account of oceanic effects. These include many intricacies to do with exchanges of water vapour, carbon dioxide and other infrared-absorbing greenhouse gases, between seawater and the air. The oceans also interact with ice at the polar margins, and release salt and sulphur that help to make clouds. Life in the sea has climatic effects too.

More generally, the oceans tend to delay climate change because their sheer mass means that they take a long time to warm up or cool down. The lineaments of the climate system are defined in no small measure by the oceanic central heating. When the currents change it is not always obvious what is cause and what is effect. And what happens deep below the surface cannot be excluded, in long-term reckonings.

Past climates are represented in parcels of warmer or cooler water that cruise like submarines at a few kilometres a day. They resurface, perhaps many years later, and play back weather remembered from far away and long ago. On a much shorter time-scale, a faltering of a cold current off the coast of Ecuador signals the notorious El Niño, when the eastern Pacific warms, with far-flung effects on weather and the global temperature.

In principle, supercomputers can calculate flows in the oceans at all depths, in much the same way as weather-forecasting computer models reckon the motions and temperatures of the air and the behaviour of water, at various altitudes. In the 1980s, in a pioneering project called FRAM, a British consortium modelled the Southern Ocean, and global efforts followed. But the task is aggravated by the small scale of the watery weather of the eddies, and 20th-century computers were barely up to the job.

In any case, the models had to be compared with actuality in all oceans and at all depths—a monumental task. Oceanographers of 30 countries therefore joined in the World Ocean Circulation Experiment, 1990–2002, to study the ocean currents more thoroughly than ever before. The main observing phase, ending in 1998, used three satellites and a multinational fleet of research ships. In addition, 1000 subsurface floats mapped the currents across entire ocean basins at a depth of one kilometre. Some of the floats gauged the variations of temperature and salinity at different depths as they surfaced, every two weeks.

The main task of the seagoing expeditions in the World Ocean Circulation Experiment was to traverse the ocean basins measuring the temperature and salinity of the water, from the surface to the ocean floor, at 10,000 places. Chemical sampling told of dissolved gases, of the supply of nutrients needed by living things, and of man-made pollution. The abundance in the water of tritium, radioactive hydrogen-3 released into the atmosphere in nuclear weapons tests, gave an impression of when deep-lying water parcels were last exposed to the air.

A critical region for investigation at great depths was the far South Atlantic. There cold water from the North Atlantic joins forces with even colder water from Antarctica, eventually spilling into deep basins of the Indian and Pacific Oceans. Shallow seas surrounding the islands of Indonesia were of special interest too. From a huge Warm Pool east of New Guinea, the hottest spot in all the oceans, water pours as if through a sluice along the Molucca Sea, the Makassar Strait and other historic seaways. A French–Indonesian effort, called the Java Australia Dynamic Experiment, studied the water's struggle to exit to the Indian Ocean.

By 2002 John Gould, who coordinated the World Ocean Circulation Experiment at its headquarters in Southampton, England, was making a positive assessment. 'Global computer models capable of representing scales as small as 10 kilometres were improved and validated by comparisons with the WOCE data,' he said. 'Models into which the data have been assimilated have enabled the evolving state of the ocean in the 1990s to be revealed, and estimates to be made of the transports of heat and fresh water by the oceans.'

The slopes of the sea

As the new century began, Gould and the ocean observers were already embarking on a successor programme called Climate Variability and Predictability, due to run till 2010. Sophisticated subsurface floats formed the basis of a new ocean monitoring system called Argo. Ocean modellers hoped to imitate the meteorologists in real-time current forecasting from routine observations, in the Global Ocean Data Assimilation Experiment.

Success in observing the oceans from space also encouraged optimism. Starting with the US Seasat (1978) a succession of satellites caressed the sea with radar beams that measured its level, and felt humps and hollows in its surface. Water flows downhill, so the currents should reveal themselves as slopes in the sea surface.

The relationship of slopes to currents is a simple one, but no more intuitive than the pressure–wind connection in the air. Winds attempting to flow from a high-pressure to a low-pressure region are made to swerve, because of the Earth's rotation, so that they finish up blowing with high pressure on one side and low pressure on the other. Similarly ocean currents flow across the slope of the sea, rather than down it.

In principle one can measure the world's ocean currents by gauging the slopes from space. During the World Ocean Circulation Experiment, the US–French Topex-Poseidon satellite and Europe's ERS-1 and ERS-2 satellites provided sea-slope data from radar altimeters. In practice, it proved very tricky to make measurements of sufficient accuracy to gauge the currents reliably.

Complicating the picture are humps and hollows of up to about 100 metres in the sea surface, produced by variations in the strength of gravity over different parts of the Earth. Sea-surface slopes associated with currents are much smaller, producing height differences of about two metres at most. Early in the 21st century a succession of gravity-measuring satellites culminating in a European project called GOCE (2005) promised to measure more exactly what the ideal sea level should be at each spot, if there were no currents.

'I've had this dream for 20 years,' said Georges Balmino, leader of the Groupe de Recherches de Géodésie Spatiale uniting eight French scientific teams. 'If we could compare the real and ideal sea levels with sufficient accuracy, we could vastly improve our knowledge of ocean currents and their role in climate. Thanks to GOCE and the improved radar satellites, that dream will soon come true.'

● 'A lunatic hypothesis'

Lest anyone should feel complacent, some leading ocean physicists thought that the computer models of the 20th century were based on a false assumption about what drove the ocean currents. Prevailing winds and differences in water density, the textbooks said. Because water density depends on temperature and dissolved salt, oceanographers called its contribution the heat-salt or thermohaline circulation.

Walter Munk of UC San Diego and Carl Wunsch of the Massachusetts Institute of Technology insisted that the heat-salt effects were far too weak, both in theory and by observation. Instead they proposed, in 1998, that the energy that drives the ocean currents comes half from the winds and half from the Moon. By the latter, they meant the lunar tides.

OCEAN CURRENTS

Inshore fishermen and yachtsmen are very familiar with tidal currents. As the sea rises and falls twice a day, under the Moon's influence, the water moves in and out of river estuaries and other coastal channels. In the open ocean, water movements produced directly by the tides are slow, whether compared with inshore tidal currents or with transoceanic currents like the Gulf Stream. But immense volumes of water are involved, and there are huge indirect effects on the current system.

Here the comparison is with the churning of the water seen inshore, when tidal currents feel the friction of shallows and headlands. The effect is to fight gravity and to bring to the surface cold, dense water. As this is rich in chemical nutrients, it fertilizes the coastal zone. In the deep ocean, as Munk and Wunsch pointed out, similar churning action occurs when tidal currents at the bottom of the open ocean encounter the sudden slopes of the continental margins, or the mid-ocean ridges where the central regions of oceans become relatively shallow. This, they say, is what continuously lifts relatively dense water against gravity to keep the subsurface circulation going—not the pussyfooting effects of weather on temperature and salinity.

The energy comes from the Earth–Moon system, and because of tidal friction the Moon is receding slowly from us. Laser ranging shows its distance to be increasing at four centimetres a year. The numbers fit well, if a third of the recession represents the Moon's contribution to the general circulation of open-ocean currents, and two-thirds to the more frenzied inshore tidal currents.

Within a few years support for what Munk and Wunsch called their 'lunatic hypothesis' came from two very different studies. An analysis of six years' tides, as observed by the Topex–Poseidon satellite, revealed intense friction at the Mid-Atlantic Ridge, around Fiji, and in the western Indian Ocean. And an historical study of the frequency of El Niño warming events in the eastern Pacific showed that it depended on the slant of the Moon's orbit, in relation to the Earth's Equator.

If the tidal story is correct, the value of 20th-century computer models of the ocean circulation, based as they were on heat-salt effects, is seriously in question. So is their use in predicting climate change. In compensation, the tides give new insight into past climate.

Tides and currents were different in the ice ages, when sea levels were low. In the more remote past, because of continental drift, the oceans had different shapes, and the Moon was closer. Wunsch said, 'It appears that the tides are, surprisingly, an intricate part of the story of climate change, as is the history of the lunar orbit.'

▶ *As a conspicuous agent of climate variation, the disturbance of Pacific currents called* EL NIÑO *merits a separate entry. See also* ICE-RAFTING EVENTS. *Other applications of gravity-measuring satellites figure in* PLATE MOTIONS.

ORIGINS

Pointers
Pointers
Pointers
Pointers

AN IMPORTANT SECTOR of NASA's space science programme is called 'Origins' for the excellent reason that a yardstick of advancing knowledge is how well, or otherwise, it accounts for human existence. In detail, that requires a narrative of the events that put us where we are in space and time. Key events figure in the following entries in this book.

Universe (*c.*13.5 billion years ago) **UNIVERSE, BIG BANG**

Milky Way Galaxy (*c.*12.5 billion years ago) **GALAXIES**

Earth (4.55 billion years ago) **EARTH**

Life (*c.*4 billion years ago) **LIFE'S ORIGIN, TREE OF LIFE**

Continents (*c.*3.8 billion years ago) **CONTINENTS AND SUPERCONTINENTS**

Free oxygen (*c.*2.2 billion years ago) **GLOBAL ENZYMES**

Modern (eukaryotic) cells (*c.*2 billion years ago) **TREE OF LIFE**

Sex (*c.*1 billion years ago) **CLONING**

Conspicuous animals (542 million years ago) **CAMBRIAN EXPLOSION**

Placental mammals (108 million years ago) **MAMMALS**

Dinosaurs' extinction (65 million years ago) **EXTINCTIONS, IMPACTS**

Grasslands (*c.*30 million years ago) **GLOBAL ENZYMES**

Bipedal primates (*c.*6 million years ago) **PRIMATE BEHAVIOUR, HUMAN ORIGINS**

Homo sapiens sapiens (*c.*100,000 years ago) **PREHISTORIC GENES, SPEECH**

Agriculture (*c.*11,000 years ago) **CEREALS**

Modern science (*c.*400 years ago) **DISCOVERY**

▶ *For more continuous processes in the story of origins, see* STARS, ELEMENTS, MINERALS IN SPACE, MOLECULES IN SPACE, COMETS AND ASTEROIDS *and* EVOLUTION.

PARTICLE FAMILIES

Completing the Standard Model of matter and its behaviour

I N 1934 A YOUNG LECTURER in Osaka, Hideki Yukawa, was having a restless night. He had chosen to become a theoretical physicist instead of a priest, though some might say there's not much difference, for a reclusive, contemplative soul like his. As a schoolboy he had come across an account of the early development of the quantum theory. 'I did not understand its meaning at all,' he admitted later, 'but I felt a mystical attraction towards the words.'

What troubled Yukawa that night, and not for the first time, was the discovery of the neutron by James Chadwick in Cambridge in 1932. This uncharged particle had about the same mass as the positively charged proton, which was already well known as the nucleus of the hydrogen atom. Thenceforward, the nuclei of all heavier atoms could be easily understood as collections of so many protons and so many neutrons.

After the neutron discovery, physicists were puzzled to know how atoms heavier than hydrogen survived at all. Why did the intense mutual repulsion between the electric charges on the protons, crowded into a very small volume, not simply burst the nucleus? Unable to sleep that night in Osaka, Yukawa set physics on a new course by imagining a novel kind of particle that could tie the protons and neutrons together with a strong nuclear force.

As its mass would fall between those of the lightweight electron and the heavy proton—on a mezzanine floor, as it were—Yukawa's predicted particle came to be called a meson. An Indian physicist, Homi Bhabha, so named it in 1938. He also pointed out that, if a meson were ever set free, in a violent nuclear reaction, it would quickly break up into an electron and a neutrino.

In the high Andes of Bolivia, in 1947, Cecil Powell of Bristol discovered a particle with just such a specification in the cosmic rays raining down from the sky. Powell's meson is called the pion. That distinguishes it from other mesons of the Yukawa kind that turned up, to plague the physicists with more than they had bargained for.

Mesons called kaons gave the first hint of a new and unexpected kind of matter. They were detected, also in 1947, in a cosmic-ray experiment on the Pic du Midi in the Pyrenees, by George Rochester of Manchester. That was when strangeness entered the world of the physicists.

Kaons and some other particles, including heavy relatives of the proton, were strange. They broke up much more slowly than expected. They had some quality, comparable with an electric charge or spin, which distinguished them from protons, neutrons and pions. The novel particles had to purge themselves of it before they could decay into familiar kinds of matter. In 1953, Murray Gell-Mann of Caltech dubbed the quality strangeness, which became a technical term.

Confusion reigned in particle physics. Cosmic-ray detectors and particle accelerators churned out a bewildering variety of proton-like and meson-like particles. All had different properties and masses, and arbitrary tags, usually a Greek letter. Before he died in the USA in 1954, the eminent Italian-born physicist Enrico Fermi complained to a student, 'Young man, if I could remember the names of these particles I would have been a botanist.'

Colourful quarks

Rochester's discovery of strange particles eventually prompted a great simplification of the picture. Gell-Mann and others first corralled the known heavy particles into families of proton-like and meson-like particles, by shuffling mathematical entities. Then, in 1963, Gell-Mann proposed that protons and mesons should no longer be regarded as elementary particles, but were composed of more fundamental subunits. The mathematical entities shuffled in the family-making scheme were, he said, real objects.

'I called them quarks after the taunting cry of the gulls, "Three quarks for Muster Mark," from *Finnegans Wake* by the Irish writer James Joyce,' Gell-Mann explained. 'Some people say *quahks*, but I think that among Joyce's multiple meanings there was a pun on the idea of quarts of beer, so I say *quawk*.'

All proton-like objects are made of three quarks. Initially there were thought to be three different kinds of quarks, called up, down and strange. The proton itself has two ups and a down, and the neutron, two downs and an up. The quarks' inherent qualities of upness, downness or strangeness came to be known as flavours. An early triumph for the theory was the prediction of a previously undiscovered particle, made of three strange quarks. Called the omega particle, it turned up in an experiment at the Brookhaven National Laboratory in 1964, shedding three doses of strangeness, step by step, as it broke up.

As for Yukawa's mesons, the binders of the atomic nucleus, each is made of a quark and an antiquark. An affinity between the force carriers and the particles on which they acted became beautifully apparent. The same thing was known from the electric force, which is carried by particles of light made of electrons and anti-electrons. Before the 1960s were out, a theory of another cosmic force, the weak force of radioactivity, would invoke force-carrying particles embodying neutrinos, ghostly particles affected only by the weak force.

Next, the strong nuclear force turned out to be a by-product of an even more fundamental interaction of particles—the colour force that holds the quarks together within a proton. Here the idea, as mooted by Oscar Greenberg of Maryland in 1964, is that the quarks have other distinctive qualities besides their flavours. Gell-Mann named them colours, not because anyone supposes that the quarks are truly coloured, but because their colour charges add together in the same manner as colours.

An electric charge can be only plus or minus, but a quark has three options for its colour charge: red, green or blue. The proton and similar real particles must have one of each, so that the combination is white. (The analogy is with coloured lights, not with mixtures of paint.) Naked colour is never to be seen, and in a deep sense that is why the proton does not have two or four quarks. Only three can make white.

Mesons, too, must be white. They have only two quarks, but one is an antiquark with an anticolour, or complementary colour, which can be turquoise, mauve or yellow. If the quark is red, and the antiquark is turquoise, the combination has the required whiteness. But whilst mesons join protons and neutrons together, they are not the force carriers that glue the quarks within the protons and neutrons.

That is the job of the colour force, carried by particles called gluons, which like mesons possess colour and anticolour, but without the encumbrance of quarks. Just as individual quarks exhibit their colour within the confines of the proton, so can the gluons. As they don't have to be white, like mesons that appear in public, any combination of colour and anticolour is allowed in the gluons.

Observe again: the colour force is conveyed by particles possessing colour charges, like the quarks on which they act. The idea of the colour force carried by gluons was perfected by a number of theorists in the early 1970s, under the formal name of quantum chromodynamics. Alongside the gluons were other new force carriers called W and Z, predicted for the weak force, in a theory that made it a variant of the electric force, in a unified electroweak force. The full repertoire of subatomic forces that would figure in the Standard Model was then available.

A peculiarity of the colour force is that it becomes weaker when the quarks are very close together. 'Well inside the proton they are free to rattle around, hardly affected by one another,' explained David Politzer of Harvard, one of the architects of the theory. 'The other side of this peculiar feature is that when quarks begin to separate they feel a stronger and stronger interaction.'

The quarks are firmly locked away, forever out of view in the ordinary world. So how to confirm the reality of quarks and gluons? The answer came in 1979 from Hamburg, where an experiment at the Deutsches Elektronen-Synchrotron laboratory collided electrons and anti-electrons (positrons). Among the results were distinctive Y-shaped patterns of three jets of particles. Each was a spray of well-known particles all heading in roughly the same direction.

The interpretation was that the original collision produced a quark and an antiquark rushing away from each other and promptly breaking up into other particles. If that were all that happened, the jets would be in opposite directions. But if one of the quarks fired off a gluon, the recoil changed its direction, and the gluon itself broke up to make a jet going off at an angle, so producing the Y. The rate and angles in such events at Hamburg were completely in line with the theory of quarks and the colour force.

'The quarks that manifest themselves indirectly in quark jets have become almost real,' commented Harald Fritzch of Munich. 'They are subjects of investigation despite the fact that they spend their lives locked inside hadrons.' (By hadrons, physicists mean proton-like particles, and mesons.) Later a Quark Liberation Front, with cells in CERN and Brookhaven, was bent on creating extremely high temperatures in collisions between heavy atomic nuclei and so briefly setting quarks free.

More quark flavours

After floundering in the mud of inexplicable particles during the 1950s, the theorists were by the early 1970s on firmer ground. Sprinting ahead of the experimentalists, some asserted that the roll call of matter particles was incomplete. For a start, there could be more than three flavours of quarks.

'Charm, in the sense of a magical device to avert evil,' Glashow said, explaining the name he gave to a new quark flavour, beyond upness, downness and strangeness. He and James Bjorken predicted it in 1964. The existence of quarks of the new kind would eliminate certain difficulties that began to show up in the theories of particles and forces.

A turning point came with the discovery of a novel particle, more than three times heavier than a proton. It was produced by accelerators at the Brookhaven National Laboratory and at the Stanford Linear Accelerator Center, in experiments led by Sam Ting and Burton Richter. The independence and near-simultaneity of the discovery became apparent when the two men met at Stanford at 8 o'clock one Monday morning in November 1974.

> 'Burt, I have some interesting physics to tell you about.'
> 'Sam, I have some interesting physics to tell _you_ about.'

In recalling the exchange, Richter commented, 'While this is not sparkling dialogue it began an astonishing conversation, as we had no idea about Ting's results.'

Ting called the particle J, Richter called it psi, and so it came to be known as J/psi or gipsy. An immediate suspicion was that it was a superheavy meson embodying charm. By 1976 Stanford had proved it to consist of a charmed quark and an anticharmed quark, and the name charmonium won favour. Three months later Fermilab found the first charmed proton.

Meanwhile another discovery at Stanford stirred further imaginings. In 1975, Martin Perl found a superheavy version of the electron, which he called the tau particle. Back in 1937 the muon, with 200 times the mass of an ordinary electron, had turned up in the cosmic rays. It was eventually characterized as the electron's bigger brother. Perl's tau was another brother, 3500 times heavier than the electron.

Theorists suspected that electrons, like quarks, were flavoursome, and that an extended family linked the two types of particles. The ordinary electron was related to the commonplace up and down quarks, and the more exotic muon to the charmed and strange quarks. In this scheme, the tau implied the existence of two more quarks. Indeed tau stood for T meaning tri, a third category of flavoured matter.

Haim Harari of Israel's Weizmann Institute had names for the two extra quarks, top and bottom. Some colleagues wanted to call them truth and beauty, or even topless and bottomless, but the austere names stuck. The discovery of the bottom quark at Fermilab in 1977 confirmed the extended picture. The ingredients of the Standard Model of matter and forces were essentially in place, even though particles containing the top quark did not materialize until 1994–95, again at Fermilab.

A well-rounded theory

Out of all the complexities and hesitations in the foregoing tale came a precise picture of the ordinary matter of the cosmos and of the forces at work within atoms. It was wonderfully economical in ideas and entities. In the Standard Model, the heavy matter most familiar in the atomic nucleus is built from just six flavours of quarks, which can have various colour charges, together with their antiquarks. Electrons, which in atoms form the clouds of negative electric charge around the positively charged nuclei, also come in six variants. The electron itself, the muon and the tau each have an uncharged neutrino of a distinctive type to go with it. Again there are antiparticles to match.

From combinations of these available particles and antiparticles of matter, the theory shows how Mother Nature creates not only protons and other composite particles, but also the various forces. All matter particles feel the weak force carried by W particles, made of an electron and antineutrino or vice versa, and by Z particles with a neutrino and antineutrino, or some other composition. Photons made of an electron and anti-electron carry the electric force, to which all charged particles respond. The strong nuclear force, felt only by proton-like matter particles and mesons, is carried by gluons (colour and anticolour) within the particles and by mesons (quark and antiquark) operating between the particles.

Mathematically, all of these forces are described by so-called gauge theories, which give the same results wherever you start from. The electric force provides a simple example of indifference to the starting point, in a pigeon perching safely on a power line while being repeatedly charged to 100,000 volts. Signals of a fraction of a volt continue to pass in a normal manner through the bird's nervous system.

Indifference to circumstances is a requirement if the various forces are to operate in exactly the same way on and within a proton, whether it is anchored in a mountain or whizzing through the Galaxy close to the speed of light, as a cosmic-ray particle. In other words, gauge theories are compatible with high-speed travel and Albert Einstein's special theory of relativity. The obligation that the force theories must be of this type strengthens the physicists' confidence in them.

Those four paragraphs sum up the Standard Model, a well-rounded theory and one of the grandest outcomes of 20th-century science. It was created and largely confirmed in an era of unremitting excitement. Almost as fast as theorists plucked ideas from their heads, experimenters manufactured the corresponding particles literally out of thin air, in the vacuum of their big machines. It was as if Mother Nature was in a mood to gossip with the physicists, about her arcane ways of running the Universe.

The frenzy lasted for about 20 years, bracketed by the materializations of the triply strange omega particle in 1964 and the Z carrier of the weak force in 1984. But after that climax came a period of hush on the subject of the fundamental particles and the forces operating between them. Most particle physicists had to content themselves with confirming the predictions of the existing theories to more and more decimal places.

If the Standard Model were complete in itself, and arguably the end of the story, Mother Nature's near-muteness at the end of the 20th century would have been unsurprising. Yet neither criterion was satisfied. As Chris Llewellyn Smith of CERN commented in 1998, 'While the Standard Model is economical in concepts, their realization in practice is baroque, and the model contains many arbitrary and ugly features.'

● Hoping for flaws

Two decades earlier, in the midst of all the excitement, Richard Feynman of Caltech played the party pooper. He put his finger on one of the gravest shortcomings of the-then emergent Standard Model. 'The problem of the masses has been swept into a corner,' he complained.

Theorists have rules of thumb that work well in estimating the masses of expected new particles, by reference to those of known particles. Yet no one can say why quarks are heavier than electrons, or why the top quark is 44,000 times more massive than the up quark. According to the pristine versions of the theories all particles should have zero intrinsic mass, yet only photons and neutrinos were thought to conform. The real masses of other particles are an arbitrary add-on, supposedly achieved by introducing extraneous particles.

By the start of the 21st century physicists were beefing up their accelerators to address the mass problem by looking for a particle called the Higgs, which might solve it. They were also very keen to find flaws in the Standard Model. Only then would the way be open to a superworld rich in other particles and forces.

The physicists dreaded the thought of entering a desert with nothing for their machines to find, by way of particle discoveries, to match the great achievements of the previous 100 years. The first hint that they might not be so unlucky came in 1998, with results from an underground experiment in Japan. These indicated that neutrinos do not have zero mass, as required by the Standard Model. Hooray!

▶ *For more about the evolution of the Standard Model, see* ELECTROWEAK FORCE, QUARK SOUP, *and* HIGGS BOSONS. *For theories looking beyond it, see* SPARTICLES *and* SUPERSTRINGS. *Other related entries are* COSMIC RAYS *and* NEUTRINO OSCILLATIONS.

PHOTOSYNTHESIS

How does your garden grow?

'**G**REEN PLANTS spread the enormous surface of their leaves and, in a still unknown way, force the energy of the Sun to carry out chemical syntheses, before it cools down to the temperature levels of the Earth's surface.' Thus, in 1866, the Austrian physicist Ludwig Boltzmann related the growth of plants to recently discovered laws of heat. By stressing the large leaf area he anticipated the 21st-century view of greenswards and the planktonic grass of the sea as two-dimensional photochemical factories equipped with natural light guides and photocells.

Botanists had been strangely slow even to acknowledge that plants need light. In 1688 Edmond Halley told the Royal Society of London that he had heard from a keeper of the Chelsea Physic Garden that a plant screened from light became white, withered and died. Halley was emboldened to suggest 'that it was necessary to the maintenance of vegetable life that light should be admitted to the plant'. But why heed such tittle-tattle from an astronomer?

The satirist Jonathan Swift came unwittingly close to the heart of the matter in 1726, in *Voyage to Laputa*, where 'projectors' were trying to extract sunbeams from cucumbers. Half a century later Jan Ingenhousz, a Dutch-born court physician in Vienna, carried out his *Experiments on Vegetables*, published in London in 1779. He not only established the importance of light, but showed that in sunshine plants inhale an 'injurious' gas and exhale a 'purifying' gas. At night this process is partially reversed.

The medic Ingenhousz is therefore considered the discoverer of the most important chemical reactions on Earth. In modern terms, plants take in carbon dioxide and water and use the radiant energy of sunlight to make sugars and other materials needed for life, releasing oxygen in the process. At night the plants consume some of the daytime growth for their own housekeeping.

Animal life could not exist without the oxygen and the nutrition provided by plants. The fact that small communities on the ocean floor subsist on volcanic rather than solar energy does not alter the big picture of a planet where the chemistry of life on its surface depends primarily on combining atoms into molecules with the aid of light—in a word, on photosynthesis. Thereby more than 100 billion tonnes of carbon is drawn from the carbon dioxide of the air every year and incorporated into living tissue.

Chlorophyll, photons and electrons

The machinery of photosynthesis gradually became clearer, in the microscopic and molecular contents of commonplace leaves. During the 19th and early 20th centuries scientists found that the natural green pigment chlorophyll is essential. It concentrates in small bodies within the leaf cells, called chloroplasts. The key chemical reaction of photosynthesis splits water into hydrogen and oxygen, and complex series of other reactions ensue.

Another preamble to further progress was the origin of photochemistry. It started with photography but was worked up by Giacomo Ciamician of Bologna into a broad study of the interactions of chemical substances and light. The physicists' discovery that light consists of particles, photons, opened the way to understanding one-on-one reactions between a photon and an individual atom or molecule. Electrons came into the story too, as detachable parts of atoms.

Chlorophyll paints the land and sea green. Its molecule is shaped like a kite, with a flat, roughly square head made mainly of carbon and nitrogen atoms, and a long wiggly tail of carbon atoms attached by an acetic acid molecule. In the centre of the head is a charged magnesium atom that puts out four struts—chemical bonds—to a ring of rings, each made of four atoms of carbon and one of nitrogen. Different kinds of chlorophyll are decorated with various attachments to the head and tail.

From the white light of the Sun, chlorophyll absorbs mainly blue and red photons, letting green light escape as the pigment's colour. Because the chlorophyll is concentrated in minute chloroplasts, leaves would appear white or transparent, did they not possess an optical design that forces light entering a leaf to ricochet about inside it many times before escaping again. This maximizes the chance that a photon will encounter a chloroplast and be absorbed. It also ensures that surviving green light eventually escapes from all over the leaf.

The pace of discovery about photosynthesis quickened in the latter half of the 20th century. Using radioactive carbon-14 to label molecules, the chemist Melvin Calvin of UC Berkeley and others were able to trace the course of chemical reactions involving carbon. Contrary to expectation, the system does not act directly on the assimilated carbon dioxide but first creates energy-rich molecules, called NADPH and ATP. These are portable chemical coins representing free energy that the living cell can spend on all kinds of constructive tasks. Conceptually they link photosynthesis to the laws of heat, as Boltzmann wanted.

Teams in Europe and the USA gradually revealed that two different molecular systems are involved. Somewhat confusingly they are called Photosystem II and Photosystem I, with II coming first in the chemical logic of the process, although it was the second to be discovered. II is where incoming light has its greatest effect, in splitting molecules of water to make oxygen molecules and dismembering the hydrogen atoms into positively charged protons and lightweight, negatively charged electrons.

Water, H_2O, is a stable compound, and splitting it needs the combined energy of two photons of sunlight. But as you'll not want highly reactive oxygen atoms rampaging among your delicate molecules, you'd better liberate two and pair them right away in a less harmful oxygen molecule. That doubles the energy required for the transaction.

To accumulate the means to buy one oxygen molecule, by splitting two water molecules at once, you need a piggy bank. In Photosystem II, this is a cluster of four charged atoms of a metallic element, manganese. Each dose of incoming energy extracts another electron from one manganese atom. When all four manganeses are thus fully charged, bingo, the system converts two water molecules into one oxygen molecule and four free hydrogen nuclei, protons. The four electrons have already left the scene.

The other unit in the operation, Photosystem I, then uses the electrons supplied by II, and others liberated by light within I itself, to set in motion a series of other chemical reactions. They convert carbon dioxide into energy-rich carbon compounds. Human beings are hard put to make sense of the jargon, never mind to understand all the details. Yet humble spinach operates its two systems without a moment's thought, merrily splitting water in one and fixing carbon from the air in the other.

Pigments as a transport system

Like other plants, spinach also runs molecular railways for photons and electrons. These are built of carefully positioned chains of pigment molecules, mainly chlorophyll. For light, they can act first like antennas to gather the photons, and then like glass fibres to guide their energy to the point of action.

It is mildly surprising to have pigment chains relaying light, but much more remarkable that they also transport free electrons at an astonishing rate. The possibility was unknown to scientists until the 1960s. Then the Canadian-born theorist Rudolph Marcus, working in the USA, showed how electrons can leap from molecule to molecule. In photosynthesis, this trick whisks the liberated electrons away along the molecular railway, before they can rejoin the wrong atoms. It delivers them very precisely to the distant molecules where their chemical action is required.

The separation of electric charges achieved by this means is the most crucial of all the steps in the photosynthetic process. It takes place in a few million-millionths of a second. Ultrafast laser systems became indispensable tools in studying photosynthesis, to capture events that are quicker than any ordinary flash. The production of oxygen within milliseconds seems relatively leisurely, while the reactions converting carbon dioxide into other materials can take several seconds.

The layout of the high-speed pigment railways became apparent in the first complete molecular structure of a natural photocell, converting light energy into electrical energy. Its elucidation was a landmark in photosynthesis research. In 1981, at the Max-Planck-Institut für Biochemie, Martinsried, Hartmut Michel succeeded in making crystals of photosynthetic reaction centres from a purple bacterium, *Rhodopseudomonas viridis*. This opened the way to X-ray analysis, and by 1985 Johann Deisenhofer, Michel and others at Martinsried had revealed the most complex molecular 3-D assembly ever seen at an atomic level, up to that time.

This photocell passes in rivet fashion through a membrane in the bacterium. When light falls on it, it creates a voltage across the membrane, sending a negative charge to the far side. The molecular analysis revealed how it works. Four protein molecules encase carefully positioned pigments, bacterial analogues of chlorophyll, which create a railway that guides the light energy to a place where two pigment molecules meet in a so-called special pair. There the light energy liberates an electron, which then travels via a branch line of the pigment railway to the dark side of the membrane. It settles with its negative charge on a ring-shaped quinone molecule that has a useful appetite for electrons.

'Although it is a purple bacterium that has first yielded the secrets of the photosynthetic reaction centre,' commented Robert Huber, who coordinated the work at Martinsried, 'there is no need to doubt its relevance to the higher green plants on which human beings depend for their nourishment.'

The gift of the blue-greens

Whilst it was certainly encouraging that so complicated a molecule could be analysed, the photosystems of the higher plants, with two different kinds of reaction centres, were a tougher proposition. They would keep scientists busy into the 21st century.

There are evolutionary reasons for the greater complexity. Purple bacteria live by scavenging pre-existing organic material, using light energy as an aid. This would be a dead end, if other organisms did not make fresh food from scratch, by reacting carbon dioxide with hydrogen. Some photosynthetic bacteria obtain their hydrogen by splitting volcanic hydrogen sulphide, but others took the big step to splitting water.

'Think about it,' said James Barber, a chemist at Imperial College London. 'Water is the solvent of life. It was very odd that bacteria should start attacking their solvent. That's like burning your house to keep warm. Only the abundance of water on the Earth made it a sustainable strategy. And of course the first thing that plants do in a drought is to stop photosynthesizing.'

The key players in this evolutionary switch were blue-green algae, or cyanobacteria, first appearing perhaps 2.4 billion years ago. Their direct descendants are still among us. Blue-greens are commonplace in ponds and oceans, and on the shore of Western Australia they build mounds called stromatolites, with new layers growing on top of dead predecessors. Fossils of similar stromatolites are known in rocks 2 billion years old.

Those remote ancestors of the present-day blue-greens possessed such an excellent kit for photosynthesis that other, larger cells, welcomed them aboard to make the first true algae. Whenever the cells reproduced themselves, they passed on stocks of blue-green guests to their daughters. Much later, some of the algae evolved into land plants. The green chloroplasts within the leaf cells of plants, where the photosynthesis is done, are direct descendants of the former blue-greens.

What was so special about them? Until the ancestral blue-greens appeared on the Earth, some photosynthetic bacteria, like the purples studied at Martinsried, had used quinones as the end-stations to receive electrons released by light. Others employed iron–sulphur clusters (Fe_4S_4) for that purpose. The blue-greens beefed up photosynthesis by putting both systems together. As a result, their descendent chloroplasts possess Photosystems II (using quinones) and I (using iron–sulphur).

Although there are many variants of photosynthesis, they are all related. Photosynthesis using chlorophyll seems to be a trick that Nature originated only once. Investigators of molecular evolution at Indiana and Kanagawa traced the whole story back in time, from the similarities and differences between proteins involved in photosynthesis, in plants, blue-greens and other photosynthetic bacteria alive today. Chlorophyll, the badge of sun-powered life, first appeared in an ancient form in a remote common ancestor of purple and green photosynthetic bacteria. Among the variants appearing later is chlorophyll a, which is exclusive to blue-greens and plants.

Engineering the photosystems

Although it is a quinone user like the purple bacterium, Photosystem II generates a higher voltage. For its key job, it also has a special water-splitting enzyme—a protein molecule whose modus operandi remains elusive. Like the purple bacterium's photocell, Photosystem II consists of a complex of protein molecules supporting pigment antennas and railways, but it is bigger, with about 45,000 atoms in all.

By 1995, at Imperial College London, James Barber's team had isolated the Photosystem II complex from a plant—spinach. The material resisted attempts to crystallize it for full X-ray examination. Nevertheless, powerful electron microscopes operating at very low temperatures gave a first impression of its molecular organization.

In Berlin, Wolfram Saenger and colleagues from the Freie Universität and Horst Tobias Witt and colleagues from the Technische Universität had better fortune with Photosystem II from a blue-green, *Synechococcus elongatus*, which lives in hot springs. Athina Zouni managed to grow small crystals. They were not good enough for very detailed analysis, but by 2001 the team had a broad-brush X-ray view of the complex.

The blue-green's Photosystem II was similar to what Barber was seeing in spinach, and reminiscent of the purple bacterium's photosynthetic machine too. The team positioned about ten per cent of the 45,000 atoms, including key metal atoms and chlorophyll molecules. They pinpointed the piggy bank—the manganese cluster that accumulates electric charges for the break-up of water.

The Berliners were also working on the blue-green's Photosystem I, and strong similarities convinced them that I and II shared a common ancestry. The picture grew clearer, of a treasured reaction centre originating long ago, spreading throughout the living world, adapting to different modes of existence, but always preserving essential structures and mechanisms in its core.

The Berlin group had better crystals of Photosystem I than they had of II. Ingrid Witt first managed to crystallize groups of three robust Photosystem I units from the blue-green *S. elongatus*, in 1988. That opened the possibility of X-ray analysis down to an atomic level.

With so formidable a complex as Photosystem I, containing 12 different proteins and about 100 chlorophyll molecules, this was no small matter. Very powerful X-rays, available at the European Synchrotron Radiation Facility in Grenoble, were essential. The crystals had to be frozen at the temperature of liquid nitrogen to reduce damage to the delicate structures by the X-rays themselves. By 2001 the Berliners' analysis of Photosystem I was triumphantly thorough.

It showed the detailed arrangement of the proteins, of which nine are riveted through the supporting membrane. Six carefully placed chlorophyll molecules provide central transport links for light and electrons and make a special pair as in the Martinsried structure. Most impressively, a great light-harvesting antenna using another 90 chlorophylls surrounds the active centre of Photosystem I. Orange carotene pigments also contribute to the antenna.

For outsiders who might wonder what value there might be in this strenuous pursuit of so much detail, down to the atomic level, Wolfram Saenger had an answer. 'We don't just satisfy our curiosity about the mechanisms and evolution of this life-giving chemistry,' he commented. 'We have already gained a new and surprising appreciation of how pigments, proteins, light and electrons work together in living systems. And the physics, chemistry, biochemistry and molecular biology, successfully marshalled in the study of photosynthesis, can now investigate these and many other related molecular machines in living cells, and find out how they really work.'

Can we improve on the natural systems?

Practical benefits can be expected too. Growing knowledge of the genetics and molecular biology of the photosynthetic apparatus, and of its natural control mechanisms, may help plant breeders to enhance growth rates in crop plants. Other scientists use biomolecules to build artificial photosynthetic systems for generating electrical energy or for releasing hydrogen as fuel. In competition with them are photochemists who prefer metal oxides or compound metals, which are also capable of splitting water into hydrogen and oxygen when exposed to light, without any need for living things.

In 1912 Ciamician of Bologna looked forward to a time when the secrets of plants 'will have been mastered by human industry which will know how to make them bear even more abundant fruit than Nature, for Nature is not in a hurry and mankind is'. In that sense, two centuries spent grasping the fundamentals of photosynthesis may be just the precursor to a new relationship between human beings and the all-nourishing energy of the Sun.

▶ *For the geological impact of photosynthesis, see* GLOBAL ENZYMES *and* TREE OF LIFE. *For its present influences, see* CARBON CYCLE *and* BIOSPHERE FROM SPACE. *For more about proteins and their structures, see* PROTEIN SHAPES. *The molecular biology of plants is dealt with more generally under* ARABIDOPSIS. *For alternative sources of energy for life, see* EXTREMOPHILES.

PLANT DISEASES

An evolutionary arms race or just trench warfare?

P OTATOES ARE EASY TO GROW, and when introduced into Ireland they meant that you could keep your family alive while spending most of your time labouring for the big landowners. This feudal social system worked tolerably until 1845, when an enemy of the potato arrived on the wind from the European continent. It was the potato blight *Phytophthora infestans*. Black spots and white mould on the leaves foretold that the potatoes would become a rotten pulp.

The Great Irish Famine, which killed and exiled millions, was neither the first nor the last case of a crop being largely wiped out by disease. The potato blight itself caused widespread hardship across Europe. Its effects reached historic dimensions in Ireland partly because landowners continued to export grain while the inhabitants starved. As Jane Francesca Wilde (Oscar's mother) put it:

> There's a proud array of soldiers—what do they round your door?
> They guard our masters' granaries from the thin hands of the poor.

At least 20 per cent of the world's crop production is still lost to pests, parasites and pathogens, and the figure rises to 40 per cent in Africa and Asia. Plant diseases can also devastate species in the wild, as when the bark-ravaging fungus *Cryphonectria parasitica* crippled every last stand of native American chestnut trees between 1904 and 1926. But cultivated crops are usually much more vulnerable to annihilating epidemics than wild plants are, because they are grown from varieties with a narrow genetic base.

In the wars between living species that have raged since life began, human beings often think that their natural enemies are big cats, bears, sharks, crocodiles and snakes. In fact, the depredations of those large animals are insignificant compared with disease-causing microbes. They either afflict people directly or starve them by attacking their food supplies.

There is no difference in principle between the conflicts of organisms of any size. All involve weapons of attack and defence, whether sharper canines versus tougher hides, or novel viruses versus molecular antibodies. Given the opportunities for improvements on both sides, biologists have called the interspecies war an evolutionary arms race.

Hereditary systems provide much natural resistance to diseases in plants, as well as animals. Many herbal medicines are borrowed from the plant kingdom's arsenal of chemical weapons. An overview of the genetic system involved in fighting disease became available in 2000, when a European–US–Japanese consortium of labs in the Arabidopsis Genome Initiative read every gene in arabidopsis, which is a small weed.

Very variable genes called R for resistance, of which arabidopsis possesses 150, provide the means of identifying various kinds of parasites and pathogens attacking the plant. Recognition of a foe triggers defence mechanisms in which signalling molecules activate various defender genes and sometimes command infected cells to die. Dozens of genes involved in these actions were tentatively pinpointed, including eight thought to be responsible for a burst of respiration that zaps the intruder with oxygen in a highly reactive form.

Plants devote a lot of energy, in the literal sense, to protection against disease. To keep up a guard against every possible enemy would, though, be far too much work for any individual creature. Instead populations share the task between individuals, by their genetic variability, especially in respect of the R genes. How this arrangement comes about is a matter of intense interest to plant breeders, and also to theorists of evolution.

For a fleeter cheetah

The contest between diseases and their victims is a case of co-evolution, which means an interaction on time-scales long enough for species to evolve together. The prettiest example concerns flowers, nectar, fruits and nuts, which evolved as lures and bribes for animals to help the plants in pollination and seed dispersal. Insects, birds and many other animals including our primate ancestors took advantage of the floral offerings in evolving in novel ways on their own account. The co-evolution of flowers and bees seems be a case where both sides have gained.

More antagonistic, and therefore perhaps more typical, is the contest between grasses and grass-eating animals. Leaves of grass toughened by minerals can ruin a casual muncher's teeth, but grazing animals have acquired teeth that keep growing throughout life, to compensate for the wear. Like the contest between plants and diseases, this is reminiscent of military engineers trying to outdo one another, with their missiles and their antimissile shields. But as with the ever-rising prices of modern armaments, the capacity for attack or defence imposes a tax on each creature's resources.

When trees compete for sunlight in a dense forest, they may grow ever taller to avoid being overshadowed. The upshot is that all of the species of trees involved in a height contest tend to become less efficient. The leaves exposed to sunlight in the canopy do not increase in total area, but they have to power the building and maintenance of elongated tree trunks that are useless to the trees except for giving them height.

Reflecting on the non-stop wars and competitions between species, Leigh van Valen at Chicago propounded a new evolutionary law in 1973. Even if physical conditions such as the climate don't change, he reasoned, every creature is being continually disadvantaged by changes in other species with which it is co-evolving. It is therefore obliged to evolve itself, if it is to maintain its relative position in the ecosystem.

Van Valen called his idea the Red Queen principle, citing Lewis Carroll's *Through the Looking-Glass*. 'Now, *here*, you see, it takes all the running *you* can do, to keep in the same place,' the breathless chess-piece explains to Alice. 'If you want to get somewhere else, you must run at least twice as fast as that!'

Another perspective came from William Hamilton at Oxford, in 1982, with special reference to diseases. The chief role of sexual reproduction, he argued, is to shuffle and share out genes for disease resistance, among the individuals in a species. Even if a disease breaks through on a broad front, there will still be well-armed individuals in strongpoints that can't be winkled out. So the defending species will survive to fight another day. The name of the game is remembering all the different kinds of adversaries encountered in the past, which might reappear in future.

Among mammalian foes, the cheetah becomes fleeter, and the gazelle sharper in its reactions and better at blending into the long grass. For Richard Dawkins, also at Oxford, the evolutionary arms race was the chief way of driving evolution onwards and upwards. His explanation in *The Blind Watchmaker* (1986) of how the world's magnificent, intricate organisms could have been created by the blind forces of physics, relied at its core on the arms-race hypothesis.

'Each new genetic improvement selected on one side of the arms race—say predators—changes the environment for the selection of genes on the other side of the arms race—prey,' Dawkins wrote. 'It is arms races of this kind that have been mainly responsible for the apparently *progressive* quality of evolution, for the evolution of ever-improved running speed, flying skill, acuity of eyesight, keenness of hearing, and so on.'

● Antique weapons

The arms-race theories remained largely speculative until very late in the 20th century, when progress in molecular biology at last began to expose them to observational tests. These began with Joy Bergelson at Chicago setting her graduate students to look closely at a gene conferring resistance in plants to infection by the small bacterium *Pseudomonas syringae*, which causes a blight on young leaves. They were able to show that the anti-pseudomonas Rpm1 gene in a small weed, arabidopsis, was nearly 10 million years old.

The molecular cunning that led them to this conclusion, in 1999, was a matter of examining the anchors that hold the gene in place in the long chain of the nucleic acid, DNA. The anchors consist of short lengths of DNA, but unlike the gene itself they carry no important messages in the genetic code. As a result they are free to accumulate random mutations in the DNA subunits as time passes. High variability in the Rpm1 anchors enabled the Chicago team to estimate the gene's age.

In the essentially progressive view of the evolutionary arms race, as proposed by Dawkins, you might expect each species to be armed to the teeth with the most modern weapons. You'd not expect to see a paratrooper carrying a bow and arrow. Yet the Rpm1 gene against the leaf-blight bacterium is, from this point of view, just such an antique-collector's piece.

'The arms race theory has been a generally accepted model for the evolution of disease-resistance genes because it is intuitive, but it's never been scientifically tested,' Bergelson commented. 'Our results were surprising in demonstrating that an arms race is not occurring for the resistance gene we studied.'

She offered instead the metaphor of trench warfare. Disease epidemics alternate with periods of high resistance in the plants, leading to ceaseless advances and retreats for both plants and pathogens. Genes that have proved their worth in the past may be retained indefinitely, while others from recent skirmishes may die out.

By 2000, when the Arabidopsis Genome Initiative had its 150 R genes for disease resistance, Bergelson and her group were able to check the evolutionary picture quite thoroughly. It confirmed the trench-warfare idea. The scientists found plenty of evidence of rapid adaptation of defences to meet new threats in the past, but also many antiques. Although the R genes show a very wide range of ages, they are far from being typically young, as would be expected in a reliably progressive kind of arms race as described by Dawkins.

After the initial molecular verdicts concerning the plant's armoury for resistance against disease, what survives of the 20th-century ideas about the evolutionary arms race? Co-evolution is strongly reconfirmed as a factor in evolution. There are one-to-one correspondences between proteins manufactured by command of the R genes and other proteins carried by disease-causing organisms, whereby the plant recognizes the enemy.

The Red Queen principle of non-stop evolution, which implies the possibility of retreat as well as advance, remains a valid basis for thinking generally about co-evolution and its weaponry. Hamilton's idea of sex as a means of sharing out responsibility for disease resistance between individuals, with wide variations in their complements of R genes, was strongly supported by the early molecular results from arabidopsis. It needs confirmation in other species, and perhaps with other molecular techniques.

A new mathematical theory will be needed to explain in detail the range of ages of R genes and how they relate to past battles, in which attacking diseases sometimes triumphed, sometimes retreated, during trench warfare lasting many millions of years. The development and testing of such a theory will probably go hand in hand with fresh research in molecular ecology. The search will be for patterns of resistance in wild plants alive today, which can be related to their recent experiences of disease.

▶ *For the background to the weed's genome, see* ARABIDOPSIS. *For Hamilton's theory, see* CLONING. *For diseases in wheat and rice, see* CEREALS. *For the use of crown gall in genetic engineering, see* TRANSGENIC CROPS. *For the arms race with human diseases, see* IMMUNE SYSTEM. *For other molecular insights into co-evolution, see* ALCOHOL *and* GLOBAL ENZYMES. *For general perspectives on evolution, see* EVOLUTION, *and cross-references therein.*

PLANTS

BOTANY WAS A POOR RELATION of zoology until recently. Animals are more fun to watch than plants are, and their relevance to human biology and medicine is plainer. Norman Borlaug's failure to win a Nobel science prize, after helping to save the world from mass starvation with his hybrid wheat, was a symptom of the academic pecking order, although he got the Nobel Peace Prize instead. For the Green Revolution that he started, *see* **CEREALS**. Other biologists modified plants by introducing new genes, with controversial consequences—*see* **TRANSGENIC CROPS**.

The leap forward associated with the reading of entire complements of genes, the genomes, puts plants on an equal footing with animals at the frontiers of discovery. First off the production lines were the genomes of a humble weed and of rice—*see* **ARABIDOPSIS** *and* **CEREALS**. At once, many aspects of plant life were illuminated—*see* **FLOWERING**, **PLANT DISEASES** *and* **GENOMES IN GENERAL**.

Plants grow using carbon dioxide and water, and the energy of sunlight. Their molecular machinery for this purpose has been largely elucidated—*see* **PHOTOSYNTHESIS**. The links between plants and other living things, and with the physical and chemical environment of the Earth, are ancient and far-reaching— *see* **TREE OF LIFE**, **GLOBAL ENZYMES** *and* **ALCOHOL**. Maize and arabidopsis have been used to demonstrate molecular mechanisms of evolution—*see* **HOPEFUL MONSTERS**.

Seasonal growth has large effects on the concentration of carbon dioxide in the air, and on the surface life of the planet—*see* **CARBON CYCLE** *and* **BIOSPHERE FROM SPACE**. Because the leaves of land plants adapt to changing carbon dioxide levels, fossil leaves can help to monitor past changes—*see* **CARBON CYCLE**.

The ecology of plant life looms large among the anxieties about the state of the planet, but fundamental issues remain in dispute—*see* **BIODIVERSITY**. Ecologists have become acutely aware of the importance of controlling the numbers of plant eaters—*see* **PREDATORS**. For relationships between plants and people in ancient and traditional settings, *see* **HUMAN ECOLOGY**. For a tidbit on the use of medicinal plants by chimpanzees, *see* **PRIMATE BEHAVIOUR**.

PLASMA CRYSTALS

How a newly found force empowers dust

'**S** O YOUR CHIMNEYS I SWEEP, and in soot I sleep,' lamented William Blake's child of the Industrial Revolution. Two centuries later, one of the world's dirtiest jobs was to clean out machines used for experiments in controlled nuclear fusion. Supposedly pointing the way to abundant energy supplies in the 21st century, the machines called tokamaks became filthy with black dust. It was manufactured, sometimes by the shovelful, as straying high-energy particles quarried atoms from the internal walls of the reaction chamber. A full-scale fusion reactor of that kind would make dust in radioactive tonnes.

Ever since they first ignited firewood, human beings have regretted the efficiency with which their fuels made soot, but no one thought that any explanation was needed. Not until late in the 20th century did physicists fully wake up to the tricks of soot and other kinds of dust. Makers of microchips created clean rooms with care and expense only to find that manufacturing processes using beams of atomic particles made silicon sawdust that ruined many chips. Like the begrimed cleaners of the fusion machines, they bore witness that something very odd was going on.

A common factor in the tokamaks and the microchip factories was the co-existence of dust grains and electrified gas, in what physicists call dusty plasmas. Astronomers and space scientists encountered dusty plasmas too. They occur in the vicinity of dying stars that puff off newly made chemical elements, and in interstellar clouds where such material accumulates. Around newborn stars, dusty plasmas provide material from which planets can form.

In our own Solar System, comets throw out dusty tails into the electrified solar wind. Dust accumulates in the plane in which the planets orbit, and it is sometimes visible after sunset as the zodiacal light. And inspections of the dusty rings of Saturn, by NASA's two Voyager spacecraft in 1980, showed very fast variations in the structure of the rings that defied explanation at that time.

In 1986 a fusion physicist at General Atomics in California, Hiroyuki Ikezi, considered what could happen when many charged dust particles were confined within an electrified gas, or plasma. He speculated that the dust grains might arrange themselves in neat rows, sheets and 3-D lattices, like atoms in an ordinary crystal, although on a much larger scale. But he did not explain why they should remain like that. Indeed, you'd expect the dust grains to accumulate electric charges and simply repel one another.

Only if the dusty plasma somehow generated a special confining force of its own, to hold the grains together, would the regular lattices proposed by Ikezi be stable. But if there were such a force, you could have a previously unknown state of matter, with liquid-like or crystal-like gatherings of dust grains. They came to be called plasma crystals.

The shadow force

The idea of a special force at work in dusty plasmas rang a loud bell with astronomers of the Max-Planck-Institut für extraterrestrische Physik at Garching near Munich. They were puzzled by a fantastically rapid production of dust near dying stars. That atoms of newly created elements puffed into space from the stars should combine to make microscopic grains of carbon, minerals and ice was only to be expected. But according to traditional ideas, the grains would grow very slowly, atom by atom, over millions of years. Although dust formation must start very slowly, something else was accelerating the later growth of grains, to cut the time required.

Of the main constituents in the dirty plasma around a dying star—electrons, positively charged atoms and the dust grains—the electrons are the most mobile. The dust therefore gathers a disproportionate number of electrons on its surfaces and acquires a mostly negative electric charge. Alternatively, strong ultraviolet light from the star, or its neighbours, might knock electrons out of the dust grains, and so generate mostly positive charges.

Either way, you would then expect the dust grains to repel one another in accordance with schoolroom laws of electrostatics. Yet mounting astronomical evidence showed that this idea was completely wrong. Dust grains near dying stars could grow as large as a millimetre in just a few decades. So far from delaying the agglomeration of dust, the plasma somehow accelerates it, circumventing the electrostatic repulsion.

The first revision of the theory is to visualize each negatively charged dust grain attracting a cloud of positively charged atoms around it, which neutralizes the charge and removes an obstacle to the grains getting together. Secondly comes the more remarkable idea that, as the dust grains approach one another in a plasma, they feel a mutual attraction. Experts now call it the shadow force.

A racing yacht creates a shadow in the wind, which can thwart a rival trying to overtake it on the leeward side. In a plasma, the equivalent of the wind blows from every direction, in the form of the randomly moving atoms that generate pressure. Each dust grain shadows its neighbours, reducing the pressure on the facing sides, so that the remaining pressure pushes the grains together. The cloud of charged atoms around each dust grain makes its sail area larger.

The strength of the shadow force depends on the sizes of the grains and the distances between them. If you double the size, the electric repulsion increases fourfold, but the shadow force driving the grains together is multiplied by 16.

Halving the distance between the grains quadruples the force. It's the same mathematical law as for Newton's force of gravity. Indeed the 18th-century Swiss physicist Georges-Louis Le Sage tried to explain gravity by a shadow force. He imagined space filled with corpuscles moving rapidly in all directions but being blocked by massive bodies, so that the bodies would be pushed towards one another.

As the grains in the dusty plasma come closer, their clouds of positively changed atoms merge and the grains eventually repel one another. Then they occupy space like atoms in a crystal, but on a vastly larger scale—typically a fraction of a millimetre, or a million times the width of an atom. That's when plasma crystals can form.

'An exhilarating experience'

Gregor Morfill at the Max-Planck-Institut in Garching wanted to make plasma crystals experimentally, but he foresaw difficulties. The dust grains fall under gravity. So in 1991 he proposed a *Plasmakristallexperiment* to be done in weightless conditions on the International Space Station, which was then being planned. Ten years later, thanks to collaborative Russians, Morfill's apparatus became the very first experiment in physical science to operate on the station.

Meanwhile a graduate student in Morfill's group, Hubertus Thomas, succeeded in making plasma crystals on the ground. He used electric levitation to oppose gravity and keep his microscopic plastic grains afloat in a plasma of electrified argon gas, in a box ten centimetres wide. The grains spontaneously arranged themselves in a neat honeycomb pattern, just like atoms in a crystal but spaced a fraction of a millimetre apart. When lit by a laser beam, the astonishing objects could be seen with the naked eye.

The Garching scientists were not alone in producing plasma crystals on the ground. Independently, other teams in Taiwan, Japan and Germany had similar success. By 1996 a team at the Russian Institute for High Energy Densities was making plasma crystals with a different technique. In place of a high-frequency generator for electrifying the gas, the Russians used a direct-current discharge.

In those pioneering experiments, the plasma crystals were flat, because of the levitation required. The Garching team then undertook preliminary trials under weightless conditions, in short-lived rocket flights and aircraft dives. These confirmed that 3-D plasma crystals could be made in space, just as Morfill had predicted in proposing the space-station experiments.

'Plasmas are the most disorganized form of matter—that was the common wisdom,' Morfill commented. 'To discover that they can also exist in crystallized form was, therefore, a major surprise. In a relatively young research field like plasma physics you have to expect surprises, of course, but somehow you always think that the major discoveries will be made by others. To actually see the plasma crystallization happen, for the first time, was an exhilarating experience.'

The co-leader of the experiment on the International Space Station, Anatoli Nefedov of Russia's Institute for High Energy Densities, died just a few weeks before space operations began in March 2001. So the project was renamed *Plasmakristallexperiment-Nefedov*. Tended by cosmonauts, dozens of experiments provided researchers on the ground with movies and measurements of the behaviour of plasma crystals in weightless conditions. They watched matter performing in ways seen only sketchily before, or not at all.

In space, plasma crystals usually form with holes in the middle, like doughnuts, and the holes are very sharp-edged. If a disturbance fills a hole, it quickly re-forms. The grains make 3-D assemblies, arranged in various symmetric patterns, similar to those shown by atoms in different crystals.

When mixed grains of two different sizes are injected into the plasma, they sort themselves out to make two plasma crystals, each with only one size of grain. Where they meet, the crystals weld together, with the boundary between them strangely bent. Hit the crystals with a puff of neutral gas, and a very sharply defined shock wave will travel through them.

If one side of the chamber is warmer than the other, a stronger wind of molecules comes from that side and pushes the plasma crystal towards the cooler side. Used on the ground, this thermal effect provides an alternative to an electric field, for countering gravity and levitating the plasma crystals. A warm floor and a cold ceiling in the experimental chamber will keep the plasma crystals floating comfortably for hours on end.

The strange phenomena made sense, thanks to theories that developed in parallel with the preparation of the experiments. Vadim Tsytovich of Russia's General Physics Institute had predicted the sharp boundaries of the plasma crystals and the separations of particles of different sizes. He and Morfill together developed a more refined theory, called the collective shadow effect, which operates through the whole plasma crystal and not just between neighbouring grains. This plays its part within a more general scenario by Morfill and Tsytovich concerning the instabilities in dusty plasmas that drive them to make structures.

Helping to make the Earth

An early surprise in the experiments on the International Space Station was that dust grains acquire electric charges even when injected into a neutral gas. Some grains gather an excess of positive charges (ions) from the gas, and others more negative charges (electrons). In effect, the grains make their own plasma.

As a result the grains attract one another by the ordinary electric force, with a clump accumulating 100,000 grains in a second. That is a million times faster than you'd expect just by the collision of uncharged grains. If this phenomenon had been noticed sooner, as an alternative explanation for the rapid growth of dust grains, then plasma crystals and the shadow force might have remained unknown. Which would have been a pity, because large areas of science and engineering will feel the effects of this discovery.

In the story of the shadow force and dust power, plasma crystals are a half-way house towards large dust grains. When the plasma pressure overwhelms the repulsion between small grains, a plasma crystal cannot survive. Instead the dust grains coalesce and grow rapidly, in the space around stars. And as a new force in the cosmos, dust power has consequences going beyond mere dust itself.

To make stars and planets, a cloud of dusty gas collapses under the pull of its own gravity. The cloud must be large and massive enough for gravity to grasp, and a theory dating from 1928, by the British astronomer James Jeans, defined the critical size. But by 2000 Robert Bingham of the UK's Rutherford Appleton Laboratory, in collaboration with Tsytovich, was pointing out that, in interstellar space, the force drawing dust grains together is initially far stronger than gravity. It operates over smaller volumes, and marshals the dust much more rapidly than gravity grabs the gas.

'We suspect that the shadow force operates in relatively dense interstellar clouds to build comets and all the small bodies used in planet-making,' Bingham said. 'If we're right, the Earth was being prefabricated when the Sun was still only a gassy possibility.'

Effects may continue today in the Earth's atmosphere. Dusty plasma—electrified gas containing small solid particles—is produced by meteors burning up in the atmosphere, and also by dust from the surface mixing with air electrified by lightning strokes, ultraviolet rays from the Sun, and cosmic rays from the Galaxy. Dust grains play a daily role in providing the nuclei on which water condenses or freezes, to make rain and snow. Whether the shadow force speeds their growth to an effective size, for cloud formation, is a now a matter for investigation.

● Smart dust

Plasma crystals give scientists the chance to study analogues of atomic latticework on a vastly enlarged scale. Fundamental processes of crystallization and melting in ordinary materials will be clarified. Perhaps research on the shadow force will help the fusion engineers and microchip manufacturers to escape from their dusty difficulties.

The plasma crystals may suggest how to make materials of new kinds. But they are already a fascinating novelty in their own right. In their ability to interact with electricity, magnetism, light, radio waves or sound waves, plasma crystals could create novel sensors or tools.

So scientists speculate about smart dust. In sizing up the consequences and opportunities of plasma crystals and dust power, the imagination is strongly challenged. In Fred Hoyle's science-fiction tale of *The Black Cloud* (1957) an intelligent interstellar medium appeared. As a leading theorist of plasma crystals, Tsytovich, too, toyed with the notion of living dust.

'Imagine a large, self-organizing structure of plasma crystals floating in an interstellar cloud,' he said. 'Feeding on the dusty plasma, it can grow and make copies of itself. The complex structure has a memory, but it can mutate and evolve very rapidly—for example in competition with similar structures. Should we not say it is alive?'

▶ *See also* MOLECULES IN SPACE. *For other discoveries provoked by dusty stars and electric devices, see* BUCKYBALLS AND NANOTUBES.

PLATE MOTIONS

What rocky machinery refurbishes the Earth's surface?

PROFITS FROM DANISH LAGER paid for a round-the-world expedition by the research ship *Dana*, from 1928 to 1930. So when, in the Indian Ocean, the onboard scientists detected a chain of underwater mountains running south-east from the Gulf of Aden at the exit from the Red Sea, they gratefully named it the Carlsberg Ridge. For investigators of the solid Earth, that obscure basaltic hump became the equivalent of Charles Darwin's Galapagos Islands, sparking a revolution in knowledge.

The Carlsberg Ridge was only the second feature of its kind to be discovered. A few years previously the German research ship *Meteor* had explored a similar ridge in the middle of the Atlantic, first encountered by ships laying telegraph cables across the ocean in the 19th century. Using ultrasound generators developed for hunting submarines, but adapted into hydrographical echo sounders, ocean scientists gradually revealed more and more mid-ocean ridges, each of them a long mountain chain. By the 1960s they were known in all the world's oceans, with a total length of 65,000 kilometres, and geography was transformed.

The Carlsberg Ridge showed more subtle features. First, in 1933–34, a British expedition in *John Murray* found that the ridge was also a rift. It was curiously like the Great Rift Valley in nearby East Africa, with bulging sides and a deep gully running down the middle.

In 1962 Drummond Matthews, a scientist from Cambridge, was in the Indian Ocean aboard a borrowed naval ship, *Owen*. It towed a magnetic instrument behind it as it passed to and fro over the Carlsberg Ridge. Sensitive magnetometers, devised initially to detect the steel hulls of submerged submarines, were at that time an innovation in geophysics.

Elsewhere the magnetometers had revealed strange patterns of stripes on the ocean floor, such that the magnetism was sometimes stronger, sometimes weaker. US expeditions surveyed large areas of the Pacific, without making sense of the patterns. Matthews decided to undertake a close inspection of part of the Carlsberg Ridge. Again he found a mixture of strong and weak fields, and when he returned to Cambridge he gave the data to a graduate student, Fred Vine, to try to interpret.

Not long before, Vine had heard a visitor from Princeton, Harry Hess, speaking at a students' geology congress in Cambridge about sea-floor spreading. The suggestion was that rock welling up at the mid-ocean ridges would spread outwards on either side, making the ocean gradually wider. It was an idea with no evidence to support it, and very few adherents, least of all in Hess's homeland. But while studying the magnetic data from the Carlsberg Ridge, Vine had a brainwave.

If molten rock emerges at a mid-ocean ridge and then cools down, it becomes magnetized by the prevailing magnetic field, thereby intensifying the magnetism measured by a ship cruising over it. Earlier in the century Bernard Brunhes in France and Motonori Matuyama in Japan had discovered that the Earth reverses its magnetism every so often, swapping around its north and south magnetic poles. Rock that cooled during a period of reversed magnetism will be magnetized in the opposite direction, so altering the Earth's field as measured by a passing ship.

To the sea floor spreading outwards from the mid-ocean ridge, as Hess proposed, Vine added this notion of magnetization on freezing. His inspiration was to see that the sea floor acts like a tape recorder, with the sectors of strong and weak magnetism telling of their formation at different times. 'If spreading of the ocean floor occurs,' Vine wrote in a landmark paper, 'blocks of alternately normal and reversely magnetized material would drift away from the centre of the ridge and lie parallel to the crest of it.'

Vine recalled later that when he showed his draft to a leading marine geophysicist at the Cambridge lab, 'he just looked at me and went on to talk about something else.' The head of the lab, Edward Bullard, was less discouraging but demurred from putting his name to the paper. If so crazy a notion from a graduate student was to have any hope of publication, respectable support was needed. Matthews, who supplied the magnetic data from the Carlsberg Ridge, agreed to be co-author and thereby earned his own place in scientific history.

The world turned upside down

On its publication in 1963, the Vine–Matthews paper was greeted at first with a stony silence from the world's experts. How could the sea floor spread unless continents moved to make room for it? Everyone except a few mavericks, mostly in Europe, knew perfectly well that the continents had been rooted to their spots since the creation of the world.

There followed the most comprehensive overthrow of previous beliefs to occur in science during the 20th century. The next few years brought vindication of Vine's idea of the magnetic tape recorder, confirmation of continental drift, and

PLATE MOTIONS

a brand-new theory called plate tectonics. A key contribution came in 1965 from
Tuzo Wilson at Toronto. He realized that some of the long fault-lines seen in
the ocean floor are made by large pieces of the Earth's outer shell sliding past
one another.

Together with the ridges where the sea floor is manufactured, and with deep
ocean trenches where old sea floor dives underground for recycling, Wilson's
transform faults help to define the outlines of great moving plates into which
the outer shell of the Earth is divided. The plate boundaries are the scenes of
most of the world's earthquakes and active volcanoes. Dan McKenzie of
Cambridge and Jason Morgan of Princeton developed the formal mathematical
theory of plate tectonics in 1967–68.

The story that began in Her Majesty's Ship *Owen* over the Carlsberg Ridge in
1962 climaxed in 1969 when another vessel, the US drilling ship *Glomar
Challenger*, began penetrating deep into the sediments of the ocean floor. The
eminent scientists who still believed that the oceans were primordial features
of the planet expected billions of years of Earth history to be recorded in thick
deposits. Instead, *Glomar Challenger*'s drill-bit hit the basaltic bedrock quite
quickly.

Near the ridges, the sediments go back only a few million years. They are
progressively older towards the ocean margins, just as you'd expect in basins
growing from the middle outwards, by sea-floor spreading. Everywhere they
date from less than 200 million years ago. The Earth's surface refurbishes itself
continuously, directly in the oceans that cover most of the planet, and by what
are literally knock-on effects in the continents.

Seven large plates account for 94 per cent of the Earth's surface. In descending
order of size they are the Pacific, African, Eurasian, Indo-Australian, North
American, Antarctic and South American Plates. Small plates make up the rest,
the main ones being the Philippine, Arabian and Caribbean Plates, lying roughly
where their names indicate, plus the Cocos and Nazca Plates, which are oceanic
plates located west of Central and South America.

The plates shuffle about at a few centimetres per year, roughly the speed at
which your fingernails grow. Even at that rate the momentum is terrific and the
plates jostle one another very forcibly. They also transport the mighty continents
in all directions, like so many lunches on cafeteria trays.

Plate motions and continental drift are directly measurable, by fixing the relative
positions of stations on different continents and seeing how they change as the
years pass. Ordinary navigational satellites, used with special care, do the job
surprisingly well. So does laser ranging to NASA's Lageos satellite, fitted with
cat's-eye reflectors. The fanciest method of gauging the plate motions compares
the exact arrival times, at radio telescopes scattered around the world, of radio

waves coming across billions of light-years of space from the quasars, which are giant black holes.

Looking for the rocky motor

After the revolution, while geologists and geophysicists were hurriedly rewriting their textbooks in terms of plate tectonics, two fundamental questions remained. The first, still totally obscure, is why the Earth's magnetism reverses, to produce the patterns spotted by Vine. Explanation is the more difficult because of great variations in the rate of reversals, from 0 to 6 per million years. If we lived in a magnetically tranquil phase, such as prevailed 100 million years ago, the tape recorder of the Carlsberg Ridge would be blank.

The second basic question is why the plates move. The idea of rocks flowing is not at all unacceptable, even though they are very viscous of course. Given time, they yield to pressure, as you can see in the crumpled strata of mountain ranges and the squashed fossils they contain. What's more, a slushy, semi-molten layer of rocks beneath the plates, called the asthenosphere, eases their motions, and lubrication at plate boundaries comes from water.

Nor is there any problem in principle about a power supply for moving the plates about on the face of the Earth. Internal heat first provided during the formation of the planet, by the amalgamation and settling of material under gravity, is sustained by energy released by radioactive materials present in the rocks of the Earth's interior. You can think of all activity at the surface as a direct or indirect result of heat trying to escape. Eventually it will succeed to such an extent that the planet will freeze, as its neighbour Mars has done already, and geological action will cease.

A pan of water carries heat from the stove to the air, by the hottest water rising and cooled water sinking back again. Convection of a similar kind must operate, however sluggishly, inside the Earth. Even so, the mechanism that translates heat flow and convection into plate motions has been a matter of much conjecture and argument ever since the dawn of plate tectonics. It's not easy to tell what's going on, deep below the ground we stand on.

The distance from the Earth's surface to the centre is 6400 kilometres. The record-breaking Kola Superdeep Borehole, near Zapolyarny in northern Russia, goes down just 12 kilometres. So everything scientists know about the interior has to be inferred from data collectable very near the surface. That includes figuring out what rocky motor propels the plates.

Earthquake waves have for long been the chief illuminators of the Earth's interior. By timing their arrivals at various stations around the world, seismologists can deduce how fast they have travelled, and by what routes. Beneath the crust, typically 40 kilometres thick, the main body of the Earth is the rocky mantle. At a depth of 2900 kilometres, not quite half-way to the centre, the mantle floats on a liquid core of molten iron and other elements. Within the liquid core is a small solid core, 5000 kilometres down.

The disagreement that arose among Earth scientists concerned the role of the mantle in driving plate motions. According to some, the whole mantle was involved. In what became the most popular view, the driving heat comes all the way from the mantle–core boundary, carried by plumes of hot rocks rising to the surface. Other scientists thought that only the uppermost part of the mantle plays any direct part in the convection that propels the plates, and that their action largely drives itself.

Seeing the Earth in slices

Advances in seismology were expected to settle this issue. The subject flourished in the late 20th century, because the Cold War brought a requirement for detecting nuclear weapons tests, which send out earthquake-like waves. A subsequent aim to monitor a comprehensive test-ban treaty ensured continuing governmental support for seismologists and their global networks of stations. Travel times for the earthquake waves detected at different stations revealed cold slabs sinking in the mantle, through which the waves went faster than usual, and warm rocks rising, where they travelled more slowly.

In the 1990s, computers became powerful enough to use data from natural earthquakes to paint very pretty 3-D pictures of the mantle. The technique, called seismic tomography, uses the same principle as the computer-aided tomography, or CAT scans, which revolutionized medical X-ray techniques in the 1980s. It builds up a 3-D image by observing the same features from different angles, in a series of slices.

The trouble was that the pictures revealed by seismic tomography were somewhat blurred, and a bit like the inkblot tests used by psychologists. What the experts saw in them depended to some extent on what they expected. And if they didn't like what they saw, or failed to see, they could try reprocessing or reinterpreting the data.

By the end of the century Don Anderson of Caltech, one of the founders of seismic tomography, took the view that whole-mantle convection was disproved. He saw no evidence for hot rocks rising from great depths through the mantle. On the contrary, the tomographic images seemed to him to show the mantle divided into layers, presumably with rocks in different chemical or physical states, which would tend to repress intermingling of the layers by convection.

'Smoke escaping through an igloo's roof from an Eskimo's fireplace identifies the cracks, not the location of the fireplace,' Anderson declared. By that he meant that heat in the form of molten rocks rising to the surface comes up wherever it can, at the mid-ocean ridges, and pushes the plates along, while pieces of plates that have cooled and are sinking back into the Earth at the ocean trenches help by dragging them along.

In Anderson's scheme, which he called top-down tectonics, the state of the deep mantle is not the cause of activity near the surface, but a result of it. Using the energy available in the uppermost part of the mantle the plate motions organize themselves, without reference to the underlying mantle, except to the extent that concentrations of mass inside the planet can create a variable gravitational field that stresses the plates. The existence of a dozen long-lived plates is not a fluke, but a natural number for a self-organizing convective system.

'Earth dynamics is probably much simpler than we think,' Anderson said. But his reasoning didn't settle the issue. The majority of theorists of the Earth's interior, who had for long favoured all-mantle convection as the driver of the plates, were not going to roll over without a fight.

Gravity opens a window from space

When geophysical theories are at odds, you need a better way of looking at the Earth. At the dawn of plate tectonics, sensitive magnetometers unexpectedly made possible the discovery of sea-floor spreading. And other methods of studying the Earth's interior still have scope for improvement too.

Supporting seismology are laboratory studies of the behaviour of rocky materials under high temperatures and pressures such as prevail deep down. Changes in the speed of seismic waves can be due, not to changes from hot to cold, but to switches in the composition or state of the rocks at different depths. Other evidence comes from measurements of heat flow from the ground. And the proportions of atoms of the same element but different atomic weights— isotopes—have much to say about the experiences of the rocks in which they are found.

In the quest for a better definition of the mantle, an innovation in a very old method of probing the Earth may tip the scales. This is the variation of the strength of gravity from place to place. Early in the 21st century, high hopes rode on a European satellite called GOCE, being prepared for launch in 2006, and using a new way to measure gravity from space. It would help to make the Earth more transparent.

The history of gravity in geophysics goes back to 1735, when Pierre Bouguer from Paris tried to measure the mass of the mountains in the Andes, by seeing them pull a plumb line sideways by their gravitational attraction. The deflection was ridiculously small—'much smaller than that to be expected from the mass represented by the mountains,' Bouguer complained. It was as if they were hollow. Not until 1851 did George Airy at the Royal Greenwich

Observatory explain correctly that the Andes and other great mountains don't pull their weight because they are supported on deep roots of relatively low density.

Measuring the local strength of gravity, and its variations from place to place, became a survey technique for geologists and geophysicists, first with pendulums and then with more convenient gravimeters using a weight on a spring, or an electronic accelerometer. Like seismology, gravimetry could reveal features hidden beneath the surface. For example, a deep-sunk basin where oil might be found stands out as a region of weak gravity because of the relatively low density of sedimentary rocks.

Outstanding among the pioneers of gravity measurements was Loránd Eötvös of Budapest. He began work in 1885 with his instrument of choice, the torsion balance, in which a horizontal rod hangs from the end of a fibre and swings from side to side. Working with exquisite accuracy (achieved at the expense of much time and patience) Eötvös measured not only the strength of gravity but also its variation in space from one side of the instrument to the other. His gradiometry, as the technique is called, detected even the variation of the variation.

In the 1920s the Diving Dutchman, Felix Vening Meinesz from Utrecht, used a pendulum in a naval submarine to measure gravity at sea. He discovered an amazing weakness south of Java, which can now be interpreted as a result of the ocean floor diving into the Earth in the deep Java Trench. Half a century later, the ocean trenches and mid-ocean ridges were plain to see in an image from the American satellite Seasat, which had a short but influential life in 1978.

Feeling the level of the sea with its radar altimeter, Seasat revealed humps and hollows corresponding with the strength of gravity in different oceanic regions. They mimicked, on a scale of metres, the humps and hollows of the ocean floor, which have a vertical scale of thousands of metres. The seawater is attracted to regions of strong gravity, like those made by the dense basalt welling up at the mid-ocean ridges, but to a small degree it shuns the weak gravity over the trenches.

To generate from the Seasat data what was virtually a diagram of the major plate boundaries under the oceans, William Haxby of Columbia had to ignore much bigger differences in sea level due to concentrations of mass and relatively 'hollow' regions, deep inside the Earth. They raise the sea by 70 metres north of New Guinea, and lower it by 100 metres south of India. These and other regional differences disturb the orbits of satellites, speeding them up as they approach the places where gravity is strongest.

An early hope in the Space Age was that the global picture of gravity variations, emerging from a combination of satellite tracking and radar altimetry, would weigh the various regions of the Earth's interior and so reveal the motor driving the plate motions. Certainly the picture that emerged seemed to show warm rocks rising and cold rocks sinking, deep inside the Earth. Yet these had no obvious connection with the manifest up-flows and down-flows seen near the surface, at plate boundaries.

Geophysicists describe the strength of gravity in terms of the local height of an imaginary ocean covering the whole planet, called the geoid. By the end of the 20th century, thanks to radar altimeters on European and US–French satellites, the geoid's shape was known with an accuracy of 50–80 centimetres, averaged over regions about 300 kilometres wide. Slightly imprecise tracking of the satellites limited the accuracy, whilst the high altitudes of the satellites (800 and 1300 kilometres) ruled out regional measurements on a smaller scale.

In 1986 Reiner Rummel of the Technische Universität München, together with Georges Balmino of the French Centre National d'Études Spatiales, urged the use of a radically different method of measuring gravity with a satellite. Instead of gauging its variations by changes in the satellite's behaviour, they said, let's measure the gravity directly with an onboard instrument.

At first hearing that seems silly, because a satellite is in a weightless state of free fall. But in fact the Earth's gravity is not exactly the same everywhere within the satellite. There are slight variations in different directions detectable by gradiometry, as first demonstrated on the ground by Eötvös a century before.

With help from a team of colleagues from several countries, and from various branches of the Earth sciences, Rummel and Balmino persuaded the European Space Agency to build the necessary satellite. Named GOCE, it was scheduled to fly in 2006, in an orbit 250 kilometres above the Earth, carrying three pairs of sensitive accelerometers half a metre apart, to gauge differences in gravity in all directions.

'By the time the satellite has completed two years of operations in orbit, the uncertainty about the gravitational shape of the Earth will be reduced to about a centimetre, over regions defined to within 80 kilometres,' Rummel said. 'GOCE will open a new window on the Earth's deep interior and reveal domains of rocks that move about far under our feet. As the seismologists don't agree about them, maybe we can help.'

No one expected GOCE or any other innovative gravity satellite of the early 21st century to solve the puzzle of the Earth's motor single-handedly. On the contrary, the idea was to pool the results with seismic and other data, to try to arrive at just one picture that agrees with all the evidence. If that's successful, the driving force of plate motions may at last become clear, 40 years after their discovery.

PREDATORS

▶ *For an interplanetary perspective, and the question of why there are no plate motions on the sister planet Venus, see* EARTH. *For the origin and status of the mantle plume theory, see* HOTSPOTS. *For another aspect of it, and a possible extraterrestrial connection with plate motions, see* FLOOD BASALTS. *Manifestations of plate motions figure in* EARTHQUAKES, VOLCANIC EXPLOSIONS *and* CONTINENTS AND SUPERCONTINENTS. *For life adapted to mid-ocean plate boundaries, see* EXTREMOPHILES. *For oceanographic uses of gravity satellites, see* OCEAN CURRENTS.

PREDATORS

Come back Brer Wolf, all is forgiven

W HEN THE ASTROPHYSICIST HERMANN BONDI accepted the invitation to head the UK's newly reorganized Natural Environment Research Council in 1980, his only complaint was about the name. With Einsteinian perspicacity he said, 'There is no natural environment in this country.' In the light of subsequent research he could have added that this was self-evident from the absence of bears, wolves or any other large, fierce animals in the British countryside.

Undisturbed wilderness is very rare on Planet Earth. When environmentalists take action to protect, for example, the flooded peat-pits or reclaimed marshes of eastern England, they are fighting for a man-made status quo. The same is true in the secondary forests of New England, or the systematically burnt grasslands of Kansas or Kenya. Almost the entire land surface of the globe has felt the human touch.

Even if it hadn't, who can confidently define what should be cherished and protected, when Nature, too, plays non-stop games? These are evident every time a volcano erupts, destroying vegetation, or bursts out of the sea as an island, creating new living space. Most drastic are the cyclical changes of climate in the current series of ice ages. While glaciers bulldoze forests at high latitudes and altitudes, reduced rainfall decimates them in the tropics. The sea level falls, uncovering new land on the continental margins, only to rise again when the ice retreats, and to leave former hilltops as remade islands with depleted wildlife.

To say so is certainly not to condone mindless damage to the living environment. Disturbances by human activity and natural change carry stern lessons about unexpected consequences. But they complicate the science for field biologists who have to try to understand how communities of plants, animals and microbes function as ecosystems.

The various communities under study around the world are in different states of disturbance. That is one reason why the fundamentals of ecology are still controversial. Generalizations are difficult, perhaps sometimes inept. In certain settings, like the great reserves of Africa or the forests of northern Canada, big cats or bears or other large predators plainly command the ecosystems. By controlling the numbers of herbivorous animals they prevent excessive destruction of the vegetation.

This is called top-down regulation. But it can be bottom-up in many other cases, where plant communities have reacted to overgrazing by replacing favoured browse species with poisonous or otherwise unpalatable ones. In another mode of response, some herbivorous animals control their destruction of vegetation by limiting their birth rates.

'Ecosystems going crazy'

Large-scale disturbances occurring in our own time provide opportunities to analyse their effects. In Venezuela, the damming of the Caroní River for a hydroelectric complex has, since 1986, turned many hilltops of a semi-deciduous, tropical dry forest into an archipelago of islands in the huge Lago Guri. Within a few years, the smallest islands became fantastic caricatures of the communities of plants and animals on the mainland and the largest islands.

'The Guri archipelago is almost unique in the world due to its topography that created so many new islands in a fertile tropical environment,' commented Mailén Riveros Caballero from the Museo de Ciencias in Caracas. 'We were fortunate, too, that experts from other countries had the opportunity for an important study. We started investigating right after the flooding, so we were able to watch ecosystems going crazy—which is regrettable but very instructive no doubt.'

The forest on one small island was reduced to a film of rodent dung. Other small islands were taken over by leaf-cutter ants. On somewhat larger islands, monkeys wiped out most of the birds. But the common feature was the absence of jaguars, pumas, harpy eagles, anteating armadillos and other predators on all of the smallest islands, letting the seed-eating rodents, leaf-cutter ants and monkeys run amok.

Riveros herself made a special study of the rodents, the diet and behaviour of which was previously unknown. 'Our goal is to observe the early effects of this great perturbation and to know how the surviving animals subsist under the new conditions,' she said. 'The disappearances of populations of fauna and flora are well known from many island studies, but this scenery provides an ideal ecological laboratory for describing what happens.'

By watching the events on the Guri archipelago, the multinational team could affirm that the crazy ecosystems were responding to the removal of top-down control—which therefore seems to be more fundamental. The implications for ecology are wholesale. Large predators have recently disappeared in most parts of the world, leaving them in an 'unnatural' bottom-up condition.

The exterminations began with the spread of the superskilled hunters of our own kind to every habitable continent during the past 50,000 years. They were aggravated by climate change and sea-level rise after the most recent ice age ended about 11,000 years ago. Many subsequent ecological changes and loss of species, hitherto blamed on climate variations or on the spread of farming, may have been due primarily to the loss of predators. The recent widespread protection of deer and other Disneyesque herbivores from human predation owes more to sentiment than to science, and has only made matters worse for the ecosystems.

The case for rewilding

'Interactions with the top predators cascade down through the ecosystem,' declared John Terborgh of Duke University, North Carolina, who led the programme in Venezuela. He called the situation on the Guri archipelago 'ecological meltdown'. And he was not slow to point to parallels in his home territory in the eastern USA, where the days when Davy Crockett could kill himself a bear in the oak–hickory forest have long-since gone. The white-tailed deer have increased about tenfold in population density, and they have fed uncurbed on the oak and hickory seeds and seedlings. Maples and tulip poplars have filled the gaps.

'The entire character of the predominant vegetation cover in the eastern half of the continent is being distorted by too few predators,' Terborgh said. 'Oaks are our prime timber species. They are worth billions of dollars, and we're losing them because we lost wolves and mountain lions.'

Will wiser generations in future restore the big carnivores, for the sake of a less unnatural environment? Whether it was fear, jealousy or just men showing off that led to their extermination in many places, circumstances have recently changed for the better in some respects. A combination of rising agricultural productivity and a slow-down in global population growth may make possible a huge reversion to semi-wild conditions in many of the world's landscapes. Tourists in vehicles resistant to tooth and claw can pick up the tabs.

No Jurassic Park is needed to bring the big jaws back to life. Canadians, for example, still co-exist cheerfully and mostly harm-free with bears and wolves.

Elsewhere, population explosions of deer or rabbits freed from predation have usually proved to be far more troublesome to rural and suburban human life than any big predators. Road accidents involving deer kill far more people than bears and rattlesnakes do, in the USA, and diseases carried by the deer now include a brain-attacking prion similar to that of mad cow disease.

Large and interconnected reserves will be required, to give the top predators the secure refuges and the extensive geographical ranges that they need. In a manifesto for such rewilding with big carnivores, Michael Soulé of UC Santa Cruz and Reed Noss of *Wild Earth* wrote: 'A cynic might describe rewilding as an atavistic obsession with the resurrection of Eden. A more sympathetic critic might label it romantic. We contend, however, that rewilding is simply scientific realism, assuming that our goal is to insure the long-term integrity of the land community.'

Action has begun, although so far in the name of species preservation rather than the ecological system. In the face of much political and legal wrangling, the US Department of the Interior authorized the reintroduction of wolves into Yellowstone National Park and by 2002 there were about 20 thriving dens. When a few wolves wandered into Sweden from Finland and Russia, the government decided to let the population grow to 200 at least, and see what happened.

▶ *For more on ecology, see* BIODIVERSITY, ECO-EVOLUTION *and* HUMAN ECOLOGY.

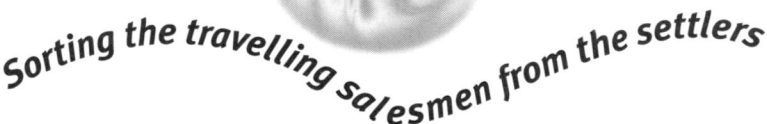

PREHISTORIC GENES

Sorting the travelling salesmen from the settlers

METEOROLOGY AND GENETICS combined to resolve an argument about the origin of the Polynesians, who during the past 2000 years populated the islands of the broad Pacific, like daring space-travellers in search of new planets to live on. In 1947, a seagoing ethnologist, Thor Heyerdahl of Norway, popularized the proposition that the Polynesians came from South America.

On *Kon-Tiki*, a balsa raft built on primitive lines, he and a small crew made a westward voyage from Peru to the island of Raroia to prove that it was possible. Related in a book and documentary movie, the adventure enchanted the public.

It annoyed the archaeologists, anthropologists and linguists who for many years had amassed evidence that the Polynesians spread eastwards from New Guinea. Called the Lapita people, they took as shipmates domesticated chickens and pigs unknown in the Americas at the time.

Science is full of tales of mavericks taking on the experts and winning, but Heyerdahl was not one of them. The strongest argument in his favour was that *Kon-Tiki* went the easy way, nautically speaking. Trade winds blowing from the east, and a west-going ocean current, carried the raft along. How could simple craft, made with stone-age tools, have gone in the other direction? In fact the trick had been explained to the 17th-century explorer James Cook, by a Polynesian canoe-pilot, Tupa'ia of Tahiti. You just waited for a wind with a bit of west in it, typically in November to January.

That became clearer when 20th-century meteorologists familiarized themselves with El Niño. The intermittent upheaval in the Pacific weather is associated with a warming of the equatorial ocean and a faltering of the trade winds. At such times a decent sailing canoe (not a balsa raft) could certainly make headway eastwards. Other seagoing ethnologists, this time from the University of Hawaii, proved the point by building a replica of a Polynesian canoe and sailing eastwards from Samoa to Tahiti in 1986.

Meanwhile the issue of origins had been settled, to the satisfaction of some, by comparisons between the blood groups of the Polynesians and other populations around the world. By the simplest interpretation these pointed to an Asian origin. Some genetic doubts remained, not unfavourable for the Heyerdahl hypothesis.

In 1990 an Oxford geneticist, Bryan Sykes, became interested in the Polynesians during a casual stopover in the Cook Islands. He begged some leftover blood samples from a local hospital. Back in his Oxford lab he used fancy new tricks to find and read genes inherited only via the mothers. A return trip to the Pacific proved necessary, but then Sykes announced overwhelming genetic evidence for the main Lapita wave of navigators spreading eastwards. In one individual he found an earlier lineage of New Guinea inhabitants who went along for the ride.

The currents of humanity

Genetic studies of human prehistory were foreshadowed during the First World War. That was when the Polish brothers Ludwik and Hann Hirszfeld noticed that the proportions of blood of different groups (A, B, AB or O) needed for treating wounded soldiers depended on where they came from. By 1964, knowing much more about both blood groups and their worldwide distributions, Luca Cavalli-Sforza and Anthony Edwards in Pavia constructed the first family tree of the human species, from statistics of the relative frequencies of the blood groups.

Big ambiguities remained, but they diminished as Cavalli-Sforza continued the work in the USA, at Stanford, using many more blood samples and the new genetic riches of tissue-typing genes called HLA. With Alberto Piazza from Turin he developed more reliable techniques for making trees, from the genetic statistics from different regions. Underpinning the analysis was the theory of random genetic drift.

If you start with a population possessing alternative versions of genes (for ABO blood groups for example), the proportions of the various alternative versions will change with time, simply by chance. When the population subdivides into dispersed groups that no longer interbreed because of geographical separation, the passage of time will make the gene frequencies different in the various groups.

The biggest differences arise if the dispersing populations are initially very small. Then some versions of genes are so scarce that they will die out. Native Americans, for example, seem to be descended from small founder bands that crossed the Bering Strait from Asia at the end of the last ice age, and left the B blood group behind. It is almost absent in Native Americans. New mutations that survive in a population are so rare that they cannot have played much part in the genetic differences between human groups.

The primary message from Cavalli-Sforza's analysis was that all the data fitted neatly with a single original population from which all human beings alive today are descended. This was in bold opposition to a still-prevalent, essentially racist idea that the major regional groupings of humankind evolved independently from primitive *Homo erectus* ancestors.

The genetic geography blew away centuries of misconceptions based on colouring and other features. Skin colour and the shapes of skulls had led anthropologists to lump Africans and Native Australians together, yet genetically they are the most widely separated of all human beings alive today. An alleged kinship of Europeans, Chinese and Native Americans was also contradicted by the genetics.

The explanation for the discrepancies between the genetics and the physical anthropology is that superficial features are exactly those most likely to adapt to local climate. Most conspicuously, dark skins give protection against skin cancer due to solar ultraviolet rays. At high latitudes dark-skinned people may be more vulnerable to rickets, a bone defect due to a lack of vitamin D, made by ultraviolet penetrating the skin.

'Here at Stanford we see a great deal of people of many different racial origins,' Cavalli-Sforza remarked in 1973. 'It's interesting to know that these differences we see are literally skin deep.'

By 1988, Cavalli-Sforza and Piazza, with Paolo Menozzi of Parma, had constructed an evolutionary tree for 42 aboriginal populations worldwide, based on an analysis of variants of 120 genes. It translated into migration routes, starting with departures from Africa perhaps 100,000 years ago. One current of modern humanity headed to China and south-east Asia, where some settled and others pressed on, to Australia and New Guinea. Others went north, and then split again. Those veering east populated Japan and north-east Asia—and also the Americas, with the most dogged travellers completing the trek from Africa in Tierra del Fuego and Greenland.

Meanwhile, north-west-heading folk became Europeans and other so-called Caucasoids, some of whom doubled back into North Africa, or trooped off to Iran and India. This history of world-encompassing derring-do, recorded in the genes, fitted rather well with archaeological evidence and also with linguistics, where there was a broad match between genetic clusters and families of languages.

Piazza and Menozzi set genetics on the road to tracing a three-way link between genes, climate and disease. Colleagues had already seen emphatic associations between the HLA tissue-typing genes and the incidence of particular medical conditions. For example, the HLA combination A3-B7-DR2 predisposes the owner of the genes to multiple sclerosis. Piazza and Menozz found that, globally, A3 is common in cold climates, while B7 is rare in very wet and humid environments.

'The relatively high prevalence of multiple sclerosis apparent in northern Europe may therefore be interpretable as a price paid for adaptation to a cooler climate during human evolution,' Piazza said. 'Thus we begin to find that the susceptibility to disease in different populations has been influenced by the environments experienced by their ancestors.'

Grandmother Eve in Africa

The impressive results of all this genetic geography concealed a technical, nay philosophical pitfall. What did 'aboriginal' mean? Common sense dictated that blood samples were collected from people who appeared to be local—for example, not from pink people in the South Seas, nor from dark-skinned Urdu-fluent folk in Europe. This method tacitly accepted the existence of races as commonly understood. To call them ethnic groups or regional populations, or to stress that the similarities between all human beings far outweighed their minor variations, still left the methodology begging the question of race.

Just across San Francisco Bay from Stanford, where Cavalli-Sforza worked, Allan Wilson and his students at UC Berkeley developed a sharper and more objective way of tracing human prehistory by genetics. They used mother-only genes, known technically as mitochondrial DNA. The little egg-shaped powerhouses inside your living cells, the mitochondria, have their own independent genes, and you inherited them exclusively from your mother.

Unlike the commonest genes of heredity, which inhabit the cell nucleus and come from both parents in ever-shuffled combinations, the mother-only genes are identical in your brothers and sisters. They do, however, accumulate mutations over many generations—much faster in fact than the nuclear genes do. And the mutations either die out for lack of female descendants, or survive from generation to generation. There are no fuzzy statistics involved, as was the case with genetic drift changing the frequencies of blood groups and tissue-typing genes, in populations. We're talking of individuals now, and unambiguous lines of descent.

The mother-only genes are like a recipe for a favourite pudding copied by the girl-children of every generation since time immemorial. The ingredients remain the same, but now and again someone makes a spelling mistake, or doodles a picture, and all her female descendants faithfully copy the changed version— errors, doodles and all. If you compared your own mother's pudding recipe with that of a friend's mother, you could tell at once how closely or distantly you and your friend are related, according to how similar or different the recipes looked. Relatedness on the fathers' sides doesn't count here, so that children of two brothers might seem to be genetic strangers by this test.

In 1987, Wilson and his colleagues examined the mother-only genes in 134 individuals from around the world. They found remarkable similarities as well as differences in all the recipes. Every one of them had exactly the same grandmother—a real-life individual—who lived an estimated 150,000 years ago. She was immediately nicknamed Eve.

She probably lived in Africa, because the most ancient mutations were found in people living in that continent today. Here was emphatic support for Cavalli-Sforza's proposition about a common origin for everyone, including the specification of Africa as the region of origin. But in other respects the mother-only genes challenged Cavalli-Sforza's picture in a startling way.

The Berkeley geneticists constructed a family tree of the 134 individuals. It grouped them according to common ancestors since Eve. Although two people from the same region had relatively recent common ancestors more often than two people from different regions, the exceptions were amazing. One recent branch of the human family, for example, turned out to unite individuals from Europe, Asia and New Guinea.

'This diagram threw a very large spanner in the works of the population tree *aficionados*,' Bryan Sykes commented. 'It shows that genetically related individuals are cropping up all over the place, in all the wrong populations.'

Who are the Europeans?

It was Sykes in Oxford, remember, who confirmed the reality of the Lapitan Polynesians using mother-genes, and found a stranger among them too. Using a variant of Wilson's method, he concentrated on a region of the mitochondrial DNA that had little functional significance and therefore tolerated a high rate of mutation. It was in effect in the margin of the ancient recipe sheets, where daughters were free to doodle.

The mutation rate meant that geneticists could study maternal relationships in greater detail, and over shorter time-scales. In particular, they could investigate an issue that has often divided prehistorians on almost ideological lines. When a new technology turns up in the archaeological record of a particular place, did invaders bring it with them as they arrived to settle there, or was the knowledge simply diffused to the pre-existing population by traders?

Longships and mobile phones illustrate the contrasting possibilities. Towards the end of the first millennium A D, distinctive longships appear in the archaeological and historical records on many of Europe's shores, and the Vikings aboard them undoubtedly colonized many of the places they visited. But when future archaeologists find great numbers of mobile phones made in Finno-Scandia appearing all over the world at the end of the second millennium A D, they will err if they infer a second Nordic rampage. Whether Ericsson's and Nokia's travelling salesmen included notable Casanovas might be a subtler question for future geneticists to address.

Open-minded archaeologists would expect cultures to spread sometimes by migrations of clans and armies, and sometimes by trade and imitation. The fusion of archaeology and genetics may help to establish what happened, case by case. Thus in the UK population, for example, Viking genes are indeed conspicuous. On the other hand, the advent of agriculture in the British Isles seems to have been more a matter of seeds and animals passing from hand to hand, like mobile phones.

That was not how it looked at first, to the geneticists. European farming originated in south-west Asia, and the archaeological evidence shows it advancing north-westwards across Europe at an average rate of a kilometre a year. Farming came first to the Balkans about 8000 years ago, when the Franchthi Cave in southern Greece shows an abrupt transition from a diet of fish to wheat, barley, sheep and goats.

Back in 1978, the Stanford–Italian team led by Cavalli-Sforza had reported genetic evidence of south-west Asian farmers of the Neolithic (New Stone Age) migrating with their crops and livestock across Europe. As agriculture can support many more people than hunter-gathering does, the farmers supposedly outnumbered the indigenous Palaeolithic (Old Stone Age) tribes and imposed their genes as well as their crops on the countryside. In this hypothesis, the south-west Asian genes were progressively diluted towards the western fringe of Europe by interbreeding with the hunter-gatherers.

When Sykes applied the improved mother-gene method to people living in Europe, he found that Cavalli-Sforza and his colleagues had overstated the Asian genetic legacy. In a masterstroke Sykes extracted DNA from a 12,000-year-old tooth of a hunter-gatherer found in England's Cheddar Gorge in 1986. The man lived at least 7000 years before farming arrived in his region. And his mother-only genes corresponded with the commonest variants found in modern Europeans. Putting that the other way, most Europeans could claim direct descent from Europe's Old Stone Age hunters.

In 1996 Sykes's team published an analysis of Palaeolithic and Neolithic ancestors in Europe, based on mother-only genes in 821 individuals from Europe and the Middle East. They distinguished five lineages indigenous to Europe since the Old Stone Age, plus two lineages coming in from the east. Harking back to Wilson's Eve of Africa, Sykes called the last shared grandmothers in each cluster of mother-genes 'the seven daughters of Eve'. In terms of numbers of individuals, the European gene pool split 80/20 between Palaeolithic incumbents and Neolithic newcomers.

And what about the grandfathers?

Father-only genes came into the scientific story a few years after the mother-only genes. Geneticists found how to detect changes in DNA carried only by men, in the Y chromosome that switches the fertilized egg away from its inherent inclination to be female, to make a boy baby. Ornella Semino of Pavia and Giuseppe Passarino of Stanford, together with a team from Russia, Ukraine, Poland, Croatia, Greece and Sweden, as well as Italy and the USA, examined the Y chromosomes of 1007 European men. Almost all belonged to ten lineages, and many appeared to be of hunter-gatherer origin, having spread widely across Europe as the last ice age came to an end.

As for the 80/20 Palaeolithic–Neolithic split deduced from mother-only genes, the father-only team concluded, 'Our data support this observation.' One of the co-authors was Cavalli-Sforza himself, so the report gracefully drew a line under years of fierce argument between the blood-gene and mother-gene scientists about what happened in Europe in the Neolithic. In the play-off between Stanford and Oxford, Oxford had won, although Cavalli-Sforza salvaged from the Y chromosomes the evidence of farmers proceeding westwards in southern Europe, perhaps by boat.

The father-only analysts began to colour in the Upper Palaeolithic. This was when fully modern humans first appeared in Europe alongside the

Neanderthalers, who were probably not their ancestors. A variant Y chromosome called M173 appeared about 40,000 years ago, apparently in Central Asia among people who were also ancestors of some present-day Siberians and Native Americans.

Half of all present-day Europeans are descended from that M173 line. Semino and her colleagues equated it with the Aurignacians, the first fully modern people in Europe, whose culture with beautifully made tools and paintings was conspicuous by 35,000 years ago. Most of the remaining Europeans trace back to a Y-chromosome variant called M170, apparently originating in south-west Asia more than 20,000 years ago. The debut of this line in Europe may correspond with the Gravettians, most famous for their obese 'Venus' figurines made of fired clay—early ceramics.

The introduction of father-only genes into prehistoric studies brought the chance to check effects on the genetic lineages of gender differences in sexual behaviour. For example, royal harems and mass rapes by conquering armies were familiar in recorded history, so why not in the unrecorded past as well? More generally, male promiscuity may tend to reduce the genetic differences between regions.

By 2001, a collaboration between the Oxford geneticists and the Decode Genetics company in Reykjavik had used both father-only and mother-only genes to disentangle the sexes in the colonization of Iceland by the Vikings around 1000 years ago. Some 80 per cent of the early male settlers of the mid-Atlantic island originated from Scandinavia, but 60 per cent of the women came from Britain. Evidently the Viking longships paused en route to Iceland to harvest brides from among the Celts of northern Scotland.

Bones brought back to life

By the beginning of the 21st century an *eminence grise* of archaeology, Colin Renfrew at Cambridge, was able to proclaim, 'Applying molecular genetics to questions of early human population history, and hence to major issues in prehistoric archaeology, is becoming so fruitful an enterprise that a new discipline—*archaeogenetics*—has recently come into being.' He saw the need for a much sharper understanding of the interactions between incomers and an indigenous population, including 'the genetic and demographic consequences of the intermarriages between the two groups.'

Here is brave new science, with most of its achievements lying in the future. It will bring the human bones in museums back to life. An example came during the making of a TV documentary, in 1997, about the work of Sykes and his Oxford group. A schoolteacher in Cheddar, living just a kilometre from the archaeological site of Cheddar Gorge, turned out to have mother-only genes very similar to those in a skeleton found there, dating from 9000 years ago.

▶ *For closely related subjects, see* SPEECH *and* LANGUAGES. *For earlier times and the transition from apes to humankind, see* HUMAN ORIGINS. *There is more about the genetics of Icelanders in* HUMAN GENOME.

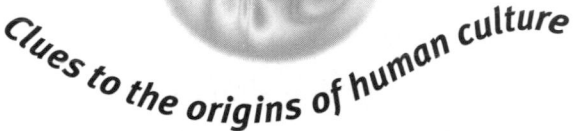

PRIMATE BEHAVIOUR

Clues to the origins of human culture

AUGMENTING POST OFFICE REVENUES by selling fancy stamps of interest to collectors is not a new phenomenon, and in 1906 the African free state of Liberia issued a five-cent postage stamp depicting a chimpanzee. Not any old chimp, but one engaged in attacking a termite nest, using a stick as a tool. The details are accurate, and the stick is of just the right size.

The picture on the stamp anticipates the discovery of the very same tool use reported in 1964 by the chimpanzee-watcher Jane Goodall, across the continent in the Gombe Stream preserve in Tanzania. She described how an animal would strip a stick of its leaves, poke it into a hole in a termite nest, and withdraw it slowly to bring some incautious termites out on the stick—from which they were licked off. How the illustrator knew about it half a century earlier was a question that teased the experts when the stamp was drawn to their attention in 2000.

Hints of human-like behaviour in other primates—monkeys and apes—have amused onlookers for thousands of years. When 19th-century science established that humans were descended from the apes, these hints acquired evolutionary significance. What features, apart from anatomy, distinguish us from the other primates? Conversely, what can our animal cousins tell us about the origins of our own behaviour?

Three possibly exclusive human talents were on offer: tool-making, culture and fully fledged language. Only the last has survived into the 21st century. The chimpanzee's preparation of a stick for termite fishing is now just one of many examples of animals using tools, but there was great resistance to the idea at first. Kenneth Oakley of London's Natural History Museum, writing in 1963, allowed that tools might be improvised on the spot, but he insisted that 'to conceive the idea of shaping a stone or stick for use in an imagined future eventuality is beyond the mental capacity of any known apes.' When chimpanzees were seen to prepare a stick and *then* to go looking for ant nests, that refuge of human superiority was lost.

The innovators of Koshima

As for the idea that only we have culture, meaning information and behaviour transmitted by social example rather than by inherited instinct, a young monkey called Imo blew that away in 1953. She was a member of a troop of Japanese macaques living on the island of Koshima and studied by Kinji Imanishi of Kyoto and his colleagues, in the first long-term monitoring of primate behaviour in the wild, anywhere in the world.

Until then some eminent scientists such as Solly Zuckerman in Oxford believed that you could learn all that you needed to know about the social behaviour of monkeys and apes just by watching them in captivity. With this was coupled hostility to anything that smacked of anthropomorphism—of giving animals human-like attributes as in fables and fairy tales. In 1929, when Zuckerman was a young researcher, studying baboons at the London Zoo, he had condemned investigators elsewhere for their 'still mainly anthropomorphic description, either in the older blatant form or in a new guise, provided with a crude behaviouristic formula'.

The Koshima monkeys were easier to observe on the beach, so the scientists from Kyoto tempted them out of the trees with sweet potatoes left on the sand. The monkeys had to brush off the sand before eating the goodies. Imo, 18 months old, found it easier to wash her sweet potato in the sea. Gradually other youngsters and mothers imitated her, and after some years 90 per cent of the troop were cleaning their food that way. Just as in human societies, the elderly males were most resistant to this cultural change.

When the scientists tried scattering wheat on the sand, sorting the edible grains by hand was a painstaking task for the monkeys. Playful Imo again found a solution. She threw the mixture of sand and wheat into the sea. The sand sank but the wheat floated and she could scoop it from the surface. Again this became the accepted method for the younger members of the troop. The oldies contented themselves with stealing the wet, ready-salted wheat that the youngsters collected.

So far from being acclaimed for these discoveries, Imanishi found himself at odds with Western colleagues. They ridiculed him for humanizing his subjects. You weren't supposed to be so fond of the animals as individuals. That smacked of anthropomorphism—not at all the mind-set that hardnosed animal behaviourists should bring to their work.

Yet for finding culture in primates, those Western inhibitions were counter-productive. They merely encouraged the interpretation of all behaviour as instinctive, while Imanishi's style of research revealed the roles of individual primates in their troops, like human beings in their societies. If one animal could learn from another, that would become apparent.

'Japanese culture does not emphasize the difference between people and animals and so is relatively free from the spell of anti-anthropomorphism,' commented Jun'ichiro Itani, Imanishi's student and colleague. Frans de Waal of Emory University, Atlanta, who chronicled this philosophical spat in his book *The Ape and the Sushi Master*, summarized the outcome by relating that the American zoologist Ray Carpenter, who had made pioneering field studies of primates since 1931, became a convert. 'He visited Japan three times, and within a decade the practice of identifying primates individually had been adopted at Western primatological field sites.'

Differences between chimpanzee troops

In 1961, Imanishi and Itani turned their attention to chimpanzees living in Tanzania, on the western slopes of the Mahale Mountains. That was a year after Jane Goodall began watching the chimpanzees by Gombe Stream, 170 kilometres to the north. She encountered great difficulties in habituating the animals to her presence, but in 1962 the turning point came when an elderly male looked in her tent. 'After all those months of despair,' Goodall wrote later, 'when the chimpanzees had fled at the mere sight of me five hundred yards away, here was one making himself at home in my very camp.'

The Kyoto scientists' problems with habituation lasted longer, and not until 1975 was their Mahale Mountains chimpanzee project fully established, with Toshisada Nishida as the leading investigator. Meanwhile Yukimaru Sugiyama was watching chimpanzees in the Budongo Forest (Uganda) and Bossou (Guinea). By that time the experts were beginning to ask whether tool use and other behaviour patterns were instinctive in the chimpanzees, or cultural in the manner of Imo's innovations among the macaques of Koshima.

The acid test would be whether the habits were common to all chimpanzees or not. By the late 1970s William McGrew of Stirling University was offering evidence for variable and therefore cultural behaviour in different chimpanzee troops. Adding zest to such studies was new genetic evidence that chimpanzees are our closest living relatives. The trouble was that establishing the *absence* of a particular habit, to prove it non-instinctive, required even more diligent and prolonged watching than detecting its presence.

Another 20 years passed. By then the chimpanzee watchers had accumulated between them 150 years of observations in seven long-term studies. Besides

Gombe, Mahale (two sites), Budongo and Bossou already mentioned, Kibale in Uganda and the Taï Forest of Ivory Coast were included in this count. Every new study identified new behaviour.

Andrew Whiten of St Andrews University decided that the time was ripe to pool this experience and to sort out, with help from all the research directors, the variations in the repertoires of chimpanzees in the different study sites. The results were conclusive. Out of 65 distinguishable habits, no fewer than 39 were judged to be cultural, in that they appeared on some sites and not in others, with no ecological reason for the differences.

Examples of unique behaviour included making meatballs from captured ants in Gombe but not elsewhere, and extracting marrow from bones with a stick, exclusively in the Taï Forest. Conversely, habits seen in most places were missing from some. Male chimpanzees perform ceremonial dances at the start of heavy rain, everywhere but Bossou.

'We know of no comparable variations in other non-human species,' Whiten and his distinguished panel concluded in 1999—adding wryly, 'although no systematic study of this kind appears to have been attempted.' The coming century may well bring evidence of invention, imitation and cultural behaviour in other species of monkeys and apes, when the necessary effort goes into looking for them.

And not just in primates. Songbirds have local dialects. Migrating animals of all kinds learn complex routes from their parents, which change with the variable climate and with geological and man-made alterations to the landscapes and rivers. We have seen only the start of the subversion of the Western view of animals as mindless automata, by the Japanese outlook that has always granted them a capacity for an intelligent culture.

Learning from mother

Chimpanzees will continue to surprise. In 1978, Kyoto's Primate Research Institute began investigating chimpanzee intelligence in a colony of captive animals. The project was named after the star of the show, a female called Ai who, with many years of tuition, communicated quasi-linguistically using symbols on a computer screen. In 1998 Ai's nine-month-old son Ayumu was watching what she did, and he suddenly reached for the computer and answered a question correctly.

Tetsuro Matsuzawa, leading this research, drew a direct parallel with the behaviour of infants in the wild at Bossou. There they learn the art of using a pair of stones as a hammer and an anvil to crack open the hard nuts of the oil palm. After watching closely how their mothers and other chimpanzees do it, at nine months they begin imitating parts of the action.

'The infant Ayumu has been observing his mother's behaviour right from birth,' Matsuzawa commented. 'He has been repeatedly exposed to the same situation day after day, until one day he suddenly decided to give the task a go. This reflects an intrinsic and strong motivation to copy the mother's behaviour—such is the chimpanzee's way of learning skills from adults.'

In 1975 there was amazement that Neanderthalers, recently extinct cousins of modern humans, knew a lot about herbal medicine, as evidenced by the simples wreathing a body buried in Iraq 60,000 years ago. Then it emerged that chimpanzees of the Mahale Mountains also use plants as remedies, for example against intestinal worms that plague them in the rainy season. One of the plants first reported in use, in 1989, is the bitterleaf tree (*Vernonia amygdalina*).

The animals pick young shoots, remove the bark and chew the pith, to suck a very bitter juice. They also fold the leaves and swallow them whole. The very hairy leaves simply scrape parasites off the gut wall. But in the bitterleaf juice, biochemists and pharmacologists around the world have since discovered various principles that make it promising for treating dysentery, malaria and bilharzia, and perhaps even for cancer prevention.

Bitterleaf is a traditional medicine in widespread use by African herbalists. Did human beings learn its virtues from their cultured cousins, the apes?

▶ *For related subjects, scc* HUMAN ORIGINS *and* MAMMALS.

PRIONS

From cannibals and mad cows to new modes of heredity and evolution

I N THE EASTERN HIGHLANDS of Papua New Guinea, the Fore people are scattered in 160 small villages, some 400 kilometres from the capital, Port Moresby. Nowadays they grow coffee and trade it with the outside world. The rugged terrain and dense forest previously kept them isolated enough to maintain their own language and ancient traditions. And the Fore had a preferred way of honouring a dead man. His relatives ate him.

An unexpected consequence was kuru, which is a Fore term for trembling. Once it started, the patient was dead within 3–9 months, by large-scale destruction of brain tissue. In the 1950s, the incidence became shockingly high, with one in a hundred of the population contracting kuru every year. Most at risk were the women who prepared the cannibalistic funeral meats and the toddlers for whom they cared. In some villages the surviving men outnumbered the women by three to one.

Enquiries into kuru set in train a new wave of medical research and, after some decades, a revolution in biology. With 21st-century hindsight, experts can say that the cause of kuru was an agent called a prion, pronounced pree-on, which is shorthand for a proteinaceous infectious particle. Half a century earlier, it was all much more mysterious. Even now, big puzzles and uncertainties remain, about kuru-like diseases.

Medically speaking, the discovery of prions extends the quite short list of types of agent known to cause infectious disease—that is to say, beyond bacteria, viruses, fungi and parasites. More broadly in the study of life, prions represent a previously unknown method of communicating information within and between organisms. Biologists have begun to get to grips with the far-reaching implications of prions for their theories about how life works and evolves.

● Mysterious 'slow viruses'

Visiting the ailing Fore people in Papua New Guinea in 1957, two medical researchers, Carleton Gajdusek and Vincent Zigas, realized that an infectious agent of kuru was passing from the brains of the dead to the brains of the living. During subsequent research spanning 20 years at the US National Institutes of

Health in Maryland, Gajdusek found he could infect a chimpanzee with kuru. He also studied its similarities to other brain-degenerating diseases, called spongiform (sponge-like) encephalopathies.

These included commonplace scrapie in sheep and a transmissible condition in mink. Also a rare but global occurrence in humans called Creutzfeldt–Jakob disease, named after two German doctors who first described the disease in 1920–21. Time and again, Gajdusek demonstrated that infected brain tissue could transmit the condition between various species of laboratory animals, including mice and monkeys.

The agents responsible for kuru and the other diseases remained elusive. Gajdusek labelled them as 'slow viruses' but he never isolated them. He conjectured that sheep scrapie was the original source of them all. Mink could have acquired the agent by scavenging dead sheep, whilst scrapie entering through cuts in kitchen accidents might be the origin of Creutzfeldt–Jakob disease in humans. The epidemic of kuru in Papua New Guinea could then have originated, he thought, from a single Creutzfeldt–Jakob case among the Fore people.

But as Gajdusek admitted in 1976, this was just 'armchair speculation'. No one knew the biological origin and means of survival of the infective agents. 'The diseases they evoke are not artificial diseases, produced by researchers tampering with cellular macromolecular structures, as some would have it,' Gajdusek commented. 'They are naturally occurring diseases, for none of which do we know the mode of dissemination or maintenance which is adequate to explain their long-term persistence.'

Fortunately for the Fore people, they gave up cannibalism in 1959 and kuru gradually died out. After 20 years there were still sporadic cases, telling of the long incubation possible with the disease, but essentially kuru was beaten, simply by abandoning an ancient custom.

From sheep to cows to humans

On the other side of the world, in Space Age England, cows were becoming carnivores. You could get higher yields and higher profits if you added animal protein to the feed of the naturally vegetarian animals. And instead of people trembling to death in the rain forest, the consequence was cows stumbling to death in the sleek countryside of Sussex.

Three days before Christmas in 1984 a vet, David Bee, was called to Pitsham Farm on the Chichester road at Midhurst. Cow 133 was unhappy. Her back was arched and she was losing weight. As the weeks passed, the animal's head began to tremble, her legs lost coordination, and in February she died.

By the summer, the farm had lost several other cows with similar symptoms. Poisonings by mercury or organophosphates were among Bee's hypotheses, but when the disease had run its course at Pitsham Farm he put the matter aside. Two years later he heard another vet, from nearby Kent, describing similar symptoms in cattle. As Bee recalled: 'He said to the conference, "I have got this new disease" and described it. And I said to him, "I have seen that," and told him what my cases had been.'

With hindsight, Cow 133 was the first known case of mad cow disease, or bovine spongiform encephalopathy, which then ran amok in the British cattle population. With the widespread use of animal-to-animal feeding, acquisition of the scrapie agent from sheep was the most likely explanation of its origin. The number of mad cows appearing each year peaked at about 37,000 in 1992.

Despite all the evidence of species-to-species transmission of brain-rotting diseases, amassed by Gajdusek and others, official experts assured an increasingly sceptical public that British beef was safe to eat. Even the chief medical officer joined in. The experts relied on the analogy with scrapie, which usually does no harm to people eating infected sheep. But this was not ordinary scrapie. The infective agent had already adapted to cattle with fatal consequences.

In 1995 the human form of mad cow disease, called variant Creutzfeldt–Jakob disease, claimed the first of dozens of victims. Guesses about the eventual human toll ranged from a few hundred to a few million. The British beef industry went into a tailspin, from which it was only gradually recovering in the early 21st century.

Nothing but a protein

By then, the basic science had moved on apace. In 1982, before mad cow disease appeared, American researchers pinned down a prion as the agent of scrapie. By inference, all kuru-like diseases had a similar cause. That story of prions had begun ten years earlier, when Stanley Prusiner at UC San Francisco was disturbed by the death of a demented patient with Creutzfeldt–Jakob disease. He undertook a trawl of all the relevant scientific literature.

'The amazing properties of the presumed causative "slow virus" captivated my imagination,' Prusiner recalled later, 'and I began to think that defining the molecular structure of this elusive agent might be a wonderful research project. The more that I read about CJD and the seemingly related diseases—kuru of the Fore people of New Guinea and scrapie of sheep—the more captivated I became.'

Setting out to find the scrapie virus, Prusiner was puzzled when his techniques for separating and characterizing it kept pointing to the presence only of a protein. There was none of the genetic material, nucleic acid, which should also be present in a virus. In 1982 he reported his results so far, and first named the protein that causes scrapie as a prion. Other experts were incredulous and even irate about this heresy, but their efforts to find the expected nucleic acid all failed too.

His contention was consolidated when Prusiner and his team isolated the protein of the prion. It was far smaller than any virus. Two years later, Leroy Hood at Caltech was able to name the 15 amino acids that made up one end of the protein chain. Thereafter, the clever tricks of molecular biology came into action to isolate the gene that codes for making the prion protein, and to track possible changes in the gene and the protein. It transpired that a harmless form of the prion protein is present in all healthy animals.

Prusiner and a widening band of associates found the normal prion protein in many tissues, including white blood cells and the surfaces of nerve cells in the brain. In some special cases, including a hereditary form of Creutzfeldt–Jakob disease, a mutant gene produces a mutant protein, thought to be more susceptible to misfolding—which is the way in which the pathogenic form arises.

Instilling a bad habit

'The protein flips into a state that the cell cannot degrade,' Prusiner said. This mode of action of the prion turned out to be just as sensational a discovery as the original identification of the protein. Like other newly assembled proteins emerging from the factories of a living cell, the prion folds itself into a certain shape required for its normal functioning. In its pathogenic form, the protein is partly unravelled. Then it can form aggregates that damage the tissue of nerve cells.

How can a pure protein replicate itself? Molecular biologists are accustomed to reading the genetic code of nucleic acid, and seeing how it commands the manufacture of a protein. To them, the method by which an infectious prion communicates its instructions for replication and causes a disease seems bizarre.

Continuous synthesis and disposal of innocuous prion proteins maintain the supply of normal molecules. But if one of them becomes misfolded into the pathogenic form, it can recruit normal molecules to fold like itself. The bad habit catches on. Each new pathogenic molecule becomes a new instructor, so the production of harmful prions accelerates, in a chain reaction.

Even so, the process happens very slowly, thus accounting for the months or years that pass between infection and the visible onset of the prion disease. The process is inexorable all the same. The immune system that normally defends the body against disease cannot distinguish the harmful form of the protein from the commonplace form. The damaged brain tissue includes long, thin protein aggregates, called fibrils, built from many of the misshapen, indestructible prion molecules.

An ever-present danger

When prion researchers compared notes with colleagues working on other disorders, they realized that the misbehaviour of proteins was a common theme.

In Alzheimer's disease, where brain damage causes memory loss, self-perpetuating assemblies of proteins appear, similar to those in prion diseases. Various other disorders involve protein aggregates.

Biochemists at Florence, collaborating with chemists at Cambridge, found that they could easily make long fibrils like those seen in prion diseases, from ordinary proteins taken from a bacterium and a mammal, and never implicated in any disorder. Monica Bucciantini, Elisa Giannoni, Fabrizio Chiti and their colleagues also tested the effects of the products on living cells. The finished fibrils were harmless, but protein clumps at an early stage of formation killed the cells. The team concluded that 'avoidance of protein aggregation is crucial for the preservation of biological function'.

Throughout the living world, the danger from misshapen proteins is ever-present. Cells employ special proteins called chaperones, just to make sure that other proteins fold correctly. And continual destruction and renewal of proteins within cells, which can sometimes seem wasteful, now looks like a necessary precaution against accumulating errors.

That being the case, the prions themselves are extremely odd. When researchers disable the gene coding for the prion protein in mice, the animals are healthy. They appear to be normal in every respect except that they are completely resistant to prion disease. Yet the prion protein must have a function. It is not credible that such a protein should survive in every animal species, if it does nothing but install a dangerous time bomb.

Another feature of prions is that special conformations can be inherited. Prion proteins can adopt distinct physical states that are self-perpetuating. Even when the genes code for the normal, harmless prion, offspring can acquire the disease-causing form from their mothers. Cow-to-calf transmission was one of the problems faced by British farmers trying to clean up their act. So this is a mode of heredity outside the normal run of genetics.

What are prions for?

Susan Lindquist at Chicago, who had been closely involved in explaining mad cow disease, pondered the general biological meaning of prions. She found an answer in baker's yeast, *Saccharomyces cerevisiae*. From 1994 onwards, Reed Wickner of the National Institutes of Health in Maryland had identified prions in this yeast and described their modes of transmission.

By 2000, Lindquist and her colleagues had shown that a prion becomes implicated in the translation of genes, during the manufacture of other proteins needed by the yeast cells. When the prion adopts the 'wrong' form, the fidelity of the translation is reduced. That will usually be harmful to individuals, but not necessarily for the yeast colony as a whole.

The resulting errors in translating genes into proteins enlarge the repertoire of active proteins—enzymes—available to the colony. And some of these enzymes enable the affected yeast to survive when researchers culture it with unusual nutrients or poisons. The Chicago team confirmed this with many different tests, some of which produced yeast colonies that looked quite different from normal baker's yeast.

Thus, in time of adversity, the prions unleash capabilities that are lurking in the yeast's genes, but which are unrealized in ordinary yeast in ordinary circumstances. In effect, the yeast evolves, and it does so far more rapidly than previously thought possible. This discovery chimed with results from the Chicago lab concerning other proteins involved in reactions to stress in animals and plants. The implications for theories of evolution were astounding.

Lindquist's perspectives broadened further when she moved to the Whitehead Institute in Massachusetts. There she developed an interest in prions as self-assembling and self-perpetuating molecular structures. She looked forward to interacting with physicists and chemists in using the fibrils, made by clumping prion proteins, as a model for inventing new engineering materials.

'As you start to probe biological processes at a very detailed level, it's really quite beautiful and extraordinary how well life works,' Lindquist remarked in 2002. 'Biology is just exploding out there. We're actually reaching a level where you find yourself imagining questions that a year ago you couldn't even formulate.'

By the following year, Lindquist's team had made the first electric wires from prions, by coating them with gold. The wires were a thousand times finer than a human hair.

▶ *For more on the significance of prions in evolutionary research, see* HOPEFUL MONSTERS. *For a related subject, see* PROTEIN SHAPES.

PROTEIN-MAKING

From an impressionistic dance to a real molecular movie

I N 1973, television producers from the BBC and Sveriges Radio borrowed a Swedish military airfield and a hundred high-school students. Special coloured smocks carried the different letters of the genetic code, or the names of various kinds of amino acids, the subunits of a protein molecule. Other colours denoted membership of molecular workforces.

Rehearsed by their teachers, and filmed from a cherry picker and from the ground, the youngsters then performed a busy dance on the runway. Its chief features were the skipping, snaking chains of children holding hands. Sequences of letters represented the code, and a chain of amino acids, a protein.

'Molecular dances like this are going on now in every part of your body,' the narrator intoned. The performance illustrated what was known at the time about the machinery in a living cell that translates the instructions of a gene into a protein. Looking back, the molecular biologists had discovered a great deal within just 20 years of the elucidation of the structure of the genetic material deoxyribonucleic acid, DNA, in 1953.

For a start, the TV audiences saw a twisted double line of dancers, the gene. It unravelled to expose the code. Too valuable to be put to work directly, the gene instead welcomed lone dancers looking for their chemical matches in the exposed sequence of DNA letters. These newcomers formed a new chain, a transcription of the gene. This 'messenger RNA' then peeled off and skipped away to another part of the runway.

There the messenger threaded itself among a different bunch of children depicting one of the living cell's protein-makers, and its raw materials. The letters in the messenger presented themselves in sequence for translation, in groups of three. Every triplet was a word of the genetic code. It had to be matched by just the right decoding group of three dancers, out of a swarm that included matches to the different possible words.

Each decoding group was like a truck, having on board the amino acid corresponding to its word. Arriving at the messenger, it delivered the amino acid for adding to a newly forming protein chain. Then the messenger moved on, to put the next triplet in the reading frame and call up the next amino acid.

Simultaneously the growing protein chain sidestepped, as if on a conveyor belt, to await the addition of its next amino acid.

In the end, the original message of the gene was faithfully translated into a protein with all its amino-acid subunits in just the right order, holding hands and prancing out of the protein-maker. As the music rose to a crescendo, these children crowded together like a rugby scrum. They curled their amino-acid chain into a compact protein molecule.

A magic spinnery

Among all the technical names for the movements and molecules represented in the dance, one worth latching onto is that of the protein-maker. The ribosome is one of the oldest machines on Earth, because bacteria were using it almost 4 billion years ago. When the Swedish dancers were filmed, ribosomes were known only as boxes through which messenger molecules threaded themselves, and out of which proteins appeared.

Electron microscopes nevertheless gave scientists quite a good view of the ribosomes, arranged like arrays of machine tools in a factory. In a book written in the early 1980s, the cell biologist Christian de Duve of Louvain guides his readers in their imagination into the deep gorges of a living cell. There he finds what he calls a magic spinnery. Silky threads of protein grow from flat, membranous walls, in which the ribosomes are embedded like rivets.

'We are enmeshed in a sea of moving silk. The rearmost thread of a row reaches its full size and drops off, and the tip of a new one emerges through the membrane somewhere in front.' As described by de Duve, this aspect of the system for mass-producing a protein should warm a factory manager's heart. Behind that special membrane within the cell, a single messenger molecule is threading its way through a dozen ribosomes at once. The first is completing one copy of the protein chain as the last is beginning to make another.

The traffic flow is less impressive. The small molecular assemblies that bring up the various amino acids crowd around each ribosome like trucks jamming a delivery bay, as they try to find the correct triplet where they can park and unload. As a result the protein grows at about four amino acids per second, which is sluggish by molecular standards.

Four billion years of evolution have done little to reduce the traffic jams. This is no oversight, but a sign of just how fundamental to all living things is the translation from gene to protein. Moment by moment it's what keeps you alive and able to read these words. So while Mother Nature felt free to invent eyes or wings or claws ad lib, the primary system of protein-making was not to be tampered with in any major way.

There are some variations in the ribosomes, all the same. Small, unimportant changes in their molecular compositions enable evolutionists to trace the whole history of life by comparing the ribosomes of organisms alive today. Some places in the molecules are never allowed to vary, and these point researchers towards key working parts of the ribosomes.

A more significant change distinguishes ribosomes in bacteria from slightly larger ones in more complicated organisms. Some antibiotics, including streptomycin and tetracycline, halt or confuse protein production in bacteria, and so kill them. Because of small differences in the ribosomes, they don't have the same effect on the patients.

The protein-maker in action

Finding out exactly how a ribosome is built and how it works took more than two decades of dogged effort, from the late 1970s onwards. By human standards it is extremely small—50,000 ribosomes side by side would make a millimetre. But it is an elephantine assembly of molecules, built of more than 400,000 atoms arranged in dozens of proteins, together with three special pieces of nucleic acid. The latter are not DNA but RNA, the ribonucleic acid that's also used in the messenger molecules that transcribe the genes.

There are two modules in a ribosome called 50S and 30S. Molecular bridges join them, and all the action of gene translation and protein-making takes place in the intervening space. To inspect it fully, molecular biologists had to make crystals of the ribosomes or their modules and analyse them with X-rays.

Experts shied away from the monstrous task until Ada Yonath of Israel's Weizmann Institute and Heinz-Günther Wittmann of the Max-Planck-Institut für molekulare Genetik in Berlin led the way. Yonath found out by trial and error how to make stable crystals of the larger 50S module, protect them at low temperatures, and decorate them with clusters of heavy atoms to provide landmarks when she X-rayed the crystals. But when she showed her early results in 1980, the pictures were very fuzzy. 'Everyone laughed at me,' Yonath recalled later.

Later she joined the Max-Planck-Arbeitsgruppen für Struktrurelle Molekularbiologie in Hamburg. Marat Yusupov and his wife Gulnara, who had followed a similar arduous path as graduate students at the Protein Research Institute in Pushchino, Russia, migrated to UC Santa Cruz in search of better facilities. There they perfected methods of crystallizing whole ribosomes, which turned out to be easier if a messenger molecule and a parked truck carrying an amino acid were in place.

At Santa Cruz, Harry Noller and his colleagues embarked on the analysis of the whole ribosome crystals by X-rays. Peter Moore and Thomas Steitz at Yale concentrated on the 50S module, while Venki Ramakrishnan and his team at the UK's Laboratory of Molecular Biology set out to do the 30S module in fine detail. The outcome was a gush of reports in 1999–2001, which revealed the blueprint of the ribosome in the bacterium *Thermus thermophilus*.

There were medical as well as technical reasons to prefer a bacterial version. Resistance to antibiotics among bacteria had reached a crisis point. 'This research not only helps us to understand how many known antibiotics work but also helps us to understand the basis of certain kinds of resistance,' Ramakrishnan commented. 'This will hopefully allow us to design new antibiotics in the future that can overcome the growing worldwide problem.'

More interesting than the precise architecture of the 54 different protein molecules and three nucleic-acid strands in the whole ribosome was the discovery of how it works as a protein-making robot. As ever-more graphic detail unfolded on their computer screens, the scientists could see exactly where the genetic messenger molecule wormed into the machine. They found the reading frame where the triplets of the code present themselves, located on an easy-to-reach bridge between modules of the ribosome. Also pinpointed were the jaws that held the growing protein chain while the truck unloaded the amino acid on to it.

With growing fascination, the molecular biologists saw the ribosome changing and moving as it worked. For example, Ramakrishnan's team found that three bases in the ribosome alter their orientation to sense the shape of the groove made between the code triplet on the messenger molecule and the decoding triplet of the truck carrying the amino acid. Only when the fit was correct would the ribosome accept its amino acid. Noller's team found that the bridges between the 50S and 30S modules also change shape during protein-making. They alter the spacing and help to control the visiting messenger molecule and the truck traffic.

'What we have at present are a few snapshots,' Noller said. 'Ultimately what we would like is a movie of the ribosome in action.' Antibiotics can halt the activity of the ribosomes at various moments in the protein-making cycle to generate the frames of the movie. Although the analyses are hard work, animation of the entire cycle is probably only a matter of time.

The emergence of a finished piece of protein silk from the ribosome is not the end of the story. Further chemical action by other molecular tools can alter the raw protein in many kinds of ways. It may be trimmed or cut in two. All kinds of special-purpose chemical groups can be attached to it at chosen places. Sugary or fatty molecules or even another entire protein may be welded onto it. Addresses are added too, to show the destination of the finished protein in the living cell.

Discovering all these possible 'post-translational' changes to proteins, and how they are accomplished, is likely to keep the biologists busy for years to come. But the late-20th-century push to understand the basics of protein-making by ribosomes shows that even a very complicated system is comprehensible in the end. It also sharpens one's sense of wonder about how clever half a million mindless atoms can be, when they are arranged the right way.

▶ *For more about molecular analysis and protein-folding, see* PROTEIN SHAPES *and* PROTEOMES. *For possible implications of the ribosome's key components, see* LIFE'S ORIGIN. *For another revelation of the workings of protein complexes, see* PHOTOSYNTHESIS.

PROTEIN SHAPES

Look forward to seeing them shimmy

B Y 2012 OR SO, scientists wanting to peer into the molecules of life with the brightest X-ray flashes in the world may find them amid the patchwork farms of Schleswig-Holstein, near Ellerhoop. The modest industrial town is thrust into the scientific limelight because it lies near the middle of a 33-kilometre line stretching north from Hamburg. That city's particle physics laboratory DESY (Deutsches Elektronen-Synchrotron) earmarked the Ellerhoop route in the hope of hosting the world's next giant particle accelerator.

The physicists dream of a big experimental hall at Ellerhoop, where beams of electrons and positrons, or anti-electrons, coming from two opposing guns 16.5 kilometres long, should collide head on. The primary task for TESLA (Teravolt Energy Superconducting Linear Accelerator) would be particle physics with electrons and positrons having combined energies equivalent to more than a million million volts. But from the project's conception there was always a semi-independent scheme to make very special X-rays available for biologists and materials scientists, to give them brilliant new views of their atomic landscapes.

The idea is that pulses of superenergetic electrons will pass through tunnels where they will run into magnetic fields that keep switching direction. Forced to wiggle, the electrons will radiate X-rays in a laser-like fashion, creating bursts of stupendous power, purity and brevity. A flash lasting less than a million-millionth of a second will illuminate a target with more than a million million X-ray particles, or photons, each with exactly the same selectable energy.

Biologists and materials scientists can learn the new tricks with a smaller X-ray laser starting up in 2004, in familiar surroundings. The Hamburg physicists have already provided them with X-rays from electrons forced to circle in a synchrotron—a different type of accelerator. This was at HASYLAB, the Hamburger Synchrotronstrahlungslabor. The European Molecular Biology Laboratory had an outpost there, where biologists could bring their samples for analysis.

'Biologists are tremendously excited about our X-ray lasers,' said Jochen Schneider, the physicist in charge of HASYLAB. 'They'll see life on the atomic scale in ways that were impossible before, and watch the shapes of molecules changing as they do their work.'

Between the early X-ray laser at Hamburg and the hoped-for Ellerhoop facility comes a big challenge from Menlo Park, California. There, by 2008, the Stanford Linear Accelerator Center is due to start up its own X-ray laser using its existing three-kilometre linear accelerator. It will be the first of the new generation of super-powerful X-ray machines.

'Stanford is definitely ahead at the moment in building a hard X-ray laser,' said Janos Hajdu of Uppsala in 2002, as a biochemist active in both the American and German projects. 'But we desperately need a big X-ray laser in Europe. Don't forget that the use of large particle accelerators for biological research began in Hamburg.'

It was in 1971 that Kenneth Holmes from the Max-Planck-Institut für medizinische Forschung first used synchrotron X-rays from a DESY accelerator to examine a protein from insect muscle. So clean and controllable were the X-rays, compared with those from ordinary machines, that Holmes' pioneering work launched a major scientific industry. Purpose-built synchrotron radiation laboratories appeared all around the world. Materials scientists benefited, as well as the investigators of biological molecules.

Motifs for three-dimensional structures

In the mid-20th century, X-ray crystallographers in the UK had begun deducing the shapes of biomolecules, using ordinary X-ray generators. Crystals of the materials scattered X-rays and produced cryptic spots on photographic film, depending on the arrangements of atoms. With primitive machinery and rudimentary computers, interpreting the spots was hard labour, but it launched both molecular biology and modern genetics.

Dorothy Hodgkin of Oxford spent four years on getting penicillin (1946) and eight years on vitamin B_{12} (1956). Her colleagues in London and Cambridge had the genetic material, DNA, by 1953. Proteins were considered particularly tough, but Cambridge came home first, in 1959, with the structure of myoglobin, a molecule that carries oxygen in muscles. It has about 10,000 atoms, and by fixing the relative positions of the 2600 non-hydrogen atoms the analysts deduced its intricate shape. The kindred haemoglobin of blood, four times more complex, followed soon after.

Life depends on the three-dimensional structures of proteins. Many are enzymes, chemical tools on a molecular scale. Each carries out a specific task like a machine tool in an assembly line. As the shapes of more and more proteins become known, biologists find out how individual enzymes and other active proteins function.

They can often see a cleft in the structure that's perfectly fashioned and chemically correct to grip the molecule that is the target of an enzyme's action. With care, the investigators can determine the combined shape of enzyme plus target, in mid-action. It looks like a vice holding a work-piece.

Enzymes with very different functions sometimes have similar chemical composition. They obviously share a genetic ancestor. Quite small evolutionary rejigs of the active parts can alter the enzyme's role, either by changing the catalytic activity at an existing binding site, or creating a new binding site.

Enlightenment about particular cases only deepens a general puzzlement. The more apt the shape, the more awe-inspiring is the ability of the protein molecule to adopt it correctly every time. An enzyme emerges as a fine fibre from the molecular machine that made it, and then spontaneously folds up into a tangled ball, with its active cleft and chemical groups positioned just so on the surface.

Power to drive the folding comes from the water in the living cell, which also influences the outcome. Some parts of a protein chain are water-friendly, and therefore suitable for exposing on the surface. Other parts are hydrophobic, like oil in water, and will try to take refuge inside the protein ball. While the folding is going on, molecular assistants called chaperones may screen the hydrophobic parts from the cell's water. The aversion to water translates into a more stable state, with lowered energy, when the folding is accomplished.

So crucial is correct protein-folding for sustained life, the rules that govern it are sometimes called the second genetic code. Throughout the latter part of the 20th century molecular biologists made a sustained effort to read it. The test would be whether they could predict a protein molecule's shape from the sequence of amino-acid subunits that make up the pristine fibre.

Clues came early on from standard features discovered in most proteins, called the alpha helix and the beta sheet. In the first, each amino acid forms a link with the fourth amino acid away from it in the protein chain, to build a spiral staircase. In a beta sheet, a row of amino acids all link to another row from a different part of the chain, like the lines in a barn dance. The adjacent row may be a nearby part of the chain folded back on itself, or from an entirely different part of the crumpled chain.

Large and important parts of the protein look altogether more disorderly. They cannot be meaningless, because evolution has protected them. Fragments of structure, called motifs, are shared by different proteins and provide a rough-and-ready basis for predicting how some pieces of a protein will shape up. The commonest motif is the TIM barrel, named after a protein (triosephosphate isomerase) in which it was discovered in 1975. Built of 250 amino acids, it turns up in very many enzymes.

Protein engineering, natural and contrived

Solving the folding problem is not just a matter of defining the final shape. It has to be understood as an active, sequential process, very complicated but repeatable on demand and accomplished in seconds or minutes. Progress was painfully slow. In 1998 Steven Chu at Stanford, who had just won the Nobel Physics Prize for cooling atoms by means of laser beams, decided that this was an essentially virgin field in which he could make a new research career. 'We're just beginning,' Chu said. 'Everyone is just beginning.'

Alan Fersht at Cambridge was more upbeat. If scientists could understand proteins and their behaviour as enzymes, then they should be able to invent new enzymes for industrial or medical purposes. Compared with man-made catalysts, natural enzymes are incredibly efficient, not least in doing exactly what they are supposed to do, nothing less and nothing more, with no unwanted side effects.

'The interaction between protein engineers, crystallographers and theoreticians will eventually provide the rules governing the three-dimensional structure of proteins,' Fersht prophesied. 'Then, when a particular reaction needs catalysing, a computer will print out the necessary gene sequence and the protein engineers will make the enzyme.'

He created the Cambridge Centre for Protein Engineering. To make progress when many fundamental questions remained unanswered, Fersht embarked on directed molecular evolution. By that he meant adapting existing natural enzymes to new purposes, as evolution has done for billions of years.

His team produced a large number of mutant versions of a TIM-barrel enzyme and tested them in cultures of bacteria, so that useful new molecules might survive. By 2000 the Cambridge team had evolved an enzyme performing a practical function different from its predecessor's. Moreover it did the work six times more efficiently than the enzyme already provided by Nature for the same purpose.

In Yokohama, protein specialists at the Genomes Research Center of RIKEN (Institute of Physical and Chemical Research) took stock of what worldwide research had revealed about the shapes of the proteins' working parts. They classified about 1000 types of basic protein folds, and about 10,000 subtypes, the molecular functions of which established each protein's way of working. This encyclopaedia, as the scientists called it, was expected to improve predictions of protein shape and function, from known sequences of amino acids.

Progress by the geneticists in reading the complete endowment of genes of more and more species—their genomes—put pressure on the protein people to speed up their work, in order to understand what all those genes did. To that end, the Yokohama team developed a way of making a protein in large quantities from the genetic instructions, in a flask, using loose ribosomes, the molecular equipment responsible for protein-making in all living cells. They also installed rows of powerful machines for finding the shapes of the proteins by nuclear magnetic resonance—another gift from physics to biology.

Nuclear magnetic resonance first came into widespread use for medical imaging, but biologists latched on to it for protein analysis. The nuclei of atoms wobble like spinning tops around the direction of the local magnetic field. If you knock them sideways with one radio wave they will spring back into alignment, emitting radio waves of their own. Each kind of nucleus broadcasts at a characteristic frequency, but the chemical environment of the atom containing it tweaks the frequency a little.

Computers can convert patterns of emitted frequencies into protein shapes. This technique has the advantage that you can analyse proteins in solution, which is a more natural environment for them than the crystals used in traditional X-ray analysis. By 2002 the Yokohama effort in protein analysis by nuclear magnetic resonance was the largest of its kind in the world.

'A wall is falling down'

X-ray analysis remained the way of getting the most precise detail about protein shapes, right down to the atomic level. Synchrotron X-rays and far better computers made many of the simpler biological molecules rapidly decipherable. Heroic efforts were reserved for very elaborate molecules and aggregations of molecules. By the end of the 20th century these included the photosynthetic apparatus by which plants grow, and the protein-making ribosomes themselves.

Great difficulties remained. Before a biomolecule can be analysed by X-rays in the conventional way it has to be crystallized. In many cases that has proved difficult or impossible. What's more, the X-rays themselves are a well-known biohazard precisely because they damage the delicate molecules of life, and the samples used in X-ray crystallography are not exempt.

The very intense X-rays from lasers will blow a molecule to pieces, but experimenters hope this will not happen before an image is obtained. And a single molecule may suffice, thus evading the problem of making crystals. Assemblies of molecules, including complete viruses, will also be analysed in a flash. One technical option is to embed whole cells in extremely cold ice. Another is to spray mixtures of proteins, viruses or pieces of cells through an electric sorter that directs the chosen item into the X-ray beam.

Most captivating is the possibility of seeing large structures and perhaps even the molecules, within their cells. There they are most likely to be in a truly natural configuration, and changing their shapes in subtle ways as they interact with other molecules. Cleverly designed experiments will take advantage of the brevity of the flashes to do for molecules what motion pictures did for animal motions a century ago, and show how a protein shimmies as it sets to work. Why, they may even solve the protein-folding problem.

'A wall is falling down to reveal a view never seen before,' said Janos Hajdu of Uppsala. 'We can only guess what we'll find, but X-ray lasers will take us into an extraordinary new world of molecular and cell biology. What we do there will be limited only by our creativity and imagination.'

▶ *For more on proteins, see* PROTEOMES, PROTEIN-MAKING, PHOTOSYNTHESIS *and* CELL TRAFFIC. *For evidence that the 'second genetic code' is more than a metaphor, see* PRIONS.

PROTEOMES

The molecular corps de ballet of living things

T HE MATTERHORN, queen of the Alps, embellishes the logo of Swiss-Prot, the world's premier bioinformatics project, although pedants point out that it is the king, Mont Blanc, which you see from Geneva where the project was born and still operates. Swiss-Prot catalogues and annotates in computer files all of the protein molecules whose composition is known to the world's scientists.

A biochemistry student and computer buff at the Université de Genève, Amos Bairoch, initiated Swiss-Prot in 1986. Here he developed computer software to analyse genes and proteins. The software was sold to the life science community by an American company, Intelligenetics. In those days, before all scientists used computers and the Internet routinely for their correspondence, the clerical tasks of creating the protein catalogue were formidable. To Bairoch it seemed nevertheless a necessary investment for the future. Events proved him right.

Whilst the genes of heredity provide a score and choreography, giving instructions for the molecular dance of life, the proteins are the *corps de ballet*. They continually appear, perform catalytic, structural, mechanical or signalling roles, and exit to be recycled. To see the full performance for the first time is a major goal for 21st-century science.

Protein molecules consist primarily of long chains of amino-acid subunits strung together in a precise sequence. In 1943 a young biochemist in Cambridge, Fred Sanger, set out to find the sequence in the medically important protein insulin, involved in sugar metabolism. It was a relatively small molecule with just 51 amino acids, but no one had fully analysed any protein before and he had to improvise his methods. The task would seem trivial half a century later, but it took Sanger 12 years and won him the first of two Nobel Prizes.

In 1950 Pehr Edman in Sweden found out how to degrade a protein step by step so as to read off the sequence of amino acids. This speeded up the work and by the mid-1980s, when Bairoch started Swiss-Prot, the compositions of about 4000 proteins or fragments of proteins were known. Others were added as they became available. The project soon joined with a related effort by the European Molecular Biology Laboratory in Heidelberg and Swiss-Prot established itself as the industry standard for bioinformatics in the world of protein research.

'In the 1980s, most laboratories were involved in the study of a single or a small group of proteins,' Bairoch reminisced in 2002. 'A well-structured database was needed to catalogue what was known as well as to perform comparative analysis. Today, new protein sequences pour in at a tremendous rate because of massive genome sequencing projects. On the one hand, such an avalanche of data renders the work of protein databases all the more difficult; on the other, their existence is even more crucial to the work of life scientists on a day to day basis.'

What were the Aussies up to?

For an impression of the protein problem, consider some humble bacteria. They are called *Mycoplasma genitalium* and you could fit a million of them on the head of a pin. As the name implies they occur in the human genital tract, among other places. They seem harmless, and they captivate scientists who wonder about creating life artificially, because they are among the smallest creatures known that can reproduce themselves and live independently, with no assistance from other cells.

Want to imitate it? The kit of parts for *genitalium* is known, at least sketchily. Within each bacterial cell, you'll find 400 million molecules of water and one molecule of genetic material, made of the nucleic acid DNA. It carries 480 genes, or a little more than one per cent of the number that you and I have. At any moment about 10,000 transcripts of the genes are milling about in the cell, in the form of strands of another kind of nucleic acid, RNA. Feeding themselves into the molecular machines called ribosomes, of which *genitalium* possesses about 400, the RNA strands command the manufacture of proteins.

A complete census of individual protein molecules in *genitalium* would total 50,000. In the early days of molecular biology it was widely believed that one gene specified one protein, and that you could predict the protein by reading the gene. Three letters in the DNA subunits do indeed code for the insertion of one type of amino-acid subunit into a protein chain. So any protein made by translating the instructions of a particular gene was expected to have the same chemical composition, shape and function.

Life is not so simple. It transpired that post-translational modifications of many kinds make crucial changes to the naked proteins coming out of the ribosomal machines. As a result there are far more protein types than there are genes, and to know what they are, the only way is to identify them one by one.

In 1995 microbiologists in Sydney University investigated the proteins of *genitalium*. They used a variety of screening techniques to identify 73 proteins and checked to see whether they were already known in catalogues of proteins of other organisms. This was a useful if unremarkable contribution to knowledge, but the research philosophy expressed in it lit a torch that the whole world would follow.

At the time, the buzzword among molecular biologists was genome, meaning the complete complement of genes in an organism. By the mid-1990s the enterprise of genomics was well under way. Reading the uncounted thousands of genes in the whole human genome still seemed a fairly distant hope, but the first complete genomes were becoming available for bacteria, including little *genitalium* with its 480 genes.

Biologists were alert to a possible 'So what?' reaction to the completion of genome projects. The meanings of all those genes would become fully apparent only when the corresponding proteins had been identified and their compositions, functions and shapes discovered. Some called this follow-up task 'functional genomics', but the Australian microbiologists had a new word, proteome, meaning the full complement of proteins in a living cell or organism. They also sketched the nature of a research programme needed for proteomics.

'Here, characterization of gene products depends upon the quickest and most economical technologies being employed initially, so as to determine if a large number of proteins are already present in . . . databases,' they wrote. 'Initial screening, which lends itself to automation and robotics, can then be followed by more time and cost intensive procedures, when necessary.'

By mid-1996, the Australian Proteome Analysis Facility was operational at Macquarie University, Sydney, as a Major National Research Centre to create the first dedicated proteome lab, anywhere. Scientific visitors came from far and wide to see what the Aussies were up to. What they found was a small group of researchers surrounded like children at Christmas with all the latest scientific toys, and technobabbling about 2-D gels and laser-desorption time-of-flight mass spectrometers that could identify thousands of proteins every week.

A bankable word

The tools of proteomics had evolved in the preceding decades. In work reported in 1975, Patrick O'Farrell of the University of Colorado distinguished 1100 proteins from a bacterium, *Escherichia coli*, using a new method called two-dimensional electrophoresis. This sorts out the proteins, first by their electric charges and then by size.

An electric field drives the proteins along a narrow jelly racetrack, specially prepared so that it changes in acidity along its length. Each protein eventually reaches a point where the local acidity cancels its electric charge and it comes to a halt. This process is called isoelectric focusing. The finishing points then become the starting points on a wide jelly track, and the proteins set off in another direction, with the smaller proteins winding their way through the jelly faster than the larger ones. In this way, each kind of protein finishes up in a spot of its own, distinct from all the others.

Identifying or characterizing the protein in each spot remained a headache for the investigators. High-tech sequencing tools still operated on Edman's principle, but in the early 1990s an alternative appeared in very precise measurements of the masses of fragments of the proteins, by mass spectrometers. These are machines that gauge the masses of charged atoms and molecules by their routes or speeds through a vacuum, under the influence of electric and magnetic fields. In one mode of operation, called electrospray, the charged protein fragments are produced from the water containing them, like perfume from an atomizer.

Innovation and automation in protein analysis were then proceeding so fast that by the time a technique had been taught to students it was probably obsolescent. Among the new tricks that kept appearing was a clever way of picking out mated pairs of interacting proteins, using yeast cells. What was invariable was the utter dependence of the proteomicists on databanks of known proteins.

If every kind of protein in every living thing from viruses to human beings had to be analysed afresh whenever it turned up, the time and cost would be forbidding. As the Australian scientists noted in their 1995 agenda for proteomics, you should start by checking the existing catalogues. To do so, they turned to Bairoch and Swiss-Prot.

The Australian Proteome Analysis Facility was able to operate with financial independence within a few years of its creation, and by then it had been widely imitated. 'Enormous investments have been made in establishing proteome facilities in the US, Canada, Europe and several locations throughout SE Asia,' the director Gary Cobon noted in 2001. 'It is very fortunate that APAF started more than 4 years earlier and is fully operational . . . and can therefore effectively compete with these start-up organizations.'

Proteomics became a bankable word among investors in biotechnology companies. The targets of medicinal drugs are almost always proteins, and new applications are patentable. Among the first patents of the Macquarie facility itself was a method of diagnosing the presence of cancer by detecting, in human teardrops, a newly discovered protein called lacryglobin.

Pointilliste pictures of protein machinery

By early in the 21st century, the situation is as follows. Biologists have the genes more or less under control, with genomes completely read in a growing list of organisms. But proteomics is a much more difficult proposition. So far from seeing the protein ballet properly, scientists don't even know how many dancers there are. They have still to discover the syntax of the post-translational modifications that create many different proteins from a single gene.

The shapes of proteins matter too. Genes are one-dimensional messages like the tickertape of old telegrams, but proteins are practical 3-D machines. The chemical sequences of amino-acid chains are useful for comparing one protein with another, but otherwise they have limited biological meaning. Only when you see how the protein chain folds itself can you begin to try to say how it works. That is another huge department of research.

Most challenging of all are the entrances, performances and exits of the protein dancers. One molecule triggers activity in another. Key actions may involve extremely brief appearances of hard-to-detect proteins. A system of zip codes can route and reroute a protein to different parts of a cell, as occasion requires.

Above all, protein behaviour responds to the exigencies of real life. The genetic choreography is not authoritarian, specifying exactly what is to happen from moment to moment. It coaches the cells in many balletic flourishes, but the dancers improvise. Whatever textbook matches can be made, between various proteins to various genes, the dance must continually change in response to events within a cell, within the whole organism, or in its surroundings.

To put it another way, if you could really define all the activity of all the proteins from moment to moment, all through the development and life of every organism, you would have life itself pretty well taped. It would be a brash biologist who thought that an early prospect. That said, proteomics is undoubtedly the signpost pointing where many molecular biologists are now going, and the automated tools under rapid development will keep accelerating the work. Surprising new discoveries are virtually certain, especially when clever techniques cut corners.

A team at the European Molecular Biology Laboratory led by Bertrand Séraphin found how to remove proteins from living cells, not as singletons or pairs but as entire complexes of many proteins linked and working together as biochemical machines. That was in 2000. Colleagues then developed 'bait' for fishing for many complexes. A start-up company on the lab's Heidelberg campus, called CellZome, provided the industrial-scale mass spectrometry needed to identify the constituents.

They soon found that dozens of different complexes use many of the same components, meaning that individual proteins can have more functions than scientists suspected. It also turns out that small machines may be integrated into a much larger complex that performs a particular task and is then dismantled again. The composition of a complex is not always exactly the same, implying that living cells are content to improvise a little.

From the largest dissection of protein complexes attempted till then, relating to one-third of the entire genome of baker's yeast *Sacharromyces cerevisiae*, Anne-Claude Gavin of CellZome and her Heidelberg colleagues announced the discovery of 134 multiprotein machines unknown to biochemists. Even in 92 other complexes that were recognizable, there were nearly always proteins lurking, that no one knew were there. On average, the complexes contained 12 proteins, but the biggest one analysed had 83. Most exciting for the analysts was the picture of cell life that emerged when they plotted all of the molecular machines on a map.

'You can link complexes by their components, or by their known cellular functions,' said CellZome's scientific director, Giulio Superti-Furga. 'You obtain a picture of a higher level of organization than we have ever been able to see before. It's somewhat like looking at a French pointilliste picture. If you stand too close, because of the technique they used in painting, all you see are single coloured dots. As you move away, you begin to see a coherent image.'

The dictionary of life

The protein databanks grow in size and importance. In 1998, Bairoch in Geneva joined with others in his homeland to create the Swiss Institute of Bioinformatics. By 2001 Swiss-Prot had combined the analytical efforts of no fewer than 150,000 individual scientists around the world, to provide annotated details of more than 100,000 amino-acid sequences, from some 7000 species. These included nearly 8000 sequences from human beings, and some 30,000 noted variations.

A Human Proteomics Initiative began in 2000 as a joint project of the Swiss Institute of Bioinformatics and the European Institute of Bioinformatics located at Hinxton in England, which is an outstation of the European Molecular Biology Laboratory. The human body contains 30,000 or so genes, but the count of proteins may be at least ten times greater. Part of the proteomicists' task is to find out what that number is.

The scientists instituting the Human Proteomics Initiative drew a parallel with the creation of the *Oxford English Dictionary* in the 19th century. They recalled how the local team appealed to English speakers around the world to send in quotes illustrating the uses of particular words and how they evolved over time. 'Today we could use their original appeal as well as the description of their goal almost verbatim, only replacing the "English language" by the "human proteome".'

If this parallel is apt, it warns us that the proteomic adventure will never be finished. The initial work on the *OED* took much longer than expected, from its initiation in 1857 to completion of the first edition in 1928. The English language was richer and subtler than any one speaker or committee of speakers could ever know. It will be disappointing if our protein language in all its dialects is not more gorgeous still.

The *OED* requires repeated updating, because human languages evolve rapidly. The proteomes of human beings and other species will reveal molecular harbingers of evolution. The protein resources of individuals, populations and species of organisms are tested by circumstantial challenges and opportunities, and the most aptly fluent ones prosper. In this perspective the stresses of life, such as changes of climate, are biomolecular elocution tests.

▶ *For the quest for 3-D structures of proteins, see* PROTEIN SHAPES. *Other related topics are* GLOBAL ENZYMES, GENOMES IN GENERAL, MOLECULES EVOLVING *and* CELL TRAFFIC.

QUANTUM TANGLES

From puzzling to spooky to useful

T HE EIFFEL TOWER was a ready-made TV mast, which Alexandre-Gustave Eiffel himself called *une antenne monumentale*. He was glad to see it used for early experiments with radio. The first main application was military, to connect Paris with the troops guarding France's eastern border. And among the army's radio telegraphists who were busy on the tower throughout the First World War was a budding scientist, Louis-Victor-Pierre-Raymond de Broglie.

In this billet de Broglie, a descendant of field marshals, escaped the bloodbaths in the trenches. Although conscientious in his technical tasks he had time to reflect on his future career. He was marked out as an *aristo* for the *corps diplomatique*, and studied history and art at the Sorbonne, before science seduced him. When the army released him he opted for theoretical physics.

In 1923, while still a graduate student, de Broglie wrote a short paper that forever altered human perceptions of the material world. It sparked the development of quantum mechanics, a theoretical scheme that made everything in the Universe jiggly and chancy. Many thought it intolerably weird, yet by the 21st century seemingly impossible long-distance quantum links would be communicating messages.

'When quite young you threw yourself into the controversy raging round the most profound problem in physics,' said a Swedish physicist, introducing de Broglie for his Nobel Prize in 1929. 'You had the boldness to assert, without the support of any known fact, that matter had not only a corpuscular nature, but also a wave nature. Experiment came later and established the correctness of your view.'

The train of thought began in Louis de Broglie's conversations with his brother Maurice, who was interested in the way X-rays interact with crystals. This phenomenon showed very plainly the dual nature of light-like radiation, as in the quantum theory initiated by Max Planck in Berlin in 1900 and pinned down by Albert Einstein in Bern in 1905. When scattered by planes of atoms in a crystal, X-rays behave like waves, but when they hit a photographic film they miraculously shrink into individual particles, called photons. The dual nature of light was perplexing enough, but de Broglie ascribed it to matter too.

'I got the idea that one had to extend this duality to material particles, especially to electrons,' de Broglie recalled later. The frequency of light is proportional to the energy of its photons, so why not also assign a wave frequency to the energy of a particle? As Einstein had shown, the energy is simply proportional to the particle's mass. For atoms, the frequency would be very high and the waves extremely short, but for lightweight electrons the wavelengths should be long enough for matter waves to be detectable.

In 1928, Clinton Davisson of the Bell Telephone Laboratories and George Thomson at Aberdeen independently confirmed the existence of matter waves. Davisson reflected electrons off a crystal of nickel. Thomson shot them through thin films of various materials. In either case, the electrons formed patterns just like those expected with light waves. Before the end of the century, physicists would be experimenting with superatoms consisting of millions of sodium atoms. They saw the matter waves behaving just like ripples on a pond. Quantum engineers were developing new kinds of atomic gyroscopes and motion sensors to exploit the wave nature of ordinary atoms, which promised to be as revolutionary as atomic clocks in timekeeping. An atomic-wave gyro operating in space could in theory be 100 billion times more sensitive than existing gyros.

And other researchers would be playing a new game with light and matter called quantum entanglement. It opened up novel and barely credible methods of communication that affect our perception of how the Universe works. Paradoxically it came about as a result of efforts to make quantum behaviour less baffling to the human mind.

'An element of chance'

Theorists did not wait for verification of de Broglie's matter waves. In the mid-1920s they snatched up the idea and constructed the theory of quantum mechanics. It swiftly overtook Einstein's relativity as the dominant concept in 20th-century physics. Niels Bohr of Copenhagen was the great coordinator, reconciling the ideas of the bright youngsters, mostly from Germany and Austria. There are quaint tales of scientists waiting on station platforms all across Europe to ask Bohr's opinion on the latest wheeze when his train passed through.

The 26-year-old Werner Heisenberg of Leipzig dreamed up the uncertainty principle while on a skiing holiday in 1928. He rejected the idea of tangible matter waves in favour of the notion of a statistical cloud. The uncertainty comes in because if you know the speed of a particle, you can't say exactly where it is. Or if you know where it is, you can't say exactly how it's travelling.

The salt crystals that form when seawater evaporates provided Heisenberg with an everyday example to illustrate the new way of thinking. 'This process retains a statistical and—one might almost say—historical element which cannot be further reduced,' he said. 'Even when the state of the liquid is completely known before crystallization, the shape of the crystal is not determined by the laws of quantum mechanics. The formation of regular shapes is just far more probable than that of a shapeless lump. But the ultimate shape owes its genesis partly to an element of chance which in principle cannot be analysed further.'

As Bohr was quick to point out, the uncertainty principle leads to the idea that scientists observing particles are unavoidably interacting with them. This prompted repeated attempts to forge links between quantum mechanics and human consciousness. One genus of interpretations comes suspiciously close to proposing that the Universe is just a Play Station for physicists.

The whole subject is a logical minefield, where non-experts should tread cautiously. But they should beware especially of bar-room philosophers who confuse physical uncertainty with human doubt or shaky science. Quantum mechanics is the most punctiliously verified theory in all of history.

Its spectacular success was already apparent by the early 1930s. For a start, it explained chemistry. By declaring that no two electrons could occupy exactly the same space in an atom, Wolfgang Pauli of Vienna made sense of the table of the chemical elements and their various properties. The nature of chemical bonds, as made clear by Linus Pauling from Caltech, gradually became comprehensible in quantum terms. By extension, chemistry incorporated biology too, in respect of the molecular processes of life. Genes, for example, are exquisite quantum-mechanical machines.

Paul Dirac in Cambridge showed that electrons must spin, and he predicted the existence of antimatter. Hideki Yukawa in Osaka set in train the search for particles that carry subatomic forces—a quest that was to keep physicists productively busy for the rest of the century. And Heisenberg's uncertainty principle fills empty space with virtual particles that can exist briefly because there was insufficient time for the laws of conservation to veto them.

The result is a very lively picture of atomic matter. Charged particles are iridescent with a swarm of virtual photons around them. When the novelist and science writer H.G. Wells expressed his reaction to quantum mechanics, he wrote, 'The atoms of our fathers seemed by contrast like a game of marbles abandoned in a corner of a muddy playground on a wet day.'

Lady Luck rules

The only trouble was that quantum mechanics made no sense to any human mind that stopped to think about it. A set of mathematical rules that successive generations of students had to learn, like the rules of chess, gives the right answers every time. 'Use it. It works, don't worry,' Isador Rabi told his students at Columbia. But the processes defy imagination.

Bright and dark stripes form whenever a beam of light of a single colour goes through a pair of narrow slits. The waves emerging from the slits reinforce one another in the bright stripes, and cancel out in between, wherever crest meets trough. The resulting pattern is a classic demonstration of the wave nature of light.

But physicists have equally good evidence that light is made of particles—the photons. So now make the source of light extremely faint, so that lone photons go through the slits individually, one after another. A naïve opinion would be that each photon can pass only through one slit or the other, and so the pattern of stripes should disappear.

Well, when the experiment is done, the arriving photons gradually build up the same old bright and dark stripes. In some sense each photon goes through both slits, which is just what the quantum theorists require. The same thing happens with electrons, travelling with de Broglie's matter waves.

In the quantum world Lady Luck rules. A wave of light or a matter wave defines a large volume of space where the associated photon or an electron might be. As soon as the particle makes its presence known, in a photographic film for example, the wave ceases to exist. It has served its purpose by defining, not where the particle will finish up, but the probability of its going to point A, or point B, or point C.

'No, you're not going to be able to understand it,' said Richard Feynman of Caltech during a lecture for a lay audience on the quantum description of the electric force. 'I can't explain why Nature behaves in this peculiar way.' Such was the orthodox view, laid down by Bohr and his shock troops and adopted by most other theorists. They offered the reassurance that quantum mechanics is about small-scale processes, and there is no contradiction with the old physics of the large scale. They're complementary.

A minority of able scientists nevertheless refused to believe that quantum mechanics was complete. They wanted a picture of subatomic events that was not only more imaginable but also less threatening to the old scientific idea of an objective, predictable reality. De Broglie himself declared: 'The statistical theories hide a completely determined and ascertainable reality behind variables which elude our experimental techniques.'

He visualized a second wave, in addition to the main light or matter wave, which might define the behaviour of a particle more narrowly. David Bohm of Birkbeck College London later developed this idea of a pilot wave. It could, for example, reconnoitre the route through the two slits, in the experiment mentioned.

The most formidable dissident was Einstein. 'God does not play dice!' he said, to which Bohr retorted: 'Stop telling God what to do!' Einstein understood perfectly well that God seems to play dice every day, in the sense that the outcome of physics experiments investigating subatomic events is indeed chancy and unpredictable. But like de Broglie he suspected that something was missing from the theory. When found, it would bring greater rationality, he hoped.

The paradox that backfired

Einstein's core complaint about quantum mechanics was that 'it cannot be reconciled with the idea that physics should represent a reality in time and space, free from spooky [*unheimlich*] action at a distance'. He used an apparent paradox of quantum theory to expose what he had in mind. In 1935 Einstein co-authored with Boris Podolsky and Nathan Rosen, young colleagues at the Institute for Advanced Study in Princeton, a paper entitled, 'Can quantum-mechanical description of physical reality be considered complete?'

The Einstein–Podolsky–Rosen Paradox concerns two particles that interact— they collide, for example—and then go off in different directions. The laws of physics govern the interaction of the particles. If you measure the position of one of the particles, the laws predict the position of the other.

But in quantum mechanics even the particles themselves don't know where they are until their positions are measured. They only have probabilities of being here rather than there, defined by their associated waves. Never mind, the interaction of the particles entangles their waves in a way that will ensure obedience to the physical laws.

Now comes the puzzle. Measure some property, perhaps the positions, first of one particle, and then of the other. Nothing is settled until the first measurement defines the position of the first particle. Only then can the second particle know where it must show up. But how does it know where to go?

The particles may be far apart by the time the measurements are made. To obtain the correct outcome, with the particles in the relative positions required by the physical laws, it is as if a message must travel faster than light, from one particle to the other. It says, 'Hi partner, they've just found me at this map reference, so please make sure you're at that one.'

Such is the action at a distance in quantum mechanics, about which Einstein complained till the end of his life. If you don't see why he called it spooky, please read the last few paragraphs again. The quantum tangles between widely separated particles are much, much weirder than a particle seeming to go through two slits at once.

Years later John Bell, a theorist from Northern Ireland working at the particle physics lab at CERN in Geneva, spent his spare time brooding about the Einstein–Podolsky–Rosen Paradox. Also about the ideas of Bohm, which he unfashionably admired. He envisaged a test of the proposition of de Broglie and Einstein that something was missing from quantum mechanics. In a paper published in 1966, Bell reasoned that if particles possessed any additional properties that determined their motions, these would alter the results in a two-particle experiment. They should make the predictions of quantum mechanics less reliable.

Back to Paris, or more precisely to the Institut d'Optique on the Paris-Sud campus in suburban Orsay. There a graduate student, Alain Aspect, put Bell's scenario to the test in a two-particle experiment. He used green and blue photons, particles of light born together like fraternal twins from excited calcium atoms.

Colour filters let green light go one way only, and blue light only the opposite way. That ensured that the twin photons flew apart. And with filters like polarizing sunglasses, Aspect measured the photons' directions of spin. The atomic physics required that the two photons should be spinning in opposite directions. When you knew the spin of the green photon, you could infer the spin of the blue, or vice versa.

Just as with positions of particles in the previous example, even the photons did not know how they were spinning until the measurement was done. It depended in part on exactly what test the experimenter made. For example, a photon spinning about a vertical axis has a 50 per cent chance of penetrating a filter that requires it to be spinning with a 45° tilt.

The experiment in Orsay had a dramatic feature. Using high-speed switching, the decision about exactly what test would be applied to the photons' spins was made only after they had set off on their journeys through the apparatus. By the time they entered the detectors they were 13 metres apart—far too far for any signal travelling at light speed to pass between them. Even so, collusion persisted between the green and blue photons, such that they showed up with appropriately matching spins on the two sides of the apparatus.

Aspect's results, announced in 1982, conformed precisely to the expectations of mainstream quantum mechanics. Nor was this a narrow victory. By Bell's predictions, if quantum mechanics were incomplete, the count of correct spin matches of green and blue photons should have been reduced by at least 25 per cent.

It might have been more amusing to find a failure of quantum mechanics. Instead, Aspect and his colleagues demonstrated exactly the action at a distance that Einstein detested. So in the end, all of those efforts to make quantum behaviour more comprehensible just made it spookier.

This long-range collusion, made possible by the entanglement of the waves associated with the photons, broke Bohr's promise that the weirdness of quantum mechanics was safely confined to highly localized, atomic-scale processes. Non-locality was the new buzzword. And by the backfiring that would make the maestro turn in his grave, the Einstein–Podolsky–Rosen Paradox became the Einstein–Podolsky–Rosen *Effect*.

Teleporting particles

In 1997, Nicolas Gisin and colleagues at the Université de Genève stretched the range of demonstrated entanglement to 11 kilometres. They used a crystal to split photons into twin, entangled photons. Two different fibre-optic telecom cables carried the photons from Geneva to detectors in the villages of Bellevue and Bernex, on either side of the city.

The energies of the photons, not their spins, were measured this time. They had to add up to a precise number, and they did. The greatly increased distance, compared with Aspect's experiment, brought no hint of any reduction in the collusion between the twin particles. By very precise measurements of the photons' arrival times, the Swiss experimenters were able to show that the news of the detection of one photon travelled to its twin at least 10 million times faster than light.

'In principle, it should make no difference whether the correlation between twin particles occurs when they are separated by a few metres or by the entire Universe,' Gisin said. So it came about that physicists entered the 21st century trying to assimilate spookiness on a cosmic scale. Imagine a photon arriving tonight from a galaxy a billion light-years away, and expiring in an owl's eye. A twin photon navigating through an intergalactic void 2 billion light-years away can experience bereavement. Not in 2 billion years' time, but instantly.

What price the prohibition against travelling faster than light? In a damage-limitation exercise, physicists insist that no real information is transferred by non-local quantum entanglement. But that gloss sits uncomfortably with technological applications that are beginning to emerge. When quantum spookiness went from bad to worse, it became useful. Swisscom supported Gisin's experiments because it was interested in unbreakable quantum codes, by which banks, for example, might transfer money with total security. Exchanges of quantum information between would-be communicators could give them unique one-time pads for use as cipher keys. Gisin's team demonstrated the idea in 1995 in an optical signal sent from Geneva to Nyon, 23 kilometres away.

Charles Bennett of IBM's Thomas J. Watson Laboratories, and Giles Brassard of the Université de Montréal had invented this scheme for quantum cryptography in 1984. By 1993 they were offering quantum entanglement as a concept for teleportation. That means destroying an object in one place and reconstituting it elsewhere, in the manner popularized in the *Star Trek* science-fiction TV series— 'Beam me up, Scottie!'—although teleporting people was not on the agenda.

Initially it was proposed for photons. The sender and receiver share a source of entangled photons. The sender then combines the photon to be teleported with an incoming entangled photon, and makes a measurement that destroys both photons. The result of the measurement goes by a normal communications channel to the receiver.

This message provides part of the information needed for adapting raw material—a spare photon at the receiving end—into a photon identical with the one being teleported. The rest of the information for the purpose, which would otherwise be denied to a scanner by the uncertainty principle, goes via the entangled photon's twin at the receiving end.

Within a few years, laboratories on both sides of the Atlantic were demonstrating teleportation of photons. For efficient transport of massive particles, including atoms, you need ways of entangling more than two particles. By 2000, physicists at the École Normale Supérieure in Paris were showing off an entangling machine for this purpose, which combined pulses from rotating atoms to entangle three particles, and then perhaps more.

A cure from gravity?

Do quantum entanglements and their awe-inspiring validation of quantum mechanics destroy all hope that some day quantum behaviour might become more acceptable to the human mind? No, they don't. The possibility of something like a pilot wave remains, although that, too, is a weird idea. And at Oxford, Roger Penrose pursued the question of whether there is a natural cut-off point beyond which quantum weirdness can no longer contaminate the familiar world.

He suspected that gravity might help to make an object of sufficient mass settle down and shed the jiggles and ambiguities of quantum behaviour. Penrose proposed an experimental test called FELIX. The name acknowledged the cat in a paradox described by Erwin Schrödinger, a leading Austrian pioneer of quantum mechanics. Schrödinger pointed out that the theory can require that a cat, hidden in a box, is simultaneously alive and dead until somebody takes off the lid to see.

In Penrose's view, the mass of Schrödinger's cat should be ample to suppress the quantum ambiguity, and save its life. The idea in the FELIX experiment is to represent the cat with a very small crystal that sometimes is, and sometimes isn't, hit by an energetic X-ray photon, which makes it recoil slightly. By quantum mechanics, it must therefore be considered both hit and not-hit, and immediate checks on the photons' behaviour will confirm the simultaneous existence of both states.

But now run the experiment between two satellites orbiting 15,000 kilometres apart. The X-rays will take a tenth of a second to shuttle between them. If Penrose's hunch is right, the delay should give the crystal time to settle down into a single, unambiguous state, so that photons revisiting it will see a difference.

There was no expectation that the space experiment would be done soon. Orthodox quantum mechanicists were inclined to regard it as wasted effort, predicting that no decay of ambiguity will be seen. The cat, they said, will remain both alive and dead in its box. But specialists in quantum computation in Penrose's own university, with individual opinions for and against his proposition, were happy to provide laboratory support for developing FELIX.

'Anything that tests the foundations of quantum mechanics experimentally is an important thing to do,' said Artur Ekert, head of Oxford's quantum computation centre. 'What Roger's trying to do is really push the limits. It's really exciting.'

▶ *For more about matter waves, see* SUPERATOMS, SUPERFLUIDS AND SUPERCONDUCTORS. *For a little more about quantum computing and cryptography, see* BITS AND QUBITS. *For the role of quantum mechanics in particle physics, see* ELECTROWEAK FORCE, PARTICLE FAMILIES *and* HIGGS BOSONS. *For attempts to reconcile quantum mechanics with Einstein's general relativity, see* GRAVITY *and* SUPERSTRINGS.

QUARK SOUP

Recreating a world without protons

I N THE LATE 1980S physicists at CERN, Europe's particle physics lab in Geneva, began a long series of experiments aimed at simulating the Big Bang in little bangs hot and dense enough to set quarks free. These are the fundamental entities that constitute the heavy matter in the atomic nucleus.

No one doubted by then that each of the protons and neutrons in a nucleus consists of three fundamental entities called quarks. Various experiments with particle accelerators had indirectly confirmed the presence of the quarks in the nuclear material. But no one had seen any free quarks.

If you try to liberate a quark in ordinary reactions between particles, you unavoidably create a new quark and an antiquark. One of them immediately replaces the extracted entity. The new antiquark handcuffs the would-be escaper in a particle called a meson. This is the trick by which Mother Nature has kept quarks in purdah since the world began.

To be more precise, the confinement of quarks began about 10 millionths of a second after the start of the Big Bang, at the supposed origin of the Universe. Before then, in unimaginably hot conditions, each quark could whizz about independently. Technically speaking, it was allowed to show its colour in public.

By the colour of a quark, physicists mean a quality similar to an electric charge. But instead of just plus and minus, the colour charge comes in three forms, labelled red, green and blue. The quarks are not really coloured, but it's a convenient way of thinking about the conditions of their confinement in ordinary matter.

In a TV screen, a red, green and blue dot together make white, and the rule nowadays is that nuclear matter, too, must be white. That's why protons and neutrons consist of three quarks apiece, and not two or four. One red, one green and one blue quark within each proton or neutron are held loosely together by particles called gluons.

The colour force carried by the gluons operates only over very short ranges. Space is opaque to the colour force, in much the same way as frozen water is impenetrable by fishes. But at a high enough temperature space melts, so to say, and lets the colour force through. Then the quarks and gluons can roam about as freely as do the individual charged atoms and electrons in the electrified gas, or plasma, of a neon lamp. The effect of the colour force is greatly weakened because immediate neighbours screen each particle from the pull of distant particles.

The resulting melee is called a quark—gluon plasma or, more colloquially, quark soup. Extremely high pressure may have the same effect as high temperatures, and physicists suspect that quark soup exists at the core of a neutron star, which is a collapsed star just one step short of a black hole. That's what the theory says, anyway, but to set the quarks free experimentally required creating a new state of matter never seen before.

'A spectacular excess of strangeness'

A multinational team of physicists working at CERN set out to make quark soup by using an accelerator, the Super Proton Synchrotron, to melt the nuclei of heavy atoms. It was a matter of whirling heavy atoms up to high energy and slamming them into a target also made of heavy atoms—lead onto lead, for example. A direct hit of one nucleus on another would create a small fireball, and might briefly produce the extreme conditions needed to liberate quarks.

The quarks would recombine almost instantly into a swarm of well-known particles and antiparticles, and fly as debris out of the target into detectors beyond. Only by oddities in the composition of the debris might one know that a peculiar state of matter had existed for a moment. For example the proportions of particles containing distinctive strange and charmed quarks might change.

Charmed quarks arc so heavy that they require a lot of energy for their formation, in the first moment of the nuclear collision. They would normally tend to pair up, as charmed and anticharmed quarks, to make a well-known particle called charmonium, or J/psi. But if conditions are so hot that plasma screening weakens the colour force, this won't happen. The charmed quarks should enjoy a brief freedom, and settle down only later, in the company of lighter quarks.

In the next moment of the nuclear collision strange quarks, somewhat lighter, are being mass-produced. By this time the colour force is much stronger, and it should corral the strange quarks, three at a time, to make a particle called omega. In short, the first signs of quark soup appearing fleetingly should be few charmoniums and many omegas.

That was exactly what the CERN experimenters saw. By 1997 they were reporting a shortage of charmoniums among the particles freezing out of the supposed soup. Within a few years they had also accumulated ample evidence for a surplus of the strange omega particles.

'A spectacular excess of strangeness, with omega production 15 times normal, is just the icing on the cake,' said Maurice Jacob of CERN, who made a theoretical analysis of the results of the nuclear collisions. 'Everything else checks too—the relative proportions of other particles, the size of the fireballs, and so on. We definitely created a new state of matter, ten times denser than nuclear matter. And the suppression of charmonium showed that we briefly let the charmed quarks out of captivity.'

For the sake of only one criterion did the CERN team hesitate to describe their 'new state of matter' as quark soup, or to claim it as a true quark–gluon plasma. The little fireballs were not sufficiently hot and long-lived for temperatures to average out. It was like deep-frozen potage microwaved but not stirred, and in Switzerland no self-respecting cook would call that soup.

A purpose-built accelerator

In 2000, colleagues at the Brookhaven National Laboratory on Long Island, New York, took over the investigation from CERN. Their new Relativistic Heavy Ion Collider was expressly built to make quark soup. Unlike the experiments at CERN, where one of the two heavy nuclei involved in an impact was a stationary target, the American machine brought two fast-moving beams of gold nuclei into collision, head-on.

It achieved full energy in 2001, and four experimental teams began to harvest the results of the unprecedented gold-on-gold impacts. Before long they were seeing evidence of better temperature stirring and other signs of soupiness. These included a reduction in the jets of particles normally produced when very energetic quarks try to escape from the throng. In quark soup, such quarks surrender much of their energy in collisions.

'It is difficult to know how the resulting insights will change and influence our technology, or even our views about Nature,' commented Thomas Kirk of Brookhaven, 'but history suggests there will be changes, and some may be profound.'

▶ *For more about quarks and gluons, see* PARTICLE FAMILIES. *The supposed sequence of events at the birth of the Universe is described in* BIG BANG.

RELATIVITY

I N A W A Y, *Relativitätstheorie* was always a poor name for Albert Einstein's ideas about space, time, motion and gravity. It seemed to make science iffy. In truth, his aim was to find out what remained reliable in physical laws *despite* confusions caused by relative motions and accelerations.

His conclusions illuminate much of physics and astronomy. Taken one by one, the ideas of relativity are not nearly as difficult as they are supposed to be, but there are quite a lot of them. One of the main theories is special relativity (1905) concerning HIGH-SPEED TRAVEL. Another is general relativity (1915) about GRAVITY.

ENERGY AND MASS appear in Einstein's famous $E = mc^2$, which was a by-product of special relativity. It reveals how to get energy from matter, notably in powering the STARS and also NUCLEAR WEAPONS, which were a fateful by-product. The equation implies that you can make new matter as a frozen form of energy, but when Paul Dirac combined special relativity with quantum theory it turned out that you inevitably get ANTIMATTER too.

General relativity is another box of tricks, among which BLACK HOLES dramatize the amazing effects on time and space of which gravity is capable. They are also very efficient converters of matter into energy. GRAVITATIONAL WAVES predicted by general relativity are being sought vigorously. More speculative are wormholes and loops in space, suggesting the possibility of TIME MACHINES.

Applied in cosmology, Einstein's general relativity could have predicted the expansion of the Universe, but he fumbled it twice. First he added a cosmological constant to prevent the expansion implied by his theory, and then he decided that was a mistake. In the outcome, his cosmological constant reappeared at the end of the 20th century when astronomers found that the cosmic expansion is accelerating, driven by DARK ENERGY.

Special relativity seems unassailable, but doubts arise about general relativity because of a mismatch to quantum theory. These are discussed in GRAVITY and SUPERSTRINGS.

SMALLPOX

The dairymaid's blessing and the general's curse

A T BOGAZKÖY IN TURKEY you can still see the Bronze Age fortifications of Hattusas, capital of the Hittites. Suppiluliumas I, who reigned there for 40 years in the 14th century BC, refurbished the city. He came to a sticky end after the widow of Tutankhamen of Egypt invited one of his sons to marry her and become pharaoh.

Opponents in Egypt thought it a bad idea and assassinated the Hittite prince. An ensuing conflict brought Egyptian prisoners of war to Anatolia. They were harbouring smallpox, long endemic in their homeland. The result was an epidemic in which Suppiluliumas I himself became the first victim of smallpox whose name history records. That was in 1350 BC.

The last person to die of smallpox was Janet Parker of Birmingham, England, in 1978. She was a medical photographer accidentally exposed to the smallpox virus retained for scientific purposes. In the previous year in Merka, Somalia, a cook named Ali Maow Maalin had been the last to catch the disease by human contagion, but he survived. In 1980, the World Health Organization in Geneva formally declared smallpox eradicated, after a 15-year programme in which vaccinators visited every last shantytown and nomadic tribe. This was arguably the greatest of all the practical achievements of science, ever.

Individual epidemics of other diseases sometimes took a high toll, including the bubonic plague that brought the Black Death to 14th-century Eurasia. Overall smallpox was the worst. Death rates in infants could approach 100 per cent, and survivors were usually disfigured by the pockmarks of the smallpox pustules, and often blinded. The historian Thomas Macaulay wrote of smallpox 'turning the babe into a changeling at which the mother shuddered, and making the eyes and cheeks of the betrothed maiden objects of horror to the lover.'

Populations in Eurasia and Africa were left with a level of naturally acquired immunity. But when European sailors and conquistadors carried smallpox and other diseases to regions not previously exposed to them, in the Americas and Oceania, they inadvertently wiped out most of the native populations. One victim was the Aztec emperor Ciutláhuac in 1520.

Nor was it always inadvertent. 'The devastating effect of smallpox gave rise to one of the first examples of biological warfare,' noted the medical historians

Nicolau Barquet and Pere Domingo of Barcelona. In 1763 General Jeffrey Amherst, commanding the British army in North America, approved a proposal by Colonel Henry Bouquet to grind the scabs of smallpox pustules into blankets that were to be distributed among disaffected tribes of Indians. 'You will do well to try to inoculate the Indians by means of blankets,' Amherst wrote, 'as well as to try every other method that can serve to extirpate this execrable race.'

By that time, many children in Eurasia were being deliberately infected with smallpox from very mild cases, in the knowledge that most would survive with little scarring and with acquired immunity. The practice of applying pus from a smallpox pustule to a child's skin, and making a small cut, may have originated among Circassian women who supplied many daughters to Turkish harems. The wife of the British ambassador in Istanbul introduced the practice to London in 1721. It killed one in 50 of the children so treated and could itself be a source of contagion for others.

'Such a wild idea'

The Circassians were not the only women with a special reputation for beauty—meaning in those days, not pockmarked. Throughout rural Europe it was common knowledge that dairymaids often escaped the smallpox. English folklore attributed their good looks to their exposure to the morning dew when they went to milk the cows. As one song had it:

> Oh, where are you going, my pretty maiden fair,
> With your rosy red cheeks and your coal-black hair?
> I'm going a-milking, kind sir, says she,
> And it's dabbling in the dew where you'll find me.

The dairymaids themselves had shrewder insight, and one of them pertly assured a Bristol doctor that she would never have the smallpox because she'd had the cowpox. This was a mild condition that produced sores on the hands of those dealing with cattle. The doctor's apprentice, Edward Jenner by name, overheard this remark and remembered it.

Three decades later, when he had his own practice in Berkeley, Gloucestershire, Jenner pursued the matter under the cloak of investigating diseases transmitted from animals to human beings. Eventually he steeled himself and his patients to see whether inoculation with the non-virulent cowpox might protect against smallpox. In 1796, in an experiment that would nowadays be called heroic, i.e. questionable, Jenner introduced matter from a sore on a dairymaid's hand into the arm of a healthy eight-year-old, James Phipps. Six weeks later he tried hard to infect the lad with smallpox. Happily for young James and the rest of us, the inoculation worked, as it did in further trials with cowpox.

'This disease leaves the constitution in a state of perfect security from the infection of the smallpox,' Jenner reported. In an early manifestation of peer review, the Royal Society of London refused to publish his manuscript. Gratuitously it added the caution, 'He had better not promulgate such a wild idea if he valued his reputation.'

When Jenner issued a monograph at his own expense, the clerics joined the medics in denouncing him. Nevertheless the treatment plainly worked, and commended itself to the likes of the French and Spanish emperors and the US president. By 1807 a grateful British parliament had rewarded Jenner with £30,000, equivalent to about £1 million today. And in less than 200 years cowpox had wholly extinguished smallpox.

A biological weapon

Or had it? Alongside the dairymaid's blessing, there remained General Amherst's curse. Nothing shows more graphically than smallpox how moral and political issues are magnified and dramatized by the power of science.

The campaign against smallpox brought out the best in people. Thomas Jefferson personally saw to it that Jenner's vaccination was demonstrated to Native Americans. And for the last big push, which occurred during the Cold War, humanity was united as never before as a single species with a common interest in eliminating smallpox from even the poorest and most remote parts of the world—and damn the cost.

Yet smallpox also brought out the worst, in governments and their scientific servants. What was superficially a scholarly argument within the World Health Organization, about what should be done with laboratory stocks of smallpox virus after eradication was certified in 1980, concealed a deeper anxiety. New generations would grow up as immunologically naïve in respect of smallpox as the Aztecs were. They would then be sitting ducks for smallpox used as a military or terrorist weapon.

Internationally approved stocks of smallpox virus were reduced to those at the Centers for Disease Control and Prevention in Atlanta, and at the Ivanovsky Institute for Viral Preparations in Moscow. The case for destroying these, too, was that as long as they existed they could escape and cause an epidemic. A minor argument for keeping them was that they might be needed for future medical research. The main objection to their destruction was that no one knew for sure if the Atlanta and Moscow stocks were the only ones. The destruction of the smallpox virus was deferred repeatedly for want of consensus in the World Health Organization's multinational executive board.

Concern about a smallpox weapon was no paranoid fantasy. That became clear when the Soviet Union collapsed. Ken Alibek (Kanatjan Alibekov) had been deputy chief of a Soviet weapons programme called Biopreparat, and in 1992 he turned up in the USA as a defector with chilling information. One of his jobs had been to work out tactics to circumvent the agreed restriction of the smallpox stock to Moscow, and to evade the Biological and Toxin Weapons Convention of 1972, which limited research to defensive measures only.

A high priority was to get international approval for moving the official stock from Moscow to a virology centre near Novosibirsk, called Vektor, which was secretly engaged in research on a smallpox weapon. To preserve all essential information against the day when the virus might have to be killed, molecular biologists embarked on a complete analysis of the genes of smallpox, and also of cowpox. The aim was then to modify the cowpox virus by genetic engineering, which could be done under the guise of vaccine research but really aimed at a virulent product.

The Soviet Union was meanwhile culturing the old-fashioned stuff on a grand scale. 'In the late 1980s and early 1990s, over 60,000 people were involved in the research, development, and production of biological weapons,' Alibek reported. 'Hundreds of tons of anthrax weapon formulation were stockpiled, along with dozens of tons of smallpox and plague.'

The risk of accidental releases was ever-present. Alibek told of anthrax escaping from a weapons facility in Sverdlovsk in 1979. In the cover-up, medical records of victims were destroyed and a peasant was arrested for allegedly supplying meat contaminated with anthrax.

Western intelligence agencies had little inkling of the Soviet programme. Unlike nuclear weapons, disease agents need no large facilities visible to spy satellites for preparing the materials. Any vaccine factory can be converted into a weapons plant overnight. The delivery system can be as simple as Amherst's contaminated blankets, or the mailed letters used in small-scale anthrax attacks on the US government in 2001.

In 1992 the Russian leader Boris Yel'tsin officially halted all activity on biological weapons. Alibek noted that the smallpox stock was nevertheless moved to Vektor in 1994. Papers subsequently appearing in the open literature about modified cowpox viruses suggested to him that the weapons programme was on track.

With the rise of international terrorism, smallpox and other bioweapons seem apt for attacks on civilian populations aimed at killing as many people as possible. Several countries began stockpiling smallpox vaccine again and vaccinating key personnel. Alibek became president of Advanced Biosystems Inc. under contract to the US Defense Advanced Projects Agency, and was soon helping to run the Center for Biodefense at George Mason University. He said,

'We need to create a new generation of scientists who will be able to work in civilian biodefence.'

▶ *For another military use of science, see* NUCLEAR WEAPONS. *For more on the biomedical side, see* IMMUNE SYSTEM.

SOLAR WIND

How it creates the heliosphere in which we live

R ADIOCARBON DATING was a nuclear chemist's great gift to the archaeologists. Willard Libby at Chicago commended it to them in 1949, giving examples of objects where his dates were in line with ages known by other means. The idea was simple. Living things absorb radioactive carbon-14 from the air, but when they die, and become building wood or charcoal or leather, the radiocarbon content gradually diminishes over thousands of years, as the radioactive atoms decay. Measure what remains, and you can tell how old the objects are.

This beautiful recipe was soon spoiled by absurdities, such as pharaohs who were dated as reigning after their known successors. The explanation came from a biophysicist, Hessel de Vries, at Groningen in 1958. The rate of production of radiocarbon in the atmosphere had varied over the centuries and millennia, he said, because of changes in the intensity of cosmic rays. These are energetic subatomic particles coming from the Galaxy, and they manufacture radiocarbon by interactions with nitrogen atoms in the air.

For the discontented archaeologists the remedy came from long-lived trees, in particular the bristlecone pines of California's White Mountains. Thanks to the work of Edmund Schulman and his successors at Arizona, the age of every ring of annual growth was known by counting, in a series of wood samples going back 8000 years. The nuclear chemist Hans Suess of UC San Diego looked to see how the tree rings' radiocarbon dates compared with their counted ages. In 1967 he published a chart showing a remarkable series of wiggles, indicating significant changes in the radiocarbon production rate.

When archaeologists used the bristlecone results to calibrate their dates, the effects were revolutionary. A cherished idea that civilization and technologies diffused outwards from Sumeria and Egypt was confounded when the corrected radiocarbon dates showed that folk in Brittany were building large stone monuments 1500 years before the first rough-stone Egyptian pyramid was constructed. As Colin Renfrew at Southampton announced in 1973: 'The whole diffusionist framework collapses, and with it the assumptions which sustained prehistoric archaeology for nearly a century.'

But why did the cosmic rays vary so much? Gradual changes in the Earth's magnetic field explained the long-term trend, but not the Suess wiggles. To begin to answer the question, an equally revolutionary change was needed, in perceptions of the Earth's relationship to the Sun. Here the big surprise was the discovery of the solar wind.

An escalator that repels cosmic rays

The Earth's magnetic field partly protects the atmosphere and surface from cosmic rays. In the equatorial zone, where it is most effective, only the most energetic cosmic-ray particles penetrate the shield. In the polar regions, the rays are funnelled towards the atmosphere by the field lines converging on the magnetic poles. The monitoring of cosmic rays worldwide therefore seemed an appropriate task for experts in terrestrial magnetism at the Carnegie Institution in Washington DC.

Scott Forbush was given the job, and in 1935–36 he set up a worldwide network of recording instruments, initially in Maryland, Peru and New Zealand. 'Study cosmic rays and see the world,' a friend recalled about Forbush. 'He carried a battered leather briefcase for many years and took a quiet pride in the dozens of stubs from airlines, shops, and hotels that he allowed to accumulate on its handle, a kind of archaeological record of his travels.'

Working almost alone for two decades, Forbush made salient discoveries about cosmic-ray variations. He found cycles of 27 days, linked to the rotation of the Sun, and cycles of 11 years, following the sunspot cycles in which the count of dark spots on the visible face waxes and wanes. He detected bursts of cosmic-ray-like energetic particles emanating from solar flares. But otherwise high sunspot counts, denoting a stormy Sun, were associated with a big reduction in cosmic rays coming from the Galaxy.

Forbush decreases are the name still given to sharp drop-offs in cosmic-ray intensities that can follow exceptional solar eruptions. These are also associated with magnetic storms on the Earth, which set compass needles wandering. The coincidence misled Forbush into an Earth-centred view of events. He thought that variations in the cosmic rays were due to changes in the magnetic environment of the Earth, when in fact both phenomena are caused by the Sun's behaviour.

John Simpson at Chicago suspected that the cosmic-ray variations were the result of magnetic effects spread much more widely in space. He invented a neutron monitor to study cosmic rays of relatively low energy, which varied the most, and he established five stations, from Huancayo in Peru to Chicago. The ways in which the changes in the count-rates depended on the energy of the particles supported his idea of variable magnetic fields pervading interplanetary space.

Then an important clue came from a completely different direction. The tail of a comet always points directly away from the Sun, regardless of which way the comet is travelling. The conventional explanation was that sunlight pushed the tail away. Whilst that was fair enough, for the fine dust grains in the tail, Ludwig Biermann at Gottingen pointed out in 1951 that the pressure of light on atoms and molecules was much too weak to account for the long, straight, gassy component of the tail.

Biermann suggested instead that the gassy tails of comets are swept away by particles coming from the Sun. These might be of the same kind as the 'solar corpuscles' thought to be responsible for buffeting the magnetic field of Earth following a burst of solar activity. Outside the world of comet science, few paid much attention to this idea that comets were responding like wind vanes to an outward flow from the Sun.

An exception was a young physicist at Chicago, Eugene Parker. He was struck by the evidence from the comet tails that matter is emitted from the Sun in all directions and at all times. Sometimes only weakly, perhaps, but never absent. A non-stop solar wind.

Parker reasoned that the story starts with the atmosphere of the Sun, which becomes visible as the corona seen during solar eclipses. As it is extremely hot, at a million degrees C or more, it should continually expand away into space, reaching speeds of hundreds of kilometres per second far out from the Sun. Thus the mysterious 'solar corpuscles', so long believed to jiggle the Earth's magnetic field, became primarily an expansion of the solar atmosphere, obeying the hydrodynamic laws of fluid motion.

The solar wind of Parker's conception also enforces magnetic laws in interplanetary space. It consists of a plasma of charged atoms and electrons, with a magnetic component too. Sweeping out through the Solar System the solar wind stretches the magnetic fields of the Sun to fill the entire space to some distance beyond the farthest planets. As the Sun rotates about its axis, the effect is to wind up the magnetic field into a large rotating spiral, later known as the Parker spiral. In the vicinity of Earth, for example, the Sun's magnetic field lines slant in from the west at about 45 degrees to the Earth–Sun line.

The outward sweep of the magnetic fields pushes back the cosmic rays to varying degrees, producing the changes in their rates studied by Forbush and

Simpson for so many years. Simpson likened the irregular magnetic field embedded in the solar wind to an upward-moving staircase, or escalator. Imagine rolling tennis balls down it, to represent cosmic rays coming from the Galaxy and trying to reach the inner Solar System and Earth. Some of them will bounce back to the top and never make it.

'Speed up the escalator to simulate increased solar activity,' Simpson said. 'Now many more of the tennis balls will come back to you, and fewer will reach the bottom of the escalator.'

Discovering the wind

Another consequence of the solar-wind theory was that the Earth's magnetic field should not simply fade away into the distance, but be bottled up by the pressure of the wind. Conversely the Earth's field acts a windscreen, keeping the solar wind at bay. So we live in a magnetic bubble, called the magnetosphere, within a huge extension of the Sun's atmosphere, called the heliosphere, which is filled by the solar wind.

Large solar eruptions have to be seen as just episodes during an unending battle between the solar wind and the Earth's field. On the sunward side, the boundary of the magnetosphere is normally about 60,000 kilometres from the Earth's surface. A strong gust in the solar wind can push the windscreen back to just 30,000 kilometres out. The squeezing of the Earth's field initiates a magnetic storm felt by detectors on the ground.

All that is now standard stuff, but when Parker mooted it in 1958, most pundits scorned his brand new picture of the hydrodynamic Sun–Earth connection. They said to him, 'If you knew anything about the subject, Parker, you could not possibly be suggesting this. We have known for decades that interplanetary space is a hard vacuum, pierced only intermittently by beams of energetic particles emitted by the Sun.'

The Space Age had just begun, and Parker was vindicated very soon. The Soviet space scientist Konstantin Gringauz saw the first hints of the solar wind with instruments on Lunik-2 and Lunik-3, bound for the Moon in 1959. In 1962 clear confirmation came from NASA's Explorer-12 satellite, which located the boundary of the Earth's magnetosphere, and from Mariner-2, which swam through the interplanetary solar wind all the way to Venus.

It became the space physicists' favourite subject. Relatively simple instruments could detect electrons and charged atoms of the solar wind, and measure the magnetic field. A long succession of dedicated satellites explored the Earth's magnetosphere and the solar wind enclosing it. During the longueurs of interplanetary spaceflight there was always something to record: for example, the planet Jupiter turned out to have a huge and highly active magnetosphere of its own.

Operating closer to the Sun, between 1974 and 1984, the German–US Helios-1 and Helios-2 spacecraft recorded many of the basic phenomena of the particles and magnetic fields of the solar wind. Other spacecraft visiting Halley's Comet in 1986 observed the interaction of its gassy component with the solar wind, as adumbrated by Biermann 35 years earlier.

The solar wind turned out to have two different speeds. In the Earth's vicinity, it is usually 350–400 kilometres per second, but fast windstreams of 750 kilometres per second sometimes hit the magnetosphere. They emanate from regions called coronal holes, which look dark in X-ray images of the Sun's atmosphere. The coronal holes are confined to the polar regions when the Sun is quiet in respect of sunspots. As activity increases, the coronal holes can spread down to the equatorial regions of the Sun, where our part of the solar wind comes from.

Clashes between fast and slow streams create shock waves in the heliosphere. Other shocks are due to gusts in the solar wind in the form of mass ejections of gas from the Sun, travelling outwards at 500–1000 kilometres per second in particular directions and spreading as they go. Intensified magnetic fields associated with the shocks help to create an obstacle course for cosmic rays entering the Solar System.

Pictorial confirmation of Parker's original meditations came in 1995, when two widely separated spacecraft tracked a burst of high-energy electrons leaving the Sun. The resulting 3-D view of the radio emissions showed the electrons swerving along a curve. Whilst the magnetic field obeys the low-energy particles of the solar wind travelling straight out from the Sun, high-energy particles from solar explosions are constrained to follow the curved magnetic field of the Parker spiral.

Exploring the heliosphere

In Dante Alighieri's *Commedia*, Ulysses the sailor tells his crew, 'Don't miss the chance to experience the unpeopled world on the far side of the Sun.' Ulysses was adopted as the name of a spacecraft built in Europe for an exploration of the solar wind, not only far from the Earth but far outside the flatland where the major planets and all other spacecraft orbit in the Sun's equatorial zone. The aim was a 3-D view of events in the heliosphere, the bubble in space blown by the solar wind.

'How could you expect to understand the Earth's weather if you lived at the Equator and were never quite sure about the climate in other latitudes?' asked Richard Marsden, the European Space Agency's project scientist. 'It's the same with the Sun. Yet astronomers and space scientists always had to make do with an equatorial view of the Sun, until Ulysses.'

Launched by a NASA space shuttle in 1990, in a joint venture that carried instruments devised by European and US teams, Ulysses swung around Jupiter in 1992. The giant planet's gravity redirected the spacecraft into an unprecedented orbit that took it over the Sun's polar regions, in 1994–95 and again in 2000–01.

Simpson in Chicago was the *éminence grise* among the Ulysses experimenters, and he took special responsibility for cosmic-ray detectors on Ulysses. He had proposed such a solar-polar mission as early as 1959. Along with a general curiosity about the untested conditions at high solar latitudes, Simpson was interested in a theoretical possibility that the cosmic rays might stream in freely along untwisted magnetic field lines over the poles of the Sun.

The first pass over the south pole, in September 1994, revealed that the solar wind smoothes out the Sun's magnetic field, cancelling the concentration of field lines expected over the poles. André Balogh of Imperial College London, who was in charge of the magnetic sensors on Ulysses, expressed the team's astonishment by saying, 'We went to the south magnetic pole of the Sun and it wasn't there!'

The observable increase in cosmic rays turned out to be small. Magnetic waves and shock waves from the polar regions batted many of them away, as effectively as in the Sun's equatorial regions. The hope of seeing cosmic rays in an unimpeded state was not fulfilled, but the Ulysses project was a big success in many other ways.

A cardinal discovery was that most of space around the Sun is filled by the fast solar wind from the coronal holes, blowing at 750 kilometres per second. The spreading out of this fast wind has the effect of making the magnetic field quite uniform in all directions. Relying on this result from Ulysses, Mike Lockwood of the UK's Rutherford Appleton Laboratory felt confident in using measurements of magnetic storms at the Earth's surface to deduce that the Sun's interplanetary magnetic field more than doubled in strength during the 20th century.

When another European–US solar spacecraft, SOHO, went into space in 1995, one of its stated tasks was to trace the sources of the solar wind, in the atmosphere of the Sun. In the relatively cool regions from which the fast solar wind comes, SOHO detected streams leaking through the corners of honeycomb-shaped magnetic fields that surround bubbles in the visible surface. It also saw gas spiralling outwards in gigantic tornadoes in the polar regions. At greater distances from the visible surface, SOHO observed charged gas atoms being accelerated out into space by magnetic waves.

The slower solar windstream, common in the Earth's vicinity, leaks out along the edges of bright wedge-shaped regions called helmets. During solar eclipses, when the Sun is quiet, the helmets are seen on the equator, but in periods of high sunspot activity they show up at odd angles. Small mass ejections, observed daily by SOHO, also contribute to the slow wind, and again magnetic waves seem to continue accelerating the slow windstream far into space.

Like the Sun itself, the solar wind consists mainly of hydrogen and helium atoms stripped of their electrons, although accompanied by the appropriate number of free electrons to keep the gas electrically neutral. Other elements present in the Sun show up in the solar wind too, and a detector on SOHO identified a large number of different masses, up to nickel-62. The proportions of the various constituents differ in the slow and fast windstreams, and give further clues to how the solar wind is heated and accelerated.

The breeze from the stars

Ulysses, SOHO and other spacecraft detected many energetic particles, called anomalous cosmic rays, accelerated inwards by distant shock waves at the frontier of the Sun's empire. Just as the Earth's magnetic field is bottled up by the solar wind, so the solar wind and the magnetism it carries are in turn brought to a halt by the thin gas that fills the space between the stars. At present the boundary is far away.

NASA's Pioneer and Voyager spacecraft have journeyed for many years beyond the farthest planets, without leaving the heliosphere. Nevertheless, like sailors hearing the noise of storm waves pounding on a distant shore, the far-flung spacecraft twice detected radio uproar, lasting about a year, that came from the distant boundary. The radio emissions were provoked by giant blast waves from the Sun.

After exceptional sunstorms in July 1982 and June 1991 the outgoing blasts washed over the spacecraft at about 800 kilometres per second. From the time when the blast waves left the Sun's vicinity, more than 13 months elapsed before the radio emissions began, implying that the boundary of the heliosphere lies at 110 to 160 times the Sun–Earth distance. Perhaps the Voyagers will reach it, and enter interstellar space, before their radioactive energy supply runs out in 2020, at about 130 times the Earth–Sun distance.

A breeze in the external interstellar gas streamlines the heliosphere. Atoms of that gas passing through the Solar System fluoresce in the Sun's ultraviolet light. A French–Finnish instrument on the SOHO spacecraft, called SWAN, was designed to see the glow of hydrogen atoms, and it fixed the track and speed of the gas, despite confusions caused by gravity.

'The solar wind destroys interstellar hydrogen atoms passing close to the Sun,' explained Jean-Loup Bertaux of France's Service d'Aéronomie, who led the SWAN team. 'Downwind we see distant survivors, whose speed is less affected by the Sun's gravity.'

The upshot is that the hydrogen in the interstellar breeze comes from the direction of the Ophiuchus constellation at 21 kilometres per second. But the interstellar helium that accompanies it travels faster through the Solar System, at 26 kilometres per second, as gauged by a German instrument, GAS, on Ulysses. Evidently the helium is less impeded than hydrogen is by its encounter with the heliospheric boundary.

The heliosphere is probably unusually large just now. A temporary reason is the increase in vigour of the solar wind, during the 20th century. On a much longer time-scale, the Sun and the Solar System are presently passing through a relatively tenuous region of interstellar space, with a density of only about 100 atoms per litre. Much greater gas densities exist in quite nearby places in the Galaxy, and when the Sun encounters them, the interstellar breeze becomes a gale that could easily compress the heliosphere to half or even one-tenth of its present size.

That must have happened in the past. Some scientists suspect that large increases in cosmic-ray intensity 60,000 and 33,000 years ago may be symptoms of encounters with small interstellar clouds of gas, conceivably with quite drastic effects on the Earth's climate. The heliosphere's size and its variations are therefore a new theme for astronomers and space scientists in the 21st century. There is even talk of sending space probes ahead of the Sun on its course among the stars, to scout for any gas clouds waiting to ambush us.

'The Sun's trajectory suggests that it will probably not encounter a large, dense cloud for at least several more million years,' commented Priscilla Frisch at Chicago. 'The consequences of such an encounter for the Earth's climate are unclear; however, one wonders whether it is a coincidence that *Homo sapiens* appeared while the Sun was traversing a region of space virtually devoid of interstellar matter.'

The realization that we live in a bubble, the magnetosphere, within another bubble, the heliosphere, and that in turn within a relatively empty bubble in the interstellar gas, completely alters humankind's perception of its relationship to the Sun and the wider Universe. Already the concept of the solar wind has extended far into mainstream astronomy. Intense stellar winds are recognized as big players in the birth, maturity and death of stars. Many climate scientists, on the other hand, have still to learn to stop regarding the Sun as if it were just a distant light in the sky.

For better or worse, its outpourings engulf us. And Eugene Parker's solar wind, scorned by experts just half a century ago, turns out to be much more than just a curious phenomenon of interplanetary space. It is one of the great connectors of modern cross-disciplinary science, from astronomy and plasma physics to meteorology and archaeology.

▶ *For more about terrestrial effects of the stormy solar wind, see* SPACE WEATHER. *For possible links between the solar wind and climate, see* EARTHSHINE *and* CLIMATE CHANGE. *An idea that the solar wind might be used as a means of propulsion crops up in* ASTRONAUTICS. *For more on cosmic rays, especially extremely energetic ones, see* COSMIC RAYS.

SPACE WEATHER

Why it is now more troublesome than in the old days

A MONG NORWAY'S LOFOTEN ISLANDS the sea goes mad in the Maelstrøm. It has scared a hundred generations of seafarers with its swift, abruptly changing currents, and sudden whirlpools that can drag a boat and its crew down into oblivion within seconds. An even stranger turmoil persists hundreds of kilometres overhead, in the electric sea called the ionosphere. Winds blowing at 200 kilometres per hour change direction abruptly, air temperatures can double in minutes, and sometimes the breathtaking displays of the aurora borealis, or Northern Lights, stretch far and wide across the sky, with rippling draperies and whirling curlicues.

Tromsø in northern Norway considers itself the Northern Lights capital of the world, for scientists and tourists alike. The town lies under the auroral zone, a wide ring that surrounds the Earth's north magnetic pole, which is currently located in northern Canada. Part of the sales pitch is that the Atlantic's Gulf Stream keeps Tromsø's climate relatively mild despite its location well inside the Arctic Circle, at almost 70 degrees north. That is just as well because winter is the best season for seeing auroras, during the long polar night.

The ancients in Scandinavia thought that the auroras were the work of warring gods, or simply the ghosts of virgins, whom one should greet by waving a white cloth. At the other end of the world, Maoris in New Zealand imagined the aurora australis, the Southern Lights, to be distress signals from fellow Polynesian navigators who had ventured too far south. There is no record of any rescue attempt.

Nowadays scientists interpret the auroras as a natural television show. Beams of atomic particles, accelerated and steered in space like the electron beams of TV tubes, hit the upper air and make the atoms glow. The kinetic art is a virtual image of plasma clouds, magnetized masses of electrons and charged atoms, which squirm and swirl in the Earth's space environment.

Grand auroras are sometimes visible far beyond the normal auroral zone. They occur when an exceptional blast of gas, which left the Sun a few days before, squeezes the magnetic field and draws out the field lines into a tail on the dark side of the Earth. There, invisible explosions send particles racing along the magnetic lines, which lead towards the north and south polar regions, where auroras occur simultaneously. Widespread auroras are the most obvious sign that the Earth is subject to the weather in space provoked by storms in the Sun's atmosphere.

The magnetic poles move, and three centuries ago the auroral zone lay over Scotland and southern Sweden. Around 1724, George Graham in London and Anders Celsius of Uppsala discovered magnetic storms, deflections of compass needles that occur at the same time as auroras. By the end of the 19th century these effects were known to be somewhat related, in frequency and severity, to the count of dark sunspots on the Sun's face, which varies in an 11-year cycle.

In 1896 in Kristiania (now called Oslo) the physicist Kristian Birkeland made a great leap of the imagination, with the aid of a toy earth. He installed an electromagnet inside the small globe, to simulate the magnetic field, and coated the outside with fluorescent paint. Then he put his model in a vacuum chamber, and bombarded the toy earth with cathode rays at 6000 volts. No one quite knew what cathode rays were, but they were all the rage in the world's physics labs at the time.

Lo and behold, glowing rings formed around the magnetic poles, just like the auroral zones. In the following year J.J. Thomson at Cambridge identified cathode rays as the first known subatomic particles—electrons. So Birkeland was able immediately to propose that auroras were due to high-energy electrons arriving at the Earth from the Sun, and hitting the air.

It was a very clever idea and it boosted auroral investigations by linking them to the most advanced laboratory physics. With hindsight, Birkeland was right in visualizing charged matter travelling to the Earth from the Sun. He was wrong in supposing that this happened in a complete vacuum, and only at times of solar explosions. Nor do the particles have quite such a clear run into the air of the auroral zone as he imagined.

A hundred years later, Birkeland's successors had a more complete but also far more complex picture, that left them less confident about the precise causes of auroras. By then Tromsø was the headquarters of a network of large scientific radars distributed across northern Scandinavia. Called EISCAT, short for European Incoherent Scatter, it is a seven-nation venture that has observed the turbulent plasma clouds in the upper atmosphere by sending radar signals from one station to another, ever since the first British campaign with the facility in 1981.

'Here in the auroral zone, scientists have spent decades using balloons, rockets and satellites, as well as radars, magnetic observatories and auroral cameras on the ground, to try to make sense of the Sun–Earth connection,' said Tony van Eyken, director of EISCAT. 'On good days, I sometimes think we may be beginning to get the hang of it. But in reality there is still much we don't understand.'

Even as knowledge of space weather was gradually advancing, practical considerations made a better understanding much more urgent. When radio came into general use, the role of the ionosphere as a convenient mirror in the sky was compromised during sunstorms, with communications blackouts occurring especially at high latitudes. In 1942, British radar operators thought that the Germans were jamming their sets, but it turned out to be the Sun emitting strong radio waves. Thereafter you could monitor the Sun's general storminess by its radio intensity, with less eyestrain than by counting sunspots.

Magnetic storms ceased to be a harmless curiosity when they encountered the long metal structures being created by 20th-century technology, and induced strong electric currents in them. Oil pipelines, for example, are liable to accelerated erosion. Particularly vulnerable to current surges are cables distributing electric power, as demonstrated in a widespread blackout in Quebec during a sunstorm in 1989.

Spacecraft are at risk. Sparks due to electrical effects in the Earth's space environment can harm equipment on satellites. The outer atmosphere also swells during a sunstorm, and it deflects satellites in low orbits or can even destroy them. Bursts of energetic subatomic particles coming from the explosions on the Sun called solar flares can damage the solar panels and other electronic equipment on satellites, and in extreme cases they can knock out computers even on the ground. As microchips become ever more micro they become increasingly vulnerable to space weather.

The greatest concern is about astronauts. At present they get about half an hour's warning, between the time when X-ray sensors in space see a flare on the Sun and the energetic particles arrive. The International Space Station has refuge bunks screened by water, but an astronaut caught in the open, for example on the surface of the Moon or Mars, could be killed by the particles, often called solar protons.

'For thousands of years my ancestors marvelled at the space weather seen in the Northern Lights, but auroras never hurt a sailor or a farmer,' commented Paal Brekke, a Norwegian solar physicist with the European Space Agency. 'It's only with our modern electrical, electronic and space technologies that the Sun's effects become damaging, and personally hazardous for astronauts. The more we do in space, the more serious and potentially costly the problems of space weather will become.'

The battle with the solar wind

The first scientific surprise of the Space Age came in 1958, when James van Allen at Iowa put a Geiger counter on the earliest American satellite, Explorer-1, and detected energetic atomic particles trapped in the magnetic field. They made a radiation belt (later, belts) around the Earth. But this was something of a red herring. Even if some of the particles were of solar origin, they did not necessarily conflict with the prevailing view that emissions from the Sun were intermittent.

The big picture changed with the discovery of the solar wind a few years later. It consists of charged particles of much less energy, but blowing continuously from the solar atmosphere and carrying the Sun's magnetic field with them. The Earth's magnetic field generally keeps the solar wind at bay, so that it flows around the planet. This creates a magnetosphere streamlined like a comet, rounded on the sunward side but stretching downwind like a comet's tail.

Changes in the solar wind disturb the magnetosphere. They often occur because of peculiar features of the solar wind, with no need for any special events on the Sun. For example, the direction of the magnetic field in the solar wind can change abruptly every few days, now to be roughly aligned with the Earth's magnetic field, now to run in the opposite direction.

This magnetic switch happens because the solar wind drags out the Sun's magnetism like bubblegum. In the Sun's equatorial zone the outgoing and return field lines come very close together. The sheet in which this happens is not flat but wavy, like a ballerina's skirt. As the Sun rotates the Earth is sometimes above and sometimes below the skirt.

Also wind-engendered are shock waves in space created by the collision of fast and slow solar windstreams, coming from different parts of the Sun's atmosphere. The same shock waves reappear every 27 days as the Sun turns, so they are known as co-rotating interaction regions. But the biggest disturbances in the solar wind are produced by giant puffs of gas called mass ejections, coming from explosions in the Sun's atmosphere.

Events in major sunstorms follow a well-known sequence. Solar flares send out X-rays that drench the Earth's outer atmosphere eight minutes later, knocking electrons out of atoms and causing sudden ionospheric disturbances. Associated bursts of energetic particles take half an hour to arrive. If a mass ejection is heading our way, it reaches the Earth 2–4 days later, and squeezes the Earth's magnetosphere.

Most vulnerable is the tail of the magnetosphere, streaming away on the dark side. The pressure of a mass ejection tweaking the tail can provoke a magnetic explosion there, which causes auroras. The Earth can also lay a magnetic egg, if part of its tail breaks off as a blob that's swept away on the solar wind.

Solar-wind particles sneak into the magnetosphere by this back door, when the magnetic fields of the Sun and Earth are suddenly joined together. In 1998 two satellites, Germany's Equator-S and Japan's Geotail, found clear evidence of such an event. Jets of solar-wind particles gushed into the magnetosphere for more than an hour.

Other solar particles enter by the front door when the magnetism of the solar wind unzips the Earth's protective field on the sunward side, in a similar fashion. And in deep cavities in the magnetosphere, over the magnetic poles, solar particles crowd like football fans without tickets, hoping for waves or other disturbances that will bounce them through the Earth's defences. Within the magnetosphere, the solar particles mix with charged atoms and electrons escaping from the Earth.

A quartet of satellites called Cluster went into space in 2000 in a special effort to make better sense of the battle between the Earth and the solar wind. Built for the European Space Agency and equipped with 11 identical sets of instruments, to detect particles and to measure electric and magnetic fields and waves, the four satellites flew in elongated orbits passing over the poles and extending 130,000 kilometres from the Earth. By skilful control the satellites adopted, in selected regions, a special formation making a three-sided pyramid or tetrahedron.

This formation flying enabled Cluster to obtain the first 3-D pictures of the electric sea in the Earth's space environment. One of the first discoveries was of surface waves on the boundary between the magnetosphere and the solar wind. Instead of being smooth, it goes up and down with waves like ocean rollers, 2000 kilometres long and travelling at more than 100 kilometres per second downwind, away from the Sun.

'Scientists wondered whether such waves might exist, but until Cluster measured their size and speed there was no proof,' commented Nicole Cornilleau-Wehrlin of France's Centre d'Étude des Environnements Terrestres et Planétaires, responsible for magnetic-wave instruments on the satellites. 'The new waves show what can be achieved by four spacecraft working together. Now we can investigate exactly what causes them, and what they do.'

Explaining solar flares

By the end of the 20th century, space weather had entered official and academic usage as a unifying term for a wide range of research, extending from the visible surface of the Sun to the far planets and beyond. An International Solar–Terrestrial Programme was in progress as a joint effort of the world's space agencies, involving some 16 spacecraft and more than 20 participating countries.

The land of the rising Sun was suitably active in solar research. In the 1990s its most conspicuous success was Yohkoh, a Japan–US–UK satellite whose name meant Sunbeam. Yohkoh astounded the public and scientists alike with movies of the seething solar atmosphere. The Sun that looks so calm and unchanging to the naked eye appeared as a wild beast, raging and spitting fire from active regions as it turned on its axis. The images came from an X-ray camera on Yohkoh, detecting emissions from gas clouds at a temperature of 2 million degrees—far hotter than the 5500 degrees of the Sun's visible surface.

By visible light, the Sun's atmosphere glows very faintly compared with the surface. During a total eclipse it appears as the streaky corona that gives the atmosphere its technical name. Telescopes called coronagraphs use a central mask to create an artificial eclipse at any time. With X-rays you need no mask, because it's the atmosphere that's bright and the Sun's visible surface is dark.

The Earth's own air blocks the solar X-rays, but they were first seen in 1948, when US scientists used a German V2 rocket to carry a detector briefly into space. By 1973 NASA's manned space station Skylab was obtaining magnificent X-ray images of the Sun, but these were limited in number by the supply of photographic film.

Yohkoh's electronic cameras were the first to provide millions of sharp X-ray images, and to monitor changes in activity in the solar atmosphere. A Japanese launcher put the satellite into orbit in 1991, at a time when the Sun was near a peak of activity. The hottest patches in the atmosphere, brightest in X-rays, were often over regions with several sunspots. In 1986, when the sunspot count was at its minimum, the solar atmosphere was less unruly yet still surprisingly busy. Yohkoh was going strong through the next period of high activity, which peaked in 2000, but the satellite died because of technical problems in 2001.

'It was exciting to see the solar weather changing day by day,' said Saku Tsuneta of the National Astronomical Observatory of Japan. 'Storms on the Sun are even more dramatic and complicated than those on the Earth, and Yohkoh's chief achievement was to show that solar flares release huge magnetic energy stored in the atmosphere.'

Flares had been known since 1859, when an amateur astronomer in England, Richard Carrington, first reported an exceptionally bright spot of visible light on the Sun's face. Seen far more frequently by X-rays, flares are like prolonged lightning flashes, lasting for some minutes at least. The explosions responsible for the strongest flares are stupendous, like a billion H-bombs going off.

Yohkoh recorded lesser flares almost daily. As solar physicists in Japan, the USA and the UK pored over the images, and the measurements of X-ray energies obtained with spectrometers on Yohkoh, they saw that magnetic fields arching high above the solar surface become tangled like spaghetti. When two magnetic loops running in different directions / and \ clash together in an ✕ their field lines can reconnect into new loops > and < with a huge release of energy.

In short, solar flares are magnetic explosions. The intense X-rays come from hot spots in the Sun's lower atmosphere, where energetic particles accelerated downwards during the reconnection slam into the gas and heat it to 30 million degrees or more. Other energetic particles, accelerated upwards at the same time, pour into space as the solar protons dreaded by astronauts, spacecraft controllers and computer operators.

Anticipating eruptions

A larger and more lavishly equipped solar spacecraft, SOHO, took up a position 1.5 million kilometres out on the sunward side of the Earth, early in 1996. Built in Europe, the Solar and Heliospheric Observatory was launched by NASA in a project of international cooperation. Among a dozen sets of instruments on SOHO provided by multinational teams, several gave new views of the solar atmosphere at ultraviolet wavelengths.

SOHO generated remarkable movies of the solar atmosphere, like Yohkoh's, but now with more detail and at various wavelengths corresponding to gas at temperatures from 80,000 to 2 million degrees. New phenomena so revealed included shock waves travelling across the Sun's face from the scene of a large explosion, and thousands of small-scale explosions occurring every day all across the Sun, even when it was ostensibly quiet. The SOHO images became highly prized by those responsible for giving early warnings of adverse space weather, to power-system engineers and satellite controllers.

The most spectacular SOHO images came from a visible-light coronagraph called LASCO. It revealed the mass ejections as colossal puffs of gas shooting off into space at 500 kilometres per second or more, and swelling as they went, until they were vastly bigger than the Sun itself. When coming straight towards the Earth, the mass ejection appeared as a huge halo around the Sun, and gave a couple of days' advance warning of its impending impact on the Earth's magnetosphere.

Will longer warnings be possible? Some solar physicists suspect that, if they are to anticipate the solar eruptions, they may need an altogether deeper understanding of the relationships between mass ejections, flares and dangerous outbursts of particles. Just as the link between earthquakes and volcanoes never quite made sense until a brand-new theory, plate tectonics, explained it, so a similar theory of the Sun's magnetic weather may be needed.

By the time a flare has detonated, the warning time is perilously short—perhaps 30 minutes, as already mentioned. As scientists scrutinized the images of the solar atmosphere, they looked for possible warning signs. They wondered if concentrations of gas detected by SOHO, or twisted magnetic fields making S-shaped structures seen by Yohkoh in the solar atmosphere, might be precursors of eruptions.

'There's no difference here between basic and applied science, because practical storm warning requires new discoveries about how the Sun's crazy atmosphere works,' said Helen Mason at Cambridge, who analysed data from Yohkoh, SOHO and other spacecraft. 'If we can find out what causes the magnetic fields in an active region of the Sun to become unstable, we may gain an hour or even a day in the prediction of dangerous eruptions—and that could be a matter of life or death for space travellers.'

Jumping croquet hoops

A task facing the SOHO scientists was to find out why the Sun's atmosphere is so hot. Alan Title of the Stanford–Lockheed Institute for Space Research in California led a team studying the patterns of magnetic fields emerging through the visible surface, as observed by SOHO. What they revealed was an amazing magnetic carpet, from which large numbers of small magnetic loops emerged and clashed with one another, before dissolving and being replaced by new loops within 40 hours. Title commented, 'We now have direct evidence for the upward transfer of magnetic energy from the Sun's surface towards the corona above.'

Later, Title and his colleagues looked in more detail at this mechanism of atmospheric heating by magnetic loops, using their small Trace satellite launched by NASA in 1998. It gave ultraviolet images sharper and more frequent than SOHO's, and showed an endless dance of magnetic loops, made visible by gas bound to the magnetic field. Gas heated to a million degrees at the footpoints of the loops travelled upwards to the top of each arch, where it acted as a heater high in the Sun's atmosphere. Here at last was the essence of a solution to the mystery of the hot atmosphere.

The Trace images were mind-boggling. They revealed the dynamic wonderland that one would see if standing on the solar surface with eyes tuned to the hot gas of the atmosphere. The magnetic loops looked like jumping croquet hoops. Their antics, and the whizzing about of packets of hot and cold gas, were so frantic and complex that it was hard to know where to start, in seeking detailed explanations for them. When Title presented movies from Trace at an international meeting of astronomers in 2000 the chairman joked: 'Counselling will be available for theorists after the session.'

The successors to Yohkoh, SOHO and Trace will have still sharper vision, and the pictures promise to become ever more complex. The crazy weather is the outcome of an endless fight between hot gas trying to break loose, and gravity and magnetic fields trying to bottle it up. One question for theorists to ponder is the ability of the active solar surface and atmosphere to generate magnetic fields for themselves, instead of relying solely on fields emerging from the Sun's interior.

Among the new solar spacecraft in prospect for the second decade of the 21st century is Europe's Solar Orbiter, due for launch in 2012. Its orbit is conceived to take it close to the Sun for about one month in every five months, approaching to within one-fifth of the Earth–Sun distance. That means the Solar Orbiter must withstand sunlight 25 times stronger than near the Earth, and concentrated blasts of energetic particles. At its fastest, the spacecraft's speed will keep it roughly positioned over the same region of the solar atmosphere, as the Sun rotates, so that it can watch storms building up in the magnetic weather over several days, and send back images ten times sharper than those of Trace.

'Go where no one's been before—that's the way to make discoveries,' said Eckart Marsch of Germany's Max-Planck-Institut für Aeronomie, who first proposed the Solar Orbiter to the European Space Agency. 'We can expect to clear up many mysteries about the Sun's behaviour. As for predicting those troublesome energetic particles, we need to find out with the Solar Orbiter exactly how the Sun creates its particle accelerators.'

▶ *For closely related subjects, see* SOLAR WIND *and* SUN'S INTERIOR. *For apparent solar effects on the Earth's weather, see* ICE-RAFTING EVENTS, CLIMATE CHANGE *and* EARTHSHINE.

SPARTICLES

A wished-for superworld of exotic matter and forces

'I SN'T IT TOO GOOD NOT TO BE TRUE?' asked Maurice Jacob, a theoretician from CERN, Europe's particle physics laboratory in Geneva. He was speaking about a theory call Grand Unification that promises to encompass all heavy and light particles of matter, and most of the forces acting upon them. Advanced versions of the theory have a feature called supersymmetry, which requires the existence of previously unseen particles. Collectively they are called supersymmetric particles, or sparticles for short.

Some fortunate traits of the Universe, without which our existence would be impossible, become explicable by Grand Unification. Why matter is electrically neutral, for example. If positive and negative charges were not exactly in balance, matter would blow up and stars and planets could not form. The theory takes care of that, yet at the same time makes it possible for matter to be far from neutral in respect of antimatter. If the proportions of matter and antimatter were as equal as the electric charges are, they would annihilate each other, leaving the Universe empty.

To get the hang of Grand Unification, first note that all ordinary matter is built from two families of particles. One consists of six kinds of heavy particles, the quarks, found in the nuclei of atoms. The other is the electron family, also with six particles, including two heavy electrons and three ghostly neutrinos. Within each family, any particle can change into any other, by the action of a cosmic alchemist called the weak force. Indeed the number of possible transmutations fixes the number of particles in the quark and electron families.

A general theory of particles that evolved in the 1970s is now known as the Standard Model. It describes the relationships within the quark family and within the electron family, but it keeps the two households quite distinct. In this theory, a quark cannot change into an electron, for example. One aim in Grand Unification is to create an extended family that includes both quarks and electrons.

A closely related aim is to unite the forces that act on the particles: the electric force, the alchemical weak force, and the strong force that binds nuclear material together. The Standard Model united the electric and weak force but it left them distinct from the strong force. In Grand Unification, this division of

SPARTICLES

the forces is to be ended too. In very hot conditions, the weak force is supposed to become stronger and the strong force weaker, so that they both converge with the electric force, in a single, ideal subatomic force.

The problem of the balance of positive and negative electric charges may be solved if there is enough kinship between quarks and electrons to ensure the right distribution of charges between them. The imbalance between matter and antimatter can make sense, within Grand Unification, if the creation of particles occurs so rapidly in an expanding Universe that there is not time to correct a slight deficit in the proportion of antiparticles.

Will matter disappear?

Preliminary notions about Grand Unification were germinating in the 1970s. Among the theorists involved were those most prominent in developing the Standard Model itself, in the same period. They included Sheldon Glashow and Steven Weinberg at Harvard, and Abdus Salam and Jogesh Pati at the International Centre for Theoretical Physics in Trieste. In 1973, Salam and Pati made the most dramatic prediction from a unified theory, namely that the stuff of the Universe should self-destruct.

If the two families of particles are related closely enough, in Grand Unification, quarks should be able to change into electrons. As a result the proton, the basic nuclear particle best known as the nucleus of the hydrogen atom, ought not to be immortal. Andrei Sakharov in Moscow had mooted the possibility in 1967, but he had no detailed theory for it.

The proton should decay into an anti-electron, a positron. That particle would then find an ordinary electron and they would annihilate each other, as particles and antiparticles do, disappearing in a puff of gamma rays. Bye-bye, atoms.

Proton decay would break a cherished elementary law of science, about the conservation of matter. Salam's daughter was warned by a schoolteacher not to mention such a heretical idea in her exams, whatever her famous father might say. Professional physicists needed some persuading, too.

'While there was considerable resistance from the theoretical community against such ideas at that point,' Pati recalled later, 'the psychological barrier against them softened over the years. The growing interest in the prospect of such a decay thus led to the building of proton-decay detectors in different parts of the world.'

Proton decay cannot happen very rapidly, or stars and planets would not have survived for so long. The simplest Grand Unification schemes predicted that half the protons in the world would decay in about a thousand billion billion billion years, compared with about 13 billion years for the age of the Universe so far. At that rate, you ought to be able to see a few protons breaking up each year, if you watched the zillions of protons present in a large enough tank of water.

Having already shifted from mountaintop cosmic-ray observatories to particle accelerators built on the plains, particle physicists then followed the miners deep underground. There they could run proton-decay experiments with as little confusion as possible from the cosmic rays. One early experiment, 900 metres down in a salt mine in Ohio, used 5000 tonnes of water and more than 2000 detectors that watched for flashes of light telling of proton decay.

They failed. By the end of the century the searchers in Ohio, Japan and elsewhere were not merely disappointed. They could testify that the proton decayed, if at all, at least a thousand times more slowly than required by the simplest extensions of the Standard Model, so these theories were obviously wrong.

Waiting for new particles

The versions of Grand Unification called supersymmetric could tolerate the longevity of the proton. Symmetry is a mathematical concept used by physicists to describe the relationships of particle families and forces, and supersymmetry is an overarching scheme that also permits the existence of particles not available in the Standard Model.

Supersymmetry became popular among physicists. Like the key to a magic garden, it invited them into a shadowy superworld of sparticles—exotic matter and forces that scarcely interact with our own world. The supermatter doesn't respond to ordinary subatomic forces, and the superforces don't affect ordinary matter. Among themselves the sparticles interact only weakly because their force-carrying particles are massive and hard to conjure up.

Matter in the ordinary world, described by the Standard Model, consists of particles that spin in a particular way that distinguishes them from force-carrying particles that spin in a different way, if at all. In Grand Unification by supersymmetry, the ordinary particles are supposed to have shadows with the other kind of spin. Thus the electrons and quarks, the particles of matter, are matched by superelectrons and superquarks, which are force carriers. These are the sparticles called selectrons and squarks.

Supermatter, in its turn, corresponds to the ordinary force carriers. Envisaged particles include photinos, shadows of the particles of light, photons, which carry the electric force. Gluinos are superequivalents of the gluons that bind quarks in protons. As the sparticles double the roster of the Standard Model, it would be tedious to recite all their individual names.

But not tedious to find them! For young physicists worried that there might be little for them to discover in the 21st century, to match the great haul of subatomic particles by previous generations, the superworld was enticing. Keen for hints that it could be real, they waited for flaws to appear in the Standard Model.

While proton decay turned out to be a very long wait, evidence came from Japan in 1998 that ordinary matter, in the form of ghostly neutrinos, changes from one variety into another in ways not directly permitted in the Standard Model. That was encouraging, although it was not in itself evidence for supersymmetry.

Meanwhile, various experiments around the world were looking for sparticles that might be present in the mysterious dark matter. This is unidentified material that is known to pervade the Universe, because of its gravitational force acting on stars and galaxies. The lightest sparticles, called neutralinos, are candidates. The belief is that any cosmic supply of other supermatter should have decayed into neutralinos long ago.

Should dark matter turn out to consist in whole or in part of sparticles, that would be wonderfully neat. Then the superworld would not after all be totally alien to ours. But the idea that gravity acts on both matter and supermatter requires that Grand Unification should be extended to include gravity. The code name is the Theory of Everything, and it requires a base in supersymmetry.

Suggestions are on offer. Most of them require an invisible framework of many mathematical dimensions, beyond the familiar three dimensions and one of time. String theory, the most popular candidate, imagines particles to be little strings vibrating in the multidimensional space. The detection of sparticles would give string theory a much-needed shot in the arm.

'At the moment supersymmetry does not have a solid experimental motivation,' said Nathan Seiberg of the Institute for Advanced Study, Princeton, in 1999. 'If it is discovered, this will be one of the biggest successes of theoretical physics— predicting such a deep notion without any experimental input!'

Unless some anchor in real observations is found, scepticism about the superworld will start to grow. A five-year search for sparticles at Fermilab near Chicago, begun in 1996, concluded only that a gluino, if it exists at all, must be at least as heavy as an atom of lead. That was beyond the capacity of Fermilab's Tevatron accelerator to manufacture.

Perhaps Europe's next accelerator, the Large Hadron Collider, will start churning out gluinos, squarks and others when it begins operations around 2007. Maybe dark-matter experiments will find the neutralinos. One of these years, decaying protons may be seen at last. Or maybe the badly needed observational facts will come from cosmic rays of extremely high energy, which provide at present the only hope of reaching directly to the heart of the wonderland where all forces become one.

These possibilities were only aspirations for the particle physicists, who entered the 21st century whistling in the dark. It was bureaucratically alarming for the funding agencies asked to pay for expensive experiments, the outcome of which was unknowable. But for scientists who remained convinced that Mother Nature was about to shed one more of her veils and reveal the superworld, the whistled tune was a merry one.

'The Large Hadron Collider is not a gamble!' insisted Maurice Jacob. 'Something has to happen in its energy range even if we cannot say exactly what.'

▶ *For the search for sparticles that may pervade the Universe, see* DARK MATTER. *For the background of the Standard Model, see* ELECTROWEAK FORCE *and* PARTICLE FAMILIES. *Its first flaw is in* NEUTRINO OSCILLATIONS. *For more about the Theory of Everything, see* SUPERSTRINGS.

SPEECH

A gene that makes us more eloquent than chimpanzees

S OME OF THE FISHERMEN who practised their art at Africa's southern tip, around 75,000 years ago, carried catfish, black musselcracker and red stumpnose, together with seafood and an occasional seal or dolphin, up to Blombos Cave. This refuge still perches 35 metres above the shore, in limestone cliffs 300 kilometres east of the Cape of Good Hope.

Archaeology in Blombos Cave began in earnest in 1997. It doubled the length of time for which people with mental faculties comparable with our own are thought to have existed. Apart from the evidence for pioneer sea fishing, presumably with spears, the inhabitants had meat from antelopes, hares and many other animals, including at least one rhino. A factory in the cave supplied stone tools and spearheads, made with a symmetry and precision not seen till much later in other parts of the world. The inventory included the oldest known finely worked bone tools.

Blombos bridged a yawning gap in prehistory. People who resembled us anatomically as the subspecies *Homo sapiens sapiens*, lightly built and with high brows, evolved in Africa more than 100,000 years ago. Yet evidence of great skill dated from only 35,000 years ago, mainly in France. The impression was that modern-looking folk remained fairly goofy for 60 millennia until they reached the western promontory of Eurasia, took courses at some prehistoric Sorbonne, and suddenly smartened up.

This delusion resulted from 200 years of archaeology in Europe, which was far more intensive than in most other parts of the world. Indirect evidence that the Eurocentric view was nonsense came from the dated arrival of *Homo sapiens sapiens* in Australia about 50,000 years ago after a daring crossing of the open ocean, the first ever made on purpose by any primate. Nevertheless the oldest artefacts attesting to skills of the modern order came only from Europe—before the finds in South Africa.

A prime discovery in Blombos Cave in 1999 and 2000 was of items of symbolic art, the oldest ever found, occurring close to two different hearths. They are small pieces of red ochre, an iron-oxide pigment long used by our ancestors to daub their skins and animal hides. In these rare cases, the ochre surfaces are ground flat and engraved with criss-cross parallel lines, to make interlocking triangles in a complex geometrical motif.

Christopher Henshilwood of the African Heritage Research Institute in Cape Town led the Blombos dig. 'I don't know what these little engravings mean, but in my opinion they are symbolic,' he commented. 'I like to imagine whoever made them explaining the patterns to their colleagues in a language of our own articulate kind.'

● People just as bright as us

In saying so, Henshilwood updated a leading hypothesis of the 20th century. This saw the transformation of human beings during the most recent ice age, from modestly successful hunter-gatherers into the dominant species of the planet, coming with the acquisition of the modern powers of language. It was supposedly the key factor that enabled the people so endowed to replace the incumbents, *Homo erectus* and the Neanderthalers.

The notion of chatterboxes taking over the world was already current in the 1950s, when William Golding in his novel *The Inheritors* imagined one of the most dramatic moments in the long history of the Earth. A Neanderthaler overhears for the first time the fluency of modern human speech, and he laughs. 'The sounds made a picture in his head of interlacing shapes, thin and complex, voluble and silly, not like the long curve of a hawk's cry, but tangled like line weed on the beach after a storm, muddled as water.'

Pity *Homo sapiens neanderthalensis*. If life were fair, that subspecies would still own Eurasia at least. The Neanderthalers were sturdy and brainy hunter-gatherers, well able to endure appalling climate changes during the ice age. They were thoughtful enough to strew a grave with flowers.

One can imagine them exchanging vehement oral signals during the hunt, and crooning to their mates and infants. The Neanderthalers' mouths and throats were less well adapted, anatomically, to making complex speech sounds, especially vowels. Opinions differ as to how important that was. You can write intelligible Hebrew without specifying any vowels.

Nevertheless it seems to be a fact that highbrowed *Homo sapiens sapiens* sauntered out of Africa and into the Eurasian wilderness, like invading aliens in a sci-fi story. The collision with the Neanderthalers is best documented in Europe, where anthropologists and archaeologists call the representatives of our own ancestors the Cro-Magnons. Whether the newcomers were friendly, disdainful or homicidal, who knows? But within a few thousand years of the first encounters, the Neanderthalers were extinct. They could be forgiven if they died of discouragement, because they were outclassed in virtually every department.

Artefacts announce the arrival of high intellect in Europe in the transition from the Middle to the Upper Palaeolithic stage. Paintings, sculptures and musical instruments appear. Lunar calendars, incised on antlers as neat circles and crescents, are the work of Palaeolithic scientists. Tools and hunting weapons became so refined that 21st-century craftsmen cannot easily imitate them. These were people just as bright as us.

The equivalent archaeological transition in Africa is from the Middle to the Later Stone Age and the Blombos discovery pushes it much farther back in time, to early in the last ice age. By the time the ice retreated, 11,000 years ago, the modern humans had occupied every continent and clime bar Antarctica. Their fearless migrations foreshadowed the time when such people would travel to the Moon and beyond. And in every part of the world, the newcomers had the same gift of speech.

The ability to utter and comprehend sentences 'muddled as water' was a persuasive explanation for humanity's sudden access of brio. Fluent speech opened the way to the sharing of complex skills and plans among large groups, and to the transmission of information, ideas and memories from generation to generation. It became the prime mediator of human social behaviour, from neighbourly gossip and discussion of handicrafts and hunting strategies, to storytelling, religion and politics.

That was a neat hypothesis, anyway. As to how language evolved, Steven Pinker of the Massachusetts Institute of Technology drew a comparison with the evolution of the elephant's trunk from a fusion of nostrils and upper-lip muscles. In his book *The Language Instinct* (1994) he suggested: 'Language could have arisen, and probably did arise, in a similar way; by a revamping of primate brain circuits that originally had no role in vocal communication, and by the addition of some new ones.'

In Pinker's view the process began 200,000 years ago or more. That was long before either the fishermen of Blombos Cave or the Cro-Magnon high noon in Golding's story. Even so, it is extremely recent on geological and evolutionary time-scales.

As an innovation, speech ranks with the inventions of animals' eyes and teeth. Yet if you let the Eiffel Tower, 300 metres tall, denote the time that has elapsed since the first animals appeared, the interval that separates us from our first eloquent ancestors is no more than the thickness of a tourist's arm on the railing. That so important a development is so close to us in geological time gives good reason for expecting quite precise explanations from scientists about what happened. Anatomy, archaeology, linguistics, brain research and genetics have all been brought to bear, in a fascinating interplay.

The tongue-tied Londoners

In right-handed individuals, and in nearly half of the left-handers too, the powers of language are concentrated in the left-hand side of the brain. Other specific areas are involved in hearing and decoding words, and in assembling words in the correct order. In adults, brain damage near the left ear may result in a permanent loss of speech. Similar damage in children will rarely result in loss of speech because of the plasticity of the young brain and its ability to reorganize functions. This much was inferred long ago, from various kinds of language disorders showing up in victims of head-wounds and strokes, and from studies of children with brain damage.

In 1964, Eric Lenneberg of Cornell had noted that some impairments of speech and language use seem to run in families. The magic of speech acquisition by what he called 'simple immersion in the sea of language' is sometimes less than perfect. When other physical or mental defects are ruled out as an explanation, a small residue of cases involves disorders of language that appear to be genetic in origin. Subsequent studies of twins confirmed this impression, yet more than 30 years passed before the identification of a particular gene which, if defective, predisposed individuals to speech and language difficulties.

In 1990 Jane Hurst, a clinical geneticist at London's Great Ormond Street Hospital for Children, reported the discovery of a family half of whom shared a severe speech disorder. They had difficulty in controlling their mouths and tongues to produce speech sounds—a condition known as verbal dyspraxia. Outsiders found it hard to understand what the affected individuals were saying, but otherwise the family flourished, with 30 members in three generations all living in the same area of London. The verbal dyspraxia showed up in 15 of them, in a pattern that indicated a classic hereditary disorder involving a mutation in a single gene.

Linguists from McGill University, in Montreal, and neuroscientists from the Institute of Child Health, in London, examined the family, which was codenamed KE. The linguists claimed that the affected members of the KE family had a specific problem with grammar. The neuroscientists reported that the speech problems were associated with more general language difficulties, affecting the identification of speech sounds and the understanding of sentences.

'The KEs were very obliging and patient about all the tests we wanted to do,' said Faraneh Vargha-Khadem of the Institute of Child Health. 'It took more than a decade to pin down the first known gene involved in speech and language, and to trace its likely role in a baby's brain development.'

A team of geneticists at Oxford led by Anthony Monaco hunted for the gene, labelled SPCH1, within the family's chromosomes—the 23 pairs of gene agglomerations in human cells. By 1998 they had found, in chromosome 7, two closely spaced segments that showed a perfect match between the affected grandmother and her linguistically impaired descendants. There was no match in unaffected family members. As SPCH1 had to lie very close to the identified segments, this narrowed the search down to about 100 genes.

Prolonged trial and error would no doubt have found the culprit in the end. By an amazing chance the task was short-circuited when Jane Hurst, who originally reported on the KEs, came across an unrelated person with the same speech disorder. A defect in the same region of chromosome 7 involved, in this case, a rearrangement of genes called a translocation, which had disrupted a single identifiable gene. It belonged to a family of genes well known to the Oxford team, called forkhead or FOX genes, so they called it FOXP2.

In the USA, the Washington University Genome Sequencing Center had already read the genetic codes of many of the genes in the relevant region of chromosome 7. These included FOXP2, so it made the quest that much easier for the Oxford laboratory. It was a clear example of how the Human Genome Project speeded up the search for genes implicated in hereditary disease.

Cecilia Lai and Simon Fisher at Oxford made the decisive discovery that FOXP2 and SPCH1 were one and the same gene. Affected members of the KE family have a mutated version, which is absent in unaffected members and in hundreds of other people tested. A single misprint in the letters of the genetic code, substituting an A for a G, results in the manufacture of a protein in which the amino acid arginine is replaced by histidine.

A forkhead protein's job is to provoke or inhibit quite different genes involved in cell-making and cell suicide. It helps in sculpting brain tissue in an infant in the womb. The identified error occurs in the region of the protein molecule directly participating in the action. Each affected individual in the KE family has one correct and one mutant version of the forkhead gene. The resulting shortage of effective forkhead proteins evidently leads to abnormal development of pathways in the brain that are important for speech and language.

'This is the first gene, to our knowledge, to have been implicated in such pathways, and it promises to offer insights into the molecular processes mediating this uniquely human trait,' Monaco and his colleagues concluded. It was stirring stuff. How breathtaking to discover that our eloquence seems to hang by so frail a biochemical thread, with a point of weakness so precisely specifiable at the molecular level!

An evolutionary history revealed

The next task was to see whether the human FOXP2 gene is noticeably different from its equivalents in other species. Were there significant changes in the recent course of evolution? In particular, how does the human version of the gene compare with that of the chimpanzee, our closest cousin among the animals? To find out, Monaco joined forces with Svante Pääbo of the Max-Planck-Institut für evolutionäre Anthropologie in Leipzig.

By 2002, the verdict was in. Pääbo's team compared human FOXP2 with the versions of the gene found in three apes (chimpanzee, gorilla, and orang-utan) and one monkey (rhesus macaque), and also in the mouse. When interpreted in terms of the forkhead proteins for which the genes provide the code, the results were emphatic.

First, forkhead proteins are so important that evolution resists significant mutations in them. The business end of the forkhead in a mouse is almost identical with that in most monkeys and apes. In the 70 million years or more since primates and mice last shared a common ancestor, in the days of the dinosaurs, their forkheads have come to differ by only a single subunit of the protein, and that change occurred in the mouse lineage. Orang-utans admitted one mutation of a single subunit, after they separated from the other apes, but not in a very important part of the molecule.

In defiance of this intense conservatism, FOXP2 in humans shows not one but two significant mutations arising since our ancestors diverged from the chimpanzees. Out of the 715 amino-acid subunits in the human form of the forkhead protein, No. 303 has changed from threonine to asparagine and No. 325 from asparagine to serine. These small changes have a big effect on the forkhead's cell-controlling functions.

The mutated human FOXP2 became universal. In genes for most other proteins, variant forms are commonplace, but a search among dozens of individuals from different parts of the world revealed not a single exception to the two-mutant configuration of the forkhead, and only a single case of another mutation, with no practical effect on molecular behaviour.

Evidently natural selection has been extremely strong in its favour. And although our pre-human ancestors diverged from the chimpanzees 5–6 million years ago, the mutations in FOXP2 are very much more recent. By a statistical inference, they almost certainly occurred during the past 120,000 years.

'This is compatible with a model in which the expansion of modern humans was driven by the appearance of a more-proficient spoken language,' the Leipzig–Oxford team reported. 'However, to establish whether FOXP2 is indeed involved in basic aspects of human culture, the normal functions of both the human and the chimpanzee FOXP2 proteins need to be clarified.'

Not *the* language gene

Gratifying though it is, this genetical backward reach into the lives of our remote ancestors is not the end of the quest for the evolution of language, but just a new beginning. Contrary to assertions of some linguists in Canada and the USA that the FOXP2 gene was directly involved in the faculty of grammar, the neuroscientists of London and the geneticists of Oxford and Leipzig were unanimous that this was not the case. The most clear-cut effect of the FOXP2 mutation was the dyspraxia.

Chimpanzees and other primates have just the same inability to control their mouths and tongues to produce clearly differentiated speech sounds. So that fits neatly with the evolutionary story of the normal FOXP2 gene revealed by the comparisons between species. But there was no reason for evolution to favour the mutations as strongly as it did unless there were a pre-existing mental apparatus for handling complex speech.

Perhaps the novelist Golding got it exactly right, nearly half a century earlier, when he described the Neanderthalers as people well endowed with language-like thought processes and simple oral communications, but lacking fluency in complex speech sounds. If so, the FOXP2 mutations may indeed have been a last, decisive step in the evolution of human language, with the enormous cultural consequences that flowed from it. The time frame is right.

But all the rest of the mental apparatus remains to be revealed, at the same genetic level. Wolfgang Enard, the graduate student at Leipzig who was the lead author of the inter-species comparisons of FOXP2, was quite clear that it was far from being the whole story. He said, 'This is hopefully the first of many language genes to be discovered.'

In a broader perspective, the genetics of speech is a pathfinding expedition into a new realm of brain research. It provides a vivid preview of what will be possible in the decades ahead, when it will no longer seem brash to look for unbroken chains of explanation from molecular evolution to human behaviour.

▶ *For related subjects, see* HUMAN ORIGINS, LANGUAGES *and* GRAMMAR.

STARBURSTS

Galactic traffic accidents and stellar baby booms

A S AN INVESTIGATOR of collisions between galaxies, the vast assemblies of stars of which our Milky Way is the prototype, the Argentine astronomer Amina Helmi made it her business to enlighten her northern colleagues about Jorge Luis Borges. She commended in particular his short story called *The Circular Ruins*. The circularity is not in the shape of the relics, she explained, but in a cycle of fiery events at long intervals. Galaxies evolve that way too.

Borges wrote that 'a remote cloud, as light as a bird, appeared on a hill; then, toward the south, the sky took on the rose colour of leopard's gums; then came clouds of smoke which rusted the metal of the nights; afterwards came the panic-stricken flight of wild animals. For what had happened many centuries before was repeating itself. The ruins of the sanctuary of the god of Fire was destroyed by fire.'

As a zoologist of imaginary beings, Borges could have added to his list the ulirgs of IRAS. They were in reality the ultraluminous infrared galaxies discovered in 1983 by the Dutch–US–UK Infrared Astronomy Satellite. These galaxies astonished the experts by giving off invisible infrared rays far more intensely than expected. Europe's Infrared Space Observatory (1995–98) then examined many of these objects in detail, and established their nature.

'This is the first time we can prove that most of the luminosity in the ulirgs comes from star formation,' Reinhard Genzel of Germany's Max-Planck-Institut für extraterrestrische Physik declared in 1999, after examining dozens of these objects. 'To understand how, and for how long, such vigorous star formation can occur in these galaxies is now one of the most interesting questions in astrophysics.'

In a word, the Infrared Space Observatory confirmed the hypothesis of starbursts. That was the proposition that dust clouds, left over from explosions of short-lived stars created during a frenzy of star-making, were the sources of the strong infrared rays. Swarming unseen in the pall of dust were vast numbers of young stars produced in a galactic baby boom. A rival suggestion, that a black hole warmed the dust, was reduced to a supplementary role, at most. So astronomers could with confidence call them starburst galaxies—and perhaps return the cryptic ulirgs to the mint of scientific jargon, for recycling.

A leading member of the team of infrared astronomers was Catherine Cesarsky, then with CEA Saclay in France. She spoke of the space observatory's 'magic' in transforming opaque clouds seen by visible light into glowing scenes in the infrared. 'The same thing happens in dust clouds hiding newborn stars, and on a huge scale in dusty starburst galaxies—which become infrared beacons lighting our way deep into the Universe.'

Cesarsky's camera obtained, for example, infrared pictures of the Antennae, a pair of spiral galaxies 60 million light-years away involved in a slow collision. Spaces between stars are so great that the galaxies can pass through each other like counter-marching soldiers, without stellar impacts. But the interstellar gas of the two galaxies is a different matter.

The gas clouds collide at high speed, causing compression and shocks that stimulate starbursts. In a spiral galaxy the gas is concentrated in the bright disk. The infrared Antennae images showed a line of star formation exactly where the disks of the two galaxies cut through each other. This was galactic science of mathematical beauty.

Other astronomers found and compared hundred of starburst galaxies. In many instances, perhaps all, a collision between two galaxies seemed to provoke the starburst events. Although very cold by earthly standards, the dust in the starburst galaxies is much warmer than it would be if the stars were not shining on it. In effect, the dust converts their intense visible light into bright infrared rays.

When the Infrared Space Observatory's cooling system gave out in 1998, team members continued to examine the galaxies with other instruments on the ground, and from high altitudes in the air. They helped to plan wider and deeper searches for starbursts with NASA's infrared observatory SIRTF, launched in 2003, and with the US–German project SOFIA to carry a variety of infrared instruments to 12 kilometres altitude aboard an adapted Boeing 747 aircraft, from 2004 onwards.

● The coolest galaxies

There's a mysterious no-man's land in the spectrum of invisible light coming from the Universe, which some astronomers call the far infrared and others, submillimetre radio. Take a nearby starburst galaxy that glows in the near (short-wavelength) infrared, and imagine it at a very great distance. The expansion rate of the cosmos shifts it into the submillimetre range. It is in this waveband that astronomers must trace the starburst galaxies out to the far reaches of the Universe.

A preview of the new era came in 1997, when the James Clerk Maxwell Telescope on the summit of Mauna Kea in Hawaii turned towards the Hercules constellation and stared intently at an extremely faint, red-coloured and distant galaxy called HR 10. This submillimetre radio telescope with a 15-metre dish, operated by a UK–Canadian–Dutch consortium, had been fitted with a new camera cooled to just one-tenth of a degree above the absolute zero of temperature.

HR 10 lies at such a distance that astronomers see it as it was when the Universe was less than half its present age. The telescope detected surprisingly strong submillimetre rays. Comparing them with weaker signals at longer wavelengths, recorded by a 30-metre millimetre-wave telescope on Pico Veleta in Spain, the astronomers figured out that galaxy HR 10 radiates most of its energy, not from stars, but from dust at a temperature 30–50 degrees above absolute zero, or −240 to −220°C.

'This galaxy looks so cool because it hides its starlight behind thick clouds of dust generated by explosions of short-lived stars,' said Andrea Cimatti of Osservatorio di Arcetri, Italy, who led an Italian–Dutch team examining HR 10. 'Hundreds of new stars are being born there every year, compared with only two or three in our own Galaxy, the Milky Way. With observations at submillimetre and millimetre wavelengths we can begin the precise analysis of such distant, very red galaxies, and find ultraluminous objects not even seen by visible light.'

The most distant galaxies show themselves to us in a juvenile state, because of the long time it has taken for their radiation to reach the Earth across the chasm of space. But starburst events were much commoner when the galaxies were young, because traffic accidents were more frequent. Indeed, the galaxies were growing by collisions and mergers. So the astronomers can't expect to see them shining brightly like the Magellanic Clouds or the Andromeda Galaxy.

'The light from most of the stars ever formed in galaxies may be hidden from view by dust generated by early stellar generations,' warned Michael Rowan-Robinson of Imperial College London. 'Perhaps two-thirds of all the starlight ever produced by all the stars in the Universe comes to us only as submillimetre radiation.'

The European Space Agency's Herschel spacecraft, due for launch in 2007 as a successor to the Infrared Space Observatory, is custom-built for exploring the Universe at submillimetre wavelengths. With it, astronomers expect to find tens of thousands of starburst galaxies. So what began as curiosities, the ulirgs of IRAS, delivered the message that most stars in the Universe were born in baby booms when galaxies collided. As a result the starburst galaxies became some of the most important objects in the sky, and prime targets for cosmic explorers in the 21st century.

▶ *For related topics, see* ELEMENTS *and* GALAXIES.

STARS

Hearing them sing and sizing them up

'WE HAD THE SKY, up there, all speckled with stars, and we used to lay on our backs and look up at them, and discuss whether they was made, or only just happened.' Thus Mark Twain's Huckleberry Finn, and in the dark ages before electric streetlights, wristwatches and navigation satellites, the stars were everyone's friends. They not only beautified the night sky and provoked musings like Huckleberry's, but they would tell you the clock time and the sowing season, or guide you to Tahiti.

Nowadays, science tightens its grip on the main form of visible matter in the cosmos. The stars are under scrutiny as never before, from mountaintop observatories or from spacecraft orbiting in the always-black sky of outer space. Sadly, for billions of mortals, the stars have faded in the electric glow of cities until you don't even notice that Betelgeuse is red.

Colours unlocked the mysteries of the lights in the night sky. 'A casket of variously coloured precious stones' was how John Herschel in Cape Town described the red, white and blue star cluster near the Southern Cross, now called the Jewel Box, when observing it in the 1830s. Early in the 20th century the Danish astronomer Ejnar Hertzsprung noticed that the brightest stars in the most famous star cluster, the Pleiades, were all blue. The middling ones were white or yellow, and the faintest ones were red. As all these stars were at roughly the same distance, a link emerged between luminosity and colour in ordinary dwarfs, which means all stars in the prime of life, neither newborn nor senile.

From this chromatic beginning, modern stellar theory evolved. Blue stars are more massive and larger than the Sun, and short-lived, whilst red stars are lighter, smaller and longer-lived. Exceptions are the red giants such as Betelgeuse and Aldebaran, which are intensely luminous though red, and the white dwarfs such as the Companion of Sirius, faint though bluish. Whilst red giants are substantial stars nearing the ends of their lives, white dwarfs are burnt-out remnants of stars. Where two stars circle around each other, on well-defined orbits, their masses can be deduced.

In the 1920s, Arthur Eddington at Cambridge described the battle inside stars, between the inward pressure of gravity and the outward pressure of radiation from an extremely hot core. He suspected that nuclear energy powered the core, but it fell to others to figure out the fusion reactions, and to go on to explain how the evolution into red giants and white dwarfs followed the exhaustion of hydrogen fuel in the core and the nuclear burning of helium and heavier elements.

Subtle variations in the links between luminosity and hue on the one hand, and mass and age on the other, arose from differences in chemical composition, as revealed by characteristic spectral colours of the elements. By the 1980s, the theory of stars seemed pretty secure. Then a European satellite called Hipparcos (1989–93) blew complacency away by measuring the distances of stars far more accurately than ever before.

The Pleiades—yes, Hertzsprung's Pleiades, dammit!—were 10 per cent closer than they were believed to be, which meant that they were 20 per cent less luminous than required by the standard reckonings. This huge discrepancy so shook the stellar theorists that some of them claimed that the Hipparcos measurements must be wrong. 'After checking it in several ways,' insisted Floor van Leeuwen in Cambridge, 'I'm sure Hipparcos gave the right answer. So don't use old theories to "correct" new data. Let's develop better theories.'

Before Hipparcos flew, astronomers used the theoretical luminosities to gauge the distances of stars. This was a bit like the Aeroflot practice, on internal flights in Soviet times, of predicting the time of take-off only after it had happened—a way to ensure perfect punctuality, or in the case of the stars, to perfect consistency between theory and observation. Such habits were no longer tolerated, after Hipparcos.

By the second decade of the 21st century its successor, called Gaia, will squeeze stellar theory further by supplying distances and luminosities for the closest 20 million stars of all kinds to better than one per cent, and for a billion other stars with lesser but still unprecedented accuracy. To be fair to all concerned, don't underestimate the difficulties. 'Astronomers have always lived by their wits,' noted a prominent member of the Hipparcos and Gaia teams, Lennart Lindegren at Lund in Sweden. 'It was never easy to extract information from those small and distant lights in the sky.'

Songs of the stars

Across the Sound, in Hertzsprung's Denmark, Jørgen Christensen-Dalsgaard of Aarhus was more severe. 'The general public may think that astronomers know how stars work,' he said in 2002. 'Even some astronomers believe it. But huge uncertainties about the ages of stars, for example, are a sign of our ignorance, and our theories make many assumptions not yet checked by any observations of the interiors of the stars. New space projects will soon improve the situation.'

Christensen-Dalsgaard was referring to a series of satellites devoted to detecting sound waves in the stars. Near or far, a star acts like a musical instrument, inside which the sounds reverberate, and the resulting tones and overtones reveal remarkably precise information about the star's interior. When promoting the space projects, Christensen-Dalsgaard naturally quoted Shakespeare's Lorenzo chatting up Jessica.

> ... Look, how the floor of heaven
> Is thick inlaid with patines of bright gold;
> There's not the smallest orb which thou behold'st
> But in his motion like an angel sings,
> Still quiring to the young-eyed cherubins ...

The interstellar vacuum, rather than the muddy vesture of decay, prevents us hearing the stellar sounds directly, and in any case the frequencies are too low for our ears. But astronomers detect the sound waves as rhythmic variations in brightness, with periods of a few minutes. If it amuses you to do so, you can convert the rhythms into audible sounds of sharply defined pitch, like notes on a musical scale.

The principle was established in the nearest star, the Sun, during the 1980s, with the rise of helioseismology as a means of probing the solar interior. Prolonged observations, for months or years on end, gave data from which experts could infer key features of the interior, such as flows of gas and the size and temperature of the nuclear core. The solar observations revealed internal complexities not anticipated in the pre-existing theories the Sun and the stars.

Applied to other stars, the technique is called asteroseismology. Distance doesn't matter, as long as the variations in brightness can be measured. By 2002, prolonged observation of a large star, with a Swiss telescope at the European Southern Observatory in Chile, had shown that reverberations in a giant star, Xi Hydrae, are, as expected, at much lower acoustic frequencies than in the Sun.

The song of the Sun was usefully recorded from the ground over many years, with networks of specialized instruments, and only later by spacecraft. But dedicated space telescopes, capable of observing many stars at once, promise to be most appropriate for the songs of the stars. A small Canadian satellite, Most (2003), and the French Corot (2005) were conceived to pioneer asteroseismology in space, by probing between them about 100 stars of a deliberately limited variety. A grander project, Europe's Eddington due for launch in 2008, has the capacity to examine 50,000 stars, from the smallest to the biggest and youngest to the oldest.

'If I tell you now that a certain star cluster is 100 million years old, I have to cross my fingers and hope it's somewhere between 80 and 120 million years,' the project scientist, Fabio Favata of the European Space Agency, noted in 2002. 'With Eddington we expect to be able to say, for example, that a certain cluster is pretty exactly 104 million years old. That gives you a simple idea of the new precision that the spacecraft will bring to astronomy.'

Sizing up the stars

On their mountaintops in Hawaii and Chile, the operators of the world's largest visible-light telescopes were not to be outdone, in the investigation of stars or anything else. During the 1990s the Hubble Space Telescope had upstaged them for a while. But they could easily beat its light-collecting power with mirrors 8 or 10 metres in diameter, compared with Hubble's 2.4 metres. Some astronomers dreamed of OWL, the Overwhelmingly Large Telescope with a mirror 100 metres in diameter. The turbulence of the air, which makes stars twinkle, nevertheless remained a problem for visible-light telescopes on the ground, and limited the sharpness of their images.

Others made the most of what they had already, to achieve OWL-like sharpness, or better, by combining simultaneous observations by arrays of smaller telescopes. Back in the 1950s, astronomers at Cambridge developed the necessary tricks, called interferometry and aperture synthesis, using two or more radio telescopes. By 1995 their successors had made the first imaging system of this kind for visible light.

Early pictures showed the bright star Capella as two stars plainly orbiting around each other, only 14 millionths of a degree apart. The Cambridge Optical Aperture Synthesis Telescope, or COAST, went on to achieve similar results in infrared light, and eventually had five 40-centimetre telescopes spaced up to 100 metres apart.

'We can expect arrays with many more telescopes, much larger collectors, and maybe even synthesizing telescope apertures up to a kilometre in size,' said John Baldwin, leader of COAST. 'Telescopes of this kind will certainly play a major role in the future evolution of astronomy, and who knows what scientific treats are in store?'

The European Southern Observatory's Very Large Telescope, with four 8.2-metre mirrors on the Chilean mountaintop of Paranal, was the first major visible-light instrument designed from the outset for interferometry. The first link between two of the main telescopes was achieved in 2001, for simultaneous observations of the same spot in the sky. Two out of four moveable 1.8-metre auxiliary telescopes were due to be in place, and the system to be fully operational, by the end of 2003. It promised stars as you never saw them before.

For centuries, stars looked like mere pinpricks of light, because of their remoteness. Early interferometers imaged the giant star Betelgeuse, 500 times wider than the Sun, and detected hotspots on the surface. The Paranal interferometer, and a similar one devised with the Americans' twin Keck 10-metre telescopes on Mauna Kea, Hawaii, will be able to image much smaller or more distant stars, with a capacity to resolve fine detail equivalent to spotting an astronaut on the Moon. The direct inspection of the faces of many stars and even of large planets orbiting around them thus becomes a realistic goal.

Sizing up the Universe

The winking Cepheids are an historic case for interferometry to pursue. They are large stars, thousands of times more luminous than the Sun, which swell and shrink like a breathing lung. The Pole Star, Polaris, happens to be a Cepheid, growing brighter and fainter every three days, but the prototype is Delta Cephei, with a five-day period discovered by the deaf-mute John Goodricke of York in the 18th century. In 1912 Henrietta Leavitt of Harvard College Observatory found that the relative luminosity of each Cepheid was related to the length of its cycle—the slower the brighter.

Cepheids then became the chief guides to cosmic distances, in the Milky Way and beyond. The Hubble Space Telescope sought them out in other galaxies and took their pulses in an effort to gauge the size and expansion rate of the whole observable Universe. The weakness in this celestial measuring rule was in its calibration, by the distances to the nearest Cepheids. Early results from the Hipparcos satellite in 1997 indicated that the Cepheids were farther away and therefore more luminous than previously supposed.

'We judge the Universe to be a little bigger and therefore a little older, by about a billion years,' declared Michael Feast of Cape Town, in interpreting the Hipparcos data. 'The oldest stars seem to be much younger than supposed, by about 4 billion years. If we can settle on an age of the Universe at, say, 12 billion years then everything will fit nicely.'

Feast's boldness spoke more of the cosmological importance of the Cepheids than the certainty of his result. The star-mapping satellite was working at the limit of its range-finding ability, far beyond the Pleiades. Another complication was that several of the stars in the survey had companions.

Still arguing about whether the most ancient stars were 10 or 17 billion years old, astronomers looked to the interferometers for clarification of the Cepheid distance scale. By 2001, a pair of 40-centimetre telescopes in the Palomar Testbed Interferometer in California had detected the pulsations of two nearby Cepheids well enough to gauge their distances to within about ten per cent, which was comparable with the Hipparcos result. Much greater accuracy was needed, and the European team at Paranal was optimistic.

'The Cepheids are a beautiful example of what we expect to do,' said Francesco Paresce, project scientist of the Very Large Telescope Interferometer. 'We'll truly see these variable stars growing or shrinking as the days pass and we'll gauge, for the first time, the distances of the nearest two dozen Cepheids to an accuracy of 1 per cent or better. Then we'll really know how far away the galaxies are!'

▶ *For more about the private lives of the stars, see* ELEMENTS *and* STARBURSTS. *For helioseismic discoveries, see* SUN'S INTERIOR.

STEM CELLS

Tissue engineering, natural and medical

B ESIDE THE KAMO RIVER, one of the grander streams that flows through the city from the surrounding mountains, stands Kyoto's university hospital. It prides itself on pushing back the frontier where fundamental biology becomes new medical science.

The distinction between pure and applied research has little meaning in the investigation of stem cells. They are living cells taken from the inner mass of a very young embryo. In principle they can develop into specialized cells of any of the different kinds needed by the animal's body. And in Kyoto's molecular genetics lab, in 2000, Shin-Ichi Nishikawa worked a little magic with stem cells from a mouse embryo.

Nishikawa's team grew the stem cells in a culture, in a dish containing collagen, which is a protein found in skin and in other parts of the body where tough fibres are required. After a few days some descendants of the original cells built smooth muscles used in blood vessels, while others made the interior linings for them. The two components then assembled themselves correctly into little tubes. Apparently the stem cells had responded to a signal from the collagen saying, 'We want blood vessels.'

The demonstration of the self-organization of cells into correctly formed tissue was accompanied by the discovery in Kyoto that both types of blood-vessel cells arise from the same precursors, during the progress from stem cells to specialized cells. Two different molecular stimuli, called growth factors, switch the precursor cells to develop either into muscle or into lining cells. Before long, other groups around the world were reporting other tissue-like products from mouse embryonic stem cells, including functional insulin-making cells and heart muscle.

Tissue engineering with embryonic stem cells appears to be an achievable goal. By tracing the precise pathways that give rise to different kinds of tissue cells, and the growth factors that steer their development, scientists hope to be able to introduce just the right cells to treat a patient who needs new tissue—new blood vessels, for example, as in Nishikawa's pioneering experiment. But sceptics, aware of how slowly the research advanced in the last half-century, warn that important medical applications may still be decades away.

Teeth in the wrong place

As so often in science, the story of embryonic stem cells began by pure chance. In 1953 Leroy Stevens, a new recruit at the Jackson Laboratory in Maine, was told to investigate the health effects of cigarette papers, as distinct from tobacco. He used laboratory mice, and one day he noticed that one of them had an enlarged scrotum. This condition was entirely unrelated to the smoking trials.

The mouse's scrotum contained a teratoma, a monstrous form of cancer containing completely misplaced tissues—in this case, teeth and hair growing in the testicles. In a strain of mice predisposed to this condition, Stevens found many other weird tissues besides teeth and hair. 'This stuff was extremely interesting,' he recalled later, 'and it sure beat studying cigarette papers!'

After many years of detailed investigation Stevens found that he could induce teratomas directly by injecting cells from the inner mass of early embryos directly into the testicles of adult mice. He gave the material its modern name: pluripotent embryonic stem cells. That was in 1970, and 11 years later competing teams at Cambridge and UC San Francisco succeeded in culturing mouse stem cells and demonstrating their ability to develop into various types of cells.

Another very long pause followed, before scientists at Wisconsin and Technion, Haifa, achieved the first similar cultures of human embryonic stem cells, in 1998. In announcing their result, James Thomson and his colleagues remarked, 'These cell lines should be useful in human developmental biology, drug discovery, and transplantation medicine.'

A great hoo-ha ensued. On the one hand, scientists and journalists speculated freely about miracle cures that might be achieved by tissue engineering. Why not use embryonic stem cells to make new tissues and organs, to repair a failing heart or kidney, replace the defective pancreatic glands of diabetics, rejuvenate the brains of sufferers from Parkinson's or Alzheimer's disease, or repair damaged spinal cords? A former Hollywood *Superman*, Christopher Reeve, who was paralysed in an accident, became a prominent advocate of stem cell research.

Between speculation and feasibility was a wide technological gap. What was to stop embryonic stem cells, injected into a patient, going berserk and producing a teratoma, just as they did in Stevens' early experiments? And even if they can be tamed, for example by doses of appropriate growth factors, stem cells cultured from an anonymous embryo will be liable, like any other transplant, to rejection by the patient's immune system.

What diabetic will want to exchange his insulin for a lifelong regime of immunosuppressive drugs, to avoid rejection of pancreatic glands grown from the stem cells of another human individual? Hence there arose the concept of making and sacrificing an embryonic clone of a patient to obtain stem cells for his treatment. If practicable, that would be technically the surest way to handle problems of tissue rejection.

But another part of the hoo-ha was the ethical and political issue about using cells from defunct human embryos for research, and perhaps eventually for medication. To compound that with hints of human cloning invited even stronger criticism of the whole idea of using embryonic stem cells. The US government banned the fresh harvesting of such cells, but permitted the continued use of existing cultures of stem cells for research.

For many experts both the medical promises and the political debate seemed premature. 'At present we do not know enough to make anything but an entirely emotional decision about future applications,' commented Davor Solter of Germany's Max-Planck-Institut für Immunobiologie. 'Every country and ultimately every individual will have to decide for themselves how they feel about the moral aspects of the use of these technologies, but strident demands to forbid them before they are fully understood are short-sighted and potentially harmful. If we are asked to give up something, it seems logical that we should know exactly what it is that we are giving up.'

To enable research to proceed more quickly, Europe's first stem cell bank opened for business at the UK's National Institute for Biological Standards and Control in Hertfordshire in 2003. Under British law it could collect stem cells from embryos up to 14 days after conception, when the embryo is the size of a pinhead. Unused embryos from test-tube baby treatments for infertility were an important source.

Adult cells can be all-powerful too

Constraints or misgivings concerning the use of embryonic stem cells encouraged closer attention to adult stem cells as an alternative for tissue engineering. Whilst embryonic stem cells appear in the inner cell mass of an embryo four or five days old, and largely disappear when the baby is fully formed, some lines of stem cells survive throughout life. Their job is to keep renewing the tissues. For example, human skin replaces every cell every few weeks, and baldness is an example of adult stem cells failing in their duty.

The best-known adult stem cells are those residing in bone marrow, which are involved in blood-making and in the immune system. Bone-marrow transplants are already used to replace them when they fail in their work, causing various diseases. Other adult stem cells were harder to find, and seemed more difficult to grow in culture. Yet by 2001 the US National Institutes of Health could report that, besides bone marrow, the known sources of adult stem cells included the blood itself, the cornea and the retina of the eye, the brain, skeletal muscle, dental pulp, the liver, the skin, the lining of the gastrointestinal tract, and the pancreas.

The adult stem cells are themselves unspecialized, but they seemed at first to be predisposed or disciplined to make special kinds of tissues. In the living body that is just as well, otherwise teratomas would be commonplace. Scientists nevertheless persisted in searching for 'pluripotent' adult stem cells that would be capable of making any kind of tissue, in the manner of embryonic stem cells.

Catherine Verfaillie at Minnesota won the race. At the end of 2001, she startled her colleagues by announcing that small cells from the bone marrow of an adult mouse contributed to almost any kind of tissue when injected into a mouse embryo. They could also be cultured outside the body in the same manner as embryonic stem cells, and showed no sign of ageing as other tissue cells do when cultured.

'They may be an ideal cell source for therapy of inherited or degenerative diseases,' claimed Verfaillie and her Minnesota team. In parallel with the mouse research, they had obtained similar pluripotent cells from human beings, and they expected rapid progress towards medical applications. However ill patients may be with other diseases, nearly all have healthy bone marrow. So the way may open up, more quickly than previously thought, towards comprehensive tissue engineering with a person's own stem cells.

▶ *For a more general view of development, see* EMBRYOS.

SUN'S INTERIOR

How sound waves made our mother star transparent

MOUNT WILSON LOOKS QUITE IMPOSING as it rises above the suburbs of Los Angeles, pushed skywards by kinks in the San Andreas Fault, where the Californian coastal strip creeps past the mainland. At 1500 metres, the mountain is only a pimple compared with some lofty peaks chosen for modern telescopes, but it was there that Edwin Hubble discovered the expansion of the Universe in the late 1920s. And Mount Wilson was also the scene of two of the three top discoveries about the Sun, made during the 20th century.

In 1908 George Hale, founder of the observatory, measured magnetic fields on the Sun by the Zeeman effect, which alters the wavelengths of light. The dark blemishes called sunspots turned out to be scenes of intense magnetism, and the bright flashes called solar flares were eventually to be understood as magnetic explosions. The fact that the count of sunspots rises, falls and rises again in a roughly 11-year cycle is linked with big changes in the Sun's magnetic field. It swaps its north and south magnetic poles around at each sunspot maximum, when general magnetic activity in the stormy atmosphere also peaks.

Half a century after Hale's pioneering discovery about the Sun's magnetic fields, and 20 years after his death in 1938, one of his old solar telescopes on Mount Wilson opened a window into the interior of our mother star. At first it was for only a glimpse. But that inspired a new science, which by the end of the century was able to seek out the sources of the magnetism and eventually to see right through the Sun.

Robert Leighton was a particle physicist from nearby Caltech, who used Mount Wilson as a convenient site for a cosmic-ray experiment. He became curious about Hale's equipment. While he tinkered with it he began to wonder whether the Sun's surface might have waves on it, like the sea. If they existed then the wavelengths of light should shorten and lengthen, by the Doppler effect, as the solar waves rose and fell, towards and away from the telescope.

Leighton looked for the waves and he found them. But instead of being merely turbulent, the Sun's entire visible surface heaved in a strangely rhythmic way. In 1959 Leighton told a graduate student, 'I know what you're going to study for your thesis. The Sun is an oscillator with a period of 300 seconds.'

In a word, it hums to itself. The solar sound waves are pitched far too low for human hearing, even if they could traverse interplanetary space, but refined observations of surface motions reveal many individual notes, as in a musical chord. They all have around one cycle per 300 seconds, as reported by Leighton. A quarter of a century after his discovery, a light meter on NASA's Solar Maximum Mission detected a strobing of the Sun's brightness, with the same five-minute period.

Leighton left it to others to work out the explanation and uses for the solar oscillations. Douglas Gough at Cambridge encapsulated the importance of what could be done with them, by naming the subject helioseismology. Helios means Sun and seismology echoes the use of earthquake waves to probe the interior of our planet. In the case of the Sun the quaking is continuous, with a steady intensity.

Reverberating through the interior, the sound waves feel the layers and movements of deep-lying hot gas. When the waves make themselves apparent at the surface, the scientists can deduce what is going on inside. Gough explained, 'It's like trying to recognize a musical instrument you've never seen, just from the tone it produces.'

A need for continuity

The helioseismologists were not starting from scratch. The Sun is a ball of gas 333,000 times more massive than the Earth and more than a million times larger by volume. But it has to obey well-known laws of gravitational compression and heat, and these enabled theorists to paint a picture, at least in broad brushstrokes, of what the Sun and other stars should be like inside.

'It is possible to work out how fast the pressure increases as we go down into the Sun, and how fast the temperature must increase to withstand the pressure,' Arthur Eddington of Cambridge explained in 1926. 'It is natural that you should feel rather sceptical about our claim that we know how hot it is in the very middle of a star—and you may be still more sceptical when I divulge the actual figure!'

Eddington suggested 40 million degrees C for the Sun's core temperature, and although that was later cut back to 15 million, it was still hot enough for nuclear reactions to occur. In 1938, in another of the great 20th-century discoveries about the Sun, Hans Bethe of Cornell figured out the source of the Sun's power, in a sequence of fusion reactions that converts hydrogen into helium.

The picture of the Sun's interior, which eventually emerged, has the very hot, dense core of the Sun surrounded with a thick layer that rotates like an almost solid ball around the north–south axis. It is called the radiative zone, and here the heat from the core works its way slowly outwards in the form of X-rays. Above the radiative zone lies the convection zone, where turbulence like a

653

boiling kettle's carries the heat to the visible surface. Observations of the surface show that it rotates faster at the equator than at the poles.

As helioseismology matured, it confirmed this general picture. The observed oscillations enabled theorists to deduce the speed of sound waves at different depths inside the Sun and compare them with the speeds expected by the theory. By 1990, an abrupt change in the variation of the speed of sound, 29 per cent of the way down towards the centre, had identified the boundary between the convection and radiative zones—somewhat deeper than expected.

Registering the solar oscillations precisely required continuous, uninterrupted observations, preferably for months on end. Eric Fossard and Gérard Grec from Nice took advantage of the midnight sun at the South Pole, and US solar physicists followed suit. Teams at Birmingham and Nice also developed instruments that could be deployed at networks of sites all around the world. These were relatively simple telescopes that observed oscillations of the whole Sun.

The US National Solar Observatory in Arizona led a more ambitious project, with support from the National Science Foundation. Instruments called Doppler imagers measured oscillations at a large number of points across the Sun's visible face, in a network of ground-based instruments called the Global Oscillation Network Group, or GONG.

Stations at Big Bear (California), Learmonth (Australia), Udaipur (India), Teide (Tenerife), Cerro Tololo (Chile) and Mauna Loa (Hawaii) began operations in 1995. Altogether 67 different institutions in 20 nations were involved in GONG. But by 2000 the GONG instruments were being upgraded, because in the meantime Stanford University stole the show with a similar instrument in space.

● Sunspots on the far side

The austerely named Michelsen Doppler Imager, or MDI, rode on the European–US spacecraft SOHO, together with simpler helioseismic instruments provided by French-led and Swiss-led teams. Developed for Stanford by Lockheed scientists and engineers, MDI measured oscillations at a million points across the visible surface. The needed continuity of observations came with SOHO's station far out in space, which enabled MDI to watch the Sun for 24 hours a day. The only limitation was the spacecraft's communication system, which restricted the abundance of data transmissible to the Earth.

As it unmasked the solar interior, from 1996 onwards, MDI on SOHO repeatedly made news in the scientific and public press. It discovered, for example, that the top 24,000 kilometres of the Sun flows slowly from the equator towards the poles. Around each polar region there circulates a huge subsurface jet stream of swiftly flowing gas. MDI gauged the depth of familiar surface features, and it revealed convergent flows of gas around the magnetic fields of sunspots.

An analytical technique called solar tomography, invented in 1993 by Thomas Duvall of NASA Goddard, aided some of the most spectacular results. It is a matter of gauging the variable speed of sound in different parts of the Sun from the time of arrival of packets of sound waves at the visible surface on the Sun's near side. Temperature, magnetic fields and gas flows all affect the speed, like the various obstacles faced by cross-country runners.

That was how MDI was able to detect stormy regions on the far side, where sunspots were developing. Charles Lindsey of the Solar Physics Research Corporation in Arizona and Douglas Braun of NorthWest Research Associates in Colorado examined wide rings of sound waves that emanate from each small region on the far side. They reach the near side after rebounding internally from the solar surface.

Sunspots depress the Sun's surface in a dimple. Their strong magnetic fields speed up the sound waves. So if there is a group of sunspots present on the far side, sound waves should arrive from it at the front side about ten seconds earlier than equivalent waves from sunspot-free regions, in a total travel time of about 4 hours. Careful analysis of the data radioed from SOHO revealed just that effect.

Detecting sunspots on the far side adds a week's early warning about stormy regions that will swing into view, as the Sun rotates, and which may then cause solar flares and mass ejections of gas, with possible effects on space weather and the Earth. Philip Scherrer of Stanford, responsible for the MDI instrument, was gratified but not surprised by this tour de force. He remarked in 2001, 'When we started work with SOHO five years ago, most experts thought it would be impossible to see right through the Sun. Now we do it regularly in real time. For practical purposes we've made the Sun transparent.'

Investigations on the near side revealed how sunspots start, and how they are maintained. The MDI scientists found sound waves beginning to travel faster and faster through a region where sunspots were about to appear. Less than half a day elapsed between these signs of unusual magnetic activity deep in the Sun's interior and the appearance of a group of dark spots on a previously unblemished surface.

'Sunspots form when intense magnetic fields break through the visible surface,' said Alexander Kosovichev of Stanford. 'We could see the magnetic field shooting upwards like a fountain, faster than we expected.' The region of strong magnetic field rose from a depth of 18,000 kilometres, at 4500 kilometres per hour, and took possession of a column of gas 20,000 kilometres wide.

Some 4000 kilometres beneath the surface, the rope-like magnetic field unravelled, and sent out strands that made individual sunspots in a group. Immediately below the largest spot was a cushion of cooler, less intensely magnetized gas.

Solar physicists already knew that the intense magnetic fields in a sunspot strangle the normal upflow of energy from the interior, leaving the sunspot cooler and therefore darker than its surroundings. MDI revealed that the ligature is a whirlpool. Hot gas near the Sun's surface converges and dives into the interior at speeds of up to 4000 kilometres per hour.

That's how the magnetic fields become concentrated, and why a sunspot can persist for days or weeks. The heat taken into the interior resurfaces elsewhere, and helps to explain why, paradoxically, the Sun is a little brighter overall when its face is freckled with spots.

Fast heartbeat or ancient field?

As mentioned before, the gas at the solar equator rotates more rapidly about the north–south axis than does the gas towards the poles. This difference occurs only in the outer part of the Sun, the convection zone. The inner part, the radiative zone, turns rigidly, at the same rate as the outlying gas 30 degrees north or south of the equator.

At other latitudes the differences in rotation rate where the two zones meet, more than 200,000 kilometres beneath the visible surface of the Sun, might in principle create a dynamo to generate the solar magnetic field. Slow pulsations in the hot gas, like a solar heartbeat, could conceivably explain the waxing and waning of the outward manifestations of the Sun's magnetic field during the 11-year sunspot cycle. To find the hypothetical dynamo was a declared aim of some helioseismologists.

Detection of a solar heartbeat, announced in 2000, nevertheless brought a disconcerting surprise. Success came from combining observations from the GONG network on the ground with results from MDI on the SOHO spacecraft. At just the depth expected for the dynamo, the analysts saw currents of gas speed up and slacken, like the blood in human arteries.

The contrast in speed between layers above and below the supposed dynamo region can change by 20 per cent in six months. When the deeper gas speeds up, the gas above slows down, and vice versa. In observations between May 1995 and November 1999, these alternations in speed occurred three times, indicating a pulse-rate much faster than expected.

'We were excited to see the first evidence of changes close to the location of the solar dynamo, the region that generates the Sun's large-scale magnetic field and is believed to drive the solar cycle,' said Rachel Howe of the US National Solar Observatory who led this work. 'It's very surprising to find that the changes have such a short period—16 months or so rather than the 11 years of the solar cycle.'

Douglas Gough at Cambridge was less put out by this result than some of his fellow solar physicists. He didn't require any dynamo to explain the Sun's magnetism. Instead he supposed that an ancient magnetic field finds its way out from the deep interior into the convection zone.

As indirect evidence he cited a slight excess in the speed of sound measured by SOHO in the supposed dynamo layer. It was only 0.2 per cent higher than expected, but he attributed the discrepancy to a stirring action that left the region with less helium gas than predicted by the theory. This is not helium made in the nuclear reactions in the core of the Sun, which stays down there, but primordial helium, built into the whole star at its formation.

'The Sun is somewhat like orange juice,' Gough explained. 'Leave it alone for a long time and the orange will settle to the bottom. Actually, the Sun is composed principally of hydrogen and helium, the hydrogen acting like the water and the heavier helium like the orange. The circulatory motion in the layer mixes the helium back into the convection zone.'

In Gough's picture, the deep-lying, rigidly rotating radiative zone is stiffened by a pervasive magnetic field shaped very like the Earth's, with magnetic field lines looping from pole to pole in an orderly way, although perhaps a thousand times as strong. This field has existed since the Sun was first formed almost 4.6 billion years ago, and it resists gas from the outer, convection zone that tries to burrow into it. The descending gas is repelled back into the convection zone, carrying with it not only the helium that gave the clue, but also a magnetic field leaking from the radiative zone.

The internal field escapes where the rotation rates of the radiative zone and the convection zone are the same, in belts 30 degrees north and south of the Sun's equator. Only there can magnetic field lines link up, between the two zones. This prediction is in contrast to the dynamo theory, which relies on differences in the rotation rates. Gough thought it no coincidence that the first sunspots in each new cycle usually appear 30 degrees from the equator.

Puzzling variations

In other respects the Sun's primordial field remains aloof from the magnetic antics of the convection zone. It doesn't flip over, swapping north and south poles around every 11 years or so, as happens in the outwardly manifest solar magnetic field. A distinct and much more dynamic regime operates in the convection zone, causing new sunspots to appear ever closer to the equator while their numbers are growing. Then, as the count diminishes, regions with a particular magnetic polarity migrate polewards, to fix the new north–south or south–north configuration and somehow to prime the next sunspot cycle.

The sunspot cycle is a magnetic cycle. In principle, the different rates of rotation of the gas at different latitudes may wind up and intensify the magnetic field within the convection zone. That creates strains, which the sunspot activity relieves and eventually dissipates. Yet nearly a century after Hale's discovery of the Sun's peculiar outward magnetism, there is no generally accepted story about exactly what happens in the convection zone, to generate the sunspot cycle.

Still less is there an explanation of why the sunspot cycles vary a lot, in intensity and duration. This ignorance is a matter of practical concern, because variations in solar magnetic activity affect the Earth. During the 20th century, sunspots became more numerous and the Sun's magnetic field in our planet's vicinity doubled in strength. Around 300 years ago, on the other hand, sunspot activity shut down almost completely.

The Mount Wilson Observatory started a project in 1966 to monitor magnetic cycles in other stars. Ten sun-like stars all showed cycles of 8–12 years in duration. In 1980 the star 54 Piscium abruptly switched off, exactly as the Sun did 300 years earlier. The cycles stopped and 54 Piscium remained magnetically calm throughout the ensuing decades.

If the variations were wholly random, they might be less mystifying. But accumulated evidence suggests that the Sun changes its magnetic behaviour quite rhythmically. A recent discovery is that sudden chills on the Earth, called ice-rafting events, occur every 1400 years or so and coincide with periods of weak magnetic activity on the Sun.

Other alternations between greater and less activity have been suggested, directly from sunspot records or indirectly from variations in the rates of production of radioactive elements in the Earth's atmosphere, which increase when the Sun is enfeebled. The most mentioned rhythm has a period of roughly 200 years. It is sometimes called the Suess Cycle, after Hans Suess of UC San Diego, who found it in variations in radiocarbon production, observed in ancient tree rings spanning thousands of years.

An explanation on offer for long-term cyclic behaviour—the only one, so far— says that the rhythms come from the gravitational influence of the planets orbiting around the Sun. The fact that planets make stars wobble became headline news in astronomy in the 1990s, when it made possible the discovery of planets orbiting other stars. But only a very few scientists were willing to argue that similar perturbations might control the Sun's magnetic behaviour.

When the planets are evenly scattered in their orbits, the centre of mass of the Solar System is close to the centre of the Sun. But when the most massive planets—Jupiter, Saturn, Uranus and Neptune—are all out to one side, the centre of mass is located outside the Sun, and the Sun is obliged to waltz around that centre. With the planets perpetually circling at different rates, the Sun's own rotary path around the centre of mass is very complicated, and it can change quite drastically in the course of a few years.

Scientists who speculate about an influence on the magnetic activity of the Sun suspect that a high rate of change of rotary motion (angular momentum) is the most likely factor. The planets' movements are well known and the wobbles and jerks are entirely computable. A basic cycle generated this way has a period of 179 years, and it may correspond with the roughly 200 years seen in the Suess cycles.

The sunspot cycles numbered 21 and 22, peaking around 1980 and 1990, respectively, were intense by the norms of the past 200 years, having been surpassed only once since 1780. Yet the consensus of experts was that the next peak around 2000 should be similarly strong. A dissenter was Ivanka Charvátová of the Czech Academy of Science's Geophysical Institute in Prague. She made a prediction based on detailed comparisons of solar behaviour, in apparent response to the wobbles, stage by stage during the most recent 179-year orbital periods.

'The current cycle 22,' Charvátová declared in 1990, 'is probably the last of the high ones. It should be followed by an epoch of about 40 years, in which the solar motion will be disordered and solar activity therefore should be low. The cycles will probably be longer and irregular.'

She may yet be right. The peak sunspot count in cycle 23, which came in 2000, was 25 per cent down on the previous cycles. Whether the next cycles will be even lower, as implied in her forecast, remains to be seen. Even if it happens, that will not prove the planetary effect, because sceptics will say that the Sun is simply returning from frenzied to more average behaviour. The only thing to do is to keep an open mind, and hope for a decent theory from either the orthodox solar physicists or the planetary-influence people, which will explain exactly how the Sun's convection zone decides how many sunspots to make this time.

▶ *For outward effects of solar magnetism in the solar atmosphere, interplanetary space and the Earth's environs, see* SOLAR WIND *and* SPACE WEATHER. *For more about solar influences on the Earth's climate, see* EARTHSHINE *and* ICE-RAFTING EVENTS. *For asteroseismology, looking into other stars by sound waves, see* STARS.

SUPERATOMS, SUPERFLUIDS AND SUPERCONDUCTORS

The march of the boson armies

U NLUCKY PUBLISHERS who reject books that later make bestsellers have their counterparts in science. Savants of Edinburgh University turned down a job application from James Clerk Maxwell, so he became the 19th century's top physicist in London instead. And in 1923 the editor of the *Philosophical Magazine* declined to publish a submission by a little-known scientist in a university no one had heard of. The rejected paper is a cornerstone of modern physics.

Dakha is now the capital of Bangladesh but in the 1920s it was a provincial centre in British India, with a newly created university. There, a young man from Calcutta called Satyen Bose mused about particles of light. Unlike particles of matter, photons can be freely created and destroyed, and they carry no identity cards. As a result, they obey rules quite different from those governing ordinary matter.

Bose found that the rules enabled him to calculate the pattern of light of different energies emitted by a glowing body. It was the same as the spectrum that Max Planck in Berlin had deduced two decades earlier, when he founded the quantum theory of light, but now obtained by a quite different route. When the *Philosophical Magazine* said No to his paper, 'Planck's law and the hypothesis of light quanta', he was sufficiently confident in his ideas to send the manuscript to Albert Einstein in Berlin.

'Respected Sir,' he wrote in the covering letter, 'I have ventured to send you the accompanying article for your perusal and opinion. You will see that I have tried to deduce the coefficient . . . in Planck's law independent of classical electrodynamics.'

All famous scientists are plagued by scatty mail but Einstein was sharp enough to spot, among the dross of unsolicited manuscripts, the gold of Bose's work. He was so impressed, in fact, that he immediately translated the paper into German himself, and forwarded it to the *Zeitschrift für Physik*. Einstein also saw much wider implications in Bose's reasoning. These are explainable more easily with hindsight than in the chronology of the 1920s.

Lasers and the getaway fluids

Nowadays physicists divide subatomic particles into two general kinds, fermions after Enrico Fermi of Italy, and bosons after Bose of India. Quarks and electrons, the building blocks of atoms, are fermions. In a word, they are loners. Two identical fermions cannot be in the same state, as defined by their location, energy and direction of spin. An atom occupies space because the electrons swarming around the nucleus all demand elbow room to preserve their individuality.

Bosons are far more sociable. They include all the particles that transmit the cosmic forces. The prototypical bosons, photons, convey the electric force. W particles engineer the weak force of radioactivity, whilst mesons and gluons carry the nuclear forces. The doubly eponymous Higgs boson, referring to Peter Higgs of Edinburgh as well as to our Satyen, was much sought-after in big accelerators at the end of the century, as a wished-for explanation of the masses of particles.

Unlike fermions, bosons can co-exist in the same state. Indeed they wish to do so if they can. The most familiar example is a laser beam, produced when many atoms release photons in precise synchrony. Einstein stated the principle that led to lasers when he pointed out that a passing photon could stimulate an atom to release a sociable photon of the same energy. Laser is an acronym for Light Amplification by Stimulated Emission of Radiation.

More than 30 years passed before the first practical lasers were developed. It is one thing to know that an effect is possible, quite another to figure out how to demonstrate it in commonplace matter. And in remarks at the Preussischen Akademie der Wissenschaften zu Berlin in 1925, Einstein predicted a laser-like effect with atoms. Here the time elapsing till its achievement in the laboratory was 70 years.

Most of the atoms in the Universe are bosons. They are therefore capable, in theory, of clubbing together like photons in a laser beam to make superatoms. Provided an atom has an even number of quarks plus electrons, it is a potentially sociable boson. For example, commonplace helium-4 is a boson, with 12 quarks and two electrons. Its lightweight sister helium-3 has nine quarks and two electrons, leaving it as a snooty fermion.

The first sign of superatomic behaviour came with superfluidity in helium-4, a very surprising phenomenon discovered in 1938 by Peter Kapitza at the Institute for Physical Problems in Moscow. When cooled to within two degrees of absolute zero (minus 271 °C) liquid helium flows completely freely, without the slightest sign of viscosity. If held in an open container within the cooling apparatus, it will defy gravity, climb up the wall, and escape over the rim. The helium-4 superfluid is assuredly some kind of bosonic superatom, as first proposed by Fritz London in Paris, in the wake of Kapitza's announcement.

Even more remarkable was superfluidity in helium-3, which is not a boson. In 1972, a sharp-eyed graduate student at Cornell, Douglas Osheroff, noticed something odd happening at a temperature just two thousandths of a degree above absolute zero, during an experiment intended to make helium-3 ice. Investigations with his senior colleagues, David Lee and Robert Richardson, then revealed the superfluidity, which was confirmed by Olli Lounasmaa at the Helsinki University of Technology.

This discovery, though accidental, was not unexpected. The possibility that fermions could, at low temperatures, lose their snootiness and pair up to make bosons, emerged from the explanation of another amazing kind of 'super' behaviour.

Resistance zero!

Heike Kamerlingh Onnes at Leiden had discovered in 1911 that mercury metal cooled to four degrees above absolute zero had no resistance whatsoever to an electric current. Once started, a current would continue to flow indefinitely with no voltage to drive it. Many other metals and alloys turned out to be superconductors at temperatures close to absolute zero.

Superconductivity was flabbergasting, and no convincing explanation was forthcoming for a long time. Ordinary currents flow in metals because individual electrons pass relatively freely between the atoms. As fermions, the electrons nevertheless feel impediments, which translate into an electrical resistance.

In 1957, John Bardeen, Leon Cooper and John Robert Schrieffer in the USA reasoned that the electrons in a superconductor could change into bosons, by joining together in pairs. At a sufficiently low temperature, interactions between the electrons and the lattice of metal atoms supposedly promote this pairing. Then, as a ghostly army of cooperative bosons, the electrons pairs simply ignore the atomic impediments. They march freely through the superconductor with zero resistance, for as long as the temperature and magnetic field remain low enough.

Many physicists were impressed by the Bardeen–Cooper–Schrieffer theory, but it failed to predict or even explain the discovery of ceramic superconductors. That story began at IBM Zurich in 1986, when Georg Bednorz and Alex Müller found that lanthanum–barium–copper oxide was superconducting, even up to 35 degrees above absolute zero. Till then, the warmest superconductor known was niobium–germanium alloy, at 23 degrees. Within two years, IBM Almaden in California had found a complex ceramic material that remained superconducting at 125 degrees absolute, or minus 148 degrees C. By the start of the new century there was no satisfactory explanation of these 'high-temperature' superconductors.

The first superatoms

Temperature trends in the opposite direction, to within a whisker of absolute zero, were needed for the superatoms predicted by Einstein. That was the main reason for the 70-year delay. At the absolute zero of temperature all heat-like motion ends. In the air you breathe, the molecules whiz about at high speeds, but at absolute zero atoms must stand still and not even shiver. It is a theoretical state that exists naturally nowhere in the Universe, and man-made cooling techniques may never reach absolute zero. But all through the 20th century they inched ever closer to it.

To make a superatom you want a gas in which thousands or billions of individual atoms travel at a few millimetres per second—literally at a snail's pace. That means a tenth of a millionth of a degree above absolute zero, or 100 nanokelvins in the physicists' units. Why so cold? Because the atoms will not club together until they can reach out to feel one another's presence, with their matter waves.

In foreseeing superatoms, back in 1925, Einstein picked up not only Bose's ideas but also the 1924 prediction of matter waves by Louis de Broglie in Paris. Just as the quantum theory welcomed the ambiguous nature of light, as both waves and particles, so it required that material particles should also have waviness associated with them. At ordinary temperatures the wavelength of an atom is smaller than the atom itself.

An ultracold atom has a matter wavelength comparable with the distances between atoms in an experimental cloud. Then, and only then, can it merge with the other atoms. In particulate terms they make a superatomic blob. In wave terms it is a single giant wave of matter.

Cryogenic engineering with liquid-helium generators and the like had attended all previous efforts to make very cold materials. Such paraphernalia became unnecessary with the realization that you could slow down a beam of atoms by hitting them head-on with a laser beam, and then trap them using other laser beams and magnetic fields. Any hot atoms could be allowed to escape, reducing the temperature still further, just as in a cooling cup of coffee.

In 1995 Eric Cornell and Carl Wiemann at JILA in Colorado made the first-ever superatoms, from the metal rubidium. (JILA is an institute, like CERN in Geneva, where the acronym remains and its origin is deliberately forgotten.) A few months later Wolfgang Ketterle, at the Massachusetts Institute of Technology, made bigger superatoms of sodium, and in 1997 Randall Hulet at Rice University, Texas, followed up with lithium. In 1998 Daniel Kleppner and Thomas Greytak at the Massachusetts Institute of Technology succeeded, after years of frustration, in making hydrogen superatoms.

Ketterle's superatoms, containing millions of sodium atoms, were the prettiest. You could see them as cigar-shaped blobs a fraction of a millimetre long—

pitch-black or transparent to light according to circumstances. You could let pieces of a superatom break off and fall away one by one, under gravity. And most gratifyingly for teachers of physics, you could demonstrate the inherent waviness by letting two superatoms spread through each other. They created interfering patterns like the ripples from two stones thrown into a pond.

'How do physicists characterize a new form of matter? They shake it, poke it, shine light on it, and see what happens!' Ketterle explained. He added, 'After decades of an elusive search, nobody expected that condensates would be so robust and relatively easy to manipulate.'

After electronics, atomics

It was playtime for the physicists, as they poked their superatoms. They confirmed a 50-year-old prediction by Nicolai Bogolyubov of Moscow that sound waves would travel through a superatom at about one centimetre per second. And there were headlines in 1999 for physicists who slowed the speed of light to just 17 metres per second in a sodium superatom. This 18-million-fold reduction in light speed was achieved at the Rowland Institute for Science in Massachusetts, when Lene Hau and her colleagues fired laser beams in two directions through a superatom. Perturbations due to one beam caused the waves of the other laser beam to keep tripping over themselves, with strong mutual interference.

By 1997 Ketterle's team was demonstrating atom lasers, by peeling off small superatoms from a large one, piece by piece, and releasing them in a series of pulses. Travelling in a straight line through a vacuum chamber, the pulses spread to a width of more than a millimetre. A combination of gravity and internal forces gave to each pulse a streamlined crescent shape, remarkable to behold.

Physicists thus had amazing manifestations of the quantum behaviour of atomic matter occurring on a large scale, to put alongside the earlier discoveries of superconductivity and superfluidity, and the invention of light lasers. The importance of bosonic and matter-wave phenomena in fundamental science was attested in a long string of Nobel Prizes from Kamerlingh Onnes in 1911 to Cornell, Ketterle and Wiemann in 2001.

By then, ultracold skills already extended to fermions. Their unsociable behaviour is not only responsible for preventing the collapse of the electrons in atoms, but also for the mutual repulsion of nuclear particles that prevents extremely dense neutron stars from collapsing further. In 1999, Deborah Jin of JILA was the first to bring fermionic potassium atoms under ultracold control. She saw them adopting a scale of different energies, like electrons in an atom. Her next experiment was to try to make superatoms of fermions and bosons co-exist in the same crucible.

SUPERATOMS, SUPERFLUIDS AND SUPERCONDUCTORS

The implications of the new ultracold states of matter are mind-boggling. As the 20th century saw the advance of electronics from primitive cathode ray tubes and thermionic valves to microchips and the Internet, the 21st century will be an era of atomics. Just what that will mean is anyone's guess, although early expectations include instruments like atomic clocks, gyroscopes, accelerometers, gravity meters and magnetic measuring devices, hundreds or even billions of times more accurate than existing devices.

Escape from the elaborate technology of the pioneering experiments will be a requirement. A preview came in 2001 when two German teams, at Tübingen and the Max-Planck-Institut für Quantenoptik in Garching, produced clouds of condensed rubidium atoms on thumbnail-sized microchips. A team in Garching succeeded in transporting matter waves along the chip surface, using a conveyor belt of undulating microwires carrying an alternating current.

Further food for thought came when experiments at the Garching institute created yet another state of matter. They altered a rubidium superatom into a peculiar ultracold solid called a Mott insulator, after a British theorist, Nevill Mott, who explained the unexpected electrical properties of ordinary materials at very low temperatures.

The physicists set up a 3-D framework of bright and dark dots in space, from intersecting interference patterns produced by three laser beams at right angles. To begin with, the superatoms moved freely through this landscape, but as the laser intensities increased the superatom suddenly disappeared. When the light–dark contrast was intense enough, the bright spots became electric traps, like the cavities in an egg carton, in which atoms absconding from the superatom took up residence. They spaced themselves out, as if in a crystal, with two or three atoms in each of more than 150,000 bright spots.

'We can switch back and forth between the superfluid and solid states just by changing the laser intensities,' commented Immanuel Bloch of the Garching team. 'And when we start thinking about applications, one of the first things that springs to mind is a new kind of quantum computer, using atoms instead of electrons.'

▶ *For more on particles as waves, see* QUANTUM TANGLES. *For the apparent role of Bose–Einstein condensates in giving mass to matter, see* HIGGS BOSONS. *Other subatomic topics include* ELECTROWEAK FORCE *and* PARTICLE FAMILIES.

SUPERSTRINGS

Retuning the cosmic imagination

'**T**HE IMPLICATIONS ARE DIZZYING,' the composer Aaron Copland wrote in 1961, in a letter to an engineer who had sent him recordings of music played by a computer. 'If I were 20, I would be really concerned at the variety of possibilities suggested. As it is, I plan to be an interested bystander, waiting to see what will happen next.'

The engineer was John Pierce of Bell Labs in New Jersey, about to become famous as the designer of the first active telecommunications satellite, Telstar, launched in 1962. His hobby was music, and his electronic efforts foreshadowed the synthesizers that simulate the classical musical instruments, and the eerie music nowadays composed for free-ranging computer-generated sounds. Pierce went back to the most basic science so that he could understand musical sounds thoroughly—to his fingertips in fact.

He experimented with 20 metres of nylon fishing line tied to a tree, just so that he could pluck it and feel the little jerks of waves travelling back and forth repeatedly along the string. More than three centuries earlier a peripatetic and polymathic Frenchman, Marin Mersenne, performed more systematic trials with strings of hemp and brass up to 40 metres long. Although better remembered now as a number theorist, Mersenne published in *Harmonie Naturelle* (1636) the formula that predicts the fundamental frequency and pitch of a string, from its tension, its length and its mass per unit length.

A worried violin dealer consulted a computer-music colleague of Pierce, about whether a steel string would overstress an instrument. The advice was simply to weigh it and compare it with the weight of the alternative gut string. If the steel string were heavier, the tension would have to increase exactly in proportion to the ratio of the masses, to achieve the same pitch.

If you raise the lid of a grand piano, the craftsmanship on display tells you plenty about the science of vibrating strings, without resort to Mersenne's mathematics. All of the strings are taut, and you can see the pins used to adjust their tensions, to fine-tune each note. But the strength of materials available in the early 18th century, when Bartolomeo Cristofori of Florence invented the piano, set limits to the musical range achievable by tension alone.

So the grand piano is lopsided. Bass notes come from long strings on the left, and the high-pitched strings on the right are short. The bass strings are also thicker, to give them more mass. What matters is how long it takes for a deflection caused by the hammer to travel along a string to the far end, where it is reflected to sustain the vibration. In a massive bass string the wave travels relatively slowly and has farther to go, and therefore makes fewer vibrations per second.

Strings too small to see

Long before science barged in, musicians learned by trial and error. They were most concerned about the impression that the notes made in the human ear and mind. A discovery in classical times, usually ascribed to Pythagoras, was a rule of intervals of pitch—in instruments in which the tension of a string was constant but its effective length could be varied. Halve the length and you go up an octave. Other exact fractions, five-sixths, four-fifths and so on, give the aesthetically approved intervals of minor third, major third, fourth and fifth.

To ancient minds, this was the music of the cosmos. If sounds pleasing to the ear had exact mathematical tie-ins, did that not speak of a divine order in the Universe? The idea persisted into medieval times, and Mersenne's contemporary, the German astronomer Johannes Kepler, used it to support the then heretical view that the Sun, not the Earth, was at the centre of the Solar System.

In the new Copernican scheme, Kepler said, the relative motions of the planets were in much better harmony with the beautiful, God-given, Pythagorean proportions. As it happened, the numbers fitted Kepler's argument quite well. Modern astronomers regard that, at best, as an approximate coincidence, possibly giving clues to the origin of the planets. They prefer to leave it to mortal composers like Gustav Holst to set the planets to music.

History nevertheless repeats itself. Since the closing decades of the 20th century, the tuning of strings and its mathematical description has become once more a preoccupation of theoretical physicists. Like Kepler, many have an intense conviction that their theory is so beautiful it must be correct, and that it truly describes the construction of the Universe. The proposed harmonious generators of everything around us are called superstrings.

Whilst Pierce's computer could make sounds corresponding with musical instruments that never existed, the theorists can calculate vibrations in strings too small to see. The starting idea is simple enough. In quantum theory, particles of light and matter have waves associated with them, so why not imagine each particle as a humming string that vibrates with the correct frequency, which corresponds with the particle's energy? Heavy particles make low-pitched notes and lightweight particles are shrill.

The strings so envisaged would not conveniently fit on your guitar. They are extremely small entities jiggling at high speed in the queer ways that quantum theory and relativity allow. Nor are they fixed at their two ends. They are like prancing caterpillars, capable of generating waves from their own internal tensions. In some theories, the two ends of a string join to make a ring.

The strings came into particle physics unbidden, around 1970, during investigations of the strong force that binds particles together to build an atomic nucleus. Theorists noticed that some of the mathematics on offer could be interpreted as if the nuclear particles were vibrating strings. But another description of the strong force, which did not need strings at that stage, elbowed the idea aside. Thereafter, the theorists were absorbed by an idea called supersymmetry, or Grand Unification, which would hopefully connect and extend the various families of particles and forces known and predicted at that time.

Onward to superstrings

One force remained stubbornly outside the scope of supersymmetry. It was gravity, for which Albert Einstein had written a powerful but feral theory all of its own. Tame gravity, and bring it within the scope of particle physics, and you might achieve what was technically called a Theory of Everything. But to do that you had to assign to gravity a new kind of force-carrying particle called a graviton, analogous to the photon, the particle of light that carries the electric force.

Among those who persevered with the idea of particles as strings were Michael Green of Queen Mary and Westfield College, London, and Joseph Schwarz of Caltech. They found that if they reinterpreted supersymmetry as a string theory, then a particle answering to the description of the graviton appeared out of the blue, as a natural by-product of the mathematics. This new composite, seeming to promise a Theory of Everything, was the first superstring theory.

'The unification of the forces is accomplished in a way determined almost uniquely by the logical requirement that the theory be internally consistent,' Green noted. 'These developments have led to an extraordinary revitalization of the interplay between mathematics and physics.'

It was 1984 before Green and Schwarz had cleared up some severe technical difficulties with their superstring theory, and colleagues seemed to have lost interest in what they were trying to do. They did not expect a dramatic reaction. But a theorist in Princeton, Edward Witten, had been monitoring their progress more closely than they realized.

'Witten got wind of what we were up to and phoned me up asking for an early copy of our paper, which I FedExed to him,' Schwarz recalled later. 'I'm told that the next day everybody in Princeton University and the Institute for Advanced Study was studying this paper. After that things went very fast.'

David Gross, Jeffrey Harvey, Emil Martinec and Ryan Rohm at Princeton quickly came up with another, even more powerful version, called heterotic string theory. This has the curious feature that waves travelling clockwise around a loopy string behave differently from those going anticlockwise. In the years that followed, theorists around the world piled onto the bandwagon, offering hundreds of refinements and variations.

Five different superstring theories turned out to be internally consistent. Also predicted were supermembranes, or branes for short. These were drumskin-like infestations of the playground of the strings, which was normally considered to have ten dimensions. So the time has come for the reader to contemplate a Universe of many dimensions, beyond the three dimensions of space and one dimension of time to which you are accustomed.

Dimensions: now you see them, now you don't

Be reassured at the outset that, if you are talking purely mathematically, there is no imaginative problem about many dimensions. With a pocket calculator you can multiply 2 by 2, which is like describing a square, by 2 again which gives a cube. But then you can go on multiplying by 2 as often as you like, and claim 100 dimensions if you wish, without blowing either your calculator or your mind.

Another approach to the puzzle is to think of an extremely versatile string in ordinary three-dimensional space. Picture it in the form of a flat tape that can vibrate up and down, which is easy, and also from side to side, which is more difficult for it to do. So you can imagine it producing two distinct notes from two directions of vibration. You might then try to construct, in your mind, a string with a more complicated cross-section that makes different notes in many directions, all around the clock.

Just as a piano-maker loads his bass strings with brass, you can attach many properties to a string representing a particle—electric charge, quark flavour or whatever—to achieve the different modes of vibration. Indeed some particle theorists like to think of the string vibrations as representing multiple freedoms of action within ordinary 3-D space.

Mainstream theorists have opted to describe the superstring vibrations as if they occur in multiple dimensions. Again this would have no imaginative significance if it were purely a mathematical fiction, like repeatedly multiplying by 2. But theorists talk as if the ten dimensions of the superstring theory are really out there, providing room for cosmic engineering behind the scenes, as it were.

Having invented the multiple dimensions, the theorists must promptly hide them from view, to leave the world looking familiar. This is done by a trick called compactification, curling up the extra dimensions like hosepipes on their reels. Also to be hidden are an infinite number of unwanted vibrations, or notional massive particles, which are conveniently smaller than the smallest pieces of observable space permitted in the theory, called the Planck length. It's all a bit like Lewis Carroll's White Knight:

> But I was thinking of a plan
> To dye one's whiskers green,
> And always use so large a fan
> That they could not be seen.

By the end of the century, many superstring theorists had come to prefer a membrane to a string, as the fundamental vibrating object. It seemed that a membrane in 11-dimensional space could incorporate all of the different kinds of superstrings. And you could think of the membrane curling up like a drinking straw, so that it even looked like a string.

Is beauty really truth?

Just to speak of superstring theory may be old hat. To a new concept, which he advanced in 1995, Witten gave the name M-theory, explaining that 'M stands for Magical, Mystery or Membrane, according to taste'. Others said that it meant the Mother of All Theories. As far as the mind's eye could see, across the chasms and hosepipes of 11-dimensional space, there was a potential for new physics and mathematics in M-theory to keep hundreds of theorists busy for many years to come.

A scandalous fact was not lost on the bystanders. This was the lack of even the smallest shred of direct evidence for the validity of either superstrings or M-theory as a description of the real world. Great swaths of particle physics and cosmology were incorporated retrospectively, but the theories were tuned to do so.

Some critics wondered whether the whole exercise of humming strings and drumskins might not turn out to be a footnote to scientific history, like Kepler's planetary tunes. Others recalled the debates about how many angels could dance on a pin—the medieval precursor of the Planck length. Non-participating theorists who were happy to see the idea of strings being investigated in depth nevertheless regretted that radically different approaches to a Theory of Everything were neglected.

As cheerleader for the protagonists, Witten commented in 2001: 'If it would turn out that string theory, which has led to so many miraculous-looking discoveries over so many decades, has nothing to do with Nature, to me this would be a remarkable cosmic conspiracy.' But note his theoretician's use of the word discoveries. This means the detection of nifty mathematical relationships, which to a hardnosed experimentalist is entirely different from discovering a new planet, a new particle or even a better guitar string. The reliance on mathematical elegance, or beauty, is reminiscent of the poet John Keats:

> 'Beauty is truth, truth, beauty,'—that is all
> Ye know on earth, and all ye need to know.

The passion for elegance has served physicists well, ever since Kepler used his strange, semi-mystical skills to find practical laws of planetary motion that are still in use today. A correct theory is likely to be mathematically beautiful, but it does not follow that a beautiful theory is necessarily correct. Slaughter by ugly facts has left detritus throughout history.

These truisms are worth recalling, because a generation of theoretical physicists has ventured farther into the unknown, without experimental or observational support, than was ever done before. No one knows what the outcome will be, when all the ugly facts are in. If the string theorists are right, it will be the greatest-ever achievement of the collective human mind in winkling out the workings of the Universe. But our species may have to wait for decades or centuries to find out.

Massive strings are quite different

A much quicker verdict can be expected on cosmic strings, which are not to be confused with the superstrings. They are visualized as huge, massive structures that concentrate primordial energy in the form of very thin hairs, so dense that a few kilometres of length would weigh as much as the Earth. If a cosmic string lay in your field of view, it might look like a crack in a window, subtly shifting the positions of stars or galaxies beyond.

The hum of a cosmic string would take the form of gravitational waves—ripples in the fabric of space itself. By their emission, the cosmic string would lose energy and tend to disappear. But as Tom Kibble of Imperial College London pointed out in 1976, cosmic strings were liable to form in the Big Bang.

They could then have played an important part in gathering matter into galaxies. If so, the cosmic strings should have influenced the patterns of matter concentration in the early Universe, seen by satellites mapping the microwave background that fills the sky. There was no evidence for them, in early results, but the jury may be out until 2010.

▶ For related subjects, see GRAVITY and SPARTICLES.

TIME MACHINES

The biggest issue in contemporary physics?

A CARTOON in Igor Novikov's book *The River of Time* (1998) drawn by the author himself shows a scientist arriving in the Garden of Eden, just in time to stop Eve picking the forbidden apple. It illustrates the problem that seems to many people to rule out the feasibility of travelling back in time. You could not visit the past without altering it, which in turn would alter the present from which you started, so creating a logical impossibility.

More succinctly, you could murder your own grandmother. The conundrum for scientists is that, even if the laws of biology might seem to rule out time machines, the laws of physics do not. On the contrary, they positively incite the idea. Antiparticles, which certainly exist, are indistinguishable from ordinary particles moving backwards in time.

In relativity theory it is trivially easy (conceptually speaking) to travel into the future by making a return flight on a high-speed rocket ship, which brings you home when your relatives are long-since dead. If you can spend a while in orbit around a black hole, where time runs very slowly, that will make the difference by your calendar even greater. These effects on time have been verified by observations, although involving particles and light, rather than time travellers.

To visit the past you must either travel faster than light, which is explicitly ruled out in relativity theory, or else use a wormhole in spacetime. This is very like the time machine of popular imagination. You go in at one point, proceed through a tunnel that is effectively outside our Universe, and reappear at a different place and/or time. Nobody knows how to construct a practical wormhole but physical laws don't exclude it. Should a prohibition turn up some day, that would itself be an important addition to the principles of physics.

If time travel is feasible, then perhaps Mother Nature already makes use of it. If so, the future can affect the past and the implications for ideas of causality are horrendous. A lazy kind of billiards illustrates the possibilities. You just hit the balls in any direction you like. Wormholes linking the pockets enable the very same balls, reappearing from the past, to collide with themselves and send themselves into the desired pockets.

The nature of time has been debated since Plato's day, yet with a strange lack of firm conclusions. For example, it has long been argued that the laws of heat provide an irreversible arrow of time, with all systems moving towards a more uniform temperature—described as an increase in entropy. Our personal experience, of past times remembered and the future unknown, is compatible with this idea of a thermodynamic arrow. Yet life itself defies entropy, and the theorists have never demonstrated that it rules out time travel.

The discovery of the expansion of the Universe was said by some experts to provide another arrow of time. If it should ever stop expanding and instead contract then, they said, time would reverse, the dead would climb out of their graves, and we should all experience our lives backwards, all the way to our mothers' wombs. The eminent theorist Yakov Zel'dovich in the Space Research Institute in Moscow dismissed this notion as being as foolish as supposing that a clock in a rocket runs backwards after it has reached its maximum height and begins to fall back to the ground.

Zel'dovich and Novikov speculated about loops in spacetime, as did John Wheeler in the USA, but it was Kip Thorne at Caltech who began to try to pin down the possibility of practical wormholes. He offered it as a means of space travel in a letter to the astronomer Carl Sagan of Cornell, who needed a plausible way of dashing about the Universe for the characters in his sci-fi novel, *Contact* (1985).

Thorne recalled later, 'It introduced to the world, to science fiction, and also reintroduced to serious scientists, the notion of a wormhole as something that is really worthy of thinking about.' To convert a space machine into a time machine would not be a trivial task, but Thorne continued to puzzle over the problem and so did Novikov, when he moved from Moscow to Copenhagen in 1991.

'Are time machines possible?' Novikov asked. 'That seems to me the most important question in contemporary physics. If they are feasible for Nature, we must look for their effects. And if wormholes ever become practicable for engineers, our descendants will no doubt want to use space machines to travel very widely in the Universe, and time machines to explore the past and the future.'

Antiparticles with anticlocks

Take a long, narrow strip of paper and paste the ends together, after putting a half-twist in one end. You then have a Möbius strip, an object popular with mathematicians ever since its description was found among the papers of August Möbius of Leipzig after his death in 1868. The innocuous-looking artefact remains a good starting point for further radical thoughts about the nature of space and time.

Suppose you live on a Möbius strip, like the ants in a well-known painting by Maurits Cornelis Escher. You find matters of orientation trouble-free as long as you don't travel very far. But take a walk all the way around the strip, and you'll come back to your starting point on the underside of the strip, separated from your friends on the topside. Up and down have become ambiguous.

Worse inconveniences occur if you live inside a Möbius strip. Then, if you set off on your travels as a right-handed person, you'll come back left-handed. Or if you're a subatomic particle spinning to the right, you'll be spinning to the left on your return. The space in the strip is said by mathematicians to be non-orientable.

A theoretical physicist at Warwick, Mark Hadley, considered what would happen if time, too, were like a Möbius strip, and non-orientable. Now a particle making the round trip comes back, not only spinning the other way but with time running backwards. The particle has changed into its own antiparticle. Hadley also imagined sending a clock around the loop and getting back an anticlock, which faithfully measures antitime.

This was no idle conjecture, or mathematician's frolic, but part of a serious campaign to probe the link between relativistic and quantum views of the world. Hadley argued that the well-known mutual annihilation that occurs when a particle meets its antiparticle actually requires that time be non-orientable—in another word, ambiguous. 'A failure of time orientability and particle–antiparticle annihilation are indistinguishable,' he concluded. 'They are alternative descriptions of the same phenomena.'

Perhaps this adds a couple of health warnings to ideas about time machines. The first is that you could go crazy thinking about them. From a more practical point of view, if you're going to try travelling through space and/or time via wormholes, be sure you don't get your personal dimensions of space and time scrambled en route, or you could finish up with arms and legs a microsecond long. Oh, and don't waste money on an expensive watch, lest it finish up running backwards.

▶ *For the well-established relativistic effects on time, see* HIGH-SPEED TRAVEL *and* GRAVITY, *the second of which includes Hadley's idea about time machines serving in a non-quantum theory of gravity. For quantum effects that seem to ensure mind-boggling simultaneity across the Universe, see* QUANTUM TANGLES. *For more about antiparticles, see* ANTIMATTER. *For a conjecture about using wormholes for space travel, see* ASTRONAUTICS.

TRANSGENIC CROPS

For better or worse, a planetary experiment has begun

T HE HEART OF GHENT in Flanders is a time machine from the 16th century. In its heyday it was one of the world's top commercial centres, offering a heady mix of cloth, Calvinism and capitalism, with gorgeous buildings to match. In the 20th century, the more sombre Rijksuniversiteit Gent to the south of the old city initiated a worldwide biotechnological revolution. It opened the way to transgenic or genetically modified (GM) crops, into which alien hereditary material is introduced by genetic engineering.

The story started with investigations of diseased plants. Crown gall produces unsightly lumps around the stems of plants at soil level. These cancerous tumours manufacture highly specialized food, peculiar chemicals called opines. They are just for the benefit of the soil bacteria, *Agrobacterium tumofaciens*, which cause the disease.

In the 1940s Amin Braun of the Rockefeller Institute in New York City established that the bacteria themselves don't infest the plants that they attack. He theorized that they insert some tumour-inducing principle into the cells of the plants and leave them to get on with the biochemical work. The pattern of attack was surprising—as if terrorist junkies could force a pharmaceutical factory to switch to making their recreational drug of choice.

Belgian scientists showed that the bacteria do the trick by natural genetic engineering. Microbiologists at Ghent had a nice collection of *Agrobacterium* strains, some of which caused crown gall whilst others didn't. By 1974 the molecular geneticists Josef Schell and Marc Van Montagu had identified and isolated a ring of the genetic material deoxyribonucleic acid, DNA. It was present in virulent strains and absent in the others, and the scientists named it the tumour-inducing plasmid.

This is the agent that the bacteria inject into a wounded plant to cause crown gall. Further investigation at Ghent and elsewhere revealed how the plasmid works. It carries genes that make the plant cells cancerous and also code for the manufacture of the bacterial food, the opines, from the amino acid arginine. The plasmid knows the appropriate signals whereby the genes become incorporated in the plant cell's own DNA and can operate efficiently there.

By coincidence, just a couple of years before the isolation of the tumour-inducing plasmid in Ghent, Paul Berg at Stanford and fellow biochemists had shown how to transfer genes at will, into bacteria. Called the recombinant-DNA technique, it took advantage of restriction enzymes. These are natural scissors that normally serve to chop up alien DNA, but the scientists showed that they could be used in a cut-and-paste operation, to snip DNA from another organism and splice it into the bacterium's own DNA, where it became inheritable.

The same technique could be used on the *Agrobacterium* plasmid, to remove the unwanted opine genes and insert other genes. In 1983, Ghent and a US team, from the University of Washington and the Monsanto company, independently accomplished the transfer of alien genes into plants. They were genes conferring resistance to antibodies, which were handy for experimental purposes because you could tell immediately whether the transferred genes were working. Only cells of the modified plants would survive in a culture exposed to the relevant antibiotic.

By 1985 Plant Genetic Systems, a spin-off company in Ghent supported with Belgian and Swedish capital, had produced its first insect-resistant and herbicide-resistant tomato, potato and tobacco plants. Monsanto in the USA was even busier. Before that decade was out, the first field trials of transgenic crops were in progress in many countries.

'Who knows what will happen when the human imagination fully grasps the potential of genetic engineering in plants?' asked Marc Van Montagu. Besides more nutritious and drought-resistant crops, he looked to plants as factories making fine chemicals, to fast growing trees for energy supplies, and to genetically engineered wood, replacing plastics. The physicist Freeman Dyson of the Princeton Institute for Advanced Study rose to the imaginative challenge by suggesting that giant trees should be engineered to grow on comets and provide abodes of life. The Greening of the Galaxy, he titled it.

In 1980–81 five different US laboratories introduced inheritable genes into mice by direct micro-injection of DNA sequences into fertilized eggs. Gene transfers in humans were by common consent a no-no. But there were promises of great benefits for farming and for health. These converged in the use of transgenic plants and animals to manufacture pharmaceutical drugs and other materia medica. That's called pharming.

Mobilized genes and promiscuous pollen

Fears of being left behind in lucrative agro-technological and pharmaceutical businesses initially tipped the political scales in favour of the genetic engineers.

But the awesome implications of gene-splicing were controversial from the outset. Objections on religious grounds, that human beings should not usurp God's function in managing life, have never ceased. Many non-religious commentators, including scientists, have been worried about the ethics, especially about the long-term prospects for genetic engineering applied in human beings.

Soon after Berg's initial success with recombinant DNA, he was chairman of a committee of the US National Academy of Sciences that, in 1974, called for a voluntary moratorium on certain kinds of experiments. In the following year he was co-convenor of a meeting at Asilomar in California, where more than 100 experts debated the issues of safety with physicians and lawyers. Gene-splicing was far too useful in basic research for experimenters to accept any general moratorium, but the deliberations provided groundwork for regulations controlling research and applications in various countries.

Arguments about safety rather than ethics also predominated when genetic modification of plants emerged as the largest application by far of the gene-splicing techniques. Could transgenic crops harm people or the environment? Although protagonists liked to say that only the ignorant worried about such things, the critics included Nobel-Prizewinning biologists.

One was Werner Arber of Biozentrum Basel, discoverer of the restriction enzymes, the DNA scissors used by genetic engineers. His concern was not the artificiality of their techniques, but their naturalness. Restriction enzymes are just one among several methods that Mother Nature has, for making genes mobile. The consequences are seen in lateral gene transfers between very different organisms that have often occurred in the course of evolution. The rapid spread of natural resistance to man-made antibiotics among bacteria, by direct injection of genes from one to another, is a recent case in point.

'Genetic engineers cannot foresee what the eventual fate of the genes may be, when natural processes have the opportunity to transfer them again to other organisms,' Arber warned in 1990. 'Even if the direct product of genetic manipulation is harmless and useful, there are grounds for caution about releasing it into the environment.'

The possibility that artificially mobilized genes in genetic modifications might remain inherently more mobile than other genes was one concern. Another was that the rather clumsy methods used in genetic engineering might disrupt other genes in unpredictable ways. Alterations of behaviour in the transgenic plants could then promote the spread of their new genes in unintended ways.

An early use of genetic engineering in crops was to make them resistant to proprietary herbicides, so that farmers could kill the weeds and spare the crop. To simulate transgenic plants of the kind being made commercially, academic researchers at Chicago carried out experiments with herbicide resistance in the small weed *Arabidopsis thaliana*, a relative of mustard much used in plant genetics, to see what happened. Like most crop plants, arabidopsis is usually self-fertilizing, without the aid of pollen from other individuals.

First the Chicago scientists did the traditional plant geneticist's thing, of making mutants of arabidopsis by treating the seeds with a gene-harming chemical, and exposing them to the herbicide chlorsulphuron as they grew. They found a resistant strain, bred from it and identified the gene responsible, which they called Csr1-1. Then they used genetic engineering twice, to introduce the gene into two separate strains of transgenic arabidopsis.

In a field in central Illinois they planted 24 each of normal arabidopsis, of the resistant weed produced by mutation, and of the two engineered strains. When the scientists gathered the seeds and planted them in the lab, they found to their surprise that many seeds of the normal arabidopsis had acquired resistance to chlorsulphuron. In nearly every case the Csr1-1 gene came from one of the engineered transgenic strains rather than the other possible source, the original resistant strain.

Somehow the engineering had accidentally promoted male promiscuity, greatly increasing the chances that the transgenic strains would pollinate other plants. The normal, wild arabidopsis thus altered had become a prototype of possible superweeds resistant to weed-killers. These could result from genes leaking from resistant crops—for example from transgenic maize into timothy grass.

'Although *A. thaliana* is unlikely to become a pernicious weed,' Joy Bergelson and her colleagues reported, 'these results show that genetic engineering can substantially increase the probability of transgene escape, even in a species considered to be almost completely selfing.'

Will there be a replay of the story of antibiotic resistance in bacteria, with weed-killer resistance in weeds? At the time of writing no one knows, but the large-scale experiment is in progress in the fields of transgenic crops. For better or worse, the gene is out of the bottle.

Good old human carelessness has already favoured the spread of transgenic material. In trial plantings of genetically modified crops, kindergarten matters like the flying range of pollinating insects or the effects of strong pollen-bearing winds were repeatedly underestimated. In Canada, pollen-induced resistance to three different herbicides showed up in the ordinary canola oilseed crop, and resulted in a lawsuit by organic farmers. In France in 2000, canola covering 600 hectares was ploughed under because it was contaminated with a genetically modified variety.

'Gene containment is next to impossible with the current generation of GM crops,' admitted an editorial in 2002 in *Nature Biotechnology*, which is virtually a trade journal for the genetic engineers. 'It is time that industry took decisive steps to address gene flow from their products. Environmental concerns surrounding GM crops are not going to go away.'

Who decides?

By the end of the 20th century large areas of the Earth, especially in the USA, Argentina and Canada, were growing genetically modified crops. Trials were widespread elsewhere, even in cautious regions like Europe. Publicly funded as well as commercial laboratories continued to extol the wonders and benefits of genetic engineering.

The controversy about transgenic crops became a test case for the relationship between science and society. It will no doubt spawn thesis subjects for students of politics or the history of science for the next 200 years. The issues turned a spotlight on the confusing state of the world, in respect of decision-making about new technologies.

At the political level, local and national governments expected to have a say in what was permissible in the planting of transgenic crops, and their use in the food chain. So did agglomerates like the European Union, which tried but failed to speak with a single voice. The United Nations came into the picture too, with its roles in agricultural development and famine relief.

Farmers expressed their viewpoints through national organizations. Whilst most tended to see benefits in the new crops, they were concerned about how they might alter the shape of their industry. Organic farmers were agitated by the risk of contamination with stray genes. Unelected lobby groups, euphemistically called non-governmental organizations, claimed special authority to speak on behalf of the planet. Here and there, activists went out and trashed experimental plantings of genetically modified crops.

Science spoke with several voices. Many academic experts could no longer be considered disinterested commentators on the risks, if any, because they had acquired ties to biotechnology companies. At a replay of the 1975 Asilomar meeting staged in 2000, David Baltimore of Caltech conceded, 'There are few pure academics left.'

Experts overseeing safety trials of transgenic crops were expected to be judiciously neutral, yet experimenters who reported possible snags, from open-minded research, were liable to be regarded by colleagues as unhelpful or worse. Scientific advisers not necessarily expert in the subject helped governments to make decisions about transgenic crops. In the United Kingdom in 1999 they and the ministers they counselled felt competent to pooh-pooh a formal proposal from the British Medical Association that there should be an open-ended moratorium on the commercial planting of transgenic crops.

The British doctors were especially worried by the 'completely unacceptable' presence of genes for antibiotic resistance in the crops, just there as markers of successful gene transfers. The lead author of their report, William Asscher, was a former chairman of the UK government's own committee on the safety of medicines. He noted that the licensing of medicines could be withdrawn, whilst for transgenic crops 'the impact on the environment is likely to be irreversible.'

In the media, environmental reporters tended to present the views of objectors, and science reporters the opinions of the genetic modifiers. Public information about transgenic crops therefore often read like public indoctrination, in either their vices or their virtues. The most gung-ho science reporters branded critics as ignorant Luddites, as if there were no technical issues worth discussing.

Transgenic crops brought out, with striking clarity, the globalization of the market on the one hand and the rise of consumer power on the other. In Europe, shoppers won the right to know what they were eating, with labelling of the presence or absence of genetically modified ingredients on the food packets in supermarkets. Some Third World governments made clear to the entrepreneurs that they were not ready to accept novel crops on the corporations' terms.

Money speaks, and the complexion of the debate changed a little. At a *Farm Journal* conference in 2000, Monsanto's chief executive officer was conciliatory. 'Our tone, our very approach, was seen as arrogant,' Hendrik Verfaillie said. 'My company had focused so much attention on getting the technology right for our customer, the grower, that we didn't fully take into account the issues and concerns it raised for others.'

Pressures favouring transgenic crops were not only commercial in origin. Public-sector plant breeders saw a necessary role for them in helping to provide the 50 per cent increase in grain production needed in the developing world in the first quarter of the 21st century. Norman Borlaug of Texas A&M, the scientific father of the Green Revolution that averted famine in the closing decades of the last century, was impatient with city-dwelling critics of modern agricultural techniques, including biotechnology.

Reviewing world food prospects, in 2000, Borlaug said that the technology was either available, or well advanced in the research pipeline, to feed 10 billion people on a sustainable basis. But would farmers and ranchers be permitted to use this new technology, he wondered? 'While the affluent nations can certainly afford to adopt ultra-low-risk positions, and pay more for food produced by the so-called "organic" methods, the one billion chronically undernourished people of the low-income, food-deficit nations cannot.'

Yet during a famine-relief operation in 2002, some low-income nations in Africa objected to receiving genetically modified maize, even to avert starvation. They cited possible risks to human health and the environment. World Food Programme officials told them that what was good enough for 280 million Americans was good enough for them. To the question, 'Who decides about transgenic crops?' the answer seemed to be no one in particular.

▶ *For more about natural gene mobility, see* TREE OF LIFE.

TREE OF LIFE

Promiscuous bacteria and the course of evolution

A STAGNANT POOL was a treat for Lynn Margulis when, as a young biologist at Boston University, she liked to descant on the little green bugs that can so quickly challenge human notions about how a nice pond should look. Her favourites included the blue-greens, often called algae but in fact bacteria, which have played an outstanding role in steering the course of life on the Earth.

Margulis became the liveliest and most stubborn advocate of the idea that we are descended from bacteria-like creatures that clubbed together in the distant past. Others had toyed with this proposition, but she pushed it hard. In 1970 she published a book, *Origin of Eukaryotic Cells*, and she followed it in 1981 with *Symbiosis in Cell Evolution*. These are now seen as landmarks in 20th-century biology, and the keywords in their titles, eukaryotic and symbiosis, go to the core of the matter.

You are the owner of eukaryotic cells. Each of the billions of microscopic units of which you're built safeguards your genes of heredity within a nucleus, or *karyon* in Greek. So, in the grandest division of living things, into just two kinds, you belong to the eukarya. That groups you with other animals, with plants, with fungi, and with single-celled creatures called protoctists, represented by 250,000 species alive today and often ambiguous in nature.

The other great bloc of living things, the prokarya, are all single-celled, and the genes just slop about within them. The earliest forms of life on the planet were all of that relatively simple kind, meaning bacteria and similar single-celled organisms called archaea. They ruled the world alone for half its history, until the eukarya appeared.

Symbiosis means living together. The proposition for which Margulis first marshalled all the available evidence is that small bacteria took up residence inside larger ones—inside archaea, one would say now—and so formed the ancestors of the eukarya. Instead of just digesting the intruders, the larger cells tolerated them as lodgers because they brought benefits.

The outcome was the microscopic equivalent of mermaids or centaurs. 'The human brain cells that conceived these creatures are themselves chimaeras,' Margulis wrote with her son Dorion Sagan, '—no less fantastic mergers of several formerly independent kinds of prokaryotes that together co-evolved.'

Oval-shaped units inside your cells, called mitochondria, are power stations that use oxygen to generate chemical energy from nutrients. They look like bacteria, they carry sloppy genetic material of their own, and they reproduce like bacteria. The same is true of chloroplasts, small green entities found in the cells of the leaves of plants. They do the work of harvesting sunlight and using water and carbon dioxide to produce energy-rich molecules that sustain plant life and growth.

A recount of the kingdoms

In the Margulis scenario, the ancestors of the mitochondria and chloroplasts were indeed bacteria that took up symbiotic residence inside other single-celled creatures. The mitochondrial forebears were bacteria that had learned to cope with oxygen. When that element first appeared unbound in the ancient sea it was deadly dangerous, like bleach poured into the bacterial–archaeal communities. So bacteria that were adapted to it could offer their hosts protection against oxygen and also the ability to exploit it in new ways of living.

Blue-greens, formally called cyanobacteria, were the ancestors of the chloroplasts. In their separate, bacterial existence, they had hit upon the most powerful way of using sunlight to grow by. It involved splitting water and releasing oxygen, and so the blue-greens were probably responsible for the oxygen crisis. But this smart photosynthesis also conferred on the hosts the capacity to generate their own food supplies.

Host cell plus mitochondria made the ancestors of fungi and of protoctists. The latter included some distinguished by their capacity for swimming about, which became the ancestors of the multicelled animals. Host cell plus mitochondria plus chloroplasts made single-celled algae, and among these were the forebears of the multicelled plants.

Aspects of the scenario are still debated. Especially uncertain is how all of these cells came to organize their cell nuclei, and how they perfected the eukaryotic kind of cell division used in multiplication, growth and sex. The origin of the capacity for movement in protozoa, and its possible survival in the swimming tails of sperm, is also controversial.

The broad brushstrokes of the symbiosis story are nevertheless accepted now. Not just as a matter of taste, but by verification. The kinship of identifiable bacteria with mitochondria and chloroplasts is confirmed by similarities in their molecules. Fossil traces of early eukaryotes are very skimpy until 1200 million years ago, but the molecular clues suggest an origin around 2 billion years ago, at a time when free oxygen was becoming a major challenge to life.

In 1859 Charles Darwin described a 'great Tree of Life, which fills with its dead and broken branches the crust of the Earth, and covers the surface with its ever branching and beautiful ramifications'. He meant a family tree, such that all extinct and living species might be placed in their relative positions on its branches and twigs. As it was pictured in those days, the plant and animal kingdoms dominated the tree. The symbiosis theory redefines the main branches of the tree, with more kingdoms.

Bacteria and archaea, sometimes lumped together as prokarya or monera, originate near the very base, when life began. Half-way up the tree, symbiosis introduces the peculiar and wonderful microbes called protoctists, which include the single-celled animal-like amoebas and plant-like algae. Other protoctists, with multifarious characters that are hard to classify, represent obvious experimentation with symbiosis. A boat-like microbe inhabiting the digestive tract of termites in Australia, and one of Margulis' prime exhibits, has recruited some 300,000 wiggly bacteria to row in unison like galley slaves.

Membership of the animal and plant kingdoms is, in this new tree, confined to multicelled creatures, so excluding amoebas and the other protoctists. The fungi, which include yeasts and moulds as well as mushrooms, get a kingdom of their own. They thus rank alongside the animals and plants, but are distinguished from them by their lack of embryos.

Fungi are very important in decomposing dead plants and weathering the rocks. But in view of the diversity of protoctists, there is something odd about singling out the fungi for special status. What about the algae, which nowadays totally dominate life on most of the Earth's surface—meaning the upper film of the wide oceans?

Bacterial sex and gene transfers

As scientists trace the course of evolution more precisely than ever before, the more confused it becomes. To Darwin's way of thinking, and for 100 years after him, the branches and twigs of the evolutionary tree of life represented distinct lines of descent. If different branches traced back to common ancestors, those existed in the past, and after them the hereditary pathways were quite separate. That was supposedly guaranteed by the fact that any mating between different species was sterile.

Organisms classified, grouped and named, according to their similarities and differences, hung on the Darwinian tree of life like Christmas presents. Each was in its proper place, with its label in Latin attached. But a bacterial guest in a symbiotic cell introduces into its host an inheritance from a completely different part of the tree. No longer do genes flow exclusively along a branch. They can also travel sideways from branch to branch, like tinsel. Some scientists call this lateral, others horizontal gene transfer.

Was gene transfer a rare event? If it concerned only the invention of cells of the modern eukaryotic kind, 2 billion years ago, it might be seen as a rare historical quirk. But even before Margulis proclaimed evolutionary symbiosis, contemporary gene transfers between different lineages had turned up in hospitals.

After antibiotics came into medicine in the 1940s, doctors were appalled by how quickly strains of harmful bacteria outwitted the miracle drugs. Pharmacologists are still in a non-stop race in which each new antibiotic soon meets resistant strains. Hospitals have become superbug factories where patients may die, if not by the infections themselves, then by toxic antibiotics given as a last resort.

Human beings did not invent antibiotics. They are ancient poisons used in conflicts among microbes. In England during the Second World War, the pioneers of penicillin therapy simply harvested the material from cultures of a well-armed mould. From the point of view of the bacteria, it was not an unprecedented challenge, and some already possessed genes that conferred resistance.

Evolve or perish—and evolve the bacteria did, at a startling rate, by distributing the genes for antibiotic resistance like insurance salesmen. Genes can pass from one bacterium to another, and even to different strains or species. In a primitive form of sexual behaviour, one bacterium simply injects genes into a neighbour. A virus invading one bacterium may pick up a gene there and carry it to another. Or a bacterium can simply graze on stray genes liberated from a dying cell.

Nor are bacteria the only organisms open to gene transfers, by natural genetic engineering. In animals, a gene can be transcribed into an RNA virus, which does not even use the usual DNA in its genetic code, and then be translated back into DNA when the virus infects a new cell. Unhappily some genes transferred by this reverse transcription cause serious diseases.

While medical concerns multiplied with these discoveries, fundamental biology was in some disarray. A basic assumption had been that organisms resemble their parents. Any alterations in the genes occurred by mutation within an organism and were passed on by the normal processes of reproduction. Evolution supposedly accumulated changes in an ancestral lineage that was in principle, if not always in practice, clearly definable. The symbiotic origin of our cells, the genetically promiscuous bacteria, and reverse transcription too, showed these assumptions to be naïve.

How important have gene transfers been, in evolutionary history? The answer to that question had to wait until molecular biologists worked out the tree of life for themselves, and examined complete sets of genes—the genomes—of present-day animals, plants and microbes. Then they could begin to trace individual genes back to their origins.

Doing without fossils

The notion that one could discover the course of evolution from molecules germinated around 1960. That was when Brian Hartley at the Laboratory of Molecular Biology in Cambridge noted that poisons analogous to military nerve gases blocked the action of a wide variety of active proteins—enzymes—besides those involved in the control of muscles by nerves, which were the prime target of the nerve agents. He suspected that the various proteins had a common genetic ancestry.

X-ray analyses showed how various proteins were shaped, and confirmed the idea. For example, three enzymes involved in human digestion, trypsin, chymotrypsin and elastase, turned out to have very similar structures. Other scientists compared proteins serving the same function, but in different species.

Richard Dickerson of Caltech studied cytochrome C, which occurs in all plants, animals and fungi as an enzyme for dealing with oxygen. To perform correctly, it must have the same properly shaped active region, built by a particular sequence of subunits, amino acids, in the protein chain. But non-critical parts of the molecule could vary, and Dickerson found that by counting the differences between one species and another he could tell how closely they were related. For example, compared with cytochrome C in pigs, the same enzyme in chicken differs in 9 amino acids, in tuna in 17, and in cauliflower in 47.

This was supermarket evolution. Instead of hammering on chilly rock faces, or wandering across searing deserts in search of fossils, you could collect your specimens in a basket at a local shop. If you felt more energetic you could catch a passing moth or frog to extend the scope of the investigation. You could then begin to construct a tree of life from the variable molecules in living organisms.

It showed how long ago, relatively speaking, these and other species shared a common ancestor.

Fossil-hunters were duly miffed. The molecular scientists needed their help to put dates on the tree of life. To know how many millions of years ago chicken and tuna had the same ancestor, you needed the evidence of fossils from rocks of dated ages. But Dickerson complained in 1972, 'The zoologists who have the best command of information on dates have maintained a reserved scepticism towards the entire protein endeavour.'

Rates of change in chemical composition during evolution differ widely from molecule to molecule, depending on how crucial its composition is for its purpose. For example, the protein histone H4 varies five per cent of its components in 2500 million years, while fibrinopeptide changes 800 times faster. A new chapter in the molecular investigation of evolution opened in the mid-1970s, with comparisons between special nucleic acids that are present in the vital equipment of every living thing, from bacteria to whales.

Ribosomes are machines used by cells to manufacture proteins, and they incorporate ribosomal ribonucleic acid, or rRNA. This became the material of choice for getting the big picture of molecular evolution. Its leading advocate, Carl Woese of Illinois, Urbana-Champaign, noted that it included slow-evolving and fast-evolving portions, so that one could investigate the entire story of life on Earth, or home in on recent details.

One of the first successes was confirmation of the symbiotic origin of the cells of animals and plants. The oval mitochondria, the power stations in the cells, have their own ribosomes with private lineages that trace back, as predicted, to oxygen-handling bacteria. Similarly, the round green chloroplasts in plants have ribosomes akin to those of the blue-green cyanobacteria. But the general-purpose ribosomes in animal and plant cells are more like those of archaea, the simple creatures similar to, but now distinguished from, the bacteria. Evidently the large host cells that found room for the bacterial lodgers were from that domain.

Counting the transferred genes

If the tree of life inferred from ribosomal ribonucleic acid is to be believed, then the history of other molecules in the same organisms should match it. This is not always the case. Analysts found that they obtained different trees for the bacteria and archaea depending on what molecular constituents they compared, from species to species. The only explanation was that genes for some of the molecules came in by transfers, either recently or in the distant past. Even the grand distinction between bacteria and archaea was compromised by discoveries of widespread exchanges of genes between them.

To make sense of the muddle, Carl Woese reflected on the universal ancestor, at the base of the tree of life. He visualized it, not as a discrete organism, but as a diverse community of very simple cells that survived and evolved as a biological unit. Rates of genetic mutation and gene transfer were very high at first, but gradually the evolutionary temperature dropped.

'Over time,' Woese wrote, 'this ancestor refined into a smaller number of increasingly complex cell types with the ancestors of the three primary groupings of organisms arising as a result.' By those he meant bacteria, archaea and eukarya. Gene exchanges were much less frequent later, he said, and 'the evolutionary dynamic became that characteristic of modern cells.'

Increasing evidence nevertheless told of gene transfers between species continuing in recent evolution. When the complete genome of the gut bacterium *Escherichia coli* became available, Jeffrey Lawrence of Pittsburgh and Howard Ochman of Rochester looked for aliens. They reported that no less than 18 per cent of the bacterium's genes had been acquired in at least 234 transfer events during the past 100 million years. These were not just miscellaneous acquisitions. They included the genes responsible for *E. coli's* distinctive appetites for lactose and citrate.

A heated debate broke out, among experts in molecular evolution. By 1999, Ford Doolittle of Dalhousie University in Canada was declaring the very concepts of species and their lineages to be obsolescent. The best one could do, he suggested, was to ask which genes have travelled together for how long, in which genomes, without being obliged to marshal the data in defence of particular evolutionary schemes.

There might be new principles waiting to be discovered about how genes become distributed between genomes. Doolittle invited biologists to consider that organisms are either less or more than the sum of their genes, and 'to rejoice in and explore, rather than regret or attempt to dismiss, the creative evolutionary role of lateral gene transfer.'

Although he cautioned that it would be rarer in animals and plants, some enthusiasts for the new picture were ready to cast doubt on the definition of species even in those kingdoms. Among the scientists who reacted angrily was Charles Kurland of Uppsala. He protested that 'Nothing in science is more self-aggrandizing than the claim that "all that went before me is wrong".'

The importance of gene transfer in the evolution of microbes was no longer in doubt, but Doolittle had good reason to query its importance in animals and plants. These are multicelled creatures, with intricate bodily organizations that would be easily disrupted by intruding genes. The fact that animals and plants often reproduce sexually also puts up a high wall against alien genes, which will be inherited in the normal way only if they get in among the genes carried by eggs or sperm.

Rare events might nevertheless become significant over long time-scales. When drafts of the entire human genome became available in 2001, molecular evolutionists pounced on them. They were looking for alien genes that might have been introduced from bacteria during 500 million years of evolution in animals with backbones.

An early claim was that bacteria introduced more than 200 of the human genes, but these were soon whittled down to about 40. Some investigators thought that those, too, might disappear from the list as comparisons with distant animal relatives continued. Even if the first figure had been correct, any influx of bacterial genes would have been very small, compared with the transfers between bacteria.

In the light of such evidence, Doolittle and his colleagues noted that 'Our multicellularity probably saved us from participating in the dirty business of lateral gene transfer so beloved by microbes.' They chose as their battleground for demonstrating the importance of gene transfer the single-celled eukaryotes— fungi, yeasts and the multifarious protoctists, half-way up the tree of life.

Thus, by the beginning of the 21st century, biologists had to consider contrasting modes of evolution during the history of life. At the base, and long since extinct, is the universal ancestor comprising a superorganism of ill-defined cells that swapped genes freely. At the top of the tree of life, robust branches of plant and animal families, genera and species preserve the most familiar features of Darwin's picture, with just a small though persistent infection with transferred genes.

The trunk of the tree, representing most of the history of life on Earth, has gone wobbly. Replacing the old hardwood is a tangled web of evolving microbes— bacteria, archaea and single-celled eukarya. It resembles the early superorganism in a continuing habit of swapping genes. But the trunk also shows prolonged persistence of clusters of genes in microbial types that foreshadow the more obvious lineages and branches of plant and animal evolution. The microbial mode of evolution continues to this day.

A neutral umpire might therefore declare the outcome a draw, in the spat between the traditionalists and the gene-transfer revolutionaries. Backed by the evidence of the human genome, the first group preserved their cherished picture of evolution in respect of plants and animals. The revolutionaries nevertheless amassed ample evidence that microbial evolution is different in character and will require a new theory to comprehend it.

Arguments are bound to continue at the interface, especially concerning the single-celled eukaryotes. Can they, with their highly organized cells, really be as promiscuous as bacteria are? And to puzzle the scientists anew is mounting evidence of molecular heredity that bypasses the genes themselves. Whether that will further disfigure the tree of life remains to be seen.

▶ *For more about molecular changes over time, see* MOLECULES EVOLVING. *For an important branch-point of the tree of life, see* CAMBRIAN EXPLOSION. *For more about blue-greens, see* PHOTOSYNTHESIS *and* GLOBAL ENZYMES.

UNIVERSE

'It must have known we were coming'

W HERE MEXICO'S SONORAN DESERT encroaches into Arizona, a volcanic plug makes the pointed peak of Baboquivari. It is the most sacred place of the Tohono O'odham Nation, formerly known as the Papagos Indians. The peak is the home of I'itoi the Creator, and it provides the axis around which the stars revolve.

This Native American idea about Baboquivari is typical of traditional cosmologies worldwide. In 1969 it served as an object lesson for the astrophysicist Philip Morrison, visiting Arizona from the Massachusetts Institute of Technology, when he ruefully acknowledged the triumph of the Big Bang theory of the Universe.

'We shall for a generation or two hold on to the most naïve cosmology,' Morrison said. 'And not unless a wiser, more experienced generation comes after us will we change it. Perhaps they will see that it, too, was a provincial preconception.'

Morrison was speaking in the aftermath of the discovery of the cosmic microwave background, announced in 1965. It told of a time when the whole of space was as hot as the Sun, and it falsified at least the pristine version of the Steady State theory that had appeared in 1948. This said that the Universe was infinite and unchanging, with new matter being continuously created to fill the growing gaps between the galaxies produced by the cosmic expansion.

Don't laugh. The most persistent advocate of the Steady State theory was Fred Hoyle at Cambridge, one of the smartest astrophysicists of the 20th century. Many of his colleagues, including Morrison himself, preferred the idea. When Science Service in Washington DC took a poll of experts in 1958, it found their beliefs almost equally divided between the Steady State and the Big Bang.

They all nevertheless gave an emphatic No to the question, 'Is a poll of this kind helpful to science?' The faint hiss of cosmic microwaves, rather than any shift in personal preferences, boosted the idea that everything began in a creative detonation at some moment of time. It also put a wrapper around the sky.

A cosy cosmos recovered

The peak-centred cosmology of the Tohono O'odham Nation was not the only belief called into question by progress in astronomy. The clever-clogs of Europe had it wrong too, when they thought that the stars revolved around the Earth.

Nearly 700 years ago the poet Dante Alighieri, in his *Commedia*, followed the scholars of his age in supposing that the stars decorated a rigid, rotating sphere just a little beyond the orbit of Saturn, the most distant planet known at the time. In this very compact cosmos, everyone could feel at home among the stars. The sky was full of invisible friendly spirits and the moderately sinful dead. It played a dynamic part in the Earth-centred order. The wheeling Sun and stars told the time of day or night, and for astrologers the dancing planets and comets were messengers telling of forthcoming events on the Earth.

Conceptual and technical advances shattered the heavenly spheres of Europe's medieval cosmology and made the Universe far bigger. Telescopes of ever-increasing power showed more and more stars populating an ever-widening Universe. By the early 19th century, when the lineaments of the Milky Way Galaxy were becoming apparent, it was plain that the Sun was a star nowhere near the centre of the Universe.

Reckoned by the time taken for light to travel the distances, the stars turned out to be some light-years or even some thousands of light-years away. Then came the revelation that many smudges of light in the night sky are vast assemblies of stars, galaxies like the Milky Way but scattered across millions of light-years of space. When millions grew to billions, it seemed by the mid-20th century that the observable Universe went on forever.

It was no place for anyone with agoraphobia. And to realize that the Earth is just a speck of dust orbiting a mediocre star, in the suburbs of an unremarkable galaxy, was humiliating. Yet this mid-century cosmos was philosophically bland, because in infinite space and time the big questions of origin and destiny became too remote to worry about.

The discovery of the cosmic microwaves closed off the observable Universe with a limit as perfectly rotund as the sphere of fixed stars at the bounds of Dante's cosmos. The microwave background is the most distant source of any light-like rays capable of reaching the Earth. It comes from the nearer edge of a fogbank, where free-range electrons block radiation from farther afield. This sphere is remote, but certainly not at infinity, and hotspots of concentrated gas seen in the very distant microwave background appear wider in the sky than the nearby Moon. Their sheer size helps to make the cosmos feel compact again— cosy even.

The Universe that the astronomers can observe is nevertheless quite large compared with the speed of light. As a result telescopes are time machines, showing distant galaxies not as they may be now but as they were billions of years ago, when the light that we see set off on its long journey. By early in the 21st century, opinions were converging on an estimate that the microwave background is about 13.5 billion light-years away, or 13.5 billion years old.

On our side of the background, the Universe since the Big Bang is laid out for our inspection like the collections in a museum. There is a Dark Age of a billion years, or perhaps much less than that, between the microwave background and the appearance of the stars and galaxies. Very distant objects are also hard to see. But improved telescopes and surveying techniques are giving more and more information about what was going on 12–13 billion years ago.

The three-way linkages of space, time and the speed of light have the curious consequence that a remote galaxy can be correctly described as very old or very young. Old because it is like a fossil from a former era, young because we see it not long after its formation. This need be no more puzzling than an archaeologist saying, 'Here's a 10,000-year-old skeleton of a small child.'

Just because the Universe is in principle observable out to 13.5 billion light-years doesn't mean that all its contents have been seen. Far from it. Some objects are too faint at a great distance. Others are hidden behind thick dust clouds, near or far. And for every star, galaxy and gas cloud that modern telescopes can register, probably ten times as much mass is in the form of so-called dark matter, the identity of which has still to be established.

Dante believed that beyond the stars, out of reach of mortal eyes, lay Paradise. In the leading hypothesis today, what hides behind the microwave background is the fireball of the Big Bang. Also concealed from us is an unknown fraction of a wider Universe to which we belong, supposedly all formed by that event. Every year a little more emerges into view from the microwave fogbank, as the Universe expands. What remains hidden may be much more substantial than the part we know. It could be infinite. It could be far more complex.

This potted history of changing outlooks, from cosy to agoraphobic to cosy again, relates to the warning that Philip Morrison gave in 1969. The microwave background is the equivalent of the horizon in Arizona that denied the local Native Americans any sight of the most southerly constellations. To avoid naïvety, scientists and commentators alike had better remember that what we see as our Universe is an essentially local view, probably much oversimplified, of something bigger.

● Fractals and kebabs

In their minds, theorists peered inwards, to what may have happened in the first split-second when the Universe was very small, at the moment of detonation. They offered a remedy for doubtful aspects of the theory by proposing that the microscopic cosmos inflated very suddenly. And all outward probing by astronomers into the far reaches of the Universe, during the closing decades of the 20th century, added support to the Big Bang.

Not everyone followed the party line. Hoyle never gave up his quest for a Steady State beyond the appearances of the Big Bang. Another dissident was the celebrated mathematician Benoit Mandelbrot. His development of fractal geometry, in Paris in the 1970s, brought the untidy, real-life shapes of Nature—clouds, coastlines, trees and so on—within the domain of picturesque new mathematics.

One of Mandelbrot's inspirations was the astronomers' recognition that objects like our own Milky Way Galaxy are gathered in groups, clusters and superclusters of vastly different sizes. 'The study of galaxy clusters has greatly stimulated the development of fractal geometry,' Mandelbrot declared. 'And today the uses of fractal geometry in the study of galaxy clusters go well beyond the tasks of streamlining and housekeeping.'

He joined battle with the cosmologists over a cherished principle, that the cosmos is tidy on a large scale. The simple mathematics used to calculate the evolution of the Universe, in the Big Bang theory, assumes that the density of matter averages out. The reckonings would be incorrect, if the principle were violated.

In fractal geometry similar shapes reappear on different scales: the twig, the branch, the whole tree. So why not also galaxy clusters, repeating their patterns on ever-larger scales until all tidiness is banished? Because trees needn't grow a kilometre high, his opponents retorted. The clustering scales would stop increasing at some point, just as the twig–branch–tree progression does, so that everything would still average out eventually.

Up to the end of the century, Mandelbrot and a circle of supporters could claim that clusters and the voids between them did indeed seem to grow in scale, the farther out the astronomers took their measurements of the distances of galaxies. But then new surveys made leaps to much greater distances, and there was no sign of the predicted super-super-superclusters or gigantic voids. On the contrary, the far Universe looked very like the near Universe, in respect of clustering.

This sameness was equally disappointing for other theorists who would have liked the clusters to be more meagre at great distances, so that they might have amassed as time passed. But an unorthodox group of German astrophysicists had already seen the little-changing nature of the clusters and voids. Indeed, they had used it to reveal that the expansion of the Universe is not slowing down, as everyone expected, but is speeding up.

Historians of science may note that Wolfgang Priester of Bonn and Dierck-Ekkehard Liebscher of Potsdam reported the cosmic acceleration in 1994. That was more than three years before other astronomers, with a great fanfare, announced the acceleration seen by observing exploding stars. The Bonn–Potsdam group had instead used the light of quasars, distant beacons of great intensity, piercing intervening galaxies like the morsels on a kebab.

The positions of more than 1000 galaxies and gas clouds, thus revealed, showed a bubbly Universe, with clusters of galaxies surrounding large voids. The bubbles grew in size as the Universe expanded, but the rate of growth at first diminished under the constraint of gravity, the German astrophysicists said. Then the rate increased as the accelerating agent—called the cosmological constant or dark energy—took charge. Colleagues in Hamburg confirmed the result.

'Nobody paid much attention,' Priester commented. 'Our Bonn–Potsdam cosmology starts with pure dark energy 30 billion years ago and today the Universe is again overwhelmingly dominated by dark energy. Also, we require no exotic dark matter. Our ideas fell outside the range of theories considered polite in the mid-1990s. But in its most important feature—the acceleration—ours was right and more popular theories were wrong.'

Narrowing the specifications

By the start of the 21st century, the Big Bang concept seemed almost unassailable. Certainly in saying that the Universe has evolved by expanding and cooling. When reflecting on the state of play, the doyen of cosmologists in the USA, James Peebles of Princeton, declared that the evidence already provided a framework, with cross-bracing tight enough to make it solid.

Peebles ticked off the main clues. The galaxies are running away from us. Thermal radiation fills space, as it should do if the Universe used to be denser and hotter. Large amounts of heavy hydrogen and helium required high temperatures for their production. Distant galaxies look distinctly younger, as they ought to do if they are closer to the time when no galaxies existed. And the expansion of the Universe conforms to predictions of Albert Einstein's theory of gravity.

'You still hear differences of opinion in cosmology, to be sure, but they concern additions to the solid part,' Peebles wrote. For example, he was personally happy with the belief that much dark matter exists in the Universe, but he reserved judgement about the then-recent discovery that the cosmic expansion is accelerating. 'Confusion is a sign that we are doing something right,' he wrote. 'It is the fertile commotion of a construction site.'

Continuing discoveries narrowed down the specifications for the observable cosmos: how big, how old, how rapidly expanding, and how massive. Rough estimates also became available, about how the mass was divided between ordinary matter, dark matter, and a huge infusion of mass from dark energy associated with the cosmic acceleration. In the process, entire genera of cosmological theories were annihilated because they no longer fitted the evidence.

Some cosmologists thought the end was in sight, for their work of characterizing the Universe. Others, including several of the younger ones, begged to differ. The contrast in opinions was evident in 2003, in reactions to results from NASA's Wilkinson-MAP spacecraft, which charted afresh the microwave hotspots populating the infant cosmos.

Accept the standard ideas, and you could read off the vital statistics of the Universe. But in interpreting the microwave patterns, you had to make assumptions that might or might not be correct. Better, the sceptics said, to look at the wonderful sky charts coming from Wilkinson-MAP and other experiments with fresh, unprejudiced eyes. Then you might find that the Universe is not at all the way you imagined it till now. For example, it could be egg-shaped, or else folded back upon itself topologically, like a paper crown.

Even when the observable cosmos comes to be almost perfectly defined, there will remain a big unanswered question: Why? Not 'Why should anything exist at all?'—a conundrum too far for science—but 'Why is the cosmos so remarkably congenial for our existence?'

Anthropic principles

'As we look out into the Universe and identify the many accidents of physics and astronomy that have worked together to our benefit, it almost seems as if the Universe must in some sense have known we were coming.' When Freeman Dyson of the Institute for Advanced Study in Princeton wrote that in 1971, scientists had already fretted about the accidents for some decades. Slight changes in the laws of physics, especially in the relative strengths of gravity, the electric force and the nuclear forces, would have left the Universe too short-lived or too uncreative for the Earth to form and human beings to appear.

The geological and biological details are not at issue here. How our planet preserved liquid water for more than 4 billion years, and how its geochemistry, modulated by impacting comets and asteroids, facilitated the appearance of quick-witted land-dwelling animals—those are local improbabilities for planetary scientists and biologists to fret about. The cosmologists' concerns run deeper. If the physics were not amazingly well tuned, the Universe would have been hard put to make carbon and oxygen atoms, never mind brainy bipeds.

Brandon Carter, a theorist at Cambridge, brought the issue into focus in a talk during an astronomical congress in Sydney in 1973. He offered the anthropic principle, the essence of which, in its mildest form, is fairly self-evident. If the Universe were not just so, we'd not be here to scrutinize it. Another universe with different characteristics would have no astronomers. 'What we can expect to observe must be restricted by the conditions necessary for our presence as observers,' Carter said.

Besides that weak anthropic principle, as he called it, he also considered whether the feasibility of life might be a precondition for any universe, along with spacetime, particles and so forth. Carter expressed the idea in the strong anthropic principle: 'The universe must be such as to admit the creation of observers within it at some stage.'

That proposition seemed to many researchers like a job for God. So although it was much discussed in a religious or quasi-religious manner, the strong anthropic principle did not fit comfortably within science. Most cosmologists left it aside.

The weak anthropic principle was more manageable. If there were any reason to suppose that ours is the only Universe there ever was or will be, the weak and strong principles would be indistinguishable. Some very clever fixing of the numbers would still be necessary, either by a designer or by biophysical laws still undiscovered.

But if there are many universes, the problem recedes, in much the same way as the existence of billions of planets scattered through our Galaxy provides some hope that intelligent life might evolve on one or two of them. Among billions of universes with various physical characteristics you might well find one or two that are alive.

One way to generate a lot of universes would be to recycle the old ones. A longstanding counterpart of the Big Bang theory was the idea that our Universe might ultimately stop expanding and collapse into a Big Crunch. Then a new big bang might materialize, like the phoenix from the ashes. That possibility was ruled out by discoveries at the end of the century showing that our Universe is set to expand forever.

Evidence that the expansion is even speeding up provoked a different idea about renewal. Andreas Albrecht of UC Davis and João Magueijo of Imperial College London proposed that, in the early moments of the Universe, light travelled much faster than it does now, until dark energy accumulated and slowed the light down. That left the dark energy more massive than its speed-of-light ticket allowed. It off-loaded the excess baggage, which appeared as the tangible energy and matter of the Universe.

'The whole thing could happen again,' Magueijo explained. 'When the expansion has scattered the present galaxies beyond sight of one another, light will first speed up, boosting the dark energy again, and then suddenly slow down, creating another universe. This could repeat again and again, in a series of big bangs.'

Other speculations generated multiple universes not serially but simultaneously. Out there, beyond the microwave fogbank, big bangs might be frequently repeatable events within an infinite and essentially unchanging cosmos. That was how Fred Hoyle was still trying to repair the Steady State theory at the time of his death in 2002. In this view, the Universe looks recent, compact and explosive only because of our provinciality.

An idea that sounds not dissimilar, yet is technically completely different, is the conjecture of the Russian astrophysicist Andrei Linde that baby universes are coming into existence in our midst, all the time. We're not aware of the newcomers, even if they sometimes grow as big as our own Universe. They supposedly slice themselves off into other dimensions of space disconnected from our own. And different baby universes can try out many variants of the physical laws.

The hospitable cosmos

For Martin Rees at Cambridge, the special tuning of those laws in our own cosmos deserved a special name. The biophilic Universe, he called it, meaning hospitable to life. As a prominent theorist of the stars and the quasars, Rees was often invited to assess progress in cosmology. He declared himself an agnostic about the competing theories of the day, but he hoped for an explanation for the biophilic Universe. Multiple universes seemed to him the best bet.

'Could there be other big bangs, sprouting into entire universes governed by different laws?' Rees asked, speaking in 2002. 'This is a key question for 21st-century science. If the answer is Yes, we'd have no reason to be surprised by the apparent fine tuning. Putting it on a firm footing must await a successful fundamental theory that tells us whether there could have been many big bangs rather than just one, and, if so, whether they're varied enough that what we call the laws of nature may be just parochial bylaws in our cosmic patch.'

Note the echo of Philip Morrison's remark about provinciality, made three decades earlier. But Rees took a positive view of the hospitable Universe produced by our private Big Bang. Within our patch, he thought, scientists should be able to integrate into cosmology not just astronomy, particle physics and chemistry, as they have done already, but biology too. And searches for living things on other worlds will assess just how biophilic the cosmos has proved to be, so far. If life isn't widespread already, then in Rees' opinion our descendants may think it their duty to make it so.

You may sense in the anthropic and biophilic views a reversion towards the Universe of Dante's time, which was centred on the Earth and humankind. The cosmos is as large as it is because its expansion till now is an exact measure of the aeons it took for us to show up after the Big Bang, and to start looking at it. The galaxies, stars, interstellar clouds and comets tell of the cosmic order that was needed to accumulate the stuff for making our planet and us.

So the Earth regains its core position, not navigationally speaking but genetically. Daily interactions between geos and cosmos, which in medieval times were mediated by angels and interpreted by astrologers, resume with the effects of lunar tides, solar storms, planet-induced wobbles of the Earth, and a non-stop influx of meteorites and cosmic rays. Human beings turn out to be just pieces of the Universe, as surely as sunbeams, Halley's Comet or the Horsehead Nebula. It's time for us to feel at home again among the stars.

BIG BANG *describes in more detail the fashionable inflation scenario and its better-established aftermath, together with Linde's baby universes.* GRAVITY *and* SUPERSTRINGS *go deeper still into fundamental theories.* DARK ENERGY *deals with the discovery of acceleration.* MICROWAVE BACKGROUND *tells of the high hopes about what that wrapper can reveal. Hints of possible ways to penetrate the fogbank, to have a more direct view of the Big Bang, appear in* GRAVITATIONAL WAVES *and* COSMIC RAYS. *Material contents of the Universe are to be found in* DARK MATTER, BLACK HOLES, GALAXIES *and* STARS. *For the opening chapters of the new biocosmology, see* ELEMENTS, MOLECULES IN SPACE, EXTRATERRESTRIAL LIFE, EARTH, LIFE'S ORIGIN *and* ASTRONAUTICS.

VOLCANIC EXPLOSIONS

Where will the next big one be?

ASH FALLING FROM THE SKY and great waves leaping from the sea afflicted Europe's first urban civilization, which was that of the Minoans on the island of Crete. Their ordeals are dismaying to contemplate, because the same things are certain to happen again some time. That is clear from the inexorable nature of the cause, which is nothing less than the gradual annihilation of the Mediterranean Sea, as Europe and Africa inch ever closer together.

The Alps, made by Italy pushing like a battering ram into Switzerland, are just a preview. Ten million years from now, mountains on a Himalayan scale will stretch from Spain to Turkey. Meanwhile, in the eastern Mediterranean, a remaining scrap of deep ocean floor still separates the continents. Its northern edge is diving to destruction under Crete, around a curved depression in the seabed called the Hellenic Trench.

In such a setting, which occurs in many parts of the world, the subducted plate slants into the Earth, and the grinding action is felt as deep earthquakes. Heat generated by the friction produces a line of active volcanoes about 200 kilometres beyond the trench. One such is Santorini, an island north of Crete, and during the Bronze Age it blew up.

'To stand at the top of the near-sheer cliff that vanishes into the Aegean is to feel you are on the edge of disaster,' noted a travel writer, Simon Calder. 'Let your gaze follow the white-flecked crescent of coastline and, when the land ends, allow your imagination to complete the circle, as it might a young moon. The lunar analogy is apt, because looming from the sea are heaps of debris straight from the NASA props department. The word "calamity" is barely appropriate for what happened here.'

Some 30 cubic kilometres of the Earth's crust were flung into the air. They left a hole in the sea floor more than 400 metres deep, to be added to 300-metre cliffs that partly ring it. Santorini, also known as Thera, is sometimes identified with Atlantis, the lost land of classical mythology.

Modern knowledge of what occurred there emerged gradually and controversially. In 1967, the archaeologist Spiridon Marinatos from Athens discovered on Santorini the remains of a thriving Bronze Age seaport buried under volcanic ash—but no bodies, because the inhabitants had fled. Recurrent

699

deposits of ash on nearby Crete and other islands indicate a series of big eruptions before the eventual explosion, so perhaps they got away in good time.

Otherwise they might have perished in a tsunami, or tidal wave, that accompanied the blast. Crete's north coast and all other shorelines of the Aegean were ravaged by tsunamis—walls of water 30 metres high or more. The playwright Euripides evidently shared a folk memory of such events on the Greek mainland when he wrote in 428 BC:

> ... And the steeds
> Pricked their ears skyward, and threw back their heads.
> And wonder came on all men, and affright,
> Whence rose that awful voice. And swift our sight
> Turned seaward, down the salt and roaring sand.
> And there, above the horizon, seemed to stand
> A wave unearthly, crested in the sky;
> Till Skiron's Cape first vanished from mine eye.

Controversy arose because some investigators wanted to blame the Santorini event for the collapse of the Minoan civilization around 1450 BC. That led to a shift of power to Mycenae on mainland Greece. But there was a discrepancy of two centuries in the dating.

Evidence came from a global climatic effect, presumably linked to the culminating eruption, which must have darkened the sky with dust thrown into the stratosphere. Ancient trees in both California and Northern Ireland showed clear signs of much reduced growth, in the tree rings, for a few years starting in 1628 BC. Radiocarbon dating of a carbonized tree under the volcanic ash of Santorini, at sometime between 1670 and 1610 BC was compatible with it.

A somewhat different date, of about 1645 BC, came from the detection of acidity due to volcanic fallout in a deep-buried layer of the ice sheet of Greenland. By 2003, small specks of glass from Santorini were identified in the ice of that age, and 1645 BC was said to be correct to within five years. Either the later tree-ring date relates to another event entirely, or one or other dating method is slightly wrong.

As is often the way with such dramatic tales from geoscience, Santorini's became more complicated as research continued. Geologists found evidence that the present-day hole, or caldera, of Santorini was formed in at least four stages. At the end of the century, Tom Pfeiffer at Aarhus concluded judiciously that 'Tsunamis, ash-fall and climatic changes by emission of aerosols into the stratosphere might have led to the decline of the Minoan civilization on Crete.' Decline, but not fall.

Chemical wedding gifts

To put Santorini into perspective: it was bigger than the famous volcanic explosion of Krakatau, an island west of Java, in 1883. That event killed 35,000 people, mainly by the tsunamis. Santorini dwarfed the late-20th-century eruptions of El Chichón (Mexico, 1982), Mount St Helens (USA, 1990) and Pinatubo (Philippines, 1991). On the other hand the culminating event at Santorini was only about half the size of the explosion of Tambora on Indonesia's Sumbawa island in 1815, which turned a mountain into a crater lake.

The caldera of Tambora is six kilometres in diameter and one kilometre deep. The dust that the 1815 event put into the stratosphere chilled the world, and in the northern hemisphere 1816 was known as a year without a summer. That was when Mary Shelley wrote *Frankenstein* while on holiday in Switzerland, with gloomy thoughts to match the atrocious weather.

A far bigger volcanic crater lake is Toba in Sumatra, 100 kilometres long and 30 wide. An explosion there about 75,000 years ago was the largest volcanic event in recent geological history. It strewed ash thickly on the bed of the Indian Ocean and it caused a miniature ice age. Worldwide pollen records show a deep chilling followed by a slow recovery.

Indonesia is volcanically active for the same reason as the Aegean Sea. In the Java Trench a narrow residue of ocean floor, between Asia on the one hand and Australia plus New Guinea on the other, is diving to destruction, in a prelude to another continental collision in 10 million years' time. Fly lengthwise above Java, parallel to the ocean trench, and you'll see volcanic cones poking through the clouds with a regularity that looks almost engineered. And when you descend through the clouds you'll find terraced farms climbing up the steep slopes of the volcanoes, as if defying them to do their worst.

Yogyakarta's first king (so the local legend goes) married the queen of the sea. They went to live inside Merapi, an ever-smoking volcano that looms over the city in central Java. The royal couple still hand out gifts to the people from their wedding feast, in the form of superfertile soil. Geochemically speaking, the tale is spot on and it explains why people crowd around volcanoes, despite the manifest dangers.

The soil's supplies of nutrient elements such as phosphorus and iron, needed for plant life, are continually lost by burial or washed away down the rivers. They have to be replaced by the weathering of rocks. Volcanic material, fresh from the bowels of the Earth, is both chemically rich and unusually easy to weather. The Javanese say that if you poke a walking stick in their soil, it will take root and grow.

For the same reason the heirs to the citizens of Pompeii still plant their vines on the slopes of Vesuvius. Inhabitants of volcanic regions strike their own bargains with Mother Nature, knowing that big eruptions are few and far between, on the scale of a human lifetime. But the threats of volcanic tsunamis and climatic chills hang over many other people living far from the scene.

Tsunamis are a complex story because earthquakes, seabed mudslides and the collapse of inactive volcanic structures in great landslides can all make waves, as well as eruptions in volcanoes rooted in the seabed. The waves are barely perceptible in the open sea, but gather height as they come ashore. They travel no faster than jet planes, so warnings are possible, in principle at least, to evacuate some of the more distant endangered shorelines. On the other hand a volcanic winter, as the severest climatic effect is sometimes called, can only be endured—until the dust settles and leaves the sunshine unimpeded again.

Volcanoes and climate

In June 1991 an eruption of Mount Pinatubo in the Philippines shot debris and gases high into the stratosphere. The significance of the altitude is that the stratosphere is above the weather, which tends to wash the air clean quite quickly. Fine dust in the stratosphere takes a long time to settle and high-altitude winds carry it to all parts of the world. Roughly speaking, mineral grains take about a year to fall out, and droplets of sulphuric acid and other chemicals persist for several years.

A ground station in Hawaii detected the Pinatubo dust by a laser beam. Satellites watched the pall spreading, until by October 1992 it covered virtually the whole globe. Other satellites monitoring air temperatures saw the stratosphere warming as the dust absorbed sunlight, and the lower atmosphere cooling as the surface received less. Between 1991 and 1992 the average temperature of the lower air dropped by 0.4°C, and it did not return to pre-Pinatubo levels until 1995. That figure can be compared with the global warming of about 0.6°C for the whole of the 20th century.

The climate signal from Pinatubo was particularly clear. The impact of the El Chichón eruption of 1982 was overwhelmed by the warming effect of an El Niño oceanic event in the eastern Pacific. The explosive eruption of Bezimianny in Kamchatka in 1955 was similarly masked, on that occasion by exceptional activity of the Sun. Confusions caused by competing natural agents affecting the climate are aggravated in the case of volcanoes by competing methods used by scientists to describe their atmospheric effects, which are often contradictory.

The Volcanic Explosivity Index, or VEI, is perhaps the most useful, like the Richter Scale used for reckoning earthquakes. It is based on the estimated volume of lava and dust released in an eruption. Dozens of volcanoes that erupt every year are in the VEI range 0–2, and their plumes don't reach very high. Those of VEI 3 or 4 inject some material into the stratosphere, and therefore have a somewhat depressing effect on the intensity of sunlight at the surface.

VEI 5 is the index point at which dramatic effects can be expected to begin to show, with the release of material exceeding one cubic kilometre. Bezimianny, El Chichón and Pinatubo all scored 5. So, by the way, did Vesuvius in A D 79, when it buried Pompeii and Herculaneum. At VEI 6, with more than ten cubic kilometres of exploded material, was Krakatau. And with more than 100 cubic kilometres vented and a VEI of 7, Tambora stands out as the biggest event known (so far) in historical times.

Normally volcanic winters are short-lived, because the dust falls out and is not replaced. But if there is a chorus of eruptions occurring at short intervals, the cooling can be protracted. Evidence for such episodes comes from the most comprehensive global record of major volcanic eruptions, which is preserved in the ice sheets of Greenland and Antarctica.

In 1977 Claus Hammer at Copenhagen discovered that chemical deposits from distant volcanoes alter the electrical conductivity of the ice, as it builds up year by year. In the decades that followed, Hammer and his colleagues were able to identify many well-known volcanoes, recorded in layers within long ice cores retrieved by drilling into the ice sheets. For example, they confirmed that the Santorini eruption occurred in the 17th century B C.

The volcanic layers proved to be very useful for cross-dating the ice in cores from Greenland and Antarctica. They also revealed eruptions previously unrecorded, and showed great variations in the rate of eruptions, from century to century and millennium to millennium. For example, there were six major events signalled in the ice in the 17th century A D, and none at all in the 14th and 15th centuries. Most striking was a cluster of big events 17,500 years ago. They came in several violent pulses spread over 170 years.

Was it a coincidence that those eruptions came just as the Earth was beginning to emerge from the last ice age, which was at its coldest about 24,000 years ago? Hammer thought not. The eruptions were in West Antarctica, and the rising sea level that accompanied the general thaw could have partly dismembered the ice sheet there. If the pressure of the ice sheet had been helping to bottle up the volcanic activity, its sudden reduction could have triggered the eruptions.

By Hammer's interpretation, not only can volcanoes affect the climate, but the climate can also influence volcanic eruptions. Just as the weight of ice sheets may tend to repress volcanoes in polar regions, so a high sea level might reduce eruptions from seabed volcanoes. The fall in sea level that comes with the onset of an ice age might therefore have a provocative effect too, but there is no evidence for that yet.

On a shorter time-scale, the natural variability in the rate of eruptions from century to century is unexplained, but it ought to be taken into account in weighing future prospects. 'After quite a busy start, the 20th century was unusually quiet in respect of large volcanic eruptions,' Hammer commented.

'Their absence certainly contributed to global warming, and we may have been lulled into a false sense of security.'

And the next big one...

The 20th century's largest eruption mysteriously darkened the skies of Washington DC and other places in 1912. Four years elapsed before it was traced to the Katmai volcano at the south-west tip of Alaska's mainland, where the remains of an event now rated at 6 on the explosivity scale provide a tourist attraction, in the Valley of Ten Thousand Smokes.

Contrast that delayed discovery with the detection in 1985 of hot rock nearing the surface of Lascar in the desert of Chile, by British geologists examining images from the US Landsat satellite, well before the volcano erupted in the following year. Earth-watching satellites spot significant eruptions easily, by their smoke plumes or the heat of their lava, and they can track the stratospheric dust and gases from the big ones.

Seismic stations, either at a distance or planted around active volcanoes, tell of earthquake rumbles that precede and accompany eruptions. Other clues to incipient activity come from magnetic instruments and detections of volcanic gases—often sulphurous. Simple TV cameras have taken over from the solitary watchmen who used to sit like shepherds on the slopes of many volcanoes, watching them smoke. Satellite navigation systems and a new technique called radar interferometry can detect movements of the ground.

Sometimes you don't need instruments to spot the ground heaving. Coral left stranded on clifftops on the Japanese island of Iwo Jima, 1200 kilometres south of the mainland, shows that the whole island has risen by 120 metres in the past 700 years. A large reservoir of molten rock is accumulating underneath it. Japanese experts keep a wary eye on Iwo Jima. It would create terrible tsunamis if it should explode, and it might conceivably attain an index of 6.

Prehistoric Japan had its own equivalent of Crete's Santorini. Around 4350 BC, Kikai in the Ryuku Islands blew up, 100 kilometres from the south-west tip of the mainland. It rates 7 on the explosivity scale, compared with 6 for Santorini. The dense ash-fall reached to Hokkaido, more than 1000 kilometres away.

Where will the next big one be? Explosive volcanoes are usually associated with ocean trenches and the convergence of tectonic plates of the Earth's outer shell—in distinction from oozier volcanoes with other origins. The Pacific Ocean is shrinking while the Atlantic grows, so it is surrounded by a Ring of Fire. And anyone going by past form, in respect of volcanic explosions, is likely to point you north-east from Japan. A succession of arc-like volcanic chains runs through the Kurile Islands, Kamchatka in eastern Russia, and thence via the Aleutian Islands to Alaska.

Every day, more than 100 passenger aircraft on polar routes fly over this northern boundary of the Ring of Fire. The top priority for the Alaska Volcano Observatory, based in Anchorage, is therefore to warn the aviation authorities of clouds of dust reaching the stratosphere. They are not kind to jet engines, and in 1989 a Boeing 747 lost power in all four engines when it encountered a plume from the Redoubt volcano. The flight crew got them going again after it had plummeted to within a kilometre of the mountaintops. Worldwide, such near disasters from volcano dust happen about once a year.

Many events with an explosivity index of 6 have occurred in these Kurile-to-Alaska chains of volcanoes in the past 10,000 years. Just as a lot of small earthquakes can relieve stresses in the crust gradually, so frequent moderate eruptions of a volcano can prevent it building up to a paroxysmal explosion. The next big one may therefore be biding its time, and not drawing attention to itself.

'At least twenty catastrophic eruptions have occurred in the Aleutian arc during the past 10,000 years that spewed tens of cubic kilometres of ejecta into the Earth's atmosphere,' said Thomas Miller of the US Geological Survey. 'Similar eruptions can be expected to occur from this region in the future. Although nothing can be done to prevent such eruptions, which can have widespread regional effects and cause global climatic changes, our modern monitoring systems have the potential to give enough warning to save lives.'

▶ *For volcanoes of the oozier kind, see* HOTSPOTS *and* FLOOD BASALTS. *For other natural disasters generated by the not-so-solid Earth, see* EARTHQUAKES.

SOURCES OF QUOTES

These sources are given here in the order in which they appear in each entry.

Introduction

Lehrer: from 'Bright College Days', in *More of Tom Lehrer*, Lehrer Records, 1959

Alcohol

Scientific board: quoted in biography of Eduard Buchner in *Nobel Lectures, Chemistry 1901–1921*, Amsterdam: Elsevier, 1966

Benner: personal communication, 2002

Altruism and aggression

Kropotkin: P. Kropotkin, *Mutual Aid: A Factor of Evolution* (1902); reprinted London: Allen & Unwin, 1984

Tajfel: in 'The Human Conspiracy', BBC-TV, Nisbett/Calder, 1975

Wilson: E.O. Wilson, *Sociobiology*, Cambridge, Mass.: Belknap Press, 1975

Fellow evolutionary theorist: John Maynard Smith, quoted by R. Dawkins, foreword to W.D. Hamilton, *Narrow Roads of Gene Land*, vol. 2, Oxford: Oxford University Press, 2001

Hamilton 1: *ibid.*

Hamilton 2: in W.D. Hamilton, *Narrow Roads of Gene Land*, vol. 1, Oxford: Oxford University Press, 1996

Trivers: in 'The Human Conspiracy', BBC-TV, Nisbett/Calder, 1975

Shakespeare: Hamlet, in *Hamlet*, Act I, scene 5

Axelrod and Hamilton: R. Axelrod and W.D. Hamilton, *Science*, vol. 211, pp. 1390–6, 1981

Axelrod: personal communication, 2002

Collins: in 'Cracking the Code of Life', PBS/WGBH/NOVA TV, Arledge/Cort, 17 April 2001

Presiding experimenter: speaking in 'The Human Conspiracy', BBC-TV, Nisbett/Calder, 1975

McGuire: J. McGuire, *Cognitive-Behavioural Approaches*, London: Home Office, July 2000

Antimatter

Sakharov jingle: autograph text on a reprint of A.D. Sakharov, *JETP Letters*, vol. 5, pp. 24–7, 1967 (Russian version); seen in a photograph circulated by the American Institute of Physics

Textbook author: J.J. Sakurai, *Principles and Elementary Particles*, Princeton, N.J.: Princeton University Press, 1964

Fitch: Nobel Lecture, Stockholm, 8 December 1980

Ellis: J. Ellis, *CERN Courier*, October 1999

Quinn: lecture at University of Michigan, Ann Arbor, 24 May 2001

Arabidopsis

Koornneef 1: quoted by Martine Segers, *Green City Wageningen* (electronic dossiers of Wageningen Agricultural University), September 1998

Arabidopsis team, Arabidopsis Genome Initiative: *Nature*, vol. 408, pp. 796–815, 2000

Koornneef 2: personal communication, 2002

Astronautics

Kyle: D. Kyle, *A Pictorial History of Science Fiction*, London: Hamlyn, 1976

Spiegelman: in 'Spaceships of the Mind', BBC-TV, Gilling/Calder, 1978

O'Neill: in *ibid*.

Ivanova: T. Ivanova, *21st Century Science and Technology*, vol. 15, no. 2, pp. 41–9, 2002

Bradbury: quoted in Oriana Fallaci, *If the Sun Dies*, trans. P. Swinglehurst, New York: Atheneum, 1966

Bernal's ladder

Bernal: J.D. Bernal, personal communication, 1958

Big Bang

Adams: introduction to J.S. Bach, *Brandenburg Concertos 1–4*, performed by the English Chamber Orchestra, conductor Benjamin Brittain, Penguin Music Classics, 1999

Lemaître: quoted by M. Rees in N. Calder, ed., *Scientific Europe*, Maastricht: Nature & Technology, 1990

Weinberg: in 'The Key to the Universe', BBC-TV, Nisbett/Calder, 1977

Linde 1: talk at Stephen Hawking's 60th Birthday Conference, Cambridge, January 2002

Linde 2: A. Linde, *Scientific American*, pp. 48–55, November 1994

Francis: lecture on Early Universe, Australian National University, Canberra, 2001

Linde 3 and 4: personal communication, 2002

Guth: in 'Parallel Universes', BBC-TV, Malcolm Clark, 2002

Biodiversity

Orwell: George Orwell, *Animal Farm*, London: Secker & Warburg, 1945

Mellanby: K. Mellanby in N. Calder, ed., *Nature in the Round*, London: Weidenfeld & Nicolson, 1973

May: R.M. May, *Science*, vol. 241, pp. 1441–9, 1988

Lugo: quoted by Charles C. Mann, *Science*, vol. 253, pp. 736–8, 1991

SOURCES OF QUOTES

Manokaran: paper at Congress of International Union of Forestry Research Organizations, Tampere, 6–12 August 1995

Hubbell: quoted by Steven Schultz, *Princeton Weekly Bulletin*, 22 February 1999

Bell: G. Bell, *Science*, vol. 293, pp. 2413–18, 2001

Connell: J.H. Connell, *Science*, vol. 199, p. 1302, 1978

Molino and Sabatier: J.-F. Molino and D. Sabatier, *Science*, vol. 294, pp. 1702–4, 2001

Molino: personal communication, 2002

European Union: press release, Brussels, 24 November 1999

Grime: J.P. Grime, *Journal of Vegetation Science*, vol. 13, pp. 709–12, 2002

Biological clocks

Djerrasi: quoted by Krishnan Rajeshwar and Walter van Schalkwijk, The Electrochemical Society, *Interface*, Fall 2000

Takahashi and Reppert: quoted by Karen Young Kreeger, *The Scientist*, 15 April 2002

Nagy and Gwinner: personal communications, 2002

Biosphere from space

Tucker: quoted in N. Calder, *Spaceship Earth*, London: Viking, 1991

Sellers: *ibid.*

Zhou: quoted in press release, American Geophysical Union, 4 September 2001

Hardy: A.C. Hardy, *The Open Sea*: *The World of Plankton*, London: Collins, 1956

Behrenfeld: personal communication, 2002

Bits and qubits

Shannon's wife Betty: quoted by M. Mitchell Waldrop, *Technology Review*, July/August 2001

Shannon 1: C.E. Shannon, 'A Symbolic Analysis of Relay and Switching Circuits', Master's dissertation, MIT, 1938

Shannon 2: A.C. Shannon, *Bell System Technical Journal*, July and October 1948

Steane: A. Steane, *Nature*, vol. 422, pp. 387–8, 2003

Deutsch: interview by Filiz Peach, *Philosophy Now*, 30 December 2000

Black holes

Stevenson: R.L. Stevenson, *In the South Seas* (1896); reprinted London: Penguin, ed. N. Rennie, 1998

Schmidt: in 'The Violent Universe', BBC-TV, Daly/Calder, 1968

Hong-yee Chiu: W. Priester, personal communication, 2000

Rees: M. Rees in N. Calder, ed., *Scientific Europe*, Maastricht: Nature & Technology, 1990

Graham: quoted in press release, Instituto de Astrofisica de Canarias, 23 November 2001

Pounds: personal communication, 2000

Tanaka: personal communication, 2002

Sako: personal communication, 2002

Schödel: quoted in press release, European Southern Observatory, 16 October 2002

Gebhart: quoted in press release, Space Telescope Science Institute, 17 September 2002

Cash and colleagues: W. Cash *et al.*, *Nature*, vol. 407, pp. 160–3, 2000

Valtaoja: personal communication, 2002

Brain images

Landau: W.M. Landau *et al.*, *Transactions of the American Neurological Association*, vol. 80, pp. 125–9, 1955

Scandinavian researchers: N. Lassen *et al.*, *Scientific American*, pp. 50–9, October 1978

Ogawa: quoted in press release, Bell Laboratories, 16 October 2000

Zassetsky (wounded soldier): trans. M. Glenny, quoted in 'The Mind of Man', BBC-TV, Daly/Calder, 1970

Luria: personal communication, 1970

Friston: personal communication, 2002

Raichle: M.E. Raichle, *Proceedings of the National Academy of Sciences* (USA), vol. 95, pp. 765–72, 1998

Brain rhythms

A visiting scientist: Philip Laurent, *Science*, vol. 45, p. 44, 1917

Smith: H.M. Smith, *Science*, vol. 82, pp. 151–2, 1935

Kopell 1: title of lecture, Harvey Mudd College, Calif., 10 April 2001, attributed to science writer Barry Cipra

Kuramoto: personal communication, 2002

Strogatz: S.H. Strogatz, *Nature*, vol. 410, pp. 268–76, 2001

Kopell 2: personal communication, 2002

Brain wiring

Cajal: S. Ramón y Cajal, *Recollections of My Life*, trans. E. Horne Craigie and Juan Cano, Philadelphia: American Philosophical Society, 1937, anthologized in John Carey, ed., *The Faber Book of Science*, London: Faber, 1995

Wiesel: T.N. Wiesel, Nobel Lecture, Stockholm, 8 December 1981

Rakic: quoted by Kaplan, requoted by Michael Specter, *The New Yorker*, 23 July 2001

Theodosis: personal communication, 2002

Buckyballs and nanotubes

Fuller: 'Prime Design', 1960, reprinted in James Meller, ed., *The Buckminster Fuller Reader*, London: Cape, 1970

Smalley 1: in 'Molecules With Sunglasses', BBC Horizon, John Lynch, 9 December 1996

Dirac: *Scientific American*, May 1963

SOURCES OF QUOTES

Smalley 2: Nobel Lecture, Stockholm, 1996

Krätschmer: personal communication, 2002

Iijima: discourse at Royal Institution, London, 1997

Dekker: personal communication, 2002

Welland: quoted in press release, Cambridge University Engineering Department, 27 April 2001

Feynman: talk at American Physical Society, 29 December 1959

Davydov: personal communication, 2002

Kroto: lecture at Schlumberger-Doll Research, Ridgefield, Connecticut, 15 October 1998

The Song of Aragorn: J.R.R. Tolkien, *The Lord of the Rings*, London: Allen & Unwin, 1954

Cambrian explosion

Gould: S.J. Gould, *Wonderful Life*, New York: Norton, 1989

Conway Morris: S. Conway Morris, *Geology Today*, pp. 88–92, May–June 1987

Hou: quoted by Richard Monastersky, *Discover*, April 1993

Collins: personal communication, 2002

Valentine and colleagues: J.W. Valentine, D. Jablonski and D.H. Erwin, *Development*, vol. 126, pp. 851–9, 1999

Carbon cycle

Revelle and Suess: R. Revelle and H.E. Suess, *Tellus*, vol. 9, pp. 18–27, 1957

Keeling: C.D. Keeling, *Proceedings of the National Academy of Sciences* (USA), vol. 94, pp. 8273–4, 1997

Lorius: quoted in press release, Centre National de la Recherche Scientifique, Paris, 3 December 2002

Wilson: personal communication, 1999

Wagner: personal communication, 1999

Ice-core scientists: A. Indermühle *et al.*, *Science*, vol. 286, p. 1815a, 1999

Intergovernmental Panel on Climate Change: J.T. Houghton *et al.*, eds., *Climate Change 2001: The Scientific Basis*, Cambridge: Cambridge University Press, 2001

Cell cycle

Weinert: quoted by Michael Balter and Gretchen Vogel, *Science*, vol. 294, pp. 502–3, 2001

Masui: quoted by Stephen Strauss, *University of Toronto Magazine*, Autumn 1999

Nurse: quoted by Tim Radford, *Guardian* (London), 9 October 2001

Scholey: personal communication, 2002

Cell death

Melville: 'The Encantadas or, Enchanted Isles', *Putnam's Monthly Magazine*, March 1854, New York: G.P. Putnam & Co.

Kerr, Wyllie and Currie: J.F.R. Kerr *et al., British Journal of Cancer*, vol. 26, pp. 239–57, 1972

Osborne: quoted by Ricki Lewis, *The Scientist*, 6 February 1995

Krammer: P.H. Krammer, *Nature*, vol. 407, pp. 789–95, 2000

Skulachev: L. Skulachev, *Life*, vol. 49, pp. 365–75, 2000

Cell traffic

Claude: Nobel Lecture, Stockholm, 12 December 1974

Simons 1: in N. Calder, ed., *Scientific Europe*, Maastricht: Nature & Technology, 1990

Vale: quoted in *Applied Genetics News*, January 2000

Simons 2: personal communication, 2002

Cereals

Chinese proverb: quoted in *The Economist*, 9 March 1991

Ehrlich: P.R. Ehrlich, *The Population Bomb*, New York: Ballantine, 1968

Borlaug 1: quoted by Aase Lionaes, Nobel Peace Prize presentation, Oslo, 1970

Khush: quoted in *Annual Report 2000–2001*, International Rice Research Institute, Manila, 2001

Zhu and colleagues: Y. Zhu *et al., Nature*, vol. 406, pp. 718–22, 2000

Borlaug 2: Lecture, Norwegian Nobel Institute, 8 September 2000

Gale: at Rockefeller Foundation's Rice Biotechnology Meeting, Tucson, 1991

Leung: quoted in *Annual Report 2000–2001*, International Rice Research Institute, Manila, 2001

Chaos

Boiteux: quoted in 'Presentation: About IHÉS', Institut des Hautes Études Scientifiques, Bures-sur-Yvette, 2001

Thom: R. Thom in M Atiyah and D Iagolnitzer, eds., *Fields Medallists' Lectures*, Singapore: World Scientific, 1997

Stewart: I. Stewart, *Nature's Numbers*, London: Weidenfeld & Nicolson, 1995

Lorenz: quoted by James Gleick in *Chaos: Making a New Science*, New York: Viking, 1987

Harrison: in 'Sunshine with Scattered Showers', BBC-TV, Chris Wells, 4 July 1996

Majerus: quoted by Greg Neale, *Sunday Telegraph* (London), 21 March 1999

Orrell: D. Orrell *et al., Nonlinear Processes in Geophysics*, vol. 8, pp. 357–71, 2001

Ruelle: D. Ruelle, *Nature*, vol. 411, p. 27, 2001

Climate change

Scriptwriter: N. Calder, *Nature*, vol. 252, pp. 216–18, 1974

Hays, Imbrie and Shackleton: J.D. Hays, J. Imbrie and N.J. Shackleton, *Science*, vol. 194, pp. 1121–32, 1976

Kukla: in 'The Weather Machine', BBC-TV, Nisbett/Calder, 1974

Shackleton: N.J. Shackleton, *Science*, vol. 289, pp. 1897–1902, 2000

SOURCES OF QUOTES

Berger: quoted by R.A. Kerr in *Science*, vol. 289, p. 1868, 2000

Bolin: in 'The Weather Machine', BBC-TV, Nisbett/Calder, 1974

Lamb: H.H. Lamb, *Climate: Present, Past and Future*, vol. 2, London: Methuen, 1977

Manabe: remarks made at the opening of Japan's Institute for Global Change Research, 1998

Kennedy: editorial in *Science*, vol. 291, p. 2515, 2001

National Academy of Sciences: *Climate Change Science: An Analysis of Some Key Questions*, Washington: National Academy of Sciences, 2001

Editors of *Science*: 'Areas to Watch in 2003', *Science*, vol. 298, p. 2298, 2002

Watson: quoted by BBC News Online, 19 April 2002

Pachauri and Love: news briefing, Geneva, quoted by Reuters, 9 August 2002

Cloning

Roslin scientists: press release, Roslin Institute, 25 February 1997

Wilmut: BBC News Online, 26 November 2001

Aldous Huxley: 'Fifth Philosopher's Song' (1920) quoted by Susan Squire in *Research/ Penn State*, September, 1996

Maynard Smith: J. Maynard Smith, *Games, Sex and Evolution*, Brighton: Harvester-Wheatsheaf, 1988

Hamilton: W.D. Hamilton, *Narrow Roads of Gene Land*, vol. 2, Oxford: Oxford University Press, 2001

Margulis: L. Margulis and D. Sagan, *What is Life?* New York: Simon & Schuster, 1995

Comets and asteroids

Whipple: in 'The Comet is Coming!', BBC-TV, Freeth/Calder, 1981

Newton: I. Newton, *Principia* (1687 and 1713), trans. A. Motte (1729); revised edition F. Cajori: University of California Press, Berkeley: 1934

Keller: personal communication, 1990

Yeomans: D.K. Yeomans, *Nature,* vol. 404, pp. 829–32, 2000

Stern: quoted in press release, Southwest Research Institute, 11 August 2000

Marsden: personal communication, 2000

Balsiger: personal communication, 2001

Shoemaker: in 'Spaceships of the Mind', BBC-TV, Gilling/Calder, 1978

Carusi: personal communication, 2001

Continents and supercontinents

Sengor 1: A. Berthelsen and A.M.C. Sengor in N. Calder, ed., *Scientific Europe*, Maastricht: Nature & Technology, 1990

Sengor 2: talk at Geological Survey of Canada, Ottawa, 11 February 1998

Scotese: 'History of the Atlas', 1998, on <http://www.scotese.com>

Guterch: personal communication, 2002

Cosmic rays

Etchegoyen: personal communication, 2002

Verse: inscription at the Ettore Majorana Centre for Scientific Culture, Erice

Auger: P. Auger, *Journal de Physique*, vol. 43, p. 12, 1982

Watson: personal communication, 2002

Cryosphere

Holmes: in A. Holmes, *Principles of Physical Geology*, London: Nelson, 1965

Denton: personal communication, 1974

Wingham: personal communication, 1999

Joughin and Tulaczyk: I. Joughin and S. Tulaczyk, *Science*, vol. 295, pp. 476–80, 2002

Lemke: personal communication, 2001

Haeberli: personal communication, 2002

Dark energy

Nørgaard-Nielsen: personal communication, 2002

Schmidt and Kolb: quoted by James Glantz, *Science*, vol. 279, pp. 1298–9, 1998

Turner: quoted by Kathy Sawyer, *Washington Post*, 3 April 2001

Efstathiou: quoted by Andrew Watson, *Science*, vol. 295, p. 2341, 2002

Einstein: in M. Born, *The Born–Einstein Letters*, London: Macmillan, 1971

Ferreira: in *CERN Courier*, vol. 39, no. 5, pp. 13–15, 1999

Clarke: quoted at Field Propulsion Workshop, University of Sussex, January 2001

Dark matter

Kipling: Rudyard Kipling (1910) in Philip Larkin, ed., *The Oxford Book of Twentieth Century English Verse*, Oxford: Oxford University Press, 1972

'The Big Blank': headline in *Scientific American*, February 1982

Croom: quoted in press release, Royal Astronomical Society, 3 April 2001

Kneib: personal communication, 2002

Dinosaurs

Xu: personal communication, 2002

Sereno: P.C. Sereno, *Science*, vol. 284, pp. 2137–47, 1999

Discovery

Freeman: talk at The Sydney Institute, Sydney, Australia, 9 July 1996

Thomas: quoted by V. Fitch, Nobel Lecture, Stockholm, 1980

Feynman: in 'The Mind of Man', BBC-TV, Daly/Calder, 1970

Ketterle: quoted in Science @ NASA, 20 March 2002

Huxley: T.H. Huxley, *Collected Essays*, vol. IX: *Evolution and Ethics, and Other Essays*, Bristol: Thoemmes Press, 2001

SOURCES OF QUOTES

Feyerabend: P.K. Feyerabend, *Against Method*, Atlantic Highlands, New Jersey: Humanities Press, 1975

Kuhn: T.S. Kuhn, *The Structure of Scientific Revolutions*, Chicago: University of Chicago Press, 1962

Weinberg: S. Weinberg, *Dreams of a Final Theory*, New York: Vintage, 1992

Smith: talk at the Royal Greenwich Observatory, Herstmonceux, 1988

Lovelock: John Preedy Memorial Lecture, Cardiff, 22 September 1989

Prusiner: Autobiography, news release, Nobel Foundation, Stockholm, 1997

Lindquist: quoted by David Cameron, *Technology Review*, 8 February 2002

Churchill: quoted by J.C. Polanyi, *United Nations Chronicle*, vol. 25, no. 4, 1998

Ryle: letter to C. Chagas, 24 February 1983, quoted by A. Rudolf and M. Rowan-Robinson, *New Scientist*, 14 February 1985

Disorderly materials

De Gennes 1: in N. Calder, ed., *Scientific Europe*, Maastricht: Nature & Technology, 1990

De Gennes 2: quoted in *Chem @ Cam*, Spring 2001

Keller: personal communication, 2002

DNA fingerprinting

Jeffreys: quoted in Australia Prize press release, Department of Industry, Science and Resources, Canberra, May 1998

Linney: personal communication, 2002

Earth

Sumerian prayer: quoted in E.C. Krupp, *Echoes of the Ancient Skies*, Oxford: Oxford University Press, 1983

Sagdeev: quoted in P. Moore, *The New Atlas of the Universe*, London: Mitchell Beazeley, 1984

Saunders: personal communication, 2002

Nimmo: personal communication, 2002

Stone: personal communication, 2002

Hoppa: quoted in *Spaceviews*, 16 September 1999

Spohn: personal communication, 2001

Grande: quoted in *SMART-1: By Sun Power to the Moon*, Noordwijk: European Space Agency BR-191, 2002

Laskar: J. Laskar in *Récents Progrès en Génie des Procédés*, vol. 11, pp. 33–46, Paris: Lavoisier, 1997

Earthquakes

Kanamori: abridged from H. Kanamori *et al.*, *Nature*, vol. 390, pp. 461–4, 1997

MacDonald: G.J.F. MacDonald in N. Calder, ed., *Unless Peace Comes*, London: Allen Lane, 1968

Dobson: quoted in press release, University College London, 15 November 2002

Hanssen: personal communication, 2002

Earthshine

Leonardo: Codex Leicester, sheet 2A, folio 2r (1506–10) owned by William H. Gates III, trans. American Museum of Natural History, 1998

Koonin: quoted by Gary Taubes, *Science*, vol. 264, pp. 1529–30, 1994

Goode: at conference 'The Solar Cycle and Terrestrial Climate', Tenerife, 25–29 September 2000

Herschel: W. Herschel, *Philosophical Transactions of the Royal Society*, vol. 91, pp. 265–83, 1801

Marsh and Svensmark: N. Marsh and H. Svensmark, *Space Science Reviews*, vol. 94, pp. 215–30, 2000

Intergovernmental Panel on Climate Change: J.T. Houghton *et al.*, *Climate Change 2001: The Scientific Basis*, Cambridge: Cambridge University Press, 2001

Kirkby: Summary in *CLOUD Proposal*, Geneva: CERN, SPSC/P317, 2000

Eco-evolution

Darwin: C. Darwin, *The Origin of Species*, London: Murray, 1859

Norberg and colleagues: J. Norberg *et al.*, *Proceedings of the National Academy of Sciences* (USA), vol. 98, pp. 11376–81, 2001

Rainey and Travisano: P.B. Rainey and M. Travisano, *Nature*, vol. 394, pp. 69–72, 1998

Bell: personal communication, 2002

Martin and Salamini: *EMBO Reports*. vol. 1, pp. 208–10, 2000

Electroweak force

Salam and reporter: quoted by N. Calder, in A.M. Hamende, ed., *Tribute to Abdus Salam*, Trieste: The Abdus Salam International Centre for Theoretical Physics, 1999

Salam and mosque: in 'The Key to the Universe', BBC-TV, Nisbett/Calder, 1977

't Hooft 1: in *ibid.*

't Hooft 2: personal communication, 2002

Musset: quoted by Gordon Fraser in *CERN Courier*, vol. 38, no. 8, p. 30, 1998

Rubbia: in N. Calder, ed., *Scientific Europe*, Maastricht: Nature & Technology, 1990

Elements

Levi: *The Periodic Table*, trans. R. Rosenthal, London: Penguin Modern Classics, 2001

Pilachowski: quoted in press release, US National Optical Astronomy Observatory, 14 November 2000

Fowler: Autobiography, news release, Nobel Foundation, Stockholm, 1983

Hoyle: F. Hoyle, *Astronomy and Cosmology*, New York: Freeman, 1975

Zinner: personal communication, 2002

SOURCES OF QUOTES

Computer of the calendar: quoted in J. Needham, *Science and Civilisation in China*, vol. 3, Cambridge: Cambridge University Press, 1959

Tycho: in *De Nova Stella* (1573), trans. in *A Treasury of World Science*, New York: Philosophical Library, 1962

Schönfelder: quoted in N. Calder, *Beyond this World*, Noordwijk: European Space Agency BR-112, 1995

Aschenbach: personal communication, 2002

Pagel: personal communication, 2002

El Niño

Trenberth, also Nierenberg: quoted by Judith Perera, Inter Press Service, 26 December 1998

Corrège: press release, Institut de Recherche pour le Développment, Paris, 27 March 2002

Landsea: quoted by R.A. Kerr, *Science*, vol. 290, pp. 257–8, 2000

Embryos

Thomas: 'On Embryology', in *The Medusa and the Snail*, New York: Viking, 1979

Nüsslein-Volhard: Autobiography, news release, Nobel Foundation, Stockholm, 1995

Britten also Davidson: in 'The Life Game', BBC-TV, Malone/Calder, 1973

Satoh: quoted by Dennis Dormile, *Science*, vol. 293, pp. 788–9, 2001

Pourquié: personal communication, 2002

Energy and mass

Gauthier-Lafaye: personal communication, 2002

Sargent: in 'Einstein's Universe', BBC-TV/WGBH, Freeth/Calder, 1979

Richter: in B. Maglich, ed., *Adventures in Experimental Physics, Epsilon Volume*, Princeton, N.J.: World Science Education, 1976

Wheeler: in 'Einstein's Universe', BBC-TV/WGBH, Freeth/Calder, 1979

Einstein: A. Einstein, *Annalen der Physik*, vol. 18, p. 639, 1905

Evolution

Jacob 1: *The Possible and the Actual*, New York: Pantheon, 1982

Darwin 1: C. Darwin, *The Origin of Species*, 6th edition, London: Murray, 1872

Lewontin: 'The Life Game', BBC-TV, Malone/Calder, 1973

Campbell: J.H. Campbell in B.J. Depew and B.H. Weber, eds., *Evolution at the Crossroads*, Cambridge, Mass.: MIT Press, 1985

Linnaeus: quoted in E. Coen, *The Art of Genes*, Oxford: Oxford University Press, 1999

Coen: quoted in press release, John Innes Centre, 8 September 1999

Dawkins: quoted by Thomas Sutcliffe, *Independent* (London), 5 July 2001

Lindquist: S. Lindquist: *Nature*, vol. 408, pp. 17–18, 2000

Jacob 2: *La Logique du Vivant*, Paris: Gallimard, 1970; trans. B.E. Spillmann, *The Logic of Life*, New York: Pantheon, 1973

Student: Jonny Firstrow on video news item, Channel 447 WFLY, November 1998

Extinctions

Darwin 2: C. Darwin, *The Origin of Species*, 6th edition, London: Murray, 1872

Gould: in D.M. Raup, *Extinction: Bad Genes or Bad Luck*, New York: Norton, 1991, introduction © Stephen Jay Gould, 1991

Lyell: *Principles of Geology* (1830–33), reprinted Chicago: University of Chicago Press, 1990

Bakker: quoted by M.W. Browne, *New York Times*, 29 October 1985

Halley: talk at Loyal Society of London, 1694

Thurber: J. Thurber, *My World and Welcome to It*, New York: Harcourt, Brace, 1942

Raup: in D.M. Raup, *Extinction: Bad Genes or Bad Luck*, New York: Norton, 1991

Extraterrestrial life

Queloz 1: in 'Hunt for Alien Worlds', PBS/Nova TV, 18 February 1997

Artymovicz: at International Astronomical Union meeting, Manchester, 8 August 2000

Guilloteau: personal communication, 2001

Bruno: *De l'infinito universo e mondi* (1584), trans. in D. Waley Singer, *Giordano Bruno: His Life and Thought*, New York, Schuman, 1950

Butler: quoted in, press-release, NASA, 13 June 2002

Queloz 2: quoted in European Space Agency news release, 18 June 2002

Brack: personal communication, 2001

Cocconi and Morrison: G. Cocconi and P. Morrison, *Nature*, vol. 184, p. 844, 1959

Shklovskii: I.S. Shklovskii, *Priroda*, no. 7, p. 21, 1960

Rees: Astronomer Royal's lecture to Royal Society of Medicine and Royal Society of Arts, London, 29 May 2002

Extremophiles

Corliss: quoted in V.A. Kaharl, *Water Baby*, New York: Oxford University Press, 1990

Ballard: interview with Douglas Colligan, *Omni*, 1998

Hempel: in N. Calder, ed., *Scientific Europe*, Maastricht: Nature & Technology 1990

Taylor: quoted by John Whitfield, *Nature Science Update*, 17 January 2002

Gold: T. Gold, *Proceedings of the National Academy of Sciences* (USA), vol. 89, pp. 6045–9, 1992

Newman and Banfield: D.K. Newman and J.F. Banfield, *Science*, vol. 296, pp. 1071–7, 2002

Wharton: in D.A. Wharton, *Life at the Limit*, Cambridge: Cambridge University Press, 2002

SOURCES OF QUOTES

Flood basalts

British–Russian team: M.K. Reichow *et al.*, *Science*, vol. 296, pp. 1846–9, 2002

Rampino and Stothers: M.R. Rampino and R.B. Stothers, *Science*, vol. 226, pp. 1427–31, 1984

Renne: P.R. Renne, *Science*, vol. 296, pp. 1812–14, 2002

Saunders: personal communication, 2002

Flowering

Blázquez: personal communication, 2002

Dean: C. Dean, *Science*, vol. 290, p. 2071, 2000

Simpson and Dean: G.G. Simpson and C. Dean, *Science*, vol. 296, pp. 285–9, 2002

Simpson: personal communication, 2002

Galaxies

Ai Guoxiang: personal communication, 2002

Strom: R. Strom, 'A New Large Aperture Radio Telescope', draft brochure, 1997

Helmi: personal communication, 2002

Gamma-ray bursts

Galama: in 'Death Star', Channel 4 TV, David Sington/David McNab, 2001

Heise: personal communication 1999

Reeves: quoted in press release, UK Particle Physics and Astronomy Research Council, 4 April 2002

Giménez: personal communication, 2001

Genes

Perutz: *Daily Telegraph* (London), 27 April 1987

Watson and Crick: J.D. Watson and F.H. Crick, *Nature*, vol. 171, pp. 737–8, 1953

Monod: Nobel Lecture, Stockholm, 11 December 1965

Director: Alan Robertson, personal communication, 1958

Mullis: Autobiography, news release, Nobel Foundation, Stockholm, 1993

Sanger: BBC Sci/Tech News Online, 26 June 2000

Haldane: J.B.S. Haldane, *Heredity and Politics*, London: Allen & Unwin, 1938

Pääbo: S. Pääbo, *Science*, vol. 291, pp. 1219–20, 2001

Genomes in general

Haiku: poet Buson, quoted by Akiko Takeda, Trade Environment Database Projects, May 1996

Venkatesh: quoted in press release, Institute of Molecular and Cell Biology, Singapore, 26 October 2001

Arabidopsis Genome Initiative: *Nature*, vol. 408, pp. 796–815, 2000

Plasterk: R.H.A. Plasterk, *Science*, vol. 296, pp. 1263–5, 2002

Bevan: M. Bevan, *Nature*, vol. 416, pp. 590–1, 2002

Global enzymes

Cloud: P. Cloud, *Science*, vol. 160, pp. 729–36, 1968

Kirschvink: personal communication, 2002

Lovelock: J. Lovelock, *Gaia: A New Look at Life on Earth*, Oxford: Oxford University Press, 1979

Benner and colleagues: S.A. Benner *et al.*, *Science*, vol. 296, pp. 864–8, 2002

Grammar

Bogolyubov: quoted in H.B.G. Casimir, *Haphazard Reality*, New York: Harper & Row, 1983

Chomsky: in 'The Mind of Man', BBC-TV, Daly/Calder, 1970

Darwin: C. Darwin, *The Descent of Man*, London: Murray, 1871

Bruner: in 'The Human Conspiracy', BBC-TV, Nisbett/Calder, 1976

Minsky: in 'Machines with Minds', BBC Radio, producer Geoff Dehan, 1983

HAL: in *2001: A Space Odyssey*, screenplay by Stanley Kubrick and Arthur C. Clarke, 1968

Lascarides: in J. Calder, A. Lascarides and K. Stenning, *Human Communication*, in preparation.

Gravitational waves

Danzmann: personal communication, 1995

Schutz: personal communication, 2002

Gravity

Einstein 1: lecture in Kyoto, 1922, quoted in M. White and J. Gribbin, *Einstein: A Life in Science*, London: Simon & Schuster, 1993

Galileo: in *De Motu*, Pisa, 1592, trans. in I.E. Drabkin and S. Drake, *Galileo Galilei on Motion and on Mechanics*, Madison: University of Wisconsin Press, 1960

Halley: 'Ode to Newton', trans. from Latin by L. Richardson in A. Cajori, *Sir Isaac Newton's Mathematical Principles of Natural Philosophy*, Berkeley: University of California Press, 1934

Newton: letter to Richard Bently, 1692, quoted in A. Cajori, *loc. cit.*

Penrose: in 'Einstein's Universe', BBC-TV, Freeth/Calder, 1979

Wheeler 1: in *ibid.*

Wheeler 2: J.A. Wheeler, *Geons, Black Holes and Quantum Foam*, New York: Norton, 1998

Witten: quoted by Michio Kaku, *New Scientist*, 18 January 1997

Baez: quoted by James Glanz, *New York Times*, 13 March 2001

Rovelli: personal communication, 2002

SOURCES OF QUOTES

Arkani-Hamed: quoted by Paul Preuss, *Science Beat*, Lawrence Berkeley Lab., 19 June 2000

Martyn: personal communication, 2002

Hadley: M.J. Hadley, talk given at the 5th UK Conference on Conceptual and Philosophical Problems in Physics, Oxford, 10–14 September 1996

Einstein 2: A. Einstein, *Out of my Later Years*, New York: Philosophical Library, 1950

Everitt 1 and 2: personal communication, 2002

Laing: quoted by Robert Matthews, *Sunday Telegraph* (London), 10 February 2002

Non-scientist: Lizzie Calder, personal communication, 2002

Handedness

Biot: quoted in R. Dubos, *Pasteur and Modern Science*, New York: Anchor, 1960

Noyori: personal communication, 2002

Pasteur: quoted in M. Gardner, *The Ambidextrous Universe*, New York: Basic Books, 1964

Feynman: quoted in N. Calder, *The Key to the Universe*, London: BBC Publications, 1977

Inoue: Project description, Inoue Photochirogenesis Project, ERATO (Exploratory Research for Advanced Technology, Japan Science and Technology Corporation), 2001

Kuroda: Project description, Kuroda Chiromorphology Project, ERATO (Exploratory Research for Advanced Technology, Japan Science and Technology Corporation), 2001

Higgs bosons

Harvard host: Sidney Coleman, quoted by P. Higgs in L. Hoddeson *et al.*, eds., *The Rise of the Standard Model*, Cambridge: Cambridge University Press, 1996

Higgs 1: *ibid.*

Higgs 2: quoted by Alison Daniels in University of Edinburgh, *Edit*, issue 7, Winter 1994–95

Miller: quoted in *Physics World*, vol. 6, no. 9, pp. 26–8, 1993

Lederman: L. Lederman, *The God Particle*, Boston: Houghton Mifflin, 1993

Rubbia: C. Rubbia in N. Calder, ed., *Scientific Europe*, Maastricht: Nature and Technology, 1990

Press release: CERN, Geneva, 16 December 1994

Womersley: Stanford Linear Accelerator Center, *SLAC Beam Line*, vol. 31, no. 1, pp. 13–20, 2001

Higgs 3: quoted by Alison Daniels in University of Edinburgh, *Edit*, issue 7, Winter 1994–95

High-speed travel

De Broglie: quoted by Frank Pellegrini, *Time*.com, article on Einstein, 2000

Kaye: 'The Square of the Hypotenuse', lyrics by Johnny Mercer and music by Saul Chaplin, in *Merry Andrew*, MGM, 1958

Einstein: remark (1911) quoted in A. Kopff, *The Mathematical Theory of Relativity*, London: Methuen, 1923

Keating: in 'Time Travel', PBS/WGBH/NOVA TV, Peter Tyson, 1999

Hafele and Keating: J.C. Hafele and R.E. Keating, *Science*, vol. 177, pp. 166–7, 1972

Brecher: personal communication, 2002

Hopeful monsters

Green: H. Green, 'In Memoriam—Barbara McClintock', Nobel Foundation, Stockholm, 1999

Kakutani: personal communication, 2002

Darwin on Lamarck: in historical sketch added to *The Origin of Species*, 3rd edition, London: Murray, 1871

Waddington 1: C.H. Waddington, *Evolution*, vol. 7, pp. 118–26, 1953

Waddington 2: C.H. Waddington, *The Strategy of the Genes*, London: Allen & Unwin, 1957

Jablonka and Lamb: E. Jablonka and M.J. Lamb, *Epigenetic Inheritance and Evolution*, Oxford: Oxford University Press, paperback edition, 1999

Lindquist: quoted in press release, University of Chicago Hospitals and Health System, 26 November 1998

British critics: L. Partridge and N.H. Barton, *Nature*, vol. 407, pp. 457–8, 2000

Sangster: personal communication, 2002

Hotspots

Schmincke: H.U. Schmincke in D.G. Smith, ed., *The Cambridge Encyclopaedia of Earth Sciences*, Cambridge: Cambridge University Press, 1983

Foulger 1: talk at Royal Astronomical Society, London, 10 May 2002

Romanowicz and Gung: B. Romanowicz and Y. Gung, *Science*, vol. 296, pp. 513–16, 2002

Foulger 2: personal communication, 2002

Human ecology

Rivera: conversation in La Paz, 1989

Kolata: in 'Living on Earth', National Public Radio (USA), 28 August 1992

Cox and Elmqvist: P.A. Cox and T. Elmqvist, *Ambio*, vol. 26, no. 2, pp. 84–9, 1997

Fa: quoted in press release, UK Natural Environment Research Council, 10 April 2002

Malthus: T. Malthus, *An Essay on the Principle of Population*, London: Johnson, 1798 (at first published anonymously)

Eckholm: E. Eckholm, *Down to Earth*, London: Pluto Press, 1982

Calder: in R. Calder, ed., *The Future of a Troubled World*, London: Heinemann, 1983

Human genome

Kent: quoted by Nicholas Wade, *New York Times*, 13 February 2001

Venter 1: PBS Newshour with Jim Lehrer, 6 April 2000 (interviewer Suzan Dentzer)

Clinton and Blair: press conference, White House, 26 June 2000 (Blair on satellite link)

Dexter: quoted in press release, Wellcome Trust, 26 June 2000

SOURCES OF QUOTES

Lander: Millennium Evening at the White House, 14 October 1999, quoted in *Science,* vol. 291, p. 1196, 2001

Celera team: J.C. Venter *et al., Science,* vol. 291, pp. 1304–51, 2001

Collins: quoted by Jonathan Amos, BBC science website, 18 February 2001

Venter 2: press conference, 18th International Congress of Biochemistry and Molecular Biology, Birmingham, UK, 16 July 2000

Stefansson: personal communication, 2002

Human origins

Pääbo 1: quoted by Steven Dickman, *Current Biology,* vol. 8, pp. R329–30, 1998

Leakey: in 'The Life Game', BBC-TV, Malone/Calder, 1973

Cheboi: in 'The First Human?', JWM Productions/Channel 4 TV, Ann Carroll/Noddy Samula, 19 November 2001

Pickford: quoted on website of Cité des Sciences et de l'Industrie, La Villette, 2001

Brunet: quoted in *Le Monde* (Paris), 11 July 2002

Wood: B. Wood, *Nature,* vol. 418, pp. 133–5, 2002

Reynolds: quoted by Natalie Angier, *New York Times,* 13 February 2001

Hong-Seog: quoted by Dennis Normile, AAAS Science News Service, 19 March 2001

Pääbo 2: *Science,* vol. 291, pp. 1219–20, 2001

Ice-rafting events

Heinrich 1: personal communication, 2002

Bond: quoted in *Columbia University Record,* 24 February 1995

Van Geel: personal communication, 1997

Bond and his colleagues: G. Bond *et al., Science,* vol. 278, pp. 1257–66, 1997

Bond's team: G. Bond *et al., Science,* vol. 294, pp. 2130–6, 2001

Heinrich 2: personal communication, 2002

Immortality

Kiel team: W. Klapper *et al., FEBS Letters,* vol. 439, pp. 143–6, 1998

Greider: C.W. Greider, *Current Biology,* vol. 8, pp. R178–81, 1998

Harley: C.B. Harley, *Mutation Research,* vol. 256, pp. 271–82, 1991

Hayflick 1: L. Hayflick, *Experimental Gerontology,* vol. 33, pp. 639–53, 1998

Kirkwood and colleague: T.B.L. Kirkwood and S.N. Austad, *Nature,* vol. 408, pp. 233–8, 2000

Shakespeare: *Julius Caesar,* Act II, scene 2

Hayflick 2: L. Hayflick, *Nature,* vol. 408, pp. 267–9, 2000

Immune System

Goodnow 1: Goodnow Laboratory website, 16 May 2001

Metchnikoff: Nobel Lecture, Stockholm, 11 December 1908

Montagnier: in N. Calder, ed., *Scientific Europe*, Maastricht: Nature & Technology, 1990

Burnet: F.M. Burnet, *Changing Patterns*, Melbourne: Heinemann, 1968

Dausset: Nobel Lecture, Stockholm, 8 December 1980

Goodnow 2: personal communication, 2002

Hacohen: personal communication, 2002

Cogoli: personal communication, 2002

Impacts

Shoemaker: in 'Crater of Death', BBC Horizon/Martin Belderson, 11 September 1997

Chicarro and Zender: in *Solar System News*, European Space Agency, September 1998

Genesis: Chapter 19, verses 24 and 25

Koeberl 1: personal communication, 2002

Koeberl 2: personal communication, 2001

Languages

Labov 1: e-mail for student enquirers, 'How I got into linguistics, and what I got out of it', 1997

Labov 2: in 'The Human Conspiracy', BBC-TV, Nisbett/Calder, 1975

Labov 3: personal communication, 2002

Weinreich: the origin of the remark is variously attributed to Uriel Weinreich or to his father Max, a Yiddish scholar

Cavalli-Sforza: L.L. Cavalli-Sforza, Balzan Prize paper, Bern, 16 November 1999

Comrie: personal communication, 2002

Labov 4: e-mail for student enquirers, 'How I got into linguistics, and what I got out of it', 1997

Life's origin

Gilbert and Sullivan: *The Mikado* in I. Bradley, ed., *The Complete Annotated Gilbert and Sullivan*, Oxford: Oxford University Press, 2001

Lugowski: W. Lugowski, *Filozoficzne podstawy protobiologii*, Warsaw: IfiS-PAN, 1995

Darwin 1: C. Darwin, *The Origin of Species*, London: Murray, 1859

Darwin 2: letter to Joseph Hooker, 1871, in F. Darwin, ed., *The Life and Letters of Charles Darwin*, vol. 3, London: Murray, 1888

Cech: T.R. Cech, *Science*, vol. 289, pp. 878–9, 2000

Lancet and colleagues: D. Segré et al., *Origins of Life and Evolution of the Biosphere*, vol. 31, pp. 119–45, 2001

Wilde: personal communication, 2002

Raulin: personal communication, 2001

Ehrenfreund: personal communication, 2002

Kissel: personal communication, 2001

SOURCES OF QUOTES

Mammals

Barsbold: personal communication, 2002

Kielan-Jaworowska: personal communication, 2002

O'Brien: quoted by Elizabeth Pennisi in *Science*, vol. 294, pp. 2266–8, 2001

Raup: D.M. Raup, *Extinction: Bad Genes or Bad Luck?*, New York: Norton, 1991

Memory

Hebb 1: in 'The Mind of Man', BBC-TV, Daly / Calder, 1970

Hebb 2: D.O. Hebb, *Organization of Behavior*, New York: Wiley, 1949

Grant: personal communication, 2000

HM: quoted by Brenda Milner, personal communication, 1970

Kandel: Autobiography, news release, Nobel Foundation, Stockholm, 2000

Mansuy: personal communication, 2002

Microwave background

Penzias: in 'The Violent Universe', BBC-TV, Daly / Calder, 1968

Dicke: D.T. Wilkinson, personal communication, 1967

Mather, Smoot and Hawking: quoted in Gordon Fraser *et al.*, *The Search for Infinity*, London: Mitchell Beazley, 1994

De Bernadis: quoted in press release, US National Science Foundation, 26 April 2000

Carlstrom: quoted in press release, University of Chicago, 29 April 2001

Kovac: quoted in press release, University of Chicago, 19 September 2002

Puget: personal communication, 2001

Minerals in space

Shakespeare: *Othello*, Act V, scene 2

Waelkens: quoted in press release, European Space Agency, 23 October 1998

Crovisier: quoted in press release, European Space Agency, 28 March 1997

Waters: personal communication, 2001

Sorby: H.C. Corby, *Nature*, vol. 15, p. 495, 1877

Hanlon: personal communication, 2001

Kemper: quoted in science website news item, European Space Agency, 17 January 2002

Anders: quoted in N. Calder, *Giotto to the Comets*, London: Presswork, 1992

Molecular partners

Huc and Lehn: I. Huc and J.-M. Lehn, *Proceedings of the National Academy of Sciences* (USA), vol. 94, pp. 2106–10, 1997

Gimzewski: personal communication, 2002

Sumper: personal communication, 2002

Lehn: J.-M. Lehn, *Science*, vol. 295, pp. 2400–3, 2002 and *Proceedings of the National Academy of Sciences* (USA), vol. 99, pp. 4763–8, 2002

Molecules evolving

Kimura 1: in 'The Life Game', BBC-TV, Malone/Calder, 1973

Kimura 2: M. Kimura, *The Neutral Theory of Molecular Evolution*, Cambridge: Cambridge University Press, 1983

Gould: S.J. Gould in *The New York Review of Books*, 12 June 1997

Reporter: Nigel Calder (1973), quoted in Kimura 2, *loc. cit.*

Ohno: at International Symposium on Network and Evolution of Molecular Information, Tokyo, 20–22 April 1996

Mewes and colleagues: H.W. Mewes *et al.*, *Nature*, Yeast Genome Supplement, 29 May 1997

Ohta 1: T. Ohta, *Theoretical Population Biology*, vol. 23, pp. 216–40, 1984

Ohta 2: T. Ohta, *Annual Reviews of Ecology and Systematics*, vol. 23, pp. 263–86, 1992

Molecules in space

Thaddeus: quoted in *Harvard News*, 11 July 1996

Léger: personal communication, 2001

Cernicharo: quoted in information note, European Space Agency, 29 April 1997

Neufeld 1: quoted in press release, Johns Hopkins University, 10 April 1998

Feuchtgruber: quoted in information note, European Space Agency, 29 April 1997

Neufeld 2: quoted by R.A. Kerr in *Science*, vol. 293, p. 407, 2001

Imai: quoted in press release, Jodrell Bank Observatory, 19 June 2002

Van Dishoeck: personal communication, 2002

Neutrino oscillations

Gold miner and Davis: in 'The Violent Universe', BBC-TV, Daly/Calder, 1969

Gold miner on cloudiness: quoted in N. Calder, *Violent Universe*, London: BBC Publications, 1969

Updike: John Updike, 'Cosmic Gall', in *Telephone Poles and other Poems*, New York: Knopf, 1963

Kirsten: personal communication, 1993

McDonald: quoted in press release, Sudbury Neutrino Observatory, 20 April 2002

Weinheimer: personal communication, 2001

Totsuka: in press release, Super-Kamiokande, 1998

Neutron stars

Bell Burnell: S.J. Bell Burnell, *Annals of the New York Academy of Science*, vol. 302, pp. 685–9, 1977

Galloway: quoted in press release, Massachusetts Institute of Technology, 23 May 2002

Ibrahim: quoted in press release, NASA Goddard, 4 November 2002

Caraveo: personal communication, 2002

Lorimer: personal communication, 2002

SOURCES OF QUOTES

Nuclear weapons

Wheeler: J.A. Wheeler with Kenneth Ford, *Geons, Black Holes, and Quantum Foam*, New York: Norton, 1998

Pincher: Chapman Pincher, letter in *Daily Telegraph* (London), 17 June 2002

Sakharov: A. Sakharov, *Memoirs*, New York: Knopf, 1990

Russell–Einstein Manifesto: text in J. Rotblat, *Scientists in the Quest for Peace*, Cambridge, Mass.: MIT Press, 1972

Rotblat: J. Rotblat, 'Science and Humanity in the Twenty-First Century', article for Nobel Foundation, Stockholm, 1999

Gusterson: quoted by Claudia Dreifus, *New York Times*, 21 May 2002

Erickson: quoted in N. Calder, *Nuclear Nightmares*, London: BBC Publications, 1979

Soviet physicist: Sergei Kapitza, personal communication, 1988

Teller: in Edward Teller with Judith L. Shoolery, *Memoirs*, Cambridge, Mass.: Perseus Publishing, 2001

Ocean currents

Nantucket skipper to Franklin: quoted in J.E. Pillsbury, *The Gulf Stream*, Washington DC: Government Printing Office, 1891

Rogachev: quoted in news release, Informnauka, Russia, 19 February 2002

Munk: lecture at International Association of Meteorology and Atmospheric Sciences/ International Association for the Physical Sciences of the Oceans Joint Assembly, Melbourne, July 1997

Broecker: US Global Change Research Program seminar, Washington DC, 24 January 1996

Gould: personal communication, 2002

Balmino: personal communication, 2001

Wunsch: C. Wunsch, *Nature*, vol. 405, pp. 743–4, 2000

Particle families

Yukawa: quoted in G. Fraser, E. Lillestøl and I. Sellevåg, *The Search for Infinity*, London: Mitchell Beazley, 1994

Fermi: remark to Leon Lederman; Lederman personal communication, 1976

Gell-Mann: in 'The Key to the Universe', BBC-TV, Nisbett/Calder, 1977

Politzer: in *ibid.*

Fritzch: H. Fritzch, in *Quarks: Urstoff unserer Welt*, Munich: R. Piper, 1981; trans. (with M. Roloff) as *Quarks: The Stuff of Matter*, New York: Basic Books, 1983

Glashow: personal communication, 1976

Richter: in B. Maglich, ed., *Adventures in Experimental Physics, Epsilon Volume*, Princeton, N.J.: World Science Education, 1976

Llewellyn Smith: C. Llewellyn Smith, *CERN Courier*, vol. 38, no. 8, pp. 33–4, 1998

Feynman: personal communication, 1976

SOURCES OF QUOTES

Photosynthesis

Boltzmann: 'Der zweite Hauptsatz der mechanischen Warmetheorie' (1886), cited by R. Huber in N. Calder, ed., *Scientific Europe*, Maastricht: Nature & Technology, 1990

Halley: cited by A. Armitage in *Edmond Halley*, London: Nelson, 1966

Huber: in N. Calder, ed., *Scientific Europe*, Maastricht: Nature & Technology, 1990

Barber: personal communication, 2002

Saenger: personal communication, 2002

Ciamician: G. Ciamician, *Science*, vol. 36, p. 385, 1912

Plant diseases

Wilde: 'The Famine Year', first published as 'The Stricken Land', in *The Nation*, 23 January 1847, quoted in P.J. Kavanagh, *Voices in Ireland*, London: Murray, 1994

Red Queen: in Lewis Carroll, *Through the Looking-Glass* (1871); reprinted in R.L. Green, ed., *Alice's Adventures in Wonderland* and *Through the Looking-Glass*, Oxford: Oxford Paperbacks, 1998

Dawkins: R. Dawkins, *The Blind Watchmaker*, Harlow: Longman, 1986

Bergelson: quoted in *Quarks and Bits*, 12 August 1999

Plasma crystals

Blake: 'The Chimney-Sweeper', in *Songs of Innocence and Experience*, 1794

Morfill: personal communication, 2001

Bingham: personal communication, 2000

Tsytovich: personal communication, 2000

Plate motions

Vine 1: F.J. Vine and D.H. Matthews, *Nature*, vol. 199, pp. 947–9, 1963

Vine 2: quoted in R. Muir Wood, *The Dark Side of the Earth*, London: Allen & Unwin, 1985

Anderson: D.L. Anderson, *Proceedings of the American Philosophical Society*, vol. 146, pp. 56–76, 2002

Bouguer: quoted by A. Holmes, *Principles of Physical Geology*, London: Nelson, 1965

Rummel: personal communication, 2002

Predators

Bondi: personal communication, 1980

Riveros: personal communication, 2002

Terborgh: quoted by Sherry Devlin in *The Missoulian*, 28 April 1999

Soulé and Noss: in *Wild Earth*, vol. 3, no. 8, Fall 1998

Prehistoric genes

Cavalli-Sforza: in 'The Life Game', BBC-TV, Malone/Calder, 1973

Piazza: in N. Calder, ed., *Scientific Europe*, Maastricht: Nature & Technology, 1990

SOURCES OF QUOTES

Sykes: B. Sykes, *The Seven Daughters of Eve*, London: Bantam, 2001

Father-only team: O. Semino *et al.*, *Science*, vol. 290, pp. 1155–9, 2000

Renfrew: C. Renfrew, *Proceedings of the National Academy of Sciences* (USA), vol. 98, pp. 4830–2, 2001

Primate behaviour

Oakley: K.P. Oakley, *Man the Tool-Maker*, 5th edition, London: British Museum (Natural History), 1963

Zuckerman: S. Zuckerman, *The Realist*, vol. 1, pp. 72–88, 1929, quoted in S. Zuckerman, *From Apes to Warlords*, London: Hamish Hamilton, 1978

Itani: quoted by F. de Waal, *New Scientist*, pp. 46–9, 13 December 2001

F. de Waal: *ibid.*

Goodall: J. van Lawick-Goodall, *In the Shadow of Man*, London: Collins, 1971

Whiten: A. Whiten *et al.*, *Nature*, vol. 399, pp. 682–5, 1999

Matsuzawa: 'Essay on Evolutionary Neighbors', Ai's Home Page, Primate Research Institute, Kyoto, 1998 <http://www.pri.kyoto-u.ac.jp/ai/index-E.htm>

Prions

Gajdusek: Nobel Lecture, Stockholm, 13 December 1976

Bee: quoted by Chris Baker, *Brighton Evening Argus*, 26 October 2000

Prusiner 1: Autobiography, news release, Nobel Foundation, Stockholm, 1997

Prusiner 2: personal communication, 2000

Bucciantini and colleagues: M. Bucciantini *et al.*, *Nature*, vol. 416, pp. 507–11, 2002

Lindquist: quoted by David Cameron, *Technology Review*, 8 February 2002

Protein-making

Narrator: Frank Bough in 'The Life Game', BBC-TV, Malone/Calder, 1973

De Duve: C. de Duve, *A Guided Tour of the Living Cell*, New York: Scientific American Books, 1984

Yonath: quoted by Elizabeth Pennisi, *Science*, vol. 285, pp. 2048–51, 1999

Ramakrishnan: quoted by Kristin Leutwyler, *Scientific American Explore*, 7 May 2001

Noller: quoted by Kristin Leutwyler, *Scientific American Explore*, 27 November 1999

Protein shapes

Schneider: personal communication, 2000

Hajdu 1: personal communication, 2002

Chu: quoted by Steve Bunk, *The Scientist*, 26 October 1998

Fersht: in N. Calder, ed., *Scientific Europe*, Maastricht: Nature & Technology, 1990

Hajdu 2: TESLA Colloquium, Hamburg, 24 March 2001

Proteomes

Bairoch: personal communication, 2002

Sydney microbiologists: V.C. Wasinger *et al.*, *Electrophoresis*, vol. 16, pp. 1090–4, 1995

Cobon: Australian Proteome Analysis Facility, Annual Report, 2000

Superti-Furga: quoted in press release, European Molecular Biology Laboratory, 9 January 2002

Human Proteomics Initiative: C. O'Donovan *et al.*, *Trends in Biotechnology*, vol. 19, pp. 178–181, 2001

Quantum tangles

Swedish physicist: C.W. Oseen, Nobel presentation speech, Stockholm, 1929

De Broglie 1: interview 1963, quoted by J.J. O'Connor and E.F. Robertson, St Andrews University website for history of mathematics, <http://www-groups.dcs.st-andrews.ac.uk/history/Mathematicians/Broglie.html>, May 2001

Heisenberg: Nobel Lecture, Stockholm, 11 December 1933

Wells: quoted in N. Calder, *The Key to the Universe*, London: BBC Publications, 1977

Rabi: quoted by Gerald Edelman, *Bright Air, Brilliant Fire: On the Matter of the Mind*, New York: Penguin, 1992

Feynman: R.P. Feynman, *QED: The Strange Theory of Light and Matter*, Princeton, N.J.: Princeton University Press, 1985

De Broglie 2: *Étude critique des bases de l'interprétation actuelle de la mécanique ondulatoire*, Paris: Gauthier-Villars, 1963

Einstein and Bohr, quoted in N. Calder, *Einstein's Universe*, London: BBC Publications, 1979

Einstein: letter to Max Born, 1947, in M. Born and A. Einstein, *The Born–Einstein Letters*, London: Macmillan, 1971

Einstein, Podolsky and Rosen: A. Einstein *et al.*, *Physical Review*, vol. 41, p. 777, 1935

Gisin: quoted by Malcolm W. Browne, *New York Times*, 22 July 1997

Ekert: quoted by Ivan Semeniuk, *New Scientist*, 9 March 2002, pp. 27–30

Quark soup

Jacob: personal communication, 2002

Kirk: Brookhaven National Laboratory, news release, 18 July 2001

Smallpox

Macaulay: T.B. Macaulay, *The History of England from the Accession of James II*, Philadelphia: Claxton, Remsen & Haffelfinger, 1880

N. Barquet and P. Domingo: *Annals of Internal Medicine*, vol. 127, pp. 635–42, 1997

Amherst: facsimile of letter of 16 July 1763 on NativeWeb, <http://www.nativeweb.org/>

Folk song: cited in I. and P. Opie, *The Oxford Dictionary of Nursery Rhymes*, Oxford: Oxford University Press, 1951

SOURCES OF QUOTES

Jenner: E. Jenner, *Inquiry into the Cause and Effects of the Variola Vaccinae*, 1798, anthologized in D.D. Runes, *A Treasury of World Science*, New York: Philosophical Press, 1962

Royal Society on Jenner: quoted by N. Barquet and P. Domingo, *Annals of Internal Medicine*, vol. 127, pp. 635–42, 1997

Alibek 1: in Boston University, *Perspective*, vol. 9, no. 1, 1998

Alibek 2: quoted by Amy Argetsinger, *Washington Post*, 14 February 2002

Solar wind

Renfrew: C. Renfrew, *Before Civilization*, London: Cape, 1973

Friend of Forbush: J.A. Van Allen, *Biographical Memoir of S.E. Forbush*, Washington DC: National Academy of Sciences, 1984

Simpson: personal communication, 1994

Pundits to Parker: E.N. Parker, personal communication, 2000

Dante: *Inferno*, canto XXVI, *Non vogliate negare l'esperienza di retro al Sol, del mondo senza gente*, trans. L. Calder

Marsden: quoted in N. Calder, *Beyond this World*, Noordwijk: European Space Agency BR-112, 1995

Balogh: personal communication, 1994

Bertaux: quoted in N. Calder, compiler, *Success Story*, Noordwijk: European Space Agency BR-147, 1999

Frisch: P.C. Frisch, *American Scientist*, vol. 88, pp. 52–9, 2000

Space weather

Van Eyken: personal communication, 2002

Brekke: quoted in press release, International Astronomical Union, 3 August 2000

Cornilleau-Wehrlin: personal communication, 2001

Tsuneta: personal communication, 2002

Mason: personal communication, 2001

Title: quoted in N. Calder, compiler, *Success Story*, Noordwijk: European Space Agency BR-147, 1999

Chairman: J. Gurman at International Astronomical Union assembly, Manchester, August 2000

Marsch: personal communication, 2001

Sparticles

Jacob 1: in A. Wilson, ed., *Fundamental Physics in Space*, Noordwijk: European Space Agency SP-420, 1997

Pati: J.C. Pati in J. Ellis *et al.*, eds., *The Abdus Salam Memorial Meeting*, Singapore: World Scientific, 1999

Seiberg: N. Seiberg in *ibid*.

Jacob 2: personal communication, 2002

Speech

Henshilwood: personal communication, 2002

Golding: William Golding, *The Inheritors*, London: Faber, 1955

Pinker: S. Pinker, *The Language Instinct*, New York: Morrow, 1994

Lenneberg, in J.A. Fodor and J.J. Katz, eds., *The Structure of Language: Readings in the Philosophy of Language*, Englewood Cliffs, N.J.: Prentice-Hall, 1964, pp. 579–603

Vargha-Khadem: personal communication, 2002

Monaco and colleagues: C.S.L. Lai *et al.*, *Nature*, vol. 413, pp. 519–23, 2001

Leipzig–Oxford team: W. Enard *et al.*, *Nature*, vol. 418, pp. 869–72, 2002

Enard: quoted by Helen Briggs, BBC News Online, 14 August 2002

Starbursts

Borges: 'The Circular Ruins', trans. J.E. Irby, in J.L. Borges, *Labyrinths*, New York: New Directions, 1964

Genzel: quoted in N. Calder, compiler, *Success Story*, Noordwijk: European Space Agency BR-147, 1999

Cesarsky: quoted in press release, European Space Agency, 7 April 1998

Cimatti: personal communication, 2001

Rowan-Robinson: personal communication, 2001

Stars

Huckleberry Finn: in Mark Twain, *Adventures of Huckleberry Finn*, E. Elliott, ed., Oxford: Oxford Paperbacks, 1999

Herschel: quoted in D. Malin and P. Murdin, *Colours of the Stars*, Cambridge: Cambridge University Press, 1984

Van Leeuwen: quoted in N. Calder, compiler, *Success Story*, Noordwijk: European Space Agency BR-147, 1999

Lindegren: personal communication, 1997

Christensen-Dalsgaard: personal communication, 2001

Shakespeare: Lorenzo, in *The Merchant of Venice*, Act V, scene 1

Favata: personal communication, 2002

Feast: quoted in press release, European Space Agency, 14 February 1997

Baldwin: adapted from handout, Cavendish Laboratory, Cambridge, 1999

Paresce: personal communication, 2002

Stem cells

Stevens: quoted by Ricki Lewis, *The Scientist*, vol. 14, p. 19, 2000

Thomson and colleagues: J.A. Thomson *et al.*, *Science*, vol. 282, pp. 1145–7, 1998

Solter: D. Solter, *Croatian Medical Journal*, vol. 40, no. 3, 1999

Verfaillie and team: Y. Jiang *et al.*, *Nature*, vol. 418, pp. 41–9, 2002

SOURCES OF QUOTES

Sun's interior

Leighton: California Institute of Technology Oral History Project, *Interviews with Robert B. Leighton* by Heidi Aspaturian, Caltech Archives, 1995

Gough 1: Lecture at US National Academy of Sciences, 1991

Eddington: discourse at British Association for the Advancement of Science, Oxford, August 1926

Scherrer: quoted in information note, European Space Agency, 27 April 2001

Kosovichev: quoted in information note, European Space Agency, 6 November 2001

Howe: quoted in press release, NASA, 30 March 2000

Gough 2: seminar at European Space Agency, Space Science Department, Noordwijk, 17 May 1999

Charvátová: I. Charvátová, *Bulletin of the Astronomical Institute of Czechoslovakia*, vol. 41, pp. 200–4, 1990

Superatoms, superfluids and superconductors

Bose: quoted by J.J. O'Connor and E.F. Robertson, St Andrews University website for history of mathematics <http://www-groups.dcs.st-andrews.ac.uk/history/Mathematicians/Bose.html> December 1996

Ketterle: W. Ketterle, *Physics Today*, pp. 30–5, December 1999

Hau: quoted by William J. Cromie, *Harvard Gazette*, 18 February 1999

Bloch: personal communication, 2002

Superstrings

Copland: quoted in J.R. Pierce, *The Science of Musical Sound*, New York: Scientific American Books, 1983

Green: M. Green, *Scientific American*, pp. 44–56, September 1986

Schwarz: interview by Patricia Schwarz, undated, on The Official String Theory Web Site <http://superstringtheory.com>

Carroll: Lewis Carroll, *Through the Looking-Glass* (1871) reprinted in R.L. Green, ed., *Alice's Adventures in Wonderland* and *Through the Looking-Glass*, Oxford: Oxford Paperbacks, 1998

Witten 1: quoted by M.J. Duff in J. Ellis *et al.*, eds., *The Abdus Salam Memorial Meeting*, Singapore: World Scientific, 1999

Witten 2: quoted by James Glanz, *New York Times*, 13 March 2001

Keats: 'Ode on a Grecian Urn', in H. Gardner, ed., *The New Oxford Book of English Verse*, Oxford: Clarendon Press, 1972

Time machines

Thorne: in 'Time Travel', PBS/WGBH/NOVA TV, Peter Tyson, 1999

Novikov: personal communication, 1999

Hadley: M.J. Hadley, *Classical and Quantum Gravity*, vol. 19, pp. 4565–71, 2002

Transgenic crops

Van Montagu: M. Van Montagu in N. Calder, ed., *Scientific Europe*, Maastricht: Nature & Technology, 1990

Arber: W. Arber in *ibid*.

Bergelson and colleagues: J. Bergelson *et al.*, *Nature*, vol. 395, p. 25, 1998

Editorial: *Nature Biotechnology*, vol. 20, p. 527, 2002

Baltimore: quoted by Marcia Barringa, *Science*, vol. 287, pp. 1584–5, 2000

Asscher: quoted by Maxine Frith and Eileen Murphy, PA News, 17 May 1999

Verfaillie: quoted by Virginia Baldwin Gilbert, *St Louis Post-Dispatch*, 12 May 2002

Borlaug: Lecture, Norwegian Nobel Institute, Oslo, 8 September 2000

Tree of life

Margulis and Sagan: L. Margulis and D. Sagan, *Microcosmos*, New York: Summit Books, 1986

Darwin: C. Darwin, *The Origin of Species*, London: Murray, 1859

Dickerson: R.E. Dickerson, *Scientific American*, April 1972

Woese: C. Woese, *Proceedings of the National Academy of Sciences (USA)*, vol. 95, pp. 6854–9, 1998

Doolittle: W.F. Doolittle, *Science*, vol. 284, p. 2124, 1999

Kurland: C.G. Kurland, *EMBO Reports*, vol. 1, pp. 92–5, 2000

Doolittle and his colleagues: J.O. Andersson *et al.*, *Science*, vol. 292, pp. 1848–50, 2001

Universe

Morrison: in 'The Violent Universe', BBC-TV, Daly / Calder, 1969

Mandelbrot: B.B. Mandelbrot, *The Fractal Geometry of Nature*, New York: Freeman, 1982

Priester: personal communication, 2002

Peebles: P.J.E. Peebles, *Scientific American* feature article on sciam.com 18 January 2001

Dyson: F. Dyson, *Scientific American*, p. 51, September 1971

Carter: B. Carter in M.S. Longair, ed., *Confrontation of Cosmological Theories with Observational Data*, Dordrecht: Reidel, 1974

Magueijo: personal communication, 2002

Rees: Astronomer Royal's lecture to Royal Society of Medicine and Royal Society of Arts, London, 29 May 2002

Volcanic explosions

Calder: Simon Calder, *Independent* (London), 31 January 1999

Euripides: in *The Hippolytus*, 428 BC, translated in Gilbert Murray, *Euripides: Collected Plays*, London: Allen & Unwin, 1954

Pfeiffer: at workshop of the European Seismological Commission, Santorini, 21–26 September 1999

Hammer: personal communication, 2002

Miller: personal communication, 2002

NAME INDEX

A

Aaby, Bent 113
Adams, Douglas 37
Ai (chimpanzee) 570
Ai Guoxiang, 308
Airy, George 553
Albrecht, Andreas 40, 696
Alibek, Ken 610–11
Alpher, Ralph 37
al-Razi 429
Altman, Joseph 94
Alvarez, Luis and Walter 278
Amherst, Jeffrey 609–11
Anders, Edward 456, 482
Anderson, Carl 16
Anderson, Don 552–3
Anderson, Philip 206, 368
Arber, Werner 677
Arkani-Hamed, Nima 356
Arrhenius, Svante 109, 145–6,
    212, 452
Artymovicz, Pawel 284
Asaro, Frank 278
Aschenbach, Bernd 250–1
Aspect, Alain 600–1
Asquith, Anthony 445
Asscher, William 680
Attardi, Domenica 92
Auger, Pierre 171–2
Auroy, Philippe 207
Avery, Oswald 317–8
Axelrod, Robert 10–12
Ayuma (chimpanzee) 570

B

Baade, Walter 504
Bacchetti, Silvia 426
Bach, Johann Sebastian 37
Baez, John 355
Baillie, Mike 442–3
Bairoch, Amos 588–9, 591,
    593
Bakker, Robert 279
Baldwin, John 646
Ballard, Robert 292
Balmino, Georges 519, 555
Balogh, André 617

Balsiger, Hans 160
Baltimore, David 320, 329
Banfield, Jillian 295
Barber, James 532, 534
Bardeen, John 662
Barquet, Nicolau 609
Barrow, Isaac 200
Barsbold, Rinchen 459
Bednorz, Georg 662
Bee, David 573–4
Beer, Juerg 421
Behrenfeld, Michael 67
Bell Burnell, Jocelyn 503
Bell, Graham 50–1, 236
Bell, John 600
Benner, Steven 5, 340–1
Bennett, Charles 602
Benzer, Seymour 57
Berg, Paul 322, 676–7
Bergelson, Joy 153, 538–9, 678
Berger, André 143
Berger, Hans 87
Bernabei, Rita 188
Bernal, Desmond 30, 35
Bernard, Claude 199
Berners-Lee, Tim 70
Bertani, Elizabeth 335
Bertaux, Jean-Loup 618
Berthold, Peter 59
Bethe, Hans 37, 653
Bevan, Michael 25, 331
Bhabha, Homi 522
Biermann, Ludwig 614, 616
Bignami, Giovanni 506
Bingham, Robert 546
Biot, Jean-Baptiste 360
Birkeland, Kristian 621
Bjerknes, Jacob 253–4, 256
Bjorken, James 525
Blackburn, Elizabeth 425
Blair, Tony 404
Blake, William 246, 542
Blázquez, Miguel 302–4
Blobel, Günter 123
Bloch, Immanuel 665
Bogolyubov, Nikolai 342, 664
Bohm, David 598, 600

Bohr, Niels 266, 509–10,
    596–9, 601
Boiteux, Marcel 133
Bolin, Bert 146, 148
Bolton, John 72
Boltzmann, Ludwig 529–30
Bond, Alan 32
Bond, Gerard 113, 419–22
Bondi, Hermann 348, 556
Bonner, William 364
Borges, Jorge Luis 640
Borlaug, Norman 129, 131,
    541, 680
Bosch, Carl 129
Bose, Satyen 367, 660–1, 663
Bouguer, Pierre 553
Bouquet, Henry 609
Boveri, Theodor 258, 261
Boynton, William 439
Brack, André 288
Bradbury, Ray 31
Bragg, Lawrence 317
Brassard, Giles 602
Braun, Amin 675
Braun, Douglas 655
Braun-Blanquet, J. 46
Brecher, Kenneth 379
Brekke, Paal 622
Brenner, Sydney 261, 325
Bretherton, Francis 232
Britten, Roy 261–2
Broca, Paul 80–1
Brochard-Wyart, Françoise 207
Broecker, Wallace 516
Brout, Robert 368
Brückner, Eduard 141
Bruner, Jerome 343–4
Brunet, Michel 413–4
Brunhes, Bernard 549
Bruno, Giordano 285
Bryson, Reid 145
Bucciantini, Monica 576
Buchner, Eduard and Hans 4
Bullard, Edward 549
Burbidge, Margaret and
    Geoffrey 246
Burnet, Macfarlane 433

NAME INDEX

Butler, Paul 286
Byars, Carlos 439

C

Caesar, Julius 427
Cajal, Santiago Ramón y
    91–2, 94
Calder, Ritchie 400
Calder, Simon 699
Calvin, Melvin 530
Camargo-Zanoguera,
    Antonio 439
Cameron, Alistair 217
Campbell, John 272–3, 276
Caraveo, Patrizia 506–7
Carlstrom, John 478
Carpenter, Ray 569
Carrel, Alexis 424
Carrington, Richard 625
Carroll, Lewis 74, 152, 538, 690
Carson, Rachel 47
Carter, Brandon 696
Carusi, Andrea 161
Cash, Webster 79
Casimir, Hendrik 186
Cavalli-Sforza, Luca 448–9, 560–5
Cech, Thomas 453
Celsius, Anders 621
Cernicharo, José 495
Cesarsky, Catherine 641
Chadwick, James 504, 522
Charvátová, Ivanka 658
Cheboi, Kiptalam 412
Chicarro, Agustin 441
Chippindale, Adam 152
Chiti, Fabrizio 576
Chiu, Hong-yee 73
Chomsky, Noam 342–4, 346
Christensen-Dalsgaard,
    Jørgen 644–5
Chu, Steven 585
Churchill, Winston 204
Ciamician, Giacomo 530, 535
Cimatti, Andrea 642
Ciutláhuac (patient) 608
Clarke, Arthur C. 187
Claude, Albert 122–3, 125
Clinton, Bill 404
Cloud, Preston 334
Cobon, Gary 591

Cocconi, Giuseppe 289
Coen, Enrico 273
Cogoli, Augusto 437
Cohen, Stanley 93
Collins, Desmond 105
Collins, Francis 12, 406
Comrie, Bernard 450
Connell, Joseph 51
Conway Morris, Simon 104–6
Cook, James 560
Cooper, Leon 662
Copernicus, Nicolaus 492
Copland, Aaron 666
Corliss, John 291–2
Cornell, Eric 663–4
Cornilleau-Wehrlin, Nicole 624
Corrège, Thierry 255
Cox, Paul 397
Crichton, Michael 409–10
Crick, Francis 317–21, 404, 452
Cristofori, Bartolomeo 666
Crockett, Davy 558
Cronin, James 19–20
Croom, Scott 192
Crovisier, Jacques 480
Curl, Bob 97, 99
Currie, Alistair 119
Cuvier, Georges 279, 464
Cyrano de Bergerac 29

D

D'Esposito, Mark 84
Daedalus (pseudonym of David
    Jones) 98
Danjon, André-Louis 227
Dansgaard, Willi 418
Dante Alighieri 616, 691–2, 698
Danzmann, Karsten 349
Darwin, Charles 6, 28, 118, 198,
    266, 273, 332, 382
  on course of evolution 683
  on ecology 235
  on mechanisms of
    evolution 9, 269–71, 275–6,
    279, 282
  on origin of life 451–2
  on speech 343
Darwin, Erasmus 270
Dashzeveg, Demberlyin 459
Dausset, Jean 434

Davidson, Eric 261–2
Davis, Raymond 498–9
Dawkins, Richard 30, 274–5,
    538–9
de Bernardis, Paolo 476
de Broglie, Louis 373, 595–6,
    598–600, 663
de Broglie, Maurice 595
de Duve, Christian 122, 579
de Gennes, Pierre-Gilles 206–7
de Vries, Hessel 612
de Waal, Frans 569
De Waele, Jean-Pierre 13–14
Dean, Caroline 304–5
Déby, Idriss 413
Deisenhofer, Johann 532
Dekker, Cees 100
Denton, George 176–7
Descartes, René 57, 270, 342
D'Esposito, Mark 84
Deutsch, David 71–2
Devos, Katrien 330–1
DeVries, Art 295
Dewey, John 163
Dexter, Michael 404
Dicke, Robert 473
Dickerson, Richard 685–6
Dimopoulos, Savas 356
Dingle, Herbert 376
Dirac, Paul 16, 98, 597, 607
Djerrasi, Carl 55
Djimdoumalbaye, Ahounta 413
Dobson, David 224
Dobzhansky, Theodosius 488
Dolly (cloned sheep) 149, 155
Domingo, Pere 609
Doolittle, Ford 697–8
Drake, Frank 289–90
Drukier, Andrzej 188
Dubois, J.E. 227–8
Duvall, Thomas 655
Dvali, Gia 356
Dyson, Freeman 32, 676, 695

E

Eckholm, Erik 399
Eddington, Arthur 643, 653
Edman, Pehr 588, 591
Edwards, Anthony 560
Efstathiou, George 184

NAME INDEX

NAME INDEX

NAME INDEX

NAME INDEX

NAME INDEX

SUBJECT INDEX

Page numbers in bold refer to main entries. The numbers span the whole entry in each of these cases, even if the subject is not dealt with directly on every page.

SUBJECT INDEX

SUBJECT INDEX